Hoover's Handbook of Private Companies 2023

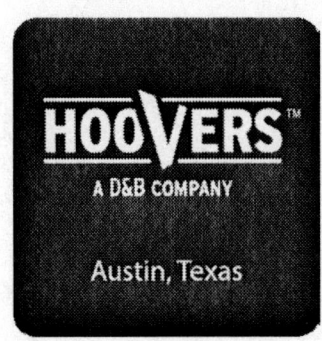

Hoover's Handbook of Private Companies 2023 is intended to provide readers with accurate and authoritative information about the enterprises covered in it. Hoover's researched all companies and organizations profiled, and in many cases contacted them directly so that companies represented could provide information. The information contained herein is as accurate as we could reasonably make it. In many cases we have relied on third-party material that we believe to be trustworthy, but were unable to independently verify. We do not warrant that the book is absolutely accurate or without error. Readers should not rely on any information contained herein in instances where such reliance might cause financial loss. The publisher, the editors, and their data suppliers specifically disclaim all warranties, including the implied warranties of merchantability and fitness for a specific purpose. This book is sold with the understanding that neither the publisher, the editors, nor any content contributors are engaged in providing investment, financial, accounting, legal, or other professional advice.

The financial data (Historical Financials sections) in this book are from a variety of sources. Mergent Inc., provided selected data for the Historical Financials sections of publicly traded companies. For private companies and for historical information on public companies prior to their becoming public, we obtained information directly from the companies or from trade sources deemed to be reliable. Hoover's, Inc., is solely responsible for the presentation of all data.

Many of the names of products and services mentioned in this book are the trademarks or service marks of the companies manufacturing or selling them and are subject to protection under US law. Space has not permitted us to indicate which names are subject to such protection, and readers are advised to consult with the owners of such marks regarding their use. Hoover's is a trademark of Hoover's, Inc.

Copyright © 2023 by Mergent, Inc. All rights reserved. No part of this book may be reproduced or transmitted in any form or by any means, electronic or mechanical, including by photocopying, facsimile transmission, recording, rekeying, or using any information storage and retrieval system, without permission in writing from Hoover's, except that brief passages may be quoted by a reviewer in a magazine, in a newspaper, online, or in a broadcast review.

10 9 8 7 6 5 4 3 2 1

Publishers Cataloging-in-Publication Data

Hoover's Handbook of Private Companies 2023

    Includes indexes.

    ISBN: 978-1-68525-304-2

    ISSN 1073-6433

    1. Business enterprises — Directories. 2. Corporations — Directories.

HF3010 338.7

U.S. AND WORLD BOOK SALES
Mergent Inc.

580 Kingsley Park Drive
Fort Mill, SC
29715
Phone: 704-559-6961
e-mail: skardon@ftserussell.com
Web: www.mergentbusinesspress.com

Mergent Inc.

Executive Managing Director: John Pedernales

Publisher/Managing Director of Print Products: Thomas Wecera

Director of Print Products: Charlot Volny

Quality Assurance Editor: Wayne Arnold

Production Research Assistant: Davie Christna

Data Manager: Jason Horvat

MERGENT CUSTOMER SERVICE-PRINT
Support and Fulfillment: Stephanie Kardon
Phone: 704-559-6961
email: skardon@ftserussell.com
Web: www.mergentbusinesspress.com

ABOUT MERGENT INC.

For over 100 years, Mergent, Inc. has been a leading provider of business and financial information on public and private companies globally. Mergent is known to be a trusted partner to corporate and financial institutions, as well as to academic and public libraries. Today we continue to build on a century of experience by transforming data into knowledge and combining our expertise with the latest technology to create new global data and analytical solutions for our clients. With advanced data collection services, cloud-based applications, desktop analytics and print products, Mergent and its subsidiaries provide solutions from top down economic and demographic information, to detailed equity and debt fundamental analysis. We incorporate value added tools such as quantitative Smart Beta equity research and tools for portfolio building and measurement. Based in the U.S., Mergent maintains a strong global presence, with offices in New York, Charlotte, San Diego, London, Tokyo, Kuching and Melbourne. Mergent, Inc. is a member of the London Stock Exchange plc group of companies. The Mergent business forms part of LSEG's Information Services Division, which includes FTSE Russell, a global leader in indexes.

Abbreviations

AFL-CIO – American Federation of Labor and Congress of Industrial Organizations
AMA – American Medical Association
AMEX – American Stock Exchange
ARM – adjustable-rate mortgage
ASP – application services provider
ATM – asynchronous transfer mode
ATM – automated teller machine
CAD/CAM – computer-aided design/computer-aided manufacturing
CD-ROM – compact disc – read-only memory
CD-R – CD-recordable
CEO – chief executive officer
CFO – chief financial officer
CMOS – complementary metal oxide silicon
COO – chief operating officer
DAT – digital audiotape
DOD – Department of Defense
DOE – Department of Energy
DOS – disk operating system
DOT – Department of Transportation
DRAM – dynamic random-access memory
DSL – digital subscriber line
DVD – digital versatile disc/digital video disc
DVD-R – DVD-recordable
EPA – Environmental Protection Agency
EPS – earnings per share
ESOP – employee stock ownership plan
EU – European Union
EVP – executive vice president
FCC – Federal Communications Commission
FDA – Food and Drug Administration
FDIC – Federal Deposit Insurance Corporation
FTC – Federal Trade Commission
GATT – General Agreement on Tariffs and Trade
GDP – gross domestic product
HMO – health maintenance organization
HR – human resources
HTML – hypertext markup language
ICC – Interstate Commerce Commission
IPO – initial public offering
IRS – Internal Revenue Service
ISP – Internet service provider
kWh – kilowatt-hour
LAN – local-area network
LBO – leveraged buyout
LCD – liquid crystal display
LNG – liquefied natural gas
LP – limited partnership
Ltd. – limited
mips – millions of instructions per second
MW – megawatt
NAFTA – North American Free Trade Agreement
NASA – National Aeronautics and Space Administration
NASDAQ – National Association of Securities Dealers Automated Quotations
NATO – North Atlantic Treaty Organization
NYSE – New York Stock Exchange
OCR – optical character recognition
OECD – Organization for Economic Cooperation and Development
OEM – original equipment manufacturer
OPEC – Organization of Petroleum Exporting Countries
OS – operating system
OSHA – Occupational Safety and Health Administration
OTC – over-the-counter
PBX – private branch exchange
PCMCIA – Personal Computer Memory Card International Association
P/E – price to earnings ratio
RAID – redundant array of independent disks
RAM – random-access memory
R&D – research and development
RBOC – regional Bell operating company
RISC – reduced instruction set computer
REIT – real estate investment trust
ROA – return on assets
ROE – return on equity
ROI – return on investment
ROM – read-only memory
S&L – savings and loan
SEC – Securities and Exchange Commission
SEVP – senior executive vice president
SIC – Standard Industrial Classification
SOC – system on a chip
SVP – senior vice president
USB – universal serial bus
VAR – value-added reseller
VAT – value-added tax
VC – venture capitalist
VoIP – Voice over Internet Protocol
VP – vice president
WAN – wide-area network

Contents

Companies Profiled vi

About *Hoover's Handbook of Private Companies 2023* xvi

Using Hoover's Handbooks xvii

A List-Lover's Compendium 1a

    The 300 Largest Companies by Sales in *Hoover's Handbook of Private Companies 2023* 2a

    The 300 Largest Employers in *Hoover's Handbook of Private Companies 2023* 4a

    The Top 100 Companies by Net Income in *Hoover's Handbook of Private Companies 2023* 6a

    The Top 100 Companies by Total Assets in *Hoover's Handbook of Private Companies 2023* 7a

The Companies 1

The Index of Company Executives 697

Companies Profiled

Company	Page
1199 SEIU NATIONAL BENEFIT FUND FOR HEALTH AND HUMAN SERVICE EMPLOYEES	1
21ST CENTURY ONCOLOGY HOLDINGS, INC	1
95 EXPRESS LANES LLC	1
A-1 SPECIALIZED SERVICES & SUPPLIES, INC.	1
AAA COOPER TRANSPORTATION	1
AARP	2
ABINGTON MEMORIAL HOSPITAL	3
ACCESS BUSINESS GROUP LLC	3
ACE HARDWARE CORPORATION	4
ADVANCED TECHNOLOGY INTERNATIONAL	5
ADVENTIST HEALTH SYSTEM/SUNBELT, INC.	5
ADVENTIST HEALTH SYSTEM/WEST, CORPORATION	6
ADVENTIST HEALTHCARE, INC.	6
ADVENTIST MIDWEST HEALTH	7
ADVOCATE HEALTH AND HOSPITALS CORPORATION	7
ADVOCATE HEALTH AND HOSPITALS CORPORATION	7
AEROTEK AFFILIATED SERVICES, INC.	8
AFFILIATED FOODS MIDWEST COOPERATIVE, INC.	9
AFFILIATED FOODS, INC.	9
AFJ, LLC	9
AG PROCESSING INC A COOPERATIVE	10
AGFIRST FARM CREDIT BANK	11
AGTEGRA COOPERATIVE	11
AHS HOSPITAL CORP.	12
AIDS HEALTHCARE FOUNDATION	12
AIR METHODS CORPORATION	12
AIRGAS, INC.	13
AKRON GENERAL MEDICAL CENTER INC	14
ALASKA NATIVE TRIBAL HEALTH CONSORTIUM	15
ALASKA PERMANENT FUND CORPORATION, AN INSTRUMENTALITY OF THE STATE OF ALASKA	15
ALBANY MED HEALTH SYSTEM	15
ALBANY MEDICAL CENTER HOSPITAL	16
ALBERICI CONSTRUCTORS, INC.	16
ALBERICI CORPORATION	16
ALBERICI GROUP, INC.	17
ALBERT EINSTEIN MEDICAL ASSOCIATES, INC.	17
ALBERTSONS COMPANIES, INC.	18
ALBUQUERQUE MUNICIPAL SCHOOL DISTRICT NUMBER 12	19
ALBUQUERQUE PUBLIC SCHOOL DISTRICT	19
ALDINE INDEPENDENT SCHOOL DISTRICT	19
ALEGENT CREIGHTON HEALTH	20
ALEGENT HEALTH - BERGAN MERCY HEALTH SYSTEM	20
ALEX LEE, INC.	20
ALFRED I.DUPONT HOSPITAL FOR CHILDREN	21
ALIEF INDEPENDENT SCHOOL DISTRICT	21
ALLAN MYERS, INC.	21
ALLEGHENY GENERAL HOSPITAL INC	22
ALLEGIS GROUP, INC.	22
ALLEGRO MICROSYSTEMS, LLC	23
ALLEN LUND COMPANY, LLC	24
ALLIANCE ENTERTAINMENT HOLDING CORPORATION	25
ALLIANCE LAUNDRY HOLDINGS LLC	25
ALLIED SECURITY HOLDINGS LLC	25
ALLIED UNIVERSAL HOLDCO LLC	26
ALLWAYS HEALTH PARTNERS, INC.	26
ALLY BANK	26
ALMOST FAMILY, INC.	26
ALPINE SCHOOL DISTRICT	27
ALRO STEEL CORPORATION	27
ALSCO INC.	28
ALSTON CONSTRUCTION COMPANY, INC.	28
ALTICOR INC.	29
ALTISOURCE SOLUTIONS, INC.	30
ALTRU HEALTH SYSTEM	30
AMC ENTERTAINMENT INC.	30
AMCAP FUND, INC.	30
AMERICA CHUNG NAM (GROUP) HOLDINGS LLC	31
AMERICAN BALANCED FUND, INC.	31
AMERICAN CAMPUS COMMUNITIES OPERATING PARTNERSHIP LP	31
AMERICAN CHEMICAL SOCIETY	31
AMERICAN CRYSTAL SUGAR COMPANY	32
AMERICAN ELECTRIC POWER SERVICE CORPORATION	32
AMERICAN FUNDS INTERNATIONAL VANTAGE FUND	33
AMERICAN FUNDS PORTFOLIO SERIES	33
AMERICAN FURNITURE WAREHOUSE CO.	33
AMERICAN HIGH INCOME TRUST	33
AMERICAN HONDA FINANCE CORPORATION	34
AMERICAN INSTITUTES FOR RESEARCH IN THE BEHAVIORAL SCIENCES	34
AMERICAN LEBANESE SYRIAN ASSOCIATED CHARITIES, INC.	35
AMERICAN MITSUBA CORPORATION	35
AMERICAN MUNICIPAL POWER, INC.	35
AMERICAN MUTUAL FUND	36
AMERICAN TIRE DISTRIBUTORS HOLDINGS, INC.	36
AMERICAN TRANSMISSION SYSTEMS, INCORPORATED	37
AMERICARES FOUNDATION, INC.	37
AMES CONSTRUCTION, INC.	37
ANC HEALTHCARE, INC.	38
ANCHORAGE SCHOOL DISTRICT	38
ANCHORAGE, MUNICIPALITY OF (INC)	38
ANMED HEALTH	39
ANN & ROBERT H. LURIE CHILDREN'S HOSPITAL OF CHICAGO	39
ANNE ARUNDEL COUNTY BOARD OF EDUCATION	40
ANOKA-HENNEPIN SCHOOL DIST NO 11	40
ANR PIPELINE COMPANY	40
API GROUP, INC.	40
APPALACHIAN REGIONAL HEALTHCARE, INC.	41
APPLE HOSPITALITY REIT, INC.	42
APPLIED MEDICAL RESOURCES CORPORATION	42
ARCTIC SLOPE REGIONAL CORPORATION	42
ARIZONA STATE LOTTERY	43
ARIZONA STATE UNIVERSITY	43
ARIZONA STATE UNIVERSITY	44
ARKANSAS ELECTRIC COOPERATIVE CORPORATION	44
ARKANSAS ELECTRIC COOPERATIVES, INC.	45
ARLINGTON INDEPENDENT SCHOOL DISTRICT (INC)	45
ASCENSION HEALTH ALLIANCE	45
ASCENSION PROVIDENCE HOSPITAL	45
ASCENSION VIA CHRISTI HOSPITALS WICHITA, INC.	46
ASI COMPUTER TECHNOLOGIES INC	46
ASPIRUS WAUSAU HOSPITAL, INC.	46
ASPIRUS, INC.	47
ASSOCIATED FOOD STORES, INC.	47
ASSOCIATED WHOLESALE GROCERS, INC.	48
ATHENE ANNUITY & LIFE ASSURANCE COMPANY	49
ATLANTIC COAST CONFERENCE	49
ATLANTIC DIVING SUPPLY, INC.	49
ATLANTIC HEALTH SYSTEM INC.	50
ATLANTICARE REGIONAL MEDICAL CENTER	50
ATLAS OIL COMPANY	50
ATLAS WORLD GROUP, INC.	51
ATMEL CORPORATION	51
ATRIUS HEALTH, INC.	52
ATTORNEY GENERAL, TEXAS	53
AU HEALTH SYSTEM, INC.	53
AUBURN UNIVERSITY	54
AUGUSTANA HEALTH CARE CENTER OF APPLE VALLEY	54
AURORA HEALTH CARE METRO, INC	54
AURORA HEALTH CARE, INC.	54
AUSTIN INDEPENDENT SCHOOL DISTRICT (INC)	55
AVANT GARDE ACADEMY FOUNDATION, INC.	55
AVAYA HOLDINGS CORP.	55
AVERITT EXPRESS, INC.	56
AVERITT INCORPORATED	56
AVI-SPL HOLDINGS, INC.	57
AVIO INC.	57
AXEL JOHNSON INC.	57
AXOS BANK	57
B.L. HARBERT HOLDINGS, L.L.C.	57
BAKERSFIELD MEMORIAL HOSPITAL	58
BALFOUR BEATTY CONSTRUCTION GROUP, INC.	58
BALFOUR BEATTY CONSTRUCTION, LLC	58
BALFOUR BEATTY, LLC	59
BALLAD HEALTH	59
BALTIMORE CITY PUBLIC SCHOOLS	59
BANNER HEALTH	59
BANNER-UNIVERSITY MEDICAL CENTER TUCSON CAMPUS LLC	60
BAPTIST HEALTH	60
BAPTIST HEALTH SOUTH FLORIDA, INC.	61
BAPTIST HEALTH SYSTEM, INC.	62
BAPTIST HEALTHCARE SYSTEM, INC.	62
BAPTIST HOSPITAL OF MIAMI, INC.	63
BAPTIST MEMORIAL HEALTH CARE CORPORATION	63
BAPTIST MEMORIAL HOSPITAL	64
BARCLAYS BANK DELAWARE	64
BARNABAS HEALTH, INC.	64
BARNES & NOBLE, INC.	65
BARNES-JEWISH HOSPITAL	66
BARRICK ENTERPRISES, INC.	66
BARRY-WEHMILLER GROUP, INC.	66
BARTON MALOW COMPANY	67
BARTON MALOW ENTERPRISES, INC.	67
BATTELLE MEMORIAL INSTITUTE	67
BAYCARE HEALTH SYSTEM, INC.	68
BAYHEALTH MEDICAL CENTER, INC.	68
BAYLOR SCOTT & WHITE HEALTH	68
BAYLOR SCOTT & WHITE HOLDINGS	69
BAYLOR UNIVERSITY	69
BAYLOR UNIVERSITY MEDICAL CENTER	69
BAYSTATE HEALTH SYSTEM HEALTH SERVICES, INC.	70

Companies Profiled (continued)

Company	Page
BAYSTATE MEDICAL CENTER, INC.	71
BCFS HEALTH AND HUMAN SERVICES	71
BEALL'S, INC.	71
BEARINGPOINT, INC.	72
BEAUMONT HEALTH	72
BEAVERTON SCHOOL DISTRICT	73
BEEBE MEDICAL CENTER, INC.	73
BENCO DENTAL SUPPLY CO.	74
BENEFIS HEALTH SYSTEM, INC	75
BENEFIS HOSPITALS, INC	75
BERGELECTRIC CORP.	75
BERRY GLOBAL FILMS, LLC	75
BEST PETROLEUM CORPORATION	76
BETH ISRAEL DEACONESS MEDICAL CENTER, INC.	77
BETH ISRAEL MEDICAL CENTER	77
BETHESDA FOUNDATION INC	78
BETHESDA HOSPITAL, INC.	78
BETHESDA, INC.	79
BI-MART ACQUISITION CORP.	79
BIG RIVER RESOURCES, LLC.	79
BIG RIVERS ELECTRIC CORPORATION	79
BIG WEST OF CALIFORNIA, LLC	79
BIG WEST OIL, LLC	79
BIG-D CONSTRUCTION CORP.	80
BILLINGS CLINIC	80
BIOURJA TRADING, LLC	81
BLACK & VEATCH HOLDING COMPANY	81
BLACK & VEATCH INTERNATIONAL COMPANY	81
BLOUNT INTERNATIONAL, INC.	82
BLUE BUFFALO PET PRODUCTS, INC.	82
BLUE CROSS & BLUE SHIELD ASSOCIATION	83
BLUE CROSS AND BLUE SHIELD OF ARIZONA, INC.	84
BLUE TEE CORP.	85
BNSF RAILWAY COMPANY	85
BOARD OF EDUCATION FOR THE CITY OF SAVANNAH AND THE COUNTY OF CHATHAM (INC)	86
BOARD OF EDUCATION OF CITY OF CHICAGO	86
BOARD OF EDUCATION-MEMPHIS CITY SCHOOLS	86
BOARD OF PUBLIC EDUCATION SCHOOL DISTRICT OF PITTSBURGH (INC)	86
BOARD OF REGENTS OF THE UNIVERSITY OF NEBRASKA	87
BOARD OF REGENTS OF THE UNIVERSITY SYSTEM OF GEORGIA	87
BOARD OF TRUSTEES OF STATE INSTITUTIONS OF HIGHER LEARNING	87
BOARDRIDERS, INC.	87
BON SECOURS MERCY HEALTH, INC.	88
BONNEVILLE POWER ADMINISTRATION	89
BOSCOV'S, INC.	90
BOSTON MEDICAL CENTER CORPORATION	90
BOSTON UNIVERSITY	91
BOZZUTO'S, INC.	91
BRAZOS ELECTRIC POWER COOPERATIVE, INC.	91
BRG SPORTS, INC.	92
BRIDGEPORT HOSPITAL	93
BRISBANE SCHOOL DISTRICT	93
BRODER BROS., CO.	93
BRONSON METHODIST HOSPITAL INC	94
BRONXCARE HEALTH SYSTEM	94
BROOKFIELD PROPERTIES RETAIL INC.	95
BROOME COUNTY	95
BROTHER INTERNATIONAL CORPORATION	95
BROWN UNIVERSITY	96
BRUCE OAKLEY, INC.	96
BRUCKNER TRUCK SALES, INC.	97
BRYAN MEDICAL CENTER	97
BUFFALO CITY SCHOOL DISTRICT	97
BVH, INC.	98
C.R. ENGLAND, INC.	98
CALGON CARBON CORPORATION	98
CALIFORNIA INSTITUTE OF TECHNOLOGY	99
CALIFORNIA STEEL INDUSTRIES, INC.	100
CALIFORNIA'S VALUED TRUST	100
CAMERON INTERNATIONAL CORPORATION	100
CAMPUS CRUSADE FOR CHRIST INC	101
CANDID COLOR SYSTEMS, INC.	101
CAPE COD HEALTHCARE, INC.	101
CAPE COD HOSPITAL	102
CAPE FEAR VALLEY MEDICAL CENTER	102
CAPISTRANO UNIFIED SCHOOL DISTRICT	102
CAPITAL DISTRICT PHYSICIANS' HEALTH PLAN, INC.	103
CAPITAL INCOME BUILDER	103
CAPITAL WORLD GROWTH AND INCOME FUND, INC.	104
CARDINAL LOGISTICS HOLDINGS, LLC	104
CARE NEW ENGLAND HEALTH SYSTEM INC	104
CAREOREGON, INC.	104
CARILION MEDICAL CENTER	105
CARILION NEW RIVER VALLEY MEDICAL CENTER	105
CARILION SERVICES, INC.	105
CARLE FOUNDATION HOSPITAL	105
CARNEGIE MELLON UNIVERSITY	106
CAROLINA HEALTHCARE CENTER OF CUMBERLAND LP	106
CAROLINAS MEDICAL CENTER NORTHEAST	106
CARTER-JONES COMPANIES, INC.	107
CARY OIL CO., INC.	107
CASE WESTERN RESERVE UNIVERSITY	107
CATHOLIC HEALTH INITIATIVES - IOWA, CORP.	107
CATHOLIC HEALTH INITIATIVES COLORADO	107
CATHOLIC MEDICAL MISSION BOARD INC	108
CATHOLIC RELIEF SERVICES - UNITED STATES CONFERENCE OF CATHOLIC BISHOPS	108
CCF BRANDS LLC	108
CEB INC.	108
CEDARS-SINAI MEDICAL CARE FOUNDATION	109
CEDARS-SINAI MEDICAL CENTER	109
CENTERPOINT ENERGY SERVICES RETAIL LLC	110
CENTIMARK CORPORATION	110
CENTRA HEALTH, INC.	110
CENTRAL CRUDE, INC.	111
CENTRAL ELECTRIC POWER COOPERATIVE, INC.	111
CENTRAL GROCERS, INC.	111
CENTRAL HUDSON GAS & ELECTRIC CORPORATION	112
CENTRAL IOWA HOSPITAL CORP	112
CENTRAL STEEL AND WIRE COMPANY, LLC	112
CERTCO, INC.	113
CFJ PROPERTIES LLC	113
CGB ENTERPRISES, INC.	114
CHALMETTE REFINING, L.L.C.	114
CHARLESTON AREA MEDICAL CENTER, INC.	114
CHARTER MANUFACTURING COMPANY, INC.	115
CHEMIUM INTERNATIONAL CORP.	116
CHENEGA CORPORATION	116
CHEROKEE NATION BUSINESSES LLC	116
CHEROKEE NATION ENTERTAINMENT, LLC	117
CHEVRON PHILLIPS CHEMICAL COMPANY LLC	117
CHEVRON PHILLIPS CHEMICAL COMPANY LP	117
CHG FOUNDATION	118
CHI ST. LUKE'S HEALTH BAYLOR COLLEGE OF MEDICINE MEDICAL CENTER CONDOMINIUM ASSOCIATION	118
CHICAGO COMMUNITY TRUST	118
CHICAGO PARK DISTRICT	118
CHILDREN'S HEALTH CARE	118
CHILDREN'S HOSPITAL	119
CHILDREN'S HOSPITAL & RESEARCH CENTER AT OAKLAND	119
CHILDREN'S HOSPITAL COLORADO	120
CHILDREN'S HOSPITAL OF ORANGE COUNTY	121
CHILDREN'S HOSPITAL OF WISCONSIN, INC	121
CHILDREN'S MEDICAL CENTER OF DALLAS	121
CHILDRENS HOSPITAL	122
CHILDRENS HOSPITAL INC	122
CHILDRENS HOSPITAL MEDICAL CENTER OF AKRON	122
CHINESE HOSPITAL ASSOCIATION	123
CHRISTIAN HEALTHCARE MINISTRIES, INC.	123
CHRISTUS NORTHEAST TEXAS HEALTH SYSTEM CORPORATION	123
CHRISTUS SANTA ROSA HEALTH CARE CORPORATION	123
CHS MCPHERSON REFINERY INC.	124
CHUGACH ALASKA CORPORATION	124
CIC GROUP, INC.	125
CIMA ENERGY, LP	125
CINCINNATI PUBLIC SCHOOLS	125
CITIZENS ENERGY GROUP	125
CITY & COUNTY OF HONOLULU	126
CITY & COUNTY OF SAN FRANCISCO	126
CITY CENTER HOLDINGS, LLC	127
CITY OF ALBUQUERQUE	127
CITY OF ALEXANDRIA	127
CITY OF ANAHEIM	127
CITY OF ATLANTA	128
CITY OF AUSTIN	128
CITY OF BAKERSFIELD	128
CITY OF BALTIMORE	129
CITY OF BATON ROUGE	129
CITY OF BIRMINGHAM	129
CITY OF CAMBRIDGE	129
CITY OF CHARLOTTE	130
CITY OF CHESAPEAKE	130
CITY OF CINCINNATI	130
CITY OF CLEVELAND	130
CITY OF COLUMBUS	131
CITY OF DALLAS	131
CITY OF EL PASO	131
CITY OF FRESNO	132
CITY OF HARTFORD	132
CITY OF HOPE NATIONAL MEDICAL CENTER	132
CITY OF JACKSONVILLE	132
CITY OF LAS VEGAS	133
CITY OF LONG BEACH	133
CITY OF LOS ANGELES	133
CITY OF MEMPHIS	133
CITY OF MESA	134
CITY OF MIAMI	134
CITY OF MINNEAPOLIS	134
CITY OF NEW HAVEN	134
CITY OF NEW ORLEANS	135
CITY OF NEW YORK	135
CITY OF NEWPORT NEWS	135
CITY OF NORFOLK	136
CITY OF OAKLAND	136
CITY OF OKLAHOMA CITY	136
CITY OF OMAHA	136
CITY OF ORLANDO	137
CITY OF PHILADELPHIA	137
CITY OF PHOENIX	137
CITY OF PITTSBURGH	138
CITY OF PORTLAND	138
CITY OF PROVIDENCE	138
CITY OF RALEIGH	138
CITY OF RICHMOND	139
CITY OF ROCHESTER	139
CITY OF SACRAMENTO	139
CITY OF SAINT PAUL	139

Companies Profiled (continued)

Company	Page
CITY OF SAN ANTONIO	140
CITY OF SAN DIEGO	140
CITY OF SAN JOSE	140
CITY OF SCOTTSDALE	140
CITY OF SEATTLE	141
CITY OF SPRINGFIELD	141
CITY OF ST. LOUIS	141
CITY OF STAMFORD	141
CITY OF SYRACUSE	141
CITY OF TAMPA	142
CITY OF TUCSON	142
CITY OF VIRGINIA BEACH	142
CITY OF WATERBURY	142
CITY OF WORCESTER	143
CITY PUBLIC SERVICES OF SAN ANTONIO	143
CITYSERVICEVALCON, LLC	143
CLARCOR INC.	144
CLARK COUNTY SCHOOL DISTRICT	145
CLARK EQUIPMENT COMPANY	145
CLEVELAND MUNICIPAL SCHOOL DISTRICT	145
CLIFTONLARSONALLEN LLP	145
CLOUD PEAK ENERGY RESOURCES LLC	146
COASTAL CHEMICAL CO., L.L.C.	146
COASTAL PACIFIC FOOD DISTRIBUTORS, INC.	146
COBANK, ACB	147
COBB COUNTY BOARD OF EDUCATION	148
COBB COUNTY MEDICAL EXAMINER'S OFFICE	148
COBB COUNTY PUBLIC SCHOOLS	148
COBB COUNTY SCHOOL DISTRICT	148
COBB ELECTRIC MEMBERSHIP CORPORATION	148
COBORN'S, INCORPORATED	149
COC PROPERTIES, INC.	149
COLORADO STATE UNIVERSITY	150
COLORADO STATE UNIVERSITY SYSTEM FOUNDATION, DELINQUENT FEBRUARY 1, 2020	150
COLUMBIA GAS OF OHIO, INC.	150
COLUMBUS CITY SCHOOL DISTRICT	151
COMENITY BANK	151
COMFORT SYSTEMS USA (ARKANSAS), INC.	151
COMMONSPIRIT HEALTH	152
COMMONSPIRIT HEALTH RESEARCH INSTITUTE	152
COMMONWEALTH CARE ALLIANCE, INC.	153
COMMONWEALTH HEALTH CORPORATION, INC.	153
COMMONWEALTH OF KENTUCKY	153
COMMONWEALTH OF MASSACHUSETTS	153
COMMONWEALTH OF VIRGINIA	154
COMMUNITY BEHAVIORAL HEALTH	154
COMMUNITY FOUNDATION OF NORTHWEST INDIANA, INC.	154
COMMUNITY HEALTH CHOICE TEXAS, INC.	154
COMMUNITY HEALTH CHOICE, INC.	154
COMMUNITY HEALTH NETWORK, INC.	154
COMMUNITY HOSPITAL OF THE MONTEREY PENINSULA	155
COMMUNITY HOSPITALS OF CENTRAL CALIFORNIA	156
COMMUNITY HOSPITALS OF CENTRAL CALIFORNIA	156
COMPASSION INTERNATIONAL INC	156
COMPUTER AID, INC.	156
COMPUTER SCIENCES CORPORATION	157
CONCORD HOSPITAL, INC.	158
CONROE INDEPENDENT SCHOOL DISTRICT	159
CONSIGLI CONSTRUCTION CO. INC.	159
CONSOLIDATED PIPE & SUPPLY COMPANY, INC.	159
CONSTELLATION ENERGY GENERATION, LLC	160
CONSUMER PRODUCT DISTRIBUTORS, LLC	161
CONTINUUM ENERGY SERVICES, L.L.C.	161
CONTINUUM MIDSTREAM, L.L.C.	162
COOK CHILDREN'S HEALTH PLAN	162
COOK CHILDREN'S MEDICAL CENTER	162
COOPERATIVE ENERGY, A MISSISSIPPI ELECTRIC COOPERATIVE	162
COOPERATIVE FOR ASSISTANCE AND RELIEF EVERYWHERE, INC. (CARE)	162
COOPERATIVE REGIONS OF ORGANIC PRODUCER POOLS	163
COPPEL CORPORATION	163
COREWELL HEALTH	163
CORNELL UNIVERSITY	164
CORONA-NORCO UNIFIED SCHOOL DISTRICT	165
CORPORATION FOR PUBLIC BROADCASTING	165
COUNTRYMARK COOPERATIVE HOLDING CORPORATION	165
COUNTY OF ADAMS	166
COUNTY OF ALAMEDA	166
COUNTY OF ALBANY	166
COUNTY OF ALLEGHENY	166
COUNTY OF ANNE ARUNDEL	166
COUNTY OF ARLINGTON	166
COUNTY OF BERGEN	167
COUNTY OF BERKS	167
COUNTY OF BEXAR	167
COUNTY OF BROWARD	167
COUNTY OF CAMDEN	167
COUNTY OF CHESTERFIELD	167
COUNTY OF CLARK	168
COUNTY OF CONTRA COSTA	168
COUNTY OF CUYAHOGA	168
COUNTY OF DALLAS	168
COUNTY OF DANE	168
COUNTY OF DEKALB	168
COUNTY OF DELAWARE	169
COUNTY OF ERIE	169
COUNTY OF ESSEX	169
COUNTY OF FORT BEND	169
COUNTY OF FRESNO	169
COUNTY OF FULTON	169
COUNTY OF GUILFORD	170
COUNTY OF HARFORD	170
COUNTY OF HARRIS	170
COUNTY OF HAWAII	170
COUNTY OF HENRICO	170
COUNTY OF HILLSBOROUGH	170
COUNTY OF JOHNSON	171
COUNTY OF KERN	171
COUNTY OF KING	171
COUNTY OF LEE	171
COUNTY OF LOS ANGELES	171
COUNTY OF MARICOPA	172
COUNTY OF MARIN	172
COUNTY OF MAUI	172
COUNTY OF MECKLENBURG	172
COUNTY OF MERCED	172
COUNTY OF MONMOUTH	172
COUNTY OF MONROE	173
COUNTY OF MONTGOMERY	173
COUNTY OF MONTGOMERY	173
COUNTY OF MULTNOMAH	173
COUNTY OF MULTNOMAH	173
COUNTY OF NASSAU	173
COUNTY OF OAKLAND	174
COUNTY OF ONONDAGA	174
COUNTY OF ORANGE	174
COUNTY OF ORANGE	174
COUNTY OF ORANGE	174
COUNTY OF PALM BEACH	174
COUNTY OF PASCO	175
COUNTY OF PIERCE	175
COUNTY OF PLACER	175
COUNTY OF PRINCE WILLIAM	175
COUNTY OF RAMSEY	175
COUNTY OF RIVERSIDE	175
COUNTY OF ROCKLAND	176
COUNTY OF SACRAMENTO	176
COUNTY OF SALT LAKE	176
COUNTY OF SAN MATEO	176
COUNTY OF SANTA BARBARA	176
COUNTY OF SANTA CLARA	176
COUNTY OF SANTA CRUZ	177
COUNTY OF SARASOTA	177
COUNTY OF SHELBY	177
COUNTY OF SNOHOMISH	177
COUNTY OF SOLANO	177
COUNTY OF SONOMA	177
COUNTY OF ST LOUIS	178
COUNTY OF STANISLAUS	178
COUNTY OF SUFFOLK	178
COUNTY OF TARRANT	178
COUNTY OF TRAVIS	178
COUNTY OF TULARE	178
COUNTY OF UNION	179
COUNTY OF VOLUSIA	179
COUNTY OF WASHINGTON	179
COUNTY OF WASHOE	179
COUNTY OF WESTCHESTER	179
COUNTY OF WYOMING	179
COUNTY OF YORK	179
COUNTY SANITATION DISTRICT NO. 2 OF LOS ANGELES COUNTY	180
COVENANT HEALTH	180
COVENANT HEALTH SYSTEM	180
COVENANT HEALTH, INC.	181
COVENANT MEDICAL CENTER, INC.	181
CREIGHTON UNIVERSITY	181
CRETE CARRIER CORPORATION	182
CROWE LLP	182
CROWLEY MARITIME CORPORATION	182
CRST INTERNATIONAL, INC.	183
CSC SUGAR, LLC	184
CUMBERLAND COUNTY HOSPITAL SYSTEM, INC.	184
CYPRESS-FAIRBANKS INDEPENDENT SCHOOL DISTRICT	184
CYRUSONE HOLDCO LLC	184
D. H. PACE COMPANY, INC.	185
D/L COOPERATIVE INC.	185
DAIRY FARMERS OF AMERICA, INC.	185
DAIRYAMERICA, INC.	186
DALLAS COUNTY HOSPITAL DISTRICT	186
DALLAS INDEPENDENT SCHOOL DISTRICT	187
DALLAS-FORT WORTH INTERNATIONAL AIRPORT FACILITY IMPROVEMENT CORPORATION	187
DANA-FARBER CANCER INSTITUTE, INC.	188
DANFOSS POWER SOLUTIONS INC.	189
DANONE US, INC.	189
DARTMOUTH COLLEGE	190
DARTMOUTH-HITCHCOCK CLINIC	190
DARTMOUTH-HITCHCOCK HEALTH	190
DATASITE GLOBAL CORPORATION	191
DATS TRUCKING, INC.	191
DAVIS SCHOOL DISTRICT	191
DAYTON CHILDREN'S HOSPITAL	191
DB US HOLDING CORPORATION	192
DBSI INC	192
DC WATER AND SEWER AUTHORITY	192
DCR WORKFORCE, INC.	192
DE PAUL UNIVERSITY	192
DEACONESS HOSPITAL INC	193
DEER PARK REFINING LIMITED PARTNERSHIP	193
DEKALB COUNTY BOARD OF EDUCATION	193
DEKALB COUNTY PUBLIC LIBRARY	194
DENNIS K. BURKE INC.	194
DENVER HEALTH AND HOSPITALS AUTHORITY INC	194
DESAROLLADORA DEL NORTE S E	194
DETROIT WAYNE MENTAL HEALTH AUTHORITY	195
DEVCON CONSTRUCTION INCORPORATED	195

Companies Profiled (continued)

Company	Page
DHPC TECHNOLOGIES, INC.	195
DIALYSIS CLINIC, INC.	195
DIGNITY HEALTH	196
DIGNITY HEALTH MEDICAL FOUNDATION	197
DIRECT RELIEF FOUNDATION	197
DISTRICT OF COLUMBIA WATER & SEWER AUTHORITY	197
DITECH HOLDING CORPORATION	198
DO IT BEST CORP.	199
DOCTOR'S ASSOCIATES INC.	199
DOCTORS HOSPITAL AT RENAISSANCE, LTD.	200
DOCTORS MEDICAL CENTER OF MODESTO, INC.	201
DON FORD SANDERSON INC	201
DORMITORY AUTHORITY - STATE OF NEW YORK	201
DOUGLAS COUNTY SCHOOL DISTRICT	201
DPR CONSTRUCTION, INC.	201
DRISCOLL CHILDRENS HEALTH PLAN	202
DRIVETIME AUTOMOTIVE GROUP, INC.	202
DST SYSTEMS, INC.	203
DUKE UNIVERSITY	204
DUKE UNIVERSITY HEALTH SYSTEM, INC.	205
DUKE UNIVERSITY HOSPITAL	206
DUTCHESS, COUNTY OF (INC)	206
DUVAL COUNTY SCHOOL BOARD (INC)	206
DYNCORP INTERNATIONAL LLC	206
EARTHLINK HOLDINGS, LLC	206
EAST BAY MUNICIPAL UTILITY DISTRICT, WATER SYSTEM	207
EAST TEXAS MEDICAL CENTER REGIONAL HEALTHCARE SYSTEM	207
EASTERN MAINE HEALTHCARE SYSTEMS	208
EASTERN MAINE MEDICAL CENTER	209
EATON CORPORATION	209
EDUCATIONAL TESTING SERVICE	209
EDWARD HOSPITAL	210
EDWARD-ELMHURST HEALTHCARE	210
EL CAMINO HEALTHCARE DISTRICT	210
EL PASO COUNTY HOSPITAL DISTRICT	211
EL PASO INDEPENDENT SCHOOL DISTRICT EDUCATION FOUNDATION	211
EL PASO NATURAL GAS COMPANY, L.L.C.	211
ELECTRIC POWER BOARD OF CHATTANOOGA	211
ELECTRIC POWER BOARD OF THE METROPOLITAN GOVERNMENT OF NASHVILLE & DAVIDSON COUNTY	212
ELEMENT14 US HOLDINGS INC	212
ELLIOT HEALTH SYSTEM	212
ELLIOT HOSPITAL OF THE CITY OF MANCHESTER	213
EMJ CORPORATION	213
EMORY UNIVERSITY HOSPITAL MIDTOWN	214
EMPIRE SOUTHWEST, LLC	214
ENGLEWOOD HOSPITAL AND MEDICAL CENTER FOUNDATION INC.	215
ENTERGY SERVICES, LLC	215
ENTERPRISE CRUDE PIPELINE LLC	215
ENTERPRISE TE PRODUCTS PIPELINE COMPANY LLC	216
EP ENERGY CORPORATION	216
EP ENERGY LLC	217
EQUINOR MARKETING & TRADING (US) INC.	217
EQUINOR NATURAL GAS LLC	217
ERIE COUNTY MEDICAL CENTER CORP.	217
ESTES EXPRESS LINES	217
EVANS GENERAL CONTRACTORS, LLC	218
EVERGY MISSOURI WEST, INC.	218
EVERSOURCE ENERGY SERVICE COMPANY	218
EXCELA HEALTH	218
EXTENDED STAY AMERICA, INC.	218
EYP STOCKBRIDGE, LLC	219
FAIRFAX COUNTY VIRGINIA	219
FAIRVIEW HEALTH SERVICES	219
FAMILY HEALTH INTERNATIONAL INC	220
FAMILY HEALTH NETWORK, INC.	220
FARM CREDIT BANK OF TEXAS	221
FARM CREDIT SERVICES OF AMERICA	221
FARM CREDIT WEST	221
FARMERS COOPERATIVE	221
FARMERS COOPERATIVE COMPANY	221
FARMERS GRAIN TERMINAL, INC.	222
FCTG HOLDINGS, INC.	222
FEDERAL-MOGUL HOLDINGS LLC	222
FERGUSON ENTERPRISES, LLC	222
FIDELITY INV CHARITABLE GIFT FUND	223
FINANCIAL INDUSTRY REGULATORY AUTHORITY, INC.	223
FINANCIAL TRADER CORPORATION	224
FLATIRON CONSTRUCTORS, INC.	224
FLORIDA CLINICAL PRACTICE ASSOCIATION, INC.	224
FLORIDA DEPARTMENT OF LOTTERY	224
FLORIDA HEALTH SCIENCES CENTER, INC.	225
FLORIDA HOSPITAL MEDICAL GROUP, INC.	225
FLORIDA MUNICIPAL POWER AGENCY	225
FLORIDA STATE UNIVERSITY	226
FLOWORKS INTERNATIONAL LLC	226
FLOWORKS USA LP	227
FONTANA UNIFIED SCHOOL DISTRICT	227
FOOD FOR THE POOR, INC.	227
FOOD GIANT SUPERMARKETS, INC.	227
FORDHAM UNIVERSITY	227
FORREST COUNTY GENERAL HOSPITAL	228
FORSYTH COUNTY BOARD OF EDUCATION	228
FORT WORTH INDEPENDENT SCHOOL DISTRICT	228
FORTERRA, INC.	229
FORTIS CONSTRUCTION, INC.	229
FRANCISCAN ALLIANCE, INC.	229
FRANCISCAN HEALTH SYSTEM	230
FRANCISCAN MISSIONARIES OF OUR LADY HEALTH SYSTEM, INC.	230
FRANKLIN COUNTY BOARD OF COMMISSIONERS	230
FRANKLIN SQUARE HOSPITAL CENTER, INC.	231
FREDERICK COUNTY, MARYLAND	231
FREEMAN HEALTH SYSTEM	231
FRESH MARK, INC.	232
FRESNO COMMUNITY HOSPITAL AND MEDICAL CENTER	232
FRESNO UNIFIED SCHOOL DISTRICT EDUCATIONAL FACILITIES CORPORATION	232
FROEDTERT HEALTH, INC.	233
FROEDTERT MEMORIAL LUTHERAN HOSPITAL, INC.	233
FRONTROW CALYPSO LLC	233
FS KKR CAPITAL CORP. II	234
FTD COMPANIES, INC.	234
FULTON COUNTY BOARD OF EDUCATION	234
FUNDAMENTAL INVESTORS, INC.	234
GARDEN GROVE UNIFIED SCHOOL DISTRICT	235
GARFF ENTERPRISES, INC.	235
GARLAND INDEPENDENT SCHOOL DISTRICT	235
GBMC HEALTHCARE, INC.	235
GCI, LLC	235
GEISINGER HEALTH	235
GEISINGER HEALTH PLAN	236
GEISINGER MEDICAL CENTER	236
GENERAL ELECTRIC INTERNATIONAL OPERATIONS COMPANY, INC.	237
GENERAL ELECTRIC INTERNATIONAL, INC.	237
GENESIS HEALTH SYSTEM	237
GENPACT LIMITED	237
GEOKINETICS INC.	238
GEORGES PRINCE COUNTY GOVERNMENT	238
GEORGIA CARESOURCE CO	238
GEORGIA TECH APPLIED RESEARCH CORPORATION	239
GERBER SCIENTIFIC PRODUCTS INC	239
GGP, INC.	239
GILBANE BUILDING COMPANY	239
GLOBAL HEALTH SOLUTIONS, INC.	240
GLU MOBILE INC.	240
GOOD SAMARITAN HOSPITAL MEDICAL CENTER	241
GOOD SAMARITAN HOSPITAL OF CINCINNATI	242
GOOD SAMARITAN HOSPITAL, L.P.	242
GOVERNMENT OF DISTRICT OF COLUMBIA	243
GPM INVESTMENTS, LLC	243
GRADY MEMORIAL HOSPITAL CORPORATION	244
GRAEBEL HOLDINGS, INC.	244
GRAHAM ENTERPRISE, INC.	244
GRAND RIVER DAM AUTHORITY	244
GRANITE SCHOOL DISTRICT	244
GRANITE TELECOMMUNICATIONS LLC	245
GREAT RIVER ENERGY	245
GREENSTONE FARM CREDIT SERVICES ACA	246
GROSSMONT HOSPITAL FOUNDATION	246
GROUP O, INC.	246
GROVE ELK UNIFIED SCHOOL DISTRICT	247
GROWMARK, INC.	247
GRUMA CORPORATION	248
GUILDNET, INC.	249
GUILFORD COUNTY SCHOOL SYSTEM	249
GUNDERSEN LUTHERAN ADMINISTRATIVE SERVICES INC.	249
GUNDERSEN LUTHERAN MEDICAL CENTER, INC.	250
GWINNETT COUNTY BOARD OF EDUCATION	250
GWINNETT HOSPITAL SYSTEM, INC.	250
H. J. BAKER SULPHUR, LLC	250
H. LEE MOFFITT CANCER CENTER AND RESEARCH INSTITUTE HOSPITAL, INC.	251
H. LEE MOFFITT CANCER CENTER AND RESEARCH INSTITUTE, INC.	251
HAGGEN, INC.	252
HAMILTON CHATTANOOGA COUNTY HOSPITAL AUTHORITY	252
HARBOR-UCLA MEDICAL CENTER	253
HARLEE MANOR, INC.	253
HARRIS COUNTY FIRE MARSHAL	253
HARRIS COUNTY HOSPITAL DISTRICT	253
HARRISON MEDICAL CENTER	254
HARTFORD HEALTHCARE CORPORATION	254
HARVARD MANAGEMENT PRIVATE EQUITY CORPORATION	254
HARVARD MEDICAL FACULTY PHYSICIANS AT BETH ISRAEL DEACONESS MEDICAL CENTER, INC.	255
HAWAI I PACIFIC HEALTH	255
HCL AMERICA INC.	255
HDR ENGINEERING, INC.	255
HDR, INC.	256
HEALTH FIRST SHARED SERVICES, INC.	256
HEALTH PARTNERS PLANS, INC.	257
HEALTH QUEST SYSTEMS, INC.	257
HEALTH RESEARCH, INC.	257
HEALTHPARTNERS, INC.	258
HEARTLAND CO-OP	258
HEARTLAND PAYMENT SYSTEMS, LLC	258
HEARTLAND REGIONAL MEDICAL CENTER	259
HELM FERTILIZER CORPORATION (FLORIDA)	259
HENDRICKS COUNTY HOSPITAL	259
HENNEPIN COUNTY	260
HENNEPIN HEALTHCARE SYSTEM, INC.	260
HENRY FORD HEALTH SYSTEM	260
HENRY MODELL & COMPANY, INC.	260
HENSEL PHELPS CONSTRUCTION CO.	261
HEXION INC.	262

Companies Profiled (continued)

HIGHER EDUCATION COORDINATING BOARD, TEXAS	263
HILAND DAIRY FOODS COMPANY., LLC	263
HILL FIRE PROTECTION, LLC	263
HILLSBOROUGH COUNTY SCHOOL DISTRICT	264
HL MANDO AMERICA CORPORATION	264
HMH HOSPITALS CORPORATION	264
HMO MINNESOTA	265
HMS HOLDINGS LLC	265
HOAG MEMORIAL HOSPITAL PRESBYTERIAN	266
HOBBY LOBBY STORES, INC.	266
HOLY CROSS HEALTH, INC.	267
HONORHEALTH	267
HOOSIER ENERGY RURAL ELECTRIC COOPERATIVE INC	267
HORRY COUNTY SCHOOL DISTRICT	268
HOSPITAL OF THE UNIVERSITY OF PENNSYLVANIA	268
HOUCHENS INDUSTRIES, INC.	268
HOUGHTON MIFFLIN HARCOURT COMPANY	268
HOUSING DEVELOPMENT AUTHORITY, MICHIGAN STATE	270
HOUSTON INDEPENDENT SCHOOL DISTRICT	270
HOUSTON METHODIST ST. JOHN HOSPITAL	271
HOWARD COUNTY OF MARYLAND (INC)	271
HPS LLC	271
HUMBLE INDEPENDENT SCHOOL DISTRICT	271
HUNTER ROBERTS CONSTRUCTION GROUP LLC	271
HUNTINGTON HOSPITAL	271
HUNTSVILLE HOSPITAL HEALTH SYSTEM	272
HUNTSVILLE UTILITIES	272
HURON HEALTH CARE CENTER, INC	272
HY-VEE, INC.	272
HYUNDAI TRANSYS GEORGIA POWERTRAIN, INC.	273
ICE DATA SERVICES, INC.	273
IDEA PUBLIC SCHOOLS	274
IDEMIA IDENTITY & SECURITY USA LLC	274
IHC HEALTH SERVICES, INC.	274
ILLINOIS HOUSING DEVELOPMENT AUTHORITY (INC)	274
ILLINOIS STATE OF TOLL HIGHWAY AUTHORITY	275
ILWU-PMA BENEFIT PLANS	275
ILWU-PMA WELFARE TRUST	275
IMPERIAL IRRIGATION DISTRICT	275
INDEPENDENT PHARMACY COOPERATIVE	276
INDIANA UNIVERSITY	276
INFIRMARY HEALTH SYSTEM, INC.	276
INLAND COUNTIES REGIONAL CENTER, INC.	276
INNOVATIVE AG SERVICES CO.	276
INOVA HEALTH CARE SERVICES	277
INOVA HEALTH SYSTEM FOUNDATION	277
INSPUR SYSTEMS, INC.	277
INTEGRIS BAPTIST MEDICAL CENTER, INC.	277
INTEGRIS HEALTH, INC.	278
INTERMOUNTAIN HEALTH CARE INC	278
INTERNATIONAL RESCUE COMMITTEE, INC.	279
INTERNATIONAL WIRE GROUP, INC.	279
INVACARE CORPORATION (TW)	280
IOWA HEALTH SYSTEM	280
IOWA PHYSICIANS CLINIC MEDICAL FOUNDATION	280
IOWA STATE UNIVERSITY OF SCIENCE AND TECHNOLOGY	280
IRVINE UNIFIED SCHOOL DISTRICT	281
J M SMITH CORPORATION	281
J.E. DUNN CONSTRUCTION COMPANY	282
J.E. DUNN CONSTRUCTION GROUP, INC.	282
JACKSON ELECTRIC MEMBERSHIP CORPORATION	283
JACKSON HEALTHCARE, LLC	284
JACKSON-MADISON COUNTY GENERAL HOSPITAL DISTRICT	284
JACKSONVILLE ELECTRIC AUTHORITY	284
JACO OIL COMPANY	285
JARDEN LLC	286
JEFFERSON COUNTY SCHOOL DISTRICT NO. R-1	286
JERSEY CENTRAL POWER & LIGHT COMPANY	286
JEWISH COMMUNAL FUND	286
JFK HEALTH SYSTEM, INC.	286
JOBSOHIO BEVERAGE SYSTEM	287
JOHN C. LINCOLN HEALTH NETWORK	287
JOHN MUIR HEALTH	288
JOHNS HOPKINS ALL CHILDREN'S HOSPITAL, INC.	288
JOHNS HOPKINS BAYVIEW MEDICAL CENTER, INC.	289
JOHNS HOPKINS HEALTHCARE LLC	290
JOHNS HOPKINS HOSPITAL	290
JOHNS HOPKINS UNIVERSITY	290
JOHNSON & JOHNSON PATIENT ASSISTANCE FOUNDATION INC	291
JOHNSON CONTROLS FIRE PROTECTION LP	291
JOHNSON CONTROLS, INC.	291
JOINT SCHOOL DISTRICT NO. 28-J OF THE COUNTIES OF ADAMS AND ARAPAHOE	292
JORDAN SCHOOL DISTRICT	292
KADLEC REGIONAL MEDICAL CENTER	293
KAISER FDN HEALTH PLAN OF COLORADO	293
KAISER FOUNDATION HOSPITALS INC	294
KALEIDA HEALTH	294
KANSAS DEPARTMENT OF TRANSPORTATION	295
KANSAS STATE UNIVERSITY	296
KATY INDEPENDENT SCHOOL DISTRICT	296
KAWEAH DELTA HEALTH CARE DISTRICT GUILD	297
KECK HOSPITAL OF USC	297
KENNESTONE HOSPITAL AT WINDY HILL, INC.	297
KENNESTONE HOSPITAL INC	297
KERN HIGH SCHOOL DST	298
KETTERING ADVENTIST HEALTHCARE	298
KETTERING MEDICAL CENTER	299
KEY FOOD STORES CO-OPERATIVE, INC.	299
KEYSTOPS, LLC	299
KFHP OF THE MID-ATLANTIC STATES INC.	299
KGBO HOLDINGS, INC	299
KIEWIT BUILDING GROUP INC.	300
KIEWIT CORPORATION	300
KIEWIT INDUSTRIAL GROUP INC	300
KIEWIT INFRASTRUCTURE CO.	300
KIEWIT INFRASTRUCTURE SOUTH CO.	301
KIEWIT INFRASTRUCTURE WEST CO.	301
KILLEEN INDEPENDENT SCHOOL DISTRICT	301
KIMBALL HILL INC	301
KING COUNTY PUBLIC HOSPITAL DISTRICT 2	301
KING'S DAUGHTERS HEALTH SYSTEM, INC.	301
KIRBY - SMITH MACHINERY, INC.	302
KLEIN INDEPENDENT SCHOOL DISTRICT	302
KMM TELECOMMUNICATIONS	302
KNIGHTS OF COLUMBUS	302
KNOXVILLE UTILITIES BOARD	303
KOOTENAI HOSPITAL DISTRICT	303
KPH HEALTHCARE SERVICES, INC.	303
KRATON POLYMERS U.S. LLC	304
KRUEGER INTERNATIONAL, INC.	304
KWIK TRIP, INC.	305
LADENBURG THALMANN FINANCIAL SERVICES INC.	305
LAHEY CLINIC HOSPITAL, INC.	306
LAKE WASHINGTON SCHOOL DISTRICT	306
LAKELAND REGIONAL HEALTH SYSTEMS, INC.	306
LAKELAND REGIONAL MEDICAL CENTER, INC.	306
LAMEX FOODS INC.	307
LANE INDUSTRIES INCORPORATED	307
LEE MEMORIAL HEALTH SYSTEM FOUNDATION, INC.	307
LEE MEMORIAL HOSPITAL, INC.	308
LEGACY EMANUEL HOSPITAL & HEALTH CENTER	308
LEGACY HEALTH	309
LEHIGH GAS CORPORATION	309
LEHIGH VALLEY HEALTH NETWORK, INC.	310
LEHIGH VALLEY HOSPITAL-COORDINATED HEALTH ALLENTOWN	310
LELAND STANFORD JUNIOR UNIVERSITY	310
LENOX HILL HOSPITAL	312
LESTER E. COX MEDICAL CENTERS	312
LEVI STRAUSS & CO.	312
LEXA INTERNATIONAL CORPORATION	314
LEXINGTON COUNTY HEALTH SERVICES DISTRICT, INC.	314
LEXINGTON MEDICAL CENTER	314
LHH CORPORATION	315
LIBERTY UNIVERSITY, INC.	316
LIFEBRIDGE HEALTH, INC.	316
LIMETREE BAY TERMINALS LLC	316
LINCOLN MEDICAL AND MENTAL HEALTH CENTER	317
LOMA LINDA UNIVERSITY CHILDREN'S HOSPITAL	317
LOMA LINDA UNIVERSITY MEDICAL CENTER	317
LONG BEACH MEDICAL CENTER	318
LONG ISLAND JEWISH MEDICAL CENTER	318
LONG ISLAND POWER AUTHORITY	318
LOS ANGELES COUNTY OFFICE OF EDUCATION	319
LOS ANGELES DEPARTMENT OF WATER AND POWER	319
LOS ANGELES LOMOD CORPORATION	319
LOS ANGELES UNIFIED SCHOOL DISTRICT	320
LOUDOUN COUNTY	320
LOUDOUN COUNTY PUBLIC SCHOOL DISTRICT	320
LOUISIANA CHILDRENS MEDICAL CENTER, INC	320
LOUISVILLE-JEFFERSON COUNTY METRO GOVERNMENT	320
LOYOLA UNIVERSITY MEDICAL CENTER	321
LOYOLA UNIVERSITY MEDICAL CENTER	321
LOYOLA UNIVERSITY OF CHICAGO INC	321
LOZIER CORPORATION	322
LUCILE SALTER PACKARD CHILDREN'S HOSPITAL AT STANFORD	322
LUKOIL PAN AMERICAS, LLC	322
LUMINIS HEALTH ANNE ARUNDEL MEDICAL CENTER, INC	322
MAGELLAN PIPELINE COMPANY, L.P.	323
MAIMONIDES MEDICAL CENTER	323
MAIN LINE HEALTH SYSTEM	324
MAIN LINE HOSPITALS, INC.	324
MAINE MEDICAL CENTER	325
MAINEGENERAL HEALTH	325
MAINEHEALTH	325
MANAGEMENT & TRAINING CORPORATION	326
MANAGEMENT-ILA MANAGED HEALTH CARE TRUST FUND	326
MANN+HUMMEL FILTRATION TECHNOLOGY INTERMEDIATE HOLDINGS INC.	327
MAP INTERNATIONAL	327
MARICOPA COUNTY SPECIAL HEALTH CARE DISTRICT	327
MARINA DISTRICT DEVELOPMENT COMPANY, LLC	327
MARQUETTE UNIVERSITY	328
MARSHFIELD CLINIC, INC.	328

Companies Profiled (continued)

Company	Page
MARTIN MEMORIAL MEDICAL CENTER, INC.	329
MARTIN PRODUCT SALES LLC	329
MARTIN RESOURCE MANAGEMENT CORPORATION	329
MARTIN'S POINT HEALTH CARE, INC.	330
MARYLAND AND VIRGINIA MILK PRODUCERS COOPERATIVE ASSOCIATION, INCORPORATED	330
MARYLAND DEPARTMENT OF TRANSPORTATION	331
MARYLAND TRANSPORTATION AUTHORITY	331
MASHANTUCKET PEQUOT GAMING ENTERPRISE INC	331
MASS GENERAL BRIGHAM INCORPORATED	332
MASSACHUSETTS DEPARTMENT OF TRANSPORTATION	332
MASSACHUSETTS HOUSING FINANCE AGENCY	332
MASSACHUSETTS INSTITUTE OF TECHNOLOGY	333
MASSACHUSETTS PORT AUTHORITY	333
MASSACHUSETTS SCHOOL BUILDING AUTHORITY	334
MASSACHUSETTS WATER RESOURCES AUTHORITY	334
MAXIFACIAL DENTAL SURGERY	334
MAXIM HEALTHCARE SERVICES, INC.	334
MAYER ELECTRIC SUPPLY COMPANY, INC.	335
MAYO FOUNDATION FOR MEDICAL EDUCATION AND RESEARCH	336
MCAFEE CORP.	336
MCCARTHY BUILDING COMPANIES, INC.	336
MCCARTHY HOLDINGS, INC.	337
MCHS HOSPITALS INC	337
MCLANE COMPANY, INC.	337
MCLEOD REGIONAL MEDICAL CENTER OF THE PEE DEE, INC.	338
MCNAUGHTON-MCKAY ELECTRIC CO.	338
MED AMERICA HEALTH SYSTEMS CORPORATION	338
MEDCO, L.L.C.	339
MEDICAL CENTER OF THE ROCKIES	339
MEDICAL UNIVERSITY HOSPITAL AUTHORITY	339
MEDSTAR HEALTH, INC.	339
MEDSTAR-GEORGETOWN MEDICAL CENTER, INC.	340
MEGLOBAL AMERICAS INC.	340
MELLANOX TECHNOLOGIES, INC.	340
MEMORIAL HEALTH CARE SYSTEM, INC.	341
MEMORIAL HEALTH SERVICES	341
MEMORIAL HEALTH SERVICES GROUP RETURN	341
MEMORIAL HEALTH, INC.	342
MEMORIAL HERMANN HEALTH SYSTEM	342
MEMORIAL HOSPITAL FOR CANCER AND ALLIED DISEASES	342
MEMORIAL MEDICAL CENTER	342
MEMORIAL SLOAN-KETTERING CANCER CENTER	342
MENTOR GRAPHICS CORPORATION	343
MERCY CARE	344
MERCY CHILDREN'S HOSPITAL	344
MERCY GENERAL HEALTH PARTNERS	345
MERCY HEALTH	345
MERCY HEALTH	346
MERCY HEALTH CORPORATION	347
MERCY HEALTH PARTNERS	347
MERCY HEALTH SERVICES-IOWA, CORP.	347
MERCY HEALTH SERVICES-IOWA, CORP.	347
MERCY HEALTH SERVICES, INC.	347
MERCY HEALTH SYSTEM CORPORATION	347
MERCY HOSPITAL OKLAHOMA CITY, INC.	348
MERCY HOSPITAL SPRINGFIELD	348
MERCY HOSPITALS EAST COMMUNITIES	348
MERCY SCRIPPS HOSPITAL	348
MERCY WOODSTOCK MEDICAL CENTER	349
MERIDIAN HOSPITALS CORPORATION	349
MESA UNIFIED SCHOOL DISTRICT 4	349
MESSER CONSTRUCTION CO.	349
METALDYNE PERFORMANCE GROUP INC.	350
METHODIST HEALTH CARE SYSTEM	350
METHODIST HEALTHCARE- MEMPHIS HOSPITALS	350
METROHEALTH MEDICAL CENTER	351
METROPOLITAN EDISON COMPANY	351
METROPOLITAN GOVERNMENT OF NASHVILLE & DAVIDSON COUNTY	351
METROPOLITAN TRANSPORTATION AUTHORITY	351
METROPOLITAN WATER RECLAMATION DISTRICT OF GREATER CHICAGO	352
MFA INCORPORATED	353
MFA OIL COMPANY	353
MHM SUPPORT SERVICES	354
MIAMI CHILDREN'S HEALTH SYSTEM MANAGEMENT SERVICES, LLC	354
MIAMI UNIVERSITY	354
MIAMI VALLEY HOSPITAL	354
MIAMI-DADE AVIATION DEPARTMENT	355
MICHIGAN MILK PRODUCERS ASSOCIATION	356
MICHIGAN STATE UNIVERSITY	356
MID-AMERICA PIPELINE COMPANY, LLC	357
MIDCOAST ENERGY PARTNERS, L.P.	357
MIDDLESEX, COUNTY OF (INC)	357
MIDMICHIGAN MEDICAL CENTER-MIDLAND	357
MILES HEALTH CARE, INC	357
MILLS-PENINSULA HEALTH SERVICES	358
MILTON HERSHEY SCHOOL & SCHOOL TRUST	359
MILWAUKEE PUBLIC SCHOOLS (INC)	359
MINERS INCORPORATED	359
MINNEAPOLIS PUBLIC SCHOOL	359
MISSION HOSPITAL REGIONAL MEDICAL CENTER INC	360
MISSION HOSPITAL, INC.	360
MISSISSIPPI STATE UNIVERSITY	360
MISSOURI BAPTIST MEDICAL CENTER	361
MISSOURI CITY OF KANSAS CITY	361
MISSOURI DEPARTMENT OF TRANSPORTATION	361
MMR CONSTRUCTORS, INC.	362
MMR GROUP, INC.	362
MODERN WOODMEN OF AMERICA	362
MODIVCARE SOLUTIONS, LLC	363
MONMOUTH MEDICAL CENTER INC.	364
MONOGRAM FOOD SOLUTIONS, LLC	364
MONONGAHELA POWER COMPANY	365
MONSTER BEVERAGE 1990 CORPORATION	365
MONTEFIORE MEDICAL CENTER	366
MONTGOMERY COUNTY, MD	366
MONUMENT HEALTH RAPID CITY HOSPITAL, INC.	367
MORENO VALLEY UNIFIED SCHOOL DISTRICT	367
MORSE OPERATIONS, INC.	367
MORTON PLANT HOSPITAL ASSOCIATION, INC.	367
MOSAIC HEALTH SYSTEM	367
MOTION PICTURE INDUSTRY HEALTH PLAN	368
MOUNT CARMEL HEALTH PLAN MEDIG	368
MOUNT CARMEL HEALTH PLAN, INC.	368
MOUNT CARMEL HEALTH SYSTEM	368
MOUNT CARMEL HEALTH SYSTEM	368
MOUNT SINAI MEDICAL CENTER OF FLORIDA, INC.	369
MPHASIS CORPORATION	370
MULTI-COLOR CORPORATION	370
MULTICARE HEALTH SYSTEM	371
MUNICIPAL ELECTRIC AUTHORITY OF GEORGIA	371
MUNSON HEALTHCARE	372
MUNSON MEDICAL CENTER	373
MUNSTER MEDICAL RESEARCH FOUNDATION, INC	373
MV TRANSPORTATION, INC.	373
MVP HEALTH PLAN, INC.	374
MWH GLOBAL, INC.	374
NANA DEVELOPMENT CORPORATION	375
NANA REGIONAL CORPORATION, INC.,	375
NARRAGANSETT ELECTRIC COMP	375
NASSUA COUNTY INTERIM FINANCE AUTHORITY	376
NATIONAL ASSOCIATION OF LETTER CARRIERS	376
NATIONAL CHRISTIAN CHARITABLE FOUNDATION, INC.	376
NATIONAL COLLEGIATE ATHLETIC ASSOCIATION	376
NATIONAL GRAPE CO-OPERATIVE ASSOCIATION, INC.	377
NATIONAL RAILROAD PASSENGER CORPORATION	377
NATURAL GAS PIPELINE COMPANY OF AMERICA LLC	379
NAVIGATE AFFORDABLE HOUSING PARTNERS, INC	379
NAVY EXCHANGE SERVICE COMMAND	379
NCH CORPORATION	380
NEBRASKA PUBLIC POWER DISTRICT	381
NEVADA SYSTEM OF HIGHER EDUCATION	381
NEW ENGLAND PETROLEUM LIMITED PARTNERSHIP	382
NEW JERSEY TRANSPORTATION TRUST FUND AUTHORITY	382
NEW JERSEY TURNPIKE AUTHORITY INC	382
NEW PRIME, INC.	382
NEW WORLD FUND	383
NEW YORK CITY HEALTH AND HOSPITALS CORPORATION	383
NEW YORK CITY SCHOOL CONSTRUCTION AUTHORITY	384
NEW YORK CITY TRANSIT AUTHORITY	384
NEW YORK HOTEL TRADES COUNCIL AND HOTEL ASSOCIATION OF NEW YORK CITY HEALTH CENTER, INC.,	385
NEW YORK POWER AUTHORITY	385
NEW YORK PRESBYTERIAN HOSPITAL WEILL CORNELL UNIVERSITY MEDICAL CENTER	386
NEW YORK STATE CATHOLIC HEALTH PLAN, INC.	387
NEW YORK STATE ENERGY RESEARCH AND DEVELOPMENT AUTHORITY	387
NEW YORK STATE ENERGY RESEARCH AND DEVELOPMENT AUTHORITY	388
NEW YORK STATE HOUSING FINANCE AGENCY	388
NEW YORK UNIVERSITY	388
NEW YORK UNIVERSITY	389
NEWARK CORPORATION	389
NEWMARK & COMPANY REAL ESTATE, INC.	390
NEWPORT CORPORATION	390
NEWYORK-PRESBYTERIAN/BROOKLYN METHODIST	391
NEWYORK-PRESBYTERIAN/QUEENS	391
NFP CORP.	392
NHK INTERNATIONAL CORPORATION	392
NICHOLAS PROPERTIES & DEVELOPMENTS, INC.	392
NIELSEN HOLDINGS PLC	393
NOBLE HOLDING (U.S.) CORPORATION	393
NORTH ADVOCATE SIDE HEALTH NETWORK	393
NORTH AMERICAN LIGHTING, INC.	393
NORTH BROWARD HOSPITAL DISTRICT	394
NORTH CAROLINA BAPTIST HOSPITAL	394
NORTH CAROLINA BAPTIST HOSPITAL FDN	395
NORTH CAROLINA ELECTRIC MEMBERSHIP CORPORATION	395

xi

Companies Profiled (continued)

Company	Page
NORTH DAKOTA UNIVERSITY SYSTEM	395
NORTH EAST INDEPENDENT SCHOOL DISTRICT	395
NORTH MISSISSIPPI HEALTH SERVICES, INC.	396
NORTH MISSISSIPPI MEDICAL CENTER, INC.	396
NORTH SHORE UNIVERSITY HEALTH SYSTEM	397
NORTH SHORE UNIVERSITY HOSPITAL	397
NORTH SHORE-LONG ISLAND JEWISH HEALTH CARE	398
NORTH TEXAS MUNICIPAL WATER DISTRICT	398
NORTH TEXAS TOLLWAY AUTHORITY	398
NORTHEAST GEORGIA MEDICAL CENTER, INC.	398
NORTHEASTERN UNIVERSITY	399
NORTHERN INDIANA PUBLIC SERVICE COMPANY LLC	399
NORTHERN NATURAL GAS COMPANY	400
NORTHSIDE HOSPITAL, INC.	400
NORTHSIDE INDEPENDENT SCHOOL DISTRICT	401
NORTHWEST DAIRY ASSOCIATION	401
NORTHWEST FARM CREDIT SERVICES	401
NORTHWESTERN MEMORIAL HOSPITAL	402
NORTHWESTERN UNIVERSITY	402
NORTON HOSPITALS, INC	403
NOVA SOUTHEASTERN UNIVERSITY, INC.	403
NOVANT MEDICAL GROUP, INC.	403
NOVARTIS PHARMACEUTICALS CORPORATION	404
NOVO CONSTRUCTION, INC.	404
NPC RESTAURANT HOLDINGS, LLC	404
NUTRISYSTEM, INC.	405
OAKLAND UNIFIED SCHOOL DISTRICT	406
OCEAN SPRAY CRANBERRIES, INC.	406
OCHSNER CLINIC FOUNDATION	407
OCHSNER HEALTH SYSTEM	407
OHIO EDISON COMPANY	407
OHIO STATE UNIVERSITY PHYSICIANS, INC.	407
OHIOHEALTH CORPORATION	408
OHIOHEALTH CORPORATION GROUP RETURN	408
OHIOHEALTH RIVERSIDE METHODIST HOSPITAL	408
OKLAHOMA STATE UNIVERSITY	409
OLD CLAIMCO, LLC	409
OLD DURA, INC.	410
OMAHA PUBLIC POWER DISTRICT	410
OMAHA PUBLIC SCHOOLS	411
ONEOK PARTNERS, L.P.	411
ORANGE AND ROCKLAND UTILITIES, INC.	412
ORANGE COUNTY HEALTH AUTHORITY, A PUBLIC AGENCY	412
ORANGE COUNTY TRANSPORTATION AUTHORITY SCHOLARSHIP FOUNDATION, INC.	412
OREGON DEPARTMENT OF TRANSPORTATION	413
OREGON HEALTH & SCIENCE UNIVERSITY	413
OREGON STATE LOTTERY	414
OREGON UNIVERSITY SYSTEM	414
ORLANDO HEALTH, INC.	414
ORLEANS PARISH SCHOOL DISTRICT	415
OSF HEALTHCARE SYSTEM	415
OU MEDICINE, INC.	416
OUR LADY OF THE LAKE HOSPITAL, INC.	416
OVERLAKE HOSPITAL ASSOCIATION	417
OVERLAKE HOSPITAL MEDICAL CENTER	417
PACE UNIVERSITY	418
PACIFIC COAST PRODUCERS	418
PACIFIC PREMIER BANK	419
PAN AMERICAN HEALTH ORGANIZATION INC	419
PANDUIT CORP.	419
PAREXEL INTERNATIONAL CORPORATION	420
PARISH OF JEFFERSON	420
PARK NICOLLET CLINIC	421
PARKLAND COMMUNITY HEALTH PLAN, INC., A PROGRAM OF DALLAS COUNTY HOSPITAL	421
PARSONS ENVIRONMENT & INFRASTRUCTURE GROUP INC.	421
PASADENA HOSPITAL ASSOCIATION, LTD.	421
PASADENA INDEPENDENT SCHOOL DISTRICT	422
PATERSON PUBLIC SCHOOL DISTRICT	422
PCL CONSTRUCTION ENTERPRISES, INC.	422
PEACEHEALTH	423
PEDERNALES ELECTRIC COOPERATIVE, INC.	424
PENNSYLVANIA - AMERICAN WATER COMPANY	424
PENNSYLVANIA ELECTRIC COMPANY	424
PENNSYLVANIA HIGHER EDUCATION ASSISTANCE AGENCY	425
PENNSYLVANIA HOUSING FINANCE AGENCY	425
PENNSYLVANIA INTERGOVERNMENTAL COOPERATION AUTHORITY	425
PEPPER CONSTRUCTION COMPANY	426
PEPPER CONSTRUCTION GROUP, LLC	426
PERISHABLE DISTRIBUTORS OF IOWA, LTD.	426
PETER KIEWIT SONS', INC.	426
PETRO STAR INC.	428
PETROCARD, INC.	428
PETROLEUM TRADERS CORPORATION	429
PGA TOUR, INC.	429
PHILADELPHIA CONSOLIDATED HOLDING CORP.	429
PHOENIX CHILDREN'S HOSPITAL, INC.	430
PHYSICIAN AFFILIATE GROUP OF NEW YORK PC	430
PIEDMONT ATHENS REGIONAL MEDICAL CENTER, INC.	431
PIEDMONT HOSPITAL, INC.	431
PIGGLY WIGGLY ALABAMA DISTRIBUTING CO., INC.	432
PIH HEALTH WHITTIER HOSPITAL	432
PIKEVILLE MEDICAL CENTER, INC.	432
PILKINGTON NORTH AMERICA, INC.	433
PIMA COUNTY	433
PINNACLE HEALTH HOSPITAL	434
PITT COUNTY MEMORIAL HOSPITAL, INCORPORATED	434
PITTSBURGH SCHOOL DISTRICT	434
PLACID HOLDING COMPANY	434
PLACID REFINING COMPANY LLC	435
PLAINS COTTON COOPERATIVE ASSOCIATION	435
PLAINS PIPELINE, L.P.	435
PLAN INTERNATIONAL, INC.	436
PLAN INTERNATIONAL, INC.	436
PLANO INDEPENDENT SCHOOL DISTRICT	436
PLY GEM HOLDINGS, INC.	436
POLK COUNTY	437
POLK COUNTY SCHOOL DISTRICT	437
POPULATION SERVICES INTERNATIONAL	437
PORT NEWARK CONTAINER TERMINAL LLC	437
PORT OF LOS ANGELES	438
PORTLAND GENERAL ELECTRIC COMP	438
PORTLAND PUBLIC SCHOOLS	438
POUDRE VALLEY HEALTH CARE, INC.	438
POWERSOUTH ENERGY COOPERATIVE	439
PRAIRIE FARMS DAIRY, INC.	439
PRATT CORRUGATED HOLDINGS, INC.	440
PRATT INDUSTRIES, INC.	440
PRECISION CASTPARTS CORP.	441
PREMIER HEALTHCARE ALLIANCE, L.P.	443
PRESBYTERIAN HOSPITAL	443
PRESBYTERIAN MEDICAL CENTER OF THE UNIVERSITY OF PENNSYLVANIA HEALTH SYSTEM	443
PRINCE GEORGE'S COUNTY PUBLIC SCHOOLS	443
PRINCE WILLIAM COUNTY PUBLIC SCHOOLS	443
PRISMA HEALTH-UPSTATE	443
PRO PETROLEUM LLC	444
PRODUCE ALLIANCE, L.L.C.	444
PRODUCTION TECHNOLOGIES, INC.	444
PROMEGA CORPORATION	445
PROVIDENCE HEALTH & SERVICES	445
PROVIDENCE HEALTH & SERVICES - OREGON	446
PSCU INCORPORATED	446
PUBLIC EMPLOYEE RETIREMENT SYSTEM, IDAHO	447
PUBLIC HEALTH FOUNDATION ENTERPRISES INCORPORATED	447
PUBLIC HOSPITAL DISTRICT 1 OF KING COUNTY	447
PUBLIC UTILITY DISTRICT 1 OF CLARK COUNTY	447
PUBLIC UTILITY DISTRICT 1 OF SNOHOMISH COUNTY	448
PUBLISHING OFFICE, US GOVERNMENT	449
QUALITY OIL COMPANY, LLC	449
R. DIRECTIONAL DRILLING & UNDERGROUND TECHNOLOGY, INC.	449
R. E. MICHEL COMPANY, LLC	450
R. M. PARKS, INC.	450
R. R. DONNELLEY & SONS COMPANY	450
R.C. WILLEY HOME FURNISHINGS	451
RADY CHILDREN'S HOSPITAL AND HEALTH CENTER	452
RADY CHILDREN'S HOSPITAL-SAN DIEGO	452
RALEIGH DUKE HOSPITAL GUILD	453
RALEY'S	453
RAYMOND JAMES & ASSOCIATES INC	454
RAYMOURS FURNITURE COMPANY, INC.	454
RDO CONSTRUCTION EQUIPMENT CO.	455
READING HOSPITAL	455
READING HOSPITAL SERVICES INC	456
REALPAGE, INC.	456
RECKSON OPERATING PARTNERSHIP, L.P.	457
RECTOR & VISITORS OF THE UNIVERSITY OF VIRGINIA	457
REDEEMER HEALTH HOLY SYSTEM	458
REDNER'S MARKETS, INC.	458
REGAL ENTERTAINMENT GROUP	459
REGENTS OF THE UNIVERSITY OF MICHIGAN	459
REGIONAL CENTER OF THE EAST BAY, INC.	460
REGIONAL TRANSPORTATION AUTHORITY	460
REGIONS HOSPITAL	460
REGIONS HOSPITAL	460
REGIONS HOSPITAL FOUNDATION	460
RESEARCH TRIANGLE INSTITUTE INC	461
REX HEALTHCARE, INC.	462
REX HOSPITAL, INC.	462
RHODE ISLAND HOSPITAL	462
RICH PRODUCTS CORPORATION	462
RICHARDSON INDEPENDENT SCHOOL DISTRICT	463
RITE-HITE HOLDING CORPORATION	463
RIVER CITY PETROLEUM, INC.	463
RIVERSIDE HEALTHCARE ASSOCIATION, INC.	463
RIVERSIDE HOSPITAL, INC.	464
RIVERSIDE REGIONAL MEDIAL CENTER	464
RIVERSIDE UNIFIED SCHOOL DISTRICT	465
RIVERVIEW HOSPITAL	465
ROBERT BOSCH LLC	465
ROBERT W BAIRD & CO INC	466
ROBERT WOOD JOHNSON UNIVERSITY HOSPITAL, INC.	467

Companies Profiled (continued)

Company	Page
ROCHESTER CITY SCHOOL DISTRICT	467
ROCHESTER GAS AND ELECTRIC CORPORATION	467
ROCHESTER INSTITUTE OF TECHNOLOGY (INC)	468
ROCHESTER REGIONAL HEALTH	468
ROCKFORD PUBLIC SCHOOLS	469
ROPER ST. FRANCIS HEALTHCARE	469
ROUND ROCK INDEPENDENT SCHOOL DISTRICT (INC)	469
ROUSE'S ENTERPRISES, L.L.C.	470
RTW RETAILWINDS, INC.	470
RUDOLPH AND SLETTEN, INC.	471
RUSH UNIVERSITY MEDICAL CENTER	471
RWJ BARNABAS HEALTH, INC.	471
RYMAN HOSPITALITY PROPERTIES, INC.	472
S & B ENGINEERS AND CONSTRUCTORS, LTD.	474
SACRAMENTO CITY UNIFIED SCHOOL DISTRICT	474
SACRAMENTO MUNICIPAL UTILITY DISTRICT	475
SADDLE BUTTE PIPELINE LLC	475
SAINT AGNES MEDICAL CENTER	476
SAINT ALPHONSUS REGIONAL MEDICAL CENTER INC	476
SAINT ALPHONSUS REGIONAL MEDICAL CENTER, INC.	476
SAINT ELIZABETH MEDICAL CENTER, INC.	477
SAINT FRANCIS HEALTHCARE SYSTEM	477
SAINT FRANCIS HOSPITAL, INC.	477
SAINT JOSEPH HOSPITAL, INC	477
SAINT LOUIS UNIVERSITY	478
SAINT LUKE'S HEALTH SYSTEM, INC.	479
SAINT LUKE'S HOSPITAL OF BETHLEHEM, PENNSYLVANIA	479
SAINT LUKE'S HOSPITAL OF KANSAS CITY	479
SAINT MARYS HOSPITAL	479
SAINT PAUL PUBLIC SCHOOLS, DISTRICT 625	480
SALEM HEALTH	480
SALT RIVER PROJECT AGRICULTURAL IMPROVEMENT AND POWER DISTRICT	480
SAMARITAN HEALTH SERVICES, INC.	481
SAMARITAN'S PURSE	481
SAN ANTONIO INDEPENDENT SCHOOL DISTRICT FAC	482
SAN BERNARDINO CITY UNIFIED SCHOOL DISTRICT	482
SAN BERNARDINO COUNTY	482
SAN BERNARDINO COUNTY TRANSPORTATION AUTHORITY	482
SAN DIEGO UNIFIED SCHOOL DISTRICT	482
SAN JUAN UNIFIED SCHOOL DISTRICT	482
SANFORD	482
SANFORD BISMARCK	483
SANFORD HEALTH	483
SANFORD HEALTH	484
SANFORD NORTH	484
SANTA CLARA VALLEY TRANSPORTATION AUTHORITY	484
SAPP BROS., INC.	484
SARASOTA COUNTY PUBLIC HOSPITAL DISTRICT	484
SAVANNAH-CHATHAM COUNTY BOARD OF EDUCATION	485
SAVE THE CHILDREN FEDERATION, INC.	485
SCAI HOLDINGS, LLC	486
SCHAUMBOND GROUP, INC.	486
SCHOOL BOARD OF BREVARD COUNTY	486
SCHOOL BOARD OF BROWARD COUNTY, THE (INC)	486
SCHOOL BOARD OF ORANGE COUNTY FLORIDA	487
SCHOOL BOARD OF PALM BEACH COUNTY	487
SCHOOL DISTRICT 1 IN THE CITY AND COUNTY OF DENVER AND THE STATE OF COLORADO	487
SCHWAB CHARITABLE FUND	487
SCL HEALTH - FRONT RANGE, INC.	487
SCOTT & WHITE MEMORIAL HOSPITAL	488
SCOTT AND WHITE HEALTH PLAN	488
SCRIPPS HEALTH	488
SCRIPPS NETWORKS INTERACTIVE, INC.	489
SEACOR HOLDINGS INC.	490
SEALASKA CORPORATION	491
SEATTLE SCHOOLS DISTRICT NO. 1 OF KING COUNTY WASHINGTON	492
SECURITY FINANCE CORPORATION OF SPARTANBURG	492
SECURITY GROUP, INC.	492
SECURITY HEALTH PLAN OF WISCONSIN, INC.	493
SEMCO ENERGY, INC.	493
SEMINOLE ELECTRIC COOPERATIVE, INC.	493
SENTARA HEALTHCARE	494
SENTARA HOSPITALS - NORFOLK	495
SERVANT FOUNDATION	495
SERVCO PACIFIC INC.	495
SES HOLDINGS, LLC	496
SEVENTY SEVEN ENERGY LLC	496
SGT, LLC	497
SHAMROCK FOODS COMPANY	498
SHANDS JACKSONVILLE HEALTHCARE, INC.	498
SHANDS JACKSONVILLE MEDICAL CENTER, INC.	498
SHANDS TEACHING HOSPITAL AND CLINICS, INC.	499
SHARP HEALTHCARE	499
SHARP MEMORIAL HOSPITAL	500
SHAWMUT WOODWORKING & SUPPLY, INC.	500
SHAWNEE MISSION MEDICAL CENTER, INC.	501
SHEA HOMES LIMITED PARTNERSHIP, A CALIFORNIA LIMITED PARTNERSHIP	502
SHELL MEDICAL PLAN	502
SHI INTERNATIONAL CORP.	502
SHOESTRING VALLEY HOLDINGS INC.	503
SHRINERS HOSPITALS FOR CHILDREN	503
SIERRA NEVADA CORPORATION	503
SIGNATURE FINANCIAL LLC	504
SINAI HOSPITAL OF BALTIMORE, INC.	504
SISTERS OF CHARITY OF LEAVENWORTH HEALTH SYSTEM, INC.	504
SKANSKA USA CIVIL INC.	505
SKANSKA USA CIVIL NORTHEAST INC.	506
SKF USA INC.	506
SMDC MEDICAL CENTER	506
SMITHSONIAN INSTITUTION	507
SMMH PRACTICE PLAN, INC.	508
SNAKE RIVER SUGAR COMPANY	508
SNYDER'S-LANCE, INC.	508
SOCORRO INDEPENDENT SCHOOL DISTRICT	509
SOLSTICE HOLDINGS INC.	509
SOUTH BROWARD HOSPITAL DISTRICT	509
SOUTH CAROLINA PUBLIC SERVICE AUTHORITY (INC)	510
SOUTH FLORIDA WATER MANAGEMENT DISTRICT LEASING CORP.	511
SOUTH NASSAU COMMUNITIES HOSPITAL	511
SOUTH SHORE HOSPITAL, INC.	511
SOUTH TEXAS ELECTRIC COOPERATIVE, INC.	511
SOUTHCOAST HOSPITALS GROUP, INC.	511
SOUTHEAST PETRO DISTRIBUTORS, INC.	512
SOUTHERN BAPTIST HOSPITAL OF FLORIDA INC.	512
SOUTHERN CAL SCHOOLS VOL EMP BENEFITS ASSOC	512
SOUTHERN ILLINOIS HEALTHCARE ENTERPRISES, INC.	512
SOUTHERN ILLINOIS UNIVERSITY INC	513
SOUTHERN INDIANA GAS & ELECTRIC COMPANY	513
SOUTHERN METHODIST UNIVERSITY INC	514
SOUTHERN NATURAL GAS COMPANY, L.L.C.	514
SOUTHERN NEW HAMPSHIRE UNIVERSITY	514
SOUTHERN NUCLEAR OPERATING COMPANY, INC.	514
SOUTHLAND INDUSTRIES	515
SOUTHWEST RESEARCH INSTITUTE INC	515
SPARROW HEALTH SYSTEM	516
SPARTANBURG REGIONAL HEALTH SERVICES DISTRICT, INC.	516
SPECTRA ENERGY, LLC	517
SPIRE MISSOURI INC.	518
SPIRIT REALTY CAPITAL, INC.	518
SPOHN INVESTMENT CORPORATION	518
SPORTS, INC.	518
SPRING BRANCH INDEPENDENT SCHOOL DISTRICT (INC)	518
SPX FLOW, INC.	519
SRCTEC, LLC	519
SSM HEALTH CARE CORPORATION	520
ST BARNABAS MEDICAL CENTER (INC)	520
ST JOHN'S UNIVERSITY, NEW YORK	521
ST LUKE'S HOSPITAL OF KANSAS CITY	521
ST LUKES-ROOSEVELT INSTITUTE	521
ST. CHARLES HEALTH SYSTEM, INC.	521
ST. FRANCIS HOSPITAL, INC.	521
ST. FRANCIS HOSPITAL, ROSLYN, NEW YORK	522
ST. JOHN HEALTH SYSTEM, INC.	522
ST. JOHN HOSPITAL AND MEDICAL CENTER	523
ST. JOHN PROVIDENCE PHYSICIANS-CMG	523
ST. JOHN'S HOSPITAL OF THE HOSPITAL SISTERS OF THE THIRD ORDER OF ST. FRANCIS	523
ST. JOSEPH HEALTH SYSTEM	524
ST. JOSEPH HOSPITAL OF ORANGE	525
ST. JOSEPH HOSPITAL, INC.	525
ST. JOSEPH'S HEALTH PARTNERS LLC	525
ST. JOSEPH'S HOSPITAL HEALTH CENTER	526
ST. JOSEPH'S HOSPITAL, INC.	527
ST. JOSEPH'S UNIVERSITY MEDICAL CENTER INC	527
ST. JUDE HOSPITAL	527
ST. LOUIS CHILDREN'S HOSPITAL	528
ST. LUKE'S HEALTH NETWORK, INC.	528
ST. LUKE'S HEALTH SYSTEM, LTD.	528
ST. LUKE'S HOSPITAL & HEALTH NETWORK	529
ST. LUKE'S REGIONAL MEDICAL CENTER, LTD.	529
ST. LUKE'S UNIVERSITY HEALTH NETWORK	529
ST. MARY'S HEALTH, INC.	529
ST. PETER'S HEALTH CARE SERVICES	530
ST. PETER'S HEALTH PARTNERS	530
ST. TAMMANY PARISH SCHOOL BOARD	530
ST. VINCENT HOSPITAL OF THE HOSPITAL SISTERS OF THE THIRD ORDER OF ST. FRANCIS	531
STAN BOYETT & SON, INC.	531
STANFORD HEALTH CARE	531
STANFORD HEALTH SERVICES	531
STAPLE COTTON COOPERATIVE ASSOCIATION	532
STATE OF ALABAMA	532
STATE OF ALASKA	532
STATE OF ARIZONA	532
STATE OF ARKANSAS	532
STATE OF CALIFORNIA	533
STATE OF COLORADO	533
STATE OF DELAWARE	533
STATE OF GEORGIA	533
STATE OF HAWAII	533
STATE OF IDAHO	533

xiii

Companies Profiled (continued)

STATE OF ILLINOIS	533	TEMPLE UNIVERSITY HEALTH SYSTEM, INC.	558	THE GEISINGER CLINIC	583
STATE OF INDIANA	533	TEMPLE UNIVERSITY-OF THE COMMONWEALTH SYSTEM OF HIGHER EDUCATION	558	THE GEORGE WASHINGTON UNIVERSITY	583
STATE OF IOWA	534			THE GEORGETOWN UNIVERSITY	584
STATE OF KANSAS	534			THE GOLUB CORPORATION	584
STATE OF LOUISIANA	534	TENASKA ENERGY, INC.	559	THE HEALTH CARE AUTHORITY OF THE CITY OF HUNTSVILLE	585
STATE OF MAINE	534	TENERITY, INC.	559		
STATE OF MARYLAND	534	TERRACON CONSULTANTS, INC.	560	THE HENRY M JACKSON FOUNDATION FOR THE ADVANCEMENT OF MILITARY MEDICINE INC	585
STATE OF MICHIGAN	534	TESLA ENERGY OPERATIONS, INC.	560		
STATE OF MINNESOTA	534	TEXAS AROMATICS, LP	561		
STATE OF MISSISSIPPI	535	TEXAS CHILDREN'S HOSPITAL	561	THE HERTZ CORPORATION	585
STATE OF MISSOURI	535	TEXAS CHRISTIAN UNIVERSITY INC	562	THE INCOME FUND OF AMERICA INC	586
STATE OF MONTANA	535	TEXAS COUNTY AND DISTRICT RETIREMENT SYSTEM	563	THE INSTITUTE OF ELECTRICAL AND ELECTRONICS ENGINEERS INCORPORATED	586
STATE OF NEBRASKA	535				
STATE OF NEVADA	535	TEXAS DEPARTMENT OF HOUSING & COMMUNITY AFFAIRS	563		
STATE OF NEW HAMPSHIRE	535			THE JAMAICA HOSPITAL	586
STATE OF NEW YORK MORTGAGE AGENCY	536	TEXAS DEPARTMENT OF TRANSPORTATION	563	THE JOHNS HOPKINS HEALTH SYSTEM CORPORATION	587
STATE OF NORTH CAROLINA	536	TEXAS EASTERN TRANSMISSION, LP	563		
STATE OF NORTH DAKOTA	536	TEXAS HEALTH HARRIS METHODIST HOSPITAL FORT WORTH	563	THE LANCASTER GENERAL HOSPITAL	588
STATE OF OKLAHOMA	536			THE LANE CONSTRUCTION CORPORATION	588
STATE OF OREGON	537	TEXAS HEALTH RESOURCES	564	THE MARY IMOGENE BASSETT HOSPITAL	589
STATE OF RHODE ISLAND	537	TEXAS STATE UNIVERSITY SYSTEM	565	THE MASSACHUSETTS GENERAL HOSPITAL	589
STATE OF SOUTH CAROLINA	537	TEXAS WORKFORCE COMMISSION	565	THE MEDICAL COLLEGE OF WISCONSIN INC	590
STATE OF SOUTH DAKOTA	537	THE ADMINISTRATORS OF THE TULANE EDUCATIONAL FUND	565		
STATE OF TENNESSEE	537			THE MEDICAL UNIVERSITY OF SOUTH CAROLINA	590
STATE OF TEXAS	537	THE AEROSPACE CORPORATION	565		
STATE OF UTAH	538	THE AMALGAMATED SUGAR COMPANY LLC	566	THE METHODIST HOSPITAL	590
STATE OF VERMONT	538	THE AMERICAN ENDOWMENT FOUNDATION	567	THE METROHEALTH SYSTEM	591
STATE OF WASHINGTON	538			THE MICHAELS COMPANIES INC	592
STATE OF WEST VIRGINIA	538	THE ANDREW W MELLON FOUNDATION	567	THE MIDDLE TENNESSEE ELECTRIC MEMBERSHIP CORPORATION	594
STATE OF WISCONSIN	538	THE ASSOCIATED PRESS	567		
STATE UNIVERSITY OF NEW YORK	538	THE BIG TEN CONFERENCE INC	568	THE MITRE CORPORATION	594
STATEN ISLAND UNIVERSITY HOSPITAL	539	THE BLOOMBERG FAMILY FOUNDATION INC	568	THE NATURE CONSERVANCY	595
STEPHEN GOULD CORPORATION	540			THE NEBRASKA MEDICAL CENTER	595
STEVENS TRANSPORT, INC.	540	THE BOARD OF EDUCATION OF FAYETTE COUNTY	568	THE NEW JERSEY TRANSIT CORPORATION	596
STEWARD HEALTH CARE SYSTEM LLC	541			THE NEW SCHOOL	596
STEWART'S SHOPS CORP.	541	THE BOLDT GROUP INC	568	THE NEW YORK AND PRESBYTERIAN HOSPITAL	597
STILLWATER MINING COMPANY	542	THE BOND FUND OF AMERICA INC	569		
STOCKTON UNIFIED SCHOOL DISTRICT	542	THE BRIGHAM AND WOMEN'S HOSPITAL INC	569	THE NORTH CAROLINA MUTUAL WHOLESALE DRUG COMPANY	598
STORMONT-VAIL HEALTHCARE, INC.	543				
STRACK AND VAN TIL SUPER MARKET INC.	543	THE BROAD INSTITUTE INC	569	THE OHIO STATE UNIVERSITY WEXNER MEDICAL CENTER	598
SUASIN CANCER CARE INC.	543	THE CHARLES STARK DRAPER LABORATORY INC	570		
SUFFOLK CONSTRUCTION COMPANY, INC.	543			THE ORANGE COUNTY PUBLIC SCHOOL DISTRICT	598
SUMMA HEALTH SYSTEM	544	THE CHARLOTTE-MECKLENBURG HOSPITAL AUTHORITY	570		
SUN COAST RESOURCES, INC.	545			THE PARSONS CORPORATION	598
SUN MAR MANAGEMENT SERVICES	546	THE CHEROKEE NATION	571	THE PENNSYLVANIA HOSPITAL OF THE UNIVERSITY OF PENNSYLVANIA HEALTH SYSTEM	600
SUN VALLEY ENERGY, INC.	546	THE CHILDREN'S HOSPITAL CORPORATION	571		
SUNDT CONSTRUCTION, INC.	546	THE CHILDREN'S HOSPITAL OF ALABAMA	572		
SUNKIST GROWERS, INC.	546	THE CHILDREN'S HOSPITAL OF PHILADELPHIA FOUNDATION	572	THE PENNSYLVANIA STATE UNIVERSITY	601
SUNOCO PIPELINE L.P.	547			THE PEPPER COMPANIES INC	601
SUNTORY INTERNATIONAL	548	THE CHILDRENS HOSPITAL LOS ANGELES	572	THE PRESIDENT AND FELLOWS OF HARVARD COLLEGE	601
SUPERIOR COMMUNICATIONS, INC.	548	THE CHRIST HOSPITAL	572		
SUTTER BAY HOSPITALS	548	THE CITY OF SEATTLE-CITY LIGHT DEPARTMENT	573	THE PRIDDY FOUNDATION	602
SUTTER BAY MEDICAL FOUNDATION	549			THE PUBLIC HEALTH TRUST OF MIAMI-DADE COUNTY	602
SUTTER HEALTH	550	THE CLEVELAND CLINIC FOUNDATION	574		
SUTTER HEALTH PLAN	551	THE CLEVELAND ELECTRIC ILLUMINATING COMPANY	574	THE QUEEN'S HEALTH SYSTEMS	602
SUTTER HEALTH SACRAMENTO SIERRA REGION	551			THE REGENTS OF THE UNIVERSITY OF COLORADO	602
		THE COMMUNITY HOSPITAL GROUP INC	575		
SUTTER ROSEVILLE MEDICAL CENTER	551	THE CONLAN COMPANY	575	THE RESEARCH FOUNDATION FOR THE STATE UNIVERSITY OF NEW YORK	603
SUTTER VALLEY HOSPITALS	551	THE COOPER HEALTH SYSTEM A NEW JERSEY NON-PROFIT CORPORATION	575		
SUTTER VALLEY MEDICAL FOUNDATION	551			THE RUDOLPH/LIBBE COMPANIES INC	604
SWEDISH HEALTH SERVICES	551	THE CORE GROUP LTD	576	THE SAINT CLOUD HOSPITAL	604
SWEETWATER UNION HIGH SCHOOL DISTRICT	552	THE COUNTY OF BUCKS	576	THE SALVATION ARMY	604
		THE DANBURY HOSPITAL	576	THE SALVATION ARMY	604
SWINERTON BUILDERS	552	THE DAVID AND LUCILE PACKARD FOUNDATION	576	THE SAVANNAH COLLEGE OF ART AND DESIGN INC	604
SWINERTON INCORPORATED	553				
TA CHEN INTERNATIONAL, INC.	553	THE DCH HEALTH CARE AUTHORITY	577	THE SCHOOL BOARD OF MIAMI-DADE COUNTY	605
TACOMA PUBLIC SCHOOLS	554	THE DREES COMPANY	577		
TALEN ENERGY SUPPLY, LLC	554	THE EMPIRE DISTRICT ELECTRIC COMPANY	578	THE SCHOOL DISTRICT OF OSCEOLA COUNTY FLORIDA	605
TALLGRASS ENERGY, LP	554				
TARRANT COUNTY HOSPITAL DISTRICT	554	THE EVANGELICAL LUTHERAN GOOD SAMARITAN SOCIETY	579	THE SCHOOL DISTRICT OF PHILADELPHIA	605
TARRANT COUNTY TEXAS (INC)	555			THE SCHOOL DISTRICT OF WEST PALM BEACH COUNTY	605
TAUBER OIL COMPANY	555	THE FINISH LINE INC	580		
TECHNIP USA, INC	555	THE FIRST DISTRICT ASSOCIATION	580	THE SCOULAR COMPANY	605
TECUMSEH PRODUCTS COMPANY LLC	556	THE FISHEL COMPANY	580	THE SIMONS FOUNDATION INC	606
TEKNOR APEX COMPANY	556	THE FORD FOUNDATION	581	THE SOUTHEASTERN CONFERENCE	606
TEKSYSTEMS, INC.	557	THE FRESH MARKET INC	582	THE ST LUKE'S-ROOSEVELT HOSPITAL CENTER	606

Companies Profiled (continued)

Company	Page
THE STAMFORD HOSPITAL	606
THE SUNDERLAND FOUNDATION	607
THE SUNDT COMPANIES INC	607
THE TOWN OF SMITHTOWN	607
THE TRUSTEES OF COLUMBIA UNIVERSITY IN THE CITY OF NEW YORK	608
THE TRUSTEES OF PRINCETON UNIVERSITY	608
THE TURNER CORPORATION	608
THE UCLA FOUNDATION	610
THE UNITED ILLUMINATING COMPANY	610
THE UNIVERSITY OF CENTRAL FLORIDA BOARD OF TRUSTEES	610
THE UNIVERSITY OF CHICAGO MEDICAL CENTER	611
THE UNIVERSITY OF DAYTON	612
THE UNIVERSITY OF IOWA	612
THE UNIVERSITY OF IOWA	613
THE UNIVERSITY OF KANSAS HOSPITAL AUTHORITY	613
THE UNIVERSITY OF NORTH CAROLINA	613
THE UNIVERSITY OF NORTH CAROLINA HEALTH SYSTEM	613
THE UNIVERSITY OF TEXAS HEALTH SCIENCE CENTER AT SAN ANTONIO	614
THE UNIVERSITY OF TOLEDO	614
THE UNIVERSITY OF UTAH	615
THE UNIVERSITY OF VERMONT MEDICAL CENTER INC	616
THE UNIVERSITY OF VIRGINIA	616
THE VALLEY HOSPITAL INC	616
THE VANDERBILT UNIVERSITY	617
THE WALSH GROUP LTD	618
THE WASHINGTON UNIVERSITY	618
THE WHITING-TURNER CONTRACTING COMPANY	619
THEDACARE, INC.	619
THOMAS JEFFERSON UNIVERSITY	620
THOMAS JEFFERSON UNIVERSITY HOSPITALS, INC.	621
THOMPSON CREEK METALS COMPANY USA	621
THRUWAY AUTHORITY OF NEW YORK STATE	622
TMH PHYSICIAN ORGANIZATION	622
TMV CORP.	623
TOLEDO PROMEDICA HOSPITAL	623
TOM LANGE COMPANY, INC.	623
TORAY TCAC HOLDING USA INC.	623
TORRANCE HEALTH ASSOCIATION, INC.	624
TORRANCE MEMORIAL MEDICAL CENTER	624
TOWN OF HEMPSTEAD	624
TOWN OF NORTH HEMPSTEAD	624
TOWNSHIP OF WOODBRIDGE	625
TRAMMO, INC.	625
TRC COMPANIES, INC.	625
TRI STAR ENERGY, LLC	627
TRIBOROUGH BRIDGE & TUNNEL AUTHORITY	627
TRICON INTERNATIONAL, LTD.	628
TRINITY HEALTH CORPORATION	628
TRINITY HEALTH OF THE MID-ATLANTIC REGION	629
TRINITY HEALTH-MICHIGAN	629
TRINITY MOTHER FRANCES HEALTH SYSTEM FOUNDATION	629
TRUMAN ARNOLD COMPANIES	630
TRUMAN MEDICAL CENTER, INCORPORATED	630
TRUSTEES OF BOSTON COLLEGE	631
TRUSTEES OF DARTMOUTH COLLEGE	631
TRUSTEES OF INDIANA UNIVERSITY	632
TRUSTEES OF THE ESTATE OF BERNICE PAUAHI BISHOP	632
TRUSTEES OF THE UNIV OF PENNA RETIREE MED AND DEATH BENEFITS TRUST	633
TRUSTEES OF TUFTS COLLEGE	633
TRUVEN HOLDING CORP.	633
TSVC, INC.	634
TUDOR INVESTMENT CORPORATION	634
TUFTS MEDICAL CENTER, INC.	634
TURNER CONSTRUCTION COMPANY INC	634
TURNPIKE COMMISSION, PA	635
TURTLE & HUGHES, INC	635
U.S. GENERAL SERVICES ADMINISTRATION	636
U.S. VENTURE, INC.	637
UAW RETIREE MEDICAL BENEFITS TRUST	637
UC HEALTH, LLC.	637
UCH-MHS	638
UFCW & EMPLOYERS TRUST LLC	638
UFCW & EMPLOYERS TRUST LLC	639
UGI UTILITIES, INC.	639
UMASS MEMORIAL HEALTH CARE INC AND AFFILIATES GROUP RETURN	639
UMASS MEMORIAL MEDICAL CENTER, INC.	639
UMASS MEMORIAL MEDICAL CENTER, INC.	639
UNIFIED SCHOOL DISTRICT 259	639
UNIPRO FOODSERVICE, INC.	640
UNIQUE DESIGNS, INC.	640
UNITED CONCORDIA LIFE AND HEALTH INSURANCE COMPANY	640
UNITED COOPERATIVE	640
UNITED DAIRYMEN OF ARIZONA	641
UNITED FOOD AND COMMERCIAL WORKERS UNIONS AND FOOD EMPLOYERS BEN FUND	641
UNITED HEALTH SERVICES HOSPITALS, INC.	642
UNITED HOSPITAL INCORPORATED	642
UNITED SPACE ALLIANCE, LLC	642
UNIVERSITY COMMUNITY HOSPITAL, INC.	643
UNIVERSITY HEALTH CARE, INC.	643
UNIVERSITY HEALTH SYSTEM SERVICES OF TEXAS, INC.	643
UNIVERSITY HOSPITAL	644
UNIVERSITY HOSPITALS HEALTH SYSTEM, INC.	644
UNIVERSITY MEDICAL CENTER INC	645
UNIVERSITY MEDICAL CENTER MANAGEMENT CORPORATION	645
UNIVERSITY OF ALABAMA	646
UNIVERSITY OF ALABAMA HEALTH SERVICES FOUNDATION, P.C.	646
UNIVERSITY OF ARKANSAS SYSTEM	646
UNIVERSITY OF CALIFORNIA	647
UNIVERSITY OF CALIFORNIA, DAVIS	647
UNIVERSITY OF CALIFORNIA, LOS ANGELES	647
UNIVERSITY OF CALIFORNIA, SAN FRANCISCO FOUNDATION	648
UNIVERSITY OF CHICAGO	648
UNIVERSITY OF CINCINNATI	648
UNIVERSITY OF COLORADO	649
UNIVERSITY OF COLORADO HEALTH	649
UNIVERSITY OF COLORADO HOSPITAL AUTHORITY	649
UNIVERSITY OF DELAWARE	649
UNIVERSITY OF DENVER	650
UNIVERSITY OF FLORIDA	651
UNIVERSITY OF GEORGIA	651
UNIVERSITY OF HAWAI'I OF MANOA	652
UNIVERSITY OF HAWAII SYSTEM	652
UNIVERSITY OF HOUSTON SYSTEM	652
UNIVERSITY OF IOWA HOSPITALS AND CLINICS	653
UNIVERSITY OF LOUISIANA SYSTEM FOUNDATION	653
UNIVERSITY OF LOUISVILLE	653
UNIVERSITY OF MARYLAND MEDICAL SYSTEM CORPORATION	654
UNIVERSITY OF MARYLAND, COLLEGE PARK	655
UNIVERSITY OF MASSACHUSETTS INCORPORATED	655
UNIVERSITY OF MINNESOTA PHYSICIANS	656
UNIVERSITY OF MISSISSIPPI MEDICAL CENTER	656
UNIVERSITY OF MISSISSIPPI MEDICAL CENTER	656
UNIVERSITY OF MISSOURI HEALTH CARE	656
UNIVERSITY OF MISSOURI SYSTEM	656
UNIVERSITY OF NEVADA, RENO	657
UNIVERSITY OF NEW MEXICO	657
UNIVERSITY OF NORTH CAROLINA AT CHAPEL HILL	657
UNIVERSITY OF NORTH TEXAS SYSTEM	658
UNIVERSITY OF OREGON	658
UNIVERSITY OF PITTSBURGH-OF THE COMMONWEALTH SYSTEM OF HIGHER EDUCATION	659
UNIVERSITY OF SAN FRANCISCO INC	660
UNIVERSITY OF SOUTH ALABAMA	660
UNIVERSITY OF SOUTH FLORIDA	661
UNIVERSITY OF TENNESSEE	661
UNIVERSITY OF UTAH HEALTH HOSPITALS AND CLINICS	662
UNIVERSITY OF VERMONT & STATE AGRICULTURAL COLLEGE	662
UNIVERSITY OF VIRGINIA	663
UNIVERSITY OF WASHINGTON INC	663
UNIVERSITY OF WISCONSIN HOSPITALS AND CLINICS AUTHORITY	663
UNIVERSITY OF WISCONSIN MEDICAL FOUNDATION, INC.	664
UNIVERSITY OF WISCONSIN SYSTEM	664
UNIVERSITY SYSTEM OF MARYLAND	665
UNIVERSITY SYSTEM OF NEW HAMPSHIRE	666
UOFL HEALTH, INC.	667
UPMC	667
UPMC MAGEE-WOMENS HOSPITAL	667
UPMC PINNACLE HOSPITALS	668
UPMC PRESBYTERIAN SHADYSIDE	668
UPSTATE NIAGARA COOPERATIVE, INC.	668
URM STORES, INC.	668
US HEALTHCARE SYSTEM	669
USG CORPORATION	669
USS-UPI, LLC	669
UTAH STATE UNIVERSITY	670
UTI, (U.S.) HOLDINGS, INC.	670
VAL VERDE UNIFIED SCH DIS	671
VALLEY CHILDREN'S HEALTHCARE FOUNDATION	671
VALLEY CHILDREN'S HOSPITAL	671
VALLEY CHILDRENS HEALTH CARE	671
VALLEY HEALTH SYSTEM GROUP RETURN	671
VALUE DRUG COMPANY	671
VAN ATLAS LINES INC	672
VANDERBILT UNIVERSITY MEDICAL CENTER	672
VANGUARD CHARITABLE ENDOWMENT PROGRAM	673
VCC, LLC	673
VCU HEALTH SYSTEM AUTHORITY	673
VEONEER, INC.	673
VIBRANTZ CORPORATION	674
VICTORY INTERNATIONAL GROUP, LLC	674
VIRGINIA COLLEGE BUILDING AUTHORITY	674
VIRGINIA COMMONWEALTH UNIVERSITY	675
VIRGINIA DEPARTMENT OF TRANSPORTATION	675
VIRGINIA HOUSING DEVELOPMENT AUTHORITY	675
VIRGINIA INTERNATIONAL TERMINALS, LLC	675
VIRGINIA MASON MEDICAL CENTER	676
VIRGINIA POLYTECHNIC INSTITUTE & STATE UNIVERSITY	676
VIRGINIA PREMIER HEALTH PLAN, INC.	676
VIRTU FINANCIAL LLC	677
VIRTUA-WEST JERSEY HEALTH SYSTEM, INC.	677
VIZIO, INC.	677

xv

Companies Profiled (continued)

Company	Page
VNS CHOICE	677
W.S. BADCOCK CORPORATION	677
WAKE COUNTY PUBLIC SCHOOL SYSTEM	678
WAKE FOREST UNIVERSITY HEALTH SCIENCES	678
WAKE, COUNTY OF NORTH CAROLINA	678
WAKEFERN FOOD CORP.	678
WAKEMED	679
WALSH CONSTRUCTION COMPANY	680
WALTON CONSTRUCTION - A CORE COMPANY, LLC	680
WALTON FAMILY FOUNDATION INC	680
WASHINGTON HEALTHCARE PHYSICIANS, MARY	680
WASHINGTON HOSPITAL CENTER CORPORATION	681
WASHINGTON SUBURBAN SANITARY COMMISSION (INC)	681
WASHOE COUNTY SCHOOL DISTRICT	681
WELCH FOODS INC., A COOPERATIVE	681
WELLMONT HEALTH SYSTEM	682
WELLS REAL ESTATE INVESTMENT TRUST II	683
WELLSPAN MEDICAL GROUP	683
WESCO AIRCRAFT HOLDINGS, INC.	683
WESLEY MEDICAL CENTER, LLC	684
WEST PENN POWER COMPANY	684
WEST VIRGINIA UNIVERSITY HOSPITALS, INC.	684
WEST VIRGINIA UNITED HEALTH SYSTEM, INC.	684
WEST VIRGINIA UNIVERSITY	685
WEST VIRGINIA UNIVERSITY	685
WESTCHESTER COUNTY HEALTH CARE CORPORATION	686
WESTERN FARMERS ELECTRIC COOPERATIVE	686
WESTERN GOVERNORS UNIVERSITY	687
WESTERN OREGON UNIVERSITY	687
WGL HOLDINGS, INC.	687
WHEATON FRANCISCAN SERVICES, INC.	688
WHITE PLAINS HOSPITAL MEDICAL CENTER	688
WHOLE FOODS MARKET, INC.	688
WILBUR-ELLIS HOLDINGS II, INC.	690
WILLIAM BEAUMONT HOSPITAL	691
WILMINGTON TRUST COMPANY	691
WINCO HOLDINGS, INC.	691
WIPRO, LLC	691
WISCONSIN MILWAUKEE COUNTY	692
WORLD WIDE TECHNOLOGY HOLDING CO., LLC	692
WORLD WIDE TECHNOLOGY, LLC	692
WORLEY & OBETZ, INC.	693
WTG GAS PROCESSING, L.P.	693
XMED OXYGEN & MEDICAL EQUIPMENT, LP	693
YAKIMA VALLEY MEMORIAL HOSPITAL ASSOCIATION INC	693
YALE NEW HAVEN HEALTH SERVICES CORPORATION	694
YALE NEW HAVEN HOSPITAL, INC.	694
YALE UNIVERSITY	695
YATES GROUP, INC.	695
YORK HOSPITAL	696
ZEN-NOH GRAIN CORPORATION	696

About Hoover's Handbook of Private Companies 2023

Finding current relevant information about nonpublic companies can be a challenge, as many of these organizations see secrecy as a competitive strategy. In this edition of Hoover's Handbook of Private Companies, we have done for you the tough work of compiling these hard-to-find facts.

We consider this volume to be one of the premier sources of business information on privately held enterprises in the US. It features the facts on 900 of the largest and most influencial of those enterprises. Entries feature overviews of company operations, up to five years of financial information, product information, and lists of company executives as found in Hoover's huge database of company information. Some larger and more visable companies will feature an additional History section.

HOOVER'S ARCHIVES FOR BUSINESS NEEDS

In addition to the 2,550 companies featured in our handbooks, comprehensive coverage of more than 6 years of Hoovers Books are published in the Hoovers Archives.. Our goal is to provide one site that offers authoritative, updated intelligence on US and global companies, industries, and the people who shape them. Stay with the Hoovers family of products and History and package the books with the archives products.

We welcome the recognition we have received as a provider of high-quality company information — online, electronically, and in print — and continue to look for ways to make our products more available and more useful to you.

Hoover's Handbook of Private Companies is one of our four-title series of handbooks that covers, literally, the world of business. The series is available as an indexed set, and also includes Hoover's Handbook of American Business, Hoover's Handbook of World Business, and Hoover's Handbook of Emerging Companies. This series brings you information on the biggest, fast-growing, and most influential enterprises in the world.

We believe that anyone who buys from, sells to, invests in, lends to, competes with, interviews with, or works for a company should know all there is to know about that enterprise. Taken together, this book and the other Hoover's products and resources represent the most complete source of basic corporate information readily available to the general public.

HOW TO USE THIS BOOK

This book has four sections:

1. "Using Hoover's Handbooks" describes the contents of our profiles and explains the ways in which we gather and compile our data.

2. "A List-Lover's Compendium" contains lists of the largest and fastest-growing private companies. The lists are based on the information in our profiles, or compiled from well-known sources.

3. The company profiles section makes up the largest and most important part of the book — 900 profiles of major private enterprises, arranged alphabetically.

4. Three indexes complete the book. The first sorts companies by industry groups, the second by headquarters location. The third index is a list of all the executives found in the Executives section of each company profile.

Using Hoover's Handbooks

SELECTION OF THE COMPANIES PROFILED

The 900 enterprises profiled in this book include the largest and most influential companies in America. Among them are:
- private companies, from the giants (Cargill and Koch) to the colorful and prominent (Bad Boy Entertainment and L.L. Bean)
- mutuals and cooperative organizations owned by their customers (State Farm Insurance, Ace Hardware, Ocean Spray Cranberries)
- not-for-profits (Red Cross, Kaiser Permanente, Smithsonian Institution)
- joint ventures (Motiva Enterprises, Dow Corning)
- partnerships (PricewaterhouseCoopers, Baker & McKenzie)
- universities (Columbia, Harvard, University of California)
- government-owned corporations (US Postal Service and New York City's Metropolitan Transportation Authority)
- and a selection of other enterprises (National Basketball Association, AFL-CIO, Texas Lottery Commission).

ORGANIZATION

The profiles are presented in alphabetical order. You will find the commonly used name of the enterprise at the beginning of the profile; the full, legal name is found in the Locations section. If a company name is also a person's name, such as Henry Ford Health System or Mary Kay, it will be alphabetized under the first name; if the company name starts with initials, for example, L.L. Bean or S.C. Johnson, look for it under the combined initials (in the above examples, LL and SC, respectively).

Basic financial data are listed under the heading Historical Financials. The annual financial information contained in the profiles is current through fiscal year-ends occuring as late as January 2022. We have included certain nonfinancial developments , such as officer changes, through January 2022.

OVERVIEW

In the first section of the profile, we have tried to give a thumbnail description of the company and what it does. The description will usually include information on the company's strategy, reputation, and ownership. We recommend that you read this section first.

HISTORY

This extended section, which is available for some of the larger and more well-known companies, reflects our belief that every enterprise is the sum of its history and that you have to know where you came from in order to know where you are going. While some companies have limited historical awareness, we think the vast majority of the enterprises in this book have colorful backgrounds. We have tried to focus on the people who made the enterprises what they are today. We have found these histories to be full of twists and ironies; they make fascinating reading.

EXECUTIVES

Here we list the names of the people who run the company, insofar as space allows. In the few cases where available, we have shown the ages and pay of key officers. In some instances the published data is for the previous year, although the company has announced promotions or retirements since year-end. The pay represents cash compensation, including bonuses, but excludes stock option programs.

Although companies are free to structure their management titles any way they please, most modern corporations follow standard practices. The ultimate power in any corporation lies with the shareholders, who elect a board of directors, usually including officers or "insiders" as well as individuals from outside the company. The chief officer, the person on whose desk the buck stops, is usually called the chief executive officer (CEO). Often, he or she is also the chairman of the board.

As corporate management has become more complex, it is common for the CEO to have a "right-hand person" who oversees the day-to-day operations of the company, allowing the CEO plenty of time to focus on strategy and long-term issues. This right-hand person is usually designated the chief operating officer (COO) and is often the president of the company. In other cases one person is both chairman and president.

A multitude of other titles exists, including chief financial officer (CFO), chief administrative officer, and vice chairman. We have always tried to include the CFO, the chief legal officer, and the chief human resources or personnel officer.

The people named in the Executives section are indexed at the back of the book.

The Executives section also includes the name of the company's auditing (accounting) firm, where available.

LOCATIONS

Here we include the company's full legal name and its headquarters, street address, telephone and fax numbers, and Web site, as available. The back of the book includes an index of companies by headquarters locations.

In some cases we have also included information on the geographic distribution of the company's business, including sales and profit data. Note that these profit numbers, like those in the Products/Operations section below, are usually operating or pretax profits rather than net profits. Operating profits are generally those before financing costs (interest income and payments) and before taxes, which are considered costs attributable to the whole company rather than to one division or part of the world. For this reason the net income figures (in the Historical Financials section) are usually much lower, since they are after interest and taxes. Pretax profits are after interest but before taxes.

Headquarters for companies that are incorporated in Bermuda, but whose operational headquarters are in the US, are listed under their US address.

PRODUCTS/OPERATIONS

This section contains selected lists of products, services, brand names, divisions, subsidiaries, and joint venture. We have tried to include a company's major lines and most familiar brand names.

The nature of this section varies by company and the amount of information contained in Hoover's storehouse of business information. If the company publishes sales and profit information by type of business, we have included it.

COMPETITORS

In this section we have listed companies that compete with the profiled company. This feature is included as a quick way to locate similar companies and compare them. The universe of competitors includes all public companies and all private companies with sales in excess of $500 million. In a few instances we have identified smaller private companies as key competitors.

HISTORICAL FINANCIALS

Here we have tried to present as much data about each enterprise's financial performance as we could compile in the allocated space. The information varies somewhat from industry to industry and is less complete in the case of private companies that do not release data. (We have always tried to provide annual sales and employment, although in some instances those numbers are simply not available). There are a few industries, venture capital and investment banking, for example, for which revenue numbers are not reported as a rule. In the case of private companies that do not publicly disclose financial information, we have statistics when reliable sources are available.

The following information is generally present.

A five-year table, with relevant annualized compound growth rates, covers:
- Sales — fiscal year sales (year-end assets for most financial companies)
- Net income — fiscal year net income (before accounting changes)
- Net profit margin — fiscal year net income as a percent of sales (as a percent of assets for most financial firms)
- Employees — fiscal year-end or average number of employees

The information on the number of employees is intended to aid the reader interested in knowing whether a company has a long-term trend of increasing or decreasing employment. As far as we know, we are the only company that publishes this information in print format.

The numbers on the left in each row of the Historical Financials section give the month and the year in which the company's fiscal year actually ends. Thus, a company with a March 31, 2020, year-end is shown as 3/20. The last item in the Financials section is a graph, which for private companies shows net income, or, if that is unavailable, sales.

Key year-end statistics are included in this section for insurance companies and companies required to file reports with the SEC. They generally show the financial strength of the enterprise, including:
- Debt ratio (long-term debt as a percent of shareholders' equity)
- Return on equity (net income divided by the average of beginning and ending common shareholders' equity)
- Cash and cash equivalents
- Current ratio (ratio of current assets to current liabilities)
- Total long-term debt (including capital lease obligations)
- Fiscal year sales for financial institutions

Hoover's Handbook of Private Companies

A List-Lover's Compendium

The 300 Largest Private Companies by Sales 2023

Rank	Company	Sales ($mil.)
1	STATE OF CALIFORNIA	$255,725
2	CHINESE HOSPITAL ASSOCIATION	$226,958
3	STATE OF TEXAS	$115,336
4	CITY OF NEW YORK	$109,744
5	COMMONWEALTH OF VIRGINIA	$62,826
6	ALBERTSONS COMPANIES, INC.	$62,455
7	STATE OF ILLINOIS	$62,451
8	STATE OF GEORGIA	$55,707
9	STATE OF MICHIGAN	$54,684
10	COMMONWEALTH OF MASSACHUSETTS	$53,391
11	STATE OF WASHINGTON	$50,993
12	STATE OF MINNESOTA	$50,689
13	NOVARTIS PHARMACEUTICALS CORPORATION	$49,436
14	STATE OF NORTH CAROLINA	$48,977
15	STATE OF MARYLAND	$48,269
16	MCLANE COMPANY, INC.	$48,016
17	UNIVERSITY OF CALIFORNIA	$38,895
18	STATE OF WISCONSIN	$38,601
19	DHPC TECHNOLOGIES, INC.	$38,584
20	STATE OF INDIANA	$38,553
21	STATE OF LOUISIANA	$37,825
22	STATE OF ARIZONA	$37,221
23	JOHNSON CONTROLS, INC.	$37,179
24	STATE OF OREGON	$36,855
25	COMMONSPIRIT HEALTH	$33,907
26	STATE OF TENNESSEE	$32,194
27	COUNTY OF WYOMING	$32,004
28	COUNTY OF LOS ANGELES	$31,698
29	STATE OF ALABAMA	$31,016
30	COMMONWEALTH OF KENTUCKY	$28,942
31	STATE OF MISSOURI	$27,080
32	STATE OF OKLAHOMA	$24,377
33	UPMC	$24,366
34	STATE OF COLORADO	$22,949
35	ASCENSION HEALTH ALLIANCE	$22,633
36	STATE OF ARKANSAS	$22,391
37	STATE OF IOWA	$21,950
38	CANDID COLOR SYSTEMS, INC.	$21,742
39	FERGUSON ENTERPRISES, LLC	$21,477
40	STATE OF SOUTH CAROLINA	$21,191
41	STATE OF MISSISSIPPI	$20,826
42	BNSF RAILWAY COMPANY	$20,747
43	U.S. GENERAL SERVICES ADMINISTRATION	$20,457
44	STATE OF UTAH	$19,735
45	CONSTELLATION ENERGY GENERATION, LLC	$19,649
46	STATE OF KANSAS	$19,473
47	GOVERNMENT OF DISTRICT OF COLUMBIA	$16,510
48	WHOLE FOODS MARKET, INC.	$16,030
49	ADVENTIST HEALTH SYSTEM/SUNBELT, INC.	$14,882
50	KAISER FOUNDATION HOSPITALS INC	$14,795
51	PROVIDENCE HEALTH & SERVICES	$14,433
52	SUTTER HEALTH	$14,225
53	GENERAL ELECTRIC INTERNATIONAL, INC.	$14,100
54	LELAND STANFORD JUNIOR UNIVERSITY	$13,939
55	STATE OF NEVADA	$13,855
56	DAIRY FARMERS OF AMERICA, INC.	$13,528
57	STATE OF HAWAII	$13,450
58	STATE OF NEBRASKA	$13,356
59	TEXAS DEPARTMENT OF TRANSPORTATION	$12,965
60	BAYLOR SCOTT & WHITE HOLDINGS	$12,718
61	BRISBANE SCHOOL DISTRICT	$12,636
62	STATE OF IDAHO	$12,566
63	STATE OF WEST VIRGINIA	$12,469
64	THE CLEVELAND CLINIC FOUNDATION	$12,440
65	STATE OF ALASKA	$12,421
66	ZEN-NOH GRAIN CORPORATION	$12,392
67	ALLEGIS GROUP, INC.	$12,269
68	STATE OF MAINE	$12,227
69	HY-VEE, INC.	$12,182
70	WAKEFERN FOOD CORP.	$11,871
71	KIEWIT CORPORATION	$11,826
72	BAYLOR SCOTT & WHITE HEALTH	$11,704
73	MASS GENERAL BRIGHAM INCORPORATED	$11,665
74	PETER KIEWIT SONS', INC.	$11,220
75	STATE OF DELAWARE	$10,960
76	BON SECOURS MERCY HEALTH, INC.	$10,877
77	INTERMOUNTAIN HEALTH CARE INC	$10,752
78	THE TURNER CORPORATION	$10,523
79	TURNER CONSTRUCTION COMPANY INC	$10,516
80	ROBERT BOSCH LLC	$10,474
81	BANNER HEALTH	$10,397
82	CAMERON INTERNATIONAL CORPORATION	$10,381
83	SHI INTERNATIONAL CORP.	$10,372
84	TMV CORP.	$10,309
85	TRICON INTERNATIONAL, LTD.	$10,239
86	LIMETREE BAY TERMINALS LLC	$10,048
87	EQUINOR MARKETING & TRADING (US) INC.	$9,959
88	DIGNITY HEALTH	$9,916
89	THE NEW YORK AND PRESBYTERIAN HOSPITAL	$9,859
90	ASSOCIATED WHOLESALE GROCERS, INC.	$9,703
91	NEW YORK CITY HEALTH AND HOSPITALS CORPORATION	$9,550
92	ALTICOR INC.	$9,459
93	LOS ANGELES UNIFIED SCHOOL DISTRICT	$9,378
94	TRUSTEES OF THE UNIV OF PENNA RETIREE MED AND DEATH BENEFITS TRUST	$9,337
95	COREWELL HEALTH	$9,179
96	FLORIDA DEPARTMENT OF LOTTERY	$9,083
97	ONEOK PARTNERS, L.P.	$8,918
98	SENTARA HEALTHCARE	$8,861
99	THE HERTZ CORPORATION	$8,803
100	THE PRIDDY FOUNDATION	$8,791
101	CHEVRON PHILLIPS CHEMICAL COMPANY LLC	$8,769
102	IHC HEALTH SERVICES, INC.	$8,693
103	JARDEN LLC	$8,603
104	ALLIED UNIVERSAL HOLDCO LLC	$8,501
105	NEW YORK UNIVERSITY	$8,500
106	CITY & COUNTY OF SAN FRANCISCO	$8,453
107	OCHSNER CLINIC FOUNDATION	$8,405
108	SOLSTICE HOLDINGS INC.	$8,235
109	THE JOHNS HOPKINS HEALTH SYSTEM CORPORATION	$8,155
110	U.S. VENTURE, INC.	$8,076
111	UPMC PRESBYTERIAN SHADYSIDE	$8,046
112	ADVANCED TECHNOLOGY INTERNATIONAL	$8,017
113	REGENTS OF THE UNIVERSITY OF MICHIGAN	$7,955
114	STATE OF VERMONT	$7,942
115	THE PENNSYLVANIA STATE UNIVERSITY	$7,867
116	STATE OF NORTH DAKOTA	$7,860
117	CFJ PROPERTIES LLC	$7,672
118	R. DIRECTIONAL DRILLING & UNDERGROUND TECHNOLOGY, INC.	$7,667
119	COMPUTER SCIENCES CORPORATION	$7,607
120	STATE OF NEW HAMPSHIRE	$7,599
121	STATE OF RHODE ISLAND	$7,547
122	GROWMARK, INC.	$7,541
123	THE CHARLOTTE-MECKLENBURG HOSPITAL AUTHORITY	$7,510
124	MERCY HEALTH	$7,469
125	JOHNS HOPKINS UNIVERSITY	$7,446
126	FEDERAL-MOGUL HOLDINGS LLC	$7,434
127	MEMORIAL HERMANN HEALTH SYSTEM	$7,358
128	MEDSTAR HEALTH, INC.	$7,279
129	CITY OF LOS ANGELES	$7,196
130	GEISINGER HEALTH	$7,121
131	CHEVRON PHILLIPS CHEMICAL COMPANY LP	$7,106
132	CGB ENTERPRISES, INC.	$7,081
133	PRECISION CASTPARTS CORP.	$7,002
134	EATON CORPORATION	$6,925
135	STATE OF MONTANA	$6,740
136	WORLD WIDE TECHNOLOGY HOLDING CO., LLC	$6,702
137	CITY OF PHILADELPHIA	$6,646
138	UNIVERSITY OF WASHINGTON INC	$6,570
139	SSM HEALTH CARE CORPORATION	$6,497
140	ALLY BANK	$6,427
141	MEMORIAL SLOAN-KETTERING CANCER CENTER	$6,398
142	PUBLIC EMPLOYEE RETIREMENT SYSTEM, IDAHO	$6,177
143	NIELSEN HOLDINGS PLC	$6,172
144	FAIRVIEW HEALTH SERVICES	$6,123
145	THE SCOULAR COMPANY	$6,004
146	STATE OF SOUTH DAKOTA	$5,968
147	STATE UNIVERSITY OF NEW YORK	$5,961
148	WORLD WIDE TECHNOLOGY, LLC	$5,927
149	AEROTEK AFFILIATED SERVICES, INC.	$5,859
150	HENRY FORD HEALTH SYSTEM	$5,853
151	THE TRUSTEES OF COLUMBIA UNIVERSITY IN THE CITY OF NEW YORK	$5,827
152	UNIVERSITY OF COLORADO HEALTH	$5,781
153	METROPOLITAN TRANSPORTATION AUTHORITY	$5,775
154	ADVOCATE HEALTH AND HOSPITALS CORPORATION	$5,672
155	ALASKA PERMANENT FUND CORPORATION, AN INSTRUMENTALITY OF THE STATE OF ALASKA	$5,671
156	HILL FIRE PROTECTION, LLC	$5,669
157	CHALMETTE REFINING, L.L.C.	$5,647
158	LEVI STRAUSS & CO.	$5,575
159	STANFORD HEALTH CARE	$5,567
160	BOARD OF REGENTS OF THE UNIVERSITY SYSTEM OF GEORGIA	$5,523
161	THE WHITING-TURNER CONTRACTING COMPANY	$5,522
162	FAIRFAX COUNTY VIRGINIA	$5,420
163	ACE HARDWARE CORPORATION	$5,388
164	HENSEL PHELPS CONSTRUCTION CO.	$5,334
165	AURORA HEALTH CARE, INC.	$5,334
166	AIRGAS, INC.	$5,304
167	NEW YORK STATE CATHOLIC HEALTH PLAN, INC.	$5,304
168	HOUSTON METHODIST ST. JOHN HOSPITAL	$5,302
169	BOARD OF EDUCATION OF CITY OF CHICAGO	$5,272
170	THE MICHAELS COMPANIES INC	$5,271
171	COUNTY OF ORANGE	$5,065
172	MARYLAND DEPARTMENT OF TRANSPORTATION	$5,058
173	UAW RETIREE MEDICAL BENEFITS TRUST	$5,050
174	R. R. DONNELLEY & SONS COMPANY	$4,963
175	ST. JOSEPH HEALTH SYSTEM	$4,955
176	VANDERBILT UNIVERSITY MEDICAL CENTER	$4,930
177	PLACID REFINING COMPANY LLC	$4,929
178	PLACID HOLDING COMPANY	$4,929
179	SPECTRA ENERGY, LLC	$4,916
180	GILBANE BUILDING COMPANY	$4,899
181	UNIVERSITY OF MARYLAND MEDICAL SYSTEM CORPORATION	$4,893
182	MONTGOMERY COUNTY, MD	$4,888
183	SCHWAB CHARITABLE FUND	$4,885
184	MERCY HEALTH	$4,860
185	TAUBER OIL COMPANY	$4,831
186	SANFORD HEALTH	$4,819
187	TEKSYSTEMS, INC.	$4,815
188	BATTELLE MEMORIAL INSTITUTE	$4,775
189	LUKOIL PAN AMERICAS, LLC	$4,745
190	MCCARTHY BUILDING COMPANIES, INC.	$4,706
191	BEAUMONT HEALTH	$4,695
192	BALFOUR BEATTY, LLC	$4,690
193	TEXAS HEALTH RESOURCES	$4,688
194	BIOURJA TRADING, LLC	$4,622
195	DUKE UNIVERSITY	$4,611
196	SHAMROCK FOODS COMPANY	$4,602
197	HOBBY LOBBY STORES, INC.	$4,544
198	COUNTY OF RIVERSIDE	$4,539
199	NEW YORK PRESBYTERIAN HOSPITAL WEILL CORNELL UNIVERSITY MEDICAL CENTER	$4,505
200	THE METHODIST HOSPITAL	$4,496
201	DUKE UNIVERSITY HEALTH SYSTEM, INC.	$4,483
202	THE SCHOOL BOARD OF MIAMI-DADE COUNTY	$4,458
203	MCCARTHY HOLDINGS, INC.	$4,440
204	THE WASHINGTON UNIVERSITY	$4,435
205	ADVENTIST HEALTH SYSTEM/WEST, CORPORATION	$4,434
206	SANFORD	$4,411
207	THE PRESIDENT AND FELLOWS OF HARVARD COLLEGE	$4,408

SOURCE: MERGENT INC., DATABASE, APRIL 2023

The 300 Largest Private Companies by Sales 2023 (continued)

Rank	Company	Sales ($mil.)
208	KAISER FDN HEALTH PLAN OF COLORADO	$4,344
209	THE INCOME FUND OF AMERICA INC	$4,332
210	J.E. DUNN CONSTRUCTION GROUP, INC.	$4,329
211	COBANK, ACB	$4,320
212	CLARK COUNTY SCHOOL DISTRICT	$4,297
213	HARTFORD HEALTHCARE CORPORATION	$4,280
214	SWINERTON BUILDERS	$4,272
215	MASSACHUSETTS INSTITUTE OF TECHNOLOGY	$4,265
216	TRAMMO, INC.	$4,161
217	IOWA HEALTH SYSTEM	$4,157
218	CEDARS-SINAI MEDICAL CENTER	$4,142
219	THE REGENTS OF THE UNIVERSITY OF COLORADO	$4,139
220	YALE UNIVERSITY	$4,105
221	WINCO HOLDINGS, INC.	$4,104
222	UNIVERSITY OF COLORADO	$4,097
223	CHS MCPHERSON REFINERY INC.	$4,081
224	AVAYA HOLDINGS CORP.	$4,081
225	XMED OXYGEN & MEDICAL EQUIPMENT, LP	$4,060
226	UNIVERSITY OF WISCONSIN HOSPITALS AND CLINICS AUTHORITY	$4,027
227	NEW YORK UNIVERSITY	$4,016
228	CORNELL UNIVERSITY	$4,013
229	SAN BERNARDINO COUNTY	$4,008
230	HMH HOSPITALS CORPORATION	$3,999
231	CAPITAL INCOME BUILDER	$3,970
232	THOMAS JEFFERSON UNIVERSITY	$3,951
233	TEMPLE UNIVERSITY-OF THE COMMONWEALTH SYSTEM OF HIGHER EDUCATION	$3,943
234	OREGON HEALTH & SCIENCE UNIVERSITY	$3,942
235	LONG ISLAND POWER AUTHORITY	$3,900
236	VCU HEALTH SYSTEM AUTHORITY	$3,895
237	BAPTIST HEALTHCARE SYSTEM, INC.	$3,885
238	ALEX LEE, INC.	$3,880
239	DANONE US, INC.	$3,866
240	BALFOUR BEATTY CONSTRUCTION GROUP, INC.	$3,852
241	AMERICAN TIRE DISTRIBUTORS HOLDINGS, INC.	$3,839
242	LEHIGH VALLEY HEALTH NETWORK, INC.	$3,833
243	MULTICARE HEALTH SYSTEM	$3,824
244	PROVIDENCE HEALTH & SERVICES - OREGON	$3,823
245	BALFOUR BEATTY CONSTRUCTION, LLC	$3,809
246	MERCY CARE	$3,796
247	MONTEFIORE MEDICAL CENTER	$3,762
248	THE UNIVERSITY OF IOWA	$3,757
249	SANFORD HEALTH	$3,741
250	SUTTER VALLEY HOSPITALS	$3,735
251	API GROUP, INC.	$3,730
252	COUNTY OF SUFFOLK	$3,698
253	AMERICAN BALANCED FUND, INC.	$3,694
254	ALRO STEEL CORPORATION	$3,682
255	THE CHILDREN'S HOSPITAL OF PHILADELPHIA FOUNDATION	$3,679
256	BARNES & NOBLE, INC.	$3,662
257	COUNTY OF CLARK	$3,662
258	KWIK TRIP, INC.	$3,640
259	SWINERTON INCORPORATED	$3,631
260	UNIVERSITY OF WISCONSIN SYSTEM	$3,613
261	FRANCISCAN ALLIANCE, INC.	$3,572
262	UTI, (U.S.) HOLDINGS, INC.	$3,567
263	SCRIPPS NETWORKS INTERACTIVE, INC.	$3,561
264	THE PARSONS CORPORATION	$3,560
265	HCL AMERICA INC.	$3,559
266	ESTES EXPRESS LINES	$3,559
267	COUNTY OF SACRAMENTO	$3,558
268	COUNTY OF HARRIS	$3,524
269	MASSACHUSETTS DEPARTMENT OF TRANSPORTATION	$3,500
270	AHS HOSPITAL CORP.	$3,494
271	BLACK & VEATCH HOLDING COMPANY	$3,479
272	SALT RIVER PROJECT AGRICULTURAL IMPROVEMENT AND POWER DISTRICT	$3,475
273	KIEWIT INDUSTRIAL GROUP INC	$3,474
274	THE SCHOOL DISTRICT OF PHILADELPHIA	$3,473
275	THE WALSH GROUP LTD	$3,462
276	BEARINGPOINT, INC.	$3,455
277	UNIVERSITY SYSTEM OF MARYLAND	$3,454
278	MAINEHEALTH	$3,451
279	THE OHIO STATE UNIVERSITY WEXNER MEDICAL CENTER	$3,433
280	THE GOLUB CORPORATION	$3,427
281	COUNTY OF NASSAU	$3,422
282	AG PROCESSING INC A COOPERATIVE	$3,410
283	BAPTIST MEMORIAL HEALTH CARE CORPORATION	$3,401
284	OHIOHEALTH CORPORATION	$3,388
285	CITY OF PHOENIX	$3,384
286	MONSTER BEVERAGE 1990 CORPORATION	$3,369
287	BVH, INC.	$3,363
288	UNIVERSITY OF CALIFORNIA, LOS ANGELES	$3,353
289	NOBLE HOLDING (U.S.) CORPORATION	$3,352
290	FRANCISCAN MISSIONARIES OF OUR LADY HEALTH SYSTEM, INC.	$3,347
291	ST. LUKE'S HEALTH SYSTEM, LTD.	$3,347
292	PRODUCTION TECHNOLOGIES, INC.	$3,289
293	COMMONSPIRIT HEALTH RESEARCH INSTITUTE	$3,283
294	RAYMOND JAMES & ASSOCIATES INC	$3,255
295	VIRGINIA DEPARTMENT OF TRANSPORTATION	$3,240
296	PHILADELPHIA CONSOLIDATED HOLDING CORP.	$3,234
297	RWJ BARNABAS HEALTH, INC.	$3,210
298	USG CORPORATION	$3,204
299	THE UNIVERSITY OF IOWA	$3,176
300	METROPOLITAN GOVERNMENT OF NASHVILLE & DAVIDSON COUNTY	$3,170

SOURCE: MERGENT INC., DATABASE, APRIL 2023

The 300 Largest Private Companies by Employees 2023

Rank	Company	Employees
1	CITY OF NEW YORK	310,000
2	ALBERTSONS COMPANIES, INC.	290,000
3	STATE OF CALIFORNIA	208,580
4	ALLIED UNIVERSAL HOLDCO LLC	188,000
5	RYMAN HOSPITALITY PROPERTIES, INC.	177,000
6	KAISER FOUNDATION HOSPITALS INC	175,668
7	ASCENSION HEALTH ALLIANCE	150,000
8	STATE OF TEXAS	144,175
9	JOHNSON CONTROLS, INC.	126,377
10	PROVIDENCE HEALTH & SERVICES - OREGON	103,036
11	COUNTY OF LOS ANGELES	101,980
12	COMMONWEALTH OF VIRGINIA	100,000
13	WHOLE FOODS MARKET, INC.	95,000
14	STATE UNIVERSITY OF NEW YORK	88,024
15	ALLEGIS GROUP, INC.	85,000
16	HY-VEE, INC.	83,000
17	STATE OF COLORADO	81,349
18	UPMC	80,000
19	COMMONSPIRIT HEALTH	72,500
20	STATE OF NORTH CAROLINA	69,869
21	STATE OF SOUTH CAROLINA	67,816
22	METROPOLITAN TRANSPORTATION AUTHORITY	67,457
23	STATE OF GEORGIA	67,139
24	MASS GENERAL BRIGHAM INCORPORATED	67,000
25	COMPUTER SCIENCES CORPORATION	66,000
26	LOS ANGELES UNIFIED SCHOOL DISTRICT	65,231
27	THE CHARLOTTE-MECKLENBURG HOSPITAL AUTHORITY	62,000
28	STATE OF ILLINOIS	59,659
29	COMMONWEALTH OF MASSACHUSETTS	59,253
30	STATE OF MARYLAND	58,020
31	STATE OF WASHINGTON	57,659
32	DIGNITY HEALTH	55,494
33	STATE OF MICHIGAN	55,416
34	THE UNIVERSITY OF NORTH CAROLINA	55,000
35	ALLIED SECURITY HOLDINGS LLC	53,760
36	FEDERAL-MOGUL HOLDINGS LLC	53,700
37	YALE NEW HAVEN HEALTH SERVICES CORPORATION	52,768
38	COREWELL HEALTH	51,996
39	STATE OF MISSOURI	51,488
40	TRINITY HEALTH CORPORATION	51,220
41	SANFORD	50,000
42	BAYLOR SCOTT & WHITE HEALTH	49,000
43	BAYLOR SCOTT & WHITE HOLDINGS	49,000
44	SUTTER HEALTH	48,000
45	NEW YORK CITY TRANSIT AUTHORITY	47,956
46	STATE OF LOUISIANA	47,937
47	ADVENTIST HEALTH SYSTEM/SUNBELT, INC.	46,960
48	THE MICHAELS COMPANIES INC	45,000
49	STATE OF HAWAII	44,201
50	THE CLEVELAND CLINIC FOUNDATION	44,000
51	THE PENNSYLVANIA STATE UNIVERSITY	44,000
52	MHM SUPPORT SERVICES	44,000
53	NIELSEN HOLDINGS PLC	43,061
54	CITY OF LOS ANGELES	41,000
55	COUNTY OF BROWARD	40,500
56	BOARD OF REGENTS OF THE UNIVERSITY SYSTEM OF GEORGIA	40,000
57	STATE OF TENNESSEE	37,737
58	STATE OF ALABAMA	37,659
59	STATE OF OKLAHOMA	37,613
60	JOHNS HOPKINS UNIVERSITY	37,600
61	CLARK COUNTY SCHOOL DISTRICT	37,361
62	STEWARD HEALTH CARE SYSTEM LLC	37,000
63	STATE OF OREGON	36,176
64	NEW YORK CITY HEALTH AND HOSPITALS CORPORATION	35,700
65	STATE OF WISCONSIN	35,522
66	STATE OF MINNESOTA	35,217
67	THE OHIO STATE UNIVERSITY WEXNER MEDICAL CENTER	35,000
68	BEAUMONT HEALTH	35,000
69	MAXIM HEALTHCARE SERVICES, INC.	35,000
70	BNSF RAILWAY COMPANY	35,000
71	BANNER HEALTH	35,000
72	INTERMOUNTAIN HEALTH CARE INC	35,000
73	REGENTS OF THE UNIVERSITY OF MICHIGAN	34,624
74	GOVERNMENT OF DISTRICT OF COLUMBIA	34,600
75	STATE OF ARIZONA	34,161
76	COMMONWEALTH OF KENTUCKY	34,000
77	RWJ BARNABAS HEALTH, INC.	34,000
78	STATE OF INDIANA	33,000
79	MEDSTAR HEALTH, INC.	33,000
80	MAYO FOUNDATION FOR MEDICAL EDUCATION AND RESEARCH	32,270
81	MOSAIC HEALTH SYSTEM	32,000
82	R. R. DONNELLEY & SONS COMPANY	32,000
83	AVANT GARDE ACADEMY FOUNDATION, INC.	31,174
84	UNIVERSITY OF MISSOURI SYSTEM	30,282
85	YALE NEW HAVEN HOSPITAL, INC.	30,278
86	PRECISION CASTPARTS CORP.	30,116
87	UNIVERSITY HOSPITALS HEALTH SYSTEM, INC.	30,099
88	AURORA HEALTH CARE, INC.	30,000
89	CITY & COUNTY OF SAN FRANCISCO	30,000
90	CITY OF PHILADELPHIA	29,862
91	STATE OF UTAH	29,821
92	NPC RESTAURANT HOLDINGS, LLC	29,000
93	STATE OF ARKANSAS	28,272
94	SENTARA HEALTHCARE	28,000
95	UNIVERSITY SYSTEM OF MARYLAND	28,000
96	STATE OF MISSISSIPPI	27,775
97	BAYCARE HEALTH SYSTEM, INC.	27,739
98	UNIVERSITY OF WASHINGTON INC	27,228
99	FERGUSON ENTERPRISES, LLC	27,000
100	CITY OF BALTIMORE	26,400
101	OREGON UNIVERSITY SYSTEM	26,000
102	REGAL ENTERTAINMENT GROUP	25,359
103	SCHOOL BOARD OF ORANGE COUNTY FLORIDA	25,000
104	HILLSBOROUGH COUNTY SCHOOL DISTRICT	25,000
105	CITY OF SCOTTSDALE	25,000
106	MCLANE COMPANY, INC.	25,000
107	DALLAS INDEPENDENT SCHOOL DISTRICT	24,937
108	BARNABAS HEALTH, INC.	24,600
109	STATE OF IOWA	24,304
110	SSM HEALTH CARE CORPORATION	24,230
111	THE ORANGE COUNTY PUBLIC SCHOOL DISTRICT	24,000
112	BARNES & NOBLE, INC.	24,000
113	THE EVANGELICAL LUTHERAN GOOD SAMARITAN SOCIETY	24,000
114	THE NEW YORK AND PRESBYTERIAN HOSPITAL	23,709
115	HOBBY LOBBY STORES, INC.	23,000
116	THE HERTZ CORPORATION	23,000
117	HENRY FORD HEALTH SYSTEM	23,000
118	ORLANDO HEALTH, INC.	23,000
119	CAMERON INTERNATIONAL CORPORATION	23,000
120	ROCHESTER REGIONAL HEALTH	22,500
121	HOUSTON INDEPENDENT SCHOOL DISTRICT	22,440
122	STATE OF KANSAS	22,375
123	PRINCE GEORGE'S COUNTY PUBLIC SCHOOLS	22,000
124	HEALTHPARTNERS, INC.	22,000
125	TEXAS HEALTH RESOURCES	21,277
126	THE SCHOOL DISTRICT OF PHILADELPHIA	21,065
127	SCHOOL BOARD OF PALM BEACH COUNTY	21,000
128	DAIRY FARMERS OF AMERICA, INC.	21,000
129	NEW YORK UNIVERSITY	21,000
130	THE VANDERBILT UNIVERSITY	21,000
131	COUNTY OF ORANGE	21,000
132	COUNTY OF RIVERSIDE	20,000
133	MV TRANSPORTATION, INC.	20,000
134	BATTELLE MEMORIAL INSTITUTE	20,000
135	AMC ENTERTAINMENT INC.	19,700
136	ADVENTIST HEALTH SYSTEM/WEST, CORPORATION	19,512
137	OREGON HEALTH & SCIENCE UNIVERSITY	19,500
138	THE GOLUB CORPORATION	19,500
139	STATE OF WEST VIRGINIA	19,357
140	VANDERBILT UNIVERSITY MEDICAL CENTER	19,000
141	BON SECOURS MERCY HEALTH, INC.	19,000
142	FRANCISCAN ALLIANCE, INC.	19,000
143	OCHSNER HEALTH SYSTEM	19,000
144	IOWA HEALTH SYSTEM	18,923
145	PAREXEL INTERNATIONAL CORPORATION	18,900
146	STATE OF NEBRASKA	18,653
147	NATIONAL RAILROAD PASSENGER CORPORATION	18,650
148	BLACK & VEATCH HOLDING COMPANY	18,568
149	BVH, INC.	18,568
150	STATE OF IDAHO	18,407
151	UNIVERSITY OF NEW MEXICO	18,362
152	WILLIAM BEAUMONT HOSPITAL	18,050
153	METROPOLITAN GOVERNMENT OF NASHVILLE & DAVIDSON COUNTY	18,000
154	THE UNIVERSITY OF UTAH	18,000
155	WHEATON FRANCISCAN SERVICES, INC.	18,000
156	FAIRVIEW HEALTH SERVICES	18,000
157	UNIVERSITY OF GEORGIA	17,800
158	UNIVERSITY OF CALIFORNIA, DAVIS	17,741
159	MAIN LINE HEALTH SYSTEM	17,485
160	OLD CLAIMCO, LLC	17,200
161	AIRGAS, INC.	17,004
162	THE UNIVERSITY OF IOWA	17,000
163	SAN DIEGO UNIFIED SCHOOL DISTRICT	17,000
164	WAKE COUNTY PUBLIC SCHOOL SYSTEM	17,000
165	JARDEN LLC	17,000
166	WAKEMED	16,933
167	AVERITT EXPRESS, INC.	16,708
168	AVERITT INCORPORATED	16,708
169	LEVI STRAUSS & CO.	16,600
170	THE SALVATION ARMY	16,168
171	UNIVERSITY OF SOUTH FLORIDA	16,165
172	UNIVERSITY SYSTEM OF NEW HAMPSHIRE	16,000
173	INOVA HEALTH SYSTEM FOUNDATION	16,000
174	TRUSTEES OF INDIANA UNIVERSITY	16,000
175	HOUCHENS INDUSTRIES, INC.	16,000
176	ALSCO INC.	16,000
177	BAPTIST HEALTH SOUTH FLORIDA, INC.	16,000
178	COUNTY OF MARICOPA	15,751
179	DST SYSTEMS, INC.	15,700
180	THE PARSONS CORPORATION	15,500
181	BEARINGPOINT, INC.	15,200
182	BOARD OF REGENTS OF THE UNIVERSITY OF NEBRASKA	15,200
183	SISTERS OF CHARITY OF LEAVENWORTH HEALTH SYSTEM, INC.	15,046
184	OHIOHEALTH CORPORATION	15,000
185	THE METHODIST HOSPITAL	15,000
186	LELAND STANFORD JUNIOR UNIVERSITY	15,000
187	THE RESEARCH FOUNDATION FOR THE STATE UNIVERSITY OF NEW YORK	15,000
188	PITT COUNTY MEMORIAL HOSPITAL, INCORPORATED	15,000
189	SCHOOL DISTRICT 1 IN THE CITY AND COUNTY OF DENVER AND THE STATE OF COLORADO	14,965
190	STATE OF NEVADA	14,790
191	TEXAS DEPARTMENT OF TRANSPORTATION	14,720
192	PETER KIEWIT SONS', INC.	14,700
193	UNIVERSITY OF CINCINNATI	14,600
194	COUNTY OF NASSAU	14,500
195	COUNTY OF SANTA CLARA	14,500
196	ALMOST FAMILY, INC.	14,200
197	MILWAUKEE PUBLIC SCHOOLS (INC)	14,154
198	STANFORD HEALTH CARE	14,100
199	UNIVERSITY OF ARKANSAS SYSTEM	14,025
200	HONORHEALTH	14,000
201	NAVY EXCHANGE SERVICE COMMAND	14,000
202	ESTES EXPRESS LINES	14,000
203	ALTICOR INC.	14,000
204	WINCO HOLDINGS, INC.	14,000
205	SOLSTICE HOLDINGS INC.	14,000
206	COUNTY OF HARRIS	14,000
207	SHARP HEALTHCARE	14,000
208	MEMORIAL HERMANN HEALTH SYSTEM	14,000
209	RALEY'S	14,000
210	CITY OF PHOENIX	14,000

SOURCE: MERGENT INC., DATABASE, APRIL 2023

The 300 Largest Private Companies by Employees 2023 (continued)

Rank	Company	Employees
211	THE HEALTH CARE AUTHORITY OF THE CITY OF HUNTSVILLE	14,000
212	NORTHSIDE INDEPENDENT SCHOOL DISTRICT	13,698
213	STATE OF RHODE ISLAND	13,535
214	THE FINISH LINE INC	13,500
215	FLORIDA STATE UNIVERSITY	13,497
216	COUNTY OF KING	13,300
217	RECTOR & VISITORS OF THE UNIVERSITY OF VIRGINIA	13,300
218	THE TRUSTEES OF COLUMBIA UNIVERSITY IN THE CITY OF NEW YORK	13,200
219	UNIVERSITY OF MASSACHUSETTS INCORPORATED	13,196
220	GEISINGER HEALTH	13,030
221	CYPRESS-FAIRBANKS INDEPENDENT SCHOOL DISTRICT	13,000
222	DUVAL COUNTY SCHOOL BOARD (INC)	13,000
223	THE JOHNS HOPKINS HEALTH SYSTEM CORPORATION	13,000
224	U.S. GENERAL SERVICES ADMINISTRATION	13,000
225	CITY OF DALLAS	13,000
226	INOVA HEALTH CARE SERVICES	13,000
227	THE PUBLIC HEALTH TRUST OF MIAMI-DADE COUNTY	12,990
228	THE REGENTS OF THE UNIVERSITY OF COLORADO	12,980
229	BAPTIST MEMORIAL HEALTH CARE CORPORATION	12,877
230	COUNTY OF SUFFOLK	12,814
231	UNIVERSITY OF HOUSTON SYSTEM	12,608
232	BAPTIST HEALTHCARE SYSTEM, INC.	12,601
233	THE FRESH MARKET INC	12,600
234	NORTH CAROLINA BAPTIST HOSPITAL	12,563
235	HARTFORD HEALTHCARE CORPORATION	12,500
236	CONSTELLATION ENERGY GENERATION, LLC	12,482
237	STATE OF NEW HAMPSHIRE	12,280
238	WESTCHESTER COUNTY HEALTH CARE CORPORATION	12,252
239	RICH PRODUCTS CORPORATION	12,224
240	CORNELL UNIVERSITY	12,207
241	UNIVERSITY OF NORTH CAROLINA AT CHAPEL HILL	12,204
242	BOARD OF EDUCATION-MEMPHIS CITY SCHOOLS	12,015
243	FAIRFAX COUNTY VIRGINIA	12,000
244	TESLA ENERGY OPERATIONS, INC.	12,000
245	THE GEISINGER CLINIC	12,000
246	METALDYNE PERFORMANCE GROUP INC.	12,000
247	UNIVERSITY OF HAWAII SYSTEM	12,000
248	JEFFERSON COUNTY SCHOOL DISTRICT NO. R-1	12,000
249	LEHIGH VALLEY HEALTH NETWORK, INC.	12,000
250	MASSACHUSETTS INSTITUTE OF TECHNOLOGY	12,000
251	UNIVERSITY OF MARYLAND MEDICAL SYSTEM CORPORATION	12,000
252	JOHNS HOPKINS HOSPITAL	12,000
253	UNIVERSITY OF TENNESSEE	12,000
254	STATE OF MAINE	12,000
255	GEORGES PRINCE COUNTY GOVERNMENT	12,000
256	ANC HEALTHCARE, INC.	12,000
257	CITY OF SAN ANTONIO	12,000
258	HCL AMERICA INC.	11,993
259	THE PRESIDENT AND FELLOWS OF HARVARD COLLEGE	11,500
260	ALBUQUERQUE PUBLIC SCHOOL DISTRICT	11,500
261	CITY OF SAN DIEGO	11,200
262	LESTER E. COX MEDICAL CENTERS	11,170
263	MICHIGAN STATE UNIVERSITY	11,100
264	VIRGINIA COMMONWEALTH UNIVERSITY	11,000
265	MONTEFIORE MEDICAL CENTER	11,000
266	YALE UNIVERSITY	11,000
267	DALLAS COUNTY HOSPITAL DISTRICT	11,000
268	COUNTY OF VOLUSIA	11,000
269	COUNTY OF SACRAMENTO	10,968
270	CITY OF AUSTIN	10,922
271	BALTIMORE CITY PUBLIC SCHOOLS	10,800
272	VIRGINIA DEPARTMENT OF TRANSPORTATION	10,737
273	MED AMERICA HEALTH SYSTEMS CORPORATION	10,700
274	LEGACY HEALTH	10,675
275	THOMAS JEFFERSON UNIVERSITY	10,625
276	KWIK TRIP, INC.	10,500
277	LOYOLA UNIVERSITY OF CHICAGO INC	10,500
278	OCHSNER CLINIC FOUNDATION	10,500
279	THE SALVATION ARMY	10,447
280	KIEWIT CORPORATION	10,441
281	FORT WORTH INDEPENDENT SCHOOL DISTRICT	10,360
282	HENNEPIN COUNTY	10,246
283	COUNTY OF ERIE	10,200
284	BEALL'S, INC.	10,179
285	THE MASSACHUSETTS GENERAL HOSPITAL	10,156
286	THE SCHOOL DISTRICT OF WEST PALM BEACH COUNTY	10,156
287	MERCY HOSPITALS EAST COMMUNITIES	10,000
288	MISSION HOSPITAL, INC.	10,000
289	NORTH EAST INDEPENDENT SCHOOL DISTRICT	10,000
290	FULTON COUNTY BOARD OF EDUCATION	10,000
291	ALEGENT CREIGHTON HEALTH	10,000
292	FARM CREDIT SERVICES OF AMERICA	10,000
293	UC HEALTH, LLC.	10,000
294	THE CHILDREN'S HOSPITAL OF PHILADELPHIA FOUNDATION	10,000
295	CITY OF SEATTLE	10,000
296	UOFL HEALTH, INC.	10,000
297	COOPERATIVE FOR ASSISTANCE AND RELIEF EVERYWHERE, INC. (CARE)	10,000
298	COVENANT HEALTH	10,000
299	CITY OF HARTFORD	10,000
300	RAYMOND JAMES & ASSOCIATES INC	10,000

SOURCE: MERGENT INC., DATABASE, APRIL 2023

The 100 Largest Private Companies by Net Income 2023

Rank	Company	Net Income ($mil.)
1	AMERICAN MUTUAL FUND	$23,814
2	AMERICAN BALANCED FUND, INC.	$22,447
3	THE BOND FUND OF AMERICA INC	$19,792
4	THE INCOME FUND OF AMERICA INC	$18,019
5	CAPITAL INCOME BUILDER	$16,978
6	AMCAP FUND, INC.	$15,952
7	AMERICAN FUNDS INTERNATIONAL VANTAGE FUND	$15,687
8	NEW WORLD FUND	$15,687
9	AMERICAN FUNDS PORTFOLIO SERIES	$13,753
10	CAPITAL WORLD GROWTH AND INCOME FUND, INC.	$12,826
11	BNSF RAILWAY COMPANY	$12,119
12	FUNDAMENTAL INVESTORS, INC.	$7,303
13	NOVARTIS PHARMACEUTICALS CORPORATION	$6,698
14	STATE OF GEORGIA	$5,578
15	ALASKA PERMANENT FUND CORPORATION, AN INSTRUMENTALITY OF THE STATE OF ALASKA	$5,109
16	PUBLIC EMPLOYEE RETIREMENT SYSTEM, IDAHO	$4,970
17	COMMONWEALTH OF VIRGINIA	$4,805
18	STATE OF CALIFORNIA	$4,798
19	THE PRESIDENT AND FELLOWS OF HARVARD COLLEGE	$4,607
20	METROPOLITAN TRANSPORTATION AUTHORITY	$4,160
21	STATE OF ALABAMA	$3,945
22	STATE OF MINNESOTA	$3,875
23	UNIVERSITY OF VIRGINIA	$3,715
24	STATE OF OREGON	$3,614
25	AMERICAN HIGH INCOME TRUST	$3,254
26	INTERMOUNTAIN HEALTH CARE INC	$2,937
27	STATE OF MARYLAND	$2,850
28	NEW YORK CITY TRANSIT AUTHORITY	$2,825
29	MCAFEE CORP.	$2,688
30	CANDID COLOR SYSTEMS, INC.	$2,534
31	IHC HEALTH SERVICES, INC.	$2,442
32	THE CLEVELAND CLINIC FOUNDATION	$2,420
33	STATE OF OKLAHOMA	$2,290
34	STATE OF ALASKA	$2,275
35	ST. JOSEPH HEALTH SYSTEM	$2,082
36	HARVARD MANAGEMENT PRIVATE EQUITY CORPORATION	$2,047
37	SUTTER HEALTH	$1,958
38	STATE OF NORTH DAKOTA	$1,955
39	STATE OF UTAH	$1,934
40	STATE OF TEXAS	$1,882
41	UPMC	$1,857
42	FERGUSON ENTERPRISES, LLC	$1,814
43	BAYLOR SCOTT & WHITE HEALTH	$1,814
44	UNIVERSITY OF COLORADO HEALTH	$1,807
45	TRUSTEES OF THE UNIV OF PENNA RETIREE MED AND DEATH BENEFITS TRUST	$1,773
46	STATE OF MISSISSIPPI	$1,761
47	TEXAS COUNTY AND DISTRICT RETIREMENT SYSTEM	$1,761
48	CHEVRON PHILLIPS CHEMICAL COMPANY LLC	$1,687
49	JOHNSON CONTROLS, INC.	$1,679
50	STATE OF IDAHO	$1,664
51	ASCENSION HEALTH ALLIANCE	$1,638
52	STATE OF NEBRASKA	$1,621
53	STATE OF WISCONSIN	$1,607
54	STATE OF ILLINOIS	$1,596
55	THE NEW YORK AND PRESBYTERIAN HOSPITAL	$1,578
56	UNIVERSITY OF PITTSBURGH-OF THE COMMONWEALTH SYSTEM OF HIGHER EDUCATION	$1,548
57	SCHWAB CHARITABLE FUND	$1,531
58	ADVENTIST HEALTH SYSTEM/SUNBELT, INC.	$1,512
59	MEMORIAL SLOAN-KETTERING CANCER CENTER	$1,480
60	STATE OF LOUISIANA	$1,454
61	THE SUNDERLAND FOUNDATION	$1,429
62	SUNOCO PIPELINE L.P.	$1,419
63	DHPC TECHNOLOGIES, INC.	$1,320
64	CHEVRON PHILLIPS CHEMICAL COMPANY LP	$1,301
65	TRUSTEES OF BOSTON COLLEGE	$1,274
66	ALLY BANK	$1,273
67	CHARLESTON AREA MEDICAL CENTER, INC.	$1,236
68	THE CHARLOTTE-MECKLENBURG HOSPITAL AUTHORITY	$1,223
69	CITY & COUNTY OF SAN FRANCISCO	$1,201
70	COBANK, ACB	$1,190
71	STATE OF KANSAS	$1,186
72	BRISBANE SCHOOL DISTRICT	$1,177
73	UAW RETIREE MEDICAL BENEFITS TRUST	$1,176
74	THE REGENTS OF THE UNIVERSITY OF COLORADO	$1,169
75	CALIFORNIA INSTITUTE OF TECHNOLOGY	$1,102
76	STATE OF IOWA	$1,083
77	CEDARS-SINAI MEDICAL CENTER	$1,083
78	STATE OF ARKANSAS	$1,077
79	ONEOK PARTNERS, L.P.	$1,072
80	STATE OF MAINE	$1,040
81	SPECTRA ENERGY, LLC	$1,020
82	BON SECOURS MERCY HEALTH, INC.	$997
83	CORNELL UNIVERSITY	$985
84	STATE OF MISSOURI	$962
85	PROVIDENCE HEALTH & SERVICES - OREGON	$946
86	RECTOR & VISITORS OF THE UNIVERSITY OF VIRGINIA	$909
87	STATE OF TENNESSEE	$902
88	STATE OF NEVADA	$872
89	HOUSTON METHODIST ST. JOHN HOSPITAL	$870
90	TEXAS HEALTH RESOURCES	$869
91	CAMERON INTERNATIONAL CORPORATION	$848
92	LELAND STANFORD JUNIOR UNIVERSITY	$845
93	STATE OF NORTH CAROLINA	$836
94	FRANCISCAN MISSIONARIES OF OUR LADY HEALTH SYSTEM, INC.	$833
95	STATE OF MICHIGAN	$832
96	METROPOLITAN GOVERNMENT OF NASHVILLE & DAVIDSON COUNTY	$830
97	EATON CORPORATION	$821
98	MONSTER BEVERAGE 1990 CORPORATION	$820
99	PRECISION CASTPARTS CORP.	$817
100	SCRIPPS NETWORKS INTERACTIVE, INC.	$814

SOURCE: MERGENT DATA APRIL 2023

The 100 Largest Private Companies by Total Assets 2023

Rank	Company	Net Income ($mil.)
1	AMERICAN MUTUAL FUND	$23,814
2	AMERICAN BALANCED FUND, INC.	$22,447
3	THE BOND FUND OF AMERICA INC	$19,792
4	THE INCOME FUND OF AMERICA INC	$18,019
5	CAPITAL INCOME BUILDER	$16,978
6	AMCAP FUND, INC.	$15,952
7	AMERICAN FUNDS INTERNATIONAL VANTAGE FUND	$15,687
8	NEW WORLD FUND	$15,687
9	AMERICAN FUNDS PORTFOLIO SERIES	$13,753
10	CAPITAL WORLD GROWTH AND INCOME FUND, INC.	$12,826
11	BNSF RAILWAY COMPANY	$12,119
12	FUNDAMENTAL INVESTORS, INC.	$7,303
13	NOVARTIS PHARMACEUTICALS CORPORATION	$6,698
14	STATE OF GEORGIA	$5,578
15	ALASKA PERMANENT FUND CORPORATION, AN INSTRUMENTALITY OF THE STATE OF ALASKA	$5,109
16	PUBLIC EMPLOYEE RETIREMENT SYSTEM, IDAHO	$4,970
17	COMMONWEALTH OF VIRGINIA	$4,805
18	STATE OF CALIFORNIA	$4,798
19	THE PRESIDENT AND FELLOWS OF HARVARD COLLEGE	$4,607
20	METROPOLITAN TRANSPORTATION AUTHORITY	$4,160
21	STATE OF ALABAMA	$3,945
22	STATE OF MINNESOTA	$3,875
23	UNIVERSITY OF VIRGINIA	$3,715
24	STATE OF OREGON	$3,614
25	AMERICAN HIGH INCOME TRUST	$3,254
26	INTERMOUNTAIN HEALTH CARE INC	$2,937
27	STATE OF MARYLAND	$2,850
28	NEW YORK CITY TRANSIT AUTHORITY	$2,825
29	MCAFEE CORP.	$2,688
30	CANDID COLOR SYSTEMS, INC.	$2,534
31	IHC HEALTH SERVICES, INC.	$2,442
32	THE CLEVELAND CLINIC FOUNDATION	$2,420
33	STATE OF OKLAHOMA	$2,290
34	STATE OF ALASKA	$2,275
35	ST. JOSEPH HEALTH SYSTEM	$2,082
36	HARVARD MANAGEMENT PRIVATE EQUITY CORPORATION	$2,047
37	SUTTER HEALTH	$1,958
38	STATE OF NORTH DAKOTA	$1,955
39	STATE OF UTAH	$1,934
40	STATE OF TEXAS	$1,882
41	UPMC	$1,857
42	FERGUSON ENTERPRISES, LLC	$1,814
43	BAYLOR SCOTT & WHITE HEALTH	$1,814
44	UNIVERSITY OF COLORADO HEALTH	$1,807
45	TRUSTEES OF THE UNIV OF PENNA RETIREE MED AND DEATH BENEFITS TRUST	$1,773
46	STATE OF MISSISSIPPI	$1,761
47	TEXAS COUNTY AND DISTRICT RETIREMENT SYSTEM	$1,761
48	CHEVRON PHILLIPS CHEMICAL COMPANY LLC	$1,687
49	JOHNSON CONTROLS, INC.	$1,679
50	STATE OF IDAHO	$1,664
51	ASCENSION HEALTH ALLIANCE	$1,638
52	STATE OF NEBRASKA	$1,621
53	STATE OF WISCONSIN	$1,607
54	STATE OF ILLINOIS	$1,596
55	THE NEW YORK AND PRESBYTERIAN HOSPITAL	$1,578
56	UNIVERSITY OF PITTSBURGH-OF THE COMMONWEALTH SYSTEM OF HIGHER EDUCATION	$1,548
57	SCHWAB CHARITABLE FUND	$1,531
58	ADVENTIST HEALTH SYSTEM/SUNBELT, INC.	$1,512
59	MEMORIAL SLOAN-KETTERING CANCER CENTER	$1,480
60	STATE OF LOUISIANA	$1,454
61	THE SUNDERLAND FOUNDATION	$1,429
62	SUNOCO PIPELINE L.P.	$1,419
63	DHPC TECHNOLOGIES, INC.	$1,320
64	CHEVRON PHILLIPS CHEMICAL COMPANY LP	$1,301
65	TRUSTEES OF BOSTON COLLEGE	$1,274
66	ALLY BANK	$1,273
67	CHARLESTON AREA MEDICAL CENTER, INC.	$1,236
68	THE CHARLOTTE-MECKLENBURG HOSPITAL AUTHORITY	$1,223
69	CITY & COUNTY OF SAN FRANCISCO	$1,201
70	COBANK, ACB	$1,190
71	STATE OF KANSAS	$1,186
72	BRISBANE SCHOOL DISTRICT	$1,177
73	UAW RETIREE MEDICAL BENEFITS TRUST	$1,176
74	THE REGENTS OF THE UNIVERSITY OF COLORADO	$1,169
75	CALIFORNIA INSTITUTE OF TECHNOLOGY	$1,102
76	STATE OF IOWA	$1,083
77	CEDARS-SINAI MEDICAL CENTER	$1,083
78	STATE OF ARKANSAS	$1,077
79	ONEOK PARTNERS, L.P.	$1,072
80	STATE OF MAINE	$1,040
81	SPECTRA ENERGY, LLC	$1,020
82	BON SECOURS MERCY HEALTH, INC.	$997
83	CORNELL UNIVERSITY	$985
84	STATE OF MISSOURI	$962
85	PROVIDENCE HEALTH & SERVICES - OREGON	$946
86	RECTOR & VISITORS OF THE UNIVERSITY OF VIRGINIA	$909
87	STATE OF TENNESSEE	$902
88	STATE OF NEVADA	$872
89	HOUSTON METHODIST ST. JOHN HOSPITAL	$870
90	TEXAS HEALTH RESOURCES	$869
91	CAMERON INTERNATIONAL CORPORATION	$848
92	LELAND STANFORD JUNIOR UNIVERSITY	$845
93	STATE OF NORTH CAROLINA	$836
94	FRANCISCAN MISSIONARIES OF OUR LADY HEALTH SYSTEM, INC.	$833
95	STATE OF MICHIGAN	$832
96	METROPOLITAN GOVERNMENT OF NASHVILLE & DAVIDSON COUNTY	$830
97	EATON CORPORATION	$821
98	MONSTER BEVERAGE 1990 CORPORATION	$820
99	PRECISION CASTPARTS CORP.	$817
100	SCRIPPS NETWORKS INTERACTIVE, INC.	$814

SOURCE: MERGENT DATA APRIL 2023

Hoover's Handbook of Private Companies

The Companies

1199 SEIU NATIONAL BENEFIT FUND FOR HEALTH AND HUMAN SERVICE EMPLOYEES

Auditors : KPMG LLP NEW YORK NY

LOCATIONS

HQ: 1199 SEIU NATIONAL BENEFIT FUND FOR HEALTH AND HUMAN SERVICE EMPLOYEES
498 7TH AVE, NEW YORK, NY 100186798
Phone: 646 473-9200
Web: WWW.1199SEIU.ORG

HISTORICAL FINANCIALS
Company Type: Private

Income Statement — FYE: December 31

	REVENUE ($mil)	NET INCOME ($mil)	NET PROFIT MARGIN	EMPLOYEES
12/17	1,642	45	2.8%	16
12/09	1,167	(19)	—	—
Annual Growth	4.4%	—	—	—

2017 Year-End Financials
Return on assets: 5.3% Cash ($ mil.): 47
Return on equity: 8.2%
Current Ratio: 8.70

21ST CENTURY ONCOLOGY HOLDINGS, INC

EXECUTIVES

CMO, Constantine A Mantz
CAO, Joseph Biscardi
US Operations President, Gary Delanois Senior V
Auditors : DELOITTE & TOUCHE LLP MIAMI

LOCATIONS

HQ: 21ST CENTURY ONCOLOGY HOLDINGS, INC
2270 COLONIAL BLVD, FORT MYERS, FL 339071412
Phone: 239 931-7254
Web: WWW.RTSX.COM

HISTORICAL FINANCIALS
Company Type: Private

Income Statement — FYE: December 31

	REVENUE ($mil)	NET INCOME ($mil)	NET PROFIT MARGIN	EMPLOYEES
12/14	1,026	(343)	—	3,930
12/13	736	(78)	—	—
12/12	693	(151)	—	—
Annual Growth	21.6%	—	—	—

2014 Year-End Financials
Return on assets: (-29.9%) Cash ($ mil.): 99
Return on equity: —
Current Ratio: 1.40

95 EXPRESS LANES LLC

EXECUTIVES

Managing Member, Michael Kulper

LOCATIONS

HQ: 95 EXPRESS LANES LLC
6440 GENERAL GREEN WAY, ALEXANDRIA, VA 223122413
Phone: 571 419-6100
Web: WWW.EXPRESSLANES.COM

HISTORICAL FINANCIALS
Company Type: Private

Income Statement — FYE: June 30

	REVENUE ($mil)	NET INCOME ($mil)	NET PROFIT MARGIN	EMPLOYEES
06/22	669	469	70.1%	1
06/20	975	722	74.1%	—
06/19	1,047	786	75.1%	—
06/18	92	32	35.6%	—
Annual Growth	64.1%	94.4%		

2022 Year-End Financials
Return on assets: 7.6% Cash ($ mil.): 142
Return on equity: 10.0%
Current Ratio: 4.30

A-1 SPECIALIZED SERVICES & SUPPLIES, INC.

Auditors : MEENA JERATH CPA MED MBA

LOCATIONS

HQ: A-1 SPECIALIZED SERVICES & SUPPLIES, INC.
347 MUNT PLSANT AVE STE 2, WEST ORANGE, NJ 07052
Phone: 215 788-9200

HISTORICAL FINANCIALS
Company Type: Private

Income Statement — FYE: December 31

	REVENUE ($mil)	NET INCOME ($mil)	NET PROFIT MARGIN	EMPLOYEES
12/10	1,359	7	0.6%	29
12/09	1,205	2	0.2%	—
12/08	2,637	15	0.6%	—
Annual Growth	(28.2%)	(28.9%)	—	—

2010 Year-End Financials
Return on assets: 1.5% Cash ($ mil.): 8
Return on equity: 12.5%
Current Ratio: 1.10

AAA COOPER TRANSPORTATION

AAA Cooper Transportation (AACT) is a trucking company offering freight hauling services primarily in the Southwest, Southeast, and Midwest along with carriers with coverage into Puerto Rico, Canada, and Mexico. AACT offers less-than-truckload (LTL), truck load, international services, freight brokerage services, dedicated contract carriage, and fleet maintenance services through 40 locations. The company's International Services division offers cross-border services to Canada and Mexico. The company's fleet includes 3,000 tractors and 6,500 trailers.

Operations

The company's five primary service offerings are LTL Services, dedicated services, international services (including port services), managed services, and fleet maintenance services.

Less than Truckload (LTL) services provides transportation to shipments typically falling between 50 and 10,000 pounds. These shipments are commingled to ensure that these small sized shipments do not solely bear the full cost of transportation. Dedicated Services provides for the provisioning and dedication of transportation resources directly to a specific logistics need. International services offer cross border service to Canada and Mexico. Its system ensures seamless service, complete control and single invoicing for shipments from origin to destination.

Managed services provides additional services which support and enhance shipping experience. These services are all offered through current sales associate. Some of fleet maintenance services include maintenance services to all type of diesel engines, including CAT, VOLVO, INTERNATIONAL, DETROIT, CUMMINS, among others, and all types of trailing equipment, PM flat rates are available based on requirements and engine part specifications, and major repair work, such as engine and transmission overhauls.

Geographic Reach

Headquartered in Alabama, AACT offers less-than-truckload (LTL) all over the Southeast and Midwest. The company also facilitates transportation in Puerto Rico, Canada, Mexico, and the US Virgin Islands, as well as some 40 fleet maintenance locations.

Sales and Marketing

The company markets their products and services through websites such less-than-truck Services (LTL), and Data Exchange. In additions, the company provides dedicated services for the provisioning and dedication of transportation resources directly to a specific logistics need such as technology, data exchange, route planning, asset tracking, reporting & customized billing and customer portal.

Company Background
ACT was founded in 1955.

EXECUTIVES

PRICING*, Brad Morris
Strategy Vice President, Lee Mcmillan

LOCATIONS

HQ: AAA COOPER TRANSPORTATION
1751 KINSEY RD, DOTHAN, AL 363035877
Phone: 334 793-2284
Web: WWW.AAACOOPER.COM

PRODUCTS/OPERATIONS

Selected Services
Dedicated
    Company branding
    Specialized equipment
International LTL
LTL
Port
    Consolidation
    Drayage
    Transloading

COMPETITORS

A&R LOGISTICS, INC.
A. DUIE PYLE INC.
AVERITT EXPRESS, INC.
C.R. ENGLAND, INC.
COMCAR INDUSTRIES, INC.
CRST INTERNATIONAL., INC.
EPES CARRIERS, INC.
ESTES EXPRESS LINES
INTERSTATE DISTRIBUTOR CO.
UPS GROUND FREIGHT, INC.

HISTORICAL FINANCIALS

Company Type: Private

Income Statement   FYE: January 1

	REVENUE ($mil)	NET INCOME ($mil)	NET PROFIT MARGIN	EMPLOYEES
01/17	592	17	3.0%	4,933
01/16*	595	14	2.4%	—
12/14	576	20	3.5%	—
Annual Growth	1.3%	(6.4%)	—	—

*Fiscal year change

2017 Year-End Financials
Return on assets: 4.9%   Cash ($ mil.): —
Return on equity: 9.9%
Current Ratio: 1.40

AARP

AARP is a nonprofit, nonpartisan organization, with a membership of nearly 38 million current members. With staffed offices in all 50 states, the District of Columbia, Puerto Rico, and the US Virgin Islands, AARP works to strengthen communities and promote the issues that matter most to families such as healthcare security, financial security and personal fulfillment. AARP also advocates for individuals in the marketplace by selecting products and services of high quality and value to carry the AARP name. It also produces the world's largest circulation magazine, AARP The Magazine and AARP Bulletin. The American Association of Retired Persons, now known as AARP, was founded in 1958 by Ethel Percy Andrus, a retired high school principal.

Operations

AARP, through its Foundation organization, serves vulnerable people 50 and older by creating and advancing effective solutions that help them secure the essentials. To this end, the organization operates Government Watch, an interactive website designed to allow older Americans to hold Congress and the President's administration accountable on key issues that affect them.

AARP oversees volunteer services as well. The AARP Foundation Experience Corps is for volunteers aged 50 and older who want to tutor and mentor youth in their communities, primarily literacy for children in kindergarten through third grade.

AARP's publications and multimedia offerings include AARP The Magazine, the nation's largest-circulation magazine; AARP Bulletin, the go-to news source for the 50-plus audience; aarp.org website; AARP television and radio programming; AARP Books; and AARP en Espanol, a bilingual news source.

Geographic Reach

Washington DC-based, AARP boasts staffed offices in all 50 US states, Puerto Rico, and the US Virgin Islands.

HISTORY

Ethel Andrus, a retired Los Angeles high school principal who founded the National Retired Teachers Association (NRTA) in 1947, founded the American Association of Retired Persons (AARP) in 1958 with the assistance of Leonard Davis, a New York insurance salesman who had helped her find an underwriter for the NRTA. The new organization's goal: to "enhance the quality of life" for older Americans and "improve the image of aging."

Andrus offered members the same low rates for health and accident insurance provided to NRTA members. She also started publishing AARP's bimonthly magazine, Modern Maturity, in 1958. The organization's first local chapter opened in Youngstown, Arizona, in 1960. Still an insurance man, Davis formed Colonial Penn Insurance in 1963 to take over the AARP account. Andrus led the AARP and its increasingly powerful lobby for the elderly until her death in 1967.

With criticism of Colonial Penn mounting in the 1970s (critics charged the organization was little more than a front for the insurance company), Prudential won AARP's insurance business in 1979. The NRTA merged with AARP in 1982, and the following year it lowered the membership eligibility age from 55 to 50. The organization continued to expand its offerings, adding an auto club and financial products such as mutual funds and expanded insurance policies. The organization also started a federal credit union for members in 1988, but despite rosy projections, it ceased operations two years later.

AARP forked over $135 million to the IRS in 1993 as part of a settlement regarding the tax status of profits from some of its activities, but the dispute remained unresolved. AARP switched insurance providers again in 1996 (New York Life) and started offering discounted legal services. Also that year, AARP said it would let HMOs offer managed-care services to members. The plan drew objections over its potential violation of Medicare anti-kickback laws and AARP developed a revised payment plan in 1997.

AARP's image was bruised in 1998 when Dale Van Atta wrote a scathing account of the organization, Trust Betrayed: Inside the AARP. The book accused the organization of operating out of lavish accommodations, acting as a shill for businesses to hawk their wares, and concealing a drop in membership. The next year, recognizing that nearly a third of its members were working, the organization dropped the American Association of Retired Persons moniker and began to refer to itself by the AARP abbreviation.

To end the long-running dispute with the IRS, AARP reached a settlement over its alleged profit-making enterprises by creating a new taxable subsidiary called AARP Services in 1999. The following year AARP initiated a five-year plan to attract aging baby boomers. AARP launched its My Generation magazine in 2001; two years later the organization combined My Generation with its Modern Maturity magazine to form a single publication: AARP The Magazine.

In 2005 the group's lobbying efforts focused on Social Security reform proposals and a new prescription drug benefit for Medicare recipients.

In 2008 the AARP celebrated its own 50th birthday.

In April 2009 A. Barry Rand, a former head of Avis Group Holdings, succeeded Bill Novelli as CEO of AARP. Novelli had held the position for eight years.

EXECUTIVES

CDO, Edna Kane-williams
Auditors : GRANT THORNTON LLP WASHINGTON

LOCATIONS

HQ: AARP
601 E ST NW, WASHINGTON, DC 200490003
Phone: 202 434-2277
Web: WWW.AARP.ORG

PRODUCTS/OPERATIONS

2016 sales

	$ mil.	% of total
Royalties	880.1	55
Membership dues	299.2	19
Publications advertising	150.5	9
Contributions	96.9	6
Grant	97.3	6
Program income	73.9	5
Other	5.8	-
Total	1,603.7	100

Selected Operations & Programs
AARP Bulletin (monthly news update)
AARP Driver Safety (classroom refresher)
AARP Foundation Experience Corps
AARP Legal Services Network
AARP Services (taxable product management, marketing and e-commerce subsidiary)
AARP The Magazine (bimonthly magazine)
Back to Work 50+
Financial Planning
Public Policy Institute
Research Information Center
Senior Community Service Employment Program (SCSEP)
Tax-Aide

COMPETITORS

AMERICAN HEART ASSOCIATION, INC.
BLUE CROSS AND BLUE SHIELD OF MASSACHUSETTS, INC.
GLOBE LIFE INC.
HABITAT FOR HUMANITY INTERNATIONAL, INC.
HUMAN RIGHTS WATCH, INC.
MUTUAL OF OMAHA INSURANCE COMPANY
TRUTH INITIATIVE FOUNDATION
UNITED STATES FUND FOR UNICEF
UNITED WAY WORLDWIDE
W. K. KELLOGG FOUNDATION

HISTORICAL FINANCIALS

Company Type: Private

Income Statement — FYE: December 31

	REVENUE ($mil)	NET INCOME ($mil)	NET PROFIT MARGIN	EMPLOYEES
12/16	1,604	141	8.8%	1,800
12/14	1,399	84	6.0%	—
12/13	1,438	408	28.4%	—
Annual Growth	3.7%	(29.8%)	—	—

2016 Year-End Financials
Return on assets: 3.6% Cash ($ mil.): 427
Return on equity: 9.8%
Current Ratio: —

ABINGTON MEMORIAL HOSPITAL

Abington Hospital?Jefferson Health (formerly Abington Memorial Hospital) brings health care to residents of southeastern Pennsylvania. The not-for-profit community hospital has some 800 beds. In addition to general medical and surgical care, the hospital offers specialized care centers for cancer and cardiovascular conditions, operates high-tech orthopedic and neurological surgery units, and serves as a regional trauma care facility. With approximately 126,000 inpatient admissions, 499,000 Emergency Department visits, and four million outpatient visits annually, it also runs an inpatient pediatric unit in affiliation with The Children's Hospital of Philadelphia. Abington?Jefferson Health operates the neighboring 140-bed Lansdale Hospital?Jefferson Health and range of inpatient and outpatient facilities.

LOCATIONS

HQ: ABINGTON MEMORIAL HOSPITAL
1200 OLD YORK RD, ABINGTON, PA 190013788
Phone: 215 481-2000
Web: WWW.ABINGTONHEALTH.ORG

PRODUCTS/OPERATIONS

Selected Facilities
Abington Health Center — Blue Bell Campus (Blue Bell, PA)
Abington Health Center — Schilling Campus (Willow Grove, PA)
Abington Health Center — Warminster Campus (Warminster, PA)
Abington Memorial Hospital (Abington, PA)
Abington Physicians at Montgomeryville (North Wales, PA)
Lansdale Hospital (Lansdale, PA)

COMPETITORS

BROOKHAVEN MEMORIAL HOSPITAL MEDICAL CENTER, INC.
CENTRA HEALTH, INC.
DOYLESTOWN HOSPITAL
ELMHURST MEMORIAL HOSPITAL
HARRINGTON MEMORIAL HOSPITAL, INC.
MONMOUTH MEDICAL CENTER INC.
PHELPS MEMORIAL HOSPITAL ASSOCIATION
PITT COUNTY MEMORIAL HOSPITAL, INCORPORATED
PROTESTANT MEMORIAL MEDICAL CENTER, INC.
WILKES-BARRE HOSPITAL COMPANY, LLC

HISTORICAL FINANCIALS

Company Type: Private

Income Statement — FYE: June 30

	REVENUE ($mil)	NET INCOME ($mil)	NET PROFIT MARGIN	EMPLOYEES
06/16	740	35	4.8%	4,018
06/15	697	28	4.1%	—
06/14	697	0	0.1%	—
06/13	708	20	2.9%	—
Annual Growth	1.5%	19.2%	—	—

2016 Year-End Financials
Return on assets: 4.5% Cash ($ mil.): 176
Return on equity: 87.7%
Current Ratio: 2.00

ACCESS BUSINESS GROUP LLC

Somehow all those Amway products have to get from factories to the sales floor, and that's where Access Business Group (ABG) comes in. The company manufactures and distributes cosmetics, nutritional supplements, home care, and personal care products for its sister company, Amway. (Both companies are units of Alticor.) It also offers contract manufacturing services for third-party consumer goods companies, but to a lesser extent. Other offerings include product packaging services, as well as catalog and direct mail printing services. In addition, the company operates R&D labs that develop and test products for Amway. Alticor is the parent company of Access Business Group, as well as Amway, and is a holding company for Amway's non-direct selling companies.

LOCATIONS

HQ: ACCESS BUSINESS GROUP LLC
7575 FULTON ST E, ADA, MI 493550001
Phone: 616 787-6000

PRODUCTS/OPERATIONS

Selected Services and Products
Beauty
  Blushes
  Eye shadows
  Lipsticks
  Mascara
  Skin care
Fulfillment
  A-Frame
  B2B & B2C
  Customized order picking at the store level
  High volume pick, pack & ship
  Pick-to-light
  Tilt tray sorter
Home Care
  Household cleaners
  Plastic bottles
  Powder and liquid dish washing detergents
  Powder and liquid laundry detergents
Nutrition
  Antioxidants/supplements/herbals
  Food bars
  Granulation
  Multiminerals/multivitamins
  OTC tableting
  Powdered drinks
Personal Care
  Bar soaps
  Bath oils
  Body mist
  Conditioners
  Lotions
  Plastic bottles
  Shampoos
  Shower gels
  Styling products
Print
  Catalogs
  Corrugated cases
  Fine printing
  Labels
  L-Boards
  Paperboard packaging

COMPETITORS

AIR PRODUCTS AND CHEMICALS, INC.
Atrium Innovations Inc
DIVERSEY, INC.
GOJO INDUSTRIES, INC.
NCH CORPORATION
NUTRACEUTICAL INTERNATIONAL CORPORATION
OIL-DRI CORPORATION OF AMERICA

TELIGENT, INC.
THE CLOROX COMPANY
THE TRANZONIC COMPANIES

HISTORICAL FINANCIALS
Company Type: Private

Income Statement — FYE: December 31

	REVENUE ($mil)	NET INCOME ($mil)	NET PROFIT MARGIN	EMPLOYEES
12/15	1,009	0	0.0%	3,000
12/14	1,068	0	0.0%	—
12/13	1,135	0	0.0%	—
Annual Growth	(5.7%)	—	—	—

ACE HARDWARE CORPORATION

Ace Hardware is the largest retailer-owned hardware cooperative in the world with more than 5,500 locally owned and operated hardware stores in approximately 65 countries. Domestically, Ace retail hardware stores operate in all 50 states and the District of Columbia. The overall home improvement industry is consists of a broad range of products and services, including lawn and garden products, paint and sundries, certain building supplies and general merchandise. Ace also provides value-added services such as advertising, market research, merchandising assistance, and store location and design services. Ace was founded in 1924 by a group of Chicago hardware store owners.

Operations
The company's wholesale revenues accounts for about 90%. Retail revenues is responsible for the remaining.

More specifically, warehouse merchandise generates nearly 70%, direct shipment merchandise about 15%, ARH revenues with around 10%, e-commerce and service revenue, together account for more than 5%. In addition, Ace Ecommerce Holdings LLC (AEH), a majority-owned and controlled subsidiary of the company, operates The Grommet, an e-commerce company that operates a website that markets and sells new and innovative products created by independent entrepreneurs.

Brands include Benjamin Moore, Weber, Yeti, Toro, and Big Green Egg, among others.

Geographic Reach
Headquartered in Brook, Illinois, its subsidiaries operate an expansive network of distribution centers in the US and have distribution capabilities in Ningbo, China; Santa Catarina, Mexico; Colon, Panama; and Dubai, United Arab Emirates.

Sales and Marketing
Aside from its e-commerce site, the company has direct shipment arrangements with various vendors to deliver products to its customer.

Gross advertising expenses amounted to approximately $264.9 million, $240.7 million, and $209.2 million in fiscal 2021, 2020, and 2019, respectively.

Financial Performance
The company's revenue for fiscal 2021 increased to $8.6 billion compared to $7.8 billion in the prior year.

Net income for fiscal 2021 increased to $330.7 million compared to $317.6 million in the prior year.

Cash held by the company at the end of fiscal 2021 increased to $37.6 million. Cash provided by operations was $317.9 million while cash used for investing and financing activities were $127.2 million and $182.0 million, respectively.

Strategy
Over the past two years, Ace has supported Higher Ground as its long-term retail growth strategy. Higher Ground replaced its former growth strategy, 20/20 Vision, due to the need to evolve with changing market conditions in the retail landscape. The strategy continues to build on Ace's commitments to enhance Retailer performance and ensure Retailer growth, not only today, but long term. Higher Ground provides Ace and its Retailers with a clear path to the future. The strategy is consumer-focused, aligned with its corporate strategy and contains two paths for growth that can be implemented separately or concurrently. The two paths for growth are Pinnacle Performance Retailing and Accelerated Store Growth. Pinnacle Performance Retailing is designed to help Ace Retailers improve their store performance by increasing sales and net profits. Accelerated Store Growth is designed to encourage Ace Retailers with the desire and ability to open new stores. It is also intended to increase store count through new investors, conversions of competitors' stores and by reducing the number of stores that leave Ace or close.

Company Background
In 2012, Ace acquired its largest customer, Kansas-based Westlake Hardward Inc. (WHI), an operator of 85 neighborhood hardware stores in Missouri, Kansas, Nebraska, Iowa, Oklahoma Texas, and New Mexico under the name Westlake Ace Hardware, for about $88 million from the private equity firm Goldner Hawn Johnson & Morrison. The purchase of WHI through a newly-formed entity, Ace Retail Holdings, added a company-owned retail component to Ace's business and preserved the Ace brand in the markets served by WHI.

HISTORY

A group of Chicago-area hardware dealers -- William Stauber, Richard Hesse, Gern Lindquist, and Oscar Fisher -- decided in 1924 to pool their hardware buying and promotional costs. In 1928 the group incorporated as Ace Stores, named in honor of the superior WWI fliers dubbed aces. Hesse became president the following year, retaining that position for the next 44 years. The company also opened its first warehouse in 1929, and by 1933 it had 38 dealers.

The organization had 133 dealers in seven states by 1949. In 1953 Ace began to allow dealers to buy stock in the company through the Ace Perpetuation Plan. During the 1960s Ace expanded into the South and West, and by 1969 it had opened distribution centers in Georgia and California -- its first such facilities outside Chicago. In 1968 it opened its first international store in Guam.

By the early 1970s the do-it-yourself market began to surge as inflation pushed up plumber and electrician fees. As the market grew, large home center chains gobbled up market share from independent dealers such as those franchised through Ace. In response, Ace and its dealers became a part of a growing trend in the hardware industry -- cooperatives.

Hesse sold the company to its dealers in 1973 for $6 million (less than half its book value), and the following year Ace began operating as a cooperative. Hesse stepped down in 1973. In 1976 the dealers took full control when the company's first Board of Dealer-Directors was elected.

After signing up a number of dealers in the eastern US, Ace had dealers in all 50 states by 1979. The co-op opened a plant to make paint in Matteson, Illinois, in 1984. By 1985 Ace had reached $1 billion in sales and had initiated its Store of the Future Program, allowing dealers to borrow up to $200,000 to upgrade their stores and conduct market analyses. Former head coach John Madden of the National Football League's Oakland Raiders signed on as Ace's mouthpiece in 1988.

A year later the co-op began to test ACENET, a computer network that allowed Ace dealers to check inventory, send and receive e-mail, make special purchase requests, and keep up with prices on commodity items such as lumber. In 1990 Ace established an International Division to handle its overseas stores. (It had been exporting products since 1975.) EVP and COO David Hodnik became president in 1995. That year the co-op added a net of 67 stores, including a three-store chain in Russia. Expanding further internationally, Ace signed a five-year joint-supply agreement in 1996 with Canadian lumber and hardware retailer Beaver Lumber. Hodnik added CEO to his title in 1996.

Ace fell further behind its old rival, True Value, in 1997 when ServiStar Coast to Coast and True Value merged to form TruServ (renamed True Value in 2005), a hardware giant that operated more than 10,000 outlets at the completion of the merger.

Late in 1997 Ace launched an expansion

program in Canada. (The co-op already operated distribution centers in Ontario and Calgary.) In 1999 Ace merged its lumber and building materials division with Builder Marts of America to form a dealer-owned buying group to supply about 2,700 retailers. Ace gained 208 member outlet stores in 2000, but saw 279 member outlets terminated. The next year it gained 220, but lost 255.

Sodisco-Howden bought all the shares of Ace Hardware Canada in February 2003. To better serve international members, Ace opened its first international buying office, in Hong Kong, in April 2004.

In all, the company added 131 new stores in 2005. That year, after 33 years with the company, David F. Hodnik retired as president and CEO of Ace Hardware. He was succeeded by COO Ray A. Griffith.

In 2007 Griffith sent a letter to Ace's retailers, saying the company was considering changing from a cooperative to a traditional corporation to become more competitive and to better fuel growth. Shortly after, the company announced an accounting shortfall of about $150 million, or nearly half of its equity, which was uncovered while Ace prepared to convert formats. The error turned out to be an accident by a mid-level employee.

In 2009 Ace launched Aisle411, a free product-location service that can be accessed via phone, similar to dialing for information. The company launched the service after learning that shoppers who were unable to find a product either left (about 20% of the time) or asked store associates for assistance (about 60%), which created a high demand for staff attention. Dedicated to pleasing its shoppers, Ace was ranked "Highest in Customer Satisfaction among Home Improvement Stores" by J.D. Power and Associates in 2007, 2008, and 2009.

In mid-2010 the hardware store chain became the first retailer -- outside of Sears and Kmart stores -- to sell Craftsman brand tools.

In January 2011 the company reorganized its international division into a stand-alone entity: Ace Hardware International Holdings. Ace Hardware owns about 78% of the newly-created entity.

In December 2012, Ace exited the paint manufacturing business with the sale of its paint manufacturing division, including two paint manufacturing plants near Chicago, to Valspar Corp. for about $45 million. Under the terms of the sale, Valspar will continue to make and supply Ace-branded paint under a long-term supply agreement. Also, it will supply a comprehensive line of Valspar-branded paints to Ace retail stores.

Auditors : ERNST & YOUNG LLP CHICAGO IL

LOCATIONS

HQ: ACE HARDWARE CORPORATION
2200 KENSINGTON CT, OAK BROOK, IL 605232100
Phone: 630 990-6600
Web: WWW.ACEHARDWARE.COM

PRODUCTS/OPERATIONS

2014 Sales

	$ mil.	% of total
Wholesale Revenues	4,466.7	95
Retail Revenues	233.8	5
Total	4700.5	100

Selected ServicesAssemblyAutomotive chip key cuttingBlade sharpeningGlass & Acrylic sheet cuttingGlass RepairHunting/Fishing licenseIn-store lock servicingSelected BrandsACCO BRANDSACEACMEADANACBIG BENBILCOEUREKAEVEREADYSelected ProductsAdhesives, Glue & TapeBuilding Materials & SuppliesCabinet HardwareChain, Cable & RopeDoor & WindowDriveway MaintenanceHandtrucksHome Safety & SecurityLaddersLetters, Numbers & Signs

COMPETITORS

DO IT BEST CORP.
GREAT LAKES ACE HARDWARE, INC.
LOWE'S COMPANIES, INC.
MENARD, INC.
ORCHARD SUPPLY COMPANY, LLC
SNAP-ON INCORPORATED
THE HOME DEPOT INC
TITAN MACHINERY INC.
TRUE VALUE COMPANY, L.L.C.
WICKES FINANCE LIMITED

HISTORICAL FINANCIALS
Company Type: Private

Income Statement — FYE: December 31

	REVENUE ($mil)	NET INCOME ($mil)	NET PROFIT MARGIN	EMPLOYEES
12/17	5,388	147	2.7%	4,500
12/16*	5,125	161	3.1%	—
01/16	5,045	156	3.1%	—
Annual Growth	3.3%	(2.9%)	—	—

*Fiscal year change

2017 Year-End Financials
Return on assets: 7.9%   Cash ($ mil.): 23
Return on equity: 26.3%
Current Ratio: 1.30

ADVANCED TECHNOLOGY INTERNATIONAL

Auditors : BDO USA LLP RALEIGH NC

LOCATIONS

HQ: ADVANCED TECHNOLOGY INTERNATIONAL
315 SIGMA DR, SUMMERVILLE, SC 294867790
Phone: 843 760-4500
Web: WWW.ATI.ORG

HISTORICAL FINANCIALS
Company Type: Private

Income Statement — FYE: September 30

	REVENUE ($mil)	NET INCOME ($mil)	NET PROFIT MARGIN	EMPLOYEES
09/21	8,017	31	0.4%	300
09/20	3,457	24	0.7%	—
09/19	2,086	7	0.3%	—
09/18	1,190	0	0.1%	—
Annual Growth	88.8%	228.8%	—	—

2021 Year-End Financials
Return on assets: 2.1%   Cash ($ mil.): 546
Return on equity: 44.5%
Current Ratio: 1.00

ADVENTIST HEALTH SYSTEM/SUNBELT, INC.

Adventist Health System Sunbelt (AdventHealth) provides full system care from everyday wellness and preventive health care to life-saving diagnostic services and innovative medical treatments in cancer, heart failure and more. It works with the world's brightest medical minds and innovators. Its integrated network of health care serves neighbors across more than 130 facilities nationwide, including hospital campuses, urgent-care centers, home-health and hospice agencies, and nursing homes across roughly 10 states. Extend the Healing Ministry of Christ, its Christian mission, shared vision, common values and focus on whole-person health is its commitment to making communities healthier with a unified system with nearly 50 hospital campuses and hundreds of care sites in diverse markets.

Operations
AdventHealth offers a whole-person care from everyday wellness and preventive health care to life-saving diagnostic services and innovative medical treatments.

Its wide array of services include allergy care, audiology care, bariatric and weight care, behavioral care, and eye care, to name a few.

Geographic Reach
Headquartered in Altamonte Springs, Florida, it has more than 130 facilities nationwide, including hospital campuses, urgent-care centers, home-health and hospice agencies, and nursing homes across around 10 states.

Auditors : ERNEST & YOUNG LLP ORLANDO

LOCATIONS

HQ: ADVENTIST HEALTH SYSTEM/SUNBELT, INC.
900 HOPE WAY, ALTAMONTE SPRINGS, FL 327141502
Phone: 407 357-1000
Web: WWW.ADVENTHEALTH.COM

Selected Facilities
Colorado
    Avista Adventist Hospital (Louisville)
    Littleton Adventist Hospital
    Parker Adventist Hospital
    Porter Adventist Hospital (Denver)
Florida
    Florida Hospital Altamonte (Altamonte Springs)
    Florida Hospital Apopka
    Florida Hospital Carrollwood (Tampa)
    Florida Hospital Celebration Health (Celebration)
    Florida Hospital DeLand
    Florida Hospital East Orlando
    Florida Hospital Fish Memorial (Orange City)
    Florida Hospital Flagler (Palm Coast)
    Florida Hospital Heartland Medical Center (Sebring)
    Florida Hospital Kissimmee
    Florida Hospital Lake Placid
    Florida Hospital Memorial Medical Center (Daytona Beach)
    Florida Hospital North Pinellas (Tarpon Springs)
    Florida Hospital Oceanside (Ormond Beach)
    Florida Hospital Orlando
    Florida Hospital Pepin Heart Institute (Tampa)
    Florida Hospital Tampa
    Florida Hospital Waterman (Tavares)
    Florida Hospital Wauchula
    Florida Hospital Winter Park Memorial Hospital
    Florida Hospital Zephyrhills
Georgia
    Gordon Hospital (Calhoun)
    Emory-Adventist Hospital (Smyrna)
Illinois
    Adventist Bolingbrook Hospital
    Adventist GlenOaks Hospital (Glendale Heights)
    Adventist Hinsdale Hospital
    Adventist La Grange Memorial Hospital
Kansas
    Shawnee Mission Medical Center
Kentucky
    Manchester Memorial Hospital
North Carolina
    Park Ridge Hospital (Fletcher)
Tennessee
    Jellico Community Hospital
    Takoma Regional Hospital (Greeneville)
Texas
    Central Texas Medical Center (San Marcos)
    Huguley Memorial Medical Center (Fort Worth)
    Metroplex Adventist Hospital (Killeen)
    Rollins Brook Community Hospital (Lampasas)
Wisconsin
    Chippewa Valley Hospital (Durand)

PRODUCTS/OPERATIONS

Selected Products
Behavioral Health
Cardiovascular
Diabetes
Digestive Health
Emergency
Eye Care Center
Family Practice
Home Health/Home Care
Imaging Services
Mammography/Breast Center/Breast Care
Minimally Invasive/Robotic Surgery
Neurology
Neurosurgery
NICU
OB/Birth Care
Oncology/Cancer
Orthopedics
Outpatient Surgery
Pain Medicine
Pediatrics
Psychology
Rehab
Senior Care
Sleep Center
Stroke Care/Stroke Center
Surgery
Therapy Services
Urology
Wellness Center
Women's Services
Wound Care

COMPETITORS

ADVENTIST HEALTH SYSTEM/WEST, CORPORATION
ADVENTIST HEALTHCARE, INC.
BAPTIST HEALTH SOUTH FLORIDA, INC.
BAPTIST HEALTHCARE SYSTEM, INC.
CENTURA HEALTH CORPORATION
COMMONSPIRIT HEALTH
HOUSTON COUNTY HEALTHCARE AUTHORITY
PROVIDENCE HEALTH & SERVICES
SANFORD
TEXAS HEALTH RESOURCES

HISTORICAL FINANCIALS

Company Type: Private

Income Statement   FYE: December 31

	REVENUE ($mil)	NET INCOME ($mil)	NET PROFIT MARGIN	EMPLOYEES
12/21	14,882	1,512	10.2%	46,960
12/20	12,623	951	7.5%	—
12/19	11,892	1,607	13.5%	—
12/09	0	0	0.0%	—
Annual Growth	201.9%	—	—	—

2021 Year-End Financials
Return on assets: 6.7%   Cash ($ mil.): 506
Return on equity: 10.5%
Current Ratio: 3.10

ADVENTIST HEALTH SYSTEM/WEST, CORPORATION

Adventist Health System/West, doing business as Adventist Health, is a faith-based, nonprofit integrated health system serving more than 80 communities on the West Coast and Hawaii. Annually, Adventist Health has more than 127,700 admissions, 682,300 emergency department visits, 246,570 home health visits, 2.4 million clinic visits, and 1.6 million outpatient visits. Adventist Health maintains strong ties to the Seventh-day Adventist Church but is independently owned. A sister organization, Adventist Health System, operates in the central and southern parts of the country.

Operations

Adventist Health offer a wide range of services, including cancer/oncology, cardiovascular, critical care, dental care, emergency services, general surgery, health education, home care services, heart and vascular, intensive care, internal medicine, maternity, mental health, orthopedics, pediatrics, pain management, rehabilitation services, urgent care, urology, women's health and wound care, among others.

Geographic Reach

Adventist Health serve patients across West Coast and Hawaii.

Sales and Marketing

Adventist Health provides care in hospitals, clinics, home care agencies, hospice agencies and joint-venture retirement centers in both rural and urban communities.

EXECUTIVES

CCO*, Joyce Newmyer

CMO*, Alex Bryan

Auditors: ERNST & YOUNG LLP ROSEVILLE

LOCATIONS

HQ: ADVENTIST HEALTH SYSTEM/WEST, CORPORATION
    1 ADVENTIST HEALTH WAY, ROSEVILLE, CA 956613266
Phone: 844 574-5686
Web: WWW.ADVENTISTHEALTH.ORG

COMPETITORS

ADVENTIST HEALTH SYSTEM/SUNBELT, INC.
ADVENTIST HEALTHCARE, INC.
AVERA HEALTH
BAPTIST HEALTH SYSTEM, INC.
BEAUMONT HEALTH
LEGACY HEALTH
MEDSTAR HEALTH, INC.
MERCY HEALTH
PROVIDENCE ST. JOSEPH HEALTH
UNIVERSITY HOSPITALS HEALTH SYSTEM, INC.

HISTORICAL FINANCIALS

Company Type: Private

Income Statement   FYE: December 31

	REVENUE ($mil)	NET INCOME ($mil)	NET PROFIT MARGIN	EMPLOYEES
12/18	4,434	544	12.3%	19,512
12/17	4,114	199	4.9%	—
12/16	3,945	185	4.7%	—
12/15	251	10	4.3%	—
Annual Growth	160.3%	267.8%	—	—

2018 Year-End Financials
Return on assets: 9.4%   Cash ($ mil.): 700
Return on equity: 19.3%
Current Ratio: 2.90

ADVENTIST HEALTHCARE, INC.

Adventist HealthCare is the first and largest provider of healthcare in Montgomery County, Maryland. The not-for-profit system, with 1,800 physicians and medical providers, is home to five acute care hospitals, and more than 414,485 outpatient visits. Its hospitals are Adventist HealthCare Shady Grove Medical Center (Rockville), White Oak Medical Center (Silver Spring), Fort Washington Medical Center (Fort Washington), Germantown Emergency Center and Adventist Rehabilitation (Rockville). Among its specialized medical services include heart and vascular car, mental health care, pregnancy care and birth and radiology and diagnostic imaging. Adventist HealthCare, which is affiliated with the Seventh-day Adventist Church, has been in operation since 1907.

Operations

Adventist HealthCare's Lourie Center for Children's Social & Emotional Wellness promotes the social and emotional health of parent-child relations through education, training, research, early prevention, and intervention. Its offerings include an early head start program to benefit low-income families, parent-child programs and therapeutic nursery. The company operates three nationally accredited acute-care hospitals, a nationally accredited rehabilitation hospital, mental health services, home health agencies, physician networks, urgent care centers, and imaging centers. In addition to cancer care, home care, and orthopedic care, the company's other specialized medical services also include rehabilitation and surgery.

Adventist HealthCare has more than 124,585 emergency visits, about 427,820 outpatient visits, approximately 120,785 home health visits, and delivers about 6,930 babies a year. It also has approximately 7,780 surgical admissions, around 13,260 outpatient surgeries, around 23,600 medical admissions and about 58,035 health and wellness encounters.

Geographic Reach

Adventist HealthCare operates facilities in Maryland, and Washington, DC. Its headquarters is located in Gaithersburg, Maryland.

Company Background

In 1907, Washington Sanitarium opens in Takoma Park later to become Washington Adventist Hospital.

Auditors : BAKER TILLY VIRCHOW KRAUSE L

LOCATIONS

HQ: ADVENTIST HEALTHCARE, INC.
820 W DIAMOND AVE STE 600, GAITHERSBURG, MD 208781469
Phone: 301 315-3030
Web: WWW.ADVENTISTHEALTHCARE.COM

PRODUCTS/OPERATIONS

Selected Home Health Services
Nursing and Home Health
    Adult nursing
    Diabetes management
    Maternal/child care
    Nutrition management
    Pediatric nursing
    Personal care
    Pre- and post-op care
    Rehabilitation
    Wound care
Home Assistance
    Laundry and linens
    Light housekeeping
    Meal preparation
    Medication reminders

Personal care

COMPETITORS

BAYLOR SCOTT & WHITE HEALTH
CENTURA HEALTH CORPORATION
CKHS, INC.
NORTHWESTERN MEMORIAL HEALTHCARE
PERSONAL TOUCH HOME CARE IPA, INC.
PROVIDENCE HEALTH & SERVICES
ST. JOSEPH HEALTH SYSTEM
STEWARD HEALTH CARE SYSTEM LLC
VISITING NURSE SERVICE OF NEW YORK
VITAS HEALTHCARE CORPORATION

HISTORICAL FINANCIALS
Company Type: Private

Income Statement   FYE: December 31

	REVENUE ($mil)	NET INCOME ($mil)	NET PROFIT MARGIN	EMPLOYEES
12/21	1,154	29	2.6%	5,236
12/20	974	42	4.3%	—
12/19	862	32	3.8%	—
12/18	820	21	2.6%	—
Annual Growth	12.0%	12.0%	—	—

2021 Year-End Financials
Return on assets: 1.7%   Cash ($ mil.): 37
Return on equity: 5.4%
Current Ratio: 1.70

ADVENTIST MIDWEST HEALTH

EXECUTIVES

NURSING, Patricia A Sutton
President Parent, Todd S Werner Junior V

LOCATIONS

HQ: ADVENTIST MIDWEST HEALTH
120 N OAK ST, HINSDALE, IL 605213829
Phone: 630 856-9000
Web: WWW.AMITAHEALTH.ORG

HISTORICAL FINANCIALS
Company Type: Private

Income Statement   FYE: December 31

	REVENUE ($mil)	NET INCOME ($mil)	NET PROFIT MARGIN	EMPLOYEES
12/19	561	(12)	—	2,470
12/16	305	10	3.4%	—
12/15	289	17	5.9%	—
12/14	287	0	0.3%	—
Annual Growth	14.3%	—	—	—

2019 Year-End Financials
Return on assets: (-1.9%)   Cash ($ mil.): 84
Return on equity: (-5.0%)
Current Ratio: 3.30

ADVOCATE HEALTH AND HOSPITALS CORPORATION

Auditors : ERNST & YOUNG US LLP CHICAGO

LOCATIONS

HQ: ADVOCATE HEALTH AND HOSPITALS CORPORATION
3075 HIGHLAND PKWY FL 6, DOWNERS GROVE, IL 605155563
Phone: 630 929-6965
Web: WWW.ADVOCATEHEALTH.COM

HISTORICAL FINANCIALS
Company Type: Private

Income Statement   FYE: December 31

	REVENUE ($mil)	NET INCOME ($mil)	NET PROFIT MARGIN	EMPLOYEES
12/19	5,672	(28)	—	4,110
12/17	5,310	243	4.6%	—
12/13	4,072	392	9.6%	—
12/12	3,645	419	11.5%	—
Annual Growth	6.5%	—	—	—

2019 Year-End Financials
Return on assets: (-0.2%)   Cash ($ mil.): 129
Return on equity: (-0.5%)
Current Ratio: 0.90

ADVOCATE HEALTH AND HOSPITALS CORPORATION

Advocate Lutheran General Hospital, also known simply as Lutheran General, provides acute and long-term medical and surgical care to the residents of Park Ridge, Illinois and the surrounding northern suburban Chicago area. As one of the largest hospitals in the region, Lutheran General boasts nearly 640 beds and a Level I trauma center. Its operations also include a complete children's hospital and pediatric critical care center. Lutheran General serves as a teaching hospital and its specialized programs include oncology, cardiology, women's health, emergency medicine, and hospice care. Lutheran General is part of the Advocate Health Care network.

Operations

Lutheran General, the sixth largest hospital in the Chicago area, is a not-for-profit, faith-based organization related to the Evangelical Lutheran Church in America and the United Church of Christ. With some 1,150 physicians, representing more than 50 specialties and subspecialties, Advocate Lutheran General saw 62,500 patients in its emergency department in 2012.

That year the company reported more than 29,000 admissions, 19,000 surgeries, and more than 4,000 births.

Geographic Reach
The hospital system is the primary academic referral hospital for northwest Chicago and north Greater Chicago.

Strategy
Increase its services to meet specific demographics, in 2012 Lutheran General opened a new South Asian Cardiovascular Center in the Midwest; it also launched Expressions, a program aimed at helping seniors in the early stages of Alzheimer's disease.

That year thee hospital introduced a new Pet Therapy program to the Adult Oncology unit. It also launched of its neuroendovascular program to expand Lutheran General's acute stroke care to provide advanced acute stroke care to patients throughout the northern Chicago area.

Company Background
Lutheran General serves those who live in the northern suburban Chicago area, specifically Park Ridge, Illinois.

The hospital was founded in 1897.

LOCATIONS
HQ: ADVOCATE HEALTH AND HOSPITALS CORPORATION
 1775 DEMPSTER ST, PARK RIDGE, IL 600681143
Phone: 847 723-6610
Web: WWW.ADVOCATEHEALTH.COM

Selected Hospitals
Advocate BroMenn Medical Center
Advocate Children's Hospital - Oak Lawn
Advocate Children's Hospital - Park Ridge
Advocate Christ Center for Breast Care
Advocate Christ Medical Center
Advocate Christ Medical Center - Physical Rehabilitation Center, Center for Hearing and Sleep Center
Advocate Christ Outpatient Center
Advocate Christ Outpatient Center - Lockport
Advocate Condell Medical Center
Advocate Eureka Hospital
Advocate Good Samaritan Hospital
Advocate Good Shepherd Hospital
Advocate Illinois Masonic Medical Center
Advocate Lutheran General Hospital
Advocate South Suburban Hospital
Advocate Trinity Hospital

PRODUCTS/OPERATIONS
Selected Services
Adult Day Hospital
Adult Down Syndrome Center
Anticoagulation Center
Behavioral Health
Caldwell Breast Center
Cancer Care
Center for Fetal Care
Children's Services
The Comprehensive Continence Center
Emergency Services
Heart and Vascular
Hyperbaric Treatment
Interventional Radiology
Joint Reconstruction & Replacement
Nutrition Services Opthamology
Outpatient Testing Prep Instructions

Pain Management Center
Rehabilitation
Senior Services
Sleep Disorders
Surgical Services
The Center for Robotic Surgery
Women's Services
Wound Care

COMPETITORS
AKRON GENERAL MEDICAL CENTER
ASCENSION PROVIDENCE HOSPITAL
FROEDTERT MEMORIAL LUTHERAN HOSPITAL, INC.
HOSPITAL SERVICE DISTRICT 1
LOMA LINDA UNIVERSITY MEDICAL CENTER

HISTORICAL FINANCIALS
Company Type: Private

Income Statement　　　　　　　　　　　　FYE: December 31

	REVENUE ($mil)	NET INCOME ($mil)	NET PROFIT MARGIN	EMPLOYEES
12/17	790	79	10.0%	4,818
12/16	785	118	15.1%	—
12/15	752	104	13.9%	—
12/14	741	107	14.5%	—
Annual Growth	2.1%	(9.6%)	—	—

2017 Year-End Financials
Return on assets: 0.9%　　　Cash ($ mil.): 229
Return on equity: 1.6%
Current Ratio: 1.00

AEROTEK AFFILIATED SERVICES, INC.

Aerotek, a unit of staffing powerhouse Allegis Group, offers commercial and technical staffing services throughout North America, Europe, and Asia Pacific. Through its several divisions, Aerotek specializes in placing light industrial, skilled trades and construction talent to support project-based, seasonal, high-volume, or niche requirements. The company also provides training and support services. Along with aerospace, auto, and engineering companies, Aerotek's clients include companies from the construction, energy, manufacturing, health care, and finance industries. Operates through more than 250 offices, the company supports over 13,000 clients across North America's leading industries.

Operations
Aerotek solutions include Staffing Services, Vendor On-Premise, Managed Resources, and Workforce Management and Solutions.

Aerotek Staffing Services provide skilled talent on a contract, contract-to-hire and direct placement basis for project-based, seasonal or niche requirements.

Its On-Premise solution brings its high level of service to facility to begin to relieve the pressure of onboarding and retention. It has more than 30,000 on-premise contractor placements annually.

Managed Resources offering reduce resource constraints while optimizing productivity and increasing visibility. Its Workforce Management & Solutions include upskilling, health and safety, master supplier, and implementation

Geographic Reach
Based in the US, Aerotek has offices in the US, Canada, Australia, China, Belgium, France, Germany, the Netherlands, Sweden, Switzerland, and in the UK. Aerotek also operates a network of more than 250 non-franchised offices.

Sales and Marketing
Aerotek serves customers in a diverse array of industries, including consumer and industrial, e-commerce, government, life sciences, transportation, energy, construction, and healthcare, among others.

Company Background
Aerotek was founded in 1983 in Baltimore, MD by entrepreneurs Steve Bisciotti and Jim Davis. It got its start by providing engineering staffing for the aerospace and defense industries and later for automotive manufacturers and suppliers. In 1990, the company formed Telecommunications Services, now known as TEKsystems, which has been recognized as the top information technology staffing firm in the US by the IT Services Business Report.

In 1993, Aerotek acquired Onsite Engineering & Management focused on environmental and energy services staffing. It later branched out to include staffing for other industries including biotechnology, pharmaceuticals, healthcare, light industrial, and light technical. It opened its first European office in 1993 and two years later, expanded into Canada with an office in Mississauga, Ontario.

In 1998, Allegis Group was formed as the parent entity of several operating companies, including Aerotek, TEKsystems, and Onsite. In 2001, Aerotek and Onsite merged to become Onsite Companies and in 2004, Onsite Companies changed its name to Aerotek, Inc., to leverage the reputation of the Aerotek name.

Auditors : PRICEWATERHOUSECOOPERS LLP B

LOCATIONS
HQ: AEROTEK AFFILIATED SERVICES, INC.
 7301 PARKWAY DR, HANOVER, MD 210761159
Phone: 410 694-5100
Web: WWW.AEROTEK.COM

PRODUCTS/OPERATIONS
INDUSTRIES SERVED
Accounting
Administrative & Support Services
Aerospace, Aviation & Defense
Architecture & Design
Automotive
Construction
Customer Service
Energy & Utilities
Engineering
Environmental

Financial Services
Government & Public Administration
Healthcare
Manufacturing
Pharmaceutical
Sciences
Warehouse & Distribution

COMPETITORS

ALLEGIS GROUP, INC.
APEX SYSTEMS, LLC
BELCAN, LLC
CENERGY INTERNATIONAL SERVICES, INC.
EDEN BROWN LIMITED
ICONMA, L.L.C.
MSX INTERNATIONAL, INC.
ROSE INTERNATIONAL, INC.
SOS STAFFING SERVICES, INC.
TECHNICAL AID CORPORATION

HISTORICAL FINANCIALS

Company Type: Private

Income Statement — FYE: December 31

	REVENUE ($mil)	NET INCOME ($mil)	NET PROFIT MARGIN	EMPLOYEES
12/20	5,859	0	0.0%	9,300
12/19	6,662	0	0.0%	—
12/18	6,586	0	0.0%	—
12/17	6,070	0	0.0%	—
Annual Growth	(1.2%)	—	—	—

2020 Year-End Financials
Return on assets: —
Return on equity: —
Current Ratio: 3.50
Cash ($ mil.): 26

AFFILIATED FOODS MIDWEST COOPERATIVE, INC.

Affiliated Foods Midwest Cooperative is a wholesale food distribution cooperative that supplies more than 800 independent grocers in some 15 states in the Midwest. From its handful of distribution centers in Kansas, Nebraska, and Wisconsin, the co-op distributes fresh produce, meats, deli items, baked goods, dairy products, and frozen foods, as well as general merchandise and equipment. It distributes goods under the Shurfine brand (from Topco Associates) and IGA labels. Additionally, Affiliated Foods Midwest provides marketing, merchandising, and warehousing support services for its members. The cooperative was formed in 1931 to make wholesale purchases for a group of retailers in Nebraska.

Geographic Reach
Norfolk, Nebraska-based Affiliated Foods Midwest Cooperative has distribution centers in Norfolk, Elwood, Kansas, and Kenosha, Wisconsin. It serves customers in 15 states across the Midwest.

Financial Performance
Affiliated Foods Midwest rang up an estimated $1.6 billion in sales in fiscal 2013 (ended June).

Auditors : BKD LLP LINCOLN NEBRASKA

LOCATIONS

HQ: AFFILIATED FOODS MIDWEST COOPERATIVE, INC.
1301 W OMAHA AVE, NORFOLK, NE 687015872
Phone: 402 371-0555
Web: WWW.AFMIDWEST.COM

PRODUCTS/OPERATIONS

Selected Private-Label Brands
CharKing
ChuckWagon (pet food)
Clear Value
Cow Belle Creamery (ice cream)
Domestix (household products)
Full Circle (organic, natural products)
IGA
PAWS Premium (pet products)
Shurfine
TopCare (OTC drugs, health and beauty)
Valu Time
Wide Awake Coffee Co. (coffee)
World Classics Trading Company

COMPETITORS

CENTRAL GROCERS, INC.
COUNTRYSIDE FOODS, LLC
LAUREL GROCERY COMPANY LLC
THE H T HACKNEY CO
THE MERCHANTS COMPANY

HISTORICAL FINANCIALS

Company Type: Private

Income Statement — FYE: June 26

	REVENUE ($mil)	NET INCOME ($mil)	NET PROFIT MARGIN	EMPLOYEES
06/15	1,527	1	0.1%	850
06/14	1,477	2	0.2%	—
06/13	1,391	2	0.2%	—
06/12	1,486	2	0.2%	—
Annual Growth	0.9%	(19.5%)	—	—

2015 Year-End Financials
Return on assets: 3.1%
Return on equity: 0.1%
Current Ratio: 0.30
Cash ($ mil.): —

AFFILIATED FOODS, INC.

This company helps keep pantries stocked in the Texas Panhandle and elsewhere. Affiliated Foods is a leading wholesale distribution cooperative that supplies grocery stores and restaurants in about a half a dozen states, including Texas, New Mexico, and Oklahoma. It distributes fresh produce, meat, and non-food products, as well as dairy products and beverages through its Plains Dairy unit. Its Tri State Baking Company supplies bread and other baked goods. In addition, Affiliated Foods owns a stake in private-label products supplier Western Family Foods. The company was founded in 1946 as Panhandle Associated Grocers, which merged with South Plains Associated Grocers to form Affiliated Foods in 1968.

Geographic Reach
Based in Amarillo, Texas, Affiliated Foods supplies grocery stores and restaurants in Texas, Oklahoma, Kansas, New Mexico, Colorado, Arizona, and Arkansas.

Financial Performance
While privately-owned Affiliated Foods doesn't report its financial results, the cooperative reported an estimated $1.5 billion in sales in fiscal 2012 (ends October).

Auditors : JOHNSON & SHELDON PLLC AMARI

LOCATIONS

HQ: AFFILIATED FOODS, INC.
1401 W FARMERS AVE, AMARILLO, TX 791186134
Phone: 806 372-3851
Web: WWW.AFIAMA.COM

PRODUCTS/OPERATIONS

Selected Subsidiaries
Affiliated Food Service (restaurant supply)
Plains Dairy (Amarillo, Texas)
Tri-State Baking Co. (Amarillo, Texas)

COMPETITORS

AFFILIATED FOODS MIDWEST COOPERATIVE, INC.
ASSOCIATED FOOD STORES, INC.
ASSOCIATED GROCERS OF THE SOUTH, INC.
BOZZUTO'S, INC.
BROOKSHIRE GROCERY COMPANY
CAITO FOODS SERVICE INC
COUNTRYSIDE FOODS, LLC
DOT FOODS, INC.
INSTITUTION FOOD HOUSE, INC.
UNIFIED GROCERS, INC.

HISTORICAL FINANCIALS

Company Type: Private

Income Statement — FYE: October 2

	REVENUE ($mil)	NET INCOME ($mil)	NET PROFIT MARGIN	EMPLOYEES
10/21	1,532	1	0.1%	1,200
10/20*	1,556	1	0.1%	—
09/19	1,450	2	0.1%	—
09/17	1,421	1	0.1%	—
Annual Growth	1.9%	10.0%	—	—

*Fiscal year change

2021 Year-End Financials
Return on assets: 0.8%
Return on equity: 2.3%
Current Ratio: 1.10
Cash ($ mil.): 6

AFJ, LLC

LOCATIONS

HQ: AFJ, LLC
1104 COUNTRY HILLS DR, OGDEN, UT 844032400
Phone: 801 624-1000

HISTORICAL FINANCIALS

Company Type: Private

Income Statement FYE: January 31

	REVENUE ($mil)	NET INCOME ($mil)	NET PROFIT MARGIN	EMPLOYEES
01/07	661	(0)	—	71
01/06	574	(2)	—	—
01/05	401	3	0.8%	—
Annual Growth	28.4%	—	—	—

2007 Year-End Financials

Return on assets: (-0.3%)   Cash ($ mil.): —
Return on equity: (-0.6%)
Current Ratio: 0.40

AG PROCESSING INC A COOPERATIVE

Soy far, soy good for Ag Processing (AGP), the largest farmer-owned soybean processor in the world, and roughly the fourth-largest soybean processor in the US based on capacity. It purchases and processes more than 5.5 million acres of members' soybeans per year. The farmer-owned cooperative is also a leading supplier of refined vegetable oil in the US. It procures, processes, markets, and transports grains and grain products, ranging from human food ingredients to livestock feed to renewable fuels. AGP is owned by about 180 local and regional cooperatives and represents more than 250,000 farmers in 15 states throughout the US.

Operations

In addition to its soybean processing and vegetable oil refining facilities, AGP operates a merchandising and trading group called Ag Products, subdivided into three areas of focus: Grain, Protein, and Export. Ag Products Grain focuses on marketing grain for members seeking to better compete in the global grain industry. Ag Products Protein markets soybean meal and soy hulls; it also manufactures AMINOPLUS, a protein that improves milk production. Ag Products Export offers international marketing of soybean meal, oilseeds, grains, and other bulk agricultural commodities. Its main gateway to the fast growing Pacific Rim market is through a West Coast export shipping terminal in Washington state.

AGP also holds investment stakes in Masterfeeds, a Canadian feed manufacturing business, and in Protinal/Proagro, Venezuela's largest poultry processor and one of country's largest animal feed producers.

Geographic Reach

AGP operates nine soybean processing plants, including six located in Iowa. Other soybean processing plants are located in Minnesota, Missouri, and Nebraska. The company operates a growing ethanol plant in Nebraska to serve the renewable fuels market and soybean methyl ester plants in Iowa and Missouri. (Soy methyl ester, an alternative to petroleum-based products, is a byproduct that is used in everything from biodiesel to solvents.)

Financial Performance

AGP recorded its fourth best earnings year in the company's history in fiscal 2011. Its earnings from continuing operations (before income taxes) nearly doubled from 2010. Soybean processing rebounded from the previous year partly due to more aggressive export efforts. The company's vegetable oil business had its most profitable year yet as a result of improved demand from the soy biodiesel market, improved oil quality, and improved plant efficiency. Its renewable fuels business (ethanol and biodiesel) started slowly but finished 2011 strong, posting improved earnings over 2010.

Strategy

With evolving EPA mandates, the potential is still strong for integrated biodiesel producers like AGP, which led it to acquire a 60-million gallon biodiesel plant in Algona, Iowa in 2011. The acquisition doubled AGP's biodiesel production capacity, now totaling about 120 million gallons.

Another major component of AGP's strategy is investing in expanding, upgrading, and modernizing various facilities for improved capacity and efficiency. In 2011 the company initiated major upgrade and modernization projects at soy processing plants in Sergeant Bluff, Iowa and Dawson, Minnesota. It also undertook a multi-million dollar expansion project at its Aberdeen, Washington-based export terminal as overseas shipments to Pacific Rim countries increases.

In 2012 Ag Processing merged its Masterfeeds subsidiary with the Canadian commercial feed business (Feed-Rite) of Ridley to form the second-largest feed provider in Canada, Masterfeeds LP. The new entity operates 22 manufacturing plants across the Quebec, Ontario, and Prairie provinces. Ridley and Ag Processing each own relative shares in Masterfeeds LP.

HISTORY

Seeking strength in numbers, Ag Processing (AGP) was formed in 1983 when agricultural cooperatives Land O' Lakes and Farmland Industries merged their money-losing soybean operations into similarly struggling Boone Valley Cooperative.

Separately, AGP's soybean mills had been unable to compete successfully against each other and larger corporations. The entire industry had been hampered by the Soviet grain embargoes imposed by the US in 1973 and 1979, and US government policies had contributed to increased competition from heavily subsidized soy producers in Argentina and Brazil. Soy exports from the US had fallen dramatically, leading to a production capacity surplus.

Collectively, AGP was able to attract a stronger management staff than its predecessors had; it hired 21-year Archer Daniels Midland (ADM) veteran James Lindsay as CEO and general manager. With operations scattered over four states, AGP placed its headquarters in Omaha, Nebraska -- chosen for its central location and close proximity to the co-op's main bank.

In its first two years, AGP cut employee rolls by 20% and scaled back production, thus trimming costs and squeezing higher prices for finished products. A turnaround came quickly, and in 1985 members received a dividend from the co-op's $8 million pretax profit. That year AGP purchased two Iowa plants from AGRI Industries.

AGP dismantled two plants in 1987. By the next year the co-op witnessed an increase in domestic demand and had resumed selling to the Soviet Union. It generated additional sales by further processing soybean oil into food-grade products like hydrogenated oil and lecithin.

With an eye on diversification and value-added products, by 1991 AGP had expanded to eight soybean plants and two vegetable oil refineries; it also acquired the feed and grain business of International Multifoods that year through an 80%-owned joint venture with ADM. The acquisition included 29 feed plants in the US and Canada, 26 retail centers, 18 grain elevators, and the brands Supersweet and Masterfeeds. In 1994 AGP formed feed manufacturer Consolidated Nutrition, a 50-50 joint venture with ADM.

Consolidated Nutrition introduced a Swine Operations program in 1996. The program quickly grew through the development of PORK PACT, a partnership to serve pork producers. (The co-op has since exited the swine business.) The next year AGP's grain division sold nine grain elevators in Ohio and Indiana to Cargill. That year the co-op gained control of Venezuelan feed manufacturer Proagro.

By 1998 passage of the Freedom to Farm Act and growing demand had spurred soybean planting. The co-op in 1998 opened an additional processing plant in Emmetsburg, Iowa, followed by another in Eagle Grove, Iowa. AGP sold off its pet food operations in 1998 to Windy Hill, which was later acquired by Doane Pet Care Enterprises. Also that year Consolidated Nutrition combined its Master Mix and Supersweet feed brands into the Consolidated Nutrition label.

In 1999 the company added the Garner-Klemme-Meservey cooperative to its grain operations. It opened a new plant late that year in St. Joseph, Missouri, to make value-added products such as hardfat (used in emulsifiers).

In 2001 AGP sold its 50% share of Consolidated Nutrition to ADM. In 2002 the co-op's Masterfeeds business acquired four feed mills and a merchandising operation from Saskatchewan Wheat Pool (now Viterra). In 2003 AGP opened the Port of Grays Harbor vessel-loading terminal in Aberdeen, Washington.

The company formed a subsidiary, AgGrowth Products, to market crop nutrients manufactured by Bio Tech Nutrients in 2005. Also that year, the company announced facility expansions for its ethanol, biodiesel, and soybean processing operations.

In 2007 the co-op's board rejected a hostile takeover bid made by Ag Processors Alliance (APA). APA was formed exclusively to take over AGP and consisted of the leadership of Ag and Food Associates of Omaha, an investment banking firm that manages the project on behalf of an investment group that has a specific interest and expertise in agricultural operations.

EXECUTIVES

CMO*, Mark Sandeen

LOCATIONS

HQ: AG PROCESSING INC A COOPERATIVE
12700 W DODGE RD, OMAHA, NE 681546102
Phone: 402 496-7809
Web: WWW.AGP.COM

PRODUCTS/OPERATIONS

Selected Brands
Masterfeeds
    AMINOPLUS (dairy cattle feed additive)
    DIRECTOR (dairy cattle feed additive)
    FUSION (horse feed additive)
Proagro/Protinal
    Corral (Prepared chicken products, Venezuela only)
SOYGOLD (bio-diesel, fuel additives, herbicides, solvents, surfactants, fuel additives)

Selected Exported Products
Barley
Corn
Distillers dried grains (DDGS)
Feeding peas
High-protein soybean meal
Lecithin
Low-protein soybean meal
Oats
Soybean hulls
Soybean oil
Soybeans
Sunflowers
Wheat

Selected Operations and Products
Animal feed
Corn processing
Corn-based ethanol
Grain processing, merchandising, and sales
Industrial products (ethanol and methyl esters)
Soybean processing
Soybean oil
Soybean biodiesel
Prepared chicken products (Venezuela only)

COMPETITORS

ADM ALLIANCE NUTRITION, INC.
BLUE BUFFALO PET PRODUCTS, INC.
Bunge Limited
CARGILL, INCORPORATED
CHS INC.
O.K. INDUSTRIES, INC.
RIDLEY CORPORATION LIMITED

Ridley Inc
SOUTHERN STATES COOPERATIVE, INCORPORATED
ZINPRO CORPORATION

HISTORICAL FINANCIALS
Company Type: Private

Income Statement   FYE: August 31

	REVENUE ($mil)	NET INCOME ($mil)	NET PROFIT MARGIN	EMPLOYEES
08/16*	3,410	134	3.9%	1,456
12/10	3	0	1.3%	—
08/06	2,360	62	2.7%	—
Annual Growth	3.7%	7.9%	—	—

*Fiscal year change

2016 Year-End Financials
Return on assets: 9.9%   Cash ($ mil.): 210
Return on equity: 15.3%
Current Ratio: 2.80

AGFIRST FARM CREDIT BANK

AgFirst Farm Credit Bank is a member of the Farm Credit System, the largest agricultural lending organization in the United States and one of the four banks in the Farm Credit Systems, and provides funding to about 20 affiliated associations and provides services to 20 associations in 18 states and Puerto Rico. Boasting $30 billion in assets, the bank provides financing to about 20 farmer-owned agricultural credit associations. The associations in turn offer mortgages and loans to some 80,000 farmers, agribusinesses, and rural homeowners in 15 Eastern states and Puerto Rico. The company also offers credit and credit-related services to qualified borrowers. AgFirst raises money by selling bonds and notes on the capital markets. AgFirst Farm Credit Bank was founded in 1916.

Auditors: PRICEWATERHOUSECOOPERS LLP MI

LOCATIONS

HQ: AGFIRST FARM CREDIT BANK
1901 MAIN ST, COLUMBIA, SC 292012443
Phone: 803 799-5000
Web: WWW.AGFIRST.COM

PRODUCTS/OPERATIONS

2014 Sales

	$ mil.	% of total
Interest		
Loans	566.5	79
Investment securities & other	127.3	18
Non-interest		
Loan fees	8.5	2
Building lease income	3.3	-
Net other-than-temporary impairment losses	(1.4)	-
Gains (losses) on called debt	(7.7)	-
Gains (losses) on investments, net	0	-
Gains (losses) on other transactions	0	-
Other	7.3	1
Total	703.8	100

COMPETITORS

BANK MUTUAL CORPORATION
CAPITAL BANK FINANCIAL CORP.
CITY HOLDING COMPANY
COBANK, ACB
FARM CREDIT EAST, ACA
FEDERAL AGRICULTURAL MORTGAGE CORPORATION
FEDERAL HOME LOAN BANK OF DALLAS
FEDERAL HOME LOAN BANK OF NEW YORK
FEDERAL HOME LOAN BANK OF PITTSBURGH
NORINCHUKIN BANK, THE

HISTORICAL FINANCIALS
Company Type: Private

Income Statement   FYE: December 31

	ASSETS ($mil)	NET INCOME ($mil)	INCOME AS % OF ASSETS	EMPLOYEES
12/17	32,487	344	1.1%	530
12/15	30,620	336	1.1%	—
Annual Growth	3.0%	1.2%	—	—

2017 Year-End Financials
Return on assets: 1.1%   Cash ($ mil.): 713
Return on equity: 15.4%
Current Ratio: —

AGTEGRA COOPERATIVE

Who loves you a bushel and a peck? South Dakota Wheat Growers may; it is an agricultural co-op comprising some 6,800 member-farmers. It provides a grain warehouse along with grain marketing services intended to compete with big food and ag companies. In addition to storage and drying, Wheat Growers offers agronomy spreading and spraying, and transportation. It supplies feed, fertilizer, chemicals, and other farm-related provisions for members in and around counties in North and South Dakota. Wheat Growers generates more than half of its revenues through marketing some 160 million bushels of grain (corn, wheat, and soybeans) each year. Remaining revenues are made through agronomy and retail sales and services.

Auditors: GARDINER THOMSEN PC DES MOIN

LOCATIONS

HQ: AGTEGRA COOPERATIVE
908 LAMONT ST S, ABERDEEN, SD 574015515
Phone: 605 225-5500
Web: WWW.AGTEGRA.COM

Selected Counties of Operation
North Dakota
    Dickey
    LaMoure
    Stutsman
South Dakota
    Aurora
    Beadle
    Brown
    Brule
    Clark

Corson
Day
Edmunds
Faulk
Hand
Hyde
Jerauld
Lyman
Marshall
Sanborn
Spink

COMPETITORS

CENTAUR GRAIN LIMITED
CHS INC.
COOPERATIVE ELEVATOR CO.
DEBRUCE GRAIN, INC.
FRONTIER AGRICULTURE LIMITED
LUCKEY FARMERS, INC.
RICELAND FOODS, INC.
THE SCOULAR COMPANY
WATONWAN FARM SERVICE, INC
WEST CENTRAL COOPERATIVE

HISTORICAL FINANCIALS

Company Type: Private

Income Statement — FYE: July 31

	REVENUE ($mil)	NET INCOME ($mil)	NET PROFIT MARGIN	EMPLOYEES
07/19	1,509	(5)	—	638
07/18	1,544	32	2.1%	—
07/17	1,275	22	1.8%	—
07/16	1,209	6	0.6%	—
Annual Growth	7.7%	—	—	—

2019 Year-End Financials
Return on assets: (-0.6%) Cash ($ mil.): 6
Return on equity: (-1.7%)
Current Ratio: 1.20

AHS HOSPITAL CORP.

Auditors : PRICEWATERHOUSECOOPERS LLP F

LOCATIONS

HQ: AHS HOSPITAL CORP.
475 SOUTH ST, MORRISTOWN, NJ 079606459
Phone: 973 660-3100
Web: WWW.ATLANTICHEALTH.ORG

HISTORICAL FINANCIALS

Company Type: Private

Income Statement — FYE: December 31

	REVENUE ($mil)	NET INCOME ($mil)	NET PROFIT MARGIN	EMPLOYEES
12/21	3,494	619	17.7%	7,300
12/20	3,069	324	10.6%	—
12/19	2,993	458	15.3%	—
12/18	2,776	30	1.1%	—
Annual Growth	8.0%	171.7%	—	—

2021 Year-End Financials
Return on assets: 10.3% Cash ($ mil.): 868
Return on equity: 19.2%
Current Ratio: 1.60

AIDS HEALTHCARE FOUNDATION

Auditors : VASQUEZ & COMPANY LLP LOS ANG

LOCATIONS

HQ: AIDS HEALTHCARE FOUNDATION
6255 W SUNSET BLVD FL 21, LOS ANGELES, CA 900287422
Phone: 323 860-5200
Web: WWW.AIDSHEALTH.ORG

HISTORICAL FINANCIALS

Company Type: Private

Income Statement — FYE: December 31

	REVENUE ($mil)	NET INCOME ($mil)	NET PROFIT MARGIN	EMPLOYEES
12/19	1,366	98	7.2%	2,331
12/16	1,163	40	3.5%	—
12/15	1,039	56	5.4%	—
12/14	879	30	3.5%	—
Annual Growth	9.2%	26.5%	—	—

2019 Year-End Financials
Return on assets: 14.4% Cash ($ mil.): 148
Return on equity: 20.2%
Current Ratio: 3.30

AIR METHODS CORPORATION

Air Methods is the leading air medical service, delivering lifesaving care to more than 70,000 people every year. Air Methods is the preferred partner for hospitals and one of the largest community-based providers of air medical services. United Rotorcraft is the company's products division specializing in the design and manufacture of aeromedical and aerospace technology. Air Methods' fleet of owned, leased, or maintained aircraft features more than 450 helicopters and fixed wing aircraft. Air Methods was founded in 1980 by Roy Morgan.

Operations

Air Methods operates through three divisions: healthcare, tourism and aerospace.

The Healthcare includes Cypheron Healthcare Solutions. Cypheron is a Revenue Cycle Management Solutions provider with a unique patient advocacy approach.

The Tourism division includes Blue Hawiian Helicopters, the leading helicopter tour company in Hawaii. Blue Hawaii serves all four majors Hawaiian Islands: Oahu, Maui, Kauai, and the Big Island.

The Aerospace division includes United RotorCraft, a leading provider of aircraft and land vehicle equipment and systems. It designs, integrates, and installs medical equipment, avionics, and vehicle accessories for emergency medical services (EMS), medevac, firefighting, airborne law enforcement (ALE), and search and rescue (SAR) operators.

Geographic Reach

Air Methods is headquartered in Greenwood Village, Colorado.

EXECUTIVES

US President*, Mike Allen
Executive Business Development Vice President*, David M Doerr
CAO*, Sharon J Keck
Auditors : KPMG LLP DENVER COLORADO

LOCATIONS

HQ: AIR METHODS CORPORATION
5500 S QUEBEC ST STE 300, GREENWOOD VILLAGE, CO 801111926
Phone: 303 792-7400
Web: WWW.AIRMETHODS.COM

PRODUCTS/OPERATIONS

2014 Sales

	$ mil.	% of total
AMS	863.9	85
Tourism	116.0	11
United Rotorcraft	36.2	4
Corporate Activities	86	0
Adjustments	(11.4)	-
Total	1,004.8	100

Fleets
AS 350
EC 135
EC 130
Bell 407
EC 145
Bell 429
BK 117
A-109
SA 365
Bell 222
Bell 430
Bell 206
MD 902
King Air
PC 12
Agusta 119Kx
Services
AirCom
Complete Billing Solutions
DirectCall
TAMMA
United Rotorcraft
LifeShield Alliance

COMPETITORS

AMERIFLIGHT, LLC
ATLAS AIR WORLDWIDE HOLDINGS, INC.
BRISTOW HOLDINGS U.S. INC.
CHC Group Limited
COLLINS INDUSTRIES, INC.
EVERGREEN HOLDINGS, INC.
LeasePlan Corporation N.V.
NETJETS INC.
SPIRIT AIRLINES, INC.
THE BOEING COMPANY

HISTORICAL FINANCIALS

Company Type: Private

Income Statement — FYE: December 31

	REVENUE ($mil)	NET INCOME ($mil)	NET PROFIT MARGIN	EMPLOYEES
12/15	1,085	109	10.1%	5,133
12/14	1,004	95	9.5%	—
12/13	881	62	7.0%	—
Annual Growth	11.0%	32.7%	—	—

2015 Year-End Financials

Return on assets: 7.0%
Return on equity: 19.0%
Current Ratio: 3.20
Cash ($ mil.): 5

AIRGAS, INC.

Airgas safely and reliably provides products, services, and expertise to industries through its more than 18,000 associates, in more than 1,400 locations, robust e-Business platform, and Airgas Total Access telesales channel. Airgas distributes argon, carbon dioxide, nitrogen, oxygen, and a variety of specialty gases as well as welding products, tools and equipment, dry ice, and safety products. The company serves more than 1 million customers in various industries. The company is owned by Air Liquide SA.

Operations

Airgas operates through five product categories: Gases, Gas equipment, Safety products, Tools and hardware, and Welding products.

Its Gases include industrial application gases such as acetylene, argon, and helium; medical gases such as carbon dioxide, nitrogen, and oxygen; and specialty gases such as gas mixtures.

Gas equipment include balloon regulators; specialty gas equipment; welding gas equipment such as torches, burning bars, spark lighters and flints; and gas equipment accessories such as adapters, cylinder carts, hoses, gas containers, and valves.

Safety products include barricades, clothing, footwear, gloves, fire equipment, first aid, and head, eye, and face protection.

Tools and hardware products include abrasives, cutting tools, industrial brushes, machine tools, air compressors, and plant maintenance equipment.

Welding products include fluxes and powders, gas welding rods, wires, solders, welders, accessories such as plasma torches and cutters, and welding support equipment such as blankets, curtains, pads, and screens.

Geographic Reach

Headquartered in Radnor, Pennsylvania, the Airgas' US network covers more than 900 retail locations and is present in over 1,400 locations in all 50 states.

Sales and Marketing

Airgas serves customers in a range of industries, including manufacturing and metal fabrication, power utilities and materials, construction, life sciences and healthcare, food, beverage and retail, energy, and chemical production. It also has government, defense, and aerospace clients. It interacts with customers through phone, online, and in physical stores.

Company Background

In the early 1980s Peter McCausland was a corporate attorney involved in mergers and acquisitions for Messer Griesheim, a large German industrial gas producer. When the German firm declined McCausland's recommendation in 1982 to buy Connecticut Oxygen, he raised money from private sources and bought it himself. He acquired other distributors and then left Messer Griesheim in 1987 to run Airgas full-time.

Since then, the company made some 500 acquisitions, becoming a nationwide company in the process.

HISTORY

In the early 1980s Peter McCausland was a corporate attorney involved in mergers and acquisitions for Messer Griesheim, a large German industrial gas producer. When the German firm declined McCausland's recommendation in 1982 to buy Connecticut Oxygen, he raised money from private sources and bought it himself. He acquired other distributors and then left Messer Griesheim in 1987 to run Airgas full-time.

Airgas began buying mostly small local and regional gas distributors in the US. By 1994 strategy shifted to purchasing larger "superregional" distributors such as Jimmie Jones Co. and Post Welding Supply of Alabama, which added about $70 million combined to the company's revenues.

Airgas then began "rolling up" additional similar businesses. In 1995 it bought more than 25 companies, and two years later it added more than 20 gas distributors. Also in 1997 Airgas expanded its manufacturing capabilities by building five plants that could fast-fill whole pallets of gas cylinders (the old, manual system rolls cylinders two at a time). By 2000 the company had about 100 cylinder fill plants.

Struggling to integrate acquisitions while dealing with softening markets, Airgas began a companywide realignment in 1998. To that end, it sold its calcium carbide and carbon products operations to former partner Elkem ASA later that year; the company also consolidated 34 hubs into 16 regional companies and sold its operations in Poland and Thailand to Germany-based Linde in 1999.

In 2000 Airgas acquired distributor Mallinckrodt's Puritan-Bennett division (gas products for medical uses) with 36 locations in the US and Canada. The company also acquired the majority of Air Products' US packaged gas business, excluding its electronic gases and magnetic resonance imaging-related helium operations, in 2002.

In 2004 and 2005 it bought units from giants like Air Products and Chemicals, BOC, and LaRoche Industries. In 2006 Airgas continued to build with the purchase of 10 businesses, including Union Industrial Gas, which supplies Texas and much of the Southwest, and then Linde's US bulk gas business for $495 million the next year. Linde, in the process of integrating its 2006 acquisition of BOC, then sold to Airgas a portion of its US packaged gas business for $310 million.

Rival Air Products had made a major bid to buy Airgas in 2010, but was rebuffed. Air Products extended its tender offer to Airgas stockholders several times, and made a "best and final offer" of $70 a share (almost $6 billion) in December 2010. Airgas said it was holding out for $78 a share and rejected that offer, too. In early 2011, a Delaware judge ruled for Airgas in a suit brought by Air Products to set aside a "poison pill" defense used by the Airgas board to fend off the takeover try. Following the verdict, Air Products dropped its bid.

Airgas acquired six businesses in 2010, including Tri-Tech, an independent distributor with 16 locations throughout Florida, Georgia, and South Carolina, and annual sales of $31 million.

In 2011 Airgas reorganized its 12 regional segments into four new business support divisions -- North, South, Central, and West -- to leverage a new SAP information systems platform in 2011. Each of the units is headed by a division president. The new company structure is designed to accelerate sales growth and pricing management, and create operating efficiencies.

In fiscal 2012 the company added eight businesses with total annual sales of about $106 million. The largest of the businesses acquired were ABCO Gases, Welding and Industrial Supply Company (ABCO); Pain Enterprises; and Industrial Welding Supplies of Hattiesburg (doing business as Nordan Smith). Connecticut-based ABCO has 12 industrial and gas welding supply locations throughout New England. Indiana-based Pain operates 20 dry ice and liquid carbon dioxide production and distribution sites. Mississippi-based Nordan Smith has 17 locations that distribute industrial, medical, and specialty gases and supplies throughout Alabama, Arkansas, and Mississippi.

In 2013 Airgas retained Chicago-based Acquity Group as a key partner in helping the company continue to provide new online digital customer platforms. As one of the leading digital marketing companies, the Acquity Group will provide its e-channel expertise in leading the design and implementation of Airgas' new content-rich website.

In 2013 Airgas acquired two US-based industrial gas and welding supply distributors that complement the Airgas portfolio of products and services. Combined annual revenues for the two acquired businesses are more than $30 million.

In fiscal 2013 the company also acquired Illinois-based The Encompass Gas Group (one of the largest privately-owned suppliers of industrial, medical, and specialty gases and related hardgoods in the US), with about $55 million in annual revenues in 2012.

Auditors : KPMG LLP PHILADELPHIA PENNSY

LOCATIONS

HQ: AIRGAS, INC.
259 N RADNOR CHESTER RD # 100, RADNOR, PA 190875240
Phone: 610 687-5253
Web: WWW.AIRGAS.COM

PRODUCTS/OPERATIONS

Selected Products and Services
Products
    Carbon dioxide
    Dry ice
    Industrial gases
    Argon
    Helium
    Hydrogen
    Liquid oxygen
    Nitrogen
    Nitrous oxide
    Oxygen
    Safety equipment
    Specialty gases
Services
    Container rental
    Welding equipment rental

Selected Subsidiaries
Airgas Canada
Airgas Carbonic
Airgas East
Airgas Great Lakes
Airgas Intermountain
Airgas Medical Services
Airgas Mid America
Airgas Mid South
Airgas Nitrous Oxide
Airgas Nor Pac
Airgas North Central
Airgas Northern California & Nevada
Airgas Refrigerant
Airgas Safety
Airgas South
Airgas Southwest
Airgas Specialty Gases
Airgas Specialty Products
Airgas West
National Welders Supply Company, dba Airgas National Welders
Nitrous Oxide Corp.
Red-D-Arc
WorldWide Welding, LLC

COMPETITORS

AIR PRODUCTS AND CHEMICALS, INC.
ASHLAND GLOBAL HOLDINGS INC.
BRENNTAG NORTH AMERICA, INC.
CHART INDUSTRIES, INC.
HARCROS CHEMICALS INC.
L'AIR LIQUIDE SOCIETE ANONYME POUR L'ETUDE ET L'EXPLOITATION DES PROCEDES GEORGES CLAUDE
NEXEO SOLUTIONS HOLDINGS, LLC
TRAMMO, INC.
UNIVAR SOLUTIONS INC.

WARWICK INTERNATIONAL GROUP LIMITED

HISTORICAL FINANCIALS
Company Type: Private

Income Statement   FYE: March 31

	REVENUE ($mil)	NET INCOME ($mil)	NET PROFIT MARGIN	EMPLOYEES
03/15	5,304	368	6.9%	17,004
03/13	4,957	340	6.9%	—
Annual Growth	3.4%	3.9%	—	—

2015 Year-End Financials
Return on assets: 6.2%   Cash ($ mil.): 50
Return on equity: 17.1%
Current Ratio: 1.30

AKRON GENERAL MEDICAL CENTER INC

Akron General Medical Center, the flagship hospital of Akron General Health System, is a not-for-profit teaching hospital that boasts more than 530 acute care beds. The hospital serves the residents of Northeast Ohio as a regional referral center in a number of medical specialties, including cardiovascular disease, heart surgery, cancer care, women's health, orthopedics, sports medicine, and trauma care. Akron General Medical also operates Edwin Shaw Rehab, the area's only rehabilitation hospital. Edwin Shaw has 35 beds and treats patients who have experienced stroke, head trauma, and other critical injuries. Akron General Medical was founded in 1914 as Peoples Hospital.

Operations
Akron General is a level I trauma center and holds the county's first certified chest pain and primary stroke centers. It also offers a level III obstetric unit, and it operates a freestanding outpatient surgery center. As a major teaching hospital with more than 1,000 physicians, as well as 3,400 professional and support staff members, Akron General Medical offers medical students about a dozen residency programs. It does so through its affiliations with Northeastern Ohio Medical University, which serves as the medical college for University of Akron, Youngstown State University, and Kent State University. Residencies include those in family medicine, OB-GYN, psychiatry, and breast cancer.

Geographic Reach
Akron General Medical Center serves communities across the counties of Summit, Medina, Portage, Stark, and Wayne located in Northeast Ohio. In addition to facilities in Akron, the hospital has satellite locations in Green, Stow, and Tallmadge. Edwin Shaw Rehab is located in the nearby town of Cuyahoga Falls. The center serves an area with a population of some 1.2 million people.

Strategy

The hospital conducts facility and equipment upgrades to meet the needs of a growing population in Northeast Ohio. Akron General enhanced its neurosurgical capabilities in 2012 as part of the establishment of its Neurosciences Institute. The center includes new Brainlab CT and MRI imaging systems for use during minimally invasive surgical procedures. The hospital is also upgrading its heart and vascular center, which was certified as a heart failure clinic in 2013. In addition, Akron General is working to upgrade IT systems to improve physician and patient resources.

Auditors : LB BLUE & CO LLC COLUMBUS OH

LOCATIONS

HQ: AKRON GENERAL MEDICAL CENTER INC
1 AKRON GENERAL AVE, AKRON, OH 443072432
Phone: 330 344-6000
Web: WWW.AKRONGENERAL.ORG

Selected Locations and Affiliates
Akron General Medical Center
Akron Health Center
Edwin Shaw Rehabilitation Institute
Green Health Center
Health and Wellness Centers (West, North, and Green)
Hospice Center
Lodi Community Hospital
Tallmadge Health Center

PRODUCTS/OPERATIONS

Selected Centers and Services
Anesthesiology
Audiology
Bariatric Surgery
Breast Health Center
Cancer Center
Community Health
Corporate Wellness
Critical Care Center
Diabetes Center
Diagnostic Services
Emergency Medicine/Level 1 Trauma Center
Endocrinology
Endoscopy
Executive Health Program
Family Medicine
Food and Nutrition Services
Gastroenterology
Health and Wellness
Heart and Vascular Center
Heartburn Center
Hyperbaric Medicine
Infectious Disease
Internal Medicine
Lab Services
Maternity Services
Nephrology
Neuroscience Institute
Nuclear Medicine
Occupational Therapy
Orthopedic Center
Osteoporosis Prevention
Pain Management
Physical Therapy
Primary Care
Psychiatry and Behavioral Sciences
Pulmonary Medicine
Radiology
Rehabilitation
Senior Services
Sleep Center
Speech and Language Pathology
Sports Medicine

Surgery
Urology
Women's Center
Wound Center

COMPETITORS

ASCENSION PROVIDENCE HOSPITAL
HOSPITAL SERVICE DISTRICT 1
MERCY HOSPITAL SOUTH
OHIO VALLEY MEDICAL CENTER, INCORPORATED
THE CHRIST HOSPITAL

HISTORICAL FINANCIALS
Company Type: Private

Income Statement — FYE: December 31

	REVENUE ($mil)	NET INCOME ($mil)	NET PROFIT MARGIN	EMPLOYEES
12/14	544	47	8.7%	875
12/13	507	22	4.4%	—
12/12	486	10	2.2%	—
12/04	0	0	—	—
Annual Growth	—	—	—	—

2014 Year-End Financials
Return on assets: 10.3%   Cash ($ mil.): 20
Return on equity: 35.3%
Current Ratio: 0.40

ALASKA NATIVE TRIBAL HEALTH CONSORTIUM

The Alaska Native Tribal Health Consortium (ANTHC) brings good health to Alaska Natives. The company is a not-for-profit, statewide health care organization managed by regional tribal governments and their respective regional health organizations. The organization connects disparate medical providers by providing a range of health programs and services, including community health care, public health advocacy and education initiatives, health research (including water and sanitation), and medical supply distribution. The nearly 175-bed Alaska Native Medical Center (ANMC), a native-owned hospital, is jointly managed by ANTHC and Southcentral Foundation, a regional health corporation based in the Cook Inlet region.

Auditors : BDO USA LLP ANCHORAGE AK

LOCATIONS

HQ: ALASKA NATIVE TRIBAL HEALTH CONSORTIUM
  4000 AMBASSADOR DR, ANCHORAGE, AK 995085909
Phone: 907 729-1900
Web: WWW.ANTHC.ORG

PRODUCTS/OPERATIONS

2014 Sales

	$ mil.	% of total
Patient revenue	213.0	33
Compact revenue	161.4	25
Grant & project revenue	109.4	17
Warehouse revenue	22.2	3
Investment income	4.3	1
Other	133.4	21
Total	643.7	100

Selected Services
Ear Nose Throat
Emergency and Trauma
Family Medicine
Imaging and Laboratory Services
Internal Medicine Clinic
Maternal Fetal Medicine
OB/GYN Services
Oncology
Orthopedics Clinic
Pediatric ICU
Pediatrics
Pharmacy Services
Pregnancy and Childbirth
Primary Care Services
Respiratory Care

COMPETITORS

ACTION FOR BOSTON COMMUNITY DEVELOPMENT, INC.
FLORIDA DEPARTMENT OF HEALTH
MARSHFIELD CLINIC HEALTH SYSTEM, INC.
NATIONAL COUNCIL ON AGING, INC.
NATIONAL SAFETY COUNCIL
NORTHSHORE UNIVERSITY HEALTHSYSTEM
SISTERS OF CHARITY OF LEAVENWORTH HEALTH SYSTEM, INC.
SPACE COAST HEALTH FOUNDATION, INC.
THE RUTLAND HOSPITAL INC ACT 220
WEST HEALTH ADVOCATE SOLUTIONS, INC.

HISTORICAL FINANCIALS
Company Type: Private

Income Statement — FYE: September 30

	REVENUE ($mil)	NET INCOME ($mil)	NET PROFIT MARGIN	EMPLOYEES
09/20	687	22	3.2%	1,850
09/16	587	72	12.4%	—
09/15	511	3	0.7%	—
09/14	(1,780)	0	0.0%	—
Annual Growth	—	1063.2%	—	—

2020 Year-End Financials
Return on assets: 2.2%   Cash ($ mil.): 194
Return on equity: 3.3%
Current Ratio: 1.40

ALASKA PERMANENT FUND CORPORATION, AN INSTRUMENTALITY OF THE STATE OF ALASKA

EXECUTIVES

CIO, Marcus Frampton
CRO, Sebastian Vadakumcherry
Auditors : KPMG LLP ANCHORAGE AK

LOCATIONS

HQ: ALASKA PERMANENT FUND CORPORATION, AN INSTRUMENTALITY OF THE STATE OF ALASKA
  801 W 10TH ST STE 302, JUNEAU, AK 998011878
Phone: 907 796-1500
Web: WWW.APFC.ORG

HISTORICAL FINANCIALS
Company Type: Private

Income Statement — FYE: June 30

	ASSETS ($mil)	NET INCOME ($mil)	INCOME AS % OF ASSETS	EMPLOYEES
06/18	67,671	5,109	7.6%	60
06/17	61,824	6,675	10.8%	—
06/16	55,346	(30)	—	—
Annual Growth	10.6%	—	—	—

ALBANY MED HEALTH SYSTEM

Albany Medical Center (AMC) provides medical care in upstate New York. Serving residents of northeastern New York and western New England, the health system has at its heart the around 765-bed Albany Medical Center Hospital. The general medical-surgical facility also provides specialty care in such areas as oncology, rehabilitation, and organ transplantation. AMC also features a children's hospital, an outpatient surgery center, and a group medical practice. It employs some 800 full-time physicians. Its Albany Medical College is one of the nation's first private medical schools.

Operations

AMC's assets includes a biomedical research enterprise and one of the region's largest physicians practices with more than 500 doctors. Its physicians have extensive training and experience in about 35 subspecialties of pediatric medicine. The system's subsidiaries include the Albany Medical Center Kidskeller Corporation, a not-for-profit day care facility, and Madison Avenue Services Corporation, a taxable corporation.

Geographic Reach

AMC offers services in 25 counties in northeastern New York and western New England. In addition to treating patients at the main site in Albany, providers also treat patients at community-based locations throughout the region including Clifton Park, Latham, Malta, North Greenbush, Delmar, and others.

Company Background

AMC, which produced Nobel prize winners in both 2009 and 2011, annually awards its own $500,000 prize, the largest monetary award in medicine and biomedical research in the US. In 2010 combined federal-state entities awarded the center $10 million, the center's largest grant since its founding, which will be used to expand research labs at Albany Medical College.

AMC's status as the Capital Region's reigning health care giant, was toppled by the 2011 merger of four locals hospitals to form St. Peter's Health Partners, with nearly 12,000 employees vs. 6,000 at AMC. Post merger, the newly-merged group has nearly 50% of the Capital Region market, while AMC has 25%. While AMC is no longer the area's largest hospital, as the region's trauma center and only medical school, it continues to draw many patients from outside the four-county area.

Albany Medical College was formed in 1839; the hospital's predecessor was formed in 1849. The two combined under the AMC umbrella in 1982.

EXECUTIVES

CSO, Courtney Burke
Auditors : KPMG LLP ALBANY NEW YORK

LOCATIONS

HQ: ALBANY MED HEALTH SYSTEM
  43 NEW SCOTLAND AVE, ALBANY, NY 122083412
Phone: 518 262-3125
Web: WWW.AMC.EDU

PRODUCTS/OPERATIONS

2013 Sales

	$ in mil.	% of total
Net patient service	720.9	96
Inter-institutional	8.8	1
Interest & dividends	2.9	-
Other	17.2	2
Net assets released from restrictions	3.0	1
Total	752.8	100

2013 Net Patient Service Revenue

	% of total
Health maintenance organizations	32
Medicare	19
Medicaid	15
Blue Cross and Blue Shield	14
Commercial carriers	9
No fault & worker's compensation	5
Private pay	2
Other third-party payors	4
Total	100

Selected Services

Cancer center
Children's Hospital
Center for Donation and Transplant
Diabetes service
Emergency medical services
Hearing center
HIV medicine
Pain management
Perinatal
Physical therapy
Radiology
Rheumatology
Surgical
Trauma center
Women's wellness center

COMPETITORS

CHARLESTON AREA MEDICAL CENTER, INC.
KALEIDA HEALTH
MISSION HOSPITAL, INC.
NASSAU HEALTH CARE CORPORATION
NORTHWELL HEALTH, INC.
ROBERT WOOD JOHNSON UNIVERSITY HOSPITAL, INC.
TEXAS CHILDREN'S HOSPITAL
THE CLEVELAND CLINIC FOUNDATION
THE PENNSYLVANIA HOSPITAL OF THE UNIVERSITY OF PENNSYLVANIA HEALTH SYSTEM
UNIVERSITY OF TEXAS MD ANDERSON CANCER CENTER

HISTORICAL FINANCIALS

Company Type: Private

Income Statement FYE: December 31

	REVENUE ($mil)	NET INCOME ($mil)	NET PROFIT MARGIN	EMPLOYEES
12/17	664	267	40.2%	8,760
12/16	317	77	24.5%	—
12/15	1,167	5	0.5%	—
12/13	980	115	11.7%	—
Annual Growth	(9.3%)	23.4%	—	—

2017 Year-End Financials
Return on assets: 36.5% Cash ($ mil.): 113
Return on equity: 84.3%
Current Ratio: 2.20

ALBANY MEDICAL CENTER HOSPITAL

Auditors : KPMG LLP ALBANY NEW YORK

LOCATIONS

HQ: ALBANY MEDICAL CENTER HOSPITAL
  43 NEW SCOTLAND AVE, ALBANY, NY 122083478
Phone: 518 262-3125
Web: WWW.AMC.EDU

HISTORICAL FINANCIALS

Company Type: Private

Income Statement FYE: December 31

	REVENUE ($mil)	NET INCOME ($mil)	NET PROFIT MARGIN	EMPLOYEES
12/17	1,017	38	3.8%	1,568
12/16	960	46	4.8%	—
12/15	893	16	1.9%	—
Annual Growth	6.7%	50.3%	—	—

2017 Year-End Financials
Return on assets: 3.5% Cash ($ mil.): 95
Return on equity: 8.4%
Current Ratio: 2.20

ALBERICI CONSTRUCTORS, INC.

LOCATIONS

HQ: ALBERICI CONSTRUCTORS, INC.
  8800 PAGE AVE, SAINT LOUIS, MO 631146106
Phone: 314 733-2000
Web: WWW.ALBERICI.COM

HISTORICAL FINANCIALS

Company Type: Private

Income Statement FYE: December 31

	REVENUE ($mil)	NET INCOME ($mil)	NET PROFIT MARGIN	EMPLOYEES
12/16	960	0	0.0%	2,000
12/15	1,028	0	0.0%	—
12/14	729	0	0.0%	—
Annual Growth	14.8%	—	—	—

2016 Year-End Financials
Return on assets: — Cash ($ mil.): 59
Return on equity: —
Current Ratio: 1.20

ALBERICI CORPORATION

Alberici helped shape the St. Louis skyline; it now sets its sights -- or its construction sites -- across North America. As the parent company of Alberici Constructors, the company encompasses a group of enterprises with a presence in North America, Central America, South America, and Europe. Operations include construction services, building materials, and steel fabrication and erection units. Alberici offers general contracting, design/build, construction management, demolition, and specialty contracting services, while also offering facilities management. Founded in 1918, the Alberici family still holds the largest share of the employee-owned firm.

Operations

The company boasts more than a dozen operating companies in the US, Canada, and Mexico that serve the automotive, energy, health care, industrial, manufacturing, and wastewater treatment markets. Its Gunther-Nash subsidiary provides construction services to the mining industry. Another division, Vertegy, specializes in construction consulting for green and sustainable projects.

Geographic Reach

Alberici is active throughout North America and has offices in St. Louis, Missouri; Detroit, Michigan; Atlanta, Georgia; Topeka, Kansas; Burlington and Cambridge, Ontario; Saskatoon, Saskatchewan; and LÃ©on, Mexico.

Sales and Marketing

Alberici serves a range of different companies, including those that are automotive, building, energy, healthcare, heavy industrial, industrial process, mining infrastructure, or water-related.

Some of Alberici's completed projects include casinos for Ameristar, modernization and new facilities for Anheuser-Busch, and factories for Boeing. Nearly 80% of its revenue comes from repeat clients.

Financial Performance

While full financial information was not available for the privately held company, Alberici reports that its annual revenue typically exceeds $1 billion. In 2013, the company took home $1.9 billion, and was ranked the 46th largest contractor in the US by the Engineering News-Record.

In 2012, the company reported more than $530 million in industrial-related revenue, thanks to a recovering economy supporting demand for major industrial projects in the US and Canada.

Strategy

In recent years, the heavy construction firm has pursued acquisitions to better diversify its business both geographically and by entering new specialty markets. In 2013, for example, Alberici purchased contractor Flintco, LLC to broaden its reach into new markets in the southern and southwestern regions of the US. In early 2012, Alberici acquired a water treatment facility specialist to expand its service offerings in the water plant construction market.

Alberici has also become a recognized contractor in recent years, which could help give the company a higher profile and thus more exposure to new potential clients. In 2013, the Associated General Contractors of St. Louis awarded Alberici with top prizes at its 16th Annual Keystone Awards for the company's work on the Seabrook Gates Complex and the Knights of Columbus Child Development Center. To date, Alberici has won 14 Keystone Awards, more than any other general contractor.

So far, its high standing hasn't hurt business. In July 2014, Alberici was chosen to lead in the engineering, procurement, and construction of a major air quality improvement project -- with the goal of installing environmental controls and reducing sulfur dioxide emissions by 90% -- at one of the generating stations owned and operated by Alliant Energy's Wisconsin utility, Wisconsin Power and Light Company.

Mergers and Acquisitions

Expanding it range of capabilities, in January 2012 Alberici acquired water treatment facility specialist CAS Construction. The addition of CAS, which has built facilities throughout the central and western US, strengthens Alberici's capabilities in the water market. The company was renamed CAS Constructors.

In early 2013, Alberici closed on its acquisition of Flintco, LLC, a century-old, Native American-owned contractor based in Tulsa, Oklahoma. With offices in Oklahoma, New Mexico, Texas, Arkansas, and California, Flintco presented an attractive geographic diversification opportunity for Alberici.

LOCATIONS

HQ: ALBERICI CORPORATION
8800 PAGE AVE, SAINT LOUIS, MO 631146106
Phone: 314 733-2000
Web: WWW.ALBERICI.COM

PRODUCTS/OPERATIONS

Selected Markets
Automotive
Building
Energy
Green building
Health care
Industrial
Manufacturing/Food and Beverage
Mining infrastructure
Steel fabrication
Water and Wastewater Treatment

Selected Subsidiaries and Brands
Alberici Global Group, GmbH
    Alberici Constructors, Ltd. (Canada)
    Alberici Construcciones S.A. de C.V. (Mexico)
Alberici Group, Inc.
    Alberici Constructors, Inc.
    Alberici Global Automotive Constructors (automotive construction)
    Alberici Healthcare Constructors
    Alberici Industrial, LLC
    CAS Construction, LLC (water, wastewater)
    Flintco, LLC (Native American-owned contractor)
    Gunther-Nash, Inc. (shaft, slope, and tunnel construction for mining industry)
    Hillsdale Fabricators (steel fabrication)
    Kienlen Constructors (structural concrete, structural steel)
    Vertegy (green building consulting)

COMPETITORS

CLAYCO, INC.
GILBANE BUILDING COMPANY
GILBANE, INC.
GRAY CONSTRUCTION, INC.
GRAYCOR, INC.
PC CONSTRUCTION COMPANY
ROSENDIN ELECTRIC, INC.
STELLAR GROUP, INCORPORATED
THE HASKELL COMPANY

WALBRIDGE ALDINGER LLC

HISTORICAL FINANCIALS

Company Type: Private

Income Statement — FYE: December 31

	REVENUE ($mil)	NET INCOME ($mil)	NET PROFIT MARGIN	EMPLOYEES
12/17	1,531	0	0.0%	2,080
12/16	1,742	0	0.0%	—
12/15	1,885	0	0.0%	—
12/14	1,532	0	0.0%	—
Annual Growth	0.0%	—	—	—

2017 Year-End Financials
Return on assets: —
Return on equity: —
Current Ratio: 1.40
Cash ($ mil.): 182

ALBERICI GROUP, INC.

LOCATIONS

HQ: ALBERICI GROUP, INC.
8800 PAGE AVE, SAINT LOUIS, MO 631146106
Phone: 314 733-2000
Web: WWW.ALBERICI.COM

HISTORICAL FINANCIALS

Company Type: Private

Income Statement — FYE: December 31

	REVENUE ($mil)	NET INCOME ($mil)	NET PROFIT MARGIN	EMPLOYEES
12/17	838	0	0.0%	2,000
12/16	1,036	0	0.0%	—
12/15	1,124	0	0.0%	—
12/14	729	0	0.0%	—
Annual Growth	4.8%	—	—	—

2017 Year-End Financials
Return on assets: —
Return on equity: —
Current Ratio: 1.20
Cash ($ mil.): 105

ALBERT EINSTEIN MEDICAL ASSOCIATES, INC.

LOCATIONS

HQ: ALBERT EINSTEIN MEDICAL ASSOCIATES, INC.
5501 OLD YORK RD STE 1, PHILADELPHIA, PA 191413018
Phone: 215 456-7890
Web: WWW.EINSTEIN.EDU

HISTORICAL FINANCIALS

Company Type: Private

Income Statement — FYE: June 30

	REVENUE ($mil)	NET INCOME ($mil)	NET PROFIT MARGIN	EMPLOYEES
06/09	670	0	0.0%	5,251
06/08	693	33	4.9%	—
06/07	785	63	8.0%	—
06/06	718	29	4.1%	—
Annual Growth	(2.3%)	—	—	—

2009 Year-End Financials

Return on assets: —
Return on equity: —
Current Ratio: 0.40
Cash ($ mil.): 82

ALBERTSONS COMPANIES, INC.

Albertsons Companies is one of the biggest supermarket retailers in the US with nearly 2,275 stores in about 35 states and the District of Columbia. In addition to traditional grocery items, many of the stores offer pharmacies and coffee shops and over 400 include adjacent gas stations. The company operates under roughly 25 banners, including Albertsons, Vons, Pavilions, Randalls, Tom Thumb, Carrs, Jewel-Osco, Shaw's, Star Market, Safeway, Market Street, Haggen, and United Supermarkets. It also owns meal kit company Plated. Albertsons, which traces its roots to 1939, owned by Cerberus Capital Management, went public in mid-2020.

Operations

Albertsons generates most of its revenue from non-perishables (about 50% of sales; general merchandise, grocery, and frozen foods) and fresh (about 35%; produce, dairy, meat, deli, floral, and seafood). Pharmacy products contribute about 10% of revenue with fuel adding about 5%.

It also operates more than 1,720 pharmacies, over 1,315 in-store branded coffee shops, and more than 400 adjacent fuel centers.

The company's nearly 14,000 high-quality products are part of its Own Brands portfolio of proprietary brands, including O Organics and Open Nature.

Geographic Reach

Boise, Idaho-based Albertsons Companies operates about 2,275 stores in about 35 US states. California is the company's largest market by far, with about 595 stores; other large markets include Washington, Texas, and Illinois.

In addition to Idaho, Albertsons Companies has corporate offices in Pleasanton, California; Phoenix, Arizona; and Plano, Texas. It also has some 20 manufacturing plants, around two dozen distribution centers, and various online platforms.

Sales and Marketing

The company serves approximately 34 million customers each week through nearly two dozen distribution centers.

Advertising costs were approximately $440.5 million, $385.1 million, and $405.6 million for fiscal 2021, fiscal 2020, and fiscal 2019, respectively.

Financial Performance

Net sales and other revenue increased $2.2 million, or 3%, from $69.7 billion in fiscal 2020 to $71.9 billion in fiscal 2021. The primary increase in Net sales and other revenue in fiscal 2021 as compared to fiscal 2020 was driven by higher fuel sales and sales related to the stores acquired and opened since fiscal 2020.

In 2022, the company had a net income of $1.6 billion, a 2% increase from the previous year's net income of $850.2 million.

The company's cash at the end of 2022 was $3 billion. Operating activities generated $3.5 billion, while investing activities used $1.5 billion, primarily for payments for property, equipment and intangibles. Financing activities used another $389.5 million, primarily for payments on long-term borrowings.

Strategy

The company's capital allocation strategy balances investing for the future, strengthening its balance sheet and returns to shareholders through a combination of dividends and opportunistic share repurchases.

Company Background

J. A. "Joe" Albertson, Leonard Skaggs (whose family ran Safeway), and Tom Cuthbert founded Albertson's Food Center in Boise, Idaho, in 1939. Albertson, who left his position as district manager for Safeway to run the store, thought big from the start. The 10,000-sq.-ft. store was not only eight times the size of the average competitor, it also offered an in-store butcher shop and bakery, one of the country's first magazine racks, and homemade "Big Joe" ice-cream cones. The men ended their partnership in 1945, the year Albertson's was incorporated, and by 1947 it operated six stores in Idaho.

The company opened its first combination food store and drugstore, a 60,000-sq.-ft. superstore, in 1951 and began locating stores in growing suburban areas. Albertson's went public to raise expansion capital in 1959 and by 1960 had 62 stores in Idaho, Oregon, Utah, and Washington.

In June 2006 Albertson's was sold to a consortium that included SUPERVALU, CVS, Cerberus Capital Management, and Kimco for about $9.7 billion. Following the acquisition and the divvying up of Albertson's assets, the surviving company went private.

HISTORY

J. A. "Joe" Albertson, Leonard Skaggs (whose family ran Safeway), and Tom Cuthbert founded Albertson's Food Center in Boise, Idaho, in 1939. Albertson, who left his position as district manager for Safeway to run the store, thought big from the start. The 10,000-sq.-ft. store was not only eight times the size of the average competitor, it also offered an in-store butcher shop and bakery, one of the country's first magazine racks, and homemade "Big Joe" ice-cream cones. The men ended their partnership in 1945, the year Albertson's was incorporated, and by 1947 it operated six stores in Idaho.

The company opened its first combination food store and drugstore, a 60,000-sq.-ft. superstore, in 1951 and began locating stores in growing suburban areas. Albertson's went public to raise expansion capital in 1959 and by 1960 had 62 stores in Idaho, Oregon, Utah, and Washington. The food retailer acquired Greater All American Markets (1964), a grocery chain based in Downey, California, and Semrau & Sons (1965) of Oakland, which aided the company's thrust into the California market.

Albertson's and the Skaggs chain (by this time run by L. S. Skaggs Jr.) reunited temporarily in 1969, financing six Skaggs-Albertson's food-and-drug-combination stores. (The partnership dissolved in 1977, with each side taking half of the units.) By 1986 the company had reached $5 billion in sales, a fivefold increase over 1975.

The company purchased 74 Jewel Osco combination food stores and drugstores (mostly in Arkansas, Florida, Oklahoma, and Texas) from American Stores in 1992. Co-founder Albertson died in 1993 at age 86.

In 1997 the United Food and Commercial Workers union, which represents supermarket employees, sued Albertson's, alleging the company forced employees to work overtime without pay. (It was settled in 1999, resulting in a $22 million charge.) Also in 1997 Albertson's began selling gasoline at a few stores. Acquisitions the next year (including Buttrey Food and Drug Stores) added stores and states. That year the company began serving online customers in the Dallas-Fort Worth area.

In 1999 the grocer revisited its roots when it acquired American Stores (Skaggs' successor), which operated more than 1,550 stores in 26 states. To obtain regulatory approval for the $12 billion deal, Albertson's sold 145 stores in overlapping markets in three states (most were in California).

In 2001 Larry Johnston, former CEO of GE Appliances, took over as chairman and CEO of Albertson's. Facing increasing competition (especially from Wal-Mart), Johnston announced in March 2002 aggressive restructuring plans that included job cuts and closing 95 stores in underperforming markets, specifically Memphis and Nashville, Tennessee, and Houston and San Antonio, Texas.

Already allowing customers to order

drugs online (from its online drugstore, Savon.com) and groceries in Seattle, Albertson's expanded its online operations to San Diego in 2001 and in early 2002 to Los Angeles, San Francisco, and parts of Oregon and Washington. Albertson's exited the New England drugstore market in 2002 when it sold 80 New England Osco stores to Brooks Pharmacy.

In February 2004 Albertson's launched its "Blue Ribbon" brand of beef, a private-label line of roasts and steaks. Also in February, the company consolidated its Southwest, Intermountain, Northwest, and Rocky Mountain divisions to form a new Intermountain West Division and combined the Acme and Florida divisions into a new Eastern Division.

A four-and-a-half month strike by grocery workers in Southern California ended in March 2004. The dispute pitted workers' demands for continued generous health care coverage vs. management's call for cost cuts to remain profitable in the face of Wal-Mart's entry into the Southern California grocery market. In April Albertson's completed the acquisition of JS USA Holdings, which runs Shaw's and Star Markets stores in New England, from UK grocer J Sainsbury. The deal to buy Shaw's was worth about $2.4 billion (cash and leases). In September Albertson's gained a toehold in the gourmet-food market with the purchase of Bristol Farms, the operator of about a dozen upscale food markets in Southern California. In October Albertson's combined its Northern and Southern California food divisions into a single business unit, the newly formed California Food Division. In an effort to improve efficiency, Albertson's reorganized its supply chain, food operations, and Six Sigma Quality functions in May 2005.

In June 2006 Albertson's was sold to a consortium that included SUPERVALU, CVS, Cerberus Capital Management, and Kimco for about $9.7 billion. Following the acquisition and the divvying up of Albertson's assets, the surviving company went private and changed its name to Albertsons LLC. Concurrently, Johnston left Albertsons and was succeeded by Robert Miller, chairman of drugstore chain Rite Aid and the former head of Fred Meyer for eight years in the 1990s. Of the company's 27 price-impact Super Saver stores, 25 closed their doors in mid-2006. Also, in June, the company put about 45 stores on the auction block. (It was announced in late 2006 that discount apparel retailer Ross Stores would acquire these stores.) In July the company shut down its online shopping service Albertsons.com. In February 2007 Albertsons sold 132 grocery stores and two distribution centers in Northern California and Nevada to Save Mart Supermarkets for an undisclosed amount. Other recent closings include stores in Texas, in the Dallas-Fort Worth, Austin, and Longview markets; Colorado; and Oklahoma.

Albertsons also sold eight of its stores in Wyoming to SUPERVALU in January 2008. The divestments continued in September with the sale of 49 supermarkets in Florida to Publix Super Markets for about $500 million. Also in 2008 Albertsons sold about 100 of its Express fuel centers in Arizona, Colorado, Florida, Louisiana, and Texas to Valero Energy and Reb Oil.

Auditors : DELOITTE & TOUCHE LLP BOISE

LOCATIONS

HQ: ALBERTSONS COMPANIES, INC.
250 E PARKCENTER BLVD, BOISE, ID 837063999
Phone: 208 395-6200
Web: WWW.ALBERTSONSCOMPANIES.COM

PRODUCTS/OPERATIONS

2018 Sales

	$ mil.	% of total
Non-perishables	26,372	44
Perishables	24,921	41
Pharmacy	4,987	8
Fuel	3,456	6
Other	799	1
Total	60,535	100

COMPETITORS

7-ELEVEN, INC
ALBERTSON'S LLC
C&S WHOLESALE GROCERS, INC.
PUBLIX SUPER MARKETS, INC.
SAFEWAY INC.
SPARTANNASH COMPANY
SUPERVALU INC.
THE GREAT ATLANTIC & PACIFIC TEA COMPANY, INC.
THE KROGER CO
THE PANTRY INC

HISTORICAL FINANCIALS

Company Type: Private

Income Statement — FYE: February 29

	REVENUE ($mil)	NET INCOME ($mil)	NET PROFIT MARGIN	EMPLOYEES
02/20	62,455	466	0.7%	290,000
02/19	60,534	131	0.2%	—
02/18	59,924	46	0.1%	—
Annual Growth	2.1%	217.4%	—	—

2020 Year-End Financials
Return on assets: 1.9% Cash ($ mil.): 470
Return on equity: 20.5%
Current Ratio: 1.00

ALBUQUERQUE MUNICIPAL SCHOOL DISTRICT NUMBER 12

Auditors : MOSS ADAMS LLP ALBUQUERQUE N

LOCATIONS

HQ: ALBUQUERQUE MUNICIPAL SCHOOL DISTRICT NUMBER 12
6400 UPTOWN BLVD NE, ALBUQUERQUE, NM 871104202
Phone: 505 880-3700
Web: WWW.APS.EDU

HISTORICAL FINANCIALS

Company Type: Private

Income Statement — FYE: June 30

	REVENUE ($mil)	NET INCOME ($mil)	NET PROFIT MARGIN	EMPLOYEES
06/21	1,083	42	3.9%	135
06/20	1,096	7	0.6%	—
06/19	1,006	(35)	—	—
06/18	954	50	5.3%	—
Annual Growth	4.3%	(5.4%)	—	—

2021 Year-End Financials
Return on assets: 1.1% Cash ($ mil.): 105
Return on equity: —
Current Ratio: 2.50

ALBUQUERQUE PUBLIC SCHOOL DISTRICT

Auditors : MOSS ADAMS LLP ALBUQUERQUE N

LOCATIONS

HQ: ALBUQUERQUE PUBLIC SCHOOL DISTRICT
6400 UPTOWN BLVD NE, ALBUQUERQUE, NM 871104202
Phone: 505 880-3700
Web: WWW.APS.EDU

HISTORICAL FINANCIALS

Company Type: Private

Income Statement — FYE: June 30

	REVENUE ($mil)	NET INCOME ($mil)	NET PROFIT MARGIN	EMPLOYEES
06/21	1,083	42	3.9%	11,500
06/09	0	0	1.5%	—
06/08	0	0	—	—
Annual Growth	—	—	—	—

2021 Year-End Financials
Return on assets: 1.0% Cash ($ mil.): 156
Return on equity: —
Current Ratio: 2.70

ALDINE INDEPENDENT SCHOOL DISTRICT

Auditors : WHITLEY PENN LLP HOUSTON TX

LOCATIONS

HQ: ALDINE INDEPENDENT SCHOOL DISTRICT
2520 WW THORNE BLVD, HOUSTON, TX 770733406
Phone: 281 449-1011

Web: WWW.ALDINEISD.ORG

HISTORICAL FINANCIALS
Company Type: Private

Income Statement — FYE: June 30

	REVENUE ($mil)	NET INCOME ($mil)	NET PROFIT MARGIN	EMPLOYEES
06/21	900	39	4.4%	7,000
06/20	814	(3)	—	—
06/19	791	106	13.5%	—
06/18	757	33	4.5%	—
Annual Growth	5.9%	5.6%	—	—

2021 Year-End Financials
Return on assets: 2.1% Cash ($ mil.): 42
Return on equity: 577.9%
Current Ratio: —

ALEGENT CREIGHTON HEALTH

CHI Health (formerly Alegent Creighton Health) pledges allegiance to medical well-being in its corner of the Midwest. The not-for-profit health care system operates 15 hospitals with about 3,000 beds in Omaha and surrounding communities in eastern Nebraska and southwestern Iowa, including Bergan Mercy Medical Center and Immanuel Medical Center. Alegent Creighton Health's hospitals provide specialty services including cardiovascular, orthopedic, and cancer care; it also operates psychiatric, long-term care, home health, and outpatient centers. The health system is sponsored by Catholic Health Initiatives and is affiliated with Creighton University.

Operations
CHI Health is the primary provider of teaching locations for the Creighton University School of Medicine, with academic programs in a number of fields including psychiatry, women's health, nursing, and pharmacy. Its hospitals have some 1,500 physicians on staff and include 10 acute care facilities and one psychiatric hospital. Specialty units include an orthopedic hospital and skilled nursing centers.

In addition to its acute care facilities, the organization provides primary and specialty outpatient care services through its CHI Health Alegent Creighton Clinic unit. The division has more than 20 specialties and operates about 100 physician practices and clinics in Omaha and surrounding areas. There are also two Express Care clinics that offer urgent care for non-life-threatening ailments and six Quick Care clinics in Omaha (located in Hy-Vee retail stores) that provide minor medical ailment treatment, as well as sports physicals and vaccinations. The idea behind the clinics is to divert patients who might otherwise end up at ERs with non-emergency symptoms (thus lowering hospital expenses).

Geographic Reach
The network's hospitals are located in Omaha (five medical centers), Papillion, Plainview, and Schuyler, Nebraska; as well as in Corning, Council Bluffs, and Missouri Valley, Iowa.

Strategy
The company has been pursuing growth to signify its presence as a unified regional health network. The efforts are intended to allow it to better compete and thrive in the changing US health care landscape by expanding its facilities, training programs, and resources in the Omaha area. Growth efforts include the formation of an intensive care partnership with Good Samaritan Hospital in 2013. The network has also opened several new community care clinics in recent years.

In 2015, CHI Health partnered with Aetna to create Nebraska's first commercial, product-based accountable care organization (ACO). The ACO offers employers a health care option that is designed to improve quality of care, outcomes, and patient experiences.

Auditors: LB CATHOLIC HEALTH INITIATIVES

LOCATIONS
HQ: ALEGENT CREIGHTON HEALTH
12809 W DODGE RD, OMAHA, NE 681542155
Phone: 402 343-4300
Web: WWW.CHIHEALTH.COM

PRODUCTS/OPERATIONS
Selected Facilities and Operations
Alegent Creighton Health Clinics (primary care, multiple locations in Iowa and Nebraska)
Alegent Creighton Health Urgent Care clinics (urgent care, three locations in Nebraska)
Alegent Creighton Health Quick Care (minor care clinics; seven locations in Omaha, Nebraska, in Hy-Vee stores)
Alegent Health at Home (home health care)
Bergan Mercy Medical Center (Omaha, Nebraska; 300 beds)
Community Memorial Hospital (Missouri Valley, Iowa; 20 beds)
Creighton University Medical Center (Omaha, Nebraska; 400 beds)
Immanuel Communities (independent and assisted living in Omaha and Lincoln)
Immanuel Fontenelle (nursing home in Omaha)
Immanuel Medical Center (Omaha, Nebraska; 280 beds)
Immanuel Rehabilitation Center (Omaha, Nebraska)
Lakeside Hospital (Omaha, Nebraska; 160 beds)
Lasting Hope Recovery Center (Omaha, Nebraska; psychiatric hospital with 120 beds)
Memorial Hospital (Schuyler, Nebraska; 25 beds)
Mercy Corning Hospital (Corning, Iowa; 20 beds)
Mercy Hospital (Council Bluffs, Iowa; 160 beds)
Midlands Hospital (Papillion, Nebraska; 50 beds)
Plainview Hospital (Plainview, Nebraska)

COMPETITORS
ATLANTIC HEALTH SYSTEM INC.
CHRISTIANA CARE HEALTH SYSTEM, INC.
HOLY SPIRIT HOSPITAL OF THE SISTERS OF CHRISTIAN CHARITY
LEGACY HEALTH
LEHIGH VALLEY HEALTH NETWORK, INC.

HISTORICAL FINANCIALS
Company Type: Private

Income Statement — FYE: June 30

	REVENUE ($mil)	NET INCOME ($mil)	NET PROFIT MARGIN	EMPLOYEES
06/20	636	12	2.0%	10,000
06/19	599	27	4.6%	—
06/13	525	63	12.2%	—
Annual Growth	2.8%	(20.5%)	—	—

2020 Year-End Financials
Return on assets: 1.4% Cash ($ mil.): 1
Return on equity: 3.0%
Current Ratio: 0.40

ALEGENT HEALTH - BERGAN MERCY HEALTH SYSTEM

LOCATIONS
HQ: ALEGENT HEALTH - BERGAN MERCY HEALTH SYSTEM
7500 MERCY RD, OMAHA, NE 681242319
Phone: 402 398-6060
Web: WWW.CHIHEALTH.COM

HISTORICAL FINANCIALS
Company Type: Private

Income Statement — FYE: June 30

	REVENUE ($mil)	NET INCOME ($mil)	NET PROFIT MARGIN	EMPLOYEES
06/20	576	31	5.4%	1
06/18	695	60	8.7%	—
06/17	727	23	3.2%	—
06/14	543	88	16.3%	—
Annual Growth	1.0%	(16.0%)	—	—

2020 Year-End Financials
Return on assets: 2.8% Cash ($ mil.): 4
Return on equity: 3.5%
Current Ratio: 0.90

ALEX LEE, INC.

The Alex Lee family of companies includes Lowes Foods and Merchants Distributors (MDI). Alex Lee grew out of Merchants Produce Company which was founded in 1931 by Alex and Lee George. MDI supplies food and general merchandise to more than 600 retailers with food and non-food items in over 10 Eastern states. The company's Consolidation Services supplies an array of warehousing and logistics services. As part of its business, Alex Lee also operates Lowes Food Stores, a chain of approximately 75 grocery stores located in the Carolinas and Virginia. The George family continues to control Alex Lee.

Operations

Alex Lee, named after Lebanese immigrant founder Moses George's two sons Alex and Lee, boasts two operating companies: Merchants Distributors (MDI) and Lowes Foods.

MDI, a privately-owned wholesale grocery store distributor, offers cold storage to manufacturers, provides digital services for retail, has a large format print facility, and exports to a wide range of stores in the US and internationally. Lowes Foods, a homegrown grocery store, offers convenient to-go meals and stellar guest services.

Geographic Reach

Alex Lee's Lowes Foods business operates some 75 stores while MDI supplies more than 600 retail food stores with food and non-food items in over 10 Eastern states.

Sales and Marketing

Alex Lee markets its products and services through its distribution companies such as Lowes Foods and MDI.

EXECUTIVES

Senior Vice President Human Resources, Robert Vipperman
Communications Vice President, Kimberly D George
Auditors : RSM US LLP CHARLOTTE NORTH C

LOCATIONS

HQ: ALEX LEE, INC.
120 4TH ST SW, HICKORY, NC 286022947
Phone: 828 725-4424
Web: WWW.ALEXLEE.COM

PRODUCTS/OPERATIONS

Selected Operations
Lowe's Food Stores, Inc.
Merchants Distributors, Inc.
  Consolidation Services, Inc.

COMPETITORS

BEN E. KEITH COMPANY
CENTRAL GROCERS, INC.
FRED MEYER STORES, INC.
George Weston Limited
HARRIS TEETER SUPERMARKETS, INC.
KEY FOOD STORES CO-OPERATIVE, INC.
LOWES FOODS, LLC
MCLANE COMPANY, INC.
THE H T HACKNEY CO
THE MERCHANTS COMPANY

HISTORICAL FINANCIALS
Company Type: Private

Income Statement				FYE: October 1
	REVENUE ($mil)	NET INCOME ($mil)	NET PROFIT MARGIN	EMPLOYEES
10/22	3,880	35	0.9%	9,550
10/21	3,556	88	2.5%	—
10/20*	3,192	56	1.8%	—
09/19	2,286	25	1.1%	—
Annual Growth	19.3%	12.3%	—	—

*Fiscal year change

ALFRED I.DUPONT HOSPITAL FOR CHILDREN

LOCATIONS

HQ: ALFRED I.DUPONT HOSPITAL FOR CHILDREN
1600 ROCKLAND RD, WILMINGTON, DE 198033607
Phone: 302 651-4000
Web: WWW.NEMOURS.ORG

HISTORICAL FINANCIALS
Company Type: Private

Income Statement				FYE: December 31
	REVENUE ($mil)	NET INCOME ($mil)	NET PROFIT MARGIN	EMPLOYEES
12/18	553	16	3.0%	3,068
12/17	525	34	6.6%	—
12/16	516	(31)	—	—
12/15	450	28	6.4%	—
Annual Growth	7.1%	(16.3%)	—	—

2018 Year-End Financials
Return on assets: 2.5%   Cash ($ mil.): —
Return on equity: 2.7%
Current Ratio: 1.90

ALIEF INDEPENDENT SCHOOL DISTRICT

Auditors : WHITLEY PENN LLP HOUSTON TE

LOCATIONS

HQ: ALIEF INDEPENDENT SCHOOL DISTRICT
4250 COOK RD, HOUSTON, TX 770721115
Phone: 281 498-8110
Web: WWW.ALIEFISD.NET

HISTORICAL FINANCIALS
Company Type: Private

Income Statement				FYE: August 31
	REVENUE ($mil)	NET INCOME ($mil)	NET PROFIT MARGIN	EMPLOYEES
08/21	566	42	7.4%	6,000
08/19	553	35	6.3%	—
08/18	535	(25)	—	—
08/17	519	(5)	—	—
Annual Growth	2.2%	—	—	—

2021 Year-End Financials
Return on assets: 4.2%   Cash ($ mil.): 252
Return on equity: 66.3%
Current Ratio: —

2022 Year-End Financials
Return on assets: 2.8%   Cash ($ mil.): 17
Return on equity: 5.0%
Current Ratio: 1.30

ALLAN MYERS, INC.

American Infrastructure provides heavy civil construction services for projects in the Mid-Atlantic. Operating as Allan A. Myers in Pennsylvania and Delaware and as American Infrastructure in Maryland and Virginia, the family-run business builds and reconstructs highways, water treatment plants, medical facilities, and shopping centers, and offers site development for homebuilders. Its quarries and asphalt plants operate under the Independence Construction Materials (ICM) subsidiary, which supplies aggregates, asphalt, and ready-mixed concrete to its construction companies. The company is ranked by Engineering News-Record as 25th on the country's Top 50 list of heavy civil contractors.

Operations

American Infrastructure builds projects ranging from $100,000 to more than $100 million per project.

As a land developer interested in conservation, American Infrastructure offers a unique all-terrain tree spade vehicle that is designed to carry large, mature trees harvested from heavily wooded sites intended to be replanted on developed sites. The process allows mature trees to be saved and relocated on a developed site.

Geographic Reach

American Infrastructure and its subsidiaries operate in the Mid-Atlantic region through about 20 locations (including quarries and plants) in Pennsylvania, Maryland, Virginia, Delaware, and Washington, DC, as well as four satellite offices in the region. The company also has 15 materials mining and/or asphalt production facilities in four states.

Sales and Marketing

American Infrastructure serves private developers, general contractors, departments of transportation, utilities, local and state governments, and federal military customers throughout the Mid-Atlantic region.

Customers include CRB Military Housing, Frederick Winchester Service Authority, O'Brien & Gere, Delaware Department of Transportation, The Goldenberg Group, Morgan-Keller Construction, Forest Park Water, Uniwest Construction, Divinity Trucking, Nardi Construction, Hunt Building Company, the City of Wilmington, and Maryland State Highway Administration.

Strategy

American Infrastructure's financial capacity is strengthened by a bonding capacity of $800 million, which allows it to tackle major projects. Selected projects includes Richmond Airport Connector, Route 715/40 Interchange, Virginia SR 29 Bridge, Jersey Shore Pump Station, Aberdeen Test Track, Argonne Drive Bridge, MARC Wedge Railyard,

Nicodemus Bridge, Route 52, Ballenger McKinney wastewater treatment plant, and Mount Holly wastewater treatment plant.

Company Background

Some past projects include Eagle Heights at Dover Air Force Base ($13.3 million), Cool Springs Reservoir ($18.6 million), and MD 43 ($46.7 million) in Baltimore County, Maryland.

The company was established in 1939 as Allan A. Myers and Son, a local hauling company in the suburbs of Philadelphia.

Auditors : PRICEWATERHOUSECOOPERS LLP PH

LOCATIONS

HQ: ALLAN MYERS, INC.
1805 BERKS RD, WORCESTER, PA 19490
Phone: 610 222-8800
Web: WWW.ALLANMYERS.COM

PRODUCTS/OPERATIONS

Selected Services
Site Development
  Concrete flatwork
  Excavation and grading
  Hauling
  Large-diameter tree relocation
  Milling and paving
  Rock drilling and blasting
  Soft dig capabilities
  Stone and curb
  Stormwater management
  Survey and stakeout
  Underground utilities
Transportation
  Asphalt paving
  Box culverts
  Bridges and structures
  Concrete paving
  Maintenance of traffic
Water Resources
  New water/wastewater treatment plants
  Reservoirs and dams
  Underground reservoirs
  Water and sewer transmission lines
  Wetland mitigation and reconstruction

Selected Subsidiaries
Allan A. Myers, Inc.
American Infrastructure-Maryland
American Infrastructure-Virginia
Independence Construction Materials

COMPETITORS

ARB, INC.
BECHTEL GROUP, INC.
CENTERPOINT PROPERTIES TRUST
CIANBRO CORPORATION
LAGAN CONSTRUCTION LIMITED
MACDONALD MOTT GROUP INC
OVERLAND CONTRACTING INC.
PC CONSTRUCTION COMPANY
RAILWORKS CORPORATION
S & B ENGINEERS AND CONSTRUCTORS, LTD.

HISTORICAL FINANCIALS

Company Type: Private

Income Statement — FYE: December 31

	REVENUE ($mil)	NET INCOME ($mil)	NET PROFIT MARGIN	EMPLOYEES
12/21	1,157	37	3.3%	2,000
12/20	1,025	33	3.3%	—
12/19	989	48	5.0%	—
12/17	751	21	2.8%	—
Annual Growth	11.4%	15.6%	—	—

2021 Year-End Financials
Return on assets: 5.5%   Cash ($ mil.): 112
Return on equity: 29.7%
Current Ratio: 1.10

ALLEGHENY GENERAL HOSPITAL INC

If there is a critical trauma anywhere near Pittsburgh, Allegheny General Hospital (AGH) is ready to take it on. The roughly 630-bed hospital is the Level I Shock Trauma Center for the five-state region surrounding Steel City. AGH offers traditional medical and surgical services as well as cardiology care and organ transplants. The hospital also is engaged in research in areas such as neuroscience, oncology, trauma, and genetics. AGH, which treats nearly 22,000 patients each year, has about 800 physicians on its staff. The hospital, which is affiliated with Philadelphia's Drexel University College of Medicine, is a subsidiary of Allegheny Health System, which itself is owned by Highmark, Inc.

Operations

AGH receives more than 50,000 emergency visits each year, as well as had 300,000 outpatient visits and more than 21,000 surgical procedures. In order to receive those emergencies in an expedient manner, the hospital also operates a LifeFlight aero medical service.

The hospital's cancer center provides programs for a wide range of diseases such as lung, breast, colon, prostate, brain, and liver cancer.

AGH also operates a smaller satellite facility in the northern Pittsburgh suburb of McCandless, as well as an outpatient facility in suburban Pittsburgh.

Strategy

In 2014 AGH proposed investing part of $175 million from Highmark Inc. in renovations and technology upgrades at its AGH and West Penn hospitals, anticipating that they will accommodate more patients when Highmark insurance subscribers lose in-network access to the University of Pittsburgh Medical Center in 2015.

Company Background
AGH first opened in 1885.

LOCATIONS

HQ: ALLEGHENY GENERAL HOSPITAL INC
320 E NORTH AVE, PITTSBURGH, PA 152124772
Phone: 412 359-3131
Web: WWW.AHN.ORG

COMPETITORS

AKRON GENERAL MEDICAL CENTER
ARKANSAS CHILDREN'S HOSPITAL
FRANKLIN SQUARE HOSPITAL CENTER, INC.
FROEDTERT MEMORIAL LUTHERAN HOSPITAL, INC.
MERCY HOSPITAL SOUTH

HISTORICAL FINANCIALS

Company Type: Private

Income Statement — FYE: June 30

	REVENUE ($mil)	NET INCOME ($mil)	NET PROFIT MARGIN	EMPLOYEES
06/16	720	73	10.2%	5,064
06/15	700	107	15.4%	—
Annual Growth	2.8%	(31.7%)	—	—

2016 Year-End Financials
Return on assets: 19.5%   Cash ($ mil.): 1
Return on equity: —
Current Ratio: 1.20

ALLEGIS GROUP, INC.

Allegis Group is one of the world's largest staffing and recruitment firms. Among its group of staffing companies are Aerotek (engineering, automotive, and scientific professionals), Aston Carter (recruitment for accounting, finance, and professional skills), and TEKsystems (information technology staffing and consulting). Other Allegis Group units include sales support outsourcer MarketSource. Allegis Group operates through more than 500 locations worldwide. Chairman Jim Davis helped found the company (originally known as Aerotek) in 1983 to provide contract engineering personnel to two clients in the aerospace industry.

Operations

Operating through a group of about a dozen companies, Allegis Group serves businesses and organizations from the engineering, automotive, finance, IT, life sciences, and other industries. The company also serves government agencies and subcontractors. Aerotek and TEKsystems are among the group's largest and most established companies; other Allegis companies provide niche services, including disability recruitment through its Getting Hired unit and legal recruitment through Major, Lindsey & Africa.

Allegis Group's core services include staffing and recruitment (screening, onboarding, and retention), search (CEO and board member services), talent advisory (executive report, data file, and segment analysis), managed delivery, and workforce management.

Geographic Reach
Hanover, Maryland-based, Allegis Group operates in more than 500 locations around the globe, including offices throughout the US, the UK and Europe as well as in the Middle East, Asia, and Asia Pacific region.

Sales and Marketing
Allegis Group has served approximately 20,000 clients.

Strategy
Allegis Group has expanded its geographical footprint and improved its position in specialist staffing markets through the use of acquisitions. The company's specialized staffing firms cater to various industries.

Mergers and Acquisitions
In 2016 Allegis Group acquired Switzerland-based staffing, recruiting, and services organization The Stamford Group. The deal increased Allegis Group's global footprint and strengthened its European presence.

Company Background
In 1983, Stephen Bisciotti and Jim Davis founded the company (originally known as Aerotek) in Maryland. At the time, the founders' firm matched job seekers with aeronautics, engineering, and light industrial positions. In the late 1980s, the company expanded into the IT application markets.

Aerotek extended its reach into commercial, environmental, and energy industries through its 2001 acquisition of Onsite Companies. The company later changed its name to Allegis Group, while the other divisions remained separate companies until eventually consolidating under the Allegis Group banner.

Auditors : PRICEWATERHOUSECOOPERS LLP B

LOCATIONS
HQ: ALLEGIS GROUP, INC.
7301 PARKWAY DR, HANOVER, MD 210761159
Phone: 410 694-5100
Web: WWW.ALLEGISGROUP.COM

PRODUCTS/OPERATIONS
Selected Subsidiaries
Aerotek
    Aerotek Aviation, LLC
    Aerotek Canada
    Aerotek Scientific, LLC
Allegis Group Canada
Allegis Group India
Major, Lindsey & Africa
MarketSource, Inc
Stephen James Associates
TEKsystems
    TEKsystems Canada
    TEKsystems Netherlands
    TEKsystems United Kingdom

COMPETITORS
AEROTEK, INC.
ASGN INCORPORATED
CORPORATE SERVICE GROUP, LTD.
GENESIS HR SOLUTIONS, INC.
GUIDANT GLOBAL, INC.
LUCAS ASSOCIATES, INC.
RANDSTAD PROFESSIONALS US, LLC
SALES CONSULTANTS OF SPARTA, NJ INC
STHREE PLC
WOODMOOR GROUP INC

HISTORICAL FINANCIALS
Company Type: Private

Income Statement   FYE: December 31

	REVENUE ($mil)	NET INCOME ($mil)	NET PROFIT MARGIN	EMPLOYEES
12/20	12,269	0	0.0%	85,000
12/19	13,583	0	0.0%	—
12/18	13,402	0	0.0%	—
12/17	12,296	0	0.0%	—
Annual Growth	(0.1%)	—	—	—

2020 Year-End Financials
Return on assets: —   Cash ($ mil.): 830
Return on equity: —
Current Ratio: 3.00

ALLEGRO MICROSYSTEMS, LLC

Allegro MicroSystems is a leading global designer, developer, fabless manufacturer and marketer of sensor integrated circuits (ICs) and application-specific analog power ICs enabling critical technologies in the automotive and industrial markets. Its solutions are based on its monolithic Hall effect and xMR technology that allows customers to develop contactless sensor solutions that reduce mechanical wear and provide greater measurement accuracy and system control. Asian markets, particularly China, generated the majority of its sales.

Operations
Allegro operates in one segment which involves the design, development, production and distribution of various integrated circuits in various markets worldwide. It is a leading supplier of power ICs and a market share leader in magnetic sensor ICs driven by its market leadership in the automotive market. Its products are foundational to automotive and industrial electronic systems. Its sensor ICs enable its customers to precisely measure motion, speed, position and current, while its power ICs include high-temperature and high-voltage capable motor driver, power management and light emitting diode (LED) driver ICs. Its photonics portfolio provides eye-safe distance measurement and 3D imaging solutions.

Overall, magnetic sensors integrated circuits (MS), account for some 65% of sales, while the power integrated circuits (PIC) accounts for the rest.

Geographic Reach
Allegro is headquartered in Manchester, New Hampshire. The company has design and applications centers located across the Americas, Europe, and Asia. Majority of the company's sales were generated in Asia with China accounting to some 25% of sales and Japan with about 20%, while the Americas generated over 15% and the EMEA region with about 20% of sales.

Sales and Marketing
Its products are sold primarily to major global OEMs and their key suppliers, primarily in the automotive and industrial markets through a sales channel that includes a direct sales force, independent sales representatives, and distributors. It also sells its products to over 10,000 end customers. Approximately half of its sales in 2022 were derived from sales to its top twenty customers.

The company's advertising expense was $452, $331, and $273 in fiscal years 2022, 2021, and 2020, respectively.

Financial Performance
Total net sales increased by $177.5 million, or 30%, to $768.7 million in the fiscal year 2022 (ended March) from $591.2 million in the fiscal year 2021. This increase was primarily due to the continued economic recovery and increases in demand for ADAS, safety, comfort and convenience, internal combustion engine (ICE) applications, xEV, wireless infrastructure, personal mobility, industrial automation, cloud computing/data center and gaming applications, partially offset by declines in personal electronics and PC printers and peripherals.

Net income for fiscal year 2022 (ended March) increased to $119.6 million compared to $18.1 million in the prior year.

Cash held by the company at the end of fiscal year 2022 increased to $289.8 million. Operating activities $156.1 million while investing and financing activities used $66.3 million and $5.3 million, respectively. Main cash uses were purchases of property and related party note receivable.

Strategy
In 2016, Allegro began a multi-year strategic transition to extend its market leadership in high-growth markets, improve its operating model through a fabless and asset-lite manufacturing strategy, increase its IC design footprint and capacity, and accelerate growth through enhanced sales operations. To date, Allegro believes that it has begun to successfully realize many of the key objectives of this transition, and the company expects to continue to benefit from measures put in place to further enhance its competitiveness, growth and profitability. As part of its strategic transformation, Allegro began to streamline manufacturing to reduce fixed costs.

The company's strategy is to provide complete IC solutions for its customers, innovate with purpose to build on leadership in its key markets and expand its presence to become a global leader in semiconductor power and sensing solutions for motion control and energy efficient systems in automotive and industrial applications.

The company's focuses are: invest in research and development that is market-aligned and focused on targeted portfolio expansion; emphasize its automotive "first" philosophy to align its product development with the most rigorous applications and safety standards; invest to lead in chosen markets and apply its intellectual property and technology to pursue adjacent growth markets; expand its sales channels and enhance its sales operations and customer relationships; continue to improve its gross margins through product innovation and cost optimization; pursue selective acquisitions and other strategic transactions; and maintain sustainability efforts.

Mergers and Acquisitions

In 2022, Allegro MicroSystems have entered into an agreement to acquire Heyday Integrated Circuits (Heyday). Heyday is a privately-held company specializing in compact, fully-integrated isolated gate drivers that enable energy conversion in high-voltage gallium nitride (GaN) and silicon carbide (SiC) wide-bandgap (WBG) semiconductor designs, headquartered in Grasse, France. The Heyday acquisition will complement Allegro's existing solutions for energy efficiency, including its market-leading current sensor solutions. Additionally, it is expected to significantly expand Allegro's addressable market for electric vehicles (xEV), solar inverters, datacenter and 5G power supplies, and broad-market industrial applications. Allegro will pay approximately $19 million in cash for the acquisition of Heyday.

LOCATIONS

HQ: ALLEGRO MICROSYSTEMS, LLC
955 PERIMETER RD, MANCHESTER, NH 031033353
Phone: 603 626-2300
Web: WWW.ALLEGROMICRO.COM

PRODUCTS/OPERATIONS

Selected Products
Current sensor integrated circuits (ICs)
    Conductor sensor chips
    High-side hot-swap Hall-effect current monitor chips
Magnetic digital position sensor chips
    Bipolar switches
    Dual-element switches
    Hall-effect latches and bipolar switches
    Hall-effect unipolar switches
    Micropower switches and latches
Magnetic linear and angular position sensor chips
    Angular position sensor chips
    Linear position sensor chips
Magnetic speed sensor ICs (camshaft, crankshaft, transmission, and wheel-speed sensor ICs)
Motor driver and interface ICs
    Bipolar stepper motor drivers
    Brushless DC motor drivers
    Photo and ion smoke detector ICs
Regulators and lighting
    LED drivers for backlighting and lighting
    Regulators (single-output, multiple output, low-noise block)
    Xenon photoflash drivers

COMPETITORS

ANALOG DEVICES, INC.
APTINA, LLC
CURTIS INSTRUMENTS, INC.
HANA MICROELECTRONICS PUBLIC COMPANY LIMITED
IXYS, LLC
MOLEX, LLC
NATIONAL SEMICONDUCTOR CORPORATION
SUPERTEX, INC.
TEXAS INSTRUMENTS AUSTIN INCORPORATED
YAZAKI NORTH AMERICA INC

HISTORICAL FINANCIALS

Company Type: Private

Income Statement   FYE: March 30

	REVENUE ($mil)	NET INCOME ($mil)	NET PROFIT MARGIN	EMPLOYEES
03/18	654	72	11.1%	3,500
03/17	600	65	10.9%	—
03/16	526	43	8.3%	—
03/13	489	45	9.3%	—
Annual Growth	6.0%	9.7%	—	—

2018 Year-End Financials
Return on assets: 12.1%   Cash ($ mil.): 114
Return on equity: 14.8%
Current Ratio: 3.40

ALLEN LUND COMPANY, LLC

The Allen Lund Company (ALC) knows loads; it matches shippers' loads with a network of truckload and less-than-truckload (LTL) carriers. (LTL carriers collect, consolidate, and haul freight from multiple shippers.) The brokerage firm arranges the transport of dry, refrigerated (predominantly produce), and flatbed cargo. It operates from 30 offices throughout more than 20 US states. ALC Logistics, ALC Perishable Logistics, and ALC International (an international division) assist shippers in managing transportation costs, tracking and tracing shipments, managing appointments, and executing freight forward management services overseas. The company was founded in 1976 by Allen Lund and his wife, Kathie Lund.

Operations
ALC has a Logistics & Software division, ALC Logistics.

Geographic Reach
The company's international division provides transportation services worldwide, along with transportation to and from the US, including Puerto Rico, Hawaii, Alaska, and ground transportation for Canada and Mexico.

Strategy
In an effort to expand its operation, in 2012, the company opened a new office in Joplin, Missouri and another in McAllen, Texas, which mainly focuses on handling heavy haul flatbed, particularly in and out of Mexico. In addition the company opened four additional offices in 2012.

Mergers and Acquisitions
In an effort to grow its business, in early 2014, ALC acquired Wisconsin based Northern Freight Service, Inc., a company provides truckload, LTL, and intermodal services to the customers ranging from small shippers to FORTUNE 500 shippers.

LOCATIONS

HQ: ALLEN LUND COMPANY, LLC
4529 ANGELES CREST HWY, LA CANADA FLINTRIDGE, CA 910113202
Phone: 818 777-6142
Web: WWW.ALLENLUND.COM

PRODUCTS/OPERATIONS

Selected Services
Software and Logistics
    LTL Freight
    Scheduling
    Spot Pricing and Bid Management
    Truck Load
Transportation Services
    Dry Van
    Flatbed Trucking
    International Freight Shipping
    LTL Freight
    Refrigerated Transportation

COMPETITORS

A&R LOGISTICS, INC.
AAA COOPER TRANSPORTATION
AERONET WORLDWIDE, INC.
ALLIANCE SHIPPERS, INC.
COMCAR INDUSTRIES, INC.
DANIEL F. YOUNG, INCORPORATED
ENGLAND GLOBAL LOGISTICS USA, INC.
FREIGHTQUOTE.COM, INC.
ODYSSEY LOGISTICS & TECHNOLOGY CORPORATION
ROCKY MOUNTAIN EXPRESS CORP.

HISTORICAL FINANCIALS

Company Type: Private

Income Statement   FYE: December 31

	REVENUE ($mil)	NET INCOME ($mil)	NET PROFIT MARGIN	EMPLOYEES
12/18	661	20	3.0%	310
12/17	515	10	2.0%	—
12/16	426	12	2.9%	—
12/15	457	13	2.9%	—
Annual Growth	13.1%	15.1%	—	—

2018 Year-End Financials
Return on assets: 19.6%   Cash ($ mil.): 32
Return on equity: 44.0%
Current Ratio: 1.70

ALLIANCE ENTERTAINMENT HOLDING CORPORATION

Auditors : BDO USA LLP MIAMI FLORIDA

LOCATIONS

HQ: ALLIANCE ENTERTAINMENT HOLDING CORPORATION
1401 NW 136TH AVE STE 100, SUNRISE, FL 333232854
Phone: 954 255-4000

HISTORICAL FINANCIALS
Company Type: Private

Income Statement — FYE: June 30

	ASSETS ($mil)	NET INCOME ($mil)	INCOME AS % OF ASSETS	EMPLOYEES
06/22	473	28	6.1%	900
06/21	388	34	8.8%	—
Annual Growth	21.6%	(16.3%)	—	—

2022 Year-End Financials
Return on assets: 6.1% Cash ($ mil.): 1
Return on equity: 26.3%
Current Ratio: 1.00

ALLIANCE LAUNDRY HOLDINGS LLC

Laundry day can't come often enough for Alliance Laundry Holdings (ALH). Through its wholly owned subsidiary, Alliance Laundry Systems, the company designs, makes, and markets commercial laundry equipment used in Laundromats, multi-housing laundry facilities (such as apartments, dormitories, and military bases), and on-premise laundries (hotels, hospitals, and prisons). Its washers and dryers are sold under the brands Speed Queen, UniMac, Huebsch, IPSO, and Cissell. They're sold primarily in the US and Canada, but also overseas. Investment firm BDT Capital Partners controls the company, which was founded in 1908.

Operations
Commercial laundry equipment, service, and parts account for 98% of the firm's revenue. It also operates an equipment financing business, which accounts for the rest.

Geographic Reach
North America is Wisconsin-based ALH's largest market, accounting for about 70% of sales. Europe and Asia each represent about 10% of sales. The remainder comes from markets in Latin America, the Middle East, and Africa. The company's manufacturing facilities are located in Wisconsin and Wevelgem, Belgium.

Sales and Marketing
ALH relies on an expansive distribution network to bring its goods to market. The company's more than 550 distributors in North America and 150-plus international distributors serve its Laundromat and on-premise laundry customers. Its multifamily housing laundry customers are served by ALH's roster of more than 100 route operators.

Financial Performance
The company's sales topped $505 million in 2012, a 10% increase compared with 2011. Net income fell 30% over the same period to $16.4 million, as a result of a loss from early retirement of debt and higher expenses. The company attributed the gain in sales (its third in as many years) to increases across all of its markets, with the exception of Europe. Increased sales volumes and price increases, primarily in the US and Canada, drove results. The strong performance over the past three years pushed sales to an all-time high following a drop-off during the recession.

Strategy
Despite difficult economic conditions globally, ALH has seen its business strengthen, driven by resilience in North America and international expansion. (The company is fortunate that consumers view clean clothes as an necessity, with economic conditions historically having limited effect on frequency of use of commercial laundry equipment.) In the US and Canada the equipment financing business is posting higher earnings and demand for commercial laundry equipment is rising. Markets in Latin America, including Colombia, Peru, and Venezuela, are driving double-digit sales growth in the region. Expansion in Asia, in such markets as Australia, China, the Philippines, and Thailand, is another growth driver.

In pursuit of future growth, in 2013 the company completed a $23 million investment to increase production capacity for current and new products and to purchase tooling and equipment for its plant in Wisconsin. The expansion added more than 20,000 square feet to the plant's existing assembly, metal stamping,and press shop facilities. The project increased ALH's production capacity for small chassis washers and dryers by more than 40%, enabling the company to meet increasing consumer demand for its products.

Auditors : PRICEWATERHOUSECOOPERS MILWAU

LOCATIONS

HQ: ALLIANCE LAUNDRY HOLDINGS LLC
221 SHEPARD ST, RIPON, WI 549711390
Phone: 920 748-3121
Web: WWW.ALLIANCELAUNDRY.COM

COMPETITORS

ASHTEAD GROUP PUBLIC LIMITED COMPANY
Adolf WÃ¼rth GmbH & Co. KG
FASTENAL COMPANY
HEADLAM GROUP PLC
LIXIL CORPORATION
TENNANT COMPANY
TITAN MACHINERY INC.
UNIFIRST CORPORATION
WESFARMERS LIMITED
WHIRLPOOL CORPORATION

HISTORICAL FINANCIALS
Company Type: Private

Income Statement — FYE: December 31

	REVENUE ($mil)	NET INCOME ($mil)	NET PROFIT MARGIN	EMPLOYEES
12/14	726	29	4.1%	1,500
12/12	505	16	3.2%	—
12/09	393	16	4.2%	—
Annual Growth	13.1%	12.3%	—	—

2014 Year-End Financials
Return on assets: 2.4% Cash ($ mil.): 48
Return on equity: 31.0%
Current Ratio: 1.40

ALLIED SECURITY HOLDINGS LLC

Better than a blanket, Allied Security Holdings gives customers a sense of security. One of the largest private contract security firms in the US, it does business as AlliedBarton Security Services. It recruits and employs trained security guards to serve thousands of customers (some of which are large FORTUNE 500 companies) and their facilities. They include government facilities, hospitals, offices, ports, residential communities, shopping centers, and universities. The firm also provides employment and background screening services through its HR Plus subsidiary. In mid-2016, AlliedBarton merged with Universal Services of America to create Allied Universal, North America's largest security services group.

Geographic Reach
Allied Security Holdings operates through more than 120 regional and district offices nationwide.

Strategy
In the last few years, the company has made strides to further build out its service offerings both organically and through acquisitions, expand its geographic footprint across the US, and increase the number of industries and types of facilities that it serves.

LOCATIONS

HQ: ALLIED SECURITY HOLDINGS LLC
161 WASHINGTON ST STE 600, CONSHOHOCKEN, PA 194282083

Phone: 484 351-1300
Web: WWW.AUS.COM

COMPETITORS

ATLANTIC DIVING SUPPLY, INC.
DELTA TUCKER HOLDINGS, INC.
GUARDSMARK, LLC
Garda World Security Corporation
INKERMAN (GROUP) LIMITED
PC SPECIALISTS, INC.
RELIANCE SECURITY GROUP LIMITED
THE DAY & ZIMMERMANN GROUP INC
UNIVERSAL SERVICES OF AMERICA, LP
WHELAN SECURITY CO.

HISTORICAL FINANCIALS
Company Type: Private

Income Statement — FYE: December 31

	REVENUE ($mil)	NET INCOME ($mil)	NET PROFIT MARGIN	EMPLOYEES
12/14	2,149	24	1.1%	53,760
12/13	2,042	51	2.5%	—
12/12	1,923	43	2.3%	—
Annual Growth	5.7%	(25.0%)	—	—

2014 Year-End Financials
Return on assets: 2.6%   Cash ($ mil.): 51
Return on equity: —
Current Ratio: 1.80

ALLIED UNIVERSAL HOLDCO LLC

EXECUTIVES
Global Chief Financial Officer, Tim Brandt

LOCATIONS
HQ: ALLIED UNIVERSAL HOLDCO LLC
1551 N TUSTIN AVE STE 650, SANTA ANA, CA 927058664
Phone: 866 877-1965
Web: WWW.AUS.COM

HISTORICAL FINANCIALS
Company Type: Private

Income Statement — FYE: December 31

	ASSETS ($mil)	NET INCOME ($mil)	INCOME AS % OF ASSETS	EMPLOYEES
12/20	7,216	(84)	—	188,000
12/19	6,432	(381)	—	—
12/17	4,451	(69)	—	—
Annual Growth	17.5%	—	—	—

2020 Year-End Financials
Return on assets: (-1.2%)   Cash ($ mil.): 970
Return on equity: (-19.5%)
Current Ratio: 2.70

ALLWAYS HEALTH PARTNERS, INC.

AllWays Health Partners, previously known as Neighborhood Health Plan (NHP), packages and delivers innovative products and programs that improve the experience of accessing care and coverage, and health outcomes. AllWays Health Partners offers health plans for small businesses, large groups, and families and individuals. The company offers Value HMO for Boston employees and retirees, ensuring access to the highest quality care. The Value HMO networks include Massachusetts General Hospital, Brigham and Women's Hospital, Beth Israel Deaconess Medical Center, Lahey Clinic, Spaulding Rehab, Mass Eye and Ear, and more.

LOCATIONS
HQ: ALLWAYS HEALTH PARTNERS, INC.
399 REVOLUTION DR, SOMERVILLE, MA 021451484
Phone: 617 772-5500
Web: WWW.MASSGENERALBRIGHAMHEALTHPLAN.ORG

COMPETITORS
ASCENSION VIA CHRISTI HEALTH, INC
CAPITAL DISTRICT PHYSICIANS' HEALTH PLAN, INC.
COMMUNITY HEALTH GROUP
HARVARD PILGRIM HEALTH CARE, INC.
HEALTH PARTNERS PLANS, INC.
HILL PHYSICIANS MEDICAL GROUP, INC.
MINISTRY HEALTH CARE, INC.
NEW YORK STATE CATHOLIC HEALTH PLAN, INC.
TUFTS ASSOCIATED HEALTH PLANS, INC.
UCARE MINNESOTA

HISTORICAL FINANCIALS
Company Type: Private

Income Statement — FYE: December 31

	ASSETS ($mil)	NET INCOME ($mil)	INCOME AS % OF ASSETS	EMPLOYEES
12/15	465	(22)	—	488
12/14	434	(108)	—	—
12/13	349	(68)	—	—
Annual Growth	15.4%	—	—	—

2015 Year-End Financials
Return on assets: (-4.9%)   Cash ($ mil.): 120
Return on equity: (-11.6%)
Current Ratio: 0.90

ALLY BANK

Ally Bank is on your side when it comes to banking. Formerly known as GMAC Bank, Ally Bank (which is a subsidiary of government-backed Ally Financial)Â offers savings and money market accounts, as well as traditionalÂ and no-penalty CDs. The online bank also offers interest checking accounts. The bankÂ offers its services online and over the phone; it operates no physical branch locations. Clients also can use any ATM in the US and Ally will reimburse any fees charged by other banks. Ally Bank was revamped and renamed in 2009 in the midst of GM's (very public) financial difficulties. Predecessor GMAC Bank had been in operation since 2001.

LOCATIONS
HQ: ALLY BANK
6985 S UNION PARK CTR # 435, MIDVALE, UT 840474177
Phone: 801 790-5005
Web: WWW.ALLY.COM

COMPETITORS
BANKINTER SOCIEDAD ANONIMA
CHASE PAYMENTECH SOLUTIONS, LLC
CREDIT SAISON CO., LTD.
FIRST NATIONAL BANK ALASKA
MANHATTAN BRIDGE CAPITAL, INC.
MITSUBISHI UFJ NICOS CO.,LTD.
NETSPEND HOLDINGS, INC.
NICHOLAS FINANCIAL, INC.
POPULUS FINANCIAL GROUP, INC
PURPOSE FINANCIAL, INC.

HISTORICAL FINANCIALS
Company Type: Private

Income Statement — FYE: December 31

	ASSETS ($mil)	NET INCOME ($mil)	INCOME AS % OF ASSETS	EMPLOYEES
12/16	123,548	1,273	1.0%	42
12/07*	28,472	291	1.0%	—
06/06	3,586	0	0.0%	—
Annual Growth	38.0%	114.3%	—	—

*Fiscal year change

2016 Year-End Financials
Return on assets: 1.0%   Cash ($ mil.): 4348
Return on equity: 7.2%
Current Ratio: —

ALMOST FAMILY, INC.

Almost Family steps in when you're more than an arm's reach from family members with health needs. With its home health nursing services, Almost Family offers senior citizens in 26 states (including Florida) an alternative to institutional care. Its Visiting Nurse unit provides skilled nursing care and therapy services at home under a variety of names, including Apex, Caretenders, Community Home Health, and Mederi-Caretenders. Its Personal Care Services segment, operating under the Almost Family banner, offers custodial care, such as housekeeping, meal preparation, and medication management. Almost Family operates 175 Visiting Nurse agencies and about 65 Personal Care Services locations.The company is merging with LHC Group.

Operations
The company's services are carried out by nurses, speech and occupational therapists, medical social workers, and home health aides. The services provided to a patient are

determined by physician's prescribed plan of care -- generally issued upon the patient's discharge from a hospital. Payments from Medicare account for 93% of revenue in the Visiting Nurse segment, making Almost Family sensitive to any changes in Medicare reimbursement policies. The Personal Care segment receives 86% of its revenues from Medicare payments, with the balance coming from private insurance, private pay, and Medicaid. This diversification of reimbursement risk is intentional, but the company is also confident that its home-based services will always be lower in cost than institutional care.

Geographic Reach

As part of its business, Kentucky-based Almost Family extends its reach to 16 states in the Northeast, Southeast, and Midwest. Florida, Ohio, and Tennessee are the company's three largest markets (in order of revenue significance).

Financial Performance

Almost Family posted a 4% rise in revenue in 2013 compared to 2012, to $357.8 million, on a 4% increase in the Visiting Nurse segment primarily due to a pair of acquisitions (both in 2013) and an increase in service revenues. The company's Personal Care business, which accounted for 23% of revenue in 2013, posted a 6% gain on incremental revenue from an acquisition as well as organic volume growth. Net income slid 52% year over year, to $8.2 million in 2013 on higher expenses due to an increase in the provision for uncollectable commercial accounts and denials by Medicare. (Medicare is the company's single largest source of revenue, accounting for about 71% of revenue in 2013.)

Strategy

As the health care industry grows and consolidates, Almost Family is looking to grow through acquisitions and continue to open home health care agencies in existing and new markets. Its expansion is focused on the eastern US. In late 2013, the company made the largest acquisition in its history: SunCrest.

Mergers and Acquisitions

In 2015 the company had its most acquisitive year ever. It acquired Willcare Health Care, adding to its operations in New York and elsewhere; it built up its operations in Ohio with the $40 million purchase of Black Stone Operations (which operates under the brand name Home Care by Black Stone). It also bought New Jersey-based Bayonne VNA Home Health Agency and Massachusetts-based Long Term Solutions (in-home nursing assessments for the insurance industry), both for undisclosed amounts.

In early 2017 Almost Family bought an 80% stake in Community Health Systems' (CHS') home health and hospice unit for $128 million. That business includes 74 home health locations and 15 hospice centers in 22 states. After that purchase, Almost Family became the third-largest Medicare home health provider in the nation. Together with CHS, the company provides services to some 50,000 patients daily.

In 2017 Almost Family agreed to merge with LHC Group. After the merger, LHC shareholders will own 58.5% of the combined entity, while Almost Family shareholders will own the rest.

HISTORY

Almost Family was founded in 1976 as National Health Industries, a Louisville, Kentucky-based home health care company. After William Yarmuth became president in 1981, he expanded the company into such service areas as home infusion and home medical equipment.

The company became Caretenders Health in 1985, and in 1991 the company merged with Senior Service Corporation, a small, public adult day care services company. The company further expanded the range of services it offered to the elderly through its home health care operations. It established beachheads in new geographic markets by opening home health offices (or buying them), and then adding day care centers. It also bought some existing care centers.

The company grew energetically following its decision to specialize in elder care. It made three acquisitions in 1997 and surpassed that feat by closing on four acquisitions in little over a month in early 1998. The company lost one of its revenue streams that year: Two home health agencies in the Louisville area that had been managed by Caretenders were sold by their owner, Columbia/HCA (now HCA). Caretenders sued Columbia/HCA for breach of contract and in 1999 won a $1.5 million settlement.

That year the company also sharpened its focus by selling its product operations (including infusion therapy, respiratory, and medical equipment) to Lincare Holdings, but decided not to discontinue its visiting nurses services.

In 2000 the company changed its name to Almost Family to underscore its focus on adult day care. The following year it bought back the 23% stake that rehabilitation titan HEALTHSOUTH had maintained in the company.

Auditors: ERNST & YOUNG LLP LOUISVILLE

LOCATIONS

HQ: ALMOST FAMILY, INC.
9510 ORMSBY STATION RD # 300, LOUISVILLE, KY 402235016
Phone: 502 891-1000
Web: WWW.ALMOSTFAMILY.COM

COMPETITORS

AMEDISYS, INC.
AMERICAN HOMEPATIENT, INC.
GENTIVA HEALTH SERVICES, INC.
LHC GROUP, INC.
MAGELLAN HEALTH, INC.
OPTION CARE HEALTH, INC.
PEDIATRIC SERVICES OF AMERICA, INC. (DE)
STEWARD HEALTH CARE SYSTEM LLC
TENET HEALTHCARE CORPORATION
TIVITY HEALTH, INC.

HISTORICAL FINANCIALS
Company Type: Private

Income Statement — FYE: December 29

	REVENUE ($mil)	NET INCOME ($mil)	NET PROFIT MARGIN	EMPLOYEES
12/17	796	20	2.6%	14,200
12/16*	623	18	2.9%	—
01/16	532	19	3.7%	—
12/14	495	13	2.7%	—
Annual Growth	17.1%	14.7%	—	—

*Fiscal year change

2017 Year-End Financials
Return on assets: 2.8%   Cash ($ mil.): 11
Return on equity: 4.0%
Current Ratio: 2.00

ALPINE SCHOOL DISTRICT

Auditors: SQUIRER & COMPANY PC OREM U

LOCATIONS

HQ: ALPINE SCHOOL DISTRICT
575 N 100 E, AMERICAN FORK, UT 840031758
Phone: 801 610-8400
Web: WWW.ALPINESCHOOLS.ORG

HISTORICAL FINANCIALS
Company Type: Private

Income Statement — FYE: June 30

	REVENUE ($mil)	NET INCOME ($mil)	NET PROFIT MARGIN	EMPLOYEES
06/22	914	56	6.2%	8,000
06/21	821	(38)	—	—
06/20	757	(78)	—	—
06/19	726	(44)	—	—
Annual Growth	8.0%	—	—	—

2022 Year-End Financials
Return on assets: 2.8%   Cash ($ mil.): —
Return on equity: 9.0%
Current Ratio: —

ALRO STEEL CORPORATION

Alro Steel runs its service centers like a grocery store for metals, keeping what customers need in easy reach. The service center operator, which has a dozen facilities in the US Northeast, Midwest, and Southeast, provides processing services such as aluminum circle cutting, CNC flame cutting,

HOOVER'S HANDBOOK OF PRIVATE COMPANIES 2023

forming, and machining. The company carries an extensive inventory of steel products, along with industrial tools and supplies. It also offers plastic sheet, rod, tube, and film through its Alro Plastics division and distributes industrial tools and materials through subsidiary Alro Industrial Supplies.

Operations
Led by its steel activities, Alro Steel operates several other businesses: Alro Metals Service Center, Alro Metals Plus (steel bars, plates, and sheet, and brass, copper, aluminum, and other products); Alro Plastics (fiberglass, acrylics, nylon, urethanes, and other); and Alro Industrial Supplies (threading, milling, boring, holemaking, reaming, and other machinery and equipment).

Geographic Reach
Alro Steel has more than 50 facilities in 12 US states (Florida, Illinois, Indiana, Kentucky, Michigan, Missouri, New York, North Carolina, Ohio, Oklahoma, Pennsylvania, and Wisconsin).

Sales and Marketing
The company distributes metals, industrial supplies, and plastics through its online store.

Strategy
Alro Steel is expanding its operations to meet demand.

In 2014 the company expanded its presence in Greensboro, North Carolina by opening a 42,000-sq.-ft. facility. It plans to potentially double the work force there within five years.

In 2013 it opened a new 70,000 sq. ft. facility in St. Louis to provide regional manufacturers with Alro's broad range of metal products and extensive processing capabilities. That year the company also opened a new 98,000 sq. ft. facility in Imperial, Pennsylvania, to serve manufacturers in western and central Pennsylvania and northern West Virginia.

Company Background
The company was established in 1948.

EXECUTIVES
Vice Chairman*, Barry Glick
Auditors: DELOITTE & TOUCHE LLP DETRO

LOCATIONS
HQ: ALRO STEEL CORPORATION
3100 E HIGH ST, JACKSON, MI 492036413
Phone: 517 787-5500
Web: WWW.ALRO.COM

COMPETITORS
BEARING DISTRIBUTORS, INC.
DILLON SUPPLY COMPANY
DOALL COMPANY
ENDRIES INTERNATIONAL, INC.
HEIDTMAN STEEL PRODUCTS, INC.
IBT, INC.
SHURTAPE TECHNOLOGIES, LLC
STEEL WAREHOUSE COMPANY LLC
TRICORBRAUN INC.
VALLEN DISTRIBUTION, INC.

HISTORICAL FINANCIALS
Company Type: Private

Income Statement — FYE: May 31

	REVENUE ($mil)	NET INCOME ($mil)	NET PROFIT MARGIN	EMPLOYEES
05/22	3,682	510	13.9%	2,400
05/19	2,213	198	9.0%	—
05/18	1,989	165	8.3%	—
Annual Growth	16.6%	32.5%	—	—

2022 Year-End Financials
Return on assets: 20.1%   Cash ($ mil.): —
Return on equity: 22.6%
Current Ratio: 7.80

ALSCO INC.

Alsco is a global leader in uniform and linen rental services. Operating from more than 180 branches in about 15 countries worldwide, the company rents and sells uniforms, linens, towels, napkins, and soft blankets to more than 355,000 customers worldwide. It also manages janitorial services, provides washroom supplies, and soap and sanitizer services. In addition, Alsco provides professional textile rental services and offers First aid that is fresh and budget friendly. The company was founded in 1889 by George Steiner and is still owned and operated by the Steiner family. It is headquartered in Utah and has locations in Australia, Brazil, Canada, China, Germany, Italy, New Zealand, Singapore, Malaysia, Thailand, and the US.

Operations
Alsco provides products and services for linens, uniforms, floorcare, washroom supplies, and first-aid, among others. In addition, the company also offers isolation gowns, face masks, clean shield, and disposable gloves.

Geographic Reach
Headquartered in Salt Lake City, Utah, Alsco operates in more than 180 locations around the world.

Sales and Marketing
Alsco serves customers in various industries, including automotive, building services, food processing, facilities, food and beverage, healthcare, restaurant, and industrial sectors. The company sell its products through its retail stores located across North America.

Strategy
In early 2022, Our Motorsports is proud to announce a partnership with Alsco Uniforms. The Utah-based company has signed a multi-race agreement with Jeb Burton and Our Motorsports. Alsco is the leader in providing rental services for uniforms, linens, floor mats, first aid cabinets and restroom supplies to many businesses across North America including Our Motorsports.

In mid-2021, Alsco Uniforms, the official uniform provider of race fans and a proud partner of Charlotte Motor Speedway (CMS), brings aboard longtime partner Darden Restaurants and its LongHorn Steakhouse brand as presenting sponsor of the May NASCAR Xfinity Series (NXS) race.

LOCATIONS
HQ: ALSCO INC.
505 E 200 S, SALT LAKE CITY, UT 841022007
Phone: 801 328-8831
Web: WWW.ALSCO.COM

PRODUCTS/OPERATIONS
Selected Products and Services
Clean room garments
Gown room management
Hospitality/restaurant apparel
Laundry services
Linens
Mats
Mops
Napkins
Restroom service
Towels
Uniform rental and sales
Vacuum filters
Washroom supplies

COMPETITORS
AMERICAN DAWN, INC.
AMERICAN HOTEL REGISTER COMPANY
AMERIPRIDE SERVICES, INC.
KRUEGER INTERNATIONAL, INC.
MARIETTA CORPORATION
MORGAN SERVICES, INC.
PRUDENTIAL OVERALL SUPPLY
RFID CORPORATION
TR INTERNATIONAL TRADING COMPANY
WESTPOINT HOME, INC.

HISTORICAL FINANCIALS
Company Type: Private

Income Statement — FYE: December 31

	REVENUE ($mil)	NET INCOME ($mil)	NET PROFIT MARGIN	EMPLOYEES
12/17	892	64	7.2%	16,000
12/16	704	38	5.5%	—
12/15	683	30	4.5%	—
Annual Growth	14.3%	45.2%	—	—

2017 Year-End Financials
Return on assets: 5.2%   Cash ($ mil.): 22
Return on equity: 8.1%
Current Ratio: 1.70

ALSTON CONSTRUCTION COMPANY, INC.

Alston Construction (formerly Panattoni Construction) offers a broad platform of general contracting, construction management, design-build services and virtual design management construction. The company serves a diverse array of industries, including healthcare, food and beverage, industrial, office, athletic facilities, and retail, among others. Refurbishing and extending buildings from its network of offices throughout the US, Alston Construction provides construction management services for such clients as Amazon.com, Bridgestone, Caterpillar, Clorox, FedEx, Petco, Helen of Troy, Under Armour, and Whirlpool. Completed approximately 6,010 projects, Alston Construction started in 1986.

Operations
Alston Construction has partnerships with designers, subcontractors, consultants, local communities, architects, engineers and construction professionals. Its construction management offer is based on shared risk and as a result, offers clients maximum flexibility. Alston offers Building Information Modeling (BIM) and Virtual Design & Construction (VDC) services in-house, and it can forecasts conflicts, minimize clashes, and avoid inevitable delays. Its VDC Specialists use the latest technology in scanning, modeling, and virtual design.

Among its projects include Aggieland Fitness, Artesian Spa, Beal Bank, Beltway 8 Interiors and Brooklyn Bedding HQ.

Geographic Reach
Based in the US, Alston Construction operates from nearly 20 offices in Arizona, California, Florida, Georgia, Illinois, Indiana and Washington, among others.

Sales and Marketing
Alston Construction serves a wide array of industries that include government, manufacturing, education, senior living, interiors, warehouse and distribution and commercial offices. Its clients include Bestbuy, Big 5, Campbells, J.Crew, Kellogs, Proctor & Gamble, Volkswagon, Disney, and more.

Auditors : CAMPBELL TAYLOR WASHBURN ROSE

LOCATIONS
HQ: ALSTON CONSTRUCTION COMPANY, INC.
  8775 FOLSOM BLVD STE 201, SACRAMENTO, CA 958263709
Phone: 916 340-2400
Web: WWW.ALSTONCO.COM

COMPETITORS
AUSTIN COMMERCIAL, INC.
CENTERPOINT PROPERTIES TRUST
DANIS BUILDING CONSTRUCTION COMPANY
DAVID E. HARVEY BUILDERS, INC.
DPR CONSTRUCTION, INC.
HOWARD BUILDING CORPORATION
RENTENBACH CONSTRUCTORS INCORPORATED
RYAN COMPANIES US, INC.
THE ALBERT M HIGLEY CO LLC
W. L. BUTLER CONSTRUCTION, INC.

HISTORICAL FINANCIALS
Company Type: Private

Income Statement   FYE: December 31

	REVENUE ($mil)	NET INCOME ($mil)	NET PROFIT MARGIN	EMPLOYEES
12/19	1,271	18	1.5%	200
12/18	909	14	1.6%	—
12/17	865	13	1.6%	—
12/15	642	6	1.1%	—
Annual Growth	18.6%	28.4%	—	—

2019 Year-End Financials
Return on assets: 5.8%   Cash ($ mil.): 50
Return on equity: 54.2%
Current Ratio: 1.10

ALTICOR INC.
Where there's a will (and an army of independent sales representatives), there's Amway. Operated through holding company Alticor, Amway is the world's top direct-selling company with millions of individual ABOs (Amway Business Owners) pitching everything from air filters to vitamins. The company makes some 450 unique products across the categories of nutrition (which generates about half of sales), beauty and personal care, and home. It is active in more than 100 countries across the globe with Asia (led by China) its largest market. Alticor is controlled by the families of Rich DeVos and Jay Van Andel, who founded Amway in 1959.

Operations
Nutrition products (supplements, skin care products, weight management programs) account for about 50% of total Amway sales. Beauty and personal care items (makeup, shampoo, toothpaste) generate about a quarter of sales and home products (water and air filters, cookware, cleaners) contribute about 20%. The company's top products include Nutrilite supplements, Artistry color cosmetics, eSpring water treatment systems, and XS energy drinks.

Geographic Reach
Based in Ada, Michigan, Amway operates in more than 100 countries. Its top markets by sales are China, the US, and South Korea; other leading markets include India, Japan, Malaysia, Russia, Taiwan, and Thailand.

The company has manufacturing facilities, farms, and warehouses in Brazil, China, Hungary, India, Japan, Mexico, the Netherlands, Poland, Russia, South Korea, Taiwan, Thailand, Vietnam, and the US.

Sales and Marketing
Amway's 450-plus products are marketing worldwide by more than 3 million independent distributors, who purchase the products and resell them. The company provides a host of support services, including personal mentors, brand centers, online learning tools, and call centers.

Financial Performance
While privately-owned Alticor doesn't report full results, Amway reported global sales of $8.6 billion in 2017, down from $8.8 billion in 2016. The company points to a challenging Chinese market for its revenue decline over the past few years

Strategy
Amway's strategy is pretty straightforward: continue to enhance and expand its line of products to serve more markets and appeal to more customers and create tools that make selling those products easier for the 3+ million ABOs (Amway Business Owners).

In 2017 Amway introduced a new formula for its Nutrilife Double X product, one of the best-selling supplements in the world, that includes a phytonutrient blend designed to help the body fight free radicals. Other additions to the company's product portfolio that year include a reformulated Essentials by Artistry skincare line and its first in-car air filtration system, Atmosphere Drive. Amway also pushed its XS brand of energy drinks into new countries in 2017, including China and India, with more launches planned for 2018. The company has more than 800 patents worldwide and another 250 pending applications.

Direct selling, of course, looks a lot different in the age of Amazon than it did some 60 years ago when Amway was founded. The company has been making significant investment in tools and technologies in recent years to enable its ABOs to better compete. It has spent some $70 million in mobile apps for ABOs, including the flagship Amway MyBiz app, which provides back office data and analytics. In addition, Amway has boosted its own customer service capabilities with instant messaging, bots, and other technologies to help it handle the more than 12 million annual customer requests. Other recent initiatives include a content sharing app for ABOs in the Philippines, a beauty app for customers in South Korea, and a one-stop product education and purchase portal in for ABOs in China.

Mergers and Acquisitions

LOCATIONS
HQ: ALTICOR INC.
  7575 FULTON ST E, ADA, MI 493550001
Phone: 616 787-1000
Web: WWW.AMWAY.COM

PRODUCTS/OPERATIONS
2017 Sales

	% of total
Nutrition	50
Beauty & personal care	26
Home	21
Other	3
Total	100

Selected Brands
Nutrition

Nutrilite
Beauty & personal care
    Artistry
    G&H
    Glister
    Satinique
Home
    Amway Home
    Atmosphere Sky
    eSpring
    iCook
Other
    XS

COMPETITORS

AMWAY CORP.
AMWAY INTERNATIONAL INC.
AVON COSMETICS LIMITED
Beijing Jingdong Century Trading Co., Ltd.
DS SERVICES OF AMERICA, INC.
LightInTheBox Holding Co., Ltd.
MARY KAY HOLDING CORPORATION
MELALEUCA, INC.
NU SKIN ENTERPRISES, INC.
USANA HEALTH SCIENCES, INC.

HISTORICAL FINANCIALS
Company Type: Private

Income Statement — FYE: December 31

	REVENUE ($mil)	NET INCOME ($mil)	NET PROFIT MARGIN	EMPLOYEES
12/15	9,459	0	0.0%	14,000
12/14	10,804	0	0.0%	—
12/13	11,754	0	0.0%	—
Annual Growth	(10.3%)	—	—	—

2015 Year-End Financials
Return on assets: — Cash ($ mil.): 1,300
Return on equity: —
Current Ratio: 1.20

ALTISOURCE SOLUTIONS, INC.

Auditors: DELOITTE & TOUCHE LLP ATLANT

LOCATIONS

HQ: ALTISOURCE SOLUTIONS, INC.
1000 ABERNATHY RD STE 200, ATLANTA, GA 303285604
Phone: 770 612-7007
Web: WWW.ALTISOURCE.COM

HISTORICAL FINANCIALS
Company Type: Private

Income Statement — FYE: December 31

	ASSETS ($mil)	NET INCOME ($mil)	INCOME AS % OF ASSETS	EMPLOYEES
12/13	724	133	18.5%	700
12/12	429	115	27.0%	—
Annual Growth	68.9%	15.4%	—	—

2013 Year-End Financials
Return on assets: 18.5% Cash ($ mil.): 130
Return on equity: 84.8%
Current Ratio: 1.90

ALTRU HEALTH SYSTEM

Altru Health System provides medical care to over 200,000 residents throughout northeastern North Dakota and northwestern Minnesota. The integrated health care network administers everything from primary care to inpatient medical and surgical care through its Altru Hospital (with more than 255 beds) and some 45 specialty centers. It also operates a cancer center, a rehabilitation center, dialysis facilities, and home health providers. For area seniors, Altru Health operates Parkwood Place, a senior living facility that provides several levels of care to residents, depending on need. A community of approximately 3,800 health professionals and support staff, the not-for-profit center was formed in 1997 by the integration of Grand Forks Clinic and United Health Services.

EXECUTIVES

Interim Chief Financial Officer*, Craig Faerber
Interim CMO*, Joshua Deere
Auditors: BRADY MARTZ & ASSOCIATES PC

LOCATIONS

HQ: ALTRU HEALTH SYSTEM
1200 S COLUMBIA RD, GRAND FORKS, ND 582014044
Phone: 701 780-5000
Web: WWW.ALTRU.ORG

PRODUCTS/OPERATIONS

2013 Sales

	$ mil	% of total
Net patient service	426.1	93
Other operating revenue	31.3	7
Total	457.4	100

2013 Net Patient Revenue

	% of total
Medicare	41
Blue Cross	31
Medicaid	11
Other third party	14
Patients	3
Total	100

Selected Centers
Bariatric Center
Breast Center
Cancer Center
Diabetes Center
Family Birthing Center
Grief Center
Hand Therapy Center
Hearing Center
Heart and Vascular Center
Joint Replacement Center
Medical Fitness Center
Outpatient Procedure Center
Pre-Admission Center
Psychiatry Center
Truyu Aesthetic Center

COMPETITORS

AGILITI HEALTH, INC.
AMERICAN HOMEPATIENT, INC.
AMERICAN SHARED HOSPITAL SERVICES
CAPE MEDICAL SUPPLY, LLC
COVENANT MEDICAL CENTER, INC.
EAST TEXAS MEDICAL CENTER REGIONAL HEALTHCARE SYSTEM
FREEDOM MEDICAL, INC.
LEE MEMORIAL HEALTH SYSTEM
THE LANCASTER GENERAL HOSPITAL
THE RUTLAND HOSPITAL INC ACT 220

HISTORICAL FINANCIALS
Company Type: Private

Income Statement — FYE: December 31

	REVENUE ($mil)	NET INCOME ($mil)	NET PROFIT MARGIN	EMPLOYEES
12/20	595	45	7.7%	3,800
12/19	589	10	1.8%	—
12/18	566	(13)	—	—
12/17	549	20	3.7%	—
Annual Growth	2.7%	31.4%	—	—

2020 Year-End Financials
Return on assets: 6.4% Cash ($ mil.): 146
Return on equity: 14.6%
Current Ratio: 6.00

AMC ENTERTAINMENT INC.

EXECUTIVES

CMO, Stephen A Colanero
CAO, Chris A Cox
CSO, Mark Peterson
Auditors: KPMG LLP KANSAS CITY MISSOUR

LOCATIONS

HQ: AMC ENTERTAINMENT INC.
11500 ASH ST, LEAWOOD, KS 662117804
Phone: 913 213-2000
Web: WWW.AMCTHEATRES.COM

HISTORICAL FINANCIALS
Company Type: Private

Income Statement — FYE: December 31

	REVENUE ($mil)	NET INCOME ($mil)	NET PROFIT MARGIN	EMPLOYEES
12/15	2,946	103	3.5%	19,700
12/14	2,695	64	2.4%	—
12/13	2,749	364	13.3%	—
12/12	811	(37)	—	—
Annual Growth	53.7%	—	—	—

2015 Year-End Financials
Return on assets: 2.0% Cash ($ mil.): 209
Return on equity: 6.7%
Current Ratio: 0.60

AMCAP FUND, INC.

Auditors: DELOITTE & TOUCHE LLP COSTA M

LOCATIONS

HQ: AMCAP FUND, INC.
  333 S HOPE ST STE LEVB, LOS ANGELES, CA 900713003
Phone: 213 486-9200

HISTORICAL FINANCIALS
Company Type: Private

Income Statement — FYE: February 28

	ASSETS ($mil)	NET INCOME ($mil)	INCOME AS % OF ASSETS	EMPLOYEES
02/21	81,181	15,952	19.6%	17
02/20	65,300	4,726	7.2%	—
02/19	65,322	1,248	1.9%	—
02/18	64,019	9,994	15.6%	—
Annual Growth	8.2%	16.9%	—	—

AMERICA CHUNG NAM (GROUP) HOLDINGS LLC

America Chung Nam (ACN) sells recovered fiber sources to Chinese paper mills where it can be converted into fiberboard, cardboard, and packaging. It also collects and exports a number of grades of post-consumer plastics. The company sources its materials through exclusive relationships with recycling facilities. Founder Yan Cheung and Ming Chung Liu own the company. It was founded in 1990.

Operations
ACN makes and supplies recovered paper (Mixed, ONP, DLK, Magazines, OCC, Office Paper and other paper grades), recyclable plastics (including PET, HDPE, LDPE, PS, ABS, Commingled Plastic, and other engineering plastics).

It annually exports more than seven million tons of paper annually. In terms of logistics services, the company has strong relationships with ocean, trucking, and transloading partners to enable access to rails, shipping routes, and ports all over the world.

ACN is partnered with Nine Dragons. It is an environmentally-friendly recovered paper based paper manufacturer based on production capacity.

The company helps the environment every year by saving 153 million trees. It also saves barrels of oil, gallons of water and acres of landfill.

Geographic Reach
The company has operations in North America, Asia, and Europe. It has offices in the US (Jersey City and California), Europe (the Netherlands and the UK), and Asia (China, South Korea and Japan).

Sales and Marketing
The relationship between ACN and its major customer, Nine Dragons Paper Group, is a tremendous advantage for the company's suppliers, enabling ACN to provide business continuity regardless of fluctuations in the global market.

Company Background
America Chung Nam was founded in 1990 by Yan Cheung and Ming Chung Liu. Recognizing the demand for packaging materials driven by China's product exports and having a ready source for fiber materials through America Chung Nam, Cheung established Nine Dragons Paper in 1996.

LOCATIONS
HQ: AMERICA CHUNG NAM (GROUP) HOLDINGS LLC
  1163 FAIRWAY DR, CITY OF INDUSTRY, CA 917892846
Phone: 909 839-8383
Web: WWW.ACNI.NET

COMPETITORS
CRANE & CO., INC.
DS SMITH PLC
JAPAN PULP AND PAPER CO., LTD.
METALICO, INC.
OMNISOURCE, LLC
RECYLEX SA
RENEWI PLC
SCHNITZER STEEL INDUSTRIES, INC.
THE DAVID J JOSEPH COMPANY
WISE RECYCLING, LLC

HISTORICAL FINANCIALS
Company Type: Private

Income Statement — FYE: December 31

	REVENUE ($mil)	NET INCOME ($mil)	NET PROFIT MARGIN	EMPLOYEES
12/19	664	83	12.6%	200
12/18	1,711	216	12.6%	—
12/09	1,125	16	1.5%	—
12/08	1,363	7	0.6%	—
Annual Growth	(6.3%)	23.9%	—	—

2019 Year-End Financials
Return on assets: 16.1%   Cash ($ mil.): 313
Return on equity: 19.7%
Current Ratio: 5.20

AMERICAN BALANCED FUND, INC.

Auditors : DELOITTE & TOUCHE LLP COSTA M

LOCATIONS
HQ: AMERICAN BALANCED FUND, INC.
  1 MARKET, SAN FRANCISCO, CA 941051596
Phone: 707 864-3945

HISTORICAL FINANCIALS
Company Type: Private

Income Statement — FYE: December 31

	ASSETS ($mil)	NET INCOME ($mil)	INCOME AS % OF ASSETS	EMPLOYEES
12/20	213,731	22,447	10.5%	9
12/19	164	25,217	15366.1%	—
12/18	129,091	2,254	1.7%	—
12/17	128,463	23,932	18.6%	—
Annual Growth	18.5%	(2.1%)	—	—

2020 Year-End Financials
Return on assets: 10.5%   Cash ($ mil.): 56
Return on equity: 12.3%
Current Ratio: —

AMERICAN CAMPUS COMMUNITIES OPERATING PARTNERSHIP LP

Auditors : ERNST & YOUNG LLP AUSTIN TEX

LOCATIONS
HQ: AMERICAN CAMPUS COMMUNITIES OPERATING PARTNERSHIP LP
  12700 HILL COUNTRY BLVD T, AUSTIN, TX 787386361
Phone: 512 732-1000
Web: WWW.AMERICANCAMPUS.COM

HISTORICAL FINANCIALS
Company Type: Private

Income Statement — FYE: December 31

	ASSETS ($mil)	NET INCOME ($mil)	INCOME AS % OF ASSETS	EMPLOYEES
12/20	7,531	69	0.9%	570
12/19	7,559	86	1.1%	—
12/18	7,038	119	1.7%	—
12/17	6,897	70	1.0%	—
Annual Growth	3.0%	(0.1%)	—	—

2020 Year-End Financials
Return on assets: 0.9%   Cash ($ mil.): 54
Return on equity: 2.2%
Current Ratio: 0.20

AMERICAN CHEMICAL SOCIETY

With more than 151,000 members, the American Chemical Society (ACS) is the world's largest scientific society. The not-for-profit organization provides information, career services, engagement programs, and educational resources to members and scientists. The company also publishes magazines, journals, and books. Its Chemical

Abstract Service provides the most comprehensive repository of research in chemistry and related sciences. ACS also serves as an advocate for its members on public policy issues. The ACS Member Insurance Program provides insurance plans to its members. The company was founded in 1876.

Operations
ACS has more than 65 journals, more than 46 million Chemical Abstracts records; over 165 million CAS REGISTRY organic and inorganic substances; some 156 million ACS journal article downloads; and it has approximately 185 local sections. The society offers members the opportunity to participate in more than 30 specialty divisions, ranging from food and agriculture to industrial and engineering chemistry.

Sales and Marketing
ACS serves client that include members and other chemistry-related practitioners, corporations, academic institutions, and government agencies. It promotes its products and services through meetings, reports, papers, and publications.

Company Background
ACS was founded in 1876 and chartered by the US Congress in 1937.

Auditors : IT KPMG LLP MC LEAN VA

LOCATIONS
HQ: AMERICAN CHEMICAL SOCIETY
 1155 16TH ST NW, WASHINGTON, DC 200364892
Phone: 202 872-4600
Web: WWW.ACS.ORG

COMPETITORS
AMERICAN ASSOCIATION FOR THE ADVANCEMENT OF SCIENCE
AMERICAN CANCER SOCIETY, INC.
AMERICAN PAYROLL INSTITUTE, INC.
AMERICAN PSYCHOLOGICAL ASSOCIATION, INC.
LONDON SCHOOL OF HYGIENE AND TROPICAL MEDICINE
MASSACHUSETTS INSTITUTE OF TECHNOLOGY
SOCIETY OF MANUFACTURING ENGINEERS
THE BRITISH DENTAL INDUSTRY ASSOCIATION
THE INSTITUTE OF ELECTRICAL AND ELECTRONICS ENGINEERS, INCORPORATED
THE JACKSON LABORATORY

HISTORICAL FINANCIALS
Company Type: Private

Income Statement — FYE: December 31

	REVENUE ($mil)	NET INCOME ($mil)	NET PROFIT MARGIN	EMPLOYEES
12/13	568	62	11.0%	2,000
12/08	451	(38)	—	—
12/05	411	26	6.4%	—
Annual Growth	4.1%	11.3%	—	—

2013 Year-End Financials
Return on assets: 4.8%   Cash ($ mil.): 37
Return on equity: 7.0%
Current Ratio: 0.60

AMERICAN CRYSTAL SUGAR COMPANY

Sugarbeet cooperative American Crystal Sugar is owned by some 2,800 growers in the Red River Valley of North Dakota and Minnesota who farms approximately 425,000 acres of cropland. The company has sugar packaging facilities located at the Moorhead, Hillsboro, Crookston, East Grand Forks and Sidney factories. The cooperative's products are sold in the US and other markets to industrial users and retail and wholesale customers under the Crystal name, as well as under private labels through marketing co-ops United Sugars and Midwest Agri-Commodities. American Crystal Sugar holds about 50% ownership interest in ProGold. It was founded by Henry Oxnard in 1890.

Operations
The company makes sugar products and agri-products from the highest quality sugar beets. Its beet sugar products are made for a variety of industries and uses. It offers its sugar in many forms ? from the fine granulated sugar, powdered sugar, and light brown sugar packages found in stores, to customized sugar varieties used by commercial bakers and food manufacturers.

In addition, American Crystal's sugar processing approach results in a variety of agri-products made from sugar beets. These agri-products include beet pulp pellets, beet pulp shreds, beet molasses and raffinate. These products are sold primarily for use in pet food manufacturing, as a feed stock enhancer in dairy production, for baker's yeast for manufacturing, for beet pulp for cattle, and for a variety of other feed-related applications.

Geographic Reach
The Moorhead, Minnesota-based cooperative has factories located in Crookston, East Grand Forks, and Moorhead, Minnesota; Drayton and Hillsboro, North Dakota; and Sidney, Montana.

Sales and Marketing
American Crystal Sugar markets its sugar through United Sugars Corporation, a marketing cooperative owned by the company and others; its agri-products are marketed by Midwest Agri-Commodities Company, which the company also owns with others. United Sugars Corporation, the company's sugar marketing agent, sells sugar primarily to industrial users such as confectioners, breakfast cereal manufacturers, and bakeries, which make up approximately 90% (by weight) of the sugar sold. The remaining portion is marketed by United Sugars to wholesalers and retailers under the "Crystal Sugar" trademark and various private labels for household consumption.

Financial Performance
From 2011 to 2012 American Crystal's revenues decreased by 4%, and its net income plummeted by 32%. Revenues decreased mainly due to a decrease in volumes of sugar and pulp, which reflect the impact of less product availability due to a smaller sugar beet crop in fiscal 2012 as compared to the previous year. The decrease in net income was attributed to an increase in operating costs, which included additional costs associated with a union labor lockout.

Company Background
In 1973 sugarbeet growers organized to acquire the business and assets of the American Crystal Sugar Company, which was a publicly held New Jersey corporation founded in 1899. It has been a cooperative ever since.

EXECUTIVES
Corporate Controller*, Teresa A Warne
Auditors : CLIFTONLARSONALLEN LLP STEVEN

LOCATIONS
HQ: AMERICAN CRYSTAL SUGAR COMPANY
 101 3RD ST N, MOORHEAD, MN 565601990
Phone: 218 236-4400
Web: WWW.CRYSTALSUGAR.COM

COMPETITORS
ARCHER-DANIELS-MIDLAND COMPANY
C&H SUGAR COMPANY, INC.
CHS INC.
Coöperatie Koninklijke Cosun U.A.
IMPERIAL SUGAR COMPANY
MICHIGAN SUGAR COMPANY
SOUTHERN MINNESOTA BEET SUGAR COOPERATIVE
THE AMALGAMATED SUGAR COMPANY LLC
THE WESTERN SUGAR COOPERATIVE
UNITED STATES SUGAR CORPORATION

HISTORICAL FINANCIALS
Company Type: Private

Income Statement — FYE: August 31

	REVENUE ($mil)	NET INCOME ($mil)	NET PROFIT MARGIN	EMPLOYEES
08/19	1,528	624	40.9%	1,365
08/18	1,515	650	43.0%	—
08/17	1,420	511	36.0%	—
08/16	1,290	561	43.5%	—
Annual Growth	5.8%	3.6%	—	—

2019 Year-End Financials
Return on assets: 61.6%   Cash ($ mil.): 1
Return on equity: 151.4%
Current Ratio: 1.20

AMERICAN ELECTRIC POWER SERVICE CORPORATION

EXECUTIVES

POLICY FIN STRAT PLANNING, Susan Tomasky
Deputy General Counsel, Jeffrey D Cross
SVCS, J Craig Baker Senior
Corporate Communication, Dale E Heydlauff

LOCATIONS

HQ: AMERICAN ELECTRIC POWER SERVICE CORPORATION
1 RIVERSIDE PLZ FL 1 # 1, COLUMBUS, OH 432152373
Phone: 614 716-1000
Web: WWW.AEP.COM

HISTORICAL FINANCIALS
Company Type: Private

Income Statement — FYE: December 31

	REVENUE ($mil)	NET INCOME ($mil)	NET PROFIT MARGIN	EMPLOYEES
12/16	1,348	0	0.0%	2,152
12/05	12,111	1,037	8.6%	
12/02	1,391	0	0.0%	
Annual Growth	(0.2%)	—	—	—

2016 Year-End Financials
Return on assets: —   Cash ($ mil.): 16
Return on equity: —
Current Ratio: 0.40

AMERICAN FUNDS INTERNATIONAL VANTAGE FUND

LOCATIONS

HQ: AMERICAN FUNDS INTERNATIONAL VANTAGE FUND
6455 IRVINE CENTER DR, IRVINE, CA 926184518
Phone: 949 975-5000

HISTORICAL FINANCIALS
Company Type: Private

Income Statement — FYE: October 31

	REVENUE ($mil)	NET INCOME ($mil)	NET PROFIT MARGIN	EMPLOYEES
10/21	802	15,687	1955.1%	4
10/20	13	13	96.6%	—
Annual Growth	5685.3%	17002.1%	—	—

2021 Year-End Financials
Return on assets: 25.4%   Cash ($ mil.): 182
Return on equity: 25.7%
Current Ratio: —

AMERICAN FUNDS PORTFOLIO SERIES

Auditors : DELOITTE & TOUCHE LLP COSTA

LOCATIONS

HQ: AMERICAN FUNDS PORTFOLIO SERIES
333 SUTH HOPE ST FL 55 FLR 55, LOS ANGELES, CA 90071
Phone: 213 486-9200

HISTORICAL FINANCIALS
Company Type: Private

Income Statement — FYE: October 31

	REVENUE ($mil)	NET INCOME ($mil)	NET PROFIT MARGIN	EMPLOYEES
10/21	871	13,753	1578.3%	5
10/20	894	5,755	643.2%	—
10/19	860	6,852	796.0%	—
10/18	684	(112)	—	—
Annual Growth	8.4%	—	—	—

2021 Year-End Financials
Return on assets: 20.4%   Cash ($ mil.): —
Return on equity: 20.5%
Current Ratio: —

AMERICAN FURNITURE WAREHOUSE CO.

Tony the Tiger hawking home furnishings might give some marketers pause, but the combination seems to work for American Furniture Warehouse. American Furniture's television commercials often spotlight white-haired president and CEO Jake Jabs (who has become a well-known personality in the state, as well as in the home furnishings industry) accompanied by baby exotic animals, mostly tigers. The company sells furniture, electronics, and decor at discounted prices. It boasts about a dozen retail locations in Colorado and Arizona and sells through its website, which also features bridal and gift registries. The company has built a reputation as a home-spun, local furniture retailer. Jabs bought the company in 1975.

Geographic Reach
American Furniture has locations in the Colorado cities of Aurora, Englewood, Centennial, Lakewood, Thornton, Westminster, Colorado Springs, Firestone/Longmont, Fort Collins, Glenwood Springs, Pueblo, and Grand Junction. In Arizona, it has locations in Phoenix, Gilbert, and Glendale. It serves customers in the neighboring states of Wyoming, Utah, Kansas, Nevada, and New Mexico.

Financial Performance
American Furniture's 2013 sales reached more than $390 million.

Strategy
In 2013 the company made its first move outside Colorado when it opened a 630,000-sq.-ft. store in Gilbert, Arizona (near Phoenix). It opens another store -- in Glendale, Arizona -- in late 2014. American Furniture hopes to net $3.4 million in direct revenue from the Glendale store during its first year in operation. The furniture retailer also has an eye on expanding into north Scottsdale.

Auditors : WIPFLI LLP DENVER COLORADO

LOCATIONS

HQ: AMERICAN FURNITURE WAREHOUSE CO.
8820 AMERICAN WAY, ENGLEWOOD, CO 801127056
Phone: 303 799-9044
Web: WWW.AFW.COM

PRODUCTS/OPERATIONS

Selected Products
Decorative accessories
Electronics
Furniture
    Bedroom
    Chairs
    Dining room
    Home office
    Indoor/outdoor
    Living room
    Occasional tables
    Sectionals
    Sofas
    Youth bedroom
Lighting
Mattresses
Rugs

COMPETITORS

AMERICAN SIGNATURE, INC.
BAER'S FURNITURE CO., INC.
BOB'S DISCOUNT FURNITURE, LLC
CITY FURNITURE, INC.
EUROMARKET DESIGNS, INC.
GANDER MOUNTAIN COMPANY
R.T.G. FURNITURE CORP.
RAYMOURS FURNITURE COMPANY, INC.
ROOM & BOARD, INC.
SLUMBERLAND, INC.

HISTORICAL FINANCIALS
Company Type: Private

Income Statement — FYE: March 31

	REVENUE ($mil)	NET INCOME ($mil)	NET PROFIT MARGIN	EMPLOYEES
03/22	992	48	4.9%	4,312
03/21	845	50	6.0%	—
03/20	740	21	2.9%	—
03/19	694	29	4.3%	—
Annual Growth	12.6%	17.6%	—	—

2022 Year-End Financials
Return on assets: 8.4%   Cash ($ mil.): 87
Return on equity: 10.6%
Current Ratio: 2.20

AMERICAN HIGH INCOME TRUST

Auditors : DELOITTE & TOUCHE LLP COSTA M

HOOVER'S HANDBOOK OF PRIVATE COMPANIES 2023

LOCATIONS

HQ: AMERICAN HIGH INCOME TRUST
333 S HOPE ST STE 5200, LOS ANGELES, CA 900713061
Phone: 949 766-6305

HISTORICAL FINANCIALS
Company Type: Private

Income Statement — FYE: September 30

	ASSETS ($mil)	NET INCOME ($mil)	INCOME AS % OF ASSETS	EMPLOYEES
09/21	20,471	3,254	15.9%	1
09/20	17,028	276	1.6%	—
09/19	16,645	25	0.2%	—
09/18	16,817	577	3.4%	—
Annual Growth	6.8%	78.0%	—	—

2021 Year-End Financials
Return on assets: 15.9% Cash ($ mil.): 75
Return on equity: 16.3%
Current Ratio: —

AMERICAN HONDA FINANCE CORPORATION

If you're fonda the idea of driving a Honda, you might want to call on American Honda Finance. Operating as Honda Financial Services, the company provides retail financing in the US for Honda and Acura automobiles, motorcycles, all-terrain vehicles, power equipment, and outboard motors. Its American Honda Service division administers service contracts, while Honda Lease Trust offers leases on new and used vehicles. Honda Financial Services also offers dealer financing and related dealer services. Ancillary services include servicing loans and securitizing and selling loans into the secondary market. A subsidiary of American Honda Motor, the company began as a wholesale motorcycle finance provider in 1980.

Operations

American Honda Finance (AHF) acquires retail installment contracts and closed-end vehicle lease contracts from purchasers and lessees, and authorized Honda and Acura dealers. It also provides these authorized dealers with wholesale flooring and commercial loans.

AHF also acquires used auto loans of non-Honda and non-Acura vehicles, and provides these third-party dealers iwth wholesale loans. Additionally, the company offers vehicle service contracts services, underwriting and pricing of consumer financing services, and incentive financing programs for Honda and Acura products.

Geographic Reach

The company is headquartered in Torrance, California and operates nine regional offices that support all authorized Honda and Acura dealers across North America.

Financial Performance

While full financials of the subsidiary were not available, American Honda Finance's (AHF) revenue has been on the uptrend as auto sales continue to strengthen along with the US economy. Revenue in fiscal 2014 (ended March 31, 2014) grew by 22% to Â¥5.97 trillion ($58.1 billion) thanks to larger revenues from its parent company's auto business and positive foreign currency exchange rates.

Despite higher selling, general, and administrative expenses and R&D expenses, AHF's operating income also increased 39% to Â¥290.9 billion ($2.83 billion) in 2014 after the company continued its cost reduction measures.

Strategy

American Honda Finance Corp. (AHFC) exists to provide stability to support sales of new and used Honda and Acura vehicles throughout North America, Honda Motor's largest market. To that end, AHFC seeks to preserve funding diversity, balanced liquidity, and maintain a prudent maturity profile. To spur growth of its US business, in 2012 the company opened its ninth regional office, a 25,000-square-foot facility in Charlotte, North Carolina, to serve Honda buyers in the Carolinas, Maryland, Tennessee, Virginia, and West Virginia.

Auditors : KPMG LLP LOS ANGELES CALIFOR

LOCATIONS

HQ: AMERICAN HONDA FINANCE CORPORATION
1919 TORRANCE BLVD, TORRANCE, CA 905012722
Phone: 310 972-2239
Web: WWW.HONDA.COM

Selected Offices
Alpharetta, GA
Charlotte, NC
Cypress, CA
Elgin, IL
Holyoke, MA
Irving, TX
San Ramon, CA
Torrance, CA
Wilmington, DE

COMPETITORS

AMERICAN EXPRESS COMPANY
BALBOA CAPITAL CORPORATION
CAPITAL ONE AUTO FINANCE, INC.
CATERPILLAR FINANCIAL SERVICES CORPORATION
CONSUMER PORTFOLIO SERVICES, INC.
FORD MOTOR CREDIT COMPANY LLC
GENERAL MOTORS FINANCIAL COMPANY, INC.
SANTANDER CONSUMER USA HOLDINGS INC.
SOR OR KOR PUBLIC COMPANY LIMITED
TOYOTA MOTOR CREDIT CORPORATION

HISTORICAL FINANCIALS
Company Type: Private

Income Statement — FYE: March 31

	ASSETS ($mil)	NET INCOME ($mil)	INCOME AS % OF ASSETS	EMPLOYEES
03/17	69,854	753	1.1%	1,000
03/16	66,653	910	1.4%	—
03/08	50,526	(45)	—	—
03/07	41,431	394	1.0%	—
Annual Growth	5.4%	6.7%	—	—

2017 Year-End Financials
Return on assets: 1.1% Cash ($ mil.): 760
Return on equity: 5.9%
Current Ratio: —

AMERICAN INSTITUTES FOR RESEARCH IN THE BEHAVIORAL SCIENCES

The American Institutes for Research (AIR) lives and breathes to enhance human performance. The not-for-profit organization conducts behavioral and social science research on topics related to education and educational assessment, health, international development, and work and training. Clients, including several federal agencies, use AIR's research in developing policies. As a major ongoing initiative, the organization provides tools to improve education both in the US and internationally, particularly in disadvantaged areas. John C. Flanagan, who developed the Critical Incident Technique personnel-selection tool to identify human success indicators in the workplace, founded the organization in 1946.

Operations

AIR has organized its group into six program areas: Analysis of Longitudinal Data in Education Research, Assessment, Education, Healthand Social Development, Workforce, and International Development, Evaluation, and Research.

AIR's assessment program focuses on score reports and online reporting tools to translate large-scale testing data on student achievement into a benchmark for school performance. International, human, and social development programs aim to improve the quality of life and education in developing areas. It works to achieve this through teacher and school administrator training, curriculum development and teaching materials coupled with mobilizing health communications, HIV/AIDS education, and raising awareness about such issues as child labor exploitation. Working with governments, private health care providers, and the general public, AIR's health programs design, implement, and evaluate the impact of health care policies.

Geographic Reach

Begun as a small research group affiliated with the University of Pittsburgh, AIR's corporate headquarters and business offices are located in Washington, DC. The group maintains about a dozen offices in the US. Domestic offices are located in San Mateo and Sacramento, California; Atlanta, Georgia; Honolulu, Hawaii; Chicago and Naperville, Illinois; Indianapolis, Indiana; Baltimore, Frederick, and Silver Spring, Maryland; Portland, Oregon; Columbus, Ohio; Chapel Hill, North Carolina; New York, New York; and Waltham, Massachusetts. AIR also operates nearly 10 international offices located in Egypt, Honduras, Kyrgyzstan, Liberia, Tajikistan, Cote d'Ivoire, and Zambia.

Strategy

The National Center for Education Statistics, a key source for statistical data about education, and AIR team up to develop large-scale databases for policymaking. Among various efforts, AIR designs surveys and assessments, develops questionnaires and tests items, as well as informational materials. It also helps in producing The Condition of Education, the agency's chief report. The organization's successes include campaigns that address public health emergencies, such as the flu and H1N1, and the prevention of HIV/AIDS, heart disease, and birth defects.

Adding to its educational research capabilities, AIR has pursued a number of strategic alliances and acquisitions. In 2015, SEDL joined forced with AIR. The combined organizations will have new and enhanced capabilities around, for example, disability research as well as an increased capacity to conduct large-scale randomized control trials and provide technical assistance to diverse populations across a broader geographic area.

In 2015 AIR awarded a $500,000 grant to Impact Network, a nonprofit seeking to make high-quality education in Zambia sustainable.

In 2014 AIR launched the Education Policy Center.

Company Background

In 2011 the National Center for Analysis of Longitudinal Data in Educational Research (CALDER) began operating as a joint project of AIR. CALDER examines how public policies and community conditions impact teacher-student results. A year earlier, AIR acquired Learning Point Associates, a Chicago-based firm that delivers research in the educational sector. Its clients include state education agencies, single-school districts, private foundations, and for-profit organizations.

Auditors : RUBINO AND COMPANY CHARTERED

LOCATIONS

HQ: AMERICAN INSTITUTES FOR RESEARCH IN THE BEHAVIORAL SCIENCES
1400 CRYSTAL DR FL 10, ARLINGTON, VA 222023289
Phone: 202 403-5000
Web: WWW.AIR.ORG

PRODUCTS/OPERATIONS

Selected Program Areas
Education
Education assessment
Health
Human development
International development
Work & training

COMPETITORS

ALTARUM INSTITUTE
AMERICAN MANAGEMENT ASSOCIATION INTERNATIONAL
FAMILY HEALTH INTERNATIONAL
NOBLIS, INC.
SOCIAL & SCIENTIFIC SYSTEMS, INC.
SOUTHERN RESEARCH INSTITUTE (INC)
SRI INTERNATIONAL
THE DEVEREUX FOUNDATION
THE MITRE CORPORATION
THE RAND CORPORATION

HISTORICAL FINANCIALS
Company Type: Private

Income Statement — FYE: December 31

	REVENUE ($mil)	NET INCOME ($mil)	NET PROFIT MARGIN	EMPLOYEES
12/19	829	398	48.0%	1,500
12/17	497	55	11.1%	—
12/16	474	43	9.2%	—
12/15	488	45	9.2%	—
Annual Growth	14.2%	72.5%	—	—

2019 Year-End Financials
Return on assets: 45.8% Cash ($ mil.): 81
Return on equity: 52.3%
Current Ratio: 1.50

AMERICAN LEBANESE SYRIAN ASSOCIATED CHARITIES, INC.

EXECUTIVES

CMO, Emily Callahan
CIO, Robert Machen
Auditors : DELOITTE & TOUCHE LLP MEMPHIS

LOCATIONS

HQ: AMERICAN LEBANESE SYRIAN ASSOCIATED CHARITIES, INC.
501 SAINT JUDE PL, MEMPHIS, TN 381051905
Phone: 901 578-2000
Web: WWW.STJUDE.ORG

HISTORICAL FINANCIALS
Company Type: Private

Income Statement — FYE: June 30

	REVENUE ($mil)	NET INCOME ($mil)	NET PROFIT MARGIN	EMPLOYEES
06/17	1,741	658	37.8%	1,300
06/16	1,161	(27)	—	—
06/15	1,182	251	21.2%	—
06/13	976	210	21.5%	—
Annual Growth	15.6%	33.0%	—	—

2017 Year-End Financials
Return on assets: 15.8% Cash ($ mil.): 178
Return on equity: 16.1%
Current Ratio: —

AMERICAN MITSUBA CORPORATION

Auditors : PLANTE & MORAN PLLC AUBURN

LOCATIONS

HQ: AMERICAN MITSUBA CORPORATION
2945 THREE LEAVES DR, MOUNT PLEASANT, MI 488584596
Phone: 989 779-4962
Web: WWW.AMERICANMITSUBA.COM

HISTORICAL FINANCIALS
Company Type: Private

Income Statement — FYE: December 31

	REVENUE ($mil)	NET INCOME ($mil)	NET PROFIT MARGIN	EMPLOYEES
12/16	697	(2)	—	765
12/15	687	9	1.4%	—
12/14	558	5	0.9%	—
12/13	557	17	3.1%	—
Annual Growth	7.7%	—	—	—

2016 Year-End Financials
Return on assets: (-0.9%) Cash ($ mil.): 24
Return on equity: (-2.0%)
Current Ratio: 1.70

AMERICAN MUNICIPAL POWER, INC.

Power to the Public is the motto of American Municipal Power (AMP). The nonprofit membership organization supplies wholesale power to more than 80 community-owned distribution utilities in Ohio, 30 in Pennsylvania, 6 in Michigan, 5 in Virginia, 3 in Kentucky, 2 in West Virginia, 1 in Indiana, and 1 in Delaware (a joint action agency). AMP and its members own and operate plants that generate more than 1500 MW of power. The company also handles projects on behalf of the Ohio Municipal Electric Generating Agency (OMEGA) Joint Ventures program (jointly owned generation and transmission projects). The power generation company is owned by its member municipalities. AMP member utilities serve some 635,000 customers.

Operations
The company provides electric capacity and energy and furnishes other services to its members on a cooperative basis. As part of its joint venture responsibilities, American Municipal Power also operates the Belleville Hydroelectric Plant, a 42 MW plant located in Belleville, West Virginia. AMP's wholly-owned subsidiary, AMPO, provides assistance in establishing electric and gas aggregation programs to benefit local consumers.

Geographic Reach
Ohio-based American Municipal Power serves 130 members - 129 member municipal electric communities in the states of Ohio, Pennsylvania, Michigan, Indiana, Virginia, Kentucky and West Virginia, as well as the Delaware Municipal Electric Corporation, a joint action agency headquartered in Smyrna, Delaware.

Financial Performance
American Municipal Power (AMP) reported $982.5 million in revenue in 2013, representing a 19% increase over 2012. Rising electric revenues and service fees, up 19% and 44%, respectively, drove growth in 2013. AMP's net margin expanded to $5.3 million from $1.9 million over the same period.

Strategy
Expanding into Indiana, in 2014 AMP gained its newest member, the city of Cannelton.

Implementing a strategy to reduce carbon emissions, the company is building six hydroelectric projects on the Ohio River. The Meldahl plant (with 105 MW of capacity) will be the largest hydroelectric plant on the Ohio River. American Municipal Power also has a deal to develop up to 300 MW of solar power with solar panel company Standard Energy. It also has wind power and landfill gas operations. Indeed, AMP members' projected energy resource mix will be approximately 21% renewable by 2015.

In 2013 American Municipal Power and the Vermont Energy Investment Corporation agreed to extend the operation of Efficiency Smart beyond the end of the year. The program provides a broad range of energy efficiency services for the power coop's member utilities. Some 49 member communities in Ohio, Pennsylvania, and Michigan participated in Efficiency Smart in 2013.

Company Background
To replace lost capacity, in 2011 it acquired the Fremont Energy Center in Fremont, Ohio from FirstEnergy for $500 million. The 707-MW natural gas combined-cycle facility commenced commercial operation in early 2012. In 2010 American Municipal Power also secured a 368-MW ownership stake in the Prairie State Energy Campus in Illinois.

Expanding geographically, American Municipal Power moved into a seventh state in 2011, when it made Delaware Municipal Electric its 129th member.

American Municipal Power was founded in 1971.

Auditors : PRICEWATERHOUSECOOPERS LLP CO

LOCATIONS
HQ: AMERICAN MUNICIPAL POWER, INC.
1111 SCHROCK RD STE 100, COLUMBUS, OH 432291155
Phone: 614 540-1111
Web: WWW.AMPPARTNERS.ORG

PRODUCTS/OPERATIONS
2013 Sales

	% of total
Electric revenues	97
Service fees	1
Programs & other	2
Total	100

Selected Services
Aggregation
Business Development
Clean Energy & Conservation
Community Outreach
Financial
Legislative, Regulatory & Legal
Power Supply / AMP Energy Control Center
Safety Programs
Scholarship Programs
Technical Services

COMPETITORS
AMERICAN ELECTRIC POWER COMPANY, INC.
ARKANSAS ELECTRIC COOPERATIVE CORPORATION
BASIN ELECTRIC POWER COOPERATIVE
EXELON GENERATION COMPANY, LLC
FIRSTENERGY CORP.
INDIANA MICHIGAN POWER COMPANY
OHIO POWER COMPANY
THE SOUTHERN COMPANY
TRI-STATE GENERATION AND TRANSMISSION ASSOCIATION, INC.
WESTERN AREA POWER ADMINISTRATION

HISTORICAL FINANCIALS
Company Type: Private

Income Statement — FYE: December 31

	REVENUE ($mil)	NET INCOME ($mil)	NET PROFIT MARGIN	EMPLOYEES
12/21	1,137	14	1.3%	229
12/20	1,091	2	0.2%	—
12/19	1,170	5	0.5%	—
12/15	1,127	5	0.5%	—
Annual Growth	0.1%	16.3%	—	—

2021 Year-End Financials
Return on assets: 0.2%   Cash ($ mil.): 189
Return on equity: 13.6%
Current Ratio: 1.40

AMERICAN MUTUAL FUND

Auditors : DELOITTE & TOUCHE LLP COSTA M

LOCATIONS
HQ: AMERICAN MUTUAL FUND
333 S HOPE ST FL 51, LOS ANGELES, CA 900711420
Phone: 213 486-9200

HISTORICAL FINANCIALS
Company Type: Private

Income Statement — FYE: October 31

	ASSETS ($mil)	NET INCOME ($mil)	INCOME AS % OF ASSETS	EMPLOYEES
10/21	85,289	23,814	27.9%	200
10/20	61,161	1,086	1.8%	—
10/19	60,172	9,524	15.8%	—
10/18	50,526	3,375	6.7%	—
Annual Growth	19.1%	91.8%	—	—

2021 Year-End Financials
Return on assets: 27.9%   Cash ($ mil.): 13
Return on equity: 28.1%
Current Ratio: —

AMERICAN TIRE DISTRIBUTORS HOLDINGS, INC.

American Tire Distributors (ATD) is the largest independent tire and service distributor in North America. Its offerings include flagship brands Yokohama, Hankook, Continental, Pirelli, and Michelin, as well as budget brands and private-label tires. ATD also markets custom wheels and tire service equipment. Its network of nearly 145 distribution centers and mixing warehouses serve independent tire dealers, retail chains, and auto service centers across the US and Canada, and has approximately 1,400 deliver vehicles on the road across the nation. In addition to some 40 million delivery miles annually, the company provides access to over 4 million tires in every style and size from the top global brands in the industry.

Operations
Passenger and light truck tires contribute most of American Tire Distributors' sales; the company also supplies tires for medium trucks, farm vehicles, and specialty vehicles.

Beyond tires, ATD distributes wheels and other automotive products. Its brands include Carlisle, Drifz, O.E. Performance, Black Rock, Dick Cepek, Schrader, and Advanti Racing.

Geographic Reach
North Carolina-based American Tire Distributors has a strong position in North America. It rings up most of its sales in the

US, where it has about 145 distribution centers. The company has nearly 25 distribution centers across Canada.

Sales and Marketing

American Tire Distributors sells tires to local, regional, and national independent tire retailers, as well as mass merchandisers, warehouse clubs, tire-manufacturer-owned stores, automotive dealerships, and web-based markets. Its private fleet of approximately 1,500 drivers hand-deliver tires, wheels, and supplies to approximately 80,000 customers across the US and Canada.

Mergers and Acquisitions

Auditors: PRICEWATERHOUSECOOPERS LLP CH

LOCATIONS

HQ: AMERICAN TIRE DISTRIBUTORS HOLDINGS, INC.
12200 HERBERT WAYNE CT # 150, HUNTERSVILLE, NC 280786335
Phone: 704 992-2000
Web: WWW.ATD.COM

PRODUCTS/OPERATIONS

Selected Brands
Tires
- Alliance
- BFGoodrich
- Continental
- Dunlop
- Firestone
- IronMan
- Michelin
- Toyo Tires
- UniRoyal

Wheels
- Center Line
- ICW Racing
- Konig
- Motiv
- Pacer
- Ultra Motorsports

Supplies
- Blaster
- Chicago Pneumatic
- Ingersoll-Rand
- Ken-Tool
- SuperSprings
- Stoner
- Western Pacific Storage Solutions

COMPETITORS

BRIDGESTONE CORPORATION
BRIDGESTONE RETAIL OPERATIONS, LLC
DEALER TIRE, LLC
Giti Tire (China) Investment Company Ltd.
TBC CORPORATION
THE CARLSTAR GROUP LLC
THE GOODYEAR TIRE & RUBBER COMPANY
TIRE GROUP INTERNATIONAL LLC
TREADWAYS CORPORATION
WHEEL PROS, LLC

HISTORICAL FINANCIALS
Company Type: Private

Income Statement — FYE: December 28

	REVENUE ($mil)	NET INCOME ($mil)	NET PROFIT MARGIN	EMPLOYEES
12/13	3,839	(6)	—	1,072
12/12	3,455	(14)	—	—
12/11	3,050	0	0.0%	—
Annual Growth	12.2%	—	—	—

2013 Year-End Financials
Return on assets: (-0.2%)   Cash ($ mil.): 35
Return on equity: (-0.9%)
Current Ratio: 1.90

AMERICAN TRANSMISSION SYSTEMS, INCORPORATED

LOCATIONS

HQ: AMERICAN TRANSMISSION SYSTEMS, INCORPORATED
76 S MAIN ST, AKRON, OH 443081812
Phone: 330 761-4370
Web: WWW.ATCLLC.COM

HISTORICAL FINANCIALS
Company Type: Private

Income Statement — FYE: December 31

	REVENUE ($mil)	NET INCOME ($mil)	NET PROFIT MARGIN	EMPLOYEES
12/17	656	165	25.2%	1
12/16	540	133	24.7%	—
Annual Growth	21.6%	23.8%	—	—

2017 Year-End Financials
Return on assets: 4.0%   Cash ($ mil.): —
Return on equity: 10.9%
Current Ratio: 0.20

AMERICARES FOUNDATION, INC.

AmeriCares Foundation provides emergency medical aid around the world. The not-for-profit charitable organization helps victims of natural disasters and supports long-term humanitarian programs by collecting medical supplies in the US and overseas and delivering them to places where they are needed. AmeriCares has provided aid in more than 90 countries worldwide. In the US, the organization offers medical assistance, runs a camp for kids with HIV/AIDS, and conducts HomeFront, a program that renovates housing for the needy in parts of Connecticut and New York. Robert C. Macauley founded AmeriCares in 1982.

Geographic Reach

The company has presence in US, Latin America, Caribbean, Asia and Eurasia, Africa and Middle East.

Financial Performance

AmeriCares' revenue decreased 9% to $572 million in 2014 due to a decline in public support, and loss on investments.

Auditors: GRANT THORNTON LLP NEW YORK

LOCATIONS

HQ: AMERICARES FOUNDATION, INC.
88 HAMILTON AVE STE 3, STAMFORD, CT 069023105
Phone: 203 658-9500
Web: WWW.AMERICARES.ORG

COMPETITORS

BRITISH RED CROSS SOCIETY
DIRECT RELIEF FOUNDATION
EASTER SEALS, INC.
HELEN KELLER INTERNATIONAL
VOLUNTEERS OF AMERICA, INC.

HISTORICAL FINANCIALS
Company Type: Private

Income Statement — FYE: June 30

	REVENUE ($mil)	NET INCOME ($mil)	NET PROFIT MARGIN	EMPLOYEES
06/20	1,440	192	13.4%	231
06/19	976	(101)	—	—
06/15	741	101	13.7%	—
06/14	560	(4)	—	—
Annual Growth	17.0%	—	—	—

2020 Year-End Financials
Return on assets: 45.7%   Cash ($ mil.): 23
Return on equity: 47.3%
Current Ratio: —

AMES CONSTRUCTION, INC.

Ames Construction aims right for the heart of heavy construction. The company is a general contractor, providing heavy civil and industrial construction services to the transportation, mining, and power industries mainly in the West and Midwest. The family-owned company works on highways, airports, bridges, rail lines, mining facilities, power plants, and other infrastructure projects. Ames also performs flood control, environmental remediation, reclamation, and landfill work. Additionally, the firm builds golf courses and undertakes commercial and residential site development projects. Ames typically partners with other companies to perform the engineering and design portion of construction jobs.

Operations

Some of Ames Construction's project include the Arlington Power Plant, Dry Fork Station Unit 1 Site Work and Substructure Construction, Rentech ClearFuels, Cortez Hills Mine and Mills Site, and Airport Extension Projects, such as its MSP International Airport work.

Geographic Reach
Ames Construction has offices in the US in Minnesota, Arizona, California, Colorado, Nevada, and Utah, as well as in Canada.

Strategy
Through its subcontracting activities Ames Construction contributed to the construction of the Minnesota Twins ballpark and served as subcontractor and partner in a joint venture with Fluor and Balfour Beatty Rail that that undertook a $1 billion design/build portion of a rail line project for the Denver Regional Transit District.

Auditors: CLIFTONLARSONALLEN LLP MINNE

LOCATIONS

HQ: AMES CONSTRUCTION, INC.
2500 COUNTY ROAD 42 W, BURNSVILLE, MN 553376911
Phone: 952 435-7106
Web: WWW.AMESCONSTRUCTION.COM

Selected Locations
Arizona
California
Canada
Colorado
Minnesota
Nevada
Utah

PRODUCTS/OPERATIONS

Selected Markets
Commercial
    Commercial site development
    Environmental remediation/ landfills
    Residential site development
Mining
    Contract mining
    Leach pad construction
    Mine development
    Mine infrastructure
    Mine reclamation/remediation
    Mine tailings dam
Power
    Coal fired
    Combined-cycle/natural gas
    Nuclear
    Transmission
    Wind
Transportation
    Airports
    Bridges
    Highways
    Railroads
Water resources
    Dams, reservoirs, and flood control
    Wastewater/water treatment
    Water delivery
    Water retention structures

COMPETITORS

BALFOUR BEATTY INFRASTRUCTURE, INC.
CLARK CONSTRUCTION GROUP, LLC
CONTI ENTERPRISES, INC.
DAVID EVANS AND ASSOCIATES, INC.
FREESEN INC.
GRIFFITH COMPANY
JUDLAU CONTRACTING, INC.
MACRO-Z-TECHNOLOGY COMPANY
MILESTONE CONTRACTORS, L.P.
THE HUBBARD GROUP INC

HISTORICAL FINANCIALS
Company Type: Private

Income Statement   FYE: November 30

	REVENUE ($mil)	NET INCOME ($mil)	NET PROFIT MARGIN	EMPLOYEES
11/20	1,308	42	3.2%	2,500
11/19	1,248	61	4.9%	—
11/16	845	2	0.3%	—
11/15	1,068	5	0.5%	—
Annual Growth	4.1%	52.5%	—	—

2020 Year-End Financials
Return on assets: 8.2%   Cash ($ mil.): 96
Return on equity: 27.8%
Current Ratio: 1.20

ANC HEALTHCARE, INC.

Auditors: GRANT THORNTON LLP CHARLOTTE

LOCATIONS

HQ: ANC HEALTHCARE, INC.
425 W NEW ENG AVE STE 300, WINTER PARK, FL 327894228
Phone: 828 213-1111
Web: WWW.MISSIONHEALTH.ORG

HISTORICAL FINANCIALS
Company Type: Private

Income Statement   FYE: September 30

	REVENUE ($mil)	NET INCOME ($mil)	NET PROFIT MARGIN	EMPLOYEES
09/18	1,799	120	6.7%	12,000
09/17	1,753	161	9.2%	—
09/16	1,632	90	5.5%	—
09/08	17	7	42.3%	—
Annual Growth	59.1%	32.3%	—	—

2018 Year-End Financials
Return on assets: 4.5%   Cash ($ mil.): 149
Return on equity: 6.7%
Current Ratio: 2.00

ANCHORAGE SCHOOL DISTRICT

Auditors: BDO USA LLP ANCHORAGE ALASK

LOCATIONS

HQ: ANCHORAGE SCHOOL DISTRICT
5530 E NTHRN LIGHTS BLVD, ANCHORAGE, AK 99504
Phone: 907 742-4000
Web: WWW.ASDK12.ORG

HISTORICAL FINANCIALS
Company Type: Private

Income Statement   FYE: June 30

	REVENUE ($mil)	NET INCOME ($mil)	NET PROFIT MARGIN	EMPLOYEES
06/12	834	(8)	—	5,039
06/11	822	(2)	—	—
06/10	774	(19)	—	—
Annual Growth	3.8%	—	—	—

2012 Year-End Financials
Return on assets: (-0.6%)   Cash ($ mil.): 162
Return on equity: (-1.3%)
Current Ratio: —

ANCHORAGE, MUNICIPALITY OF (INC)

Anchorage is Alaska's largest city in both size and population. The city encompasses almost 2,000 sq. mi. of land -- almost the size of Delaware. Anchorage had a 2010 population of about 290,000 residents, or about a quarter of the state's population. Anchorage is located in the south central part of the state and sits on the Gulf of Alaska.

Auditors: BDO USA LLP ANCHORAGE ALASKA

LOCATIONS

HQ: ANCHORAGE, MUNICIPALITY OF (INC)
632 W 6TH AVE STE 810, ANCHORAGE, AK 995012225
Phone: 907 343-6610
Web: WWW.MUNI.ORG

COMPETITORS

CITY OF ALBUQUERQUE
CITY OF BROWNSVILLE
CITY OF CORPUS CHRISTI
CITY OF HIALEAH
CITY OF SHREVEPORT

HISTORICAL FINANCIALS
Company Type: Private

Income Statement   FYE: December 31

	REVENUE ($mil)	NET INCOME ($mil)	NET PROFIT MARGIN	EMPLOYEES
12/21	1,018	(22)	—	3,680
12/20	956	272	28.5%	—
12/19	800	21	2.7%	—
12/18	740	26	3.6%	—
Annual Growth	11.2%	—	—	—

2021 Year-End Financials
Return on assets: (-0.3%)   Cash ($ mil.): 399
Return on equity: (-0.5%)
Current Ratio: 3.00

ANMED HEALTH

Auditors: DIXON HUGHES GOODMAN LLP GRE

LOCATIONS
HQ: ANMED HEALTH
800 N FANT ST, ANDERSON, SC 296215708
Phone: 864 512-1000
Web: WWW.ANMED.ORG

HISTORICAL FINANCIALS
Company Type: Private

Income Statement — FYE: December 31

	REVENUE ($mil)	NET INCOME ($mil)	NET PROFIT MARGIN	EMPLOYEES
12/21	611	124	20.4%	2,600
12/20	546	77	14.1%	
12/18	543	(15)	—	—
12/17	513	40	8.0%	—
Annual Growth	4.5%	32.1%	—	—

2021 Year-End Financials
Return on assets: 10.0%   Cash ($ mil.): 90
Return on equity: 14.4%
Current Ratio: 1.40

ANN & ROBERT H. LURIE CHILDREN'S HOSPITAL OF CHICAGO

When it comes to caring for kids, Ann & Robert H. Lurie Children's Hospital of Chicago has the Windy City covered. Founded in 1882, the not-for-profit hospital provides a full range of pediatric services with acute and specialty care. Lurie Children's provides services through its main hospital campus with about 300 beds and outpatient centers in Chicago's Lincoln Park neighborhood and through more than a dozen suburban outpatient centers and outreach partner locations in the greater Chicago area. A leader in pediatric research, the hospital operates the Children's Hospital of Chicago Research Center and is the pediatric teaching facility of Northwestern University's Feinberg School of Medicine.

Operations
Lurie Children's serves roughly 150,000 patients each year and employs some 1,350 pediatric specialists with expertise in 70 different specialties. The hospital is one of only about a dozen children's hospitals nationwide to perform more than 1,000 liver transplants. The center performs on average 50 solid organ and 50 stem cell transplants annually.

A major research center, Lurie Children's is one of nearly 30 interdisciplinary research centers and institutes belonging to the hospital's academic partner -- Feinberg School of Medicine. Its research arm, Stanley Manne Children's Research Institute, employs some 200 physician-scientists and research investigators who in 2014 were awarded more than $40 million in external funding.

Geographic Reach
Based in Chicago, Lurie Children's has cared for patients from throughout the US and about 50 countries around the globe.

Financial Performance
Lurie Children's saw revenues increase by 8% to $826 million in fiscal 2014 (ended August). That growth was attributed to a rise in patient care revenues and other earnings. Net income increased 198% to $128 million that year, largely due to the higher revenue as well as strong investment returns.

Cash flow from operations rose 36% to $124.5 million in fiscal 2014.

Strategy
The hospital has all-private rooms, even in the neonatal intensive care unit; private rooms are said to speed healing by reducing hospital-acquired infection and minimize noise. Lurie Children's is working to enhance its specialist services and has upgraded its information technology systems. In 2013 it implemented a Voalte system that allows nurses to communicate through rapid-response systems including text messages and high-definition voice calls. Also that year, it opened the first pediatric gender identity clinic. In 2015 the hospital acquired the fourth-generation da Vinci Xi robotic system for use in minimally invasive surgery.

In 2014, Lurie Children's Health Partners (composed of Lurie Children's and two groups of pediatricians) launched the Clinically Integrated Network, the first health care network in Chicago to focus exclusively on children and their families. Its areas of focus include care coordination, obesity, asthma, immunizations, and child development.

LOCATIONS
HQ: ANN & ROBERT H. LURIE CHILDREN'S HOSPITAL OF CHICAGO
225 E CHICAGO AVE, CHICAGO, IL 606112991
Phone: 312 227-4000
Web: WWW.LURIECHILDRENS.ORG

Selected Illinois Locations
Lurie Children's at Cadence Health (Winfield)
Main Hospital (Chicago)
Outpatient Center in Arlington Heights (Arlington Heights)
Outpatient Center in Glenview (Glenview)
Outpatient Center in Lake Forest (Lake Forest)
Outpatient Center in Lincoln Park (Chicago)
Outpatient Center in New Lenox (New Lenox)
Outpatient Center in Westchester (Westchester)
Outpatient Services in Grayslake (Grayslake)
Outpatient Services in Gurnee (Gurnee)
Outpatient Services in Lincoln Square (Chicago)
Pediatrics - Uptown (Chicago)
Rehabilitation Services at Westbrook (Westchester)

PRODUCTS/OPERATIONS
2014 Sales

	$ mil	% of total
Patient care revenues	706.2	85
Grants, gifts & endowment income	62.4	8
Other revenues	57.2	7
Total	825.8	100

Selected Services
Adolescent Medicine
Allergy and Immunology
Anesthesiology
Audiology
Autonomic Medicine
Brain Tumor
Cancer and Blood Disorders
Cardiology (Heart Center)
Child Abuse Pediatrics
Child and Adolescent Psychiatry
Clinical Nutrition
Convenient Care
Critical Care
Cystic Fibrosis
Dentistry and Oral Surgery
Dermatology
Emergency Medicine
Endocrinology
Epilepsy
Fetal Health
Gastroenterology, Hepatology and Nutrition (Digestive Disorders)
Gender and Sex Development
General Pediatric Surgery
General Pediatrics
Genetics, Birth Defects and Metabolism
Heart Failure and Transplants
HIV/AIDS Prevention
Infectious Diseases
Intestinal Transplants
Kidney Diseases
Kidney Transplants
Liver Transplants
Medical Imaging (Radiology)
Neonatology
Neurology
Neurosurgery
Occupational Therapy
Ophthalmology
Orthopaedic Surgery
Orthotics/Prosthetics
Otolaryngology (ENT)
Palliative Care
Pathology and Laboratory Medicine
Physical Therapy
Plastic and Reconstructive Surgery
Pulmonary Medicine
Rehabilitative Services
Rheumatology
Speech-Language Pathology
Spina Bifida Center
Sports Medicine
Stem Cell Transplants
Transitioning to Adult Care
Transplantation
Urology

COMPETITORS
BILLINGS CLINIC
CHILDREN'S HEALTH CLINICAL OPERATIONS
CHILDREN'S HOSPITAL & RESEARCH CENTER AT OAKLAND
H. LEE MOFFITT CANCER CENTER AND RESEARCH INSTITUTE HOSPITAL, INC.
SHANDS TEACHING HOSPITAL AND CLINICS, INC.
SONIC HEALTHCARE LIMITED
SWEDISH HEALTH SERVICES
TEXAS CHILDREN'S HOSPITAL
THE CHILDREN'S MERCY HOSPITAL
THE MASSACHUSETTS GENERAL HOSPITAL

HISTORICAL FINANCIALS
Company Type: Private

Income Statement   FYE: August 31

	REVENUE ($mil)	NET INCOME ($mil)	NET PROFIT MARGIN	EMPLOYEES
08/13	694	28	4.2%	2,800
08/10	599	52	8.8%	—
08/09	533	(5)	—	—
Annual Growth	6.8%	—	—	—

2013 Year-End Financials
Return on assets: 1.4%   Cash ($ mil.): 92
Return on equity: 2.0%
Current Ratio: 2.90

ANNE ARUNDEL COUNTY BOARD OF EDUCATION

Auditors: CLIFTONLARSONALLEN LLP BALTIM

LOCATIONS
HQ: ANNE ARUNDEL COUNTY BOARD OF EDUCATION
2644 RIVA RD, ANNAPOLIS, MD 214017427
Phone: 410 222-5000

HISTORICAL FINANCIALS
Company Type: Private

Income Statement   FYE: June 30

	REVENUE ($mil)	NET INCOME ($mil)	NET PROFIT MARGIN	EMPLOYEES
06/13	1,147	3	0.3%	435
06/04	712	0	0.1%	—
06/03	701	50	7.1%	—
Annual Growth	5.1%	(23.0%)	—	—

2013 Year-End Financials
Return on assets: 0.3%   Cash ($ mil.): 166
Return on equity: 0.6%
Current Ratio: —

ANOKA-HENNEPIN SCHOOL DIST NO 11

Auditors: MALLOY MONTAGUE KARNOWSKI RA

LOCATIONS
HQ: ANOKA-HENNEPIN SCHOOL DIST NO 11
2727 N FERRY ST, ANOKA, MN 553031650
Phone: 763 506-1000
Web: WWW.AHSCHOOLS.US

HISTORICAL FINANCIALS
Company Type: Private

Income Statement   FYE: June 30

	REVENUE ($mil)	NET INCOME ($mil)	NET PROFIT MARGIN	EMPLOYEES
06/21	591	(50)	—	6,100
06/20	585	59	10.1%	—
06/19	574	(88)	—	—
06/18	550	151	27.5%	—
Annual Growth	2.4%	—	—	—

2021 Year-End Financials
Return on assets: (-4.3%)   Cash ($ mil.): 342
Return on equity: —
Current Ratio: —

ANR PIPELINE COMPANY

ANR Pipeline keeps natural gas in line, a pipeline that is. The company operates one of the largest interstate natural gas pipeline systems in the US. A subsidiary of TransCanada Corp., ANR controls about 10,350 miles of pipeline and delivers more than 1 trillion cu. ft. of natural gas per year. The company primarily serves customers in the Midwest, but through its network is capable of connecting to all major gas basins in North America. In tandem with its ANR Storage and Blue Lake Gas Storage subsidiaries, ANR Pipeline also provides natural gas storage services and has ownership interests in more than 250 billion cu. ft. of underground natural gas storage capacity.

Operations
The ANR System is part of TransCanada's network 37,000 miles of wholly owned and 4,900 miles of partially owned pipelines, connecting major supply basins with major markets all across North America.

Geographic Reach
ANR transports natural gas from producing fields in Texas and Oklahoma, from offshore and onshore regions of the Gulf of Mexico, and from the US midcontinent, for delivery mainly to Illinois, Indiana, Michigan, Ohio, and Wisconsin.

Strategy
To create greater operating efficiency, in 2012 ANR Pipeline Company sold assets and certain related onshore facilities to its wholly owned subsidiary, TC Offshore LLC.

To support the growing natural gas production in the Haynesville Shale play in Texas and Louisiana, the company is developing the ANR Haynesville Lateral Project to transport up to 1.8 billion cu. ft. of natural gas a day. The Haynesville Lateral pipeline enables producers to transport shale gas to markets in the Southeast, Midwest, and Northeast.

Company Background
ANR Pipeline was founded as Michigan-Wisconsin Pipe Line Company in 1945 and adopted its current name in 1984.

El Paso Corp. sold ANR Pipeline to TransCanada in 2007. The deal gave TransCanada a regulated natural gas pipeline and storage assets that complemented its other North American gas transmission operations.

EXECUTIVES
Commercial Vice President, Gary C Charette
Commercial Vice President, Dean Patry

LOCATIONS
HQ: ANR PIPELINE COMPANY
700 LOUISIANA ST STE 700 # 700, HOUSTON, TX 770022873
Phone: 832 320-2000
Web: WWW.ANRPL.COM

COMPETITORS
ONEOK PARTNERS, L.P.
PANHANDLE EASTERN PIPE LINE COMPANY, LP
TENNESSEE GAS PIPELINE COMPANY, L.L.C.
TEXAS GAS TRANSMISSION, LLC
WBI ENERGY TRANSMISSION, INC

HISTORICAL FINANCIALS
Company Type: Private

Income Statement   FYE: December 31

	REVENUE ($mil)	NET INCOME ($mil)	NET PROFIT MARGIN	EMPLOYEES
12/17	758	139	18.5%	1,000
12/16	686	54	8.0%	—
12/06	540	152	28.1%	—
12/05	548	147	26.8%	—
Annual Growth	2.7%	(0.4%)	—	—

2017 Year-End Financials
Return on assets: 4.6%   Cash ($ mil.): —
Return on equity: 10.4%
Current Ratio: 1.30

API GROUP, INC.

Holding company APi Group has a piece of the action in two main sectors: fire protection systems and industrial and specialty construction services. APi boasts about 40 subsidiaries, which operate as independent companies across the US (nearly half of them in Minnesota), the UK, and Canada. Services provided by the company's construction subsidiaries include HVAC and plumbing system installation; electrical, industrial, and mechanical contracting; industrial insulation; and garage door installation. Safety-focused units install a host of fire sprinkler, detection, security, and alarm systems. The family-owned company was founded in 1926 by Reuben Anderson, father of chairman Lee Anderson.

Operations

Through its various companies, APi Group is involved in engineering, designing, constructing, and installing LEED green-building certification program projects. Its divisions include Architectural Roofing and Mechanical, Classic Industrial Services, APi Construction, APi Distribution, and Industrial Fabricators, among others.

Geographic Reach
Minnesota-based APi Group operates companies throughout North America and the UK.

Sales and Marketing
APi Group serves several sectors, such as security and defense, education, commercial, industrial, medical, oil and gas, and residential.

Strategy
Although APi Group companies are independent, they often pool resources and work together to service clients.

Mergers and Acquisitions
The highly acquisitive APi Group regularly acquires new companies to strengthen its growing group.

In 2013, the company's Western States Fire Protection (WSFP) acquired Advanced Fire, an Oklahoma City-based fire-suppression company that specializes in military work. Buying Advanced Fire extends the company's reach in the fire protection industry and boosts its market share within Oklahoma City and the surrounding area. APi Group's Delta Fire Systems acquired Idaho's 3-D Fire, which provides full-fire-system design, fabrication, installation, testing, and certification capabilities for commercial and private projects.

APi Group previous purchases include Dynamic Fire Protection LLC (DFP), Omlid & Swinney Fire Protection and Security, Canada-based Fire Stop Enterprises, Ohio-based 3S, and Kansas-based mainline pipeline contractor Jomax Construction.

EXECUTIVES
CLO, Paul W Grunau
Auditors : KPMG

LOCATIONS
HQ: API GROUP, INC.
  1100 OLD HIGHWAY 8 NW, NEW BRIGHTON, MN 551126447
Phone: 651 636-4320
Web: WWW.APIGROUPINC.COM

PRODUCTS/OPERATIONS
Selected Subsidiaries
Fire Protection Systems
  Alliance Fire Protection, Inc.
  APi National Service Group
  Davis-Ulmer Sprinkler Company
  Delta Fire Systems, Inc.
  Grunau Company
  Halon Banking Systems
  International Fire Protection, Inc.
  Island Fire Sprinkler, Inc.
  Reliance Fire Protection
  Rich Fire Protection Co, Inc.
  Security Fire Protection Company
  United States Fire Protection Company
  VFP Fire Systems, Inc.
  Viking Automatic Sprinkler Company
  Vipond Fire Protection, Inc. (Canada)
  Vipond Fire Protection, Ltd. (UK)
  Western States Fire Protection, Inc.
Industrial and Specialty Construction Services
  3S Incorporated
  Anco Products, Inc.
  APi CAD Services
  APi Construction Company
  APi Distribution, Inc.
  APi Electric
  APi Supply, Inc.
  Classic Industrial Services, Inc.
  Doody Mechanical, Inc.
  Garage Door Store
  Grunau Company, Inc.
  Industrial Contractors, Inc.
  Industrial Fabricators, Inc.
  Jamar Company
  Jomax Construction Co.
  LeJeune Steel Company
  NYCO, Inc.
  Tessier's Inc.
  Twin City Garage Door Company
Low Voltage
  APi Systems Group, Inc.
  APi Systems Integrators
  Vipond Systems Group

COMPETITORS
ACCO ENGINEERED SYSTEMS, INC.
CONTI LLC
EMCOR GROUP (UK) PLC
ISS TECHNICAL SERVICES HOLDINGS LIMITED
MCKINSTRY CO., LLC
MURPHY COMPANY MECHANICAL CONTRACTORS AND ENGINEERS
THE KLEINFELDER GROUP INC
THE WALDINGER CORPORATION
WAYNE J. GRIFFIN ELECTRIC, INC.
WESTERN STATES FIRE PROTECTION COMPANY

HISTORICAL FINANCIALS
Company Type: Private

Income Statement   FYE: December 31

	REVENUE ($mil)	NET INCOME ($mil)	NET PROFIT MARGIN	EMPLOYEES
12/18	3,730	122	3.3%	4,237
12/17	3,046	112	3.7%	—
12/16	2,608	104	4.0%	—
12/15	2,448	106	4.3%	—
Annual Growth	15.1%	5.0%	—	—

2018 Year-End Financials
Return on assets: 6.2%   Cash ($ mil.): 54
Return on equity: 21.3%
Current Ratio: 1.10

APPALACHIAN REGIONAL HEALTHCARE, INC.

Under-the-weather coal miners (and their daughters) can turn to Appalachian Regional Healthcare (ARH) for medical services. The not-for-profit health system serves residents of eastern Kentucky and southern West Virginia through a dozen hospitals with more than 1,000 beds, as well as dozens of clinics, home health care agencies, HomeCare Stores, and retail pharmacies. Its largest hospital in Hazard, Kentucky, has 310 beds and features an inpatient psychiatric unit that serves as the state mental health facility. Several of the system's hospitals are Critical Access Hospitals, a federal government designation for rural community hospitals that operate in medically underserved areas.

Operations
ARH's HomeCare Stores provide home medical equipment and oxygen delivery as well as 24-hour support through eight respiratory therapists. Its HomeCare Stores are supported by the ARH Home Health Agencies, which provide access to nursing care, occupational and physical therapy, and social services.

Among the system's hospitals are Beckley ARH Hospital, a not-for-profit, 173-bed acute-care facility; Harlan ARH Hospital, a state-licensed, 150-bed acute-care facility; and Mary Breckinridge ARH Hospital, a critical access facility.

ARH is the largest provider of care and single largest employer in southeastern Kentucky and the third-largest private employer in southern West Virginia. It employs almost 5,000 people and has a network of more than 600 medical staff members. In 2013 the system had 153,000 emergency department visits, 482,000 outpatient visits, some 1,500 births, and about 12,000 outpatient surgeries.

Geographic Reach
ARH serves residents of eastern Kentucky and southern West Virginia. It has hospitals in Harlan, Hazard, Hyden, Martin, McDowell, Middlesboro, Morgan County, South Williamson, and Whitesburg, Kentucky; and in Beckley and Summers County, West Virginia.

Strategy
As the primary provider of health care to medically underserved populations, ARH doles out millions of dollars in uncompensated care each year to un- or underinsured residents of the Appalachian region.

Along with a larger population of uninsured patients and the resulting unpaid medical bills that come along with them, rural health care providers face a number of hardships not encountered by their urban brethren. For example, physician recruitment is more difficult at rural hospitals, especially for some higher-risk specialties such as obstetrics. In order to attract and retain doctors, ARH and other rural health care providers have to offer more competitive compensation packages, pay for relocation, and invest in technology and facility upgrades.

Also, patients in rural areas are more

likely to suffer from chronic health problems such as diabetes and obesity, which can become a significant drain on a health system's resources. ARH is one of many health care providers looking to benefit from changes to the health care system outlined in Affordable Care Act, especially the requirement that all US citizens carry health insurance.

To keep up with patient demand, ARH also focuses on building and acquiring new facilities as well as investing in new technology and medical capacities.

Beckley ARH Hospital is undergoing a nearly $7 million renovation project that will add 19 more private rooms, decrease utility costs and improve patient flow processes. In 2014 ARH completed a $47 million expansion project at the Hazard ARH Regional Medical Center that added an additional 100,000 sq. ft. to the medical center, including a new patient tower, a new 24-bed emergency department on the first floor, a dedicated 16-bed cardiac critical care unit, and 34 private rooms. Hazard ARH is now the largest hospital in southeastern Kentucky.

Mergers and Acquisitions

In 2018 Appalachian Regional Healthcare acquired its twelfth hospital -- the 25-bed Saint Joseph Martin Hospital -- and its clinics. That facility now operates as ARH Our Lady of the Way.

Company Background

Appalachian Regional Healthcare was formed in 1956 by the United Mine Workers of America but became an independent, not-for-profit entity in the early 1960s.

Auditors : MCM CPA'S & ADVISORS LLP LOU

LOCATIONS

HQ: APPALACHIAN REGIONAL HEALTHCARE, INC.
2260 EXECUTIVE DR, LEXINGTON, KY 405054808
Phone: 859 226-2440
Web: WWW.ARH.ORG

PRODUCTS/OPERATIONS

Selected Facilities
Beckley ARH Hospital (Beckley, West Virginia)
Hazard ARH Regional Medical Center (Hazard, Kentucky)
Harlan ARH Hospital (Harlan, Kentucky)
McDowell ARH Hospital (McDowell, Kentucky)
Middlesboro ARH Hospital (Middlesboro, Kentucky)
Morgan County ARH Hospital (West Liberty, Kentucky)
Summers County ARH Hospital (Hinton, West Virginia)
Tug Valley ARH Regional Medical Center (South Williamson, Kentucky)
Whitesburg ARH Hospital (Whitesburg, Kentucky)

Selected Services
Bariatrics
Behavioral Health
Cancer Care
Clinics
Emergency
Heart Care
Home Health
HomeCare Stores
Imaging
Laboratory
Medical Spa
Nephrology
Obstetrics and Gynecology
Pediatrics
Pharmacy
Rehabilitation Therapy
Respiratory Therapy
Rheumatology
Senior Care
Skilled Nursing
Sleep Lab
Surgery
Swing Beds

COMPETITORS

ALLINA HEALTH SYSTEM
AVERA HEALTH
CAROMONT HEALTH, INC.
CHRISTUS HEALTH
DENVER HEALTH AND HOSPITALS AUTHORITY
HOLY SPIRIT HOSPITAL OF THE SISTERS OF CHRISTIAN CHARITY
HOUSTON COUNTY HEALTHCARE AUTHORITY
LEHIGH VALLEY HEALTH NETWORK, INC.
MEDSTAR HEALTH, INC.
WELLSTAR HEALTH SYSTEM, INC.

HISTORICAL FINANCIALS
Company Type: Private

Income Statement FYE: June 30

	REVENUE ($mil)	NET INCOME ($mil)	NET PROFIT MARGIN	EMPLOYEES
06/21	993	275	27.7%	4,520
06/20	868	23	2.7%	—
06/19	760	1	0.2%	—
06/18	689	65	9.4%	—
Annual Growth	13.0%	61.8%		

2021 Year-End Financials
Return on assets: 19.6%   Cash ($ mil.): 292
Return on equity: 47.9%
Current Ratio: 1.20

APPLE HOSPITALITY REIT, INC.

EXECUTIVES

CAO, Rachel S Labrecque
CLO, Matthew P Rash
Auditors : ERNST & YOUNG LLP RICHMOND V

LOCATIONS

HQ: APPLE HOSPITALITY REIT, INC.
814 E MAIN ST, RICHMOND, VA 232193306
Phone: 804 344-8121
Web: WWW.APPLEHOSPITALITYREIT.COM

HISTORICAL FINANCIALS
Company Type: Private

Income Statement FYE: December 31

	REVENUE ($mil)	NET INCOME ($mil)	NET PROFIT MARGIN	EMPLOYEES
12/14	803	6	0.8%	66
12/13	387	115	29.7%	—
12/12	365	75	20.6%	—
12/11	320	69	21.8%	—
Annual Growth	35.9%	(54.0%)	—	—

2014 Year-End Financials
Return on assets: 6.9%   Cash ($ mil.): —
Return on equity: 0.8%
Current Ratio: —

APPLIED MEDICAL RESOURCES CORPORATION

EXECUTIVES

Group President*, Stephen E Stanley
Group President*, Nabil Hilal
Group President*, Gary Johnson

LOCATIONS

HQ: APPLIED MEDICAL RESOURCES CORPORATION
22872 AVENIDA EMPRESA, RCHO STA MARG, CA 926882650
Phone: 949 713-8000
Web: WWW.APPLIEDMEDICAL.COM

HISTORICAL FINANCIALS
Company Type: Private

Income Statement FYE: December 31

	REVENUE ($mil)	NET INCOME ($mil)	NET PROFIT MARGIN	EMPLOYEES
12/21	649	34	5.2%	4,902
12/20	544	31	5.8%	—
12/19	585	47	8.1%	—
Annual Growth	5.3%	(15.5%)		

2021 Year-End Financials
Return on assets: 4.8%   Cash ($ mil.): —
Return on equity: 7.8%
Current Ratio: 3.80

ARCTIC SLOPE REGIONAL CORPORATION

The Inupiat-owned Arctic Slope Regional Corporation (ASRC) is a locally owned and operated business in Alaska. It gets the bulk of its sales from energy services (ASRC Energy Services) and petroleum refining and marketing unit (Petro Star). Other operations include construction (ASRC Construction Holding), governmental services (ASRC Federal Holding), economic development (Alaska Growth Capital BIDCO), local services (Eskimos, Inc.) and tourism (Tundra Tours).

Operations

ASRC own titles to nearly 5 million acres of land on Alaska's North Slope which contain a high potential for oil, gas, coal and base metal sulfides.

It operates in six diverse major business segments: petroleum refining and marketing, government contract services, energy support services, industrial services, resource development, and construction industries. Petro Star has two refineries (strategically positioned along the Trans-Alaska Pipeline) and serves Interior Alaska, South Central Alaska, Kodiak and Dutch Harbor. Its North Pole facility supplies the mining industry in the interior region of Alaska and provides home heating oil to several communities.

ASRC Federal Holding Company provides professional and technical services to the federal government (including defense and intelligence agencies, engineering, IT, infrastructure support, professional and technical services to civil).

ASRC Energy Services offers oilfield engineering, operations, maintenance, construction, fabrication, regulation and permitting, and other services to oil and gas companies. The company provides services to the energy industry throughout Alaska, and the Gulf of Mexico.

ASRC Construction Holding Company provides construction services to commercial and government clients in Alaska, the Lower 48, and in other countries.

ASRC Industrial Services (AIS) is a people-oriented organization of complementary yet diverse services, focusing on the industrial end-use customers nationwide.

Geographic Reach

ASRC represents approximately 13,000 Iñupiat shareholders in the villages of Point Hope, Point Lay, Wainwright, Atqasuk, Utqiagvik, Nuiqsut, Kaktovik and Anaktuvuk Pass. ASRC has its offices in Anchorage. It has other subsidiary offices in the Lower 48 states.

ASRC was set up to own and manage 5 million acres on Alaska's North Slope after the Alaska Native Claims Settlement Act in 1971 cleared the way for oil development in the area.

Strategy

In 2017, the ASRC board of directors and executive management undertook an intensive strategic planning process focused on successfully mitigating risk factors and growing the corporation over the next five years. The 2018-2023 Strategic Plan takes an integrated approach to grow and diversify ASRC's core base of businesses and includes some ambitious benchmark goals, including its overarching measure of success to become one of the top 100 largest private companies in the US.

The ultimate goal is to provide the greatest amount of benefit to the greatest number of shareholders, and its Pillar Strategies describe how the company is focusing its efforts to maximize shareholder impact. The company's strategic focus: financial performance, shareholder & employee growth; and community economic development.

Company Background

ASRC was set up to own and manage 5 million acres on Alaska's North Slope after the Alaska Native Claims Settlement Act in 1971 cleared the way for oil development in the area.

In 2010 ASRC protested the US Fish and Wildlife Service's designation of Alaskan North Slope oil-producing areas as a critical habitat for endangered polar bears, claiming it would cost ASRC millions of dollars in lost oil revenues. In 2011 it led a coalition of Native groups to sue the Department of the Interior over this issue.

In 2012 ASRC Construction Holding expanded into southeast Alaska with the acquisition of native-Alaskan owned McGraw's Custom Construction.

EXECUTIVES

Vice Chairman*, George Sielak

LOCATIONS

HQ: ARCTIC SLOPE REGIONAL CORPORATION
3900 C ST STE 801, ANCHORAGE, AK 995035963
Phone: 907 339-6000
Web: WWW.ASRC.COM

PRODUCTS/OPERATIONS

Selected Businesses
Energy Services
    ASRC Energy Services, Inc.
    Arctic Inupiat Offshore LLC.
Petroleum Refining and Marketing
    Petro Star Inc.
Government Services
    ASRC Federal Holding Company
Construction
    ASRC Construction Holding Company, LLC
Resource Development
    Little Red Services
    Petrochem

COMPETITORS

DOYON, LIMITED
GEOKINETICS INC.
HALLIBURTON COMPANY
KEY ENERGY SERVICES, INC.
NEWPARK RESOURCES INC.
Petrofac Limited
RPC, INC.
SEACOR HOLDINGS INC.
STALLION OILFIELD SERVICES LTD.
Schlumberger N.V.

HISTORICAL FINANCIALS

Company Type: Private

Income Statement   FYE: December 31

	REVENUE ($mil)	NET INCOME ($mil)	NET PROFIT MARGIN	EMPLOYEES
12/08	2,297	151	6.6%	6,700
12/07	1,777	207	11.7%	—
12/06	1,700	206	12.1%	—
12/05	1,566	127	8.1%	—
Annual Growth	13.6%	5.8%	—	—

2008 Year-End Financials
Return on assets: 11.7%   Cash ($ mil.): 302
Return on equity: 19.0%
Current Ratio: 1.70

ARIZONA STATE LOTTERY

EXECUTIVES

Department Director, Karen Emery
Auditors: HENRY & HORNE LLP CASA GRAND

LOCATIONS

HQ: ARIZONA STATE LOTTERY
4740 E UNIVERSITY DR, PHOENIX, AZ 850347400
Phone: 480 921-4400
Web: WWW.ARIZONALOTTERY.COM

HISTORICAL FINANCIALS

Company Type: Private

Income Statement   FYE: June 30

	REVENUE ($mil)	NET INCOME ($mil)	NET PROFIT MARGIN	EMPLOYEES
06/22	1,368	6	0.4%	112
06/21	1,439	9	0.7%	—
06/20	1,097	5	0.5%	—
06/19	1,076	9	0.9%	—
Annual Growth	8.3%	(14.1%)	—	—

2022 Year-End Financials
Return on assets: 3.0%   Cash ($ mil.): 136
Return on equity: 16.3%
Current Ratio: 1.10

ARIZONA STATE UNIVERSITY

LOCATIONS

HQ: ARIZONA STATE UNIVERSITY
951 S PALM WALK, TEMPE, AZ 852870001
Phone: 480 965-4385
Web: WWW.ASU.EDU

HISTORICAL FINANCIALS

Company Type: Private

Income Statement   FYE: June 30

	REVENUE ($mil)	NET INCOME ($mil)	NET PROFIT MARGIN	EMPLOYEES
06/15	1,482	92	6.2%	26
06/14	1,348	103	7.7%	—
Annual Growth	9.9%	(10.7%)	—	—

2015 Year-End Financials
Return on assets: 6.4%   Cash ($ mil.): 47
Return on equity: 6.2%
Current Ratio: 0.60

ARIZONA STATE UNIVERSITY

Arizona State University (ASU) is a comprehensive public research university that offers more than 850 degree programs for undergraduate and degree pursuing a master's degree or doctoral program. The university offers nearly 300 undergraduate and graduate degree programs and certificates are also offered 100% online. It has 54,000 students enrolled. ASU is ranked top 10 nationally for best online bachelor's programs by US News & World Report. It offers nearly 300 online degree and certificate programs taught by award-winning ASU faculty. ASU was founded in 1885.

Operations
From engineering, journalism and business to sustainability, nursing, education and beyond, ASU offers 16 colleges and schools, including the W. P. Carey School of Business, Mary Lou Fulton Teachers College, College of Nursing and Health Innovation, and the Ira A. Fulton School of Engineering.

The university's extensive research programs cover a variety of fields in life science, medicine, and Physics and more.

Geographic Reach
ASU's four campuses in the greater Phoenix metropolitan region, in locations across Arizona, and at centers in Los Angeles and Washington, D.C.

EXECUTIVES

CIO, Lev Gonick
Auditors : LINDSEY A PERRY CPA CFE PHO

LOCATIONS

HQ: ARIZONA STATE UNIVERSITY
300 E UNIVERSITY DR # 410, TEMPE, AZ 852812061
Phone: 480 965-2100
Web: WWW.ASU.EDU

PRODUCTS/OPERATIONS

2014 Sales

	$ mil	% of total
Tuition & fees	896.9	67
Research grants and contracts	244.3	18
Auxiliary enterprises	140.5	10
Other operating revenues	66.9	5
Total	1,348.6	100

Selected Colleges and Schools
Barrett Honors College
College of Health Solutions
College of Liberal Arts and Sciences
College of Nursing and Health Innovation
College of Public Programs
College of Technology and Innovation
Graduate College
Herberger Institute for Design and the Arts
Ira A. Fulton Schools of Engineering
Mary Lou Fulton Teachers College
New College of Interdisciplinary Arts and Sciences
Sandra Day O'Connor College of Law
School of Letters and Sciences
School of Sustainability
Thunderbird School of Global Management
University College
Walter Cronkite School of Journalism and Mass Communication
W.P. Carey School of Business

COMPETITORS

BOISE STATE UNIVERSITY
CLARK ATLANTA UNIVERSITY INC
EASTERN MICHIGAN UNIVERSITY
FAIRFIELD UNIVERSITY
NEW MEXICO STATE UNIVERSITY
PURDUE UNIVERSITY
THE COLLEGE OF WILLIAM & MARY
UNIVERSITY OF THE PACIFIC
VILLANOVA UNIVERSITY IN THE STATE OF PENNSYLVANIA
WICHITA STATE UNIVERSITY

HISTORICAL FINANCIALS
Company Type: Private

Income Statement — FYE: June 30

	REVENUE ($mil)	NET INCOME ($mil)	NET PROFIT MARGIN	EMPLOYEES
06/21	2,220	247	11.2%	8,000
06/20	2,180	6	0.3%	—
06/19	2,048	85	4.2%	—
06/18	1,915	63	3.3%	—
Annual Growth	5.0%	57.8%	—	—

2021 Year-End Financials
Return on assets: 4.4%   Cash ($ mil.): 370
Return on equity: 15.4%
Current Ratio: 1.10

ARKANSAS ELECTRIC COOPERATIVE CORPORATION

Having access to power is the natural state in the Natural State, thanks to Arkansas Electric Cooperative Corporation (AECC), the sole wholesale power provider for 17 Arkansas electric distribution cooperatives. The company operates power plants with 3,418 MW of generating capacity, owns transmission assets, and buys wholesale power to meet its members' demands. Affiliate Arkansas Electric Cooperatives, Inc. (AECI) provides administrative and maintenance services to the distribution companies. The distribution utilities serve about 500,000 customers in more than 60% of Arkansas. AECC and AECI, along with the state's 17 electric distribution cooperatives, are known as the Electric Cooperatives of Arkansas.

Operations
AECC's diverse generation assets include three hydropower plants, three natural gas/oil-based plants, and three natural gas-based-only plants. It also co-owns portions of four low-cost coal-based plants and has a long-term power purchase agreement for 51 MW wind energy. The coop also has four transmission lines.

Sales and Marketing
In fiscal 2013 co-op members Mississippi County Electric Cooperative, First Electric Cooperative, Carroll Electric Cooperative, and Arkansas Valley Electric Corporation together accounted for 59% of AECC's total revenues.

Financial Performance
Thanks to a rebounding economy and growing demand for power, the company saw its revenues grow by 13% in fiscal 2013.

Net income declined by 37% in fiscal 2013 due to higher operations, maintenance, generation, and transmission expenses, as well as an increase in administration and general expenses.

Strategy
AECC is ramping up its renewable energy resources in order to meet state and federal clean energy power requirements.

In 2013 the company signed a long-term deal to buy 150 MW of wind energy from RES America Developments Inc., a subsidiary of Renewable Energy Systems Americas Inc.

In 2012 it reached a long-term purchase power agreement for 51 MW of wind energy from the Flat Ridge 2 South Wind Farm in Kansas. AECC's 51 MW of capacity is part of 470 MW of potential generation provided by the farm's 294 GE wind turbines. BP and Sempra U.S. Gas & Power are equal joint venture partners for the facility, which has a combined investment of more than $800 million. A wholly-owned affiliate of BP Wind Energy will monitor and maintain the farm

Mergers and Acquisitions
In another move to cut back on the use of coal-fired power plants, in 2012 AECC bought a 746-MW combined cycle natural gas-fired power plant near Magnet Cove for $240 million.

Company Background
The first electric cooperative in Arkansas was formed in Jacksonville in 1938 as part of the Roosevelt Administration's national rural electrification drive.

Auditors : BKD LLP LITTLE ROCK ARKANSA

LOCATIONS

HQ: ARKANSAS ELECTRIC COOPERATIVE CORPORATION
1 COOPERATIVE WAY, LITTLE ROCK, AR 722095493
Phone: 501 570-2200
Web: WWW.AECC.COM

COMPETITORS

ASSOCIATED ELECTRIC COOPERATIVE, INC.
SEMINOLE ELECTRIC COOPERATIVE, INC.
THE SOUTHERN COMPANY
TRI-STATE GENERATION AND TRANSMISSION ASSOCIATION, INC.
WESTERN FARMERS ELECTRIC COOPERATIVE

HISTORICAL FINANCIALS
Company Type: Private

Income Statement — FYE: October 31

	REVENUE ($mil)	NET INCOME ($mil)	NET PROFIT MARGIN	EMPLOYEES
10/19	790	24	3.1%	220
10/18*	827	38	4.7%	—
12/15	462	35	7.7%	—
12/14	455	30	6.6%	—
Annual Growth	11.7%	(3.8%)	—	—

*Fiscal year change

2019 Year-End Financials
Return on assets: 1.4%
Return on equity: 4.1%
Current Ratio: 0.90
Cash ($ mil.): 154

ARKANSAS ELECTRIC COOPERATIVES, INC.

Auditors: BKD LLP LITTLE ROCK ARKANSA

LOCATIONS

HQ: ARKANSAS ELECTRIC COOPERATIVES, INC.
1 COOPERATIVE WAY, LITTLE ROCK, AR 722095493
Phone: 501 570-2200
Web: WWW.AECC.COM

HISTORICAL FINANCIALS
Company Type: Private

Income Statement — FYE: December 31

	REVENUE ($mil)	NET INCOME ($mil)	NET PROFIT MARGIN	EMPLOYEES
12/18	679	50	7.4%	840
12/17	564	44	7.8%	—
12/15	462	35	7.7%	—
12/13	416	32	7.7%	—
Annual Growth	10.3%	9.4%	—	—

2018 Year-End Financials
Return on assets: 13.8%
Return on equity: 18.5%
Current Ratio: 3.60
Cash ($ mil.): 101

ARLINGTON INDEPENDENT SCHOOL DISTRICT (INC)

Auditors: WHITLEY PENN LLP FORT WORTH

LOCATIONS

HQ: ARLINGTON INDEPENDENT SCHOOL DISTRICT (INC)
690 E LAMAR BLVD STE 110, ARLINGTON, TX 760113869
Phone: 682 867-4611
Web: WWW.AISD.NET

HISTORICAL FINANCIALS
Company Type: Private

Income Statement — FYE: June 30

	REVENUE ($mil)	NET INCOME ($mil)	NET PROFIT MARGIN	EMPLOYEES
06/21	742	91	12.4%	8,000
06/20	732	248	33.9%	—
06/19	688	(87)	—	—
06/18	680	(28)	—	—
Annual Growth	2.9%	—	—	—

2021 Year-End Financials
Return on assets: 4.6%
Return on equity: 88.6%
Current Ratio: —
Cash ($ mil.): 765

ASCENSION HEALTH ALLIANCE

EXECUTIVES

Executive Adviser, Sister Bernice Coreil D.c. Sen ior
Auditors: ERNST & YOUNG LLP ST LOUIS

LOCATIONS

HQ: ASCENSION HEALTH ALLIANCE
101 S HANLEY RD STE 450, SAINT LOUIS, MO 631053463
Phone: 314 733-8000
Web: WWW.ASCENSION.ORG

HISTORICAL FINANCIALS
Company Type: Private

Income Statement — FYE: June 30

	ASSETS ($mil)	NET INCOME ($mil)	INCOME AS % OF ASSETS	EMPLOYEES
06/17	34,320	1,638	4.8%	150,000
06/16	32,469	(339)	—	—
06/15	30,963	(42)	—	—
Annual Growth	5.3%	—	—	—

2017 Year-End Financials
Return on assets: 4.8%
Return on equity: 8.0%
Current Ratio: 1.00
Cash ($ mil.): 857

ASCENSION PROVIDENCE HOSPITAL

Providence Hospital and Medical Centers provides health care in the Motor City and surrounding areas. The main Providence Hospital is a 408-bed teaching facility that has been recognized for its cardiology program and clinical expertise in behavioral medicine. It offers a variety of other services ranging from cancer treatment and neurosurgery to orthopedics and women's health. The network also includes dozens of affiliated general practice and specialty health clinics. The not-for-profit medical center, founded in 1845 as St. Vincent's Hospital in Detroit by the Daughters of Charity, is part of Catholic health ministry St. John Health (itself a subsidiary of Ascension Health).

Operations

As part of its health care system, Providence Hospital and Medical Centers operates a host of hospitals and medical centers across the metropolitan Detroit area. They include Providence Southfield and four namesake Providence Medical Center locations in Farmington Hills, Livonia, Dearborn Heights, and South Lyon. Across its system, the medical facilities employ some 1,500 physicians and enlist the help of about 300 active volunteers.

Carroll Manor is a skilled nursing center that provides short- and long-term medical care and rehabilitation services. The system's behavioral health division, Seton House, provides alcohol and addiction treatment in Washington, DC.

Providence Hospital and Medical Centers had more than 41,600 emergency department visits in 2013.

Strategy

In order to provide better services, the hospital renovated and expanded its emergency department in 2014. Also that year, its family medicine division opened a new office in the Glenn Dale/Bowie area.

Auditors: DELOITTE TAX LP CINCINNATI O

LOCATIONS

HQ: ASCENSION PROVIDENCE HOSPITAL
16001 W 9 MILE RD, SOUTHFIELD, MI 480754818
Phone: 248 849-3000
Web: WWW.PULMCCMPROV.ORG

Selected Hospitals and Medical Centers
Providence Southfield-Southfield
Providence Medical Center-Farmington Hills
Providence Medical Center-Livonia
Providence Medical Center-Dearborn Heights
Providence Medical Center-South Lyon

PRODUCTS/OPERATIONS

Selected Primary Services
Cancer clinical trials
Cardiac rehabilitation
Childbirth
Congenital heart disease clinic
Emergency
Oncology
Orthopedics
Senior services
Surgery
Women's health

COMPETITORS

ASCENSION SOUTHEAST MICHIGAN
ATLANTIC HEALTH SYSTEM INC.
HOSPITAL SERVICE DISTRICT 1
PHELPS MEMORIAL HOSPITAL ASSOCIATION
PROVIDENCE HOSPITAL

HISTORICAL FINANCIALS
Company Type: Private

Income Statement   FYE: June 30

	REVENUE ($mil)	NET INCOME ($mil)	NET PROFIT MARGIN	EMPLOYEES
06/16	703	21	3.1%	4,700
06/15	654	25	3.9%	—
06/14	659	53	8.1%	—
06/11	706	27	3.9%	—
Annual Growth	(0.1%)	(4.9%)	—	—

2016 Year-End Financials
Return on assets: 0.5%   Cash ($ mil.): 3
Return on equity: 3.2%
Current Ratio: 1.20

ASCENSION VIA CHRISTI HOSPITALS WICHITA, INC.

LOCATIONS

HQ: ASCENSION VIA CHRISTI HOSPITALS WICHITA, INC.
  929 N ST FRANCIS ST, WICHITA, KS 672143821
Phone: 316 268-5880
Web: HEALTHCARE.ASCENSION.ORG

HISTORICAL FINANCIALS
Company Type: Private

Income Statement   FYE: June 30

	REVENUE ($mil)	NET INCOME ($mil)	NET PROFIT MARGIN	EMPLOYEES
06/19*	597	64	10.7%	4,100
09/14	534	68	12.9%	—
09/13	534	24	4.5%	—
09/12	(855)	0	0.0%	—
Annual Growth	—	515.2%	—	—

*Fiscal year change

2019 Year-End Financials
Return on assets: 17.1%   Cash ($ mil.): —
Return on equity: 22.8%
Current Ratio: —

ASI COMPUTER TECHNOLOGIES INC

ASI Computer Technologies is a national distributor of IT software and hardware products. It offers more than 10,000 products, including PCs, scanners, security, surveillance, and data storage devices. The company has rapidly grown to become the partner of choice for over 10,000 VARs throughout North America. Its vendor partners include companies the likes of AMD, Intel, Micron, Samsung, and Viewsonic. ASI's services include custom systems integration. Furthermore, it caters to various industries such as retail and the SMB market. The company was established in 1987 by president and owner Cristine Liang.

Operations
ASI offers an extensive line of products, components, and services, and also provides ISO-9001 compliant system integration and value add contract assembly. More specifically, it has other products including, but not limited to cables, drones, desktops, mount, USBs, software, hard drives, and printers.

The company has services such as hardware and software testing, pre-sales system design and configuration assistance and bios, and driver updates, among others. The company has partnerships with Intel, ASUS, NVIDIA, MSI, Samsung, Supermicro, Micron, AMD, Viewsonic, and Toshiba, to name a few.

Geographic Reach
Headquartered in Fremont, California, ASI has regional US offices in Atlanta, Chicago, Dallas, Los Angeles, and New Jersey, as well as Canada offices in Montreal, Toronto, and Vancouver.

Sales and Marketing
ASI's diverse portfolio of products and services allow it to service a broad customer base (it counts more than 10,000 customers), which includes VARs, systems integrators, OEMs, and retailers.

Auditors : MARCUM LLP SAN FRANCISCO CA

LOCATIONS

HQ: ASI COMPUTER TECHNOLOGIES INC
  48289 FREMONT BLVD, FREMONT, CA 945386510
Phone: 510 226-8000
Web: WWW.ASIPARTNER.COM

PRODUCTS/OPERATIONS
Selected Products
Accessories
Cables
Cameras
Cases
CD-ROM drives
Central processing units
Controller cards
DVD drives
Fans
Floppy drives
Hard drives
Keyboards
Memory
Mice
Modems
Monitors
Motherboards
MP3 players
Multimedia products
Network connectivity products
Notebooks
Optical drives
PCs
Power supplies
Printers
Projectors
Removable drives and media
Scanners
Software
Sound cards
Speakers
Storage devices
Tape back-up products
Video cards
Zip drives

COMPETITORS
CONTINENTAL RESOURCES, INC.
D & H DISTRIBUTING COMPANY
DAIWABO INFORMATION SYSTEM CO., LTD.
EXPRESSPOINT TECHNOLOGY SERVICES, INC.
KORBER SUPPLY CHAIN US, INC.
NEC CORPORATION OF AMERICA
SED INTERNATIONAL HOLDINGS, INC.
SUPPLIES NETWORK, INC.
TALLEY INC.
WORLD DATA PRODUCTS, INC.

HISTORICAL FINANCIALS
Company Type: Private

Income Statement   FYE: December 31

	REVENUE ($mil)	NET INCOME ($mil)	NET PROFIT MARGIN	EMPLOYEES
12/13	1,746	17	1.0%	76
12/04	1,057	12	1.2%	—
12/03	982	13	1.3%	—
12/02	865	10	1.2%	—
Annual Growth	6.6%	4.9%	—	—

2013 Year-End Financials
Return on assets: 5.4%   Cash ($ mil.): 28
Return on equity: 1.0%
Current Ratio: 1.10

ASPIRUS WAUSAU HOSPITAL, INC.

Auditors : WIPFLI LLP EAU CLAIRE WISCON

LOCATIONS

HQ: ASPIRUS WAUSAU HOSPITAL, INC.
  425 PINE RIDGE BLVD # 1, WAUSAU, WI 544014121
Phone: 715 847-2019
Web: WWW.ASPIRUS.ORG

HISTORICAL FINANCIALS
Company Type: Private

Income Statement   FYE: June 30

	REVENUE ($mil)	NET INCOME ($mil)	NET PROFIT MARGIN	EMPLOYEES
06/20	564	7	1.3%	3,500
06/19	543	70	12.9%	—
06/18	497	8	1.7%	—
06/16	456	51	11.4%	—
Annual Growth	5.5%	(38.6%)	—	—

2020 Year-End Financials
Return on assets: 1.2%   Cash ($ mil.): 4
Return on equity: 2.0%
Current Ratio: 1.80

ASPIRUS, INC.

Aspirus is a non-profit, community-directed health system based in Wausau, Wisconsin. The health system provides a comprehensive range of health and medical services to communities through four hospitals in Upper Michigan and about 15 hospitals in Wisconsin, some 75 clinics, home health and hospice care, pharmacies, critical care and air-medical transport, medical goods, nursing homes and a broad network of physicians. In addition to its four hospitals in Michigan, Aspirus operates the Aspirus Wausau Hospital, a 325-bed and staffed by 350 physicians in 35 specialties. With approximately 15,000 admissions per year, outpatient visits exceed 50,000 and there are also more than 24,000 annual emergency department visits.

Operations
Aspirus offers services that includes behavioral health & counseling, hospice services, sleep medicine, and birthing services. It also offers inpatient rehabilitation, spine and neurosciences, breast care and mammography, and NICU, to name a few.

Its Aspirus Network is a Clinically Integrated Network of leading primary and specialty care physicians, hospitals and allied health care professionals. Aspirus Network negotiates contracts on behalf of its members with employers and health plans. ANI works closely with Aspirus' health plan, Aspirus Health Plan, to help deliver direct access to high-value, personalized health care that aims to improve the health and well-being through all health care needs.

Geographic Reach
Headquartered in Wausau, Wisconcin, it has operations in Amherst, Antigo, Hancock, Athens, and Stevens Point, all in Wisconsin.

Sales and Marketing
Aspirus serves communities through four hospitals in Upper Michigan and thirteen hospitals in Wisconsin, seventy-five clinics, home health and hospice care, pharmacies, critical care and air-medical transport, medical goods, nursing homes and a broad network of physicians.

Auditors : WIPFLI LLP EAU CLAIRE WISCO

LOCATIONS
HQ: ASPIRUS, INC.
 2200 WESTWOOD DR, WAUSAU, WI 544017806
Phone: 715 847-2121
Web: WWW.ASPIRUS.ORG

Selected FacilitiesU.P. of MichiganAspirus Grand View Aspirus Keweenaw HospitalAspirus Ontonagon HospitalNORTHSTAR Health System WisconsinAspirus Wausau HospitalAspirus Langlade HospitalAspirus Medford HospitalRiverview Hospital

PRODUCTS/OPERATIONS
Selected Services
Alzheimer's & Memory Disorders
Anesthesia Services
Angioplasty
Anticoagulation Clinic
Cardiac Electrophysiology
Cardiac Rehab
Cardioversion
Dentistry
Oral & Maxillofacial Surgery
Prosthodontics
Psychiatry
Psychology
Pulmonary Medicine
Sleep Disorders

COMPETITORS
ALEGENT CREIGHTON HEALTH
AULTMAN HEALTH FOUNDATION
CAROMONT HEALTH, INC.
CENTRACARE HEALTH - PAYNESVILLE, LLC
CHRISTUS SPOHN HEALTH SYSTEM CORPORATION
EXCELA HEALTH HOLDING COMPANY, INC.
HOLY SPIRIT HOSPITAL OF THE SISTERS OF CHRISTIAN CHARITY
LEHIGH VALLEY HEALTH NETWORK, INC.
REGIONAL CARE HOSPITAL PARTNERS, INC.
SPACE COAST HEALTH FOUNDATION, INC.

HISTORICAL FINANCIALS
Company Type: Private

Income Statement — FYE: June 30

	REVENUE ($mil)	NET INCOME ($mil)	NET PROFIT MARGIN	EMPLOYEES
06/22	1,687	34	2.1%	7,100
06/20	1,090	169	15.5%	—
06/19	996	102	10.3%	—
06/18	911	78	8.6%	—
Annual Growth	16.7%	(18.2%)	—	—

2022 Year-End Financials
Return on assets: 1.4% Cash ($ mil.): 261
Return on equity: 2.2%
Current Ratio: 3.30

ASSOCIATED FOOD STORES, INC.

This business makes sure there's plenty of grub for the Wild West. Associated Food Stores (AFS) is a leading regional cooperative wholesale distributor that supplies groceries and other products to some 500 independent supermarkets in about eight Western states. It also offers support services for its member-owners, including market research, real estate analysis, store design, technology procurement, and training. In addition, AFS owns a stake in Western Family Foods, a grocery wholesalers' partnership that produces Western Family private-label goods. The co-op, formed in 1940, also operates 40-plus corporate stores in Utah under five different banners, including Fresh Market.

Operations
In addition to its wholesale business, AFS's retail arm -- Associated Retail Operations -- owns and operates corporate stores in Utah under five different formats and banners: Macey's; Fresh Market; Dan's Fresh Market in Salt Lake City; Lin's Fresh Market; and Dick's Fresh Market. The retail business accounts for about 35% of AFS's annual revenue.

The grocery distributor supplies independent supermarkets with over 3,600 products. Products comprise a wide array including baking, breakfast cereals, frozen foods, household supplies, and even pet food and supplies. In early 2013 Associated closed its distribution centers in Helena and Billings, Montana and consolidated warehouse operations for its nearly 100 Montana and Wyoming customers at its facility in Farr West, Utah.

Geographic Reach
Salt Lake City-based Associated Food Stores has operations in Arizona, Colorado, Idaho, Montana, Nevada, Oregon, Utah, and Wyoming. The

Financial Performance
While privately-owned Associated Food Stores doesn't report its financial results, the company logged an estimated $2.2 billion in sales in fiscal 2013 (ended March), versus $2.1 billion in sales the previous year.

Auditors : DELOITTE & TOUCHE LLP SALT L

LOCATIONS
HQ: ASSOCIATED FOOD STORES, INC.
 1850 W 2100 S, SALT LAKE CITY, UT 841191304
Phone: 801 973-4400
Web: WWW.AFSTORES.COM

PRODUCTS/OPERATIONS
Selected Brands
Western Family
Full Circle
Shur Saving

Selected Retail Banners
Dan's Fresh Market
Dick's Fresh Market
Fresh Market
Lin's Fresh Market
Macey's

COMPETITORS
CENTRAL GROCERS, INC.
DISCOUNT DRUG MART, INC.
FOUR B CORP.
NAVARRO DISCOUNT PHARMACIES, LLC
SHOPKO STORES OPERATING CO., LLC
Shoppers Drug Mart Corporation
THE MIDCOUNTIES CO-OPERATIVE LIMITED
UNIFIED GROCERS, INC.
URM STORES, INC.
WALGREENS BOOTS ALLIANCE, INC.

HISTORICAL FINANCIALS
Company Type: Private

Income Statement   FYE: March 31

	REVENUE ($mil)	NET INCOME ($mil)	NET PROFIT MARGIN	EMPLOYEES
03/12	2,011	5	0.3%	300
03/11	1,953	(6)	—	—
03/10	1,785	(2)	—	—
Annual Growth	6.1%	—	—	—

2012 Year-End Financials
Return on assets: 1.0%   Cash ($ mil.): 105
Return on equity: 5.4%
Current Ratio: 0.90

ASSOCIATED WHOLESALE GROCERS, INC.

Associated Wholesale Grocers (AWG) is one of the largest grocery wholesalers in the US and the nation's oldest grocery cooperative. AWG supplies more than 1,100 member companies and over 3,100 locations throughout nearly 30 states. In addition to its cooperative wholesale grocery operations, AWG also offers a variety of business services to its members, including certain real estate and supermarket development services, print and digital marketing services, health and beauty care, general merchandise, pharmaceutical products, specialty foods, and natural and organic products. AWG was founded by a group of independent grocers in 1924.

Operations
Associated Wholesale Grocers predominantly operates on a cooperative basis procuring grocery merchandise for distribution to its retailer/shareholders throughout the mid-western, southwestern, and southeastern US. Non-Cooperative businesses include nonfood distribution centers and retail supermarkets that operate under the banners of Cash Saver and Price Chopper. The cooperative represents around 90% of total net sales.

AWG's subsidiary, VMC that provides procurement and marketing of health, beauty and wellness, general and seasonal merchandise, natural, organic, and specialty food, and pharmacy programs. The company's other services include Real Estate and Store Development and Market Research. Real Estate provides customer origin surveys, overall market strategies, site selection / acquisition, contract negotiations, Supermarket Developers (SMD), Project / Self Development Company, and financial feasibility performas. Market Research includes market studies ? forecast sales, evaluate sites and competition, identify population and growth trends, understanding customer's, demographic characteristics, and more.

Geographic Reach
Kansas City-headquartered AWG began in Missouri and its operations are generally centered on that state. It operates from eight full-line wholesale divisions in Missouri, Nebraska, Kansas, Oklahoma, Louisiana, Tennessee, and Wisconsin. Its distribution activities extend into another nearly 30 states.

AWG's Valu Merchandisers subsidiary supplies stores in more than half the states in the country.

As a cooperative, AWG serves about 10 modern and efficient distribution centers, totaling more than 7.0 million square feet.

Sales and Marketing
AWG serves up several private label brands to stores. These bands include Superior Selections, Clearly Organic, Best Choice, Always Save, and IGA.

The company's advertising expenses for the fiscal years 2021, 2020, and 2019 were approximately $0.5 million, $0.8 million, and $4.6 million, respectively.

Financial Performance
The company's net sales for 2021 was $10.8 billion, a 2% increase from the previous year's net income of $10.6 billion.

In 2021, the company had a net income of $259.7 million, a 9% decrease from the previous year's net income of $284.4 million.

The company's cash at the end of 2021 was $185.8 million. Operating activities generated $325.8 million, while investing activities used $129.9 million, mainly for purchase of property and equipment. Financing activities used another $184 million, mainly for year-end patronage distributions.

Company Background
Associated Wholesale Grocers (AWG) was founded in 1924.

HISTORY

About 20 Kansas City, Kansas-area grocers met in a local grocery in 1924 and organized the Associated Grocers Company to get better deals on purchases and advertising. They elected J. C. Harline president, and each chipped in a few hundred dollars to make their first purchases. It took a while to find a manufacturer who would sell directly to them; a local soap maker was finally convinced, and others gradually followed.

In 1926 the group was incorporated as Associated Wholesale Grocers (AWG). It outgrew two warehouses in four years, finally moving to a 16,000-sq.-ft. facility big enough to add new lines and more products. Membership doubled between 1930 and 1932 as grocers moved from ordering products a year ahead to the new wholesale concept, and members took seriously the slogan: "Buy, Sell, Buy Some More." They met every week to plan how to sell their products, and buyer and advertising manager Harry Small gave sales presentations and advertising ideas (his trade-in plan for old brooms sold more than two train-carloads of brooms in two weeks). Heavy newspaper advertising also paid off; AWG topped $1 million in sales in 1933.

The cooperative made its first acquisition in 1936, buying Progressive Grocers, a warehouse in Joplin, Missouri; a second warehouse named Associated Grocers was acquired the next year in Springfield, Missouri. AWG continued building and expanding warehouses, and annual sales were at $11 million by 1951.

Louis Fox became CEO in 1956. Fox maximized year-end rebates for members, led several acquisitions, and formed a new subsidiary for financing stores and small shopping centers where AWG members had a presence (Supermarket Developers). Sales increased nearly 15-fold to over $200 million in his first 15 years.

James Basha, who succeeded Fox when he retired in 1984, saw sales reach $2.4 billion by the time of his own retirement in 1992.

Basha was followed by former COO Mike DeFabis, once a deputy mayor of Indianapolis. DeFabis orchestrated several acquisitions, including 41 Kansas City-area stores -- most of which were quickly bought by members -- from bankrupt Food Barn Stores in 1994 and 29 Oklahoma stores and a warehouse from Safeway spinoff Homeland Stores in 1995 (members bought all the stores).

AWG's non-food subsidiary, Valu Merchandisers, was established in 1995; its new Kansas warehouse began shipping health and beauty aids and housewares the following year to help members battle big discounters. Members narrowly defeated a proposal in late 1996 to convert the cooperative into a public company. Proponents promptly petitioned for a second vote, which was defeated early the next year.

AWG veteran Doug Carolan succeeded DeFabis in 1998, becoming only the fifth CEO in the cooperative's history. The company bought five Falley's and 33 Food 4 Less stores in Kansas and Missouri from Fred Meyer in 1998 for $300 million. In a break with tradition, AWG began operating the stores rather than selling them to members.

In 2000, after a months-long labor dispute with the Teamsters was resolved, Carolan left AWG. The company's CFO, Gary Phillips, was named president and CEO later that year. In 2001 the company debuted a new format, ALPS (Always Low Price Stores) -- small stores that carry a limited selection of grocery top-sellers. Also that year AWG's Kansas City division began distributing to more than 10 new stores that had formerly been served by Fleming, at the time the #1 US wholesale food distributor.

In 2002 supermarket operator Homeland Stores, which operates stores in Oklahoma, emerged from bankruptcy as a fully owned subsidiary of AWG. AWG formed a new subsidiary, Associated Retail Grocers, to oversee Homeland and its Falley's chain.

As a result of the 2003 sale of Fleming Companies' wholesale distribution business, AWG picked up food distribution centers in Nebraska (two), Oklahoma (one), and Tennessee (two) and general-merchandise distribution centers in Tennessee and Kansas.

Introducing a "dollar" section in its stores in 2004 proved successful, leading AWG to expand the category to more than 1,000 food and non-food items. The following year it merged the corporate offices of its Homeland and Food 4 Less chains.

AWG took steps to expand its capacity and its territory in 2007 when it acquired a distribution center in Fort Worth from Albertsons. The cooperative also took on supply operations for Albertsons locations in Arkansas, Louisiana, and Texas.

In 2009 AWG acquired the assets of Little Rock, Arkansas-based Affiliated Foods Southwest in 2009, adding about a dozen new stores.

During 2010 the firm introduced a paperless coupon program.

In December 2011, AWG sold its corporate supermarkets to a group of employees. The corporate stores included 76 retail locations operating under the Homeland, United of Oklahoma, and Country mart banners in Oklahoma, and the Super Saver banner in northern Texas.

In late 2012 AWG completed a 35,000-square-foot addition to its corporate headquarters in Kansas City. The location is also home to AWG's Kansas City distribution centers and its Valu Merchandisers division.

Auditors : GRANT THORTON LLP KANSAS CIT

LOCATIONS

HQ: ASSOCIATED WHOLESALE GROCERS, INC.
5000 KANSAS AVE, KANSAS CITY, KS 661061135
Phone: 913 288-1000
Web: WWW.AWGINC.COM

COMPETITORS

99 CENTS ONLY STORES LLC
ASSOCIATED GROCERS OF NEW ENGLAND, INC.
C&S WHOLESALE GROCERS, INC.
FAREWAY STORES, INC.
REDNER'S MARKETS, INC.
SPARTANNASH COMPANY
SUPERVALU INC.
UNIFIED GROCERS, INC.
WAKEFERN FOOD CORP.
WEIS MARKETS, INC.

HISTORICAL FINANCIALS
Company Type: Private

Income Statement — FYE: December 31

	REVENUE ($mil)	NET INCOME ($mil)	NET PROFIT MARGIN	EMPLOYEES
12/17	9,703	199	2.1%	2,997
12/15	8,935	198	2.2%	—
12/14	8,934	226	2.5%	—
12/13	8,380	192	2.3%	—
Annual Growth	3.7%	0.8%	—	—

2017 Year-End Financials
Return on assets: 12.3% Cash ($ mil.): 166
Return on equity: 39.4%
Current Ratio: 1.20

ATHENE ANNUITY & LIFE ASSURANCE COMPANY

LOCATIONS

HQ: ATHENE ANNUITY & LIFE ASSURANCE COMPANY
2000 WADE HAMPTON BLVD, GREENVILLE, SC 296151037
Phone: 864 609-1000
Web: WWW.ATHENE.COM

HISTORICAL FINANCIALS
Company Type: Private

Income Statement — FYE: December 31

	ASSETS ($mil)	NET INCOME ($mil)	INCOME AS % OF ASSETS	EMPLOYEES
12/13	11,775	49	0.4%	120
12/12	10,481	11	0.1%	—
Annual Growth	12.3%	330.4%	—	—

ATLANTIC COAST CONFERENCE

Auditors : SHARRARD MCGEE & CO PA HIGH P

LOCATIONS

HQ: ATLANTIC COAST CONFERENCE
4512 WEYBRIDGE LN, GREENSBORO, NC 274077876
Phone: 336 854-8787
Web: WWW.THEACC.COM

HISTORICAL FINANCIALS
Company Type: Private

Income Statement — FYE: June 30

	REVENUE ($mil)	NET INCOME ($mil)	NET PROFIT MARGIN	EMPLOYEES
06/21	578	5	1.0%	42
06/20	496	(2)	—	—
06/17	418	0	0.1%	—
06/15	403	(1)	—	—
Annual Growth	6.2%	—	—	—

2021 Year-End Financials
Return on assets: 2.5% Cash ($ mil.): 2
Return on equity: 13.4%
Current Ratio: —

ATLANTIC DIVING SUPPLY, INC.

Atlantic Diving Supply (doing business as ADS) is geared toward gearing up the military. Serving agencies in the Federal Government, the company specializes in helping customers procure tactical and operational military equipment. The Company is serving the local and military diving community and Defense Logistics Agency (DLA) as a prime vendor for marine and lifesaving, diving, and search and rescue equipment. The Company holds more than 50 Indefinite Delivery, Indefinite Quantity (IDIQ) contracts and Blanket Purchase Agreement (BPAs) and has grown to be a top 5 DLA Supplier and Top 50 Federal Government Contractor.

Operations
ADS, Inc. provides equipment, procurement, logistics, and supply chain solutions. Products include apparel, nylon equipment, surveillance and sensors, robotics and aviation equipment, among others.

Geographic Reach
The company is headquartered in Virginia.

Sales and Marketing
ADS' customers are within the Department of Defense and the Federal Government, other customers are Air Force, Army and Army Reserves, Coast Guard, Marine Corps, National Guardm Navy, Space Force and U.S. Partner Nation.

EXECUTIVES

Vice Chairman*, Daniel J Clarkson
CGO*, Julie Cooke
CSO*, Mark Libonate

LOCATIONS

HQ: ATLANTIC DIVING SUPPLY, INC.
621 LYNNHVEN PKWY STE 160, VIRGINIA BEACH, VA 23452
Phone: 757 481-7758
Web: WWW.ADSINC.COM

PRODUCTS/OPERATIONS

Selected Products
Apparel
Bags, packs, and cases
Eyewear
Footwear
Hydration systems
Knives
Lighting
Medical
Tools
Training aids

COMPETITORS

BERETTA U.S.A. CORP.
DAIWA CORPORATION
HII MISSION DRIVEN INNOVATIVE SOLUTIONS INC.
LESLIE'S POOLMART, INC.
MAURICE SPORTING GOODS OF DELAWARE, INC.
MICROTECHNOLOGIES LLC
POOL CORPORATION
RAWLINGS SPORTING GOODS COMPANY, INC.
THE DAY & ZIMMERMANN GROUP INC
WILSON SPORTING GOODS CO.

HISTORICAL FINANCIALS

Company Type: Private

Income Statement — FYE: December 31

	REVENUE ($mil)	NET INCOME ($mil)	NET PROFIT MARGIN	EMPLOYEES
12/10	1,327	77	5.8%	360
12/09	938	54	5.8%	—
12/08	650	40	6.2%	—
Annual Growth	42.8%	38.7%	—	—

2010 Year-End Financials
Return on assets: 28.7%   Cash ($ mil.): 1
Return on equity: 676.2%
Current Ratio: 1.10

ATLANTIC HEALTH SYSTEM INC.

The not-for-profit Atlantic Health System (AHS) operates about dozen urgent care hospital providing general medical and surgical services to residents of northern New Jersey. Its flagship Morristown Medical Center is a nationally-recognized leader in cardiology, orthopedics, nursing, critical care and geriatrics. AHS is a member of AllSpire Health Partners ? an alliance of five hospital systems that addresses quality, population health management, best practices and medical research in the Northeast region. Atlantic Health System also has medical school affiliation with the Sidney Kimmel Medical College at Thomas Jefferson University, and is the official health care partner of the New York Jets.

Operations

Atlantic Medical Group is a multispecialty physician network that provides high-quality, comprehensive medical care with more than 1,000 doctors, nurse practitioners and physician assistants at more than 300 locations throughout Northern and Central New Jersey and Northeast Pennsylvania. Its integrated physician network offers an efficient, coordinated patient care experience, as well as a state-of-the art electronic medical record system that provides patients enhanced, secure access to their medical data.

Atlantic Health System is home to a regional campus of Jefferson's Sidney Kimmel Medical College (SKMC) at Morristown Medical Center and Overlook Medical Center. SKMC offers a Longitudinal Integrated Clerkship (LIC), a unique model of medical education that reinforces continuity of care and patient-centered treatment unique in northern New Jersey. With more than 250 medical residents, and several technologist and technician certificate programs, Atlantic Health is training its state's future health care professionals.

Geographic Reach

Atlantic Health System hospitals provides services to New Jersey, where it is headquartered, and surrounding areas.

Sales and Marketing

Atlantic Health System serves more than half the state of New Jersey, including about a dozen counties and about 4.9 million people.

EXECUTIVES

CDO*, Armond Kinsey
CIO*, Sylvia Romm
CIO*, Sunil Dadlani
CMO*, Eric Steinberger
Executive Vice President COS*, Scott Leighty
Auditors : PRICEWATERHOUSECOOPERS LLP FL

LOCATIONS

HQ: ATLANTIC HEALTH SYSTEM INC.
475 SOUTH ST, MORRISTOWN, NJ 079606459
Phone: 973 660-3100
Web: WWW.ATLANTICHEALTH.ORG

PRODUCTS/OPERATIONS

Selected Operations
Atlantic Home Care
Atlantic Hospice
Atlantic Neuroscience Institute (Overlook Hospital)
Carol G. Simon Cancer Center (Morristown and Overlook hospitals)
Chilton Medical Center
Gagnon Cardiovascular Institute (Morristown Hospital)
Goryeb Children's Hospital
Morristown Medical Center
Newton Medical Center
Overlook Medical Center

COMPETITORS

ASCENSION PROVIDENCE HOSPITAL
CENTRASTATE HEALTHCARE SYSTEM INC
CONEMAUGH HEALTH COMPANY, LLC
HOSPITAL SERVICE DISTRICT 1
KENNEDY HEALTH SYSTEM, INC.
MARSHFIELD CLINIC HEALTH SYSTEM, INC.
PHELPS MEMORIAL HOSPITAL ASSOCIATION
PITT COUNTY MEMORIAL HOSPITAL, INCORPORATED
SHELBY COUNTY HEALTH CARE CORPORATION
YORK HOSPITAL

HISTORICAL FINANCIALS

Company Type: Private

Income Statement — FYE: December 31

	REVENUE ($mil)	NET INCOME ($mil)	NET PROFIT MARGIN	EMPLOYEES
12/19	3,163	476	15.0%	3,100
12/17	0	(0)	—	—
Annual Growth	8917.8%	—	—	—

2019 Year-End Financials
Return on assets: 11.0%   Cash ($ mil.): 465
Return on equity: 19.8%
Current Ratio: 2.10

ATLANTICARE REGIONAL MEDICAL CENTER

LOCATIONS

HQ: ATLANTICARE REGIONAL MEDICAL CENTER
65 W JIMMIE LEEDS RD, POMONA, NJ 082409102
Phone: 609 652-1000
Web: WWW.ATLANTICARE.ORG

HISTORICAL FINANCIALS

Company Type: Private

Income Statement — FYE: December 31

	REVENUE ($mil)	NET INCOME ($mil)	NET PROFIT MARGIN	EMPLOYEES
12/14	718	64	9.0%	249
12/08	560	(58)	—	—
12/05	457	51	11.3%	—
Annual Growth	5.1%	2.5%	—	—

2014 Year-End Financials
Return on assets: 6.4%   Cash ($ mil.): —
Return on equity: 14.0%
Current Ratio: 0.50

ATLAS OIL COMPANY

Auditors : ERNST & YOUNG LLP DETROIT M

LOCATIONS

HQ: ATLAS OIL COMPANY
335 E MAPLE RD STE 200, BIRMINGHAM, MI 480096314
Phone: 313 292-5500
Web: WWW.ATLASOIL.COM

HISTORICAL FINANCIALS
Company Type: Private

Income Statement　　　　　　　　　　　FYE: December 31

	REVENUE ($mil)	NET INCOME ($mil)	NET PROFIT MARGIN	EMPLOYEES
12/08	1,153	1	0.1%	453
12/07	717	1	0.1%	—
12/06	617	0	0.1%	—
Annual Growth	36.7%	99.7%	—	—

2008 Year-End Financials
Return on assets: 1.6%　　Cash ($ mil.): 3
Return on equity: 8.6%
Current Ratio: 1.00

ATLAS WORLD GROUP, INC.

Willing to carry the weight of a moving world, agent-owned Atlas World Group is the holding company for Atlas Van Lines, one of the largest moving companies in the US. Atlas Van Lines' more than 500 agents transport household goods domestically and between the US and Canada; it also offers specialized transportation of items such as trade show exhibits, fine art, and electronics. Atlas Van Lines International provides international corporate relocation and freight forwarding services. Its Atlas Canada unit moves household goods in that country while American Red Ball International specializes in military relocations and serves van lines outside Atlas' network.

Operations
Atlas World Group oversees a family of companies that deliver transportation and related services globally through a network agents and select service partners. Several of its key locations are concentrated in Evansville, Indiana.

Strategy
The company continues to grow by adding offices and regional moving agents. In 2013 Atlantic Relocation Systems, the second largest agency group within the Atlas Van Lines' US network, expanded both its national footprint as well as its local service area in Colorado by opening a new office in Colorado Springs.

Auditors : ERNST & YOUNG LLP INDIANAPOL

LOCATIONS
HQ: ATLAS WORLD GROUP, INC.
　1212 SAINT GEORGE RD, EVANSVILLE, IN 477112364
Phone: 812 424-2222
Web: WWW.ATLASWORLDGROUPINC.COM

PRODUCTS/OPERATIONS
Selected Companies
American Red Ball International (international freight forwarding)
American Vanpac Carriers (international freight forwarding)
Atlas Terminal Company (relocation-related supplies and equipment)
Atlas Van Lines (transportation services)
Atlas Van Lines (Canada) (transportation services)
Atlas Van Lines International (transportation services)
Atlas World Class Travel (travel agency)
Avail Move Management (management programs)
AWG Logistics (transportation, warehousing and distribution)
Cornerstone Relocation Group (relocation services)
Smart Move Transportation (containerized shipping)
Titan Global Distribution (logistics)

COMPETITORS
ACE RELOCATION SYSTEMS, INC.
ATLAS VAN LINES, INC.
HELLMANN WORLDWIDE LOGISTICS, INC.
PANALPINA, INC.
PICKFORDS LIMITED
PITT-OHIO EXPRESS, LLC
STEVENS TRANSPORT, INC.
UNIGROUP, INC.
UNITED VAN LINES, LLC
VAN WHEATON LINES INC

HISTORICAL FINANCIALS
Company Type: Private

Income Statement　　　　　　　　　　　FYE: December 31

	REVENUE ($mil)	NET INCOME ($mil)	NET PROFIT MARGIN	EMPLOYEES
12/21	973	16	1.7%	726
12/20	805	8	1.0%	—
12/19	906	9	1.1%	—
12/18	900	10	1.1%	—
Annual Growth	2.6%	18.8%	—	—

2021 Year-End Financials
Return on assets: 5.9%　　Cash ($ mil.): 17
Return on equity: 10.9%
Current Ratio: 2.00

ATMEL CORPORATION

Atmel is a leading maker of microcontrollers, which are used in a wide range of products, from computers and mobile devices (smartphones, tablets, e-readers) to automobile motor control systems, television remote controls, and solid-state lighting. In addition, the company offers touchscreen controllers and sensors, nonvolatile memory devices, and radio frequency (RF) and wireless components. Its chips are used worldwide in consumer, communications, industrial, military, and networking applications. Most of Atmel's sales come from customers outside the US. In mid-2016 the company was bought by Microchip, a chip maker, for $3.6 billion.

Operations
In 2014 Atmel realigned its business segments for allocation of resources and focus on core its markets. The company created the Multi-Market and Other segment while eliminating the former Application Specific Integrated Circuit (ASIC) segment.

But it's the Microcontroller segment that leads the way for Atmel, accounting for 70% of the company's sales. The segment includes Atmel's general purpose microcontroller and microprocessor families, AVR 8-bit and 32-bit products, SMART ARM-based products, Atmel's 8051 8-bit products, and designated commercial wireless products, including low power radio and SOC products.

The Nonvolatile Memory segment, 12% of sales, includes electrically erasable programmable read-only, erasable programmable read-only memory ('EPROM') devices and secure cryptographic products. The Automotive segment, 11%, makes devices for automotive electronics, including products using radio frequency technology. The new segment, Multi-Market and Other, is 7% of sales, and includes application specific and standard products for aerospace applications and legacy products.

Geographic Reach
The company generates about 60% of its sales from Asia, including about a third from China and Hong Kong. After China and Hong Kong, the US is Atmel's largest market, accounting for 15% of sales with sales in Germany at 14%.

Sales and Marketing
Atmel markets its products to original equipment manufacturers (OEMs) via a direct sales force, as well as through distribution partners; each method accounts for about half of revenue. Arrow Electronics and Samsung Electronics each account for more than 10% of sales.

End-market customers include some of the leading names in the fields of communications (Alcatel Lucent, Cisco, Ericsson), computer and consumer electronics (Acer, Dell, Motorola, Nokia), automotive (Delphi, Visteon), and military and aerospace (BAE Systems, Airbus, Honeywell, Lockheed Martin).

Financial Performance
Revenue rose 2% to $1.4 billion in 2014 from $1.39 billion in 2013, boosted by a 4% increase in microcontroller sales. The unit experienced demand from industrial, automotive, and communications markets. The addition of Newport Media, acquired in mid-2014, also abetted microcontroller revenue. Sales in the nonvolatile memory segment were up 9% for the year.

On the bottom line, Atmel went from a $22 million loss in 2013 to a $32 million profit in 2014. Profit was pushed by revenue growth as well as a lack of charges the company contended with in 2013. Cash flow from operations jumped 41% higher in 2014 to about $180 billion from $127 million in 203.

Strategy
Looking to pursue a "fab-lite" strategy of streamlining existing facilities and relying more on silicon foundries (contract manufacturers of semiconductors), Atmel has sold most of its manufacturing plants and now operates only one fab, located in Colorado. Wafer fabs are highly expensive to build and

maintain, mostly due to the cost of semiconductor production equipment, and pushing some of those costs off on the foundries, many of which have state-of-the-art plants, is attractive.

Atmel has increased the release of new products in the past three years, aiming to provide customers with high performing microcontrollers than use little power. The company has found a place for its products within the Internet of Things, the conglomeration of devices that communicate through the Internet.

The company also has pushed its line of maXTouch products for touchscreens in smartphones and tables. The products have found acceptance in automotive, consumer, and industrial markets. While that line thrives, Atmel sold its XSense line of touch sensors to UniPixel in 2015. Atmel maintained possession of the XSense patent portfolio, which it licensed to UniPixel.

With its sale to Dialog, Atmel gets access to a range of new customers within Atmel's portfolio. Dialog expects to benefit from Atmel's products primed for the Internet of Things. The combined company would have about $2.7 billion sales annually. The deal is expected to close in the 2016 first quarter.

Mergers and Acquisitions

In agreeing to be bought by Microchip, Atmel ended a deal to be purchased by Dialog. Atmel management said company shareholders would get a better return from the Microchip deal. Atmel was on the hook for a $137 million termination fee to be paid to Dialog. The Dialog offer had been valued at $4.6 billion when it was made, but the value of Atmel stock has declined since then. The Atmel-Microchip deal enables the companies to gather competitive strength with complementary technologies and products.

In 2014 Atmel acquired Newport Media Inc., a provider of advanced Wi-Fi and Bluetooth products. This acquisition expands Atmel's wireless portfolio with the addition of 802.11n Wi-Fi and Bluetooth. Those product should speed up Atmel's introduction of low-energy Bluetooth products.

HISTORY

George Perlegos -- a former Intel design engineer and co-founder of chip maker SEEQ Technology (later acquired by LSI Logic, now LSI Corp.) -- founded Atmel in 1984. (The name was short for Advanced Technology for Memory and Logic.) The enterprise started with a $30,000 investment and a $5.1 million design contract from General Instrument; it soon added military and corporate contracts. In 1991 the company went public and introduced the first three-volt flash memory.

Atmel built its business by developing fast, power-efficient chips -- perfect for portable electronics. It acquired Concurrent Logic, a maker of field-programmable gate arrays (user-programmable chips), in 1993.

One year later Atmel became the #1 producer of EEPROMs (electrically erasable programmable ROM chips) when it bought SEEQ's chip business.

To strengthen its product line, in 1995 Atmel licensed SRAM (static random-access memory) technology in an alliance with Paradigm Technology (now part of IXYS) for use in creating multimedia chips. It purchased RISC chip technology (which uses shorter instruction sets for faster processing) from Norwegian chip maker Nordic VLSI in 1996.

LOCATIONS

HQ: ATMEL CORPORATION
  1600 TECHNOLOGY DR, SAN JOSE, CA 951101382
Phone: 408 735-9110
Web: WWW.MICROCHIP.COM

2014 Sales

	$ mil.	% of total
Asia/Pacific		
China (including Hong Kong)	435.9	31
South Korea	119.9	9
Taiwan	60.6	4
Singapore	55.5	4
Japan	37.1	3
Other countries	102.6	7
Europe		
Germany	204.3	14
France	15.5	1
Other countries	139.5	10
US	211.5	15
Other regions	30.9	2
Total	**1,413.3**	**100**

PRODUCTS/OPERATIONS

2014 Sales

	$ mil.	% of total
Microcontrollers	994.1	70
Nonvolatile memory	166.7	12
Automotive	153.2	11
Multi-Market and others	99.3	7
Total	**1,413.3**	**100**

Selected Products and Applications

Application-Specific Integrated Circuits (ASICs)
  Cell-based ASICs
  Complex ASIC cores
  Gate arrays/embedded arrays
Application-Specific Standard Products (ASSPs)
  Aerospace and military
  Communications
  Cellular, corded, and cordless phones
  Internet appliances and voice over Internet Protocol (VoIP)
  Wireless datacom
  Industrial
  Industrial controls
  Power metering
  Multimedia
  Audio
  Video
  Power management
  Security and smart card
  Biometrics
  PC security
  Radio-frequency identification (RFID)
  Secure memories
  Secure microcontrollers
  USB controllers
Logic
  Field-programmable gate arrays (FPGAs)
  Programmable logic devices (PLDs)
Microcontrollers (MCUs)
  4-, 8-, 16-, and 32-bit microcontrollers

  ARM microprocessor architecture-based MCUs
  Flash MCUs
Nonvolatile Memory
  EPROMs (erasable programmable read-only memories)
  Flash memory chips
  Parallel EEPROMs (electrically erasable PROMs)
  Serial EEPROMs

COMPETITORS

ALTERA CORPORATION
AVAGO TECHNOLOGIES LIMITED
INTEL CORPORATION
IXYS, LLC
MICROCHIP TECHNOLOGY INCORPORATED
MOSYS, INC.
QUICKLOGIC CORPORATION
RAMTRON INTERNATIONAL CORPORATION
RENESAS ELECTRONICS AMERICA INC.
SEMTECH CORPORATION

HISTORICAL FINANCIALS

Company Type: Private

Income Statement FYE: December 31

	REVENUE ($mil)	NET INCOME ($mil)	NET PROFIT MARGIN	EMPLOYEES
12/14	1,413	35	2.5%	5,200
12/13	1,386	(22)	—	—
12/12	1,432	30	2.1%	—
Annual Growth	(0.7%)	7.5%	—	—

2014 Year-End Financials

Return on assets: 2.6%   Cash ($ mil.): 206
Return on equity: 4.0%
Current Ratio: 2.70

ATRIUS HEALTH, INC.

Atrius Health, an innovative nonprofit healthcare leader, delivers an effective system of connected care for adult and pediatric patients at some 30 medical practice locations in eastern Massachusetts. Atrius Health's physicians and primary care providers, along with additional clinicians, work in close collaboration with hospital partners, community specialists and skilled nursing. Atrius Health provides high-quality, patient-centered, coordinated, cost effective care to every patient it serves. Atrius Health was founded in 2004 by medical groups including Dedham Medical Associates and Harvard Vanguard Medical Associates; Granite Medical Group joined a short time later in 2005.

Operations

Atrius Health's network of doctors represent more than 50 medical specialties including primary care, oncology, cardiology and neurology. In addition to providing health care services, the company operates the Center for Clinical Research which focuses on patient-centered models of care, provider well-being and burnout prevention, health technologies, quality improvement, and implementation science.

Atrius Health has primary/tertiary hospital affiliations with Emerson Hospital, Lahey Hospital & Medical Center, Lowell General Hospital, Mount Auburn Hospital,

South Shore Hospital and Winchester Hospital. Specialty affiliations include Massachusetts Eye and Ear Infirmary, an international center for treatment and home to the world's largest vision and hearing research centers, and New England Baptist Hospital, a premier regional provider for orthopedic surgery and the treatment of musculoskeletal diseases and disorders.

Atrius Health has an affiliation with Firefly Health, a tech-enabled primary care and behavioral health provider, which enables Firefly Health to contract through Atrius Health's value-based collaboration with Blue Cross Blue Shield of Massachusetts servicing HMO and PPO patients.

Geographic Reach
Atrius Health has four locations in the City of Boston, about 30 locations in Greater Boston, and two administrative offices in Newton and Needham.

Sales and Marketing
Atrius Health accepts insurance from most major health plans, including Aetna, Blue Cross and Blue Shield of Massachusetts, CIGNA, Coventry Health Care, Harvard Pilgrim Health Care, AllWays Health Partners, and Tufts Health Plan, among others.

Company Background
Atrius Health was founded in 2004 by medical groups including Dedham Medical Associates and Harvard Vanguard Medical Associates; Granite Medical Group joined a short time later in 2005.The companies work together to coordinate care in a number of ways, including sharing an electronic medical records system. In 2015 the groups merged to create one not-for-profit group named Atrius Health. Reliant Medical Group, Southboro Medical Group, and South Shore Medical Center were no longer affiliated with the group after the transformation. In 2017, PMG Physician Associates joined Atrius Health adding seven new office locations to our practice.

Auditors : PKF PC QUINCY MA

LOCATIONS
HQ: ATRIUS HEALTH, INC.
  275 GROVE ST STE 3300, AUBURNDALE, MA 024662274
Phone: 617 559-8444
Web: WWW.ATRIUSHEALTH.ORG

PRODUCTS/OPERATIONS
Selected Specialty Affiliations
Massachusetts Eye and Ear Infirmary
New England Baptist Hospital
Selected OB/GYN Affiliations
Beth Israel Deaconess Medical Center
Beth Israel Deaconess Hospital - Milton
Emerson Hospital
Lowell General Hospital
Mount Auburn Hospital
Newton-Wellesley Hospital
South Shore Hospital
Selected Services
Allergy
Andrology
Audiology
Behavioral Health
Cardiology
Central Patient Registration
Complex Chronic Care Program
Cosmetic Dermatology
Dermatology
Developmental and Behavioral Pediatrics
Ear, Nose, & Throat
Endocrinology
Endoscopy
Eye Care
Family Medicine
Fertility & Reproductive Health
Gastroenterology
Genetics
Geriatrics
Hematology/Oncology
Imaging/Radiology
Infectious Disease
Internal Medicine
Interpreter Services
Laboratory
Medical Billing
Medical Records
Minimally-Invasive GYN Surgery
Nephrology
Neurology
Nutrition
Obstetrics/Gynecology
Occupational
Hand Therapy
Orthopedics & Sports Medicine
Pain Management
Palliative Care
Pediatrics
Pharmacy
Physical Therapy
Podiatry
Pulmonology
Rheumatology
Speech and Language Therapy
Surgery
Travel Medicine
Urgent Care
Urology
Weight Management/HMR® Program

COMPETITORS
ALEGENT CREIGHTON HEALTH
ASCENSION VIA CHRISTI HEALTH, INC
AULTMAN HEALTH FOUNDATION
BOSTON MEDICAL CENTER CORPORATION
HEALTH PARTNERS PLANS, INC.
INTERMOUNTAIN HEALTH CARE, INC.
LEHIGH VALLEY HEALTH NETWORK, INC.
MARSHFIELD CLINIC, INC.
MINISTRY HEALTH CARE, INC.
SWEDISH HEALTH SERVICES

HISTORICAL FINANCIALS
Company Type: Private

Income Statement — FYE: December 31

	REVENUE ($mil)	NET INCOME ($mil)	NET PROFIT MARGIN	EMPLOYEES
12/19	2,167	5	0.3%	3,906
12/17	1,872	39	2.1%	—
12/15	1,577	(28)	—	—
12/14	28	(0)	—	—
Annual Growth	137.6%	—	—	—

2019 Year-End Financials
Return on assets: 0.6%   Cash ($ mil.): 174
Return on equity: 2.1%
Current Ratio: 0.80

ATTORNEY GENERAL, TEXAS

The Office of the Attorney General of Texas defends the state Constitution, represents the state in litigation, and approves public bond issues. The office is legal counsel to state government boards and agencies and issues legal opinions when requested by the Governor and agency heads. The Attorney General also sits as an ex-officio member of state committees and commissions and defends state laws and suits against agencies and state employees. Other roles include enforcing health, safety, and consumer regulations; protecting elderly and disabled residents' rights; collecting court-ordered child support; and administering the Crime Victims' Compensation Fund. Greg Abbott was elected Attorney General in 2002.

LOCATIONS
HQ: ATTORNEY GENERAL, TEXAS
  300 W 15TH ST, AUSTIN, TX 787011649
Phone: 512 475-4375
Web: WWW.TEXASATTORNEYGENERAL.GOV

COMPETITORS
CRIMINAL DIVISION
STATE PUBLIC DEFENDER, CALIFORNIA OFFICE OF THE
TRUSTEE PROGRAM, UNITED STATES
UNITED STATES ATTORNEYS, EXECUTIVE OFFICE FOR
UNITED STATES DEPARTMENT OF JUSTICE

HISTORICAL FINANCIALS
Company Type: Private

Income Statement — FYE: August 31

	REVENUE ($mil)	NET INCOME ($mil)	NET PROFIT MARGIN	EMPLOYEES
08/16	659	45	6.8%	4,200
08/15	561	8	1.5%	—
08/14	571	(6)	—	—
08/06	0	0	—	—
Annual Growth	—	—	—	—

2016 Year-End Financials
Return on assets: 13.1%   Cash ($ mil.): 87
Return on equity: 16.5%
Current Ratio: 4.20

AU HEALTH SYSTEM, INC.

LOCATIONS
HQ: AU HEALTH SYSTEM, INC.
  1120 15TH ST B8255, AUGUSTA, GA 309120004
Phone: 706 721-9439
Web: WWW.AUGUSTAHEALTH.ORG

HISTORICAL FINANCIALS
Company Type: Private

Income Statement   FYE: June 30

	REVENUE ($mil)	NET INCOME ($mil)	NET PROFIT MARGIN	EMPLOYEES
06/20	955	(4)	—	99
06/19	866	(36)	—	—
Annual Growth	10.3%	—	—	—

2020 Year-End Financials
Return on assets: (-0.6%)   Cash ($ mil.): 154
Return on equity: (-1.6%)
Current Ratio: 1.50

AUBURN UNIVERSITY

Most of us bleed red, but students and alumni of this university bleed auburn. One of the largest schools in the South, Auburn University has an enrollment of more than 30,000 students on two campuses and offers bachelors, master's, and doctoral degrees in more than 140 different fields of study through about a dozen colleges and schools. Fields of study include agriculture, business, education, construction, forestry, and mathematics and science, as well as medical fields including nursing, pharmacy, and veterinary medicine. Auburn has 1,200 faculty members and a student-to-teacher ratio of 18:1.

Operations
Unique research institutes at Auburn include the Space Research Institute, the National Center for Asphalt Technology, the Alabama Agricultural Experiment Station, and the Canine and Detection Research Institute.

Geographic Reach
Auburn's main campus is in Auburn, Alabama. The university also has a branch campus in Montgomery, Alabama. More than 800 students participate in the university's study abroad programs each year.

Financial Performance
Auburn reported a 5% rise in revenues to some $602 million in 2012 due to increased income from tuition and fees, state and local grants and contracts, and sales and services from educational departments. Net income fell 12% to $87 million in 2012, however, due to higher operating expenses from benefits and compensation, as well as due to the absence of federal stimulus funds (streamed through the state during 2011).

Company Background
Auburn was founded by the Alabama Conference of the Methodist Episcopal Church in 1856 as the East Alabama Male College. It became a state land-grant institution in 1872 (known as the Agricultural and Mechanical College of Alabama) and adopted its current name in 1960. The university is governed by a board of trustees appointed by the Alabama governor.

Auditors: PRICEWATERHOUSECOOPERS LLP BI

LOCATIONS

HQ: AUBURN UNIVERSITY
107 SAMFORD HALL, AUBURN, AL 368490001
Phone: 334 844-4650
Web: WWW.AUBURN.EDU

PRODUCTS/OPERATIONS

Selected Colleges and Schools
College of Agriculture
College of Architecture, Design and Construction
College of Business
College of Education
College of Human Sciences
College of Liberal Arts
College of Sciences and Mathematics
College of Veterinary Medicine
Graduate School
Harrison School of Pharmacy
Honors College
Samuel Ginn College of Engineering
School of Forestry and Wildlife Sciences
School of Nursing

COMPETITORS

DELAWARE STATE UNIVERSITY
MARSHALL UNIVERSITY
MICHIGAN STATE UNIVERSITY
MISSOURI STATE UNIVERSITY
MONTANA STATE UNIVERSITY, INC
NORTH CAROLINA STATE UNIVERSITY
RECTOR & VISITORS OF THE UNIVERSITY OF VIRGINIA
THE UNIVERSITY OF MEMPHIS
UNIVERSITY OF ARKANSAS SYSTEM
UNIVERSITY OF OKLAHOMA

HISTORICAL FINANCIALS
Company Type: Private

Income Statement   FYE: September 30

	REVENUE ($mil)	NET INCOME ($mil)	NET PROFIT MARGIN	EMPLOYEES
09/21*	975	225	23.2%	6,000
12/20	5	0	6.3%	—
09/20	888	109	12.3%	—
09/19	897	78	8.8%	—
Annual Growth	4.2%	69.2%	—	—

*Fiscal year change

2021 Year-End Financials
Return on assets: 4.8%   Cash ($ mil.): 181
Return on equity: 14.1%
Current Ratio: 0.90

AUGUSTANA HEALTH CARE CENTER OF APPLE VALLEY

LOCATIONS

HQ: AUGUSTANA HEALTH CARE CENTER OF APPLE VALLEY
14650 GARRETT AVE, SAINT PAUL, MN 551247543
Phone: 952 431-7700
Web: WWW.APPLEVALLEYCAMPUS.ORG

HISTORICAL FINANCIALS
Company Type: Private

Income Statement   FYE: September 30

	REVENUE ($mil)	NET INCOME ($mil)	NET PROFIT MARGIN	EMPLOYEES
09/09	1,505	30	2.0%	280
09/05	6	(0)	—	—
Annual Growth	287.7%	—	—	—

2009 Year-End Financials
Return on assets: 162.5%   Cash ($ mil.): 1
Return on equity: 784.9%
Current Ratio: 3.10

AURORA HEALTH CARE METRO, INC

LOCATIONS

HQ: AURORA HEALTH CARE METRO, INC
2900 W OKLAHOMA AVE, MILWAUKEE, WI 532154330
Phone: 414 649-6000
Web: WWW.AURORAHEALTHCARE.ORG

HISTORICAL FINANCIALS
Company Type: Private

Income Statement   FYE: December 31

	REVENUE ($mil)	NET INCOME ($mil)	NET PROFIT MARGIN	EMPLOYEES
12/17	1,428	141	9.9%	4,000
12/16	1,416	164	11.6%	—
Annual Growth	0.8%	(14.0%)	—	—

2017 Year-End Financials
Return on assets: 5.4%   Cash ($ mil.): 1,804
Return on equity: 6.2%
Current Ratio: 19.70

AURORA HEALTH CARE, INC.

Auditors: DELOITTE & TOUCHE LLP MILWAUK

LOCATIONS

HQ: AURORA HEALTH CARE, INC.
750 W VIRGINIA ST, MILWAUKEE, WI 532041539
Phone: 800 326-2250
Web: WWW.AURORAHEALTHCARE.ORG

HISTORICAL FINANCIALS
Company Type: Private

Income Statement — FYE: December 31

	REVENUE ($mil)	NET INCOME ($mil)	NET PROFIT MARGIN	EMPLOYEES
12/17	5,334	437	8.2%	30,000
12/16	5,124	385	7.5%	—
12/15	4,930	428	8.7%	—
Annual Growth	4.0%	1.1%	—	—

2017 Year-End Financials
Return on assets: 7.7%   Cash ($ mil.): 192
Return on equity: 14.4%
Current Ratio: 3.50

AUSTIN INDEPENDENT SCHOOL DISTRICT (INC)

Auditors: RSM US LLP AUSTIN TEXAS

LOCATIONS
HQ: AUSTIN INDEPENDENT SCHOOL DISTRICT (INC)
4000 S IH 35 FRONTAGE RD, AUSTIN, TX 78704
Phone: 512 414-1700
Web: WWW.AUSTINISD.ORG

HISTORICAL FINANCIALS
Company Type: Private

Income Statement — FYE: June 30

	REVENUE ($mil)	NET INCOME ($mil)	NET PROFIT MARGIN	EMPLOYEES
06/21	1,788	(6)	—	9,200
06/20	1,670	(343)	—	—
06/19	1,703	208	12.3%	—
06/18	1,534	(117)	—	—
Annual Growth	5.3%	—	—	—

2021 Year-End Financials
Return on assets: (-0.2%)   Cash ($ mil.): 16
Return on equity: (-5.2%)
Current Ratio: —

AVANT GARDE ACADEMY FOUNDATION, INC.

LOCATIONS
HQ: AVANT GARDE ACADEMY FOUNDATION, INC.
600 SE 3RD AVE, FORT LAUDERDALE, FL 333013125
Phone: 754 321-0000
Web: WWW.BROWARDSCHOOLS.COM

HISTORICAL FINANCIALS
Company Type: Private

Income Statement — FYE: June 30

	REVENUE ($mil)	NET INCOME ($mil)	NET PROFIT MARGIN	EMPLOYEES
06/16	2,630	(37)	—	31,174
06/15	2,536	186	7.3%	—
06/11	2,515	(37)	—	—
Annual Growth	0.9%	—	—	—

2016 Year-End Financials
Return on assets: (-0.9%)   Cash ($ mil.): 671
Return on equity: (-6.4%)
Current Ratio: 1.50

AVAYA HOLDINGS CORP.

Avaya provides software and equipment for contact centers, unified communications, and workflow automation. The company's software, offered via the cloud, and hardware products provide workers with one place for communicating with colleagues and customers. Avaya's customers range from small and medium-sized businesses and organizations to Fortune 100 companies in financial services, hospital, government, and other industries. More than half of its sales are to customers in the US. A descendant company of the old AT&T, Avaya still sells phones, but has shifted to sell mostly software and services.

Operations
Avaya operates in two segments, Product & Solutions, more than 40% of revenue, and Services, about 60% of revenue. Products & Solutions primarily develops, markets, and sells unified communications and contact center solutions, offered on premises, in the cloud, or as a hybrid solution. These integrate multiple forms of communications includes telephony, email, instant messaging and video.

Services segment consists of three business areas: Global Support Services, Enterprise Cloud and Managed Services and Professional Services. Global Support Services provide offerings that address the risk of system outages and help businesses protect their technology investments. Enterprise Cloud and Managed Services enable customers to take advantage of technology via the cloud, on premises, or a hybrid of both. Professional Services enable businesses worldwide to take full advantage of their IT and communications solution investments.

The company relies on third-party contract manufacturers, component suppliers and partners (some of which are sole source and limited source suppliers) and warehousing and distribution logistics providers.

Geographic Reach
Avaya is based in Santa Clara, California and has operations in about 60 countries. It has about a dozen research and development facilities in Canada, Czech Republic, India, Ireland, Italy and the US.

About 55% of Avaya's sales were generated in the US, and more than 25% came from Europe. Asia Pacific contributed over 10% of the company's sales, while the Americas outside of US accounted for almost 10% of the sales.

Sales and Marketing
About 70% of Avaya's sales are brokered through over 4,000 channel partners while its direct sales staff is responsible for the remaining sales. The company's customers are in financial services, manufacturing, retail, transportation, energy, media and communications, hospitality, health care, education, and government.

Avaya serves its customers directly with the company, or through its sales channel, which includes its global network of channel alliance partners, distributors, dealers, value-added resellers, telecommunications service providers and system integrators. The company's sales organizations are equipped with a broad product and software portfolio, complemented with services offerings including product support, integration and other professional services, and Enterprise Cloud and Managed Services.

Avaya's advertising expenses were $39 million, $27 million, and $53 million for 2019, 2018 and 2017, respectively.

Financial Performance
Avaya's had a rough time financially in recent years. Revenue stood at $4.1 billion in 2015, but tumbled, year by year, to $2.9 billion in 2019 (ended September), with a stop in Chapter 11 bankruptcy along the way. In the past five years, 2018 is the only year the company managed to post a profit, as it fell to a loss again in 2019.

In 2019 (ended September), revenue remained virtually unchanged at $2.9 billion, only increasing by about $36 million. The increase was primarily driven by a lower impact of applying fresh start accounting upon emergence from bankruptcy, which was partially offset by lower demand for Avaya's unified communications and contact center products, lower professional services revenue, a decline in maintenance services revenue, and the unfavorable impact of foreign currency exchange rates.

Net loss was $671 million for fiscal 2019 compared to a net income of $3.3 billion for fiscal 2018 as a result of a $473 million operating loss, a $659 million impairment charge, higher amortization of intangible assets due to the application of fresh start accounting upon the emergence from bankruptcy, and from costs incurred in connection with certain legal matters of $37 million for fiscal 2018.

Avaya held $756 million in cash and cash

equivalents at the end of fiscal 2019. Its operating activities provided $241 million. While investing activities used $124 million, mostly for capital expenditures. Financing activities used another $61 million for debt repayments, acquisition-related payments, and payments related to sale-leaseback transactions.

Strategy

Avaya believes it is well-positioned to capitalize on the disruption and opportunity presented by digital transformation to create long-term sustainable value. It is investing significantly in its people and technology and has established four strategic pillars: innovate in its core business solutions; bring emerging technologies to market; deliver breadth and depth of cloud; and deliver high-value services.

Avaya is integrating artificial intelligence capabilities, chatbot and virtual assistance, machine learning, security, and mobility into its products. In 2020, Avaya announced the global expansion and general availability of Avaya Cloud Office in Australia, Canada, and the UK along with the availability of several key features and capabilities including tools to help migrate customers more efficiently and effectively.

It also signed Master Agent agreements with Tradewinds Brokerage and Westcon. Avaya's agreement with Tradewinds extended its brokerage portfolio with the new Avaya Cloud Office, alongside Avaya's open SIP, multi-platform devices plus professional services. Meanwhile Westcon intends to build on the successful launch of Avaya Cloud Office in the UK, by both enabling its partner community and creating end user demand in the Irish market.

Furthermore, Avaya has secured over 120,000 subscription seats from Teleperformance. Avaya has worked with Teleperformance since early 2020, only now it supports Teleperformance's global footprint, helping to modernize its customer's communications environment. The new three-year subscription spans all world regions.

Mergers and Acquisitions

Avaya acquired Spoken Communications, a developer of cloud-based contact center tools using artificial intelligence, for $172 million. Avaya integrated Spoken technologies in its offerings.

EXECUTIVES

CRO, Eric Koza
CPO, Anthony F Bartolo
CAO, Kevin Speed
Auditors : PRICEWATERHOUSECOOPERS LLP NE

LOCATIONS

HQ: AVAYA HOLDINGS CORP.
 2605 MERIDIAN PKWY # 200, DURHAM, NC 277135253
Phone: 908 953-6000
Web: WWW.AVAYA.COM

COMPETITORS

ACI WORLDWIDE, INC.
ARIBA, INC.
ARRIS GROUP, INC.
ASURE SOFTWARE, INC.
BRAVOSOLUTION US, INC.
CERIDIAN LLC
MICRO FOCUS SOFTWARE INC.
Nortel Networks Limited
SS&C TECHNOLOGIES HOLDINGS, INC.
WILHELMINA INTERNATIONAL, INC.

HISTORICAL FINANCIALS
Company Type: Private

Income Statement — FYE: September 30

	REVENUE ($mil)	NET INCOME ($mil)	NET PROFIT MARGIN	EMPLOYEES
09/15	4,081	(168)	—	8,063
09/14	4,371	(253)	—	—
09/13	4,708	(376)	—	—
09/11	5,547	(863)	—	—
Annual Growth	(7.4%)	—	—	—

2015 Year-End Financials
Return on assets: (-2.5%)   Cash ($ mil.): 323
Return on equity: —
Current Ratio: 0.80

AVERITT EXPRESS, INC.

Small loads add up at Averitt Express. The company provides less-than-truckload (LTL) freight transportation service. (LTL carriers combine freight from multiple shippers into a single trailer.) . Averitt Express directly serves the southern US and Mexico, and it provides service elsewhere in North America through partnerships with other carriers such as Lakeville Motor Express and DATS. The company also offers truckload and expedited freight transportation, along with logistics, warehousing, and international freight forwarding.

Geographic Reach

Averitt Express has a total of about 100 facilities that serve thousands of points throughout the Southern US (in around 20 states), Canada, Mexico, and the Caribbean.

Auditors : CARR RIGGS & INGRAM LLC COOK

LOCATIONS

HQ: AVERITT EXPRESS, INC.
 1415 NEAL ST, COOKEVILLE, TN 385014328
Phone: 931 526-3306
Web: WWW.AVERITT.COM

PRODUCTS/OPERATIONS

Selected Services

Cross-border/domestic offshore (Canada, Mexico, Puerto Rico/Virgin Islands)
Dedicated
Expedited
Intermodal
International ocean/air (ocean/air, Asia-Memphis Express)
LTL (regional, nationwide, distribution/consolidation)
Portside
Retail specialized services
Transportation management
Truckload (dry van, flatbed, brokerage)
Warehousing

COMPETITORS

A. DUIE PYLE INC.
BEKINS HOLDING CORP.
BELTMANN GROUP INCORPORATED
FREIGHTQUOTE.COM, INC.
PRK CORPORATION PTY LTD
SANKYU INC.
THE SUDDATH COMPANIES
TRANSPLACE TEXAS, LP
TTS, LLC
UPS GROUND FREIGHT, INC.

HISTORICAL FINANCIALS
Company Type: Private

Income Statement — FYE: December 31

	REVENUE ($mil)	NET INCOME ($mil)	NET PROFIT MARGIN	EMPLOYEES
12/21	1,531	142	9.3%	16,708
12/20	1,204	77	6.4%	—
12/18	1,292	77	6.0%	—
12/16	1,088	45	4.1%	—
Annual Growth	7.1%	26.0%	—	—

2021 Year-End Financials
Return on assets: 10.1%   Cash ($ mil.): 344
Return on equity: 12.7%
Current Ratio: 5.40

AVERITT INCORPORATED

Auditors : DUNCAN WHEELER & WILKERSON P

LOCATIONS

HQ: AVERITT INCORPORATED
 1415 NEAL ST, COOKEVILLE, TN 385014328
Phone: 931 526-3306
Web: WWW.AVERITT.COM

HISTORICAL FINANCIALS
Company Type: Private

Income Statement — FYE: December 31

	REVENUE ($mil)	NET INCOME ($mil)	NET PROFIT MARGIN	EMPLOYEES
12/18	1,292	86	6.7%	16,708
12/17	1,157	93	8.1%	—
12/16	1,097	52	4.8%	—
12/15	1,104	52	4.8%	—
Annual Growth	5.4%	17.7%	—	—

2018 Year-End Financials
Return on assets: 7.6%   Cash ($ mil.): 96
Return on equity: 9.9%
Current Ratio: 3.20

AVI-SPL HOLDINGS, INC.

Auditors: ERNST & YOUNG LLP TAMPA FL

LOCATIONS

HQ: AVI-SPL HOLDINGS, INC.
6301 BENJAMIN RD STE 101, TAMPA, FL 336345115
Phone: 866 708-5034
Web: WWW.AVISPL.COM

HISTORICAL FINANCIALS
Company Type: Private

Income Statement				FYE: December 31
	REVENUE ($mil)	NET INCOME ($mil)	NET PROFIT MARGIN	EMPLOYEES
12/11	555	5	1.1%	4,936
12/10	505	(0)	0.0%	—
12/09	421	3	0.7%	—
Annual Growth	14.8%	38.5%	—	—

2011 Year-End Financials
Return on assets: 1.8%   Cash ($ mil.): 2
Return on equity: 4.2%
Current Ratio: 1.50

AVIO INC.

LOCATIONS

HQ: AVIO INC.
270 SYLVAN AVE STE 130, ENGLEWOOD CLIFFS, NJ 076322545
Phone: 201 816-2720

HISTORICAL FINANCIALS
Company Type: Private

Income Statement				FYE: December 31
	REVENUE ($mil)	NET INCOME ($mil)	NET PROFIT MARGIN	EMPLOYEES
12/12	1,310	7	0.6%	34
12/05	293	0	0.2%	—
12/04	387	8	2.1%	—
12/03	(1,817)	0	0.0%	—
Annual Growth	—	—	—	—

2012 Year-End Financials
Return on assets: 12.3%   Cash ($ mil.): 42
Return on equity: 0.6%
Current Ratio: 0.60

AXEL JOHNSON INC.

The Johnson family of Stockholm, Sweden, has an investment arm that stretches across the ocean. Axel Johnson owns and operates North American businesses on behalf of the Johnson dynasty. The investment firm focuses on several industries, such as energy, medical device manufacturing, and water treatment. Its portfolio includes Sprague Energy, Parkson Corp., and Kinetico Incorporated. Axel Johnson's companies boast about $4 billion in annual revenues. Axel Johnson, along with Axel Johnson AB, and AXFast are all affiliated with Sweden-based Axel Johnson Group but are independent. Established in 1873, the Johnson family of companies is in its fourth generation of family ownership.

Operations

Axel Johnson, which was formed in 1920, is a long-term investor that typically holds on to its companies for about 20 years. Some companies have been a part of Axel Johnson's portfolio for more than 40 years. Two of its holdings, Parkson and Kinetico, are part of Axel Johnson's AxWater Group, which was formed in 2000.

Financial Performance

Following the economic downturn, the company has seen sales increase for several years. Axel Johnson's revenue rose by 6% in 2012 to $4.2 billion as compared to 2011. Energy product sales generated the largest portion of the company's revenue. The results were powered by higher commodity prices and growth at Kinetico, Cadence, and Mountain Lumber; the first two, along with ConforMis and Walk2Campus, reported record sales in 2012.

Strategy

Through NewtrAX, Axel Johnson makes minority investments in smaller businesses. NewtrAX has stakes in Cadence, a manufacturer of cutting and piercing instruments used for the medical and industrial applications. It also owns portions of wood reclamation company Mountain Lumber Co., and Walk2Campus, a real estate management and acquisition company. The company in late 2011 invested some $15 million in ConforMIS, which develops and markets customized medical devices for the treatment of osteoarthritis and joint damage.

Auditors: ERNST & YOUNG LLP NEW YORK N

LOCATIONS

HQ: AXEL JOHNSON INC.
155 SPRING ST FL 6, NEW YORK, NY 100125254
Phone: 646 291-2445
Web: WWW.AXELJOHNSON.COM

PRODUCTS/OPERATIONS

Selected Portfolio Companies
Cadence Incorporated
ConforMIS, Inc.
Decisyon, Inc.
Kinetico Incorporated
Mountain Lumber Company
Parkson Corporation
Sprague Energy Corp.
Walk2Campus Holdings, LLC

COMPETITORS

ALON USA ENERGY, INC.
Axel Johnson AB
CITGO PETROLEUM CORPORATION
LANGLEY HOLDINGS PLC
MARTIN MIDSTREAM PARTNERS L.P.
MATTHEWS INTERNATIONAL CORPORATION
MIDSTREAM MAGELLAN PARTNERS L P
SOUTHERN COUNTIES OIL CO.
U.S. VENTURE, INC.
WORLD POINT TERMINALS, LP

HISTORICAL FINANCIALS
Company Type: Private

Income Statement				FYE: December 31
	REVENUE ($mil)	NET INCOME ($mil)	NET PROFIT MARGIN	EMPLOYEES
12/10	2,982	15	0.5%	1,200
12/09	2,598	11	0.5%	—
12/08	4,312	8	0.2%	—
Annual Growth	(16.8%)	35.5%	—	—

2010 Year-End Financials
Return on assets: 1.4%   Cash ($ mil.): 9
Return on equity: 5.2%
Current Ratio: 1.70

AXOS BANK

EXECUTIVES

REGLT, Tom Constantine

LOCATIONS

HQ: AXOS BANK
4350 LA JOLLA VILLAGE DR # 100, SAN DIEGO, CA 921221244
Phone: 858 350-6200
Web: WWW.AXOSBANK.COM

HISTORICAL FINANCIALS
Company Type: Private

Income Statement				FYE: December 31
	ASSETS ($mil)	NET INCOME ($mil)	INCOME AS % OF ASSETS	EMPLOYEES
12/17	8,908	150	1.7%	102
12/16	8,162	137	1.7%	—
12/15	6,656	104	1.6%	—
12/14	5,190	71	1.4%	—
Annual Growth	19.7%	28.1%	—	—

2017 Year-End Financials
Return on assets: 1.7%   Cash ($ mil.): 617
Return on equity: 17.3%
Current Ratio: —

B.L. HARBERT HOLDINGS, L.L.C.

EXECUTIVES

CAO, James Stewart
Risk Management Vice-President, William Lalor
Auditors: CROWE HORWATH LLP ATLANTA GE

LOCATIONS

HQ: B.L. HARBERT HOLDINGS, L.L.C.
820 SHADES CREEK PKWY # 3000, BIRMINGHAM, AL 352094564

HOOVER'S HANDBOOK OF PRIVATE COMPANIES 2023

Phone: 205 802-2800
Web: WWW.BLHARBERT.COM

HISTORICAL FINANCIALS
Company Type: Private

Income Statement				FYE: December 31
	REVENUE ($mil)	NET INCOME ($mil)	NET PROFIT MARGIN	EMPLOYEES
12/14	807	53	6.7%	2,000
12/05	361	0	0.0%	—
12/04	203	0	0.0%	—
Annual Growth	14.8%	—	—	—

2014 Year-End Financials
Return on assets: 6.8% Cash ($ mil.): 191
Return on equity: 6.7%
Current Ratio: 0.60

BAKERSFIELD MEMORIAL HOSPITAL

Auditors: KPMG LLP SAN FRANCISCO CA

LOCATIONS

HQ: BAKERSFIELD MEMORIAL HOSPITAL
420 34TH ST, BAKERSFIELD, CA 933012237
Phone: 661 327-1792
Web: WWW.DIGNITYHEALTH.ORG

HISTORICAL FINANCIALS
Company Type: Private

Income Statement				FYE: June 30
	REVENUE ($mil)	NET INCOME ($mil)	NET PROFIT MARGIN	EMPLOYEES
06/20	540	16	3.0%	1,100
06/16	401	19	4.8%	—
06/15	423	71	16.9%	—
06/14	373	45	12.1%	—
Annual Growth	6.4%	(15.4%)	—	—

2020 Year-End Financials
Return on assets: 2.2% Cash ($ mil.): 75
Return on equity: 2.8%
Current Ratio: 1.70

BALFOUR BEATTY CONSTRUCTION GROUP, INC.

Balfour Beatty Construction is deep in the heart of Texas -- and beyond. The company provides start-to-finish project management, pre-construction, and related services for commercial construction projects. Offerings include site evaluation and analysis, general contracting, cost consulting, process equipment installation, turnkey medical facility development, capital equipment planning, and closeout services. The company works on a range of facilities including hotels, office buildings, civic centers, airports, hospitals, schools, public buildings, and retail locations. UK firm Balfour Beatty plc acquired the company, then named Centex Construction, from Centex Corp. in 2007.

Operations
Balfour Beatty Construction ranks as the fifth largest general builder in the US. The firm is also active in the construction services, infrastructure investment, and professionals and support services markets.

Geographic Reach
Dallas-based Balfour Beatty Construction has locations in the West, Mid-Atlantic, and Southeast.

Strategy
The US arm of the international infrastructure group, Balfour Beatty Construction is poised to profit from the recovery of the US economy. Indeed, the US market has seen a quicker return to growth that its UK counterpart, with more private and complex construction projects coming to the market. To that end, the construction service firm is expanding its Houston Division to capitalize on growing demand from the energy and multifamily housing markets in the Houston area. To build its Campus Solutions business, which specializes in the construction of education facilities, Balfour Beatty Construction absorbed Charter Builders, a specialist in educational facilities, in 2012. Recent student housing projects include a 1,274-bed student housing project at Texas A&M University. Construction of the $104 million project began in mid-2014 with completion and occupancy set for August 2015.

Some of the company's more notable projects include NASA Mission Control (Houston), Texas Stadium (home of the Dallas Cowboys), the Mayo Clinic, The James Madison Library of Congress, One America Plaza, Miami International Airport, and Cinderella's Castle at Walt Disney World.

Auditors: KPMG LLP DALLAS TX

LOCATIONS

HQ: BALFOUR BEATTY CONSTRUCTION GROUP, INC.
3100 MCKINNON ST FL 10, DALLAS, TX 752017007
Phone: 214 451-1000
Web: WWW.BALFOURBEATTYUS.COM

PRODUCTS/OPERATIONS

Selected Key Markets
Airports
Defense housing
Education
Health care
Judicial & institutional
Rail
Roads

Selected Projects
Air Force Memorial (Arlington, VA)
Army/Air Force Exchange Shopping Center (Fort Jackson, SC)
Bank of America (Charlotte, NC)
Broward County Convention Center (Fort Lauderdale, FL)
Burger King, corporate headquarters (Miami)
Cape Coral Parkway Expansion (Cape Coral, FL)
Carnival Cruise Lines, corporate headquarters (Miami)
Children's Hospital & Health Center (San Diego, CA)
Cisco Systems, corporate headquarters (Research Triangle Park, NC)
Disney's Wilderness Lodge Resort (Lake Buena Vista, FL)
Duke University Levine Science Research Center (Durham, NC)
Harrah's Casino (New Orleans)
Harris Methodist Hospital (Fort Worth, TX)
James Madison Memorial Building, Library of Congress (Washington, DC)
J.P. Morgan International Plaza (Dallas)
Lucayan Beach Resort (Grand Bahama Island, Bahamas)
Mescalero Apache K-12 (Mescalero, NM)
Music City Central MTA Bus Facility (Nashville, TN)
NASA Space Station Control Center (Houston)
Osceoloa County Courthouse (Kissimmee, FL)
Port of Miami (Miami)
Southwest Airlines, corporate headquarters (Dallas)
United Spirit Arena (Lubbock, TX)
Vanderbilt University Medical Center (Nashville, TN)
Walter Reed Army Medical Center, military housing (Silver Spring, MD)
White Sands Missile Range, military housing (White Sands, NM)

COMPETITORS

CBRE HEERY, INC.
CLARK CONSTRUCTION GROUP, LLC
GILBANE BUILDING COMPANY
GILBANE, INC.
HOLDER CONSTRUCTION COMPANY
J.E. DUNN CONSTRUCTION COMPANY
LECHASE CONSTRUCTION SERVICES, LLC
MCCARTHY BUILDING COMPANIES, INC.
SUFFOLK CONSTRUCTION COMPANY, INC.
TURNER CONSTRUCTION COMPANY

HISTORICAL FINANCIALS
Company Type: Private

Income Statement				FYE: December 31
	REVENUE ($mil)	NET INCOME ($mil)	NET PROFIT MARGIN	EMPLOYEES
12/15	3,852	(14)	—	2,495
12/14	3,932	17	0.4%	—
12/13	3,816	24	0.6%	—
12/12	3,459	19	0.6%	—
Annual Growth	3.7%	—	—	—

2015 Year-End Financials
Return on assets: (-0.9%) Cash ($ mil.): 69
Return on equity: (-3.0%)
Current Ratio: 1.20

BALFOUR BEATTY CONSTRUCTION, LLC

EXECUTIVES

CLO*, David Hodnett
Auditors: KPMG LLP DALLAS TX

LOCATIONS

HQ: BALFOUR BEATTY CONSTRUCTION, LLC
3100 MCKINNON ST FL 3, DALLAS, TX 752011044
Phone: 214 451-1000
Web: WWW.BALFOURBEATTYUS.COM

HISTORICAL FINANCIALS
Company Type: Private

Income Statement — FYE: December 31

	REVENUE ($mil)	NET INCOME ($mil)	NET PROFIT MARGIN	EMPLOYEES
12/16	3,809	13	0.3%	2,495
12/13	3,816	23	0.6%	—
12/12	3,365	8	0.3%	—
12/10	0	0	—	—
Annual Growth	—	—	—	—

2016 Year-End Financials
Return on assets: 0.8% Cash ($ mil.): 53
Return on equity: 2.8%
Current Ratio: 1.20

BALFOUR BEATTY, LLC

Auditors: KPMG LLP DALLAS TX

LOCATIONS
HQ: BALFOUR BEATTY, LLC
1011 CENTRE RD STE 322, WILMINGTON, DE 198051266
Phone: 302 573-3873
Web: WWW.BALFOURBEATTYUS.COM

HISTORICAL FINANCIALS
Company Type: Private

Income Statement — FYE: December 31

	REVENUE ($mil)	NET INCOME ($mil)	NET PROFIT MARGIN	EMPLOYEES
12/15	4,690	(18)	—	2,495
12/12	4,378	43	1.0%	—
12/11	4,078	58	1.4%	—
Annual Growth	3.6%	—	—	—

2015 Year-End Financials
Return on assets: (-0.5%) Cash ($ mil.): 391
Return on equity: (-1.0%)
Current Ratio: 1.70

BALLAD HEALTH

EXECUTIVES
CIO*, Pam Austin
Auditors: PYA PC KNOXVILLE TN

LOCATIONS
HQ: BALLAD HEALTH
400 N STATE OF FRNKLIN RD, JOHNSON CITY, TN 376046035
Phone: 423 230-8200
Web: WWW.BALLADHEALTH.ORG

HISTORICAL FINANCIALS
Company Type: Private

Income Statement — FYE: June 30

	REVENUE ($mil)	NET INCOME ($mil)	NET PROFIT MARGIN	EMPLOYEES
06/22	2,312	(135)	—	6,114
06/21	2,191	267	12.2%	—
06/20	2,077	(69)	—	—
06/19	2,106	99	4.7%	—
Annual Growth	3.2%	—	—	—

2022 Year-End Financials
Return on assets: (-3.9%) Cash ($ mil.): 148
Return on equity: (-9.2%)
Current Ratio: 1.10

BALTIMORE CITY PUBLIC SCHOOLS

EXECUTIVES
SCHOOL SUPPORTS, Karl E Perry
Auditors: CLIFTONLARSONALLEN LLP BALTIM

LOCATIONS
HQ: BALTIMORE CITY PUBLIC SCHOOLS
200 E NORTH AVE, BALTIMORE, MD 212025984
Phone: 443 984-2000
Web: WWW.BALTIMORECITYSCHOOLS.ORG

HISTORICAL FINANCIALS
Company Type: Private

Income Statement — FYE: June 30

	REVENUE ($mil)	NET INCOME ($mil)	NET PROFIT MARGIN	EMPLOYEES
06/12	1,480	(18)	—	10,800
06/02	988	(23)	—	—
Annual Growth	4.1%	—	—	—

2012 Year-End Financials
Return on assets: (-2.0%) Cash ($ mil.): 183
Return on equity: (-3.6%)
Current Ratio: —

BANNER HEALTH

Banner Health is one of the largest secular not-for-profit health systems in the US. The organization operates about 30 acute-care hospitals, as well as clinics, medical labs, nursing homes, home health agencies, physician groups, and ambulatory surgery and urgent care centers. Banner Health also provides health insurance through Medicaid, Medicare, and commercial plans, largely through partnerships. Banner Health participates in medical research in areas such as Alzheimer's disease and digestive diseases and disorders through its Banner - University Medicine Digestive Diseases Institute.

Operations
The multi-specialty system offers a Medicaid managed care plan; it also manages a Medicare Advantage plan through a partnership with Blue Cross and Blue Shield of Arizona. The company also operates the Banner Health Network, an integrated network for Medicare and private health plans. It is comprised of 3,000 Banner Health-affiliated physicians and advanced practice providers, 15 Phoenix-area Banner Health hospitals and a variety of other medical facilities.

Banner ? University Medicine is the new academic medicine division of Banner Health, anchored in Phoenix and Tucson. This division includes three academic medical centers: Banner ? University Medical Center Tucson, Banner ? University Medical Center Phoenix and Banner ? University Medical Center South.

Geographic Reach
Banner Health operates in Arizona (headquarter), California, Colorado, Nebraska, Nevada, and Wyoming.

Sales and Marketing
Banner Health serves more than one million members.

Company Background
Banner Health was formed in 1999 through the merger of the Samaritan Health System and the Lutheran Health System. Samaritan Health System traced its roots to the opening of the Good Samaritan Medical Center as a 20-bed hospital in 1911. Lutheran Health System dated back to 1938.

New hospital construction includes Banner Estrella Medical Center (2005), Banner Gateway (2007), Banner Ironwood (2010), and Banner Fort Collins (2015).

The company has expanded through acquisitions over the years. Casa Grande Regional Medical Center joined the system in 2014 and Banner Payson Medical Center was added in 2015. The company acquired The University of Arizona Health Network (now Banner - University Medicine) in 2015, adding three academic medical centers. In mid-2016 the company acquired more than 30 Arizona urgent-care centers from Urgent Care Extra. In 2017, Banner Health acquired Medicare-certified home health agency SunLife Home Health.

Banner Health managed th Fairbanks Memorial Hospital in Alaska until 2017 when the facility transitioned to management by the Greater Fairbanks Community Hospital Foundation.

EXECUTIVES
CAO*, Ron Bunnell
CMO*, John Hensing
Development*, Rebecca Kuhn
CIO*, Deanna Wise
CLO*, Jean Fitterer Lance
Auditors: ERNST & YOUNG LLP PHOENIX AZ

LOCATIONS

HQ: BANNER HEALTH
2901 N CENTRAL AVE # 160, PHOENIX, AZ 850122702
Phone: 602 747-4000
Web: WWW.BANNERHEALTH.COM

FEATURED SERVICES
Academic Medicine
Alzheimer's
Cancer
Heart
Insurance (Networks)
Maternity
Orthopedics
Pediatrics
Pharmacy
Physicians & Specialists
Research
Women's Health

COMPETITORS

ADVOCATE AURORA HEALTH, INC.
ADVOCATE HEALTH CARE NETWORK
ENCOMPASS HEALTH CORPORATION
INDIANA UNIVERSITY HEALTH, INC.
MASS GENERAL BRIGHAM INCORPORATED
NORTHWELL HEALTH, INC.
NORTON HEALTHCARE, INC.
NOVANT HEALTH, INC.
ORLANDO HEALTH, INC.
WELLMONT HEALTH SYSTEM

HISTORICAL FINANCIALS

Company Type: Private

Income Statement — FYE: December 31

	REVENUE ($mil)	NET INCOME ($mil)	NET PROFIT MARGIN	EMPLOYEES
12/20	10,397	711	6.8%	35,000
12/19	9,426	753	8.0%	—
Annual Growth	10.3%	(5.6%)	—	—

2020 Year-End Financials
Return on assets: 4.5%   Cash ($ mil.): 1,145
Return on equity: 9.7%
Current Ratio: 1.30

BANNER-UNIVERSITY MEDICAL CENTER TUCSON CAMPUS LLC

Banner - University Medicine (formerly The University of Arizona Health Network) heals Arizonans and trains Wildcats. It operates three academic medical centers in Phoenix and Tucson, serving as the primary teaching hospital for the University of Arizona (UA) and offering medical treatment, research, and education services. The not-for-profit center provides cancer, cardiology, geriatric, respiratory, transplant, and dialysis care, as well as general practice and home health services. Specialty services include burn care, behavioral health, integrative medicine, sports medicine, and level I trauma care. The network merged with Banner Healthcare in 2015.

Operations

The University of Arizona Health Network merged with Banner Health to create Banner - University Medicine. The division includes three hospitals: Banner - University Medical Center Tucson, Banner - University Medical Center South, and Banner - University Medical Center Phoenix. The network also includes Banner - University Medical Group (formerly named University of Arizona Physicians), a group of Tucson-based physicians.

Geographic Reach

Banner - University Medicine serves patients in and around Phoenix and Tucson, Arizona.

Strategy

In 2015, Banner - University Medical Center Phoenix broke ground on a new $160 million emergency department that will have the capacity to serve an additional 20,000 patients each year. Expected to open in mid-2017, the new facility will include 60 private exam rooms, a new trauma unit, and 40 observation beds.

Company Background

The University of Arizona Health Network was formed in 2010 when University Physicians Hospital merged with University Medical Center.

LOCATIONS

HQ: BANNER-UNIVERSITY MEDICAL CENTER TUCSON CAMPUS LLC
1501 N CAMPBELL AVE, TUCSON, AZ 857240001
Phone: -
Web: WWW.UAHEALTH.IXT.COM

COMPETITORS

COLUMBUS REGIONAL HEALTHCARE SYSTEM, INC
EL PASO COUNTY HOSPITAL DISTRICT
PRINCETON HEALTHCARE SYSTEM HOLDING INC.
THE UNIVERSITY OF VERMONT MEDICAL CENTER INC.
TRINITAS REGIONAL MEDICAL CENTER A NEW JERSEY NONPROFIT CORPORATION

HISTORICAL FINANCIALS

Company Type: Private

Income Statement — FYE: June 30

	REVENUE ($mil)	NET INCOME ($mil)	NET PROFIT MARGIN	EMPLOYEES
06/09	541	0	0.0%	3,000
06/08	512	27	5.3%	—
06/05	708	0	0.0%	—
Annual Growth	(6.5%)	—	—	—

2009 Year-End Financials
Return on assets: 16.3%   Cash ($ mil.): 3
Return on equity: —
Current Ratio: —

BAPTIST HEALTH

For those seeking medical salvation, Baptist Health may be the answer to their prayers. The organization provides health services through about 175 points of care scattered throughout in Arkansas. Its facilities include seven hospitals and a number of rehabilitation facilities, family clinics, and therapy and wellness centers. Arkansas Health Group, a division of Baptist Health, runs more than 20 physician clinics across the state. Specialized services include cardiology, women's health, orthopedics, rehabilitation, and home and hospice care. Baptist Health's Parkway Village is a 90-acre retirement community for active seniors located close to Baptist Health Medical Center - Little Rock.

Operations

In addition to its hospitals, the company has 47 physician clinics, 20 therapy centers, and 53 other centers and service locations. Its Baptist Health Mobile Health Unit travels the state to provide a temporary facility for health screenings, health education, and first-aid (emergent care) services.

Along with the standard roster of health care services, Baptist Health also offers Little Rock residents nine programs of health care study through its Baptist Health Schools Little Rock division. The school coordinates with Arkansas Tech University to offer Baptist Health RN graduates an online option to complete their Bachelor of Science in Nursing degree. Its average enrollment is about 900 students each semester.

Geographic Reach

Baptist Health serves patients across Arkansas. Baptist Health's hospitals include Baptist Health Extended Care Hospital, Baptist Health Medical Center - Arkadelphia, Baptist Health Medical Center - Heber Springs, Baptist Health Medical Center - Little Rock, Baptist Health Medical Center - North Little Rock, Baptist Health Medical Center - Stuttgart, and Baptist Health Medical Center - Hot Spring County.

Sales and Marketing

Baptist Health works with a number of insurance policies and organizations, including Aetna, AMCO PPO, Arkansas Blue Cross and Blue Shield, Arkansas Municipal League, Care Improvement Plus, CIGNA, Coventry/First Health PPO and GEHA.

Strategy

The hospital system has been growing to meet the needs of its customers. In 2013 it began leasing Hot Spring County Medical Center in Malvern. The 72-bed acute care hospital was renamed Baptist Health Medical Center, Hot Spring County. Baptist Health also bought nearly 40 acres in Conway and began construction on a medical center to serve Faulkner county.

To improve operating efficiency, in 2013 Baptist Health formed a new organization -- Baptist Health Physician Partners, a clinical integration program with more than 200 physician partners.

BAPTIST HEALTH SOUTH FLORIDA, INC.

Faith-based, non-for-profit, Baptist Health South Florida (BHSF) is the largest healthcare organization in the region, With more than 1.5 million patient visits every year. Baptist Hospital is its flagship facility that offers a full range of medical and technological services and home to three Centers of Excellence ? Miami Cardiac & Vascular Institute, Miami Neuroscience Institute and Miami Cancer Institute. Baptist Children's Hospital provides neonatal intensive care, inpatient pediatric oncology services and pediatric care, among other services.

Operations
BHSF's group of hospitals include Baptist Health Hospital, Baptist Hospital, Baptist Hospital of Miami, Baptist Children's Hospital, Bethesda Hospital East, Bethesda Hospital West, Boca Raton Regional Hospital, Doctors Hospital, Fishermen's Community Hospital, Homestead Hospital, Mariners Hospital, West Kendall Baptist Hospital and South Miami Hospital.

BHSF offers an extensive range of medical, surgical and technological services ? including cancer, neuroscience, cardiovascular, sports medicine and orthopedics.

BHSF International offers a full range of services for international patients, including access to multilingual patient coordinators who provide personalized concierge service, outpatient diagnostics and procedures, medical second opinions, and special rates for hotel accommodations at the recently opened Hilton Miami Dadeland on the main campus of Baptist Hospital.

Geographic Reach
Headquartered in Coral Gables, Florida, BHSF operates a dozen of hospitals, more than 100 outpatient facilities and physician practice locations.

Sales and Marketing
Baptist Health Care On Demand, a telehealth app, allows people to see its BHSF's urgent doctor from their phone or computer- any time, day, or night, nationwide.

Company Background
Baptist Hospital opened in 1960, and the Baptist Health organization was formed in 1990.

The company added a number of hospitals through acquisitions and construction efforts over the years. It opened the West Kendall Baptist Hospital in 2011. In 2017 the system merged with the not-for-profit Bethesda Health, adding two hospitals (Bethesda East and Bethesda West) in Boynton Beach. It also added the Fishermen's Community Hospital that year.

EXECUTIVES
Chief Development Officer*, Lena Moore
CCO*, Marea Aspillaga
CMO*, David Rice
Auditors : BKD LLP LITTLE ROCK ARKANSA

LOCATIONS
HQ: BAPTIST HEALTH
9601 BAPTIST HEALTH DR # 109, LITTLE ROCK, AR 722056323
Phone: 501 202-2000
Web: WWW.BAPTIST-HEALTH.COM

Selected Locations in Arkansas
Arkansas Health Group (statewide)
BH Extended Care (Little Rock)
BHMC Arkadelphia
BHMC Heber Springs
BHMC Hot Spring County
BHMC Little Rock
BHMC North Little Rock
BHMC Stuttgart
Baptist Health Rehabilitation Institute (Little Rock)
Parkway Village (Little Rock)

PRODUCTS/OPERATIONS

Selected Services
Behavioral Health
Cardiac Rehab
Diabetes Treatment & Management
Eye Center
Hospice & Home Health
Home Infusion Services
Imaging Services
Laboratory
MedFlight
Men's Health
Pastoral Care
Sleep Disorder
Transplant
Weight Loss Program
Wound Care Center

COMPETITORS
ALDEN MANAGEMENT SERVICES, INC.
BAPTIST HEALTH CARE CORPORATION
BAPTIST MEMORIAL HEALTH CARE SYSTEM, INC.
DOYLESTOWN HOSPITAL
ELLIS HOSPITAL
LEVINDALE HEBREW GERIATRIC CENTER AND HOSPITAL, INC.
MADONNA REHABILITATION HOSPITAL
MIAMI JEWISH HEALTH SYSTEMS, INC.
ST MARGARET MERCY HEALTHCARE CENTERS INC
STATESVILLE HMA, LLC

HISTORICAL FINANCIALS
Company Type: Private

Income Statement — FYE: December 31

	REVENUE ($mil)	NET INCOME ($mil)	NET PROFIT MARGIN	EMPLOYEES
12/21	1,872	98	5.2%	7,000
12/20	1,650	155	9.4%	—
12/18	1,215	(45)	—	—
12/17	875	49	5.6%	—
Annual Growth	20.9%	18.7%	—	—

2021 Year-End Financials
Return on assets: 4.7%
Return on equity: 8.6%
Current Ratio: 1.70
Cash ($ mil.): 204

EXECUTIVES
MEDICAL CLINICAL TRANSFORMATION*, Jack A Ziffer
Chief Digital Officer*, Tony Ambrozie
Auditors : DELOITTE TAX LLP TAMPA FL

LOCATIONS
HQ: BAPTIST HEALTH SOUTH FLORIDA, INC.
6855 S RED RD, SOUTH MIAMI, FL 331433647
Phone: 305 596-1960
Web: WWW.BAPTISTHEALTH.NET

PRODUCTS/OPERATIONS

2013 Sales

	$ mil.	% of total
Managed Care	1,655.6	69
Medicare	278.3	12
Medicaid	122.5	5
Other	331.8	14
Total		100

Selected Florida Facilities
Baptist Hospital of Miami (Kendall)
    Baptist Cardiac & Vascular Institute
    Baptist Children's Hospital
Doctors Hospital (Coral Gables)
Homestead Hospital (Homestead)
Mariners Hospital (Tavernier)
South Miami Hospital (South Miami)
West Kendall Baptist Hospital (Kendall)

Selected Services
Addiction treatment
Behavioral medicine
Blood conservation program
Cancer services
Cardiovascular services
Care and counseling services
Children's health
Community wellness
Critical care center
Diabetes
eICU LifeGuard
Emergency
Endoscopy
Executive health
Gamma knife center
Heart surgery
Home care
Hyperbaric services
Imaging
Intensive care unit
International services
Interventional/surgical Services
Laboratory
Maritime medical services
Neonatal
Neuroscience
Nutrition counseling services
Occupational health
Online appointments
Orthopedics
Outpatient/diagnostic services
Pain center
Pastoral care
Pediatric
Pelvic health
Physical and speech therapy
Pregnancy and childbirth
Progressive care unit
Prostate cancer
Pulmonary services
Radiation oncology
Rehabilitation services
Robotic surgery
Senior services
Sleep diagnostic center
Sports medicine and orthopedic programs

Stroke services
Surgery
Weight-loss surgery
Wellness Center
Women's health
Wound care

COMPETITORS

BORGESS HEALTH ALLIANCE, INC.
BRRH CORPORATION
CATHOLIC MEDICAL CENTER
HCA-HEALTHONE LLC
HOUSTON COUNTY HEALTHCARE AUTHORITY
HUNTINGTON HOSPITAL DOLAN FAMILY HEALTH CENTER, INC.
LEHIGH VALLEY HEALTH NETWORK, INC.
MEDSTAR HEALTH, INC.
ORLANDO HEALTH, INC.
SOUTH MIAMI HOSPITAL, INC.

HISTORICAL FINANCIALS
Company Type: Private

Income Statement — FYE: September 30

	REVENUE ($mil)	NET INCOME ($mil)	NET PROFIT MARGIN	EMPLOYEES
09/19	1,294	598	46.3%	16,000
09/17	608	244	40.2%	—
09/15	846	137	16.2%	—
09/09	616	121	19.7%	—
Annual Growth	7.7%	17.3%	—	—

2019 Year-End Financials
Return on assets: 8.8%   Cash ($ mil.): 132
Return on equity: 12.7%
Current Ratio: 0.90

BAPTIST HEALTH SYSTEM, INC.

Founded in 1955, Baptist Health serves the Jacksonville, Florida area through four acute care hospitals and a children's hospital with a combined total of more than 1,200 physicians in about 90 specialties. Baptist MD Anderson Cancer Center is a regional destination for world-renowned cancer care which is clinically integrated with MD Anderson Cancer Center in Houston Across the street, Wolfson Children's Hospital also cares for the city's youngest residents. The system's satellite acute-care facilities include Baptist Medical Center Beaches, Baptist Medical Center Nassau, and Baptist Medical Center South.

Operations
Baptist Health's flagship tertiary care hospital, Baptist Medical Center, is centrally located in Jacksonville and is a full-service medical center representing nearly all major health care specialties. Its Baptist Heart Hospital offers comprehensive cardiovascular care. Baptist Health has more than 200 primary care and specialty physician practices, children's specialty clinics, home health care, behavioral health, occupational health, rehabilitation services and urgent care.

Its Health Care for Women provides a comprehensive health services for issues of concern to women such as breast health, pregnancy, childbirth, gynecology and senior issues such as osteoporosis.

In addition, Baptist Research Institute is currently overseeing more than 50 clinical research studies in a wide range of areas. Its primary areas of interest include endovascular, neurology and cardiovascular and pediatrics.

Geographic Reach
Baptist Health is headquartered in Jacksonville, Florida.

Company Background
A major construction project was completed in late 2012 with the opening of a new 11-story patient tower at Baptist Jacksonville. The new $200 million tower features all private patient rooms and high-tech surgical suites.

Baptist Health was founded in 1955.

Auditors : ERNEST & YOUNG LLP JACKSONVI

LOCATIONS

HQ: BAPTIST HEALTH SYSTEM, INC.
841 PRUDENTIAL DR # 1802, JACKSONVILLE, FL 322078329
Phone: 904 202-2000
Web: WWW.BAPTISTJAX.COM

PRODUCTS/OPERATIONS

Selected facilities
Baptist Medical Center Beaches (Jacksonville Beach, Florida)
Baptist Medical Center Jacksonville (Jacksonville, Florida)
  Baptist Heart Hospital
Baptist Medical Center Nassau (Fernandina Beach, Florida)
Baptist Medical Center South (Jacksonville, Florida)
Wolfson Children's Hospital (Jacksonville, Florida)

COMPETITORS

BEAUMONT HEALTH
BRONXCARE HEALTH SYSTEM
MEDSTAR HEALTH, INC.
MERCY HOSPITAL SPRINGFIELD
PASADENA HOSPITAL ASSOCIATION, LTD.
SHANDS JACKSONVILLE MEDICAL CENTER, INC.
UNIVERSITY HOSPITALS HEALTH SYSTEM, INC.
VALLEY HEALTH SYSTEM
WELLMONT HEALTH SYSTEM
WELLSPAN HEALTH

HISTORICAL FINANCIALS
Company Type: Private

Income Statement — FYE: September 30

	REVENUE ($mil)	NET INCOME ($mil)	NET PROFIT MARGIN	EMPLOYEES
09/21	2,408	570	23.7%	7,000
09/20	2,022	95	4.7%	—
09/19	1,923	176	9.2%	—
09/18	1,736	252	14.5%	—
Annual Growth	11.5%	31.2%	—	—

2021 Year-End Financials
Return on assets: 11.1%   Cash ($ mil.): 260
Return on equity: 17.6%
Current Ratio: 1.10

BAPTIST HEALTHCARE SYSTEM, INC.

Baptist Health owns eight acute-care hospitals in Kentucky with a total capacity of more than 2,700 beds. The not-for-profit health system's largest facility is Baptist Health Louisville, a 519-bed hospital in Louisville that provides a wide range of health services, with special expertise in cardiology, rehabilitation, and women's health. In addition to its owned facilities, Baptist Health manages Baptist Health Lexington, a 434-bed tertiary care facility, and Baptist Health Richmond with approximately 105 beds. The growing Baptist Health was founded as a single hospital in Louisville in 1924.

Operations
Along with inpatient acute care services, Baptist Health offers home health care services, more than 250 outpatient facilities and services, including urgent care and retail-based clinics, outpatient diagnostic and surgery centers, occupational medicine, physical therapy clinics and fitness centers. The Baptist Health Medical Group is a comprehensive network that includes more than 1,100 physicians and advanced practice clinicians across Kentucky and southern Indiana, and represents over 75 specialties, including primary care and family medicine, internal medicine, osteopathic medicine, emergency medicine, general surgery and a wide range of surgical specialties offering advanced treatments and care.

In addition to its nine hospitals that include Baptist Health Hardin, Baptist Health Floyd, Baptist Health Richmond, Baptist Health Madisonville, Baptist Health Paducah, Baptist Health Louisville, Baptist Health La Grange, Baptist Health Lexington and Baptist Health Corbin, Baptist Health's clinicians are engaged in over 200 clinical studies throughout its network of hospitals, working to advance treatments in oncology, cardiology, orthopedics, neuroscience, epidemiology, diabetes and other areas.

Geographic Reach
Headquartered in Louisville, the Baptist Health's home care is available in about 40 Kentucky counties, four counties in Illinois and seven counties in Southern Indiana.

EXECUTIVES

CIO, David J Bensema
CMO, Timothy Jahn
Auditors : DELOITTE & TOUCHE LLP LOUISVI

LOCATIONS

HQ: BAPTIST HEALTHCARE SYSTEM, INC.
2701 EASTPOINT PKWY, LOUISVILLE, KY 402234166

Phone: 502 896-5000
Web: WWW.BAPTISTHEALTH.COM

PRODUCTS/OPERATIONS

Selected Facilities and Operations (Kentucky)
Hospitals
    Managed
        Baptist Health Corbin
        Baptist Health La Grange
        Baptist Health Lexington
        Baptist Health Louisville
        Baptist Health Richmond
        Baptist Health Madisonville
        Baptist Health Paducah
        ContinueCARE Hospital (Corbin)
    Owned
        Hardin Memorial Hospital (Elizabethtown)
        Russell County Hospital (Russell Springs)
Other operations
    Baptist East Milestone Wellness Center (Louisville)
    Baptist Express Care (various Walmarts in state)
    Baptist Medical Associates (medical practice group, Louisville area)
    Baptist Urgent Care (Louisville)
    Bluegrass Family Health (provider-sponsored insurance)

COMPETITORS

ADVENTIST HEALTH SYSTEM/SUNBELT, INC.
AHS MEDICAL HOLDINGS LLC
BAPTIST HEALTH SOUTH FLORIDA, INC.
BAPTIST HEALTH SYSTEM, INC.
HEALTH FIRST, INC.
HOUSTON COUNTY HEALTHCARE AUTHORITY
MEDSTAR HEALTH, INC.
PROSPECT WATERBURY, INC.
UNIVERSITY HEALTH SERVICES, INC.
YAKIMA VALLEY MEMORIAL HOSPITAL ASSOCIATION

HISTORICAL FINANCIALS

Company Type: Private

Income Statement   FYE: August 31

	REVENUE ($mil)	NET INCOME ($mil)	NET PROFIT MARGIN	EMPLOYEES
08/21	3,885	373	9.6%	12,601
08/20	2,994	199	6.7%	—
08/19	2,878	122	4.2%	—
08/18	2,725	149	5.5%	—
Annual Growth	12.6%	35.6%	—	—

2021 Year-End Financials
Return on assets: 7.5%
Return on equity: 14.6%
Current Ratio: 2.60
Cash ($ mil.): 531

BAPTIST HOSPITAL OF MIAMI, INC.

Baptist Hospital of Miami can treat many vices for Miami residents. The flagship facility of the Baptist Health South Florida health system provides residents of the city with a full range of health care services, including pediatric, cancer, home health, rehabilitation, neurology, and cardiovascular care. The hospital has more than 680 beds and includes the Baptist Children's Hospital, which offers a pediatric emergency room and a neonatal intensive care unit. Baptist Hospital of Miami also includes the Baptist Cardiac & Vascular Institute, a regional cancer program, and a diabetes care center. Baptist Hospital of Miami was founded in 1960.

Operations

Baptist Children's Hospital offers 24-hour emergency care, as well as two intensive care units and specialist services including pediatric cancer care. Baptist Hospital of Miami also contains the Baptist Cardiac and Vascular Institute, which conducts treatment and research programs. The hospital's international care unit provides services to patients from the Caribbean, Latin America, and other regions. Other specialist divisions include a sleep diagnostic center and a spine care facility, as well as a maternity ward. Baptist Hospital of Miami also operates several wellness centers.

As part of Baptist Health South Florida, the Baptist Hospital of Miami is part of a network of six hospitals, including South Miami Hospital, Doctors Hospital, and the West Kendall Baptist Hospital. In addition, the health system includes outpatient care clinics including emergency, surgery, imaging, and primary care centers.

Strategy

Controlling expenses through data management, quality and wellness initiatives, and other measures becomes increasingly important for the hospital and its affiliates as the cost of medical care in the US market continues to skyrocket. Maintaining an efficient organization is also imperative as the level of charity care provided by the system's facilities continues to rise in the face of economic difficulties.

As the largest hospital in the Baptist Health system, Baptist Hospital of Miami takes a leading role in technology programs such as medical equipment and data management system upgrades. The Baptist Health network is in the process of installing an electronic health record (EHR) system to connect patient records across its facilities.

In 2012 Baptist Hospital of Miami launched a $90 million construction effort to expand the Cardiac and Vascular Institute. The new, expanded institute facility will open in 2016 and will include centers for aneurysm treatment, structural heart therapy, and endovascular therapy. The project also includes expansion efforts on the hospital's surgery center, which will have enhanced capabilities for neurological, cardiac, and robotic surgery procedures.

LOCATIONS

HQ: BAPTIST HOSPITAL OF MIAMI, INC.
  8900 N KENDALL DR, MIAMI, FL 331762197
Phone: 786 596-1960
Web: WWW.BAPTISTHEALTH.NET

PRODUCTS/OPERATIONS

Selected Centers and Services
Baptist Cardiac & Vascular Institute (Heart Care)
Baptist Children's Hospital (Pediatrics)
Breast Care
Cancer Services
Center for Spine Care
Children's Cancer Services
Children's Emergency Center
Clinical Research Trials
Community Wellness
Critical Care/eICU LifeGuard
Diabetes Care
Diagnostic Imaging
Emergency Services
Endoscopy
Gynecology
Home Care
Intensive Care
International Services
Interventional
Maternity
Neonatal Intensive Care Unit
Neuroscience Center
Neurosurgery
Orthopedic Services
Pain Management
Physical & Speech Therapy
Pulmonary Services
Rehabilitation Services
Robotic Surgery
Senior Services
Sleep Diagnostic Center
Spine Care
Stroke Services
Surgery
Women's Services

COMPETITORS

BRYAN MEDICAL CENTER
GENESIS HEALTHCARE SYSTEM
MERCY HOSPITAL AND MEDICAL CENTER
SOUTH MIAMI HOSPITAL, INC.
ST. ANTHONY'S HOSPITAL, INC.

HISTORICAL FINANCIALS

Company Type: Private

Income Statement   FYE: September 30

	REVENUE ($mil)	NET INCOME ($mil)	NET PROFIT MARGIN	EMPLOYEES
09/20	1,310	161	12.3%	4,200
09/19	1,717	282	16.4%	—
09/18*	1,169	143	12.3%	—
12/17	1,004	73	7.3%	—
Annual Growth	9.3%	30.1%	—	—

*Fiscal year change

2020 Year-End Financials
Return on assets: 13.6%
Return on equity: 42.2%
Current Ratio: 0.40
Cash ($ mil.): —

BAPTIST MEMORIAL HEALTH CARE CORPORATION

EXECUTIVES

Chief Development Officer*, Robbie Johnson
Chief Marketing*, Ayoka Pond

LOCATIONS

HOOVER'S HANDBOOK OF PRIVATE COMPANIES 2023   63

HQ: BAPTIST MEMORIAL HEALTH CARE CORPORATION
350 N HUMPHREYS BLVD, MEMPHIS, TN 381202177
Phone: 901 226-4640
Web: WWW.BAPTISTONLINE.ORG

HISTORICAL FINANCIALS
Company Type: Private

Income Statement — FYE: September 30

	REVENUE ($mil)	NET INCOME ($mil)	NET PROFIT MARGIN	EMPLOYEES
09/21	3,401	186	5.5%	12,877
09/20	3,089	(29)	—	—
Annual Growth	10.1%	—	—	—

2021 Year-End Financials
Return on assets: 4.5%   Cash ($ mil.): 606
Return on equity: 9.0%
Current Ratio: 1.60

BAPTIST MEMORIAL HOSPITAL

When most of us think of Memphis, we think of Elvis Presley. When doctors think of Memphis, they think of Elvis and Baptist Memorial Hospital-Memphis. As the flagship facility of Baptist Memorial Health Care, the 710-bed hospital, often simply called Baptist Memphis, offers patients the full spectrum of health care services, including cancer treatment, orthopedics, surgical services, and neurology. The campus also features the Baptist Heart Institute for cardiovascular care and research, a pediatric emergency room, a skilled nursing facility, and the Plaza Diagnostic Pavilion for outpatient health care. Baptist Memphis, established in 1979, is one of the state's highest volume hospitals.

Operations
Doctors at the hospital see more than 27,000 admissions, 54,000 emergency department visits and nearly 116,000 outpatient visits each year. The emergency department houses more than 30 treatment bays. In addition, Baptist Memphis' skilled nursing center includes 30 beds. The hospital also operates a 30-bed rehabilitation hospital and a 165,000 sq. ft. heart institute for diagnostic and surgical cardiac care. The facility boasts advanced surgical systems including the CyberKnife radiation system for cancerous and non-cancerous tumor removal.

LOCATIONS
HQ: BAPTIST MEMORIAL HOSPITAL
6019 WALNUT GROVE RD, MEMPHIS, TN 381202113
Phone: 901 226-5000
Web: WWW.BAPTISTONLINE.ORG

COMPETITORS
BAPTIST HOSPITAL OF MIAMI, INC.
KIMBALL DAY HEALTHCARE INC

NEWTON MEMORIAL HOSPITAL (INC)
NEWYORK-PRESBYTERIAN/BROOKLYN METHODIST
ST. ANTHONY'S HOSPITAL, INC.

HISTORICAL FINANCIALS
Company Type: Private

Income Statement — FYE: September 30

	REVENUE ($mil)	NET INCOME ($mil)	NET PROFIT MARGIN	EMPLOYEES
09/15	690	(1)	—	6,000
09/14	663	(47)	—	—
09/13	504	17	3.4%	—
09/12	697	15	2.2%	—
Annual Growth	(0.3%)	—	—	—

2015 Year-End Financials
Return on assets: (-0.2%)   Cash ($ mil.): 28
Return on equity: (-0.5%)
Current Ratio: 1.40

BARCLAYS BANK DELAWARE

Barclays Bank Delaware (doing business as Barclays US) is a leading co-branded credit card issuer and financial services partner in the US that creates highly customized programs to drive customer loyalty and engagement for some of the country's most successful travel, entertainment, retail and affinity institutions. The company, a division of Barclays, issues Visa and MasterCard credit cards, in addition to co-branded credit cards through partnerships with over 25 top companies, including Priceline, Choice Privileges, Carnival World, and JetBlue. Founded as Juniper Financial in 2000; it became a part of Barclays in 2004.

Operations
The company creates customized, co-branded credit card programs for some of the country's most successful travel, entertainment, retail, cashback, business expenses, and financial institutions. Barclays also offer personal loans by invitation to some customers.

Geographic Reach
Barclays US is headquartered in Wilmington, Delaware, and has customers and clients across some 40 countries.

Sales and Marketing
Barclays US collaborates with over 25 top companies to deliver an array of consumer and small business credit card programs uses partnerships to expand its business. Some of its major partners include Barnes & Noble, Frontier Airlines, Priceline.com, Wyndham, Holland America, and Diamond Resorts World.

Company Background
In 1966, Barclays launches Barclaycard, the first credit card in the UK. Following that year, it introduces the world's first ATM. Barclays acquires Juniper Bank, a credit card company formed in 2000, and creating Barclaycard US in 2004. In 2009, Barclaycard becomes a top-10 credit card issuer in the U.S. It launches the first mobile app for card members in 2011. In 2018, Barclaycard rebrands to Barclays in the U.S., offering a range of personal banking products to U.S. consumers.

LOCATIONS
HQ: BARCLAYS BANK DELAWARE
100 S WEST ST, WILMINGTON, DE 198015015
Phone: 302 255-8000
Web: CARDS.BARCLAYCARDUS.COM

PRODUCTS/OPERATIONS
Selected Card Partnerships
Ameriprise
Bank Atlantic
Barnes & Noble
BJ's
Frontier
L.L. Bean
US Airways
Best Western
Priceline.com
Payless
Travelocity
Virgin America

COMPETITORS
AMERICAN EXPRESS COMPANY
ATHENS BANCSHARES CORPORATION
BANKUNITED, INC.
DOLLAR BANK, FEDERAL SAVINGS BANK
FEDFIRST FINANCIAL CORPORATION
MASTERCARD INCORPORATED
NETSPEND HOLDINGS, INC.
PEOPLE'S UNITED FINANCIAL, INC.
PRINCIPAL BANK
UMPQUA HOLDINGS CORPORATION

HISTORICAL FINANCIALS
Company Type: Private

Income Statement — FYE: December 31

	ASSETS ($mil)	NET INCOME ($mil)	INCOME AS % OF ASSETS	EMPLOYEES
12/14	25,012	239	1.0%	349
12/13	19,055	331	1.7%	—
12/08	12,418	20	0.2%	—
12/07	7,470	0	0.0%	—
Annual Growth	18.8%	—	—	—

2014 Year-End Financials
Return on assets: 1.0%   Cash ($ mil.): 2956
Return on equity: 7.5%
Current Ratio: 1.10

BARNABAS HEALTH, INC.

EXECUTIVES
CAO*, Stephen Jones
Auditors: KPMG LLP SHORT HILLS NJ

LOCATIONS

HQ: BARNABAS HEALTH, INC.
95 OLD SHORT HILLS RD, WEST ORANGE, NJ 070521008
Phone: 973 322-5000
Web: WWW.RWJBH.ORG

HISTORICAL FINANCIALS
Company Type: Private

Income Statement — FYE: December 31

	REVENUE ($mil)	NET INCOME ($mil)	NET PROFIT MARGIN	EMPLOYEES
12/18	730	(131)	—	24,600
12/17	624	293	47.0%	—
12/02	2,159	(92)	—	—
Annual Growth	(6.6%)	—	—	—

2018 Year-End Financials
Return on assets: (-3.0%)   Cash ($ mil.): 626
Return on equity: —
Current Ratio: 0.20

BARNES & NOBLE, INC.

Barnes & Noble is one of the largest bookstore chains in the US operating more than 600 Barnes & Noble superstores in all 50 states, and one of the Web's premier e-commerce sites, BN.com. Carrying about 3,000 magazine titles and more than 400 newspaper titles, the company sold more than 190 million physical books between its retail stores and online operations annually. In addition, Barnes & Noble has approximately 1 million unique physical book titles sold per year. The company's NOOK brand, develops, supports, and creates digital content and products for the digital reading and digital education markets. Founded in 1971 by bookseller Leonard Riggio, Barnes & Noble is now owned by Elliott Advisors (UK) Limited.

Operations
Barnes & Noble offers content, digital media and educational products. Its Nook Digital business offers a lineup of NOOK tablets and e-Readers and an expansive collection of digital reading content through the NOOK Store. The company's offering categories include book annex, books for teens, kid's books, toys and games and textbooks.

Geographic Reach
Headquartered in New York, Barnes & Noble operates approximately 600 retail bookstores in all 50 states.

Sales and Marketing
Barnes & Noble distributes its own books through retail bookstores in regional shopping malls, major strip centers and freestanding locations, as well as online. It serves more than serves more than 600 communities.

Company Background
Barnes & Noble dates back to 1873 when Charles Barnes went into the used-book business in Wheaton, Illinois.

After growing organically and through acquisitions and changing hands several times, Barnes & Noble -- by then a booming book superstore chain -- went public in 1993.

In 2019, after years of struggle brought on by online book giant Amazon and other retail headwinds, Barnes & Noble was purchased by private equity firm Elliott Management.

HISTORY

Barnes & Noble dates back to 1873 when Charles Barnes went into the used-book business in Wheaton, Illinois. By the turn of the century, he was operating a thriving bookselling operation in Chicago. His son William took over as president in 1902. William sold his share in the firm in 1917 (to C. W. Follett, who built Follett Corp.) and moved to New York City, where he bought an interest in established textbook wholesalers Noble & Noble. The company was soon renamed Barnes & Noble. It first sold mainly to colleges and libraries, providing textbooks and opening a large Fifth Avenue shop. Over the next three decades, Barnes & Noble became one of the leading booksellers in the New York region.

Enter Leonard Riggio, who worked at a New York University bookstore to help pay for night school. He studied engineering but got the itch for bookselling. In 1965, at age 24, he borrowed $5,000 and opened Student Book Exchange NYC, a college bookstore. Beginning in the late 1960s, he expanded by buying other college bookstores.

In 1971 Riggio paid $1.2 million for the Barnes & Noble store on Fifth Avenue. He soon expanded the store, and in 1974 he began offering jaw-dropping, competitor-maddening discounts of up to 40% for best-sellers. Acquiring Marlboro Books five years later, the company entered the mail-order and publishing business.

By 1986 Barnes & Noble had grown to about 180 outlets (including 142 college bookstores). Along with Dutch retailer Vendex, that year it bought Dayton Hudson's B. Dalton mall bookstore chain (about 800 stores), forming BDB Holding Corp. (Vendex had sold its shares by 1997.) In 1989 the company acquired the Scribner's Bookstores trade name and the Bookstop/Bookstar superstore chain. BDB began its shift to superstore format and streamlined its operations to integrate Bookstop and Doubleday (acquired in 1990) into its business.

BDB changed its name to Barnes & Noble in 1991. With superstore sales booming, the retailer went public in 1993 (the college stores remained private). It bought 20% of Canadian bookseller Chapters (now Indigo Books) in 1996 (sold in 1999).

The bookseller went online in 1997, and in 1998 sold a 50% stake in its Web operation subsidiary to Bertelsmann (which it re-purchased in 2003) in an attempt to strengthen both companies in the battle against online rival Amazon.com.

Also in 1998 Barnes & Noble agreed to buy #1 US book distributor Ingram Book Group, but the deal was called off in 1999 because of antitrust concerns. Also in 1999 barnesandnoble.com went public and Barnes & Noble bought small book publisher J.B. Fairfax International USA, which included coffee-table book publisher Michael Friedman Publishing Group. Later that year the company bought a 49% stake in book publishing portal iUniverse.com (later reduced to 22%). It also bought Riggio's financially struggling Babbage's Etc., a chain of about 500 Babbage's, Software Etc., and GameStop stores, for $215 million.

Subsidiary Babbage's Etc. (renamed GameStop, Inc.) acquired video game retailer Funco for $161.5 million in 2000. In 2001 Barnes & Noble joined barnesandnoble.com in acquiring a majority stake in magazine subscription seller enews.com.

The company completed an IPO of its GameStop unit in 2003, reducing its ownership interest to about 63%. Leonard also handed over the CEO title to his brother, Steve Riggio. Another development during that busy year included shutting down enews.com due to repeated quarterly losses.

In 2003 the company beefed up its self-publishing efforts with the purchase of Sterling Publishing, a specialist in how-to and craft books. In addition, Barnes & Noble's half-owned BOOK magazine shut down. The next year saw Barnes & Noble exit the video game retailing business when it spun off its remaining shares in GameStop.

In 2009 the firm sold its majority interest in Calendar Club for $7 million.

CEO Steve Riggio was replaced by William Lynch, president of Barnes&Noble.com, in 2010. Riggio remained chairman of the company. Barnes & Noble closed the last of its small-format B. Dalton bookstores in early 2010. (B. Dalton, which once numbered more than 900 stores, had been closing stores since 1989.) Later in the year hedge fund manager William Ackman offered to finance a $960 million merger of Barnes & Noble and its smaller rival Borders but nothing came of it.

CEO Lynch resigned in mid-2013 following an earnings report that underscored Barnes & Noble's failed attempt at building up its Nook division. CFO Michael Huseby was appointed chief executive of the Nook division and president of Barnes & Noble.

EXECUTIVES

CAO, Peter M Herpich
Corporate Secretary, Bradley A Feuer

HOOVER'S HANDBOOK OF PRIVATE COMPANIES 2023

Auditors : ERNST & YOUNG LLP NEW YORK N

LOCATIONS

HQ: BARNES & NOBLE, INC.
122 5TH AVE FL 2, NEW YORK, NY 100115634
Phone: 212 633-3300
Web: WWW.BARNESANDNOBLEINC.COM

2018 Stores

	No.
California	69
Texas	51
Florida	39
New York	38
Illinois	26
Pennsylvania	26
Virginia	25
New Jersey	22
North Carolina	21
Other states	310
Total	627

PRODUCTS/OPERATIONS

2019 Sales

	$ mil.	% of total
Retail	3,481.9	97
NOOK	92.1	3
Adjustments	(21.3)	—
Total	3,552.7	100

COMPETITORS

BAKER & TAYLOR HOLDINGS, LLC
BARNES & NOBLE COLLEGE BOOKSELLERS, LLC
BARNES & NOBLE EDUCATION, INC.
BOOKS-A-MILLION, INC.
FOLLETT CORPORATION
FOLLETT HIGHER EDUCATION GROUP, INC.
NOOK DIGITAL, LLC
PAPERCHASE PRODUCTS LIMITED
TARGET CORPORATION
THE MICHAELS COMPANIES INC

HISTORICAL FINANCIALS
Company Type: Private

Income Statement   FYE: April 28

	REVENUE ($mil)	NET INCOME ($mil)	NET PROFIT MARGIN	EMPLOYEES
04/18	3,662	(125)	—	24,000
04/17	3,894	22	0.6%	—
04/16	4,163	(24)	—	—
Annual Growth	(6.2%)	—	—	—

2018 Year-End Financials
Return on assets: (-7.2%)   Cash ($ mil.): 10
Return on equity: (-30.5%)
Current Ratio: 1.10

BARNES-JEWISH HOSPITAL

LOCATIONS

HQ: BARNES-JEWISH HOSPITAL
1 B J HOSPITAL PLAZA DR, SAINT LOUIS, MO 63110
Phone: 314 747-3000
Web: WWW.BARNESJEWISH.COM

HISTORICAL FINANCIALS
Company Type: Private

Income Statement   FYE: December 31

	REVENUE ($mil)	NET INCOME ($mil)	NET PROFIT MARGIN	EMPLOYEES
12/15	1,726	68	4.0%	30
12/14	1,664	83	5.0%	—
Annual Growth	3.7%	(18.2%)	—	—

2015 Year-End Financials
Return on assets: 5.1%   Cash ($.mil.): —
Return on equity: 5.7%
Current Ratio: 3.00

BARRICK ENTERPRISES, INC.

Auditors : CROSKEY LANNI PC ROCHESTER

LOCATIONS

HQ: BARRICK ENTERPRISES, INC.
4338 DELEMERE BLVD, ROYAL OAK, MI 480731876
Phone: 248 549-3737
Web: WWW.BARRICKENT.COM

HISTORICAL FINANCIALS
Company Type: Private

Income Statement   FYE: December 31

	REVENUE ($mil)	NET INCOME ($mil)	NET PROFIT MARGIN	EMPLOYEES
12/18	573	2	0.5%	35
12/17	534	0	0.1%	—
12/16	491	3	0.6%	—
12/15	552	3	0.7%	—
Annual Growth	1.2%	(8.8%)	—	—

2018 Year-End Financials
Return on assets: 8.5%   Cash ($ mil.): 10
Return on equity: 11.4%
Current Ratio: 2.00

BARRY-WEHMILLER GROUP, INC.

Barry-Wehmiller manufactures and supplies packaging, corrugating, paper converting, filling, and labeling automation equipment for a broad range of industries. It conducts business around the world through some 20 operating companies such as Accraply (labeling machinery), Design Group (automation and control systems), Winkler and Dunnebier (postage services and tissue and hygiene), and Synerlink (ultra-clean packaging for milk products and desserts). Other divisions manufacture paper converting machinery and offer engineering/IT consulting services. Berry-Wehmiller is privately owned by the Chapman family, who took over from Fred Wehmiller in 1963.

Operations
Barry-Wehmiller's operations comprise six segments and about 20 divisions: Packaging Equipment & Solutions (Accraply, BW Flexible Systems, BW Integrated systems, Pneumatic Scale Angelus, and Synerlink); Corrugating, Sheeting & Paper Processing Solutions (BW Papersystems and Alliance Machine Systems); Converting & Packaging of tissue, film & envelopes; flexographic printing (Paper Converting Machine Company, Winkler + Dünnebier, STAX Technologies, Hudson-Sharp and Northern Engraving); Engineering and IT Consulting (Design Group); Leadership & Culture Training & Consulting (Chapman & Co Leadership Institute; and BW Forsyth Partners (Afinitas, Baldwin Technology, Cor Partners and Machine Solutions).

Geographic Reach
Barry-Wehmiller is based in St. Louis, Missouri.

Sales and Marketing
Barry-Wehmiller's manufacturing technology and services serve a wide range of industries including packaging, paper converting, sheeting, corrugating, engineering, and IT consulting.

Financial Performance
Through its aggressive acquisition strategy and the opening of new locations, Barry-Wehmiller generated revenues of about $2 billion in 2014. The company has seen 18% compound revenue growth since 1987.

Mergers and Acquisitions
Barry-Wehmiller is highly acquisitive, making several bolt-ons each year for a total of nearly 100.

Company Background
Originally a provider of conveying equipment to St. Louis malt houses, Barry-Wehmiller was founded by Thomas Barry and Alfred Wehmiller in 1885. Ownership passed from the Wehmiller family to the Chapman family in 1963, and the Chapmans continue as the majority owners.

Auditors : ERNST & YOUNG LLP ST LOUIS

LOCATIONS

HQ: BARRY-WEHMILLER GROUP, INC.
8020 FORSYTH BLVD, SAINT LOUIS, MO 631051707
Phone: 314 862-8000
Web: WWW.BARRYWEHMILLER.COM

PRODUCTS/OPERATIONS

Selected Operations
BW Engineering and IT Consulting
   Design Group
BW Converting Platform
   Paper Converting Machine Company (PCMC)
   Winkler + Dunnebier
BW Packaging Systems
   Accraply, Inc. (packaging label machinery)
   PneumaticScaleAngelus (fillers, cappers, seamers, and labelers)
   BW Flexible Systems
   BW Integrated Systems
   Synerlink
BW Papersystems

COMPETITORS

BELVAC PRODUCTION MACHINERY, INC.
DELTA SYSTEMS & AUTOMATION LLC
ESSENTRA PLC
HUHTAMAKI, INC.
KEY TECHNOLOGY, INC.
KRONES AG
KRONES, INC.
MTS MEDICATION TECHNOLOGIES, INC.
ROCKWELL AUTOMATION, INC.
SPEEDLINE TECHNOLOGIES, INC.

HISTORICAL FINANCIALS

Company Type: Private

Income Statement — FYE: September 30

	REVENUE ($mil)	NET INCOME ($mil)	NET PROFIT MARGIN	EMPLOYEES
09/19	2,856	77	2.7%	4,500
09/18	3,037	85	2.8%	—
09/11	1,240	0	0.0%	—
09/10	1,097	0	0.0%	—
Annual Growth	11.2%	—	—	—

2019 Year-End Financials
Return on assets: 4.0%   Cash ($ mil.): 199
Return on equity: 17.6%
Current Ratio: 1.40

BARTON MALOW COMPANY

Barton Malow is a construction management and general contracting company, which has built its share of sporting facilities, also focuses on projects such as schools, hospitals, offices, and metals. Across the US and Canada, the company offers design/build and program management services ranging from the pre-planning stage to completion. Projects have included the Middletown Distribution Hub, the McLaren Greater Lansing Replacement Hospital, IBio: The Integrative Biosciences Center, Water Treatment Plant Expansion, Orlando Health ER and Medical Pavilion ? Lake Mary and the American Legion Memorial Stadium. Carl Osborn Barton founded the employee-owned firm as C.O. Barton Company in 1924.

Operations

In addition to preconstruction and planning, construction and delivery, virtual design and construction solutions and self-perform trades, Barton Malow also provides integrated technology services with a single source of responsibility for design and project, eliminating the headaches of multiple vendors. Other services include boilermaker, civil/concrete, constructive management, general contracting, refractory, steel, and more.

Geographic Reach

Michigan-based Barton Malow has operations in about 15 offices across North Carolina, Maryland, Ohio, Indiana, Illinois, Tennessee, Florida and Pennsylvania, among others.

Sales and Marketing

Barton Malow serves a wide range of industries, including automotive, commercial, energy, healthcare, higher education, industrial, infrastructure, K12 education, and sports and entertainment.

EXECUTIVES

CLO*, Maryann Kanary

Auditors : PRICEWATERHOUSECOOPERS LLP DE

LOCATIONS

HQ: BARTON MALOW COMPANY
26500 AMERICAN DR, SOUTHFIELD, MI 480342252
Phone: 248 436-5000
Web: WWW.BARTONMALOW.COM

Selected Locations
Atlanta
Baltimore
Charlottesville
Chicago
Columbus
Fairfax
Jacksonville
Oak Park
Orlando
Richmond
Southfield

PRODUCTS/OPERATIONS

Selcted Services
Architecture and planning
Building Information Management (BIM)
Concrete trade services
Construction management
Design/build
Facility audits
Facility services
   Administration
   Engineering
   Maintenance, repair, and operations
General contracting
Interior design
Interior trade services
Preconstruction
Program management
Rigging
Special projects
Technology consulting

COMPETITORS

CLAYCO, INC.
GILBANE BUILDING COMPANY
LPCIMINELLI, INC.
MIRON CONSTRUCTION CO., INC.
SHAWMUT WOODWORKING & SUPPLY, INC.
SUMMIT ENERGY SERVICES, INC.
THE CHRISTMAN COMPANY
THE MORGANTI GROUP INC
TISHMAN CONSTRUCTION CORPORATION
VJS CONSTRUCTION SERVICES, INC.

HISTORICAL FINANCIALS

Company Type: Private

Income Statement — FYE: March 31

	REVENUE ($mil)	NET INCOME ($mil)	NET PROFIT MARGIN	EMPLOYEES
03/20	1,971	11	0.6%	1,600
03/19	1,634	8	0.5%	—
03/18	2,502	11	0.4%	—
03/17	2,361	0	0.0%	—
Annual Growth	(5.8%)	202.9%	—	—

2020 Year-End Financials
Return on assets: 1.7%   Cash ($ mil.): 94
Return on equity: 15.3%
Current Ratio: 1.10

BARTON MALOW ENTERPRISES, INC.

Auditors : PRICEWATERHOUSECOOPERS LLP DE

LOCATIONS

HQ: BARTON MALOW ENTERPRISES, INC.
26500 AMERICAN DR, SOUTHFIELD, MI 480342252
Phone: 248 436-5000
Web: WWW.BARTONMALOW.COM

HISTORICAL FINANCIALS

Company Type: Private

Income Statement — FYE: March 31

	REVENUE ($mil)	NET INCOME ($mil)	NET PROFIT MARGIN	EMPLOYEES
03/20	1,972	19	1.0%	2,000
03/18	2,502	18	0.7%	—
03/17	2,361	14	0.6%	—
03/16	1,777	9	0.6%	—
Annual Growth	2.6%	17.6%	—	—

2020 Year-End Financials
Return on assets: 2.6%   Cash ($ mil.): 111
Return on equity: 17.1%
Current Ratio: 1.10

BATTELLE MEMORIAL INSTITUTE

Auditors : DELOITTE & TOUCHE LLP COLUMBU

LOCATIONS

HQ: BATTELLE MEMORIAL INSTITUTE
2555 INTERNATIONAL ST, COLUMBUS, OH 432284604
Phone: 800 201-2011
Web: WWW.BATTELLE.ORG

BAYCARE HEALTH SYSTEM, INC.

BayCare Health System is the leading, not-for-profit health care system that connects individuals and families to a wide range of services at hundreds of locations in the Tampa Bay and West Central Florida regions. The system's member hospitals boast approximately 4,000 beds; the facilities offer a variety of specialty services ranging from orthopedics to cancer care to women's services. BayCare has about 6,000 physicians and medical professionals. Established in 1997, the health system operates approximately 15 not-for-profit hospitals, nearly 15 outpatient imaging facilities and about 20 urgent care centers.

Operations

BayCare's family of hospitals includes Morton Plant (about 600 beds), St. Joseph's (approximately 600 beds), Winter Haven (about 450), St. Anthony's (about 400 beds), Mease Countryside (about 310 beds), St. Joseph's Children's (nearly 220 beds), St. Joseph's Women's (about 125 beds), Winter Haven Women's Hospital (about 60 beds), Morton Plant North Bay (approximately 150 beds), South Florida Baptist (more than 145 beds), Mease Dunedin (approximately 120 beds), St. Joseph's Hospital-North (about 215 beds), St. Joseph's Hospital-South (over 210 beds), and Bartow Regional Medical Center (more than 70 beds).

Winter Haven Hospital serves as the major medical center for east Polk County.

BayCare has about 6,000 physicians and medical professionals and reported about 80,000 outpatient surgeries, and about 600,000 emergency room visits.

Geographic Reach

BayCare serves the residents of Florida's greater Tampa Bay area, consisting of the Hillsborough, Polk, Pasco, and Pinellas counties.

Financial Performance
Mergers and Acquisitions

EXECUTIVES

Vice Chairman*, Jeff Lyash
TRANSFORMATION*, Emily Allinder Scott
Auditors: CROWE LLP FORT LAUDERDALE FL

LOCATIONS

HQ: BAYCARE HEALTH SYSTEM, INC.
2985 DREW ST, CLEARWATER, FL 337593012
Phone: 727 820-8200
Web: WWW.BAYCARE.ORG

Selected Locations
Baycare Alliant Hospital (Dunedin, Florida)
Mease Countryside Hospital (Safety Harbor, Florida)
Mease Dunedin Hospital (Mease Dunedin, Florida)
Morton Plant Hospital (Clearwater, Florida)
Morton Plant North Bay Hospital (New Port Richey, Florida)
St. Anthony's Hospital (St. Petersburg, Florida)
St. Joseph's Children's Hospital (Tampa, Florida)
St. Joseph's Hospital (Tampa, Florida)
St. Joseph's Hospital-North (Lutz, Florida)
St. Joseph's Women's Hospital (Tampa, Florida)
South Florida Baptist Hospital (Plant City, Florida)
Winter Haven Hospital (Plok, Florida)

PRODUCTS/OPERATIONS

Selected Services
Advance Care Planning
BayCare Behavioral Health
BayCare HomeCare
BayCare Outpatient Imaging
Breast Health
Behavioral Health Services
Patient Secure Identity
Pediatric Specialty Centers
Physician Office EMR
Robotic Surgery
Wellness Centers

COMPETITORS

BILL & MELINDA GATES FOUNDATION
CATHOLIC CHARITIES USA
EXCLUSIVE RESORTS, LLC
MOUNTAIN STATES HEALTH ALLIANCE
SOUTHCOAST HOSPITALS GROUP, INC.
TEXAS MEDICAL ASSOCIATION LIBRARY
THE RALPH M PARSONS FOUNDATION
UNBOUND
UNIVERSITY OF SUSSEX(THE)
WEST VIRGINIA UNITED HEALTH SYSTEM, INC.

HISTORICAL FINANCIALS
Company Type: Private

Income Statement — FYE: December 31

	REVENUE ($mil)	NET INCOME ($mil)	NET PROFIT MARGIN	EMPLOYEES
12/19	818	228	27.9%	27,739
12/14	463	163	35.3%	—
Annual Growth	12.0%	6.9%	—	—

2019 Year-End Financials
Return on assets: 3.7%   Cash ($ mil.): 83
Return on equity: 21.2%
Current Ratio: 0.10

HISTORICAL FINANCIALS
Company Type: Private

Income Statement — FYE: September 30

	REVENUE ($mil)	NET INCOME ($mil)	NET PROFIT MARGIN	EMPLOYEES
09/14	4,775	(95)	—	20,000
09/13	4,795	(7)	—	—
09/12	5,228	(20)	—	—
Annual Growth	(4.4%)	—	—	—

2014 Year-End Financials
Return on assets: 2.7%   Cash ($ mil.): 117
Return on equity: (-2.0%)
Current Ratio: 0.70

BAYHEALTH MEDICAL CENTER, INC.

Auditors: GRANT THORNTON LLP PHILADELP

LOCATIONS

HQ: BAYHEALTH MEDICAL CENTER, INC.
640 S STATE ST, DOVER, DE 199013530
Phone: 302 674-4700
Web: WWW.BAYHEALTH.ORG

HISTORICAL FINANCIALS
Company Type: Private

Income Statement — FYE: June 30

	REVENUE ($mil)	NET INCOME ($mil)	NET PROFIT MARGIN	EMPLOYEES
06/21	782	218	28.0%	2,790
06/20	725	35	4.9%	—
06/19	677	58	8.7%	—
06/18	615	87	14.2%	—
Annual Growth	8.3%	35.8%	—	—

2021 Year-End Financials
Return on assets: 13.7%   Cash ($ mil.): 130
Return on equity: 18.9%
Current Ratio: 1.10

BAYLOR SCOTT & WHITE HEALTH

Baylor Scott & White Health is the largest not-for-profit health care system in Texas. The Christian-based organization includes more than 50 hospitals and more than 800 patient care sites (including primary care clinics, retail pharmacies, and ambulatory surgery centers). Baylor Scott & White Health employs some 7,000 active physicians, and its specialties include allergy and immunology, cancer care, dermatology, endocrinology, neuroscience and primary care. The system also operates the Scott & White Health Plan, which provides individual and family plans, fully insured and self-funded plans for small and large employers, Medicare Advantage and Prescription Drug plans, and a Medicaid plan, primarily in the Central Texas region.

Operations

Baylor Scott & White provides full-range, inpatient, outpatient, rehabilitation and emergency medical services. It has more than 7.8 million annual patient encounters, about 250 satellite outpatient facilities, roughly 600 specialty care clinics and about 160 primary care clinics, delivers nearly 31,370 babies, more than 5,000 licensed beds and over 7,300 active physicians. In addition to more than 900,000 emergency department visits, it has nearly 208,790 hospital admissions and about 35 retail pharmacies.

Its affiliate HealthTexas Provider Network

is a multi-specialty medical group with more than 1,300 providers, practicing in more than 360 care-sites in the North Texas area.

Geographic Reach

Baylor Scott & White Health is based in Texas.

Company Background

Baylor Scott & White Health was formed from the 2013 merger between Baylor Health Care System and Scott & White Healthcare.

EXECUTIVES

CMO*, Alejandro Arroliga
CIO*, Lavone Arthur
CIO*, Matthew Chambers
CMO*, Glen Couchman
Auditors : PRICEWATERHOUSECOOPERS LLP DA

LOCATIONS

HQ: BAYLOR SCOTT & WHITE HEALTH
  301 N WASHINGTON AVE, DALLAS, TX 752461754
Phone: 214 820-3151
Web: WWW.BSWHEALTH.COM

COMPETITORS

ADVENTIST HEALTHCARE, INC.
MEDSTAR HEALTH, INC.
MEMORIAL HERMANN HEALTHCARE SYSTEM
NORTHWESTERN MEMORIAL HEALTHCARE
PEDIATRIC SERVICES OF AMERICA, INC. (DE)
REX HEALTHCARE, INC.
ROBERT WOOD JOHNSON UNIVERSITY HOSPITAL, INC.
ST. JOSEPH HEALTH SYSTEM
VISITING NURSE SERVICE OF NEW YORK
WELLMED MEDICAL MANAGEMENT, INC.

HISTORICAL FINANCIALS

Company Type: Private

Income Statement — FYE: June 30

	REVENUE ($mil)	NET INCOME ($mil)	NET PROFIT MARGIN	EMPLOYEES
06/21	11,704	1,814	15.5%	49,000
06/20	416	51	12.5%	—
06/19	982	(17)	—	—
Annual Growth	245.1%	—	—	—

2021 Year-End Financials
Return on assets: 10.4%   Cash ($ mil.): 1,424
Return on equity: 20.9%
Current Ratio: 1.30

BAYLOR SCOTT & WHITE HOLDINGS

Auditors : PRICEWATERHOUSECOOPERS LLP DA

LOCATIONS

HQ: BAYLOR SCOTT & WHITE HOLDINGS
  301 N WASHINGTON AVE, DALLAS, TX 752461754
Phone: 214 820-3151
Web: WWW.BSWHEALTH.COM

HISTORICAL FINANCIALS

Company Type: Private

Income Statement — FYE: June 30

	REVENUE ($mil)	NET INCOME ($mil)	NET PROFIT MARGIN	EMPLOYEES
06/22	12,718	95	0.7%	49,000
06/21	11,704	1,814	15.5%	—
06/20	72	(58)	—	—
06/19	62	(130)	—	—
Annual Growth	488.0%	—	—	—

2022 Year-End Financials
Return on assets: 0.6%   Cash ($ mil.): 1,624
Return on equity: 1.1%
Current Ratio: 1.60

BAYLOR UNIVERSITY

Don't mess with Texas, and don't mess around at Baylor University. The world's largest Baptist institution of higher learning requires its more than 15,000 students to follow a strict code of conduct. The university has approximately 150 undergraduate degree programs, as well as about 75 masters and more than 30 doctoral programs. With a student-to-faculty ratio of 15:1, the private, co-educational university also offers degrees from its law school (juris doctor) and theological seminary (master of divinity and doctor of ministry), as well as extensive research programs. Founded in 1845, the college is affiliated with the Baptist General Convention of Texas.

Geographic Reach

Baylor University has a 1,000-acre campus on the banks of the Brazos River in Waco, Texas. Its students hail from across the US and some 90 international countries.

Financial Performance

Baylor University reported an 18% increase in revenues to $561 million in 2012 due to higher tuition, fees, and gifts. Net income fell by 101% (to a loss of some $2 million) due to higher program and support expenses.

The university's market endowment value was some $960 million as of mid-2012.

Auditors : GRANT THORTNTON LLP DALLAS

LOCATIONS

HQ: BAYLOR UNIVERSITY
  700 S UNIV PKS DR STE 67, WACO, TX 767061003
Phone: 254 710-1561
Web: WWW.BAYLOR.EDU

PRODUCTS/OPERATIONS

Selected Colleges and Schools
College of Arts and Sciences
George W. Truett Theological Seminary
Graduate School
Hankamer School of Business
Honors College
Law School
Louise Herrington School of Nursing
School of Education
School of Engineering and Computer Science
School of Music
School of Social Work

Selected Institutes
Allbritton Art Institute
Institute for Air Science
Institute for Faith and Learning
Institute for Oral History
Institute of Biblical and Related Languages
Institute of Biomedical Studies
J. M. Dawson Institute of Church-State Studies

COMPETITORS

BEAUMONT HEALTH
INDIANA UNIVERSITY HEALTH, INC.
MCLAREN HEALTH CARE CORPORATION
PROMEDICA HEALTH SYSTEMS, INC.
RITE AID CORPORATION
SSM HEALTH CARE CORPORATION
THE CLEVELAND CLINIC FOUNDATION
THE COLLEGE OF WILLIAM & MARY
TRUSTEES OF CLARK UNIVERSITY
UNIVERSITY OF DELAWARE

HISTORICAL FINANCIALS

Company Type: Private

Income Statement — FYE: May 31

	REVENUE ($mil)	NET INCOME ($mil)	NET PROFIT MARGIN	EMPLOYEES
05/22	925	281	30.4%	2,500
05/21	920	524	56.9%	—
05/20	791	142	18.0%	—
05/19	710	19	2.8%	—
Annual Growth	9.2%	142.2%	—	—

2022 Year-End Financials
Return on assets: 7.2%   Cash ($ mil.): 311
Return on equity: 9.7%
Current Ratio: —

BAYLOR UNIVERSITY MEDICAL CENTER

Baylor University Medical Center at Dallas is the flagship institution of the Baylor Health Care System. The medical center (known as Baylor Dallas) serves more than 300,000 patients annually with more than 1,000 inpatient beds and some 1,200 physicians. It offers general medical and surgical services to specialty care in a wide range of fields, including oncology, cardiovascular disease, and neuroscience. The hospital also features a Level I trauma center, neonatal ICU, and organ transplantation center. Founded in 1903, the Baylor Dallas campus includes the Charles A. Sammons Cancer Center and the Baylor Research Institute, which conducts basic and clinical research across numerous medical specialties.

Operations

The Baylor University Medical Center campus consists of 20 specialty centers for treating a range of medical conditions. Primary facilities include the Charles A. Sammons Cancer Center, Neuroscience Center, Annette C. and Harold C. Simmons

Transplant Institute, James M. and Dorothy D. Collins Womens and Children's Center, and the George Truett James Orthopaedic Institute, as well as a top trauma center, digestive care program, and heart and vascular unit. The Heart and Vascular Institute conducts more than 50 research studies a year.

Strategy

The hospital received a boost in 2011 when Texas A&M's Health Science Center struck an affiliation with Baylor Health Care System. The two parties agreed to make Baylor Dallas a primary teaching hospital for A&M's third and fourth-year medical students. No hospital in the Baylor Health Care System held such a designation after it became independent from Baylor University in 1997.

As one of only two adult Level 1 trauma centers in the region, Baylor Dallas has worked to bolster its emergency services to keep up with increasing demand. To this end, it has broadened its Level 1 trauma capabilities, increased the size of its minor emergency care area, and added more patient care areas. The Riggs Emergency Department treats some 67,000 patients each year.

Baylor Dallas' transplant program is considered a national leader in solid organ transplantation and, in partnership with the program at Baylor All Saints Medical Center, is one of only three programs worldwide to have performed more than 3,000 adult liver transplants. The program is also known for its kidney, pancreas, heart and lung, small bowel, and blood and marrow transplants.

LOCATIONS

HQ: BAYLOR UNIVERSITY MEDICAL CENTER
2001 BRYAN ST STE 2200, DALLAS, TX 752013024
Phone: 214 820-3151
Web: WWW.BSWHEALTH.COM

Selected Locations
A. Webb Roberts Hospital
Baylor Charles A. Sammons Cancer Center
Baylor Jack and Jane Hamilton Heart and Vascular Hospital
Carr P. Collins Hospital
Erik and Margaret Jonsson Medical and Surgical Hospital
George W. Truett Memorial Hospital
Karl and Esther Hoblitzelle Memorial Hospital
Baylor Specialty Hospital
Our Children's House at Baylor

PRODUCTS/OPERATIONS

Selected Speciality Centers
Baylor Cancer Hospital
Baylor Center for Pain Management
Baylor Diagnostic Imaging Centers
Baylor George Truett James Orthopaedic Institute
Baylor Geriatric and Senior Center
Baylor Heart and Vascular Institute
Baylor Heart Failure Program
Baylor Motion and Sports Performance Center
Baylor Neuroscience Center
Baylor Radiosurgery Center
Baylor Ruth Collins Diabetes Center
Baylor Sammons Bone Tumor Center
Baylor Sammons Lung Cancer Center
Baylor Spine Center
Baylor SportsCare
Comprehensive Wound Center
Darlene G. Cass Women's Imaging Center
Digestive Care Services
Ernie's Appearance Center
Gastrointestinal and Endoscopy Laboratory
Hereditary Cancer Risk Program
Infectious Disease Center
James M. and Dorothy D. Collins Women and Children's Center
Kimberly H. Courtwright and Joseph W. Summers Institute of Metabolic Disease
Louise Gartner Center for Hyperbaric Medicine
Martha Foster Lung Care Center
Non-invasive Heart and Vascular Laboratory
Reuben H. Adams Family Health Center
Simply Mom's Mother and Baby Boutique
Sleep Center
TINY TOTS Clinic
Virginia R. Cvetko Cancer Patient Education Center
Visual Function Testing Center
W.H. and Peggy Smith Baylor Sammons Breast Center
Weight Loss Surgery Program

COMPETITORS

AKRON GENERAL MEDICAL CENTER
TEXAS HEALTH PRESBYTERIAN HOSPITAL DALLAS
THE BRIGHAM AND WOMEN'S HOSPITAL INC
THE CHRIST HOSPITAL
THOMAS JEFFERSON UNIVERSITY HOSPITALS, INC.

HISTORICAL FINANCIALS

Company Type: Private

Income Statement FYE: June 30

	NET REVENUE ($mil)	NET INCOME ($mil)	NET PROFIT MARGIN	EMPLOYEES
06/15	1,394	378	27.2%	5,003
06/09	1,072	0	0.0%	—
06/08	155	16	10.3%	—
06/06	937	114	12.2%	—
Annual Growth	4.5%	14.3%	—	—

2015 Year-End Financials
Return on assets: 18.8%
Return on equity: 19.5%
Current Ratio: 3.10
Cash ($ mil.): —

BAYSTATE HEALTH SYSTEM HEALTH SERVICES, INC.

Patients in need of medical care can dock at this bay. Not-for-profit Baystate Health is the largest health care services provider in western Massachusetts. The system operates five acute-care and specialty hospitals with a total of approximately 1,000 beds, including the flagship Baystate Medical Center, which operates a Level 1 Trauma Center and a specialized children's hospital. Baystate Health also offers ancillary medical services such as cancer care, respiratory care, infusion therapy, visiting nurse, and hospice services through its regional clinics and agencies. The system controls for-profit health plan provider Health New England, as well as clinical pathology firm Baystate Reference Laboratories.

Operations

Baystate Medical Center accounts for more than 700 of the system's beds. Its other four acute care hospitals are Baystate Franklin Medical Center (89 beds), Baystate Wing Hospital (74 beds), Baystate Noble Hospital (97 beds), and Baystate Mary Lane Hospital (25 beds). The system also runs a physicians group, Baystate Medical Practices, which operates more than two dozen physician practices in several surrounding counties and towns. Other outpatient centers include surgery centers, imaging and radiology clinics, and neighborhood health centers. Altogether, its facilities serve a population of 750,000 western New England residents and admit more than 45,000 inpatients, perform some 34,000 surgeries, handle about 4,500 births, and conduct 1.4 million outpatient visits each year.

Baystate Health provides academic and community educational programs, as well as conducting basic, clinical, and biomedical research. For instance, the Baystate Medical Center is a teaching hospital that serves as the western campus of the Tufts University School of Medicine. Baystate Health also partners with a number of regional colleges to offer nursing programs.

In the research realm, Tufts and Baystate Health work on biomedical studies through the Tufts Clinical and Translational Science Institute. Baystate Medical Center also has a partnership with the University of Massachusetts that forms the Pioneer Valley Life Sciences Institute. Areas of research include clinical care, quality of care, and diabetes and metabolism. The Baystate Health system receives about $10 million per year in research funding from the National Institutes of Health and other agencies.

Geographic Reach

Baystate Health has some 60 locations serving western Massachusetts, including Berkshire, Franklin, Hampden, Hampshire, and Worcester counties.

Sales and Marketing

Patient service revenue accounts for a majority (about 60%) of the hospital system's sales; Medicare and Medicaid reimbursements make up 57% of patient service payments. Other sources include commercial insurers and private-pay customers.

Financial Performance

In fiscal 2015 (ended September), Baystate Health revenues grew 17% to $1.2 billion; this was driven by a growth in premiums as well as net patient service revenue. However, that year the system reported a net loss of $78 million due to higher medical claims and capitation, as well as losses on investments and pension adjustments.

Following net income's suit, cash flow from operations dropped 38% to $51 million in fiscal 2015.

Strategy

Baystate Health has been conducting expansion and renovation efforts at its facilities in recent years, including medical technology and information system upgrades. The system's largest effort was the construction of a $300 million clinical building on the Baystate Medical Center Campus.

Other facilities and divisions are undergoing expansion as well: The system is adding new space to house a pharmacy and nearly 100 modern inpatient rooms at its flagship campus, while a new surgical center is being added to Baystate Franklin Medical Center in Greenfield. Baystate Medical Practices continues to grow by adding new practices on a regular basis. Baystate Health is also upgrading its medical equipment and its information technology systems.

Mergers and Acquisitions

Baystate Health acquired Noble Hospital (now Baystate Noble Hospital), a 97-bed not-for-profit community hospital, in 2015. The year before that, it added another acute care facility when it bought the 74-bed Wind Memorial Hospital (now Baystate Wing Hospital) from UMass Memorial Healthcare.

Auditors: ERNST & YOUNG LLP BOSTON MAS

LOCATIONS

HQ: BAYSTATE HEALTH SYSTEM HEALTH SERVICES, INC.
280 CHESTNUT ST, SPRINGFIELD, MA 011991000
Phone: 413 794-9939

Selected Locations
Baystate Medical Center (Springfield)
    Baystate Children's Hospital (Springfield)
Baystate Franklin Medical Center (Greenfield)
Baystate Mary Lane Hospital (Ware)
Baystate Noble Hospital (Westfield)
Baystate Wing Hospital (Palmer)
Outpatient Centers
    Baystate Home Infusion & Respiratory Services
    Baystate Medical Practices
    Baystate Radiology and Imaging (BRI)
    Baystate Reference Laboratories (BRL)
    Baystate Visiting Nurse Association & Hospice
    Brightwood Health Center
    Chestnut Surgery Center
    D'Amour Center for Cancer Care
    High Street Center (adult and pediatrics)
    Mason Square Neighborhood Health Center
    Neurodiagnostics & Sleep Center
    Orthopedic Surgery Center
    Wesson Women & Infants Health Center

PRODUCTS/OPERATIONS

2015 Sales

	$ mil	% of total
Net patient service revenue	1,222.0	57
Premiums	822.0	39
Other	94.5	4
Total	2,138.5	100

Selected Services
Ambulance
Anesthesiology
Behavioral health services
Birthing services
Cancer
Cardiovascular
Emergency medicine
Endoscopy
Home care and home medical supplies
Hospital medicine
Neurosciences
Obstetrics and gynecology
Pain management center
Pathology
Pediatrics
Radiology
Rehabilitation care
Reproductive medicine
Sleep program
Surgery
Weight management
Women's health

COMPETITORS

CAREGROUP, INC.
INSPIRA HEALTH NETWORK, INC.
NORTON HEALTHCARE, INC.
SOUTHCOAST HEALTH SYSTEM, INC.
TRIHEALTH, INC.

HISTORICAL FINANCIALS
Company Type: Private

Income Statement   FYE: September 30

	REVENUE ($mil)	NET INCOME ($mil)	NET PROFIT MARGIN	EMPLOYEES
09/07	1,286	125	9.7%	5,000
09/06	1,209	83	6.9%	—
09/05	0	0	—	—
09/04	0	0	—	—
Annual Growth	—	—	—	—

2007 Year-End Financials
Return on assets: 5.4%   Cash ($ mil.): 61
Return on equity: 9.7%
Current Ratio: 0.70

BAYSTATE MEDICAL CENTER, INC.

LOCATIONS

HQ: BAYSTATE MEDICAL CENTER, INC.
759 CHESTNUT ST, SPRINGFIELD, MA 011990001
Phone: 413 794-0000
Web: WWW.BAYSTATEHEALTH.ORG

HISTORICAL FINANCIALS
Company Type: Private

Income Statement   FYE: September 30

	REVENUE ($mil)	NET INCOME ($mil)	NET PROFIT MARGIN	EMPLOYEES
09/20	1,257	95	7.6%	6,000
09/19	1,389	119	8.6%	—
Annual Growth	(9.5%)	(20.1%)	—	—

2020 Year-End Financials
Return on assets: 5.1%   Cash ($ mil.): 530
Return on equity: 11.3%
Current Ratio: 2.30

BCFS HEALTH AND HUMAN SERVICES

EXECUTIVES

Vice Chairman, George Cowden Iii Board
Auditors: BKD LLP DALLAS TX

LOCATIONS

HQ: BCFS HEALTH AND HUMAN SERVICES
1506 BEXAR CROSSING ST, SAN ANTONIO, TX 782321587
Phone: 210 832-5000
Web: WWW.DISCOVERBCFS.NET

HISTORICAL FINANCIALS
Company Type: Private

Income Statement   FYE: August 31

	REVENUE ($mil)	NET INCOME ($mil)	NET PROFIT MARGIN	EMPLOYEES
08/20	873	23	2.7%	96
08/19	86	1	2.2%	—
08/13	70	(1)	—	—
08/12	72	3	4.8%	—
Annual Growth	36.6%	27.1%	—	—

2020 Year-End Financials
Return on assets: 11.1%   Cash ($ mil.): —
Return on equity: 79.9%
Current Ratio: —

BEALL'S, INC.

Residents of the Sun Belt have been known to leave their homes with Beall's on. The retail holding company operates through subsidiaries Beall's Department Stores, Beall's Outlet, and Burke's Outlet Stores in a dozen states. The multi-brand retailer has more than 530 department and outlet stores (about 200 are in Florida) located throughout states in the southern and western US, including Arizona, California, Georgia, Louisiana, and Texas. Products range from off-price clothing and footwear for men and women to cosmetics, gifts, and housewares. Each chain has its own online shopping destination. The family-owned company was founded in 1915 by the grandfather of chairman Robert Beall (pronounced "bell").

Operations

Beall's Inc. oversees operations of its three operating companies. Beall's Florida operates some 190 stores in the Sunshine State. Beall's Outlet operates about 300 stores in Arizona, Florida, Texas, and Georgia, while Burke's Outlet operates more than 190 stores in 16 states.

Geographic Reach

Beall's trio of chain's operate stores in Alabama, Arkansas, Arizona, California, Florida, Georgia, Kentucky, Louisiana, Mississippi, Nevada, New Mexico, North

Carolina, South Carolina, Tennessee, Texas, Virginia, and West Virginia.

Financial Performance
Privately-owned Beall's rings ups more than $1 billion in sales annually.

Strategy
The company has aspirations to transform itself into a major discount retailer, much like its larger rivals TJX and Ross Stores. To that end, the company plans to add new stores outside its traditional markets, with an eye on establishing a national retail presence. Targets include adding 30 to 50 stores a year for the next several years and raising brand awareness beyond Florida.

With many of its stores in Arizona, Florida, and California (three of the states hit hardest by the housing crisis and deep recession) Beall's Inc. should have been in a heap of retail trouble. However, its largest chain -- Beall's Outlet --proved to be quite popular during this recession. Indeed, the budget-priced outlet chain outperformed its two sister chains, as well as more moderately priced department stores. The retailer has also benefited from the demise of other retailers, including Goody's, Linens 'n Things, and Mervyn's.

The three operating companies share resources provided by Beall's Inc., such as distribution, finance, loss prevention, and information systems. Conversely, each chain is responsible for its purchasing, product development, real estate, and advertising activities.

Company Background
Stores operating under the Bealls name in Alabama, New Mexico, and Texas are owned by Stage Stores and are not affiliated with Beall's, Inc.

Auditors : CHRISTOPHER SMITH LEONARD B

LOCATIONS
HQ: BEALL'S, INC.
 E R BALL CTR 700 13TH AVE, BRADENTON, FL 34208
Phone: 941 747-2355
Web: WWW.BEALLSINC.COM

PRODUCTS/OPERATIONS
Selected Retail Operations
Bealls Department Stores (Florida)
Bealls Outlet (deep-discount outlet stores in Arizona, Florida, Georgia)
Burke's Outlet (11 southern states)

COMPETITORS
ACADEMY, LTD.
ADIR INTERNATIONAL, LLC
BELK, INC.
BLOOMINGDALE'S, INC.
BOSCOV'S DEPARTMENT STORE, LLC
GABRIEL BROTHERS, INC.
MACY'S, INC.
RACETRAC PETROLEUM, INC.
SCHOTTENSTEIN STORES CORPORATION
Sears Canada Inc

HISTORICAL FINANCIALS
Company Type: Private

Income Statement   FYE: August 1

	REVENUE ($mil)	NET INCOME ($mil)	NET PROFIT MARGIN	EMPLOYEES
08/15*	1,321	25	1.9%	10,179
07/12	1,232	14	1.1%	—
07/11	1,166	15	1.3%	—
Annual Growth	3.2%	12.8%	—	—

*Fiscal year change

2015 Year-End Financials
Return on assets: 4.5%   Cash ($ mil.): 107
Return on equity: 8.7%
Current Ratio: 1.60

BEARINGPOINT, INC.

Auditors : ERNST & YOUNG LLP MCLEAN VI

LOCATIONS
HQ: BEARINGPOINT, INC.
 100 CRESCENT CT STE 700, DALLAS, TX 752012112
Phone: 214 459-2770

HISTORICAL FINANCIALS
Company Type: Private

Income Statement   FYE: December 31

	REVENUE ($mil)	NET INCOME ($mil)	NET PROFIT MARGIN	EMPLOYEES
12/07	3,455	(362)	—	15,200
12/06	3,444	(177)	—	—
Annual Growth	0.3%	—	—	—

2007 Year-End Financials
Return on assets: (-18.3%)   Cash ($ mil.): 468
Return on equity: —
Current Ratio: 1.40

BEAUMONT HEALTH

Beaumont Health is an eight-hospital regional health system in southeastern Michigan. The health system boasts about 3,400 hospital beds, 150 outpatient sites, and 5,000 affiliated physicians. Outpatient facilities include community medical centers, nursing homes, a home health agency, a research institute, and primary and specialty care clinics, as well as rehabilitation, cardiology, and cancer centers. Beaumont is the exclusive clinical teaching site for the Oakland University William Beaumont School of Medicine; it also has affiliations with Michigan State University College of Osteopathic Medicine and Wayne State University School of Medicine. In 2019 it agreed to acquire Ohio hospital operator Summa Health.

OperationsBeaumont holds a Level I trauma designation in Oakland and Macomb counties. The system's Children's Hospital has more than 80 pediatric subspecialists. Its research institute has more than 1,000 active clinical studies, including interventional clinical research trials. A teaching hospital, Beaumont has 40 residency and fellowship programs with more than 450 participants. The system is also the exclusive clinical partner of William Beaumont School of Medicine, providing more than 1,500 physicians to the school's faculty. The system handles about 180,000 admissions, some 18,000 infant births, more than 550,000 emergency department visits annually.

Geographic Reach
Beaumont Health operates health care facilities throughout suburban Detroit (in Oakland, Macomb, and Wayne counties).

Strategy
Beaumont Health expands its care offerings by partnering with other service providers (such as insurance groups), adding new facilities to its network, and by taking advantage of government initiatives to modernize its systems.

Mergers and Acquisitions
In 2019, Beaumont Health agreed to acquire Akron, Ohio-based Summa Health, which operates three acute care hospitals, a rehab hospital, a health plan, and other health resources in northeastern Ohio. Summa, with $1.4 billion in revenue, will operate as a wholly owned subsidiary of Beaumont ($4.7 billion in revenue) and will retain its name and local leadership. In the face of reimbursement changes, rising expenses, and intensifying competition, the deal aims to allow for continued expansion and growth while improving care for patients in the two states. No financial transaction will occur between Beaumont and Summa, but the two companies will buy out Summa's minority shareholder Mercy Health (now part of Bon Secours Mercy Health).

Company Background
Beaumont Health system traces its roots to Dr. William Beaumont, an army doctor who conducted groundbreaking research on the human digestive system on Mackinac Island, Michigan, in the 1820s. The first Beaumont Hospital was opened in Royal Oak in 1955; the Troy facility was opened in 1977; and its third hospital in Grosse Pointe was acquired in 2007 from Bon Secours Health System. In 2014, Beaumont merged with hospital operators Oakwood Healthcare and Botsford Hospital, creating a $3.8 billion not-for-profit organization to provide improved care services across combined communities.

EXECUTIVES
Chief Medical Officer, Barbara Ducatman
Auditors : ERNST & YOUNG LLP DETROIT M

LOCATIONS
HQ: BEAUMONT HEALTH
 3601 W 13 MILE RD, ROYAL OAK, MI 480736712
Phone: 248 898-5000
Web: WWW.BEAUMONT.ORG

Selected Michigan Locations
Lake Orion
Macomb
Rochester Hills
Royal Oak
St. Clair Shores
Sterling Heights
Warren
West Bloomfield

PRODUCTS/OPERATIONS

Selected Michigan Facilities
Health, Wellness, and Outpatient Care
    Beaumont Bon Brae Center (fitness; St. Clair Shores)
    Beaumont Health and Wellness Center (Rochester Hills)
    Beaumont Health Center (outpatient services; Royal Oak)
    Beaumont Medical Centers
Hospitals
    Beaumont Hospital, Grosse Pointe
    Beaumont Hospital, Royal Oak
    Beaumont Hospital, Troy
Nursing and Rehabilitation
    Evergreen Health and Living Center (Southfield)
    Shelby Nursing Center (Shelby Township)
    ShorePointe Nursing Care (St. Clair Shores)
    ShorePointe Village Assisted Living (St. Clair Shores)
    West Bloomfield Nursing Center
    Woodward Hills Nursing Center (Bloomfield Hills)
Research and Education
    Oakland University William Beaumont School of Medicine (Royal Oak)

Selected Centers of Excellence
Cancer
Children's Hospital
Digestive health
Heart and vascular
Neuroscience
Orthopedics
Women's health

COMPETITORS

BAPTIST HEALTH SYSTEM, INC.
INDIANA UNIVERSITY HEALTH, INC.
MEDSTAR HEALTH, INC.
MERCY HEALTH
PASADENA HOSPITAL ASSOCIATION, LTD.
SANFORD
SUMMA HEALTH
THE CLEVELAND CLINIC FOUNDATION
UNIVERSITY HOSPITALS HEALTH SYSTEM, INC.
WILLIAM BEAUMONT HOSPITAL

HISTORICAL FINANCIALS
Company Type: Private

Income Statement — FYE: December 31

	REVENUE ($mil)	NET INCOME ($mil)	NET PROFIT MARGIN	EMPLOYEES
12/21	4,695	500	10.6%	35,000
12/20	4,580	318	7.0%	—
12/19	4,703	401	8.5%	—
12/18	4,659	142	3.0%	—
Annual Growth	0.3%	52.1%	—	—

2021 Year-End Financials
Return on assets: 7.5%   Cash ($ mil.): 1,175
Return on equity: 13.2%
Current Ratio: 2.40

BEAVERTON SCHOOL DISTRICT

EXECUTIVES

CIO*, Stephen Langford
Auditors : GROVE MUELLER & SWANK PC SA

LOCATIONS

HQ: BEAVERTON SCHOOL DISTRICT
1260 NW WATERHOUSE AVE # 100, BEAVERTON, OR 970065794
Phone: 503 591-8000
Web: WWW.BEAVERTON.K12.OR.US

HISTORICAL FINANCIALS
Company Type: Private

Income Statement — FYE: June 30

	REVENUE ($mil)	NET INCOME ($mil)	NET PROFIT MARGIN	EMPLOYEES
06/20	625	(54)	—	4,000
06/19	611	(93)	—	—
06/18	584	(97)	—	—
06/17	529	119	22.5%	—
Annual Growth	5.7%	—	—	—

2020 Year-End Financials
Return on assets: (-3.5%)   Cash ($ mil.): —
Return on equity: —
Current Ratio: —

BEEBE MEDICAL CENTER, INC.

Sea shells on the sea shore can be found near Beebe Medical Center. The health care provider offers emergency, inpatient, long-term care, women's health, and other medical services to residents of Sussex County, Delaware. The hospital is located in the town of Lewes, near Rehoboth Beach. It hasÂ approximatelyÂ 210 beds and offers specialized services including cardiology, orthopedic, rehabilitation, and oncology treatments. Beebe Medical Center offers outpatientÂ services includingÂ woundÂ care, diabetes management,Â surgery, radiology, and sleep disorder diagnosis. It alsoÂ operatesÂ senior care centers, home health agencies,Â medical laboratories, and a nursing school.

Operations
Beebe Medical Center has a staff of some 1,400 health professionals, including about 300 doctors. It handles some 50,000 emergency room visits per year. In addition to the primary hospital facilities, the health care provider operates the Beebe Health Campus (outpatient services) and theÂ nearby Millville Emergency Center (a summertime clinic near Bethany Beach).

Strategy
Beebe Medical Center has expanded its facilities over the years to better serve area residents. It began an expansion aiming to double enrollment of the nursing school in 2012.Â Construction efforts at the main hospital facility include a new emergency and critical care wing added in 2008.

Company Background
Beebe Medical Center was founded in 1916 by two brothers, Dr. James Beebe and Dr. Richard Beebe. The Beebe School of NursingÂ opened in 1921, and the outpatient Beebe Health Campus was completed in 2003.

EXECUTIVES

Interim Chief Executive Officer, Rick Schaffner
Auditors : GRANT THORNTON LLP PHILADELPH

LOCATIONS

HQ: BEEBE MEDICAL CENTER, INC.
424 SAVANNAH RD, LEWES, DE 199581462
Phone: 302 645-3300
Web: WWW.BEEBEHEALTHCARE.ORG

Selected Delaware Locations
Beebe Health Campus (Rehoboth Beach)
Beebe Lab Express (Milton)
Beebe School of Nursing (Lewes)
Diabetes Management and Wound Care Center (Long Neck)
Georgetown Professional Park (Georgetown)
Gull House Adult Activities Center (Lewes)
Home Health Agency (Lewes)
Millville Walk-in Health Center (Millville)
Sleep Disorders Center (Rehoboth Beach)
Tunnell Cancer Center (Rehoboth Beach)

PRODUCTS/OPERATIONS

Selected Services
Bariatric
Cancer care
Cardiac & vascular
Community health
Diabetes management
Emergency
Home health
Hospitalist program
Imaging
Integrative health
Orthopedics
Rehabilitation
Senior care
Sleep Disorder
Surgical
Walk-in Healthcare
Wellness
Women's Health
Wound Care

COMPETITORS

COLUMBIA HOSPITAL (PALM BEACHES) LIMITED PARTNERSHIP
HARRINGTON MEMORIAL HOSPITAL, INC.
HUNTINGTON HOSPITAL DOLAN FAMILY HEALTH CENTER, INC.
MONMOUTH MEDICAL CENTER INC.
NEWTON MEMORIAL HOSPITAL (INC)
OHIO VALLEY MEDICAL CENTER, INCORPORATED
PRIME HEALTHCARE SERVICES - GARDEN CITY, LLC
SUBURBAN HOSPITAL, INC.
WAKEMED
WHITE COUNTY MEDICAL CENTER

BENCO DENTAL SUPPLY CO.

Benco Dental Supply is a one-stop shop for the tooth doc. Through regional showrooms and distribution centers, Benco provides dental and dentistry supplies to more than 30,000 dental professionals throughout the US. Its offerings include dental hand pieces, furniture, and disposable supplies. Its BencoNET division develops and distributes custom computers and proprietary programming and networking systems for dentists. Other services include dental office design, practice consulting, financing and real estate planning, wealth management, and equipment repairs.

Operations
Benco offerings range from large equipment to small supplies made by a broad range of manufacturers. The company supplies more than 80,000 products including dental cement, impression supplies, and curing lights made by manufacturers such as 3M, Dentsply Sirona, Sybron (Kerr), Hu-Friedy, and more. It also sells products under its own Benco Dental brand.

Support services include offers inventory management services and hand piece, equipment, and upholstery repair.

Benco Dental's practice management services include staff recruitment assistance, product training programs for dentists, peer-to-peer networking solutions, and continuing medical education programs.

Geographic Reach
Benco Dental's main headquarters and showroom is located in Pittston, Pennsylvania. It also operates another CenterPoint Experience (large-scale) showroom in Costa Mesa, California, and it has a network of about 50 smaller regional showrooms and five distribution centers (in Pittston; Dallas; Fort Wayne, Indiana; Jacksonville, Florida; and Reno, Nevada) across the US that serve customers in all 50 US states.

Although most of its operations are in the US, the company also ships products to overseas customers.

Sales and Marketing
Benco markets its products and services directly to dental practices. It also increasing the number of orders placed through its online ordering system (Painless), and it promotes services to dentists through affiliations with dental organizations and associations (including the American Academy of Dental Group Practice and the American Association of Orthodontists). The company has more than 400 sales representatives. To support sales, it also has about 300 factory-trained service technicians.

Financial Performance
Benco increased net sales by 9% in 2012 due to new product sales launches and increased sales of existing products in fields including 3D imaging equipment and digital sensors.

Strategy
Benco tends to expand its operations through organic growth initiatives, including offering new products and services to a wider customer base. In addition, the company grows through acquisitions in key growth regions. The company launched 14 Benco branded products during 2012, as well as 3,800 new products made by its vendor partners. It also added about 50 new sales reps that year to meet rising customer demands. The company estimated that it grew market share to some 11% of the US market that year (placing itself among the top three dental supply distributors).

Benco increased sales to community health centers that year through its partnership with PSS. To expand its educational programs, in 2012 the company also formed a partnership with the Kois Center, which offers a nine-course program on topics including aesthetic and restorative dentistry.

To reach additional customers and expand its capacity, the company opened its fifth distribution center -- a 120,000-sq. ft. facility in Reno, Nevada -- in 2011. It also opened a new sales branch office in Los Angeles to serve the Southern California market in 2012.

Benco Dental moved into its CenterPoint headquarters and showroom in Pittston, Pennsylvania, in early 2010. The facility is one of the largest dental equipment showrooms in the US with exhibits including more than two dozen dental rooms, 14 digital X-ray units, three sterilization centers, and other oral surgery and orthodontic units, as well as an office design concept suite and a training and education center. Following the success of that location, the company opened a second CenterPoint Experience showroom in Costa Mesa, California, in 2012.

Auditors : COHEN AND CO CLEVELAND OHIO

LOCATIONS

HQ: BENCO DENTAL SUPPLY CO.
295 CENTERPOINT BLVD, PITTSTON, PA 186406136
Phone: 570 602-7781
Web: WWW.BENCO.COM

Selected Distribution Center Locations
Dallas, Texas
Fort Wayne, Indiana
Jacksonville, Florida
Pittston, Pennsylvania
Reno, Nevada

PRODUCTS/OPERATIONS

Selected Brands
Large Equipment
   A-dec
   Belmont
   BIOLASE
   Cadent
   Gendex
   Instrumentarium
   Marus
   Midmark
   Pelton & Crane
   Sirona
   Soredex
   Vatech
Small Equipment
   Accutron
   Aceton
   Air Techniques
   Cadent
   KaVo
   Midmark
   Midwest
   Tuttnauer
   W&H
Supplies and technology (Benco brands)
   BencoNET
   BluChip rewards
   BluPrint (dental impression material)
   fas-TRACT
   HD
   Iris (dental pit and fissure sealant)
   Natural Extensions (nitrile gloves)
   Painless
   ValuGrip (latex gloves)
   Vision XR (oral x-ray film)
   XLR8 (dental equipment)
   Z3

COMPETITORS

AMERISOURCEBERGEN CORPORATION
CHINDEX INTERNATIONAL, INC.
COOPERSURGICAL, INC.
DEROYAL INDUSTRIES, INC.
HENRY SCHEIN, INC.
MEDLINE INDUSTRIES, INC.
OWENS & MINOR, INC.
PATTERSON COMPANIES, INC.
TRIVIDIA HEALTH, INC.
YOUNG INNOVATIONS, INC.

HISTORICAL FINANCIALS
Company Type: Private

Income Statement   FYE: June 30

	REVENUE ($mil)	NET INCOME ($mil)	NET PROFIT MARGIN	EMPLOYEES
06/22	581	44	7.6%	1,606
06/21	500	65	13.1%	—
06/20	450	(8)	—	—
06/19	447	21	4.7%	—
Annual Growth	9.1%	27.7%	—	—

2022 Year-End Financials
Return on assets: 6.0%   Cash ($ mil.): 118
Return on equity: 12.5%
Current Ratio: 2.10

HISTORICAL FINANCIALS
Company Type: Private

Income Statement   FYE: January 4

	REVENUE ($mil)	NET INCOME ($mil)	NET PROFIT MARGIN	EMPLOYEES
01/14*	620	8	1.4%	1,600
12/12	600	7	1.2%	—
12/07	389	5	1.3%	—
Annual Growth	8.1%	10.0%	—	—

*Fiscal year change

2014 Year-End Financials
Return on assets: 4.9%   Cash ($ mil.): —
Return on equity: —
Current Ratio: 1.60

BENEFIS HEALTH SYSTEM, INC

Auditors : MOSS ADAMS LLP PORTLAND OR

LOCATIONS

HQ: BENEFIS HEALTH SYSTEM, INC
1101 26TH ST S, GREAT FALLS, MT 594055161
Phone: 406 455-5000
Web: WWW.BENEFIS.ORG

HISTORICAL FINANCIALS
Company Type: Private

Income Statement — FYE: December 31

	REVENUE ($mil)	NET INCOME ($mil)	NET PROFIT MARGIN	EMPLOYEES
12/21	588	90	15.3%	94
12/19	69	5	8.2%	—
12/16	413	15	3.8%	—
12/15	69	7	10.5%	—
Annual Growth	42.9%	52.1%	—	—

2021 Year-End Financials
Return on assets: 7.9%   Cash ($ mil.): —
Return on equity: 12.3%
Current Ratio: 1.80

BENEFIS HOSPITALS, INC

Auditors : MOSS ADAMS LLP SEATTLE WASHI

LOCATIONS

HQ: BENEFIS HOSPITALS, INC
1101 26TH ST S, GREAT FALLS, MT 594055161
Phone: 406 455-5000
Web: WWW.BENEFIS.ORG

HISTORICAL FINANCIALS
Company Type: Private

Income Statement — FYE: December 31

	REVENUE ($mil)	NET INCOME ($mil)	NET PROFIT MARGIN	EMPLOYEES
12/21	546	49	9.1%	2,419
12/19	1,147	49	4.3%	—
12/16	865	26	3.0%	—
12/15	860	20	2.4%	—
Annual Growth	(7.3%)	16.0%	—	—

2021 Year-End Financials
Return on assets: 4.5%   Cash ($ mil.): (-5)
Return on equity: 16.9%
Current Ratio: 1.30

BERGELECTRIC CORP.

One of the nation's top electrical contractors, Bergelectric provides design/build and design/assist services on projects that include office buildings, public-sector facilities, bioscience labs, entertainment complexes, hotels, data centers, and hospitals. Its projects also consist of parking garages, water treatment plants, residential towers, and correctional facilities. The company boasts expertise in building information modeling, fire alarms and security, and telecommunications and data infrastructure. Bergelectric operates mainly in the western and southeastern US from about a dozen offices.

Operations
The electrical company keeps a lengthy list of projects, past and current. More recent projects have included the San Ysidro Land Port of Entry, Lackland Ambulatory Care Center, Northwest Water Reclamation Facility, Naval Hospital Camp Pendleton, Fort Riley Community Replacement Hospital, Wilshire Boulevard Temple, California Health Care Facility, Visitors Center at King Gillette Ranch, Variety Special Education School, Greenlaw Partners, and Sandy High School.

The company has more than $550 million in backlog.

Geographic Reach
From its headquarters in Los Angeles, Bergelectric maintains a presence in California through a handful of offices in San Diego, Los Angeles, Orange County, Sacramento, and Ventura. It also serves as an electrical contractor in half a dozen cities, including Austin, Texas; Denver, Colorado; Las Vegas, Nevada; Orlando, Florida; Phoenix, Arizona; Portland, Oregon; and Raleigh, North Carolina.

Strategy
The company is also focused on green initiatives, completing Leadership in Energy and Environmental Design (LEED) construction projects for the likes of Sony, the FBI, the EPA, and the University of Oregon. To this end, the company formed the Fire-Alarm/Security Division, which provides projects and clients with comprehensive electrical services for such fire alarm projects as the Morongo Casino & Hotel, Pechanga Hotel & Casino, and San Manuel Indian Bingo & Casino.

Bergelectric has extended the reach of its traditional electrical contracting operations by expanding into new markets, including sustainable building structures and renewable energy systems such as wind farms. Through a partnership with telecommunications firm Teo, Bergelectric provides communications services to wind energy producers. As part of the agreement, Bergelectric designs and installs fiber connections and equipment while Teo supplies phones, switches, and other hardware.

To simplify the integration of complex systems, Bergelectric established a national Technology Systems group, which serves to consolidate all of the company's existing low-voltage divisions under one management umbrella. The move aims to differentiate Bergelectric from the traditionally fragmented industry of electrical and systems components.

Company Background
Bergelectric was founded in 1946.

Auditors : MOSS LEVY & HARTZHEIM LLP B

LOCATIONS

HQ: BERGELECTRIC CORP.
3182 LIONSHEAD AVE, CARLSBAD, CA 920104701
Phone: 760 638-2374
Web: WWW.BERGELECTRIC.COM

Selected Locations
Agoura Hills, CA
Austin, TX
Costa Mesa, CA
Denver
Durham, NC
Escondido, CA
Los Angeles
North Las Vegas, NV
Orlando, FL
Portland, OR
Rancho Cordova, CA
Tempe, AZ

COMPETITORS

CUPERTINO ELECTRIC, INC.
DAVID EVANS AND ASSOCIATES, INC.
GUARANTEE ELECTRICAL COMPANY INC
MMR GROUP, INC.
MORROW-MEADOWS CORPORATION
ROSENDIN ELECTRIC, INC.
SASCO
SWINERTON BUILDERS, INC.
TDINDUSTRIES, INC.
WAYNE J. GRIFFIN ELECTRIC, INC.

HISTORICAL FINANCIALS
Company Type: Private

Income Statement — FYE: January 31

	REVENUE ($mil)	NET INCOME ($mil)	NET PROFIT MARGIN	EMPLOYEES
01/22	705	7	1.0%	2,600
01/21	667	9	1.4%	—
01/20	521	6	1.2%	—
01/14	525	4	0.9%	—
Annual Growth	3.8%	4.9%	—	—

2022 Year-End Financials
Return on assets: 2.8%   Cash ($ mil.): 6
Return on equity: 14.5%
Current Ratio: 1.30

BERRY GLOBAL FILMS, LLC

Making plastic cling is this company's thing. AEP Industries manufactures plastic packaging films -- more than 15,000 types -- including stretch wrap for industrial pallets, packaging for foods and beverages, and films for agricultural uses, such as wrap for hay bales. AEP also makes dispenser-boxed plastic wraps, which are sold to consumers as well as institutions ranging from schools to hospitals. Other industries courted by AEP are packaging, transportation, food, autos, chemicals, textiles, and electronics. The company operates in the US and in Canada. In the summer of 2016, AEP agreed to be acquired by rival Berry Plastics Group.

Geographic Reach
AEP conducts about 95% of its business in the US market. Remaining sales take place in Canada. It has about 15 manufacturing facilities in the US (about 11 states) and Canada. The company also exports its products to Latin America through its office in Waxahachie, Texas.

Sales and Marketing
About two-thirds of AEP's sales are made to distributors, and the remainder, directly to end-users of its products. It serves about 3,000 customers. The company works to maintain customer relationships, and it provides technical training to its sales personal so that they are able to provide customer support and communicate customer needs to the company's product development team. Distribution functions are mostly contracted to third parties.

Financial Performance
AEP's revenues have fluctuated over the years. After peaking at $1.19 billion in 2014, revenues fell by 4% to $1.14 billion in 2015. The revenue decrease for 2015 was fueled by a 3% dip in average selling prices, primarily due to the pass-through of lower resin costs negatively affecting net sales by $31 million.

The company in 2015 also experienced a 1% decrease in sales volumes attributed to volatility in the resin markets. This resulted in soft customer demand in certain stock product lines, customer bankruptcies, and the impact of exiting certain low-margin businesses during fiscal 2014.

After experiencing a net loss of $6 million in 2014, AEP posted positive net income of $29 million in 2015. This was the result of a decline in costs coupled with a larger amount of income tax benefits.

Strategy
With little product differentiation among plastic film producers, AEP positions itself as the low-cost source, with technological expertise to customize value-added flexible films to satisfy myriad manufacturing and processing applications. The company aims to provide long-term value to shareholders by becoming the preferred provider of flexible packaging products in the North American market.

To strengthen its finances and increase manufacturing output and productivity, AEP is investing heavily in capital improvements. During the last decade it has purchased or leased new equipment and made equipment upgrades intended to optimize its manufacturing footprint in high-growth product categories.

The company looks for success in its sales and distribution model by establishing long-term relationships with its customers. To mitigate the volatility of raw material prices, the company pursues volume raw material rebates by making most of its purchases from three primary suppliers.

Company Background
Brendan Barba, a former salesman for polyethylene film maker PPD, formed Flexible Plastics in 1967 in Lodi, New Jersey. In 1970 his partner bought him out. That year Barba founded AEP Industries, briefly called Automatically Extruded Products. In 1982 the company moved into the specialty and premium films market. It established a plant in Waxahachie, Texas, in 1985, and went public a year later.

LOCATIONS
HQ: BERRY GLOBAL FILMS, LLC
95 CHESTNUT RIDGE RD, MONTVALE, NJ 076451801
Phone: 201 641-6600
Web: WWW.BERRYGLOBAL.COM

2015 Sales
	$ mil.	% of total
US	1,073.4	94
Canada	68.0	6
Total	1,141.4	100

PRODUCTS/OPERATIONS
2015 Sales
	$ mil.	% of total
Custom films	357.7	31
Stretch (pallet) wrap	332.9	29
Food contact	165.6	14
Canliners	144.4	13
PROformance films	63.2	6
Printed & converted films, specialty films & other	77.6	7
Total	1,141.4	100

Selected Products
Canliners
Kitchen and standard garbage bags
Custom films (polyethylene co-extruded and monolayer custom designed film)
    Drum, box, carton, pail liners
    Films to cover high value products
    Furniture and mattress bags
    Magazine overwrap
PROformance films (co-extruded and monolayer polyolefin films)
    Cereal box liners
    Fresh cut produce packaging
    Frozen foods
    Medical
Polyvinyl chloride wrap
    Food and freezer wrap
Printed and converted films (polyethylene)
    Printed, laminated, converted films for flexible packaging to consumer markets
    Printed shrink films
Stretch (pallet) wrap (polyethylene)
    Pallet wrap
Other products and specialty films (unplasticized polyvinyl chloride, polyethylene)
    Agricultural films
    Battery labels
    Canliners
    Credit card laminate
    Retail and institutional films and products
    Table covers, aprons, bibs and gloves
    Twist wrap

COMPETITORS
ALBEMARLE CORPORATION
BLUELINX HOLDINGS INC.
Covestro Deutschland AG
HUNTSMAN CORPORATION
HUNTSMAN INTERNATIONAL LLC
LYONDELLBASELL ADVANCED POLYMERS INC.
SOLUTIA INC.
SONOCO PRODUCTS COMPANY
STR HOLDINGS, INC.
THE DOW CHEMICAL COMPANY

HISTORICAL FINANCIALS
Company Type: Private

Income Statement   FYE: October 31

	REVENUE ($mil)	NET INCOME ($mil)	NET PROFIT MARGIN	EMPLOYEES
10/15	1,141	28	2.5%	2,600
10/14	1,192	(5)	—	—
10/13	1,143	10	0.9%	—
Annual Growth	(0.1%)	63.8%	—	—

2015 Year-End Financials
Return on assets: 6.6%   Cash ($ mil.): 20
Return on equity: 32.2%
Current Ratio: 2.10

BEST PETROLEUM CORPORATION

Auditors: JESUS OYOLA CUADRADO BAYAMON

LOCATIONS
HQ: BEST PETROLEUM CORPORATION
KM 20 HM 5 RR 2, TOA BAJA, PR 00951
Phone: 787 251-6218
Web: WWW.BESTPETROLEUMCORP.COM

HISTORICAL FINANCIALS
Company Type: Private

Income Statement   FYE: December 31

	REVENUE ($mil)	NET INCOME ($mil)	NET PROFIT MARGIN	EMPLOYEES
12/18	673	32	4.8%	130
12/17	547	26	4.8%	—
12/16	439	16	3.7%	—
12/15	479	11	2.4%	—
Annual Growth	12.0%	41.5%	—	—

2018 Year-End Financials
Return on assets: 18.8%   Cash ($ mil.): 110
Return on equity: 21.2%
Current Ratio: 8.10

BETH ISRAEL DEACONESS MEDICAL CENTER, INC.

Beth Israel Deaconess Medical Center (BIDMC) is part of Beth Israel Lahey Health, a new health care system that brings together academic medical centers and teaching hospitals, community and specialty hospitals with more than 4,000 physicians and 35,000 employees. BIDMC has about 675 beds, including around 495 medical/surgical beds, more than 75 critical care beds, and more than 60 OB/GYN beds. It also provides a full range of emergency services, including a Level 1 Trauma Center and roof-top heliport. BIDMC a patient care, teaching and research affiliate of Harvard Medical School. The health system traces its roots to Deaconess Hospital, founded in 1896, and Beth Israel Hospital, established in 1916.

Operations

BIDMC constantly rank as national leader among independent hospitals in National Institutes of health funding. The company research funding totally over $229.8 million annually, 850 active sponsored projects, 500 founded, and non-founded clinical trials.

Beth Israel Deaconess Medical Center shares important clinical and research programs with institutions such as the Dana-Farber/Harvard Cancer Center, Joslin Diabetes Center and Children's Hospital. It has some 1,250 physicians on the active medical staff (including more than 800 full-time staff physicians). Most of these physicians hold faculty appointments at Harvard Medical School. In addition to its medical students, Beth Israel Deaconess Medical Center provides clinical education to students in nursing; social work; radiologic technology, ultrasound and nuclear medicine; and physical, occupational, speech and respiratory therapies.

The Carl J. Shapiro Institute for Education and Research provides medical students and physicians in training with an on-site centralized educational facility, a state-of-the-art computer lab, and a variety of educational resources that let students diagnose, manage, and learn technical skills on simulated patients.

Geographic Reach

BIDMC is located in Boston, Massachusetts and has a growing presence in Eastern Massachusetts.

Sales and Marketing

BIDMC market its products and services through websites such as providing extraordinary care, world-renowned experts provide care from patients call home from Newburyport to Plymouth, from Lexington to Quincy.

LOCATIONS

HQ: BETH ISRAEL DEACONESS MEDICAL CENTER, INC.
330 BROOKLINE AVE, BOSTON, MA 022155400
Phone: 617 667-7000
Web: WWW.BIDMC.ORG

PRODUCTS/OPERATIONS

Centers and Departments
Cancer Center
CardioVascular Institute
Digestive Disease Center
Spine Center
Transplant Institute
Clinical Departments
Anesthesia, Critical Care and Pain Medicine
Dermatology
Emergency Medicine
Medicine
Neonatology
Neurology
Obstetrics and Gynecology
Orthopedic Surgery
Pathology
Psychiatry
Radiation Oncology
Radiology
Rehabilitation Services
Surgery
Selected Facilities
Beth Israel Deaconess HealthCare-Chelsea
Beth Israel Deaconess HealthCare-Chestnut Hill
Beth Israel Deaconess HealthCare-Lexington
Beth Israel Deaconess Hospital-Milton
Beth Israel Deaconess Hospital-Needham
Beth Israel Deaconess Hospital-Plymouth

COMPETITORS

ATLANTIC HEALTH SYSTEM INC.
CAREGROUP, INC.
CONTINUUM HEALTH PARTNERS, INC.
JOHNS HOPKINS MEDICINE INTERNATIONAL, L.L.C.
KENNEDY HEALTH SYSTEM, INC.
OHIOHEALTH CORPORATION
THE CHILDREN'S HOSPITAL CORPORATION
THE UNIVERSITY OF VERMONT MEDICAL CENTER INC.
VHS HARPER-HUTZEL HOSPITAL, INC.
YORK HOSPITAL

HISTORICAL FINANCIALS

Company Type: Private

Income Statement   FYE: September 30

	REVENUE ($mil)	NET INCOME ($mil)	NET PROFIT MARGIN	EMPLOYEES
09/20	1,359	99	7.4%	6,500
09/19	1,945	67	3.5%	—
09/17	1,335	37	2.8%	—
09/16	1,279	28	2.3%	—
Annual Growth	1.5%	36.4%	—	—

2020 Year-End Financials
Return on assets: 4.0%
Return on equity: 9.4%
Current Ratio: 2.20
Cash ($ mil.): 192

BETH ISRAEL MEDICAL CENTER

Residents of New York City's Lower East Side look to Mount Sinai Beth Israel (formerly Beth Israel Medical Center) to keep them healthy. A member of Mount Sinai Health System, the tertiary care medical facility has about 800 inpatient beds located in Manhattan. It emphasizes its services in heart disease, cancer, neurology, orthopedics, gastrointestinal disease, chemical dependency, psychiatric disorders, pain management and palliative care, and HIV/AIDS research and treatment. It is notable for its unique approach to combining medical excellence with clinical innovation. Its wide array of services have included addiction, emergency department, heart (cardiology), lung and pulmonology, musictherapy, neurology, orthopedics, pediatric emergency care, psychiatry, radiology, surgery and urology. Headquartered in New York, Mount Sinai Beth Israel has played an important role in providing health care to New Yorkers since the mid-20th century. The company traces its roots back in 1889.

Auditors : PRICEWATERHOUSECOOPERS LLP NE

LOCATIONS

HQ: BETH ISRAEL MEDICAL CENTER
281 1ST AVE, NEW YORK, NY 100032925
Phone: 212 420-2000
Web: WWW.MOUNTSINAI.ORG

PRODUCTS/OPERATIONS

Selected Centers and Services
AIDS Services
Allergy and Immunology
Anesthesiology
Appel-Venet Comprehensive Breast Service
Asian Services
Beth Israel ALS Center
Beth Israel Hernia Center
Beth Israel Medical Group
Betty & Morton Yarmon Stroke Center
Brief Psychotherapy Research Program
Cancer Center (Oncology)
Center for Blood Management and Bloodless Medicine and Surgery
Center for Endovascular Surgery
Center for Health and Healing
Craniofacial and Cleft Palate Center
Cystic Fibrosis Center
Dermatology
Endocrinology and Metabolism
Epilepsy
Friedman Diabetes Institute
Genetics
Geriatrics
Heart Institute (Cardiology)
Hematology
Hospice
Hyman Newman Institute for Neurology and Neurosugery (INN)
The Chris and Morton P. Hyman Patient Care Unit
Hyperhidrosis Program
Incontinence
Integrative Medicine
Interventional Neuroradiology

Israeli Health Program
Karpas Health Information Center
Latino Health Institute
Live Well New York
Louis Armstrong Center for Music and Medicine:
Lung Nodule Center
Maternity Services
Methadone Maintenance Treatment Program
Midwifery
Nephrology
Neurology
Orthopedics
Ostomy Program
Pain Medicine and Palliative Care
Pediatrics
Phillips Beth Israel School of Nursing
Primary Care
Psychiatry
Pulmonary and Critical Care Medicine
Radiation Oncology
Radiology
Rheumatology
Senior Health
Sleep Health
Speech-Language and Learning Center
Spine Institute
Sports Medicine
Stroke Centers
Styuvesant Square Chemical Dependency Services
Surgery
Urology
Vascular and Birthmarks Institute of New York
Women's Health
Women's Heart NY
Wound Healing Center

COMPETITORS

ASCENSION PROVIDENCE HOSPITAL
ATLANTIC HEALTH SYSTEM INC.
CENTRASTATE HEALTHCARE SYSTEM INC
MERCY HOSPITAL AND MEDICAL CENTER
MONMOUTH MEDICAL CENTER INC.
NEWYORK-PRESBYTERIAN/BROOKLYN METHODIST
NYU WINTHROP HOSPITAL
PHELPS MEMORIAL HOSPITAL ASSOCIATION
PRINCETON HEALTHCARE SYSTEM HOLDING INC.
THE JAMAICA HOSPITAL

HISTORICAL FINANCIALS
Company Type: Private

Income Statement — FYE: December 31

	REVENUE ($mil)	NET INCOME ($mil)	NET PROFIT MARGIN	EMPLOYEES
12/09	1,256	15	1.2%	8,100
12/08	932	(59)	—	—
Annual Growth	34.8%	—	—	—

2009 Year-End Financials
Return on assets: 1.6%   Cash ($ mil.): 98
Return on equity: 5.6%
Current Ratio: 0.50

BETHESDA FOUNDATION INC

Auditors: BKD LLP CINCINNATI OH

LOCATIONS

HQ: BETHESDA FOUNDATION INC
619 OAK ST, CINCINNATI, OH 452061613
Phone: 513 569-6575

Web: WWW.TRIHEALTH.COM

HISTORICAL FINANCIALS
Company Type: Private

Income Statement — FYE: June 30

	REVENUE ($mil)	NET INCOME ($mil)	NET PROFIT MARGIN	EMPLOYEES
06/21	853	159	18.7%	33
06/20	0	(1)	—	—
06/19	0	2	394.9%	—
06/18	0	5	821.1%	—
Annual Growth	1011.8%	215.0%	—	—

2021 Year-End Financials
Return on assets: 11.9%   Cash ($ mil.): —
Return on equity: 26.1%
Current Ratio: —

BETHESDA HOSPITAL, INC.

From modest beginnings as a informal cottage hospital, Bethesda North Hospital has grown into the fourth largest medical center in Cincinnati, Ohio. Bethesda North is a full-service acute care hospital with some 360 beds for adults and 60 for children. It provides comprehensive medical and surgical care, including maternity and fertility services, emergency care, and diagnostic imaging. The hospital joined with fellow Cincinnati health care provider Good Samaritan Hospital in 1995 to form TriHealth. Together, the two hospitals offer care at some 80 locations, including primary care offices, fitness centers, and occupational health facilities.

Operations
The full-service, 420-bed acute care hospital handles some 24,000 inpatient admissions each year, as well as 260,000 outpatient visits, 77,000 emergency room visits, and 4,000 births. It employs 165 full-time doctors and dentists and provides more than $30 million in community outreach efforts (including charity care programs) each year.

Specialty units at Bethesda North Hospital include institutes for cancer, heart, surgical, and digestive care, as well as centers for outpatient imaging, breast, stroke, obstetrics-gynecology, orthopedics, and emergency trauma care. As a regional teaching center, the hospital offers residency programs in a number of specialties including family medicine, internal medicine, OB-GYN, and surgery.

Geographic Reach
Bethesda North is located in northern Cincinnati, Ohio, and serves as a regional trauma center, as well as a major teaching hospital in the area.

Strategy
Parent organization TriHealth has aligned skilled physicians, specialists, surgeons, and its staff to create specialty institutes offering best-of-class medical assistance in fields including heart and cancer care. To further enhance its facilities, in 2013 the organization renovated the labor and delivery wing at Bethesda North Hospital. Other recent projects include the addition of a seven-story patient tower and a new outpatient imaging center.

Additionally, the company has invested in TriHealth Connect, the electronic medical records system that will help access accurate patient information.

Company Background
In early 2012 TriHealth unveiled a new logo.

Bethesda North traces it roots to 1896 and a cottage occupied by seven German Methodist deaconesses ministering to the poor and sick.

Auditors: ERNST & YOUNG LLP CINCINNATI

LOCATIONS

HQ: BETHESDA HOSPITAL, INC.
4750 WESLEY AVE, CINCINNATI, OH 452122244
Phone: 513 569-6100
Web: WWW.TRIHEALTH.COM

PRODUCTS/OPERATIONS

List of Selected Services
Breast health
Cancer care
Digestive diseases
Heart and vascular care
Maternity (OB-GYN, childbirth)
Orthopedics
Outpatient imaging
Palliative Care
Pharmacy
Robotic-assisted surgery
Stroke care
Trauma/Emergency services

COMPETITORS

FIRSTHEALTH OF THE CAROLINAS, INC.
FRANKLIN SQUARE HOSPITAL CENTER, INC.
FROEDTERT MEMORIAL LUTHERAN HOSPITAL, INC.
OHIO VALLEY MEDICAL CENTER, INCORPORATED
WAKEMED

HISTORICAL FINANCIALS
Company Type: Private

Income Statement — FYE: June 30

	REVENUE ($mil)	NET INCOME ($mil)	NET PROFIT MARGIN	EMPLOYEES
06/22	815	(2)	—	3,000
06/21	744	66	9.0%	—
06/20	643	(36)	—	—
06/19	624	32	5.2%	—
Annual Growth	9.3%	—	—	—

2022 Year-End Financials
Return on assets: (-0.2%)   Cash ($ mil.): —
Return on equity: (-0.4%)
Current Ratio: 1.10

BETHESDA, INC.

EXECUTIVES

CIO, Chip Crowther
Vice Chairman, Michael F Haverkamp
Auditors : ERNST & YOUNG LLP CINCINNATI

LOCATIONS

HQ: BETHESDA, INC.
619 OAK ST 7N, CINCINNATI, OH 452061613
Phone: 513 569-6400
Web: 29829.THANKYOU4CARING.ORG

HISTORICAL FINANCIALS

Company Type: Private

Income Statement — FYE: June 30

	REVENUE ($mil)	NET INCOME ($mil)	NET PROFIT MARGIN	EMPLOYEES
06/22	840	(44)	—	5,543
06/21	809	157	19.5%	—
06/20	667	(37)	—	—
06/19	651	28	4.4%	—
Annual Growth	8.9%	—	—	—

2022 Year-End Financials
Return on assets: (-2.6%) Cash ($ mil.): —
Return on equity: (-4.3%)
Current Ratio: 1.20

BI-MART ACQUISITION CORP.

Auditors : DELOITTE & TOUCHE LLP PORTLAN

LOCATIONS

HQ: BI-MART ACQUISITION CORP.
220 SENECA RD, EUGENE, OR 974022725
Phone: 541 344-0681

HISTORICAL FINANCIALS

Company Type: Private

Income Statement — FYE: February 23

	REVENUE ($mil)	NET INCOME ($mil)	NET PROFIT MARGIN	EMPLOYEES
02/08	721	10	1.4%	3,300
02/07	694	11	1.7%	—
02/06	665	6	1.0%	—
02/05	648	7	1.1%	—
Annual Growth	3.6%	12.8%	—	—

2008 Year-End Financials
Return on assets: 5.6% Cash ($ mil.): 3
Return on equity: 105.3%
Current Ratio: 1.90

BIG RIVER RESOURCES, LLC.

Auditors : CHRISTIANSON PLLP WILLMAR M

LOCATIONS

HQ: BIG RIVER RESOURCES, LLC.
211 N GEAR AVE STE 200, WEST BURLINGTON, IA 526551027
Phone: 319 753-1100
Web: WWW.BIGRIVERRESOURCES.COM

HISTORICAL FINANCIALS

Company Type: Private

Income Statement — FYE: December 31

	REVENUE ($mil)	NET INCOME ($mil)	NET PROFIT MARGIN	EMPLOYEES
12/19	823	17	2.2%	250
12/18	802	20	2.5%	—
12/17	817	33	4.2%	—
12/16	851	74	8.8%	—
Annual Growth	(1.1%)	(38.1%)	—	—

2019 Year-End Financials
Return on assets: 5.0% Cash ($ mil.): 40
Return on equity: 5.9%
Current Ratio: 2.70

BIG RIVERS ELECTRIC CORPORATION

EXECUTIVES

Vice Chairman*, Larry Elder
Finance*, Donna Windhaus

LOCATIONS

HQ: BIG RIVERS ELECTRIC CORPORATION
201 3RD ST, HENDERSON, KY 424202979
Phone: 270 827-2561
Web: WWW.BIGRIVERS.COM

HISTORICAL FINANCIALS

Company Type: Private

Income Statement — FYE: December 31

	REVENUE ($mil)	NET INCOME ($mil)	NET PROFIT MARGIN	EMPLOYEES
12/12	568	11	2.0%	400
12/11	561	5	1.0%	—
12/10	527	6	1.3%	—
Annual Growth	3.8%	27.0%	—	—

2012 Year-End Financials
Return on assets: 0.7% Cash ($ mil.): —
Return on equity: 2.8%
Current Ratio: 1.70

BIG WEST OF CALIFORNIA, LLC

LOCATIONS

HQ: BIG WEST OF CALIFORNIA, LLC
1104 COUNTRY HILLS DR, OGDEN, UT 844032400
Phone: 801 296-7890

HISTORICAL FINANCIALS

Company Type: Private

Income Statement — FYE: January 31

	REVENUE ($mil)	NET INCOME ($mil)	NET PROFIT MARGIN	EMPLOYEES
01/07	1,438	(32)	—	310
01/06	1,109	23	2.1%	—
Annual Growth	29.6%	—	—	—

2007 Year-End Financials
Return on assets: (-6.7%) Cash ($ mil.): (-1)
Return on equity: (-27.2%)
Current Ratio: 1.10

BIG WEST OIL, LLC

Big West Oil keeps the wagon trains rolling across the big West -- at least the station wagons. The company is in the oil processing and products business, centered around its 35,000 barrels-a-day refinery in North Salt Lake, Utah, to its fleet of tanker trucks that gather crude oil from the refinery and other purchases and deliver to wholesale customers and gas station/convenience stores in seven Western states, including Colorado, Idaho, Nevada, Utah, and Wyoming. The company's refinery processes crude oil produced in Utah, Wyoming and Canada. Big West Oil is a subsidiary ofÂ FJ Management.

EXECUTIVES

Managing Member, Fred Greener

LOCATIONS

HQ: BIG WEST OIL, LLC
333 W CENTER ST, NORTH SALT LAKE, UT 840542805
Phone: 801 624-1000
Web: WWW.BIGWESTOIL.COM

COMPETITORS

ALON USA PARTNERS, LP
BIG WEST OIL PARTNERS, LP
Irving Oil Limited
PARAMOUNT PETROLEUM CORPORATION
THE SINCLAIR COMPANIES

HISTORICAL FINANCIALS
Company Type: Private

Income Statement   FYE: January 31

	REVENUE ($mil)	NET INCOME ($mil)	NET PROFIT MARGIN	EMPLOYEES
01/08	3,053	191	6.3%	460
01/07	2,399	89	3.7%	—
01/06	2,014	102	5.1%	—
01/05	735	50	6.9%	—
Annual Growth	60.7%	55.6%	—	—

2008 Year-End Financials
Return on assets: 19.9%   Cash ($ mil.): 6
Return on equity: 50.4%
Current Ratio: 1.20

BIG-D CONSTRUCTION CORP.

Founded in 1967 by Dee Livingood (who carried the nickname "Big-Dee"), the family-run construction firm offers design/build services to customers in nine states from Minnesota to California. Known for its work on projects in the food and beverage sector, Big-D also works on light commercial, office and retail properties, manufacturing, health care, and hospitality projects, among others. Other owned affiliates include Martin Harris in Las Vegas and Reno, Nevada; Dovetail in Bozeman, Montana; McAlvain Companies Inc. in Boise, Idaho; and CFC Construction in Golden, Colorado.

Geographic Reach
The Salt Lake City-based contractor serves clients with offices in nine states from Minnesota to California. Regional offices are in Salt Lake City, Ogden, Lindon and Park City, Utah; Jackson, Wyoming; Pleasanton and Irvine, California; St. Paul, Minnesota; Idaho Falls, Idaho; and Tempe, Arizona.

Sales and Marketing
Big-D serves industries from industrial/mining, hospitality, federal/state, technology, retail, commercial, education, healthcare, warehouse/distribution, manufacturing, and food/beverage.

Mergers and Acquisitions
In 2022, Big-D Construction acquired CFC Construction. Based in Golden, Colorado, CFC Construction has served the state for 45 years. Under new ownership, the company will continue to be locally managed and operate under the same name. Chairman and Founder, EJ Olbright, will continue in his role with CFC, along with CFC President Pat Smith. "This acquisition is part of Big-D's vision to strengthen our company through alliances with premier builders and talented project teams in selected markets. CFC has a reputation for providing clients innovative solutions and strong leadership. We are honored to be partners and excited to be a part of their future," said Chairman Jack Livingood, Big-D Construction.

Company Background
Big-D courted more government projects as a way to weather the economic downturn, which has put a halt on many commercial jobs. Among those public projects was the Utah Museum of Natural History at The University of Utah and the Wallace F. Bennett Federal Building in Salt Lake City. Big-D also is focusing on developing its eco-friendly construction business.

Auditors: GRANT THORNTON LLP SALT LAKE

LOCATIONS

HQ: BIG-D CONSTRUCTION CORP.
404 W 400 S, SALT LAKE CITY, UT 841011108
Phone: 801 415-6000
Web: WWW.BIG-D.COM

Selected Markets
Arizona
Arkansas
California
Colorado
Georgia
Hawaii
Idaho
Montana
Nevada
New Mexico
North Carolina
North Dakota
Oklahoma
Oregon
South Dakota
Tennessee
Texas
Utah
Washington

PRODUCTS/OPERATIONS

Selected Services
Construction management
Design/build
Field services
    Architectural concrete
    Finish carpentry
    Rough framing
    Structural concrete
General contracting
Green and Leadership in Energy and Environmental Design

Selected Industry Specializations
Commercial/public spaces (governmental, educational, and office complexes; mixed-use projects)
Food processing and distribution
Health care
Hospitality and resort
Manufacturing
Retail

COMPETITORS

ALBERICI CORPORATION
CLAYCO, INC.
GILBANE, INC.
HOAR CONSTRUCTION, LLC
J.E. DUNN CONSTRUCTION COMPANY
LECHASE CONSTRUCTION SERVICES, LLC
MCCARTHY BUILDING COMPANIES, INC.
S. M. WILSON & CO.
THE PIKE COMPANY INC
WALBRIDGE ALDINGER LLC

HISTORICAL FINANCIALS
Company Type: Private

Income Statement   FYE: December 31

	REVENUE ($mil)	NET INCOME ($mil)	NET PROFIT MARGIN	EMPLOYEES
12/12	541	0	0.0%	1,384
12/11	554	0	0.0%	—
12/10	259	0	0.0%	—
Annual Growth	44.4%	—	—	—

2012 Year-End Financials
Return on assets: —   Cash ($ mil.): 38
Return on equity: —
Current Ratio: 1.40

BILLINGS CLINIC

Through a group of more than 450 doctors and other providers, Billings Clinic caters a vast region covering much of Montana, Wyoming and the western Dakotas. It offers more than 80 specialties, such as emergency and trauma, cancer, orthopedics, birthing, cardiovascular, neurosciences, dialysis, and pediatrics. Its operations include a more than 300-bed hospital and the organization's main clinic. Additionally, Billings Clinic has more than 15 regional partnerships, including management agreements with about a dozen of Critical Access Hospitals and one outpatient clinic. The not-for-profit health care system is owned by the community.

Operations
With its vast service area, the health care system provides a MedFlight advanced life support fixed-wing aircraft service that transports critically ill or injured patients from rural communities.

As part of its operations, Billings Clinic runs a Level II emergency and trauma center, 20-suite family birthing center, Level III neonatal intensive care unit, inpatient cancer care unit, and surgery centers. The health care system's cancer center provides both inpatient and outpatient care in Billings.

Billings Clinic is led by a physician CEO, and is governed by a board of community members, nurses and physicians.

Billings Clinic's Community Benefit totaled more than $43 million, including $18.4 million in financial assistance provided to more than 14,600 patients.

Geographic Reach
As the largest health care organization in the area, Billings Clinic's service area extends 260,000 sq. miles to provide specialty care for residents of rural Montana (headquarters), Wyoming, and North Dakota.

Company Background
The Billings Clinic evolved from the general practice of Dr. Arthur J. Movius who founded his Billings practice in 1911.

It expanded its capacity for infusions in 2012 when its Billings Clinic Cody location opened an infusion center. In late 2012 the organization also opened a new Stillwater Billings Clinic medical facility, which combines Stillwater Community Hospital and Billings Clinic Columbus and integrates the billing process for the two health care facilities.

EXECUTIVES

Interim Chief Executive Officer, Clint Seger
CMO, Toni Green-cheatwood

LOCATIONS

HQ: BILLINGS CLINIC
2800 10TH AVE N, BILLINGS, MT 591010703
Phone: 406 657-4000
Web: WWW.BILLINGSCLINIC.COM

PRODUCTS/OPERATIONS

Selected Services
Advance Medical Directives
Allergy, Asthma, Immunology
Aspen Meadows - Skilled Nursing and Assisted Living
Anticoagulation Clinic
Breast Center
Cancer Center
Cardiovascular Services
Cardiovascular Surgery
Children's Services
Continence Center
Community Training Center
Cosmetic Surgery
da Vinci Surgical System
Dermatology Center
Diabetes Management Center
Diagnostic Imaging
Diabetes
Dialysis Center
Eldercare Solutions
Emergency & Trauma Center
Emmi Educational Videos
Employer Services - Occupational Health
Endocrinology
Eye Center
Facial Plastic Surgery
Family Medicine
Family Birth Center
Gastroenterology
General Surgery
Genetic Counseling
Geriatric Assessment Program
Gynecologic Cancer
Heart Services
Heart Surgery
Home Oxygen & Medical Equipment
Hospitalist Program
Infectious Diseases
Insurance Finder
Internal Medicine
Laboratory Services
LifeFit
Maternal-Fetal Medicine
MedFlight Air Ambulance
Mental Health Services
Metabolism Center
Mohs Surgery
Nutrition Services
Neurosciences
Obstetrics & Gynecology
Occupational Health - Employer Services
Ophthalmology
Orthopedics & Sports Medicine
Palliative Care
Pediatrics
    Pediatric Center
    Pediatric Cancer
    Pediatric Diabetes
    Pediatric Gastroenterology
    Pediatric Pulmonology
    Rehabilitation (Therapy)
Pharmacy
Physical Medicine & Rehabilitation
Plastic Surgery
Primary Care for Adults
Pulmonary Rehabilitation Program
Radiology Services
Reproductive Medicine and Fertility Care
Robotic Surgery
SameDay Care
Senior Services
Sleep Disorders Center
Sports Medicine
Sports Specific Camps
Stroke Care
Surgery Center
Transitional Care Unit
Urology Services
Vascular Surgery
Vein Clinic
Women's Free Screenings
Women's and Children's Services

Selected Affiliate Hospitals and Clinics
Beartooth Billings Clinic - Red Lodge
Colstrip Medical Center - Colstrip
Daniels Memorial Healthcare - Scobey
Livingston HealthCare - Livingston
North Big Horn Hospital - Lovell
Pioneer Medical Center - Big Timber
Roundup Memorial Healthcare - Roundup
Sheridan Memorial Hospital Association
Stillwater Billings Clinic

COMPETITORS

AULTMAN HEALTH FOUNDATION
MARSHFIELD CLINIC, INC.
PARK NICOLLET HEALTH SERVICES
PROMEDICA TOLEDO HOSPITAL
SHAWNEE MISSION MEDICAL CENTER, INC.
SWEDISH HEALTH SERVICES
TALLAHASSEE MEMORIAL HEALTHCARE, INC.
TEXAS CHILDREN'S HOSPITAL
THE MASSACHUSETTS GENERAL HOSPITAL
UNIVERSITY HOSPITALS HEALTH SYSTEM, INC.

HISTORICAL FINANCIALS

Company Type: Private

Income Statement   FYE: June 30

	REVENUE ($mil)	NET INCOME ($mil)	NET PROFIT MARGIN	EMPLOYEES
06/16	586	(2)	—	3,300
06/15	565	30	5.4%	—
06/14	593	38	6.6%	—
06/13	560	14	2.6%	—
Annual Growth	1.6%	—	—	—

2016 Year-End Financials
Return on assets: (-0.3%)   Cash ($ mil.): 13
Return on equity: (-0.6%)
Current Ratio: 1.80

BIOURJA TRADING, LLC

Auditors : CARR RIGGS & INGRAM LLC HOUST

LOCATIONS

HQ: BIOURJA TRADING, LLC
1500 CITYWEST BLVD # 700, HOUSTON, TX 770422558
Phone: 832 775-9000

Web: WWW.BIOURJA.COM

HISTORICAL FINANCIALS

Company Type: Private

Income Statement   FYE: December 31

	REVENUE ($mil)	NET INCOME ($mil)	NET PROFIT MARGIN	EMPLOYEES
12/13	4,622	26	0.6%	214
12/12	2,992	11	0.4%	—
12/11	3,842	13	0.4%	—
Annual Growth	9.7%	38.6%	—	—

2013 Year-End Financials
Return on assets: 16.9%   Cash ($ mil.): 15
Return on equity: 57.0%
Current Ratio: 1.40

BLACK & VEATCH HOLDING COMPANY

Auditors : KPMG LLP KANSAS CITY MISSOUR

LOCATIONS

HQ: BLACK & VEATCH HOLDING COMPANY
11401 LAMAR AVE, OVERLAND PARK, KS 662111598
Phone: 913 458-2000
Web: WWW.BV.COM

HISTORICAL FINANCIALS

Company Type: Private

Income Statement   FYE: December 28

	REVENUE ($mil)	NET INCOME ($mil)	NET PROFIT MARGIN	EMPLOYEES
12/18	3,479	80	2.3%	18,568
12/17	3,364	87	2.6%	—
12/16*	3,207	75	2.3%	—
01/16	2,955	109	3.7%	—
Annual Growth	5.6%	(9.7%)	—	—

*Fiscal year change

2018 Year-End Financials
Return on assets: 4.9%   Cash ($ mil.): 383
Return on equity: 54.7%
Current Ratio: 1.10

BLACK & VEATCH INTERNATIONAL COMPANY

Auditors : KPMG LLP KANSAS CITY MO

LOCATIONS

HQ: BLACK & VEATCH INTERNATIONAL COMPANY
11401 LAMAR AVE, OVERLAND PARK, KS 662111598
Phone: 913 458-2000
Web: WWW.BV.COM

HISTORICAL FINANCIALS
Company Type: Private

Income Statement — FYE: December 31

	REVENUE ($mil)	NET INCOME ($mil)	NET PROFIT MARGIN	EMPLOYEES
12/09	711	43	6.1%	283
12/08	711	43	6.1%	—
12/07	1	(0)	—	—
12/06	1	(0)	—	—
Annual Growth	754.9%	—	—	—

2009 Year-End Financials
Return on assets: 8.5%   Cash ($ mil.): 39
Return on equity: 37.5%
Current Ratio: 1.10

BLOUNT INTERNATIONAL, INC.

Formerly Blount International, Oregon Tool produces cutting chain, guide bars, sprockets, and accessories for chainsaws, concrete-cutting equipment, and lawnmower blades. Oregon Tool's lineup is sold under brands Oregon, Carlton, and KOX to dealers and consumers in key markets. End users are professionals and consumers engaged in forestry, lawn and garden, farming, and construction activities. Oregon Tool was founded in 1947 as Oregon Saw Chain Company by Joe Cox. In 2021, Blount International, Inc. is renamed to Oregon Tool, Inc. to honor the company's legacy and unite all of its brands under one name moving forward.

Operations
The company produces saw chains, bars and sprockets and outdoor equipment accessories and parts for the garden and landscape industry. Blount offers these products under the brand names OREGON, Carlton, and KOX.

Oregon Tool manufactures high-quality attachments and implements, finish mowers, seeders and other agriculture-related products. These products are marketed under the brand name Woods.

The company also manufactures and markets diamond-cutting chains, assembles and markets concrete cutting chain saws, and purchases other concrete cutting products that are marketed to the construction and utility industries.

Geographic Reach
Oregon-based, Oregon Tool sells its products in more than 100 countries around the world.

Sales and Marketing
Oregon Tool's sales, distribution and manufacturing network serves the forestry; lawn & garden; farm; ranch & agriculture; and construction industries; delivering products to a diverse range of consumer and professional end users

Company Background
Blount was founded in 1947 as Oregon Saw Chain Company by Joe Cox.

EXECUTIVES
Corporate Controller*, Mark Allred
Auditors : KPMG LLP PORTLAND OREGON

LOCATIONS
HQ: BLOUNT INTERNATIONAL, INC.
4909 SE INTERNATIONAL WAY, PORTLAND, OR 972224679
Phone: 503 653-8881
Web: WWW.BLOUNT.COM

PRODUCTS/OPERATIONS

Selected Products
Chain drive sprockets
Chainsaw guide bars
Concrete-cutting chainsaws and circular saws (gasoline and hydraulic powered)
Cutting chain (for chainsaws)
Diamond-segmented chain (for cutting concrete)
Farm accessories
Lawn and garden cutting attachments
Lawnmower and edger cutting blades
Log splitters
Maintenance tools (for chainsaws and mechanical timber harvesting equipment)
Tractor driven post-hole diggers
Tractor three-point linkage parts

COMPETITORS
AGCO CORPORATION
ALAMO GROUP INC.
Buhler Industries Inc
CNH INDUSTRIAL N.V.
FASTENAL COMPANY
KUBOTA CORPORATION
LINDSAY CORPORATION
OXBO INTERNATIONAL CORPORATION
THE TORO COMPANY
TITAN MACHINERY INC.

HISTORICAL FINANCIALS
Company Type: Private

Income Statement — FYE: December 31

	REVENUE ($mil)	NET INCOME ($mil)	NET PROFIT MARGIN	EMPLOYEES
12/15	828	(49)	—	4,000
12/14	944	36	3.9%	—
12/13	900	4	0.5%	—
12/12	927	39	4.3%	—
Annual Growth	(3.7%)	—	—	—

2015 Year-End Financials
Return on assets: (-7.2%)   Cash ($ mil.): 25
Return on equity: (-45.1%)
Current Ratio: 2.60

BLUE BUFFALO PET PRODUCTS, INC.

Blue Buffalo makes natural dog and cat food using whole meats, fruits, and vegetables with no by-products or artificial ingredients; some products are also grain-free. The company's products undergo a robust formulation, manufacturing and testing process to ensure they are safe, effective and compliant with all nutrient requirements outlined by AAFCO and the Global Nutrition Committee of the World Small Animal Veterinary Association (WSAVA). BLUE's exclusive LifeSource Bits are "cold-formed" to minimize heat exposure which can degrade the potency of many vitamins, minerals, antioxidants and enzymes. Blue Buffalo started in 2003.

IPO

Operations
Blue Buffalo offers dry foods, wet foods, and treats for puppies, adults, kittens, and senior/mature cats and dogs.

Geographic Reach
Blue Buffalo has two manufacturing facilities ? one in Joplin, Missouri and one in Richmond, Indiana.

Sales and Marketing
Blue Buffalo products are sold through its website and online retailers such as PetSmart, Petco, Chewy, Target, Walmart, Amazon, and more.

Auditors : KPMG LLP STAMFORD CONNECTICU

LOCATIONS
HQ: BLUE BUFFALO PET PRODUCTS, INC.
11 RIVER RD STE 103, WILTON, CT 068976011
Phone: 203 762-9751
Web: WWW.BLUEBUFFALO.COM

PRODUCTS/OPERATIONS

2017 Sales

	$ mil.	% of total
Dry foods	1,013.5	80
Wet foods, treats, and other	261.1	20
Total	1,274.6	100

Selected Product Lines
BLUE Life Protection Formula
BLUE Wilderness
BLUE Basics
BLUE Freedom
BLUE Natural Veterinary Diet

COMPETITORS
ADM ALLIANCE NUTRITION, INC.
AG PROCESSING INC A COOPERATIVE
CASEY'S GENERAL STORES, INC.
CORE-MARK HOLDING COMPANY, INC.
O.K. INDUSTRIES, INC.
PERFORMANCE FOOD GROUP COMPANY
RIDLEY CORPORATION LIMITED
ROYAL CANIN SAS
Ridley Inc
SOUTHERN STATES COOPERATIVE, INCORPORATED

HISTORICAL FINANCIALS

Company Type: Private

Income Statement — FYE: December 31

	REVENUE ($mil)	NET INCOME ($mil)	NET PROFIT MARGIN	EMPLOYEES
12/17	1,274	193	15.2%	1,800
12/16	1,149	130	11.3%	—
12/15	1,027	89	8.7%	—
Annual Growth	11.4%	47.1%	—	—

2017 Year-End Financials

Return on assets: 22.8%
Return on equity: 64.7%
Current Ratio: 3.70
Cash ($ mil.): 282

BLUE CROSS & BLUE SHIELD ASSOCIATION

The Blue Cross and Blue Shield Association is a national federation of about 35 independent, community-based and locally operated Blue Cross and Blue Shield companies that collectively provide health care coverage for one in three Americans across all 50 US states, the District of Columbia and Puerto Rico. The association owns and manages the Blue Cross and Blue Shield trademarks and names in more than 170 countries. In addition, the BCBS Federal Employee Program insures over 5.8 million federal employees, retirees and their families. The company traces its roots back to 1929.

Operations

Blue Cross and Blue Shield companies are the oldest, most experienced providers of health coverage in America. As community-based companies, the Blues understand their local markets and offer customized products and services that are tailored to meet local needs. BCBS companies also partner with more than 1.7 million doctors and hospitals nationwide to provide high-quality care at the best possible price. BCBS companies offer coverage through the Affordable Care Act marketplaces, and it also provides coverage through the Office of Personnel Management's multi-state plan.

Geographic Reach

Based in Chicago, BCBSA has additional office in Washington, DC and provides coverage in all 50 US states, the District of Columbia and Puerto Rico.

Sales and Marketing

The BCBS companies cover 74 of America's Fortune 100 employers, including some of America's top companies like Microsoft, Walmart, General Motors and UPS, and 6.8 million people who work for small employers and are committed to helping small businesses manage their healthcare costs.

HISTORY

Blue Cross was born in 1929, when Baylor University official Justin Kimball offered schoolteachers 21 days of hospital care for $6 a year. A major plan feature was a community rating system that based premiums on the community claims experience rather than members' conditions.

The Blue Cross symbol was devised in 1933 by Minnesota plan executive E. A. van Steenwyck. By 1935 many of the 15 plans in 11 states used the symbol. Many states gave the plans not-for-profit status, and in 1936 the American Hospital Association formed the Committee on Hospital Service (renamed the Blue Cross Association in 1948) to coordinate them.

As Blue Cross grew, state medical societies sponsored prepaid plans to cover doctors' fees. In 1946 they united under the aegis of the American Medical Association (AMA) as the Associated Medical Care Plans (later the Association of Blue Shield Plans).

In 1948 the AMA thwarted a Blue Cross attempt to merge with Blue Shield. But the Blues increasingly cooperated on public policy matters while competing for members, and each Blue formed a not-for-profit corporation to coordinate its plan's activities.

Blue Cross insured about a third of the US by 1960. Over the next decade the Blues started administering Medicare and other government health plans, and by 1970 half of Blue Cross' premiums came from government entities.

In the 1970s the Blues adopted such cost-control measures as review of hospital admissions; many plans even abandoned the community rating system. Most began emphasizing preventive care in HMOs or PPOs. The two Blues finally merged in 1982 to form the Blue Cross and Blue Shield Association (BCBSA), but this had little effect on the associations' bottom lines as losses grew.

By the 1990s the Blues were big business. Some of the state associations offered officers high salaries and perks but still insisted on special regulatory treatment.

But as lower-cost plans attracted the hale and hearty, the Blues' customers became older, sicker, and more expensive. With their quasi-charitable status and outdated rate structures, many Blues plans lost market share.

The Blues fought back by updating their technology and rate structures, merging among themselves, creating for-profit subsidiaries, forming alliances with for-profit enterprises, or (in some cases) dropping their not-for-profit status and going public -- while still using the Blue Cross Blue Shield name.

Blue Cross of California became the first chapter to give up its tax-free status when it was bought by WellPoint Health Networks, a managed care subsidiary it had founded in 1992. In a 1996 deal, WellPoint became the chapter's parent and converted it to for-profit status, assigning all of the stock to a public charitable foundation which received the proceeds of its subsequent IPO. WellPoint also bought the group life and health division of Massachusetts Mutual Life Insurance.

The for-profit switches picked up in 1997. Blue Cross of Connecticut merged with insurance provider Anthem, and other mergers followed. Half the nation's Blues formed an alliance called BluesCONNECT (now BlueCard), competing with national health plans by offering employers one nationwide benefits organization. BCBSA also pursued overseas licensing agreements in Europe, South America, and Asia, assembling a network of Blue Cross-friendly caregivers aiming for worldwide coverage.

In 1998 Blues in more than 35 states sued the nation's big cigarette companies to recoup costs of treating smoking-related illnesses. In a separate lawsuit, Blue Cross and Blue Shield of Minnesota received nearly $300 million from the tobacco industry. In 1999 Anthem moved to acquire or affiliate with Blues in Colorado, Maine, Nevada, and New Hampshire.

After years of discussions, in 2000 the New York attorney general permitted Empire Blue Cross and Blue Shield to convert to for-profit status. The pace of for-profit conversions slowed down in following years, however, as state regulators became increasingly wary of signing off on the procedure. The improved financial situation of most of the not-for-profit Blues also took away a key incentive for for-profit conversion -- access to capital markets.

In 2004 Anthem and WellPoint Health Networks merged and Anthem's name changed to Wellpoint (though it continued to use the Anthem brand name in certain markets), becoming the largest for-profit health insurer in the nation. WellPoint acquired Empire Blue Cross and its parent WellChoice, as well as non-Blue consumer-driven plan provider Lumenos, in 2005. In addition to snapping up Blues providers, the for-profit WellPoint acquired a number of non-Blue subsidiaries, such as American Imaging Management, while meeting the requirement that it get two-thirds of its insurance revenue from Blue products to keep its BCBSA license. (Wellpoint changed its name back to Anthem in 2012.)

Consolidation among Blues plans continued when Health Care Service Corporation added its fourth not-for-profit Blues plan (Blue Cross and Blue Shield of Oklahoma) in 2005.

In 2007 BCBSA was approved under a Federal Savings Bank charter to provide health-related banking services through its Blue Healthcare Bank.

Two licensees, Highmark and Independence Blue Cross, had agreed to merge in 2008, but the deal was terminated in early 2009 after long delays and heavy regulatory concern that the merger would create an unfair advantage in the Pennsylvania market. Some consolidation continued, however, as Triple-S, which operates under the Blue Shield brand in Puerto Rico, acquired and absorbed Blue Cross licensee La Cruz Azul from Independence Blue Cross in 2009.

Highmark reached a formal affiliation agreement (including shared administrative and IT resources) with Blue Cross Blue Shield of Delaware in 2011.

Another regional Blues provider, Cambia Health Solutions (formerly Regence Group), changed its name in 2011 to signify its diversification efforts, though its BCBS subsidiaries continue to operate under the Regence name.

Three Blues companies -- Anthem, Health Care Service Corp. (HCSC), and BCBS of Michigan-- joined together in 2011 to invest in a commercial insurance exchange (Bloom Health) designed to allow businesses to contribute to employees' selected health coverage. The venture was part of the Blues' efforts to meet the changing US insurance needs under health reform laws.

BCBSA launched a new wellness rewards program for FEP participants in 2012.

EXECUTIVES

CLINICAL TRANSFORMATION*, Adam Myers
Auditors : PRICEWATERHOUSECOOPERS LLP PH

LOCATIONS

HQ: BLUE CROSS & BLUE SHIELD ASSOCIATION
  225 N MICHIGAN AVE FL 5, CHICAGO, IL 606017658
Phone: 312 297-6000
Web: WWW.BCBS.COM

PRODUCTS/OPERATIONS

Selected Blue Cross and Blue Shield Licensees
Arkansas Blue Cross and Blue Shield
Blue Cross and Blue Shield of Alabama
Blue Cross and Blue Shield of Arizona
Blue Cross and Blue Shield of Delaware
Blue Cross and Blue Shield of Florida
Blue Cross and Blue Shield of Kansas
Blue Cross and Blue Shield of Kansas City
Blue Cross and Blue Shield of Louisiana
Blue Cross and Blue Shield of Massachusetts
Blue Cross and Blue Shield of Michigan
Blue Cross and Blue Shield of Minnesota
Blue Cross and Blue Shield of Mississippi
Blue Cross and Blue Shield of Montana
Blue Cross and Blue Shield of Nebraska
Blue Cross and Blue Shield of North Carolina
Blue Cross and Blue Shield of North Dakota
Blue Cross and Blue Shield of Rhode Island
Blue Cross and Blue Shield of South Carolina
Blue Cross and Blue Shield of Tennessee
Blue Cross and Blue Shield of Vermont
Blue Cross and Blue Shield of Wyoming
Blue Cross of Idaho Health Service
Blue Cross of Northeastern Pennsylvania
California Physicians' Service (dba Blue Shield of California)
Cambia Health Solutions, Inc. (formerly The Regence Group)
  Regence BlueCross and BlueShield of Oregon
  Regence BlueCross BlueShield of Utah
  Regence BlueShield of Idaho
  Regence BlueShield (Washington)
Capital BlueCross (Pennsylvania)
CareFirst
  CareFirst Blue Cross and Blue Shield (District of Columbia)
  CareFirst Blue Cross and Blue Shield of Maryland
Excellus BlueCross BlueShield of New York
Hawaii Medical Service Association
Health Care Service Corporation
  Blue Cross and Blue Shield of Illinois
  Blue Cross and Blue Shield of New Mexico
  Blue Cross and Blue Shield of Oklahoma
  Blue Cross and Blue Shield of Texas
HealthNow New York
  BlueCross and BlueShield of Western New York
  BlueShield of Northeastern New York
Highmark Blue Cross Blue Shield (Pennsylvania)
  Mountain State Blue Cross and Blue Shield (West Virginia)
Horizon Healthcare Services (dba Horizon Blue Cross and Blue Shield of New Jersey)
Independence Blue Cross (Pennsylvania)
Premera Blue Cross (Alaska and Washington)
Triple-S (Puerto Rico)
Wellmark
  Wellmark Blue Cross and Blue Shield of Iowa
  Wellmark Blue Cross and Blue Shield of South Dakota
WellPoint
  Anthem Blue Cross and Blue Shield of Colorado
  Anthem Blue Cross and Blue Shield of Connecticut
  Anthem Blue Cross and Blue Shield of Indiana
  Anthem Blue Cross and Blue Shield of Kentucky
  Anthem Blue Cross and Blue Shield of Maine
  Anthem Blue Cross and Blue Shield of Nevada
  Anthem Blue Cross and Blue Shield of New Hampshire
  Anthem Blue Cross and Blue Shield of Ohio
  Anthem Blue Cross and Blue Shield of Virginia
  Blue Cross and Blue Shield of Georgia
  Blue Cross and Blue Shield of Missouri (dba Anthem Blue Cross and Blue Shield)
  BlueCross BlueShield of Wisconsin (dba Anthem Blue Cross and Blue Shield)
  California Blue Cross (Anthem Blue Cross)
  Empire Blue Cross and Blue Shield of New York
International plans
  Blue Cross & Blue Shield de Uruguay
  BlueCross BlueShield of Panama

COMPETITORS

AMERICAN CANCER SOCIETY, INC.
AMERICAN DENTAL ASSOCIATION
AMERICAN DENTAL PARTNERS, INC.
AMERICAN HOSPITAL ASSOCIATION
AMERICAN MEDICAL ASSOCIATION
BLUE CROSS AND BLUE SHIELD OF MASSACHUSETTS, INC.
BLUE CROSS BLUE SHIELD OF MICHIGAN MUTUAL INSURANCE COMPANY
HEALTH CARE SERVICE CORPORATION, A MUTUAL LEGAL RESERVE COMPANY
THE BRITISH DENTAL INDUSTRY ASSOCIATION
UNITED KINGDOM ACCREDITATION SERVICE

HISTORICAL FINANCIALS

Company Type: Private

Income Statement — FYE: December 31

	NET REVENUE ($mil)	NET INCOME ($mil)	NET PROFIT MARGIN	EMPLOYEES
12/17	591	(1)	—	1,880
12/06	320	14	4.5%	—
12/05	275	8	3.0%	—
12/04	270	11	4.3%	—
Annual Growth	6.2%	—	—	—

2017 Year-End Financials
Return on assets: (-0.2%)   Cash ($ mil.): 486
Return on equity: (-1.5%)
Current Ratio: 1.00

BLUE CROSS AND BLUE SHIELD OF ARIZONA, INC.

Blue Cross Blue Shield of Arizona (BCBSAZ) provides health insurance products and services to more than 1.9 million Arizonans. The not-for-profit company offers a variety of managed care plans to small and large employer groups, individuals, and families, including PPO, HMO, and high-deductible health plans. It also provides dental, vision, and prescription drug coverage, as well as supplemental health plans for Medicare beneficiaries. Founded in 1933, the company is an independent licensee of the Blue Cross and Blue Shield Association.

Operations
Geographic Reach
BCBSAZ serves customers throughout the state of Arizona (headquarters) from its offices in Flagstaff, Phoenix, and Tucson.

Sales and Marketing
BCBSAZ offers insurance services to individuals and families, seniors, employers, brokers and consultants, and health care professionals through agents.

EXECUTIVES

Chief Medical Officer, Woodrow Myers Junior
CGO, Paige Rothermel

LOCATIONS

HQ: BLUE CROSS AND BLUE SHIELD OF ARIZONA, INC.
  2444 W LAS PALMARITAS DR, PHOENIX, AZ 850214860
Phone: 602 864-4100
Web: WWW.AZBLUE.COM

PRODUCTS/OPERATIONS

Selected Plans
Family and Individual Medical Plans
  BlueBasic Plus PPO
  BlueEssential Plus PPO
  BlueOptimum Plus PPO
  BluePortfolio Plus (high deductible PPO with HSA)
  BlueValue Plus PPO
  Medicare Part D
  Medicare Supplement
Group Medical Plans
  BlueAlliance benefit
  BluePreferred PPO
  BluePreferred HSA Plus (high deductable PPO with HSA)
  BlueSelect HMO
  Dental plans
  Eyewear plans
  GeoBlue Expat

COMPETITORS

AVMED, INC.
CAMBIA HEALTH SOLUTIONS, INC.
COMMUNITYCARE MANAGED HEALTHCARE PLANS OF OKLAHOMA, INC.
HEALTH ALLIANCE PLAN OF MICHIGAN
HEALTHNOW NEW YORK INC.

KEYSTONE FAMILY HEALTH PLAN
PRIORITY HEALTH MANAGED BENEFITS, INC.
SECURITY HEALTH PLAN OF WISCONSIN, INC.
TUFTS ASSOCIATED HEALTH PLANS, INC.
WELLMARK, INC.

HISTORICAL FINANCIALS
Company Type: Private

Income Statement — FYE: December 31

	ASSETS ($mil)	NET INCOME ($mil)	INCOME AS % OF ASSETS	EMPLOYEES
12/09	1,059	64	6.1%	1,278
12/08	975	71	7.4%	—
Annual Growth	8.6%	(9.9%)	—	—

2009 Year-End Financials
Return on assets: 6.1%   Cash ($ mil.): (-10)
Return on equity: 9.0%
Current Ratio: 3.60

BLUE TEE CORP.

Handling a variety of steel products and scrap materials suits Blue Tee to a tee. The holding company, which operates through two primary subsidiaries, distributes steel building materials and scrap metal. Blue Tee's Brown-Strauss Steel subsidiary is one of the largest distributors of wide flange beam and structural steel products (beams, pipe, and tubing) in North America. The metal distributor's other primary business is Azcon, a leading scrap processor, broker, and mill services management company which handles scrap metal sales, rail cars, and other steel parts.

Operations
Azcon is a major scrap processor, broker, and mill services management company. Brown-Strauss Steel distributes steel products.

Azcon buys, collects, warehouses, and distributes a wide variety of rail and track accessories for the railroad industry across North America. Its core businesses include Processing Yard, Mill Scrap Management, and Brokerage. Other product lines include Relaying and Re-rolling Rail, Railroad Equipment, and Railroad Parts.

Brown-Strauss Steel's focus is on the distribution of new steel (wide flange beam and structural steel tubing) across the US.

Geographic Reach
The company has major offices in Denver, Kansas City, Longview (Washington), New York City, Phoenix, Salt Lake City, and Stockton and Fontana (California). It has additional locations in Alton, Chicago, and Sterling, (Illinois); Austin, Texas; Duluth, Minnesota; and Sharpsburg, Pennsylvania.

In Canada Blue Tee has offices in Edmonton, Calgary, Grande Prairie, Grimshaw, Kamloops, Prince George, and Red Deer.

Sales and Marketing
Blue Tee serves a range of industries including construction, forestry, road building, mining, farming, power, oil and gas, solid waste, water, waste management, highway transportation, environmental, and groundwater monitoring.

Strategy
The company is focusing its resources developing Azcon and Brown-Strauss Steel. Brown-Strauss is looking to grow its product offerings to include structural tubing; it also plans to expand its facilities. In this regard, in 2012, Blue Tee Corp (through Brown-Strauss) purchased a 69,190 sq. ft. industrial building in Aurora, Colorado from The Lowenberg Corp. for $6 million.

Company Background
Blue Tee is owned by its employees through an employee stock ownership plan.

In 2011 Blue Tee divested subsidiaries GEFCO (an OEM of portable drilling rigs and other industrial equipment), and STECO (transfer and dump-truck trailers) to Astec Industries for about $30.8 million.

The move to axe its GEFCO and STECO subsidiaries followed another sale. Blue Tee sold its pump parts subsidiary, Texas-based Standard Alloys, to German pump manufacturer KSB in mid-2010.

The Blue Tee holding company was founded in 1986. Azcon was formed in 1863 and Brown-Strauss Steel was established in 1905.

Auditors: DELOITTE & TOUCHE LLP NEW YO

LOCATIONS
HQ: BLUE TEE CORP.
387 PARK AVE S FL 5, NEW YORK, NY 100161495
Phone: 212 598-0880
Web: WWW.BLUETEE.COM

PRODUCTS/OPERATIONS

Selected Subsidiaries
Azcon Corporation (ferrous and nonferrous scrap; rail cars, locomotives, and parts; relay and reroll rail)
Brown-Strauss Steel (steel distribution, including angles, beams, channels, pipe, and tubing)

Selected Azcon Services
Barge Services
Brokerage Services
Demolition Services
Foundries - Scrap Management
Industrial Plants - Scrap Management
Mill Service
Mine Services
Railroad Industry Services
Steel Mills - Scrap Management

Selected Brown-Strauss Steel Products and Services
Products:
Structural Angle
Structural Channels
Structural Pipe
Structural Tubing
Wide Flange Beams
Services:
Cambering
Inventory Stocking program
Length/cutting optimization program
Mill Brokerage
Saw Cutting
Track Torch Cutting

COMPETITORS
BAKER HUGHES HOLDINGS LLC
HARBISON-FISCHER, INC.
PREMIER PIPE LLC
ROBBINS & MYERS, INC.
SPM OIL & GAS INC.

HISTORICAL FINANCIALS
Company Type: Private

Income Statement — FYE: December 31

	REVENUE ($mil)	NET INCOME ($mil)	NET PROFIT MARGIN	EMPLOYEES
12/10	809	14	1.8%	900
12/09	564	(10)	—	—
12/08	1,549	33	2.1%	—
Annual Growth	(27.7%)	(34.4%)	—	—

2010 Year-End Financials
Return on assets: 3.7%   Cash ($ mil.): 8
Return on equity: 8.2%
Current Ratio: 2.10

BNSF RAILWAY COMPANY

BNSF Railway is one of North America's leading freight transportation companies. A wholly-owned subsidiary of Burlington Northern Santa Fe, itself is a unit of Berkshire Hathaway, the company provides freight transportation over a network of approximately 32,500 route miles of track across nearly 30 US states and three provinces in Canada. BNSF Railway owns or leases a fleet of about 8,000 locomotives. It also has some 25 intermodal facilities that help to transport agricultural, consumer, and industrial products, as well as coal. In addition to major cities and ports, BNSF Railway is one of the top transporters of the products and materials that help feed, clothe, supply and power communities throughout America and the world.

Operations
BNSF Railway transports a wide range of products and commodities through its three main product segments.

The Consumer Products segment transports approximately 5.6 million intermodal shipments (truck trailers or containers) on BNSF's rail lines instead of on the nation's congested highways. It also has approximately 1.3 million feet of track in intermodal facilities alone. If spread end to end, it would be the length of 9 ½ Boston Marathons. The Industrial Products segment hauls some 3.2 million carloads of industrial products.

Agricultural Products segment hauls approximately 1.2 million carloads of agricultural commodities. It moves enough grain to supply some 900 million people with a year's supply of bread and transports enough wheat flour in a year to bake more than 23 billion dozens of cookies.

Geographic Reach

Headquartered in Fort Worth, Texas, BNSF Railway's network spreads across about 30 US states and three Canadian provinces.

Company Background

BNSF's traces its roots to 1849 when the Aurora Branch Railroad was founded in Illinois with 12 miles of track. Over the years, additional rail lines were built, including Atchison, Topeka & Santa Fe;Burlington Northern; Chicago, Burlington & Quincy; Frisco; Great Northern; Northern Pacific; and Spokane, Portland & Seattle.

BNSF was created in 1995 when Burlington Northern, Inc. (the parent company of Burlington Northern Railroad) merged with Santa Fe Pacific Corporation (parent company of the Atchison, Topeka & Santa Fe Railway). The company was acquired by Berkshire Hathaway in 2010 and BNSF now operates as a subsidiary of that company.

EXECUTIVES

CAO*, Jon I Stevens

Auditors : DELOITTE & TOUCHE LLP FORT WO

LOCATIONS

HQ: BNSF RAILWAY COMPANY
  2650 LOU MENK DR, FORT WORTH, TX 761312830
Phone: 800 795-2673
Web: WWW.BNSF.COM

PRODUCTS/OPERATIONS

2018 Sales

	$ mil.	% of total
Consumer Products	7,902	33
Industrial Products	5,967	25
Agricultural Products	4,697	20
Coal	4,012	17
Other revenues	1,277	5
Total	23,855	100

COMPETITORS

BURLINGTON NORTHERN SANTA FE, LLC
CSX CORPORATION
Compagnie des Chemins de Fer Nationaux du Canada
EXPEDITORS INTERNATIONAL OF WASHINGTON, INC.
GENESEE & WYOMING INC.
HUB GROUP, INC.
J. B. HUNT TRANSPORT SERVICES, INC.
THE BRINK'S COMPANY
UNIVERSAL LOGISTICS HOLDINGS, INC.
XPO LOGISTICS, INC.

HISTORICAL FINANCIALS

Company Type: Private

Income Statement — FYE: December 31

	REVENUE ($mil)	NET INCOME ($mil)	NET PROFIT MARGIN	EMPLOYEES
12/17	20,747	12,119	58.4%	35,000
12/16	19,278	4,260	22.1%	—
12/14	22,714	4,397	19.4%	—
12/13	21,552	4,271	19.8%	—
Annual Growth	(0.9%)	29.8%	—	—

2017 Year-End Financials
Return on assets: 14.6%   Cash ($ mil.): 516
Return on equity: 19.3%
Current Ratio: 1.00

BOARD OF EDUCATION FOR THE CITY OF SAVANNAH AND THE COUNTY OF CHATHAM (INC)

Auditors : KRT CPAS PC SAVANNAH GEORG

LOCATIONS

HQ: BOARD OF EDUCATION FOR THE CITY OF SAVANNAH AND THE COUNTY OF CHATHAM (INC)
  208 BULL ST, SAVANNAH, GA 314013843
Phone: 912 395-1000
Web: SPWWW.SCCPSS.COM

HISTORICAL FINANCIALS

Company Type: Private

Income Statement — FYE: June 30

	REVENUE ($mil)	NET INCOME ($mil)	NET PROFIT MARGIN	EMPLOYEES
06/20	587	41	7.1%	4,781
06/19	569	86	15.2%	—
06/18	525	41	7.8%	—
06/17	500	(30)	—	—
Annual Growth	5.5%			

2020 Year-End Financials
Return on assets: 3.1%   Cash ($ mil.): 117
Return on equity: 9.0%
Current Ratio: 2.30

BOARD OF EDUCATION OF CITY OF CHICAGO

Auditors : RSM US LLP CHICAGO ILLINOIS

LOCATIONS

HQ: BOARD OF EDUCATION OF CITY OF CHICAGO
  42 W MADISON ST FL 2, CHICAGO, IL 606024309
Phone: 773 553-1600
Web: WWW.cpsboe.org

HISTORICAL FINANCIALS

Company Type: Private

Income Statement — FYE: June 30

	REVENUE ($mil)	NET INCOME ($mil)	NET PROFIT MARGIN	EMPLOYEES
06/16	5,272	(381)	—	1,007
06/12	5,760	324	5.6%	—
06/11	5,659	238	4.2%	—
06/08	17	(0)	—	—
Annual Growth	103.8%	—	—	

2016 Year-End Financials
Return on assets: (-4.0%)   Cash ($ mil.): —
Return on equity: —
Current Ratio: 1.50

BOARD OF EDUCATION- MEMPHIS CITY SCHOOLS

LOCATIONS

HQ: BOARD OF EDUCATION-MEMPHIS CITY SCHOOLS
  160 S HOLLYWOOD ST, MEMPHIS, TN 381124801
Phone: 901 416-5300

HISTORICAL FINANCIALS

Company Type: Private

Income Statement — FYE: June 30

	REVENUE ($mil)	NET INCOME ($mil)	NET PROFIT MARGIN	EMPLOYEES
06/13	1,157	(12)	—	12,015
06/12	1,169	(2)	—	—
06/11*	1,173	(5)	—	—
12/09	449	(64)	—	—
Annual Growth	37.1%	—	—	

*Fiscal year change

2013 Year-End Financials
Return on assets: —   Cash ($ mil.): 177
Return on equity: (-1.1%)
Current Ratio: —

BOARD OF PUBLIC EDUCATION SCHOOL DISTRICT OF PITTSBURGH (INC)

Auditors : MAHER DUESSEL PITTSBURGH PEN

LOCATIONS

HQ: BOARD OF PUBLIC EDUCATION SCHOOL DISTRICT OF PITTSBURGH (INC)
341 S BELLEFIELD AVE, PITTSBURGH, PA 152133552
Phone: 412 622-3500
Web: WWW.PGHSCHOOLS.ORG

HISTORICAL FINANCIALS
Company Type: Private

Income Statement				FYE: December 31
	REVENUE ($mil)	NET INCOME ($mil)	NET PROFIT MARGIN	EMPLOYEES
12/13	624	19	3.1%	634
12/12	613	3	0.6%	—
12/11	631	(14)	—	—
Annual Growth	(0.6%)	—	—	—

2013 Year-End Financials
Return on assets: 2.6%   Cash ($ mil.): 88
Return on equity: 8.0%
Current Ratio: 2.60

BOARD OF REGENTS OF THE UNIVERSITY OF NEBRASKA

The University of Nebraska has sprouted four campuses out in the fields of the Cornhusker State. Founded in 1869, the university confers bachelor's, master's, and doctoral degrees in more than 200 majors including agriculture, business, education, and engineering at its campuses in Kearney, Lincoln, and Omaha. The university's Medical Center in Omaha trains doctors, performs research, and is affiliated with a nearly 720-bed teaching hospital. The school also operates research and extension services across the state. More than 51,420 students attend classes in the system that has a student-teacher ratio of about 17:1. It was founded as a land-grant university just two years after the Nebraska became a state.

Operations

Undergraduate and graduate students can find research opportunities in all six of colleges (arts and sciences, business administration, communication, fine arts and media, education, information science & technology, public affairs and community services). Its many research centers and labs provide a wealth of opportunity for students to work with faculty members who are known nationally for having expertise in their respective field. Agencies like the NIH, US Department of Defense, and NASA award millions of dollars to UNO annually.

Geographic Reach

The university campus size 856 acres and is located in Lincoln, Nebraska.

Strategy

The resulting strategy is built around several key principles: the value of higher education is clear and growing; students come first; "our people are our greatest asset"; make the best use of every dollar; themes of equity and inclusion touch everything the company does; and Nebraskans should know what to expect from their University.

Auditors : MARK AVERY CPA LINCOLN NEBR

LOCATIONS

HQ: BOARD OF REGENTS OF THE UNIVERSITY OF NEBRASKA
3835 HOLDREGE ST, LINCOLN, NE 685031435
Phone: 402 472-3906
Web: WWW.NEBRASKA.EDU

PRODUCTS/OPERATIONS

University Campuses
The University of Nebraska at Kearney
The University of Nebraska-Lincoln
The University of Nebraska Medical Center
The University of Nebraska at Omaha

COMPETITORS

AUBURN UNIVERSITY
HAMPTON UNIVERSITY
IDAHO STATE UNIVERSITY
MISSOURI STATE UNIVERSITY
NORTHWESTERN UNIVERSITY
PHILADELPHIA UNIVERSITY
THE UNIVERSITY OF CHICAGO
THE UNIVERSITY OF IOWA
UNIVERSITY OF ARKANSAS SYSTEM
UNIVERSITY OF CINCINNATI

HISTORICAL FINANCIALS
Company Type: Private

Income Statement				FYE: June 30
	REVENUE ($mil)	NET INCOME ($mil)	NET PROFIT MARGIN	EMPLOYEES
06/16	1,490	215	14.5%	15,200
06/15	1,405	221	15.8%	—
06/14	1,333	222	16.7%	—
06/13	1,313	254	19.4%	—
Annual Growth	4.3%	(5.4%)	—	—

2016 Year-End Financials
Return on assets: 4.3%   Cash ($ mil.): 613
Return on equity: 6.0%
Current Ratio: 2.80

BOARD OF REGENTS OF THE UNIVERSITY SYSTEM OF GEORGIA

EXECUTIVES

FOR GRANTS Accounting*, Jennifer Shaw
FOR*, Juanita Hicks
Auditors : GREG S GRIFFIN STATE AUDITOR

LOCATIONS

HQ: BOARD OF REGENTS OF THE UNIVERSITY SYSTEM OF GEORGIA
270 WASHINGTON ST SW, ATLANTA, GA 303349056
Phone: 404 962-3050
Web: WWW.USG.EDU

HISTORICAL FINANCIALS
Company Type: Private

Income Statement				FYE: June 30
	REVENUE ($mil)	NET INCOME ($mil)	NET PROFIT MARGIN	EMPLOYEES
06/20	5,523	(116)	—	40,000
06/19	5,532	426	7.7%	—
06/18	5,210	221	4.3%	—
06/17	5,100	57	1.1%	—
Annual Growth	2.7%	—	—	—

2020 Year-End Financials
Return on assets: (-0.8%)   Cash ($ mil.): 1,628
Return on equity: (-6.0%)
Current Ratio: 3.10

BOARD OF TRUSTEES OF STATE INSTITUTIONS OF HIGHER LEARNING

Auditors : CLIFTONLARSONALLEN LLP BALTI

LOCATIONS

HQ: BOARD OF TRUSTEES OF STATE INSTITUTIONS OF HIGHER LEARNING
3825 RIDGEWOOD RD, JACKSON, MS 392116453
Phone: 601 432-6198
Web: WWW.MISSISSIPPI.EDU

HISTORICAL FINANCIALS
Company Type: Private

Income Statement				FYE: June 30
	REVENUE ($mil)	NET INCOME ($mil)	NET PROFIT MARGIN	EMPLOYEES
06/21	2,786	233	8.4%	65
06/20	2,752	41	1.5%	—
06/19	2,720	103	3.8%	—
06/18	2,588	(5)	—	—
Annual Growth	2.5%	—	—	—

2021 Year-End Financials
Return on assets: 2.9%   Cash ($ mil.): 961
Return on equity: 9.6%
Current Ratio: 2.30

BOARDRIDERS, INC.

Boardriders (formerly known as Quiksilver) is a leading action sports and lifestyle company that designs, produces and distributes branded apparel, footwear and accessories for board riders around the world. The company caters to the young and athletic with surfwear, snowboard wear, sportswear, and swimwear sold under the Quiksilver, Billabong, Element, VonZipper, and Roxy names, among others. It also owns the DC Shoes brand of footwear and apparel for young men and juniors. It sells its apparel, footwear, and accessories in specialty and department stores worldwide, as well as through its own network of approximately 570 retail stores. It emerged from Chapter 11 bankruptcy protection in 2016 and is now owned by Oaktree Capital Management; in 2018 it bought rival Billabong.

Operations
Boardriders operates some 15 flagship stores, approximately 570 retail stores, over 7,000 wholesale accounts and e-com platforms in approximately 35 countries.

Geographic Reach
Boardriders has presence in more than 55 countries; it has e-commerce capabilities in approximately 35 countries with some 570 retail stores. The company's global and Americas headquarters is located in Huntington Beach, California.

Sales and Marketing
Financial Performance

HISTORY

Australian surfers Alan Green and John Law started Quiksilver in 1969 to make "boardshorts" for surfers. In 1976 surfers Jeff Hakman and Bob McKnight bought the US rights to the Quiksilver name -- Hakman displayed his enthusiasm for the line by eating a doily at a dinner with Green -- and established Quiksilver, USA. The firm went public in 1986.

The recession of the early 1990s and the dominance of grunge as the fashion du jour hurt Quiksilver and prompted it to restructure. It acquired French affiliate Na Pali in 1991 and began building its European operations. To gain surer footing in the fickle teen fashion market, Quiksilver broadened its product offerings. It added the Roxy women's swimwear line in 1991, expanding it to clothing in 1993. It also launched the Boardriders Club concept -- stores featuring Quiksilver merchandise but owned by independent retailers. In 1994 the company acquired swimwear maker The Raisin Company. In 1997 Quiksilver began advertising nationally and entered the snowboard market, buying Mervin Manufacturing, maker of Lib Technologies, Gnu, and Bent Metal snowboard products.

With its women's lines making waves and a strong current from European sales, Quiksilver began opening its own Boardriders Club stores in 1998. In 1999 it launched the Quik Jeans and Roxy Jeans denim lines, and the next year it added the Alex Goes line for women 25 to 40. Riding a tide of rising profits, in 2000 the company acquired Fidra men's golf apparel; Freestyle, the European licensee of rival youth wear label Gotcha; and pro-skateboarder Tony Hawk's apparel and accessories business. In a tail-that-wags-the-dog move, the company bought its progenitor, Quiksilver International, the same year; in doing so, Quiksilver gained sole possession of the Quiksilver name worldwide.

In June 2002 Quiksilver launched Quiksilver Entertainment, a production company that creates actionsport-based programming for the entertainment industry. Later that year Quiksilver acquired Ug Manufacturing in Australia and Quiksilver Japan, in an effort to gain control over nearly all its global business, with the exception of a few licenses in small niche markets. At about the same time, the company purchased and integrated Beach Street, the owner and operator of 26 Quiksilver outlet stores.

The company formed a 50-50 joint venture in 2003 with Glorious Sun Enterprises to expand into China.

Quiksilver's entertainment unit in 2004 launched an actionsport film distribution company, Union, which is a supplier to more than 1,000 retail locations in Australia, China, Europe, Japan, and the US. In 2004 Quiksilver completed its purchase of DC Shoes and bought the footwear firm's Canadian distributor, Centre Skateboard Distribution, in 2005. The footwear company's popularity in the skate and surf community serves to embed Quiksilver further in that market, while ensuring its ability to compete with Nike and adidas in the footwear arena.

In 2005 Quiksilver flipped its board in a new direction, however, and broadened its reach into the mainstream. The company announced it has signed an exclusive licensing deal with Kohl's and Tony Hawk to give traction to its apparel, outerwear, and accessories. As part of the agreement, Quiksilver will continue to design the Tony Hawk clothing brand and Kohl's will do the rest, including sourcing, distributing, marketing, and other functions.

Quiksilver exited the sports equipment manufacturing business in November 2008 when it sold its Rossignol unit.

It emerged from Chapter 11 bankruptcy protection in 2016 and changed its name to Boardriders.

EXECUTIVES

INTERIM PRESIDENT EMEA*, Thomas Chambolle

CRO*, Stephen Coulombe

Auditors : DELOITTE & TOUCHE LLP COSTA M

LOCATIONS

HQ: BOARDRIDERS, INC.
  5600 ARGOSY AVE STE 100, HUNTINGTON BEACH, CA 926491063
Phone: 714 889-5404
Web: WWW.BOARDRIDERS.COM

PRODUCTS/OPERATIONS

Selected Brands
Billabong
DC Shoes
Element
Kustom
Palmers
Quiksilver
Roxy
RVCA
VonZipper
Xcel

COMPETITORS

CLARUS CORPORATION
COLUMBIA SPORTSWEAR COMPANY
CUTTER & BUCK INC.
DC SHOES, INC.
PENTLAND GROUP LIMITED
PERRY ELLIS INTERNATIONAL INC
PUMA SE
SPEEDO USA INC.
UNDER ARMOUR, INC.
VF OUTDOOR, LLC

HISTORICAL FINANCIALS

Company Type: Private

Income Statement   FYE: October 31

	REVENUE ($mil)	NET INCOME ($mil)	NET PROFIT MARGIN	EMPLOYEES
10/14	1,570	(320)	—	600
10/13	1,810	(233)	—	—
10/12	2,013	(9)	—	—
Annual Growth	(11.7%)	—	—	—

2014 Year-End Financials
Return on assets: (-25.5%)   Cash ($ mil.): 46
Return on equity: (-556.7%)
Current Ratio: 2.10

BON SECOURS MERCY HEALTH, INC.

Bon Secours Mercy Health is one of the 20 largest health systems in the US and the fifth-largest Catholic health system in the country. The ministry's quality, compassionate care is provided by more than 60,000 associates serving communities in Florida, Kentucky, Maryland, New York, Ohio, South Carolina, Virginia, and throughout Ireland.

Operations
Bon Secours Mercy Health operates in 50 hospitals with 60,000 associates, including some 3,000 providers in the US and 450 consultants in Ireland.

Geographic Reach
Bon Secours Mercy Health has hospitals in Florida, Kentucky, Maryland, New York, Ohio, South Carolina, Virginia and Ireland.

Strategy
In mid-2021, Trilliant Health, a health care analytics company that helps providers develop strategies for increasing market share growth and predicting consumer preferences to improve patient experience, announced it

has added Bon Secours Mercy Health as a strategic growth investor. The investment will help the company accelerate the development of its predictive analytics platform and joins previous investments made by Primus Capital, Providence Ventures, Martin Ventures, Noro-Moseley Partners and Nashville Capital Network.

As part of the investment, Deepesh Chandra, chief analytics officer at Bon Secours Mercy Health, will join Trilliant Health's Board of Directors as an observer.

EXECUTIVES

CCO*, Wael Haidar
CSO*, David Cannady
CDO*, Jason Szczuk
Auditors : KPMG LLP CINCINNATI OHIO

LOCATIONS

HQ: BON SECOURS MERCY HEALTH, INC.
  1701 MERCY HEALTH PL, CINCINNATI, OH 452376147
Phone: 513 952-5000
Web: WWW.BONSECOURS.COM

Selected Facilities
Florida
  Bon Secours St. Petersburg Health System
  Bon Secours - Maria Manor Nursing Care and Rehabilitation Center
  Bon Secours Place at St. Petersburg
  Bon Secours St. Petersburg Home Care Services
Kentucky
  Bon Secours Kentucky Health System
  Our Lady of Bellefonte Hospital (Ashland)
Maryland
  Bon Secours Baltimore Health System
  Bon Secours Hospital
  Bon Secours Washington Village
  Community Institute of Behavioral Sciences
  Hollins Terrace/Benet House
New York
  Bon Secours Charity Health System
  Bon Secours Community Hospital (Port Jervis)
  Good Samaritan Hospital (Suffern)
  St. Anthony Community Hospital (Warwick)
  Bon Secours New York Health System
  Schervier Nursing Care Center (Riverdale)
Pennsylvania
  Altoona Regional Health System (joint venture)
South Carolina
  Bon Secours St. Francis Health System, Inc.
  St. Francis Hospital (Downtown and Eastside Campuses, Greenville)
  Roper St. Francis Healthcare (Charleston, joint venture)
Virginia
  Bon Secours Hampton Roads Health System
  Bon Secours Maryview Nursing Care Center (Suffolk)
  DePaul Medical Center (Norfolk)
  Mary Immaculate Hospital (Newport News)
  Maryview Medical Center (Portsmouth)
  Province Place (Norfolk and Portsmouth)
  St. Francis Nursing Care Center (Newport News)
  Bon Secours Richmond Health System (joint venture)
  Memorial Regional Medical Center (Mechanicsville)
  Richmond Community Hospital
  St. Francis Medical Center (Midlothian)
  St. Mary's Hospital (Richmond)

Selected Affiliations
Cosponsoring Congregational Relationships
  Bernardine Sisters of the Third Order of St. Francis (Newport News, Virginia)
  Sisters of Charity of Saint Elizabeth of Convent Station (New Jersey and New York)

Affiliated Organizations
  Health Corporation of Virginia (Richmond)
  Medical Society of South Carolina and Carolinas Health Care System (Charleston)
  Life Care Services (Florida and Virginia)

PRODUCTS/OPERATIONS

2014 Sales

	$ mil.	% of total
Net Patient Service Revenue	3,328.5	96
Other revenue	133.3	4
Total	3,461.8	100

COMPETITORS

ADVOCATE AURORA HEALTH, INC.
ADVOCATE HEALTH CARE NETWORK
COMMONSPIRIT HEALTH
MERCY HEALTH
MERCY HEALTH
NOVANT HEALTH, INC.
SPECTRUM HEALTH SYSTEM
ST. JOSEPH HEALTH SYSTEM
TRINITY HEALTH CORPORATION
WELLMONT HEALTH SYSTEM

HISTORICAL FINANCIALS
Company Type: Private

Income Statement
FYE: December 31

	REVENUE ($mil)	NET INCOME ($mil)	NET PROFIT MARGIN	EMPLOYEES
12/21	10,877	997	9.2%	19,000
12/20	9,969	609	6.1%	—
12/19*	8,717	2,593	29.7%	—
08/10	3,084	(41)	—	—
Annual Growth	12.1%	—	—	—

*Fiscal year change

2021 Year-End Financials
Return on assets: 5.6%   Cash ($ mil.): 402
Return on equity: 10.1%
Current Ratio: 0.90

BONNEVILLE POWER ADMINISTRATION

Bonneville Power Administration (BPA) keeps the lights on in the Pacific Northwest. The US Department of Energy power marketing agency operates a transmission grid (with more than 15,000 miles of high-voltage lines) that delivers about 30% of the electrical power consumed in the region. The electricity that BPA wholesales is generated primarily by around 30 federal hydroelectric dams (operated by the US Army Corp of Engineers) and one nonfederal nuclear facility and several small nonfederal power plants.

Operations
BPA operates and maintains about three-fourths of the high-voltage transmission in its service territory. It promotes energy efficiency, renewable resources and new technologies. The agency also funds regional efforts to protect and rebuild fish and wildlife populations affected by hydroelectric power development in the Columbia River Basin.

Overall, power accounts to about 70% of total sales, transmission accounts for some 25%, and US Treasury credits and others account for the rest.

Geographic Reach
Headquartered in Portland, Oregon, BPA's service territory includes Idaho, Oregon, Washington, western Montana and small parts of eastern Montana, California, Nevada, Utah and Wyoming.

Sales and Marketing
The company serves consumer-owned electric cooperatives, municipalities, public utility districts, and tribal utilities.

It also sells wholesale power and transmission to entities that buy and sell non-federal power in the region, in-region purchasers of federal power, generators, marketers, and utilities that seek to transmit power into, out of, or through the region.

Financial Performance
BPA's 2019 revenue is similar to its 2018 revenue ($3.7 billion).

Cash and cash equivalents at the end of the year were $846.5 million, 62% higher than in the previous year. Cash provided by operating activities was $972.3 million. Investing activities used $543.9 million primarily for Investment in utility plant, including AFUDC, while financing activities used $105.8 million primarily for repayment of borrowings from US Treasury.

Strategy
Technology and energy markets are changing rapidly, impacting how BPA operates the transmission grid and hydropower plants it, together with its federal partners, are entrusted with managing. Its asset management program maximizes the value it derives from these and other assets, including facilities and IT equipment. NIE is continually growing and updating its program to help maintain Bonneville's competitive edge in the marketplace, enable industry change, deliver on its public responsibilities, and strengthen financial health by effectively managing asset lifecycle costs. This year NIE strengthened the tie between its strategic asset management plans and its financial planning process, and it began implementing a common risk methodology to base all asset decisions on five dimensions of risk: financial, reliability, compliance, safety and environmental.

It is also making significant headway in its effort to modernize BPA's systems and operations in response to new and changing markets. Out of a portfolio of 35 grid modernization projects, six were completed this year, three were completed in FY 2019, and all but one of the others are in flight. This work is essential for the agency to remain the region's wholesale power provider of choice by helping the company identify surplus capacity available on the power and transmission systems for additional sales, manage grid congestion more efficiently and reliably, and provide valuable insights into how best to invest in the system. Projects are already delivering significant value to BPA and our customers, such as through a new program called One BPA Outage.

Company Background

In 2012 BPA bought electricity from a number of wind projects and had more than 4,000 MW of wind power capacity tied in to its transmission grid. BPA harnessed and integrated about 6,000 MW of wind power by the end of 2013.

BPA is also expanding its transmission grid, building three new 500-kilovolt transmission lines to cater to expanding Columbia Gorge wind power. In this regard, in 2011 the company began building a new high-voltage transmission line and substation (the Big Eddy-Knight Transmission Project) that would add more than 1,150 MW of capacity to its transmission grid and accommodate new wind energy sources. In 2012 it completed a separate 79-mile, $216-million line along the Columbia River east of the gorge.

BPA was founded in 1937.

Auditors: PRICEWATERHOUSECOOPERS LLP PO

LOCATIONS

HQ: BONNEVILLE POWER ADMINISTRATION
905 NE 11TH AVE, PORTLAND, OR 972324169
Phone: 503 230-3000
Web: WWW.BPA.GOV

PRODUCTS/OPERATIONS

2014 Sales

	$ mil.	% of total
Power	2,572	71
Transmission	892	25
US Treasury credits for fish	104	3
Other	70	1
Adjustments	(38)	-
Total	3,600	100

COMPETITORS

CALIFORNIA INDEPENDENT SYSTEM OPERATOR CORPORATION
CITY OF DALTON
CITY OF PASADENA
FEDERAL COMMUNICATIONS COMMISSION
FEDERAL ELECTION COMMISSION
GREAT RIVER ENERGY
MUNICIPAL ELECTRIC AUTHORITY OF GEORGIA
NUCLEAR REGULATORY COMMISSION, UNITED STATES
PUBLIC UTILITY DISTRICT 1 OF SNOHOMISH COUNTY
THE GOVERNMENT PUBLIC RELATIONS DEPARTMENT

HISTORICAL FINANCIALS

Company Type: Private

Income Statement FYE: September 30

	REVENUE ($mil)	NET INCOME ($mil)	NET PROFIT MARGIN	EMPLOYEES
09/10	3,055	(127)	—	3,100
09/09	2,870	(101)	—	—
09/08	3,036	264	8.7%	—
Annual Growth	0.3%	—	—	—

2010 Year-End Financials
Return on assets: (-0.6%)   Cash ($ mil.): 1,078
Return on equity: (-0.9%)
Current Ratio: 1.20

BOSCOV'S, INC.

EXECUTIVES

CAO, Russell C Diehm
Auditors: KPMG LLP PHILADELPHIA PENNS

LOCATIONS

HQ: BOSCOV'S, INC.
4500 PERKIOMEN AVE, READING, PA 196063946
Phone: 610 779-2000
Web: LOCATIONS.BOSCOVS.COM

HISTORICAL FINANCIALS

Company Type: Private

Income Statement FYE: January 29

	REVENUE ($mil)	NET INCOME ($mil)	NET PROFIT MARGIN	EMPLOYEES
01/22	1,225	98	8.0%	6,311
01/21*	882	(1)	—	—
02/20	1,241	41	3.3%	—
02/19	1,215	47	3.9%	—
Annual Growth	0.3%	27.5%	—	—

*Fiscal year change

2022 Year-End Financials
Return on assets: 15.4%   Cash ($ mil.): 230
Return on equity: 26.9%
Current Ratio: 2.70

BOSTON MEDICAL CENTER CORPORATION

Boston Medical Center (BMC) offers a full spectrum of health care services, from prenatal care and obstetrics to surgery and rehabilitation. BMC is also the city's largest provider of indigent care, spending millions of dollars annually on care for uninsured patients and offering free screenings and other community outreach programs. The not-for-profit hospital boasts more than 500 licensed beds, about 880 physicians, and includes a Level 1 trauma center, acute rehabilitation facilities, and neonatal and pediatric intensive care units. BMC is the primary teaching hospital of Boston University's School of Medicine.

Operations

BMC also operates Boston HealthNet, a network affiliation of the medical center, Boston University School of Medicine, and more than a dozen community health centers. Boston HealthNet provides outreach, prevention, primary care and specialty care, and dental services at sites located throughout the community.

Hand-in-hand with being a major teaching hospital is engaging in extensive medical research. BMC oversees more than 570 research and service projects and conducts both biomedical and clinical research programs exploring infectious disease, cardiology, vascular biology, Parkinson's disease, geriatrics, and endocrinology, among other areas.

BMC had more than 1.3 million outpatient clinic visits, 120,800 emergency department visits, and 24,365 admissions.

Sales and Marketing

Nearly 75% of its patients come from underserved populations, such as the low-income and elderly, who rely on government payers such as Medicaid, the Health Safety Net, and Medicare for their coverage.

Auditors: BMC HEALTH SYSTEM INC BOSTO

LOCATIONS

HQ: BOSTON MEDICAL CENTER CORPORATION
1 BOSTON MEDICAL CTR PL # 1, BOSTON, MA 021182999
Phone: 617 414-5000
Web: WWW.BMC.ORG

PRODUCTS/OPERATIONS

Selected Services and Programs
Alzheimer's Disease Center
Anesthesiology
Boston HealthNet
Boston University Affiliated Physicians
Boston University Cosmetic and Laser Center
Cardiovascular Center
Care Management
Dermatology
Diabetes
Elders Living at Home Program
Emergency Medicine
Facial Plastic and Reconstructive Surgery
General Internal Medicne / Primary Care
Geriatrics
Head and Neck Cancer Center of Excellence
Hematology & Medical Oncology
Immigrant & Refugee Health Program
Integrative Medicine
LocoMotor Training
Mattapan Community Health Center
Melanoma Program
Neurosurgery
Nursing
Ophthalmology
Oral and Maxillofacial Surgery
Pediatrics - bWell Center
Pediatrics - Cardiology
Rehabilitation Therapies
Renal Medicine
South End Community Health Center
Special Kids Special Help
Thoracic Surgery
Transplant Surgery
Uphams Corner Health Center
Urology
Vascular Center
Vascular and Endovascular Surgery
Weight Loss Surgery (Bariatric Surgery)
Whittier Street Health Center

COMPETITORS

ATRIUS HEALTH, INC.

CHILDREN'S HOSPITAL MEDICAL CENTER
H. LEE MOFFITT CANCER CENTER AND RESEARCH INSTITUTE HOSPITAL, INC.
LAHEY HEALTH SYSTEM, INC.
PALO ALTO MEDICAL FOUNDATION FOR HEALTH CARE, RESEARCH AND EDUCATION
SWEDISH HEALTH SERVICES
TEXAS CHILDREN'S HOSPITAL
THE CHILDREN'S HOSPITAL CORPORATION
THE CHILDREN'S HOSPITAL OF PHILADELPHIA
THE MASSACHUSETTS GENERAL HOSPITAL

HISTORICAL FINANCIALS
Company Type: Private

Income Statement — FYE: September 30

	REVENUE ($mil)	NET INCOME ($mil)	NET PROFIT MARGIN	EMPLOYEES
09/17	1,089	12	1.2%	4,200
09/15	1,004	7	0.8%	—
09/12	886	2	0.3%	—
Annual Growth	4.2%	38.0%	—	—

2017 Year-End Financials
Return on assets: 0.6% Cash ($ mil.): 125
Return on equity: 1.0%
Current Ratio: 1.90

BOSTON UNIVERSITY

Auditors: KMPG LLP BOSTON MA

LOCATIONS

HQ: BOSTON UNIVERSITY
590 COMMONWEALTH AVE # 255, BOSTON, MA 022152521
Phone: 617 353-2600
Web: WWW.BU.EDU

HISTORICAL FINANCIALS
Company Type: Private

Income Statement — FYE: June 30

	REVENUE ($mil)	NET INCOME ($mil)	NET PROFIT MARGIN	EMPLOYEES
06/18	2,018	517	25.6%	70
06/17	1,895	507	26.8%	—
Annual Growth	6.5%	2.0%	—	—

2018 Year-End Financials
Return on assets: 8.1% Cash ($ mil.): 148
Return on equity: 13.2%
Current Ratio: —

BOZZUTO'S, INC.

Bozzuto's is a leading wholesale grocery distribution company that supplies food and household products to retailers in New Jersey, New York, Pennsylvania, and in New England. The company distributes a full line of grocery items, including meat products, produce and floral, grocery, dairy and frozen food, bakery and deli, fresh meat and seafood, as well as seasonal and GM/HBC and specialty and organics. It carries goods sold under both the IGA and Hy-Top labels, in addition to national brands. Bozzuto's also owns about five distribution centers in Connecticut and Pennsylvania. The company was founded in 1945.

Operations
Bozzuto's is a total service wholesale distributor of food and household products to retailers. It provides retail sales support, grocery and perishable, retail technology, retail accounting and payroll, creative custom design and store development, merchandising and category management support and transportation ? logistics services.

In terms of brands, the customers can choose from IGA brand products or Hy-Top brand products. The company also offers a growing line of store brand organics, called Seven Farms.

Geographic Reach
Cheshire, Connecticut-based Bozzuto's operates a pair of distribution centers in Cheshire, as well as facilities in North Haven, Connecticut, and Allentown, Pennsylvania. In terms of its clients, it also has its presence in New England.

Sales and Marketing
Bozzuto's has sales associates and distributes its products to retailers.

Company Background
The company, founded in 1945, is owned and operated by the Bozzuto family, including chairman and CEO Michael Bozzuto.

Auditors: FEDERMAN LALLY & REMIS LLC F

LOCATIONS

HQ: BOZZUTO'S, INC.
275 SCHOOLHOUSE RD, CHESHIRE, CT 064101257
Phone: 203 272-3511
Web: WWW.BOZZUTOS.COM

PRODUCTS/OPERATIONS

Selected Services
New store site and demographic analysis
Retail merchandising specialists and sales support
Retail financial services, accounting and payroll
Operational analysis
Shelf management programs
Market/pricing strategies
Employee training, seminars and workshops
Profit building ideas
Retail technology

COMPETITORS

AFFILIATED FOODS, INC.
ASSOCIATED GROCERS OF NEW ENGLAND, INC.
BROOKSHIRE GROCERY COMPANY
CERTCO, INC.
CONSUMER PRODUCT DISTRIBUTORS, LLC
DOT FOODS, INC.
LINEAGE FOODSERVICE SOLUTIONS, LLC
THE H T HACKNEY CO
UNIFIED GROCERS, INC.
URM STORES, INC.

HISTORICAL FINANCIALS
Company Type: Private

Income Statement — FYE: September 27

	REVENUE ($mil)	NET INCOME ($mil)	NET PROFIT MARGIN	EMPLOYEES
09/08	1,243	(5)	—	3,100
09/07	1,180	(0)	0.0%	—
09/06	955,449	0	0.0%	—
Annual Growth	(96.4%)	—	—	—

2008 Year-End Financials
Return on assets: 7.0% Cash ($ mil.): 1
Return on equity: (-0.5%)
Current Ratio: 0.60

BRAZOS ELECTRIC POWER COOPERATIVE, INC.

Brazos means "arms" in Spanish, and the generation and transmission arms of Brazos Electric Power Cooperative reach across 68 Texas counties. It serves 16 member/owner distribution cooperatives and one municipality in Northern and Central Texas. Brazos Electric Power annually generates (through its four power stations) and/or accesses from other power marketers some 3,655 MW of electric power. The cooperative's members include Comanche Electric Cooperative Association, Heart of Texas Electric Co-op (McGregor), Mid-South Synergy (Navasota), United Coop Services (Cleburne), and Wise Electric (Decatur).

Auditors: PRICEWATERHOUSECOOPERS LLP KA

LOCATIONS

HQ: BRAZOS ELECTRIC POWER COOPERATIVE, INC.
7616 BAGBY AVE, WACO, TX 767126924
Phone: 254 750-6500
Web: WWW.BRAZOSELECTRIC.COM

Brazos Electric Power Cooperative has operations in 68 counties in northern and Central Texas.

PRODUCTS/OPERATIONS

Member/Owners
Barlett Electric Cooperative
BEPC
Comanche Electric Cooperative
Cooke County Electric Cooperative
CoServ Electric
Fort Belknap Electric Cooperative
Hamilton County Electric Cooperative
Heart of Texas Electric Cooperative
HILCO Electric Cooperative
J-A-C Electric Cooperative
Mid-South Synergy
Navarro County Electric Cooperative
Navasota Valley Electric Cooperative
South Plains Electric Cooperative
Tri-County Electric Cooperative
United Cooperative Services
Wise Electric Cooperative

COMPETITORS
CUIVRE RIVER ELECTRIC COOPERATIVE, INC.
MIDDLE TENNESSEE ELECTRIC MEMBERSHIP CORPORATION (THE)
OHIO VALLEY ELECTRIC CORPORATION
RAYBURN COUNTRY ELECTRIC COOPERATIVE, INC
SEQUACHEE VALLEY ELECTRIC COOPERATIVE

HISTORICAL FINANCIALS
Company Type: Private

Income Statement — FYE: December 31

	REVENUE ($mil)	NET INCOME ($mil)	NET PROFIT MARGIN	EMPLOYEES
12/17	905	58	6.5%	366
12/09	963	56	5.9%	—
12/99	307	6	2.3%	—
Annual Growth	6.2%	12.6%	—	—

2017 Year-End Financials
Return on assets: 1.9%   Cash ($ mil.): 353
Return on equity: 7.4%
Current Ratio: 15.30

BRG SPORTS, INC.

BRG Sports is a corporate holding company of leading brands that design, develop and market innovative sports equipment, smart helmet technology, team apparel, and accessories. The company's Riddell brand is a premier designer and developer of football helmets, protective sports equipment, head impact monitoring technologies, apparel and related accessories. A recognized leader in helmet technology and innovation, Riddell is the leading manufacturer of football helmets and shoulder pads, and a top provider of reconditioning services (cleaning, repairing, repainting and recertifying existing equipment).

Operations
BRG offers innovative sports equipment, smart helmet technology, team apparel, and accessories under Riddel brand. It offers varsity and youth helmets such as Speedflex and Victor; shoulder pads; accessories such as face masks, chin straps, and hardware, as well as back plates and rib protectors; and apparel including padded shirts and jerseys, and padded girdle and pants.

Geographic Reach
BRG Sports is based in Illinois and has approximately 10 facilities worldwide.

Sales and Marketing
BRG serves youth sports equipment and apparel, institutional/scholastic sports equipment and apparel, professional football equipment industries.

Financial Performance

HISTORY

The company traces its roots to the Los Angeles suburb of Bell, a hotbed of auto racing, and Roy Richter, a racer who operated Bell Auto Parts. Richter began making racing helmets in 1954 and became a leading maker of motorcycle and ski helmets during the 1960s. In 1975 Bell Helmets introduced the Bell Biker, the first hard-shell bicycle helmet.

Phil Matthews, a former executive with Wilson Sporting Goods, and Terry Lee, an executive with bankrupt motorcycle accessory maker Vetter Products, purchased Bell Helmets with several partners in 1983 (the group merged Vetter and Bell). Motorcycle helmet sales slowed, but sales of bicycle helmets (including lines for infants and children) propelled the company during the 1980s. Bell Helmets began selling products in Europe in 1988, and in 1991 it sold its motorcycle helmet business to Italian manufacturer Bieffe for $15 million.

The company went public in 1992 as Bell Sports and began benefiting from new state laws requiring children to wear helmets while bicycling. Also that year it acquired Blackburn, a maker of pumps, racks, packs, and accessories, but by 1995 competition began cutting into sales and profits.

To protect its market share, in 1995 the company acquired American Recreation, the nation's #2 helmet maker. To reduce debt Bell sold its Mongoose bicycle unit in 1997 for $22 million. Investment firms Charlesbank Capital Partners and Brentwood Associates Buyout Fund II took the firm private the next year and installed Mary George as CEO.

In 1999 Bell narrowed its focus, selling its auto-racing helmet business and closing or selling all but one of its factories. Investment firm Chartwell bought Bell in 2000, and moved Mary George to executive chairman. Bell moved its headquarters in 2001 to Irving, Texas.

The company broadened its product offerings when it bought Bollinger Industries' fitness accessory product line in 2002; products range from yoga mats to jump ropes and weightlifting belts.

Fenway Partners acquired Bell Sports for $240 million in September 2004. Fenway combined the company with its Riddell Sports Group (football helmets) to form Riddell Bell Holdings. Under this umbrella Fenway created one of the top global suppliers of helmets. Bell Sports and Riddell were once a combined company when William Zimmerman (then president of Zimmerman Holdings) and James Marshall Galbraith purchased Bell Helmets and Riddell to form Bell-Riddell. The companies were sold separately in 1984.

In December 2004 Riddell Bell purchased Sports Instruments, an athletic performance technology company. Sports Instruments' products, which include heart rate monitors and sports watches, were absorbed into Riddell Bell's specialty retail division. In January 2005 the company purchased auto racing helmets maker Bell Racing.

Easton-Bell Sports was formed in 2006 when Easton Sports and Riddell Bell Holdings merged their operations. Tony Palma, Easton's former chief executive, took over as CEO upon completion of the deal. He held that position until March 2008, when he departed the firm. Bill Fry, Riddell Bell's top executive, was named EBS's president. Fry left the company in early 2007, following the merger transition. Palma was replaced by former Reebok CEO Paul Harrington in April 2008.

EXECUTIVES

Senior Vice President Human Resources,
Jackelyn E Werblo
Auditors: ERNST & YOUNG LLP LOS ANGELE

LOCATIONS

HQ: BRG SPORTS, INC.
1700 E HIGGINS RD STE 500, DES PLAINES, IL 600183800
Phone: 224 585-5200
Web: CONTENT.RIDDELL.COM

2013 Sales

	$ mil.	% of total
North America	667.5	85
Europe	84.7	11
Other	28.2	4
Total	780.4	100

PRODUCTS/OPERATIONS

Selected Products
Riddell helmets
Riddell shoulder pads
Riddell padded shirts
Riddell game pants
Riddell compression shirts and pants

COMPETITORS

CYCLING SPORTS GROUP, INC.
DUCATI MOTOR HOLDING SPA
EDELBROCK, LLC
FOX FACTORY HOLDING CORP.
HARLEY-DAVIDSON, INC.
HUFFY CORPORATION
PIAGGIO & C. SPA
RAWLINGS SPORTING GOODS COMPANY, INC.
RUSSELL BRANDS, LLC
YAMAHA MOTOR CO., LTD.

HISTORICAL FINANCIALS
Company Type: Private

Income Statement — FYE: December 29

	REVENUE ($mil)	NET INCOME ($mil)	NET PROFIT MARGIN	EMPLOYEES
12/12	827	(3)	—	2,370
12/11*	834	10	1.2%	—
01/11	772	8	1.1%	—
Annual Growth	3.5%	—	—	—

*Fiscal year change

2012 Year-End Financials
Return on assets: (-0.3%)   Cash ($ mil.): 40
Return on equity: (-0.9%)
Current Ratio: 2.50

BRIDGEPORT HOSPITAL

EXECUTIVES

Medical Vice President, Bruce Mc Donald Md Senior
Chief Medical Officer*, Victor Morris

LOCATIONS

HQ: BRIDGEPORT HOSPITAL
267 GRANT ST, BRIDGEPORT, CT 066102870
Phone: 203 384-3000
Web: WWW.BRIDGEPORTHOSPITAL.ORG

HISTORICAL FINANCIALS
Company Type: Private

Income Statement — FYE: September 30

	REVENUE ($mil)	NET INCOME ($mil)	NET PROFIT MARGIN	EMPLOYEES
09/20	595	(8)	—	200
09/19	626	39	6.3%	—
09/18	550	72	13.2%	—
09/17	482	25	5.4%	—
Annual Growth	7.3%	—	—	—

2020 Year-End Financials
Return on assets: (-2.4%)   Cash ($ mil.): 94
Return on equity: (-11.1%)
Current Ratio: 1.70

BRISBANE SCHOOL DISTRICT

Auditors : RT DENNIS ACCOUNTANCY RANCHO

LOCATIONS

HQ: BRISBANE SCHOOL DISTRICT
1 SOLANO ST, BRISBANE, CA 940051342
Phone: 415 467-0550
Web: WWW.BRISBANESD.ORG

HISTORICAL FINANCIALS
Company Type: Private

Income Statement — FYE: June 30

	REVENUE ($mil)	NET INCOME ($mil)	NET PROFIT MARGIN	EMPLOYEES
06/21	12,636	1,177	9.3%	82
06/20	9,940	10,131	101.9%	—
06/19	9	0	9.8%	—
06/18	8	0	3.7%	—
Annual Growth	1037.5%	1445.3%	—	—

2021 Year-End Financials
Return on assets: 842.1%   Cash ($ mil.): 20
Return on equity: —
Current Ratio: —

BRODER BROS., CO.

Selling clothes had been in the genes of sportswear distributor Broder Bros. for years. Begun as a haberdashery in 1919, the company evolved from making hats and gloves into a leading distributor of imprintable sportswear, distributing 40,000-plus SKUs across more than 40 retail brands, including adidas Golf, Champion, Russell Athletic, alternative, Dickies, and private labels. It operates under the Broder, Alpha, and NES divisions. Private labels include Devon & Jones, Chestnut Hill, and Harriton. Customers, mostly small US retailers, order merchandise through seasonal catalogs or online. Private investment firm Bain Capital has held a majority interest in the company since 2000, when the Broder family sold the company.

Operations
Broder Bros.' business comprises eight distribution facilities nationwide, as well as 10 Express locations that offer pickup services to customers. Express facilities ship through ground parcel service to more than 80% of the continental US population within one business day and to more than 98% of the continental US population within two business days.

Its two primary markets are imprintable sportswear and accessories. Typically, undecorated or blank items, such as sweatshirts, polo shirts, fleece, outerwear, caps, bags, and other imprintable accessories are bought from Broder Bros. and decorated for the purposes of advertising and promotion. Decorator customers are offered value-added merchandising, marketing, and promotional support to help them grow their businesses.

Geographic Reach
Based in Pennsylvania, Broder Bros. boasts the industry's largest distribution network. It provides its products to customers across the continental US.

Sales and Marketing
The company, which caters to more than 70,000 customers, relies on a handful of suppliers such as Gildan, Hanes, and Fruit of the Loom.

In general, Broder Bros. clients include advertising specialty companies, screen printers, embroiderers, and specialty retailers that purchase Broder Bros. products (blank T-shirts, sweatshirts, polo shirts, outerwear, caps, bags, and more) to embellish for their own clients. Broder Bros. distributes popular brands such as Anvil, Jerzees, Hanes, Fruit of the Loom, and Gildan.

Strategy
Broder Bros. has seen its business pick up on the heels of a tough selling environment. One way it has turned its business around is by ensuring that it had in stock the most popular products while it rebuilt its inventory of proprietary brands. It also strengthened its commitment not to be undersold by rivals. To ensure that its dozen distribution centers were bustling with business, Broder Bros. also recruited a senior sales and marketing executive to review and fine-tune how the company sells its products, help to decide which product assortment is ideal going forward, and figure out how to attract a wider customer base from the imprintable sportswear market.

Mergers and Acquisitions
Looking to post more than $900 million in sales and $50 million in pro forma EBITDA in 2013, Broder Bros. bought Denver-based Imprints Wholesale, one of the top wholesale clothing distributors in the Rocky Mountain region. The deal is Broder Bros.' first acquisition since 2006 and first since private investment firm Littlejohn & Co. took over control of the board of directors in mid-2012.

LOCATIONS

HQ: BRODER BROS., CO.
6 NESHAMINY INTERPLEX DR, TREVOSE, PA 190536964
Phone: 215 291-0300
Web: WWW.ALPHABRODER.COM

PRODUCTS/OPERATIONS

Selected Products
Accessories
Bags
Decoration supplies
Fleece
Headwear
Pants
Shorts
Sport shirts
T-shirts
Woven shirts

Selected Brands
Trade
    Adams Cap
    American Apparel
    Anvil
    Bella
    Canvas
    Cross Creek
    Fruit of the Loom
    Gildan
    Hanes
    Izod
    Outer Banks
    Van Heusen
    Weatherproof
    Yupoong
Retail
    adidas Golf
    Champion
    Dickies Chef
    Dickies Workwear
    Rossignol Pure Mountain Company
Private-label
    Chestnut Hill
    Harriton
    Devon & Jones
    HYP
    Harvard Square

COMPETITORS

ANVIL HOLDINGS, INC.
BENSUSSEN DEUTSCH & ASSOCIATES, LLC
CHANEL

COLUMBIA SPORTSWEAR COMPANY
FOX HEAD, INC.
HANESBRANDS INC.
INDUSTRIA DE DISEA'O TEXTIL SA
R. G. BARRY CORPORATION
SAN MAR CORPORATION
TOMMY BAHAMA GROUP, INC.

HISTORICAL FINANCIALS
Company Type: Private

Income Statement — FYE: December 26

	REVENUE ($mil)	NET INCOME ($mil)	NET PROFIT MARGIN	EMPLOYEES
12/09	705	(13)	—	3,101
12/08	926	(68)	—	—
12/07	929	(124)	—	—
Annual Growth	(12.9%)	—	—	—

2009 Year-End Financials
Return on assets: (-4.5%)   Cash ($ mil.): 2
Return on equity: —
Current Ratio: 2.10

BRONSON METHODIST HOSPITAL INC

From your leg bone to your knee bone; your neck bone to your head bone, Bronson Methodist Hospital has the specialists to cure what ails you. The 435-bed hospital is the flagship facility of the Bronson Healthcare Group, a not-for-profit health care system. Bronson Methodist provides care in just about every specialty including orthopedics, surgery, and oncology. The hospital also contains specialist units for critical care (level I trauma center), neurology (primary stroke center), cardiology (Chest pain emergency center), women's health (BirthPlace), and pediatrics (children's hospital).

Operations
In addition to providing general, emergency, and specialty inpatient care to privately insured or self-paying customers, the hospital serves a large percentage of Medicaid patients and provides charity care to uninsured patients. Altogether, Bronson Methodist's charity and community outreach program contributions total more than $55 million annually.

The hospital contains the Bronson Children's Hospital, which offers burn and wound, neonatal development, and newborn pulmonary services, among others.

Geographic Reach
Bronson Methodist serves patients throughout southwestern Michigan from its main facility in Kalamazoo.

Strategy
All of the hospital's inpatient rooms are private; this transition was made to reduce infection rates and increase privacy for Bronson Methodist patients.

Bronson Methodist began participation in the bundled payment program of the Centers for Medicare and Medicaid Services in 2013. The program is designed to improve the quality of care delivery for Medicare patients by changing the way that providers are reimbursed for services.

Auditors : PLANTE & MORAN PLLC CHICAGO

LOCATIONS
HQ: BRONSON METHODIST HOSPITAL INC
  601 JOHN ST STE E-012, KALAMAZOO, MI 490075346
Phone: 269 341-7654
Web: WWW.BRONSONHEALTH.COM

PRODUCTS/OPERATIONS
Selected Services
Anticoagulation
Bereavement
Breast Health
Burn
Cancer Care
Critical Care
Diabetes
Flu
Heart and Vascular
Home Health
Hyperbaric Oxygen Therapy
Infusion
Laboratory
Medical and Surgical Weight Management
Neurosciences
Nutrition
Occupational Health
Orthopedics
Palliative Care
Pediatrics
Pharmacy
Pregnancy and Childbirth
Rehabilitation
Respiratory Care
Sleep
Surgery
Stomal Therapy
Testing and Imaging
Trauma and Emergency
Women's Health
Wound

COMPETITORS
CHILDRENS HOSPITAL & MEDICAL CENTER
MERCY HEALTH - ST. RITA'S MEDICAL CENTER, LLC
PROVIDENCE HEALTH & SERVICES-WASHINGTON
SAINT JOSEPH HOSPITAL, INC
YAKIMA VALLEY MEMORIAL HOSPITAL ASSOCIATION

HISTORICAL FINANCIALS
Company Type: Private

Income Statement — FYE: December 31

	REVENUE ($mil)	NET INCOME ($mil)	NET PROFIT MARGIN	EMPLOYEES
12/19	952	2	0.3%	2,861
12/18	864	26	3.1%	—
12/17	864	85	9.8%	—
12/15	726	69	9.5%	—
Annual Growth	7.0%	(55.6%)	—	—

2019 Year-End Financials
Return on assets: 0.2%   Cash ($ mil.): 552
Return on equity: 0.4%
Current Ratio: 1.70

BRONXCARE HEALTH SYSTEM

Bronx-Lebanon Hospital Center cares for patients in the central and south Bronx, no doubt while rooting for the Yankees a few blocks away. The health care provider maintains more than 970 beds across its two campuses, as well as psychiatric and nursing home facilities. Hospital specialty units include chest pain, orthopedic, cancer, and women's health centers. Bronx-Lebanon also manages a network of about 70 owned and affiliated medical practices (under the BronxCare brand). This network includes primary care doctors and specialty clinics, as well as rehabilitation facilities. The hospital is also a primary teaching hospital for the Albert Einstein College of Medicine.

Operations
Aside from its two major hospitals, Bronx-Lebanon operates a psychiatric facility, a pair of specialized long-term care facilities, and the BronxCare network of medical practices that include Dr. Martin Luther King Jr. Health Center and a 51-unit facility to house seniors and low-income residents. Bronx-Lebanon cares for those with mental or substance abuse problems through the Family Wellness Center. It also operates a 240-bed Special Care Center and the 90-bed Highbridge Woodycrest Center to provide long term health care to geriatric, AIDS, and disabled residents. Its ER Department responds to about 141,000 patient visits a year.

Geographic Reach
The hospital system's 37 locations serve residents of central and south Bronx in New York.

Sales and Marketing
In 2013 the company spent about $144,000 on advertising.

Financial Performance
The Hospital Center is supported primarily by patient service fees paid by Medicaid, Medicare and commercial insurance carriers. In 2013, the Medicaid contributed 63% of the revenue, whereas Medicare contributed 28%, and the rest 9% was contributed other third-party insurance carriers.

In 2013 Bronx-Lebanon's net revenues increased by about 5% due to a rise in patient service revenues and grants, partially offset by a decrease in auxiliary services.

The company's net income increased by more than 790% in 2013 as the result of an increase in revenues.

Bronx-Lebanon's operating cash flows increased by 53%, thanks to higher income.

Strategy
Bronx-Lebanon emphasizes its role as a community health care provider, not only

through its BronxCare network, but through a number of community outreach and service efforts, including school-based programs, mobile health units, free health screening, and even a weekly live television show that discusses health issues.

To accommodate the growing population in and around the Bronx, the hospital system has expanded in recent years with a new children's wing for inpatient and outpatient services; a nine-story ambulatory care facility; and an extensive emergency room modernization. Bronx-Lebanon also maintains a short stay observation unit in the emergency room area to monitor and evaluate patients in cardiac distress prior to admission or discharge.

Bronx-Lebanon is one of many hospital organizations to have joined a regional health information organization (RHIO) to allow medical professionals to access a patient's medical records at any number of health care locations. Other members of the Bronx RHIO include Montefiore Medical Center, Jacobi Medical Center, St. Barnabas Hospital, and Hebrew Home at Riverdale.

Bronx-Lebanon is also one of the few hospitals in New York that is fully computerized, with a complete inpatient and outpatient electronic medical record.

The hospital center's expansion plans include a $42 million, 60,000 sq. ft ambulatory care facility and a $34 million, 56,000 sq. ft. life recovery center for chemical dependency services.

In 2014 the company completed the construction of its Health and Wellness Center, a new state-of-the-art outpatient facility with general and specialty services, and new treatment rooms and diagnostic equipment. It also completed the construction of its Life Recovery Center, to combine inpatient, outpatient, and residential services for individuals suffering from chemical dependency.

The company also expanded its Emergency room adding a new 11-bay treatment area.

In the same year, it also relocated and expanded its main Dentistry Practice, adding 39 dental chairs (a 50% increase).

Auditors : LOEB & TROPER LLP NEW YORK N

LOCATIONS

HQ: BRONXCARE HEALTH SYSTEM
1276 FULTON AVE, BRONX, NY 104563402
Phone: 718 590-1800
Web: WWW.BRONXCARE.ORG

PRODUCTS/OPERATIONS

Selected Services
Anesthesiology
Asthma
   Adult
     Pediatric
Cardiology
Dentistry
Diabetes
   Adult
     Pediatric
Ear, Nose & Throat
Gastroenterology
Hematology & Oncology
Neonatology
Neurology
Ophthalmology
Orthopaedics
Pediatrics
Physical Medicine
Psychiatry
Radiology
Special Care Center
Urology & Men's Health

Selected Academic Affiliations
Albert Einstein College of Medicine
Bronx Community College
Hostos Community College
Lehman College, City University of New York
State University of New York at Stony Brook

COMPETITORS

ALLINA HEALTH SYSTEM
KALEIDA HEALTH
THE LANCASTER GENERAL HOSPITAL
THE PENNSYLVANIA HOSPITAL OF THE UNIVERSITY OF PENNSYLVANIA HEALTH SYSTEM
WELLSTAR HEALTH SYSTEM, INC.

HISTORICAL FINANCIALS
Company Type: Private

Income Statement   FYE: December 31

	REVENUE ($mil)	NET INCOME ($mil)	NET PROFIT MARGIN	EMPLOYEES
12/17	750	12	1.6%	4,000
12/16	641	6	1.0%	—
12/15	631	18	3.0%	—
12/14	598	(34)	—	—
Annual Growth	7.9%	—	—	—

2017 Year-End Financials
Return on assets: 2.4%   Cash ($ mil.): 117
Return on equity: 19.6%
Current Ratio: 0.70

BROOKFIELD PROPERTIES RETAIL INC.

Auditors : DELOITTE & TOUCHE LLP CHICAGO

LOCATIONS

HQ: BROOKFIELD PROPERTIES RETAIL INC.
350 N ORLEANS ST STE 300, CHICAGO, IL 606541607
Phone: 312 960-5000
Web: WWW.BROOKFIELDPROPERTIES.COM

HISTORICAL FINANCIALS
Company Type: Private

Income Statement   FYE: December 31

	REVENUE ($mil)	NET INCOME ($mil)	NET PROFIT MARGIN	EMPLOYEES
12/19	1,563	480	30.7%	235
12/18	2,064	4,163	201.7%	—
Annual Growth	(24.2%)	(88.5%)	—	—

2019 Year-End Financials
Return on assets: 2.2%   Cash ($ mil.): 197
Return on equity: 14.6%
Current Ratio: —

BROOME COUNTY

Auditors : DRESCHER & MALECKI LLP BUFFAL

LOCATIONS

HQ: BROOME COUNTY
5 S COLLEGE DR STE 201, BINGHAMTON, NY 139051346
Phone: 607 778-2452
Web: WWW.GOBROOMECOUNTY.COM

HISTORICAL FINANCIALS
Company Type: Private

Income Statement   FYE: December 31

	REVENUE ($mil)	NET INCOME ($mil)	NET PROFIT MARGIN	EMPLOYEES
12/21	601	47	7.9%	2,503
12/20	365	(0)	—	—
12/19	385	(1)	—	—
12/18	378	11	3.2%	—
Annual Growth	16.8%	58.3%	—	—

2021 Year-End Financials
Return on assets: 6.5%   Cash ($ mil.): 120
Return on equity: 51.6%
Current Ratio: —

BROTHER INTERNATIONAL CORPORATION

Brother International is a leading supplier of innovative products for the home sewing and crafting enthusiast. A subsidiary of Japan-based Brother Industries, Brother International sells a host of products ? including inkjet and laser printers, fax machines, scanners, typewriters, sewing machines, gear motors, and machine tools ? manufactured by its parent company. Its products are marketed to consumers and businesses in North America and across Latin America. Through its subsidiaries, Brother International operates production and sales facilities in more than 30 countries worldwide, and it serves customers in over 100 countries.

The business was formed in 1954.

Operations
Brother International creates high-quality, feature-rich printers, scanners, fax machines, mobile solutions, home sewing and embroidery machines and more.

Geographic Reach
Brother International is headquartered in Bridgewater, New Jersey. In addition, Brother has facilities in California, Illinois, and Tennessee, as well as subsidiaries in Canada, Brazil, Chile, Argentina, Peru, and Mexico.

Sales and Marketing
Brother International serves customers in agriculture, education, food/restaurant, healthcare, industrial, manufacturing and retail industries.

Financial Performance
Thanks to exchange rate benefits and rising demand for both equipment and consumables, Brother International's printing and solutions segment revenue rose some 23% in fiscal 2014 as compared to 2013.

EXECUTIVES
Senior Vice President Product Development, Roger T Nakagawa

LOCATIONS
HQ: BROTHER INTERNATIONAL CORPORATION
200 CROSSING BLVD FL 1, BRIDGEWATER, NJ 088072861
Phone: 908 704-1700
Web: WWW.BROTHER-USA.COM

PRODUCTS/OPERATIONS
Selected Services
Brother Business Solutions
Brother Cloud

Selected Products
Fax machines
Garment printers
Gear motors
Home sewing & embroidery
Industrial printing & sewing
Labeling systems
Machine tools
Mobile products (portable scanners, printers, industrial labelers)
Printers
Scanners
Sewing and embroidery machines
Stamp-making systems
Typewriters
Web conferencing

COMPETITORS
KONICA MINOLTA BUSINESS SOLUTIONS U.S.A., INC.
KORBER SUPPLY CHAIN US, INC.
MIMEO.COM, INC.
PRINTRONIX, LLC
RICOH AMERICAS CORPORATION
RICOH USA, INC.
TELLERMATE, INC.
TOSHIBA AMERICA BUSINESS SOLUTIONS, INC.
WESTCOAST (HOLDINGS) LIMITED
XEROX BUSINESS SOLUTIONS INC

HISTORICAL FINANCIALS
Company Type: Private

Income Statement — FYE: March 31

	REVENUE ($mil)	NET INCOME ($mil)	NET PROFIT MARGIN	EMPLOYEES
03/18	1,751	33	1.9%	2,000
03/15	1,852	3	0.2%	—
03/14	1,826	26	1.5%	—
Annual Growth	(1.0%)	6.1%	—	—

2018 Year-End Financials
Return on assets: 4.2%   Cash ($ mil.): 29
Return on equity: 6.0%
Current Ratio: 3.30

BROWN UNIVERSITY

Brown is a leading research university distinct for its student-centered learning and deep sense of purpose. The University's academic programs include: undergraduate, graduate and professional, schools and colleges, academic departments, centers and institutes, libraries and collections, global education, as well as non-degree programs. The University, founded in 1764, is located in Providence, Rhode Island ? Brown's home for more than two and a half centuries.

Auditors: KPMG LLP PROVIDENCCE RI

LOCATIONS
HQ: BROWN UNIVERSITY
1 PROSPECT ST, PROVIDENCE, RI 029129127
Phone: 401 369-0294
Web: WWW.BROWN.EDU

PRODUCTS/OPERATIONS
2015 Revenues

	$ mil.	% of total
Net tuition & fees	289.1	36
Grants & contracts	151.5	18
Endowment income	142.7	18
Contributions	98.7	12
Auxiliary enterprises	90.0	11
Other	36.7	5
Total	808.7	100

Selected Programs
Africana Studies, Department of
American Studies, Department of
Anthropology, Department of
Applied Mathematics, Division of
Archaeology and the Ancient World, Joukowsky Institute for
Behavioral and Social Sciences, Department of
Biology & Medicine, Division of
Biomedical Engineering, Center for
Biostatistics, Department of
Biotechnology Graduate Program
Brown-Pfizer MA Program in Biology
Chemistry, Department of
Classics, Department of
Cognitive, Linguistic, and Psychological Sciences, Department of
Commerce, Organizations, & Entrepreneurship, C.V. Starr Program in
Comparative Literature, Department of
Computational Biology, Center for
Computer Science, Department of
Development Studies, Program in

COMPETITORS
AMERICAN PUBLIC EDUCATION, INC.
PURDUE UNIVERSITY
Queen's University At Kingston
ROCHESTER INSTITUTE OF TECHNOLOGY (INC)
THE QUEEN'S UNIVERSITY OF BELFAST
UNIVERSITY OF DELAWARE
UNIVERSITY OF NORTH CAROLINA AT GREENSBORO
UNIVERSITY OF THE PACIFIC
VIRGINIA POLYTECHNIC INSTITUTE AND STATE UNIVERSITY
ZOVIO INC

HISTORICAL FINANCIALS
Company Type: Private

Income Statement — FYE: June 30

	REVENUE ($mil)	NET INCOME ($mil)	NET PROFIT MARGIN	EMPLOYEES
06/13	732	289	39.6%	5,100
06/12	704	(69)	—	—
06/11	666	359	53.9%	—
Annual Growth	4.8%	(10.2%)	—	—

2013 Year-End Financials
Return on assets: 6.6%   Cash ($ mil.): 14
Return on equity: 8.4%
Current Ratio: —

BRUCE OAKLEY, INC.

From little acorns, mighty Oakleys grow. Bruce Oakley provides road and river (barge) transportation of dry bulk commodities, as well as grain storage and bulk fertilizer sales. The company's trucking division, which uses both end-dump and pneumatic tank trailers, serves the continental US and Canada. Overall Bruce Oakley operates some 450 trailers. It maintains about half a dozen ports in Arkansas, Louisiana, and Missouri on the Arkansas, Mississippi, and Red rivers, and the company's river barge transportation unit operates on those and other inland and intracoastal waterways. Grain storage services are available in five ports in Arkansas. Bruce Oakley was founded in 1968.

LOCATIONS
HQ: BRUCE OAKLEY, INC.
3400 GRIBBLE ST, NORTH LITTLE ROCK, AR 721146406
Phone: 501 945-0875
Web: WWW.BRUCEOAKLEY.COM

PRODUCTS/OPERATIONS
Selected Products and Services
Bagging
Barges
Bulk fertilizer
Grain and grain storage
Oakley vessel freight
River ports and stevedoring
Trucking

COMPETITORS
AMERICAN COMMERCIAL LINES, INC.

Hamburg Südamerikanische Dampfschifffahrts-Gesellschaft A/S & Co KG
INGRAM BARGE COMPANY LLC
KIRBY INLAND MARINE, LP
TRANSTAR, LLC

HISTORICAL FINANCIALS
Company Type: Private

Income Statement — FYE: September 25

	REVENUE ($mil)	NET INCOME ($mil)	NET PROFIT MARGIN	EMPLOYEES
09/08	1,160	31	2.8%	800
09/07	526	11	2.2%	—
09/06	419	13	3.2%	—
Annual Growth	66.3%	53.6%	—	—

2008 Year-End Financials
Return on assets: 21.7%   Cash ($ mil.): 3
Return on equity: 34.6%
Current Ratio: 2.50

BRUCKNER TRUCK SALES, INC.

Auditors: CLIFTON LARSON ALLEN LLP DALL

LOCATIONS

HQ: BRUCKNER TRUCK SALES, INC.
9471 E INTERSTATE 40, AMARILLO, TX 791186960
Phone: 806 376-6273
Web: WWW.BRUCKNERTRUCK.COM

HISTORICAL FINANCIALS
Company Type: Private

Income Statement — FYE: June 30

	REVENUE ($mil)	NET INCOME ($mil)	NET PROFIT MARGIN	EMPLOYEES
06/15	580	10	1.8%	900
06/14	490	10	2.1%	—
06/10	200	2	1.1%	—
Annual Growth	23.8%	37.9%	—	—

2015 Year-End Financials
Return on assets: 3.5%   Cash ($ mil.): 31
Return on equity: 12.9%
Current Ratio: 1.20

BRYAN MEDICAL CENTER

Bryan Medical Center is the centerpiece of a not-for-profit health care system serving residents of Lincoln, Nebraska, and surrounding communities. The medical center, which operates as part of Bryan Health, features two acute-care hospitals (Bryan East and Bryan West) housing a combined 670 beds. In addition to providing general medical and surgical care, it serves as a regional trauma center and provides specialty care in areas such as cancer, orthopedics, and cardiology. The Bryan Health organization also includes a rural hospital and several outpatient clinics, and it provides medical training, home health care services, and wellness programs.

Operations
In addition to Bryan Medical Center, the Bryan Health organization operates the Crete Area Medical Center, a 25-bed community hospital. Outpatient facilities include the Bryan Heart Institute (cardiology and cardiothoracic surgery), the Bryan Physician Network (family practice, urgent care, and specialist locations), and Bryan LifePointe (wellness and fitness programs). In addition, the network includes the Bryan College of Health Sciences, which provides bachelor's and master's degrees in nursing and health professional fields, and the Bryan Foundation. It also conducts community education activities.

In the latest year for which data is available, the hospital had 5,912 inpatient visits; 6,650 outpatient surgeries; and 68,352 emergency department visits.

Geographic ReachBryan Medical Center serves patients throughout Nebraska, as well as portions of neighboring states including Kansas, Iowa, and Missouri, with clinics in more than 30 communities including Lincoln, Columbus, and Hastings.

Sales and Marketing
Bryan Medical Center advertises through magazines and through the Internet.

Strategy
In 2015 the hospital became the first in Nebraska to utilize the CardioMEMS HF System, a miniaturized and wireless monitoring device to manage heart failure and reduce hospital admissions. That year, it also began using the Kiva VCF Treatment System for the treatment of patients with vertebral compression fractures.

Company Background
The BryanLGH system was formed through the 1997 combination of Bryan Memorial Hospital (named after populist firebrand William Jennings Bryan) and Lincoln General Hospital. Bryan Health is part of the Heartland Health Alliance, a group of about 40 Nebraska hospitals that work together to improve rural health care services through shared services and best practices.

In 2012 the health organization rebranded itself to reflect its expanded position in the region's health care market. BryanLGH Medical Center was renamed Bryan Medical Center, and the broader health organization changed its name from the BryanLGH Health System to simply Bryan Health.

Auditors: CROWE HORWATH LLP SIMSBURY C

LOCATIONS

HQ: BRYAN MEDICAL CENTER
1600 S 48TH ST, LINCOLN, NE 685061227
Phone: 402 481-1111
Web: WWW.BRYANHEALTH.COM

PRODUCTS/OPERATIONS

Selected Services
Bariatrics
Cardiac Services
Cancer
Cardiothoracic Surgery
Childbirth/Family Birthplace
Corporate & Community Wellness
Diabetes Center
Early Detection
Emergency Department
Heart Valve Center of Excellence
Hospitalists
Independence Center
Inpatient Rehabilitation
Neuroscience
Mental Health
Orthopedics
Outpatient Specialty Clinic
Radiation Oncology
Radiology
Rehabilitation/Therapy
Robotic Surgery
Sleep Medicine
StarCare Air Ambulance
Substance Abuse
Trauma Center
Urgent Care
Vascular Services
Women's & Children's

COMPETITORS
ATLANTIC HEALTH SYSTEM INC.
MERCY HOSPITAL AND MEDICAL CENTER
MOSAIC HEALTH SYSTEM
SAVANNAH HEALTH SERVICES, LLC
SHELBY COUNTY HEALTH CARE CORPORATION

HISTORICAL FINANCIALS
Company Type: Private

Income Statement — FYE: December 31

	REVENUE ($mil)	NET INCOME ($mil)	NET PROFIT MARGIN	EMPLOYEES
12/21	839	(51)	—	3,970
12/19	785	129	16.5%	—
12/17	606	74	12.3%	—
12/16	586	60	10.3%	—
Annual Growth	7.4%	—	—	—

2021 Year-End Financials
Return on assets: (-4.6%)   Cash ($ mil.): 59
Return on equity: (-6.1%)
Current Ratio: 1.30

BUFFALO CITY SCHOOL DISTRICT

Auditors: FREEDMAXICK CPAS PC BUFFALO

LOCATIONS

HQ: BUFFALO CITY SCHOOL DISTRICT
712 CITY HALL, BUFFALO, NY 142027537
Phone: 716 816-3575
Web: WWW.BUFFALOSCHOOLS.ORG

HISTORICAL FINANCIALS
Company Type: Private

Income Statement   FYE: June 30

	REVENUE ($mil)	NET INCOME ($mil)	NET PROFIT MARGIN	EMPLOYEES
06/12	868	(194)	—	5,386
06/05	0	0	1.4%	
Annual Growth	215.8%	—	—	—

2012 Year-End Financials
Return on assets: (-11.2%)   Cash ($ mil.): 348
Return on equity: —
Current Ratio: —

BVH, INC.

Auditors: KPMG LLP KANSAS CITY MO

LOCATIONS
HQ: BVH, INC.
  11401 LAMAR AVE, OVERLAND PARK, KS 662111508
Phone: 913 458-2000
Web: WWW.BV.COM

HISTORICAL FINANCIALS
Company Type: Private

Income Statement   FYE: December 29

	REVENUE ($mil)	NET INCOME ($mil)	NET PROFIT MARGIN	EMPLOYEES
12/17	3,363	87	2.6%	18,568
12/16*	3,207	75	2.4%	—
01/16	2,955	108	3.7%	—
01/15	3,029	113	3.7%	—
Annual Growth	3.6%	(8.3%)	—	—

*Fiscal year change

2017 Year-End Financials
Return on assets: 5.6%   Cash ($ mil.): 344
Return on equity: 73.5%
Current Ratio: 1.10

C.R. ENGLAND, INC.

C.R. England is a leader in transportation solutions with a rich heritage built on an entrepreneurial spirit. The family-owned company's fleet includes more than 4,500 tractors, over 6,000 trailers, and some 6,000 containers. The most reliable refrigerated carrier in the nation also has more than 6,200 drivers. Besides for-hire freight hauling, C.R. England offers dedicated contract carriage, in which drivers and equipment are assigned to a customer long-term; logistics services, including freight brokerage; and intermodal railroad service. The company was founded in 1920.

Operations
C.R. England's operations include over the road solutions, regional solutions, Mexico solutions, dedicated solutions, and intermodal solutions.

The company's national service offering is the largest, most expensive refrigerated transportation solution in the industry, spanning the entire continental US.

C.R. England provides flexible, short haul transportation services through its regional division.

The company is well equipped to handle transportation needs into and out of Mexico. It delivers a team of quality people, late model equipment, and innovative technology that makes transnational shipping across the US-Mexico border seamless.

Its intermodal solution offers rail service using the next generation of transportation, the company's TempStack technology, across a long-established railroad.

C.R. England's business also benefits from operating five truck driving schools in the US, and a course on becoming a freight broker. The school helps improve driver safety as well as provides a pool of qualified truck drivers for hire.

Geographic Reach
Based in Salt Lake City, Utah, the company operates primarily in California, Indiana, Texas, and Utah.

Company Background
C.R. England was founded in 1920 by Chester Rodney England and is run by his descendants.

EXECUTIVES
CSO*, Brandon Harrison

Auditors: TANNER LLC SALT LAKE CITY UT

LOCATIONS
HQ: C.R. ENGLAND, INC.
  4701 W 2100 S, SALT LAKE CITY, UT 841201223
Phone: 800 421-9004
Web: WWW.CRENGLAND.COM

PRODUCTS/OPERATIONS
Selected Operations
Trucking
  National - Long haul truckload service
  Mexico - Shipments in and out of Mexico
  Regional - Short haul truckload service positioned in the West, Midwest, and Texas and surrounding areas (AR, LA, OK)
  Dedicated - Tailor-made services dedicating trucks and drivers to specific customer needs
  Intermodal - Expedited priority rail service using TempStack, 53' refrigerated containers
England Logistics

COMPETITORS
A&R LOGISTICS, INC.
A. DUIE PYLE INC.
AAA COOPER TRANSPORTATION
COMCAR INDUSTRIES, INC.
CRST INTERNATIONAL, INC.
DART TRANSIT COMPANY
GORDON TRUCKING, INC.
KLLM TRANSPORT SERVICES, LLC
STEVENS TRANSPORT, INC.
UPS GROUND FREIGHT, INC.

HISTORICAL FINANCIALS
Company Type: Private

Income Statement   FYE: December 31

	REVENUE ($mil)	NET INCOME ($mil)	NET PROFIT MARGIN	EMPLOYEES
12/12	1,579	56	3.6%	6,500
12/11	1,315	55	4.3%	—
12/07	829	41	5.0%	—
Annual Growth	13.7%	6.2%	—	—

2012 Year-End Financials
Return on assets: 7.4%   Cash ($ mil.): 15
Return on equity: 24.7%
Current Ratio: 1.40

CALGON CARBON CORPORATION

Calgon Carbon is a global leader in activated carbons and purification systems. It offers purification and a variety of industrial and commercial manufacturing processes. Services include ballast water treatment, ultraviolet light disinfection, and advanced ion-exchange technologies used in the treatment of drinking water, wastewater, odor control, pollution abatement, and a variety of industrial and commercial manufacturing processes. With more than 240 patents, its products find usage in more than 700 discrete market applications including air, drinking water, foods, and pharmaceuticals purification, and the removal of mercury emissions from coal-powered electrical plants.

Operations
Calgon Carbon operates in three division ? Activated Carbon, Applications, and Products.

Activated Carbon makes granular and powdered activated carbon to remove organic compounds from liquids and gases.

Products include Granular Activated Carbon, Reactivation Services, UV Technologies, ION Exchange, Activated Carbon Pellets, Activated Carbon Cloth, and Equipment.

Applications services include Environmental Air Treatment, Mercury Removal, Industrial Processes, Food and Beverage, Personal Protection Equipment, Metals Recovery, Medical/Pharmaceutical, and Energy Storage.

Geographic Reach
Pennsylvania-based, Calgon Carbon operates in a geographically diverse array of markets. It operates approximately 25 global offices and more than 15 manufacturing and reactivation facilities.

Sales and Marketing
Calgon Carbon offer carbon technologies used in over 700 distinct market applications from purifying air and drinking water, to purifying foods and pharmaceuticals, to

separating gas and removing mercury emissions from coal-fired power plants.

Strategy

In mid-2021, Calgon Carbon Corporation announced today that it has entered into a definitive Securities and Asset Purchase Agreement with De Nora Water Technologies LLC to sell its Ultraviolet Technologies (UVT) business to De Nora. This agreement, which is expected to close at the end of June 2021, includes the products, brands and assets of Hyde Marine, a world-leader in UV ballast water treatment systems, as well as municipal and industrial disinfection brands such as RAYOX, SENTINEL and C3 SERIES UV.

Calgon Carbon decided to expand its Mississippi activated carbon plant in mid-2020. The expansion is expected to add 38 jobs at the plant when complete. The estimated investment in the additional production line will be $185 million. When completed, Calgon Carbon's virgin granular activated carbon capacity will exceed 200 million pounds per year. the expansion enables its activated carbon products to be more broadly used to clean the world's air and water on an even larger scale.

Company Background

In 1942, the Company produced an activated carbon product using bituminous coal, and that was the beginning of the firm now known as Calgon Carbon Corporation.

Auditors : DELOITTE & TOUCHE LLP PITTSBU

LOCATIONS

HQ: CALGON CARBON CORPORATION
3000 GSK DR, MOON TOWNSHIP, PA 151081381
Phone: 412 787-6700
Web: WWW.CALGONCARBON.COM

2015 sales

	$ mil.	% of total
United States	288.6	53
United Kingdom	43.2	8
Japan	35.8	7
France	20.9	4
China	17.9	3
Germany	17.8	3
Canada	17.1	3
South Korea	12.2	2
Belgium	10.4	2
Singapore	9.9	2
Netherlands	5.2	1
Denmark	4.3	1
Switzerland	3.3	1
Spain	3.3	1
Thailand	3.3	1
Other	41.8	8
Total	535	100

PRODUCTS/OPERATIONS

2015 Sales

	$ mil.	% of total
Activated Carbon & Service	486.5	91
Equipment	39.3	7
Consumer	9.2	2
Total	535	100

Selected Products
Ballast Water Treatment
Energy Storage
Environmental Air Treatment
Environmental Water Treatment
Food and Beverage
Industrial Processes
Medical
Mercury Removal
Metals Recovery
Municipal Water Treatment
Personal Protection Equipment
Residential Point of Use/Entry

COMPETITORS

3M PURIFICATION INC.
ASAHI KASEI CORPORATION
CABOT CORPORATION
CELANESE CORPORATION
EVONIK CORPORATION
MINERALS TECHNOLOGIES INC.
ROCKWOOD HOLDINGS, INC.
UOP LLC
VENATOR MATERIALS PLC
W. R. GRACE & CO.

HISTORICAL FINANCIALS

Company Type: Private

Income Statement   FYE: December 31

	REVENUE ($mil)	NET INCOME ($mil)	NET PROFIT MARGIN	EMPLOYEES
12/17	619	21	3.4%	1,334
12/16	514	13	2.7%	—
12/15	535	43	8.1%	—
12/14	555	49	8.9%	—
Annual Growth	3.7%	(24.7%)	—	—

2017 Year-End Financials
Return on assets: 2.5%   Cash ($ mil.): 42
Return on equity: 5.0%
Current Ratio: 2.60

CALIFORNIA INSTITUTE OF TECHNOLOGY

The California Institute of Technology (Caltech) is a world-renowned science and engineering institute that marshals some of the world's brightest minds and most innovative tools to address fundamental scientific questions and pressing societal challenge. The institute enrolls over 2,395 students and offers about 30 majors across six academic divisions focused on biology, chemistry, engineering, geology, humanities, and physics. Caltech has a very low student-teacher ratio of 3:1. Caltech operates the Jet Propulsion Laboratory (JPL), which supervises robotic Mars exploration programs and other interplanetary missions, under contract to NASA. The school was founded in 1891.

Operations

CalTech's most popular majors are chemical engineering, computer science, electrical engineering, mechanical engineering, and physics. The school's primary research focus areas include energy, medical science, information science, the universe, the environment, and nanoscience.

The JPL lab is responsible for about two dozen spacecraft missions in a given year.

Geographic Reach

Caltech is headquartered in Pasadena, California. In addition to its facilities in California, the institute has a network of about a dozen astronomy observatories across the US and in Antarctica and Chile.

Sales and Marketing

The university caters to over 985 undergraduate, and some 1,410 graduate students.

Company Background

Caltech's professors and graduates have snared more than 30 Nobel Prizes. Other alumni include filmmaker Frank Capra and Apollo 17 astronaut Harrison Schmitt.

Auditors : PRICEWATERHOUSECOOPERS LLP L

LOCATIONS

HQ: CALIFORNIA INSTITUTE OF TECHNOLOGY
1200 E CALIFORNIA BLVD, PASADENA, CA 911250001
Phone: 626 395-6811
Web: WWW.CALTECH.EDU

PRODUCTS/OPERATIONS

Selected Academic Divisions
Academics
  Biology
  Chemistry and Chemical Engineering
  Engineering and Applied Science
  Geological and Planetary Sciences
  Humanities and Social Sciences
  Physics, Mathematics, and Astronomy
Jet Propulsion Laboratory (NASA partnership)
  Galaxy Evolution Explorer Science Center
  Infrared Processing and Analysis Center
  NASA Exoplanet Science Institute
  NASA Herschel Science Center
  Spitzer Space Telescope Science Center

COMPETITORS

CORNELL UNIVERSITY
ILLINOIS INSTITUTE OF TECHNOLOGY
MASSACHUSETTS INSTITUTE OF TECHNOLOGY
NORTH CAROLINA STATE UNIVERSITY
STEVENS INSTITUTE OF TECHNOLOGY (INC)
UNIVERSITY OF CALIFORNIA, BERKELEY
UNIVERSITY OF CALIFORNIA, SAN DIEGO
UNIVERSITY OF CALIFORNIA, SANTA CRUZ
UNIVERSITY OF LEICESTER
UNIVERSITY OF TEXAS AT DALLAS

HISTORICAL FINANCIALS

Company Type: Private

Income Statement   FYE: September 30

	REVENUE ($mil)	NET INCOME ($mil)	NET PROFIT MARGIN	EMPLOYEES
09/21	3,145	1,102	35.1%	6,567
09/20	3,354	82	2.5%	—
09/19	3,434	(11)	—	—
09/18	3,303	165	5.0%	—
Annual Growth	(1.6%)	88.2%	—	—

2021 Year-End Financials
Return on assets: 15.2%   Cash ($ mil.): 62
Return on equity: 25.2%
Current Ratio: —

CALIFORNIA STEEL INDUSTRIES, INC.

California Steel Industries (CSI) doesn't use forensic evidence, but its work does involve a steel slab. The company uses steel slab produced by third parties to manufacture steel products such as hot-rolled and cold-rolled steel, galvanized coils and sheets, and electric resistance weld (ERW) pipe. Its customers include aftermarket automotive manufacturers, oil and gas producers, roofing makers, tubing manufacturers, and building suppliers. CSI serves the western region of the US. The company operates slitting, shearing, coating, and single-billing services for third parties. Japan's JFE Holdings and Brazilian iron ore miner Vale SA each own 50% of CSI.

Operations
CSI has an annual production capacity of 2.8 million metric tons of flat rolled steel and pipe. It is the leading producer of flat rolled steel in the Western US, and the only West Coast steel supplier capable of producing more than 2 million tons of steel in five different product lines: hot rolled, pickled and oiled, galvanized, and cold rolled sheet, and electric resistance welded pipe.

Geographic Reach
At its California plant the company processes steel slab purchased from suppliers around the world, including Brazil, Mexico, Australia, Japan, Europe, and the US.

CSI buys more than two-thirds of its steel slab from ArcelorMittal subsidiary Lazaro Cardenas, in Mexico; ArcelorMittal TubarÃ£o, in Brazil; and Australia's Bluescope Steel. The purchased slab is transported to the Port of Los Angeles and then sent by train to CSI's facilities.

Sales and Marketing
Most of CSI's product lines are also sold to service distribution centers throughout the Western and Midwestern US, with some product also sold worldwide through the export market. Its steel framing studs, roofing, decking and metal lath products are used in the home and commercial building industries. Other uses include water, gas, and oil pipelines, automotive pans, tubing (used by construction and furniture makers), and heating and cooling parts.

Strategy
In 2014 CSI built a new pipe mill on its site near Fontana, California. The mill produces high-strength electrical resistance welded pipe, up to 24 inches in diameter and up to 80 feet in length. Its existing pipe mill was limited to 16-inch diameter and 60-foot lengths.

Since 1992 CSI has invested more than $1 billion on its facilities to maintain, modernize, and expand operations.

Company Background
The company was formed in 1983.

EXECUTIVES
Executive Commercial Vice President*, Ricardo Bernardes
Executive Vice President Finance & Administration*, Brett Guge
Auditors: ERNST & YOUNG LLP LOS ANGELES

LOCATIONS
HQ: CALIFORNIA STEEL INDUSTRIES, INC.
14000 SAN BERNARDINO AVE, FONTANA, CA 923355259
Phone: 909 350-6300
Web: WWW.CALIFORNIASTEEL.COM

PRODUCTS/OPERATIONS
Selected Steel Products
Cold Rolled
ERW Pipe
Galvanized
Hot Rolled
Pickled and Oiled

COMPETITORS
A. FINKL & SONS CO.
AMERICAN CAST IRON PIPE COMPANY
CHARLOTTE PIPE AND FOUNDRY COMPANY
Grupo Simec, S.A.B. de C.V.
KEYSTONE CONSOLIDATED INDUSTRIES, INC.
NUCOR - YAMATO STEEL COMPANY (LIMITED PARTNERSHIP)
REPUBLIC STEEL
STEEL TECHNOLOGIES LLC
USS-POSCO INDUSTRIES, A CALIFORNIA JOINT VENTURE
Wugang Group Co., Ltd.

HISTORICAL FINANCIALS
Company Type: Private

Income Statement — FYE: December 31

	REVENUE ($mil)	NET INCOME ($mil)	NET PROFIT MARGIN	EMPLOYEES
12/09	551	(13)	—	1,095
12/08	1,510	13	0.9%	
Annual Growth	(63.5%)	—	—	—

2009 Year-End Financials
Return on assets: (-2.2%)   Cash ($ mil.): 61
Return on equity: (-4.4%)
Current Ratio: 4.30

CALIFORNIA'S VALUED TRUST

LOCATIONS
HQ: CALIFORNIA'S VALUED TRUST
520 E HERNDON AVE, FRESNO, CA 937202907
Phone: 559 437-2960
Web: WWW.CVTRUST.ORG

HISTORICAL FINANCIALS
Company Type: Private

Income Statement — FYE: September 30

	ASSETS ($mil)	NET INCOME ($mil)	INCOME AS % OF ASSETS	EMPLOYEES
09/18	157	(3)	—	20
09/17	157	21	13.3%	—
09/15	136	(5)	—	—
Annual Growth	4.9%	—	—	—

CAMERON INTERNATIONAL CORPORATION

Cameron International has been a Schlumberger company since 2016 that provides state-of-the-art wellhead, surface, and flow control products, systems, and services to oil, gas, and process companies around the world. It offers the industry's most complete portfolio of drilling and production systems backed by expertise in instrumentation, data processing, control software, and system integration. Cameron is committed to solving the industry's most sophisticated problems and is helping forge a new era of environmental stewardship and safety in an ever-evolving industry. It was founded in 1920 by Harry Cameron and James Abercrombie as Cameron Iron Works.

Operations
The company designs, manufactures, and services the most comprehensive and reliable portfolio of pressure control equipment in the industry.

Its products have included Wellhead Systems (conventional and compact solutions for onshore and platform applications); Fracturing and Flowback Equipment & Services (reliable technology to maximize stimulation efficiency); Rig Equipment (comprehensive suite of onshore and offshore rig equipment); Pressure Control (vomplete systems for containing wellbore pressure and diverting formation fluids); Valves (comprehensive solutions for global energy and industrial markets); Processing and Separation (treatment solutions from the wellhead to the refinery); Production Trees (innovative designs to streamline operations and enhance safety); Safety Systems (customized technologies and services to achieve ultimate valve control and well safety); and Measurement (custody transfer, allocation, and quality sampling and analysis systems).

Geographic Reach
Cameron has various operations in Canada located in Alberta, British Columbia,

and Ontario, as well as in the US, Saudi Arabia, Norway, Mexico, and Brazil.

Sales and Marketing
Company Background

In 2013 Cameron and Schlumberger formed OneSubsea (60% owned by Cameron International) to manufacture and develop products, systems, and services for the subsea oil and gas market. The creation of OneSubsea allows the company to bring together Schlumberger's expertise in subsea processing and platform integration with its own capabilities in subsea equipment to allow customers to greatly increase their subsea reservoir recovery rates. (In 2014 OneSubsea, Helix Energy Solutions, and Schlumberger formed an alliance to develop technologies and deliver services to optimize the cost and efficiency of subsea well intervention systems.)

Cameron moved into the lucrative shale market in the US Northeast in 2011 through the acquisition of West Virginia-based Industrial Machine & Fabrication, a leading aftermarket service provider for reciprocating engines and compressors.

That year it also expanded its drilling equipment portfolio, buying LeTourneau Technologies Drillings Systems and Offshore Products divisions from Joy Global for $375 million.

In 2010 a BP rig in the Gulf of Mexico exploded and sank, spewing oil into the Gulf. The blowout preventer on the system, made by Cameron International, failed to work properly. A board of inquiry was set up to find out the cause of the disaster, and a separate government report found that the company's blowout preventer proved incapable of stopping the high-pressure flow from the doomed well. The company claimed that its equipment met industry standards, and it was not found liable in any legal proceeding, although it did pay $82.5 million to settle with BP. (BP accounted for 12% of the company's revenues in 2010).

Cameron traces its roots to the mid-1800s when it made steam engines to generate power for plants and textile and rolling mills.

EXECUTIVES

CAO, Dennis Baldwin
Auditors : ERNST & YOUNG LLP HOUSTON TE

LOCATIONS

HQ: CAMERON INTERNATIONAL CORPORATION
1333 WEST LOOP S STE 1700, HOUSTON, TX 770279118
Phone: 713 939-2282
Web: WWW.SLB.COM

PRODUCTS/OPERATIONS

Selected Mergers and Acquisitions
2012
OneSubsea, (60%-owned joint venture with Schlumberger; products, systems, and services for the subsea oil and gas market)
TTS Energy Division (from TTS Group ASA)
2011
Industrial Machine & Fabrication (West Virginia, aftermarket service provider for reciprocating engines and compressors)
LeTourneau Technologies Drilling Systems and Offshore Products ($375 million; drilling equipment)

COMPETITORS

DRESSER-RAND GROUP INC.
Enerflex Ltd
GRAHAM CORPORATION
KSB SE & Co. KGaA
LUFKIN GEARS LLC
NORDSON CORPORATION
PIPELINE ENGINEERING & SUPPLY CO. LIMITED
ROPER TECHNOLOGIES, INC.
SUNDYNE, LLC
VETCO GRAY, LLC

HISTORICAL FINANCIALS
Company Type: Private

Income Statement — FYE: December 31

	REVENUE ($mil)	NET INCOME ($mil)	NET PROFIT MARGIN	EMPLOYEES
12/14	10,381	848	8.2%	23,000
12/13	9,838	724	7.4%	—
12/12	8,502	750	8.8%	—
Annual Growth	10.5%	6.3%	—	—

2014 Year-End Financials
Return on assets: 6.6%   Cash ($ mil.): 1,513
Return on equity: 15.6%
Current Ratio: 1.80

CAMPUS CRUSADE FOR CHRIST INC

LOCATIONS

HQ: CAMPUS CRUSADE FOR CHRIST INC
100 LAKE HART DR, ORLANDO, FL 328320100
Phone: 407 826-2000
Web: WWW.CRU.ORG

HISTORICAL FINANCIALS
Company Type: Private

Income Statement — FYE: August 31

	REVENUE ($mil)	NET INCOME ($mil)	NET PROFIT MARGIN	EMPLOYEES
08/17	598	26	4.4%	7,688
08/08	7	1	25.1%	—
08/05	0	0	—	—
08/04	423	414	97.7%	—
Annual Growth	2.7%	(19.0%)	—	—

2017 Year-End Financials
Return on assets: 7.4%   Cash ($ mil.): 45
Return on equity: 10.8%
Current Ratio: 0.70

CANDID COLOR SYSTEMS, INC.

LOCATIONS

HQ: CANDID COLOR SYSTEMS, INC.
1300 METROPOLITAN AVE, OKLAHOMA CITY, OK 731082042
Phone: 405 947-8747
Web: WWW.CANDID.COM

HISTORICAL FINANCIALS
Company Type: Private

Income Statement — FYE: July 31

	REVENUE ($mil)	NET INCOME ($mil)	NET PROFIT MARGIN	EMPLOYEES
07/07	21,742	2,534	11.7%	300
07/05	22	1	8.3%	—
07/04	21	2	10.9%	—
07/03	21	1	9.4%	—
Annual Growth	467.2%	498.3%	—	—

2007 Year-End Financials
Return on assets: 999.9%   Cash ($ mil.): 2
Return on equity: 999.9%
Current Ratio: 2.30

CAPE COD HEALTHCARE, INC.

Cape Cod Healthcare (CCHC) is a not-for-profit healthcare organization that operates two acute care hospitals (Cape Cod Hospital and Falmouth Hospital). Specializations include heart and vascular, women's health, bones and muscles, cancer care, and brain, spine, and nerves. CCHC also operates a home health services agency (Visiting Nurse Association of Cape Cod), more than 130-bed skilled nursing and rehabilitation facility (JML Care Center), and assisted living facility (Heritage at Falmouth). The health care system has affiliations with UMass Medical School, Boston University, University of New England and Cape Cod Community College. CCHC is the Cape's largest private employer with more than 5,300 staff members, 450 physicians and 790 volunteers.

Auditors : PRICEWATERHOUSECOOPERS LLP BO

LOCATIONS

HQ: CAPE COD HEALTHCARE, INC.
27 PARK ST, HYANNIS, MA 026015230
Phone: 508 862-5030
Web: WWW.CAPECODHEALTH.ORG

PRODUCTS/OPERATIONS

Selected Massachusetts Facilities
Bourne Health Center
Cape Cod Hospital (Hyannis)
Davenport Mugar Cancer Center (Hyannis)

Falmouth Hospital
  Clark Cancer Center
Fontaine Medical Center (Harwich)
Heritage at Falmouth
JLM Care Center (Falmouth)
Mashpee Health Center
Sandwich Health Center
Wilkins Outpatient Medical Complex (Hyannis)

COMPETITORS

ALLINA HEALTH SYSTEM
ENCOMPASS HEALTH CORPORATION
INTEGRIS HEALTH, INC.
LEGACY LIFEPOINT HEALTH, INC.
NORTHSHORE UNIVERSITY HEALTHSYSTEM
OVERLAKE HOSPITAL MEDICAL CENTER
PRESBYTERIAN HEALTHCARE SERVICES
SISTERS OF CHARITY OF LEAVENWORTH HEALTH SYSTEM, INC.
THE CLEVELAND CLINIC FOUNDATION
THE RUTLAND HOSPITAL INC ACT 220

HISTORICAL FINANCIALS

Company Type: Private

Income Statement — FYE: September 30

	REVENUE ($mil)	NET INCOME ($mil)	NET PROFIT MARGIN	EMPLOYEES
09/20	931	27	2.9%	1,850
09/19	978	29	3.0%	—
09/18	921	80	8.7%	—
09/17	872	74	8.5%	—
Annual Growth	2.2%	(28.4%)	—	—

2020 Year-End Financials
Return on assets: 2.0% Cash ($ mil.): 75
Return on equity: 3.2%
Current Ratio: 1.20

CAPE COD HOSPITAL

Get too much sun or eat too much lobster while visiting Cape Cod? Never fear, Cape Cod Hospital can treat whatever ails you. Cape Cod Hospital, a subsidiary of Cape Cod Healthcare, is a 260-bed acute care hospital that serves the Cape Cod, Massachusetts area. Its specialty services include pediatrics, maternity care, cancer treatment, and infectious disease therapeutics. The not-for-profit Cape Cod Hospital also includes a specialty cardiovascular center, a psychiatry unit, a surgical pavilion, and a diagnostic imaging facility, as well as outpatient medical offices.

Operations

Cape Cod Hospital's emergency department treats about 85,000 patients each year. The medical center also performs more than 12,500 surgeries and 1,000 birth procedures each year, as well as about 2 million laboratory tests. Its 20-bed Cape Psych Center provides inpatient and outpatient mental and behavioral services. The campus also includes more than a dozen medical offices buildings and a community health center. Cape Cod Hospital's staff includes about 300 physicians.

Geographic Reach

Cape Cod Hospital is located on a 40-acre campus on the shoreline of Hyannis, Massachusetts.

Strategy

To keep its facilities modern and efficient, in 2015 the company opened a new emergency center, located adjacent to the existing emergency center. The 18-month, $22 million project added 25,000 sq. ft. of space and 72 patient treatment rooms.

In 2013 Cape Cod Hospital reopened the renovated and expanded Intensive Care Unit. That project cost $4.9 million and doubled the size of the original area.

To control the cost of providing hospital care, parent Cape Cod Healthcare has also been expanding its outpatient and ambulatory care services. It is adding new urgent care centers and surgery centers, both near the hospital and in surrounding communities.

Company Background

Cape Cod Hospital was established in Hyannis in 1920.

Auditors : POWERHOUSECOOPERS LLP BOSTON

LOCATIONS

HQ: CAPE COD HOSPITAL
27 PARK ST, HYANNIS, MA 026015203
Phone: 508 771-1800
Web: WWW.CAPECODHEALTH.ORG

PRODUCTS/OPERATIONS

Selected Services
Allergy and Immunology
Behavioral Health
Blood Center
Dermatology
Foot Care & Surgery
Hand Surgery
Orthopedics
Pregnancy & Birth
Sports Medicine
Women's Health

COMPETITORS

BAY COUNTY HEALTH SYSTEM, LLC
CENTRAL SUFFOLK HOSPITAL
DOCTORS HOSPITAL OF AUGUSTA; LLC
HUNTINGTON HOSPITAL DOLAN FAMILY HEALTH CENTER, INC.
WINTER HAVEN HOSPITAL, INC.

HISTORICAL FINANCIALS

Company Type: Private

Income Statement — FYE: September 30

	REVENUE ($mil)	NET INCOME ($mil)	NET PROFIT MARGIN	EMPLOYEES
09/20	569	12	2.2%	1,700
09/19	599	25	4.3%	—
09/18	564	46	8.3%	—
09/17	526	47	9.0%	—
Annual Growth	2.7%	(36.3%)	—	—

2020 Year-End Financials
Return on assets: 1.6% Cash ($ mil.): 15
Return on equity: 2.5%
Current Ratio: 1.40

CAPE FEAR VALLEY MEDICAL CENTER

LOCATIONS

HQ: CAPE FEAR VALLEY MEDICAL CENTER
1638 OWEN DR, FAYETTEVILLE, NC 283043424
Phone: 910 615-4000
Web: WWW.CAPEFEARVALLEY.COM

HISTORICAL FINANCIALS

Company Type: Private

Income Statement — FYE: September 30

	REVENUE ($mil)	NET INCOME ($mil)	NET PROFIT MARGIN	EMPLOYEES
09/15	630	23	3.8%	2,711
09/14	590	40	6.8%	—
09/13	823	398	48.4%	—
Annual Growth	(12.5%)	(75.5%)	—	—

2015 Year-End Financials
Return on assets: 2.6% Cash ($ mil.): 38
Return on equity: 5.1%
Current Ratio: 2.80

CAPISTRANO UNIFIED SCHOOL DISTRICT

EXECUTIVES

BRD*, Jane Boss
Managing Member*, Joel Drew
Auditors : NIGRO & NIGRO PC MURRIETA

LOCATIONS

HQ: CAPISTRANO UNIFIED SCHOOL DISTRICT
33122 VALLE RD, SAN JUAN CAPISTRANO, CA 926754859
Phone: 949 234-9200
Web: CALPREP.CAPOUSD.ORG

HISTORICAL FINANCIALS

Company Type: Private

Income Statement — FYE: June 30

	REVENUE ($mil)	NET INCOME ($mil)	NET PROFIT MARGIN	EMPLOYEES
06/21	651	29	4.5%	4,500
06/20	549	(29)	—	—
06/19	2	0	9.2%	—
Annual Growth	1461.3%	994.6%	—	—

2021 Year-End Financials
Return on assets: 2.5% Cash ($ mil.): —
Return on equity: 9.0%
Current Ratio: —

CAPITAL DISTRICT PHYSICIANS' HEALTH PLAN, INC.

Capital District Physicians' Health Plan (CDPHP) is an independent, not-for-profit health plan serving some 448,000 members in two dozen New York counties. It offers employer-sponsored and individual managed care plans (including HMO, PPO, and consumer-directed plans), as well as a Medicare Advantage plan for seniors. The company's coverage include full coverage for some preventative medical services, as well as options for covering prescription drugs, dental work, and vision services. CDPHP also provides wellness programs that help members with weight loss, smoking cessation, and chronic disease management.

Operations
In addition to its commercial and Medicare offerings, CDPHP provides health plans under several state-subsidized insurance programs, including Family Health Plus and Child Health Plus (intended for residents who don't qualify for Medicaid) and Healthy NY (intended for small businesses and sole proprietors). Altogether, the CDPHP provider network includes more than 10,000 physicians and facilities.

The company's classifies its products in three lines of business: Health Maintenance Organization (HMO) products (which includes Healthy New York, Medicare Choices, Medicaid, Child Health Plus, and Family Health Plus) provided by CDPHP; Preferred Provider Organization (PPO) products (which include PPO, High Deductible PPO, Medicare Choices, Exclusive Provider Organization - EPO-, and High Deductible EPO products) provided by CDPHP Universal Benefits, Inc.; and the Administrative Services Organization (ASO) plans (which includes ASO and self-insured plans) provided by Capital District Physicians' Healthcare Network, Inc.

In 2013 CDPHP's membership increased by about 38,000.

Geographic Reach
CDPHP serves customers in 24 New York counties: Albany, Broome, Chenango, Columbia, Delaware, Dutchess, Essex, Fulton, Greene, Hamilton, Herkimer, Madison, Montgomery, Oneida, Orange, Otsego, Rensselaer, Saratoga, Schenectady, Schoharie, Tioga, Ulster, Warren, and Washington.

Financial Performance
CDPHP reported a 13% increase in revenues in 2013 due to an increase in membership and in earned premiums.

The company suffered a loss of $43 million in 2013 (a decrease of more than 375%) due to an increase in claims and general expenses.

Strategy
CDPHP's self-proclaimed strategy is to use the majority of its premium income to pay out medical claims, while maintaining necessary reserve levels to keep its solid financial performance and to comply with federal medical loss-ratio guidelines. It earmarks a small amount of income for operational expenses, as well as to fund growth and wellness initiatives.

In mid-2014, the company teamed upewith Independent Health, to build innovative products, tools and services for providers, employers and individuals across New York State. The partnership will focus on developing new tools, technology and products, along with recruiting new physicians.

In the early 2013, the company opened a new CDPHP Service Center location at Latham, New York, and a health and fitness center inside an Albany supermarket.

CDPHP also works to lower medical expenses by partnering with other regional care and plan providers.

Company Background
In 2011 CDPHP partnered with Trendshift in 2011 to provide a new group funding management system for employers.

An association of local Albany physicians founded CDPHP in 1984.

EXECUTIVES
Chief Medical Officer*, Elizabeth Warner

LOCATIONS
HQ: CAPITAL DISTRICT PHYSICIANS' HEALTH PLAN, INC.
500 PATROON CREEK BLVD, ALBANY, NY 122061057
Phone: 518 641-3700
Web: WWW.CDPHP.COM

PRODUCTS/OPERATIONS
Selected Products
Dental and Vision Health Plans
    CVS ExtraCare Health Card
    Delta Dental
Government Plans
    Child Health Plus
    Family Health Plus
    Medicaid Select Plan
    Medicare Choices (HMO)
Group Health Plans
    Embrace Health
    Exclusive Provider Organization (EPO)
    Group Medicare
    High Deductible Health Plans (HDHP)
    Health Maintenance Organization (HMO)
    Healthy Direction
    Lifestyle Riders
    Preferred Provider Organization (PPO)
    Transitional Health Plans
    Health Funding Arrangements
    Flexible Spending Accounts
    Health Reimbursement Arrangement
    Health Savings Account
Individual Health Plans
    Healthy New York
    Non-Group Health Plans

COMPETITORS
ALLWAYS HEALTH PARTNERS, INC.
HEALTH ALLIANCE PLAN OF MICHIGAN
HILL PHYSICIANS MEDICAL GROUP, INC.
INDEPENDENT HEALTH ASSOCIATION, INC.
IPC HEALTHCARE, INC.
MERCY CARE
MVP HEALTH PLAN, INC.
NEW YORK STATE CATHOLIC HEALTH PLAN, INC.
SCOTT AND WHITE HEALTH PLAN
SECURITY HEALTH PLAN OF WISCONSIN, INC.

HISTORICAL FINANCIALS
Company Type: Private

Income Statement — FYE: December 31

	ASSETS ($mil)	NET INCOME ($mil)	INCOME AS % OF ASSETS	EMPLOYEES
12/13	526	22	4.4%	700
12/09	457	33	7.3%	—
12/03	237	(1)	—	—
Annual Growth	8.3%	—	—	—

2013 Year-End Financials
Return on assets: 4.4% Cash ($ mil.): 61
Return on equity: 7.0%
Current Ratio: 0.80

CAPITAL INCOME BUILDER

EXECUTIVES
Vice Chairman, Rob Lovelace
Auditors : PRICEWATERHOUSECOOPERS LLP LO

LOCATIONS
HQ: CAPITAL INCOME BUILDER
333 S HOPE ST FL 55, LOS ANGELES, CA 900713061
Phone: 213 486-9200

HISTORICAL FINANCIALS
Company Type: Private

Income Statement — FYE: October 31

	ASSETS ($mil)	NET INCOME ($mil)	INCOME AS % OF ASSETS	EMPLOYEES
10/21	113,600	16,978	14.9%	19
10/19	107	5,826	5441.8%	—
10/18	102,649	(7,919)	—	—
10/16	100,287	2,628	2.6%	—
Annual Growth	2.5%	45.2%	—	—

2021 Year-End Financials
Return on assets: 14.9% Cash ($ mil.): 16
Return on equity: 15.4%
Current Ratio: —

CAPITAL WORLD GROWTH AND INCOME FUND, INC.

Auditors : PRICEWATERHOUSECOOPERS LLP LO

LOCATIONS

HQ: CAPITAL WORLD GROWTH AND INCOME FUND, INC.
  333 S HOPE ST FL 55, LOS ANGELES, CA 900713061
Phone: 213 486-9200

HISTORICAL FINANCIALS
Company Type: Private

Income Statement   FYE: November 30

	REVENUE ($mil)	NET INCOME ($mil)	NET PROFIT MARGIN	EMPLOYEES
11/19	2,646	12,826	484.7%	11
11/18	2,878	(5,381)	—	—
11/17	2,407	19,764	820.9%	—
11/15	1,658	(5,120)	—	—
Annual Growth	12.4%	—	—	—

2019 Year-End Financials
Return on assets: 12.8%   Cash ($ mil.): 33
Return on equity: 12.9%
Current Ratio: —

CARDINAL LOGISTICS HOLDINGS, LLC

EXECUTIVES

Chief Risk Officer, Jeff Lester
Auditors : KPMG LLP CHARLOTTE NORTH CA

LOCATIONS

HQ: CARDINAL LOGISTICS HOLDINGS, LLC
  5333 DAVIDSON HWY, CONCORD, NC 280278478
Phone: 704 789-2000
Web: WWW.CARDLOG.COM

HISTORICAL FINANCIALS
Company Type: Private

Income Statement   FYE: December 31

	REVENUE ($mil)	NET INCOME ($mil)	NET PROFIT MARGIN	EMPLOYEES
12/18	804	(16)	—	3,040
12/17	791	(10)	—	—
Annual Growth	1.7%	—	—	—

2018 Year-End Financials
Return on assets: (-6.7%)   Cash ($ mil.): 56
Return on equity: (-12.7%)
Current Ratio: 1.60

CARE NEW ENGLAND HEALTH SYSTEM INC

Care New England Health System take pains to ease its patients' pain. The system operates four hospitals: Kent Hospital, a general acute care facility with about 360 beds; the 290-bed Memorial Hospital of Rhode Island; psychiatric facility Butler Hospital; and Women & Infants Hospital of Rhode Island, which specializes in obstetrics, gynecology, and newborn pediatrics. All told, the system has more than 963 licensed beds. Care New England, formed in 1996 by three member hospitals, also operates a home health agency and outpatient care facilities. In late 2016 the system dropped its plans to merge with Southcoast Health. The following year it agreed to be acquired by Partners HealthCare, which is expanding outside of Massachusetts.

Operations

Three of the Care New England hospitals -- Memorial Hospital, Women & Infants, and Butler -- are teaching hospitals for Brown University's Warren Alpert Medical School. Altogether, the organization's facilities handle more than 40,000 inpatient discharges each year, as well as 129,000 emergency room visits and 9,800 births.

The organization's VNA of Care New England unit administers home health and hospice care, as well as private duty nursing services for the elderly, new mothers, and terminally ill patients. The Care New England Wellness Center offers fitness and rehabilitation services. The health care network also includes physician practice locations and an adult day care center.

Geographic Reach

Based in Providence, Rhode Island, Care New England serves southeastern New England communities including Central Falls and Pawtucket, Rhode Island, and Plainville, Massachusetts.

Financial Performance

In 2014 the system posted revenue of $1.1 billion.

Strategy

The Care New England system is focused on five key initiatives: system strength, clinical excellence, physician alignment, strategic partnerships, and academic excellence. It is working to strengthen operations in clinical fields including cardiology, emergency medicine, behavioral health, pathology, pediatrics, and women's health. In 2013 the company enhanced its mental health services by forming an affiliation with The Providence Center. In addition, Kent Hospital launched the construction of a new ambulatory surgery and primary care center.

Mergers and Acquisitions

The Care New England organization added its fourth hospital in 2013 through the acquisition of Memorial Hospital of Rhode Island. The purchase added acute care and primary care capacity and expanded the organization's regional presence.

In late 2015, Care New England and Southcoast Health signed a letter of intent to merge. The deal will create a new parent organization to oversee both health systems.

EXECUTIVES

Chief Clinical Officer, Raymond Powrie
Auditors : PRICEWATERHOUSECOOPERS LLP B

LOCATIONS

HQ: CARE NEW ENGLAND HEALTH SYSTEM INC
  4 RICHMOND SQ, PROVIDENCE, RI 029065117
Phone: 401 453-7900
Web: WWW.CARENEWENGLAND.ORG

COMPETITORS

CATHOLIC MEDICAL CENTER
HALLMARK HEALTH CORPORATION
HOLY SPIRIT HOSPITAL OF THE SISTERS OF CHRISTIAN CHARITY
KENNEDY HEALTH SYSTEM, INC.
MEDSTAR HEALTH, INC.
ONTRAK, INC.
PROVIDENCE HEALTH & SERVICES-WASHINGTON
RUSSELL COUNTY MEDICAL CENTER INC
TELECARE CORPORATION
THE MCLEAN HOSPITAL CORPORATION

HISTORICAL FINANCIALS
Company Type: Private

Income Statement   FYE: September 30

	REVENUE ($mil)	NET INCOME ($mil)	NET PROFIT MARGIN	EMPLOYEES
09/21	1,248	119	9.5%	6,500
09/20	1,123	(26)	—	—
09/19	1,146	(30)	—	—
09/17	1,132	21	1.9%	—
Annual Growth	2.5%	52.7%	—	—

2021 Year-End Financials
Return on assets: 10.8%   Cash ($ mil.): 18
Return on equity: 34.9%
Current Ratio: 1.20

CAREOREGON, INC.

Auditors : LB KPMG LLP SEATTLE WA

LOCATIONS

HQ: CAREOREGON, INC.
  315 SW 5TH AVE STE 900, PORTLAND, OR 972041703
Phone: 503 416-4100
Web: WWW.CAREOREGON.ORG

HISTORICAL FINANCIALS
Company Type: Private

Income Statement				FYE: December 31
	REVENUE ($mil)	NET INCOME ($mil)	NET PROFIT MARGIN	EMPLOYEES
12/19	1,240	64	5.2%	140
12/16	886	(9)	—	—
12/14	851	87	10.3%	—
12/13	564	(0)	—	—
Annual Growth	14.0%	—	—	—

2019 Year-End Financials
Return on assets: 13.1% Cash ($ mil.): 96
Return on equity: 19.6%
Current Ratio: 4.20

CARILION MEDICAL CENTER

Auditors: DELOITTE & TOUCHE LLP CHARLOT

LOCATIONS
HQ: CARILION MEDICAL CENTER
1906 BELLEVIEW AVE SE, ROANOKE, VA 240141838
Phone: 540 981-7000
Web: WWW.CARILIONCLINIC.ORG

HISTORICAL FINANCIALS
Company Type: Private

Income Statement				FYE: September 30
	REVENUE ($mil)	NET INCOME ($mil)	NET PROFIT MARGIN	EMPLOYEES
09/19	1,380	(137)	—	6,390
09/18	1,281	134	10.5%	—
09/17	1,232	134	10.9%	—
09/16	1,177	4	0.4%	—
Annual Growth	5.4%	—	—	—

2019 Year-End Financials
Return on assets: (-9.0%) Cash ($ mil.): 2
Return on equity: (-26.4%)
Current Ratio: 1.30

CARILION NEW RIVER VALLEY MEDICAL CENTER

LOCATIONS
HQ: CARILION NEW RIVER VALLEY MEDICAL CENTER
2900 LAMB CIR STE 150, CHRISTIANSBURG, VA 240736341
Phone: 540 731-2000

HISTORICAL FINANCIALS
Company Type: Private

Income Statement				FYE: September 30
	REVENUE ($mil)	NET INCOME ($mil)	NET PROFIT MARGIN	EMPLOYEES
09/13	896	116	12.9%	48
09/05	30	2	6.5%	—
09/04	115	18	16.0%	—
09/03	88	11	13.5%	—
Annual Growth	26.1%	25.5%	—	—

2013 Year-End Financials
Return on assets: 10.9% Cash ($ mil.): —
Return on equity: 27.1%
Current Ratio: 1.20

CARILION SERVICES, INC.

Auditors: DELOITTE & TOUCHE LLP CHARLOT

LOCATIONS
HQ: CARILION SERVICES, INC.
213 S JEFFERSON ST # 633, ROANOKE, VA 240111705
Phone: 540 981-7000
Web: WWW.CARILIONCLINIC.ORG

HISTORICAL FINANCIALS
Company Type: Private

Income Statement				FYE: September 30
	REVENUE ($mil)	NET INCOME ($mil)	NET PROFIT MARGIN	EMPLOYEES
09/08	1,221	(147)	—	935
09/05	87	(2)	—	—
09/04	228	(23)	—	—
09/03	205	17	8.3%	—
Annual Growth	42.8%	—	—	—

2008 Year-End Financials
Return on assets: (-8.4%) Cash ($ mil.): 1
Return on equity: (-18.4%)
Current Ratio: 0.90

CARLE FOUNDATION HOSPITAL

Carle Foundation Hospital is a nearly 435-bed acute-care facility that serves the residents of east central Illinois. The hospital includes the region's only Level I trauma center, as well as a Level III perinatal center, a neonatal ICU, and centers devoted to cardiac and cancer care. It also runs a handful of specialty centers in the region. Carle Foundation Hospital is the primary teaching hospital for the University of Illinois College of Medicine at Urbana-Champaign. With more than 20 primary care locations throughout the region, it is controlled by the not-for-profit Carle Foundation; sister company Carle Physician Group, which boasts approximately 280 physicians representing early 75 specialties, is one of the nation's largest private physician groups.

LOCATIONS
HQ: CARLE FOUNDATION HOSPITAL
611 W PARK ST, URBANA, IL 618012529
Phone: 217 326-2900
Web: WWW.CARLE.ORG

PRODUCTS/OPERATIONS
2014 Sales

	$ mil	% of total
Net premium revenue-health insurance	1,296.2	63
Net patient service revenue	709.7	34
Rental income	15.6	1
Net assets released from restrictions	1.6	-
Other	34.6	2
Loss on the disposal of property & equipment	(2.8)	-
Total	2,054.9	100

Selected Medical Services
Bariatrics
Cancer
Cancer
Cardiology & Heart Surgery
Diabetes & Endocrinology
Ear, Nose & Throat
Gastroenterology & GI Surgery
Geriatrics
Gynecology
Heart
Nephrology
Neurology & Neurosurgery
Sports Medicine
Stroke
Women's Health

COMPETITORS
ALBANY MEDICAL CENTER
ANN & ROBERT H. LURIE CHILDREN'S HOSPITAL OF CHICAGO
CHARLESTON AREA MEDICAL CENTER, INC.
CHILDREN'S HOSPITAL & RESEARCH CENTER AT OAKLAND
JOHN T. MATHER MEMORIAL HOSPITAL OF PORT JEFFERSON, NEW YORK, INC.
PASADENA HOSPITAL ASSOCIATION, LTD.
ROBERT WOOD JOHNSON UNIVERSITY HOSPITAL, INC.
TEXAS CHILDREN'S HOSPITAL
THE PENNSYLVANIA HOSPITAL OF THE UNIVERSITY OF PENNSYLVANIA HEALTH SYSTEM
WOMAN'S HOSPITAL FOUNDATION

HISTORICAL FINANCIALS
Company Type: Private

Income Statement				FYE: December 31
	REVENUE ($mil)	NET INCOME ($mil)	NET PROFIT MARGIN	EMPLOYEES
12/20	1,038	181	17.5%	2,500
12/18	937	216	23.1%	—
12/17	900	247	27.5%	—
12/16	812	185	22.8%	—
Annual Growth	6.3%	(0.4%)	—	—

2020 Year-End Financials
Return on assets: 94.5% Cash ($ mil.): (-26)
Return on equity: 78.3%
Current Ratio: —

CARNEGIE MELLON UNIVERSITY

Carnegie Mellon University is a private, global research university, and one of the world's most renowned educational institutions. Carnegie Mellon enrolls approximately 14,190 students and granted some 5,150 bachelor's, master's and doctoral degrees. About 80% of undergraduate students are from the US. International student comprise some 20% of undergraduate, 60% of master's and more than 50% of PH.D. students. Carnegie Mellon was founded by philanthropist and industrialist Andrew Carnegie, who established the Carnegie Technical Schools in 1900 for the sons and daughters of Pittsburgh's blue-collar workers.

Operations
In addition to the hundreds of programs offered by the schools and colleges, Carnegie Mellon also offers dozens of interdisciplinary programs, which are designed especially for students who want to work beyond just one discipline.

Carnegie Mellon has become a model for economic development in forming partnerships with companies such as Uber, Google and Disney. Carnegie's CyLab is one of the largest university-based cybersecurity education and research centers in the country. Cylab consists of over 100 faculty and more than 30 graduate students, who collaborate across some 15 different departments across Carnegie Mellon, and it is currently focusing on about 50 courses in security and privacy.

The school's alumni network includes about 20 Nobel Prize laureates, more than 140 Emmy Award winners and a dozen of Academy Award winners.

Geographic Reach
The school's main campus is located in Pittsburgh, Pennsylvania. With more than a dozen degree-granting locations, and more than 20 research partnerships, Carnegie Mellon also has branch campuses in Africa, Australia, Qatar and Silicon Valley.

Company Background
Carnegie Tech merged with the Mellon Institute of Research to become Carnegie Mellon University in 1967.

Auditors: KPMG LLP PITTSBURGH PENNSYLV

LOCATIONS

HQ: CARNEGIE MELLON UNIVERSITY
5000 FORBES AVE, PITTSBURGH, PA 152133890
Phone: 412 268-2000
Web: WWW.CMU.EDU

Selected Locations
Adelaide, Australia
Athens, Greece
Aveiro and Coimbra, Portugal
Doha, Qatar
Kobe, Japan
Lisbon, Portugal
Los Angeles
Madeira, Portugal
Minho and Porto, Portugal
Mexico
Silicon Valley
Singapore

PRODUCTS/OPERATIONS

2015 Sales

	$ mil	% of total
Tuition and other educational fees revenue, net of financial aid	450.7	39
Sponsored projects revenue	376.8	32
Contributions revenue	136.6	12
Auxiliary services revenue	57.9	5
Investment income	37.1	3
Other sources	109.3	9
Total	1,168.4	100

Selected Departments
Chemical Engineering
Civil and Environmental Engineering
Energy Science, Technology & Policy
Electrical and Computer Engineering
Engineering and Public Policy
Engineering & Technology Innovation Management
Information Networking Institute
Materials Science Engineering
Mechanical Engineering
Software Engineering and
Software Management
Architecture
Art
Design
Drama
Master of Arts Management
Master of Entertainment Industry Management
Music
English
History
Modern Languages
Philosophy
Psychology
Social and Decision Sciences
Statistics

Selected Schools
Carnegie Institute of Technology
School of Computer Science
College of Fine Arts
College of Humanities & Social Sciences
H. John Heinz III College
Mellon College of Science
Tepper School of Business

COMPETITORS

IMPERIAL COLLEGE LONDON LIMITED
NORTHEASTERN UNIVERSITY
ROCHESTER INSTITUTE OF TECHNOLOGY (INC)
THE COLLEGE OF WILLIAM & MARY
TRUSTEES OF BOSTON COLLEGE
UNIVERSITY OF LEICESTER
UNIVERSITY OF NOTTINGHAM (THE)
UNIVERSITY OF THE PACIFIC
UNIVERSITY OF WARWICK
UNIVERSITY SYSTEM OF MARYLAND

HISTORICAL FINANCIALS

Company Type: Private

Income Statement — FYE: June 30

	REVENUE ($mil)	NET INCOME ($mil)	NET PROFIT MARGIN	EMPLOYEES
06/22	1,642	134	8.2%	4,913
06/21	1,672	1,525	91.2%	—
06/20	1,850	411	22.2%	—
06/19	1,363	207	15.2%	—
Annual Growth	6.4%	(13.4%)	—	—

2022 Year-End Financials
Return on assets: 2.1%   Cash ($ mil.): 765
Return on equity: 2.6%
Current Ratio: —

CAROLINA HEALTHCARE CENTER OF CUMBERLAND LP

Auditors: RSM MCGLADREY CHARLOTTE NC

LOCATIONS

HQ: CAROLINA HEALTHCARE CENTER OF CUMBERLAND LP
4600 CUMBERLAND RD, FAYETTEVILLE, NC 283062412
Phone: 910 429-1690
Web: WWW.CAROLINA-HEALTH.COM

HISTORICAL FINANCIALS

Company Type: Private

Income Statement — FYE: September 30

	REVENUE ($mil)	NET INCOME ($mil)	NET PROFIT MARGIN	EMPLOYEES
09/09	1,019	62	6.2%	150
09/03	6	(0)	—	—
Annual Growth	132.0%	—	—	—

2009 Year-End Financials
Return on assets: 771.0%   Cash ($ mil.): —
Return on equity: 999.9%
Current Ratio: 0.60

CAROLINAS MEDICAL CENTER NORTHEAST

LOCATIONS

HQ: CAROLINAS MEDICAL CENTER NORTHEAST
920 CHURCH ST N, CONCORD, NC 280252927
Phone: 704 783-3000
Web: WWW.ATRIUMHEALTH.ORG

HISTORICAL FINANCIALS

Company Type: Private

Income Statement — FYE: December 31

	REVENUE ($mil)	NET INCOME ($mil)	NET PROFIT MARGIN	EMPLOYEES
12/17	576	158	27.4%	4,500
12/16	552	130	23.6%	—
12/15	557	117	21.0%	—
Annual Growth	1.7%	16.3%	—	—

2017 Year-End Financials
Return on assets: 10.1%   Cash ($ mil.): —
Return on equity: 10.3%
Current Ratio: 23.20

CARTER-JONES COMPANIES, INC.

Auditors: BDO USA LLP CLEVELAND OH

LOCATIONS

HQ: CARTER-JONES COMPANIES, INC.
601 TALLMADGE RD, KENT, OH 442407331
Phone: 330 673-6100
Web: WWW.DOITBEST.COM

HISTORICAL FINANCIALS

Company Type: Private

Income Statement — FYE: December 31

	REVENUE ($mil)	NET INCOME ($mil)	NET PROFIT MARGIN	EMPLOYEES
12/21	2,565	158	6.2%	3,225
12/20	1,750	70	4.0%	—
12/19	1,504	45	3.0%	—
12/18	1,482	39	2.7%	—
Annual Growth	20.1%	59.0%	—	—

2021 Year-End Financials
Return on assets: 13.5%   Cash ($ mil.): 25
Return on equity: 23.7%
Current Ratio: 2.60

CARY OIL CO., INC.

Auditors: BATCELOR TILLERY & ROBERTS L

LOCATIONS

HQ: CARY OIL CO., INC.
110 MACKENAN DR STE 300, CARY, NC 275117901
Phone: 919 462-1100
Web: WWW.CARYOIL.COM

HISTORICAL FINANCIALS

Company Type: Private

Income Statement — FYE: December 31

	REVENUE ($mil)	NET INCOME ($mil)	NET PROFIT MARGIN	EMPLOYEES
12/12	1,647	2	0.2%	100
12/11	1,608	2	0.1%	—
12/10	1,177	1	0.1%	—
Annual Growth	18.3%	28.2%	—	—

2012 Year-End Financials
Return on assets: 4.8%   Cash ($ mil.): 4
Return on equity: 25.1%
Current Ratio: 1.00

CASE WESTERN RESERVE UNIVERSITY

Case Western Reserve University (CWRU) is an independent research school with an enrollment of about 12,070 students from all US states and around 90 countries, more than half of whom are graduate and professional students. CWRU offers approximately 260 undergraduate, graduate and professional options, and almost 145 dual-degree programs from its eight colleges and schools ? management, engineering, law, arts and sciences, dentistry, social work, nursing, and medicine ? as well as a graduate school at its campus in Cleveland. The university has more than 3,655 faculty members and a student-to-teacher ratio of 11:1.

Operations

CWRU receives approximately $390 million in external funding each year to pay for its various research enterprises.

In addition to the university's approximately 100 undergraduate degree choices, about 160 graduate and professional options, and almost 145 dual-degree programs, CWRU also has more than 100 interdisciplinary academic and research centers and institutes.

Geographic Reach

CWRU is located at more than 265-acre campus in Cleveland's University Circle; and houses approximately 60 educational, medical, cultural, social, and religious institutions. CWRU's students come from all 50 US states and around 90 countries.

Company Background

The university's origins date back to 1826 in the Ohio region then known as the Western Reserve of Connecticut; its current structure was formed in 1967 with the combination of neighboring Case Institute of Technology and Western Reserve College.

Auditors: PRICEWATERHOUSECOOPERS LLP CL

LOCATIONS

HQ: CASE WESTERN RESERVE UNIVERSITY
10900 EUCLID AVE, CLEVELAND, OH 441064901
Phone: 216 368-6062
Web: WWW.CASE.EDU

PRODUCTS/OPERATIONS

2014 Sales

	$ mil	% of total
Grants and contracts	249.2	27
Student tuition and fees	218.5	24
Gifts and pledges	85.2	9
CCLCM grants and contracts	83.0	9
Facilities and administrative cost recovery	72.5	8
Others	217.9	23
Total	926.3	100

Selected Schools and Programs

Case School of Engineering
College of Arts and Sciences
Cleveland Clinic (part of the School of Medicine)
Frances Payne Bolton School of Nursing
Mandel Center for Nonprofit Organizations
Mandel School of Applied Social Sciences
School of Dental Medicine
School of Graduate Studies
School of Law
School of Medicine
Weatherhead School of Management

COMPETITORS

NORTHEASTERN UNIVERSITY
PURDUE UNIVERSITY
Queen's University At Kingston
THE WASHINGTON UNIVERSITY
TRUSTEES OF BOSTON UNIVERSITY
UNIVERSITY OF GLASGOW
UNIVERSITY OF KANSAS
UNIVERSITY OF LEICESTER
UNIVERSITY OF THE PACIFIC
UNIVERSITY OF YORK

HISTORICAL FINANCIALS

Company Type: Private

Income Statement — FYE: June 30

	REVENUE ($mil)	NET INCOME ($mil)	NET PROFIT MARGIN	EMPLOYEES
06/22	1,132	(140)	—	6,599
06/21	1,101	679	61.7%	—
06/20	1,075	(49)	—	—
06/18	1,016	111	10.9%	—
Annual Growth	2.7%	—	—	—

2022 Year-End Financials
Return on assets: (-3.5%)   Cash ($ mil.): 551
Return on equity: (-4.9%)
Current Ratio: —

CATHOLIC HEALTH INITIATIVES - IOWA, CORP.

Auditors: KPMG LLP DENVER CO

LOCATIONS

HQ: CATHOLIC HEALTH INITIATIVES - IOWA, CORP.
1111 6TH AVE, DES MOINES, IA 503142613
Phone: 515 247-3121
Web: WWW.MERCYONE.ORG

HISTORICAL FINANCIALS

Company Type: Private

Income Statement — FYE: June 30

	REVENUE ($mil)	NET INCOME ($mil)	NET PROFIT MARGIN	EMPLOYEES
06/20	817	14	1.7%	6,100
06/16	804	58	7.3%	—
06/14	733	(14)	—	—
06/10	691	39	5.8%	—
Annual Growth	1.7%	(9.9%)	—	—

2020 Year-End Financials
Return on assets: 1.4%   Cash ($ mil.): 149
Return on equity: 2.2%
Current Ratio: 2.00

CATHOLIC HEALTH INITIATIVES COLORADO

Auditors: CROWE LLP WASHINGTON DC

LOCATIONS

HQ: CATHOLIC HEALTH INITIATIVES COLORADO
9100 E MINERAL CIR, CENTENNIAL, CO 801123401
Phone: 303 290-6500
Web: WWW.CATHOLICHEALTHINITIATIVES.ORG

HISTORICAL FINANCIALS
Company Type: Private

Income Statement — FYE: June 30

	REVENUE ($mil)	NET INCOME ($mil)	NET PROFIT MARGIN	EMPLOYEES
06/21	2,304	273	11.9%	8,000
06/20	2,251	251	11.2%	—
06/19	2,190	203	9.3%	—
Annual Growth	2.6%	16.0%	—	—

2021 Year-End Financials
Return on assets: 8.8% Cash ($ mil.): 398
Return on equity: 10.9%
Current Ratio: 2.60

CATHOLIC MEDICAL MISSION BOARD INC

Auditors: MARKS PANETH LLP NEW YORK NY

LOCATIONS

HQ: CATHOLIC MEDICAL MISSION BOARD INC
100 WALL ST FL 9, NEW YORK, NY 100055765
Phone: 212 242-7757
Web: WWW.MEDICSONAMISSION.ORG

HISTORICAL FINANCIALS
Company Type: Private

Income Statement — FYE: September 30

	REVENUE ($mil)	NET INCOME ($mil)	NET PROFIT MARGIN	EMPLOYEES
09/18	740	105	14.2%	38
09/17	603	19	3.2%	—
09/16	371	(12)	—	—
09/15	290	(3)	—	—
Annual Growth	36.7%	—	—	—

2018 Year-End Financials
Return on assets: 48.2% Cash ($ mil.): 5
Return on equity: 49.6%
Current Ratio: —

CATHOLIC RELIEF SERVICES - UNITED STATES CONFERENCE OF CATHOLIC BISHOPS

Auditors: RSM US LLP GAITHERSBURG MD

LOCATIONS

HQ: CATHOLIC RELIEF SERVICES - UNITED STATES CONFERENCE OF CATHOLIC BISHOPS
228 W LEXINGTON ST, BALTIMORE, MD 212013422
Phone: 410 625-2220
Web: WWW.CRS.ORG

HISTORICAL FINANCIALS
Company Type: Private

Income Statement — FYE: September 30

	REVENUE ($mil)	NET INCOME ($mil)	NET PROFIT MARGIN	EMPLOYEES
09/19	940	(21)	—	7,100
09/18	989	(3)	—	—
09/17	978	20	2.1%	—
09/16	917	(47)	—	—
Annual Growth	0.8%	—	—	—

2019 Year-End Financials
Return on assets: (-4.2%) Cash ($ mil.): 64
Return on equity: (-13.2%)
Current Ratio: 1.00

CCF BRANDS LLC

Auditors: FROST PLLC LITTLE ROCK ARKAN

LOCATIONS

HQ: CCF BRANDS LLC
5211 W VILLAGE PKWY # 101, ROGERS, AR 727588104
Phone: 479 464-0544
Web: WWW.CCFBRANDS.COM

HISTORICAL FINANCIALS
Company Type: Private

Income Statement — FYE: April 30

	REVENUE ($mil)	NET INCOME ($mil)	NET PROFIT MARGIN	EMPLOYEES
04/22	551	2	0.5%	58
04/21	453	1	0.4%	—
04/20	444	0	0.1%	—
Annual Growth	11.5%	167.2%	—	—

2022 Year-End Financials
Return on assets: 3.1% Cash ($ mil.): 14
Return on equity: 21.9%
Current Ratio: 0.90

CEB INC.

Don't fear the competition; learn from it. So says CEB, a provider of business research and analysis services to more than 10,000 companies worldwide. Its program areas cover "best practices" in such topics as finance, human resources, information technology, operations, and sales and marketing. Unlike consulting firms, which engage with one client at a time, CEB operates on a membership-based business model. Members subscribe to one or more of the company's programs and participate in the research and analysis, thus sharing expertise with others. Besides reports on best practices, CEB offers seminars, customized research briefs, and decision-support tools.

Operations

The company operates through two segments: CEB (79% of net sales) and CEB Talent Assessment (21%). The CEB segment provides data analysis, research, and advisory services that align to executive leadership roles and key recurring decisions and enable members to focus efforts to address emerging and recurring business challenges. CEB Talent Assessment segment includes its SHL product and services of cloud-based products for talent assessment, development, strategy, analytics, decision support, and professional services.

Geographic Reach

CED has offices in almost 20 locations through the US and almost 15 in Europe. The US accounts for 62% of its net sales; Europe generates 20%, and other countries account for the remainder.

Financial Performance

CEB achieved unprecedented growth in 2015, with revenues peaking at a record-setting $928 million in 2015. The historic growth was fueled by a 4% bump in CEB segment sales and a 4% increase in the US. CEB was also helped by an increase in 2014 sales bookings and the positive impact of acquisitions.

Profits also skyrocketed by 80% to reach $93 million in 2015, another company milestone, primarily due to the absence of an impairment loss which it incurred the previous year. After years of posting steadily increasing cash flow, CEB saw its operating cash flow decrease by $34 million from 2014 to 2015, primarily due to unfavorable changes in deferred revenue and other liabilities.

Mergers and Acquisitions

One of the ways in which CEB posted milestone revenue growth for 2015 was through the use of acquisitions. In 2016 CEB agreed to acquire Evanta Ventures for $275 million. Portland, Oregon-based Evanta offers best practices data for information technology, human resources, and finance executives through nearly 200 annual events, online, and offline learning platforms and subscription information offerings.

In 2015 CEB picked up Wanted Technologies Corporation, a provider of real-time market intelligence and analytics for staffing and talent sourcing professionals. The same year, CEB, acquired Australia-based CEO Forum Group, a provider of membership-based peer group briefing services serving senior executives of foreign-owned multinational organizations doing business in Australia.

EXECUTIVES

CAO*, J Barron Anschutz
Auditors : ERNST & YOUNG LLP MCLEAN VIR

LOCATIONS

HQ: CEB INC.
1201 WILSON BLVD STE 1800, ARLINGTON, VA 222092316
Phone: 571 303-3000
Web: WWW.CEBGLOBAL.COM

2015 Sales

	$ mil.	% of total
US	579.7	62
Europe	184.1	20
Other regions	164.6	18
Total	928.4	100

PRODUCTS/OPERATIONS

2015 Sales

	$ mil	% of total
CEB	731.8	79
CEB Talent Assessment	196.6	21
Total	928.4	100

Selected Practice Areas
Communications
Financial services
General management
Human resources
Information technology
Legal and compliance
Operations and procurement
Sales and marketing
Strategy and research and development

COMPETITORS

CORNERSTONE ONDEMAND, INC.
EDELMAN FINANCIAL ENGINES, LLC
FTI CONSULTING, INC.
GARTNER, INC.
GUIDEHOUSE INC.
HEALTHSTREAM, INC.
HURON CONSULTING GROUP INC.
KORN FERRY
PREMIER, INC.
RESOURCES CONNECTION, INC.

HISTORICAL FINANCIALS
Company Type: Private

Income Statement   FYE: December 31

	REVENUE ($mil)	NET INCOME ($mil)	NET PROFIT MARGIN	EMPLOYEES
12/16	949	(34)	—	4,600
12/15	928	92	10.0%	—
12/14	908	51	5.6%	—
12/13	820	31	3.9%	—
Annual Growth	5.0%	—	—	—

2016 Year-End Financials
Return on assets: (-2.5%)   Cash ($ mil.): 134
Return on equity: —
Current Ratio: 0.80

CEDARS-SINAI MEDICAL CARE FOUNDATION

Auditors : ERNST & YOUNG LLP LOS ANGELES

LOCATIONS

HQ: CEDARS-SINAI MEDICAL CARE FOUNDATION
200 N ROBERTSON BLVD # 101, BEVERLY HILLS, CA 902111704
Phone: 800 700-6424
Web: WWW.CEDARS-SINAI.ORG

HISTORICAL FINANCIALS
Company Type: Private

Income Statement   FYE: June 30

	REVENUE ($mil)	NET INCOME ($mil)	NET PROFIT MARGIN	EMPLOYEES
06/21	560	42	7.6%	4
06/20	447	(114)	—	—
06/19	441	127	28.9%	—
06/18	394	8	2.2%	—
Annual Growth	12.4%	70.6%	—	—

2021 Year-End Financials
Return on assets: 7.6%   Cash ($ mil.): 92
Return on equity: 13.7%
Current Ratio: 1.80

CEDARS-SINAI MEDICAL CENTER

Cedars-Sinai is a nonprofit academic healthcare organization serving the diverse Los Angeles community and beyond. Cedars-Sinai is consistently listed as a top-ranked hospital by US News & World Report in such specialties as cancer, cardiology, endocrinology, gastrointestinal disorders, gynecology, heart surgery, kidney disease, neurology, orthopedics, and respiratory disorders. Cedars-Sinai is a partner institution in the UCLA Clinical and Translational Science Institute (CTSI), an academic-clinical-community partnership and is engaged in hundreds of research programs in areas such as cancer, neuroscience, and genetics. It also partners with some 30 leading community service organizations, advocacy groups, health delivery networks, churches and schools.

Operations

Cedars-Sinai ranks among the nation's top non-university hospitals for competitive research funding from the National Institutes of Health and currently has more than 1,845 research projects, many led by physician-scientists.

The hospital sees some 1.6 million outpatient visits and more than 111,000 emergency department visits each year.

Geographic Reach

Cedars-Sinai serves more than one million people each year in over 40 locations.

EXECUTIVES

Senior Vice President Human Resources, Jeanne Flores
Senior Vice President Legal Affairs, Peter E Braveman
Auditors : ERNST & YOUNG LLP LOS ANGELES

LOCATIONS

HQ: CEDARS-SINAI MEDICAL CENTER
8700 BEVERLY BLVD, WEST HOLLYWOOD, CA 900481804
Phone: 310 423-3277
Web: WWW.CEDARS-SINAI.ORG

PRODUCTS/OPERATIONS

Selected Centers and Services
Ambulatory Care Center
Cedars-Sinai Center for Chest Disease
Cedars-Sinai Center for Digestive Diseases
Cedars-Sinai Heart Institute
Cedars-Sinai Institute Spine Center
Cedars-Sinai Health Associates (affiliated independent physician association)
Cedars-Sinai Medical Group (multi-specialty physicians group)
Cedars-Sinai Orthopedic Center
Diagnostic imaging center
Emergency department and trauma center
Hospice services
Kidney and pancreas transplant center
Neuroscience services
Pediatric services
Psychiatry and mental health services
Samuel Oschin Comprehensive Cancer Institute
Surgical services
Organ and bone marrow transplantation
Radiation therapy
Radiology
Stroke program
Pain management services
Women's health services

COMPETITORS

ARKANSAS CHILDREN'S HOSPITAL
CHILDREN'S HOSPITAL MEDICAL CENTER
FROEDTERT MEMORIAL LUTHERAN HOSPITAL, INC.
MOUNT SINAI HOSPITAL MEDICAL CENTER OF CHICAGO
MOUNT SINAI MEDICAL CENTER OF FLORIDA, INC.
SAINT JOSEPH HOSPITAL, INC
THE CHILDREN'S HOSPITAL CORPORATION
THE CHILDREN'S HOSPITAL OF PHILADELPHIA
THE PENNSYLVANIA HOSPITAL OF THE UNIVERSITY OF PENNSYLVANIA HEALTH SYSTEM
THE UNIVERSITY OF CHICAGO MEDICAL CENTER

HISTORICAL FINANCIALS
Company Type: Private

Income Statement   FYE: June 30

	REVENUE ($mil)	NET INCOME ($mil)	NET PROFIT MARGIN	EMPLOYEES
06/21	4,142	1,083	26.2%	8,000
06/20	3,647	443	12.2%	—
06/19	3,649	389	10.7%	—
06/18	3,470	417	12.0%	—
Annual Growth	6.1%	37.4%	—	—

2021 Year-End Financials
Return on assets: 12.8%   Cash ($ mil.): 1,077
Return on equity: 17.6%
Current Ratio: 5.30

CENTERPOINT ENERGY SERVICES RETAIL LLC

Auditors : GRANT THORNTON LLP TULSA OKL

LOCATIONS

HQ: CENTERPOINT ENERGY SERVICES RETAIL LLC
1111 LA ST FL 20 FLR 20, HOUSTON, TX 77002
Phone: 800 752-8036
Web: WWW.INFUSEENERGY.COM

HISTORICAL FINANCIALS
Company Type: Private

Income Statement   FYE: December 31

	REVENUE ($mil)	NET INCOME ($mil)	NET PROFIT MARGIN	EMPLOYEES
12/14	695	8	1.2%	35
12/13	549	9	1.7%	—
Annual Growth	26.6%	(11.9%)	—	—

2014 Year-End Financials
Return on assets: 4.7%   Cash ($ mil.): —
Return on equity: 9.7%
Current Ratio: 1.20

CENTIMARK CORPORATION

Centimark is one of the commercial and industrial roofing contractors in the US, Canada, and Mexico. The company provides roof installation, inspection, repair, and emergency leak service. Centimark typically works on flat roofs using EPDM rubber, thermoplastic, bitumen, metal, and coatings. Its QuestMark division offers commercial, industrial, and retail flooring, do-it-yourself (DIY) products, and floor maintenance and cleaning products. The company has more than 95 offices throughout US, Canada, and Mexico.

Operations
The company offers roof services, roof replacement, roof repairs, roof cleaning, preventative maintenance programs, asset alert and asset management. Centimark also provides systems, such as thermoplastic solutions, sprayed polyurethane foams, roof coatings, modified bitumen and built-up roofing, metal products, and steep slope products.

QuestMark, a division of Centimark, offers materials for commercial, retail and industrial floors. It specializes in DiamondQuest polished concrete flooring, epoxy flooring, floor repair materials, floor maintenance, and floor cleaning products.

Centimark's Asset Management service provides extensive roof surveys, roof life expectancy models, return-on-investment analysis for roof repairs and evaluations for roof repair or roof replacement.

Geographic Reach
Canonsburg, Pennsylvania-based, Centimark also does business in Canada through subsidiary Centimark Ltd., which has eight offices throughout Canada.

Sales and Marketing
The company serves customers in different segments, including retail, industrial, general contractors, and education.

Company Background
Chairman and CEO Edward Dunlap founded Centimark as an industrial cleaning business in 1967. Centimark is owned by its employees.

EXECUTIVES

Executive Land Vice President*, Robert Penney
QM FL*, John Scanlon
ETN*, Mark Cooper
S*, Keith Battenfield
Auditors : SCHNEIDER DOWNS & CO INC P

LOCATIONS

HQ: CENTIMARK CORPORATION
12 GRANDVIEW CIR, CANONSBURG, PA 153178533
Phone: 724 514-8700
Web: WWW.CENTIMARK.COM

PRODUCTS/OPERATIONS

Selected Operations
CentiMark (roofing)
CentiMark ltd. (Canada, roofing)
QuestMark (flooring)

Selected Systems
Roof Systems
EPDM
Green Roofing
Metal Roofs
Modified Bitumen and Built-Up Roofs
Roof Coatings
SPF
Steep Slope
TPO & PVC
Floor Systems
Chemical Resistant Systems
Decorative Broadcast
Decorative Concrete
Electric Static Dissipative
Heavy Duty Resurfacer
High Build Coating
Polished Concrete
Thin Mil

COMPETITORS

CABRAL ROOFING & WATERPROOFING CORPORATION
CUSTOM BUILDING PRODUCTS
D. C. TAYLOR CO.
EUROWINDOWS LIMITED
G-I HOLDINGS INC.
HOLLAND ROOFING, INC.
PICKENS ROOFING, INC.
SAHCO AMERICA, INC.
TECTA AMERICA CORP.
THL ENTERPRISES, INC.

HISTORICAL FINANCIALS
Company Type: Private

Income Statement   FYE: April 30

	REVENUE ($mil)	NET INCOME ($mil)	NET PROFIT MARGIN	EMPLOYEES
04/21	783	73	9.4%	3,500
04/18	670	54	8.1%	—
04/17	625	51	8.2%	—
04/15	(817)	0	0.0%	—
Annual Growth	—	952.3%	—	—

2021 Year-End Financials
Return on assets: 10.7%   Cash ($ mil.): 309
Return on equity: 13.8%
Current Ratio: 4.80

CENTRA HEALTH, INC.

Centra Health is a regional nonprofit healthcare system based in Lynchburg, Virginia. Its entity's core are two acute care facilities in Lynchburg: The Lynchburg General, which is the region's main emergency center and specializes in orthopedic, pediatric, and cardiac care; and Virginia Baptist, facility focused on surgery, women's health, infant care, mental health, and rehabilitation. With nearly 800 physicians and medical staff, Centra Health provides care to over 500,000 people in some 50 locations throughout central and southern Virginia. It was founded on 1987.

Operations
Centra Lynchburg General Hospital is home to the Centra Stroobants Heart Center and Stroobants Cardiovascular Pavilion, a national benchmark facility for cardiac care. Heart Center specialists perform more than 6,000 major cardiac procedures each year. LGH is also a Level II Trauma Center, providing emergency and critical care services to more than 85,000 patients per year. LGH has a pediatric center, outpatient surgery center, and provides orthopaedic, neurology, neurosurgery, diabetes and pulmonary services.

Centra Virginia Baptist Hospital is home to The Birth Center, Women's and Children's Health, and the region's neonatal intensive care unit. VBH also serves as the primary regional provider of children and adult mental health services. Virginia Baptist operates an outpatient surgery center and provides skilled care, rehabilitation, physical therapy, and ambulatory surgery. VBH is home to a variety of specialty services including the Breast Imaging Center, Heartburn Treatment Center, Center for Wound Care and Hyperbaric Medicine, Sleep Disorders Center and the Center for Pain Management.

Centra Southside Community Hospital in Farmville is an around 115-bed acute care facility. Its hospital inpatient services include obstetrics, general medicine intensive care, surgical services, and general medicine. It serves as a medical hub for an eight-county region. Each year Southside has approximately 4,000 admissions and sees more than 33,000 patients through its emergency department.

Centra Bedford Memorial Hospital in Bedford is a full-service medical facility with special emphasis on women's health, outpatient surgery, emergency services, cardiology care, and rehabilitative services. The facility offers 24-hour emergency care to the local community of approximately 60,000 residents. Centra Bedford Memorial Hospital has about 50 beds and a 111 bed long-term care facility.

The Centra Healthcare System includes the Centra Medical Group; a network of local family practices, primary care physicians, and medical and surgical specialists. Centra Medical Group provides the community with primary care physicians, cardiologists, cardiothoracic surgeons, gerontologists, neurosurgeons, physiatrists, psychiatrists, therapists and urologists.

Geographic Reach
Centra Health serves Lynchburg and surrounding communities in central Virginia including Farmville (located in Prince Edward County), Bedford, Burkeville, Cumberland, Forest, Gretna, Keysville and Moneta.

Company Background
Centra Health was founded in 1987 through the merger of Lynchburg General and Virginia Baptist. Southside Community Hospital joined the network in 2006.

LOCATIONS

HQ: CENTRA HEALTH, INC.
1920 ATHERHOLT RD, LYNCHBURG, VA 245011120
Phone: 434 200-3204
Web: WWW.CENTRAHEALTH.COM

PRODUCTS/OPERATIONS

Selected Facilities
Bedford Memorial Hospital (Bedford, Virginia; partnership with Carilion Health System)
Lynchburg General Hospital (Lynchburg, Virginia)
Virginia Baptist Hospital (Lynchburg, Virginia)
Southside Community Hospital (Farmville, Virginia)
Physician Practices
　Altavista Medical Center (Altavista, Virginia)
　Big Island Medical Center (North Big Island, Virginia)
　Brookneal Family Medical Center (Brookneal, Virginia)
　Gretna Medical Center (Gretna, Virginia)
　Lynchburg Family Medicine Center (Lynchburg, Virginia)
Other Facilities
　Bridges Treatment Center (Lynchburg, Virginia)
　Fairmont Crossing Health and Rehabilitation Center (Amherst, Virginia)
　Guggenheimer Health and Rehabilitation Center (Lynchburg, Virginia)
　Piedmont Psychiatric Center (Lynchburg, Virginia)
　Rivermont Schools (regional)
　The Summit (regional)

COMPETITORS

ASCENSION PROVIDENCE HOSPITAL
ASCENSION SOUTHEAST MICHIGAN
BAPTIST MEMORIAL HEALTH CARE SYSTEM, INC.
CAROMONT HEALTH, INC.
CHRISTUS SPOHN HEALTH SYSTEM CORPORATION
MARION COMMUNITY HOSPITAL, INC.
MCLEOD HEALTH SERVICES, INC.
PITT COUNTY MEMORIAL HOSPITAL, INCORPORATED
PROVIDENCE HOSPITAL
WINTER HAVEN HOSPITAL, INC.

HISTORICAL FINANCIALS
Company Type: Private

Income Statement　　　　　　　　　　　FYE: December 31

	REVENUE ($mil)	NET INCOME ($mil)	NET PROFIT MARGIN	EMPLOYEES
12/20	836	285	34.1%	6,000
12/19	1,078	8	0.8%	—
12/15	742	25	3.4%	—
12/14	553	63	11.5%	—
Annual Growth	7.1%	28.5%	—	—

2020 Year-End Financials
Return on assets: 22.4%　　Cash ($ mil.): 90
Return on equity: 82.8%
Current Ratio: 1.20

CENTRAL CRUDE, INC.

Auditors: MCELROY QUIRK & BURCH

LOCATIONS

HQ: CENTRAL CRUDE, INC.
4187 HIGHWAY 3059, LAKE CHARLES, LA 706153310
Phone: 337 436-1000
Web: WWW.CENTRALCRUDE.COM

HISTORICAL FINANCIALS
Company Type: Private

Income Statement　　　　　　　　　　　FYE: March 31

	REVENUE ($mil)	NET INCOME ($mil)	NET PROFIT MARGIN	EMPLOYEES
03/09	637	1	0.2%	50
03/08	635	0	0.1%	—
03/06	280	0	0.1%	—
Annual Growth	31.5%	56.2%	—	—

2009 Year-End Financials
Return on assets: 2.4%　　Cash ($ mil.): —
Return on equity: 40.0%
Current Ratio: 1.00

CENTRAL ELECTRIC POWER COOPERATIVE, INC.

Auditors: BAUKNIGHT PIETRAS & STORMER PA

LOCATIONS

HQ: CENTRAL ELECTRIC POWER COOPERATIVE, INC.
20 COOPERATIVE WAY, COLUMBIA, SC 292103112
Phone: 803 779-4975
Web: WWW.CEPCI.ORG

HISTORICAL FINANCIALS
Company Type: Private

Income Statement　　　　　　　　　　　FYE: December 31

	REVENUE ($mil)	NET INCOME ($mil)	NET PROFIT MARGIN	EMPLOYEES
12/15	1,220	0	0.0%	54
12/14	1,254	0	0.0%	—
12/13	1,198	0	0.0%	—
12/09	1,037	1	0.2%	—
Annual Growth	2.8%	(33.9%)	—	—

2015 Year-End Financials
Return on assets: —　　Cash ($ mil.): 8
Return on equity: 0.4%
Current Ratio: —

CENTRAL GROCERS, INC.

In a city of big stores, Central Grocers helps keep neighborhood markets stocked. Founded in 1917, the cooperative wholesale food distributor is owned by some 225 members. It supplies 40,000 food items and general merchandise to more than 400 independent grocery stores, serving several states such as Illinois, Indiana, Iowa, Michigan, and Wisconsin. Central Grocers distributes products under both national brands and its own Centrella brand, which is marketed exclusively to its member stores. The co-op also operates about 30 stores under a handful of banner names, including Strack & Van Til, Town & Country, Key Market, and the low-cost Ultra Foods chain.In 2017 the company filed for Chapter 11 bankruptcy protection.

Bankruptcy
In May 2017 Central Grocers filed for Chapter 11 bankruptcy protection. The company intends to sell its Strack & Van Tilstores and its Joliet, Ill. distribution warehouse as its seeks to exit its wholesale distribution business.

Operations
As part of its business, Central Grocers caters to its customers with the help of a fleet of 100 refrigerated trucks, 300 dry trailers,

and about 70 Freightliner tractors.

Sales and Marketing
Central Grocers services a wide variety of store formats and ethnic groups including Hispanic, Italian, and African Americans. Besides older and smaller 5,000-sq.-ft. stores, its clients include large-scale warehouse discount stores that measure 75,000 sq. ft. and large conventional stores that average 70,000 sq. ft.

Financial Performance
While privately-owned Central Grocers doesn't report financial results. The co-op rings up an estimated $2 billion in sales and it returns (in the form of dividends) to its members about $243 million.

Strategy
Central Grocers, the 7th largest grocery cooperative in the US, boasts the second-largest market share in the Chicago area. It specializes in serving Chicago independent supermarkets. Central Grocers supplies them with a comprehensive menu of groceries, produce, fresh meat, service deli items, frozen foods, ice cream, and items from its own Centrella brand.

Central Grocers expanded its distribution center by 15,000-sq.-ft. to 940,000-sq.-ft. of storage capacity in 2011. The reason for expansion was due to demand for produce and fresh meats.

LOCATIONS
HQ: CENTRAL GROCERS, INC.
2600 HAVEN AVE, JOLIET, IL 604338467
Phone: 815 553-8800
Web: WWW.CENTRAL-GROCERS.COM

PRODUCTS/OPERATIONS
Selected Products
Fresh meat
Frozen foods
Groceries
Ice cream
Produce
Service deli items

COMPETITORS
CORE-MARK HOLDING COMPANY, INC.
HYPERAMA PLC
MCLANE COMPANY, INC.
METCASH LIMITED
TOPCO ASSOCIATES, LLC

HISTORICAL FINANCIALS
Company Type: Private

Income Statement — FYE: July 28

	REVENUE ($mil)	NET INCOME ($mil)	NET PROFIT MARGIN	EMPLOYEES
07/07	1,197	(10)	—	2,300
07/06	1,108	5	0.5%	—
07/05	1,103	4	0.4%	—
07/04	1,047	3	0.3%	—
Annual Growth	4.5%	—	—	—

2007 Year-End Financials
Return on assets: (-3.8%)
Cash ($ mil.): —
Return on equity: (-35.2%)
Current Ratio: 1.00

CENTRAL HUDSON GAS & ELECTRIC CORPORATION

LOCATIONS
HQ: CENTRAL HUDSON GAS & ELECTRIC CORPORATION
284 SOUTH AVE DEPT 100, POUGHKEEPSIE, NY 126014839
Phone: 845 452-2700
Web: WWW.CENHUD.COM

HISTORICAL FINANCIALS
Company Type: Private

Income Statement — FYE: December 31

	REVENUE ($mil)	NET INCOME ($mil)	NET PROFIT MARGIN	EMPLOYEES
12/17	671	55	8.2%	869
12/16	640	52	8.2%	—
12/11	700	45	6.4%	—
Annual Growth	(0.7%)	3.4%	—	—

2017 Year-End Financials
Return on assets: 2.5%
Cash ($ mil.): 14
Return on equity: 8.8%
Current Ratio: 1.80

CENTRAL IOWA HOSPITAL CORP

EXECUTIVES
Executive Director Finance*, Kara Dunham

LOCATIONS
HQ: CENTRAL IOWA HOSPITAL CORP
1200 PLEASANT ST, DES MOINES, IA 503091406
Phone: 515 241-6212

HISTORICAL FINANCIALS
Company Type: Private

Income Statement — FYE: December 31

	REVENUE ($mil)	NET INCOME ($mil)	NET PROFIT MARGIN	EMPLOYEES
12/17	832	3	0.4%	3,495
12/16	573	153	26.8%	—
12/15	548	152	27.9%	—
12/14	534	145	27.2%	—
Annual Growth	15.9%	(71.6%)	—	—

2017 Year-End Financials
Return on assets: 0.3%
Cash ($ mil.): 2
Return on equity: 0.4%
Current Ratio: 3.20

CENTRAL STEEL AND WIRE COMPANY, LLC

When it comes to metal, service center Central Steel & Wire Company (CS&W) can shape up and ship out. CS&W distributes ferrous and nonferrous metals in a variety of shapes and forms, including bars, coils, plates, sheets, structurals, tubing, and wire. Among the company's processing services are annealing, blanking, computer numerical control (CNC) laser cutting, galvanizing, and structural fabrication. CS&W distributes its products throughout North America from five facilities that are located primarily in the Midwestern US. The company has metallurgical engineers on its staff to support customers with metal specifications and interpretation expertise.

Operations
The company distributes processed and unprocessed ferrous and nonferrous metals which are are generally obtained from rolling mills in many forms and distributed from CS&W's warehouses.

Geographic Reach
CS&W is based in Chicago. It has stocking facilities in Cincinnati, Detroit, Milwaukee, Greensboro (North Carolina). Its Central Coil Processing unit is in Portage, Indiana.

Financial Performance
In 2013 CS&W's revenues decreased by 10% due to lower prices caused by excess mill capacity and a 4% drop in tons shipped caused by lower net sales.

The company's net income decreased by 79% that year primarily due to a decline in revenues.

CS&W's operating cash inflow increased to $11 million (compared to $10 million in 2012) due to cash generated from inventories and receivables.

Strategy
In 2013 the company launched a new web based material test reporting feature, increasing its ability to service customers more efficiently through an additional channel when material certifications are required.

Company Background
In 2011 CS&W added pre-painted steel and aluminum coil to its full-line inventory of metal products. The pre-paint program includes material stocked and processed to customer specific specifications for next day delivery. The main intent of this expansion is to develop inventory management programs to reduce total costs and support short-dated delivery requirements.

CS&W was founded in 1909. The company is majority-owned by a trust set up by a former chairman, the late James Lowenstein.

LOCATIONS

HQ: CENTRAL STEEL AND WIRE COMPANY, LLC
3000 W 51ST ST, CHICAGO, IL 606322198
Phone: 773 471-3800
Web: WWW.CENTRALSTEEL.COM

PRODUCTS/OPERATIONS

Selected Products
Alloy bars
Aluminum
Bar and structural shapes
Brass and copper
CF bars/flat wire
Grating/Morton products
HR bars
Steel plates
Steel sheets/strapping
Stainless steel
Steel tubing/pipe
Wire/drill rod/tool steel

Selected Processing Capabilities
Angle Rings
Annealing
Annodizing
Band Saw Cutting
Beam Splitting
Blanking
Burning - Oxyfuel
Centerless Grinding
Circle Shearing
CNC Laser Cutting
CNC Plasma Cutting
CNC Punching
CNC Waterjet Cutting
Coil Blanking
Coil Cut To Length
Cold Sawing Bar
Cold Sawing Plate
Contour Sawing
Deep Hole Drilling
Drilling & Tapping
F&D Heads
Facing & Centering
Forming
Galvanizing
Grinding
Heat Treating
Honing
Lathe Cut Tube/Pipe
Machining
Mech Descale and Oil
Miter Cutting
Normalizing
Painting
Perforating
Pickling & Oiling
Plate and Struct Rolling
Plating
Polishing
Precision Plasma
Precision Sawing
Protex Covering
Sand/Shot Blasting
SCS Finishing
Seam Planishing
Seam Welding
Shearing
Slitting
Straightening
Stress Relieving
Struct Fabrication
Threading
Tube/Pipe Fabrication
Tumble Deburring
Ultrasonic Testing
Welding
Wire Brush Deburr

COMPETITORS

AMPCO-PITTSBURGH CORPORATION
BEKAERT CORPORATION
DAYTON SUPERIOR CORPORATION
INSTEEL INDUSTRIES, INC.
KAISER ALUMINUM CORPORATION
MASTER-HALCO, INC.
OLYMPIC STEEL, INC.
SUNCOAST POST-TENSION, LTD.
THE HEICO COMPANIES L L C
voestalpine Wire Rod Austria GmbH

HISTORICAL FINANCIALS

Company Type: Private

Income Statement — FYE: December 31

	REVENUE ($mil)	NET INCOME ($mil)	NET PROFIT MARGIN	EMPLOYEES
12/14	698	(2)	—	1,075
12/13	678	2	0.3%	—
12/12	750	10	1.4%	—
Annual Growth	(3.6%)	—	—	—

2014 Year-End Financials
Return on assets: (-1.3%)   Cash ($ mil.): 28
Return on equity: (-1.8%)
Current Ratio: 7.10

CERTCO, INC.

Certco has built a business serving about 200 independent grocers in Minnesota, Wisconsin, Iowa, and Illinois. The food distribution cooperative offers customers an inventory of more than 57,000 items, including bakery goods, frozen foods, meat products, produce, and general merchandise. It distributes products under the Shurfine, Shurfresh, and Top Care labels. Additionally, Certco offers its member-operators such services as advertising, accounting, client data services, warehousing, merchandising, store planning and design, and other business support services. The cooperative was founded in 1930 as Central Wisconsin Cooperative Food Stores.

Operations
To support its business, Certco operates a nearly 1 million-sq.-ft. distribution center. Its brands include Shurfine, Shurfresh, Value Time, Full Circle, Topco, and Top Care.

Geographic Reach
Based in Madison, Wisconsin, Certco operates in Minnesota and Wisconsin, with an extended reach into parts of Iowa and Illinois.

Sales and Marketing
Many of Certco's clients are Fortune 500 companies. It distributes the national brands of major companies, such as Kraft, General Mills, Procter & Gamble, and Johnson & Johnson. The company also distributes specialty items under the names Amy's, Hodgson Mills, Bob's Red Mill, and Annie's, that are only available through direct-store-delivery suppliers.

Company Background
Certco was established in 1930 when five Madison-area retailers formed an alliance to boost their combined purchasing muscle.

Auditors: SATTELL JOHNSON APPEL & CO

LOCATIONS

HQ: CERTCO, INC.
5321 VERONA RD, FITCHBURG, WI 537116050
Phone: 608 271-4500
Web: WWW.CERTCOINC.COM

PRODUCTS/OPERATIONS

Selected Brands
Full Circle
Shurfine
Shurfresh
Top Care
Topco
Value Time

Selected Services
Advertising
Client data services
Retail accounting
Retail meetings/seminars
Retail support
Retail technology
Store planning & design
Trade shows
Value added services
Warehouses
Web architecture

COMPETITORS

ASSOCIATED GROCERS OF FLORIDA, INC.
BOZZUTO'S, INC.
CJ LOGISTICS AMERICA, LLC
CONSUMER PRODUCT DISTRIBUTORS, LLC
DOT FOODS, INC.
LAUREL GROCERY COMPANY LLC
THE HOME CITY ICE COMPANY
UNIFIED GROCERS, INC.
UNITED HARDWARE DISTRIBUTING COMPANY
URM STORES, INC.

HISTORICAL FINANCIALS

Company Type: Private

Income Statement — FYE: April 30

	REVENUE ($mil)	NET INCOME ($mil)	NET PROFIT MARGIN	EMPLOYEES
04/22	980	4	0.5%	325
04/14	640	5	0.9%	—
04/13	607	5	0.9%	—
04/12	1,027	0	0.0%	—
Annual Growth	(0.5%)	187.4%	—	—

2022 Year-End Financials
Return on assets: 3.1%   Cash ($ mil.): 27
Return on equity: 4.8%
Current Ratio: 2.00

CFJ PROPERTIES LLC

EXECUTIVES

Executive Committee Member*, Andre Lortz
Executive Committee Member*, Richard D Peterson

Auditors: KPMG LLP SALT LAKE CITY UTAH

LOCATIONS

HQ: CFJ PROPERTIES LLC
  5508 LONAS DR, KNOXVILLE, TN 379093221
Phone: 801 624-1000
Web: WWW.PILOTFLYINGJ.COM

HISTORICAL FINANCIALS
Company Type: Private

Income Statement — FYE: January 31

	REVENUE ($mil)	NET INCOME ($mil)	NET PROFIT MARGIN	EMPLOYEES
01/09	7,672	157	2.1%	6,250
01/07	6,769	50	0.7%	—
01/06	6,166	48	0.8%	—
Annual Growth	7.6%	47.7%	—	—

2009 Year-End Financials
Return on assets: 18.7%   Cash ($ mil.): 37
Return on equity: 47.1%
Current Ratio: 0.60

CGB ENTERPRISES, INC.

CGB Enterprises is a leader in the grain and transportation industries. Located in Louisiana, the agricultural company provides US farmers with a range of services, including grain handling, storage, lending, and merchandising. It offers inland grain transportation by barge, rail, and truck and also markets and sells seeds, agricultural products, and insurance. CGB's Consolidated Terminals and Logistics Co. (CTLC) subsidiary provides transportation, logistics, and bulk commodity services for both agricultural and non-agricultural customers. The company operates more than 125 locations across the US. Japanese trading conglomerates ITOCHU and ZEN-NOH own CGB.

Operations
CGB Enterprises provides an array of services for grain farmers, from buying, storing, selling and shipping of agricultural products, to global supply chain solutions.

The company operates an enterprise overseeing a diverse family of businesses that provide an array of services for producers and logistics services.

CGB's divisions include Consolidated Grain and Barge Co., AgriFinancial (services more than $2 billion in loans and leases for agricultural producers across the country), Diversified Services, Soybean Processing, CTLC, CGB Marine (an operating business unit under the CTLC division directly involved in more than 10,000 barge loads of cargo annually), Feed Ingredients (source Dried Distiller's Grains (DDGs) and other feed ingredients for export and domestic markets), and Container Shipping.

Geographic Reach
From its headquarters in the city of Covington, Louisiana, CGB operates its business through more than 125 locations nationwide, including over 125 grain facilities. CGB Marine has facilities located on the Lower Mississippi River near the Gulf of Mexico, the St. Louis Harbor, Cairo, and various other locations on the Mississippi, the Ohio, and the Illinois Rivers.

Sales and Marketing
Besides its core services of inland grain transportation via barge, rail, and truck, CGB markets and sells its products beyond the agricultural industry. Its Soybean Processing provides high quality soybean products to a global base of meal and oil customers. Its Trucking business serves multiple industries such as wine, beer and spirits, agribusiness, food and beverage, and plastics and packaging, among others.

Mergers and Acquisitions
In late 2021, Consolidated Grain and Barge Co., a wholly-owned subsidiary of CGB Enterprises acquired Agspring Logistics' business assets operated under the trade name Agforce Transport Services (Agforce). "The acquisition of Agforce business assets is a complement to our existing freight transportation company, River Bend Brokerage, and to our overall strategic business portfolio. We are excited to welcome new team members to CGB and to begin servicing a new customer base through expanded supply chain services," said Hector Orellana, Senior Director of Inland Terminals and River Bend Brokerage at CGB. Terms of the agreement were not disclosed.

EXECUTIVES
OF, Michael T Merkel
GA Division President, Gregory A Beck V
SOYBEAN PROCESSING, Stephen B O'nan
Auditors : KPMG LLP NEW ORLEANS LOUISI

LOCATIONS
HQ: CGB ENTERPRISES, INC.
  1127 HWY 190 E SERVICE RD, COVINGTON, LA 704334929
Phone: 985 867-3500
Web: WWW.CGB.COM

PRODUCTS/OPERATIONS
Selected Business Units
Feed Ingredients
Fertilizer
Financial Services
Grain
Marine
Premium Grains
Risk Management
Soybean Processing
Terminals & Logistics

COMPETITORS
A&R LOGISTICS, INC.
AMERICAN COMMERCIAL LINES, INC.
ASH GROVE CEMENT COMPANY
BARTLETT AGRI ENTERPRISES, INC.
CONTANDA LLC
FLEETPRIDE, INC.
GRAINCORP LIMITED
J. D. HEISKELL HOLDINGS, LLC
MFA INCORPORATED
OMNITRAX, INC.

HISTORICAL FINANCIALS
Company Type: Private

Income Statement — FYE: May 31

	REVENUE ($mil)	NET INCOME ($mil)	NET PROFIT MARGIN	EMPLOYEES
05/21	7,081	116	1.6%	3,250
05/20	5,955	50	0.8%	—
05/19	6,498	67	1.0%	—
05/18	6,801	110	1.6%	—
Annual Growth	1.4%	1.8%	—	—

2021 Year-End Financials
Return on assets: 4.9%   Cash ($ mil.): 251
Return on equity: 20.0%
Current Ratio: 1.00

CHALMETTE REFINING, L.L.C.

LOCATIONS
HQ: CHALMETTE REFINING, L.L.C.
  500 W SAINT BERNARD HWY, CHALMETTE, LA 700434821
Phone: 504 281-1212
Web: WWW.CHALMETTEREFINING.COM

HISTORICAL FINANCIALS
Company Type: Private

Income Statement — FYE: December 31

	REVENUE ($mil)	NET INCOME ($mil)	NET PROFIT MARGIN	EMPLOYEES
12/07	5,647	364	6.4%	600
12/06	5,020	423	8.4%	—
12/05	3,462	264	7.6%	—
12/04	3,130	221	7.1%	—
Annual Growth	21.7%	18.1%	—	—

2007 Year-End Financials
Return on assets: —   Cash ($ mil.): 302
Return on equity: 6.4%
Current Ratio: 0.50

CHARLESTON AREA MEDICAL CENTER, INC.

CAMC Health System is a catalyst for care in Charleston. The health network includes flagship facility Charleston Area Medical Center (CAMC), which is the largest hospital in West Virginia and consists of three campuses with some 840 beds total. The system also includes the CAMC Health Education and Research Institute, which coordinates education programs for medical students from West Virginia University. In addition, the health system operates smaller rural hospital CAMC Teays Valley and several urgent care and family practice clinics. CAMC Health System operates an online medical information system and physician services company Integrated Health Care Providers.

Operations

The three campuses of CAMC include CAMC General Hospital, CAMC Memorial Hospital, and CAMC Women and Children's Hospital, all of which are located in Charleston. Specialty services at the hospitals include cardiology, kidney transplants, trauma, and pediatrics. The CAMC Institute conducts graduate and continuing education courses; it also connects education and health care through clinical research projects in areas such as cancer and cardiovascular clinical science studies. The Teays Valley Hospital is a 70-bed facility located in nearby Hurricane, West Virginia.

CAMC General Hospital is home to the highest level Trauma Center, nationally-accredited Medical Rehabilitation and Stroke Centers, The Center for Joint Replacement, Neurosciences Center, one of two Facial Surgery Centers, Charleston's only accredited Sleep Center, and West Virginia's only kidney transplant program, affiliated with the Cleveland Clinic.

CAMC Memorial Hospital hosts one of highest volume heart programs in the US, which performs 8,000 procedures in the cardiac catheterization labs and more than 1,600 open-heart bypass surgeries a year.

CAMC Women and Children's Hospital facilitates the birth of more than 3,000 babies (including many high-risk births) per year.

Teays Valley Hospital is a not-for-profit, 70-bed hospital. More than 100 doctors are authorized to practice at the hospital.

CAMC serves as a clinical training site for 700 additional learners per year through educational affiliations with regional colleges and universities.

Sales and Marketing

Commercial insurance providers and other third parties accounted for more than half of CAMC's net patient revenue in 2013; Medicare and Medicaid account for 30% and 13%, respectively.

Financial Performance

The company's revenue grew by 4% to $969 million in 2013 due to higher net patient revenues and investment income. Net income fell 8% to $86 million, though, as expenses including salaries and employee benefits rose. Cash flow from operations dropped 48% to $33 million, both as a result of the lower net income and an increase in cash used in short-term trading investments.

Strategy

In 2013 CAMC teamed up with The Ohio State University, University of Michigan, and West Virginia University to raise awareness and educate the community about cervical cancer. Community Awareness Resources and Education (CARE) is one of OSU Cancer Center's programs sponsored by the National Cancer Institute that focuses on an important health disparity among an underserved Appalachian population.

The following year, CAMC teamed with Alliance Oncology, a division of Alliance HealthCare Services, to work on establishing a department of radiation therapy at CAMC Cancer Center.

Upgrading its infrastructure, in 2013 Teays Valley Hospital completed a $3.7 million ICU expansion project.

Auditors: DELOITTE TAX LLP CHICAGO IL

LOCATIONS

HQ: CHARLESTON AREA MEDICAL CENTER, INC.
  501 MORRIS ST, CHARLESTON, WV 253011326
Phone: 304 348-5432
Web: WWW.CAMC.ORG

PRODUCTS/OPERATIONS

2013 Net Patient Revenue

	% of total
Commercial insurance & other third-party payment programs	51
Medicare	30
Medicaid	13
Self-pay	1
PEIA	5
Total	100

2013 Sales

	$ mil	% of total
Net patient revenue less provision for bad debts	876.2	91
Investment income	49.8	5
Other revenue	41.0	4
Net assets released from restrictions	1.8	-
Total	968.8	100

Selected Service Areas
Behavioral health
Cancer
Cardiac
Children's medicine
Craniofacial surgery
Endoscopy
Fertility
Gynecology
Hemophilia
Kidney transplant
Orthopedics
Palliative care
Perinatal
Plastic surgery
Stroke
Trauma
Urology
Vascular

COMPETITORS

KALEIDA HEALTH
NORTHWELL HEALTH, INC.
ORLANDO HEALTH, INC.
THE PENNSYLVANIA HOSPITAL OF THE UNIVERSITY OF PENNSYLVANIA HEALTH SYSTEM
WELLMONT HEALTH SYSTEM

HISTORICAL FINANCIALS

Company Type: Private

Income Statement — FYE: December 31

	REVENUE ($mil)	NET INCOME ($mil)	NET PROFIT MARGIN	EMPLOYEES
12/20	2,439	1,236	50.7%	4,000
12/19	1,273	40	3.2%	—
12/16	1,044	(17)	—	—
12/15	932	36	4.0%	—
Annual Growth	21.2%	101.8%	—	—

2020 Year-End Financials
Return on assets: 84.1%   Cash ($ mil.): 39
Return on equity: 164.6%
Current Ratio: 2.20

CHARTER MANUFACTURING COMPANY, INC.

Charter Manufacturing's magna carta calls for it to make steel products. The family-owned company manufactures such steel products as special bar quality (SBQ) bar, rod, wire, and stainless steel rod. The company also supplies precision cold-rolled custom profiles and engineered components, including driveline, engine, and transmission parts, for the automotive industry. It operates primarily in the US, but also in Europe and Asia through subsidiaries Charter Steel (general steel products), Charter Wire (precision, cold-rolled custom profiles, flat wire and standard shapes), Charter Dura-Bar (cast iron bar and bronze alloys), and Charter Automotive (engineered components for automotive applications).

Operations

The company manufactures special bar quality bar, rod, and wire, as well as precision cold-rolled custom profiles, flat wire and standard shapes, and engineered components for use in engines, transmissions and drivelines. Charter Steel is an integrated producer of special bar quality bar, rod and wire products has an annual coil-making capacity of 1.2 million tons; Charter Dura-Bar is a leading producer of continuous cast iron bar stock and a distributor (through Dura-Bar Metal Services) of Dura-Bar products and bronze alloys; Charter Wire supplies precision, cold-rolled custom profiles, flat wire, and standard shapes; while Charter Automotive supplies of engineered components for engine, driveline, and transmission applications.

Geographic Reach

Charter Manufacturing serves customers around the world and has plants in the US (Illinois, North Carolina, Ohio, Pennsylvania, and Wisconsin), China (one plant), and the UK (two plants).

Sales and Marketing

Charter Manufacturing sells its products through its operating subsidiaries and sales representatives.

Strategy

The company is looking to expand both geographically and in terms of product offerings. Growing its global footprint, in 2012 the company expanded its European operations with the purchase of a 57,000 sq.-ft. manufacturing plant in Burntwood, UK. The expansion strengthens Charter Automotive's position as a global supplier to OEM automotive and powertrain industries and helps it meet the growing demands of customers in Europe and elsewhere.

Mergers and Acquisitions

In 2012 the company acquired Wells Manufacturing Company (owner of Dura-Bar and DuraBar Metal Services). The acquired assets (which added a fourth division to Charter Manufacturing's family of companies -- Charter Dura-Bar) focus on producing specialty iron bar and distributing bronze alloy products.

Company Background

Facing tough market conditions, Charter Automotive closed part of its steelmaking operations in Milwaukee, Wisconsin in 2010. The company ceased making steel dipsticks and tubes for cars and trucks as part of a wider response to global market trends. The company, which kept its engine components operations elsewhere in Milwaukee active, sold the Heather Avenue plant idled by this move.

Charter Manufacturing was established in 1936 and is owned by the family of founder Alfred Mellowes.

Auditors: DELOITTE & TOUCHE LLP MILWAU

LOCATIONS

HQ: CHARTER MANUFACTURING COMPANY, INC.
12121 CORPORATE PKWY, MEQUON, WI 530923332
Phone: 262 243-4700
Web: WWW.CHARTERMFG.COM

PRODUCTS/OPERATIONS

Selected Operating Units
Charter Automotive
Charter Dura-Bar
Charter Steel
Charter Wire

Selected Mergers and Acquisitions
2012
Wells Manufacturing Company (owner of Dura-Bar--specialty iron bar, and DuraBar Metal Services--bronze alloys)

COMPETITORS

A. FINKL & SONS CO.
CALIFORNIA STEEL INDUSTRIES, INC.
HEIDTMAN STEEL PRODUCTS, INC.
HITCHINER MANUFACTURING CO., INC.
KEYSTONE CONSOLIDATED INDUSTRIES, INC.
REPUBLIC STEEL
STEEL TECHNOLOGIES LLC
Samuel, Son & Co., Limited
ThyssenKrupp Steel Europe AG
Wugang Group Co., Ltd.

HISTORICAL FINANCIALS

Company Type: Private

Income Statement — FYE: December 31

	REVENUE ($mil)	NET INCOME ($mil)	NET PROFIT MARGIN	EMPLOYEES
12/10	903	74	8.3%	2,000
12/09	517	2	0.4%	—
12/08	996	26	2.7%	—
Annual Growth	(4.8%)	66.8%	—	—

2010 Year-End Financials
Return on assets: 14.4%   Cash ($ mil.): 85
Return on equity: 24.7%
Current Ratio: 1.60

CHEMIUM INTERNATIONAL CORP.

LOCATIONS

HQ: CHEMIUM INTERNATIONAL CORP.
3773 RICHMOND AVE STE 600, HOUSTON, TX 770463725
Phone: 713 622-7766
Web: WWW.CHEMIUMCORP.COM

HISTORICAL FINANCIALS

Company Type: Private

Income Statement — FYE: December 31

	REVENUE ($mil)	NET INCOME ($mil)	NET PROFIT MARGIN	EMPLOYEES
12/15	2,015	3	0.2%	24
12/06	450	3	0.9%	—
12/03	103	0	0.0%	—
Annual Growth	28.1%	—	—	—

2015 Year-End Financials
Return on assets: 2.9%   Cash ($ mil.): 5
Return on equity: 0.2%
Current Ratio: 0.80

CHENEGA CORPORATION

An Alaska Native Corporation, Chenega Corporation has gone from landowner to business titan. Representing the Chenega people residing in the central Alaskan Prince William Sound region, it operates mostly through its subsidiaries. Chenega Integrated Systems and Chenega Technology Services offer information technology, security training, manufacturing, research and development, network engineering, and military operation support services. Chenega Corporation's clients have included the Department of Defense, Department of Homeland Security and EPA.

Geographic Reach

The company's headquarters are located in Anchorage, Alaska. Chenega Corporation and its subsidiaries operate in 45 states and 11 countries.

Strategy

Government contracts are a source of revenue growth. Chenega Corporation began to participate in the Government Services marketplace in 1997. By 2012 it was performing on more than 158 prime contracts and 100 principal sub-contracts, through a combination of competitive and negotiated best-value awards.

LOCATIONS

HQ: CHENEGA CORPORATION
3000 C ST STE 301, ANCHORAGE, AK 995033975
Phone: 907 277-5706
Web: WWW.CHENEGA.COM

PRODUCTS/OPERATIONS

Selected Services
Base operations and maintenance
Environmental management
Information technology
Intel and military operations
Light manufacturing
Logistics support
Telecommunications
Tourism and hospitality
Training services
Security services

COMPETITORS

ARCADIS U.S., INC.
CHOICE HOTELS INTERNATIONAL, INC.
CIVEO U.S. HOLDINGS LLC
DIAMOND RESORTS HOLDINGS, LLC
DYNAMICS RESEARCH CORPORATION
GOLDBERG LINDSAY & CO. LLC
INTERNATIONAL ENTERTAINMENT CORPORATION
LOWE ENTERPRISES, INC.
OXFORD DEVELOPMENT COMPANY
PC SPECIALISTS, INC.

HISTORICAL FINANCIALS

Company Type: Private

Income Statement — FYE: September 30

	REVENUE ($mil)	NET INCOME ($mil)	NET PROFIT MARGIN	EMPLOYEES
09/20	948	19	2.0%	4,500
09/19	871	19	2.3%	—
09/18	829	19	2.3%	—
09/17	875	12	1.4%	—
Annual Growth	2.7%	16.7%	—	—

2020 Year-End Financials
Return on assets: 4.5%   Cash ($ mil.): 48
Return on equity: 8.1%
Current Ratio: 1.90

CHEROKEE NATION BUSINESSES LLC

Auditors: BKD LLP TULSA OKLAHOMA

LOCATIONS

HQ: CHEROKEE NATION BUSINESSES LLC
777 W CHEROKEE ST, CATOOSA, OK 740153235
Phone: 918 384-7474
Web: WWW.CHEROKEENATIONBUSINESSES.COM

HISTORICAL FINANCIALS
Company Type: Private

Income Statement — FYE: September 30

	REVENUE ($mil)	NET INCOME ($mil)	NET PROFIT MARGIN	EMPLOYEES
09/21	1,964	254	13.0%	3,117
09/19	1,183	48	4.1%	—
09/18	1,098	65	5.9%	—
09/17	1,018	40	4.0%	—
Annual Growth	17.8%	58.4%	—	—

2021 Year-End Financials
Return on assets: 16.6%   Cash ($ mil.): 643
Return on equity: 21.9%
Current Ratio: 2.40

CHEROKEE NATION ENTERTAINMENT, LLC

Auditors: BKD LLP TULSA OK

LOCATIONS

HQ: CHEROKEE NATION ENTERTAINMENT, LLC
777 W CHEROKEE ST, CATOOSA, OK 740153235
Phone: 918 384-7800
Web: WWW.CHEROKEECASINO.COM

HISTORICAL FINANCIALS
Company Type: Private

Income Statement — FYE: September 30

	REVENUE ($mil)	NET INCOME ($mil)	NET PROFIT MARGIN	EMPLOYEES
09/19	686	(14)	—	3,100
09/17	666	25	3.9%	—
Annual Growth	1.5%	—	—	—

2019 Year-End Financials
Return on assets: (-1.9%)   Cash ($ mil.): 55
Return on equity: (-2.1%)
Current Ratio: 2.30

CHEVRON PHILLIPS CHEMICAL COMPANY LLC

Chevron Phillips Chemical (CPChem) is one of the top suppliers of polyethylene in the world today. It produces high-density (HDPE), medium-density (MDPE), low-density (LDPE), linear low-density (LLDPE), metallocene and masterbatches for a wide range of applications ? including pressure pipe, soap and detergent bottles, flexible packaging, coating and laminations, films, and more. Chevron Phillips Chemical also produces aromatics such as benzene and styrene, specialty chemicals for dozens of applications, from aerosols and fluid additives to textiles and water treatment products. CPChem is 50% owned by Chevron USA Inc., an indirect wholly-owned subsidiary of Chevron Corporation, and 50% by wholly-owned subsidiaries of Phillips 66.

Operations
CPChem is a leading global producer of olefins and a major supplier of aromatics, alpha olefins, styrenics, specialty chemicals, as well as piping material and other proprietary plastics. It is the Western Hemisphere's largest producer of high-density polyethylene -- used in automotive, film, coating and laminating, packaging, and sheet extrusions. CPChem also is near the top in styrene, ethylene, and aromatics production.

CPChem has several petrochemical joint ventures in the Middle East, including Saudi Chevron Phillips Company (50%) and Qatar Chemical Company (not quite 50%). Subsidiary Chevron Oronite produces fuel additives.

The company's chemical products are used in more than 70,000 consumer and industrial products.

Geographic Reach
Headquartered in The Woodlands, Texas, CPChem operates administrative offices in Singapore, Australia, China, Dubai Germany, Italy, Japan, Malaysia, Spain, Turley and UK.

Sales and Marketing
The company serves a range of markets, including Automotive, Energy & Chemical, Food & Agriculture, Home & Electronics, Medical & Pharmaceutical, Personal Care, Recreational, and Industrial.

Company Background
A coin toss determined whose name would go first when Chevron and Phillips Petroleum (now Phillips 66) formed 50-50 joint venture Chevron Phillips Chemical Company in 2000.

EXECUTIVES

Care Vice President, Greg G Maxwell Senior
Auditors: ERNST & YOUNG LLP HOUSTON TX

LOCATIONS

HQ: CHEVRON PHILLIPS CHEMICAL COMPANY LLC
10001 SIX PINES DR, THE WOODLANDS, TX 773801498
Phone: 832 813-4100
Web: WWW.CPCHEM.COM

PRODUCTS/OPERATIONS

Selected Products
Olefins and polyolefins
   Ethylene
   Polyethylene
   Polyethylene pipe
   Polypropylene
   Propylene
Aromatics and styrenics
   Benzene
   Cumene
   Cyclohexane
   Paraxylene
   Styrene
Specialty products
   Acetylene black
   Alpha olefins
   Dimethyl sulfide
   Drilling specialty chemicals
   High-purity hydrocarbons and solvents
   Mining chemicals
   Neohexene
   Performance and reference fuels
   Polyalpha olefins
   Polystyrene

Selected Joint Ventures
Americas Styrenics (50%)
Chevron Phillips Singapore Chemicals (Private) Limited (50%)
KR Copolymer, Co., Ltd. (60%, South Korea)
Qatar Chemical Company Ltd. (Q-Chem, 49%)
Saudi Chevron Phillips Company (50%)
Shanghai Golden Phillips Petrochemical Co. Ltd. (40%)

COMPETITORS

CHEVRON CORPORATION
CHEVRON PIPE LINE COMPANY
CHEVRON U.S.A. INC.
EXXON MOBIL CORPORATION
JOHNSON MATTHEY PLC
OXY CHEMICAL CORPORATION
SASOL CHEMICALS (USA) LLC
SHELL OIL COMPANY
TOTAL PETROCHEMICALS & REFINING USA, INC.
UNITED REFINING COMPANY

HISTORICAL FINANCIALS
Company Type: Private

Income Statement — FYE: December 31

	REVENUE ($mil)	NET INCOME ($mil)	NET PROFIT MARGIN	EMPLOYEES
12/16	8,769	1,687	19.2%	6,472
12/15	9,859	2,651	26.9%	—
12/14	14,148	3,288	23.2%	—
Annual Growth	(21.3%)	(28.4%)	—	—

2016 Year-End Financials
Return on assets: 10.9%   Cash ($ mil.): 587
Return on equity: 14.7%
Current Ratio: 1.90

CHEVRON PHILLIPS CHEMICAL COMPANY LP

EXECUTIVES

Parent Chief Executive Officer, Bruce Chinn
Auditors: ERNST & YOUNG LLP HOUSTON T

LOCATIONS

HQ: CHEVRON PHILLIPS CHEMICAL COMPANY LP
10001 SIX PINES DR, THE WOODLANDS, TX 773801498
Phone: 832 813-4100

Web: WWW.CPCHEM.COM

HISTORICAL FINANCIALS
Company Type: Private

Income Statement — FYE: December 31

	REVENUE ($mil)	NET INCOME ($mil)	NET PROFIT MARGIN	EMPLOYEES
12/16	7,106	1,301	18.3%	6,737
12/15	7,990	2,020	25.3%	—
12/14	11,758	2,444	20.8%	—
Annual Growth	(22.3%)	(27.0%)	—	—

2016 Year-End Financials
Return on assets: 11.1%   Cash ($ mil.): 422
Return on equity: 13.5%
Current Ratio: 1.30

CHG FOUNDATION

Auditors: MOSS ADAMS LLP LOS ANGELES C

LOCATIONS
HQ: CHG FOUNDATION
740 BAY BLVD, CHULA VISTA, CA 919105254
Phone: 619 422-0422
Web: WWW.CHGSD.COM

HISTORICAL FINANCIALS
Company Type: Private

Income Statement — FYE: December 31

	REVENUE ($mil)	NET INCOME ($mil)	NET PROFIT MARGIN	EMPLOYEES
12/19	943	(25)	—	372
12/16	1,098	206	18.8%	—
12/14	622	34	5.5%	—
12/13	323	(11)	—	—
Annual Growth	19.5%	—	—	—

2019 Year-End Financials
Return on assets: (-4.1%)   Cash ($ mil.): 460
Return on equity: (-5.7%)
Current Ratio: 4.20

CHI ST. LUKE'S HEALTH BAYLOR COLLEGE OF MEDICINE MEDICAL CENTER CONDOMINIUM ASSOCIATION

Auditors: LB CATHOLIC HEALTH INIATNES E

LOCATIONS
HQ: CHI ST. LUKE'S HEALTH BAYLOR COLLEGE OF MEDICINE MEDICAL CENTER CONDOMINIUM ASSOCIATION
6720 BERTNER AVE, HOUSTON, TX 770302604
Phone: 832 355-1000
Web: WWW.STLUKESHEALTH.ORG

HISTORICAL FINANCIALS
Company Type: Private

Income Statement — FYE: June 30

	REVENUE ($mil)	NET INCOME ($mil)	NET PROFIT MARGIN	EMPLOYEES
06/21	1,041	(17)	—	6,000
06/20	972	(29)	—	—
06/15*	15	(4)	—	—
12/08	1,078	1,155	107.2%	—
Annual Growth	(0.3%)	—	—	—

*Fiscal year change

2021 Year-End Financials
Return on assets: (-1.6%)   Cash ($ mil.): 6
Return on equity: (-2.5%)
Current Ratio: 1.70

CHICAGO COMMUNITY TRUST

You can trust this group to do the giving thing. The Chicago Community Trust gave more than $105 million in 2008 to not-for-profit organizations, such as social services agencies, schools, health centers, museums, and theaters in the Chicago area. The grant program targets groups working in arts and culture, basic human needs, community development, education, and health. Past projects have included after-school programs for impoverished children, funding a senior citizens center, and health services for people with AIDS. Chicago Community Trust gets its funds from corporate and private donations. It was founded in 1915.

Auditors: IT RSM US LLP CHICAGO IL

LOCATIONS
HQ: CHICAGO COMMUNITY TRUST
33 S STATE ST STE 700, CHICAGO, IL 606032809
Phone: 312 616-8000
Web: WWW.CCT.ORG

COMPETITORS
BOYS & GIRLS CLUBS OF AMERICA
COOPERATIVE FOR ASSISTANCE AND RELIEF EVERYWHERE, INC. (CARE)
JUNIOR ACHIEVEMENT USA
THE ASSOCIATION OF JUNIOR LEAGUES INTERNATIONAL, INC.
THE INTERNATIONAL ASSOCIATION OF LIONS CLUBS INCORPORATED

HISTORICAL FINANCIALS
Company Type: Private

Income Statement — FYE: September 30

	REVENUE ($mil)	NET INCOME ($mil)	NET PROFIT MARGIN	EMPLOYEES
09/19	564	194	34.4%	100
09/16	389	135	34.8%	—
09/15	363	136	37.5%	—
09/14	291	105	36.3%	—
Annual Growth	14.1%	12.9%	—	—

2019 Year-End Financials
Return on assets: 6.0%   Cash ($ mil.): 17
Return on equity: 6.1%
Current Ratio: 1.00

CHICAGO PARK DISTRICT

EXECUTIVES
General*, David Doig

LOCATIONS
HQ: CHICAGO PARK DISTRICT
541 N FAIRBANKS CT # 300, CHICAGO, IL 606113653
Phone: 312 742-7529
Web: WWW.CHICAGOPARKDISTRICT.COM

HISTORICAL FINANCIALS
Company Type: Private

Income Statement — FYE: December 31

	REVENUE ($mil)	NET INCOME ($mil)	NET PROFIT MARGIN	EMPLOYEES
12/21	551	37	6.7%	3,100
12/20	449	20	4.5%	—
12/19	501	(46)	—	—
12/18	504	(9)	—	—
Annual Growth	3.0%	—	—	—

2021 Year-End Financials
Return on assets: 1.2%   Cash ($ mil.): 266
Return on equity: —
Current Ratio: —

CHILDREN'S HEALTH CARE

Children's Hospitals and Clinics of Minnesota (also known as Children's Minnesota) is one of the largest pediatric health organizations in the US, with two full-service hospital campuses in St. Paul, and Minneapolis, as well as a number of specialty clinics in the region. It is the only health system and Level I Trauma Center in Minnesota to provide care exclusively to children from before birth through young adulthood. It specializes in diagnosing, treating, and researching diseases that afflict babies and children, including epilepsy, diabetes, cancers, and cystic fibrosis. Children's Minnesota is a member of Children's Health Network, Minnesota's largest pediatric health collaborative.

Operations
Children's Minnesota reports some 391,100 outpatient visits; more than 20,520 surgical procedures; and 75,900 rehabilitation visits. Overall, Children's Minnesota generates some 95% of revenue from patient care reimbursement.

Geographic Reach
In addition to its two full-service hospitals in St. Paul, and Minneapolis, Children's Minnesota has nine primary and specialty care clinics and six rehab sites in Maple Grove, Minnetonka, Roseville, and Woodbury, Minnesota.

Financial Performance
The company generates around $977.9 million annually.

Company Background
The prolonged downturn in the economy in the late 2000s and resultant increase in the use of Medicaid for health coverage combined with cuts to Medicaid funding took a toll on Children's Hospitals and Clinics of Minnesota, forcing the organization to take cost-cutting measures. Still, like the patients it serves, the hospital operator is continuing to grow. At its hospital in Minneapolis it recently completed a three-year, multi-million-dollar, 90,000-square-foot expansion that includes a new surgery and cardiovascular center, emergency department, renovated neonatal and pediatric intensive care units, an expansive family resource center and sibling play areas, and an in-hospital Ronald McDonald House, the only such facility in the Upper Midwest. In 2012 the Peter J. King Pediatric Emergency Department debuted on the St. Paul Campus, following the opening of a 12-room Level II Neonatal Intensive Care Unit there.

Children's Hospitals and Clinics of Minnesota was founded in 1924.

EXECUTIVES
Chief Strategy Officer, Carol Koenecke-grant
Senior Vice President Patient Care Service, Caroline Njau
Auditors : DELOITTE TAX LLP MINNEAPOLIS

LOCATIONS
HQ: CHILDREN'S HEALTH CARE
2525 CHICAGO AVE, MINNEAPOLIS, MN 554044518
Phone: 612 813-6000
Web: WWW.CHILDRENSMN.ORG

PRODUCTS/OPERATIONS

Selected Services
Anesthesiology
Apnea
Asthma
Audiology
Behavioral Health
Cancer and Blood Disorders
Cardiovascular Program
Cleft and Craniofacial
Concussion
Cystic Fibrosis
Developmental Pediatrics
Developmental & Rehabilitation Services
Diabetes / Endocrinology
Dietitians
Down Syndrome
Ear, Nose & Throat
Eating Disorders
ECMO
Emergency and Trauma
Epilepsy
Feeding Clinic
Gastroenterology
Genetics Clinic
Gynecology
Home Care
Hospitalist
Immunology
Influenza
Infectious Diseases
Integrative Medicine
Intensive Care (PICU, Intensivists)
Lab and Pathology
Midwest Children's Resource Center
Midwest Fetal Care Center
Neonatal
Nephrology
Neurocutaneous Syndromes Clinic
Neurology
Neurosurgery
Nutrition
Occupational Therapy
Orthopedics
Pain Program
Palliative and Hospice Program
Pharmacy
Primary Care/General Pediatrics
Pulmonary and Respiratory
Radiology
Rehabilitation Services
Rheumatology
Sleep Disorders
Special Diagnostics
Speech-Language Pathology
Surgery
Trauma Program
Vascular Anomalies

COMPETITORS
CHILDREN'S HEALTH CLINICAL OPERATIONS
CHILDREN'S HEALTHCARE OF ATLANTA, INC.
CHILDREN'S HOSPITAL AND HEALTH SYSTEM, INC.
CHILDRENS HOSPITAL & MEDICAL CENTER
COOK CHILDREN'S HEALTH CARE SYSTEM
FROEDTERT MEMORIAL LUTHERAN HOSPITAL, INC.
JOHNS HOPKINS ALL CHILDREN'S HOSPITAL, INC.
SEATTLE CHILDREN'S HOSPITAL
THE CHILDREN'S HOSPITAL OF PHILADELPHIA
VHS CHILDREN'S HOSPITAL OF MICHIGAN, INC.

HISTORICAL FINANCIALS
Company Type: Private

Income Statement — FYE: December 31

	REVENUE ($mil)	NET INCOME ($mil)	NET PROFIT MARGIN	EMPLOYEES
12/20	740	35	4.8%	4,285
12/19	10	2	25.3%	—
12/17	11	2	25.0%	—
12/16	843	55	6.6%	—
Annual Growth	(3.2%)	(10.9%)	—	—

2020 Year-End Financials
Return on assets: 2.2% Cash ($ mil.): 28
Return on equity: 3.3%
Current Ratio: 1.50

CHILDREN'S HOSPITAL

Auditors : GRANT THORNTON LLP MC LEAN V

LOCATIONS
HQ: CHILDREN'S HOSPITAL
111 MICHIGAN AVE NW, WASHINGTON, DC 200102916
Phone: 202 232-0521
Web: WWW.CHILDRENSNATIONAL.ORG

HISTORICAL FINANCIALS
Company Type: Private

Income Statement — FYE: June 30

	REVENUE ($mil)	NET INCOME ($mil)	NET PROFIT MARGIN	EMPLOYEES
06/20	1,276	38	3.0%	6,000
06/15	1,076	118	11.0%	—
06/14	983	43	4.4%	—
Annual Growth	4.4%	(2.1%)	—	—

2020 Year-End Financials
Return on assets: 2.1% Cash ($ mil.): 58
Return on equity: 5.0%
Current Ratio: 0.60

CHILDREN'S HOSPITAL & RESEARCH CENTER AT OAKLAND

Children's Hospital & Research Center at Oakland (operating as Children's Hospital Oakland) does just what its name says, provides medical care for children and performs research to advance the treatment of pediatric diseases. The freestanding hospital has about 190 beds and a staff of some more than 200 hospital-based physicians professionals with more than 30 medical specialties. Its services include orthopedics, neurology, oncology, and cardiology, as well as surgery, trauma, neonatal, and intensive care. Additionally, the hospital operates several satellite outpatient clinics providing general and specialized care. Children's Hospital Oakland also conducts teaching and community outreach programs.

Operations
The organization's research division, Children's Hospital Oakland Research Institute, conducts research programs on transmittable diseases, vaccines, cancer, immune system diseases, diabetes, asthma, and obesity. It receives funding from the National Institutes of Health. The research center has more than 300 scientists working on 150 clinical trials.

Children's Hospital Oakland is a teaching hospital and is one of only two solely designated California Level 1 pediatric trauma centers in the region (and has one of the largest pediatric intensive care units in Northern California).

In 2012 it had 236,877 outpatient visits (of which 46,142 were emergency visits); 10,183 inpatient admissions; and 8,640 surgical cases.

Financial Performance

The hospitals' revenues declined by 6% in 2012 due to a drop in net patient service fees, fundraising, investments, and other revenue sources.

Some 47% of 2012 revenues came from Medi-Cal/California Children's Services and Medicare/Supplemental funds; 36% from other insurance, private insurance (contract and commercial), and self-pay; and 12% from research programs.

Children's Hospital Oakland's net income decreased by 74% in 2012 due to lower revenues and an increase in expenses (including salaries, benefits, supplies and services).

In 2013 the hospital had an annual operating budget of more than $350 million.

Strategy

To boost coverage and resources, in 2014 Children's Hospital Oakland and UCSF's Benioff Children's Hospital (also in the Bay area) formed an affiliation. Together, the hospitals will be among the top ten largest children's health care providers in the US when the new UCSF Benioff Children's Hospital opens in 2015. In 2012 UCSF had 1,230 physicians on staff, including 150 clinicians at its current Benioff Children's Hospital location.

Previously the Oakland hospital held unsuccessful merger talks with Lucile Packard Children's Hospital at Stanford and Sutter Health network.

The hospital is also developing a master plan to maximize the use of existing property and buildings, modernize facilities, and provide individual rooms so that families can stay with their child during hospitalization.

In 2013 the Children's Hospital Oakland's Walnut Creek Campus completed a large-scale expansion, and now include a Sports Medicine Center for Young Athletes and comprehensive Speech and Hearing Center.

Children's Hospital Oakland has had its share of financial troubles over the years. Along with a weak economy, reduced reimbursement rates from both public and private payers and increasing health care costs added to the company's financial losses.

Company Background

In 2011 it received $532.8 million in research funding from the National Institutes of Health.

The hospital's research institute provided 85% of the DNA used for the Human Genome Project.

Children's Hospital Oakland was founded in 1942 and opened for business in 1914.

LOCATIONS

HQ: CHILDREN'S HOSPITAL & RESEARCH CENTER AT OAKLAND
747 52ND ST, OAKLAND, CA 946091809
Phone: 510 428-3000
Web: WWW.UCSFBENIOFFCHILDRENS.ORG

PRODUCTS/OPERATIONS

Selected Services
Anesthesiology
Blood and Marrow Transplant (BMT) Program
Cardiology and Cardiothoracic Surgery
Center for Child Protection (CCP)
Center for the Vulnerable Child (CVC)
Clinical Laboratory Medicine & Pathology
Clinical Nutrition Department
Clinical Pathology Lab
Craniofacial Center
Cryopreservation Lab
Cytogenetics Laboratory
Developmental and Behavioral Pediatrics
Diagnostic Imaging/Radiology
Early Childhood Mental Health
Endocrinology/Diabetes
Family Outreach Clinic
Gastroenterology/Hepatology/Nutrition
Hematology/Oncology
Neonatology
Neuro-Oncology
Neurosurgery
Oncology/Hematology
Ophthalmology
Orthopedics
Otorhinolaryngology
Respiratory Care Services
Speech and Language Center
Sports Medicine Center
Urology

COMPETITORS

CHARLESTON AREA MEDICAL CENTER, INC.
CHILDRENS HOSPITAL & MEDICAL CENTER
KALEIDA HEALTH
NATIONWIDE CHILDREN'S HOSPITAL
THE PENNSYLVANIA HOSPITAL OF THE UNIVERSITY OF PENNSYLVANIA HEALTH SYSTEM

HISTORICAL FINANCIALS

Company Type: Private

Income Statement — FYE: June 30

	REVENUE ($mil)	NET INCOME ($mil)	NET PROFIT MARGIN	EMPLOYEES
06/20	661	(8)	—	2,000
06/15*	178	34	19.5%	—
12/13	541	44	8.3%	—
12/05	313	15	5.0%	—
Annual Growth	5.1%	—	—	—

*Fiscal year change

2020 Year-End Financials
Return on assets: (-1.0%)
Return on equity: (-2.3%)
Current Ratio: 1.70
Cash ($ mil.): 180

CHILDREN'S HOSPITAL COLORADO

Children's Hospital Colorado is a private, nonprofit pediatric healthcare network dedicated to caring for kids at all ages and stages of growth. With more than 3,000 pediatric specialists, the company provides comprehensive pediatric care at its hospital on Anschutz Medical Campus and at several locations throughout the region. Children's Hospital Colorado also operates some 15 satellite locations in and around Denver that specialize in providing children with emergency and specialty care. Its affiliation with the University of Colorado School of Medicine means that its doctors are not only expert clinicians, but also active researchers working toward better ways to care for kids.

Operations

Children's Hospital Colorado's hospital on Anschutz Medical Campus in Aurora was designed and built to enhance its care for kids. Children's Colorado is the only dedicated Level 1 trauma center in its seven-state region, handling the most challenging emergencies. It offers emergency and urgent care at multiple locations as well as numerous specialty care centers and clinics. In addition to these locations, it brings its expertise to doctors and families throughout the Rocky Mountain region with more than 400 outreach clinics every year.

Children's Hospital Colorado also specializes in baby care, bone and joint care, brain and behavior, endocrinology, digestive issues, cancer treatment, fetal care, heart health and respiratory issues.

The health care facility's research initiatives are conducted at the Children's Hospital Colorado Research Institute. Along with its affiliation with the university, the Children's Hospital works with the Pediatric Clinical Translational Research Center to conduct research and clinical trials in a number of fields including cardiology, pulmonology, and psychiatry.

Geographic Reach

Based in Aurora, Colorado, Children's Hospital Colorado operates through some 15 locations.

EXECUTIVES

CSO*, Raphe Schwartz

LOCATIONS

HQ: CHILDREN'S HOSPITAL COLORADO
13123 E 16TH AVE, AURORA, CO 800457106
Phone: 720 777-1234
Web: WWW.CHILDRENSCOLORADO.ORG

Selected Locations
Children's Hospital Colorado Main Campus
Children's Hospital Colorado at Saint Joseph Hospital
Children's Hospital Colorado, KidStreet

Children's Hospital Colorado Orthopedic Care, Centennial
Children's Hospital Colorado Outpatient Specialty Care, Centennial
Children's Hospital Colorado Outpatient Specialty Care, Colorado Springs
Children's Hospital Colorado Outpatient Specialty Care, Parker
Children's Hospital Colorado Therapy Care, Parker
Children's Hospital Colorado Therapy Care, Pueblo
Children's Hospital Colorado, Urgent and Outpatient Specialty Care, Wheat Ridge

PRODUCTS/OPERATIONS

Selected Departments
Adolescent Medicine Program
Adult Congenital Heart Disease Program
Aerodigestive Program
Allergy Program
Arrhythmia Center
Asthma Program
Audiology, Speech and Learning Program
Bill Daniels Center for Children's Hearing
Bone Marrow Transplant Program
Breathing Institute
Burn program
Cardiac Anesthesia
Cardiac Catheterization
Cardiology Clinic
Cardiology Outreach Programs
Cardiomyopathy Program
Center for Cancer and Blood Disorders
Center for Celiac Disease
Child Abuse Services
Child Development Unit
Child Health Clinic
Colorado Fetal Care Center
Colorado Institute for Maternal and Fetal Health
Colorectal and Complex Pelvic Floor Disorders Program
Complex Congenital Heart Disease and Development Clinic
Craniofacial Center
Critical Care
Cystic Fibrosis Research and Care Center
Dental
Dermatology
Digestive Health Institute
Ear, Nose and Throat
Eating Disorder Program
Emergency Department
Endocrinology
Endoscopy Clinic (ATECh)
Experimental Therapeutics Program
Extracorporeal Membrane Oxygenation (ECMO) Program
Eye
Fetal Cardiology Program
Fiberoptic Endoscopic Evaluation of Swallowing (FEES) Clinic
Flight for Life
Gastroenterology
Gastrointestinal Eosinophilic Diseases
Genetics Program
Gynecology
Healthy Expectations Perinatal Mental Health Program
Heart Institute
Heart Surgery
Heart Transplant Program
HOPE Clinic for Cancer Survivors
Hospitalist Services

COMPETITORS
COMMUNITY HOSPITALS OF CENTRAL CALIFORNIA
FROEDTERT MEMORIAL LUTHERAN HOSPITAL, INC.
OHIO VALLEY MEDICAL CENTER, INCORPORATED
PITT COUNTY MEMORIAL HOSPITAL, INCORPORATED
ST. LUKE'S HOSPITAL OF DULUTH
THE CHILDREN'S HOSPITAL CORPORATION
THE CHILDREN'S HOSPITAL OF PHILADELPHIA
THE JAMAICA HOSPITAL
UNIVERSITY OF VIRGINIA MEDICAL CENTER

WINTER HAVEN HOSPITAL, INC.

HISTORICAL FINANCIALS
Company Type: Private

Income Statement — FYE: December 31

	REVENUE ($mil)	NET INCOME ($mil)	NET PROFIT MARGIN	EMPLOYEES
12/19	1,327	63	4.8%	2,200
12/18	1,102	138	12.6%	—
12/17	960	76	8.0%	—
12/16	911	50	5.5%	—
Annual Growth	13.3%	8.0%	—	—

2019 Year-End Financials
Return on assets: 3.1%   Cash ($ mil.): 55
Return on equity: 6.5%
Current Ratio: 0.40

CHILDREN'S HOSPITAL OF ORANGE COUNTY

Auditors: KPMG LLP LOS ANGELES CA

LOCATIONS

HQ: CHILDREN'S HOSPITAL OF ORANGE COUNTY
1201 W LA VETA AVE, ORANGE, CA 928684203
Phone: 714 997-3000
Web: WWW.CHOC.ORG

HISTORICAL FINANCIALS
Company Type: Private

Income Statement — FYE: June 30

	REVENUE ($mil)	NET INCOME ($mil)	NET PROFIT MARGIN	EMPLOYEES
06/20	992	76	7.7%	3,200
06/16	523	10	2.0%	—
06/15	518	20	3.9%	—
06/14	517	(15)	—	—
Annual Growth	11.5%	—	—	—

2020 Year-End Financials
Return on assets: 5.6%   Cash ($ mil.): 497
Return on equity: 11.0%
Current Ratio: 1.20

CHILDREN'S HOSPITAL OF WISCONSIN, INC

EXECUTIVES

CIO*, Michael Jones

Corporate Vice President*, Marge Nienen

LOCATIONS

HQ: CHILDREN'S HOSPITAL OF WISCONSIN, INC
999 N 92ND ST STOP 1, MILWAUKEE, WI 532264876
Phone: 414 266-2000
Web: WWW.CHILDRENSWI.ORG

HISTORICAL FINANCIALS
Company Type: Private

Income Statement — FYE: December 31

	REVENUE ($mil)	NET INCOME ($mil)	NET PROFIT MARGIN	EMPLOYEES
12/13	600	57	9.6%	2,045
12/12	34	(0)	—	—
12/09	588	74	12.7%	—
Annual Growth	0.5%	(6.2%)	—	—

2013 Year-End Financials
Return on assets: 4.1%   Cash ($ mil.): 86
Return on equity: 5.8%
Current Ratio: 3.20

CHILDREN'S MEDICAL CENTER OF DALLAS

Children's Medical Center of Dallas one of the largest and most prestigious pediatric health care providers and the leading pediatric health system in North Texas. Through the academic affiliation with UT Southwestern and leader in life changing treatments, innovative technology and groundbreaking research. Among the campus Children's Health is licensed for around 600 beds, including 490 beds at the main campus in the Southwestern Medical District and over 70 beds at Children's House facility in Dallas. Around 800 patients visits annually for 50 estates around the world. It was founded in 1913 when a group of nurses led by public health nurse May Forster Smith organized the Dallas Baby Camp.

Operations

Children's Medical Center of Dallas has licensed 490 beds for inpatient portion of the hospitals that provides all rooms a place for the family to spend for the night with the child. The hospital has critical care unites 47 bed level IV Neonatal Intensive Care Unit (NICU), Pediatric Intensive Care Unit (PICU), Cardiac Intensive Care Unit and the main campus home for pediatric level I trauma center.

Children's Health's specialty Dallas campus provides surgery center and includes eight operating rooms where outpatient surgical services are provided.

Children's Medical Center of Dallas provides pediatric sickle cell disease program that focus on the prevention of disease complications and management using newest treatment strategies. Children's Medical Center provides Level IV Neonatal Intensive Care Unit (NICU) specifically designed to meet the needs of premature and critically ill newborns. In additions, providing respiratory support to surgical procedures, renowned neonatologists, surgeons, and pediatric sub-specialist from UT Southwestern can care for all neonatal health issues.

Geographic Reach
Children's main hospital campuses are in Dallas (headquarters) and Plano, Texas.

Sales and Marketing
Children's Medical Center of Dallas market its product and services through its website such as specialty care centers recognized pediatric care close to home families offering a wide array of outpatient pediatric specialties outpatient surgery, lab services and rehabilitation, Children's Health Specialty Centers have a wealth of resources under one roof.

Company Background
In the four-year period between 2001 and 2005, the center spent more than $250 million on new construction and expansion projects. It opened a 72-bed Children's Legacy Hospital in nearby Plano in 2008, and in 2009 Children's completed construction of a new $150 million tower on its main Dallas campus to house its heart center, cancer center, and neonatal intensive care unit.

The company was founded in 1913.

LOCATIONS

HQ: CHILDREN'S MEDICAL CENTER OF DALLAS
1935 MEDICAL DISTRICT DR, DALLAS, TX 752357701
Phone: 214 456-7000
Web: WWW.CHILDRENS.COM

Children's Medical Center Selected Locations
Chase Bank Building Specialty Center (Dallas)
Children's Medical Center and Ambulatory Care Pavilion at Legacy (Plano)
Children's Medical Center of Dallas Main Campus
Dallas Ambulatory Care Pavilion
Irving Specialty Center
Mesquite Specialty Center
MyChildren's Primary Care (about 16 locations)
Pediatric Urology Clinic at Rockwall
Southlake Specialty Care Center
Walnut Hill Urology Clinic

PRODUCTS/OPERATIONS

Children's Medical Center Selected Services
Allergy/Immunology/Asthma
Audiology
Cystic fibrosis
Day surgery
Dentistry
Dermatology
Diabetes
Ear/Nose/Throat
Endocrinology
Gastroenterology
General surgery
Genetics/Metabolism
International adoption medicine
Laboratory services
Neurology
Nutrition
Obesity program
Occupational therapy
Ophthalmology
Orthodontics
Orthopaedics
Physical therapy
Plastic Surgery

Pulmonary function lab
Pulmonology
Radiology
Rheumatology
Sickle cell treatment
Sleep disorders
Speech therapy
Trauma
Urology

COMPETITORS
ARKANSAS CHILDREN'S HOSPITAL
CHILDREN'S HEALTHCARE OF ATLANTA, INC.
CHILDREN'S HOSPITAL AND HEALTH SYSTEM, INC.
CHILDRENS HOSPITAL & MEDICAL CENTER
COOK CHILDREN'S HEALTH CARE SYSTEM
JOHNS HOPKINS ALL CHILDREN'S HOSPITAL, INC.
SEATTLE CHILDREN'S HOSPITAL
TEXAS CHILDREN'S HOSPITAL
THE CHILDREN'S HOSPITAL OF PHILADELPHIA
THE CHILDREN'S MERCY HOSPITAL

HISTORICAL FINANCIALS
Company Type: Private

Income Statement — FYE: December 31

	REVENUE ($mil)	NET INCOME ($mil)	NET PROFIT MARGIN	EMPLOYEES
12/15	712	(185)	—	5,318
12/14	1,120	135	12.1%	
12/13	1,111	166	15.0%	
12/08	744	(4)	—	
Annual Growth	(0.6%)	—	—	—

2015 Year-End Financials
Return on assets: (-7.7%)   Cash ($ mil.): 9
Return on equity: (-6.6%)
Current Ratio: 4.70

CHILDRENS HOSPITAL

Auditors: GRANT THORNTON LLP MC LEAN V

LOCATIONS

HQ: CHILDRENS HOSPITAL
1917 C ST NE, WASHINGTON, DC 200026753
Phone: 202 476-5000
Web: WWW.CHILDRENSNATIONAL.ORG

HISTORICAL FINANCIALS
Company Type: Private

Income Statement — FYE: June 30

	REVENUE ($mil)	NET INCOME ($mil)	NET PROFIT MARGIN	EMPLOYEES
06/13	970	24	2.5%	17
06/10	805	66	8.2%	—
Annual Growth	6.4%	(28.3%)	—	—

2013 Year-End Financials
Return on assets: 2.5%   Cash ($ mil.): 59
Return on equity: 6.0%
Current Ratio: 0.50

CHILDRENS HOSPITAL INC

LOCATIONS

HQ: CHILDRENS HOSPITAL INC
1513 4TH AVE S, BIRMINGHAM, AL 352331612
Phone: 205 251-3430
Web: WWW.CHILDRENSAL.ORG

HISTORICAL FINANCIALS
Company Type: Private

Income Statement — FYE: December 31

	REVENUE ($mil)	NET INCOME ($mil)	NET PROFIT MARGIN	EMPLOYEES
12/13	684	47	7.0%	5
12/12	576	34	5.9%	—
Annual Growth	18.7%	39.8%	—	—

2013 Year-End Financials
Return on assets: 5.9%   Cash ($ mil.): 111
Return on equity: 12.3%
Current Ratio: 0.60

CHILDRENS HOSPITAL MEDICAL CENTER OF AKRON

Akron Children's Hospital is the largest pediatric health care system in northeast Ohio. The health system operates through approximately 50 urgent, primary and specialty care locations scattered around the state. Among Children's specialized services are cardiology, orthopedics, rehabilitation, and home care. It added two new pediatric primary care locations: Akron Children's Hospital Pediatrics, East Liverpool, and Akron Children's Health Center, Wooster The main hospital's emergency department treats nearly 70,000 patients each year. With about 16,445 urgent care visits, the health system also has more than 337,245 specialty visits per year. Akron Children's Hospital started as a nursery more than 100 years ago.

Operations
Each year, Akron Children's Hospital sees more than 1 million outpatients, performs about 15,345 surgeries, and admits more than 8,045 inpatients.

Geographic Reach
Akron Children's Hospital is a major teaching facility, affiliated with Northeastern Ohio Medical University and offering nearly a dozen subspecialty fellowship training programs. Children's also runs two children's hospitals, approximately pediatrician offices and some 50 primary and specialty locations.

Sales and Marketing

Medicaid/Medicaid Managed Care payments account for about 55% of gross patient service revenue, while commercial payments account for about 40%. Medicare/other governmental and other account for the remaining.

Strategy

Beyond the tremendous efforts devoted to COVID-19, the company made significant progress advancing its strategic goals in 2020. Akron's Children opened the Portage Health Center and new primary care offices in Lorain County and East Liverpool. The company started construction on a health center in Amherst and are looking forward to expanding access to pediatric care to families in this new region. The company added programs and specialty care services in many areas and set the stage to launch our Centers of Excellence in Spine, Mitochondrial Disease and Vision, which will offer the highest levels of quality care, patient experience and research.

In 2020, there was also a focused spotlight on the inequities that exist within its society and health care systems, bringing renewed urgency to its diversity and inclusion programs.

EXECUTIVES

CAO, Craig Mcghee
Auditors : ERNST & YOUNG LLP CLEVELAND

LOCATIONS

HQ: CHILDRENS HOSPITAL MEDICAL CENTER OF AKRON
  1 PERKINS SQ, AKRON, OH 443081063
Phone: 330 543-1000
Web: WWW.AKRONCHILDRENS.ORG

COMPETITORS

CHILDREN'S HEALTH CLINICAL OPERATIONS
CHILDREN'S HEALTHCARE OF CALIFORNIA
CHILDREN'S HOSPITAL AND HEALTH SYSTEM, INC.
CHILDRENS HOSPITAL LOS ANGELES
JOHNS HOPKINS ALL CHILDREN'S HOSPITAL, INC.
NATIONWIDE CHILDREN'S HOSPITAL
ST. LUKE'S EPISCOPAL-PRESBYTERIAN HOSPITALS
TEXAS CHILDREN'S HOSPITAL
THE CHILDREN'S HOSPITAL OF PHILADELPHIA
THE CHILDREN'S MERCY HOSPITAL

HISTORICAL FINANCIALS
Company Type: Private

Income Statement — FYE: December 31

	REVENUE ($mil)	NET INCOME ($mil)	NET PROFIT MARGIN	EMPLOYEES
12/20	853	95	11.1%	4,763
12/19	1,014	107	10.6%	—
12/14	701	93	13.3%	—
12/13	623	80	13.0%	—
Annual Growth	4.6%	2.3%	—	—

2020 Year-End Financials
Return on assets: 5.2%   Cash ($ mil.): 145
Return on equity: 7.6%
Current Ratio: 1.80

CHINESE HOSPITAL ASSOCIATION

Auditors : MOSS & ADAMS LLP SAN FRANCISC

LOCATIONS

HQ: CHINESE HOSPITAL ASSOCIATION
  845 JACKSON ST, SAN FRANCISCO, CA 941334899
Phone: 415 982-2400
Web: WWW.CHINESEHOSPITAL-SF.ORG

HISTORICAL FINANCIALS
Company Type: Private

Income Statement — FYE: December 31

	REVENUE ($mil)	NET INCOME ($mil)	NET PROFIT MARGIN	EMPLOYEES
12/19	226,958	(10,648)	—	285
12/19	226,958	(10,648)	—	—
12/18	216	(28)	—	—
12/17	123	(11)	—	—
Annual Growth	4180.6%	—	—	—

2019 Year-End Financials
Return on assets: (-2.9%)   Cash ($ mil.): 21,386
Return on equity: (-6.2%)
Current Ratio: 1.10

CHRISTIAN HEALTHCARE MINISTRIES, INC.

LOCATIONS

HQ: CHRISTIAN HEALTHCARE MINISTRIES, INC.
  127 HAZELWOOD AVE, BARBERTON, OH 442031316
Phone: 330 848-1511
Web: WWW.CHMINISTRIES.ORG

HISTORICAL FINANCIALS
Company Type: Private

Income Statement — FYE: December 31

	REVENUE ($mil)	NET INCOME ($mil)	NET PROFIT MARGIN	EMPLOYEES
12/20	633	(3)	—	40
12/16	220	27	12.7%	—
Annual Growth	30.2%	—	—	—

2020 Year-End Financials
Return on assets: (-2.4%)   Cash ($ mil.): 54
Return on equity: (-2.5%)
Current Ratio: 18.10

CHRISTUS NORTHEAST TEXAS HEALTH SYSTEM CORPORATION

EXECUTIVES

CMO, Steve Keuer Md
Auditors : ERNST & YOUNG LLP DALLAS TX

LOCATIONS

HQ: CHRISTUS NORTHEAST TEXAS HEALTH SYSTEM CORPORATION
  800 E DAWSON ST, TYLER, TX 757012036
Phone: 903 593-8441
Web: WWW.CHRISTUSHEALTH.ORG

HISTORICAL FINANCIALS
Company Type: Private

Income Statement — FYE: June 30

	REVENUE ($mil)	NET INCOME ($mil)	NET PROFIT MARGIN	EMPLOYEES
06/17	789	42	5.4%	4,000
06/15	752	48	6.4%	—
Annual Growth	2.5%	(5.6%)	—	—

2017 Year-End Financials
Return on assets: 5.0%   Cash ($ mil.): —
Return on equity: 10.1%
Current Ratio: 1.20

CHRISTUS SANTA ROSA HEALTH CARE CORPORATION

Auditors : ERNST & YOUNG US LLP INDIANAP

LOCATIONS

HQ: CHRISTUS SANTA ROSA HEALTH CARE CORPORATION
  2827 BABCOCK RD, SAN ANTONIO, TX 782294813
Phone: 210 704-2011
Web: WWW.CHRISTUSHEALTH.ORG

HISTORICAL FINANCIALS
Company Type: Private

Income Statement — FYE: June 30

	REVENUE ($mil)	NET INCOME ($mil)	NET PROFIT MARGIN	EMPLOYEES
06/19	702	(12)	—	3,700
06/15	656	(14)	—	—
06/14	635	6	1.1%	—
06/13	612	2	0.4%	—
Annual Growth	2.3%	—	—	—

2019 Year-End Financials
Return on assets: (-2.1%)   Cash ($ mil.): —
Return on equity: (-16.2%)
Current Ratio: 2.50

CHS MCPHERSON REFINERY INC.

Cooperation is a refined art and refining a cooperative art for the National Cooperative Refinery Association (NCRA), which provides its member owners, farm supply cooperatives CHS, GROWMARK, and MFA Oil, with gasoline and diesel fuel through its oil refinery in McPherson, Kansas. The refinery's production rate is 85,000 barrels per day. Fuel from the refinery is allocated to member/owners on the basis of ownership percentages. In addition to the refinery, NCRA owns Jayhawk Pipeline, stakes in two other pipeline companies, and an underground oil storage facility.

Operations
NCRA's logistical system includes 76 trucks. (In 2012 almost 40,000 barrels per day of crude was gathered from more than 6,000 oil wells, mainly in Kansas, and transported to the McPherson refinery by truck.)

The system also includes more than 1,000 miles of pipelines to move crude oil and finished products from its refinery to tanks and terminals. Its Conway, Texas underground storage facility has 1.5 million barrels of refined products capacity. NCRA also has two refined products terminals (in McPherson, Kansas and Council Bluffs, Iowa).

Strategy
The cooperative's primary strategy is to gather oil and gas and make diesel and gasoline to serve it members (and the farms of rural America) while maintaining and upgrading its systems in order to stay competitive with better resourced private sector refining rivals.

In 2011 NCRA announced a $555 million investment to build a new Delayed Coking Unit at its McPherson refinery. The new facility will allow the refiner to process a larger variety of crude oils. It is scheduled to be completed in 2015 and will replace a unit that was built in 1952.

In 2012 the company agreed to pay $700,000 in federal and state penalties to settle violations of environmental laws at its McPherson petroleum refinery and underground storage facility.

Company Background
The enterprise has its origins in 1943, when five regional farm supply cooperatives, tired of wartime fuel shortages, created the NCRA to buy the Globe oil refinery in McPherson, Kansas.

Auditors : PRICEWATERHOUSECOOPERS LLP MI

LOCATIONS
HQ: CHS MCPHERSON REFINERY INC.
 2000 S MAIN ST, MCPHERSON, KS 674609402
Phone: 620 241-2340

COMPETITORS
HEARTLAND EXPRESS, INC.
QUALITY DISTRIBUTION, INC.
RIO VISTA ENERGY PARTNERS L.P.
TFI International Inc
TURNERS (SOHAM) LIMITED

HISTORICAL FINANCIALS
Company Type: Private

Income Statement — FYE: August 31

	REVENUE ($mil)	NET INCOME ($mil)	NET PROFIT MARGIN	EMPLOYEES
08/13	4,081	686	16.8%	700
08/12	4,045	705	17.4%	—
08/11	3,405	378	11.1%	—
Annual Growth	9.5%	34.7%	—	—

2013 Year-End Financials
Return on assets: 32.8%   Cash ($ mil.): 386
Return on equity: 51.0%
Current Ratio: 1.60

CHUGACH ALASKA CORPORATION

At the heart of Chugach Alaska Corporation is a vision of indigenous people running their own businesses on their own land. Chugach Alaska was formed following the activation of the Alaska Native Claims Settlement Act (which was passed by the US Congress in 1971), to provide land management services for the 928,000-acre Chugach region of Alaska. The company derives the bulk of its sales from oil and gas production, mining, commercial timber, and tourist activities that occur in the region and from its engagement in military base construction projects at more than 30 locations in Alaska, the US Pacific Northwest, and the Western Pacific. Chugach Alaska's shareholders consist of Aleut, Eskimo, and Indian natives.

Operations
In 2011 the company's Chugach World Services unit secured a $32 million contract (with the option for an additional $33 million) for housing and maintenance operations at Naval Base Guam and Andersen Air Force Base Guam.

In late 2010 the Chugach Alaska Services unit won a renewal of its existing oil spill prevention and response contract with Alyeska Pipeline Service Company. The new contract to service the Alaska Pipeline runs from 2011 to 2016.

Geographic Reach
With operations in Alaska, the Pacific Northwest, and the Western Pacific, the company has major offices in Alabama, Alaska, Hawaii, and Nevada.

Financial Performance
To raise cash, in 2013 Chugach Alaska sold its three-story former headquarters building in downtown Anchorage.

Strategy
Developing and sustaining multiple revenues streams has been a key to the company's growth. Chugach Alaska is looking to continue to grow its Alaskan gas natural gas projects while diversifying into markets that are not traditional for the company, such as the niche market of environmentally responsible guided tourism.

Expanding its global engineering footprint, in 2012 the company acquired bankrupt Hawaii-based engineering firm Heide & Cook, LLC.

Company Background
Chugach Alaska was founded in 1972 as an Alaska Native Claims Settlement Act Corporation. A nine-person board of directors, elected from the corporation's more than 2,300 shareholders oversees Chugach Alaska's management and operations. The company has gone from filing bankruptcy protection in 1990 (in the wake of the Exxon Valdez oil spill and a major cannery fire) to generating about $1 billion in annual revenues.

EXECUTIVES
Interim Chief Executive Officer, Sheri Buretta

LOCATIONS
HQ: CHUGACH ALASKA CORPORATION
 3800 CNTRPINT DR STE 1200, ANCHORAGE, AK 99503
Phone: 907 563-8866
Web: WWW.CHUGACH.COM

PRODUCTS/OPERATIONS
Selected Services
Base Operating Services
Construction Services
Educational Services
Engineering Services
IT/Telecommunications
Manufacturing Services
Oil and Gas Services

Selected Subsidiaries
Chugach Alaska Services Inc. (CASI)
Chugach Education Services Inc. (CESI)
Chugach Federal Solutions Inc. (CFSI)
Chugach Government Services Inc. (CGSI)
Chugach Industries Inc. (CII)
Chugach Information Technology, Inc. (CITI)
Chugach Management Services Inc. (CMSI)
Chugach McKinley Inc. (CMI)
Chugach Support Services Inc. (CSSI)
Chugach Systems Integration, Llc (CSI)
Chugach World Services Inc. (CWSI)
Heide & Cook, LLC. (H&C)
Wolf Creek Federal Services, Inc. (WCFS)

COMPETITORS
ARCTIC SLOPE REGIONAL CORPORATION
AVALON CORRECTIONAL SERVICES, INC.
DOYON, LIMITED
G4S SECURE SOLUTIONS (USA) INC.

HEALTH CARE CORPORATION OF AMERICA
J H M RESEARCH & DEVELOPMENT INC
JOULE INC
MANAGEMENT & TRAINING CORPORATION
MCDERMOTT INTERNATIONAL INC
NORTH WIND PORTAGE, INC.

HISTORICAL FINANCIALS
Company Type: Private

Income Statement — FYE: December 31

	REVENUE ($mil)	NET INCOME ($mil)	NET PROFIT MARGIN	EMPLOYEES
12/17	919	20	2.3%	4,822
12/16	842	35	4.2%	—
12/15	758	22	3.0%	—
12/14	7	(12)	—	—
Annual Growth	387.6%	—	—	—

2017 Year-End Financials
Return on assets: 4.5% Cash ($ mil.): 66
Return on equity: 6.5%
Current Ratio: 2.60

CIC GROUP, INC.

CIC Group can see clearly that its future (like its present) is in heavy manufacturing and construction. Its group of commercial and industrial subsidiaries specialize in the manufacture, maintenance, and repair of equipment for the crude oil, natural gas, coal, and other energy industries. Its largest subsidiary is Nooter/Eriksen, which supplies heat recovery steam generators for combustion gas turbines worldwide. CIC's Nooter Construction is a construction contractor serving the refining, petrochemical, pulp and paper, and power industries, among others. The employee-owned holding company was formed in 2002.

Operations
CIC, through its 20 subsidiaries, is engaged in the heavy industrial construction of refineries and petrochemical and power plants. It also designs and builds heat recovery systems for power plants.

Sales and Marketing
Some of the company's largest customers include Ameren, Calpine, Chevron, ConocoPhillips, Exxon Mobil, Florida Power & Light, and Royal Dutch Shell.

Financial Performance
Although privately held, the company reported 2012 revenue of $1.2 billion, up 30% from 2011. CIC anticipates revenue of $2 billion by 2017 or 2018.

Strategy
The company is taking advantage of the low price and abundance of natural gas in the US which has encouraged companies to shift the manufacture of petrochemical plants to the US from the Middle East and Asia.

However, CIC is also strengthening its position in the growth markets of Eastern Europe and Asia. In 2012, the company announced plans to work on photovoltaic projects for Chinese solar manufacturer LDK Solar, and to act as a distributor for the company.

LOCATIONS
HQ: CIC GROUP, INC.
1509 OCELLO DR, FENTON, MO 630262406
Phone: 314 682-2900
Web: WWW.CICGROUP.COM

PRODUCTS/OPERATIONS
Selected Subsidiaries
ArcMelt
Delta Nooter
Megamet Sold Metals Co.
Nooter Construction
Nooter/Eriksen s.r.l.
Pressline Services
RMF Nooter
Schoeller Bleckmann Nooter GmbH
St. Louis Metallizing
Superior Corporate Travel
Wyatt Field Service Co.
Wyatt Virgin Islands

COMPETITORS
AMERON INTERNATIONAL CORPORATION
CHIYODA CORPORATION
Chicago Bridge & Iron Company N.V.
EDGEN GROUP INC.
IDEMITSU KOSAN CO.,LTD.
JABIL SILVER CREEK, INC.
JOHN CRANE INC.
Kuhl Machine Shop Ltd
MARUBENI CORPORATION
ROSE CITY MANUFACTURING, INC.

HISTORICAL FINANCIALS
Company Type: Private

Income Statement — FYE: November 30

	REVENUE ($mil)	NET INCOME ($mil)	NET PROFIT MARGIN	EMPLOYEES
11/11	838	0	0.0%	1,500
11/10	758	0	0.0%	—
11/08	1,120	0	0.0%	—
Annual Growth	(9.2%)	—	—	—

2011 Year-End Financials
Return on assets: — Cash ($ mil.): 136
Return on equity: —
Current Ratio: 1.70

CIMA ENERGY, LP

Auditors: DELOITTE & TOUCHE LLP HOUSTON

LOCATIONS
HQ: CIMA ENERGY, LP
1221 MCKINNEY ST STE 3700, HOUSTON, TX 770102046
Phone: 713 209-1112
Web: WWW.CIMA-ENERGY.COM

HISTORICAL FINANCIALS
Company Type: Private

Income Statement — FYE: December 31

	REVENUE ($mil)	NET INCOME ($mil)	NET PROFIT MARGIN	EMPLOYEES
12/07	1,195	8	0.7%	140
12/06	902	11	1.3%	—
12/05	872	0	0.0%	—
12/04	569	4	0.8%	—
Annual Growth	28.0%	19.1%	—	—

2007 Year-End Financials
Return on assets: 5.6% Cash ($ mil.): 16
Return on equity: 26.2%
Current Ratio: 1.20

CINCINNATI PUBLIC SCHOOLS

Auditors: PLATTENBURG & ASSOCIATES INC

LOCATIONS
HQ: CINCINNATI PUBLIC SCHOOLS
2651 BURNET AVE, CINCINNATI, OH 452192551
Phone: 513 363-0000
Web: WWW.CPS-K12.ORG

HISTORICAL FINANCIALS
Company Type: Private

Income Statement — FYE: June 30

	REVENUE ($mil)	NET INCOME ($mil)	NET PROFIT MARGIN	EMPLOYEES
06/17	703	17	2.5%	7,070
06/16	650	13	2.1%	—
06/15	654	(0)	—	—
06/05	402	0	0.0%	—
Annual Growth	4.8%	—	—	—

2017 Year-End Financials
Return on assets: 1.0% Cash ($ mil.): —
Return on equity: 28.3%
Current Ratio: —

CITIZENS ENERGY GROUP

Hoosiers are happy to have their homes provided with gas and water services by Public Utilities of the City of Indianapolis (dba Citizens Energy, and CWA Authority, public charitable trusts). Its Citizens Water unit provides water and wastewater services to 300,000 customers in Indianapolis; Citizens Gas serves more than 266,000 gas customers. Citizens Energy also provides steam heating and chilled water cooling services to about 250 customers through Citizens Thermal Energy. The regional utility also has a small oil production unit (Citizens Oil Division). Its Citizens Resources unit has joint venture stakes in some companies not regulated by the Indiana Utility Regulatory Commission, such as ProLiance Energy.

Operations
Citizens Energy operates six business segments: Citizens Gas, Water, Steam, Chilled Water, Oil and Citizens Resources, Steam and Chilled Water. Citizen Resources holds affiliate joint venture interests, including ProLiance Energy, and a number of subsidiaries, including Westfield Gas, a regulated natural gas distribution utility. Citizens Oil has produced more than 6 million barrels of oil since 1969 from Greene County, Indiana. CWA Authority provides wastewater services.

Financial Performance
The company's revenues increased by 50% in 2012 due to an increase in water and wastewater revenues. (The water and wastewater segments which were acquired in August 2011). This growth was offset by a decrease in Westfield Gas and Citizens Gas revenues due to lower usage driven by a warmer winter lower gas cost recovery revenues.

Strategy
In 2012 Citizens Energy filed a plan with the Indiana Utility Regulatory Commission to create a multistate transportation and industrial fueling business Using liquefied natural gas (LNG), the new Citizens Energy subsidiary will market and sell LNG as a competitive alternative to diesel fuel for use by heavy-duty vehicles and by drilling rigs, marine vessels, and railway locomotives.

Mergers and Acquisitions
Expanding its water and wastewater coverage, in 2013 Citizens Energy (with the cooperation of The Indiana Office of Utility Consumer Counselor, and the City of Westfield, agreed to transfer Westfield Utilities to Citizens Energy for $91 million.

Responding to the company's efficient operation of its gas utility, in 2011 the Indianapolis City/County Council sold its debt-laden water and wastewater utility (CWA Authority) to Citizens Energy in a $1.9 billion deal. The transaction reshaped the utility's business organization and transformed Citizens Energy into a multiutility.

Company Background
The company was first organized as a public charitable trust in 1887. In a 2008 rebranding, Citizens Gas & Coke Utility changed its operating name to Citizens Energy Group to reflect the company's closing of its old smokestack industry (coke manufacturing operations for steelmakers and smelter) and its new strategic emphasis on energy conservation.

LOCATIONS
HQ: CITIZENS ENERGY GROUP
  2020 N MERIDIAN ST, INDIANAPOLIS, IN 462021306
Phone: 317 924-3341
Web: INFO.CITIZENSENERGYGROUP.COM

PRODUCTS/OPERATIONS
2012 Sales

	$ mil.	% of total
Utility	650.6	93
Non-utility	45.8	7
Total	696.4	100

2012 Sales

	% of total
Citizens Gas	37
Water	24
Wastewater	22
Steam	9
Chilled Water	6
Oil	1
Resources	1
Total	100

COMPETITORS
ALLETE, INC.
DTE ENERGY COMPANY
GENIE ENERGY LTD.
NATIONAL FUEL GAS COMPANY
POWERSOUTH ENERGY COOPERATIVE
SOUTHERN COMPANY GAS
SPIRE ALABAMA INC.
TENASKA, INC.
VECTREN CORPORATION
YANKEE GAS SERVICES COMPANY

HISTORICAL FINANCIALS
Company Type: Private

Income Statement   FYE: September 30

	REVENUE ($mil)	NET INCOME ($mil)	NET PROFIT MARGIN	EMPLOYEES
09/12	696	(11)	—	1,100
09/11	463	32	7.0%	
09/10	440	(1)	—	—
Annual Growth	25.7%	—	—	—

2012 Year-End Financials
Return on assets: (-0.3%)   Cash ($ mil.): 393
Return on equity: (-10.5%)
Current Ratio: 1.50

CITY & COUNTY OF HONOLULU

With a population of almost 1 million people, Honolulu County, located on the island of Oahu, is the largest city and county in Hawaii. The city and county are governed by a mayor and a nine-member legislative council. Honolulu's largest industry is tourism, but the city is also the financial center of Hawaii.

Auditors : ACCUITY LLP HONOLULU HAWAII

LOCATIONS
HQ: CITY & COUNTY OF HONOLULU
  530 S KING ST RM 300, HONOLULU, HI 968133006
Phone: 808 768-4141
Web: WWW.ELDERLYAFFAIRS.COM

COMPETITORS
CITY OF BELLEVUE
CITY OF NEWARK, NEW JERSEY
CITY OF NORFOLK
CITY OF OXNARD
CITY OF PHOENIX

HISTORICAL FINANCIALS
Company Type: Private

Income Statement   FYE: June 30

	REVENUE ($mil)	NET INCOME ($mil)	NET PROFIT MARGIN	EMPLOYEES
06/21	2,557	231	9.1%	8,000
06/20	2,211	336	15.2%	—
06/19	2,013	315	15.6%	—
06/18	1,848	482	26.1%	—
Annual Growth	11.4%	(21.7%)	—	—

2021 Year-End Financials
Return on assets: 1.1%   Cash ($ mil.): 405
Return on equity: 4.4%
Current Ratio: —

CITY & COUNTY OF SAN FRANCISCO

The City of San Francisco is the 14th largest in the US, and its dense population, geographic detachment, and cultural diversity have made San Francisco a favorite with both tourists and residents. San Francisco's government is a consolidated city-county bureaucracy, with both entities led by an elected mayor. The government includes an executive branch led by the mayor and consisting of other elected officials and city departments, and a legislative branch consisting of an 11-member Board of Supervisors. The city is also home to several federal institutions, including the Federal Reserve Bank and the US Mint.

EXECUTIVES
Assessor*, Doris M Ward
City Attorney*, Louise Renne
District Attorney*, Terence Hallian
Public Defender*, Jeff Brown
City Administrator*, William Lee
City Attorney*, Dennis Herrera
Auditors : MACIAS GINI & O'CONNELL LLP

LOCATIONS
HQ: CITY & COUNTY OF SAN FRANCISCO
  1 DR CARLTON B GOODLETT P, SAN FRANCISCO, CA 941024604
Phone: 415 554-7500
Web: WWW.SF.GOV

COMPETITORS
CITY & COUNTY OF DENVER
CITY OF BERKELEY
CITY OF LOS ANGELES
CITY OF NEWARK, NEW JERSEY

CITY OF OXNARD
CITY OF PHOENIX
CITY OF SACRAMENTO
CITY OF ST LOUIS
CITY OF TAMPA
GOVERNMENT OF DISTRICT OF COLUMBIA

HISTORICAL FINANCIALS
Company Type: Private

Income Statement — FYE: June 30

	REVENUE ($mil)	NET INCOME ($mil)	NET PROFIT MARGIN	EMPLOYEES
06/21	8,453	1,201	14.2%	30,000
06/20	7,181	(100)	—	—
06/19	7,561	563	7.4%	—
06/18	6,411	1,172	18.3%	—
Annual Growth	9.7%	0.8%	—	—

2021 Year-End Financials
Return on assets: 2.5%   Cash ($ mil.): —
Return on equity: 11.2%
Current Ratio: 2.50

CITY CENTER HOLDINGS, LLC

Auditors: DELOITTE & TOUCHE LLP LAS VE

LOCATIONS
HQ: CITY CENTER HOLDINGS, LLC
3950 LAS VEGAS BLVD S, LAS VEGAS, NV 891191005
Phone: 702 632-9800
Web: WWW.CITIZENSLASVEGAS.COM

HISTORICAL FINANCIALS
Company Type: Private

Income Statement — FYE: December 31

	REVENUE ($mil)	NET INCOME ($mil)	NET PROFIT MARGIN	EMPLOYEES
12/12	1,189	(510)	—	0
12/11	1,081	(502)	—	—
Annual Growth	10.0%	—	—	—

2012 Year-End Financials
Return on assets: (-5.6%)   Cash ($ mil.): 252
Return on equity: (-8.3%)
Current Ratio: 1.20

CITY OF ALBUQUERQUE

Albuquerque is by far New Mexico's largest city, with a 2015 estimated population of 561,380 (about 970,680 in the greater metropolitan area). Albuquerque is located in the central part of the state and is home to The University of New Mexico. While Pueblo Indians lived in the general area for several centuries, Spanish explorers arrived in the 16th century. The city of Albuquerque was founded in 1706 and named after the Spanish town of Albuquerque (with an extra "r"). The City of Albuquerque is administered by a Mayor and a nine-person City Council.

Auditors: MOSS ADAMS LLLP ALBUQUERQUE

LOCATIONS
HQ: CITY OF ALBUQUERQUE
400 MARQUETTE AVE NW, ALBUQUERQUE, NM 871022117
Phone: 505 768-3000
Web: WWW.CABQ.GOV

COMPETITORS
CITY OF BROCKTON
CITY OF CHESAPEAKE
CITY OF MESA
CITY OF TRENTON
CITY OF YONKERS

HISTORICAL FINANCIALS
Company Type: Private

Income Statement — FYE: June 30

	REVENUE ($mil)	NET INCOME ($mil)	NET PROFIT MARGIN	EMPLOYEES
06/21	1,040	47	4.6%	6,500
06/20	913	209	23.0%	—
06/19	825	20	2.5%	—
06/18	722	45	6.2%	—
Annual Growth	12.9%	1.7%	—	—

2021 Year-End Financials
Return on assets: 0.8%   Cash ($ mil.): —
Return on equity: 1.4%
Current Ratio: 2.90

CITY OF ALEXANDRIA

Historically a wartime victim of occupying forces, modern Alexandria is home to many Defense Department contractors and employees. It uses a council-manager form of government wherein the mayor is part of the six-member city council (all elected at large), which determines city policy. The city manager works to carry out the policy and run the day-to-day operations of Alexandria. In addition to the city manager, the council also appoints the city attorney, city clerk, and members of various commissions and boards. Alexandria's more than 30 departments operate on an annual budget of about $400 million and serve about 130,000 citizens. The city was founded in 1749.

EXECUTIVES
Deputy City Manager*, Emily A Baker
Auditors: CLIFTONLARSONALLEN LLP ARLING

LOCATIONS
HQ: CITY OF ALEXANDRIA
301 KING ST, ALEXANDRIA, VA 223143211
Phone: 703 746-4000
Web: WWW.ALEXANDRIAVA.GOV

COMPETITORS
CITY OF AUSTIN
CITY OF LOS ANGELES
CITY OF OXNARD
CITY OF SACRAMENTO
CITY OF TAMPA

HISTORICAL FINANCIALS
Company Type: Private

Income Statement — FYE: June 30

	REVENUE ($mil)	NET INCOME ($mil)	NET PROFIT MARGIN	EMPLOYEES
06/21	924	(75)	—	2,375
06/20	910	167	18.4%	—
06/19	880	(8)	—	—
06/18	842	108	12.9%	—
Annual Growth	3.2%	—	—	—

2021 Year-End Financials
Return on assets: (-3.2%)   Cash ($ mil.): 551
Return on equity: (-19.4%)
Current Ratio: —

CITY OF ANAHEIM

Anaheim is a city in sunny southern Orange County, California. The state's 10th largest city is home to Disneyland Resort, one of Walt Disney Parks and Resorts' theme parks. The city also features a number of professional sports franchises, such as the Anaheim Ducks hockey team and the Angels baseball team. Anaheim was founded in 1857.

Auditors: KPMG LLP LOS ANGELES CALIFOR

LOCATIONS
HQ: CITY OF ANAHEIM
200 S ANAHEIM BLVD, ANAHEIM, CA 928053820
Phone: 714 765-5162
Web: WWW.ANAHEIM.NET

COMPETITORS
ARCHITECT OF THE CAPITOL
CITY OF BERKELEY
CITY OF ST LOUIS
HOUSE OF REPRESENTATIVES, HAWAII
LEGISLATURE OF THE VIRGIN ISLANDS

HISTORICAL FINANCIALS
Company Type: Private

Income Statement — FYE: June 30

	REVENUE ($mil)	NET INCOME ($mil)	NET PROFIT MARGIN	EMPLOYEES
06/21	547	91	16.7%	3,100
06/20	574	(100)	—	—
06/19	592	12	2.2%	—
06/18	566	27	4.9%	—
Annual Growth	(1.1%)	48.9%	—	—

2021 Year-End Financials
Return on assets: 1.7%   Cash ($ mil.): 257
Return on equity: 4.9%
Current Ratio: 3.20

CITY OF ATLANTA

City of Atlanta leaders have a dream to improve Atlantans' quality of life. The birthplace of civil rights activist Martin Luther King, Jr., Atlanta is run by a mayor and a 16-member council. With a metropolitan population of more than 5 million, Atlanta is the most populous city in Georgia. It's also the state capital and home to such major companies as The Coca-Cola Company, The Home Depot, and UPS. In addition, Atlanta has a number of professional sports franchises, namely the Atlanta Braves, Hawks, and Falcons.

EXECUTIVES

City Attorney*, Nina Hickson
RESILIENCE*, Stephanie Stuckey Benfield
ACTING CHIEF PROCUREMENT OFFICER*, Angela Hinton
Chief of Staff, Odie Donald Ii
Auditors : KPMG LLP ATLANTA GA

LOCATIONS

HQ: CITY OF ATLANTA
55 TRINITY AVE SW # 3900, ATLANTA, GA 303033543
Phone: 404 330-6100
Web: WWW.ATLANTAGA.GOV

COMPETITORS

CITY OF BALTIMORE
CITY OF CHARLOTTE
CITY OF CINCINNATI
CITY OF HOUSTON
CITY OF MILWAUKEE
CITY OF OAKLAND
CITY OF OMAHA
CITY OF RALEIGH
CITY OF RICHMOND
CITY OF TUCSON

HISTORICAL FINANCIALS

Company Type: Private

Income Statement — FYE: June 30

	REVENUE ($mil)	NET INCOME ($mil)	NET PROFIT MARGIN	EMPLOYEES
06/17	1,044	146	14.0%	8,885
06/15	920	274	29.8%	—
06/14	883	9	1.0%	—
06/13	850	14	1.7%	—
Annual Growth	5.3%	79.0%	—	—

2017 Year-End Financials
Return on assets: 0.8%   Cash ($ mil.): 48
Return on equity: 2.0%
Current Ratio: 3.20

CITY OF AUSTIN

Deep in the heart of Texas you'll find Austin, the capital of the state and self-proclaimed Live Music Capital of the World. The city, covering more than 300 square miles, follows the council/manager model where the mayor and six city council members, all elected to three-year terms, enact policy and the city manager carries it out. The manager's office oversees about 30 departments/offices, the municipal court system, city utilities, and the city's airport. Austin has a city population of more than 820,000 and a greater metro population of more than 1.8 million. Stephen F. Austin brought the first Anglo settlers to the area in 1821.

EXECUTIVES

Mayor Pro-tem, Mike Martinez
Auditors : DELOITTE & TOUCHE LLP AUSTIN

LOCATIONS

HQ: CITY OF AUSTIN
301 W 2ND ST, AUSTIN, TX 787014652
Phone: 512 974-2000
Web: WWW.AUSTINTEXAS.GOV

Selected Departments and Offices
Austin Resource Recovery
Animal Services Office
Austin Convention Center Department
Austin Water Utility
Aviation Department
Capital Planning Office
Code Compliance Department
Communications and Public Information Office
Contract Management Department
Economic Growth and Redevelopment Services Office
Emergency Medical Services Department
Fire Department
Health and Human Services Department/Medical Director
Human Resources
Labor Relations Office
Law Department
Library Department
Neighborhood Housing and Community Development
Office of Homeland Security and Emergency Management
Office of Police Monitor
Office of Real Estate Services
Parks and Recreation Department
Planning and Development Review Department
Police Department
Public Works Department
Small and Minority Business Resources Department
Sustainability Office
Transportation Department
Watershed Protection Department

COMPETITORS

CITY OF ALEXANDRIA
CITY OF BELLEVUE
CITY OF CHICAGO
CITY OF DENTON
CITY OF HOUSTON
CITY OF LOS ANGELES
CITY OF NEWARK, NEW JERSEY
CITY OF PHOENIX
CITY OF SACRAMENTO
MISSOURI CITY OF KANSAS CITY

HISTORICAL FINANCIALS

Company Type: Private

Income Statement — FYE: September 30

	REVENUE ($mil)	NET INCOME ($mil)	NET PROFIT MARGIN	EMPLOYEES
09/21	1,712	(25)	—	10,922
09/20	1,449	(34)	—	—
09/19	1,352	33	2.5%	—
09/18	1,279	67	5.2%	—
Annual Growth	10.2%	—	—	—

2021 Year-End Financials
Return on assets: (-0.1%)   Cash ($ mil.): 230
Return on equity: (-0.8%)
Current Ratio: 2.10

CITY OF BAKERSFIELD

Californians can enjoy sunny weather with fewer crowds in the City of Bakersfield. With a population of about 350,000, Bakersfield is the 9th largest city in the state. Governed by the mayor and seven city council members (elected for four-year terms), the City of Bakersfield operates through 15 departments, including water resources, animal services, and recreation and parks. Bakersfield was founded in 1858 and named after early settler Colonel Thomas Baker. The city is home to the Bakersfield Panthers, California State University, and the Rabobank Arena.

Auditors : BROWN ARMSTRONG BAKERSFIELD

LOCATIONS

HQ: CITY OF BAKERSFIELD
1600 TRUXTUN AVE FL 5TH, BAKERSFIELD, CA 933015104
Phone: 661 326-3000
Web: WWW.BAKERSFIELDCITY.US

COMPETITORS

CITY OF CHESAPEAKE
CITY OF HOUSTON
CITY OF INDEPENDENCE
CITY OF PHOENIX
CITY OF TAMPA

HISTORICAL FINANCIALS

Company Type: Private

Income Statement — FYE: June 30

	REVENUE ($mil)	NET INCOME ($mil)	NET PROFIT MARGIN	EMPLOYEES
06/21	572	143	25.1%	1,570
06/20	448	27	6.0%	—
06/19	359	12	3.5%	—
06/18	334	2	0.6%	—
Annual Growth	19.7%	310.7%	—	—

2021 Year-End Financials
Return on assets: 4.7%   Cash ($ mil.): —
Return on equity: 6.6%
Current Ratio: 6.30

CITY OF BALTIMORE

Although it is the birthplace of the National Anthem, home to the first commercial ice cream factory in the US, and among the nation's oldest cities, Baltimore is more than an asterisk to history. With a population of about 620,000, the city -- Maryland's largest -- supports a major seaport, and is part of the Baltimore-Washington metropolis. The city's economy is founded on shipping, transportation, auto manufacturing, and steel processing. It is, however, shifting to a diverse service base attractive to tourists. Baltimore is home to two professional sports teams, the Baltimore Orioles and the Baltimore Ravens.

EXECUTIVES

CIO CDO*, Frank Johnson
Auditors : SB & COMPANY LLC OWINGS MILL

LOCATIONS

HQ: CITY OF BALTIMORE
100 HOLLIDAY ST STE 250, BALTIMORE, MD 212023459
Phone: 410 396-3835
Web: WWW.BALTIMORECITY.GOV

COMPETITORS

CITY OF ATLANTA
CITY OF BUFFALO
CITY OF HOUSTON
CITY OF MIAMI
CITY OF MILWAUKEE
CITY OF RICHMOND
CITY OF RICHMOND
CITY OF ROCHESTER
CITY OF SYRACUSE
CITY OF TUCSON

HISTORICAL FINANCIALS
Company Type: Private

Income Statement — FYE: June 30

	REVENUE ($mil)	NET INCOME ($mil)	NET PROFIT MARGIN	EMPLOYEES
06/21	2,436	(54)	—	26,400
06/20	2,391	(5)	—	—
06/19	2,413	133	5.5%	—
06/18	2,147	126	5.9%	—
Annual Growth	4.3%	—	—	—

2021 Year-End Financials
Return on assets: (-0.3%)   Cash ($ mil.): 1,997
Return on equity: (-1.2%)
Current Ratio: —

CITY OF BATON ROUGE

The capital of Louisiana sits along the Mississippi River about 80 miles upstream from New Orleans. Baton Rouge (which means "red stick" in French) counts a population of about 230,000. The city is home to a number of companies in the oil, gas, and chemical industries; it also has a thriving film industry. The Louisiana State University System and its beloved LSU Tigers football team are also located in Baton Rouge.

Auditors : POSTLETHWAITE & NETTERVILLE B

LOCATIONS

HQ: CITY OF BATON ROUGE
222 SAINT LOUIS ST RM 301, BATON ROUGE, LA 708025814
Phone: 225 389-3000
Web: WWW.BRLA.GOV

COMPETITORS

CITY OF BUFFALO
CITY OF HOUSTON
CITY OF MONTGOMERY
CITY OF ROCHESTER
CITY OF SYRACUSE

HISTORICAL FINANCIALS
Company Type: Private

Income Statement — FYE: December 31

	REVENUE ($mil)	NET INCOME ($mil)	NET PROFIT MARGIN	EMPLOYEES
12/21	692	20	3.0%	4,400
12/18	559	35	6.4%	—
12/17	583	11	2.0%	—
12/16	569	(0)	0.0%	—
Annual Growth	4.0%	—	—	—

2021 Year-End Financials
Return on assets: 0.4%   Cash ($ mil.): 816
Return on equity: 37.0%
Current Ratio: —

CITY OF BIRMINGHAM

Birmingham is the largest city in Alabama with a city population of more than 242,000 people and a metro population of more than 1 million. The namesake University of Alabama at Birmingham is located in Birmingham, as is one Fortune 500 company, Regions Financial.

Auditors : CARR RIGGS & INGRAM LLC BIR

LOCATIONS

HQ: CITY OF BIRMINGHAM
710 20TH ST N STE 600, BIRMINGHAM, AL 352032281
Phone: 205 254-2000
Web: WWW.BIRMINGHAMAL.GOV

COMPETITORS

CITY OF ALBUQUERQUE
CITY OF DURHAM
CITY OF IRVING
CITY OF MONTGOMERY
CITY OF PHOENIX

HISTORICAL FINANCIALS
Company Type: Private

Income Statement — FYE: June 30

	REVENUE ($mil)	NET INCOME ($mil)	NET PROFIT MARGIN	EMPLOYEES
06/21	595	112	18.9%	4,000
06/20	539	11	2.1%	—
06/19	0	50	—	—
06/18	506	(42)	—	—
Annual Growth	5.6%	—	—	—

2021 Year-End Financials
Return on assets: 5.0%   Cash ($ mil.): 23
Return on equity: —
Current Ratio: 3.80

CITY OF CAMBRIDGE

The City of Cambridge houses an abundance of prominent minds. Part of the Greater Boston area, it is home to prestigious universities Harvard and the Massachusetts Institute of Technology (MIT). With a population of more than 100,000, the city covers just seven square miles. Most of its commercial districts are major street intersections (which act as neighborhood centers), which has given rise to its nickname "City of Squares." They include: Central, Harvard, Inman, Kendall, Lechmere, and Porter Squares. Cambridge's city government is a bit unusual. The city manager (appointed by its nine city council members), rather than the mayor (also elected by the council), serves as the chief executive of the city.

Auditors : KPMG LLP BOSTON MASSACHUSET

LOCATIONS

HQ: CITY OF CAMBRIDGE
795 MASSACHUSETTS AVE, CAMBRIDGE, MA 021393219
Phone: 617 349-4260
Web: WWW.CAMBRIDGEMA.GOV

COMPETITORS

CITY OF CHICAGO
CITY OF CLEVELAND
CITY OF PITTSBURGH
CITY OF ROCHESTER
MISSOURI CITY OF KANSAS CITY

HISTORICAL FINANCIALS
Company Type: Private

Income Statement — FYE: June 30

	REVENUE ($mil)	NET INCOME ($mil)	NET PROFIT MARGIN	EMPLOYEES
06/21	825	31	3.8%	2,000
06/20	782	25	3.3%	—
06/19	754	38	5.1%	—
06/18	726	65	9.0%	—
Annual Growth	4.3%	(21.9%)	—	—

2021 Year-End Financials
Return on assets: 0.9%   Cash ($ mil.): —
Return on equity: 2.8%
Current Ratio: —

CITY OF CHARLOTTE

You can bank on Charlotte ...Â the nation's second-largest banking center (behind New York City). The City of CharlotteÂ delivers public services andÂ promotesÂ safety and health among residents.Â Policies are set by a mayor and 11 council members elected for two-year terms.Â The day-to-day operations are handled byÂ a city manager. Charlotte hasÂ a population of more thanÂ 750,000 andÂ coversÂ about 280 square miles. It'sÂ home to a handful of Fortune 500 companies, including Bank of America, Family Dollar, and Duke Energy, as well as the Carolina Panthers and Charlotte Motor Speedway. It also boastsÂ some 700 places of worship, earning itÂ the nickname "The City of Churches."

Auditors : CHERRY BEKAERT LLP CHARLOTTE

LOCATIONS

HQ: CITY OF CHARLOTTE
600 E 4TH ST, CHARLOTTE, NC 282022816
Phone: 704 336-7600
Web: WWW.CHARLOTTENC.GOV

COMPETITORS

CITY OF AUSTIN
CITY OF BELLEVUE
CITY OF DAYTON
CITY OF DENTON
CITY OF HOUSTON
CITY OF PITTSBURGH
CITY OF RALEIGH
CITY OF RICHMOND
CITY OF SAN JOSE
CITY OF TAMPA

HISTORICAL FINANCIALS
Company Type: Private

Income Statement   FYE: June 30

	REVENUE ($mil)	NET INCOME ($mil)	NET PROFIT MARGIN	EMPLOYEES
06/21	1,219	(215)	—	5,011
06/20	1,102	(83)	—	—
06/19	1,065	148	13.9%	—
06/18	997	(10)	—	—
Annual Growth	6.9%	—	—	—

2021 Year-End Financials
Return on assets: (-1.1%)   Cash ($ mil.): 1,963
Return on equity: (-1.8%)
Current Ratio: —

CITY OF CHESAPEAKE

The City of Chesapeake attracts both beachcombers and history buffs. Located about 20 miles from Virginia Beach, Chesapeake was established in 1963 through the merging of the city of South Norfolk and Norfolk County, which was created in 1691. The first English settlement in the area began around 1620 along the banks of the Elizabeth River. The mayor, vice mayor, and seven city council members (elected for four-year terms) govern the city, which has a population of more than 233,370. The third-largest city in Virginia, Chesapeake is home to the College of William and Mary and Hampton University.

EXECUTIVES

City Treasurer*, Barbara O Carraway
Auditors : CHERRY BEKAERT LLP VIRGINIA B

LOCATIONS

HQ: CITY OF CHESAPEAKE
306 CEDAR RD, CHESAPEAKE, VA 233225597
Phone: 757 382-6586
Web: WWW.CITYOFCHESAPEAKE.NET

COMPETITORS

CITY OF BAKERSFIELD
CITY OF BELLEVUE
CITY OF NEWARK, NEW JERSEY
CITY OF NORFOLK
CITY OF TAMPA

HISTORICAL FINANCIALS
Company Type: Private

Income Statement   FYE: June 30

	REVENUE ($mil)	NET INCOME ($mil)	NET PROFIT MARGIN	EMPLOYEES
06/21	775	90	11.7%	2,893
06/20	703	54	7.7%	—
06/16	621	14	2.4%	—
06/15	595	4	0.8%	—
Annual Growth	4.5%	64.5%	—	—

2021 Year-End Financials
Return on assets: 2.3%   Cash ($ mil.): —
Return on equity: 4.8%
Current Ratio: —

CITY OF CINCINNATI

Founded in 1788, Cincinnati is home to almost 300,000 people and covers roughly 80 square miles. It is the third-largest city in Ohio, trailing behind Columbus and Cleveland. The city's government consists of the mayor and nine city council members (elected at large). Council committees deal with a wide range of issues including public education, health, economic concerns, and community development. The city is also home to two major-league sports franchises -- baseball's Cincinnati Reds andÂ football's Cincinnati Bengals.

Auditors : DAVE YOST COLUMBUS OHIO

LOCATIONS

HQ: CITY OF CINCINNATI
801 PLUM ST RM 246, CINCINNATI, OH 452025704
Phone: 513 352-3221
Web: WWW.CINCINNATI-OH.GOV

COMPETITORS

CITY OF CHARLOTTE
CITY OF DENTON
CITY OF HOUSTON
CITY OF RALEIGH
CITY OF TAMPA

HISTORICAL FINANCIALS
Company Type: Private

Income Statement   FYE: June 30

	REVENUE ($mil)	NET INCOME ($mil)	NET PROFIT MARGIN	EMPLOYEES
06/21	998	218	21.9%	5,964
06/19	769	25	3.3%	—
06/18	728	(22)	—	—
06/17	708	10	1.5%	—
Annual Growth	9.0%	111.7%	—	—

2021 Year-End Financials
Return on assets: 4.3%   Cash ($ mil.): 528
Return on equity: 29.4%
Current Ratio: 3.40

CITY OF CLEVELAND

It's only rock and roll, butÂ Cleveland residentsÂ like it. The City of Cleveland, Ohio (C-Town), isÂ home to the Rock and Roll Hall of Fame,Â and isÂ the nation'sÂ 45th largest city and Ohio's second largest (behind Columbus). C-Town, with more than 390,000 residents, is run by a mayor-council form of government. The legislative branchÂ consists of a 21-member council and the executive branch comprisesÂ the mayor, his adjunct offices, advisors, and the city's administrative departments. The mayor is the city's CEOÂ and is elected to enforce itsÂ charter,Â ordinances, and stateÂ laws. The Village of Cleveland was incorporatedÂ in 1814.

EXECUTIVES

City Treasurer*, Algernon Walker
Lead Director*, Subodh Chandra
Clerk of Council*, Valerie Mc Call
Auditors : KEITH FABER COLUMBUS OH

LOCATIONS

HQ: CITY OF CLEVELAND
601 LAKESIDE AVE E RM 210, CLEVELAND, OH 441141015
Phone: 216 664-2000
Web: WWW.CLEVELANDOHIO.GOV

COMPETITORS

CITY OF BELLEVUE
CITY OF NEWARK, NEW JERSEY
CITY OF OXNARD
CITY OF SACRAMENTO
MISSOURI CITY OF KANSAS CITY

CITY OF DALLAS

Big D, with a population of 1.2 million, is actually Texas' third-largest city (behind Houston and San Antonio) and the nation's ninth largest. The city operates through 14 districts, each represented by a council member, and about 40 city departments, including the Trinity River Corridor Project and the CityDesign Studio. The city is home to Southern Methodist University, the Dallas Market Center, and the Dallas Cowboys.

Auditors : GRANT THORNTON DALLAS TEXAS

LOCATIONS

HQ: CITY OF DALLAS
1500 MARILLA ST, DALLAS, TX 752016390
Phone: 214 670-3146
Web: WWW.DALLASCITYHALL.COM

PRODUCTS/OPERATIONS

Selected Departments and Offices
Animal Services
Aviation
Building Inspection Engineering
Business Development and Procurement Services
CityDesign Studio
Civil Service Board
Communication and Information Services
Community Development
Convention and Event Services
Court and Detention Services
Cultural Affairs
Fire-Rescue
Economic Development
Employees' Retirement Fund
Equipment and Building Services
Fair Housing
Housing/Community Services
Human Resources
Intergovernmental Services
Judiciary
Library
Office of Emergency Management
Office of Environmental Quality
Office of Financial Services
Office of Risk Management
Park and Recreation
Police
Public Information Office
Public Works
Sanitation Services
Stormwater
Strategic Customer Services
Street Services
Sustainable Development and Construction
Trinity River Corridor Project
Trinity Watershed Management
Water Utilities
WRR Radio
Zoo

COMPETITORS

CITY OF BROWNSVILLE
CITY OF CINCINNATI
CITY OF DENTON
CITY OF FORT WORTH
CITY OF HOUSTON
CITY OF INDIANAPOLIS
CITY OF MESA
CITY OF PHILADELPHIA
CITY OF PHOENIX
CITY OF PLANO

HISTORICAL FINANCIALS

Company Type: Private

Income Statement — FYE: December 31

	REVENUE ($mil)	NET INCOME ($mil)	NET PROFIT MARGIN	EMPLOYEES
12/21	972	200	20.6%	8,073
12/20	816	8	1.1%	—
12/19	839	31	3.7%	—
12/17	801	75	9.5%	—
Annual Growth	5.0%	27.4%	—	—

2021 Year-End Financials
Return on assets: 2.8% Cash ($ mil.): 1,787
Return on equity: 6.7%
Current Ratio: —

CITY OF COLUMBUS

So what if European explorer Christopher Columbus didn't sail the Scioto River? Columbus, the capital of Ohio, is located smack dab in the middle of the state. With a population of almost 836,000 people, Columbus is the largest city in the Buckeye State. (Cleveland and Cincinnati, however, have larger populations in their greater metropolitan areas.) Columbus is home to a handful of Fortune 500 companies, including Nationwide Insurance and retailer L Brands. While the area had been home to European fur trappers since the 1700s and Native Americans for centuries, Columbus became a city in 1812.

Auditors : PLANTE & MORAN PLLC COLUMBUS

LOCATIONS

HQ: CITY OF COLUMBUS
90 W BROAD ST RM B33, COLUMBUS, OH 432159061
Phone: 614 645-7671
Web: WWW.COLUMBUS.GOV

COMPETITORS

CITY OF BALTIMORE
CITY OF BUFFALO
CITY OF OMAHA
CITY OF PEORIA
CITY OF TULSA

HISTORICAL FINANCIALS

Company Type: Private

Income Statement — FYE: December 31

	REVENUE ($mil)	NET INCOME ($mil)	NET PROFIT MARGIN	EMPLOYEES
12/21	1,727	105	6.1%	8,385
12/20	1,805	(72)	—	—
12/19	1,630	29	1.8%	—
12/18	1,478	94	6.4%	—
Annual Growth	5.3%	3.8%	—	—

2021 Year-End Financials
Return on assets: 1.0% Cash ($ mil.): 1,643
Return on equity: 3.1%
Current Ratio: —

CITY OF EL PASO

Out in the West Texas Town of El Paso, the sprawling metropolis is administered by the City of El Paso. The sixth-largest city in Texas with a population of about 650,000 (2.5 million in the region, including Ciudad Juárez, Mexico), El Paso is built around the base of the Franklin Mountains, across the Rio Grande from Juárez. Its city government consists of the mayor and eight council members (elected to four-year terms), along with a hired city manager. US Army post Fort Bliss and The University of Texas at El Paso are among the city's largest employers.

Financial Performance

In the budget of 2015, the City of El Paso had estimated revenues of $841.1 million, with a major increase in Franchises Fees, and Service Revenues, offsetting a decline in Intergovernmental Revenues.

The increase in Franchises Fees was due to increase in the customer base (including El Paso Water Utilities, International Bridges Crossing Fees) offset by lower decreases in the AT&T, Electric Company, and Gas Franchise Fees.

Service revenues grew thanks to higher mass transit revenues (due to an increase in fares and new transit projects), and higher revenues from solid waste services (thanks to a growth in customer accounts).

Strategy

The City is looking to leverage the region's position as one of the largest manufacturing centers in North America (with the largest bilingual and bi-cultural workforce in the Western Hemisphere) to further attract industries and new job growth. It is also seeking to boost tourism.

Auditors : BKD LLP DALLAS TX

LOCATIONS

HQ: CITY OF EL PASO
300 N CAMPBELL ST, EL PASO, TX 799011402
Phone: 915 212-0000
Web: WWW.ELPASOTEXAS.GOV

HISTORICAL FINANCIALS

Company Type: Private

Income Statement — FYE: September 30

	REVENUE ($mil)	NET INCOME ($mil)	NET PROFIT MARGIN	EMPLOYEES
09/20	2,067	45	2.2%	13,000
09/19	1,898	147	7.7%	—
09/18	1,802	258	14.3%	—
09/17	1,678	(58)	—	—
Annual Growth	7.2%	—	—	—

2020 Year-End Financials
Return on assets: 0.3% Cash ($ mil.): 1,524
Return on equity: 3.8%
Current Ratio: —

COMPETITORS

CITY OF FRESNO
CITY OF HOUSTON
CITY OF IRVING
CITY OF NEW YORK
CITY OF PHOENIX

HISTORICAL FINANCIALS
Company Type: Private

Income Statement — FYE: August 31

	REVENUE ($mil)	NET INCOME ($mil)	NET PROFIT MARGIN	EMPLOYEES
08/21	827	120	14.6%	6,500
08/20	679	83	12.2%	—
Annual Growth	21.8%	45.4%	—	—

2021 Year-End Financials
Return on assets: 2.1%   Cash ($ mil.): 110
Return on equity: 7.5%
Current Ratio: —

CITY OF FRESNO

Fresno (which means "ash" or "ash tree" in Spanish) is California's fifth-largest city. Located in the fertile San Joaquin Valley, Fresno counts about 500,000 residents in the city and about 940,000 residents across Fresno County. The City's residents represent more than 80 different nationalities. Centrally located, Fresno is the financial, industrial, trade, and commercial capital of the Central San Joaquin Valley. The area is home to many agricultural concerns, including Sun-Maid Raisins, Valley Fig Growers, and Zacky Farms. Fresno was founded by the Central Pacific Railroad Company in 1872.

Financial Performance

For fiscal 2015, the City had a budget $996 million, a decrease of 4% from fiscal 2014 levels, due to lower budgets allotted to minor capitals and contingencies, offset by higher budgets for operations and maintenance.

Strategy

In 2015 Fresno City Council approved a proposed water rate plan to pay for the City's amended water infrastructure project.

Auditors : BROWN ARMSTRONG BAKERSFIELD

LOCATIONS

HQ: CITY OF FRESNO
2600 FRESNO ST, FRESNO, CA 937213620
Phone: 559 621-7001
Web: WWW.FRESNO.GOV

COMPETITORS

CITY OF DURHAM
CITY OF EL PASO
CITY OF HOUSTON
CITY OF IRVING
CITY OF PHOENIX

HISTORICAL FINANCIALS
Company Type: Private

Income Statement — FYE: June 30

	REVENUE ($mil)	NET INCOME ($mil)	NET PROFIT MARGIN	EMPLOYEES
06/21	573	35	6.2%	2,600
06/20	462	23	5.0%	—
06/19	436	22	5.1%	—
06/18	397	(12)	—	—
Annual Growth	13.0%	—	—	—

2021 Year-End Financials
Return on assets: 0.8%   Cash ($ mil.): —
Return on equity: 1.4%
Current Ratio: —

CITY OF HARTFORD

EXECUTIVES

City Treasurer*, Kathleen Plam
Auditors : CLIFTONLARSONALLEN LLP WEST H

LOCATIONS

HQ: CITY OF HARTFORD
550 MAIN ST STE 1, HARTFORD, CT 061032913
Phone: 860 757-9311
Web: WWW.HARTFORDCT.GOV

HISTORICAL FINANCIALS
Company Type: Private

Income Statement — FYE: June 30

	REVENUE ($mil)	NET INCOME ($mil)	NET PROFIT MARGIN	EMPLOYEES
06/21	989	25	2.6%	10,000
06/20	1,013	(10)	—	—
06/19	948	5	0.6%	—
06/18	940	(11)	—	—
Annual Growth	1.7%	—	—	—

2021 Year-End Financials
Return on assets: 1.0%   Cash ($ mil.): 270
Return on equity: 3.9%
Current Ratio: —

CITY OF HOPE NATIONAL MEDICAL CENTER

Auditors : IT ERNST & YOUNG US LLP IRVI

LOCATIONS

HQ: CITY OF HOPE NATIONAL MEDICAL CENTER
1500 DUARTE RD, DUARTE, CA 910103012
Phone: 626 256-4673

HISTORICAL FINANCIALS
Company Type: Private

Income Statement — FYE: September 30

	REVENUE ($mil)	NET INCOME ($mil)	NET PROFIT MARGIN	EMPLOYEES
09/20	1,345	33	2.5%	1,900
09/19	1,357	41	3.1%	—
09/15	860	107	12.5%	—
09/14	0	0	—	—
Annual Growth	—	—	—	—

2020 Year-End Financials
Return on assets: 1.1%   Cash ($ mil.): 492
Return on equity: 4.4%
Current Ratio: 1.10

CITY OF JACKSONVILLE

In Jacksonville, residents and visitors can enjoy the Florida wilderness. The city, which offers some 57,000 acres of parks, provides more land for recreation than any other city in the US. ItsÂ 19 city council members (five at-large members and 14 representing geographic districts) enact the legislation for theÂ Jacksonville. Elected for four-year terms, the mayor oversees the administration of the central government and appoints directors for its 10 departments. The 14th-largest city in the US, Jacksonville has a population ofÂ more thanÂ 850,000 residents.

EXECUTIVES

State Attorney*, Melissa Nelson
Auditors : CARR RIGGS & INGRAM JACKSONVI

LOCATIONS

HQ: CITY OF JACKSONVILLE
117 W DUVAL ST, JACKSONVILLE, FL 322023700
Phone: 904 630-1776
Web: WWW.COJ.NET

COMPETITORS

CITY OF ALEXANDRIA
CITY OF MINNEAPOLIS
CITY OF PHOENIX
CITY OF SACRAMENTO
CITY OF TAMPA

HISTORICAL FINANCIALS
Company Type: Private

Income Statement — FYE: September 30

	REVENUE ($mil)	NET INCOME ($mil)	NET PROFIT MARGIN	EMPLOYEES
09/18	1,599	64	4.0%	7,908
09/17	1,560	12	0.8%	—
09/16	1,493	33	2.3%	—
09/15	1,414	50	3.6%	—
Annual Growth	4.2%	8.7%	—	—

2018 Year-End Financials
Return on assets: 0.4% Cash ($ mil.): 187
Return on equity: 2.5%
Current Ratio: —

CITY OF LAS VEGAS

Some 585,000 people call Sin City home. Las Vegas, Nevada's largest city, is the gaming capital of the US. The city is overseen by a mayor, an appointed city manager, and six elected city council members. Its largest industry is tourism; the casino resorts attract visitors seeking business and pleasure -- Las Vegas hosts almost 20,000 conventions every year.

EXECUTIVES

Deputy City Manager*, Steve Houchens
Deputy City Manager*, Betsy Fretwell
Auditors : BDO LLP LAS VEGAS NEVADA

LOCATIONS

HQ: CITY OF LAS VEGAS
495 S MAIN ST, LAS VEGAS, NV 891012986
Phone: 702 229-6321
Web: WWW.LASVEGASNEVADA.GOV

COMPETITORS

CITY OF LOS ANGELES
CITY OF MIAMI
CITY OF RALEIGH
CITY OF SACRAMENTO
MISSOURI CITY OF KANSAS CITY

HISTORICAL FINANCIALS
Company Type: Private

Income Statement — FYE: June 30

	REVENUE ($mil)	NET INCOME ($mil)	NET PROFIT MARGIN	EMPLOYEES
06/21	967	55	5.7%	2,500
06/20	999	(94)	—	—
06/19	857	58	6.9%	—
06/18	782	69	8.9%	—
Annual Growth	7.3%	(7.3%)	—	—

2021 Year-End Financials
Return on assets: 0.9% Cash ($ mil.): 915
Return on equity: 1.2%
Current Ratio: 8.40

CITY OF LONG BEACH

It's a city, it's a port, it's Long Beach. The City of Long Beach boasts the Port of Long Beach, one of the busiest ports in the nation. With a population of more than 460,000, Long Beach is part of the greater Los Angeles metropolitan area. The city uses a charter form of government with an elected mayor and city council, as well as an appointed city manager. It's also known for its large oil reserves managed by the Long Beach Gas & Oil Department.

EXECUTIVES

City Treasurer*, David Nakamoto
Auditors : KPMG LLP LOS ANGELES CA

LOCATIONS

HQ: CITY OF LONG BEACH
1800 E WARDLOW RD, LONG BEACH, CA 908074931
Phone: 562 570-6450
Web: WWW.LONGBEACH.GOV

COMPETITORS

CITY & COUNTY OF DENVER
CITY OF CHICAGO
CITY OF HENDERSON
CITY OF LONG BEACH
CITY OF MIAMI
CITY OF MINNEAPOLIS
CITY OF NORFOLK
CITY OF ROCHESTER
CITY OF SEATTLE
CITY OF SYRACUSE

HISTORICAL FINANCIALS
Company Type: Private

Income Statement — FYE: September 30

	REVENUE ($mil)	NET INCOME ($mil)	NET PROFIT MARGIN	EMPLOYEES
09/21	1,056	83	7.9%	5,028
09/20	889	19	2.2%	—
09/19	864	36	4.3%	—
09/18	779	26	3.4%	—
Annual Growth	10.7%	46.4%	—	—

2021 Year-End Financials
Return on assets: 0.7% Cash ($ mil.): 454
Return on equity: 1.4%
Current Ratio: 1.90

CITY OF LOS ANGELES

Los Angeles may be a Mecca for the rich and famous, but there is little glamour in running a city of more than 4 million people. Governing responsibilities are shared among the city's mayor and city council, while various commissions, departments, and bureaus see to the daily operations that keep the wheels spinning. Elected every four years, the mayor appoints most commission members (subject to approval by the city council) and serves as the city's executive officer. The City of Los Angeles is located in the County of Los Angeles.

LOCATIONS

HQ: CITY OF LOS ANGELES
200 N SPRING ST STE 303, LOS ANGELES, CA 900123239
Phone: 213 978-0600
Web: WWW.LACITY.ORG

COMPETITORS

CITY OF ALEXANDRIA
CITY OF AUSTIN
CITY OF CHICAGO
CITY OF MIAMI
CITY OF NEWARK, NEW JERSEY
CITY OF OXNARD
CITY OF PITTSBURGH
CITY OF SACRAMENTO
CITY OF TAMPA
MISSOURI CITY OF KANSAS CITY

HISTORICAL FINANCIALS
Company Type: Private

Income Statement — FYE: June 30

	REVENUE ($mil)	NET INCOME ($mil)	NET PROFIT MARGIN	EMPLOYEES
06/16	7,196	231	3.2%	41,000
06/09*	6,281	(285)	—	—
12/08	0	0	0.0%	—
Annual Growth	217.6%	—	—	—

*Fiscal year change

2016 Year-End Financials
Return on assets: 0.4% Cash ($ mil.): 7,446
Return on equity: 1.2%
Current Ratio: —

CITY OF MEMPHIS

Home to Graceland and Beale Street, Memphis has both feet entrenched in the world of music. With a population of more than 670,000, it is located in the southwestern corner of the state and stretches over 300 square miles. Serving the largest urban population in Tennessee, it is run by a mayor and 13 city council members (elected from nine districts). City government is responsible for economic development, public education, housing, public utilities, homeland security, and landmark preservation. Set atop the eastern bank of the Mississippi River and named after the ancient capital of Egypt, Memphis was founded in 1820.

Auditors : BANKS FINLEY WHITE & CO ME

LOCATIONS

HQ: CITY OF MEMPHIS
125 N MAIN ST STE 628, MEMPHIS, TN 381032032
Phone: 901 676-6657
Web: WWW.MEMPHISTN.GOV

COMPETITORS

CITY & COUNTY OF DENVER
CITY OF BAKERSFIELD
CITY OF BERKELEY
CITY OF BROCKTON
CITY OF CHESAPEAKE
CITY OF FORT WORTH
CITY OF INDEPENDENCE
CITY OF MINNEAPOLIS
CITY OF PHOENIX
CITY OF ST LOUIS

HISTORICAL FINANCIALS
Company Type: Private

Income Statement   FYE: June 30

	REVENUE ($mil)	NET INCOME ($mil)	NET PROFIT MARGIN	EMPLOYEES
06/16	906	8	0.9%	6,000
06/15	863	1	0.2%	—
06/14	840	26	3.2%	—
06/13	845	(25)	—	—
Annual Growth	2.3%	—	—	—

2016 Year-End Financials
Return on assets: 0.1%   Cash ($ mil.): 285
Return on equity: 0.3%
Current Ratio: —

CITY OF MESA

This city, which literally covers a "mesa" or plateau, stands roughly 100 feet higher than Phoenix and spreads across 130 square miles. With a population of more than 468,000, the City of Mesa is the third-largest city in Arizona, behind Phoenix and Tucson. Its city government consists of the mayor, six city council members (elected to four-year terms), and a city manager. Mesa is also home to the Chicago Cubs baseball team during spring training. The city was founded in 1878 by Mormon (Latter-day Saint or LDS) pioneers, who gave it its name; Mesa still has a large Mormon population. It was incorporated in 1883.

Auditors: CLIFTON LARSON ALLEN LLP PHOE

LOCATIONS

HQ: CITY OF MESA
   20 E MAIN ST, MESA, AZ 852017425
Phone: 480 644-2011
Web: WWW.MESAAZ.GOV

COMPETITORS

CITY OF BELLEVUE
CITY OF DALLAS
CITY OF DENTON
CITY OF HENDERSON
CITY OF TUCSON

HISTORICAL FINANCIALS
Company Type: Private

Income Statement   FYE: June 30

	REVENUE ($mil)	NET INCOME ($mil)	NET PROFIT MARGIN	EMPLOYEES
06/21	725	175	24.2%	4,068
06/20	646	89	13.9%	—
06/19	539	50	9.3%	—
06/18	515	47	9.1%	—
Annual Growth	12.1%	55.3%	—	—

2021 Year-End Financials
Return on assets: 3.3%   Cash ($ mil.): —
Return on equity: 18.2%
Current Ratio: —

CITY OF MIAMI

Thankfully, the City of Miami is much more than Dolphins, sound-machines, and vice cops. With a population of more than 400,000 the city has little trouble attracting tourists and residents alike to the bustling international hub of business, entertainment, and culture. Thanks to its status as a transportation hub and the businesses that make the city home to international operations, the city is also known as the Gateway to Latin America. The city government consists of its elected mayor, five commissioners, a city manager, and the heads of Miami's various public services departments.

Auditors: RSM US LLP MIAMI FLORIDA

LOCATIONS

HQ: CITY OF MIAMI
   3500 PAN AMERICAN DR FL 2, MIAMI, FL 331335595
Phone: 305 250-5300
Web: WWW.MIAMIGOV.COM

COMPETITORS

CITY & COUNTY OF DENVER
CITY OF CHICAGO
CITY OF DETROIT
CITY OF LOS ANGELES
CITY OF SYRACUSE

HISTORICAL FINANCIALS
Company Type: Private

Income Statement   FYE: September 30

	REVENUE ($mil)	NET INCOME ($mil)	NET PROFIT MARGIN	EMPLOYEES
09/15	792	(1)	—	3,000
09/12	675	(18)	—	—
09/09	691	(30)	—	—
Annual Growth	2.3%	—	—	—

2015 Year-End Financials
Return on assets: (-0.1%)   Cash ($ mil.): 401
Return on equity: —
Current Ratio: —

CITY OF MINNEAPOLIS

One half of Minnesota's famed Twin Cities, Minneapolis is a combination of the Sioux word for water with the Greek word for city. With 20 lakes and wetlands plus the Mississippi River waterfront and many creeks and streams, the City of Minneapolis is known as the City of Lakes. It is governed by a mayor and city council with 13 members representing the city's wards. The mayor appoints the chief of police but has little other power. Independent boards oversee public housing, the tax office, and public parks and libraries. The city's more than 80 parks serve as a model for city park systems nationwide. Formed in 1856, Minneapolis is now home to a population of almost 400,000.

EXECUTIVES

City Clerk*, Steve Ristuben
Chief of Staff*, Mychal Vlatkovich
INTERIM CITY AUDITOR*, Ryan Patrick
Auditors: JULIE BLAHA ST PAUL MN

LOCATIONS

HQ: CITY OF MINNEAPOLIS
   350 S 5TH ST STE 325M, MINNEAPOLIS, MN 554151306
Phone: 612 673-3000
Web: WWW.MINNEAPOLISMN.GOV

COMPETITORS

CITY & COUNTY OF DENVER
CITY OF HOUSTON
CITY OF PHOENIX
CITY OF TAMPA
MISSOURI CITY OF KANSAS CITY

HISTORICAL FINANCIALS
Company Type: Private

Income Statement   FYE: December 31

	REVENUE ($mil)	NET INCOME ($mil)	NET PROFIT MARGIN	EMPLOYEES
12/21	817	(22)	—	5,000
12/20	903	(21)	—	—
12/19	916	85	9.3%	—
12/18	858	84	9.8%	—
Annual Growth	(1.6%)	—	—	—

2021 Year-End Financials
Return on assets: (-0.4%)   Cash ($ mil.): —
Return on equity: (-0.8%)
Current Ratio: —

CITY OF NEW HAVEN

Auditors: MCGLADREY LLP NEW HAVEN CONN

LOCATIONS

HQ: CITY OF NEW HAVEN
   165 CHURCH ST FL 2, NEW HAVEN, CT 065102010
Phone: 203 946-8200
Web: WWW.NEWHAVENCT.GOV

HISTORICAL FINANCIALS
Company Type: Private

Income Statement   FYE: June 30

	REVENUE ($mil)	NET INCOME ($mil)	NET PROFIT MARGIN	EMPLOYEES
06/18	776	10	1.3%	4,500
06/17	819	5	0.7%	—
06/16	811	10	1.3%	—
06/15	738	3	0.5%	—
Annual Growth	1.7%	45.2%	—	—

2018 Year-End Financials
Return on assets: 0.5%   Cash ($ mil.): 96
Return on equity: —
Current Ratio: —

CITY OF NEW ORLEANS

New Orleans is a city with a story. The city was founded in 1718 and became famous for its architecture, music, food, and parties. The city is home to a major port, the New Orleans Saints, the French Quarter, and is the regarded as the birthplace of jazz. Devastated by Hurricane Katrina and the flooding which ensued in 2005, the city has undertaken a massive rebuilding and recovery effort utilizing state and federal assistance. The city of New Orleans is governed by a city council consisting of seven members and an elected mayor.

Auditors : POSTLETHWAITE & NETTERVILLE N

LOCATIONS

HQ: CITY OF NEW ORLEANS
1300 PERDIDO ST BSMT FL2, NEW ORLEANS, LA 701122128
Phone: 504 658-4900
Web: WWW.NOLA.GOV

COMPETITORS

CITY OF CHICAGO
CITY OF MINNEAPOLIS
CITY OF SYRACUSE
CITY OF TAMPA
CITY OF TOLEDO

HISTORICAL FINANCIALS
Company Type: Private

Income Statement — FYE: December 31

	REVENUE ($mil)	NET INCOME ($mil)	NET PROFIT MARGIN	EMPLOYEES
12/18	1,056	1	0.1%	6,658
12/17	901	(74)	—	—
12/16	881	39	4.5%	—
12/15	905	65	7.2%	—
Annual Growth	5.2%	(71.4%)	—	—

2018 Year-End Financials
Return on assets: — Cash ($ mil.): 318
Return on equity: 0.1%
Current Ratio: —

CITY OF NEW YORK

The City That Never Sleeps, the Big Apple, Gotham -- NYC by any name is a unique place. With a population of 8.2 million packed into more than 300 square miles, New York City is run by the mayor and 51 city council members (elected to four-year terms) along with the public advocate, comptroller, and presidents of the five boroughs. The city government is responsible for welfare services, public education, water supply/sanitation, correctional institutions, recreational facilities, public safety, and libraries. It uses about $65 to $70 billion a year to manage those departments. First settled by Europeans around 1614, New York took its current name when the English conquered it in 1664.

Operations
Tourism, media production, and construction have reached records levels for the City over the years. NYC & Company, a tourism partnership for the City of New York, works to attract some 50 million tourists who annually spend about $32 billion. Through such efforts as brokering between local vendors and media production companies and media career development programs, the City of New York helps to attract about $5 billion in annual media industry expenditures.

Financial Performance
The City's budget for 2012 was $66 billion. This number was almost $510 million less than its budget for 2011.

Strategy
In 2013 city officials announced an agreement to sell two City-owned buildings for nearly $250 million as a part of the city's plan to reduce City government office space by 1.2 million square feet by 2014. The properties are on Chambers Street and Broadway, and the move is part of the administration's efforts to increase efficiency by eliminating underused office space and relocating employees to office environments that better serve the City's needs. It plans to generate an estimated $120 million in net revenue for the City, after the costs of relocating various agencies and the creation of a space for public use for the community. The City states it will also save about $120 million in operating expenses over the next two decades.

EXECUTIVES
CMPTRLR, Scott Stringer
PUBLIC ADVOCATE, Letitia James
Chief of Staff, Thomas G Snyder
Auditors : GRANT THORTON LLP NEW YORK N

LOCATIONS
HQ: CITY OF NEW YORK
CITY HALL PARK, NEW YORK, NY 10007
Phone: 212 788-3000
Web: WWW.NYC.GOV

COMPETITORS
CITY OF ALEXANDRIA
CITY OF DAYTON
CITY OF EL PASO
CITY OF HOUSTON
CITY OF IRVING
COUNTY OF LOS ANGELES
HILL INTERNATIONAL, INC.
KANSAS DEPARTMENT OF TRANSPORTATION
METROPOLITAN TRANSPORTATION AUTHORITY
TALLAHASSEE, CITY OF (INC)

HISTORICAL FINANCIALS
Company Type: Private

Income Statement — FYE: June 30

	REVENUE ($mil)	NET INCOME ($mil)	NET PROFIT MARGIN	EMPLOYEES
06/22	109,744	(147)	—	310,000
06/20	98,235	819	0.8%	—
06/18	90,568	1,348	1.5%	—
Annual Growth	4.9%	—	—	—

2022 Year-End Financials
Return on assets: (-0.1%) Cash ($ mil.): 14,067
Return on equity: —
Current Ratio: —

CITY OF NEWPORT NEWS

There are nearly as many theoriesÂ on where the unusual city name came from as there are citizens of Newport News, Virginia. Whether it was founded on land chosen by Sir William Newce or the point where Captain Newport delivered good news to early settlers, Newport News today boasts a population ofÂ some 193,000. The mayor and six-member city council (representing three districts)Â work together toÂ serveÂ residents and visitorsÂ backed byÂ an annual budget ofÂ about $750 million. The council sets up city policies and controls funding while the city manager, attorney, and clerk carry out the day-to-dayÂ administration of Newport News. The city, which was settled around 1621,Â is well known as a military shipbuilding hub.

Auditors : CHERRY BEKAERT LLP RICHMOND

LOCATIONS
HQ: CITY OF NEWPORT NEWS
2400 WASHINGTON AVE MAIN, NEWPORT NEWS, VA 236074300
Phone: 757 926-8411
Web: WWW.NNVA.GOV

COMPETITORS
CITY OF ALEXANDRIA
CITY OF CHICAGO
CITY OF RICHMOND
CITY OF SEATTLE
CITY OF TAMPA

HISTORICAL FINANCIALS
Company Type: Private

Income Statement — FYE: June 30

	REVENUE ($mil)	NET INCOME ($mil)	NET PROFIT MARGIN	EMPLOYEES
06/21	653	99	15.2%	5,000
06/20	598	(30)	—	—
06/19	602	50	8.4%	—
06/17	563	33	5.9%	—
Annual Growth	3.8%	31.5%	—	—

2021 Year-End Financials
Return on assets: 3.7%   Cash ($ mil.): 447
Return on equity: 13.3%
Current Ratio: —

CITY OF NORFOLK

You could say that the City of Norfolk, Virginia, is at home on the water. The second-largest city in Virginia with a population of more than 245,400, Norfolk sports miles of lake, river, and bay front as well as a bustling international port and the world's largest naval base. The city was founded in 1682 and offers such attractions as the battleship USS Wisconsin, the National Maritime Center, and Old Dominion University. Norfolk Southern Railway's corporate headquarters are also located in the city. Norfolk city government consists of its seven-member city council and mayor. The city manager serves as the city's COO and is appointed by the city council.

EXECUTIVES

CMO*, Michael G Brown
Auditors : CLIFTONLARSONALLEN LLP ARLIN

LOCATIONS

HQ: CITY OF NORFOLK
  810 UNION ST STE 508, NORFOLK, VA 235108048
Phone: 757 664-7300
Web: WWW.NORFOLK.GOV

COMPETITORS

CITY & COUNTY OF DENVER
CITY OF BELLEVUE
CITY OF CHESAPEAKE
CITY OF NEWARK, NEW JERSEY
MISSOURI CITY OF KANSAS CITY

HISTORICAL FINANCIALS
Company Type: Private

Income Statement — FYE: June 30

	REVENUE ($mil)	NET INCOME ($mil)	NET PROFIT MARGIN	EMPLOYEES
06/21	835	28	3.4%	4,364
06/20	749	(15)	—	—
06/19	751	162	21.6%	—
06/18	730	73	10.0%	—
Annual Growth	4.6%	(27.2%)	—	—

2021 Year-End Financials
Return on assets: 0.8%   Cash ($ mil.): —
Return on equity: 5.8%
Current Ratio: —

CITY OF OAKLAND

Joining San Francisco and San Jose, Oakland makes up one-third of Northern California's Golden Triangle. Founded in 1852, Oakland boasts of a diverse population, numbering more than 390,000 residents, a Mediterranean climate and thriving hip arts scene. The city is a hub for the port of San Francisco Bay, as well as for the business elite and the higher educated. Environmental policies have helped propel Oakland to stand among the top green economies in the US. The city is served by a mayor and eight council members, who oversee a budget of almost $1 billion. It is home to the NBA's Golden State Warriors, NFL's Oakland Raiders and national landmark, Lake Merritt.

Auditors : MACIAS GINI & O'CONNELL LLP W

LOCATIONS

HQ: CITY OF OAKLAND
  1 FRANK H OGAWA PLZ 2ND, OAKLAND, CA 946121904
Phone: 510 238-3280
Web: WWW.OAKLANDCA.GOV

COMPETITORS

CITY OF BELLEVUE
CITY OF PEORIA
CITY OF RICHMOND
CITY OF SAN DIEGO
CITY OF TUCSON

HISTORICAL FINANCIALS
Company Type: Private

Income Statement — FYE: June 30

	REVENUE ($mil)	NET INCOME ($mil)	NET PROFIT MARGIN	EMPLOYEES
06/21	1,401	(13)	—	4,000
06/20	1,239	163	13.2%	—
06/19	1,211	28	2.3%	—
06/18	1,164	184	15.8%	—
Annual Growth	6.4%	—	—	—

2021 Year-End Financials
Return on assets: (-0.2%)   Cash ($ mil.): —
Return on equity: (-0.9%)
Current Ratio: —

CITY OF OKLAHOMA CITY

Oklahoma City was born overnight as a boomtown named Oklahoma Station in 1889 during the celebrated land rush in Oklahoma Territory. It became in time the state capital and largest city (with a population approaching 600,000) and is headquarters of oil and gas companies Chesapeake Energy and Devon Energy as well as electric utility OGE Energy and service station operator Love's Truck Stops. City government is headed by a mayor and council members representing eight wards. The city captured its first top-rank sports franchise when the Oklahoma City Thunder NBA team began play in 2008.

EXECUTIVES

City Clerk*, Frances Kersey
Auditors : ALLEN GIBBS & HOULIK LC W

LOCATIONS

HQ: CITY OF OKLAHOMA CITY
  100 N WALKER AVE, OKLAHOMA CITY, OK 731022230
Phone: 405 297-2506
Web: WWW.OKC.GOV

COMPETITORS

CITY OF BELLEVUE
CITY OF HOUSTON
CITY OF INDIANAPOLIS
CITY OF LUBBOCK
CITY OF PEORIA

HISTORICAL FINANCIALS
Company Type: Private

Income Statement — FYE: June 30

	REVENUE ($mil)	NET INCOME ($mil)	NET PROFIT MARGIN	EMPLOYEES
06/21	1,031	157	15.3%	4,500
06/18	865	112	13.0%	—
06/17	806	(21)	—	—
06/16	800	26	3.3%	—
Annual Growth	5.2%	43.2%		

2021 Year-End Financials
Return on assets: 1.9%   Cash ($ mil.): 89
Return on equity: 3.6%
Current Ratio: 5.00

CITY OF OMAHA

Owing it name to one the tribes living in the area, the City Omaha was once bypassed by the Lewis and Clark expedition. Founded in 1854, Omaha has become the 42nd largest city in the U.S. with a population of almost 409,000 in an area measuring little more than 130 square miles. The city is ruled by a mayor-council consisting of of an "at-large" mayor and 7 district councilmembers. The City of Omaha is home for megacompanies Berkshire Hathaway, ConAgra, Peter Kiewit Sons, Mutual of Omaha, TD Ameritrade, Union Pacific, West Corporation, Valmont Industries, and Werner Enterprises.

Auditors : RSM US LLP OMAHA NEBRASKA

LOCATIONS

HQ: CITY OF OMAHA
  1819 FARNAM ST RM 300, OMAHA, NE 681831000
Phone: 402 444-5000
Web: WWW.CITYOFOMAHA.ORG

COMPETITORS

CITY OF BELLEVUE
CITY OF CHESAPEAKE
CITY OF FORT WORTH
CITY OF MEMPHIS
CITY OF PLANO

HISTORICAL FINANCIALS

Company Type: Private

Income Statement — FYE: December 31

	REVENUE ($mil)	NET INCOME ($mil)	NET PROFIT MARGIN	EMPLOYEES
12/21	805	44	5.5%	2,800
12/20	707	4	0.7%	—
12/19	636	1	0.2%	—
12/18	593	(29)	—	—
Annual Growth	10.7%	—	—	—

2021 Year-End Financials

Return on assets: 1.1% Cash ($ mil.): —
Return on equity: 7.9%
Current Ratio: —

CITY OF ORLANDO

The City of Orlando offers its own fountain of youth for tourists from around the globe. The young and the young at heart all flock to Orlando, home to Disney World and other popular theme parks. The fast-growing Orlando, which is in the geographic center of Florida, offers a wide variety of attractions for kids of all ages, including Sea World, Universal Studios, and Epcot. The mayor and six city commissioners (elected for four-year terms) make up its city council, which enacts policy for Orlando. Warm and sunny year-round, the city has over 240,000 residents. Incorporated in 1885, the City of Orlando, which operates through some 50 departments, has an annual budget of more than $950 million.

EXECUTIVES

E-Business Point of Contact, Rose Flores
Auditors : MOORE STEPHENS LOVELACE PA

LOCATIONS

HQ: CITY OF ORLANDO
1 CITY CMMONS 400 S ORNGE, ORLANDO, FL 32801
Phone: 407 246-2121
Web: WWW.ORLANDO.GOV

COMPETITORS

CITY OF CHARLOTTE
CITY OF HOUSTON
CITY OF IRVING
CITY OF PHILADELPHIA
CITY OF SAN DIEGO

HISTORICAL FINANCIALS

Company Type: Private

Income Statement — FYE: September 30

	REVENUE ($mil)	NET INCOME ($mil)	NET PROFIT MARGIN	EMPLOYEES
09/21	783	(9)	—	3,000
09/17	567	17	3.1%	—
09/16	556	26	4.8%	—
09/15	493	77	15.7%	—
Annual Growth	8.0%	—	—	—

2021 Year-End Financials

Return on assets: (-0.2%) Cash ($ mil.): 1,081
Return on equity: (-0.4%)
Current Ratio: —

CITY OF PHILADELPHIA

Known as the City of Brotherly Love, Philadelphia is the fifth largest city in the nation, with a population of more than 1.5 million. The city, which covers 135 square miles, operates through some 50 departments, boards, offices, and other units that include emergency medical services, sanitation services, and street maintenance. Founded in 1682 by William Penn, Philadelphia has a mayor, 10 districts and 17 council members. The city, which hosts millions of tourists each year, is home to the Phillies, the Eagles, the Flyers, the 76ers, Bryn Mawr College, the Liberty Bell, and the National Constitution Center. The City of Philadelphia has an annual budget of more than $3.5 billion.

EXECUTIVES

Mayor, Jim Kenney
Staff, Frank Galioto
Coordinator, Francesco Cerrai
Scientist, Anne Harvey
Solicitor, Marcel S Pratt
Procurement Manager, Anita Sharpe
Information Technology Trainin, Nick Demarco
Senior Appeals, Elise Bruhl
Judge, Anne Lazarus
Paralegal, Debbie Decolli
Senior Deputy Director of Comm, Duane Bumb
Auditors : CHRISTY BRADY CPA PHILADELPH

LOCATIONS

HQ: CITY OF PHILADELPHIA
215 CITY HALL, PHILADELPHIA, PA 191073214
Phone: 215 686-2181
Web: WWW.PHILA.GOV

PRODUCTS/OPERATIONS

Selected Units
Behavioral Health
Board of Pensions and Retirement
Board of Revision of Taxes
City Controllers Office
City Planning Commission
City Treasurer
Civil Service Commission
Commerce
Department of Human Services
Ethics Board
Finance
Fire
Fleet Management
Health Department
Historical Commission
Human Relations
Inspector General
Labor Relations
Law
Library
Licenses and Inspections
Parking Authority
Philadelphia International Airport
Police
Procurement
Recreation
Records Department
Redevelopment Authority
Water Revenue Bureau

COMPETITORS

CITY OF CAMBRIDGE
CITY OF CHARLOTTE
CITY OF DALLAS
CITY OF DAYTON
CITY OF DETROIT
CITY OF FORT WORTH
CITY OF HOUSTON
CITY OF OXNARD
CITY OF PHOENIX
LOWELL, CITY OF (INC)

HISTORICAL FINANCIALS

Company Type: Private

Income Statement — FYE: June 30

	REVENUE ($mil)	NET INCOME ($mil)	NET PROFIT MARGIN	EMPLOYEES
06/17	6,646	20	0.3%	29,862
06/16	6,264	(64)	—	—
06/15	6,070	(92)	—	—
06/14	5,947	(10)	—	—
Annual Growth	3.8%	—	—	—

2017 Year-End Financials

Return on assets: 0.1% Cash ($ mil.): 1,744
Return on equity: —
Current Ratio: —

CITY OF PHOENIX

Phoenix, the capital of Arizona, has a population of about 1.4 million and is the sixth largest city in the US. Located in the south-central portion of the state, Phoenix covers a sprawling 500 square miles and is geographically larger than Los Angeles. The City of Phoenix operates through some 30 departments, including street transportation, water services, human services, and public transit. Eight city council members (representing eight districts) and the mayor make up the city council, which develop laws and policy for governing the city. Phoenix was incorporated in 1881.

Auditors : BKD LLP DALLAS TEXAS

LOCATIONS

HQ: CITY OF PHOENIX
200 W WASHINGTON ST FL 11, PHOENIX, AZ 850031611
Phone: 602 262-7111
Web: WWW.PHOENIX.GOV

COMPETITORS

CITY & COUNTY OF DENVER
CITY OF AUSTIN

CITY OF BERKELEY
CITY OF FORT WORTH
CITY OF HOUSTON
CITY OF IRVING
CITY OF MEMPHIS
CITY OF NEWARK, NEW JERSEY
CITY OF OXNARD
LOWELL, CITY OF (INC)

HISTORICAL FINANCIALS
Company Type: Private

Income Statement — FYE: June 30

	REVENUE ($mil)	NET INCOME ($mil)	NET PROFIT MARGIN	EMPLOYEES
06/21	3,384	259	7.7%	14,000
06/20	2,786	27	1.0%	—
06/19	2,588	54	2.1%	—
06/18	2,521	(34)	—	—
Annual Growth	10.3%	—	—	—

2021 Year-End Financials
Return on assets: 1.2%   Cash ($ mil.): 928
Return on equity: 3.9%
Current Ratio: —

CITY OF PITTSBURGH

Take one look at the skyline and it's no wonder Pittsburgh's been nicknamed "The City of Bridges." With more than 440 bridges, 150 skyscrapers, and a countless number of steel behemoths, Pittsburgh is Pennsylvania's second largest city (behind Philadelphia) with a population of more than 305,700. The city is composed of nine districts, each represented by a council member, while the mayor rounds out the executive side. Its annual budget goes toward enhancements to health care and retirement as well as hiring police and fire prevention personnel; most of its revenue comes from real estate taxes. Pittsburgh was founded in 1758.

Auditors : MAHER DUESSEL PITTSBURGH PEN

LOCATIONS

HQ: CITY OF PITTSBURGH
414 GRANT ST, PITTSBURGH, PA 152192409
Phone: 412 255-2640
Web: WWW.PITTSBURGHPA.GOV

COMPETITORS
CITY OF CHICAGO
CITY OF DAYTON
CITY OF HOUSTON
CITY OF RICHMOND
CITY OF SEATTLE

HISTORICAL FINANCIALS
Company Type: Private

Income Statement — FYE: December 31

	REVENUE ($mil)	NET INCOME ($mil)	NET PROFIT MARGIN	EMPLOYEES
12/21	705	62	8.9%	3,500
12/19	651	48	7.4%	—
12/18	635	2	0.3%	—
12/14	537	22	4.2%	—
Annual Growth	4.0%	15.7%	—	—

2021 Year-End Financials
Return on assets: 2.4%   Cash ($ mil.): 546
Return on equity: —
Current Ratio: 2.10

CITY OF PORTLAND

"A rose by any other name would smell as sweet" may be only way to tell this city from 18 other Portlands in the US. Portland has been known as the City of Roses since 1888 and has hosted an annual rose festival since 1905.

EXECUTIVES

City Commissioner*, Steve Novick
Chief of Staff*, Tera Pierce
Deputy Chief of Staff*, Diana Nunez
Auditors : MOSS ADAMS PORTLAND OREGON

LOCATIONS

HQ: CITY OF PORTLAND
1221 SW 4TH AVE RM 340, PORTLAND, OR 972041900
Phone: 503 823-4120
Web: WWW.PORTLAND.GOV

COMPETITORS
CITY OF CHICAGO
CITY OF MILWAUKEE
CITY OF NEWPORT NEWS
CITY OF SEATTLE
CITY OF SYRACUSE

HISTORICAL FINANCIALS
Company Type: Private

Income Statement — FYE: June 30

	REVENUE ($mil)	NET INCOME ($mil)	NET PROFIT MARGIN	EMPLOYEES
06/22	1,969	216	11.0%	5,684
06/21	1,768	(9)	—	—
06/20	1,648	269	16.3%	—
06/19	1,604	138	8.6%	—
Annual Growth	7.1%	16.1%	—	—

2022 Year-End Financials
Return on assets: 1.8%   Cash ($ mil.): —
Return on equity: 8.9%
Current Ratio: 3.10

CITY OF PROVIDENCE

Auditors : CLIFTONLARSONALLEN LLP CRANST

LOCATIONS

HQ: CITY OF PROVIDENCE
25 DORRANCE ST UNIT 1, PROVIDENCE, RI 029031738
Phone: 401 421-7740
Web: WWW.PROVIDENCERI.GOV

HISTORICAL FINANCIALS
Company Type: Private

Income Statement — FYE: June 30

	REVENUE ($mil)	NET INCOME ($mil)	NET PROFIT MARGIN	EMPLOYEES
06/21	951	161	17.0%	2,800
06/20	849	(4)	—	—
06/19	853	7	0.8%	—
06/18	836	15	1.9%	—
Annual Growth	4.4%	116.8%	—	—

2021 Year-End Financials
Return on assets: 6.7%   Cash ($ mil.): 568
Return on equity: —
Current Ratio: 1.70

CITY OF RALEIGH

Raleigh offers the culture of a city with theÂ character of a small town. As North Carolina's capital, itÂ boasts a variety of arts, parks,Â and historic sites. It joins Durham and Chapel Hill to form Research Triangle Park , the nation's largestÂ hub for research and economic development.Â A city council, comprising seven members and a mayor (elected for two-year terms), sets policy and enacts ordinancesÂ forÂ itsÂ 400,000 residents. The City of Raleigh, whose operations areÂ directed by a city manager,Â has an annual budget ofÂ about $860 million. Founded in 1792, Raleigh is home to the NHL's Carolina Hurricanes and NC State. Notable residents include former US president Andrew Johnson and US senator Jesse Helms.

Auditors : CHERRY BEKAERT LLP RALEIGH

LOCATIONS

HQ: CITY OF RALEIGH
222 W HARGETT ST, RALEIGH, NC 276011316
Phone: 919 996-3000
Web: WWW.RALEIGHNC.GOV

PRODUCTS/OPERATIONS

Selected Top Employers
State of North Carolina
Wake County Public School System
North Carolina State University
WakeMed
Rex Hospital
Red Hat
Wake County
City of Raleigh
Progress Energy
First Citizens BancShares
Duke Raleigh Hospital

COMPETITORS
CITY OF DURHAM
CITY OF FORT WORTH
CITY OF HOUSTON
CITY OF OXNARD
CITY OF RICHMOND

HISTORICAL FINANCIALS
Company Type: Private

Income Statement — FYE: June 30

	REVENUE ($mil)	NET INCOME ($mil)	NET PROFIT MARGIN	EMPLOYEES
06/21	572	19	3.4%	4,000
06/19	564	14	2.6%	—
06/18	0	(14)	—	—
Annual Growth	—	—	—	—

2021 Year-End Financials
Return on assets: 0.4%   Cash ($ mil.): 1,144
Return on equity: 0.7%
Current Ratio: —

CITY OF RICHMOND

Music legends Joan Baez and Jerry Garcia both sang about seeing Richmond fall but these days Richmond is rising. The city, which made its living on tobacco and slave trading early in its history, now thrives on business, law, and the research center at the Virginia Biotechnology Research Park. Richmond is home to several major corporations including CarMax, Dominion Resources, Genworth Financial, and MeadWestvaco. It's also home to more than 200,000 people, who are governed by a city council representing nine districts along with an at-large mayor. The city follows a council-manager system and the mayor is not part of the council. Richmond, which was founded in 1737, has an annual budget of about $1.4 billion.

Auditors: CLIFTONLARSONALLEN LLP ARLING

LOCATIONS

HQ: CITY OF RICHMOND
900 E BROAD ST STE 201, RICHMOND, VA 232191907
Phone: 804 646-7970
Web: WWW.RICHMONDGOV.COM

COMPETITORS

CITY OF DURHAM
CITY OF HOUSTON
CITY OF NEWPORT NEWS
CITY OF RALEIGH
TALLAHASSEE, CITY OF (INC)

HISTORICAL FINANCIALS
Company Type: Private

Income Statement — FYE: June 30

	REVENUE ($mil)	NET INCOME ($mil)	NET PROFIT MARGIN	EMPLOYEES
06/21	878	65	7.5%	5,315
06/20	824	(6)	—	—
06/19	800	72	9.0%	—
06/18	757	(41)	—	—
Annual Growth	5.1%	—	—	—

2021 Year-End Financials
Return on assets: 1.5%   Cash ($ mil.): 711
Return on equity: 6.2%
Current Ratio: 2.00

CITY OF ROCHESTER

Known as "The World's Image Center," the City of Rochester, situated on the south of Lake Ontario, encompasses some 37 sq. mi. The city, incorporated in 1703, was one of the first "boomtowns" in the US due to a large number of flour mills. Rochester is now a center of higher education, medical and technological research with University of Rochester, Rochester Institute of Technology, Bausch & Lomb, and Kodak calling it home. Xerox still has a large presence in the city. A population of over 200,000 makes the city the third largest in the state. The government is a "strong mayor" style with 4 district and 5 at-large council members. Previously known as "The Flower City," it hosts an annual lilac festival.

Auditors: FREED MAXICK CPA PC ROCHESTE

LOCATIONS

HQ: CITY OF ROCHESTER
30 CHURCH ST, ROCHESTER, NY 146141206
Phone: 585 428-6755
Web: WWW.CITYOFROCHESTER.GOV

COMPETITORS

CITY OF BROCKTON
CITY OF CAMBRIDGE
CITY OF HENDERSON
CITY OF MILWAUKEE
CITY OF SYRACUSE

HISTORICAL FINANCIALS
Company Type: Private

Income Statement — FYE: June 30

	REVENUE ($mil)	NET INCOME ($mil)	NET PROFIT MARGIN	EMPLOYEES
06/21	645	6	1.0%	3,200
06/20	559	(44)	—	—
06/19	577	(3)	—	—
06/18	584	16	2.9%	—
Annual Growth	3.4%	(28.6%)	—	—

2021 Year-End Financials
Return on assets: 0.2%   Cash ($ mil.): 489
Return on equity: —
Current Ratio: —

CITY OF SACRAMENTO

With its Mediterranean climate and location at the foot of the Sierra Nevadas, living in the city of Sacramento is no sacrifice. Founded in 1849, Sacramento is theÂ oldest incorporated city in the state, and itsÂ seventh most populated comprising about 470,000 residents. California's capital city uses a council-manager form of government, with council members from eight districtsÂ elected to four-year terms.Â The councilÂ sets up city policies, approvesÂ contracts and a budget ofÂ nearly $800 million, as well asÂ hears appeals of city decisions. The four council-appointed officers that carry out the city's business are the city manager, attorney, treasurer, and clerk.Â A Legislative Affairs Unit supports the council.

EXECUTIVES

Chief Innovation Officer*, Louis Stewart
Auditors: VAVRINEK TRINE DAY & CO LL

LOCATIONS

HQ: CITY OF SACRAMENTO
915 I ST FL 5, SACRAMENTO, CA 958142622
Phone: 916 808-5300
Web: WWW.CITYOFSACRAMENTO.ORG

COMPETITORS

CITY OF ALEXANDRIA
CITY OF AUSTIN
CITY OF OXNARD
CITY OF TAMPA
MISSOURI CITY OF KANSAS CITY

HISTORICAL FINANCIALS
Company Type: Private

Income Statement — FYE: June 30

	REVENUE ($mil)	NET INCOME ($mil)	NET PROFIT MARGIN	EMPLOYEES
06/19	838	86	10.3%	4,500
06/18	723	2	0.3%	—
06/17	694	46	6.7%	—
06/16	709	91	12.9%	—
Annual Growth	5.7%	(1.9%)	—	—

2019 Year-End Financials
Return on assets: 1.7%   Cash ($ mil.): —
Return on equity: 4.2%
Current Ratio: —

CITY OF SAINT PAUL

In a Pig's Eye once referred to the City of Saint Paul. Founded in 1849 in the Territory of Minnesota, the city of 285,000 has gone through a few other name changes, finally settling on its current name in 1854. Saint Paul is located on the east bank of the Mississippi River and with its twin city Minneapolis forms the 16th largest metropolis in the US. The mayor-council government consists of an "at large" mayor and seven ward councilmembers. Minnesota's capital, Saint Paul is home to professional sports teams Minnesota Wild of the NHL and Minnesota Swarm of the National Lacrosse League (NLL).

Auditors: REBECCA OTTO/GREG HIERLINGER

LOCATIONS

HQ: CITY OF SAINT PAUL
15 KELLOGG BLVD W STE 390, SAINT PAUL, MN 551021615
Phone: 651 266-8500
Web: WWW.STPAUL.GOV

COMPETITORS

CITY OF BELLEVUE

CITY OF BROCKTON
CITY OF INDIANAPOLIS
CITY OF PEORIA
CITY OF TRENTON

HISTORICAL FINANCIALS
Company Type: Private

Income Statement — FYE: December 31

	REVENUE ($mil)	NET INCOME ($mil)	NET PROFIT MARGIN	EMPLOYEES
12/20	544	(41)	—	3,358
12/19	509	36	7.2%	—
12/18	488	(24)	—	—
12/17	454	(10)	—	—
Annual Growth	6.2%	—	—	—

2020 Year-End Financials
Return on assets: (-1.2%) Cash ($ mil.): —
Return on equity: (-2.5%)
Current Ratio: —

CITY OF SAN ANTONIO

When you "Remember the Alamo," don't forget San Antonio! The second-largest Texas city (behind Houston), with a population of about 1.5 million, San Antonio was the site of the Battle of the Alamo. Today, it's home to major tourist attractions like the River Walk, SeaWorld, and Six Flags Fiesta Texas, as well as the San Antonio Spurs NBA franchise and more than 50 golf courses. It has a huge military presence, with three major Army and Air Force bases. San Antonio is run by a mayor and 10 district representatives who pass laws and establish policies for the city. Its city manager oversees day-to-day operations, including nearly 40 departments. San Antonio has an annual budget of more than $2 billion.

Auditors : GRANT THORNTON LLP HOUSTON T

LOCATIONS

HQ: CITY OF SAN ANTONIO
100 W HOUSTON ST STE 1800, SAN ANTONIO, TX 782051414
Phone: 210 207-6000
Web: WWW.SANANTONIO.GOV

COMPETITORS

CITY OF COLORADO SPRINGS
DEPARTMENT OF CORRECTIONS GUAM
HIGHLANDS & ISLANDS ENTERPRISE
National Health Service
REMEMBRANCE, WHITE HOUSE COMMISSION ON

HISTORICAL FINANCIALS
Company Type: Private

Income Statement — FYE: September 30

	REVENUE ($mil)	NET INCOME ($mil)	NET PROFIT MARGIN	EMPLOYEES
09/20	2,167	(15)	—	12,000
09/19	2,150	192	9.0%	—
09/18	2,056	284	13.8%	—
09/16	0	0	—	—
Annual Growth	—	—	—	—

2020 Year-End Financials
Return on assets: (-0.1%) Cash ($ mil.): 591
Return on equity: (-0.2%)
Current Ratio: 3.30

CITY OF SAN DIEGO

The City of San Diego offers more than just warm weather and beautiful beaches. The second-largest city in California (with a population of more than 1.3 million), known as Telecom Valley, is also one of the centers in the US for technological manufacturing. Its council members each represent one of its nine districts. Founded in 1769, San Diego is the home to 3 universities as well as professional sports teams Padres of MLB and Chargers of the NFL. The city operates through some 50 programs and departments, including environmental services, homeland security, parks and recreation, and the commission for arts and culture. The City of San Diego has an annual budget of approximately $3 billion.

Auditors : MACIAS GINI & O'CONNELL LLP S

LOCATIONS

HQ: CITY OF SAN DIEGO
202 C ST, SAN DIEGO, CA 921013860
Phone: 619 236-6330
Web: WWW.SANDIEGO.GOV

COMPETITORS

CITY OF HOUSTON
CITY OF IRVING
CITY OF ORLANDO
CITY OF TUCSON
TALLAHASSEE, CITY OF (INC)

HISTORICAL FINANCIALS
Company Type: Private

Income Statement — FYE: June 30

	REVENUE ($mil)	NET INCOME ($mil)	NET PROFIT MARGIN	EMPLOYEES
06/21	2,362	113	4.8%	11,200
06/20	2,237	(103)	—	—
06/19	2,283	62	2.7%	—
06/18	2,021	(82)	—	—
Annual Growth	5.3%	—	—	—

2021 Year-End Financials
Return on assets: 0.6% Cash ($ mil.): —
Return on equity: 1.2%
Current Ratio: —

CITY OF SAN JOSE

Do you know the way to San José? If so, you're probably a high tech worker, and hopefully one with a salary to match its real estate prices. The city is known for its Silicon Valley location and technology-driven economy. More than 500 tech firms are the major employers in the area, which is also known for its premium home prices (median $495,000). San José was founded in 1777 and incorporates some 180 square miles. 950,000 residents make San José the third largest city in the state. The city government uses the council/manager model wherein the council, made up of the mayor (elected at large) and the 10 council members (one from each district), sets policy and the council-appointed city manager carries it out.

EXECUTIVES

City Clerk, Patricia O'hearn
Auditors : MACIAS GINI & O'CONNELL LLP

LOCATIONS

HQ: CITY OF SAN JOSE
200 E SANTA CLARA ST 13TH, SAN JOSE, CA 951131905
Phone: 408 535-3500
Web: WWW.SANJOSECA.GOV

COMPETITORS

CITY OF ALEXANDRIA
CITY OF CHARLOTTE
CITY OF DAYTON
CITY OF HOUSTON
CITY OF NEWPORT NEWS

HISTORICAL FINANCIALS
Company Type: Private

Income Statement — FYE: June 30

	REVENUE ($mil)	NET INCOME ($mil)	NET PROFIT MARGIN	EMPLOYEES
06/21	1,894	3	0.2%	7,500
06/20	1,868	309	16.6%	—
06/19	1,731	134	7.8%	—
06/18	1,629	9	0.6%	—
Annual Growth	5.1%	(24.3%)	—	—

2021 Year-End Financials
Return on assets: — Cash ($ mil.): —
Return on equity: 0.1%
Current Ratio: —

CITY OF SCOTTSDALE

EXECUTIVES

City Auditor*, Cheryl Barcala
Auditors : HEINFELD MEECH & CO PC P

LOCATIONS

HQ: CITY OF SCOTTSDALE
7447 E INDIAN SCHOOL RD, SCOTTSDALE, AZ 852513915
Phone: 480 312-7859
Web: WWW.SCOTTSDALEAZ.GOV

HISTORICAL FINANCIALS
Company Type: Private

Income Statement   FYE: June 30

	REVENUE ($mil)	NET INCOME ($mil)	NET PROFIT MARGIN	EMPLOYEES
06/21	546	119	21.8%	25,000
06/20	533	67	12.6%	—
06/15	412	27	6.7%	—
06/12	413	4	1.1%	—
Annual Growth	3.2%	43.7%	—	—

2021 Year-End Financials
Return on assets: 1.6%   Cash ($ mil.): —
Return on equity: 2.1%
Current Ratio: —

CITY OF SEATTLE

In the Emerald City, it's not just the name that's green. The City of Seattle is knownÂ forÂ rain-fed lush greenery but also for its environmentalism. It uses aÂ charter form of government, which features an elected mayor and city council along with a city attorney.Â The nine council members are electedÂ at large annually. AmongÂ some 25Â other departments, Seattle has an Office of Sustainability and Environment, it's restoring salmon habitat,Â andÂ it celebrates Earth Month rather than just Earth Day. The city serves a population ofÂ more thanÂ 600,000 with an annual budget of around $4 billion. It was first settled by Europeans in 1851, and takes its name from Chief Seattle, a local tribal leader.

Auditors : PAT MCCARTHY PAT MCCARTHY

LOCATIONS

HQ: CITY OF SEATTLE
700 5TH AVE STE 5500, SEATTLE, WA 981045016
Phone: 206 684-7999
Web: WWW.SEATTLE.GOV

COMPETITORS

CITY & COUNTY OF DENVER
CITY OF CHICAGO
CITY OF HENDERSON
CITY OF MILWAUKEE
CITY OF MINNEAPOLIS
CITY OF NEWPORT NEWS
CITY OF OXNARD
CITY OF PITTSBURGH
CITY OF RICHMOND
CITY OF SYRACUSE

HISTORICAL FINANCIALS
Company Type: Private

Income Statement   FYE: December 31

	REVENUE ($mil)	NET INCOME ($mil)	NET PROFIT MARGIN	EMPLOYEES
12/21	3,077	388	12.6%	10,000
12/20	2,583	(83)	—	—
12/19	0	0	—	—
12/18	2,395	44	1.9%	—
Annual Growth	8.7%	105.5%	—	—

2021 Year-End Financials
Return on assets: 2.2%   Cash ($ mil.): —
Return on equity: 5.2%
Current Ratio: 3.50

CITY OF SPRINGFIELD

Auditors : POWERS & SULLIVAN LLC WAKEFI

LOCATIONS

HQ: CITY OF SPRINGFIELD
36 COURT ST, SPRINGFIELD, MA 011031687
Phone: 413 736-3111
Web: WWW.SPRINGFIELD-MA.GOV

HISTORICAL FINANCIALS
Company Type: Private

Income Statement   FYE: June 30

	REVENUE ($mil)	NET INCOME ($mil)	NET PROFIT MARGIN	EMPLOYEES
06/17	813	40	5.0%	6,107
06/14	764	(10)	—	—
06/13	751	(19)	—	—
06/12	0	0	—	—
Annual Growth	—	—	—	—

2017 Year-End Financials
Return on assets: 3.6%   Cash ($ mil.): 207
Return on equity: —
Current Ratio: 2.50

CITY OF ST. LOUIS

"The Gateway to the West" is bordered by the Mississippi River on the east and occupiesÂ approximately 62 square miles with a population of more than 300,000.Â The government of the City of St. LouisÂ is comprised ofÂ the city's mayor andÂ a Board of Aldermen (made up of 28 electedÂ members, in addition to the board president). Unlike most city governments, the mayor shares executive authority with other independent citywide elected officials, such as the treasurer and comptroller. During the 21st century, St. LouisÂ has transitioned fromÂ a manufacturing and industrial economy to one heavily dependent on medicine, biotechnology, and other sciences. It is home to MLB's St. Louis Cardinals and NFL's St. Louis Rams.

EXECUTIVES

Chief of Staff, Tim O'connell
Auditors : KPMG LLP ST LOUIS MO

LOCATIONS

HQ: CITY OF ST. LOUIS
1200 MARKET ST RM 212, SAINT LOUIS, MO 631032802
Phone: 314 622-3201
Web: WWW.STLOUIS-MO.GOV

COMPETITORS

CITY OF BERKELEY
HOUSE OF REPRESENTATIVES, MASSACHUSETTS
HOUSE OF REPRESENTATIVES, NEW HAMPSHIRE
HOUSE OF REPRESENTATIVES, RHODE ISLAND
SENATE, MASSACHUSETTS

HISTORICAL FINANCIALS
Company Type: Private

Income Statement   FYE: June 30

	REVENUE ($mil)	NET INCOME ($mil)	NET PROFIT MARGIN	EMPLOYEES
06/21	899	121	13.5%	4,500
06/20	863	8	1.0%	—
06/19	870	111	12.8%	—
06/18	848	50	5.9%	—
Annual Growth	2.0%	34.1%	—	—

2021 Year-End Financials
Return on assets: 2.9%   Cash ($ mil.): 436
Return on equity: 26.4%
Current Ratio: —

CITY OF STAMFORD

Auditors : BLUM SHAPIRO & COMPANY PC W

LOCATIONS

HQ: CITY OF STAMFORD
888 WASHINGTON BLVD, STAMFORD, CT 069012924
Phone: 203 977-4150
Web: WWW.STAMFORDCT.GOV

HISTORICAL FINANCIALS
Company Type: Private

Income Statement   FYE: June 30

	REVENUE ($mil)	NET INCOME ($mil)	NET PROFIT MARGIN	EMPLOYEES
06/18	709	(6)	—	2,878
06/17	678	5	0.8%	—
06/16	648	29	4.5%	—
06/15	627	19	3.0%	—
Annual Growth	4.2%	—	—	—

2018 Year-End Financials
Return on assets: (-0.5%)   Cash ($ mil.): 67
Return on equity: (-3.9%)
Current Ratio: —

CITY OF SYRACUSE

Syracuse, New York is located in the center of the state but it is a world apart from the " Big Apple". Named after the Sicilian city of Syracuse, the city owes much of its growth and history to two things-- salt and the Erie Canal. Although neither is as important as it once was to the city, Syracuse is still a regional transportation hub and the city has managed to weather the economic trends supplanting a salt-centricÂ economy with industrial manufacturing, before evolvingÂ toÂ a service industry centered economy. The city has a population of about

150,000 and is governed by its mayor and a ten-person Common Council.

Auditors : BONADIO & CO LLP SYRACUSE

LOCATIONS

HQ: CITY OF SYRACUSE
233 E WSHNGTN ST STE 231, SYRACUSE, NY 132021423
Phone: 315 448-8005
Web: WWW.SYRGOV.NET

COMPETITORS

CITY & COUNTY OF DENVER
CITY OF CHICAGO
CITY OF MILWAUKEE
CITY OF SEATTLE
CITY OF TOLEDO

HISTORICAL FINANCIALS
Company Type: Private

Income Statement — FYE: June 30

	REVENUE ($mil)	NET INCOME ($mil)	NET PROFIT MARGIN	EMPLOYEES
06/20	779	21	2.7%	6,456
06/19	775	16	2.1%	—
06/18	758	122	16.2%	—
06/17	741	6	0.8%	—
Annual Growth	1.7%	51.2%	—	—

2020 Year-End Financials
Return on assets: 1.1%   Cash ($ mil.): 172
Return on equity: —
Current Ratio: —

CITY OF TAMPA

Disregarded by its first owners, the Spanish in 1517 and the British in 1763, Tampa is now a thriving city on the Gulf Coast of Florida. It joins Clearwater and St. Petersburg in forming the Tampa Bay Area. The city uses a mayor-council form of government with seven council members, one from each of four districts and three at-large. The mayor and council members are elected to four year terms. They set policy and the chief of staff carries it out by running the day-to-day operations of the city. In addition to tourism and the port of Tampa, major area industry includes agriculture, construction, health care, and military operations. Tampa, which has a population of about 350,000, was incorporated in 1855.

Auditors : RSM US LLP TAMPA FLORIDA

LOCATIONS

HQ: CITY OF TAMPA
306 E JACKSON ST, TAMPA, FL 336025223
Phone: 813 274-8211
Web: WWW.TAMPA.GOV

COMPETITORS

CITY OF BELLEVUE
CITY OF HOUSTON
CITY OF OXNARD

CITY OF RICHMOND
CITY OF SACRAMENTO

HISTORICAL FINANCIALS
Company Type: Private

Income Statement — FYE: September 30

	REVENUE ($mil)	NET INCOME ($mil)	NET PROFIT MARGIN	EMPLOYEES
09/21	698	73	10.5%	4,500
09/20	652	43	6.7%	—
09/19	610	33	5.5%	—
09/18	558	64	11.5%	—
Annual Growth	7.7%	4.3%	—	—

2021 Year-End Financials
Return on assets: 1.7%   Cash ($ mil.): —
Return on equity: 2.8%
Current Ratio: —

CITY OF TUCSON

There's no such thing as too much sun in Tucson. The City of Tucson, Arizona, enjoys 360 sunny days a year, is divided into six wards, each represented by a council member. Together with the mayor, the members form the Tucson City Council, which sets city policies; a city manager leads all departments in implementing these policies. Tucson has about half a million residents and a culture that blends Native American and Mexican influences. It's home to The University of Arizona, Davis-Monthan Air Force Base, and The National Optical Astronomy Observatories. The Arizona Diamondbacks are based in Tucson and the Chicago White Sox hold spring training here. The city has an annual budget of greater than $2 billion.

Auditors : CLIFTON LARSON ALLEN LLP TUCS

LOCATIONS

HQ: CITY OF TUCSON
255 W ALAMEDA ST, TUCSON, AZ 857011362
Phone: 520 791-4561
Web: WWW.TUCSONAZ.GOV

COMPETITORS

CITY OF HOUSTON
CITY OF OAKLAND
CITY OF RICHMOND
CITY OF SAN DIEGO
CITY OF TAMPA

HISTORICAL FINANCIALS
Company Type: Private

Income Statement — FYE: June 30

	REVENUE ($mil)	NET INCOME ($mil)	NET PROFIT MARGIN	EMPLOYEES
06/19	903	58	6.4%	5,900
06/16	763	19	2.5%	—
06/15	723	(16)	—	—
06/14	728	31	4.4%	—
Annual Growth	4.4%	12.8%	—	—

2019 Year-End Financials
Return on assets: 1.2%   Cash ($ mil.): 392
Return on equity: 3.2%
Current Ratio: 2.40

CITY OF VIRGINIA BEACH

Whether you're looking for seaside peace and seclusion or bustling boardwalk adventure, Virginia Beach is the spot. With nearly 40 miles of Chesapeake Bay and Atlantic Ocean coastline, the city's economy thrives largely on travel and tourism and supports a population of more than 435,000 people. Virginia Beach's city council consists of 11 elected members (including its mayor) and is responsible for legislative duties including levying taxes, adopting an annual budget, and appointing a city manager. The city manager carries out executive and administrative tasks in this city's Council-Manager government.

Auditors : CLIFTONLARSONALLEN LLP ARLING

LOCATIONS

HQ: CITY OF VIRGINIA BEACH
2401 COURTHOUSE DR # 9001, VIRGINIA BEACH, VA 234569120
Phone: 757 385-3111
Web: WOODSTOCKES.VBSCHOOLS.COM

COMPETITORS

CITY & COUNTY OF DENVER
CITY OF OXNARD
CITY OF RALEIGH
CITY OF SACRAMENTO
CITY OF TAMPA

HISTORICAL FINANCIALS
Company Type: Private

Income Statement — FYE: June 30

	REVENUE ($mil)	NET INCOME ($mil)	NET PROFIT MARGIN	EMPLOYEES
06/21	1,463	(12)	—	7,500
06/20	1,412	156	11.1%	—
06/19	1,379	(70)	—	—
06/18	1,356	61	4.5%	—
Annual Growth	2.6%	—	—	—

2021 Year-End Financials
Return on assets: (-0.2%)   Cash ($ mil.): —
Return on equity: (-0.3%)
Current Ratio: —

CITY OF WATERBURY

Auditors : BLUM SHAPIRO & COMPANY PC

LOCATIONS

HQ: CITY OF WATERBURY
235 GRAND ST, WATERBURY, CT 067021915

Phone: 203 574-6712
Web: WWW.WATERBURYCT.ORG

HISTORICAL FINANCIALS
Company Type: Private

Income Statement   FYE: June 30

	REVENUE ($mil)	NET INCOME ($mil)	NET PROFIT MARGIN	EMPLOYEES
06/17	558	(16)	—	3,200
06/16	536	22	4.1%	—
06/15	530	(20)	—	—
06/08	505	(15)	—	—
Annual Growth	1.1%	—	—	—

2017 Year-End Financials
Return on assets: (-1.7%)   Cash ($ mil.): 25
Return on equity: —
Current Ratio: 3.90

CITY OF WORCESTER

Auditors: CLIFTONLARSONALLEN LLP BOSTON

LOCATIONS

HQ: CITY OF WORCESTER
455 MAIN ST RM 112, WORCESTER, MA 016081805
Phone: 508 799-1049

HISTORICAL FINANCIALS
Company Type: Private

Income Statement   FYE: June 30

	REVENUE ($mil)	NET INCOME ($mil)	NET PROFIT MARGIN	EMPLOYEES
06/13	726	9	1.3%	5,637
06/12	703	(15)	—	—
06/11	720	21	3.0%	—
Annual Growth	0.4%	(33.2%)	—	—

2013 Year-End Financials
Return on assets: 0.7%   Cash ($ mil.): 145
Return on equity: 4.0%
Current Ratio: —

CITY PUBLIC SERVICES OF SAN ANTONIO

CPS Energy (formerly City Public Service of San Antonio) is owned by the City of San Antonio. It is the largest municipally-owned gas and electric utility in the US. It provides customers in San Antonio and surrounding areas with affordable and reliable power while being sensitive to the environment. From grid optimization to solar power, it is also building valuable partnerships with companies who share its belief in clean energy, innovation and energy efficiency. It serves around 907,525 electricity customers and about 374,000 natural gas customers in the greater San Antonio, Texas area. The company traces its roots back in 1860.

Operations
CPS Energy's plant-in-service includes four power stations that are solely owned and operated by the company. In total, there are more than 15 generating units at these four power stations, two of which are coal-fired and some 15 of which are gas-fired. CPS Energy also has two solar generating units, one which also includes battery storage.

Approximately 90% of sales were generated from electric sales, while gas and non-operating sales account for the rest.

Geographic Reach
CPS Energy serves customers in the greater San Antonio, Texas area where it is headquartered, including Bexar County.

Sales and Marketing
Throughout its service territory, CPS Energy provides electric and natural gas services for residential and commercial customers. It serves around 907,525 electric customers and about 374,000 natural gas customers.

Financial Performance
The company had revenues amounting to $2.8 billion in 2022, a 10% increase from the previous year's revenue of $2.5 billion.

The company's cash at the end of FY2021 was $494.8 million. Operating activities generated $571.3 million, while financing activities used $597.9 million, mainly for cash paid for additions to utility plant and net removal costs. Investing activities used another $7.1 million.

Strategy
In support of CPS Energy's commitment to provide world-class energy solutions to meet the diverse and unique needs of its customers, CPS Energy is focused on dialog with the community regarding power generation options and resource planning.

CPS Energy's goals include integrating new and emerging technologies like battery storage and electric vehicles, renewable energy resources, and adding more programs and services like energy efficiency and demand response. Strategic and operational flexibility will allow the company to remain successful with a diverse generation portfolio that focuses on the environment as well as traditional generation assets that continue to be an important bridge to the future while ensuring value and reliability to customers. This strategy ultimately positions CPS Energy to embrace the changing utility landscape while serving its customers.

Company Background
A venerable company, CPS Energy traces its roots to the 1860s, when its predecessor opened a manufactured gas plant on Houston Street.

EXECUTIVES

Chief Administrator, Frank Almaraz
Customer Management, Felicia Etheridge
SECURITY SAFETY GAS SOLUTIONS, Fred Bonewell
CIO, Vivan Bouet
Interim Chief Legal ETHICS, Shanna Ramirez
Auditors: GARZA PREIS & CO LLC/BAKER

LOCATIONS

HQ: CITY PUBLIC SERVICES OF SAN ANTONIO
500 MCCULLOUGH AVE, SAN ANTONIO, TX 782152104
Phone: 210 353-2222
Web: WWW.CPSENERGY.COM

PRODUCTS/OPERATIONS

2015 Sales

	$ mil.	% of total
Electric	2,320.0	92
Gas	175.3	7
Other	36.0	1
Total	2,531.3	100

COMPETITORS

ALLETE, INC.
CMS ENERGY CORPORATION
CONSOLIDATED EDISON, INC.
CONSUMERS ENERGY COMPANY
GEORGIA POWER COMPANY
PUBLIC SERVICE COMPANY OF NEW HAMPSHIRE
PUBLIC SERVICE ENTERPRISE GROUP INCORPORATED
SACRAMENTO MUNICIPAL UTILITY DISTRICT
SAN DIEGO GAS & ELECTRIC COMPANY
UNION ELECTRIC COMPANY

HISTORICAL FINANCIALS
Company Type: Private

Income Statement   FYE: January 31

	REVENUE ($mil)	NET INCOME ($mil)	NET PROFIT MARGIN	EMPLOYEES
01/12	2,258	21	0.9%	3,100
01/11	2,068	78	3.8%	—
01/10	1,930	107	5.6%	—
Annual Growth	8.1%	(55.5%)	—	—

2012 Year-End Financials
Return on assets: 0.2%   Cash ($ mil.): 148
Return on equity: 0.6%
Current Ratio: 1.30

CITYSERVICEVALCON, LLC

You don't have to live in the city to get the services of CityServiceValcon, which markets and distributes petroleum products throughoutÂ the Inland Northwest, and Rocky Mountain regions of the US, as well as in the adjacent Plains states. Its products include gasoline, diesel, aviation fuels, lubricants, propane, and heating oil. The company has diesel, gasoline, and heating oils for delivery through its network of bulk plants. CityServiceValcon also operates cardlock fueling facilities under the Pacific Pride brand name. Regional independent petroleum marketers City Service and Valcon merged their operations in 2003 to form CityServiceValcon.

EXECUTIVES

Managing Member, Dallas Herron

LOCATIONS

HQ: CITYSERVICEVALCON, LLC
   640 W MONTANA ST, KALISPELL, MT 599013834
Phone: 406 755-4321
Web: WWW.CITYSERVICEVALCON.COM

COMPETITORS

CHEVRON PIPE LINE COMPANY
ENGLEFIELD, INC.
GULF OIL LIMITED PARTNERSHIP
THE SOCO GROUP INC
UNITED REFINING COMPANY

HISTORICAL FINANCIALS

Company Type: Private

Income Statement — FYE: September 30

	NET REVENUE ($mil)	NET INCOME ($mil)	NET PROFIT MARGIN	EMPLOYEES
09/08	625	3	0.6%	50
09/07	490	3	0.6%	—
09/06	459	4	1.0%	—
Annual Growth	16.6%	(8.0%)	—	—

2008 Year-End Financials
Return on assets: 9.3%   Cash ($ mil.): 1
Return on equity: 19.2%
Current Ratio: 1.30

CLARCOR INC.

CLARCOR cleans up with filters. The company's industrial and environmental filtration unit makes air and antimicrobial filters for commercial, industrial, and residential buildings, along with filters used in industrial processes. Brands include Airguard, Facet, ATI, Transweb, UAS, Keddeg, MKI, TFS, and Purolator. Companies in CLARCOR's engine and mobile filtration business make products under brands such as Baldwin, Hastings Filters, and Clark that filter the air, oil, fuel, coolant, and hydraulic fluids. In 2017, in order to expand its filtration portfolio, Parker-Hannifin acquired CLARCOR for about $4.3 billion.

Operations

CLARCOR operates in two industry segments: Engine/Mobile Filtration, and Industrial/Environmental Filtration.

The Engine/Mobile Filtration segment (about 60% of total revenue) makes and sells filtration products for engines used in stationary power generation and for engines in mobile equipment applications, including trucks, automobiles, buses and locomotives, and marine, construction, industrial, mining and agricultural equipment. The company manufactures and sells both 'First-fit' filtration systems and replacement products such as oil, air, fuel, coolant, transmission and hydraulic filters.

The company's Industrial/Environmental Filtration segment (about 40%) centers around the manufacturing and marketing of filtration products used in industrial and commercial processes, and in buildings and infrastructures of various types. Its liquid process filtration products include specialty industrial process liquid filters; filters for pharmaceutical processes and beverages; and filtration systems and filters for the oil and natural gas industry, sewage treatment and water recycling, and other industrial uses.

Its air filtration products represent air filters and systems, including advanced medias and treatments and high efficiency first-fit systems used in gas turbine power generation systems, heavy industrial manufacturing processes, thermal power plants, commercial buildings, hospitals, general factories, residential buildings, paint spray booths, medical devices and facilities, motor vehicle systems, aircraft cabins, clean rooms, compressors and compressor stations.

Geographic Reach

CLARCOR makes and sells its products worldwide, and more than 30% of the company's sales come from outside the US. The company has manufacturing, distribution and service facilities in US, Brazil, China, France, Germany, India, Italy, Malaysia, Netherlands, the UAE, the UK, Japan, and Mexico.

Sales and Marketing

The company's filtration products are sold through independent distributors and dealers for OEMs, as well as directly to end users.

The 10 largest customers of the Engine/Mobile Filtration segment accounted for 35% of 2016 fiscal year (November year end) segment sales.

The 10 largest customers of the Industrial/Environmental Filtration segment accounted for more than 15% of that segment's revenue.

Financial Performance

In fiscal 2016 CLARCOR's revenue declined by 6% ($91 million) due to a number of factors, including the 2015 divestiture of J.L. Clark (the former Packaging Segment) which accounted for $40.9 million; decreased net sales volume (due to lower industrial demand) of $26.3 million in the Industrial/Environmental Filtration segment; and $25.1 from a negative currency exchange rate impact due to the strong dollar.

CLARCOR's net income grew by 3.4% to $139.3 million, primarily due to Other, net income of $20.7 million (flat in 2015), which primarily reflected $27.3 million from 3M to settle a patent litigation case.

Net cash provided by operating activities increased by $131.7 million in 2016 to $285.4 million. Some $18.1 million of this increase came from the 3M patent litigation award and the remainder primarily from cost cutting activities, including lowering inventory levels by $36.4 million (resulting in a $58.5 million improvement in cash from operations). The company also reported a $26 million impact from lower cash taxes paid, driven by the timing of tax payments in 2016 and 2015.

Strategy

Following the closing of its acquisition by Parker Hannifin in 2017, CLARCOR will be combined with Parker's Filtration Group to form a diverse global filtration business.

Restructuring to focus on two core business lines, in 2015 CLARCOR sold its J.L. Clark business (the former Packaging Segment) to CC Industries.

Mergers and Acquisitions

In addition to organic growth, CLARCOR has pursued a strategy of expanding its portfolio through acquisitions.

To support its global growth and innovation activities, in 2016 the company acquired certain assets of US-based FibeRio Technology (a technology company focused on the research, development, and commercialization of performance fabric and filtration media) for $11.9 million. That year its CLARCOR Industrial Air division acquired TDC Filter Manufacturing, a top US manufacturer and supplier of pleated filter bags, dust collection cartridges and gas turbine air filters, for $11 million.

In 2014 the company acquired Stanadyne's diesel fuel filtration business for $327.7 million and changed its name to CLARCOR Engine Mobile Solutions. That year it also bought Filter Resources, Inc., Filtration, Inc. and Fabrication Specialties, Inc. for $21.9 million.

Company Background

In 2013 CLARCOR purchased the air filtration business of General Electric's power and water division for $260.3 million.

In 2013 CLARCOR announced plans to invest $40 million for subsidiary Baldwin Filters, Inc. to build a new 400,000 sq. ft. warehouse and distribution center adjacent to Baldwin's manufacturing facility in Kearney, Nebraska.

In 2012 the company acquired Modular Engineering Pty Ltd., an Australian manufacturer of natural gas filtration products as well as a distributor of aftermarket elements. Modular, a longtime supplier to CLARCOR's PECOFacet division, became part of the division. PECOFacet is included in the company's Industrial/Environmental Filtration segment. Modular produces skid-mounted equipment for the natural gas industry in the Asia/Pacific region and expands CLARCOR's presence in that region in both manufacturing and aftermarket sales.

In 2011 the company purchased one of its suppliers of filtration media, Transweb LLC. New Jersey-based Transweb manufactures and supplies media used in end-market applications, including respirators and HVAC filters.

CLARCOR was founded in 1904 and reincorporated in 1969.

Auditors : PRICEWATERHOUSECOOPERS LLP NA

LOCATIONS

HQ: CLARCOR INC.
840 CRESCENT CENTRE DR # 600, FRANKLIN, TN 370674687
Phone: 615 771-3100
Web: WWW.PARKER.COM

Sales 2016

	$ mil.	% of total
United States	944.3	68
Europe	152.7	11
Asia	144.1	10
Other International	148.5	11
Total	1,389.6	100

PRODUCTS/OPERATIONS

sales 2016

	$ mil	% of total
Industrial/Environmental Filtration	803.6	58
Engine/Mobile Filtration	586.0	42
Total	1,389.6	100

COMPETITORS

BALDWIN FILTERS, INC.
BORGWARNER INC.
CHART INDUSTRIES, INC.
COLFAX CORPORATION
COOPER-STANDARD HOLDINGS INC.
CUMMINS FILTRATION INC
CUMMINS INC.
DONALDSON COMPANY, INC.
GENTHERM INCORPORATED
TENNECO INC.

HISTORICAL FINANCIALS
Company Type: Private

Income Statement   FYE: November 30

	REVENUE ($mil)	NET INCOME ($mil)	NET PROFIT MARGIN	EMPLOYEES
11/16	1,389	139	10.0%	5,773
11/15	1,481	134	9.1%	—
11/14	1,512	144	9.5%	—
11/13	1,130	118	10.5%	—
Annual Growth	7.1%	5.6%	—	—

2016 Year-End Financials
Return on assets: 8.0%   Cash ($ mil.): 134
Return on equity: 12.2%
Current Ratio: 3.10

CLARK COUNTY SCHOOL DISTRICT

Auditors : EIDE BAILLY LLP LAS VEGAS N

LOCATIONS

HQ: CLARK COUNTY SCHOOL DISTRICT
2832 E FLAMINGO RD, LAS VEGAS, NV 891215295
Phone: 702 794-9238

Web: WWW.CCSD.NET

HISTORICAL FINANCIALS
Company Type: Private

Income Statement   FYE: June 30

	REVENUE ($mil)	NET INCOME ($mil)	NET PROFIT MARGIN	EMPLOYEES
06/22	4,297	471	11.0%	37,361
06/20	3,616	285	7.9%	—
06/19	3,519	274	7.8%	—
Annual Growth	6.9%	19.8%	—	—

2022 Year-End Financials
Return on assets: 5.0%   Cash ($ mil.): —
Return on equity: 53.6%
Current Ratio: —

CLARK EQUIPMENT COMPANY

Auditors : DELOITTE & TOUCHE LLP MINNEA

LOCATIONS

HQ: CLARK EQUIPMENT COMPANY
250 E BEATON DR, WEST FARGO, ND 580782656
Phone: 701 241-8700
Web: WWW.BOBCAT.COM

HISTORICAL FINANCIALS
Company Type: Private

Income Statement   FYE: December 31

	REVENUE ($mil)	NET INCOME ($mil)	NET PROFIT MARGIN	EMPLOYEES
12/17	2,543	174	6.9%	5,822
12/16	2,415	166	6.9%	—
12/15	0	0	—	—
12/14	2,539	492	19.4%	—
Annual Growth	0.1%	(29.3%)	—	—

2017 Year-End Financials
Return on assets: 6.1%   Cash ($ mil.): 127
Return on equity: 24.8%
Current Ratio: 1.40

CLEVELAND MUNICIPAL SCHOOL DISTRICT

Auditors : KEITH FABER COLUMBUS OH

LOCATIONS

HQ: CLEVELAND MUNICIPAL SCHOOL DISTRICT
1111 SUPERIOR AVE E # 1800, CLEVELAND, OH 441142500
Phone: 216 838-0000
Web: WWW.MC2STEMHIGHSCHOOL.ORG

HISTORICAL FINANCIALS
Company Type: Private

Income Statement   FYE: June 30

	REVENUE ($mil)	NET INCOME ($mil)	NET PROFIT MARGIN	EMPLOYEES
06/21	990	82	8.3%	9,500
06/20	896	(35)	—	—
06/19	941	(119)	—	—
06/18	957	(49)	—	—
Annual Growth	1.2%	—	—	—

2021 Year-End Financials
Return on assets: 4.4%   Cash ($ mil.): 253
Return on equity: 42.2%
Current Ratio: —

CLIFTONLARSONALLEN LLP

CliftonLarsonAllen (CLA) exists to create opportunities for its clients, its people, and its communities through industry-focused wealth advisory, outsourcing, audit, tax, and consulting services. CLA is a network member of CLA Global, an international organization of independent accounting and advisory firms. The firm has operations in more than 120 locations across the US.

Operations

The company's services include audit, accounting, tax, consulting, outsourcing, and wealth advisory. Its investment advisory services are conducted through CliftonLarsonAllen Wealth Advisors, LLC.

Other services include cybersecurity and risk management, data analytics, employee benefit plans, M&A advisory and investment banking, talent solutions, and tax educations for CPAs.

Geographic ReachMinnesota-based, CLA boasts more than 120 locations across the US.

Sales and Marketing

CLA, which has more than 232,000 clients, serves privately-held businesses, individuals, not-for-profits, and governmental entities. Its major client groups include agribusiness and cooperatives, dealerships, employee benefit plans, federal government, financial institutions, healthcare, manufacturing and distribution companies, as well as state and local governments.

Company Background

CLA was formed in 2011 by the merger of Clifton Gunderson and LarsonAllen. Prior to the pairing, both companies had been active in expanding across the country by purchasing smaller firms and parts of other firms.

EXECUTIVES

CSO, John Richter
CPO, Larry Taylor

Chief Executive Officer Emeritus, Denny Schleper

LOCATIONS

HQ: CLIFTONLARSONALLEN LLP
220 S 6TH ST STE 300, MINNEAPOLIS, MN 554021418
Phone: 612 376-4500
Web: BLOGS.CLACONNECT.COM

Selected Locations
Arizona
California
Colorado
Florida
Idaho
Illinois
Indiana
Iowa
Maryland
Massachusetts
Michigan
Minnesota
Mississippi
Missouri
New Jersey
New Mexico
New York
North Carolina
Ohio
Pennsylvania
Texas
Virginia
Washington
Wisconsin

PRODUCTS/OPERATIONS

Selected Services: Audit and assuranceConsultingCLA Intuition financial modelingEmployee benefit plansExecutive searchForensicInformation securityIntacct softwareLitigation supportRisk managementTechnologyTransaction supportValuationInternationalOutsourcingPrivate client tax and wealth advisoryTaxTax education for CPAsIndustries
Selected: AgribusinessArchitecture and engineering firmsConstruction and real estateCooperativesCraft brewers and distillersDealershipsEmployee benefit plansFinancial institutionsGovernmentGovernment contractorsHigher educationManufacturing and distributionNonprofitTechnology and emerging companiesTrucking and transportation

COMPETITORS

ALVAREZ & MARSAL HOLDINGS, LLC
BKD, LLP
BUCK GLOBAL, LLC
CRA INTERNATIONAL, INC.
EISNERAMPER LLP
HORNE LLP
MAYFIELD CONSULTING, INC.
PROTIVITI INC.
THE SEGAL GROUP INC
WIPFLI LLP

HISTORICAL FINANCIALS
Company Type: Private

Income Statement — FYE: December 4

	REVENUE ($mil)	NET INCOME ($mil)	NET PROFIT MARGIN	EMPLOYEES
12/15	650	170	26.3%	4,786
12/14	598	163	27.3%	—
12/13	563	154	27.5%	—
Annual Growth	7.5%	5.1%	—	—

2015 Year-End Financials
Return on assets: 68.4%   Cash ($ mil.): 12
Return on equity: 95.9%
Current Ratio: 3.50

CLOUD PEAK ENERGY RESOURCES LLC

Auditors: PRICEWATERHOUSECOOPERS LLP DE

LOCATIONS

HQ: CLOUD PEAK ENERGY RESOURCES LLC
505 S GILLETTE AVE, GILLETTE, WY 827164203
Phone: 303 956-7596
Web: WWW.CLOUDPEAKENERGY.COM

HISTORICAL FINANCIALS
Company Type: Private

Income Statement — FYE: December 31

	REVENUE ($mil)	NET INCOME ($mil)	NET PROFIT MARGIN	EMPLOYEES
12/13	1,396	58	4.2%	1,200
12/12	1,516	155	10.3%	—
12/11	1,553	201	13.0%	—
12/10	1,370	170	12.4%	—
Annual Growth	0.6%	(29.8%)	—	—

2013 Year-End Financials
Return on assets: 2.5%   Cash ($ mil.): 231
Return on equity: 5.5%
Current Ratio: 1.80

COASTAL CHEMICAL CO., L.L.C.

LOCATIONS

HQ: COASTAL CHEMICAL CO., L.L.C.
3520 VETERANS MEMORIAL DR, ABBEVILLE, LA 705105708
Phone: 337 898-0001
Web: WWW.COASTALCHEM.COM

HISTORICAL FINANCIALS
Company Type: Private

Income Statement — FYE: December 31

	REVENUE ($mil)	NET INCOME ($mil)	NET PROFIT MARGIN	EMPLOYEES
12/14	736	33	4.6%	964
12/09	386	10	2.6%	—
12/08	635	16	2.6%	—
Annual Growth	2.5%	12.9%	—	—

2014 Year-End Financials
Return on assets: 10.3%   Cash ($ mil.): 3
Return on equity: 88.0%
Current Ratio: 0.90

COASTAL PACIFIC FOOD DISTRIBUTORS, INC.

Coastal Pacific Food Distributors (CPF) fuels the military forces from facility to fork. The company is one of the top wholesale food distributors that primarily serves the US armed forces across the Western US and in the Far East. As part of its business, CPF provides a full line of groceries to military bases run by the US Army, Navy, Air Force, and Marines. It delivers a variety of products from distribution centers located in California, Washington, and Hawaii. CPF also offers information system programming services for its customers to track sales and shipping, as well as procurement and logistics through partnerships in Iraq, Kuwait, and Saudi Arabia. The company was founded in 1986.

Operations
CPF has grown to become the second-largest worldwide military distributor of food and related products.

As part of its business, CPF operates distribution centers in California, Washington, Hawaii, and Canada. In California, its largest Stockton facility spans more than 500,000 sq. ft. while its Ontario center boasts 429,000 sq. ft. Its distribution center in Fife, Washington, is 153,000 sq. ft. A 45,000-sq.-ft. facility in Hawaii delivers food to four military commissaries.

Geographic Reach
California-based CPF caters to the Western US, as well as Alaska, Hawaii, Guam, Japan, Okinawa, Korea, Singapore, Kwajalein, Diego Garcia, and the Philippines. Its business extends to the Middle East through partnerships for procurement and logistics with other companies. These additional areas include Iraq, Kuwait, and Saudi Arabia.

Sales and Marketing
Industry partners that keep CPF busy include the Defense Logistics Agency, the Defense Commissary Agency, Air Force NAF

Purchasing Office, Navy Exchange (NEXCOM), Army and Air Force Exchange Service (AAFES), and the American Logistics Association, to name a few.

The company counts on food manufacturers to keep its customers happy. They include Kraft Foods, Tyson Foods, Procter & Gamble, General Mills, Nestle, ConAgra, Unilever, Frito-Lay, Campbell, J.M. Smucker, Global Military Marketing, Mars, S&K Sales, Del Monte Corp., Georgia-Pacific, Johnson & Johnson, and Alder Foods.

Strategy

The company works to support its existing markets. In 2013 CPF opened a new prime vendor platform in Calamba, Luguna, Philippines as it looks to serve future growth there. The platform supports Naval ships with dry, chill, and frozen items.

EXECUTIVES

Vice Chairman, David Jared
Auditors : DIXON HUGHES GOODMAN LLP NORF

LOCATIONS

HQ: COASTAL PACIFIC FOOD DISTRIBUTORS, INC.
1015 PERFORMANCE DR, STOCKTON, CA 952064925
Phone: 909 947-2066
Web: WWW.CPFD.COM

PRODUCTS/OPERATIONS

Selected Products
Bakery
Candy
Deli
Fresh & frozen meats
Frozen foods
Pet foods
Refrigerated items
Sushi

Selected Brokers
Acosta Sales & Marketing
Alder Foods, Inc.
Bisek & Co., Inc.
Dixon Marketing, Inc.
Dunham & Smith Agencies
Elite Brands
Finnegan International Sales
First Wave Sales
Gateway Military, LLC
Global Office Building
HI-PAC, Ltd
Mid Valley
Overseas Service Corporation
Otis McAllister
Parra Sales, Inc
Reese Group
S&K
S. Schwartz Sales, Inc.
Turnkey Management
WEBCO General Partnership

COMPETITORS

BURRIS LOGISTICS
CERTCO, INC.
CJ LOGISTICS AMERICA, LLC
COWAN SYSTEMS, LLC
CROWLEY MARITIME CORPORATION
DOT FOODS, INC.
LOGISTICS PLUS, INC.
MAINFREIGHT, INC.
URM STORES, INC.
YUSEN LOGISTICS (UK) LIMITED

HISTORICAL FINANCIALS

Company Type: Private

Income Statement — FYE: December 29

	REVENUE ($mil)	NET INCOME ($mil)	NET PROFIT MARGIN	EMPLOYEES
12/12	1,212	15	1.2%	459
12/11*	1,162	25	2.2%	—
01/11	1,113	17	1.6%	—
Annual Growth	4.4%	(7.6%)	—	—

*Fiscal year change

2012 Year-End Financials
Return on assets: 6.7%   Cash ($ mil.): 5
Return on equity: 50.6%
Current Ratio: 2.60

COBANK, ACB

CoBank is one of the largest private providers of credit to the US rural economy. The bank delivers loans, leases and other financial services to agribusiness, rural infrastructure and Farm Credit customers in all 50 states. Primary products and services include term loans, revolving lines of credit, trade finance, capital markets services, as well as risk management, cash management, leasing and investment products. Its Farm Credit Banking has some 20 affiliated associations operating in about 25 states serving the Northwest, West, Southwest, Rocky Mountains, Mid-Plains, and Northeast regions of the US. Its core agribusiness customers range from local and single facility grain cooperatives to national global food, beverage and agribusiness companies. Formed in 1989, CoBank merged with US AgBank in early 2012.

Operations

CoBank operates three main business segments: Agribusiness (about 55% of total revenue), Rural Infrastructure (some 30%) and Farm Credit Banking (about 30%).

Agribusiness provides lending to regional and corporate business customers, export finance customers and leasing customers. It serves cooperatives and other customers involved in a wide variety of industries, including grain handling and marketing, farm supply, food processing, dairy livestock, fruits, nuts vegetables, cotton, biofuels and forest products.

Rural Infrastructure provides lending to rural infrastructure borrowers across in the US and its serves rural utilities and other customers across a wide variety of industries, including electric generation, transmission and distribution cooperatives, midstream energy and gas pipeline providers, water and wastewater companies, broadband and more.

Farm Credit banking provides loans and financial services to more than 76,000 farmers, ranchers, and other rural borrowers in about 25 states. It serves a diverse array of industries from fruits, nuts and vegetables to grains, and other row crops, to dairy, beef, poultry and forest products.

Overall, net interest income generates some 90% of total revenue and non-interest income accounts for the remaining 10% of CoBank's revenue.

Geographic Reach

Based in Colorado, CoBank operates nearly 15 regional offices throughout the US, including locations in Iowa, Georgia, Texas, Connecticut, North Dakota, Minnesota, Nebraska, California, Kansas, Missouri, Kentucky, and Washington. It also has an international office in Singapore.

Sales and Marketing

CoBank mainly serves clients in the agribusiness, water and waste disposal, communications, and power sectors.

Financial Performance

The company had a net interest income of $1.7 billion, a 10% increase from the previous year's net interest income of $1.4 billion.

In 2021, the company had a net income of $1.3 billion, a 4% increase from the previous year's net income. The primary driver of the increase was higher net interest income, which resulted from the increase in average loan volume described above, as well as improved lending spreads, strong fee income and other favorable factors.

The company's cash at the end of 2021 was $3.2 billion. Operating activities generated $1.6 billion, while investing activities used $12.1 billion, mainly for purchases of investment securities. Financing activities provided another $11.4 million.

EXECUTIVES

Chief Business Officer*, Eric Itambo
Auditors : PRICEWATERHOUSECOOPERS LLP D

LOCATIONS

HQ: COBANK, ACB
6340 S FIDDLERS GREEN CIR, GREENWOOD VILLAGE, CO 801114951
Phone: 303 740-6527
Web: WWW.COBANK.COM

Selected Regional Offices
Ames, IA
Atlanta, GA
Austin, TX
Enfield, CT
Fargo, ND
Louisville, KY
Lubbock, TX
Minneapolis, MN
Omaha, NE
Roseville, CA
Spokane, WA
St. Louis, MO
Washington , D.C.
Wichita, KS

COMPETITORS

AGFIRST FARM CREDIT BANK
BANKIA SA
BRITISH ARAB COMMERCIAL BANK PUBLIC LIMITED COMPANY
CAIXABANK SA

FARM CREDIT EAST, ACA
FEDERAL AGRICULTURAL MORTGAGE CORPORATION
FEDERAL HOME LOAN BANK OF DALLAS
MIDSOUTH BANCORP, INC.
NORINCHUKIN BANK, THE
WESTERN ALLIANCE BANCORPORATION

HISTORICAL FINANCIALS
Company Type: Private

Income Statement — FYE: December 31

	ASSETS ($mil)	NET INCOME ($mil)	INCOME AS % OF ASSETS	EMPLOYEES
12/18	139,016	1,190	0.9%	500
12/17	129,211	1,125	0.9%	—
12/16	126	945	749.8%	—
12/15	117,471	936	0.8%	—
Annual Growth	5.8%	8.3%	—	—

2018 Year-End Financials
Return on assets: 0.9%   Cash ($ mil.): 1368
Return on equity: 12.5%
Current Ratio: —

COBB COUNTY BOARD OF EDUCATION

Auditors: MAULDIN & JENKINS LLC ATLANT

LOCATIONS
HQ: COBB COUNTY BOARD OF EDUCATION
514 GLOVER ST SE, MARIETTA, GA 300602750
Phone: 770 426-3300
Web: WWW.COBBK12.ORG

HISTORICAL FINANCIALS
Company Type: Private

Income Statement — FYE: June 30

	REVENUE ($mil)	NET INCOME ($mil)	NET PROFIT MARGIN	EMPLOYEES
06/17	1,299	(13)	—	293
06/16	1,238	(1)	—	—
06/15	1,166	(28)	—	—
06/14	532	67	12.6%	—
Annual Growth	34.7%	—	—	—

2017 Year-End Financials
Return on assets: (-0.6%)   Cash ($ mil.): 247
Return on equity: (-1.6%)
Current Ratio: —

COBB COUNTY MEDICAL EXAMINER'S OFFICE

EXECUTIVES
County Manager*, David Hanerkson
Auditors: MOORE & CUBBEDGE LLP MARIETT

LOCATIONS
HQ: COBB COUNTY MEDICAL EXAMINER'S OFFICE
122 WADDELL ST NE, MARIETTA, GA 30060
Phone: 770 528-3300
Web: WWW.COBBCOUNTY.ORG

HISTORICAL FINANCIALS
Company Type: Private

Income Statement — FYE: September 30

	REVENUE ($mil)	NET INCOME ($mil)	NET PROFIT MARGIN	EMPLOYEES
09/21	990	137	13.9%	5,000
09/20	924	68	7.5%	—
09/19	834	57	6.9%	—
09/18	793	4	0.6%	—
Annual Growth	7.7%	210.0%	—	—

2021 Year-End Financials
Return on assets: 2.0%   Cash ($ mil.): 164
Return on equity: 2.7%
Current Ratio: 12.10

COBB COUNTY PUBLIC SCHOOLS

Auditors: MAULDIN & JENKINS ATLANTA GE

LOCATIONS
HQ: COBB COUNTY PUBLIC SCHOOLS
4575 WADE GREEN RD NW, ACWORTH, GA 301023407
Phone: 678 594-8320
Web: WWW.COBBK12.ORG

HISTORICAL FINANCIALS
Company Type: Private

Income Statement — FYE: June 30

	REVENUE ($mil)	NET INCOME ($mil)	NET PROFIT MARGIN	EMPLOYEES
06/22	1,698	131	7.7%	3,026
06/21	1,581	130	8.3%	—
06/20	1,503	(21)	—	—
06/17	1,299	(13)	—	—
Annual Growth	5.5%	—	—	—

2022 Year-End Financials
Return on assets: 4.2%   Cash ($ mil.): 678
Return on equity: 24.7%
Current Ratio: —

COBB COUNTY SCHOOL DISTRICT

Auditors: MAULDIN & JENKINS LLC ATLANT

LOCATIONS
HQ: COBB COUNTY SCHOOL DISTRICT
514 GLOVER ST SE, MARIETTA, GA 300602706
Phone: 770 426-3300
Web: WWW.COBBK12.ORG

HISTORICAL FINANCIALS
Company Type: Private

Income Statement — FYE: June 30

	REVENUE ($mil)	NET INCOME ($mil)	NET PROFIT MARGIN	EMPLOYEES
06/20	1,503	(21)	—	64
06/19	1,407	24	1.7%	—
06/17	0	0	0.0%	—
06/16	0	(0)	—	—
Annual Growth	1310.5%	—	—	—

2020 Year-End Financials
Return on assets: (-0.8%)   Cash ($ mil.): 458
Return on equity: (-12.1%)
Current Ratio: —

COBB ELECTRIC MEMBERSHIP CORPORATION

Cobb Electric Membership Corporation (Cobb EMC) makes sure that Cobb County, Georgia residents can cook corn on the cob (and anything else) using either electric power or natural gas. The utility distributes electricity to more than 200,000 meters (more than 177,000 residential, commercial, and industrial members) in Cobb County and four other north metro Atlanta counties. Cobb EMC operates about 10,000 miles of power lines. The company's Gas South unit markets natural gas to customers who receive their service on Atlanta Gas & Light's natural gas distribution pipelines in Georgia.

Operations

Its Cobb Energy Management provides administrative and labor support to Cobb EMC and offers phone and Internet services to Cobb EMC's customers primarily through subsidiaries. Cobb Energy Management provides call center, training, tree trimming, and billing software services and other ancillary support to EMC's core activities.

Geographic Reach

One of the largest of Georgia's 41 EMCs, Cobb EMC's distribution system covers approximately 1,434 square miles (Cobb, Bartow, Cherokee, Fulton, and Paulding counties in the north metro Atlanta area and Randolph, Calhoun, Quitman and Clay counties in Southwest Georgia).

Financial Performance

In 2012 the company reported a 46% increase in revenues thanks to a 10% rise in natural gas sales which outpaced a 2% decline in electric revenues. Net income grew by 194% in 2012 as a result of higher net sales and lower operating costs.

Strategy

Cobb EMC is a partner in Power4Georgians, a consortium of six Georgia

EMCs that collectively is developing a comprehensive strategy to provide reliable and affordable energy to the EMC members.

In 2013 as part of its ongoing transition out of non-energy businesses, Cobb EMC announced today plans to cut its workforce by up to 20% percent through a company-wide offer of voluntary separation packages.

In 2012 Smart Energy Capital, LLC and Jacoby Development, Inc., signed a power purchase deal with Cobb EMC to provide power from the Azalea Solar Facility, the largest solar power plant (10MW) in Georgia, and one of the largest in the Southeast.

Company Background

The cooperative has been embroiled in litigation in recent years, and in 2011 a Cobb County grand jury indicted Cobb EMC Dwight Brown on 31 counts of theft and racketeering. Brown was replaced as CEO by W.T. "Chip" Nelson.

The gas and support companies were merged into EMC as wholly owned units in 2009 as a way to streamline EMC's overall operations. The company has also sold a number of former assets to raise cash, including Cooperative Business Ventures in 2009 for $2 million, and the health and welfare brokerage business of Cooperative Benefits and Financial Services for a gain of $470,000 in 2010.

Formed in 1938, Cobb EMC began life as an electric utility with 489 residential members and 14 commercial customers.

Auditors : MCNAIR MCLEMORE MIDDLEBROOKS

LOCATIONS

HQ: COBB ELECTRIC MEMBERSHIP CORPORATION
1000 EMC PKWY NE, MARIETTA, GA 300607908
Phone: 770 429-2100
Web: WWW.COBBEMC.COM

COMPETITORS

AMBIT ENERGY HOLDINGS, LLC
AMERICAN MUNICIPAL POWER, INC.
CLAY ELECTRIC COOPERATIVE, INC.
COLUMBIA GAS OF OHIO, INC.
GREYSTONE POWER CORPORATION, AN ELECTRIC MEMBERSHIP CORPORATION
JACKSON ELECTRIC MEMBERSHIP CORPORATION
LEE COUNTY ELECTRIC COOPERATIVE, INC.
SOUTHERN MARYLAND ELECTRIC COOPERATIVE, INC.
SOUTHERN UNION GAS COMPANY, INC.
THE SOUTHERN COMPANY

HISTORICAL FINANCIALS
Company Type: Private

Income Statement — FYE: December 31

	REVENUE ($mil)	NET INCOME ($mil)	NET PROFIT MARGIN	EMPLOYEES
12/20*	802	49	6.1%	548
04/18	849	25	3.0%	—
12/13	416	(8)	—	—
04/09	641	3	0.6%	—
Annual Growth	1.9%	24.4%	—	—

*Fiscal year change

2020 Year-End Financials
Return on assets: 3.7% Cash ($ mil.): 2
Return on equity: 11.1%
Current Ratio: 1.00

COBORN'S, INCORPORATED

Coborn's operates more than 120 stores across Midwest of the US under the Coborn's, Cash Wise, Captain Jack's, Marketplace Foods and Hornbacher's. Coborn's operates its own central bakery, fuel and convenience division, pharmacy division, in-house grocery warehouse and distribution center and tops cleaners. Along with its grocery stores, the firm owns and operates pharmacies and convenience, and liquor stations. The company manages the delivery logistics of hundreds of grocery products for its entire family of stores throughout the upper Midwest. Founded in 1921, Coborn's is a fourth generation business managed by its CEO Chris Coborn.

Operations

As part of its business, Coborn's operates under several banner names, including Cash Wise, Marketplace Foods, Hornbacher's, and namesake Coborn's. These supermarkets are supported by their own central bakery, fuel and convenience division, pharmacy division, in-house grocery warehouse and distribution center, and tops cleaners. The company also runs convenience, pharmacy, and liquor stores under the brands Coborn's Liquor, Cash Wise Liquor, and Captain Jack's.

Geographic Reach

Based in Minnesota, Coborn's operates two support center offices in North Dakota and Wisconsin.

Sales and Marketing

Coborn's distribution channel includes grocery, convenience, liquor, retail stores, and online.

Strategy

In mid-2021, Associated Wholesale Grocers, Inc. (AWG) and Coborn's, Inc. (Coborn's) announced they have reached an agreement for AWG to serve as the primary wholesale supplier to Coborn's. AWG will commence supply of grocery products to the Coborn's stores in January 2022 from AWG's new Upper Midwest Division in St Cloud, Minnesota situated in the former Creative Memories warehouse facility located in St. Cloud's I-94 Business Park at Opportunity Drive and I-94. Fresh and frozen products will temporarily ship from AWG's Nebraska and Great Lakes Divisions.

Later in 2022, AWG will complete a new fresh and frozen warehouse at a location still to be determined. Once completed, these warehouses will provide more than 650,000 square feet of warehouse space and accommodate the full-line distribution of products to Coborn's and other AWG member stores in the region. Additionally, once a site is selected for the new fresh and frozen warehouse and completed, AWG plans a future expansion into a single state-of-the-art facility with automated high-tech operations and with up to one million square feet of space, based on retail demand. In total, AWG expects this project to create over 400 new jobs.

Company Background

Founded in 1921 when Chester Coborn started a single produce market, the company opened its first Cash Wise Foods store in 1979 and its first convenience store in 1986.

EXECUTIVES

OF ORG Development*, Rebecca Estby
Auditors : RSM US LLP MINNEAPOLIS MINNE

LOCATIONS

HQ: COBORN'S, INCORPORATED
1921 COBORN BLVD, SAINT CLOUD, MN 563012100
Phone: 320 252-4222
Web: WWW.COBORNSINC.COM

PRODUCTS/OPERATIONS

Selected Store Formats
Convenience stores (Little Dukes, Holiday)
Hardware stores (Ace)
Liquor stores
Pharmacies
Restaurants (Subway)
Supermarkets (Coborn's, Cash Wise Foods, JK Markets, Save-A-Lot)
Video stores

COMPETITORS

FAREWAY STORES, INC.
FOUR B CORP.
GRISTEDE'S FOODS, INC.
HOUCHENS INDUSTRIES, INC.
MSM HOLDCO, LLC
SAVE MART SUPERMARKETS DISC
SHAW'S SUPERMARKETS, INC.
STEWART'S SHOPS CORP.
UNITED SUPERMARKETS, L.L.C.
WAWA, INC.

HISTORICAL FINANCIALS
Company Type: Private

Income Statement — FYE: December 28

	REVENUE ($mil)	NET INCOME ($mil)	NET PROFIT MARGIN	EMPLOYEES
12/13	1,246	30	2.5%	7,200
12/12	1,220	32	2.7%	—
Annual Growth	2.1%	(5.0%)	—	—

2013 Year-End Financials
Return on assets: 8.8% Cash ($ mil.): 21
Return on equity: 17.7%
Current Ratio: 1.10

COC PROPERTIES, INC.

Auditors : BATCHELOR TILLERY & ROBERTS

LOCATIONS

HQ: COC PROPERTIES, INC.
110 MACKENAN DR STE 300, CARY, NC 275117901
Phone: 919 462-1100

HISTORICAL FINANCIALS
Company Type: Private

Income Statement — FYE: December 31

	ASSETS ($mil)	NET INCOME ($mil)	INCOME AS % OF ASSETS	EMPLOYEES
12/21	133	13	9.8%	230
12/20	117	13	11.4%	—
12/19	110	13	12.5%	—
12/18	102	8	8.8%	—
Annual Growth	9.4%	13.5%	—	—

2021 Year-End Financials
Return on assets: 9.8%   Cash ($ mil.): 22
Return on equity: 18.3%
Current Ratio: 1.30

COLORADO STATE UNIVERSITY

Colorado State University (CSU) got its start as an agricultural college in 1870, six years before Colorado was even a state. The school still has agricultural and forestry programs, as well as a veterinary medicine school, but it also offers degrees in liberal arts, business, engineering, and the sciences. True to its roots as a land-grant college, CSU engages the larger community in research and outreach through statewide Cooperative Extension programs and centers like the Colorado Agricultural Experiment Station. More than 30,000 students are enrolled at CSU, about 80% of whom are Colorado residents. It employs about 1,500 faculty members and has aÂ student-to-teacher ratioÂ of 19:1.

Operations

The school's student body is largely composed of undergraduate students (more than 80%), but also includes some graduate and professional veterinary medicine students. CSU'sÂ most popularÂ undergraduate majors are business, health and exercise science, psychology, biological science, construction management, and human development and family studies. Overall, the university offers about 150 undergraduate, graduate, and professional degree programs through eight colleges.

CSU has extensive research programs in fields including atmospheric science, clean energy, the environment, biomedicine, and infectious diseases. The university's research programs attract some $300 million in external funding each year.

Geographic Reach

CSU's main campusÂ and itsÂ nearby foothills, agricultural, and mountain campusesÂ are located on about 5,000 acres in Fort Collins, Colorado.Â The universityÂ has more than 1,200 international students and scholars from about 90 countries on its campus. Additionally, about 900 CSU students travel abroad every year to participate in educational programs.

Financial Performance

CSU's revenues increased 8% in 2012 to $827 million from higher earnings on student tuition and fees, grants and contracts, auxiliary enterprises, and other education activity sales and service income. Net income increased by 63% to $67 millionÂ that year as a result of theÂ university's revenue growth.

CSU has primarily experienced an increase in revenues over the last five years, with the exception a slight dip during 2010 caused by decreased state capital contributions and grants and contracts.

Student tuition and feesÂ run at about $9,000 per year for Colorado residents and $24,000 for out-of-state students.

LOCATIONS

HQ: COLORADO STATE UNIVERSITY
6003 CAMPUS DELIVERY, FORT COLLINS, CO 805236003
Phone: 970 491-1372
Web: WWW.COLOSTATE.EDU

PRODUCTS/OPERATIONS

Selected Colleges, Schools and Programs
Colleges
- College of Agricultural Sciences
- College of Applied Human Sciences
- College of Business
- College of Engineering
- College of Liberal Arts
- College of Natural Sciences
- College of Veterinary Medicine and Biomedical Sciences
- Warner College of Natural Resources

Schools and Programs
- Graduate School
- International Programs
- Online Degrees and Courses (Online Plus)
- School of the Arts
- School of Biomedical Engineering
- School of Education
- School of Global Environmental Sustainability
- School of Social Work

COMPETITORS

BOISE STATE UNIVERSITY
CALIFORNIA POLYTECHNIC STATE UNIVERSITY
CLARK ATLANTA UNIVERSITY INC
PURDUE UNIVERSITY
ROCHESTER INSTITUTE OF TECHNOLOGY (INC)
SOUTH DAKOTA STATE UNIVERSITY
THE RUTGERS STATE UNIVERSITY
UNIVERSITY OF OREGON
UNIVERSITY OF THE PACIFIC
WILLAMETTE UNIVERSITY

HISTORICAL FINANCIALS
Company Type: Private

Income Statement — FYE: June 30

	REVENUE ($mil)	NET INCOME ($mil)	NET PROFIT MARGIN	EMPLOYEES
06/08	740	(44)	—	6,701
06/06	562	26	4.7%	—
Annual Growth	14.7%	—	—	—

2008 Year-End Financials
Return on assets: (-3.6%)   Cash ($ mil.): 249
Return on equity: (-6.6%)
Current Ratio: 4.20

COLORADO STATE UNIVERSITY SYSTEM FOUNDATION, DELINQUENT FEBRUARY 1, 2020

EXECUTIVES

Vice Chairman, Armando Valdez
Auditors: BKD LLP DENVER COLORADO

LOCATIONS

HQ: COLORADO STATE UNIVERSITY SYSTEM FOUNDATION, DELINQUENT FEBRUARY 1, 2020
555 17TH ST STE 1000, DENVER, CO 802023910
Phone: 303 534-6290
Web: WWW.CSUSYSTEM.EDU

HISTORICAL FINANCIALS
Company Type: Private

Income Statement — FYE: June 30

	REVENUE ($mil)	NET INCOME ($mil)	NET PROFIT MARGIN	EMPLOYEES
06/15	1,011	33	3.3%	6,701
06/14	938	(5)	—	—
06/13	884	22	2.6%	—
Annual Growth	6.9%	21.7%	—	—

2015 Year-End Financials
Return on assets: 1.5%   Cash ($ mil.): 352
Return on equity: 7.5%
Current Ratio: 2.40

COLUMBIA GAS OF OHIO, INC.

Columbia Gas of Ohio takes pride in the fact that it can deliver gas first class, en masse, without impasse to the working class, the middle class, and the upper class. The utility is the largest natural gas utility in the state, serving 1.4 million customers (including about 1.3 million residential, 112,000 commercial, and 2,600 industrial customers in more than 1,030 communities in more than 60 of Ohio's 88 counties). The NiSource subsidiary offers a customer choice program, which allows customers to choose their energy suppliers while Columbia Gas of Ohio continues to deliver the gas.

Operations
In addition to operating more than 19,160 miles of distribution mains, the company also provides other gas products, services, and programs across its 25,400-sq.-mi. service area. Columbia Gas of Ohio is part of the NiSource's Gas Distribution segment, which contributed about 54% of the total sales in fiscal 2013.

Geographic Reach
Columbia Gas of Ohio distributes natural gas to residential, commercial, and industrial customers in Columbus, Mansfield, Parma, Springfield, and Toledo. It is one of a handful of NiSource's distribution companies, which collectively serve about 3.4 million gas and electric customers in seven states and operates about 58,000 miles of pipeline.

Financial Performance
Columbia Gas of Ohio is part of the NiSource's Gas Distribution segment which reported an increase of 9% in 2013, due primarily to an increase for regulatory and service programs (including the impact from the rate cases at Columbia of Pennsylvania and Columbia of Massachusetts and the implementation of rates under Columbia of Ohio's approved infrastructure replacement program); the effects of colder weather which increased residential, commercial and industrial usage; and an increase in the numbers of residential and commercial customers.

Strategy
The company's strategy includes spending about $2 billion over 25 years to improve its underground pipeline system.

In 2014 it asked state regulators for permission to replace a mile-long, 12-inch diameter pipeline that crosses the Maumee River between Maumee and Perrysburg with a new 20-inch pipeline.

Upgrading its main offices in order to be more efficient, in 2013 Columbia Gas of Ohio announced plans to relocated to the Arena District of Columbus, taking about 208,000 sq. ft. of a planned 288,000-sq.-ft. office complex.

In 2012 Columbia Gas of Ohio has finished work on its $14 million Ackerman Road natural gas pipeline replacement project in Columbus.

That year it moved more than 722,000 customers to independent suppliers as part of a decade-long deregulation plan by the state.

Company Background
In 2011 Columbia Gas of Ohio announced plans to secure permission from the Public Utilities Commission of Ohio for a five year extension of its energy efficiency programs (home energy audits, weatherization, and other initiatives) aimed at bringing down energy costs for individual customers.

In 2010 Columbia Gas of Ohio commenced a $1.3 million gas mains upgrade in two neighborhoods in Toledo.

EXECUTIVES
CRO, Devit Vajda

LOCATIONS
HQ: COLUMBIA GAS OF OHIO, INC.
290 W NATIONWIDE BLVD # 1, COLUMBUS, OH 432151082
Phone: 614 460-6000

COMPETITORS
EVERSOURCE ENERGY
NEW JERSEY NATURAL GAS COMPANY
NEW JERSEY RESOURCES CORPORATION
NICOR INC.
ORANGE AND ROCKLAND UTILITIES INC

HISTORICAL FINANCIALS
Company Type: Private

Income Statement				FYE: December 31
	REVENUE ($mil)	NET INCOME ($mil)	NET PROFIT MARGIN	EMPLOYEES
12/17	908	96	10.7%	2,500
12/16	854	114	13.4%	—
12/15	872	113	13.0%	—
12/14	993	102	10.3%	—
Annual Growth	(3.0%)	(1.9%)	—	—

2017 Year-End Financials
Return on assets: 2.3%   Cash ($ mil.): 7
Return on equity: 7.9%
Current Ratio: 0.40

COLUMBUS CITY SCHOOL DISTRICT

Auditors : DAVE YOST COLUMBUS OHIO

LOCATIONS
HQ: COLUMBUS CITY SCHOOL DISTRICT
270 E STATE ST FL 3, COLUMBUS, OH 432154312
Phone: 614 365-5000
Web: WWW.CCSOH.US

HISTORICAL FINANCIALS
Company Type: Private

Income Statement				FYE: June 30
	REVENUE ($mil)	NET INCOME ($mil)	NET PROFIT MARGIN	EMPLOYEES
06/20	966	(90)	—	10,000
06/18	1,087	66	6.2%	—
06/17	1,038	106	10.3%	—
06/16	972	(13)	—	—
Annual Growth	(0.1%)	—	—	—

2020 Year-End Financials
Return on assets: (-4.3%)   Cash ($ mil.): 608
Return on equity: —
Current Ratio: —

COMENITY BANK

World Financial Network National Bank (WFNNB) will take credit for the credit it extends. The company is the private-label and co-branded credit card banking subsidiary of Alliance Data Systems. Along with affiliate World Financial Capital Bank, the company underwrites cards on behalf of more than 85 businesses. The company's largest clients include apparel retailers L Brands and Redcats USA. WFNNB oversees about 120 million cardholder accounts and roughly $4 billion in receivables. Private equity giant Blackstone planned to acquire parent Alliance Data Systems for more than $6 billion, but that deal was terminated in 2008.

LOCATIONS
HQ: COMENITY BANK
12921 S VISTA STATION BLV, DRAPER, UT 840202377
Phone: 614 729-4000
Web: WWW.BREADFINANCIAL.COM

COMPETITORS
BANK OF THE WEST
CITIZENS FINANCIAL GROUP, INC.
COLUMBIA BANKING SYSTEM, INC.
DISCOVER FINANCIAL SERVICES
FIRST NATIONAL OF NEBRASKA, INC.

HISTORICAL FINANCIALS
Company Type: Private

Income Statement				FYE: December 31
	ASSETS ($mil)	NET INCOME ($mil)	INCOME AS % OF ASSETS	EMPLOYEES
12/14	9,149	389	4.3%	200
12/13	7,453	350	4.7%	—
12/05	332	10	3.2%	—
12/03	672	88	13.2%	—
Annual Growth	26.8%	14.4%	—	—

2014 Year-End Financials
Return on assets: 4.3%   Cash ($ mil.): 392
Return on equity: 30.8%
Current Ratio: 1.10

COMFORT SYSTEMS USA (ARKANSAS), INC.

Auditors : ERNST & YOUNG LLP HOUSTON TE

LOCATIONS
HQ: COMFORT SYSTEMS USA (ARKANSAS), INC.
9924 LANDERS RD, NORTH LITTLE ROCK, AR 721171588

Phone: 501 834-3320
Web: WWW.COMFORTAR.COM

HISTORICAL FINANCIALS
Company Type: Private

Income Statement   FYE: December 31

	REVENUE ($mil)	NET INCOME ($mil)	NET PROFIT MARGIN	EMPLOYEES
12/15	1,580	49	3.1%	102
12/14	1,410	28	2.0%	—
12/13	1,357	28	2.1%	—
Annual Growth	7.9%	31.5%	—	—

2015 Year-End Financials
Return on assets: 7.1%   Cash ($ mil.): 56
Return on equity: 13.5%
Current Ratio: 1.40

COMMONSPIRIT HEALTH

Formed in 2019 through the merger of Catholic hospital systems Catholic Health Initiatives and Dignity Health, CommonSpirit Health is a not-for-profit organization with more than 140 hospitals in about 20 states. Its hospitals range from large urban medical centers (many with educational and research programs) to small hospitals in rural areas. The company also operates clinics, long-term care, assisted-living, and senior residential facilities (totaling more than 1,500 care sites) and provides home-based care services.

Geographic Reach
CommonSpirit operates in Arizona, Arkansas, California, Colorado, Georgia, Indiana, Iowa, Kansas, Kentucky, Minnesota, Nebraska, Nevada, New Mexico, North Dakota, Ohio, Oregon, Pennsylvania, Tennessee, Texas, and Wisconsin.
CommonSpirit national office is located in Illinois.

Sales and Marketing
Managed care accounted for about half of patient revenue and Medicare accounted for about 40%.

Financial Performance
The company's revenue for fiscal 2021 increased to $33.3 billion compared with $29.6 billion.
Cash held by the company at the end of fiscal 2021 increased to $3.3 billion. Cash used for operations, investing and financing activities were $2.1 billion, $267 million, and $194 million, respectively. Main cash uses were purchases of property and equipment, repayments and investment in health-relates activities.

Strategy
CommonSpirit's strategic vision encompasses five transformative strategies: advocate for health populations; coordinate and customize care; address unique needs of the communities it serves; enhance consumer engagement; and inspire the CommonSpirit workforce.

HISTORY

In 1860 the Sisters of St. Francis established a hospital in Philadelphia, laying the foundation for a larger health care organization. In 1981 Franciscan Health System was formally established to be a national holding company for Catholic hospitals and related organizations. By the mid-1990s the system consisted of 12 member and two affiliate hospitals and 11 long-term-care facilities located in the mid-Atlantic states and the Pacific Northwest.

Sisters of Charity of Cincinnati and the Sisters of St. Francis Perpetual Adoration of Colorado Springs co-sponsored The Sisters of Charity Health Care Systems, incorporated in 1979 as a multi-institutional health care network. By the mid-1990s the system included 20 hospitals in Colorado, Kentucky, Nebraska, New Mexico, and Ohio.

Three congregations collaborated to form Catholic Health Corporation in 1980, one of the first such health care partnerships between religious communities within the Roman Catholic Church in the US. By 1996 this coalition operated 100 health care facilities in 12 states.

The development of modern managed care health care systems put pressure on the smaller Catholic hospital operations, so the three systems established Catholic Health Initiatives (CHI) in 1996 as a national entity serving five geographic regions. Patricia Cahill, a lay health care veteran who previously served the Archdiocese of New York, was appointed president and CEO of CHI. The following year CHI absorbed the 10-hospital Sisters of Charity of Nazareth Health Care System, based in Bardstown, Kentucky (founded in a log cabin in 1812).

That year CHI continued to seek new partnerships to improve efficiency. With Alegent Health it formed provider network Midwest Select with nearly 200 hospitals, marketing discounted rates to businesses. CHI allied with the Daughters of Charity to form for-profit joint venture Catholic Healthcare Audit Network to provide operational, financial, compliance, and information systems audits, as well as due diligence reviews. CHI also joined insurance joint venture NewCap Insurance with the Daughters of Charity and Catholic Health East; the firm allowed CHI to operate independently of commercial insurers.

CHI made a secular tie-in with the University of Pennsylvania Health System in 1998, whereby the university's system would offer care through five Catholic hospitals (CHI made plans to transfer these hospitals to Catholic Health East in 2001). The next year CHI announced its first loss, due to lackluster performance in the Midwest. During 2000 the company responded by streamlining operations and changing management, resulting in a positive bottom line. In 2001 it sold three hospitals in Pennsylvania, one in Delaware, and one in New Jersey to Catholic Health East.

Auditors: ERNST & YOUNG LLP IRVINE CA

LOCATIONS

HQ: COMMONSPIRIT HEALTH
444 W LAKE ST STE 2500, CHICAGO, IL 606060097
Phone: 312 741-7000
Web: WWW.COMMONSPIRIT.ORG

COMPETITORS

ADVOCATE AURORA HEALTH, INC.
ADVOCATE HEALTH CARE NETWORK
ASCENSION HEALTH
DIGNITY HEALTH
HOSPITAL SISTERS HEALTH SYSTEM
JEWISH HOSPITAL & ST. MARY'S HEALTHCARE, INC.
PROVIDENCE HEALTH & SERVICES
ST. JOSEPH HEALTH SYSTEM
TRINITY HEALTH CORPORATION
WHEATON FRANCISCAN SERVICES, INC.

HISTORICAL FINANCIALS
Company Type: Private

Income Statement   FYE: June 30

	REVENUE ($mil)	NET INCOME ($mil)	NET PROFIT MARGIN	EMPLOYEES
06/22	33,907	(1,847)	—	72,500
06/21	33,253	8,303	25.0%	—
06/19	7,170	9,008	125.6%	—
06/18	14,982	222	1.5%	—
Annual Growth	22.7%	—	—	—

2022 Year-End Financials
Return on assets: (-3.7%)   Cash ($ mil.): 2,592
Return on equity: (-8.8%)
Current Ratio: 1.20

COMMONSPIRIT HEALTH RESEARCH INSTITUTE

Auditors: CATHOLIC HEALTH INITIATIVES E

LOCATIONS

HQ: COMMONSPIRIT HEALTH RESEARCH INSTITUTE
198 INVERNESS DR W, ENGLEWOOD, CO 801125202
Phone: 303 383-2733
Web: WWW.CATHOLICHEALTHINITIATIVES.ORG

HISTORICAL FINANCIALS
Company Type: Private

Income Statement   FYE: June 30

	REVENUE ($mil)	NET INCOME ($mil)	NET PROFIT MARGIN	EMPLOYEES
06/21	3,283	128	3.9%	43
06/18	4	(5)	—	—
06/15	1	(7)	—	—
06/14	1	(8)	—	—
Annual Growth	205.6%	—	—	—

2021 Year-End Financials
Return on assets: 1.7%   Cash ($ mil.): 820
Return on equity: —
Current Ratio: 0.50

COMMONWEALTH CARE ALLIANCE, INC.

Auditors: GRANT THORNTON LLP HARTFORD

LOCATIONS
HQ: COMMONWEALTH CARE ALLIANCE, INC.
30 WINTER ST, BOSTON, MA 021084720
Phone: 617 426-0600
Web: WWW.COMMONWEALTHCAREALLIANCE.ORG

HISTORICAL FINANCIALS
Company Type: Private

Income Statement   FYE: December 31

	REVENUE ($mil)	NET INCOME ($mil)	NET PROFIT MARGIN	EMPLOYEES
12/19	1,544	21	1.4%	30
12/18	1,259	14	1.1%	—
Annual Growth	22.6%	52.4%	—	—

2019 Year-End Financials
Return on assets: 5.3%   Cash ($ mil.): 17
Return on equity: 16.6%
Current Ratio: 6.60

COMMONWEALTH HEALTH CORPORATION, INC.

For care in Kentucky, Bluegrass Staters can turn to Commonwealth Health Corporation. The holding company houses a full spectrum of health care facilities and services including The Medical Center, a 415-bed regional health care system comprised of four hospitals, long-term health care providers, and senior care, among other services. Commonwealth's outpatient offerings include nutrition therapy, a women's center, diabetes programs, and adult day care. The corporation's Center Care Health Benefits Program supplies employers with products and services to support the distribution and administration of employee benefits and healthcare services.

Operations
The company's four hospitals include Commonwealth Regional Specialty Hospital (28 beds); The Medical Center (Bowling Green) (337 beds); The Medical Center at Franklin (25 beds) critical access acute care hospital providing both inpatient and outpatient services including a 24-hour, full service emergency room; and The Medical Center (Scottsville; 135 beds).

Commonwealth also runs two companies designed to help health care providers get paid. Commonwealth Financial Services supplies medical billing services for hospitals, physicians, and other care givers, while Hillcrest Credit Agency operates as a collection agency assisting providers in recouping payment for medical services.

The Commonwealth Health Free Clinic operates two programs designed to accommodate patients who are employed, but do not have insurance or other forms of social assistance and cannot otherwise afford healthcare. The Medical Clinic offers free medical services to the working uninsured, while The Dental Clinic offers a low cost alternative to locals in need of basic dental care.

Company Background
The corporation started out in 1926 as a 35-bed hospital. In 1984, Commonwealth Health Corporation was formed as a not-for-profit holding company for The Medical Center at Bowling Green, Franklin, and Scottsville, Commonwealth Regional Specialty Hospital, and other health related businesses.

EXECUTIVES
Chief Development Officer*, Cornelio Catena
Auditors: BLUE & CO LLC INDIANAPOLIS I

LOCATIONS
HQ: COMMONWEALTH HEALTH CORPORATION, INC.
800 PARK ST, BOWLING GREEN, KY 421012347
Phone: 270 745-1500
Web: WWW.MEDCENTERHEALTH.ORG

PRODUCTS/OPERATIONS
Selected Operations (Kentucky)
Barren River Adult Day Care (Bowling Green)
Barren River Regional Cancer Center (Glasgow)
Bluegrass Outpatient Center (Bowling Green)
Bone & Joint Center (Bowling Green)
Cal Turner Extended Care Pavilion (Bowling Green)
Center Care Health Benefit Programs (Bowling Green)
Commonwealth Health Free Clinic (Bowling Green)
Commonwealth Regional Specialty Hospital (Bowling Green)
Corpcare (Bowling Green)
MedEquip (Bowling Green)
The Medical Center at Bowling Green
The Medical Center at Franklin
The Medical Center at Scottsville
Quick Care Clinic (Bowling Green)
Scottsville Medical Plaza (Scottsville)
Urgentcare (Bowling Green)
Women's Health Specialists (Bowling Green)

COMPETITORS
ALEGENT CREIGHTON HEALTH
HARTFORD HEALTHCARE CORPORATION
LEHIGH VALLEY HEALTH NETWORK, INC.
NORTHEAST HEALTH SYSTEMS INC.
ROGER WILLIAMS MEDICAL CENTER

HISTORICAL FINANCIALS
Company Type: Private

Income Statement   FYE: March 31

	REVENUE ($mil)	NET INCOME ($mil)	NET PROFIT MARGIN	EMPLOYEES
03/21	598	150	25.2%	2,700
03/20	531	18	3.5%	—
03/15	68	2	4.0%	—
Annual Growth	43.5%	94.9%	—	—

2021 Year-End Financials
Return on assets: 15.7%   Cash ($ mil.): 54
Return on equity: 21.7%
Current Ratio: 1.60

COMMONWEALTH OF KENTUCKY

Auditors: MIKE HARMON FRANKFORT KY

LOCATIONS
HQ: COMMONWEALTH OF KENTUCKY
700 CAPITAL AVE STE 100, FRANKFORT, KY 406013410
Phone: 502 564-2611
Web: WWW.KENTUCKY.GOV

HISTORICAL FINANCIALS
Company Type: Private

Income Statement   FYE: June 30

	REVENUE ($mil)	NET INCOME ($mil)	NET PROFIT MARGIN	EMPLOYEES
06/20	28,942	578	2.0%	34,000
06/19	27,091	3	0.0%	—
06/18	25,692	338	1.3%	—
Annual Growth	6.1%	30.8%	—	—

2020 Year-End Financials
Return on assets: 0.9%   Cash ($ mil.): 5,634
Return on equity: —
Current Ratio: —

COMMONWEALTH OF MASSACHUSETTS

Auditors: KPMG LLP BOSTON MA

LOCATIONS
HQ: COMMONWEALTH OF MASSACHUSETTS
1 ASHBURTON PL FL 9, BOSTON, MA 021081518
Phone: 617 727-5000
Web: WWW.MASS.GOV

HISTORICAL FINANCIALS
Company Type: Private

Income Statement — FYE: June 30

	REVENUE ($mil)	NET INCOME ($mil)	NET PROFIT MARGIN	EMPLOYEES
06/17	53,391	323	0.6%	59,253
06/16	52,992	(31)	—	—
06/15	50,609	685	1.4%	—
06/14	47,709	(250)	—	—
Annual Growth	3.8%	—	—	—

2017 Year-End Financials
Return on assets: 0.4%   Cash ($ mil.): 7,580
Return on equity: —
Current Ratio: 1.40

HISTORICAL FINANCIALS
Company Type: Private

Income Statement — FYE: December 31

	REVENUE ($mil)	NET INCOME ($mil)	NET PROFIT MARGIN	EMPLOYEES
12/17	935	0	0.0%	270
12/16	919	0	0.0%	—
12/15	811	0	0.0%	—
12/02	453	(0)	0.0%	—
Annual Growth	4.9%	—	—	—

2017 Year-End Financials
Return on assets: —   Cash ($ mil.): 42
Return on equity: —
Current Ratio: —

HISTORICAL FINANCIALS
Company Type: Private

Income Statement — FYE: February 28

	REVENUE ($mil)	NET INCOME ($mil)	NET PROFIT MARGIN	EMPLOYEES
02/21	1,232	139	11.3%	696
02/20	976	(17)	—	—
02/19	959	2	0.2%	—
Annual Growth	13.3%	723.3%	—	—

2021 Year-End Financials
Return on assets: 36.5%   Cash ($ mil.): 310
Return on equity: 64.9%
Current Ratio: 2.20

COMMONWEALTH OF VIRGINIA

EXECUTIVES
Press Secretary, Crystal Carson
Auditors : STACI A HENSHAW CPA RICHMON

LOCATIONS
HQ: COMMONWEALTH OF VIRGINIA
101 N 14TH JMES MNROE BLD, RICHMOND, VA 23219
Phone: 804 225-3131
Web: WWW.VIRGINIA.GOV

HISTORICAL FINANCIALS
Company Type: Private

Income Statement — FYE: June 30

	REVENUE ($mil)	NET INCOME ($mil)	NET PROFIT MARGIN	EMPLOYEES
06/21	62,826	4,805	7.6%	100,000
06/20	53,086	4,811	9.1%	—
06/19	40,939	1,480	3.6%	—
06/18	38,725	1,353	3.5%	—
Annual Growth	17.5%	52.6%	—	—

2021 Year-End Financials
Return on assets: 3.1%   Cash ($ mil.): 19,005
Return on equity: 6.6%
Current Ratio: —

COMMUNITY BEHAVIORAL HEALTH

Auditors : MITCHELL & TITUS LLP PHILADEL

LOCATIONS
HQ: COMMUNITY BEHAVIORAL HEALTH
801 MARKET ST STE 7000, PHILADELPHIA, PA 191073158
Phone: 215 413-3100
Web: WWW.CBHPHILLY.ORG

COMMUNITY FOUNDATION OF NORTHWEST INDIANA, INC.

LOCATIONS
HQ: COMMUNITY FOUNDATION OF NORTHWEST INDIANA, INC.
905 RIDGE RD, MUNSTER, IN 463211773
Phone: 219 836-0130

HISTORICAL FINANCIALS
Company Type: Private

Income Statement — FYE: June 30

	REVENUE ($mil)	NET INCOME ($mil)	NET PROFIT MARGIN	EMPLOYEES
06/22	1,294	(49)	—	2,000
06/21	1,248	350	28.1%	—
06/20	1,133	87	7.7%	—
06/19	1,125	104	9.3%	—
Annual Growth	4.8%	—	—	—

2022 Year-End Financials
Return on assets: (-2.3%)   Cash ($ mil.): 35
Return on equity: (-3.6%)
Current Ratio: 1.00

COMMUNITY HEALTH CHOICE TEXAS, INC.

Auditors : BKD LLP DALLAS TEXAS

LOCATIONS
HQ: COMMUNITY HEALTH CHOICE TEXAS, INC.
2636 S LOOP W STE 125, HOUSTON, TX 770542600
Phone: 713 295-6704
Web: WWW.COMMUNITYHEALTHCHOICE.ORG

COMMUNITY HEALTH CHOICE, INC.

Auditors : I KPMG LLP OKLAHOMA CITY OK

LOCATIONS
HQ: COMMUNITY HEALTH CHOICE, INC.
2636 S LOOP W STE 700, HOUSTON, TX 770545630
Phone: 713 295-2200
Web: WWW.COMMUNITYHEALTHCHOICE.ORG

HISTORICAL FINANCIALS
Company Type: Private

Income Statement — FYE: December 31

	ASSETS ($mil)	NET INCOME ($mil)	INCOME AS % OF ASSETS	EMPLOYEES
12/15	239	1	0.5%	700
12/14	192	16	8.6%	—
12/13	166	(3)	—	—
12/12	172	(17)	—	—
Annual Growth	11.6%	—	—	—

2015 Year-End Financials
Return on assets: 0.5%   Cash ($ mil.): 138
Return on equity: 1.2%
Current Ratio: 16.00

COMMUNITY HEALTH NETWORK, INC.

As a non-profit health system with more than 200 sites of care and affiliates throughout Central Indiana, Community's full continuum of care integrates hundreds of physicians, specialty and acute care hospitals, surgery centers, home care services, MedChecks, behavioral health and employer health services. Its state-of-the-art emergency departments are open 24/7 to treat emergency medical conditions, including stroke, head trauma, heart attack, chest pain, broken bones, wounds and more. Community Health has partnership with Marian University's College of Osteopathic Medicine. Community Health has been deeply committed to the communities it serves since opening its first hospital, Community Hospital East, in 1956.

Operations
Community Health provide health services, including breast care, cancer care, children's health, heart and vascular, genetic testing and counseling, medical imaging, post-acute care, plastic and reconstructive surgery, primary care, and sleep wake services, among others.

Community Health hospitals are Community Heart Vascular Hospital, Community Fairbanks Recovery Centers, Community Hospital Anderson, Community Hospital East, Community Hospital North, Community Hospital South, Community Howard Regional Health, Community Rehabilitation Hospital North and Community Rehabilitation Hospital South.

Geographic Reach
Community Health is based in Indianapolis, Indiana.

Auditors: KSM BUSINESS SERVICES INC IND

LOCATIONS
HQ: COMMUNITY HEALTH NETWORK, INC.
1500 N RITTER AVE, INDIANAPOLIS, IN 462193027
Phone: 317 355-1411
Web: WWW.ECOMMUNITY.COM

PRODUCTS/OPERATIONS

2014 Sales

	$ mil	% of total
Net patient service revenue less provision for bad debts	1,815.9	94
Service fee revenue	25.5	1
Other revenue	100.7	5
Total	1,942.1	100

Selected Services
Advanced Wound Center
Assisted Fertility Services
Bariatric Services
Behavioral Health
Breast Care Services
Cancer Care Services
Children's Health
Clinical Research Trials
Community Home Health
Diet and Nutrition Services
Digestive Health Services
Emergency Services
Heart and Vascular
Inpatient Rehabilitation
Interventional Radiology
Maternity Services
Mid America Clinical Labs
Neuroscience Services
Orthopedic Services
Physical Therapy and Rehab
Radiology/Imaging Services
Sleep Wake Services
Sports Medicine
Surgical Services
Symptom Management Group
Weight Loss and Wellness
Women's Services

Selected Facilities and Affiliates
Community Health Pavilions
Community Heart and Vascular Hospital
Community Hospital Anderson
Community Hospital East
Community Hospital North
Community Hospital South
Community Imaging Centers
Community Physicians of Indiana network
Community Spine Center
Community Westview Hospital
Hook Rehabilitation Center
Indiana Surgery Centers
Indianapolis Endoscopy Center
MedCheck walk-in clinics
MedCheck Express clinics
Wellspring Pharmacy chain

COMPETITORS
INTEGRIS HEALTH, INC.
LEGACY LIFEPOINT HEALTH, INC.
LEHIGH VALLEY HEALTH NETWORK, INC.
OVERLAKE HOSPITAL MEDICAL CENTER
READING HOSPITAL
SHANDS TEACHING HOSPITAL AND CLINICS, INC.
THE LANCASTER GENERAL HOSPITAL
THE RUTLAND HOSPITAL INC ACT 220
UNIVERSITY HEALTH SYSTEMS OF EASTERN CAROLINA, INC.
UNIVERSITY HOSPITALS HEALTH SYSTEM, INC.

HISTORICAL FINANCIALS
Company Type: Private

Income Statement — FYE: December 31

	REVENUE ($mil)	NET INCOME ($mil)	NET PROFIT MARGIN	EMPLOYEES
12/19	1,645	413	25.1%	5,000
12/14	1,942	(0)	0.0%	—
12/13	1,763	179	10.2%	—
Annual Growth	(1.1%)	15.0%	—	—

2019 Year-End Financials
Return on assets: 10.4%   Cash ($ mil.): 191
Return on equity: 15.5%
Current Ratio: 0.60

COMMUNITY HOSPITAL OF THE MONTEREY PENINSULA

Community Hospital of the Monterey Peninsula has a sunny disposition when it comes to medical care. The not-for-profit health care facility provides general medical and surgical services to residents of Monterey, California. It has about 235 acute care and skilled nursing beds and offers specialty services including cardiac and cancer care, obstetrics, orthopedics, and rehabilitation. In addition to its main facility, the hospital operates several ancillary centers, including a mental health clinic, an inpatient hospice, medical laboratory branches, and several outpatient centers offering diagnostic imaging, diabetes care, and other services.

Operations
Community Hospital offers a broad range of healthcare services at 15 locations, including the main hospital, outpatient facilities, satellite laboratories, a mental health clinic, a short-term skilled nursing facility, Hospice of the Central Coast, and business offices.

In 2012 the hospital systems served 12,130 in-patients in 2012. It also had 49,565 emergency visits, 283,181 outpatient visits, and assisted in 1,193 births.

Geographic Reach
The company has facilities in Carmel, Marina, Monterey, and Seaside counties in California.

Financial Performance
Medicare accounted for 53% of Community Hospital of the Monterey Peninsula's revenues in 2012; commercial insurance, 23%, and Medi-Cal, 10%.

Strategy
To improve care in its service territory, the hospital is working to increase best-practice sharing among physicians. It is also supporting information sharing by coordinating electronic health records (EHRs).

In 2014 the hospital received a $200,000 contribution from the Auxiliary of Community Hospital of the Monterey Peninsula, completing a five-year, $1 million pledge by the service organization to support the hospital.

Company Background
As health care costs skyrocket in the US, Community Hospital of the Monterey Peninsula has worked to lower its expenses. Between 2008 and 2011 the organization lowered annual costs by about $44 million.

Community Hospital of the Monterey Peninsula was founded in 1934.

Auditors: MOSS ADAMS LLP SAN FRANCISCO

LOCATIONS
HQ: COMMUNITY HOSPITAL OF THE MONTEREY PENINSULA
23625 HOLMAN HWY, MONTEREY, CA 939405902
Phone: 831 624-5311
Web: WWW.MONTAGEHEALTH.ORG

PRODUCTS/OPERATIONS

Selected Community Hospital Service Locations
Community Hospital of the Monterey Peninsula: Monterey
Carol Hatton Breast Care Center: Monterey
Development/Patient Business Services: Monterey
Hartnell Professional Center: Monterey Peninsula
Primary Care/Satellite Laboratory: Carmel
Peninsula Wellness Center: Marina
Ryan Ranch Outpatient Campus: Monterey
Seaside Satellite Laboratory: Seaside
Westland House: Monterey

Selected Services
Bariatric Surgery
Behavioral Health Services
Carol Hatton Breast Care Center
Comprehensive Cancer Center
Diabetes
Diagnostic and Interventional Radiology
Emergency
Family Birth Center
Hospice of the Central Coast
Intermediate Intensive Care Nursery

Laboratory Services
Nutrition Therapy Program
Orthopedics
Outpatient Immunology Services
Outpatient Surgery Center
Pulmonary Wellness Services
Radiation Oncology
Rehabilitation Services
Sleep disorders
Social Services
Stroke Program
Tyler Heart Institute (Cardiac Care)
Westland House Skilled Nursing Facility
Wound Care and Hyperbaric Healing

COMPETITORS

CENTURA HEALTH CORPORATION
CHILDREN'S HEALTHCARE OF CALIFORNIA
CHILDREN'S HOSPITAL AND HEALTH SYSTEM, INC.
JOHNS HOPKINS ALL CHILDREN'S HOSPITAL, INC.
THE CHILDREN'S HOSPITAL OF PHILADELPHIA

HISTORICAL FINANCIALS
Company Type: Private

Income Statement — FYE: December 31

	REVENUE ($mil)	NET INCOME ($mil)	NET PROFIT MARGIN	EMPLOYEES
12/21	739	110	14.9%	1,947
12/16	526	71	13.7%	—
12/15	560	66	11.9%	—
12/12	(1,452)	0	0.0%	—
Annual Growth	—	279.7%	—	—

2021 Year-End Financials
Return on assets: 11.2% Cash ($ mil.): 106
Return on equity: 30.4%
Current Ratio: 2.00

COMMUNITY HOSPITALS OF CENTRAL CALIFORNIA

Community Medical Centers helps California's San Joaquin Valley stay healthy. The not-for-profit system operates four hospitals ? along with nursing homes and freestanding outpatient facilities ? in the greater Fresno area. Its Community Regional Medical Center is a roughly 685-bed academic hospital that provides advanced care in areas such as trauma, cardiac care, neuroscience, and orthopedics. Clovis Community Medical Center (nearly 210 beds) provides general medical-surgical care, with expertise in women's health and bariatric surgery. Specialty hospitals Fresno Heart & Surgical Hospital and Community Behavioral Health Center (the largest psychiatric care facility in the area) each have about 60 beds.

EXECUTIVES

CLO, Robin Van Patton
Auditors : MOSS ADAMS LLP SAN FRANCISCO

LOCATIONS

HQ: COMMUNITY HOSPITALS OF CENTRAL CALIFORNIA
2823 FRESNO ST, FRESNO, CA 937211324
Phone: 559 459-6000
Web: WWW.COMMUNITYMEDICAL.ORG

PRODUCTS/OPERATIONS

Selected Locations
Hospitals
 Clovis Community Medical Center (Fresno)
 Community Regional Medical Center (Fresno)
 Community behavioral Health Center (Fresno)
 Fresno Heart & Surgical Care (Fresno)
Outpatient centers
 Advanced Medical Imaging
 California Cancer Center
 Community Medical Center-SierraDeran Koligian
Ambulatory Care Center

COMPETITORS

FLAGSTAFF MEDICAL CENTER, INC.
HCA-HEALTHONE LLC
LEHIGH VALLEY HEALTH NETWORK, INC.
MEMORIAL HEALTH SERVICES
SHAWNEE MISSION MEDICAL CENTER, INC.
THE NEBRASKA MEDICAL CENTER
UNIVERSITY HEALTH SYSTEM SERVICES OF TEXAS, INC.
UNIVERSITY HOSPITALS HEALTH SYSTEM, INC.
WELLSTAR HEALTH SYSTEM, INC.
YAKIMA VALLEY MEMORIAL HOSPITAL ASSOCIATION

HISTORICAL FINANCIALS
Company Type: Private

Income Statement — FYE: August 31

	REVENUE ($mil)	NET INCOME ($mil)	NET PROFIT MARGIN	EMPLOYEES
08/21	2,016	94	4.7%	6,200
08/20	1,857	100	5.4%	—
08/19	1,813	117	6.5%	—
08/18	1,667	108	6.5%	—
Annual Growth	6.5%	(4.6%)	—	—

2021 Year-End Financials
Return on assets: 3.2% Cash ($ mil.): 79
Return on equity: 6.2%
Current Ratio: 1.00

COMMUNITY HOSPITALS OF CENTRAL CALIFORNIA

Auditors : MOSS ADAMS LLP STOCKTON CA

LOCATIONS

HQ: COMMUNITY HOSPITALS OF CENTRAL CALIFORNIA
2823 FRESNO ST, FRESNO, CA 937211324
Phone: 559 459-6000
Web: WWW.COMMUNITYMEDICAL.ORG

HISTORICAL FINANCIALS
Company Type: Private

Income Statement — FYE: August 31

	REVENUE ($mil)	NET INCOME ($mil)	NET PROFIT MARGIN	EMPLOYEES
08/17	1,529	48	3.1%	1,000
08/14	127	0	0.5%	—
Annual Growth	128.9%	320.6%	—	—

2017 Year-End Financials
Return on assets: 2.4% Cash ($ mil.): 64
Return on equity: 4.3%
Current Ratio: 1.60

COMPASSION INTERNATIONAL INC

EXECUTIVES

Vice Chairman*, Laurent Mbanda
Auditors : CAPIN CROUSE LP COLORADO SPRI

LOCATIONS

HQ: COMPASSION INTERNATIONAL INC
12290 VOYAGER PKWY, COLORADO SPRINGS, CO 809213694
Phone: 719 487-7000
Web: WWW.COMPASSION.COM

HISTORICAL FINANCIALS
Company Type: Private

Income Statement — FYE: June 30

	REVENUE ($mil)	NET INCOME ($mil)	NET PROFIT MARGIN	EMPLOYEES
06/16	800	13	1.6%	2,002
06/15	768	(8)	—	—
06/14	719	8	1.2%	—
06/13	659	15	2.3%	—
Annual Growth	6.6%	(4.4%)	—	—

2016 Year-End Financials
Return on assets: 4.4% Cash ($ mil.): 95
Return on equity: 6.2%
Current Ratio: 1.30

COMPUTER AID, INC.

Computer Aid Inc. (CAI) is a leading business technology services company committed to helping private and public organizations drive value, improve productivity and enhance customer experience. The company specializes in digital transformation services, including application management, strategy and consulting, intelligent automation, contingent workforce solutions, IT service management, and business analytics. Its strategic consulting encompasses business analytics, intelligent automation, and testing, to name a few. It has partnership with ServiceNow. CAI also offers application maintenance. It serves such markets as financial, utilities, health care, and retail, as well as the public sector. The company was founded in 1981. It has offices throughout the US and the Asia-Pacific region.

Operations
The company specializes in digital transformation services, including application management, strategy and consulting, intelligent automation, contingent workforce solutions, IT service management, and business analytics. It also offers enterprise and operational services such as application maintenance, Autism2Work, cybersecurity, as well as flexible contract staffing, service desk and ServiceNow offerings.

Geographic Reach
Headquartered in Allentown, Pennsylvania, CAI has offices throughout the US and the Asia-Pacific region.

Sales and Marketing
CAI caters to various industries such as financial services, leisure, entertainment, manufacturing & supply chain, retail, utilities and healthcare.

LOCATIONS
HQ: COMPUTER AID, INC.
1390 RIDGEVIEW DR STE 300, ALLENTOWN, PA 181049065
Phone: 610 530-5000
Web: WWW.CAI.IO

PRODUCTS/OPERATIONS
Selected Services
Best Practices Consulting
Application Support
Application Development
Desktop Services
Application Knowledge Capture
Staff Augmentation
Managed Staffing Services
Industry Expertise
QA and Testing
Outsourcing
    Global Delivery
    Staffing Services
    Desktop Services

COMPETITORS
ADVANCED BUSINESS SOFTWARE AND SOLUTIONS LIMITED
CLIENT NETWORK SERVICES, LLC
FINANCIAL AND MANAGEMENT INFORMATION SYSTEMS LIMITED
INTERSYSTEMS CORPORATION
LIAISON TECHNOLOGIES, INC.
QUILOGY, INC.
SABA SOFTWARE, INC.
SERENA SOFTWARE, INC.
SYNCSORT INCORPORATED
YARDI SYSTEMS, INC.

HISTORICAL FINANCIALS
Company Type: Private

Income Statement — FYE: December 31

	REVENUE ($mil)	NET INCOME ($mil)	NET PROFIT MARGIN	EMPLOYEES
12/20	874	0	0.0%	1,411
12/19	733	0	0.0%	—
12/18	603	0	0.0%	—
Annual Growth	20.4%	—	—	—

COMPUTER SCIENCES CORPORATION

Computer Sciences Corporation (CSC) has been one of the world's leading providers of systems integration and other information technology services. It offers application development, data center management, communications and networking development, IT systems management, and business consulting. It also provides business process outsourcing (BPO) services in such areas as billing and payment processing, customer relationship management (CRM), and human resources. CSC boasts 2,500 clients in more than 70 countries. In 2017 CSC merged with the Enterprise Services segment of Hewlett-Packard Enterprise to form DXC Technology Co. This report is based on CSC's last year as an independent company.

Operations
Prior to the creation of DXC, CSC conducted business in through Global Business Services (GBS) and Global Infrastructure Services (GIS). GBS (55% of revenue) addresses key business challenges, such as consulting, applications services, and software. GIS (45% of revenue) provides IT infrastructure services such as managed and virtual desktop solutions, unified communications and collaboration services, data center management, cyber security, and cloud-based offerings.

Geographic Reach
CSC has major operations throughout North America, Europe, Asia, and Australia. The company has clients in more than 70 countries. About 40% of sales are made in the US and about 20% are in the UK, the second biggest market.

Sales and Marketing
CSC's clients have included AboveNet Communications, Deutsche Telekom, DirecTV, Vodafone, and Ryman Hospitality Properties (formerly Gaylord Entertainment).

Financial Performance
After seven straight years of revenue declines, CSC's sales rebounded in 2017 (ended March) to $7.6 billion, a 7% increase from 2016. The increase was driven by the Global Business Services unit's business processing services offerings and contributions from recent acquisitions in the Digital Applications business. The Global Infrastructure Services unit posted a small revenue increase from new business and sales from acquisitions.

CSC lost about $123 million in 2017, down from a $251 million profit in 2016, mainly due to large restructuring charges.

Cash flow from operating activities rose to $978 million in 2017 from $802 million in 2016. The increase flowed from an increase in trade payables and a decrease in net account receivables.

Strategy
After going through corporate breakups, DXC Technology bets that bigger will be better and stronger in competing in the worldwide market for IT services. The companies have a wide footprint and, with some $26 billion in annual revenue, and will have some weight to throw around. A question will be if the company can effectively compete with companies that provide similar services such as Cognizant, WiPro, Accenture, IBM Global Service, and Dell Technologies.

DXC has bulked up to ride the wave of digital transformation that its customers and potential customers are going through. The company's range of services could lead customers from legacy systems to private or public or hybrid cloud systems.

Mergers and Acquisitions
In 2016 CSC acquired Xchanging plc, provider of technology-enabled business services, for $633 million. Xchanging brings its Xuber software, which is used by commercial insurance companies around the world.

Also in 2016 CSC acquired Aspediens, a European provider in the service-management sector and a preferred partner of ServiceNow. The deal extended CSC's reach in software-as-a-service in Europe.

HISTORY
Computer Sciences Corporation (CSC) was founded in Los Angeles in 1959 by Fletcher Jones and Roy Nutt to write software for manufacturers such as Honeywell. In 1963 CSC became the first software company to go public. Three years later it signed a $5.5 million contract to support NASA's computation laboratory. Annual sales had climbed to just over $53 million by 1968.

In 1969 CSC agreed to merge with Western Union, but the deal ultimately fell through. When Jones died in a plane crash in 1972, William Hoover, a former NASA executive who had come aboard eight years earlier, became chairman and CEO. Under Hoover, CSC began transforming itself into a systems integrator. In 1986, when federal contracts still accounted for 70% of sales, the company started diversifying into the commercial sector.

CSC signed a 10-year, $3 billion contract in 1991 with defense supplier General Dynamics. In 1995 Hoover, after more than three decades with CSC, stepped down as CEO (remaining chairman until 1997); he was succeeded by president and COO Van Honeycutt. Also that year CSC bought Germany's largest independent computer services company, Ploenzke. In 1996 CSC acquired insurance services provider Continuum Company for $1.5 billion.

EXECUTIVES

Operations INTEGRATION, Eric Harmon
Chief Human Resource Officer, Jo Mason
Auditors : DELOITTE & TOUCHE LLP MCLEAN

LOCATIONS

HQ: COMPUTER SCIENCES CORPORATION
    1775 TYSONS BLVD FL 8, TYSONS, VA 221024251
Phone: 855 716-0853
Web: WWW.DXC.COM

2017 Sales

	$ mil.	% of total
United States	2,986	40
United Kingdom	1,482	19
Australia	921	12
Other Europe	1,594	21
Other International	624	8
Total	7,607	100

PRODUCTS/OPERATIONS

2017 Sales

	$ mil.	% of total
Global Business Services	4,173	55
Global Infrastructure Services	3,434	45
Total	7,607	100

Selected Service Areas
Application outsourcing
Business process outsourcing
Customer relationship management
Data hosting
Enterprise application integration
Knowledge management
Management consulting
Risk management
Security
Supply chain management

Selected Solutions
Application Services
Big Data & Analytics
Business & Technology Consulting
Cloud Solutions & Services
Cybersecurity
Industry Software & Solutions
Infrastructure Services
Managed Services & Outsourcing
Mobility Solutions

COMPETITORS

ACCRUENT, LLC
ARCONTECH GROUP PLC
CAPGEMINI
DXC TECHNOLOGY COMPANY
FULCRUM IT SERVICES, LLC
ONENECK IT SERVICES CORPORATION
PERSPECTA ENTERPRISE SOLUTIONS LLC
SECURE-24, LLC
TELENT LIMITED
TietoEVRY Oyj

HISTORICAL FINANCIALS
Company Type: Private

Income Statement   FYE: March 31

	REVENUE ($mil)	NET INCOME ($mil)	NET PROFIT MARGIN	EMPLOYEES
03/17*	7,607	(100)	—	66,000
04/16	7,106	263	3.7%	—
04/15	12,173	7	0.1%	—
03/14	12,998	690	5.3%	—
Annual Growth	(16.4%)	—	—	—

*Fiscal year change

2017 Year-End Financials
Return on assets: (-1.2%)   Cash ($ mil.): 1,263
Return on equity: (-4.6%)
Current Ratio: 1.10

CONCORD HOSPITAL, INC.

Concord Hospital is agreeably an acute care regional hospital serving central New Hampshire. The hospital has some 300 licensed beds and provides general inpatient and outpatient medical care, as well as specialist centers for cardiology, orthopedics, cancer care, urology, and women's health. Concord Hospital operates other medical facilities either on its main campus or nearby, including surgery, imaging, diagnostic, hospice, and rehabilitation facilities, as well as physician practice locations. With roots reaching back to 1884, Concord Hospital is part of the Capital Region Health Care system, which also offers mental health and home health care services.

Operations
With a staff of some 350 doctors, Concord Hospital sees about 18,000 patients (including some 9,000 rehabilitation patients), performs more than 9,600 surgeries, and handles about 65,000 emergency room visits and 1,200 births each year. The hospital provides services in about 40 specialty medical fields.

As part of Capital Region Health Care, Concord Hospital shares education, purchasing, and outpatient service functions (and expenses) with its network sister entities, which include the Concord Regional Visiting Nurse Association and the Riverbend Community Mental Health center. Through Capital Regional Health Care, Concord Hospital also has affiliations with area organizations including Dartmouth-Hitchcock Medical Center, Concord Ambulatory Center, and Concord Imaging Center.

Concord Hospital is also part of a collaborative network, the Granite Healthcare Network, with four regional New Hampshire health care providers: Elliot Health System (which operates the Elliot Hospital), LRGHealthcare (consisting of Lakes Region General Hospital and Franklin Regional Hospital), Southern New Hampshire Health System (operating the Southern New Hampshire Medical Center), and Wentworth-Douglass Hospital. Hospitals in the network remain independently managed and owned and have the option to participate or not participate in each of the group efforts.

Geographic Reach
Concord Hospital is located on a 110-acre campus in Concord, New Hampshire. It provides services in area communities including Allenstown, Andover, Barnstead, Boscawen, Bow, Bradford, Canterbury, Chichester, Deering, Dunbarton, Epsom, Henniker, Hillsboro, Hopkinton, Loudon, Northwood, Pembroke, Pittsfield, Salsibury, Warner, Washington, Weare, Webster, and Windsor.

Sales and Marketing
Medicare and Medicaid accounted for some 27% and 3% of net patient revenues, respectively, in 2014.

Financial Performance
Annual operating revenues increased 3% to some $440 million due to higher net patient revenues in 2014. However, net income fell 72% to $18 million due to factors including loss from pension adjustments and declines in net unrealized gains. Cash flow from operations rose 14% to $32 million as less cash was used in accounts receivable and towards supplies and other assets.

Strategy
To help control the spiraling costs of medical care in the US, as well as to meet health reform mandates, Concord and its affiliated facilities are launching programs to share technology and administrative resources, such as claims management software, data storage, linen service, liability insurance pooling, and Medicare patient management.

Concord Hospital has also launched independent initiatives to improve quality and patient safety programs, including putting infection reduction protocols in place, consolidating electronic health record (EHR) consolidation efforts, and enacting medication management practices.

EXECUTIVES

CCO, Matthew Gibb
Auditors : BAKER NEWMAN & NOYES LLC MAN

LOCATIONS

HQ: CONCORD HOSPITAL, INC.
    250 PLEASANT ST, CONCORD, NH 033012598
Phone: 603 227-7000
Web: WWW.CONCORDHOSPITAL.ORG

PRODUCTS/OPERATIONS

2014 Sales

	$ mil	% of total
Net patient service revenue	410.5	93
Other revenue	23.4	6
Disproportionate share revenue	5.1	1
Net assets released from restrictions for operations	1.3	—
Total	440.3	100

Selected Services
Ambulatory Care Center
Behavioral Health
Breast Care Center
Cancer
Cardiac
Center for Health Promotion
Child Life
Clinical Decision Unit
Day Surgery Center
Diabetes Self-Management Education
Concord Hospital Medical Group
Emergency Services
End Of Life
Family Health Centers
Infectious Disease
Intensive Care
Laboratory Services
Maternity
Neurology
Occupational Health
Orthopedics
Pediatrics
Primary Care
Radiology
Rehabilitation
Sleep Center
Surgery
Urology
Walk-in Urgent Care
Women's Health
Wound Care

COMPETITORS
BJC HEALTH SYSTEM
EXCELA HEALTH HOLDING COMPANY, INC.
LEGACY HEALTH
LEHIGH VALLEY HEALTH NETWORK, INC.
SOUTH MIAMI HOSPITAL, INC.

HISTORICAL FINANCIALS
Company Type: Private

Income Statement   FYE: September 30

	REVENUE ($mil)	NET INCOME ($mil)	NET PROFIT MARGIN	EMPLOYEES
09/21	657	90	13.8%	2,000
09/20	516	9	1.9%	—
09/19	528	9	1.8%	—
09/18	500	23	4.6%	—
Annual Growth	9.5%	58.0%	—	—

2021 Year-End Financials
Return on assets: 9.6%   Cash ($ mil.): 37
Return on equity: 17.2%
Current Ratio: 1.10

CONROE INDEPENDENT SCHOOL DISTRICT

LOCATIONS
HQ: CONROE INDEPENDENT SCHOOL DISTRICT
3205 W DAVIS ST, CONROE, TX 773042039
Phone: 936 709-7751
Web: WWW.CONROEISD.NET

HISTORICAL FINANCIALS
Company Type: Private

Income Statement   FYE: August 31

	REVENUE ($mil)	NET INCOME ($mil)	NET PROFIT MARGIN	EMPLOYEES
08/21	773	81	10.6%	6,223
08/20	719	70	9.8%	—
08/19	683	(80)	—	—
08/18	637	57	9.0%	—
Annual Growth	6.7%	12.6%	—	—

2021 Year-End Financials
Return on assets: 3.9%   Cash ($ mil.): 13
Return on equity: —
Current Ratio: 5.30

CONSIGLI CONSTRUCTION CO. INC.

LOCATIONS
HQ: CONSIGLI CONSTRUCTION CO. INC.
72 SUMNER ST, MILFORD, MA 017571663
Phone: 508 473-2580
Web: WWW.CONSIGLI.COM

HISTORICAL FINANCIALS
Company Type: Private

Income Statement   FYE: December 31

	REVENUE ($mil)	NET INCOME ($mil)	NET PROFIT MARGIN	EMPLOYEES
12/12	616	34	5.6%	500
12/11	297	12	4.3%	—
12/10	0	0	—	—
12/09	297	12	4.3%	—
Annual Growth	27.5%	39.6%	—	—

2012 Year-End Financials
Return on assets: 21.7%   Cash ($ mil.): 29
Return on equity: 120.7%
Current Ratio: 1.20

CONSOLIDATED PIPE & SUPPLY COMPANY, INC.

Consolidated Pipe and Supply lives up to its name: Its nine divisions supply pipe and pipeline materials to a swath of industries, from energy to water and waste treatment, chemical, mining, nuclear, oil and gas, and pulp and paper. Its industrial unit specializes in carbon and stainless alloy pipe, valves, and fittings. Vulcan makes all types of PVC. Corrosion resistant coatings are offered by a Line Pipe and Tubular unit, and liquid applied coatings by Specialty Coatings. Its Consolidated Power Supply is the largest in the business of safety related metallic materials for commercial nuclear generation. Another unit caters to utilities. Consolidated also provides engineering services and inventory systems.

Operations

Consolidated Pipe and Supply is one of nearly 20 US Steel distributors authorized to sell seamless and electric resistance welded products in North America. Not limited to its branch and sales centers, Consolidated Pipe and Supply's fitted semi-trailers, complete with area, row and bin, and bar coded shelving, serve as mobile warehouses for construction customers requiring on-site materials management.

The company operates through nine divisions: Industrial, Line Pipe, Structural, Pipeline Coatings, Utility Products, Specialty Coatings, Consolidated Power, Vulcan Plastics, and Consolidated Controls.

Geographic Reach

The company's reach extends to 19 US states, including Alabama, Arkansas, Florida, Georgia, Illinois, Indiana, Kentucky, Missouri, Mississippi, North Carolina, Pennsylvania, South Carolina, Tennessee, Texas, and Virginia. It has nearly 50 sales offices in 15 states.

Auditors : WARREN AVERETT CPAS AND ADVISO

LOCATIONS
HQ: CONSOLIDATED PIPE & SUPPLY COMPANY, INC.
1205 HILLTOP PKWY, BIRMINGHAM, AL 352045002
Phone: 205 323-7261
Web: WWW.CONSOLIDATEDPIPE.COM

PRODUCTS/OPERATIONS

Selected Industries Served
Chemical
Energy
Mining
Nuclear Generation
Oil and Gas
Petro-Chemical
Pulp and Paper
Water and Waste Treatment

Selected Divisions

Consolidated Controls (valves)
Consolidated Power (provides materials to energy industries)
Industrial (provides materials construction, commercial energy, pulp and paper, chemical, petro-chemical, mining, and fabrication industries)
Line Pipe (line pipe and tubular products)
Pipeline Coatings
Specialty Coatings (specialty linings for use in jet fuel and military applications)
Structural (1/8" through 48" structural and prime grades of carbon steel pipe)
Utility Products (provides utilities with products such as steel, ductile iron, PVC, polyethylene, and brass fittings and valves and steel, PVC, and polyethylene pipe)
Vulcan Plastics (water and sewer pipe)

COMPETITORS

ALRO STEEL CORPORATION
COLUMBIA PIPE & SUPPLY LLC
DILLON SUPPLY COMPANY
ENERGY ALLOYS, L.L.C.
KLOECKNER METALS CORPORATION
O'NEAL STEEL, LLC
STEEL WAREHOUSE COMPANY LLC
SUNSHINE METALS, INC.
THYSSENKRUPP MATERIALS NA, INC.
ZEKELMAN INDUSTRIES, INC.

HISTORICAL FINANCIALS
Company Type: Private

Income Statement — FYE: December 31

	REVENUE ($mil)	NET INCOME ($mil)	NET PROFIT MARGIN	EMPLOYEES
12/19	808	25	3.2%	900
12/18	810	44	5.4%	—
12/16	550	17	3.3%	—
12/15	575	7	1.3%	—
Annual Growth	8.9%	36.9%	—	—

2019 Year-End Financials
Return on assets: 7.7%   Cash ($ mil.): 7
Return on equity: 12.4%
Current Ratio: 2.70

CONSTELLATION ENERGY GENERATION, LLC

Exelon Generation Company has built an excellent reputation by generating electricity. The company, a subsidiary of Exelon Corporation, is one of the largest electric wholesale and retail power generation companies in the US. In 2013 Exelon Generation had a generation capacity of more than 44,560 MW (primarily nuclear, but also fossil-fired and hydroelectric and other renewable energy-based plants). Subsidiary Exelon Nuclear operates the largest fleet of nuclear power plants in the US. Exelon Generation's Exelon Power unit oversees a fleet of more than 100 fossil- and renewable-fueled plants (more than 15,875 MW of capacity) in Illinois, Maryland, Massachusetts, Pennsylvania, and Texas.

Operations

The company operates as an integrated business, leveraging its owned and contracted electric generation capacity to market and sell power to wholesale and retail customers. It has ownership interests in eleven nuclear generating stations currently in service, consisting of 19 units with an aggregate of 17,263 MW of capacity. It also owns a 50% interest in CENG, a joint venture with EDF. CENG is governed by a board of ten directors, five of which are appointed by Generation and five by EDF.

Geographic Reach

The Mid-Atlantic represents operations in the eastern half of PJM, and accounted for 37% of Exelon Generation's generating capacity in 2013; Midwest (western half of PJM, the entire US footprint of MISO, 34%); New England (the operations within the ISO-NE, 8%); New York (ISO-NY, 3%); ERCOT (Texas) 12%; and Other areas, 6%).

The Mid-Atlantic region includes Pennsylvania, New Jersey, Maryland, Virginia, West Virginia, Delaware, the District of Columbia and parts of North Carolina. Midwest includes portions of Illinois, Indiana, Ohio, Michigan, Kentucky and Tennessee; and the United States footprint of MISO excluding MISO's Southern Region, which covers all or most of North Dakota, South Dakota, Nebraska, Minnesota, Iowa, Wisconsin, and the remaining parts of Illinois, Indiana, Michigan and Ohio not covered by PJM; and parts of Montana, Missouri and Kentucky.New England represents the operations within ISO-NE covering the states of Connecticut, Maine, Massachusetts, New Hampshire, Rhode Island and Vermont. New York represents the operations within ISO-NY, which covers the state of New York in its entirety. ERCOT represents operations within Electric Reliability Council of Texas, covering most of the state of Texas. "Other Regions" is an aggregate of other geographic regions not considered individually significant.

Sales and Marketing

Exelon Generation's customers include distribution utilities, municipalities, cooperatives, financial institutions, and commercial, industrial, governmental, and residential customers in competitive markets. The company also sells natural gas and renewable energy and other energy-related products and services, and engages in natural gas exploration and production activities.

Financial Performance

The company's revenues increased by 8% in 2013 primarily due to increased capacity prices and higher nuclear volume, partially offset by lower realized energy prices, higher nuclear fuel costs, and lower mark-to-market gains.

Net income increased by 90% in 2013 primarily due to higher revenues, net of purchased power and fuel expense, lower operating and maintenance expense, and higher earnings from Exelon Generation's interest in CENG; partially offset by impairment of certain generating assets, and higher depreciation costs, property taxes, and interest expenses.

Strategy

Exelon Generation leverages owned and contracted electric generation capacity to market and sell power wholesale. The company's integrated business operations include the physical delivery and marketing of power obtained through its generation capacity and through long-term, intermediate-term and short-term contracts. Exelon Generation maintains an effective supply strategy through ownership of generation assets and power purchase and lease agreements. The company has also contracted for access to additional generation through bilateral long-term power agreements.

Exelon Generation's electricity generation strategy is to pursue opportunities that provide generation to load matching and that diversify the generation fleet by expanding Generation's regional and technological footprint. The company leverages its energy generation portfolio to ensure delivery of energy to both wholesale and retail customers under long-term and short-term contracts, and in wholesale power markets.

In 2012 a subsidiary of Exelon Generation sold three coal-fired plants (Brandon Shores and H.A. Wagner generating station in Anne Arundel County, Maryland, and the C.P. Crane plant in Baltimore County, Maryland) to Raven Power Holdings LLC, a subsidiary of Riverstone Holdings LLC to comply with certain of the regulatory approvals required by the company's merger with Constellation Energy, for net proceeds of $371 million, which resulted in a pre-tax loss of $272 million.

Exelon Nuclear operates the largest nuclear fleet in the US (10 stations with 17 nuclear units) and has about 20% of the industry's total capacity. Exelon Generation has submitted an application to the Nuclear Regulatory Commission to build a new nuclear generating facility in Texas. The company hasn't made the decision to build the facility but wanted to get a start on the potentially onerous process. The last license to result in the construction of a new nuclear facility in the US was granted in 1973. However, the Fukushima nuclear plant disaster in early 2011 placed nuclear power expansion plans under serious scrutiny from regulators.

Mergers and Acquisitions

In a major move to grow its retail operations, in 2012 parent Exelon Corporation bought Constellation Energy in a $7.9 billion stock deal. The purchase of Constellation Energy (which gets 17% of its power from nuclear plants) helped the company boost its nuclear-generated power plant assets.

Company Background

Growing its cleaner-burning plant fleet in Texas, in 2011 Exelon Corporation bought the 720 MW capacity Wolf Hollow plant in north Texas, from Sequent Wolf Hollow, for $305 million.

In 2010, to grow its renewable energy unit, the company acquired wind power developer John Deere Renewables for about $860 million. The purchase adds 735 MW of operating wind power capacity to its generation capacity.

EXECUTIVES

GENERATION, Bryan C Hanson
Auditors : PRICEWATERHOUSECOOPERS LLP BA

LOCATIONS

HQ: CONSTELLATION ENERGY GENERATION, LLC
  200 EXELON WAY, KENNETT SQUARE, PA 193482442
Phone: 610 765-5959
Web: WWW.CONSTELLATIONENERGY.COM

PRODUCTS/OPERATIONS

2013 Sales

	$ in mil.	% of total
Mid-Atlantic	5.2	33
Midwest	4.3	27
New England	1.2	8
ERCOT	1.2	8
Other Regions	1.0	6
New York	0.7	5
Others	2.0	13
Total	15.6	100

COMPETITORS

ALLETE, INC.
AMERICAN ELECTRIC POWER COMPANY, INC.
ARKANSAS ELECTRIC COOPERATIVE CORPORATION
DOMINION ENERGY, INC.
ENTERGY CORPORATION
EXELON CORPORATION
FIRSTENERGY CORP.
NEXTERA ENERGY, INC.
TALEN ENERGY CORPORATION
THE SOUTHERN COMPANY

HISTORICAL FINANCIALS
Company Type: Private

Income Statement FYE: December 31

	REVENUE ($mil)	NET INCOME ($mil)	NET PROFIT MARGIN	EMPLOYEES
12/21	19,649	(83)	—	12,482
12/20	17,603	579	3.3%	—
12/19	18,924	1,217	6.4%	—
12/18	20,437	443	2.2%	—
Annual Growth	(1.3%)	—	—	—

2021 Year-End Financials
Return on assets: (-0.2%)   Cash ($ mil.): 504
Return on equity: (-0.7%)
Current Ratio: 1.00

CONSUMER PRODUCT DISTRIBUTORS, LLC

Consumer Product Distributors helps convenience stores provide convenient services to their customers. The company, which operates as J. Polep Distribution Services, is a leading wholesale supplier serving more than 4,000 convenience retailers in New York, Pennsylvania, and the New England states. J. Polep distributes a variety of products, including cigarettes and other tobacco items, candy, dairy products, frozen foods, snack items, and general merchandise, as well as alcohol and other beverages. As part of its business, J. Polep provides merchandising, sales and marketing, and technology services. The family-owned company was founded as Polep Tobacco in 1898 by Charles Polep.

Operations
Consumer Product Distributors ranks as one of the nation's top 12 convenience store distributors. To support its operations, the company supplies customers with products through distribution centers located in Massachusetts (in Chicopee and Woburn), in Rhode Island (in Providence), and in Connecticut (in West Haven).

Geographic Reach
The distribution company serves chain and independent retailers in six New England states, as well as New York, and Pennsylvania. Its distribution centers are located in Massachusetts, Rhode Island, and Connecticut.

Mergers and Acquisitions
Company subsidiary Rachael's Food Corporation, based in Chicopee, Massachusetts, entered the meat manufacturing business in late 2012 when the company acquired 122-year-old family-owned Grote and Weigel, a hot dog and meat processor based in Bloomfield, Connecticut. Soon after, Rachael's Food Corporation also purchased family-owned meat processor Mucke's and transferred its operations to the Grote and Weigel unit. The 2012 purchases followed the company's acquisition of Springfield Smoked Fish. The food corporation's facilities are USDA-inspected and HACCP-certified.

EXECUTIVES
DATA PROC*, Lori Polep Saffer
Auditors : MEYERS BROTHERS KALICKA PC

LOCATIONS
HQ: CONSUMER PRODUCT DISTRIBUTORS, LLC
  705 MEADOW ST, CHICOPEE, MA 010134820
Phone: 413 592-4141

PRODUCTS/OPERATIONS
Selected Products
Alcohol
  Spirits
  Wine
Automotive
  Branded Motor Oils
  Mag 1
  Additives
  Cleaning Supplies
Bakery/Pastry
  Rachael's Gourmet
  Mrs. Freshley's
  Dolly Madison
  Bon Appetite
  Bellow's House
  Diana's
  Table Talk
Beverages
  Poland Springs (Nestle Waters)
  Adirondack Soda
  Arizona
  Florida's Natural
  Simply Juices
  Sweet Leaf Tea
  Trade Winds
  Daily Juice

Selected Services
Credit & Return Policy
Management Information Systems
Merchandising Support
Sales and Marketing Support

COMPETITORS
AMCON DISTRIBUTING COMPANY
BOZZUTO'S, INC.
CENTURY DISTRIBUTORS, INC.
CHAS. M. SLEDD COMPANY
EBY-BROWN COMPANY, LLC
HOLIDAY WHOLESALE, INC.
LINEAGE FOODSERVICE SOLUTIONS, LLC
S. ABRAHAM & SONS, INC.
THE GEORGE J FALTER COMPANY
THE MERCHANTS COMPANY

HISTORICAL FINANCIALS
Company Type: Private

Income Statement FYE: September 29

	REVENUE ($mil)	NET INCOME ($mil)	NET PROFIT MARGIN	EMPLOYEES
09/18	1,248	1	0.1%	400
09/17*	1,101	5	0.5%	—
10/16	1,005	5	0.6%	—
10/15	968	2	0.3%	—
Annual Growth	8.8%	(14.4%)	—	—

*Fiscal year change

2018 Year-End Financials
Return on assets: 0.9%   Cash ($ mil.): 6
Return on equity: 5.0%
Current Ratio: 3.20

CONTINUUM ENERGY SERVICES, L.L.C.

Auditors : GRANT THORNTON LLP TULSA OKL

LOCATIONS
HQ: CONTINUUM ENERGY SERVICES, L.L.C.
  1323 E 71ST ST STE 100, TULSA, OK 741365036

Phone: 918 492-2840
Web: WWW.CONTINUUMENERGYSERVICES.COM

HISTORICAL FINANCIALS
Company Type: Private

Income Statement				FYE: December 31
	REVENUE ($mil)	NET INCOME ($mil)	NET PROFIT MARGIN	EMPLOYEES
12/13	2,092	5	0.2%	159
12/12	1,558	16	1.0%	—
12/11	2,021	26	1.3%	—
Annual Growth	1.7%	(56.3%)	—	—

2013 Year-End Financials
Return on assets: 1.0%   Cash ($ mil.): 11
Return on equity: 3.3%
Current Ratio: 1.10

CONTINUUM MIDSTREAM, L.L.C.

Auditors : GRANT THORNTON LLP TULSA OKL

LOCATIONS

HQ: CONTINUUM MIDSTREAM, L.L.C.
1323 E 71ST ST STE 100, TULSA, OK 741365036
Phone: 918 492-2840
Web: WWW.SEMINOLEENERGY.COM

HISTORICAL FINANCIALS
Company Type: Private

Income Statement				FYE: December 31
	REVENUE ($mil)	NET INCOME ($mil)	NET PROFIT MARGIN	EMPLOYEES
12/14	1,153	(2)	—	75
12/13	296	0	0.2%	—
12/02	17	0	5.3%	—
12/01	13	1	11.9%	—
Annual Growth	40.8%	—	—	—

2014 Year-End Financials
Return on assets: (-1.7%)   Cash ($ mil.): 3
Return on equity: (-2.2%)
Current Ratio: 0.70

COOK CHILDREN'S HEALTH PLAN

Auditors : BKD LLP HOUSTON TX

LOCATIONS

HQ: COOK CHILDREN'S HEALTH PLAN
801 7TH AVE, FORT WORTH, TX 761042733
Phone: 817 334-2247
Web: WWW.COOKCHILDRENS.ORG

HISTORICAL FINANCIALS
Company Type: Private

Income Statement				FYE: September 30
	REVENUE ($mil)	NET INCOME ($mil)	NET PROFIT MARGIN	EMPLOYEES
09/19	567	1	0.3%	27
09/18	547	5	0.9%	—
09/17	484	(8)	—	—
09/15	307	17	5.8%	—
Annual Growth	16.6%	(44.5%)	—	—

2019 Year-End Financials
Return on assets: 1.0%   Cash ($ mil.): 100
Return on equity: 2.0%
Current Ratio: 11.60

COOK CHILDREN'S MEDICAL CENTER

LOCATIONS

HQ: COOK CHILDREN'S MEDICAL CENTER
801 7TH AVE, FORT WORTH, TX 761042796
Phone: 682 885-4000
Web: WWW.COOKCHILDRENS.ORG

HISTORICAL FINANCIALS
Company Type: Private

Income Statement				FYE: September 30
	REVENUE ($mil)	NET INCOME ($mil)	NET PROFIT MARGIN	EMPLOYEES
09/20	1,113	233	21.0%	2,000
09/19	230	2	1.3%	—
09/15	753	159	21.1%	—
09/14	753	107	14.2%	—
Annual Growth	6.7%	13.9%	—	—

2020 Year-End Financials
Return on assets: 13.0%   Cash ($ mil.): 786
Return on equity: 20.8%
Current Ratio: 6.80

COOPERATIVE ENERGY, A MISSISSIPPI ELECTRIC COOPERATIVE

LOCATIONS

HQ: COOPERATIVE ENERGY, A MISSISSIPPI ELECTRIC COOPERATIVE
7037 U S HIGHWAY 49, HATTIESBURG, MS 394029128
Phone: 601 268-2083
Web: WWW.COOPERATIVEENERGY.COM

HISTORICAL FINANCIALS
Company Type: Private

Income Statement				FYE: December 31
	REVENUE ($mil)	NET INCOME ($mil)	NET PROFIT MARGIN	EMPLOYEES
12/16	822	0	0.0%	238
12/13	811	0	0.0%	—
12/12	771	0	0.0%	—
12/11	766	0	0.0%	—
Annual Growth	1.4%	—	—	—

2016 Year-End Financials
Return on assets: —   Cash ($ mil.): 41
Return on equity: —
Current Ratio: 1.50

COOPERATIVE FOR ASSISTANCE AND RELIEF EVERYWHERE, INC. (CARE)

The Cooperative for Assistance and Relief Everywhere (CARE) strives to be the beginning of the end of poverty. The organization works to reduce poverty in about 85 countries by helping communities in areas such as health, education, economic development, emergency relief, and agriculture. CARE supports more than 1,100 projects to combat poverty.Â It also operates a small economic activity development (SEAD) unit that supports moneymaking activities. Through SEAD, CAREÂ provides technical training and savings and loans programs to help people -- particularlyÂ women --Â open or expand small businesses. CARE was founded in 1945 to give aid to WWII survivors.

Operations

In addition to its home office in Georgia, CARE maintains field offices in about 10 US cities, including Boston, Chicago, Miami, New York, and Washington, DC. The group'sÂ internationalÂ field offices are located inÂ more than 55 countries.

CARE's 1,100 projects reach 122 million people, more than half of which are women. About 90% of the funds that CARE receives go toward its aid efforts. The organization helps people in the poorest communities of developing nations. (It does not provide assistance in the US.)

Geographic Reach

From its headquarters in Atlanta, CARE serves poor communities in nearly 85 countries. It does not provide assistance in the US.

Financial Performance

CARE's revenue increased a modest 1% to $590 million in fiscal 2011 as compared to 2010. While it logged a drop in revenues from the US government, the organization saw a boost in private contributions -- totaling $310 million -- from CARE international members.

Strategy

CARE is supported by donations from thousands of individuals and dozens of corporations, foundations, and other charitable organizations in the US. Some of the participating organizations include World Wildlife Fund, Covance, Merck, Meredith Corporation, and the Wal-Mart Foundation. The group also receives funding and supplies from government agencies, including the United Nations and European Union. As a result of the economic downturn, CARE has been working to raise contribution levels as governments, businesses, and individuals cut back their spending, including charitable donations.

Auditors : WARREN AVERETT LLC BIRMINGHAM

LOCATIONS

HQ: COOPERATIVE FOR ASSISTANCE AND RELIEF EVERYWHERE, INC. (CARE)
151 ELLIS ST NE, ATLANTA, GA 303032420
Phone: 404 681-2552
Web: WWW.CARE.ORG

PRODUCTS/OPERATIONS

Selected International Partner Organizations
Covance Inc.
Merck Foundation
Meredith Corporation
The Wal-mart Foundation
WWF

COMPETITORS

DUCKS UNLIMITED, INC.
NATURE CONSERVANCY (THE)
THE CHICAGO COMMUNITY TRUST
THE INTERNATIONAL ASSOCIATION OF LIONS CLUBS INCORPORATED
UNIHEALTH FOUNDATION

HISTORICAL FINANCIALS
Company Type: Private

Income Statement — FYE: June 30

	REVENUE ($mil)	NET INCOME ($mil)	NET PROFIT MARGIN	EMPLOYEES
06/20	609	(37)	—	10,000
06/19	620	16	2.7%	—
06/18	604	15	2.6%	—
06/16	530	(21)	—	—
Annual Growth	3.5%	—	—	—

2020 Year-End Financials
Return on assets: (-7.5%)   Cash ($ mil.): 95
Return on equity: (-11.4%)
Current Ratio: 1.60

COOPERATIVE REGIONS OF ORGANIC PRODUCER POOLS

Cooperative Regions of Organic Producers Pool (CROPP) is the largest organic farming cooperative in North America. The cooperative's more than 2,000 farmer/members produce the co-op's Organic Valley Family of Farms and Organic Prairie brands of fluid and shelf-stable milk, along with cheese, butter, and soy milk. Beyond the dairy barn, the cooperative also offers organic citrus juices, produce, eggs, meats, and poultry. Its Organic Valley products are sold by food retailers, and its ingredients are marketed to other organic food processors. Wisconsin-headquartered CROPP's farmer/members are located throughout North America and Australia. The co-op was founded in 1988.

Geographic Reach

The Wisconsin-based cooperative's farmer members are located in about 35 US states, Canada, and Australia.

EXECUTIVES

Interim Chief Executive Officer, Bob Kirchoff

LOCATIONS

HQ: COOPERATIVE REGIONS OF ORGANIC PRODUCER POOLS
1 ORGANIC WAY, LA FARGE, WI 546396604
Phone: 608 625-2602
Web: WWW.ORGANICVALLEY.COOP

PRODUCTS/OPERATIONS

Selected Products
Butter
Cheese
Cottage cheese
Cream
Cream cheese
Eggs
Healthy snacks
Juice
Meat
Milk
Sour cream
Soy
Yogurt

COMPETITORS

CALIFORNIA DAIRIES, INC.
CITRUS WORLD, INC.
DAIRY FARMERS OF AMERICA, INC.
FOREMOST FARMS USA, COOPERATIVE
McCain Foods Limited
NATIONAL FROZEN FOODS CORPORATION
NORTH PACIFIC CANNERS & PACKERS, INC.
SMITH FROZEN FOODS, INC.
THE PICTSWEET COMPANY
TWIN CITY FOODS, INC.

HISTORICAL FINANCIALS
Company Type: Private

Income Statement — FYE: December 31

	REVENUE ($mil)	NET INCOME ($mil)	NET PROFIT MARGIN	EMPLOYEES
12/10	619	12	2.0%	764
12/08	527	3	0.7%	—
12/07	432	6	1.4%	—
Annual Growth	12.7%	24.6%	—	—

2010 Year-End Financials
Return on assets: 7.5%   Cash ($ mil.): 29
Return on equity: 12.8%
Current Ratio: 2.20

COPPEL CORPORATION

Auditors : BEACHFLEISCHMAN PLLC TUCSON

LOCATIONS

HQ: COPPEL CORPORATION
503 SCARONI AVE, CALEXICO, CA 922319791
Phone: 760 357-3707

HISTORICAL FINANCIALS
Company Type: Private

Income Statement — FYE: December 31

	REVENUE ($mil)	NET INCOME ($mil)	NET PROFIT MARGIN	EMPLOYEES
12/21	826	17	2.2%	75
12/17	329	2	0.8%	—
12/16	335	3	1.0%	—
12/15	(128)	0	0.0%	—
Annual Growth	—	—	—	—

2021 Year-End Financials
Return on assets: 12.5%   Cash ($ mil.): 5
Return on equity: 57.4%
Current Ratio: 1.30

COREWELL HEALTH

Spectrum Health is an integrated health system, with award winning health plan, teams of nationally recognized doctors, providers and network of hospitals and care facilities serving dozen of counties in West Michigan. The not-for-profit network operates some 15 hospitals, including Spectrum Health Ludington Hospital, Spectrum Health Zeeland Community Hospital, Spectrum Health Lakeland Medical Center, Spectrum Health Hospitals Butterworth Hospital and Spectrum Health Ludington Hospital. The nation's third-largest provider-sponsored health plan, Priority Health, currently serving over one million members across the state of Michigan. In early 2022, Spectrum Health and Beaumont Health are moving forward to create a new health system that is For Michigan, By Michigan.

Operations

Spectrum Health operates three rehabilitation and nursing centers, about 120 outpatient sites, and telehealth services. Spectrum Health Helen DeVos Children's Hospital provides expert care from 350-plus pediatric specialists in more than 70 specialties and programs. Spectrum Health's other hospitals include Blodgett Hospital, Butterworth Hospital, Kelsey Hospital, Reed City Hospital, and United Hospital.

Spectrum Health works with 4,000 physicians and advanced practice providers, including Spectrum Health Medical Group, one of the largest and most comprehensive multispecialty physician groups in West Michigan.

Geographic Reach

Spectrum Health is based in Grand Rapids, Michigan.

Mergers and Acquisitions

In early 2022, Spectrum Health and Beaumont Health are moving forward to create a new health system that is For Michigan, By Michigan. Its focus, as its launch its new health system, is to continue to provide excellent health care and coverage in its communities. The new system, which will be temporarily known as BHSH System, will launch Feb. 1, 2022. While Spectrum Health and Beaumont Health create this new health system, patients and health plan members are encouraged to access care in the same ways they currently do. All patients will continue to have access to their same sites of care, physicians and health providers, and insurance plans.

Company Background

Spectrum Health was formed through the 1997 merger of Blodgett Hospital and Butterworth Hospital. Kent Community Hospital joined the organization in 1999, and the United Memorial Health System (Kelsey Hospital and United Hospital) became a member in 2003.

Auditors : ERNST & YOUNG LLP GRAND RAPID

LOCATIONS

HQ: COREWELL HEALTH
100 MICHIGAN ST NE, GRAND RAPIDS, MI 495032560
Phone: 616 391-1774
Web: WWW.SPECTRUMHEALTH.ORG

PRODUCTS/OPERATIONS

2014 Sales

	$ mil	% of total
Health plan	2,136.3	52
Net patient service revenue	1,868.6	45
Other	102.9	3
Total	4,107.8	100

Selected Services

Cancer
Continuing care
Digestive disease
Heart & vascular
Neurosciences
Orthopedics
Outpatient
Pediatric
Rehabilitation
Transplant
Women's health

Selected Operations

Helen DeVos Children's Hospital
Priority Health
Spectrum Health Blodgett Hospital
Spectrum Health Butterworth Hospital
Spectrum Health Continuing Care
Spectrum Health Kent Community Campus
Spectrum Health Gerber Memorial Hospital
Spectrum Health Pennock Hospital
Spectrum Health Reed City Hospital
Spectrum Health Special Care Hospital
Spectrum Health United Memorial
 Kelsey Hospital
 United Hospital

COMPETITORS

ADVOCATE AURORA HEALTH, INC.
ADVOCATE HEALTH CARE NETWORK
EAST TEXAS MEDICAL CENTER REGIONAL HEALTHCARE SYSTEM
NORTHWELL HEALTH, INC.
NORTON HEALTHCARE, INC.
NOVANT HEALTH, INC.
PEACEHEALTH
ST. JOSEPH HEALTH SYSTEM
THE CLEVELAND CLINIC FOUNDATION
WELLMONT HEALTH SYSTEM

HISTORICAL FINANCIALS

Company Type: Private

Income Statement   FYE: December 31

	REVENUE ($mil)	NET INCOME ($mil)	NET PROFIT MARGIN	EMPLOYEES
12/21	9,179	599	6.5%	51,996
12/20*	8,299	714	8.6%	—
06/19	6,884	332	4.8%	—
06/18	6,004	332	5.5%	—
Annual Growth	11.2%	15.9%	—	—

*Fiscal year change

2021 Year-End Financials

Return on assets: 6.2%   Cash ($ mil.): 1,080
Return on equity: 9.3%
Current Ratio: 1.50

CORNELL UNIVERSITY

Cornell is the federal land-grant institution of New York State, a private endowed university, a member of the ivy League/Ancient Eight, and a partner of the State University of New York. The Ivy League school's some 25,580 students can select undergraduate, graduate, and professional courses from around 16 colleges and schools. In addition to its Ithaca, New York, campus, the university has medical and professional programs in New York City and Doha, Qatar. Cornell's faculty includes some 1,730 of regular and part time employee. It was founded 1865 by Ezra Cornell and Andrew Dickson White.

Operations

Cornell is deeply involved in research with more than 100 interdisciplinary research organizations, 18 Cornell research centers and national research centers. Cornell offers nearly 80 formal major fields, including agricultural sciences, astronomy, biological engineering, chemistry, civil engineering, computer literature, earth and atmospheric science and more. Cornell has dozens of research centers, such as the Cornell High Energy Synchrotron Source (CHESS), the Cornell Electroacoustic Music Center (CEMC), the Cornell Wildlife Health Center (CWHC), the National Biomedical Center for Advanced ESR Technology (ACERT), and the Laboratory of Elementary-Particle Physics (LEPP).

Geographic Reach

Cornell's main campus in Ithaca, New York is composed of endowed colleges and contract colleges (operated on behalf of the state) spanning a 2,300-acre campus in New York State's Finger Lakes region. In New York City, Cornell operates Weill Medical College, which has an extension campus in Doha, Qatar, and the Graduate School of Medical Sciences. Also in New York City is Cornell Tech, is a diverse environment of academics and practitioners who excel at imagining, researching and building digitally-enabled products and services to directly address societal and commercial needs. It is operated with Israel's Technion University.

Sales and Marketing

Cornell University is a private research university providing an exceptional education for undergraduates and graduate and professional students. Cornell's colleges and schools includes four contract colleges (operated by Cornell under contract with New York state) encompassing 100-field study. It has locations in Ithaca, New York, New York City and Doha, Qatar.

Company Background

The Ivy League university was founded in 1865 as a land grant university as set out in the Morrill Act, passed by the US Congress in 1862.

Auditors : PRICEWATERHOUSECOOPERS LLP R

LOCATIONS

HQ: CORNELL UNIVERSITY
260 DAY HALL, ITHACA, NY 148532801
Phone: 607 254-4636
Web: WWW.CORNELL.EDU

COMPETITORS

MICHIGAN STATE UNIVERSITY
NORTH CAROLINA STATE UNIVERSITY
PURDUE UNIVERSITY
THE COLLEGE OF WOOSTER
THE RUTGERS STATE UNIVERSITY
TRUSTEES OF BOSTON UNIVERSITY
The Governing Council of The University of Toronto
UNIVERSITY OF KANSAS
UNIVERSITY SYSTEM OF MARYLAND
VIRGINIA POLYTECHNIC INSTITUTE AND STATE UNIVERSITY

HISTORICAL FINANCIALS
Company Type: Private

Income Statement — FYE: June 30

	REVENUE ($mil)	NET INCOME ($mil)	NET PROFIT MARGIN	EMPLOYEES
06/17	4,013	985	24.6%	12,207
06/16	3,809	(442)	—	—
06/12	2,956	(341)	—	—
06/11	2,955	814	27.5%	—
Annual Growth	5.2%	3.2%	—	—

2017 Year-End Financials
Return on assets: 7.5% Cash ($ mil.): 181
Return on equity: 9.8%
Current Ratio: —

CORONA-NORCO UNIFIED SCHOOL DISTRICT

Auditors: EIDE BAILLY LLP RANCHO CUCAMO

LOCATIONS
HQ: CORONA-NORCO UNIFIED SCHOOL DISTRICT
2820 CLARK AVE, NORCO, CA 928601903
Phone: 951 736-5000
Web: WWW.CNUSD.K12.CA.US

HISTORICAL FINANCIALS
Company Type: Private

Income Statement — FYE: June 30

	REVENUE ($mil)	NET INCOME ($mil)	NET PROFIT MARGIN	EMPLOYEES
06/21	756	38	5.1%	614
06/20	696	20	3.0%	—
06/19	717	(47)	—	—
06/18	658	42	6.5%	—
Annual Growth	4.7%	(3.2%)	—	—

2021 Year-End Financials
Return on assets: 2.4% Cash ($ mil.): —
Return on equity: 186.6%
Current Ratio: —

CORPORATION FOR PUBLIC BROADCASTING

This organization is made possible by a grant from the federal government and by support from viewers like you. The Corporation for Public Broadcasting (CPB) is a private, not-for-profit corporation created by the federal government that receives appropriations from Congress to help fund programming for more than 1,000 locally-owned public TV and radio stations. CPB-funded programs are distributed by the Public Broadcasting Service (PBS), National Public Radio (NPR), and Public Radio International (PRI). Funds are also used for research on media and education. CPB was created by Congress in 1967.

HISTORY

As commercial radio began to fill the radio dial, the FCC in 1945 reserved 20 channels from 88 FM to 92 FM for noncommercial, educational broadcasts. The first public television station started broadcasting in 1953, and by 1965 there were 124 public TV stations across the country. To help allocate government funds to these public TV and radio stations, Congress created the Corporation for Public Broadcasting (CPB) in 1967. CPB created the Public Broadcasting Service (PBS) in 1969 and National Public Radio (NPR) in 1970.

CPB has always been politically controversial; critics have often charged it with elitism, cultural bias, and liberalism. When Republicans gained control of Congress in 1994, their laundry list of grievances included government cultural spending. They were foiled in their effort to eliminate funding for CPB, however, in part because of public support for public television. Congress still cut funding by $100 million, forcing CPB to reduce its staff by almost 25% and introduce performance criteria for stations seeking grant money, including listenership and community financial support minimums.

Robert Coonrod was promoted to CEO in 1997. The following year Congress approved additional funding to help public television's transition from analog to digital broadcasting. Frank Cruz was appointed chairman of CPB in 1999. At about the same time, increased funding for 2003 (funding is approved two years in advance) was threatened when it was discovered that some PBS stations were giving their mailing lists to the Democratic party for fundraising purposes. Nevertheless, funding for CPB was increased in the 2001 budget.

In late 2001 businesswoman Katherine Milner Anderson was voted in as chairman, taking over for Cruz (who remained on the board). After serving two consecutive terms as chairman, Anderson was replaced by veteran journalist Kenneth Tomlinson in 2003.

CPB's funding was approved at $350 million for 2002 and $365 million for 2003. Coonrod left the company the following year. Former COO Kathleen Cox and CPB agreed to a one-year contract for her to serve as president and CEO. However, she left the post after nine months.

Chairman Tomlinson resigned in 2005 amid allegations that he violated CPB policies by using his position to get funding for programs with a conservative political view. That same year, former Republican National Committee co-chairwoman Patricia Harrison was named the new CEO of the CPB.

EXECUTIVES
Vice Chairman*, Patricia Cahill
Auditors: GRANT THORNTON LLP ARLINGTON

LOCATIONS
HQ: CORPORATION FOR PUBLIC BROADCASTING
401 9TH ST NW STE 200, WASHINGTON, DC 200042129
Phone: 202 879-9600
Web: WWW.CPB.ORG

COMPETITORS
Canadian Broadcasting Corporation
ION MEDIA NETWORKS, INC.
PUBLIC BROADCASTING SERVICE
SINCLAIR BROADCAST GROUP, INC.
UNIVISION COMMUNICATIONS INC.

HISTORICAL FINANCIALS
Company Type: Private

Income Statement — FYE: September 30

	REVENUE ($mil)	NET INCOME ($mil)	NET PROFIT MARGIN	EMPLOYEES
09/20	570	29	5.2%	99
09/19	498	17	3.5%	—
09/18	493	(55)	—	—
09/16	510	31	6.1%	—
Annual Growth	2.8%	(1.1%)	—	—

2020 Year-End Financials
Return on assets: 11.8% Cash ($ mil.): 153
Return on equity: 22.6%
Current Ratio: 1.40

COUNTRYMARK COOPERATIVE HOLDING CORPORATION

LOCATIONS
HQ: COUNTRYMARK COOPERATIVE HOLDING CORPORATION
225 S EAST ST STE 144, INDIANAPOLIS, IN 462024059
Phone: 800 808-3170
Web: WWW.COUNTRYMARK.COM

HISTORICAL FINANCIALS
Company Type: Private

Income Statement — FYE: December 31

	REVENUE ($mil)	NET INCOME ($mil)	NET PROFIT MARGIN	EMPLOYEES
12/08	1,325	26	2.0%	425
12/07	964	56	5.9%	—
12/05	774	40	5.2%	—
Annual Growth	19.6%	(12.7%)	—	—

2008 Year-End Financials
Return on assets: 7.7% Cash ($ mil.): 8
Return on equity: 13.5%
Current Ratio: 1.60

HOOVER'S HANDBOOK OF PRIVATE COMPANIES 2023

COUNTY OF ADAMS

Auditors : CLIFTONLARSONALLEN LLP BROOMF

LOCATIONS

HQ: COUNTY OF ADAMS
4430 S ADAMS, BRIGHTON, CO 80601
Phone: 720 523-6100
Web: WWW.ADCOGOV.ORG

HISTORICAL FINANCIALS

Company Type: Private

Income Statement — FYE: December 31

	REVENUE ($mil)	NET INCOME ($mil)	NET PROFIT MARGIN	EMPLOYEES
12/21	541	13	2.4%	1,740
12/20	589	24	4.2%	—
12/18	427	46	10.9%	—
12/16	0	(29)	—	—
Annual Growth	—	—	—	—

2021 Year-End Financials
Return on assets: 0.8% Cash ($ mil.): —
Return on equity: 1.5%
Current Ratio: —

COUNTY OF ALAMEDA

Just east of San Francisco Bay lies Alameda County. Governed by a five-member board of supervisors, it includes 14 cities, among them Hayward, Oakland, and San Leandro. Nearly 60 departments handle services like behavioral health care, emergency medical, and human resources along with law enforcement, property tax assessment and collection, and community development for a population of more than 1.5 million. The county also serves as the keeper of birth, death, and marriage certificates and other public records. Its budget is more than $2.7 billion; most of it goes to public assistance, public protection, and health care. Alameda was incorporated in 1853 from parts of neighboring Contra Costa and Santa Clara counties.

EXECUTIVES

County Administrator, Susan Moranishi
Supervisor District 1*, Scott Haggerty
Supervisor District 2*, Gail Steele
Supervisor District 4*, Nate Miley
Supervisor District 5*, Keith Carson
Supervisor District 3, Ellis Lai-bitker
Auditors : MACIAS GINI & O'CONNELL LLP O

LOCATIONS

HQ: COUNTY OF ALAMEDA
1221 OAK ST STE 555, OAKLAND, CA 946124224
Phone: 510 272-6691
Web: WWW.ACGOV.ORG

COMPETITORS

CITY OF HOUSTON
CITY OF OXNARD
COUNTY OF LOS ANGELES
GOVERNMENT OF DISTRICT OF COLUMBIA
WILL COUNTY

HISTORICAL FINANCIALS

Company Type: Private

Income Statement — FYE: June 30

	REVENUE ($mil)	NET INCOME ($mil)	NET PROFIT MARGIN	EMPLOYEES
06/15	2,714	(26)	—	8,000
06/14	2,579	203	7.9%	—
06/13	2,622	65	2.5%	—
06/12	2,403	(155)	—	—
Annual Growth	4.1%	—	—	—

2015 Year-End Financials
Return on assets: (-0.5%) Cash ($ mil.): —
Return on equity: (-2.3%)
Current Ratio: 4.20

COUNTY OF ALBANY

EXECUTIVES

County Executive, Daniel P Mccoy
Auditors : BST & CO CPAS LLP ALBANY

LOCATIONS

HQ: COUNTY OF ALBANY
112 STATE ST RM 1200, ALBANY, NY 122072023
Phone: 518 447-7040
Web: WWW.ALBANYCOUNTY.COM

HISTORICAL FINANCIALS

Company Type: Private

Income Statement — FYE: December 31

	REVENUE ($mil)	NET INCOME ($mil)	NET PROFIT MARGIN	EMPLOYEES
12/21	699	32	4.7%	2,567
12/20	552	(21)	—	—
12/19	587	14	2.4%	—
12/18	582	63	10.9%	—
Annual Growth	6.3%	(19.8%)	—	—

2021 Year-End Financials
Return on assets: 1.9% Cash ($ mil.): 175
Return on equity: 8.9%
Current Ratio: —

COUNTY OF ALLEGHENY

EXECUTIVES

County Manager, William Mckey
Auditors : ZELENKOFSKE AXELROD LLC PITTS

LOCATIONS

HQ: COUNTY OF ALLEGHENY
436 GRANT ST STE 104, PITTSBURGH, PA 152195403
Phone: 412 350-5300

Web: WWW.ALLEGHENYCOUNTY.US

HISTORICAL FINANCIALS

Company Type: Private

Income Statement — FYE: December 31

	REVENUE ($mil)	NET INCOME ($mil)	NET PROFIT MARGIN	EMPLOYEES
12/20	2,004	111	5.6%	7,013
12/19	1,768	(51)	—	—
12/18	1,722	53	3.1%	—
12/17	1,640	(40)	—	—
Annual Growth	6.9%	—	—	—

2020 Year-End Financials
Return on assets: 2.3% Cash ($ mil.): —
Return on equity: —
Current Ratio: —

COUNTY OF ANNE ARUNDEL

EXECUTIVES

County Executive, Steuart Pittman
Budget Officer, John Hammond
Auditors : CLIFTONLARSONALLEN LLP BALTIM

LOCATIONS

HQ: COUNTY OF ANNE ARUNDEL
44 CALVERT ST STE 1, ANNAPOLIS, MD 214011930
Phone: 410 222-1166
Web: WWW.AACOUNTY.ORG

HISTORICAL FINANCIALS

Company Type: Private

Income Statement — FYE: June 30

	REVENUE ($mil)	NET INCOME ($mil)	NET PROFIT MARGIN	EMPLOYEES
06/20	1,858	58	3.2%	4,600
06/19	1,700	(20)	—	—
06/18	1,635	3	0.2%	—
06/17	1,573	40	2.6%	—
Annual Growth	5.7%	13.0%	—	—

2020 Year-End Financials
Return on assets: 0.8% Cash ($ mil.): —
Return on equity: —
Current Ratio: 2.40

COUNTY OF ARLINGTON

EXECUTIVES

County Manager*, James Schwartz
Auditors : CLIFTONLARSONALLEN LLP ARLIN

LOCATIONS

HQ: COUNTY OF ARLINGTON
2100 CLARENDON BLVD # 500, ARLINGTON, VA 222015447

Phone: 703 228-3130
Web: WWW.ARLINGTONVA.US

HISTORICAL FINANCIALS
Company Type: Private

Income Statement — FYE: June 30

	REVENUE ($mil)	NET INCOME ($mil)	NET PROFIT MARGIN	EMPLOYEES
06/19	1,409	71	5.1%	4,000
06/18	1,349	(14)	—	—
06/17	1,321	99	7.5%	—
06/16	1,261	(10)	—	—
Annual Growth	3.8%	—	—	—

2019 Year-End Financials
Return on assets: 1.3%   Cash ($ mil.): —
Return on equity: 3.2%
Current Ratio: —

COUNTY OF BERGEN

EXECUTIVES
County Executive, James Tedesco

LOCATIONS
HQ: COUNTY OF BERGEN
1 BERGEN COUNTY PLZ RM 1 # 1, HACKENSACK, NJ 076017075
Phone: 201 336-6000
Web: WWW.CO.BERGEN.NJ.US

HISTORICAL FINANCIALS
Company Type: Private

Income Statement — FYE: December 31

	REVENUE ($mil)	NET INCOME ($mil)	NET PROFIT MARGIN	EMPLOYEES
12/17	565	26	4.7%	2,347
12/16	604	22	3.8%	—
12/02	369	19	5.1%	—
12/01	18	0	0.0%	—
Annual Growth	23.9%	—	—	—

2017 Year-End Financials
Return on assets: 1.0%   Cash ($ mil.): 248
Return on equity: 1.8%
Current Ratio: —

COUNTY OF BERKS

EXECUTIVES
OF BUDGET Finance*, Robert Petizio
Auditors : RKL LLP WYOMISSING PENNSYLVA

LOCATIONS
HQ: COUNTY OF BERKS
633 COURT ST FL 2, READING, PA 196013552
Phone: 610 478-6640
Web: CO.BERKS.PA.US

HISTORICAL FINANCIALS
Company Type: Private

Income Statement — FYE: December 31

	REVENUE ($mil)	NET INCOME ($mil)	NET PROFIT MARGIN	EMPLOYEES
12/21	549	20	3.7%	2,500
12/17	434	6	1.5%	—
12/16	431	(10)	—	—
12/15	390	(2)	—	—
Annual Growth	5.9%	—	—	—

2021 Year-End Financials
Return on assets: 2.2%   Cash ($ mil.): 69
Return on equity: 3.9%
Current Ratio: 2.20

COUNTY OF BEXAR

EXECUTIVES
District Attorney*, Susan Reed
Auditors : GARZA/GONZALEZ & ASSOCIATES S

LOCATIONS
HQ: COUNTY OF BEXAR
101 W NUEVA STE 1019, SAN ANTONIO, TX 782053400
Phone: 210 335-2626
Web: WWW.BEXAR.ORG

HISTORICAL FINANCIALS
Company Type: Private

Income Statement — FYE: September 30

	REVENUE ($mil)	NET INCOME ($mil)	NET PROFIT MARGIN	EMPLOYEES
09/21	748	(98)	—	4,200
09/20	776	96	12.5%	—
09/19	703	131	18.7%	—
09/18	672	(103)	—	—
Annual Growth	3.7%	—	—	—

2021 Year-End Financials
Return on assets: (-1.3%)   Cash ($ mil.): 1,192
Return on equity: (-5.7%)
Current Ratio: 3.20

COUNTY OF BROWARD

EXECUTIVES
Assistant County Administrator, Monica Cepero
Assistant County Administrator, Alphonso Jefferson Junior
Auditors : CROWE HORWATH LLP FORT LAUDER

LOCATIONS
HQ: COUNTY OF BROWARD
115 S ANDREWS AVE STE 409, FORT LAUDERDALE, FL 333011817
Phone: 954 357-7050
Web: WWW.BROWARD.ORG

HISTORICAL FINANCIALS
Company Type: Private

Income Statement — FYE: September 30

	REVENUE ($mil)	NET INCOME ($mil)	NET PROFIT MARGIN	EMPLOYEES
09/11	1,525	(76)	—	40,500
09/09	1,693	(28)	—	—
09/06	1,799	116	6.5%	—
Annual Growth	(3.3%)	—	—	—

2011 Year-End Financials
Return on assets: (-1.0%)   Cash ($ mil.): 593
Return on equity: (-1.6%)
Current Ratio: 3.60

COUNTY OF CAMDEN

Auditors : BOWMAN & COMPANY LLP-MICHAEL D

LOCATIONS
HQ: COUNTY OF CAMDEN
520 MARKET ST FL 11, CAMDEN, NJ 081021300
Phone: 856 225-5000
Web: WWW.CAMDENCOUNTY.COM

HISTORICAL FINANCIALS
Company Type: Private

Income Statement — FYE: December 31

	REVENUE ($mil)	NET INCOME ($mil)	NET PROFIT MARGIN	EMPLOYEES
12/20	585	24	4.2%	2,100
12/19	465	(1)	—	—
12/18	467	35	7.6%	—
12/17	438	29	6.8%	—
Annual Growth	10.1%	(6.3%)	—	—

2020 Year-End Financials
Return on assets: 1.8%   Cash ($ mil.): 299
Return on equity: 9.5%
Current Ratio: —

COUNTY OF CHESTERFIELD

EXECUTIVES
Acting Deputy Administrator*, Rebecca T Dickson
Auditors : KPMG LLP RICHMOND VA

LOCATIONS
HQ: COUNTY OF CHESTERFIELD
9901 LORI RD, CHESTERFIELD, VA 238326626
Phone: 804 748-1000
Web: WWW.CIVICPLUS.HELP

HISTORICAL FINANCIALS
Company Type: Private

Income Statement — FYE: June 30

	REVENUE ($mil)	NET INCOME ($mil)	NET PROFIT MARGIN	EMPLOYEES
06/21	1,022	186	18.2%	4,618
06/20	894	75	8.5%	—
06/19	841	80	9.6%	—
06/18	857	(30)	—	—
Annual Growth	6.1%	—	—	—

2021 Year-End Financials
Return on assets: 4.0%   Cash ($ mil.): 571
Return on equity: 9.0%
Current Ratio: —

COUNTY OF CLARK

EXECUTIVES

County Manager, Don Burnette
County Manager*, Don Burnett
Auditors : CROWE LLP COSTA MESA CALIFOR

LOCATIONS

HQ: COUNTY OF CLARK
500 S GRAND CENTRAL PKWY # 6, LAS VEGAS, NV 891554502
Phone: 702 455-3530
Web: WWW.CLARKCOUNTYNV.GOV

HISTORICAL FINANCIALS
Company Type: Private

Income Statement — FYE: June 30

	REVENUE ($mil)	NET INCOME ($mil)	NET PROFIT MARGIN	EMPLOYEES
06/21	3,662	152	4.2%	8,528
06/20	3,398	107	3.2%	—
06/19	3,301	625	18.9%	—
06/18	3,021	89	3.0%	—
Annual Growth	6.6%	19.6%	—	—

2021 Year-End Financials
Return on assets: 0.5%   Cash ($ mil.): —
Return on equity: 1.2%
Current Ratio: —

COUNTY OF CONTRA COSTA

Auditors : MACIAS GINI & O'CONNELL LLP W

LOCATIONS

HQ: COUNTY OF CONTRA COSTA
625 COURT ST STE 100, MARTINEZ, CA 945531204
Phone: 925 957-5280
Web: CONTRACOSTA.CA.GOV

HISTORICAL FINANCIALS
Company Type: Private

Income Statement — FYE: June 30

	REVENUE ($mil)	NET INCOME ($mil)	NET PROFIT MARGIN	EMPLOYEES
06/20	2,514	47	1.9%	7,193
06/19	2,438	98	4.0%	—
06/18	2,259	84	3.7%	—
06/17	2,182	215	9.9%	—
Annual Growth	4.8%	(39.7%)	—	—

2020 Year-End Financials
Return on assets: 1.1%   Cash ($ mil.): —
Return on equity: 4.2%
Current Ratio: —

COUNTY OF CUYAHOGA

Auditors : KEITH FABER AUDITOR OF STATE

LOCATIONS

HQ: COUNTY OF CUYAHOGA
1215 W 3RD ST, CLEVELAND, OH 441131532
Phone: 216 443-7022
Web: COC.CUYAHOGACOUNTY.US

HISTORICAL FINANCIALS
Company Type: Private

Income Statement — FYE: December 31

	REVENUE ($mil)	NET INCOME ($mil)	NET PROFIT MARGIN	EMPLOYEES
12/21	1,561	146	9.4%	9,800
12/20	1,452	52	3.6%	—
12/18	1,371	(118)	—	—
12/17	1,325	64	4.9%	—
Annual Growth	4.2%	22.6%	—	—

2021 Year-End Financials
Return on assets: 2.2%   Cash ($ mil.): 1,821
Return on equity: 9.9%
Current Ratio: —

COUNTY OF DALLAS

EXECUTIVES

PREC 1st*, Jimmy L Jackson
PREC 2*, Mike Cantrell
Commissioner PET 3*, John Wiley Price
Auditors : DELOITTE & TOUCHE LLP DALLAS

LOCATIONS

HQ: COUNTY OF DALLAS
900 JACKSON ST STE 680, DALLAS, TX 752024425
Phone: 214 653-7099
Web: WWW.DALLASCOUNTY.ORG

HISTORICAL FINANCIALS
Company Type: Private

Income Statement — FYE: September 30

	REVENUE ($mil)	NET INCOME ($mil)	NET PROFIT MARGIN	EMPLOYEES
09/21	1,144	(15)	—	6,600
09/20	1,081	(34)	—	—
09/19	931	(34)	—	—
09/18	871	4	0.5%	—
Annual Growth	9.5%	—	—	—

2021 Year-End Financials
Return on assets: (-0.2%)   Cash ($ mil.): —
Return on equity: (-0.6%)
Current Ratio: —

COUNTY OF DANE

EXECUTIVES

Site Executive, Kathleen Falk
Auditors : BAKER TILLY VIRCHOW KRAUSE LL

LOCATIONS

HQ: COUNTY OF DANE
210 M LTHR KNG JR BLV 425, MADISON, WI 53703
Phone: 608 266-4114
Web: WWW.COUNTYOFDANE.COM

HISTORICAL FINANCIALS
Company Type: Private

Income Statement — FYE: December 31

	REVENUE ($mil)	NET INCOME ($mil)	NET PROFIT MARGIN	EMPLOYEES
12/21	571	12	2.1%	1,568
12/20	544	6	1.2%	—
12/19	456	27	6.1%	—
12/18	463	22	4.9%	—
Annual Growth	7.2%	(18.7%)	—	—

2021 Year-End Financials
Return on assets: 0.6%   Cash ($ mil.): —
Return on equity: 1.6%
Current Ratio: —

COUNTY OF DEKALB

EXECUTIVES

Interim Chief Executive Officer*, Lee May
CPO*, Talisa R Clark
Auditors : KPMG LLP ATLANTA GA

LOCATIONS

HQ: COUNTY OF DEKALB
1300 COMMERCE DR, DECATUR, GA 300303222
Phone: 404 371-2881
Web: WWW.DEKALBCOUNTYGA.GOV

HISTORICAL FINANCIALS
Company Type: Private

Income Statement				FYE: December 31
	REVENUE ($mil)	NET INCOME ($mil)	NET PROFIT MARGIN	EMPLOYEES
12/19	749	34	4.6%	7,300
12/18	698	49	7.1%	—
12/17	628	20	3.2%	—
12/16	577	15	2.7%	—
Annual Growth	9.1%	30.2%	—	—

2019 Year-End Financials
Return on assets: 0.8%   Cash ($ mil.): 561
Return on equity: 2.7%
Current Ratio: —

COUNTY OF DELAWARE

Auditors : BAKER TILLY VIRCHOW KRAUSE LL

LOCATIONS

HQ: COUNTY OF DELAWARE
201 W FRONT ST FRNT, MEDIA, PA 190632700
Phone: 610 891-4000
Web: WWW.DELAWARECOUNTYPA.COM

HISTORICAL FINANCIALS
Company Type: Private

Income Statement				FYE: December 31
	REVENUE ($mil)	NET INCOME ($mil)	NET PROFIT MARGIN	EMPLOYEES
12/21	687	(36)	—	3,100
12/20	651	45	7.0%	—
12/19	583	(16)	—	—
12/18	584	40	7.0%	—
Annual Growth	5.6%	—	—	—

2021 Year-End Financials
Return on assets: (-3.7%)   Cash ($ mil.): 227
Return on equity: —
Current Ratio: —

COUNTY OF ERIE

EXECUTIVES

County Executive, Mark Poloncarz
Auditors : DRESCHER & MALECKI LLP·BUFFAL

LOCATIONS

HQ: COUNTY OF ERIE
95 FRANKLIN ST RM 1603, BUFFALO, NY 142023914
Phone: 716 858-8500
Web: WWW.ERIE.GOV

HISTORICAL FINANCIALS
Company Type: Private

Income Statement				FYE: December 31
	REVENUE ($mil)	NET INCOME ($mil)	NET PROFIT MARGIN	EMPLOYEES
12/20	1,767	(6)	—	10,200
12/19	1,693	23	1.4%	—
12/18	1,646	34	2.1%	—
12/17	1,630	48	3.0%	—
Annual Growth	2.7%	—	—	—

2020 Year-End Financials
Return on assets: (-0.2%)   Cash ($ mil.): 303
Return on equity: —
Current Ratio: —

COUNTY OF ESSEX

EXECUTIVES

Acting City Treasurer*, Ron Weitz
City Administrator*, Vincent A Dimauro
Auditors : SAMUEL KLEIN AND COMPANY-JOSEP

LOCATIONS

HQ: COUNTY OF ESSEX
465 MARTIN LUTHER KING, NEWARK, NJ 071021735
Phone: 973 621-4454
Web: WWW.ECDPW.ORG

HISTORICAL FINANCIALS
Company Type: Private

Income Statement				FYE: December 31
	REVENUE ($mil)	NET INCOME ($mil)	NET PROFIT MARGIN	EMPLOYEES
12/16	862	31	3.6%	5,300
12/09	784	25	3.2%	—
12/97	478	7	1.6%	—
12/95	1,107	0	0.0%	—
Annual Growth	(1.2%)	—	—	—

2016 Year-End Financials
Return on assets: 1.2%   Cash ($ mil.): 182
Return on equity: 1.7%
Current Ratio: —

COUNTY OF FORT BEND

EXECUTIVES

County Auditor, Robert Grayless
Auditors : WHITLEY PENN LLP HOUSTON TEX

LOCATIONS

HQ: COUNTY OF FORT BEND
301 JACKSON ST, RICHMOND, TX 774693108
Phone: 281 341-8608
Web: WWW.FORTBENDCOUNTYTX.GOV

HISTORICAL FINANCIALS
Company Type: Private

Income Statement				FYE: September 30
	REVENUE ($mil)	NET INCOME ($mil)	NET PROFIT MARGIN	EMPLOYEES
09/21*	643	(3)	—	1,800
12/20	0	(0)	—	—
09/20	546	47	8.6%	—
09/19	466	(20)	—	—
Annual Growth	17.4%	—	—	—

*Fiscal year change

2021 Year-End Financials
Return on assets: (-0.1%)   Cash ($ mil.): 625
Return on equity: (-0.2%)
Current Ratio: —

COUNTY OF FRESNO

EXECUTIVES

County Administrative Officer, Paul Nerland
Auditors : BROWN ARMSTRONG ACCOUNTANCY CO

LOCATIONS

HQ: COUNTY OF FRESNO
2281 TULARE ST STE 304, FRESNO, CA 937212101
Phone: 559 600-1710
Web: FRESNO.COURTS.CA.GOV

HISTORICAL FINANCIALS
Company Type: Private

Income Statement				FYE: June 30
	REVENUE ($mil)	NET INCOME ($mil)	NET PROFIT MARGIN	EMPLOYEES
06/21	2,032	69	3.4%	7,000
06/20	1,781	19	1.1%	—
06/19	1,649	30	1.9%	—
06/18	1,538	5	0.3%	—
Annual Growth	9.7%	139.6%	—	—

2021 Year-End Financials
Return on assets: 2.2%   Cash ($ mil.): —
Return on equity: 11.7%
Current Ratio: —

COUNTY OF FULTON

Auditors : PJC GROUP LLC ATLANTA GEORG

LOCATIONS

HQ: COUNTY OF FULTON
141 PRYOR ST SW STE 7001, ATLANTA, GA 303033468
Phone: 404 612-4000
Web: WWW.FULTONCOUNTYGA.GOV

HISTORICAL FINANCIALS
Company Type: Private

Income Statement — FYE: December 31

	REVENUE ($mil)	NET INCOME ($mil)	NET PROFIT MARGIN	EMPLOYEES
12/20	947	(11)	—	5,000
12/19	816	3	0.5%	—
12/18	843	70	8.3%	—
12/15	760	1	0.3%	—
Annual Growth	4.5%	—	—	—

2020 Year-End Financials
Return on assets: (-0.2%) Cash ($ mil.): 952
Return on equity: (-1.0%)
Current Ratio: —

HISTORICAL FINANCIALS
Company Type: Private

Income Statement — FYE: June 30

	REVENUE ($mil)	NET INCOME ($mil)	NET PROFIT MARGIN	EMPLOYEES
06/22	785	64	8.2%	1,400
06/21	790	40	5.1%	—
06/20	692	(5)	—	—
06/18	630	22	3.5%	—
Annual Growth	5.6%	30.7%	—	—

2022 Year-End Financials
Return on assets: 1.7% Cash ($ mil.): —
Return on equity: 9.2%
Current Ratio: —

HISTORICAL FINANCIALS
Company Type: Private

Income Statement — FYE: June 30

	REVENUE ($mil)	NET INCOME ($mil)	NET PROFIT MARGIN	EMPLOYEES
06/21	681	80	11.8%	2,000
06/20	578	25	4.4%	—
06/19	524	10	2.0%	—
06/18	475	50	10.6%	—
Annual Growth	12.8%	16.8%	—	—

2021 Year-End Financials
Return on assets: 3.3% Cash ($ mil.): 149
Return on equity: 20.2%
Current Ratio: 2.70

COUNTY OF GUILFORD

Auditors: CHERRY BEKAERT & HOLLAND LLP

LOCATIONS
HQ: COUNTY OF GUILFORD
301 W MARKET ST, GREENSBORO, NC 274012514
Phone: 336 641-3836
Web: WWW.COUNTYWEB.CO.GUILFORD.NC.US

HISTORICAL FINANCIALS
Company Type: Private

Income Statement — FYE: June 30

	REVENUE ($mil)	NET INCOME ($mil)	NET PROFIT MARGIN	EMPLOYEES
06/16	596	3	0.6%	2,700
06/15	584	(21)	—	—
06/08	577	(70)	—	—
06/07	548	67	12.3%	—
Annual Growth	0.9%	(28.4%)	—	—

2016 Year-End Financials
Return on assets: 0.6% Cash ($ mil.): —
Return on equity: —
Current Ratio: —

COUNTY OF HARFORD

EXECUTIVES
County Executive, David Craig
Auditors: SB & COMPANY LLC HUNT VALLEY

LOCATIONS
HQ: COUNTY OF HARFORD
220 S MAIN ST, BEL AIR, MD 210143820
Phone: 410 638-3000
Web: WWW.HARFORDCOUNTYMD.GOV

COUNTY OF HARRIS

EXECUTIVES
1st, Rodney Ellis Precinct
Commissioner Precinct #2*, Adrian Garcia
Commissioner Precinct #3*, Tom Ramsey
Commissioner Precinct #4*, R Jack Cagle
Auditors: DELOITTE & TOUCHE LLP HOUSTON

LOCATIONS
HQ: COUNTY OF HARRIS
201 CAROLINE ST FL 4, HOUSTON, TX 770021902
Phone: 713 274-8600
Web: WWW.HARRISCOUNTYTX.GOV

HISTORICAL FINANCIALS
Company Type: Private

Income Statement — FYE: February 28

	REVENUE ($mil)	NET INCOME ($mil)	NET PROFIT MARGIN	EMPLOYEES
02/22	3,524	43	1.2%	14,000
02/21	3,477	319	9.2%	—
02/20	3,076	176	5.7%	—
Annual Growth	7.0%	(50.3%)	—	—

2022 Year-End Financials
Return on assets: 0.2% Cash ($ mil.): 2,928
Return on equity: 0.3%
Current Ratio: —

COUNTY OF HAWAII

Auditors: N&K CPAS INC HONOLULU HAWAI

LOCATIONS
HQ: COUNTY OF HAWAII
25 AUPUNI ST STE 107, HILO, HI 967204245
Phone: 808 961-8211
Web: WWW.HAWAIICOUNTY.GOV

COUNTY OF HENRICO

EXECUTIVES
County Manager, John A Vithoulkas
Auditors: KPMG LLP RICHMOND VA

LOCATIONS
HQ: COUNTY OF HENRICO
4301 E PARHAM RD, HENRICO, VA 232282745
Phone: 804 501-4000
Web: WWW.HENRICO.US

HISTORICAL FINANCIALS
Company Type: Private

Income Statement — FYE: June 30

	REVENUE ($mil)	NET INCOME ($mil)	NET PROFIT MARGIN	EMPLOYEES
06/21	979	112	11.5%	9,178
06/20	935	74	8.0%	—
06/19	906	72	8.0%	—
06/18	853	(13)	—	—
Annual Growth	4.7%	—	—	—

2021 Year-End Financials
Return on assets: 2.1% Cash ($ mil.): —
Return on equity: 4.2%
Current Ratio: —

COUNTY OF HILLSBOROUGH

EXECUTIVES
County Administrator, Bonnie M Wise
Deputy County Administrator*, Gregory Horwedel
Development SVS*, Lucia Garsys
OF HUMAN SVS*, Carl Harness
Branch Administrator*, Wayne Finley
Auditors: RSM US LLP TAMPA FLORIDA

LOCATIONS
HQ: COUNTY OF HILLSBOROUGH
601 E KENNEDY BLVD, TAMPA, FL 336024156
Phone: 813 276-2720

Web: WWW.HILLSBOROUGHCOUNTY.ORG

HISTORICAL FINANCIALS
Company Type: Private

Income Statement FYE: September 30

	REVENUE ($mil)	NET INCOME ($mil)	NET PROFIT MARGIN	EMPLOYEES
09/21	2,364	241	10.2%	10,000
09/20	2,072	129	6.2%	—
09/19	1,933	421	21.8%	—
09/18	1,737	66	3.9%	—
Annual Growth	10.8%	53.4%	—	—

2021 Year-End Financials
Return on assets: 1.8% Cash ($ mil.): 421
Return on equity: 2.3%
Current Ratio: 5.50

COUNTY OF JOHNSON

Auditors : ALLEN GIBBS & HOULIK LC WIC

LOCATIONS

HQ: COUNTY OF JOHNSON
111 S CHERRY ST STE 1200, OLATHE, KS 660613451
Phone: 913 715-0435
Web: WWW.JOCOGOV.ORG

HISTORICAL FINANCIALS
Company Type: Private

Income Statement FYE: December 31

	REVENUE ($mil)	NET INCOME ($mil)	NET PROFIT MARGIN	EMPLOYEES
12/21	579	31	5.4%	2,242
12/20	658	97	14.8%	—
12/18	487	13	2.7%	—
12/17	464	19	4.1%	—
Annual Growth	5.7%	13.2%	—	—

2021 Year-End Financials
Return on assets: 1.0% Cash ($ mil.): —
Return on equity: 3.0%
Current Ratio: —

COUNTY OF KERN

Auditors : BROWN ARMSTRONG ACCOUNTANCY CO

LOCATIONS

HQ: COUNTY OF KERN
1115 TRUXTUN AVE RM 505, BAKERSFIELD, CA 933014630
Phone: 661 868-3690
Web: WWW.KERNCOUNTY.COM

HISTORICAL FINANCIALS
Company Type: Private

Income Statement FYE: June 30

	REVENUE ($mil)	NET INCOME ($mil)	NET PROFIT MARGIN	EMPLOYEES
06/16	1,561	1	0.1%	8,000
06/15	1,546	94	6.1%	—
06/11	1,365	21	1.6%	—
06/06	1,141	13	1.2%	—
Annual Growth	3.2%	(21.8%)	—	—

2016 Year-End Financials
Return on assets: — Cash ($ mil.): 1
Return on equity: 0.6%
Current Ratio: —

COUNTY OF KING

EXECUTIVES

County Executive, Dow Constantine
Auditors : PAT MCCARTHY OLYMPIA WA

LOCATIONS

HQ: COUNTY OF KING
201 S JACKSON ST, SEATTLE, WA 981043854
Phone: 206 296-4040
Web: WWW.KINGCOUNTY.GOV

HISTORICAL FINANCIALS
Company Type: Private

Income Statement FYE: December 31

	REVENUE ($mil)	NET INCOME ($mil)	NET PROFIT MARGIN	EMPLOYEES
12/20	2,765	(25)	—	13,300
12/19	2,367	61	2.6%	—
12/18	2,295	16	0.7%	—
12/17	2,191	121	5.5%	—
Annual Growth	8.1%	—	—	—

2020 Year-End Financials
Return on assets: (-0.2%) Cash ($ mil.): 4,080
Return on equity: (-0.3%)
Current Ratio: —

COUNTY OF LEE

EXECUTIVES

County Manager, Roger Desjarlais
Auditors : CLIFTONLARSONALLEN LLP FORT M

LOCATIONS

HQ: COUNTY OF LEE
2115 SECOND ST, FORT MYERS, FL 339013012
Phone: 239 533-2236
Web: WWW.LEEGOV.COM

HISTORICAL FINANCIALS
Company Type: Private

Income Statement FYE: September 30

	REVENUE ($mil)	NET INCOME ($mil)	NET PROFIT MARGIN	EMPLOYEES
09/21	937	78	8.4%	3,000
09/20	804	76	9.5%	—
09/19	726	(4)	—	—
09/18	693	0	0.1%	—
Annual Growth	10.6%	434.3%	—	—

2021 Year-End Financials
Return on assets: 1.4% Cash ($ mil.): —
Return on equity: 2.5%
Current Ratio: —

COUNTY OF LOS ANGELES

The County of Los Angeles could easily be its own country; all it really needs is just an "r." It encompasses more than 4,000 square miles, 88 cities, two islands, and has a population of more than 10 million. The regional level of state government provides such services as law enforcement, property assessment, tax collection, public health protection, and other social services within its boundaries (sometimes sharing and often providing municipal services for unincorporated cities). The county's elected Board of Supervisors provide political direction, filling executive, legislative, and judicial roles, while the various departments manage daily operations. LA County has an annual budget of nearly $30 billion.

Financial Performance

The county's 2014 budget proposal of $24.7 billion was the first in five years to not include major cuts or include a deficit as the economy improves. It has weathered the economic recession better than many, but most departments were trimmed an average of 15% over the last five years. In addition, the county dipped into its reserves and froze pay for most of its employees.

EXECUTIVES

Supervisor #1*, Gloria Molina
Supervisor 2*, Yvonne Brathwaite Burke
THIRD District*, Zev Yaroslavsky
FOURTH District*, Don Knabe
Supervisor #1*, Michael D Antonovich
Auditors : MACIAS GINI & O'CONNELL LLP L

LOCATIONS

HQ: COUNTY OF LOS ANGELES
500 W TEMPLE ST STE 437, LOS ANGELES, CA 900122706
Phone: 213 974-1101
Web: WWW.LACOUNTY.GOV

COMPETITORS

CITY OF DAYTON
CITY OF HOUSTON
CITY OF IRVING
CITY OF NEW YORK
CITY OF PITTSBURGH
CORECIVIC, INC.
EXECUTIVE OFFICE OF THE GOVERNMENT OF THE US VIRGIN ISLANDS
SCIENCE APPLICATIONS INTERNATIONAL CORPORATION
TALLAHASSEE, CITY OF (INC)
THE NATIONAL TRUST FOR PLACES OF HISTORIC INTEREST OR NATURAL BEAUTY

HISTORICAL FINANCIALS
Company Type: Private

Income Statement — FYE: June 30

	REVENUE ($mil)	NET INCOME ($mil)	NET PROFIT MARGIN	EMPLOYEES
06/21	31,698	(481)	—	101,980
06/20	25,198	323	1.3%	—
06/19	23,510	915	3.9%	—
06/18	21,191	403	1.9%	—
Annual Growth	14.4%	—	—	—

2021 Year-End Financials
Return on assets: (-0.8%)   Cash ($ mil.): —
Return on equity: —
Current Ratio: —

COUNTY OF MARICOPA

Auditors : LINDSEY A PERRY CPA CFE PH

LOCATIONS

HQ: COUNTY OF MARICOPA
 301 W JEFFERSON ST # 960, PHOENIX, AZ 850032111
Phone: 602 506-3561
Web: WWW.MARICOPA.GOV

HISTORICAL FINANCIALS
Company Type: Private

Income Statement — FYE: June 30

	REVENUE ($mil)	NET INCOME ($mil)	NET PROFIT MARGIN	EMPLOYEES
06/21	2,872	292	10.2%	15,751
06/20	2,444	278	11.4%	—
06/19	2,266	21	1.0%	—
06/18	2,136	25	1.2%	—
Annual Growth	10.4%	125.2%	—	—

2021 Year-End Financials
Return on assets: 3.9%   Cash ($ mil.): 93
Return on equity: 7.1%
Current Ratio: —

COUNTY OF MARIN

Auditors : CLIFTONLARSONALLEN LLP ROSEVI

LOCATIONS

HQ: COUNTY OF MARIN
 3501 CIVIC CENTER DR # 225, SAN RAFAEL, CA 949034163
Phone: 415 473-6358
Web: WWW.MARINCOUNTY.ORG

HISTORICAL FINANCIALS
Company Type: Private

Income Statement — FYE: June 30

	REVENUE ($mil)	NET INCOME ($mil)	NET PROFIT MARGIN	EMPLOYEES
06/21	772	80	10.4%	2,122
06/20	656	41	6.2%	—
06/19	651	69	10.7%	—
06/18	608	32	5.4%	—
Annual Growth	8.3%	35.0%	—	—

2021 Year-End Financials
Return on assets: 3.2%   Cash ($ mil.): —
Return on equity: 4.8%
Current Ratio: —

COUNTY OF MAUI

Auditors : N&K CPAS INC HONOLULU HAWA

LOCATIONS

HQ: COUNTY OF MAUI
 200 S HIGH ST, WAILUKU, HI 967932155
Phone: 808 270-7855
Web: WWW.MAUICOUNTY.GOV

HISTORICAL FINANCIALS
Company Type: Private

Income Statement — FYE: June 30

	REVENUE ($mil)	NET INCOME ($mil)	NET PROFIT MARGIN	EMPLOYEES
06/20	621	14	2.3%	2,000
06/16	463	3	0.8%	—
06/15	445	4	1.0%	—
06/14	429	(117)	—	—
Annual Growth	6.4%	—	—	—

2020 Year-End Financials
Return on assets: 0.7%   Cash ($ mil.): —
Return on equity: 3.0%
Current Ratio: —

COUNTY OF MECKLENBURG

Auditors : CHERRY BEKAERT LLP RALEIGH N

LOCATIONS

HQ: COUNTY OF MECKLENBURG
 600 E 4TH ST, CHARLOTTE, NC 282022816
Phone: 704 336-2108
Web: WWW.MECKNC.GOV

HISTORICAL FINANCIALS
Company Type: Private

Income Statement — FYE: June 30

	REVENUE ($mil)	NET INCOME ($mil)	NET PROFIT MARGIN	EMPLOYEES
06/16	1,603	(46)	—	4,800
06/15	1,469	17	1.2%	—
06/14	1,485	41	2.8%	—
06/13	1,433	109	7.7%	—
Annual Growth	3.8%	—	—	—

2016 Year-End Financials
Return on assets: (-1.9%)   Cash ($ mil.): —
Return on equity: (-12.7%)
Current Ratio: —

COUNTY OF MERCED

EXECUTIVES

County Administrator, Demitrios Tatum
Auditors : BROWN ARMSTRONG BAKERSFIELD

LOCATIONS

HQ: COUNTY OF MERCED
 2222 M ST, MERCED, CA 953403729
Phone: 209 385-7511
Web: WWW.COUNTYOFMERCED.COM

HISTORICAL FINANCIALS
Company Type: Private

Income Statement — FYE: June 30

	REVENUE ($mil)	NET INCOME ($mil)	NET PROFIT MARGIN	EMPLOYEES
06/21	578	45	7.8%	2,700
06/20	551	12	2.3%	—
06/19	518	16	3.1%	—
06/18	477	(3)	—	—
Annual Growth	6.6%	—	—	—

2021 Year-End Financials
Return on assets: 3.7%   Cash ($ mil.): —
Return on equity: 12.4%
Current Ratio: —

COUNTY OF MONMOUTH

Auditors : HOLMAN FRENIA ALLISON PC-ROB

LOCATIONS

HQ: COUNTY OF MONMOUTH
 1 E MAIN ST, FREEHOLD, NJ 077282273
Phone: 732 431-7000
Web: WWW.VISITMONMOUTH.COM

HISTORICAL FINANCIALS
Company Type: Private

Income Statement   FYE: December 31

	REVENUE ($mil)	NET INCOME ($mil)	NET PROFIT MARGIN	EMPLOYEES
12/20	670	33	4.9%	3,800
12/19	589	38	6.6%	—
12/18	563	38	6.9%	—
12/17	563	41	7.3%	—
Annual Growth	6.0%	(7.2%)	—	—

2020 Year-End Financials
Return on assets: 1.2%   Cash ($ mil.): 314
Return on equity: 2.0%
Current Ratio: —

HISTORICAL FINANCIALS
Company Type: Private

Income Statement   FYE: December 31

	REVENUE ($mil)	NET INCOME ($mil)	NET PROFIT MARGIN	EMPLOYEES
12/19	661	17	2.6%	3,278
12/17	635	5	0.8%	—
12/15	525	(27)	—	—
12/12	542	(16)	—	—
Annual Growth	2.9%	—	—	—

2019 Year-End Financials
Return on assets: 1.7%   Cash ($ mil.): 167
Return on equity: 52.2%
Current Ratio: —

HISTORICAL FINANCIALS
Company Type: Private

Income Statement   FYE: June 30

	REVENUE ($mil)	NET INCOME ($mil)	NET PROFIT MARGIN	EMPLOYEES
06/21	1,687	530	31.5%	297
06/20	14	2	17.9%	—
06/18	13	0	1.4%	—
06/16	10	(1)	—	—
Annual Growth	174.5%	—	—	—

2021 Year-End Financials
Return on assets: 18.2%   Cash ($ mil.): —
Return on equity: 56.7%
Current Ratio: 3.20

COUNTY OF MONROE

EXECUTIVES

County Executive, Adam J Bello
Auditors : KPMG LLP ROCHESTER NY

LOCATIONS

HQ: COUNTY OF MONROE
39 W MAIN ST STE 110, ROCHESTER, NY 146141408
Phone: 585 753-1700
Web: WWW.MONROECOUNTY.GOV

HISTORICAL FINANCIALS
Company Type: Private

Income Statement   FYE: December 31

	REVENUE ($mil)	NET INCOME ($mil)	NET PROFIT MARGIN	EMPLOYEES
12/18	1,353	21	1.6%	4,800
12/15	1,299	39	3.0%	—
Annual Growth	1.4%	(18.2%)	—	—

2018 Year-End Financials
Return on assets: 0.8%   Cash ($ mil.): 248
Return on equity: 10.6%
Current Ratio: 1.30

COUNTY OF MONTGOMERY

Auditors : MAILLIE LLP OAKS PENNSYLVAN

LOCATIONS

HQ: COUNTY OF MONTGOMERY
530 PORT INDIAN RD, NORRISTOWN, PA 194033502
Phone: 610 630-2252
Web: WWW.MONTCOPA.ORG

COUNTY OF MONTGOMERY

EXECUTIVES

County Administrator, Michael B Colbert
Auditors : KEITH FABER COLUMBUS OHIO

LOCATIONS

HQ: COUNTY OF MONTGOMERY
451 W 3RD ST, DAYTON, OH 454220001
Phone: 937 225-4000
Web: WWW.MCOHIO.ORG

HISTORICAL FINANCIALS
Company Type: Private

Income Statement   FYE: December 31

	REVENUE ($mil)	NET INCOME ($mil)	NET PROFIT MARGIN	EMPLOYEES
12/21	603	23	3.9%	5,000
12/20	654	13	2.0%	—
12/19	559	25	4.5%	—
12/18	528	12	2.3%	—
Annual Growth	4.5%	25.3%	—	—

2021 Year-End Financials
Return on assets: 1.1%   Cash ($ mil.): 719
Return on equity: 1.8%
Current Ratio: —

COUNTY OF MULTNOMAH

Auditors : WILCOX ARREDONDO & CO CANBY

LOCATIONS

HQ: COUNTY OF MULTNOMAH
35800 E HISTRC COLMB RIV, CORBETT, OR 970199687
Phone: 503 261-4200
Web: WWW.CORBETT.K12.OR.US

COUNTY OF MULTNOMAH

EXECUTIVES

City Chairman, Jeff Cogen
Auditors : MOSS ADAMS LLP EUGENE OREGON

LOCATIONS

HQ: COUNTY OF MULTNOMAH
501 SE HAWTHORNE BLVD # 5, PORTLAND, OR 972143587
Phone: 503 988-3511
Web: WWW.MULTCO.US

HISTORICAL FINANCIALS
Company Type: Private

Income Statement   FYE: June 30

	REVENUE ($mil)	NET INCOME ($mil)	NET PROFIT MARGIN	EMPLOYEES
06/19	1,469	(56)	—	5,000
06/18	1,273	93	7.3%	—
06/17	1,238	(19)	—	—
Annual Growth	9.0%	—	—	—

2019 Year-End Financials
Return on assets: (-2.5%)   Cash ($ mil.): —
Return on equity: (-5.9%)
Current Ratio: 2.70

COUNTY OF NASSAU

EXECUTIVES

County Executive, Laura Curran
Auditors : MARKS PANETH LLP NEW YORK N

LOCATIONS

HQ: COUNTY OF NASSAU
1 WEST ST, MINEOLA, NY 115014813
Phone: 516 571-3131
Web: WWW.NASSAUCOUNTYNY.GOV

HISTORICAL FINANCIALS
Company Type: Private

Income Statement — FYE: December 31

	REVENUE ($mil)	NET INCOME ($mil)	NET PROFIT MARGIN	EMPLOYEES
12/20	3,422	15	0.5%	14,500
12/19	3,522	150	4.3%	—
12/18	3,442	111	3.2%	—
12/17	3,401	(115)	—	—

Annual Growth 0.2% — — —

2020 Year-End Financials
Return on assets: 0.2% Cash ($ mil.): 1,055
Return on equity: —
Current Ratio: 1.10

COUNTY OF OAKLAND

EXECUTIVES
County Executive, L Brooks Patterson
Auditors : PLANTE & MORAN PLLC DETROIT

LOCATIONS
HQ: COUNTY OF OAKLAND
1200 N TELEGRAPH RD STE 1, PONTIAC, MI 483411043
Phone: 248 858-1000
Web: WWW.OAKGOV.COM

HISTORICAL FINANCIALS
Company Type: Private

Income Statement — FYE: September 30

	REVENUE ($mil)	NET INCOME ($mil)	NET PROFIT MARGIN	EMPLOYEES
09/21	699	28	4.0%	4,229
09/20	620	(6)	—	—
09/18	500	(11)	—	—
09/17	483	(8)	—	—

Annual Growth 9.7% — — —

2021 Year-End Financials
Return on assets: 0.6% Cash ($ mil.): —
Return on equity: 0.8%
Current Ratio: —

COUNTY OF ONONDAGA

EXECUTIVES
County Executive*, Nicholas J Pirro
Auditors : BONADIO & CO LLP SYRACUSE

LOCATIONS
HQ: COUNTY OF ONONDAGA
1000 ERIE BLVD W, SYRACUSE, NY 132042748
Phone: 315 435-8683
Web: WWW.ONGOV.NET

HISTORICAL FINANCIALS
Company Type: Private

Income Statement — FYE: December 31

	REVENUE ($mil)	NET INCOME ($mil)	NET PROFIT MARGIN	EMPLOYEES
12/21	1,098	142	12.9%	508
12/20	947	34	3.7%	—
12/19	981	26	2.7%	—
12/18	964	(0)	0.0%	—

Annual Growth 4.4% — — —

2021 Year-End Financials
Return on assets: 5.0% Cash ($ mil.): —
Return on equity: 34.7%
Current Ratio: —

COUNTY OF ORANGE

Auditors : EIDE BAILLY LLP LAGUNA HILLS

LOCATIONS
HQ: COUNTY OF ORANGE
333 W SANTA ANA BLVD, SANTA ANA, CA 927014084
Phone: 714 834-6200
Web: WWW.OCGOV.COM

HISTORICAL FINANCIALS
Company Type: Private

Income Statement — FYE: June 30

	REVENUE ($mil)	NET INCOME ($mil)	NET PROFIT MARGIN	EMPLOYEES
06/21	5,065	62	1.2%	21,000
06/20	4,387	40	0.9%	—
06/19	4,105	152	3.7%	—
06/18	4,045	(78)	—	—

Annual Growth 7.8% — — —

2021 Year-End Financials
Return on assets: 0.4% Cash ($ mil.): 4,546
Return on equity: 1.2%
Current Ratio: 18.80

COUNTY OF ORANGE

EXECUTIVES
County Executive, Edward A Diana
Finance*, Joel Kleiman

LOCATIONS
HQ: COUNTY OF ORANGE
255 MAIN ST STE 1055, GOSHEN, NY 109241641
Phone: 845 291-2480
Web: WWW.ORANGECOUNTYGOV.COM

HISTORICAL FINANCIALS
Company Type: Private

Income Statement — FYE: December 31

	REVENUE ($mil)	NET INCOME ($mil)	NET PROFIT MARGIN	EMPLOYEES
12/21	771	75	9.8%	2,700
12/20	680	10	1.6%	—
12/19	724	12	1.7%	—
12/18	699	(33)	—	—

Annual Growth 3.3% — — —

2021 Year-End Financials
Return on assets: 5.5% Cash ($ mil.): 257
Return on equity: —
Current Ratio: —

COUNTY OF ORANGE

EXECUTIVES
County Administrator*, Christopher R Testerman
District #1*, Nicole H Wilson
District #2*, Christine Moore
District #3*, Mayra Uribe
District #4*, Maribel Gomez Cordero
District #5*, Emily Bonilla
District 6*, Victoria P Siplin
Auditors : CHERRY BEKAERT LLP ORLANDO F

LOCATIONS
HQ: COUNTY OF ORANGE
201 S ROSALIND AVE FL 5, ORLANDO, FL 328013527
Phone: 407 836-7350
Web: WWW.ORANGECOUNTYFL.NET

HISTORICAL FINANCIALS
Company Type: Private

Income Statement — FYE: September 30

	REVENUE ($mil)	NET INCOME ($mil)	NET PROFIT MARGIN	EMPLOYEES
09/21	2,560	192	7.5%	7,315
09/20	1,970	113	5.7%	—
09/19	1,822	205	11.3%	—
09/18	1,694	126	7.5%	—

Annual Growth 14.8% 14.8% — —

2021 Year-End Financials
Return on assets: 1.7% Cash ($ mil.): —
Return on equity: 2.6%
Current Ratio: —

COUNTY OF PALM BEACH

Auditors : RSM US LLP WEST PALM BEACH

LOCATIONS
HQ: COUNTY OF PALM BEACH
301 N OLIVE AVE FRNT, WEST PALM BEACH, FL 334014703
Phone: 561 355-4950

Web: DISCOVER.PBCGOV.ORG

HISTORICAL FINANCIALS
Company Type: Private

Income Statement — FYE: September 30

	REVENUE ($mil)	NET INCOME ($mil)	NET PROFIT MARGIN	EMPLOYEES
09/20	2,366	153	6.5%	5,500
09/18	2,081	134	6.5%	—
09/17	1,960	28	1.5%	—
09/16	1,821	68	3.8%	—
Annual Growth	6.8%	22.5%	—	—

2020 Year-End Financials
Return on assets: 1.6%   Cash ($ mil.): —
Return on equity: 3.8%
Current Ratio: —

COUNTY OF PASCO

Auditors : KPMG LLP TAMPA FL

LOCATIONS

HQ: COUNTY OF PASCO
8731 CITIZENS DR, NEW PORT RICHEY, FL 346545572
Phone: 727 847-2411
Web: WWW.PASCOCOUNTYFL.NET

HISTORICAL FINANCIALS
Company Type: Private

Income Statement — FYE: September 30

	REVENUE ($mil)	NET INCOME ($mil)	NET PROFIT MARGIN	EMPLOYEES
09/21	773	152	19.7%	1,540
09/18	577	41	7.1%	—
09/17	520	58	11.3%	—
09/16	475	48	10.2%	—
Annual Growth	10.2%	25.8%	—	—

2021 Year-End Financials
Return on assets: 3.7%   Cash ($ mil.): 700
Return on equity: 5.7%
Current Ratio: 10.10

COUNTY OF PIERCE

Auditors : PAT MCCARTHY STATE AUDITOR O

LOCATIONS

HQ: COUNTY OF PIERCE
950 FAWCETT AVE STE 100, TACOMA, WA 984025603
Phone: 253 798-7285
Web: WWW.PIERCECOUNTYWA.GOV

HISTORICAL FINANCIALS
Company Type: Private

Income Statement — FYE: December 31

	REVENUE ($mil)	NET INCOME ($mil)	NET PROFIT MARGIN	EMPLOYEES
12/20	839	35	4.2%	2,270
12/19	647	107	16.6%	—
12/18	606	34	5.7%	—
12/17	582	27	4.7%	—
Annual Growth	13.0%	8.5%	—	—

2020 Year-End Financials
Return on assets: 1.2%   Cash ($ mil.): 251
Return on equity: 1.7%
Current Ratio: —

COUNTY OF PLACER

Auditors : VAVRINEK TRINE DAY & CO LL

LOCATIONS

HQ: COUNTY OF PLACER
2986 RICHARDSON DR, AUBURN, CA 956032640
Phone: 530 889-4200
Web: PLACER.CA.GOV

HISTORICAL FINANCIALS
Company Type: Private

Income Statement — FYE: June 30

	REVENUE ($mil)	NET INCOME ($mil)	NET PROFIT MARGIN	EMPLOYEES
06/21	780	80	10.4%	3,024
06/20	700	(11)	—	—
06/19	638	18	3.0%	—
06/18	596	7	1.2%	—
Annual Growth	9.4%	124.7%	—	—

2021 Year-End Financials
Return on assets: 3.9%   Cash ($ mil.): —
Return on equity: 8.7%
Current Ratio: —

COUNTY OF PRINCE WILLIAM

EXECUTIVES

County Executive, Melissa S Peacor
Auditors : CHERRY BEKAERT LLP TYSONS CO

LOCATIONS

HQ: COUNTY OF PRINCE WILLIAM
1 COUNTY COMPLEX CT, WOODBRIDGE, VA 221929202
Phone: 703 792-4640
Web: WWW.PWCVA.GOV

HISTORICAL FINANCIALS
Company Type: Private

Income Statement — FYE: June 30

	REVENUE ($mil)	NET INCOME ($mil)	NET PROFIT MARGIN	EMPLOYEES
06/21	1,565	45	2.9%	2,700
06/20	1,417	33	2.3%	—
06/19	1,366	10	0.7%	—
06/18	1,261	(42)	—	—
Annual Growth	7.5%	—	—	—

2021 Year-End Financials
Return on assets: 1.0%   Cash ($ mil.): —
Return on equity: 3.9%
Current Ratio: —

COUNTY OF RAMSEY

Auditors : REBECCA OTTO SAINT PAUL MN

LOCATIONS

HQ: COUNTY OF RAMSEY
121 7TH PL E STE 4000, SAINT PAUL, MN 551012419
Phone: 651 266-8044
Web: WWW.RAMSEYCOUNTY.US

HISTORICAL FINANCIALS
Company Type: Private

Income Statement — FYE: December 31

	REVENUE ($mil)	NET INCOME ($mil)	NET PROFIT MARGIN	EMPLOYEES
12/21	954	2	0.3%	4,000
12/20	1,087	129	12.0%	—
12/19	934	39	4.2%	—
12/18	725	91	12.5%	—
Annual Growth	9.6%	(70.2%)	—	—

2021 Year-End Financials
Return on assets: 0.1%   Cash ($ mil.): —
Return on equity: 0.2%
Current Ratio: 6.40

COUNTY OF RIVERSIDE

EXECUTIVES

First District Superintendent, Bob Buster
District Superintendent, John Tavaglinoe Ii
Third District Superintendent*, Jeff Stone
Auditors : BROWN ARMSTRONG ACCOUNTANCY CO

LOCATIONS

HQ: COUNTY OF RIVERSIDE
4080 LEMON ST FL 11, RIVERSIDE, CA 925013609
Phone: 951 955-1110
Web: WWW.COUNTYOFRIVERSIDE.US

HISTORICAL FINANCIALS
Company Type: Private

Income Statement — FYE: June 30

	REVENUE ($mil)	NET INCOME ($mil)	NET PROFIT MARGIN	EMPLOYEES
06/21	4,539	184	4.1%	20,000
06/20	4,044	76	1.9%	—
06/19	3,727	26	0.7%	—
Annual Growth	10.4%	164.7%	—	—

2021 Year-End Financials
Return on assets: 1.8%   Cash ($ mil.): —
Return on equity: 8.5%
Current Ratio: —

COUNTY OF ROCKLAND

EXECUTIVES

County Executive, Edwin Day
Auditors : MARKS PANETH LLP NEW YORK NY

LOCATIONS

HQ: COUNTY OF ROCKLAND
11 NEW HEMPSTEAD RD # 10, NEW CITY, NY 109563664
Phone: 845 638-5122
Web: WWW.ROCKLANDGOV.COM

HISTORICAL FINANCIALS
Company Type: Private

Income Statement — FYE: December 31

	REVENUE ($mil)	NET INCOME ($mil)	NET PROFIT MARGIN	EMPLOYEES
12/21	869	86	9.9%	3,100
12/20	612	30	5.0%	—
12/19	624	34	5.6%	—
12/18	616	61	10.0%	—
Annual Growth	12.1%	11.8%	—	—

2021 Year-End Financials
Return on assets: 2.4%   Cash ($ mil.): 277
Return on equity: 4.7%
Current Ratio: —

COUNTY OF SACRAMENTO

Auditors : VAVRINEK TRINE DAY & CO LL

LOCATIONS

HQ: COUNTY OF SACRAMENTO
700 H ST STE 7650, SACRAMENTO, CA 958141280
Phone: 916 874-8515
Web: WWW.SACCOUNTY.NET

HISTORICAL FINANCIALS
Company Type: Private

Income Statement — FYE: June 30

	REVENUE ($mil)	NET INCOME ($mil)	NET PROFIT MARGIN	EMPLOYEES
06/22	3,558	251	7.1%	10,968
06/20	3,114	98	3.2%	—
06/19	2,857	(17)	—	—
06/18	2,801	62	2.2%	—
Annual Growth	6.2%	41.7%	—	—

2022 Year-End Financials
Return on assets: 3.1%   Cash ($ mil.): —
Return on equity: 12.4%
Current Ratio: 2.80

COUNTY OF SALT LAKE

Auditors : SQUIRE & COMPANY PC OREM UT

LOCATIONS

HQ: COUNTY OF SALT LAKE
2001 S STATE ST STE 2-200, SALT LAKE CITY, UT 841900001
Phone: 801 468-3225
Web: WWW.SLCO.ORG

HISTORICAL FINANCIALS
Company Type: Private

Income Statement — FYE: December 31

	REVENUE ($mil)	NET INCOME ($mil)	NET PROFIT MARGIN	EMPLOYEES
12/20	1,284	29	2.3%	4,200
12/15	972	35	3.7%	—
12/10	564	79	14.1%	—
12/09	504	27	5.5%	—
Annual Growth	8.9%	0.4%	—	—

2020 Year-End Financials
Return on assets: 1.5%   Cash ($ mil.): —
Return on equity: 3.1%
Current Ratio: —

COUNTY OF SAN MATEO

EXECUTIVES

County Manager*, John L Maltbie
Auditors : WALNUT CREEK CALIFORNIA WALN

LOCATIONS

HQ: COUNTY OF SAN MATEO
555 COUNTY CTR FL 4, REDWOOD CITY, CA 940631665
Phone: 650 363-4123
Web: WWW.SMCGOV.ORG

HISTORICAL FINANCIALS
Company Type: Private

Income Statement — FYE: June 30

	REVENUE ($mil)	NET INCOME ($mil)	NET PROFIT MARGIN	EMPLOYEES
06/21	1,795	160	9.0%	5,800
06/20	1,731	190	11.0%	—
06/19	1,721	443	25.7%	—
06/18	1,475	84	5.7%	—
Annual Growth	6.8%	23.9%	—	—

2021 Year-End Financials
Return on assets: 2.7%   Cash ($ mil.): —
Return on equity: 4.9%
Current Ratio: —

COUNTY OF SANTA BARBARA

EXECUTIVES

City Administrator*, Michael Brown
Auditors : EIDE BAILLY LLP RANCHO CUCAM

LOCATIONS

HQ: COUNTY OF SANTA BARBARA
105 E ANAPAMU ST RM 406, SANTA BARBARA, CA 931012065
Phone: 805 568-3400
Web: WWW.COUNTYOFSB.ORG

HISTORICAL FINANCIALS
Company Type: Private

Income Statement — FYE: June 30

	REVENUE ($mil)	NET INCOME ($mil)	NET PROFIT MARGIN	EMPLOYEES
06/20	1,007	44	4.4%	4,582
06/19	987	53	5.4%	—
06/18	930	15	1.7%	—
06/17	889	21	2.4%	—
Annual Growth	4.3%	27.5%	—	—

2020 Year-End Financials
Return on assets: 2.1%   Cash ($ mil.): —
Return on equity: 6.5%
Current Ratio: —

COUNTY OF SANTA CLARA

EXECUTIVES

County Executive, Jeffrey V Smith
Auditors : MACIAS GINI & O'CONNELL LLP W

LOCATIONS

HQ: COUNTY OF SANTA CLARA
70 W HEDDING ST 2WING, SAN JOSE, CA 951101768
Phone: 408 299-5200
Web: WWW.SCCGOV.ORG

HISTORICAL FINANCIALS
Company Type: Private

Income Statement — FYE: June 30

	REVENUE ($mil)	NET INCOME ($mil)	NET PROFIT MARGIN	EMPLOYEES
06/15	2,866	183	6.4%	14,500
06/14	2,660	12	0.5%	—
06/13	2,395	147	6.2%	—
06/11	2,408	54	2.2%	—
Annual Growth	4.5%	35.7%	—	—

2015 Year-End Financials
Return on assets: 2.9%   Cash ($ mil.): —
Return on equity: —
Current Ratio: —

COUNTY OF SANTA CRUZ

EXECUTIVES

Administrative Officer, Susan Mauriello
District #1*, Janet K Beautz
District #2*, Ellen Pirie
District #3*, Mardi Wormoudt
District #4*, Tony Campos
District #5*, Jeff Almquist
Auditors : BROWN ARMSTRONG ACCOUNTANCY CO

LOCATIONS

HQ: COUNTY OF SANTA CRUZ
701 OCEAN ST RM 520, SANTA CRUZ, CA 950604002
Phone: 831 454-2100
Web: CO.SANTA-CRUZ.CA.US

HISTORICAL FINANCIALS
Company Type: Private

Income Statement — FYE: June 30

	REVENUE ($mil)	NET INCOME ($mil)	NET PROFIT MARGIN	EMPLOYEES
06/21	719	3	0.5%	1,654
06/20	602	(2)	—	—
06/19	583	18	3.2%	—
06/18	544	0	0.0%	—
Annual Growth	9.8%	244.3%	—	—

2021 Year-End Financials
Return on assets: 0.3%   Cash ($ mil.): —
Return on equity: 1.2%
Current Ratio: —

COUNTY OF SARASOTA

EXECUTIVES

City Administrator, James Ley
County Administrator, James Ley
Auditors : CLIFTONLARSONALLEN LLP TAMPA

LOCATIONS

HQ: COUNTY OF SARASOTA
1660 RINGLING BLVD, SARASOTA, FL 342366808
Phone: 941 861-5165
Web: WWW.SCGOV.NET

HISTORICAL FINANCIALS
Company Type: Private

Income Statement — FYE: September 30

	REVENUE ($mil)	NET INCOME ($mil)	NET PROFIT MARGIN	EMPLOYEES
09/18	547	12	2.3%	3,600
09/16	482	(43)	—	—
09/15	482	(23)	—	—
Annual Growth	4.3%	—	—	—

2018 Year-End Financials
Return on assets: 0.4%   Cash ($ mil.): —
Return on equity: 0.6%
Current Ratio: 5.50

COUNTY OF SHELBY

EXECUTIVES

Finance*, James Huntzicker
OF Finance*, Micheal A Swift
Auditors : BANKS FINLEY WHITE & CO ME

LOCATIONS

HQ: COUNTY OF SHELBY
160 N MAIN ST FL 4, MEMPHIS, TN 381031866
Phone: 901 222-2050
Web: WWW.SHELBYCOUNTYTN.GOV

HISTORICAL FINANCIALS
Company Type: Private

Income Statement — FYE: June 30

	REVENUE ($mil)	NET INCOME ($mil)	NET PROFIT MARGIN	EMPLOYEES
06/21	1,189	89	7.5%	7,990
06/20	1,125	(83)	—	—
06/19	1,125	39	3.5%	—
06/18	1,113	(10)	—	—
Annual Growth	2.2%	—	—	—

2021 Year-End Financials
Return on assets: 2.0%   Cash ($ mil.): 525
Return on equity: 69.0%
Current Ratio: —

COUNTY OF SNOHOMISH

EXECUTIVES

County Executive*, Aaron Reardon
Auditors : PAT MCCARTHY OLYMPIA WA

LOCATIONS

HQ: COUNTY OF SNOHOMISH
3000 ROCKEFELLER AVE MS508, EVERETT, WA 982014071
Phone: 425 388-3460
Web: WWW.SNOHOMISHCOUNTYWA.GOV

COUNTY OF SOLANO

HISTORICAL FINANCIALS
Company Type: Private

Income Statement — FYE: December 31

	REVENUE ($mil)	NET INCOME ($mil)	NET PROFIT MARGIN	EMPLOYEES
12/21	750	102	13.7%	2,500
12/20	699	(2)	—	—
12/18	532	(4)	—	—
12/17	502	25	5.1%	—
Annual Growth	10.6%	41.6%	—	—

2021 Year-End Financials
Return on assets: 3.7%   Cash ($ mil.): 496
Return on equity: 5.3%
Current Ratio: 3.30

EXECUTIVES

Co-Administrator, Michael Johnson
County Administrator, Michael Johnson
Chief Officer*, Philis Taynton
Auditors : MACIAS GINI & O'CONNELL LLP S

LOCATIONS

HQ: COUNTY OF SOLANO
675 TEXAS ST STE 2600, FAIRFIELD, CA 945336301
Phone: 707 784-6706
Web: WWW.SOLANOCOUNTY.COM

HISTORICAL FINANCIALS
Company Type: Private

Income Statement — FYE: June 30

	REVENUE ($mil)	NET INCOME ($mil)	NET PROFIT MARGIN	EMPLOYEES
06/21*	856	79	9.3%	2,600
12/20	0	(0)	—	—
06/20	740	13	1.9%	—
06/19	739	36	4.9%	—
Annual Growth	7.6%	48.9%	—	—

*Fiscal year change

2021 Year-End Financials
Return on assets: 5.6%   Cash ($ mil.): —
Return on equity: 16.9%
Current Ratio: 3.40

COUNTY OF SONOMA

EXECUTIVES

Collector*, Rodney Dole
Auditors : EIDE BAILLY LLP RANCHO CUCAM

LOCATIONS

HQ: COUNTY OF SONOMA
585 FISCAL DR 100, SANTA ROSA, CA 954032824
Phone: 707 565-2431
Web: SONOMACOUNTY.CA.GOV

HISTORICAL FINANCIALS
Company Type: Private

Income Statement — FYE: June 30

	REVENUE ($mil)	NET INCOME ($mil)	NET PROFIT MARGIN	EMPLOYEES
06/21	1,365	250	18.3%	5,260
06/20	1,017	7	0.8%	—
06/19	1,019	77	7.6%	—
06/18	984	26	2.7%	—
Annual Growth	11.5%	112.3%	—	—

2021 Year-End Financials
Return on assets: 6.6%   Cash ($ mil.): —
Return on equity: 10.7%
Current Ratio: —

HISTORICAL FINANCIALS
Company Type: Private

Income Statement — FYE: June 30

	REVENUE ($mil)	NET INCOME ($mil)	NET PROFIT MARGIN	EMPLOYEES
06/20	1,234	21	1.8%	4,972
06/18	940	18	2.0%	—
06/17	0	0	—	—
06/16	882	18	2.1%	—
Annual Growth	8.7%	4.1%	—	—

2020 Year-End Financials
Return on assets: 1.3%   Cash ($ mil.): —
Return on equity: 3.6%
Current Ratio: —

HISTORICAL FINANCIALS
Company Type: Private

Income Statement — FYE: September 30

	REVENUE ($mil)	NET INCOME ($mil)	NET PROFIT MARGIN	EMPLOYEES
09/16	597	5	1.0%	139
09/15	580	52	9.1%	—
09/14	0	0	—	—
09/13	537	20	3.8%	—
Annual Growth	3.6%	(33.8%)	—	—

2016 Year-End Financials
Return on assets: 0.3%   Cash ($ mil.): —
Return on equity: 0.7%
Current Ratio: —

COUNTY OF ST LOUIS

EXECUTIVES
County Executive, Charles Dooley
OF Personnel, Kirk Mccarley
Auditors : HOCHCHILD BLOOM & COMPANY LL

LOCATIONS
HQ: COUNTY OF ST LOUIS
41 S CENTRAL AVE, SAINT LOUIS, MO 631051703
Phone: 314 615-7016
Web: WWW.STLOUISCOUNTYMO.GOV

HISTORICAL FINANCIALS
Company Type: Private

Income Statement — FYE: December 31

	REVENUE ($mil)	NET INCOME ($mil)	NET PROFIT MARGIN	EMPLOYEES
12/21	991	174	17.6%	4,100
12/20	856	(5)	—	—
12/19	810	49	6.1%	—
12/18	804	49	6.2%	—
Annual Growth	7.2%	52.0%	—	—

2021 Year-End Financials
Return on assets: 7.3%   Cash ($ mil.): —
Return on equity: 13.3%
Current Ratio: 3.40

COUNTY OF STANISLAUS

Auditors : BROWN ARMSTRONG ACCOUNTANCY CO

LOCATIONS
HQ: COUNTY OF STANISLAUS
1010 10TH ST STE 5100, MODESTO, CA 953540872
Phone: 209 525-6398
Web: WWW.STANCOUNTY.COM

COUNTY OF SUFFOLK

EXECUTIVES
County Executive, Steven Bellone
Auditors : DELOITTE & TOUCHE LLP JERICHO

LOCATIONS
HQ: COUNTY OF SUFFOLK
100 VETERANS HWY, HAUPPAUGE, NY 117885402
Phone: 631 853-4000
Web: WWW.SUFFOLKCOUNTYNY.GOV

HISTORICAL FINANCIALS
Company Type: Private

Income Statement — FYE: December 31

	REVENUE ($mil)	NET INCOME ($mil)	NET PROFIT MARGIN	EMPLOYEES
12/21	3,698	304	8.2%	12,814
12/20	3	0	7.2%	—
12/19	3,378	36	1.1%	—
12/18	3,257	(69)	—	—
Annual Growth	4.3%	—	—	—

2021 Year-End Financials
Return on assets: 3.6%   Cash ($ mil.): 1,188
Return on equity: —
Current Ratio: 1.80

COUNTY OF TARRANT

Auditors : KPMG LLP DALLAS TX

LOCATIONS
HQ: COUNTY OF TARRANT
100 E WEATHERFORD ST, FORT WORTH, TX 761960206
Phone: 817 884-1205
Web: WWW.ACCESS.TARRANTCOUNTY.COM

COUNTY OF TRAVIS

Auditors : ATCHLEY & ASSOCIATES LLP AUST

LOCATIONS
HQ: COUNTY OF TRAVIS
700 LAVACA ST FL 11, AUSTIN, TX 787013101
Phone: 512 854-9125
Web: WWW.TRAVISCOUNTYTX.GOV

HISTORICAL FINANCIALS
Company Type: Private

Income Statement — FYE: September 30

	REVENUE ($mil)	NET INCOME ($mil)	NET PROFIT MARGIN	EMPLOYEES
09/21	999	45	4.5%	3,900
09/20	940	41	4.4%	—
09/19	846	384	45.4%	—
09/17	758	(41)	—	—
Annual Growth	7.2%	—	—	—

2021 Year-End Financials
Return on assets: 1.2%   Cash ($ mil.): 1,301
Return on equity: 6.9%
Current Ratio: —

COUNTY OF TULARE

EXECUTIVES
County Administrative Officer, Jean M Rousseau
Auditors : BROWN ARMSTRONG ACCOUNTANCY CO

LOCATIONS
HQ: COUNTY OF TULARE
2800 W BURREL AVE, VISALIA, CA 932914517
Phone: 559 636-5005
Web: WWW.TULARECOUNTYLIBRARY.ORG

HISTORICAL FINANCIALS
Company Type: Private

Income Statement — FYE: June 30

	REVENUE ($mil)	NET INCOME ($mil)	NET PROFIT MARGIN	EMPLOYEES
06/21	993	87	8.8%	4,485
06/20	882	45	5.2%	—
06/19	882	80	9.1%	—
06/18	814	30	3.7%	—
Annual Growth	6.9%	42.4%	—	—

2021 Year-End Financials
Return on assets: 3.0%   Cash ($ mil.): 1
Return on equity: 4.8%
Current Ratio: —

COUNTY OF UNION

LOCATIONS
HQ: COUNTY OF UNION
10 ELIZABETH AVE, ELIZABETH, NJ 07206
Phone: 908 659-7407
Web: WWW.UCNJ.ORG

HISTORICAL FINANCIALS
Company Type: Private

Income Statement — FYE: December 31

	REVENUE ($mil)	NET INCOME ($mil)	NET PROFIT MARGIN	EMPLOYEES
12/21	701	77	11.1%	2,700
12/20	685	58	8.6%	—
12/18	561	36	6.5%	—
12/17	550	47	8.6%	—
Annual Growth	6.2%	13.3%	—	—

2021 Year-End Financials
Return on assets: 3.2%   Cash ($ mil.): 622
Return on equity: 5.1%
Current Ratio: —

COUNTY OF VOLUSIA

Auditors: JAMES MOORE & CO PL DAYTON

LOCATIONS
HQ: COUNTY OF VOLUSIA
123 W INDIANA AVE STE A, DELAND, FL 327204615
Phone: 386 736-2700
Web: WWW.VOLUSIA.ORG

HISTORICAL FINANCIALS
Company Type: Private

Income Statement — FYE: September 30

	REVENUE ($mil)	NET INCOME ($mil)	NET PROFIT MARGIN	EMPLOYEES
09/20	573	77	13.5%	11,000
09/18	497	18	3.6%	—
09/17	462	12	2.7%	—
09/16	428	19	4.7%	—
Annual Growth	7.6%	40.3%	—	—

2020 Year-End Financials
Return on assets: 3.9%   Cash ($ mil.): —
Return on equity: 6.3%
Current Ratio: —

COUNTY OF WASHINGTON

EXECUTIVES
County Administrator, Robert Davis
Auditors: TALBOT KORVOLA & WARWICK LLP

LOCATIONS
HQ: COUNTY OF WASHINGTON
155 N 1ST AVE STE 300, HILLSBORO, OR 971243001
Phone: 503 846-8685
Web: WWW.WASHINGTONCOUNTYOR.GOV

HISTORICAL FINANCIALS
Company Type: Private

Income Statement — FYE: June 30

	REVENUE ($mil)	NET INCOME ($mil)	NET PROFIT MARGIN	EMPLOYEES
06/21	734	(8)	—	1,800
06/20	624	(50)	—	—
06/19	577	(7)	—	—
06/18	522	(35)	—	—
Annual Growth	12.1%	—	—	—

2021 Year-End Financials
Return on assets: (-0.2%)   Cash ($ mil.): —
Return on equity: (-0.3%)
Current Ratio: 2.70

COUNTY OF WASHOE

Auditors: EIDE BAILLY LLP RENO NEVADA

LOCATIONS
HQ: COUNTY OF WASHOE
1001 E 9TH ST, RENO, NV 895122845
Phone: 775 328-2552
Web: WWW.WASHOECOUNTY.GOV

HISTORICAL FINANCIALS
Company Type: Private

Income Statement — FYE: June 30

	REVENUE ($mil)	NET INCOME ($mil)	NET PROFIT MARGIN	EMPLOYEES
06/21	618	79	12.8%	2,800
06/20	542	18	3.5%	—
06/19	518	30	5.9%	—
06/18	500	7	1.6%	—
Annual Growth	7.3%	115.0%	—	—

2021 Year-End Financials
Return on assets: 5.7%   Cash ($ mil.): —
Return on equity: 25.0%
Current Ratio: —

COUNTY OF WESTCHESTER

Auditors: PKF OCONNOR DAVIES LLP HARRIS

LOCATIONS
HQ: COUNTY OF WESTCHESTER
148 MARTINE AVE, WHITE PLAINS, NY 106013311
Phone: 914 995-2000
Web: WWW.WESTCHESTERGOV.COM

HISTORICAL FINANCIALS
Company Type: Private

Income Statement — FYE: December 31

	REVENUE ($mil)	NET INCOME ($mil)	NET PROFIT MARGIN	EMPLOYEES
12/21	2,670	148	5.6%	5,927
12/20	2	0	1.2%	—
12/19	2,412	5	0.2%	—
12/18	2,268	1	0.0%	—
Annual Growth	5.6%	418.9%	—	—

2021 Year-End Financials
Return on assets: 2.5%   Cash ($ mil.): 522
Return on equity: —
Current Ratio: 1.40

COUNTY OF WYOMING

Auditors: HALLOCKSHANNON PC TUNKHANNOC

LOCATIONS
HQ: COUNTY OF WYOMING
1 COURT HOUSE SQ OFC, TUNKHANNOCK, PA 18657
Phone: 570 836-3200
Web: WWW.WYCOPA.ORG

HISTORICAL FINANCIALS
Company Type: Private

Income Statement — FYE: December 31

	REVENUE ($mil)	NET INCOME ($mil)	NET PROFIT MARGIN	EMPLOYEES
12/19	32,004	(675)	—	167
12/17	25	1	6.6%	—
12/15*	25	3	12.5%	—
06/05	0	0	—	—
Annual Growth	—	—	—	—

*Fiscal year change

2019 Year-End Financials
Return on assets: (-2.1%)   Cash ($ mil.): 9,610
Return on equity: (-5.3%)
Current Ratio: —

COUNTY OF YORK

Auditors: ZELENKOFSKE AXELORD LLC HARRI

LOCATIONS
HQ: COUNTY OF YORK
28 E MARKET ST RM 216, YORK, PA 174011587

Phone: 717 771-9964
Web: WWW.YORKCOUNTYPA.GOV

HISTORICAL FINANCIALS
Company Type: Private

Income Statement — FYE: December 31

	REVENUE ($mil)	NET INCOME ($mil)	NET PROFIT MARGIN	EMPLOYEES
12/21	599	22	3.8%	2,600
12/20	541	35	6.6%	—
12/19	481	(3)	—	—
12/18	475	32	6.9%	—
Annual Growth	8.1%	(11.7%)	—	—

2021 Year-End Financials
Return on assets: 2.5% Cash ($ mil.): 124
Return on equity: 6.4%
Current Ratio: —

COUNTY SANITATION DISTRICT NO. 2 OF LOS ANGELES COUNTY

Auditors: MOSS LEVY & HARTZHEIM LLP CU

LOCATIONS
HQ: COUNTY SANITATION DISTRICT NO. 2 OF LOS ANGELES COUNTY
1955 WORKMAN MILL RD, WHITTIER, CA 906011415
Phone: 562 699-7411
Web: WWW.LACSD.ORG

HISTORICAL FINANCIALS
Company Type: Private

Income Statement — FYE: June 30

	REVENUE ($mil)	NET INCOME ($mil)	NET PROFIT MARGIN	EMPLOYEES
06/19	627	211	33.8%	1,700
06/16	545	144	26.4%	—
06/15	555	92	16.7%	—
06/12	550	74	13.6%	—
Annual Growth	1.9%	16.0%	—	—

2019 Year-End Financials
Return on assets: 3.5% Cash ($ mil.): 519
Return on equity: 5.0%
Current Ratio: 14.10

COVENANT HEALTH

Covenant Health has made a pact to provide good health to the good people of Tennessee. The not-for-profit health care system, established in 1996, provides a variety of medical services through seven acute care hospitals, a psychiatric hospital and a number of specialty outpatient centers offering geriatrics, pediatric care, cancer services, weight management, and diagnostics. Covenant Health also operates home health and hospice agencies and a physician practice management company. Covenant Health provides staffing and medical management services to its affiliated facilities, and to make itself a really well-rounded health care provider, it operates the Covenant Health Federal Credit Union.

LOCATIONS
HQ: COVENANT HEALTH
100 FORT SANDERS W BLVD, KNOXVILLE, TN 379223353
Phone: 865 531-5555
Web: WWW.COVENANTHEALTH.COM

PRODUCTS/OPERATIONS
Selected Tennessee Facilities
Fort Loudon Medical Center (Lenoir City, TN)
Fort Sanders Regional Medical Center (Knoxville, TN)
LeConte Medical Center (formerly Fort Sanders Sevier Medical Center; Sevierville, TN)
Methodist Medical Center of Oak Ridge (Oak Ridge, TN)
Parkwest Medical Center (Knoxville, TN)
Peninsula Hospital (behavioral health care, Louisville, TN)
Roane Medical Center (Harriman, TN)

COMPETITORS
ALEGENT CREIGHTON HEALTH
AULTMAN HEALTH FOUNDATION
COMMONWEALTH HEALTH CORPORATION, INC.
FRANKLIN COMMUNITY HEALTH NETWORK
HARTFORD HEALTHCARE CORPORATION
HUNTERDON HEALTHCARE SYSTEM
NORTHEAST HEALTH SYSTEMS INC.
ROGER WILLIAMS MEDICAL CENTER
UNION HEALTH SERVICE INC
VIRTUA HEALTH, INC.

HISTORICAL FINANCIALS
Company Type: Private

Income Statement — FYE: December 31

	REVENUE ($mil)	NET INCOME ($mil)	NET PROFIT MARGIN	EMPLOYEES
12/21	1,572	178	11.4%	10,000
12/20	1,470	158	10.8%	—
12/19	1,407	183	13.1%	—
12/18	1,296	(49)	—	—
Annual Growth	6.6%	—	—	—

2021 Year-End Financials
Return on assets: 5.6% Cash ($ mil.): 179
Return on equity: 9.4%
Current Ratio: 1.40

COVENANT HEALTH SYSTEM

Covenant Health System ties West Texas and Eastern New Mexico together with quality health care. The health services provider offers some 1,100 beds in its five primary acute-care and specialty hospitals; it also manages about a dozen affiliated community hospitals. Covenant Health System, part of Providence St. Joseph Health, also maintains a network of family health care and medical clinics. Covenant Health System's major facilities are Covenant Medical Center, Covenant Specialty Hospital, and Covenant Women's and Children's Hospital. The health system also includes some 20 clinics and 50 physician practices, and its extensive outreach programs target isolated rural communities with mobile services.

Operations
The system's five hospitals include Covenant Medical Center, Covenant Medical Center-Lakeside, Covenant Specialty Hospital, and Covenant Children's Hospital. It also operates three schools for healthcare careers in nursing, radiography, and surgical technology, respectively.

Strategy
The Christian-based system, which calls itself a ministry, focuses on providing benefits to the community. Its key priorities include mental health, dentistry, diabetes, home health management, and childhood obesity.

Company Background
Covenant Health System was founded when two Lubbock hospitals, St. Mary of the Plains Hospital (now known as Covenant Medical Center-Lakeside) and the Lubbock Methodist Hospital System (including the flagship Methodist Hospital, which is now known as Covenant Medical Center) merged in 1998.

EXECUTIVES
OF*, Denise Saenz
Auditors: ERNST & YOUNG US LLP IRVINE

LOCATIONS
HQ: COVENANT HEALTH SYSTEM
3615 19TH ST, LUBBOCK, TX 794101209
Phone: 806 725-1011
Web: WWW.COVENANTHEALTH.ORG

COMPETITORS
ALEGENT CREIGHTON HEALTH
ASCENSION PROVIDENCE HOSPITAL
BAPTIST MEMORIAL HEALTH CARE SYSTEM, INC.
BRYAN MEDICAL CENTER
GENESIS HEALTHCARE SYSTEM
MAYO CLINIC HEALTH SYSTEM-FRANCISCAN HEALTHCARE, INC.
MOSES TAYLOR HOSPITAL
PROVIDENCE HOSPITAL
SCL HEALTH - FRONT RANGE, INC.
THE JOHNS HOPKINS HEALTH SYSTEM CORPORATION

HISTORICAL FINANCIALS
Company Type: Private

Income Statement — FYE: June 30

	REVENUE ($mil)	NET INCOME ($mil)	NET PROFIT MARGIN	EMPLOYEES
06/15	703	76	10.9%	5,000
06/13	552	35	6.5%	—
06/09	1,185	(38)	—	—
Annual Growth	(8.3%)	—	—	—

2015 Year-End Financials
Return on assets: 10.5% Cash ($ mil.): 39
Return on equity: 14.7%
Current Ratio: 3.20

COVENANT HEALTH, INC.

Auditors: BAKER NEWMAN & NOYES LLC BOST

LOCATIONS

HQ: COVENANT HEALTH, INC.
100 AMES POND DR STE 102, TEWKSBURY, MA
018761240
Phone: 978 312-4300
Web: WWW.COVENANTHEALTH.NET

HISTORICAL FINANCIALS

Company Type: Private

Income Statement — FYE: December 31

	REVENUE ($mil)	NET INCOME ($mil)	NET PROFIT MARGIN	EMPLOYEES
12/20	718	10	1.4%	6,500
12/18	666	(74)	—	—
12/17	670	38	5.8%	—
12/16	645	18	2.9%	—
Annual Growth	2.7%	(13.8%)	—	—

2020 Year-End Financials

Return on assets: 1.1%
Return on equity: 1.9%
Cash ($ mil.): 66
Current Ratio: 1.50

COVENANT MEDICAL CENTER, INC.

Covenant Medical Center (operating as Covenant HealthCare) has made a pact with Wolverine Staters to try to keep them in good health. The not-for-profit health care provider operates more than 20 inpatient and outpatient care facilities, including its two main Covenant Medical Center campuses. It serves residents in a 20-county area of east-central Michigan, with additional facilities in Bay City, Frankenmuth, and Midland. Specialized care services include cardiovascular health, cancer treatment, and obstetrics. The regional health care system has more about 650 beds.

Operations

Covenant HealthCare programs and services range from high-risk obstetrics and neonatal/pediatric intensive care to acute care. Its assets include cardiology, oncology, orthopaedics, robotic surgery, and Level II Adult and Pediatric Trauma Center.

The health system has more than 20 inpatient and outpatient facilities and a trauma/emergency department that provides 85,000 visits per year. The system employs more than 500 physicians from 52 medical specialties.

Sales and Marketing

Covenant HealthCare markets its services via social media.

Financial Performance

In 2014 the company's revenue increased 4% to $528 million as patient service revenue rose; this gain was partially offset by a decline in realized gain and other revenues. An increase in salaries and wages, as well as higher supplies expenses, led to a 12% decline in net income (to $57 million).

Cash flow from operations also fell, slipping 20% to $48 million as accounts receivable increased.

Strategy

Expanding its infrastructure to keep up with demand, in 2014 Covenant HealthCare added 11,456 sq. ft. to its Emergency Department. The addition allows for more efficient triage, enhanced patient waiting areas, and additional space for current technology. It added 18 treatment bays to the existing 47 and also brought a dedicated CT scanner and mini-laboratory within the department.

Also that year, it opened the assisted living community of Covenant Glen in Frankenmuth. The 35,000 sq. ft. structure has 45 rooms (15 dedicated to memory care and 30 with assisted living beds).

Company Background

Covenant HealthCare was formed in 1998 through the merger of Saginaw General and St. Luke's Hospitals.

LOCATIONS

HQ: COVENANT MEDICAL CENTER, INC.
1447 N HARRISON ST, SAGINAW, MI 486024727
Phone: 989 583-0000
Web: WWW.COVENANTHEALTHCARE.COM

PRODUCTS/OPERATIONS

2014 Revenues

	% of total
Net patient service revenues	95
Other revenues	5
Total	100

Selected services

Bariatrics
Birth Center
Cancer Care
Cardiology - Center for the Heart
Childbirth Classes
da Vinci Robotic Surgery
Diabetes Self-Management Program
Emergency Care Center
Imaging and Diagnostics
Neonatal Intensive Care
Neurology
Osteoporosis
Orthopedics
Pediatrics
Physical Medicine and Rehab.
Pulmonary/Respiratory Care
Sleep Center
Surgical Services
Trauma
Urologic Surgery
Women's Health
Wound Healing Center

COMPETITORS

EVANGELICAL COMMUNITY HOSPITAL
INTEGRIS HEALTH, INC.
OVERLAKE HOSPITAL MEDICAL CENTER
SALINAS VALLEY MEMORIAL HEALTHCARE SYSTEMS
THE LANCASTER GENERAL HOSPITAL

HISTORICAL FINANCIALS

Company Type: Private

Income Statement — FYE: June 30

	REVENUE ($mil)	NET INCOME ($mil)	NET PROFIT MARGIN	EMPLOYEES
06/21	776	(29)	—	4,000
06/16	579	40	7.0%	—
06/15	535	31	5.8%	—
06/14	566	34	6.1%	—
Annual Growth	4.6%	—	—	—

2021 Year-End Financials

Return on assets: (-2.9%)
Return on equity: (-5.2%)
Cash ($ mil.): 169
Current Ratio: 1.00

CREIGHTON UNIVERSITY

Consistently ranked among the top universities in the Midwest, Creighton University is a Jesuit Catholic university with an enrollment of approximately 8,000 undergraduate, graduate, and professional students. With a student-to-faculty ratio of 11:1, it offers more than 70 majors through nine schools and colleges, including institutions focused on arts and sciences, business, law, medicine, dentistry, pharmacy, and nursing. Its 130-acre campus is adjacent to the downtown business district of Omaha, Nebraska. Creighton University was founded in 1878 and named after Omaha businessman Edward Creighton.

Operations

In addition to core curriculum, the university has a long history of providing medical education. Many of its on-site medical training programs are provided at the facilities of medical care provider Alegent Creighton Health (formerly Alegent Health). Creighton University also has a partnership with the St. Joseph's Hospital and Medical Center in Phoenix, Arizona. In addition, the university conducts research programs in various scientific fields.

Following student tuition and fees, which account for about 53% of annual revenue, health services bring in about 18% of sales.

Financial Performance

Revenue fell 11.5% to $371 million in 2014 from lower health services revenue and grant and contract revenues, which was partly offset by increased tuition and fee income. Net income increased 9%.

Strategy

To expand its services for students, Creighton University looks to launch new degree programs, enhance facilities, and

HOOVER'S HANDBOOK OF PRIVATE COMPANIES 2023

increase partnerships with other educational, medical, and research institutions. In 2012 the university launched its first 100% online degree program (for a Bachelor of Science in Integrated Leadership), and in 2013 it opened the Creighton Business Institute to improve its business leadership development offerings.

In 2014, Creighton University and Alegent Creighton Health made plans for a new medical complex next to the campus in downtown Omaha. The 90,000-sqquare-foot building will serve area residents with outpatient, emergency, and diagnostic services.

Creighton previously sold its 26% stake in the 400-bed Creighton University Medical Center (CUMC) in Omaha to Alegent. Tenet Healthcare owned a majority stake in the hospital, which was also acquired by Alegent. The transaction also made Alegent's network of care centers the primary teaching sites for Creighton University's School of Medicine and other health-related schools. Creighton University already partnered with Alegent on a number of health-related professional education and research programs prior to the deal, and the university believes that its students will benefit from the expanded relationship.

Geographic Reach

In addition to teaching international students from about 40 countries at its Omaha campus, Creighton University offers hands-on service and learning programs in the Dominican Republic and the Middle East. It also has international affiliate or exchange programs with institutions in about 55 countries.

LOCATIONS

HQ: CREIGHTON UNIVERSITY
2500 CALIFORNIA PLZ, OMAHA, NE 681780002
Phone: 402 280-2900
Web: WWW.CREIGHTON.EDU

PRODUCTS/OPERATIONS

2013 Revenue

	$ mil.	% of total
Student tuition & fees	190.3	46
Health care services	115.3	28
Auxiliary enterprises	31.7	8
Grants & contracts	27.0	7
Investment income	14.6	4
Contributions	11.9	3
Released assets	11.9	3
Other	5.2	1
Total	407.9	100

COMPETITORS

ARIZONA STATE UNIVERSITY
FAIRFIELD UNIVERSITY
UNIVERSITY OF KENTUCKY
UNIVERSITY OF MISSOURI SYSTEM
UNIVERSITY OF OKLAHOMA

HISTORICAL FINANCIALS

Company Type: Private

Income Statement — FYE: June 30

	REVENUE ($mil)	NET INCOME ($mil)	NET PROFIT MARGIN	EMPLOYEES
06/20	563	61	10.9%	5,000
06/19	567	62	11.0%	—
06/17	394	107	27.4%	—
Annual Growth	12.6%	(17.2%)	—	—

2020 Year-End Financials

Return on assets: 4.4%   Cash ($ mil.): 95
Return on equity: 6.2%
Current Ratio: 0.50

CRETE CARRIER CORPORATION

Holding company Crete Carrier Corporation's flagship business, Crete Carrier, provides dry van truckload freight transportation services in the 48 contiguous states. It operates from some two dozen terminals, mainly in the mid-western and southeastern US. The company's Shaffer Trucking unit transports temperature-controlled cargo, and Hunt Transportation (no relation to J.B. Hunt Transport Services) hauls heavy equipment and other cargo on flatbed trailers. Overall, the companies operate more than 5,400 tractors and 13,000 trailers. Family-owned Crete Carrier was founded in 1966 by chairman Duane Acklie; president and CEO Tonn Ostergard is his son-in-law.

LOCATIONS

HQ: CRETE CARRIER CORPORATION
400 NW 56TH ST, LINCOLN, NE 685288843
Phone: 800 998-4095
Web: WWW.CRETECARRIER.COM

COMPETITORS

CELADON GROUP, INC.
COMCAR INDUSTRIES, INC.
DATS TRUCKING, INC.
EMPIRE TRUCK LINES, INC.
GORDON TRUCKING, INC.
LAKEVILLE MOTOR EXPRESS, INC.
LONE STAR TRANSPORTATION, LLC
MCO TRANSPORT, INC.
MIDWEST PARTS & EQUIPMENT CO.
SEINO TRANSPORTATION CO.,LTD.

HISTORICAL FINANCIALS

Company Type: Private

Income Statement — FYE: September 30

	REVENUE ($mil)	NET INCOME ($mil)	NET PROFIT MARGIN	EMPLOYEES
09/18	1,150	139	12.1%	6,000
09/16	984	95	9.7%	—
09/15	0	0	—	—
09/14	1,034	127	12.3%	—
Annual Growth	2.7%	2.3%	—	—

2018 Year-End Financials

Return on assets: 13.3%   Cash ($ mil.): 128
Return on equity: 15.8%
Current Ratio: 2.20

CROWE LLP

Auditors : CROWE LLP

LOCATIONS

HQ: CROWE LLP
225 W WACKER DR STE 2600, CHICAGO, IL 606061228
Phone: 312 899-7000
Web: WWW.CROWE.COM

HISTORICAL FINANCIALS

Company Type: Private

Income Statement — FYE: March 31

	REVENUE ($mil)	NET INCOME ($mil)	NET PROFIT MARGIN	EMPLOYEES
03/15	700	204	29.2%	3,130
03/14	670	163	24.4%	—
03/13	0	0	—	—
Annual Growth	—	—	—	—

2015 Year-End Financials

Return on assets: 71.1%   Cash ($ mil.): 6
Return on equity: 260.7%
Current Ratio: 2.00

CROWLEY MARITIME CORPORATION

Crowley, founded in 1892, is a privately-held, US-owned and operated logistics, government, marine and energy solutions company headquartered in Jacksonville, Florida. Crowley owns, operates and/or manages a fleet of more than 200 vessels, consisting of RO/RO (roll-on-roll-off) vessels, LO/LO (lift-on-lift-off) vessels, articulated tug-barges (ATBs), LNG-powered container/roll-on, roll-off ships (ConRos) and multipurpose tugboats and barges. Land-based facilities and equipment include port terminals, warehouses, tank farms, gas stations, office buildings, trucks, trailers, containers, chassis, cranes and other specialized vehicles.

Operations

Crowley owns, operates and/or manages a fleet of more than 200 vessels, consisting of RO/RO (roll-on-roll-off) vessels, LO/LO (lift-on-lift-off) vessels, articulated tug-barges (ATBs), LNG-powered container/roll-on, roll-off ships (ConRos) and multipurpose tugboats and barges. Land-based facilities and equipment include port terminals, warehouses, tank farms, gas stations, office buildings, trucks, trailers, containers, chassis, cranes and other specialized vehicles.

Services are provided worldwide by four primary business units ? Crowley Logistics,

Crowley (Government) Solutions, Crowley Shipping and Crowley Fuels.

Crowley Logistics, a singular supply chain division, serves more than 12,000 customers and manages more than one million shipments annually on a global scale. The group blends company-owned assets and services with its worldwide network of service providers to reduce complexity and add velocity to customers' supply chains.

Crowley Shipping owns, operates and manages conventional and dual fuel (LNG) vessels for Crowley and other customers. These vessels include tankers, articulated tug barges (ATBs), container ships, LNG-powered container/roll-on, roll-off ships (ConRos) and multipurpose tugboats and barges.

Crowley Solutions is a key partner for the Department of Defense (DoD), Department of Homeland Security (DHS) and other government agencies.

Crowley Fuels is a leader in Alaska's fuel industry, providing safe, dependable transportation, distribution and sales of petroleum products to more than 280 communities across the state.

Company Background
Crowley traces its historical roots back to 1892.

EXECUTIVES

Deputy General Counsel*, Tim Bush

LOCATIONS

HQ: CROWLEY MARITIME CORPORATION
9487 REGENCY SQUARE BLVD # 101, JACKSONVILLE, FL 322257800
Phone: 904 727-2200
Web: WWW.CROWLEY.COM

PRODUCTS/OPERATIONS

Selected Services
Energy industry support services
Fuel sales and distribution
Liner services
Logistics
Ocean towing and transportation
Petroleum and chemical transportation
Project management
Salvage and emergency response
Ship assist and escort
Ship management
Vessel construction and naval architecture
Alaska fuel sales and distribution
Arctic all-terrain transportation
Harbor ship assist and tanker escort
Marine salvage, wreck removal and emergency response
Ocean towing and barge transportation
OPA 90 compliance
Petroleum and chemical transportation
Ship management
Shipping And Logistics
Vessel design and construction management

COMPETITORS

APEX OIL COMPANY, INC.
Compania Sud Americana de Vapores S.A
INTERNATIONAL SHIPHOLDING CORPORATION
KAWASAKI KISEN KAISHA, LTD.
LOGISTICS PLUS, INC.
LYNDEN INCORPORATED

MAINFREIGHT, INC.
Odfjell Se
SEACOR HOLDINGS INC.
WAN HAI LINES LTD.

HISTORICAL FINANCIALS
Company Type: Private

Income Statement   FYE: December 31

	REVENUE ($mil)	NET INCOME ($mil)	NET PROFIT MARGIN	EMPLOYEES
12/08	1,955	86	4.4%	4,329
12/07	1,622	122	7.5%	—
12/06	1,467	38	2.6%	—
12/05	1,190	38	3.3%	—
Annual Growth	18.0%	30.3%	—	—

2008 Year-End Financials
Return on assets: 6.2%   Cash ($ mil.): 64
Return on equity: 18.2%
Current Ratio: 1.40

CRST INTERNATIONAL, INC.

CRST International promises f-a-s-t freight transportation through its operating units. CRST Expedited provides standard dry van truckload transportation, primarily on long-haul routes, along with dedicated and expedited transportation services. CRST Malone hauls steel and other freight requiring flatbed trailers or trailers with removable sides, and CRST Logistics arranges freight transportation and provides other third-party logistics services. The family-owned business' other operations include CRST Dedicated Services and Specialized Transportation. Overall, the companies operate a fleet of about 4,500 tractors and 7,300 van trailers.

Operations
CRST operates through seven distinct operations. CRST Expedited is a long-haul truckload carrier and CRST Malone is a flatbed carrier serving customers in North America. The company's CRST Dedicated Services unit offers tailor-made, specialized transportation services, while CRST Logistics helps customers reduce costs and optimize their performance.

CRST Specialized Transportation provides multi-modal logistics supported by distribution centers located throughout the US and Canada. Other operations include Temperature Controlled Team Service (TCTS) (expedited transcontinental transportation of perishable products) and BESL Transfer Company (provider of short haul, flatbed services).

Geographic Reach
Based in Cedar Rapids, Iowa, CRST operates more than 50 distribution centers, terminals, and offices across North America.

Sales and Marketing
The company targets the business and retail, industrial, metals, building products, technology, telecommunications, automotive, government, tradeshows and events, health care, transportation, and residential markets.

Strategy
In 2015 CRST broke ground on its new $37 million world headquarters in downtown Cedar Rapids, Iowa.

In 2013 CRST Expedited opened a training and repair facility in Riverside, California.

Mergers and Acquisitions
CRST also continues to grow through the use of acquisitions.

In 2015 the company bought privately-held Pegasus Transportation, based in Louisville, Kentucky. The acquisition allows CRST to expand its temperature controlled operations nationwide footprint through its expanded customer base.

In early 2014, CRST obtained a privately held short haul and flatbed services provider, BESL Transfer Co., based in Cincinnati, Ohio, in a transaction that fortified its CRST Malone operations. The acquisition of BESL allowed CRST to expand its flatbed operations nationwide footprint through its short haul, regional services, and expanded agent base.

In 2013 it picked up the Allied Special Products Division of Allied Van Lines, based in Fort Wayne, Indiana. The deal enabled its Specialized Transportation operations to further develop its distribution center network and provide better service and faster transit to its customers. That year subsidiary CRST Logistics, added Top Shelf Logistics, LLC, to its rapidly growing agency network.

Company Background
CRST was founded in 1955 by Herald Smith, father of chairman John Smith.

Auditors : DELOITTE & TOUCHE LLP CEDAR R

LOCATIONS

HQ: CRST INTERNATIONAL, INC.
201 1ST ST SE STE 400, CEDAR RAPIDS, IA 524011423
Phone: 319 396-4400
Web: WWW.CRST.COM

PRODUCTS/OPERATIONS

Selected Services
Expedited Team Service
Dry Van
Flatbed
Dedicated
High Value/White Glove
Temperature Controlled
Transportation Management
Brokerage
Home Delivery/First & Final Mile
Warehousing/Inventory Solutions
LTL
Intermodal
Equipment Sales

COMPETITORS

A&R LOGISTICS, INC.
AAA COOPER TRANSPORTATION

ATLANTIC AUTOMOTIVE CORP.
AUTONATION, INC.
CARDINAL LOGISTICS MANAGEMENT CORPORATION
CARS.COM, LLC
CENTRAL STATES BUS SALES, INC.
KENCO GROUP, INC.
RYGOR GROUP LIMITED
TOYOTA TSUSHO AMERICA, INC.

HISTORICAL FINANCIALS
Company Type: Private

Income Statement — FYE: December 31

	REVENUE ($mil)	NET INCOME ($mil)	NET PROFIT MARGIN	EMPLOYEES
12/12	1,257	75	6.0%	5,960
12/11	1,143	81	7.1%	—
Annual Growth	10.1%	(7.8%)	—	—

2012 Year-End Financials
Return on assets: 13.7% Cash ($ mil.): 71
Return on equity: 45.2%
Current Ratio: 2.70

CSC SUGAR, LLC

Auditors : GRANT THORNTON LLP MINNEAPOLI

LOCATIONS
HQ: CSC SUGAR, LLC
    33 RIVERSIDE AVE STE 101, WESTPORT, CT 068804226
Phone: 203 846-5610
Web: WWW.CSCSUGAR.COM

HISTORICAL FINANCIALS
Company Type: Private

Income Statement — FYE: December 31

	REVENUE ($mil)	NET INCOME ($mil)	NET PROFIT MARGIN	EMPLOYEES
12/09	574	18	3.2%	300
12/08	790	5	0.7%	—
12/07	515	6	1.2%	—
Annual Growth	5.6%	74.5%	—	—

2009 Year-End Financials
Return on assets: 24.8% Cash ($ mil.): 4
Return on equity: 104.6%
Current Ratio: 1.20

CUMBERLAND COUNTY HOSPITAL SYSTEM, INC.

Don't fear for a lack of medical services at Cumberland County Hospital System (doing business as Cape Fear Valley Health System). The medical provider comprises five acute-care and specialty hospitals, with about 915 total beds, serving a six-county region of Southeastern North Carolina and more than 935,000 patients annually. The hospital system serves residents of coastal North Carolina, providing general and specialized medical services such as cancer treatment, open-heart surgery, psychiatric care, and rehabilitation. It also operates the HealthPlex fitness and wellness facility that has over 140 pieces of next-generation cardiovascular and strength-building equipment, and provides home health and hospice services. Among its medical facilities include Cape Fear Valley Medical Center, Highsmith-Rainey Specialty Hospital, Cape Fear Valley Rehabilitation Center, Bladen County Hospital and Hoke Hospital.

EXECUTIVES
Chief Human Resource Officer, Denver Hopkins
CCO, Michael Zappa
Auditors : CLIFTONLARSONALLEN LLP RALEIG

LOCATIONS
HQ: CUMBERLAND COUNTY HOSPITAL SYSTEM, INC.
    1638 OWEN DR, FAYETTEVILLE, NC 283043424
Phone: 910 609-4000
Web: WWW.CAPEFEARVALLEY.COM

PRODUCTS/OPERATIONS
2014 Sales

	$ in mil.	% of total
Net patient service revenue	621.1	96
Other revenue	25.8	4
Total	646.9	100

Selected Services
Birth center
Healthplex
Heart and vascular
Imaging/diagnostics
Minority health
Neuroscience
Orthopedics
Outpatient services
Pediatrics
Physician practice
Rehabilitation
Scancer treatment
Surgical services
Weight loss surgery

COMPETITORS
ALLINA HEALTH SYSTEM
APPALACHIAN REGIONAL HEALTHCARE, INC.
BAPTIST HEALTH SYSTEM, INC.
ELLIS HOSPITAL
FLOYD HEALTHCARE MANAGEMENT, INC.
SPARTANBURG REGIONAL HEALTH SERVICES DISTRICT, INC.
THE EAST ALABAMA HEALTH CARE AUTHORITY
TRI-CITY HOSPITAL DISTRICT (INC)
VALLEY HEALTH SYSTEM
WELLMONT HEALTH SYSTEM

HISTORICAL FINANCIALS
Company Type: Private

Income Statement — FYE: September 30

	REVENUE ($mil)	NET INCOME ($mil)	NET PROFIT MARGIN	EMPLOYEES
09/21	1,117	140	12.6%	5,000
09/20	779	50	6.4%	—
09/19	1,149	30	2.7%	—
09/07	504	23	4.6%	—
Annual Growth	5.8%	13.8%	—	—

2021 Year-End Financials
Return on assets: 8.8% Cash ($ mil.): 317
Return on equity: 18.5%
Current Ratio: 1.50

CYPRESS-FAIRBANKS INDEPENDENT SCHOOL DISTRICT

Auditors : WEAVER AND TIDWELL LLP CONROE

LOCATIONS
HQ: CYPRESS-FAIRBANKS INDEPENDENT SCHOOL DISTRICT
    10300 JONES RD, HOUSTON, TX 770654208
Phone: 281 897-4000
Web: WWW.CFISD.NET

HISTORICAL FINANCIALS
Company Type: Private

Income Statement — FYE: June 30

	REVENUE ($mil)	NET INCOME ($mil)	NET PROFIT MARGIN	EMPLOYEES
06/22	1,506	(214)	—	13,000
06/21	1,410	161	11.5%	—
06/20	1,331	208	15.7%	—
06/19	1,342	32	2.4%	—
Annual Growth	3.9%	—	—	—

2022 Year-End Financials
Return on assets: (-5.1%) Cash ($ mil.): 5
Return on equity: —
Current Ratio: —

CYRUSONE HOLDCO LLC

Auditors : DELOITTE & TOUCHE LLP DALLAS

LOCATIONS
HQ: CYRUSONE HOLDCO LLC
    2850 N HARWOOD ST # 2200, DALLAS, TX 752012640
Phone: 972 350-0060
Web: WWW.CYRUSONE.COM

HISTORICAL FINANCIALS
Company Type: Private

Income Statement — FYE: December 31

	REVENUE ($mil)	NET INCOME ($mil)	NET PROFIT MARGIN	EMPLOYEES
12/21	1,205	25	2.1%	456
12/20	1,033	41	4.0%	—
12/19	981	41	4.2%	—
12/18	821	1	0.1%	—
Annual Growth	13.6%	176.3%	—	—

2021 Year-End Financials
Return on assets: 0.3% Cash ($ mil.): 346
Return on equity: 0.9%
Current Ratio: —

D. H. PACE COMPANY, INC.

EXECUTIVES

President Overhead Door Division*, Steve Pascuzzi
CIO*, Chris Mann

LOCATIONS

HQ: D. H. PACE COMPANY, INC.
 1901 E 119TH ST, OLATHE, KS 660619502
Phone: 816 221-0543
Web: WWW.DHPACE.COM

HISTORICAL FINANCIALS
Company Type: Private

Income Statement — FYE: December 31

	REVENUE ($mil)	NET INCOME ($mil)	NET PROFIT MARGIN	EMPLOYEES
12/20	711	26	3.7%	2,800
12/19	677	28	4.1%	—
12/07	0	0	—	—
12/06	140	0	0.0%	—
Annual Growth	12.3%	—	—	—

2020 Year-End Financials
Return on assets: 9.4%   Cash ($ mil.): —
Return on equity: 22.9%
Current Ratio: 1.50

D/L COOPERATIVE INC.

Yes, the farmer takes a wife, then hi-ho, the dairy-o, the farmer takes membership in milk-marketing organizations such as Dairylea Cooperative. Owned by some 2,000 dairy farmers in the northeastern US, Dairylea processes and markets 6.3 billion pounds of milk for its farmers annually to dairy-product customers including food manufacturers. Its Agri-Services holding company provides members with a full range of financial and farm-management services, as well as insurance. Its Empire Livestock Marketing unit operates regional livestock auction locations. Dairylea, which was established in 1907 by New York dairy farmers, merged with the US's largest milk marketing coop, Dairy Farmers of America, in 2014.

Operations

Through its DMS partnership with Dairy Farmers of America, Dairylea sells and distributes raw milk. DMS serves both organizations, as well as independent producers and cooperatives that produce 16 billion pounds of milk each year.

Geographic Reach

Dairylea sells 6 billion pounds of raw milk annually through a milk-marketing network that stretches from Maine to Ohio to Maryland.

Services provided by holding company Agri-Services, LLC, include insurance coverage, information management, livestock marketing, loan programs, milk price risk management services, business planning and consulting services, purchasing programs, and investment and retirement planning advice.

Financial Performance

Dairylea has annual sales of about $1 billion.

Auditors : HERBEIN COMPANY INC READING

LOCATIONS

HQ: D/L COOPERATIVE INC.
 5001 BRITTONFIELD PKWY, EAST SYRACUSE, NY 130579201
Phone: 315 233-1000
Web: WWW.DAIRYLEA.COM

PRODUCTS/OPERATIONS

Selected Affiliates & Subsidiaries
Agri-Edge Development
Agri-Max Financial Services
Agri-Services Agency
Dairy Risk Management Services
Eagle Dairy Direct
Empire Livestock Marketing Services

COMPETITORS

Agropur Cooperative
DALE FARM CO-OPERATIVE LIMITED
MULLER DAIRY (U.K.) LIMITED
NATIONAL DAIRY, LLC
US DAIRY EXPORT COUNCIL

HISTORICAL FINANCIALS
Company Type: Private

Income Statement — FYE: March 31

	REVENUE ($mil)	NET INCOME ($mil)	NET PROFIT MARGIN	EMPLOYEES
03/11	1,333	1	0.1%	107
03/10	1,066	1	0.1%	—
Annual Growth	25.1%	7.6%	—	—

2011 Year-End Financials
Return on assets: 9.2%   Cash ($ mil.): 14
Return on equity: 0.1%
Current Ratio: 0.60

DAIRY FARMERS OF AMERICA, INC.

Dairy Farmers of America (DFA) is one of the world's largest dairy cooperatives, with more than 12,500 member farmers across the US. Along with fresh and shelf-stable fluid milk, the co-op produces cheese, butter, powders, and sweetened condensed milk for industrial, wholesale, and retail customers. It also offers contract manufacturing services. The company's brands include Borden and Cache Valley for consumer cheese; Keller's Creamery, Plugrá, Breakstone's, Falfurrias, and Oakhurst Dairy; and other dairy products under Sport Shake (sports beverage), La Vaquita (queso), Kemps, Guida's, and Cass Clay. The company owns around 85 production plants nationwide.

Operations

In addition to DFA's fresh and wholesome dairy products that include butter, cheese, ice cream, milk, and yogurt, the company also offers services such as DFA Risk Management, DFA Grazing, DFA Insurance, DFA Farm Supplies, DFA Energy, DFA Financing, Empire Livestock, Dairy One, and Member Savings Network.

Geographic Reach

DFA is based in Kansas City, Missouri, and divides the US into seven areas: Central (which shares the main headquarters), Mideast (Medina, Ohio), Mountain (Salt Lake City, Utah), Northeast (East Syracuse, New York), Southeast (Knoxville, Tennessee), Southwest (Grapevine, Texas), and Western (Ripon, California).

Sales and Marketing

DFA's customers include food manufacturers, school cafeterias, large restaurants, and retailers, among others.

Company Background

DFA was established in 1998 by leaders of four of the nation's leading milk cooperatives: Associated Milk Producers, Mid-America Dairymen, Milk Marketing, and Western Dairymen Cooperative.

HISTORY

Mid-America Dairymen (Mid-Am), the largest of the cooperatives that merged to form Dairy Farmers of America (DFA), was born in 1968. At that time, several Midwestern dairy co-ops banded together to attack common economic problems, such as reduced government subsidies, price drops resulting from a rising milk surplus, dealer consolidation, and improvements in production, processing, and packaging. The merging organizations -- representing 15,000 dairy farmers -- were Producers Creamery Company (Springfield, Missouri), Sanitary Milk Producers (St. Louis), Square Deal Milk Producers (Highland, Illinois), Mid-Am (Kansas City, Missouri), and Producers Creamery Company of Chillicothe (north central Missouri).

During the early 1970s Mid-Am struggled with internal restructuring. Most dairy farmers and co-ops were hit hard by the energy crisis and the government's decision to allow increased dairy imports in 1973, the same year the US Justice Department filed an antitrust suit against Mid-Am. (A judge cleared the co-op 12 years later.)

In 1974 Mid-Am lost almost $8 million on revenues of $625 million, chalked up to record-high feed prices, a weakened economy, a milk surplus, and a massive inventory loss.

Co-op veteran Gary Hanman was named CEO that year. Over the next two years, Mid-Am cut costs, sold corporate frills, downsized management, and began marketing more of its own products under the Mid-America Farms label, thus reducing dependency on commodity sales.

Mid-Am expanded its research and development efforts throughout the 1980s. The co-op opened its services to farmers in California and New Mexico in 1993, and a series of mergers in 1994 and 1995 nearly doubled its size. In 1997 it purchased some of Borden's dairy operations, including rights to the valuable Elsie the Cow and Borden's trademarks.

Wary of falling milk prices, Mid-Am merged with Western Dairymen Cooperative, Milk Marketing, and the Southern Region of Associated Milk Producers at the end of 1997 to form DFA. Hanman moved into the seat of CEO at the new co-op. DFA began a series of joint ventures with the #1 US dairy processor, Suiza Foods (now Dean Foods).

DFA added California Gold (more than 330 farmers, 1998) and Independent Cooperative Milk Producers Association (730 dairy farmer members in Michigan and parts of Ohio and Indiana, 1999). In another joint venture with Suiza, in early 2000 DFA sold its 50% stake in the US's #3 fluid milk processor, Southern Foods, in exchange for 34% of a new company named Suiza Dairy Group.

After mollifying the government's antitrust fears, DFA acquired the butter operations of Sodiaal North America in 2000. It then molded all its butter businesses into a new entity, Keller's Creamery. However, another acquisition did not fare as well. The same year, DFA acquired controlling interest in Southern Belle Dairy only to have the merger challenged three years later by the Department of Justice. Arguing that the merger formed a monopoly in school milk sales in several states, the Department of Justice filed suit which a federal judge later dismissed.

During 2001 the cooperative went in with Land O'Lakes 50/50 to purchase a cheese plant from Kraft. Later in the year as Suiza Foods acquired Dean Foods (and took on its name), DFA sold back its stake in Suiza Dairy Group to the new Dean Foods. DFA then teamed up with a group of dairy investors to form a new 50/50 joint venture, National Dairy Holdings, which received 11 processing plants from Dean Foods as part of the exchange for Suiza Dairy.

Auditors : KPMG LLP KANSAS CITY MISSOU

LOCATIONS

HQ: DAIRY FARMERS OF AMERICA, INC.
1405 N 98TH ST, KANSAS CITY, KS 661111865
Phone: 816 801-6455
Web: WWW.DFAMILK.COM

PRODUCTS/OPERATIONS
Selected Products and Brands
Consumer brands
    Borden cheese
    Breakstone's butter
    Cache Valley cheese
    Keller's Creamery butter
    Plugrá butter
    Sport Shake energy milk shake
Contract manufacturing
    Cheese dips
    Cheese powders & flavors
    Coffee-based flavored drinks
    Instant formula
    Sour cream
    Sports drinks
Dairy ingredients
    Cheeses (American & Italian)
    Nonfat dry milk powder
    Skim milk powder
    Sweetened condensed milk

COMPETITORS
ASSOCIATED MILK PRODUCERS, INC.
DANONE
DARIGOLD, INC.
DEAN FOODS COMPANY
Grupo Lala, S.A.B. de C.V.
LAND O'LAKES, INC.
NESTLE USA, INC.
NORTHWEST DAIRY ASSOCIATION
SYNUTRA INTERNATIONAL, INC.
THE HAIN CELESTIAL GROUP INC

HISTORICAL FINANCIALS
Company Type: Private

Income Statement   FYE: December 31

	REVENUE ($mil)	NET INCOME ($mil)	NET PROFIT MARGIN	EMPLOYEES
12/16	13,528	136	1.0%	21,000
12/15	13,803	98	0.7%	—
12/14	17,856	48	0.3%	—
Annual Growth	(13.0%)	67.6%	—	—

2016 Year-End Financials
Return on assets: 3.8%   Cash ($ mil.): 85
Return on equity: 14.1%
Current Ratio: 1.10

DAIRYAMERICA, INC.

Auditors : DELOITTE & TOUCHE LLP FRESNO

LOCATIONS

HQ: DAIRYAMERICA, INC.
7815 N PALM AVE STE 250, FRESNO, CA 937115528
Phone: 559 251-0992
Web: WWW.DAIRYAMERICA.COM

HISTORICAL FINANCIALS
Company Type: Private

Income Statement   FYE: December 31

	REVENUE ($mil)	NET INCOME ($mil)	NET PROFIT MARGIN	EMPLOYEES
12/12	1,222	21	1.8%	51
12/11	1,319	19	1.5%	—
12/10	1,514	19	1.3%	—
Annual Growth	(10.2%)	5.5%	—	—

2012 Year-End Financials
Return on assets: 12.8%   Cash ($ mil.): 1
Return on equity: 108.5%
Current Ratio: 1.80

DALLAS COUNTY HOSPITAL DISTRICT

Parkland Health & Hospital System (PHHS) is one of the largest public hospital systems and a level I Trauma Center and second largest civilian burn center in the U.S. and Level III Neonatal Intensive Care Unit. Parkland Memorial sits at the heart of the health system and is Dallas' only public hospital. PHHS also manages a network of about 20 community clinics, as well as Parkland Community Health Plan, a regional HMO for Medicaid and CHIP (Children's Health Insurance Program) members. Additionally, the system offers Parkland Financial Assistance, a program to help residents of Dallas County pay for health care services. Founded in 1894.

Operations
PHHS is one of the largest public hospital systems in the US. In addition to its community-based clinics, it offers a number of outreach and education programs to improve wellness in its service area.

Parkland Memorial Hospital has 878 single-patient rooms and is a Level I trauma center. Each year, the hospital has some 66,595 inpatient discharges and about 205,550 emergency department visits. Its Specialty, community, and women's clinic outpatient visits total more than 1.1 million.

The system also manages the health system for Lew Sterrett -- Dallas County Jail, one of the nation's largest jails.

Its sales were generate from patients services (about 45% of sales), property taxes (around 25%), government programs (roughly 20%), grants and contributions (less than 5%), and other (about 10%).

Geographic Reach
PHHS is based in Dallas, Texas.

Sales and Marketing
PHHS markets its products and services through its websites. Majority of its sales were generated from charity (about 35% of sales), Medicaid (roughly 30%), Medicare (about 20%), commercial insurance (about 10%), and self-pay and other (around 5% each).

Financial Performance
Strategy
Parkland's strategic plan includes an emphasis on priorities common to all health systems: improving quality and safety; staff engagement; sound business functions; and as an academic medical center, teaching and research. Leadership also identified areas where Parkland is positioned to make unique, meaningful contributions and encourage

innovative thinking throughout the organization to develop those ideas.

And, to meet the needs of Dallas County's most vulnerable residents, Parkland has created programs to deliver care beyond the walls of its hospital and clinics. The strategic plan furthers that effort.

Parkland has made significant investments to develop a sophisticated infrastructure for obtaining and using data to improve health. The Parkland Center for Clinical Innovation (PCCI) developed predictive models that help save lives of patients with sepsis and that personalize asthma care to improve well-being and reduce hospital costs. PCCI's population health modeling allowed the company to target COVID-19 immunizations to reduce disparities in vaccination rates among racial and ethnic groups in the communities the company serve. Parkland will leverage those investments further over the next 5 years to create a comprehensive digital health program to improve the health and experience of care for Dallas County residents.

Auditors : BKD LLP DALLAS TEXAS

LOCATIONS

HQ: DALLAS COUNTY HOSPITAL DISTRICT
5200 HARRY HINES BLVD, DALLAS, TX 752357709
Phone: 214 590-8000
Web: WWW.PARKLANDHEALTH.ORG

PRODUCTS/OPERATIONS

Selected Facilities
Bluitt Flowers Health Center
de Haro-Saldivar Health Center
East Dallas Health Center
Garland Health Center
Oak West Health Center
Pediatric Primary Care Center
Simmons Ambulatory Surgery Center
Southeast Dallas Health Center
Vickery Health Center

COMPETITORS

ATLANTICARE HEALTH SYSTEM INC.
BRONXCARE HEALTH SYSTEM
CKHS, INC.
DENVER HEALTH AND HOSPITALS AUTHORITY
GREATER BALTIMORE MEDICAL CENTER, INC.
READING HOSPITAL
UNIVERSITY HEALTH SYSTEM SERVICES OF TEXAS, INC.
UNIVERSITY HEALTH SYSTEMS OF EASTERN CAROLINA, INC.
UNIVERSITY HOSPITALS HEALTH SYSTEM, INC.
WELLSTAR HEALTH SYSTEM, INC.

HISTORICAL FINANCIALS
Company Type: Private

Income Statement — FYE: September 30

	REVENUE ($mil)	NET INCOME ($mil)	NET PROFIT MARGIN	EMPLOYEES
09/21	2,669	321	12.0%	11,000
09/20	1,850	297	16.1%	—
09/19	1,600	208	13.0%	—
09/18	1,456	17	1.2%	—
Annual Growth	22.4%	164.8%	—	—

2021 Year-End Financials
Return on assets: 9.0% Cash ($ mil.): 694
Return on equity: 17.9%
Current Ratio: 2.60

DALLAS INDEPENDENT SCHOOL DISTRICT

Auditors : WEAVER AND TIDWELL LLP DALLA

LOCATIONS

HQ: DALLAS INDEPENDENT SCHOOL DISTRICT
9400 N CNTL EXPY STE 1510, DALLAS, TX 75231
Phone: 972 925-3700
Web: WWW.DALLASISD.ORG

HISTORICAL FINANCIALS
Company Type: Private

Income Statement — FYE: June 30

	REVENUE ($mil)	NET INCOME ($mil)	NET PROFIT MARGIN	EMPLOYEES
06/21	2,324	321	13.8%	24,937
06/20	2,248	240	10.7%	—
06/19	2,241	(17)	—	—
Annual Growth	1.8%	—	—	—

2021 Year-End Financials
Return on assets: 5.5% Cash ($ mil.): 1,442
Return on equity: 117.5%
Current Ratio: —

DALLAS-FORT WORTH INTERNATIONAL AIRPORT FACILITY IMPROVEMENT CORPORATION

Many things are bigger in Texas, and Dallas/Fort Worth International Airport (DFW) is no exception. Covering some 30 square miles, DFW is one of the world's largest airports by land mass. The facility includes seven runways, two active control towers, five terminals, and 165 gates. Some 65 million passengers pass through DFW annually to destinations domestic and international. Aside from airport fare, DFW provides private warehouse and distribution centers to tenants and features Grand Hyatt and Hyatt Regency hotels. Opened in 1974, DFW is owned by the cities of Dallas and Fort Worth; it is situated halfway between them and within about a four-hour flight time of most US destinations.

Operations

DFW's primary operating goal is the facilitation of movement of people, cargo, and airplanes. Beyond that it leases land to travel-related businesses (car rental agencies), provide parking, coordinates concessions, and permits hotels to operate within its confines. About 45% of revenue comes from airlines (landing fees, terminal usage fees) and 55% comes from non-airline activities.

With about 1800 flights per day serving 65 million customers a year, DFW is the world's fourth busiest airport. Airlines flying out of DFW provide nonstop service to 163 domestic and 55 international non-stop destinations through about 25 passenger carriers and nearly 20 cargo carriers.

DFW is the home airport for the world's largest carrier, American Airlines (AA), which operates 745 flights per day to nearly 200 domestic destinations and some 50 international destinations. AA is constructing a new headquarters on a 300-acre campus on DFW property.

Financial Performance

In FY2016 (ended September 30, 2016), Dallas Fort Worth International Airport generated revenue of $745 million, a 10% increase from the prior year.

The airport's earnings in FY2016 had a hard landing, losing almost $94 million. Although its operations incurred a relatively small $4.6 million loss, the big contributor was massive interest expense on its revenue bonds. The interest is a recurring, annual charge and the airport has recently been running at an annual loss.

Strategy

DFW is in the midst of a $2.34 billion terminal improvement project that's expected to be completed in late 2018. Improvements include new gates and a new concourse, light rail connections to downtown Dallas, and renovations to existing terminals. Improvements to Terminals A, B, and E completed in 2017 and work on Terminal C is on hold due to financing decisions. The physical airfield is also on tap to receive capital funding: runway 17C to get $250 million and end-around taxiways to get $430 million.

The airport has excellent connectivity to Latin & South America and to Asia, and believes it is well positions to serve as a gateway between the two world regions. It is geographically situated in an advantageous place and already has an extensive network of destinations into Mexico and Latin & South America.

Auditors : DELOITTE & TOUCHE LLP DALLAS

LOCATIONS

HQ: DALLAS-FORT WORTH INTERNATIONAL AIRPORT FACILITY IMPROVEMENT CORPORATION
2400 AVIATION DR, DFW AIRPORT, TX 75261
Phone: 972 973-5400
Web: WWW.DFWAIRPORT.COM

HOOVER'S HANDBOOK OF PRIVATE COMPANIES 2023

COMPETITORS

AENA S.M.E. SA.
AIRCRAFT SERVICE INTERNATIONAL, INC.
JETBLUE AIRWAYS CORPORATION
MASSACHUSETTS PORT AUTHORITY
SIGNATURE FLIGHT SUPPORT CORPORATION
SOUTHWEST AIRLINES CO.
SYDNEY AIRPORT HOLDINGS PTY LIMITED
Swissport International AG
THE PORT AUTHORITY OF NEW YORK & NEW JERSEY
UNITED AIRLINES, INC.

HISTORICAL FINANCIALS

Company Type: Private

Income Statement — FYE: September 30

	REVENUE ($mil)	NET INCOME ($mil)	NET PROFIT MARGIN	EMPLOYEES
09/18	929	54	5.9%	1,700
09/16	745	(88)	—	—
09/07	567	28	5.0%	—
09/06	388	140	36.2%	—
Annual Growth	7.5%	(7.6%)	—	—

2018 Year-End Financials

Return on assets: 0.7%
Return on equity: 16.1%
Current Ratio: 1.70
Cash ($ mil.): 154

DANA-FARBER CANCER INSTITUTE, INC.

The Dana-Farber Cancer Institute fights cancer on two fronts: It provides treatment to cancer patients, young and old, and researches new cancer diagnostics, treatments, and preventions. The organization's scientists also research AIDS treatments and cures for a host of other deadly diseases. Patients receive treatment from Dana-Farber through its cancer centers operated in conjunction with Brigham and Women's Hospital, Boston Children's Hospital, and Massachusetts General Hospital. The institute is also a principal teaching affiliate of Harvard Medical School. Dana-Farber is funded by the National Cancer Institute, the National Institute of Allergy and Infectious Diseases, and private contributions.

Operations

Dana-Farber reports more than 640,000 annual outpatient visits, more than 1,000 hospital discharges per year, and is involved in over 1,100 clinical trials.

Dana-Farber provides care to children and adults with cancer while advancing the understanding, diagnosis, treatment, cure, and prevention of cancer and related diseases. As an affiliate of Harvard Medical School and a Comprehensive Cancer Center designated by the National Cancer Institute, the institute also provides training for new generations of physicians and scientists, designs programs that promote public health particularly among high-risk and underserved populations, and disseminates innovative patient therapies and scientific discoveries to target community across the US and around the world.

Dana-Farber researchers have contributed to the development of 35 of 75 cancer drugs recently approved by the FDA for use in cancer patients.

Patients services generates about 70% of total sales, research accounts for nearly 25%, while unrestricted contributions and bequests and other revenue account for the remaining.

Geographic Reach

Based in Boston, Massachusetts, Dana-Farber has two main campuses ? Boston's Longwood Medical Area and provides care for adult and pediatric cancer patients. The other campus is located in Chestnut Hill, Massachusetts and provides care for adult cancer patients. It also has facilities in Brighton, Milford, South Weymouth, and Methuen (all in Massachusetts); Londonderry, New Hampshire; and Foxborough, Massachusetts (open in late summer 2022).

Financial Performance

Total operating revenues grew by 16% in fiscal year 2021 and included $23.5 million in relief received through the federal CARES Act (Coronavirus Aid, Relief, and Economic Security Act).

Strategy

The development of better preventive strategies treatments has become a top priority in medicine and the pharmaceutical industry. More scientists are now working on the problem, with more promising leads and potential therapies than at any time in the stem-cell transplant era.

The research has one overriding goal: to reduce the risk and severity of GVHD without diminishing the GVT effect. DanaFarber physician-scientists have been at the center of the effort. Cutler led a clinical trial that demonstrated the effectiveness and staying power of the drug belumosudil in patients with chronic GVHD.

Company Background

In 2013 the institute and Lawrence + Memorial Cancer Center opened a $34.5 million, 47,000 sq.-ft. cancer facility in Waterford, Connecticut.

The Yawkey Center for Cancer Care, named in honor of long-time contributor The Yawkey Foundation, opened in 2011 to serve a growing number of patients. The 275,000-sq.-ft center's 14-stories house most of Dana-Farber's adult outpatient care. The building has more than 100 exam rooms, about 140 infusion chairs, and a number of consultation rooms for family and patients. It also connected Dana-Farber to other campus buildings and to its clinical partners, Brigham and Women's Hospital and Children's Hospital Boston.

Dana-Farber Cancer Institute was founded as a children's cancer research foundation in 1947 by Dr. Sidney Farber. The institute later expanded its services to provide programs for adults as well as children.

EXECUTIVES

CIO*, Lesley Solomon
CRO*, Kevin Haigis
CGO*, John Ryan

LOCATIONS

HQ: DANA-FARBER CANCER INSTITUTE, INC.
450 BROOKLINE AVE, BOSTON, MA 022155450
Phone: 617 632-3000
Web: WWW.DANA-FARBER.ORG

PRODUCTS/OPERATIONS

2014 Sales

	% of total
Patients Services	62
Research	30
Unrestricted Contributions and Bequests	6
Other revenue	2
Total	100

Selected Clinical Affiliations

Dana-Farber/Brigham and Women's Cancer Center (outpatient services for adult cancer patients provided by Dana-Farber; and inpatient care provided by Brigham and Women's Hospital)
Dana-Farber/Children's Hospital Cancer Center (Dana-Farber Cancer Institute and Children's Hospital Boston outpatient care for children provided at Dana-Farber's Jimmy Fund Clinic)
Dana-Farber/Harvard Cancer Center (Beth Israel Deaconess Medical Center, Brigham and Women's Hospital, Children's Hospital Boston, and Massachusetts General Hospital collaborate on research, cancer prevention, and treatments and therapies for cancer patients)
Dana-Farber/Lawrence + Memorial Cancer Center (cancer facility, Waterford, Connecticut).
Dana-Farber/Partners Cancer Care (consolidated adult oncology programs and clinical research of Dana-Farber Cancer Institute, Brigham and Women's Hospital, and Massachusetts General Hospital)

Selected Satellite Centers

Dana-Farber/Brigham and Women's Cancer Center at Faulkner Hospital in Jamaica Plain (southwest Boston area)
Dana-Farber/Brigham and Women's Cancer Center at Milford Regional Medical Center (Massachusetts)
Dana-Farber/Brigham and Women's Cancer Center in clinical affiliation with South Shore Hospital (South Weymouth, Massachusetts)
Dana-Farber/New Hampshire Oncology-Hematology (Londonderry)
Adult Treatment Centers and Clinical Services
Blood Cancers
Breast Cancer
Cancer Genetics and Prevention
Cutaneous (Skin) Cancer
Gastrointestinal Cancer
Genitourinary Cancer
Gynecologic Cancer
Head and Neck Cancer
Hematology
Melanoma
Neuro-Oncology
Sarcoma
Thoracic (Lung) Cancer
Pediatric Treatment Centers and Clinical Services
Blood Disorders Center
Brain Tumor Center
Hematologic Malignancies Center
Solid Tumors Center
Stem Cell Transplant Center

COMPETITORS

CHILDREN'S HOSPITAL MEDICAL CENTER
MEMORIAL SLOAN-KETTERING CANCER CENTER
PUBLIC HEALTH SOLUTIONS
SANFORD BURNHAM PREBYS MEDICAL DISCOVERY INSTITUTE
ST. JUDE CHILDREN'S RESEARCH HOSPITAL, INC.
THE CHILDREN'S HOSPITAL CORPORATION
THE FOX CHASE CANCER CENTER FOUNDATION
THE JACKSON LABORATORY
THE SCRIPPS RESEARCH INSTITUTE
WHITEHEAD INSTITUTE FOR BIOMEDICAL RESEARCH

HISTORICAL FINANCIALS

Company Type: Private

Income Statement — FYE: September 30

	REVENUE ($mil)	NET INCOME ($mil)	NET PROFIT MARGIN	EMPLOYEES
09/20	1,282	50	4.0%	3,000
09/19	1,985	102	5.1%	—
09/14	672	34	5.1%	—
09/13	635	56	8.8%	—
Annual Growth	10.5%	(1.4%)	—	—

2020 Year-End Financials
Return on assets: 1.8%
Return on equity: 5.0%
Current Ratio: 1.10
Cash ($ mil.): 181

DANFOSS POWER SOLUTIONS INC.

Danfoss Power Solutions (formerly known as Sauer-Danfoss) is one of the largest companies in the mobile hydraulics industry. It designs, manufactures and sells a complete range of engineered hydraulic, electronic and electric components and solutions. The mobile equipment manufacturers rely on its expertise for the most innovative, propel, control, work function and steering solutions around the world. Its solutions have included motors, pumps, valves, and software, among others. Danfoss Power Solutions is a wholly-owned subsidiary of Denmark-based industrial company Danfoss A/S.

Operations
The company offers a complete range of engineered hydraulic, electronic and electric components and solutions including motors (hydrostatic, gear, orbtal, and electric), pumps (hydrostatic, gear, and digital displacement), valves (PVG proportional valve, DCV directional control valves, and ICS cartridge valves and HICs), and steering components and systems (hydraulic, and electrohydraulic), as well as electronic controls, electrical systems, and software. Under its separate brand Hydro-Gear, it supplies hydrostatic drive systems to a number of markets.

Geographic Reach
Danfoss Power Solutions operates throughout the Americas, Asia-Pacific, and Europe.

Sales and Marketing
The company serves a diverse array of industries, including automotive, commercial, residential, energy, food and beverage, marine and offshore, and water and wastewater, among others.

EXECUTIVES

CAO, Kenneth D Mccuskey
CMO, Marc A Weston
Auditors : KPMG LLP DES MOINES IOWA

LOCATIONS

HQ: DANFOSS POWER SOLUTIONS INC.
2800 E 13TH ST, AMES, IA 500108600
Phone: 515 239-6000
Web: WWW.DANFOSS.COM

PRODUCTS/OPERATIONS

Selected Products
Controls
    Control valves
    Mobile electronics
Propel
    Hydrostatic transmissions
    Open circuit piston pumps
Stand-Alone
    Cartridge valves and HICs
    Directional control valves
    Investors
    Light duty hydrostatic transmissions
    Open circuit gear pumps and motors
Work Function
    Low speed high torque motors
    Open circuit gear pumps and motors
    Steering units

Selected Markets
Agriculture and turf care
Construction and road building
Material handling
Specialty vehicles

COMPETITORS

Danfoss A/S
ITT INC.
ITT LLC
KOCH ENTERPRISES, INC.
MCNALLY INDUSTRIES, LLC
MOTION INDUSTRIES, INC.
NATIONAL OILWELL VARCO, INC.
TENNECO INC.
THE GORMAN-RUPP COMPANY
THE OILGEAR COMPANY

HISTORICAL FINANCIALS

Company Type: Private

Income Statement — FYE: December 31

	REVENUE ($mil)	NET INCOME ($mil)	NET PROFIT MARGIN	EMPLOYEES
12/11	2,057	259	12.6%	6,400
12/10	1,640	246	15.0%	—
12/09	1,159	(332)	—	—
Annual Growth	33.2%	—	—	—

2011 Year-End Financials
Return on assets: 20.3%
Return on equity: 45.0%
Current Ratio: 2.30
Cash ($ mil.): 251

DANONE US, INC.

Danone North America is a purpose-driven company with a portfolio of dairy and plant-based foods. As the world's largest Certified B Corporation, Danone North America is committed to the creation of both economic and social value, while nurturing natural ecosystems through sustainable agriculture. Its portfolio of brands includes Activia, DanActive, Danimals, Dannon, Good Plants, Horizon Organic, International Delight, Light + Fit, Oikos, Silk, So Delicious Dairy Free, SToK, Two Good, Vega, Wallaby Organic and YoCrunch. Danone North America was formed in April 2017, when Danone acquired WhiteWave Foods and united two companies in North America. Danone North America is a business unit of Danone and one of the top 15 food and beverage companies in the US.

Operations
Danone North America offers fresh dairy; organic dairy; plant-based; fresh foods; and coffee creamers and beverages under Activia, DanActive, Danimals, Dannon, Danonino, Light & Fit, Oikos, Silk, So Delicious, Alpro, Horizon, Wallaby Organic and International Delight.

Geographic Reach
Danone North America has offices in Broomfield, Colorado; White Plains, New York; Boucherville, Quebec; and Mississauga, Ontario.

Auditors : DELOITTE & TOUCHE LLP DENVER

LOCATIONS

HQ: DANONE US, INC.
12002 AIRPORT WAY, BROOMFIELD, CO 800212546
Phone: 303 635-4000
Web: WWW.DANONENORTHAMERICA.COM

2016 Sales

	% of total
North America	86
Europe	14
Total	100

PRODUCTS/OPERATIONS

Selected Products and Brands
Europe
    Plant-based foods and beverages (Alpro, Provamel)
    Almond
    Hazelnut
    Oat
    Rice
    Soy
North America
    Coffee creamers and beverages (Land O Lakes, International Delight)
    Flavored coffee creamers
    Half & Half
    Iced coffee
    Unflavored coffee creamers
    Plant-based foods and beverages (Silk)
    Almond
    Coconut
    Soy
    Premium dairy (Horizon Organic)
    Organic milk

Other organic dairy
Other premium milk

COMPETITORS

CLOVER INDUSTRIES LTD
DEAN FOODS COMPANY
INVENTURE FOODS, INC.
KALLO FOODS LIMITED
KERRY GROUP PUBLIC LIMITED COMPANY
LIFEWAY FOODS, INC.
Lactalis Canada Inc
NESTLE USA, INC.
NORTHWEST DAIRY ASSOCIATION
THE HAIN CELESTIAL GROUP INC

HISTORICAL FINANCIALS
Company Type: Private

Income Statement — FYE: December 31

	REVENUE ($mil)	NET INCOME ($mil)	NET PROFIT MARGIN	EMPLOYEES
12/15	3,866	168	4.4%	500
12/14	3,436	140	4.1%	—
12/13	2,542	99	3.9%	—
Annual Growth	23.3%	30.4%	—	—

2015 Year-End Financials
Return on assets: 4.0%   Cash ($ mil.): 38
Return on equity: 13.9%
Current Ratio: 1.00

DARTMOUTH COLLEGE

Auditors : PRICEWATERHOUSECOOPERS LLP BO

LOCATIONS

HQ: DARTMOUTH COLLEGE
  6193 HINMAN, HANOVER, NH 037554007
Phone: 603 646-2191
Web: HOME.DARTMOUTH.EDU

HISTORICAL FINANCIALS
Company Type: Private

Income Statement — FYE: June 30

	REVENUE ($mil)	NET INCOME ($mil)	NET PROFIT MARGIN	EMPLOYEES
06/19	927	314	34.0%	409
06/18	893	739	82.8%	—
06/17	887	691	77.9%	—
06/16	859	(301)	—	—
Annual Growth	2.6%	—	—	—

2019 Year-End Financials
Return on assets: 3.7%   Cash ($ mil.): 293
Return on equity: 4.7%
Current Ratio: 1.50

DARTMOUTH-HITCHCOCK CLINIC

The New England Alliance for Health (NEAH) brings together health care facilities and professionals looking to improve health in the New England region. Members of the alliance include about 20 community hospitals, home health care agencies, and mental health centers in New Hampshire, Vermont, and Massachusetts. While the members collaborate on wellness, quality, and communication initiatives, each member of the alliance is an independently owned and operated not-for-profit organization with its own board of directors. Collaborative services provided by NEAH include procurement, staff training, information technology, quality control, and finance, as well as the coordination of facility policies and planning.

Operations
NEAH's core services are provided to and funded by all of its member organizations. In addition, the alliance provides some voluntary services (such as licensing and insurance services) that are funded only by the participating members.

An affiliated organization, the New England Pharmacy Collaborative (NEPC), handles drug purchases for the health care members.

Geographic Reach
New Hampshire holds the largest number of NEAH members (11), while the organization has seven participants in Vermont and one in Massachusetts.

Company Background
NEAH was formerly known as Dartmouth-Hitchcock Alliance; it changed its name in 2009.

Auditors : PRICEWATERHOUSE LLP BOSTON

LOCATIONS

HQ: DARTMOUTH-HITCHCOCK CLINIC
  1 MEDICAL CENTER DR, LEBANON, NH 037560001
Phone: 603 650-5000
Web: WWW.DARTMOUTH-HITCHCOCK.ORG

PRODUCTS/OPERATIONS

Selected Services
Core Services
  Financial Planning and Benchmarking
  Information Services
  Materials Management and Pharmacy Services
  Professional Staff Education and Development
  Program Administration
  Quality Improvement/Loss Prevention
Other Services
  Licenses
  Property/Casualty Insurance Program

Selected Alliance Members
Massachusetts
  Cooley Dickinson Health Care (Northampton)
New Hampshire
  Alice Peck Day Memorial Hospital (Lebanon)
  Cheshire Medical Center (Keene)
  Cottage Hospital (Woodsville)
  Dartmouth-Hitchcock Medical Center (Lebanon, includes Mary Hitchcock Memorial Hospital)
  Monadnock Community Hospital
  New London Hospital
  Upper Connecticut Valley Hospital (Colebrook)
  Valley Regional Hospital (Claremont)
  Weeks Medical Center (Lancaster)
  West Central Behavioral Health (Lebanon)
Vermont
  Brattleboro Memorial Hospital
  Grace Cottage Hospital (Townshend)
  Mt. Ascutney Hospital (Windsor)
  Northeastern Vermont Regional Hospital (St. Johnsbury)
  Southwestern Vermont Medical Center (Bennington)
  Springfield Hospital
  VNA and Hospice of VT and NH

COMPETITORS

COMMONSPIRIT HEALTH
DIGNITY HEALTH
DUKE UNIVERSITY HEALTH SYSTEM, INC.
JEWISH HOSPITAL & ST. MARY'S HEALTHCARE, INC.
THE RUTLAND HOSPITAL INC ACT 220

HISTORICAL FINANCIALS
Company Type: Private

Income Statement — FYE: June 30

	REVENUE ($mil)	NET INCOME ($mil)	NET PROFIT MARGIN	EMPLOYEES
06/19	1,888	21	1.2%	7,999
06/15	6	0	0.0%	—
Annual Growth	313.1%	—	—	—

2019 Year-End Financials
Return on assets: 1.3%   Cash ($ mil.): 47
Return on equity: 4.9%
Current Ratio: 1.50

DARTMOUTH-HITCHCOCK HEALTH

EXECUTIVES

CAO, Stephen Leblanc
CMO, Jennifer Gilkie
Auditors : PRICEWATERHOUSECOOPERS LLP

LOCATIONS

HQ: DARTMOUTH-HITCHCOCK HEALTH
  1 MEDICAL CENTER DR, LEBANON, NH 037560001
Phone: 603 653-1118
Web: WWW.DARTMOUTH-HITCHCOCK.ORG

HISTORICAL FINANCIALS
Company Type: Private

Income Statement — FYE: June 30

	REVENUE ($mil)	NET INCOME ($mil)	NET PROFIT MARGIN	EMPLOYEES
06/22	2,870	(109)	—	8,000
06/21	2,663	359	13.5%	—
06/20	2,344	(119)	—	—
06/19	2,299	40	1.8%	—
Annual Growth	7.7%	—	—	—

2022 Year-End Financials
Return on assets: (-3.7%)   Cash ($ mil.): 191
Return on equity: (-13.1%)
Current Ratio: 1.20

DATASITE GLOBAL CORPORATION

Datasite, formerly known as Merrill Corporation, is a leading SaaS provider for the M&A industry, empowering dealmakers around the world with the tools they need to succeed across the entire deal lifecycle. As the premiere virtual data room for M&A due diligence globally, Datasite is consistently recognized for breakthrough technologies like its AI/ML-enabled capabilities and automated redaction tools. Beyond due diligence, Datasite provides transaction and document management solutions for investment banks, corporate development, private equity, and law firms across industries.

Operations

Datasite provides secure software solutions for managing the full spectrum of financial transactions ? including M&A, restructuring & administration, and capital raising. Its intuitive platform offers ironclad security enabling file sharing and collaboration within and across organizations. More than a virtual data room (VDR), Datasite supports advisors and their clients across the entire deal lifecycle with secure collaborative software that shortens timelines for buy-side and sell-side teams from deal sourcing and deal preparation to post-merger integration (PMI) while meeting regulatory compliance ? including GDPR and CCPA requirements.

Sales and Marketing

Datasite serves investment banking, corporate development, private equity and law firms.

HISTORY

Kenneth Merrill founded K. F. Merrill with his wife Lorraine in 1968 and grew the company into a major regional printer. He turned over the reins in 1984 to John Castro, who had worked his way up from production manager. The company went public two years later.

EXECUTIVES

Legal Finance*, Rodney D Johnson
CRO*, Todd R Albright
CPO*, Thomas Fredell
CIO*, Dixon Gould
Auditors : PRICE WATER HOUSE COOPER LLP

LOCATIONS

HQ: DATASITE GLOBAL CORPORATION
733 MARQUETTE AVE STE 600, MINNEAPOLIS, MN 554022302
Phone: 651 632-4000
Web: WWW.DATASITE.COM

PRODUCTS/OPERATIONS

SERVICES
Capital Transactions
Contract Management
Data Warehousing
Elections
Financial Services Marketing & Communications
Healthcare Member Communications
Intellectual Property Management
M&A, Reorganizations & Exchange Offers
Merrill IFN
Portfolio Management
Regulatory Disclosure

COMPETITORS

ADVANCED COMPUTER SOFTWARE GROUP LIMITED
ADVANSTAR COMMUNICATIONS INC.
BANCTEC, INC.
DELOITTE TOUCHE TOHMATSU LIMITED
EISNERAMPER LLP
INTRADO CORPORATION
IPREO HOLDINGS LLC
MORRIS BUSINESS DEVELOPMENT COMPANY
PMSI UK LTD
WIPFLI LLP

HISTORICAL FINANCIALS

Company Type: Private

Income Statement — FYE: January 31

	REVENUE ($mil)	NET INCOME ($mil)	NET PROFIT MARGIN	EMPLOYEES
01/17	609	53	8.9%	6,010
01/16	579	78	13.5%	—
01/15	691	64	9.3%	—
Annual Growth	(6.1%)	(8.5%)	—	—

2017 Year-End Financials
Return on assets: 17.4%   Cash ($ mil.): 62
Return on equity: —
Current Ratio: 2.30

DATS TRUCKING, INC.

DATS Trucking specializes in less-than-truckload (LTL) freight transportation in the western US, but that's not all there is to the company's operations. In addition to its LTL operations, in which freight from multiple shippers is combined into a single trailer, DATS Trucking provides truckload transportation. The company's tanker division, Overland Petroleum, transports gasoline, diesel fuel, and other petroleum products. Overall, DATS Trucking operates a fleet of about 500 tractors and 2,500 trailers. It offers LTL service outside its home territory via The Reliance Network, a group of regional carriers that covers the US and Canada. President and CEO Don Ipson founded DATS Trucking in 1988.

LOCATIONS

HQ: DATS TRUCKING, INC.
321 N OLD HIGHWAY 91, HURRICANE, UT 847373194
Phone: 435 673-1886
Web: WWW.DATSTRUCKING.COM

COMPETITORS

CRETE CARRIER CORPORATION
EMPIRE TRUCK LINES, INC.
LAKEVILLE MOTOR EXPRESS, INC.
MCO TRANSPORT, INC.
MIDWEST PARTS & EQUIPMENT CO.

HISTORICAL FINANCIALS

Company Type: Private

Income Statement — FYE: December 31

	REVENUE ($mil)	NET INCOME ($mil)	NET PROFIT MARGIN	EMPLOYEES
12/07	717	1	0.3%	475
12/06	658	7	1.2%	—
12/05	600	1	0.2%	—
12/04	391	1	0.4%	—
Annual Growth	22.3%	4.6%	—	—

2007 Year-End Financials
Return on assets: 4.9%   Cash ($ mil.): —
Return on equity: 13.6%
Current Ratio: 1.40

DAVIS SCHOOL DISTRICT

Auditors : SQUIRE & COMPANY PC OREM UT

LOCATIONS

HQ: DAVIS SCHOOL DISTRICT
45 E STATE ST, FARMINGTON, UT 840252344
Phone: 801 402-5261
Web: WWW.DAVIS.K12.UT.US

HISTORICAL FINANCIALS

Company Type: Private

Income Statement — FYE: June 30

	REVENUE ($mil)	NET INCOME ($mil)	NET PROFIT MARGIN	EMPLOYEES
06/18	645	(15)	—	6,310
06/14	509	12	2.5%	—
06/13	500	(6)	—	—
06/11	482	1	0.4%	—
Annual Growth	4.2%	—	—	—

2018 Year-End Financials
Return on assets: (-1.2%)   Cash ($ mil.): —
Return on equity: (-9.0%)
Current Ratio: —

DAYTON CHILDREN'S HOSPITAL

LOCATIONS

HQ: DAYTON CHILDREN'S HOSPITAL
1 CHILDRENS PLZ, DAYTON, OH 454041815
Phone: 937 641-3000
Web: WWW.CHILDRENSDAYTON.ORG

HISTORICAL FINANCIALS
Company Type: Private

Income Statement   FYE: June 30

	REVENUE ($mil)	NET INCOME ($mil)	NET PROFIT MARGIN	EMPLOYEES
06/21	553	125	22.7%	3,300
06/20	509	90	17.7%	—
06/16	253	24	9.7%	—
06/15	233	17	7.3%	—
Annual Growth	15.5%	39.5%	—	—

2021 Year-End Financials
Return on assets: 9.9%   Cash ($ mil.): 16
Return on equity: 12.7%
Current Ratio: 1.50

DB US HOLDING CORPORATION

Auditors: PRICEWATERHOUSECOOPERS LLP N

LOCATIONS
HQ: DB US HOLDING CORPORATION
81 MAIN ST UNIT 504, WHITE PLAINS, NY 106011719
Phone: 914 366-7200
Web: WWW.DBUSHOLDING.COM

HISTORICAL FINANCIALS
Company Type: Private

Income Statement   FYE: December 31

	REVENUE ($mil)	NET INCOME ($mil)	NET PROFIT MARGIN	EMPLOYEES
12/16	914	(2)	—	6,300
12/15	1,766	(10)	—	—
12/10	2,198	(47)	—	—
Annual Growth	(13.6%)	—	—	—

2016 Year-End Financials
Return on assets: (-2.2%)   Cash ($ mil.): 122
Return on equity: (-2.3%)
Current Ratio: 102.70

DBSI INC

LOCATIONS
HQ: DBSI INC
12426 W EXPLORER DR # 100, BOISE, ID 837131560
Phone: 208 955-9800
Web: WWW.DBSI-INC.COM

HISTORICAL FINANCIALS
Company Type: Private

Income Statement   FYE: December 31

	ASSETS ($mil)	NET INCOME ($mil)	NET INCOME AS % OF ASSETS	EMPLOYEES
12/07	244	15	6.4%	53
12/06	168	2	1.6%	—
12/05	150	25	17.0%	—
12/04	70	49	69.9%	—
Annual Growth	51.2%	(31.7%)	—	—

2007 Year-End Financials
Return on assets: 6.4%   Cash ($ mil.): 19
Return on equity: 14.9%
Current Ratio: 1.50

DC WATER AND SEWER AUTHORITY

EXECUTIVES
CIO, Omer Siddiqui
Auditors: KPMG LLP WASHINGTON DC

LOCATIONS
HQ: DC WATER AND SEWER AUTHORITY
5000 OVERLOOK AVE SW, WASHINGTON, DC 200325212
Phone: 202 787-2000
Web: WWW.DCWATER.COM

HISTORICAL FINANCIALS
Company Type: Private

Income Statement   FYE: September 30

	REVENUE ($mil)	NET INCOME ($mil)	NET PROFIT MARGIN	EMPLOYEES
09/18	684	187	27.4%	1,000
09/06	0	0	18.4%	—
09/05	272	48	17.6%	—
Annual Growth	7.3%	11.0%	—	—

2018 Year-End Financials
Return on assets: 2.4%   Cash ($ mil.): 123
Return on equity: 9.0%
Current Ratio: 1.40

DCR WORKFORCE, INC.

EXECUTIVES
CGO*, Daniel Weinfurter
Auditors: JOHN KAMMERER BOCA RATON FLO

LOCATIONS
HQ: DCR WORKFORCE, INC.
7795 NW BCN SQ BLVD # 201, BOCA RATON, FL 334871394
Phone: 561 998-3737

HISTORICAL FINANCIALS
Company Type: Private

Income Statement   FYE: December 31

	REVENUE ($mil)	NET INCOME ($mil)	NET PROFIT MARGIN	EMPLOYEES
12/12	548	2	0.5%	82
12/11	464	2	0.6%	—
12/01	12	0	6.3%	—
Annual Growth	41.0%	11.9%	—	—

2012 Year-End Financials
Return on assets: 16.9%   Cash ($ mil.): —
Return on equity: 21.1%
Current Ratio: 3.80

DE PAUL UNIVERSITY

In the land of da Bulls and da Bears, there's DePaul. One of the largest private, not-for-profit universities in the US, DePaul has more than 21,920 students attending classes at its Chicago-area campuses, and its increasing offerings of online learning courses. The university offers more than 300 undergraduate and graduate programs through 10 colleges and schools, including the Driehaus College of Business, and the College of Communication. It has a student teacher ratio of 16 to 1. One of the country's largest Catholic institutions of higher learning, DePaul was founded in 1898 by the Vincentian religious community and is named after 17th century French priest St. Vincent de Paul.

Operations

The university's more than 130 undergraduate majors include accountancy, acting, animation, chemistry, criminology, data science, history, journalism, and marketing. Its more than 175 graduate programs include Counseling: Clinical Mental Health Counseling (MEd), Creative Producing (MFA), Early Childhood Education (EdD), Healthcare Markets & Analytics (MBA), Information Systems (MS), and Marketing Strategy and Planning (MBA), among its graduate programs. These programs are offered in School and Colleges of Business, Communication, Education, Law, Liberal Arts and Social Sciences, Science and Health, Music, Continuing and Professional Studies, as well as in Driehaus College of Business and The Theatre School.

Geographic Reach

DePaul's Chicago-area campuses are located in Lincoln Park (which is home to five colleges/schools), the Loop (for another five DePaul colleges and schools). DePaul's student body hosts learners from about 50 US states and more than 135 countries. In addition, it study abroad programs are offered in more than 30 countries.

Auditors: KPMG LLP CHICAGO IL

LOCATIONS

HQ: DE PAUL UNIVERSITY
1 E JACKSON BLVD, CHICAGO, IL 606042287
Phone: 312 362-6714
Web: WWW.DEPAUL.EDU

COMPETITORS

DREW UNIVERSITY
JOHN CARROLL UNIVERSITY
NORTHERN ILLINOIS UNIVERSITY
OAKLAND UNIVERSITY
TEXAS CHRISTIAN UNIVERSITY
TRUSTEES OF BOSTON COLLEGE
UNIVERSITY AT ALBANY
UNIVERSITY OF SAN DIEGO
UNIVERSITY OF SAN FRANCISCO
WILLAMETTE UNIVERSITY

HISTORICAL FINANCIALS
Company Type: Private

Income Statement — FYE: June 30

	REVENUE ($mil)	NET INCOME ($mil)	NET PROFIT MARGIN	EMPLOYEES
06/22	597	(125)	—	3,895
06/21	568	254	44.7%	
06/20	595	67	11.3%	
06/19	580	45	7.9%	
Annual Growth	1.0%	—	—	—

2022 Year-End Financials
Return on assets: (-7.0%)   Cash ($ mil.): 25
Return on equity: (-9.4%)
Current Ratio: —

DEACONESS HOSPITAL INC

Deaconess Hospital provides benevolent medical assistance to residents of southern Indiana, western Kentucky, and southeastern Illinois. The not-for-profit hospital is a 365-bed acute care medical facility that is the flagship hospital of the Deaconess Health System. Specialized services include cardiovascular surgery, cancer treatment, orthopedics, neurological, and trauma care. The hospital also offers home health care, hospice services, and medical equipment rental, and it operates outpatient family practice, surgery, wellness, and community outreach centers. Founded in 1892, Deaconess Hospital is a teaching and research facility affiliated with the Indiana University School of Medicine.

Operations
Deaconess handles about 18,000 inpatient visits per year. It also sees about 350,000 outpatients and 65,000 emergency room visitors, and it handles about 7,500 annual surgery procedures.

Geographic Reach
Deaconess Hospital is located in Evansville, Indiana, and provides services to about 26 surrounding counties.

Strategy
To improve services to area residents, Deaconess Hospital is expanding its outpatient care facilities and enhancing its IT resources. For instance, in 2013 it moved its urgent care center to a larger, more efficient facility. The hospital is also pursuing recognition for specialist programs, such as its stroke center, which was certified as a level one facility in 2013.

Auditors: IT BLUE & CO LLC INDIANAPOLI

LOCATIONS

HQ: DEACONESS HOSPITAL INC
600 MARY ST, EVANSVILLE, IN 477101674
Phone: 812 450-5000
Web: WWW.DEACONESS.COM

Selected Services
24-hour Emergency Center
Cancer Services
Corporate Wellness
Family Medicine Clinic
Heart Services
Home Medical Equipment
Home-based Medical Care
Hospice Care
Inpatient and Outpatient Surgery
Mental Health Services
Neuro Services
Orthopedics
Pediatrics
Physician Referral Service
Radiology Services
Residency Program
Support Groups and Programs
Women's Hospital

COMPETITORS

BETHESDA HOSPITAL, INC.
BLESSING HOSPITAL
FROEDTERT MEMORIAL LUTHERAN HOSPITAL, INC.
HOLY SPIRIT HOSPITAL OF THE SISTERS OF CHRISTIAN CHARITY
NEW LIBERTY HOSPITAL DISTRICT

HISTORICAL FINANCIALS
Company Type: Private

Income Statement — FYE: September 30

	REVENUE ($mil)	NET INCOME ($mil)	NET PROFIT MARGIN	EMPLOYEES
09/20	987	196	19.9%	5,300
09/19	1,047	159	15.2%	—
09/18	823	153	18.6%	—
09/17	725	94	13.0%	—
Annual Growth	10.8%	27.8%	—	—

2020 Year-End Financials
Return on assets: 10.3%   Cash ($ mil.): 222
Return on equity: 16.4%
Current Ratio: 2.20

DEER PARK REFINING LIMITED PARTNERSHIP

Auditors: ERNST & YOUNG LLP HOUSTON TE

LOCATIONS

HQ: DEER PARK REFINING LIMITED PARTNERSHIP
5900 HIGHWAY 225, DEER PARK, TX 775362434
Phone: 713 246-7280

HISTORICAL FINANCIALS
Company Type: Private

Income Statement — FYE: December 31

	REVENUE ($mil)	NET INCOME ($mil)	NET PROFIT MARGIN	EMPLOYEES
12/17	867	97	11.2%	51
12/16	897	154	17.2%	—
Annual Growth	(3.3%)	(36.9%)	—	—

2017 Year-End Financials
Return on assets: 4.7%   Cash ($ mil.): 77
Return on equity: 6.7%
Current Ratio: 1.90

DEKALB COUNTY BOARD OF EDUCATION

EXECUTIVES

Vice Chairman*, Marshall D Orson
Auditors: RUSSELL W HINTON CPA CGFM

LOCATIONS

HQ: DEKALB COUNTY BOARD OF EDUCATION
1701 MOUNTAIN INDUS BLVD, STONE MOUNTAIN, GA 300831027
Phone: 678 676-1200
Web: WWW.DEKALBSCHOOLSGA.ORG

HISTORICAL FINANCIALS
Company Type: Private

Income Statement — FYE: June 30

	REVENUE ($mil)	NET INCOME ($mil)	NET PROFIT MARGIN	EMPLOYEES
06/07	1,128	350	31.1%	270
06/06	1,055	10	0.9%	—
Annual Growth	7.0%	3405.8%	—	—

2007 Year-End Financials
Return on assets: 22.9%   Cash ($ mil.): 116
Return on equity: 33.3%
Current Ratio: 3.60

DEKALB COUNTY PUBLIC LIBRARY

Auditors : KPMG LLP ATLANTA GA

LOCATIONS

HQ: DEKALB COUNTY PUBLIC LIBRARY
215 SYCAMORE ST FL 4, DECATUR, GA 300303413
Phone: 404 370-3070
Web: WWW.DEKALBLIBRARY.ORG

HISTORICAL FINANCIALS
Company Type: Private

Income Statement — FYE: December 31

	REVENUE ($mil)	NET INCOME ($mil)	NET PROFIT MARGIN	EMPLOYEES
12/07	622	(124)	—	228
12/06	622	186	30.0%	—
12/05	564	56	10.0%	—
Annual Growth	5.1%	—	—	—

2007 Year-End Financials
Return on assets: (-3.8%)   Cash ($ mil.): 536
Return on equity: (-6.5%)
Current Ratio: —

DENNIS K. BURKE INC.

Auditors : TONNESON & COMPANY INC WAKE

LOCATIONS

HQ: DENNIS K. BURKE INC.
555 CONSTITUTION DR, TAUNTON, MA 027807365
Phone: 617 884-7800
Web: WWW.BURKEOIL.COM

HISTORICAL FINANCIALS
Company Type: Private

Income Statement — FYE: April 30

	REVENUE ($mil)	NET INCOME ($mil)	NET PROFIT MARGIN	EMPLOYEES
04/12	929	3	0.3%	110
04/11	807	0	0.1%	—
04/10	(2,050)	0	0.0%	—
Annual Growth	—	25724.5%	—	—

2012 Year-End Financials
Return on assets: 5.3%   Cash ($ mil.): 1
Return on equity: 21.3%
Current Ratio: 1.20

DENVER HEALTH AND HOSPITALS AUTHORITY INC

Denver Health was founded as City Hospital in 1860 to serve the health care needs of the rapidly developing city of Denver. As a comprehensive, integrated organization, Denver Health provides hospital and emergency care to the public, regardless of ability to pay. The health system delivers preventative, primary and acute care services. Denver Health sees nearly 930,000 total patient visits annually. As Colorado's primary safety-net institution, Denver Health has provided billions of dollars in uncompensated care and serves as a model for other safety net institutions across the nation.

Operations
Denver Health is Colorado's second largest graduate medical education training site. As an affiliate of the University of Colorado School of Medicine (CUSOM), Denver Health welcomes CUSOM medical students, physician assistant students, interns, residents, and fellows from a wide variety of clinical specialties. Denver Health sponsors its own accredited residencies and fellowships in general and pediatric dentistry, emergency medicine (EM), emergency medical services (EMS), oral and maxillofacial surgery, pharmacy, psychology, and toxicology. It also sponsor fellowship programs in areas such as EM ultrasound and research, integrated behavioral health, emergency psychiatry.

Company Background
Denver Health traces its beginnings back to territorial days in 1860. As Denver General Hospital, it operated as an agency of Denver's city and county governments until 1997, when it became a freestanding authority.

Denver Health's flagship medical center joined forces with Children's Hospital Colorado in late 2010 to share best practices and resources to expand and improve pediatric care throughout the region. Through the collaboration the two have increased access to pediatric mental health services; they also coordinate recruitment and sharing of highly specialized pediatric providers.

LOCATIONS

HQ: DENVER HEALTH AND HOSPITALS AUTHORITY INC
777 BANNOCK ST, DENVER, CO 802044597
Phone: 720 956-2580
Web: WWW.DENVERHEALTH.ORG

PRODUCTS/OPERATIONS

2013 Sales

	$ mil	% of total
Net patient service	368.6	46
Captation earned net of reinsurance expense	129.2	16
Medicaid disproportionate share & other safety net reimbursements	125.0	16
Federal, state & other grants	71.7	9
Others	98.8	13
Total	793.3	100

Selected Medical Centers, Clinics, and Affiliates
Denver Emergency Center for Children
Denver Health Dental Care Clinics
Denver Health Medical Center
Denver Health Medical Plan (for Denver Health employees)
Denver Health Primary Care Clinics
Denver Paramedics
Denver Public Health
Rocky Mountain Center for Medical Response to Terrorism, Mass Casualties and Epidemics
Rocky Mountain Poison & Drug Center
Rocky Mountain Regional Trauma Center

COMPETITORS

ALLINA HEALTH SYSTEM
ATLANTICARE HEALTH SYSTEM INC.
BRONXCARE HEALTH SYSTEM
DALLAS COUNTY HOSPITAL DISTRICT
KALEIDA HEALTH
MERCY HEALTH - ST. RITA'S MEDICAL CENTER, LLC
NORTHSHORE UNIVERSITY HEALTHSYSTEM
TALLAHASSEE MEMORIAL HEALTHCARE, INC.
TRUMAN MEDICAL CENTER, INCORPORATED
WELLSTAR HEALTH SYSTEM, INC.

HISTORICAL FINANCIALS
Company Type: Private

Income Statement — FYE: December 31

	REVENUE ($mil)	NET INCOME ($mil)	NET PROFIT MARGIN	EMPLOYEES
12/21	1,219	14	1.2%	3,541
12/19	1,111	127	11.4%	—
12/18	1,119	62	5.6%	—
12/17	1,056	14	1.3%	—
Annual Growth	3.7%	0.9%	—	—

2021 Year-End Financials
Return on assets: 1.1%   Cash ($ mil.): 34
Return on equity: 2.2%
Current Ratio: 1.20

DESAROLLADORA DEL NORTE S E

LOCATIONS

HQ: DESAROLLADORA DEL NORTE S E
200 COCO BCH BLVD HWY 955, RIO GRANDE, PR 00745
Phone: 787 657-1026

HISTORICAL FINANCIALS
Company Type: Private

Income Statement — FYE: December 31

	REVENUE ($mil)	NET INCOME ($mil)	NET PROFIT MARGIN	EMPLOYEES
12/16	1,801	102	5.7%	500
12/15	1,738	0	0.0%	—
Annual Growth	3.7%	—	—	—

2016 Year-End Financials
Return on assets: 3.1%   Cash ($ mil.): 366
Return on equity: 6.6%
Current Ratio: 0.90

DETROIT WAYNE MENTAL HEALTH AUTHORITY

LOCATIONS

HQ: DETROIT WAYNE MENTAL HEALTH AUTHORITY
707 W MILWAUKEE ST, DETROIT, MI 482022943
Phone: 313 833-2500
Web: WWW.DWIHN.ORG

HISTORICAL FINANCIALS
Company Type: Private

Income Statement — FYE: September 30

	REVENUE ($mil)	NET INCOME ($mil)	NET PROFIT MARGIN	EMPLOYEES
09/16	736	4	0.6%	99
09/15	701	19	2.8%	—
Annual Growth	5.0%	(77.0%)	—	—

2016 Year-End Financials
Return on assets: 2.1% Cash ($ mil.): 176
Return on equity: 4.7%
Current Ratio: 1.70

DEVCON CONSTRUCTION INCORPORATED

Devcon Construction has built a sturdy business from building in the Bay Area. One of the area's top general building contractors, Devcon has constructed more than 30 million sq. ft. of office, industrial, and commercial space. Its focus is on Northern California, mainly in the San Francisco Bay Area and Silicon Valley. The company provides engineering, design/build, and interior design services. It specializes in high-tech projects, including data centers, and industrial research and development facilities. In addition to building company facilities and offices, Devcon works on such projects as hotels, restaurants, parking structures, retail stores, sports facilities, and schools.

Geographic Reach
Based in Milpitas, California, Devcon maintains several satellite offices in California in Petaluma, Stockton, and Santa Cruz, as well as an office in Reno, Nevada.

Strategy
Although most of Devcon's work is in California, the company also has completed projects in Nevada, Oregon, Idaho, Texas, Massachusetts, and Florida. Recent projects in the San Francisco Forty Niners Stadium in Santa Clara, San Jose Sharks Ice Center in Pleasanton, and the Stanford Research Computing Facility.

The company partnered with US-based Central Concrete in 2012 to supply its high-performing, low-CO2 concrete for the new San Francisco 49er Stadium. The move showcases Devcon's focus on sustainability as part of its projects.

Auditors: JOHANSON & YAU ACCOUNTANCY COR

LOCATIONS

HQ: DEVCON CONSTRUCTION INCORPORATED
690 GIBRALTAR DR, MILPITAS, CA 950356317
Phone: 408 942-8200
Web: WWW.DEVCON-CONST.COM

PRODUCTS/OPERATIONS

Selected Projects
1880 Mission Street, San Francisco
3333 Scott Blvd., Buildings A, B, & C, Santa Clara
Anderson Collection At Stanford University, Stanford
Barnes & Nobles, Palo Alto
Cisco Parking Structure 1, San Jose
Cisco Parking Structure 2, San Jose
Downtown Sunnyvale Town Center, Sunnyvale
El Camino Family Housing, South San Francisco
Fresno Hyatt Place Hotel, Fresno
Friedenrich Center For Translational Research At 800 Welch Road
Lawson Lane East - Buildings A & B, Santa Clara
Oakland Air Traffic Control Tower (ATCT), Oakland
San Francisco 49ers Stadium, Santa Clara
San Jose Earthquakes - MLS Soccer Stadium, San Jose
SanDisk, Milpitas
Santa Clara University Admissions & Enrollment Services Building, Santa Clara
Sharks Ice Center, Pleasanton
Stanford Research Computing Facility, Stanford
The Plaza At Triton Park, Foster City
University Plaza, Palo Alto
Villa Siena Nursing Care Units, Mountain View

COMPETITORS

DAVID E. HARVEY BUILDERS, INC.
FAULKNERUSA, INC.
JAYNES CORPORATION
O'NEIL INDUSTRIES, INC.
RUDOLPH AND SLETTEN, INC.

HISTORICAL FINANCIALS
Company Type: Private

Income Statement — FYE: December 31

	REVENUE ($mil)	NET INCOME ($mil)	NET PROFIT MARGIN	EMPLOYEES
12/14	1,181	20	1.7%	550
12/13	1,012	12	1.2%	—
12/12	779	3	0.5%	—
Annual Growth	23.1%	138.8%	—	—

2014 Year-End Financials
Return on assets: 6.0% Cash ($ mil.): 64
Return on equity: 54.9%
Current Ratio: 1.10

DHPC TECHNOLOGIES, INC.

LOCATIONS

HQ: DHPC TECHNOLOGIES, INC.
10 WODBRDGE CTR DR STE 65, WOODBRIDGE, NJ 07095
Phone: 732 791-5400
Web: WWW.PERATON.COM

HISTORICAL FINANCIALS
Company Type: Private

Income Statement — FYE: May 11

	REVENUE ($mil)	NET INCOME ($mil)	NET PROFIT MARGIN	EMPLOYEES
05/17*	38,584	1,320	3.4%	150
12/09	11	1	9.0%	—
12/07	6	1	29.2%	—
06/06	1,726	0	0.0%	—
Annual Growth	32.6%	179.9%	—	—

*Fiscal year change

2017 Year-End Financials
Return on assets: 14.5% Cash ($ mil.): 2,039
Return on equity: 21.9%
Current Ratio: 2.80

DIALYSIS CLINIC, INC.

Dialysis Clinic, Inc., or DCI, is dedicated to caring for patients with end-stage renal disease (ESRD). The not-for-profit company, which operates a network of more than 210 dialysis centers serving more than 14,000 patients in 27 states, also provides kidney transplant assistance services. Affiliate DCI Donor Services is an organ and tissue procurement agency. DCI also funds kidney-related research and educational programs and is affiliated with various universities and teaching hospitals throughout the US, including Tufts University, the University of Arizona, and Tulane University.

Geographic Reach
The company has its locations in Alabama, Arizona, Arkansas, California, Colorado, Connecticut, Florida, Georgia, Indiana, Iowa, Kentucky, Louisiana, Maine, Massachusetts, Missouri, Montana, Nebraska, Nevada, New Jersey, New Mexico, New York, North Carolina, Ohio, Pennsylvania, South Carolina, Tennessee, and Texas.

Strategy
DCI grows its network of facilities by forming partnerships with health care providers and other organizations. The company provides funding for construction and operation of the facility, and it provides clinic support services including supply procurement and central laboratory services (through its DCI Lab subsidiary).

In 2012 the company opened a dialysis clinic in Albuquerque, its first dialysis clinic in the South Valley region of New Mexico.

Company Background

DCI was established in 1971 by nephrologist Keith Johnson.

Auditors : DELOITTE & TOUCHE LLP NASHVIL

LOCATIONS

HQ: DIALYSIS CLINIC, INC.
1633 CHURCH ST STE 500, NASHVILLE, TN 372032948
Phone: 615 327-3061
Web: WWW.DCIINC.ORG

COMPETITORS

ADOLFSON & PETERSON, INC.
CARIDIANBCT, INC.
DAVITA INC.
IOWA HEALTH SYSTEM
PATHOLOGY ASSOCIATES MEDICAL LABORATORIES, LLC
PIEDMONT ATHENS REGIONAL MEDICAL CENTER, INC.
RENAL ADVANTAGE INC.
SHERIDAN HEALTHCARE, INC.
U.S. RENAL CARE, INC.
WISCONSIN PHYSICIANS SERVICE INSURANCE CORPORATION

HISTORICAL FINANCIALS

Company Type: Private

Income Statement — FYE: September 30

	REVENUE ($mil)	NET INCOME ($mil)	NET PROFIT MARGIN	EMPLOYEES
09/19	739	7	1.1%	5,000
09/18	760	5	0.7%	—
09/17	736	23	3.3%	—
09/16	719	22	3.2%	—
Annual Growth	0.9%	(30.0%)	—	—

2019 Year-End Financials

Return on assets: 1.1%
Return on equity: 1.3%
Current Ratio: 26.90
Cash ($ mil.): 127

DIGNITY HEALTH

Dignity Health is the largest hospital provider in California and the fifth largest health system in the US. The not-for-profit health care provider operates a network of more than 400 care centers, including nearly 40 hospitals, urgent and occupational care, imaging and surgery centers, home health, and primary care clinics in more than 20 states. Dignity Health is the official health care provider of the San Francisco Giants. With more than 60,000 caregivers and staff who deliver excellent care to diverse communities, the company has more than 10,000 active physicians.

Operations

Dignity Health offers inpatient, outpatient, sub-acute, and home health care services, as well as physician services through affiliates.

Geographic Reach

Headquartered in San Francisco, Dignity Health operates some 40 hospitals, urgent care centers, clinics, emergency rooms, and specialty care centers in California, Nevada, and Arizona.

Company Background

Dignity Health traces its roots to 1857. The Sisters of Mercy Catholic order was established in Dublin in 1831. In the 1850s, eight Sisters arrived in San Francisco and began caring for residents with cholera, typhoid, and influenza. They established St. Mary's Hospital, now that city's oldest continuously operating hospital. The order merged operations with another community of Sisters of Mercy in 1986 to create Catholic Healthcare West. The combined system had one retirement home and 10 hospitals throughout California.

The system changed its name to Dignity Health in early 2012 as part of a governance restructuring program. While the firm remained a not-for-profit organization with Catholic roots, and its Catholic hospitals continued to be sponsored by their founding congregations (and governed by the Catholic health care directives), the parent organization itself was no longer an official ministry of the Catholic church. In 2019, Dignity Health joined forces with Catholic Health Initiatives to create CommonSpirit Health, the nation's largest not-for-profit health system.

HISTORY

Dignity Health, formerly Catholic Healthcare West (CHW), traces its roots to 1857, when the Sisters of Mercy founded St. Mary's Hospital in San Francisco. The order expanded in that area, and in 1986 two different communities of the Sisters of Mercy merged their hospitals into an organization with one retirement home and 10 hospitals from the Bay Area to San Diego. Declining membership in Roman Catholic religious orders, combined with consolidation in the field, led the orders to see merger as their only route to survival.

CHW continued to add facilities, including AMI Community Hospital in Santa Cruz, California, in 1990. Since CHW already owned the area's only other acute care hospital, Dominican Santa Cruz Hospital, CHW in 1993 was ordered not to acquire any more acute care hospitals in Santa Cruz County without FTC approval.

As the trend to managed care became a stampede in the 1990s, CHW moved more into preventive care and began reigning in costs through productivity improvement plans. It continued to add hospitals, including tax-supported institutions trying to compete with national for-profit systems.

The network increased its medical clout in 1994 by allying with San Diego-based Scripps, one of the state's largest HMO systems. In 1995 the Daughters of Charity Province of the West realigned its six-hospital operation with CHW. The next year the Dominican Sisters (California), the Dominican Sisters of St. Catherine of Siena (Wisconsin), and the Sisters of Charity of the Incarnate Word allied their California hospitals with CHW. New community hospitals included Bakersfield Memorial, Sierra Nevada Memorial (Grass Valley), Sequoia Hospital (Redwood City), and Woodland Healthcare.

Charity and cost-consciousness clashed in 1996 when union members staged a walkout to protest nonunion outsourcing of vocational nursing, housekeeping, and kitchen jobs. This dispute was settled, but CHW continued to be a target for union organizers, with a bitter battle against the Service Employees International Union (SEIU) starting in 1998.

The year 2000 brought CHW more problems with labor relations: SEIU argued that the organization was resistant to unionization. Continued losses led the organization to implement major restructuring the following year, as its 10 regional divisions were consolidated into four.

The company parted ways with one of its sponsoring organizations, the Franciscan Sisters of the Sacred Heart of Frankfort, Illinois, in 2003. The sponsorship ended when CHW closed St. Francis Medical Center of Santa Barbara. However, the hospital operator that fiscal year posted its first operating profit in seven years.

The company changed its name from Catholic Healthcare West (CHW) to Dignity Health in early 2012 as part of a governance restructuring program. While the firm remained a not-for-profit organization with Catholic roots, and its Catholic hospitals continued to be sponsored by their founding congregations (and governed by the Catholic health care directives), the parent organization itself was no longer an official ministry of the Catholic church.

The company's rebranding and restructuring aimed to give it more flexibility to pursue its growth strategy of widening its presence into additional regions of the US, while lowering the overall cost of care (a desire of most large hospital operators as the US government works to reform its ailing health system). At the time of the governance shift, Dignity Health operated 25 Catholic hospitals and 15 non-Catholic hospitals.

Auditors : IT KPMG LLP SAN FRANCISCO C

LOCATIONS

HQ: DIGNITY HEALTH
185 BERRY ST STE 200, SAN FRANCISCO, CA 941071777
Phone: 415 438-5500
Web: WWW.DIGNITYHEALTH.ORG

Selected Facilities

Arizona
    Barrow Neurological Institute (Phoenix)
    Chandler Regional Medical Center

Mercy Gilbert Medical Center
St. Joseph's Hospital and Medical Center (Phoenix)
California
Arroyo Grande Community Hospital
Bakersfield Memorial Hospital
California Hospital Medical Center (Los Angeles)
Community Hospital of San Bernardino
Dominican Hospital (Santa Cruz)
French Hospital Medical Center (San Luis Obispo)
Glendale Memorial Hospital and Health Center
Marian Medical Center (Santa Maria)
Mark Twain St. Joseph's Hospital (San Andreas)
Mercy General Hospital (Sacramento)
Mercy Hospital of Bakersfield
Mercy Hospital of Folsom
Mercy Medical Center Merced Community Campus
Mercy Medical Center Merced Dominican Campus
Mercy Medical Center Mt. Shasta
Mercy Medical Center Redding
Mercy San Juan Medical Center (Carmichael)
Mercy Southwest Hospital (Bakersfield)
Methodist Hospital of Sacramento
Northridge Hospital Medical Center
Oak Valley Hospital (Oakdale)
Saint Francis Memorial Hospital (San Francisco)
Sequoia Hospital (Redwood City)
Sierra Nevada Memorial Hospital (Grass Valley)
St. Bernardine Medical Center (San Bernardino)
St. Elizabeth Community Hospital (Red Bluff)
St. John's Pleasant Valley Hospital (Camarillo)
St. John's Regional Medical Center (Oxnard)
St. Joseph's Behavioral Health Center (Stockton)
St. Joseph's Medical Center (Stockton)
St. Mary Medical Center (Long Beach)
St. Mary's Medical Center (San Francisco)
Woodland Healthcare
Nevada
St. Rose Dominican Hospital Rose de Lima Campus (Henderson)
St. Rose Dominican Hospital San Martín Campus (Las Vegas)
St. Rose Dominican Hospital Siena Campus (Henderson)

PRODUCTS/OPERATIONS

Sponsoring Organizations
Congregation of the Dominican Sisters of St. Catherine of Siena of Kenosha (Kenosha, Wisconsin)
Congregation of the Sisters of Charity of the Incarnate Word (Houston, Texas)
Sisters of Mercy of the Americas, West Midwest Community (Omaha, Nebraska; formerly Auburn Regional Community of the Sisters of Mercy and Burlingame Regional Community of the Sisters of Mercy in California)
Sisters of St. Dominic, Congregation of the Most Holy Rosary (Adrian, Michigan)
Sisters of St. Francis of Penance and Christian Charity, St. Francis Province (Redwood City, California)
Sisters of the Third Order of St. Dominic, Congregation of the Most Holy Name (San Rafael, California)

COMPETITORS

ALEXIAN BROTHERS HEALTH SYSTEM
ASCENSION HEALTH
COMMONSPIRIT HEALTH
HOSPITAL SISTERS HEALTH SYSTEM
JEWISH HOSPITAL & ST. MARY'S HEALTHCARE, INC.
NEW YORK CITY HEALTH AND HOSPITALS CORPORATION
PROVIDENCE HEALTH & SERVICES
SISTERS OF CHARITY OF LEAVENWORTH HEALTH SYSTEM, INC.
ST. JOSEPH HEALTH SYSTEM
UNIHEALTH FOUNDATION

HISTORICAL FINANCIALS
Company Type: Private

Income Statement — FYE: June 30

	REVENUE ($mil)	NET INCOME ($mil)	NET PROFIT MARGIN	EMPLOYEES
06/19	9,916	119	1.2%	55,494
06/09	8,957	(799)	—	—
Annual Growth	1.0%	—	—	—

2019 Year-End Financials
Return on assets: 0.8%   Cash ($ mil.): 1,845
Return on equity: 2.3%
Current Ratio: 1.00

DIGNITY HEALTH MEDICAL FOUNDATION

Auditors: KPMG LLP SAN FRANCISCO CA

LOCATIONS

HQ: DIGNITY HEALTH MEDICAL FOUNDATION
3400 DATA DR, RANCHO CORDOVA, CA 956707956
Phone: 916 851-2000
Web: WWW.DIGNITYHEALTH.ORG

HISTORICAL FINANCIALS
Company Type: Private

Income Statement — FYE: June 30

	REVENUE ($mil)	NET INCOME ($mil)	NET PROFIT MARGIN	EMPLOYEES
06/14	570	17	3.1%	1,000
06/09	297	0	0.1%	—
Annual Growth	13.9%	120.7%	—	—

2014 Year-End Financials
Return on assets: 9.4%   Cash ($ mil.): 31
Return on equity: 19.7%
Current Ratio: 1.40

DIRECT RELIEF FOUNDATION

Direct Relief International wants to relieve the health problems of people around the world. The not-for-profit organization is dedicated to providing health care support and emergency relief to people in developing countries, as well as victims of disasters and war. Active in 50 US states and 70 countries, it gives medicine, supplies, and equipment through partnerships with local groups that make specific requests and coordinates distribution. The group also has partnered with nonprofit clinics and community health centers to provide medical care and medicine for homeless and low-income people in California. Direct Relief was founded in 1948 by Estonian immigrant William Zimdin.

LOCATIONS

HQ: DIRECT RELIEF FOUNDATION
6100 WALLACE BECKNELL RD, SANTA BARBARA, CA 931173265
Phone: 805 964-4767
Web: WWW.DIRECTRELIEF.ORG

COMPETITORS

AMERICARES FOUNDATION, INC.
BRITISH RED CROSS SOCIETY
CANCER CARE, INC.
HELEN KELLER INTERNATIONAL
VOLUNTEERS OF AMERICA, INC.

HISTORICAL FINANCIALS
Company Type: Private

Income Statement — FYE: June 30

	REVENUE ($mil)	NET INCOME ($mil)	NET PROFIT MARGIN	EMPLOYEES
06/21	1,942	20	1.0%	2
06/20	3	(4)	—	—
06/19	21	10	47.3%	—
06/17	1,114	105	9.5%	—
Annual Growth	14.9%	(33.9%)	—	—

2021 Year-End Financials
Return on assets: 2.0%   Cash ($ mil.): 185
Return on equity: 2.1%
Current Ratio: —

DISTRICT OF COLUMBIA WATER & SEWER AUTHORITY

Auditors: KPMG LLP WASHINGTON DC

LOCATIONS

HQ: DISTRICT OF COLUMBIA WATER & SEWER AUTHORITY
5000 OVERLOOK AVE SW, WASHINGTON, DC 200325212
Phone: 202 787-2000
Web: WWW.DCWATER.COM

HISTORICAL FINANCIALS
Company Type: Private

Income Statement — FYE: September 30

	REVENUE ($mil)	NET INCOME ($mil)	NET PROFIT MARGIN	EMPLOYEES
09/21	770	187	24.4%	1,100
09/20	736	222	30.3%	—
09/19	705	165	23.4%	—
09/17	643	194	30.2%	—
Annual Growth	4.6%	(0.9%)	—	—

2021 Year-End Financials
Return on assets: 2.2%   Cash ($ mil.): 193
Return on equity: 7.1%
Current Ratio: 1.40

DITECH HOLDING CORPORATION

Walter Investment Management does its best to collect from the credit-challenged. The firm owns and services residential mortgages (particularly those of the subprime and nonconforming variety) for itself as well as for government sponsored entities, government agencies, third-party securitization trusts, and other credit owners. Operating through subsidiaries Walter Mortgage Company; Hanover Capital; Marix Servicing; Ditech; and third-party credit servicer Green Tree, Walter Investment Management services 2 million residential loan accounts with unpaid balances of $256 billion, making it one of the 10 largest mortgage servicers in the US. The firm also originates residential loans, including reverse loans.The firm filed for Chapter 11 bankruptcy in 2017 and is expected to emerged from it, less $800 million in debt overhang, in early 2018.

Operations

Walter Investment Management operates three main business segments. Its Servicing segment, which generates more than 50% of Walter's revenue, mostly services mortgage loans for third-party creditors and its own mortgage loan portfolio, on a fee-for-service basis. Following the simplification of its business in 2015, the segment also consists of an insurance agency serving residential loan borrowers and credit owners, and a collections agency that performs collections of post charge-off deficiency balances for third parties and Walter's own portfolio. It also holds the assets and mortgage-backed debt of the Residual Trusts.

As one of the US' top 20 largest mortgage loan originators, Walter's Origination segment (32% of revenue) purchases and originates mortgage loans that are sold to third parties, with servicing rights generally retained. The Reverse Mortgage segment (10% of revenue) purchases and originates securitized loans backed by secured borrowings, services loans for third-party credit owners and its portfolio, and also provides complementary reverse mortgage services like property management and dispositions.

Geographic Reach

The Tampa-based firm has offices across the US.

Sales and Marketing

Walter's origination business sells nearly all of its mortgage loans into the secondary market for securitization or private investors as whole loans. It sells conventional conforming and government-backed mortgage loans through agency-sponsored securitizations where mortgage-backed securities are made and sold to third-party investors. Its non-conforming mortgage loans are sold to private investors.

The firm's consumer direct retail channel originates reverse loans through call centers, and purchases leads from lead purveyors or through advertising campaigns. The wholesale channel sources reverse loans from a broker network. The correspondent channel buys reverse loans from a correspondents network in the marketplace.

Financial Performance

Walter Investment Management's revenues and profits have mostly trended higher over the past few years, thanks to regular loan portfolio acquisitions as well as acquisitions of other servicing companies and financial firms.

The firm's revenue reversed course in 2014, however, diving 18% to $1.49 billion for the year. Most of the decline came from the Servicing division, which suffered from a $278 million decrease in fair value of servicing rights due to market-driven changes. The Origination segment's income fell by 24% on lower loan sales due to a shift in volume from the higher-margin consumer retention channel to the lower-margin correspondent lending channel.

Revenue declines coupled with an $82.3 million- impairment charge caused Walter to suffer a net loss of $110.33 million in 2014. The impairment charge came after an evaluation found its reverse mortgage's goodwill was less than its carrying value. Walter's operations continued to use more cash than it produced -- operations used $204 million -- though its cash levels improved greatly from the year before as it sold a higher volume of loans in relation to originated loans given the ramp up of its mortgage loan originations business in 2013.

Strategy

Walter Investment hopes to tap into growing demand from big lenders looking to shift their debt servicing functions to outside firms. A rise in borrower delinquencies and foreclosures following the recession has forced traditional loan servicers and owners, such as banks, to look for third-party assistance. Accordingly, part of Walters' growth strategy focuses on acquiring and servicing large loan portfolios that other banks and other financial companies haven't been able to successfully collect on.

The firm also hopes to grow its consumer-facing origination business, seeking more cross-sell opportunities as well as opportunities to grow its consumer direct and consumer retail channels to meet demand for low-cost mortgage loans in the market. To this end, in 2015, it planned to leverage its well known Ditech brand (while saving $75 million in annual costs) by consolidating its Ditech and Green Tree Servicing into a single company: Ditech, a Walter company.

In early 2017 the company agreed to sell Green Tree Insurance Agency to Assurant for $125 million, thereby focusing further on its core operations.

Mergers and Acquisitions

In early 2013, in taking advantage of the opportunity to further expand its servicing portfolio, Walter closed on two separate purchases (from Bank of America and Residential Capital, LLC) of Fannie Mae mortgage serving rights for loans totaling $132 billion in unpaid principal balance.

Also in 2013, Walter Investment Management acquired a $12 billion reverse mortgage servicing portfolio from Wells Fargo. The portfolio, with $12.2 billion in unpaid balance, houses more than 76,000 loans. The portfolio transferred to Walter's wholly-owned subsidiary, Reverse Mortgage Solutions, and doubled the size of its serviced book.

Company Background

The company entered the reverse mortgage business in late 2012 with the purchase of Reverse Mortgage Solutions (RMS) for some $120 million. RMS provided servicing, origination, asset management, and technology services to the fast-growing reverse mortgage industry.

In 2011, Walter Investment Management increased its loan portfolio and transformed into a fee-based service provider when it paid $1 billion for GTCS Holdings, the parent of Green Tree Servicing. As a result, Walter Investment Management no longer qualified as a real estate investment trust (REIT). The Green Tree acquisition represented a dramatic increase the size and scope of Walter Investment Management's business. The company's servicing portfolio grew by 50% and nearly 2,000 employees were added. Green Tree also increased Walter Investment Management's geographic footprint by adding 27 offices in the US.

Walter Investment Management was created in 2009 when Hanover Capital Mortgage merged with the home financing business of Walter Industries (now Walter Energy). Walter Energy was spun off after the closure of troubled homebuilder Jim Walter Homes.

EXECUTIVES

RISK, Alfred W Young Junior
Chief Human Resources Officer*, Elizabeth F Monahan
CLO*, John J Haas
Auditors : ERNST & YOUNG LLP PHILADELPHI

LOCATIONS

HQ: DITECH HOLDING CORPORATION
500 OFFICE CENTER DR # 400, FORT WASHINGTON, PA 190343219
Phone: 844 714-8603
Web: WWW.DITECH.COM

PRODUCTS/OPERATIONS

2014 Sales

	$ in mil.	% of total
Servicing	563.5	37
Originations	481.8	32
Reverse Mortage	157.2	10
ARM	58.2	4
Insurance	71.0	5
Loans & Residuals	134.5	9
Other	41.2	3
Elliminations	(20.2)	-
Total	1,487.2	100

COMPETITORS

ARLINGTON ASSET INVESTMENT CORP.
FIRST EAGLE PRIVATE CREDIT, LLC
GUILD MORTGAGE COMPANY
NATIONSTAR MORTGAGE HOLDINGS INC.
OCWEN FINANCIAL CORPORATION
PENNYMAC MORTGAGE INVESTMENT TRUST
PHH CORPORATION
PNMAC HOLDINGS, INC.
REDWOOD TRUST, INC.
THE SOUTHERN BANC COMPANY INC

HISTORICAL FINANCIALS
Company Type: Private

Income Statement — FYE: December 31

	REVENUE ($mil)	NET INCOME ($mil)	NET PROFIT MARGIN	EMPLOYEES
12/18	658	(205)	—	3,800
12/17	831	(426)	—	—
12/16	995	(529)	—	—
12/15	1,274	(263)	—	—
Annual Growth	(19.7%)	—	—	—

2018 Year-End Financials
Return on assets: (-1.8%)   Cash ($ mil.): 187
Return on equity: —
Current Ratio: —

DO IT BEST CORP.

Do it Best is a member-owned wholesaler of hardware, lumber, builder supplies, and related products, operating as a wholesaler cooperative. Members are located principally in the US, with some member locations abroad. Only dealers in hardware, lumber, builder supplies, and related products are eligible to hold shares in the company. Besides the usual tools and building materials, merchandise includes automotive items, bicycles, camping gear, housewares, office supplies, and small appliances. Customers also can have products specially shipped to their local stores through Do it Best's e-commerce site. The company only ships to nearly 50 contiguous US, as well as Alaska, Hawaii, and Washington DC. The company was founded in 1945.

Operations
Do it Best offers a wide variety of products, including hardware, outdoor living, farm and ranch, holiday decoration and supplies, building materials, sporting goods, cleaning supplies, clothing and apparel, electronics, food and snacks, and hand tools, among others. Its popular categories include caulk and sealant, cleaning chemicals, lawn and plant care, wall materials, canning equipment and supplies, circuit breakers, power equipment parts and accessories, and pipe fittings. The company has a large network of more than 3,800 independently owned retailers.

Geographic Reach
Based in Fort Wayne, Indiana, Do it Best operates warehouses in Illinois, South Carolina, Ohio, Nevada, New York, Missouri, Texas, and Oregon. The company also has regional lumber centers located in Minnesota, Indiana, South Carolina, New York, and Oregon.

Sales and Marketing
Nearly all of the Do it Best's sales are to dealer-members. Members are required to buy 20 voting common shares at $50 per share on becoming a member and, in some cases, shares of nonvoting common stock. The company participates in cooperative advertising arrangements with its vendors. Its advertising and promotion costs, net, charged to operation in 2022, 2021, and 2020 were approximately $10.4 million, $10.1 million, and $11.9 million, respectively.

Company Background
Formerly named Hardware Wholesalers, Do it Best was founded in 1945 in Fort Wayne, Indiana, by Arnold Gerberding. The company launched its doitbest.com e-commerce site in 1996.

EXECUTIVES
Business Development*, Nick Talarico
Auditors: CLIFTONLARSONALLEN LLP INDIAN

LOCATIONS
HQ: DO IT BEST CORP.
1626 BROADWAY, FORT WAYNE, IN 468024377
Phone: 260 748-5300
Web: WWW.DOITBESTONLINE.COM

COMPETITORS
ACE HARDWARE CORPORATION
AMERIMARK HOLDINGS, LLC
CENTRAL PURCHASING, LLC
GREAT LAKES ACE HARDWARE, INC.
MENARD, INC.
NORTHERN TOOL & EQUIPMENT COMPANY, INC.
ORCHARD SUPPLY COMPANY, LLC
SNAP-ON INCORPORATED
UNITED HARDWARE DISTRIBUTING COMPANY
W. E. AUBUCHON CO., INC.

HISTORICAL FINANCIALS
Company Type: Private

Income Statement — FYE: June 25

	REVENUE ($mil)	NET INCOME ($mil)	NET PROFIT MARGIN	EMPLOYEES
06/16	2,925	0	0.0%	1,519
06/11	2,328	0	0.0%	—
06/10	2,296	0	0.0%	—
Annual Growth	4.1%	(5.7%)	—	—

2016 Year-End Financials
Return on assets: 0.1%   Cash ($ mil.): 20
Return on equity: 0.2%
Current Ratio: 1.40

DOCTOR'S ASSOCIATES INC.

Doctor's Associates owns the Subway chain of sandwich shops, the world's largest quick-service restaurant chain by number of locations, surpassing burger giant McDonald's. The company boasts more than 44,000 restaurants in greater than 110 countries. Virtually all Subway restaurants are franchised and offer such fare as hot and cold sub sandwiches, turkey wraps, and salads. The widely recognized eateries are in freestanding buildings, as well as in airports, convenience stores, sports facilities, and other locations.

Operations
With the ability to fit one of its restaurants almost anywhere, Subway can offer franchisees lower startup costs as compared to other concepts that require large areas for food preparation or dining space. Many of Subway's franchisees operate just a single location, but a few oversee a large estate.

Local operators, who own the individual restaurants, use the Subway name in exchange for royalties and other fees. This allows Doctor's Associates to expand its sandwich business without the cost of construction and operation. (Domiciled in Florida, the company operates its franchising business largely through Connecticut-based affiliate World Franchise Headquarters.)

Geographic Reach
The company's network of eateries, stretching from Afghanistan to Zambia, is a testament to how effectively the franchising model can be used to expand a dining concept. Part of the reason for Subway's success is the portability and adaptability of the dining concept. The sandwich restaurants can be found in a vast array of locations, including shopping center food courts, suburban strip malls, and even military bases. The company is particularly focused on expanding its international presence in Asia and Central Europe.

Sales and Marketing
Like its fast-food brethren, Subway relies heavily on continuous television advertising and sponsorships to promote itself. It has marketing partnerships with dozens of companies and celebrity spokespeople.

Strategy
The Subway chain has tapped into the health food and weight loss zeitgeist in the US, prominently featuring in its advertising Jared Fogle, a man who famously lost nearly 250 lbs. by switching to a Subway sandwich

diet. The chain continues to tout the health benefits of its sandwiches over traditional burgers and fries by introducing new low-fat menu items.

Subway has been developing an upscale concept called Subway CafÃ©. The new format, conceived for office buildings and other high-end locations, is larger than the average Subway restaurant and features coffee, espresso, lattes, and hot chocolate along with an expanded breakfast menu.

The company also seeks partnerships with other food brands to generate buzz around its products. In 2019 the company partnered with Halo Top Creamery to introduce Halo Top milkshakes at almost 1,000 Subway restaurants. That year it also collaborated with Hubert's Lemonade to offer the company's drinks at its locations. The company also began testing a Kings Hawaiian-branded bread offering at three cities.

The company is investing in improving the look of its operations. It has remodeled nearly 1,400 franchise locations and has around 900 remodels underway. In 2019 Subway announced a grant program that will cover 25% of remodeling costs for more than 10,500 restaurants.

Company Background

Co-founders DeLuca and Buck opened the first Subway in 1965.

HISTORY

In 1965 17-year-old Fred DeLuca dreamed of becoming a doctor while working as a stock boy in a Bridgeport, Connecticut, hardware store to earn college tuition. It wasn't enough, so he cornered family friend Peter Buck at a backyard barbecue and asked for advice. Buck, a nuclear physicist, suggested DeLuca open a submarine sandwich shop and put up $1,000 to get him started.

As the summer of 1965 was coming to an end, DeLuca rented a small location in a remote area of Bridgeport, opened Pete's Super Submarines, and there he sold foot-long sandwiches. On the first day the sandwiches were so popular that DeLuca hired his own customers to work behind the counter; by the end of the day, he had sold out of all his supplies. The sandwiches continued to be popular for a while, but within a few months the shop started losing money, and DeLuca and Buck found that selling submarine sandwiches was a seasonal business. They decided they could create an illusion of success by opening a second location and then a third. The third store was finally successful, partly because of its more visible location and increased marketing and partly because of a new name -- Subway.

DeLuca and Buck had set a goal of 32 shops opened by 1975, but they had only 16 by 1974. They realized that the only way they could reach their goal in one year was to license the Subway name. The first franchise opened that year in Wallingford, Connecticut, and they opened 32 by the end of 1975. The partners hit 100 by 1978, then 200 by 1983, and DeLuca set a new goal: 5,000 Subway shops by 1994. The first international Subway opened in Bahrain in 1984, and DeLuca achieved his goal of 5,000 shops by 1990.

During the 1990s DeLuca experimented with several other franchise concepts, including We Care Hair (budget styling salons), Cajun Joe's (spicy fried chicken), and Q Burgers. But none of these ventures fared as well as his sandwich empire. As Subway grew, however, controversy surrounding its treatment of franchisees began to surface. A Federal Trade Commission investigation of the company was dropped in 1993, but Subway continued to battle franchisees complaining about broken contracts, market over-saturation (and, therefore, too much competition and self-cannibalization), and what the franchisees viewed as unreasonably high royalty fees.

In spite of its franchising troubles, Subway kept growing. It expanded into Russia and China in the mid-1990s, and opened its 11,000th restaurant in 1995. In 1997 Subway inked deals with the Army, Navy, and Air Force exchange services to bring Subway units to military bases. Two years later the company opened its 14,000th restaurant in Mount Gambier, Australia, an event that coincided with Subway's renewed push to expand internationally.

The company got some unexpected publicity in 1999 when 22-year-old Jared Fogle claimed that he dropped 245 pounds from his 425-pound frame by subsisting on a diet of Subway turkey sandwiches. Subway helped Fogle extend his 15 minutes of fame by featuring him and his oversized pants in a TV commercial. (The company has since built an entire campaign around Fogle that features other weight watchers attributing their success to Jared and Subway.) Subway introduced its largest menu initiative ever in 2000 when it unveiled its Subway Selects Gourmet Sandwiches, adding 13 items to the menu. In April 2001 the company opened its 15,000th store.

Also that year Buck retired as chairman, but stayed on as a member of the board of directors. Becoming one of the fastest-growing franchises in the world, Subway expanded from 16,000 locations in 2002 to more than 22,000 stores by the end of 2004.

All US Subway outlets switched from Pepsi to Coke products in 2005. Two years later the chain surpassed 21,000 locations in the US.

LOCATIONS

HQ: DOCTOR'S ASSOCIATES INC.
  325 SUB WAY, MILFORD, CT 064613081
Phone: 203 877-4281
Web: ORDER.SUBWAY.COM

COMPETITORS

CAESAR LITTLE ENTERPRISES INC
CHECKERS DRIVE-IN RESTAURANTS, INC.
DINE BRANDS GLOBAL, INC.
DOMINO'S PIZZA, INC.
FRIENDLY'S ICE CREAM, LLC
KAHALA BRANDS, LTD.
MCDONALD'S CORPORATION
SBARRO INC.
SONIC CORP.
WHATABURGER RESTAURANTS LLC

HISTORICAL FINANCIALS

Company Type: Private

Income Statement — FYE: December 31

	REVENUE ($mil)	NET INCOME ($mil)	NET PROFIT MARGIN	EMPLOYEES
12/10	1,049	7	0.7%	650
12/08	926	6	0.7%	—
12/07	780	5	0.7%	—
Annual Growth	10.4%	9.8%	—	—

2010 Year-End Financials
Return on assets: 6.5%   Cash ($ mil.): 43
Return on equity: 49.4%
Current Ratio: 1.00

DOCTORS HOSPITAL AT RENAISSANCE, LTD.

LOCATIONS

HQ: DOCTORS HOSPITAL AT RENAISSANCE, LTD.
  5501 S MCCOLL RD, EDINBURG, TX 785395503
Phone: 956 362-8677
Web: WWW.DHRHEALTH.COM

HISTORICAL FINANCIALS

Company Type: Private

Income Statement — FYE: December 31

	REVENUE ($mil)	NET INCOME ($mil)	NET PROFIT MARGIN	EMPLOYEES
12/16	580	80	13.9%	176
12/14	436	63	14.4%	—
Annual Growth	15.3%	13.1%	—	—

2016 Year-End Financials
Return on assets: 17.7%   Cash ($ mil.): 49
Return on equity: 44.6%
Current Ratio: 2.00

DOCTORS MEDICAL CENTER OF MODESTO, INC.

LOCATIONS
HQ: DOCTORS MEDICAL CENTER OF MODESTO, INC.
1441 FLORIDA AVE, MODESTO, CA 953504404
Phone: 209 578-1211
Web: WWW.DMC-MODESTO.COM

HISTORICAL FINANCIALS
Company Type: Private

Income Statement — FYE: May 31

	REVENUE ($mil)	NET INCOME ($mil)	NET PROFIT MARGIN	EMPLOYEES
05/16	587	86	14.6%	2,000
05/09	306	4	1.4%	—
Annual Growth	9.8%	52.8%	—	—

2016 Year-End Financials
Return on assets: 28.1% Cash ($ mil.): —
Return on equity: 41.1%
Current Ratio: 2.30

DON FORD SANDERSON INC

LOCATIONS
HQ: DON FORD SANDERSON INC
6400 N 51ST AVE, GLENDALE, AZ 853014600
Phone: 623 842-8600
Web: WWW.SANDERSONFORD.COM

HISTORICAL FINANCIALS
Company Type: Private

Income Statement — FYE: December 31

	REVENUE ($mil)	NET INCOME ($mil)	NET PROFIT MARGIN	EMPLOYEES
12/14	671	4	0.7%	416
12/13	692	5	0.8%	—
12/12	590	3	0.6%	—
Annual Growth	6.6%	11.2%	—	—

2014 Year-End Financials
Return on assets: 4.1% Cash ($ mil.): 6
Return on equity: 14.1%
Current Ratio: 1.50

DORMITORY AUTHORITY - STATE OF NEW YORK

EXECUTIVES
Chief Administrator*, Maryanne Gridley
PUBLIC Finance*, Cheryl Ishmael
POLICY Program Developer*, Thomas E Guiley
Deputy Executive Director*, Micheal Coorigan
Chief of Staff*, Caroline Griffin
Auditors : KPMG LLP ALBANY NY

LOCATIONS
HQ: DORMITORY AUTHORITY - STATE OF NEW YORK
515 BROADWAY STE 100, ALBANY, NY 122072964
Phone: 518 257-3000
Web: WWW.DASNY.ORG

HISTORICAL FINANCIALS
Company Type: Private

Income Statement — FYE: March 31

	REVENUE ($mil)	NET INCOME ($mil)	NET PROFIT MARGIN	EMPLOYEES
03/11	2,075	(115)	—	625
03/06	1,693	(40)	—	—
03/05	0	0	—	—
Annual Growth	—	—	—	—

2011 Year-End Financials
Return on assets: (-0.3%) Cash ($ mil.): 452
Return on equity: (-27.6%)
Current Ratio: 1.10

DOUGLAS COUNTY SCHOOL DISTRICT

Auditors : CLIFTONLARSONALLEN LLP GREENW

LOCATIONS
HQ: DOUGLAS COUNTY SCHOOL DISTRICT
620 WILCOX ST, CASTLE ROCK, CO 801041730
Phone: 303 387-0100
Web: WWW.DCSDK12.ORG

HISTORICAL FINANCIALS
Company Type: Private

Income Statement — FYE: June 30

	REVENUE ($mil)	NET INCOME ($mil)	NET PROFIT MARGIN	EMPLOYEES
06/13	562	(0)	—	8,000
06/10	551	(11)	—	—
06/08	480	(48)	—	—
06/07	0	0	—	—
Annual Growth	—	—	—	—

2013 Year-End Financials
Return on assets: 4.8% Cash ($ mil.): —
Return on equity: (-0.1%)
Current Ratio: —

DPR CONSTRUCTION, INC.

DPR is one of the nation's leading general contractors and ranks among the top general contractors in the nation. The employee-owned firm provides general contracting and construction management services for the advanced technology/mission-critical life sciences, health care, higher education, and corporate office markets. The construction firm specializes in developing retail stores, hospitals, data centers, clean rooms, laboratories, manufacturing facilities, and green buildings. Altogether, DPR Construction boasts more than 25 regional offices nationwide. Company head Doug Woods, former CEO Peter Nosler, and secretary/treasurer Ron Davidowski (the D, P, and R in DPR Construction) founded the firm in 1990.

Operations
DPR Construction has expertise in collaborative virtual building and Building Information Modeling (BIM), Integrating Project Delivery (IPD), sustainability, preconstruction, prefabrication, and other niche areas. DPR's Special Services Group focuses on small- to mid-size projects including building core upgrades, hospital renovations, office reconfigurations, roof replacements, and site improvements, among others.

Geographic Reach
To maintain a presence near customers, DPR boasts about 30 regional offices. Its operations span around 15 states, including Arizona, California, Colorado, North Carolina, Florida, Georgia, Maryland, Texas, Virginia, and Washington, DC. DPR also includes three international offices located in Netherlands, South Korea, and Singapore.

Sales and Marketing
DPR serves several core markets, including advanced technology, corporate offices, healthcare, higher education, and life sciences. Customers include Adobe Systems, AT&T, EVA Airways, Baptist Health Medical Center, CHRISTUS Health, Clif Bar & Company, Intuit, Facebook, and Kaiser Permanente.

Company Background
Company head Doug Woods, former CEO Peter Nosler, and secretary/treasurer Ron Davidowski (the D, P, and R in DPR Construction) founded the firm in 1990 with offices in Redwood City, CA and Sacramento, CA. In 1993, DPR ranks #1 on both San Francisco Business Times' and San Jose/Silicon Valley Business Journal's Fastest-Growing Private Companies in the bay Area lists.

Auditors : PRICEWATERHOUSECOOPERS LLP LO

LOCATIONS

HQ: DPR CONSTRUCTION, INC.
   1450 VETERANS BLVD, REDWOOD CITY, CA 940632617
Phone: 650 474-1450
Web: WWW.DPR.COM

Selected Offices
Atlanta
Austin, TX
Baltimore
Denver
Houston
Newport Beach, CA
Orlando, Florida
Pasadena, CA
Phoenix
Raleigh-Durham, NC
Redwood City, CA
Richmond, VA
Sacramento, CA
San Diego, CA
San Francisco, CA
San Jose, CA
Tampa, Florida
Washington, DC
West Palm Beach, FL

COMPETITORS

EMJ CORPORATION
GILBANE, INC.
HITT CONTRACTING, INC.
JAMES G. DAVIS CONSTRUCTION CORPORATION
LECHASE CONSTRUCTION SERVICES, LLC
MESSER CONSTRUCTION CO.
RENTENBACH CONSTRUCTORS INCORPORATED
RYAN COMPANIES US, INC.
SUFFOLK CONSTRUCTION COMPANY, INC.
THE YATES COMPANIES INC

HISTORICAL FINANCIALS
Company Type: Private

Income Statement — FYE: December 31

	REVENUE ($mil)	NET INCOME ($mil)	NET PROFIT MARGIN	EMPLOYEES
12/08	1,836	68	3.7%	8,002
12/00	1,958	25	1.3%	—
Annual Growth	(0.8%)	13.0%	—	—

2008 Year-End Financials
Return on assets: 13.0%   Cash ($ mil.): 162
Return on equity: 37.9%
Current Ratio: 1.50

DRISCOLL CHILDRENS HEALTH PLAN

Auditors: BKD LLP HOUSTON TX

LOCATIONS

HQ: DRISCOLL CHILDRENS HEALTH PLAN
   4525 AYERS ST, CORPUS CHRISTI, TX 784151401
Phone: 361 694-6432
Web: WWW.DRISCOLLHEALTHPLAN.COM

HISTORICAL FINANCIALS
Company Type: Private

Income Statement — FYE: December 31

	REVENUE ($mil)	NET INCOME ($mil)	NET PROFIT MARGIN	EMPLOYEES
12/19	711	(59)	—	49
12/14	385	(9)	—	—
12/13	317	1	0.4%	—
12/09	135	(0)	—	—
Annual Growth	18.0%	—	—	—

2019 Year-End Financials
Return on assets: (-32.3%)   Cash ($ mil.): 71
Return on equity: (-69.2%)
Current Ratio: —

DRIVETIME AUTOMOTIVE GROUP, INC.

In this story the ugly duckling changes into DriveTime Automotive Group. Formerly known as Ugly Duckling, the company is a used-car dealership chain that primarily targets low-income customers and those with less-than-stellar credit. To cater to subprime clients, it's a "buy here-pay here" dealer, meaning it finances and services car loans, rather than using outside lenders. DriveTime operates more than 125 dealerships in 50 US metropolitan areas in 24 mostly southern and western states. The company provides customers with a comprehensive end-to-end solution for their automotive needs, including the sale, financing, and maintenance of their vehicle.

Operations
The company's activities includes vehicle acquisition, vehicle reconditioning and distribution, vehicle sales, underwriting and finance, loan servicing and after sale support. DriveTime has sold more than 750,000 used cars to consumers of all credit types and services a $2 billion loan portfolio.

DriveTime's financing business operates under the name DT Acceptance Corporation. The unit generates about a quarter of the company's total revenues

The company also offers DriveCare, a 36-month/36,000 miled (5-Year/50,000 miled in some states) vehicle protection plan and extended powertrain coverage.

Geographic Reach
Phoenix-based DriveTime operates dealerships in 47 US metro areas throughout 24 states. More than a third of the dealerships are located in Florida and Texas.

Sales and Marketing
DriveTime markets its automotive products and services through TV commercials.

Strategy
DriveTime's long-term strategic goal is to expand its network of dealerships throughout the US, targeting metropolitan areas with populations of 500,000 to 3 million residents. In 2015 the company opened its first New Jersey location, in Williamstown. In 2014 it established its presence in the Chicago area with the opening of the Lombard location; it also opened first location in the Washington, DC, area.

The used car dealer is also expanding in Texas, opening a dealership in Corpus Christi in late 2013, its 20th in the Lone Star State.

As part of its business model, DriveTime acquires used vehicles at auction. In 2013 the company purchased more than 96,000 vehicles nationwide, primarily from used vehicle auctions.

That year DriveTime teamed up with fellow car dealer Manheim to form Go Auto Exchange, a new separate and independent wholesale auction company focused on independent dealers and the low-end vehicle segment.

Company venture Carvana (launched in early 2013), allows customers to buy its used cars online. Carvana expands the company's customer base by targeting customers outside its traditional credit-impaired, low-income cohort.

Company Background
Chairman Ernest Garcia III owns the company through his Verde Investments firm. In 2012 the company abandoned plans to split its finance and used vehicle retail operations by selling the financing arm to Santander Consumer USA and the used car dealerships to a group of third-party investors. Prior to that, DriveTime in early 2010 filed to go public, but withdrew the proposed offering seven months later. It with drew a second IPO attempt in 2014.

EXECUTIVES

Accounting Operations*, Maripaz Perez
Auditors: GRANT THORNTON LLP PHOENIX A

LOCATIONS

HQ: DRIVETIME AUTOMOTIVE GROUP, INC.
   1720 W RIO SALADO PKWY, TEMPE, AZ 852816590
Phone: 602 852-6600

2014 Stores	No.
Alabama	5
Arkansas	1
Arizona	6
California	5
Colorado	2
Delaware	1
Florida	21
Georgia	9
Illinois	2
Indiana	2
Kentucky	2
Maryland	2
Missouri	4
Mississippi	1
North Carolina	9
New Jersey	1
New Mexico	3
Nevada	2
Ohio	7
Oklahoma	3
South Carolina	4
Tennessee	6
Texas	22
Virginia	7
Total	127

COMPETITORS

AMERICA'S CAR-MART INC.
AUTONATION, INC.
AUTOTRADER.COM, INC.
CAR GIANT LIMITED
CARMAX, INC.
CARVANA CO.
COPART, INC.
FIRST ACCEPTANCE CORPORATION
MOTORPOINT GROUP PLC
UNITED ROAD SERVICES, INC.

HISTORICAL FINANCIALS

Company Type: Private

Income Statement — FYE: December 31

	REVENUE ($mil)	NET INCOME ($mil)	NET PROFIT MARGIN	EMPLOYEES
12/21	2,655	594	22.4%	2,021
12/17	3,267	(16)	—	—
12/15	2,372	32	1.4%	—
Annual Growth	1.9%	62.6%	—	—

2021 Year-End Financials
Return on assets: 11.1%   Cash ($ mil.): 108
Return on equity: 49.1%
Current Ratio: 1.30

DST SYSTEMS, INC.

Financial firms and health institutions focus on making clients wealthy and healthy, respectively. So, they might be wise to turn to DST Systems to handle their information processing tasks. The company provides information processing software and services to the mutual fund, insurance, retirement, and healthcare industries. The company's financial services segment offers software and systems used to handle a wide range of tasks including shareowner recordkeeping, investment management, and business process management. Among the healthcare offerings are claims adjudication and benefit and care management. DST makes most of its sales to customers in the US. The company was acquired by SS&C Technologies Holdings in 2018.

Operations

DST Systems' Domestic Financial Services business produces about 55% of revenue. The segment supports direct and intermediary sales of mutual funds, alternative investments, securities brokerage accounts, and retirement plans. Its software also handles reports to investors for confirmations, statements and tax forms, web access, and electronic delivery of documents. Systems include TA 2000 and TRAC. The company offers its AWD workflow software to clients and licenses it to third parties.

The International Financial Services segment, which accounts for almost a quarter of its revenue, offers investor and policyholder administration and technology services on a Remote and BPO basis in the UK and in Canada, Ireland, and Luxembourg through the IFDS joint venture.

The Healthcare Services segment, which provides medical and pharmacy claims administration, generates about a fifth of sales. The segment provides healthcare organizations with pharmacy and healthcare administration software and health outcomes optimization services. Specific tasks handled by DST software include claims adjudication, benefit management, care management, and business intelligence.

DST sold its North American Customer Communications business in 2016 for about $410 million, followed by the sale of its UK counterpart in 2017 for about $45 million.

DST operates its own data centers that provide secure infrastructure for its products and services.

Geographic Reach

The US is DST Systems' largest market, accounting for about 75% of sales. The UK is its largest international market with about 25% of sales. The Kansas City, Missouri-based company also has customers in Australia, Canada, and several other geographic markets.

Sales and Marketing

DST Systems markets its products directly and through subsidiaries, joint venture affiliates, and strategic alliances. The Domestic Financial Services business works in some areas through joint ventures with State Street Corp. In the US, the companies work through Boston Financial Data Services and through International Financial Data Services overseas.

DST's five largest customers overall account for about 25% of its revenue. The healthcare business is the more heavily concentrated with its five largest customers generating almost half of revenue, including nearly 20% from one customer. International Financial Services' five largest customers supply almost 55% of the segment's revenue with the largest customer generating nearly 25%.

Primary customers for Financial Services are mutual fund managers, insurers, and platform providers. The main healthcare customers are managed care organizations, preferred provider organizations, third-party administrators, dental, vision, and behavioral health organizations. The company also works with government sponsored programs such as the Health Insurance Exchanges that operate under the Patient Protection and Affordable Care Act, Medicare Advantage, Medicare Part D, and Medicaid.

Financial Performance

Charting DST Systems' five-year revenue record shows a dip to about $1.4 billion in 2015 before rebounding in 2015 and 2016, following a series of divestments and acquisitions.

In 2017 revenue jumped about 42% to $2.2 billion, which include reimbursements for out-of-pocket expenses (about 6% of total revenue). A good chunk of the increase came from BFDS and IFDS UK, in which DST took controlling interest in 2017.

Net income increased about 6% to $451 million in 2017 from 2016 due to the acquired interests in BFDS and IFDS UK. The company also recorded a gain on the sale of securities in 2017.

DST's cash fell to about $80 million in 2017 from $199 million in 2016. A difference was that the company had about $248 million from discontinued operations that it didn't have in 2017.

Strategy

The acquisition by DST Systems by SS&C Technologies unites two major players in financial software. The combined product portfolios cover a wide range of financial services and it provides SS&C with DST's healthcare component. The deal doesn't do much, however, to expand their geographic reach other than to deepen their UK business. The companies are not strangers. SS&C bought DST's Global Solutions subsidiary in 2014.

Mergers and Acquisitions

DST Systems has been active on the acquisition front to complement its product line and expand into new geographic areas. DST has balanced its acquisition strategy by purchasing technology providers and service providers, with an emphasis on business process outsourcing concerns and consulting firms.

In 2017 DST acquired the remaining interests in IFDS UK and BFDS that it didn't own for about $330 million. The businesses have been strategically important to DST, which intends to make enhancements as full owner.

In 2016 DST bought Kaufman Rossin Fund Services, a provider of administration services to the investment community, for $95 million. This acquisition provides DST with products for the alternative investment market.

HISTORY

After expanding into mutual funds during the early 1960s, Kansas City Southern Industries (KCSI) formed an electronic computer data processing unit to handle its mutual fund transactions, using technology designed originally for tracking railroad cars and their revenues.

In 1968 KCSI incorporated its data processing unit as DST Systems and began offering its services to the financial industry. To establish itself on the East Coast, in 1974 DST formed Boston Financial Data Services, a joint venture with State Street. Also during the 1970s DST entered the insurance market with a system for variable annuity policyholders.

In 1983 KCSI bought a majority stake in Janus Capital, a Denver-based mutual funds company. DST went public later that year; KCSI kept an 86% stake. Thomas McDonnell, president since the early 1970s, was named CEO in 1984.

EXECUTIVES

GENCOUNSEL, Paul G Igoe
Auditors : PRICEWATERHOUSECOOPERS LLP K

LOCATIONS

HQ: DST SYSTEMS, INC.
333 W 11TH ST FL 5, KANSAS CITY, MO 641051628
Phone: 816 654-6067
Web: WWW.DSTSYSTEMSINC.COM

COMPETITORS

BROADRIDGE FINANCIAL SOLUTIONS, INC.
CASTLIGHT HEALTH, INC.
CONDUENT INCORPORATED
EXAMWORKS GROUP, INC.
FIS CAPITAL MARKETS US LLC
FISERV, INC.
INNODATA INC.
SS&C TECHNOLOGIES HOLDINGS, INC.
STARTEK, INC.
TOTAL SYSTEM SERVICES, INC.

HISTORICAL FINANCIALS
Company Type: Private

Income Statement — FYE: December 31

	REVENUE ($mil)	NET INCOME ($mil)	NET PROFIT MARGIN	EMPLOYEES
12/17	2,218	452	20.4%	15,700
12/16	1,556	426	27.4%	—
12/15	2,825	358	12.7%	—
12/14	2,749	593	21.6%	—
Annual Growth	(6.9%)	(8.7%)	—	—

2017 Year-End Financials
Return on assets: 15.4%   Cash ($ mil.): 80
Return on equity: 36.4%
Current Ratio: 1.10

DUKE UNIVERSITY

Duke University has 15,551 undergraduate and graduate students. Duke School and Colleges includes Trinity College of Art and Sciences, the Fuqua School of Business, and the Pratt School of Engineering and more. The private institution, which boasts some 3,956 faculty members, also operates the Duke University Health System (DUHS). Duke was founded in 1924 but traces its roots to 1838.

Operations

Undergraduates at Duke enter either the Trinity College of Arts and Sciences or the Pratt School of Engineering. Top majors for Duke undergraduates include computer science, economics, public policy, biology, and biomedical engineering. The university's eight graduate schools cover law, divinity, medicine, nursing, business, public policy, the environment, and other fields. Academic sources of revenue include government and private grants and contracts, investment returns, tuition and fees, auxiliary enterprises, and contributions.

Duke's operating revenue come from Grants and Contracts (27%), Investment return designated for current operations (22%), Tuition and fees (16%), Private grants, contracts (12%), support from clinical operation (6%), auxiliary enterprises (6%) and other income (4%). Duke University Health System consists of Duke University Hospital, Duke Regional Hospital, Duke Raleigh Hospital, Duke University Affiliated Physicians, Inc. and Durham Casualty Company, Ltd.

Other Duke programs include student athletics (27 NCAA Division I teams), about a dozen research institutes, Duke Libraries (one of the top US private library systems), the Duke Marine Laboratory, and Duke University Press (publishes some 120 new books annually).

Like most universities, Duke is governed by a board of trustees, which serves as the institution's fiduciary. The board manages and oversees long-term financial health, strategic direction, educational policy, finances, and operations.

Geographic Reach

Most of Duke's operations occur in the heart of Durham, North Carolina. Its facilities include iconic architecture and classic landscape design. It covers 1,300 acres, which includes West Campus, East Campus, and Central Campus. Another 7,000 acres are designated as Duke Forest. At the heart of Duke Quest Campus lies Abele Quad and includes a Marine Lab campus located in Beaufort NC.

The Duke Kunshan University is a partnership campus between Duke and China's Wuhan University. Duke also partners with the National University of Singapore to operate the Duke-NUS Medical School in Singapore.

Sales and Marketing

Duke University provide campus tours for student applicants and its academic offerings are found in the school website.

Financial Performance

Total operating revenues for the University declined $18 million to $3 billion in fiscal 2021.

Duke's consolidated net asset base increased $7.9 billion in fiscal 2021 to $22.2 billion as of June 30, 2021. The increase is driven by strong investment performance.

Cash held by the University at the end of 2021 was $445.6 million. Cash provided by operations and financing activities were $174.7 million and $134.8 million, respectively. Cash used for investing activities was $445.4 billion, mainly for purchases of investments.

Strategy

Investment strategies employed by DUMAC and investment managers retained by DUMAC incorporate the use of various derivative financial instruments. DUMAC uses these instruments for a number of investment purposes, including hedging or altering exposure to certain asset classes and cost-effectively adding exposures to portions of the portfolio.

During fiscal 2021 and 2020, Duke, or external investment managers on Duke's behalf, entered into swap agreements, futures contracts, or forward contracts, and acquired warrants or rights to increase, reduce or otherwise modify investment exposures.

Company Background

Duke traces its roots to the founding of Union Institute in Randolph County, North Carolina, in 1838. Union Institute later became Trinity College, which in 1892 moved to Durham, where the Duke family became a primary benefactor. In 1924 American Tobacco Co. magnate James B. Duke established the Duke Endowment, which allowed Trinity College to expand into Duke University.

The original Durham campus became known as the East Campus, and a new West Campus opened in 1930. The East Campus served as a women's college until 1972, when the undergraduate colleges merged. The East Campus was transformed into a home for first-year students in 1995.

Auditors : KPMG LLP GREENSBORO NC

LOCATIONS

HQ: DUKE UNIVERSITY
324 BLACKWELL ST, DURHAM, NC 277013658
Phone: 919 684-8111
Web: WWW.DUKE.EDU

PRODUCTS/OPERATIONS

Selected Institutes
Center for the Study of Aging and Human Development
Duke Cancer Institute
Duke Global Health Institute
Duke Institute for Brain Sciences
Duke Science & Society Initiative
Duke University Energy Initiative
Institute for Genomic & Computational Biology
Interdisciplinary Studies

John Hope Franklin Humanities Institute
Kenan Institute for Ethics
Nicholas Institute for Environmental Policy Solutions
Trent Center for Bioethics, Humanities, and History of Medicine
Social Science Research Institute

Selected Schools and Colleges
Divinity School (Since 1926)
Duke Kunshan University (Since 2014; China)
Duke-NUS Medical School (Since 2005)
Fuqua School of Business (Since 1969)
Graduate School (Since 1926)
Nicholas School of the Environment (Since 1938)
Pratt School of Engineering (Since 1939)
Sanford School of Public Policy (Since 1971)
School of Law (Since 1904)
School of Medicine (Since 1930)
School of Nursing (Since 1931)
Trinity College of Arts & Sciences (Since 1859)

COMPETITORS

GWYNEDD MERCY UNIVERSITY
IMPERIAL COLLEGE LONDON LIMITED
KENT STATE UNIVERSITY
SYRACUSE UNIVERSITY
THE AMERICAN UNIVERSITY
THE COLLEGE OF WILLIAM & MARY
THE GEORGE WASHINGTON UNIVERSITY
THE JOHNS HOPKINS UNIVERSITY
UNIVERSITY OF ABERDEEN
UNIVERSITY SYSTEM OF MARYLAND

HISTORICAL FINANCIALS

Company Type: Private

Income Statement — FYE: June 30

	REVENUE ($mil)	NET INCOME ($mil)	NET PROFIT MARGIN	EMPLOYEES
06/12	4,611	(507)	—	8,852
06/05	1,832	246	13.5%	—
06/04	2,806	679	24.2%	—
Annual Growth	6.4%	—	—	—

2012 Year-End Financials
Return on assets: (-3.6%)   Cash ($ mil.): 526
Return on equity: (-5.2%)
Current Ratio: —

DUKE UNIVERSITY HEALTH SYSTEM, INC.

Duke University Health System is a world-class hospital and health care network supported by outstanding and renowned clinical faculty, nurses and care teams. In addition to its hospitals, Duke Health has an extensive, geographically dispersed network of outpatient facilities that include primary care offices, urgent care centers, multi-specialty clinics and outpatient surgery centers. Its Duke Health & Well-Being includes a medically-based weight loss program, medically-based fitness, wellness and rehabilitation programs at the Duke Health & Fitness Center and Duke Integrative Medicine, which combines evidence-based treatment with proven complementary therapies.

Operations

The health system operates through three hospitals: Duke University Hospital (DUH); Duke Regional Hospital (DRH); and Duke Raleigh Hospital (DRaH).

DUH is a quarternary care teaching hospital located on the campus of University in Durham, North Carolina, licensed for about 1,050 acute and specialty care beds, leased from Duke University, operated by the health system and providing patient care and serving as a site for medical education and clinical research provided by the Duke University School of Medicine. DUH generates more than 65% health system's total revenue.

DRaH (about 15% of revenue) is a community hospital located Raleigh, North Carolina, licensed for about 185 acute care beds, leased from the university operated by health system and providing patient care.

DRH (around 10% of revenue) is a full-service community hospital located in Durham, North Carolina, licensed for about 390 acute and specialty care beds and providing patient care; DRH is owned by Durham County, North Carolina and leased to the Durham County Corporation in which has in turn subleased DRH to the health system.

Duke HomeCare & Hospice offers hospice, home health and infusion services. Hospice care is offered to terminally ill patients in their home, skilled-nursing facilities, assisted-living facilities, and at our two inpatient facilities located in Hillsborough and Durham, North Carolina. Home health services are available to patients who are homebound and in need of nursing services, physical therapy, speech therapy, or occupational therapy. Infusion services are provided at home or at work for individuals who need intravenous therapy.

Geographic Reach

The Private Diagnostic Clinic owns and operates more than 140 primary and specialty care clinics in 10 counties in central and eastern North Carolina.

Financial Performance

The company's revenue increased by 8% from $4 billion in 2020 to $4.3 billion in 2021. This was primarily due to a higher sales volume across all of the patient revenue services' components.

In 2021, the company had net assets of $5.7 billion, a 63% increase from the previous year's net assets of $3.5 billion. This was mainly due to a higher sales volume for the year.

The company's cash at the end of 2021 was $98.5 million. Operating activities generated $285.2 million, while investing activities used $174.3 million, primarily for purchases of investments. Financing activities used another $170.2 million, mainly for transfers to the university.

Auditors: KPMG LLP WINSTON-SALEM NC

LOCATIONS

HQ: DUKE UNIVERSITY HEALTH SYSTEM, INC.
2301 ERWIN RD, DURHAM, NC 277054699

Phone: 919 684-8111
Web: WWW.DUKEHEALTH.ORG

Selected Facilities
Duke Clinic (Durham, North Carolina)
Duke Raleigh Hospital (Raleigh, North Carolina)
Duke University Hospital (Durham, North Carolina)
   Duke Children's Hospital & Health Center
Durham Regional Hospital (Durham, North Carolina)

PRODUCTS/OPERATIONS

2014 Sales

	$ mil	% of total
Patient service	2,437.7	50
Grants & contracts	1,097.9	22
Tuition & fees	408.6	8
Investment return	384.8	8
Auxiliary enterprises	186.5	5
Contributions	92.1	4
Net assets released from restrictions	46.5	2
Other	228.5	1
Total	4,882.6	100

Selected Services
AIDS Research and Treatment Center (DART)
Anesthesiology
Aortic Disease
Asthma and Allergies
Attention Deficit Hyperactivity Disorder
Breast Cancer
Cardiac Rehabilitation
Children's Health
Coronary Artery Disease
Dermatology
Developmental and Behavioral Pediatrics
Diabetes
Diet & Fitness Center
Duke Heart Center
Duke Medicine
Ear, Nose, Throat, Head & Neck Surgery
Eating Disorders
Endocrinology
Esophageal Cancer
Executive Health
Eye Center
Foot and Ankle
Gastroenterology
Gastrointestinal Cancer
General Orthopaedics
General and Consultative Heart Care
Geriatrics
Gynecologic Cancer
Gynecology
Health & Fitness Center
Health and Wellness
Healthy Lifestyles for Children
Heart Rhythm Services
Hematology
Hereditary Cancer
Hyperbaric, Diving, and Altitude Medicine
Infectious Diseases
Integrative Medicine
Knee Treatments
Leukemias, Lymphomas, and Myelomas
Lung Cancer
Men's Health
Neurological Disorders
Neuroscience
Obstetrics and Gynecology
Pain Disorders
Peripheral Vascular Disease
Prostate Cancer
Psychiatry
Pulmonology and Respiratory Medicine
Radiology
Research
Rheumatology and Immunology
Skin Cancer
Sleep Disorders
Smoking/Smoking Cessation
Speech and Audiology

Sports Medicine
Stroke Center
Transplants
Urologic Cancer
Valvular Heart Disease
Vascular Diseases
Women's Health
Women's Heart Care

COMPETITORS
CHARLESTON AREA MEDICAL CENTER, INC.
CHILDREN'S HOSPITAL MEDICAL CENTER
HMH HOSPITALS CORPORATION
NASSAU HEALTH CARE CORPORATION
NORTHWELL HEALTH, INC.
OHIOHEALTH CORPORATION
STANFORD HEALTH CARE
THE PENNSYLVANIA HOSPITAL OF THE UNIVERSITY OF PENNSYLVANIA HEALTH SYSTEM
UNIVERSITY HEALTH SYSTEMS OF EASTERN CAROLINA, INC.
UNIVERSITY HOSPITALS HEALTH SYSTEM, INC.

HISTORICAL FINANCIALS
Company Type: Private

Income Statement — FYE: June 30

	REVENUE ($mil)	NET INCOME ($mil)	NET PROFIT MARGIN	EMPLOYEES
06/22	4,483	123	2.7%	2,400
06/21	4,269	2,194	51.4%	—
06/20	3,951	(296)	—	—
06/19	3,836	160	4.2%	—
Annual Growth	5.3%	(8.4%)	—	—

2022 Year-End Financials
Return on assets: 1.4% Cash ($ mil.): 161
Return on equity: 2.1%
Current Ratio: 2.00

DUKE UNIVERSITY HOSPITAL

LOCATIONS
HQ: DUKE UNIVERSITY HOSPITAL
1 DUKE MEDICAL CTR, DURHAM, NC 277100007
Phone: 919 684-8111
Web: WWW.DUKEHEALTH.ORG

HISTORICAL FINANCIALS
Company Type: Private

Income Statement — FYE: June 30

	REVENUE ($mil)	NET INCOME ($mil)	NET PROFIT MARGIN	EMPLOYEES
06/19	2,597	25	1.0%	25
06/18	2,467	(0)	0.0%	—
Annual Growth	5.3%	—	—	—

2019 Year-End Financials
Return on assets: 2.0% Cash ($ mil.): —
Return on equity: 2.4%
Current Ratio: 1.40

DUTCHESS, COUNTY OF (INC)

EXECUTIVES
County Executive, Marcus J Molinaro
Auditors : DRESCHER & MALECKI LLP BUFFAL

LOCATIONS
HQ: DUTCHESS, COUNTY OF (INC)
626 DUTCHESS TPKE, POUGHKEEPSIE, NY 126031906
Phone: 845 486-2000
Web: CO.DUTCHESS.NY.US

HISTORICAL FINANCIALS
Company Type: Private

Income Statement — FYE: December 31

	REVENUE ($mil)	NET INCOME ($mil)	NET PROFIT MARGIN	EMPLOYEES
12/21	563	58	10.5%	1,852
12/20	564	4	0.8%	—
12/19	511	6	1.3%	—
12/18	549	9	1.8%	—
Annual Growth	0.8%	82.5%	—	—

2021 Year-End Financials
Return on assets: 4.5% Cash ($ mil.): 170
Return on equity: —
Current Ratio: —

DUVAL COUNTY SCHOOL BOARD (INC)

Auditors : MSL PA ORLANDO FLORIDA

LOCATIONS
HQ: DUVAL COUNTY SCHOOL BOARD (INC)
1701 PRUDENTIAL DR, JACKSONVILLE, FL 322078182
Phone: 904 390-2000
Web: DCPS.DUVALSCHOOLS.ORG

HISTORICAL FINANCIALS
Company Type: Private

Income Statement — FYE: June 30

	REVENUE ($mil)	NET INCOME ($mil)	NET PROFIT MARGIN	EMPLOYEES
06/21	1,443	76	5.3%	13,000
06/20	1,310	45	3.5%	—
06/19	1,279	22	1.8%	—
06/18	1,231	(7)	—	—
Annual Growth	5.4%	—	—	—

2021 Year-End Financials
Return on assets: 4.0% Cash ($ mil.): 115
Return on equity: 18.8%
Current Ratio: —

DYNCORP INTERNATIONAL LLC

Auditors : FRYE & COMPANY CPAS MANASSAS

LOCATIONS
HQ: DYNCORP INTERNATIONAL LLC
4800 WESTFIELDS BLVD # 400, CHANTILLY, VA 201514231
Phone: 571 722-0210
Web: WWW.DYNCORPINTERNATIONAL.COM

HISTORICAL FINANCIALS
Company Type: Private

Income Statement — FYE: April 3

	REVENUE ($mil)	NET INCOME ($mil)	NET PROFIT MARGIN	EMPLOYEES
04/09*	3,101	69	2.2%	100
03/08	2,139	47	2.2%	—
Annual Growth	44.9%	45.5%	—	—

*Fiscal year change

2009 Year-End Financials
Return on assets: 4.5% Cash ($ mil.): 200
Return on equity: 14.0%
Current Ratio: 2.00

EARTHLINK HOLDINGS, LLC

Auditors : ERNST & YOUNG LLP ATLANTA GE

LOCATIONS
HQ: EARTHLINK HOLDINGS, LLC
4001 N RODNEY PARHAM RD, LITTLE ROCK, AR 722122442
Phone: 501 748-7000

HISTORICAL FINANCIALS
Company Type: Private

Income Statement — FYE: December 31

	REVENUE ($mil)	NET INCOME ($mil)	NET PROFIT MARGIN	EMPLOYEES
12/16	959	7	0.8%	8
12/15	1,097	(43)	—	—
12/14	1,176	(72)	—	—
Annual Growth	(9.7%)	—	—	—

2016 Year-End Financials
Return on assets: 1.2% Cash ($ mil.): 51
Return on equity: 38.0%
Current Ratio: 1.00

EAST BAY MUNICIPAL UTILITY DISTRICT, WATER SYSTEM

It is part of the job description of East Bay Municipal Utility District (EBMUD) to keep the mud out of the drinking water. The utility provides potable water to 1.3 million people in a 331-square-mile area (which includes the cities of Alameda, Berkeley, and Oakland). Its wastewater system serves about 650,000 people in an 88-square-mile area of Alameda and Contra Costa counties along San Francisco Bay's east shore. EBMUD operates a wastewater treatment plant that treats wastewater collected by nine East Bay cities and cleans it before discharge to the San Francisco Bay.

Operations
EBMUD has three business segments: The Water System (the collection, transmission and distribution of water within Alameda and Contra Costa countries of California); The Wastewater System (the treatment of wastewater in Alameda, Albany, Berkeley, Emeryville, Oakland, Piedmont, and the Stege Sanitary District); and The Pension and Other Employee Benefit Trust, which manages the Employees' Retirement System (retirement benefits of the company employees).

Geographic Reach
EBMUD serves the cities and towns of Alameda, Albany, Berkeley, Danville, El Cerrito, Emeryville, part of Hayward, Hercules, Lafayette, Moraga, Oakland, Orinda, Piedmont, Pinole, part of Pleasant Hill, Richmond, San Leandro, San Pablo, San Ramon, part of Walnut Creek and the unincorporated communities of Alamo, Ashland, Blackhawk, Castro Valley, Cherryland, Crockett, Diablo, El Sobrante, Fairview, Kensington, North Richmond, Oleum, Rodeo, San Lorenzo and Selby.

Financial Performance
The company's overall fiscal 2014 revenues increased by 8%. Water sales grew by 9% due to a 10% increase in water rates and wastewater revenues increased by 6% resulting from a 9% rate increase. Offsetting these gains, EBMUD's power sales decreased by 42% as the result of lower precipitation and run-off of power generation.

In fiscal 2014 the company's net income decreased by 5% due to major increase raw water expenses and higher sewer treatment plant costs. This was offset by higher revenues and lower administration expenses.

EBMUD's operating cash flows increased by 14% in fiscal 2014 due to a rise in cash inflows from cash received from customers, offset by an increase in payments to suppliers.

Strategy
EBMUD's mission is to provide reliable, high quality water and wastewater services at fair and reasonable rates for the people of the East Bay. The company's 2010-2040 strategic plan calls for the company to obtain an additional 32 million gallons a day of supply. Future activities include infrastructure expansion, maintaining fiscal stability, and increasing rationing to preserve long term water supply. It is also committed to green energy. Some 90% of the electricity needed to power its main wastewater facility comes from a biomass-fired plant that uses waste from food, wineries, fats, greases, and oils.

The company has planned a two year budget (fiscal 2016 and 2017) of $1.8 billion that will fund needed water and wastewater capital projects that replace aging pipelines and rehab aging reservoirs, continue to pay for long-term water supply infrastructure, and account for the increasing costs of drought. Its active projects include Summit Reservoir Replacement; Round Hill Reservoir/Oakshire Place; Danville Pumping Plant Upgrades; Eden Reservoir Replacement; 39th and Bayo Street Pumping Plant; and Crossroads Reservoir.

Company Background
Formed in 1923 by residents of the San Francisco Bay area, EBMUD gets most of its water supply from the Mokelumne River watershed. The Sacramento River provides the balance.

EXECUTIVES
Corporate Secretary*, Rischa Cole
Auditors : LANCE SOLL & LUNGHARD LLP S

LOCATIONS
HQ: EAST BAY MUNICIPAL UTILITY DISTRICT, WATER SYSTEM
375 11TH ST, OAKLAND, CA 946074246
Phone: 866 403-2683
Web: WWW.EBMUD.COM

PRODUCTS/OPERATIONS
2013 Sales

	% of total
Water	79
Wastewater	16
Wet weather facilities charges	4
Electricity	1
Total	100

COMPETITORS
ARTESIAN RESOURCES CORPORATION
BRISTOL WATER HOLDINGS UK LIMITED
SAN ANTONIO WATER SYSTEM
SAN DIEGO COUNTY WATER AUTHORITY
SJW GROUP

HISTORICAL FINANCIALS
Company Type: Private

Income Statement FYE: June 30

	REVENUE ($mil)	NET INCOME ($mil)	NET PROFIT MARGIN	EMPLOYEES
06/22*	769	284	37.0%	1,511
09/21	228	94	41.6%	—
06/21	625	212	34.1%	—
06/20	693	244	35.2%	—
Annual Growth	5.3%	8.0%	—	—

*Fiscal year change

2022 Year-End Financials
Return on assets: 4.0%   Cash ($ mil.): 167
Return on equity: 10.7%
Current Ratio: 3.40

EAST TEXAS MEDICAL CENTER REGIONAL HEALTHCARE SYSTEM

East Texas Medical Center (ETMC) Regional Healthcare System works to meet the health care needs of residents of the Piney Woods. The not-for-profit health system operates more than a dozen hospitals across eastern Texas, along with behavioral, rehabilitation, and home health care businesses. Its flagship 450-bed Tyler location serves as the hub and referral center for satellite medical centers located in more rural locations. The system also runs numerous primary care and outpatient clinics throughout the region. Serving more than 300,000 patients each year, ETMC operates an emergency ambulance service subsidiary and a clinical laboratory, which provide services to the ETMC Regional Healthcare System.

Operations
The flagship ETMC Tyler facility offers specialized care for cancer and cardiovascular and neurological conditions. It is a Level I regional trauma center and provides diagnostic and outpatient surgery services.

The system is organized so that primary care is provided in the rural health clinics. Secondary care is also provided locally in the ETMC affiliate hospitals. High-level secondary and tertiary care is provided at ETMC Tyler.

Geographic Reach
ETMC serves the more than 1 million people who reside in East Texas communities. It caters to nearly 20 Texas counties, including Anderson, Camp, Cherokee, Ellis, Franklin, Freestone, Henderson, Hopkins, Houston, Panola, Red River, Rusk, Shelby, Smith, Trinity, Upshur, Van Zandt, and Wood. These communities range in size from fewer than 500 residents to more than 50,000.

Sales and Marketing
The Medicare program accounted for 50% of net patient revenues in 2012; Medicaid

contributed 12% of the same. Some 16% of total net patient service revenue came from commercial insurance carriers and preferred provider organizations.

Financial Performance

Due to an increase in patient service revenue, ETMC's revenue rose by 6% to $942 million in 2012 from $888 million in 2011. Net income for the same reporting period dropped some 92% to $1.1 million from $16 million due to rising salaries and wages and employee benefits expenses, as well as from an increase in loss from defined benefit pension adjustment.

Strategy

To keep up with the needs of its residents, the ETMC Regional Healthcare System works to expand its operations.

In 2013 ETMC Pittsburg broke ground on a 5,000-sq.-ft. expansion of the hospital's surgery department. Its East Texas Medical Center Regional Healthcare System also added a pair of emergency transport helicopters, valued at more than $9 million.

In 2012 the company completed $30-million expansion and renovation project at East Texas Medical Center Henderson, including a new emergency department, grand lobby, and clinic space. It also wrapped up the second phase of an expansion project at ETMC Fairfield that involved adding a new entrance, lobby, clinic space, cardiopulmonary rehabilitation facility, and administrative suite.

Its 100-bed Henderson Memorial Hospital joined the network in 2009 as ETMC Henderson. Soon after becoming part of the network, ETMC assisted its new affiliate with facility upgrades that included building new emergency department facilities, renovating old rooms, and installing new electrical and HVAC systems, all completed in 2011. ETMC also expanded its Trinity facility with a 15-bed patient wing at the cost of $7.4 million and expanded its mammography services at ETMC Cedar Creek Lake. A $35 million ETMC Quitman facility is expected to be completed in 2013.

ETMC also concentrates on upgrading its information systems. The healthcare system's data exchange organization, FirstNet Exchange, received a grant from the state of Texas in 2011 to develop and operate a secure health information network to support hospitals and clinicians.

LOCATIONS

HQ: EAST TEXAS MEDICAL CENTER REGIONAL HEALTHCARE SYSTEM
 1000 S BECKHAM AVE, TYLER, TX 757011908
Phone: 903 596-3267
Web: WWW.UTHEALTHEASTTEXAS.COM

PRODUCTS/OPERATIONS

Selected Health and Medical Services
Bariatric Surgery Center
Behavioral Health Center
Cancer Institute
Cardiovascular Institute
Digestive Disease Center
Emergency Services
Fitness Centers
Home Health
Neurological Institute
Orthopedic Institute
Plastic Surgery
Podiatry Care
Radiology and Imaging
Rehabilitation Center
Sleep Disorders Center
Specialty Hospital
Transplant Center
Urology Institute
Women's Health
Wound Healing Center

Selected East Texas Medical Center Hospitals
ETMC Athens
ETMC Carthage
ETMC Clarksville
ETMC Crockett
ETMC Fairfield
ETMC Gilmer
ETMC Henderson
ETMC Jacksonville
ETMC Lake Palestine
ETMC Mount Vernon
ETMC Pittsburg
ETMC Quitman
ETMC Rehabilitation Hospital (Tyler)
ETMC Specialty Hospital (Tyler)
ETMC Trinity
ETMC Tyler

COMPETITORS

ALTRU HEALTH SYSTEM
IASIS HEALTHCARE LLC
LEE MEMORIAL HEALTH SYSTEM
NOVANT HEALTH, INC.
SALINAS VALLEY MEMORIAL HEALTHCARE SYSTEMS
THE CLEVELAND CLINIC FOUNDATION
THE LANCASTER GENERAL HOSPITAL
THE RUTLAND HOSPITAL INC ACT 220
UNIVERSITY HEALTH SYSTEMS OF EASTERN CAROLINA, INC.
WELLMONT HEALTH SYSTEM

HISTORICAL FINANCIALS

Company Type: Private

Income Statement — FYE: October 31

	REVENUE ($mil)	NET INCOME ($mil)	NET PROFIT MARGIN	EMPLOYEES
10/08	876	30	3.4%	7,600
10/07	827	40	4.8%	—
10/06	837	0	0.0%	—
10/05	837	17	2.1%	—
Annual Growth	1.5%	20.4%	—	—

2008 Year-End Financials
Return on assets: 4.0%
Return on equity: 11.1%
Current Ratio: 3.20
Cash ($ mil.): 175

EASTERN MAINE HEALTHCARE SYSTEMS

Eastern Maine Healthcare Systems (EMHS) keeps the folks in the Pine Tree State feeling fine. With more than a dozen member hospitals and multiple medical practices and clinics, the organization offers patients emergency, primary, mental-health, laboratory, and other specialty services. It primarily serves eastern, central, and northern portions of rural Maine. Some hospitals include Eastern Maine Medical Center (410 beds), Acadia Hospital (100 beds), Aroostook Medical Center (75 beds), and Inland Hospital (50 beds). The system also operates long-term care, hospice, and home health facilities, as well as emergency transportation and administrative services businesses.

Operations

Besides its Acadia Hospital, Aroostook Medical Center, Eastern Maine Medical Center, and Inland Hospital, EMHS operates three smaller community hospitals with 15 to 30 beds each: Blue Hill Memorial Hospital, Charles A. Dean Memorial Hospital, and Sebasticook Valley Hospital. The system has affiliations with the Houlton Regional Hospital and Millinocket Regional Hospital.

Subsidiaries of EMHS include Affiliated Healthcare Systems (medical communications and retirement ventures), Affiliated Laboratory (pathology services), Affiliated Material Services (medical supplies distribution and pharmacies), and Affiliated Healthcare Management (transcription and employee services).

As part of its operations, EMHS also runs the Eastern Maine Medical Center Clinical Research Center, which performs clinical studies in several medical disciplines and diseases including cancer, hospital-acquired infections, heart disease, and physician best practices.

In fiscal 2014 EMHS had 105,629 emergency room visits; 32,964 inpatient and outpatient surgeries; 3,017 births; and 388,920 primary care visits.

The company's total Community Benefit that year was about $200 million, and its philanthropy giving was nearly $3 million.

Geographic Reach

Despite its name Eastern Maine Healthcare System serves those in eastern, central, and northern portions of rural Maine.

Strategy

EMHS continues to work collaboratively at the national level, looking at not only making a difference in healthcare in Maine, but to be a change leader throughout the country. The Northern New England Accountable Care Collaborative is creating resources necessary to propel the reinvention of care model. In addition, their work in the High Value Healthcare Collaborative (co-owned with Dartmouth, MaineHealth, and the University of Vermont Medical Center) this past year has been focused on sepsis care and prevention, patient engagement, and shared decision-making pilot projects.

In fiscal 2015, Maine's largest health insurer teamed up with Eastern Maine Healthcare Systems under a new venture aimed at keeping patients healthier while reducing costs. The deal involves Anthem Blue Cross and Blue Shield in Maine, EMHS, and an EMHS-led coalition of hospitals and physician practices across the state. EMHS and its partners have agreed to avoid any cost increase for services they deliver to 40,000 Anthem policyholders.

In mid-2014, EMHS completed a community health needs assessment of the northern two-thirds of Maine, including the counties of Aroostook, Cumberland, Hancock, Kennebec, Penobscot, Piscataquis, Somerset, and Washington. This report was seen as foundational to the company achieving its mission of improving the health and well-being of the communities it serves.

Company Background
The system was established in 1982.

Auditors : BERRY DUNN MCNEIL & PARKER LL

LOCATIONS

HQ: EASTERN MAINE HEALTHCARE SYSTEMS
43 WHITING HILL RD # 500, BREWER, ME 044121016
Phone: 207 973-7000
Web: WWW.NORTHERNLIGHTHEALTH.ORG

PRODUCTS/OPERATIONS

Selected Strategic Affiliates
Houlton Regional Hospital
Millinocket Regional Hospital
Member Hospitals
Acadia Hospital
Affiliated Healthcare Systems
Aroostook Medical Center
Beacon Health
Blue Hill Memorial Hospital
Charles A. Dean Memorial Hospital and Nursing Home
Dirigo Pines Retirement Community
Eastern Maine HomeCare
Eastern Maine Medical Center
Healthcare Charities
Inland Hospital
Rosscare
Sebasticook Valley Hospital

COMPETITORS

AMERICAN DENTAL PARTNERS, INC.
AMERICAN HOSPITAL ASSOCIATION
AMERICAN STAFFING ASSOCIATION
BLUE CROSS AND BLUE SHIELD ASSOCIATION
CEP AMERICA-CALIFORNIA
CHILD HEALTH CORPORATION OF AMERICA
HERITAGE VALLEY HEALTH SYSTEM, INC.
LEHIGH VALLEY HEALTH NETWORK, INC.
MEDIMPACT HEALTHCARE SYSTEMS, INC.
NORTHWESTERN MEMORIAL HEALTHCARE

HISTORICAL FINANCIALS
Company Type: Private

Income Statement — FYE: September 30

	REVENUE ($mil)	NET INCOME ($mil)	NET PROFIT MARGIN	EMPLOYEES
09/21	2,027	116	5.8%	8,175
09/20	1,753	(77)	—	—
09/19	1,744	16	0.9%	—
09/18	1,672	8	0.5%	—
Annual Growth	6.6%	136.3%	—	—

2021 Year-End Financials
Return on assets: 5.4%   Cash ($ mil.): 152
Return on equity: 13.9%
Current Ratio: 1.50

EASTERN MAINE MEDICAL CENTER

Auditors : BERRY DUNN MCNEIL & PARKER LL

LOCATIONS

HQ: EASTERN MAINE MEDICAL CENTER
489 STATE ST, BANGOR, ME 044016674
Phone: 207 973-7000
Web: WWW.NORTHERNLIGHTHEALTH.ORG

HISTORICAL FINANCIALS
Company Type: Private

Income Statement — FYE: September 30

	REVENUE ($mil)	NET INCOME ($mil)	NET PROFIT MARGIN	EMPLOYEES
09/20	803	(15)	—	1,119
09/19	932	53	5.7%	—
09/16	776	23	3.0%	—
09/15	720	41	5.8%	—
Annual Growth	2.2%	—	—	—

2020 Year-End Financials
Return on assets: (-1.6%)   Cash ($ mil.): 165
Return on equity: (-6.7%)
Current Ratio: 3.00

EATON CORPORATION

EXECUTIVES

Senior Vice President Corporate Development, David Foster
CIO, Katrina R Redmond Scp
Auditors : ERNST & YOUNG LLP CLEVELAND

LOCATIONS

HQ: EATON CORPORATION
1000 EATON BLVD, CLEVELAND, OH 441226058
Phone: 440 523-5000
Web: WWW.EATONELECTRICAL.COM

HISTORICAL FINANCIALS
Company Type: Private

Income Statement — FYE: December 31

	REVENUE ($mil)	NET INCOME ($mil)	NET PROFIT MARGIN	EMPLOYEES
12/15	6,925	821	11.9%	736
12/14	6,990	170	2.4%	—
Annual Growth	(0.9%)	382.9%	—	—

2015 Year-End Financials
Return on assets: 3.0%   Cash ($ mil.): —
Return on equity: 7.7%
Current Ratio: 0.30

EDUCATIONAL TESTING SERVICE

ETS is the world's largest private educational testing and measurement organization. It develops and administers the Graduate Record Examinations (GRE) and Test of English as a Foreign Language (TOEFL). The company develops and administers more than 50 million achievements, admissions, academic, and professional tests a year at more than 9,000 locations in more than 180 countries.

Operations
ETS Global B.V. is an assessment service provider delivering ETS's assessment solutions and expertise to educational and business communities. ETS Global deploys, among others, the TOEIC tests, the TOEFL tests and the GRE General Test to Europe, Middle East, Africa, Asia and South America. Its subsidiary Pipplet offers digital multi-language assessment that is used by recruiters and companies for screening and internal audits. Together, ETS Global and Pipplet cover all assessments needs of academic institutions, language schools, corporates and individuals in more than 30 languages.

Its EdAgree subsidiary offers a free platform and services to help students identify universities for international students. Edusoft Ltd., a foreign subsidiary, is a global leader in technology-based, comprehensive English Language Learning solutions, serving a range of educational, government and corporate sectors worldwide.

ETS Canada supports the ETS mission and ETS tests by providing ongoing research, development and innovation through psychometricians and experts in artificial intelligence and natural language processing.

Geographic Reach
Based in Princeton, New Jersey, ETS has US offices in Concord, Sacramento and San Francisco, California; Ewing, New Jersey; San Antonio, Texas and Washington, D.C. ETS has also operations in Asia Pacific (Korea and China), Canada, Europe, Middle East and Africa.

Sales and Marketing
The company serves students, educators, schools, businesses, and governments.

Company Background
In 2011 the company opened several new customer support centers to support international customers seeking to take the TOEFL test.

The company bulked up its testing technology in early 2011 with the acquisition of Computerized Assessments and Learning (CAL). Operating as a subsidiary of ETS, CAL offers assessment products for K-12 education systems.

To move beyond assessment and into actual education, ETS acquired Edusoft, an English language learning firm, in 2011. The 2011 acquisition brought in Edusoft's English Discoveries Online product used around the world. The online product is designed to accompany and support classroom instruction with courses for general and technical English language instruction. Edusoft operates as a for-profit subsidiary.

ETS was founded in 1947.

EXECUTIVES

Corporate Secretary, David Hobson
Auditors : DELOITTE & TOUCHE LLP

LOCATIONS

HQ: EDUCATIONAL TESTING SERVICE
660 ROSEDALE RD, PRINCETON, NJ 085402218
Phone: 609 921-9000
Web: WWW.ETS.ORG

PRODUCTS/OPERATIONS

Selected Testing Programs
Advanced Placement (AP)
Algebra end of course assessment (EOC)
California High School Exit Examination (CAHSEE)
California State University Placement Test (EPT/ELM)
College-Level Examination Program (CLEP)
ETS Literacy
ETS Proficiency Profile
EXADEP
Graduate Record Examinations (GRE)
High Schools That Work Assessment
iSkills Assessment
Major Field Tests (MFT)
Middle Grades Assessment (MGA)
National Assessment of Educational Progress (NAEP)
ParaPro Assessment
The Praxis Series: Professional Assessments for Beginning Teachers
Preliminary SAT/National Merit Scholarship Qualifying Test (PSAT/NMSQT)
Scholastic Aptitude Test (SAT)
School Leaders Licensure Assessment (SLLA)
School Leadership Series (SLS)
School Superintendent Assessment (SSA)
Secondary Level English Proficiency Test (SLEP)
Test Link Test Collection
TFI Test
Test of English as a Foreign Language (TOEFL)
Test of English for International Communication (TOEIC)

Selected Acquisitions
2011
Computerized Assessments and Learning (CAL, assessment products for K-12 education systems)
Edusoft (English language learning programs)

COMPETITORS

ACT, INC.
EDMENTUM, INC.
EDUCATE, INC.
EDUCATION HOLDINGS 1, INC.
KAPLAN, INC.
PROMETRIC LLC
QUESTAR ASSESSMENT, INC.
THE DEGARMO GROUP INC
THE LEARNING KEY INC
TLT GROUP INC

HISTORICAL FINANCIALS
Company Type: Private

Income Statement   FYE: September 30

	REVENUE ($mil)	NET INCOME ($mil)	NET PROFIT MARGIN	EMPLOYEES
09/21	1,071	168	15.7%	2,756
09/20	1,050	(85)	—	—
09/19	1,358	(22)	—	—
09/18	1,392	686	49.3%	—
Annual Growth	(8.4%)	(37.4%)	—	—

2021 Year-End Financials
Return on assets: 8.1%   Cash ($ mil.): 101
Return on equity: 10.0%
Current Ratio: 0.80

EDWARD HOSPITAL

EXECUTIVES

Physician AMBULATORY NETWORK Development*, Bill Kottman
Vice President Facilities*, Gary Mielak
CIO*, Bobbie Byrne
CMO*, Brian Davis
CMO*, Robert Payton

LOCATIONS

HQ: EDWARD HOSPITAL
801 S WASHINGTON ST, NAPERVILLE, IL 605407499
Phone: 630 527-3000
Web: WWW.EEHEALTH.ORG

HISTORICAL FINANCIALS
Company Type: Private

Income Statement   FYE: June 30

	REVENUE ($mil)	NET INCOME ($mil)	NET PROFIT MARGIN	EMPLOYEES
06/21	761	118	15.6%	4,700
06/20	665	21	3.2%	—
06/16	592	2	0.5%	—
06/15	567	39	7.0%	—
Annual Growth	5.0%	19.9%	—	—

2021 Year-End Financials
Return on assets: 25.1%   Cash ($ mil.): (-11)
Return on equity: 48.7%
Current Ratio: 1.50

EDWARD-ELMHURST HEALTHCARE

EXECUTIVES

CLO*, Chris Mollet
SOUTH REGION*, Mary Lou Mastro
EDWARD HOSPITAL*, Joe Dant
ELMHURST HOSPITAL*, Pamela Dunley
Auditors : KPMG LLP CHICAGO IL

LOCATIONS

HQ: EDWARD-ELMHURST HEALTHCARE
4201 WINFIELD RD, WARRENVILLE, IL 605554025
Phone: 630 527-3000
Web: WWW.EEHEALTH.ORG

HISTORICAL FINANCIALS
Company Type: Private

Income Statement   FYE: June 30

	REVENUE ($mil)	NET INCOME ($mil)	NET PROFIT MARGIN	EMPLOYEES
06/21	1,650	358	21.7%	6,500
06/20	1,487	(107)	—	—
06/19	1,514	76	5.1%	—
06/18	1,474	119	8.1%	—
Annual Growth	3.8%	44.1%	—	—

2021 Year-End Financials
Return on assets: 11.9%   Cash ($ mil.): 167
Return on equity: 25.0%
Current Ratio: 1.10

EL CAMINO HEALTHCARE DISTRICT

Auditors : MOSS ADAMS LLP SAN FRANCISCO

LOCATIONS

HQ: EL CAMINO HEALTHCARE DISTRICT
2500 GRANT RD, MOUNTAIN VIEW, CA 940404302
Phone: 650 940-7000
Web: WWW.ELCAMINOHEALTHCAREDISTRICT.ORG

HISTORICAL FINANCIALS
Company Type: Private

Income Statement   FYE: June 30

	REVENUE ($mil)	NET INCOME ($mil)	NET PROFIT MARGIN	EMPLOYEES
06/22	1,346	58	4.3%	10
06/21	1,150	354	30.8%	—
06/20	1,031	129	12.6%	—
Annual Growth	14.3%	(32.9%)	—	—

2022 Year-End Financials
Return on assets: 1.8%   Cash ($ mil.): 207
Return on equity: 2.5%
Current Ratio: 3.10

EL PASO COUNTY HOSPITAL DISTRICT

University Medical Center is a community, not-for-profit health care system serving West Texas and southern New Mexico. The network includes the 330-bed University Medical Center of El Paso (formerly also known as Thomason General Hospital), several neighborhood primary care clinics, and the El Paso First Health Plans HMO. The hospital is an acute-care teaching hospital affiliated with Texas Tech. It specializes in emergency/trauma care, obstetrics, pediatric medicine, and orthopedics. The hospital district, through its affiliates, provides a range of outpatient services including physical rehabilitation, speech therapy, family planning, dental care, cancer treatment, diagnostics, and pharmacy services.

Company Background

University Medical Center of El Paso opened in 1915. The hospital was rebranded under the University Medical Center name in 2009 when Texas Tech opened a full four-year medical school on the Thomason General campus.

Auditors: BKD LLP DALLAS TEXAS

LOCATIONS

HQ: EL PASO COUNTY HOSPITAL DISTRICT
4815 ALAMEDA AVE, EL PASO, TX 799052705
Phone: 915 544-1200
Web: WWW.UMCELPASO.ORG

PRODUCTS/OPERATIONS

Selected Services
After Hours Pediatrics
Aquatic Therapy
Cardiac Cath
CAT Scan
Case Management
Dental Clinic
Diabetes Management
Diagnostic Radiology
Echocardiograms
Electrocardiograms
Emergency Department
Endoscopy/Special Procedures
Family Planning
Infusion Center
Interventional Radiology
Laboratory Services
Labor and Delivery
Laparoscopic Surgery
Lithotripsy
Mammography
Medical Unit
Mother/Baby Unit
MRI
Neonatal Intensive Care
Neonatal Intermediate Care
Neonatal Continuing Care
Newborn Nursery
Neurosurgery
Nuclear Medicine
Nutritional Care
Occupational Health
Occupational Therapy
Patient Financial Services
Pediatric Unit
Pediatric Rehabilitation
Pharmacy
Physical Therapy
Poison Control Center
Prenatal Services
Primary Care Clinics
Public Affairs
Rehabilitative Services
Respiratory Services
Special Care Nurseries
Speech Therapy
Surgical Services
Surgical Unit
Telemetry Unit
Trauma - Level 1
Ultrasound
West Texas Regional Poison Control Center
Wound Care

COMPETITORS

CENTEGRA HEALTH SYSTEM
COLUMBUS REGIONAL HEALTHCARE SYSTEM, INC
NORTH MISSISSIPPI MEDICAL CENTER, INC.
PRIME HEALTHCARE SERVICES - GARDEN CITY, LLC
ST DAVID'S SOUTH AUSTIN MEDICAL CENTER

HISTORICAL FINANCIALS

Company Type: Private

Income Statement — FYE: September 30

	REVENUE ($mil)	NET INCOME ($mil)	NET PROFIT MARGIN	EMPLOYEES
09/21	918	63	7.0%	1,898
09/20	769	30	4.0%	—
09/19	679	(10)	—	—
09/18	599	(31)	—	—
Annual Growth	15.3%	—	—	—

2021 Year-End Financials
Return on assets: 7.5%   Cash ($ mil.): 175
Return on equity: 33.8%
Current Ratio: 1.40

EL PASO INDEPENDENT SCHOOL DISTRICT EDUCATION FOUNDATION

Auditors: GIBSON RUDDOCK PATTERSON LLC

LOCATIONS

HQ: EL PASO INDEPENDENT SCHOOL DISTRICT EDUCATION FOUNDATION
1014 N STANTON ST, EL PASO, TX 799024109
Phone: 915 230-2000
Web: WWW.EPISD.ORG

HISTORICAL FINANCIALS

Company Type: Private

Income Statement — FYE: June 30

	REVENUE ($mil)	NET INCOME ($mil)	NET PROFIT MARGIN	EMPLOYEES
06/21	685	(213)	—	9,000
06/20	688	44	6.4%	—
06/19	648	196	30.3%	—
06/18	625	(34)	—	—
Annual Growth	3.1%	—	—	—

2021 Year-End Financials
Return on assets: (-12.3%)   Cash ($ mil.): 283
Return on equity: —
Current Ratio: —

EL PASO NATURAL GAS COMPANY, L.L.C.

EXECUTIVES

CAO, Rosa P Jackson

LOCATIONS

HQ: EL PASO NATURAL GAS COMPANY, L.L.C.
1001 LOUISIANA ST, HOUSTON, TX 770025089
Phone: 713 420-2600
Web: WWW.KINDERMORGAN.COM

HISTORICAL FINANCIALS

Company Type: Private

Income Statement — FYE: December 31

	REVENUE ($mil)	NET INCOME ($mil)	NET PROFIT MARGIN	EMPLOYEES
12/17	648	141	21.8%	525
12/16	627	128	20.5%	—
12/10	517	83	16.1%	—
Annual Growth	3.3%	7.9%	—	—

2017 Year-End Financials
Return on assets: 5.2%   Cash ($ mil.): —
Return on equity: 9.9%
Current Ratio: 1.30

ELECTRIC POWER BOARD OF CHATTANOOGA

Pardon me .... is that the Electric Power Board (EPB) of Chattanooga? EPB keeps on choo-chooin' along by providing electricity to more than 167,410 residents and businesses. The utility (a non-profit agency of the City of Chattanooga) distributes energy in a 600 sq.-ml. area that includes greater Chattanooga, as well as parts of surrounding counties in Georgia and Tennessee. It gets its wholesale power supply from the Tennessee Valley

Authority. EPB also provides telecommunications (telephone and Internet) services to area homes and businesses through its EPB Fiber Optics unit.

Operations
In addition to its electric distribution business, the company's all-fiber Internet product gives 50,000 businesses and residences access to up to 500 Mbps of bandwidth, a capacity 300 times faster than standard DSL, cable, or T1 connections. This service gives all EFB customers internet bandwidth capacity and service on a par with or superior to that offered in Atlanta, Chicago, and Los Angeles.

Geographic Reach
EPB serves greater Chattanooga and parts of surrounding counties (Bledsoe, Bradley, Marion, Rhea, and Sequatchie) and North Georgia (parts of Catoosa, Dade, and Walker counties).

Financial Performance
The company saw its operating revenues rise by 1% in 2013, thanks to an increase of $12.4 million in Fiber Optics residential services sales.

Strategy
EFB is pushing technological innovation and the modernization of its systems as a way to increase value and efficiency.

To help reduce power outages, in 2013 the company added 200 smart switches to its 46 Kv system (in addition to its 1,200 smart swtiches on the 12kV system already in place.

Company Background
During 2009 the company received a $111 million federal stimulus grant to build and operate a Smart Grid (an automated electric system with communication capabilities to help improve response time, reduce outages, cut down on theft, and help clients take charge of their own power use). In 2012 EFB completed the installation of the 1,170 IntelliRupter® PulseCloser (smart switches) making EPB's Smart Grid the most automated system of its size in the US.

The utility was established in 1935 to provide electric power to the people of the greater Chattanooga area.

Auditors : MAULDIN & JENKINS LLC CHATTA

LOCATIONS
HQ: ELECTRIC POWER BOARD OF CHATTANOOGA
10 W MRTIN LTHER KING BLV, CHATTANOOGA, TN 374021832
Phone: 423 756-2706
Web: WWW.EPB.COM

PRODUCTS/OPERATIONS
2013 Sales

	% of total
Electric	86
Fiber Optics	12
Other	2
Total	100

COMPETITORS
CENTRAL MAINE POWER COMPANY
MIDCONTINENT INDEPENDENT SYSTEM OPERATOR, INC.
PPL ELECTRIC UTILITIES CORPORATION
SOUTHERN MARYLAND ELECTRIC COOPERATIVE, INC.
THE CITY OF SEATTLE-CITY LIGHT DEPARTMENT

HISTORICAL FINANCIALS
Company Type: Private

Income Statement FYE: June 30

	REVENUE ($mil)	NET INCOME ($mil)	NET PROFIT MARGIN	EMPLOYEES
06/21	721	47	6.6%	400
06/19	741	36	5.0%	—
06/18	729	43	6.0%	—
06/17	716	35	4.9%	—
Annual Growth	0.2%	8.0%	—	—

2021 Year-End Financials
Return on assets: 4.6%   Cash ($ mil.): 173
Return on equity: 9.4%
Current Ratio: 1.80

ELECTRIC POWER BOARD OF THE METROPOLITAN GOVERNMENT OF NASHVILLE & DAVIDSON COUNTY

The Electric Power Board of the Metropolitan Government of Nashville and Davidson County is a mouthful. Its operating name, Nashville Electric Service (NES), sounds much better. And talking of sound, the legendary "Nashville Sound" would be hard to hear without the resources of this power distributor, which serves more thanÂ 360,000 customers in central Tennessee. NES is one of the largest government-owned utilities in the US. The company is required to purchase all its power from another government-owned operator, the Tennessee Valley Authority (TVA).

EXECUTIVES
Vice Chairman, Robert Campbell Junior
Auditors : PRICEWATERHOUSECOOPERS LLP NA

LOCATIONS
HQ: ELECTRIC POWER BOARD OF THE METROPOLITAN GOVERNMENT OF NASHVILLE & DAVIDSON COUNTY
1214 CHURCH ST, NASHVILLE, TN 372460001
Phone: 615 747-3831
Web: WWW.NESPOWER.COM

COMPETITORS
CALIFORNIA INDEPENDENT SYSTEM OPERATOR CORPORATION
CITY OF FORT COLLINS
ELECTRIC POWER BOARD OF CHATTANOOGA
SOUTHERN MARYLAND ELECTRIC COOPERATIVE, INC.
TEXAS-NEW MEXICO POWER COMPANY

HISTORICAL FINANCIALS
Company Type: Private

Income Statement FYE: June 30

	REVENUE ($mil)	NET INCOME ($mil)	NET PROFIT MARGIN	EMPLOYEES
06/19	1,342	90	6.7%	950
06/18	380	94	24.7%	—
06/16	1,203	28	2.4%	—
06/15	1,246	55	4.5%	—
Annual Growth	1.9%	12.7%	—	—

2019 Year-End Financials
Return on assets: 4.8%   Cash ($ mil.): 387
Return on equity: 14.7%
Current Ratio: 2.50

ELEMENT14 US HOLDINGS INC

LOCATIONS
HQ: ELEMENT14 US HOLDINGS INC
4180 HIGHLANDER PKWY, RICHFIELD, OH 442869352
Phone: 330 523-4280

HISTORICAL FINANCIALS
Company Type: Private

Income Statement FYE: February 1

	REVENUE ($mil)	NET INCOME ($mil)	NET PROFIT MARGIN	EMPLOYEES
02/16	598	9	1.6%	1,043
02/15	717	48	6.7%	—
02/14	698	35	5.1%	—
Annual Growth	(7.5%)	(48.4%)	—	—

2016 Year-End Financials
Return on assets: 3.0%   Cash ($ mil.): 70
Return on equity: 4.2%
Current Ratio: 6.40

ELLIOT HEALTH SYSTEM

Auditors : BAKER NEWMAN & NOYES LLC MANC

LOCATIONS
HQ: ELLIOT HEALTH SYSTEM
1 ELLIOT WAY, MANCHESTER, NH 031033502
Phone: 603 663-1600
Web: WWW.ELLIOTHOSPITAL.ORG

HISTORICAL FINANCIALS
Company Type: Private

Income Statement				FYE: June 30
	REVENUE ($mil)	NET INCOME ($mil)	NET PROFIT MARGIN	EMPLOYEES
06/22	705	37	5.4%	3,400
06/21	657	153	23.3%	—
06/20	582	6	1.0%	—
06/19	592	0	0.1%	—
Annual Growth	6.0%	312.0%	—	—

2022 Year-End Financials
Return on assets: 4.9%
Return on equity: 9.6%
Current Ratio: 1.70
Cash ($ mil.): 148

ELLIOT HOSPITAL OF THE CITY OF MANCHESTER

Elliot Health System provides medical care to southern New Hampshire. The health care organization operates Elliot Hospital, an acute care hospital with nearly 300 beds that is home to a regional cancer center, a designated regional trauma center, and a level III neonatal intensive care unit (NICU). In addition to general and surgical care, the hospital offers rehabilitation, behavioral health, obstetrics, cardiology, and lab services. The system also operates the Elliot Physician Network, which operates primary care centers, specialty clinics, and surgery centers in various regional communities. Elliot Hospital was founded in 1890.

Operations
Elliot Hospital is Manchester's designated Regional Trauma Center. Additional facilities include the Elliot Breast Health Center, Elliot Urgent Care, Elliot Senior Health Center, and New Hampshire's Hospital for Children.

Strategy
Elliot Health System has expanded throughout the region by constructing new outpatient care centers in nearby towns. Most recently Elliot Health completed construction of satellite facilities including an ambulatory care center and a senior health center. In 2015, it partnered with Northeast Rehabilitation Hospital to create a new rehabilitation floor within its Elliot Hospital.

Auditors: BAKER NEWMAN & NOYES LLC MANC

LOCATIONS
HQ: ELLIOT HOSPITAL OF THE CITY OF MANCHESTER
1 ELLIOT WAY, MANCHESTER, NH 031033502
Phone: 603 669-5300
Web: WWW.ELLIOTHOSPITAL.ORG

PRODUCTS/OPERATIONS
Selected Centers and Services
Aeronautics Medicine
Adult Day Programs
Bariatric Surgery
Behavioral Health
Breast Health Center
Cardiology Services
Center for Sleep Evaluation
Center for Wound Care & Hyberbaric Medicine
Childbirth And Family Education
Community Health and Wellness
Critical Care at The Elliot
Diabetes and Outpatient Nutrition Services
Diagnostic Imaging
Elliot 1-Day Surgery Center
The Elliot at Hooksett
Elliot Behavioral Health Services
Elliot Endocrinology Associates
Elliot Gastroenterology
Elliot General Surgical Specialists
Elliot Maternal Fetal Medicine
Elliot Medical Center at Londonderry
Elliot Neurology Associates
Elliot Obstetrics and Gynecology
Elliot Orthopaedic Surgical Specialists
Elliot Physician Network
Elliot Regional Cancer Center
Elliot Sports Medicine
Elliot Trauma Center
Elliot Wellness Center
Endoscopy Center
Health Education Library
Home Medical Equipment
Hospitalist Program
Infection Control Department
Inpatient Care/Nursing Units
Laboratory Services
Max K. Willscher Urology Center
Neurophysiology
New England EMS Institute
New Hampshire Arthritis Center
Nursing Units/Inpatient Care
Nutrition Services
Occupational Health & Wellness
Oral Maxillofacial Surgery Center
Oxygen Therapy
Pain Management Center
Pediatric Surgery
Pharmacy Services
Pulmonary Medicine
Pulmonary Rehabilitation
Physical Therapy
Rehabilitation
Respiratory Care
Senior Health Center
Sports Medicine
Surgery
Speech Therapy
Urgent Care - Londonderry
Urgent Care - Manchester
Visiting Nurse Association of Manchester & So. NH, Inc.
Weight Management
Wellness Center
Women's & Children's Services
Wound Center

COMPETITORS
CENTEGRA HEALTH SYSTEM
CHILTON HOSPITAL
PORTER FOUNDATION, INC.
UPSON COUNTY HOSPITAL, INC.
WILKES-BARRE HOSPITAL COMPANY, LLC

HISTORICAL FINANCIALS
Company Type: Private

Income Statement				FYE: June 30
	REVENUE ($mil)	NET INCOME ($mil)	NET PROFIT MARGIN	EMPLOYEES
06/22	672	9	1.5%	2,000
06/21	621	139	22.5%	—
06/20	549	(27)	—	—
06/19	560	(4)	—	—
Annual Growth	6.3%	—	—	—

2022 Year-End Financials
Return on assets: 1.5%
Return on equity: 3.4%
Current Ratio: 1.50
Cash ($ mil.): 115

EMJ CORPORATION

EMJ does it all for the mall. Founded in 1968 by namesake Edgar M. Jolley, the company specializes in building and renovating retail outlets and shopping centers throughout the US. It is also known for other building projects, such as offices, warehouses, churches, hotels, multifamily residences, hospitals, and wind farms. Working from five offices nationwide, EMJ provides general construction and construction management. The company's pre-construction services include creating detailed budgets and construction schedules and coordinating permitting, utility companies, and municipal requirements. To track a project's progress and monitor costs, EMJ offers quality control and safety and warranty management.

Operations
EMJ owns several operating divisions, including Signal Energy, which engineers and builds renewable energy projects such as wind farms and solar and biomass energy projects. Another division, Accent Construction Management, provides site selection, budgeting, scheduling, and other services. Its RedStone Construction Services builds commercial, retail, hospitality, healthcare, government facilities, and others. It is focused on fostering economic growth in Native American communities.

Geographic Reach
From its base in Chattanooga, Tennessee, EMJ serves clients through a handful of US offices in Massachusetts, Tennessee, Texas, and California.

Sales and Marketing
EMJ has built more than 500 million sq. ft. of construction projects. Its client roster includes Academy, Barnes & Noble, Bed Bath & Beyond, Blue Cross and Blue Shield, Home Depot, PetSmart, and Winn-Dixie.

The company serves several sectors, such as airports, education, entertainment, government and civic, grocery, healthcare, hospitality, industrial and warehouse, and Native American tribal communities, office buildings, parking, lifestyle and mixed use development, retail, renewable energy, renovations, and worship centers.

Strategy
The company is working on projects for Whole Foods Market, TownPlace Suites, Silverdale Baptist student center, and Dick's Sporting Goods. Inked in 2013, EMJ's $250-million deal with Native American Chris Samples, operating under the name RedStone Construction Services, is building a 500-room hotel and expanding a casino in Tulsa, Oklahoma.

EXECUTIVES
CLO*, Colby Cox

LOCATIONS
HQ: EMJ CORPORATION
2034 HAMILTON PLACE BLVD # 400, CHATTANOOGA, TN 374216102
Phone: 423 855-1550
Web: WWW.EMJCORP.COM

PRODUCTS/OPERATIONS
Selected Projects
Airports
Education
Entertainment
Government/civic
Grocery
Healthcare
Hospitality
Industrial/warehouse
Lifestyle/mixed use development and retail
Native American tribal communities
Office buildings
Parking
Renewable energy
Renovations
Worship centers

Selected Services
Construction
Construction management
General contracting
Pre-construction services
Quality control
Safety consultation
Site evaluation
Warranty

COMPETITORS
AUSTIN COMMERCIAL, INC.
DPR CONSTRUCTION, INC.
GILBANE, INC.
HITT CONTRACTING, INC.
HUNZINGER CONSTRUCTION COMPANY
JAMES G. DAVIS CONSTRUCTION CORPORATION
KITCHELL CORPORATION
SWINERTON BUILDERS, INC.
THE WALDINGER CORPORATION
THE YATES COMPANIES INC

HISTORICAL FINANCIALS
Company Type: Private

Income Statement — FYE: March 7

	REVENUE ($mil)	NET INCOME ($mil)	NET PROFIT MARGIN	EMPLOYEES
03/17*	960	4	0.5%	210
12/11	437	0	0.1%	—
12/08	821	7	1.0%	—
12/07	959	10	1.1%	—
Annual Growth	0.0%	(7.9%)	—	—

*Fiscal year change

2017 Year-End Financials
Return on assets: 2.3%   Cash ($ mil.): 29
Return on equity: 18.5%
Current Ratio: 1.10

EMORY UNIVERSITY HOSPITAL MIDTOWN

LOCATIONS
HQ: EMORY UNIVERSITY HOSPITAL MIDTOWN
550 PEACHTREE ST NE, ATLANTA, GA 303082212
Phone: 404 686-4411
Web: WWW.EMORYHEALTHCARE.ORG

HISTORICAL FINANCIALS
Company Type: Private

Income Statement — FYE: August 31

	REVENUE ($mil)	NET INCOME ($mil)	NET PROFIT MARGIN	EMPLOYEES
08/16	735	64	8.7%	2,500
08/15	641	(21)	—	—
Annual Growth	14.8%	—	—	—

2016 Year-End Financials
Return on assets: 9.9%   Cash ($ mil.): 269
Return on equity: 38.5%
Current Ratio: 2.50

EMPIRE SOUTHWEST, LLC

Empire Southwest is a third-generation family-owned Cat Dealer that sells, rents and services heavy equipment, tractors, and power generation equipment to clients throughout Arizona and Southeastern California. One of the largest Caterpillar dealerships in the US, Empire Southwest operates through four divisions: hydraulic service, fluid labs, precision machining, and rebuilds. The company's equipment includes backhoe loaders, compactors, dozers, electric rope shovels, track loaders, pipelayers, telehandlers, and tractors. It also handles equipment used for mining and forestry projects. The company was founded by Jack Whiteman in 1950 as Empire Machinery, an Eastern Oregon Caterpillar dealer.

Operations
Empire Southwest consists of four operating divisions. Empire Machinery sells, rents, and provides product support for Caterpillar equipment and other brands.

Its Empire Fluids Lab can detect potential problems long before they materialize. Its Scheduled Oil Sampling (SOS) is a regular maintenance program designed to monitor the overall condition of all equipment brands and machine types. Empire Precision Machining is fully equipped to work on small to large components used in today's top industries including mining, construction, and agriculture. Empire Hydraulic Service specializes in repairing and rebuilding of hydraulic cylinders, pumps and motors.

Geographic Reach
Headquartered in Mesa, Arizona, Empire has carved out a territory that includes about 30 communities in Arizona, southeastern California, and portions of northern Mexico.

Sales and Marketing
The company targets the agriculture, mining, demo and scrap, forestry and logging, on-highway truck, general construction, heavy construction, electric power, and waste management industries.

Company Background
The company was founded in 1950 when Jack Whiteman acquired Empire Machinery (which held the Caterpillar and John Deere dealerships in eastern Oregon). In 1959 he relocated to Arizona and took over a Caterpillar dealership there.

LOCATIONS
HQ: EMPIRE SOUTHWEST, LLC
1725 S COUNTRY CLUB DR, MESA, AZ 852106099
Phone: 480 633-4000
Web: WWW.EMPIRE-CAT.COM

PRODUCTS/OPERATIONS
Selected Industries Served
Agriculture
Demo and Scrap
Forestry
General Construction
Governmental
Heavy Construction
Landscaping
Marine
Mining
Oil and Gas
On-Highway Truck
Paving
Pipeline
Quarry and Aggregates
Waste

COMPETITORS
AMERAMEX INTERNATIONAL, INC.
CAROLINA TRACTOR & EQUIPMENT COMPANY
CARTER MACHINERY COMPANY, INCORPORATED
FOLEY INCORPORATED
MACALLISTER MACHINERY CO INC
OHIO MACHINERY CO.
PUCKETT MACHINERY COMPANY
RING POWER CORPORATION
WAUKESHA-PEARCE INDUSTRIES, LLC
WYOMING MACHINERY COMPANY

ENGLEWOOD HOSPITAL AND MEDICAL CENTER FOUNDATION INC.

Englewood Hospital and Medical Center is a 520-bed acute care hospital serving New Jersey's Bergen County, which is part of the New York City metro area. The not-for-profit health care provider offers general medical and surgical care, along with specialty services in areas such as oncology, cardiovascular disease, wound care, women's health, joint replacement, and pediatrics. It also maintains a short-term inpatient behavioral health program for adults. The hospital is affiliated with the Mount Sinai School of Medicine and the Mount Sinai Consortium for Graduate Medical Education and provides residency programs to doctors from the Mount Sinai School of Medicine.

Operations

Englewood Hospital and Medical Center has a nursing staff of 800 and medical staff of 380. It serves more than 23,000 admitted patients and nearly 47,000 emergency cases a year. It conducted some 8,000 operations and helped deliver 2,000 babies in 2014.

As a teaching hospital, it offers education and research programs including Grand Rounds, CME Online, an Internal Medicine Residency Program, a Vascular Surgery Fellowship, a Pharmacy Residency Program, and a School of Radiography.

Along with the typical acute and chronic medical care services, the hospital maintains an infusion center for patients requiring chemotherapy, and also offers hyperbaric oxygen treatments for divers with the bends and other patients who will benefit from having oxygen administered under pressure.

To better serve patients for whom blood transfusions are not an option, the hospital had established a program for bloodless medicine and surgery. The Institute for Patient Blood Management & Bloodless Medicine and Surgery serves as a leading resource for training health professionals in working in environments where blood transfusions are not readily available.

Geographic Reach

The company operates the largest voluntary acute care hospital in Bergen County and the third largest in New Jersey.

Company Background

The hospital was founded in 1890.

EXECUTIVES

Information Technology Vice President*, Dimitri J Cruz

LOCATIONS

HQ: ENGLEWOOD HOSPITAL AND MEDICAL CENTER FOUNDATION INC.
350 ENGLE ST, ENGLEWOOD, NJ 076311808
Phone: 201 894-3725
Web: WWW.ENGLEWOODHEALTHFOUNDATION.ORG

PRODUCTS/OPERATIONS

Selected ServicesMedical ServicesAMI of EnglewoodAnesthesiologyAntepartum Testing CenterBerrie Center Same Day SurgeryBariatric SurgeryBloodless Medicine & SurgeryBreast Care CenterBreast Surgical ServicesCancer Center ResourcesCardiac RehabCardiac SurgeryCardiology ServicesCenter for Integrative MedicineClinical Research CenterColorectal SurgeryConcussion CenterContinence Control CenterDiabetesEMS/Ambulance ServicesER/ Emergency MedicineGastroenterologyHome Health & TeleHealthHospice Care Hospitalist ProgramHybrid Operating RoomHyperbaric MedicineInfectious DiseaseInflammatory Bowel Disease CtrInfusion CenterJoint Replacement CenterLaboratory Services & PathologyMaternity/Family Birth PlaceNeurosciencesNutrition CounselingObstetrics & GynecologyOccupational TherapyOncologyOrthopedic SurgeryPain ManagementPalliative CarePancreas, Biliary & Liver Center.PediatricsPharmacyPhysical TherapyPost-Polio InstitutePulmonary/ Respiratory MedicinePsychiatry/Behavioral HealthRadiologyRehabilitation MedicineRobotic SurgerySame Day SurgerySleep MedicineSpeech TherapySpine CenterStroke CenterVascular/Vein ServicesWound Healing CenterProfessional servicesAnesthesiology CardiologyEKG/EEG/EMG LaboratoryPathology Pulmonary functionRadiation therapyRadiologyRehabilitation Stress testing Vascular studies

COMPETITORS

NEWYORK-PRESBYTERIAN/BROOKLYN METHODIST
ROSE MEDICAL GROUP
THE JAMAICA HOSPITAL
THE UNION MEMORIAL HOSPITAL
YORK HOSPITAL

HISTORICAL FINANCIALS
Company Type: Private

Income Statement — FYE: October 31

	REVENUE ($mil)	NET INCOME ($mil)	NET PROFIT MARGIN	EMPLOYEES
10/11	683	38	5.6%	1,450
10/10	528	22	4.3%	—
10/09	448	7	1.6%	—
Annual Growth	23.5%	127.0%	—	—

2011 Year-End Financials
Return on assets: 7.6%
Return on equity: 18.8%
Current Ratio: 1.80
Cash ($ mil.): —

ENTERGY SERVICES, LLC

EXECUTIVES

Executive President, Marcus V Brown

LOCATIONS

HQ: ENTERGY SERVICES, LLC
639 LOYOLA AVE STE 300, NEW ORLEANS, LA 701133121
Phone: 504 576-4000
Web: WWW.ENTERGY.COM

HISTORICAL FINANCIALS
Company Type: Private

Income Statement — FYE: December 31

	REVENUE ($mil)	NET INCOME ($mil)	NET PROFIT MARGIN	EMPLOYEES
12/16	1,112	10	0.9%	1,325
12/04	10,123	933	9.2%	—
Annual Growth	(16.8%)	(31.2%)	—	—

2016 Year-End Financials
Return on assets: 0.8%
Return on equity: —
Current Ratio: 0.70
Cash ($ mil.): 51

ENTERPRISE CRUDE PIPELINE LLC

LOCATIONS

HQ: ENTERPRISE CRUDE PIPELINE LLC
1100 LOUISIANA ST # 1000, HOUSTON, TX 770025227
Phone: 713 381-6500
Web: WWW.ENTERPRISEPRODUCTS.COM

HISTORICAL FINANCIALS
Company Type: Private

Income Statement — FYE: December 31

	REVENUE ($mil)	NET INCOME ($mil)	NET PROFIT MARGIN	EMPLOYEES
12/19	770	45	5.8%	38
12/17	11	7	66.8%	—
12/16	552	19	3.5%	—
12/15	480	12	2.5%	—
Annual Growth	12.5%	38.6%	—	—

2019 Year-End Financials
Return on assets: 7.2%
Return on equity: 14.2%
Current Ratio: 0.40
Cash ($ mil.): 21

HISTORICAL FINANCIALS
Company Type: Private

Income Statement   FYE: December 31

	REVENUE ($mil)	NET INCOME ($mil)	NET PROFIT MARGIN	EMPLOYEES
12/17	596	378	63.5%	300
12/16	472	284	60.2%	—
Annual Growth	26.2%	33.1%	—	—

2017 Year-End Financials
Return on assets: 11.1%   Cash ($ mil.): —
Return on equity: 11.6%
Current Ratio: 1.10

ENTERPRISE TE PRODUCTS PIPELINE COMPANY LLC

LOCATIONS
HQ: ENTERPRISE TE PRODUCTS PIPELINE COMPANY LLC
1100 LOUISIANA ST # 1600, HOUSTON, TX 770025227
Phone: 713 381-6500

HISTORICAL FINANCIALS
Company Type: Private

Income Statement   FYE: December 31

	REVENUE ($mil)	NET INCOME ($mil)	NET PROFIT MARGIN	EMPLOYEES
12/17	659	337	51.1%	5
12/16	628	275	43.9%	—
Annual Growth	5.0%	22.3%	—	—

2017 Year-End Financials
Return on assets: 11.7%   Cash ($ mil.): —
Return on equity: 12.2%
Current Ratio: 1.10

EP ENERGY CORPORATION

EP Energy is into the (E)xploration and (P)roduction of oil and gas. The company's primary operations are at the Eagle Ford Shale in South Texas, Northeastern Utah (NEU) in the Uinta basin, and the Permian basin in West Texas. It owns proved reserves of around 190 million barrels of oil equivalent, about 75% of which is oil and NGLs (natural gas liquids). In early 2020, EP Energy emerged from Chapter 11 bankruptcy protection. EP Energy was formed in 2012 when the former El Paso Corporation sold its exploration and production assets to an investment group for $7.2 billion.

Bankruptcy

The company and certain of its direct and indirect subsidiaries (collectively with the company, the debtors) filed voluntary petitions (the "Chapter 11 Cases") in the United States Bankruptcy Court for the Southern District of Texas (the "Bankruptcy Court") seeking relief under Chapter 11 of title 11 of the United States Code (the "Bankruptcy Code"). To ensure ordinary course operations, the debtors obtained approval from the Bankruptcy Court for a variety of "first day" motions, including motions to obtain customary relief intended to assure the company's ability to continue its ordinary course operations after the filing date. In addition to this, the debtors received authority to use cash collateral of the lenders under the RBL Facility.

The company will reduce its debt by approximately $3.3 billion, will receive approximately $629 million in senior secured exit financing from the company's existing revolving loan lenders, and approximately $325 million of new-money equity financing from certain of its existing noteholders, upon emergence.

Operations

Of EP Energy's 190MMboe (millions of barrels of oil equivalent) of proved reserves, around 90% are oil reserves, more than 5% of sales from natural gas liquids and approximately 5% of sales from natural gas.

It produces around 70,850 boe each day via nearly 1,560 producing wells.

Geographic Reach

Headquartered in Houston, Texas, the company operates in three areas: the Eagle Ford Shale (in South Texas), Northeastern Utah (NEU) (in the Uinta basin), and the Permian (basin in West Texas).

Sales and Marketing

EP Energy sells oil and natural gas to third parties in the US at spot market prices. NGLs are sold at market prices under monthly or long-term contracts.

Nine purchasers account for about 90% of the company's oil revenues. The top two purchasers are: Shell Trading U.S. Co. (an affiliate of Shell Oil Company) and Flint Hills Resources, LP (an affiliate of Koch Industries), which together accounted for approximately 45% of our oil revenues.

The majority of its produced gas flows are on the Camino Real gas gathering system via pipelines. The gas is then redelivered into interconnects with ETC Texas Pipeline LTD, Enterprise Hydrocarbons LP, Regency Energy Partners LP and Eagle Ford Gathering LLC. Wax crude is sold to Salt Lake City refineries under long-term sales agreements.

Financial Performance

EP Energy's revenue has been fluctuating in the last five years with an overall decline of 57% between 2015 and 2019. The company's revenue declined 38% from $1.3 billion in 2018 to $820 million in 2019.

EP Energy suffered a $943 million net loss in 2019 due to decrease in revenue.

The company's cash at the end of 2019 was $33 million, 6$ million more than the previous year. Operating activities generated $227 million while investing activities used $518 million. Financing activities provided another $297 million mainly from proceeds from issuance of long-term debt.

Strategy

EP Energy's strategy is to invest in opportunities that provide the highest return across our asset base, continually seek out operating and capital efficiencies, effectively manage costs, and identify accretive acquisition opportunities and divestitures, all with the objective of enhancing our portfolio, growing asset value, improving cash flow and increasing financial flexibility.

Mergers and Acquisitions

EXECUTIVES
Non-Executive Chairman of the Board, Alan R Crain Junior
Corporate Secretary, Jace D Locke
Auditors : ERNST & YOUNG LLP HOUSTON TE

LOCATIONS
HQ: EP ENERGY CORPORATION
601 TRAVIS ST STE 1400, HOUSTON, TX 770023001
Phone: 713 997-5000
Web: WWW.VERDUNOILCO.COM

PRODUCTS/OPERATIONS
2016 sales

	in million	% of total
Oil	653	78
Natural gas	122	14
NGLs	65	8
Financial derivatives	(73)	-
Total	767	100

COMPETITORS
ABRAXAS PETROLEUM CORPORATION
CIMAREX ENERGY CO.
DIAMONDBACK ENERGY, INC.
EOG RESOURCES, INC.
LINN ENERGY, LLC
MARATHON OIL CORPORATION
NORTHERN OIL AND GAS, INC.
OVINTIV EXPLORATION INC.
SOUTHWESTERN ENERGY COMPANY
WPX ENERGY, INC.

HISTORICAL FINANCIALS
Company Type: Private

Income Statement   FYE: December 31

	REVENUE ($mil)	NET INCOME ($mil)	NET PROFIT MARGIN	EMPLOYEES
12/18	1,324	(1,003)	—	372
12/17	1,066	(194)	—	—
12/16	767	(27)	—	—
Annual Growth	31.4%	—	—	—

2018 Year-End Financials
Return on assets: (-24.0%)   Cash ($ mil.): 27
Return on equity: —
Current Ratio: 0.90

EP ENERGY LLC

Auditors : ERNST & YOUNG LLP HOUSTON T

LOCATIONS

HQ: EP ENERGY LLC
601 TRAVIS ST STE 1400, HOUSTON, TX 770023001
Phone: 713 997-1000
Web: WWW.VERDUNOILCO.COM

HISTORICAL FINANCIALS
Company Type: Private

Income Statement — FYE: December 31

	REVENUE ($mil)	NET INCOME ($mil)	NET PROFIT MARGIN	EMPLOYEES
12/19	820	(943)	—	372
12/18	1,324	(1,003)	—	—
12/17	1,066	(203)	—	—
12/16	767	(21)	—	—
Annual Growth	2.3%	—	—	—

2019 Year-End Financials
Return on assets: (-25.4%)   Cash ($ mil.): 32
Return on equity: —
Current Ratio: 0.10

EQUINOR MARKETING & TRADING (US) INC.

Check the stats. Oil. Hundreds of thousands of barrels of oil, gasoline, and more. Statoil Marketing & Trading is a wholesaler of oil and petroleum products. The company is the US trading arm of Statoil,Â the leading Scandinavian oil and gas enterprise. Statoil Marketing & Trading delivers about 600,000 barrels a day in the form of crude oil, gasoline, liquefied petroleum gas (LPG), propane, and butane to the North American market. In addition to supplying Norwegian crude, the company trades crude oil from Africa, South America, and North America.Â Statoil Marketing & Trading sells itÂ oil products primarilyÂ to customers in Northeastern Canada, the US East Coast and Gulf Coast.

EXECUTIVES

ENERGY TRADING, Stein-erling Brekke
CRUDE OIL TRADING, Oddgeir Wskeland
Auditors : KPMG LLP STAMFORD CONNECTICU

LOCATIONS

HQ: EQUINOR MARKETING & TRADING (US) INC.
600 WSHINGTON BLVD FL 8 FLR 8, STAMFORD, CT 06902
Phone: 203 978-6900

COMPETITORS
KUNLUN ENERGY COMPANY LIMITED
PETROBRAS AMERICA INC.
RS ENERGY K.K.
TAUBER OIL COMPANY

Tidal Energy Marketing Inc

HISTORICAL FINANCIALS
Company Type: Private

Income Statement — FYE: December 31

	REVENUE ($mil)	NET INCOME ($mil)	NET PROFIT MARGIN	EMPLOYEES
12/20	9,959	209	2.1%	5
12/19	13,594	88	0.7%	—
12/18	14,852	139	0.9%	—
12/17	9,874	(28)	—	—
Annual Growth	0.3%	—	—	—

2020 Year-End Financials
Return on assets: 9.6%   Cash ($ mil.): 97
Return on equity: 28.4%
Current Ratio: 1.60

EQUINOR NATURAL GAS LLC

EXECUTIVES

TAX, Kathleen Parchinski
Auditors : ERNST & YOUNG LLP NEW YORK N

LOCATIONS

HQ: EQUINOR NATURAL GAS LLC
600 WSHINGTON BLVD FL 8 FLR 8, STAMFORD, CT 06902
Phone: 203 978-6900

HISTORICAL FINANCIALS
Company Type: Private

Income Statement — FYE: December 31

	REVENUE ($mil)	NET INCOME ($mil)	NET PROFIT MARGIN	EMPLOYEES
12/19	1,964	32	1.6%	15
12/15	1,967	722	36.7%	—
12/13	3,507	(127)	—	—
12/10	1,614	149	9.3%	—
Annual Growth	2.2%	(15.7%)	—	—

2019 Year-End Financials
Return on assets: 3.1%   Cash ($ mil.): 23
Return on equity: 7.9%
Current Ratio: 2.60

ERIE COUNTY MEDICAL CENTER CORP.

EXECUTIVES

Chief Human Resource Officer, Joseph T Giglia Ii
Auditors : RSM US LLP

LOCATIONS

HQ: ERIE COUNTY MEDICAL CENTER CORP.
462 GRIDER ST, BUFFALO, NY 142153098
Phone: 716 898-3000
Web: WWW.ECMC.EDU

HISTORICAL FINANCIALS
Company Type: Private

Income Statement — FYE: December 31

	REVENUE ($mil)	NET INCOME ($mil)	NET PROFIT MARGIN	EMPLOYEES
12/21	689	(21)	—	3,300
12/20	638	(64)	—	—
12/19	750	12	1.7%	—
12/18	661	1	0.2%	—
Annual Growth	1.4%	—	—	—

2021 Year-End Financials
Return on assets: (-2.0%)   Cash ($ mil.): 69
Return on equity: —
Current Ratio: 1.20

ESTES EXPRESS LINES

Estes Express is the largest, privately-owned freight shipping company in North America. Its fleet of over 7,000 tractors and some 30,000 trailers operates via a network of more than 260 terminals dotting the US. The company provides reliable Less Than Truckload (LTL) freight solutions to and from all 50 states, Canada, Mexico and the Caribbean, as well as asset-based and brokered Volume LTL and Truckload shipping to regional, national, international and offshore destinations. The company was founded in 1931 when W.W. Estes bought a used Chevrolet truck to haul livestock to market for his neighbors in rural Virginia.

Operations

Estes offers asset-based and brokered Volume LTL and Truckload shipping to regional, national, international and offshore destinations. It also offers comprehensive freight forwarding options that make it easy to ship anywhere on the globe with confidence, residential and commercial non-dock delivery solutions to take freight the final mile, and custom shipping and logistics including dedicated delivery, flatbed, truckload, warehousing, supply chain management, pick and pack, and other special services.

The company operates through several divisions and companies. Divisions include Estes Time-Critical (offering guaranteed and time-sensitive service for maximum shipping flexibility), Estes Logistics (helps create B2B and B2C shipping solutions), Estes Specialized Truckload and Delivery Services, and Estes SureMove (customers load shipments themselves and Estes provides transportation). Companies include Estes Forwarding Worldwide, Estes Leasing, and Big E Transportation.

Geographic Reach

Headquartered in Richmond, Virginia, Estes Express offers regional service to all 50

US states. It also offers direct service to Canada, Mexico, and the Caribbean.

Company Background
The company was formed in 1931.

LOCATIONS

HQ: ESTES EXPRESS LINES
3901 W BROAD ST, RICHMOND, VA 232303962
Phone: 804 353-1900
Web: WWW.ESTES-EXPRESS.COM

PRODUCTS/OPERATIONS

Selected Services
Global (airfreight, ocean, international consolidation/deconsolidation, customs brokerage, international freight forwarding)
Less-than-truckload (regional, national, international/offshore)
Time critical (expedited, guaranteed, time/date definite)
Volume & truckload (LTL, full loads, backhaul services, truckload brokerage, dedicated truckload)

COMPETITORS

A. DUIE PYLE INC.
AAA COOPER TRANSPORTATION
AERONET WORLDWIDE, INC.
CRST INTERNATIONAL, INC.
EXEL INC.
LYNDEN INCORPORATED
PITT-OHIO EXPRESS, LLC
R & L CARRIERS, INC.
STEVENS TRANSPORT, INC.
U.S. XPRESS ENTERPRISES, INC.

HISTORICAL FINANCIALS
Company Type: Private

Income Statement — FYE: December 31

	REVENUE ($mil)	NET INCOME ($mil)	NET PROFIT MARGIN	EMPLOYEES
12/20	3,559	494	13.9%	14,000
12/19	3,259	251	7.7%	—
12/18	3,159	252	8.0%	—
12/17	2,731	231	8.5%	—
Annual Growth	9.2%	28.9%	—	—

2020 Year-End Financials
Return on assets: 26.0%   Cash ($ mil.): 99
Return on equity: 56.0%
Current Ratio: 1.70

EVANS GENERAL CONTRACTORS, LLC

EXECUTIVES
OK Vice President, Jared W Heald Senior

LOCATIONS

HQ: EVANS GENERAL CONTRACTORS, LLC
3050 NORTHWINDS PKWY # 20, ALPHARETTA, GA 300092564
Phone: 678 713-7216
Web: WWW.EVANSGENERALCONTRACTORS.COM

HISTORICAL FINANCIALS
Company Type: Private

Income Statement — FYE: December 31

	REVENUE ($mil)	NET INCOME ($mil)	NET PROFIT MARGIN	EMPLOYEES
12/21	1,166	33	2.9%	145
12/20	650	13	2.2%	—
12/10	55	1	2.2%	—
12/08	89	2	2.4%	—
Annual Growth	21.8%	23.5%	—	—

2021 Year-End Financials
Return on assets: 9.3%   Cash ($ mil.): 102
Return on equity: 87.2%
Current Ratio: 1.10

EVERGY MISSOURI WEST, INC.

LOCATIONS

HQ: EVERGY MISSOURI WEST, INC.
1200 MAIN ST FL 30, KANSAS CITY, MO 641052122
Phone: 816 556-2200

HISTORICAL FINANCIALS
Company Type: Private

Income Statement — FYE: December 31

	REVENUE ($mil)	NET INCOME ($mil)	NET PROFIT MARGIN	EMPLOYEES
12/18	833	27	3.3%	1,088
12/17	818	(40)	—	—
12/16	801	60	7.6%	—
Annual Growth	2.0%	(32.8%)	—	—

2018 Year-End Financials
Return on assets: 0.8%   Cash ($ mil.): 1
Return on equity: 2.3%
Current Ratio: 2.50

EVERSOURCE ENERGY SERVICE COMPANY

Northeast Utilities Service Company (NUSCO) provides support and reports for its cohorts. The company was created in 1966 to centralize corporate activities for Northeast Utilities (renamed Eversource Energy). NUSCO acts as an agent and offers centralized administrative services not only for its parent company, Northeast Utilities, but all of its subsidiaries (Connecticut Light and Power, Public Service Company of New Hampshire, Western Massachusetts Electric, and Yankee Gas Services Company) as well. NUSCO duties include accounting, financial, legal, operational, information technology, engineering, planning, and purchasing services.

LOCATIONS

HQ: EVERSOURCE ENERGY SERVICE COMPANY
56 PROSPECT ST, HARTFORD, CT 061032818
Phone: 800 286-5000
Web: WWW.EVERSOURCE.COM

COMPETITORS

ALLIANCE FOR COOPERATIVE ENERGY SERVICES POWER MARKETING, LLC
AMERESCO SOUTHWEST, INC.
DUQUESNE LIGHT HOLDINGS, INC.
ENTERPRISE GROUP HOLDINGS LIMITED
GEXA ENERGY, LP
Hafslund Produksjon Holding AS
MANILA ELECTRIC COMPANY
PREFERRED ENERGY SERVICES, INC.
ROSE INTERNATIONAL, INC.
STONEBRIDGE ACQUISITION, INC.

HISTORICAL FINANCIALS
Company Type: Private

Income Statement — FYE: December 31

	REVENUE ($mil)	NET INCOME ($mil)	NET PROFIT MARGIN	EMPLOYEES
12/16	831	11	1.4%	4,550
12/08	5,800	260	4.5%	—
12/07	5,822	246	4.2%	—
12/05	0	0	—	—
Annual Growth	—	—	—	—

2016 Year-End Financials
Return on assets: 0.8%   Cash ($ mil.): 11
Return on equity: 8.2%
Current Ratio: 0.60

EXCELA HEALTH

Auditors: BAKER TILLY US LLP PITTSBURG

LOCATIONS

HQ: EXCELA HEALTH
56 CLUB LN STE 101, BLAIRSVILLE, PA 157177957
Phone: 724 459-0595

HISTORICAL FINANCIALS
Company Type: Private

Income Statement — FYE: June 30

	REVENUE ($mil)	NET INCOME ($mil)	NET PROFIT MARGIN	EMPLOYEES
06/21	662	127	19.3%	19
06/20	575	(38)	—	—
Annual Growth	15.1%	—	—	—

2021 Year-End Financials
Return on assets: 15.7%   Cash ($ mil.): 65
Return on equity: 29.6%
Current Ratio: 1.30

EXTENDED STAY AMERICA, INC.

Guests at this hotel chain need not worry about wearing out their welcome. The company owns and operates some 680 Extended Stay hotels. Extended Stay brands include Extended Stay America, Extended Stay Canada, and Crossland Economy Studios. A hybrid between a hotel and an apartment, its lodgings offer all-suite accommodations targeting business and leisure travelers looking for a temporary place to call home. The rooms feature separate living and dining areas and fully-equipped kitchens. Extended Stay can charge lower rates than hotels by eliminating room service and daily maid services. The company went public in 2013.

IPO

Extended Stay America raised $565 million, which it will use to buy stock in its real estate investment trust, the tax-free entity that owns its hotels' properties. Any remainder will be used to pay down debt and for general corporate purposes.

Geographic Reach

The company manages hotel properties in 44 US states and Canada. California is home to 85 properties, Texas has about 70, and Florida has more than 50. All other states have less than 35 hotels. There are only three Extended Stay Canada properties.

Sales and Marketing

Extended Stay hotels cater mostly to business travelers; its average length of stay is 28 days, while the average stay at a regular hotel is 2.5 days. As such, the company's sales team focuses on building relationships with certain companies to attract repeat guests. While it does not offer a loyalty program, it does use its customer database for targeted marketing and promotional campaigns.

Most of its reservations are made directly with the property, less than 10% of stays are booked through third-party hotel booking websites. Extended Stay outsources its reservation system, call center operations, and the management of its website.

Financial Performance

Overall revenues increased 7% in 2012 to $1 billion, up from $942,000 in 2011. Room sales were up due to a 10% increase in the average daily rate the company charged, despite occupancy being down 2%. The company also lost about $2 million in other revenue by offering free WiFi Internet access in 2012, but it justified the loss through customer satisfaction.

Strategy

In order to achieve brand consistency, the company recently consolidated most of its brands under the Extended Stay America. Previously, almost 300 hotels were branded as Homestead Studio Suites, Studio Plus, and Extended Stay Deluxe.

The company is also in the process of renovating 90% its hotels for a total cost of almost $380 million. About 300 hotels are being treated to a million-dollar renovation, which includes remodeling of common areas, new paint, carpet, signs, floors and counters in bathrooms and kitchens, as well as new mattresses and flat screen TVs, artwork, lighting, bedspreads, and refurbished furniture. The company is spending $150,000 a pop on renovations at 300 other hotels, which includes new mattresses, flat screen TVs, lighting, bedspreads, and signs.

EXECUTIVES

Corporate Secretary, Christopher Dekle
Auditors : DELOITTE & TOUCHE LLP CHARLOT

LOCATIONS

HQ: EXTENDED STAY AMERICA, INC.
11525 N CMNITY HSE RD, CHARLOTTE, NC 282773609
Phone: 980 345-1600
Web: WWW.EXTENDEDSTAYAMERICA.COM

COMPETITORS

CHOICE HOTELS INTERNATIONAL, INC.
HOMEAWAY, INC.
INTERCONTINENTAL HOTELS GROUP PLC
MARRIOTT INTERNATIONAL, INC.
MOTEL 6 OPERATING L.P.
PARK HOTELS & RESORTS INC.
PEBBLEBROOK HOTEL TRUST
PREFERRED HOTEL GROUP, INC.
RED LION HOTELS CORPORATION
TRAVELODGE HOTELS LIMITED

HISTORICAL FINANCIALS

Company Type: Private

Income Statement — FYE: December 31

	REVENUE ($mil)	NET INCOME ($mil)	NET PROFIT MARGIN	EMPLOYEES
12/20	1,042	96	9.2%	8,400
12/19	1,218	165	13.6%	—
12/18	1,275	211	16.6%	—
12/17	1,282	172	13.4%	—
Annual Growth	(6.7%)	(17.6%)	—	—

2020 Year-End Financials
Return on assets: 2.4%   Cash ($ mil.): 396
Return on equity: 8.5%
Current Ratio: —

EYP STOCKBRIDGE, LLC

Auditors : KAUFMAN ROSSIN AND CO

LOCATIONS

HQ: EYP STOCKBRIDGE, LLC
3200 SW 42ND ST, FORT LAUDERDALE, FL 333126813
Phone: 954 797-4000

HISTORICAL FINANCIALS

Company Type: Private

Income Statement — FYE: September 25

	REVENUE ($mil)	NET INCOME ($mil)	NET PROFIT MARGIN	EMPLOYEES
09/10	800	7	0.9%	28
09/09	826	8	1.0%	—
Annual Growth	(3.2%)	(12.4%)	—	—

2010 Year-End Financials
Return on assets: 2.4%   Cash ($ mil.): 2
Return on equity: 4.4%
Current Ratio: 1.00

FAIRFAX COUNTY VIRGINIA

EXECUTIVES

County Executive, Bryan Hill
County Executive*, Christopher Leonard
County Executive*, Rachel Flynn
County Executive, Ellicia Seard-mccormick
County Executive*, Thomas G Arnold
Chief Security Officer*, Karla Bruce
Auditors : CHERRY BEKAERT LLP TYSONS CO

LOCATIONS

HQ: FAIRFAX COUNTY VIRGINIA
12000 GVRNMENT CTR PKWY S, FAIRFAX, VA 220350002
Phone: 703 324-3126
Web: WWW.FAIRFAXCOUNTY.GOV

HISTORICAL FINANCIALS

Company Type: Private

Income Statement — FYE: June 30

	REVENUE ($mil)	NET INCOME ($mil)	NET PROFIT MARGIN	EMPLOYEES
06/21	5,420	96	1.8%	12,000
06/20	5,201	(75)	—	—
06/18	4,806	71	1.5%	—
06/17	4,695	171	3.6%	—
Annual Growth	3.7%	(13.4%)	—	—

2021 Year-End Financials
Return on assets: 0.5%   Cash ($ mil.): 1,942
Return on equity: 9.3%
Current Ratio: —

FAIRVIEW HEALTH SERVICES

It's fair to say that when it comes to health care, Fairview Health Services takes the long view. The not-for-profit system serves Minnesota's Twin Cities and nearby communities. Fairview Health is affiliated with the medical school of the University of

Minnesota and counts among its 10 hospitals the University of Minnesota Medical Center. The hospitals house more than 2,500 beds and provide comprehensive medical and surgical services. The system also operates primary and specialty care clinics that provide preventive and wellness care. Additionally, it operates retail pharmacies and nursing homes and provides home health care and rehabilitation. Merger talks with University of Minnesota Physicians have stalled.

Operations

Fairview operates more than 40 primary care clinics, seven urgent care clinics, more than 55 specialty service centers, some 50 senior housing locations, and 30-plus retail pharmacies scattered across the state. It employs more than 2,300 physicians. The health system was one of the first in the nation to initiate a pay scheme for clinic doctors that rewards them for the manner in which they treat patients, favorable satisfaction surveys, and their ability to keep patients healthy and out of the hospital rather than simply for the number of tests run.

Fairview provides a host of senior care options through its Ebenezer unit that include assisted and independent living, adult day care, and health services designed specifically for the elderly and administered by specialists that include geriatricians.

The company's affiliated physician organizations include Behavioral Healthcare Providers, University of Minnesota Physicians, and Fairview Physician Associates.

Sales and Marketing

Negotiated contracts and commercial channels account for about two-thirds of the company's revenues, while Medicare accounts for about a quarter of revenues. Medicaid and self-pay channels round out the sales.

Financial Performance

Fairview's revenues grew by 5% to $3.4 billion in 2013 due to an increase in revenues from net patient services and other operating revenues; this was slightly offset by a decrease in revenue from net assets released from restriction. Net income grew 51% that year to $244.3 million, led by the increase in revenues and investment returns. Also contributing to the improvement was the absence of disaffiliation loss of subsidiaries which had occurred the prior year.

Cash flow from operations grew by $8 million to $79.3 million in 2013; the rise in net income and changes in current liabilities and other assets led to the inflow.

Strategy

Fairview has grown through organic initiatives and via acquisitions. It has recently made several improvements to its new specialty center including adding a physical therapy gym, refurbishing its pediatric floor, renovating the neonatal intensive care unit, and adding a larger laboratory.

In 2013 the University of Minnesota proposed taking over Fairview, which would have then been combined with South Dakota's Sanford Health. That deal ultimately fell through, but in 2015 Fairview announced plans to instead merge with the school's private physician network University of Minnesota Physicians. The combined company is to be named University of Minnesota Health. (That brand was launched in early 2014, prior to organizations' announced intention to combine forces.)

Company Background

Fairview was founded in 1906.

EXECUTIVES

CIO*, Sameer Badlani

Auditors : ERNST & YOUNG LLP MINNEAPOLIS

LOCATIONS

HQ: FAIRVIEW HEALTH SERVICES
1700 UNIVERSITY AVE W, SAINT PAUL, MN 551043727
Phone: 612 672-6300
Web: WWW.FAIRVIEW.ORG

COMPETITORS

APTIV PLC
DELTEX MEDICAL GROUP PLC
FEEDBACK PLC
KIRKLAND'S, INC.
LEGACY LIFEPOINT HEALTH, INC.
ROTECH HEALTHCARE INC.
SISTERS OF CHARITY OF LEAVENWORTH HEALTH SYSTEM, INC.
THE CLEVELAND CLINIC FOUNDATION
ULTA SALON, COSMETICS & FRAGRANCE, INC.
VCA INC.

HISTORICAL FINANCIALS

Company Type: Private

Income Statement — FYE: December 31

	REVENUE ($mil)	NET INCOME ($mil)	NET PROFIT MARGIN	EMPLOYEES
12/20	6,123	(18)	—	18,000
12/19	6,049	13	0.2%	—
12/18	5,709	5	0.1%	—
12/17	5,275	511	9.7%	—
Annual Growth	5.1%	—	—	—

2020 Year-End Financials
Return on assets: (-0.3%)   Cash ($ mil.): 94
Return on equity: (-0.7%)
Current Ratio: 1.50

FAMILY HEALTH INTERNATIONAL INC

Known as FHI 360, Family Health International believes that health is wealth. From a handful of offices located in the US, Asia-Pacific, and South Africa, FHI 360 funds and manages public health programs, research, education, and other resources in more than 60 countries. Founded in 1971 as the International Fertility Research Program of the University of North Carolina at Chapel Hill, FHI 360 primarily focuses on and supports HIV/AIDS prevention research, reproductive health services, and maternal and neonatal health programs. The organization works with governments, private agencies, and non-governmental organizations to develop the most appropriate programs for different areas.

Auditors : ERNST & YOUNG US LLP TAMPA F

LOCATIONS

HQ: FAMILY HEALTH INTERNATIONAL INC
359 BLACKWELL ST STE 200, DURHAM, NC 277012477
Phone: 919 544-7040
Web: WWW.FHI360.ORG

PRODUCTS/OPERATIONS

Selected Services
Behavior-change communication
Capacity-building
Clinical trials services
Creative services
Data analysis
Quality assurance
Research services
Social marketing
Training and technical assistance

COMPETITORS

ALTARUM INSTITUTE
AMERICAN INSTITUTES FOR RESEARCH IN THE BEHAVIORAL SCIENCES
CHILDREN'S HOSPITAL MEDICAL CENTER
HEALTH RESEARCH, INC.
LONDON SCHOOL OF HYGIENE AND TROPICAL MEDICINE
Organisation Mondiale de la Santé (OMS)
PATHFINDER INTERNATIONAL
THE JACKSON LABORATORY
THE POPULATION COUNCIL INC
THE RAND CORPORATION

HISTORICAL FINANCIALS

Company Type: Private

Income Statement — FYE: September 30

	REVENUE ($mil)	NET INCOME ($mil)	NET PROFIT MARGIN	EMPLOYEES
09/19	781	0	0.1%	4,000
09/14	653	(3)	—	—
09/13	664	10	1.5%	—
09/09	327	2	0.9%	—
Annual Growth	9.1%	(10.2%)	—	—

2019 Year-End Financials
Return on assets: 0.4%   Cash ($ mil.): 123
Return on equity: 1.1%
Current Ratio: 1.60

FAMILY HEALTH NETWORK, INC.

LOCATIONS

HQ: FAMILY HEALTH NETWORK, INC.
222 MERCHANDISE MART PLZ # 960, CHICAGO, IL 606541236
Phone: 312 243-5235

Web: WWW.CHICAGOFAMILYHEALTH.ORG

HISTORICAL FINANCIALS
Company Type: Private

Income Statement				FYE: December 31
	REVENUE ($mil)	NET INCOME ($mil)	NET PROFIT MARGIN	EMPLOYEES
12/17	549	(23)	—	30
12/09	60	2	4.9%	—
12/08	56	0	0.0%	—
Annual Growth	28.7%	—	—	—

2017 Year-End Financials
Return on assets: (-15.2%)   Cash ($ mil.): 59
Return on equity: (-341.2%)
Current Ratio: —

FARM CREDIT BANK OF TEXAS

The largest member of the federal Farm Credit System, the Farm Credit Bank of Texas provides loans and financial services to about 20 lending cooperatives and financial institutions in Alabama, Louisiana, Mississippi, New Mexico and Texas. These include agricultural credit associations, which provide agricultural production loans, agribusiness financing, and rural mortgage financing; and federal land credit associations, which offer real estate loans on farms, ranches, and other rural property. Farm Credit Bank of Texas is owned by the lending cooperatives it serves.

EXECUTIVES
CCO*, Steven H Fowlkes
Operations Officer*, Thomas W Hill
Auditors : PRICEWATERHOUSECOOPERS LLP A

LOCATIONS
HQ: FARM CREDIT BANK OF TEXAS
4801 PLZ ON THE LK # 1200, AUSTIN, TX 787461081
Phone: 512 465-0400
Web: WWW.FARMCREDITBANK.COM

COMPETITORS
AGRIBANK, FCB
FEDERAL HOME LOAN BANK OF ATLANTA
FEDERAL HOME LOAN BANK OF CHICAGO
FEDERAL HOME LOAN BANK OF CINCINNATI
FEDERAL HOME LOAN BANK OF SAN FRANCISCO
FEDERAL HOME LOAN BANK OF TOPEKA
MICHIGAN COMMUNITY BANCORP LIMITED
NORTHWEST FARM CREDIT SERVICES
WELLS FINANCIAL CORP.
ZIONS BANCORPORATION, NATIONAL ASSOCIATION

HISTORICAL FINANCIALS
Company Type: Private

Income Statement				FYE: December 31
	ASSETS ($mil)	NET INCOME ($mil)	INCOME AS % OF ASSETS	EMPLOYEES
12/16	21,222	192	0.9%	200
12/13	16,212	179	1.1%	—
12/07	13,520	74	0.5%	—
Annual Growth	5.1%	11.2%	—	—

2016 Year-End Financials
Return on assets: 0.9%   Cash ($ mil.): 195
Return on equity: 11.9%
Current Ratio: —

FARM CREDIT SERVICES OF AMERICA

Auditors : PRICEWATERHOUSECOOPERS LLP M

LOCATIONS
HQ: FARM CREDIT SERVICES OF AMERICA
5015 S 118TH ST, OMAHA, NE 681372210
Phone: 800 884-3276
Web: WWW.FCSAMERICA.COM

HISTORICAL FINANCIALS
Company Type: Private

Income Statement				FYE: December 31
	ASSETS ($mil)	NET INCOME ($mil)	INCOME AS % OF ASSETS	EMPLOYEES
12/15	24,772	514	2.1%	10,000
12/04	8,475	294	3.5%	—
12/03	7,633	114	1.5%	—
12/02	0	132	—	—
Annual Growth	—	11.0%	—	—

2015 Year-End Financials
Return on assets: 2.1%   Cash ($ mil.): 60
Return on equity: 11.9%
Current Ratio: —

FARM CREDIT WEST

EXECUTIVES
BICA Vice President, Ernest M Hodges
Auditors : PRICEWATERHOUSECOOPERS LLP SA

LOCATIONS
HQ: FARM CREDIT WEST
3755 ATHERTON RD, ROCKLIN, CA 957653701
Phone: 916 724-4800
Web: WWW.AGWESTFC.COM

HISTORICAL FINANCIALS
Company Type: Private

Income Statement				FYE: December 31
	ASSETS ($mil)	NET INCOME ($mil)	INCOME AS % OF ASSETS	EMPLOYEES
12/12	6,668	151	2.3%	165
12/11	6,282	176	2.8%	—
12/10	6,129	0	0.0%	—
Annual Growth	4.3%	—	—	—

2012 Year-End Financials
Return on assets: 2.3%   Cash ($ mil.): 35
Return on equity: 12.5%
Current Ratio: —

FARMERS COOPERATIVE

Auditors : GARDINER THOMSEN LINCOLN NE

LOCATIONS
HQ: FARMERS COOPERATIVE
208 W DEPOT ST, DORCHESTER, NE 683432375
Phone: 402 946-2211
Web: WWW.FARMERSCO-OPERATIVE.COM

HISTORICAL FINANCIALS
Company Type: Private

Income Statement				FYE: August 31
	REVENUE ($mil)	NET INCOME ($mil)	NET PROFIT MARGIN	EMPLOYEES
08/14	830	19	2.3%	470
08/12	918	22	2.5%	—
08/11	695	21	3.1%	—
08/10	636	0	0.0%	—
Annual Growth	6.9%	1803.9%	—	—

2014 Year-End Financials
Return on assets: 7.6%   Cash ($ mil.): 28
Return on equity: 11.5%
Current Ratio: 1.80

FARMERS COOPERATIVE COMPANY

The importance of cooperation -- it's one of life's most important lessons. Dating back to the early 1900s, the Farmers Cooperative Company (FCC) learned that lesson early on. The 5,500-member-plus co-op offers agronomy and grain marketing services to its members, who oversee some 3 million acres of farmland in central and north central Iowa. The largest of its kind in Iowa, FCC operates 40 grain elevators and provides soil testing and mapping services. It sells supplies including seed, feed, and fertilizer to its members. The coop merged with another Iowa coop, West Central Cooperative in 2016 to form Landus Cooperative.

Operations
Farmers Cooperative (FCC) operates four departments: Agronomy, Feed, Grain, and Seed. Agronomy serves customers at some 40 locations across central Iowa and is one of largest agronomy divisions in the state. The Feed department has six manufacturing locations across central, north central, and northwest Iowa. FCC's feed mills produce more than 900,000 tons of complete feed annually. FCC has 40 grain elevators across its membership area. More than 118 million bushels of grain are handled annually. FCC also has grain storage capacity of 75 million bushels. The cooperative's Seed department works closely with the Agronomy division since both serve the same customers.

Auditors : MERIWETHER WILSON & COMPANY

LOCATIONS
HQ: FARMERS COOPERATIVE COMPANY
105 GARFIELD AVE, FARNHAMVILLE, IA 505386712
Phone: 515 817-2100
Web: WWW.LANDUS.AG

PRODUCTS/OPERATIONS
Selected Departments
Agronomy
Feed
Grain
Seed

COMPETITORS
CHS INC.
COUNTRY PRIDE COOPERATIVE, INC.
FIVE STAR COOPERATIVE
NEW COOPERATION COMPANY
WEST CENTRAL COOPERATIVE

HISTORICAL FINANCIALS
Company Type: Private

Income Statement — FYE: August 31

	REVENUE ($mil)	NET INCOME ($mil)	NET PROFIT MARGIN	EMPLOYEES
08/10	779	10	1.3%	450
08/09	894	13	1.5%	—
Annual Growth	(12.8%)	(19.9%)	—	—

2010 Year-End Financials
Return on assets: 5.6%   Cash ($ mil.): —
Return on equity: 1.3%
Current Ratio: —

FARMERS GRAIN TERMINAL, INC.

Auditors : HUDSON CISNE & CO LLP LITT

LOCATIONS
HQ: FARMERS GRAIN TERMINAL, INC.
1977 HARBOR FRONT RD, GREENVILLE, MS 387019588

Phone: 662 332-0987
Web: WWW.FGTCOOP.COM

HISTORICAL FINANCIALS
Company Type: Private

Income Statement — FYE: July 31

	REVENUE ($mil)	NET INCOME ($mil)	NET PROFIT MARGIN	EMPLOYEES
07/13	929	19	2.1%	102
07/12	615	12	2.1%	—
07/11	471	8	1.8%	—
Annual Growth	40.4%	53.0%	—	—

2013 Year-End Financials
Return on assets: 15.6%   Cash ($ mil.): 63
Return on equity: 30.0%
Current Ratio: 2.20

FCTG HOLDINGS, INC.

LOCATIONS
HQ: FCTG HOLDINGS, INC.
10250 SW GREENBURG RD # 200, PORTLAND, OR 972235461
Phone: 503 246-8500
Web: WWW.FCTG.COM

HISTORICAL FINANCIALS
Company Type: Private

Income Statement — FYE: January 31

	REVENUE ($mil)	NET INCOME ($mil)	NET PROFIT MARGIN	EMPLOYEES
01/09	1,535	2	0.2%	406
01/08	2,055	1	0.1%	—
01/07	2,798	(0)	0.0%	—
Annual Growth	(25.9%)	—	—	—

2009 Year-End Financials
Return on assets: 2.7%   Cash ($ mil.): 3
Return on equity: 11.0%
Current Ratio: 1.20

FEDERAL-MOGUL HOLDINGS LLC

Auditors : GRANT THORNTON LLP SOUTHFIELD

LOCATIONS
HQ: FEDERAL-MOGUL HOLDINGS LLC
27300 W 11 MILE RD # 101, SOUTHFIELD, MI 480346193
Phone: 248 354-7700
Web: WWW.FEDERALMOGUL.COM

HISTORICAL FINANCIALS
Company Type: Private

Income Statement — FYE: December 31

	REVENUE ($mil)	NET INCOME ($mil)	NET PROFIT MARGIN	EMPLOYEES
12/16	7,434	90	1.2%	53,700
12/15	7,419	(104)	—	—
12/14	7,317	(161)	—	—
Annual Growth	0.8%	—	—	—

2016 Year-End Financials
Return on assets: 1.3%   Cash ($ mil.): 300
Return on equity: 10.2%
Current Ratio: 1.70

FERGUSON ENTERPRISES, LLC

Ferguson Enterprises is the largest wholesale distributor of plumbing supplies, pipes, valves, and fittings in the US. It is also a major distributor of HVAC equipment for heating and cooling, waterworks (water hydrants and meters), kitchen and bath, lighting, safety equipment, appliances, and tools. The company's major brands include: KOHLER, Fujitsu, Delta, Jacuzzi, Samsung, Westcraft, and PROFLO, among others. Ferguson has greater than 1,600 locations and about 10 distribution centers across the US. It has customers in all 50 states, the Caribbean, Puerto Rico, and Mexico. Formed in 1953, Ferguson is a subsidiary of UK-based Ferguson plc (formerly Wolseley) and has more than 31,000 associates in 1,600 locations.

Operations
Ferguson raises the bar for industry standards as the top-rated wholesale supplier of commercial and residential plumbing supplies. The diverse distributor that spans multiple businesses including pipe, valves and fittings (PVF); heating and cooling equipment (HVAC); kitchen, bath, lighting and appliances; and maintenance, repair and operations (MRO) products provides expert advice and a range of products and services to its customers to improve their construction, renovation and maintenance projects.

Geographic Reach
Based in Newport News, Virginia, Ferguson operates in approximately 1,600 locations nationwide. In addition to its approximately ten distribution centers throughout the US and one in Canada, the company serves customers in all 50 states, the Caribbean, Canada, Puerto Rico, and Mexico.

Sales and Marketing
Ferguson serves customers in residential plumbing, commercial mechanical, HVAC, builder, fire and fabrication, waterworks and industrial industries.

Mergers and Acquisitions
Ferguson made three major purchases in

2014. In December it purchased HP Products Corporation, a distributor of janitorial, packaging, safety, laundry and dietary, lighting, equipment, food, and textile products, adding all 450 employees, 5 distribution centers, 3 cross-decks and 500,000 square feet of warehouse space located in the Midwest. In April, Ferguson bought Factory Direct Appliance, Inc., including five showrooms in Kansas City, and two more in Des Moines and Omaha. In January, the company purchased Karl's appliance, adding six showrooms in northern New Jersey to its retail network.

In February 2013, Ferguson expanded its waterworks business with the acquisition of Fluid Systems Hawaii, which operates a single location near Honolulu and distributes underground water supply and wastewater drainage products to Oahu, Maui, and other Hawaiian islands. Ferguson also bought Chicago-based Power Equipment Direct, a business-to-consumer business selling generators and power tools.

In 2012, the company acquired four businesses -- two in its Blended Branches business and one in each of the Waterworks and Industrial businesses -- for a total consideration of about $44.2 million. In April 2012 it acquired Reese Kitchens, Inc., a cabinet designer in Indianapolis that caters to the residential remodeling market. In October the company bought Davis & Warshow, a residential and commercial plumbing supplier based in Maspeth, New York. With eight wholesale and seven showroom locations in the metro New York market, the purchase of Davis & Warshow marked Ferguson's entry into the competitive and lucrative New York market.

Auditors : DELOITTE & TOUCHE LLP RICHMON

LOCATIONS

HQ: FERGUSON ENTERPRISES, LLC
12500 JEFFERSON AVE, NEWPORT NEWS, VA 236024314
Phone: 757 874-7795
Web: WWW.FERGUSON.COM

PRODUCTS/OPERATIONS

2016 Sales by Segment

	% of total
Blended branches	62
Waterworks	16
Industrial	7
HVAC	7
B2C	6
Other	2
Total	100

Selected Products
HVAC parts and supplies (coils, diffusers, furnaces, pumps, refrigerants)
Pipes (ductile iron, PVC)
Plumbing (bath accessories, faucets, fixtures, water heaters)
Safety products (foot, hand, hearing, and respiratory protection, protective clothing, signs)
Tools (batteries, flashlights, hand tools, ladders, paints, power tools)

Waterworks (backflow prevention devices, hydrants, meters, pipes, valves)

COMPETITORS

APPLIED INDUSTRIAL TECHNOLOGIES, INC.
FASTENAL COMPANY
HD SUPPLY HOLDINGS, INC.
LAWSON PRODUCTS, INC.
MOTION INDUSTRIES, INC.
MSC INDUSTRIAL DIRECT CO., INC.
STANDEX INTERNATIONAL CORPORATION
TRICORBRAUN, INC.
W. W. GRAINGER, INC.
WESCO INTERNATIONAL, INC.

HISTORICAL FINANCIALS
Company Type: Private

Income Statement — FYE: July 31

	REVENUE ($mil)	NET INCOME ($mil)	NET PROFIT MARGIN	EMPLOYEES
07/21	21,477	1,814	8.4%	27,000
07/20	18,856	1,266	6.7%	—
07/19	18,356	1,005	5.5%	—
07/18	16,669	819	4.9%	—
Annual Growth	8.8%	30.4%	—	—

2021 Year-End Financials
Return on assets: 16.1%   Cash ($ mil.): 304
Return on equity: 41.7%
Current Ratio: 1.60

FIDELITY INV CHARITABLE GIFT FUND

EXECUTIVES

Vp, Krystal Kiley
Vice President, Philanthropic, Nageeb Sumar
Director, Institutional Relati, Colin Roth

LOCATIONS

HQ: FIDELITY INV CHARITABLE GIFT FUND
200 SEAPORT BLVD STE 1, BOSTON, MA 022102000
Phone: 617 392-8679
Web: WWW.FIDELITYCHARITABLE.ORG

HISTORICAL FINANCIALS
Company Type: Private

Income Statement — FYE: June 30

	REVENUE ($mil)	NET INCOME ($mil)	NET PROFIT MARGIN	EMPLOYEES
06/11	1,874	599	32.0%	1
06/10	1,274	147	11.6%	—
Annual Growth	47.1%	306.7%	—	—

2011 Year-End Financials
Return on assets: 10.7%   Cash ($ mil.): 77
Return on equity: 10.8%
Current Ratio: 1.90

FINANCIAL INDUSTRY REGULATORY AUTHORITY, INC.

FINRA is dedicated to protecting investors and safeguarding market integrity in a manner that facilitates vibrant capital markets. It is a not-for-profit organization that ? working under the supervision of the SEC ? actively engages with and provides essential tools for investors, member firms and policymakers. In addition, it is authorized by the congress to protect America's investors by making sure the broker-dealer industry operates fairly and honestly. FINRA oversee more than 624,000 brokers across the country and analyze billion dollars of market events. FINRA was formed in 2007 from the consolidation of the National Association of Securities Dealers and certain regulatory and enforcement elements of the NYSE.

Operations
FINRA regulates the Broker-Dealers, Capital Acquisition Brokers, and Funding Portals. In additions, Broker Dealer is in the business of buying or selling securities on behalf of its customers or its own account or both. A Capital Acquisition Broker is a Broker Dealer subject to a narrower rule book. A Funding Portal is a crowd-funding intermediary. FINRA plays a critical role in ensuring the integrity of America's financial system. It writes and enforces rules governing the ethical activities of all registered broker-dealer firms and registered brokers in the US, examines firms for compliance with rules, fosters market transparency, and educates investors.

Its operating revenues include regulatory revenues (approximately 35% of sales), activity assessment revenues (about 5%), user revenue (over 20%), contract services revenue (roughly 15%), and fines (around 5%).

Geographic Reach
FINRA operates from Washington, DC, where it is headquartered, and New York, with about 20 regional offices around the US.

Sales and Marketing
FINRA markets its services through conference and events, virtual conference Panels, and Webinars.

Financial Performance
In 2021, the company had a net revenue of $1.4 billion, a 21% increase from the previous year's net revenue of $1.2 billion.

FINRA reported net income of $218.8 million in 2021 versus a net income of $19.8 million in 2020, an increase of $199 million year over year. The company's 2021 net income was driven by operating income of $112 million, investment gains of $105.3 million and other income of $1.5 million.

The company's cash at the end of 2021

was $322.3 million. Operating activities used $10.8 million, while investing activities used $251.4 million, mainly for net purchases of fixed income securities. Financing activities used another $12.8 million for debt principal payments.

Strategy

FINRA's Enterprise Risk Management (ERM) program is designed to provide a consolidated, organization-wide view of the risks that FINRA faces in the execution of its mission, strategic goals and key business objectives. The program covers a broad spectrum of risks in various risk categories, such as strategic, operational, legal and compliance, and financial, and provides transparency for senior management and the Board regarding FINRA's enterprise-level risks and how they are being managed. The chart below shows the governance structure FINRA has in place to oversee and manage enterprise risk.

In determining a benchmarking strategy for key executives, the Committee and its advisor (see next section) engaged in substantial research and consideration of the functions and operations of several potential comparisons as well as general competitive conditions. Ultimately, the Committee approved a benchmarking process for key executives that focused on the following sources: Public comparison group composed of a blend of public financial services organizations engaged in brokerage or other related banking activities; Public exchanges and regulators; Financial services industry survey data; Legal industry survey data; and Other not-for-profit sector data.

Company Background

FINRA was founded in 2007 by NASD and NYSE.

EXECUTIVES

CAO*, Todd Diganci
Senior Vice President Human Resources*, Tracy Johnson
Auditors : ERNST & YOUNG LLP MCLEAN VIR

LOCATIONS

HQ: FINANCIAL INDUSTRY REGULATORY AUTHORITY, INC.
  1735 K ST NW, WASHINGTON, DC 200061506
Phone: 301 590-6500
Web: WWW.FINRA.ORG

PRODUCTS/OPERATIONS

2015 Sales

	$ mil.	% of total
Regulatory revenue	444.9	45
User revenue	218.1	22
Contract services revenue	125.5	13
Fines	93.8	6
Transparency services revenue	63.8	4
Dispute resolution revenue	41.0	1
Other revenue	5.4	9
Total	992.5	100

COMPETITORS

AMERICAN BANKERS ASSOCIATION
AMERICAN BUSINESS CONFERENCE INC
COUNCIL OF BETTER BUSINESS BUREAUS, INC.
INSTITUTE OF INTERNATIONAL FINANCE, INC. (THE)
NATIONAL RURAL ELECTRIC COOPERATIVE ASSOCIATION
PERFORMANT FINANCIAL CORPORATION
PINNACOL ASSURANCE
SECURITY INDUSTRY ASSOCIATION
SOFTWARE PUBLISHERS ASSOC (INC)
U.S. SECURITIES AND EXCHANGE COMMISSION

HISTORICAL FINANCIALS

Company Type: Private

Income Statement   FYE: December 31

	REVENUE ($mil)	NET INCOME ($mil)	NET PROFIT MARGIN	EMPLOYEES
12/21	1,404	218	15.6%	3,400
12/20	1,162	19	1.7%	—
12/19	938	(45)	—	—
12/12	878	10	1.2%	—
Annual Growth	5.4%	40.1%	—	—

2021 Year-End Financials
Return on assets: 8.6%   Cash ($ mil.): 322
Return on equity: 12.5%
Current Ratio: 3.80

FINANCIAL TRADER CORPORATION

LOCATIONS

HQ: FINANCIAL TRADER CORPORATION
  5743 LONGMONT LN, HOUSTON, TX 770572510
Phone: 713 206-4600

HISTORICAL FINANCIALS

Company Type: Private

Income Statement   FYE: December 31

	ASSETS ($mil)	NET INCOME ($mil)	INCOME AS % OF ASSETS	EMPLOYEES
12/13	398	6	1.7%	1
12/11	10	0	5.6%	—
Annual Growth	525.1%	243.5%	—	—

FLATIRON CONSTRUCTORS, INC.

Auditors : DELOITTE & TOUCHE LLP DENVER

LOCATIONS

HQ: FLATIRON CONSTRUCTORS, INC.
  385 INTERLOCKEN BLVD, BROOMFIELD, CO 800218067
Phone: 303 485-4050
Web: WWW.FLATIRONCORP.COM

HISTORICAL FINANCIALS

Company Type: Private

Income Statement   FYE: December 31

	REVENUE ($mil)	NET INCOME ($mil)	NET PROFIT MARGIN	EMPLOYEES
12/12	941	(96)	—	611
12/11	1,017	39	3.9%	—
Annual Growth	(7.5%)	—	—	—

2012 Year-End Financials
Return on assets: (-18.5%)   Cash ($ mil.): 123
Return on equity: (-55.9%)
Current Ratio: 1.60

FLORIDA CLINICAL PRACTICE ASSOCIATION, INC.

Auditors : PYA PC TAMPA FL

LOCATIONS

HQ: FLORIDA CLINICAL PRACTICE ASSOCIATION, INC.
  1329 SW 16TH ST STE 4250, GAINESVILLE, FL 326081128
Phone: 352 265-8017
Web: COMFS.UFL.EDU

HISTORICAL FINANCIALS

Company Type: Private

Income Statement   FYE: June 30

	REVENUE ($mil)	NET INCOME ($mil)	NET PROFIT MARGIN	EMPLOYEES
06/21	827	30	3.6%	2
06/20	741	(10)	—	—
06/18	667	11	1.8%	—
06/17	642	(1)	—	—
Annual Growth	6.5%	—	—	—

2021 Year-End Financials
Return on assets: 9.4%   Cash ($ mil.): —
Return on equity: 17.2%
Current Ratio: 3.70

FLORIDA DEPARTMENT OF LOTTERY

The State of Florida Department of the Lottery runs instant-play scratch tickets and lotto games, including Florida Lotto, Mega Money, Fantasy 5, and Cash 3. In addition to its own games, Florida is part of the Multi-State Lottery Association, which operates the popular Powerball drawing. Proceeds from the games are contributed to Florida's Educational Enhancement Trust Fund, which provides funding for a variety of education programs from pre-kindergarten up to the state university level. The lottery has returned more than $19 billion to the state since starting in 1988.

Auditors : SHERRILL F NORMAN CPA TALLA

LOCATIONS

HQ: FLORIDA DEPARTMENT OF LOTTERY
250 MARRIOTT DR, TALLAHASSEE, FL 323012983
Phone: 850 487-7777
Web: WWW.FLALOTTERY.COM

COMPETITORS

CALIFORNIA STATE LOTTERY COMMISSION
LOTTERY AGENCY, MARYLAND STATE
LOTTERY COMMISSION, OHIO
LOTTERY COMMISSION, WASHINGTON STATE
VIRGINIA DEPARTMENT OF LOTTERY

HISTORICAL FINANCIALS
Company Type: Private

Income Statement — FYE: June 30

	REVENUE ($mil)	NET INCOME ($mil)	NET PROFIT MARGIN	EMPLOYEES
06/21	9,083	(37)	—	400
06/20	7,511	4	0.1%	—
06/19	7,157	36	0.5%	—
06/03	2,872	117	4.1%	—
Annual Growth	6.6%	—	—	—

2021 Year-End Financials
Return on assets: (-4.6%)   Cash ($ mil.): 389
Return on equity: (-72.0%)
Current Ratio: 0.90

FLORIDA HEALTH SCIENCES CENTER, INC.

Florida Health Sciences Center, which does business as Tampa General Hospital (TGH), is a private, not-for-profit hospital and one of the most comprehensive medical facilities in Florida serving a dozen counties with a population in excess of four million. The hospital offers general medical and surgical care, as well as tertiary offerings including a Level 1 trauma center, a burn unit, a pediatric ward, women's and cardiovascular centers, and an organ transplant unit. The hospital has more than 1,000 acute-care beds, as well as some 60 beds in its rehabilitation unit, which specializes in helping patients recover from stroke, head or spine trauma, and other neuromuscular conditions. TGH is the primary teaching hospital for USF Health Morsani College of Medicine.

Operations
TGH division Tampa General Medical Group (TGMG) is a multispecialty physician group with locations in Florida's Hillsborough, Pnellas and Pasco counties. Specialties include family practice, internal medicine, pediatrics, transplant cardiology, endocrinology, hepatology, nephrology, oncology and surgery.

TGH's off-campus hospital outpatient services include Specialty Care Center, Genesis Women's Center, Pediatric Center, TGH Family Care Centers, TGH Brandon Healthplex, TGH Medical Village and TGH Urgent Care.

Each year, TGH treats more than 124,960 patients in its emergency department. This includes pediatric, chest pain, minor emergency, and trauma center patients. The hospital also operates a regional helicopter medical transport program.

Geographic Reach
The main hospital campus is located on Davis Islands in Tampa.

Sales and Marketing
TGH offers secure online health services through MyChart, an electronic medical record connects patients to their health information, and TGH EpicLink, which allows physicians to access real-time information about their patients receiving services at TGH.

EXECUTIVES

Vice Chairman*, Jim Warren

LOCATIONS

HQ: FLORIDA HEALTH SCIENCES CENTER, INC.
1 TAMPA GENERAL CIR, TAMPA, FL 336063571
Phone: 813 844-7000
Web: WWW.TGH.ORG

COMPETITORS

AKRON GENERAL MEDICAL CENTER
ASCENSION BORGESS HOSPITAL
BETHESDA HOSPITAL, INC.
CENTRAL SUFFOLK HOSPITAL
DOCTORS HOSPITAL OF AUGUSTA, LLC
NORTH FLORIDA REGIONAL MEDICAL CENTER, INC.
PIKEVILLE MEDICAL CENTER, INC.
THE BROOKDALE HOSPITAL MEDICAL CENTER
THE CHRIST HOSPITAL
TRIHEALTH, INC.

HISTORICAL FINANCIALS
Company Type: Private

Income Statement — FYE: September 30

	REVENUE ($mil)	NET INCOME ($mil)	NET PROFIT MARGIN	EMPLOYEES
09/21	1,840	182	9.9%	8,000
09/20	1,590	146	9.2%	—
09/19	1,447	57	4.0%	—
09/18	1,325	79	6.0%	—
Annual Growth	11.6%	32.1%	—	—

2021 Year-End Financials
Return on assets: 6.2%   Cash ($ mil.): 235
Return on equity: 13.3%
Current Ratio: 1.30

FLORIDA HOSPITAL MEDICAL GROUP, INC.

LOCATIONS

HQ: FLORIDA HOSPITAL MEDICAL GROUP, INC.
2600 WESTHALL LN, MAITLAND, FL 327517102
Phone: 407 200-2700
Web: WWW.ADVENTHEALTH.COM

HISTORICAL FINANCIALS
Company Type: Private

Income Statement — FYE: December 31

	REVENUE ($mil)	NET INCOME ($mil)	NET PROFIT MARGIN	EMPLOYEES
12/19	595	(4)	—	2,911
12/18	562	2	0.4%	—
12/15	421	0	0.2%	—
12/14	363	(17)	—	—
Annual Growth	10.4%	—	—	—

2019 Year-End Financials
Return on assets: (-2.3%)   Cash ($ mil.): 57
Return on equity: (-5.6%)
Current Ratio: 1.80

FLORIDA MUNICIPAL POWER AGENCY

Unlike some politicians, Florida Municipal Power Agency (FMPA) doesn't believe in holding on to power. The non-profit public agency generates and supplies electric power to 31 county or municipally owned distribution utilities, which in turn serve 2 million Florida residents and businesses. Each of the distribution utilities appoints one representative to FMPA's board of directors, which governs the Agency's activities. The Agency is authorized to undertake joint power supply projects for its members and to issue tax-exempt bonds to finance the costs of such projects. It is also empowered to implement a pooled financing program for utility-related projects.

Operations
FMPA has five distinct power supply projects and has stakes in 15 operating power plants. Each of its members have the option of whether or not to participate in a power supply project. Some members receive all their power from FMPA, some receive part of their power and others receive no power. Agency members may participate in more than one project, although each project is independent from the others.

FMPA supplies all of the power needs for 13 of its members and some of the power supply needs of seven others. All together, FMPA supplies more than 40% of its members' total power needs.

Strategy

The Agency is looking to diversify its fuel mix in the long term, adding nuclear and renewable energy powered plants to reduce the carbon emission output from its generation activities.

Company Background

FMPA has also been modernizing its power plant fleet since 2003, and in 2011 it opened a new low-emission, high efficiency generator known as Cane Island Unit 4. Plant modernization has led to lower power costs, enabling Florida Municipal Power Agency to reduce its wholesale rates to a number of members' cities in 2011 by 20% over 2009 levels.

The Agency was formed in 1978 to support the activities of Florida's locally owned and operated municipal utilities in projects requiring joint action, such as the development of large power plants to serve a number of municipalities.

Auditors: PURVIS GRAY & COMPANY LLP OC

LOCATIONS

HQ: FLORIDA MUNICIPAL POWER AGENCY
8553 COMMODITY CIR, ORLANDO, FL 328199002
Phone: 407 355-7767
Web: WWW.FMPA.COM

COMPETITORS

ELECTRIC RELIABILITY COUNCIL OF TEXAS, INC.
NEW YORK POWER AUTHORITY
OMAHA PUBLIC POWER DISTRICT
POWERSOUTH ENERGY COOPERATIVE
PUERTO RICO ELECTRIC POWER AUTHORITY

HISTORICAL FINANCIALS
Company Type: Private

Income Statement — FYE: September 30

	REVENUE ($mil)	NET INCOME ($mil)	NET PROFIT MARGIN	EMPLOYEES
09/21	628	51	8.1%	67
09/20	582	(0)	—	—
09/19	620	0	0.1%	—
09/18	604	32	5.3%	—
Annual Growth	1.3%	16.8%	—	—

2021 Year-End Financials
Return on assets: 3.0%   Cash ($ mil.): 74
Return on equity: 542.6%
Current Ratio: 2.60

FLORIDA STATE UNIVERSITY

Home to the Florida State Seminoles, Florida State University offers more than 300 undergraduate, graduate, and professional programs, including M.D. (medicine) and J.D. (law) programs. The educational institution has 16 colleges dedicated to academic fields ranging from liberal arts, music, visual arts, and education, to criminology, engineering, social work, and information. A major research institution, the university is home to the National High Magnetic Field Laboratory, or "Mag Lab," the only national lab in Florida and the only such high-magnetic facility in the US. Florida State was founded in 1851 and is part of the 11-school State University System of Florida.

Operations

Florida State boasts more than 41,000 students and has a student/faculty ratio of 26:1. The school's reputation as a top-notch research school stems from its extensive network of research facilities that cover areas such as biological medicine, social sciences, and energy. Its facilities also include the Center for Advanced Power Systems, which is supported by the US Department of Defense and the Department of Energy. The Mag Lab is funded by the National Science Foundation. Florida State also operates the John and Mable Ringling Museum of Art in Sarasota, Florida.

Geographic Reach

The main Florida State University campus in Tallahassee covers about 450 acres. The university also offers degree programs in Sarasota, Florida, and in the Republic of Panama. It boasts instructional programs in London, Florence, and Valencia as well as programs in research, development, and/or services in Costa Rica, Croatia, and Italy.

Sales and Marketing

The Florida university enrolls students from more than 120 foreign countries.

Auditors: SHERRILL F NORMAN CPA TALLA

LOCATIONS

HQ: FLORIDA STATE UNIVERSITY
600 W COLLEGE AVE, TALLAHASSEE, FL 323061096
Phone: 850 644-5482
Web: WWW.FSU.EDU

PRODUCTS/OPERATIONS

Selected Colleges
College of Applied Studies
College of Arts and Sciences
College of Business
College of Communication and Information
College of Criminology and Criminal Justice
College of Education
College of Engineering
College of Human Sciences
College of Law
College of Medicine
College of Motion Picture Arts
College of Music
College of Nursing
College of Social Sciences and Public Policy
College of Social Work
College of Visual Arts, Theatre, and Dance

COMPETITORS

CALIFORNIA STATE UNIVERSITY, LOS ANGELES
CLARKSON UNIVERSITY
FLORIDA A & M UNIVERSITY
NATIONAL UNIVERSITY
THE JOHNS HOPKINS UNIVERSITY
THE UNIVERSITY OF CENTRAL FLORIDA BOARD OF TRUSTEES
THE UNIVERSITY OF IOWA
THE UNIVERSITY OF TOLEDO
TROY UNIVERSITY
UNIVERSITY OF ILLINOIS

HISTORICAL FINANCIALS
Company Type: Private

Income Statement — FYE: June 30

	REVENUE ($mil)	NET INCOME ($mil)	NET PROFIT MARGIN	EMPLOYEES
06/12	654	40	6.1%	13,497
06/11	607	188	31.0%	—
06/10	567	121	21.4%	—
Annual Growth	7.4%	(42.4%)	—	—

2012 Year-End Financials
Return on assets: 1.2%   Cash ($ mil.): 48
Return on equity: 1.4%
Current Ratio: 6.00

FLOWORKS INTERNATIONAL LLC

EXECUTIVES

Distributor SERVICES, John Higgins Pres Fabrication
IPVF*, Michael Stanwood
Executive Corporate Strategy Vice President*, Rob Broyles
Chief Human Resource Officer*, Herbert Allen
Corporate Controller*, Michael Goldberg
IPVF*, Jeff Legrand
VALVES & AUTOMATION*, Keith Barnard
Auditors: PRICEWATERHOUSECOOPERS LLP HO

LOCATIONS

HQ: FLOWORKS INTERNATIONAL LLC
3750 HWY 225, PASADENA, TX 77503
Phone: 713 672-2222
Web: WWW.GOFLOWORKS.COM

HISTORICAL FINANCIALS
Company Type: Private

Income Statement — FYE: February 2

	REVENUE ($mil)	NET INCOME ($mil)	NET PROFIT MARGIN	EMPLOYEES
02/14*	805	(30)	—	808
06/12	222	(5)	—	—
Annual Growth	90.5%	—	—	—

*Fiscal year change

2014 Year-End Financials
Return on assets: (-5.2%)   Cash ($ mil.): 12
Return on equity: (-12.6%)
Current Ratio: 4.70

FLOWORKS USA LP

LOCATIONS

HQ: FLOWORKS USA LP
  3750 HWY 225, PASADENA, TX 77503
Phone: 713 672-2222
Web: WWW.GOFLOWORKS.COM

HISTORICAL FINANCIALS
Company Type: Private

Income Statement — FYE: January 31

	REVENUE ($mil)	NET INCOME ($mil)	NET PROFIT MARGIN	EMPLOYEES
01/14	657	24	3.8%	677
01/13	668	28	4.3%	—
Annual Growth	(1.6%)	(14.5%)	—	—

2014 Year-End Financials
Return on assets: 4.8%   Cash ($ mil.): (-2)
Return on equity: 5.8%
Current Ratio: 5.30

FONTANA UNIFIED SCHOOL DISTRICT

Auditors: NIGRO NIGRO & WHITE PC TEMEC

LOCATIONS

HQ: FONTANA UNIFIED SCHOOL DISTRICT
  9680 CITRUS AVE, FONTANA, CA 923355571
Phone: 909 357-7600
Web: WWW.FUSD.NET

HISTORICAL FINANCIALS
Company Type: Private

Income Statement — FYE: June 30

	REVENUE ($mil)	NET INCOME ($mil)	NET PROFIT MARGIN	EMPLOYEES
06/21	724	175	24.3%	3,627
06/20	574	7	1.3%	—
06/19	589	(0)	0.0%	—
06/18	543	31	5.7%	—
Annual Growth	10.1%	78.1%	—	—

2021 Year-End Financials
Return on assets: 13.4%   Cash ($ mil.): —
Return on equity: 125.2%
Current Ratio: —

FOOD FOR THE POOR, INC.

Food For The Poor feeds spiritual and physical hunger. The Christian charity provides health, social, economic, and religious services for impoverished people in 17 countries in Latin America and the Caribbean. Food For The Poor believes its organization serves God by helping those most in need, distributing requested goods through local churches and charities. The group works through Caritas, the American-Nicaraguan Foundation, and others to provide vocational training, clinic and school construction, educational materials, feeding programs, and medical supplies. Food For The Poor has distributed more than $3 billion in goods since its 1982 inception; the group uses 96% of its funds on programs.

EXECUTIVES

CMO*, Angel Aloma
Project, Frederick Khouri Evp Special
Auditors: MAYER HOFFMAN MCCANN PC BOCA

LOCATIONS

HQ: FOOD FOR THE POOR, INC.
  6401 LYONS RD, COCONUT CREEK, FL 330733602
Phone: 954 427-2222
Web: WWW.FOODFORTHEPOOR.ORG

COMPETITORS

CATHOLIC CHARITIES USA
SABRE FOUNDATION INC
THE AMERICAN SOCIETY FOR THE PREVENTION OF CRUELTY TO ANIMALS
UNBOUND
WORLD VISION INTERNATIONAL

HISTORICAL FINANCIALS
Company Type: Private

Income Statement — FYE: December 31

	REVENUE ($mil)	NET INCOME ($mil)	NET PROFIT MARGIN	EMPLOYEES
12/19	914	13	1.5%	418
12/18	942	(10)	—	—
12/17	948	(1)	—	—
12/16	994	14	1.5%	—
Annual Growth	(2.8%)	(1.7%)	—	—

2019 Year-End Financials
Return on assets: 31.2%   Cash ($ mil.): 23
Return on equity: 35.9%
Current Ratio: 5.00

FOOD GIANT SUPERMARKETS, INC.

LOCATIONS

HQ: FOOD GIANT SUPERMARKETS, INC.
  120 INDUSTRIAL DR, SIKESTON, MO 638015216
Phone: 573 471-3500
Web: WWW.FOODGIANT.COM

HISTORICAL FINANCIALS
Company Type: Private

Income Statement — FYE: October 1

	REVENUE ($mil)	NET INCOME ($mil)	NET PROFIT MARGIN	EMPLOYEES
10/16	725	22	3.1%	4,500
10/15	757	25	3.4%	—
10/10*	616	21	3.6%	—
09/06	468	108	23.1%	—
Annual Growth	4.5%	(14.6%)	—	—

*Fiscal year change

2016 Year-End Financials
Return on assets: 12.8%   Cash ($ mil.): 18
Return on equity: 14.0%
Current Ratio: 1.70

FORDHAM UNIVERSITY

A private Catholic university, Fordham offers its nearly 16,365 students numerous degree programs through nine graduate and undergraduate schools. Called the Jesuit University of New York, Fordham has multiple locations including the original Rose Hill campus in the Bronx (often the scene of location shooting for movies, TV shows, and commercials), the Westchester campus, and the Lincoln Center campus in Manhattan. It also operates a biological field station in Armonk, New York, and an international center in the UK. With about 755 full-time instructors, the university has a 13:1 undergraduate student-to-faculty ratio. Fordham was founded in 1841.

Auditors: KPMG LLP NEW YORK NY

LOCATIONS

HQ: FORDHAM UNIVERSITY
  441 E FORDHAM RD, BRONX, NY 104589993
Phone: 718 817-1000
Web: WWW.FORDHAM.EDU

PRODUCTS/OPERATIONS

2017 Sales

	$ mil.	% of total
Net tuition & fees	424.7	71
Net auxiliary enterprises	78.3	13
Investments	27.8	5
Contributions & private grants	27.5	4
Government grants	17.0	3
Net assets released from restrictions	4.5	1
Other	16.7	3
Total	596.5	100

Selected Colleges

Graduate and Professional
  Graduate School of Arts and Sciences
  Graduate School of Business
  Graduate School of Education
  Graduate School of Religion and Religious Education
  Graduate School of Social Services
  School of Law
Undergraduate
  Fordham College at Lincoln Center

Fordham College at Rose Hill
Gabelli School of Business
School of Professional and Continuing Studies

COMPETITORS

CLEVELAND STATE UNIVERSITY
LAFAYETTE COLLEGE
MARSHALL UNIVERSITY
OAKLAND UNIVERSITY
PACE UNIVERSITY
TRUSTEES OF INDIANA UNIVERSITY
UNIVERSITY OF NEW HAVEN, INCORPORATED
WAYNE STATE UNIVERSITY
WICHITA STATE UNIVERSITY
WILLAMETTE UNIVERSITY

HISTORICAL FINANCIALS
Company Type: Private

Income Statement — FYE: June 30

	REVENUE ($mil)	NET INCOME ($mil)	NET PROFIT MARGIN	EMPLOYEES
06/20	665	(20)	—	4,070
06/19	933	59	6.4%	—
06/18	631	41	6.6%	—
06/16	588	(52)	—	—
Annual Growth	3.1%	—	—	—

2020 Year-End Financials
Return on assets: (-1.0%) Cash ($ mil.): 25
Return on equity: (-1.5%)
Current Ratio: —

FORREST COUNTY GENERAL HOSPITAL

Forrest General Hospital is the hub of health care in Hattiesburg, Mississippi. Founded in 1952, the regional medical center serves southern Mississippi and its "Hub City," so named for its importance to early rail and lumber interests in the Pine Belt area. With some 400 acute care beds, Forrest General offers general medical and surgical care, as well as specialty care in heart disease, cancer, and women's health. Other facilities include the 90-bed Pine Grove behavioral health center for psychiatric and substance abuse treatment, a 25-bed inpatient rehabilitation facility, and an outpatient surgery center. The hospital system also operates a home health care agency and two nearby community hospitals.

Operations
In addition to the main inpatient and outpatient facilities, Forrest General operates the nearby 100-bed Highland Community Hospital in Picayune. It also manages the Walthall County General Hospital in Tylertown through a lease management agreement. Within the Forrest General inpatient building, a 30-bed long-term acute care hospital is operated by partner Regency Hospital Company. Altogether, the system handles about 30,000 inpatient visits and 100,000 emergency room visits each year.

Company Background
Forrest General claims many area and state wide firsts including, in 1969, the area's first emergency helicopter patient transport service. It is now the nation's longest continuously operating air ambulance. The hospital purchased Highland Community Hospital in 2006, and then constructed a new $76 million version of the hospital on a main state highway in 2009.

Auditors : BKD CPAS & ADVISORS JACKSON

LOCATIONS

HQ: FORREST COUNTY GENERAL HOSPITAL
6051 U S HIGHWAY 49, HATTIESBURG, MS 394017200
Phone: 601 288-7000
Web: WWW.FORRESTHEALTH.ORG

PRODUCTS/OPERATIONS

Selected Services
Behavioral Health
Critical Care
Emergency
Heart and Vascular
Home Care
Hospice
Lithotripsy Center
Lifeline
LiveWell Center
Medicine
Neurology
Occupational Health
Oncology
Organ and Tissue Donation
Orthopedic
Radiology
Rehabilitation
Spirit of Women
Surgery
Trauma
Women and Children

COMPETITORS

BEAUFORT MEMORIAL HOSPITAL
DIMENSIONS HEALTH CORPORATION
PARMA COMMUNITY GENERAL HOSPITAL
SHAWNEE MISSION MEDICAL CENTER, INC.
WINTER HAVEN HOSPITAL, INC.

HISTORICAL FINANCIALS
Company Type: Private

Income Statement — FYE: September 30

	REVENUE ($mil)	NET INCOME ($mil)	NET PROFIT MARGIN	EMPLOYEES
09/21	595	43	7.2%	4,030
09/20	556	18	3.4%	—
09/19	546	9	1.7%	—
09/18	0	0	—	—
Annual Growth	—	—	—	—

2021 Year-End Financials
Return on assets: 5.6% Cash ($ mil.): 139
Return on equity: 8.1%
Current Ratio: 3.20

FORSYTH COUNTY BOARD OF EDUCATION

Auditors : MAULDIN & JENKINS LLC ATLANT

LOCATIONS

HQ: FORSYTH COUNTY BOARD OF EDUCATION
1120 DAHLONEGA HWY, CUMMING, GA 300404536
Phone: 770 887-2461
Web: WWW.FORSYTH.K12.GA.US

HISTORICAL FINANCIALS
Company Type: Private

Income Statement — FYE: June 30

	REVENUE ($mil)	NET INCOME ($mil)	NET PROFIT MARGIN	EMPLOYEES
06/21	648	(77)	—	4,160
06/20	622	80	13.0%	—
06/19	582	127	21.9%	—
06/17	526	(16)	—	—
Annual Growth	5.3%	—	—	—

2021 Year-End Financials
Return on assets: (-4.5%) Cash ($ mil.): 283
Return on equity: (-123.3%)
Current Ratio: —

FORT WORTH INDEPENDENT SCHOOL DISTRICT

Auditors : WEAVER AND TIDWELL LLP FO

LOCATIONS

HQ: FORT WORTH INDEPENDENT SCHOOL DISTRICT
100 N UNIVERSITY DR, FORT WORTH, TX 761071360
Phone: 817 871-2000
Web: WWW.FWISD.ORG

HISTORICAL FINANCIALS
Company Type: Private

Income Statement — FYE: June 30

	REVENUE ($mil)	NET INCOME ($mil)	NET PROFIT MARGIN	EMPLOYEES
06/17	924	133	14.4%	10,360
06/16	909	(101)	—	—
06/15	843	64	7.7%	—
06/12	777	(98)	—	—
Annual Growth	3.5%	—	—	—

2017 Year-End Financials
Return on assets: 7.2% Cash ($ mil.): —
Return on equity: 35.1%
Current Ratio: 3.80

FORTERRA, INC.

EXECUTIVES

Corporate Secretary, Lori M Browne
Auditors : ERNST & YOUNG LLP DALLAS TX

LOCATIONS

HQ: FORTERRA, INC.
511 E JOHN CARPENTER FWY # 600, IRVING, TX 750623958
Phone: 469 458-7973
Web: WWW.RINKERPIPE.COM

HISTORICAL FINANCIALS

Company Type: Private

Income Statement — FYE: December 31

	REVENUE ($mil)	NET INCOME ($mil)	NET PROFIT MARGIN	EMPLOYEES
12/21	1,858	116	6.3%	4,729
12/20	1,594	64	4.0%	—
12/19	1,529	(7)	—	—
12/18	1,479	(24)	—	—
Annual Growth	7.9%	—	—	—

2021 Year-End Financials
Return on assets: 6.6%
Return on equity: 36.5%
Current Ratio: 2.20
Cash ($ mil.): 56

FORTIS CONSTRUCTION, INC.

Fortis Construction isn't afraid to get its hands dirty. TheÂ fast-growing US construction company offers general contracting, preconstruction, construction management, and environmentally-friendly green building services to customers primarily inÂ Portland, OregonÂ and others in the Pacific Northwest. It specializes in remodeling and upgrading corporate offices, health care facilities,Â retail complexes, and schools; it also conducts seismic and structural upgrades. Customers have included Oregon State University, Portland State University, PPG Industries, and StanCorp.

Auditors : ALDRICH CPAS AND ADVISORS LLP

LOCATIONS

HQ: FORTIS CONSTRUCTION, INC.
1705 SW TAYLOR ST STE 200, PORTLAND, OR 972051922
Phone: 503 459-4477
Web: WWW.FORTISCONSTRUCTION.COM

PRODUCTS/OPERATIONS

Selected Services
Construction management
General contracting
Green building
Preconstruction
Web-based collaboration and electronic document management

COMPETITORS

AUSTIN COMMERCIAL, INC.
CAPE ENVIRONMENTAL MANAGEMENT INC.
DPR CONSTRUCTION, INC.
EMJ CORPORATION
JAMES G. DAVIS CONSTRUCTION CORPORATION

HISTORICAL FINANCIALS

Company Type: Private

Income Statement — FYE: December 31

	REVENUE ($mil)	NET INCOME ($mil)	NET PROFIT MARGIN	EMPLOYEES
12/16	782	30	3.9%	175
12/15	468	18	3.9%	—
12/14	282	14	5.0%	—
Annual Growth	66.6%	48.0%	—	—

2016 Year-End Financials
Return on assets: 20.5%
Return on equity: 75.8%
Current Ratio: 1.40
Cash ($ mil.): 41

FRANCISCAN ALLIANCE, INC.

Franciscan Alliance is a not-for-profit organization operating more than a dozen hospitals in Indiana and south suburban Chicago. The hospitals include specialist centers for cancer care, heart and vascular care, weight loss, pediatrics, and women's health. In addition to inpatient acute care services, they operate numerous outpatient facilities and medical practices within their local service areas. Other subsidiaries and affiliates perform clinical laboratory tests, offer home health services, and provide support services to the system. Franciscan Alliance was founded and is sponsored by the Sisters of St. Francis of Perpetual Adoration.

Operations

Along with providing a wide range of health care services, Franciscan Alliance educates future health care providers through affiliations with area universities. The schools offer a variety of degree programs in fields including nursing, medical technician, and pharmacy residency.

Geographic Reach

Franciscan Alliance's hospitals are located in more than ten communities in Indiana, as well as in southern Chicago suburbs. The facilities serve patients in parts of Michigan as well. The organization also operates outpatient clinics and physician offices in the area, as well as a data center in Beech Grove, Indiana.

EXECUTIVES

SYSTEM*, Agnes Therady
Auditors : PRICEWATERHOUSECOOPERS LLP CH

LOCATIONS

HQ: FRANCISCAN ALLIANCE, INC.
1515 W DRAGOON TRL, MISHAWAKA, IN 465444710
Phone: 574 256-3935
Web: WWW.FRANCISCANHEALTH.ORG

PRODUCTS/OPERATIONS

Selected Operations
St. Anthony Health (Crown Point and Michigan City, Indiana)
St. Elizabeth Health (Crawfordsville, Lafayette Central, Lafayette East, Indiana)
St. Francis Health (Carmel, Indianapolis, and Mooresville, Indiana)
St. James Health (Chicago Heights and Olympia Fields, Illinois)
St. Margaret Health (Hammond and Dyer, Indiana)
Franciscan Healthcare Munster (formerly Physicians Hospital; Munster, Indiana)

Selected Services
Anticoagulation Clinics
Behavioral Health
Cancer Care
Colon and Rectal Surgery
Diabetes Care
Ear, Nose, and Throat
Emergency Medicine
Heart & Vascular
Home Health Care
Hospice
Imaging
Joint & Spine Care
Laboratory Services
Neurology
Neurosurgery
Occupational Health
Ophthalmology
Pain Management
Palliative Medicine
Pediatrics
Plastic Surgery
Primary Care Physicians
Pulmonary Medicine
Registered Dietitians
Rehabilitation Services
Robotic Surgery
Senior Services
Sleep Disorders
Sports Medicine
Surgical Services
Urgent Care
Weight Loss/Bariatrics
Women's Health/OBGYN
Wound Care

Selected Hospitals
Franciscan St. Anthony - Crown Point
Franciscan St. Anthony - Michigan City
Franciscan St. Elizabeth - Lafayette Central
Franciscan St. Elizabeth - Lafayette East
Franciscan St. Elizabeth - Crawfordsville
Franciscan St. Francis - Carmel
Franciscan St. Francis - Indianapolis
Franciscan St. Francis - Mooresville
Franciscan St. James - Chicago Heights
Franciscan St. James - Olympia Fields
Franciscan St. Margaret - Dyer
Franciscan St. Margaret - Hammond
Franciscan Healthcare - Munster

COMPETITORS

AVERA HEALTH
BEACON MEDICAL GROUP, INC.
CARILION CLINIC
CONTINUUM HEALTH PARTNERS, INC.
HMH HOSPITALS CORPORATION
MEDSTAR HEALTH, INC.
MEMORIAL HERMANN HEALTHCARE SYSTEM
PASADENA HOSPITAL ASSOCIATION, LTD.

SPARROW HEALTH SYSTEM
UNIVERSITY HOSPITALS HEALTH SYSTEM, INC.

HISTORICAL FINANCIALS
Company Type: Private

Income Statement — FYE: December 31

	REVENUE ($mil)	NET INCOME ($mil)	NET PROFIT MARGIN	EMPLOYEES
12/21	3,572	572	16.0%	19,000
12/18	3,144	14	0.5%	—
12/15	2,731	250	9.2%	—
Annual Growth	4.6%	14.8%	—	—

2021 Year-End Financials
Return on assets: 8.4%   Cash ($ mil.): 274
Return on equity: 13.1%
Current Ratio: 1.30

FRANCISCAN HEALTH SYSTEM

St. Francis himself may have hailed from Italy, but his followers look after the health of the residents of the South Puget Sound area through the Franciscan Health System. The not-for-profit system includes five full-service hospitals. The oldest and largest hospital is St. Joseph Medical Center in Tacoma, Washington, a 320-bed facility. Its facilities include community hospitals St. Clare Hospital (in Lakewood) and St. Francis Hospital (in Federal Way), as well as a hospice program, and numerous primary and specialty care clinics. Its St. Anthony Hospital is an 80-bed full service pharmacy and home medical equipment retail location at Gig Harbor.

Geographic Reach
Franciscan Health System serves patients in Tacoma, Washington, and surrounding areas.

Financial Performance
The company gets most of its revenues from patient services. Other sources of income includes foundation gifts and investment, community benefit, charity care, and uncompensated care (unreimbursed costs of serving patients enrolled in Medicaid and other state-subsidized programs).

Strategy
Franciscan Health System and Harrison Medical Center are looking to join forces, while Franciscan's parent continues in talks to combine its Northwest operations with PeaceHealth of Vancouver, Washington. If both plans are approved by regulators, Harrison will become part of the largest community hospital system in the Northwest, with facilities in Alaska, Washington, and Oregon. Both the Harrison-Franciscan affiliation and that of Franciscan's parent, Catholic Health Initiatives, with PeaceHealth is slated to be approved in 2013.

In addition, Franciscan Health System is collaborating with the MultiCare Health System and TRA Medical Imaging to build a women's imaging and breast cancer care center.

St. Elizabeth Hospital opened its doors in 2011 in Enumclaw, replacing Enumclaw Regional Hospital as that community's acute-care facility.

Company Background
St. Joseph Medical Center in Tacoma (the health system's oldest facility) was founded by the Sisters of St. Francis in 1891.

LOCATIONS

HQ: FRANCISCAN HEALTH SYSTEM
1717 S J ST, TACOMA, WA 984054933
Phone: 253 426-4101
Web: WWW.VMFH.ORG

PRODUCTS/OPERATIONS

Key Facilities and Services
Carol Milgard Breast Center, Tacoma
Franciscan Center for Weight Management, Federal Way
Franciscan Dialysis Center Eastside, Tacoma
Franciscan Medical Group primary-care and specialty-care clinics
Franciscan Hospice House, University Place
Franciscan Port Clinic, Tacoma
Gig Harbor Medical Pavilion, Gig Harbor
Gig Harbor Ambulatory Surgery Clinic, Gig Harbor
St. Anthony Hospital, Gig Harbor
St. Clare Hospital, Lakewood
St. Clare Specialty Center, Lakewood
St. Clare Medical Pavilion, Lakewood
St. Elizabeth Hospital, Enumclaw
St. Francis Hospital, Federal Way
St. Francis Outpatient Center, Federal Way
St. Joseph Medical Center, Tacoma
St. Joseph Outpatient Center, Tacoma
St. Joseph Heart & Vascular Center, Tacoma
St. Joseph Dialysis Center, Tacoma
St. Joseph Dialysis Center, Gig Harbor
St. Joseph Dialysis Center, Puyallup
St. Joseph Medical Clinic, Tacoma
St. Joseph Medical Pavilion, Tacoma
Milgard Medical Pavilion at St. Anthony, Gig Harbor
Women's Health & Breast Center, Federal Way

COMPETITORS

ASCENSION PROVIDENCE HOSPITAL
GREATER LAFAYETTE HEALTH SERVICES, INC.
JOHN C. LINCOLN HEALTH NETWORK
SAINT ELIZABETH REGIONAL MEDICAL CENTER
SAINT LUKE'S HEALTH SYSTEM, INC.
ST LUKE'S HOSPITAL
ST. MARY'S HEALTH CARE SYSTEM, INC.
ST. VINCENT ANDERSON REGIONAL HOSPITAL, INC.
SYLVANIA FRANCISCAN HEALTH
WHEATON FRANCISCAN SERVICES, INC.

HISTORICAL FINANCIALS
Company Type: Private

Income Statement — FYE: June 30

	REVENUE ($mil)	NET INCOME ($mil)	NET PROFIT MARGIN	EMPLOYEES
06/16	637	51	8.0%	3,183
06/15	610	56	9.2%	—
06/14	1,190	(106)	—	—
06/10	1,093	71	6.5%	—
Annual Growth	(8.6%)	(5.4%)	—	—

2016 Year-End Financials
Return on assets: 11.2%   Cash ($ mil.): 113
Return on equity: 13.8%
Current Ratio: 3.10

FRANCISCAN MISSIONARIES OF OUR LADY HEALTH SYSTEM, INC.

Auditors: KPMG LLP BATON ROUGE LA

LOCATIONS

HQ: FRANCISCAN MISSIONARIES OF OUR LADY HEALTH SYSTEM, INC.
4200 ESSEN LN, BATON ROUGE, LA 708092158
Phone: 225 923-2701
Web: WWW.FMOLHS.ORG

HISTORICAL FINANCIALS
Company Type: Private

Income Statement — FYE: June 30

	REVENUE ($mil)	NET INCOME ($mil)	NET PROFIT MARGIN	EMPLOYEES
06/21	3,347	833	24.9%	9,000
06/20	3,007	44	1.5%	—
06/19	2,296	27	1.2%	—
06/18	2,029	106	5.3%	—
Annual Growth	18.1%	98.3%	—	—

2021 Year-End Financials
Return on assets: 16.4%   Cash ($ mil.): 1,105
Return on equity: 32.5%
Current Ratio: 2.20

FRANKLIN COUNTY BOARD OF COMMISSIONERS

Auditors: KEITH FABER COLUMBUS OHIO

LOCATIONS

HQ: FRANKLIN COUNTY BOARD OF COMMISSIONERS
373 S HIGH ST FL 26, COLUMBUS, OH 432154591
Phone: 614 525-3322
Web: WWW.FRANKLINCOUNTYOHIO.GOV

HISTORICAL FINANCIALS
Company Type: Private

Income Statement — FYE: December 31

	REVENUE ($mil)	NET INCOME ($mil)	NET PROFIT MARGIN	EMPLOYEES
12/20	1,403	12	0.9%	6,000
12/19	1,348	(48)	—	—
12/17	1,281	85	6.7%	—
12/16	1,226	48	3.9%	—
Annual Growth	3.4%	(28.5%)	—	—

2020 Year-End Financials
Return on assets: 0.4%   Cash ($ mil.): 1,332
Return on equity: 1.2%
Current Ratio: 17.20

FRANKLIN SQUARE HOSPITAL CENTER, INC.

Franklin Square Hospital Center has made a declaration to care for the residents of eastern Baltimore County, Maryland. The facility offers a wide range of specialties through some 700 doctors and about 380 beds. Since 1998 the hospital has been part of MedStar Health, the region's largest integrated health system. As a teaching hospital, Franklin Square offers a number of residency programs, including internal and family medicine, OB-GYN, and surgery. The not-for-profit hospital offers its medical services through half a dozen primary service lines: Medicine, Surgery, Women's and Children's Care, Oncology, Behavioral Health, and Community Health and Wellness.

Operations
Franklin Square Hospital boasts more than 3,000 skilled professions, including 1,000-plus nurses and 400 staff physicians and more than 750 independently practicing physicians.

Geographic Reach
The only one of its kind in the region, Franklin Square's Cancer Institute serves oncology patients by offering education and prevention services, research, and diagnostic treatment.

Strategy
The hospital, which logs one of the highest numbers of cancer admissions in Maryland, is working to expand its cancer services as it anticipates admissions to grow.

In fact, the company is expanding other services as well, also in anticipation of future patient demand. The hospital built a 300-bed patient tower on the campus that includes an expanded emergency department, dedicated pediatric and inpatient suites, and an expanded 50-bed critical care unit.

LOCATIONS

HQ: FRANKLIN SQUARE HOSPITAL CENTER, INC.
9000 FRANKLIN SQUARE DR, BALTIMORE, MD 212373901
Phone: 410 933-2777
Web: WWW.MEDSTARHEALTH.ORG

PRODUCTS/OPERATIONS

Selected Services
Ambulatory & Minimally Invasive Surgery
Cancer Services
Cyberknife
da Vinci Robotic Surgery
Diagnostic Imaging and Radiology
Obstetrics & Neonatology
Orthopedics & Joint Replacement Therapies
Sleep Disorders
Women's Services

COMPETITORS
BETHESDA HOSPITAL, INC.
CENTRAL SUFFOLK HOSPITAL
FROEDTERT MEMORIAL LUTHERAN HOSPITAL, INC.
GREATER BALTIMORE MEDICAL CENTER, INC.
NORTH SHORE UNIVERSITY HOSPITAL

HISTORICAL FINANCIALS
Company Type: Private

Income Statement   FYE: June 30

	REVENUE ($mil)	NET INCOME ($mil)	NET PROFIT MARGIN	EMPLOYEES
06/20	605	56	9.2%	3,019
06/16	506	10	2.1%	—
06/15	492	17	3.5%	—
06/11	452	18	4.0%	—
Annual Growth	3.3%	13.4%	—	—

2020 Year-End Financials
Return on assets: 15.9%   Cash ($ mil.): 4
Return on equity: 30.4%
Current Ratio: 2.40

FREDERICK COUNTY, MARYLAND

EXECUTIVES
County Manager, Lori Depies
Auditors: SB & COMPANY LLC OWINGS MILL

LOCATIONS

HQ: FREDERICK COUNTY, MARYLAND
12 E CHURCH ST, FREDERICK, MD 217015402
Phone: 301 600-9000
Web: WWW.FREDERICKCOUNTYMD.GOV

HISTORICAL FINANCIALS
Company Type: Private

Income Statement   FYE: June 30

	REVENUE ($mil)	NET INCOME ($mil)	NET PROFIT MARGIN	EMPLOYEES
06/21	900	54	6.1%	1,800
06/20	744	1	0.2%	—
06/19	723	22	3.1%	—
06/18	662	21	3.2%	—
Annual Growth	10.7%	36.8%	—	—

2021 Year-End Financials
Return on assets: 1.5%   Cash ($ mil.): 603
Return on equity: 3.9%
Current Ratio: —

FREEMAN HEALTH SYSTEM

Freeman Health System (FHS) offers comprehensive health and behavioral health services to the residents of Arkansas, Kansas, Missouri, and Oklahoma through three hospitals with a total of more than 500 beds. Specialty facilities include a full-service cardiothoracic and vascular program at the Freeman Heart Institute, and behavioral health services through its Ozark Health Center. Community-owned, not-for-profit FHS also operates two urgent care centers, a separate sleep center, several doctors' office buildings, and serves as a teaching hospital with three residency programs (ear, nose, and throat; emergency medicine; and internal medicine). FHS employs more than 300 physicians in 60 specialties.

Operations
FHS operates three Missouri hospitals - Freeman Hospital West and Freeman Hospital East in Joplin and Freeman Neosho in Neosho. Its Ozark Center provides behavioral health services to patients from Missouri, Arkansas, Oklahoma, and Kansas.

Strategy
Like most health care providers, FHS has been working to update it facilities and expand it offerings. To that end, in 2013 it opened a transitional living and life skills assistance center for homeless teens and teamed with an autism support group to design an autism treatment program for its Ozark Center. The prior year it christened Will's Place behavioral health center for children and opened a $2 million sports and rehabilitation center.

Company Background
Located in Joplin, Missouri -- the site of the deadly E5 tornado that killed 161 people in May 2011-- Freeman Health System was the only fully functional hospital in the aftermath of the disaster. Rival St. John's Regional Medical Center, just two miles away, was destroyed. However, Ozark Health Center, FHS's behavioral health division, lost nine buildings in the disaster.

EXECUTIVES
CRO*, Kevin Gaudette
CCO*, Jeff Thompson
Auditors: BKD LLP SPRINGFIELD MISSOUR

LOCATIONS

HQ: FREEMAN HEALTH SYSTEM
1102 W 32ND ST, JOPLIN, MO 648043503
Phone: 417 347-1111
Web: WWW.FREEMANHEALTH.COM

PRODUCTS/OPERATIONS

Selected Services
Autism Services
Behavioral/mental health
Bladder care
Cancer care
Children's Miracle Network Hospitals
Clinical trials
Cosmetic/reconstructive surgery
Critical Care (ICU)
Diabetes education
Digestive care
Emergency medicine
Family care
Family counseling
Geriatric medicine

Health screenings
Hearing services
Home care
Internal medicine
Internet Addiction Services
Kidney Care
Lung care
Maternity
Neonatal intensive care
Nephrology & dialysis
Neurology & neurosurgery
Occupational medicine
Orthopedics
Pain management
Palliative care
QuickMeds Pharmacy™
Radiology
Rehabilitation
Senior Services
Skilled nursing
Sleep disorders
Sports medicine
Substance abuse services
Surgery
Tobacco cessation
Transitional Care Unit (TCU)
Urgent care
Women's Services
Wound care

Selected Facilities
Freeman Hospital West - Joplin, MO
Freeman Hospital East - Joplin, MO
Freeman Neosho Hospital - Neosho, MO
Freeman Business Center - Joplin, MO
Ozark Center - Joplin, Missouri

COMPETITORS

BAPTIST HEALTH SYSTEM, INC.
BEAUMONT HEALTH
BRONSON HEALTH CARE GROUP, INC.
MEDSTAR HEALTH, INC.
MEMORIAL HERMANN HEALTHCARE SYSTEM

HISTORICAL FINANCIALS
Company Type: Private

Income Statement — FYE: March 31

	REVENUE ($mil)	NET INCOME ($mil)	NET PROFIT MARGIN	EMPLOYEES
03/22	721	55	7.7%	4,500
03/21	676	164	24.3%	—
03/20	562	16	3.0%	—
03/19	624	57	9.2%	—
Annual Growth	4.9%	(1.0%)	—	—

2022 Year-End Financials
Return on assets: 5.8%   Cash ($ mil.): 104
Return on equity: 7.7%
Current Ratio: 1.80

FRESH MARK, INC.

Fresh Mark is a leading producer of smoked and processed pork products for the domestic and international retail and foodservice industries. From its four plants in Ohio, the company makes and markets such products as bacon (raw, par-cooked, and cooked), dry sausage, ham (natural and smoked), hot dogs, and lunch meats under the Sugardale and Superior's brands. Sugardale label is available in all 50 states and over 20 countries. The company also produces private-label processed meat products for others and supplies the foodservice industry through its Sugardale Food Service business. Founded in 1920, Ohio-based Fresh Mark is owned and operated by the Genshaft family.

Operations
Fresh Mark makes and supplies smoked and processed meats for the US retail and foodservice industries. Products include bacon, ham, wieners, dry sausages, specialty meat items, and deli and luncheon meats. All of its products are gluten-free and free of the Big-8 allergenic foods, including milk, eggs, fish, crustacean shellfish, tree nuts, peanuts, wheat and soybeans.

Some of its brands include Superior's Brand and Sugardale.

Geographic Reach
Headquartered in Ohio, Fresh Mark has facilities in Canton, Massillon, and Salem.

Sales and Marketing
The company markets its products through restaurants, delis, grocers, retailers and food service operators.

Strategy
One of the largest privately owned companies in its industry, Fresh Mark has grown from a regional supplier of smoked and processed meats to a leading supplier nationwide. It's ranked among the top 40 of the nation's leading 150 meat and poultry companies, as measured by National Provisioner magazine.

Auditors : ERNST & YOUNG LLP AKRON OH

LOCATIONS

HQ: FRESH MARK, INC.
1888 SOUTHWAY ST SW, MASSILLON, OH 446469429
Phone: 330 832-7491
Web: WWW.FRESHMARK.COM

PRODUCTS/OPERATIONS

Selected Products
Bacon
Deli meats
Dry sausage
Ham
Luncheon meats
Specialty meat items
Weiners

COMPETITORS

ADVANCEPIERRE FOODS, INC.
HOLTEN MEAT, INC.
JTM PROVISIONS COMPANY, INC
KENOSHA BEEF INTERNATIONAL, LTD.
LAKESIDE FOODS, INC.
LOPEZ FOODS, INC.
MICHAEL'S FINER MEATS, LLC
OBERTO SNACKS INC.
PATRICK CUDAHY, LLC
ZWEIGLE'S, INC.

HISTORICAL FINANCIALS
Company Type: Private

Income Statement — FYE: January 1

	REVENUE ($mil)	NET INCOME ($mil)	NET PROFIT MARGIN	EMPLOYEES
01/11*	795	59	7.5%	2,300
12/07	534	31	5.8%	—
12/06	481	21	4.5%	—
12/05	481	23	4.9%	—
Annual Growth	10.6%	20.4%	—	—

*Fiscal year change

2011 Year-End Financials
Return on assets: 3.9%   Cash ($ mil.): 4
Return on equity: 7.5%
Current Ratio: 0.90

FRESNO COMMUNITY HOSPITAL AND MEDICAL CENTER

Auditors : MOSS ADAMS LLP STOCKTON CA

LOCATIONS

HQ: FRESNO COMMUNITY HOSPITAL AND MEDICAL CENTER
2823 FRESNO ST, FRESNO, CA 937211324
Phone: 559 459-3948
Web: WWW.COMMUNITYMEDICAL.ORG

HISTORICAL FINANCIALS
Company Type: Private

Income Statement — FYE: August 31

	REVENUE ($mil)	NET INCOME ($mil)	NET PROFIT MARGIN	EMPLOYEES
08/15	1,571	139	8.9%	5,045
08/10	1,027	9	0.9%	—
08/09	1,010	65	6.5%	—
Annual Growth	7.6%	13.3%	—	—

2015 Year-End Financials
Return on assets: 7.8%   Cash ($ mil.): 62
Return on equity: 13.3%
Current Ratio: 0.50

FRESNO UNIFIED SCHOOL DISTRICT EDUCATIONAL FACILITIES CORPORATION

EXECUTIVES

Operations*, Rick Hausman
Auditors : PERRY SMITH SACRAMENTO CALIF

LOCATIONS

HQ: FRESNO UNIFIED SCHOOL DISTRICT
EDUCATIONAL FACILITIES CORPORATION
2309 TULARE ST, FRESNO, CA 937212266
Phone: 559 457-3000
Web: WWW.FRESNOUNIFIED.ORG

HISTORICAL FINANCIALS
Company Type: Private

Income Statement — FYE: June 30

	REVENUE ($mil)	NET INCOME ($mil)	NET PROFIT MARGIN	EMPLOYEES
06/10	692	(13)	—	8,400
06/09	757	0	0.1%	—
06/08	771	(40)	—	—
06/07	781	74	9.5%	—
Annual Growth	(3.9%)	—	—	—

2010 Year-End Financials
Return on assets: (-1.5%) Cash ($ mil.): 221
Return on equity: (-4.6%)
Current Ratio: —

FROEDTERT HEALTH, INC.

Auditors : KPMG LLP COLUMBUS OH

LOCATIONS

HQ: FROEDTERT HEALTH, INC.
9200 W WISCONSIN AVE, MILWAUKEE, WI 532263522
Phone: 414 805-3666
Web: WWW.FROEDTERT.COM

HISTORICAL FINANCIALS
Company Type: Private

Income Statement — FYE: June 30

	REVENUE ($mil)	NET INCOME ($mil)	NET PROFIT MARGIN	EMPLOYEES
06/21	881	91	10.4%	3,458
06/20	675	55	8.2%	—
06/14	362	66	18.4%	—
06/13	269	13	5.2%	—
Annual Growth	16.0%	26.6%	—	—

2021 Year-End Financials
Return on assets: 2.7% Cash ($ mil.): 125
Return on equity: 4.7%
Current Ratio: 0.10

FROEDTERT MEMORIAL LUTHERAN HOSPITAL, INC.

The 702-bed Froedtert Memorial Lutheran Hospital (also known as Froedtert Hospital) is an academic medical center and a leading referral resource for advanced medical care. Froedtert Hospital also operates the region's only adult Level I Trauma Center. It is the primary adult teaching affiliate of the Medical College of Wisconsin, Froedtert Hospital is a major training facility for more than 1,000 medical, nursing and health technical students annually. Froedtert Hospital is part of the Froedtert & MCW health network, which includes eight hospital locations, over 2,000 physicians and more than 45 health centers and clinics. It is also a respected research center, participating in some 2,000 research studies, including clinical trials, every year.

Operations
Its medical services include treatment for cancer, diabetes and endocrinology, heart and vascular, plastic and reconstructive surgery, sleep disorder, transplant, vision services, weight management and bariatrics, and women's health.

In 2021, outpatient visits were nearly 1.5 million, inpatient admissions to its hospitals were about 55,085 and visits to its network physicians exceeded 1.1 million.

Geographic Reach
Froedtert Hospital is located on the Milwaukee Regional Medical Center campus.

Auditors : KPMG LLP COLUMBUS OH

LOCATIONS

HQ: FROEDTERT MEMORIAL LUTHERAN HOSPITAL, INC.
9200 W WISCONSIN AVE, MILWAUKEE, WI 532263522
Phone: 414 805-3000
Web: WWW.FROEDTERT.COM

PRODUCTS/OPERATIONS

Selected Departments, Centers, and Programs
Clinical Cancer Center
    Blood and Lymph Node Cancer Program
    Blood and Marrow Transplant Program
    Bone and Connective Tissue Cancer Program
    Brain and Spine Tumor Program
    Breast Cancer Program
    Cancer Genetics Screening Program
    Colorectal Cancer Program
    Endocrine Cancer Program
    Eye/Orbital Cancer Program
    Geriatric Oncology
    Gynecologic Cancer Program
    Head and Neck Cancer Program
    Liver, Pancreas and Bile Duct Cancer Program
    Neuro-oncology Cognitive Clinic
    Palliative Care Program
    Plastic Surgery Center
    Prostate and Urologic Cancer Program
    Skin Cancer Center
    Thoracic Cancer Program (Lung and Esophageal Cancers)
Heart and Vascular Center
    Adult Congenital Heart Disease
    Advanced Heart Failure and Cardiac Transplantation
    Aortic Disease
    Arrhythmia and Atrial Fibrillation
    Coronary Artery Disease (CAD)
    Hereditary Hemorrhagic Telangiectasia (HHT)
    Hypertrophic Cardiomyopathy (HCM)
    Preventive Cardiology and Lipid Therapy
    Peripheral Arterial Disease (PAD)
    Pulmonary Hypertension
    Valvular Disease
    Venous Thrombotic Disease
    Venous and Vein Disease
    Women and Heart Disease
Neurosciences Center
    Brain Injury Program
    Brain and Spine Tumor Program
    Comprehensive Epilepsy Program
    Comprehensive Spasticity Management Program
    Memory Disorders Program
    Neuro-Oncology Cognitive Clinic
    Normal Pressure Hydrocephalus
    Parkinson's and Movement Disorders Program
    Sleep Disorders Program
    SpineCare Program
    Spinal Cord Injury Center
    Stroke and Neurovascular Program

COMPETITORS

BETHESDA HOSPITAL, INC.
CHILDRENS HOSPITAL & MEDICAL CENTER
FRANKLIN SQUARE HOSPITAL CENTER, INC.
HOLY SPIRIT HOSPITAL OF THE SISTERS OF CHRISTIAN CHARITY
LEHIGH VALLEY HEALTH NETWORK, INC.
MEMORIAL HEALTH SERVICES
PROVIDENCE HEALTH & SERVICES-WASHINGTON
THE CHILDREN'S HOSPITAL OF PHILADELPHIA
WINTER HAVEN HOSPITAL, INC.
YAKIMA VALLEY MEMORIAL HOSPITAL ASSOCIATION

HISTORICAL FINANCIALS
Company Type: Private

Income Statement — FYE: June 30

	REVENUE ($mil)	NET INCOME ($mil)	NET PROFIT MARGIN	EMPLOYEES
06/20	1,958	143	7.3%	3,400
06/14	1,164	92	7.9%	—
06/11	980	79	8.1%	—
06/10	894	59	6.7%	—
Annual Growth	8.2%	9.2%	—	—

2020 Year-End Financials
Return on assets: 11.6% Cash ($ mil.): 2
Return on equity: 15.2%
Current Ratio: 3.20

FRONTROW CALYPSO LLC

LOCATIONS

HQ: FRONTROW CALYPSO LLC
1690 CORPORATE CIR, PETALUMA, CA 949546912
Phone: 800 277-0735
Web: WWW.GOFRONTROW.COM

HISTORICAL FINANCIALS
Company Type: Private

Income Statement — FYE: December 31

	REVENUE ($mil)	NET INCOME ($mil)	NET PROFIT MARGIN	EMPLOYEES
12/08	1,009	128	12.7%	61
12/07	1,083	214	19.8%	—
12/04	21	(1)	—	—
Annual Growth	162.1%	—	—	—

2008 Year-End Financials
Return on assets: 17.4%   Cash ($ mil.): 26
Return on equity: 126.6%
Current Ratio: 0.80

FS KKR CAPITAL CORP. II

Auditors: DELOITTE & TOUCHE LLP SAN FRA

LOCATIONS
HQ: FS KKR CAPITAL CORP. II
201 ROUSE BLVD, PHILADELPHIA, PA 191121902
Phone: 215 495-1150
Web: WWW.FSKKRCAPITALCORP.COM

HISTORICAL FINANCIALS
Company Type: Private

Income Statement — FYE: December 31

	ASSETS ($mil)	NET INCOME ($mil)	INCOME AS % OF ASSETS	EMPLOYEES
12/20	8,522	(376)	—	9
12/19	8,970	238	2.7%	—
12/18	4,554	(37)	—	—
12/17	5,110	189	3.7%	—
Annual Growth	18.6%	—	—	—

2020 Year-End Financials
Return on assets: (-4.4%)   Cash ($ mil.): 160
Return on equity: (-8.8%)
Current Ratio: —

FTD COMPANIES, INC.

Mercury, the Roman god of speed and commerce with winged feet, comes bearing flowers. FTD is a leader in the floral industry for over a century supported by the iconic Mercury Man logo displayed in more than 30,000 floral shops in over 125 countries. The company works with local florists to handcraft floral arrangements available for same-day delivery on FTD.com and ProFlowers.com. In addition, the company provides technology, marketing, and digital services to members of its florist network. The company was founded by John A. Valentine in 1910.

Operations
Product revenue for FTD comes from selling floral, gift, and related items to consumers through its web sites and by phone, as well as through its floral network members.

Geographic Reach
Based in Downers Grove, Illinois, FTD serves consumers across the US, Canada, and India through its floral network members, web sites, and by phone.

Sales and Marketing
FTD markets its products through FTD.com, ProFlowers.com and ProPlants.com, and also in social media including Facebook and Instagram.

Auditors: DELOITTE & TOUCHE LLP CHICAGO

LOCATIONS
HQ: FTD COMPANIES, INC.
3113 WOODCREEK DR, DOWNERS GROVE, IL 605155420
Phone: 630 719-7800
Web: WWW.FTDCOMPANIES.COM

2014 Sales

	% of total
US	72
International	28
Total	100

2014 Sales

	Revenue by Segments (in million)	% Contribution
Product Revenues:		
Consumer	318.5	48
International	155.7	24
Florist	46	7
Service Revenues:		
Florist	116.2	18
International	22.1	3
Intersegment Elimination		(18)
Total	640.5	100

PRODUCTS/OPERATIONS
Selected Businesses
Consumer
  US
    1-800-SEND-FTD
    www.ftd.com
  Canada
    www.ftd.ca
  Ireland
    www.interflora.ie
  UK
    www.drakealgar.com
    www.interflora.uk
    www.flyingflowers.co.uk
    www.flowersdirect.co.uk
Floral Network
  US
  Canada
  Ireland
  UK

COMPETITORS
C-USA, INC.
ENESCO, LLC
ETSY, INC.
EVENT NETWORK, LLC
GROUPON, INC.
HALLMARK CARDS, INCORPORATED
PARTY CITY HOLDCO INC.

RESIDUAL PUMPKIN ENTITY, LLC
SCHURMAN FINE PAPERS
TUESDAY MORNING CORPORATION

HISTORICAL FINANCIALS
Company Type: Private

Income Statement — FYE: December 31

	REVENUE ($mil)	NET INCOME ($mil)	NET PROFIT MARGIN	EMPLOYEES
12/18	1,014	(224)	—	1,501
12/17	1,084	(234)	—	—
12/16	1,121	(83)	—	—
12/15	1,219	(78)	—	—
Annual Growth	(6.0%)	—	—	—

2018 Year-End Financials
Return on assets: (-58.1%)   Cash ($ mil.): 16
Return on equity: —
Current Ratio: 0.20

FULTON COUNTY BOARD OF EDUCATION

Auditors: MAULDIN & JENKINS LLC ATLANT

LOCATIONS
HQ: FULTON COUNTY BOARD OF EDUCATION
6201 POWERS FERRY RD, ATLANTA, GA 303392926
Phone: 404 768-3600
Web: WWW.FULTONSCHOOLS.ORG

HISTORICAL FINANCIALS
Company Type: Private

Income Statement — FYE: June 30

	REVENUE ($mil)	NET INCOME ($mil)	NET PROFIT MARGIN	EMPLOYEES
06/21	1,402	42	3.1%	10,000
06/20	1,392	18	1.3%	—
06/19	1,351	32	2.4%	—
06/18	1,268	40	3.2%	—
Annual Growth	3.4%	1.8%	—	—

2021 Year-End Financials
Return on assets: 1.3%   Cash ($ mil.): 533
Return on equity: 4.5%
Current Ratio: 3.50

FUNDAMENTAL INVESTORS, INC.

Auditors: DELOITTE & TOUCHE LLP COSTA M

LOCATIONS
HQ: FUNDAMENTAL INVESTORS, INC.
1 MARKET, SAN FRANCISCO, CA 941051596
Phone: 800 421-0180

HISTORICAL FINANCIALS
Company Type: Private

Income Statement — FYE: December 31

	REVENUE ($mil)	NET INCOME ($mil)	NET PROFIT MARGIN	EMPLOYEES
12/20	2,137	7,303	341.6%	6
12/19	2,262	24,161	1068.1%	—
12/18	2,151	(8,234)	—	—
Annual Growth	(0.3%)	—	—	—

2020 Year-End Financials
Return on assets: 6.3% Cash ($ mil.): 63
Return on equity: 6.3%
Current Ratio: —

GARDEN GROVE UNIFIED SCHOOL DISTRICT

LOCATIONS
HQ: GARDEN GROVE UNIFIED SCHOOL DISTRICT
  10331 STANFORD AVE, GARDEN GROVE, CA 928406351
Phone: 714 663-6000
Web: WWW.GGUSD.US

HISTORICAL FINANCIALS
Company Type: Private

Income Statement — FYE: June 30

	REVENUE ($mil)	NET INCOME ($mil)	NET PROFIT MARGIN	EMPLOYEES
06/20	658	(38)	—	5,000
06/19	655	2	0.4%	—
06/18	613	(90)	—	—
06/17	602	7	1.2%	—
Annual Growth	3.0%	—	—	—

2020 Year-End Financials
Return on assets: (-2.1%) Cash ($ mil.): —
Return on equity: (-7.9%)
Current Ratio: —

GARFF ENTERPRISES, INC.

Auditors : MAYER HOFFMAN MC CANN PC SAL

LOCATIONS
HQ: GARFF ENTERPRISES, INC.
  111 E BROADWAY STE 900, SALT LAKE CITY, UT 841112304
Phone: 801 257-3400
Web: WWW.KENGARFF.COM

HISTORICAL FINANCIALS
Company Type: Private

Income Statement — FYE: December 31

	REVENUE ($mil)	NET INCOME ($mil)	NET PROFIT MARGIN	EMPLOYEES
12/13	576	14	2.5%	855
12/03	481	10	2.1%	—
12/02	270	4	1.5%	—
12/01	189	0	0.0%	—
Annual Growth	9.7%	—	—	—

2013 Year-End Financials
Return on assets: 1.4% Cash ($ mil.): 26
Return on equity: 2.5%
Current Ratio: 0.20

GARLAND INDEPENDENT SCHOOL DISTRICT

Auditors : WHITLEY PENN LLP DALLAS TEX

LOCATIONS
HQ: GARLAND INDEPENDENT SCHOOL DISTRICT
  501 S JUPITER RD, GARLAND, TX 750427108
Phone: 972 494-8201
Web: WWW.GARLANDISD.NET

HISTORICAL FINANCIALS
Company Type: Private

Income Statement — FYE: June 30

	REVENUE ($mil)	NET INCOME ($mil)	NET PROFIT MARGIN	EMPLOYEES
06/21	654	(10)	—	7,307
06/20	669	5	0.9%	—
08/18	648	(25)	—	—
Annual Growth	0.3%	—	—	—

2021 Year-End Financials
Return on assets: (-0.8%) Cash ($ mil.): 392
Return on equity: (-3.6%)
Current Ratio: —

GBMC HEALTHCARE, INC.

Auditors : KPMG LLP BALTIMORE MARYLAND

LOCATIONS
HQ: GBMC HEALTHCARE, INC.
  6701 N CHARLES ST, BALTIMORE, MD 212046808
Phone: 443 849-2000
Web: WWW.GBMC.ORG

HISTORICAL FINANCIALS
Company Type: Private

Income Statement — FYE: June 30

	REVENUE ($mil)	NET INCOME ($mil)	NET PROFIT MARGIN	EMPLOYEES
06/22	667	(85)	—	3,900
06/21	666	160	24.1%	—
06/20	605	26	4.4%	—
06/19	602	40	6.7%	—
Annual Growth	3.5%	—	—	—

2022 Year-End Financials
Return on assets: (-7.4%) Cash ($ mil.): 25
Return on equity: (-12.7%)
Current Ratio: 1.50

GCI, LLC

Auditors : KPMG LLP DENVER COLORADO

LOCATIONS
HQ: GCI, LLC
  2550 DENALI ST STE 1000, ANCHORAGE, AK 995032751
Phone: 907 868-5400
Web: WWW.GCI.COM

HISTORICAL FINANCIALS
Company Type: Private

Income Statement — FYE: December 31

	REVENUE ($mil)	NET INCOME ($mil)	NET PROFIT MARGIN	EMPLOYEES
12/18	739	(917)	—	7
12/17	919	31	3.4%	—
12/16	933	(1)	—	—
12/15	978	(10)	—	—
Annual Growth	(8.9%)	—	—	—

2018 Year-End Financials
Return on assets: (-11.2%) Cash ($ mil.): 170
Return on equity: (-20.5%)
Current Ratio: 0.40

GEISINGER HEALTH

Geisinger Health System serves more than 1 million residents. Founded more than 100 years ago by Abigail Geisinger, the system includes ten hospital campuses, a health plan with more than half a million members, a research institute and the Geisinger Commonwealth School of Medicine. With nearly 24,000 employees and more than 1,600 employed physicians, Geisinger offers women's health, sleep services, surgery, senior health, dental medicine, and addiction treatment, among others. Its Geisinger Health Plan is an integrated health system that provides its member and patients with exceptional healthcare.

Operations
Geisinger Commonwealth School of Medicine offers a community-based model of undergraduate medical education, as well as

doctor of medicine program, master of Biomedical Sciences and a portfolio of graduate programs. Geisinger Commonwealth School of Medicine is also home to around 585 residents and fellows, comprising more than 35 accredited residency programs and about 30 subspecialty fellowships, which encompass Accreditation Council for Graduate Medical Education physician programs as well as dental, podiatry, pharmacy and more.

Geographic Reach
Geisinger Health is based in Danville, Pennsylvania. Its Geisinger Commonwealth School of Medicine has regional campuses in Atlantic City, Danville, Lewistown, Sayre, Scranton and Wilkes-Barre.

Sales and Marketing
Its health plan serves more than 500,000 residents throughout central, south-central and northeast Pennsylvania, and works with affiliates in Delaware and Maine.

EXECUTIVES

Chief Medical Officer, Bruce H Hamory Md
CSO, Dominic Moffa
CIO, David Tilton
Auditors : KPMG LLP PHILADELPHIA PA

LOCATIONS

HQ: GEISINGER HEALTH
100 N ACADEMY AVE, DANVILLE, PA 178229800
Phone: 800 275-6401
Web: WWW.GEISINGER.ORG

PRODUCTS/OPERATIONS

Selected Services
Adolescent & Young Adult Medicine
Allergy
Anesthesia
Audiology
Bariatric Surgery
Cancer Institute
Cardiology
Colorectal Surgery
Cosmetics Program
Critical Care
Dental Medicine
Dermatology
Ear, Nose & Throat
Emergency Medicine
Endocrinology & Metabolism
Fertility Center
Gastroenterology
Gynecology
Gynecologic Oncology
Heart Services
Hip & Knee Center
Imaging Services
Infectious Disease
Internal Medicine
Joint Replacement
Laboratory Medicine
LASIK Surgery
Mammography
Maternal Fetal Medicine
Mental Health
Minimally Invasive Surgery
Mohs Surgery
Neonatology
Nephrology
Neurodevelopmental Pediatrics
Neuroscience Institute
Neurology
Neurosurgery
Obstetrics
Ophthalmology
Orthopaedics
Osteoporosis
Pain Management
Palliative Medicine
Pediatrics (General)
Pediatric Allergy & Immunology
Pediatric Anesthesia & Sedation
Pediatric Cardiology
Pediatric Dental Surgery
Pediatric Dentistry
Pediatric Dermatology
Pediatric Endocrinology
Pediatric Gastroenterology
Pediatric General Surgery
Pediatric Genetics
Pediatric Hematology/Oncology
Pediatric Hospitalists
Pediatric Infectious Disease
Pediatric Intensive Care
Pediatric Interventional Radiology
Pediatric Nephrology
Pediatric Neurology
Pediatric Neuropsychology
Pediatric Neurosurgery
Pediatric Ophthalmology
Pediatric Orthopaedics
Pediatric Otolaryngology
Pediatric Plastic Surgery
Pediatric Psychology & Psychiatry
Pediatric Pulmonology
Pediatric Rehabilitation
Pediatric Rheumatology
Pediatric Transplant Surgery
Pediatric Trauma
Pediatric Urology
Pediatric Weight Management & Nutrition
Plastic & Reconstructive Surgery
Podiatry
Psychiatry
Pulmonary Medicine
Radiology
Rehabilitation
Rheumatology
Sleep Services
Spine Medicine
Sports Medicine
Surgery
Thoracic Surgery
Transplant Surgery
Trauma Center
Urogynecology
Urology
Vascular Surgery
Weight Management Clinic
Women's Health

Selected Facilities
Geisinger HealthSouth Rehabilitation Hospital (Danville)
Geisinger Medical Center (Danville)
  The Janet Weis Children's Hospital
Geisinger Wyoming Valley Medical Center (Wilkes-Barre)
  Pearsall Heart Hospital
Geisinger South Wilkes-Barre Outpatient Center
Shamokin Area Community Hospital

COMPETITORS

AMERIHEALTH CARITAS HEALTH PLAN
APS HEALTHCARE, INC.
ASCENSION HEALTH
AVERA HEALTH
CENTRASTATE HEALTHCARE SYSTEM INC
CORIZON HEALTH, INC.
DEAN HEALTH SYSTEMS, INC.
UNIVERSITY HEALTH SYSTEMS OF EASTERN CAROLINA, INC.
UNIVERSITY HOSPITALS HEALTH SYSTEM, INC.
WHEATON FRANCISCAN SERVICES, INC.

HISTORICAL FINANCIALS
Company Type: Private

Income Statement — FYE: June 30

	REVENUE ($mil)	NET INCOME ($mil)	NET PROFIT MARGIN	EMPLOYEES
06/20	7,121	(190)	—	13,030
06/19	7,145	174	2.4%	—
06/18	6,536	359	5.5%	—
06/17	6,337	552	8.7%	—
Annual Growth	4.0%	—	—	—

2020 Year-End Financials
Return on assets: (-2.1%)   Cash ($ mil.): 1,125
Return on equity: (-4.5%)
Current Ratio: 1.60

GEISINGER HEALTH PLAN

Auditors : GEISINGER SYSTEM SERVICES INC

LOCATIONS

HQ: GEISINGER HEALTH PLAN
100 N ACADEMY AVE, DANVILLE, PA 178229800
Phone: 570 271-8778
Web: HEALTHPLAN.GEISINGER.ORG

HISTORICAL FINANCIALS
Company Type: Private

Income Statement — FYE: June 30

	REVENUE ($mil)	NET INCOME ($mil)	NET PROFIT MARGIN	EMPLOYEES
06/19	2,704	107	4.0%	900
06/18	2,638	55	2.1%	—
06/17	2,337	79	3.4%	—
06/10	875	35	4.0%	—
Annual Growth	13.4%	13.2%	—	—

2019 Year-End Financials
Return on assets: 16.9%   Cash ($ mil.): 15
Return on equity: 25.1%
Current Ratio: —

GEISINGER MEDICAL CENTER

EXECUTIVES

Chief Medical Officer*, Rosemary Leeming
CIO*, Karen Murphy

LOCATIONS

HQ: GEISINGER MEDICAL CENTER
100 N ACADEMY AVE, DANVILLE, PA 178220001
Phone: 570 271-6211
Web: WWW.GEISINGER.ORG

GENERAL ELECTRIC INTERNATIONAL OPERATIONS COMPANY, INC.

Auditors: KPMG LLP CINCINNATI OHIO

LOCATIONS

HQ: GENERAL ELECTRIC INTERNATIONAL OPERATIONS COMPANY, INC.
  191 ROSA PARKS ST, CINCINNATI, OH 452022573
Phone: 513 813-9133

HISTORICAL FINANCIALS
Company Type: Private

Income Statement — FYE: June 30

	REVENUE ($mil)	NET INCOME ($mil)	NET PROFIT MARGIN	EMPLOYEES
06/20	1,356	98	7.3%	8,000
06/16	1,095	108	9.9%	—
06/15	1,058	120	11.4%	—
06/10	815	79	9.7%	—
Annual Growth	5.2%	2.3%	—	—

2020 Year-End Financials
Return on assets: 8.5% Cash ($ mil.): 174
Return on equity: 67.9%
Current Ratio: —

GENERAL ELECTRIC INTERNATIONAL, INC.

Auditors: KPMG LLP CINCINNATI OHIO

LOCATIONS

HQ: GENERAL ELECTRIC INTERNATIONAL, INC.
  1 RIVER RD, SCHENECTADY, NY 123456000
Phone: 617 443-3000
Web: WWW.GE.COM

HISTORICAL FINANCIALS
Company Type: Private

Income Statement — FYE: December 31

	REVENUE ($mil)	NET INCOME ($mil)	NET PROFIT MARGIN	EMPLOYEES
12/17	966	192	19.9%	944
12/16	925	(55)	—	—
12/15	925	(22)	—	—
12/14	760	(8)	—	—
Annual Growth	8.3%	—	—	—

2017 Year-End Financials
Return on assets: 1.9% Cash ($ mil.): 101
Return on equity: 2.1%
Current Ratio: 0.60

GENESIS HEALTH SYSTEM

Genesis Health System operates three acute care hospitals in Iowa and Illinois that have more than 660 beds total and employ some 700 doctors. Genesis Medical Center in Davenport, Iowa, with more than 500 beds, is the system's flagship facility; the hospital offers a range of general, surgical, and specialist health services. The system's Illini Campus in Silvis, Illinois, features an assisted-living center. The Genesis Medical Center Dewitt Campus serves that Iowa town and the surrounding area with its 13-bed hospital, nursing home, and related care facilities. Genesis Health System also operates physician practices, outpatient centers, and a home health agency.

Operations
Altogether, Genesis Health System has more than 100 locations, including hospitals, convenient care locations, Genesis Health Group sites, physical rehabilitation clinics, and outpatient service centers.

Strategy
In 2014, the system invested $15 million in the new Genesis HealthPlex in Bettendorf.

The following year, Genesis Health System entered into a partnership with technology vendor Cerner Corporation to improve its patient care enterprise management systems.

Company Background
Genesis Health System had its genesis in 1869 with the establishment of Mercy Hospital (one of the first hospitals west of the Mississippi), and in the 1895 founding of St. Luke's Hospital. The two hospitals merged in 1994 to form the health system.

Auditors: RSM US LLP DAVENPORT IOWA

LOCATIONS
HQ: GENESIS HEALTH SYSTEM
  1227 E RUSHOLME ST, DAVENPORT, IA 528032459
Phone: 563 421-1000
Web: WWW.GENESISHEALTH.COM

PRODUCTS/OPERATIONS

Selected Services
Bariatric Surgery
Behavioral Health
Birthing Services
Cancer
Cardiology
Home Health/Hospice
Neuroscience
Nursing Homes
Physical Medicine & Rehab
Senior Services

COMPETITORS

AKRON GENERAL HEALTH SYSTEM
CAROMONT HEALTH, INC.
CKHS, INC.
GENESIS HEALTHCARE SYSTEM
HERITAGE VALLEY HEALTH SYSTEM, INC.
JFK HEALTH SYSTEM, INC.
MERITER HEALTH SERVICES, INC.
OHIOHEALTH CORPORATION
ROCKFORD HEALTH SYSTEM
TRIHEALTH, INC.

HISTORICAL FINANCIALS
Company Type: Private

Income Statement — FYE: December 31

	REVENUE ($mil)	NET INCOME ($mil)	NET PROFIT MARGIN	EMPLOYEES
12/17	14,100	685	4.9%	125
12/16	13,364	1,339	10.0%	—
12/15	13,288	82	0.6%	—
12/14	12,884	(304)	—	—
Annual Growth	3.1%	—	—	—

2017 Year-End Financials
Return on assets: 3.5% Cash ($ mil.): 961
Return on equity: 10.5%
Current Ratio: 1.50

Income Statement — FYE: June 30

	REVENUE ($mil)	NET INCOME ($mil)	NET PROFIT MARGIN	EMPLOYEES
06/22	721	(83)	—	5,000
06/21	706	73	10.5%	—
06/20	648	4	0.7%	—
06/19	646	13	2.1%	—
Annual Growth	3.7%	—	—	—

2022 Year-End Financials
Return on assets: (-7.7%) Cash ($ mil.): 93
Return on equity: (-11.7%)
Current Ratio: 1.40

GENPACT LIMITED

LOCATIONS

HQ: GENPACT LIMITED
  1155 AVENUE OF THE AMERIC, NEW YORK, NY 100362711
Phone: 212 896-6600
Web: WWW.GENPACT.COM

HISTORICAL FINANCIALS
Company Type: Private

Income Statement — FYE: December 31

	REVENUE ($mil)	NET INCOME ($mil)	NET PROFIT MARGIN	EMPLOYEES
12/11	1,600	191	11.9%	325
12/10	1,258	149	11.8%	—
12/09	1,120	134	12.0%	—
Annual Growth	19.5%	19.0%	—	—

2011 Year-End Financials
Return on assets: 1.3% Cash ($ mil.): 408
Return on equity: 11.9%
Current Ratio: 1.20

GEOKINETICS INC.

Using kinetic energy to assess the Earth's hydrocarbon sources, Geokinetics is a global provider of geophysical services to the oil and gas industry. It acquires seismic data in North America and internationally and processes and interprets that data at processing centers in the US and the UK. The company's seismic crews work in a range of terrains, including land, marsh, swamp, shallow water, and difficult transition zones (between land and water). Not dependent on any one customer, its client base consists of international and national oil companies, as well as smaller independent oil and gas exploration and production companies.

Bankruptcy
Hurt by project delays and a 2011 incident in which three employers were killed on a mapping expedition, in 2013 the company filed for Chapter 11 bankruptcy protection, citing assets of $12 million and liabilities of $351 million.

Operations
The company is an industry leader in land, transition zone, and shallow water environments, with more than 30 seismic crews with 200,000 channels of seismic data acquisition equipment and five data processing centers around the world and 10,443 square miles of multi-client data. Geokinetics offers two types of contracts: proprietary (individual contracts controlled by the client) and multi-client (pre-funded contracts managed by Geokinetics). It has a multi-client data library with data covering areas in the Brazil, Canada, and the US.

Geographic Reach
Geokinetics has offices in 29 major countries and operations in Angola, Brazil, Canada, Colombia, Libya, Mexico, Singapore, Suriname, Tunisia, the UAE, the UK, and the US. The company focuses on seismic acquisition activities in the US (Gulf Coast, Mid-Continent and Rocky Mountain regions) and in Canada.

Sales and Marketing
The company's customers include independent, international, and state-owned national oil companies.

Financial Performance
In 2012 Geokinetic's revenue declined by 22% primarily due to lower activity in North America, Africa and Asia Pacific, offset by higher activity in Latin America. North America proprietary revenue decreased by 30% due to decreased crew activity in the US because of postponed projects. Multi-Client revenues dropped by 31% as the result of permit delays in certain areas of the US and a drop in new projects due to lower gas prices.

The company reported a net loss $82.9 million (compared to a net loss of $222 million in 2011). In 2011 Geokinetic's net loss increased dramatically led by costs related to a suspended contract, a lost liftboat vessel and related fatalities in the Gulf of Mexico and subsequent litigation and a credit rating downgrade.

Strategy
A key part of Geokinetics' growth strategy is to offer a broad range of seismic services. To this end, it plans to pursue strategic acquisitions to complement its existing acquisition, processing, and interpretation products and services and to expand its geographic footprint. It also hopes to partner with oil and gas exploration and production companies on multi-client library projects. Together, these integrated set of services can help customers better evaluate known oil and gas deposits and improve the amount of recoverable hydrocarbons.

Company Background
In 2010 Geokinetics purchased the onshore seismic data acquisition and multi-client library business of Petroleum Geo-Services (PGS). The acquisition of PGS Onshore made Geokinetics the second largest provider of onshore seismic data acquisition services in the world in terms of crew count and the largest based in the West. The $183 million acquisition built on Geokinetics' expertise in transition zone and ocean bottom cable (OBC) environments, two areas that the company believes are underserved but growing within the overall seismic services market. The acquisition also added new operating areas, such as Alaska, Mexico, and certain countries in the Middle East and North Africa.

LOCATIONS
HQ: GEOKINETICS INC.
1500 CITYWEST BLVD # 800, HOUSTON, TX 770422300
Phone: 713 850-7600
Web: WWW.GEOKINETICSINC.COM

COMPETITORS
C&J ENERGY SERVICES, INC.
Cequence Energy Ltd
DAWSON OPERATING LLC
EVOLUTION PETROLEUM CORPORATION
EXPRO INTERNATIONAL GROUP LIMITED
HARVEST NATURAL RESOURCES, INC.
KEY ENERGY SERVICES, INC.
PIONEER ENERGY SERVICES CORP.
SCHLUMBERGER OMNES, INC.
WORLEY LIMITED

HISTORICAL FINANCIALS
Company Type: Private

Income Statement — FYE: December 31

	REVENUE ($mil)	NET INCOME ($mil)	NET PROFIT MARGIN	EMPLOYEES
12/11	763	(222)	—	5,695
12/10	558	(138)	—	—
12/09	510	(5)	—	—
Annual Growth	22.3%	—	—	—

2011 Year-End Financials
Return on assets: (-43.2%)   Cash ($ mil.): 44
Return on equity: —
Current Ratio: 1.10

GEORGES PRINCE COUNTY GOVERNMENT

EXECUTIVES
County Executive*, Angela Alsobrooks
Auditors : CLIFTONLARSONALLEN LLP BALTIM

LOCATIONS
HQ: GEORGES PRINCE COUNTY GOVERNMENT
1301 MCCORMICK DR # 4200, LARGO, MD 207745416
Phone: 301 952-3300
Web: WWW.PRINCEGEORGESCOUNTYMD.GOV

HISTORICAL FINANCIALS
Company Type: Private

Income Statement — FYE: June 30

	REVENUE ($mil)	NET INCOME ($mil)	NET PROFIT MARGIN	EMPLOYEES
06/21	2,601	150	5.8%	12,000
06/20	2,251	(17)	—	—
06/18	2,109	550	26.1%	—
Annual Growth	7.2%	(35.0%)	—	—

2021 Year-End Financials
Return on assets: 1.6%   Cash ($ mil.): 46
Return on equity: —
Current Ratio: —

GEORGIA CARESOURCE CO

LOCATIONS
HQ: GEORGIA CARESOURCE CO
600 GALLERIA PKWY SE # 400, ATLANTA, GA 303398146
Phone: 678 214-7500
Web: WWW.CARESOURCE.COM

HISTORICAL FINANCIALS
Company Type: Private

Income Statement — FYE: December 31

	REVENUE ($mil)	NET INCOME ($mil)	NET PROFIT MARGIN	EMPLOYEES
12/18	669	(20)	—	2,384
12/17	307	15	5.0%	—
Annual Growth	117.6%	—	—	—

2018 Year-End Financials
Return on assets: (-15.7%)   Cash ($ mil.): 42
Return on equity: (-81.1%)
Current Ratio: —

GEORGIA TECH APPLIED RESEARCH CORPORATION

Auditors : CHERRY BEKAERT LLP ATLANTA G

LOCATIONS

HQ: GEORGIA TECH APPLIED RESEARCH CORPORATION
926 DALNEY ST NW, ATLANTA, GA 303186395
Phone: 404 894-6934
Web: GTRC.GATECH.EDU

HISTORICAL FINANCIALS
Company Type: Private

Income Statement				FYE: June 30
	REVENUE ($mil)	NET INCOME ($mil)	NET PROFIT MARGIN	EMPLOYEES
06/20	567	8	1.4%	1,100
06/19	491	7	1.5%	—
06/16	358	(0)	—	—
06/15	340	0	0.1%	—
Annual Growth	10.7%	87.0%	—	—

2020 Year-End Financials
Return on assets: 5.0%
Return on equity: 19.6%
Current Ratio: 2.40
Cash ($ mil.): 57

GERBER SCIENTIFIC PRODUCTS INC

LOCATIONS

HQ: GERBER SCIENTIFIC PRODUCTS INC
83 GERBER RD W, SOUTH WINDSOR, CT 060743230
Phone: 860 648-8300

HISTORICAL FINANCIALS
Company Type: Private

Income Statement				FYE: April 30
	REVENUE ($mil)	NET INCOME ($mil)	NET PROFIT MARGIN	EMPLOYEES
04/07	574	13	2.4%	300
04/06	530	0	0.0%	—
Annual Growth	8.4%	—	—	—

2007 Year-End Financials
Return on assets: 4.0%
Return on equity: 9.3%
Current Ratio: 1.70
Cash ($ mil.): 8

GGP, INC.

Auditors : DELOITTE & TOUCHE LLP CHICAGO

LOCATIONS

HQ: GGP, INC.
350 N ORLEANS ST STE 300, CHICAGO, IL 606541607
Phone: 312 960-5000
Web: WWW.GGP.COM

HISTORICAL FINANCIALS
Company Type: Private

Income Statement				FYE: December 31
	ASSETS ($mil)	NET INCOME ($mil)	INCOME AS % OF ASSETS	EMPLOYEES
12/12	27,282	(471)	—	1,500
12/11	29,518	(306)	—	—
12/10	32,367	(256)	—	—
12/09	28,149	(1,304)	—	—
Annual Growth	(1.0%)	—	—	—

2012 Year-End Financials
Return on assets: (-1.7%)
Return on equity: (-6.1%)
Current Ratio: —
Cash ($ mil.): 624

GILBANE BUILDING COMPANY

Gilbane Building Company provides construction services, consulting, subcontracting, and facilities management to commercial, institutional, and governmental markets. Operating as the construction arm of Gilbane, the company builds schools, hospitals, laboratories, and prisons, serving both the public and private sectors. Its completed projects include the Stroh Center at Bowling Green State University and the National WWII Memorial in Washington, DC. Founded in 1870 as a carpentry and general contracting shop, the family-owned Gilbane Building Company operates from more than 45 offices around the world.

Operations
The company offers Building Information Modeling (BIM) and Virtual Design and Construction (VDC), construction, design-build, disaster recovery & reconstruction, environmental services, facilities management, fueling facilities construction & repair, interdisciplinary document coordination, multimedia studio, multi-site project delivery systems, preconstruction, schedule risk analysis, and transition planning & management. Its delivery methods include construction management; Integrated Project Delivery (IPD) a delivery model based on lean construction that collaborates and involve the owner, A/E, builders, trade contractors, facility managers, end users; lump sum contracting, and program/project management.

Geographic Reach
Rhode Island-based, the company has more than 45 offices and 1,000 projects underway around the world, some of its domestic locations are in Arizona, California, Colorado, Connecticut, Florida, Georgia, New York, and South Carolina. Gilbane Building Company enjoys a geographic footprint that extends from the US to Japan, Guam, Ireland, Saudi Arabia, and the UAE.

Sales and Marketing
Gilbane Building Company serves several sectors, such as healthcare, higher education, K-12 schools, federal and public entities, mission critical, corporate, and sports and recreation. The company reported over 75% of its work comes from repeat clients.

Company Background
In 1870, William Gilbane founded a carpentry firm and in 1871, Thomas Gilbane apprenticed with his brother William. Together the brothers worked tirelessly to found Gilbane Building Company in 1870.

EXECUTIVES

Vice Chairman, William J Gilbane Junior
CMO*, Karen Medeiros
Auditors : RSM US LLP BOSTON MASSACHUSE

LOCATIONS

HQ: GILBANE BUILDING COMPANY
7 JACKSON WALKWAY STE 2, PROVIDENCE, RI 029033694
Phone: 401 456-5800
Web: WWW.GILBANECO.COM

PRODUCTS/OPERATIONS

Selected Markets
Convention/cultural
Corporate
Criminal justice
Federal/public
Health care
    Children's hospitals
    Women's centers
    Cardiac-care centers
    Cancer centers
    Clinical and research facilities
Higher education
    Research laboratories
    Academic facilities
    Admissions buildings
    Residence halls
    Performing arts centers
    Sports and recreational centers
    Libraries and technology centers
    Student unions
K-12 schools
Life sciences
Mission critical
Sports/recreation
Transportation
Water/wastewater

Selected Services
Pre-construction
    Transition planning and management
    Building information modeling
    Conceptual cost modeling
    High-performance building & energy modeling
    Interdisciplinary document coordination
Consulting
    CAT-response
    Facilities management services
    Schedule & risk analysis
    Transition planning & management
Construction
    Construction management at risk
    Construction management as agent

Lump sum general contracting
Integrated project delivery

COMPETITORS

CBRE HEERY, INC.
E.W. HOWELL CO., LLC
GILBANE, INC.
HENSEL PHELPS CONSTRUCTION CO.
J.E. DUNN CONSTRUCTION COMPANY
KITCHELL CORPORATION
LECHASE CONSTRUCTION SERVICES, LLC
SWINERTON INCORPORATED
THE PIKE COMPANY INC
TURNER CONSTRUCTION COMPANY

HISTORICAL FINANCIALS

Company Type: Private

Income Statement — FYE: December 31

	REVENUE ($mil)	NET INCOME ($mil)	NET PROFIT MARGIN	EMPLOYEES
12/17	4,899	63	1.3%	2,500
12/14	3,840	0	0.0%	—
12/13	4,100	0	0.0%	—
Annual Growth	4.5%	—	—	—

2017 Year-End Financials
Return on assets: 3.9%   Cash ($ mil.): 252
Return on equity: 22.6%
Current Ratio: 1.20

GLOBAL HEALTH SOLUTIONS, INC.

LOCATIONS

HQ: GLOBAL HEALTH SOLUTIONS, INC.
325 SWANTON WAY, DECATUR, GA 300303001
Phone: 404 592-1430

HISTORICAL FINANCIALS

Company Type: Private

Income Statement — FYE: August 31

	REVENUE ($mil)	NET INCOME ($mil)	NET PROFIT MARGIN	EMPLOYEES
08/15	1,609	0	0.0%	2
08/14	1,790	0	0.0%	—
08/13	1,574	0	0.0%	—
08/10	1,120	0	0.0%	—
Annual Growth	7.5%	—	—	—

GLU MOBILE INC.

Glu Mobile develops, publishes, and markets a portfolio of free-to-play mobile games designed to appeal to a broad cross section of users who download and make purchases within its games through direct-to-consumer digital storefronts, such as the Apple App Store, Google Play Store, and others. Glu's portfolio includes Cooking Dash, Covet Fashion, Deer Hunter, Design Home, and Diner DASH Adventures. The company has approximately 2.5 million daily active users and some 11.2 million active monthly users. The company gets around 80% of sales in the US. In 2021, Electronic Arts Inc., a global leader in interactive entertainment, completed the acquisition of Glu Mobile Inc. for $2.1 billion in enterprise value.

Operations

Glu Mobile's in-house developed games are aimed at the social, free-to-play (or "freemium") space. In-App Purchases conducted to make in-game purchases account for around 90% of Glu Mobile's revenue. Although users can download and play its games free of charge, they can purchase virtual currency, virtual items, other virtual benefits like time and energy or subscriptions to receive any of these benefits, to enhance their gameplay experience. In addition to in-app purchases of virtual currency, it also monetize its games through offers and in-game advertising which account for some 10%.

The company devotes all its resources to developing games exclusively for smartphones and tablets, such as those running Google's Android OS, and Apple's iPhone and iPad. It develops and publishes a portfolio of mobile games designed to appeal to a broad cross section of the users of smartphones and tablet devices. These products have included Design Home, Covet Fashion, and Table & Taste for lifestyle genre; Diner DASH, Kim Kardashian, and Cooking Dash for casual genre; Disney Sorcere's Arena for RPG; and MLB Tap Sports, and Deer Hunter for sports and outdoors genre.

Geographic Reach

Headquartered in San Francisco, California, the company has gaming development studios in San Francisco and Foster City, California; Orlando, Florida and Toronto, Canada. It also has additional locations in Hyderabad, India.. Customers in the US account for around 80% of sales.

Sales and Marketing

Glu Mobile doesn't need salespeople - it has the Internet. Its games are sold online in direct-to-consumer digital storefronts, such as Apple's App Store, the Google Play Store, and others. Major customers include Apple (over 60% of revenue) and Google (about 35% of revenue).

Advertising expense was $146,207 $117,979, and $95,037 in the years 2020, 2019, and 2018, respectively

Financial Performance

Revenue for 2020 was $540.5 million, a 31% increase compared to 2019, in which the company reported revenue of $411.4 million. The increase in total revenue was primarily related to a $120.7 million increase in the company's revenue from micro-transactions (in-app purchases) and an $8.3 million increase in its revenue from advertisements and offers.

The net income in 2020 was $20.4 million versus a net income of $8.9 million in 2019. This change was primarily due to an increase in revenue of $129.1 million. This change was partially offset by an increase in cost of sales of $46.1 million, an increase in sales and marketing expenses of $36.9 million, an increase in research and development expenses of $24.6 million, and an increase in general and administrative expenses of $8.3 million.

Cash and cash equivalents at the end of the period were $364.4 million. Net cash generated from operating activities was $76.1 million while investing activities used $7.1 million. Financing activities generated another $364.4 million. Main cash uses were for purchases of property and equipment.

Strategy

The company goal is to become the leading developer and publisher of free-to-play mobile games. Its strategy for achieving this goal is comprised of three parts:

Building Growth Games and Maximizing the Value of Catalog Games- This strategy is to build growth games for smartphones and tablets as well as maximize the value it derives from its catalog games. Growth games are titles that it continues to update with additional content and features and which it expects to grow revenue year over year.

Attracting and Fostering Creative Leaders, Including Potentially by Selective Acquisitions- This strategy is to attract, cultivate and retain proven creative leaders who will develop and update its growth and catalog games. Each creative leader is responsible for the long-term planning of his or her titles and to identify and invest in long-term opportunities and concepts that have the potential to become growth games. Its talent model is to attract the industry's finest and provide them with world-class infrastructure, tools, funding and the support to create hit games. It has made, and plan to make, significant investment in its creative leaders. In addition, it recently announced that it intends to increase its focus on potentially acquiring companies or individual game teams in order to complement its existing portfolio and augment its roster of creative leaders.

Cultivating Highly Creative Environments- The company believes a key part of building growth games and attracting and cultivating creative leaders is providing them with highly creative environments that are optimal for creating hit games. In December 2017, it moved into its new headquarters in San Francisco that were designed to foster collaboration among its game teams and focus the company around its core values and creative-led vision. Creative environments that support its creative leaders and other game development personnel are also needed to attract the level of talent that will support its growth and catalog games.

EXECUTIVES

CRO*, Chris Akhavan
Corporate Secretary*, Scott J Leichtner
Auditors : PRICEWATERHOUSECOOPERS LLP SA

LOCATIONS

HQ: GLU MOBILE INC.
  875 HOWARD ST STE 100, SAN FRANCISCO, CA
  941033032
Phone: 415 800-6100
Web: WWW.GLU.COM

2014 Sales

	$ mil.	% of total
America		
United States	132.4	59
Others	9.7	4
Europe, Middle East, & Africa	43.5	20
Asia/Pacific		
China	11.8	5
Others	25.7	12
Total	223.1	100

PRODUCTS/OPERATIONS

2014 Sales

	$ mil.	% of total
Micro-Transaction	182.2	81
Offers	23.0	10
Advertisement	14.5	7
Feature phone	1.4	1
Others	2.0	1
Total	223.1	100

Selected Titles
Poker Hold'em Challenge
Rogue Racing
Small Street
Samurai vs. Zombies Defense
Deer Hunter Reloaded Lil' Kingdom
Mutant Roadkill
Blood & Glory Legend
Eternity Warriors 2
Gears & Guts
Ham on the Run Tavern Quest
Bombshells: Hell's Belles
Campers!
Enchant U
Indestructible
My Dragon
Contract Killer 2
Death Dome
Call of Duty Black Ops Zombies (licensed)
Contract Killer: Zombies 2 Dragon Slayer

COMPETITORS

ALPHABET INC.
ELECTRONIC ARTS INC.
GOOGLE LLC
KING DIGITAL ENTERTAINMENT LIMITED
NATURALMOTION LIMITED
REALNETWORKS, INC.
Rovio Entertainment Oyj
SNAP INC.
TAKE-TWO INTERACTIVE SOFTWARE, INC.
ZYNGA INC.

HISTORICAL FINANCIALS
Company Type: Private

Income Statement — FYE: December 31

	REVENUE ($mil)	NET INCOME ($mil)	NET PROFIT MARGIN	EMPLOYEES
12/20	540	20	3.8%	715
12/19	411	8	2.2%	—
12/18	366	(13)	—	—
12/17	286	(97)	—	—
Annual Growth	23.5%	—	—	—

2020 Year-End Financials
Return on assets: 3.1%
Return on equity: 4.9%
Current Ratio: 2.60
Cash ($ mil.): 364

GOOD SAMARITAN HOSPITAL MEDICAL CENTER

The folks at Good Samaritan Hospital Medical Center have plenty of reasons to feel good about their efforts. The hospital is part of Catholic Health Services of Long Island (CHS) and serves the south shore community of West Islip, New York. The full-service medical center boasts 900 physicians and 440 acute care beds, offering a complete range of health care, counseling, and rehabilitation services. Good Samaritan provides emergency medicine and trauma care, in addition to oncology, cardiology, pediatric, woman's health, diagnostic, and surgical care. It also operates the Good Samaritan Nursing Home, a 100-bed skilled nursing facility, as well as satellite clinics and a home health care agency.

Operations
Good Samaritan, which contributes about 28% of its parent's revenue, logged more than 95,000 emergency department visits in 2012. Its ambulatory surgery department treats an average of nearly 300 patients weekly as part of its focus on same-day procedures. Additionally, the medical facility in 2012 admitted 27,615 patients and logged 2,820 births, 66,000 rehabilitation inpatient visits, and 49,640 dialysis treatments.

The hospital's outpatient services include same day surgeries, pulmonary rehabilitation, pediatric specialty visits, and physical, occupational, and speech therapy sessions; it also has satellite locations that provide dialysis treatment. Good Samaritan's palliative care program offers an 11-bed dedicated acute palliative care inpatient unit.

Geographic Reach
Good Samaritan Hospital Medical Center serves those in and around West Islip, New York.

Financial Performance
Net patient revenue dragged down Good Samaritan's revenue increases in fiscal 2012 vs. 2011. During the reporting period, the medical center posted $579 million in revenue, representing a marginal $260,000 rise. Net income dropped some 77% to $8.3 million in 2012 vs. 2011, thanks to rising operating expenses from increases in CHS Services.

Strategy
Good Samaritan is recognized for its cancer care and radiology programs, as well as its cardiac, pediatric, and women's health services, all of which it has been expanding and enhancing in recent years. For instance, the hospital added a nephrology unit in 2011 within its pediatric division to evaluate and treat children with kidney disease. It expanded its pediatric nephrology unit in 2012 by opening a new 16-bed surgical intensive care unit (SICU). Good Samaritan also added a new diagnostic imaging center in 2012 that provides radiology services, including breast imaging.

In addition, Good Samaritan is working to add an open-heart surgery program to its cardiology division through a partnership with St. Francis Hospital, another member of the CHS organization also known as The Heart Center. In 2013, Good Samaritan became the first facility in the New York metropolitan region to install and offer the GE Innova IGS 530 digital cardiovascular and interventional imaging system in its cardiac catheterization laboratory.

The not-for-profit facility's growth measures are supported in part by its charitable organization, The Guilds of Good Samaritan Hospital Medical Center. The Good Samaritan hospital provides some $50 million in community service and charity care each year.

Company Background
Founded in 1959, Good Samaritan became part of the CHS organization in 1997.

EXECUTIVES

CAO, Thomas Ockers
Quality Vice President*, Vincent Angeloro
Risk Management Vice-President*, Gail Donheiser
OF PATIENT SERV*, Gara Edelstein
Assistant Vice President Finance*, Christine Stehlik
Auditors : PRICEWATERHOUSECOOPERS LLP NE

LOCATIONS

HQ: GOOD SAMARITAN HOSPITAL MEDICAL CENTER
  1000 MONTAUK HWY, WEST ISLIP, NY 117954927
Phone: 631 376-3000
Web: WWW.CHSLI.ORG

PRODUCTS/OPERATIONS

Selected Premier Services
Cancer Care
Cardiac Care

Children's Care
Emergency Services
Satellites
Surgery
Women's Care

Selected Services
Ambulatory Surgery Unit
Audiology/Hearing Aids
BirthPlace
Breast Health Center
Cancer Care
Cancer Surgery
Cardiac Rehabilitation
Cardiology Services
Center for Pediatric Specialty Care
Care Management and Social Work
Child Life Services
da Vinci Surgery
Dentistry
Dermatology
Dialysis Services
Ear, Nose and Throat
Emergency Department
Endocrinology
Family Practice
Gastroenterology
Good Samaritan Hospital Foundation
Good Samaritan Nursing Home
Hematology and Oncology
Imaging Services
Infectious Diseases
Inpatient Dialysis
Internal Medicine
Laboratory
Long Term Home Health Care
Managed Care
Martin Luther King, Jr., Community Health Center
Maternal Fetal Medicine
Medical Education
Neonatology
Nephrology
Neurosurgery
Nursing at Good Sam
Nutrition and Food Services
Obstetrics and Gynecology
Oncology
Ophthalmology
Oral Surgery
Orthopaedics
Osteoporosis
Palliative Care
Pain Management
Pastoral/Spiritual Care Department
Pathology
Pediatric Services
Perinatal Education
Plastic and Reconstructive Services
Podiatry
Pre-Surgical Testing
Psychiatry
Pulmonary Rehabilitation
Radiation Oncology Center
Rehabilitation Services
Respiratory Care
Safe Haven Program
Sleep Apnea Center
Special Care
Support Groups
Surgery
Thoracic Surgery
Trauma Services
Urology
Vascular Suite
Vascular Surgery
Weight Loss Surgery/Bariatric Surgery
Women's Imaging Center

COMPETITORS

GOOD SAMARITAN HOSPITAL
SAINT JOSEPH HOSPITAL, INC
SWEDISH COVENANT HOSPITAL

THE BROOKDALE HOSPITAL MEDICAL CENTER
THE PENNSYLVANIA HOSPITAL OF THE UNIVERSITY OF PENNSYLVANIA HEALTH SYSTEM

HISTORICAL FINANCIALS
Company Type: Private

Income Statement — FYE: December 31

	REVENUE ($mil)	NET INCOME ($mil)	NET PROFIT MARGIN	EMPLOYEES
12/19	725	20	2.8%	3,774
12/15	505	28	5.7%	—
12/14	488	36	7.5%	—
12/13	534	(28)	—	—
Annual Growth	5.2%	—	—	—

2019 Year-End Financials
Return on assets: 3.6%   Cash ($ mil.): 96
Return on equity: 7.4%
Current Ratio: 2.10

GOOD SAMARITAN HOSPITAL OF CINCINNATI

Auditors: ERNST & YOUNG LLP CINCINNATI

LOCATIONS

HQ: GOOD SAMARITAN HOSPITAL OF CINCINNATI
375 DIXMYTH AVE, CINCINNATI, OH 452202489
Phone: 513 569-6251
Web: WWW.TRIHEALTH.COM

HISTORICAL FINANCIALS
Company Type: Private

Income Statement — FYE: June 30

	REVENUE ($mil)	NET INCOME ($mil)	NET PROFIT MARGIN	EMPLOYEES
06/22	793	(22)	—	3,452
06/21	743	157	21.1%	—
06/20	563	(60)	—	—
06/19	563	33	5.9%	—
Annual Growth	12.1%	—	—	—

2022 Year-End Financials
Return on assets: (-2.0%)   Cash ($ mil.): —
Return on equity: (-2.4%)
Current Ratio: 1.10

GOOD SAMARITAN HOSPITAL, L.P.

Good Samaritan Hospital lends a hand to help Silicon Valley's techies and their neighbors stay healthy. The facility, part of the HCA family of for-profit hospitals, administers care through campuses in San José (the main campus) and Los Gatos, California. Good Samaritan Hospital provides general acute care as well as a host of tertiary services that include cardiology and cardiovascular surgery; oncology; obstetrics and gynecology; and psychiatry (both inpatient and outpatient care). The main campus hospital has some 408 patient beds and 600 physicians, and the Los Gatos outpatient and short-stay facility houses approximately 100 beds.

Operations
Each year Good Samaritan admits 17,000 patients (excluding newborns) and handles more than 93,500 outpatient visits. More than 4,000 deliveries and 8,000 surgeries are performed annually in 18 surgical suites.

Strategy
In addition to being a community hospital, Good Samaritan is a world-class academic medical center affiliated with both USC and UCLA Schools of Medicine. To cater to the diverse urban population the hospital system serves, Good Samaritan's medical staff and employees speak more than 54 languages/dialects.

Company Background
Good Samaritan Hospital opened its doors in 1965 as an acute care hospital with a staff of about 400.

EXECUTIVES

Chief Medical Officer, Paul Deaupre

LOCATIONS

HQ: GOOD SAMARITAN HOSPITAL, L.P.
2425 SAMARITAN DR, SAN JOSE, CA 951243985
Phone: 408 559-2011
Web: WWW.GOODSAMSANJOSE.COM

PRODUCTS/OPERATIONS

Selected Services and Departments
Cardiology
Cardiac Surgery
Comprehensive Sleep Center
Diagnostic Imaging (Radiology)
ENT (Ear, Nose & Throat)
Emergency Services
Gamma Knife
Gastroenterology
Laboratory
Neurosciences
Oncology (Cancer)
Opthalmology & Retinal Medicine
Orthopedics
Podiatry
Physical Medicine
Pulmonary Medicine & Respiratory Care
Radiation Oncology
Surgery
Women's Health & Newborn Services
Urology

COMPETITORS

COMMUNITY HOSPITALS OF CENTRAL CALIFORNIA
GLENDALE ADVENTIST MEDICAL CENTER
GOOD SAMARITAN HOSPITAL
NORTHWEST COMMUNITY HOSPITAL
WHITE MEMORIAL MEDICAL CENTER

HISTORICAL FINANCIALS
Company Type: Private

Income Statement   FYE: January 31

	REVENUE ($mil)	NET INCOME ($mil)	NET PROFIT MARGIN	EMPLOYEES
01/17	618	141	22.8%	1,800
01/09*	413	30	7.3%	—
05/05	170	0	0.0%	—
12/03	0	0	—	—
Annual Growth	—	—	—	—

*Fiscal year change

2017 Year-End Financials
Return on assets: 53.2%   Cash ($ mil.): —
Return on equity: 37.7%
Current Ratio: 2.10

GOVERNMENT OF DISTRICT OF COLUMBIA

Government of the District of Columbia manages ticket and tax payments, housing and property issues, children and youth services, and motor vehicles registration, among other duties for Washington, DC. More than 689,000 people live in Washington DC, and many more commute to the city every day to work for the federal government. Washington, DC is overseen by a mayor and a 13-member city council. It acquires contracts with more than 30 local government agencies. The Government of the District of Columbia was created in 1790 with donated land from Maryland and Virginia as part of the Residence Act.

EXECUTIVES
CPO*, George Schutter
Auditors: MCCONNELL JONES WASHINGTON D

LOCATIONS
HQ: GOVERNMENT OF DISTRICT OF COLUMBIA
441 4TH ST NW, WASHINGTON, DC 200012714
Phone: 202 727-0252
Web: WWW.DC.GOV

PRODUCTS/OPERATIONS
Selected Services
311 Service Request Online
Children and Youth Services
District Neighborhoods
Emergency Preparedness
Health and Human Services
Housing and Property
Pay a Ticket
Public Safety
Public Works, Sanitation and Utilities
Taxpayer Service Center
Transportation and Motor Vehicles

COMPETITORS
CITY OF ALEXANDRIA
CITY OF BERKELEY
CITY OF HOUSTON
CITY OF OXNARD
CITY OF RICHMOND
CITY OF SACRAMENTO
CITY OF TAMPA
EXECUTIVE OFFICE OF THE STATE OF ALASKA
HOUSING AND COMMUNITY RENEWAL, NEW YORK STATE DIVISION OF
NATIONAL CAPITAL PLANNING COMMISSION

HISTORICAL FINANCIALS
Company Type: Private

Income Statement   FYE: September 30

	REVENUE ($mil)	NET INCOME ($mil)	NET PROFIT MARGIN	EMPLOYEES
09/20	16,510	(504)	—	34,600
09/16	12,095	(78)	—	—
09/15	11,637	583	5.0%	—
09/11	9,822	102	1.0%	—
Annual Growth	5.9%	—	—	—

2020 Year-End Financials
Return on assets: (-1.7%)   Cash ($ mil.): 1,838
Return on equity: (-6.0%)
Current Ratio: —

GPM INVESTMENTS, LLC

Convenience is key for GPM Investments, which operates or supplies fuel to more than 1,100 convenience stores in about 20 US states. The stores sell BP, Exxon, Marathon, and Valero brand gas, among others, as well as the usual beer, smokes, and snacks. Some locations also offer fresh, made-to-order salads, sandwiches, and other items, or offer branded food from Subway, Taco Bell, and others. The company, which primarily serves the Midwest and eastern US, operates or supplies stores under a host of names, including Fas Mart, Shore Stop, Jiffi Stop, Young's, and Roadrunner Markets.

Operations
In addition to convenience stores, GPM also operates 15 Subway franchises, one Taco Bell franchise, and 50 restaurants that serve Southern fried chicken.

Geographic Reach
Richmond, Virginia-based GPM operates more than 600 convenience stores in Virginia, North Carolina, Delaware, Maryland, Pennsylvania, New Jersey, Connecticut, Rhode Island, South Carolina, and Tennessee.

Strategy
To help fund investments in new capital improvement projects and in acquisitions, GPM entered into a $35 million credit facility with PNC Bank N.A. in 2012. Maturing in November 2016, the credit facility allows GPM to open new stores and improve existing locations. To this end, the convenience store operator has offered to buy a 50% stake in EZ Energy Ltd. based in Ramat Gan, Israel, for $15 million. The company typically uses funding received through credit facilities to improve its locations with brighter interior and exterior lighting, wider aisles, and cleaner stores. It is also increasing its marketing efforts through social media to target younger shoppers.

Fast-growing GPM Investments in growing through acquisitions. Indeed, in 2013 the company made its largest acquisition to date, propelling its store count to more than 600 locations in 10 states.

Mergers and Acquisitions
In August 2013 GPM acquired the Southeastern division of VPS Convenience Store Group from Sun Capital Partners. The regional division operates more than 260 stores and 33 dealer sites and was cobbled together from acquisitions that included the Scotchman, Young's, Li'l Cricket, Everyday Shop, and Cigarette City banners. Most of the newly-acquired stores are in the Carolinas, where GPM's retail presence is thin. Earlier in August, GPM purchased five stores operating under the Get & Zip banner in Virginia. Most of the

Auditors: GRANT THORNTON LLP RALEIGH

LOCATIONS
HQ: GPM INVESTMENTS, LLC
8565 MAGELLAN PKWY # 400, RICHMOND, VA 232271167
Phone: 276 328-3669
Web: WWW.GPMINVESTMENTS.COM

Selected Locations
Connecticut
Delaware
Maryland
New Jersey
North Carolina
Pennsylvania
Rhode Island
South Carolina
Tennessee
Virginia

COMPETITORS
HOLIDAY COMPANIES
HOUCHENS INDUSTRIES, INC.
KUM & GO, L.C.
RACETRAC PETROLEUM, INC.
SHEETZ, INC.
SPEEDWAY LLC
STEWART'S SHOPS CORP.
THE PANTRY INC
THE SPINX COMPANY LLC
TOWN PUMP, INC.

HISTORICAL FINANCIALS
Company Type: Private

Income Statement   FYE: December 31

	REVENUE ($mil)	NET INCOME ($mil)	NET PROFIT MARGIN	EMPLOYEES
12/08	1,249	(1)	—	2,150
12/07	891	3	0.4%	—
Annual Growth	40.2%	—	—	—

2008 Year-End Financials
Return on assets: 1.7% Cash ($ mil.): 12
Return on equity: (-0.1%)
Current Ratio: 0.40

GRADY MEMORIAL HOSPITAL CORPORATION

Auditors: KPMG LLP ATLANTA GA

LOCATIONS

HQ: GRADY MEMORIAL HOSPITAL CORPORATION
80 JESSE HILL JR DR SE, ATLANTA, GA 303033050
Phone: 404 616-4360
Web: WWW.GRADYHEALTH.ORG

HISTORICAL FINANCIALS
Company Type: Private

Income Statement — FYE: December 31

	REVENUE ($mil)	NET INCOME ($mil)	NET PROFIT MARGIN	EMPLOYEES
12/20	978	131	13.5%	270
12/19	2,032	29	1.5%	—
12/17	1,494	42	2.9%	—
12/16	1,444	47	3.3%	—
Annual Growth	(9.3%)	28.9%	—	—

2020 Year-End Financials
Return on assets: 11.4% Cash ($ mil.): 164
Return on equity: 16.8%
Current Ratio: 1.70

GRAEBEL HOLDINGS, INC.

Auditors: WIPFLI LLP WAUSAU WISCONSIN

LOCATIONS

HQ: GRAEBEL HOLDINGS, INC.
16346 AIRPORT CIR, AURORA, CO 800111558
Phone: 303 214-6683
Web: WWW.GRAEBEL.COM

HISTORICAL FINANCIALS
Company Type: Private

Income Statement — FYE: December 31

	REVENUE ($mil)	NET INCOME ($mil)	NET PROFIT MARGIN	EMPLOYEES
12/20	912	7	0.8%	1,771
12/17	96	1	1.2%	—
12/16	90	3	3.6%	—
12/15	94	5	5.9%	—
Annual Growth	57.5%	6.1%	—	—

2020 Year-End Financials
Return on assets: 5.6% Cash ($ mil.): 13
Return on equity: 24.8%
Current Ratio: 1.20

GRAHAM ENTERPRISE, INC.

Auditors: FGMK LLC BANNOCKBURN ILLINO

LOCATIONS

HQ: GRAHAM ENTERPRISE, INC.
750 BUNKER CT STE 100, VERNON HILLS, IL 600611864
Phone: 847 837-0777
Web: WWW.GRAHAMEI.COM

HISTORICAL FINANCIALS
Company Type: Private

Income Statement — FYE: December 31

	REVENUE ($mil)	NET INCOME ($mil)	NET PROFIT MARGIN	EMPLOYEES
12/17	638	12	2.0%	350
12/16	596	6	1.1%	—
12/15	662	11	1.7%	—
12/14	866	8	0.9%	—
Annual Growth	(9.7%)	16.5%	—	—

2017 Year-End Financials
Return on assets: 32.4% Cash ($ mil.): 6
Return on equity: 47.9%
Current Ratio: 1.90

GRAND RIVER DAM AUTHORITY

It took the dam authority of the State of Oklahoma to create the body that would dam the Grand River. The resulting power provider, the Grand River Dam Authority, is responsible for supplying wholesale electricity to municipal and cooperative utilities and industrial customers in its service territory, which encompasses 24 counties in northeastern Oklahoma. It also sells excess power to customers across a four-state region. The state-owned utility has 1,480 MW of generating capacity from hydroelectric and fossil-fueled power plants and operates a 2,090-mile transmission system. Grand River Dam Authority also manages two lakes and a total of 70,000 surface acres of water in Northeast Oklahoma.

Sales and Marketing
The company sells power to sixteen municipal customers in Oklahoma (serving 500,000 homes) as well as customers in Arkansas, Kansas, and Missouri.

Financial Performance
In 2012 the Grand River Dam Authority's revenues increased by 4% due to improved sales (thanks to an improving economy pushing up demand) and higher electricity rates. Sales increases were led by growth in the industrial and off-system segments

The company's net income decreased by 7% in 2012 due to higher operating costs.

Strategy
The Grand River Dam Authority's long-term strategy is to balance ensuring low-cost supply with maintaining reliable electrical service (through infrastructure maintenance and upgrades), while delivering financial stability.

Honoring a promise to keep rates low and competitive while addressing environmental needs, in 2013 the Authority lowered rates to 2009 levels.

Company Background
The Grand River Dam Authority was created by state legislation in 1935. It began construction on the Pensacola Dam across the Grand River in 1938. The dam was inaugurated in 1940. A second smaller dam (Robert S. Kerr Dam) downstream was completed in 1962.

Auditors: BAKER TILLY US LLP MADISON

LOCATIONS

HQ: GRAND RIVER DAM AUTHORITY
8142 S 412 B, CHOUTEAU, OK 74337
Phone: 918 256-5545
Web: WWW.GRDA.COM

COMPETITORS

LOWER COLORADO RIVER AUTHORITY
MODESTO IRRIGATION DISTRICT (INC)
NORTHWESTERN CORPORATION
SALT RIVER PROJECT AGRICULTURAL IMPROVEMENT AND POWER DISTRICT
TENNESSEE VALLEY AUTHORITY

HISTORICAL FINANCIALS
Company Type: Private

Income Statement — FYE: December 31

	REVENUE ($mil)	NET INCOME ($mil)	NET PROFIT MARGIN	EMPLOYEES
12/21	579	68	11.9%	468
12/20	397	33	8.5%	—
12/19	424	53	12.7%	—
12/18	437	30	6.9%	—
Annual Growth	9.8%	31.7%	—	—

2021 Year-End Financials
Return on assets: 3.5% Cash ($ mil.): 17
Return on equity: 8.8%
Current Ratio: 2.60

GRANITE SCHOOL DISTRICT

Auditors: SQUIRE & COMPANY PC OREM UT

LOCATIONS

HQ: GRANITE SCHOOL DISTRICT
2500 S STATE ST STE 500, SOUTH SALT LAKE, UT 841153195
Phone: 385 646-5000
Web: WWW.GRANITESCHOOLS.ORG

HISTORICAL FINANCIALS
Company Type: Private

Income Statement   FYE: June 30

	REVENUE ($mil)	NET INCOME ($mil)	NET PROFIT MARGIN	EMPLOYEES
06/22	764	(3)	—	8,000
06/21	709	32	4.6%	—
06/20	693	0	0.0%	—
06/19	678	52	7.7%	—
Annual Growth	4.0%	—	—	—

2022 Year-End Financials
Return on assets: (-0.2%)   Cash ($ mil.): —
Return on equity: (-0.6%)
Current Ratio: —

GRANITE TELECOMMUNICATIONS LLC

Granite Telecommunications carves out an increasing block of telecommunications services to commercial clients in the US and Canada. The company is a wholesaler of local and long distance telephone service, as well as broadband internet connections, with approximately 1.75 million lines provided by network operators. It serves corporate clients, many of whom run offices in multiple states, offering them no account transfer charges and no term or volume contracts on telephone service. Granite also designs and installs network cabling and security systems and provides loss prevention and risk management services.

Operations
The company offer its products in six categories: Mobility; Granite Merged Voice; Advanced Services; Access; Granite Guardian; and Granite Grid.

Granite Mobility offers all four major US and multiple Canadian/International Mobile Operators available on one platform along with a full end to end Managed Solution to address the needs of the Mobile Enterprises. Through Daily Dashboard, customers have the ability to manage their plans and data pools for their entire inventory of mobility services, regardless of carrier, in one centralized portal. A dedicated Premier support team helps its customers manage their data usage through Cross Carrier Pooling, Proactive alerts and the ability to backdate billing to the beginning of the month. Granite Marketplace offers its customers the flexibility to amortize any device purchases on up to 5-year terms.

Granite Merged Voice is an all-encompassing VoIP portfolio that provides stable, scalable telephony solutions ranging from emulated POTS, to Cloud PBX to traditional hand-off options like Primary Rate Interface (PRI) or Business SIP Trunking which seamlessly integrates with clients' existing phone systems.

Advanced Services includes services related to SD-WAN, security and Wi-Fi and Switching.

Access provides services related to Internet Access; Multiprotocol Label Switching; and WAN Wireless Access.

Granite Guardian is the new exclusive managed service offerings to enhance network operations and to dramatically increase uptime. Through industry leading development and integration it can offer monitored or fully managed network services for all of its customers telecommunication needs. The company's customers take comfort in the industry leading MTTR and customer service.

Granite Grid is the first telecommunications product to offer management companies and their tenants a reliable one-stop-shop solution. Granite Grid offers affordable voice and data services along with a certified support team.

Geographic Reach
Granite serves clients across Canada and the US from offices in Florida, Pennsylvania, Virginia, Tennessee, California, Massachusetts, Georgia, Illinois, New York, Texas, and Rhode Island. It is based in Quincy, Massachusetts.

EXECUTIVES
Managing Member, Robert Hale Junior
Managing Member, Rand Currier
Managing Member, Paul Stutzman
Managing Member, John Prinner
Managing Member, Mark Prendergast
Deputy General Counsel, Sana Sheikh

LOCATIONS
HQ: GRANITE TELECOMMUNICATIONS LLC
100 NEWPORT AVENUE EXT # 1, QUINCY, MA 021712126
Phone: 617 933-5500
Web: WWW.GRANITENET.COM

PRODUCTS/OPERATIONS
Products and Services
Voice
Managed Solutions
Data
Network Integration
Granite Grid

COMPETITORS
CEQUEL COMMUNICATIONS HOLDINGS, LLC
CHARTER COMMUNICATIONS, INC.
CONSOLIDATED COMMUNICATIONS HOLDINGS, INC.
ELECTRIC LIGHTWAVE COMMUNICATIONS, INC.
FUSION CLOUD SERVICES, LLC
LEVEL 3 PARENT, LLC
LUMOS NETWORKS CORP.
MULTIBAND CORPORATION
TELKONET, INC.
UNITEK GLOBAL SERVICES, INC.

HISTORICAL FINANCIALS
Company Type: Private

Income Statement   FYE: December 31

	REVENUE ($mil)	NET INCOME ($mil)	NET PROFIT MARGIN	EMPLOYEES
12/12	736	187	25.5%	2,116
12/11	609	143	23.5%	—
12/10	517	109	21.2%	—
Annual Growth	19.3%	31.0%	—	—

2012 Year-End Financials
Return on assets: 110.5%   Cash ($ mil.): 45
Return on equity: 394.1%
Current Ratio: 1.40

GREAT RIVER ENERGY

Great River Energy is not-for-profit wholesale electric power cooperative serving 28 member-owner distribution cooperatives. The utility provides wholesale electric service to member distribution cooperatives engaged in the retail sale of electricity to member consumers in Minnesota and a small section of Wisconsin. It operates about 4,790 miles of transmission lines. Approximately one-third of the people in Minnesota receive their electricity from a cooperative. Just like their counterparts in agriculture or housing, cooperative utilities are owned by the members they serve.

Operations
Great River Energy serves members through a diverse portfolio of power supply resources and dependable transmission system, all of which are part of the region's energy market.

As part of its efforts to increase its green energy output, Great River owns Blue Flint Ethanol, which includes of approximately 75-80 million-gallon ethanol refinery that uses process steam produced at Great River Energy Coal Creek Station.

Overall, electric revenue account for about 95% of the company's sales while other operating revenue accounts for the rest.

Geographic Reach
The company provides power to cooperatives, which in turn serve customers in Minnesota (headquarters) and Wisconsin.

Sales and Marketing
Great River Energy provides reliable, affordable and environmentally responsible wholesale electricity to 28 member-owner cooperatives that serve around 1.7 million people.

In all, members generated some 85% of sales. The rest were generated from non-members, nonutility operations excluding non-controlling interest, non-operating and others.

Financial Performance
The company's revenue in 2021 increased by $49.3 million to $1.0 billion compared with $980.9 million in the prior year. Electric

revenue increased $49.4 million or 5.5% to $954.0 million in 2021 from $904.6 million in 2020. Of the $49.4 million increase, $27.1 million was due to electric revenue from member cooperatives.

Net income in 2021 was $53.5 million compared to a net loss of $129.1 million in the prior year.

Cash held by the company at the end of 2021 increased to $251.0 million. Operating activities provided $256.1 million while investing and financing activities used $78.6 million and $158.1 million, respectively. Main cash uses were utility plant additions and repayments of long-term obligations.

Company Background

In 2013 the company signed a deal with Tangshan Shenzhou Manufacturing Company to make Great River Energy's DryFining technology (for more efficient coal use in power stations) available to utilities in China.

It is also cut costs and increasing efficiency at its own power plants. In 2012 these measures saved Great River Energy more than $8 million.

In 2012 Great River bought the remaining 51% of Blue Flint Ethanol it didn't already own. The move added to its production capabilities and helped push the company to record production that year.

The utility was formed in 1999 through the combination of two Minnesota utilities, Cooperative Power and United Power Association.

EXECUTIVES

Vice Chairman, Bruce Leino Board
Board Treasurer, Robert Thompson
Auditors : DELOITTE & TOUCHE LLP MINNEA

LOCATIONS

HQ: GREAT RIVER ENERGY
12300 ELM CREEK BLVD N, MAPLE GROVE, MN 553694718
Phone: 763 445-5000
Web: WWW.GREATRIVERENERGY.COM

PRODUCTS/OPERATIONS

2014 Sales

	% of total
Member	83
Non-member	7
Other	7
Nonutility operations Excluding non-controlling Interest	3
Total	100

2014 Sales

	$mil	% of total
Electric revenue	952.0	93
Other operating revenue	68.2	7
Total	1020.2	100

COMPETITORS

ASSOCIATED ELECTRIC COOPERATIVE, INC.
BONNEVILLE POWER ADMINISTRATION
GEORGIA POWER COMPANY
LOS ANGELES DEPARTMENT OF WATER AND POWER
OMAHA PUBLIC POWER DISTRICT
PUBLIC SERVICE COMPANY OF NEW HAMPSHIRE
PUBLIC UTILITY DISTRICT 1 OF SNOHOMISH COUNTY
ROCHESTER GAS AND ELECTRIC CORPORATION
SACRAMENTO MUNICIPAL UTILITY DISTRICT
SEMINOLE ELECTRIC COOPERATIVE, INC.

HISTORICAL FINANCIALS
Company Type: Private

Income Statement — FYE: December 31

	REVENUE ($mil)	NET INCOME ($mil)	NET PROFIT MARGIN	EMPLOYEES
12/18	1,295	8	0.7%	850
12/17	1,270	18	1.4%	—
12/16	1,022	21	2.1%	—
12/15	983	15	1.5%	—
Annual Growth	9.6%	(17.8%)	—	—

2018 Year-End Financials
Return on assets: 0.2% Cash ($ mil.): 276
Return on equity: 1.0%
Current Ratio: 1.30

GREENSTONE FARM CREDIT SERVICES ACA

One of the largest associations in the Farm Credit System, GreenStone offers FARM CREDIT SERVICES (FCS) providesÂ short, intermediate, and long-term loans; equipment and building leases; appraisal services; and life and crop insurance to farmers in Michigan and Wisconsin. ItÂ serves about 15,000 members and has nearlyÂ 40 locations. Through an alliance with AgriSolutions, a farm software and consulting company, Greenstone provides income tax planning and preparation services, farm business consulting, and educational seminars. FCS Mortgage provides residential loans for rural properties, as well as loans for home improvement, construction, and refinancing.

Auditors : PRICEWATERHOUSECOOPERS LLP MI

LOCATIONS

HQ: GREENSTONE FARM CREDIT SERVICES ACA
3515 WEST RD, EAST LANSING, MI 488237312
Phone: 517 324-0213
Web: WWW.GREENSTONEFCS.COM

COMPETITORS

AGRIBANK, FCB
CDC SMALL BUSINESS FINANCE CORP.
FARM CREDIT EAST, ACA
FEDERAL HOME LOAN BANK OF DES MOINES
NORTHWEST FARM CREDIT SERVICES

HISTORICAL FINANCIALS
Company Type: Private

Income Statement — FYE: December 31

	ASSETS ($mil)	NET INCOME ($mil)	INCOME AS % OF ASSETS	EMPLOYEES
12/20	10,967	270	2.5%	380
12/07	4,317	69	1.6%	—
12/06	3,691	63	1.7%	—
Annual Growth	8.1%	10.8%	—	—

GROSSMONT HOSPITAL FOUNDATION

Auditors : ERNST & YOUNG US LLP SAN DIEG

LOCATIONS

HQ: GROSSMONT HOSPITAL FOUNDATION
5555 GROSSMONT CENTER DR, LA MESA, CA 919423077
Phone: 619 740-4200
Web: WWW.SHARP.COM

HISTORICAL FINANCIALS
Company Type: Private

Income Statement — FYE: September 30

	REVENUE ($mil)	NET INCOME ($mil)	NET PROFIT MARGIN	EMPLOYEES
09/16	737	65	8.9%	6
09/09	5	0	8.5%	—
09/08	5	0	16.8%	—
09/01	1	3	314.9%	—
Annual Growth	54.5%	21.8%	—	—

2016 Year-End Financials
Return on assets: 6.9% Cash ($ mil.): 43
Return on equity: 8.5%
Current Ratio: 2.40

GROUP O, INC.

The "O" in Group O stands for optimization. It also stands for Ontiveros, the family that leads this company. Founded by chairman Robert Ontiveros, Group O is one of the largest Hispanic-owned companies in the US. It helps big businesses improve their operations through three divisions: marketing, packaging, and supply chain. It offers everything from direct mail creation to shrink wrap procurement to warehousing and distribution, and business intelligence. It has served clients from various industries, including food and beverage (Kerry), consumer goods (P&G), manufacturing (Johnson Controls), pharmaceutical (Bristol-Myers Squibb), and telecommunications (AT&T).

Operations

Group O is a diversified business process outsourcing provider specializing in marketing, supply chain, packaging, and business analytics products.

The company's supply chain division mainly serves heavy equipment and high technology OEMs, while its packaging division targets manufacturers and distributors in need of streamlining their packaging processes. It procures and distributes bags, stretch films, tapes, and other materials and also repairs, calibrates, and upgrades equipment to optimize performance.

Its SMART Audit reporting tool provides real-time reports that monitor production and spending across a plant network so that companies can take appropriate cost reduction actions. Meanwhile, its marketing division offers a range of service offerings, including marketing analytics, customer rewards programs, direct mail and e-mail marketing, outsourced printing, and a customer call center.

The company's Business Analytics unit has experts that can guide companies that seek to make sense out of unstructured and structured data - providing strategists and decision-makers with new insights into customer behavior while maximizing both new and existing channels. The team guides the creation, implementation and management of tools in the latest applications and platforms, across a comprehensive spectrum of existing systems.

Geographic Reach

Group O maintains a national network of more than 20 facilities mostly concentrated in the Midwest (Illinois, Iowa, and Minnesota) and Texas. Other sales offices and warehouses are located in California, Nevada, Pennsylvania, and various southern states. It also works with more than 7,000 suppliers in more than 30 countries.

Sales and Marketing

The company serves FORTUNE 500 clients across a broad range of industries including food and beverage, telecommunications, manufacturing, consumer packaged goods, retail, financial services, pharmaceutical, healthcare, technology, energy, and the public sector.

Strategy

In 2014 Group O launched a new website for its O-vations service offering which is aimed at helping companies optimize the design and operation of enterprise-scale reward programs. Key services range from program design and management, technology integration, operations and communications, value-added services, and reporting and analytics.

That year the company also opened its Business Analytics unit, in Hyderabad, India. The team helps generate customer acquisition and loyalty marketing insights that clients can then use to make better business decisions.

Company Background

Ontiveros established Group O in 1974 as Bi-State Packaging, which sold packaging materials and equipment to manufacturers. Today it is one of the top 15 Hispanic-owned businesses in the nation.

Auditors : HONKAMP KRUEGER & CO PC MO

LOCATIONS

HQ: GROUP O, INC.
4905 77TH AVE E, MILAN, IL 612643250
Phone: 309 736-8100
Web: WWW.GROUPO.COM

PRODUCTS/OPERATIONS

Selected Services
Marketing
    Analytics
    Consumer and trade fulfillment
    Customer call center and workforce management
    Direct mail and e-mail optimization
    Print management outsourcing
    Rewards and loyalty programs
Packaging
    Equipment supply and repair (bagging, case handling, labeling, shrinking and stretch wrapping systems)
    Materials supply (labels, poly bags, protective packaging, sanitation products, shrink and stretch films and tape)
    Stretch film equipment auditing
Supply chain
    Business process outsourcing
    Distribution
    Global sourcing
    Inventory management
    Order management
    Supplier management
    Warehousing

Selected Industries Served
Food and Beverage
Telecommunications
Manufacturing
Consumer Packaged Goods
Financial Services
Pharmaceutical
Health care
Technology

COMPETITORS

ADVANCED BUSINESS SOFTWARE AND SOLUTIONS LIMITED
ASG TECHNOLOGIES GROUP, INC.
COLLABERA INC.
CROSSMARK, INC.
DEMATIC CORP.
ENGIE INSIGHT SERVICES INC.
MARKETSTAR QOZ BUSINESS LLC
SCHOENECKERS, INC.
STAYINFRONT, INC.
TRANSPORTATION INSIGHT, LLC

HISTORICAL FINANCIALS

Company Type: Private

Income Statement   FYE: December 31

	REVENUE ($mil)	NET INCOME ($mil)	NET PROFIT MARGIN	EMPLOYEES
12/13	569	5	1.0%	1,066
12/05	240	5	2.2%	—
Annual Growth	11.4%	0.9%	—	—

2013 Year-End Financials
Return on assets: 87.9%   Cash ($ mil.): 7
Return on equity: 1.0%
Current Ratio: 0.90

GROVE ELK UNIFIED SCHOOL DISTRICT

EXECUTIVES

Associate Superintendent*, Richard Odegaard
Auditors : CROWE HORWATH LLP SACRAMENTO

LOCATIONS

HQ: GROVE ELK UNIFIED SCHOOL DISTRICT
9510 ELK GROVE FLORIN RD, ELK GROVE, CA 956241801
Phone: 916 686-5085
Web: WWW.EGUSD.NET

HISTORICAL FINANCIALS

Company Type: Private

Income Statement   FYE: June 30

	REVENUE ($mil)	NET INCOME ($mil)	NET PROFIT MARGIN	EMPLOYEES
06/17	741	65	8.8%	5,600
06/07	560	(30)	—	—
06/06	0	0	—	—
06/03	454	19	4.4%	—
Annual Growth	3.6%	8.9%		

2017 Year-End Financials
Return on assets: 5.6%   Cash ($ mil.): —
Return on equity: 44.4%
Current Ratio: —

GROWMARK, INC.

GROWMARK is an agricultural cooperative serving about 400,000 customers across North America. It provides agronomy, energy, facility engineering and construction products and services, as well as grain marketing and risk management services. It owns the FS trademark, which is used by member cooperatives. Handles more than 3.2 million tons annually, the company also operates a full-line seed company, SEEDWAY, and provides grain facility planning and grain marketing services. In addition to secure warehousing in facilities, GROWMARK also provides truck, barge and rail transport, unloading and inventory control. The company has an extensive network of fertilizer terminals throughout the Midwest and Ontario.

Operations

GROWMARK delivers high quality agronomy and energy products, as well as premium services from expert advisors. Its long-term relationships with manufacturers and refiners, coupled with the company's extensive terminal network, means

GROWMARK has access to a broad and reliable supply of fertilizers, fuel, and propane. The company also offers private label crop protection products and proprietary brands of corn and soybean seeds.

In addition, GROWMARK also provides grain marketing services through its subsidiary, MID-CO COMMODITIES, and has partnership with COFCO International. Its commercial construction provides equipment, facilities, and services that improve the operating efficiency of the company's customers. It is equipped to provide system consultations through complete turnkey construction services, such as consultation, development, planning, construction and operation. GROWMARK logistics includes brokerage services specializing in transporting and storing liquid fuel, propane, anhydrous ammonia, bulk and packaged motor oils, and crop inputs including seed, liquid and dry fertilizer and bulk and packaged crop protection products, while its Electronic Payments Network keeps pace with regulatory and market demands for bank cards, fleet cards, DEBIT cards, gift cards, ACH/electronic check conversion, and PC/web-based payments. Lastly, GROWMARK Agronomy Equipment has national account relationships with John Deere, Case IH, AGCO, and Caterpillar to provide its customers with competitive pricing and service from local dealer on application equipment, tractors, loaders, construction equipment, and small equipment.

GROWMARK's high performing product lines include proprietary brands FS InVISION, FS HiSOY, FS Wheat, FS Alfalfa, as well as distribution agreements with DEKALB, Asgrow, and NK.

Geographic Reach
GROWMARK is headquartered in Bloomington, Illinois, and serves customers in about 35 US states and Ontario, Canada.

Its SEEDWAY business has about 25 office and warehouse locations in California, Vermont, South Carolina, Mexico, New York, Pennsylvania, Texas, and Florida, among others.

Sales and Marketing
GROWMARK is serving agriculture and energy cooperatives, retailers, grain companies, and other business customers of all industries, including freight brokerage and credit card processing.

Mergers and Acquisitions
In early 2022, GROWMARK acquired the remaining ownership interest in AgriVisor, a full-service agricultural risk management and marketing services firm. This comes after GROWMARK purchased Illinois Agricultural Association's ownership interest in AgriVisor in late 2021. AgriVisor delivers in-depth market analysis and recommendations to more than 1,000 producers across North America. Using extensive relationships with grain elevators, farm insurance brokerages, farm bureaus, ag research firms and other ag advisory firms to stay ahead of industry trends, the company leverages collective buying power and pricing strategies on crop insurance and other innovative services such as its Crossover Solutions.

Company Background
GROWMARK traces its history back to 1920 and the establishment of local cooperatives by Farm Bureau members. One of those cooperatives, Farm Bureau Service Company of Iowa, in the early 1960s merged with Illinois Farm Supply Company (founded in 1927) to form the foundation of what is today GROWMARK. The GROWMARK name started being used in 1980.

EXECUTIVES
ENERGY & LOGISTICS, Carol Kitchen
Retail Vice President, Barry Schmidt
AGRONOMY, Mark Orr
Strategy Officer, Ann Kafer
MIDWEST, Mike Turner
Auditors : RSM US LLP PEORIA ILLINOIS

LOCATIONS
HQ: GROWMARK, INC.
1701 TOWANDA AVE, BLOOMINGTON, IL 617012057
Phone: 309 557-6000
Web: WWW.GROWMARK.COM

COMPETITORS
ARMSTRONG GARDEN CENTERS, INC.
CAPITAL NURSERY COMPANY
DIVERSEY, INC.
FLORIKAN-CAROLINA, INC.
MEADOWS FARMS, INC.
MILES FARM SUPPLY, LLC
MOLBAK'S LLC
STELLAR GROUP, INCORPORATED
SUMMERWINDS GARDEN CENTERS, INC.
THE GAVILON GROUP LLC

HISTORICAL FINANCIALS
Company Type: Private

Income Statement — FYE: August 31

	REVENUE ($mil)	NET INCOME ($mil)	NET PROFIT MARGIN	EMPLOYEES
08/20	7,541	68	0.9%	8,641
08/19	8,745	75	0.9%	—
08/18	8,522	65	0.8%	—
08/17	7,291	115	1.6%	—
Annual Growth	1.1%	(16.0%)	—	—

2020 Year-End Financials
Return on assets: 2.6% Cash ($ mil.): 78
Return on equity: 6.1%
Current Ratio: 1.80

GRUMA CORPORATION

Gruma Corporation is one of the main producers of tortillas and related products throughout the US as well as one of the main producers of nixtamalized corn flour in the US. Its tortilla business operates approximately 20 plants producing tortillas, tortilla chips, and other related products and the main brands include Mission, Guerrero, and Calidad. Through its corn flour business, GRUMA operates six plants and the main brand is Maseca. Its food service customers include major chain restaurants, food service distributors, schools, hospitals, and the military. The vast majority of nixtamalized corn flour produced by Azteca Milling in the US is sold to tortilla and tortilla chip manufacturers and is delivered directly from its plants to the customers' manufacturing facilities by third parties. Gruma is the American subsidiary of giant Mexican food company Gruma, S.A.B. de C.V.

Operations
Gruma, which generates about 55% of its parent company's revenue, operates primarily through its Mission Foods division, which produces tortillas and related products mainly under the MISSION, GUERRERO, and CALIDAD brand names in the US, and through Azteca Milling, which produces nixtamalized corn flour in the US under the MASECA brand, and, to a lesser extent, under the company's value brand TORTIMASA. In addition, Mission Foods has approximately 20 tortilla and other related products plants throughout the US.

Geographic Reach
Based in the US, Gruma produces nixtamalized corn flour at six plants located in Amarillo, Edinburg and Plainview, Texas; Evansville, Indiana; Henderson, Kentucky; and Madera, California. The majority of its plants are located within important corn growing areas.

Sales and Marketing
Mission Foods, a division of Gruma, distributes its products mainly through independent distributors, who supply tortillas and other related products directly to retail chains (Independent Distributors). Mission Foods' products are marketed in both retail and food service channels. In the US, retail customers represented nearly 80% of the company's sales volume in 2021, including supermarkets, mass merchandisers, membership stores, and smaller independent stores. Azteca Milling's third-party customers consist largely of other tortilla manufacturers, corn chip producers, retail customers, and wholesalers. Azteca Milling sold more than 20% of its nixtamalized corn flour sales volume to Mission Foods' plants in the US.

Financial Performance
Company's revenue for fiscal 2021 increased to MXN 94.3 billion compared from the prior year with MXN 91.1 billion.

Net income for fiscal 2021 increased to MXN 9.6 billion compared from the prior year with MXN 8.5 billion.

Cash held by the company at the end of fiscal 2021 decreased to MXN 5.2 billion. Cash provided by operations was MXN 11.4 billion while cash used for investing and financing activities were MXN 5.3 billion and MXN 7.0 billion, respectively. Main uses of cash were for acquisitions of property, plant and equipment; and payment of debt.

Strategy

Gruma's strategy is to focus on its core business?nixtamalized corn flour and tortilla? as well as to expand its product portfolio towards the flatbreads category in general and flavored corn chips, with emphasis in healthier and higher added value products. The company will continue taking advantage of the increasing popularity of Mexican food and, more importantly, tortillas, in the US, European, Asian and Oceanian markets. The company will also continue taking advantage of the adoption of tortillas by the consumers of several regions of the world for the preparation of different recipes other than Mexican food.

Gruma's strategy includes the following key elements: expand in the Tortilla Market in the United States; expand in the tortilla, flatbread markets and flavored corn chips in Europe, Asia and Oceania; gradually enter the flat bread and flavored corn chips markets in the United States and Mexico; maintain MISSIONÂ® and GUERREROÂ® tortilla brands as the first and second national brands in the United States and position its mission brand in other regions of the world; encourage transition from the traditional cooked-corn method to the nixtamalized corn flour method as well as new uses for nixtamalized corn flour; and invest in its core business and focus on optimizing operational matters.

LOCATIONS

HQ: GRUMA CORPORATION
5601 EXECUTIVE DR STE 800, IRVING, TX 750382508
Phone: 972 232-5000
Web: WWW.MISSIONFOODS.COM

PRODUCTS/OPERATIONS

Selected Brands and Products
Guerrero
 Chicharron de Cerdo
 Tortillas de Harina (Original and Butter)
 Tortillas de Maíz Blanco
 Tostadas Norte?as Clásicas
 Tostadas Caseras Doraditas
Mission Foods
 96% Fat Free Heart Healthy tortillas
 All Natural Spicy Bean dip
 Caramel Twists
 Carb Balance tortillas
 Cheddar Cheese dip
 Chicharrones (Original, BBQ, Habanero, and Picante)
 Cinnamon Twists
 Chunky Salsa, Medium
 Corn tortilla
 Flour tortillas
 Guacamole dip
 Jumbo Taco shells
 Life Balance tortillas
 Multi-Grain Flour tortillas
 Organic Stone-Ground tortilla chips
 Pork Cracklins Plain Tenders
 Restaurant Style Tortilla Triangles (Cilantro Lime, Premium White Corn, and Salsa Roja)
 Restaurant Style Tortilla Rounds
 Salsa Con Queso
 Salsa Verde, Medium
 Sliced Nacho Jalape?o Peppers
 Taco and tostada shells
 Wraps (Original, Garden Spinach, Jalapeno Cheddar, Multi-Grain, Sun-dried Tomato Basil, and Zesty Garlic Herb)

COMPETITORS

CALAVO GROWERS, INC.
CENTAUR GRAIN LIMITED
EARTHBOUND FARM, LLC
FRONTIER AGRICULTURE LIMITED
Fresh Del Monte Produce Inc.
Gruma, S.A.B. de C.V.
LIMONEIRA COMPANY
SUN WORLD INTERNATIONAL, INC.
THE ANDERSONS INC
THE WONDERFUL COMPANY LLC

HISTORICAL FINANCIALS

Company Type: Private

Income Statement — FYE: December 31

	REVENUE ($mil)	NET INCOME ($mil)	NET PROFIT MARGIN	EMPLOYEES
12/21	2,598	266	10.2%	7,000
12/19	2,202	224	10.2%	—
12/16	2,023	179	8.9%	—
12/15	2,086	152	7.3%	—
Annual Growth	3.7%	9.7%	—	—

2021 Year-End Financials
Return on assets: 15.9%   Cash ($ mil.): 58
Return on equity: 25.3%
Current Ratio: 1.80

GUILDNET, INC.

Auditors: KPMG LLP NEW YORK NY

LOCATIONS

HQ: GUILDNET, INC.
15 W 65TH ST, NEW YORK, NY 100236601
Phone: 212 769-6200
Web: WWW.LIGHTHOUSEGUILD.ORG

HISTORICAL FINANCIALS

Company Type: Private

Income Statement — FYE: December 31

	REVENUE ($mil)	NET INCOME ($mil)	NET PROFIT MARGIN	EMPLOYEES
12/15	950	(24)	—	377
12/14	826	1	0.1%	—
12/13	672	45	6.8%	—
12/12	433	42	9.8%	—
Annual Growth	29.9%	—	—	—

2015 Year-End Financials
Return on assets: (-8.5%)   Cash ($ mil.): 12
Return on equity: (-19.4%)
Current Ratio: 1.40

GUILFORD COUNTY SCHOOL SYSTEM

EXECUTIVES

Interim Superintendent, Nora K Carr Co
CIO*, Terrance Young

LOCATIONS

HQ: GUILFORD COUNTY SCHOOL SYSTEM
712 N EUGENE ST, GREENSBORO, NC 274011622
Phone: 336 370-8100
Web: WWW.GCSNC.COM

HISTORICAL FINANCIALS

Company Type: Private

Income Statement — FYE: June 30

	REVENUE ($mil)	NET INCOME ($mil)	NET PROFIT MARGIN	EMPLOYEES
06/11	692	(0)	—	10,000
06/09	0	(0)	—	—
06/03	0	0	—	—
06/02	546	69	12.8%	—
Annual Growth	2.7%	—	—	—

2011 Year-End Financials
Return on assets: —   Cash ($ mil.): 28
Return on equity: (-0.1%)
Current Ratio: 1.10

GUNDERSEN LUTHERAN ADMINISTRATIVE SERVICES INC.

Auditors: ERNST & YOUNG US LLP CHICAGO

LOCATIONS

HQ: GUNDERSEN LUTHERAN ADMINISTRATIVE SERVICES INC.
1900 SOUTH AVE, LA CROSSE, WI 546015467
Phone: 608 782-7300
Web: WWW.GUNDERSENHEALTH.ORG

HISTORICAL FINANCIALS

Company Type: Private

Income Statement — FYE: December 31

	REVENUE ($mil)	NET INCOME ($mil)	NET PROFIT MARGIN	EMPLOYEES
12/19	771	(59)	—	6,000
12/18	841	40	4.8%	—
12/17	716	(38)	—	—
Annual Growth	3.8%	—	—	—

2019 Year-End Financials
Return on assets: (-5.8%)   Cash ($ mil.): 136
Return on equity: —
Current Ratio: 0.40

GUNDERSEN LUTHERAN MEDICAL CENTER, INC.

At the heart of the Gundersen Lutheran health system, Gundersen Lutheran Medical Center serves residents of nearly 20 counties that stretch across the upper Midwest. The clinical campus for the University of Wisconsin's medical and nursing schools operates a 325-bed teaching hospital with a Level II Trauma and Emergency Center. Focused on caring for patients in western Wisconsin, the hospital boasts several specialty services, such as bariatrics, behavioral health, cancer care, orthopedics, palliative care, pediatrics, rehabilitation, and women's health. The physician-led, not-for-profit medical center is affiliated with a group of regional clinics and specialty centers.

Operations
Gundersen Lutheran Medical Center has a staff of some 800 doctors, dentists, and other professionals. As part of Gundersen Lutheran (also known as Gundersen Health System), the hospital's sister entities include the Gundersen Clinic and the Gundersen Lutheran Administrative Services entity.

In 2013 the Gundersen Health System reported 1,437 births, 17,000 surgeries, and 278,000 outpatient hospital visits.

Geographic Reach
From its main campus in La Crosse, Wisconsin, as well as a satellite outpatient center in Onalaska, the hospital serves communities located in 19 counties throughout western Wisconsin, northeastern Iowa, and southeastern Minnesota.

Strategy
The Gundersen Lutheran organization expands though partnerships, such as an alliance with the Allen Hospital in Iowa to enhance regional cardiovascular services in 2013. The medical center is also working to upgrade its infrastructure to enable 100% energy independence in 2014.

To offer advanced training to residents and physicians, Gundersen Lutheran Medical Center developed and opened a high-tech training center in 2012. The Cleary Kumm Simulation and Training Labs offer mock operating rooms and simulation labs for use by local doctors and nationwide medical professionals for training or conferences. Gundersen Lutheran Medical Center is banking on the simulation and training facility to draw interest, talent, and outside funds.

Company Background
Gundersen Lutheran Medical Center was founded in 1995 through the merger of Gunderson Clinic and Lutheran Hospital-La Crosse. The Lutheran Hospital opened in 1902.

Auditors : KPMG-LLP MINNEAPOLIS MN

LOCATIONS

HQ: GUNDERSEN LUTHERAN MEDICAL CENTER, INC.
1900 SOUTH AVE, LA CROSSE, WI 546015467
Phone: 608 782-7300
Web: WWW.GUNDERSENHEALTH.ORG

PRODUCTS/OPERATIONS

Selected Services
Advance care planning
Apnea
Audiology
Autism Spectrum Disorder
BioBank
Brain disorders
Cardiac services
Children's health
Cleft Lip & Palate Clinic
Endocrinology
Hospice
Eye care
Gynecology
Hand surgery
Heart Institute
LASIK eye surgery
Massage
Neck surgery
Neurosciences
Oral and maxillofacial surgery
Pediatrics
Radiation oncology
Rehabilitation
Urgent care
Urology
Weight management
Wound care

COMPETITORS

ASCENSION PROVIDENCE HOSPITAL
CENTEGRA HEALTH SYSTEM
GENESYS HEALTH SYSTEM
JEFFERSON HOSPITAL
PITT COUNTY MEMORIAL HOSPITAL, INCORPORATED

HISTORICAL FINANCIALS
Company Type: Private

Income Statement — FYE: December 31

	REVENUE ($mil)	NET INCOME ($mil)	NET PROFIT MARGIN	EMPLOYEES
12/19	1,275	216	17.0%	4,500
12/18	1,073	117	10.9%	—
12/17	1,071	112	10.5%	—
12/15	980	60	6.1%	—
Annual Growth	6.8%	37.9%	—	—

2019 Year-End Financials
Return on assets: 13.1%   Cash ($ mil.): —
Return on equity: 13.2%
Current Ratio: 30.20

GWINNETT COUNTY BOARD OF EDUCATION

Auditors : MAULDIN & JENKINS LLC ATLANT

LOCATIONS

HQ: GWINNETT COUNTY BOARD OF EDUCATION
437 OLD PEACHTREE RD NW, SUWANEE, GA
300242978
Phone: 678 301-6000
Web: PUBLISH.GWINNETT.K12.GA.US

HISTORICAL FINANCIALS
Company Type: Private

Income Statement — FYE: June 30

	REVENUE ($mil)	NET INCOME ($mil)	NET PROFIT MARGIN	EMPLOYEES
06/21	2,284	123	5.4%	261
06/20	2,263	14	0.7%	—
06/19	2,071	118	5.7%	—
06/18	1,973	(55)	—	—
Annual Growth	5.0%	—	—	—

2021 Year-End Financials
Return on assets: 2.7%   Cash ($ mil.): 141
Return on equity: —
Current Ratio: 3.00

GWINNETT HOSPITAL SYSTEM, INC.

Auditors : KPMG LLP ATLANTA GA

LOCATIONS

HQ: GWINNETT HOSPITAL SYSTEM, INC.
1000 MEDICAL CENTER BLVD, LAWRENCEVILLE, GA
300467694
Phone: 678 343-3428
Web: WWW.GWINNETTMEDICALCENTER.ORG

HISTORICAL FINANCIALS
Company Type: Private

Income Statement — FYE: June 30

	REVENUE ($mil)	NET INCOME ($mil)	NET PROFIT MARGIN	EMPLOYEES
06/18	731	12	1.7%	2,050
06/17	729	29	4.1%	—
06/16	735	(31)	—	—
06/15	698	15	2.2%	—
Annual Growth	1.5%	(6.3%)	—	—

2018 Year-End Financials
Return on assets: 1.4%   Cash ($ mil.): 54
Return on equity: 2.6%
Current Ratio: 2.60

H. J. BAKER SULPHUR, LLC

Auditors : GRANT THORNTON LLP HOUSTON T

LOCATIONS

HQ: H. J. BAKER SULPHUR, LLC
1450 LAKE ROBBINS DR # 500, THE WOODLANDS, TX
773803258
Phone: 346 372-3455

HISTORICAL FINANCIALS

Company Type: Private

Income Statement — FYE: December 31

	REVENUE ($mil)	NET INCOME ($mil)	NET PROFIT MARGIN	EMPLOYEES
12/08	878	26	3.0%	27
12/07	273	4	1.5%	—
12/05	170	(0)	—	—
Annual Growth	72.8%	—	—	—

2008 Year-End Financials

Return on assets: 17.3%   Cash ($ mil.): 19
Return on equity: 75.7%
Current Ratio: 1.40

H. LEE MOFFITT CANCER CENTER AND RESEARCH INSTITUTE HOSPITAL, INC.

The H. Lee Moffitt Cancer Center and Research Institute, founded in 1986, is a National Cancer Institute-designated Comprehensive Cancer Center located on the Tampa campus of the University of South Florida. The institute carries it out its stated mission of "contributing to the prevention and cure of cancer" through patient care, research, and education. It operates a 210-bed medical and surgical facility, as well as outpatient treatment programs and a blood and marrow transplant program. Its research programs include study in the areas of molecular oncology, immunology, risk assessment, health outcomes, and experimental therapeutics.

Operations

The Moffitt Cancer Center sees more than 9,000 cancer inpatients each year; it also handles some 328,000 outpatient visits annually. In addition to its 40-bed blood and marrow transplant center, which performs 400 annual transplants, the hospital includes more than a dozen operating rooms and extensive diagnostic radiology and radiation therapy labs. The Cancer Screening and Prevention Center offers genetic testing for certain kinds of hereditary cancers (breast, ovarian, colon, and melanoma).

The Moffitt Research Institute conducts a wide range of cancer studies, and some of its drug discovery research programs are managed through partnerships with pharmaceutical companies and other research laboratories. The research institute also relies on funding grants from organizations such as the National Institutes of Health. It has received more than $80 million in grant funding and participated in some 300 clinical trials.

The Moffitt Cancer Center likewise has educational and health care alliances with a number of Florida hospitals and colleges, including a three-way cancer care and research partnership with Shands HealthCare and the University of Florida. Through its affiliated network program (the Moffitt Oncology Network), Moffitt works with community doctors and centers across Florida to provide enhanced cancer services throughout the state. It also operates a number of outpatient clinics in surrounding areas.

Geographic Reach

Through its main campus and numerous outpatient sites, Moffitt Cancer Center primarily serves residents of seven Florida counties: Hernando, Hillsborough, Manatee, Pasco, Pinellas, Polk, and Sarasota. It also serves patients from other areas of Florida and neighboring states.

Sales and Marketing

HMO and PPO plans account for about 65% of patient service revenues, while reimbursements from Medicare and Medicaid plans account for another 32% of sales.

Financial Performance

Revenue at Moffitt Cancer Center and Research Institute increased 1% to $779 million in 2013, from $772 the previous year, due to higher patient service revenues. After a net loss in 2012, the institute reported net income of $26 million due to an increase in net assets and non-operating gains. Cash from operations also grew, by $77 million, due to the net income increase and cash generated from an estimated third-party settlement.

Strategy

Moffitt Cancer Center conducts expansion and facility improvement projects to enhance services for its cancer patients. For instance, it launched construction of a new $74 million outpatient facility at the current McKinley office site in 2013; the location is near the main campus and will provide surgery, infusion, imaging, research, and other services. It also formed a partnership with Space Coast Cancer Center, Boca Raton Regional Hospital, Advinus Therapeutics, and Lehigh Valley Health Network to improve cancer care for all the organizations.

EXECUTIVES

Center Director*, Thomas Sellers
Auditors : GRANT THORNTON LLP TAMPA FL

LOCATIONS

HQ: H. LEE MOFFITT CANCER CENTER AND RESEARCH INSTITUTE HOSPITAL, INC.
  12902 USF MAGNOLIA DR, TAMPA, FL 336129416
Phone: 813 745-4673
Web: WWW.MOFFITT.ORG

PRODUCTS/OPERATIONS

Selected Services
Chemotherapy
Diagnosis
Emotional Support
Integrative Medicine
Labwork, Scans and Biopsy
Other Patient Services
Pain Management
Radiation
Screening and Genetics
Spiritual Support
Surgical Care
Well-Being

Selected Research Fields
Basic Science Division
  Cancer Imaging and Metabolism
  Drug Discovery
  Immunology
  Integrated Mathematical Oncology
  Molecular Oncology
  Tumor Biology
Population Science Division
  Biostatistics and Bioinformatics
  Cancer Epidemiology
  Health Outcomes & Behavior

COMPETITORS

BILLINGS CLINIC
BOSTON MEDICAL CENTER CORPORATION
SHANDS TEACHING HOSPITAL AND CLINICS, INC.
SWEDISH HEALTH SERVICES
TEXAS CHILDREN'S HOSPITAL

HISTORICAL FINANCIALS

Company Type: Private

Income Statement — FYE: June 30

	REVENUE ($mil)	NET INCOME ($mil)	NET PROFIT MARGIN	EMPLOYEES
06/21	1,515	295	19.5%	4,200
06/20	1,353	287	21.3%	—
06/18	1,020	167	16.4%	—
06/14	855	50	5.9%	—
Annual Growth	8.5%	28.9%	—	—

2021 Year-End Financials

Return on assets: 96.4%   Cash ($ mil.): —
Return on equity: 156.3%
Current Ratio: 2.10

H. LEE MOFFITT CANCER CENTER AND RESEARCH INSTITUTE, INC.

EXECUTIVES

CIO, Elizabeth Lindsay-wood
CIO, Joyce Oh
Auditors : GRANT THORNTON LLP TAMPA FLO

LOCATIONS

HQ: H. LEE MOFFITT CANCER CENTER AND RESEARCH INSTITUTE, INC.
  12902 USF MAGNOLIA DR, TAMPA, FL 336129416
Phone: 813 745-4673
Web: WWW.MOFFITT.ORG

HAGGEN, INC.

HISTORICAL FINANCIALS
Company Type: Private

Income Statement — FYE: June 30

	REVENUE ($mil)	NET INCOME ($mil)	NET PROFIT MARGIN	EMPLOYEES
06/22	2,070	130	6.3%	1,007
06/21	1,827	186	10.2%	—
06/20	1,655	121	7.3%	—
06/19	1,509	111	7.4%	—
Annual Growth	11.1%	5.5%	—	—

2022 Year-End Financials
Return on assets: 5.5% Cash ($ mil.): 498
Return on equity: 9.6%
Current Ratio: 2.70

Haggen showers shoppers in the Pacific Northwest with salmon, coffee, and other essentials. Formerly one of the area's largest independent grocers, Haggen operated some 130 supermarkets in Washington and Oregon, as well as California, Nevada, and Arizona. Most of the stores were acquired from Albertsons in late 2014. In late 2015 Haggen filed for Chapter 11 bankruptcy protection to allow it to reorganize around a reduced number of locations, and in 2016 the company agreed to sell its remaining core stores to Albertsons. The chain was founded in 1933 in Bellingham, Washington.

Operations
Haggen runs its retail business under two banner names: Haggen Food & Pharmacy and TOP Food & Drug.

Geographic Reach
Haggen serves customers primarily in Washington, but also in Oregon.

Strategy
In late 2014 the company announced it would purchase 146 Vons, Pavilions, Albertsons, and Safeway stores being sold as part of the pending merger of Albertsons and Safeway. More than 80 of the new stores are located in California.

Aiming to boost its business and strengthen its competitive position, the grocery operator whittled down its stores portfolio in 2013 to about 20 locations from 30 by shuttering underperforming stores. It's also rebranding many of its TOP Food & Drug stores as Northwest Fresh. The Northwest Fresh theme emphasizes local products, new service departments, and departments named after local geographic references. The supermarket chain is rebannering all of its TOP stores under the Haggen name and new theme to reinforce its local roots and differentiate itself from its national competition.

Having been a customer since 2007, Haggen also extended a supply partnership with Unified Grocers through 2018.

Focused on brick-and-mortar efforts, Haggen had set aside its e-commerce initiative. To keep up with the Joneses of supermarket fortune, Haggen partnered with ShopEaze.com (an e-commerce service provider), which failed, leaving Haggen without an online store. Awards and Recognition

Industry publication Supermarket News ranks Haggen one of the 75 largest grocery chains in the US. It's also the Northwest's largest independent grocer.

Company Background
Haggen traces its roots back to 1933, when Ben Haggen, alongside his wife, Dorothy, and brother-in-law, Doug Clark, launched the Economy Food Store in Bellingham, Washington, with a combined investment of $1,100. They later moved and changed the name to White House Market before moving to yet another location in 1957 and adopting the name Haggen's Thriftway.

Auditors: MOSS ADAMS LLP

LOCATIONS
HQ: HAGGEN, INC.
2211 RIMLAND DR STE 300, BELLINGHAM, WA 982265699
Phone: 360 733-8720
Web: WWW.HAGGEN.COM

2014 Stores
Washington	15
Oregon	2
Total	17

COMPETITORS
AHOLD U.S.A., INC.
ALBERTSONS COMPANIES, INC.
C&S WHOLESALE GROCERS, INC.
DEMOULAS SUPER MARKETS, INC.
GIANT EAGLE, INC.
SPARTANNASH COMPANY
THE GREAT ATLANTIC & PACIFIC TEA COMPANY, INC.
UNIFIED GROCERS, INC.
UNITED SUPERMARKETS, L.L.C.
WAKEFERN FOOD CORP.

HISTORICAL FINANCIALS
Company Type: Private

Income Statement — FYE: December 31

	REVENUE ($mil)	NET INCOME ($mil)	NET PROFIT MARGIN	EMPLOYEES
12/07	787	8	1.1%	3,900
12/06	758	6	0.9%	—
12/05	(164)	0	0.0%	—
Annual Growth	—	20237.1%	—	—

2007 Year-End Financials
Return on assets: 4.9% Cash ($ mil.): 6
Return on equity: 1.1%
Current Ratio: 0.30

HAMILTON CHATTANOOGA COUNTY HOSPITAL AUTHORITY

The Chattanooga-Hamilton County Hospital Authority (dba Erlanger Health System) offers a broad range of health service operations, including the T.C. Thompson Children's Hospital, a cancer treatment facility, and centers devoted to heart treatment, trauma, and eye care. The system comprises five hospital campuses in Tennessee with some 810 acute care beds, as well as 50 long-term care beds. A teaching center for the University of Tennessee College of Medicine, Erlanger provides tertiary care for a region that includes southeastern Tennessee, northern Georgia, northern Alabama, and western North Carolina.

Operations
Erlanger is the tri-state region's only Level One Trauma Center, providing the highest level of trauma care for adults. The Children's Hospital at Erlanger houses the region's only Level III Neonatal Intensive Care Unit, as well as a pediatric trauma team, Emergency Center and Pediatric Intensive Care Unit

The hospital system treats more than 300,000 patients every year. In 2014 Erlanger had 30,394 inpatient admissions, 230,765 outpatient visits to physician practices, and 28,810 surgical patients. Some 3,067 children were admitted to Children's Hospital and 43,192 received treatment in the Emergency Department and outpatient surgery.

The LIFE FORCE air ambulance service is is equipped with two EC-135 aircraft, capable of single pilot IFR, and two Bell 407 aircraft. LIFE FORCE transported 1,419 patients in 2014.

Geographic Reach
The Erlanger Health System is a multi-hospital system with five hospitals based in Chattanooga: the University Hospital, Children's Hospital at Erlanger, Erlanger North Hospital, Erlanger East Hospital, and Erlanger Bledsoe Hospital, located in Pikeville, Tennessee. Its LIFE FORCE air ambulance service is stationed in Chattanooga and Sparta in Tennessee, and in Calhoun and Blue Ridge in Georgia.

Financial Performance
Medicare accounted for 33% of Erlanger's net patient revenues in fiscal 2014; Commercial insurance, 31%; and Medicaid 22%.

Company Background
To extend its patient reach, Erlanger entered into a management contract with

Hutcheson Hospital located in North Georgia in 2011.

Erlanger was founded in 1889 through the generosity of French nobleman Baron Frederic Emile d'Erlanger, who held financial interests in a number of railroads in the region. He donated $5,000 (more than $4 million in today's dollars) for a new hospital. It opened with 72 beds in 1899.

EXECUTIVES

Vice Chairman, Sheila Boyington
Interim Chief Financial Officer, Lynn Dejaco
Auditors : PYA PC KNOXVILLE TENNESSEE

LOCATIONS

HQ: HAMILTON CHATTANOOGA COUNTY HOSPITAL AUTHORITY
975 E 3RD ST, CHATTANOOGA, TN 374032173
Phone: 423 778-7000
Web: WWW.ERLANGER.ORG

PRODUCTS/OPERATIONS

Selected Campuses
Dodson Avenue Community Health Center
Erlanger Bledsoe Campus
Erlanger East Campus
Erlanger Medical Center
Erlanger North Campus
Southside Community Health Center
T.C. Thompson Children's Hospital

Selected Medical Services
Breast Imaging
Cancer Services
Cardiology
Chattanooga Lifestyle Center
Community Health Centers
Craniofacial Center
Erlanger Metabolic and Bariatric Surgery Center
Erlanger Pharmacy
Gastroenterology
Heart
Home Health (ContinuCare)
HouseCalls
Hypertension Management Center
Imaging Services
LIFE FORCE
Neurobehavioral and Memory Services
Orthopedics
Radiology
Respiratory Services
Rheumatology
Robotic Surgery
Sleep Disorders Center
Stroke
The Weight Loss Program
Trauma Services
Urgent Care - Adult
Urology
UT Erlanger Kidney Transplant Center
Weight Management
Women's Services
WorkForce Corporate Health
Wound Care and Hyperbaric Oxygen center

COMPETITORS

BAPTIST HEALTH SYSTEM, INC.
FREEMAN HEALTH SYSTEM
MERCY HOSPITAL SPRINGFIELD
PASADENA HOSPITAL ASSOCIATION, LTD.
VALLEY HEALTH SYSTEM

HISTORICAL FINANCIALS
Company Type: Private

Income Statement — FYE: June 30

	REVENUE ($mil)	NET INCOME ($mil)	NET PROFIT MARGIN	EMPLOYEES
06/22	1,155	18	1.6%	4,700
06/21	1,044	37	3.6%	—
06/20	1,021	29	2.9%	—
06/18	973	26	2.8%	—
Annual Growth	4.4%	(8.4%)	—	—

2022 Year-End Financials
Return on assets: 1.9% Cash ($ mil.): 225
Return on equity: 4.8%
Current Ratio: 1.60

HARBOR-UCLA MEDICAL CENTER

LOCATIONS

HQ: HARBOR-UCLA MEDICAL CENTER
1000 W CARSON ST, TORRANCE, CA 905022059
Phone: 310 222-2301
Web: WWW.EMEDHARBOR.EDU

HISTORICAL FINANCIALS
Company Type: Private

Income Statement — FYE: June 30

	REVENUE ($mil)	NET INCOME ($mil)	NET PROFIT MARGIN	EMPLOYEES
06/16	637	(268)	—	3,000
06/15	607	(287)	—	—
Annual Growth	5.0%	—	—	—

2016 Year-End Financials
Return on assets: (-33.1%) Cash ($ mil.): 9
Return on equity: —
Current Ratio: 1.40

HARLEE MANOR, INC.

LOCATIONS

HQ: HARLEE MANOR, INC.
218 N DIAMOND ST, CLIFTON HEIGHTS, PA 190181507
Phone: 610 544-2200
Web: WWW.HARLEEMANOR.COM

HISTORICAL FINANCIALS
Company Type: Private

Income Statement — FYE: June 30

	REVENUE ($mil)	NET INCOME ($mil)	NET PROFIT MARGIN	EMPLOYEES
06/09	1,164	62	5.4%	151
06/98	8	0	6.3%	—
Annual Growth	55.9%	53.6%	—	—

2009 Year-End Financials
Return on assets: 48.8% Cash ($ mil.): —
Return on equity: 821.7%
Current Ratio: 1.80

HARRIS COUNTY FIRE MARSHAL

Auditors : DELOITTE & TOUCHE LLP HOUSTON

LOCATIONS

HQ: HARRIS COUNTY FIRE MARSHAL
7701 WILSHIRE PLACE DR, HOUSTON, TX 770405326
Phone: 713 587-7800
Web: WWW.HCFMO.NET

HISTORICAL FINANCIALS
Company Type: Private

Income Statement — FYE: February 28

	REVENUE ($mil)	NET INCOME ($mil)	NET PROFIT MARGIN	EMPLOYEES
02/19	829	310	37.4%	3
02/18	740	224	30.4%	—
Annual Growth	12.1%	38.1%	—	—

2019 Year-End Financials
Return on assets: 6.7% Cash ($ mil.): 325
Return on equity: 17.0%
Current Ratio: 4.80

HARRIS COUNTY HOSPITAL DISTRICT

Auditors : BKD LLP DALLAS TEXAS

LOCATIONS

HQ: HARRIS COUNTY HOSPITAL DISTRICT
4800 FOURNACE PL, BELLAIRE, TX 774012324
Phone: 713 634-1000
Web: WWW.HARRISHEALTH.ORG

HISTORICAL FINANCIALS
Company Type: Private

Income Statement — FYE: February 28

	REVENUE ($mil)	NET INCOME ($mil)	NET PROFIT MARGIN	EMPLOYEES
02/22	1,425	294	20.6%	5,532
02/21	1,293	323	25.0%	—
Annual Growth	10.2%	(9.0%)	—	—

2022 Year-End Financials
Return on assets: 11.5% Cash ($ mil.): 708
Return on equity: 26.5%
Current Ratio: 5.60

HARRISON MEDICAL CENTER

Auditors: KPMG LLP DENVER CO

LOCATIONS

HQ: HARRISON MEDICAL CENTER
2520 CHERRY AVE, BREMERTON, WA 983104229
Phone: 360 744-6510

HISTORICAL FINANCIALS
Company Type: Private

Income Statement — FYE: June 30

	REVENUE ($mil)	NET INCOME ($mil)	NET PROFIT MARGIN	EMPLOYEES
06/20	610	133	21.9%	2,400
06/16	433	45	10.6%	—
06/15*	398	56	14.1%	—
04/12	345	(22)	—	—
Annual Growth	7.4%	—	—	—

*Fiscal year change

2020 Year-End Financials
Return on assets: 12.0% Cash ($ mil.): 146
Return on equity: 16.1%
Current Ratio: 1.70

HARTFORD HEALTHCARE CORPORATION

Hartford Health Care provides a variety of health services to the descendants of our founding fathers. Founded in 1854, the health care system operates a network of hospitals, behavioral health centers, nursing and rehabilitation facilities, medical labs, and numerous community programs for residents in northern Connecticut. Medical specialties range from orthopedics and women's health to cancer and heart care. Hartford Health Care's flagship facility is the Hartford Hospital, an 870-bed teaching hospital affiliated with the University of Connecticut Medical School. Its network also includes MidState Medical Center (some 155 beds), Windham Hospital (145 beds), and The Hospital of Central Connecticut (415 beds).

Operations

Hartford Health Care provides primary and specialty care services through partnerships with several physician practice organizations and specialist facilities including diagnostic imaging centers and mental health facilities. The company provides medical laboratory services including pathology, genetic testing, and other diagnostic services through its Clinical Laboratory Partners affiliate. It also provides long-term care through Central Connecticut Senior Health Services, as well as home health services through VNA HealthCare.

Financial Performance

In 2013 Hartford Health Care reported a 2% rise in revenue, from $1.7 million to $2.1 million, due to increased patient service revenue.

Strategy

As it becomes increasingly challenging for hospitals to remain independently profitable in an unstable economic climate, especially as health reform changes take effect, Hartford has been working to expand its footprint in the Connecticut health care market. In 2012 Hartford Health Care formed an alliance with Backus Corporation, which operates the Backus Hospital and other medical care centers in eastern Connecticut. Backus gained access to Hartford's broader resources, but continues to manage its own day-to-day operations.

In 2014 Hartford Health Care broke ground on a new, 90,000-square-foot cancer center at The Hospital of Central Connecticut.

Auditors: ERNST & YOUNG LLP HARTFORD C

LOCATIONS

HQ: HARTFORD HEALTHCARE CORPORATION
100 PEARL ST FL 2, HARTFORD, CT 061034506
Phone: 860 263-4100
Web: WWW.HARTFORDHEALTHCARE.ORG

PRODUCTS/OPERATIONS

2013 Sales

	$ mil	% of total
Net patient revenue	1,906.3	90
Other operating revenue	211.7	10
Net assets released from restrctions for operations	10.3	-
Total	2,128.3	100

Selected Facilities
Alliance Occupational Health
Central Connecticut Senior Health Services
Clinical Laboratory Partners
Eastern Rehabilitation Network
Hartford Hospital (acute care)
Hartford Medical Group (primary care)
The Hospital of Central Connecticut (acute care)
Institute of Living (research and psychiatric care)
MidState Medical Center (acute care)
Natchaug Hospital (mental health facility)
Rushford (mental health treatment centers)
VNA HealthCare (home health)
Windham Hospital (acute care)

COMPETITORS

ALEGENT CREIGHTON HEALTH
ASCENSION VIA CHRISTI HEALTH, INC
AULTMAN HEALTH FOUNDATION
CHRISTIANA CARE HEALTH SYSTEM, INC.
EXCELA HEALTH HOLDING COMPANY, INC.
HALLMARK HEALTH CORPORATION
LEGACY HEALTH
LEHIGH VALLEY HEALTH NETWORK, INC.
THE BRISTOL HOSPITAL INCORPORATED
WESTERN CONNECTICUT HEALTH NETWORK, INC.

HISTORICAL FINANCIALS
Company Type: Private

Income Statement — FYE: September 30

	REVENUE ($mil)	NET INCOME ($mil)	NET PROFIT MARGIN	EMPLOYEES
09/20	4,280	108	2.5%	12,500
09/19	3,541	(101)	—	—
09/18	3,072	410	13.4%	—
09/15	297	(37)	—	—
Annual Growth	70.4%	—	—	—

2020 Year-End Financials
Return on assets: 1.9% Cash ($ mil.): 724
Return on equity: 4.5%
Current Ratio: 1.70

HARVARD MANAGEMENT PRIVATE EQUITY CORPORATION

Auditors: RSM MCGLADREY INC CHICAGO IL

LOCATIONS

HQ: HARVARD MANAGEMENT PRIVATE EQUITY CORPORATION
600 ATLANTIC AVE STE 1500, BOSTON, MA 022102203
Phone: 617 523-4400

HISTORICAL FINANCIALS
Company Type: Private

Income Statement — FYE: June 30

	REVENUE ($mil)	NET INCOME ($mil)	NET PROFIT MARGIN	EMPLOYEES
06/21	2,446	2,047	83.7%	6
06/20	2,389	2,025	84.7%	—
06/17	663	477	71.9%	—
06/10	1,661	(611)	—	—
Annual Growth	3.6%	—	—	—

2021 Year-End Financials
Return on assets: 4.1% Cash ($ mil.): —
Return on equity: 4.1%
Current Ratio: —

HARVARD MEDICAL FACULTY PHYSICIANS AT BETH ISRAEL DEACONESS MEDICAL CENTER, INC.

Auditors : LB DELOITTE TAX LLP JERICHO

LOCATIONS

HQ: HARVARD MEDICAL FACULTY PHYSICIANS AT BETH ISRAEL DEACONESS MEDICAL CENTER, INC.
375 LONGWOOD AVE STE 3, BOSTON, MA 022155395
Phone: 617 632-9755
Web: WWW.HMFPHYSICIANS.ORG

HISTORICAL FINANCIALS
Company Type: Private

Income Statement — FYE: September 30

	REVENUE ($mil)	NET INCOME ($mil)	NET PROFIT MARGIN	EMPLOYEES
09/19	553	8	1.6%	800
09/15	487	1	0.3%	—
09/14	460	14	3.2%	—
09/08	22	2	11.6%	—
Annual Growth	33.8%	11.8%	—	—

2019 Year-End Financials
Return on assets: 3.5%   Cash ($ mil.): 32
Return on equity: 5.4%
Current Ratio: 2.00

HAWAI'I PACIFIC HEALTH

Hawaii may be paradise, but even in paradise's some residents get sick. That's when Hawai'i Pacific Health (HPH) surfs in to save the day. HPH is a not-for-profit health care system consisting of four hospitals (Kapi'olani Medical Center for Women & Children, Pali Momi Medical Center, Straub Clinic & Hospital, and Wilcox Memorial Hospital) across the islands with a combined capacity of 550 beds. The system offers a full array of tertiary, specialty, and acute care services through its hospitals, which also serve as teaching and research centers, as well as about 50 outpatient centers. Specialized services offered by HPH include cardiac care, maternity services, oncology, orthopedics, and pediatric care.

Operations
HPH supplies a wide range of primary and specialty medical services through its physician organizations. The Kapi'olani Medical Specialists group, for instance, comprises more than 100 physicians and partners with Kapi'olani Medical Center for Women & Children to care for patients from infancy through adulthood. The center also functions as the women's health and pediatric teaching hospital for the University of Hawaii School of Medicine. Its Visiting Specialists group provides care to the islands where HPH doesn't have primary care facilities.

Strategy
The system has partnered with Surgical Care Affiliates to build an outpatient surgical center in Honolulu in an effort to meet growing demand there. The center, dubbed Surgicare of Hawai'i, offers an array of medical services, including orthopedics, pain management, ophthalmology, general surgery, and podiatry.

In 2010, the hospital system embarked on a 6-year, $580 million master facility plan to expand and improve some of its primary hospital locations. The first stage included new intensive care units and parking capacity at the Kapi'olani Medical Center.

Company Background
The organization was formed through the 2001 merger of three entities: Kapi'olani Health, Straub Clinic & Hospital, and Wilcox Health System. Committed to supporting Hawaiian culture and values, HPH and its member hospitals honor the Hawaiian language and its use of diacritical marks, the glottal stop and the macron (okina and kahako).

EXECUTIVES

CMO*, Kenneth B Robbins
CIO*, Steve Robertson
Auditors : ERNST & YOUNG LLP HONOLULU

LOCATIONS

HQ: HAWAI I PACIFIC HEALTH
55 MERCHANT ST STE 2500, HONOLULU, HI 968134306
Phone: 808 949-9355
Web: WWW.HAWAIIPACIFICHEALTH.ORG

PRODUCTS/OPERATIONS

Selected Facilities
Kapi'olani Medical Center for Women & Children (Honolulu)
Kaua'i Medical Clinics (Kaua'i)
Pali Momi Medical Center (Aiea)
Straub Clinic & Hospital (Honolulu)
Straub Family Health Centers (Honolulu)
Visiting Specialists (Hilo, Kaua'i, Lana'i, Maui, Moloka'i, Walmea)
Wilcox Memorial Hospital (Lihue, Kaua'i)

COMPETITORS

CENTRAL SUFFOLK HOSPITAL
FLAGSTAFF MEDICAL CENTER, INC.
FRANKLIN SQUARE HOSPITAL CENTER, INC.
HOLY SPIRIT HOSPITAL OF THE SISTERS OF CHRISTIAN CHARITY
LEHIGH VALLEY HEALTH NETWORK, INC.
LONG BEACH MEDICAL CENTER
MAINEHEALTH
NORTH SHORE UNIVERSITY HOSPITAL
PROVIDENCE HEALTH & SERVICES-WASHINGTON
TRIHEALTH, INC.

HISTORICAL FINANCIALS
Company Type: Private

Income Statement — FYE: June 30

	REVENUE ($mil)	NET INCOME ($mil)	NET PROFIT MARGIN	EMPLOYEES
06/20	1,369	(48)	—	5,400
06/18	1,351	130	9.7%	—
06/17	1,290	153	11.9%	—
06/15	159	0	0.3%	—
Annual Growth	53.8%	—	—	—

2020 Year-End Financials
Return on assets: (-2.3%)   Cash ($ mil.): 284
Return on equity: (-4.8%)
Current Ratio: 1.80

HCL AMERICA INC.

Auditors : SR BATLIBOI & CO LLP CAMAC

LOCATIONS

HQ: HCL AMERICA INC.
330 POTRERO AVE, SUNNYVALE, CA 940854194
Phone: 408 733-0480
Web: WWW.HCL.COM

HISTORICAL FINANCIALS
Company Type: Private

Income Statement — FYE: March 31

	REVENUE ($mil)	NET INCOME ($mil)	NET PROFIT MARGIN	EMPLOYEES
03/17*	3,559	130	3.7%	11,993
06/15	2,815	53	1.9%	—
06/14	2,353	0	0.0%	—
06/13	2,075	35	1.7%	—
Annual Growth	14.4%	37.9%	—	—

*Fiscal year change

2017 Year-End Financials
Return on assets: 8.8%   Cash ($ mil.): 4
Return on equity: 20.2%
Current Ratio: 1.10

HDR ENGINEERING, INC.

Auditors : ERNST & YOUNG LLP CHICAGO I

LOCATIONS

HQ: HDR ENGINEERING, INC.
1917 S 67TH ST, OMAHA, NE 681062973
Phone: 402 399-1000
Web: WWW.HDRINC.COM

HISTORICAL FINANCIALS
Company Type: Private

Income Statement   FYE: December 29

	REVENUE ($mil)	NET INCOME ($mil)	NET PROFIT MARGIN	EMPLOYEES
12/18	1,399	107	7.7%	6,111
12/17	1,707	73	4.3%	—
12/16	1,748	89	5.1%	—
12/15	1,218	100	8.2%	—
Annual Growth	4.7%	2.3%	—	—

2018 Year-End Financials
Return on assets: 9.7%   Cash ($ mil.): 25
Return on equity: 13.1%
Current Ratio: 3.90

HDR, INC.

HDR specializes in engineering, architecture, environmental and construction services. The company is most well-known for adding beauty and structure to communities through high-performance buildings and smart infrastructure. The company also provides mechanical and plumbing services, construction and project management, and utilities planning. It has operations in nearly 15 countries and has offices in more than 200 global locations. The employee-owned company was founded as Henningson Engineering in 1917 to build municipal plants in the rural Midwest.

Operations
HDR's offers architecture services such as branding, infrastructure, interior, landscape & site, as well as lighting designs. Other programs and services include asset management, facility management, economics and finance services, and environmental sciences services (which includes acoustics, noise, vibration, and ecosystem restoration), among others.

Geographic Reach
Headquartered in Omaha, Nebraska, HDR has operations in the Americas (US and Canada), Asia Pacific (Australia, China, and Singapore), Europe (Germany and the UK), and the Middle East (Saudi Arabia and the UAE).

Sales and Marketing
HDR's markets include defense & intelligence, education, health, power, justice, power & energy, tech, transportation, and urban community, among others.

Auditors : ERNST & YOUNG LLP CHICAGO IL

LOCATIONS

HQ: HDR, INC.
1917 S 67TH ST, OMAHA, NE 681062965
Phone: 402 399-1000
Web: WWW.HDRINC.COM

PRODUCTS/OPERATIONS

Selected Mergers and Acquisitions
FY2015
   Brentwood, Tennessee-based Infrastructure Corporation of America (ICA)
FY2103
   Rice Daubney (Australia, architecture design for healthcare, retail, defense markets)
FY2012
   Stetson Engineering (Wyoming, projects in water, sewer, storm water, hydrology, and transportation)
FY2011
   Amnis Engineering (Canada)
   Cooper Medical (Healthcare design/build specialist)
   HydroQual (New Jersey, water resource management)
   Schiff Associates (California, engineering)
FY2009
   Devine Tarbell & Associates (Maine, now named HDR|DTA)
   iTrans Consulting (Toronto-based engineering firm)

Selected Markets
Architecture
   Academic
   Civic
   Corporate
   Healthcare
   Justice
   Science and Technology
Energy
   Oil and Gas
   Power Delivery
   Power Generation
   Renewable Energy
Federal
   Federal Architecture
   Federal Engineering
   Federal Planning
   Federal Environmental
   Federal Energy
   Federal Construction
   HDR SeaPort-e
Private Land Development
   Commercial
   Industrial
   Institutional
   Residential
   Resorts and Hotels
Resource Management
   Community Planning & Consulting
   Environmental Sciences & Permitting
   Fisheries Science & Design
   Mining
   Natural Resource Management
   Waste Management and Industrial
Transportation
   Aviation
   Freight Rail
   Highways and Local Roads
   Maritime
   Transit
Water
   Water
   Wastewater
   Water Planning
   Industrial

Selected Services
Analytical consulting
Architectural design
Coastal engineering and restoration
Consulting
Design/build
Environmental monitoring
Finished water storage facility services
Interior design
Landscape architecture
Master planning
Power facility engineering
Pump stations and flow control
Security services
Utility master planning and modeling
Water resources
Water treatment systems

COMPETITORS

AIKEN REALISATIONS LIMITED
ARCADIS U.S., INC.
AUKETT SWANKE GROUP PLC
CALLISONRTKL INC.
HKS, INC.
M. ARTHUR GENSLER JR. & ASSOCIATES, INC.
PERKINS EASTMAN ARCHITECTS, D.P.C.
S & B ENGINEERS AND CONSTRUCTORS, LTD.
STV GROUP, INCORPORATED
Stantec Inc

HISTORICAL FINANCIALS
Company Type: Private

Income Statement   FYE: December 29

	REVENUE ($mil)	NET INCOME ($mil)	NET PROFIT MARGIN	EMPLOYEES
12/18	1,762	115	6.5%	10,000
12/17	2,362	82	3.5%	—
12/16	2,230	90	4.0%	—
12/15	2,132	74	3.5%	—
Annual Growth	(6.1%)	15.9%	—	—

2018 Year-End Financials
Return on assets: 7.8%   Cash ($ mil.): 283
Return on equity: 20.1%
Current Ratio: 2.00

HEALTH FIRST SHARED SERVICES, INC.

Health First is Central Florida's only fully integrated delivery network (IDN). The not-for-profit health system operates four hospitals in Brevard County. Health First's biggest hospital is Holmes Regional Medical Center in Melbourne, with 514 beds. Its Cape Canaveral Hospital and Palm Bay Community Hospital have 150 and 120 beds, respectively. Its Viera Hospital is an 84-bed acute-care hospital. The system also runs outpatient clinics, a home health service, and a physicians group. Health First also offers numerous outpatient and wellness services, including Health First Aging Services, Health First Pro-Health & Fitness Center, Home Care and Hospice of Health First.

Operations
The company operates four hospitals (Holmes Regional Medical Center, Palm Bay Hospital, Cape Canaveral Hospital and Viera Hospital) and offers a wide range of services including aging services, ENT, diagnostic/lab, general surgery, home care, physical therapy, pastoral care, plastic and reconstructive surgery and urgent care, among others.

Geographic Reach
Health First operates four hospitals and a health insurance company in Brevard County, Florida.

Company Background
In 2011 Health First partnered with

Nemours to expand pediatric care in Brevard County. That year Health First Health Plans opened a new Vero Beach office to serve residents of Indian River County and launch its Medicare Advantage plans to the rest of Indian River County.

Despite an ongoing lawsuit with Wuesthoff Health System (which claims that Health First has an unfair monopoly of hospital services in Brevard County), the company forged ahead with construction of its fourth hospital in the county, the Viera hospital campus. The Medical Plaza at Viera Health Park, which will includes offices for multi-specialty physicians and a diagnostic/imaging center, opened in 2010. And, the park's centerpiece, Viera Hospital, a 100-bed acute-care hospital, opened in 2011.

Health First was founded in 1995 through a merger of regional hospitals. The Brevard Hospital (now Holmes Regional Medical Center) first opened in 1937.

EXECUTIVES

Care Vice President, Roberta B Stoner
CIO, William Walders
Auditors : RSM US LLP CHICAGO IL

LOCATIONS

HQ: HEALTH FIRST SHARED SERVICES, INC.
6450 US HIGHWAY 1, ROCKLEDGE, FL 329555747
Phone: 321 434-4300
Web: WWW.HF.ORG

Selected facilities
Cape Canaveral Hospital (Cocoa Beach)
Holmes Regional Medical Center (Melbourne)
Palm Bay Community Hospital (Palm Bay)
Viera Hospital (Viera)

COMPETITORS

ADVENTIST HEALTH SYSTEM/SUNBELT, INC.
ATLANTICARE HEALTH SYSTEM INC.
BAPTIST HEALTH SOUTH FLORIDA, INC.
BORGESS HEALTH ALLIANCE, INC.
HACKENSACK MERIDIAN HEALTH, INC.
ORLANDO HEALTH, INC.
PROSPECT WATERBURY, INC.
THE PUBLIC HEALTH TRUST OF MIAMI-DADE COUNTY
THEDACARE, INC.
WEST FLORIDA REGIONAL MEDICAL CENTER, INC.

HISTORICAL FINANCIALS
Company Type: Private

Income Statement — FYE: September 30

	REVENUE ($mil)	NET INCOME ($mil)	NET PROFIT MARGIN	EMPLOYEES
09/15	1,255	19	1.6%	6,900
09/14	1,136	90	7.9%	—
09/13	1,059	51	4.8%	—
09/11	129	(0)	—	—
Annual Growth	76.5%	—	—	—

2015 Year-End Financials
Return on assets: 1.2% Cash ($ mil.): 152
Return on equity: 2.7%
Current Ratio: 4.30

HEALTH PARTNERS PLANS, INC.

Health Partners wants to partner up with Pennsylvanians in need of health care. It is one of a few hospital-owned health maintenance organizations in the nation providing free and low-cost high-quality health insurance through its Medicaid, Medicare and CHIP plans. The company is a not-for-profit health plan that provides health benefits to over 280,000 members in the Philadelphia area. Its Health Partners Medicare plans offer three Medicare Advantage plans in the twelve-county area, all of which provide more benefits than Original Medicare with no or low monthly plan premiums. Its KidzPartners program is provided in partnership with the state of Pennsylvania's Children's Health Insurance Program (CHIP). Its provider network includes over 6,400 primary and specialty care doctors and more than 40 hospitals in the region. Health Partners was founded in 1984 by a group of hospitals in the Philadelphia area.

EXECUTIVES

Operations, Lisa Getzfrid Coosvp
Auditors : KPMG LLP PHILADELPHIA PENNSY

LOCATIONS

HQ: HEALTH PARTNERS PLANS, INC.
901 MARKET ST STE 500, PHILADELPHIA, PA 191074496
Phone: 215 849-9606
Web: WWW.HEALTHPARTNERSPLANS.COM

COMPETITORS

ALLWAYS HEALTH PARTNERS, INC.
ASCENSION VIA CHRISTI HEALTH, INC
ATLANTICARE HEALTH SYSTEM INC.
ATRIUS HEALTH, INC.
CENTURA HEALTH CORPORATION
MARSHFIELD CLINIC, INC.
MINISTRY HEALTH CARE, INC.
NEW YORK STATE CATHOLIC HEALTH PLAN, INC.
TOTAL HEALTH CARE, INC.
UCARE MINNESOTA

HISTORICAL FINANCIALS
Company Type: Private

Income Statement — FYE: December 31

	REVENUE ($mil)	NET INCOME ($mil)	NET PROFIT MARGIN	EMPLOYEES
12/14	910	(8)	—	620
12/13	1,000	(0)	0.0%	—
12/12	1,034	(1)	—	—
Annual Growth	(6.2%)	—	—	—

2014 Year-End Financials
Return on assets: (-2.9%) Cash ($ mil.): 60
Return on equity: (-10.8%)
Current Ratio: 0.90

HEALTH QUEST SYSTEMS, INC.

Auditors : PRICEWATERHOUSECOOPERS LLP N

LOCATIONS

HQ: HEALTH QUEST SYSTEMS, INC.
54 PAGE PARK DR, POUGHKEEPSIE, NY 126032584
Phone: 845 475-9500
Web: WWW.NUVANCEHEALTH.ORG

HISTORICAL FINANCIALS
Company Type: Private

Income Statement — FYE: December 31

	REVENUE ($mil)	NET INCOME ($mil)	NET PROFIT MARGIN	EMPLOYEES
12/14	796	5	0.6%	2,000
12/13	706	103	14.6%	—
12/12	692	8	1.2%	—
Annual Growth	7.3%	(21.3%)	—	—

2014 Year-End Financials
Return on assets: 0.6% Cash ($ mil.): 75
Return on equity: 1.2%
Current Ratio: 3.10

HEALTH RESEARCH, INC.

Health Research, Inc. (HRI) knows where the money is. The group is a not-for-profit organization that helps the New York State Department of Health and its affiliated Roswell Park Cancer Institute solicit, evaluate, and administer financial support. Sources of that support come from federal and state government sources, other non-profits, and businesses. HRI's Technology Transfer office also assists the Department of Health in sharing its research findings with other public and private institutions and finding ways to create biomedical technologies through private sector development. HRI was founded in 1953 and has administered $7 billion over its lifetime.

Auditors : BONADIO & CO LLP ALBANY NE

LOCATIONS

HQ: HEALTH RESEARCH, INC.
150 BROADWAY STE 280, MENANDS, NY 122042732
Phone: 518 431-1200
Web: WWW.HEALTHRESEARCH.ORG

COMPETITORS

HOWARD HUGHES MEDICAL INSTITUTE
THE JACKSON LABORATORY
THE MITRE CORPORATION
THE RESEARCH FOUNDATION FOR THE STATE UNIVERSITY OF NEW YORK
THE ROCKEFELLER UNIVERSITY

HISTORICAL FINANCIALS
Company Type: Private

Income Statement			FYE: March 31
	REVENUE ($mil)	NET INCOME ($mil)	NET PROFIT MARGIN	EMPLOYEES
03/20	1,326	506	38.2%	1,400
03/15	677	22	3.3%	—
03/14	703	13	1.9%	—
03/13	665	25	3.9%	—
Annual Growth	10.3%	52.8%	—	—

2020 Year-End Financials
Return on assets: 66.5%   Cash ($ mil.): 154
Return on equity: 82.0%
Current Ratio: —

HEALTHPARTNERS, INC.

Auditors: KPMG LLP MINNEAPOLIS MINNESO

LOCATIONS
HQ: HEALTHPARTNERS, INC.
8170 33RD AVE S, BLOOMINGTON, MN 554254516
Phone: 952 883-6000
Web: WWW.HEALTHPARTNERS.COM

HISTORICAL FINANCIALS
Company Type: Private

Income Statement			FYE: December 31
	REVENUE ($mil)	NET INCOME ($mil)	NET PROFIT MARGIN	EMPLOYEES
12/21	2,596	96	3.7%	22,000
12/20	7,033	374	5.3%	—
12/19	7,251	278	3.8%	—
12/18	7,061	143	2.0%	—
Annual Growth	(28.4%)	(12.5%)	—	—

2021 Year-End Financials
Return on assets: 6.9%   Cash ($ mil.): 383
Return on equity: 14.1%
Current Ratio: 2.60

HEARTLAND CO-OP

Heartland Co-op has no need to go against the grain. The cooperative offers agricultural products and services for its central Iowa member/farmers. Heartland operates more than 50 grain elevators and service centers. It offers agronomy products and services, such as seed treatments and alfalfa fertilization; grain drying, storage, and merchandising; petroleum products for farm vehicles and home heating; livestock and pet feed; and personal and crop credit and financing. Headquartered in West Des Moines, Heartland was formed in 1987 when cooperatives in Dallas Center, Minburn, and Panora merged. Heartland, which has grown to more than 5,400-members, merged with Farm Service Company of Council Bluffs in 2013.

Operations
Heartland Co-op operates more than 60 cooperatives in Iowa.

Geographic Reach
Iowa-based Heartland Co-op operates across its home state in the cities of Blairstown, Luzerne, Chelsea, Elberon, Conroy, Hartwick, Marengo, Malcom and Montezuma.

Strategy
Heartland Co-op has grown through consolidation and mergers with many smaller cooperatives.

Mergers and Acquisitions
Heartland Co-op acquired Farm Service Company (FSC) in Council Bluffs, Iowa, in August 2013. The combination of the two extended Heartland's reach westward in Iowa. The corporate offices of the combined operation remains in West Des Moines in Central Iowa.

It sold its service station business in 2012, as it was deemed non-core.

Auditors: BERGAN PAULSEN & COMPANY PC

LOCATIONS
HQ: HEARTLAND CO-OP
2829 WESTOWN PKWY STE 350, WEST DES MOINES, IA 502661340
Phone: 515 225-1334
Web: WWW.HEARTLANDCOOP.COM

PRODUCTS/OPERATIONS
Selected Products & Services
Crop Nutrition
Seed Solutions
Precision Ag Services
Agronomy Services
Crop Protection Products

COMPETITORS
BARTLETT AGRI ENTERPRISES, INC.
COUNTRY PRIDE COOPERATIVE, INC.
NEW COOPERATION COMPANY
WATONWAN FARM SERVICE, INC
WEST CENTRAL COOPERATIVE

HISTORICAL FINANCIALS
Company Type: Private

Income Statement			FYE: June 30
	REVENUE ($mil)	NET INCOME ($mil)	NET PROFIT MARGIN	EMPLOYEES
06/19	867	17	2.0%	678
06/18	901	20	2.2%	—
06/17	932	17	1.9%	—
06/16	854	15	1.9%	—
Annual Growth	0.5%	3.5%	—	—

2019 Year-End Financials
Return on assets: 3.1%   Cash ($ mil.): —
Return on equity: 7.3%
Current Ratio: 1.50

HEARTLAND PAYMENT SYSTEMS, LLC

Heartland Payment Systems (HPS), a wholly owned subsidiary of Global Payments Inc., makes sure plastic-card transactions don't get lost along their way. The company performs credit, debit, and prepaid card processing services at some 300,000 locations nationwide. Its client list includes restaurants, retailers, convenience stores, and professional service providers. The Heartland Payroll Solutions segment provides payroll processing such as check printing and direct deposit for more than 10,000 customers. Other markets for the firm include K-12 school nutrition programs and payment processing for colleges and universities. Global Payments bought Heartland for $4.3 billion in 2016.

Sales and Marketing
Heartland Payment Systems clients include small businesses, midsize companies, enterprise organizations, restaurants, retailers, convenience stores, and professional service providers.

Mergers and Acquisitions

Auditors: DELOITTE & TOUCHE LLP PHILADE

LOCATIONS
HQ: HEARTLAND PAYMENT SYSTEMS, LLC
10 GLENLAKE PKWY STE 324, ATLANTA, GA 303283495
Phone: 609 683-3831
Web: WWW.HEARTLANDPAYMENTSYSTEMS.COM

PRODUCTS/OPERATIONS
Products:
Billing Solutions
E-Commerce
Gift Cards
Internet of Things
Lending
Loyalty Program
Mobile Ordering
Mobile Payment
Payroll Services
Point of Sale
Processing
School Nutrition
School Payment

COMPETITORS
BANCTEC, INC.
ELECTRIC LIGHTWAVE COMMUNICATIONS, INC.
GLOBAL PAYMENTS INC.
Moneris Solutions Corporation
PAYMENT PROCESSING, INC.
PAYPOINT PLC
UNITED BANK CARD, INC.
WORLDPAY (UK) LIMITED
WORLDPAY, INC.
Wirecard AG

HISTORICAL FINANCIALS
Company Type: Private

Income Statement   FYE: December 31

	REVENUE ($mil)	NET INCOME ($mil)	NET PROFIT MARGIN	EMPLOYEES
12/15	2,682	84	3.2%	3,734
12/14	2,311	31	1.4%	—
12/13	2,135	78	3.7%	—
12/12	2,013	66	3.3%	—
Annual Growth	10.0%	8.4%	—	—

2015 Year-End Financials
Return on assets: 5.5%   Cash ($ mil.): 56
Return on equity: 25.2%
Current Ratio: 0.90

HEARTLAND REGIONAL MEDICAL CENTER

Heartland Regional Medical Center strives for healthy hearts, minds, and bodies in the US heartland. The acute care hospital, a subsidiary of Heartland Health, provides medical services to residents of St. Joseph, Missouri, and some 20 surrounding counties in northwest Missouri, southeast Nebraska, and northeast Kansas. Heartland Regional Medical Center encompasses specialty centers for trauma and long-term care, acute rehabilitation, cancer, heart disease, and birthing. As part of the services provided by the medical center, Heartland Regional Medical Center offers services such as arthritis, pain, and wound treatments, as well as home health and hospice care.

Geographic Reach
Operating in Missouri, Heartland Regional Medical Center serves the residents and visitors of its home state, as well as those in Nebraska and Kansas. Altogether, the medical center caters to a more than 20-county area.

Financial Performance
In fiscal 2012, as compared to 2011, Heartland Regional Medical Center's revenue rose some 8% and its net income saw a 31% boost.

Strategy
As part of its operations, Heartland Regional Medical Center partners with several managed care organizations, such as Aetna, CCN Managed Care, Coventry Healthcare, and Blue Cross Blue Shield of Kansas City, to give its patients payment options for its health services. In 2012 Heartland Regional Medical Center developed an accountable care organization. It's a participant in the Medicare Shared Savings Program and enters into other similar shared savings arrangements with commercial, self-insured, or other third-party payors.

In recent years, the medical facility has been investing in growing its footprint. Heartland Regional Medical Center is funding a $55-million expansion project that includes adding a handful of new operating rooms and renovating 10 more.

Auditors: BLD LLP KANSAS CITY MISSOUR

LOCATIONS
HQ: HEARTLAND REGIONAL MEDICAL CENTER
5325 FARAON ST, SAINT JOSEPH, MO 645063488
Phone: 816 271-6000
Web: WWW.MYMLC.COM

PRODUCTS/OPERATIONS
Selected Services
Appendectomy
Cholecystectomy
Colon Resection
Hernia Repair
Nephrectomy
Assisted Vaginal Hysterectomy
Peritoneal Dialysis Catheter Placement
Pyloromyotomy
Tubal Ligation
Abdominal Perineal Resection
Adrenalectomy
Colostomy
Gastric Banding
Gastric Bypass
Gastric Sleeve
Gastrostomy Tube Placement
Laser Lysis of Adhesions/Endometriosis
Nissan Fundoplication
Salpingo-Oophorectomy
Prostatectomy

COMPETITORS
FIRSTHEALTH OF THE CAROLINAS, INC.
HOUSTON COUNTY HEALTHCARE AUTHORITY
LEGACY HEALTH
PEACEHEALTH
POUDRE VALLEY HEALTH CARE, INC.

HISTORICAL FINANCIALS
Company Type: Private

Income Statement   FYE: June 30

	REVENUE ($mil)	NET INCOME ($mil)	NET PROFIT MARGIN	EMPLOYEES
06/21	672	47	7.1%	4,000
06/20	714	84	11.8%	—
06/19	645	38	5.9%	—
06/18	639	64	10.1%	—
Annual Growth	1.7%	(9.6%)	—	—

2021 Year-End Financials
Return on assets: 9.4%   Cash ($ mil.): —
Return on equity: 12.1%
Current Ratio: 0.80

HELM FERTILIZER CORPORATION (FLORIDA)

Auditors: ISRAELOFF TRATTNER & CO PC

LOCATIONS
HQ: HELM FERTILIZER CORPORATION (FLORIDA)
401 E JACKSON ST STE 1400, TAMPA, FL 336025264
Phone: 813 621-8846
Web: US.HELMCROP.COM

HISTORICAL FINANCIALS
Company Type: Private

Income Statement   FYE: December 31

	REVENUE ($mil)	NET INCOME ($mil)	NET PROFIT MARGIN	EMPLOYEES
12/13	611	5	0.9%	28
12/12	947	11	1.2%	—
12/11	1,056	10	1.0%	—
12/10	667	6	1.0%	—
Annual Growth	(2.9%)	(6.7%)	—	—

2013 Year-End Financials
Return on assets: 7.6%   Cash ($ mil.): —
Return on equity: 24.4%
Current Ratio: 1.40

HENDRICKS COUNTY HOSPITAL

Auditors: BLUE & CO LLC INDIANAPOLIS

LOCATIONS
HQ: HENDRICKS COUNTY HOSPITAL
1000 E MAIN ST, DANVILLE, IN 461221991
Phone: 317 745-4451
Web: WWW.HENDRICKS.ORG

HISTORICAL FINANCIALS
Company Type: Private

Income Statement   FYE: December 31

	REVENUE ($mil)	NET INCOME ($mil)	NET PROFIT MARGIN	EMPLOYEES
12/19	747	13	1.8%	1,700
12/18	605	(25)	—	—
12/17	550	39	7.1%	—
12/16	530	43	8.2%	—
Annual Growth	12.1%	(32.5%)	—	—

2019 Year-End Financials
Return on assets: 1.9%   Cash ($ mil.): 20
Return on equity: 3.1%
Current Ratio: 1.30

HENNEPIN COUNTY

EXECUTIVES

County Administrator, David Hough
Auditors : RSM US LLP MINNEAPOLIS MINNE

LOCATIONS

HQ: HENNEPIN COUNTY
300 S 6TH ST STE A1700, MINNEAPOLIS, MN 554870999
Phone: 612 348-3000
Web: WWW.HENNEPIN.US

HISTORICAL FINANCIALS

Company Type: Private

Income Statement — FYE: December 31

	REVENUE ($mil)	NET INCOME ($mil)	NET PROFIT MARGIN	EMPLOYEES
12/21	1,852	150	8.1%	10,246
12/20	1,897	(4)	—	—
12/18	17	38	222.5%	—
12/17	1,618	(95)	—	—
Annual Growth	3.4%	—	—	—

2021 Year-End Financials
Return on assets: 2.8%   Cash ($ mil.): —
Return on equity: 10.9%
Current Ratio: 2.60

HENNEPIN HEALTHCARE SYSTEM, INC.

EXECUTIVES

CMO*, Dan Hoody
PEOPLE CULTURE*, Tonya Jackman Hampton
HEALTH EQUITY*, Nneka O Sederstrom
Health Officer, Wendy Chief Ambulatory Population Stulac-motzel
CAO*, Meghan Walsh

LOCATIONS

HQ: HENNEPIN HEALTHCARE SYSTEM, INC.
701 PARK AVE, MINNEAPOLIS, MN 554151623
Phone: 612 873-3000
Web: WWW.HENNEPINHEALTHCARE.ORG

HISTORICAL FINANCIALS

Company Type: Private

Income Statement — FYE: December 31

	REVENUE ($mil)	NET INCOME ($mil)	NET PROFIT MARGIN	EMPLOYEES
12/18	950	13	1.4%	5,000
12/17	1,011	(19)	—	—
Annual Growth	(6.0%)	—	—	—

2018 Year-End Financials
Return on assets: 1.7%   Cash ($ mil.): 38
Return on equity: 55.5%
Current Ratio: 2.00

HENRY FORD HEALTH SYSTEM

Founded in 1915 by auto pioneer Henry Ford, Henry Ford Health System is one of the leading healthcare provider and not-for-profit corporation and is comprised of hospitals, medical centers, and the Henry Ford Medical Group, which includes more than 1,200 physicians practicing in over 40 specialties. The system's five hospitals -- including the flagship Henry Ford Hospital (877-bed), the Henry Ford Wyandotte Hospital (360-bed), and Henry Ford Allegiance Health (420-bed). Health Alliance Plan (HAP), a Henry Ford subsidiary, is a Michigan-based nonprofit health plan that provides health coverage to individuals and companies of all sizes.

Operations

Henry Ford Health System is comprised of hospitals, medical centers, and the largest in the Henry Ford Medical Group, which includes 1,200 physicians practicing over 40 specialties.

The system flagship is the Henry Ford Hospital in Detroit, a level 1 Trauma Center recognized for clinical excellence in cardiology, cardiovascular surgery, neurology, neurosurgery, orthopedics, sports medicine, multi-organ transplants and cancer treatment. Henry Ford Allegiance Health is a Level II Trauma Center and a teaching hospital center with a thriving Graduate Medical Education program. Henry Ford Macomb Hospital - Clinton Township provides comprehensive acute and tertiary care; specialty services include a Heart & Vascular Institute, Joint Replacement Center, Henry Ford Cancer Institute, a Women's Health Center, with a Birthing Center that features roughly 20 labor delivery and post-partum suites. Henry Ford West Bloomfield Hospital provides the highest quality safety, clinical excellence integrative services, and innovation a unique environment that encourages wellness and provides access information to support and wellness offerings such as Demonstration Kitchen, Live Well Shoppe, and Greenhouse. Henry Ford Wyandotte Hospital offers a full range of services such as 24-hours emergency care, adult mental health services, birthing center, general medicine, neurosurgical services, physical therapy and rehabilitation, surgery, and more.

Geographic Reach

Henry Ford Health System is based in Detroit, Michigan.

Company Background

Automaker Henry Ford founded Henry Ford Hospital in 1915.

The Health Alliance Plan became part of the Henry Ford Health System in 1986.

In 2016 Allegiance Health, which operated a hospital and other health facilities in Jackson, joined the Henry Ford Health System and began operating as Henry Ford Allegiance Health.

EXECUTIVES

Chief Human Resources Officer*, Kathy Oswald
CSO*, Carladenise Edwards
Chief Marketing EXP*, Heather Geisler
Auditors : DELOITTE & TOUCHE LLP DETROIT

LOCATIONS

HQ: HENRY FORD HEALTH SYSTEM
1 FORD PL, DETROIT, MI 482023450
Phone: 313 916-2600
Web: WWW.HENRYFORD.COM

HOSPITAL LOCATIONS
Henry Ford Allegiance Health
Henry Ford Hospital
Henry Ford Kingswood Hospital
Henry Ford Macomb Hospital - Clinton Township
Henry Ford West Bloomfield Hospital
Henry Ford Wyandotte Hospital

PRODUCTS/OPERATIONS

SELECTED SERVICES
Bariatric Surgery
Cancer
Heart & Vascular
Neurology & Neurosurgery
OptimEyes
Orthopedic Surgery
Primary Care
Transplant Services

COMPETITORS

ALLINA HEALTH SYSTEM
BEAUMONT HEALTH
BRONXCARE HEALTH SYSTEM
KALEIDA HEALTH
PASADENA HOSPITAL ASSOCIATION, LTD.
ROBERT WOOD JOHNSON UNIVERSITY HOSPITAL, INC.
SAINT JOSEPH HOSPITAL, INC
THE COOPER HEALTH SYSTEM
WELLSTAR HEALTH SYSTEM, INC.
WILLIAM BEAUMONT HOSPITAL

HISTORICAL FINANCIALS

Company Type: Private

Income Statement — FYE: December 31

	REVENUE ($mil)	NET INCOME ($mil)	NET PROFIT MARGIN	EMPLOYEES
12/18	5,853	89	1.5%	23,000
12/17	5,977	203	3.4%	—
12/14	1,513	(13)	—	—
12/13	4,517	135	3.0%	—
Annual Growth	5.3%	(8.0%)	—	—

2018 Year-End Financials
Return on assets: 2.0%   Cash ($ mil.): 556
Return on equity: 4.2%
Current Ratio: 1.50

HENRY MODELL & COMPANY, INC.

Operating as Modell's Sporting Goods, retailer Henry Modell & Company sells sporting goods, fitness equipment, apparel, and brand-name athletic footwear. It is America's oldest family-owned and -operated sporting goods retailer. Its top brands are Asics, Champion, FILA and Smith's, to name a few. It also offers fan gear such as jerseys for football. It also boasts an online presence at Modells.com.

Operations
The company offers various products including but not limited to: sports and activities, sporting goods, athletic footwear, active apparel, accessories and fan shop. It also offers equipment used for strength, cardio, bikes, outdoor activities, games, and more.

Sales and Marketing
Modell's markets and sells its products through its stores and online.

Company Background
Hungarian immigrant Morris Modell first sold menswear from a Lower East Side pushcart in New York City before he founded Henry Modell & Company in 1889. Led by CEO Mitchell Modell, the company is operated by the fourth generation of the Modell family.

Auditors : BDO USA LLP NEW YORK NY

LOCATIONS
HQ: HENRY MODELL & COMPANY, INC.
498 7TH AVE FL 20, NEW YORK, NY 100186738
Phone: 212 822-1000
Web: WWW.MODELLS.COM

2016 Locations

	No.
New York	71
New Jersey	38
Pennsylvania	18
Maryland	9
Connecticut	6
Massachusetts	7
Virginia	5
District of Columbia	2
New Hampshire	2
Delaware	1
Rhode Island	1
Total	160

PRODUCTS/OPERATIONS

Selected Product Categories
Accessories
Apparel
Baseball
Basketball
Boxing/martial arts
Camping/hiking
Cycling
Electronics/optics
Fan shop-pro/college
Field hockey
Fishing
Fitness
Football
Footwear
Games
Golf
Ice/roller hockey
In-Line/roller skating
Lacrosse
Optics/telescopes
Outdoor recreation
Paintball
Pilates
Racquetball/squash
Roller hockey
Rugby
Running
Scooters
Skateboarding
Snow sports
Soccer
Softball
Tennis
Water recreation
Winter recreation
Wrestling
Yoga

COMPETITORS
DOVER SADDLERY, INC.
FGL Sports Ltd
FRASERS GROUP PLC
GOLF GALAXY, LLC
OSC SPORTS, INC.
P.C. RICHARD & SON, INC.
PENTLAND GROUP LIMITED
SCHOTTENSTEIN STORES CORPORATION
SPORT CHALET LLC
TSAWD, INC.

HISTORICAL FINANCIALS
Company Type: Private

Income Statement   FYE: February 2

	REVENUE ($mil)	NET INCOME ($mil)	NET PROFIT MARGIN	EMPLOYEES
02/13*	607	0	0.1%	5,430
01/12	570	(3)	—	—
01/11	558	(7)	—	—
Annual Growth	4.3%	—	—	—

*Fiscal year change

2013 Year-End Financials
Return on assets: 0.3%   Cash ($ mil.): 3
Return on equity: 1.7%
Current Ratio: 1.10

HENSEL PHELPS CONSTRUCTION CO.

Hensel Phelps Construction is a proven industry leader and trusted advisor. The employee-owned general contractor provides a full range of development, pre-construction, construction, and renovation services for commercial, institutional, and government projects throughout the US. Its project portfolio includes prisons, airports, arenas, laboratories, government complexes, offices, and more. Major public and private clients include the US Intercontinental San Diego, Masonic Temple Hotel, NASA, Samsung, US Air Force, and Cinépolis Luxury Cinema. Hensel Phelps founded the eponymous company as a homebuilder in 1937.

Operations
The company also offers virtual design and construction (VDC), life-cycle cost analysis, prefabrication and modularization, as well as specialized construction solutions for small projects, including renovations and retrofitting of existing facilities. Its facility services include asset management and preservation, integrated facility management (FM), and it offers mobile maintenance service that dispatched technicians perform thorough inspections, preventative maintenance, and repair of building systems.

Geographic Reach
Colorado-based Hensel Phelps Construction has ten regional offices located in California, Colorado, Tennessee, Florida, Texas, Arizona, Washington DC and Hawaii.

Sales and Marketing
The company serves a wide range of industries including aviation, commercial, education, government, health care, hospitality, infrastructure and transportation, technology and technology, and water and wastewater. Its public and private clients include the University of Texas, Hotel Indigo, United Airlines, Los Angeles International Airport, and Universal Studios.

Company Background
Hensel Phelps founded the eponymous company as a homebuilder in 1937. Operations initially were limited to home building and remodeling, after which competitive contract work was undertaken on a limited scale.

Auditors : KPMG LLLP DENVER COLORADO

LOCATIONS
HQ: HENSEL PHELPS CONSTRUCTION CO.
420 6TH AVE, GREELEY, CO 806312332
Phone: 970 352-6565
Web: WWW.HENSELPHELPS.COM

PRODUCTS/OPERATIONS

Selected Projects
Hilton Hokulani - Waikiki
Aegis Ashore Missile Defense Test Complex - PMRF
Regional Operations Center - Guam
Guam NAVFAC Bachelor Enlisted Quarters (BEQ)
Mamizu Utilities and Site Improvements Phase I
Samaritan MOB and Parking Structure
Santa Clara Valley Medical Center Receiving and Support Center
Santa Clara Family Justice Center
Santa Clara Valley Medical Center Receiving and Support Center
Rotary PlayGarden
Norman Y. Mineta San José International Airport Terminal Area Improvement Program (TAIP)
Vantage Data Center V2
Vantage Data Center V1

Selected Services
Construction
    Change management
    Construction waste management
    LEED project registration
    Quality control
    Safety management
    Scheduling
    Self-perfoming concrete
    Status reporting
    Subcontractor management
    Sustainability audits
    Quality control
Development
    Feasibility studies
    Financing
    Green building planning/education
    Land acquisition

Leasing
Pro forma review
Post-construction
    As-built documentation
    Building operations
    Certificate of occupancy
    Commissioning and warranty programs
    LEED project certification
    Moving services
Preconstruction
    Bid packaging
    Budgeting/cost modeling
    Design management
    Estimating
    Green building and planning/education
    Phasing plans
    Regulatory investigation
    Scheduling
    Status reporting
    Subcontractor prequalification
    Value engineering

Selected Markets
Commercial
Education
High technology
Industrial
International
Justice
Leisure
Medical
Multiresidence
Public
Transportation

COMPETITORS

BECK INTERNATIONAL, LLC
BERGER GROUP HOLDINGS, INC.
GILBANE BUILDING COMPANY
GILBANE, INC.
HITT CONTRACTING, INC.
JAMES G. DAVIS CONSTRUCTION CORPORATION
SUFFOLK CONSTRUCTION COMPANY, INC.
T & G CORPORATION
THE WALSH GROUP LTD
WALBRIDGE ALDINGER LLC

HISTORICAL FINANCIALS

Company Type: Private

Income Statement   FYE: December 31

	REVENUE ($mil)	NET INCOME ($mil)	NET PROFIT MARGIN	EMPLOYEES
12/21	5,334	186	3.5%	2,065
12/20	5,868	181	3.1%	—
12/19	5,676	177	3.1%	—
Annual Growth	(3.1%)	2.5%	—	—

2021 Year-End Financials
Return on assets: 7.7%
Return on equity: 45.3%
Current Ratio: 1.30
Cash ($ mil.): 549

HEXION INC.

When it comes to making resins, Hexion is on it. Hexion (formerly Momentive Specialty Chemicals) is the world's largest thermosetting resins (or thermosets) maker, ahead of competitor Georgia-Pacific. Thermosets add a desired quality (heat resistance, gloss, adhesion, etc.) to a number of different paints, coatings, and adhesives. They include an array of resins: phenolic, epoxy, polyester, acrylic, and urethane. The company also is a leading producer of adhesive and structural resins and coatings. It serves several markets, including paints, consumer products, and automotive coatings. In 2022, the parent company of Hexion Inc. (Hexion Holdings Corp.) was acquired by affiliates of American Securities.

Operations

Hexion's products play an integral role across a wide variety of applications from adhesives to coatings and building materials. The company's products are used for: adhesive, chemical intermediates, civil engineering, coatings, crop protection, engineered wood, fertilizers and pesticides, furniture, oilfield, oriented strand board, particle board and fiber board.

Geographic Reach

Based in Columbus, Ohio, Hexion Inc. has approximately 25 production and manufacturing facilities around the world.

Sales and Marketing

The diverse markets include forest products, architectural and industrial paints, packaging, consumer products, and automotive coatings, as well as higher growth markets, such as composites and electrical components. Major industry sectors served by Hexion include industrial/marine, construction, consumer/durable goods, automotive, wind energy, aviation, electronics, architectural, civil engineering, repair/remodeling, and oil and gas field support.

Mergers and Acquisitions

HISTORY

Growing its global footprint, in 2013 the company opened new curing agent manufacturing capabilities at a plant in Tianjin, China. The facility expands its regional capacity to produce amine curing agents for that fast growing market. That year the company signed a deal with Kanoria Chemicals & Industries Limited to form a formaldehyde and phenolic specialty resins joint venture in India, and a joint venture to construct a phenolic specialty resins manufacturing facility in China.

In 2013 Momentive Specialty Chemicals) and MicroBlend, based in Gilbert, Arizona, agreed to form a joint venture company located in Cali, Colombia, to support MicroBlend's revolutionary 'Automated Paint Machine System' with the necessary liquid components for making fresh paint at the point of sale in Colombian home center stores.

That year the company also teamed up with the Fraunhofer Project Center for Composites Research at Western University to develop high-volume, lightweight composites for the North American automotive market.

In 2013 Momentive Specialty Chemicals acquired Dynea Chemical OY's stake in the Dynea Australia's joint venture with the Laminex Group (the leading marketer and manufacturer of premium decorative surfaces in Australia and New Zealand). The new joint venture, known as Momentive Specialty Chemicals Australia, is 50% owned by Momentive Specialty Chemicals and 50% by Laminex. The JV provides formaldehyde and urea formaldehyde resins to Laminex, as well as other products to industrial customers in Western Australia.

In 2012 the company's joint venture with China-based Shanxi Sanwei Group began production at a VeoVa-brand vinyl ester plant that supplies Momentive's monomer products for the coatings and adhesives industry. The monomer is used to provide a variety of qualities to water-based paints, wood stains, and coatings, as well as to adhesives and powders used in construction.

That year the company also announced that it is building a new plant in Thailand to expand its production of acrylic-based resins, used in coatings, adhesives, and building applications, in the Southeast Asia region. The plant is part of the company's strategy for global growth.

In another expansion move, in 2012 Momentive Speciality Chemicals and sister company Momentive Performance Materials opened a new research and development center and business headquarters in Bangalore to serve the India, Middle East, and Africa markets.

Momentive Specialty Chemicals also opened a joint venture plant in 2011 with China-based UPC Technology Corporation, a maker of specialty chemicals and materials, to produce specialty phenolic resins. The plant in Zhenjiang, in Jiangsu Province, produces specialty novolac and resole phenolic resins used in refractories, friction, and abrasives applications.

To raise cash, in early 2011 Momentive Specialty Chemicals sold its IAR business, which produced naturally derived resins for a variety of applications, to Japan's Harima Chemicals for about $120 million. The unit had been one of the company's Coating and Inks' segments.

That year Momentive Specialty Chemicals also sold its North American composites and coating resins business to a subsidiary of Investindustrial, a European investment group specializing in chemicals, resins, and intermediates.

The company was created after the former Hexion merged with Momentive Performance Materials in 2010. Under the terms of the merger, Momentive Performance Materials and Momentive Specialty Chemicals became subsidiaries of the newly formed Momentive Performance Materials Holdings. The capital and legal structures of both companies remain separate entities under the holding company.

Auditors : PRICEWATERHOUSECOOPERS LLP CO

LOCATIONS

HQ: HEXION INC.
  180 E BROAD ST, COLUMBUS, OH 432153707

Phone: 614 225-4000
Web: WWW.HEXION.COM

2016 Sales	$ mil.	% of total
U.S.	1,389	40
Netherlands	583	17
Other international	526	15
Canada	302	9
China	296	9
Germany	180	5
Brazil	162	5
Total	3,438	100

PRODUCTS/OPERATIONS

2016 Sales

	$ mil.	% of total
Epoxy, Phenolic and coating reigns	2,094	61
Forest products reigns	1,344	39
Total	3,438	100

COMPETITORS

AVIENT CORPORATION
AXIALL CORPORATION
CELANESE CORPORATION
Evonik Industries AG
HEXION TOPCO, LLC
HUNTSMAN CORPORATION
KRATON CORPORATION
KRATON POLYMERS LLC
LANXESS SOLUTIONS US INC.
THE DOW CHEMICAL COMPANY

HISTORICAL FINANCIALS
Company Type: Private

Income Statement   FYE: December 31

	REVENUE ($mil)	NET INCOME ($mil)	NET PROFIT MARGIN	EMPLOYEES
12/20	2,510	(230)	—	4,000
12/19	1,596	(88)	—	—

Annual Growth   57.3%   —   —   —

2020 Year-End Financials
Return on assets: (-5.7%)   Cash ($ mil.): 204
Return on equity: (-27.9%)
Current Ratio: 1.40

HIGHER EDUCATION COORDINATING BOARD, TEXAS

Auditors : KPMG LLP AUSTIN TX

LOCATIONS

HQ: HIGHER EDUCATION COORDINATING BOARD, TEXAS
   1200 E ANDERSON LN, AUSTIN, TX 787521706
Phone: 512 427-6100
Web: THECB.STATE.TX.US

HISTORICAL FINANCIALS
Company Type: Private

Income Statement   FYE: August 31

	REVENUE ($mil)	NET INCOME ($mil)	NET PROFIT MARGIN	EMPLOYEES
08/21	1,862	52	2.8%	290
08/18	1,732	73	4.2%	—
08/03	1,116	(42)	—	—
08/02	0	0	—	—

Annual Growth   —   —   —   —

2021 Year-End Financials
Return on assets: 2.4%   Cash ($ mil.): —
Return on equity: 8.9%
Current Ratio: 5.00

HILAND DAIRY FOODS COMPANY., LLC

Hiland Dairy Foods is a farmer-owned dairy foods company that offers dairy products, including ice cream, milk, butter, cheese, and eggnog. It has expanded beyond dairy and has a wide variety of other beverages, such as Red Diamond Tea, lemonade, and fresh juices. Hiland runs more than 15 processing plants and has over 50 distribution centers across the region. It partners with a larger dairy co-operative, Prairie Farms Dairy, to market and sell products. Beyond dairy, Hiland supplies juices, bottled milk and coffee, as well as tea, water, and other to-go drinks. It features limited-run specialty items, such as peanut butter banana ice cream. Hiland was founded in 1938.

Operations
It is a full-service dairy with a bulging products portfolio that includes the ubiquitous milk cartons as well as ice cream, yogurt, cheese, sour cream, dairy-based dips, whipping cream, butter, cheese, and orange juice. The company's products are free of antibiotics and artificial growth hormones.

Geographic Reach
Springfield, MO-based Hiland serves customers in several states, including Arkansas, Kansas, Iowa, Missouri, Nebraska, Oklahoma, and Texas. To support its operations, the cooperative boasts more than 15 plants in Arkansas, Kansas, Missouri, Nebraska, Oklahoma, and Texas and operates over 50 distribution centers.

Sales and Marketing
Hiland uses social media such as Facebook, Twitter, Instagram and Pinterest to connect with its consumers and to promote dairy foods through blog posts, photography and other original content.

Auditors : BKD LLP SPRINGFIELD MO

LOCATIONS

HQ: HILAND DAIRY FOODS COMPANY., LLC
   1133 E KEARNEY ST, SPRINGFIELD, MO 658033435

Phone: 417 862-9311
Web: WWW.HILANDDAIRY.COM

Selected Plant Locations
Chandler, Oklahoma
Fayetteville, Arkansas
Fort Smith, Arkansas
Kansas City, Missouri
Little Rock, Arkansas
Norfolk, Nebraska
Norman, Oklahoma
Omaha, Nebraska
Springfield, Missouri
Tyler, Texas
Wichita, Kansas

PRODUCTS/OPERATIONS

Selected Products
Butter
Cheese
Cottage cheese
Cravélatté (milk and coffee)
Creams/Half-and-Half
Dips
Egg nog
Egg substitute
Fruit-flavored drinks
Ice cream
Juice
Lactose-free milk
Lemonade
Milk
Sour cream
Tea
To-go drinks
Water
Yogurt

COMPETITORS

AGRI-MARK, INC.
BERKELEY FARMS, LLC
GARELICK FARMS, LLC
MAYFIELD DAIRY FARMS, LLC
MICHIGAN MILK PRODUCERS ASSOCIATION
PRAIRIE FARMS DAIRY, INC.
ROBERTS DAIRY COMPANY, LLC
SCHREIBER FOODS, INC.
STREMICKS HERITAGE FOODS, LLC
UNITED DAIRYMEN OF ARIZONA

HISTORICAL FINANCIALS
Company Type: Private

Income Statement   FYE: September 30

	REVENUE ($mil)	NET INCOME ($mil)	NET PROFIT MARGIN	EMPLOYEES
09/11	958	8	0.9%	1,350
09/10	588	24	4.2%	—
09/09	559	39	7.0%	—

Annual Growth   30.8%   (53.0%)   —   —

2011 Year-End Financials
Return on assets: 2.7%   Cash ($ mil.): 19
Return on equity: 3.9%
Current Ratio: 2.30

HILL FIRE PROTECTION, LLC

LOCATIONS

HQ: HILL FIRE PROTECTION, LLC
11045 GAGE AVE, FRANKLIN PARK, IL 601311437
Phone: 847 288-5100
Web: WWW.HILLGRP.COM

HISTORICAL FINANCIALS
Company Type: Private

Income Statement — FYE: December 31

	REVENUE ($mil)	NET INCOME ($mil)	NET PROFIT MARGIN	EMPLOYEES
12/11	5,669	185	3.3%	100
12/10	2,568	80	3.1%	—
Annual Growth	120.7%	130.7%	—	—

2011 Year-End Financials
Return on assets: 7.3%   Cash ($ mil.): 480
Return on equity: 11.4%
Current Ratio: 2.60

HILLSBOROUGH COUNTY SCHOOL DISTRICT

EXECUTIVES

Vice Chairman*, Cindy Stuart
Auditors : KPMG LLP TAMPA FL

LOCATIONS

HQ: HILLSBOROUGH COUNTY SCHOOL DISTRICT
901 E KENNEDY BLVD, TAMPA, FL 336023502
Phone: 813 272-4000
Web: WWW.HILLSBOROUGHSCHOOLS.ORG

HISTORICAL FINANCIALS
Company Type: Private

Income Statement — FYE: June 30

	REVENUE ($mil)	NET INCOME ($mil)	NET PROFIT MARGIN	EMPLOYEES
06/16	2,133	(59)	—	25,000
06/15	2,042	(110)	—	—
06/14	1,984	(45)	—	—
06/13	1,878	(44)	—	—
Annual Growth	4.3%	—	—	—

2016 Year-End Financials
Return on assets: (-1.8%)   Cash ($ mil.): 113
Return on equity: (-7.6%)
Current Ratio: —

HL MANDO AMERICA CORPORATION

Auditors : PRICEWATERHOUSECOOPERS LLP AT

LOCATIONS

HQ: HL MANDO AMERICA CORPORATION
4201 N PARK DR, OPELIKA, AL 368019667
Phone: 334 364-3600
Web: WWW.MANDO.COM

HISTORICAL FINANCIALS
Company Type: Private

Income Statement — FYE: December 31

	REVENUE ($mil)	NET INCOME ($mil)	NET PROFIT MARGIN	EMPLOYEES
12/21	818	14	1.8%	1,458
12/20	747	14	2.0%	—
Annual Growth	9.5%	1.2%	—	—

2021 Year-End Financials
Return on assets: 3.2%   Cash ($ mil.): 4
Return on equity: 7.2%
Current Ratio: 1.40

HMH HOSPITALS CORPORATION

Hackensack University Medical Center (HUMC) is an acute care teaching and research hospital that serves northern New Jersey and parts of New York. The hospital has about 775 beds and staffs more than 2,200 medical professionals. HUMC administers general medical, surgical, emergency, and diagnostic care. The center also includes specialized treatment centers including a children's hospital, a women's hospital, a cancer center, and a heart and vascular hospital. HUMC is part of the Hackensack University Health Network, which also includes a physician practice group and a joint venture that operates two community hospitals. In 2016 the network merged with Meridian Health to create Hackensack Meridian Health.

Operations

HUMC helps train future dentists and doctors through its affiliation with the University of Medicine and Dentistry of New Jersey. It expanded its education programs in 2012 by partnering with the Stevens Institute of Technology to offer joint biomedical training programs.

The hospital also performs research through the David Joseph Jurist Research Center for Tomorrow's Children. The center has roughly 475 research programs in operation at any given time.

Financial Performance

Medicare accounts for 29.5% of HUMC's funding; HMOs, 28%; and Blue Cross, 28%.

Strategy

The company grows organically and through acquisitions, partnerships, and affiliations.

To expand its services, HUMC broke ground on a $35 million project to expand and renovate its trauma and emergency facilities in 2012 (scheduled to open in 2015).

Hackensack University Health Network is increasing its partnerships and affiliations with other regional care providers, following the trend of US hospitals seeking to improve and lower the cost of health care through shared services and resources. The network partnered up with Texas-based LPH Hospital Group in 2012 to reenovate the Pascack Valley Hospital (now HackensackUMC Pascack) in Westwood, New Jersey. Hackensack took over the bankrupt facility's ER back in 2007, and in 2012 the joint venture launched a $90 million project to revamp the rest of the 130-bed acute-care community hospital. It reopened in 2013.

Hackensack University Health Network also formed a joint venture with an area physician group to open two ambulatory surgery centers in 2012, and it entered a collaboration with CVS Health's MinuteClinic to open new urgent care centers.

That year HUMC formed a joint venture partnership with community physicians and United Surgical Partners International to buy and operate ambulatory surgery centers in Bergen County: Hackensack Endoscopy Center and the Endoscopy Center of Bergen County.

Mergers and Acquisitions

In 2015 the Hackensack University Health Network agreed to merge with fellow New Jersey care provider Meridian Health. The combined system, to be named Hackensack Meridian Health, will have 11 hospitals and two children's hospitals. The deal, which is one of a number of consolidation efforts by hospitals in the state, is pending regulatory approval.

Company Background

To simplify its operations, HUMC sold its hospice operations to Amedisys in 2011. The health provider previously sold its home health agency to Amedisys in 2009 to generate revenue and control costs after struggling with financial losses throughout the year due to declining admissions.

HUMC completed construction of its new John Theurer Cancer Center in late 2010, giving it one of the largest comprehensive cancer centers in the US. The center includes diagnostic and treatment units that focus on specific types of cancers.

HUMC was founded as a hospital in 1888 with 12 beds.

EXECUTIVES

VPRE*, Ketul J Patel
Auditors : PRICEWATERHOUSECOOPERS LLP NE

LOCATIONS

HQ: HMH HOSPITALS CORPORATION
343 THORNALL ST, EDISON, NJ 088372206
Phone: 201 996-2000

PRODUCTS/OPERATIONS

Selected Services
Donna A. Sanzari Women's Hospital

Emergency Services
Heart & Vascular Hospital
Hospital Services
John Theurer Cancer Center
Joseph M. Sanzari Children's Hospital
Medical
Specialized
Surgical
Tackle Kids Cancer

Selected Facilities
Donna A. Sanzari Women's Hospital
Hackensack University Medical Center Mountainside
Hackensack University Medical Center Pascack
Heart & Vascular Hospital
John Theurer Cancer Center
Joseph M. Sanzari Children's Hospital
   Tomorrows Children's Institute for Cancer and Blood Disorders

COMPETITORS

ATLANTICARE HEALTH SYSTEM INC.
CONTINUUM HEALTH PARTNERS, INC.
HACKENSACK MERIDIAN HEALTH, INC.
KALEIDA HEALTH
KENNEDY HEALTH SYSTEM, INC.
NASSAU HEALTH CARE CORPORATION
NORTHWELL HEALTH, INC.
ORLANDO HEALTH, INC.
TALLAHASSEE MEMORIAL HEALTHCARE, INC.
UNIVERSITY HOSPITALS HEALTH SYSTEM, INC.

HISTORICAL FINANCIALS
Company Type: Private

Income Statement — FYE: December 31

	REVENUE ($mil)	NET INCOME ($mil)	NET PROFIT MARGIN	EMPLOYEES
12/18	3,999	220	5.5%	1,100
12/16	1,707	41	2.4%	—
12/15	1,357	83	6.1%	—
12/14	1,309	106	8.1%	—
Annual Growth	32.2%	19.9%	—	—

2018 Year-End Financials
Return on assets: 5.7%   Cash ($ mil.): 202
Return on equity: 8.6%
Current Ratio: 1.50

HMO MINNESOTA

LOCATIONS

HQ: HMO MINNESOTA
   3535 BLUE CROSS RD, SAINT PAUL, MN 551221154
Phone: 952 456-8434

HISTORICAL FINANCIALS
Company Type: Private

Income Statement — FYE: December 31

	REVENUE ($mil)	NET INCOME ($mil)	NET PROFIT MARGIN	EMPLOYEES
12/16	1,839	(156)	—	51
12/15	918	52	5.7%	—
12/14	850	85	10.1%	—
12/09	978	30	3.1%	—
Annual Growth	9.4%	—	—	—

2016 Year-End Financials
Return on assets: (-18.2%)   Cash ($ mil.): 108
Return on equity: (-36.2%)
Current Ratio: —

HMS HOLDINGS LLC

HMS Holdings is an industry-leading provider of cost containment and analytical solutions in the healthcare marketplace. The company provides solutions such as Coordination of Benefits (COB), Payment Integrity (PI), and Payment Health Management (PHM). Through subsidiary Health Management Systems, the company also assist in identifying third party insurance and recovering medical expenses where a number is involved in a casualty or tort incident. HMS Holdings serves state Medicaid agencies and Children's Health Insurance Programs, as well as federal agencies, health plans and PBMs, healthcare exchanges, employers, at-risk providers and ACOs, and other healthcare organizations.

Operations
HMS generate about 70% of its revenue from Coordination of benefits which derived from contracts with state governments and Medicaid managed care plans. Payment integrity services generate more than 20% of revenue. It is derived from contracts with federal and state governments, commercial health plans and other at-risk entities and the rest comes from population health management.

Geographic Reach
Texas-based, HMS has offices located in Texas, Nevada, Massachusetts, New York, Minnesota, and Ohio. It also has office space in India and Australia.

Sales and Marketing
HMS provide solutions across a broad range of entities within the healthcare industry, including state and federal government agencies, health plans and PBMS, healthcare exchanges, employers, at risk providers and ACOS and other healthcare organization.

Although no customer accounts for 10% or more of revenue, the company's top 10 customers collectively brought in about 40% of revenue.

Financial Performance
In 2020, revenue was $673.3 million, an increase of $46.9 million or 7.5% compared to $626.4 million in 2019. By solution, Coordination of benefits revenue increased $65.1 million or 16.1% largely driven by Accent related revenue of $43.3 million, partially offset by a 6% and 13% decrease in payment integrity and population health management, respectively.

Net income in 2020 decreased by 20% to $70.1 million compared with $87.2 million in 2019.

Cash held by the company at the end of fiscal 2020 increased by $207.1 million. Cash provided by operations was $99.0 million, while investing and financing activities used $29.7 million and $1.4 million, respectively. Main cash uses were Investment in capitalized software and payments of tax withholdings on behalf of employees for net-share settlements.

Strategy
During the fiscal year 2020, HMS' business continued to evolve through a combination of targeted acquisitions and strategic investments. In November 2020, The company made an additional investment in MedAdvisor, an Australian-based digital medication adherence company, reinforcing its strategic relationship and efforts to expand internationally and into new markets.

HMS also believes these factors present growth opportunities for its PHM services. The company is ocused on growing its business over the course of 2021 and beyond, both organically and inorganically, by leveraging existing key assets and pursuing a number of strategic objectives and initiatives, including expanding the scope of its relationship with existing customers; adding new customers; entering new markets for diversification and growth; introducing new innovative solutions and services; utilizing technology tools and innovation; and strategic deployment of capital.

EXECUTIVES

Corporate Secretary, Meredith W Bjorck
Chief Marketing, Maria Perrin
Auditors : GRANT THORNTON LLP DALLAS TE

LOCATIONS

HQ: HMS HOLDINGS LLC
   5615 HIGH POINT DR, IRVING, TX 750382453
Phone: 214 453-3000
Web: WWW.GAINWELLTECHNOLOGIES.COM

PRODUCTS/OPERATIONS

Selected Services
Coordination of Benefits
Customer Service Operations
Eligibility and Enrollment
Healthstone Data Analytics
Pharmacy Services
Program Integrity

COMPETITORS

ALORICA GLOBAL SOLUTIONS, INC.
BILATERAL CREDIT CORP, LLC
COMMERCIAL CLAIMS INC.
CONVERGENT COMMERCIAL, INC.
EXAMWORKS GROUP, INC.
GRANT MERCANTILE AGENCY
IQOR US INC.
MOLINA HEALTHCARE, INC.
PRA GROUP, INC.
UNIVERSAL AMERICAN CORP.

HISTORICAL FINANCIALS
Company Type: Private

Income Statement — FYE: December 31

	REVENUE ($mil)	NET INCOME ($mil)	NET PROFIT MARGIN	EMPLOYEES
12/20	673	70	10.4%	3,100
12/19	626	87	13.9%	—
12/18	598	54	9.2%	—
12/17	521	40	7.7%	—
Annual Growth	8.9%	20.5%	—	—

HOAG MEMORIAL HOSPITAL PRESBYTERIAN

Serving California's Orange County population, Hoag Memorial Hospital Presbyterian boasts several hospitals and even more clinics to cater to area residents. The not-for-profit health care system is home to two acute care hospitals, nine health centers, nearly 15 urgent care centers, and a network of more than 1,700 physicians. Its hospitals include Hoag Hospital Irvine, Hoag Orthopedic Institute and Hoag Hospital Newport Beach in Southern California. Combined, these hospitals have some 600 beds and provide a comprehensive range of medical and surgical services, with specialized expertise in a number of areas, such as cancer, heart and vascular, neurosciences, women's health, and orthopedics.

Operations
As part of its operations, Hoag operates a pair of hospitals ? Hoag Hospital Irvine and Hoag Hospital Newport Beach ? as well as nine health centers located in Aliso Viejo, Costa Mesa, Foothill Ranch, Huntington Beach, Irvine, Tustin, and Newport Beach.

Hoag offers a comprehensive blend of health care services that includes six institutes providing specialized services in the following areas: cancer, heart and vascular, neurosciences, women's health, digestive health and orthopedics through Hoag's affiliate, Hoag Orthopedic Institute.

Hoag Medical Group is a physician group with specialties in Internal Medicine, Family Medicine, Pediatrics, Geriatrics, Diabetes, Endocrinology, Sports Medicine, Rheumatology, Allergy & Immunology, Infectious Disease and HIV Medicine. The group offers same day appointments, provides access to the Hoag network of services and specialists, and accepts most major insurance plans. With approximately 100 allied health members, more than 30,000 inpatients and 450,000 outpatients choose Hoag each year.

Geographic Reach
Based in California, Hoag operates in about 40 locations.

Company Background
In 2013 Hoag formed an affiliation with St. Joseph Health, a Catholic-sponsored health network with operations in three states. The two Hoag hospitals were combined into a new regional network known as Covenant Health Network, which also includes five nearby St. Joseph facilities. The Hoag and St. Joseph facilities retain their independent identities and religious affiliations.

Hoag was Founded in 1952.

LOCATIONS
HQ: HOAG MEMORIAL HOSPITAL PRESBYTERIAN
1 HOAG DR, NEWPORT BEACH, CA 926634162
Phone: 949 764-4624
Web: WWW.HOAG.ORG

COMPETITORS
ASCENSION PROVIDENCE HOSPITAL
ASCENSION SOUTHEAST MICHIGAN
BAPTIST MEMORIAL HEALTH CARE SYSTEM, INC.
BRRH CORPORATION
CALVERTHEALTH MEDICAL CENTER, INC.
PHELPS MEMORIAL HOSPITAL ASSOCIATION
RADY CHILDREN'S HOSPITAL-SAN DIEGO
SADDLEBACK MEMORIAL MEDICAL CENTER
SAINT ELIZABETH REGIONAL MEDICAL CENTER
THE MEMORIAL HOSPITAL

HISTORICAL FINANCIALS
Company Type: Private

Income Statement — FYE: June 30

	REVENUE ($mil)	NET INCOME ($mil)	NET PROFIT MARGIN	EMPLOYEES
06/16	894	100	11.2%	3,800
06/15	822	107	13.1%	—
09/13	784	155	19.8%	—
Annual Growth	4.4%	(13.7%)	—	—

2016 Year-End Financials
Return on assets: 3.0%   Cash ($ mil.): 189
Return on equity: 5.1%
Current Ratio: 1.20

2020 Year-End Financials
Return on assets: 5.3%   Cash ($ mil.): 207
Return on equity: 7.4%
Current Ratio: 4.90

HOBBY LOBBY STORES, INC.

Hobby Lobby is the largest privately-owned arts-and-crafts retailer in the world. The craft-and-fabric company operates more than 900 stores in more than 45 US states. It is primarily an arts-and-crafts store but also includes hobbies, picture framing, jewelry making, fabrics, floral and wedding supplies, cards and party ware, baskets, wearable art, home decor and holiday merchandise. Hobby Lobby also maintains offices in Hong Kong, Shenzhen, and Yiwu, China. In addition, the company operates Mardel Christian and Education Supply, which sells Christian, educational, and homeschooling products. CEO David Green, who owns the company, founded Hobby Lobby in 1972 and operates it according to biblical principles, including closing shop on Sunday.

Operations
Hobby Lobby offers more than 70,000 items featuring home decor, seasonal decor, tableware, floral, art supplies, craft supplies, yarn, fabric, jewelry making, and hobbies, among others. The company works with trusted brands, such as DMC, Vintaj, Crayola, Revell, Tim Holtz, and more. Its affiliate company, Mardel Christian and Education Supply, offers books, Bibles, gifts, church and education supplies as well as homeschooling curriculum.

Geographic Reach
Hobby Lobby's headquarters include more than 10 million-square-feet of manufacturing, distribution, and an office complex in Oklahoma City.

LOCATIONS
HQ: HOBBY LOBBY STORES, INC.
7707 SW 44TH ST, OKLAHOMA CITY, OK 731794899
Phone: 405 745-1100
Web: WWW.HOBBYLOBBY.COM

PRODUCTS/OPERATIONS

Selected Products
Arts and crafts supplies
Baskets
Candles
Cards
Furniture
Home accent pieces
Jewelry-making supplies
Needlework
Party supplies
Picture frames and framing
Scrapbooking supplies
Seasonal items
Sewing materials (fabric, patterns, notions)
Silk flowers
Toys
Wearable art

Selected Affiliates
Hemispheres (home furnishings and accessories stores)
Mardel Christian Office & Educational Supply (Christian materials, office supplies, and educational products)

COMPETITORS
A.C. MOORE ARTS & CRAFTS, INC.
AMERICAN GIRL BRANDS, LLC
ANN SUMMERS LTD.
BUILD-A-BEAR WORKSHOP, INC.
DREAMS, INC.
EUROMARKET DESIGNS, INC.
LIFETIME PRODUCTS INC.
NORTHERN TOOL & EQUIPMENT COMPANY, INC.
THE MICHAELS COMPANIES INC
TOYS "R" US LIMITED

HISTORICAL FINANCIALS
Company Type: Private

Income Statement — FYE: December 31

	REVENUE ($mil)	NET INCOME ($mil)	NET PROFIT MARGIN	EMPLOYEES
12/17	4,544	352	7.8%	23,000
12/06	196	58	29.5%	—
12/04	1,363	88	6.5%	—
12/03	150	58	39.0%	—
Annual Growth	27.5%	13.7%	—	—

2017 Year-End Financials
Return on assets: 11.2%   Cash ($ mil.): —
Return on equity: 20.8%
Current Ratio: 2.10

HOLY CROSS HEALTH, INC.

LOCATIONS

HQ: HOLY CROSS HEALTH, INC.
1500 FOREST GLEN RD, SILVER SPRING, MD 209101460
Phone: 301 754-7000
Web: WWW.HOLYCROSSHEALTH.ORG

HISTORICAL FINANCIALS
Company Type: Private

Income Statement — FYE: June 30

	REVENUE ($mil)	NET INCOME ($mil)	NET PROFIT MARGIN	EMPLOYEES
06/20	628	48	7.7%	3,270
06/18	561	43	7.7%	—
06/16	434	28	6.6%	—
Annual Growth	9.7%	13.9%	—	—

2020 Year-End Financials
Return on assets: 4.7%
Return on equity: 10.2%
Current Ratio: 1.30
Cash ($ mil.): —

HONORHEALTH

Auditors: ERNST & YOUNG US LLP PHOENIX

LOCATIONS

HQ: HONORHEALTH
8125 N HAYDEN RD, SCOTTSDALE, AZ 852582463
Phone: 480 324-7215
Web: WWW.HONORHEALTH.COM

HISTORICAL FINANCIALS
Company Type: Private

Income Statement — FYE: December 31

	REVENUE ($mil)	NET INCOME ($mil)	NET PROFIT MARGIN	EMPLOYEES
12/17	1,817	44	2.5%	14,000
12/14*	900	25	2.9%	—
09/09	847	4	0.5%	—
09/08	812	(17)	—	—
Annual Growth	9.4%	—	—	—

*Fiscal year change

2017 Year-End Financials
Return on assets: 2.1%
Return on equity: 3.9%
Current Ratio: —
Cash ($ mil.): 96

HOOSIER ENERGY RURAL ELECTRIC COOPERATIVE INC

Who's yer daddy? In terms of providing electricity, for many Indianans (and some residents of Illinois) that would be Hoosier Energy Rural Electric Cooperative, which provides wholesale electric power to 18 member distribution cooperatives in 59 central and southern Indiana counties, and 11 counties in southeastern Illinois. These electric cooperatives serve 300,000 consumers (650,000 residents, businesses, industries and farms) in a 18,000 sq. ml. service area. Hoosier Energy operates six power plants and a 1,720-mile transmission system, and maintains the Tuttle Creek Reservoir in Southwest Indiana. Hoosier Energy is part of the Touchstone Energy network of electric cooperatives.

Operations
Hoosier Energy operates coal-, natural gas-, and renewable energy-generation plants. It delivers electricity via a 1,720-mile transmission network, including 21 major substations, and more than 350 delivery points.

Geographic Reach
The company delivers power to member distribution cooperatives in central and southern Indiana and southeastern Illinois.

Financial Performance
In 2013 the power coop's revenues increased by 3% due to higher member revenues and increased sales of electricity. Net income grew by 1% as the result of higher revenues and slight decrease in maintenance costs.

Strategy
To advance its push for more renewable sources Hoosier Energy is pursuing cost-effective generating projects and supply contracts including the Clark-Floyd Landfill Methane Generation plant, which has four landfill/coal bed methane projects and which has purchased power agreements for wind and hydropower. These measures are expected to provide 7% of member energy sales annually.

Its recent capital projects include a $400 million multi-year upgrade of the Merom Station, investing $18 million in power delivery projects to support growth and reliability, and continuing progress toward renewable energy goals with the commercial operation of the Osprey Point coalbed methane plant, and the Livingston landfill-methane plant.

Company Background
In 2011 the coop was operating a 2.5 MW landfill methane generation facility in addition to buying 25 MW of wind energy.

Expanding its geographic coverage, in 2011 Hoosier Energy began to supply power to the Wayne-White Counties Electric Cooperative, when that coop's contract with an independent power supplier ended. The distribution coop serves 13,500 residential, farm, and business consumers in 11 counties in southeastern Illinois.

Hoosier Energy was formed in 1948 as part of the nationwide rural electrification drive initiated by the Roosevelt administration in the 1930s.

Auditors: DELOITTE & TOUCHE LLP INDIAN

LOCATIONS

HQ: HOOSIER ENERGY RURAL ELECTRIC COOPERATIVE INC
2501 S COOPERATIVE WAY, BLOOMINGTON, IN 474035175
Phone: 812 876-2021
Web: WWW.HOOSIERENERGY.COM

PRODUCTS/OPERATIONS

2012 Sales

	$ mil.	% of total
Members	532.5	82
Nonmembers	115.2	18
Other	0.2	-
Total	647.9	100

Member Cooperatives
Bartholomew County REMC
Clark County REMC
Decatur County REMC
Daviess-Martin County REMC
Dubois REC, Inc.
Harrison REMC
Henry County REMC
Jackson County REMC
Johnson County REMC
Orange County REMC
RushShelby Energy
South Central Indiana REMC
Southeastern Indiana REMC
Southern Indiana Power
Utilities District of Western Indiana REMC
Wayne-White Counties Electric Cooperative
WIN Energy REMC
Whitewater Valley REMC

COMPETITORS

ALLETE, INC.
ARKANSAS ELECTRIC COOPERATIVE CORPORATION
ASSOCIATED ELECTRIC COOPERATIVE, INC.
DAIRYLAND POWER COOPERATIVE
GREAT RIVER ENERGY
POWERSOUTH ENERGY COOPERATIVE
SALT RIVER PROJECT AGRICULTURAL IMPROVEMENT AND POWER DISTRICT
SEMINOLE ELECTRIC COOPERATIVE, INC.
THE SOUTHERN COMPANY
WESTERN FARMERS ELECTRIC COOPERATIVE

HISTORICAL FINANCIALS
Company Type: Private

Income Statement — FYE: December 31

	REVENUE ($mil)	NET INCOME ($mil)	NET PROFIT MARGIN	EMPLOYEES
12/12	647	27	4.3%	475
12/11	649	30	4.7%	—
12/09	575	16	2.9%	—
Annual Growth	4.1%	18.9%	—	—

2012 Year-End Financials
Return on assets: 1.6% Cash ($ mil.): 50
Return on equity: 11.0%
Current Ratio: 1.50

HORRY COUNTY SCHOOL DISTRICT

Auditors : MCGREGOR & COMPANY LLP COLUM

LOCATIONS

HQ: HORRY COUNTY SCHOOL DISTRICT
335 FOUR MILE RD, CONWAY, SC 295264506
Phone: 843 488-6700
Web: WWW.HORRYCOUNTYSCHOOLS.NET

HISTORICAL FINANCIALS
Company Type: Private

Income Statement — FYE: June 30

	REVENUE ($mil)	NET INCOME ($mil)	NET PROFIT MARGIN	EMPLOYEES
06/21	663	20	3.0%	5,000
06/19	585	(8)	—	—
06/18	548	(42)	—	—
06/17	520	(140)	—	—
Annual Growth	6.3%	—	—	—

2021 Year-End Financials
Return on assets: 1.4% Cash ($ mil.): 294
Return on equity: —
Current Ratio: —

HOSPITAL OF THE UNIVERSITY OF PENNSYLVANIA

LOCATIONS

HQ: HOSPITAL OF THE UNIVERSITY OF PENNSYLVANIA
3400 SPRUCE ST OFC, PHILADELPHIA, PA 191044208
Phone: 215 662-4000
Web: WWW.PENNMEDICINE.ORG

HISTORICAL FINANCIALS
Company Type: Private

Income Statement — FYE: June 30

	REVENUE ($mil)	NET INCOME ($mil)	NET PROFIT MARGIN	EMPLOYEES
06/16	2,236	283	12.7%	2,737
06/15	2,164	320	14.8%	—
Annual Growth	3.3%	(11.5%)	—	—

2016 Year-End Financials
Return on assets: 9.3% Cash ($ mil.): 1,091
Return on equity: 13.2%
Current Ratio: 9.90

HOUCHENS INDUSTRIES, INC.

Houchens Industries is listed by Forbes as one of the largest 100% employee-owned companies in the world. The diversified company runs more than 300 retail grocery, convenience, and neighborhood markets across around 15 US states. That includes grocery and convenience stores under the Houchens, Crossroads Express, Food Giant, IGA, Price Less, Shell Fuel & Convenience, and Save-A-Lot banners. In addition, Houchens' diversified portfolio includes retail, insurance, manufacturing, construction, restaurant, utilities, and fast food, among others. Houchens was originally founded in Glasgow, Kentucky by Ervin G. Houchens in 1917 as Houchens Foods.

Operations
Houchens operates about 25 companies, including Cohen's Fashion Optical, Food Giant, IGA, Save-a-Lot, and more. It also operates about 10 franchises such as Schlotzsky's, Cinnabon, Carvel, Ace, and Subway to name a few.

The company's manufacturing businesses include Stephens Pipe & Steel, a leading maker and distributor of fence materials.

Geographic Reach
Based in Kentucky, Houchens operates more than 300 retail grocery, convenience, and neighborhood market stores across around 15 states.

Mergers and Acquisitions
In early 2021, Houchens acquired Lee Masonry Products, and subsequent merger of the existing Lee Masonry ESOP into the Houchens ESOP. Lee Masonry is a manufacturer of concrete block and specialty concrete products and a distributor of clay masonry products for commercial and residential use.

Company Background
Founded by Ervin Houchens as BG Wholesale in rural Kentucky in 1917, Houchens has been owned by its employees since 1988.

Auditors : BKD LLP BOWLING GREN KENTUC

LOCATIONS

HQ: HOUCHENS INDUSTRIES, INC.
700 CHURCH ST, BOWLING GREEN, KY 421011816
Phone: 270 843-3252
Web: WWW.HOUCHENS.COM

PRODUCTS/OPERATIONS

Selected Operations
American Sun Systems (tanning salon supplier)
Blake, Hart Taylor & Wiseman (insurance)
Buehler's Buy Low (grocery retail)
Cohen's Fashion Optical (optical stores)
Food Giant (grocery retail)
Hilliard Lyons (financial services)
Houchens Markets (grocery retail)
IGA (licensed, grocery retail)
Insurance Specialists (insurance)
Jr. Food Stores (convenience stores)
Price Less Foods (grocery retail)
Save-A-Lot (licensed, grocery retail)
Scotty's (asphalt paving)
Sheldon's Express Pharmacy (drugstores)
Southern Recycling Inc. (recycling)
Stewart-Richey Construction, Inc. (construction management)
Taco Del Mar (fast-food)
Tampico (juice)
TS Trucking (hauling)
Van Meter Insurance (insurance, benefits)
White's Fresh Foods (grocery retail)

COMPETITORS

CENTRAL GROCERS, INC.
DIERBERGS MARKETS, INC.
GROCERY OUTLET INC.
KUM & GO, L.C.
SCHNUCK MARKETS, INC.
SHOPPERS FOOD WAREHOUSE CORP.
STEWART'S SHOPS CORP.
THE FRESH MARKET INC
UNITED SUPERMARKETS, L.L.C.
URM STORES, INC.

HISTORICAL FINANCIALS
Company Type: Private

Income Statement — FYE: October 1

	REVENUE ($mil)	NET INCOME ($mil)	NET PROFIT MARGIN	EMPLOYEES
10/16	2,987	104	3.5%	16,000
10/15	3,212	99	3.1%	—
Annual Growth	(7.0%)	4.1%	—	—

2016 Year-End Financials
Return on assets: 5.3% Cash ($ mil.): 259
Return on equity: 8.0%
Current Ratio: 2.00

HOUGHTON MIFFLIN HARCOURT COMPANY

Houghton Mifflin Harcourt Company (HMH) is a leading provider of Kindergarten through 12th grade (K-12) core curriculum, supplemental and intervention solutions, and professional learning services, HMH partners with educators and school districts to uncover solutions that unlock students' potential and extend teachers' capabilities. HMH estimates that it serves more than 50 million students and three million educators in about 150 countries. The company specializes in comprehensive core curriculum, supplemental and intervention solutions, and provides ongoing support in professional learning and coaching for educators and administrators. In 2021, HMH completed the sales of HMH Books & Media segment, its consumer publishing business. HMH generates most of its revenue in the US.

IPO
In late 2013 the company launched an IPO, and most of the $219 million in proceeds it earned went to its shareholders.

Bankruptcy

HMH filed for Chapter 11 bankruptcy protection in May 2012 and emerged a few months later. Houghton Mifflin was stung by the ill effects of the global financial crisis, which caused massive spending cuts in the US school budget, its main market. Education accounts for about 90% of the company's revenues, and struggling state and local governments had been forced to cut back on education-related purchases, causing HMH to file for Chapter 11.

Operations

HMH offers its products and services through Core Solutions and Extensions.

The core solutions offerings include education programs in disciplines including Reading, Literature, Math, Science and Social Studies that serve as primary sources of classroom instruction and accounts for more than 50% of total revenue.

Its extensions offerings include supplemental solutions, intervention solutions, professional services, and our Heinemann brand that provides professional resources and educational services for teachers. Extensions account for about 50% of total revenue.

Geographic Reach

Headquartered in Boston, Massachusetts, HMH operates over 130,000 school districts in some 150 countries. The company also has several offices and warehouse located in Florida, Illinois, New Hampshire, New York, Texas and Ireland.

The US generates about 95% of HMH's total revenue.

Sales and Marketing

The company operates predominantly within the US K-12 education market. The US education market comprises of approximately 13,000 K-12 public school districts, 130,000 public and private schools, more than 3.7 million teachers and 56.4 million total student enrollment across public, private and charter schools.

Internationally, the company exports and sells K-12 English language education products to premium private schools that utilize the US curriculum, who are located primarily in Asia, the Pacific, the Middle East, Latin America, the Caribbean and Africa.

HMH's advertising costs were $0.7 million, $1.1 million and $1.3 million for the years 2021, 2020 and 2019, respectively.

Financial Performance

Net sales in 2021 increased $210.3 million, or 25.0%, from $840.5 million in 2020 to $1,050.8 million. Core Solutions increased by $91.0 million from $459.0 million in 2020 to $550.0 million, driven by strong open territory demand resulting from the strength of its connected solutions and the continued market recovery, as well as the success of its digital first, connected strategy. Further, net sales in Extensions, consisting of its Heinemann brand, intervention and supplemental products as well as professional services, increased by $120.0 million from $381.0 million in 2020 to $501.0 million. Within Extensions, net sales of its Heinemann products increased due to strong demand across most product portfolios.

Net income in 2021 was $213.6 million compared to a net loss of $479.8 million in the prior year.

Cash held by the company at the end of fiscal 2021 increased to $463.1 million. Operating and investing activities contributed $267.7 million and $249.6 million, respectively. Financing activities used $335.4 million, mainly for payments of long-term debt.

HISTORY

In 1848 printer Henry Houghton bought part of a printing company started in 1832. The company acquired other printers' booklists, but by 1880 it was deep in debt. George Mifflin became a partner, and the company, then known as Houghton Osgood, became Houghton Mifflin. In the following decades the bookmaker prospered primarily on the strength of its nonfiction trade and educational lines.

Houghton Mifflin's sales from the 1950s to the 1970s followed the curve of the baby boom, from elementary and high school to college publishing. In the 1980s and 1990s, the company moved to strengthen its position in the education market, acquiring Rand McNally's education unit (1980) and textbook publishers McDougal, Littell & Co. (1994) and D.C. Heath (1995).

The costs of the acquisitions, a failed attempt to outsource distribution, and disarray in the trade book area sent Houghton Mifflin into the red in 1995. However, the consolidation of Heath paid off in 1996, as sales and earnings rebounded. Acquisitions continued in 1997 (cookbook imprint Chapters Publishing) and 1998 (Pearson's Discovery Works unit).

In 1998 Houghton Mifflin took an interest in OnlineLearning.net (distance learning) and acquired Computer Adaptive Technologies, a producer of computer-based testing materials. Strengthening its new media education lines, the company bought video and software developer Sunburst Communications in 1999.

Houghton Mifflin increased its online presence in 2000 with the acquisition of Internet testing company Virtual Learning Technologies and through several strategic agreements. The next year the company was acquired for $2.2 billion (including the assumption of $500 million in debt) by French conglomerate Vivendi Universal (now just Vivendi). Houghton Mifflin was placed under Vivendi Universal's publishing unit, which in 2002 decided to sell off most of its assets as part of Vivendi Universal's $9.8 billion divestiture. A group of investors (including affiliates of Thomas H. Lee and Bain Capital) bought Houghton Mifflin that year for some $2 billion.

In 2002 the publisher settled a dispute with the estate of Margaret Mitchell over the book The Wind Done Gone, a retelling of the historical bestseller Gone With the Wind from a slave's point of view. That year Hans Gieskes, formerly chairman of Monster.com, replaced Nader Darehshori as CEO of the company. The company was sold to two investment firms in 2002. Gieskes left the company in 2003.

Anthony Lucki took over as CEO. In 2006 the company was sold to a new parent company (which later became Education Media Publishing Group), for some $5 billion. The following year Houghton Mifflin acquired several Harcourt brands to form Houghton Mifflin Harcourt Publishing Company.

Harcourt traces its roots to 1919, when Alfred Harcourt and Donald Brace, former classmates at Columbia University, quit their jobs at Henry Holt & Co. and joined Will Howe to begin their own publishing firm in New York called Harcourt, Brace and Howe. Howe left after less than a year and the name became Harcourt, Brace and Co. The company published such notable works as The Economic Consequences of Peace by John Maynard Keynes and Main Street and Arrowsmith by Sinclair Lewis. During the 1920s, Harcourt, Brace diversified into religious works and high school and college textbooks. Harcourt turned the company over to Brace in 1942.

William Jovanovich, who had joined the company as a salesman, became president of the firm in 1955 following the deaths of Harcourt (1954) and Brace (1955). (Jovanovich died in 2001). The company merged with World Book Company in 1960 to become the largest publisher of educational materials in the US. Renamed Harcourt, Brace & World, Inc., the company went public that year. Jovanovich became chairman in 1970. Renamed Harcourt Brace Jovanovich (HBJ), the company continued its acquisition spree throughout the 1970s and 1980s, buying The Psychological Corporation in 1970 and Sea World in 1976 (sold in 1989). Jovanovich retired as chairman in 1990. In 1991 General Cinema acquired HBJ.

Movie-theater pioneer General Cinema was founded in 1922 as Philip Smith Theatrical Enterprises. Smith's son Richard became CEO in 1961 and renamed the company in 1964. GC bought 37% of Carter Hawley Hale in 1984, which owned the Neiman Marcus Group (founded 1907). Three years later GC traded its interest in Carter Hawley for a 44% stake in the retailer. After buying HBJ, General Cinema was renamed Harcourt General in 1993 and spun off its theaters as GC Companies. (GC was bought by rival AMC Entertainment in 2002.)

In 1995 Harcourt General acquired Assessment Systems, a provider of computerized testing and licensing services. Two years later it bought National Education Corporation for about $854 million, topping a bid from Sylvan Learning Systems. Also in 1997 it became a majority owner of Steck-Vaughn, but the acquisition put Harcourt into the red that year. In early 1998 the company bought the remaining 18% stake in Steck-Vaughn it didn't already own for $42.8 million. It also paid $415 million for Mosby, Inc., the health sciences unit of Times Mirror (later acquired by rival Tribune).

In 1999 Harcourt expanded its professional development titles by buying Knowledge Communication, which it merged into Drake Beam Morin. Later the company spun off most of its stake in Neiman Marcus, retaining a 10% interest. Smith stepped down as CEO, turning those duties over to his son, Robert, and son-in-law, Brian Knez.

Dutch legal and medical publishing giant Reed Elsevier bought Harcourt in 2001 and sold some of its businesses (such as its higher education and corporate training operations) to Thomson Learning to alleviate antitrust concerns. Reed Elsevier later changed the company's name from Harcourt General to Harcourt Education. In 2003 the company cut several hundred jobs through layoffs and early retirement citing a difficult business climate.

Following the tough times, the publisher began to gain its stride and strengthened its operations with acquisitions such as Saxon Publishing in 2004 and UK-based textbook publisher Payne-Gallway in 2005. In 2004 the company changed the name of its Harcourt Supplemental Education unit to Harcourt Achieve.

Educational publisher Houghton Mifflin purchased several Harcourt brands from Reed Elsevier to form Houghton Mifflin Harcourt in 2007. The deal included the acquisition of US-based text book publishing giant Harcourt Education, as well as the Harcourt Trade Publishers and Greenwood-Heinemann (now Heinemann) businesses, for some $4 billion. Houghton Mifflin's purchase of the Harcourt brands formed a leader in the US education publishing market. (In tandem with this deal, Reed Elsevier sold its international education publishing business Harcourt Education Ltd. to education firm Pearson for some for $950 million.)

Reflecting a slowdown in book sales, in 2008 the company briefly stopped acquiring new manuscripts in its consumer books division. The move, unusual in the publishing industry, was a result of an overall slump in the global economy. Also in 2008 Houghton Mifflin streamlined operations when it sold its College Division for $750 million in cash to Cengage Learning (formerly Thomson Learning) in order to focus on K-12, trade, and reference titles.

Education Media Publishing Group head Barry O'Callaghan replaced Lucki as CEO of the company in 2009 following a financial restructuring. O'Callaghan resigned from the position in 2011. The following year Houghton Mifflin filed for bankruptcy.

EXECUTIVES

CRO, Michael E Evans
CPO, Alejandro Reyes
Auditors : PRICEWATERHOUSECOOPERS LLP BO

LOCATIONS

HQ: HOUGHTON MIFFLIN HARCOURT COMPANY
125 HIGH ST STE 900, BOSTON, MA 021102777
Phone: 617 351-5000
Web: IR.HMHCO.COM

2016 Sales

	$mil	%of total
United States	1,284.6	94
International	88.1	6
Total	1,372.7	100

PRODUCTS/OPERATIONS

2016 Sales

	% of total
Education	88
Trade Publishing	12
Total	100

Selected Divisions
Classroom Connect (online instructional materials for K-12 school districts)
Heinemann (materials for teachers)
Houghton Mifflin Harcourt International Publishers (foreign sales)
Hold, Rinehart and Winston (textbooks)
Houghton Mifflin Harcourt Trade and Reference Publishers (fiction, nonfiction, and reference titles)
The Learning Company (educational software brands)
Riverdeep (interactive educational and personal publishing products)
Riverside Publishing (professional testing products)
Steck-Vaughn (educational materials)
Holt McDougal
Classwell Learning Group
Edusoft And Advanced Learning

COMPETITORS

AMERICAN EDUCATIONAL PRODUCTS LLC
JOHN WILEY & SONS, INC.
PARTYLITE WORLDWIDE, LLC
PEARSON PLC
RELX GROUP PLC
REMGRO LTD
SCHOOL ZONE PUBLISHING COMPANY
THE BELLEEK POTTERY LIMITED
THE YANKEE CANDLE COMPANY INC
WMS INDUSTRIES INC

HISTORICAL FINANCIALS
Company Type: Private

Income Statement   FYE: December 31

	REVENUE ($mil)	NET INCOME ($mil)	NET PROFIT MARGIN	EMPLOYEES
12/21	1,050	213	20.3%	2,300
12/20	1,031	(479)	—	—
12/19	1,390	(213)	—	—
12/18	1,322	(94)	—	—
Annual Growth	(7.4%)	—	—	—

2021 Year-End Financials
Return on assets: 10.8%   Cash ($ mil.): 463
Return on equity: 64.6%
Current Ratio: 1.40

HOUSING DEVELOPMENT AUTHORITY, MICHIGAN STATE

EXECUTIVES

Vice Chairman*, Bernard Glieberman
Auditors : PLANTE & MORAN PLLC EAST LAN

LOCATIONS

HQ: HOUSING DEVELOPMENT AUTHORITY, MICHIGAN STATE
735 E MICHIGAN AVE, LANSING, MI 489121474
Phone: 517 373-8370
Web: WWW.MICHIGAN.GOV

HISTORICAL FINANCIALS
Company Type: Private

Income Statement   FYE: June 30

	REVENUE ($mil)	NET INCOME ($mil)	NET PROFIT MARGIN	EMPLOYEES
06/22	1,457	20	1.4%	320
06/21	875	35	4.1%	—
06/20	701	26	3.7%	—
06/19	684	25	3.7%	—
Annual Growth	28.6%	(7.7%)	—	—

2022 Year-End Financials
Return on assets: 0.4%   Cash ($ mil.): 506
Return on equity: 2.5%
Current Ratio: —

HOUSTON INDEPENDENT SCHOOL DISTRICT

EXECUTIVES

Interim Chief Financial Officer*, Glenn Reed
Interim CAO*, Yolanda Rodriguez
Auditors : WEAVER AND TIDWELL LLP HO

LOCATIONS

HQ: HOUSTON INDEPENDENT SCHOOL DISTRICT
4400 W 18TH ST, HOUSTON, TX 770928501
Phone: 713 556-6000
Web: WWW.HOUSTONISD.ORG

HISTORICAL FINANCIALS
Company Type: Private

Income Statement				FYE: June 30
	REVENUE ($mil)	NET INCOME ($mil)	NET PROFIT MARGIN	EMPLOYEES
06/21	2,846	(7)	—	22,440
06/20	2,699	(131)	—	—
06/18	2,695	(250)	—	—
06/17	2,329	(39)	—	—
Annual Growth	5.1%	—	—	—

2021 Year-End Financials
Return on assets: (-0.1%) Cash ($ mil.): 4
Return on equity: (-0.4%)
Current Ratio: —

HOUSTON METHODIST ST. JOHN HOSPITAL

Auditors : DELOITTE & TOUCHE LLP HOUSTO

LOCATIONS

HQ: HOUSTON METHODIST ST. JOHN HOSPITAL
18300 HOUSTON METHDST DR, HOUSTON, TX 770586302
Phone: 281 333-5503
Web: WWW.HOUSTONMETHODIST.ORG

HISTORICAL FINANCIALS
Company Type: Private

Income Statement				FYE: December 31
	REVENUE ($mil)	NET INCOME ($mil)	NET PROFIT MARGIN	EMPLOYEES
12/20	5,302	870	16.4%	4
12/19	5,225	1,275	24.4%	—
12/17	3,887	681	17.5%	—
12/16	3,746	338	9.0%	—
Annual Growth	9.1%	26.7%	—	—

2020 Year-End Financials
Return on assets: 6.9% Cash ($ mil.): 995
Return on equity: 9.8%
Current Ratio: 1.20

HOWARD COUNTY OF MARYLAND (INC)

EXECUTIVES

County Executive, Calvin Ball
Chief Administrator*, Raquel Sanodo
Deputy Chief of Staff, Candace Dodson-reed
Auditors : CLIFTONLARSONALLEN LLP BALTIM

LOCATIONS

HQ: HOWARD COUNTY OF MARYLAND (INC)
3430 COURT HOUSE DR, ELLICOTT CITY, MD 210434300
Phone: 410 313-2195
Web: WWW.HOWARDCOUNTYMD.GOV

HISTORICAL FINANCIALS
Company Type: Private

Income Statement				FYE: June 30
	REVENUE ($mil)	NET INCOME ($mil)	NET PROFIT MARGIN	EMPLOYEES
06/22	1,665	4	0.3%	3,463
06/21	1,588	218	13.7%	—
06/19	1,335	(25)	—	—
06/18	1,298	76	5.9%	—
Annual Growth	6.4%	(50.6%)	—	—

2022 Year-End Financials
Return on assets: 0.1% Cash ($ mil.): 7
Return on equity: 0.2%
Current Ratio: —

HPS LLC

EXECUTIVES

Managing Member, Matt Thompson
Auditors : MEYNARD TOLMAN & VENLET PC

LOCATIONS

HQ: HPS LLC
3275 N M 37 HWY, MIDDLEVILLE, MI 493339126
Phone: 269 795-3308
Web: WWW.HPSGPO.COM

HISTORICAL FINANCIALS
Company Type: Private

Income Statement				FYE: June 30
	REVENUE ($mil)	NET INCOME ($mil)	NET PROFIT MARGIN	EMPLOYEES
06/19	899	0	0.1%	38
06/18	782	0	0.1%	—
06/16	1,032	0	0.1%	—
06/15	960	0	0.1%	—
Annual Growth	(1.6%)	(4.7%)	—	—

2019 Year-End Financials
Return on assets: 4.0% Cash ($ mil.): 4
Return on equity: 5.3%
Current Ratio: 2.00

HUMBLE INDEPENDENT SCHOOL DISTRICT

Auditors : WHITLEY PENN LLP HOUSTON TEX

LOCATIONS

HQ: HUMBLE INDEPENDENT SCHOOL DISTRICT
10203 BIRCHRIDGE DR, HUMBLE, TX 773382200
Phone: 281 641-1000
Web: WWW.HUMBLE.K12.TX.US

HISTORICAL FINANCIALS
Company Type: Private

Income Statement				FYE: June 30
	REVENUE ($mil)	NET INCOME ($mil)	NET PROFIT MARGIN	EMPLOYEES
06/21	612	63	10.4%	5,000
06/20	559	90	16.1%	—
06/19	546	132	24.3%	—
06/18	490	(67)	—	—
Annual Growth	7.7%	—	—	—

2021 Year-End Financials
Return on assets: 4.1% Cash ($ mil.): —
Return on equity: 82.2%
Current Ratio: —

HUNTER ROBERTS CONSTRUCTION GROUP LLC

EXECUTIVES

OF Purchasing*, Tim Dillon
NY*, Paul Andersen
Auditors : GRASSI & CO JERICHO NEW YOR

LOCATIONS

HQ: HUNTER ROBERTS CONSTRUCTION GROUP LLC
55 WATER ST FL 51, NEW YORK, NY 100413201
Phone: 212 321-6800
Web: WWW.HRCG.COM

HISTORICAL FINANCIALS
Company Type: Private

Income Statement				FYE: December 31
	REVENUE ($mil)	NET INCOME ($mil)	NET PROFIT MARGIN	EMPLOYEES
12/13	762	3	0.4%	260
12/12	706	1	0.2%	—
12/10	458	7	1.7%	—
Annual Growth	18.4%	(26.8%)	—	—

2013 Year-End Financials
Return on assets: 1.4% Cash ($ mil.): 61
Return on equity: 6.4%
Current Ratio: 1.20

HUNTINGTON HOSPITAL

LOCATIONS

HQ: HUNTINGTON HOSPITAL
100 W CALIFORNIA BLVD, PASADENA, CA 911053010
Phone: 626 397-5000
Web: WWW.HUNTINGTONHOSPITAL.ORG

HISTORICAL FINANCIALS
Company Type: Private

Income Statement — FYE: December 31

	REVENUE ($mil)	NET INCOME ($mil)	NET PROFIT MARGIN	EMPLOYEES
12/17	654	15	2.3%	3,500
12/16	646	6	0.9%	—
12/15	551	3	0.7%	—
12/14	513	1	0.4%	—
Annual Growth	8.4%	102.0%	—	—

2017 Year-End Financials
Return on assets: 1.7%   Cash ($ mil.): 11
Return on equity: 2.6%
Current Ratio: 3.30

HUNTSVILLE HOSPITAL HEALTH SYSTEM

LOCATIONS

HQ: HUNTSVILLE HOSPITAL HEALTH SYSTEM
101 SIVLEY RD SW, HUNTSVILLE, AL 358014470
Phone: 256 265-1000
Web: WWW.HUNTSVILLEHOSPITAL.ORG

HISTORICAL FINANCIALS
Company Type: Private

Income Statement — FYE: June 30

	REVENUE ($mil)	NET INCOME ($mil)	NET PROFIT MARGIN	EMPLOYEES
06/16	864	98	11.4%	143
06/15	799	100	12.6%	—
Annual Growth	8.1%	(2.4%)	—	—

2016 Year-End Financials
Return on assets: 7.0%   Cash ($ mil.): 186
Return on equity: 9.7%
Current Ratio: 2.10

HUNTSVILLE UTILITIES

Auditors: JACKSON THORNTON & CO PC FRA

LOCATIONS

HQ: HUNTSVILLE UTILITIES
112 SPRAGINS ST NW, HUNTSVILLE, AL 358014902
Phone: 256 535-1200
Web: WWW.HSVUTIL.ORG

HISTORICAL FINANCIALS
Company Type: Private

Income Statement — FYE: September 30

	REVENUE ($mil)	NET INCOME ($mil)	NET PROFIT MARGIN	EMPLOYEES
09/21	643	67	10.5%	634
09/20	604	36	6.1%	—
09/19	629	32	5.1%	—
09/18	525	18	3.6%	—
Annual Growth	7.0%	53.2%	—	—

2021 Year-End Financials
Return on assets: 5.9%   Cash ($ mil.): 62
Return on equity: 10.0%
Current Ratio: 2.90

HURON HEALTH CARE CENTER, INC

LOCATIONS

HQ: HURON HEALTH CARE CENTER, INC
1920 CLEVELAND RD W, HURON, OH 448391211
Phone: 419 433-4990

HISTORICAL FINANCIALS
Company Type: Private

Income Statement — FYE: December 31

	REVENUE ($mil)	NET INCOME ($mil)	NET PROFIT MARGIN	EMPLOYEES
12/09	584	58	10.0%	45
12/98	3	0	0.0%	—
12/97	3	3	97.8%	—
12/96	3	0	0.0%	—
Annual Growth	48.0%	—	—	—

2009 Year-End Financials
Return on assets: 999.9%   Cash ($ mil.): —
Return on equity: 999.9%
Current Ratio: 2.20

HY-VEE, INC.

Hy-Vee is one of the largest privately-owned US supermarket chains, despite serving some modestly sized towns in the Midwest. The company runs more than 280 stores in eight Midwestern states. It distributes products to its stores through several subsidiaries, including Amber Pharmacy, D & D Foods, Florist Distributing, Hy-Vee Construction, Midwest Heritage, Perishable Distributors of Iowa, and Vivid Clear RX. Hy-Vee is synonymous with quality, variety, convenience, healthy lifestyles, culinary expertise and superior customer service. Charles Hyde and David Vredenburg founded the employee-owned company in 1930. It takes its name from a combination of its founders' names.

Operations

Hy-Vee offers beverages, fresh, frozen, health and beauty, household and laundry, ready to go meals, pastries, cakes, and baby products. Through its subsidiaries, Hy-Vee established a distribution system that secures the highest quality merchandise and transports its products quickly and efficiently to its customers.

Geographic Reach

Iowa-based, Hy-Vee operates more than 280 retail stores in Illinois, Iowa, Kansas, Minnesota, Missouri, Nebraska, South Dakota, and Wisconsin. The company has distribution centers in Chariton, Iowa, and Cherokee, Iowa, with a third perishable operation in Ankeny, Iowa.

Sales and Marketing

Hy-Vee sell its products through online, and its own groceries located in eight Midwestern states in the US.

EXECUTIVES

Vice Chairman, Jay Marshall
Chief Merchandising Officer, Darren Baty
CDO, Jason Buhrow
CMO, Daniel Fick

LOCATIONS

HQ: HY-VEE, INC.
5820 WESTOWN PKWY, WEST DES MOINES, IA 502668223
Phone: 515 267-2800
Web: WWW.HY-VEE.COM

PRODUCTS/OPERATIONS

Selected Subsidiaries
D & D Foods, Inc. (salads, dips, and meats)
Florist Distributing, Inc. (flowers, plants, and florist supplies)
Hy-Vee Construction, L.C. (construction)
Hy-Vee Pharmacy Solutions (specialty pharmacy services)
Hy-Vee Weitz Construction, L.C. (construction)
Lomar Distributing, Inc. (specialty foods)
Midwest Heritage Bank, FSB (banking)
Perishable Distributors of Iowa, Ltd. (meat, fish, seafood, and ice cream)

COMPETITORS

AMERICAN ITALIAN PASTA COMPANY
BAXTERS FOOD GROUP LIMITED
GENERAL MILLS, INC.
HOUCHENS INDUSTRIES, INC.
K-VA-T FOOD STORES, INC.
LAND O'FROST, INC.
MCCORMICK & COMPANY, INCORPORATED
NORTHERN TOOL & EQUIPMENT COMPANY, INC.
OSI GROUP, LLC
Premium Brands Holdings Corporation

HISTORICAL FINANCIALS
Company Type: Private

Income Statement   FYE: September 30

	REVENUE ($mil)	NET INCOME ($mil)	NET PROFIT MARGIN	EMPLOYEES
09/21	12,182	0	0.0%	83,000
09/20	11,449	0	0.0%	—
09/19	10,672	0	0.0%	—
09/18	10,290	0	0.0%	—
Annual Growth	5.8%	—	—	—

2021 Year-End Financials
Return on assets: —
Return on equity: —
Current Ratio: 0.90
Cash ($ mil.): 84

HYUNDAI TRANSYS GEORGIA POWERTRAIN, INC.

Auditors: PK LLP OPELIKA ALABAMA

LOCATIONS
HQ: HYUNDAI TRANSYS GEORGIA POWERTRAIN, INC.
6801 KIA PKWY, WEST POINT, GA 318334937
Phone: 706 902-6800
Web: WWW.HYUNDAIUSA.COM

HISTORICAL FINANCIALS
Company Type: Private

Income Statement   FYE: December 31

	REVENUE ($mil)	NET INCOME ($mil)	NET PROFIT MARGIN	EMPLOYEES
12/16	1,134	7	0.6%	500
12/15	1,230	12	1.0%	—
12/14	1,250	11	0.9%	—
12/13	1,220	11	0.9%	—
Annual Growth	(2.4%)	(14.3%)	—	—

2016 Year-End Financials
Return on assets: 2.5%
Return on equity: 6.0%
Current Ratio: 1.70
Cash ($ mil.): 22

ICE DATA SERVICES, INC.

Interactive Data Corporation has something vital to the information superhighway -- the information. Its subscription services provide financial market data, analytics, and related services to financial institutions, active traders, and individual investors. Interactive Data conducts business through two segments: Institutional Services and Active Trader Services. Products include Interactive Data Fixed Income Analytics (fixed-income portfolio analytics for institutions), Interactive Data Pricing and Reference Data (securities information for institutions), and Interactive Data Desktop Solutions (real-time market data for individuals). Private-equity firms Silver Lake and Warburg Pincus agreed to sell IDC to Intercontinental Exchange in 2015.

Operations
The company conducts business through two segments: Pricing and Reference Data and Trading Solutions. Its Pricing and Reference Data segment accounted for about 70% of its revenue in fiscal 2012, while its Trading Solutions segment contributed the other 30% of revenue.

Geographic Reach
Interactive Data has operations in the US, Europe, and Asia Pacific. About 30% of sales come from outside the US.

Sales and Marketing
To support the sales efforts of its businesses, the company implemented a range of promotional and lead-generating campaigns such as publishing white papers, direct mail and email initiatives, advertising in leading industry publications, participating in targeted industry conferences, and other public relations tactics.

Financial Performance
In fiscal 2012 the company's total revenue increased by about $12.4 million, or 1.4%, compared to fiscal 2011. Interactive Data reported slightly more than $880 million in revenue for fiscal 2012 after it claimed $867.7 million for fiscal 2011.

HISTORY
Data Broadcasting was formed in 1992 as the successor to the Financial News Network, a bankrupt financial cable TV network. Alan Hirschfield, former CEO of Twentieth Century Fox and Columbia Pictures, and Allan Tessler, experienced in restructuring businesses, were brought in; they sold many of Financial News' assets but held onto two information services, DBC West (stock data for private investors) and Shark Information Services (serving professional traders).

The company expanded its services and markets through key acquisitions. In 1994 it bought Computer Sports World (online sports data) and Capital Management Sciences (fixed-income data and analysis). The following year Data Broadcasting bought and merged with its chief rival (Broadcast International), bought a stake in Internet Financial Network (online distributor of SEC filings), and sold Shark. These transactions also hurt earnings in 1996.

Data Broadcasting acquired international news provider Federal News Service Group in 1997. It also put its InStore Satellite Network and CheckRite International business services divisions up for sale to focus on information services and fund future acquisitions. National Data Corporation, a provider of transaction processing services, bought CheckRite International in 1998; InStore Satellite was a tougher sell, but finally went to Muzak in 1999. Also that year MarketWatch.com, a financial news Web site operated by Data Broadcasting and CBS, went public (each company retained a 34% stake). (MarketWatch.com later changed its name to MarketWatch in 2004 and was sold to Dow Jones & Company in 2005.) Data Broadcasting later sold its AgCast business to closely held agricultural publisher The Farm Journal.

In 2000 UK media company Pearson took a 60% stake in Data Broadcasting in exchange for its global equities information business, Financial Times Asset Management. Former Pearson executives Stephen Hill and Stuart Clark took over as chairman and CEO, respectively. Data Broadcasting later sold its DBC Sports unit (including odds maker Las Vegas Sports Consultants) to former SportsLine.com subsidiary VegasInsider. Also that year Data Broadcasting acquired Thomson Financial's security data business (Muller Data Corporation).

In early 2001 Data Broadcasting sold its stake in MarketWatch.com to Pearson. It later changed its name to Interactive Data Corporation. The following year the company purchased Merrill Lynch's security data business (Merrill Lynch Securities Pricing Service). Interactive Data purchased McGraw-Hill's S&P ComStock (now called Interactive Data Real-Time Services), a provider of financial data, news, historical information, and software applications, for $115 million in cash, and added Hyperfeed Technologies' consolidated data feed business in 2003.

The following year Interactive Data acquired the assets of FutureSource, a provider of real-time futures and commodities data, and in 2005 it bought IS.Teledata, a provider of customized financial information portals and terminals. IS.Teledata was subsequently renamed Interactive Data Managed Solutions.

In a move to expand its revenue from consumer-oriented services, the company acquired online stock information provider Quote.com from search portal Lycos (owned by Korea's Daum Communication) for about $30 million in 2006. The acquired business, which includes investment community message board Raging Bull, operates as part of Interactive Data's eSignal division.

In 2007 the company grew when it acquired the market data division of Xcitek. The purchase added North American corporate actions information, such as reorganization, cost basis, and class action data, to its In

LOCATIONS
HQ: ICE DATA SERVICES, INC.
32 CROSBY DR STE 100, BEDFORD, MA 017301448
Phone: 781 687-8500

COMPETITORS

AMDOCS LIMITED
CLYDESDALE BANK PLC
DBRS Limited
FACTSET RESEARCH SYSTEMS INC.
FROG CAPITAL LIMITED
LIGHTHOUSE GROUP LIMITED
PRIMARY CAPITAL LIMITED
SCHRODERS PLC
THOMSON REUTERS CORPORATION
YORKSHIRE BANK PUBLIC LIMITED COMPANY

HISTORICAL FINANCIALS

Company Type: Private

Income Statement — FYE: December 31

	ASSETS ($mil)	NET INCOME ($mil)	INCOME AS % OF ASSETS	EMPLOYEES
12/13	3,968	33	0.8%	2,600
12/12	3,962	1	—	—
12/11	4,093	(29)	—	—
Annual Growth	(1.5%)	—	—	—

2013 Year-End Financials
Return on assets: 0.8%   Cash ($ mil.): 356
Return on equity: 2.8%
Current Ratio: 2.60

IDEA PUBLIC SCHOOLS

EXECUTIVES

Acting Chief Operating Officer*, Collin Sewell
Auditors: RSM US LLP SAN ANTONIO TEXA

LOCATIONS

HQ: IDEA PUBLIC SCHOOLS
2115 W PIKE BLVD, WESLACO, TX 785960054
Phone: 956 377-8000
Web: WWW.IDEAPUBLICSCHOOLS.ORG

HISTORICAL FINANCIALS

Company Type: Private

Income Statement — FYE: June 30

	REVENUE ($mil)	NET INCOME ($mil)	NET PROFIT MARGIN	EMPLOYEES
06/21	850	79	9.3%	2,381
06/20	677	57	8.5%	—
06/19	532	39	7.4%	—
06/18	422	31	7.6%	—
Annual Growth	26.3%	35.3%	—	—

2021 Year-End Financials
Return on assets: 4.3%   Cash ($ mil.): 276
Return on equity: 24.5%
Current Ratio: 2.30

IDEMIA IDENTITY & SECURITY USA LLC

Idemia Identity & Security USA (formerly MorphoTrust USA) has operated in the US for nearly half a century, developing technologies and products that enhance national security while simplifying lives of Americans. It is a global leader in Augmented Identity for an increasingly digital world. It is administered, managed and operated by US staff on US soil for all services provided to US government customers at the federal, state, local, and tribal levels.

Operations

The company is the leading driver's license provider in the US. It ensures prevention of fraudulent duplicate licenses and provides secure identity documents meeting federal requirements. It also offers public safety through its biometric systems and customer support center. In addition it also offers enrollment services as well as identity-related solutions.

Geographic Reach

Headquartered in Reston, Virginia, the company also has office locations in Billerica and Anaheim, California; Brentwood, Tennessee; Bloomington Minnesota; Fort Wayne, Indiana; and Des Moines, Iowa.

Sales and Marketing

The company caters to US government customers at the federal, state, local, and tribal levels.

LOCATIONS

HQ: IDEMIA IDENTITY & SECURITY USA LLC
11951 FREEDOM DR STE 1800, RESTON, VA 201905642
Phone: 703 775-7800
Web: WWW.IDEMIA.COM

PRODUCTS/OPERATIONS

Selected Products and Services
Biometric-based access control to buildings and restricted areas
Biometric recognition technologies that accurately identify individuals
Enrollment centers for processing pre-employment background checks
Secure credentials that serve as proof of identity
Solving critical issues facing US intelligence and national security

COMPETITORS

APPRISS INC.
CYBERSOURCE CORPORATION
DST SYSTEMS, INC.
HEALTH MANAGEMENT SYSTEMS, INC.
MANTECH INTERNATIONAL CORPORATION
NATIONAL INFORMATION SOLUTIONS COOPERATIVE, INC.
PC SPECIALISTS, INC.
PERSPECTA ENTERPRISE SOLUTIONS LLC
TYLER TECHNOLOGIES, INC.
VERTAFORE, INC.

HISTORICAL FINANCIALS

Company Type: Private

Income Statement — FYE: December 31

	REVENUE ($mil)	NET INCOME ($mil)	NET PROFIT MARGIN	EMPLOYEES
12/16	708	(7)	—	1,600
12/15	604	0	0.0%	—
Annual Growth	17.1%	—	—	—

2016 Year-End Financials
Return on assets: (-0.5%)   Cash ($ mil.): 73
Return on equity: (-0.7%)
Current Ratio: 1.70

IHC HEALTH SERVICES, INC.

Auditors: KPMG LLP SALT LAKE CITY UTA

LOCATIONS

HQ: IHC HEALTH SERVICES, INC.
1380 E MEDICAL CENTER DR, ST GEORGE, UT 847902123
Phone: 435 251-2992
Web: WWW.DIXIEREGIONAL.COM

HISTORICAL FINANCIALS

Company Type: Private

Income Statement — FYE: December 31

	REVENUE ($mil)	NET INCOME ($mil)	NET PROFIT MARGIN	EMPLOYEES
12/21	8,693	2,442	28.1%	4,000
12/20	7,742	1,335	17.2%	—
12/19	6,947	888	12.8%	—
12/18	6,037	317	5.3%	—
Annual Growth	12.9%	97.4%	—	—

2021 Year-End Financials
Return on assets: 13.8%   Cash ($ mil.): 305
Return on equity: 20.8%
Current Ratio: 1.20

ILLINOIS HOUSING DEVELOPMENT AUTHORITY (INC)

The Illinois Housing Development Authority (IHDA) wants every Illinoisan to have a safe, comfortable place to lay their head. The authority finances the construction and preservation of affordable housing for low- and moderate-income families throughout the state. Since its inception in 1967 the IHDA has allocated more than $6 billion and financed roughly 150,000 units of affordable housing. An independent and self-supporting authority, the IHDA raises private capital from bond markets and administers and manages a number of federal and state funding programs, including the Illinois Affordable Housing Trust Fund and the Illinois Affordable Housing Tax Credit Fund.

Auditors : CLIFTONLARSONALLEN LLP OAK BR

LOCATIONS

HQ: ILLINOIS HOUSING DEVELOPMENT AUTHORITY (INC)
111 E WACKER DR STE 1000, CHICAGO, IL 606014306
Phone: 312 836-5200
Web: WWW.IHDA.ORG

COMPETITORS

APPALACHIAN REGIONAL COMMISSION
ARCADIS U.S., INC.
CEG SOLUTIONS LLC
ECOLOGY AND ENVIRONMENT INC.
VIRGINIA ECONOMIC DEVELOPMENT PARTNERSHIP

HISTORICAL FINANCIALS
Company Type: Private

Income Statement — FYE: June 30

	REVENUE ($mil)	NET INCOME ($mil)	NET PROFIT MARGIN	EMPLOYEES
06/21	578	56	9.7%	200
06/20	38	(61)	—	—
06/19	191	64	33.8%	—
06/18	57	(122)	—	—
Annual Growth	115.7%	—	—	—

2021 Year-End Financials
Return on assets: 1.4%   Cash ($ mil.): 1,151
Return on equity: 4.1%
Current Ratio: 2.30

ILLINOIS STATE OF TOLL HIGHWAY AUTHORITY

The Illinois State Toll Highway Authority (ISTHA) is trying to give Illinois drivers a little relief from congestion, making their morning and afternoon commutes easier to swallow. The department maintains and operates about 275 miles of interstate tollways in 12 Northern Illinois counties. ISTHA is mid-way through its 10-year, $6.3 billion Congestion-Relief Program, which is conducting major improvements, including rebuilding, widening, and extending tollway segments; converting toll plazas to provide non-stop toll collection for I-PASS users; opening additional tollway oases; and adding electronic over-the-road signs to improve communication with tollway users.

EXECUTIVES

Acting Executive Director*, Michael King
Auditors : MCGLADREY & PULLEN LLP SCHAU

LOCATIONS

HQ: ILLINOIS STATE OF TOLL HIGHWAY AUTHORITY
2700 OGDEN AVE, DOWNERS GROVE, IL 605151703
Phone: 630 241-6800
Web: WWW.ILLINOISTOLLWAY.COM

COMPETITORS

COLORADO DEPARTMENT OF TRANSPORTATION
FEDERAL TRANSIT ADMINISTRATION
INDIANA DEPARTMENT OF TRANSPORTATION
OHIO DEPARTMENT OF TRANSPORTATION
OKLAHOMA DEPARTMENT OF TRANSPORTATION

HISTORICAL FINANCIALS
Company Type: Private

Income Statement — FYE: December 31

	REVENUE ($mil)	NET INCOME ($mil)	NET PROFIT MARGIN	EMPLOYEES
12/21	1,459	299	20.5%	1,750
12/20	1,260	124	9.8%	—
12/19	1,484	374	25.2%	—
12/18	1,436	353	24.6%	—
Annual Growth	0.5%	(5.4%)	—	—

2021 Year-End Financials
Return on assets: 2.2%   Cash ($ mil.): 1,042
Return on equity: 8.9%
Current Ratio: 1.80

ILWU-PMA BENEFIT PLANS

LOCATIONS

HQ: ILWU-PMA BENEFIT PLANS
1188 FRANKLIN ST STE 300, SAN FRANCISCO, CA 941096852
Phone: 415 673-8500
Web: WWW.BENEFITPLANS.ORG

HISTORICAL FINANCIALS
Company Type: Private

Income Statement — FYE: June 30

	REVENUE ($mil)	NET INCOME ($mil)	NET PROFIT MARGIN	EMPLOYEES
06/21	811	0	0.1%	18
06/08	468	3	0.7%	—
Annual Growth	4.3%	(8.7%)	—	—

2021 Year-End Financials
Return on assets: 0.5%   Cash ($ mil.): 5
Return on equity: 0.8%
Current Ratio: 2.00

ILWU-PMA WELFARE TRUST

EXECUTIVES

Prin, Michael Ouchida

Auditors : PRICEWATERHOUSECOOPERS LLP SA

LOCATIONS

HQ: ILWU-PMA WELFARE TRUST
1188 FRANKLIN ST STE 101, SAN FRANCISCO, CA 941096852
Phone: 415 673-8500
Web: WWW.BENEFITPLANS.ORG

HISTORICAL FINANCIALS
Company Type: Private

Income Statement — FYE: June 30

	REVENUE ($mil)	NET INCOME ($mil)	NET PROFIT MARGIN	EMPLOYEES
06/18	738	(4)	—	10
06/17	738	5	0.8%	—
06/15	676	27	4.1%	—
06/14	624	(21)	—	—
Annual Growth	4.3%	—	—	—

2018 Year-End Financials
Return on assets: (-2.4%)   Cash ($ mil.): 5
Return on equity: (-4.6%)
Current Ratio: 1.80

IMPERIAL IRRIGATION DISTRICT

Imperial Irrigation District (IID) keeps the lights on and the water flowing. A public agency, IID is the six largest public power utility in the state of California, providing generation, transmission, and distribution services to more than 145,000 residential, commercial, and industrial customers. It is also the largest irrigation district in the US, with more than 3,000 miles of canals and drains delivering water to active farmland and providing wholesale water to local municipalities primarily in the Southern California desert corridors of Imperial Valley and Coachella Valley. The district is governed by a five-member board of directors elected by district residents.

Financial Performance

IID saw its revenues increase 6% from $530 million in 2011 to $562 million in 2012. The growth was driven by a 12% surge in water revenue; this was due to a rise in water transfer rates and a volume increase in water transferred to the San Diego County Water Authority and the Coachella Valley Water District of about $5 million. Power revenues also climbed 4% in 2012 due to a spike in energy sales, mainly from residential customers.

Strategy

In the area of renewable energy, IID is part of a statewide effort to significantly increase solar energy development and production by the year 2017. In 2011 it announced a public-private partnership with renewable energy generators. The partnership involves the signing of interconnection and transmission service agreements among IID, CalEnergy Generation, 8minuteenergy, Ormat Technologies, and the Los Angeles Department of Water and Power. It's the first step in a renewable energy transmission expansion plan to increase capacity enough to support more than a dozen renewable energy construction projects.

In addition, IID offers a variety of programs to assist its customers in reducing their personal energy consumption, including rebates for buying select energy efficient products, online home energy audits, and funding for residential projects that involve installing solar technologies, such as photovoltaic (PV) systems.

Company Background

Founded in 1911, IID acquired properties from the financially struggling California Development Company and its Mexican subsidiary. By 1922 it had purchased 13 mutual water companies, each of which had developed and operated distribution canals in the Imperial Valley. Principal water customers today include farm operators and municipalities that treat the water and resell it to their residential and business customers. The district entered the power business in 1936 to utilize the hydroelectric generation of the All-American Canal. Since that time, IID has added geothermal, natural gas, coal, and solar to its energy generation portfolio. Its electric services account for majority of IID's annual revenues.

Auditors : MOSS ADAMS LLP PORTLAND OREG

LOCATIONS

HQ: IMPERIAL IRRIGATION DISTRICT
333 E BARIONI BLVD, IMPERIAL, CA 922511773
Phone: 800 303-7756
Web: WWW.IID.COM

COMPETITORS

OMAHA PUBLIC POWER DISTRICT
PUBLIC UTILITY DISTRICT 1 OF SNOHOMISH COUNTY
SACRAMENTO MUNICIPAL UTILITY DISTRICT
SALT RIVER PROJECT AGRICULTURAL IMPROVEMENT AND POWER DISTRICT
THE CITY OF SEATTLE-CITY LIGHT DEPARTMENT

HISTORICAL FINANCIALS
Company Type: Private

Income Statement — FYE: December 31

	REVENUE ($mil)	NET INCOME ($mil)	NET PROFIT MARGIN	EMPLOYEES
12/21	795	107	13.5%	1,300
12/20	705	115	16.4%	—
12/19	642	51	8.0%	—
12/18	615	48	7.9%	—
Annual Growth	8.9%	30.4%	—	—

2021 Year-End Financials
Return on assets: 3.7%   Cash ($ mil.): 94
Return on equity: 5.6%
Current Ratio: 2.30

INDEPENDENT PHARMACY COOPERATIVE

Auditors : GRANT THORNTON LLP APPLETON

LOCATIONS

HQ: INDEPENDENT PHARMACY COOPERATIVE
1550 COLUMBUS ST, SUN PRAIRIE, WI 535903901
Phone: 800 755-1531
Web: WWW.IPCRX.COM

HISTORICAL FINANCIALS
Company Type: Private

Income Statement — FYE: December 31

	REVENUE ($mil)	NET INCOME ($mil)	NET PROFIT MARGIN	EMPLOYEES
12/16	1,427	30	2.1%	160
12/14	1,052	2	0.2%	—
12/13	1,058	2	0.2%	—
12/11	806	1	0.2%	—
Annual Growth	12.1%	73.9%	—	—

2016 Year-End Financials
Return on assets: 12.5%   Cash ($ mil.): 40
Return on equity: 60.7%
Current Ratio: 1.20

INDIANA UNIVERSITY

LOCATIONS

HQ: INDIANA UNIVERSITY
1020 E KIRKWOOD AVE, BLOOMINGTON, IN 474057103
Phone: 812 855-7581
Web: WWW.IU.EDU

HISTORICAL FINANCIALS
Company Type: Private

Income Statement — FYE: June 30

	REVENUE ($mil)	NET INCOME ($mil)	NET PROFIT MARGIN	EMPLOYEES
06/14	2,195	201	9.2%	31
06/13	2,146	189	8.8%	—
Annual Growth	2.3%	6.3%	—	—

2014 Year-End Financials
Return on assets: 10.0%   Cash ($ mil.): 313
Return on equity: 9.2%
Current Ratio: 1.10

INFIRMARY HEALTH SYSTEM, INC.

LOCATIONS

HQ: INFIRMARY HEALTH SYSTEM, INC.
5 MOBILE INFIRMARY CIR, MOBILE, AL 366073513
Phone: 251 435-3030
Web: WWW.INFIRMARYHEALTH.ORG

HISTORICAL FINANCIALS
Company Type: Private

Income Statement — FYE: March 31

	REVENUE ($mil)	NET INCOME ($mil)	NET PROFIT MARGIN	EMPLOYEES
03/21	902	192	21.3%	5,000
03/20	839	(65)	—	—
03/19	783	(4)	—	—
03/18	727	35	4.8%	—
Annual Growth	7.5%	76.0%	—	—

2021 Year-End Financials
Return on assets: 17.1%   Cash ($ mil.): 145
Return on equity: 36.2%
Current Ratio: 3.70

INLAND COUNTIES REGIONAL CENTER, INC.

Auditors : WINDES INC LONG BEACH CA

LOCATIONS

HQ: INLAND COUNTIES REGIONAL CENTER, INC.
1365 S WATERMAN AVE, SAN BERNARDINO, CA 924082804
Phone: 909 890-3000
Web: WWW.INLANDRC.ORG

HISTORICAL FINANCIALS
Company Type: Private

Income Statement — FYE: June 30

	REVENUE ($mil)	NET INCOME ($mil)	NET PROFIT MARGIN	EMPLOYEES
06/21	686	0	0.1%	586
06/20	641	15	2.3%	—
06/19	557	(0)	—	—
06/18	502	(0)	0.0%	—
Annual Growth	11.0%	—	—	—

2021 Year-End Financials
Return on assets: 0.6%   Cash ($ mil.): 51
Return on equity: —
Current Ratio: 1.00

INNOVATIVE AG SERVICES CO.

Auditors : MERIWETHER WILSON & COMPANY

LOCATIONS

HQ: INNOVATIVE AG SERVICES CO.
2010 S MAIN ST, MONTICELLO, IA 523107707
Phone: 319 465-3501
Web: WWW.INNOVATIVEAG.COM

HISTORICAL FINANCIALS
Company Type: Private

Income Statement — FYE: August 31

	REVENUE ($mil)	NET INCOME ($mil)	NET PROFIT MARGIN	EMPLOYEES
08/19	597	9	1.6%	500
08/18	649	11	1.8%	—
08/17	615	15	2.6%	—
08/16	682	10	1.6%	—
Annual Growth	(4.4%)	(4.6%)	—	—

2019 Year-End Financials
Return on assets: 3.2%   Cash ($ mil.): 1
Return on equity: 6.0%
Current Ratio: 1.80

INOVA HEALTH CARE SERVICES

LOCATIONS

HQ: INOVA HEALTH CARE SERVICES
8110 GATEHOUSE RD 200E, FALLS CHURCH, VA 220421217
Phone: 703 289-2000
Web: WWW.INOVA.ORG

HISTORICAL FINANCIALS
Company Type: Private

Income Statement — FYE: December 31

	REVENUE ($mil)	NET INCOME ($mil)	NET PROFIT MARGIN	EMPLOYEES
12/13	2,134	145	6.8%	13,000
12/09	1,663	200	12.0%	—
12/03	1,012	46	4.6%	—
12/02	1	(0)	—	—
Annual Growth	96.8%	—	—	—

2013 Year-End Financials
Return on assets: 3.9%   Cash ($ mil.): 203
Return on equity: 7.8%
Current Ratio: 0.30

INOVA HEALTH SYSTEM FOUNDATION

Inova Health Foundation provides financial support and assistance to the Inova Health System, which operates a network of not-for-profit community hospitals in northern Virginia. It also supports home health services, heart care programs, clinical research and trials, emergency and urgent care centers, outpatient services and destination institutes. Inova Health serves more than 2 million individuals annually. Its five hospitals are consistently recognized by the Centers for Medicare and Medicaid Services (CMS), US News & World Report Best Hospitals and Leapfrog Hospital Safety Grades for excellence in healthcare. The organization is home to Northern Virginia's only Level 1 Trauma Center and Level 4 Neonatal Intensive Care Unit. Its hospitals have a total of more than 1,950 licensed beds.

Operations
Money raised by the foundation supports programs at Inova Health. As the leading nonprofit healthcare system in the region, it welcomes partnerships with individuals and organizations who share its commitment to providing world-class healthcare to each person in every community it has the privilege to serve. In addition to the organization's areas of research that include cancer, heart and vascular disease, obesity, trauma surgery, pediatrics, and neuroscience, Inova Health offers a diverse array of services, including acupuncture treatment, bariatric surgery, cancer care, diagnostic imaging, electroconvulsive therapy (ECT), geriatrics, and behavioral health services, among others.

Geographic Reach
Virginia-based, Inova Health operates five health facilities in Virginia.

EXECUTIVES
CAO*, Kylenne Green
Auditors: II ERNST & YOUNG US LLP CINC

LOCATIONS
HQ: INOVA HEALTH SYSTEM FOUNDATION
8095 INNOVATION PARK DR, FAIRFAX, VA 220314868
Phone: 703 289-2069
Web: FOUNDATION.INOVA.ORG

COMPETITORS
CAREGROUP, INC.
CITY OF HOPE
CKHS, INC.
INSPIRA HEALTH NETWORK, INC.
NORTHSHORE UNIVERSITY HEALTHSYSTEM
SINAI HEALTH SYSTEM
SOUTHCOAST HEALTH SYSTEM, INC.
SWEDISH COVENANT HOSPITAL
THE CLEVELAND CLINIC FOUNDATION
WASHINGTON HOSPITAL CENTER CORPORATION

HISTORICAL FINANCIALS
Company Type: Private

Income Statement — FYE: December 31

	REVENUE ($mil)	NET INCOME ($mil)	NET PROFIT MARGIN	EMPLOYEES
12/19	821	762	92.9%	16,000
12/17	765	717	93.6%	—
12/15	2,972	234	7.9%	—
Annual Growth	(27.5%)	34.3%	—	—

2019 Year-End Financials
Return on assets: 13.3%   Cash ($ mil.): 1
Return on equity: 23.0%
Current Ratio: 12.40

INSPUR SYSTEMS, INC.

Auditors: CG UHLENBERG LLP FREMONT C

LOCATIONS

HQ: INSPUR SYSTEMS, INC.
1501 MCCARTHY BLVD, MILPITAS, CA 950357420
Phone: 800 697-5893
Web: WWW.INSPURSYSTEMS.COM

HISTORICAL FINANCIALS
Company Type: Private

Income Statement — FYE: December 31

	REVENUE ($mil)	NET INCOME ($mil)	NET PROFIT MARGIN	EMPLOYEES
12/20	617	5	0.9%	300
12/18	410	3	0.8%	—
12/17	180	(0)	—	—
12/16	65	(0)	—	—
Annual Growth	75.1%	—	—	—

2020 Year-End Financials
Return on assets: 2.9%   Cash ($ mil.): 22
Return on equity: 49.5%
Current Ratio: 1.00

INTEGRIS BAPTIST MEDICAL CENTER, INC.

INTEGRIS Baptist Medical Center seeks integrity by caring for citizens from across the state of Oklahoma. The Oklahoma City-based medical center is the flagship hospital of the not-for-profit INTEGRIS Health system. With about 510 beds, INTEGRIS Baptist is home to specialty care facilities for burns, women's and children's health, infertility, stroke treatment, cardiac care, organ transplantation, cancer treatment, and more. The company also has centers for wellness, hearing, sleep disorders, senior health, and weight loss, and it provides medical training and residency programs. INTEGRIS Baptist Medical Center opened its doors in 1959 with 200 beds.

LOCATIONS

HQ: INTEGRIS BAPTIST MEDICAL CENTER, INC.
3300 NW EXPRESSWAY, OKLAHOMA CITY, OK 731124418
Phone: 405 949-3011
Web: WWW.INTEGRISOK.COM

PRODUCTS/OPERATIONS

Selected Centers and Services
Advanced Cardiac Care
Anticoagulation Clinics

Bariatrics
Bennett Fertility Institute
Bones and Joints
Breast Care
Burn Center
Cancer Care
Cardiology
Case Management
Children's Health
Comprehensive Breast Center of Oklahoma
Continuing Medical Education
Corporate Assistance Program
Diabetes
Diagnostic Services
Digestive Health
Emergency Department
Fertility
General Heart Care
General Pediatrics
Home Care
Hospice
Hospitalist Program
Hough Ear Institute
Hyperbaric Medicine and Wound Care
James R. Daniel Cerebrovascular and Stroke Center
Jim Thorpe Rehabilitation Center
Labor and Delivery
Men's Health
Nazih Zuhdi Transplant Institute
Neonatal Intensive Care Unit (NICU)
Orthopedics
PACER Fitness Center
Pastoral Care
Pediatric Intensive Care Unit (PICU)
Pediatric Neurology
Pharmacy
Radiology Services
Senior Health
Sleep Disorders Center of Oklahoma
Stroke Center
Surgical Services
TeleHealth
Urogynecology
Weight Loss

COMPETITORS

CARSON TAHOE REGIONAL HEALTHCARE
CHRISTUS SAINT CATHERINE HOSPITAL
LEXINGTON MEDICAL CENTER
MERCY MEDICAL CENTER
SAINT FRANCIS MEDICAL CENTER

HISTORICAL FINANCIALS
Company Type: Private

Income Statement — FYE: June 30

	REVENUE ($mil)	NET INCOME ($mil)	NET PROFIT MARGIN	EMPLOYEES
06/22	1,049	(33)	—	2,700
06/21	1,051	192	18.3%	—
06/20	950	(14)	—	—
06/18	814	67	8.3%	—
Annual Growth	6.6%	—	—	—

2022 Year-End Financials
Return on assets: (-1.7%)   Cash ($ mil.): 100
Return on equity: (-4.7%)
Current Ratio: 5.80

INTEGRIS HEALTH, INC.

INTEGRIS Health is Oklahoma's largest not-for-profit and owned health care systems, with hospitals, specialty clinics, family care practices and centers of excellence. Its flagship hospital, INTEGRIS Baptist Medical Center is a center of leading-edge medicine, housing nine Centers of Excellence, including a full-service heart hospital, a comprehensive transplant institute and one of the nation's foremost burn centers. Its Lakeside Women's Hospital is a fully Licensed Joint Commission accredited hospital designed exclusively for women. The hospitals provide services including primary care, breast health, cancer care, gynecology, surgery, lung care, transplant, and rehabilitation & physical care and more.

Operations

INTEGRIS Heart Hospital and INTEGRIS Cardiovascular Physicians are focused on delivering the highest quality of cardiac services in Oklahoma and beyond. INTEGRIS Health offers a comprehensive heart care to more than more than 40 rural heart clinics and services including interventional cardiology, valve repair, emergent heart failure treatment, LVADs, live-saving ECMO, artificial hearts, heart transplants, cardiac rehabilitation and more.

EXECUTIVES

CIO*, Bill Hudson
Auditors : KPMG LLP OKLAHOMA CITY OKLA

LOCATIONS

HQ: INTEGRIS HEALTH, INC.
3300 NW EXPWY, OKLAHOMA CITY, OK 731124418
Phone: 405 949-6066
Web: WWW.INTEGRISOK.COM

PRODUCTS/OPERATIONS

2015 Sales

	$ mil	% of total
INTEGRIS Baptist Medical Center, Inc.	635.4	39
INTEGRIS South Oklahoma City Hospital Corporation	244.0	15
INTEGRIS Rural Health, Inc.	227.5	14
INTEGRIS Health Edmond	48.1	3
All others	459.4	29
Eliminations	(229.7)	-
Total	1,384.7	100

Selected Facilities
Baptist Medical Center
Baptist Regional Health Center
Bass Baptist Health Center
Blackwell Regional Hospital
Canadian Valley Regional Hospital
Cancer Institute of Oklahoma
Clinton Regional Hospital
Grove General Hospital
Health Edmond
Hospice House
Jim Thorpe Rehabilitation
Marshall County Medical Center
Mayes County Medical Center
Mental Health Spencer
Seminole Medical Center
Southwest Medical Center

COMPETITORS

ACADIA HEALTHCARE COMPANY, INC.
ALLINA HEALTH SYSTEM
COMMUNITY HEALTH NETWORK, INC.
COVENANT MEDICAL CENTER, INC.
MERITUS HEALTH, INC.
OVERLAKE HOSPITAL MEDICAL CENTER
PROVIDENCE ST. JOSEPH HEALTH
THE LANCASTER GENERAL HOSPITAL
THE RUTLAND HOSPITAL INC ACT 220
WELLMONT HEALTH SYSTEM

HISTORICAL FINANCIALS
Company Type: Private

Income Statement — FYE: June 30

	REVENUE ($mil)	NET INCOME ($mil)	NET PROFIT MARGIN	EMPLOYEES
06/22	2,346	(40)	—	9,500
06/21	2,250	300	13.3%	—
06/20	2,077	(172)	—	—
06/19	1,950	11	0.6%	—
Annual Growth	6.4%	—	—	—

2022 Year-End Financials
Return on assets: (-1.2%)   Cash ($ mil.): 118
Return on equity: (-3.0%)
Current Ratio: 2.00

INTERMOUNTAIN HEALTH CARE INC

Intermountain Healthcare is a nonprofit system composed of 42,000 caregivers that serve the healthcare needs of people across the Intermountain West, primarily in Utah, Idaho, and Nevada. Intermountain includes some 25 hospitals, a Medical Group with more than 2,400 physicians and advanced practice clinicians at about 160 clinics, a health plans division called SelectHealth, and other health services. SelectHealth covers approximately 940,000 people in three states; recognized for superior member satisfaction.

Geographic Reach

Salt Lake City, Utah-based Intermountain Healthcare serves the health care needs of Utah, Nevada, and Idaho residents.

Company Background

Intermountain was formed in 1975 when the Church of Jesus Christ of Latter Day Saints donated 15 hospitals to local communities.

EXECUTIVES

CLO, Greg Matis
Auditors : KPMG LLP SALT LAKE CITY UT

LOCATIONS

HQ: INTERMOUNTAIN HEALTH CARE INC
36 S STATE ST STE 1600, SALT LAKE CITY, UT 841111633
Phone: 801 442-2000
Web: WWW.INTERMOUNTAINHEALTHCARE.ORG

PRODUCTS/OPERATIONS

2016 Sales

	$ mil.	% of total
Net patient services	4,368.9	57
Non-patient activities	3,010.7	40
Non-operating income	237.5	3
Total	7,617.1	100

Selected Hospitals
Alta View Hospital (Sandy, UT)
American Fork Hospital (Utah)
Bear River Valley Hospital (Tremonton, UT)
Cassia Regional Medical Center (Burley, ID)
Delta Community Medical Center (Utah)
Dixie Regional Medical Center (St. George, UT)
Fillmore Community Medical Center (Utah)
Garfield Memorial Hospital (Panguitch, UT)
Heber Valley Medical Center (Heber City, UT)
Intermountain Medical Center (Murray, UT)
LDS Hospital (Salt Lake City)
Logan Regional Hospital (Orem, UT)
McKay-Dee Hospital Center (Ogden, UT)
    McKay-Dee Behavioral Health Institute
Orem Community Hospital (Utah)
Park City Medical Center (Park City, UT)
Primary Children's Medical Center (Salt Lake City)
Riverton Hospital (Riverton, UT)
Sanpete Valley Hospital (Mt. Pleasant, UT)
Sevier Valley Hospital (Richfield, UT)
TOSH - The Orthopedic Specialty Hospital (Murray, UT)
Utah Valley Regional Medical Center (Provo, UT)
Valley View Medical Center (Cedar City, UT)

COMPETITORS
AHS MEDICAL HOLDINGS LLC
CENTURA HEALTH CORPORATION
LEGACY HEALTH
LEHIGH VALLEY HEALTH NETWORK, INC.
NORTHSHORE UNIVERSITY HEALTHSYSTEM
OHIOHEALTH CORPORATION
READING HOSPITAL
UNIVERSITY HEALTH SYSTEMS OF EASTERN CAROLINA, INC.
UNIVERSITY HOSPITALS HEALTH SYSTEM, INC.
WELLSTAR HEALTH SYSTEM, INC.

HISTORICAL FINANCIALS
Company Type: Private

Income Statement — FYE: December 31

	REVENUE ($mil)	NET INCOME ($mil)	NET PROFIT MARGIN	EMPLOYEES
12/21	10,752	2,937	27.3%	35,000
12/20	10,082	1,571	15.6%	—
12/19	8,812	1,212	13.8%	—
12/18	7,724	420	5.4%	—
Annual Growth	11.7%	91.1%	—	—

2021 Year-End Financials
Return on assets: 15.0%
Return on equity: 21.6%
Current Ratio: 1.10
Cash ($ mil.): 396

INTERNATIONAL RESCUE COMMITTEE, INC.

Auditors: KPMG LLP NEW YORK NY

LOCATIONS
HQ: INTERNATIONAL RESCUE COMMITTEE, INC.
122 E 42ND ST, NEW YORK, NY 101680002
Phone: 212 551-3000
Web: WWW.RESCUE.ORG

HISTORICAL FINANCIALS
Company Type: Private

Income Statement — FYE: September 30

	REVENUE ($mil)	NET INCOME ($mil)	NET PROFIT MARGIN	EMPLOYEES
09/19	785	10	1.3%	8,000
09/18	744	2	0.3%	—
09/17	753	44	5.9%	—
09/14	562	9	1.7%	—
Annual Growth	6.9%	1.9%	—	—

2019 Year-End Financials
Return on assets: 2.7%
Return on equity: 4.6%
Current Ratio: 1.60
Cash ($ mil.): 126

INTERNATIONAL WIRE GROUP, INC.

International Wire Group (IWG) bares it all in the wire business. Through three divisions -- Bare Wire Products, Engineered Products - Europe, and High Performance Conductors -- IWG makes multi-gauge bare, silver-, nickel-, and tin-plated copper wire, as well as engineered wire products and performance conductors. The company's customers (General Cable is one of its largest) include suppliers and OEMs. IWG's wire products are used in industrial/energy, consumer electronics, aerospace and defense, medical electronics, automotive, and appliance applications.

Operations
The company's Bare Wire Products (or conductors) are used to transmit digital, video and audio signals or conduct electricity and are sold to more than 1,000 insulated wire manufacturers and various industrial OEMs for use in computer and data communications products, general industrial, energy, appliances, automobiles, and other applications.

IWG's Engineered Products - Europe makes bare copper wire products which are sold to a diverse customer base of various OEMs in Europe.

Its High Performance Conductors include tin, nickel, and silver plated copper and copper alloy conductors, including standard and customized conductors as well as specialty film insulated conductors and miniature tubing products.

Subsidiaries include US-based Continental Cordage, a leading maker of braided wire for a wide range of commercial, military, and industrial applications, and Tresse Metallique J. Forissier SAS, and Italtrecce, leading European makerd of bare copper wire products.

Geographic Reach
The company maintains 18 manufacturing plants and two distribution facilities in the US and Europe (Belgium, France, Italy and Poland). IWG makes the majority of its sales in the US.

Sales and Marketing
IWG serves customers in the electrical appliances, power supplies, aircraft, railway and automotive system sectors. The volatile pricing of raw materials, especially copper, is a lingering concern for IWG. The company depends on four leading suppliers for copper, and does not have long-term supply contracts with any of them, creating concern about the reliability of IWG's copper supply chain. Many of the company's customers have their own captive (in-house) wire production facilities, and they could exclusively turn to those facilities, reducing orders to IWG.

Mergers and Acquisitions
In late 2019, International Wire Group (IWG) bought New York-based Owl Wire & Cable (Owl) from Marmon Holdings. The deal expands IWG's copper wire manufacturing footprint.

EXECUTIVES
LOGISTICS*, Geoff Kent

LOCATIONS
HQ: INTERNATIONAL WIRE GROUP, INC.
12 MASONIC AVE, CAMDEN, NY 133161202
Phone: 315 245-3800
Web: WWW.INTERNATIONALWIRE.COM

PRODUCTS/OPERATIONS

Selected Products
Bare wire products
  Bare and tin-plated copper wire (or conductors)
Engineered products - Europe
  Bare copper wire (to conduct electricity)
High performance conductors
  Conductors

COMPETITORS
AMERCABLE INCORPORATED
BEKAERT CORPORATION
CHROMALOX, INC.
ENCORE WIRE CORPORATION
KALAS MFG. INC.
RSCC WIRE & CABLE LLC
SOUTHWIRE COMPANY, LLC
SUPERIOR ESSEX INC.
THE OKONITE COMPANY INC
W. L. GORE & ASSOCIATES, INC.

HISTORICAL FINANCIALS
Company Type: Private

Income Statement — FYE: December 31

	REVENUE ($mil)	NET INCOME ($mil)	NET PROFIT MARGIN	EMPLOYEES
12/08	736	6	0.9%	1,600
12/07	730	15	2.2%	—
12/06	(1,789)	0	0.0%	—
Annual Growth	—	13597.3%	—	—

INVACARE CORPORATION (TW)

LOCATIONS

HQ: INVACARE CORPORATION (TW)
39400 TAYLOR PKWY, NORTH RIDGEVILLE, OH 440356270
Phone: 440 329-6000
Web: WWW.INVACARE.COM

HISTORICAL FINANCIALS

Company Type: Private

Income Statement — FYE: December 31

	REVENUE ($mil)	NET INCOME ($mil)	NET PROFIT MARGIN	EMPLOYEES
12/11	1,801	(4)	—	45
12/10	1,722	25	1.5%	—
12/09	1,693	41	2.4%	—
Annual Growth	3.1%	—	—	—

2011 Year-End Financials
Return on assets: (-0.3%)   Cash ($ mil.): 34
Return on equity: (-0.7%)
Current Ratio: 1.80

2008 Year-End Financials
Return on assets: 1.8%   Cash ($ mil.): 7
Return on equity: 3.6%
Current Ratio: 2.10

IOWA HEALTH SYSTEM

Iowa Health System (IHS), which does business as UnityPoint Health, is the nations' fifth largest non-denominational health system. This overall system name also includes the UnityPoint Clinic (formerly known as Iowa Health Physicians & Clinic) and UnityPoint at Home and UnityPoint Hospice (formerly Iowa Health Home Care). As an industry leader in the Midwest, the system provides care throughout Iowa, Illinois, and Wisconsin through partnerships with more than 1,100 physicians and providers working in more than 280 UnityPoint Clinics, about 30 hospitals in metropolitan and rural communities, and home care services throughout its eight regions. UnityPoint Health was founded in 1993.

Operations

UnityPoint Health provides genetics, internal medicine, mental health, OB/GYN, palliative care, pediatrics, primary care, specialty pharmacy, telehealth, urgent care, hospitals, and home health services, among others.

Geographic Reach

With corporate office in West Des Moines, Iowa, UnityPoint Health includes nearly 30 hospitals in Iowa, Illinois, and Wisconsin. Its largest geographic markets served are Anamosa, Cedar Rapids, Des Moines, Dubuque, Fort Dodge, Grinnell, Sioux City, and Waterloo, Iowa; the Quad Cities/Muscatine region in Iowa and Illinois; Peoria, Illinois; and Madison, Wisconsin.

Company Background

Iowa Health System (IHS) was founded in 1993. In 2013 the network rebranded itself UnityPoint to showcase its mission to be a point of unity for patient care and its expansion to include health care facilities in other states including Illinois and Wisconsin.

EXECUTIVES

CSO, Dan Carpenter
CCO, Andrea Eklund
Auditors: KPMG LLP MINNEAPOLIS MN

LOCATIONS

HQ: IOWA HEALTH SYSTEM
1776 WEST LAKES PKWY # 400, WEST DES MOINES, IA 502668377
Phone: 515 241-6161
Web: WWW.UNITYPOINT.ORG

PRODUCTS/OPERATIONS

Selected Facilities
Metropolitan Hospitals
  Allen Memorial Hospital Corporation (Waterloo, Iowa)
  Iowa Lutheran Hospital (Des Moines, Iowa)
  Iowa Methodist Medical Center (Des Moines, Iowa)
  Blank Children's Hospital (Des Moines, Iowa)
  Methodist Medical Center of Illinois (Peoria, Illinois)
  Methodist West Hospital (West Des Moines, Iowa)
  St. Luke's Hospital (Cedar Rapids, Iowa)
  St. Luke's Regional Medical Center (Sioux City, Iowa)
  Jones Regional Medical Center (Anamosa, Iowa)
  The Finley Hospital (Dubuque, Iowa)
  Trinity Bettendorf (Bettendorf, Iowa)
  Trinity Moline (Moline, Illinois)
  Trinity Muscatine (Muscatine, Iowa)
  Trinity Regional Medical Center (Fort Dodge, Iowa)
  Trinity Rock Island (Rock Island, Illinois)
Rural Hospitals
  Buena Vista Regional Medical Center (Storm Lake, Iowa)
  Clarke County Hospital (Osceola, Iowa)
  Community Memorial Hospital (Sumner, Iowa)
  Greater Regional Medical Center (Creston, Iowa)
  Greene County Medical Center (Jefferson, Iowa)
  Grundy County Memorial Hospital (Grundy Center, Iowa)
  Guthrie County Hospital (Guthrie Center, Iowa)
  Guttenberg Municipal Hospital (Guttenberg, Iowa)
  Humboldt County Memorial Hospital (Humboldt, Iowa)
  Loring Hospital (Sac City, Iowa)
  Pocahontas Community Hospital (Pocahantas, Iowa)

COMPETITORS

ADVENTIST HEALTH SYSTEM/SUNBELT, INC.
CHRISTUS HEALTH
COMMONSPIRIT HEALTH
EASTERN MAINE HEALTHCARE SYSTEMS
HEARTLAND REGIONAL MEDICAL CENTER
HERITAGE VALLEY HEALTH SYSTEM, INC.
HOUSTON COUNTY HEALTHCARE AUTHORITY
MERCY HEALTH
MERCY HEALTH NETWORK, INC.
SANFORD

HISTORICAL FINANCIALS

Company Type: Private

Income Statement — FYE: December 31

	REVENUE ($mil)	NET INCOME ($mil)	NET PROFIT MARGIN	EMPLOYEES
12/17	4,157	229	5.5%	18,923
12/16	4,054	148	3.7%	—
Annual Growth	2.5%	54.4%	—	—

2017 Year-End Financials
Return on assets: 4.1%   Cash ($ mil.): 251
Return on equity: 6.8%
Current Ratio: 1.50

IOWA PHYSICIANS CLINIC MEDICAL FOUNDATION

LOCATIONS

HQ: IOWA PHYSICIANS CLINIC MEDICAL FOUNDATION
8101 BIRCHWOOD CT UNIT N, JOHNSTON, IA 501312930
Phone: 515 471-9200
Web: WWW.UNITYPOINT.ORG

HISTORICAL FINANCIALS

Company Type: Private

Income Statement — FYE: December 31

	REVENUE ($mil)	NET INCOME ($mil)	NET PROFIT MARGIN	EMPLOYEES
12/17	600	17	3.0%	1,000
12/00	76	(13)	—	—
12/99	8	2	31.3%	—
12/98	61	(19)	—	—
Annual Growth	12.8%	—	—	—

2017 Year-End Financials
Return on assets: 8.6%   Cash ($ mil.): 11
Return on equity: 26.0%
Current Ratio: 2.30

IOWA STATE UNIVERSITY OF SCIENCE AND TECHNOLOGY

Home to the Cyclones athletics teams, Iowa State University of Science and Technology (ISU) can be a whirlwind experience for some. ISU is a public land-grant institution offering higher education courses and programs with an emphasis on science, technology, and related areas. ISU's eight colleges offer more than 100 undergraduate degrees and nearly 200 fields of study leading to graduate and professional degrees. The university has an enrollment of more than 31,000 students and charges more than $7,720 in tuition and fees for resident students for two semesters.

Operations

In fiscal 2012 Iowa State received $360.2 million in grants, contracts, co-operative agreements and gifts of which about 60% is utilized for research purpose. The university's research park has about 20,000 square feet of incubators space including office and laboratories.

Geographic Reach

The university enrolls students from 50 states and more than 100 countries.

Financial Performance

The 6% increase in revenues in 2012 was due to higher tuition and fees, sales and services of educational activities, and auxiliary enterprise revenues. The tuition revenue increase was to a 5% hike in the resident tuition rate coupled with record enrollments. The increase in sales and services of educational activities was due to large one-time events, ISU farms, and the Vet Diagnostic Lab. ISU's auxiliary enterprises reported revenue growth thanks to new revenue sources and a record number of students in the residence system.

ISU's net income increased by 47% in 2012 thanks to higher operating expenses and a decline in non-operating revenues. Non-operating revenues decreased $24.4 million, thanks to an $11 million decrease in funding from education appropriations. Investment income also dropped $16.3 million, or 49%, mainly due to an unrealized loss in the value of investments.

Company Background

Chartered as Iowa Agriculture College in 1858, the school first officially opened for classes in 1869. Among ISU's notable alumni is scientist and inventor George Washington Carver.

Auditors : MARLYS K GASTON CPA DES MOI

LOCATIONS

HQ: IOWA STATE UNIVERSITY OF SCIENCE AND TECHNOLOGY
515 MORRILL RD, AMES, IA 500112105
Phone: 515 294-6162
Web: WWW.IASTATE.EDU

PRODUCTS/OPERATIONS

Colleges
Agriculture and Life Sciences
Business
Design
Engineering
Graduate
Human Sciences
Liberal Arts and Sciences
Veterinary Medicine

COMPETITORS

BOURNEMOUTH UNIVERSITY
MONTANA STATE UNIVERSITY, INC
Queen's University At Kingston
TRUSTEES OF THE COLORADO SCHOOL OF MINES
UNIVERSITY OF NORTH CAROLINA AT GREENSBORO
WELLESLEY COLLEGE
WEST VIRGINIA UNIVERSITY
WRIGHT STATE UNIVERSITY
YOUNGSTOWN STATE UNIVERSITY
ZOVIO INC

HISTORICAL FINANCIALS

Company Type: Private

Income Statement — FYE: June 30

	REVENUE ($mil)	NET INCOME ($mil)	NET PROFIT MARGIN	EMPLOYEES
06/21	895	44	5.0%	5,800
06/20	936	43	4.6%	—
06/19	952	97	10.2%	—
06/18	948	58	6.2%	—
Annual Growth	(1.9%)	(8.8%)	—	—

2021 Year-End Financials
Return on assets: 1.7%   Cash ($ mil.): 82
Return on equity: 2.5%
Current Ratio: 1.80

IRVINE UNIFIED SCHOOL DISTCT

Auditors : VAVRINEK TRINE DAY & CO LL

LOCATIONS

HQ: IRVINE UNIFIED SCHOOL DISTICT
5050 BARRANCA PKWY, IRVINE, CA 926044652
Phone: 949 936-5000
Web: WWW.IUSD.ORG

HISTORICAL FINANCIALS

Company Type: Private

Income Statement — FYE: June 30

	REVENUE ($mil)	NET INCOME ($mil)	NET PROFIT MARGIN	EMPLOYEES
06/21	684	134	19.7%	2,212
06/20	672	85	12.6%	—
06/19	513	4	0.9%	—
06/18	497	(1)	—	—
Annual Growth	11.2%	—	—	—

2021 Year-End Financials
Return on assets: 5.2%   Cash ($ mil.): —
Return on equity: 7.7%
Current Ratio: —

J M SMITH CORPORATION

J M Smith Corporation is the third-largest privately-held company in South Carolina, operating industry-leading healthcare and technology business units including Smith Drug Company, which provides purchasing and distribution services in more than 30 US states, and RxMedic Systems, a pharmacy automation manufacturer. Founded in 1925 by James M. Smith Sr. as a single community pharmacy in Asheville, North Carolina, the company supplies services and technology to organizations across the US.

Operations

J M Smith operates industry-leading healthcare and technology business units: Smith Drug Company and RxMedic Systems.

Smith Drug Company, a full-line distributor of pharmaceuticals, medical equipment (HME/DME), over-the-counter medicines, gifts and sundries to pharmacies and long-term care facilities.

Rxmedic Systems is a pharmacy automation manufacturer driven to provide the best products that pharmacy automation has to offer.

Geographic Reach

Based in Spartanburg, South Carolina, J M Smith's headquarters and regional offices span the entire US. Smith Drug has five distribution centers in more than 30 states, primarily in the southern US, as well as Washington, DC, and the Virgin Islands.

Company Background

In 2010 Smith expanded by acquiring health equipment manufacturing firm RxMedic. Through the purchase, the company entered the automated dispensing system market.

J M Smith was founded in 1943 by drugstore proprietor James Smith and is run by the Smith family.

LOCATIONS

HQ: J M SMITH CORPORATION
101 W SAINT JOHN ST # 305, SPARTANBURG, SC 293065150
Phone: 864 542-9419
Web: WWW.JMSMITH.COM

Selected Office Locations
Altamonte Springs, FL
Brandon, MS
Columbia, SC
Dallas, TX
Fairmont, WV
Gray, ME
Hermitage, PA
Houston, TX
Indianapolis, IN
Lexington, KY
Mechanicsburg, PA
Miami, FL
Morrisville, GA
Paragould, AR
Perry, GA
Pleasant Hill, MO
Richmond, VA
Seattle, WA
Spartanburg, SC
St. Paul, MN
Sturbridge, MA
Valdosta, GA
Valencia, CA

Wake Forest, NC

PRODUCTS/OPERATIONS

Selected Divisions
Integral Solutions Group
Norgenix Pharmaceuticals
QS/1
RxMedic
Smith Drug Company
Smith Premier Services

COMPETITORS

CARDINAL HEALTH, INC.
H. D. SMITH, LLC
HOSPIRA, INC.
MAWDSLEY-BROOKS & COMPANY LIMITED
MCKESSON CORPORATION
MCKESSON MEDICAL-SURGICAL TOP HOLDINGS INC.
MEDLINE INDUSTRIES, INC.
OMNICARE, INC.
SUZUKEN CO., LTD.
TRIPLEFIN LLC

HISTORICAL FINANCIALS

Company Type: Private

Income Statement — FYE: February 28

	REVENUE ($mil)	NET INCOME ($mil)	NET PROFIT MARGIN	EMPLOYEES
02/15	2,566	47	1.8%	235
02/14	2,370	38	1.6%	—
02/13	2,362	26	1.1%	—
Annual Growth	4.2%	33.8%	—	—

2015 Year-End Financials
Return on assets: 8.1%   Cash ($ mil.): 142
Return on equity: 16.0%
Current Ratio: 1.60

J.E. DUNN CONSTRUCTION COMPANY

From first building designs to the last brick, J.E. Dunn Construction helps make building plans a done deal. The contractor offers general construction services, construction management, and design/build services nationwide. It's known for its work on campus, health care, and commercial projects, including the BayCare Health System, CHI Health - Creighton University Medical Center - Bergan Mercy, Seaton Hall/Regnier Hall, Decatur High School and Ron Clark Academy. Founded in 1924, the company is one of Kansas City's top commercial construction firms and has been listed as one of the nation's top 20 general building companies. It operates as a subsidiary of J.E. Dunn Construction Group.

Operations

JE Dunn has ranked as one of the top 20 largest general building companies in the US. It offers services such as virtual design & construction, augmented reality, smart building solutions, robotics, as well as wearable technology including tool assist, personal safety, access to data as job aids, and visualization. JE Dunn also operates a real estate investment through its subsidiary JE Dunn Capital Partners.

It counts several noteworthy projects among its portfolio, such as Cerner Innovations Campus, Omaha Capitol District, Restoration Hardware, The Thompson Hotel, Minnesota State Capitol, Lenexa Civic Center, and Minnesota Children's Museum Renovation and Addition.

Geographic Reach

Based in Kansas City, Missouri, JE Dunn operates nearly 25 offices throughout the US.

Sales and Marketing

JE Dunn works on projects for clients in several sectors, including projects related to: science and technology, corporate environments, healthcare, hospitality, government and military, energy and utility, education, and multifamily residential properties, among others.

Financial Performance

While full financial information of the privately-held company were not available, the company reported that it brings in annual revenue of $3.6 billion as of early 2019. Its revenues in 2019 rose to $4.3 billion, representing the company's consistent revenue growth over the years.

Strategy

J.E. Dunn Construction Company has been busy working on a variety of different projects in recent years. In 2020, J.E. Dunn completed the seven-story, 350,000-square-foot new Johnson County Courthouse, which replaced the aging, overcrowded existing courthouse by consolidating the Tenth Judicial District Court, District Attorney, and supporting spaces into a distinctive civic building. The team plans to finish installing systems and ancillary furniture in November. Johnson County staff will begin occupying the courthouse by September, and the building is intended to open to the public in the first quarter of 2021.

Earlier that year, it started construction on the new General Leonard Wood Army Community Hospital, a $295 million, state-of-the-art, 52-acre hospital complex that, when completed in 2024, will replace the current hospital facility.

J.E. Dunn also worked on the $40 million Minnehaha County Jail expansion, which added 329 beds and new administration space, which will solve a long-standing space problem. J.E. Dunn worked with Henry Carlson Construction, JLG Architects, and BWBR Architects for this project.

Company Background

John Ernest Dunn (Ernie) founded JE Dunn Construction Company in Kansas City, Missouri in 1924. In the past, JE Dunn grew through acquisitions, purchasing RJ Griffin & Co. (Atlanta) in 2000, Witcher Construction (Minneapolis) in 1990, and Drake Construction (Portland, Oregon) in 1992.

EXECUTIVES

CLO, Casey S Halsey
Auditors : KPMG LLP KANSAS CITY MO

LOCATIONS

HQ: J.E. DUNN CONSTRUCTION COMPANY
  1001 LOCUST ST, KANSAS CITY, MO 641061904
Phone: 816 474-8600
Web: WWW.JEDUNN.COM

PRODUCTS/OPERATIONS

Selected Project Delivery Methods
Competitive Bid
Construction Management (Agency)
Design-Build
General Contracting/CM At Risk
Integrated Project Delivery
Project Management

COMPETITORS

BIG-D CONSTRUCTION CORP.
BRASFIELD & GORRIE, L.L.C.
GILBANE BUILDING COMPANY
GILBANE, INC.
J.E. DUNN CONSTRUCTION GROUP, INC.
MCCARTHY BUILDING COMPANIES, INC.
MIRON CONSTRUCTION CO., INC.
SWINERTON INCORPORATED
TDINDUSTRIES, INC.
THE PIKE COMPANY INC

HISTORICAL FINANCIALS

Company Type: Private

Income Statement — FYE: December 31

	REVENUE ($mil)	NET INCOME ($mil)	NET PROFIT MARGIN	EMPLOYEES
12/17	2,945	0	0.0%	1,635
12/16	2,909	0	0.0%	—
12/15	2,909	0	0.0%	—
12/14	2,242	0	0.0%	—
Annual Growth	9.5%	—	—	—

2017 Year-End Financials
Return on assets: —   Cash ($ mil.): 29
Return on equity: —
Current Ratio: 1.10

J.E. DUNN CONSTRUCTION GROUP, INC.

Owned by descendants of founder John Ernest Dunn, J.E. Dunn Construction Group operates as the holding company for a group of construction firms that includes flagship J.E. Dunn Construction and JE Dunn Capital Partners. With expertise across corporate environments, courthouse and justice, federal and military, education, life sciences, local and state government, and mixed use and retail industries, the company builds institutional, commercial, and industrial structures nationwide. It also provides construction and program management and design/build services. J.E. Dunn Construction, which is among the largest US general builders, is one of the first contractors to offer the construction management delivery method. Some of its major projects have included an IRS facility and the world headquarters for H&R Block, both located in Kansas City, Missouri. The company was founded in 1924.

Operations
J.E. Dunn provides virtual design and construction, augmented reality, and aptitude. From programming, through preconstruction and construction, Building Information Modeling (BIM), and Virtual Design Construction (VDC) play a major role in all projects. Every project J.E. Dunn undertakes involves a multitude of moving parts such as equipment commissioning, delivery scheduling, construction process coordination, safety planning, and others. In addition, the company's Dunn Dashboard also provides collaboration and efficiency when it comes to utilizing VDC in real time. This technology provides web-based collaboration on design documents, digital models, victual estimates, and other project documentation.

Geographic Reach
Headquartered in Kansas City, Missouri, J.E. Dunn operates nearly 25 offices across the nation. It has offices in Austin, Dallas, Colorado Houston, Minneapolis, Raleigh, and Oklahoma, among others.

Sales and Marketing
The company serves customers across a diverse array of industries, including aviation, healthcare, hospitality, industrial, religious, senior living, sports and recreation, and advanced industries.

Company Background
A bigwig particularly in the Midwest, the group regularly bids on federal government projects. J.E. Dunn won a major contract from the US Army Corps of Engineers to build a regional correctional facility at Fort Leavenworth, Kansas, that replaced smaller prisons in Texas, Kentucky, and Oklahoma.

In 2012 the company earned the designation of having the first ever LEED Gold Certified building in downtown Kansas City.

The descendants of John Ernest Dunn hold a majority stake in the company.

EXECUTIVES
Vice Chairman, William H Dunn Senior
CLO, Casey S Halsey
Auditors : KPMG LLP KANSAS CITY MISSOUR

LOCATIONS
HQ: J.E. DUNN CONSTRUCTION GROUP, INC.
 1001 LOCUST ST, KANSAS CITY, MO 641061904
Phone: 816 474-8600
Web: WWW.JEDUNN.COM

PRODUCTS/OPERATIONS
Selected Group Companies
JE Dunn Midwest
JE Dunn North Central
JE Dunn Northwest
JE Dunn Rocky Mountain
JE Dunn South Central
R.J. Griffin & Company

Selected Services
Preconstruction
 Constructability review
 Feasibility studies
 Market analysis
 Mechanical, electrical, plumbing review
 Preconstruction estimating
 Quality control
 Risk management
 Scheduling
Construction
 Change order management
 Labor relations
 Progress monitoring
 Quality control and testing
Post Construction
 Commissioning
 Final closeout
 Lien releases
 One-year walkthrough
 Operations and maintenance manuals

COMPETITORS
BRASFIELD & GORRIE, L.L.C.
GILBANE BUILDING COMPANY
HOAR CONSTRUCTION, LLC
HUNT CONSTRUCTION GROUP, INC.
J.E. DUNN CONSTRUCTION COMPANY
M. A. MORTENSON COMPANY
MANHATTAN CONSTRUCTION COMPANY
MCCARTHY BUILDING COMPANIES, INC.
RIVER CITY CONSTRUCTION, L.L.C.
S. M. WILSON & CO.

HISTORICAL FINANCIALS
Company Type: Private

Income Statement — FYE: December 31

	REVENUE ($mil)	NET INCOME ($mil)	NET PROFIT MARGIN	EMPLOYEES
12/19	4,329	0	0.0%	2,080
12/15	2,910	0	0.0%	—
12/14	2,243	0	0.0%	—
12/13	2,243	0	0.0%	—
Annual Growth	11.6%	—	—	—

JACKSON ELECTRIC MEMBERSHIP CORPORATION

Jackson EMC distributes electricity to more than 197,800 individual customers (more than 210,200 meters) in 10 counties around Atlanta and in northeastern Georgia. The majority of customers are residential, with commercial and industrial customers accounting for 42% of fiscal year 2013 revenues. One of the largest nonprofit power cooperatives in the US and the largest electric cooperative in Georgia, Jackson EMC is owned by its members. The cooperative's generation and transmission partners include Oglethorpe Power Corp., Georgia Systems Operation, and Georgia Transmission Corp.

Operations
Jackson EMC operates 86 substations and more than 13,550 miles of power line.

Financial Performance
In fiscal 2013 the coop reported a revenue increased of 1%. Net income declined slightly by 0.3%. That year the non-profit coop returned $5.5 million in margin refunds to nearly 201,000 members.

Strategy
Among other initiatives, Jackson EMC is promoting conservation and green energy options as a way to slow energy growth and reduce greenhouse gas emissions. Initiatives include advocating the use of more efficient light bulbs, and the widespread use of solar panels for power generation.

Company Background
Although the county of Jackson is named after a Georgia statesman from the Revolutionary War era, Jackson Electric Membership Corporation (Jackson EMC) can trace its roots more directly to US president Franklin Roosevelt, whose frequent trips to Warm Springs alerted him to the shortage of affordable electric power outside of major cities. Jackson EMC was founded in 1938 as part of the Roosevelt government's national rural electrification drive.

Auditors : MCNAIR MCLEMORE MIDDLEBROOKS

LOCATIONS
HQ: JACKSON ELECTRIC MEMBERSHIP CORPORATION
 850 COMMERCE RD, JEFFERSON, GA 305493329
Phone: 706 367-5281
Web: WWW.JACKSONEMC.COM

COMPETITORS
COBB ELECTRIC MEMBERSHIP CORPORATION
LEE COUNTY ELECTRIC COOPERATIVE, INC.
NEW YORK POWER AUTHORITY
PEDERNALES ELECTRIC COOPERATIVE, INC.
SOUTHERN MARYLAND ELECTRIC COOPERATIVE, INC.

HISTORICAL FINANCIALS
Company Type: Private

Income Statement — FYE: May 31

	REVENUE ($mil)	NET INCOME ($mil)	NET PROFIT MARGIN	EMPLOYEES
05/21	593	36	6.2%	445
05/20	585	37	6.4%	—
05/19	571	29	5.1%	—
05/18	548	37	6.8%	—
Annual Growth	2.7%	(0.8%)	—	—

2021 Year-End Financials
Return on assets: 3.1%   Cash ($ mil.): 58
Return on equity: 6.8%
Current Ratio: 1.60

HOOVER'S HANDBOOK OF PRIVATE COMPANIES 2023

JACKSON HEALTHCARE, LLC

Jackson Healthcare is a family of highly specialized healthcare staffing, search and technology companies. Its companies provide healthcare systems, hospitals and medical facilities of all sizes with the skilled and specialized labor and technologies they need to deliver high quality patient care and achieve the best possible outcomes ? while connecting healthcare professionals to the temporary engagements, contract assignments and permanent placement employment opportunities they desire. Jackson Healthcare allows to help health systems, hospitals and other healthcare facilities with temporary and permanent workforce needs. . Richard Jackson formed the company in 2000.

Operations

Jackson Healthcare operates about 15 subsidiaries and operations units and serves more than 10 million patients spread throughout thousands of health care facilities.

Subsidiaries and divisions include Premier Anesthesia, Jackson Therapy Partners, LucumTenens.com, Jackson Nurse Professionals, and Jackson & Coker. Other operations include USAntibiotics, Sullivan Healthcare Consulting, Jackson Pharmacy Professionals, Tyler & Company, and Parker Staffing.

Its health care software and technology portfolio is managed by Care Logistics and Healthcare Workforce Logistics.

Geographic Reach

The company is headquartered in Alpharetta, Georgia. It is backed by over 15,000 clinician providers covering all 50 US states.

Sales and Marketing

The company helps thousands of healthcare facilities that serve over 10 million patients annually.

EXECUTIVES

CIO, Ryan Esparza

LOCATIONS

HQ: JACKSON HEALTHCARE, LLC
2655 NORTHWINDS PKWY, ALPHARETTA, GA 300092280
Phone: 770 643-5500
Web: WWW.JACKSONHEALTHCARE.COM

PRODUCTS/OPERATIONS

Selected Subsidiaries and Operating Units
Jackson Healthcare Staffing
    AdvancedPractice.com (a full-service locum tenens agency dedicated to physician assistants and nurse practitioners)
    Healthcare Staffing Technologies (provider of career concierge sites in the healthcare market)
    HealthIT Project Managers (provider of experienced IT project management contractors to hospitals)
    Jackson & Coker (locum tenens and permanent recruitment firm for physicians)
    Jackson Nurse Professionals (specializes in the placement of registered nurses in healthcare settings nationwide)
    Jackson Pharmacy Professionals (national pharmacy-only staffing and recruiting company)
    Jackson Surgical Assistants (staffing of certified surgical assistants to surgeons and hospitals)
    Jackson Therapy Partners (staffing of rehabilitation therapists and other allied healthcare professionals)
    LocumTenens.com (locum tenens physician recruitment agency)
    Parker HealthcareIT (provider of supplemental IT staffing)
    Premier Anesthesia (anesthesia department management company)
Jackson Healthcare Technology
    Care Logistics (firm that helps hospitals transform their operations to deliver hospital efficiency)
    Patient Placement Systems (supplier of continuing care provider software)

COMPETITORS

AMN HEALTHCARE SERVICES, INC.
ATRIUS HEALTH, INC.
CHG COMPANIES, INC.
CROSS COUNTRY HEALTHCARE, INC.
DNA SEARCH INC.
ENVISION HEALTHCARE CORPORATION
MEDSTAFF INC
ONWARD HEALTHCARE, INC.
SHERIDAN HEALTHCARE, INC.
SOLIANT HEALTH, LLC

HISTORICAL FINANCIALS

Company Type: Private

Income Statement   FYE: December 31

	REVENUE ($mil)	NET INCOME ($mil)	NET PROFIT MARGIN	EMPLOYEES
12/17	949	99	10.5%	949
12/16	838	92	11.1%	—
12/15	696	70	10.2%	—
12/07	384	18	4.8%	—
Annual Growth	9.5%	18.4%	—	—

2017 Year-End Financials
Return on assets: 25.6%   Cash ($ mil.): 65
Return on equity: 132.6%
Current Ratio: 3.60

JACKSON-MADISON COUNTY GENERAL HOSPITAL DISTRICT

LOCATIONS

HQ: JACKSON-MADISON COUNTY GENERAL HOSPITAL DISTRICT
620 SKYLINE DR, JACKSON, TN 383013923
Phone: 731 541-5000
Web: WWW.WTH.ORG

HISTORICAL FINANCIALS

Company Type: Private

Income Statement   FYE: June 30

	REVENUE ($mil)	NET INCOME ($mil)	NET PROFIT MARGIN	EMPLOYEES
06/16	597	10	1.8%	6,000
06/15	554	20	3.7%	—
06/04	429	37	8.6%	—
06/03	307	247	80.4%	—
Annual Growth	5.3%	(21.4%)	—	—

2016 Year-End Financials
Return on assets: 1.2%   Cash ($ mil.): 20
Return on equity: 2.3%
Current Ratio: 3.70

JACKSONVILLE ELECTRIC AUTHORITY

As long as sparks are flying in Jacksonville, everything is A-OK with JEA. The community-owned, not-for-profit utility provides electricity to 438,000 customers in Jacksonville and surrounding areas in northeastern Florida. Managing an electric system that dates back to 1895, JEA has a net generating capacity of 3,747 MW. It owns an electric system with five primarily fossil-fueled generating plants. JEA also gets 12.8 MW of generating capacity from two methane-fueled landfill plants. The company resells electricity to other utilities, including NextEra Energy. JEA also provides water and wastewater services; it serves 321,600 water customers and 247,500 wastewater customers.

Operations

JEA is the largest community-owned utility in Florida and the eighth largest in the US.

The company operates in four segments: the Electric System and Bulk Power Supply System; the St. Johns River Power Park System System; the Water and Sewer System; and the District Energy System.

The Electric System operates five generating plants in Florida (and holds a stake in a power plant in Georgia) and all transmission and distribution facilities, including more than 745 miles of transmission lines and more than 6,500 miles of distribution lines. It purchases power locally from a solar field and a landfill gas facility. This segment accounted for 77% of the company's 2014 revenues.

JEA's Water System consists of 134 artesian wells that tap into the Floridan aquifer. Water is distributed through 37 water treatment plants and more than 4,300 miles of water lines. Wastewater is collected through more than 3,800 miles of wastewater collection lines and treated at seven regional treatment plants.

The company's operations are funded by

three enterprise funds: the Electric Enterprise Fund, the Water and Sewer Fund, and the District Energy System, The Electric Enterprise Fund is comprised of the JEA Electric System, Bulk Power Supply System, and St. Johns River Power Park System.

Geographic Reach
The cooperative serves customers in Northeast Florida.

Financial Performance
In 2014 JEA's revenues increased by 3% due to a 3% growth in electric sales as the result of higher consumption (primarily 4.3% in residential sales). Water and sewer sales increased by 1% related to a rise in customers, and District Energy System sales increased by 2%. Approximately 47% of JEA's electric 2014 revenues came from its 375,000 residential customers, 50% from 48,000 commercial and industrial customers, and 3% from one wholesale customer.

The company's net income increased by 97% due to higher investment returns and a decline in loss from interest on debt.

JEA's operating cash flow decreased by 4% due to higher payments to suppliers.

Strategy
To help meet state regulations for carbon emission control, JEA plans to get 10% of its energy requirements from nuclear energy by 2018, and 30% by 2030. In this regard JEA has signed a purchase power agreement to get 206 MW from a nuclear plant beginning in 2016 and is pursuing additional purchased power contracts.

JEA is also building out more fossil fuel capacity.

Company Background
The electric utility grew from a department of city of Jacksonville into an independent authority created by city and county government consolidation in 1967. In 1997 the water and sewer systems (which had been operated by the city since 1880) were also placed under JEA management.

In 2011 it completed the Greenland Energy Center, which included two 175-MW natural gas-fired combustion turbines.

EXECUTIVES
Executive President*, James Chancellor
CIO*, Ron Baker
Interim Chief COMP*, Steve Tuten
Auditors : ERNST & YOUNG LLP JACKSONVIL

LOCATIONS
HQ: JACKSONVILLE ELECTRIC AUTHORITY
21 W CHURCH ST FL 1, JACKSONVILLE, FL 322023152
Phone: 904 665-6000
Web: WWW.JEA.COM

PRODUCTS/OPERATIONS

2014 Sales
	$ mil.	% of total
Electric	1,431.2	77
Water & wastewater	383.6	21
District Energy System	8.7	-
Other	38.4	2
Total	1,861.9	100

COMPETITORS
GAINESVILLE REGIONAL UTILITIES (INC)
GREAT RIVER ENERGY
KNOXVILLE UTILITIES BOARD
LOS ANGELES DEPARTMENT OF WATER AND POWER
OMAHA PUBLIC POWER DISTRICT
ORLANDO UTILITIES COMMISSION (INC)
POWERSOUTH ENERGY COOPERATIVE
PUBLIC UTILITY DISTRICT 1 OF SNOHOMISH COUNTY
SACRAMENTO MUNICIPAL UTILITY DISTRICT
SEMINOLE ELECTRIC COOPERATIVE, INC.

HISTORICAL FINANCIALS
Company Type: Private

Income Statement   FYE: September 30

	REVENUE ($mil)	NET INCOME ($mil)	NET PROFIT MARGIN	EMPLOYEES
09/18	1,789	126	7.1%	2,356
09/17	1,875	254	13.6%	—
09/16	1,782	210	11.8%	—
Annual Growth	0.2%	(22.4%)	—	—

2018 Year-End Financials
Return on assets: 1.5%   Cash ($ mil.): 441
Return on equity: 4.6%
Current Ratio: 4.20

JACO OIL COMPANY

Jaco Oil Company is jockeying for its piece of the convenience store pie. The company's Fastrip Food Stores subsidiary operates more than 50 convenience stores and gas stations primarily in and around Bakersfield, California, but also in Arizona. Besides offering customers traditional convenience-store fare, which includes coffee, milk, beer, snacks, tobacco, and the like, the Fastrip chain stocks a full range of grocery items and provides in-store financial service centers. Financial services include check cashing, payday loans, wire transfer services via The Western Union Company, refund anticipation loans, and other services, at many locations. Jaco Oil Company was founded in 1970.

Operations
The company operates nearly 50 stores in Bakersfield and Kern counties, as well as in Fresno, Sacramento, and the Chico area. It also has four stores in Arizona, located in Bullhead, Casa Grande, and Nogales. As part of its business, Jaco Oil offers food, beverages, and financial services, such as payday loans, wire transfer services, and tax preparation services.

Geographic Reach
Jaco Oil owns and operates gasoline service stations and convenience stores in the Western US.

Strategy
Fastrip works to distinguish itself from other convenience store chains by stocking a complete assortment of grocery items, including such staples as sugar, flour, salt, cake mix, and even green beans. The chain bills itself as a Mini Grocery Store, a strategy that other retailers, including Dollar General and drugstore-giant Walgreen, have adopted. It's also always open (24/7/365).

Auditors : MOSS ADAMS LLP LOS ANGELES

LOCATIONS
HQ: JACO OIL COMPANY
3101 STATE RD, BAKERSFIELD, CA 933084931
Phone: 661 393-7000
Web: WWW.JACO.COM

2013 Stores
	No.
California	49
Arizona	4
Total	53

PRODUCTS/OPERATIONS

Selected Services
Check cashing
EBT
Ice
Liquor
Lottery
Money orders
Money transfers
Phone cards
Quick serve restaurant
Restrooms
WIC

Selected Products
Alcoholic beverages
Beverages
Coffee
Dairy
Food
Fountain drinks
Groceries
Snacks
Tobacco products

COMPETITORS
COBORN'S, INCORPORATED
FOOD 4 LESS OF SOUTHERN CALIFORNIA, INC.
GROCERY OUTLET INC.
HOUCHENS INDUSTRIES, INC.
SUPER CENTER CONCEPTS, INC.

HISTORICAL FINANCIALS
Company Type: Private

Income Statement   FYE: December 31

	REVENUE ($mil)	NET INCOME ($mil)	NET PROFIT MARGIN	EMPLOYEES
12/21	993	18	1.8%	350
12/20	555	20	3.7%	—
12/19	657	25	3.9%	—
12/18	636	19	3.1%	—
Annual Growth	16.0%	(2.2%)	—	—

2021 Year-End Financials
Return on assets: 8.9%   Cash ($ mil.): 89
Return on equity: 10.6%
Current Ratio: 4.60

JARDEN LLC

Auditors : PRICEWATERHOUSECOOPERS LLP NE

LOCATIONS

HQ: JARDEN LLC
221 RIVER ST, HOBOKEN, NJ 070305989
Phone: 201 610-6600
Web: WWW.NEWELLBRANDS.COM

HISTORICAL FINANCIALS
Company Type: Private

Income Statement — FYE: December 31

	REVENUE ($mil)	NET INCOME ($mil)	NET PROFIT MARGIN	EMPLOYEES
12/15	8,603	146	1.7%	17,000
12/14	8,287	242	2.9%	—
12/13	7,355	203	2.8%	—
12/12	6,696	243	3.6%	—
Annual Growth	8.7%	(15.6%)	—	—

2015 Year-End Financials
Return on assets: 1.0%   Cash ($ mil.): 1,298
Return on equity: 3.6%
Current Ratio: 2.00

JEFFERSON COUNTY SCHOOL DISTRICT NO. R-1

Auditors : CLIFTONLARSONALLEN LLP GREEN

LOCATIONS

HQ: JEFFERSON COUNTY SCHOOL DISTRICT NO. R-1
1829 DENVER WEST DR # 27, GOLDEN, CO 804013120
Phone: 303 982-6500
Web: WWW.JEFFCOPUBLICSCHOOLS.ORG

HISTORICAL FINANCIALS
Company Type: Private

Income Statement — FYE: June 30

	REVENUE ($mil)	NET INCOME ($mil)	NET PROFIT MARGIN	EMPLOYEES
06/20	1,016	(55)	—	12,000
06/19	960	368	38.4%	—
06/18	848	(4)	—	—
06/17	808	(40)	—	—
Annual Growth	7.9%	—	—	—

2020 Year-End Financials
Return on assets: (-2.7%)   Cash ($ mil.): 17
Return on equity: —
Current Ratio: —

JERSEY CENTRAL POWER & LIGHT COMPANY

New Jersey native son Bruce Springsteen may be The Boss, but Jersey Central Power & Light (JCP&L) electrifies more fans than he does every day. The company, a subsidiary of multi-utility holding company FirstEnergy, transmits and distributes electricity to 1.1 million homes and businesses in 13 counties in central and northern New Jersey. JCP&L operates 22,670 miles of distribution lines; its 2,550-mile transmission system is overseen by regional transmission organization (RTO) PJM Interconnection. The utility also has some power plant interests.

Operations
The company provides regulated electric transmission and distribution services. JCP&L also has an ownership interest in a hydroelectric generating facility.

Geographic Reach
JCP&L conducts business in 3,200 square miles of east central, northern, and western New Jersey. The area it serves has a population of approximately 2.7 million.

Financial Performance
Revenues decreased by 18% in 2011 due to a rate adjustment for all customer classes and lower power deliveries. The lower power delivery to residential customers was the result of decreased weather-related usage in 2011. Lower distribution deliveries to commercial and industrial customers that year reflected the impact of economic conditions in JCP&L's service territory. A decrease in retail generation revenues was due to lower generation power sales in all customer classes primarily due to an increase in customers shopping around for alternative providers. Wholesale generation revenues decreased due to a drop in PJM spot market energy sales.

JCP&L's net income decreased by 39% in 2011 due to lower revenues offset by reductions in purchased power costs and amortization of regulatory assets.

Company Background
The utility was organized under the laws of the State of New Jersey in 1925.

EXECUTIVES

CAO*, Marlene A Barwood
Auditors : PRICEWATERHOUSECOOPERS LLP C

LOCATIONS

HQ: JERSEY CENTRAL POWER & LIGHT COMPANY
76 S MAIN ST, AKRON, OH 443081812
Phone: 800 736-3402
Web: WWW.FIRSTENERGYCORP.COM

PRODUCTS/OPERATIONS

Selected Services
Electrical services
Outdoor lighting
Professional tree services

COMPETITORS

OMAHA PUBLIC POWER DISTRICT
ONCOR ELECTRIC DELIVERY COMPANY LLC
PPL ELECTRIC UTILITIES CORPORATION
SACRAMENTO MUNICIPAL UTILITY DISTRICT
TUCSON ELECTRIC POWER COMPANY

HISTORICAL FINANCIALS
Company Type: Private

Income Statement — FYE: December 31

	REVENUE ($mil)	NET INCOME ($mil)	NET PROFIT MARGIN	EMPLOYEES
12/17	1,801	115	6.4%	1,413
12/16	1,787	80	4.5%	—
12/11	2,495	144	5.8%	—
12/10	3,027	192	6.3%	—
Annual Growth	(7.1%)	(7.1%)	—	—

2017 Year-End Financials
Return on assets: 1.3%   Cash ($ mil.): 251
Return on equity: 3.6%
Current Ratio: 2.20

JEWISH COMMUNAL FUND

Auditors : EISNERAMPER LLP NEW YORK NY

LOCATIONS

HQ: JEWISH COMMUNAL FUND
575 MADISON AVE STE 703, NEW YORK, NY 100228591
Phone: 212 752-8277
Web: WWW.JCFNY.ORG

HISTORICAL FINANCIALS
Company Type: Private

Income Statement — FYE: June 30

	REVENUE ($mil)	NET INCOME ($mil)	NET PROFIT MARGIN	EMPLOYEES
06/21	678	140	20.7%	14
06/20	585	36	6.2%	—
06/19	822	355	43.3%	—
06/18	511	65	12.9%	—
Annual Growth	9.9%	28.6%	—	—

2021 Year-End Financials
Return on assets: 5.8%   Cash ($ mil.): 83
Return on equity: 5.8%
Current Ratio: 64.90

JFK HEALTH SYSTEM, INC.

JFK Health System provides medical services in a tri-county area in central New

Jersey through flagship facility JFK Medical Center. The hospital has about 500 acute care beds and is one of the Garden State's major health care facilities. Included in the medical center complex are JFK Johnson Rehabilitation Institute, JFK New Jersey Neuroscience Institute, and a number of outpatient care and imaging centers. Other JFK Health System facilities provide primary and specialty services, as well as senior living, home health, and hospice care. In 2017 JFK Health agreed to merge with Hackensack Meridian; the combined system will operate 15 hospitals in New Jersey.

Operations
JFK Health System's Hartwyck Nursing, Convalescent, and Rehabilitation Centers, are located at three additional sites. Combined, they house more than 500 beds for nursing home, sub-acute, rehabilitation, and respite-care patients. One of the units is the only center in the state and one of very few in the country offering specialty care for Huntington's disease patients.

Geographic Reach
JFK Health System serves patients in the central New Jersey counties of Middlesex, Union, and Somerset.

Strategy
JFK Health System regularly expands and upgrades its facilities and its medical equipment to keep pace with modern health care needs. For instance, in 2011 JFK Medical Center began construction of a three-story ER pavilion on top of its existing emergency department.

Company Background
Formerly Solaris Health, the not-for-profit system took the JFK Health System name in 2011 to align with its flagship facility. It previously took on the Solaris name in 1997 when JFK Medical Center (founded in 1967) and Muhlenberg Regional Medical Center (founded in 1894) merged. The Muhlenberg inpatient operations were discontinued in 2008, victim of an economically declining population base. JFK sold Muhlenberg to Community Healthcare Associates in 2018.

LOCATIONS
HQ: JFK HEALTH SYSTEM, INC.
80 JAMES ST, EDISON, NJ 088203938
Phone: 732 321-7000
Web: WWW.JFKHEALTHSYSTEM.ORG

COMPETITORS
ATLANTIC HEALTH SYSTEM INC.
BORGESS HEALTH ALLIANCE, INC.
CAPITAL HEALTH SYSTEM, INC.
CARE NEW ENGLAND HEALTH SYSTEM
CONEMAUGH HEALTH COMPANY, LLC
GENESIS HEALTH SYSTEM
HACKENSACK MERIDIAN HEALTH, INC.
KENNEDY HEALTH SYSTEM, INC.
SPACE COAST HEALTH FOUNDATION, INC.
THEDACARE, INC.

HISTORICAL FINANCIALS
Company Type: Private

Income Statement — FYE: December 31

	REVENUE ($mil)	NET INCOME ($mil)	NET PROFIT MARGIN	EMPLOYEES
12/18	591	128	21.7%	6,735
12/17	0	(0)	—	—
12/15	0	0	—	—
12/14	0	0	—	—
Annual Growth	—	—	—	—

2018 Year-End Financials
Return on assets: 33.7% Cash ($ mil.): 35
Return on equity: 74.5%
Current Ratio: 0.70

JOBSOHIO BEVERAGE SYSTEM

LOCATIONS
HQ: JOBSOHIO BEVERAGE SYSTEM
41 S HIGH ST STE 150, COLUMBUS, OH 432156115
Phone: 614 224-6446
Web: WWW.JOBSOHIO.COM

HISTORICAL FINANCIALS
Company Type: Private

Income Statement — FYE: June 30

	REVENUE ($mil)	NET INCOME ($mil)	NET PROFIT MARGIN	EMPLOYEES
06/21	699	3	0.4%	13
06/20	596	(17)	—	—
06/19	1,284	(126)	—	—
06/17	444	4	1.0%	—
Annual Growth	12.0%	(9.4%)	—	—

2021 Year-End Financials
Return on assets: 0.2% Cash ($ mil.): 229
Return on equity: —
Current Ratio: 1.90

JOHN C. LINCOLN HEALTH NETWORK

John C. Lincoln Health Network takes care of the health of John Q. Public in Arizona. The not-for-profit health care network serves the northern Phoenix area and is home to two hospitals: John C. Lincoln Deer Valley Hospital, with more than 200 beds, and John C. Lincoln North Mountain Hospital, with roughly 260 beds (the Valley's first Magnet nursing hospital, an accredited Chest Pain Center, and the host of a Level 1 Trauma Center). The system also features a children's care facility, various physician and dental clinics, a food bank, and assisted living facilities for the elderly all operating under the Desert Mission moniker. John C. Lincoln Health Network is part of the Scottsdale Lincoln Health Network, along with Scottsdale Healthcare.

Operations
John C. Lincoln Health Network has a staff of about 1,100 physicians.

In addition to its hospital locations, the network includes physician practices for primary and specialty care, as well as medical imaging and research centers. John C. Lincoln's facilities serve about 750,000 patients each year and provide specialty services in fields including cardiology, pulmonary care, neuroscience, and women's health. The Deer Valley Hospital is also home to Mendy's Place, the North Valley's only 24-hour hospital emergency center exclusively for children, and an accredited Chest Pain Center.

In 2012 John C. Lincoln Health Network had 748,019 patient visits to its hospitals and physicians and specialty practices; 26,868 exams at the breast health and research center; and 8,719 adult day health care visits.

Its specialized medical services includes heart care, pulmonary care, neurosciences, emergency care, and a Breast Health and Research Center. Community services include Desert Mission Food Bank, a dental clinic for uninsured children, a resource center for families in crisis, and a child care center. The John C. Lincoln Health Foundation conducts philanthropic efforts.

The health system's Desert Mission Food Bank distributed roughly 41,000 emergency food boxes to members of its community in 2012. Other locations providing community outreach services include the Community Health Center, Children's Dental Clinic, Lincoln Learning Center, Adult Day Health Care, and Neighborhood Renewal. The Marley House Behavioral Health Clinic provides mental health and related services for children and adults on a sliding scale basis in English and Spanish.

Strategy
In 2013 John C. Lincoln expanded its infrastructure, opening the John C. Lincoln Sonoran Health and Emergency Center, a new emergency center and outpatient clinic in Phoenix. The $18 million project includes an emergency department, medical practice, and diagnostic imaging facilities.

Upgrading its technology, in 2012 John C. Lincoln Deer Valley Hospital added the da Vinci Si Robotic Surgical System. To help it improve its medical record keeping, that year, the health system's primary care offices launched JCL Connect electronic health records software.

Mergers and Acquisitions
To strengthen its footing in the Arizona marketplace, in 2014 John C. Lincoln formed an affiliation with Scottsdale Healthcare. The combined networks, operating under the

moniker Scottsdale Lincoln Health Network, include five hospitals with some 3,700 affiliated physicians and an extensive outpatient services network.

Company Background

The hospital gained its first real funding in 1933 from millionaire entrepreneur John C. Lincoln, the founder of Lincoln Electric.

LOCATIONS

HQ: JOHN C. LINCOLN HEALTH NETWORK
2500 E DUNLAP AVE, PHOENIX, AZ 85020
Phone: 602 870-6060

Hospitals
Deer Valley Hospital: Phoenix, Arizona
North Mountain Hospital: Phoenix, Arizona

PRODUCTS/OPERATIONS

Selected Centers and Services
Breast Health and Research Center
Cancer Treatment
Cardiac Care
Deep Vein Thrombosis Program
Emergency Care
Heartburn Program
Level I Trauma Center
Medical Imaging
Neurosciences
Orthopedics
Outpatient Surgery Centers
Pediatrics
Pulmonary Program
Reconstructive Plastic Surgery
Scarless Surgery
Uterine Fibroid Treatment
Varicose Vein Treatment

COMPETITORS

ASCENSION PROVIDENCE HOSPITAL
ASCENSION SOUTHEAST MICHIGAN
BRYAN MEDICAL CENTER
JOHN MUIR HEALTH
ST LUKE'S HOSPITAL

HISTORICAL FINANCIALS
Company Type: Private

Income Statement			FYE: December 31
	REVENUE ($mil)	NET INCOME ($mil)	NET PROFIT MARGIN	EMPLOYEES
12/13	584	44	7.6%	3,500
12/12	509	32	6.4%	—
12/11	486	17	3.6%	—
12/10	551	19	3.5%	—
Annual Growth	2.0%	31.3%	—	—

2013 Year-End Financials
Return on assets: 4.7% Cash ($ mil.): 40
Return on equity: 7.6%
Current Ratio: 1.30

JOHN MUIR HEALTH

John Muir Health provides health care throughout the scenic San Francisco Bay area. The John Muir Health Walnut Creek Medical Center has about 555 beds and that serves as Contra Costa County's only designated trauma center. The John Muir Health Concord Medical Center has about 245 beds. Both are recognized as the finest centers for neurosciences, orthopedics, cancer care, cardiovascular care and high-risk obstetrics. The John Muir Behavioral Health Center is a nearly 75-bed psychiatric hospital. John Muir Health also offers home health, rehabilitation, and wellness programs.

Operations

John Muir Health's network of outpatient facilities include physical therapy and occupational therapy centers, as well as specialty pediatric, women's health, and diabetes centers. The system also includes medical imaging centers.

John Muir Health's other areas of specialty include general surgery, robotic surgery, weight-loss surgery, rehabilitation and critical care.

The system has more than 1,000 physicians associated with the John Muir Health Physician Network. The John Muir Medical Group's approximately 350 clinician members work within the John Muir Health System's hospitals, urgent care and outpatient clinics in multiple specialties, mostly in primary care.

John Muir Health partners include Optum, Canopy Health, UCSF Medical Center, San Ramon Regional Medical Center, Stanford Children's Health, Blue Cross Blue Shield of California, and Health Net of California.

Geographic Reach

John Muir Health's facilities are located throughout Contra Costa county and part of Alameda and Solano counties.

Company Background

John Muir Health was formed from the 1997 merger of the John Muir Medical Center (the Walnut Creek Campus, which dates back to 1965) and the Mt. Diablo Medical Center (now the Concord Campus, dating back to 1930 as the Concord Hospital).

Auditors: KPMG LLP SAN FRANCISCO CA

LOCATIONS

HQ: JOHN MUIR HEALTH
1601 YGNACIO VALLEY RD, WALNUT CREEK, CA 945983122
Phone: 925 947-4449
Web: WWW.JOHNMUIRHEALTH.COM

PRODUCTS/OPERATIONS

Selected California Locations
Behavioral Health Center (Concord)
Breast Health Center (Walnut Creek)
Caring Hands Volunteer Program (Walnut Creek)
Clinical Research Centers (Concord)
Diabetes Center (Walnut Creek)
Garret Thrift Shop (Walnut Creek)
John Muir Medical Center (Concord)
John Muir Medical Center (Walnut Creek)
John Muir Outpatient Center (Brentwood, Tice Valley/Rossmoor)
Medical Imaging (Brentwood, Concord, San Ramon, Walnut Creek)
MuirLab (Regional)
Occupational Medicine (Brentwood, Concord, Walnut Creek)
Physical Rehabilitation Center (Concord, Pleasant Hill)
Urgent Care Centers (Brentwood, Concord, San Ramon, Walnut Creek)
Women's Health Center (Walnut Creek)
Wound Care Center (Walnut Creek)

Selected Services
Behavioral Health
Cancer
Cardiovascular Services
Chemical Dependency
Children's Services
Emergency Services
Lab Services
Medical Imaging
Orthopedics
Neurosciences
Physical Rehabilitation
Pregnancy & New Parent
Primary Care
Urgent Care

COMPETITORS

ATLANTIC HEALTH SYSTEM INC.
BRYAN MEDICAL CENTER
EMANATE HEALTH MEDICAL GROUP
HOSPITAL SERVICE DISTRICT 1
JEFFERSON HOSPITAL
JOHN C. LINCOLN HEALTH NETWORK
KENNEDY HEALTH SYSTEM, INC.
ORLANDO HEALTH, INC.
PALOMAR HEALTH
POUDRE VALLEY HEALTH CARE, INC.

HISTORICAL FINANCIALS
Company Type: Private

Income Statement			FYE: December 31
	REVENUE ($mil)	NET INCOME ($mil)	NET PROFIT MARGIN	EMPLOYEES
12/21	2,340	239	10.2%	2,200
12/20	2,106	178	8.5%	—
12/17	1,831	92	5.0%	—
12/16	1,734	107	6.2%	—
Annual Growth	6.2%	17.4%	—	—

2021 Year-End Financials
Return on assets: 6.0% Cash ($ mil.): 129
Return on equity: 9.4%
Current Ratio: 1.20

JOHNS HOPKINS ALL CHILDREN'S HOSPITAL, INC.

Johns Hopkins All Children's Hospital has about 260 beds, all dedicated to the health of west-central Florida's children. With over 590 pediatric physician specialists on board, the hospital offers its young patients (infants, children, and teens) a variety of services including a Neonatal Intensive Care Unit for premature and "at-risk" infants. Its heart, bone marrow, and kidney transplant programs are nationally renowned. The teaching hospital is also affiliated with the University of South Florida College of Medicine. All Children's Hospital is a member of the Johns Hopkins Medicine network.

Operations

The hospital handles over 6,200 inpatient visits each year, as well as more than 48,000 emergency room and over 312,000 outpatient visits. Johns Hopkins All Children's Hospital has expanded its services over the years to include specialty cancer, cystic fibrosis, cardiology, neurology, and cleft and craniofacial programs. In all, it provides igh quality care in more than 50 pediatric medical and surgical subspecialties. The hospital also includes several satellite outpatient care centers.

Geographic Reach
The hospital is headquartered in St. Petersburg, Florida. It has outpatient care facilities in Tampa and Sarasota, as well as other locations in Brandon, East Lake, Ft. Myers, Lakeland, Pasco, and North Port.

Company Background
The hospital became a fully integrated part of the Johns Hopkins Health System (the operating health organization of Johns Hopkins Medicine) through a non-cash transaction in 2011. Under terms of the agreement, Florida residents remained a majority of the All Children's governing board, thereby ensuring local control and staffing, and day-to-day operations would not change drastically. The deal gave All Children's access to the Johns Hopkins extensive educational and research resources. It also gave Johns Hopkins a dedicated pediatric facility, something it previously lacked.

The hospital traces its roots to the American Legion Hospital for Crippled Children, which was opened in 1927 in St. Petersburg to treat children suffering from polio and other diseases.

LOCATIONS

HQ: JOHNS HOPKINS ALL CHILDREN'S HOSPITAL, INC.
 501 6TH AVE S, SAINT PETERSBURG, FL 337014634
Phone: 727 898-7451
Web: WWW.HOPKINSALLCHILDRENS.ORG

PRODUCTS/OPERATIONS

Selected Affiliates
ACHPOB, Inc.
All Children's Hospital Foundation, Inc.
All Children's Research Institute, Inc. (ACRI)
Kids Home Care, Inc.
Pediatric Physician Services, Inc.
SurgiKid of Florida, Inc.
West Coast Neonatology, Inc.

Selected Services
Acute Care Rehabilitation
Allergy/ Immunology
Anesthesiology
Applied Behavior Analysis (ABA)
Asthma Coalition
Audiology: Hearing and Hearing Aid Services
Autism Center
Blood and Marrow Transplant (BMT)
Cancer and Blood Disorders
CanSurvive Clinic
Cardiology and Cardiovascular Surgery
Child Life Services
Craniofacial and Craniomaxillofacial
Critical Care
Early Steps
Emergency Medicine
Endocrinology & Diabetes
Fit4AllKids
Fit4AllMoms
Gastroenterology, Nutrition and Hepatology
General Pediatrics
Genetics
Healthy Start
Hematology/ Oncology
Hospitalists
Infectious Disease
Kids Home Care
Minimally Invasive Surgery
Music Therapy at All Children's Hospital
Neonatal Surgery
Neonatology
Nephrology
Neurology
Neuropsychiatry
Neuroscience Institute
Nutrition
Obstetrics/ Gynecology
Occupational Therapy Services
Ophthalmology
Orthopaedic and Scoliosis Surgery
Otolaryngology and Cochlear Implant Program
Pathology and Laboratory Medicine
Pediatric Developmental Medicine
Pediatric General Surgery
Perinatology
Physical Therapy Services
Plastic and Reconstructive Surgery
Psychiatry
Pulmonology
Radiology and Neuroradiology
Rehabilitation Services
Retail Pharmacy
Rheumatology
SAFE KIDS
Safe Routes to School
Speech-Language Pathology Services
Sports Medicine
STEPS to a Healthier Florida
Stroke Program
Thoracic Surgery
Thrombosis Program
Transport Team
Trauma Services
Urology

COMPETITORS

CHILDREN'S HEALTH CARE
CHILDREN'S HEALTH CLINICAL OPERATIONS
CHILDREN'S HEALTHCARE OF ATLANTA, INC.
CHILDREN'S HOSPITAL & RESEARCH CENTER AT OAKLAND
CHILDREN'S HOSPITAL AND HEALTH SYSTEM, INC.
CHILDRENS HOSPITAL & MEDICAL CENTER
SEATTLE CHILDREN'S HOSPITAL
TEXAS CHILDREN'S HOSPITAL
THE CHILDREN'S HOSPITAL OF PHILADELPHIA
THE CHILDREN'S MERCY HOSPITAL

HISTORICAL FINANCIALS
Company Type: Private

Income Statement — FYE: June 30

	REVENUE ($mil)	NET INCOME ($mil)	NET PROFIT MARGIN	EMPLOYEES
06/21	540	144	26.8%	2,325
06/16	400	21	5.4%	—
06/15	408	(1)	—	—
Annual Growth	4.8%	—	—	—

2021 Year-End Financials
Return on assets: 12.5%
Return on equity: 18.8%
Current Ratio: 1.50
Cash ($ mil.): 46

JOHNS HOPKINS BAYVIEW MEDICAL CENTER, INC.

If you've just been pulled from the bay like an old emptyÂ crab trap, Johns Hopkins Bayview might be the first place you're taken. One of five member institutions in the Johns Hopkins Health System, Johns Hopkins Bayview Medical Center is a community teaching hospital. Its Baltimore-based operations include a neonatal intensive care unit, as well as centers devoted to trauma, geriatrics, sleep disorders, and weight management. It also features the state's onlyÂ regional burn center.Â The facilityÂ includes a meditation labyrinth for patients, families, and staff to walk. Established in 1773, the medical center has more than 560 beds.

Operations
As an academic teaching hospital, all of the physicians at Johns Hopkins Bayview are also full-time faculty at the Johns Hopkins School of Medicine. Students from TheÂ Johns Hopkins University School of Nursing also come to the medical center for hospital-based instruction in acute and long term care.

Auditors : PRICEWATERHOUSECOOPERS LLP BA

LOCATIONS

HQ: JOHNS HOPKINS BAYVIEW MEDICAL CENTER, INC.
 4940 EASTERN AVE, BALTIMORE, MD 212242735
Phone: 410 550-0100
Web: WWW.HOPKINSMEDICINE.ORG

PRODUCTS/OPERATIONS

Selected services
Primary Care Services
 General Internal Medicine
 Obstetrics/Gynecology
 Pediatrics
Specialty Services
 Bariatrics
 Burn
 Cardiology
 Clinical Nutrition
 Dermatology
 Endocrinology
 Gastroenterology
 General Surgery
 Hematology/Oncology
 Imaging (X-ray, mammography, ultrasound, etc)
 Minor Surgery
 Neurodiagnostic Lab
 Neurology
 Ophthalmology
 Otolaryngology (ear, nose and throat)
 Orthopaedics
 Plastic Surgery
 Podiatry
 Urology
 Vascular Lab

COMPETITORS

ELLIS HOSPITAL
LEVINDALE HEBREW GERIATRIC CENTER AND HOSPITAL, INC.
MADONNA REHABILITATION HOSPITAL
MCDONOUGH COUNTY HOSPITAL DISTRICT
MIAMI JEWISH HEALTH SYSTEMS, INC.

HISTORICAL FINANCIALS

Company Type: Private

Income Statement — FYE: June 30

	REVENUE ($mil)	NET INCOME ($mil)	NET PROFIT MARGIN	EMPLOYEES
06/22	749	18	2.5%	3,300
06/21	716	91	12.7%	—
06/20	669	(41)	—	—
06/19	648	(39)	—	—
Annual Growth	4.9%	—	—	—

2022 Year-End Financials
Return on assets: 4.6% Cash ($ mil.): 22
Return on equity: 21.3%
Current Ratio: 1.20

JOHNS HOPKINS HEALTHCARE LLC

LOCATIONS

HQ: JOHNS HOPKINS HEALTHCARE LLC
7231 PARKWAY DR STE 100, HANOVER, MD 210762331
Phone: 410 424-4400
Web: WWW.HOPKINSMEDICINE.ORG

HISTORICAL FINANCIALS

Company Type: Private

Income Statement — FYE: June 30

	REVENUE ($mil)	NET INCOME ($mil)	NET PROFIT MARGIN	EMPLOYEES
06/22	2,667	14	0.5%	520
06/21	2,580	30	1.2%	—
06/20	2,412	26	1.1%	—
06/19	2,248	(18)	—	—
Annual Growth	5.9%	—	—	—

2022 Year-End Financials
Return on assets: 2.6% Cash ($ mil.): 96
Return on equity: 7.4%
Current Ratio: 0.90

JOHNS HOPKINS HOSPITAL

Auditors: PRICEWATERHOUSECOOPERS LLP BA

LOCATIONS

HQ: JOHNS HOPKINS HOSPITAL
1800 ORLEANS ST, BALTIMORE, MD 212870010
Phone: 410 550-0730
Web: WWW.HOPKINSMEDICINE.ORG

HISTORICAL FINANCIALS

Company Type: Private

Income Statement — FYE: June 30

	REVENUE ($mil)	NET INCOME ($mil)	NET PROFIT MARGIN	EMPLOYEES
06/22	3,042	(3)	—	12,000
06/20	2,617	(202)	—	—
06/19	2,527	(64)	—	—
06/18	2,422	98	4.1%	—
Annual Growth	5.9%	—	—	—

2022 Year-End Financials
Return on assets: (-0.1%) Cash ($ mil.): 157
Return on equity: (-0.2%)
Current Ratio: 1.10

JOHNS HOPKINS UNIVERSITY

Founded in 1876, The Johns Hopkins University is a premier, privately endowed institution that provides education and related services to students and others, research and related services to sponsoring organizations, and professional medical services to patients. While renowned for its School of Medicine, the private university offers more than 400 academic programs spanning fields of study including arts and sciences, business, engineering, and international studies. The university enrolls more than 24,000 full- and part-time students throughout nine academic divisions. Johns Hopkins has about a half-dozen campuses in Maryland and Washington, DC, as well as facilities in China and Italy. The student-teacher ratio is 7:1. Jhpiego, a nonprofit health organization is affiliated with the university.

Operations

Johns Hopkins University actively prepares students to be global leaders and citizens, to take part in international learning activities. With a proud tradition of leadership in education, research, service, and patient care around the globe, the university promotes intellectual discovery through academic exchanges, programs abroad, collaborative research, and cooperative agreements.

Keenly focused on research, Johns Hopkins is engaged in a range of disciplines, including health and medicine, social sciences, humanities, the arts, natural sciences, engineering, and technology. Projects include researching alternatives to animal testing, disease treatments, and chemical and biomolecular engineering topics, among others.

The Johns Hopkins University offers graduate programs in business, finance, and real estate through its relatively new Carey Business School.

Notable alumni of the school include 28th US president Woodrow Wilson, Michael Bloomberg, and horror film director Wesley Craven.

Geographic Reach

Johns Hopkins University boasts four campuses in Baltimore as well as single campus locations in (Montgomery County) Maryland and Washington, DC. Johns Hopkins also operates facilities in the Baltimore-Washington area and abroad in Nanjing, China and Bologna, Italy.

Financial Performance

Auditors: KPMG LLP BALTIMORE MARYLAND

LOCATIONS

HQ: JOHNS HOPKINS UNIVERSITY
3400 N CHARLES ST, BALTIMORE, MD 212182680
Phone: 410 516-8000
Web: WWW.JHU.EDU

PRODUCTS/OPERATIONS

Selected Schools and Colleges
Bloomberg School of Public Health
Carey Business School
Krieger School of Arts and Sciences
Peabody Institute
School of Advanced International Studies
School of Education
School of Medicine
School of Nursing
Whiting School of Engineering

Selected Centers and Institutes
American Institute for Contemporary German Studies
Bloomberg School of Public Health, Department of Health Policy and Management Fall Institute in Barcelona, Spain
Bloomberg School of Public Health Research Centers
Center for Africana Studies
Center for Communication Programs
Center for Constitutional Studies and Democratic Development
Center for Clinical Global Health Education
Center for Global Health
Center for International Business and Public Policy
Center for Language Education
Center for Talented Youth
Center for Transatlantic Relations
Central Asia Caucasus Institute
Foreign Policy Institute
Hopkins Nanjing Center
Institute for Global Studies in Culture, Power and History
Institute for Policy Studies
Johns Hopkins SAIS Bologna Center
Office of Global Nursing
SAIS Research Centers
Summer Language Institute
The Institute for Johns Hopkins Nursing
Yeung Center for Collaborative China Studies

Selected Campuses
Columbia Center - Columbia, Maryland
East Baltimore Campus - Baltimore
Harbor East - Downtown Baltimore
Homewood Campus - Baltimore
Hopkins-Nanjing Center - Nanjing Jiangsu Province, People's Republic of China
Johns Hopkins University Applied Physics Laboratory - Laurel, MD; Baltimore and Washington
Johns Hopkins University Zanvyl Krieger School of Arts & Sciences Advanced Academic Programs - Washington, DC
Montgomery County Center - Rockville, Maryland
Nitze School of Advanced International Studies (SAIS) - Washington, D.C
Peabody Campus - Baltimore

School of Advanced International Studies - Bologna, Italy

COMPETITORS
CLARK ATLANTA UNIVERSITY INC
DESALES UNIVERSITY
DUKE UNIVERSITY
GWYNEDD MERCY UNIVERSITY
THE UNIVERSITY OF HARTFORD
THE UNIVERSITY OF IOWA
THE UNIVERSITY OF PITTSBURGH
UNIVERSITY OF ILLINOIS
UNIVERSITY OF KENTUCKY
UNIVERSITY OF LIVERPOOL

HISTORICAL FINANCIALS
Company Type: Private

Income Statement — FYE: June 30

	REVENUE ($mil)	NET INCOME ($mil)	NET PROFIT MARGIN	EMPLOYEES
06/22	7,446	(273)	—	37,600
06/21	6,659	3,427	51.5%	—
06/20	6,470	903	14.0%	—
06/19	6,410	2,017	31.5%	—
Annual Growth	5.1%	—	—	—

2022 Year-End Financials
Return on assets: (-1.5%)   Cash ($ mil.): 770
Return on equity: (-2.1%)
Current Ratio: —

JOHNSON & JOHNSON PATIENT ASSISTANCE FOUNDATION INC

LOCATIONS
HQ: JOHNSON & JOHNSON PATIENT ASSISTANCE FOUNDATION INC
1 JOHNSON AND JOHNSON PLZ, NEW BRUNSWICK, NJ 089330001
Phone: 732 524-1394
Web: WWW.JJPAF.ORG

HISTORICAL FINANCIALS
Company Type: Private

Income Statement — FYE: December 31

	REVENUE ($mil)	NET INCOME ($mil)	NET PROFIT MARGIN	EMPLOYEES
12/14	787	(16)	—	19
12/13	741	13	1.8%	—
12/10	425	(6)	—	—
12/09	355	(2)	—	—
Annual Growth	17.2%	—	—	—

2014 Year-End Financials
Return on assets: (-23.4%)   Cash ($ mil.): 31
Return on equity: (-23.4%)
Current Ratio: —

JOHNSON CONTROLS FIRE PROTECTION LP

SimplexGrinnell handles emergencies well. The company provides integrated security alarm, fire suppression, healthcare communications, and emergency lighting systems. SimplexGrinnell reaches some 1 million customers in the US and Canada through more than 150 district offices located in the Americas, Europe, Asia, and other regions. In addition to providing security and fire related products, SimplexGrinnell operates a service division devoted to test and inspection, preventive maintenance, central station monitoring, and emergency services. The company's clients include members of local, state, and federal government agencies, corporations, oil and gas companies, hospitals, and educational facilities.

Operations
The company's communications segment provides mass notification and commercial paging, as well as intercom and other sound systems. The company also provides healthcare communications such as infant security, nurse call, and emergency alert units.

Strategy
SimplexGrinnell launched a new website to give its customers a fast and convenient way to purchase many of its products that do not require installation support.

LOCATIONS
HQ: JOHNSON CONTROLS FIRE PROTECTION LP
6600 CONGRESS AVE, BOCA RATON, FL 334871213
Phone: 561 988-7200
Web: WWW.JOHNSONCONTROLS.COM

PRODUCTS/OPERATIONS
Selected Products and Services
Fire Detection and Alarm
  Control Panels
  Notification
  Network Solutions
  Smoke Detector and Carbon Monoxide Detection
Sound and Communication
  Healthcare Communications
  Emergency Communications
  Public Address and Intercom
  Sound Reinforcement
  Telephone Networks
Integrated Security
  Access Control
  Intrusion Detection
  Property Surveillance
  Mass Notification
Fire Sprinkler and Suppression
  Fire Extinguisher
  Special Hazards
  Sprinkler

COMPETITORS
AUSTIN TASK, INC.
BROOKS EQUIPMENT COMPANY, LLC
CASTLEROCK SECURITY, INC
FIRST CITY CARE (LONDON) LIMITED
FORTEK COMPUTERS LIMITED
HART INTERCIVIC, INC.
HD SUPPLY HOLDINGS, INC.
LAGASSE, INC.
NIKKEN GLOBAL INC.
PWS, INC.

HISTORICAL FINANCIALS
Company Type: Private

Income Statement — FYE: September 30

	REVENUE ($mil)	NET INCOME ($mil)	NET PROFIT MARGIN	EMPLOYEES
09/16	1,871	182	9.7%	9,500
09/09	1,750	0	0.0%	—
Annual Growth	1.0%	—	—	—

2016 Year-End Financials
Return on assets: 6.8%   Cash ($ mil.): (-11)
Return on equity: 8.2%
Current Ratio: 1.40

JOHNSON CONTROLS, INC.

Climate control for offices, Johnson Controls manufactures, installs, and services energy-efficient heating, ventilation, and air conditioning (HVAC) systems. Its products cover everything needed to make a place of work comfortable and safe to be in, extending to fire detection and suppression and security measures such as electronic card site access. Originally an American company, Johnson Controls completed a reverse merger with Cork-based Tyco International and is now domiciled in Ireland (although the US remains its largest market by far). The company sold its car battery manufacturing operations in 2018 to Brookfield Business Partners.

Operations
JCI operates through 230 wholly- and majority-owned manufacturing or assembly plants. Its building efficiency business segment designs control systems and mechanical equipment, as well as services non-residential properties in about 52 countries. About 65% of this segment's sales are derived from HVAC products and control systems for construction and retrofit markets, and the other half from services. Branded products include the Metasys control system and York chillers. This segment is looking to such emerging markets as China and the Middle East for strong sales.

The company's power solutions business claims it is the largest lead-acid automotive battery producer in the world. JCI holds an edge over other battery companies, as it is not locked into an alliance with any specific automaker, allowing it to play the field. Its 60 manufacturing and assembly facilities are located in about 22 countries and produce lead-acid batteries, as well as AGM (absorbent glass mat) battery technology and lithium-ion batteries used in hybrid vehicles. About 75% of the company's batteries are sold in the automotive replacement sector, with the rest going to OEMs. Power solutions is ready to benefit from vertical integration for lead recycling and a shift in its product mix to AGM technology.

Automotive experience designs and manufactures interior products and systems for passenger cars and light trucks, including vans, pick-up trucks and sport/crossover utility vehicles. The business produces automotive interior systems for OEMs and operates approximately 230 wholly- and majority-owned manufacturing or assembly plants, with operations in 32 countries worldwide.

Geographic Reach

JCI operates through more than 1,500 locations worldwide. Nearly 45% of its total sales come from the US; other major markets include Germany (9%) and other countries in Europe (20%).

Sales and Marketing

JCI's main customers include the biggest names in the industry: Ford, Daimler, Fiat Chrysler, Toyota, and GM. The company sells its control systems, mechanical equipment, and services through its extensive global network of sales and service offices. Some building controls, products, and mechanical systems are also sold to distributors of air-conditioning, refrigeration, and commercial heating systems throughout the world.

Financial Performance

JCI's revenues dipped 1% to $36.9 billion in 2016 as it posted its first net loss in seven years. The marginal revenue decrease for 2016 was driven by lower sales from its automotive experience business and the unfavorable impact of foreign currency translation of $754 million.

The net loss of $847 million JCI suffered in 2016 was due to an increase in the income tax provision, additional separation and transaction costs, and mounting restructuring and impairment costs. Most of these costs were affiliated with the company's $16.5 billion purchase of Tyco International in late 2016.

Strategy

JCI is looking to streamline its business by selling and spinning off non-core operations. In late 2015 it completed the sale of its Global Workplace Solutions (GWS) business to CBRE Group for $1.5 billion. GWS is a worldwide provider of facilities management services.

In addition, the company spun off its global automotive seating components and systems operations into a publicly traded company called Adient Inc. in October 2016.

Mergers and Acquisitions

The company often grows its product portfolio through the use of acquisitions. In a sweeping move for the home-products industry, in early 2016, JCI purchased Tyco International for $16.5 billion. The combined company will boast revenues of up to $32 billion.

HISTORY

Professor Warren Johnson developed the electric telethermoscope in 1880 so that janitors at Whitewater, Wisconsin's State Normal School could regulate room temperatures without disturbing classrooms. His device, the thermostat, used mercury to move a heat element that opened and shut a circuit. Milwaukee hotelier William Plankinton believed in the invention and invested $150,000 to start production.

The two men formed Johnson Electric Service Company in 1885. They sold the marketing, installation, and service rights to concentrate on manufacturing. Johnson also invented other devices such as tower clocks, and he experimented with the telegraph before becoming intrigued with the automobile and beginning production of steam-powered cars. He won the US Postal Service's first automotive contract, but never gained support within his own company. Johnson continued to look elsewhere for financing until his death in 1911.

The renamed Johnson Services regained full rights to its thermostats in 1912 and sold its other businesses. During the Depression it produced economy systems that regulated building temperatures. Johnson Services became a public company in 1940. During WWII it aided the war effort, building weather-data gatherers and radar test sets.

In the 1960s Johnson Services began developing centralized control systems for temperature, fire alarm, lighting, and security regulation. The company was renamed Johnson Controls in 1974.

EXECUTIVES

Corporate Controller*, Suzanne M Vincent
CPO*, Michael Bartschat
Chief Commercial Officer*, Rodney Clark
Auditors : PRICEWATERHOUSECOOPERS LLP MI

LOCATIONS

HQ: JOHNSON CONTROLS, INC.
5757 N GREEN BAY AVE, MILWAUKEE, WI 532094408
Phone: 414 524-1200
Web: WWW.JOHNSONCONTROLS.COM

COMPETITORS

AMERICAN RESIDENTIAL SERVICES, L.L.C.
ELECTROCOMPONENTS PUBLIC LIMITED COMPANY
ENERPAC TOOL GROUP CORP.
ISS TECHNICAL SERVICES HOLDINGS LIMITED
JOHNSON CONTROLS INTERNATIONAL PUBLIC LIMITED COMPANY
LIME ENERGY CO.
LORNE STEWART PLC
MURPHY COMPANY MECHANICAL CONTRACTORS AND ENGINEERS
SSE PLC
TESLA ENERGY OPERATIONS, INC.

HISTORICAL FINANCIALS
Company Type: Private

Income Statement — FYE: September 30

	REVENUE ($mil)	NET INCOME ($mil)	NET PROFIT MARGIN	EMPLOYEES
09/15	37,179	1,679	4.5%	126,377
09/14	42,828	1,335	3.1%	—
09/13	42,730	1,297	3.0%	—
Annual Growth	(6.7%)	13.8%	—	—

2015 Year-End Financials
Return on assets: 5.7%   Cash ($ mil.): 597
Return on equity: 15.9%
Current Ratio: 1.10

JOINT SCHOOL DISTRICT NO. 28-J OF THE COUNTIES OF ADAMS AND ARAPAHOE

Auditors : FORVIS LLP DENVER COLORADO

LOCATIONS

HQ: JOINT SCHOOL DISTRICT NO. 28-J OF THE COUNTIES OF ADAMS AND ARAPAHOE
15701 E 1ST AVE STE 106, AURORA, CO 800119037
Phone: 303 365-5810
Web: WWW.AURORAK12.ORG

HISTORICAL FINANCIALS
Company Type: Private

Income Statement — FYE: June 30

	REVENUE ($mil)	NET INCOME ($mil)	NET PROFIT MARGIN	EMPLOYEES
06/22	687	69	10.1%	6,000
06/21	680	39	5.8%	—
06/20	608	24	4.0%	—
06/19	555	6	1.2%	—
Annual Growth	7.4%	115.9%	—	—

2022 Year-End Financials
Return on assets: 5.2%   Cash ($ mil.): 238
Return on equity: —
Current Ratio: 2.50

JORDAN SCHOOL DISTRICT

EXECUTIVES

Business Administrator*, Burke Jolley
Auditors : SQUIRE & COMPANY PC OREM UT

LOCATIONS

HQ: JORDAN SCHOOL DISTRICT
7387 S CAMPUS VIEW DR, WEST JORDAN, UT
840845500
Phone: 801 280-3689
Web: WWW.JORDANDISTRICT.ORG

HISTORICAL FINANCIALS

Company Type: Private

Income Statement — FYE: June 30

	REVENUE ($mil)	NET INCOME ($mil)	NET PROFIT MARGIN	EMPLOYEES
06/22	622	0	0.1%	5,900
06/20	535	(17)	—	—
06/19	503	(32)	—	—
Annual Growth	7.3%	—	—	—

2022 Year-End Financials
Return on assets: — Cash ($ mil.): —
Return on equity: 0.1%
Current Ratio: —

KADLEC REGIONAL MEDICAL CENTER

Kadlec Regional Medical Center is an acute care hospital facility serving southeastern Washington and northeastern Oregon. In addition to providing comprehensive medical, surgical, and emergency services, the hospital provides neonatal intensive care, cardiopulmonary rehabilitation, interventional cardiology, neurology, cancer care, and other specialist services. Not-for-profit Kadlec Regional has some 270 inpatient beds, including pediatric, intensive, intermediate, and critical care capacity. It also operates outpatient physician offices and clinics in surrounding areas.

Operations

Kadlec Regional's cardiovascular programs include open heart surgery and interventional cardiology. The hospital also operates an all-digital outpatient imaging center and the region's only level III neonatal intensive care unit (NICU). Kadlec was is also designated as a Level 1 Cardiac Center and a Level 2 Stroke Center. Area specialist practices include centers for dermatology, colorectal surgery, nephrology, pediatrics, women's health, ENT (ear, nose, and throat), and foot and ankle practices. Kadlec Regional also operates satellite urgent care and family practice clinics.

The Kadlec Neuroscience Center offers a wide range of services to treat and diagnose conditions related to the brain, spine, spinal cord, & peripheral nervous system.

In 2013 the hospital reported more than 2,700 births, 66,000 emergency department visits, and about 15,000 admissions.

That year Kadlec Regional provided $27 million in charity care.

Geographic Reach

Kadlec Regional has hospital and clinic locations in Hermiston, Kennewick, Pasco, Pendleton, Prosser, and Richland.

Financial Performance

The hospital reported revenue of $312 million in 2012, consisting of $305 million in net patient service earnings and other revenue of some $7.5 million. Kadlec Regional brought in profits of some $29 million.

Strategy

The hospital has undergone aggressive expansion efforts, adding a new patient tower with diagnostic, outpatient and intermediate care, and surgery rooms. Kadlec Regional is enhancing its specialty service units in fields to attract specialists and increase revenue. The organization launched a $10 million project to expand its NICU unit in 2013. It will add 27 private and semi-private rooms and new observation, gathering, and lactation areas.

It is also expanding outpatient service facilities, such as a new $19 million, three-story specialty physician practice office that opened in Richland in 2013. The new building increases collaboration between various surgical and medical specialists in the Kadlec Regional clinic network.

The year the company also expanded its emergency room offerings through the opening of the Kadlec ER in Kennewick. The new 15-bed ER is the first in the region to operate as a freestanding facility, like traditional hospital-based ERs.

Mergers and Acquisitions

Kadlec Regional also absorbs other area providers. In 2013 Inland Cardiology Associates become part of the Kadlec Regional health system. The region's largest independent group of experienced cardiologists, Inland provides comprehensive invasive, noninvasive and interventional services throughout southeast Washington and northeast Oregon.

Company Background

In 2011 it partnered with the nearby PMH Medical Center to increase collaboration and specialist referrals between the two hospitals. The partnership extends the reach of Kadlec Regional's medical specialists to additional communities and brings PMH online with Kadlec Regional's electronic health record system. Both hospitals remained independently run.

The hospital system was founded in 1944.

EXECUTIVES

Co-Vice President*, Bill Wingo

LOCATIONS

HQ: KADLEC REGIONAL MEDICAL CENTER
888 SWIFT BLVD, RICHLAND, WA 993523514
Phone: 509 946-4611
Web: WWW.KADLEC.ORG

PRODUCTS/OPERATIONS

Selected Services
The Birth Center
Bloodless Medicine and Surgery
Cancer Care
Cardiac Care
Cardiac Catheterization
CardioPulmonary Rehabilitation
Cardiovascular and Thoracic Surgery
CaringBridge
Clinical Decision Unit
Coumadin Clinic
Diabetes Learning Center
Diagnostic Imaging
Don and Lori Watts Pediatric Center
Emergency Department
Emergency Room-Kennewick
Home Health Care
Imaging
Inpatient Rehabilitation and Therapy
Intensive Care Unit
Joint Care Center
Kadlec Academy
Kadlec Healthy Ages
Kadlec Medical Associates
Neonatal Intensive Care Unit
Occupational Medicine
Occupational Therapy
Ostomy Support Group
Outpatient Imaging Center
Outpatient Procedures
Physical Therapy
Planetree
Rehabilitation and Therapy Services
Speech Therapy
Urgent Care
Water Therapy
Wound Healing Center

COMPETITORS

ARROWHEAD REGIONAL MEDICAL CENTER
CENTRAL SUFFOLK HOSPITAL
COOKEVILLE REGIONAL MEDICAL CENTER
LEHIGH VALLEY HEALTH NETWORK, INC.
MARION COMMUNITY HOSPITAL, INC.

HISTORICAL FINANCIALS

Company Type: Private

Income Statement — FYE: December 31

	REVENUE ($mil)	NET INCOME ($mil)	NET PROFIT MARGIN	EMPLOYEES
12/20	675	72	10.8%	2,668
12/18	640	51	8.0%	—
12/17	595	87	14.7%	—
12/16	534	9	1.9%	—
Annual Growth	6.0%	64.7%	—	—

2020 Year-End Financials
Return on assets: 9.1% Cash ($ mil.): 163
Return on equity: 19.8%
Current Ratio: 2.80

KAISER FDN HEALTH PLAN OF COLORADO

Auditors: PRICEWATERHOUSECOOPERS LLP PH

LOCATIONS

HQ: KAISER FDN HEALTH PLAN OF COLORADO
1 KAISER PLZ STE 15L, OAKLAND, CA 946123610

Phone: 510 271-6611

HISTORICAL FINANCIALS
Company Type: Private

Income Statement FYE: December 31

	REVENUE ($mil)	NET INCOME ($mil)	NET PROFIT MARGIN	EMPLOYEES
12/19	4,344	258	6.0%	17
12/13	3,197	115	3.6%	—
12/09	2,374	32	1.4%	—
Annual Growth	6.2%	23.1%	—	—

2019 Year-End Financials
Return on assets: 15.5%   Cash ($ mil.): 10
Return on equity: 41.2%
Current Ratio: 0.20

KAISER FOUNDATION HOSPITALS INC

Kaiser Foundation Hospitals is on a roll. The hospital group operates nearly 40 acute care hospitals and 680 medical offices in eight states (California, Colorado, Georgia, Hawaii, Maryland, Oregon, Virginia, and Washington) and Washington D.C. The company's largest presence is in California, where the majority of its hospitals are located. Kaiser Foundation Hospitals employs more than 21,000 physicians, representing all medical specialties. Kaiser Foundation Hospital's doctors group is controlled by Permanente Medical Groups, and its HMO is offered through Kaiser Foundation Health Plan. Altogether, the group provides care for about 11.7 million members.

Operations
Kaiser Foundation Hospitals works with other organizations to tackle such issues as obesity, access to care, and violence. It also works to promote health in the communities it serves through wellness programs.

In 2016, Kaiser Foundation Hospitals logged 44 million office visits. It facilitated 106,000 births, performed 129,000 surgeries, and filled 90 million prescriptions.

Sales and Marketing
Company Background
Kaiser Foundation Hospitals was founded in 1945.

EXECUTIVES
Group President*, Janet Liang
CCO*, Catherine Hernandez

LOCATIONS
HQ: KAISER FOUNDATION HOSPITALS INC
1 KAISER PLZ, OAKLAND, CA 946123610
Phone: 510 271-6611
Web: WWW.KAISERCENTER.COM

PRODUCTS/OPERATIONS
Selected Hospitals
Antioch Medical Center
Fremont Medical Center
Fresno Medical Center
Hayward Medical Center
Manteca Medical Center
Modesto Medical Center
Oakland Medical Center
Redwood City Medical Center
Richmond Medical Center
Roseville Women and Children's Center
San Jose Medical Center
Santa Clara Medical Center
Sacramento Medical Center
South San Francisco Medical Center
South Sacramento Trauma Center
Santa Rosa Medical Center
San Francisco Medical Center
San Rafael Medical Center
Vacaville Medical Center
Vallejo Medical Center
Walnut Creek Medical Center
Baldwin Park Medical Center
Downey Medical Center
Fontana Medical Center
Los Angeles Medical Center
Moreno Valley Community Hospital
Orange County - Anaheim Medical Center
Orange County - Irvine Medical Center
Panorama City Medical Center
Riverside Medical Center
San Diego Medical Center
Harbor City (South Bay Medical Center)
Woodlands Hills Medical Center
West Los Angeles Medical Center
Sunnyside Medical Center (Portland, Oregon area)
Moanalua Medical Center (Hawaii)

COMPETITORS
ADVENTIST HEALTH SYSTEM/WEST, CORPORATION
ALEGENT CREIGHTON HEALTH
BEAUMONT HEALTH
CHRISTIANA CARE HEALTH SYSTEM, INC.
FROEDTERT MEMORIAL LUTHERAN HOSPITAL, INC.
LEGACY HEALTH
MEDSTAR HEALTH, INC.
MERCY HEALTH
SANFORD
WILLIAM BEAUMONT HOSPITAL

HISTORICAL FINANCIALS
Company Type: Private

Income Statement FYE: December 31

	REVENUE ($mil)	NET INCOME ($mil)	NET PROFIT MARGIN	EMPLOYEES
12/09	14,795	429	2.9%	175,668
12/08	0	0	99.0%	—
12/05	9,852	774	7.9%	—
Annual Growth	10.7%	(13.7%)	—	—

2009 Year-End Financials
Return on assets: —   Cash ($ mil.): 57
Return on equity: 2.9%
Current Ratio: —

KALEIDA HEALTH

Kaleida Health provides a kaleidoscope of services to residents of western New York. The health system operates five acute care hospitals including Buffalo General Hospital and Gates Vascular Institute (combined with about 550 beds), The Women & Children's Hospital of Buffalo (200), DeGraff Memorial Hospital (70), and Millard Fillmore Suburban Hospital (260). Community health needs are met through a network of some 80 medical clinics. Kaleida Health also operates skilled nursing care facilities and provides home health care through its Visiting Nursing Association. To help train future medical professionals, Buffalo General Hospital is a teaching affiliate of the State University of New York.

Operations
Kaleida Health is also home to the Deaconess Center and Waterfront long-term care facilities. Along with primary care, the system's network of outpatient centers offers medical and surgical subspecialty care, dental and oral surgery services, and behavioral health and outpatient alcohol treatment services. Kaleida Health also operates the Pediatric Trauma Center and Pediatric HIV/AIDS Center for the Western New York (WNY).

In 2012 the health system had 55,125 inpatient discharges, 158,902 emergency department visits, and 2.3 million clinic and lab visits.

Financial Performance
The company's revenues grew by 3% to $1.2 billion in 2012 thanks to higher net patient service revenues and other revenues (including increases from a medical resident tax refund and HITECH incentive funds). It reported that 37% of net patient service revenues came from Medicare; 21% from New York State Medicaid; and 38% from commercial insurance plans.

Kaleida Health saw net income of $52 million in 2012 (compared to a net loss in 2011) as the result of higher revenues and an increase in investment returns (including a gain from a net change in unrealized gains and losses on investments).

Strategy
In an effort to draw in more patients to the eight communities in which it already operates in the US, Kaleida Health has become one of a handful of US medical providers to market itself to patients north of the border in Canada. The organization launched a marketing campaign in Ontario over the years that included a website aimed at pulling in Canadian patients seeking bariatric care for obesity, gastrointestinal services (such as colonoscopies), joint replacement or spinal surgery, pediatric care, and radiology services. Overall, Kaleida is focused on attracting Canadian patients who can either pay out-of-pocket or patients seeking non-emergency services covered in the US by the Ontario Health Insurance Program.

Growing its operations, in 2013 The Kaleida Health Laboratories (which performs more than 4 million tests a year) opened four new patient service centers in New York (Tonawanda, Lancaster, Buffalo, and

Cheektowaga).

Teaming up with Olean General Hospital (OGH), in 2013 Kaleida Health and OGH opened their new interventional cardiac catheterization lab joint-venture in the Southern Tier of New York.

Kaleida Health and The University at Buffalo opened a new 10-story vascular institute and research building in 2012. The $291 million Gates Vascular Institute and the University at Buffalo's Clinical and Translational Research Center, integrates Kaleida Health's physicians and UB researchers in a collaborative effort to deliver clinical care, investigate the causes of a wide range of human diseases, and spin-off new biotechnology businesses and jobs.

In 2012 Kaleida Health's Visiting Nursing Association of Western New York received regulatory approval to expand into four additional counties.

To raise cash, in 2013 Kaleida Health sold the former Millard Fillmore Gates Circle Hospital to TM Montante Development for commercial development.

Mergers and Acquisitions

In 2013 The Visiting Nursing Association of Western New York was selected as the provider of choice to buy the Livingston County Certified Home Health Agency. In 2012 it was selected as the provider of choice to purchase the Wyoming Certified Home Health Agency.

Company Background

Along with trying to grab a share of the Canadian market, Kaleida is working to renovate and refurbish its current locations to draw in more patients. In late 2011 the system completed renovations of its maternity services at Women & Children's Hospital of Buffalo. The new Mother-Baby Unit offers 14 additional single rooms with private showers and enhanced amenities. The health system underwent another complete renovation that serves as an additional Mother-Baby Unit as well as inpatient beds for the Perinatal Center, gynecology and other women's services.

EXECUTIVES

CMO*, David P Hughes
Chief of Staff*, Michael P Hughes
Executive Vice President COS*, Cheryl Klass
Chief Human Resources Officer*, Jerry Venable
CIO*, Robert Diamond
Auditors : KPMG LLP ALBANY NY

LOCATIONS

HQ: KALEIDA HEALTH
726 EXCHANGE ST, BUFFALO, NY 142101484
Phone: 716 859-5600
Web: WWW.KALEIDAHEALTH.ORG

PRODUCTS/OPERATIONS

Selected Facilities
Buffalo General Hospital (Buffalo)
Deaconess Center (Buffalo)
DeGraff Memorial Hospital (North Tonawanda)
Gates Vascular Institute (Buffalo)
Millard Fillmore Suburban Hospital (Williamsville)
VNA Home Care Services (Allegany County, Chautauqua County, Erie County, Genesee County, Niagara County)
Women and Children's Hospital of Buffalo (Buffalo)

Selected Services
Admissions
Adult Day Services
Allergy & Immunology Clinic
Anesthesia
Bariatric Program
Bereavement Services
Blood Draw Labs
Breast Reconstruction Surgery Information
Buffalo Niagara MRI Center
Cardiac Program
Center for Asthma & Environmental Exposure
Center for Wound Care
Chest Pain Center
Colorectal Surgery
Community Health Department
DeGraff Skilled Nursing Facility
Diabetes-Endocrinology Center of Western New York
Dialysis Treatments
Diversity & Inclusion
Ear, Nose, and Throat Center/Otolaryngology
Easy Referrals
Emergency Department
Epilepsy Family Planning Center
Gastroenterology
Geriatric Center of Western New York
Hernia Center
Imaging Services
Immunology Laboratory
Laboratory and Pathology
Maternity Services
Minimally Invasive Surgery
Minor Surgery
Multiple Sclerosis
Neonatology
Neuropsychology
Neurosciences
Neurosurgery and Procedures
Obstetrics and Gynecology
Occupational Therapy
Orthopedics
Parkinson's Disease Comprehensive Movement Disorder Center
Pastoral Care
Personal Care Services
Personal Response System (Lifeline)
Pharmacy - High Street
Pharmacy Pharmacy - Suburban Family Pharmacy
Pharmacy Residency Program
Physical Therapy Prenatal Testing
Primary Care
Rehabilitation Medicine - Acute Medical
Rehabilitation Rehabilitation Services
Retinal
Surgical Services
Robotic Surgery
School Based Health Centers
Security
Speech Therapy - Outpatient
Spirit of Women
Stroke Program
Subacute Rehabilitation
Surgical Services
Telehealth Home Monitoring
The Greater Buffalo
United Accountable Healthcare
Urology Services
Vascular Lab
Vascular Services
Visiting Nursing Association of WNY
VNA Diabetes Program
Women's Services
Wound Care

COMPETITORS

ALLINA HEALTH SYSTEM
BRONXCARE HEALTH SYSTEM
CHARLESTON AREA MEDICAL CENTER, INC.
NASSAU HEALTH CARE CORPORATION
NORTHSHORE UNIVERSITY HEALTHSYSTEM
ROBERT WOOD JOHNSON UNIVERSITY HOSPITAL, INC.
SOUTHCOAST HEALTH SYSTEM, INC.
THE PENNSYLVANIA HOSPITAL OF THE UNIVERSITY OF PENNSYLVANIA HEALTH SYSTEM
UNIVERSITY HOSPITALS HEALTH SYSTEM, INC.
WELLSTAR HEALTH SYSTEM, INC.

HISTORICAL FINANCIALS

Company Type: Private

Income Statement FYE: December 31

	REVENUE ($mil)	NET INCOME ($mil)	NET PROFIT MARGIN	EMPLOYEES
12/17	1,331	60	4.5%	9,000
12/13	1,139	(14)	—	—
12/09	1,155	75	6.5%	—
Annual Growth	1.8%	(2.7%)	—	—

2017 Year-End Financials
Return on assets: 4.3%   Cash ($ mil.): 16
Return on equity: 19.6%
Current Ratio: 1.40

KANSAS DEPARTMENT OF TRANSPORTATION

The Kansas Department of Transportation (KDOT) helps connect the dots with residents who love to travel the 140,000-plus miles across the Sunflower State. The agency focuses on providing a transportation system for citizens in the state by offering a wide range of services such as maintaining roads and bridges, transportation planning, and designing construction projects. The department also provides federal fund program administration, as well as administrative support, travel information, and programs in traffic safety. KDOT traces its roots to the organization of interstate travel in 1917.

Strategy

The agency hopes to bring in additional revenue and preserve and expand its state's road, bridge, and highway infrastructure through its $7.8 billion T-WORKS program, in effect from fiscal year end 2011 through 2020. It includes $2.7 billion in new revenues from registration fees for heavy trucks and a sales tax deposit that begins in 2014. KDOT will spend at least $8 million in each of Kansas' 105 counties during T-WORKS' administration. KDOT plans for the program to create 175,000 jobs over the course of the next 10 years.

Auditors : CLIFTONLARSONALLEN LLP BROOM

LOCATIONS

HQ: KANSAS DEPARTMENT OF TRANSPORTATION
700 SW HARRISON ST # 500, TOPEKA, KS 666033964
Phone: 785 296-3501
Web: WWW.KSDOT.ORG

COMPETITORS

ALABAMA DEPT OF TRANSPORTATION
COLORADO DEPARTMENT OF TRANSPORTATION
FEDERAL AVIATION ADMINISTRATION
FEDERAL HIGHWAY ADMINISTRATION
OHIO DEPARTMENT OF TRANSPORTATION

HISTORICAL FINANCIALS

Company Type: Private

Income Statement — FYE: June 30

	REVENUE ($mil)	NET INCOME ($mil)	NET PROFIT MARGIN	EMPLOYEES
06/22	1,804	145	8.1%	3,000
06/21	1,624	21	1.3%	—
06/20	1,540	104	6.8%	—
06/19	1,583	312	19.7%	—
Annual Growth	4.5%	(22.4%)	—	—

2022 Year-End Financials
Return on assets: 1.0%   Cash ($ mil.): 445
Return on equity: 1.2%
Current Ratio: —

KANSAS STATE UNIVERSITY

K-State is a big deal in the Little Apple. Located in Manhattan, Kansas (aka the Little Apple), Kansas State University (K-State) is a land grant institution that has an enrollment of some 24,000 students. It offers more than 250 undergraduate majors, 65 master's degrees, 45 doctoral degrees, and more than 20 graduate certificate programs. Major fields of study include agriculture, technology, and veterinary medicine. Notable alumni include former White House press secretary Marlin Fitzwater and actor Gordon Jump. Along with the University of Kansas and other universities, technical schools, and community colleges in the state, K-State is governed by The Kansas Board of Regents.

Operations

With a student-to-faculty ratio of 20:1, K-State ranks among top US colleges and has one of the highest levels of prestigious scholarship winners (including Rhodes, Marshall, and Truman scholars) in the US. The university also has several notable research organizations in fields including agriculture and genetic science.

K-State is also big on sports and is part of the Big 12 Conference of collegiate athletics.

Geographic Reach

K-State has its main campus on 670-acres in Manhattan, Kansas. It also has satellite campuses in Salina and Olathe. It also has agricultural and research centers at five Kansas locations. The university's students come from all 50 US states and more than 90 countries.

Financial Performance

K-State increased revenues by 9% to $541 million in 2012 due to higher income from student fees; government and non-government grants and contracts (for research and athletic activities); and auxiliary enterprises. Net income decreased 24% to $47 million due to higher operating expenses and lower non-operating revenues, which was attributed to lower state appropriation levels and higher interest expenses.

Strategy

K-State is expanding its facilities and programs to meet the needs of its students. It completed the first $22 million phase of its National Bio and Agro-Defense Facility in 2012, as well as work on a new student recreational, housing, classroom, and athletics facilities. In 2011 it added a new bachelor's degree program in social work. It also expanded its partnership with the Chinese scholarship council to allow additional students from China to study at K-State.

Company Background

K-State was established in 1858 as Bluemont Central College; five years later it was one of the first colleges in the US to be designated a land-grant school.

LOCATIONS

HQ: KANSAS STATE UNIVERSITY
ANDERSON HALL 110 1301 MI, MANHATTAN, KS 66506
Phone: 785 532-6011
Web: WWW.K-STATE.EDU

PRODUCTS/OPERATIONS

Selected Colleges and Departments
College of Agriculture
    Agricultural Economics
    Agronomy
    Animal Sciences and Industry
    Entomology
    Food Science Institute
    Grain Science and Industry
    Plant Pathology
College of Architecture, Planning, and Design
    Architecture
    Interior Architecture and Product Design
    Landscape Architecture/Regional and Community Planning
College of Arts and Sciences
    Aerospace Studies
    American Ethnic Studies
    Art
    Biochemistry
    Chemistry
    Economics
    English
    Geography
    Geology
    History
    International and Area Studies
    Journalism and Mass Communications
    Kinesiology
    Mathematics
    Military Science
    Modern Languages
    Music
    Philosophy
    Physics
    Political Science
    Psychology
    Statistics
    Women's Studies
College of Business Administration
    Accounting
    Finance
    Management
    Marketing
College of Education
    Educational Leadership
    Elementary Education
    Secondary Education
    Special Education, Counseling, and Student Affairs
College of Engineering
    Architectural Engineering and Construction Science
    Biological and Agricultural Engineering
    Chemical Engineering
    Computing and Information Science
    Electrical and Computer Engineering
    Mechanical and Nuclear Engineering
College of Human Ecology
    Apparel, Textiles, and Interior Design
    Gerontology
    Human Nutrition
College of Technology and Aviation
    Arts, Sciences, and Business
    Aviation Technology
College of Veterinary Medicine
    Anatomy and Physiology
    Clinical Sciences

COMPETITORS

DELAWARE STATE UNIVERSITY
MICHIGAN STATE UNIVERSITY
MISSOURI STATE UNIVERSITY
THE COLLEGE OF WILLIAM & MARY
UNIVERSITY OF DELAWARE

HISTORICAL FINANCIALS

Company Type: Private

Income Statement — FYE: June 30

	REVENUE ($mil)	NET INCOME ($mil)	NET PROFIT MARGIN	EMPLOYEES
06/17	620	50	8.2%	5,168
06/10	459	50	11.0%	—
06/09	420	10	2.6%	—
Annual Growth	5.0%	21.4%	—	—

2017 Year-End Financials
Return on assets: 3.5%   Cash ($ mil.): 150
Return on equity: 6.8%
Current Ratio: 1.90

KATY INDEPENDENT SCHOOL DISTRICT

LOCATIONS

HQ: KATY INDEPENDENT SCHOOL DISTRICT
6301 S STADIUM LN, KATY, TX 774941057
Phone: 281 396-6000
Web: WWW.KATYISD.ORG

HISTORICAL FINANCIALS
Company Type: Private

Income Statement — FYE: August 31

	REVENUE ($mil)	NET INCOME ($mil)	NET PROFIT MARGIN	EMPLOYEES
08/21	1,095	(89)	—	6,631
08/20	1,060	47	4.5%	—
08/19	993	17	1.8%	—
08/18	922	0	0.1%	—
Annual Growth	5.9%	—	—	—

2021 Year-End Financials
Return on assets: (-3.0%) Cash ($ mil.): 437
Return on equity: (-107.4%)
Current Ratio: —

KAWEAH DELTA HEALTH CARE DISTRICT GUILD

Auditors: MOSS ADAMS LLP STOCKTON CAL

LOCATIONS
HQ: KAWEAH DELTA HEALTH CARE DISTRICT GUILD
400 W MINERAL KING AVE, VISALIA, CA 932916237
Phone: 559 624-2000
Web: WWW.KAWEAHHEALTH.ORG

HISTORICAL FINANCIALS
Company Type: Private

Income Statement — FYE: June 30

	REVENUE ($mil)	NET INCOME ($mil)	NET PROFIT MARGIN	EMPLOYEES
06/22	857	(20)	—	3,200
06/21	776	13	1.8%	—
06/20	734	(6)	—	—
06/19	751	28	3.8%	—
Annual Growth	4.5%	—	—	—

2022 Year-End Financials
Return on assets: (-2.2%) Cash ($ mil.): 21
Return on equity: (-4.4%)
Current Ratio: 1.90

KECK HOSPITAL OF USC

LOCATIONS
HQ: KECK HOSPITAL OF USC
1500 SAN PABLO ST, LOS ANGELES, CA 900335313
Phone: 800 872-2273
Web: WWW.KECKMEDICINE.ORG

HISTORICAL FINANCIALS
Company Type: Private

Income Statement — FYE: September 30

	REVENUE ($mil)	NET INCOME ($mil)	NET PROFIT MARGIN	EMPLOYEES
09/20	1,130	(31)	—	264
09/14	685	(47)	—	—
09/13	611	(17)	—	—
Annual Growth	9.2%	—	—	—

2020 Year-End Financials
Return on assets: (-2.9%) Cash ($ mil.): 236
Return on equity: (-4.2%)
Current Ratio: —

KENNESTONE HOSPITAL AT WINDY HILL, INC.

Kennestone cures kidney stones and other ailments for residents of Cobb County, Georgia. WellStar Kennestone Hospital has more than 630 beds and a full range of specialty services. The hospital's physicians provide cardiac care, inpatient and outpatient surgery and rehabilitation, trauma, diabetes care, oncology, dialysis, and home health care. The hospital also operates centers specializing in women's health, senior living facilities, diagnostic clinics, and a wellness and fitness center. WellStar Kennestone Hospital is part of the not-for-profit WellStar Health System, which operates hospitals and other medical facilities throughout Georgia.

Operations
WellStar Kennestone Hospital is the anchor of the group's WellStar Kennestone Regional Medical Center division. WellStar Kennestone Hospital handles about 37,000 inpatient admissions each year, as well as more than 400,000 outpatient appointments and 120,000 emergency room visits. It also conducts about 23,000 inpatient and outpatient surgeries and 9,000 births annually and operates a level II regional trauma center. The hospital has been recognized in a number of specialist fields such as orthopedics, neurology, and gastroenterology.

Geographic Reach
Located in Marietta, Georgia, WellStar Kennestone Hospital primary serves northern and central Cobb County.

Strategy
The hospital is undergoing renovation and expansion efforts, including construction of a new hospital tower with all private patient rooms; the tower was completed and opened in early 2013. Two years later, the hospital opened a new inpatient pediatric unit. It also began renovations of its cancer center.

WellStar Kennestone also regularly upgrades its medical technology systems and tools, such as robotic surgery systems and data management programs.

LOCATIONS
HQ: KENNESTONE HOSPITAL AT WINDY HILL, INC.
677 CHURCH ST NE, MARIETTA, GA 300601101
Phone: 770 793-5000
Web: WWW.WELLSTAR.ORG

COMPETITORS
BETHESDA HOSPITAL, INC.
DOCTORS HOSPITAL OF AUGUSTA, LLC
HAYS MEDICAL CENTER, INC.
THE JAMAICA HOSPITAL
WAKEMED

HISTORICAL FINANCIALS
Company Type: Private

Income Statement — FYE: June 30

	REVENUE ($mil)	NET INCOME ($mil)	NET PROFIT MARGIN	EMPLOYEES
06/15	821	106	12.9%	2,950
06/05	481	54	11.2%	—
06/04	877	50	5.7%	—
06/03	792	24	3.1%	—
Annual Growth	0.3%	12.9%	—	—

2015 Year-End Financials
Return on assets: 20.5% Cash ($ mil.): —
Return on equity: 38.2%
Current Ratio: 8.90

KENNESTONE HOSPITAL INC

Auditors: PRICEWATERHOUSECOOPERS LLP PH

LOCATIONS
HQ: KENNESTONE HOSPITAL INC
805 SANDY PLAINS RD, MARIETTA, GA 300666340
Phone: 770 792-5023
Web: WWW.WELLSTAR.ORG

HISTORICAL FINANCIALS
Company Type: Private

Income Statement — FYE: June 30

	REVENUE ($mil)	NET INCOME ($mil)	NET PROFIT MARGIN	EMPLOYEES
06/15	948	182	19.2%	15
06/14	836	113	13.5%	—
06/13	791	123	15.6%	—
06/10	800	123	15.5%	—
Annual Growth	3.5%	8.0%	—	—

2015 Year-End Financials
Return on assets: 29.0% Cash ($ mil.): —
Return on equity: 48.5%
Current Ratio: 8.60

KERN HIGH SCHOOL DST

Auditors: CROWE LLP SACRAMENTO CALIFO

LOCATIONS

HQ: KERN HIGH SCHOOL DST
5801 SUNDALE AVE, BAKERSFIELD, CA 933097908
Phone: 661 827-3100
Web: WWW.KERNHIGH.ORG

HISTORICAL FINANCIALS
Company Type: Private

Income Statement — FYE: June 30

	REVENUE ($mil)	NET INCOME ($mil)	NET PROFIT MARGIN	EMPLOYEES
06/21	734	71	9.7%	2,000
06/20	676	(51)	—	—
06/19	677	(43)	—	—
06/18	557	40	7.3%	—
Annual Growth	9.7%	20.5%	—	—

2021 Year-End Financials
Return on assets: 4.1% Cash ($ mil.): —
Return on equity: 15.1%
Current Ratio: —

KETTERING ADVENTIST HEALTHCARE

Kettering Adventist Healthcare, dba Kettering Health Network and named for famed inventor Charles F. Kettering, is an Ohio-based health care system. It comprises about 120 outpatient facilities, including seven acute care hospitals: Kettering Medical Center, Grandview Medical Center, Sycamore Medical Center, Southview Medical Center, Fort Hamilton Hospital, Greene Memorial Hospital, and Soin Medical Center. Other facilities include Kettering Behavioral Hospital and multiple outpatient, diagnostic, senior care, and urgent care clinics. Among its specialized services are heart care, rehabilitation, orthopedics, women's health, and emergency medicine.

Operations

Several times in recent years, Kettering Health has been named by Thomson Reuters as one of the Top 10 US Healthcare Systems.

The system operates nine radiology centers, 10 pharmacies, eight outpatient rehab centers, seven sleep centers, 13 sports medicine centers, and five wound centers.

Kettering Health provides community care benefits including health screenings, education programs, charity care for uninsured patients, and coverage of Medicare/Medicaid shortfalls for under-insured patients.

Geographic Reach

Kettering Health's facilities are located in Dayton, Ohio, and the surrounding towns of Beavercreek, Centerville, Hamilton, Kettering, Miamisburg, and Xenia.

Financial Performance

Revenue totaled $1.4 billion in 2014.

Strategy

Kettering makes capital investments in its medical centers to better serve its communities. It works to improve specialty units and equipment at its existing inpatient hospitals as well, as technologically advanced hospitals tend to attract better physicians (and therefore patients). Kettering is adding new freestanding emergency room facilities in Franklin and in Eaton to the tune of $19 million. In 2015 it broke ground on a $49 million, five-story cancer center at Kettering Medical Center.

The health network is also intent on expanding its outpatient facility network.

It's expanding in Ohio, as well, through a 2014 collaboration with Health Innovations of Ohio. To keep its database up to date, Kettering in 2014 enlisted the help of ProVation Order Sets to oversee its clinical content management system.

Auditors: ERNST & YOUNG LLP CINCINNATI

LOCATIONS

HQ: KETTERING ADVENTIST HEALTHCARE
3535 SOUTHERN BLVD, DAYTON, OH 454291221
Phone: 937 298-4331
Web: WWW.KETTERINGHEALTH.ORG

PRODUCTS/OPERATIONS

Selected Ohio Facilities
Acute Care Hospitals
  Fort Hamilton Hospital (Hamilton)
  Grandview Medical Center (Dayton)
  Greene Memorial Hospital (Xenia)
  Kettering Medical Center (Kettering)
  Soin Medical Center (Beavercreek)
  Southview Medical Center (Dayton)
  Sycamore Medical Center (Miamisburg)
Other
  Adolescent Recovery Center of Hope
  Beavercreek Health Center
  Beavercreek Health Park
  Charles H. Huber Health Center
  Corwin M. Nixon Health Center
  Englewood Community Medical Center
  Kettering Behavioral Hospital (Dayton)
  Sugarcreek Health Center
  Sycamore Glen Health Center
  Sycamore Glen Retirement Center
  Sycamore Primary Care Center
  Urgent Care Centers (regional)

Selected Services
Assisted Living
Back Pain
Bariatric
Behavioral Health
Bladder Confidence
Breast Health
Cancer Care
Cardiovascular
Corporate Wellness
Community Outreach
Counseling
Diabetes
Emergency
Epilepsy
Executive Health
Fertility
Gamma Knife
Heart Care
Home Care
Hyperbaric Medicine
Imaging
Independent Living
Mammography
Maternity
Mental Health
Minimally Invasive Surgery
Neonatal Care
Neuroscience
NeuroRehab
Nutrition Counseling
Obstetrics
Oncology
Orthopedics
Pain Management
Palliative Care
Pastoral Care
Pelvic Control
Physical Therapy
Pulmonary Rehab
Radiology
Rehab Therapy
Reproductive
Robotic Surgery
Senior Living
Short-term Rehab
Skilled Nursing
Sleep
Spine
Spiritual Services
Sports Medicine
Stroke
Surgery
Urgent Care
Weight Loss
Wound Care

COMPETITORS

ADVENTIST HEALTH SYSTEM/WEST, CORPORATION
ASCENSION SOUTHEAST MICHIGAN
BAPTIST HEALTH SYSTEM, INC.
BEAUMONT HEALTH
BRONSON HEALTH CARE GROUP, INC.
LESTER E. COX MEDICAL CENTERS
MEDSTAR HEALTH, INC.
MEMORIAL HERMANN HEALTHCARE SYSTEM
RIVERVIEW HOSPITAL
UNIVERSITY HOSPITALS HEALTH SYSTEM, INC.

HISTORICAL FINANCIALS
Company Type: Private

Income Statement — FYE: December 31

	REVENUE ($mil)	NET INCOME ($mil)	NET PROFIT MARGIN	EMPLOYEES
12/21	2,375	192	8.1%	6,800
12/19	40	2	7.3%	—
12/17	1,753	171	9.8%	—
12/16	1,577	98	6.2%	—
Annual Growth	8.5%	14.5%	—	—

2021 Year-End Financials
Return on assets: 5.8% Cash ($ mil.): 84
Return on equity: 10.6%
Current Ratio: 1.60

KETTERING MEDICAL CENTER

Auditors: CLARK SCHAEFER HACKETT & CO M

LOCATIONS

HQ: KETTERING MEDICAL CENTER
3535 SOUTHERN BLVD, KETTERING, OH 454291298
Phone: 937 298-4331
Web: WWW.KETTERINGHEALTH.ORG

HISTORICAL FINANCIALS

Company Type: Private

Income Statement — FYE: December 31

	REVENUE ($mil)	NET INCOME ($mil)	NET PROFIT MARGIN	EMPLOYEES
12/19	946	122	13.0%	3,100
12/09	531	40	7.6%	—
12/04	628	40	6.4%	—
12/03	568	561	98.6%	—
Annual Growth	3.2%	(9.1%)	—	—

2019 Year-End Financials
Return on assets: 8.0%   Cash ($ mil.): 5
Return on equity: 14.1%
Current Ratio: 0.20

KEY FOOD STORES CO-OPERATIVE, INC.

Key Food Stores Co-Operative is a friend to independent New York area grocers. The co-op provides retail support and other services to 150 independently owned food retailers in the New York City area. Key Food's member-owners run stores mainly in Brooklyn and Queens, but also in the other boroughs and surrounding counties. It operates stores primarily under the Key Food banner, but it also has Key Food Marketplace locations that feature expanded meat, deli, and produce departments. In addition, the co-op supplies Key Foods-branded products to member stores. Among its members are Pick Quick Foods, Dan's Supreme Super Markets, Gemstone Supermarkets, and Queens Supermarkets. Key Foods was founded in 1937.

Geographic Reach

Staten Island-based Key Food Stores Co-Operative operates supermarkets across the five boroughs, and on Long Island, in upstate New York, and in New Jersey, and Pennsylvania.

Financial Performance

Key Foods Stores has annual sales of about $1.5 billion.

Strategy

Key Food has been expanding in Queens and Brooklyn and on Long Island, after scaling back in Manhattan -- where many of its stores were converted to Duane Reade drugstores as the pharmacy chain expanded and took over individual locations. To that end, in late 2013 the regional grocer launched a new banner called Urban Market in Brooklyn. The 16,000-square foot store in Williamsburg was the co-op's 150th location. The cooperative is expanding aggressively, adding more than 30 locations under the Key Food, Key Fresh & Natural, and Food Dynasty banners, including stores in Harlem and the Bronx. It also recently reopened a store in Coney Island that was destroyed by Hurricane Sandy in 2012.

Auditors: ANCHIN BLOCK & ANCHIN LLP N

LOCATIONS

HQ: KEY FOOD STORES CO-OPERATIVE, INC.
100 MATAWAN RD STE 100 # 100, MATAWAN, NJ 077473913
Phone: 718 370-4200
Web: WWW.KEYFOOD.COM

PRODUCTS/OPERATIONS

Selected Banners
Food Dynasty
Food World
Holiday Farms
Key Food
Key Food Marketplace
Key Fresh & Natural
Locust Valley
Milford Farms
Urban Market
Vitelio's Marketplace

COMPETITORS

ALEX LEE, INC.
CENTRAL GROCERS, INC.
FORREST CITY GROCERY CO.
GRISTEDE'S FOODS, INC.
George Weston Limited
HYPERAMA PLC
KINGS SUPER MARKETS, INC.
METCASH LIMITED
TOPCO ASSOCIATES, LLC
WALDBAUM, INC.

HISTORICAL FINANCIALS

Company Type: Private

Income Statement — FYE: April 25

	REVENUE ($mil)	NET INCOME ($mil)	NET PROFIT MARGIN	EMPLOYEES
04/15	893	(0)	—	84
04/14	753	0	0.0%	—
04/11	537	(0)	0.0%	—
04/10	0	0	—	—
Annual Growth	—	—	—	—

2015 Year-End Financials
Return on assets: (-0.6%)   Cash ($ mil.): 4
Return on equity: (-2.7%)
Current Ratio: 1.10

KEYSTOPS, LLC

Auditors: BKD LLP BOWRLING GREEN KENTU

LOCATIONS

HQ: KEYSTOPS, LLC
376 REASONOVER AVE, FRANKLIN, KY 421344003
Phone: 270 586-8283
Web: WWW.KEYSTOPS.COM

HISTORICAL FINANCIALS

Company Type: Private

Income Statement — FYE: September 30

	REVENUE ($mil)	NET INCOME ($mil)	NET PROFIT MARGIN	EMPLOYEES
09/21	584	13	2.2%	200
09/20	462	3	0.8%	—
09/19	561	5	1.0%	—
09/18	578	0	0.1%	—
Annual Growth	0.4%	176.8%	—	—

2021 Year-End Financials
Return on assets: 10.8%   Cash ($ mil.): 2
Return on equity: 16.8%
Current Ratio: 2.30

KFHP OF THE MID-ATLANTIC STATES INC.

Auditors: PRICEWATERHOUSECOOPERS LLP PH

LOCATIONS

HQ: KFHP OF THE MID-ATLANTIC STATES INC.
1 KAISER PLZ 15L, OAKLAND, CA 946123610
Phone: 510 271-6611

HISTORICAL FINANCIALS

Company Type: Private

Income Statement — FYE: December 31

	REVENUE ($mil)	NET INCOME ($mil)	NET PROFIT MARGIN	EMPLOYEES
12/13	2,511	(13)	—	2
12/09	2,089	(10)	—	—
Annual Growth	4.7%	—	—	—

2013 Year-End Financials
Return on assets: 7.1%   Cash ($ mil.): 7
Return on equity: (-0.5%)
Current Ratio: 0.60

KGBO HOLDINGS, INC

Total Quality Logistics sets a high standard for moving merchandise. The third-party logistics (non-asset based) provider specializes in arranging freight transportation using reefers (refrigerated trucks), vans, and flatbeds -- moving in excess of 500,000 loads each year. The trucking brokerage company serves more than 7,000 clients across the US, Canada, and Mexico, ranging from small businesses to Fortune 500 organizations. Founded in 1997 by company president Ken Oaks, Total Quality Logistics (TQL) has contracts with carriers that include single owner operators and large fleets. Customers have included Kroger, Dole Food, and Laura's

Lean Beef.

Operations

The company began as a produce shipper -- not a popular item for most brokers because it is perishable -- and expanded into flatbed shipments and other dry freight. As a non-asset-based business, TQL does not own trucks or warehouses, nor does it employ drivers. Rather, it arranges for independent carrier companies and owner/operators to transport its customers' freight; TQL manages the shipment while it is on the road. Additionally, the company has no expensive overhead and is not limited by fleet size, equipment, or shipping routes, allowing more flexibility for its customers.

Geographic Reach

TQL largely caters to customers in the Greater Cincinnati Area, where it has nearly five offices. It has about 25 satellite locations located in Chicago; Cleveland; Charlotte, North Carolina; Charleston, South Carolina; Detroit; Indianapolis; Denver; Columbus, Ohio; Houston; Lexington, Kentucky; Louisville; Nashville, Tennessee; Orlando, Florida; Dayton, Ohio; Erlanger, Kentucky; Pittsburgh; Tampa; and Austin, Texas.

Sales and Marketing

The company serves more than 10,000 customers and 50,000 carriers across North America to move more than 800,000 loads each year. Customers include Dole Food, Wholesalers, and Kroger.

Financial Performance

TOL posted $1.6 billion in annual sales for 2013, up from the $1.4 billion it posted the previous year. With no expense overhead to bog down its balance sheet, the company has enjoyed three straight years of sizable growth.

Strategy

TQL grows its business by gradually launching additional locations and sales offices in key cities across the country. In 2013 it expanded its sales office in Charlotte, North Carolina and moved its operations in Lexington, Kentucky to a larger space. Also that year, TQL launched a new sales office in Orlando, Florida. In 2012 the company opened new offices in the key metropolitan areas of Cleveland, Detroit, and Pittsburgh. In 2014 it announced plans to launch a new office in Nashville, Tennessee.

Auditors : BARNES DENNIG & CO LTD CI

LOCATIONS

HQ: KGBO HOLDINGS, INC
4289 IVY POINTE BLVD, CINCINNATI, OH 452450002
Phone: 513 831-2600

COMPETITORS

C.H. ROBINSON FREIGHT SERVICES, LTD.
C.H. ROBINSON WORLDWIDE, INC.
COYOTE LOGISTICS, LLC
FORWARD AIR CORPORATION
MAINFREIGHT, INC.

ODYSSEY LOGISTICS & TECHNOLOGY CORPORATION
OLD DOMINION FREIGHT LINE, INC.
PITT-OHIO EXPRESS, LLC
ULINE, INC.
UNIVERSAL LOGISTICS HOLDINGS, INC.

HISTORICAL FINANCIALS

Company Type: Private

Income Statement — FYE: December 30

	REVENUE ($mil)	NET INCOME ($mil)	NET PROFIT MARGIN	EMPLOYEES
12/12	1,387	0	0.0%	4,077
12/11	1,046	0	0.0%	—
12/10	762	0	0.0%	—
Annual Growth	34.9%	—	—	—

KIEWIT BUILDING GROUP INC.

Auditors : KPMG LLP OMAHA NE

LOCATIONS

HQ: KIEWIT BUILDING GROUP INC.
10055 TRAINSTATION CIR, LITTLETON, CO 801245700
Phone: 402 977-4500
Web: WWW.KIEWIT.COM

HISTORICAL FINANCIALS

Company Type: Private

Income Statement — FYE: December 29

	REVENUE ($mil)	NET INCOME ($mil)	NET PROFIT MARGIN	EMPLOYEES
12/12	649	12	1.9%	1,047
12/11	860	85	10.0%	—
12/10	1,280	124	9.7%	—
Annual Growth	(28.8%)	(68.3%)	—	—

2012 Year-End Financials
Return on assets: 4.5%   Cash ($ mil.): 47
Return on equity: 9.2%
Current Ratio: 1.80

KIEWIT CORPORATION

Auditors : KPMG LLP OMAHA NE

LOCATIONS

HQ: KIEWIT CORPORATION
1550 MIKE FAHEY ST, OMAHA, NE 681024722
Phone: 402 342-2052
Web: WWW.KIEWIT.COM

HISTORICAL FINANCIALS

Company Type: Private

Income Statement — FYE: December 28

	REVENUE ($mil)	NET INCOME ($mil)	NET PROFIT MARGIN	EMPLOYEES
12/13	11,826	796	6.7%	10,441
12/12	11,220	512	4.6%	—
12/11	10,381	796	7.7%	—
Annual Growth	6.7%	0.0%	—	—

2013 Year-End Financials
Return on assets: 12.0%   Cash ($ mil.): —
Return on equity: 20.2%
Current Ratio: 2.10

KIEWIT INDUSTRIAL GROUP INC

Auditors : KPMG LLP OMAHA NE

LOCATIONS

HQ: KIEWIT INDUSTRIAL GROUP INC
3555 FARNAM ST, OMAHA, NE 681313311
Phone: 402 342-2052
Web: WWW.KIEWIT.COM

HISTORICAL FINANCIALS

Company Type: Private

Income Statement — FYE: December 28

	REVENUE ($mil)	NET INCOME ($mil)	NET PROFIT MARGIN	EMPLOYEES
12/13	3,474	241	6.9%	20
12/12	3,397	110	3.2%	—
12/11	2,445	118	4.8%	—
12/10	2,546	173	6.8%	—
Annual Growth	10.9%	11.5%	—	—

2013 Year-End Financials
Return on assets: 13.8%   Cash ($ mil.): 324
Return on equity: 26.4%
Current Ratio: 1.80

KIEWIT INFRASTRUCTURE CO.

LOCATIONS

HQ: KIEWIT INFRASTRUCTURE CO.
1550 MIKE FAHEY ST, OMAHA, NE 681024722
Phone: 402 346-8535
Web: WWW.KIEWIT.COM

HISTORICAL FINANCIALS
Company Type: Private

Income Statement   FYE: December 31

	REVENUE ($mil)	NET INCOME ($mil)	NET PROFIT MARGIN	EMPLOYEES
12/12	857	55	6.5%	9,000
12/11	1,127	74	6.6%	—
12/10	3,516	269	7.7%	—
Annual Growth	(50.6%)	(54.6%)	—	—

2012 Year-End Financials
Return on assets: 6.9%   Cash ($ mil.): —
Return on equity: 10.3%
Current Ratio: 2.30

KIEWIT INFRASTRUCTURE SOUTH CO.

Auditors: KPMG LLP OMAHA NEBRASKA

LOCATIONS

HQ: KIEWIT INFRASTRUCTURE SOUTH CO.
2050 ROANOKE RD, KELLER, TX 762629616
Phone: 817 337-7000
Web: WWW.KIEWIT.COM

HISTORICAL FINANCIALS
Company Type: Private

Income Statement   FYE: December 29

	REVENUE ($mil)	NET INCOME ($mil)	NET PROFIT MARGIN	EMPLOYEES
12/12	549	85	15.6%	333
12/11	901	135	15.0%	—
12/10	1,009	126	12.6%	—
Annual Growth	(26.2%)	(17.8%)	—	—

2012 Year-End Financials
Return on assets: 21.0%   Cash ($ mil.): 127
Return on equity: 39.7%
Current Ratio: 2.00

KIEWIT INFRASTRUCTURE WEST CO.

Auditors: KPMG LLP OMAHA NEBRASKA

LOCATIONS

HQ: KIEWIT INFRASTRUCTURE WEST CO.
2200 COLUMBIA HOUSE BLVD, VANCOUVER, WA 986617753
Phone: 402 342-2052
Web: WWW.KIEWIT.COM

HISTORICAL FINANCIALS
Company Type: Private

Income Statement   FYE: December 29

	REVENUE ($mil)	NET INCOME ($mil)	NET PROFIT MARGIN	EMPLOYEES
12/12	1,512	(126)	—	2,625
12/11	1,209	85	7.1%	—
12/10	945	31	3.3%	—
Annual Growth	26.5%	—	—	—

2012 Year-End Financials
Return on assets: (-13.5%)   Cash ($ mil.): 152
Return on equity: (-47.1%)
Current Ratio: 1.20

KILLEEN INDEPENDENT SCHOOL DISTRICT

Auditors: LOTT VERNON & COMPANY PC K

LOCATIONS

HQ: KILLEEN INDEPENDENT SCHOOL DISTRICT
200 N W S YOUNG DR, KILLEEN, TX 765434025
Phone: 254 336-0000
Web: WWW.KILLEENISD.ORG

HISTORICAL FINANCIALS
Company Type: Private

Income Statement   FYE: August 31

	REVENUE ($mil)	NET INCOME ($mil)	NET PROFIT MARGIN	EMPLOYEES
08/21	560	(91)	—	6,200
08/20	524	(122)	—	—
08/19	494	113	23.0%	—
08/18	456	316	69.3%	—
Annual Growth	7.1%	—	—	—

2021 Year-End Financials
Return on assets: (-7.1%)   Cash ($ mil.): 54
Return on equity: (-21.9%)
Current Ratio: —

KIMBALL HILL INC

LOCATIONS

HQ: KIMBALL HILL INC
5999 NEW WILKE RD STE 306, ROLLING MEADOWS, IL 600084503
Phone: 847 364-7300

HISTORICAL FINANCIALS
Company Type: Private

Income Statement   FYE: September 30

	REVENUE ($mil)	NET INCOME ($mil)	NET PROFIT MARGIN	EMPLOYEES
09/07	900	(220)	—	900
09/05	1,146	86	7.6%	—
09/04	927	55	6.0%	—
09/03	786	37	4.8%	—
Annual Growth	3.4%	—	—	—

2007 Year-End Financials
Return on assets: (-25.0%)   Cash ($ mil.): 31
Return on equity: (-144.4%)
Current Ratio: —

KING COUNTY PUBLIC HOSPITAL DISTRICT 2

Auditors: KPMG LLP SEATTLE WASHINGTON

LOCATIONS

HQ: KING COUNTY PUBLIC HOSPITAL DISTRICT 2
12040 NE 128TH ST, KIRKLAND, WA 980343013
Phone: 425 899-2769
Web: WWW.EVERGREENHEALTH.COM

HISTORICAL FINANCIALS
Company Type: Private

Income Statement   FYE: December 31

	REVENUE ($mil)	NET INCOME ($mil)	NET PROFIT MARGIN	EMPLOYEES
12/17	713	14	2.0%	2,400
12/16	597	(3)	—	—
12/15	565	3	0.7%	—
12/06	273	16	6.2%	—
Annual Growth	9.1%	(1.4%)	—	—

2017 Year-End Financials
Return on assets: 2.1%   Cash ($ mil.): 44
Return on equity: 4.4%
Current Ratio: 1.70

KING'S DAUGHTERS HEALTH SYSTEM, INC.

Auditors: BAKER TILLY VIRCHOW KRAUSE LLP

LOCATIONS

HQ: KING'S DAUGHTERS HEALTH SYSTEM, INC.
2201 LEXINGTON AVE, ASHLAND, KY 411012843
Phone: 606 408-4000
Web: WWW.KINGSDAUGHTERSHEALTH.COM

HISTORICAL FINANCIALS
Company Type: Private

Income Statement   FYE: September 30

	REVENUE ($mil)	NET INCOME ($mil)	NET PROFIT MARGIN	EMPLOYEES
09/20	547	14	2.7%	4,200
09/19	505	(4)	—	—
09/18	485	(1)	—	—
09/17	475	3	0.8%	—
Annual Growth	4.8%	59.6%	—	—

2020 Year-End Financials
Return on assets: 2.1% Cash ($ mil.): 37
Return on equity: 5.4%
Current Ratio: 1.00

KIRBY - SMITH MACHINERY, INC.

Auditors : EIDE BAILLY OKLAHOMA CITY OK

LOCATIONS

HQ: KIRBY - SMITH MACHINERY, INC.
6715 W RENO AVE, OKLAHOMA CITY, OK 731276590
Phone: 888 861-0219
Web: WWW.KIRBY-SMITH.COM

HISTORICAL FINANCIALS
Company Type: Private

Income Statement   FYE: December 31

	REVENUE ($mil)	NET INCOME ($mil)	NET PROFIT MARGIN	EMPLOYEES
12/21	575	55	9.7%	516
12/20	517	39	7.6%	—
12/19	575	47	8.3%	—
12/18	666	52	7.9%	—
Annual Growth	(4.8%)	1.8%	—	—

2021 Year-End Financials
Return on assets: 11.8% Cash ($ mil.): —
Return on equity: 18.7%
Current Ratio: 1.60

KLEIN INDEPENDENT SCHOOL DISTRICT

Auditors : HEREFORD LYNCH SELLARS & KIR

LOCATIONS

HQ: KLEIN INDEPENDENT SCHOOL DISTRICT
7200 SPRING CYPRESS RD, SPRING, TX 773793215
Phone: 832 249-4000
Web: WWW.KLEINISD.NET

HISTORICAL FINANCIALS
Company Type: Private

Income Statement   FYE: June 30

	REVENUE ($mil)	NET INCOME ($mil)	NET PROFIT MARGIN	EMPLOYEES
06/21*	634	(34)	—	5,691
08/19	622	39	6.3%	—
08/18	594	2	0.4%	—
08/17	548	8	1.5%	—
Annual Growth	3.7%	—	—	—

*Fiscal year change

2021 Year-End Financials
Return on assets: (-1.9%) Cash ($ mil.): 314
Return on equity: (-118.3%)
Current Ratio: —

KMM TELECOMMUNICATIONS

Auditors : DORFMAN ABRAMS MUSIC LLC SAD

LOCATIONS

HQ: KMM TELECOMMUNICATIONS
1900 LAKEWAY DR STE 100, LEWISVILLE, TX 750576012
Phone: 888 566-2677
Web: WWW.KMMCORP.NET

HISTORICAL FINANCIALS
Company Type: Private

Income Statement   FYE: December 31

	REVENUE ($mil)	NET INCOME ($mil)	NET PROFIT MARGIN	EMPLOYEES
12/08	868	13	1.5%	190
12/07	789	17	2.2%	—
12/06	483	0	0.0%	—
Annual Growth	34.0%	30961.0%	—	—

2008 Year-End Financials
Return on assets: 13.3% Cash ($ mil.): 3
Return on equity: 57.5%
Current Ratio: 1.30

KNIGHTS OF COLUMBUS

Good Knight! The Knights of Columbus are men who lead, serve, protect, and defend, whether it is giving out Coats for Kids, lending a hand in disaster relief efforts, supporting local pregnancy centers by donating ultrasound machines, or providing top-quality financial products. The fraternal organization is also a force to be reckoned with in the insurance world, providing life insurance, annuities, and long-term care insurance to its members and their families. In addition, the group manages the Knights of Columbus Museum in New Haven, Connecticut. The group was founded in 1882 by Father Michael J. McGivney.

Operations
The company offers charity, insurance, investments, programs, scholarships, and ChurchLoans to its members. Charity is at the heart of its work and faith. One hundred percent of the donation goes directly to support the Knights of Columbus charitable cause of choice. Its insurance products have included permanent life insurance, term life insurance, retirement annuities, long-term care, and disability insurance. It also offers a suite of faith-based investment solutions specifically designed for Catholic investors such as mutual funds, separate accounts, model portfolios, and target date portfolios. In addition, the Knights of Columbus has been helping young people. It provided nearly $1 million in scholarships to students attending colleges, universities, and seminaries. It also offers ChurchLoan to any Church institution that is affiliated with the Catholic community in the United States, United States Territories, and Canada.

Geographic Reach
The Knights of Columbus is headquartered in New Haven, Connecticut.

Company Background
The Knights of Columbus was founded in New Haven by Father Michael J. McGivney in 1882 and has been selling insurance since its founding.

Auditors : SEWARD AND MONDE CPA'S NORTH

LOCATIONS

HQ: KNIGHTS OF COLUMBUS
1 COLUMBUS PLZ STE 1700, NEW HAVEN, CT 065103326
Phone: 203 752-4000
Web: WWW.KOFC.ORG

COMPETITORS
AARP
AIA GROUP LIMITED
CHURCH MUTUAL INSURANCE COMPANY
CNA FINANCIAL CORPORATION
ECCLESIASTICAL INSURANCE GROUP PLC
PAN-AMERICAN LIFE MUTUAL HOLDING COMPANY
ROYAL LONDON MUTUAL INSURANCE SOCIETY,LIMITED(THE)
ROYAL NEIGHBORS OF AMERICA
UNITED WAY WORLDWIDE
VOLUNTEERS OF AMERICA, INC.

HISTORICAL FINANCIALS
Company Type: Private

Income Statement   FYE: December 31

	ASSETS ($mil)	NET INCOME ($mil)	INCOME AS % OF ASSETS	EMPLOYEES
12/13	20,534	113	0.6%	2,300
12/12	19,401	127	0.7%	—
12/11	18,026	80	0.4%	—
12/10	16,861	86	0.5%	—
Annual Growth	6.8%	9.5%	—	—

2013 Year-End Financials
Return on assets: 0.6%   Cash ($ mil.): 192
Return on equity: 6.0%
Current Ratio: 0.10

KNOXVILLE UTILITIES BOARD

Providing utility services to residential and business customers has proven to be an excellent idea for Knoxville Utilities Board (KUB), an independent agency that serves the city of Knoxville, and surrounding areas. The multi-utility provides services to 196,500 electric, 96,920 gas, 77,600 water, and 68,740 wastewater customers. The company accesses electric power from the Tennessee Valley Authority. KUB's natural gas supply comes from the East Tennessee Natural Gas pipeline. It also maintains five treatment plants, which provide water and wastewater services.

Operations
In 2013 the company was operating 1,324 miles of wastewater mains, 1,407 miles of water mains, 5,265 miles of electric service lines and 69 substations, and 2,295 miles of natural gas mains.

Geographic Reach
The company serves 440,000 customers in Knoxville, and parts of seven surrounding counties.

Financial Performance
In 2013 KUB's operating revenues grew by 7%. Electric Division operating revenue increased $27.4 million, thanks to a 1% rise in sales volumes and electric rate increases. Gas Division revenues grew 20% thanks to 14% rise in natural gas sales volumes. Water Divisionrevenue increased by 1.4% due tomwater rate increases. The Wastewater Division revenues were $4.1 million higher than in 2012, thanks to a rate increase.

Strategy
KUB is engaged in a long term plan to renovate its aging infrastructure. The push began the mid-1990s with a focus on upgrading Knoxville's water tanks, distribution pipelines, and the its water treatment plants.

Company Background
The agency was founded by the City of Knoxville in 1939. The utility's electric system is one of the nation's most dependable, reporting a 99.9% uninterrupted service rating.

Auditors : COULTER & JUSTUS PC KNOXVI

LOCATIONS
HQ: KNOXVILLE UTILITIES BOARD
445 S GAY ST, KNOXVILLE, TN 379021125
Phone: 865 594-7501
Web: WWW.KUB.ORG

COMPETITORS
FAYETTEVILLE PUBLIC WORKS COMMISSION
JACKSONVILLE ELECTRIC AUTHORITY
PECO ENERGY COMPANY
SALT RIVER PROJECT AGRICULTURAL IMPROVEMENT AND POWER DISTRICT
UNITIL CORPORATION

HISTORICAL FINANCIALS
Company Type: Private

Income Statement   FYE: June 30

	REVENUE ($mil)	NET INCOME ($mil)	NET PROFIT MARGIN	EMPLOYEES
06/22	905	77	8.6%	500
06/21	822	75	9.2%	—
06/20	803	78	9.7%	—
06/19	815	65	8.0%	—
Annual Growth	3.6%	6.0%		

2022 Year-End Financials
Return on assets: 2.8%   Cash ($ mil.): 146
Return on equity: 5.7%
Current Ratio: 1.40

KOOTENAI HOSPITAL DISTRICT

LOCATIONS
HQ: KOOTENAI HOSPITAL DISTRICT
2003 KOOTENAI HEALTH WAY, COEUR D ALENE, ID 838146051
Phone: 208 625-4000
Web: WWW.KH.ORG

HISTORICAL FINANCIALS
Company Type: Private

Income Statement   FYE: December 31

	REVENUE ($mil)	NET INCOME ($mil)	NET PROFIT MARGIN	EMPLOYEES
12/20	693	48	7.0%	2,776
12/18	550	17	3.1%	—
12/17	506	35	6.9%	—
12/16	467	15	3.4%	—
Annual Growth	10.4%	32.4%	—	—

2020 Year-End Financials
Return on assets: 5.5%   Cash ($ mil.): 169
Return on equity: 8.7%
Current Ratio: 2.50

KPH HEALTHCARE SERVICES, INC.

Founded by Burt Orrin Kinney, who opened the company's first drugstore in 1903, Kinney Drugs has grown to number about 100 stores in central and northern New York and Vermont. Most of the company's stores are free-standing units, with pharmacies, one-hour photo developing services, and a growing selection of convenience foods. The 100%-employee-owned company maintains its own distribution warehouse and offers about 800 different products, including Kinney-branded over-the-counter medicines. Pharmacy accounts for 75% of sales. Besides retail stores, the firm operates ProAct prescription benefit management firm, HealthDirect institutional pharmacy services, and HealthDirect mail order pharmacy services.

Geographic Reach
Upstate New York-based Kinney Drugs operates more than 75 stores in New York and about two dozen locations in Vermont, as well as a distribution warehouse.

Financial Performance
The employee-owned company rings up more than $800 million in annual sales. Prescription drugs sales account for about three-quarters of Kinney Drugs' total sales.

Strategy
To distinguish itself from its national competitors, including Walgreen, CVS, and Wal-Mart, the regional retailer strives to maintain a hometown feel. To that end, it launched the KinneyCare Discount Prescription Plan for its insured and uninsured pharmacy customers. Under the plan more than 350 generic prescriptions are available for $12 for a 90-day supply. The plans costs $10 a year to enroll. The chain's ReadyScripts automated refill program sends messages to remind patients to pick up their prescriptions and offers free delivery to the mobility-impaired customers. Taking a page from its large rivals Kinney is moving to provide health care services, in addition to filling prescriptions. In 2014, Kinney teamed with a local health care organization to open a Healthy You Wellness Center to treat lung problems at a store in Syracuse, New York. The wellness center is staffed by specialists from Pulmonary Health Physicians, PC and will focus on disease management and immediate care of certain health concerns. Kinney Drugs national rivals Walgreen and CVS both operate a growing number of in-store clinics. The regional drugstore chain hopes to open more Health You Wellness Centers in the near future.

With the worst of the recession -- and concurrent decrease in spending on health care and prescription drugs -- behind it, Kinney acquired four independent pharmacies in central New York and Vermont in mid-2012, and has since added about a half a dozen more, bringing its store count to about 100 locations.

Auditors : DANNIBLE & MCKEE LLP SYRACUS

LOCATIONS
HQ: KPH HEALTHCARE SERVICES, INC.
29 E MAIN ST, GOUVERNEUR, NY 136421401
Phone: 315 287-3600
Web: WWW.KPHHEALTHCARESERVICES.COM

2013 Stores

New York	77
Vermont	23
Total	100

COMPETITORS

CVS HEALTH CORPORATION
DISCOUNT DRUG MART, INC.
EXPRESS SCRIPTS HOLDING COMPANY
FRED'S, INC.
Katz Group Inc
MAXOR NATIONAL PHARMACY SERVICES, LLC
OPTUMRX, INC.
PHARMACA INTEGRATIVE PHARMACY, INC.
WALGREEN CO.
WALGREENS BOOTS ALLIANCE, INC.

HISTORICAL FINANCIALS
Company Type: Private

Income Statement — FYE: December 31

	REVENUE ($mil)	NET INCOME ($mil)	NET PROFIT MARGIN	EMPLOYEES
12/21	1,760	42	2.4%	4,300
12/20	1,589	41	2.6%	—
12/19	1,542	51	3.3%	—
Annual Growth	6.8%	(9.1%)	—	—

2021 Year-End Financials
Return on assets: 7.2%   Cash ($ mil.): 22
Return on equity: 17.5%
Current Ratio: 1.80

KRATON POLYMERS U.S. LLC

EXECUTIVES

Managing Member, Kevin Fogarty
CPO*, Suzanne Pesgens
Chief Accounting Officer*, Christopher Gingrich

LOCATIONS

HQ: KRATON POLYMERS U.S. LLC
15710 JOHN F KENNEDY BLVD # 300, HOUSTON, TX 770322347
Phone: 281 504-4700
Web: WWW.KRATON.COM

HISTORICAL FINANCIALS
Company Type: Private

Income Statement — FYE: December 31

	REVENUE ($mil)	NET INCOME ($mil)	NET PROFIT MARGIN	EMPLOYEES
12/08	1,226	28	2.3%	520
12/07	1,089	(43)	—	—
12/06	0	0	—	—
12/05	975	166	17.1%	—
Annual Growth	7.9%	(44.6%)	—	—

2008 Year-End Financials
Return on assets: 6.1%   Cash ($ mil.): 101
Return on equity: 2.3%
Current Ratio: 1.10

KRUEGER INTERNATIONAL, INC.

Krueger International is one of the world's leading contract furniture manufacturers in the industry. The company, which does business as KI, makes ergonomic seating, cabinets, sleepers, occasional tables, and other furniture used by businesses, healthcare organizations, government agencies, and educational institutions. It offers everything from benches and beds to desks and tables, not to mention shelving, filing systems, and movable walls. KI markets its products through sales representatives, furniture dealers, architects, and interior designers worldwide. Founded in 1941, KI is 100% employee-owned.

Operations
KI operates a variety of subsidiaries, including KI Europe, KI Canada, KI India, KI China and KI Australia (Sebel). The company provides delivery and furniture installation services worldwide. Its service program includes space planning, on-site project management, furniture reconfiguration, special inside delivery and coordination of product staging and a dedicated transportation fleet. KI also offers the option to purchase furniture according to what fits to its clients' ordering and fulfillment process, whether direct or via a third party.

KI also owns Pallas Textiles and Spacesaver. Pallas Textiles, which operates out of Wisconsin, creates textile products for contract upholstery, panel systems and wall-coverings, healthcare environments, and casements. Spacesaver, also located in Wisconsin, makes high-density mobile storage systems for office, institutional, and industrial applications, and is a major supplier of steel shelving systems, rotary storage systems, and storage accessories.

KI's products include seating, tables, desks, architectural walls, pods, files and storage, casegoods, dormitory furniture, school library furniture, auditorium and lecture hall furniture, and accessories, among others.

Geographic Reach
Based in Wisconsin, KI sells its products worldwide, and operates manufacturing facilities, showrooms and sales offices in the US, Canada, China, and India, as well as throughout Europe, Middle East, America, and Asia. It currently operates six manufacturing facilities in the US and Canada. The company has subsidiaries based in Europe, Canada, India, Australia, and China. Its showrooms are in several metropolitan areas across the US, Toronto, and London.

Sales and Marketing
KI sells its products globally through furniture dealers, sales representatives, architects, and interior designers. It primarily serves the educational, university, workplace, healthcare, business, and government markets.

The company has district sales offices around the world, and also boasts showrooms in metropolitan areas to display its products to potential business and individual customers.

Strategy
KI's entries into foreign markets are varied. Entries include exporting, licensing, joint ventures, and foreign direct investments where appropriate. Services are provided through fulfillment partners in established and emerging markets.

KI continues to differentiate itself and establish enduring relationships throughout the world by personalizing products and service solutions to the specific needs of each customer through its unique design and "Market of One" manufacturing philosophy.

Company Background
The company has expanded its network of showrooms in the US and abroad over the years. KI added a showroom in Houston in 2010 to boost its US presence, which includes about 10 locations in half a dozen states. To better serve its Asian and European customers, the company operates through a showroom in Shanghai, China. KI has international showrooms in London, Malaysia, Mexico, Puerto Rico, and Toronto. To support its growth, KI completed a $3.3-million, 100,000-sq.-ft. plant expansion in 2012 to reduce costs and streamline its business. The move boosts its manufacturing, shipping, receiving, and warehousing space.

As its showroom presence grew, KI also formed new sales partnerships. The company tapped Heartland Furniture Group, a contract furniture representative, in 2011 to take care of existing customer accounts and broker sales in Kansas, Missouri, and southern Illinois.

It's also looked to acquisitions to extend the reach of its business. In 2011 KI purchased Sebel Furniture Limited from GWA Group Ltd., a top supplier of building fixtures in Australia. The $24 million deal has given KI a foothold in the commercial furniture business in Australia, New Zealand, the UK, and Hong Kong.

Auditors : BAKER TILLY VIRCHOW KRAUSE LL

LOCATIONS

HQ: KRUEGER INTERNATIONAL, INC.
1330 BELLEVUE ST, GREEN BAY, WI 543022197
Phone: 920 468-8100
Web: WWW.KI.COM

PRODUCTS/OPERATIONS

Selected Products
Auditorium seating
Beds
Benches
Bookcases
Carrels

Chairs
Desks
File cabinets
Lecterns
Movable walls
Planters
Power and data connections
Receptacles
Recliners
Residence hall furniture
Sleepers
Special events seating
Stools
Tables

COMPETITORS

CANO CORPORATION
ERGOGENESIS WORKPLACE SOLUTIONS, LLC
FELLOWES, INC.
HAWORTH, INC.
HUMANSCALE CORPORATION
INTERMETRO INDUSTRIES CORPORATION
OFS BRANDS HOLDINGS INC.
PETER PEPPER PRODUCTS, INC.
STEELCASE INC.
Teknion Corporation

HISTORICAL FINANCIALS

Company Type: Private

Income Statement — FYE: December 31

	REVENUE ($mil)	NET INCOME ($mil)	NET PROFIT MARGIN	EMPLOYEES
12/15	617	53	8.6%	2,300
12/11	649	56	8.8%	—
12/10	(40)	0	0.0%	—
Annual Growth	—	1047.2%	—	—

2015 Year-End Financials
Return on assets: 19.5% Cash ($ mil.): 4
Return on equity: 92.6%
Current Ratio: 1.10

KWIK TRIP, INC.

Kwik Trip is a privately owned family company. Midwesterners who need to make a quick trip to get gas or groceries, cigarettes or donuts, race on over to Kwik Trip stores. Adding approximately 40 new stores each year, the company's more than 30,000 co-workers serve guests at more than 800 Kwik Trip, Kwik Star, Stop-N-Go, Tobacco Outlet Plus Grocery, and Tobacco Outlet Plus convenience stores throughout Iowa, Illinois, Minnesota, and Wisconsin. With its own bakery (bakes between 25 and 30 different items each day), kitchens, dairy, distribution, and transportation divisions, the company produces quality products for its customers. Kwik Trip opened its first store in 1965.

Operations
Kwik Trip vertically integrates by processing its own gasoline and producing and packaging products to be sold in its convenience stores.

Geographic Reach
The company is based in La Crosse, Wisconsin.

Mergers and Acquisitions

In late 2021, Kwik Trip completed the acquisition of Pritzl's. In addition to more fueling stations, it will feature all the values and convenient products and service Kwik Trip guests love.

In mid-2021, Kwik Trip is acquiring four Dells Travel Mart locations from Travel Mart Inc. Wisconsin-based Travel Mart is a unit of Holiday Wholesale, a broad-line distributor serving more than 6,500 customers in Wisconsin and parts of Illinois, Iowa, Michigan and Minnesota.

Company Background
The John Hansen family founded Kwik Trip in Eau Claire, Wisconsin in 1965. In 2000, the Hansens sold their interest in Kwik Trip to the Zietlow family for $120 million. The two families had jointly owned Kwik Trip since 1972.

Auditors : MCGLADREY & PULLEN LLP MINNE

LOCATIONS

HQ: KWIK TRIP, INC.
1626 OAK ST, LA CROSSE, WI 546032308
Phone: 608 781-8988
Web: WWW.KWIKTRIP.COM

PRODUCTS/OPERATIONS

Selected Banners
Hearty Platter
Kwik Star
Kwik Trip
Tobacco Outlet Plus

COMPETITORS

FAREWAY STORES, INC.
FRY'S FOOD STORES OF ARIZONA, INC.
SCHWAN'S COMPANY
SHEETZ, INC.
SPARTANNASH COMPANY
STEWART'S SHOPS CORP.
THE HOME CITY ICE COMPANY
UNIFIED GROCERS, INC.
URM STORES, INC.
WEGMANS FOOD MARKETS, INC.

HISTORICAL FINANCIALS

Company Type: Private

Income Statement — FYE: September 27

	REVENUE ($mil)	NET INCOME ($mil)	NET PROFIT MARGIN	EMPLOYEES
09/08	3,640	23	0.7%	10,500
09/04	1,887	24	1.3%	—
09/03	1,651	24	1.5%	—
Annual Growth	17.1%	(0.2%)	—	—

2008 Year-End Financials
Return on assets: 3.6% Cash ($ mil.): 1
Return on equity: 20.3%
Current Ratio: 0.70

LADENBURG THALMANN FINANCIAL SERVICES INC.

Ladenburg Thalmann Financial Services is a wholly-owned subsidiary of Advisor Group Holdings, Inc., which is owned by private investment funds sponsored by Reverence Capital Partners, LLC. Ladenburg's subsidiaries include industry-leading independent advisory and brokerage (IAB) firms Securities America, Triad Advisors, Securities Service Network, Investacorp and KMS Financial Services, as well as Premier Trust, Ladenburg Thalmann Asset Management, Highland Capital Brokerage, a leading independent life insurance brokerage company and full-service annuity processing and marketing company, and Ladenburg Thalmann & Co. Inc., an investment bank.

Operations
Ladenburg Thalmann offers a full suite of investment banking and capital markets products and services, including proprietary equity research and a fixed-income trading desk.

Geographic Reach
Based in New York, Ladenburg Thalmann has branch offices in Boca Raton and Naples Florida; and Melville, New York.

Sales and Marketing
Ladenburg Thalmann has relationships with over 1,000 institutional investors and provide targeted, results-driven corporate access through non-deal road shows, one-day forums, one-on-one meetings, specialized industry events, conference calls and site visits for its corporate clients.

Ladenburg Thalmann serves also middle-market public companies across various industry vertical, including healthcare & life sciences, yield-oriented securities (BDCs, REITs, MLPs), energy, power & infrastructure, and telecom, media & technology.

EXECUTIVES

CAO, Ahmed Hassanein

Auditors : EISNERAMPER LLP NEW YORK NEW

LOCATIONS

HQ: LADENBURG THALMANN FINANCIAL SERVICES INC.
4400 BISCAYNE BLVD FL 12, MIAMI, FL 331373212
Phone: 305 572-4100
Web: WWW.LADENBURG.COM

PRODUCTS/OPERATIONS

2017 Sales

	$ mil.	% of total
Commissions	536.0	42
Advisory fees	560.9	44
Investment banking	46.5	4
Interest & dividends	25.0	2
Principal transactions	0.9	-
Service fees & other	98.9	8
Total	1,268.2	100

2017 Sales

	$ mil.	% of total
Independent Advisory & Brokerage	1,140.4	90
Ladenburg	66.7	5
Insurance Brokerage	57.1	5
Corporate	4.0	-
Total	1,268.2	100

COMPETITORS

BRC MERGER SUB, LLC
FIRST EAGLE PRIVATE CREDIT, LLC
FRANKLIN RESOURCES, INC.
INVESTEC PLC
LPL FINANCIAL HOLDINGS INC.
OPPENHEIMER HOLDINGS INC.
PIPER SANDLER COMPANIES
STIFEL FINANCIAL CORP.
VOYA FINANCIAL, INC.
WADDELL & REED FINANCIAL, INC.

HISTORICAL FINANCIALS

Company Type: Private

Income Statement   FYE: December 31

	REVENUE ($mil)	NET INCOME ($mil)	NET PROFIT MARGIN	EMPLOYEES
12/19	1,469	22	1.5%	1,512
12/18	1,391	33	2.4%	—
12/17	1,268	7	0.6%	—
12/16	1,106	(22)	—	—
Annual Growth	9.9%	—	—	—

2019 Year-End Financials
Return on assets: 2.7% Cash ($ mil.): 248
Return on equity: 9.4%
Current Ratio: —

LAHEY CLINIC HOSPITAL, INC.

EXECUTIVES

Vice Chairman, John Libertino

LOCATIONS

HQ: LAHEY CLINIC HOSPITAL, INC.
41 MALL RD, BURLINGTON, MA 018050002
Phone: 781 273-5100
Web: WWW.LAHEY.ORG

HISTORICAL FINANCIALS

Company Type: Private

Income Statement   FYE: September 30

	REVENUE ($mil)	NET INCOME ($mil)	NET PROFIT MARGIN	EMPLOYEES
09/15	816	(17)	—	1
09/14	800	(0)	0.0%	—
09/13	774	228	29.5%	—
09/12	796	192	24.1%	—
Annual Growth	0.8%	—	—	—

2015 Year-End Financials
Return on assets: (-2.3%) Cash ($ mil.): 105
Return on equity: (-12.0%)
Current Ratio: 2.40

LAKE WASHINGTON SCHOOL DISTRICT

LOCATIONS

HQ: LAKE WASHINGTON SCHOOL DISTRICT
16250 NE 74TH ST, REDMOND, WA 980527817
Phone: 425 936-1200
Web: WWW.LWSD.ORG

HISTORICAL FINANCIALS

Company Type: Private

Income Statement   FYE: August 31

	REVENUE ($mil)	NET INCOME ($mil)	NET PROFIT MARGIN	EMPLOYEES
08/21	595	(76)	—	3,100
08/20	583	38	6.7%	—
08/16	385	176	45.7%	—
Annual Growth	9.1%	—	—	—

2021 Year-End Financials
Return on assets: (-4.2%) Cash ($ mil.): 196
Return on equity: (-11.2%)
Current Ratio: —

LAKELAND REGIONAL HEALTH SYSTEMS, INC.

EXECUTIVES

Public Relations, Timothy J Boynton
Chief Nurse, Janet Fansler
Chief Analytics Officer, Caroline Gay
Chief Strategy Officer, Deana Nelson
Auditors: II PYA PC TAMPA FL

LOCATIONS

HQ: LAKELAND REGIONAL HEALTH SYSTEMS, INC.
1324 LAKELAND HILLS BLVD, LAKELAND, FL 338054543

Phone: 863 687-1100
Web: WWW.MYLRH.ORG

HISTORICAL FINANCIALS

Company Type: Private

Income Statement   FYE: September 30

	REVENUE ($mil)	NET INCOME ($mil)	NET PROFIT MARGIN	EMPLOYEES
09/14	685	67	9.9%	3,124
09/13	24	(13)	—	—
09/12	582	67	11.6%	—
Annual Growth	8.5%	0.4%	—	—

2014 Year-End Financials
Return on assets: 7.2% Cash ($ mil.): 22
Return on equity: 10.9%
Current Ratio: 1.40

LAKELAND REGIONAL MEDICAL CENTER, INC.

Lakeland Regional Medical Center (LRMC) serves Florida's Polk County (roughly between Kissimmee and Tampa) through an acute care hospital with approximately 850 beds. Among its specialty services are cardiac care, cancer treatment, senior care, urology, emergency medicine, orthopedics, women's and children's health care, and surgery. LRMC also operates general care and specialty outpatient clinics. Additionally, the hospital provides medical training programs for radiology specialists. Its LRMC Foundation offers financial support for indigent patients facing ongoing treatment.

Operations

LRMC is part of Lakeland Regional Health System, a not-for-profit organization that also includes Lakeland Regional Cancer Center, Lakeland Regional Family Health Center, and Lakeland Regional Health Medical Group.

Annually, LRMC has more than 41,000 admissions and performs more than 15,000 surgeries. Its emergency department treats more than 200,000 patients each year.

Financial Performance

Revenue in 2014 totaled $633 million (representing 92% of Lakeland Regional Health System's revenue), while net income totaled $67 million.

LRMC funds its activities through charges to patients for inpatient and outpatient services, as well as from non-hospital activities, such as its cafeteria, gift and uniform shops, and physicians' answering service. Although the hospital also receives payment from federal agencies, such as Medicaid and Medicare, they, along with other managed care entities, have cut their reimbursement levels causing LRMC's charity care levels to increase.

Strategy

The hospital has been undergoing facility and data systems improvement efforts to enhance care and increase efficiencies. It recently expanded its intensive care department and upgraded technology in areas including radiology, orthopedics, and chemotherapy.

In 2014, Lakeland Regional Health System announced plans to build an eight-story women and children pavilion at LRMC. The $250 million addition will include 300,000 sq. ft. of space, including 32 private rooms for mothers and newborns, a 30-bed neonatal intensive care unit, 64 private rooms for women's surgical and medical care, three surgical suites, and 12 private suites for labor, delivery, and recovery. It will also have an education and conference center. The pavilion is expected to open in 2017.

Auditors: PERSHING YOAKLEY & ASSOCIATES

LOCATIONS

HQ: LAKELAND REGIONAL MEDICAL CENTER, INC.
1324 LAKELAND HILLS BLVD, LAKELAND, FL 338054500
Phone: 863 687-1100
Web: WWW.MYLRH.ORG

PRODUCTS/OPERATIONS

Selected Facilities
Lakeland Regional Cancer Center
Lakeland Regional Medical Center (LRMC) Foundation
Lakeland Regional Orthopedics Associates
Lakeland Regional Rehabilitation and Sports Medicine Clinic

Selected Services and Centers
Emergency
Family health center
Gastroenterology
Heart center
Mental health & addictions
Neurosurgery
Nursing
Oncology care
Orthopedic care
Palliative care
Pharmacy
Rehabilitation and sports medicine clinic
Robotic surgery
School of radiologic technology
Stroke center
Surgery
Trauma services
Women and children
Wound center

COMPETITORS

ARROWHEAD REGIONAL MEDICAL CENTER
BJC HEALTH SYSTEM
COMMUNITY HEALTH NETWORK, INC.
FLOYD HEALTHCARE MANAGEMENT, INC.
INTEGRIS HEALTH, INC.
LEHIGH VALLEY HEALTH NETWORK, INC.
OVERLAKE HOSPITAL MEDICAL CENTER
SWEDISH COVENANT HOSPITAL
WELLSTAR HEALTH SYSTEM, INC.
YAKIMA VALLEY MEMORIAL HOSPITAL ASSOCIATION

HISTORICAL FINANCIALS
Company Type: Private

Income Statement — FYE: September 30

	REVENUE ($mil)	NET INCOME ($mil)	NET PROFIT MARGIN	EMPLOYEES
09/19	905	65	7.3%	3,100
09/16	790	84	10.7%	—
09/15	674	68	10.2%	—
09/14	618	66	10.8%	—
Annual Growth	7.9%	(0.3%)	—	—

2019 Year-End Financials
Return on assets: 7.7%   Cash ($ mil.): —
Return on equity: 16.4%
Current Ratio: 0.40

LAMEX FOODS INC.

LOCATIONS

HQ: LAMEX FOODS INC.
8500 NORMANDALE LAKE BLVD # 800, BLOOMINGTON, MN 554373813
Phone: 952 844-0585
Web: WWW.LAMEXFOODS.EU

HISTORICAL FINANCIALS
Company Type: Private

Income Statement — FYE: March 31

	REVENUE ($mil)	NET INCOME ($mil)	NET PROFIT MARGIN	EMPLOYEES
03/15	592	7	1.3%	80
03/05	103	1	1.0%	—
03/04	76	0	0.9%	—
Annual Growth	20.4%	24.8%	—	—

2015 Year-End Financials
Return on assets: 7.2%   Cash ($ mil.): —
Return on equity: 20.8%
Current Ratio: 1.50

LANE INDUSTRIES INCORPORATED

Auditors: KPMG LLP HARTFORD CT

LOCATIONS

HQ: LANE INDUSTRIES INCORPORATED
90 FIELDSTONE CT, CHESHIRE, CT 064101212
Phone: 203 235-3351

HISTORICAL FINANCIALS
Company Type: Private

Income Statement — FYE: December 31

	REVENUE ($mil)	NET INCOME ($mil)	NET PROFIT MARGIN	EMPLOYEES
12/18	856	(68)	—	4,500
12/17	1,592	14	0.9%	—
12/16	1,292	36	2.8%	—
12/15	1,197	(13)	—	—
Annual Growth	(10.6%)	—	—	—

2018 Year-End Financials
Return on assets: (-6.9%)   Cash ($ mil.): 137
Return on equity: (-13.8%)
Current Ratio: 1.80

LEE MEMORIAL HEALTH SYSTEM FOUNDATION, INC.

Not feeling so bright in the Sunshine State? Lee Memorial Health System can help. Serving residents of Fort Myers and surrounding areas in Southwestern Florida's Lee County, the community-owned, not-for-profit health care system is home to four acute care hospitals (with a total of more than 1,400 beds), a home health agency, a 112-bed nursing home, and numerous outpatient treatment and diagnostic centers. The flagship Lee Memorial Hospital also houses a 60-bed inpatient rehabilitation hospital, and the HealthPark Medical Center location includes a dedicated 100-bed children's hospital. Lee Memorial Health Systems' corporate services include pre-employment screenings, drug screens, and wellness programs.

Operations

The system's facilities include the flagship Lee Memorial Hospital (355 beds), HealthPark Medical Center (270 beds), Gulf Coast Medical Center (350 beds), and Cape Coral Hospital (290 beds). Lee Memorial Health System employs more than 1,200 doctors, including primary and specialty care practitioners that are members of the affiliated Lee Physician Group. Patient service revenues account for nearly all of the company's revenues.

Lee Memorial Hospital is the only level II trauma center between Tampa and Miami.

Altogether, the system has more than 1 million patient contacts each year.

Geographic Reach

Three of the systems' hospitals are located in Fort Myers, Florida. Its fourth hospital (Cape Coral Hospital) is located in Cape Coral, Florida.

Sales and Marketing

Medicare payments accounted for a third of the system's net patient service revenues in fiscal 2014, while Medicaid accounted for 15%. Self-pay accounted for 26%, followed by managed care (20%) and commercial insurance (6%).

Financial Performance
Revenue increased 8% to $1.4 billion in fiscal 2014 (ended September) as net patient service revenues grew. This in turn led to an increase in net income, which grew 31% to $158 million. Decreased interest expenses also helped boost profits.

Cash flow from operations increased 49% to $225 million that year, largely due to cash received from patient care services.

Strategy
Lee Memorial Health System is a not-for-profit organization that proclaims its fiscal mission is to reinvest its profits back into the community it serves through facility and equipment upgrades and other measures. The system has undertaken a number of expansion projects at its hospitals in recent years to add specialty services and private patient rooms, and has also opened a number of new community outpatient centers. In addition, it is enhancing existing facilities to improve quality, safety, and financial performance.

In 2015, the system approved a $315 million expansion plan that will add 275 patient beds to Gulf Coast Medical Center. Construction on the project is expected to begin in 2017.

Lee Memorial Health System is also upgrading its IT systems to provide coordinated and efficient care. It has installed electronic health record programs (using EHR software from Epic Systems) at most of its facilities, and it is improving other tools to streamline business systems and improve health care delivery processes.

Company Background
Tracing its roots to 1916, Lee Memorial Health System is a public health care system created by special act of the Florida Legislature in 1963. Its governing board is composed of 10 members elected by the public.

EXECUTIVES

Strategy Officer*, C B Rebsamen
CIO*, Rick Schooler
EQUITY INCLUSION*, Selynto Anderson
Chief Officer*, Kristine Fay
Chief Officer*, Armando Llechu
STRATEGY Innovation*, Lisa Martinez
Auditors : PRICEWATERHOUSECOOPERS LLP

LOCATIONS

HQ: LEE MEMORIAL HEALTH SYSTEM FOUNDATION, INC.
2776 CLEVELAND AVE, FORT MYERS, FL 339015864
Phone: 239 343-2000
Web: WWW.LEEHEALTH.ORG

PRODUCTS/OPERATIONS

2014 Sales by Segment

	$ mil.	% of total
Lee Memorial Hospital	682.1	50
Gulf Coast Memorial Center	302.1	22
Cape Memorial Hospital	206.4	15
Physicians	133.4	10
Health Park Care Center	13.0	1
Lee Memorial Home Health	8.5	1
Lee Memorial Health System Foundation	3.5	—
Lee County Trauma Services District	3.2	—
Lee Community Health Care	1.7	—
Other	9.9	1
Total	1,363.8	100

Selected Florida Hospitals
Blood Centers
Cardiac Care (Heart Services)
Community Health Centers/United Way Houses
Convenient Care
Emergency Services
Home Health Services
The Kidney Transplant Center
Lee Physician Group
Mental Health Services
Neuroscience Services
Nursing Home
Occupational Health Services
Orthopedic and Spine Services
Palliative Services
Patient Services
Pediatric Services
Pulmonary Services
Rehabilitation Services
Sleep Disorder Center
Surgical Services
Volunteer Services
Wellness and Nutrition Services
Women's Health Services
Wound Care and Hyperbaric Medicine

COMPETITORS

ALTRU HEALTH SYSTEM
CAREGROUP, INC.
CATHOLIC HEALTH SYSTEM, INC.
EAST TEXAS MEDICAL CENTER REGIONAL HEALTHCARE SYSTEM
INSPIRA HEALTH NETWORK, INC.
MILES HEALTH CARE, INC
NORTH MISSISSIPPI HEALTH SERVICES, INC.
NORTON HEALTHCARE, INC.
SOUTHCOAST HEALTH SYSTEM, INC.
THE LANCASTER GENERAL HOSPITAL

HISTORICAL FINANCIALS
Company Type: Private

Income Statement — FYE: September 30

	REVENUE ($mil)	NET INCOME ($mil)	NET PROFIT MARGIN	EMPLOYEES
09/18	1,789	101	5.6%	7,870
09/04	585	46	8.0%	—
09/03	522	50	9.8%	—
09/02	477	7	1.6%	—
Annual Growth	8.6%	17.4%	—	—

2018 Year-End Financials
Return on assets: 4.1% Cash ($ mil.): 33
Return on equity: 6.6%
Current Ratio: 5.40

LEE MEMORIAL HOSPITAL, INC.

LOCATIONS

HQ: LEE MEMORIAL HOSPITAL, INC.
2776 CLEVELAND AVE, FORT MYERS, FL 339015855
Phone: 239 343-2000
Web: WWW.LEEHEALTH.ORG

HISTORICAL FINANCIALS
Company Type: Private

Income Statement — FYE: September 30

	REVENUE ($mil)	NET INCOME ($mil)	NET PROFIT MARGIN	EMPLOYEES
09/14	688	163	23.8%	1,159
09/13	632	135	21.4%	—
09/12	613	105	17.3%	—
Annual Growth	6.0%	24.4%	—	—

2014 Year-End Financials
Return on assets: 10.8% Cash ($ mil.): 32
Return on equity: 21.1%
Current Ratio: 7.30

LEGACY EMANUEL HOSPITAL & HEALTH CENTER

Legacy Emanuel Hospital and Health Center, part of the Legacy Health System, provides acute and specialized health care to residents of Portland, Oregon, and surrounding communities. The 420-bed teaching hospital's operations include centers devoted to trauma treatment, burn care, oncology, birthing, neurosurgery, orthopedics, and cardiology. It also houses a pediatric hospital and operates the region's Life Flight Network service, which is owned by a consortium of local hospitals. Legacy Emanuel's emergency department handles more than 15,600 visits every year.

Operations
Legacy Emanuel's trauma and burn centers are level I designated facilities, meaning they receive severe trauma and burn cases from other area hospitals. The hospital's burn center is the only one of its kind in an area stretching from Seattle to Sacramento and Salt Lake City. Other specialist facilities at Legacy Emanuel include its maternity center and its diagnostic imaging and screening units.

The medical center sees more than 18,000 inpatients each year. Its staff includes about 140 full-time doctors and dentists, as well as 700 full-time registered nurses. The Randall Children's Hospital, located within

Legacy Emanuel, has about 600 affiliated pediatricians and specialists on its staff and handles about 100,000 patient encounters each year, including 20,000 emergency room visits.

Strategy

The hospital has undergone massive expansion efforts. The hospital has completed construction of the new Randall Children's Hospital facilities, making it one of the largest pediatric facilities in the state. The new pediatric center is four times as large as the past facilities. Other expansion efforts in recent years include new acute and intensive care capacity.

Company Background

To expand its medical transportation services, Legacy Emanuel and other owners of LFN teamed up to purchase 15 new helicopters in 2012.

Legacy Emanuel Hospital was established in 1912 by the Lutheran Church.

LOCATIONS

HQ: LEGACY EMANUEL HOSPITAL & HEALTH CENTER
2801 N GANTENBEIN AVE, PORTLAND, OR 972271623
Phone: 503 413-2200
Web: WWW.LEGACYHEALTH.ORG

PRODUCTS/OPERATIONS

Selected Centers and Services
Burn care
Cancer care
Children's care
Diabetes and nutrition
Emergency services
Family birth center
Gardens
High-risk obstetrics
Imaging
Injury prevention
Intensive care
Interventional and diagnostic cardiology
Level I trauma center
Life flight network
Maternal-fetal medicine
Neurology and neurosurgery including spine surgery
Orthopedics
Pediatrics
Rehabilitation (inpatient and outpatient)
Radiation oncology
Stroke
Surgery (including minimally invasive surgery)
Vascular clinic
Wound and ostomy clinic
Wound care and outpatient burn clinic

COMPETITORS

FRANKLIN SQUARE HOSPITAL CENTER, INC.
LOMA LINDA UNIVERSITY MEDICAL CENTER
MEMORIAL HEALTH SERVICES
REGIONS HOSPITAL FOUNDATION
SHAWNEE MISSION MEDICAL CENTER, INC.

HISTORICAL FINANCIALS

Company Type: Private

Income Statement FYE: March 31

	REVENUE ($mil)	NET INCOME ($mil)	NET PROFIT MARGIN	EMPLOYEES
03/20	977	(49)	—	3,619
03/17	778	(12)	—	—
03/15	705	29	4.2%	—
03/14	649	30	4.8%	—
Annual Growth	7.0%	—	—	—

2020 Year-End Financials
Return on assets: (-11.2%) Cash ($ mil.): (-2)
Return on equity: —
Current Ratio: 1.60

LEGACY HEALTH

Legacy Health is a locally owned, nonprofit health system that offers a unique blend of health services across the Portland/Vancouver metro area and mid-Willamette Valley. Its services range from wellness and urgent care to dedicated children's services and advanced medical centers for patients of all ages. It operates half a dozen hospitals, including Legacy Emanuel Medical Center and Legacy Good Samaritan Medical Center, as well as the Randall Children's Hospital at Legacy Emanuel. Legacy Health has more than 70 primary care, specialty and urgent care clinics and its facilities provide such services as behavioral health, and outpatient and health education programs.

Operations

Legacy Health has nearly 3,000 doctors and providers. Its hospitals include Legacy Emanuel Medical Center, Randall Children's Hospital, Legacy Good Samaritan Medical Center, Legacy Meridian Park Medical Center, Legacy Mount Hood Medical Center, Legacy Silverton Medical Center, and Legacy Salmon Creek Medical Center in Washington.

Geographic Reach

Portland, Oregon-based, Legacy Health operates six advanced medical centers in Portland, Vancouver, Gresham, Tualatin and Silverton.

Company Background

Legacy Health was founded through the 1989 merger of HealthLink and Good Samaritan Hospital.

Auditors: KPMG LLP PORTLAND OREGON

LOCATIONS

HQ: LEGACY HEALTH
1919 NW LOVEJOY ST, PORTLAND, OR 972091503
Phone: 503 415-5600
Web: WWW.LEGACYHEALTH.ORG

PRODUCTS/OPERATIONS

Selected Facilities
Hospitals
    Legacy Emanuel Medical Center (Portland, Oregon)
    Legacy Good Samaritan Medical Center (Portland, Oregon)
    Legacy Meridian Park Medical Center (Tualatin, Oregon)
    Legacy Mount Hood Medical Center (Gresham, Oregon)
    Legacy Salmon Creek Medical Center (Vancouver, Washington)
    Randall Children's Hospital At Legacy Emanuel (Portland, Oregon)
Clinics
    Legacy Medical Group - Bridgeport
    Legacy Medical Group - Broadway
    Legacy Medical Group - Canby
    Legacy Medical Group - Cornell
    Legacy Medical Group - Firwood
    Legacy Medical Group - Fisher's Landing
    Legacy Medical Group - Good Samaritan
    Legacy Medical Group - Lake Oswego
    Legacy Medical Group - Northeast
    Legacy Medical Group - Northwest
    Legacy Medical Group - Salmon Creek Family Medicine (Vancouver, Washington)
    Legacy Medical Group - Salmon Creek Internal Medicine (Vancouver, Washington)
    Legacy Medical Group - Tualatin
    Legacy Medical Group - West Linn
    Legacy Medical Group - Woodburn

COMPETITORS

ARROWHEAD REGIONAL MEDICAL CENTER
CAROMONT HEALTH, INC.
HCA-HEALTHONE LLC
HOLY SPIRIT HOSPITAL OF THE SISTERS OF CHRISTIAN CHARITY
LEHIGH VALLEY HEALTH NETWORK, INC.
MEDSTAR HEALTH, INC.
TALLAHASSEE MEMORIAL HEALTHCARE, INC.
UNIVERSITY HEALTH SYSTEMS OF EASTERN CAROLINA, INC.
UNIVERSITY HOSPITALS HEALTH SYSTEM, INC.
WELLSTAR HEALTH SYSTEM, INC.

HISTORICAL FINANCIALS

Company Type: Private

Income Statement FYE: March 31

	REVENUE ($mil)	NET INCOME ($mil)	NET PROFIT MARGIN	EMPLOYEES
03/21	2,265	363	16.0%	10,675
03/20	2,336	(42)	—	—
03/19	2,219	84	3.8%	—
03/18	2,117	100	4.7%	—
Annual Growth	2.3%	53.6%	—	—

2021 Year-End Financials
Return on assets: 10.2% Cash ($ mil.): 563
Return on equity: 16.9%
Current Ratio: 2.30

LEHIGH GAS CORPORATION

LOCATIONS

HQ: LEHIGH GAS CORPORATION
702 HAMILTON ST STE 203, ALLENTOWN, PA 181012469
Phone: 610 791-3800

LEHIGH VALLEY HEALTH NETWORK, INC.

Lehigh Valley Health Network (LVHN) is a not-for-profit health care provider operates through nine full-service hospital campuses. LVHN serves as a regional referral center for trauma and burn care and organ transplantation, as well as specialty care such as cardiology, women's health, and pediatric surgery. LVHN also boasts a network of physician practices and community health centers, as well as home health and hospice units. Through Lehigh Valley Physician Group, LVHN has more than 2,000 primary care and specialty physicians, as well as more than 800 advanced practice clinicians. HNL Lab Medicine provides an extensive range of laboratory tests from the most critical medical applications to simple pre-employment drug screenings.

Operations

The company's hospitals provide care in about 95 specialist fields, including pediatric care, burn treatment, trauma care, organ transplant, emergency care, general surgery and neurology. Its children's hospital includes inpatient, emergency, and specialist units. LVHN conducts medical training programs and performs research in a range of different areas including cancer, cardiovascular, and infectious disease; a number of these programs are conducted through partnership with University of South Florida's Morsani College of Medicine. In addition, LVHN offers a full-time three-year non-resident RN diploma nursing program at Joseph F. McCloskey School of Nursing at Lehigh Valley Health Network in Schuylkill County.

Lehigh Valley Reilly Children's Hospital is the only children's hospital in the Lehigh Valley. The Children's Hospital offers both inpatient and ambulatory care, a children's ER, the J.B. and Kathleen Reilly Children's Surgery Center in Salisbury Township, more than 30 pediatric specialists and numerous child-specific services such as rehab and burn care.

Overall, net patient service generates some 95% of total revenue and other supporting operations account for the remaining 5%.

Geographic Reach

LVHN operates more than 20 offices and lab and imaging services located in an eight-county territory in Pennsylvania.

Its HNL Lab Medicine is located in a dozens of convenient locations in Pennsylvania.

Financial Performance

The company's revenue for fiscal 2021 increased to $3.4 billion compared from the prior year with $3.1 billion.

EXECUTIVES

Support Services Vice President, Stuart Paxton
Auditors : KPMG LLP PHILADELPHIA PENNSY

LOCATIONS

HQ: LEHIGH VALLEY HEALTH NETWORK, INC.
2100 MACK BLVD, ALLENTOWN, PA 181035622
Phone: 610 402-8000
Web: WWW.LVHN.ORG

PRODUCTS/OPERATIONS

Selected Facilities
Community Health Centers
    Hamburg Community Health Center
    Lehigh Valley Health Center at Bath
    Lehigh Valley Health Center at Bethlehem Township
    Lehigh Valley Health Center at Hellertown
    Lehigh Valley Health Center at Kutztown
    Lehigh Valley Health Center at Saucon Valley
    Lehigh Valley Health Center at Trexlertown
    Upper Bucks Health & Diagnostic Center (in partnership with Grand View Hospital, Quakertown)
Hospitals
    Lehigh Valley Hospital - 17th St. (short-stay hospital, Salisbury Township in Allentown)
    Lehigh Valley Hospital - Cedar Crest (Allentown)
    Lehigh Valley Hospital - Muhlenberg (Bethlehem)

COMPETITORS

ARROWHEAD REGIONAL MEDICAL CENTER
HCA-HEALTHONE LLC
HOLY SPIRIT HOSPITAL OF THE SISTERS OF CHRISTIAN CHARITY
KINGSBROOK JEWISH MEDICAL CENTER
LEGACY HEALTH
READING HOSPITAL
TRIHEALTH, INC.
UNIVERSITY HEALTH SYSTEMS OF EASTERN CAROLINA, INC.
UNIVERSITY HOSPITALS HEALTH SYSTEM, INC.
WELLSTAR HEALTH SYSTEM, INC.

HISTORICAL FINANCIALS
Company Type: Private

Income Statement — FYE: December 31

	REVENUE ($mil)	NET INCOME ($mil)	NET PROFIT MARGIN	EMPLOYEES
12/07	1,034	4	0.5%	200
12/05*	53	(0)	—	—
06/04	116	1	1.2%	—
Annual Growth	72.5%	36.5%	—	—

*Fiscal year change

2007 Year-End Financials
Return on assets: 2.5%   Cash ($ mil.): 1
Return on equity: 46.7%
Current Ratio: 0.80

LEHIGH VALLEY HOSPITAL-COORDINATED HEALTH ALLENTOWN

LOCATIONS

HQ: LEHIGH VALLEY HOSPITAL-COORDINATED HEALTH ALLENTOWN
1503 N CEDAR CREST BLVD, ALLENTOWN, PA 181042310
Phone: 484 884-0130
Web: WWW.LVHN.ORG

HISTORICAL FINANCIALS
Company Type: Private

Income Statement — FYE: June 30

	REVENUE ($mil)	NET INCOME ($mil)	NET PROFIT MARGIN	EMPLOYEES
06/21	2,362	104	4.4%	1
06/20	2,200	117	5.4%	—
Annual Growth	7.4%	(11.3%)	—	—

2021 Year-End Financials
Return on assets: 3.4%   Cash ($ mil.): 170
Return on equity: 7.0%
Current Ratio: 0.40

HISTORICAL FINANCIALS
Company Type: Private

Income Statement — FYE: June 30

	REVENUE ($mil)	NET INCOME ($mil)	NET PROFIT MARGIN	EMPLOYEES
06/22	3,833	(102)	—	12,000
06/21	3,437	700	20.4%	—
06/20	3,129	2	0.1%	—
06/19	2,978	118	4.0%	—
Annual Growth	8.8%	—	—	—

2022 Year-End Financials
Return on assets: (-2.1%)   Cash ($ mil.): 212
Return on equity: (-4.1%)
Current Ratio: 1.40

LELAND STANFORD JUNIOR UNIVERSITY

The Leland Stanford Junior University, better known as simply Stanford University, is one of the top universities in the US. It boasts respected programs across seven schools and about 20 interdisciplinary institutes, such as business, engineering, law, and medicine, among others. Stanford serves about 17,000 students (taught by nearly 2,280 faculty members). Its student-teacher ratio sits at about 5:1. A private institution, Stanford is supported through an endowment of some $37.8 billion, one of the largest in the US. The university was established in 1885 by Leland Stanford Sr. It was named after his son, Leland Stanford Jr.

Geographic Reach

Stanford is located in the heart of California's Silicon Valley, known worldwide as an epicenter for technology and research ventures.

The university is located on 8,180 contiguous acres and has almost 700 major buildings.

Strategy

To further widen its student resources, Stanford has recently completed renovation and construction efforts on some 40 campus buildings and added a number of new faculty and fellowship positions. The university is also exploring options to establish a satellite-applied science and engineering campus in another US city. In addition, Stanford is examining whether it might begin to offer courses through an online platform.

In 2017 Stanford launched a new major in aeronautics and astronautics (allowing students to work with unmanned aerial vehicles, satellites, autonomous systems, and other flight technologies).

HISTORY

In 1885 Leland Stanford Sr. and his wife, Jane, established Leland Stanford Junior University in memory of their son Leland Jr., who had died of typhoid at age 15. Stanford made his fortune selling provisions to California gold miners and as a major investor in the Central Pacific Railroad, one of the two companies that built the first transcontinental railway. It was Stanford who connected the tracks laid eastward by Central Pacific and westward by Union Pacific with a gold railway spike in 1869. He also served as California's governor and as a US senator.

The Stanfords donated more than 8,000 acres of land from their own estate to establish an unconventional university, one that was coeducational and nondenominational with a focus on preparing students for a profession. Stanford opened its doors in 1891 to a freshman class of 559 students. It awarded its first degrees four years later, and among the graduates was future US president Herbert Hoover.

Leland Stanford Sr. died in 1893, and in 1903 Jane Stanford turned the university over to the board of trustees. After weathering significant damage in 1906 from the Great San Francisco Earthquake, the university established a law school in 1908 and its medical school five years later.

During WWI the university mobilized half of its students into the Students' Army Training Corps. The School of Education was established in 1917, followed by the School of Engineering and Graduate School of Business eight years later. In 1933 a rule limiting the number of women admitted to Stanford was abolished.

Wallace Sterling, who became president of the university after WWII, initiated the transformation of Stanford into a world-class institution with a reputation for teaching and research. Under Sterling the university initiated development on the Stanford Research Park.

In 1958 Stanford opened its first overseas campus (near Stuttgart, Germany), and the Stanford Medical Center was completed the following year. The university created a computer science department in 1965 and two years later opened the Stanford Linear Accelerator Center dedicated to physics research.

Donald Kennedy became president in 1980. The next year students voted to abandon the university's official mascot, the "Indians," in response to concerns raised by Native American students. The nickname "Cardinal" was adopted in its place. The term refers to the school's color, cardinal red.

Also during Kennedy's tenure, it was revealed that Stanford had overcharged the Office of Naval Research for indirect costs associated with research. The scandal led to Kennedy's resignation in 1992, and in 1994 the Office of Naval Research and the university settled a related lawsuit for $1.2 million and a stipulation that Stanford had not committed any wrongdoing. Gerhard Casper succeeded Kennedy as president.

In 1997 Stanford and the University of California at San Francisco combined their teaching hospitals in a public/private merger. Two years later, after the controversial experiment had harmed both hospitals' financial pictures, the merger was terminated, and the two hospitals agreed to go their separate ways.

In 1999 Casper announced his intention to resign as president. The school tapped provost John Hennessy as his replacement. Soon after his appointment in 2000, Hennessey launched a campaign to raise $1 billion. Former Stanford professor and Netscape co-founder Jim Clark donated $150 million later that year to support Stanford's biomedical engineering and sciences program. The school also launched a new company, SKOLAR, which developed an online search engine for the medical industry.

Auditors : PRICEWATERHOUSECOOPERS LLP SA

LOCATIONS

HQ: LELAND STANFORD JUNIOR UNIVERSITY
450 JANE STANFORD WAY, STANFORD, CA 943052004
Phone: 650 723-2300
Web: WWW.STANFORD.EDU

PRODUCTS/OPERATIONS

2014 Sales

	$ mil	% of total
Healthcare services	3,942.5	50
Sponsored reseach support	1,266.1	16
Investment income	1,181.4	15
Student income	533.7	7
Special program fee and other income	641.5	7
Gifts	212.5	3
Net assets released from restrictions	146.4	2
Total	7,924.1	100

Selected Schools

Undergraduate
    School of Earth Sciences
    School of Engineering
    School of Humanities and Sciences
Graduate
    School of Business
    School of Earth Sciences
    School of Education
    School of Engineering
    School of Humanities and Sciences
    School of Law
    School of Medicine

Selected Interdisciplinary Research Centers

Alliance for Innovative Manufacturing at Stanford
Center for Computer Research in Music and Acoustics
Center for Integrated Facility Engineering
Center for Integrated Systems

Selected Laboratories, Centers, and Institutes

Center for Research on Information Storage Materials
Center for the Study of Language and Information
Edward L. Ginzton Laboratory
Institute for International Studies
Institute for Research on Women and Gender
John and Terry Levin Center for Public Service and Public Interest Law
Stanford Center for Buddhist Studies
Stanford Humanities Center
Stanford Institute for Economic Policy Research
W.W. Hansen Experimental Physics Laboratory

Selected Medical Research Facilities

Center for Biomedical Ethics
Center for Research in Disease Prevention
Human Genome Center
Richard M. Lucas Center for Magnetic Resonance Spectroscopy & Imaging
Sleep Disorders Center

Other Selected Research Facilities

Hoover Institution on War, Revolution and Peace
Hopkins Marine Station
Martin Luther King, Jr. Papers Project
Stanford Linear Accelerator Center

COMPETITORS

CALIFORNIA STATE UNIVERSITY SYSTEM
NEW YORK UNIVERSITY
NORTHWESTERN UNIVERSITY
PRESIDENT AND FELLOWS OF HARVARD COLLEGE
THE OHIO STATE UNIVERSITY
THE REGENTS OF THE UNIVERSITY OF CALIFORNIA
THE UNIVERSITY OF CHICAGO
THE UNIVERSITY OF TEXAS SYSTEM
UNIVERSITY OF CINCINNATI
UNIVERSITY OF SOUTHERN CALIFORNIA

HISTORICAL FINANCIALS

Company Type: Private

Income Statement
FYE: August 31

	REVENUE ($mil)	NET INCOME ($mil)	NET PROFIT MARGIN	EMPLOYEES
08/21	13,939	845	6.1%	15,000
08/20	12,455	1,983	15.9%	—
08/19	12,262	1,961	16.0%	—
08/18	11,311	2,653	23.5%	—
Annual Growth	7.2%	(31.7%)	—	—

LENOX HILL HOSPITAL

LOCATIONS

HQ: LENOX HILL HOSPITAL
210 E 64TH ST FL 4, NEW YORK, NY 100657471
Phone: 212 472-8872
Web: WWW.LENOXHILL.ORG

HISTORICAL FINANCIALS
Company Type: Private

Income Statement			FYE: December 31
	REVENUE ($mil)	**NET INCOME** ($mil)	**NET PROFIT MARGIN**	**EMPLOYEES**
12/16	960	21	2.3%	41
12/15	885	6	0.7%	—
Annual Growth	8.5%	244.8%	—	—

2016 Year-End Financials
Return on assets: 1.8%
Return on equity: 4.7%
Cash ($ mil.): —
Current Ratio: 0.80

LESTER E. COX MEDICAL CENTERS

Lester E. Cox Medical Centers (dba CoxHealth) is the area leader in health care and community involvement. CoxHealth's network includes six acute care hospitals (with about 1,195 licensed beds), five ERs, and more than 80 physician clinics. Centers for cardiac care, cancer treatment, orthopedics, and women's health are among CoxHealth's specialized care options. In addition to a wide range of treatments and services, CoxHealth contributes millions each year to community outreach, medical education and research, foundation grants, donations and other contributions to the community. The organization was named after its primary fundraiser in 1949.

Operations

Each year, CoxHealth handles about 1.5 million clinic visits; approximately 295,885 emergency, urgent care, and trauma visits; around 41,535 ambulance services; and more than 4,220 births. Its hospitals include Cox Medical Center South, Cox Medical Center Branson, Cox North Hospital, Cox Monett Hospital, Meyer Orthopedic and Rehabilitation Hospital, CoxHealth at Home, Home Parenteral Services and Ferrell-Duncan Clinic. Its specialty clinics include centers for cancer, orthopedics, cardiovascular care, women's and children's health, outpatient surgery, and diagnostic imaging.

Geographic Reach

Springfield, Missouri-based, CoxHealth has primary and specialty care providers located in more than 80 clinics across the region. Serving approximately 25 counties, CoxHealth's major facilities are in Branson, Monett, and Springfield, Missouri.

Company Background

CoxHealth was founded as Burge Deaconess Hospital in 1908. It became Lester E. Cox Medical Centers in 1968 following the death of Cox, a St. Louis businessman who led a series of major fundraising campaigns in the 1940s critical to the survival and growth of the hospital.

EXECUTIVES

Vice Chairman, William Turner

LOCATIONS

HQ: LESTER E. COX MEDICAL CENTERS
1423 N JEFFERSON AVE, SPRINGFIELD, MO 658021917
Phone: 417 269-3000
Web: WWW.COXHEALTH.COM

PRODUCTS/OPERATIONS

Selected Services
Air Care
Alzheimer's Disease
Behavioral Health
Brain and Spine Disorders
Breast Care
Cancer Services
Children's Health
Diabetes
Dialysis
Ear, Nose and Throat (ENT)
Emergency Department
Fitness Centers
Food and Nutrition
Heart and Vascular
Home Health
Hyperbaric Medicine and Wound Care
Neuroscience
Occupational Medicine
Orthopedics
Parenting
Parkinson's Clinic
Pharmacy
Physical Medicine
Pregnancy
Radiology
Rehabilitation
Respiratory Care
Robotic Surgery
Sleep Disorders
Smoking Cessation
Specialty Services
Sports Medicine
Stroke
Trauma Services
Urgent Care
Weight Loss
Wellness Consultations
Women's Health
Workers' Compensation

COMPETITORS

ASCENSION SOUTHEAST MICHIGAN
BAPTIST MEMORIAL HEALTH CARE SYSTEM, INC.
BAXTER COUNTY REGIONAL HOSPITAL, INC.
BORGESS HEALTH ALLIANCE, INC.
BRYAN MEDICAL CENTER
CHRISTUS SPOHN HEALTH SYSTEM CORPORATION
FIRSTHEALTH OF THE CAROLINAS, INC.
FROEDTERT MEMORIAL LUTHERAN HOSPITAL, INC.
LEGACY HEALTH
THE JOHNS HOPKINS HEALTH SYSTEM CORPORATION

HISTORICAL FINANCIALS
Company Type: Private

Income Statement			FYE: September 30
	REVENUE ($mil)	**NET INCOME** ($mil)	**NET PROFIT MARGIN**	**EMPLOYEES**
09/14	898	50	5.6%	11,170
09/13	858	105	12.3%	—
09/12	843	66	7.9%	—
Annual Growth	3.2%	(13.0%)	—	—

2014 Year-End Financials
Return on assets: 3.6%
Return on equity: 7.3%
Cash ($ mil.): 61
Current Ratio: 2.00

LEVI STRAUSS & CO.

Levi Strauss & Co. (LS&CO) is a global manufacturer of brand-name clothing, LS&CO sells jeans and sportswear under the Levi's, Dockers, Signature by Levi Strauss, and Denizen labels in more than 110 countries. The company distributes its brand products through approximately 50,000 retail stores worldwide, which includes 3,100 brand-dedicated stores and shop-in-shops. It designs, markets and sells ? directly or through third parties and licensees ? products that include jeans, pants, tops, shorts, skirts, dresses, jackets, footwear, and related accessories for men, women and children. About 45% of the company total revenue comes from US operation. Founded In 1853, Levi Strauss opened a wholesale dry goods business in San Francisco that became known as Levi Strauss & Co.

Operations

In fiscal year 2021, LS&CO simplified its organization structure and created an integrated global commercial organization to continue to elevate and strengthen its Levi's commercial business. changed our segment reporting. Its Levi's Brands business, which includes the Levi's, Signature by Levi Strauss & Co. and Denizen brands, is presented in its financial statements under the caption of Levi's Brands and is defined geographically in three reportable segments: Americas, Europe and Asia. The Dockers business, which is managed separately, is no longer reported in the geographical regions of Americas, Europe and Asia.

Sales of the Levi's brand accounts for more than 85% of the total while sales of Signature by Levi Strauss & Co. and Denizen Brands account for over 5%, and sales of Dockers Brand represent some 5% of sales as well.

The wholesale channel generates nearly

2021 Year-End Financials (Lenox Hill top):
Return on assets: 1.1%
Return on equity: 1.4%
Cash ($ mil.): 1,672
Current Ratio: —

65% of LS&CO's sales while within the direct channel accounts for more than 35% of sales.

Geographic Reach

LS&CO sells its products in more than 110 countries. It operates manufacturing, distribution, and finishing facilities in the Americas, Europe, and Asia/Pacific regions. The company's Americas segment contributes more than 50% of total revenue, while its Europe and Asia (which includes the Middle East and North Africa) segments contributed about 30% and 15%, respectively.

Its global headquarters and the headquarters are both located in San Francisco, California, while its Europe and Asia headquarters are located in Diegem, Belgium and Singapore, respectively. Its finance shared service centers in Eugene, Oregon and Bangalore, India. It also operates two back- up data centers located in Carrollton and Westlake, Texas.

Sales and Marketing

A multi-channel marketer, LS&CO sells its products in more than 50,000 retail locations worldwide. Its brands lend themselves to a variety of retail formats, including chain retailers, department stores, and company-operated e-commerce sites and online stores of other retailers. Sales to its top 10 wholesale customers account for more than 30% of revenues.The company distributes its products through a wide variety of retail formats around the world, including chain and department stores, franchise stores and shop-in-shops, company-operated retail network, multi-brand specialty stores, mass channel retailers, and both company-operated and retailer ecommerce sites.

Advertising expenses were $434.5 million, $331.4 million, and $399.3 million for 2021, 2020, and 2019, respectively.

Financial Performance

Compared to fiscal year 2020, consolidated net revenues increased 29.5% on a reported basis and 27.1% on a constant-currency basis. The increase was primarily due to demand increasing to pre-pandemic levels, in comparison to adverse impacts of the COVID-19 pandemic in fiscal 2020, including temporary store closures of company-operated and wholesale customer retail locations.

The company recognized net income of $553.5 million compared to a net loss of $127.1 million in fiscal year 2020. The increase was primarily due to the increase in operating income, offset by $36.5 million in incremental costs in the current year related to the early extinguishment of debt.

LS&CO's cash on hand loss $687.1 million, ending the year at $810.3 million. The company's operations generated $737.3 million, offset by $571.8 million used in its investing activities and $840.9 million were used by financing activities. LS&CO's main cash uses were for repayments of long-term debt including extinguishment costs.

Strategy

In fiscal 2021, LS&CO shifted its focus to prioritize the most important areas that it believes will drive long-term success.

The following three "where to play" choices serve as our strategic framework for what it intends to achieve: Brand Led, direct-to-consumer (DTC) First, and Further Diversify Portfolio. The company's three strategic choices are supported by a foundation of the following three "how to win" choices: Digital Transformation, Operational Excellence, and Financial Discipline.

The company continues to invest in its direct-to-consumer business, which accounts for about 40% of the company's sales. The DTC channels enables the company to connect directly with consumers to offer the best experience and elevate consumer experiences on store and online. The company also plans to further diversify its portfolio, specifically growing its international segments, focusing on China.

In addition, the company is incorporating and continuing to develop improved consumer experience through digital transformation. The company aims to use various technology such as data and artificial intelligence (AI). Omnichannels and digital shopping platforms will be further invested on as well.

Mergers and Acquisitions

In 2021, LS&CO completed the acquisition of Beyond Yoga, a fast-growing, premium athletic and lifestyle U.S.-based apparel brand. The acquisition establishes LS&CO's presence in the fast-growing activewear segment with a brand with tremendous growth potential.

Company Background

Founded In 1853, Levi Strauss opened a wholesale dry goods business in San Francisco that became known as Levi Strauss & Co. Seeing a need for work pants that could hold up under rougher conditions, he and Jacob Davis, a tailor, created the first jean. In 1873, they received a U.S. patent for "waist overalls" with metal rivets at points of strain. The first product line designated by the lot number "501" was created in 1890.

HISTORY

Levi Strauss arrived in New York City from Bavaria in 1847. In 1853 he joined his brother-in-law, David Stern, in San Francisco, selling dry goods to the gold rushers. Shortly after, a prospector told Strauss of miners' problems in finding sturdy pants. Strauss made a pair out of canvas for the prospector; word of the rugged pants spread quickly.

Strauss continued his dry-goods business in the 1860s. During this time he switched the pants' fabric to a durable French cloth called serge de Nimes, soon known as denim. He colored the fabric with indigo dye and adopted the idea from Nevada tailor Jacob Davis of reinforcing the pants with copper rivets. In 1873 Strauss and Davis produced their first pair of waist-high overalls (later known as jeans). The pants soon became de rigueur for lumberjacks, cowboys, railroad workers, oil drillers, and farmers.

Strauss continued to build his pants and wholesaling business until he died in 1902. Levi Strauss & Co. passed to four Stern nephews who carried on their uncle's jeans business while maintaining the company's philanthropic reputation.

After WWII Walter Haas and Peter Haas (a fourth-generation Strauss family member) assumed leadership of LS&CO. In 1948 they ended the company's wholesaling business to concentrate on Levi's clothing. In the 1950s Levi's jeans ceased to be merely functional garments for workers; they became the uniform of American youth. In the 1960s LS&CO. added women's attire and expanded overseas.

The company went public in 1971. That year it added a women's career line and bought Koret sportswear (sold in 1984). By the mid-1980s profits declined. Peace Corps-veteran-turned-McKinsey-consultant Robert Haas (Walter's son) grabbed the reins of LS&CO. in 1984 and took the company private the next year (he became chairman in 1989). He also instilled a touchy-feely corporate culture often at odds with the bottom line.

In 1986 LS&CO. introduced Dockers casual pants. The company's sales began rising in 1991 as consumers forsook the designer duds of the 1980s for more practical clothes. LS&CO. says seven out of every 10 American men own a pair of Dockers. However, LS&CO. missed out on the birth of another trend: the split between the fashion sense of US adolescents and their Levi's-loving, baby boomer parents.

In 1996 the company introduced Slates dress slacks. That year LS&CO. bought back nearly one-third of its stock from family and employees for $4.3 billion. Grappling with slipping sales and debt from the buyout, in 1997 LS&CO. closed 11 of its 37 North American plants, laying off 6,400 workers and 1,000 salaried employees; it granted generous severance packages even to those earning minimum wage.

In 1998, citing improved labor conditions in China, LS&CO. announced it would step up its use of Chinese subcontractors. Further restructuring added a third of its European plants to the closures list that year. LS&CO.'s sales fell 13% in fiscal 1998. Also that year Haas handed his CEO title to Pepsi executive Philip Marineau; Haas remained chairman.

LS&CO. closed 11 of 22 remaining North American plants in 1999. It also unleashed several new jeans brands that eschewed the company's one-style-fits-all approach of old.

In April 2002 LS&CO. announced it would close six of its last eight US plants and cut 20% of its worldwide staff (3,300 workers). In September 2003 it cut another 5% of its global staff (650 workers). That month the company opened its first girls-only store, located in Paris. In December LS&CO. replaced CFO Bill Chiasson with an outside turnaround specialist.

Pinpointing 2006 as the best time to step down as the company's chief executive, Philip Marineau retired at the end of 2006. John Anderson, president of LS&CO.'s Asia/Pacific division and head of the firm's global supply chain unit, replaced Marineau as president and CEO.

Levi Strauss chairman Robert Haas retired in 2008 after 18 years in that role. His successor was Dryer's ice cream executive T. Gary Rogers, who became the first leader in the company's history who was not a descendant of the founder. In August 2008 CFO Hans Ploos van Amstel left the company the and was replaced by Heidi Manes, its corporate controller and principal accounting officer.

Looking to gain a more active role in its store business, LS&CO. in July 2009 bought the operating rights for more than 70 Levi's and Dockers Outlet locations from store operator Anchor Blue Retail Group, which had filed for bankruptcy, for $72 million. Anchor Blue said the US recession and drop in consumer spending, especially among teens, severely affected its financial performance. LS&CO. said the acquisition will enable it to better manage its brands' positioning.

Rogers retired in late 2009, and Richard Kauffman became chairman.

EXECUTIVES

CCO, Seth Ellison
Auditors : PRICEWATERHOUSECOOPERS LLP SA

LOCATIONS

HQ: LEVI STRAUSS & CO.
1155 BATTERY ST, SAN FRANCISCO, CA 941101264
Phone: 415 501-6000
Web: WWW.LEVISTRAUSS.COM

2018 Stores#

Europe region	300
Asia/Pacific region	256
Total	697

2018 Sales

	$ mil.	% of total
Americas	3,042.7	55
Europe	1,646.2	29
Asia/Pacific region	886.5	17
Total	5,575.4	100

PRODUCTS/OPERATIONS

2018 Sales

	% of total
Levi's brand	86
Dockers brand	7
Signature by Levi Strauss & Denizen brands	7
Total	100

Selected Brands
Denizen
Dockers
    Dockers Alpha Khaki
    Dockers for Men
    Dockers for Women
Levi's
    Levi's 501 Original
    Levi's 505 Straight
    Levi's 511 Skinny
    Levi's 513 Slim
    Levi's 514 Slim Straight
    Levi's Curve ID
Signature by Levis Strauss & Co.
Intro
Waterless
Wellthread
Wasteless

COMPETITORS

AALFS MANUFACTURING, INC.
CHRISTIAN CASEY LLC
GUESS ?, INC.
J. CREW GROUP, INC.
PERRY ELLIS INTERNATIONAL INC
RALPH LAUREN CORPORATION
TAILORED BRANDS, INC.
THE GAP INC
TRUE RELIGION APPAREL, INC.
V.F. CORPORATION

HISTORICAL FINANCIALS

Company Type: Private

Income Statement   FYE: November 25

	REVENUE ($mil)	NET INCOME ($mil)	NET PROFIT MARGIN	EMPLOYEES
11/18	5,575	285	5.1%	16,600
11/17	4,904	284	5.8%	—
11/16	4,552	291	6.4%	—
11/15	4,494	209	4.7%	—
Annual Growth	7.4%	10.8%	—	—

2018 Year-End Financials
Return on assets: 8.1%   Cash ($ mil.): 713
Return on equity: 42.7%
Current Ratio: 2.20

LEXA INTERNATIONAL CORPORATION

Auditors : CITRIN COOPERMAN & COMPANY LL

LOCATIONS

HQ: LEXA INTERNATIONAL CORPORATION
1 LANDMARK SQ STE 407, STAMFORD, CT 069012601
Phone: 203 326-5200

HISTORICAL FINANCIALS

Company Type: Private

Income Statement   FYE: December 31

	REVENUE ($mil)	NET INCOME ($mil)	NET PROFIT MARGIN	EMPLOYEES
12/09	2,598	6	0.2%	1,204
12/08	4,312	4	0.1%	—
12/07	4,003	(21)	—	—
Annual Growth	(19.4%)	—	—	—

2009 Year-End Financials
Return on assets: 0.6%   Cash ($ mil.): 43
Return on equity: 3.1%
Current Ratio: 1.80

LEXINGTON COUNTY HEALTH SERVICES DISTRICT, INC.

Auditors : KPMG LLP ATLANTA GA

LOCATIONS

HQ: LEXINGTON COUNTY HEALTH SERVICES DISTRICT, INC.
2720 SUNSET BLVD, WEST COLUMBIA, SC 291694810
Phone: 803 791-2000
Web: WWW.LEXMED.COM

HISTORICAL FINANCIALS

Company Type: Private

Income Statement   FYE: September 30

	REVENUE ($mil)	NET INCOME ($mil)	NET PROFIT MARGIN	EMPLOYEES
09/10	576	59	10.4%	6,000
09/09	528	57	10.9%	—
09/08	491	35	7.2%	—
Annual Growth	8.3%	29.8%	—	—

2010 Year-End Financials
Return on assets: 7.3%   Cash ($ mil.): 170
Return on equity: 11.6%
Current Ratio: 4.70

LEXINGTON MEDICAL CENTER

Lexington Medical Center is a not-for-profit health care organization serving the residents of South Carolina's Lexington County. Established in 1971, the medical center has some 415 beds and provides general, emergency, surgical, and diagnostic services. Specialty services include cancer treatment, cardiovascular care, women's health, and rehabilitation. Lexington Medical Center also operates a skilled nursing center, as well as a network of affiliated community health centers, urgent care clinics, and affiliated physician practices. The hospital is managed by the Lexington County Health Service District.

Operations

The 414-bed facility is home to the largest extended-care facility in the Carolinas. It sees about 100,000 emergency department visits each year.

Altogether, the Lexington Medical Center's network of facilities -- which includes six community clinics, an occupational health center, an Alzheimer's care center, and 60 doctors' offices -- employs some 5,900 health professionals.

Strategy

Lexington Medical Center is expanding its facilities to better serve the growing population in its service territory. In 2015, it opened a new cardiac rehabilitation program at its Irmo Medical Park campus. The program -- the first of its kind in the area -- provides services to patients with a history of heart attack, angioplasty, heart failure, heart transplant, bypass surgery, or the like.

In 2014, Lexington's physician practice opened a third sleep lab where clinicians can diagnose such conditions as hypersomnia, insomnia, narcolepsy, restless leg syndrome, snoring, and sleep apnea.

EXECUTIVES

Chief Medical Officer, Doctor Brent Powers Senior
Auditors : KPMG LLP ATLANTA GA

LOCATIONS

HQ: LEXINGTON MEDICAL CENTER
2720 SUNSET BLVD, WEST COLUMBIA, SC 291694810
Phone: 803 791-2000
Web: WWW.LEXMED.COM

PRODUCTS/OPERATIONS

Selected Services
Patient Care
Alzheimer's Care
Birth Center
Extended Care
Family Medicine
General Surgery
Imaging
Laboratory & Pathology
Occupational Health
Weight-Loss Surgery
Health & Wellness
Community Health Screenings
Health Directions Wellness Center
Nutrition Therapy
Sleep Solutions

Selected Facilities
Community Medical Centers
    LMC Batesburg-Leesville
    LMC Chapin
    LMC Gilbert
    LMC Irmo
    LMC Lexington
    LMC Swansea
Hospital Units
    Alzheimers Care Center
    Birth Center
    Cancer Center
    Emergency Care
    Extended Care
    Heart Center
    Obesity Surgery Center
    Urgent Care
    Women's Services

COMPETITORS

BLESSING HOSPITAL
BORGESS HEALTH ALLIANCE, INC.
CAROMONT HEALTH, INC.
FIRSTHEALTH OF THE CAROLINAS, INC.
FROEDTERT MEMORIAL LUTHERAN HOSPITAL, INC.
HOLY SPIRIT HOSPITAL OF THE SISTERS OF CHRISTIAN CHARITY
LONG BEACH MEDICAL CENTER
MERCY HOSPITAL AND MEDICAL CENTER
MERITER HEALTH SERVICES, INC.
WHITE COUNTY MEDICAL CENTER

HISTORICAL FINANCIALS
Company Type: Private

Income Statement   FYE: September 30

	REVENUE ($mil)	NET INCOME ($mil)	NET PROFIT MARGIN	EMPLOYEES
09/20	1,166	24	2.1%	5,616
09/17	953	(9)	—	—
09/16	906	21	2.3%	—
09/15	863	86	10.0%	—
Annual Growth	6.2%	(22.0%)	—	—

2020 Year-End Financials
Return on assets: 1.3%   Cash ($ mil.): 374
Return on equity: 7.0%
Current Ratio: 2.50

LHH CORPORATION

When Manhattanites are looking for health care, many of them head for the hill: Lenox Hill Hospital, to be exact. The 650-bed facility provides care to patients on Manhattan's Upper East Side -- about 45% of its patient base is from Manhattan, the rest from surrounding boroughs. Services include cardiac care, high-risk obstetrics, pediatrics, and orthopedics and sports medicine. Lenox Hill serves as a teaching affiliate for NYU Medical Center and also owns Manhattan Eye, Ear and Throat Hospital, a provider of specialty care for vision, hearing, and speech disorders. Today it's part of North Shore-Long Island Jewish Health System.

Operations

As part of the North Shore-LIJ system, Lenox Hill has access to the larger organization's resources. North Shore-LIJ one of the largest health care providers in New York State; Lenox Hill is its first hospital in the New York metropolitan area.

Lenox Hill Hospital operates a handful of outpatient locations that provide medical, surgical, and specialized services. Its center for mental health administers a wide range of inpatient and ambulatory psychiatric services for adults and children. To provide quality services to a diverse population, Lenox Hill provides multi-lingual translators.

The hospital treats more than 325,000 patients a year.

Geographic Reach

The hospital serves patients from Manhattan and surrounding neighborhoods from two campuses in New York City and one in Westchester County.

Financial Performance

In 2012 Lenox Hill reported revenues of $729 million and a net loss of $37 million.

Strategy

Lenox Hill Hospital has also expanded in recent years by opening primary care center and urgent care centers in Manhattan and upgrading and enhancing some of its existing facilities, such as its emergency care center, to accommodate a growing number of patients.

In 2012 it opened a new pediatric inpatient care unit for general and surgical care, as well as new head and neck and cranial base surgery centers. In 2013 it opened a new reproduction clinic for fertility services.

Expanding its medical services outside of North Shore-LIJ system's 16 hospitals and into community settings, in 2013 Lenox Hill opened the 3,200-sq.-ft. Heart and Vascular Institute in Yorktown Heights -- the first facility for the hospital system in Westchester County.

In 2012 Lenox Hill became the first in the New York area to perform minimally invasive heart valve replacement.

Company Background

US News & World Report has ranked Lenox Hill as one the top 50 in Cardiology and Heart Surgery, and Ear, Nose and Throat facilities in the US, and among the top 10 hospitals in New York state.

In 2010, the hospital expanded its service offerings by adding palliative care to its medical roster. The services are aimed at relieving pain, symptoms, and stress related to serious illness. In many cases palliative care specialists provide care to patients who are not eligible for, or don't want, hospice care when facing a fatal illness.

It performed the first coronary angioplasty in the US (in 1978) and the first angiocardiogram (in 1938).

The hospital was established in 1857 as the German Dispensary.

LOCATIONS

HQ: LHH CORPORATION
100 E 77TH ST, NEW YORK, NY 100751850
Phone: 212 434-2000
Web: WWW.NORTHWELL.EDU

PRODUCTS/OPERATIONS

Selected Services
Bariatric surgery
Cardiothoracic surgery
Cardiovascular care
Colorectal surgery
Critical care
Maternal and child health
Manhattan Ear, Eye and Throat Institute
Mental health
Neurosurgery
Palliative care
Pathology
Plastic and reconstructive surgery
Primary care
Radiology
Rehabilitation
Robotic surgery

COMPETITORS

DIMENSIONS HEALTH CORPORATION
HUNTINGTON HOSPITAL DOLAN FAMILY HEALTH CENTER, INC.
JERSEY CITY MEDICAL CENTER (INC)
THE UNIVERSITY OF CHICAGO MEDICAL CENTER
VALLEY HEALTH SYSTEM, INC.

HISTORICAL FINANCIALS
Company Type: Private

Income Statement   FYE: December 31

	REVENUE ($mil)	NET INCOME ($mil)	NET PROFIT MARGIN	EMPLOYEES
12/18	1,064	73	6.9%	2,955
12/16	960	21	2.3%	—
12/14	790	3	0.4%	—
Annual Growth	7.7%	119.1%	—	—

2018 Year-End Financials
Return on assets: 5.8%   Cash ($ mil.): 2
Return on equity: 12.9%
Current Ratio: 1.10

LIBERTY UNIVERSITY, INC.

EXECUTIVES
CAO*, Ronald E Hawkins
Auditors : BDO USA LLP ATLANTA GA

LOCATIONS
HQ: LIBERTY UNIVERSITY, INC.
   1971 UNIVERSITY BLVD, LYNCHBURG, VA 245150002
Phone: 434 582-2000
Web: WWW.LIBERTY.EDU

HISTORICAL FINANCIALS
Company Type: Private

Income Statement   FYE: June 30

	REVENUE ($mil)	NET INCOME ($mil)	NET PROFIT MARGIN	EMPLOYEES
06/22	1,210	66	5.5%	7,200
06/21	1,153	551	47.8%	—
06/20	1,043	213	20.4%	—
06/19	989	316	32.0%	—
Annual Growth	6.9%	(40.7%)	—	—

2022 Year-End Financials
Return on assets: 1.7%   Cash ($ mil.): 427
Return on equity: 1.9%
Current Ratio: —

LIFEBRIDGE HEALTH, INC.

LifeBridge Health links patients to healthcare. Serving the Baltimore region, the not-for-profit company operates two general hospitals -- Sinai Hospital of Baltimore and Northwest Hospital -- with specialties including oncology, neurology, pediatrics, and sports medicine. The LifeBridge Health network also provides long-term care at the Levindale Hebrew Geriatric Center and Hospital (nursing, subacute, and adult day care services) and the Courtland Gardens Nursing & Rehabilitation Center. Altogether, the health system boasts some 1,190 beds. LifeBridge's Health Wellness division includes a health and fitness program and community fitness center.

Operations
Sinai Hospital is a teaching hospital with residency programs for medical students training at Johns Hopkins University and University of Maryland. Levindale also serves as a teaching facility for medical, dental, nursing, and social work students pursuing training to serve geriatric populations.

Auditors : KPMG LLP BALTIMORE MD

LOCATIONS
HQ: LIFEBRIDGE HEALTH, INC.
   2401 W BELVEDERE AVE, BALTIMORE, MD 212155216
Phone: 410 601-5653
Web: WWW.LIFEBRIDGEHEALTH.ORG

PRODUCTS/OPERATIONS
Selected Locations
Courtland Gardens Nursing & Rehabilitation Center
Levindale Hebrew Geriatric Center and Hospital
Northwest Hospital
Sinai Hospital

Selected Services
Bariatric and Minimally Invasive Surgery
Brain & Spine Institute
Cancer Institute
Hospitalist Program
Rubin Institute for Advanced Orthopedics
Vascular Institute

COMPETITORS
BRIGHAM AND WOMEN'S FAULKNER HOSPITAL, INC.
EVANSTON HOSPITAL CORPORATION
NEBRASKA METHODIST HEALTH SYSTEM, INC.
NEWARK BETH ISRAEL MEDICAL CENTER INC.
OHIO VALLEY MEDICAL CENTER, INCORPORATED
PRINCETON COMMUNITY HOSPITAL ASSOCIATION, INC.
REGINA MEDICAL CENTER
RIVERVIEW HOSPITAL
SAINT LUKE'S HOSPITAL OF BETHLEHEM, PENNSYLVANIA
UNIVERSITY OF CALIFORNIA, SAN DIEGO

HISTORICAL FINANCIALS
Company Type: Private

Income Statement   FYE: June 30

	REVENUE ($mil)	NET INCOME ($mil)	NET PROFIT MARGIN	EMPLOYEES
06/20	1,662	54	3.3%	6,000
06/19	1,610	65	4.1%	—
06/17	1,527	111	7.3%	—
06/15	145	0	0.5%	—
Annual Growth	62.8%	134.1%	—	—

2020 Year-End Financials
Return on assets: 2.1%   Cash ($ mil.): 251
Return on equity: 4.1%
Current Ratio: 2.00

LIMETREE BAY TERMINALS LLC

HOVENSA brings together US and Latin American know-how and operations to handle oil products in the US Virgin Islands. HOVENSA is a joint venture of Hess and Venezuelan oil giant PDVSA (its major crude oil supplier). Once the largest private employer in the US Virgin Islands, the company operated a 500,000-barrels-per-day crude oil refinery on St. Croix, along with two specialized oil processing complexes, a 150,000-barrels-per-day fluid catalytic cracking unit, and a 58,000-barrels-per-day delayed coker unit. However, the St. Croix refinery had run up losses for years; it was shut down in 2012 and was put up for sale in 2013.

Strategy
Citing high operating and maintenance costs (the refinery was fueled by oil, not the cheaper natural gas) and the growth of lower-cost refineries in emerging markets, HOVENSA has posted $1.3 billion in losses since 2009. As a result the company decided to cut its losses by converting the refinery into an oil storage terminal, which can take advantage of St. Croix's strategic location. Its 55-ft. deep harbor enables it to receive crude oil tanker deliveries from Venezuela and around the world. The storage terminal employs about 100 workers. The shutdown of the refinery resulted in more than 2,000 employes being laid off.

Company Background
In 2009 the global economic downturn depressed demand for oil, caused a dip in production, and prompted the company to lay off 270 employees (about 21% of its total contract workers).

Crude thoughput has declined steadily at HOVENSA due to weaker refining margins and planned and unplanned maintenance, from 402,000 barrels per day (bpd) in 2009, to 390,000 bpd in 2010, to 284,000 bpd in 2011.

Auditors : ERNST & YOUNG LLP NEW YORK N

LOCATIONS
HQ: LIMETREE BAY TERMINALS LLC
   1 ESTATE HOPE, CHRISTIANSTED, VI 00820
Phone: 340 692-3000

COMPETITORS
Cenovus Energy Inc
NORTHERN OIL AND GAS, INC.
PETROQUEST ENERGY, INC.
SAUDI ARABIAN OIL COMPANY
TALOS PETROLEUM LLC

HISTORICAL FINANCIALS
Company Type: Private

Income Statement				FYE: December 31
	REVENUE ($mil)	NET INCOME ($mil)	NET PROFIT MARGIN	EMPLOYEES
12/09	10,048	(451)	—	1,300
12/08	17,479	94	0.5%	—
Annual Growth	(42.5%)	—	—	—

2009 Year-End Financials
Return on assets: 3.2%   Cash ($ mil.): 77
Return on equity: (-4.5%)
Current Ratio: 0.20

LINCOLN MEDICAL AND MENTAL HEALTH CENTER

LOCATIONS
HQ: LINCOLN MEDICAL AND MENTAL HEALTH CENTER
234 E 149TH ST, BRONX, NY 104515504
Phone: 718 579-5000

HISTORICAL FINANCIALS
Company Type: Private

Income Statement				FYE: June 30
	REVENUE ($mil)	NET INCOME ($mil)	NET PROFIT MARGIN	EMPLOYEES
06/16	616	120	19.6%	951
06/15	530	20	3.9%	—
Annual Growth	16.2%	488.5%	—	—

2016 Year-End Financials
Return on assets: 14.0%   Cash ($ mil.): —
Return on equity: 50.4%
Current Ratio: 1.40

LOMA LINDA UNIVERSITY CHILDREN'S HOSPITAL

Auditors: ERNST & YOUNG LLP IRVINE CA

LOCATIONS
HQ: LOMA LINDA UNIVERSITY CHILDREN'S HOSPITAL
11234 ANDERSON ST, LOMA LINDA, CA 923542804
Phone: 909 558-8000
Web: WWW.LLUCH.ORG

HISTORICAL FINANCIALS
Company Type: Private

Income Statement				FYE: June 30
	REVENUE ($mil)	NET INCOME ($mil)	NET PROFIT MARGIN	EMPLOYEES
06/22	584	17	2.9%	44
06/21	523	52	10.1%	—
06/20*	508	39	7.7%	—
12/15	4	1	24.8%	—
Annual Growth	102.7%	49.4%	—	—

*Fiscal year change

2022 Year-End Financials
Return on assets: 1.1%   Cash ($ mil.): 46
Return on equity: 3.4%
Current Ratio: 1.30

LOMA LINDA UNIVERSITY MEDICAL CENTER

Loma Linda University Medical Center is widely respected as a healthcare leader, known for advances in many disciplines. These include pioneering work in organ transplants, proton treatment for cancers, cardiac care, physical rehabilitation, neurology, neurosurgery and acute care. LLUMC is the largest and only Level I Trauma Center in the San Bernardino, Riverside, Inyo, and Mono counties. With a total of 507 beds, Loma Linda University Medical Center sees over 16,000 inpatients and about 470,000 outpatient visits a year.

Strategy
Loma Linda University Medical Center is widely respected as a healthcare leader, known for advances in many disciplines. These include pioneering work in organ transplants, proton treatment for cancers, cardiac care, physical rehabilitation, neurology, neurosurgery and acute care. LLUMC is the largest and only Level I Trauma Center in the San Bernardino, Riverside, Inyo, and Mono counties. With a total of 507 beds, Loma Linda University Medical Center sees over 16,000 inpatients and about 470,000 outpatient visits a year.

Auditors: ERNST & YOUNG LLP IRVINE CA

LOCATIONS
HQ: LOMA LINDA UNIVERSITY MEDICAL CENTER
11234 ANDERSON ST, LOMA LINDA, CA 923542871
Phone: 909 558-4000
Web: WWW.LLUH.ORG

Selected Facilities
Beaumont, California
    Highland Springs Medical Plaza (in collaboration with Redlands Community Hospital and Beaver Medical Group)
Loma Linda, California
    Loma Linda University Children's Hospital
    Loma Linda University Health Care
    Loma Linda University Medical Center
    Loma Linda University Medical Center East Campus Hospital
    Loma Linda University Outpatient Rehabilitation Center
    Loma Linda University Outpatient Surgery Center
Redlands, California
    Loma Linda University Behavioral Medicine Center
    Loma Linda University Heart & Surgical Hospital

PRODUCTS/OPERATIONS
Selected Facilities
University Hospital
Loma Linda University Children's Hospital
Loma Linda University East Campus
Loma Linda University Heart & Surgical Hospital
Loma Linda University Behavioral Medicine Center

Selected Services and Centers
Allergy, Asthma and Immunology
Allergy Laboratory
Cancer Center
Clinical Trial Center
Dentistry
Diabetes Treatment Center
Ears, Nose and Throat (ENT)
Emergency and Trauma Services
Family Medicine
Fertility and In Vitro Fertilization
Gastroenterology
Heart and Vascular
Home Care
Metabolic and Bariatric Surgery
Nephrology
Neurology
Neurosurgery
Obstetrics and Gynecology
Ophthalmology
Orthopedics
Pediatrics
Perinatal Institute
Pharmacy
Plastic Surgery
Pulmonology
Radiology
Transplantation Institute and Liver Center
Urogynecology
Urology

COMPETITORS
DIMENSIONS HEALTH CORPORATION
GREATER BALTIMORE MEDICAL CENTER, INC.
HOSPITAL SERVICE DISTRICT 1
JERSEY CITY MEDICAL CENTER (INC)
LEGACY EMANUEL HOSPITAL & HEALTH CENTER
OUR LADY OF THE LAKE HOSPITAL, INC.
PARMA COMMUNITY GENERAL HOSPITAL
PITT COUNTY MEMORIAL HOSPITAL, INCORPORATED
SHAWNEE MISSION MEDICAL CENTER, INC.
THE UNIVERSITY OF CHICAGO MEDICAL CENTER

HISTORICAL FINANCIALS
Company Type: Private

Income Statement				FYE: June 30
	REVENUE ($mil)	NET INCOME ($mil)	NET PROFIT MARGIN	EMPLOYEES
06/22	1,587	(26)	—	5,766
06/21	1,511	145	9.6%	—
06/20*	1,439	71	4.9%	—
12/16	1,776	128	7.3%	—
Annual Growth	(2.2%)	—	—	—

*Fiscal year change

2022 Year-End Financials
Return on assets: (-0.7%)   Cash ($ mil.): 124
Return on equity: (-2.6%)
Current Ratio: 1.70

LONG BEACH MEDICAL CENTER

Long Beach Medical Center (LBMC) is an old-timer in the Long Beach health care market. A subsidiary of Memorial Care, LBMC provides a full range of health services to residents of the Long Beach, California, area. Services include primary, emergency, diagnostic, surgical, therapeutic, and rehabilitative care. The hospital is home to centers for treatment of cancer, heart, stroke, and women's and children's health concerns. It also provides home and hospice care programs, as well as occupational health services. Through Outpatient Wound Healing Center, LBMC provides full-services wound care for adults and children in Los Angeles County and Orange County.

EXECUTIVES

CIO*, Scott Joslyn
CPO*, Wendy Dorchester

LOCATIONS

HQ: LONG BEACH MEDICAL CENTER
2801 ATLANTIC AVE FL 2, LONG BEACH, CA 908061701
Phone: 562 933-2000
Web: WWW.MEMORIALCARE.ORG

PRODUCTS/OPERATIONS

Selected Institutes and Centers
Certified Comprehensive Stroke Center
Long Beach Adult & Pediatric Sleep Center
MemorialCare Breast Center at Long Beach Medical Center
MemorialCare Heart & Vascular Institute
MemorialCare Imaging Center
MemorialCare Joint Replacement Center
MemorialCare Rehabilitation Institute
MemorialCare Todd Cancer Institute
Spine Center at Long Beach Memorial
Trauma Center at Long Beach Medical Center

Selected Services
Blood Donation Center
Diabetes Care
Digestive Care
Emergency Department
Gynecological Care at Long Beach Medical Center
Lung & Respiratory Care
Minimally Invasive Surgery at Long Beach Memorial
Palliative Care Program at Long Beach Medical Center
Pharmacy at Long Beach Medical Center
Robotic-Assisted Surgery at Long Beach Memorial
Surgical Care
Wound Healing & Hyperbaric Medicine at Long Beach Medical Center

COMPETITORS

BLESSING HOSPITAL
CENTRAL SUFFOLK HOSPITAL
CENTRASTATE HEALTHCARE SYSTEM INC
CONEMAUGH HEALTH COMPANY, LLC
FLAGSTAFF MEDICAL CENTER, INC.
FRANKLIN SQUARE HOSPITAL CENTER, INC.
HAWAI'I PACIFIC HEALTH
MAINEHEALTH
MERCY HOSPITAL AND MEDICAL CENTER
YORK HOSPITAL

HISTORICAL FINANCIALS
Company Type: Private

Income Statement — FYE: June 30

	REVENUE ($mil)	NET INCOME ($mil)	NET PROFIT MARGIN	EMPLOYEES
06/18	633	63	10.1%	6,000
06/16	618	88	14.4%	—
06/15	624	93	15.0%	—
06/11	1,083	63	5.9%	—
Annual Growth	(7.4%)	0.1%	—	—

2018 Year-End Financials
Return on assets: 4.8%   Cash ($ mil.): —
Return on equity: 5.3%
Current Ratio: 11.70

LONG ISLAND JEWISH MEDICAL CENTER

Long Island Jewish Medical Center serves the western edge of Long Island and the eastern edge of the greater metropolitan New York area. The medical center campus includes Long Island Jewish Hospital, a general acute care hospital; Cohen Children's Medical Center of New York Hospital, which provides a full range of pediatric care services; and The Zucker Hillside Hospital, a psychiatric hospital for patients of all ages. The medical center's staff includes 1,200 physicians. Long Island Jewish Medical Center is the primary clinical and medical training facility of Northwell Health.

Operations
The Long Island Jewish Medical Center's main activities are centered at the Long Island Jewish Hospital, which provides emergency, diagnostic, surgical, inpatient, and outpatient services. The hospital has centers for cancer treatment, cardiac surgery, and women's health, as well as units specializing in hearing loss, stroke recovery, sleep disorders, and hemophilia treatment. As an affiliate of Hofstra University, the Long Island Jewish Hospital also provides graduate medical education programs.

Geographic Reach
Long Island Jewish Medical Center is located on a 48-acre campus on the border of New York's Queens and Nassau counties, about 15 miles east of Manhattan.

Strategy
To enhance services provided to residents of the growing New York City metropolitan area, Long Island Jewish Medical Center is conducting expansion efforts on its facilities. In 2012 it opened a new $300 million, 10-story inpatient tower (containing 160 private patient rooms) at the Long Island Jewish Hospital. The project increased the hospital's overall capacity and added women's health, cardiovascular care, and wellness centers.

LOCATIONS

HQ: LONG ISLAND JEWISH MEDICAL CENTER
27005 76TH AVE, NEW HYDE PARK, NY 110401496
Phone: 516 465-2600
Web: WWW.LIJED.COM

PRODUCTS/OPERATIONS

Selected Facilities
Long Island Jewish Hospital (490 beds)
The Steven and Alexandra Cohen Children's Medical Center (160 beds)
The Zucker Hillside Hospital (240 beds)

Selected Services
Anesthesiology
Cardiac Services
Center for Maternal-Fetal Health
Dental Medicine
Emergency Medicine
Medicine
Neurosciences
Obstetrics
Ophthalmology
Orthopaedic Surgery
Otolaryngology
Pathology
Radiation Oncology
Radiology
Rehabilitation
Surgery
Thoracic Surgery
Urogynecology
Urology: The Arthur Smith Insitute for Urology

COMPETITORS

BETH ISRAEL MEDICAL CENTER
BROOKHAVEN MEMORIAL HOSPITAL MEDICAL CENTER, INC.
HUNTINGTON HOSPITAL DOLAN FAMILY HEALTH CENTER, INC.
STATEN ISLAND UNIVERSITY HOSPITAL, INC
THE JAMAICA HOSPITAL

HISTORICAL FINANCIALS
Company Type: Private

Income Statement — FYE: December 31

	REVENUE ($mil)	NET INCOME ($mil)	NET PROFIT MARGIN	EMPLOYEES
12/18	2,448	56	2.3%	1,214
12/17	2,222	154	6.9%	—
12/16	2,093	162	7.8%	—
12/15	1,524	44	2.9%	—
Annual Growth	17.1%	7.6%	—	—

2018 Year-End Financials
Return on assets: 2.0%   Cash ($ mil.): 1
Return on equity: 8.4%
Current Ratio: 2.00

LONG ISLAND POWER AUTHORITY

The long and short of it is that Long Island Power Authority (LIPA) owns the electric transmission and distribution system on Long Island that delivers power to more than 1.1 million retail customers. The company's network, which is managed and operated by the National Grid USA consists of nearly 14,000 miles of overhead and underground lines. LIPA offers energy conservation products and services, as well as incentive programs to encourage customers to purchase energy from "green" (environmentally friendly) power generation sources. LIPA is a municipally owned, not-for-profit utility company.

EXECUTIVES

ENVRNM AFFRS*, Michael Deering
Auditors : KPMG LLP NEW YORK NEW YORK

LOCATIONS

HQ: LONG ISLAND POWER AUTHORITY
333 EARLE OVINGTON BLVD # 403, UNIONDALE, NY 115533606
Phone: 516 222-7700
Web: WWW.LIPOWER.ORG

PRODUCTS/OPERATIONS

Energy Conservation Products and Services
Commercial energy analysis
Construction and renovation incentives
Energy Star labeled homes program
Geothermal rebates
HVAC upgrades
Lighting and appliance solutions
Peak demand reduction programs
Residential energy affordability program
Residential energy audit
Solar Pioneer program
Wind energy development initiatives

COMPETITORS

CALIFORNIA INDEPENDENT SYSTEM OPERATOR CORPORATION
Hydro One Inc
PUERTO RICO ELECTRIC POWER AUTHORITY
SACRAMENTO MUNICIPAL UTILITY DISTRICT
TERRAFORM POWER, INC.

HISTORICAL FINANCIALS
Company Type: Private

Income Statement — FYE: December 31

	REVENUE ($mil)	NET INCOME ($mil)	NET PROFIT MARGIN	EMPLOYEES
12/20	3,900	18	0.5%	100
12/19	3,516	24	0.7%	—
12/18	3,576	22	0.6%	—
12/16	3,399	(26)	—	—
Annual Growth	3.5%	—	—	—

2020 Year-End Financials
Return on assets: 0.1%   Cash ($ mil.): 266
Return on equity: 3.5%
Current Ratio: 1.50

LOS ANGELES COUNTY OFFICE OF EDUCATION

Auditors : EIDEBAILLY LLP RANCHO CUCAMON

LOCATIONS

HQ: LOS ANGELES COUNTY OFFICE OF EDUCATION
9300 IMPERIAL HWY, DOWNEY, CA 902422813
Phone: 562 922-6111
Web: WWW.LACOE.EDU

HISTORICAL FINANCIALS
Company Type: Private

Income Statement — FYE: June 30

	REVENUE ($mil)	NET INCOME ($mil)	NET PROFIT MARGIN	EMPLOYEES
06/19	621	38	6.2%	4,000
06/18	657	22	3.4%	—
06/17	646	17	2.6%	—
06/16	661	7	1.2%	—
Annual Growth	(2.1%)	71.2%	—	—

2019 Year-End Financials
Return on assets: 6.7%   Cash ($ mil.): —
Return on equity: —
Current Ratio: —

LOS ANGELES DEPARTMENT OF WATER AND POWER

The Los Angeles Department of Water and Power (LADWP) keeps the movie cameras running and the swimming pools full. The largest municipally owned utility in the US, LADWP provides electricity to approximately 1.4 million residential and business customers and water to some 681,000 customers. The company has net dependable capacity of about 8,010 MW from a diverse mix of energy resources; it also buys and sells wholesale power. As a revenue-producing proprietary department, the LADWP transfers a portion of its annual estimated electric revenues to the City of Los Angeles general fund.

Operations

LADWP's operations are financed solely by the sale of water and electric services. The department has about 115 tanks and reservoirs, ranging in size of approximately 400 million gallons, and a storage capacity of approximately 323,820 acre feet. Nine aqueduct reservoirs provide some 95% of the Water system's storage capacity while major and minor distribution reservoirs and tanks provide the remaining nearly 5%. It also has about 85 pump stations, a distribution main of around 7,335 miles of pipe.

The company has about 35 generation plants with some 1.6 MW of city-owned energy storage, approximately 21.5 MW of utility-scale battery energy storage, and some 1,244 MW of pumped hydro storage. About 35% of power resources come from renewable energy, over 25% from natural gas, about 25% from nuclear, around 20% from coal, and nearly 5% from large hydroelectric.

Geographic Reach

The company is based in Los Angeles, California.

Sales and Marketing

LADWP also provides its around 681,000 water customers and some 1.4 million electric customers with quality service at competitive prices.

Company Background

LADWP was founded in 1902.

Auditors : KPMG LLP LOS ANGELES CA

LOCATIONS

HQ: LOS ANGELES DEPARTMENT OF WATER AND POWER
111 N HOPE ST, LOS ANGELES, CA 900122607
Phone: 213 367-1320
Web: WWW.LADWP.COM

COMPETITORS

AMERICAN WATER WORKS COMPANY, INC.
ARTESIAN RESOURCES CORPORATION
LOWER COLORADO RIVER AUTHORITY
OMAHA PUBLIC POWER DISTRICT
ORLANDO UTILITIES COMMISSION (INC)
PUBLIC UTILITY DISTRICT 1 OF SNOHOMISH COUNTY
SAN ANTONIO WATER SYSTEM
SAN DIEGO COUNTY WATER AUTHORITY
SJW GROUP
THE EMPIRE DISTRICT ELECTRIC COMPANY

HISTORICAL FINANCIALS
Company Type: Private

Income Statement — FYE: June 30

	REVENUE ($mil)	NET INCOME ($mil)	NET PROFIT MARGIN	EMPLOYEES
06/17	1,118	140	12.6%	9,500
06/11	3,125	57	1.8%	—
06/10	812	67	8.3%	—
Annual Growth	4.7%	11.1%	—	—

2017 Year-End Financials
Return on assets: 1.4%   Cash ($ mil.): 320
Return on equity: 4.5%
Current Ratio: 1.20

LOS ANGELES LOMOD CORPORATION

Auditors : MACIAS GINI & O'CONNELL LLP L

LOCATIONS

HQ: LOS ANGELES LOMOD CORPORATION
2600 WILSHIRE BLVD, LOS ANGELES, CA 900573400

Phone: 213 252-2510
Web: WWW.LOMOD.ORG

HISTORICAL FINANCIALS
Company Type: Private

Income Statement   FYE: December 31

	REVENUE ($mil)	NET INCOME ($mil)	NET PROFIT MARGIN	EMPLOYEES
12/18	575	14	2.5%	44
12/17	534	12	2.4%	—
12/13	405	6	1.5%	—
12/09	356	5	1.4%	—
Annual Growth	5.5%	12.3%	—	—

2018 Year-End Financials
Return on assets: 34.9%   Cash ($ mil.): 37
Return on equity: 35.2%
Current Ratio: —

LOS ANGELES UNIFIED SCHOOL DISTRICT

LOCATIONS
HQ: LOS ANGELES UNIFIED SCHOOL DISTRICT
333 S BEAUDRY AVE STE 209, LOS ANGELES, CA 900175141
Phone: 213 241-1000
Web: WWW.LAUSD.NET

HISTORICAL FINANCIALS
Company Type: Private

Income Statement   FYE: June 30

	REVENUE ($mil)	NET INCOME ($mil)	NET PROFIT MARGIN	EMPLOYEES
06/20	9,378	160	1.7%	65,231
06/09	0	0	0.0%	—
06/06	0	0	—	—
06/05	0	0	20.1%	—
Annual Growth	92.6%	63.5%	—	—

2020 Year-End Financials
Return on assets: 0.7%   Cash ($ mil.): 5,888
Return on equity: —
Current Ratio: —

LOUDOUN COUNTY

EXECUTIVES
County Administrator, Tim Hemstreet
Deputy County Administrator*, Charles Yudd
Auditors : CHERRY BEKAERT LLP TYSONS CO

LOCATIONS
HQ: LOUDOUN COUNTY
1 HARRISON ST SE FL 1 # 1, LEESBURG, VA 201753102
Phone: 703 777-0100
Web: WWW.LOUDOUN.GOV

HISTORICAL FINANCIALS
Company Type: Private

Income Statement   FYE: June 30

	REVENUE ($mil)	NET INCOME ($mil)	NET PROFIT MARGIN	EMPLOYEES
06/21	2,161	95	4.4%	6,999
06/19	1,797	133	7.4%	—
06/18	1,716	71	4.2%	—
06/17	1,638	126	7.7%	—
Annual Growth	7.2%	(6.7%)	—	—

2021 Year-End Financials
Return on assets: 1.2%   Cash ($ mil.): 1,595
Return on equity: 4.5%
Current Ratio: —

LOUDOUN COUNTY PUBLIC SCHOOL DISTRICT

Auditors : CHERRY BEKAERT LLP TYSONS COR

LOCATIONS
HQ: LOUDOUN COUNTY PUBLIC SCHOOL DISTRICT
21000 EDUCATION CT, BROADLANDS, VA 201485526
Phone: 571 252-1000
Web: WWW.LCPS.ORG

HISTORICAL FINANCIALS
Company Type: Private

Income Statement   FYE: June 30

	REVENUE ($mil)	NET INCOME ($mil)	NET PROFIT MARGIN	EMPLOYEES
06/16	1,130	14	1.3%	6,900
06/15	1,080	19	1.8%	—
Annual Growth	4.7%	(28.6%)	—	—

2016 Year-End Financials
Return on assets: 0.7%   Cash ($ mil.): —
Return on equity: 1.7%
Current Ratio: —

LOUISIANA CHILDRENS MEDICAL CENTER, INC

Auditors : LAPORTE APAC METAIRE LA

LOCATIONS
HQ: LOUISIANA CHILDRENS MEDICAL CENTER, INC
1100 POYDRAS ST STE 2500, NEW ORLEANS, LA 701632500
Phone: 504 896-9581
Web: WWW.LCMCHEALTH.ORG

HISTORICAL FINANCIALS
Company Type: Private

Income Statement   FYE: December 31

	REVENUE ($mil)	NET INCOME ($mil)	NET PROFIT MARGIN	EMPLOYEES
12/21	2,288	44	1.9%	6,100
12/18	1,617	(34)	—	—
12/14	21	0	0.0%	—
12/13	926	285	30.8%	—
Annual Growth	12.0%	(20.8%)	—	—

2021 Year-End Financials
Return on assets: 1.2%   Cash ($ mil.): 175
Return on equity: 2.2%
Current Ratio: 1.20

LOUISVILLE-JEFFERSON COUNTY METRO GOVERNMENT

Louisville is so much more than bourbon, baseball bats, and horse races. The largest city in Kentucky, Louisville counts about 600,000 people in the urban area, which has the same parameters as Jefferson County. Louisville is home to liquor company Brown-Forman; Hillerich & Bradsby, maker of Louisville Slugger baseball bats; and Churchill Downs, where the Kentucky Derby is held. In addition, Louisville has a few Fortune 500 companies in the city - fast food operator YUM! Brands and health care companies Humana and Kindred.

Auditors : STROTHMAN & COMPANY LOUISVILL

LOCATIONS
HQ: LOUISVILLE-JEFFERSON COUNTY METRO GOVERNMENT
527 W JEFFERSON ST # 400, LOUISVILLE, KY 402022814
Phone: 502 574-2003
Web: WWW.LOUISVILLE-POLICE.ORG

COMPETITORS
CITY OF ARLINGTON
CITY OF ATLANTA
CITY OF BALTIMORE
CITY OF COLUMBUS
CITY OF TUCSON

HISTORICAL FINANCIALS
Company Type: Private

Income Statement   FYE: June 30

	REVENUE ($mil)	NET INCOME ($mil)	NET PROFIT MARGIN	EMPLOYEES
06/21	1,037	60	5.8%	6,500
06/20	860	26	3.1%	—
06/19	873	(38)	—	—
06/18	825	14	1.8%	—
Annual Growth	7.9%	59.7%	—	—

2021 Year-End Financials
Return on assets: 0.7%   Cash ($ mil.): 436
Return on equity: 2.5%
Current Ratio: —

LOYOLA UNIVERSITY MEDICAL CENTER

LOCATIONS

HQ: LOYOLA UNIVERSITY MEDICAL CENTER
2160 S 1ST AVE, MAYWOOD, IL 601533328
Phone: 708 216-9000
Web: WWW.LOYOLAMEDICINE.ORG

HISTORICAL FINANCIALS
Company Type: Private

Income Statement — FYE: June 30

	REVENUE ($mil)	NET INCOME ($mil)	NET PROFIT MARGIN	EMPLOYEES
06/20	1,581	81	5.2%	1
06/15	1,210	19	1.6%	—
Annual Growth	5.5%	33.3%	—	—

2020 Year-End Financials
Return on assets: 4.6%   Cash ($ mil.): 14
Return on equity: 35.7%
Current Ratio: 1.00

LOYOLA UNIVERSITY MEDICAL CENTER

Auditors: PRICEWATERHOUSECOOPERS LLP WA

LOCATIONS

HQ: LOYOLA UNIVERSITY MEDICAL CENTER
2160 S 1ST AVE, MAYWOOD, IL 601533328
Phone: 708 216-9000
Web: WWW.LOYOLAHEALTH.ORG

HISTORICAL FINANCIALS
Company Type: Private

Income Statement — FYE: June 30

	REVENUE ($mil)	NET INCOME ($mil)	NET PROFIT MARGIN	EMPLOYEES
06/11	938	14	1.6%	4
06/10	917	8	0.9%	—
Annual Growth	2.3%	75.7%	—	—

2011 Year-End Financials
Return on assets: —   Cash ($ mil.): 65
Return on equity: 1.6%
Current Ratio: 0.30

LOYOLA UNIVERSITY OF CHICAGO INC

Loyola University is a Jesuit, Catholic university with a reach that extends far beyond the Windy City. In addition to its three Chicago-area campuses, the university also maintains an undergraduate campus in Italy and a study center in Beijing, China. Loyola University's nearly 14,765 students can choose from more than 80 undergraduate, nearly 100 master's, a dozen doctoral, and more than 140 graduate, professional, and certificate programs. With nearly 1,390 full-time faculty and staff members, the not-for-profit school has a 15:1 student-teacher ratio. Notable alumni include actor Bob Newhart and writer Sandra Cisneros. Established in 1870 by a group of Jesuit priests, the university turned its medical center into a separate subsidiary in 1995.

Operations
The university's undergraduate offers major and minor programs including accounting, advertising and public relations, biochemistry, criminal justice and criminology, economics, film and digital media, and theology among others. It also offers graduate and professional education such as arts and sciences biomedical sciences & medicine, business, continuing and professional studies (adult), education, law, nursing, pastoral studies, and social work.

Undergraduate students work with advisors in Academic Advising. Graduate students are advised differently depending on their school and program. These schools include The Graduate School, Quinlan School of Business, Institute of Pastoral Studies, Marcella Niehoff School of Nursing, School of Continuing and Professional Studies, School of Education, and School of Social Work.

Geographic Reach
Headquartered in Illinois, Loyola University three Chicago campuses include Lake Shore, Water Tower, and Health Sciences, as well as the John Felice Rome Center in Italy. It is home to a dozen schools and colleges that include arts and sciences, business administration, communication, education, graduate studies, law, medicine, nursing, continuing and professional studies, and social work.

Loyola also features course locations in Beijing, China and Saigon-Ho Chi Minh City, Vietnam.

Sales and Marketing
Loyola University uses social media channels such as Facebook, Twitter, and YouTube to connect with the students, faculty, staff, and Alumni.

Strategy
The Loyola University Chicago created Plan 2020. Plan 2020 is a framework to focus its energies on improving the quality of education, so its students are prepared to be agents of change affecting their families, careers, and communities.

Plan 2020 has four institutional priorities: student access and success, faculty development, programs for societal needs, and local and global partnerships.

For the first institutional priority, strategies include recruitment of and retaining underserved students and making programs for student success.

For the second priority, recruitment, retaining, and development of faculty for social justice will be of focus.

For the third priority, strategies include collaboration for the reduction of health disparities, the advancement of STEM and sustainability, and addressing injustice and violence.

Lastly, to promote local and global partnerships, the university will develop community outreach programs and expand global engagement.

Company Background
Founded in 1870 by Arnold Damen, S.J., as St. Ignatius College, the college was originally located at West Twelfth Street, next to Holy Family Church, the current location of St. Ignatius College Prep. In 1909, St. Ignatius College was re-chartered by the State of Illinois as Loyola University, and in 1922 the University moved operations from West Twelfth Street to Sheridan and Devon in the Rogers Park neighborhood. College classes had been offered at the Rogers Park campus since 1912, and Loyola Academy opened on the property in 1909.

Auditors: DELOITTE & TOUCHE LLP CHICAGO

LOCATIONS

HQ: LOYOLA UNIVERSITY OF CHICAGO INC
1032 W SHERIDAN RD, CHICAGO, IL 606601537
Phone: 773 274-3000
Web: WWW.LUC.EDU

PRODUCTS/OPERATIONS

Selected Schools & Colleges
College of Arts and Sciences
Graduate School of Business
Institute of Pastoral Studies
Marcella Niehoff School of Nursing
Quinlan School of Business
School of Communication
School of Continuing and Professional Studies
School of Education
School of Law
School of Social Work
Stritch School of Medicine
The Graduate School

COMPETITORS

ADELPHI UNIVERSITY
DRAKE UNIVERSITY
FAIRLEIGH DICKINSON UNIVERSITY
GEORGETOWN UNIVERSITY (THE)
HAMPTON UNIVERSITY
QUINNIPIAC UNIVERSITY
ST LAWRENCE UNIVERSITY (INC)

TEMPLE UNIVERSITY-OF THE COMMONWEALTH SYSTEM OF HIGHER EDUCATION
THE UNIVERSITY OF IOWA
UNIVERSITY OF ILLINOIS

HISTORICAL FINANCIALS
Company Type: Private

Income Statement — FYE: June 30

	REVENUE ($mil)	NET INCOME ($mil)	NET PROFIT MARGIN	EMPLOYEES
06/21	554	301	54.5%	10,500
06/20	611	23	3.8%	—
06/19	614	78	12.8%	—
06/18	594	109	18.4%	—
Annual Growth	(2.3%)	40.2%	—	—

2021 Year-End Financials
Return on assets: 12.0% Cash ($ mil.): 106
Return on equity: 15.2%
Current Ratio: —

LOZIER CORPORATION

Lozier is a leader in the manufacturing store fixtures industry. The company makes retail store fixtures, including gondolas, display shelving and freestanding displays, for pharmacy, groceries, food service, convenience store, and hardware. It has manufacturing facilities and a distribution center in Alabama, Indiana, Missouri, Nebraska, and Pennsylvania. Lozier distributes fixtures across the US, as well as internationally. The company maintains a sales and service network for its international retailers. In addition to selling fixtures, Lozier also offers installation services. To expedite parcel pickup and simplify the order fulfillment process, the company offers Buy Online Pick up In Store (BOPIS) products and solutions.

Operations
Lozier specializes in making and marketing agility conveyor, display shelving, multi-function, counters and checkouts, gondolas, storage shelving, tubular, wood products, and pharmacy line. Its services include design and engineering, manufacturing, import and export, support and logistics, and installation.

Geographic Reach
Based in Nebraska, Lozier operates seven manufacturing and distribution facilities in Pennsylvania, Indiana, Alabama, Missouri, and Nebraska.

Sales and Marketing
As part of its business, Lozier serves discounters, apparel, food service, grocery, chain drug stores, and convenience stores for multiple markets, such as automotive, farm, home, office, computer, pet, toys, and sporting goods.

The company leverages its approximately 6,500 sq. ft. showroom in Omaha for its sales and marketing efforts. The facility features display shelving configurations, accessories, colors, and finishes to provide retail customers with a variety of ideas and solutions.

Company Background
The company was founded in 1956.

Auditors : RSM US LLP OMAHA NEBRASKA

LOCATIONS
HQ: LOZIER CORPORATION
6336 JOHN J PERSHING DR, OMAHA, NE 681101122
Phone: 402 457-8000
Web: WWW.LOZIER.COM

PRODUCTS/OPERATIONS
Services
Design & Engineering
Manufacturing
Import/Export
Support & Logistics
Installation

COMPETITORS
DAVACO, INC.
Expedit A/S
HUSSMANN INTERNATIONAL, INC.
INDOFF, INCORPORATED
LOAD KING MANUFACTURING CO.
LYON WORKSPACE PRODUCTS, L.L.C.
MADIX, INC.
NPARALLEL, LLC
TRION INDUSTRIES, INC.
VIRA MANUFACTURING INC

HISTORICAL FINANCIALS
Company Type: Private

Income Statement — FYE: December 25

	REVENUE ($mil)	NET INCOME ($mil)	NET PROFIT MARGIN	EMPLOYEES
12/21	573	0	0.0%	2,210
12/20	451	0	0.0%	—
12/19	525	0	0.0%	—
12/18	552	0	0.0%	—
Annual Growth	1.3%	—	—	—

LUCILE SALTER PACKARD CHILDREN'S HOSPITAL AT STANFORD

Auditors : PRICEWATERHOUSECOOPERS LLP SA

LOCATIONS
HQ: LUCILE SALTER PACKARD CHILDREN'S HOSPITAL AT STANFORD
725 WELCH RD, PALO ALTO, CA 943041601
Phone: 650 497-8000
Web: WWW.STANFORDCHILDRENS.ORG

HISTORICAL FINANCIALS
Company Type: Private

Income Statement — FYE: August 31

	REVENUE ($mil)	NET INCOME ($mil)	NET PROFIT MARGIN	EMPLOYEES
08/20	2,064	95	4.6%	1,100
08/19	1,959	99	5.1%	—
08/18	1,637	22	1.4%	—
08/17	1,486	227	15.3%	—
Annual Growth	11.6%	(25.2%)	—	—

2020 Year-End Financials
Return on assets: 2.3% Cash ($ mil.): 354
Return on equity: 3.6%
Current Ratio: 2.20

LUKOIL PAN AMERICAS, LLC

EXECUTIVES
Managing Member, Stephen Wolfe

LOCATIONS
HQ: LUKOIL PAN AMERICAS, LLC
3200 KIRBY DR STE 900, HOUSTON, TX 770983279
Phone: 713 929-6775
Web: WWW.LITASCO.COM

HISTORICAL FINANCIALS
Company Type: Private

Income Statement — FYE: December 31

	REVENUE ($mil)	NET INCOME ($mil)	NET PROFIT MARGIN	EMPLOYEES
12/08	4,745	5	0.1%	77
12/07	4,717	3	0.1%	—
12/06	3,021	23	0.8%	—
12/05	2,788	21	0.8%	—
Annual Growth	19.4%	(37.8%)	—	—

2008 Year-End Financials
Return on assets: — Cash ($ mil.): 1
Return on equity: 0.1%
Current Ratio: 0.40

LUMINIS HEALTH ANNE ARUNDEL MEDICAL CENTER, INC

The ill and infirm get the royal treatment at Anne Arundel Medical Center. The full-service, acute-care hospital serves the residents of Anne Arundel, Calvert, Prince George's, and Queen Anne counties in Maryland. With about 425 beds, the hospital administers care for women's health, oncology, pediatrics (it has a level III neonatal intensive care unit), neurology, orthopedics, and cardiovascular care. The medical center also has weight loss, sleep disorder, and rehabilitation centers. Anne Arundel, which opened its doors in 1902 and is part of the Anne Arundel Health System, has expanded its service offerings through various affiliations with regional specialty and primary care clinics. It also has a partnership with Johns Hopkins Medicine.

Operations
With more than 1,000 staff members, Anne Arundel handles some 26,000 inpatient visits and 102,000 outpatient visits per year. It also manages more than 5,000 births and 93,000 emergency room visits.

Johns Hopkins and the not-for-profit Anne Arundel share some services, faculty, and patients through their collaboration. They also operate a joint outpatient urgent-care facility. Additionally, the two organizations work together to perform clinical research projects and conduct physician graduate medical education programs.

Geographic Reach
In addition to its 57-acre Annapolis campus, Anne Arundel has outpatient centers in Bowie, Kent Island, Odenton, Pasadena, and Waugh Chapel.

Sales and Marketing
In 2014, Medicare payments accounted for about one-third of net patient revenues.

Financial Performance
In 2014 revenue grew 3% to $591 million as net patient services revenues increased. However, net income fell 23% to $42 million due to a decline in non-operating income (investment earnings). Cash flow from operations spike 188% to $56 million as cash generated from patient receivables, prepaid expenses, and other sources rose.

Strategy
Anne Arundel has, in recent years, added new facilities to better keep up with a continued growth in demand for health care services throughout its service area. In 2015 it opened the second phase of its Pasadena Pavilion, adding physical therapy, orthopedics, and sports medicine capabilities. It also opened a new FastCare walk-in clinic in a grocery store/pharmacy in Annapolis. In 2014 the system opened an outpatient mental health clinic in Annapolis, which provides services for patients 13 years of age and older.

In 2013 Anne Arundel opened a training center -- the James and Sylvia Earl Simulation to Advance Innovation and Learning (SAIL) Center -- to enhance its medical education programs and improve the quality and safety of care in the region. It also opened the Hackerman-Patz House that year to provide an affordable and convenient housing option for families of patients.

Also in 2013 the organization was designated as a Medicare accountable care organization (ACO) by the US government. ACOs work to coordinate care for Medicare patients to improve quality and reduce expenses.

EXECUTIVES
CSO*, Paula Widerlite
Auditors: SC&H TAX & ADVISORY SERVICES L

LOCATIONS
HQ: LUMINIS HEALTH ANNE ARUNDEL MEDICAL CENTER, INC
2001 MEDICAL PKWY, ANNAPOLIS, MD 214013773
Phone: 443 481-1000
Web: WWW.LUMINISHEALTH.ORG

PRODUCTS/OPERATIONS
Selected Centers and Services
Blood Donor Center
Breast Center
Cardiac Cath Lab
Chest Pain Center
DeCesaris Cancer Institute
Diabetes, Wound and Hyperbaric Center
Diagnostic Imaging
Heart and Vascular Institute
Joint Center
Laboratory
Pediatrics
Rehabilitation
Research Institute
Sleep Disorder Center
Spine Center
Stroke Center
Surgery
Women's and Children's Center

COMPETITORS
BRONXCARE HEALTH SYSTEM
FLOYD HEALTHCARE MANAGEMENT, INC.
JUPITER MEDICAL CENTER, INC.
OVERLAKE HOSPITAL MEDICAL CENTER
THE LANCASTER GENERAL HOSPITAL

HISTORICAL FINANCIALS
Company Type: Private

Income Statement — FYE: June 30

	REVENUE ($mil)	NET INCOME ($mil)	NET PROFIT MARGIN	EMPLOYEES
06/21	650	59	9.2%	1,890
06/19	579	17	2.9%	—
06/15	525	39	7.6%	—
06/14	492	20	4.1%	—
Annual Growth	4.1%	16.8%	—	—

2021 Year-End Financials
Return on assets: 5.2%   Cash ($ mil.): 132
Return on equity: 10.6%
Current Ratio: 0.70

MAGELLAN PIPELINE COMPANY, L.P.

LOCATIONS
HQ: MAGELLAN PIPELINE COMPANY, L.P.
1 WILLIAMS CTR STE 2800, TULSA, OK 741720140
Phone: 918 574-7000
Web: WWW.MAGELLANLP.COM

HISTORICAL FINANCIALS
Company Type: Private

Income Statement — FYE: December 31

	REVENUE ($mil)	NET INCOME ($mil)	NET PROFIT MARGIN	EMPLOYEES
12/17	828	396	47.9%	435
12/16	911	339	37.2%	
Annual Growth	(9.1%)	17.0%	—	—

2017 Year-End Financials
Return on assets: 18.5%   Cash ($ mil.): 15
Return on equity: 20.9%
Current Ratio: 0.60

MAIMONIDES MEDICAL CENTER

Maimonides Medical Center, a not-for-profit hospital, offers emergency medicine, surgical procedures, psychiatric treatment, and other traditional hospital services to patients in Brooklyn, New York. Its Maimonides Children's Hospital provides full array of pediatric subspecialties. Maimonides is home to the most advanced team of orthopedic specialists in the region at its Bone and Joint Center. It also manages pain for patients in ways that minimize the risk of opioid addiction. Its Acute Care for the Elderly (ACE) Geriatric Unit, provides an interdisciplinary approach to care for older patients, helping to ease their hospitalization.

Sales and Marketing
Maimonides is the hometown hospital of Brooklyn Nets and the Brooklyn Cyclones.

Company Background
Maimonides Medical Center traces its roots to the New Utrecht Dispensary, which opened in 1911. The medical center later merged with Beth Moses and United Israel Zion hospitals in 1947. It is named after 12th-century philosopher Rabbi Moshe Ben Maimon.

LOCATIONS
HQ: MAIMONIDES MEDICAL CENTER
4802 10TH AVE, BROOKLYN, NY 112192916
Phone: 718 581-0598
Web: WWW.MAIMO.ORG

PRODUCTS/OPERATIONS

2014 Sales

	$ mil	% of total
Net patient revenue, less provision for bad debts	1,001.8	95
Net assets released from restrictions	0.9	-
Other revenue	48.5	5
Total	1,051.2	100

Selected Services
Adult Primary Care
Ambulatory Health Services
Bay Parkway Multi-Specialty
Manfredi Family Health Center

Newkirk Family Health Center
Outpatient Eye Clinic
Pediatric Primary Care
Primary Health Services
Sheepshead Bay
Women's Primary Care Services

COMPETITORS

BRONXCARE HEALTH SYSTEM
COVENANT MEDICAL CENTER, INC.
LEE MEMORIAL HEALTH SYSTEM
LEGACY LIFEPOINT HEALTH, INC.
NORTHWELL HEALTH, INC.
OVERLAKE HOSPITAL MEDICAL CENTER
PRESBYTERIAN HEALTHCARE SERVICES
THE CLEVELAND CLINIC FOUNDATION
THE LANCASTER GENERAL HOSPITAL
THE RUTLAND HOSPITAL INC ACT 220

HISTORICAL FINANCIALS
Company Type: Private

Income Statement — FYE: December 31

	REVENUE ($mil)	NET INCOME ($mil)	NET PROFIT MARGIN	EMPLOYEES
12/19	1,304	7	0.6%	6,382
12/17	958	19	2.0%	—
12/16	940	20	2.2%	—
12/15	890	(1)	—	—
Annual Growth	10.0%	—	—	—

2019 Year-End Financials
Return on assets: 0.5% Cash ($ mil.): 77
Return on equity: 1.6%
Current Ratio: 1.40

MAIN LINE HEALTH SYSTEM

Main Line Health is a not-for-profit network that includes four acute care hospitals, a drug and alcohol recovery treatment center, home care, outpatient centers, a physician network, and a biomedical research organization, all serving the greater Philadelphia area. Its hospitals -- Lankenau Medical Center, Bryn Mawr Hospital, Paoli Hospital, and Riddle Hospital -- are accredited as primary stroke care centers, comprehensive breast centers, and chest pain centers. Other specialties include diabetes and endocrinology, orthopedics, and cardiovascular care. Bryn Mawr Hospital offers residency programs in family practice, radiology, and surgical podiatry. Main Line Health was founded in 1985.

Operations

Main Line Hospitals include The Bryn Mawr Hospital; The Lankenau Hospital; Paoli Hospital); Lankenau Institute of Medical Research; Main Line Diversified Services; Bryn Mawr Rehabilitation Hospital, and other related organizations. TJUH includes Thomas Jefferson University Hospitals (Thomas Jefferson University Hospital and its subsidiaries; the Jefferson Hospital for Neuroscience and the Methodist Hospital Division.)

Thomas Jefferson University Hospitals has 969 licensed acute care beds and provides services in at five locations - the main hospital facility and Jefferson Hospital for Neuroscience, both in Center City Philadelphia; Methodist Hospital in South Philadelphia; Jefferson at the Navy Yard, just past the sports complex; and Jefferson-Voorhees in South Jersey. Magee Rehabilitation Hospital is a physical rehabilitation hospital specializing in the treatment of spinal cord injury, brain injury, stroke and orthopedic. Main Line Health offers a range of medical, surgical, obstetric, pediatric, psychiatric and emergency services.

Financial Performance

The company's revenues increased by 5% in fiscal 2012 due to a growth in patient services and other revenues. The patient services revenues increase was primarily due to a growth in Medicare and Medical Assistance fee-for-service program revenues. The increase in other income was due to receipts received for the initial payment of the incentive relating to Main Line Health implementing an electronic health records program as part of the American Recovery and Reinvestment Act of 2009.

Net income increased by 2% in fiscal 2012, primarily due to higher revenues.

Strategy

Jefferson Health System has realigned its relationship with former member Aria Health (formerly Frankford Health Care System) after the two organizations decided they too could better serve customers as separate entities. While Aria Health is no longer a direct member of the Jefferson Health System, the two health networks maintain an affiliate relationship through which they collaborate in some areas of care.

Auditors : PRICEWATERHOUSECOOPERS LLP PH

LOCATIONS

HQ: MAIN LINE HEALTH SYSTEM
240 N RADNOR CHESTER RD, RADNOR, PA 190875170
Phone: 610 225-6200
Web: WWW.MAINLINEHEALTH.ORG

COMPETITORS

ALBERT EINSTEIN HEALTHCARE NETWORK
BRYAN MEDICAL CENTER
CAPITAL HEALTH SYSTEM, INC.
CHRISTIANA CARE HEALTH SYSTEM, INC.
ELLIS HOSPITAL
GENESIS HEALTHCARE SYSTEM
MERCY HOSPITAL AND MEDICAL CENTER
SAINT JOSEPH HOSPITAL, INC
THE PENNSYLVANIA HOSPITAL OF THE UNIVERSITY OF PENNSYLVANIA HEALTH SYSTEM
TRIHEALTH, INC.

HISTORICAL FINANCIALS
Company Type: Private

Income Statement — FYE: June 30

	REVENUE ($mil)	NET INCOME ($mil)	NET PROFIT MARGIN	EMPLOYEES
06/21	1,984	510	25.7%	17,485
06/20	1,781	(17)	—	—
06/19	1,769	21	1.2%	—
06/18	1,742	267	15.4%	—
Annual Growth	4.4%	24.0%		

2021 Year-End Financials
Return on assets: 10.4% Cash ($ mil.): 138
Return on equity: 16.0%
Current Ratio: 2.30

MAIN LINE HOSPITALS, INC.

Bryn Mawr Hospital, a member of the Main Line not-for-profit health network, is an acute care facility providing a variety of inpatient and outpatient services in the western suburbs of Philadelphia. With some 320 beds, Bryn Mawr Hospital is recognized nationally for its orthopedic program. Founded in 1893 by Dr. George Gerhard, the teaching hospital also provides cancer, cardiac, surgical, pediatric, reproductive health, diagnostic imaging, psychiatric, bariatric, and wound care services. The hospital also operates the Main Line Health Center outpatient facility (which includes a comprehensive breast center) in Newtown Square.

Operations

Based in Bryn Mawr, Pennsylvania, Bryn Mawr Hospital boasts specialized departments, such as a Comprehensive Breast Center; Wound Healing Center at Bryn Mawr Hospital; Outpatient Imaging Center; Center for Reproductive Medicine; Cancer Center; Main Line Health Heart Center; Center for Addictive Diseases; Level III Neonatal Intensive Care Unit; and Nemours Pediatric Partners at Bryn Mawr Hospital. The hospital also operates an outpatient health center in Newton Square, Pennsylvania.

Bryn Mawr Hospital admits some 18,000 patients annually, performing around 4,800 inpatient and 6,800 outpatient surgeries. It provides care to more than 2,000 newborns and receives some 47,000 emergency department visits each year.

Strategy

Main Line Health in 2015 announced plans to invest $200 million to modernize Bryn Mawr Hospital. The initiative is the most significant renovation ever for the hospital, and it includes plans to build a five-story patient-care pavilion and convert all patient rooms to private rooms.

Like many hospitals, Bryn Mawr

Hospital aims to expand its outpatient services and connect to medical practices. The practice helps to boost the number of referrals to its facility and grow physician relations throughout the community.

Bryn Mawr Hospital collaborates with Nemours/Alfred I. duPont Hospital for Children to provide 24/7 pediatric care for the pediatric inpatient unit and the pediatric emergency department with added board-certified emergency medicine physicians. In 2015 the hospital formed a partnership with Lifecycle WomanCare to provide specialized care to pregnant and postpartum families in the community.

LOCATIONS

HQ: MAIN LINE HOSPITALS, INC.
130 S BRYN MAWR AVE, BRYN MAWR, PA 190103121
Phone: 610 526-3000
Web: WWW.MAINLINEHEALTH.ORG

COMPETITORS

HAYS MEDICAL CENTER, INC.
KENNESTONE HOSPITAL AT WINDY HILL, INC.
MAIN LINE HEALTH SYSTEM
ST PATRICK HOSPITAL CORPORATION
TAS-CNH, INC.

HISTORICAL FINANCIALS
Company Type: Private

Income Statement — FYE: June 30

	REVENUE ($mil)	NET INCOME ($mil)	NET PROFIT MARGIN	EMPLOYEES
06/21	1,485	194	13.1%	5,840
06/20	1,345	11	0.8%	—
06/19	1,323	58	4.4%	—
06/18	1,193	100	8.4%	—
Annual Growth	7.6%	24.6%	—	—

2021 Year-End Financials
Return on assets: 4.8%   Cash ($ mil.): 75
Return on equity: 6.7%
Current Ratio: 3.40

MAINE MEDICAL CENTER

Auditors : BAKER NEWMAN & NOYES LLC PORT

LOCATIONS

HQ: MAINE MEDICAL CENTER
576 SAINT JOHN ST, PORTLAND, ME 041022710
Phone: 207 780-0020
Web: WWW.MAINEHEALTH.ORG

HISTORICAL FINANCIALS
Company Type: Private

Income Statement — FYE: September 30

	REVENUE ($mil)	NET INCOME ($mil)	NET PROFIT MARGIN	EMPLOYEES
09/20	1,671	(5)	—	14
09/19	1,622	74	4.6%	—
09/18	1,564	164	10.5%	—
Annual Growth	3.3%	—	—	—

2020 Year-End Financials
Return on assets: (-0.4%)   Cash ($ mil.): 1
Return on equity: (-1.7%)
Current Ratio: 2.50

MAINEGENERAL HEALTH

If you're aching or ailing within shouting distance of the Kennebec River in Maine, then MaineGeneral Health is the place to head. The comprehensive health care organization features acute care hospitals, outpatient clinics and physicians' practices, long-term care centers, and home health and hospice agencies. Its flagship facilities are the three main campuses (in state capital Augusta and Waterville farther north) of MaineGeneral Medical Center, together featuring about 290 inpatient beds. MaineGeneral Health also runs nursing homes with some 270 beds in all, as well as senior living apartments, lab and imaging centers, and inpatient rehabilitation and mental health facilities.Operations

Strategy

In 2009 MaineGeneral announced plans to build a new 225-bed medical center in north Augusta that would consolidate the inpatient operations of its hospital campuses. Two of the medical center campuses would close (Augusta Campus and Seton Campus), while the third (Thayer Campus) would become an outpatient/emergency care facility. Construction of the $322 million hospital began in 2011, with a completion date in late 2013.

Auditors : BAKER NEWMAN NOYES LLC PORTLA

LOCATIONS

HQ: MAINEGENERAL HEALTH
35 MEDICAL CENTER PKWY # 20, AUGUSTA, ME 043308160
Phone: 207 626-1000
Web: WWW.MAINEGENERAL.ORG

COMPETITORS

MEMORIAL HEALTH SERVICES
MOUNTAIN STATES HEALTH ALLIANCE
MULTICARE HEALTH SYSTEM
SHAWNEE MISSION MEDICAL CENTER, INC.
WAKEMED

HISTORICAL FINANCIALS
Company Type: Private

Income Statement — FYE: June 30

	REVENUE ($mil)	NET INCOME ($mil)	NET PROFIT MARGIN	EMPLOYEES
06/20	575	31	5.5%	3,800
06/17	10	1	14.8%	—
06/15	11	0	4.5%	—
06/12	440	(1)	—	—
Annual Growth	3.4%	—	—	—

2020 Year-End Financials
Return on assets: 4.2%   Cash ($ mil.): 29
Return on equity: 11.5%
Current Ratio: 1.10

MAINEHEALTH

Maine Medical Center (MMC) is the flagship hospital of MaineHealth, which is an integrated health network comprising a dozen local hospital and other health facilities that touch central, southern, and western Maine and eastern New Hampshire. MMC is a not-for-profit medical center consists of a tertiary care community hospital, The Barbara Bush Children's Hospital, and outpatient clinics. Specialty services include cancer care, geriatrics, emergency medicine, cardiovascular care, rehabilitation, neurology, orthopedics, and women's health. Through its partnership with the Tufts University School of Medicine, the 640-bed teaching hospital provides a variety of medical education and training programs. MMC also conducts research through the Maine Medical Center Research Institute. The medical center was founded in 1874.

Operations

MMC boasts a large, ever-expanding outpatient segment that provides day surgery, cardiac catheterization, laboratory services, and rehabilitation services. It also operates about 20 inpatient and outpatient clinics. MMC provides preventive and consultation services, including the MMC Pre-Operative Readiness Education Program ? Preadmission Testing Unit, MMC Wound Healing & Hyperbarics and NorDx laboratory services.

The medical center is one of the largest employers in its service territory, with a workforce of some 9,600. Its Maine Medical Partners is a group of primary care and specialty medical practices. Its The Barbara Bush Children's Hospital is a full-service children's hospital with some 115 beds. MMC also provides more than 20% of charity care for uninsured or underinsured patients in the state.

Geographic Reach

Located in Portland, the MMC serves the northern New England area.

EXECUTIVES

CIO, Daniel Nigrin
Auditors : KPMG LLP BOSTON MA

LOCATIONS

HQ: MAINEHEALTH
  22 BRAMHALL ST, PORTLAND, ME 041023134
Phone: 207 662-0111
Web: WWW.MAINEHEALTH.ORG

PRODUCTS/OPERATIONS

Selected Specialty Centers
Cancer Institute
Cardiovascular Institute
Emergency Medicine
Family Birth Center
Joint Replacement Center
Neuroscience Institute
The Barbara Bush Children's Hospital

COMPETITORS

CENTRAL SUFFOLK HOSPITAL
CENTRASTATE HEALTHCARE SYSTEM INC
FLAGSTAFF MEDICAL CENTER, INC.
HCA-HEALTHONE LLC
KINGSBROOK JEWISH MEDICAL CENTER
LEHIGH VALLEY HEALTH NETWORK, INC.
LONG BEACH MEDICAL CENTER
RARITAN BAY MEDICAL CENTER, A NEW JERSEY NONPROFIT CORPORATION
UNITED REGIONAL HEALTH CARE SYSTEM, INC.
YORK HOSPITAL

HISTORICAL FINANCIALS

Company Type: Private

Income Statement — FYE: September 30

	REVENUE ($mil)	NET INCOME ($mil)	NET PROFIT MARGIN	EMPLOYEES
09/21	3,451	492	14.3%	2,000
09/20	2,884	283	9.8%	—
09/19	2,717	5	0.2%	—
09/18	2,523	205	8.2%	—
Annual Growth	11.0%	33.8%	—	—

2021 Year-End Financials
Return on assets: 10.6%   Cash ($ mil.): 435
Return on equity: 19.4%
Current Ratio: 3.10

MANAGEMENT & TRAINING CORPORATION

Management & Training Corporation (MTC) prepares prison inmates for re-entry into society. It provides a variety of academic, vocational, and social-skills training in rehabilitation-oriented private prisons. Its holistic education model offers programs to help inmates avoid substance abuse as they also boost their engagement in community service, find work, and increase their cognitive skills. As part of its services, MTC operates about 25 Job Corps centers, more than 20 correctional facilities, nearly 15 prison and detention medical departments, some five detention centers, and two workforce development sites around the world.

Operations

MTC operates through four divisions: Correctional, Education & Training, MTC Medical, and Economic & Social Development. It currently educates and trains more than 14,000 students, provides safe and secure rehabilitation and transition services to nearly 29,000 residents and detainees, and provides healthcare to more than 16,000 residents and detainees.

The company's MTC Medical unit provides vital healthcare and wellness services to people at its correctional facilities and detention centers. It is comprised of doctors, nurses, and other healthcare professionals, and provides approximately 47,450 dental evaluations and services to promote proper dental hygiene. It conducts some 37,160 comprehensive mental health visits to provide appropriate services and about 53,060 physicals performed to promote overall health and wellness. Its Economic & Social Development division provides training in entrepreneurship and innovation to more than 20,740 technical school students.

Geographic Reach

The company's main offices are located in Centerville, Utah, and has regional office in Texas and Washington, DC. MTC operates correctional facility contracts in Arizona, Florida, Idaho, Ohio, Mississippi, and Texas. It also operates two international corrections in Rainsbrook Secure Training Centre (in the UK) and Parklea Correctional Centre in Australia.

Sales and Marketing

MTC clients including the Federal Bureau of Prisons, Immigration & Customs Enforcement, US Marshals Service, and state departments of corrections. It also provided workforce training to USAID, the World Bank, the United Nations, regional development banks, and national governments.

Company Background

MRC was founded in 1981.

EXECUTIVES

Vice Chairman*, Jane Marquardt
TRAINING PROGRAMS*, Jeffrey Barton
Auditors : KPMG LLP PORTLAND OREGON

LOCATIONS

HQ: MANAGEMENT & TRAINING CORPORATION
  500 N MARKET PLACE DR # 100, CENTERVILLE, UT 840141711
Phone: 801 693-2600
Web: WWW.MTCTRAINS.COM

PRODUCTS/OPERATIONS

Selected Services
Communicate through formal and informal channels
Develop custom training for students, clients & offenders
Manage facilities
Provide community connections
Provide data solutions

COMPETITORS

AVALON CORRECTIONAL SERVICES, INC.
COMMUNITY EDUCATION CENTERS, INC.
G4S SECURE SOLUTIONS (USA) INC.
HEALTH CARE CORPORATION OF AMERICA
J H M RESEARCH & DEVELOPMENT INC
L&M TECHNOLOGIES, INC.
MHM SERVICES, INC.
NORTH WIND PORTAGE, INC.
STG INTERNATIONAL, INC.
U.S. HEALTHWORKS, INC.

HISTORICAL FINANCIALS

Company Type: Private

Income Statement — FYE: December 31

	REVENUE ($mil)	NET INCOME ($mil)	NET PROFIT MARGIN	EMPLOYEES
12/21	857	59	6.9%	9,500
12/20	907	54	6.0%	—
12/15	753	30	4.0%	—
12/13	735	50	6.9%	—
Annual Growth	1.9%	2.0%	—	—

2021 Year-End Financials
Return on assets: 17.0%   Cash ($ mil.): 53
Return on equity: 26.0%
Current Ratio: 2.30

MANAGEMENT-ILA MANAGED HEALTH CARE TRUST FUND

Auditors : DESENA & COMPANY CPAS EAST HA

LOCATIONS

HQ: MANAGEMENT-ILA MANAGED HEALTH CARE TRUST FUND
  111 BROADWAY FL 5, NEW YORK, NY 100062021
Phone: 212 766-5700
Web: WWW.MILAMHCTF.COM

HISTORICAL FINANCIALS

Company Type: Private

Income Statement — FYE: December 31

	REVENUE ($mil)	NET INCOME ($mil)	NET PROFIT MARGIN	EMPLOYEES
12/17	675	64	9.6%	3
12/14	492	(39)	—	—
12/13	491	24	5.0%	—
Annual Growth	8.3%	27.3%	—	—

2017 Year-End Financials
Return on assets: 6.9%   Cash ($ mil.): 28
Return on equity: 7.5%
Current Ratio: 1.90

MANN+HUMMEL FILTRATION TECHNOLOGY INTERMEDIATE HOLDINGS INC.

Affinia Group Intermediate Holdings caters to car drivers with a natural affinity for parts. The company is a leading designer, manufacturer, and distributor of aftermarket vehicular components. Affinia's slew of products -- primarily oil and air filters, ball joints, idler arms, steering components, and suspension parts -- are made for passenger cars; SUVs; light, medium, and heavy trucks; and off-highway vehicles. Its well-known brand names, including McQuay-Norris, Nakata, ecoLAST, Raybestos, and WIX, are sold in 70 countries. It primarily serves the US and South American markets.

Geographic Reach

Affinia has operations in North and South America, Europe, and Asia spanning nearly 12 countries. It manufactures and distributes products in 11 countries and sells into more than 70 countries. The US accounts for 42% of the company's sales; Brazil is its second-largest market, generating 30%.

Sales and Marketing

Affinia's largest customers include aftermarket distributors NAPA (22% of total sales) and CARQUEST (6%). Other customers include AutoZone , O'Reilly Auto Parts, and Canadian Tire . The company derived 97% of its 2013 net sales from the on and off-highway replacement products and services industry.

Financial Performance

The company saw its revenues jump 8% from 2012 to 2013. The growth for 2013 was driven by a 9% increase in its filtration segment due to increased sales in its North American and Asia operations driven by increased volume as a result of market growth and new business with existing customers. European sales increased in 2013 due to higher sales in Poland along with favorable currency translation effects in Poland. Increased Venezuela filter sales were the main contributor to the increase in South America sales.

Affinia posted net income of $10 million in 2013 after posting net losses in 2011 and 2012. The positive net income for 2013 was attributed to the absence of losses from discontinued operations, as opposed to other years.

Strategy

With the sale of its Brake North America and Asia group in 2012, and the announced signing of an agreement to sell its Chassis group in 2014, the company is focused on operating strictly as a Filtration segment and Affinia South America segment company. (Affinia agreed to sell its chassis operations to Federal-Mogul in January 2014.)

Company Background

Affinia got its start in 2004. Private-equity firm Cypress and OMERS (Ontario Municipal Employees Retirement System), a Canadian pension fund, bought the auto replacement parts business of Dana Holding Corporation to form Affinia. In mid-2010 Affinia filed to go public, but remains privately owned.

EXECUTIVES

CIO, Karl J Westrick
Senior Vice President Human Resources, Kay Teixeira
Auditors : DELOITTE & TOUCHE LLP CHARLOT

LOCATIONS

HQ: MANN+HUMMEL FILTRATION TECHNOLOGY INTERMEDIATE HOLDINGS INC.
1 WIX WAY, GASTONIA, NC 280546142
Phone: 704 869-3300
Web: WWW.WIXFILTERS.COM

COMPETITORS

ALLISON TRANSMISSION HOLDINGS, INC.
AUTOLIV, INC.
LEAR CORPORATION
MOTORCAR PARTS OF AMERICA, INC.
WABCO HOLDINGS INC.

HISTORICAL FINANCIALS
Company Type: Private

Income Statement — FYE: December 31

	REVENUE ($mil)	NET INCOME ($mil)	NET PROFIT MARGIN	EMPLOYEES
12/15	899	(71)	—	5,574
12/14	1,396	82	5.9%	—
12/13	1,361	10	0.7%	—
12/12	1,453	(102)	—	—
Annual Growth	(14.8%)	—	—	—

2015 Year-End Financials
Return on assets: (-12.2%)   Cash ($ mil.): 28
Return on equity: —
Current Ratio: 0.90

MAP INTERNATIONAL

Auditors : BATTS MORRISON WALES & LEE PA

LOCATIONS

HQ: MAP INTERNATIONAL
4700 GLYNCO PKWY, BRUNSWICK, GA 315256901
Phone: 800 225-8750
Web: WWW.MAP.ORG

MARICOPA COUNTY SPECIAL HEALTH CARE DISTRICT

EXECUTIVES

Chief Human Resources Officer*, Jenny Marchiniak

LOCATIONS

HQ: MARICOPA COUNTY SPECIAL HEALTH CARE DISTRICT
2601 E ROOSEVELT ST, PHOENIX, AZ 850084973
Phone: 602 344-5011
Web: WWW.VALLEYWISEHEALTH.ORG

HISTORICAL FINANCIALS
Company Type: Private

Income Statement — FYE: June 30

	REVENUE ($mil)	NET INCOME ($mil)	NET PROFIT MARGIN	EMPLOYEES
06/20	548	19	3.6%	4,000
06/19	507	51	10.1%	—
06/18	510	93	18.3%	—
Annual Growth	3.7%	(54.0%)	—	—

2020 Year-End Financials
Return on assets: 1.5%   Cash ($ mil.): 210
Return on equity: 7.1%
Current Ratio: 3.00

HISTORICAL FINANCIALS
Company Type: Private

Income Statement — FYE: September 30

	REVENUE ($mil)	NET INCOME ($mil)	NET PROFIT MARGIN	EMPLOYEES
09/20	588	(129)	—	200
09/19	590	28	4.8%	—
09/18	575	11	2.1%	—
09/17	598	(40)	—	—
Annual Growth	(0.6%)	—	—	—

2020 Year-End Financials
Return on assets: (-131.5%)   Cash ($ mil.): 3
Return on equity: (-132.9%)
Current Ratio: 105.90

MARINA DISTRICT DEVELOPMENT COMPANY, LLC

LOCATIONS

HQ: MARINA DISTRICT DEVELOPMENT COMPANY, LLC
1 BORGATA WAY, ATLANTIC CITY, NJ 084011946

Phone: 609 317-1000
Web: BORGATA.MGMRESORTS.COM

HISTORICAL FINANCIALS
Company Type: Private

Income Statement   FYE: December 31

	REVENUE ($mil)	NET INCOME ($mil)	NET PROFIT MARGIN	EMPLOYEES
12/10	738	44	6.0%	7,000
12/09	777	108	13.9%	—
12/08	830	83	10.0%	—
Annual Growth	(5.7%)	(27.1%)	—	—

2010 Year-End Financials
Return on assets: 3.1%   Cash ($ mil.): 42
Return on equity: 9.6%
Current Ratio: 0.80

MARQUETTE UNIVERSITY

A member of the Association of Jesuit Colleges and Universities, Marquette University provides undergraduate, graduate, and professional courses and programs. It specializes in business, engineering, arts and sciences, nursing, law, dentistry, and other fields. The university offers undergraduates some 75 majors and 65 minors and postgraduate students about 50 doctoral and master's degree programs. With an enrollment of more than 11,700 students, Marquette University boasts a student/faculty ratio of 14:1. Its student population consists of students from all 50 US states and nearly 70 countries. Founded in 1881, the university is named after French missionary explorer Father Jacques Marquette.

Operations
Marquette University, an independent, coeducational, and not-for-profit institution of higher learning and research, consists of a dozen separate colleges and schools.

Geographic Reach
Based in Milwaukee, Wisconsin, the Marquette University campus attracts students across the nation and from nearly 70 countries worldwide.

Financial Performance
The educational institution logged a marginal 1% increase in revenue in fiscal 2012 as compared to 2011 due to rising tuition and fees, contributions, government and private grants, and endowment income used in operations. Net income during the same reporting period dropped some 90%, thanks to increases in operating expenses and declines in endowment gains in excess of the amount designated for current operations (net other).

Strategy
To boost its healthcare presence, the Marquette University College of Nursing opened the Wheaton Franciscan Healthcare Center for Clinical Simulation in late 2012. The facility features a six-bed hospital suite with a pair of intensive care rooms, two medical surgical rooms, one pediatrics room, and one labor and delivery suite.

Auditors: KPMG LLP MILWAUKEE WI

LOCATIONS
HQ: MARQUETTE UNIVERSITY
1250 W WISCONSIN AVE, MILWAUKEE, WI 532332225
Phone: 414 288-7250
Web: WWW.MARQUETTE.EDU

PRODUCTS/OPERATIONS
Selected Schools and Colleges
College of Business Administration
College of Education
College of Engineering
College of Health Sciences
College of Nursing
College of Professional Studies
Graduate School
Graduate School of Management
Helen Way Klingler College of Arts and Sciences
J. William and Mary Diederich College of Communications
Law School
School of Dentistry

COMPETITORS
DESALES UNIVERSITY
FAIRFIELD UNIVERSITY
MISSOURI STATE UNIVERSITY
RECTOR & VISITORS OF THE UNIVERSITY OF VIRGINIA
THE COLLEGE OF WILLIAM & MARY

HISTORICAL FINANCIALS
Company Type: Private

Income Statement   FYE: June 30

	REVENUE ($mil)	NET INCOME ($mil)	NET PROFIT MARGIN	EMPLOYEES
06/20	679	53	7.9%	3,000
06/18	463	57	12.4%	—
06/17	434	67	15.4%	—
06/15	548	48	8.8%	—
Annual Growth	4.4%	2.2%	—	—

2020 Year-End Financials
Return on assets: 3.2%   Cash ($ mil.): 211
Return on equity: 4.7%
Current Ratio: 0.90

MARSHFIELD CLINIC, INC.

Marshfield Clinic is a private group medical practice that operates more than 50 medical locations across Wisconsin. The network provides primary and tertiary care through its more than 700 physicians who represent about 80 medical specialties. Through two hospitals -- the 25-bed Flambeau Hospital and the 40-bed Lakeview Medical Center -- and dozens of clinics Marshfield annually serves roughly 380,000 patients and handles 3.8 million patient encounters. Other parts of the network include Marshfield Laboratories and Security Health Plan of Wisconsin, as well as medical education and research organizations.

Operations
Marshfield Clinic's Security Health Plan of Wisconsin provides a variety of health insurance options to more than 200,000 members in much of central, northern, and western Wisconsin. The Marshfield Clinic organization also includes Marshfield Labs, one of the largest private practice full-service laboratory systems in the nation conducting more than 25 million tests annually.

Flambeau Hospital is a 25-bed, Critical Access Hospital and provides 24-hour care for inpatient and outpatient services, emergency ambulance services, and home health & hospice service. Flambeau Hospital is jointly sponsored by Ministry Health Care and Marshfield Clinic.

Lakeview Medical Center is a 40-bed, nonprofit community hospital and provides 24-hour care for inpatient and outpatient services and emergency ambulance services. Lakeview Medical Center integrates modern design and technology with a calm, healing environment.

Marshfield Clinic runs about 50 general and specialty medical clinics and dental offices in its service territory. It also has an outreach services program that collaborates with 1,200 medical sites to provide care in surrounding regions.

The Marshfield Clinic Education Foundation programs for medical school graduates are internal medicine, pediatrics, dermatology, and surgery. The company's research division, Marshfield Clinic Research Foundation, focuses on clinical research, health and safety, human genetics, epidemiology, and biomedical informatics.

Geographic Reach
Marshfield Clinic operates about 50 clinic locations and two hospitals in central, western, and northern Wisconsin. Its main hospital campuses are located in Park Falls and Rice Lake.

Sales and Marketing
Features of the Security Health Plan include contacting members through reminder mailings and personal phone calls to aid with their health maintenance. Additionally, affiliated home health nurses visit members at home or in the hospital to answer their questions about their medications or care and to provide needed resources for their recuperation.

Strategy
In 2015 CareCloud and Marshfield Clinic Information Services, a healthcare IT company established from within the Marshfield Clinic, announced a partnership to deliver a joint, cloud-based solution to help improve the clinical, financial, and administrative outcomes of large ambulatory

medical practices. The two parties have joined together MCIS' clinical solutions - including a physician-designed electronic health record (EHR), patient portal, and population health management tool, with CareCloud's practice management and medical billing software and services. The integrated solution, which also includes unified customer implementation and support, is optimized for the requirements of large practices across dozens of specialties. MCIS has collaborated with Marshfield Clinic to build a physician-designed, cloud-based clinical solution that reflects our successful experiences supporting a renowned multi-specialty group of more than 700 physicians.

Marshfield Clinic has a rich history in health information technology and software development. The Clinic has used a computer-based electronic health record for more than 20 years. Cattails Software Suite, Marshfield Clinic's homegrown electronic health record, was developed in conjunction with Clinic providers and the Information Systems Department. Cattails Software Suite played a significant role in the Clinic's success in the Centers for Medicare and Medicaid Services' Physician Group Practice project. Marshfield Clinic improved patient care while lowering health care costs during the five-year project - saving the Medicare program more than $118 million.

In 2015 the company expanded outpatient services provided in the Ambulatory Surgery Center in Marshfield, adding skilled nursing care in the East Wing of its Marshfield campus. Similar plans to lower the total cost of care have been designed for all of its mission-critical centers.

The second phase of the plan includes construction of a new hospital of the future in Marshfield. A smaller, more smartly-designed and more energy efficient high-tech facility will allow for highly-specialized care that requires a hospital setting.

The organization also advances its patient care through a collaboration with Cleveland Clinic. Together, the organizations conduct research and development programs on new medical innovations.

Company Background

Marshfield Clinic announced the formation of a new subsidiary, Marshfield Clinic Information Services, in 2013. The unit will use the organizations health IT expertise to help other care providers implement electronic health record (EHR) systems and other population health management software programs and services.

The clinic was founded in 1916.

Auditors : KPMG LLP MINNEAPOLIS MN

LOCATIONS

HQ: MARSHFIELD CLINIC, INC.
 1000 N OAK AVE, MARSHFIELD, WI 544495702
Phone: 715 387-5511
Web: WWW.MARSHFIELDCLINIC.ORG

COMPETITORS

ATRIUS HEALTH, INC.
AULTMAN HEALTH FOUNDATION
BILLINGS CLINIC
GREENWICH PERINATOLOGY SERVICES, P.C.
PARK NICOLLET HEALTH SERVICES

HISTORICAL FINANCIALS
Company Type: Private

Income Statement — FYE: September 30

	REVENUE ($mil)	NET INCOME ($mil)	NET PROFIT MARGIN	EMPLOYEES
09/15	1,211	24	2.0%	363
09/09	1,062	78	7.4%	—
09/08*	102	6	5.9%	—
06/06	813	23	2.9%	—
Annual Growth	4.5%	0.5%	—	—

*Fiscal year change

2015 Year-End Financials
Return on assets: 2.3% Cash ($ mil.): 96
Return on equity: 4.5%
Current Ratio: 0.70

MARTIN MEMORIAL MEDICAL CENTER, INC.

LOCATIONS

HQ: MARTIN MEMORIAL MEDICAL CENTER, INC.
 200 SE HOSPITAL AVE, STUART, FL 349942346
Phone: 772 287-5200
Web: WWW.MARTINHEALTH.ORG

HISTORICAL FINANCIALS
Company Type: Private

Income Statement — FYE: September 30

	REVENUE ($mil)	NET INCOME ($mil)	NET PROFIT MARGIN	EMPLOYEES
09/19	599	31	5.2%	2,972
09/18	506	20	4.0%	—
09/17	490	26	5.3%	—
09/14	910	545	59.9%	—
Annual Growth	(8.0%)	(43.6%)	—	—

2019 Year-End Financials
Return on assets: 4.5% Cash ($ mil.): 23
Return on equity: 11.2%
Current Ratio: 0.30

MARTIN PRODUCT SALES LLC

LOCATIONS

HQ: MARTIN PRODUCT SALES LLC
 4200 STONE RD, KILGORE, TX 756626935
Phone: 903 983-6200

HISTORICAL FINANCIALS
Company Type: Private

Income Statement — FYE: December 31

	REVENUE ($mil)	NET INCOME ($mil)	NET PROFIT MARGIN	EMPLOYEES
12/07	1,204	8	0.7%	206
12/02*	156	1	0.7%	—
06/01	260	3	1.4%	—
06/99	132	0	0.2%	—
Annual Growth	27.8%	46.7%	—	—

*Fiscal year change

2007 Year-End Financials
Return on assets: 2.0% Cash ($ mil.): 5
Return on equity: 21.2%
Current Ratio: 1.80

MARTIN RESOURCE MANAGEMENT CORPORATION

Martin Resource Management likes to push around petroleum products. The employee-owned company's flagship affiliate, Martin Midstream Partners, offers transportation, storage, marketing, and logistics management services for petroleum products, including sulfur, sulfur derivatives, fuel oil, liquefied petroleum gas, asphalt and other bulk tank liquids, primarily in the southern US. Martin Resource also manufactures and markets fertilizer and other processed sulfur products. Through its Martin Energy Services unit the company offers inland marine fuel supply and offshore support services. Other units include The Brimrock Group (sulfur), Cross Oil Refining & Marketing, and Martin Asphalt.

Operations

Each year the company markets more than 250 million gallons of diesel fuel and lubricants along the Gulf Coast and 1.5 million barrels of naphthenic lubricants and base oils across the US. In addition, Martin Resource also provides surface transportation services for products such as molten sulfur, sulfuric acid, fuel oil, natural gas liquids (NGLs), asphalt, paper mill liquids, and other bulk tank liquids.

The company's more than $550 million of assets include a fleet of truck trailers and tractors. Its Martin Transport subsidiary has about 25 terminals in the Southeast and Southern US, with more than 850 trucks and 1,200 trailers. Martin Product Sales LLC markets and distributes petroleum-based products including asphalt, fuel oil, and sulfuric acid.

Martin Resource owns a 28.0% limited

partnership interest and a 2% general partnership interest in its flagship operating company Martin Midstream Partners. Its Martin Energy Services subsidiary offers marine fuel supply and offshore support services.

Sales and Marketing
The company's customers include agriculture, petrochemical, petroleum, and utility companies.

Strategy
Martin Resource markets oil and gas and by-products through facilities located throughout the Gulf Coast region. It acquires other companies or forms joint ventures to develop its portfolio. It also redistributes operating assets to its major subsidiaries to improve their performance.

In 2013 Canadian subsidiary Brimrock signed an engineering service agreement with Keyera to act as the engineering management and technology provider for Keyera's planned sulphur forming and materials handling facilities upgrade.

That year Martin Resource sold a 49% voting interest in MMGP Holdings LLC, a newly-formed sole member of Martin Midstream GP LLC, the general partner of Martin Midstream Partners to Alinda Capital Partners.

In 2012 Martin Midstream Partners also sold its East Texas and Northwest Louisiana natural gas gathering and processing assets to CenterPoint Energy Field Services for $275 million.

Streamlining its businesses, in 2012 the company formed Martin Energy Services LLC, combining the entities of Midstream Fuel Service LLC, L & L Oil and Gas Services L.L.C., and PEPCO into one entity for improved service and growth.

Mergers and Acquisitions
In 2013 Martin Midstream Partners' subsidiary Martin Operating Partnership L.P bought Kansas City, Missouri-based NL Grease, LLC, a grease manufacturer that specializes in private-label packaging of commercial and industrial greases.

Boosting its NGL handling capabilities, that year Martin Midstream Partners purchased six liquefied petroleum gas pressure barges and two commercial push boats from affiliates of Florida Marine Transporters for $51 million.

In 2012 Martin Midstream Partners acquired Gulf Coast fuels and lubricants provider Talen's Marine & Fuel, LLC. The transactions boosted the company's marine terminal infrastructure, adding ten marine terminals between Houston/Galveston, and Port Fourchon, in Louisiana with total tankage of 300,000 barrels and an additional 4,000 feet of water-accessible bulkhead.

In 2012 Martin Midstream Partners bought the remaining equity interests in Redbird Gas Storage LLC for $150 million. (In 2011 Martin Resource and Martin Midstream Partners formed the Redbird Gas Storage natural gas storage joint venture to invest in Cardinal Gas Storage Partners, a joint venture between Redbird and Energy Capital Partners focused on the development of natural gas storage facilities across North America).

Company Background
The acquisition of L & L Oil and Gas L.L.C. by Midstream Fuel Service in 2011 increased Martin Resources' capability along the U.S. Gulf Coast to 31 facilities for offshore fuels, lubricants, and logistical services, including land based commercial and industrial fuels and lubricants.

In 2011 Martin Resource and Martin Midstream Partners formed the Redbird Gas Storage natural gas storage joint venture to invest in Cardinal Gas Storage Partners. Cardinal is a joint venture between Redbird and Energy Capital Partners that is focused on the development, construction, operation and management of natural gas storage facilities across North America.

To raise cash and boost the Martin Midstream Partners' storage segment, in 2011 Martin Resource sold 13 terminals to that unit for $36.5 million.

Founded in 1951 by R. S. Martin Jr., Martin Resource also holds a stake in Ican Energy, an LPG distributor. To raise cash and increase its financial flexibility, in 2002 the company spun off a portion of its assets.

Auditors : KPMG LLP DALLAS TEXAS

LOCATIONS
HQ: MARTIN RESOURCE MANAGEMENT CORPORATION
4200 STONE RD, KILGORE, TX 756626935
Phone: 903 983-6200

PRODUCTS/OPERATIONS
Selected Companies
Altec Environmental Consulting
Commercial & Industrial Fuels & Lubricants
Commercial & Industrial Tanks & Equipment
Cross Oil Refining & Marketing, Inc.
Marine Lubricants & Specialty Products
Martin Crude Marketing Company
Martin Energy Services LLC
Martin Product Sales LLC
Martin Transport, Inc
Roddey engineering services, Inc.

COMPETITORS
DELEK US HOLDINGS, INC.
ENTERPRISE PRODUCTS PARTNERS L.P.
ERGON, INC.
HOLLYFRONTIER CORPORATION
IDEMITSU KOSAN CO.,LTD.
MARTIN MIDSTREAM PARTNERS L.P.
NORTHERN TIER ENERGY LP
Suncor Energy Inc
TRANSMONTAIGNE PARTNERS LLC
WESTERN REFINING, INC.

HISTORICAL FINANCIALS
Company Type: Private

Income Statement — FYE: December 31

	REVENUE ($mil)	NET INCOME ($mil)	NET PROFIT MARGIN	EMPLOYEES
12/15	2,493	27	1.1%	2,300
12/11	2,985	37	1.3%	—
12/09	1,537	23	1.5%	—
12/08	2,903	5	0.2%	—
Annual Growth	(2.1%)	24.9%	—	—

2015 Year-End Financials
Return on assets: 1.5%   Cash ($ mil.): 13
Return on equity: 6.9%
Current Ratio: 1.80

MARTIN'S POINT HEALTH CARE, INC.

Auditors : BAKER NEWMAN & NOYES PORTLAND

LOCATIONS
HQ: MARTIN'S POINT HEALTH CARE, INC.
331 VERANDA ST STE 1, PORTLAND, ME 041035544
Phone: 207 774-5801
Web: WWW.MARTINSPOINT.ORG

HISTORICAL FINANCIALS
Company Type: Private

Income Statement — FYE: December 31

	ASSETS ($mil)	NET INCOME ($mil)	INCOME AS % OF ASSETS	EMPLOYEES
12/16	386	17	4.6%	839
12/14	351	3	1.0%	—
12/13	345	10	3.0%	—
12/09	247	30	12.2%	—
Annual Growth	6.6%	(7.2%)	—	—

2016 Year-End Financials
Return on assets: 4.6%   Cash ($ mil.): 36
Return on equity: 6.6%
Current Ratio: 3.30

MARYLAND AND VIRGINIA MILK PRODUCERS COOPERATIVE ASSOCIATION, INCORPORATED

Milk is "Mar-VA-lous" for the members of the Maryland & Virginia Milk Producers Cooperative Association. Known as Maryland

& Virginia, the co-op processes and sells milk for nearly 1,500 member/farmers with dairy herds in the southeastern US and mid-Atlantic region. Maryland & Virginia produces fluid milk, ice cream, and cultured dairy products for retail sale under the Marva Maid, Maola, and Valley Milk brands. Its butter, condensed milk, and milk-powder products are sold primarily to food manufacturers. As a co-op, it also offers agricultural supplies to its members. Maryland & Virginia operates three fluid-milk processing plants, a manufacturing plant, and an equipment-supply warehouse.

Operations

Maryland & Virginia operates three fluid processing plants, a single manufacturing plant, and a farm supply equipment division. It also owns a majority stake in Valley Milk LLC. The co-op transports more than 300 tanker truckloads of milk daily to nearly 30 different plants. Member farms range in size from fewer than 100 cows to more than 2,000. Combined, Maryland & Virginia members produce three billion pounds of milk annually.

Geographic Reach

The co-op gets its milk from member farmers in Delaware, Florida, Georgia, Kentucky, Maryland, North Carolina, Ohio, Pennsylvania, South Carolina, Tennessee, Virginia, and West Virginia. Its fluid processing plants are located in Newport News, Virginia; Landover, Maryland; and New Bern, North Carolina. It has manufacturing facilities in Laurel, Maryland, and Strasburg, Virginia, and a warehouse in Frederick, Maryland.

Sales and Marketing

In addition to supermarkets, the co-op counts customers such as Walgreens, Starbucks, Sheetz convenience stores, and Dairy Queen among its customers.

Financial Performance

The co-op's revenue decreased by 5% to $1.3 billion in 2012 versus $1.4 billion in 2011, due to a decline in milk, dairy, and other products as well as sales of equipment and supplies, partially offset by an increase in sales of its members' and nonmembers' raw milk. Despite the decline in sales, the Maryland & Virginia reported a profit of $5.5 million in 2012, versus a loss of $2.8 million the prior year. Like other milk producers, Maryland & Virginia has been contending with sluggish milk sales due to decreasing milk consumption beginning in the 1970s.

EXECUTIVES

Corporate Secretary*, Barbara Campbell
Auditors : HERLIEM & COMPANY INC READING

LOCATIONS

HQ: MARYLAND AND VIRGINIA MILK PRODUCERS COOPERATIVE ASSOCIATION, INCORPORATED
 1985 ISAAC NEWTON SQ W, RESTON, VA 201905031
Phone: 703 742-6800

Web: WWW.MDVAMILK.COM

COMPETITORS

Agropur Cooperative
COOPERATIVE REGIONS OF ORGANIC PRODUCER POOLS
D/L COOPERATIVE INC.
DALE FARM CO-OPERATIVE LIMITED
MAYFIELD DAIRY FARMS, LLC
MICHIGAN MILK PRODUCERS ASSOCIATION
MULLER DAIRY (U.K.) LIMITED
NATIONAL DAIRY, LLC
PRAIRIE FARMS DAIRY, INC.
SWISS VALLEY FARMS COOPERATIVE

HISTORICAL FINANCIALS
Company Type: Private

Income Statement — FYE: December 31

	REVENUE ($mil)	NET INCOME ($mil)	NET PROFIT MARGIN	EMPLOYEES
12/12	1,296	5	0.4%	550
12/11	1,362	(2)	—	—
12/10	1,219	8	0.7%	—
Annual Growth	3.1%	(20.4%)	—	—

2012 Year-End Financials
Return on assets: 3.4% Cash ($ mil.): —
Return on equity: 14.9%
Current Ratio: 0.80

MARYLAND DEPARTMENT OF TRANSPORTATION

Traveling in Maryland? You can thank (or curse) the Maryland Department of Transportation (MDOT). MDOT is responsible for building, operating, and maintaining a safe and seamless transportation network that includes highway, transit, maritime, and aviation facilities. TheÂ Department of Transportation is organized along various administrative groups including the Maryland Motor Vehicle Administration, Transit Administration, Port Administration, Aviation Administration, and Highway Administration. MDOT annual budget of about $1.5 billion is funded through the state's Transportation Trust Fund and federal aid.

Auditors : CLIFTONLARSONALLEN LLP BALTI

LOCATIONS

HQ: MARYLAND DEPARTMENT OF TRANSPORTATION
 7201 CORPORATE CENTER DR, HANOVER, MD 210761415
Phone: 410 865-1037
Web: MDOT.MARYLAND.GOV

COMPETITORS

AMERICAN SERVICES TECHNOLOGY, INC.
APPALACHIAN REGIONAL COMMISSION
ARCADIS U.S., INC.
S C & A, INC.
THE SHIPLEY GROUP INC

HISTORICAL FINANCIALS
Company Type: Private

Income Statement — FYE: June 30

	REVENUE ($mil)	NET INCOME ($mil)	NET PROFIT MARGIN	EMPLOYEES
06/21	5,058	232	4.6%	1,000
06/20	4,791	(210)	—	—
06/19	4,609	229	5.0%	—
06/18	4,407	(189)	—	—
Annual Growth	4.7%	—	—	—

2021 Year-End Financials
Return on assets: 1.0% Cash ($ mil.): —
Return on equity: 1.5%
Current Ratio: —

MARYLAND TRANSPORTATION AUTHORITY

LOCATIONS

HQ: MARYLAND TRANSPORTATION AUTHORITY
 2310 BROENING HWY STE 150, BALTIMORE, MD 212246673
Phone: 410 537-7833
Web: MDTA.MARYLAND.GOV

HISTORICAL FINANCIALS
Company Type: Private

Income Statement — FYE: June 30

	REVENUE ($mil)	NET INCOME ($mil)	NET PROFIT MARGIN	EMPLOYEES
06/21	727	118	16.3%	77
06/20	733	210	28.7%	—
06/19	862	321	37.2%	—
06/18	862	309	35.9%	—
Annual Growth	(5.5%)	(27.4%)	—	—

2021 Year-End Financials
Return on assets: 1.4% Cash ($ mil.): 118
Return on equity: 2.3%
Current Ratio: 2.70

MASHANTUCKET PEQUOT GAMING ENTERPRISE INC

Auditors : DELOITTE & TOUCHE LLP HARTFO

LOCATIONS

HQ: MASHANTUCKET PEQUOT GAMING ENTERPRISE INC
 350 TROLLEY LINE BLVD, MASHANTUCKET, CT 063383830
Phone: 860 312-3465

HOOVER'S HANDBOOK OF PRIVATE COMPANIES 2023

Web: WWW.FOXWOODSMEETINGSANDEVENTS.COM

HISTORICAL FINANCIALS
Company Type: Private

Income Statement — FYE: September 30

	REVENUE ($mil)	NET INCOME ($mil)	NET PROFIT MARGIN	EMPLOYEES
09/19	787	(40)	—	2
09/18	828	(46)	—	—
Annual Growth	(5.0%)	—	—	—

2019 Year-End Financials
Return on assets: (-5.8%)   Cash ($ mil.): 47
Return on equity: (-7.1%)
Current Ratio: 0.80

MASS GENERAL BRIGHAM INCORPORATED

Mass General Brigham is an integrated academic healthcare system. Mass General Brigham connects a full continuum of care across a system of academic medical centers, community and specialty hospitals, a health insurance plan, physician networks, community health centers, home care, and long-term care services. Mass General Brigham is a non-profit organization that is committed to patient care, research, teaching, and service to the community. In addition, Mass General Brigham is one of the nation's leading biomedical research organizations and a principal teaching affiliate of Harvard Medical School.

Operations
The nearly 15-member institutions encompass a range of health care organizations, including Brigham and Women's Hospital which is comprised of nearly 795 bed teaching hospitals of Harvard Medical School; Brigham and Women's Faulkner Hospital which is comprised of a 171-bed non-profit, community teaching hospital offering complete medical, surgical, and psychiatric care, as well as a full complement of emergency, ambulatory, and diagnostic services; and Martha's Vineyard Hospital is a critical access, not-for-profit, community hospital on the island of Martha's Vineyard.

In addition to its academic medical centers, Mass General also operates COVID-19 vaccination centers, rehabilitation, community health centers, urgent care, and outpatient healthcare centers.

Sales and Marketing
Mass General Brigham serves 1.5 million patients.

Strategy
In late 2021, Mass General Brigham joined with leaders from Kraft Sports + Entertainment to announce Mass General Brigham will now serve as the official sports medicine sponsor of the New England Patriots, New England Revolution and Gillette Stadium. As part of this expanded relationship, Mass General Brigham is opening the Mass General Performance and Research Center at Patriot Place in 2022. Representatives from Mass General Brigham and Kraft Sports + Entertainment gathered at Gillette Stadium on December 15 as part of this announcement.

Company Background
Partners HealthCare was founded in 1994 through the merger of Brigham and Women's Hospital and Massachusetts General Hospital.

EXECUTIVES
Legal Counsel*, Brent L Henry

LOCATIONS
HQ: MASS GENERAL BRIGHAM INCORPORATED
800 BOYLSTON ST STE 1100, BOSTON, MA 021998123
Phone: 617 278-1000
Web: WWW.MASSGENERAL.ORG

PRODUCTS/OPERATIONS
2014 Sales

	$ mil	% of total
Net patient service revenue	7,042.5	65
Premium revenue	1,622.4	15
Direct academic and research	1,225.8	11
Indirect academic and research	353.0	3
Other revenue	662.4	6
Total	10,906.1	100

COMPETITORS
ADVOCATE AURORA HEALTH, INC.
BANNER HEALTH
ENCOMPASS HEALTH CORPORATION
INDIANA UNIVERSITY HEALTH, INC.
NORTHWELL HEALTH, INC.
STANFORD HEALTH CARE
THE CLEVELAND CLINIC FOUNDATION
THE RUTLAND HOSPITAL INC ACT 220
UPMC
WELLMONT HEALTH SYSTEM

HISTORICAL FINANCIALS
Company Type: Private

Income Statement — FYE: September 30

	REVENUE ($mil)	NET INCOME ($mil)	NET PROFIT MARGIN	EMPLOYEES
09/15	11,665	(916)	—	67,000
09/10	8	(0)	—	—
09/08	551	(44)	—	—
Annual Growth	54.7%	—	—	—

2015 Year-End Financials
Return on assets: (-6.1%)   Cash ($ mil.): 621
Return on equity: (-15.1%)
Current Ratio: 2.30

MASSACHUSETTS DEPARTMENT OF TRANSPORTATION

The Massachusetts Department of Transportation (MassDOT) oversees the operations essential for the massive job of moving people and goods throughout the Commonwealth. In 2009 the former Massachusetts Executive Office of Transportation merged with other state agencies to form MassDOT. The unified organization operates in four divisions: highway; transit; aeronautics; and the registry of motor vehicles. In addition to its regulatory responsibility, MassDOT also provides research, planning, and information services relevant to the state's transportation system.

LOCATIONS
HQ: MASSACHUSETTS DEPARTMENT OF TRANSPORTATION
10 PARK PLZ STE 4160, BOSTON, MA 021163979
Phone: 857 368-4636
Web: WWW.MASS.GOV

COMPETITORS
ARKANSAS DEPARTMENT OF TRANSPORTATION
NEW JERSEY DEPT OF TRANSPORTATION
NEW YORK DEPARTMENT OF TRANSPORTATION
TEXAS DEPARTMENT OF TRANSPORTATION
TRANSPORTATION, UNITED STATES DEPARTMENT OF

HISTORICAL FINANCIALS
Company Type: Private

Income Statement — FYE: June 30

	REVENUE ($mil)	NET INCOME ($mil)	NET PROFIT MARGIN	EMPLOYEES
06/21	3,500	13	0.4%	6,100
06/20	3,114	58	1.9%	—
06/18	2,957	1	0.1%	—
06/17	2,984	(107)	—	—
Annual Growth	4.1%	—	—	—

2021 Year-End Financials
Return on assets: —   Cash ($ mil.): 802
Return on equity: —
Current Ratio: 1.50

MASSACHUSETTS HOUSING FINANCE AGENCY

LOCATIONS
HQ: MASSACHUSETTS HOUSING FINANCE AGENCY
1 BEACON ST FL 4, BOSTON, MA 021083132

Phone: 617 854-1000
Web: WWW.MASSHOUSING.COM

HISTORICAL FINANCIALS
Company Type: Private

Income Statement   FYE: June 30

	ASSETS ($mil)	NET INCOME ($mil)	INCOME AS % OF ASSETS	EMPLOYEES
06/22	6,266	(18)	—	325
06/21	6,316	39	0.6%	—
06/20	5,948	149	2.5%	—
06/18	5,460	6	0.1%	—
Annual Growth	3.5%	—	—	—

2022 Year-End Financials
Return on assets: (-0.3%)   Cash ($ mil.): 768
Return on equity: (-1.2%)
Current Ratio: 3.60

MASSACHUSETTS INSTITUTE OF TECHNOLOGY

Massachusetts Institute of Technology (MIT) is an academic community for undergraduate and graduate for education, research, and innovation. MIT is providing its students with an education that combines rigorous academic study and discovery of support of intellectual stimulation of a diverse campus community. MIT has more than 11,250 students from all 50 states and the District of Columbia, three territories, and about 120 foreign nations in the academic year ending 2020-2021. The school's student teacher ratio is 3:1 (undergraduates). Founded in 1865, MIT is integral part of host city Cambridge.

Operations
Research flourishes in its 30 departments across five schools and one college, as well as in dozens of centers, labs, and programs that convene experts across disciplines to explore new intellectual frontiers and attack important societal problems. MIT's on-campus research capabilities are enhanced through the work of MIT Lincoln Laboratory, the Woods Hole Oceanographic Institution, active research relationships with industry, and a wide range of global collaborations. In this work, the MIT Libraries serve as a crucial partner and a source of important research in their own right.

MITx, the Institute's portfolio of massively open online courses, offers flexible access to a range of interactive courses developed and taught by instructors from MIT. Another MIT innovation ? the MicroMasters credential ? is increasingly recognized by industry leaders hiring new talent. And MIT's original digital learning option, OpenCourseWare, continues to offer teachers and learners worldwide the materials for more than 2,450 MIT courses, freely available online.

Geographic Reach
MIT is based in Cambridge, Massachusetts.

Company Background
MIT has some extraordinary alumni who include former chairman of the Federal Reserve Ben Bernanke, former US Representative Pete Stark, former National Economic Council chairman Lawrence H. Summers, and former Council of Economic Advisors chairwoman Christina Romer. Outside of politics MIT alumni founded or co-founded several notable companies, such as Intel, Hewlett-Packard, Texas Instruments, Qualcomm, Bose, and Campbell Soup.

Auditors : PRICEWATERHOUSECOOPERS LLP BO

LOCATIONS
HQ: MASSACHUSETTS INSTITUTE OF TECHNOLOGY
77 MASSACHUSETTS AVE, CAMBRIDGE, MA 021394307
Phone: 617 253-1000
Web: WEB.MIT.EDU

PRODUCTS/OPERATIONS
2014 Sales

	$ mil	% of total
Reseach revenue	1,528.9	49
Support from investment	625.4	20
Tuition and similar revenue	324.5	10
Fee and services	176.3	6
Gifts	162.1	5
Auxiliary enterprises	120.1	4
Other program	117.5	4
Net asset reclassification	69.5	2
Total	3,124.3	100

Schools and Areas of Study
School of Architecture and Planning
    Architecture
    Media Arts and Sciences
    Urban Studies and Planning
School of Engineering
    Aeronautics and Astronautics
    Biological Engineering
    Chemical Engineering
    Civil and Environmental Engineering
    Electrical Engineering and Computer Science
    Engineering Systems Division
    Materials Science and Engineering
    Mechanical Engineering
    Nuclear Science and Engineering
School of Humanities, Arts, and Social Sciences
    Anthropology
    Comparative Media Studies
    Economics
    Foreign Languages and Literatures
    History
    Humanities
    Linguistics and Philosophy
    Literature
    Music and Theater Arts
    Political Science
    Science, Technology, and Society
    Writing and Humanistic Studies
Sloan School of Management
    Management
School of Science
    Biology
    Brain and Cognitive Sciences
    Chemistry
    Earth, Atmospheric, and Planetary Sciences
    Mathematics
    Physics
Whitaker College of Health Sciences and Technology

Harvard-MIT Division of Health Sciences and Technology
MIT-WHOI Joint Program in Oceanography and Applied Ocean Science and Engineering
Degrees Offered
Bachelor of Science (SB)
Master of Architecture (MArch)
Master of Business Administration (MBA)
Master in City Planning (MCP)
Master of Engineering (MEng)
Master of Finance (MFin)
Master of Science (SM)
Engineer (degree designates the field)
Doctor of Philosophy (PhD)
Doctor of Science (ScD)

COMPETITORS
CASE WESTERN RESERVE UNIVERSITY
CLARK ATLANTA UNIVERSITY INC
LONDON SCHOOL OF ECONOMICS & POLITICAL SCIENCE
NORTHEASTERN UNIVERSITY
PURDUE UNIVERSITY
ROCHESTER INSTITUTE OF TECHNOLOGY (INC)
TRUSTEES OF BOSTON UNIVERSITY
UNIVERSITY OF LEICESTER
UNIVERSITY OF NOTTINGHAM (THE)
VIRGINIA POLYTECHNIC INSTITUTE AND STATE UNIVERSITY

HISTORICAL FINANCIALS
Company Type: Private

Income Statement   FYE: June 30

	REVENUE ($mil)	NET INCOME ($mil)	NET PROFIT MARGIN	EMPLOYEES
06/22	4,265	(3,215)	—	12,000
06/21	3,945	12,229	310.0%	—
06/20	3,950	1,447	36.7%	—
06/19	3,931	1,252	31.8%	—
Annual Growth	2.7%	—	—	—

2022 Year-End Financials
Return on assets: (-8.1%)   Cash ($ mil.): 374
Return on equity: (-9.7%)
Current Ratio: —

MASSACHUSETTS PORT AUTHORITY

Massachusetts Port Authority (Massport) operates three airports: Boston Logan International, Hanscom Field, and Worcester Regional. Logan is home to 50 airlines and is New England's largest airport and the first port of call for many international flights entering the US. (It accounts for the majority of Massport's revenues.) Hanscom Field operates as the region's main aviation airport and offers niche commercial services, while Worcester Regional primarily supports commercial flight services. Massport also oversees various waterfront properties of the Port of Boston. The agency was created by the Commonwealth of Massachusetts in 1956. The governor of Massachusetts appoints the agency's board members.

Operations
Massport's business consists of two distinct operating departments: Aviation and

the Port. Logan airport catered to 29.4 million aviation passengers and 369,000 cruise passengers in 2013. Its shipping operations serviced more than 110,000 containers of products at its port.

Financial Performance

Massport's net revenues have steadily climbed over the years. Revenues jumped 2% from $1.78 billion in 2012 to $1.83 billion in 2013 thanks mainly to parking, concession, ground services, and other revenue from nearly 125,000 more passengers at Logan. The overall revenue increase for 2013 was generated by operating revenues exceeding operating expenses by $2.4 million.

EXECUTIVES

CSO*, Harold H Shaw
Auditors : ERNST & YOUNG LLP BOSTON MA

LOCATIONS

HQ: MASSACHUSETTS PORT AUTHORITY
 1 HARBORSIDE DR STE 200, BOSTON, MA 021282905
Phone: 617 561-1600
Web: WWW.MASSPORT.COM

COMPETITORS

AENA S.M.E. SA.
DALLAS/FORT WORTH INTERNATIONAL AIRPORT
METROPOLITAN WASHINGTON AIRPORTS AUTHORITY
SIGNATURE FLIGHT SUPPORT CORPORATION
Swissport International AG

HISTORICAL FINANCIALS
Company Type: Private

Income Statement — FYE: June 30

	REVENUE ($mil)	NET INCOME ($mil)	NET PROFIT MARGIN	EMPLOYEES
06/20	824	104	12.6%	1,102
06/15	662	107	16.2%	—
Annual Growth	4.5%	(0.6%)	—	—

2020 Year-End Financials
Return on assets: 1.8% Cash ($ mil.): 82
Return on equity: 4.1%
Current Ratio: 3.10

MASSACHUSETTS SCHOOL BUILDING AUTHORITY

Auditors : RSM US LLP BOSTON MASSACHUS

LOCATIONS

HQ: MASSACHUSETTS SCHOOL BUILDING AUTHORITY
 40 BROAD ST STE 500, BOSTON, MA 021094371
Phone: 617 720-4466
Web: WWW.MASSSCHOOLBUILDINGS.ORG

MASSACHUSETTS WATER RESOURCES AUTHORITY

Auditors : CLIFTONLARSONALLEN LLP BOSTON

LOCATIONS

HQ: MASSACHUSETTS WATER RESOURCES AUTHORITY
 100 1ST AVE, BOSTON, MA 021292043
Phone: 617 242-6000
Web: MWRA.APPLICANTPRO.COM

HISTORICAL FINANCIALS
Company Type: Private

Income Statement — FYE: June 30

	REVENUE ($mil)	NET INCOME ($mil)	NET PROFIT MARGIN	EMPLOYEES
06/21	1,073	61	5.7%	8
06/19	998	270	27.0%	—
06/18	891	252	28.3%	—
06/17	828	148	17.9%	—
Annual Growth	6.7%	(19.8%)	—	—

2021 Year-End Financials
Return on assets: 3.2% Cash ($ mil.): —
Return on equity: —
Current Ratio: 4.40

HISTORICAL FINANCIALS
Company Type: Private

Income Statement — FYE: June 30

	REVENUE ($mil)	NET INCOME ($mil)	NET PROFIT MARGIN	EMPLOYEES
06/22	811	79	9.7%	1,200
06/21	786	(39)	—	—
06/20	778	(40)	—	—
Annual Growth	2.1%	—	—	—

2022 Year-End Financials
Return on assets: 1.1% Cash ($ mil.): 73
Return on equity: 5.0%
Current Ratio: 2.10

MAXIFACIAL DENTAL SURGERY

Auditors : ERNST & YOUNG US LLP INDIAN

LOCATIONS

HQ: MAXIFACIAL DENTAL SURGERY
 1 MEDICAL CENTER DR, LEBANON, NH 037561000
Phone: 603 650-5000
Web: WWW.HITCHCOCK.ORG

HISTORICAL FINANCIALS
Company Type: Private

Income Statement — FYE: September 30

	REVENUE ($mil)	NET INCOME ($mil)	NET PROFIT MARGIN	EMPLOYEES
09/09	1,147	27	2.4%	7,500
09/06	913	15	1.7%	—
Annual Growth	7.9%	20.7%	—	—

2009 Year-End Financials
Return on assets: 2.3% Cash ($ mil.): 40
Return on equity: 10.6%
Current Ratio: 1.30

MAXIM HEALTHCARE SERVICES, INC.

Maxim Healthcare Services aims to promote good health by offering home health care, as well as immunizations and other wellness services, to clients nationwide. The company offers private duty nursing, skilled nursing, physical rehabilitation, companion care, respite care, and behavioral care for individuals with chronic and acute illnesses and disabilities. It delivers patient care through private duty nursing, at-home behavioral health care and personal caregiving services. While the company specializes in caring for medically-fragile pediatric patients, it is expanding its focus on Applied Behavioral Analysis (ABA) therapy and companion care services, as well as launching technology to enable its nurses to document notes electronically. The company, which operates from more than 150 locations nationwide, was established in 1988.

Operations

Maxim Healthcare Services' LPNs, LVNs, and RNs provide private duty care and treatment for chronic and acute illnesses and disabilities for pediatric and adult patients. Its services include tracheostomy and ventilator management; enteral care and management; seizure management; diabetic management; complex intravenous therapy management; and intermittent skilled nursing and therapy visits. It also offers unskilled in-home care services such as personal care; companion care; respite care; and home health care.

Geographic Reach

Maryland-based, Maxim Healthcare Services has more than 150 offices in about 35 US states.

Sales and Marketing

Maxim Healthcare Services' compassionate patient care experienced healthcare professionals has made the company as an established resource in the healthcare industry. The company provides its services to elderly, chronically ill, disabled, recuperating, and pediatric patients. It partners with local agencies and referral sources to provide quality care services for adults and children across the US.

EXECUTIVES

CIO*, Kevin Apperson
Chief Experience Officer*, Julie Judge
Auditors : PRICEWATERHOUSECOOPERS LLP BA

LOCATIONS

HQ: MAXIM HEALTHCARE SERVICES, INC.
  7227 LEE DEFOREST DR, COLUMBIA, MD 210463236
Phone: 410 910-1500
Web: WWW.MAXIMHEALTHCARE.COM

PRODUCTS/OPERATIONS

Selected Services
Allied Health staffing
Facility nurse staffing
Flu and wellness services
Government services
Health information services
International nursing
Home healthcare
HME/pharmacy services
Habilitation services
Physician services
Travel nursing

Selected Divisions
CareFocus
CareFocus Companion Services
Centrus Premier Homecare
Logix Healthcare Search Partners
Maxim Coders
Maxim Government Services
Maxim Health Information Services
Maxim Health Systems
Maxim Healthcare Services (Homecare)
Maxim Home Health Resources
Maxim Pediatric Services
Maxim Physician Resources
Maxim Staffing Solutions - Administrative Staffing
Maxim Staffing Solutions - Allied Health
Maxim Staffing Solutions - Nurse Staffing
Orbis Clinical
Reflectx Services
StaffAssist
TimeLine Recruiting
TravelMax

COMPETITORS

ADVENTIST HEALTHCARE, INC.
ALLIED HEALTHCARE INTERNATIONAL INC.
CRASSOCIATES, INC.
DELTA-T GROUP, INC.
HEALTH DIALOG SERVICES CORPORATION
MEDSEARCH STAFFING SERVICES, INC.
PROFESSIONAL PLACEMENT RESOURCES, LLC
SHERIDAN HEALTHCARE, INC.
VITAS HEALTHCARE CORPORATION
WELLMED MEDICAL MANAGEMENT, INC.

HISTORICAL FINANCIALS
Company Type: Private

Income Statement FYE: December 31

	REVENUE ($mil)	NET INCOME ($mil)	NET PROFIT MARGIN	EMPLOYEES
12/17	1,510	38	2.5%	35,000
12/15	1,382	11	0.8%	—
12/14	1,269	4	0.4%	—
12/13	1,226	(1)	—	—
Annual Growth	5.3%	—	—	—

2017 Year-End Financials
Return on assets: 14.2%   Cash ($ mil.): 8
Return on equity: 71.1%
Current Ratio: 1.40

MAYER ELECTRIC SUPPLY COMPANY, INC.

Mayer Electric Supply helps to light up those southern nights. The company is one of the nation's largest distributors of electrical supplies, with about 50 branch locations in the southeastern US. It offers some 40,000 items made by leading manufacturers, such as 3M, GE, Littelfuse, and Schneider Electric. Products include conduit, circuit breakers, controls and switches, fire and safety products, LED and low-voltage lighting systems, motors, power tools, transformers, and wire and cable. Mayer Electric supplies customers in the construction, datacomm, government, industrial, and utility industries. The Collat family, including CEO Nancy Collat Goedecke, owns Mayer Electric.

Operations
Besides distributing electrical supplies, Mayer Electric offers several services. Its Mayer Project Management group works to lower cost for construction contractors by providing on-site storage and inventory management. Other services include lamp and battery recycling, conduit bending and threading, and wire and cable cutting. The company also specializes in factory automation, energy efficiency, and datacomm systems.

Geographic Reach
Mayer Electric serves customers through locations in Alabama, Florida, Georgia, Mississippi, the Carolinas, Texas, Tennessee, and Virginia.

Sales and Marketing
The electrical supplies distributor serves multiple customer segments, including those in the construction, government, industrial, datacomm, and utility industries through about 51 branch locations across US Southeast.

Strategy
Growing its geographic presence, in 2013 Mayer Electric opened a branch location in the Houston area.

Mergers and Acquisitions
Looking to expand further in the southeastern US, Mayer Electric in 2012 acquired Mustang Electric Supply, based outside Dallas in Lewisville, Texas. Established in 1998, Mustang Electric serves commercial and residential contractors across the Dallas and Fort Worth area, allowing Mayer Electric to expand to the dynamic and lucrative Dallas market. The purchase included Mustang Electric's 40,000-sq.-ft. facility in Lewisville.

Company Background
The recession hit companies like Mayer Electric hard as residential and commercial construction efforts were backburnered. Sales for Mayer Electric dropped by about 21% in 2009 compared to the prior year. Rather than responding by laying off employees or shuttering branches, the company planned for break-even results or a small loss for the year. Indeed, the company made a small profit in 2009.

Mayer Electric was founded in 1930.

Auditors : WARREN AVERETT BIRMINGHAM AL

LOCATIONS

HQ: MAYER ELECTRIC SUPPLY COMPANY, INC.
  3405 4TH AVE S, BIRMINGHAM, AL 352222300
Phone: 205 583-3500
Web: WWW.MAYERELECTRIC.COM

PRODUCTS/OPERATIONS

Selected Services
Basic distributor services
Construction partner
Maintenance, repair and operations

Selected Products
Ballasts
Batteries
Cable and wire
Circuit breakers
Conduit
Factory automation products
Fan boxes
Fasteners
Fuses
LED lighting systems
Lenses
Lighting fixtures
Locks
Low-voltage lighting systems
Meters
Motors
Panelboards
Power supplies
Relays
Switches
Surge protection devices
Terminal blocks
Tools
Transformers
Voltage regulators

COMPETITORS

BORDER STATES INDUSTRIES, INC.
CRESCENT ELECTRIC SUPPLY COMPANY
ELECTRICAL EQUIPMENT COMPANY
ELLIOTT ELECTRIC SUPPLY, INC.
FACILITY SOLUTIONS GROUP, INC.
HAJOCA CORPORATION
REVERE ELECTRIC SUPPLY CO.
ROSENDIN ELECTRIC, INC.
THE OKONITE COMPANY INC
WALTERS WHOLESALE ELECTRIC CO.

HISTORICAL FINANCIALS
Company Type: Private

Income Statement   FYE: January 2

	REVENUE ($mil)	NET INCOME ($mil)	NET PROFIT MARGIN	EMPLOYEES
01/21*	1,067	11	1.1%	900
12/19	1,138	14	1.2%	—
12/18	1,072	11	1.1%	—
12/17	911	11	1.2%	—
Annual Growth	5.4%	0.9%	—	—

*Fiscal year change

2021 Year-End Financials
Return on assets: 3.3%   Cash ($ mil.): —
Return on equity: 12.0%
Current Ratio: 1.10

MAYO FOUNDATION FOR MEDICAL EDUCATION AND RESEARCH

LOCATIONS
HQ: MAYO FOUNDATION FOR MEDICAL EDUCATION AND RESEARCH
  200 1ST ST SW, ROCHESTER, MN 559050001
Phone: 507 284-2511
Web: WWW.MAYO.EDU

HISTORICAL FINANCIALS
Company Type: Private

Income Statement   FYE: December 31

	REVENUE ($mil)	NET INCOME ($mil)	NET PROFIT MARGIN	EMPLOYEES
12/13	1,069	6	0.6%	32,270
12/05	5,802	505	8.7%	—
12/03	4,822	348	7.2%	—
12/02	0	0	—	—
Annual Growth	—	—	—	—

2013 Year-End Financials
Return on assets: 75.4%   Cash ($ mil.): 496
Return on equity: 0.6%
Current Ratio: 0.70

MCAFEE CORP.

Mcafee Corp. is primarily engaged in the design, development, and production of prepackaged computer software. Important products of this industry include operating, utility, and applications programs. Establishments of this industry may also provide services such as preparation of software documentation for the user-installation of software for the user; and training the user in the use of the software. The company provides its products to approximately 110 million customers on their over 600 million devices.

Operations
The company's products includes all-in-one protection, device protection, web protection, free antivirus trial, device security scan, pc optimizer, techmaster concierge, and virus removal.

Geographic Reach
McAfee's North America and Latin America locale site was McAfee, LLC located at San Jose, California. For EMEA and APAC locale site was McAfee Ireland Limited and also located at San Jose, California.

HISTORY
John McAfee, a former systems consultant for Lockheed (now part of Lockheed Martin), started McAfee Associates in 1989 to sell his antivirus software. Normal retail channels were too difficult for a small entrepreneur to crack, so he marketed his product on computer bulletin boards as shareware, depending on the honesty of users to pay for the product if they found it useful. Enough of them did, and the success was compounded as satisfied individual users recommended it for their companies' systems.

McAfee Associates went public in 1992. The next year former Apple and Sun Microsystems marketer William Larson became CEO. He built a suite of products through more than a dozen acquisitions, bundled them to reap higher returns, and stretched the company's sales and marketing efforts.

EXECUTIVES
PRODUCT, Gagan Singh
Auditors : PRICEWATERHOUSECOOPERS LLP DA

LOCATIONS
HQ: MCAFEE CORP.
  6220 AMERICA CENTER DR, SAN JOSE, CA 950022563
Phone: 866 622-3911
Web: WWW.MCAFEE.COM

HISTORICAL FINANCIALS
Company Type: Private

Income Statement   FYE: December 25

	REVENUE ($mil)	NET INCOME ($mil)	NET PROFIT MARGIN	EMPLOYEES
12/21	1,920	2,688	140.0%	2,262
12/20	2,906	(289)	—	—
Annual Growth	(33.9%)	—	—	—

2021 Year-End Financials
Return on assets: 78.6%   Cash ($ mil.): 816
Return on equity: —
Current Ratio: 0.80

MCCARTHY BUILDING COMPANIES, INC.

McCarthy Building Companies is one of the top privately-held builders in the US. McCarthy Building Companies, Inc. has a long history of building facilities that drive greater value. From exceptional levels of quality and safety to ease of maintenance over time, It is firmly committed to helping its clients and partners achieve the short- and long-term strategic goals of every project it does. Contracts include heavy construction projects and transportation expertise (bridges and highways and road construction), commercial projects (retail and office buildings), and more. Founded by Timothy McCarthy in 1864, the company is 100% employee owned.

Operations
The company builds a wide array of projects including advanced technology & manufacturing, aviation, commercial, education, government, healthcare, heavy civil & transportation, hospitality & entertainment, industrial, parking, ports & marine terminals, renewable energy, research laboratory, and water & wastewater projects.

Geographic Reach
Headquartered in Saint Louis, McCarthy Building Companies has offices in Atlanta, Georgia; Austin, Dallas, Houston, Texas; Denver, Colorado; Collinsville, Illinois; Overland Park, Kansas; Las Vegas, Nevada; Los Angeles, Newport Beach, Sacramento, San Diego, San Francisco, and San Jose, California; Omaha, Nebraska; and Phoenix, Arizona.

Sales and Marketing
The company's clients include some of the well-known companies such as Banner Health, Ameren, Cornell University, Dairy Farmers of America, Delta Airlines, Eli Lilly & Company, Genetech, Kaiser Permanente, Lifescan, Metropolitan Transit Authority, NRG Energy, Occidental Petroleum, Pfizer, Sigma-Aldrich, Toyota, University of Arizona, Walt Disney Imagineering, and Yuma Regional Medical Center, and among others.

EXECUTIVES
BI Division President*, Justin Kelton
CALIFORNIA DIV*, Michael Myers
NOPAC DIV*, Shaun Sleeth
Central Division*, John Buescher
SOUTHERN DIVISION*, Joe Jouvenal
Auditors : RUBINBROWN LLP SAINT LOUIS M

LOCATIONS
HQ: MCCARTHY BUILDING COMPANIES, INC.
  12851 MANCHESTER RD, SAINT LOUIS, MO 631311802
Phone: 314 968-3300
Web: WWW.MCCARTHY.COM

PRODUCTS/OPERATIONS

Selected Markets
Commercial
Education K-12
Health care
Heavy/civil/transportation
Higher education
High performance/green
Hospitality/entertainment
Industrial
Native American
Parking structures
Science and technology
Water/wastewater

Selected Services
Negotiated general contracting
Construction management
Hard bid (lump sum contract for services)
Design/build
Construction management/general contracting

COMPETITORS

ALBERICI CORPORATION
BIG-D CONSTRUCTION CORP.
BRASFIELD & GORRIE, L.L.C.
GILBANE BUILDING COMPANY
H. J. RUSSELL & COMPANY
J.E. DUNN CONSTRUCTION COMPANY
ROSENDIN ELECTRIC, INC.
THE PIKE COMPANY INC
THE TURNER CORPORATION
TURNER CONSTRUCTION COMPANY

HISTORICAL FINANCIALS
Company Type: Private

Income Statement — FYE: December 31

	REVENUE ($mil)	NET INCOME ($mil)	NET PROFIT MARGIN	EMPLOYEES
12/20	4,706	0	0.0%	4,783
12/19	4,513	0	0.0%	—
12/18	3,852	0	0.0%	—
12/17	3,574	0	0.0%	—
Annual Growth	9.6%	—	—	—

2020 Year-End Financials
Return on assets: —   Cash ($ mil.): 706
Return on equity: —
Current Ratio: 1.40

MCCARTHY HOLDINGS, INC.

Auditors : RUBINBROWN LLP SAINT LOUIS M

LOCATIONS

HQ: MCCARTHY HOLDINGS, INC.
12851 MANCHESTER RD, SAINT LOUIS, MO 631311802
Phone: 314 968-3300
Web: WWW.MCCARTHY.COM

HISTORICAL FINANCIALS
Company Type: Private

Income Statement — FYE: December 31

	REVENUE ($mil)	NET INCOME ($mil)	NET PROFIT MARGIN	EMPLOYEES
12/21	4,440	0	0.0%	5,342
12/20	4,783	0	0.0%	—
12/19	4,591	0	0.0%	—
12/18	3,925	0	0.0%	—
Annual Growth	4.2%	—	—	—

2021 Year-End Financials
Return on assets: —   Cash ($ mil.): 150
Return on equity: —
Current Ratio: 1.30

MCHS HOSPITALS INC

LOCATIONS

HQ: MCHS HOSPITALS INC
1000 N OAK AVE, MARSHFIELD, WI 544495703
Phone: 715 389-3258

HISTORICAL FINANCIALS
Company Type: Private

Income Statement — FYE: September 30

	REVENUE ($mil)	NET INCOME ($mil)	NET PROFIT MARGIN	EMPLOYEES
09/18	629	17	2.8%	16
09/17	82	(4)	—	—
Annual Growth	665.0%	—	—	—

2018 Year-End Financials
Return on assets: 2.6%   Cash ($ mil.): 10
Return on equity: 17.8%
Current Ratio: —

MCLANE COMPANY, INC.

McLane Company is one of the largest wholesale suppliers of grocery and food products in the US, serving some 46,000 retail locations. It buys, sells and delivers more than 50,000 different consumer products to customers and nearly 110,000 locations across the US such as convenience and discount stores, mass merchandisers, wholesale clubs, and drug stores, among others. Through McLane Grocery and McLane Foodservice, the company operates more than 80 distribution centers and one of the nation's largest private fleets. In addition, McLane provides spirits, wine, beer, and nonalcoholic beverages distribution through its subsidiary, Empire Distributors, Inc. McLane is a wholly owned unit of Berkshire Hathaway Inc.

Operations

McLane offers a wide range of industry-leading supply chain solutions. It operates through three business units: grocery distribution, foodservice distribution, and alcoholic beverage distribution. In addition, the company also offers proven, third-party supply chain management solutions.

McLane's grocery and foodservice divisions, along with numerous subsidiaries, deliver more than 10 billion pounds of merchandise to customers annually. Through Empire Distributors, the company offers more than 15,000 unique products and sells over 10 million cases of beverages annually.

Geographic Reach

McLane has an extensive distribution network of some 80 facilities across the country. Its headquarters and grocery operations are based in Temple, Texas, while its foodservice operation is based in Carrollton, Texas.

The company supplies alcoholic beverages throughout the southeastern US and in Colorado through distribution centers in Colorado, Georgia, North Carolina, and Tennessee.

Sales and Marketing

McLane is a leading supplier to convenience stores; other customers include discount and drug stores, bars, chain restaurants, mass merchants, wholesale clubs, and more.

Strategy

McLane continues to strengthen its business partnerships. In 2020, the company renewed its multi-year service agreement with RaceTrac Petroleum, Inc. The relationship dates back to 1996, and McLane's distribution services encompass all convenience store categories including tobacco, grocery, candy, snacks, and store supplies. McLane helps RaceTrac pursue its growth strategy by leveraging its purchasing power, geographic distribution, and product assortment, allowing RaceTrac to offer competitive pricing across all of its stores.

McLane also renewed its multi-year contract with EG America. EG America will continue to utilize McLane's scale of 24 grocery distribution centers across the US to provide excellent service to all of its locations, except for Cumberland Farms and Fastrac which self-distribute.

Company Background

Starting as a family-owned grocery store in 1894, McLane expanded into wholesale distribution in the early 1900s. The McLane family, including former Houston Astros owner Drayton McLane, sold the business to Wal-Mart Stores in the 1990s. Conglomerate Berkshire Hathaway acquired McLane Company in 2003 for about $1.5 billion.

EXECUTIVES

President Grocery Distribution, Christopher Smith
President Food Service Distribution, Susan Adzick

CIO, Bradly Kimbrough

LOCATIONS

HQ: MCLANE COMPANY, INC.
4747 MCLANE PKWY, TEMPLE, TX 765044854
Phone: 254 771-7500
Web: WWW.MCLANECO.COM

COMPETITORS

AMCON DISTRIBUTING COMPANY
CENTRAL GROCERS, INC.
CORE-MARK HOLDING COMPANY, INC.
METCASH LIMITED
PERFORMANCE FOOD GROUP COMPANY
SMART & FINAL STORES LLC
SPARTANNASH COMPANY
THE MERCHANTS COMPANY
TOPCO ASSOCIATES, LLC
UNIFIED GROCERS, INC.

HISTORICAL FINANCIALS
Company Type: Private

Income Statement — FYE: December 30

	REVENUE ($mil)	NET INCOME ($mil)	NET PROFIT MARGIN	EMPLOYEES
12/16*	48,016	0	0.0%	25,000
01/16	48,144	0	0.0%	—
12/12	37,389	0	0.0%	—
01/09	29,800	0	0.0%	—
Annual Growth	6.1%	—	—	—

*Fiscal year change

2016 Year-End Financials
Return on assets: — Cash ($ mil.): 122
Return on equity: —
Current Ratio: 1.40

MCLEOD REGIONAL MEDICAL CENTER OF THE PEE DEE, INC.

Auditors : KPMG LLP GREENSBORO NC

LOCATIONS

HQ: MCLEOD REGIONAL MEDICAL CENTER OF THE PEE DEE, INC.
555 E CHEVES ST, FLORENCE, SC 295062617
Phone: 843 777-2000
Web: WWW.MCLEODHEALTH.ORG

HISTORICAL FINANCIALS
Company Type: Private

Income Statement — FYE: September 30

	REVENUE ($mil)	NET INCOME ($mil)	NET PROFIT MARGIN	EMPLOYEES
09/20	700	75	10.8%	5,000
09/19	784	91	11.7%	—
09/15	607	72	11.8%	—
Annual Growth	2.9%	1.0%	—	—

2020 Year-End Financials
Return on assets: 3.4% Cash ($ mil.): 184
Return on equity: 4.4%
Current Ratio: 3.20

MCNAUGHTON-MCKAY ELECTRIC CO.

McNaughton-McKay is a wholesale distributor of electrical supplies through its office in Germany and several offices in the US. One of the largest employee-owned companies in the US, McNaughton-McKay distributes an array of product lines from manufacturers such as nVent Hoffman, Sylvania, Panduit, Appleton, Sola HD, and Rockwell Automation, to name a few. It is a full line electrical distributor of products ranging from pipe and wire to complex automation control systems for everyone from small electrical contractors to large scale manufacturers. It sells to the construction, lighting, motion, networking, and industrial automation markets.

Operations
The company offers products such as Rockwell automation, alarms, security & signaling, audio & video, batteries & accessories, cable trays & struts, chemicals, lubricants & paints, conduit fittings, and more. Its services and solutions include predictive and preventive maintenance, mechatronics, lighting, renewable energy, visualization, and enclosure modification, among others.

Geographic Reach
McNaughton-McKay Electric Company is headquartered in Madison Heights, Michigan with over 25 locations across five states and one sale office in Germany.

Sales and Marketing
In addition to industrial automation, commercial markets, McNaughton-McKay supports construction, drives, lighting, motion, networking, safety, and visualization. McNaughton-McKay's customers include supplyFORCE, Edge Global Supply, and Vantage Group, to name a few.

Company Background
Founded in 1910, the Bull and McNaughton families ran McNaughton-McKay until 2006. It established a sales office in Germany in 2004.

EXECUTIVES
Sales & Marketing*, J Christopher Majni
Auditors : KPMG LLP

LOCATIONS

HQ: MCNAUGHTON-MCKAY ELECTRIC CO.
1357 E LINCOLN AVE, MADISON HEIGHTS, MI 480714126
Phone: 248 399-7500
Web: WWW.MC-MC.COM

PRODUCTS/OPERATIONS

Selected Products
Bar code scanners and systems
Communication input/output (I/O) networks
Computers and peripherals
Convenience panels (cables and equipment)
Cordsets
Data-collection terminals and software
Drives and motor controllers
Engineered products
I/O products (AC/DC modules)
Motion-control products
 CNC controls
 Servos
 Spindles
Motors (AC)
PLC processors
Radio-frequency identification (RFID) products
Safety products
 Gate switches
 Light curtains
 Mats
 Relays
Sensors
Software
Vision products (inspection equipment)

COMPETITORS

ALLIED ELECTRONICS, INC.
AVI SYSTEMS, INC.
CRESCENT ELECTRIC SUPPLY COMPANY
DISCOVERIE GROUP PLC
ELLIOTT ELECTRIC SUPPLY, INC.
FACILITY SOLUTIONS GROUP, INC.
Future Electronics (CDA) Ltd
HIS COMPANY, INC.
N. F. SMITH & ASSOCIATES, L.P.
TALLEY INC.

HISTORICAL FINANCIALS
Company Type: Private

Income Statement — FYE: December 31

	REVENUE ($mil)	NET INCOME ($mil)	NET PROFIT MARGIN	EMPLOYEES
12/21	1,651	0	0.0%	1,700
12/20	1,335	0	0.0%	—
12/19	1,515	0	0.0%	—
12/16	724	0	0.0%	—
Annual Growth	17.9%	—	—	—

2021 Year-End Financials
Return on assets: — Cash ($ mil.): 8
Return on equity: —
Current Ratio: 3.00

MED AMERICA HEALTH SYSTEMS CORPORATION

LOCATIONS

HQ: MED AMERICA HEALTH SYSTEMS CORPORATION
1 WYOMING ST, DAYTON, OH 454092722
Phone: 937 223-6192

HISTORICAL FINANCIALS
Company Type: Private

Income Statement				FYE: December 31
	REVENUE ($mil)	NET INCOME ($mil)	NET PROFIT MARGIN	EMPLOYEES
12/11	919	24	2.7%	10,700
12/10	843	67	8.1%	—
12/08	790	(153)	—	—
Annual Growth	5.1%	—	—	—

2011 Year-End Financials
Return on assets: 1.7% Cash ($ mil.): 42
Return on equity: 3.5%
Current Ratio: 1.90

MEDCO, L.L.C.

LOCATIONS

HQ: MEDCO, L.L.C.
3701 DADEVILLE RD, ALEXANDER CITY, AL 350109075
Phone: 256 215-3889
Web: WWW.MEDCOLLC.COM

HISTORICAL FINANCIALS
Company Type: Private

Income Statement				FYE: June 30
	REVENUE ($mil)	NET INCOME ($mil)	NET PROFIT MARGIN	EMPLOYEES
06/09*	854	(173)	—	225
09/02	4	0	13.6%	—
09/00	2	0	13.7%	—
12/99	0	0	—	—
Annual Growth	—	—	—	—

*Fiscal year change

2009 Year-End Financials
Return on assets: (-999.9%) Cash ($ mil.): —
Return on equity: (-999.9%)
Current Ratio: 1.40

MEDICAL CENTER OF THE ROCKIES

EXECUTIVES
General*, Emily Weber

LOCATIONS
HQ: MEDICAL CENTER OF THE ROCKIES
2500 ROCKY MOUNTAIN AVE, LOVELAND, CO 805389004
Phone: 970 624-2500
Web: WWW.UCHEALTH.ORG

HISTORICAL FINANCIALS
Company Type: Private

Income Statement				FYE: June 30
	REVENUE ($mil)	NET INCOME ($mil)	NET PROFIT MARGIN	EMPLOYEES
06/21	639	154	24.1%	4,000
06/20	552	84	15.3%	—
06/16	421	61	14.6%	—
06/15	403	68	16.9%	—
Annual Growth	8.0%	14.5%	—	—

2021 Year-End Financials
Return on assets: 23.9% Cash ($ mil.): 31
Return on equity: 46.3%
Current Ratio: 0.40

MEDICAL UNIVERSITY HOSPITAL AUTHORITY

Auditors : KPMG LLP ATLANTA GA

LOCATIONS
HQ: MEDICAL UNIVERSITY HOSPITAL AUTHORITY
169 ASHLEY AVE, CHARLESTON, SC 294258905
Phone: 843 792-1414
Web: WWW.MUSCHEALTH.ORG

HISTORICAL FINANCIALS
Company Type: Private

Income Statement				FYE: June 30
	REVENUE ($mil)	NET INCOME ($mil)	NET PROFIT MARGIN	EMPLOYEES
06/08	821	(19)	—	4,000
06/07	749	26	3.5%	—
06/06	0	0	—	—
Annual Growth	—	—	—	—

2008 Year-End Financials
Return on assets: (-2.2%) Cash ($ mil.): 14
Return on equity: (-8.3%)
Current Ratio: 1.50

MEDSTAR HEALTH, INC.

MedStar Health is a not-for-profit, regional healthcare system based in Columbia, Maryland, and one of the largest employers in the region. MedStar Health runs ten hospitals and about 35 other health-related businesses across Maryland and the Washington, DC, area. MedStar Health has one of the largest graduate medical education programs in the country, training 1,150 medical residents annually, and is the medical education and clinical partner of Georgetown University. With more than 31,000 physicians, nurses, and many other clinical and non-clinical associates, MedStar has a comprehensive service offering, including emergency services, home health care, and rehabilitation.

Operations
MedStar operates ten hospitals (MedStar Harbor Hospital, MedStar St. Mary's Hospital and MedStar Washington Hospital Center), two clinical research and innovation (MedStar Health Research Institute and MedStar Institute Nurse Association), two home health care (MedStar Health Infusion and MedStar Health Home Care), two managed care (MedStar Family Choice and MedStar Medicare Choice), and two independent senior living (Belverde Green and Woodbourne Woods).

Geographic Reach
MedStar has operations in Maryland and Washington, D.C.

Auditors : KMPG LLP BALTIMORE MD

LOCATIONS
HQ: MEDSTAR HEALTH, INC.
10980 GRANTCHESTER WAY WA, COLUMBIA, MD 210446097
Phone: 410 772-6500
Web: WWW.MEDSTARHEALTH.ORG

Selected Facilities
Maryland
    Franklin Square Hospital Center (Baltimore)
    Good Samaritan Hospital (Baltimore)
    Harbor Hospital (Baltimore)
    Montgomery General Hospital (Olney)
    St. Mary's Hospital (Leonardtown)
    Union Memorial Hospital (Baltimore)
Washington, DC
    Georgetown University Hospital
    National Rehabilitation Hospital
    Washington Hospital Center

PRODUCTS/OPERATIONS

Selected Affiliates/Operations
Clinical Research
    Georgetown University Medical Center (Washington, DC)
    MedStar Research Institute (Hyattsville, Maryland)
Home Health Care
    MedStar Health VNA (Washington, DC)
    MedStar Health Infusion (Elkridge, Maryland)
    MGH Community Health (Olney, Maryland)
Managed Care
    MedStar Family Choice (Baltimore, Maryland)
Nursing Homes/Senior Living
    Franklin Woods (Rosedale, Maryland)
    Good Samaritan Nursing Center (Baltimore, Maryland)
    Belvedere Green (Baltimore, Maryland)
    Woodbourne Woods (Baltimore, Maryland)
Primary Care
    MedStar Physician Partners (Washington, DC)
Outpatient Surgery Centers
    MedStar Surgery Center (Washington, DC)
    Harbor Hospital HealthPark (Pasadena, Maryland)
    SurgiCenter at Pasadena (Pasadena, Maryland)

COMPETITORS

ADVENTIST HEALTH SYSTEM/WEST, CORPORATION
AVERA HEALTH
BEAUMONT HEALTH
FRANCISCAN ALLIANCE, INC.
INSPIRA HEALTH NETWORK, INC.
LEGACY HEALTH
LEHIGH VALLEY HEALTH NETWORK, INC.
MEMORIAL HERMANN HEALTHCARE SYSTEM

SPARROW HEALTH SYSTEM
UNIVERSITY HOSPITALS HEALTH SYSTEM, INC.

HISTORICAL FINANCIALS
Company Type: Private

Income Statement   FYE: June 30

	REVENUE ($mil)	NET INCOME ($mil)	NET PROFIT MARGIN	EMPLOYEES
06/22	7,279	(199)	—	33,000
06/21	6,725	774	11.5%	—
06/20	5,788	136	2.4%	—
06/19	5,690	187	3.3%	—
Annual Growth	8.6%	—	—	—

2022 Year-End Financials
Return on assets: (-2.6%)   Cash ($ mil.): 846
Return on equity: (-6.6%)
Current Ratio: 1.40

MEDSTAR-GEORGETOWN MEDICAL CENTER, INC.

Medstar-Georgetown Medical Center (dba as Medstar Georgetown University Hospital as a part of MedStar Health) is a 609-bed acute care teaching hospital serving residents of the greater Washington, DC, area, including Maryland and Virginia. The hospital's staff of more than 1,100 physicians represents a wide range of medical specializations including cardiology, oncology, neurology/neurosurgery, and surgical transplantation. Medstar Georgetown provides a comprehensive array of inpatient, outpatient, surgical, and rehabilitative care services. The hospital is part of a local network of affiliated primary care providers.

Operations
Medstar Georgetown's Transplant Institute is one of a handful of centers in the US that offers living-donor liver transplants; it opened a new medical space in 2014. Also, Georgetown Neurosciences is the sixth unit nationwide to provide CyberKnife stereotactic radiosurgery for the treatment of tumors and lesions of the brain, neck, and spine.

Strategy
In 2015 Medstar Georgetown submitted a letter of intent with the District of Columbia State Health Planning and Development Agency seeking approval to modernize its existing medical facility by constructing a new state-of-the-art medical surgical pavilion. The pavilion will house surgical, critical care and emergency departments, as well as related administrative functions.

In 2014 MedStar Georgetown became the first center in Washington, DC to perform a two-level artificial disc replacement in a patient's neck.

Company Background
In 2011 Medstar Georgetown became the first health system in the area to offer bloodless surgery to patients who prefer not to receive someone else's blood, usually for religious reasons. There are three primary approaches to performing bloodless surgeries: before, during, and after surgery. Before surgery the hospital gives the patient medications such as iron supplements or epoprotein to boost the blood's hemoglobin level. During surgery the hospital is precise as it can be with its surgical techniques to limit blood loss, and there are anesthesia techniques to lower blood pressure so patients bleed less. There is also a machine called Cell Saver that is used during surgery that collects blood lost, suctions it into a canister, washes and filters it and then returns it directly into the patient as a product that is about 60-percent pure red blood cells. After surgery medications are used to raise blood levels and medical providers avoid taking multiple blood draws for blood tests.

The hospital was founded in 1898 to promote health through education, research, and patient care. The current hospital/medical center was opened in 1947.

LOCATIONS
HQ: MEDSTAR-GEORGETOWN MEDICAL CENTER, INC.
  3800 RESERVOIR RD NW, WASHINGTON, DC 200072113
Phone: 202 444-2000
Web: WWW.MEDSTARHEALTH.ORG

PRODUCTS/OPERATIONS
Selected Services
Anesthesiology
Audiology
Bloodless Medicine and Surgery Program
Bone Marrow Transplant
Breast Cancer
Breast Health Program
Cancer Care
Cardiology
Cerebrovascular Center
Colon and Rectal Surgery
Ear, Nose and Throat (ENT)
Emergency, Urgent Care and Trauma
Endocrinology
Epilepsy
Family Medicine
Fracture Liaison
Head and Neck Cancer
Headache Center
Hematology
Hospital Medicine
Huntington Disease Center
Hyperbaric Oxygen Therapy
Ophthalmology
Orthopaedics
Ostomy Clinic
Otolaryngology
Pastoral Care
Pediatrics
Pharmacy
Physical Medicine
Plastic Surgery
Primary Care
Prostate Cancer

COMPETITORS
BAYLOR COLLEGE OF MEDICINE
OREGON HEALTH & SCIENCE UNIVERSITY MEDICAL GROUP
SUNY DOWNSTATE MEDICAL CENTER
TEMPLE UNIVERSITY HEALTH SYSTEM, INC.
UNIVERSITY OF VIRGINIA MEDICAL CENTER

HISTORICAL FINANCIALS
Company Type: Private

Income Statement   FYE: June 30

	REVENUE ($mil)	NET INCOME ($mil)	NET PROFIT MARGIN	EMPLOYEES
06/16	801	104	13.1%	4,000
06/15	774	98	12.7%	—
06/11	809	43	5.4%	—
06/10	782	45	5.8%	—
Annual Growth	0.4%	15.0%	—	—

2016 Year-End Financials
Return on assets: 23.6%   Cash ($ mil.): 5
Return on equity: 31.3%
Current Ratio: 1.90

MEGLOBAL AMERICAS INC.

LOCATIONS
HQ: MEGLOBAL AMERICAS INC.
  2150 TOWN SQUARE PL # 750, SUGAR LAND, TX 774791465
Phone: 844 634-5622
Web: WWW.MEGLOBAL.BIZ

HISTORICAL FINANCIALS
Company Type: Private

Income Statement   FYE: December 31

	REVENUE ($mil)	NET INCOME ($mil)	NET PROFIT MARGIN	EMPLOYEES
12/13	596	10	1.7%	15
12/12	597	13	2.2%	—
12/11	743	20	2.7%	—
Annual Growth	(10.4%)	(29.9%)	—	—

2013 Year-End Financials
Return on assets: 13.6%   Cash ($ mil.): 5
Return on equity: 107.6%
Current Ratio: 1.10

MELLANOX TECHNOLOGIES, INC.

EXECUTIVES
West Chief Executive Officer, Eyal Waldman
Auditors : KOST FORER GABBAY AND KASIERER

LOCATIONS

HQ: MELLANOX TECHNOLOGIES, INC.
2530 ZANKER RD, SAN JOSE, CA 951311127
Phone: 408 970-3400

HISTORICAL FINANCIALS
Company Type: Private

Income Statement — FYE: December 31

	REVENUE ($mil)	NET INCOME ($mil)	NET PROFIT MARGIN	EMPLOYEES
12/19	1,330	205	15.4%	876
12/18	1,088	134	12.3%	—
12/17	863	(19)	—	—
12/16	857	18	2.2%	—
Annual Growth	15.8%	122.9%	—	—

2019 Year-End Financials
Return on assets: 9.7%   Cash ($ mil.): 77
Return on equity: 12.4%
Current Ratio: 3.70

MEMORIAL HEALTH CARE SYSTEM, INC.

Auditors: CATHOLIC HEALTH INITIATIVES E

LOCATIONS

HQ: MEMORIAL HEALTH CARE SYSTEM, INC.
2525 DESALES AVE, CHATTANOOGA, TN 374041161
Phone: 423 495-2525
Web: WWW.MEMORIAL.ORG

HISTORICAL FINANCIALS
Company Type: Private

Income Statement — FYE: June 30

	REVENUE ($mil)	NET INCOME ($mil)	NET PROFIT MARGIN	EMPLOYEES
06/20	564	(30)	—	8,800
06/16	545	22	4.1%	—
06/15	527	34	6.6%	—
06/14	557	25	4.6%	—
Annual Growth	0.2%	—	—	—

2020 Year-End Financials
Return on assets: (-3.7%)   Cash ($ mil.): 33
Return on equity: (-6.1%)
Current Ratio: 1.40

MEMORIAL HEALTH SERVICES

MemorialCare is a nonprofit integrated delivery system which includes four premier hospitals ? Long Beach Medical Center, Miller Children's & Women's Hospital Long Beach, Orange Coast Medical Center and Saddleback Medical Center; medical groups ? MemorialCare Medical Group and Greater Newport Physicians; a health plan ? Seaside Health Plan; and numerous outpatient health centers, imaging centers, surgery centers and dialysis centers throughout Orange and Los Angeles Counties. The MemorialCare 55+ Program is a unique program for adults 55 and older that provides easy access to health and wellness information, resources and exclusive perks free of cost to members.

Operations
MemorialCare Medical Group includes 1,700 physicians specializing in internal medicine, family medicine, obstetrics-gynecology and pediatrics; specialties like oncology, cardiology, pulmonology, gastroenterology, surgery and urgent care.

Geographic Reach
MemorialCare has convenient outpatient health centers, urgent care centers, imaging centers, breast centers, surgical centers, physical therapy centers and dialysis centers throughout Orange and Los Angeles Counties.

Sales and Marketing
In addition to multiple locations throughout Orange County, MemorialCare Medical Group offers Urgent Care Centers that are open 365 days a year, Telephone Advice Nurses available 24 hours a day, 7 days a week; and Lab and X-ray services available on-site at most locations.

EXECUTIVES

CIO*, Rick Graniere
Auditors: PRICEWATERHOUSECOOPERS LLP LO

LOCATIONS

HQ: MEMORIAL HEALTH SERVICES
17360 BROOKHURST ST # 160, FOUNTAIN VALLEY, CA 927083720
Phone: 714 377-2900
Web: WWW.MEMORIALCARE.ORG

Selected Facilities
Long Beach Memorial Medical Center (Long Beach, California)
Miller Children's Hospital (Long Beach, California)
Community Hospital (Long Beach, California)
Orange Coast Memorial Medical Center (Fountain Valley, California)
Saddleback Memorial Medical Center (San Clemente, California)
Saddleback Memorial Medical Center (Laguna Hills, California)
MemorialCare Medical Group (regional)
MemorialCare HealthExpress (regional)
MemorialCare Imaging Centers (regional)
Memorial Prompt Care (regional)

PRODUCTS/OPERATIONS

Selected Services
Blood Donation
Diabetes Care
Heart and Vascular Care
Joint Replacement
Neonatal Intensive Care
Rehabilitation and Therapy
Wellness Care
Cancer Care
Gynecological Care
Imaging and Radiology
Maternity Care
Orthopedic Care
Stroke Care
Wound Healing
Breast Care
Express Care
Hyperbaric Medicine
Laboratory Services
Pediatric Care
Surgical Care
Women's Care

COMPETITORS

ARROWHEAD REGIONAL MEDICAL CENTER
ASCENSION PROVIDENCE ROCHESTER HOSPITAL
FIRSTHEALTH OF THE CAROLINAS, INC.
FROEDTERT MEMORIAL LUTHERAN HOSPITAL, INC.
HCA-HEALTHONE LLC
LEHIGH VALLEY HEALTH NETWORK, INC.
REGIONS HOSPITAL FOUNDATION
SHORE MEMORIAL HOSPITAL
UNIVERSITY HOSPITALS HEALTH SYSTEM, INC.
WELLSTAR HEALTH SYSTEM, INC.

HISTORICAL FINANCIALS
Company Type: Private

Income Statement — FYE: June 30

	REVENUE ($mil)	NET INCOME ($mil)	NET PROFIT MARGIN	EMPLOYEES
06/22	2,688	(249)	—	6,000
06/21	2,580	770	29.8%	—
06/20	2,556	(52)	—	—
06/19	2,438	208	8.6%	—
Annual Growth	3.3%	—	—	—

2022 Year-End Financials
Return on assets: (-5.1%)   Cash ($ mil.): 133
Return on equity: (-8.1%)
Current Ratio: 1.00

MEMORIAL HEALTH SERVICES GROUP RETURN

EXECUTIVES

Senior Manager, Ryan Gil
Research Analyst, Dena Freeman
Director, Robert Hunn
Corporate Accounting Manager, Laline Gutierrez
Auditors: MOSS ADAMS LLP SAN FRANCISCO

LOCATIONS

HQ: MEMORIAL HEALTH SERVICES GROUP RETURN
17360 BROOKHURST ST, FOUNTAIN VALLEY, CA 927083720
Phone: 714 377-3002
Web: WWW.MEMORIALCARE.ORG

HISTORICAL FINANCIALS
Company Type: Private

Income Statement — FYE: June 30

	REVENUE ($mil)	NET INCOME ($mil)	NET PROFIT MARGIN	EMPLOYEES
06/21	2,641	121	4.6%	6
06/18	2,340	73	3.1%	—
06/17	2,253	87	3.9%	—
06/15	2,302	135	5.9%	—
Annual Growth	2.3%	(1.8%)	—	—

2021 Year-End Financials
Return on assets: 4.1%   Cash ($ mil.): 54
Return on equity: 5.5%
Current Ratio: 0.90

MEMORIAL HEALTH, INC.

Auditors: DIXON HUGHES GOODMAN LLP ASHE

LOCATIONS

HQ: MEMORIAL HEALTH, INC.
4700 WATERS AVE, SAVANNAH, GA 314046220
Phone: 912 350-8000
Web: WWW.MEMORIALHEALTH.COM

HISTORICAL FINANCIALS
Company Type: Private

Income Statement — FYE: December 31

	REVENUE ($mil)	NET INCOME ($mil)	NET PROFIT MARGIN	EMPLOYEES
12/16	581	(38)	—	4,500
12/14	42	(11)	—	—
12/13	24	0	0.0%	—
Annual Growth	185.6%	—	—	—

2016 Year-End Financials
Return on assets: (-6.8%)   Cash ($ mil.): 16
Return on equity: (-28.3%)
Current Ratio: 1.50

MEMORIAL HERMANN HEALTH SYSTEM

EXECUTIVES
EQUITY DIVERSITY INCLUSION*, Toi B Harris
Auditors: ERNST & YOUNG LLP HOUSTON TX

LOCATIONS
HQ: MEMORIAL HERMANN HEALTH SYSTEM
929 GESSNER RD STE 1900, HOUSTON, TX 770242317
Phone: 713 242-3000
Web: WWW.MEMORIALHERMANN.ORG

HISTORICAL FINANCIALS
Company Type: Private

Income Statement — FYE: June 30

	REVENUE ($mil)	NET INCOME ($mil)	NET PROFIT MARGIN	EMPLOYEES
06/22	7,358	195	2.7%	14,000
06/21	6,924	1,511	21.8%	—
06/20	5,792	248	4.3%	—
06/19	5,528	270	4.9%	—
Annual Growth	10.0%	(10.3%)	—	—

2022 Year-End Financials
Return on assets: 1.9%   Cash ($ mil.): 525
Return on equity: 3.3%
Current Ratio: 1.10

MEMORIAL HOSPITAL FOR CANCER AND ALLIED DISEASES

LOCATIONS
HQ: MEMORIAL HOSPITAL FOR CANCER AND ALLIED DISEASES
1275 YORK AVE, NEW YORK, NY 100656094
Phone: 212 639-2000
Web: WWW.MSKCC.ORG

HISTORICAL FINANCIALS
Company Type: Private

Income Statement — FYE: December 31

	REVENUE ($mil)	NET INCOME ($mil)	NET PROFIT MARGIN	EMPLOYEES
12/14	2,035	71	3.5%	5,000
12/08	1,236	(51)	—	—
Annual Growth	8.7%	—	—	—

2014 Year-End Financials
Return on assets: 3.5%   Cash ($ mil.): —
Return on equity: 7.4%
Current Ratio: 0.90

MEMORIAL MEDICAL CENTER

If you've lost the spring in your step and need a little care, Memorial Medical Center will be there. As the flagship facility for Memorial Health System in Springfield, Illinois, this acute care and teaching hospital provides a wide range of medical and surgical services as well as emergency medicine and outpatient care. Its myriad specialties include cardiovascular, maternity, cancer care, behavioral health, orthopedic, rehabilitation, and burn treatment services. The hospital, which sees 25,000 inpatients per year, also has special surgical divisions for bariatric procedures and organ transplants. The 500-bed hospital is a teaching affiliate of the Southern Illinois University (SIU) School of Medicine.

Auditors: ERNST & YOUNG LLP ST LOUIS

LOCATIONS
HQ: MEMORIAL MEDICAL CENTER
701 N 1ST ST, SPRINGFIELD, IL 627810001
Phone: 217 788-3000
Web: WWW.MEMORIAL.HEALTH

PRODUCTS/OPERATIONS

Selected Services
Bariatric Services
Behavioral Health
Regional Burn Center
Regional Cancer Center
Da Vinci Robotic Surgery
EEG
Emergency Department
Express Care
Family Maternity
Food Nutrition Counseling
Healthcare Psychology
Hearing Center
Heart and Vascular Services
Intensive Care Unit
Industrial Rehab
JointWorks
Lab Services
Medical Imaging Services
Neurosciences
Orthopedic Services
Palliative Care
Rehab Services
Sleep Disorder Center
SpineWorks
SportsCare
Stroke Center
Surgical Services
Transplant Services
Would Healing Center

COMPETITORS
FROEDTERT MEMORIAL LUTHERAN HOSPITAL, INC.
KIMBALL DAY HEALTHCARE INC
NEWYORK-PRESBYTERIAN/BROOKLYN METHODIST
PACIFIC ALLIANCE MEDICAL CENTER, INC.
ST. ANTHONY'S HOSPITAL, INC.

HISTORICAL FINANCIALS
Company Type: Private

Income Statement — FYE: September 30

	REVENUE ($mil)	NET INCOME ($mil)	NET PROFIT MARGIN	EMPLOYEES
09/20	647	39	6.1%	2,849
09/19	734	(13)	—	—
09/18	711	58	8.3%	—
09/17	682	63	9.3%	—
Annual Growth	(1.7%)	(14.6%)	—	—

2020 Year-End Financials
Return on assets: 4.2%   Cash ($ mil.): 25
Return on equity: 7.4%
Current Ratio: 2.20

MEMORIAL SLOAN-KETTERING CANCER CENTER

Memorial Sloan-Kettering Cancer Center (MSKCC) one of the oldest and largest private cancer center for patient care, innovative research, and outstanding educational program. The center includes about 500 inpatient beds, and more than 1,400 physicians, more than 3,900 nurses, more than 22,800 inpatient stays and more than 781,900 outpatient visits. Memorial Hospital specializes in bone-marrow transplants, radiation therapy, and chemotherapy. It also offers programs in cancer prevention, diagnosis, treatment, research, and education. The Sloan Kettering Institute hosts more than

100 laboratory investigators, 400 postdoctoral research fellows (including clinical fellows), and 300 PhD and MD/PhD graduate students.

Geographic Reach
MSKCC is based in New York and has cancer care facilities are located in New York City, Long Island, Westchester County and New Jersey.

The company maintains one of the world's most dynamic programs of cancer research, with more than 120 research laboratories that are focused on better understanding every type of the disease. Memorial Sloan Kettering is also home to about 40 state-of-the-art core facilities.

Company Background
Memorial Hospital was founded in 1884 as the New York Cancer Center by a group that included John and Charlotte Astor. Sloan Kettering Institute was founded in 1945 by Alfred Sloan and Charles Kettering to research new cancer cures; the institute was located adjacent to Memorial Hospital. The two entities formed a coordinating corporate entity (Memorial Sloan Kettering Cancer Center) in 1960 and officially merged in 1980.

EXECUTIVES
Senior Vice President Legal, Jorge Lopez
CDO, Claus Torp Jensen
CIO, Atefeh Riazi
Auditors : ERNST & YOUNG US LLP INDIANAP

LOCATIONS
HQ: MEMORIAL SLOAN-KETTERING CANCER CENTER
1275 YORK AVE, NEW YORK, NY 100656007
Phone: 212 639-2000
Web: WWW.MSKCC.ORG

PRODUCTS/OPERATIONS
2013 Sales

	$ mil.	% of total
Patient care	2,367.7	78
Grants and contracts	202.1	7
Other	455.7	15
Total	3,025.5	100

COMPETITORS
CHILDREN'S HEALTHCARE OF ATLANTA, INC.
CHILDREN'S HEALTHCARE OF CALIFORNIA
CHILDREN'S HOSPITAL MEDICAL CENTER
DANA-FARBER CANCER INSTITUTE, INC.
H. LEE MOFFITT CANCER CENTER AND RESEARCH INSTITUTE HOSPITAL, INC.
ROSWELL PARK CANCER INSTITUTE CORPORATION
SHEPHERD CENTER, INC.
THE CHILDREN'S HOSPITAL OF PHILADELPHIA
THE FOX CHASE CANCER CENTER FOUNDATION
UNIVERSITY OF TEXAS MD ANDERSON CANCER CENTER

HISTORICAL FINANCIALS
Company Type: Private

Income Statement — FYE: December 31

	REVENUE ($mil)	NET INCOME ($mil)	NET PROFIT MARGIN	EMPLOYEES
12/21	6,398	1,480	23.1%	9,325
12/19	5,561	302	5.4%	—
12/17	4,499	314	7.0%	—
12/13	582	0	0.2%	—
Annual Growth	34.9%	149.6%	—	—

2021 Year-End Financials
Return on assets: 9.9%   Cash ($ mil.): 742
Return on equity: 15.1%
Current Ratio: 1.90

MENTOR GRAPHICS CORPORATION

Mentor Graphics lends a hand to guide engineers who design electronic components. The company is a leading global developer of electronic design automation (EDA) software and systems used by engineers to design, simulate, and test electronic components, such as integrated circuits (IC's), wire harness systems, and printed circuit boards (PCBs). Products include PADS (PCB design), Nucleus (operating system), and Calibre (IC design). Its software is used to design components for such products as computers and wireless handsets. Clients come from the aerospace, IT, telecommunications, and, increasingly, transportation industries. Mentor Graphics was acquired by Siemens for $4.5 billion in 2017.

Operations
Mentor Graphics creates system and software products, most of which are sold through term software license contracts. It also provides service and support, including professional services, consulting, training, and other services.

Geographic Reach
Based in Wilsonville, Oregon, Mentor Graphics has US research and development operations in Colorado, Washington, Alabama, and Massachusetts. It also conducts R&D in Armenia, Egypt, France, Germany, Hungary, India, Israel, Pakistan, Poland, Russia, Taiwan, and the UK.

Sales and Marketing
Financial Performance
Mentor Graphics reported increases in revenue and profit in 2017 (ended January). The company's sales rose 9% to $1.3 billion in 2017 from 2016 and profit shot up 60% to $155 million for the year. The company had robust growth in all geographic markets except for the US, its biggest market with about 40% of sales. Japan was particularly strong in 2017 with sales jumping more than 35% while sales rose about 15% each in the Pacific Rim and Europe. The company credited the overseas growth to the timing of contract renewals and blamed the North America decline of 3% on weaker sales of emulation hardware systems and a slower rate of contract renewals for the year.

The 60% rise in profit to $1.3 billion in 2017 resulted from higher sales combined with lower special charges in 2017 from 2016. The higher profit helped boost cash flow from operations to $322 million in 2017 from $228 million in 2016.

Strategy
Mentor Graphics is moving to apply its processes to new businesses. The automotive business is one example. It has grown to 20% of Mentor Graphics' revenue in several years. The company is keen on driving its products into other transportation areas such as the design of electronic components in airplanes and trains.

Mergers and Acquisitions

HISTORY
Mentor Graphics was founded in 1981 by a group from instrument maker Tektronix to market desktop computers to design engineers. Throughout the 1980s the company was a leader in electronic design automation (EDA) software, but the early 1990s found it in trouble. Revenues fell because of delays in upgrade releases and a worldwide recession.

In 1992 Mentor Graphics began phasing out hardware sales, further disrupting operations. Texas Instruments veteran Walden Rhines became CEO in 1993. That year the company acquired CheckLogic, a maker of testing software for integrated circuit (IC) design. By 1994 cost-cutting and product line restructuring returned Mentor to profitability.

The company bought ANACAD, which developed design software for analog and mixed-signal ICs, and Model Technology, a very-high-density logic simulation tool firm, in 1994. It acquired 14 more companies in 1995 and 1996, including embedded software tool developer Microtec Research (1996), which moved Mentor into the market for software development tools.

Auditors : KPMG LLP PORTLAND OREGON

LOCATIONS
HQ: MENTOR GRAPHICS CORPORATION
8005 SW BOECKMAN RD, WILSONVILLE, OR 970707777
Phone: 503 685-7000
Web: WWW.NEW.SIEMENS.COM

2016 Sales

	$ mil.	% of total
United States	488.2	41
Europe	254.8	22
Japan	87.1	7
Pacific Rim	335.8	29
Other	15.1	1
Total	1,181	100

PRODUCTS/OPERATIONS

2017 Sales

	$ mil.	% of total
System and software	794.5	62
Service & support	488	38
Total	1,282.5	100

Selected Products
Embedded software development
    Compilers
    Debugger
    Real-time operating system
Integrated circuit (IC) design and verification
    Analog/mixed signal
    Custom design
    Design-for-test
    Field-programmable gate array/application-specific
IC design
    Formal verification
    High-capacity circuit simulation
    Interconnect modeling
    Physical optimization
    Physical verification & manufacturability
    Resolution enhancement technologies
    Static timing
    Synthesis
Printed circuit board design and analysis
    Design tools
    Digital high-speed
    Integration, interfaces, and viewers
    Layout
    Library management
    Radio-frequency/mixed-signal
    Simulation and analysis
System-level design and verification
    Accelerated system verification
    Cabling design and analysis
    Design creation
    Digital simulation
    Hardware emulation and simulation
    Intellectual property
    Process management
    System-on-a-chip
    Web-based development system

COMPETITORS

ASPEN TECHNOLOGY, INC.
CADENCE DESIGN SYSTEMS, INC.
DXC TECHNOLOGY COMPANY
F5 NETWORKS, INC.
FUJITSU LIMITED
JACK HENRY & ASSOCIATES, INC.
NEC CORPORATION
PTC INC.
SYNOPSYS, INC.
UNISYS CORPORATION

HISTORICAL FINANCIALS
Company Type: Private

Income Statement   FYE: January 31

	REVENUE ($mil)	NET INCOME ($mil)	NET PROFIT MARGIN	EMPLOYEES
01/17	1,282	154	12.1%	5,700
01/16	1,180	94	8.0%	—
01/15	1,244	145	11.7%	—
01/14	1,156	153	13.3%	—
Annual Growth	3.5%	0.3%	—	—

2017 Year-End Financials
Return on assets: 6.8%
Return on equity: 11.3%
Current Ratio: 1.30
Cash ($ mil.): 441

MERCY CARE

Mercy Care is a not-for-profit provider of managed health care services in Arizona. The Mercy Care Plan provides these services under a contract with the Arizona Health Care Cost Containment System, the state of Arizona's Medicaid program. The plan provides health coverage and prescription drug benefits to some 300,000 members. The company, founded in 1985, is affiliated with St. Joseph's Hospital & Medical Center (which is part of Catholic Healthcare West), Dignity Health, and Carondelet Health Network. The plan is administered by health care management firm Schaller Anderson.

Operations
Mercy Care provides coverage to families, children, the elderly, and the developmentally disabled. In addition to traditional HMO coverage, the company also offers disease management and preventative health care services.

Along with the Centers for Medicare & Medicaid Services (CMS), Mercy Care provides qualified members with medical and prescription drug benefits. Its Mercy Care Long Term Care (MCLTC) offers services to those covered by the AHCCCS Arizona Long Term Care System (ALTCS), which accounts for 22% of revenue.

The Division of Developmental Disabilities Long Term Care serves members who are enrolled through the Arizona Department of Economic Security/Division of Development Disabilities (DES/ DDD), which generates approximately 2% of SCHN's revenue. Through a contract with the DES/DDD, the company provides medical care to qualified members.

Geographic Reach
Mercy Care serves the Arizona counties of Maricopa, Pima, Graham, Greenlee, and Cochise, providing covered services to enrolled members.

Sales and Marketing
As part of its business, Mercy Care provides patients with prescriptions through retail pharmacies, mail order pharmacies, home infusion pharmacies, long-term care pharmacies, and Indian Health Service/Tribal/Urban Indian Health Program (I/T/U) pharmacies.

Financial Performance
Mercy Care logged a 10% decline in revenue in 2012 as compared to 2011. The provider points to a decrease in capitation premiums, delivery/HIV AIDS supplement, reinsurance, and third-party recoveries for the double-digit drop. During the same reporting period, SCHN posted a $7.5 million net loss, thanks to revenue decreases paired with increases in investment fees and unrealized losses on investments incurred by the company during 2012.

LOCATIONS
HQ: MERCY CARE
4500 E COTTON CENTER BLVD, PHOENIX, AZ 850408895
Phone: 602 263-3000
Web: WWW.MERCYCAREAZ.ORG

COMPETITORS

ASCENSION VIA CHRISTI HEALTH, INC
CAPITAL DISTRICT PHYSICIANS' HEALTH PLAN, INC.
DAVITA MEDICAL MANAGEMENT, LLC
HILL PHYSICIANS MEDICAL GROUP, INC.
IPC HEALTHCARE, INC.

HISTORICAL FINANCIALS
Company Type: Private

Income Statement   FYE: June 30

	REVENUE ($mil)	NET INCOME ($mil)	NET PROFIT MARGIN	EMPLOYEES
06/20	3,796	65	1.7%	500
06/14	1,808	41	2.3%	—
06/12	1,747	28	1.6%	—
06/11	1,939	58	3.0%	—
Annual Growth	7.7%	1.2%	—	—

2020 Year-End Financials
Return on assets: 8.6%
Return on equity: 17.8%
Current Ratio: —
Cash ($ mil.): 188

MERCY CHILDREN'S HOSPITAL

Children's Mercy Kansas City is a not-for-profit health system and a leading independent children's health organization dedicated to holistic care, translational research, breakthrough innovation, and educating the next generation of caregivers. Among its specialized services are diabetes and endocrinology, genetics, heart surgery, neonatology, and rehabilitation. Children's Mercy also offers several research education opportunities for healthcare professionals, researchers, and students. Founded in 1897, the system today has about 484,850 patient visits annually.

Operations
Children's Mercy has a medical staff of roughly 785 pediatric specialists. Its main campus Children's Mercy Adele Hall which is home to the region's highest-level neonatal intensive care unit (NICU) and the region's only Level I pediatric trauma center; there are an additional locations at the Children's Mercy Hospital Kansas suburban campus.

The system performs roughly 19,290 surgeries annually; it has about 131,755 emergency room visits each year.

Geographic Reach
Children's Mercy Adele Hall is the only Level I pediatric trauma center between Kansas, and Missouri, where it is headquartered.

Company Background

Children's Mercy is a not-for-profit, freestanding pediatric health system that offers low-income families a low- or no-cost health plan through the Take CARE benefit plans.

Auditors : KPMG LLP KANSAS CITY MISSOUR

LOCATIONS

HQ: MERCY CHILDREN'S HOSPITAL
2401 GILLHAM RD, KANSAS CITY, MO 641084619
Phone: 816 234-3000
Web: WWW.CHILDRENSMERCY.ORG

Selected locations
Children's Mercy Adele Hall Campus (Kansas City, MO)
Children's Mercy Blue Valley (Overland Park, KS)
Children's Mercy Broadway (Kansas City)
Children's Mercy College Boulevard (Overland Park, KS)
Children's Mercy East (Independence, MO)
Children's Mercy Hospital Kansas (Overland Park, KS)
Children's Mercy Northland (Kansas City, MO)
Children's Mercy Olathe (Olathe, KS)
Children's Mercy West (Kansas City, KS)
Children's Mercy Sports Medicine Center at Village West (Kansas City, KS)

COMPETITORS

ANN & ROBERT H. LURIE CHILDREN'S HOSPITAL OF CHICAGO
CHILDREN'S HEALTH CLINICAL OPERATIONS
CHILDREN'S HEALTHCARE OF CALIFORNIA
ENCOMPASS HEALTH CORPORATION
JOHNS HOPKINS ALL CHILDREN'S HOSPITAL, INC.
NORTHSHORE UNIVERSITY HEALTHSYSTEM
SEATTLE CHILDREN'S HOSPITAL
TEXAS CHILDREN'S HOSPITAL
THE CHILDREN'S HOSPITAL OF PHILADELPHIA
The Hospital For Sick Children

HISTORICAL FINANCIALS
Company Type: Private

Income Statement — FYE: June 30

	REVENUE ($mil)	NET INCOME ($mil)	NET PROFIT MARGIN	EMPLOYEES
06/21	1,754	175	10.0%	7,000
06/20	1,614	91	5.7%	—
06/16	1,020	35	3.5%	—
06/15	978	79	8.1%	—
Annual Growth	10.2%	14.2%	—	—

2021 Year-End Financials
Return on assets: 6.5% Cash ($ mil.): 69
Return on equity: 8.7%
Current Ratio: 0.80

MERCY GENERAL HEALTH PARTNERS

LOCATIONS

HQ: MERCY GENERAL HEALTH PARTNERS
1500 E SHERMAN BLVD, MUSKEGON, MI 494441849
Phone: 231 728-4032
Web: WWW.MERCYHEALTH.COM

HISTORICAL FINANCIALS
Company Type: Private

Income Statement — FYE: June 30

	REVENUE ($mil)	NET INCOME ($mil)	NET PROFIT MARGIN	EMPLOYEES
06/20	692	(30)	—	2,000
06/09	215	(0)	—	—
Annual Growth	11.2%	—	—	—

2020 Year-End Financials
Return on assets: (-3.7%) Cash ($ mil.): —
Return on equity: (-14.5%)
Current Ratio: 0.60

MERCY HEALTH

Mercy Health (formerly Catholic Health Partners) performs acts of healing in Kentucky and Ohio. One of the nation's largest not-for-profit health systems, Mercy Health offers health care services through about 450 facilities, including 23 hospitals, eight homes for the elderly, five hospice programs, and seven home health agencies. It also operates more than 150 clinics, a number of physician practices, and a health insurance plan. The system is co-sponsored by the Sisters of Mercy South Central and Mid-Atlantic communities; the Sisters of the Humility of Mary; the Franciscan Sisters of the Poor; and Covenant Health Systems. Mercy Health merged with Maryland-based Bon Secours Health System to create the 43-hospital system Bon Secours Mercy Health in 2018.

Operations

Mercy Health organizes its operations into regions to better serve the communities where its facilities are located. Its acute and non-acute inpatient facilities have a total of more than 6,300 beds. The system is affiliated with more than 1,800 physicians of various medical and surgical specialties.

Hospitals include St. Elizabeth and St. Joseph Health Centers near Youngstown, Ohio; seven Mercy locations in the Toledo, Ohio, area; Mercy Regional Medical Center near Cleveland; St. Rita's Medical Center in Lima, Ohio; Springfield Regional Medical Center and Mercy Memorial Hospital in Springfield, Ohio; Anderson, Clermont, Fairfield, Mt. Airy, Jewish, West, and Western Hills hospitals in Cincinnati; and Lourdes Hospital in Paducah, Kentucky.

Its specialized health care services include cancer, cardiology, radiology, laboratory, surgical, and women's health care. The company also operates HealthSpan, a PPO health insurance plan that covers nearly 273,000 lives.

Geographic Reach

Mercy Health divides its operations into seven regional markets. North Markets include Mercy in Toledo and Lorain, Ohio, and Humility of Mary Health Partners in Youngstown, Ohio. South Markets include St. Rita's Health Partners, Community Mercy Health Partners, and Mercy Health Partners in Ohio as well as Mercy Health Partners - Kentucky.

Financial Performance

Mercy Health's revenue increased 14% to $4.5 billion in 2014 on growing net patient service revenue and other revenue. However, the system lost a net $6.5 million that year due to interest rate swap agreement losses, lower investment earnings, and higher operating expenses.

Cash flow from operations dropped in 2014 to $354 million.

Strategy

In 2014, after the Affordable Care Act (which requires insurance companies to provide access to abortion and birth control) took effect, Mercy Health spun off its HealthSpan insurance arm to avoid a conflict with church doctrine.

The following year, Mercy Health partnered with Akron, Ohio-based Summa Health to create Advanced Health Select, a network of doctors and medical caregivers, in an effort to attract large employers and insurance companies.

Mergers and Acquisitions

In 2018, Mercy Health and Maryland-based Bon Secours Health System merged to create a system with 43 hospitals in seven states. The combined entity has more than 2,100 physicians and clinicians working in more than 1,000 locations.

Auditors : KPMG LLP CINCINNATI OHIO

LOCATIONS

HQ: MERCY HEALTH
12621 ECKEL JUNCTION RD, PERRYSBURG, OH 435511304
Phone: 513 639-2800
Web: WWW.MERCY.COM

COMPETITORS

ADVENTIST HEALTH SYSTEM/SUNBELT, INC.
BON SECOURS MERCY HEALTH, INC.
COMMONSPIRIT HEALTH
IOWA HEALTH SYSTEM
MERCY HEALTH
MINISTRY HEALTH CARE, INC.
PROVIDENCE HEALTH & SERVICES
SAINT LUKE'S HEALTH SYSTEM, INC.
TRINITY HEALTH CORPORATION
WHEATON FRANCISCAN SERVICES, INC.

HISTORICAL FINANCIALS
Company Type: Private

Income Statement — FYE: December 31

	REVENUE ($mil)	NET INCOME ($mil)	NET PROFIT MARGIN	EMPLOYEES
12/18	4,860	(978)	—	1,000
12/17	4,737	456	9.6%	—
Annual Growth	2.6%	—	—	—

2018 Year-End Financials
Return on assets: (-14.8%)   Cash ($ mil.): —
Return on equity: (-40.3%)
Current Ratio: 1.00

MERCY HEALTH

Mercy Health, formerly known as the Sisters of Mercy Health System, provides a range of health care and social services through its network of facilities and service organizations. The organization operates some 35 acute care hospitals (including four specialty heart hospitals and two children's hospitals) with more than 4,200 licensed beds, as well as 700 clinics and outpatient facilities in four Midwestern states. Its hospital groups include facilities for nursing homes, medical practices, and outpatient centers. Mercy Health also operates Resource Optimization & Innovation (ROi), its industry-leading health care supply chain organization, and health outreach organizations in Louisiana, Mississippi, and Texas.

Operations
Mercy Health also operates three rehabilitation hospitals and two orthopedic hospitals. The system has more than 2,000 Mercy Clinic physicians.

In 2014 Mercy Health had 150,696 acute inpatient discharges; 158,911 inpatient and outpatient surgeries; 631,444 emergency department visits; 23,213 births; and nearly 8.4 million outpatient visits.

Geographic Reach
The system operates in Arkansas, Kansas, Missouri, and Oklahoma.

Mercy Health's outreach efforts include Mercy Ministries of Laredo, a group providing primary health care and social services to residents of Laredo, Texas. In New Orleans, Mercy Health sponsors Mercy Family Center, which provides mental health services; in Mississippi it funds a health care advocacy group.

Sales and Marketing
Commercial and other third-party payments accounted for 44% of net patient service revenue, while Medicare and Medicaid combined accounted for 51%.

Financial Performance
Mercy Health's operating revenue increased 14% to $4.5 billion in 2014 as net patient and other revenues grew. However, the system reported a net loss of $6.5 million that year (versus net income in 2013) as a result of interest rate swap agreement losses and higher expenses, as well as lower investment earnings.

Cash flow from operations fell 46% to $354 million in 2014.

Strategy
In 2013, Mercy Health opened new facilities in Missouri (St. Charles and Wentzville), as well as a new heart and vascular center that centralized its outpatient heart and vascular offerings. The following year, it opened a new orthopedic hospital in Fort Smith and a 60-bed rehabilitation hospital.

The system acquired Lincoln County Medical Center (renamed Mercy Hospital Lincoln) and its eight affiliated clinics in 2015, expanding its presence in eastern Missouri.

Despite its various expansions, the Mercy system experienced the same industry challenges as its health care brethren, including escalating medical and pharmaceutical costs and increasing self-pay bad debts (uninsured patients who leave their medical bills unpaid). Several of the health system's facilities have seen a decline in discharges.

Company Background
The organization was founded by the Sisters of Mercy of the St. Louis Regional Community in 1986 and operated under that model until 2008, when its sponsorship was transferred from the Sisters of Mercy of the St. Louis Regional Community to a new entity, Mercy Health Ministry. The shift to the new sponsorship organization was made to allow lay members to join the Sisters of Mercy in sponsoring the ministry. It also reflected the growing number of lay people holding executive positions at the system's hospitals and on the board of directors.

Auditors: ERNST & YOUNG LLP ST LOUIS

LOCATIONS

HQ: MERCY HEALTH
615 S NEW BALLAS RD, SAINT LOUIS, MO 631418221
Phone: 314 579-6100
Web: WWW.MERCY.NET

Selected Locations
Arkansas
    Berryville
    Fort Smith
    Hot Springs
    Ozark
    Paris
    Rogers
    Waldron
Kansas
    Columbus
    Fort Scott
    Independence
Missouri
    Aurora
    Cassville
    Joplin
    Lebanon
    Mountain View
    St. Louis
    Springfield
    Washington
Oklahoma
    Ada
    Ardmore
    El Reno
    Guthrie
    Healdton
    Kingfisher
    Marietta
    Oklahoma City
    Tishomingo
    Watonga

PRODUCTS/OPERATIONS

2014 Sales

	$ mil	% of total
Net patient service revenue less provision for bad debts	3,838.2	85
Member revenue	477.4	11
Other revenue	194.6	4
Total	4,510.2	100

Selected Facilities
Arkansas
    Mercy Hospital Berryville
    Mercy Hospital Fort Smith
    Mercy Hospital Hot Springs
    Mercy Hospital Northwest Arkansas
    Mercy Hospital of Scott County
    Mercy Hospital Ozark
    Mercy Hospital Paris
    Mercy Hospital Waldron
Kansas
    Mercy Health Center
    Mercy Hospital Fort Scott
    Mercy Hospital Independence
    Mercy Maude Norton Hospital Columbus
Missouri
    Mercy Hospital Aurora
    Mercy Hospital Cassville
    Mercy Hospital Joplin
    Mercy Hospital Lebanon
    Mercy Hospital St. Louis
    Mercy Children's Hospital St. Louis
    Mercy Heart and Vascular Hospital St. Louis
    Mercy Heart Hospital St. Louis
    Mercy Rehabilitation Hospital St. Louis
    Mercy Hospital Springfield
    Mercy Children's Hospital Springfield
    Mercy Hospital Washington
    Mercy McCune-Brooks Hospital
    Mercy St. Francis Hospital
Oklahoma
    Arbuckle Memorial Hospital
    Mercy Health Love County
    Mercy Hospital Ardmore
    Mercy Hospital El Reno
    Mercy Hospital Healdton
    Mercy Hospital Logan County
    Mercy Hospital Oklahoma City
    Mercy Hospital - Tishomingo
    Valley View Regional Hospital
    Watonga Municipal Hospital

COMPETITORS

ASCENSION HEALTH
DIGNITY HEALTH
INDIANA UNIVERSITY HEALTH, INC.
MERCY HOSPITAL SPRINGFIELD
PROVIDENCE ST. JOSEPH HEALTH
SSM HEALTH CARE CORPORATION
ST. JOSEPH HEALTH SYSTEM
THE CLEVELAND CLINIC FOUNDATION
UNIVERSITY HOSPITALS HEALTH SYSTEM, INC.
WELLSPAN HEALTH

HISTORICAL FINANCIALS
Company Type: Private

Income Statement FYE: June 30

	REVENUE ($mil)	NET INCOME ($mil)	NET PROFIT MARGIN	EMPLOYEES
06/22	7,469	(231)	—	8,800
06/21	7,422	1,330	17.9%	—
06/20	6,519	(325)	—	—
06/19	6,509	(32)	—	—
Annual Growth	4.7%	—	—	—

2022 Year-End Financials
Return on assets: (-2.4%) Cash ($ mil.): 766
Return on equity: (-4.8%)
Current Ratio: 1.20

MERCY HEALTH CORPORATION

Auditors: WIPFLI LLP MILWAUKEE WISCON

LOCATIONS

HQ: MERCY HEALTH CORPORATION
2400 N ROCKTON AVE, ROCKFORD, IL 611033655
Phone: 815 971-5000
Web: WWW.MERCYHEALTHSYSTEM.ORG

HISTORICAL FINANCIALS
Company Type: Private

Income Statement — FYE: June 30

	REVENUE ($mil)	NET INCOME ($mil)	NET PROFIT MARGIN	EMPLOYEES
06/21	1,163	210	18.1%	2,200
06/19	1,152	50	4.4%	—
06/18	1,014	68	6.7%	—
Annual Growth	4.7%	45.4%	—	—

2021 Year-End Financials
Return on assets: 9.1% Cash ($ mil.): 345
Return on equity: 17.3%
Current Ratio: 2.10

MERCY HEALTH PARTNERS

LOCATIONS

HQ: MERCY HEALTH PARTNERS
1675 LEAHY ST STE 101, MUSKEGON, MI 494425538
Phone: 231 728-4032
Web: WWW.MERCYHEALTH.COM

HISTORICAL FINANCIALS
Company Type: Private

Income Statement — FYE: June 30

	REVENUE ($mil)	NET INCOME ($mil)	NET PROFIT MARGIN	EMPLOYEES
06/18	666	36	5.5%	1,500
06/08	0	0	81.1%	—
06/06	0	0	50.7%	—
06/04	0	(0)	—	—
Annual Growth	96.2%	—	—	—

2018 Year-End Financials
Return on assets: 7.1% Cash ($ mil.): —
Return on equity: 14.8%
Current Ratio: 2.40

MERCY HEALTH SERVICES-IOWA, CORP.

LOCATIONS

HQ: MERCY HEALTH SERVICES-IOWA, CORP.
20555 VICTOR PKWY, LIVONIA, MI 481527031
Phone: 734 343-1000
Web: WWW.TRINITY-HEALTH.ORG

HISTORICAL FINANCIALS
Company Type: Private

Income Statement — FYE: June 30

	REVENUE ($mil)	NET INCOME ($mil)	NET PROFIT MARGIN	EMPLOYEES
06/18	969	31	3.3%	2,471
06/14	665	2	0.4%	—
06/05	546	23	4.3%	—
Annual Growth	4.5%	2.3%	—	—

2018 Year-End Financials
Return on assets: 2.6% Cash ($ mil.): —
Return on equity: 3.9%
Current Ratio: 2.70

MERCY HEALTH SERVICES-IOWA, CORP.

LOCATIONS

HQ: MERCY HEALTH SERVICES-IOWA, CORP.
1000 4TH ST SW, MASON CITY, IA 504012800
Phone: 641 428-7000
Web: WWW.MERCYNORTHIOWA.COM

HISTORICAL FINANCIALS
Company Type: Private

Income Statement — FYE: June 30

	REVENUE ($mil)	NET INCOME ($mil)	NET PROFIT MARGIN	EMPLOYEES
06/11	649	17	2.7%	0
06/10	632	19	3.0%	—
Annual Growth	2.7%	(7.9%)	—	—

2011 Year-End Financials
Return on assets: 2.2% Cash ($ mil.): 10
Return on equity: 3.5%
Current Ratio: 0.40

MERCY HEALTH SERVICES, INC.

Auditors: DIXON HUGHES GOODMAN LLP CHA

LOCATIONS

HQ: MERCY HEALTH SERVICES, INC.
301 SAINT PAUL ST, BALTIMORE, MD 212022102
Phone: 410 332-9000
Web: WWW.MDMERCY.COM

HISTORICAL FINANCIALS
Company Type: Private

Income Statement — FYE: June 30

	REVENUE ($mil)	NET INCOME ($mil)	NET PROFIT MARGIN	EMPLOYEES
06/22	895	(3)	—	1
06/21	861	132	15.4%	—
06/20	774	8	1.0%	—
06/19	766	30	4.0%	—
Annual Growth	5.3%	—	—	—

2022 Year-End Financials
Return on assets: (-0.3%) Cash ($ mil.): 283
Return on equity: (-0.6%)
Current Ratio: 1.80

MERCY HEALTH SYSTEM CORPORATION

Auditors: WIPFLI LLP MILWAUKEE WISCONS

LOCATIONS

HQ: MERCY HEALTH SYSTEM CORPORATION
1000 MINERAL POINT AVE, JANESVILLE, WI 535482940
Phone: 608 741-6891
Web: WWW.MERCYHEALTHSYSTEM.ORG

HISTORICAL FINANCIALS
Company Type: Private

Income Statement — FYE: June 30

	REVENUE ($mil)	NET INCOME ($mil)	NET PROFIT MARGIN	EMPLOYEES
06/21	633	89	14.1%	2,200
06/20	592	50	8.5%	—
06/16	559	19	3.5%	—
06/15	523	12	2.3%	—
Annual Growth	3.2%	39.7%	—	—

2021 Year-End Financials
Return on assets: 11.5% Cash ($ mil.): 259
Return on equity: 22.3%
Current Ratio: 3.70

MERCY HOSPITAL OKLAHOMA CITY, INC.

Auditors : PLEUS AND COMPANY LLC CHESTER

LOCATIONS

HQ: MERCY HOSPITAL OKLAHOMA CITY, INC.
4300 W MEMORIAL RD, OKLAHOMA CITY, OK 731208304
Phone: 405 755-1515
Web: WWW.MERCY.NET

HISTORICAL FINANCIALS
Company Type: Private

Income Statement — FYE: June 30

	REVENUE ($mil)	NET INCOME ($mil)	NET PROFIT MARGIN	EMPLOYEES
06/20	583	71	12.3%	2,302
06/10	312	16	5.2%	—
06/09	287	7	2.7%	—
06/08	1	0	34.7%	—
Annual Growth	60.5%	47.3%	—	—

2020 Year-End Financials
Return on assets: 17.2%   Cash ($ mil.): 12
Return on equity: 28.0%
Current Ratio: 6.30

MERCY HOSPITAL SPRINGFIELD

Mercy Hospital Springfield is an 890-bed acute-care hospital in the Mercy Health system. The facility provides health care to southwestern Missouri and northwestern Arkansas and includes the Mercy Children's Hospital Springfield. Other hospital specialties include cardiology and stroke care, as well as women's and seniors' health, cancer, emergency, trauma, burn, neuroscience, rehabilitation, and sports medicine. In addition to its hospital in Springfield, Mercy Hospital Springfield operates a number of community clinics and specialty care centers in the area.

Operations
Mercy Hospital Springfield has about 700 doctors on its medical staff. The center sees some 441,000 outpatient visits per year, as well as 94,000 emergency room visits and 37,000 surgeries. It also enables more than 3,000 births, Specialty units feature a level I trauma and burn center (the highest ranking in the US), a neonatal intensive care unit, a nationally certified stroke center, and high-tech surgery suites (including da Vinci robotic surgery and CyberKnife radiosurgery centers). It also operates an air ambulance service.

Geographic Reach
The hospital serves patients in southwest Missouri and northwest Arkansas.

Financial Performance
The hospital's revenues decreased by 1% in 2014, due to 1% drop in net patient service revenue (which contributed 98% of the revenue) and a 11% decrease in revenues from other sources.

In 2014 the company provided charity care of about $26 million, along with unreimbursed Medicaid expenses of around $17 million.

Strategy
That year Mercy Hospital Springfield opened the 60-bed Mercy Rehabilitation Hospital Springfield, which is spread across a 63,000-square-feet facility. The new $28 million building allows for more options for patient rehabilitation and will also serve as the region's only burn unit.

In 2014 the company also opened Phase II of its Betty and Bobby Allison Neonatal Intensive Care Unit (NICU), which expands the number of beds under NICU to 46. With this final phase complete, Mercy permanently closed its former NICU.

Company Background
Formerly St. John's Regional Health Center, the hospital's name changed to Mercy Hospital Springfield in 2012; the move coincided with the parent organization's efforts to to unify its brand identity. (The parent group's named changed as well, from Sisters of Mercy Health System to Mercy Health.)

The hospital was founded in 1891 by the Sisters of Mercy.

LOCATIONS

HQ: MERCY HOSPITAL SPRINGFIELD
1235 E CHEROKEE ST, SPRINGFIELD, MO 658042203
Phone: 417 820-2000
Web: WWW.MERCY.NET

PRODUCTS/OPERATIONS

Selected Services
Bariatric Surgery
Cancer Care
Children's Care
Heart Care
Integrative Medicine
Mother and Baby Care
Neurosciences
Orthopedic and Sport Care
Palliative Care
Pastoral Care
Senior Care
Trauma and Burn Care
Women's Care

COMPETITORS

BAPTIST HEALTH SYSTEM, INC.
MERCY HEALTH
PASADENA HOSPITAL ASSOCIATION, LTD.
UNIVERSITY HOSPITALS HEALTH SYSTEM, INC.
VALLEY HEALTH SYSTEM

HISTORICAL FINANCIALS
Company Type: Private

Income Statement — FYE: June 30

	REVENUE ($mil)	NET INCOME ($mil)	NET PROFIT MARGIN	EMPLOYEES
06/21	1,115	165	14.8%	4,400
06/16	1,024	104	10.2%	—
06/15	948	93	9.9%	—
06/14	964	42	4.4%	—
Annual Growth	2.1%	21.4%	—	—

2021 Year-End Financials
Return on assets: 30.2%   Cash ($ mil.): 23
Return on equity: 34.3%
Current Ratio: 2.50

MERCY HOSPITALS EAST COMMUNITIES

LOCATIONS

HQ: MERCY HOSPITALS EAST COMMUNITIES
615 S NEW BALLAS RD, SAINT LOUIS, MO 631418221
Phone: 314 251-6000
Web: WWW.MERCY.NET

HISTORICAL FINANCIALS
Company Type: Private

Income Statement — FYE: June 30

	REVENUE ($mil)	NET INCOME ($mil)	NET PROFIT MARGIN	EMPLOYEES
06/21	1,636	299	18.3%	10,000
06/16	1,023	184	18.0%	—
06/15	940	132	14.1%	—
06/14	1,177	118	10.1%	—
Annual Growth	4.8%	14.1%	—	—

2021 Year-End Financials
Return on assets: 44.7%   Cash ($ mil.): 32
Return on equity: 49.2%
Current Ratio: 4.50

MERCY SCRIPPS HOSPITAL

LOCATIONS

HQ: MERCY SCRIPPS HOSPITAL
4077 5TH AVE MER35, SAN DIEGO, CA 921032105
Phone: 619 294-8111
Web: WWW.SCRIPPS.ORG

HISTORICAL FINANCIALS
Company Type: Private

Income Statement   FYE: September 30

	REVENUE ($mil)	NET INCOME ($mil)	NET PROFIT MARGIN	EMPLOYEES
09/20	835	49	6.0%	95
09/15	750	44	5.9%	—
09/14	623	3	0.6%	—
09/13	700	41	5.9%	—
Annual Growth	2.6%	2.8%	—	—

2020 Year-End Financials
Return on assets: 8.1%
Return on equity: 10.9%
Current Ratio: 1.20
Cash ($ mil.): 24

MERCY WOODSTOCK MEDICAL CENTER

Auditors: WIPFLI LLP MILWAUKEE WISCON

LOCATIONS

HQ: MERCY WOODSTOCK MEDICAL CENTER
2000 LAKE AVE, WOODSTOCK, IL 600987401
Phone: 815 337-7100

HISTORICAL FINANCIALS
Company Type: Private

Income Statement   FYE: June 30

	REVENUE ($mil)	NET INCOME ($mil)	NET PROFIT MARGIN	EMPLOYEES
06/19	592	23	3.9%	156
06/18	584	25	4.4%	—
Annual Growth	1.4%	(8.6%)	—	—

2019 Year-End Financials
Return on assets: 4.0%
Return on equity: 9.0%
Current Ratio: 3.10
Cash ($ mil.): 84

MERIDIAN HOSPITALS CORPORATION

Auditors: PRICEWATERHOUSECOOPERS LLP NE

LOCATIONS

HQ: MERIDIAN HOSPITALS CORPORATION
1945 ROUTE 33, NEPTUNE, NJ 077534859
Phone: 732 751-7500

HISTORICAL FINANCIALS
Company Type: Private

Income Statement   FYE: December 31

	REVENUE ($mil)	NET INCOME ($mil)	NET PROFIT MARGIN	EMPLOYEES
12/16	1,667	244	14.7%	5,200
12/15	674	64	9.5%	—
12/09	929	94	10.2%	—
12/08	873	(140)	—	—
Annual Growth	8.4%	—	—	—

2016 Year-End Financials
Return on assets: 9.6%
Return on equity: 18.4%
Current Ratio: 2.80
Cash ($ mil.): 257

MESA UNIFIED SCHOOL DISTRICT 4

Auditors: HEINFELD MEECH & CO PC P

LOCATIONS

HQ: MESA UNIFIED SCHOOL DISTRICT 4
63 E MAIN ST STE 101, MESA, AZ 852017431
Phone: 480 472-0200
Web: WWW.MPSAZ.ORG

HISTORICAL FINANCIALS
Company Type: Private

Income Statement   FYE: June 30

	REVENUE ($mil)	NET INCOME ($mil)	NET PROFIT MARGIN	EMPLOYEES
06/21	711	39	5.6%	9,621
06/20	642	35	5.5%	—
06/19	617	39	6.5%	—
06/18	580	8	1.4%	—
Annual Growth	7.0%	69.9%	—	—

2021 Year-End Financials
Return on assets: 3.5%
Return on equity: 36.2%
Current Ratio: 3.70
Cash ($ mil.): 343

MESSER CONSTRUCTION CO.

Messer Construction provides unmatched leadership of complex, commercial construction projects. The builder provides commercial construction services (including design/build and project management) for projects in Indiana (Indianapolis), Kentucky (Louisville and Lexington), Ohio (Cincinnati, Columbus and Dayton), North Carolina (Charlotte and Raleigh), and Tennessee (Knoxville and Nashville). It has clients in the life sciences, higher education, senior living, manufacturing/industrial, public, and health care sectors, among others. Its projects have included the renovation of Michaelman, Inc., Advanced Materials Collboration Center & Corporate Campus and Cook Regentec Build-Out & Renovations. Founded in 1932, employee-owned Messer became employee-owned in 1990.

Operations

Messer offers a range of commercial construction services, including building systems/MEP, cost planning and estimating, self-performed work, equipment rental, lean construction, preconstruction, risk management, real estate development, and virtual design and construction. It also offers prefabrication services referred to as off-site manufacturing which is the assembly of building units or components at a workshop or factory separate from the jobsite.

Geographic Reach

Based in Cincinnati, Ohio, Messer operates regional offices in North Carolina (Charlotte and Raleigh), Ohio (Cincinnati, Columbus, and Dayton), Indiana (Indianapolis), Tennessee (Knoxville and Nashville), and Kentucky (Lexington and Louisville).

Sales and Marketing

Messer has served customers from a variety of industries, including aviation, federal/military, healthcare, education, industrial, and science and technology.

Company Background

Formerly known as Frank Messer & Sons, Inc., the company changed its name to Messer Construction Co. in March 2002.

Auditors: DELOITTE & TOUCHE LLP CINCINN

LOCATIONS

HQ: MESSER CONSTRUCTION CO.
643 W COURT ST, CINCINNATI, OH 452031511
Phone: 513 242-1541
Web: WWW.MESSER.COM

PRODUCTS/OPERATIONS

Selected Projects
Health Care
    Norton Healthcare
    Knoxville Orthopedic Clinic
Life Sciences
    Indiana University
    University of Kentucky
Higher Education
    Xavier University
    Western Kentucky University
Senior Living
    Graceworks Lutheran Services
    Episcopal Retirement Homes
Commercial
    IGS Energy
    Penn National Gaming
Manufacturing & Industrial
    Aisin Automotive Casting Tennessee, Inc.
    DHL Express Inc.
Public/Institutional
    The Ohio Building Authority
    Commonwealth of Kentucky

COMPETITORS

ADOLFSON & PETERSON, INC.
BERNARDS BROS. INC.
BRASFIELD & GORRIE, L.L.C.

DAVID E. HARVEY BUILDERS, INC.
DPR CONSTRUCTION, INC.
GILBANE, INC.
HOWARD S. WRIGHT CONSTRUCTION CO.
JAMES G. DAVIS CONSTRUCTION CORPORATION
JOHN E. GREEN COMPANY
VJS CONSTRUCTION SERVICES, INC.

HISTORICAL FINANCIALS
Company Type: Private

Income Statement — FYE: September 30

	REVENUE ($mil)	NET INCOME ($mil)	NET PROFIT MARGIN	EMPLOYEES
09/17	1,092	0	0.0%	1,390
09/15	1,167	0	0.0%	—
09/14	1,029	0	0.0%	—
09/13	831	0	0.0%	—
Annual Growth	7.0%	—	—	—

2017 Year-End Financials
Return on assets: —
Return on equity: —
Current Ratio: 1.20
Cash ($ mil.): 83

METALDYNE PERFORMANCE GROUP INC.

Metaldyne designs and supplies a slew of products for engine, transmission, and driveline applications. The company focuses on powertrain products, such as balance shaft modules, differential assemblies, clutch modules, and exhaust components. Other business units make vibration control (dampers, isolation pulleys), sintered (connecting rods, bearing caps), and forged parts. Customers have included OEMs Chrysler, Ford, GM, and Toyota. Metaldyne in 2017 was acquired by American Axle & Manufacturing (AAM) for $3.3 billion.

Operations
Metaldyne operates in three segments including HHI Holding LLC (HHI; 38% of sales), Metaldyne (32%), and Grede (30%). Metaldyne manufactures highly-engineered metal-based powertrain components for the global light vehicle markets. HHI manufactures highly-engineered metal-based components for the North American light vehicle market.

Grede manufactures cast, machined and assembled components for the light, commercial and industrial (agriculture, construction, mining, rail, wind energy and oil field) vehicle and equipment end-markets.

Geographic Reach
Metaldyne's business is supported by 61 locations dotting 13 countries in Asia, Europe, South America, and North America. The US accounts for 77% of net sales; other major markets include Europe (12%) and other international countries (11%).

Sales and Marketing
Metaldyne targets the global light, commercial and industrial vehicle markets. In 2015 Ford Motor, General Motors, and Fiat Chrysler Automobiles (FCA) accounted for approximately 24%, 21%, and 15%, of its end-customer sales, respectively. Other customers included Daimler AG, Toyota, and Hyundai, which together accounted for approximately 9% of its end-customer sales for the year.

Financial Performance
The company has experienced strong revenue growth the last three years. In 2015 revenues climbed by 12% to peak at $3 billion, primarily due to a 59% surge in its Grede segment, partially offset by declines in its Metaldyne segment. Net income also surged by 72% in 2015 mainly due to a decline in losses related to paying down debt.

The growth in its Grede segment was fueled by its Grede acquisition which contributed approximately $409 million of extra revenue and increased volumes, mainly due to light vehicle production volumes. Also a 2% increase in HHI net sales was primarily attributable to increased volumes due to higher North American light vehicle production levels. The decrease in Metaldyne net sales was attributable to unfavorable foreign currency movements, net price decreases, and lower raw material pass-through.

Mergers and Acquisitions

EXECUTIVES
CAO, Gary Ford
Auditors: DELOITTE & TOUCHE LLP DETROIT

LOCATIONS
HQ: METALDYNE PERFORMANCE GROUP INC.
 1 DAUCH DR, DETROIT, MI 482111115
Phone: 248 727-1800
Web: WWW.AAM.COM

COMPETITORS
AMERICAN AXLE & MANUFACTURING HOLDINGS, INC.
BORGWARNER INC.
COMMERCIAL VEHICLE GROUP, INC.
COOPER-STANDARD HOLDINGS INC.
MERITOR, INC.
SIFCO INDUSTRIES, INC.
STONERIDGE, INC.
VISHAY PRECISION GROUP, INC.
WABCO HOLDINGS INC.
ZF AUTO HOLDINGS US INC.

HISTORICAL FINANCIALS
Company Type: Private

Income Statement — FYE: December 31

	REVENUE ($mil)	NET INCOME ($mil)	NET PROFIT MARGIN	EMPLOYEES
12/16	2,790	96	3.5%	12,000
12/15	3,047	125	4.1%	—
12/14	2,717	73	2.7%	—
Annual Growth	1.3%	15.0%	—	—

2016 Year-End Financials
Return on assets: 3.0%
Return on equity: 14.3%
Current Ratio: 2.00
Cash ($ mil.): 209

METHODIST HEALTH CARE SYSTEM

Auditors: GRANT THORNTON LLP DALLAS TX

LOCATIONS
HQ: METHODIST HEALTH CARE SYSTEM
 6565 FANNIN ST D200, HOUSTON, TX 770302703
Phone: 713 793-1602
Web: WWW.HOUSTONMETHODIST.ORG

HISTORICAL FINANCIALS
Company Type: Private

Income Statement — FYE: September 30

	REVENUE ($mil)	NET INCOME ($mil)	NET PROFIT MARGIN	EMPLOYEES
09/17	1,536	161	10.5%	30
09/14*	1,199	151	12.6%	—
06/05	17	0	1.9%	—
Annual Growth	45.4%	67.8%	—	—

*Fiscal year change

2017 Year-End Financials
Return on assets: 6.8%
Return on equity: 10.0%
Current Ratio: 9.10
Cash ($ mil.): 58

METHODIST HEALTHCARE- MEMPHIS HOSPITALS

Auditors: DIXON HUGHES GOODMAN LLP ASHE

LOCATIONS
HQ: METHODIST HEALTHCARE- MEMPHIS HOSPITALS
 1265 UNION AVE, MEMPHIS, TN 381043415
Phone: 901 516-7000
Web: WWW.METHODISTHEALTH.ORG

HISTORICAL FINANCIALS
Company Type: Private

Income Statement — FYE: December 31

	REVENUE ($mil)	NET INCOME ($mil)	NET PROFIT MARGIN	EMPLOYEES
12/17	2,101	101	4.8%	7,000
12/02	784	(26)	—	—
12/01	717	(28)	—	—
Annual Growth	6.9%	—	—	—

2017 Year-End Financials
Return on assets: 8.9%
Return on equity: 10.3%
Current Ratio: 2.00
Cash ($ mil.): (-10)

METROHEALTH MEDICAL CENTER

LOCATIONS

HQ: METROHEALTH MEDICAL CENTER
2500 METROHEALTH DR, CLEVELAND, OH 441091900
Phone: 216 778-7800
Web: WWW.METROHEALTH.ORG

HISTORICAL FINANCIALS

Company Type: Private

Income Statement — FYE: December 31

	REVENUE ($mil)	NET INCOME ($mil)	NET PROFIT MARGIN	EMPLOYEES
12/16	883	(8)	—	6,000
12/15	795	35	4.5%	—
12/14	782	32	4.2%	—
Annual Growth	6.3%	—	—	—

2016 Year-End Financials
Return on assets: (-0.8%) Cash ($ mil.): 11
Return on equity: (-4.9%)
Current Ratio: 1.30

METROPOLITAN EDISON COMPANY

Metropolitan Edison is an electric company, and it knows a thing or two about serving cities and surrounding communities. The company, a subsidiary of holding company FirstEnergy, provides electric services to a population of 1.3 million in a 3,300-sq. ml. service area in south central and eastern Pennsylvania. Metropolitan Edison, or Met-Ed as it is sometimes referred to, operates almost 16,500 miles of power transmission and distribution lines. Although the company's primary source of electricity is derived from oil-and gas-fired units, its York Haven Power Company generates hydroelectric power.

EXECUTIVES

CAO, Harvey L Wagner
Auditors : PRICEWATERHOUSECOOPERS LLP CL

LOCATIONS

HQ: METROPOLITAN EDISON COMPANY
76 S MAIN ST, AKRON, OH 443081812
Phone: 800 736-3402
Web: WWW.FIRSTENERGYCORP.COM

COMPETITORS

DUKE ENERGY FLORIDA, LLC
NSTAR LLC
PENNSYLVANIA ELECTRIC COMPANY
SOUTH CENTRAL POWER COMPANY
THE SOUTHERN COMPANY

HISTORICAL FINANCIALS

Company Type: Private

Income Statement — FYE: December 31

	REVENUE ($mil)	NET INCOME ($mil)	NET PROFIT MARGIN	EMPLOYEES
12/17	837	97	11.6%	678
12/16	865	87	10.1%	—
12/10	1,818	58	3.2%	—
12/09	1,688	55	3.3%	—
Annual Growth	(8.4%)	7.3%	—	—

2017 Year-End Financials
Return on assets: 2.7% Cash ($ mil.): —
Return on equity: 10.4%
Current Ratio: 1.50

METROPOLITAN GOVERNMENT OF NASHVILLE & DAVIDSON COUNTY

Memphis may have the blues but Nashville has that country sound. Tennessee's second-largest city (with about 600,000 people) is home to many recording studios, music labels, and thousands of working musicians. The city also has a large health care community, with two Fortune 500 companies - HCA and Community Health Systems- employing thousands of people.

EXECUTIVES

Chief of Staff*, Debby D Mason
Auditors : CROSSLIN PLLC NASHVILLE TEN

LOCATIONS

HQ: METROPOLITAN GOVERNMENT OF NASHVILLE & DAVIDSON COUNTY
100 METRO COURTHOUSE, NASHVILLE, TN 37201
Phone: 615 862-5000
Web: WWW.NASHVILLE.GOV

COMPETITORS

CITY OF CHARLOTTE
CITY OF HOUSTON
CITY OF MILWAUKEE
CITY OF NEWPORT NEWS
CITY OF RICHMOND

HISTORICAL FINANCIALS

Company Type: Private

Income Statement — FYE: June 30

	REVENUE ($mil)	NET INCOME ($mil)	NET PROFIT MARGIN	EMPLOYEES
06/21	3,170	830	26.2%	18,000
06/20	2,572	(315)	—	—
06/19	2,605	416	16.0%	—
06/18	2,462	(517)	—	—
Annual Growth	8.8%	—	—	—

2021 Year-End Financials
Return on assets: 4.6% Cash ($ mil.): 1,809
Return on equity: 82.0%
Current Ratio: —

METROPOLITAN TRANSPORTATION AUTHORITY

Metropolitan Transportation Authority (MTA) is North America's largest transportation network, serving a population of 15.3 million people across a 5,000-square-mile travel area surrounding New York City through Long Island, southeastern New York State, and Connecticut. The MTA network comprises the nation's largest bus fleet and more subway and commuter rail cars than all other US transit systems combined. The MTA's operating agencies are MTA New York City Transit, MTA Bus, Long Island Rail Road, Metro-North Railroad, and MTA Bridges and Tunnels.

Operations

The MTA comprises six agencies: MTA New York City Transit, MTA Bus Company, MTA Long Island Rail Road, MTA Metro-North Railroad, MTA Bridges and Tunnels, and MTA Construction & Development.

Its projects have included the 42 street Connection Project, East End Gateway, LIRR Expansion Project, and Penn Station Reconstruction, among others.

Geographic Reach

The MTA is headquartered in Manhattan, New York. It operates in a 5,000-square-mile travel area surrounding New York City through Long Island, southeastern New York State, and Connecticut.

Sales and Marketing

The company serves a population of 15.3 million people.

HISTORY

Mass transit began in New York City in the 1820s with the introduction of horse-drawn stagecoaches run by small private firms. By 1832 a horse-drawn railcar operating on Fourth Avenue offered a smoother and faster ride than its street-bound rivals.

By 1864 residents were complaining that horsecars and buses were overcrowded and that drivers were rude. (Horsecars were transporting 45 million passengers annually.) In 1870 a short subway under Broadway was opened, but it remained a mere amusement. Elevated steam railways were built, but people avoided them because of the smoke, noise, and danger from explosions. Cable cars arrived in the 1880s, and by the 1890s electric streetcars had emerged.

Construction of the first commercial

subway line was completed in 1904. The line was operated by Interborough Rapid Transit (IRT), which leased the primary elevated rail line in 1903 and had effective control of rail transit in Manhattan and the Bronx. In 1905 IRT merged with the Metropolitan Street Railway, which ran most of the surface railways in Manhattan, giving the firm almost complete control of the city's rapid transit. Public protests led the city to grant licenses to Brooklyn Rapid Transit (later BMT), creating the Dual System. The two rail firms covered most of the city.

By the 1920s the transit system was again in crisis, largely because the two lines were not allowed to raise their five-cent fares. With the IRT and BMT in receivership in 1932, the city decided to own and operate part of the rail system and organized the Independent (IND) rail line. Pressure for public ownership and operation of the transit system resulted in the city's purchase of all of IRT's and BMT's assets in 1940 for $326 million.

In 1953 the legislature created the New York City Transit Authority, the first unified system. In 1968, two years after striking transit workers left the city in a virtual gridlock, the Metropolitan Transit Authority began to coordinate the city's transit activities with other commuter services.

The 1970s and 1980s saw the city's transit infrastructure and service deteriorate as crime, accidents, and fares rose. But by the early 1990s a modernization program had begun to make improvements: Subway stations were repaired, graffiti was removed from trains, and service was extended. By 1994 the agency said subway crime was down 50% from 1990, and ridership had increased.

The MTA set up a five-year plan in 1995 to cut expenses by $3 billion. Only 18 months later and already two-thirds of the way to reaching the goal, the authority said it would cut another $230 million and return the savings to customers as fare discounts. The agency agreed in 1996 to sell Long Island Rail Road's freight operations. The next year it began selling its one-fare/free-transfer MetroCard Gold.

In 1998 the MTA capital program completed the $200 million restoration of the Grand Central Terminal. The next year the MTA ordered 500 new clean-fuel buses. But the agency suffered a setback when New York State's $3.8 billion Transportation Infrastructure Bond Act, which included $1.6 billion for MTA improvements, was rejected by voters in 2000.

MTA subway lines in lower Manhattan suffered extensive damage from the September 11, 2001, terrorist attacks that destroyed the World Trade Center's twin towers. The attacks left the MTA, which was already seeking billions of dollars for improvements, faced with $530 million worth of damage.

Confronted with a budget gap for the 2003 fiscal year, the MTA authorized the sale of nearly $2.9 billion worth of transportation bonds, the largest bond issue in the agency's history. The MTA had hoped the eventual proceeds from the bonds would help stave off a fare increase, but in 2003 the agency raised subway and bus fares from $1.50 to $2, among other fare and toll increases.

Angered by issues involving wage hikes, health care, retirement age, and pension costs, members of the Transportation Workers Union walked off the job mere days before Christmas in 2005. The strike stranded commuters and stymied New Yorkers eager to shop and celebrate during the holiday season. The strike was estimated to cause a loss of $300 million per day to the city. In the face of heavy fines, possible jail terms, and the growing ire of would-be commuters, the 33,000 striking union members agreed to go back to work without a contract after three days of picketing, and negotiations resumed. The Metropolitan Transportation Authority and the transit union later reached a contract agreement in which workers pay a portion of their health care costs.

In May 2009 the New York Legislature passed a $2.3 billion bailout package for the MTA, which outlines fare increases of 10% in 2009 and 7.5% in 2011 and 2013. The bailout also requires management changes including combining the agency's chairman and CEO positions. Within days after the bailout was passed, CEO Elliot Sander stepped down and was replaced on an interim basis by Long Island Rail Road President Helena Williams. New York Governor David Paterson picked Jay Walder, a former executive with the London transit system and MTA's former CFO, to succeed Sander and Chairman H. Dale Hemmerdinger. Walder was confirmed by the New York Senate in September 2009.

After five years of working toward bringing in cash by selling naming rights, the MTA made a $4 million deal with Barclays in June 2009 to have the British bank's moniker added to the Atlantic Avenue-Pacific Street subway station in Brooklyn. The MTA also hopes to sell naming rights on its bus lines, bridges, and tunnels, and to expand other corporate sponsorship and advertising opportunities. In 2008 the agency reached a $1 billion deal with Related Companies for the rights to build a 26-acre office and apartment complex above railyards on Manhattan's West Side but the deal's closing was pushed back to 2010 due to the financial slump. The MTA also sold an eight-acre plot above the Long Island Rail Road's Brooklyn railyard for $100 million to Forest City Ratner.

EXECUTIVES

Acting Executive Director*, Veronique Hakim
Chief of Staff*, Zeb Voss
CAO*, Quemuel Arroyo
Auditors: DELOITTE & TOUCHE LLP NEW YOR

LOCATIONS

HQ: METROPOLITAN TRANSPORTATION AUTHORITY
2 BROADWAY, NEW YORK, NY 100042207
Phone: 212 878-7000
Web: NEW.MTA.INFO

PRODUCTS/OPERATIONS

Selected Operations
Bus
    Long Island Bus
    MTA Bus Company
    New York City Transit
Commuter Rail
    Long Island Rail Road
    Metro-North Railroad
    Staten Island Railway

COMPETITORS

CHICAGO TRANSIT AUTHORITY (INC)
DELAWARE RIVER PORT AUTHORITY
FIRSTGROUP PLC
LONDON UNDERGROUND LIMITED
NATIONAL RAILROAD PASSENGER CORPORATION
NORTHEAST ILLINOIS REGIONAL COMMUTER RAILROAD CORPORATION
REGIONAL TRANSPORTATION DISTRICT
SAN FRANCISCO BAY AREA RAPID TRANSIT DISTRICT
THE GO-AHEAD GROUP PLC
THE PORT AUTHORITY OF NEW YORK & NEW JERSEY

HISTORICAL FINANCIALS

Company Type: Private

Income Statement   FYE: December 31

	REVENUE ($mil)	NET INCOME ($mil)	NET PROFIT MARGIN	EMPLOYEES
12/21	5,775	4,160	72.0%	67,457
12/20	4,728	532	11.3%	—
12/19	9,043	498	5.5%	—
12/18	8,736	(145)	—	—
Annual Growth	(12.9%)	—	—	—

2021 Year-End Financials
Return on assets: 3.7%   Cash ($ mil.): 526
Return on equity: 45.5%
Current Ratio: 1.30

METROPOLITAN WATER RECLAMATION DISTRICT OF GREATER CHICAGO

Auditors: BAKER TILLY US LLP CHICAGO

LOCATIONS

HQ: METROPOLITAN WATER RECLAMATION DISTRICT OF GREATER CHICAGO
100 E ERIE ST, CHICAGO, IL 606113154
Phone: 312 751-5600
Web: WWW.MWRD.ORG

HISTORICAL FINANCIALS
Company Type: Private

Income Statement   FYE: December 31

	REVENUE ($mil)	NET INCOME ($mil)	NET PROFIT MARGIN	EMPLOYEES
12/21	820	214	26.1%	2,259
12/20	782	88	11.4%	—
12/19	792	116	14.7%	—
12/18	755	107	14.2%	—
Annual Growth	2.8%	26.0%	—	—

2021 Year-End Financials
Return on assets: 2.2%   Cash ($ mil.): 259
Return on equity: 4.3%
Current Ratio: 0.30

MFA INCORPORATED

Agricultural cooperative MFA brings together 45,000 farmers in Missouri and adjacent states. It is a primary manufacturer of livestock feed, holding a major market share within its trade territory. It is also a supplier and marketer of plant food and crop protection products. The co-op also provides its members with animal feeds, animal-health products, and farm supplies. The company's some 145 company-owned MFA Agri Services Centers combined with nearly 25 locally owned MFA affiliates and approximately 400 independent dealers. The company was founded in 1914.

Operations
MFA's services include credit and finance, crop insurance, health track, powercalf, precision agronomy, among others. MFA's Animal Health division provides its retail operations a good mix of over-the-counter (OTC) labeled medications and vaccines, along with the staff at the dealer locations. The crop protection division sells roughly 850 products from over 40 different vendors to meet the demand of producers. This division's products include, but are not limited to pesticides - row crops, aquatic, range/pasture, stored grain, vineyards, and lawn/garden, foliar nutrition, fertilizer stabilizers, adjuvants and seed treatments and biological. Other product offerings include equine, farm supply, feed, lawn and garden, and pets, among others.

With the combination of its core business, subsidiaries and joint ventures the company delivers sales of about one billion dollars annually.

Geographic Reach
The company's corporate office is located in Columbia, Missouri. The coop has fertilizer terminals on the Mississippi River, as well as on the Missouri and Arkansas rivers.

Sales and Marketing
The coop sells through 400 independent dealers. MFA offers the best products and state-of-the-art services through its MFA Agri Services, affiliates and partners.

Company Background
Expanding its assets, in 2013 MFA acquired Producers Grain Company's assets in El Dorado Springs, Walker, Bronaugh, and Nevada in Missouri.

The co-op was established in 1914 when seven Missouri farmers got together to buy binder twine.

Auditors : WILLIAMS KEEPERS LLC JEFFERS

LOCATIONS
HQ: MFA INCORPORATED
201 RAY YOUNG DR, COLUMBIA, MO 652013599
Phone: 573 874-5111
Web: WWW.MFA-INC.COM

COMPETITORS
Bodisen Biotech, Inc.
CENTAUR GRAIN LIMITED
CHS INC.
Copebras Industria Ltda
FRUIT GROWERS SUPPLY COMPANY
GROWMARK, INC.
Kingenta Ecological Engineering Group Co., Ltd.
MFA OIL COMPANY
TENNESSEE FARMERS COOPERATIVE
WEST CENTRAL COOPERATIVE

HISTORICAL FINANCIALS
Company Type: Private

Income Statement   FYE: August 31

	REVENUE ($mil)	NET INCOME ($mil)	NET PROFIT MARGIN	EMPLOYEES
08/18	1,367	6	0.5%	1,393
08/17	1,373	14	1.0%	—
08/16	1,192	4	0.3%	—
Annual Growth	7.1%	30.1%	—	—

2018 Year-End Financials
Return on assets: 1.4%   Cash ($ mil.): —
Return on equity: 3.9%
Current Ratio: 1.40

MFA OIL COMPANY

Many farmers appreciate MFA Oil. The energy cooperative, controlled by its 40,000 farmer-members, produces fuel and lubrication products and manages bulk petroleum and propane plants in the Central and Western US. Operating 140 propane plants, the company sells more propane for farm use and home heating than any other company in Missouri. It also operates nearly 100 oil and lubricant bulk plants and serves customers in Arkansas, Iowa, Kansas, and Oklahoma. Additionally, the company operates 76 convenience stores under the Break Time brand (in Arkansas and Missouri), more than 160 Petro-Card 24 fueling locations, and owns 10 Jiffy Lube and a dozen Big O Tire franchises.

Geographic Reach
MFA Oil serves customers in Arkansas, Colorado, Kansas, Kentucky, Indiana, Iowa, Missouri, Nebraska, Oklahoma, Virginia, and Wyoming.

Strategy
While not a pure vertically integrated enterprise, over time the cooperative has developed multiple complementary business lines to enable it to respond to a wide range of its members' fuel, transportation, and food service needs. In this tradition, in 2011 MFA Oil teamed up with biofuel developer Aloterra Energy to form MFA Oil Biomass LLC. The partnership aims to help farmers to produce a renewable energy crop that can be used as biomass for an alternative cleaner burning energy supply for use in power generation plants, as well as a liquid fuel. In 2011 about 250 farmers had signed letters of intent to grow miscanthus (a perennial grass) on more than 21,000 acres as part of this initiative.

Mergers and Acquisitions
Expanding its geographic network, in 2013 MFA Oil acquired Kansas-based American Petroleum Marketers, which distributes fuel to more than 60 Cenex branded sites, along with unbranded fuel, in six states.

Company Background
MFA Oil has grown well beyond its Missouri roots, where it was founded by farmers in 1929. The company's first bulk plant was located at Wright City, Missouri.

EXECUTIVES
OF ENTERPRISE RISK MGT, Ed Harper
Auditors : WILLIAMS-KEEPERS LLC COLUMBIA

LOCATIONS
HQ: MFA OIL COMPANY
1 RAY YOUNG DR STE 1 # 1, COLUMBIA, MO 652013506
Phone: 573 442-0171
Web: WWW.MFAOIL.COM

COMPETITORS
ENI USA R&M CO. INC.
ENVIRONMENTAL SYSTEMS PRODUCTS, INC.
JIFFY LUBE INTERNATIONAL, INC.
LUCOR, INC.
VALVOLINE INC.

HISTORICAL FINANCIALS
Company Type: Private

Income Statement   FYE: August 31

	REVENUE ($mil)	NET INCOME ($mil)	NET PROFIT MARGIN	EMPLOYEES
08/17	900	8	0.9%	2,110
08/16	800	24	3.1%	—
08/15	1,045	48	4.6%	—
Annual Growth	(7.2%)	(58.4%)	—	—

2017 Year-End Financials
Return on assets: 2.1%   Cash ($ mil.): 22
Return on equity: 2.7%
Current Ratio: 2.20

MHM SUPPORT SERVICES

Auditors: ERNST & YOUNG US LLP CLAYTON

LOCATIONS

HQ: MHM SUPPORT SERVICES
14528 SOUTH OUTER 40 RD # 100, CHESTERFIELD, MO 630175785
Phone: 314 628-3513

HISTORICAL FINANCIALS
Company Type: Private

Income Statement — FYE: June 30

	REVENUE ($mil)	NET INCOME ($mil)	NET PROFIT MARGIN	EMPLOYEES
06/20	1,018	(86)	—	44,000
06/18	867	0	0.1%	—
06/10	326	(39)	—	—
Annual Growth	12.0%	—	—	—

2020 Year-End Financials
Return on assets: (-10.1%) Cash ($ mil.): 136
Return on equity: —
Current Ratio: —

MIAMI CHILDREN'S HEALTH SYSTEM MANAGEMENT SERVICES, LLC

LOCATIONS

HQ: MIAMI CHILDREN'S HEALTH SYSTEM MANAGEMENT SERVICES, LLC
3100 SW 62ND AVE, MIAMI, FL 331553009
Phone: 305 666-6511
Web: WWW.NICKLAUSHEALTH.ORG

HISTORICAL FINANCIALS
Company Type: Private

Income Statement — FYE: December 31

	REVENUE ($mil)	NET INCOME ($mil)	NET PROFIT MARGIN	EMPLOYEES
12/19	754	(38)	—	27
12/16	688	72	10.5%	—
Annual Growth	3.1%	—	—	—

2019 Year-End Financials
Return on assets: (-2.9%) Cash ($ mil.): 153
Return on equity: (-5.8%)
Current Ratio: 1.90

MIAMI UNIVERSITY

Not that Miami, the other one. Named for the Miami Indian Tribe that inhabited the area now known as the Miami Valley Region of Ohio, Miami University emphasizes undergraduate study at its main campus in Oxford (35 miles north of Cincinnati) as well as at commuter campuses in Hamilton, Middletown, and West Chester, Ohio, and a European Center in Luxembourg. The school offers bachelors, masters, and doctoral programs in areas including business administration, arts and sciences, engineering, and education. Its student body includes more than 15,000 undergraduates on the Oxford campus; 2,500 graduate students; and another 5,700 students attending satellite campuses. Miami University was established in 1809.

Financial Performance
Miami University's 2011 revenue increased 3% vs. 2010, due to a corresponding increase in undergraduate tuition on its three campuses and a rising rates for room and board. Net income at the public university rose 25% over the same period on higher revenue and lower operating expenses, due primarily to a reduction in the number of positions and no salary increases. The rise in tuition for Ohio residents in 2011 was the first in four years. Also, investment income rose in 2011 for the second consecutive year.

Company Background
Miami University celebrated its bicentennial in 2009. The school was chartered in February of 1809 by the State of Ohio, but the first classses were not held until 1824.

EXECUTIVES

Co-Vice President*, Jessica Rivinius
Auditors: MCGLADREY LLP CLEVELAND OHIO

LOCATIONS

HQ: MIAMI UNIVERSITY
501 E HIGH ST, OXFORD, OH 450561846
Phone: 513 529-1809
Web: WWW.MIAMIOH.EDU

COMPETITORS

AUBURN UNIVERSITY
CLEVELAND STATE UNIVERSITY
GRAND VALLEY STATE UNIVERSITY
LAFAYETTE COLLEGE
MARSHALL UNIVERSITY
MISSOURI STATE UNIVERSITY
NORWICH UNIVERSITY
OAKLAND UNIVERSITY
PACE UNIVERSITY
UNIVERSITY OF RHODE ISLAND

HISTORICAL FINANCIALS
Company Type: Private

Income Statement — FYE: June 30

	REVENUE ($mil)	NET INCOME ($mil)	NET PROFIT MARGIN	EMPLOYEES
06/18	551	184	33.5%	4,925
06/17	544	83	15.4%	—
06/16	522	65	12.5%	—
06/12	440	32	7.5%	—
Annual Growth	3.8%	33.3%	—	—

2018 Year-End Financials
Return on assets: 7.7% Cash ($ mil.): 85
Return on equity: 15.7%
Current Ratio: 6.20

MIAMI VALLEY HOSPITAL

Don't go to Florida looking for this hospital! Miami Valley Hospital (MVH) is an acute care facility serving the residents of Dayton, Ohio and surrounding areas through two campuses. MVH and MVH South have roughly 950 beds and offer 50 primary and specialty care practices through its Regional Adult Burn Center, the MVH Cancer Center, MVH Sports Medicine Center, and behavioral health units for outpatient and inpatient chemical dependency therapy and other psychiatric services. MVH also offers Level I trauma services, Level III-B NICU, adult burn center, an air ambulance program, and blood, marrow, and kidney transplant services. The hospital is part of the Premier Health Partners network.

Operations
In addition to MVH, the Premier Health Partners network consists of Good Samaritan Hospital (also stationed in Dayton, Ohio), Atrium Medical Center in nearby Middletown, and Upper Valley Medical Center in Troy. Collectively, the multi-hospital health system houses about 1,800 inpatient beds and around 65 facilities.

MVH have more than 1,100 physicians in more than 70 primary and specialty medical practice areas. It was a 2012 recipient of the HealthGrades Distinguished Hospital Award for Clinical Excellence, placing it among the top 5% of hospitals in the US.

In 2012 it had 41,555 inpatient admissions; 164,140 outpatient visits; 125,622 emergency department visits; and oversaw 4,000 births.

Financial Performance
Medicare accounted for 40% of the company's 2012 revenues; Medicaid, 20%.

Strategy
Over the past few years, MVH has focused on upgrading its infrastructure. It has built a $135 million 440,000-sq. ft., 11-story heart tower on the south side of the campus

and spent $19 million on renovating and expanding its neonatal intensive care unit.

In 2013 it opened its new $6 million 24-hour Emergency Center in Jamestown, Ohio to meet the growing demand for emergency care.

In 2013 MVH South opened a $20 million Comprehensive Cancer Center and (in 2012) a new maternity center which includes five labor and delivery suites, two surgical suites for c-section deliveries and 16 private after-birthing suites.

Company Background
MVH was formed in 1890.

LOCATIONS

HQ: MIAMI VALLEY HOSPITAL
1 WYOMING ST, DAYTON, OH 454092711
Phone: 937 208-8000
Web: WWW.PREMIERHEALTH.COM

PRODUCTS/OPERATIONS

Campus Locations
Miami Valley Hospital - Dayton, OH
Miami Valley Hospital South - Centerville, Ohio

Selected Services and Specialties
Ablation (Cardiology)
Access and Transfer Center (physicians)
Alcoholism, Drug Dependency and Addiction Treatment
Aneurysm (Neurosciences)
Ankle Surgery
Arterial Interventions
Audiology
Bariatrics/Weight Loss Surgery
Behavioral Services
Biotherapy/Targeted Therapy
Blood and Marrow Transplant Program
Brachytherapy
Brain Conditions and Treatments
Brain Injury Rehabilitation
Breast Cancer Navigators
Breast Center
Breast Center
Brethen Center for Surgical Advancement (physicians)
Bull Family Diabetes Center
Burn Center
Cancer Care
Cancer Care (Oncology)
Cardiac Electrophysiology Lab
Cardiac Rehabilitation
Cardiology
Cardiology
Cardiothoracic Surgery
CareFlight - Medical Transportation
Catheterization Lab Procedures
Center for Sleep and Wake Disorders
Chemoembolization
Chemotherapy and Infusion Therapy
Childbirth Education
Colon Cancer
Colorectal Cancer
Complementary Medicine (Cancer)
Comprehensive Outpatient Rehab Program (CORP)
Counseling/Pastoral Care
Craniectomy (Neuroscience)
Craniotomy (Neuroscience)
Cryoablation
CT scan (Imaging)
Dental Center
Depression/Anxiety Treatment
Diabetes
Dialysis Services
Discectomy
Drug Addiction Treatment
Elder Care
Emergency & Trauma Center (ETC)
Foot Surgery
Fractures (Athletes)
Fusion (spinal treatment)
Gastric Bypass
Genetic Testing
Gynecologic Cancer
Gynecology
Hand Therapy
Head and Neck Cancer
Heart Care
Heart Surgery
High Risk Breast Cancer Center
Hip Surgery
Hormone Therapy
Hospitalists/Medical Professionals
Hyperbaric Oxygen Therapy Center
Image Guided Radiation Therapy (IGRT)
Injury Prevention Center
Inpatient Rehabilitation
Intensity Modulated Radiation Therapy (IMRT)
Intensive Care Unit (ICU)
Interventional Radiology
Joint replacements
Kidney Transplant
Knee Surgery
Kyphoplasty
Leukemia
Lung Cancer
Lymphoma
Mammography Screenings
Maternal-Fetal Medicine
Maternity
Maternity
Medical Professionals/Hospitalists
Medical Transportation - CareFlight
Mental Health Services
Minimally Invasive Surgery
Mother and Baby Services
MRI (Imaging)
Nanoknife
Neonatal Intensive Care
Neuro Rehabilitation
NeuroInterventional Center
Neuroscience
Neurosciences
Nutrition Services
OB-GYN
Obstetrics
Occupational Rehabilitation
Occupational Therapy
Oncology
Organ Transplant
Orthopedics
Orthopedics
Outpatient Physical Therapy
Pain Management
Palliative Care
Pancreatic Cancer
Perinatal Intensive Care
PET Scan (Imaging)
Pharmacy
Physiatry
Physical Therapy
Pre-Admission Testing
Premier HeartWorks
Preventive Cardiology
Prostate Cancer
Pulmonary Services
Radiofrequency ablation
Radiology
Radionuclide scan
Rehabilitation
Rehabilitation Institute of Ohio
Respiratory Care
Robotic Surgery
Shoulder Surgery
Shunt (Neuroscience)
Skin Cancer
Sleep Center
Solitaire Revascularization Device (Neurosciences)
Speech-Language Pathology
Spinal decompression surgery
Spinal disc replacement
Spinal fracture treatment
Spinal tumor surgery
Spine and back injuries (Orthopedics)
Spine Conditions and Treatments (Neuroscience)
Sports Medicine
Sports Medicine
Stereotaxis
Stomach Cancer
Stroke Treatments
Surgery Center
Surgical Oncology
Thoracic Surgery
Throat Cancer
Trauma
Ultrasound (Imaging)
Urological Cancer
Urology
Vascular Services
Venous Interventions
Vertebroplasty
Weight Loss Surgery (Bariatrics)
Weight Loss Surgery/Bariatrics
Wheelchair Clinic
Women's Health
Women's Heart Services
Women's Services
Wound Therapy
X-rays (Imaging)
Y-90 Radioembolization

COMPETITORS

ASCENSION PROVIDENCE ROCHESTER HOSPITAL
GOOD SAMARITAN HOSPITAL
MOUNTAIN STATES HEALTH ALLIANCE
MULTICARE HEALTH SYSTEM
NATIONWIDE CHILDREN'S HOSPITAL

HISTORICAL FINANCIALS

Company Type: Private

Income Statement — FYE: December 31

	REVENUE ($mil)	NET INCOME ($mil)	NET PROFIT MARGIN	EMPLOYEES
12/16	809	35	4.4%	8,403
12/15	827	37	4.5%	—
12/14	785	37	4.8%	—
12/07	622	44	7.1%	—
Annual Growth	3.0%	(2.3%)	—	—

2016 Year-End Financials
Return on assets: 2.3%
Return on equity: 5.2%
Current Ratio: 10.00
Cash ($ mil.): 42

MIAMI-DADE AVIATION DEPARTMENT

EXECUTIVES

Aviation Director, Lester Sola
Chief of Staff, Arlyn Rull
Auditors : CHERRY BEKAERT TAMPA FLORIDA

LOCATIONS

HQ: MIAMI-DADE AVIATION DEPARTMENT
13344 SW 108TH STREET CIR, MIAMI, FL 331863424
Phone: 305 876-7000

Web: WWW.AIAMIAMI.ORG

HISTORICAL FINANCIALS
Company Type: Private

Income Statement FYE: September 30

	REVENUE ($mil)	NET INCOME ($mil)	NET PROFIT MARGIN	EMPLOYEES
09/16	830	(29)	—	40
09/15	794	(15)	—	—
Annual Growth	4.6%	—	—	—

2016 Year-End Financials
Return on assets: (-0.4%) Cash ($ mil.): 171
Return on equity: (-3.1%)
Current Ratio: 2.00

MICHIGAN MILK PRODUCERS ASSOCIATION

Ice cream and other dairy products might be missing a major ingredient without Michigan Milk Producers Association (MMPA). The dairy cooperative, whichÂ servesÂ more than 2,100Â farmers in Michigan, Ohio, Indiana, and Wisconsin, produces some 3.9 billion pounds of milk each year. Milk products include sweetened condensed milk, instant nonfat milk, and dried buttermilk, as well as other items the likes of cream, cheese, butter, and ice-cream mixes. With no consumer brands or products, MMPA sells its products as ingredients to foodÂ makers whoÂ sell baby formulas, candy, ice cream, and yogurt. Founded in 1916, the co-op operates a pair of Michigan plants and a merchandise facility.

Operations
As part of its business of serving member-farmers, MMPA provides themÂ with product quality incentives, testing, and customized blending, as well as protection against loss from disaster.

Geographic Reach
From its headquarters in Novi, Michigan, MMPA operates solely in the state of Michigan, where it has manufacturing plants in the villages of Ovid and Constantine and a merchandise facility in the Michigan city of Saint Louis. Its farmers are located in Michigan, Ohio, Indiana, and Wisconsin.

Auditors : CLIFTONLARSONALLEN LLP

LOCATIONS
HQ: MICHIGAN MILK PRODUCERS ASSOCIATION
  41310 BRIDGE ST, NOVI, MI 483751302
Phone: 248 474-6672
Web: WWW.MIMILK.COM

PRODUCTS/OPERATIONS
Selected Products
Condensed skim milk
Condensed whole milk
Dried buttermilk
Dried whole milk
Ice cream mixes
Instant nonfat dry milk
Nonfat dry milk
Standardized cream
Standardized milk
Sweet condensed milk
Sweet cream butter

COMPETITORS
CALIDAD PASCUAL SAU
DAIRY FARMERS PTY LIMITED
DALE FARM CO-OPERATIVE LIMITED
FARMLAND DAIRIES LLC
GREAT LAKES CHEESE CO., INC.
HILAND DAIRY FOODS COMPANY, LLC
MARYLAND AND VIRGINIA MILK PRODUCERS COOPERATIVE ASSOCIATION, INCORPORATED
MAYFIELD DAIRY FARMS, LLC
PRAIRIE FARMS DAIRY, INC.
SWISS VALLEY FARMS COOPERATIVE

HISTORICAL FINANCIALS
Company Type: Private

Income Statement FYE: September 30

	REVENUE ($mil)	NET INCOME ($mil)	NET PROFIT MARGIN	EMPLOYEES
09/11	870	6	0.7%	200
09/10	698	6	1.0%	—
09/09	556	6	1.1%	—
Annual Growth	25.1%	3.2%	—	—

2011 Year-End Financials
Return on assets: 3.8% Cash ($ mil.): 5
Return on equity: 13.4%
Current Ratio: 1.50

MICHIGAN STATE UNIVERSITY

Founded in 1855, Michigan State University (MSU) was the model of a land-grant institution made into law in 1862. MSU and its nearly 49,700 students cover a lot of land in East Lansing. The university offers more than 200 programs of study through more than 15 colleges and unrivaled opportunities for undergraduate research. It has extensive programs in core fields including education, physics, psychology, medicine, and communications. It is also a leading research university with top-ranked international studies programs. As a highly ranked research university, MSU is awarded millions of dollars in research grants each year from public and private entities.

Operations
Michigan State University has more than 100 active research centers and institutes on campus, as well as field research sites throughout the state of Michigan.

With more than 12,000 faculty and academic staff members and a student-teacher ratio of about 16:1, MSU is noted by US. News & World Report for its programs in graduate-level elementary and secondary education, nuclear physics, and industrial and organizational psychology. Its more than 200 undergraduates, masters, doctoral, and certificate programs include accounting, biomedical engineering, communication, finance, and educational technology (online program).

Geographic Reach
MSU's 5,300-acre main campus is in East Lansing, three miles east of Lansing (the capital city of Michigan).

MSU's students hail from all 50 US states, as well as 125 other countries.

Company Background
MSU was founded in 1855, a forerunner of the land-grant college concept, under the name Agricultural College of the State of Michigan. The Morrill Act, which codified land-grant institutions, became law in 1862. MSU became a full university in 1955 as Michigan State University of Agriculture and Applied Science. It changed its name to Michigan State University in 1964.

EXECUTIVES
Academic Affairs Vice President, Thomas Jeitschko Int
CIO*, Melissa Woo
HEALTH SCIENCES, Norman J Beauchamp Junior
Acting Chief*, Brian Quinn
Auditors : PLANTE & MORAN PLLC EAST LAN

LOCATIONS
HQ: MICHIGAN STATE UNIVERSITY
  426 AUDITORIUM RD, EAST LANSING, MI 488242600
Phone: 517 355-1855
Web: WWW.MSU.EDU

PRODUCTS/OPERATIONS
Selected Colleges and Divisions
College of Agriculture and Natural Resources
College of Arts and Letters
College of Communication Arts and Sciences
College of Education
College of Engineering
College of Human Medicine
College of Law (affiliated)
College of Music
College of Natural Science
College of Nursing
College of Osteopathic Medicine
College of Social Science
College of Veterinary Medicine
Eli Broad College of Business and Eli Broad Graduate School of Management
Honors College
James Madison College
Lyman Briggs College
Residential College in the Arts and Humanities
Undergraduate University Division

COMPETITORS
AUBURN UNIVERSITY
CORNELL UNIVERSITY
KANSAS STATE UNIVERSITY
NORTH CAROLINA STATE UNIVERSITY
NORTHEASTERN UNIVERSITY
PURDUE UNIVERSITY
REGENTS OF THE UNIVERSITY OF MINNESOTA
UNIVERSITY OF KANSAS

UNIVERSITY OF OKLAHOMA
UNIVERSITY OF TEXAS AT DALLAS

HISTORICAL FINANCIALS
Company Type: Private

Income Statement — FYE: June 30

	REVENUE ($mil)	NET INCOME ($mil)	NET PROFIT MARGIN	EMPLOYEES
06/18	1,986	(246)	—	11,100
06/17	1,931	481	25.0%	—
06/16	1,811	71	3.9%	—
Annual Growth	4.7%	—	—	—

2018 Year-End Financials
Return on assets: (-3.7%)   Cash ($ mil.): 384
Return on equity: (-10.5%)
Current Ratio: 0.50

MID-AMERICA PIPELINE COMPANY, LLC

EXECUTIVES
Managing Member, J M Collingsworth

LOCATIONS
HQ: MID-AMERICA PIPELINE COMPANY, LLC
1100 LA ST STE 1000, HOUSTON, TX 77002
Phone: 713 880-6500
Web: WWW.ENTERPRISEPRODUCTS.COM

HISTORICAL FINANCIALS
Company Type: Private

Income Statement — FYE: December 31

	REVENUE ($mil)	NET INCOME ($mil)	NET PROFIT MARGIN	EMPLOYEES
12/17	591	361	61.1%	250
12/16	591	366	62.0%	—
Annual Growth	0.0%	(1.4%)	—	—

2017 Year-End Financials
Return on assets: 23.8%   Cash ($ mil.): —
Return on equity: 24.4%
Current Ratio: 2.90

MIDCOAST ENERGY PARTNERS, L.P.

Midcoast Energy Partners was formed by Enbridge Energy Partners in 2013 as an investment vehicle to own and grow its natural gas and NGL midstream business. It has minority stakes in Enbridge's network of natural gas and natural gas liquids (NGLs) gathering and transportation systems, natural gas processing and treating facilities, and NGL fractionation plants in Texas and Oklahoma. Organized as a limited partnership, Midcoast Energy Partners is exempt from paying income tax as long as it distributes quarterly dividends to shareholders. It went public in 2013, raising $333 million. In 2017 Enbridge Energy Partners agreed to acquire control of Midcoast Energy Partners.

Auditors : PRICEWATERHOUSECOOPERS LLP HO

LOCATIONS
HQ: MIDCOAST ENERGY PARTNERS, L.P.
1100 LA ST STE 3300, HOUSTON, TX 77002
Phone: 800 755-5400
Web: WWW.MIDCOASTENERGY.COM

COMPETITORS
Direct Energy Marketing Limited
EMERGE ENERGY SERVICES LP
EQT CORPORATION
QEP RESOURCES, INC.
WILLIAMS PARTNERS L.P.

HISTORICAL FINANCIALS
Company Type: Private

Income Statement — FYE: December 31

	REVENUE ($mil)	NET INCOME ($mil)	NET PROFIT MARGIN	EMPLOYEES
12/16	1,966	(157)	—	1,250
12/15	2,842	(284)	—	—
12/14	5,894	144	2.4%	—
12/13	5,593	53	1.0%	—
Annual Growth	(29.4%)	—	—	—

2016 Year-End Financials
Return on assets: (-3.2%)   Cash ($ mil.): 7
Return on equity: (-4.2%)
Current Ratio: 0.50

MIDDLESEX, COUNTY OF (INC)

EXECUTIVES
County Administrator, John Pulomena
Auditors : HODULIK & MORRISON PA CRANF

LOCATIONS
HQ: MIDDLESEX, COUNTY OF (INC)
75 BAYARD ST, NEW BRUNSWICK, NJ 089012112
Phone: 732 745-3000
Web: WWW.MIDDLESEXCOUNTYNJ.GOV

HISTORICAL FINANCIALS
Company Type: Private

Income Statement — FYE: December 31

	REVENUE ($mil)	NET INCOME ($mil)	NET PROFIT MARGIN	EMPLOYEES
12/21	693	10	1.5%	2,100
12/20	689	18	2.7%	—
12/19	522	6	1.2%	—
12/17	497	9	2.0%	—
Annual Growth	8.7%	1.9%	—	—

2021 Year-End Financials
Return on assets: 0.6%   Cash ($ mil.): 205
Return on equity: 1.2%
Current Ratio: —

MIDMICHIGAN MEDICAL CENTER-MIDLAND

Auditors : ANDREWS HOOPER PAVLIK PLC SAG

LOCATIONS
HQ: MIDMICHIGAN MEDICAL CENTER-MIDLAND
4000 WELLNESS DR, MIDLAND, MI 486702000
Phone: 989 839-3000
Web: WWW.MYMICHIGAN.ORG

HISTORICAL FINANCIALS
Company Type: Private

Income Statement — FYE: June 30

	REVENUE ($mil)	NET INCOME ($mil)	NET PROFIT MARGIN	EMPLOYEES
06/21	550	173	31.4%	1,404
06/20	519	41	8.0%	—
06/19	476	62	13.0%	—
06/18	427	37	8.7%	—
Annual Growth	8.8%	66.8%	—	—

2021 Year-End Financials
Return on assets: 16.0%   Cash ($ mil.): 10
Return on equity: 23.3%
Current Ratio: 1.10

MILES HEALTH CARE, INC

Miles Health Care provides acute and specialty health care service to the residents of Maine's Lincoln County. The not-for-profit company operates Miles Memorial Hospital -- known as LincolnHealth Miles Campus -- a rural medical center with about 40 beds and has emergency, intensive care, surgery, and birthing departments. In addition, Miles Health Care operates outpatient and specialty practice clinics, physician practice offices, and home health, rehabilitation, and hospice programs. It also provides long-term senior care through its nursing, assisted, and independent living facilities. Miles Health Care is a member of Lincoln County Healthcare (LincolnHealth), which is part of the MaineHealth network.

Operations

In addition to the two main hospital campuses, LincolnHealth includes physician practices operated by the Lincoln Medical Partners, as well as family care and urgent care centers. It also continues to operate nursing, home health, hospice, and assisted-living organizations.

Geographic Reach
The LincolnHealth Miles Campus is located in Lincoln County, Maine, in the town of Damariscotta (which is north of Portland). The LincolnHealth St. Andrews Campus is located in Boothbay Harbor.

Strategy
Both the Miles and St. Andrews medical centers began using electronic health record (EHR) systems in 2010, which allows doctors to access a patient's past medical and diagnostic experiences to make the best decisions on current treatment plans and avoid duplication. Such EHR systems are part of an initiative to lower the cost of medical care in the US.

Company Background
Miles Health Care was established in 1941. Miles has historically been governed by a board of trustees (the Lincoln County Healthcare Board of Trustees) that also oversee the nearby St. Andrews Hospital; as an independently governed member of MaineHealth, Miles has received planning, consulting, capital, and group purchasing benefits. In 2013 St. Andrews Hospital and Miles Memorial Hospital were officially merged to serve as dual campuses of the single LincolnHealth hospital.

LOCATIONS
HQ: MILES HEALTH CARE, INC
35 MILES ST, DAMARISCOTTA, ME 045434047
Phone: 207 563-1234
Web: WWW.MAINEHEALTH.ORG

PRODUCTS/OPERATIONS
Selected Centers and Services
Chase Point Adult Day Services
Chase Point Assisted Living
Cove's Edge
Emergency Services
Family Support Services
General Surgery
Internal Medicine
Mammography
Miles & St. Andrews Home Health & Hospice
Miles Family Medicine
MMH BabyNet
Obstetrics
Orthopedic Services
Pediatric Services
Schooner Cove
Senior Services
Waldoboro Family Medicine
Wellness and Rehabilitation
Wiscasset Family Medicine
Women's Services

COMPETITORS
BEACON MEDICAL GROUP, INC.
CKHS, INC.
INSPIRA HEALTH NETWORK, INC.
MAINEHEALTH SERVICES
SOUTHCOAST HEALTH SYSTEM, INC.

HISTORICAL FINANCIALS
Company Type: Private

Income Statement   FYE: September 30

	REVENUE ($mil)	NET INCOME ($mil)	NET PROFIT MARGIN	EMPLOYEES
09/09	1,042	12	1.2%	800
09/08	14	0	3.9%	—
09/06	58	3	5.9%	—
09/05	52	(0)	—	—
Annual Growth	111.6%	—	—	—

2009 Year-End Financials
Return on assets: 112.3%   Cash ($ mil.): —
Return on equity: 494.4%
Current Ratio: 1.30

MILLS-PENINSULA HEALTH SERVICES

With health facilities south of San Francisco, Mills-Peninsula Health Services provides care to communities in and around Burlingame, California. The not-for-profit health care group includes the 240-bed Mills-Peninsula Medical Center, an acute-care hospital in Burlingame; Mills Health Center, an outpatient diagnostic, surgery, and rehabilitation facility in San Mateo; and physician practice offices in surrounding areas. The facilities provide specialty services such as cancer care, cardiovascular therapy, behavioral health, radiology, respiratory care, and senior services. Mills-Peninsula Health Services is part of the Sutter Health network.

Operations
Along with sister company Palo Alto Medical Foundation, Mills-Peninsula forms the Peninsula Coastal Region division of Sutter Health. Together, the organizations operate collaborative medical clinic and physician practice locations.

Geographic Reach
Mills-Peninsula Health Services operates facilities in Burlingame and San Mateo in California.

Financial Performance
Mills-Peninsula Health Services reported revenues of $611 million (7% of the parent company's net revenues) in 2013.
Its net income in 2013 was $53 million.

Strategy
Through the contribution of donors, in 2014 the Mills-Peninsula Women's Center replaced all its digital mammography units with digital breast tomosynthesis, allowing it to provide 3D mammography for breast cancer screenings at no extra cost to patients.
The hospital enhanced its surgical capabilities in 2013 with the addition of a da Vinci Si robotic system for surgical procedures.
That year Mills-Peninsula's Dorothy E. Schneider Cancer Center introduced a new cancer treatment, Xofigo (Radium-223 dichloride), for patients with advanced-stage prostate cancer that has metastasized to the bones, but not other organs.

Company Background
The organization opened the doors on its newly constructed Mills-Peninsula Medical Center in Burlingame in 2011. The $618 million project added a new 240-bed main hospital facility (to replace the aging Peninsula Medical Center facility) with all private patient rooms, as well as a 180,000 sq. ft. medical office building and a parking garage. The new hospital is compliant with California's new earthquake safety requirements.
The Peninsula facility was founded as a public hospital district in 1954. The two hospitals merged in 1985 and became part of Sutter Health the following year.
Founded in 1908, the Mills hospital was named for philanthropist Elizabeth Mills Reid, who helped to fund the medical facility.

Auditors: ERNST & YOUNG US LLP SAN DIEG

LOCATIONS
HQ: MILLS-PENINSULA HEALTH SERVICES
1501 TROUSDALE DR, BURLINGAME, CA 940104506
Phone: 650 696-5400
Web: WWW.MILLS-PENINSULA.ORG

PRODUCTS/OPERATIONS
Selected Services
Arthritis & Osteoporosis
Behavioral Health
Birth Center
Cancer Center
Cardiovascular
Children's Services
Psychiatric Emergency
Senior Services
Obesity Surgery
Orthopedic Surgery
Women's Center

COMPETITORS
BAPTIST HEALTH SOUTH FLORIDA, INC.
BORGESS HEALTH ALLIANCE, INC.
HUNTINGTON HOSPITAL DOLAN FAMILY HEALTH CENTER, INC.
MEMORIAL HEALTH SYSTEM OF EAST TEXAS
MULTICARE HEALTH SYSTEM

HISTORICAL FINANCIALS
Company Type: Private

Income Statement   FYE: December 31

	REVENUE ($mil)	NET INCOME ($mil)	NET PROFIT MARGIN	EMPLOYEES
12/13	609	54	8.9%	2,200
12/09	533	56	10.6%	—
12/02	274	18	6.6%	—
12/01	398	0	0.0%	—
Annual Growth	3.6%	172.8%	—	—

2013 Year-End Financials
Return on assets: 12.6%   Cash ($ mil.): 20
Return on equity: 8.9%
Current Ratio: 0.10

MILTON HERSHEY SCHOOL & SCHOOL TRUST

Auditors : PRICEWATERHOUSECOOPERS LLP PH

LOCATIONS

HQ: MILTON HERSHEY SCHOOL & SCHOOL TRUST
711 CREST LN, HERSHEY, PA 170338903
Phone: 717 520-1100
Web: WWW.HERSHEYTRUST.COM

HISTORICAL FINANCIALS

Company Type: Private

Income Statement — FYE: July 31

	REVENUE ($mil)	NET INCOME ($mil)	NET PROFIT MARGIN	EMPLOYEES
07/18	1,069	784	73.4%	13
07/17	469	198	42.2%	—
07/12	386	180	46.7%	—
07/10	211	3	1.6%	—
Annual Growth	22.4%	97.8%	—	—

2018 Year-End Financials
Return on assets: 5.6%   Cash ($ mil.): 72
Return on equity: 5.7%
Current Ratio: —

MILWAUKEE PUBLIC SCHOOLS (INC)

Auditors : BAKER TILLY VIRCHOW KRAUSE LL

LOCATIONS

HQ: MILWAUKEE PUBLIC SCHOOLS (INC)
5225 W VLIET ST, MILWAUKEE, WI 532082698
Phone: 414 475-8393
Web: MPS.MILWAUKEE.K12.WI.US

HISTORICAL FINANCIALS

Company Type: Private

Income Statement — FYE: June 30

	REVENUE ($mil)	NET INCOME ($mil)	NET PROFIT MARGIN	EMPLOYEES
06/21	1,294	26	2.1%	14,154
06/19	1,199	(22)	—	—
06/18	1,196	2	0.2%	—
06/17	1,182	9	0.8%	—
Annual Growth	2.3%	28.9%	—	—

2021 Year-End Financials
Return on assets: 1.9%   Cash ($ mil.): —
Return on equity: —
Current Ratio: 1.70

MINERS INCORPORATED

Miner's is a family-owned chain of about 30 grocery stores in Michigan, North Dakota, northern Minnesota, and Wisconsin. Most of the company's stores fly the Super One Foods banner, but there are a few under the U-Save Foods and Marketplace Foods names. Following the acquisition of seven Jubilee and Festival Foods stores in Minnesota from Plaza Holding Co., Miner's converted the stores to its Super One Foods banner, most of which are located in Minnesota. Miner's also has a wholesale grocery operation in Duluth. Miner's was founded by Anton and Ida Miner, who started out selling groceries out of their tavern in Grand Rapids, Michigan in the 1930s. In 1943 they built the family's first store, Miner's Market.

Geographic Reach

Minnesota is the regional grocery chain's largest market, home to 21 of its 31 stores. Wisconsin and Michigan are each home to about five locations. The grocery chain has a single store North Dakota.

Financial Performance

Miner's rang up an estimated $437 million in sales in fiscal 2013 (ended June).

Strategy

Miner's takes a measured approach to growth, combining occasional acquisitions with organic growth. Its newest location is a 59,000-square-foot Super One Foods store slated to open in 2014 in Superior, Wisconsin.

Mergers and Acquisitions

In May 2011 Miner's upped its store count with the acquisition of four family-owned Paulson's Super Valu grocery stores in northern Minnesota and Wisconsin.

Prevented by Minnesota law from selling alcohol in grocery stores, the company recently bought two liquor stores, in Cloquet and Duluth.

Auditors : RSM US LLP DULUTH MINNESOTA

LOCATIONS

HQ: MINERS INCORPORATED
5065 MILLER TRUNK HWY, HERMANTOWN, MN 558111442
Phone: 218 729-5882
Web: WWW.SUPERONEFOODS.COM

2014 Stores

	No.
Minnesota	21
Michigan	5
Wisconsin	4
North Dakota	1
Total	31

PRODUCTS/OPERATIONS

2014 Stores

	No.
Super One Foods	27
U-Save Foods	2
Country Market	1
Marketplace Foods	1
Total	31

COMPETITORS

ARDEN GROUP, INC.
DEMOULAS SUPER MARKETS, INC.
HARP'S FOOD STORES, INC.
LOWES FOODS, LLC
ROUNDY'S, INC.

HISTORICAL FINANCIALS

Company Type: Private

Income Statement — FYE: June 24

	REVENUE ($mil)	NET INCOME ($mil)	NET PROFIT MARGIN	EMPLOYEES
06/17	548	26	4.8%	2,300
06/12	501	31	6.3%	—
06/11	475	30	6.4%	—
06/10	463	27	5.8%	—
Annual Growth	2.4%	(0.5%)	—	—

2017 Year-End Financials
Return on assets: 10.7%   Cash ($ mil.): 7
Return on equity: 15.4%
Current Ratio: 1.80

MINNEAPOLIS PUBLIC SCHOOL

EXECUTIVES

Acting Superintendent, Michael Goar
Auditors : BERGAN KDV LTD MINNEAPOLIS

LOCATIONS

HQ: MINNEAPOLIS PUBLIC SCHOOL
1250 W BROADWAY AVE, MINNEAPOLIS, MN 554112533
Phone: 612 668-0200
Web: WWW.MPLS.K12.MN.US

HISTORICAL FINANCIALS

Company Type: Private

Income Statement — FYE: June 30

	REVENUE ($mil)	NET INCOME ($mil)	NET PROFIT MARGIN	EMPLOYEES
06/16	709	(25)	—	9,000
06/15	685	116	17.1%	—
06/05	441	18	4.2%	—
06/04	632	(42)	—	—
Annual Growth	1.0%	—	—	—

2016 Year-End Financials
Return on assets: (-1.9%)   Cash ($ mil.): —
Return on equity: —
Current Ratio: —

MISSION HOSPITAL REGIONAL MEDICAL CENTER INC

Auditors : ERNST & YOUNG US LLP SAN DIEG

LOCATIONS

HQ: MISSION HOSPITAL REGIONAL MEDICAL CENTER INC
27700 MEDICAL CENTER RD, MISSION VIEJO, CA 926916426
Phone: 949 364-1400
Web: M.MISSION4HEALTH.COM

HISTORICAL FINANCIALS

Company Type: Private

Income Statement — FYE: June 30

	REVENUE ($mil)	NET INCOME ($mil)	NET PROFIT MARGIN	EMPLOYEES
06/16	547	28	5.3%	2,600
06/15	516	23	4.5%	—
06/10	500	50	10.1%	—
06/09	355	12	3.5%	—
Annual Growth	6.4%	13.0%	—	—

2016 Year-End Financials

Return on assets: 4.9%   Cash ($ mil.): 38
Return on equity: 10.5%
Current Ratio: 1.40

MISSION HOSPITAL, INC.

Its mission is clear and bold: Improve the health of all in western North Carolina. Mission Hospital is a 760-bed regional referral center serving the western quarter of North Carolina and portions of adjoining states. A not-for-profit community hospital system, Mission is located in Asheville on two adjoining campuses: Memorial and St. Joseph's. It provides tertiary-level services in neurosciences, cardiac care, trauma care, surgery, pediatric medicine, and women's services and has a medical staff of more than 540. It also includes the Mission Children's Hospital. Mission Hospital is the flagship hospital of Mission Health System, which is being acquired by HCA Healthcare for $1.5 billion.

Geographic Reach

Mission Health System serves patients in western North Carolina.

Sales and Marketing

Medicare accounts for some 40% of Mission Hospital's net patient service revenue; Medicaid account for around for 30%, and self-pay and other third-party payors account for the rest.

Financial Performance

Revenue increased 6% to $119 million in 2014 on higher net patient service earnings. Those gains, plus higher investment returns, led to a 12% increase in net income to $1.2 million.

After posting an operating cash outflow in 2013, Mission Hospital had a cash inflow of $0.9 million in 2014 as less cash was used towards net patient accounts receivable.

Strategy

Mission Hospital has been actively expanding and modernizing its facilities in recent years. It built a surgery registration and waiting area to ease patient comfort as they wait to be seen at the Memorial Campus. It also opened a four-story facility to provide more surgery suites and patient beds for Mission Hospital. In order to increase patient satisfaction, the hospital opened a new surgery registration and waiting area at its Memorial Campus.

Mission Hospital places great focus on genetic medicine. It has an entire department dedicated to the study of genetics, genetic therapy, and the study of fetal alcohol spectrum disorders.

Mission Health partnered with Western Carolina University to provide a graduate certification program in Healthcare Innovation Management. The program, which began in 2013, is a component of Mission Health's budding Center for Innovation, established to foster a spirit of advancement in healthcare throughout western North Carolina. The program consists of four courses over a period of 21 months and is open to all Mission Health employees. Students who complete the program, which is fully funded by Mission Health, will earn credit towards bachelor's and master's degrees.

Company Background

Mission Hospital was formed in 1996 from the partnership (and eventual merger) of Memorial and St. Joseph's hospitals.

LOCATIONS

HQ: MISSION HOSPITAL, INC.
509 BILTMORE AVE, ASHEVILLE, NC 288014601
Phone: 828 213-1111
Web: WWW.MISSIONHEALTH.ORG

PRODUCTS/OPERATIONS

Surgical Services
General Surgery
Minimally Invasive Surgery
Outpatient Surgery
Prepare for Surgery
Robotic Surgery
Surgery at Mission Hospital
Surgery Guide
Programs of Service
Endoscopy
Genetics
Integrative Healthcare
Mother and Baby
Outpatient Care Centers
Sleep Center
Urology
Weight Management Center
Wound Healing and Hyperbarics
Support Services
Chronic Medical Conditions
Long-Term Acute Care
Laboratory
Pastoral Care Services
Pharmacy
Psychiatric Services
Radiology (Imaging) Services
Rehabilitation Services
Research Institute
Respiratory Therapy
Senior Services and Geriatrics

COMPETITORS

ADENA HEALTH SYSTEM
CHARLESTON AREA MEDICAL CENTER, INC.
JOHN T. MATHER MEMORIAL HOSPITAL OF PORT JEFFERSON, NEW YORK, INC.
NORTHSHORE UNIVERSITY HEALTHSYSTEM
THE RUTLAND HOSPITAL INC ACT 220

HISTORICAL FINANCIALS

Company Type: Private

Income Statement — FYE: September 30

	REVENUE ($mil)	NET INCOME ($mil)	NET PROFIT MARGIN	EMPLOYEES
09/15	1,019	91	9.0%	10,000
09/14	936	64	6.9%	—
09/13	942	71	7.6%	—
09/12	861	86	10.0%	—
Annual Growth	5.8%	2.0%	—	—

2015 Year-End Financials

Return on assets: 7.5%   Cash ($ mil.): —
Return on equity: 8.4%
Current Ratio: 3.70

MISSISSIPPI STATE UNIVERSITY

While agriculture is at its roots, Mississippi State University's (MSU) is today a four-year university offering approximately 150 undergraduate majors and pre-professional programs, as well as master's, educational specialist, and doctorate degree programs at a dozen colleges and schools. It confers more than 4,300 degrees annually and has an enrollment of more than 20,870 students at its main campus in Starkville and a regional campus in Meridian. More than three-quarters of its student body hail from Mississippi. MSU was created by the Mississippi Legislature in 1878 as The Agricultural and Mechanical College of the State of Mississippi.

EXECUTIVES

Chief Human Resource Officer*, Nancy L Siegert
Budget Director*, June Dempsey

LOCATIONS

HQ: MISSISSIPPI STATE UNIVERSITY
245 BARR AVE MCRTHUR HL MCARTHUR HALL, MISSISSIPPI STATE, MS 39762

Phone: 662 325-2302
Web: WWW.MSSTATE.EDU

COMPETITORS

BOARD OF REGENTS OF THE UNIVERSITY OF NEBRASKA
MIDWESTERN STATE UNIVERSITY
NORFOLK STATE UNIVERSITY
NORTHERN ILLINOIS UNIVERSITY
OREGON STATE UNIVERSITY

HISTORICAL FINANCIALS
Company Type: Private

Income Statement — FYE: June 30

	REVENUE ($mil)	NET INCOME ($mil)	NET PROFIT MARGIN	EMPLOYEES
06/21	572	58	10.3%	4,500
06/20	547	68	12.6%	—
06/19	525	71	13.6%	—
06/18	489	29	6.0%	—
Annual Growth	5.4%	25.8%	—	—

2021 Year-End Financials
Return on assets: 3.3%   Cash ($ mil.): 298
Return on equity: 8.6%
Current Ratio: 3.50

MISSOURI BAPTIST MEDICAL CENTER

LOCATIONS

HQ: MISSOURI BAPTIST MEDICAL CENTER
3015 N BALLAS RD, SAINT LOUIS, MO 631312329
Phone: 314 996-5155
Web: WWW.MISSOURIBAPTIST.ORG

HISTORICAL FINANCIALS
Company Type: Private

Income Statement — FYE: December 31

	REVENUE ($mil)	NET INCOME ($mil)	NET PROFIT MARGIN	EMPLOYEES
12/20	613	51	8.5%	1,670
12/18	584	15	2.6%	—
12/17	600	18	3.0%	—
12/16	570	25	4.5%	—
Annual Growth	1.8%	19.5%	—	—

2020 Year-End Financials
Return on assets: 15.4%   Cash ($ mil.): —
Return on equity: 22.7%
Current Ratio: 1.00

MISSOURI CITY OF KANSAS CITY

You may not be in Kansas anymore, but you could still be in Kansas City. Situated opposite Kansas City, Kansas, is the city of Kansas City, Missouri, the state's largest city, with a population of about 460,000. Its council-manager form of government is made up of 12 members presided over by the mayor. The city manager serves and advises the council and prepares the annual budget for council consideration, as well as enforces municipal laws and ordinances and manages city operations. With more than 200 fountains within 320 square miles, its official nickname is the "City of Fountains." Incorporated in 1850, it is home to the Chiefs and Royals and is famous for barbeque.

Auditors : ALLEN GIBBS & HOULIK LC WIC

LOCATIONS

HQ: MISSOURI CITY OF KANSAS CITY
414 E 12TH ST STE 105, KANSAS CITY, MO 641062705
Phone: 816 513-1313
Web: WWW.KCMO.GOV

COMPETITORS

CITY OF AUSTIN
CITY OF CLEVELAND
CITY OF LOS ANGELES
CITY OF OXNARD
CITY OF SACRAMENTO

HISTORICAL FINANCIALS
Company Type: Private

Income Statement — FYE: April 30

	REVENUE ($mil)	NET INCOME ($mil)	NET PROFIT MARGIN	EMPLOYEES
04/21	1,171	28	2.4%	8,000
04/20	1,150	42	3.7%	—
04/19	1,150	(22)	—	—
04/18	1,085	13	1.2%	—
Annual Growth	2.6%	28.8%	—	—

2021 Year-End Financials
Return on assets: 0.3%   Cash ($ mil.): —
Return on equity: 0.7%
Current Ratio: —

MISSOURI DEPARTMENT OF TRANSPORTATION

Missouri has come a long way since its first byway, Three Notch Road, was built in 1735, and MoDOT has had a lot to do with the progress. The Missouri Department of Transportation (MoDOT) oversees one of the nation's largest state highway systems. Specifically, it designs, builds, and maintains the 32,000-plus miles of highway and some 10,000 bridges, and administers federal and state programs that affect public transit and air, water, and rail transportation throughout the state. MoDOT is governed by the six-member Missouri Highways and Transportation Commission. The agency that became MoDOT got its start when the Missouri Legislature established a job for a state highway engineer in 1907.

Auditors : BKD LLP SPRINGFIELD MO

LOCATIONS

HQ: MISSOURI DEPARTMENT OF TRANSPORTATION
105 W CAPITOL AVE, JEFFERSON CITY, MO 651016811
Phone: 573 751-2551
Web: WWW.MODOT.ORG

PRODUCTS/OPERATIONS

Selected Services and Operations
Commnity Services
    Adopt-A-Highway
    Being Green
    Economic Impact Analysis
    Local Programs
    Memorial Designation Programs
    Partnership Development
    Planning and Policy Group
    Request a Speaker
    Roadside Vegetation Management
    Scenic Byways
    Sponsor-A-Highway
    Stormwater Pollution Reporting
    Transportation Enhancements
    Work-Zone Safety Awareness
Engineering Services
    Bridge Engineering Assistance Program
    Traffic Engineering Assistance Program
Travel Services
    Carpool Connections
    Commuter Lots
    Gateway Guide
    Intelligent Transportation Systems
    Kansas City Scout
    Missouri Rest Area Guide
    Motorist Assist
    Online Traveler Information Map
    Ozark Traffic Information
    Snow Plowing info -- priorities, driving tips and more

COMPETITORS

ARIZONA DEPARTMENT OF TRANSPORTATION
NEW YORK DEPARTMENT OF TRANSPORTATION
OHIO DEPARTMENT OF TRANSPORTATION
TEXAS DEPARTMENT OF TRANSPORTATION
TRANSPORTATION, SOUTH CAROLINA DEPARTMENT OF

HISTORICAL FINANCIALS
Company Type: Private

Income Statement — FYE: June 30

	REVENUE ($mil)	NET INCOME ($mil)	NET PROFIT MARGIN	EMPLOYEES
06/17	2,213	(107)	—	6,295
06/09	2,142	(357)	—	—
06/05	0	0	—	—
Annual Growth	—	—	—	—

2017 Year-End Financials
Return on assets: (-0.3%)   Cash ($ mil.): 735
Return on equity: (-0.4%)
Current Ratio: 2.60

MMR CONSTRUCTORS, INC.

Auditors : MADDOX & ASSOCIATES APC BATO

LOCATIONS

HQ: MMR CONSTRUCTORS, INC.
15961 AIRLINE HWY, BATON ROUGE, LA 708177412
Phone: 225 756-5090
Web: WWW.MMRGRP.COM

HISTORICAL FINANCIALS

Company Type: Private

Income Statement — FYE: December 31

	REVENUE ($mil)	NET INCOME ($mil)	NET PROFIT MARGIN	EMPLOYEES
12/20	556	42	7.6%	4,000
12/19	772	30	3.9%	—
12/18	775	25	3.3%	—
12/17	581	16	2.9%	—
Annual Growth	(1.5%)	36.6%	—	—

2020 Year-End Financials
Return on assets: 7.8%   Cash ($ mil.): 2
Return on equity: 15.3%
Current Ratio: 3.90

MMR GROUP, INC.

That murmur you hear could be the gentle hum of a properly functioning power system. MMG Group provides electrical and instrumentation construction, maintenance, management, and technical services for clients in the oil and gas, manufacturing, chemical, and power generation industries around the world. It also offers services in offshore marine and platform environments. Its Power Solutions division constructs onsite power-generation systems in industrial plants and other facilities. The group primarily operates in the Gulf of New Mexico. Founded in 1990, MMG is 100% management owned and has served such clients as Chevron, Shell, BP, Merck, Air Liquide, DuPont, and 3M.

Operations

MMR Group's provides four main services: electrical and instrumentation contracting, safety services, panel fabrication, and communications.

MMR's electrical and instrumentation contractors work on projects throughout the US and overseas. To ensure its projects are completed on time and within budget, its personnel has support and management control systems, and emphasizes planning, scheduling, progress tracking, and labor analysis.

The MMR Offshore Safety Services division specializes in disaster prevention and safety, helping with navigation, fire and gas detection, suppression products, paging and alarm systems, level one cathodic protection, inspections, and other related services.

For panel fabrication services, MMR stages, tests, and designs control systems that best fit client needs.

The MMR ProCom division is in charge of pre-commissioning, commissioning, and start-Up activities for both MMR Group construction projects and for outside clients interested in turning their facilities construction into a safe and reliable operation, seamlessly.

Geographic Reach

MMR operates out of some 20 offices spread across North and South America, with most of its offices in Texas, Louisiana, and California. The company works on projects all over the world, with foreign affiliate offices in Calgary, Canada; Cartagena, Colombia; Puerto la Cruz, Venezuela; and Port of Spain, Trinidad & Tobago.

Sales and Marketing

MMR serves a variety of markets including: alternative energy exploration and production, chemical and petrochemical, industrial and manufacturing, oil and gas, power generation, and waste and water treatment, among others.

Some of the company's panel fabrication clients have included Shell Pipeline, Chevron Pipeline, Enbridge Pipeline, AGI Services, Cimitation Engineering, ExxonMobil, Keystone Engineering, W.S. Nelson Engineering, and Entergy, among others.

Depending on the project and client's preference, MMR operates on all types of fixed-price and cost-plus contracts.

Strategy

The company continues to expand its operations to accommodate more projects. In 2014, the company built a 19-office administration building along with a 6,000 square-foot warehouse facility to support the influx of new projects going on in the Golden Triangle area between Beaumont, TX and Lake Charles, LA.

Auditors : MADDOX & ASSOCIATES APC BATO

LOCATIONS

HQ: MMR GROUP, INC.
15961 AIRLINE HWY, BATON ROUGE, LA 708177412
Phone: 225 756-5090
Web: WWW.MMRGRP.COM

PRODUCTS/OPERATIONS

Selected Services
Instrumentation
   Air supply installation
   Control room equipment installation
   Instrument installation
   Process leads
   Panel fabrication
   Signal wiring
Electrical
   Controls
   Electrical equipment setting
   Grounding
   Lighting
   Power distribution
Technical
   Calibration
   Commissioning
   Detail design
   High voltage testing
   Instrument procurement
   Loop check
   Maintenance
   Start up assistance
   System analysis

Selected Divisions
MMR Constructors
MMR International
MMR Power Solutions
MMR Offshore Services
MMR Technical Services
Southwestern Power Group

COMPETITORS

ATLAS INDUSTRIAL CONTRACTORS, L.L.C.
BERGELECTRIC CORP.
CHRISTENSON ELECTRIC, INC.
KENTZ CORPORATION LIMITED
ROSENDIN ELECTRIC, INC.
SARGENT & LUNDY, L.L.C.
SCHWEITZER ENGINEERING LABORATORIES, INC.
THE KLEINFELDER GROUP INC
THE NEWTRON GROUP L L C
WAYNE J. GRIFFIN ELECTRIC, INC.

HISTORICAL FINANCIALS

Company Type: Private

Income Statement — FYE: December 31

	REVENUE ($mil)	NET INCOME ($mil)	NET PROFIT MARGIN	EMPLOYEES
12/21	687	35	5.2%	4,000
12/20	564	36	6.4%	—
12/19	783	23	3.0%	—
12/18	786	17	2.2%	—
Annual Growth	(4.4%)	26.6%	—	—

2021 Year-End Financials
Return on assets: 6.2%   Cash ($ mil.): 3
Return on equity: 13.1%
Current Ratio: 1.50

MODERN WOODMEN OF AMERICA

One of the largest fraternal benefit societies in the US, Modern Woodmen of America provides annuities, life insurance, and other financial savings products to nearly 730,000 members through more than 1,000 agents. The organization, founded in 1883, is organized into "camps" (or chapters) that provide financial, social, recreational, and service benefits to members. Founder Joseph Cullen Root chose the society's name to compare pioneering woodmen clearing forests to men using life insurance to remove the financial burdens their families could face upon their deaths.

Operations

The organization claims some approximately 2,400 chapters nationwide provide opportunities for members to take part in educational, social and volunteer activities; nearly 300 summit chapters offer activities for members age 55 and over; and more than 600 youth service clubs, which are led by adult member volunteers.

In addition to financial services, the organization offers life insurance for member families include term life insurance, plans specifically designed for children and young adults, and permanent life insurance plans. Its annuities services include MaxProvider for retirement savings, variable annuity for multiple investment options, and single premium immediate annuity. In addition to life insurance and annuities, the company offers retirement accounts, including IRAs, college savings plans, investment assistance, and other insurance products. Modern Woodmen has $42.78 million in life insurance in force.

Subsidiary MWA Financial Services offers securities and advisory products. The MWABank (dba Modern Woodmen Bank) division provides retail banking services.

Geographic Reach
Based in Rock Island, Illinois, the organization has nearly 500 home offices and operates throughout the US. It has agents in more than 45 regions throughout some 45 states.

Company Background
Although Modern Woodmen's roots are tangled with Woodmen of the World Life Insurance Society, the two fraternal benefit societies are not related. Modern Woodmen of America was founded in 1883.

LOCATIONS

HQ: MODERN WOODMEN OF AMERICA
1701 1ST AVE, ROCK ISLAND, IL 612018779
Phone: 309 793-5537
Web: WWW.MODERNWOODMEN.ORG

PRODUCTS/OPERATIONS

Selected Products
Annuities (fixed, immediate, and variable; through MWA Financial Services)
Banking (MWABank)
    Certificates of Deposit
    Checking and savings accounts
    Credit cards and gift cards
    First mortgage and refinancing home loans
    Home equity loans
Insurance (through MWAGIA)
    Dental and vision insurance
    Disability income insurance
    Group employee benefits
    Group voluntary benefits
    Impaired risk life insurance
    International life and health insurance
    Long-term care insurance
    Major medical insurance
    Medicare supplement insurance
Investment (through MWA Financial Services)
    Brokerage services
    College savings plans
    Mutual funds
    Retirement plans
Life Insurance
    Term life insurance
    Term life insurance for children
    Universal life insurance
    Whole life insurance

COMPETITORS

AIG RETIREMENT SERVICES
CITIZENS, INC.
GLOBE LIFE INC.
LINCOLN NATIONAL CORPORATION
LIVERPOOL VICTORIA FRIENDLY SOCIETY LTD
MASSACHUSETTS MUTUAL LIFE INSURANCE COMPANY
SYMETRA FINANCIAL CORPORATION
T&D HOLDINGS, INC.
THE GUARDIAN LIFE INSURANCE COMPANY OF AMERICA
WOODMEN OF THE WORLD LIFE INSURANCE SOCIETY

HISTORICAL FINANCIALS
Company Type: Private

Income Statement   FYE: December 31

	ASSETS ($mil)	NET INCOME ($mil)	INCOME AS % OF ASSETS	EMPLOYEES
12/07	8,318	96	1.2%	480
12/06	7,928	99	1.3%	—
Annual Growth	4.9%	(2.6%)	—	—

2007 Year-End Financials
Return on assets: 1.2%   Cash ($ mil.): 40
Return on equity: 8.2%
Current Ratio: —

MODIVCARE SOLUTIONS, LLC

LogistiCare is a go-between for getting from your house to the doctor's office and back. The company brokers non-emergency transportation services for commercial health plans, government entities (such as state Medicaid agencies), and hospitals throughout the US. Using its nearly 20 call centers and a network of some 1,500 independent, contracted transportation providers, the company coordinates the medical-related travel arrangements of its clients' members. In addition, it contracts with local school boards to coordinate transportation for special needs students. The company provides more than 26 million trips each year for clients in some 40 states. LogistiCare is a subsidiary of Providence Service.

Operations
LogistiCare, also known as Charter LCI, has contracts with clients including metro transit authorities, HMOs, and commercial insurance firms. Other services include finance and consulting to help companies with billing management and claims adjudication, customer reimbursement, risk management, and discount programs for patients requesting noncovered services. LogistiCare's eligibility and authorization services include call screening to determine client-provided benefit criteria, as well as screening to determine type of transport needed.

The company operates more than a dozen regional call centers that match incoming requests with subcontracted transportation providers, including local taxi and ambulance companies. Transportation customers often include the elderly or those with disabilities that prevent self-transportation.

Strategy
A major part of LogistiCare's growth strategy is to secure contracts with state and local authorities to become the sole Medicaid or Medicare transportation provider. It scored one such contract in late 2010 with Sussex County, Delaware. Under terms of that agreement, LogistiCare became the statewide broker for all Medicaid medical transportation.

EXECUTIVES

CIO, Walt Meffert
CCO, Jody Kepler
Auditors : KPMG LLP ATLANTA GEORGIA

LOCATIONS

HQ: MODIVCARE SOLUTIONS, LLC
6900 E LAYTON AVE # 1200, DENVER, CO 802373656
Phone: 404 888-5831
Web: WWW.MODIVCARE.COM

PRODUCTS/OPERATIONS

Selected Services
Billing and claims management
Call center management
Credentialing
Data management and reporting
Eligibility and authorization services
Logistics
Non-emergency transportation management (ambulatory/livery vans, wheel chair vans, stretcher vans)
Provider payment
Quality assurance

COMPETITORS

AMERICAN MEDICAL RESPONSE, INC.
CORVEL CORPORATION
CRST LOGISTICS, INC.
ENVISION HEALTHCARE HOLDINGS, INC.
FREIGHTQUOTE.COM, INC.
HUB GROUP, INC.
INTERCONEX, INC.
MI Group Ltd, The
MILLENNIUM TRANSPORTATION, INC.
NEWGISTICS, INC.

HISTORICAL FINANCIALS
Company Type: Private

Income Statement   FYE: December 31

	REVENUE ($mil)	NET INCOME ($mil)	NET PROFIT MARGIN	EMPLOYEES
12/17*	1,318	35	2.7%	3,794
04/17	1,234	44	3.6%	—
12/15	1,083	40	3.7%	—
12/14	884	71	8.1%	—
Annual Growth	14.2%	(21.0%)	—	—

*Fiscal year change

2017 Year-End Financials
Return on assets: 19.1%   Cash ($ mil.): 26
Return on equity: 73.8%
Current Ratio: 1.10

MONMOUTH MEDICAL CENTER INC.

Monmouth Medical Center is a 530-bed, tertiary care teaching hospital providing comprehensive health care to residents of central New Jersey. The not-for-profit medical center offers services ranging from orthopedics, diagnostics, and obstetric care to surgery, dentistry, and geriatric services. The medical center campus also includes a children's hospital, a cancer center, a neuroscience institute, an outpatient care clinic, and hospice and home health facilities. Monmouth Medical Center is a teaching affiliate of the Rutgers-Robert Wood Johnson Medical School. The hospital is part of the RWJBarnabas Health network.

Operations
Monmouth Medical Center handles 19,000 inpatient admissions each year, as well as 49,000 emergency room visits. Its outpatient clinic handles some 126,000 appointments annually. The hospital has 700 doctors representing 60 specialties on its staff.

Geographic Reach
Monmouth Medical Center is located on about 20 acres in Long Branch, New Jersey, near the Atlantic Ocean. The campus includes the main, 16-wing hospital and and about 16 other buildings including resident physician dwellings, a day care center, a medical education and training facility, and a Ronald McDonald House.

The hospital serves a territory consisting of Monmouth, Ocean, and Middlesex counties, with a total of about one million residents. It has outpatient locations in Colts Neck, Howell, Long Branch, Ocean Township, and Shrewsbury.

Strategy
The hospital has conducted recent expansion projects including additions of new a new cancer center, surgical suites, and a family center. In 2013 it opened a new postpartum wing and newborn nursery, as well as a larger neonatal ICU. Monmouth Medical Center also extended its pediatric and oncology programs by forming partnerships with other area hospitals in 2012.

Company Background
Monmouth Medical Center was founded in 1887. It has expanded over the years to provide a number of specialist services, including high-tech offerings such as robotic surgery. Parent Barnabas Health merged with Robert Wood Johnson Health in 2016 to form RWJBarnabas.

Auditors: KPMG LLP SHORT HILLS NJ

LOCATIONS
HQ: MONMOUTH MEDICAL CENTER INC.
300 2ND AVE, LONG BRANCH, NJ 077406395

Phone: 732 222-5200
Web: WWW.RWJBH.ORG

PRODUCTS/OPERATIONS
Selected Centers and Services
Anesthesiology Services
Behavioral Health Network
Brain Tumor Center (David S. Zocchi)
The Breast Center (Jacqueline M. Wilentz Comprehensive)
Burn Center
Cancer Services
Cardiac Services
Cardiac Surgery
Children's Hospital at Monmouth (Pediatrics)
Cleft Palate Center
Cord Blood Banking Program
Cosmetic Surgery
Cranmer Ambulatory Surgery Center
Critical Care Services
Diabetes Education - Center for Diabetes Education
Dental Medicine
Diagnostic Imaging Services
The Eisenberg Family Center
Emergency Services
Epilepsy Monitoring Program
Extracorporeal Membrane Oxygenation Program (ECMO)
The Gamma Knife Center
Geriatric Emergency Medicine (GEM) Unit
Geriatric Health Center
Head & Neck Surgery
Hernias Repair, Institute for the Treatment of Complex
HIV/AIDS Program
Home Health Care
Home Infusion Care
Hospice
Hyperbaric Oxygen Therapy
Integrative Medicine (Center for)
Joint Replacement and Spine Center
Medical Records
Medical Alert/Lifeline
Medicine (Department of)
Minimally Invasive Surgery
Monmouth Family Health Center
Neonatal Intensive Care Unit (Regional Newborn Center)
Neuroscience Institute
Nutritional Counseling
Obstetrics/Gynecological Services
Occupational Medicine
Orthopaedic Services
Outpatient Services Location
Pain Management Program
Palliative Care
Pastoral Care
Pathology & Laboratory Services
Pediatric Services
Pediatric Subspecialty Center at Toms River, The
Pediatric Surgery
Pharmacy Department
Plastic Surgery
Podiatry Services
Pre-Admission Testing Services
Psychiatric Services
Pulmonary Services
Radiation Oncology
Rehabilitation Services
Renal Services
Renal Transplantation
Respiratory Services
Robotic Surgery
Senior Services Program
Sleep Disorders Center
Spine Center
Surgical Services
Total Joint Replacement
Urogynecology
Urology
Valerie Fund Cancer Center (Pediatrics)
Vascular Surgery
The Weight Loss Institute of New Jersey
Wound Treatment Center

COMPETITORS
BAPTIST MEMORIAL HEALTH CARE SYSTEM, INC.
CATHOLIC HEALTH SYSTEM OF LONG ISLAND, INC.
PALO ALTO MEDICAL FOUNDATION FOR HEALTH CARE, RESEARCH AND EDUCATION
PROMEDICA TOLEDO HOSPITAL
THE MASSACHUSETTS GENERAL HOSPITAL

HISTORICAL FINANCIALS
Company Type: Private

Income Statement — FYE: December 31

	REVENUE ($mil)	NET INCOME ($mil)	NET PROFIT MARGIN	EMPLOYEES
12/19	556	5	1.0%	2,400
12/18	546	43	8.0%	—
12/17	529	52	10.0%	—
12/16	399	46	11.5%	—
Annual Growth	11.7%	(50.5%)	—	—

2019 Year-End Financials
Return on assets: 0.7%   Cash ($ mil.): —
Return on equity: 1.6%
Current Ratio: 2.90

MONOGRAM FOOD SOLUTIONS, LLC

Monogram Food Solutions is focused on M, E, A, and T. As a manufacturer of meat and meat snack products, the company produces beef jerky, sausage, hot dogs, bacon, and other processed food items. Its brands include Circle B, King Cotton, and Trail's Best Meat Snacks. Through several special licensing agreements, Monogram Food Solutions also sells Jeff Foxworthy Jerky Products, NASCAR Jerky and Steak Strips, and Bass Pro Uncle Buck's Licensed Products. The company, which distributes its products nationwide, operates facilities in Minnesota, Indiana, and Virginia. Founded in 2004, Monogram Food Solutions was formed through the merger of assets (King Cotton and Circle B) previously owned by Sara Lee Corp.

Geographic Reach
From its headquarters in Memphis, Tennessee, Monogram Food Solutions directs the operation of additional facilities in (Chandler) Minnesota, (Muncie and Bristol) Indiana, and (Martinsville) Virginia. The company distributes its products nationwide.

Strategy
Licensing agreements have helped Monogram Food Solutions build a firm foundation for its business. Aside from its deal with Bass Pro Shops and Jeff Foxworthy, the company enjoys licensing partnerships with Johnsonville Sausage and Glory Foods. Its alliance with Johnsonville Sausage, inked in 2012, gave Monogram Food Solutions the go-ahead to produce and market Johnsonville Deli Bites, Bacon Jerky, and other meat snacks innovations.

Beginning in 2010, the company began manufacturing and selling meat snacks for the energy drink maker, DNA Beverages Corporation, under the DNA brand. Geared toward a younger consumer, the DNA beef products gives Monogram a larger demographic for its products.

Mergers and Acquisitions

Since its founding, the company has quickly built itself up by buying established meat product manufacturers and processing plants. In 2009 it acquired three companies, including beef jerky maker Wild Bill's Foods and Al Pete's Meats (and the Pete's Pride brand name). It also acquired the Hannah's, Bull's, O'Brien's, and Dakota meat snack brands from meat processing company American Foods Group.

In late 2012 Monogram Food Solutions purchased Hinsdale Farms of Bristol, Indiana. As one of the nation's largest makers of corn dogs, Hinsdale also has a hand in serving retail private label customers and co-packing for other manufacturers. The deal added a fourth manufacturing plant for processing meat. As part of the acquisition, Monogram Food Solutions is working to integrate the Hinsdale business into its manufacturing and sales systems.

EXECUTIVES

Senior Analyst*, Jocelyn Brown
Auditors : MAYER HOFFMAN MCCANN PC MEM

LOCATIONS

HQ: MONOGRAM FOOD SOLUTIONS, LLC
530 OAK COURT DR STE 400, MEMPHIS, TN 381173735
Phone: 901 685-7167
Web: WWW.MONOGRAMFOODS.COM

PRODUCTS/OPERATIONS

Selected Brands
Circle B
Hannah's
King Cotton
O'Brien's Meat Snacks/Sausages
Wild Bill's

COMPETITORS

ADVANCEPIERRE FOODS, INC.
COLORADO BOXED BEEF CO.
GOYA FOODS, INC.
LINEAGE FOODSERVICE SOLUTIONS, LLC
LOPEZ FOODS, INC.
MITSUBISHI SHOKUHIN CO.,LTD.
NEWPORT MEAT NORTHERN CALIFORNIA, INC.
OMAHA STEAKS INTERNATIONAL, INC.
PDNC, LLC
ZWEIGLE'S, INC.

HISTORICAL FINANCIALS

Company Type: Private

Income Statement — FYE: January 2

	REVENUE ($mil)	NET INCOME ($mil)	NET PROFIT MARGIN	EMPLOYEES
01/21*	819	25	3.1%	790
12/19	747	(4)	—	—
12/18	647	11	1.7%	—
12/17	640	2	0.4%	—
Annual Growth	8.5%	114.8%	—	—

*Fiscal year change

2021 Year-End Financials
Return on assets: 6.6%   Cash ($ mil.): —
Return on equity: 19.1%
Current Ratio: 1.30

MONONGAHELA POWER COMPANY

Electricity flows from Monongahela Power (Mon Power) just like the river the utility was named after. The company services approximately 388,000 residential and commercial customers in a service area of 13,000 sq. mi. in West Virginia. Mon Power, along with West Penn Power and Potomac Edison, comprise the Allegheny Power arm of Allegheny Energy, which is now part of FirstEnergy. In 2013 Mon Power owned or controlled 3,580 MW of generating capacity. The company is contractually obligated to supply Potomac Edison with sufficient power to meet that company's power load obligations in West Virginia.

Operations

Mon Power provides generation, transmission and distribution services. Its infrastructure includes 25,390 miles of distribution lines and more than 2,125 miles of transmission lines.

Geographic Reach

The utility's service area includes Northern, Central, and Southeastern West Virginia.

Strategy

In 2013, the parent company invested about $131 million in Mon Power and planned to invest about $233 million more in 2014 to help Mon Power expand its operations.

In a transfer of assets within FirstEnergy's West Virginia-based operations to improve efficiencies, in 2013 Mon Power sold its 8% share of the Pleasants power plant at its fair market value of $73 million to Allegheny Energy Supply. In return Allegheny Energy Supply sold its 80% stake in the Harrison plant to Mon Power at its book value of $1.2 billion.

To lower carbon emissions, in 2012 Mon Power shut down three aging coal-fired power plants in West Virginia: Albright, Willow Island, and Rivesville.

Company Background

The company is a subsidiary of Allegheny Energy, which is owned by FirstEnergy.

Mon Power was incorporated in Ohio in 1924.

Auditors : PRICEWATERHOUSECOOPERS LLP CL

LOCATIONS

HQ: MONONGAHELA POWER COMPANY
5001 NASA BLVD, FAIRMONT, WV 265548248
Phone: 800 686-0022

COMPETITORS

ARIZONA PUBLIC SERVICE COMPANY
DUKE ENERGY CORPORATION
EAST KENTUCKY POWER COOPERATIVE, INC.
INDIANA MICHIGAN POWER COMPANY
THE SOUTHERN COMPANY

HISTORICAL FINANCIALS

Company Type: Private

Income Statement — FYE: December 31

	REVENUE ($mil)	NET INCOME ($mil)	NET PROFIT MARGIN	EMPLOYEES
12/17	1,619	69	4.3%	4,000
12/16	1,613	66	4.1%	—
Annual Growth	0.3%	4.5%	—	—

2017 Year-End Financials
Return on assets: 1.6%   Cash ($ mil.): 76
Return on equity: 5.4%
Current Ratio: 1.80

MONSTER BEVERAGE 1990 CORPORATION

LOCATIONS

HQ: MONSTER BEVERAGE 1990 CORPORATION
1 MONSTER WAY, CORONA, CA 928797101
Phone: 951 739-6200
Web: WWW.MONSTERBEVCORP.COM

HISTORICAL FINANCIALS

Company Type: Private

Income Statement — FYE: December 31

	REVENUE ($mil)	NET INCOME ($mil)	NET PROFIT MARGIN	EMPLOYEES
12/17	3,369	820	24.4%	2,001
12/16	3,049	712	23.4%	—
12/15	2,722	546	20.1%	—
12/14	2,464	483	19.6%	—
Annual Growth	11.0%	19.3%	—	—

2017 Year-End Financials
Return on assets: 17.1%   Cash ($ mil.): 528
Return on equity: 21.1%
Current Ratio: 3.70

MONTEFIORE MEDICAL CENTER

The primary teaching hospital of the Albert Einstein College of Medicine, Montefiore offers medical education programs. Montefiore Medical Center attends to the health care needs of residents across the Bronx, Westchester and the Hudson Valley. Montefiore Einstein Center for Cancer Care, a Montefiore Center of Excellence, delivers advanced patient-centered, multidisciplinary care designed to maximize treatment outcomes while optimizing the quality of life for each patient. Children's Hospital at Montefiore (CHAM), a premier academic children's hospital, nationally renowned for its clinical excellence, innovative research and commitment to training the next generation of pediatricians and pediatric subspecialists. Montefiore Medical Center was founded in 1884 by Jewish philanthropists.

Operations

As the teaching hospital for Albert Einstein College of Medicine, Montefiore provides postgraduate training for more than 1,250 residents across some 90 accredited residency and fellowship programs.

Through Montefiore Care Management, the company uses a global prepayment or similar strategies to manage care for 200,000 individuals for hospital care, rehabilitation, outpatient care, professional services, home care, mental health counseling, community-based services, remote patient monitoring, and other programs.

Montefiore and Einstein are among about three dozen academic medical centers nationwide to be awarded the Clinical and Translational Science Award (CTSA) by the National Institutes of Health.

Geographic Reach

Montefiore operations throughout the Bronx, Westchester and the Hudson Valley. It has nearly 50 primary care locations throughout the New York metropolitan area.

Strategy

Montefiore's partnership with Einstein advances clinical and translational research to accelerate the pace at which new discoveries become the treatments and therapies that benefit patients. Together, the two institutions are among 38 academic medical centers nationwide to be awarded a prestigious Clinical and Translational Science Award (CTSA) by the National Institutes of Health.

The second-largest medical residency program in the country, with 1,251 residents and fellows across 89 programs, Montefiore provides the doctors of tomorrow a unique opportunity for education and training in one of the most diverse urban areas in the country ? one where the population is global, the disease burden is high, and the need for quality care is great.

The partnership is further strengthened by the dual appointments of faculty and physicians across both organizations? enhancing synergies and collaborations for research, teaching and patient care.

Company Background

Founded in 1884 to treat tuberculosis patients, Montefiore has a long history of responding to community health crises, including lead poisoning and AIDS. In response to rising needs in the community, Montefiore opened a community clinic with the aim of vaccinating young women for HPV, a sexually transmitted disease that can cause cervical cancer.

Auditors : ERNST & YOUNG US LLP NEW YORK

LOCATIONS

HQ: MONTEFIORE MEDICAL CENTER
111 E 210TH ST, BRONX, NY 104672401
Phone: 718 920-4321
Web: WWW.MONTEFIORE.ORG

PRODUCTS/OPERATIONS

Selected Services
Allergy & Immunology
Arthritis & Joint Disease (Rheumatology)
Blood (Hematology)
Bones, Muscles & Joints Orthopaedics
Brain (Neurology)
Centers of Excellence
Dentistry & Oral Surgery
Dermatology
Diabetes, Hormones, Metabolism (Endocrinology)
Diagnostics & Testing (Pathology)
Digestive & Liver Dieases (Gastroenterology)
Elder Care (Geriatrics)
Emergency Medicine
Eyes (Opthalmology and Visual Sciences)
Family and Social Medicine
General Internal Medicine
Headache Center
HIV/AIDS
Home Care
ICU (Critical Care Medicine)
Infectious Diseases
Internal Medicine
Kidney Disease (Nephrology)
Lungs (Pulmonary Medicine)
Neurosurgery
OB/GYN & Women's Health
Otorhinolaryngology - Head and Neck Surgery
Pain Management & Anesthesiology
Pediatrics
Pharmacy Services
Primary Care
Psychiatry and Behavioral Sciences
Radiology
Rehabilitation Medicine
Sleep-Wake Disorders Center
Surgery
Surgical Services (All)
Urology
Wound Care (Hyperbaric Medicine)

Selected Facilities
Greene Medical Arts Pavilion (outpatient care)
Mercy Community Care (outpatient care)
Montefiore Medical Group (23 Bronx and Westchester locations)
Montefiore Medical Park (outpatient care)
Moses Division Hospital (or Henry and Lucy Moses Division)
The Children's Hospital at Montefiore
North Division (formerly Our Lady of Mercy Medical Center)
Weiler Division Hospital (or Jack D. Weiler Hospital)

COMPETITORS

CHILDREN'S HOSPITAL MEDICAL CENTER
DALLAS COUNTY HOSPITAL DISTRICT
HOLY SPIRIT HOSPITAL OF THE SISTERS OF CHRISTIAN CHARITY
LEHIGH VALLEY HEALTH NETWORK, INC.
SAINT JOSEPH HOSPITAL, INC
SINAI HEALTH SYSTEM
UNIVERSITY HOSPITALS HEALTH SYSTEM, INC.
UNIVERSITY OF WISCONSIN HOSPITALS AND CLINICS AUTHORITY
WELLSTAR HEALTH SYSTEM, INC.
WYCKOFF HEIGHTS MEDICAL CENTER

HISTORICAL FINANCIALS

Company Type: Private

Income Statement — FYE: December 31

	REVENUE ($mil)	NET INCOME ($mil)	NET PROFIT MARGIN	EMPLOYEES
12/17	3,762	43	1.2%	11,000
12/16	2,690	42	1.6%	—
Annual Growth	39.9%	2.7%	—	—

2017 Year-End Financials
Return on assets: 1.2%   Cash ($ mil.): 253
Return on equity: 5.1%
Current Ratio: 1.70

MONTGOMERY COUNTY, MD

EXECUTIVES

County Executive, Marc Elrich
Auditors : SB & COMPANY LLC OWINGS MILLS

LOCATIONS

HQ: MONTGOMERY COUNTY, MD
101 MONROE ST FL 15, ROCKVILLE, MD 208502503
Phone: 240 777-8220
Web: WWW.MONTGOMERYCOUNTYMD.GOV

HISTORICAL FINANCIALS

Company Type: Private

Income Statement — FYE: June 30

	REVENUE ($mil)	NET INCOME ($mil)	NET PROFIT MARGIN	EMPLOYEES
06/21	4,888	442	9.0%	7,400
06/20	4,464	(248)	—	—
06/18	4,203	217	5.2%	—
06/17	4,191	52	1.3%	—
Annual Growth	3.9%	70.0%	—	—

2021 Year-End Financials
Return on assets: 2.6%   Cash ($ mil.): 197
Return on equity: 17.2%
Current Ratio: —

MONUMENT HEALTH RAPID CITY HOSPITAL, INC.

Auditors: EIDE BAILLY LLP MINNEAPOLIS

LOCATIONS

HQ: MONUMENT HEALTH RAPID CITY HOSPITAL, INC.
353 FAIRMONT BLVD, RAPID CITY, SD 577017375
Phone: 605 755-1000
Web: WWW.MONUMENT.HEALTH

HISTORICAL FINANCIALS
Company Type: Private

Income Statement — FYE: June 30

	REVENUE ($mil)	NET INCOME ($mil)	NET PROFIT MARGIN	EMPLOYEES
06/20	799	31	4.0%	4,258
06/19	808	49	6.2%	—
06/09	0	0	0.0%	—
Annual Growth	89.5%	—	—	—

2020 Year-End Financials
Return on assets: 2.5%   Cash ($ mil.): 151
Return on equity: 4.2%
Current Ratio: 0.70

MORENO VALLEY UNIFIED SCHOOL DISTRICT

Auditors: EIDE BAILLY RANCHO CUCAMONGA

LOCATIONS

HQ: MORENO VALLEY UNIFIED SCHOOL DISTRICT
25634 ALESSANDRO BLVD, MORENO VALLEY, CA 925534916
Phone: 951 571-7500
Web: WWW.MVUSD.NET

HISTORICAL FINANCIALS
Company Type: Private

Income Statement — FYE: June 30

	REVENUE ($mil)	NET INCOME ($mil)	NET PROFIT MARGIN	EMPLOYEES
06/21	544	57	10.6%	3,500
06/20	504	(25)	—	—
06/19	498	39	7.8%	—
06/18	443	(50)	—	—
Annual Growth	7.1%	—	—	—

2021 Year-End Financials
Return on assets: 5.2%   Cash ($ mil.): —
Return on equity: 29.0%
Current Ratio: —

MORSE OPERATIONS, INC.

Morse Operations (dba Ed Morse Automotive Group) has been selling cars and trucks long enough to know the code of the road. It owns about a dozen new car dealerships across Florida, most of them operating under the Ed Morse name. Dealerships house more than 15 franchises and 10 domestic and import car brands, including Cadillac, Fiat, Chevrolet, Buick, GMC, Scion, Honda, Mazda, and Toyota. The company's Bayview Cadillac in Fort Lauderdale is one of the world's largest volume sellers of Cadillacs. Morse Operations also sells used cars, provides parts and service, and operates a fleet sales division. Founder and auto magnate, the late Ed Morse, entered the automobile business in 1946 with a 20-car rental fleet.

Operations
Ed Morse Fleet Sales offers vehicles from about 10 different brands, including Honda, Cadillac, Fiat, Chevrolet, Buick, GMC, Scion, Mazda, and Toyota. To date, annual fleet sales have reached 100,000 vehicles.

Fleet customers include daily rental companies, such as National Car Rental, Avis, and Alamo Rent A Car.

Geographic Reach
The dealership network serves customers throughout Florida, along the East and West coasts and in Central Florida.

Auditors: CROWE LLP FORT LAUDERDALE FL

LOCATIONS

HQ: MORSE OPERATIONS, INC.
2850 S FEDERAL HWY, DELRAY BEACH, FL 334833216
Phone: 561 276-5000
Web: WWW.EDMORSE.COM

PRODUCTS/OPERATIONS

Selected Dealerships
Brandon Auto Mall
Ed Morse Auto Plaza - Port Richey
Ed Morse Bayview Cadillac
Ed Morse Cadillac - Delray Beach
Ed Morse Cadillac - Tampa
Ed Morse Cadillac - Brandon
Ed Morse Delray Toyota/Scion
Ed Morse Honda Blue Heron
Ed Morse Mazda - Lakeland
Ed Morse Sawgrass

COMPETITORS

ANCIRA ENTERPRISES INCORPORATED
HOLMAN ENTERPRISES INC.
MARTY FRANICH FORD LINCOLN MERCURY INC
OURISMAN CHEVROLET CO., INC.
ROHR-ETTE MOTORS INC

HISTORICAL FINANCIALS
Company Type: Private

Income Statement — FYE: December 31

	REVENUE ($mil)	NET INCOME ($mil)	NET PROFIT MARGIN	EMPLOYEES
12/20	1,290	17	1.4%	925
12/18	1,125	(0)	—	—
12/17	1,019	4	0.4%	—
12/16	1,334	9	0.7%	—
Annual Growth	(0.8%)	16.8%	—	—

2020 Year-End Financials
Return on assets: 2.8%   Cash ($ mil.): 54
Return on equity: 17.1%
Current Ratio: 1.20

MORTON PLANT HOSPITAL ASSOCIATION, INC.

Auditors: CROWE LLP FORT LAUDERDALE FL

LOCATIONS

HQ: MORTON PLANT HOSPITAL ASSOCIATION, INC.
300 PINELLAS ST, CLEARWATER, FL 337563892
Phone: 727 462-7000
Web: WWW.BAYCARE.ORG

HISTORICAL FINANCIALS
Company Type: Private

Income Statement — FYE: December 31

	REVENUE ($mil)	NET INCOME ($mil)	NET PROFIT MARGIN	EMPLOYEES
12/19	852	67	7.9%	3,000
12/16	555	83	14.9%	—
12/15	107	(8)	—	—
12/13	598	49	8.3%	—
Annual Growth	6.1%	5.2%	—	—

2019 Year-End Financials
Return on assets: 5.6%   Cash ($ mil.): —
Return on equity: 5.8%
Current Ratio: 3.10

MOSAIC HEALTH SYSTEM

Heartland Health provides medical care in the heart of the Midwest. The integrated health care system serves residents of northwest Missouri, as well as bordering areas of Kansas and Nebraska. Its flagship facility is Heartland Regional Medical Center, a 350-bed acute-care hospital that features an emergency room and Level II trauma center, as well as specialty care programs in heart disease, cancer, and obstetrics. Heartland Health also provides primary care through a multi-specialty medical practice (Heartland Clinic), and it offers home health, hospice, and long-term care services from the primary medical center facility. The company's Community Health Improvement Solutions unit is an HMO health insurer.

Strategy

In 2012 Heartland Health joined the Mayo Clinic Care Network, which will enable to it to tap the knowledge and expertise of Mayo Clinic physicians to better serve its patients.

Company Background

Heartland Health was formed in 1984 through the merger of two St. Joseph, Missouri hospital: Methodist Medical Center and St. Joseph's Hospital. The two facilities trace their roots back to 1924 and 1861, respectively.

EXECUTIVES

CMO*, Robert Permet
Auditors : RSM US LLP DAVENPORT IOWA

LOCATIONS

HQ: MOSAIC HEALTH SYSTEM
5325 FARAON ST, SAINT JOSEPH, MO 645063488
Phone: 816 271-6000
Web: WWW.MYMLC.COM

PRODUCTS/OPERATIONS

Selected Affiliates
Atchison Hospital (Atchison, KS)
Community Hospital (Fairfax, MO)
Community Medical Center (Falls City, NE)
Dental Clinic (St. Joseph, MO)
Laser Cosmedic Center (Platte City, MO)
North Kansas City Hospital (North Kansas City, MO)
The Surgery Center (St. Joseph, MO)

COMPETITORS

ASCENSION PROVIDENCE HOSPITAL
BAPTIST MEMORIAL HEALTH CARE SYSTEM, INC.
BORGESS HEALTH ALLIANCE, INC.
BRYAN MEDICAL CENTER
CENTEGRA HEALTH SYSTEM
GENESIS HEALTHCARE SYSTEM
MERCY HOSPITAL AND MEDICAL CENTER
MERITER HEALTH SERVICES, INC.
PROVIDENCE HOSPITAL
THE MEMORIAL HOSPITAL

HISTORICAL FINANCIALS

Company Type: Private

Income Statement			FYE: June 30
	REVENUE ($mil)	NET INCOME ($mil)	NET PROFIT MARGIN	EMPLOYEES
06/22	820	(104)	—	32,000
06/21	780	221	28.4%	—
06/20	778	75	9.6%	—
06/19	688	85	12.4%	—
Annual Growth	6.0%	—	—	—

2022 Year-End Financials
Return on assets: (-7.6%) Cash ($ mil.): 64
Return on equity: (-11.6%)
Current Ratio: 7.10

MOTION PICTURE INDUSTRY HEALTH PLAN

Auditors : MILLER KAPLAN ARASE LLP NORTH

LOCATIONS

HQ: MOTION PICTURE INDUSTRY HEALTH PLAN
11365 VENTURA BLVD, STUDIO CITY, CA 916043148
Phone: 818 769-0007

HISTORICAL FINANCIALS

Company Type: Private

Income Statement			FYE: December 31
	ASSETS ($mil)	NET INCOME ($mil)	INCOME AS % OF ASSETS	EMPLOYEES
12/13	856	60	7.1%	48
12/09	543	(75)	—	—
Annual Growth	12.0%	—	—	—

2013 Year-End Financials
Return on assets: 7.1% Cash ($ mil.): 158
Return on equity: 18.7%
Current Ratio: 24.90

MOUNT CARMEL HEALTH PLAN MEDIG

LOCATIONS

HQ: MOUNT CARMEL HEALTH PLAN MEDIG
6150 E BROAD ST, COLUMBUS, OH 432131574
Phone: 614 546-3138
Web: WWW.MOUNTCARMELHEALTH.COM

HISTORICAL FINANCIALS

Company Type: Private

Income Statement			FYE: December 31
	REVENUE ($mil)	NET INCOME ($mil)	NET PROFIT MARGIN	EMPLOYEES
12/16	571	(20)	—	17
12/13	423	37	8.8%	—
Annual Growth	10.5%	—	—	—

2016 Year-End Financials
Return on assets: (-7.1%) Cash ($ mil.): 55
Return on equity: (-14.2%)
Current Ratio: 3.40

MOUNT CARMEL HEALTH PLAN, INC.

LOCATIONS

HQ: MOUNT CARMEL HEALTH PLAN, INC.
6150 E BROAD ST, COLUMBUS, OH 432131574
Phone: 614 546-4300
Web: WWW.MOUNTCARMELHEALTH.COM

HISTORICAL FINANCIALS

Company Type: Private

Income Statement			FYE: December 31
	REVENUE ($mil)	NET INCOME ($mil)	NET PROFIT MARGIN	EMPLOYEES
12/18	582	47	8.1%	32
12/17	614	32	5.3%	—
Annual Growth	(5.3%)	44.2%	—	—

2018 Year-End Financials
Return on assets: 14.0% Cash ($ mil.): 99
Return on equity: 21.8%
Current Ratio: 2.30

MOUNT CARMEL HEALTH SYSTEM

LOCATIONS

HQ: MOUNT CARMEL HEALTH SYSTEM
5300 N MEADOWS DR, GROVE CITY, OH 431232546
Phone: 614 234-5000
Web: WWW.MOUNTCARMELHEALTH.COM

HISTORICAL FINANCIALS

Company Type: Private

Income Statement			FYE: June 30
	REVENUE ($mil)	NET INCOME ($mil)	NET PROFIT MARGIN	EMPLOYEES
06/16	743	33	4.5%	1
06/15	707	47	6.7%	—
Annual Growth	5.1%	(29.5%)	—	—

2016 Year-End Financials
Return on assets: 6.6% Cash ($ mil.): 39
Return on equity: 7.6%
Current Ratio: 3.00

MOUNT CARMEL HEALTH SYSTEM

Mount Carmel Health System cares for the sick in the greater Columbus area and central Ohio. The health care system boasts 1,500 physicians at three general hospitals and a specialty surgical hospital, offering a comprehensive range of medical and surgical services including cardiovascular care. Mount Carmel Health also operates outpatient centers including primary care and specialty physicians' practices, and it offers home health care services. The hospital group is part of Trinity Health, one of the largest Catholic health care systems in the US.

Operations

Mount Carmel's facilities include the acute care Mount Carmel East, Mount Carmel West, and Mount Carmel St. Ann's hospitals, as well as the Mount Carmel New Albany, a surgical hospital specializing in orthopedic, neurological, and musculoskeletal treatments. The system also operates several freestanding emergency and surgery centers, and other outpatient and community care centers. Its HealthProviders subsidiary manages about two dozen primary care and specialty practices with more than 100 physicians in central Ohio.

In the realm of education, Mount Carmel Health operates six medical residency programs for physicians, and its Mount Carmel College of Nursing is one of the largest in the state.

Strategy

In 2015 Mount Carmel announced that it was investing more than $700 million in a major expansion. The investment includes big projects at three Mount Carmel campuses: Mount Carmel East, Mount Carmel Grove City and Mount Carmel West. Mount Carmel East will begin a $310 million modernization in 2015, to be completed in phases through 2019.

That year the company signed an agreement with HealthSouth to begin construction on a new inpatient rehabilitation hospital in Westerville, Ohio. The 60-bed hospital will be a joint venture between HealthSouth and Mount Carmel and will provide specialized rehabilitative care to patients who have experienced stroke, trauma, brain and orthopedic injuries or other major illnesses or injuries. Construction on the 60,000-square-foot hospital is expected to be completed in early 2017. When the new hospital opens, Mount Carmel will relocate its existing 24-bed unit at Mount Carmel West to the new facility.

Company Background

In 2012 the company launched a $110 million facilities improvement project (Project GRACE), which includes the renovation of the St. Ann's hospital. Mount Carmel Health plans for the upgraded St. Ann's facility to serve as a regional medical center.

In 2010 Mount Carmel completed construction of a new freestanding emergency center in the town of Canal Winchester through a partnership with Fairfield Medical Center. The center features both general emergency and pediatric urgent care facilities. In time the center might expand into a larger hospital facility.

Mother M. Angela and Sister M. Rufina Dunn of the Congregation of the Sisters of the Holy Cross of Notre Dame founded Mount Carmel in 1886.

EXECUTIVES

Interim Chief Executive Officer, Michael Englehart

LOCATIONS

HQ: MOUNT CARMEL HEALTH SYSTEM
6150 E BROAD ST, COLUMBUS, OH 432131574
Phone: 614 234-6000
Web: WWW.MOUNTCARMELHEALTH.COM

PRODUCTS/OPERATIONS

Selected Facilities
Hospitals
    Mount Carmel East
    Mount Carmel New Albany
    Mount Carmel St. Ann's
    Mount Carmel West
Other Facilities
    Anticoagulation Centers
    Atrial Fibrillation Center
    Cardiac Rehabilitation
    Diley Ridge Medical Center
    Mount Carmel Grove City Medical Center
    Geriatrics Center
    Health Centers
    Heart Failure Centers
    Home Medical Equipment
    Imaging Centers
    Mount Carmel Medical Group
    Occupational Health Centers
    Outpatient Cancer Treatment
    Outpatient Labs
    Physician Offices
    Rehab and Sports Medicine Services
    Sleep Medicine
    Surgery Centers
    Urgent Care Centers
    Women's Health Centers
    Wound Centers

COMPETITORS

FAIRFIELD MEDICAL CENTER
FRANCISCAN ALLIANCE, INC.
JOHN MUIR HEALTH
LHH CORPORATION
PALOMAR HEALTH
PASADENA HOSPITAL ASSOCIATION, LTD.
PHELPS MEMORIAL HOSPITAL ASSOCIATION
SILVER CROSS HOSPITAL AND MEDICAL CENTERS
ST LUKE'S HOSPITAL
UPPER CHESAPEAKE HEALTH FOUNDATION, INC.

HISTORICAL FINANCIALS

Company Type: Private

Income Statement   FYE: June 30

	REVENUE ($mil)	NET INCOME ($mil)	NET PROFIT MARGIN	EMPLOYEES
06/20	1,345	1	0.1%	8,000
06/18	1,911	157	8.2%	—
06/15	1,267	131	10.4%	—
06/14	1,223	94	7.7%	—
Annual Growth	1.6%	(50.3%)	—	—

2020 Year-End Financials
Return on assets: 0.1%   Cash ($ mil.): 6
Return on equity: 0.1%
Current Ratio: —

MOUNT SINAI MEDICAL CENTER OF FLORIDA, INC.

Mount Sinai Medical Center is the largest private independent not-for-profit teaching hospital in South Florida. The medical center, which boasts more than 670 licensed beds, provides general medical and surgical care, as well as specialty care in cardiology (Mount Sinai Heart Institute), neuroscience, oncology, orthopedics, pulmonology, radiology, and other fields. It also participates in clinical research studies and drug trials with an emphasis on cancer, heart, and lung conditions. It maintains an inpatient behavioral health unit and houses the Wien Center for Alzheimer's disease and memory disorders diagnosis and research, the largest such facility in the region.

Operations

Mount Sinai Medical Center has about 25 operating suites and more than 700 physicians. Its medical specialties include cardiology, endocrinology, urology, internal medicine, cancer diagnostics and care, gastroenterology and sleep lab. Mount Sinai's Centers of Excellence combine technology, research and academics to provide innovative and comprehensive care in cardiology, neuroscience, oncology and orthopaedics. It works together with New York's prestigious Columbia University to create the Mount Sinai Heart Institute and the Columbia University Division of Urology at Mount Sinai, the only Ivy League-affiliated programs in South Florida. These programs combine the strengths of two leaders in cardiovascular and urological care, enhancing the outstanding level of service and providing greater access to state-of-the-art technology, research and treatment options.

Geographic Reach

Reaching beyond its main South Florida campus, the Mount Sinai Medical Center also operates a multi-specialty physicians' clinic, emergency care, and diagnostic center in nearby Aventura. It also operates physicians' clinics in Key Biscayne, Hialeah, Key West, Marathon, Miami Shores, Midtown, Skylake, Sunny Isles Beach and two satellite locations in Coral Gables.

Company Background

Mount Sinai Medical Center of Florida was founded in 1949 by a group of philanthropists and concerned citizens.

LOCATIONS

HQ: MOUNT SINAI MEDICAL CENTER OF FLORIDA, INC.
4300 ALTON RD, MIAMI BEACH, FL 331402948
Phone: 305 674-2121

Web: WWW.MSMC.COM

PRODUCTS/OPERATIONS

Florida Locations
MOUNT SINAI MEDICAL CENTER (MAIN CAMPUS): Miami Beach
MOUNT SINAI AVENTURA EMERGENCY ROOM, PHYSICIAN OFFICES, CANCER CENTER AND DIAGNOSTIC CENTER: Aventura
MOUNT SINAI KEY BISCAYNE PHYSICIAN OFFICES: Key Biscayne
MOUNT SINAI CORAL GABLES DIAGNOSTIC CATHETERIZATION LAB: Coral Gables
MOUNT SINAI PRIMARY & SPECIALTY CARE CORAL GABLES: Coral Gables
MOUNT SINAI HIALEAH: Hialeah

COMPETITORS

ALBERT EINSTEIN HEALTHCARE NETWORK
CHARLESTON AREA MEDICAL CENTER, INC.
JUPITER MEDICAL CENTER, INC.
MOUNT SINAI HOSPITAL MEDICAL CENTER OF CHICAGO
ORLANDO HEALTH, INC.
PASADENA HOSPITAL ASSOCIATION, LTD.
SHANDS JACKSONVILLE MEDICAL CENTER, INC.
SINAI HEALTH SYSTEM
TEMPLE UNIVERSITY HEALTH SYSTEM, INC.
THE PENNSYLVANIA HOSPITAL OF THE UNIVERSITY OF PENNSYLVANIA HEALTH SYSTEM

HISTORICAL FINANCIALS

Company Type: Private

Income Statement — FYE: December 31

	REVENUE ($mil)	NET INCOME ($mil)	NET PROFIT MARGIN	EMPLOYEES
12/20	648	(3)	—	3,225
12/16	560	19	3.5%	—
12/15	533	38	7.2%	—
12/14	530	17	3.2%	—
Annual Growth	3.4%	—	—	—

2020 Year-End Financials
Return on assets: (-0.4%)
Return on equity: (-1.4%)
Cash ($ mil.): 276
Current Ratio: 2.00

MPHASIS CORPORATION

Auditors: GRANT THORNTON BHARAT LLP BEN

LOCATIONS

HQ: MPHASIS CORPORATION
460 PARK AVE S RM 1101, NEW YORK, NY 100167315
Phone: 212 686-6655
Web: WWW.MPHASIS.COM

HISTORICAL FINANCIALS

Company Type: Private

Income Statement — FYE: March 31

	REVENUE ($mil)	NET INCOME ($mil)	NET PROFIT MARGIN	EMPLOYEES
03/20	597	15	2.6%	2,000
03/19	584	29	5.0%	—
Annual Growth	2.3%	(47.5%)	—	—

2020 Year-End Financials
Return on assets: 5.0%
Return on equity: 12.2%
Current Ratio: 1.30
Cash ($ mil.): 16

MULTI-COLOR CORPORATION

Multi-Color Corporation is a global label solution supporting a number of the world's most prominent brands including leading producers of home and personal care, wine and spirits, food and beverage, healthcare and specialty consumer products. The company serves international brand owners in the North American, Latin American, EMEA and Asia Pacific regions with a comprehensive range of the latest label technologies. With operations in more than 25 countries worldwide, Multi-Color also provides specialized label solutions including pressure sensitive shack, cut and stack, and heat transfer.

Operations

Multi-Color provides a wide range of products for the packaging needs of customers and is one of the world's largest producers of high-quality pressure sensitive, in-mold and heat transfer labels and a major manufacturer of cut and stack, roll fed, aluminum and shrink sleeve labels.

The company also offers the right label solution, including creative development, label production and application and packaging durability. It also provides custom durables and technical such as customer foams, gaskets and insulator, decal and digital braille. In addition to in-mold labels, pressure sensitive labels and shrink sleeves, Multi-Color also offers premium label solutions that will differentiate its clients' products from the competition and attract more customers. Lastly, the company also provides extended text labels, security label and smart label solutions.

Geographic Reach

Headquartered in Ohio, Multi-Color also has more than 100 manufacturing facilities located in North America, Latin America, EMEA, and Asia Pacific.

Sales and Marketing

Multi-Color sells a broad range of automotive and chemicals, beverages, durables and technical, food and dairy, personal care and beauty, healthcare, wine and spirits, home care and laundry.

Mergers and Acquisitions

In 2022, Multi-Color acquired Skanem Group's label operations in Europe and Thailand. Seven of Skanem Group's facilities in Denmark, Norway, Poland, Sweden, the UK and Thailand are part of Multi-Color Corporation, giving MCC an enhanced footprint in Europe and Thailand.

In 2021, Multi-Color acquired Hexagon Label Group in Australia and New Zealand. The acquisition includes Hexagon subsidiaries Hally Labels AU, Label Partners AU, Adhesif Labels NZ, Hally Labels NZ, Kiwi Labels NZ & Rapid Labels NZ. The acquisition enhanced Multi-Color's footprint and offerings to its ANZ customers with comprehensive Label Solutions in Adelaide, Brisbane, Griffith, Melbourne, Perth, Sydney, Auckland and Christchurch.

In early 2021, Multi-Color acquired Melbourne, Australia-based Herrods, a leading provider of in-mould label (IML) solutions in Australia and New Zealand. The acquisition expands MCC's in-mould labeling network, creates new foothold for growth in the Asia Pacific region. Financial terms of the transaction were not disclosed.

Auditors: GRANT THORNTON LLP DETROIT M

LOCATIONS

HQ: MULTI-COLOR CORPORATION
4053 CLOUGH WOODS DR, BATAVIA, OH 451032587
Phone: 513 381-1480
Web: WWW.MCCLABEL.COM

2015 Sales

	$ mil.	% of total
US	512.4	58
Australia	63.2	7
Italy	57.4	5
Other International	177.8	30
Total	810.8	100

PRODUCTS/OPERATIONS

Selected Products and Services
Labels
- Heat transfer
- In-mold
- Neck bands
- Peel-away
- Pressure sensitive
- Re-sealable
- Shrink sleeve

COMPETITORS

CCL Industries Inc
ELECTRONICS FOR IMAGING, INC.
IMAGELINX PLC
JELD-WEN HOLDING, INC.
KIN AND CARTA PLC
LABELCORP HOLDINGS, INC.
LASER MASTER INTERNATIONAL, INC.
MIMEO.COM, INC.
R. R. DONNELLEY & SONS COMPANY
SONOCO PRODUCTS COMPANY

HISTORICAL FINANCIALS

Company Type: Private

Income Statement — FYE: March 31

	REVENUE ($mil)	NET INCOME ($mil)	NET PROFIT MARGIN	EMPLOYEES
03/19	1,725	(28)	—	8,400
03/18	1,300	71	5.5%	—
03/17	923	61	6.6%	—
03/16	870	47	5.5%	—
Annual Growth	25.6%	—	—	—

2019 Year-End Financials
Return on assets: (-1.1%)   Cash ($ mil.): 57
Return on equity: (-4.6%)
Current Ratio: 1.90

MULTICARE HEALTH SYSTEM

MultiCare Health System is a not-for-profit health system that serves the residents in the southern Puget Sound region and southwestern Washington. Altogether, the system's some 10 hospitals have more than 1,785 beds. The largest facility, Tacoma General, boasts more than 435 beds and provides specialized cancer, cardiac, orthopedic, and trauma care, in addition to general medical and surgical care. Other medical centers include Good Samaritan Hospital (with approximately 375 beds), Allenmore Hospital (some 130 beds), Auburn Regional Medical Center (approximately 195 beds), and Mary Bridge Children's Hospital (more than 80 beds). Wellfound Behavioral Health Hospital is an independently operated joint venture of MultiCare and CHI Franciscan Health.

Operations

MultiCare has more than 1,800 staff physician specialists. In addition to its more than 10 hospitals, the health system also operates numerous inpatient care, primary care, virtual care, urgent care, dedicated pediatric care and specialty services ? including MultiCare Behavioral Health Network, MultiCare Indigo Urgent Care, Mary Bridge Children's Hospital & Health Network, a comprehensive regional network of health services for children, Pulse Heart Institute, MultiCare Rockwood Clinic, the largest multispecialty clinic in the Inland Northwest region.

Tacoma General Hospital operates a wide range of essential health care services including a 24-hour Emergency Department, the MultiCare Regional Cancer Center, Family Birth Center and the region's largest, most advanced NICU, as well as leading-edge cardiac, neurological, orthopedic, robotic and traditional surgical care. Tacoma General also offers Level II Adult Trauma Center and Level IV NICU. The nationally accredited in neonatal transport services and provides care and transportation for more than 750?800 premature infants annually. Mary Bridge Children's Hospital & Health Center operates a Pediatric Intensive Care Unit, Pediatric Heart Center, Center for Childhood Safety, Child Abuse Intervention Programs, and outpatient specialty clinics.

Geographic Reach

MultiCare serves patients in more than 230 primary care, specialty care and urgent care clinics in Pierce, King, Kitsap, Thurston, Snohomish and Spokane counties.

Auditors : KPMG LLP SEATTLE WASHINGTON

LOCATIONS

HQ: MULTICARE HEALTH SYSTEM
316 MRTIN LTHER KING JR W, TACOMA, WA 984054252
Phone: 253 403-1000
Web: WWW.MARYBRIDGE.ORG

PRODUCTS/OPERATIONS

Selected Facilities
Hospitals
　　Allenmore Hospital (Tacoma)
　　Auburn Medical Center (Auburn)
　　Good Samaritan Hospital (Puyallup)
　　Mary Bridge Children's Hospital and Health Center (Tacoma)
　　Tacoma General Hospital (Tacoma)
Other facilities
　　Allenmore Medical Center
　　Auburn MultiCare Clinic
　　Covington MultiCare Clinic
　　Lakewood Urgent Care Clinic
　　Kent MultiCare Clinic
　　MultiCare Home Services
　　Spanaway MultiCare Clinic
　　Tacoma Family Medicine
　　University Place Urgent Care Clinic
　　Westgate Urgent Care Clinic

Selected Services
Adult Day Health
Behavioral Health
Boutique
Breast Health
Cancer Center
Center for Healthy Living
Children's Therapy Unit
Community Programs
CyberKnife Radiosurgery
Diabetes Services
Ear, Nose and Throat
Emergency and Urgent Care
Family Birth Centers
Geriatric Psychiatric Center
Health Care Resource Center
Heart Care
Home Health and Hospice
Immunization Clinic
Infusion Center
Institute for Research & Innovation
Laboratories Northwest
Maternal-Fetal Medicine
Medical Imaging
Nephrology
Neonatal Intensive Care Unit
Neurosciences
Nutrition
OB/GYN
Occupational Medicine
Orthopedics
Pain Management
Palliative Medicine
Perinatal Outreach Program
Pharmacy
Physical Therapy
Podiatry
Primary Care Clinics
Pulmonary Care
Pulmonary Rehabilitation
Rehabilitation
Robotic Technology
Senior Services
Sexual Assault Services
Spa
Sports Medicine
Surgical Services
Tobacco Cessation
Transfusion Free Medical and Surgical Program
Urology
Weight Loss and Wellness
Wound Healing Center

COMPETITORS

ARROWHEAD REGIONAL MEDICAL CENTER
ASCENSION PROVIDENCE ROCHESTER HOSPITAL
CENTRAL SUFFOLK HOSPITAL
CHILDRENS HOSPITAL & MEDICAL CENTER
FROEDTERT MEMORIAL LUTHERAN HOSPITAL, INC.
GOOD SAMARITAN HOSPITAL
MOUNTAIN STATES HEALTH ALLIANCE
NATIONWIDE CHILDREN'S HOSPITAL
PROVIDENCE HEALTH & SERVICES-WASHINGTON
YAKIMA VALLEY MEMORIAL HOSPITAL ASSOCIATION

HISTORICAL FINANCIALS
Company Type: Private

Income Statement　　　　　　　　　　　　FYE: December 31

	REVENUE ($mil)	NET INCOME ($mil)	NET PROFIT MARGIN	EMPLOYEES
12/21	3,824	352	9.2%	6,510
12/20	3,367	311	9.2%	—
12/19	3,234	336	10.4%	—
12/18	2,922	34	1.2%	—
Annual Growth	9.4%	117.2%	—	—

2021 Year-End Financials
Return on assets: 5.5%　　Cash ($ mil.): 308
Return on equity: 9.8%
Current Ratio: 1.30

MUNICIPAL ELECTRIC AUTHORITY OF GEORGIA

With more juice than a ripe Georgia peach, the Municipal Electric Authority of Georgia (MEAG Power) supplies wholesale electric power. The authority has a generating capacity of 2,069 MW through its interests in nuclear and fossil-fueled plants. Some 49% of the energy MEAG Power delivered in 2012 came from its nuclear plants. MEAG Power transmits electricity to 48 municipal and one county distribution systems across Georgia that in turn serve some 600,000 consumers. It utilizes a transmission network that is co-owned by all the power suppliers in Georgia, although it is considering joining a regional transmission organization (RTO) to further defray costs.

Operations

MEAG Power owns more than 1,300 miles of high-voltage transmission lines and almost 200 substations. It also provides value-added services, including management, infrastructure, and marketing support, to its member municipalities, energy marketers, and other utilities.

The company generates most of its revenues from Project One (ownership stakes in nine generating units, other owned transmission plants, and working capital).

Higher member billings for operating expenses related to fuel and nuclear operations lifted MEAG Power's revenues and net income in 2010.

Geographic Reach
The company serves 49 communities across Georgia.

Financial Performance
In 2012 MEAG Power's revenues increased by 8% thanks to higher participant billings related to a planned reduction in trust transfers, as well as an increase in debt service related to environmental improvements to the coal operations, and higher contract energy sales. These gains were partially offset by lower participant billings for maintenance and fuel expenses.

That year the company's net income increased by 351% as the result of higher net sales and decreased operating costs.

Strategy
With Georgia restricted in its natural potential for solar and wind power development, MEAG Power is pushing hard for the expansion of nuclear power as a clean energy alternative to coal.

In a major breakthrough, in 2012 the Nuclear Regulatory Commission approved a Combined Construction and Operating License for units 3 and 4 of the Vogtle plant (near Waynesboro, Georgia) the first such license ever approved for a US nuclear plant, and the first federal go-ahead for nuclear plant construction since 1978.

In 2013 MEAG Power completed a basemat of structural concrete for the nuclear island at the Vogtle Unit 4 nuclear expansion site, the second of two units under construction at Plant Vogtle.

Company Background
In 2009 the Georgia Public Service Commission gave the go ahead for the expansion of the nuclear-powered Vogtle Electric Generating Plant, which is co-owned by MEAG Power, and in 2010 MEAP Power sold $2.7 billion in bonds to fund this expansion.

Auditors : PRICEWATERHOUSECOOPERS LLP AT

LOCATIONS
HQ: MUNICIPAL ELECTRIC AUTHORITY OF GEORGIA
1470 RIVEREDGE PKWY, ATLANTA, GA 303284640
Phone: 770 563-0300

COMPETITORS
AEGION CORPORATION
DYCOM INDUSTRIES, INC.
JGC HOLDINGS CORPORATION
MYR GROUP INC.
PRIMORIS SERVICES CORPORATION

HISTORICAL FINANCIALS
Company Type: Private

Income Statement FYE: December 31

	REVENUE ($mil)	NET INCOME ($mil)	NET PROFIT MARGIN	EMPLOYEES
12/21	714	77	10.8%	150
12/20	639	23	3.6%	—
12/19	648	17	2.7%	—
12/18	681	(4)	—	—
Annual Growth	1.6%	—	—	—

2021 Year-End Financials
Return on assets: 0.6%   Cash ($ mil.): 1,138
Return on equity: —
Current Ratio: 1.40

MUNSON HEALTHCARE

Munson Healthcare is a not-for-profit health care system serving residents in northern Michigan. Its flagship facility is Munson Medical Center in Traverse City, a regional referral hospital with about 390 beds offering specialty services including cancer treatment, behavioral health, cardiac care, and orthopedics. Munson Healthcare also has management agreements and other types of affiliations with about a dozen other hospitals in the region. In addition, Munson Healthcare operates urgent care and community clinics, home health care and hospice agencies, an ambulance service, and the Northern Michigan Supply Alliance, a supply chain management group co-owned with Trinity Health.

Operations
Munson Healthcare is composed of eight hospitals located throughout northern Michigan - Charlevoix Area Hospital (Charlevoix), Kalkaska Memorial Health Center (Kalkaska), Mercy Hospital Cadillac (Cadillac), Mercy Hospital Grayling (Grayling), Munson Medical Center (Traverse City), Otsego Memorial Hospital (Gaylord), Paul Oliver Memorial Hospital (Frankfort), and West Shore Medical Center (Manistee). Services are also available at Munson Community Health Center (Traverse City) and Mercy Community Health Center (Prudenville). Munson Healthcare also works closely with Alpena General Hospital in Alpena and War Memorial Hospital in Sault St. Marie.

In addition to its hospital operations, Munson Healthcare also offers in-home care through Munson Home Health and Munson Hospice and Palliative Care. Other specialty services and resources include speech and hearing clinics, physical rehabilitation, CAT scans, magnetic resonance imaging, and cardiac catheterization.

Munson Healthcare provides direct access to nearly 800 physicians, representing more than 50 specialties.

Eah year, the system sees some 22,500 admissions, performs some 8,000 inpatient and 7,000 outpatient surgeries, and has some 51,000 emergency department visits.

Geographic Reach
The health care system offers a continuum of health care services to people in 24 Michigan counties.

Strategy
To better provide services to region residents, Munson Healthcare partnered with critical access hospital Mackinac Straits Health System in 2015. The affiliation is focused on improving health care services in rural northern Michigan.

Munson Healthcare is also forming an air ambulance joint venture between its North Flight EMS Air Division and Spectrum Health's Aero Med. The venture, to be named North Flight Aero Med, will provide critical care air emergency transport services in northern Michigan. It will begin operating in 2016.

Company Background
Munson Healthcare was founded in 1915.

EXECUTIVES
CMO, Walt Noble
Auditors : PLANTE & MORAN PLLC TRAVERSE

LOCATIONS
HQ: MUNSON HEALTHCARE
1105 SIXTH ST, TRAVERSE CITY, MI 496842345
Phone: 800 252-2065
Web: WWW.MUNSONHEALTHCARE.ORG

PRODUCTS/OPERATIONS
Selected Michigan Facilities
Charlevoix Area Hospital - Charlevoix
Kalkaska Memorial Health Center - Kalkaska
Mercy Hospital Cadillac - Cadillac
Mercy Hospital Grayling - Grayling
Munson Community Health Center - Traverse City
Munson Hospice House - Traverse City
Munson Manor Hospitality House - Traverse City
Munson Medical Center - Traverse City
Northwest Michigan Surgery Center - Traverse City
Otsego Memorial Hospital - Gaylord
Paul Oliver Memorial Hospital - Frankfort
Smith Family Breast Health Center - Traverse City
West Shore Medical Center - Manistee
Medical Specialties
Bariatric Surgery
Behavioral Health
Bleeding Disorders Center
Cancer Services
Diabetes
Dialysis
Emergency Services
Hearing Clinic
Heart and Vascular Services
Hospice and Palliative Care
Occupational Health and Medicine
Orthopedics
Senior's Health
Sleep Disorders Center
Stroke Care
Teen's Health
Urgent Care

Urology
Women and Children

COMPETITORS

ASCENSION SOUTHEAST MICHIGAN
ASPIRUS, INC.
BRONSON HEALTH CARE GROUP, INC.
CENTEGRA HEALTH SYSTEM
HARRINGTON MEMORIAL HOSPITAL, INC.
METHODIST HEALTHCARE SYSTEM OF SAN ANTONIO, LTD., L.L.P.
SOUTHERN ILLINOIS HEALTHCARE ENTERPRISES, INC.
UNITED HEALTH SERVICES HOSPITALS, INC.
WEST FLORIDA REGIONAL MEDICAL CENTER, INC.
WILKES-BARRE HOSPITAL COMPANY, LLC

HISTORICAL FINANCIALS
Company Type: Private

Income Statement — FYE: June 30

	REVENUE ($mil)	NET INCOME ($mil)	NET PROFIT MARGIN	EMPLOYEES
06/22	1,284	(48)	—	4,000
06/21	1,258	260	20.7%	—
06/20	1,144	39	3.4%	—
06/18	1,039	142	13.7%	—
Annual Growth	5.4%	—	—	—

2022 Year-End Financials
Return on assets: (-2.7%)
Return on equity: (-4.0%)
Current Ratio: 2.50
Cash ($ mil.): 120

MUNSON MEDICAL CENTER

Auditors: PLANTE & MORAN PLLC CHICAGO

LOCATIONS

HQ: MUNSON MEDICAL CENTER
1105 SIXTH ST, TRAVERSE CITY, MI 496842386
Phone: 231 935-6000
Web: WWW.MUNSONHEALTHCARE.ORG

HISTORICAL FINANCIALS
Company Type: Private

Income Statement — FYE: June 30

	REVENUE ($mil)	NET INCOME ($mil)	NET PROFIT MARGIN	EMPLOYEES
06/20	704	66	9.5%	3,100
06/16	533	67	12.7%	—
06/15	509	60	11.9%	—
06/10	441	28	6.4%	—
Annual Growth	4.8%	9.0%	—	—

2020 Year-End Financials
Return on assets: 5.9%
Return on equity: 10.5%
Current Ratio: 2.40
Cash ($ mil.): 391

MUNSTER MEDICAL RESEARCH FOUNDATION, INC

Auditors: ERNST & YOUNG LLP

LOCATIONS

HQ: MUNSTER MEDICAL RESEARCH FOUNDATION, INC
901 MACARTHUR BLVD, MUNSTER, IN 463212901
Phone: 219 836-1600

HISTORICAL FINANCIALS
Company Type: Private

Income Statement — FYE: June 30

	REVENUE ($mil)	NET INCOME ($mil)	NET PROFIT MARGIN	EMPLOYEES
06/21	607	(9)	—	2,000
06/20	541	(104)	—	—
06/19	537	1	0.2%	—
06/18	548	74	13.5%	—
Annual Growth	3.4%	—	—	—

2021 Year-End Financials
Return on assets: (-3.2%)
Return on equity: (-5.6%)
Current Ratio: 1.00
Cash ($ mil.): —

MV TRANSPORTATION, INC.

Need to supply transportation by bus? MV Transportation will run your bus system so you don't have to. The company operates more than 200 contracts to offer fixed-route and shuttle bus services, as well as paratransit (transportation of people with disabilities) and transportation of Medicaid beneficiaries. Its customers consist primarily of transit authorities and other state and local government agencies responsible for public transportation. MV Transportation operates in more than 130 locations spanning 28 US states and in British Columbia, Canada and Saudi Arabia; overall, the company maintains a fleet of about 7,000 vehicles. MV Transportation was founded in 1975.

Geographic Reach
MV Transportation and its subsidiaries, joint ventures, partnerships, and affiliates operate more than 130 locations in 28 states, the District of Columbia, two Canadian Provinces, and Saudi Arabia.

Sales and Marketing
The company provides its transportation services to cities, counties, municipalities, and other jurisdictional entities, as well as for private corporations, non-profit agencies, and community organizations. Some of its customers include Corpus Christi Regional Transportation Authority (B-Line paratransit and shuttle services), Ashland Public Transit (the curb-to-curb demand response transit service), Capital Area Transit System, and Ashtabula County Transportation System (paratransit services).

Strategy
The company relies on the signing of year-long contracts and joint ventures for growth. In 2013 MV Transportation received a four-year contract to continue operation of the City of Irvine's iShuttle service; Irvine's iShuttle provides morning and evening peak-hour service along four routes connecting the Irvine Metrolink Station, the Tustin Metrolink Station, John Wayne Airport, Irvine Spectrum, and the Irvine Business Complex (IBC).

To expand its presence and experience in Qatar, MV Transportation in 2013 opened its newest business venture in Doha, Qatar: MV Global Transport Logistics WLL (MVGTL). In addition, MVGTL signed an agreement with passenger transportation provider Mowasalat to provide planning, scheduling, and event management for the numerous events in Doha.

In early 2012, MV Transportation signed its first contract to manage a bus system outside North America when it made a two-year agreement to coordinate an operation of more than 400 buses carrying Saudi Arabian Oil employees in the Middle Eastern kingdom. Striving to extend its international reach even further, the company purchased Transportation Management Services UK Limited (TMSUK) a few months later. The deal allowed MV Transportation to enter a niche market as TMSUK designs and operates transportation systems for special events worldwide.

EXECUTIVES

Interim Chief Financial Officer, Erin Niewinski Co
Interim Chief Financial Officer, Gary Richardson Co

LOCATIONS

HQ: MV TRANSPORTATION, INC.
2711 N HASKELL AVE # 150, DALLAS, TX 752042911
Phone: 972 391-4600
Web: WWW.MVTRANSIT.COM

PRODUCTS/OPERATIONS

Selected Services
Bid committee consultation
Emergency evacuation planning
Global mobility and unique technology assets
International transport and logistics solutions
Logistics and security staffing
Paratransit and multimodal transport
Parking management and valet services
Sustainability transport initiatives
Traffic control planning, staffing, and consultation
Transport planning and operations
VIP fleet services

COMPETITORS

CAPITAL METROPOLITAN TRANSPORTATION AUTHORITY
FIRSTGROUP AMERICA, INC.
FIRSTGROUP PLC
HNTB CORPORATION
LOS ANGELES COUNTY METROPOLITAN TRANSPORTATION AUTHORITY
NETWORK RAIL LIMITED
ORANGE COUNTY TRANSPORTATION AUTHORITY
PILOT AIR FREIGHT, LLC
REGIONAL TRANSPORTATION DISTRICT
THE NEW JERSEY TRANSIT CORPORATION

HISTORICAL FINANCIALS
Company Type: Private

Income Statement   FYE: December 31

	REVENUE ($mil)	NET INCOME ($mil)	NET PROFIT MARGIN	EMPLOYEES
12/09	706	23	3.3%	20,000
12/08	645	(2)	—	—
12/07	422	0	0.0%	—
Annual Growth	29.3%	—	—	—

2009 Year-End Financials
Return on assets: 12.3%   Cash ($ mil.): 6
Return on equity: 94.1%
Current Ratio: 1.50

MVP HEALTH PLAN, INC.

MVP Health Plan, also know as MVP Health Care, provides health insurance and employee benefits to its more than 700,000 members in upstate New York, New Hampshire, and Vermont. MVP, a not-for-profit organization, offers a variety of plans including HMO, PPO, and indemnity coverage, as well as dental plans, health accounts, and Medicare Advantage plans. Subsidiary MVP Select Care provides third-party administration (TPA) services for self-insured employers. MVP Health Care was founded in 1983 as Mohawk Valley Physicians' Health Plan.

Geographic Reach
MVP Health Care operates regional service and support offices across New York, Vermont, and New Hampshire. New York State is its largest service area. The firm has offices in Binghamton, Fishkill, Schenectady, Syracuse, Rochester, and Utica, New York, as well as in Manchester, New Hampshire; and Williston, Vermont.

The company's provider network includes 19,000 doctors in its three-state service territory; the firm also provides its members with access to about 500,000 providers in other states through a partnership with CIGNA.

Sales and Marketing
The company uses a direct sales force, as well as brokerages and call centers, to sell its products. Its customers include individuals, Medicare and Medicaid participants, and employer groups.

Financial Performance
MVP Health Care revenue increased 18% to $2.9 billion in 2014; that growth was bolstered by the integration of Hudson Health Plan (acquired in 2013), as well as commercial and government membership growth. Medicaid Managed Care membership grew 21% that year.

Despite that growth, the company lost a net $13.6 million.

Strategy
In addition to acquiring other area providers, MVP Health Care widens its product offerings to attract a diversified customer base, adding new non-employer group options (individual and high-deductible plans) and new small employer group products. It is has also launched new financial and preventative care tools including flexible spending accounts and disease management programs. Cutting policy prices has helped boost membership numbers, as well.

The company also partners with health care providers to provide better care for its members, as well as developing programs to target specific segments of the population.

MVP Health Care utilizes new technologies to cut its own operating costs. Recent initiatives include launching an e-commerce/plan administration platform, creating virtual medical records with area health information organizations, and supporting the Taconic Health Information Network and Community (an independent physician practice association).

EXECUTIVES

Executive President*, Patrick Glavey
Auditors : PRICEWATERHOUSECOOPERS LLP HA

LOCATIONS

HQ: MVP HEALTH PLAN, INC.
625 STATE ST, SCHENECTADY, NY 123052260
Phone: 518 370-4793
Web: WWW.MVPHEALTHCARE.COM

PRODUCTS/OPERATIONS

Selected Products
Alternative Funding Arrangements
Deferred Deductible Plans
Defined Contribution Plans
EPOs and PPOs
Health Spending Accounts
High-Deductible Health Plans
HMOs
Medicare Advantage Plans
Regional Plan Options

COMPETITORS

AVMED, INC.
BLUECROSS BLUESHIELD OF TENNESSEE, INC.
CAPITAL DISTRICT PHYSICIANS' HEALTH PLAN, INC.
CORESOURCE, INC.
FALLON COMMUNITY HEALTH PLAN, INC.
HARVARD PILGRIM HEALTH CARE, INC.
HEALTH ALLIANCE PLAN OF MICHIGAN
HORIZON HEALTHCARE SERVICES, INC.
INDEPENDENT HEALTH ASSOCIATION, INC.
TUFTS ASSOCIATED HEALTH PLANS, INC.

HISTORICAL FINANCIALS
Company Type: Private

Income Statement   FYE: December 31

	ASSETS ($mil)	NET INCOME ($mil)	INCOME AS % OF ASSETS	EMPLOYEES
12/15	589	11	1.9%	1,500
12/14	540	(26)	—	—
Annual Growth	9.2%	—	—	—

2015 Year-End Financials
Return on assets: 1.9%   Cash ($ mil.): 6
Return on equity: 2.7%
Current Ratio: —

MWH GLOBAL, INC.

MWH Global is an environmental engineering, construction, and management firm that specializes in water-related projects or "wet infrastructure." The company's typical projects include building water treatment or desalination plants, water transmission systems, or storage facilitates. MWH also provides general building services for transportation, energy, mining, ports and waterways, and industrial projects. The company is active in some 35 countries and serves governments, public utilities, and private sector clients. Affiliates of the employee-owned company include software provider Innovyze, and business and government relations firm mCapitol. Canadian Engineering firm Stantec acquired MWH Global for $795 million in May 2016.

Geographic Reach
When it comes to projects, MWH Global lives up to its name. The Colorado-based firm operates from 180 offices in 35 countries on six continents in the Americas, the Asia/Pacific region, the Middle East, Africa, and Europe.

Sales and Marketing
MWH Global seeks projects in five main markets, including: the energy and power; water and wastewater; natural resources and mining; ports, waterways and coastal; industrial and commercial, transportation; and oil and gas markets.

It also does work for local, regional and federal governments; US federal clients; public and private utilities; financial institutions; and insurance companies.

Strategy
MWH Global has kept busy in recent years, working on a series of high-profile, design and construction projects around the globe.

In 2015, the company continued its design-build work on the $7 billion Panama Canal Third Set of Locks project, which will double the canal's capacity by the time its completed at the end of the year. The company also continued working with international electricity and gas company National Grid on the largest energy infrastructure program in the UK.

In late-2014, through a joint venture with Costain, MWH Global signed on to a £200 million ($325 million) contract to provide design and build services for Southern Water's water and wastewater infrastructure and non-infrastructure assets program in Southeast England; part of Southern Waters' £3 billion ($5 billion) business plan for 2015-2020. Around the same time, MWH Global completed its nearly two-decade-long Huanza Hydroelectric project in the Andes Mountains, which now provides 92 Megawatts of electricity to some 90,000 households in Peru.

In mid-2014, the South Florida Water Management District awarded MWH Global with a master services agreement to help implement the $880 million Restoration Strategies Regional Water Quality Plan, which is part of the state's long-term strategy to restore the Everglades. In 2012, the Qatar Public Works Authority appointed MWH to design a drainage master plan in Qatar, which will provide a road map for future investment into water and wastewater treatment and other water-related infrastructure programs over the next 50 years.

EXECUTIVES

CLO, Jeffrey D'agosta
Chief Communication Officer*, Meg Vanderlaan
Chief Strategy Officer*, David A Smith
Auditors : DELOITTE & TOUCHE LLP DENVER

LOCATIONS

HQ: MWH GLOBAL, INC.
370 INTERLOCKEN BLVD # 30, BROOMFIELD, CO 800218009
Phone: 303 533-1900
Web: WWW.MWHCONSTRUCTORS.COM

PRODUCTS/OPERATIONS

Selected Services
Construction
    Airports
    General building
    Industrial
    Highways, bridges, roads
    Marine and port facilities
Engineering and technical services
Facilities development
Government relations
Program management and management consulting
Research and testing
Renewable energy and sustainability
    Chemical and soil remediation
    Hazardous waste
    Hydroelectric power
    Non-hydro renewable energy
    Power distribution and transmission lines
    Thermal power
Risk assessment
Specialized consulting services
Water and environment
    Dams and reservoirs
    Landfills, biosolids
    Sanitary/storm sewers, conveyance, pumping stations
    Water resources, planning management
    Water treatment and desalination plants
    Water transmission lines, aqueducts
    Waste water planning and management

COMPETITORS

AMERESCO, INC.
ARCADIS U.S., INC.
BLACK & VEATCH CORPORATION
CDM SMITH INC.
CH2M HILL COMPANIES, LTD.
COSTAIN GROUP PLC
GRANITE CONSTRUCTION INCORPORATED
ORION GROUP HOLDINGS, INC.
SNC-Lavalin Group Inc
Stantec Inc

HISTORICAL FINANCIALS

Company Type: Private

Income Statement — FYE: January 1

	REVENUE ($mil)	NET INCOME ($mil)	NET PROFIT MARGIN	EMPLOYEES
01/16*	1,318	35	2.7%	6,700
12/05	946	0	0.0%	—
01/03	975	942	96.6%	—
12/01	774	19	2.6%	—
Annual Growth	3.9%	4.3%	—	—

*Fiscal year change

2016 Year-End Financials
Return on assets: 5.4%   Cash ($ mil.): 68
Return on equity: 19.1%
Current Ratio: 1.40

NANA DEVELOPMENT CORPORATION

Auditors : KPMG LLP ANCHORAGE AK

LOCATIONS

HQ: NANA DEVELOPMENT CORPORATION
909 W 9TH AVE, ANCHORAGE, AK 995013322
Phone: 907 265-4100
Web: WWW.NANA-DEV.COM

HISTORICAL FINANCIALS

Company Type: Private

Income Statement — FYE: September 30

	REVENUE ($mil)	NET INCOME ($mil)	NET PROFIT MARGIN	EMPLOYEES
09/08	1,018	1	0.2%	3,000
09/07	833	7	0.8%	—
09/06	30	31	104.1%	—
09/00	119	0	0.6%	—
Annual Growth	30.7%	11.4%	—	—

2008 Year-End Financials
Return on assets: 0.3%   Cash ($ mil.): 37
Return on equity: 4.0%
Current Ratio: 2.10

NANA REGIONAL CORPORATION, INC.,

LOCATIONS

HQ: NANA REGIONAL CORPORATION, INC.,
3150 C ST STE 150, KOTZEBUE, AK 99752
Phone: 907 442-3301
Web: WWW.NANA.COM

HISTORICAL FINANCIALS

Company Type: Private

Income Statement — FYE: September 30

	REVENUE ($mil)	NET INCOME ($mil)	NET PROFIT MARGIN	EMPLOYEES
09/09	1,257	17	1.4%	4,650
09/08	1,175	29	2.5%	—
09/07	975	37	3.8%	—
Annual Growth	13.6%	(32.4%)	—	—

2009 Year-End Financials
Return on assets: 2.3%   Cash ($ mil.): 23
Return on equity: 7.0%
Current Ratio: 1.60

NARRAGANSETT ELECTRIC COMP

LOCATIONS

HQ: NARRAGANSETT ELECTRIC COMP
642 GEORGE WASHINGTON HWY, LINCOLN, RI 028654244
Phone: 401 335-6238

HISTORICAL FINANCIALS

Company Type: Private

Income Statement — FYE: December 31

	REVENUE ($mil)	NET INCOME ($mil)	NET PROFIT MARGIN	EMPLOYEES
12/17	1,387	121	8.8%	5
12/16	1,269	84	6.7%	—
Annual Growth	9.3%	43.0%	—	—

2017 Year-End Financials
Return on assets: 2.6%   Cash ($ mil.): 8
Return on equity: 6.1%
Current Ratio: 0.70

NASSUA COUNTY INTERIM FINANCE AUTHORITY

EXECUTIVES

Exec Dir, Richard Luke
Executive Director, Evan Cohen
Auditors : RSM US LLP NEW YORK NEW YORK

LOCATIONS

HQ: NASSUA COUNTY INTERIM FINANCE AUTHORITY
170 OLD COUNTRY RD # 205, MINEOLA, NY 115014322
Phone: 516 248-2828
Web: WWW.NASSAUCOUNTYNY.GOV

HISTORICAL FINANCIALS
Company Type: Private

Income Statement			FYE: December 31	
	REVENUE ($mil)	NET INCOME ($mil)	NET PROFIT MARGIN	EMPLOYEES
12/19	1,173	(2)	—	6
12/18	1,133	(0)	0.0%	—
12/17	1,095	(5)	—	—
12/16	1	1	140128 31.1%	—
Annual Growth	924.2%	—	—	—

2019 Year-End Financials
Return on assets: (-1.3%) Cash ($ mil.): —
Return on equity: —
Current Ratio: —

NATIONAL ASSOCIATION OF LETTER CARRIERS

Auditors : BOND BEEBE PC BETHESDA MD

LOCATIONS

HQ: NATIONAL ASSOCIATION OF LETTER CARRIERS
100 INDANA AVE NW STE 709, WASHINGTON, DC 20001
Phone: 202 393-4695
Web: WWW.NALC.ORG

HISTORICAL FINANCIALS
Company Type: Private

Income Statement			FYE: March 31	
	REVENUE ($mil)	NET INCOME ($mil)	NET PROFIT MARGIN	EMPLOYEES
03/14*	1,406	97	6.9%	533
12/13	0	0	17.9%	—
12/11	0	0	67.4%	—
03/10	1	0	28.8%	—
Annual Growth	436.7%	275.8%	—	—

*Fiscal year change

2014 Year-End Financials
Return on assets: 10.5% Cash ($ mil.): 245
Return on equity: 20.1%
Current Ratio: —

NATIONAL CHRISTIAN CHARITABLE FOUNDATION, INC.

Auditors : NATIONAL CHRISTIAN CHARITABLE

LOCATIONS

HQ: NATIONAL CHRISTIAN CHARITABLE FOUNDATION, INC.
11625 RAINWATER DR # 500, ALPHARETTA, GA 300098674
Phone: 404 252-0100
Web: WWW.NCFGIVING.COM

HISTORICAL FINANCIALS
Company Type: Private

Income Statement			FYE: December 31	
	REVENUE ($mil)	NET INCOME ($mil)	NET PROFIT MARGIN	EMPLOYEES
12/16	1,413	306	21.7%	2
12/11	665	141	21.3%	—
12/09	396	50	12.7%	—
Annual Growth	19.9%	29.4%	—	—

2016 Year-End Financials
Return on assets: 14.9% Cash ($ mil.): 457
Return on equity: 15.1%
Current Ratio: —

NATIONAL COLLEGIATE ATHLETIC ASSOCIATION

The National Collegiate Athletic Association (NCAA) supports the intercollegiate sports activities of around 1,000 member colleges and universities. A not-for-profit organization, the NCAA administers scholarship and grant programs, enforces conduct and eligibility rules, and works to support and promote the needs of student athletes. The association is known for its lucrative branding and television deals, such as those surrounding the popular "March Madness" tournament for Division I men's basketball. Seeking reform of athletics rules and regulations, officials from 13 schools formed the Intercollegiate Athletic Association of the United States in 1906. The organization took its current name in 1910.

Financial Performance

NCAA revenue in fiscal 2013 (ended August) was $913 million, up 5% versus the prior year, most of which came from the rights agreement with CBS Sports and Turner Broadcasting. Indeed, about 80% of the NCAA's revenue come from television and marketing rights fees generated primarily from the Division I men's basketball championship. Another 12% comes from championships and NIT tournaments, including ticket and merchandise sales.

About 96% of NCAA revenue is distributed directly to the Division I membership or to support championships or programs that benefit student-athletes. The remaining 4% goes for central services, such as building operations and salaries not related to particular programs.

Strategy

In a major shift, the NCAA in 2019 allowed student-athletes to receive compensation when their names, images or likenesses are used for commercial purposes. The organization changed its rules on student-athletes aftere California passed a law allowing compensation (effective in 2023) following a lawsuit. The NCAA has long adamantly prohibited any payment of college athletes (other than scholarships) to preserve their amateur status. The NCAA's three major divisions were left to set rules governing compensation.

Auditors : CROWE LLP INDIANAPOLIS IN

LOCATIONS

HQ: NATIONAL COLLEGIATE ATHLETIC ASSOCIATION
700 W WASHINGTON ST, INDIANAPOLIS, IN 462042710
Phone: 317 917-6222
Web: WWW.NCAA.ORG

PRODUCTS/OPERATIONS

2013 Revenues

	% of total
Television & marketing rights fees	80
Championships & NIT tournaments	12
Investments	4
Sales & services	3
Contributions, facilities & other	1
Total	100

COMPETITORS

APOLLO EDUCATION GROUP, INC.
CARNEGIE CORPORATION OF NEW YORK
Gambling Commission
KANSAS STATE UNIVERSITY
NATIONAL RIFLE ASSOCIATION OF AMERICA
TEXAS MEDICAL ASSOCIATION LIBRARY
UNITED STATES GOLF ASSOCIATION, INC.
UNITED STATES OLYMPIC COMMITTEE
USA TRACK & FIELD, INC.
ZOVIO INC

HISTORICAL FINANCIALS
Company Type: Private

Income Statement — FYE: August 31

	REVENUE ($mil)	NET INCOME ($mil)	NET PROFIT MARGIN	EMPLOYEES
08/19	1,118	70	6.3%	508
08/18	1,064	27	2.5%	—
08/17	1,061	104	9.9%	—
08/16	995	(403)	—	—
Annual Growth	3.9%	—	—	—

2019 Year-End Financials
Return on assets: 11.5%
Return on equity: 15.7%
Current Ratio: 0.50
Cash ($ mil.): 15

NATIONAL GRAPE CO-OPERATIVE ASSOCIATION, INC.

Well, of course grape growers want to hang out in a bunch! The more than 1,090 grower/owner-members of the National Grape Cooperative harvest Concord and Niagara grapes from almost 50,000 acres of vineyards. The plucked produce supplies the coop's wholly owned subsidiary Welch Foods. Welch Foods makes and sells fruit-based juices, jams, jellies, and spreads under the Welch's and Bama brands in the US and nearly 50 other countries. Offerings include fresh eating grapes, distributed by C.H. Robinson Worldwide, as well as dried fruit and frozen juice pops. The grape growers own vineyards in Pennsylvania, Michigan, New York, Ohio, Washington, and Ontario, Canada, which produce some 300,000 tons of grapes annually.

HISTORY

Looking for a steady supply of grapes for his processing plant, in 1945 Russian immigrant Jack Kaplan convinced 900 grape growers to join the newly formed National Grape Cooperative. Also that year Welch Foods' parent company decided to spin off its purple fruit interests, and Kaplan purchased a controlling interest. Welch's -- a competitor at the time -- had been started in 1869 when Dr. Thomas Welch, a tee totaling dentist, created an unfermented Concord grape wine to be used for nonalcoholic communions. The juice was coolly received at first, but the advent of Prohibition helped push the company to the forefront of the fruit-drink industry.

While Kaplan had purchased his interest in Welch's with the intention of combining it with the National Grape Co-op, it wasn't until the mid-1950s that the two could agree on the acquisition. Welch's product line grew throughout the 1960s and 1970s, including the 1972 introduction of red grape and white grape juices. A glut of grapes depressed prices in the 1980s, but the co-op rebounded by the 1990s.

In 1994 the co-op acquired jam and jelly maker BAMA Foods from Borden. Daniel Dillon became CEO of Welch's in 1995, and Fredrick Kalian was named president of the co-op the next year. Yakima Valley Grape Producers joined National Grape Co-op in 1997, adding new growers and more grapes to meet a growing demand, spurred, in part, by newly discovered health benefits of purple and white grape juice. (Welch's helped fund the research.)

New products and increased advertising helped boost juice sales dramatically in 1998 and 1999. Fresh table grapes, distributed by C.H. Robinson Worldwide, were also introduced in 1999 and by 2000 were available nationwide. In 2001 the company announced it would be cutting up to 100 jobs -- its first layoffs in more than two decades -- due to slowing sales.

In 2003 the company introduced new variations of its products including single-serving juices (Welsh Squeezables). This along with increased marketing and new packaging, have seen its sales growing during the last two years. Expansion in grocery channels and the introduction of low-calorie items and shrink-pack products led to further sales gains in 2004.

Auditors: KPMG LLP BOSTON MA

LOCATIONS

HQ: NATIONAL GRAPE CO-OPERATIVE ASSOCIATION, INC.
71 E MAIN ST, WESTFIELD, NY 147871342
Phone: 716 326-5200
Web: WWW.WELCHS.COM

COMPETITORS

BELL-CARTER FOODS, LLC
J. R. SIMPLOT COMPANY
MOTT'S LLP
ODWALLA, INC.
PACIFIC COAST PRODUCERS
SENECA FOODS CORPORATION
SUNKIST GROWERS, INC.
THE J M SMUCKER COMPANY
THE WONDERFUL COMPANY LLC
WELCH FOODS INC., A COOPERATIVE

HISTORICAL FINANCIALS
Company Type: Private

Income Statement — FYE: August 31

	REVENUE ($mil)	NET INCOME ($mil)	NET PROFIT MARGIN	EMPLOYEES
08/12	649	74	11.5%	1,325
08/11	640	74	11.6%	—
08/10	658	82	12.6%	—
Annual Growth	(0.7%)	(5.1%)	—	—

2012 Year-End Financials
Return on assets: 19.8%
Return on equity: 999.9%
Current Ratio: 1.50
Cash ($ mil.): 4

NATIONAL RAILROAD PASSENGER CORPORATION

National Railroad Passenger Corporation, better known as Amtrak, has been riding the rails for more than 40 years. Amtrak is the US' intercity passenger rail provider and its only high-speed rail operator. More than 30 million passengers travel on Amtrak every year on more than 300 daily trains. It connects 46 states, Washington, DC, and three provinces in Canada. Its network consists of about 21,000 route miles of track, most of which is owned by freight railroads. Amtrak also operates commuter rail systems on behalf of several states and transit agencies. Owned by the US government through the US Department of Transportation, Amtrak depends on subsidies from the federal government to operate.

Geographic Reach

With 21,000 route miles in 46 states, Washington, DC, and three Canadian provinces, Amtrak operates daily services to more than 500 destinations. Amtrak also is the operator of choice for state-supported corridor services in 15 states and for four commuter rail agencies.

Formally known as the National Railroad Passenger Corporation, Amtrak is governed by a nine member board of directors appointed by the President of the US and confirmed by the US Senate.

Sales and Marketing

The company's national promotional campaign includes radio, print, digital, mobile and out-of-home media elements. Advertising expenses were $36.8 million and $35.5 million for fiscal 2014 and fiscal 2013, respectively.

Financial Performance

In fiscal 2014 Amtrak's revenues increased by 8% thanks to higher revenues from commuter services and passenger related services.

The company posted net loss of $1.08 billion in fiscal 2014 compared to a net loss of $1.28 billion in fiscal 2013, thanks to higher revenues.

Amtrak posted cash outflow of $459.72 million (compared to $364.81 million in fiscal 2013) due to changes in working capital items.

Strategy

The operation and maintenance of its national passenger rail system and underlying infrastructure is largely funded by subsidies from the US government that are received through annual appropriations. Over the years, some government officials have called for Amtrak to be self-sufficient, and the railroad's annual requests for federal money tend to be the subject of considerable debate in Congress. Over the years, some government officials have called for Amtrak to be self-sufficient. After a Bush administration proposal to end subsidies, break up Amtrak, and turn over passenger rail operations to local authorities failed to gain traction, rising gas prices led some lawmakers to push for an increase in Amtrak appropriations.

As far as infrastructure, Amtrak is investing in improvements in the northeastern US, where the company owns most of the track that it runs on in the Boston-Washington, DC, corridor. Another focus has been a route between Philadelphia and Harrisburg, Pennsylvania, where Amtrak has worked with state authorities to make the improvements necessary to enable the railroad to offer high-speed service. High-demand routes in California, the Chicago area, and the Pacific Northwest region also have been targeted for upgrades. Wyoming, South Dakota, Alaska, and Hawaii are excluded from Amtrak's service in the US.

Still, ridership rates and passenger related revenues, which includes tickets, state contributions, and food and beverages, continue to increase for Amtrak partly as a result of growing difficulties associated with air travel -- higher airfare prices and baggage fees, delayed flights, and reduced capacity. Airlines carrying passengers across the continental US continue to be Amtrak's largest set of competitors.

HISTORY

US passenger train travel peaked in 1929, with 20,000 trains in operation. But the spread of automobiles, bus service, and air travel cut into business, and by the late 1960s only about 500 passenger trains remained running in the country. In 1970 the combined losses of all private train operations exceeded $1.8 billion in today's dollars. That year Congress passed the Rail Passenger Service Act, which created Amtrak to preserve America's passenger rail system. Although railroads were offered stock in the corporation for their passenger equipment, most just wrote off the loss.

Amtrak began operating in 1971 with 1,200 cars, most built in the 1950s. Although the company lost money from the outset ($153 million in 1972), it continued to be bankrolled by Uncle Sam, despite much criticism. Amtrak ordered its first new equipment in 1973, the year it also began taking over stations, yards, and service staff. The company didn't own any track until 1976, when it purchased hundreds of miles of right-of-way track from Boston to Washington, DC.

After a 1979 study showed Amtrak passengers to be by far the most heavily subsidized travelers in the US, Congress ordered the company to better utilize its resources. The 1980s saw Amtrak leasing its rights-of-way along its tracks in the Northeast corridor to telecommunications companies, which installed fiber-optic cables, and beginning mail and freight services for extra revenue.

In the early 1990s Amtrak faced a number of challenges: Midwest flooding, falling airfares, and safety concerns over a number of rail accidents, particularly the 1993 wreck of the Sunset Limited near Mobile, Alabama, in which 47 people were killed (the worst accident in Amtrak's history). In 1994 Amtrak's board of directors (at Congress' behest) adopted a plan to be free of federal support by 2002. In 1995 the company began planning high-speed trains for its heavily traveled East Coast routes.

In 1997 Amtrak finalized agreements to buy the high-speed cars and locomotives central to its self-sufficiency plan. It also began increasing its freight hauling and had its first profitable offering: the Metroliner route between New York and Washington, DC.

Amtrak's board of directors was replaced by Congress in 1997 with a seven-member Reform Board appointed by President Clinton. Chairman and president Thomas Downs resigned that year, and Tommy Thompson, then governor of Wisconsin, took over as chairman. Former Massachusetts governor Michael Dukakis was named vice chairman, and George Warrington stepped in as Amtrak's president and CEO.

Technical problems in 1999 delayed Amtrak's introduction of the Acela high-speed train in the Northeast until late 2000, when service began in the Boston-Washington corridor. In 2001 Amtrak pitched a 20-year plan, involving an annual outlay of $1.5 billion in federal funds, for expanding and modernizing its passenger service to help alleviate highway and airport congestion nationwide.

Thompson left the Amtrak board in 2001 after he was named US secretary of health and human services.

Realizing Amtrak would not meet its end-of-the-year deadline to be self-sufficient, in 2002 the Amtrak Reform Council sent a proposal to Congress that Amtrak be divided into three groups: one to oversee operations and funding, a second to maintain certain Amtrak-owned tracks and properties, and a third to operate trains. It also called for competition to be allowed on some passenger routes within two to three years.

Also in 2002 Warrington resigned and was replaced by David Gunn, who formerly headed the metropolitan transit systems in New York and Toronto. Gunn began moving to cut costs, and he worked to secure new federal money to avert a threatened shutdown of rail service in July 2002. In 2004 the company exited the mail-carrying business, which had not been profitable.

Gunn was fired in November 2005, however, and chief engineer David Hughes was named interim president and CEO. He left the company after Alexander Kummant was made president and CEO in September 2006.

The Passenger Rail Investment and Improvement Act of 2008 gives five annual grants to Amtrak amounting to $9.8 billion for fiscal years 2009 through 2013. Another boon came in the form of $1.3 billion of stimulus money earmarked for Amtrak by the American Recovery and Reinvestment Act (ARRA) of 2009, which authorizes the Federal Railroad Administration to make the funds available to Amtrak by grant agreement. About $446.8 million will be used for capital security grants, including life safety improvements. Another $884 million will go toward the repair, rehabilitation, or upgrade of railroad assets and infrastructure and toward capital projects that expand rail capacity, including the rehabilitation of rolling stock. The Obama administration promised an ongoing investment of about $1 billion annually for high-speed rail projects.

A record 28.7 million passengers rode on Amtrak in fiscal 2010. While impressive, the company also had a history of recurring operating losses. Although total revenues increased about 7% in 2010 compared to 2009, Amtrak reported fairly comparable net losses in both years.

EXECUTIVES

Corporate Secretary, Eleanor D Acheson
Chief Marketing, J Timothy Griffin
Chief Safety Officer, Kenneth Hylander
CAO, Dj Stadtler
CIO, Christian Zacariassen
Chief Marketing, Roger Harris
Auditors : ERNST & YOUNG LLP TYSONS VA

LOCATIONS

HQ: NATIONAL RAILROAD PASSENGER CORPORATION
 1 MASSACHUSETTS AVE NW, WASHINGTON, DC 200011401
Phone: 202 906-3000
Web: WWW.AMTRAKOIG.GOV

PRODUCTS/OPERATIONS

2014 Sales

	% of total
Passenger related	78
Commuter	4
Other	18
Total	100

2014 Sales

	% of total
Ticket	69
State Contribution	7
Food Beverage	4
Others	20
Total	100

COMPETITORS

CONRAIL, INC
CSX CORPORATION
Compagnie des Chemins de Fer Nationaux du Canada
EAST JAPAN RAILWAY COMPANY
FIRSTGROUP PLC
GENESEE & WYOMING INC.

GREYHOUND LINES, INC.
KANSAS CITY SOUTHERN
METROPOLITAN TRANSPORTATION AUTHORITY
UNION PACIFIC CORPORATION

HISTORICAL FINANCIALS
Company Type: Private

Income Statement — FYE: September 30

	REVENUE ($mil)	NET INCOME ($mil)	NET PROFIT MARGIN	EMPLOYEES
09/21	2,081	(2,007)	—	18,650
09/20	2,430	(1,679)	—	—
09/19	3,503	(880)	—	—
09/18	3,386	(817)	—	—
Annual Growth	(15.0%)	—	—	—

2021 Year-End Financials
Return on assets: (-9.3%)   Cash ($ mil.): 491
Return on equity: (-13.7%)
Current Ratio: 2.40

NATURAL GAS PIPELINE COMPANY OF AMERICA LLC

EXECUTIVES
Managing Member*, Richard D Kinder

LOCATIONS
HQ: NATURAL GAS PIPELINE COMPANY OF AMERICA LLC
  1001 LOUISIANA ST, HOUSTON, TX 770025089
Phone: 713 369-9000
Web: WWW.KINDERMORGAN.COM

HISTORICAL FINANCIALS
Company Type: Private

Income Statement — FYE: December 31

	REVENUE ($mil)	NET INCOME ($mil)	NET PROFIT MARGIN	EMPLOYEES
12/17	679	130	19.2%	1,747
12/16	613	121	19.7%	—
Annual Growth	10.8%	8.0%	—	—

2017 Year-End Financials
Return on assets: 6.7%   Cash ($ mil.): 15
Return on equity: 9.7%
Current Ratio: 1.50

NAVIGATE AFFORDABLE HOUSING PARTNERS, INC

Auditors: KASSOUF & CO PC BIRMINGHAM A

LOCATIONS
HQ: NAVIGATE AFFORDABLE HOUSING PARTNERS, INC
  1827 1ST AVE N STE 100, BIRMINGHAM, AL 352033137
Phone: 205 445-2800
Web: WWW.NAVIGATEHOUSING.COM

HISTORICAL FINANCIALS
Company Type: Private

Income Statement — FYE: December 31

	REVENUE ($mil)	NET INCOME ($mil)	NET PROFIT MARGIN	EMPLOYEES
12/19	605	9	1.5%	49
12/17	573	8	1.5%	—
12/16	540	(12)	—	—
12/13	498	(6)	—	—
Annual Growth	3.3%	—	—	—

2019 Year-End Financials
Return on assets: 21.2%   Cash ($ mil.): 33
Return on equity: 21.4%
Current Ratio: 105.80

NAVY EXCHANGE SERVICE COMMAND

Before Old Navy, there was the Navy Exchange Service Command (NEXCOM). Active-duty military personnel, reservists, retirees, and their family members can shop and gas up at more than 100 Navy Exchange (NEX) retail stores (brand-name and private-label merchandise ranging from apparel to home electronics), more than 150 NEXCOM Ships Stores (basic necessities), and its 100-plus Uniform Support Centers (the sole source of authorized uniforms). NEXCOM also runs about 40 Navy Lodges (motels) in the US and about half a dozen foreign countries. NEXCOM receives tax dollars for its shipboard stores, but it is otherwise self-supporting. Most of the profits fund morale, welfare, and recreational programs (MWR) for sailors.

Geographic Reach
Navy Exchange Service Command has more than 100 NEX stores on land in the US, Cuba, Africa, Europe, the Middle East, Japan, and China.

Strategy
Since the government lifted restrictions on the types of items sold at the stores, allowing more expensive furniture, jewelry, and televisions, sales have been on the rise at NEX stores. NEXCOM has also been adding stores at home and abroad. In fall 2013 it opened a Fleet Store in Jebel Ali, Dubai to serve sailors stationed in and around Dubai, as well as military personnel passing through the area aboard ship.

To better compete with online rivals Walmart.com, Target.com, Amazon.com, BestBuy.com, and others, in 2013 NEX expanded its Price Match Policy to match their prices.

LOCATIONS
HQ: NAVY EXCHANGE SERVICE COMMAND
  3280 VIRGINIA BEACH BLVD, VIRGINIA BEACH, VA 234525799
Phone: 757 463-6200
Web: WWW.MYNAVYEXCHANGE.COM

PRODUCTS/OPERATIONS

2014 Sales

	% of total
Total Sales	95
Income from Concessions, net	2
Contributed Services	3
Other Revenue	0
Total	100

PRODUCT DEPARTMENTS
For The Home
Electronics
Shoes
Beauty
Women
Men
Kids
Navy pride
Handbags and accessories

COMPETITORS
ARMY & AIR FORCE EXCHANGE SERVICE
BI-MART CORPORATION
BJ'S WHOLESALE CLUB, INC.
COSTCO WHOLESALE CORPORATION
CUMBERLAND GENERAL STORE LLC
DO IT BEST CORP.
GIFI
JOHN LEWIS PARTNERSHIP PLC
ROSS STORES, INC.
SAM'S WEST, INC.

HISTORICAL FINANCIALS
Company Type: Private

Income Statement — FYE: January 28

	REVENUE ($mil)	NET INCOME ($mil)	NET PROFIT MARGIN	EMPLOYEES
01/17	2,574	45	1.8%	14,000
01/16	2,635	73	2.8%	—
01/11	2,749	68	2.5%	—
Annual Growth	(1.1%)	(6.5%)	—	—

2017 Year-End Financials
Return on assets: 3.2%   Cash ($ mil.): —
Return on equity: 6.8%
Current Ratio: 1.70

NCH CORPORATION

NCH Corporation is a global leader in industrial, commercial, and institutional maintenance products and services, and one of the largest companies in the world to sell such products through direct marketing. The company makes and sells chemical, maintenance, repair, and supply products, including all kinds of cleaners, for customers in more than 50 countries throughout the world. NCH markets its products through a direct sales force to companies in industrial, commercial and infrastructure markets. Other products include pet care supplies, plumbing parts. Founded in 1919, leadership of the company remains in the hands of the Levy family, descendants of the founding father, Milton P. Levy, Senior.

Operations

The company's divisions include: water treatment solutions, plumbing, industrial and institutional maintenance.

Subsidiaries in NCH's Chemical Specialties division produce cleaners, degreasers, lubricants, grounds care, housekeeping, and water treatment products. Its plumbing products group provides plumbing supplies that include thousands of parts and products for repair, replacement, remodeling and new construction. Other subsidiaries include Pure Solve, a parts washing service.

NCH sells its products directly through a number of wholly owned subsidiaries, many of which are engaged in the maintenance products business. It include Certified, Chemsearch, Chem-Aqua, and Danco.

Geographic Reach

Headquartered in Irving, Texas, NCH has offices and manufacturing plants on six continents and serve clients in about 55 countries across the globe.

Sales and Marketing

NCH sells to industrial, commercial and institutional customers. Its products are distributed nationally through home centers and hardware stores. The company has organization of direct sales representatives and it sells its products through direct marketing. The Plumbing Products group provides supplies for the do-it-yourself consumer and the OEM market.

Company Background

Founded in 1919, NCH Corporation is a global leader in industrial, commercial, and institutional maintenance products and services, and one of the largest companies in the world to sell such products through direct marketing.

HISTORY

NCH was established in 1919.

Salesman Milton Levy founded National Disinfectant Co. in Dallas in 1919 to make disinfectants, insecticides, and soaps. The company's offerings grew in the 1930s to include Everbrite, a top-selling industrial floor wax. Levy's sons, Irvin, Lester, and Milton Jr., worked for the company as teenagers and took over its management after their father's death in 1946.

National Disinfectant expanded geographically in the 1950s and 1960s, opening its first branch office in St. Louis in 1956. The company changed its name to National Chemsearch in 1960 to reflect its diversity. It also expanded into Europe and Latin America. National Chemsearch went public in 1965. Acquisitions boosted its product line to about 250 items by 1970. The company shortened its name to NCH in 1978.

NCH expanded its marketing to include catalog sales, direct mail, and telemarketing in 1986. It opened a South Korean plant in 1992. Troubled economies in Mexico and Venezuela hurt profits in 1994, and the next year NCH began work on a long-term business strategy that envisioned third-generation Levy family members moving into higher executive ranks.

Softened currency rates in Europe and Asia contributed to a decrease in profits for fiscal 1999. That year NCH focused on strengthening its customer relationships by boosting sales staff training and implementing an Internet-based corporate network.

In 2000 Irvin Levy became the company's chairman and NCH sold its electronic components business. The next year the company shut down its direct broadcast satellite equipment operations. In February 2002 the Levys took the company private by purchasing the 43% of the company that they didn't already own. The brothers originally offered a 20% premium to buy the shares but were greeted by lawsuits from shareholders who claimed they were taking advantage of a depressed market. The Levys settled the suits by upping the offer by $120 million.

In 2012 subsidiaries Chem-Aqua and Nephros signed a non-exclusive distributor agreement for Chem-Aqua to distribute Nephros's innovative ultrafilters in North America. The addition of Nephros ultrafilters to Chem-Aqua's product line allows both companies to offer their institutional customers a comprehensive multi-barrier approach for the prevention of waterborne infection.

Auditors : PRICEWATERHOUSECOOPERS LLP DA

LOCATIONS

HQ: NCH CORPORATION
2727 CHEMSEARCH BLVD, IRVING, TX 750626454
Phone: 972 438-0211
Web: WWW.NCH.COM

PRODUCTS/OPERATIONS

Selected Operations and Products
Chemical Specialties
    Cleaning chemicals
    Deodorizers
    Floor and carpet care products
    HVAC products
    Lubricants
    Oil production facility chemicals
    Paint
    Paint removers
    Water-treatment chemicals
Landmark Direct
    First-aid supplies
    Workplace signage and productivity products
Pet Care
Partsmaster Group
    Cutting tools
    Electrical products
    Fasteners
    Welding alloys
Plumbing Products Group
    Plumbing products for new construction
    Plumbing repair and replacement parts
Industrial and Institutional Maintenance
Industrial and commercial cleaning
Industrial Repair and maintenance
Drains, Grease Traps and lift stations
Lubrication and coolants
Equipment and supplies
Parts washing
Grounds Care
Personal hygiene
Pet Care
Training pads
Stain and Odor Removers
Cleaners and Disinfectants
Allergy Relief and shed Control
Grooming products
Plumbing
Sinks
Faucets
Tub & Showers
Toilets
Drains
Specialty Industrial Supply
High Performance Cutting Tools
Welding
Abrasives
Compounds
Fasteners
Electrical and Automotive
Shop Supplies
Storage Hardware
Tools
Water Treatment Solutions
Boiler
Cooling Towers
Colsed Recirculation Systems
Biocides and Algaecides
Cleaner/Descalers
Equipment
Wastewater and Bio Remediation

COMPETITORS

ACCESS BUSINESS GROUP LLC
AIR PRODUCTS AND CHEMICALS, INC.
DIVERSEY, INC.
GOJO INDUSTRIES, INC.
HARCROS CHEMICALS INC.
HILLYARD, INC.
MACDERMID, INCORPORATED
OIL-DRI CORPORATION OF AMERICA
THE TRANZONIC COMPANIES
TUTHILL CORPORATION

HISTORICAL FINANCIALS
Company Type: Private

Income Statement   FYE: April 30

	REVENUE ($mil)	NET INCOME ($mil)	NET PROFIT MARGIN	EMPLOYEES
04/19	1,005	26	2.6%	8,500
04/12	1,045	6	0.6%	—
04/11	952	6	0.7%	—
Annual Growth	0.7%	18.5%	—	—

2019 Year-End Financials
Return on assets: 4.3%   Cash ($ mil.): 26
Return on equity: 13.5%
Current Ratio: 2.20

NEBRASKA PUBLIC POWER DISTRICT

Nebraska Public Power District (NPPD) electrifies the Cornhusker State. The government-owned electric utility, the largest in the state, provides power in 86 of the state's 93 counties. The firm has a generating capacity of about 3,130 MW and operates more than 5,200 miles of transmission lines. NPPD distributes electricity to about 89,000 retail customers in 81 cities and towns; it also provides power to about 1 million customers through wholesale power contracts with more than 50 towns and 25 public power districts. In addition, NPPD purchases electricity from the federally owned Western Area Power Administration and operates a surface water irrigation system.

Operations
The company uses multiple sources, including nuclear, steam, mixed, wind, hydro, and diesel, to generate power.

NPPD's revenues comes from wholesale power supply agreements with 50 towns and 25 rural public power districts and rural cooperatives who rely totally or partially on NPPD's electrical system. NPPD also serves about 81 communities at the retail level.

Financial Performance
Revenues for 2013 increased by 2% due mostly to rate increases and sales to other utilities. Net income jumped 30% on the revenue increase and reduced costs. Cash from operations followed suit and rose nearly $100 million.

Strategy
Faced with growing long-term demand for electricity, along with pressure to keep prices low, NPPD has implemented plans to increase transmission capacity. With a goal of getting of 15% it energy from renewable sources by 2025, the company is exploring alternative fuel sources for future plants. With 45% of NPPD's energy supply coming from coal in 2011, the company was looking to cleaner alternatives, such as wind power and biomass in order to meet stricter environmental regulations. In 2014 it signed a deal to purchase wind power from Sempra, a move that put it within sight of its goal to have 10% of its power generation come from renewable sources.

Company Background
NPPD was formed in 1970 through the merger of three public utilities: Consumers Public Power District, Platte Valley Public Power and Irrigation District, and Nebraska Public Power System.

EXECUTIVES
CCO, Ken Curry
Corporate Strategy Vice President, Tim Arlt
CIO, Robyn Tweedy
Auditors : PRICEWATERHOUSECOOPERS LLP C

LOCATIONS
HQ: NEBRASKA PUBLIC POWER DISTRICT
1414 15TH ST, COLUMBUS, NE 686015226
Phone: 877 275-6773
Web: WWW.NPPD.COM

PRODUCTS/OPERATIONS
2013 Sales

	$ mil.	% of total
Wholesale	584.1	53
Retail	294.2	27
Other	227.9	20
Total	1,106.1	100

COMPETITORS
CONSUMERS ENERGY COMPANY
GEORGIA POWER COMPANY
GREAT RIVER ENERGY
LOS ANGELES DEPARTMENT OF WATER AND POWER
LOWER COLORADO RIVER AUTHORITY
OMAHA PUBLIC POWER DISTRICT
POWERSOUTH ENERGY COOPERATIVE
PUBLIC UTILITY DISTRICT 1 OF SNOHOMISH COUNTY
SACRAMENTO MUNICIPAL UTILITY DISTRICT
SEMINOLE ELECTRIC COOPERATIVE, INC.

HISTORICAL FINANCIALS
Company Type: Private

Income Statement   FYE: December 31

	REVENUE ($mil)	NET INCOME ($mil)	NET PROFIT MARGIN	EMPLOYEES
12/21	1,221	133	10.9%	1,900
12/20	1,103	95	8.7%	—
12/19	1,074	89	8.3%	—
12/18	1,144	82	7.2%	—
Annual Growth	2.2%	17.2%	—	—

2021 Year-End Financials
Return on assets: 2.8%   Cash ($ mil.): 34
Return on equity: 7.1%
Current Ratio: 5.70

NEVADA SYSTEM OF HIGHER EDUCATION

You can gamble on a solid academic foundation with The Nevada System of Higher Education (NSHE). The system oversees Nevada's public colleges and institutions. NSHE encompasses eight institutions: the University of Nevada, Las Vegas; the University of Nevada, Reno; Nevada State College; community colleges Truckee Meadows, Great Basin College, College of Southern Nevada, and Western Nevada College; and environmental research arm Desert Research Institute (DRI). The system, which enrolls some 106,000 students, is governed by the Nevada Board of Regents, consisting of 13 members elected for six-year terms.

Financial Performance
Total operating revenue fell 4% in 2012 as an increase in NSHE's largest segment (student tuition and fees) was not enough to offset double-digit declines in federal, state, and local grants and contracts. The rise in tuition and fees resulted from an increase in tuition rates to offset an enrollment decrease.

Strategy
In late 2013 NSHE announced a partnership to establish medical schools at the University of Nevada, Las Vegas and Reno campuses.

Auditors : GRANT THORNTON LLP SAN JOSE

LOCATIONS
HQ: NEVADA SYSTEM OF HIGHER EDUCATION
2601 ENTERPRISE RD, RENO, NV 895121666
Phone: 775 784-4901
Web: NSHE.NEVADA.EDU

COMPETITORS
AUBURN UNIVERSITY
CONNECTICUT STATE UNIVERSITY SYSTEM
MARSHALL UNIVERSITY
MISSOURI STATE UNIVERSITY
UNIVERSITY OF ALASKA SYSTEM

HISTORICAL FINANCIALS
Company Type: Private

Income Statement   FYE: June 30

	REVENUE ($mil)	NET INCOME ($mil)	NET PROFIT MARGIN	EMPLOYEES
06/19	982	(6)	—	8,000
06/18	953	116	12.2%	—
06/17	1,115	140	12.6%	—
06/16	1,055	48	4.6%	—
Annual Growth	(2.4%)	—	—	—

2019 Year-End Financials
Return on assets: (-0.2%)   Cash ($ mil.): 175
Return on equity: (-0.4%)
Current Ratio: 2.90

NEW ENGLAND PETROLEUM LIMITED PARTNERSHIP

Auditors : PRICEWATERHOUSECOOPERS LLP B

LOCATIONS

HQ: NEW ENGLAND PETROLEUM LIMITED PARTNERSHIP
6 KIMBALL LN STE 400, LYNNFIELD, MA 019402685
Phone: 617 660-7400

HISTORICAL FINANCIALS
Company Type: Private

Income Statement — FYE: December 31

	REVENUE ($mil)	NET INCOME ($mil)	NET PROFIT MARGIN	EMPLOYEES
12/12	1,081	4	0.4%	25
12/11	998	3	0.3%	—
12/10	568	2	0.5%	—
Annual Growth	37.9%	32.5%	—	—

2012 Year-End Financials
Return on assets: 7.7% Cash ($ mil.): 1
Return on equity: 13.5%
Current Ratio: 2.40

NEW JERSEY TRANSPORTATION TRUST FUND AUTHORITY

Auditors : MERCADIEN PC PRINCETON NJ

LOCATIONS

HQ: NEW JERSEY TRANSPORTATION TRUST FUND AUTHORITY
1035 PARKWAY AVE, EWING, NJ 086182309
Phone: 609 530-2035

HISTORICAL FINANCIALS
Company Type: Private

Income Statement — FYE: June 30

	REVENUE ($mil)	NET INCOME ($mil)	NET PROFIT MARGIN	EMPLOYEES
06/21	2,059	(560)	—	1
06/20	2,348	(362)	—	—
06/19	2,272	(364)	—	—
06/18	1,676	(859)	—	—
Annual Growth	7.1%	—	—	—

2021 Year-End Financials
Return on assets: (-2.6%) Cash ($ mil.): 1,283
Return on equity: (-111.2%)
Current Ratio: —

NEW JERSEY TURNPIKE AUTHORITY INC

The New Jersey Turnpike Authority operates two toll-supported highways, the New Jersey Turnpike and the Garden State Parkway. The New Jersey Turnpike runs for 148 miles, from the Delaware River Bridge at the southern end of the state to the George Washington Bridge that connects New Jersey with New York. The turnpike includes about 10 rest stops, or service areas, named for former New Jersey residents such as Alexander Hamilton, Vince Lombardi, and Walt Whitman. The Garden State Parkway runs for 173 miles and spans the length of New Jersey's Atlantic coastline.

HISTORY

After almost seven years of construction, Garden State Parkway's Driscoll Bridge was opened in May 2009. The $225 million project included constructing a new span and rehabilitating two existing spans, bumping the Driscoll Bridge up to 15 lanes -- more than any other US bridge. The Driscoll Bridge connects Woodbridge Township to Sayreville and is traveled by some 300,000 vehicles daily.

New Jersey Turnpike Authority, New Jersey Transit, the Port Authority of New York and New Jersey had committed $5.7 billion toward an $8.7 billion new mass transit tunnel beneath the Hudson River -- the first such project in a century. Work began in 2009 on the almost four-mile tunnel known as the Mass Transit Tunnel (MTT), which was to double the rail capacity between New Jersey and New York, but the project was cancelled in 2010.

Auditors : KPMG LLP SHORT HILLS NJ

LOCATIONS

HQ: NEW JERSEY TURNPIKE AUTHORITY INC
1 TURNPIKE PLZ, WOODBRIDGE, NJ 070955195
Phone: 732 750-5300
Web: WWW.NJTA.COM

COMPETITORS

HAWAII DEPARTMENT OF PUBLIC SAFETY
HIGHWAY PATROL, CALIFORNIA
SOUTHERN COMMAND, UNITED STATES
STATE POLICE, RHODE ISLAND
WASHINGTON STATE PATROL

HISTORICAL FINANCIALS
Company Type: Private

Income Statement — FYE: December 31

	REVENUE ($mil)	NET INCOME ($mil)	NET PROFIT MARGIN	EMPLOYEES
12/21	2,185	412	18.9%	2,400
12/20	1,528	(50)	—	—
12/19	1,743	191	11.0%	—
12/18	1,753	209	12.0%	—
Annual Growth	7.6%	25.3%	—	—

2021 Year-End Financials
Return on assets: 2.5% Cash ($ mil.): 396
Return on equity: 43.4%
Current Ratio: 2.30

NEW PRIME, INC.

Specialized carrier New Prime (which does business simply as Prime) provides refrigerated, flatbed, tanker, and intermodal trucking services throughout North America through over 11,600 remotely monitored, temperature-controlled trailers. Prime has been an innovative regional and Over the Road (OTR) trucking company, paving the way for the rest of the trucking industry. A subsidiary, Prime Floral, uses the parent company's refrigerated equipment and facilities to serve the flower industry. In addition to its freight-hauling operations, Prime provides logistics services, including freight brokerage. The company was founded in 1970.

Operations

Prime, with a fleet of over 6,100 trucks, operates through four divisions.

Prime's liquid bulk fleet (Tanker Division) consists of over 300 trucks and over 500 tank trailers with capacities of 6,800, 7,000 or 7,250 gallons. The company's Refrigerated Division has over 6,500 trucks and over 11,700 remotely monitored, temperature-controlled trailers. It is a carrier that can ship fresh produce, fresh cut floral, pharmaceuticals, fresh or frozen meats or any other dry or temperature-controlled freight. Flatbed division is focused on hauling freight from pipe and steel to drywall and roofing materials and more. Prime's Intermodal fleet is a direct link to virtually every market across the continent.

The company also offers two leasing options, lease and lease purchase.

Geographic Reach

The company serves customers in North America. Based in Springfield, Missouri, Prime operates US terminals in Colorado, Texas, Pennsylvania and Utah. Additionally, it has facilities in Indiana, Georgia, Florida, Oregon, and California.

Sales and Marketing

Company Background

Prime was founded in 1970 by Robert Low, who continues to serve as Prime's president.

LOCATIONS

HQ: NEW PRIME, INC.
2740 N MAYFAIR AVE, SPRINGFIELD, MO 658035084
Phone: 800 321-4552
Web: WWW.PRIMEINC.COM

COMPETITORS

ABF FREIGHT SYSTEM, INC.
AMERICOLD LOGISTICS, LLC
CASESTACK LLC
KLLM TRANSPORT SERVICES, LLC
LIQUID TRANSPORT CORP.
ROEHL TRANSPORT, INC.
RUAN TRANSPORTATION MANAGEMENT SYSTEMS, INC.
SCHNEIDER NATIONAL, INC.
STEVENS TRANSPORT, INC.
THE RAYMOND CORPORATION

HISTORICAL FINANCIALS

Company Type: Private

Income Statement — FYE: March 31

	REVENUE ($mil)	NET INCOME ($mil)	NET PROFIT MARGIN	EMPLOYEES
03/17*	1,653	116	7.1%	6,775
04/16	1,598	133	8.3%	—
03/12	1,022	60	6.0%	—
04/11	941	47	5.0%	—
Annual Growth	9.8%	16.2%	—	—

*Fiscal year change

2017 Year-End Financials
Return on assets: 12.7% Cash ($ mil.): —
Return on equity: 32.2%
Current Ratio: 0.40

NEW WORLD FUND

LOCATIONS

HQ: NEW WORLD FUND
333 S HOPE ST FL 53, LOS ANGELES, CA 900711418
Phone: 213 486-9200

HISTORICAL FINANCIALS

Company Type: Private

Income Statement — FYE: October 31

	REVENUE ($mil)	NET INCOME ($mil)	NET PROFIT MARGIN	EMPLOYEES
10/21	802	15,687	1955.1%	2
10/20	595	3,579	601.2%	—
10/19	792	8,314	1049.1%	—
10/18	404	(94)	—	—
Annual Growth	25.6%	—	—	—

2021 Year-End Financials
Return on assets: 25.4% Cash ($ mil.): 182
Return on equity: 25.7%
Current Ratio: —

NEW YORK CITY HEALTH AND HOSPITALS CORPORATION

New York City Health and Hospitals Corporation (NYC Health + Hospitals) is the largest public health care system in the nation serving more than a million New Yorkers annually in more than 70 patient care locations across the city's five boroughs. A robust network of outpatient, neighborhood-based primary and specialty care centers anchors care coordination with the system's trauma centers, nursing homes, post-acute care centers, home care agency, and MetroPlus health plan?all supported by more than 10 essential hospitals. Its health plan, MetroPlus, offers low to no-cost health insurance to eligible people living in Manhattan, Brooklyn, Queens, Staten Island, and the Bronx. NYC Health + Hospitals/Community Care offers comprehensive care management and better access to social support services in patients' homes and communities.

Operations

NYC H+H has five facilities:

NYC Health + Hospitals/Cooler, which provides high quality short-term rehabilitation therapy and long-term skilled nursing services and from specialized rehabilitation equipment to expert wound care.

The NYC Health + Hospitals/Gouverneur is the 295-bed skilled nursing facility that provides medical, nursing, and rehabilitative care in an atmosphere of dignity and compassion and provides a full spectrum of care for children and adults.

NYC Health + Hospitals/Carter provides safe and superior quality care across the continuum of long-term acute and skilled nursing care, with clinical excellence and patient focused philosophy.

NYC Health + Hospitals/McKinney offer short-term rehabilitation services, long-term skilled nursing care, specialized care for serious injuries and medically complex services.

NYC Health + Hospitals/Sea View provides 24-hour medical and nursing care, patients, and residents have access to specialty services and highest quality of rehabilitation and long-term skilled nursing services.

Geographic Reach

NYC Health + Hospital operates health care facilities in New York's Manhattan, Brooklyn, Queens, Bronx, and Staten Island boroughs.

Sales and Marketing

NYC Health + Hospital's MetroPlus health plan provides low to no-cost insurance to more than 500,000 customers in New York. It insures many New York City government employees.

HISTORY

The City of New York in 1929 created a department to manage its hospitals for the poor. During the Depression, more than half of the city's residents were eligible for subsidized care, and its public hospitals operated at full capacity.

Four new hospitals opened in the 1950s, but the city was already having trouble maintaining existing facilities and attracting staff (young doctors preferred private, insurance-supported hospitals catering to the middle class). Meanwhile, technological advances and increased demand for skilled nurses made hospitals more expensive to operate. The advent of Medicaid in 1965 was a boon for the system because it brought in federal money.

In 1969 the city created the New York City Health and Hospitals Corporation (HHC) to manage its public health care system -- and, it was hoped, to distance it from the political arena. But HHC was still dependent on the city for funds, arousing criticism from those who had hoped for more autonomy. A 1973 state report claimed "the people of New York City are not materially better served by the Health and Hospitals Corporation than by its predecessor agencies."

City budget shortfalls in the mid-1970s led to cutbacks at HHC, including nearly 20% of staff. Later in the decade several hospitals closed and some services were discontinued. Ed Koch became mayor in 1978 and gained more control over HHC's operations. Struggles between his administration and the system led three HHC presidents to resign by 1981. That year Koch crony Stanley Brezenoff assumed the post and helped transform HHC into a city pseudo-department.

The early 1980s brought greater prosperity to the system. Reimbursement rates and collections procedures improved, allowing HHC to upgrade its record-keeping and its ambulatory and psychiatric care programs. In the late 1980s sharp increases in AIDS and crack addiction cases strained the system and a sluggish economy decreased city funding. Criticism mounted in the early 1990s, with allegations of wrongful deaths, dangerous facilities, and lack of Medicaid payment controls. HHC lost patients to managed care providers, and revenues plummeted. In 1995 a city panel recommended radically revamping the system.

Faced with declining revenues and criticism from Mayor Rudolph Giuliani that HHC was "a jobs program," the company began cutting jobs and consolidating facilities in 1996. Under Giuliani's direction, HHC made plans to sell its Coney Island, Elmhurst,

HOOVER'S HANDBOOK OF PRIVATE COMPANIES 2023

and Queens hospital centers. In 1997 the New York State Supreme Court struck down Giuliani's privatization efforts, saying the city council had a right to review and approve each sale. In 1998 Giuliani continued to seek to restructure HHC, and the agency itself contended it was making progress toward its restructuring goals, which were aimed at giving HHC more autonomy as well as more fiscal responsibility. In anticipation of a budget shortfall that year, the system laid off some 900 support staff employees. In 1999 the state court of appeals ruled HHC could not legally lease or sell its hospitals.

In 2000 HHC launched an effort to improve its physical infrastructure by beginning the rebuilding and renovation of facilities in Brooklyn, Manhattan, and Queens. The organization also began converting to an electronic (and thus more efficient) clinical information system. In 2001 HHC forged ahead with further restructuring initiatives. It introduced the Open Access plan, a cost-cutting measure designed to expedite the processes involved in outpatient visits.

In 2006 Mayor Michael Bloomberg committed $16 million in funds toward the treatment of those affected by exposure to toxic fumes and dust from the 2001 attacks on the World Trade Center. Together with the city, HHC established the WTC Environmental Health Center at Bellevue Hospital; treatment was made available at little or no charge to the patient.

Auditors : KPMG LLP NEW YORK NY

LOCATIONS

HQ: NEW YORK CITY HEALTH AND HOSPITALS CORPORATION
  125 WORTH ST RM 514, NEW YORK, NY 100134006
Phone: 212 788-3321
Web: WWW.NYCHEALTHANDHOSPITALS.ORG

HHC Networks
Central Brooklyn Family Health Network
  Dr. Susan Smith McKinney Nursing and Rehabilitation Center
    East New York Diagnostic & Treatment Center
    Kings County Hospital Center
Generations Plus Northern Manhattan Health Network
  Harlem Hospital Center
  Lincoln Medical and Mental Health Center
  Metropolitan Hospital Center
  Morrisania Diagnostic & Treatment Center
  Renaissance Health Care Network Diagnostic & Treatment Center
  Segundo Ruiz Belvis Diagnostic & Treatment Center
North Bronx Healthcare Network
  Jacobi Medical Center
  North Central Bronx Hospital
North Brooklyn Health Network
  Cumberland Diagnostic & Treatment Center
  Woodhull Medical and Mental Health Center
Queens Health Network
  Elmhurst Hospital Center
  Queens Hospital Center
South Brooklyn and Staten Island Health Network
  Coney Island Hospital
  Sea View Hospital Rehabilitation Center & Home
South Manhattan Healthcare Network
  Bellevue Hospital Center
  Gouverneur Healthcare Services

PRODUCTS/OPERATIONS

2018 Sales

	$ mil.	% of total
Net patient services	6,216.7	80
Net appropriations from City of New York	787.3	10
Grants	652.0	9
Other	105.0	1
Total	7,761.0	100

Selected Services

Alcohol and Opioid Use Disorder
Asthma Care
Bariatric Services
Breast Health
Burn Care
Cancer Care
Cardiology
Child Health and Pediatrics
Colon Cancer Screening
Deaf and Hard-of-Hearing
Dental Care
Depression
Diabetes Care
Farmers Market
Flu Vaccination
Geriatric Services
HIV/AIDS Care
HPV Vaccine
Hypertension
Language/Translation Services
LGBTQ Services
Men's Health
Mental Health
Neonatal Intensive Care
Obstetrics & Gynecology
Palliative Care
Parkinson's Disease
Pediatrics
Quit Smoking
Rehab Services
Victims of Domestic Violence
Sexual Response Assault Teams
Sickle Cell Disease
Sleep Disorder Labs
Stroke Prevention and Care
Telehealth Initiatives
Trauma Centers
Vision Care
Women's Health
WTC Environmental Health Center
Youth Health

COMPETITORS

ASCENSION HEALTH
DIGNITY HEALTH
FAIRVIEW HEALTH SERVICES
HCA HEALTHCARE, INC.
IASIS HEALTHCARE LLC
PRESBYTERIAN HEALTHCARE SERVICES
SISTERS OF CHARITY OF LEAVENWORTH HEALTH SYSTEM, INC.
SUNLINK HEALTH SYSTEMS, INC.
TENET HEALTHCARE CORPORATION
UNIHEALTH FOUNDATION

HISTORICAL FINANCIALS
Company Type: Private

Income Statement   FYE: June 30

	REVENUE ($mil)	NET INCOME ($mil)	NET PROFIT MARGIN	EMPLOYEES
06/17	9,550	(193)	—	35,700
06/02	4,285	(118)	—	—
06/01	4,287	(71)	—	—
06/00	4,083	9	0.2%	—
Annual Growth	5.1%	—	—	—

2017 Year-End Financials
Return on assets: (-2.8%)   Cash ($ mil.): 1,184
Return on equity: —
Current Ratio: 1.00

NEW YORK CITY SCHOOL CONSTRUCTION AUTHORITY

Auditors : PRICEWATERHOUSECOOPER LLP NE

LOCATIONS

HQ: NEW YORK CITY SCHOOL CONSTRUCTION AUTHORITY
  3030 THOMSON AVE FL 3, LONG ISLAND CITY, NY 111013019
Phone: 718 472-8000
Web: WWW.NYCSCA.ORG

HISTORICAL FINANCIALS
Company Type: Private

Income Statement   FYE: June 30

	REVENUE ($mil)	NET INCOME ($mil)	NET PROFIT MARGIN	EMPLOYEES
06/14	2,190	(410)	—	600
06/13	1,840	(494)	—	—
Annual Growth	19.0%	—	—	—

2014 Year-End Financials
Return on assets: (-16.8%)   Cash ($ mil.): 74
Return on equity: (-24.4%)
Current Ratio: —

NEW YORK CITY TRANSIT AUTHORITY

New York City Transit Authority has your ticket to ride in the Big Apple. Known as MTA New York City Transit, it provides subway and bus transportation throughout New York City's five boroughs. It is the primary agency of the MTA and the largest public transportation system in North America. Its subway system -- which includes more than 6,300 subway cars, 468 stations, and 660 miles of track -- serves more than 5.5 million passengers a day day on 238 local, six select bus service, and 61 express routes in the five boroughs. Its more than 5,700 buses transport some 2.6 million riders each day. The agency also operates the Staten Island Railway system.

Operations
New York City Subways and Buses is comprised of two agencies of the MTA regional transportation network - MTA New York City

Transit Transit and MTA Bus. The regional network also includes MTA Staten Island Railway (part of NYC Transit's Department of Subways), MTA Long Island Rail Road, MTA Metro-North Railroad, MTA Bridges and Tunnels, and MTA Capital Construction.

MTA New York City Transit and its subsidiary, Manhattan and Bronx Surface Transit Operating Authority, provide subway and public bus service within New York City's five boroughs.

In 2013 MTA New York City Transit's total ridership was 2.4 billion, up 62 million, or 2.7% from 2012. After including 44 million of lost ridership from Superstorm Sandy in 2012, the company's 2013 ridership increased by 0.8%, with a subway ridership increase of 19 million, or 1.1%, and no change in bus ridership.

Geographic Reach
The company serves customers in Brooklyn, the Bronx, Manhattan, and Queens, and Staten Island

Financial Performance
Rebounding from the effects of Superstorm Sandy on ridership (which resulted in lost revenues of $52 million), in 2013 MTA New York City Transit's revenues from fares increased by 9%. In 2014 its operating budget was $10.1 billion.

Strategy
MTA New York City Transit's parent company, the MTA, has been plagued by operating losses. To mitigate its losses, the MTA has in recent years raised fares, cut jobs, and decreased service on its buses and subway lines. It has also sought to raise its non-operating revenues by seeking increased government funding.

With the help of federal stimulus and other funding, MTA New York City Transit has been making capital improvements to its systems. Projects have included the construction of the Second Avenue Subway and renovations at the Fulton Street Transit Center and other stations throughout the system.

In 2013 the company broke ground on a new MTA Staten Island Railway station. The 27-month construction project, the first such project to include a parking lot, will replace the existing Atlantic and Nassau Stations in the Tottenville section of the borough.

Company Background
New York City Transit Authority was formed in the 1950s by New York's legislature; the city's transit system dates back to the early 1900s.

Auditors : PRICEWATERHOUSECOOPERS LLP ST

LOCATIONS
HQ: NEW YORK CITY TRANSIT AUTHORITY
2 BROADWAY FL 18, NEW YORK, NY 100043357
Phone: 718 330-1234
Web: NEW.MTA.INFO

COMPETITORS
CHICAGO TRANSIT AUTHORITY (INC)
HARRIS COUNTY, METROPOLITAN TRANSIT AUTHORITY OF
LOS ANGELES COUNTY METROPOLITAN TRANSPORTATION AUTHORITY
METRO-NORTH COMMUTER RAILROAD COMPANY
METROPOLITAN TRANSPORTATION AUTHORITY
NORTHEAST ILLINOIS REGIONAL COMMUTER RAILROAD CORPORATION
SOUTHEASTERN PENNSYLVANIA TRANSPORTATION AUTHORITY
THE LONG ISLAND RAILROAD CO
THE NEW JERSEY TRANSIT CORPORATION
WASHINGTON METROPOLITAN AREA TRANSIT AUTHORITY

HISTORICAL FINANCIALS
Company Type: Private

Income Statement   FYE: December 31

	REVENUE ($mil)	NET INCOME ($mil)	NET PROFIT MARGIN	EMPLOYEES
12/21	2,815	2,825	100.4%	47,956
12/19	5,060	1,049	20.7%	—
12/18	4,892	985	20.1%	—
12/17	4,911	(287)	—	—
Annual Growth	(13.0%)	—	—	—

2021 Year-End Financials
Return on assets: 5.4%   Cash ($ mil.): 27
Return on equity: 11.5%
Current Ratio: 0.70

NEW YORK HOTEL TRADES COUNCIL AND HOTEL ASSOCIATION OF NEW YORK CITY HEALTH CENTER, INC.,

Auditors : MSPC CPAS & ADVISORS PC CRA

LOCATIONS
HQ: NEW YORK HOTEL TRADES COUNCIL AND HOTEL ASSOCIATION OF NEW YORK CITY HEALTH CENTER, INC.,
305 W 44TH ST, NEW YORK, NY 100365407
Phone: 212 586-6400
Web: WWW.HOTELFUNDS.ORG

HISTORICAL FINANCIALS
Company Type: Private

Income Statement   FYE: December 31

	REVENUE ($mil)	NET INCOME ($mil)	NET PROFIT MARGIN	EMPLOYEES
12/19	540	(21)	—	1,000
12/18	500	12	2.5%	—
12/17	272	44	16.3%	—
12/16	565	121	21.5%	—
Annual Growth	(1.5%)	—	—	—

2019 Year-End Financials
Return on assets: (-5.8%)   Cash ($ mil.): 14
Return on equity: (-6.5%)
Current Ratio: 560.30

NEW YORK POWER AUTHORITY

The New York Power Authority (NYPA) is America's largest state power organization, with around 15 generating facilities. Some 80% of the power that NYPA produces is from hydropower resources. The company generates and transmits some 20% of New York's electricity. NYPA owns hydroelectric and fossil-fueled generating facilities, and it operates more than 1,400 circuit-miles of transmission lines. State and federal regulations shape NYPA's diverse customer base, which includes large and small businesses, not-for-profit organizations, community-owned electric systems and rural electric cooperatives and government entities. NYPA is owned by the State of New York.

Operations
The company's principal operating revenues are generated from the power sales (over 60% of sales), wheeling of power (around 25%), and transmission (over 10%). Revenues are recorded when power is delivered or service is provided. Customers' meters are read, and bills are rendered, monthly. Wheeling charges are for costs the Authority incurred for the transmission and/or delivery of power and energy to customers over transmission lines owned by other utilities.

Geographic Reach
The company serves customers throughout New York State, various public corporations in Southeastern New York within the metropolitan area of New York City (SENY Governmental Customers), and certain out-of-state customers.

Financial Performance
Company's revenue for fiscal 2021 increased by 21% to $2.7 billion compared from the prior year with $2.3 billion.

Cash held by the company at the end of fiscal 2021 decreased to $591 million. Cash provided by operations and financing activities were $364 million and $17 million, respectively. Cash used for investing activities was $527 million, mainly for gross additions to capital assets.

Strategy

The company's strategic priorities are: preserve and enhance the value of our hydropower assets as a core source of carbon-free power in New York State, and as a source of flexibility and resilience as the state's grid evolves; pioneer the path to decarbonization by acting as a testbed for innovation while ensuring reliability, resilience and affordability of New York State's energy grid; be the leading transmission developer, owner and operator for New York State and its changing needs; be the leading transmission developer, owner and operator for New York State and its changing needs; repurpose the New York State Canal System for the economic and recreational benefit of New Yorkers while driving operational efficiency.

HISTORY

The Power Authority of the State of New York (aka New York Power Authority, or NYPA) was established in 1931 by Gov. Franklin Roosevelt to gain public control of New York's hydropower resources. The utility's major power plants came on line with the opening of the St. Lawrence-Franklin D. Roosevelt Power Project (1958) and the Niagara Power Project (1961). The Blenheim-Gilboa Pumped Storage Power Project opened in 1973.

In the mid-1970s NYPA shifted to nuclear power when it opened the James A. FitzPatrick Nuclear Power Plant (1975) and the Indian Point 3 Nuclear Power Plant (1976). The company then opened gas- and oil-powered plants: the Charles Poletti Power Project (1977) and the Richard M. Flynn Power Plant (1994).

In 1998 the authority allocated low-cost electricity to five companies that planned to invest $104 million in business expansions in western New York. The company suffered a loss in 1999 in part from reduced hydro generation and a drop in investment earnings. In 2000 NYPA sold its two nuclear plants (1,800 MW of capacity) to utility holding company Entergy for $967 million.

The company completed the installation of 11 gas-powered turbines at various locations in New York City and on Long Island in 2001; the program was initiated to prevent expected energy shortages that summer, but it also helped maintain power in areas of the city during the September 11 terrorist attacks.

In 2013 The Village of Lake Placid unveiled a new hybrid-electric shuttle bus that will make commuting on public transportation quieter and cleaner. Financing for the bus was made possible through NYPA's Municipal Electric-Drive Vehicle Program, which provides financial assistance to New York municipal utilities to facilitate the replacement of less fuel-efficient vehicles in order to advance the state's clean energy goals. That year NYPA added seven more hybrids and one more EV to its fleet, bringing the total number of electric drive vehicles to 79. It also purchased just over 40,000 gallons of B20 biodiesel, which earned the Power Authority 17 Alternative Fuel Vehicle credits under the Department of Energy's Energy Policy Act that will be used to purchase additional hybrid and plug-in hybrid vehicles.

EXECUTIVES

Senior Vice President Internal Audit, Jennifer Faulkner
Senior Vice President Human Resources, Kristine Pizzo
COMMERCIAL Operations, Jill C Anderson Senior
Chief Risk Officer, Soubhagya Parija
Senior Advisor, Rocco Iannarelli
Auditors : KPMG LLP NEW YORK NY

LOCATIONS

HQ: NEW YORK POWER AUTHORITY
250 MARTINE AVE APT 2E, WHITE PLAINS, NY 106013410
Phone: 914 681-6200
Web: WWW.NYPA.GOV

PRODUCTS/OPERATIONS

2014 Sales

	$ mil.	% of total
Power sales	2,396	76
Wheeling charges	614	19
Transmission charges	165	5
Total	3,175	100

Selected Operations
Transmission Control Facility
    Frederick R. Clark Energy Center (Oneida County)
Fossil-Fueled Plants
    Charles Poletti Power Project (New York City)
    Richard M. Flynn Power Plant (Suffolk County)
    PowerNow! Turbines (11 units in New York City and Long Island)
Hydropower Plants
    Blenheim-Gilboa Pumped Storage Power Project (Schoharie County)
    Niagara Power Project (Niagara County)
    St. Lawrence-Franklin D. Roosevelt Power Project (St. Lawrence County)
Small Hydropower Plants
    Ashokan Project (Ulster County)
    Crescent Plant (Albany and Saratoga Counties)
    Gregory B. Jarvis Plant (Oneida County)
    Kensico Project (Westchester County)
    Vischer Ferry Plant (Saratoga and Schenectady counties)

COMPETITORS

CONSOLIDATED EDISON, INC.
GREAT RIVER ENERGY
ISO NEW ENGLAND INC.
MUNICIPAL ELECTRIC AUTHORITY OF GEORGIA
OMAHA PUBLIC POWER DISTRICT
PUBLIC SERVICE COMPANY OF NEW HAMPSHIRE
PUBLIC UTILITY DISTRICT 1 OF SNOHOMISH COUNTY
ROCHESTER GAS AND ELECTRIC CORPORATION
THE CITY OF SEATTLE-CITY LIGHT DEPARTMENT
THE NEW YORK INDEPENDENT SYSTEM OPERATOR, INC.

HISTORICAL FINANCIALS

Company Type: Private

Income Statement   FYE: December 31

	REVENUE ($mil)	NET INCOME ($mil)	NET PROFIT MARGIN	EMPLOYEES
12/20	2,265	(17)	—	2,237
12/19	2,370	26	1.1%	—
12/18	2,689	102	3.8%	—
12/17	2,573	119	4.6%	—
Annual Growth	(4.2%)	—	—	—

2020 Year-End Financials
Return on assets: (-0.2%)   Cash ($ mil.): 219
Return on equity: (-0.4%)
Current Ratio: 1.10

NEW YORK PRESBYTERIAN HOSPITAL WEILL CORNELL UNIVERSITY MEDICAL CENTER

EXECUTIVES

CMO*, Craig Albanese
Senior Vice President Cash*, Jennings Aske
CIO*, Daniel Barchi
CLO, Mary Beth Claus S

LOCATIONS

HQ: NEW YORK PRESBYTERIAN HOSPITAL WEILL CORNELL UNIVERSITY MEDICAL CENTER
525 E 68TH ST, NEW YORK, NY 100654870
Phone: 212 746-8115
Web: WWW.NYP.ORG

HISTORICAL FINANCIALS

Company Type: Private

Income Statement   FYE: December 31

	REVENUE ($mil)	NET INCOME ($mil)	NET PROFIT MARGIN	EMPLOYEES
12/15	4,505	265	5.9%	5,387
12/12	75	21	28.2%	—
Annual Growth	290.4%	131.8%	—	—

2015 Year-End Financials
Return on assets: 3.9%   Cash ($ mil.): 227
Return on equity: 7.6%
Current Ratio: 2.20

NEW YORK STATE CATHOLIC HEALTH PLAN, INC.

Fidelis Care hopes for always faithful health plan members. The New York State Catholic Health Plan, which does business as Fidelis Care, serves more than 921,000 residents in some 60 counties across the state, including the New York City area. The church-sponsored plan's provider network includes more than 63,000 physicians, hospitals, and other health care professionals and facilities. Fidelis Care provides managed Medicaid, Medicare, and state-sponsored family and children's Health Plus plans, as well as long-term care and behavioral health coverage.

Operations
The company boasts an overall statewide member retention rate of more than 78%, with a s Child Health Plus retention rate of more than 85%.

Geographic Reach
Fidelis Care's regional offices are located in Rego Park, Queens (Greater Metropolitan); Albany (Northeast); Syracuse (Central); and Buffalo (Western), with satellite offices in Poughkeepsie, Rochester and Suffern.

Sales and Marketing
The health plan has expanded its membership by seeking new low-income patients who lack coverage. In addition to direct sales efforts, Fidelis Care tries to maintain a presence at health centers frequented by its target audience, partnering with neighborhood clinics to hold free health screenings and Health Plus enrollment information sessions.

Enroll NY, a new website sponsored by not-for-profit organization Hudson Center for Health Equity & Quality, is also connecting Fidelis Care and other Medicaid providers with potential customers. In 2013, Fidelis Care began selling through the New York State of Health insurance exchange marketplace.

To bosst membership, in 2013 the company ran the "I Want Fidelis Care,' campaign (which promoted Fidelis Care as a health care resource) in English and Spanish. TV was added to the media buy in the New York City and Buffalo regions. It also established a social media presence on Facebook, Twitter, YouTube, and Google+.

Financial Performance
Fidelis Care reported gross revenues of $4.1 billion in 2013, up from $3.3 billion in 2012.

Strategy
The company is expanding its office to keep up with demand. In 2014 it opened Ridgewood Community Office; in 2013 it completed of?ce expansion projects in the Albany and Syracuse regional of?ces, and the satellite of?ce in Suffern, and opened new community of?ces in Flushing (Queens), the Bronx, and Bath (Steuben County).

Forecasting substantial growth in 2014 with the enrollment of more than 120,000 new members, the company announced plans to add more than 75 new information technology jobs at its Buffalo regional office.

In 2013 Fidelis Care moved into 12 new counties with the Medicare Advantage program, highlighted by the opportunity to serve residents of western New York for the ?rst time. It also made plans to expand into Seneca, Yates, and Jefferson counties in 2014, and served additional Managed Long Term Care members as part of the State's phased-in expansion of mandatory enrollment in counties beyond New York City.

Fidelis Care has grown by expanding rapidly into new counties in New York, including a number of growth measures in the Medicare marketplace during 2012 and 2013. The health plan's recent activity includes completing construction of Fidelis Care's new operations center and offices in Getzville (Erie County) and the launch of its new provider portal (Provider Access Online). Other growth measures include a 2012 partnership with DentaQuest to promote dental checkups; it also launched a new member portal for members to access benefit information. In 2013 the company gained approval to be a qualified health plan provider on the official New York State of Health marketplace.

Fidelis Care regularly evaluates and broadens its plan offerings. Recent additions include its Fidelis Care at Home managed long-term care offering; the behavioral health and developmental disabilities coverage options; and its fully integrated dual advantage plans (for consumers with both Medicare and Medicaid coverage).

Company Background
The church-sponsored plan was founded in 1993 by the bishops of New York's Roman Catholic dioceses and the Catholic Medical Center of Brooklyn and Queens.

Auditors : LB DELOITTE TAX LLP JERICHO

LOCATIONS

HQ: NEW YORK STATE CATHOLIC HEALTH PLAN, INC.
9525 QUEENS BLVD, REGO PARK, NY 113744510
Phone: 888 343-3547
Web: WWW.FIDELISCARE.ORG

PRODUCTS/OPERATIONS

Selected Plans
Child Health Plus
Dual Advantage
Family Health Plus
Fidelis Care at Home (managed long-term care)
Medicaid Advantage Plus (managed long-term care)
Medicaid Managed Care
Medicare Advantage
New York State of Health

COMPETITORS

ALLWAYS HEALTH PARTNERS, INC.
AMERIGROUP CORPORATION
ASCENSION VIA CHRISTI HEALTH, INC
BLUE CROSS AND BLUE SHIELD OF KANSAS, INC.
CAPITAL DISTRICT PHYSICIANS' HEALTH PLAN, INC.
EMBLEMHEALTH, INC.
HEALTH PARTNERS PLANS, INC.
IPC HEALTHCARE, INC.
MINISTRY HEALTH CARE, INC.
MOLINA HEALTHCARE, INC.

HISTORICAL FINANCIALS
Company Type: Private

Income Statement — FYE: December 31

	ASSETS ($mil)	NET INCOME ($mil)	INCOME AS % OF ASSETS	EMPLOYEES
12/14	2,199	271	12.4%	1,625
12/10	585	51	8.8%	—
12/09	490	27	5.7%	—
12/08	0	3	—	—
Annual Growth	—	103.1%	—	—

2014 Year-End Financials
Return on assets: 12.4%   Cash ($ mil.): 948
Return on equity: 22.3%
Current Ratio: 9.10

NEW YORK STATE ENERGY RESEARCH AND DEVELOPMENT AUTHORITY

The New York State Energy Research and Development Authority (NYSERDA) uses technological innovation to solve the state's energy and environmental problems. The public benefit corporation funds energy supply and conservation research and energy-related environmental issues. It also conducts research projects that help state and city groups solve their energy problems. Its Energy Efficiency Services group works helps more than 450 schools, businesses, and municipalities find ways to reduce their energy costs. Investor-owned electric and gas utilities, grants, and contributions from the New York Power Authority and the Long Island Power Authority fund NYSERDA, which was created in 1975.

EXECUTIVES

Program Vice President*, Robert G Callender
Auditors : KPMG LLP ALBANY NY

LOCATIONS

HQ: NEW YORK STATE ENERGY RESEARCH AND DEVELOPMENT AUTHORITY
17 COLUMBIA CIR, ALBANY, NY 122035156
Phone: 518 862-1090
Web: NYSERDA.NY.GOV

COMPETITORS

CITY OF INDEPENDENCE
FLORIDA DEPARTMENT OF ELDER AFFAIRS
GOVERNOR'S OFFICE, NEW MEXICO
NATURAL RESOURCES, LOUISIANA DEPARTMENT OF
OFFICE OF SCIENCE AND TECHNOLOGY POLICY

HISTORICAL FINANCIALS
Company Type: Private

Income Statement — FYE: March 31

	REVENUE ($mil)	NET INCOME ($mil)	NET PROFIT MARGIN	EMPLOYEES
03/22	1,614	258	16.0%	345
03/19	1,091	51	4.7%	—
03/17	0	(0)	—	—
Annual Growth	502.1%	—	—	—

2022 Year-End Financials
Return on assets: 12.1% Cash ($ mil.): —
Return on equity: 15.3%
Current Ratio: 4.40

NEW YORK STATE ENERGY RESEARCH AND DEVELOPMENT AUTHORITY

LOCATIONS
HQ: NEW YORK STATE ENERGY RESEARCH AND DEVELOPMENT AUTHORITY
17 COLUMBIA CIR, ALBANY, NY 122035156
Phone: 518 862-1090
Web: WWW.NYSERDA.NY.GOV

HISTORICAL FINANCIALS
Company Type: Private

Income Statement — FYE: March 31

	REVENUE ($mil)	NET INCOME ($mil)	NET PROFIT MARGIN	EMPLOYEES
03/21	1,204	(1)	—	1
03/20	1,287	32	2.5%	—
Annual Growth	(6.4%)	—	—	—

2021 Year-End Financials
Return on assets: (-0.1%) Cash ($ mil.): —
Return on equity: (-0.1%)
Current Ratio: 4.50

NEW YORK STATE HOUSING FINANCE AGENCY

Auditors : ERNST & YOUNG LLP NEW YORK N

LOCATIONS
HQ: NEW YORK STATE HOUSING FINANCE AGENCY
641 LEXINGTON AVE FL 4, NEW YORK, NY 100224503
Phone: 212 688-4069
Web: HCR.NY.GOV

HISTORICAL FINANCIALS
Company Type: Private

Income Statement — FYE: October 31

	REVENUE ($mil)	NET INCOME ($mil)	NET PROFIT MARGIN	EMPLOYEES
10/20	549	90	16.5%	131
10/18	553	187	33.9%	—
10/17	400	112	28.0%	—
10/16	279	77	27.7%	—
Annual Growth	18.4%	4.1%	—	—

2020 Year-End Financials
Return on assets: 0.5% Cash ($ mil.): 52
Return on equity: 8.2%
Current Ratio: 2.60

NEW YORK UNIVERSITY

The setting and heritage of New York University (NYU) make it one of the nation's most popular educational institutions. With about 53,600 students attending its nearly 20 schools and colleges, NYU is among the largest private schools in the US. Its Tisch School of the Arts is well-regarded, and its law school and Leonard N. Stern School of Business are among the foremost in the country. One of the most prominent and respected research universities in the world, featuring top-ranked academic programs and accepting fewer than one-in-eight undergraduates, NYU's students come from nearly every state and about 135 countries. NYU was founded in 1831.

Operations

NYU reports its financials in two segments ? NYU Langone Health and University. The latter segment is composed of the NYU Langone Health System (Health System) and its two medical schools: the NYU Robert I. Grossman School of Medicine (NYUGSoM) and NYU Long Island School of Medicine (collectively the NYU Schools of Medicine).

NYU Langone Health operates two hospitals, Kimmel Pavilion and Tisch Hospital, which together have nearly 845 beds. It also operates the 225-bed NYU Langone Orthopedic Hospital; the 450-bed NYU Langone Hospital in Brooklyn; NYU Langone Hospital-Long Island, a 591-bed acute care facility; and several ambulatory care facilities. The segment brings in about 75% of NYU's total revenue.

The University includes about 20 colleges and divisions, including schools of art and sciences, law, dentistry, business, mathematical sciences, fine arts, professional studies, public services, social work, and engineering. NYU also operates NYU Abu Dhabi and NYU Shanghai, a joint venture with East China Normal University. The University segment accounts for about 25% of NYU's total revenue.

Overall, patient care accounts for about 60% of NYU's total revenue.

Geographic Reach

Along with its campuses in New York, NYU operates degree-granting campuses in Abu Dhabi and Shanghai. It also has more than 10 global academic centers in Africa, Asia, Europe, and the Americas, and research programs in more than 25 countries.

Sales and Marketing

Financial Performance

Company's revenue for fiscal 2021 increased to $13.5 billion compared from the prior year with $12.8 billion.

Cash held by the company at the end of fiscal 2021 increased to $3.9 billion. Cash provided by operations was $1.7 billion while cash used for investing and financing activities were $1.2 billion and $74.0 million, respectively.

Company Background

In 1831, Albert Gallatin, who'd served as Secretary of the Treasury under Thomas Jefferson and James Madison, announced his plans to establish NYU. His vision was to create a center of higher learning that would be available to all, regardless of nationality, religion, or social background. In 1832, NYU's first classes were held at Clinton Hill in Lower Manhattan.

HISTORY

New York University was founded by several prominent New Yorkers in 1831. The school held its first classes the following year in rented rooms on the corner of Beekman and Nassau streets, then moved to a building in Washington Square in 1835. It established its law school that year. NYU started its school of medicine in 1841, followed by the school of engineering and science (1854). Postgraduate studies in arts and science (its first coeducational program) began in 1886.

NYU's enrollment jumped from fewer than 2,000 in 1900 to 28,000 in 1930. After a lull during the Depression and WWII, the campus boomed again in the postwar years. During the 1950s the university began focusing on improving academics rather than on increasing enrollment. It created a school of the arts in 1965, and in the early 1970s it completed the Elmer Holmes Bobst Library. However, a cash crunch that decade almost forced the school into bankruptcy.

President Jay Oliva took the reins in 1981 and focused on transforming NYU from a largely commuter college into a global university. The school began a campaign to raise $1 billion in 1984, but earmarked the funds for campus improvements rather than swelling its endowment. During the late 1980s NYU opened several new dormitories and conference spaces. In 1994 British historian and collector Sir Harold Acton bequeathed to the school his Tuscany estate -- five art-filled villas overlooking Florence, Italy.

In 1996 NYU's Medical Center began talks with Mount Sinai Medical Center aimed at merging their hospitals and medical schools. The talks fell apart in early 1997, but the following year the two sides agreed to merge hospitals and keep their medical schools distinct. Also in 1998 NYU formed NYU On-Line, Inc., a for-profit subsidiary to develop and sell specialized Internet courses to other schools, training centers, and students; the venture was subsequently folded in late 2001. During 1999 contributions to the school approached $250 million. That year, however, two upper-level school officials were fired following allegations of improper use of university money.

Oliva retired as president in 2002 and was replaced by John Sexton, former School of Law dean. In 2004 Sexton announced that NYU would give $1 million to New York City towards renovation of Washington Square Park (the school annually gives some $200,000 for the park's ongoing maintenance).

EXECUTIVES

CIO, Kathleen E Jacobs
CIO, Len Peters
Auditors : PRICEWATERHOUSECOOPERS LLP NE

LOCATIONS

HQ: NEW YORK UNIVERSITY
  70 WASHINGTON SQ S, NEW YORK, NY 100121019
Phone: 212 998-1212
Web: WWW.NYU.EDU

PRODUCTS/OPERATIONS

2018 Sales

	$ mil.	% of total
Patient care	6,981.9	60
Tuition & fees	1,852.0	16
Grants & contracts	1,011.6	9
Auxiliary enterprises	505.3	4
Hospital affiliations	342.7	3
Endowment distribution	169.1	2
Contributions	168.2	2
Net assets from restrictions	121.5	1
Insurance premiums earned	115.6	1
Return on short-term investments	16.1	-
Programs & other	272.2	2
Total	11,556.2	100

2018 Sales

	$ mil.	% of total
NYU Langone Health	8,298.8	72
University	3,267.7	28
Adjustments	(10.3)	-
Total	11,556.2	100

Selected Schools and Colleges

College of Arts and Science (founded 1832)
College of Dentistry (1865)
Courant Institute of Mathematical Sciences (1934)
Gallatin School of Individualized Study (1972)
Graduate School of Arts and Science (1886)
Leonard N. Stern School of Business (1900)
Robert F. Wagner Graduate School of Public Service (1938)
School of Continuing and Professional Studies (1934)
School of Law (1835)
School of Medicine (1841)
School of Social Work (1960)
Steinhardt School of Culture, Education, and Human Development (1890)
Tisch School of the Arts (1965)

COMPETITORS

MARSHALL UNIVERSITY
NORTHWESTERN UNIVERSITY
PRESIDENT AND FELLOWS OF HARVARD COLLEGE
THE LELAND STANFORD JUNIOR UNIVERSITY
THE OHIO STATE UNIVERSITY
THE REGENTS OF THE UNIVERSITY OF CALIFORNIA
THE TRUSTEES OF THE UNIVERSITY OF PENNSYLVANIA
THE UNIVERSITY OF CHICAGO
TRUSTEES OF BOSTON COLLEGE
UNIVERSITY OF SOUTHERN CALIFORNIA

HISTORICAL FINANCIALS

Company Type: Private

Income Statement — FYE: August 31

	REVENUE ($mil)	NET INCOME ($mil)	NET PROFIT MARGIN	EMPLOYEES
08/16	8,500	177	2.1%	21,000
08/11	5,172	563	10.9%	—
08/06	2,148	195	9.1%	—
Annual Growth	14.7%	(1.0%)	—	—

2016 Year-End Financials

Return on assets: 1.1%   Cash ($ mil.): 1,033
Return on equity: 2.4%
Current Ratio: —

NEW YORK UNIVERSITY

Auditors : PRICEWATERHOUSECOOPERS LLP NE

LOCATIONS

HQ: NEW YORK UNIVERSITY
  433 1ST AVE RM 619, NEW YORK, NY 100104067
Phone: 212 998-5813
Web: WWW.HEARTBREAKDREAMS.COM

HISTORICAL FINANCIALS

Company Type: Private

Income Statement — FYE: August 31

	REVENUE ($mil)	NET INCOME ($mil)	NET PROFIT MARGIN	EMPLOYEES
08/12	4,016	53	1.3%	30
08/10	3,376	149	4.4%	—
08/09	2,970	(172)	—	—
Annual Growth	10.6%	—	—	—

2012 Year-End Financials

Return on assets: 0.7%   Cash ($ mil.): 982
Return on equity: 1.4%
Current Ratio: 0.70

NEWARK CORPORATION

Newark offers all sorts of electronic goods in one place, and in places all across the Americas. The company, doing business as Newark element14, distributes some 4.4 million electronic components and supplies, including semiconductors, passive devices, electrical equipment, connectors, wire and cable, optoelectronics, test and measurement instruments, and tools. It is also a source for companies needing parts compliant with the Restrictions of Hazardous Substances order in the European Union. Customers are electronics design engineers, maintenance technicians, and other electronics buyers. Newark element14 is a subsidiary of Premier Farnell, a top UK electronic and industrial parts supplier.

Operations

Newark element14 also offers such services as re-calibration, custom panel meters and cable assemblies, and re-reeling, as well as procurement and stockroom services.

The company stocks more than 500 brands from companies the likes of Analog Devices, AVX, Cypress Semiconductor, Freescale, Microchip, and Texas Instruments.

Geographic Reach

The company operates in North America.

Sales and Marketing

Like its parent, Newark element14 maximizes the Internet for selling and customer service purposes, with a growing emphasis on electronics design engineering (EDE). Newark element14's EDE customers can access a website that offers collaborative design tools; the company also maintains a dedicated website just for US federal government customers. In addition to its websites, Newark element14 operates a customer contact center, has a dedicated sales force, and offers a print catalog of its products.

Strategy

As part of its business, Newark element14 regularly rolls out new products through partnerships with other companies. In 2014, for instance, it launched the MagniV S12ZVML-MINIBRD variable-speed motor-control development kit alongside Freescale, as well as the Tektronix TBS1000B Series digital storage oscilloscopes. Newark element14 also introduced three new Fluke Thermal Image cameras to its test and measurement portfolio to help boost a technician's productivity while in the field.

Expanding its distribution agreements also keeps Newark element14 growing. In 2014 the company became an authorized distributor of Wurth Electronics items. Wurth specializes in components, circuit boards, and intelligent systems.

Company Background
Newark was originally established in 1934 as Newark Electric Company, a supplier of radio parts -- the name of the Chicago-based company's way of recognizing Newark, New Jersey, as the home of the the first radio station in the US. Newark Electric first published a catalog of parts in 1948. The company went public in 1960 on the American Stock Exchange (now NYSE MKT), changing its name to Newark Electronics Corporation. In 1968 the company was acquired by Premier Industrial Corporation, a Cleveland-based distributor. Premier Industrial merged in 1996 with Farnell Electronics plc to become Premier Farnell. Newark and element14 (another Premier Farnell company) combined in 2011 to create Newark element14.

LOCATIONS
HQ: NEWARK CORPORATION
300 S RIVERSIDE PLZ # 220, CHICAGO, IL 606066613
Phone: 773 784-5100
Web: WWW.NEWARK.COM

PRODUCTS/OPERATIONS
Selected Product Categories
Automation and process control
Batteries and chargers
Cable, wire, and assemblies
Chemicals and adhesives
Circuit protection
Connectors
Crystals and oscillators
Electrical
Enclosures, racks, and cabinets
Fans, heat sinks, and HVAC
Fasteners and mechanical
LED technologies
Office and computer
Optoelectronics and displays
Passive components
Power and line protection
Security and audio visual
Semiconductors
Sensors and transducers
Static control and site safety
Switches and relays
Test, measurement, and inspection
Tools and production supplies
Transformers

COMPETITORS
ALLIED ELECTRONICS, INC.
HIS COMPANY, INC.
N. F. SMITH & ASSOCIATES, L.P.
SAGER ELECTRICAL SUPPLY COMPANY INC.
TALLEY INC.

HISTORICAL FINANCIALS
Company Type: Private

Income Statement — FYE: February 1

	REVENUE ($mil)	NET INCOME ($mil)	NET PROFIT MARGIN	EMPLOYEES
02/15	543	24	4.5%	834
02/14	541	23	4.4%	—
02/13	580	20	3.5%	—
Annual Growth	(3.2%)	9.6%	—	—

2015 Year-End Financials
Return on assets: 10.5%   Cash ($ mil.): —
Return on equity: 15.2%
Current Ratio: 4.80

NEWMARK & COMPANY REAL ESTATE, INC.

Newmark & Company Real Estate, Inc. and certain of its affiliates, via the Newmark Knight Frank, NKF and NGKF brands, provides real estate brokerage, appraisal and valuation, portfolio and property management, mortgage brokerage, loan servicing, consultancy, advisory, and facilities and construction management services.

Geographic Reach
The company is based in New York.

Company Background

LOCATIONS
HQ: NEWMARK & COMPANY REAL ESTATE, INC.
125 PARK AVE, NEW YORK, NY 100175529
Phone: 212 372-2000
Web: WWW.NMRK.COM

Selected Locations
North America
  US
  Canada
  Mexico
Europe
Asia-Pacific
Africa
Middle East

PRODUCTS/OPERATIONS
Selected Services
Leasing Advisory
Global Corporate Services
Investment Sales and Capital Markets
Retail
Industrial
Consulting
Program and Project Management
Facilities Management
Property Management
Landauer Valuation & Advisory
Residential Construction Services
Specialty Practice Groups
    Data Center Consulting
    Global Gaming Group
    Global Healthcare
    Government
    Hotels

Law Firm Advisory
Loan Sale Advisory
Multi-Housing Group
Not-For-Profit Advisory
Retail Occupier Services
Self Storage Group

COMPETITORS
ALVAREZ & MARSAL HOLDINGS, LLC
ARONOV REALTY COMPANY, INC
CORNISH & CAREY COMMERCIAL
DRAPER AND KRAMER, INCORPORATED
MITSUBISHI ESTATE COMPANY, LIMITED
MURRAY HILL PROPERTIES LLC
NOVOGRADAC & COMPANY LLP
PM REALTY GROUP, L.P.
THE WOODMONT COMPANY
TRANSWESTERN COMMERCIAL SERVICES, L.L.C.

HISTORICAL FINANCIALS
Company Type: Private

Income Statement — FYE: December 31

	ASSETS ($mil)	NET INCOME ($mil)	INCOME AS % OF ASSETS	EMPLOYEES
12/16	860	53	6.3%	2,250
12/15	694	139	20.1%	—
12/14	234	0	0.0%	—
Annual Growth	91.7%	—	—	—

2016 Year-End Financials
Return on assets: 6.3%   Cash ($ mil.): 33
Return on equity: 10.2%
Current Ratio: —

NEWPORT CORPORATION

Newport delivers innovative products in the areas of lasers, photonics instrumentation, sub-micron positioning systems, vibration isolation, and optical components and subsystems to enhance the capabilities and productivity of its customers' manufacturing, engineering and research applications. In addition, Newport has built a strong history of partnering with OEM customers, delivering solutions from subassemblies to full solutions including design, testing and manufacturing. Established in 1969 as Newport Research Corporation, the company is a wholly owned subsidiary of MKS Instruments, Inc.

Operations
Newport offers products such as motion, opto-mechanics, optics, light, light analysis, tables and isolation, and vacuum instruments under leading brands such as ILX Lightwave, New Focus, Oriel Instruments, Ophir, Richardson Gratings, MKS Instruments, and Spectra-Physics.

Geographic Reach
Newport's corporate headquarters is located in Irvine, California, and has a significant worldwide presence, with about 15 manufacturing facilities located in the US, Austria, China, France, Germany, Israel, and Romania. It serve its customers through

direct sales offices located in the US, Austria, China, France, Germany, Japan, Israel, Singapore, South Korea, Taiwan, and the United Kingdom.

Sales and Marketing
Newport uses a direct sales force as well as an international network of independent distributors and sales representatives.

Auditors : DELOITTE & TOUCHE LLP COSTA M

LOCATIONS

HQ: NEWPORT CORPORATION
1791 DEERE AVE, IRVINE, CA 926064814
Phone: 949 863-3144
Web: WWW.NEWPORT.COM

2016 Sales

	$ mil.	% of total
US	231.5	38
Asia	170.1	28
Europe	157.1	26
Other regions	44	8
Total	602.7	100

PRODUCTS/OPERATIONS

2016 Sales

	$ mil.	% of total
Photonics & precision technologies	249.2	41
Lasers	192.8	32
Optics	160.6	27
Total	602.7	100

COMPETITORS

ARTHUR H. THOMAS COMPANY
BECKMAN COULTER, INC.
COHERENT, INC.
EPPENDORF, INC.
Fabrinet
HARVARD BIOSCIENCE, INC.
KEWAUNEE SCIENTIFIC CORPORATION
OCLARO, INC.
SCIENTIFIC INDUSTRIES, INC.
WRIGHT LINE LLC

HISTORICAL FINANCIALS
Company Type: Private

Income Statement   FYE: January 3

	REVENUE ($mil)	NET INCOME ($mil)	NET PROFIT MARGIN	EMPLOYEES
01/15*	605	35	5.8%	2,480
12/13	560	15	2.8%	—
12/12	595	(89)	—	—
Annual Growth	0.8%	—	—	—

*Fiscal year change

2015 Year-End Financials
Return on assets: 6.1%   Cash ($ mil.): 46
Return on equity: 9.9%
Current Ratio: 2.90

NEWYORK-PRESBYTERIAN/ BROOKLYN METHODIST

New York Methodist Hospital is a not-for-profit, acute-care teaching hospital serving Brooklyn residents. Established in 1881 as the Methodist Episcopal Hospital, the facility has more than 650 licensed beds. It offers a full range of medical services, including primary and emergency care, as well as specialty services such as women's health, cancer, cardiovascular, pediatric, geriatric, and behavioral health. The hospital also operates satellite clinics in surrounding areas. A member of New York-Presbyterian Healthcare System, New York Methodist is a teaching hospital affiliated with Cornell University's Weill Medical College.

Operations
New York Methodist Hospital handles about 40,000 inpatient admissions and 100,000 emergency department visits each year, as well as 24,000 surgeries and 5,000 births. It also processes about 200,000 laboratory sample processes annually.

New York Methodist Hospital includes specialty institutes in about 10 fields including pulmonary medicine, cancer care, and vascular health. In addition to providing inpatient care, the organization operates some 10 primary and specialty outpatient centers. It also runs a number of graduate medical programs, including programs affiliated with professional training schools in the areas of radiography, medical technology, radiation therapy, and paramedics.

Geographic Reach
New York Methodist Hospital's main campus is in the Park Slope neighborhood of Brooklyn. It has several outpatient centers in other parts of Brooklyn as well.

Strategy
To expand care for area residents, New York Methodist is adding new specialist programs and equipment. For instance in 2012 the hospital added a robotic-assisted surgery program for bariatric procedures. It also opened a new wound care and hyperbaric oxygen therapy center for hard-to-heal wounds. In addition, in 2013 the hospital moved its sleep disorder center into a new facility.

Auditors : ERNST & YOUNG LLP NEW YORK N

LOCATIONS

HQ: NEWYORK-PRESBYTERIAN/BROOKLYN METHODIST
506 6TH ST, BROOKLYN, NY 112153609
Phone: 718 780-3000
Web: WWW.NYP.ORG

COMPETITORS

ASCENSION SOUTHEAST MICHIGAN
FROEDTERT MEMORIAL LUTHERAN HOSPITAL, INC.
NEWTON MEMORIAL HOSPITAL (INC)
NYU WINTHROP HOSPITAL
THE JAMAICA HOSPITAL

HISTORICAL FINANCIALS
Company Type: Private

Income Statement   FYE: December 31

	REVENUE ($mil)	NET INCOME ($mil)	NET PROFIT MARGIN	EMPLOYEES
12/19	962	123	12.8%	4,929
12/16	788	145	18.5%	—
12/15	732	88	12.1%	—
Annual Growth	7.1%	8.6%	—	—

2019 Year-End Financials
Return on assets: 6.3%   Cash ($ mil.): 74
Return on equity: 11.6%
Current Ratio: 1.20

NEWYORK-PRESBYTERIAN/ QUEENS

The New York Hospital Medical Center of Queens aims to provide care that's fit for royalty. Better known as the New York Hospital Queens, the acute care hospital has about 520 beds and provides both primary and tertiary care. Specialist services include cancer, cardiovascular, pediatric, obstetric, surgical, and dental care. The medical center also operates about a dozen outpatient clinics and care centers that offer such services as family health, kidney dialysis, rehabilitation, and dental care, as well as home health care services. New York Hospital Queens is part of the NewYork-Presbyterian Healthcare System.

Auditors : ERNST & YOUNG LLP NEW YORK N

LOCATIONS

HQ: NEWYORK-PRESBYTERIAN/QUEENS
5645 MAIN ST, FLUSHING, NY 113555045
Phone: 718 670-2000
Web: WWW.NYP.ORG

PRODUCTS/OPERATIONS

Selected Services and Centers
Ambulatory Patient Care Facilities
Anesthesiology
Cancer Center
Cardiothoracic Surgery
Center for Dental and Oral Medicine
Children's Health (Pediatrics)
Emergency Medicine
Heart and Vascular Center
Neuroscience Institute
Obstetrics and Gynecology
Orthopaedics and Rehabilitation

Pathology and Laboratories
Primary Care and Specialties
Radiation Oncology
Radiology
Surgery
Women's Health

COMPETITORS

CHRISTUS SAINT CATHERINE HOSPITAL
JEFFERSON HOSPITAL ASSOCIATION, INC.
NEWTON MEMORIAL HOSPITAL (INC)
PARKWEST MEDICAL CENTER
PORTER FOUNDATION, INC.

HISTORICAL FINANCIALS
Company Type: Private

Income Statement — FYE: December 31

	REVENUE ($mil)	NET INCOME ($mil)	NET PROFIT MARGIN	EMPLOYEES
12/19	841	(2)	—	2,380
12/17	846	5	0.6%	—
12/14	669	14	2.1%	—
12/05	457	10	2.3%	—
Annual Growth	4.4%	—	—	—

2019 Year-End Financials
Return on assets: (-0.3%)   Cash ($ mil.): 13
Return on equity: (-3.1%)
Current Ratio: 1.10

NFP CORP.

Through a network of subsidiaries and affiliates, NFP provides commercial and personal insurance, corporate benefits products, and wealth management services to businesses and individuals in the US, Puerto Rico, Canada, and the Europe. NFP enables client success through the expertise of over 6,600 global employees, investments in innovative technologies, and enduring relationships with highly rated insurers, vendors, and financial institutions. NFP is the 5th largest benefits broker by global revenue.

Operations
NFP is organized along three business segments. Its Individual Solutions provides life insurance, wealth management and personal risk. Corporate Benefits offers employee, executive, and retirement benefits products and HR consulting services to commercial clients. Property and Casualty provides claims management, reinsurance, occupational health and safety, professional liability, and workers' compensations.

Geographic Reach
New York-headquartered NFP has offices throughout the US and Puerto Rico, Canada, and Europe.

Sales and Marketing
NFP serves a wide range of industries, including aviation, communication, media and technology, healthcare and life sciences, municipalities and public entities, education, financial institutions, real estate, nonprofit organizations, power and utility companies, and transportation, logistics and distribution.

Mergers and Acquisitions
In late 2021, NFP acquired Improved Funding Techniques Inc. (IFTI), a third-party administrator (TPA), with an internal RIA, offering a consolidated solution for designing, implementing and administering retirement plans for privately owned business. The acquisition adds scale to its retirement business and expands its footprint in the New York metro area and around the country. The acquisition also advances NFP's existing internal TPA expertise, while adding complementary defined benefit plan capabilities that can be leveraged across the entire organization.

In 2021, NFP acquired Foster Park Brokers Inc. (Foster Park). With the addition of Foster Park, one of Western Canada's largest independent insurance brokerages, NFP is adhering to its strategic plan of building a unified national platform that provides superior expertise and advice to clients and reinforcing our people first culture for all employees.

Also in late 2021, NFP acquired Connecticut-based Insurance Provider Group, LLC (IPG), a P&C insurance broker that provides commercial brokerage services primarily to small to medium sized businesses. In acquiring IPG, NFP adds scale as it expands its P&C presence in its Northeast region, particularly in Connecticut. IPG will complement NFP's existing expertise and capabilities in commercial risk management, personal lines P&C and employee benefits.

Company Background
In 2013 Chicago-based private equity investment firm Madison Dearborn Partners took NFP private in a $1.4 billion deal.

EXECUTIVES

Head OF INSURANCE BROKERAGE*, Ed Omalley
Associate General Counsel*, Suzanne Spradley

LOCATIONS

HQ: NFP CORP.
  340 MADISON AVE FL 21, NEW YORK, NY 101730401
Phone: 212 301-4000
Web: WWW.NFP.COM

COMPETITORS

BANKERS FINANCIAL CORPORATION
BENEFICIAL LIFE INSURANCE COMPANY
BOLTON & COMPANY
FORTEGRA FINANCIAL CORPORATION
HUB INTERNATIONAL LIMITED
KEENAN & ASSOCIATES
NATIONWIDE LIFE INSURANCE COMPANY
STANCORP FINANCIAL GROUP, INC.
THE NEW ENGLAND LIFE INSURANCE COMPANY
VOYA SERVICES COMPANY

HISTORICAL FINANCIALS
Company Type: Private

Income Statement — FYE: December 31

	ASSETS ($mil)	NET INCOME ($mil)	INCOME AS % OF ASSETS	EMPLOYEES
12/11	894	36	4.1%	5,124
12/10	893	42	4.8%	—
12/09	970	(493)	—	—
12/08	1,543	14	1.0%	—
Annual Growth	(16.6%)	35.5%	—	—

2011 Year-End Financials
Return on assets: 4.1%   Cash ($ mil.): 210
Return on equity: 9.1%
Current Ratio: 1.60

NHK INTERNATIONAL CORPORATION

Auditors: ERNST & YOUNG LLP LOUISVILLE

LOCATIONS

HQ: NHK INTERNATIONAL CORPORATION
  46855 MAGELLAN DR, NOVI, MI 483772451
Phone: 248 926-0111
Web: WWW.NHKINTERNATIONAL.COM

HISTORICAL FINANCIALS
Company Type: Private

Income Statement — FYE: March 31

	REVENUE ($mil)	NET INCOME ($mil)	NET PROFIT MARGIN	EMPLOYEES
03/16	894	12	1.4%	200
03/15	842	(13)	—	—
03/14	739	17	2.4%	—
03/13	688	14	2.1%	—
Annual Growth	9.1%	(4.4%)	—	—

2016 Year-End Financials
Return on assets: 2.8%   Cash ($ mil.): 3
Return on equity: 6.1%
Current Ratio: 1.00

NICHOLAS PROPERTIES & DEVELOPMENTS, INC.

Auditors: HW & COMPANY LPA

LOCATIONS

HQ: NICHOLAS PROPERTIES & DEVELOPMENTS, INC.
  160 E WASHINGTON ST # 194, CHAGRIN FALLS, OH 440223060
Phone: 216 296-9469

HISTORICAL FINANCIALS
Company Type: Private

Income Statement — FYE: December 31

	ASSETS ($mil)	NET INCOME ($mil)	INCOME AS % OF ASSETS	EMPLOYEES
12/20*	656	494	75.4%	10
11/18	77	32	41.8%	—
12/16	118	23	19.8%	—
12/14	19	0	1.3%	—
Annual Growth	79.4%	250.9%	—	—

*Fiscal year change

2020 Year-End Financials
Return on assets: 75.4% Cash ($ mil.): 470
Return on equity: 134.8%
Current Ratio: 2.30

NIELSEN HOLDINGS PLC

LOCATIONS
HQ: NIELSEN HOLDINGS PLC
85 BROAD ST, NEW YORK, NY 100042434
Phone: 646 654-5000

HISTORICAL FINANCIALS
Company Type: Private

Income Statement — FYE: December 31

	REVENUE ($mil)	NET INCOME ($mil)	NET PROFIT MARGIN	EMPLOYEES
12/15	6,172	575	9.3%	43,061
12/14	6,288	381	6.1%	—
12/13	5,703	736	12.9%	—
12/12	5,612	273	4.9%	—
Annual Growth	3.2%	28.2%	—	—

2015 Year-End Financials
Return on assets: 16.4% Cash ($ mil.): 357
Return on equity: 9.3%
Current Ratio: 0.90

NOBLE HOLDING (U.S.) CORPORATION

Auditors: PRICEWATERHOUSECOOPERS LLP H

LOCATIONS
HQ: NOBLE HOLDING (U.S.) CORPORATION
3135 S DAIRY ASHFORD, SUGAR LAND, TX 77478
Phone: 281 276-6100
Web: WWW.NOBLECORP.COM

HISTORICAL FINANCIALS
Company Type: Private

Income Statement — FYE: December 31

	REVENUE ($mil)	NET INCOME ($mil)	NET PROFIT MARGIN	EMPLOYEES
12/15	3,352	607	18.1%	3,744
12/14	3,232	83	2.6%	—
12/13	4,234	935	22.1%	—
Annual Growth	(11.0%)	(19.4%)	—	—

2015 Year-End Financials
Return on assets: 4.7% Cash ($ mil.): 511
Return on equity: 8.2%
Current Ratio: 1.40

NORTH ADVOCATE SIDE HEALTH NETWORK

EXECUTIVES
Chief Executive, Kenneth J Rojek

LOCATIONS
HQ: NORTH ADVOCATE SIDE HEALTH NETWORK
836 W WELLINGTON AVE, CHICAGO, IL 606575147
Phone: 773 296-5699
Web: WWW.ADVOCATEHEALTH.COM

HISTORICAL FINANCIALS
Company Type: Private

Income Statement — FYE: December 31

	REVENUE ($mil)	NET INCOME ($mil)	NET PROFIT MARGIN	EMPLOYEES
12/19	776	116	15.0%	1,600
12/15	487	97	19.9%	—
12/08	317	29	9.3%	—
Annual Growth	8.5%	13.3%	—	—

2019 Year-End Financials
Return on assets: 12.9% Cash ($ mil.): 15
Return on equity: 14.7%
Current Ratio: —

NORTH AMERICAN LIGHTING, INC.

North American Lighting offers travelers a beacon of safety through the fog. The company is an independent manufacturer of vehicle lighting products in North America. Operating through four assembly plants and one technology center, the company produces a line-up of headlamps, signal lamps, and fog lamps. Its forward-lighting products include mercury-free, high intensity discharge (HID) headlamps and the Adaptive Front Lighting System (AFS). Among its signal lamps are rear-combo and license plate lamps. Its products are tailored to the designs of large auto makers and local Japanese automakers. Founded in 1983, North American Lighting is a subsidiary of Japan-based KOITO MANUFACTURING.

Geographic Reach
North American Lighting is stationed in Paris, Illinois, and has four manufacturing plants in Illinois and one in Alabama. Its technology research center resides in Michigan, while a tool plan is located in Indiana.

Sales and Marketing
North American Lighting sells its products primarily to vehicle manufacturers in North America. It provides headlights and taillights to Toyota, Nissan, General Motors, and Honda.

Financial Performance
The company generated 16% of its parent's revenue total in 2014. Revenues for the North American segment also skyrocketed by almost 20% in 2014 due to higher demand in the auto sector which resulted in increased automobile production.

Strategy
Like most players in the manufacturing sector, North American Lighting's strategy for growth involves the expansion of its manufacturing capacity. It also attracts additional clients through new product launches. In 2013 the company invested $50 million to expand its plant in Edgar County, Illinois, by building a 200,000 sq. ft. addition and purchasing new equipment for added production lines.

In 2014 the company also began production at its North American Lighting Mexico, S.A. de C.V. (Mexican manufacturing plant), which was established in 2012 to expand automobile production throughout Mexico.

LOCATIONS
HQ: NORTH AMERICAN LIGHTING, INC.
2275 S MAIN ST, PARIS, IL 619442963
Phone: 217 465-6600
Web: WWW.NAL.COM

COMPETITORS
FEDERAL SIGNAL CORPORATION
G N U INC
ICHIKOH INDUSTRIES,LTD.
KOITO MANUFACTURING CO., LTD.
LUMINESCENT SYSTEMS, INC.
MAGNA MIRRORS OF AMERICA, INC.
MARELLI EUROPE SPA
PETERSON MANUFACTURING COMPANY
STREET GLOW INC
THE GENLYTE GROUP INCORPORATED

HISTORICAL FINANCIALS
Company Type: Private

Income Statement — FYE: December 31

	REVENUE ($mil)	NET INCOME ($mil)	NET PROFIT MARGIN	EMPLOYEES
12/17	1,466	111	7.6%	2,200
12/11	297	13	4.4%	—
12/10	297	13	4.4%	—
Annual Growth	25.6%	35.6%	—	—

2017 Year-End Financials
Return on assets: 16.2%   Cash ($ mil.): 77
Return on equity: 22.9%
Current Ratio: 2.10

NORTH BROWARD HOSPITAL DISTRICT

North Broward Hospital District, which operates as Broward Health, takes care of shark bites and more. The taxpayer-supported, not-for-profit health system serves the coastal city of Fort Lauderdale and the northern two-thirds of Broward County, Florida, with four acute care hospitals and a host of community-based centers. Flagship hospital Broward General Medical Center has more than 700 beds and features the Chris Evert Children's Hospital; all of the hospitals together have more than 1,500 beds. Broward Health boasts about 30 additional facilities, including family health and surgery centers and home health and hospice programs.

Operations
The Broward Health system also includes teaching hospital Broward Health Medical Center, facilities such as Broward Health North and Broward Health Imperial Point, Broward Health Community Services, and Broward Health Physician Group. The company also operates urgent care clinics.

With more than 1,200 physicians, Broward Health typically sees some 62,500 admissions, 283,000 emergency department visits, 267,000 outpatient visits, and 17,000 outpatient clinic visits each year. It also delivers some 6,000 babies annually.

Broward Health is controlled by a seven-member board of commissioners appointed by Florida's governor. As a safety-net health provider in its service territory, the system's hospitals receive property tax-based funding for the charity care they provide. The rest of Broward County is served by a second public hospital system, South Broward Hospital District. (The county's dual structure goes back to the 1950s.)

Geographic Reach
The company has more than 50 locations across Broward County.

Sales and Marketing
Managed care accounts for more than half of Broward Health's net patient revenues; Medicare and Medicaid combined make up more than 20%.

Financial Performance
In fiscal 2014, revenue grew 2% to $971 million due to growth in net patient service revenues. Net income rose 20% that year on higher investment gains and a decline in interest expenses. The system reported an operating cash outflow to $80 million (versus $27 million in 2013) as less cash was generated from third-party payers and patients.

Strategy
Broward Health looks to improve services by adding new or renovating existing facilities in its system. For example, in 2014 it opened a new Adult Cancer Infusion Center at Broward Health Medical Center (featuring an outdoor healing garden); it also opened AJ Acker Virtual Hospital with interactive patient simulators at Broward Health North for training purposes. It broke ground on a $70 million renovation of Broward Health North that will add more operating rooms and expand the emergency department. In 2015, it was given approval to expand Broward Health Coral Springs.

EXECUTIVES

Human Resources Officer, Kiera Page Corporate
Compliance*, Nicholas Hartfield
Chief Human Resources Officer*, Deven Silverman
Auditors : WARREN AVERETT LLC BIRMINGHA

LOCATIONS

HQ: NORTH BROWARD HOSPITAL DISTRICT
1800 NW 49TH ST, FORT LAUDERDALE, FL 333093092
Phone: 954 473-7010
Web: WWW.BROWARDHEALTH.ORG

PRODUCTS/OPERATIONS

2014 Sales

	$ mil.	% of total
Patient care		
Broward Health Medical Center	432.8	44
Broward Health North	207.2	21
Broward Health Imperial Point	100.4	10
Broward Health Coral Springs	140.0	15
Other	96.7	10
Eliminations	(5.9)	7
Total	971.2	100

Selected Services
Bariatric Surgery
Barrett's Esophagus
Behavioral Health
Broward Health Complete
Cancer Services
Cardiac Services
Children's Diagnostic & Treatment Center
Clinical Trials
Colorectal Services
Concussion Care
Diabetes
Digestive Health
Dysphagia
Emergency Services
Endoscopic Sinus Surgery
Home Health & Hospice Services
International Services
Liver Transplant
Maternity Place
Men's Health
Neurology
Orthopedic Services
Ostomy
Outpatient Services
Pediatric Services
Pharmacy
Primary Care
Senior Services
Sickle Cell Day Unit
Single Incision Laparoscopic Surgery (SILS)

Selected Facilities
Hospitals
　Broward General Medical Center (Fort Lauderdale)
　Coral Springs Medical Center (Coral Springs)
　Imperial Point Medical Center (Fort Lauderdale)
　North Broward Medical Center (Deerfield Beach)
Other Facilities
　Chris Evert Children's Hospital (Fort Lauderdale)
　Broward Health Physician Group (Fort Lauderdale)
　Broward Health Weston (Weston)
　Gold Coast Home Health & Hospice Services (Fort Lauderdale)
　Seventh Avenue Family Health Center (Fort Lauderdale)

COMPETITORS

ALLINA HEALTH SYSTEM
LEE MEMORIAL HEALTH SYSTEM
NOVANT HEALTH, INC.
SARASOTA COUNTY PUBLIC HOSPITAL DISTRICT
SHANDS TEACHING HOSPITAL AND CLINICS, INC.
SPECTRUM HEALTH SYSTEM
THE LANCASTER GENERAL HOSPITAL
WELLMONT HEALTH SYSTEM
WELLSPAN HEALTH
WELLSTAR HEALTH SYSTEM, INC.

HISTORICAL FINANCIALS
Company Type: Private

Income Statement — FYE: June 30

	REVENUE ($mil)	NET INCOME ($mil)	NET PROFIT MARGIN	EMPLOYEES
06/18	1,035	120	11.6%	7,000
06/17	1,025	33	3.3%	—
06/16	1,014	(12)	—	—
06/08	1,335	67	5.0%	—
Annual Growth	(2.5%)	6.0%	—	—

2018 Year-End Financials
Return on assets: 7.1%   Cash ($ mil.): 121
Return on equity: 13.3%
Current Ratio: 3.60

NORTH CAROLINA BAPTIST HOSPITAL

Auditors : KPMG LLP GREENSBORO NORTH CA

LOCATIONS

HQ: NORTH CAROLINA BAPTIST HOSPITAL
MEDICAL CENTER BLVD, WINSTON SALEM, NC 271570001
Phone: 336 716-2011
Web: WWW.WAKEHEALTH.EDU

HISTORICAL FINANCIALS
Company Type: Private

Income Statement   FYE: June 30

	REVENUE ($mil)	NET INCOME ($mil)	NET PROFIT MARGIN	EMPLOYEES
06/21	2,062	319	15.5%	12,563
06/20	1,887	8	0.5%	—
06/19	1,762	8	0.5%	—
06/18	1,633	60	3.7%	—
Annual Growth	8.1%	73.7%	—	—

2021 Year-End Financials
Return on assets: 12.4%   Cash ($ mil.): 73
Return on equity: 20.7%
Current Ratio: 1.60

NORTH CAROLINA BAPTIST HOSPITAL FDN

Auditors : DIXON HUGHES GOODMAN LLP ASHE

LOCATIONS

HQ: NORTH CAROLINA BAPTIST HOSPITAL FDN
MEDICAL CTR BLVD, WINSTON SALEM, NC 271570001
Phone: 336 716-4445

HISTORICAL FINANCIALS
Company Type: Private

Income Statement   FYE: June 30

	REVENUE ($mil)	NET INCOME ($mil)	NET PROFIT MARGIN	EMPLOYEES
06/18	1,795	(6)	—	13
06/17	0	(0)	—	—
06/15	1	0	33.5%	—
06/11	1	0	32.2%	—
Annual Growth	170.8%	—	—	—

2018 Year-End Financials
Return on assets: (-0.4%)   Cash ($ mil.): 35
Return on equity: (-0.6%)
Current Ratio: —

NORTH CAROLINA ELECTRIC MEMBERSHIP CORPORATION

It's a cooperative effort: North Carolina Electric Membership Corporation (NCEMC) generates and transmits electricity to the state's 26 electric cooperatives (more than 2.5 million people) in 93 of 100 North Carolina counties. The co-op owns more than 600 MW of generating capacity through four primarily natural gas peak load generators, plus a 61.5% stake in Catawba Nuclear Station Unit 1, and a 31% stake in the Catawba Nuclear Station in South Carolina. It also buys power from Progress Energy, American Electric Power, and other for-profit utilities. NCEMC's member cooperatives serve more than 950,000 metered businesses and homes in North Carolina. The wholesale co-op also operates an energy operations center.

Auditors : ERNST & YOUNG LLP RALEIGH NC

LOCATIONS

HQ: NORTH CAROLINA ELECTRIC MEMBERSHIP CORPORATION
3400 SUMNER BLVD, RALEIGH, NC 276162950
Phone: 919 872-0800
Web: WWW.NCELECTRICCOOPERATIVES.COM

PRODUCTS/OPERATIONS
Subsidiaries
North Carolina Association of Electric Cooperatives (NCAEC, training programs)
The Tarheel Electric Membership Association, Inc. (TEMA, purchasing and materials supply)
North Carolina Cooperatives
Albemarle Electric Membership Corporation
Blue Ridge Electric Membership Corporation
Brunswick Electric Membership Corporation
Cape Hatteras Electric Cooperative
Carteret-Craven Electric Cooperative
Central Electric Membership Corporation
Edgecombe-Martin County Electric Membership Corporation
EnergyUnited
Four County Electric Membership Corporation
French Broad Electric Membership Corporation
Halifax Electric Membership Corporation
Haywood Electric Membership Corporation
Jones-Onslow Electric Membership Corporation
Lumbee River Electric Membership Corporation
Pee Dee Electric Membership Corporation
Piedmont Electric Membership Corporation
Pitt & Greene Electric Membership Corporation
Randolph Electric Membership Corporation
Roanoke Electric Cooperative
Rutherford Electric Membership Corporation
South River Electric Membership Corporation
Surry-Yadkin Electric Membership Corporation
Tideland Electric Membership Corporation
Tri-County Electric Membership Corporation
Union Power Cooperative
Wake Electric Membership Corporation

COMPETITORS
ARKANSAS ELECTRIC COOPERATIVE CORPORATION
EAST KENTUCKY POWER COOPERATIVE, INC.
SEMINOLE ELECTRIC COOPERATIVE, INC.
SOUTH CAROLINA PUBLIC SERVICE AUTHORITY (INC)
THE SOUTHERN COMPANY

HISTORICAL FINANCIALS
Company Type: Private

Income Statement   FYE: December 31

	REVENUE ($mil)	NET INCOME ($mil)	NET PROFIT MARGIN	EMPLOYEES
12/21	1,128	32	2.9%	188
12/20	1,092	29	2.7%	—
12/19	1,219	30	2.5%	—
12/18	1,188	30	2.5%	—
Annual Growth	(1.7%)	3.1%	—	—

2021 Year-End Financials
Return on assets: 1.4%   Cash ($ mil.): 283
Return on equity: 10.3%
Current Ratio: 1.70

NORTH DAKOTA UNIVERSITY SYSTEM

Auditors : ROBERT R PETERSON STATE AUDI

LOCATIONS

HQ: NORTH DAKOTA UNIVERSITY SYSTEM
2000 44TH ST S STE 301, FARGO, ND 581037197
Phone: 701 231-6326
Web: WWW.NDUS.EDU

HISTORICAL FINANCIALS
Company Type: Private

Income Statement   FYE: June 30

	REVENUE ($mil)	NET INCOME ($mil)	NET PROFIT MARGIN	EMPLOYEES
06/21	758	90	11.9%	19
06/20	690	(11)	—	—
06/19	709	8	1.2%	—
06/18	713	19	2.8%	—
Annual Growth	2.0%	65.8%	—	—

2021 Year-End Financials
Return on assets: 3.5%   Cash ($ mil.): 274
Return on equity: 5.9%
Current Ratio: 3.40

NORTH EAST INDEPENDENT SCHOOL DISTRICT

EXECUTIVES

Board Vice President, Susan Galindo
Auditors : ABIP SAN ANTONIO TEXAS

LOCATIONS

HQ: NORTH EAST INDEPENDENT SCHOOL DISTRICT
8961 TESORO DR, SAN ANTONIO, TX 782176209
Phone: 210 407-0359
Web: WWW.NEISD.NET

HISTORICAL FINANCIALS
Company Type: Private

Income Statement   FYE: June 30

	REVENUE ($mil)	NET INCOME ($mil)	NET PROFIT MARGIN	EMPLOYEES
06/21	780	27	3.5%	10,000
06/20	768	38	5.0%	—
06/19	744	(41)	—	—
06/18	759	23	3.0%	—
Annual Growth	0.9%	5.8%	—	—

2021 Year-End Financials
Return on assets: 1.3%   Cash ($ mil.): 315
Return on equity: —
Current Ratio: —

NORTH MISSISSIPPI HEALTH SERVICES, INC.

North Mississippi Health Services (NMHS) isn't contained by its name: The health system also provides health care to residents of northwestern Alabama. NMHS includes half a dozen community hospitals, including its flagship North Mississippi Medical Center in Tupelo. North Mississippi Medical Clinics, a regional network of more than 30 primary and specialty clinics; and nursing homes. Combined, the facilities have nearly 1,000 beds, designated for acute, long term, and nursing care. Specialty services include home health and long-term care, inpatient and outpatient behavioral health, and treatment centers for cancer and digestive disorders. NMHS also operates outpatient care and wellness clinics in the region.

Operations
During 2014 NMHS handled about 30,000 inpatient visits, as well as more than 128,000 emergency room visits and some 345,000 outpatient care visits. It also conducted about 24,000 surgeries at its various facilities. Its outpatient centers include more than 30 primary and specialty care clinics in Mississippi and Alabama operated through the North Mississippi Medical Clinics division, as well as more than half a dozen wellness centers.

Geographic Reach
In all, NMHS serves two dozen counties across the two states. In addition to its main hospital in Tupelo, NMHS operates health centers in communities including Eupora, Iuka, Pontotoc, and West Point, Mississippi, and in Hamilton, Alabama. It also manages a center in Calhoun City, Mississippi. Its Baldwyn Nursing Facility is located in Baldwyn, Mississippi.

Financial Performance
Flagship North Mississippi Medical Center (NNMC)'s revenues increased by 6% due to a growth in net patient revenues. Medicare and Medicaid together accounted for about 50% of net patient revenues; managed care and commercial, 25%; Blue Cross, 14%; self-pay, 10%; and Health Link 1%.

NNMC reported net loss of $14 million in 2014 over net income in 2013 due to pension-related changes.

NNMC's operating cash flow increased by 256% that year.

Mergers and Acquisitions
In 2018, North Mississippi Health Services agreed to buy Gilmore Memorial Hospital out of bankruptcy. It will pay $10.5 million for the Armory, Mississippi, hospital, including the assumption of liabilities and financial commitments.

LOCATIONS

HQ: NORTH MISSISSIPPI HEALTH SERVICES, INC.
830 S GLOSTER ST, TUPELO, MS 388014934
Phone: 662 377-3000
Web: WWW.NMHS.NET

Selected Locations
Baldwyn Nursing Facility (Baldwyn, Mississippi)
Calhoun County Medical Clinic (managed facility; Calhoun, Mississippi)
NMMC-Eupora (Eupora, Mississippi)
NMMC-Hamilton (Hamilton, Alabama)
NMMC-Iuka (Iuka, Mississippi)
NMMC-Pontotoc (Pontotoc, Mississippi)
NMMC-Tupelo (Tupelo, Mississippi)
NMMC-West Point (West Point, Mississippi)
North Mississippi Medical Clinics (NMMCI, regional)

PRODUCTS/OPERATIONS

Selected Facilities and Services
Acute Stroke Unit
Advanced Wound Center and Hyperbarics
Bariatric Center
Behavioral Health Center
Breast Care Center
Cancer Center
Center for Digestive Health
Community Health
Critical Care Unit
CRNA Program
Diabetes Treatment Center
Emergency Services
Family Medicine Residency Center
Heart Institute
Home Health and Hospice
Hospitalists
Joint Replacement Center
Le Bonheur Specialty Clinics
Medical Imaging
North Mississippi Surgery Center
Outpatient Infusion
Pain Management Center
Pastoral Care
Physician Specialties
Radiology
Rehabilitation Services
Respiratory Therapy
Skilled Nursing Facility
Sleep Disorders Center
Surgical Services
Tupelo Wellness Center
Vein Center
Volunteer Services
Women's Hospital
Women's and Children Services

COMPETITORS

HERITAGE VALLEY HEALTH SYSTEM, INC.
INSPIRA HEALTH NETWORK, INC.
LEE MEMORIAL HEALTH SYSTEM
NORTON HEALTHCARE, INC.
SOUTHCOAST HEALTH SYSTEM, INC.

HISTORICAL FINANCIALS
Company Type: Private

Income Statement FYE: September 30

	REVENUE ($mil)	NET INCOME ($mil)	NET PROFIT MARGIN	EMPLOYEES
09/17	898	26	3.0%	6,000
09/16	893	30	3.4%	—
09/15	860	19	2.2%	—
09/14	779	(14)	—	—
Annual Growth	4.9%	—	—	—

2017 Year-End Financials
Return on assets: 2.2%   Cash ($ mil.): 36
Return on equity: 3.4%
Current Ratio: 4.00

NORTH MISSISSIPPI MEDICAL CENTER, INC.

At North Mississippi Medical Center you might get some Mississippi Mud ice cream after your tonsils are removed. The full-service, 650-bed regional referral hospital in Tupelo, Mississippi, is part of the North Mississippi Health Services system, an affiliation of hospitals and clinics serving northern Mississippi, northwestern Alabama, and parts of Tennessee. It's the largest, private, not-for-profit hospital in Mississippi and the largest non-metropolitan hospital in America. Specialty services at the medical center include cancer treatment, women's health care, cardiology, and behavioral health care. The hospital also operates a skilled-nursing facility and home health and hospice organizations.

Operations
Besides being a Mississippi State Department of Health-designated Level II trauma center, North Mississippi Medical Center offers more than 40 specialties, as well as centers for excellence in cardiac surgery, cardiology, research, neurology, neurosurgery, pulmonology, rehabilitation, cancer treatment, chemical dependency, and neonatal programs.

The medical center's Home Health Agency canvases 17 counties in north Mississippi and provides complex and extremely high-tech procedures that can be performed in the home setting. It also operates Baldwyn Nursing Facility.

Geographic Reach
North Mississippi Medical Center serves more than 700,000 people across 24 counties in north Mississippi, northwestern Alabama, and portions of Tennessee.

Strategy
In 2012 North Mississippi Medical Center - Hamilton opened a new pulmonary

rehabilitation unit. Also, the medical center's Outpatient Rehabilitation Center in 2012 became the first outpatient rehabilitation center in Mississippi to offer Fiberoptic Endoscopic Evaluation of Swallowing (FEES) to assess swallowing function. Awards and Recognition

North Mississippi Medical Center's hospitalist program has been recognized by The American Journal of Medicine for providing cost-effective care to patients in the hospital. The program, begun in 1997, serves hospitalized patients who do not have a primary care physician or whose primary care physicians do not have hospital practices.

Auditors : MMWINKLER & ASSOCIATES CPAS T

LOCATIONS

HQ: NORTH MISSISSIPPI MEDICAL CENTER, INC.
830 S GLOSTER ST, TUPELO, MS 388014934
Phone: 662 377-3000
Web: WWW.NMHS.NET

Selected Locations
Baldwyn Nursing Facility - Baldwyn, Mississippi
NMMC - Eupora - Mississippi
NMMC - Hamilton - Alabama
NMMC - Iuka - Mississippi
NMMC - Pontotoc - Pontotoc, Mississippi
NMMC - Tupelo - Tupelo, Mississippi
NMMC - West Point - West Point, Mississippi

PRODUCTS/OPERATIONS

Selected Programs & Services
Acute Stroke Unit
Advanced Wound Center and Hyperbarics
Bariatric Center
Behavioral Health Center
Breast Care Center
Cancer Center
Center for Digestive Health
Community Health
Critical Care Unit
CRNA Program
Diabetes Treatment Center
Emergency Services
Family Medicine Residency Center
Gift & Floral Shop
Heart Institute
Home Health and Hospice
Hospitalists
Joint Replacement Center
Le Bonheur Specialty Clinics
Medical Imaging
North Mississippi Surgery Center
Outpatient Infusion
Pain Management Center
Pastoral Care
Physician Specialties
Radiology
Rehabilitation Services
Respiratory Therapy
Skilled Nursing Facility
Sleep Disorders Center
Surgical Services
Tupelo Wellness Center
Vein Center
Volunteer Services
West Bedtower Project
Women's Hospital
Women's and Children Services

COMPETITORS

AKRON GENERAL MEDICAL CENTER
CENTEGRA HEALTH SYSTEM
HOSPITAL SERVICE DISTRICT 1
SHELBY COUNTY HEALTH CARE CORPORATION
SOUTHWEST MISSISSIPPI REGIONAL MEDICAL CENTER

HISTORICAL FINANCIALS
Company Type: Private

Income Statement — FYE: September 30

	REVENUE ($mil)	NET INCOME ($mil)	NET PROFIT MARGIN	EMPLOYEES
09/20*	680	56	8.3%	6,000
12/19	0	0	46.4%	—
09/14	633	52	8.3%	—
09/13	537	2	0.5%	—
Annual Growth	3.4%	56.3%	—	—

*Fiscal year change

2020 Year-End Financials
Return on assets: 4.1%   Cash ($ mil.): 27
Return on equity: 6.6%
Current Ratio: 0.60

NORTH SHORE UNIVERSITY HEALTH SYSTEM

LOCATIONS

HQ: NORTH SHORE UNIVERSITY HEALTH SYSTEM
2650 RIDGE AVE, EVANSTON, IL 602011700
Phone: 847 570-2640
Web: WWW.NORTHSHORE.ORG

HISTORICAL FINANCIALS
Company Type: Private

Income Statement — FYE: September 30

	REVENUE ($mil)	NET INCOME ($mil)	NET PROFIT MARGIN	EMPLOYEES
09/15	1,419	55	3.9%	3
09/14	1,397	148	10.6%	—
09/13	1,815	238	13.1%	—
Annual Growth	(11.6%)	(51.7%)	—	—

2015 Year-End Financials
Return on assets: 1.7%   Cash ($ mil.): 62
Return on equity: 3.0%
Current Ratio: 0.60

NORTH SHORE UNIVERSITY HOSPITAL

North Shore University Hospital (NSUH) knows you shouldn't have to leave the island for quality health care. The Long Island hospital has more than 800 beds devoted to adult and pediatric medicine, rehabilitation, stroke care, women's health, orthopedics, urology, wound healing, dentistry, and trauma emergency services, among other areas. The hospital is home to specialist institutes for cancer care and cardiology. It also serves as a campus for the Hofstra Northwell Shool of Medicine. NSUH is part of Northwell Health.

Operations
The not-for-profit NSUH operates numerous satellite community health centers that provide primary, surgery, psychiatric, dental, and specialty care, including the Schwartz Ambulatory Surgery Center. Its Stern Family Center for Extend Care and Rehabilitation has about 250 beds; NSUH also includes a Katz Women's Hospital (one of two in the system). The hospital provides comprehensive care in all health care specialties, including organ transplant services. In addition, the hospital operates mobile health vehicles and conducts educational and wellness programs for area residents.

NSUH has a staff of more than 6,000 specialist and subspecialist physicians, nurses, and other medical workers. It handles about 50,000 inpatient visits, 90,000 emergency room visits, 20,000 surgeries, and 6,000 births each year.

NSUH has medical, health professional, and nursing school affiliations with about 15 colleges and universities. Programs include residencies, post-graduate training, and fellowships.

Geographic Reach
Strategy
NSUH and the larger Northwell Health system tend to grow through the acquisitions of smaller campuses and mergers with other systems. This allows the hospital to gain operating efficiency through vertical integration, bargaining power with vendors, and a more diversified revenue stream.

In 2017 NSUH opened the Sandra Atlas Bass Heart Hospital for advanced cardiac care. The facility will be the first on Long Island to offer heart transplants and the sixth in New York State (which has a very high number of transplant candidates on its waiting list).

As part of its efforts to bring cutting-edge health care to the community it serves, the hospital began offering 3D-printed titanium spinal implants in 2017.These synthetic implants, approved in the US in 2016, are made with titanium powder rather than from a donor or from the patient's own body, and manufactured using a 3D-printing process.

LOCATIONS

HQ: NORTH SHORE UNIVERSITY HOSPITAL
300 COMMUNITY DR, MANHASSET, NY 110303876
Phone: 516 562-0100
Web: WWW.NORTHWELL.EDU

PRODUCTS/OPERATIONS

Selected Centers and Services
Bariatric Services
Cancer Institute
Cardiovascular and Thoracic Services
Colorectal Surgery
Emergency Department / Trauma Services
Fertility and Reproductive Services
Geriatric and Palliative Medicine
Infectious Diseases / AIDS Research
Kidney Transplantation
Laparoendoscopic Single-Site Surgery
Military/Veterans Services
Minimally Invasive Robotic Surgery
Neuroscience
Obstetrics and Gynecology
Orthopaedics
Pain Management
Pediatric Services
Radiation Medicine
Travel Immunization
Urology Services
Wound Care

COMPETITORS

FRANKLIN SQUARE HOSPITAL CENTER, INC.
HOLY SPIRIT HOSPITAL OF THE SISTERS OF CHRISTIAN CHARITY
JUPITER MEDICAL CENTER, INC.
LEHIGH VALLEY HEALTH NETWORK, INC.
UNITED REGIONAL HEALTH CARE SYSTEM, INC.

HISTORICAL FINANCIALS

Company Type: Private

Income Statement   FYE: December 31

	REVENUE ($mil)	NET INCOME ($mil)	NET PROFIT MARGIN	EMPLOYEES
12/18	1,883	38	2.1%	5,000
12/17	1,826	191	10.5%	—
12/16	1,795	171	9.6%	—
12/15	1,617	37	2.3%	—
Annual Growth	5.2%	1.3%	—	—

2018 Year-End Financials
Return on assets: 1.9%   Cash ($ mil.): 31
Return on equity: 3.8%
Current Ratio: 3.00

NORTH SHORE-LONG ISLAND JEWISH HEALTH CARE

EXECUTIVES

Prin, Filippo Petti
Information Technology/Interne, Phil Leonardi
Project Manager, Cathlyn Fagan
Director Research, Michael Ryan

LOCATIONS

HQ: NORTH SHORE-LONG ISLAND JEWISH HEALTH CARE
972 BRUSH HOLLOW RD 5TH, WESTBURY, NY 115901740
Phone: 516 876-6611

HISTORICAL FINANCIALS

Company Type: Private

Income Statement   FYE: December 31

	REVENUE ($mil)	NET INCOME ($mil)	NET PROFIT MARGIN	EMPLOYEES
12/14	719	(34)	—	2
12/13	633	(33)	—	—
12/09	351	(2)	—	—
Annual Growth	15.4%	—	—	—

2014 Year-End Financials
Return on assets: (-1.9%)   Cash ($ mil.): 74
Return on equity: (-7.7%)
Current Ratio: 0.50

NORTH TEXAS MUNICIPAL WATER DISTRICT

Auditors : CROWE LLP DALLAS TEXAS

LOCATIONS

HQ: NORTH TEXAS MUNICIPAL WATER DISTRICT
501 E BROWN ST, WYLIE, TX 750984406
Phone: 972 442-5405
Web: WWW.NTMWD.COM

HISTORICAL FINANCIALS

Company Type: Private

Income Statement   FYE: September 30

	REVENUE ($mil)	NET INCOME ($mil)	NET PROFIT MARGIN	EMPLOYEES
09/21	565	74	13.2%	670
09/20	572	134	23.5%	—
09/19	516	167	32.4%	—
09/18	484	117	24.3%	—
Annual Growth	5.3%	(14.0%)	—	—

2021 Year-End Financials
Return on assets: 1.2%   Cash ($ mil.): 126
Return on equity: 4.1%
Current Ratio: 0.40

NORTH TEXAS TOLLWAY AUTHORITY

The North Texas Tollway Authority (NTTA) operates a toll system consisting of about 90 miles of roadway. Facilities include the Dallas North Tollway, the President George Bush Turnpike, the Addison Airport Toll Tunnel, the Mountain Creek Lake Bridge, and the Sam Rayburn Tollway. The authority serves four counties in the Dallas-Fort Worth area. A predecessor agency, the Texas Turnpike Authority, was created by the Texas Legislature in 1953; the NTTA was created by the Legislature in 1997 to take over for the turnpike authority in Collin, Dallas, Denton, and Tarrant counties.

EXECUTIVES

Interim Executive Director*, Gerry Carrigan
Auditors : CROWE LLP DALLAS TX

LOCATIONS

HQ: NORTH TEXAS TOLLWAY AUTHORITY
5900 W PLANO PKWY STE 100, PLANO, TX 750934695
Phone: 214 461-2000
Web: WWW.NTTA.ORG

COMPETITORS

CITY OF ARLINGTON
CITY OF CHESAPEAKE
CITY OF DALLAS
CITY OF FORT WORTH
CITY OF PEORIA

HISTORICAL FINANCIALS

Company Type: Private

Income Statement   FYE: December 31

	REVENUE ($mil)	NET INCOME ($mil)	NET PROFIT MARGIN	EMPLOYEES
12/21	979	190	19.4%	733
12/20	785	(1)	—	—
12/16	741	93	12.6%	—
12/13	551	(99)	—	—
Annual Growth	7.4%	—	—	—

2021 Year-End Financials
Return on assets: 1.7%   Cash ($ mil.): 45
Return on equity: 39.0%
Current Ratio: 2.30

NORTHEAST GEORGIA MEDICAL CENTER, INC.

Auditors : PYA P C KNOXVILLE TN

LOCATIONS

HQ: NORTHEAST GEORGIA MEDICAL CENTER, INC.
743 SPRING ST NE, GAINESVILLE, GA 305013715
Phone: 770 219-9000
Web: WWW.NGHS.COM

HISTORICAL FINANCIALS

Company Type: Private

Income Statement   FYE: September 30

	REVENUE ($mil)	NET INCOME ($mil)	NET PROFIT MARGIN	EMPLOYEES
09/20	1,134	25	2.3%	3,053
09/19	1,328	162	12.2%	—
09/18	1,266	113	9.0%	—
09/17	1,152	7	0.7%	—
Annual Growth	(0.5%)	49.1%	—	—

2020 Year-End Financials
Return on assets: 1.3%   Cash ($ mil.): 67
Return on equity: 3.7%
Current Ratio: 1.00

NORTHEASTERN UNIVERSITY

Founded in 1898, Northeastern University is one of the largest private urban universities in North America. It is a world leader in experiential education, a learning approach that integrates classroom instruction and professional experience. The university is also a leader in the production of use-inspired research to solve global problems. The graduate programs offer professional doctorates, masters, certificates and all other programs. Undergraduate education offers accounting, biology, business administration, computer science, engineering and more. The university attracts students from all 50 states within the US and more than 125 countries, with campuses in Boston, Charlotte, Seattle, Portland, the San Francisco Bay Area, Toronto, Vancouver, and London.

Geographic Reach

Northeastern's students hail from about 150 countries. The university has study abroad programs, in locations including Argentina, Costa Rica, France, China, Germany, and the UK (among many others).

In addition to its main campus in Boston, Northeastern has satellite graduate schools in Charlotte, North Carolina, Seattle, California, London, Silicon Valley, Portland Maine, Vancouver and Toronto.

Strategy

Northeastern University has launched a new academic plan to strengthen its vision for learning and discovery. As a result of ongoing global events, the university has evaluated its traditional approach to higher education, rethinking its classrooms, campuses, and communities as a global university system of unbound spaces to experience, understand, and solve challenges in the evolving contexts. The university's goal is to be the indispensable university for learners and innovators who want to be see their work make a direct impact on the world; and restore trust in higher education's capacity to solve the world's hardest problems and prepare learners for lives of accomplishment.

EXECUTIVES

Chief of Staff*, James R Hackney
Auditors : PRICEWATERHOUSECOOPERS LLP BO

LOCATIONS

HQ: NORTHEASTERN UNIVERSITY
   360 HUNTINGTON AVE, BOSTON, MA 021155000
Phone: 617 373-2000
Web: WWW.NORTHEASTERN.EDU

PRODUCTS/OPERATIONS

Selected Schools & Colleges
Bouvé College of Health Sciences
College of Arts, Media, and Design
College of Computer and Information Science
College of Engineering
College of Professional Studies
College of Science
College of Social Sciences and Humanities
D'Amore-McKim School of Business
School of Law

COMPETITORS

EASTERN MICHIGAN UNIVERSITY
LONDON SCHOOL OF ECONOMICS & POLITICAL SCIENCE
REGENTS OF THE UNIVERSITY OF MINNESOTA
ROCHESTER INSTITUTE OF TECHNOLOGY (INC)
TRUSTEES OF BOSTON COLLEGE
TRUSTEES OF BOSTON UNIVERSITY
UNIVERSITY OF OREGON
UNIVERSITY OF THE PACIFIC
VIRGINIA POLYTECHNIC INSTITUTE AND STATE UNIVERSITY
WILLAMETTE UNIVERSITY

HISTORICAL FINANCIALS
Company Type: Private

Income Statement — FYE: June 30

	REVENUE ($mil)	NET INCOME ($mil)	NET PROFIT MARGIN	EMPLOYEES
06/22	1,812	730	40.3%	4,175
06/21	1,551	53	3.4%	—
06/20	1,523	193	12.7%	—
06/19	1,405	229	16.4%	—
Annual Growth	8.9%	47.0%	—	—

2022 Year-End Financials
Return on assets: 13.4%   Cash ($ mil.): 311
Return on equity: 21.0%
Current Ratio: —

NORTHERN INDIANA PUBLIC SERVICE COMPANY LLC

Northern Indiana Public Service Company (NIPSCO) can shine a little light on the topic of Hoosiers. The largest subsidiary of utility holding company NiSource, NIPSCO has more than 457,000 electricity customers and more than 786,000 natural gas customers. The utility has three coal-fired power plants with 2,540 MW of generating capacity. On the power side of the business, NIPSCO generates, transmits, and distributes electricity to the northern part of Indiana, and engages in electric wholesale and transmission transactions. The company operates approximately 13,000 miles of electric transmission and distribution lines and 16,000 miles of gas mains.

Operations

NIPSCO's three operating power facilities have a net capability of 2,540 MW. It also owns and operates Sugar Creek, a combined cycle gas turbine plant with a 535 MW capacity, four gas-fired generating units with a net capability of 206 MW and two hydroelectric generating plants with a net capability of 10 MW. During 2012, NIPSCO generated 74.1% and purchased 25.9% of its electric requirements.

Geographic Reach

NIPSCO Gas is the largest natural gas distribution company in Indiana and NIPSCO Electric, which serves customers in 20 counties, is the state's #2 power distribution company behind Duke Energy Indiana.

Strategy

NIPSCO is promoting incentive plans to help customers save money through energy efficiency programs, including appliance rebates for the installation of more energy efficient water heaters and other electric appliances, and for automated air-conditioning cycling (cutting use for limited periods during peak loads). Other incentives are available for weatherizing, energy audits, and green construction projects.

In 2011 the company increased residential customer rates by 5%. The rate increase was, in part, a way to compensate for a decline in usage and revenues as a result of the global recession.

In 2011 NiSource companies Northern Indiana Fuel & Light and Kokomo Gas were consolidated with and into NIPSCO in order to improve operating efficiencies.

EXECUTIVES

TRANS & ENG'G*, Timothy A Dehring
FL Vice President*, Gary W Pottorff

LOCATIONS

HQ: NORTHERN INDIANA PUBLIC SERVICE COMPANY LLC
   801 E 86TH AVE, MERRILLVILLE, IN 464106271
Phone: 800 464-7726

PRODUCTS/OPERATIONS

Selected Services
Call 811 Before You Dig
Commercial and Industrial Services
DependaBill
Dusk to Dawn Streetlights
Extra Service Protection
Green Power
IN-Charge Electric Vehicle Program
Meter Reading
NIPSCO Choice Program
NIPSCO Connect
Price Protection Service
Residential Builder and Developer Services
Selling Your Clean Energy
Smart Grid Technology
Start or Stop Gas and Electric Services
Trees and Power Lines
Wood Stove Changeout Program

COMPETITORS

DTE GAS COMPANY
NEW JERSEY RESOURCES CORPORATION
SOUTHERN CALIFORNIA GAS COMPANY
VECTREN CORPORATION
YANKEE GAS SERVICES COMPANY

HISTORICAL FINANCIALS
Company Type: Private

Income Statement — FYE: December 31

	REVENUE ($mil)	NET INCOME ($mil)	NET PROFIT MARGIN	EMPLOYEES
12/17	2,418	226	9.3%	3,096
12/16	2,251	178	7.9%	—
12/06	2,209	157	7.1%	—
Annual Growth	0.8%	3.3%	—	—

2017 Year-End Financials
Return on assets: 3.2% Cash ($ mil.): 7
Return on equity: 9.0%
Current Ratio: 0.50

NORTHERN NATURAL GAS COMPANY

Northern Natural Gas (NNG) keeps the pipes gassed up. The company operates 14,600 miles of natural gas pipeline stretching from the Permian Basin in Texas to Michigan's Upper Peninsula. It also provides transportation and storage services to more than 80 utilities and a number of other customers. The company has 6.3 billion cu. ft. per day market area peak capacity, and its three natural gas storage facilities have a total capacity of 75 billion cu. ft., including 4 billion cu. ft. of liquefied natural gas (LNG). NNG, which was formed in 1930, is an indirect subsidiary of Berkshire Hathaway Energy.

Operations
The company provides cross-haul and grid transportation between other interstate and intrastate pipelines in the Permian, Anadarko, Hugoton and Midwest areas.

NNG offers firm and interruptible transportation services, storage services, as well as other transportation related services that are available to customers as a reliable and flexible supply source to meet short-and long-term market demands.

Geographic Reach
Omaha, Nebraska-bsed, NNG accesses natural gas supply in the Mid-Continent, Rocky Mountain, and Western Canadian basins. Its northern service unit (Market Area) delivers gas supply to customers in Illinois, Iowa, Kansas, Michigan, Minnesota, Nebraska, South Dakota, and Wisconsin.

The company's pipeline system stretches across over 10 states, from the Permian Basin in Texas to Michigan's Upper Peninsula, providing access to five of the major natural gas supply regions in North America.

Sales and Marketing
NNG offers its products for utilities and numerous producers, energy marketing companies, and industrial end-users.

Company Background
NNG was established in 1930 in Omaha to serve 44 communities in Iowa, Kansas, and Nebraska. Its more recent history includes a takeover by Dynegy in 2002 from the pipeline unit's former parent, bankrupt energy giant Enron. The deal was part of Dynegy's proposed acquisition of Enron, which was subsequently called off. To strengthen its own balance sheet, Dynegy ended up selling NNG to MidAmerican Energy (which later became Berkshire Hathaway Energy) that year.

In 2011 NNG brought in 13 billion cu. ft. of new gas supply to its northern system from tight sand formations in Oklahoma and Texas.

LOCATIONS
HQ: NORTHERN NATURAL GAS COMPANY
  1111 S 103RD ST, OMAHA, NE 681241072
Phone: 402 398-7700
Web: WWW.NORTHERNNATURALGAS.COM

COMPETITORS
BOARDWALK PIPELINE PARTNERS, LP
ENABLE OKLAHOMA INTRASTATE TRANSMISSION, LLC
ENERGY TRANSFER LP
ENLINK MIDSTREAM PARTNERS, LP
ENTERPRISE PRODUCTS PARTNERS L.P.
ETP LEGACY LP
NORTHWESTERN CORPORATION
SOUTHERN COMPANY GAS
THE EMPIRE DISTRICT ELECTRIC COMPANY
THE WILLIAMS COMPANIES INC

HISTORICAL FINANCIALS
Company Type: Private

Income Statement — FYE: December 31

	REVENUE ($mil)	NET INCOME ($mil)	NET PROFIT MARGIN	EMPLOYEES
12/17	693	170	24.6%	1,055
12/16	636	159	25.0%	—
12/07	663	161	24.3%	—
12/06	633	142	22.5%	—
Annual Growth	0.8%	1.7%	—	—

2017 Year-End Financials
Return on assets: 4.6% Cash ($ mil.): 20
Return on equity: 10.8%
Current Ratio: 1.00

NORTHSIDE HOSPITAL, INC.

Northside Hospital is committed to health wellness community and offers all benefits of high-touch quality care close to home and the best in class health care delivery, including: North Side Hospital Cancer Institute (NHCI) top two community cancer programs and the largest and most comprehensive cancer hospital network in Georgia. NHCI Cancer Research Program is one of the largest community-based oncology/hematology programs. Northside Hospital Atlanta is system's flagship hospital with 621 beds and more than 12,000 employees.

Operations
Northside hospitals has grown over the years, expanding across 25 counties with five acute-care hospitals over 250 outpatient facilities, some 4,100 providers, and 25,500 employees.

Geographic Reach
Northside Hospital's operates five hospitals located in Atlanta, Cherokee, Duluth, Forsyth and Lawrenceville, Georgia.

Sales and Marketing
Northside Hospital offers their products services through its MyOneChart patient portal, to which patients can easily access their personal health information.

LOCATIONS
HQ: NORTHSIDE HOSPITAL, INC.
  1000 JOHNSON FERRY RD, ATLANTA, GA 303421611
Phone: 404 851-8000
Web: WWW.NORTHSIDE.COM

Selected Locations
Alpharetta Medical Campus
Dunwoody Cancer Center
Imaging at Peachtree Dunwoody
Medlock Bridge Imaging
Meridian Park Plaza
Northside Hospital Doctors Center
Northside Hospital-Atlanta
Northside Hospital-Cherokee
Northside Hospital-Forsyth
Northside-Forsyth Outpatient Surgery Center
Northside Sugar Hill Imaging (Buford)
Pediatric Center at Northside/Alpharetta
Roswell Cancer Center
Townelake Medical Office/Riverstone Imaging

COMPETITORS
BAXTER COUNTY REGIONAL HOSPITAL, INC.
CAROMONT HEALTH, INC.
CENTRA HEALTH, INC.
CHRISTUS SPOHN HEALTH SYSTEM CORPORATION
FROEDTERT MEMORIAL LUTHERAN HOSPITAL, INC.
HOSPITAL AUTHORITY OF VALDOSTA AND LOWNDES COUNTY, GEORGIA
KENNESTONE HOSPITAL AT WINDY HILL, INC.
MARION COMMUNITY HOSPITAL, INC.
SUBURBAN HOSPITAL, INC.
WINTER HAVEN HOSPITAL, INC.

HISTORICAL FINANCIALS
Company Type: Private

Income Statement — FYE: September 30

	REVENUE ($mil)	NET INCOME ($mil)	NET PROFIT MARGIN	EMPLOYEES
09/20	2,228	238	10.7%	8,000
09/18	2,081	265	12.8%	—
09/17	2,002	301	15.0%	—
09/16	1,897	157	8.3%	—
Annual Growth	4.1%	10.9%	—	—

2020 Year-End Financials
Return on assets: 7.5% Cash ($ mil.): 945
Return on equity: 12.0%
Current Ratio: 3.80

NORTHSIDE INDEPENDENT SCHOOL DISTRICT

Auditors : WEAVER & TIDWELL LLP SAN ANT

LOCATIONS

HQ: NORTHSIDE INDEPENDENT SCHOOL DISTRICT
5900 EVERS RD, SAN ANTONIO, TX 782381606
Phone: 210 397-8770
Web: WWW.NISD.NET

HISTORICAL FINANCIALS
Company Type: Private

Income Statement — FYE: August 31

	REVENUE ($mil)	NET INCOME ($mil)	NET PROFIT MARGIN	EMPLOYEES
08/21	1,236	118	9.6%	13,698
08/20	1,292	(150)	—	—
08/19	1,223	4	0.3%	—
08/18	1,203	57	4.8%	—
Annual Growth	0.9%	27.3%	—	—

2021 Year-End Financials
Return on assets: 3.5%   Cash ($ mil.): 711
Return on equity: —
Current Ratio: —

NORTHWEST DAIRY ASSOCIATION

Northwest Dairy Association (NDA) members milk a lot of cows. The dairy cooperative's 550-plus member/farmers ship 7.2 billion pounds of milk annually, which is processed by the co-op's subsidiary Darigold and packaged and sold under the Darigold label. NDA produces fluid and cultured dairy products, including milk, butter, cottage cheese, sour cream, and yogurt that altogether generate some $2 billion in sales. It also makes bulk butter and cheese, milk powder, and whey products. The co-op caters to several sectors nationwide. Its customers include food retailers and wholesalers, as well as foodservice and food-manufacturing companies. The association's membership spans half a dozen US states.

Operations
The cooperative's Darigold subsidiary operates a dozen processing facilities across the Northwestern US.

Geographic Reach
NDA members are located in Washington, Oregon, Idaho, Montana, California, and Utah.

Sales and Marketing
Through Darigold, NDA makes and markets a full line of dairy-based products for retail, foodservice, and commodity and specialty markets.

Financial Performance
The dairy cooperative logged nearly $2.5 billion in revenue in 2012, up from just shy of $2.1 billion the prior year. While NDA earned more revenue, its assets declined from $579 million to $548 million.

Mergers and Acquisitions
NDA added Country Classic Dairies to its operations in 2010. Its Montana-based business churn out Darigold-branded products with help from its 30 member/farmers. Securing the Country Classics business added some 160 million pounds of milk a year (more than half of Montana's milk supply) to the co-op's total production. NDA and Country Classic's union was the culmination of the two businesses' longtime working relationship (at one time, Country Classic used the Darigold name to market its products).

LOCATIONS

HQ: NORTHWEST DAIRY ASSOCIATION
5601 6TH AVE S STE 300, SEATTLE, WA 981082545
Phone: 206 284-7220
Web: WWW.DARIGOLD.COM

PRODUCTS/OPERATIONS

Selected Products
Consumer
  Butter
  Buttermilk
  Cottage cheese
  Cream
  Half and half
  Milk
  Sour cream
  Whipping cream
  Yogurt
Ingredients
  Bleached sweet dry whey
Colored cheddar cheese
Cultured skim milk powder
Milk protein concentrate
Monterey Jack cheese
Nonfat dry milk
Salted sweet cream butter
Skim milk powder
Sweet cream buttermilk powder
Unsalted butter
Whey protein concentrate

COMPETITORS

ASSOCIATED MILK PRODUCERS, INC.
Agropur Cooperative
DAIRY FARMERS OF AMERICA, INC.
DARIGOLD, INC.
DEAN FOODS COMPANY
LAND O'LAKES, INC.
LIFEWAY FOODS, INC.
MULLER DAIRY (U.K.) LIMITED
SYNUTRA INTERNATIONAL, INC.
THE HAIN CELESTIAL GROUP INC

HISTORICAL FINANCIALS
Company Type: Private

Income Statement — FYE: March 31

	REVENUE ($mil)	NET INCOME ($mil)	NET PROFIT MARGIN	EMPLOYEES
03/08	2,207	87	4.0%	1,300
03/07	1,450	12	0.9%	—
03/04	1,297	(6)	—	—
03/03	1,140	2	0.2%	—
Annual Growth	14.1%	107.0%	—	—

2008 Year-End Financials
Return on assets: 17.7%   Cash ($ mil.): 10
Return on equity: 41.5%
Current Ratio: 1.80

NORTHWEST FARM CREDIT SERVICES

Customer-owned financial cooperative Northwest Farm Credit Services is an agricultural lender that provides financial services to farmers, ranchers, agribusinesses, commercial fishermen, timber producers, and rural home owners in Alaska, Idaho, Montana, Oregon, and Washington. The company has a network of around 45 branches and offers a broad range of flexible loan programs to meet the needs of people in the agriculture business. Northwest Farm Credit also provides leasing services, appraisal services, and life, mortgage, disability, and crop insurance, as well as legal advocacy and assistance to customers in need. It is part of the Farm Credit System, a network of lenders serving the US agriculture industry.

Operations
The credit union provides financing and related services to farmers, ranchers, agribusinesses, commercial fishermen, timber producers, rural homeowners and crop insurance customers. Northwest Farm Credit provides $10.3 billion in loans. Farm Credit System, a nationwide network of borrower-owned lending institutions of which it is part, provides $205 billion in loans to rural America.

Geographic Reach
Northwest Farm Credit serves customers through 45 offices located in Idaho, Alaska, Montana, Oregon, and Washington.

Sales and Marketing
Northwest Farm Credit finances farmers, ranchers, agribusinesses, commercial fishermen, timber producers and rural homeowners as well as farm-related businesses, agricultural cooperatives and rural utilities.

Financial Performance
In 2015 the company's net revenue increased by 5% due to higher net interest income, driven by increased loan volume.

Northwest Farm Credit's net income

rose by 12% due to higher net revenues and a decrease in income tax expense.

In 2015 the company's operating cash inflow increased by 19%.

Strategy
The company plans to continue to fund lending operations primarily through its borrowing relationship with CoBank (a fellow Farm Credit System member) and from retained earnings.

Mergers and Acquisitions
In 2014 the company expanded its operations in Montana by buying Culbertson State Agency's crop insurance portfolio.

Company Background
The US Congress created the Farm Credit System in 1916 to meet the financial needs of farmers, ranchers, and cooperatives, who invest as well as borrow from the institutions within the system. All Farm Credit System members are regulated by the Farm Credit Administration.

Auditors : PRICEWATERHOUSECOOPERS LLP S

LOCATIONS

HQ: NORTHWEST FARM CREDIT SERVICES
2001 S FLINT RD, SPOKANE, WA 992249198
Phone: 509 838-2429
Web: WWW.AGWESTFC.COM

PRODUCTS/OPERATIONS

2015 Sales

	$ mil.	% of total
Interest Income	412.1	82
Patronage income	52.5	11
Financially Related Services	19.3	4
loans and other fee	6.5	1
Other non-interest income	11.8	2
Total	502.2	100

COMPETITORS

AGFIRST FARM CREDIT BANK
AGRIBANK, FCB
COBANK, ACB
FARM BUREAU PROPERTY & CASUALTY INSURANCE COMPANY
FARM CREDIT EAST, ACA
FARM CREDIT MID-AMERICA FLCA
FEDERAL AGRICULTURAL MORTGAGE CORPORATION
FEDERAL HOME LOAN BANK OF DES MOINES
NORINCHUKIN BANK, THE
STATE FARM MUTUAL AUTOMOBILE INSURANCE COMPANY

HISTORICAL FINANCIALS
Company Type: Private

Income Statement   FYE: December 31

	ASSETS ($mil)	NET INCOME ($mil)	INCOME AS % OF ASSETS	EMPLOYEES
12/13	9,604	236	2.5%	500
12/12	9,471	187	2.0%	—
12/11	8,696	159	1.8%	—
Annual Growth	5.1%	22.0%	—	—

2013 Year-End Financials
Return on assets: 2.5%   Cash ($ mil.): 39
Return on equity: 13.5%
Current Ratio: —

NORTHWESTERN MEMORIAL HOSPITAL

LOCATIONS

HQ: NORTHWESTERN MEMORIAL HOSPITAL
251 E HURON ST, CHICAGO, IL 606113055
Phone: 312 926-2000
Web: WWW.NM.ORG

HISTORICAL FINANCIALS
Company Type: Private

Income Statement   FYE: August 31

	REVENUE ($mil)	NET INCOME ($mil)	NET PROFIT MARGIN	EMPLOYEES
08/15	1,337	198	14.8%	5,800
08/10	1,380	64	4.7%	—
08/09	1,304	4	0.3%	—
Annual Growth	0.4%	87.7%	—	—

2015 Year-End Financials
Return on assets: 4.7%   Cash ($ mil.): —
Return on equity: 8.4%
Current Ratio: 0.70

NORTHWESTERN UNIVERSITY

With its main campus in the Chicago suburb of Evanston, Northwestern University (NU) serves over 22,000 students through about a dozen schools and colleges such as the Medill School of Journalism and the McCormick School of Engineering and Applied Sciences. Its Chicago campus houses the schools of law and medicine, as well as several hospitals of the McGaw Medical Center. With a faculty of more than 3,300, the school has a student-to-teacher ratio of about 6:1. NU is home to several research centers and community outreach programs; it also has a branch in Qatar. It is the only private member of the Big 10 conference; varsity sports include baseball, football, basketball, and fencing.

Operations
Among NU's top-ranked programs are its law school, medical school, and its engineering program. Its Kellogg Graduate School of Management consistently ranks among the nation's top five business schools. Its prestigious journalism and drama programs produced such alumni as Charlton Heston, Gary Marshall, and Julia Louis-Dreyfus.

NU has about $893 million in sponsored research funds performing research at over 40university research centers (and some 90 school-based research centers) in areas such as materials science, biomedical engineering, African studies, performance studies, and marketing.

Geographic Reach
NU's main campus in Chicago encompasses about 240 acres in Evanston. The university operates another 25-acre campus in Chicago, as well as its education center in Qatar.

Company Background
Northwestern University's Methodist founders met in 1850 to create an institution of higher learning serving the original Northwest Territory. The university was chartered in 1851, and two years later it acquired 379 acres of property north of Chicago on Lake Michigan. The town of Evanston was later named after John Evans, one of the school's founders.

HISTORY

Northwestern University's Methodist founders met in 1850 to create an institution of higher learning serving the original Northwest Territory. The university was chartered in 1851, and two years later it acquired 379 acres of property north of Chicago on Lake Michigan. The town of Evanston was later named after John Evans, one of the school's founders.

Classes began in the fall of 1855 with two professors and 10 students. By 1869 Northwestern had more than 100 students and began to admit women. In 1870 Northwestern signed an affiliation agreement with the Chicago Medical College (founded 1859), and three years later it joined with the original University of Chicago (no relation to the current institution) to create the Union College of Law. When the University of Chicago closed in 1886 due to financial difficulties, Northwestern took control of the law school. The university reorganized in 1891, consolidating its affiliated professional schools (dentistry, law, medicine, and pharmacy) into the university.

By 1900 Northwestern had become the third-largest university in the US (after Harvard and Michigan), with an enrollment of 2,700. During the 1920s the university created the Medill School of Journalism, named for Joseph Medill, founder of the Chicago Tribune. In 1924 the school's athletic teams adopted the nickname Wildcats, and two years later the university completed the primary buildings that form its Chicago campus. Northwestern suffered a drop in enrollment during the Depression, but after WWII it saw student numbers swell as veterans took advantage of the GI Bill. Expansion continued throughout the 1960s and 1970s.

In 1985 the school and the City of Evanston began developing a research center to attract more high-tech industries to the area. The university's graduate school of business achieved national prominence in 1988 after it was ranked #1 in the US by

Business Week. In 1995 Northwestern's football team, forever the doormat of the Big 10, achieved national fame when it won the conference championship.

In 1998 faculty member Professor John Pople won the Nobel Prize in Chemistry, the first Nobel Prize awarded to a faculty member while teaching at the university.

Northwestern won a significant legal battle in 1998 when a judge ruled that the university was not obligated to pay a faculty member simply because he had been granted tenure.

The university's dental school closed its doors in 2001, citing the difficulties posed for private schools in providing a competitive dental education.

Auditors : KPMG LLP CHICAGO IL

LOCATIONS

HQ: NORTHWESTERN UNIVERSITY
633 CLARK ST, EVANSTON, IL 602080001
Phone: 847 491-3741
Web: WWW.NORTHWESTERN.EDU

PRODUCTS/OPERATIONS

Selected Programs
Continuing and Professional Programs
Graduate Programs
Pre-Collegiate Programs
Undergraduate Programs

Selected Schools and Colleges
Bienen School of Music
Feinberg School of Medicine
The Graduate School
Kellogg School of Management
McCormick School of Engineering and Applied Science
Medill School of Journalism, Media, Integrated Marketing Communications
Northwestern in Qatar
School of Communication
School of Continuing Studies
School of Education and Social Policy
School of Law
Weinberg College of Arts and Science

COMPETITORS

CALIFORNIA STATE UNIVERSITY SYSTEM
NEW YORK UNIVERSITY
PRESIDENT AND FELLOWS OF HARVARD COLLEGE
THE LELAND STANFORD JUNIOR UNIVERSITY
THE OHIO STATE UNIVERSITY
THE REGENTS OF THE UNIVERSITY OF CALIFORNIA
THE UNIVERSITY OF CHICAGO
THE UNIVERSITY OF TEXAS SYSTEM
UNIVERSITY OF CINCINNATI
UNIVERSITY OF SOUTHERN CALIFORNIA

HISTORICAL FINANCIALS
Company Type: Private

Income Statement — FYE: August 31

	REVENUE ($mil)	NET INCOME ($mil)	NET PROFIT MARGIN	EMPLOYEES
08/18	2,464	560	22.7%	5,954
08/17	2,309	668	29.0%	—
Annual Growth	6.7%	(16.2%)	—	—

2018 Year-End Financials
Return on assets: 3.6%   Cash ($ mil.): 185
Return on equity: 4.6%
Current Ratio: —

NORTON HOSPITALS, INC

LOCATIONS

HQ: NORTON HOSPITALS, INC
200 E CHESTNUT ST, LOUISVILLE, KY 402021831
Phone: 502 629-8000
Web: WWW.NORTONHEALTHCARE.COM

HISTORICAL FINANCIALS
Company Type: Private

Income Statement — FYE: December 31

	REVENUE ($mil)	NET INCOME ($mil)	NET PROFIT MARGIN	EMPLOYEES
12/15	1,712	137	8.0%	1,500
12/14	1,577	187	11.9%	—
Annual Growth	8.6%	(26.7%)	—	—

2015 Year-End Financials
Return on assets: 8.0%   Cash ($ mil.): —
Return on equity: 8.6%
Current Ratio: 2.20

NOVA SOUTHEASTERN UNIVERSITY, INC.

A dynamic, private research university, Northeast Southeastern University (NSU) is providing high-quality educational and research programs at the undergraduate, graduate, and professional degree levels. Established in 1964, the university includes some 15 colleges, the "theme park" for start-ups, scale-ups, and entrepreneurs, the Alan B. Levan | NSU Broward Center of Innovation, the 215,000-square-foot Center for Collaborative Research, the private PK1-12 grade University School, the world-class NSU Art Museum Fort Lauderdale, and the Alvin Sherman Library, Research and Information Technology Center, one of Florida's largest public libraries. NSU students learn at its campuses in Fort Lauderdale, Fort Myers, Jacksonville, Miami, Miramar, Orlando, Palm Beach, and Tampa, Florida, as well as San Juan, Puerto Rico, and online globally.

Operations

In addition to its more than 150 undergraduate and graduate programs, NSU also operates The University School, a pre-K through 12th grade college preparatory day school. The university's Mailman Segal Institute for Early Childhood Studies is a multidisciplinary demonstration and professional training center for education, research, and the advancement of knowledge in early childhood, parenting, and autism across the life span. Located at the Jim & Jan Moran Family Center Village, the center offers educational programs, clinical services, and academic programs in collaboration with other NSU divisions.

Geographic Reach

NSU is a distance education pioneer (it was the one of the first US university to offer graduate programs online), offering classes on the Internet as well as at nine regional campuses in Florida and Puerto Rico.

Company Background

Founded in 1964, Nova University merged with Southeastern University of the Health Sciences in 1994 to become Nova Southeastern University.

Auditors : LB KPMG LLP GREENSBORO NC

LOCATIONS

HQ: NOVA SOUTHEASTERN UNIVERSITY, INC.
3301 COLLEGE AVE, DAVIE, FL 333147796
Phone: 954 262-7300
Web: WWW.NOVA.EDU

COMPETITORS

BOISE STATE UNIVERSITY
EASTERN MICHIGAN UNIVERSITY
FAIRFIELD UNIVERSITY
FLORIDA INTERNATIONAL UNIVERSITY
KENT STATE UNIVERSITY
MISSOURI STATE UNIVERSITY
NEW MEXICO STATE UNIVERSITY
THE UNIVERSITY OF IOWA
UNIVERSITY OF MIAMI
UNIVERSITY OF OKLAHOMA

HISTORICAL FINANCIALS
Company Type: Private

Income Statement — FYE: June 30

	REVENUE ($mil)	NET INCOME ($mil)	NET PROFIT MARGIN	EMPLOYEES
06/20	777	24	3.1%	2,500
06/15	678	45	6.7%	—
Annual Growth	2.8%	(11.9%)	—	—

2020 Year-End Financials
Return on assets: 1.5%   Cash ($ mil.): 70
Return on equity: 2.6%
Current Ratio: 0.30

NOVANT MEDICAL GROUP, INC.

LOCATIONS

HQ: NOVANT MEDICAL GROUP, INC.
2085 FRONTIS PLAZA BLVD, WINSTON SALEM, NC 271035614
Phone: 336 718-2803

HISTORICAL FINANCIALS
Company Type: Private

Income Statement   FYE: December 31

	REVENUE ($mil)	NET INCOME ($mil)	NET PROFIT MARGIN	EMPLOYEES
12/17	852	(76)	—	14
12/15	708	(63)	—	—
12/14	641	(39)	—	—
12/13	591	(41)	—	—
Annual Growth	9.6%	—	—	—

2017 Year-End Financials
Return on assets: (-51.0%)   Cash ($ mil.): —
Return on equity: —
Current Ratio: 1.10

NOVARTIS PHARMACEUTICALS CORPORATION

As part of the Innovative Medicines Division of Swiss drug giant Novartis AG, Novartis Pharmaceuticals Corporation (NPC) helps with the development, manufacturing, marketing, and sales of its parent company's products in the US. Its product lines address a range of ailments including cardiovascular and respiratory diseases, central nervous system disorders, cancers, bone and skin conditions, infectious diseases, and organ transplant complications. NPC's key products include tumor growth inhibitor Gleevec, high blood pressure drug Diovan, and attention deficit disorder therapies Focalin and Ritalin. NPC markets its products through an in-house sales team.

Operations
NPC is part of Novartis' Innovative Medicines Division, which handles the group's growing portfolio of patented medicines. The Innovative Medicines Division is further divided into two global business units: Novartis Oncology and Novartis Pharmaceuticals. Novartis Pharmaceuticals is composed of six divisions: Ophthalmology; Established Medicines; Neuroscience; Immunology, Hepatology, and Dermatology; Respiratory; and Cardio-Metabolic.

Geographic Reach
NPC parent Novartis AG operates some 65 manufacturing sites around the world. US sales account for around 35% of its total revenue.

Sales and Marketing
NPC and the broader Innovative Medicines Division have some 3,000 field force representatives including supervisors and administrative staff. In general, Novartis sells its prescription drugs to wholesale distributors, retail distributors, hospitals and clinics, government entities, and managed care organizations. It markets certain products in the US through online, television, newspaper, and magazine advertising.

Strategy
NPC widens its offerings in the US market through a number of methods including internal research programs, licensing agreements, and acquisitions. In 2015, the company received approval from the US FDA for its Cosentyx product for the treatment of moderate-to-severe plaque psoriasis in adults eligible for systemic therapy (drug absorbed through the bloodstream) or phototherapy (light therapy).

As part of its parent's efforts to focus on eye care, generics, and innovative pharmaceuticals, NPC remains a vital part of Novartis' growth strategy. One area of growing interest is oncology; in 2015 Novartis acquired certain cancer-fighting products and pipeline compounds from GlaxoSmithKline.

Mergers and Acquisitions
In 2016, Novartis acquired the Oklahoma-based Selexys Pharmaceuticals, which specializes in hematologic and inflammatory disorder treatments, for some $665 million.

Company Background
In 2016, Novartis AG restructured its Pharmaceuticals Division, creating two business units: Novartis Pharmaceuticals and Novartis Oncology. Those units now comprise the group's Innovative Medicines Division, of which NPC is a part.

EXECUTIVES
CMO, Nancy Lurker
Auditors : PRICEWATERHOUSECOOPERS LLP-BR

LOCATIONS
HQ: NOVARTIS PHARMACEUTICALS CORPORATION
1 HEALTH PLZ, EAST HANOVER, NJ 079361016
Phone: 862 778-8300
Web: WWW.NOVARTIS.COM

COMPETITORS
ASTELLAS PHARMA US, INC.
ASTRAZENECA PHARMACEUTICALS LP
BAYER HEALTHCARE PHARMACEUTICALS INC.
KYOWA KIRIN CO., LTD.
MGI PHARMA, INC.
NOVARTIS CORPORATION
NOVARTIS UK LIMITED
Novartis AG
SUMITOMO DAINIPPON PHARMA CO., LTD.
U C B

HISTORICAL FINANCIALS
Company Type: Private

Income Statement   FYE: December 31

	REVENUE ($mil)	NET INCOME ($mil)	NET PROFIT MARGIN	EMPLOYEES
12/16	49,436	6,698	13.5%	7,000
12/15	49,440	17,794	36.0%	—
12/13	58,831	9,292	15.8%	—
Annual Growth	(5.6%)	(10.3%)	—	—

2016 Year-End Financials
Return on assets: 5.1%   Cash ($ mil.): 7,007
Return on equity: 8.9%
Current Ratio: 1.10

NOVO CONSTRUCTION, INC.

LOCATIONS
HQ: NOVO CONSTRUCTION, INC.
1460 OBRIEN DR, MENLO PARK, CA 940251432
Phone: 650 701-1500
Web: WWW.NOVOCONSTRUCTION.COM

HISTORICAL FINANCIALS
Company Type: Private

Income Statement   FYE: October 31

	REVENUE ($mil)	NET INCOME ($mil)	NET PROFIT MARGIN	EMPLOYEES
10/19	872	8	1.0%	133
10/18	684	7	1.1%	—
10/17	603	5	0.9%	—
10/16	577	6	1.1%	—
Annual Growth	14.8%	11.4%	—	—

2019 Year-End Financials
Return on assets: 2.4%   Cash ($ mil.): 93
Return on equity: 95.0%
Current Ratio: 1.00

NPC RESTAURANT HOLDINGS, LLC

NPC International is the prince of pepperoni in a pizza empire. The world's largest franchisee of Pizza Hut restaurants, NPC owns and operates more than 1,275 pizza restaurants and delivery kitchens in about 30 states. The quick-service eateries, located mostly in such southern states as Alabama, Florida, Georgia, and Tennessee, serve a variety of pizza styles, as well as such items as buffalo wings and pasta. The pizza parlors are franchised from YUM! Brands, the world's largest fast-food restaurant company. NPC was founded in 1962 by former chairman Gene Bicknell, who was one of the first Pizza Hut franchisees. The company was acquired by private equity group NPC International Holdings in late 2011.

Operations
NPC runs more than 20 Wendys restaurants in addition to its large stable of pizza places. As a franchisee, NPC gets the benefit of operating restaurants under a popular and well known name. It pays YUM! Brands royalties and fees in exchange for the right to use the Pizza Hut brand and other intellectual property. Typically, local operators

are also held to certain standards regarding food and service quality.

Strategy

NPC has grown to such a large size primarily through a series of acquisitions, mostly corporate-run locations. In 2012 it snapped up 36 Pizza Hut units located primarily in Florida for roughly $19 million from Pizza Hut, Inc. The deal enabled NPC to strengthen its position in its largest geographical market.

While NPC doesn't own the Pizza Hut chain, as its largest franchisee the company can exert a certain amount of influence in how the fast-food business operates. It called upon YUM! Brands to improve its Pizza Hut marketing strategy while sales were slumping amid the economic downturn. The company spends 6% of its revenue on national and local advertising, demonstrating its commitment to Pizza Hut operations and advertising strategy.

NPC's revenue improved in 2010 and 2011 partly as a result of promoting its value-priced menu items as a way to gain market share from competing chains including Domino's and Papa John's. (Within its local markets, NPC competes against #1 Domino's franchisee RPM Pizza and Papa John's operator PJ United.)

EXECUTIVES

Head OF Operations, D Blayne Vaughn
CAO, Jason P Poenitske
Auditors : KPMG LLP KANSAS CITY MISSOUR

LOCATIONS

HQ: NPC RESTAURANT HOLDINGS, LLC
  7300 W 129TH ST, OVERLAND PARK, KS 662132631
Phone: 913 327-5555
Web: WWW.NPCINTERNATIONAL.COM

COMPETITORS

PAPA JOHN'S INTERNATIONAL, INC.
PAPA MURPHY'S HOLDINGS, INC.
PIZZA HUT, INC.
THE KRYSTAL COMPANY
YUM BRANDS, INC.

HISTORICAL FINANCIALS
Company Type: Private

Income Statement				FYE: December 27
	REVENUE ($mil)	NET INCOME ($mil)	NET PROFIT MARGIN	EMPLOYEES
12/16	1,236	8	0.7%	29,000
12/15	1,223	6	0.5%	—
12/14	1,179	1	0.1%	—
12/13	1,094	29	2.7%	—
Annual Growth	4.2%	(33.5%)	—	—

2016 Year-End Financials
Return on assets: 0.7%   Cash ($ mil.): 13
Return on equity: 3.1%
Current Ratio: 0.40

NUTRISYSTEM, INC.

Nutrisystem is a leader in the weight loss industry, having helped millions of people lose weight for nearly 50 years. It sells prepared meals and grocery items that are delivered directly to US consumers. With up to more than 150 menu choices, the company offers a variety of breakfasts, lunches, dinners, and snacks made with real, quality ingredients. It also offers individualized calorie plans, one-on-one diet counseling, behavior modification, and exercise education and maintenance plans. Nutrisystem meals and snacks, along with fresh grocery additions, deliver a nutritionally balanced meal plan that provides customers the flexibility to align their diet with the US Healthy Eating Meal Pattern, as recommended by the USDA Dietary Guidelines.

Operations

Nutrisystem offers safe, effective, and scientifically backed weight loss plans, with a distinguished Science Advisory Board and strong clinical studies. All plans include comprehensive support and counseling options from trained weight loss coaches, registered dietitians, and certified diabetes educators available seven days a week from an award-winning contact center.

The All-New Nutrisystem is an easy-to-follow weight loss program tailored to a person's unique metabolism. The personal plan adapts calorie goals as the individual progresses through their weight loss journey. The All-New Nutrisystem integrates the science of metabolic adaptation to support sustainable, healthy weight loss, and helps avoid plateaus and yo-yo dieting. It includes delicious foods created with the right balance of carbs, proteins, and fats that are delivered directly to the customer's door. Nutrisystem also adds approximately 25 new on-trend foods to its menu of more than 150 delicious, nutritious meals and snacks, including zesty pizza bowls, flatbreads, and plant-based favorites.

An integral part of the All-New Nutrisystem is the brand new NuMi SmartAdapt feature of the NuMi app. NuMi SmartAdapt recalculates the customer's choice goal and meal plan when weight loss milestones are reached. In addition, NuMi provides personalized meal plans, grocery guides, content, and recipes to support customers along their journey.

The Nutrisystem plans align with national guidelines for total fat, saturated fat, trans fat, sodium, carbohydrates, fiber, protein, and added sugars. The available weight loss plans can accommodate specific dietary needs and preferences, including the Nutrisystem D program for people living with Type 2 diabetes or pre-diabetes. For customers transitioning to maintenance, there are Nutrisystem Success Plan options. The company also has select products available at retail.

Sales and Marketing

A variety of membership plans are available with Nutrisystem Advantage for customers who just want their favorite meal selections at a discounted rate with free shipping.

Financial Performance

After several years of sale declines, Nutrisystem's revenue in 2014 rebounded by 12% to $403.08 million, thanks to growth from new customers, retail, and on-program revenue. The company also benefited from a higher average sales prices. Sales from reactivation and QVC declined, offsetting some of the company's potential top-line gains.

Higher revenue caused profit to spike for a second year, with net income skyrocketing by 162% to $19.31 million in 2014. Operations provided $32.81 million, or 7% less cash than in 2013, mostly because of an increase in receivables and timing of accrued payroll and benefits.

Company Background

The Company was founded in the early 1970s by Harold Katz

EXECUTIVES

CMO, Keira Krausz
Auditors : KPMG LLP PHILADELPHIA PENNSY

LOCATIONS

HQ: NUTRISYSTEM, INC.
  600 OFFICE CENTER DR, FORT WASHINGTON, PA 190343232
Phone: 215 706-5300
Web: WWW.NUTRISYSTEM.COM

PRODUCTS/OPERATIONS

2014 Sales

	% of total
Direct	91
Retail	7
QVC	2
Total	100

Selected Food Programs
Men's Program
Men's Silver Program
My Plan
SUCCESS
Women's Diabetic Program
Women's Program
Women's Silver Program
Vegetarian

COMPETITORS

ANGI HOMESERVICES INC.
COINSTAR, LLC
GAIA, INC.
JENNY CRAIG, INC.
MEDIFAST, INC.
NATURAL GROCERS BY VITAMIN COTTAGE, INC.
VISA PAYMENTS LIMITED
WAYFAIR INC.
WW INTERNATIONAL, INC.
XO GROUP INC.

HISTORICAL FINANCIALS

Company Type: Private

Income Statement — FYE: December 31

	REVENUE ($mil)	NET INCOME ($mil)	NET PROFIT MARGIN	EMPLOYEES
12/18	691	58	8.5%	606
12/17	696	57	8.3%	—
12/16	545	35	6.5%	—
12/15	462	26	5.7%	—
Annual Growth	14.3%	30.9%	—	—

2018 Year-End Financials
Return on assets: 28.7%
Return on equity: 40.0%
Current Ratio: 2.90
Cash ($ mil.): 22

OAKLAND UNIFIED SCHOOL DISTRICT

LOCATIONS

HQ: OAKLAND UNIFIED SCHOOL DISTRICT
 1000 BROADWAY STE 450, OAKLAND, CA 946074039
Phone: 510 879-8000
Web: WWW.OUSD.ORG

HISTORICAL FINANCIALS

Company Type: Private

Income Statement — FYE: June 30

	REVENUE ($mil)	NET INCOME ($mil)	NET PROFIT MARGIN	EMPLOYEES
06/21	849	30	3.5%	7,200
06/20	721	106	14.8%	—
06/19	731	(69)	—	—
06/18	677	(45)	—	—
Annual Growth	7.9%	—	—	—

2021 Year-End Financials
Return on assets: 1.6%
Return on equity: —
Current Ratio: —
Cash ($ mil.): —

OCEAN SPRAY CRANBERRIES, INC.

Known for its blue-and-white wave logo, Ocean Spray Cranberries is a top US maker of canned, bottled, and shelf-stable juice drinks. Structured as a cooperative, Ocean Spray is owned by more than 700 cranberry and grapefruit growers in North and South America. It produces juice drinks by blending cranberries with other fruits, typically ranging from apples to blueberries, at its processing facilities. The company's other products include fresh and dried cranberries, sauces, snacking, energy, sparkling, and supplements, along with fresh citrus fruits. Ocean Spray sells its products through food retailers, foodservice providers, distributors, and food makers worldwide. The vibrant agricultural company was founded in 1930.

Operations

The world's leading producer of cranberry juices, juice drinks and dried cranberries and the best-selling brand in the North American bottled juice category's original products remain most popular: Ocean Spray Jellied Cranberry Sauce and Ocean Spray Cranberry Juice Cocktail.

The company partners with key stakeholders, including Feeding America and others.

Geographic Reach

Headquartered in Massachusetts, Ocean Spray has operations in Pennsylvania, Nevada, Wisconsin, Washington, Texas and Chile.

While it primarily harvests in the Northeast, cranberries also grow in other parts of North and South America, from Massachusetts to New Jersey, Oregon to Washington, Wisconsin, parts of British Columbia and Quebec, and Chile.

Through its global network of distributors across North America, Europe, Africa, South America, Middle East, Asia and Australia, the company sells its products to more than 70 countries worldwide.

Sales and Marketing

In addition to healthcare, restaurants and bars, the company also serves in retail, schools, and travel and leisure sectors. The company's variety of product offerings are available in grocery, convenience, drug and club stores throughout the world, as well as on various online retailers.

HISTORY

Ocean Spray Cranberries traces its roots to Marcus Urann, president of the Cape Cod Cranberry Company. In 1912 Urann, who became known as the "Cranberry King," began marketing a cranberry sauce that was packaged in tins and could be served year-round. Inspired by the sea spray that drifted off the Atlantic and over his cranberry bogs, Urann dubbed his concoction Ocean Spray Cape Cod Cranberry Sauce.

It didn't take long for other cranberry growers to make their own sauces, and rather than compete, the Cranberry King consolidated. In 1930 Urann merged his company with A.D. Makepeace Company and with Cranberry Products, forming a national cooperative called Cranberry Canners. During the 1940s it added growers in Wisconsin, Oregon, and Washington and, to reflect its new scope, changed its name to National Cranberry Association.

Canadian growers were added to the fold in 1950. Urann retired in 1955, and two years later the co-op introduced its first frozen products. To take advantage of the popular Ocean Spray brand name, in 1959 the company changed its name to Ocean Spray Cranberries.

EXECUTIVES

CCO, Celina Li
Auditors : PRICEWATERHOUSECOOPERS LLP BO

LOCATIONS

HQ: OCEAN SPRAY CRANBERRIES, INC.
 1 OCEAN SPRAY DR, MIDDLEBORO, MA 023490001
Phone: 508 946-1000
Web: WWW.OCEANSPRAY.COM

PRODUCTS/OPERATIONS

Selected Brands & Products
Dried fruit
  Craisins Blueberry Juice Infused Dried Cranberries
  Craisins Cherry Juice Infused Dried Cranberries
  Craisins Original Dried Cranberries
  Craisins Pomegranate Juice Infused Dried
Cranberries
  Craisins Snack Packs
  Craisins Trail Mix - Cranberry & Chocolate
  Craisins Trail Mix - Cranberry, Fruit & Nut
Fresh Produce
  Clementines
  Cranberries
  Grapefruit
  Lemons
  Limes
  Oranges
  Tangerines
Instant oatmeal
  Cranberry
  Cranberry Honey Multigrain
  Cranberry Orange Muffin
  Cranberry Pomegranate
Juice
  100% Juice Blends
  Blueberry Juice Drinks
  Cran•Energy Energy Juice Drinks
  Cranberry Juice Cocktails
  Cranberry Juice Drink Blends
  Diet Juice Drinks
  Fruit & Veggie Juice
  Fruit & Veggie Juice Drinks
  Grapefruit Juice
  Grapefruit Juice Drinks
  Juice Drinks
  Light Juice Drinks
  On the Go Juice
  On the Go Juice Drinks
  Sugar-Free Drink Mixes
  White Cranberry Juice Drinks
Sauces
  Jellied cranberry sauce
  Whole berry cranberry sauce

COMPETITORS

BLUE DIAMOND GROWERS
CHERRY CENTRAL COOPERATIVE, INC.
HORNELL BREWING CO., INC.
KNOUSE FOODS COOPERATIVE, INC.
NORTHLAND CRANBERRIES, INC.
ODWALLA, INC.
RED GOLD, INC.
TREE TOP, INC.
TROPICANA PRODUCTS, INC.
WELCH FOODS INC., A COOPERATIVE

HISTORICAL FINANCIALS
Company Type: Private

Income Statement				FYE: August 31
	REVENUE ($mil)	NET INCOME ($mil)	NET PROFIT MARGIN	EMPLOYEES
08/17	1,660	272	16.4%	2,000
08/16	1,706	334	19.6%	—
08/15	1,719	317	18.5%	—
Annual Growth	(1.7%)	(7.4%)	—	—

2017 Year-End Financials
Return on assets: 16.1%   Cash ($ mil.): 11
Return on equity: 81.6%
Current Ratio: 2.30

OCHSNER CLINIC FOUNDATION

Auditors : ERNST & YOUNG US LLP FORT WOR

LOCATIONS

HQ: OCHSNER CLINIC FOUNDATION
1514 JEFFERSON HWY, JEFFERSON, LA 701212429
Phone: 866 624-7637
Web: WWW.OCHSNER.ORG

HISTORICAL FINANCIALS
Company Type: Private

Income Statement				FYE: December 31
	REVENUE ($mil)	NET INCOME ($mil)	NET PROFIT MARGIN	EMPLOYEES
12/17	8,405	128	1.5%	10,500
12/14	2,196	(16)	—	—
12/13	5,550	52	0.9%	—
12/12	4,829	12	0.3%	—
Annual Growth	11.7%	60.1%	—	—

2017 Year-End Financials
Return on assets: 4.9%   Cash ($ mil.): 306
Return on equity: 13.3%
Current Ratio: 0.60

OCHSNER HEALTH SYSTEM

Auditors : ERNST & YOUNG LLP NEW ORLEANS

LOCATIONS

HQ: OCHSNER HEALTH SYSTEM
1516 JEFFERSON HWY, NEW ORLEANS, LA 701212429
Phone: 504 842-3483
Web: WWW.OCHSNER.ORG

HISTORICAL FINANCIALS
Company Type: Private

Income Statement				FYE: December 31
	REVENUE ($mil)	NET INCOME ($mil)	NET PROFIT MARGIN	EMPLOYEES
12/16	2,812	55	2.0%	19,000
12/15	2,592	63	2.5%	—
Annual Growth	8.5%	(13.2%)	—	—

2016 Year-End Financials
Return on assets: 2.4%   Cash ($ mil.): 121
Return on equity: 7.8%
Current Ratio: 1.40

OHIO EDISON COMPANY

Ohio Edison has taken a shine to the folks in the Buckeye state. The company distributes electricity to a population of about 2.3 million (more than 1 million customers) in a 7,000 sq. ml. area of central and northeastern Ohio. Ohio Edison, a unit of FirstEnergy, also has 5,955 MW of generating capacity from interests in primarily fossil-fueled and nuclear generation facilities, and it sells excess power to wholesale customers. The utility's power plants are operated by sister companies FirstEnergy Nuclear and FirstEnergy Generation. Subsidiary Pennsylvania Power Company provides electric service to communities in a 1,100 sq. ml. area of western Pennsylvania, which has a population of approximately 400,000.

Operations
Ohio Edison and Pennsylvania Power provide regulated electric distribution services and procure of generation services. Ohio Edison operates more than 30,460 miles of distribution lines and 500 miles of transmission lines.

Geographic Reach
Ohio Edison and Pennsylvania Power conduct business in portions of Ohio and Pennsylvania.

Financial Performance
Revenues decreased by 11% in 2011 due to lower retail generation revenues, partially offset by higher distribution and wholesale generation revenues. Retail generation revenues decreased primarily due to a drop in energy sales caused from an increase in customers shopping for alternative power providers and lower average prices across all customer classes.

Ohio Edison's net income decreased by 17% in 2011 due to lower revenues, partially offset by lower purchased power costs.

Strategy
In 2011 parent FirstEnergy acquired Allegheny Energy in a $8.5 billion deal that grew FirstEnergy's generation capacity and dramatically boosted the company's position as a leading regional energy provider.

Company Background
FirstEnergy and Ohio Edison reached a settlement in 2005 with the federal government to reduce harmful emissions from its Ohio power generating plants; in addition to fines, Ohio Edison has been mandated to pledge $25 million for wind power, biomass, and other alternative energy sources. In 2009 Ohio Edison began retrofitting two units at its Shadyside, Ohio power plant to burn wood and other biomass materials in order to lower its greenhouse gas output.

Auditors : PRICEWATERHOUSECOOPES LP CLEV

LOCATIONS

HQ: OHIO EDISON COMPANY
76 S MAIN ST BSMT, AKRON, OH 443081817
Phone: 800 736-3402

COMPETITORS

DUKE ENERGY INDIANA, LLC
INDIANA MICHIGAN POWER COMPANY
INTERSTATE POWER AND LIGHT COMPANY
NEVADA POWER COMPANY
OHIO POWER COMPANY

HISTORICAL FINANCIALS
Company Type: Private

Income Statement				FYE: December 31
	REVENUE ($mil)	NET INCOME ($mil)	NET PROFIT MARGIN	EMPLOYEES
12/16	1,394	150	10.8%	1,190
12/11	1,633	128	7.8%	—
12/10	1,836	157	8.6%	—
12/09	2,516	122	4.9%	—
Annual Growth	(8.1%)	3.0%	—	—

2016 Year-End Financials
Return on assets: 4.0%   Cash ($ mil.): —
Return on equity: 13.4%
Current Ratio: 2.40

OHIO STATE UNIVERSITY PHYSICIANS, INC.

LOCATIONS

HQ: OHIO STATE UNIVERSITY PHYSICIANS, INC.
700 ACKERMAN RD STE 600, COLUMBUS, OH 432021559
Phone: 614 947-3700
Web: WWW.OSUPHYSICIANS.COM

HISTORICAL FINANCIALS
Company Type: Private

Income Statement   FYE: June 30

	REVENUE ($mil)	NET INCOME ($mil)	NET PROFIT MARGIN	EMPLOYEES
06/20	606	8	1.4%	99
06/17	500	29	6.0%	—
Annual Growth	6.7%	(35.0%)	—	—

2020 Year-End Financials
Return on assets: 2.9%   Cash ($ mil.): 182
Return on equity: 4.0%
Current Ratio: —

OHIOHEALTH CORPORATION

OhioHealth is a nationally recognized, not-for-profit, charitable, healthcare outreach of the United Methodist Church. The not-for-profit system runs a dozen of hospitals including OhioHealth Riverside Methodist Hospital, OhioHealth Grant Medical Center, and OhioHealth Doctors Hospital. All told, OhioHealth has 200-plus ambulatory sites, hospice, home health, medical equipment and other services spanning more than 45 Ohio counties. OhioHealth offers urgent care, physical rehabilitation, diagnostic imaging, and sleep diagnostics services. OhioHealth Physician Group includes 800 primary care physicians and 400 advance practice providers in more than 50 specialties.

Operations
In addition to offering patient care, OhioHealth also operates the OhioHealth Research & Innovation Institute, which coordinates research throughout the health system, including conducting clinical trials of new drugs and medical devices. The system also operates The Center for Medical Education, a medical training facility that, among other technologies, offers human patient simulators on which medical professionals can practice new procedures in various clinical situations.

OhioHealth has some 35,000 associates, physicians, and volunteers.

Geographic Reach
Based in Ohio, OhioHealth provide health services in more than 45 counties.

Strategy
In late 2021, OhioHealth Doctors Hospital purchased the medical office building across the street from the hospital, located at 5109 West Broad Street. Renovations for that building will follow. Starting in January 2022, OhioHealth will begin planning and design work for a complete renovation within the recently purchased medical office building attached to the hospital located at 5131 Beacon Hill Road. The investment will bring more outpatient services to the west side, allowing Doctors Hospital to recruit new physicians, and improve the patient experience.

This investment brings the OhioHealth commitment to nearly $75 million dollars over a little more than a decade, ensuring patients have access to the right care at the right time, and most importantly at the right place.

Company Background
The health system traces its roots back to 1892 when Protestant Hospital (now known as Riverside Methodist Hospital) opened. The system, initially organized as U.S. Health Corporation in 1984, later took on the OhioHealth name in 1997.

Auditors: DELOITTE TAX LLP INDIANAPOL

LOCATIONS
HQ: OHIOHEALTH CORPORATION
3430 OHHALTH PKWY FL 5 FLR 5, COLUMBUS, OH 43202
Phone: 614 788-8860
Web: WWW.OHIOHEALTH.COM

PRODUCTS/OPERATIONS
Selected Facilities
Owned
    Doctors Hospital (Columbus)
    Doctors Hospital Nelsonville (Nelsonville)
    Dublin Methodist Hospital (Dublin)
    Grady Memorial Hospital (Delaware)
    Grant Medical Center (Columbus)
    Hardin Memorial Hospital (Kenton)
    Marion General Hospital (Marion)
    O'Bleness Memorial Hospital (Athens)
    Riverside Methodist Hospital (Columbus)
Affiliated
    Blanchard Valley Medical Center
    Galion Community Hospital (Galion)
    Genesis Healthcare System (Zanesville)
    Knox Community Hospital
    Morrow County Hospital (Mt. Gilead)
    Samaritan Regional Health System (Ashland)
    Southern Ohio Medical Center (Portsmouth)

COMPETITORS
ATLANTICARE HEALTH SYSTEM INC.
CKHS, INC.
HCA-HEALTHONE LLC
HOLY SPIRIT HOSPITAL OF THE SISTERS OF CHRISTIAN CHARITY
LEHIGH VALLEY HEALTH NETWORK, INC.
NORTHWELL HEALTH, INC.
READING HOSPITAL
UNIVERSITY HEALTH SYSTEMS OF EASTERN CAROLINA, INC.
UNIVERSITY HOSPITALS HEALTH SYSTEM, INC.
YORK HOSPITAL

HISTORICAL FINANCIALS
Company Type: Private

Income Statement   FYE: June 30

	REVENUE ($mil)	NET INCOME ($mil)	NET PROFIT MARGIN	EMPLOYEES
06/19	3,388	542	16.0%	15,000
06/18	4,045	519	12.8%	—
06/17	3,792	631	16.6%	—
06/14	2,179	354	16.3%	—
Annual Growth	9.2%	8.9%	—	—

2019 Year-End Financials
Return on assets: 7.8%   Cash ($ mil.): 132
Return on equity: 11.5%
Current Ratio: 0.40

OHIOHEALTH CORPORATION GROUP RETURN

Auditors: DELOITTE TAX LLP CINCINNATI

LOCATIONS
HQ: OHIOHEALTH CORPORATION GROUP RETURN
180 E BROAD ST, COLUMBUS, OH 432153707
Phone: 614 544-4052

HISTORICAL FINANCIALS
Company Type: Private

Income Statement   FYE: June 30

	REVENUE ($mil)	NET INCOME ($mil)	NET PROFIT MARGIN	EMPLOYEES
06/18	1,334	(98)	—	20
06/17	1,204	(77)	—	—
06/14	600	(85)	—	—
06/13	563	(55)	—	—
Annual Growth	18.8%	—	—	—

2018 Year-End Financials
Return on assets: (-9.0%)   Cash ($ mil.): 42
Return on equity: (-14.1%)
Current Ratio: 1.40

OHIOHEALTH RIVERSIDE METHODIST HOSPITAL

LOCATIONS
HQ: OHIOHEALTH RIVERSIDE METHODIST HOSPITAL
3535 OLENTANGY RIVER RD, COLUMBUS, OH 432143908
Phone: 614 566-5000
Web: WWW.OHIOHEALTH.COM

HISTORICAL FINANCIALS
Company Type: Private

Income Statement   FYE: June 30

	REVENUE ($mil)	NET INCOME ($mil)	NET PROFIT MARGIN	EMPLOYEES
06/16	1,207	190	15.8%	944
06/15*	19	0	2.3%	—
12/01	49	(1)	—	—
12/00	0	0	—	—
Annual Growth	—	—	—	—

*Fiscal year change

2016 Year-End Financials
Return on assets: 28.3% Cash ($ mil.): —
Return on equity: —
Current Ratio: 0.50

OKLAHOMA STATE UNIVERSITY

Oooooklahoma where the... students come to learn! Oklahoma State University is the flagship campus of its namesake (OSU) system, which also includes OSU-Tulsa, OSU-Oklahoma City, OSU-Okmulgee, the OSU Center for Health Sciences in Tulsa, the OSU College of Veterinary Medicine, and the Oklahoma Agricultural Experiment Station. OSU offers courses in a variety of disciplines and confers undergraduate, graduate, doctoral, and professional degrees in everything from agriculture and the arts to business and engineering. Altogether, the system boasts an enrollment of about 36,000 students across its five campuses; its student-teacher ratio is about 17:1.

Geographic Reach
Operating across Oklahoma, OSU's several campus locations include three branch campuses, a Center for Health Sciences, College of Veterinary Medicine, and Oklahoma Agricultural Experiment Station.

Financial Performance
The Oklahoma university has seen its revenue rise for the past several years due to organic growth. OSU logged an 11% increase in revenue in 2012 as compared to 2011, thanks to increases from tuition and fees, grants and contracts, auxiliary enterprises, and other operating revenue. Net income, meanwhile, slipped by 14% during the same reporting period attributable to increases in compensation and employee benefits, contractual services, scholarships and fellowships, depreciation expense, supplies and materials, and other operating expenses.

Strategy
One of OSU's biggest financial contributors is alumnus and oil and gas tycoon T. Boone Pickens, who over the years has given the school more than $500 million. Pickens' 2010 donation of $100 million went toward the school's $1 billion fundraising campaign that was used to endow scholarships and fellowships for students, as well as attract and retain professors, upgrade facilities, and create new programs. Pickens is the campaign's honorary chairman.

Company Background
OSU was founded in 1890 as the Oklahoma Territorial Agricultural and Mechanical College (A&M). The first students were enrolled the following year; the school operated as Oklahoma A&M until 1957 when it changed its name to Oklahoma State University to reflect the fact that its curriculum had grown to include a wide range of subjects. Following the name change, the OSU began establishing campuses starting with the Stillwater campus and then the OSU-Institute of Technology in Okmulgee (1946), OSU-Oklahoma City (1961), OSU-Tulsa (1984), and the Center for Health Sciences also in Tulsa (1988).

Auditors : BKD LLP SPRINGFIELD MISSOUR

LOCATIONS
HQ: OKLAHOMA STATE UNIVERSITY
  401 WHITEHURST HALL, STILLWATER, OK 740781030
Phone: 405 744-5000
Web: AGRICULTURE.OKSTATE.EDU

PRODUCTS/OPERATIONS
Selected Colleges
Agricultural Sciences and Natural Resources
Arts and Sciences
Education
Engineering, Architecture and Technology
Human Sciences
Spears School of Business
Center for Veterinary Health Sciences
Graduate College
Honors College

COMPETITORS
AUBURN UNIVERSITY
MARSHALL UNIVERSITY
MICHIGAN STATE UNIVERSITY
MISSOURI STATE UNIVERSITY
NORTH CAROLINA STATE UNIVERSITY
OREGON STATE UNIVERSITY
UNIVERSITY OF ARKANSAS SYSTEM
UNIVERSITY OF KANSAS
UNIVERSITY OF MISSOURI SYSTEM
UNIVERSITY OF OKLAHOMA

HISTORICAL FINANCIALS
Company Type: Private

Income Statement FYE: June 30

	REVENUE ($mil)	NET INCOME ($mil)	NET PROFIT MARGIN	EMPLOYEES
06/20	842	115	13.8%	8,882
06/19	904	95	10.6%	—
06/18	802	8	1.1%	—
06/17	815	40	5.0%	—
Annual Growth	1.1%	42.1%		—

2020 Year-End Financials
Return on assets: 4.5% Cash ($ mil.): 134
Return on equity: 10.6%
Current Ratio: 2.70

OLD CLAIMCO, LLC

Don't let the mouse mascot fool you: This amusement kingdom is founded on the power of pizza. CEC Entertainment operates the Chuck E. Cheese's chain of pizza parlors with more than 610 locations in over 45 states and approximately 15 foreign countries and territories. The restaurants cater mostly to families with children and feature a broad array of entertainment offerings including arcade-style and skill-oriented games, rides, live entertainment shows. Entertainment and merchandise account for some 55% of sales. The menu features pizzas, wings, appetizers, salads, and desserts. CEC Entertainment owns and operates more than 550 of the pizza and fun joints, while the rest are franchised.

Bankruptcy
CEC Entertainment, Inc., a nationally recognized leader in family entertainment and dining, announced that, in order to overcome the financial strain resulting from prolonged COVID-19 related venue closures and position the company for long-term success, CEC Entertainment and its domestic affiliates have filed for voluntary protection under Chapter 11 of the U.S. Bankruptcy Code. The company expects to use the time and legal protections made available through the Chapter 11 process to continue discussions with financial stakeholders, as well as critical conversations with its landlords, to achieve a comprehensive balance sheet restructuring that supports its re-opening and longer-term strategic plans.

Operations
Chuck E. Cheese is a highly recognized brand that appeals to primary guest base of families with children between below 5 and 12 years of age. Each venue includes approximately 75 games, rides and attractions for kids of all ages, including classic skill games, such as arcade basketball, skee-ball and Whack-a-Mole, along with the Ticket Blaster machine. Chuck E. Cheese menu features fresh, hand-made pizza, boneless and bone-in chicken wings, desserts and beverages, including beer and wine at most locations.

Peter Piper Pizza serves fresh, handcrafted food and beverages, including craft beer and wine, and offers state-of-the-art games for all ages. Venues feature a bold design and contemporary layout, with open kitchens such as fresh mozzarella being shredded off the block, vegetables being hand-chopped, wings being hand-tossed and its Certified Dough Masters crafting pizzas with made-from-scratch dough. The company's open dining areas provide an enjoyable atmosphere for families and group events, with attentive staff dedicated to providing an enjoyable and memorable experience to each guest.The company's entertainment and merchandise generate approximately 55% of sales, food and beverage generate about 45% of sales, and franchise fees and royalties generate the remaining.

Geographic Reach
The company and its franchisees operate a system of more than 600 Chuck E. Cheese and more than 120 Peter Piper Pizza venues, with locations in over 45 states and more than 15 foreign countries and territories.

Peter Piper Pizza's office is located in Phoenix, Arizona. The company also has a warehouse building in Topeka, Kansas, which primarily serves as a storage, distribution and refurbishing facility for venue fixtures and game equipment. The company's headquarter is located in Irving, Texas.

Sales and Marketing
The Chuck E. Cheese's concept has successfully cemented a place in the family dining market by focusing on the entertainment options available at its restaurants and marketing itself as a safe and convenient place for parents to take the kids. The company's advertising expenses were $45 million and $48.2 million for 2019 and 2018, respectively.

Financial Performance
After a dip in revenue in 2017, the company was back on its tracks and have increased revenue for three consecutive years. The net income for the last five years has been mostly in black. Only in 2017 did they reported a positive income. Net revenue in 2019 increased by 2% to $890 million. The increase in company venue sales was primarily attributable to a 2.7% increase in comparable venue sales, partially offset by a $2.6 million decrease in company venue sales from its non-comparable venues, primarily due to a net reduction of seven company-operated venues over the last two years. Net income loss incurred by the company in 2019 was $28.9 million. The decrease in income were due to higher operating costs and expenses and higher interest expense. Cash at the end of 2019 was $34.8 million. Cash generated by operations was $111.1 million. Investing and financing activities used $87.6 and $52.1 million, respectively. Main cash uses for 2019 were for property and equipment purchases, repayments of loans and repurchases of senior notes.

Strategy
The company's strategic objectives are focused on becoming "the world's leading family - friendly entertainment restaurant brands" by entertaining and inspiring kids around the world and ensuring that every guest is happy. This strategic plan is centered on the following six growth pillars: Increasing traffic to its venues through marketing and sales promotions; Drive in-store guest spending; Pursuing a programmatic approach to our domestic remodel program; Expanding the global franchise network; Launching a division to focus on entertainment & licensing efforts; and Increasing efficiencies and lower operating costs with tight controls.

Also, as part of its long-term growth strategy, the company plans to upgrade the games, rides and entertainment in most of its existing venues, remodel certain of its existing venues and open additional new venues in selected markets. Over the years, the company has made significant changes to its marketing and advertising strategy, including the introduction of an updated Chuck E. Cheese character; change in the mix of its media expenditures, increase in advertising directed to parents, and promoting its brand and reasons to visit on television and online.

Company Background
The Chuck E. Cheese's concept was created by Nolan Bushnell, founder of video game pioneer Atari Corporation, in 1977. Showbiz Pizza acquired the chain in 1984 and changed its name to CEC Entertainment 1998.

Auditors : DELOITTE & TOUCHE LLP DALLAS

LOCATIONS
HQ: OLD CLAIMCO, LLC
 1707 MARKET PL STE 200, IRVING, TX 750638049
Phone: 972 258-8507
Web: WWW.CHUCKECHEESE.COM

2016
 Company-Owned Stores◻ Franchised Stores◻Total ◻

 Domestic◻◻◻
  Chuck E. Cheese's 512◻ 29◻ 541◻
  Peter Piper Pizza 32◻ 62◻ 94◻
 International◻◻◻
  Chuck E. Cheese's 12◻ 39◻ 51◻
  Peter Piper Pizza- ◻46◻ 46◻
 Total 556◻ 176◻ 732◻

PRODUCTS/OPERATIONS
2016 Sales

	$ mil.	% of total
Company store sales		
Entertainment and merchandise sales	497.0	54
Food and beverage sales	408.1	44
Franchise fees and royalties	17.5	2
Total	922.6	100

COMPETITORS
BRINKER INTERNATIONAL, INC.
DOMINO'S PIZZA, INC.
IGNITE RESTAURANT GROUP, INC.
JACK IN THE BOX INC.
MCDONALD'S CORPORATION
PAPA JOHN'S INTERNATIONAL, INC.
RUTH'S HOSPITALITY GROUP, INC.
SONIC CORP.
THE CHEESECAKE FACTORY INCORPORATED
YUM BRANDS, INC.

HISTORICAL FINANCIALS
Company Type: Private

Income Statement　　　　　　　　　　FYE: December 29

	REVENUE ($mil)	NET INCOME ($mil)	NET PROFIT MARGIN	EMPLOYEES
12/19	912	(28)	—	17,200
12/18	896	(20)	—	—
12/17*	886	53	6.0%	—
01/17	923	(3)	—	—
Annual Growth	(0.4%)	—	—	—

*Fiscal year change

2019 Year-End Financials
Return on assets: (-1.4%)　　Cash ($ mil.): 34
Return on equity: (-13.5%)
Current Ratio: 0.60

OLD DURA, INC.

LOCATIONS
HQ: OLD DURA, INC.
 1780 POND RUN, AUBURN HILLS, MI 483262752
Phone: 248 299-7500
Web: WWW.DURAAUTO.COM

HISTORICAL FINANCIALS
Company Type: Private

Income Statement　　　　　　　　　　FYE: December 31

	REVENUE ($mil)	NET INCOME ($mil)	NET PROFIT MARGIN	EMPLOYEES
12/07	1,894	(472)	—	3
12/06	2,090	(910)	—	—
12/05	2,344	1	0.1%	—
12/04	2,492	11	0.5%	—
Annual Growth	(8.7%)	—	—	—

2007 Year-End Financials
Return on assets: (-45.1%)　　Cash ($ mil.): 93
Return on equity: —
Current Ratio: 1.20

OMAHA PUBLIC POWER DISTRICT

Thirteen's the lucky number for Omaha Public Power District (OPPD). A subdivision of the Nebraska state government, OPPD generates and distributes electricity to residents and businesses in 13 counties in southeastern Nebraska. It operates and maintains its facilities without tax revenues and raises money for major construction through bonds. OPPD serves more than 853,000 customers in an area covering 5,000 sq. mi. The utility has a generating capacity of approximately 2,700 MW, which is powered by primarily nuclear, coal, oil, and natural gas sources. It sells wholesale power to other utilities and offers energy consulting and management services.

Operations
The majority of OPPD's power comes from three baseload power plants: North Omaha Station and Nebraska City Station (both coal-fired), and the Fort Calhoun Station nuclear power plant.

Geographic Reach
OPPD is headquartered in Omaha, Nebraska; and serves people in approximately 15 counties within 5,000 sq. miles.

Company Background
It 2011 the utility announced that it was studying how to support both the auto industry and customers regarding the larger numbers of electric cars being introduced into its service region.

OPPD was organized as a self-supporting subdivision of the State of Nebraska in 1946, although state power operations date back to 1917.

EXECUTIVES
Vice Chairman*, Del B Weber
Auditors : BKD LLP OMAHA NEBRASKA

LOCATIONS

HQ: OMAHA PUBLIC POWER DISTRICT
444 S 16TH ST, OMAHA, NE 681022247
Phone: 402 636-2000
Web: WWW.OPPD.COM

COMPETITORS

GEORGIA POWER COMPANY
LOS ANGELES DEPARTMENT OF WATER AND POWER
MUNICIPAL ELECTRIC AUTHORITY OF GEORGIA
OGLETHORPE POWER CORPORATION
PINNACLE WEST CAPITAL CORPORATION
POWERSOUTH ENERGY COOPERATIVE
PPL ELECTRIC UTILITIES CORPORATION
PUBLIC SERVICE COMPANY OF NEW HAMPSHIRE
SACRAMENTO MUNICIPAL UTILITY DISTRICT
TUCSON ELECTRIC POWER COMPANY

HISTORICAL FINANCIALS

Company Type: Private

Income Statement — FYE: December 31

	REVENUE ($mil)	NET INCOME ($mil)	NET PROFIT MARGIN	EMPLOYEES
12/21	1,496	27	1.9%	2,300
12/20	1,083	74	6.8%	—
12/19	1,160	86	7.5%	—
Annual Growth	13.6%	(43.3%)	—	—

2021 Year-End Financials
Return on assets: 0.5%   Cash ($ mil.): 37
Return on equity: 2.1%
Current Ratio: 3.10

OMAHA PUBLIC SCHOOLS

Auditors: SEIM JOHNSON LLP OMAHA NEBR

LOCATIONS

HQ: OMAHA PUBLIC SCHOOLS
3215 CUMING ST, OMAHA, NE 681312000
Phone: 402 557-2120
Web: WWW.OPS.ORG

HISTORICAL FINANCIALS

Company Type: Private

Income Statement — FYE: August 31

	REVENUE ($mil)	NET INCOME ($mil)	NET PROFIT MARGIN	EMPLOYEES
08/18	763	20	2.7%	8,000
08/17	720	33	4.7%	—
08/16	693	(41)	—	—
08/15	626	126	20.3%	—
Annual Growth	6.9%	(45.4%)	—	—

2018 Year-End Financials
Return on assets: 1.4%   Cash ($ mil.): 305
Return on equity: —
Current Ratio: —

ONEOK PARTNERS, L.P.

For ONEOK Partners it's OK to have three businesses: natural gas pipelines; gas gathering and processing; and natural gas liquids (NGLs). Its pipelines include Midwestern Gas Transmission, Guardian Pipeline, Viking Gas Transmission, and OkTex Pipeline. The ONEOK affiliate operates 17,100 miles of gas-gathering pipeline and 7,600 miles of transportation pipeline, as well as gas processing plants and storage facilities (with 52 billion cu. ft. of capacity). It also owns one of the US's top natural NGL systems (more than 7,200 miles of pipeline). In 2017, 41%-owner ONEOK agreed to buy the stock of ONEOK Partners that it did not already own for $9.3 billion in a stock deal. Operations ONEOK Partners operates in three business segments: natural gas gathering and processing; natural gas pipelines; and natural gas liquids. Geographic Reach The company gathers and processes natural gas in the Mid-Continent region, which includes the NGL-rich Cana-Woodford Shale and Granite Wash formations, the Mississippian Lime formation of Oklahoma and Kansas, and the Hugoton and Central Kansas Uplift Basins of Kansas. The Natural Gas Pipelines segment owns and operates regulated natural gas transmission pipelines, natural gas storage facilities and natural gas gathering systems for nonprocessed gas. It also provide interstate natural gas transportation and storage service. The company's interstate natural gas pipeline assets transport natural gas through pipelines in North Dakota, Minnesota, Wisconsin, Illinois, Indiana, Kentucky, Tennessee, Oklahoma, Texas and New Mexico. Its Natural gas liquids assets provide nondiscretionary services to producers that consist of facilities that gather, fractionate, and treat NGLs and store NGL products primarily in Oklahoma, Kansas and Texas. It also owns or has stakes in natural gas liquids gathering and distribution pipelines in Oklahoma, Kansas, Texas, Wyoming and Colorado, and terminal and storage facilities in Missouri, Nebraska, Iowa and Illinois. In addition it owns natural gas liquids distribution and refined petroleum products pipelines in Kansas, Missouri, Nebraska, Iowa, Illinois and Indiana that connect the company's Mid-Continent assets with Midwest markets, including Chicago.

Financial Performance

Revenues decreased by 10% in 2012 due to lower net realized natural gas and NGL product prices, offset partially by higher natural gas and NGL sales volumes from completed capital projects. The increase in natural gas supply resulting from the development of nonconventional resource areas in North America and a warmer than normal winter caused natural gas prices to drop. NGL prices, particularly ethane and propane, also decreased in 2012 due primarily to increased NGL production and an increase in available supply. Propane prices also were affected by a warmer than normal winter.

ONEOK Partners' net income grew by 7% in 2012, thanks to lower costs of sales and fuels and lower interest expenses.

Strategy

The company pursues a strategy of building up its fee-based earnings coupled with organic growth and complementary acquisitions, in both conventional oil and gas and unconventional (shale plays).

It is looking to increase NGL volumes gathered and fractionated in its NGL segment and natural gas volumes processed in its natural gas gathering and processing segment, as producers continue to develop NGL-rich resource plays in the Mid-Continent and Rocky Mountain areas.

In 2012 ONEOK Partners announced plans to invest up to $360 million to grow its projects in the Woodford Shale formation.

Company Background

ONEOK Partners was formed in 2006 when ONEOK spun off its gathering and processing, NGLs, pipelines, and storage businesses for $3 billion, following that company's acquisition of Northern Border Partners (which was founded in 1993). Building out its assets in 2007 the company acquired an interstate pipeline system from Kinder Morgan Energy Partners for $300 million.

LOCATIONS

HQ: ONEOK PARTNERS, L.P.
100 W 5TH ST STE LL, TULSA, OK 741034298
Phone: 918 588-7000
Web: WWW.ONEOK.COM

PRODUCTS/OPERATIONS

Natural Gas Pipelines
Midwestern Gas Transmission Company
Viking Gas Transmission Company
Guardian Pipeline
OkTex Pipeline Company
ONEOK Gas Transportation
ONEOK Gas Gathering
ONEOK Gas Storage
ONEOK WesTex Transmission
ONEOK Texas Gas Storage
Mid Continent Market Center
ONEOK Transmission Company
Natural Gas Gathering & Processing
Crestone Energy Ventures
ONEOK Field Services
ONEOK Rockies Midstream

COMPETITORS

ENERGY TRANSFER LP
ENTERPRISE PRODUCTS PARTNERS L.P.
ETP LEGACY LP
MARKWEST ENERGY PARTNERS, L.P.
TARGA RESOURCES PARTNERS LP

ORANGE AND ROCKLAND UTILITIES, INC.

Orange and Rockland Utilities (O&R) operates under the auspices of its big city cousin, holding company Consolidated Edison (Con Edison). O&R's subsidiaries, Rockland Electric and Pike County Power & Light, operate in southeastern New York and adjacent portions of New Jersey and Pennsylvania. The utilities distribute electricity to more than 301,800 customers in about 100 communities in those three states, and deliver natural gas more than to 128,000 customers in New York and Pennsylvania. O&R's transmission and distribution facilities include 5,550 miles of overhead and underground power distribution lines, 560 miles of transmission lines, and more than 1,850 miles of gas pipeline.

Operations
O&R and its two utility subsidiaries, Rockland Electric Company and Pike County Light & Power Co., deliver power and gas to customers in three states. The electricity O&R sold to its customers in 2011 was purchased under firm power contracts or through the wholesale electricity markets administered by the NYISO and PJM Interconnection LLC.

Geographic Reach
The company serves a population of approximately 750,000 in seven counties in New York, northern New Jersey, and northeastern Pennsylvania. About 75% of O&R's power customers are in the state of New York.

Financial Performance
O&R's revenues increased by 5% in 2011, mainly due to lower purchased power costs and a decrease in gas purchased for resale.

Strategy
As a way to attract more businesses to its New York service area, in 2011 O&R doubled the discount on its electric delivery rate (up from 10% to 20% for five years) for qualified companies.

The company is investing heavily in upgrading its aging infrastructure. In late 2010 the company announced plans to invest $2.6 million over a 13 month period to replace 11,800 feet of 60-year-old, 4-inch steel gas underground distribution pipe with 8-inch, plastic gas pipe across Orange and Rockland counties.

Company Background
When deregulation arrived in O&R's territory in 1999, the energy company exited its power generation activities and sold itself to Con Edison.

LOCATIONS
HQ: ORANGE AND ROCKLAND UTILITIES, INC.
1 BLUE HILL PLZ STE 20, PEARL RIVER, NY 109653100
Phone: 845 352-6000
Web: WWW.ORU.COM

PRODUCTS/OPERATIONS
2011 Sales

	$ mil.	% of total
Electric	641	75
Gas	214	25
Total	855	100

Subsidiaries
Pike County Light & Power Company
Rockland Electric Company

COMPETITORS
CENTERPOINT ENERGY, INC.
COLUMBIA GAS OF OHIO, INC.
EVERSOURCE ENERGY
NEW JERSEY RESOURCES CORPORATION
TECO ENERGY, INC.

HISTORICAL FINANCIALS
Company Type: Private

Income Statement — FYE: December 31

	REVENUE ($mil)	NET INCOME ($mil)	NET PROFIT MARGIN	EMPLOYEES
12/16	653	59	9.1%	1,060
12/05	824	50	6.1%	—
12/04	703	46	6.5%	—
12/03	727	45	6.2%	—
Annual Growth	(0.8%)	2.1%	—	—

2016 Year-End Financials
Return on assets: 2.1%
Return on equity: 9.2%
Current Ratio: 0.50
Cash ($ mil.): —

ORANGE COUNTY HEALTH AUTHORITY, A PUBLIC AGENCY

EXECUTIVES
Chief Medical Officer, Richard Helmer

LOCATIONS
HQ: ORANGE COUNTY HEALTH AUTHORITY, A PUBLIC AGENCY
505 CITY PKWY W, ORANGE, CA 928682924
Phone: 714 246-8500
Web: WWW.CALOPTIMA.ORG

HISTORICAL FINANCIALS
Company Type: Private

Income Statement — FYE: June 30

	REVENUE ($mil)	NET INCOME ($mil)	NET PROFIT MARGIN	EMPLOYEES
06/09	1,078	(17)	—	432
06/05	812	(24)	—	—
06/04	0	0	—	—
06/03	756	1	0.2%	—
Annual Growth	6.1%	—	—	—

2009 Year-End Financials
Return on assets: (-5.2%)
Return on equity: (-13.3%)
Current Ratio: 1.00
Cash ($ mil.): 81

ORANGE COUNTY TRANSPORTATION AUTHORITY SCHOLARSHIP FOUNDATION, INC.

Public transportation in sunny Orange County, California is overseen by the Orange County Transportation Authority (OCTA). The OCTA is the main provider of bus services in its 800-sq.-mi. territory, which is home to more than 3 million people. In cooperation with the Southern California Regional Rail Authority, the OCTA oversees Metrolink commuter rail service in Orange County. The agency also operates a 10-mile toll road and issues permits to taxi operators. Revenue from a half-cent local sales tax allows the agency to pay for road improvement and mass transit projects.

Operations
OCTA builds, designs, operates, plans, maintains, and regulates the robust transportation network within Orange County. In addition to the four modes of transportation (transit, driving, bicycling, and walking) OCTA oversees paratransit services, taxi services, light rail, commuter rail, and high-occupancy managed lanes.

It operates rail service for OCTA centers on Metrolink, Southern California's commuter rail system linking residential communities to employment and activity centers. Metrolink is operated by the Southern California Regional Rail Authority- a

---

HISTORICAL FINANCIALS (Orange and Rockland Utilities)
Company Type: Private

Income Statement — FYE: December 31

	REVENUE ($mil)	NET INCOME ($mil)	NET PROFIT MARGIN	EMPLOYEES
12/16	8,918	1,072	12.0%	2,364
12/15	7,761	597	7.7%	—
12/14	12,191	911	7.5%	—
Annual Growth	(14.5%)	8.5%	—	—

2016 Year-End Financials
Return on assets: 6.9%
Return on equity: 17.4%
Current Ratio: 0.40
Cash ($ mil.): —

joint powers authority of five member agencies representing the counties of Los Angeles, Orange, Riverside, San Bernardino, and Ventura. OCTA is one of the five member agencies that administers Orange County Metrolink activities.

The 91 Express Lanes is a four-lane, 10-mile toll road built in the median of California's Riverside Freeway (SR-91) between the Orange/Riverside County line and the SR-55.

Geographic Reach
The company is located in Southern California - south of Los, Angeles County, north of San Diego, County, and west of Riverside, and San Bernardino counties.

Financial Performance
OCTA's rail budget for fiscal year 2015-16 consists of both operating and capital expenses. Operating expenses in FY 2015-16 are budgeted at $31.6 million, while capital expenditures are anticipated to reach $100.4 million. The FY 2015-16 rail capital projects. The organization saw a decline in its budget for FY 2015-16 due to drop in passenger fares and state assistance federal capital assistance grants.

(OCTA uses its revenue primarily in salaries and benefits, professional services and capital expenditure).

Strategy
The 2014 - 2019 OCTA Strategic Plan takes a comprehensive, forward-looking approach to address Orange County's transportation needs during the next five years.(OCTA maintains a Long-Range Transportation Plan updated every four years to account for new planning efforts, as well as changes in demographics, economic conditions, and available sources of transportation funding).

In the FY 2015-16 budget, $6.9 million of Measure M funds deposited in the General Fund are being used to fund the final work on the West County Connectors project.

After four years in the making, OCTA marked the completion of the $297 million West County Connector project in 2014, which will bring congestion relief where three major freeways (Interstate 405, Interstate 605 and State Route 22) converge.

In 2014 OCTA purchased 400 new buses for fixed-route and ACCESS services. This purchase, combined with the in-process repainting of the existing fleet, presents a cost-effective opportunity to explore new branding concepts for Orange County bus services.

Company Background
OCTA was formed in 1991 in a consolidation of seven transportation agencies.

Auditors : VAVRINEK TRINE DAY & CO LL

LOCATIONS
HQ: ORANGE COUNTY TRANSPORTATION AUTHORITY SCHOLARSHIP FOUNDATION, INC.
550 S MAIN ST, ORANGE, CA 928684506
Phone: 714 636-7433
Web: WWW.OCTA.NET

PRODUCTS/OPERATIONS
2014 Sales

	$ mil	% of total
Sales taxes	451.1	93
Unrestricted investment earning	18.5	4
Property taxes	12.4	3
Other	0.7	-
Total	482.7	100

Selected Services
91 Express Lanes toll facility
Bus transit service
Freeway improvements funding
Freeway Service Patrol
Long-range planning
Measure M2 administration
Metrolink rail service
Rideshare options
Street and road improvements grants
Taxi administration program
Vanpool subsidies

COMPETITORS
CAPITAL METROPOLITAN TRANSPORTATION AUTHORITY
LOS ANGELES COUNTY METROPOLITAN TRANSPORTATION AUTHORITY
MV TRANSPORTATION, INC.
REGIONAL TRANSPORTATION DISTRICT
WASHINGTON METROPOLITAN AREA TRANSIT AUTHORITY

HISTORICAL FINANCIALS
Company Type: Private

Income Statement   FYE: June 30

	REVENUE ($mil)	NET INCOME ($mil)	NET PROFIT MARGIN	EMPLOYEES
06/21	721	(83)	—	1,050
06/20	708	(87)	—	—
06/18	634	(53)	—	—
06/17	611	54	9.0%	—
Annual Growth	4.2%	—	—	—

2021 Year-End Financials
Return on assets: (-2.4%)   Cash ($ mil.): —
Return on equity: (-4.5%)
Current Ratio: 6.20

OREGON DEPARTMENT OF TRANSPORTATION

The Oregon Department of Transportation (ODOT) helps move people and goods across the state. The agency strives to provide a safe and efficient transportation system -- including highway, rail, and public transit -- for its residents. The department is responsible for construction and maintenance of highways and bridges, improving public transportation services, reducing traffic crashes, and ensuring equal access for low-income and elderly citizens, as well as people with disabilities. Its division of driver and motor vehicles (DMV) provides vehicle registration, driver licenses, and ID cards. The agency also tries to decrease the impact that its transportation system has on air and water quality.

LOCATIONS
HQ: OREGON DEPARTMENT OF TRANSPORTATION
355 CAPITOL ST NE MS21, SALEM, OR 973013871
Phone: 503 378-5849
Web: WWW.OREGON.GOV

COMPETITORS
ARKANSAS DEPARTMENT OF TRANSPORTATION
DEPARTMENT OF TRANSPORTATION CALIFORNIA
FEDERAL MOTOR CARRIER SAFETY ADMINISTRATION
NEW JERSEY DEPT OF TRANSPORTATION
NEW MEXICO DEPARTMENT OF TRANSPORTATION

HISTORICAL FINANCIALS
Company Type: Private

Income Statement   FYE: June 30

	REVENUE ($mil)	NET INCOME ($mil)	NET PROFIT MARGIN	EMPLOYEES
06/19	2,260	56	2.5%	4,800
06/18	2,017	23	1.2%	—
06/05	0	0	—	—
06/03	461	(198)	—	—
Annual Growth	10.4%	—	—	—

2019 Year-End Financials
Return on assets: 3.6%   Cash ($ mil.): 958
Return on equity: 5.7%
Current Ratio: 2.40

OREGON HEALTH & SCIENCE UNIVERSITY

Oregon Health & Science University (OHSU) is Oregon's only academic health center and distinguished nationally as a research university dedicated solely to advancing health sciences. OHSU focuses on discoveries to prevent and cure diseases, on education that prepares the health care and health science professionals of the future, and on patient care that incorporates the latest advances. OSHU operates OSHU Hospital; OHSU Doernbecher Children's Hospital Hillsboro Medical Center (formerly Tuality Healthcare); Adventist Health Portland; and clinics across Oregon. OHSU traces its roots to 1867, when members of the medical department at Willamette University began the first formal medical students to its Salem campus.

Geographic Reach
OSHU has facilities in Marquam Hill Campus, Portland (with more than 35 major buildings, OHSU Hospital, Kohler Pavilion and Doernbecher Children's Hospital), South Waterfront Campus, Portland (includes five major buildings) and West Campus, Hillsboro

(OHSU's Oregon National Primate Research Center and The Vaccine and Gene Therapy Institute).

Sales and Marketing

About 95% of its health care patients are from Oregon.

Auditors: KPMG LLP PORTLAND OREGON

LOCATIONS

HQ: OREGON HEALTH & SCIENCE UNIVERSITY
3181 SW SAM JACKSON PK RD, PORTLAND, OR 972393011
Phone: 503 494-8311
Web: WWW.OHSU.EDU

PRODUCTS/OPERATIONS

Selected schools
School of Dentistry
School of Medicine
School of Nursing
School of Pharmacy (with Oregon State University)
School of Science & Engineering

COMPETITORS

BAYLOR COLLEGE OF MEDICINE
CHARLESTON AREA MEDICAL CENTER, INC.
EASTERN VIRGINIA MEDICAL SCHOOL
REGENTS OF THE UNIVERSITY OF MICHIGAN
STONY BROOK UNIVERSITY
UNIVERSITY OF CALIFORNIA, SAN FRANCISCO
UNIVERSITY OF KANSAS
UNIVERSITY OF TEXAS MD ANDERSON CANCER CENTER
UPSTATE MEDICAL UNIVERSITY
VANDERBILT UNIVERSITY MEDICAL CENTER

HISTORICAL FINANCIALS
Company Type: Private

Income Statement — FYE: June 30

	REVENUE ($mil)	NET INCOME ($mil)	NET PROFIT MARGIN	EMPLOYEES
06/22	3,942	(150)	—	19,500
06/20	3,313	(13)	—	—
06/19	3,178	251	7.9%	—
06/18	3,050	259	8.5%	—
Annual Growth	6.6%	—	—	—

2022 Year-End Financials
Return on assets: (-2.2%)   Cash ($ mil.): 262
Return on equity: (-3.8%)
Current Ratio: 2.00

OREGON STATE LOTTERY

The Oregon State Lottery operates the Beaver State's lottery and other state-run games of chance. It offers traditional lotto numbers games and instant-win tickets, and it operates video lottery and video poker machines. Oregon also takes part in the multistate Powerball drawing. About 65% of the lottery's profits are channeled into public education programs, while the rest is used to fund economic development projects, state parks, and other government programs. Oregon created its lottery in 1984.

LOCATIONS

HQ: OREGON STATE LOTTERY
500 AIRPORT RD SE, SALEM, OR 973015068
Phone: 503 540-1000
Web: WWW.OREGONLOTTERY.ORG

COMPETITORS

Atlantic Lottery Corporation Inc
GEORGIA LOTTERY CORPORATION
KENTUCKY LOTTERY CORPORATION
LOUISIANA LOTTERY CORPORATION
MULTI-STATE LOTTERY ASSOCIATION

HISTORICAL FINANCIALS
Company Type: Private

Income Statement — FYE: June 30

	REVENUE ($mil)	NET INCOME ($mil)	NET PROFIT MARGIN	EMPLOYEES
06/20	1,145	(11)	—	420
06/19	1,347	7	0.5%	—
06/18	1,302	(14)	—	—
06/16	1,230	61	5.0%	—
Annual Growth	(1.8%)	—	—	—

2020 Year-End Financials
Return on assets: (-1.8%)   Cash ($ mil.): 172
Return on equity: (-4.3%)
Current Ratio: 1.40

OREGON UNIVERSITY SYSTEM

Auditors: CLIFTONLARSONALLEN LLP GREENW

LOCATIONS

HQ: OREGON UNIVERSITY SYSTEM
, EUGENE, OR 97403
Phone: 541 737-0827
Web: WWW.OUS.EDU

HISTORICAL FINANCIALS
Company Type: Private

Income Statement — FYE: June 30

	REVENUE ($mil)	NET INCOME ($mil)	NET PROFIT MARGIN	EMPLOYEES
06/14	1,782	83	4.7%	26,000
06/13	1,701	14	0.8%	—
06/12	1,657	10	0.6%	—
06/08	1,251	80	6.4%	—
Annual Growth	6.1%	0.6%	—	—

2014 Year-End Financials
Return on assets: 9.8%   Cash ($ mil.): 456
Return on equity: 4.7%
Current Ratio: 1.30

ORLANDO HEALTH, INC.

Orlando Health Orlando Health is a not-for-profit healthcare organization with $7.6 billion of assets under management that serves the southeastern US. It has about 3,200 beds that includes some15 wholly-owned hospitals and emergency departments; rehabilitation services, cancer institutes, heart institutes, physician offices for adults and pediatrics and more. Its flagship facility, the Orlando Regional Medical Center, is a Level 1 trauma center and provides comprehensive acute care services in a range of specialties. Orlando Health is also home to the only state-accredited Level 2 Adult Trauma Center in the St. Petersburg region at Bayfront Health St. Petersburg. Orlando Health Winnie Palmer Hospital for Women & Babies houses the nation's largest neonatal intensive care unit.

Operations

Diagnostic services include pathology and laboratory medicine, radiology and diagnostic imaging, and nuclear medicine, with an array of invasive and noninvasive testing, such as angiography, bone density scan, CT scan, mammography, MRI, ultrasound and X-ray.

In addition to diagnostic services, Orlando Health provide a comprehensive range of outpatient medical services in an environment that offers more convenience and less stress for its patients and families. Outpatient services include advanced catheterization, surgical and endoscopic procedures, neurodiagnostics, cardiology, wound care, and rehabilitation therapy.

Orlando Health hospitals are Bayfront Health St. Petersburg, Orlando Health Arnold Palmer Hospital for Children, Orlando Health Dr. P. Phillips Hospital, Orlando Health ? Health Central Hospital, Orlando Health Horizon West Hospital, Orlando Health Orlando Regional Medical Center; Orlando Health South Lake Hospital; Orlando Health South Seminole Hospital, Orlando Health St. Cloud Hospital and Orlando Health Winnie Palmer Hospital for Women & Babies.

Orlando Health operates the National Training Center for Olympic athletes and the Orlando Health Network, which is recognized as one of the largest and highest performing clinically integrated networks in the region. The system's Graduate Medical Education (GME) program hosts more than 350 residents and fellows including more than 40 who are enrolled at Bayfront Health St. Petersburg.

Geographic Reach

Based in Orlando, Florida, Orlando Health has eight primary facility locations within Central Florida.

Sales and Marketing

Orlando Health served nearly 160,000 inpatients and nearly 3.6 million outpatients.

Mergers and Acquisitions

In 2021, Orlando Health acquires Leesburg-based FHV health for undisclosed price. The multispecialty medical group has 19 physicians and 10 locations, including primary care, cardiology practices and urgent care facilities in Lake, Sumton Marion counties. The acquisition will expand its presence in those three counties and advance FHV Health's ability.

Company Background

In 2012 Arnold Palmer Hospital added an outpatient rehabilitation center.

The health system expanded its network in 2012 by acquiring the 170-bed Health Central Hospital and its associated facilities in Ocoee, Florida, for $181 million. Orlando Health further expanded through the purchase of Physician Associates, a professional practice organization, in 2013.

Orlando Health was founded in 1918.

Auditors : GRANT THORNTON LLP ORLANDO F

LOCATIONS

HQ: ORLANDO HEALTH, INC.
52 W UNDERWOOD ST, ORLANDO, FL 328061110
Phone: 407 841-5111
Web: WWW.ORLANDOHEALTH.COM

PRODUCTS/OPERATIONS

2014 Sales

	$ mil	% of total
Net patient service revenue less provision for bad debts	2,010.9	95
Other revenue	103.7	5
Net assets released from restrictions	4.0	-
Total	2,118.6	100

Selected Facilities
Arnold Palmer Hospital for Children (Orlando)
Dr. P. Phillips Hospital (formerly Orlando Regional Sand Lake Hospital, Orlando)
Health Central Hospital (Ocoee)
Lucerne Pavilion (Orlando)
M. D. Anderson Cancer Center Orlando
Orlando Health Heart Institute
Orlando Health Rehabilitation Institute
Orlando Regional Medical Center
South Lake Hospital (50%, affiliate, Clermont)
South Seminole Hospital (Longwood)
St. Cloud Regional Medical Center (20%, affiliate)
Winnie Palmer Hospital for Women & Babies (Orlando)

Selected Specialties
Cancer care (at M. D. Anderson Cancer Center Orlando)
Emergency and trauma care
Heart and vascular
Neurosciences
Oncology/hematology
Orthopedic and sports medicine
Surgery
Women's services

Selected Services
Anesthesiology
Brain Injury Rehabilitation Center (BIRC)
Endocrinology (diabetes)
Endoscopy
Epilepsy care
Home health care
Infectious diseases
Internal medicine
Laboratory and pathology Services
Mammography
Memory Disorder Center
MRI
Multiple sclerosis treatment
Nephrology
Nuclear medicine
Ophthalmology
Otolaryngology (Ears, Nose, Throat)
Pain management
Patient and family counseling
Pediatric outpatient surgery
Pulmonary medicine
Radiology and diagnostic imaging
Rehabilitation and physical therapy

COMPETITORS

BAPTIST HEALTH SOUTH FLORIDA, INC.
CHARLESTON AREA MEDICAL CENTER, INC.
NASSAU HEALTH CARE CORPORATION
NORTHWELL HEALTH, INC.
SHANDS JACKSONVILLE MEDICAL CENTER, INC.
TALLAHASSEE MEMORIAL HEALTHCARE, INC.
UNIVERSITY HEALTH SYSTEM SERVICES OF TEXAS, INC.
UNIVERSITY HEALTH SYSTEMS OF EASTERN CAROLINA, INC.
UNIVERSITY HOSPITALS HEALTH SYSTEM, INC.
WELLMONT HEALTH SYSTEM

HISTORICAL FINANCIALS
Company Type: Private

Income Statement   FYE: September 30

	REVENUE ($mil)	NET INCOME ($mil)	NET PROFIT MARGIN	EMPLOYEES
09/20	2,561	652	25.5%	23,000
09/19	2,756	508	18.5%	—
09/14	1,663	231	13.9%	—
09/13	1,576	115	7.3%	—
Annual Growth	7.2%	28.0%	—	—

2020 Year-End Financials
Return on assets: 12.8%   Cash ($ mil.): 492
Return on equity: 25.2%
Current Ratio: 1.50

ORLEANS PARISH SCHOOL DISTRICT

Auditors : LA PORTE METAIRIE LA

LOCATIONS

HQ: ORLEANS PARISH SCHOOL DISTRICT
3520 GEN DE GAULLE STE 5, NEW ORLEANS, LA 70114
Phone: 504 304-3520
Web: PREVIOUS.OPSB.US

HISTORICAL FINANCIALS
Company Type: Private

Income Statement   FYE: June 30

	REVENUE ($mil)	NET INCOME ($mil)	NET PROFIT MARGIN	EMPLOYEES
06/19	626	10	1.6%	7,062
06/17	433	(0)	0.0%	—
06/16	473	46	9.8%	—
06/05	419	19	4.7%	—
Annual Growth	2.9%	(4.7%)	—	—

2019 Year-End Financials
Return on assets: 0.5%   Cash ($ mil.): 33
Return on equity: 0.6%
Current Ratio: —

OSF HEALTHCARE SYSTEM

OSF Healthcare helps patients who are feeling oh-so-frail in northern Illinois and southwestern Michigan. OSF Healthcare system includes 11 acute care hospitals and one long-term care facility that combined are home to more than 1,500 beds and offer a full spectrum of inpatient and outpatient medical and surgical services. The system's primary care physician network consists of about 650 physicians at more than 105 locations throughout its service area. Subsidiary OSF Home Care provides hospice, home visit, and equipment services, and OSF Saint Francis provides ambulance, pharmacy, and health care management services. The not-for-profit system is a subsidiary of the Sisters of The Third Order of St. Francis.

Operations

Along with its various acute care hospitals, OSF Healthcare provides urgent care through its OSF PromptCare locations. PromptCare administers a range of services including labs, MRI, ultrasound, and primary and specialty care.

The company also has two colleges of nursing -- Saint Francis Medical Center College of Nursing in Peoria, Illinois; and the Saint Anthony College of Nursing in Rockford, Illinois.

The system had some 58,000 inpatient admissions; 1.3 million outpatient visits; and 254,000 emergency department visits in 2014.

Financial Performance

In 2014, gross patient services revenue totaled $6.9 billion.

Strategy

OSF Healthcare has an incubation collaboration with the University of Illinois College of Medicine at Peoria. The venture, dubbed Jump Trading Simulation and Education Center, was established in 2013 to focus on advances in education, research, and innovation. It has been involved in such activities as funding 3-D printing for surgical procedures and exposing high school students to medical training experiences.

EXECUTIVES

CMO*, Harley Brooks
Auditors : KPMG LLP CHICAGO ILLINOIS

LOCATIONS

HQ: OSF HEALTHCARE SYSTEM
124 SW ADAMS ST, PEORIA, IL 616021308

Phone: 309 655-2850
Web: WWW.OSFHEALTHCARE.ORG

PRODUCTS/OPERATIONS

Selected Clinical Services
Cancer Care
Diabetes & Endocrinology
Emergency Services
Heart & Vascular
Home Health
Hospice
Neurosciences
Pediatrics
Primary Care
Rehabilitation
Surgery
Transplant Services
Weight Loss Management
Women's Health

Selected Support Services
Advance Care Planning
Clinical Research
Equipment Technology Services
Home Infusion Pharmacy
Home Medical Equipment
Mobile Medical Systems
OSF Life Flight
Retail Services
Skilled Nursing Network
System Laboratory
Telehealth

Selected Facilities
OSF Holy Family Medical Center (Monmouth, IL)
OSF Saint Anthony Medical Center (Rockford, IL)
OSF Saint Clare Home (Peoria Heights, IL)
OSF Saint Elizabeth Medical Center (formerly Ottowa Regional Hospital, Ottowa, IL)
OSF Saint Francis Medical Center (Peoria, IL)
OSF Saint James - John W. Albrecht Medical Center (Pontiac, IL)
OSF St. Mary Medical Center (Galesburg, IL)
OSF St. Francis Hospital (Escanaba, MI)
OSF St. Joseph Medical Center (Bloomington, IL)

COMPETITORS

ATLANTIC HEALTH SYSTEM INC.
BEAUMONT HEALTH
HALLMARK HEALTH CORPORATION
MARSHFIELD CLINIC HEALTH SYSTEM, INC.
MEDSTAR HEALTH, INC.
SAINT JOSEPH HOSPITAL, INC
THE JOHNS HOPKINS HEALTH SYSTEM CORPORATION
THE NEBRASKA MEDICAL CENTER
TRINITAS REGIONAL MEDICAL CENTER A NEW JERSEY NONPROFIT CORPORATION
WILLIAM BEAUMONT HOSPITAL

HISTORICAL FINANCIALS
Company Type: Private

Income Statement — FYE: September 30

	REVENUE ($mil)	NET INCOME ($mil)	NET PROFIT MARGIN	EMPLOYEES
09/19	2,622	354	13.5%	4,360
09/18	2,826	155	5.5%	—
09/17	2,561	144	5.7%	—
09/16	2,422	99	4.1%	—
Annual Growth	2.7%	52.9%	—	—

2019 Year-End Financials
Return on assets: 9.3%   Cash ($ mil.): 136
Return on equity: 24.2%
Current Ratio: 2.50

OU MEDICINE, INC.

Auditors: ERNST & YOUNG LLP OKLAHOMA C

LOCATIONS

HQ: OU MEDICINE, INC.
700 NE 13TH ST, OKLAHOMA CITY, OK 731045004
Phone: 405 271-6035
Web: WWW.OUHEALTH.COM

HISTORICAL FINANCIALS
Company Type: Private

Income Statement — FYE: June 30

	REVENUE ($mil)	NET INCOME ($mil)	NET PROFIT MARGIN	EMPLOYEES
06/22	1,944	22	1.2%	2,900
06/21	1,415	(27)	—	—
06/20	1,298	48	3.7%	—
06/19	1,213	12	1.0%	—
Annual Growth	17.0%	23.4%	—	—

2022 Year-End Financials
Return on assets: 1.1%   Cash ($ mil.): 263
Return on equity: 9.3%
Current Ratio: 1.80

OUR LADY OF THE LAKE HOSPITAL, INC.

Our Lady of the Lake Regional Medical Center reaches out to Baton Rouge residents with a helping hand. Participating in teaching programs for LSU and Tulane medical schools, the medical center has some 800 inpatient beds and includes trauma emergency, surgery, general medical, and specialty care centers for conditions including heart disease, cancer, orthopedics, and ENT (ear, nose, and throat) disorders. Our Lady of the Lake also includes a Children's Hospital, two nursing homes, and an independent-living facility, and it offers outpatient services at its main campus and at satellite facilities throughout the greater Baton Rouge area.

Operations
The hospital's family of services include an 800-bed Regional Medical Center; a dedicated Children's Hospital; a 350-provider Physician Group primary care network, free-standing emergency room in Livingston Parish; an outpatient imaging and surgery centers; Assumption Community Hospital; a network of urgent care clinics; and Our Lady of the Lake College.

Our Lady of the Lake is a primary teaching site for graduate medical education programs and serves 45,000 inpatients and 350,000 outpatients a year.

The company has more than 850 doctors. Some 70% of its physicians and other professional medical staff members are board certified, and in nearly one-third of the hospital system's medical specialty areas, 100% of the physicians and other professionals are board certified.

Strategy
As a major facility in the Baton Rouge area, Our Lady of the Lake has been expanding its services in the region in recent years. In 2015, Our Lady of the Lake Children's Hospital opened its first pediatric specialty clinic outside of the Baton Rouge area, offering specialized outpatient care for pediatric gastroenterology patients.

In 2014 the company opened a new children's emergency room and expanded its adult emergency department.

Company Background
In 2012 the hospital constructed a freestanding emergency room facility in the suburban community of Livingston, Louisiana. It is also building a new nine-story patient tower to the main hospital campus; the tower will house the heart and vascular center, as well as an expanded ER and a new level 1 regional trauma center, and will be completed in late 2013.

Our Lady of the Lake has also expanded its education programs. For instance, it added a pediatric residency program in 2010. The hospital also moved to extend its relationship with LSU that year by agreeing to become the primary clinical site for the LSU medical school. The agreement came as LSU considered whether to build a replacement hospital for its aging teaching facility and coincides with the Our Lady of the Lake expansion projects. The partnership launched a new psychiatric residency program in 2012.

Our Lady of the Lake was founded in 1923 by the Franciscan Missionaries of Our Lady.

Auditors: KPMG LLP BATON ROUGE LOUISI

LOCATIONS

HQ: OUR LADY OF THE LAKE HOSPITAL, INC.
5000 HENNESSY BLVD, BATON ROUGE, LA 708084375
Phone: 225 765-6565
Web: WWW.OLOLRMC.COM

PRODUCTS/OPERATIONS

Selected Services
Advanced Wound and Ostomy Clinic
Cancer
Children's Hospital
Critical Care
Diabetes & Nutrition Center
Emergency Services
Endoscopy Center
Hearing and Balance Center
Heart & Vascular Institute
Imaging Services
Laboratory and Diagnostics
Lake Express Check-In
LSU Health Baton Rouge
Mental and Behavioral Health
Neurology, Neurosurgery and Stroke
Orthopedics
Palliative Care
Pharmacy
Rehabilitation Center
Respiratory Care

Senior Services
St. Anthony's Home
Surgery
Trauma Center
Urgent Care
Voice Center
Weight Loss

COMPETITORS

EISENHOWER MEDICAL CENTER
JERSEY CITY MEDICAL CENTER (INC)
LOMA LINDA UNIVERSITY MEDICAL CENTER
THE UNIVERSITY OF CHICAGO MEDICAL CENTER
VIRTUA OUR LADY OF LOURDES HOSPITAL, INC.

HISTORICAL FINANCIALS
Company Type: Private

Income Statement — FYE: June 30

	REVENUE ($mil)	NET INCOME ($mil)	NET PROFIT MARGIN	EMPLOYEES
06/20	1,526	(18)	—	1,800
06/19	1,467	33	2.3%	—
06/18	1,254	103	8.2%	—
06/16	895	(89)	—	—
Annual Growth	14.3%	—	—	—

2020 Year-End Financials
Return on assets: (-0.7%)   Cash ($ mil.): 383
Return on equity: (-1.6%)
Current Ratio: 1.90

OVERLAKE HOSPITAL ASSOCIATION

Auditors: KPMG LLP SEATTLE WA

LOCATIONS

HQ: OVERLAKE HOSPITAL ASSOCIATION
1035 116TH AVE NE, BELLEVUE, WA 980044604
Phone: 425 688-5000
Web: WWW.OVERLAKEHOSPITAL.ORG

HISTORICAL FINANCIALS
Company Type: Private

Income Statement — FYE: June 30

	REVENUE ($mil)	NET INCOME ($mil)	NET PROFIT MARGIN	EMPLOYEES
06/22	642	(134)	—	100
06/21	607	91	15.1%	—
06/20	579	(0)	—	—
06/19	574	48	8.4%	—
Annual Growth	3.8%	—	—	—

2022 Year-End Financials
Return on assets: (-12.4%)   Cash ($ mil.): 16
Return on equity: (-23.6%)
Current Ratio: 1.00

OVERLAKE HOSPITAL MEDICAL CENTER

Over the lake and through the sound to Overlake Hospital Medical Center we go! The not-for-profit hospital provides health care services to residents of Bellevue, Washington, in the Puget Sound region. The nearly 350-bed facility provides comprehensive inpatient and outpatient services ranging from cancer care and surgery to specialized senior care. Overlake also operates a number of outpatient clinics providing primary care, urgent care, and specialty care such as weight loss surgery. The organization also provides patients with health and wellness programs, addressing issues like women's and children's health.

Operations
The medical center has more than 1,000 physicians on staff and runs Centers of Excellence in cardiac care, cancer care, surgical services, women's and infants' care, and emergency and Level III trauma care. The facility is home to a 24-hour urgent care clinic, an anticoagulation clinic, and a breast screening center. Overlake also operates numerous outpatient clinics providing primary care, urgent care, and specialty care.

Geographic Reach
Overlake provides health care services to residents of Bellevue, Washington, and the entire Puget Sound region. It operates clinics on its main campus in Bellevue, as well as in Redmond and in Issaquah and on Mercer Island.

Sales and Marketing
In 2014, Medicare payments accounted for 27% of net patient revenues, followed by group health organizations (17%), Premera (13%), and Regence (12%).

Financial Performance
Overlake's revenues increased by 2% to $433 million in 2014 as the result of higher net patient revenues and contribution revenues.

Net income rose 50% to $60 million that year, primarily due to income from change in net unrealized gains on investments. Cash flow from operations fell 3% to $47 million as more cash was used in net clinic accounts receivable, pledges receivable, prepaid expenses, and other long-term receivables.

Strategy
Increasing demand in the region has led the hospital to invest in expansions and equipment upgrades that include more emergency treatment capabilities and an on-campus helistop for trauma patients being airlifted to the area.

Along with its expansion and construction projects, Overlake is investing in new technology to keep the health system in line with its competitors and to improve patient care. It is adding endoscopic video towers to its operating rooms to facilitate improved views of surgical procedures and is also moving to digitize all of its facilities with electronic health records.

In 2013 it opened the new $17.4 million David and Shelley Hovind Heart & Vascular center. The new 19,200-sq.-ft. facility brings cardiac and vascular services together in one location.

Overlake has also focused on adding new primary care clinics and expanding its physician network to serve patients in locations closer to where they live and work.

Company Background
Overlake, founded in 1960, is led by CEO Craig Hendrickson, a veteran health care executive.

Auditors: KPMG LLP SEATTLE WA

LOCATIONS

HQ: OVERLAKE HOSPITAL MEDICAL CENTER
1035 116TH AVE NE, BELLEVUE, WA 980044604
Phone: 425 688-5000
Web: WWW.OVERLAKEHOSPITAL.ORG

Selected Locations
Outpatient Rehabilitation Services
Outpatient Surgery (park in the West Garage; Outpatient Surgery is located on the first floor of the West Garage.)
Overlake Bellevue Campus and Overlake Medical Clinics Medical Tower
Overlake Medical Clinics Downtown Bellevue
Overlake Medical Clinics Issaquah
Overlake Medical Clinics Kirkland
Overlake Medical Clinics Redmond
Urgent Care Clinic in Issaquah
Urgent Care Clinic in Redmond

PRODUCTS/OPERATIONS

2014 Sales

	$ mil	% of total
Net patient service revenue	419.7	97
Other operating revenue	11.2	3
Contribution revenue	2.3	-
Total	433.2	100

Selected Medical Services
Breast Health Services
Cancer Center at Overlake
Cardiac Center at Overlake
Clinical Trials
Emergency & Trauma Center
Medical Imaging
Overlake Medical Clinics
Surgical Services
Weight Loss Surgery
Women's & Infants' Center

COMPETITORS

COVENANT MEDICAL CENTER, INC.
INTEGRIS HEALTH, INC.
THE LANCASTER GENERAL HOSPITAL
THE RUTLAND HOSPITAL INC ACT 220
WELLSTAR HEALTH SYSTEM, INC.

HISTORICAL FINANCIALS
Company Type: Private

Income Statement — FYE: June 30

	REVENUE ($mil)	NET INCOME ($mil)	NET PROFIT MARGIN	EMPLOYEES
06/21	601	86	14.4%	2,450
06/20	574	(3)	—	—
06/19	570	45	8.0%	—
06/18	555	39	7.1%	—
Annual Growth	2.7%	30.1%	—	—

PACE UNIVERSITY

Students can learn at their own pace at Pace University, which offers certificate programs as well as undergraduate, graduate, and doctoral degrees through half a dozen schools: arts and sciences, business, computer science and information systems, education, law, and nursing. Altogether, the school is home to 100 undergraduate majors offering roughly 30 undergraduate and graduate degrees, 50 master's programs, and four doctoral programs. Nearly 13,000 students attend the university's three New York campuses (Lower Manhattan, Pleasantville-Briarcliff, and White Plains). Pace was founded in 1906 by the brothers Homer and Charles Pace as a co-educational business school called Pace Institute.

Operations
The school has an endowment of more than $100 million. Besides its three New York campuses, the university also offers courses online and at a location in midtown Manhattan.

Geographic Reach
Pace boasts campus locations in New York City and in Westchester County.

Financial Performance
The university logged a 3% increase in revenue in 2012 as compared to 2011 due to a boost in contributions as well as tuition and fees net government grants and contracts. Net income, meanwhile, dropped by 160% during the same reporting period thanks to rises in expenses and unrealized depreciation in fair value of derivative instruments in 2012 vs. appreciation in 2011.

Company Background
In 1948 Pace began its transformation into its current incarnation as a liberal arts and sciences college.

EXECUTIVES
Legal Counsel*, Stephen Brodsky
DIVERSITY*, Tiffany Hamilton
Auditors: KPMG LLP NEW YORK NY

LOCATIONS
HQ: PACE UNIVERSITY
1 PACE PLZ, NEW YORK, NY 100381598
Phone: 212 346-1956
Web: WWW.PACE.EDU

COMPETITORS
CHAPMAN UNIVERSITY
DELAWARE STATE UNIVERSITY
MANHATTANVILLE COLLEGE
OAKLAND UNIVERSITY
UNIVERSITY OF NEW HAVEN, INCORPORATED

2021 Year-End Financials
Return on assets: 7.5% Cash ($ mil.): 22
Return on equity: 12.8%
Current Ratio: 1.00

PACIFIC COAST PRODUCERS

Fruits, seafood sauces, and organic tomato puree -- rather than movies -- are the creative output of this particular group of Pacific Coast Producers. The cooperative markets the apricots, grapes, peaches, pears, and tomatoes grown by its approximately 160 California-based members. It turns the produce into private-label canned fruit, sauces, and juices and sells them to the retail and foodservice industries. Pacific Coast Producers typically serves retailers the likes of Albertson's, Aldi, Kroger, Safeway, SUPERVALU, Whole Foods, and Wal-Mart, as well as the US Department of Agriculture. The company, founded in 1971, operates three production sites and one distribution center in California.

Operations
The cooperative boasts three food-processing facilities in California, as well as distribution centers in California and Washington.

Geographic Reach
From its base in Lodi, California, Pacific Coast Producers grows its fruits in California and sells them nationwide.

Sales and Marketing
Pacific Coast Producers sells the products it grows and processes to retailers and foodservice operators nationwide, as well as to the US Department of Agriculture.

Financial Performance
As one of California's premier private label packers, Pacific Coast Producers has logged annual sales in excess of $535 million, plus $100 million in alliance income.

Strategy
Pacific Coast Producers has expanded its warehouse space in Lodi to improve efficiency and boost capacity. The move cost the company $23 million. It expanded its distribution center by 50% to meet rising demand for canned food.

The cooperative serves tomato processor Morning Star through a sales and marketing alliance it formed with the company in 2009. As part of the collaboration, Pacific Coast Producers provides canned tomatoes to the retail and foodservice industries.

Auditors: KPMG LLP SACRAMENTO CALIFORN

LOCATIONS
HQ: PACIFIC COAST PRODUCERS
631 N CLUFF AVE, LODI, CA 952400756
Phone: 209 367-8800
Web: WWW.PACIFICCOASTPRODUCERS.COM

PRODUCTS/OPERATIONS
Selected Products
Apricots
Catsup
Chili Sauces
Chunky Mixed Fruit
Concentrated Crushed Tomatoes
Diced Style Tomatoes
Extra Heavy Concentrated Crushed Round Tomato Puree
Formulated Pizza Sauces
Fruit Cocktail
Fruit for Salad
Fruit Mix
Ground Tomatoes
Marinara Sauces
Non-Formulated Pizza Sauce
Organic Tomatoes
Peaches
Pears
Random Cut / Strip Style Tomatoes
Seafood Sauces
Stewed Style Tomatoes
Tomato Juice
Whole Peeled Tomatoes

COMPETITORS
BELL-CARTER FOODS, LLC
CHERRY CENTRAL COOPERATIVE, INC.
COUNTRY PURE FOODS, INC.
FURMAN FOODS, INC.
Fresh Del Monte Produce Inc.
JOHANNA FOODS, INC.
LAKESIDE FOODS, INC.
NORTH PACIFIC CANNERS & PACKERS, INC.
SEABOARD FOODS LLC
SENECA FOODS CORPORATION

HISTORICAL FINANCIALS
Company Type: Private

Income Statement — FYE: June 30

	REVENUE ($mil)	NET INCOME ($mil)	NET PROFIT MARGIN	EMPLOYEES
06/20	597	14	2.5%	1,862
06/16	393	14	3.7%	—
06/14	492	26	5.4%	—
06/13	326	20	6.2%	—
Annual Growth	9.0%	(4.4%)	—	—

2020 Year-End Financials
Return on assets: 2.1% Cash ($ mil.): 22
Return on equity: 4.7%
Current Ratio: 0.20

Income Statement — FYE: May 31

	REVENUE ($mil)	NET INCOME ($mil)	NET PROFIT MARGIN	EMPLOYEES
05/21	864	47	5.5%	1,000
05/20	911	27	3.0%	—
05/19	806	-14	1.8%	—
05/18	668	22	3.4%	—
Annual Growth	9.0%	27.5%	—	—

2021 Year-End Financials
Return on assets: 8.6% Cash ($ mil.): 2
Return on equity: 17.7%
Current Ratio: 1.80

PACIFIC PREMIER BANK

EXECUTIVES

CRO*, Michael Karr
CCO*, Donn Jakosky
Chief Accounting Officer*, Lori Wright

LOCATIONS

HQ: PACIFIC PREMIER BANK
17901 VON KARMAN AVE # 1, IRVINE, CA 926146253
Phone: 714 431-4000
Web: WWW.PPBI.COM

HISTORICAL FINANCIALS
Company Type: Private

Income Statement — FYE: December 31

	ASSETS ($mil)	NET INCOME ($mil)	INCOME AS % OF ASSETS	EMPLOYEES
12/17	8,022	68	0.9%	104
12/16	4,035	44	1.1%	—
12/15	2,782	29	1.1%	—
12/14	2,033	18	0.9%	—
Annual Growth	58.0%	54.0%	—	—

2017 Year-End Financials
Return on assets: 0.9%   Cash ($ mil.): 200
Return on equity: 5.1%
Current Ratio: —

PAN AMERICAN HEALTH ORGANIZATION INC

LOCATIONS

HQ: PAN AMERICAN HEALTH ORGANIZATION INC
525 23RD ST NW, WASHINGTON, DC 200372825
Phone: 202 974-3000
Web: WWW.PAHO.ORG

HISTORICAL FINANCIALS
Company Type: Private

Income Statement — FYE: December 31

	REVENUE ($mil)	NET INCOME ($mil)	NET PROFIT MARGIN	EMPLOYEES
12/09	1,268	101	8.0%	1,288
12/06	541	84	15.7%	—
Annual Growth	32.9%	6.2%	—	—

2009 Year-End Financials
Return on assets: 0.9%   Cash ($ mil.): 351
Return on equity: 8.0%
Current Ratio: 14.00

PANDUIT CORP.

Panduit creates leading-edge physical, electrical, network infrastructure and AV solutions for enterprise-wide environments, from the data center to the telecom room, from the desktop to the plant floor. Products include cabling, connectors, copper wire, fiber-optic components, cabinets and racks, grounding systems, outlets, terminals, and other electrical components. Panduit's products are used in data centers, office buildings, single pair Ethernet, wire harness and other settings. With approximately 2,000 patents, the privately held company also serves about 90% of the Fortune 100 companies.

Operations
Panduit provides infrastructure products and services for data networks and electrical power applications. Its industrial electrical and network infrastructure ensures smart, scalable, and efficient connectivity solutions. The company designs, builds, installs, and services innovative solutions ranging from data centers and office facilities to plant floors and processing lines.

In addition to wire termination, fiber optic systems, power, environmental, security and connectivity hardware and wire routing, management and protection, Panduit also offers audio visual, monitoring, signs, labels and identification, among others.

With nearly 20 laboratories, the company's world-class innovation center houses research, design, analysis, prototyping, testing, and manufacturing capabilities that lead to smarter solutions.

Geographic Reach
Headquartered in Illinois, Panduit operates across the US, Canada, Europe, Middle East and Africa, Latin America, and Asia Pacific.

Sales and Marketing
Panduit serves customers in education, healthcare, oil and gas, renewable energy, transportation, food and beverage and financial industries.

Strategy
In early 2021, as bandwidth speeds continue to increase, 200G/400G applications are becoming commonplace in high performance data center environments, requiring enhanced capabilities at the rack level. Panduit launched the CSConnector, a high-density fiber connector solution that optimizes the data center for next generation applications. Its compact size enables breakout mode options and improves compute density for 25G-400G deployments. The CS Connector is available for unitary Singlemode and Multimode fiber options.

Around the same time, Panduit Corp. signed a partner agreement with Cailabs, a French deep tech company and global leader in light beam shaping, for the global rights to integrate Cailabs technology within Panduit's innovative OneModeTM product portfolio. This is a far-reaching partnership that includes, among other elements of the relationship, exclusive use of the technology for the K-12 (kindergarten through 12th grade) education market in the United States.

Panduit's OneMode is a passive media converter allowing the deployment of 10 Gbps, 50 Gbps, and faster, using existing multimode fibers, by eliminating modal dispersion. This innovation provides a flexible and affordable solution that reduces the investment in upgrading the multimode cabling infrastructure. Regardless of the network topology, OneMode can transport 10 Gbps or more, and can support the evolution in network traffic, without long, complex, and expensive new cable deployment. OneMode is attractive to the K-12, university, healthcare, enterprise, industrial, and other campus markets because they do not need to trench or rip and replace with new fiber to upgrade their network infrastructure.

Company Background
Panduit was established in 1955 by Jack Caveney, Sr. Its first product was the Panduct Wiring Duct.

EXECUTIVES

Chief Commercial Officer*, Marc Naese
Auditors : GRANT THORNTON LLP CHICAGO I

LOCATIONS

HQ: PANDUIT CORP.
18900 PANDUIT DR, TINLEY PARK, IL 604873600
Phone: 708 532-1800
Web: WWW.PANDUIT.COM

PRODUCTS/OPERATIONS

PRODUCTS
Cabinets, Thermal Management, Racks and Enclosures
Cable and Wire Bundling
Cable Routing and Pathways
Copper Systems
Fiber Systems
Grounding
Identification
Japan Market Only Products
Power Distribution and Environmental Monitoring
Product Promotions
Safety and Security
Software and Hardware
Tools
Wire Routing, Protection and Insulation
Wire Termination
SOFTWARE/INTELLIGENCE
DCIM
6 Zone™ Methodology
Data Center Management
Enterprise Management
Intelligent Hardware
Intelligent Software
SmartZone Overview
PROFESSIONAL SERVICES
Case Studies
Industrial Automation Services
Safety Services

COMPETITORS

AMPLICON LIVELINE LIMITED

APOLLO FIRE DETECTORS LIMITED
COMPX INTERNATIONAL INC.
ECHELON CORPORATION
HUBBELL INCORPORATED
IPG PHOTONICS CORPORATION
March Networks Corporation
SOUTHWIRE COMPANY, LLC
TT ELECTRONICS IOT SOLUTIONS LIMITED
VERTIV CORPORATION

HISTORICAL FINANCIALS
Company Type: Private

Income Statement — FYE: December 31

	REVENUE ($mil)	NET INCOME ($mil)	NET PROFIT MARGIN	EMPLOYEES
12/16	937	0	0.0%	5,110
12/15	924	0	0.0%	—
12/14	973	0	0.0%	—
Annual Growth	(1.9%)	—	—	—

PAREXEL INTERNATIONAL CORPORATION

Parexel is a leading global clinical research organization (CRO) focused on development and delivery of innovative new therapies to advance patient health. It provides the clinical development capabilities and integrated consulting expertise it takes to streamline development every step of the way ? faster and more cost-effectively. Parexel has operations in North and South America, Europe, Middle and Africa, and Asia. In 2021, Parexel announced the completion of its acquisition by EQT IX fund (EQT Private Equity) and funds managed by the Private Equity business within Goldman Sachs Asset Management from Pamplona Capital Management LP for $8.5 billion.

Operations
Parexel solutions include clinical research services, consulting, outsourcing services, medical communications, medical affairs and real-world data sciences.

In clinical research services, Parexel provides the comprehensive clinical development services, from First-in-Human through Phase IV and post-marketing follow-through. It also has the regulatory consulting expertise, clinical trial operations management, payer and market access planning, medical communications and education capabilities.

With Parexel's Regulatory & Access consulting organization client can get access to industry luminaries, including ~100 Former regulators/HTA Professionals. Its Real-World Data Sciences solutions help customers identify fit-for-purpose data to solve problems at each stage of development, including business and strategy consulting, genomics/translational medicine, study optimization, market access planning and real-world evidence generation.

In medical affairs solutions, The Medical Affairs Company is the industry's leading provider of comprehensive outsourced medical affairs solutions.

Geographic Reach
Headquartered in Newton, Massachusetts, Parexel has a global presence ? about 75 locations in more than 40 countries on six continents.

Company Background
Founders Josef von Rickenbach, a health care and international products specialist, and Anne Sayigh, a chemist and regulatory affairs specialist, started PAREXEL in 1982 to provide regulatory consulting services to pharmaceutical firms. Its name referred to 16th-century Swiss physician Theophrastus Bombastus von Hohenheim -- better known as Paracelsus, the father of empirical chemistry.

Through a series of acquisitions, PAREXEL entered new markets, including biostatistics and data management, medical marketing, and health consulting.

The company went public in 1995 and was taken private again in 2017.

HISTORY

Founders Josef von Rickenbach, a health care and international products specialist, and Anne Sayigh, a chemist and regulatory affairs specialist, started PAREXEL in 1982 to provide regulatory consulting services to pharmaceutical firms. Its name referred to 16th-century Swiss physician Theophrastus Bombastus von Hohenheim -- better known as Paracelsus, the father of empirical chemistry.

In 1988 PAREXEL bought Consulting Statisticians and moved into the biostatistics and data management market. The next year it went international with the purchase of the biostatistics and data management division of McDonnell Douglas Information Systems. In 1991 PAREXEL augmented its European operations with the acquisition of German contract researcher AFB Arzneimittelforschung -- a move that paid off in rising sales.

PAREXEL went public in 1995. In the following two years it bought six health consulting firms, including State and Federal Associates and medical marketing firm Rescon, with the intention of boosting its ability to get its clients' products on the market. The company continued its acquisition spree in 1998; this time European marketing and research companies were on the shopping list. Competitor Covance was set to buy PAREXEL in 1999, then called off the deal when investors balked.

The company announced in 2000 that it would lay off more than 400 workers after Novartis cancelled a major contract. That year the company formed new alliances with such companies as NeuroRecovery Research, Phenome Sciences, and Prevention Concepts. PAREXEL also bought a full-service clinical pharmacology unit in the UK from GlaxoWellcome (now GlaxoSmithKline), as well as a majority stake in FARMOVS, a clinical pharmacology research business and laboratory in South Africa.

In 2001 the company formed Perceptive Informatics, a subsidiary focused on developing Internet-based information management systems. To strengthen its clinical trial management services, PAREXEL bought software developer FW Pharma Systems in 2003. In 2006 it purchased US-based Behavioral and Medical Research LLC for $69 million to expand its research services.

Auditors : ERNST & YOUNG LLP BOSTON MAS

LOCATIONS

HQ: PAREXEL INTERNATIONAL CORPORATION
275 GROVE ST STE 3101, AUBURNDALE, MA 024662281
Phone: 617 454-9300
Web: WWW.PAREXEL.COM

COMPETITORS

AQUILANT LIMITED
CHARLES RIVER LABORATORIES INTERNATIONAL, INC.
COVANCE INC.
IQVIA HOLDINGS INC.
MEDIDATA SOLUTIONS, INC.
PPD DEVELOPMENT, L.P.
PRA HEALTH SCIENCES, INC.
PRA INTERNATIONAL, LLC
SYNEOS HEALTH, INC.
SYNEOS HEALTH, LLC

HISTORICAL FINANCIALS
Company Type: Private

Income Statement — FYE: June 30

	REVENUE ($mil)	NET INCOME ($mil)	NET PROFIT MARGIN	EMPLOYEES
06/16	2,426	154	6.4%	18,900
06/15	2,330	147	6.3%	—
06/14	2,266	129	5.7%	—
Annual Growth	3.5%	9.5%	—	—

2016 Year-End Financials
Return on assets: 7.6%   Cash ($ mil.): 248
Return on equity: 24.5%
Current Ratio: 1.50

PARISH OF JEFFERSON

Auditors : POSTLEHWAITE & NETTERVILLE NE

LOCATIONS

HQ: PARISH OF JEFFERSON
200 DERBIGNY ST, GRETNA, LA 700535812
Phone: 504 364-2600
Web: WWW.JEFFPARISH.NET

PARK NICOLLET CLINIC

Auditors: DELOITTE TAX LLP MINNEAPOLIS

LOCATIONS

HQ: PARK NICOLLET CLINIC
3800 PARK NICOLLET BLVD, MINNEAPOLIS, MN 554162527
Phone: 952 993-3123
Web: WWW.PARKNICOLLET.COM

HISTORICAL FINANCIALS

Company Type: Private

Income Statement — FYE: December 31

	REVENUE ($mil)	NET INCOME ($mil)	NET PROFIT MARGIN	EMPLOYEES
12/21	647	(39)	—	3,217
12/20	641	111	17.3%	—
12/19	588	281	47.8%	—
12/18	561	(4)	—	—
Annual Growth	4.8%	—	—	—

2021 Year-End Financials
Return on assets: (-0.9%)
Return on equity: (-1.6%)
Current Ratio: 8.10
Cash ($ mil.): 68

PARKLAND COMMUNITY HEALTH PLAN, INC., A PROGRAM OF DALLAS COUNTY HOSPITAL

Auditors: BRUCE E BERNSTEIN & ASSOC PC

LOCATIONS

HQ: PARKLAND COMMUNITY HEALTH PLAN, INC., A PROGRAM OF DALLAS COUNTY HOSPITAL
1341 W MOCKINGBIRD LN 1150E, DALLAS, TX 752476913
Phone: 214 266-2100
Web: WWW.PARKLANDHEALTHPLAN.COM

HISTORICAL FINANCIALS

Company Type: Private

Income Statement — FYE: December 31

	REVENUE ($mil)	NET INCOME ($mil)	NET PROFIT MARGIN	EMPLOYEES
12/18	577	(9)	—	2
12/17	541	17	3.3%	—
12/15	527	(31)	—	—
12/13	519	27	5.2%	—
Annual Growth	2.1%	—	—	—

2018 Year-End Financials
Return on assets: (-6.4%)
Return on equity: (-10.7%)
Current Ratio: 2.50
Cash ($ mil.): 138

PARSONS ENVIRONMENT & INFRASTRUCTURE GROUP INC.

A unit of Parsons Corporation, Parsons Commercial Technology Group (PARCOMM) provides project management, engineering, construction, design, maintenance, and related services for industrial and commercial projects. The company's clients include firms in the telecommunications, health care, manufacturing, defense, petroleum, and chemical industries. PARCOMM also completes projects for schools, colleges, and government entities. Specialized services include industrial environmental remediation, factory modernization, and developing state vehicle inspection and compliance programs. PARCOMM operates throughout the US and the world.

LOCATIONS

HQ: PARSONS ENVIRONMENT & INFRASTRUCTURE GROUP INC.
4701 HEDGEMORE DR, CHARLOTTE, NC 282093281
Phone: 704 529-6246

COMPETITORS

AFRY Group Finland Oy
GEOSYNTEC CONSULTANTS, INC.
LEIDOS ENGINEERING, LLC
MANROCHEM LIMITED
MICHAEL BAKER INTERNATIONAL, INC.

PASADENA HOSPITAL ASSOCIATION, LTD.

No need to hunt for medical care if you're near Huntington Hospital. The not-for-profit Pasadena Hospital Association, which does business as Huntington Hospital, provides health care to residents of the San Gabriel Valley in Southern California. The hospital boasts some 625 beds and offers acute medical and surgical care and community services in a number of specialties, including cardiology, gastroenterology, women's and children's health, orthopedics, and neurology. It engages in clinical cancer research (as well as diagnosis and treatment) through the Huntington Cancer Center. The hospital is also a teaching facility for the University of Southern California (USC) Keck School of Medicine.

Operations

As part of its operations, the California hospital runs The Stroke Center, Heart and Vascular Center, Huntington Hospital Cancer Center, Regional Neonatal Intensive Care Unit, Prenatal High Risk Unit, and Pediatric Intensive Care Unit. The hospital is the only level II trauma center and level III NICU in the San Gabriel Valley.

Through its partnership with USC, Huntington Hospital offers graduate medical education in areas such as general surgery and internal medicine. Its Huntington Cancer Center partners with area physicians (including some affiliated with USC and UCLA) and the City of Hope medical center to provide comprehensive oncology services and research potential new cancer treatments.

The hospital has 900 physicians and more than 1,200 nurses. In 2013 it had about 26,000 inpatient admissions, more than 216,000 outpatient visits, and helped deliver more than 3,300 babies. Huntington Hospital provided a $92.9 million in community benefits that year.

Geographic Reach

Huntington Hospital serves the health

HISTORICAL FINANCIALS

Company Type: Private

Income Statement — FYE: July 29

	REVENUE ($mil)	NET INCOME ($mil)	NET PROFIT MARGIN	EMPLOYEES
07/14*	684	(12)	—	1,205
12/12	684	(12)	—	—
12/11	443	(57)	—	—
Annual Growth	15.6%	—	—	—

*Fiscal year change

2014 Year-End Financials
Return on assets: (-1.9%)
Return on equity: (-3.1%)
Current Ratio: 1.30
Cash ($ mil.): 24

HISTORICAL FINANCIALS (Park Nicollet – continued page data)

Company Type: Private

Income Statement — FYE: December 31

	REVENUE ($mil)	NET INCOME ($mil)	NET PROFIT MARGIN	EMPLOYEES
12/21	1,018	63	6.2%	1,300
12/20	858	(24)	—	—
12/19	921	13	1.5%	—
Annual Growth	5.2%	114.6%	—	—

2021 Year-End Financials
Return on assets: 12.5%
Return on equity: 20.5%
Current Ratio: 1.80
Cash ($ mil.): —

care needs of those who reside in and around Southern California's San Gabriel Valley.

Sales and Marketing
The medical center is working to upgrade its information technology systems, including the addition of an electronic health record (EHR) system.

Financial Performance
Huntington Hospital's revenues rose by 3% in 2013 thanks to an increase in patient services and revenues.

The hospital recorded a net loss of $10 million that year due to higher expenses (including salaries, employees benefits, and other costs).

Strategy
The company is pursuing infrastructure and services expansion and innovation to keep up with demand.

In 2014 Huntington Hospital collaborated with Anthem Blue Cross and six of its fellow leading hospitals in Los Angeles and Orange counties to form Anthem Blue Cross Vivity, a new insurance entity.

In 2013 the hospital signed a deal with Shriners Hospitals for Children- Southern California to provide inpatient surgical services for its pediatric patients.

Huntington Hospital completed renovating its existing emergency facility in 2013. The project to increase patient capacity up to 80,000 and increase diagnostic facilities came about in response to growing levels of ER visits.

Company Background
Huntington Hospital broke ground several years ago on an $80-million expansion effort to double the size of its emergency department. The project has included building a new portion that was completed in 2012.

Upgrading its technology to increase efficiency, in 2012 Huntington Hospital launched a multi-year project to replace and upgrade its computer information system with new system (Huntington Access Network Knowledge) to manage the hospital's clinical and financial software.

In a medical innovation, in 2012 the hospital became the first hospital in Southern California to offer an Ekso Bionics' technology enabling patients with lower-extremity paralysis or weakness to stand and walk.

Huntington Hospital was founded in 1892.

Auditors : ERNST & YOUNG US LLP IRVINE

LOCATIONS
HQ: PASADENA HOSPITAL ASSOCIATION, LTD.
100 W CALIFORNIA BLVD, PASADENA, CA 911053010
Phone: 626 397-5000
Web: WWW.HUNTINGTONHEALTH.ORG

PRODUCTS/OPERATIONS
Selected Services
Ambulatory Care/Dispensary
Angiography
Anticoagulation Clinic
Asthma Education and Management
Bariatric Surgery
Breast Cancer Program
Cardiac Catheterization Lab
Cardiac Electrophysiology (EP)
Cardiac Rehabilitation
Cardiac Screening and Diagnostics
Cardiothoracic Surgery
Community Outreach
CT Scanning (Type 2) Diabetes Prevention and Management
Epilepsy and Brain Mapping
Gastroenterology
Genetic Counseling
Geriatric Assessment Clinic
Gynecological Cancer Program
Heart and Vascular Services
Neurophysiology
Neuroradiology
Neurosciences
Neurosurgery
Obstetrics
Orthopedics
Ostomy Clinic
Pediatric Obesity Prevention
Prenatal High Risk Unit
Prostate Cancer Program
Radiation Oncology
Urology
Uterine Artery Embolization (UAE)

COMPETITORS
BEAUMONT HEALTH
CARILION CLINIC
FRANCISCAN ALLIANCE, INC.
MERCY HOSPITAL SPRINGFIELD
UNIVERSITY HOSPITALS HEALTH SYSTEM, INC.

HISTORICAL FINANCIALS
Company Type: Private

Income Statement — FYE: December 31

	REVENUE ($mil)	NET INCOME ($mil)	NET PROFIT MARGIN	EMPLOYEES
12/16	695	8	1.2%	2,800
12/15	593	0	0.0%	—
Annual Growth	17.2%	3278.7%	—	—

2016 Year-End Financials
Return on assets: 0.9%   Cash ($ mil.): 12
Return on equity: 1.5%
Current Ratio: 0.60

PASADENA INDEPENDENT SCHOOL DISTRICT

Auditors : WHITLEY PENN HOUSTON TEXAS

LOCATIONS
HQ: PASADENA INDEPENDENT SCHOOL DISTRICT
1515 CHERRYBROOK LN, PASADENA, TX 775024048
Phone: 713 740-0000
Web: WWW.PASADENAISD.ORG

HISTORICAL FINANCIALS
Company Type: Private

Income Statement — FYE: August 31

	REVENUE ($mil)	NET INCOME ($mil)	NET PROFIT MARGIN	EMPLOYEES
08/21	682	(6)	—	5,000
08/20	660	(29)	—	—
08/19	696	30	4.3%	—
08/18	680	99	14.7%	—
Annual Growth	0.1%	—	—	—

2021 Year-End Financials
Return on assets: (-0.4%)   Cash ($ mil.): —
Return on equity: (-9.3%)
Current Ratio: —

PATERSON PUBLIC SCHOOL DISTRICT

Auditors : LERCH VINCI & HIGGINS LLP F

LOCATIONS
HQ: PATERSON PUBLIC SCHOOL DISTRICT
90 DELAWARE AVE, PATERSON, NJ 075031804
Phone: 973 321-0980
Web: PS5-PPS-NJ.SCHOOLLOOP.COM

HISTORICAL FINANCIALS
Company Type: Private

Income Statement — FYE: June 30

	REVENUE ($mil)	NET INCOME ($mil)	NET PROFIT MARGIN	EMPLOYEES
06/20	661	(12)	—	3,055
06/19	642	(6)	—	—
06/18	602	(4)	—	—
06/17	601	1	0.3%	—
Annual Growth	3.2%	—	—	—

2020 Year-End Financials
Return on assets: (-2.9%)   Cash ($ mil.): 21
Return on equity: (-9.7%)
Current Ratio: —

PCL CONSTRUCTION ENTERPRISES, INC.

PCL Construction Enterprises is the contractor to call on for commercial and civil construction concerns. The company serves as the parent to half a dozen US construction companies: PCL Construction Services, PCL Civil Constructors, PCL Construction, PCL Industrial Services, PCL Industrial Construction, and Nordic PCL Construction. The companies serve as the operating entities for PCL, one of Canada's largest general contracting groups. Having completed projects in nearly every US state, PCL Construction Enterprises is active in the commercial, institutional, multi-family residential, heavy industrial, and civil construction sectors. PCL first entered the US construction market in 1975.

Operations
PCL Construction Enterprises and its subsidiaries work on a variety of projects. PCL Construction Enterprises has completed bridges, water and wastewater systems, manufacturing plants, office buildings, and restaurants nationwide.

Like many construction companies, PCL was hit by the economic recession. Backlogs were lacking and new projects became tougher to win due to an increase in competition. Contracts with water, wastewater, and renewable energy projects, and universities have helped PCL Construction Enterprises through the downturn.

Geographic Reach
Denver-based PCL Construction Enterprises, through its half a dozen operating units, concentrates on commercial, civil, and industrial construction projects located in the US.

Its parent's work spans the US, Canada, the Caribbean, and Australia.

Sales and Marketing
PCL caters to customers in three primary sectors: commercial buildings, civil infrastructure, and heavy industrial construction. Clients have included the Alaska Railroad Corporation, US Army Corps of Engineers, Shaw Constructors, and OUC-The Reliable One.

Its markets span big cities in Alaska, Georgia, California, North Carolina, Texas, Colorado, Hawaii, Minnesota, Florida, Arizona, and Washington.

LOCATIONS
HQ: PCL CONSTRUCTION ENTERPRISES, INC.
2000 S COLO BLVD STE 2-50, DENVER, CO 80222
Phone: 303 365-6500

PRODUCTS/OPERATIONS
Selected Operating Companies
Nordic PCL Construction, Inc.
PCL Civil Constructors, Inc.
PCL Construction, Inc.
PCL Construction Services, Inc.
PCL Industrial Construction Co.
PCL Industrial Services, Inc.

COMPETITORS
AMES CONSTRUCTION, INC.
AUSTIN COMMERCIAL, INC.
BALFOUR BEATTY CONSTRUCTION GROUP, INC.
CAPE ENVIRONMENTAL MANAGEMENT INC.
CLARK CONSTRUCTION GROUP, LLC
HENSEL PHELPS CONSTRUCTION CO.
JAMES G. DAVIS CONSTRUCTION CORPORATION
PCL Constructors Inc
PCL Employees Holdings Ltd
SUFFOLK CONSTRUCTION COMPANY, INC.

HISTORICAL FINANCIALS
Company Type: Private

Income Statement   FYE: October 31

	REVENUE ($mil)	NET INCOME ($mil)	NET PROFIT MARGIN	EMPLOYEES
10/10	1,616	23	1.5%	3,300
10/09	2,182	52	2.4%	—
10/08	2,315	84	3.7%	—
Annual Growth	(16.4%)	(47.2%)	—	—

2010 Year-End Financials
Return on assets: 4.2%   Cash ($ mil.): 95
Return on equity: 17.6%
Current Ratio: 1.20

PEACEHEALTH

PeaceHealth is a not-for-profit Catholic health system that serves residents in Washington, Oregon and Alaska. In all, PeaceHealth has some 16,000 caregivers and a multi-specialty medical group practice with more than 1,100 physicians. It also has ten medical centers in both rural and urban communities throughout the Northwest. Its medical centers include PeaceHealth Ketchikan Medical Center, PeaceHealth St. Joseph Medical Center, PeaceHealth St. John Medical Center, Sacred Heart Medical Center (two campuses), Cottage Grove Community Hospital, Peace Harbor Hospital, PeaceHealth Peace Island Medical Center, and PeaceHealth Southwest Medical Center.

Operations
PeaceHealth reported more than 66,800 inpatient admissions and roughly 1.5 million outpatient registrations, as well as almost 2 million patient encounters with its medical group. It had more than 7,000 infant births and more than 309,500 emergency department visits annually.

Geographic Reach
Based in Vancouver, Washington, PeaceHealth has operations in Washington, Oregon, and Alaska.

Company Background
PeaceHealth was formed in 1923 by the Sisters of St. Joseph of Peace who opened the Little Flower Hospital in Ketchikan, named after Saint Teresa. The Sisters of St. Joseph of Peace had previously opened St. Joseph Hospital in Bellingham in 1891.

PeaceHealth and Southwest Washington Health System merged in early 2011, boosting PeaceHealth's hospital holdings from six to eight with the addition of the two-campus Southwest Washington Medical Center in Vancouver, Washington.

Under terms of the affiliation, Southwest Washington Health System became part of PeaceHealth, allowing Southwest to benefit from its larger peer's medical and financial resources. The move allows both health systems to increase the scope of services they offer in Washington State, where Southwest Washington Health System also operates clinics, a medical group, and a foundation through which it conducts fundraising efforts.

EXECUTIVES
CDO, Anne Rassmussen

LOCATIONS
HQ: PEACEHEALTH
1115 SE 164TH AVE, VANCOUVER, WA 986839324
Phone: 360 788-6841
Web: WWW.PEACEHEALTH.ORG

PRODUCTS/OPERATIONS
2013 Sales

	$ mil.	% of total
Patient service revenue	1,984	92
Premium revenue	93	4
Other operating revenue	94	4
Total	2,171	100

Selected Hospitals
PeaceHealth Ketchikan Medical Center (Ketchikan, Alaska)
Cottage Grove Community Hospital (Cottage Grove, Oregon)
Peace Harbor Hospital (Florence, Oregon)
PeaceHealth Peace Island Medical Center (Friday Harbor, Washington)
PeaceHealth Southwest Medical Center (Vancouver, Washington)
PeaceHealth St. John Medical Center (Longview, Washington)
PeaceHealth St. Joseph Medical Center (Bellingham, Washington)
Sacred Heart Medical Center at RiverBend (Springfield, Oregon)
Sacred Heart Medical Center University District (Eugene, Oregon)
Other Operations
PeaceHealth Laboratories (locations throughout Oregon and Washington)
PeaceHealth Medical Group (operates in Alaska, Oregon, and Washington)

COMPETITORS
ALLINA HEALTH SYSTEM
BRONXCARE HEALTH SYSTEM
COMMUNITY HEALTH NETWORK, INC.
NORTHWESTERN MEMORIAL HEALTHCARE
NOVANT HEALTH, INC.
REGIONS HOSPITAL FOUNDATION
SPECTRUM HEALTH SYSTEM
ST. JOSEPH HEALTH SYSTEM
VALLEY HEALTH SYSTEM
WELLMONT HEALTH SYSTEM

HISTORICAL FINANCIALS
Company Type: Private

Income Statement   FYE: June 30

	REVENUE ($mil)	NET INCOME ($mil)	NET PROFIT MARGIN	EMPLOYEES
06/14	2,249	114	5.1%	6,690
06/09	1,372	(88)	—	—
06/06	1,048	103	9.8%	—
Annual Growth	10.0%	1.3%	—	—

2014 Year-End Financials
Return on assets: 3.3%   Cash ($ mil.): 549
Return on equity: 6.5%
Current Ratio: 0.70

HOOVER'S HANDBOOK OF PRIVATE COMPANIES 2023

PEDERNALES ELECTRIC COOPERATIVE, INC.

Created by Texas ranchers and business owners, Pedernales Electric Cooperative provides electricity services in the Texas Hill Country. The company, the largest electric cooperative in the US, purchases its electricity from wholesale providers, primarily the Lower Colorado River Authority (LCRA), and transmits and distributes it to about 209,350 cooperative members (or more than 247,810 individual customer meters). Pedernales Electric Cooperative operates more than 17,450 miles of power line and maintains 290,000 wooden utility poles in its service area.

Geographic Reach
The cooperative serves a customer base spread across 24 counties in Central Texas (8,100 sq. miles, an area larger than the state of Massachusetts).

Financial Performance
In 2012 the company's revenues decreased by 3% as the result of unfavorable weather conditions weakening demand for power (despite an increase of 5,500 new customers). Net income decreased 24%, driven by lower net sales.

Strategy
A member of the American Wind Energy Association, Pedernales Electric Cooperative is committed to move toward conservation and cleaner energy (to meet clean air standards) and has a renewable energy goal of 30% of energy from renewable sources by 2020. The coop contracts with AEP Energy Partners to buy wind power produced at the South Trent Wind Farm near Sweetwater, Texas. In all, the wind-power purchase is expected to power up 22,000 to 27,000 homes.

In 2013 company upgraded the electric system in the Canyon Lake area, manually converting more than 1,900 transformers to accept higher voltage to better serve the growing energy needs of nearly 2,600 coop members in the Clear Water Estates, Tamarack Shores, Scenic Terrace, Linda Ledges, Hancock Oak Hills, and Rocky Creek Ranch subdivisions.

Company Background
As part of reforming its operations following a financial scandal, in 2009 Pedernales Electric Cooperative became one of the first electric distribution cooperatives in the US to broadcast its Board meetings live on the Internet. In 2009 the cooperative ratified the first member advisory panel (on energy conservation and renewable energy use) in Pedernales Electric Cooperative's history.

Pedernales Electric Cooperative was founded in 1938 with the help of local landowner (and later US president) Lyndon Johnson.

Auditors: BOLINGER SEGARS GILBERT AND MO

LOCATIONS
HQ: PEDERNALES ELECTRIC COOPERATIVE, INC.
201 S AVENUE F, JOHNSON CITY, TX 786362072
Phone: 830 868-7155
Web: WWW.PEC.COOP

COMPETITORS
ARKANSAS ELECTRIC COOPERATIVE CORPORATION
DENTON COUNTY ELECTRIC COOPERATIVE, INC.
DUKE ENERGY FLORIDA, LLC
GREAT RIVER ENERGY
IMPERIAL IRRIGATION DISTRICT
SALT RIVER PROJECT AGRICULTURAL IMPROVEMENT AND POWER DISTRICT
SOUTH CAROLINA PUBLIC SERVICE AUTHORITY (INC)
SOUTHERN MARYLAND ELECTRIC COOPERATIVE, INC.
THE SOUTHERN COMPANY
WESTERN FARMERS ELECTRIC COOPERATIVE

HISTORICAL FINANCIALS
Company Type: Private

Income Statement — FYE: December 31

	REVENUE ($mil)	NET INCOME ($mil)	NET PROFIT MARGIN	EMPLOYEES
12/11	589	6	1.1%	741
12/10	550	53	9.8%	—
12/09	578	57	10.0%	—
Annual Growth	0.9%	(66.5%)	—	—

2011 Year-End Financials
Return on assets: 0.5%   Cash ($ mil.): 27
Return on equity: 1.6%
Current Ratio: 0.20

PENNSYLVANIA - AMERICAN WATER COMPANY

Pennsylvania-American Water distributes water and provides wastewater services to a population of more than 2 million people in some 390 communities across Pennsylvania. The company serves 635,000 water customers and 17,500 wastewater customers. It operates about 35 water treatment plants, six wastewater facilities, and 9,800 miles of pipeline. Pennsylvania-American Water's service territory covers some three dozen Pennsylvania counties. The utility, the largest regulated water and wastewater service provider in Pennsylvania, is a subsidiary of New Jersey-based American Water Works.

Operations
Pennsylvania-American Water also has 85 well stations and treats and delivers about 216 millions of gallons of water each day. In addition, it also operates 70 groundwater treatment facilities, which process water sourced from more than 100 groundwater wells, and maintains 250 treated water storage facilities, 280 pumping stations, and 60 dams.

Geographic Reach
The utility's primarily service areas include Mechanicsburg, Mon Valley, Norristown, Pittsburgh, Scranton, Washington, and Wilkes-Barre.

Financial Performance
Pennsylvania-American Water represents about a fifth of its parent company's sales; in 2011 it reported $516 million in revenue from Pennsylvania.

Mergers and Acquisitions
The utility expands its reach in Pennsylvania by picking up smaller water systems; in 2012 it completed six such acquisitions, including a Monroe County system serving the Fernwood Resort and a Pike County system serving about 100 residents.

Auditors: PRICEWATERHOUSECOOPERS LLP PH

LOCATIONS
HQ: PENNSYLVANIA - AMERICAN WATER COMPANY
852 WESLEY DR, MECHANICSBURG, PA 170554436
Phone: 800 565-7292
Web: WWW.AMWATER.COM

COMPETITORS
DENVER BOARD OF WATER COMMISSIONERS
MIDDLESEX WATER COMPANY
SUEZ ENVIRONNEMENT
THE YORK WATER COMPANY
VEOLIA WATER NORTH AMERICA OPERATING SERVICES, LLC

HISTORICAL FINANCIALS
Company Type: Private

Income Statement — FYE: December 31

	REVENUE ($mil)	NET INCOME ($mil)	NET PROFIT MARGIN	EMPLOYEES
12/17*	661	160	24.3%	1,007
06/14	589	127	21.7%	—
03/14	584	128	22.0%	—
12/13	571	122	21.4%	—
Annual Growth	3.7%	7.1%	—	—

*Fiscal year change

2017 Year-End Financials
Return on assets: 3.5%   Cash ($ mil.): 3
Return on equity: 5.6%
Current Ratio: 0.20

PENNSYLVANIA ELECTRIC COMPANY

Pennsylvania Electric (Penelec) has elected to provide power to the people of the Keystone State. The company distributes power to a population of 1.6 million in a 17,600-square-mile portion of northern, western, and south-central Pennsylvania. The utility operates more than 20,170 miles of distribution and more than 2,700 transmission lines. The Waverly Electric Light & Power Company, a subsidiary of Penelec, provides electric services to a population of about 8,400 in Waverly, New York. Penelec is an operating subsidiary of regional utility power player FirstEnergy.

EXECUTIVES

CAO, Harvey L Wagner

Auditors : PRICEWATERHOUSECOOPERS LLP CL

LOCATIONS

HQ: PENNSYLVANIA ELECTRIC COMPANY
2800 POTTSVILLE PIKE, AKRON, OH 44308
Phone: 800 545-7741
Web: WWW.FIRSTENERGYCORP.COM

COMPETITORS

DUKE ENERGY FLORIDA, LLC
METROPOLITAN EDISON COMPANY
MONONGAHELA POWER COMPANY
SOUTHERN MARYLAND ELECTRIC COOPERATIVE, INC.
SOUTHWESTERN ELECTRIC POWER COMPANY

HISTORICAL FINANCIALS

Company Type: Private

Income Statement — FYE: December 31

	REVENUE ($mil)	NET INCOME ($mil)	NET PROFIT MARGIN	EMPLOYEES
12/17	893	95	10.7%	896
12/16	904	88	9.8%	—
12/10	1,539	59	3.9%	—
12/09	1,448	65	4.5%	—
Annual Growth	(5.9%)	4.9%	—	—

2017 Year-End Financials
Return on assets: 2.2%   Cash ($ mil.): —
Return on equity: 7.8%
Current Ratio: 1.20

PENNSYLVANIA HIGHER EDUCATION ASSISTANCE AGENCY

PHEAA is a national provider of student financial aid services, serving millions of students and thousands of schools through its loan guaranty, loan servicing, financial aid processing, outreach, and other student aid programs. PHEAA conducts its student loan servicing operations nationally as FedLoan Servicing and American Education Services (AES). PHEAA operates its digital technology division as Avereo. PHEAA's earnings are used to support its public service mission and to pay its operating costs, including administration of the PA State Grant and other state-funded student aid programs. Created in 1963 by the Pennsylvania General Assembly, the Pennsylvania Higher Education Assistance Agency (PHEAA) has evolved into one of the nation's leading student aid organizations.

Auditors : ERNST & YOUNG LLP MCLEAN VA

LOCATIONS

HQ: PENNSYLVANIA HIGHER EDUCATION ASSISTANCE AGENCY
1200 N 7TH ST, HARRISBURG, PA 171021419
Phone: 717 720-2700
Web: WWW.PHEAA.ORG

PRODUCTS/OPERATIONS

2015 sales

	$ mil.	% of total
Non-interest		
Servicing fees	308.0	50
Retention of collections on defaulted loans, net	130.9	21
Federal fees	20.6	3
Other	(1.2)	-
Interest		
Loans	155.0	25
Investments	5.7	1
Total	619.0	100

COMPETITORS

CHILDREN & FAMILIES, FLORIDA DEPARTMENT OF
COGNITION FINANCIAL CORPORATION
FLORIDA DEPARTMENT OF EDUCATION
KANSAS DEPT OF EDUCATION
NAVIENT CORPORATION
NELNET, INC.
OREGON DEPARTMENT OF EDUCATION
UNITED STATES DEPT OF EDUCATION
UNITED STATES DEPT OF EDUCATION
WISCONSIN DEPT OF PUBLIC INSTRUCTION

HISTORICAL FINANCIALS

Company Type: Private

Income Statement — FYE: June 30

	REVENUE ($mil)	NET INCOME ($mil)	NET PROFIT MARGIN	EMPLOYEES
06/13*	671	155	23.2%	2,700
03/12	436	68	15.7%	—
Annual Growth	53.8%	127.6%		—

*Fiscal year change

2013 Year-End Financials
Return on assets: 1.7%   Cash ($ mil.): 88
Return on equity: 16.4%
Current Ratio: 5.60

PENNSYLVANIA HOUSING FINANCE AGENCY

Pennsylvania Housing Finance Agency (PHFA) helps residents of the Keystone State obtain keys to their dream homes. The government-owned agency provides financing for low-income homebuyers, including the elderly and disabled, and participates in rental housing development initiatives. It generates funding from state and federal grants, interest earned on investments and loans, and the sale of its own securities to private investors. The agency is run by a board which includes Pennsylvania's secretary of banking, secretary of community and economic development, secretary of public welfare, and the state treasurer. The PHFA has funded more than 130,000 houses and 54,000 apartment units since its founding in 1972.

LOCATIONS

HQ: PENNSYLVANIA HOUSING FINANCE AGENCY
211 N FRONT ST, HARRISBURG, PA 171011406
Phone: 717 780-3800
Web: WWW.PHFA.ORG

COMPETITORS

HOME DEVELOPMENT MUTUAL FUND
HOUSING AND URBAN DEVELOPMENT, UNITED STATES DEPT OF
HOUSING AND URBAN DEVELOPMENT, UNITED STATES DEPT OF
HOUSING AND URBAN DEVELOPMENT, UNITED STATES DEPT OF
HOUSING FINANCE AGENCY, CALIFORNIA

HISTORICAL FINANCIALS

Company Type: Private

Income Statement — FYE: June 30

	ASSETS ($mil)	NET INCOME ($mil)	INCOME AS % OF ASSETS	EMPLOYEES
06/22	5,548	(41)	—	250
06/21	4,667	9	0.2%	—
06/20	4,542	14	0.3%	—
06/19	4,366	22	0.5%	—
Annual Growth	8.3%	—	—	—

2022 Year-End Financials
Return on assets: (-0.7%)   Cash ($ mil.): 502
Return on equity: (-5.5%)
Current Ratio: 3.40

PENNSYLVANIA INTER GOVERNMENTAL COOPERATION AUTHORITY

Auditors : MAHER DUESSEL HARRISBURG PEN

LOCATIONS

HQ: PENNSYLVANIA INTERGOVERNMENTAL COOPERATION AUTHORITY
1500 WALNUT ST STE 1600, PHILADELPHIA, PA 191023501
Phone: 215 561-9160
Web: WWW.PICAPA.ORG

PEPPER CONSTRUCTION COMPANY

HISTORICAL FINANCIALS
Company Type: Private

Income Statement — FYE: June 30

	REVENUE ($mil)	NET INCOME ($mil)	NET PROFIT MARGIN	EMPLOYEES
06/22	578	(2)	—	11
06/21	536	20	3.9%	—
06/20	531	(38)	—	—
Annual Growth	4.3%	—	—	—

2022 Year-End Financials
Return on assets: (-6.1%)   Cash ($ mil.): 9
Return on equity: (-15.0%)
Current Ratio: —

EXECUTIVES
Executive President, James A Nissen
Auditors: BKD LLP OAKBROOK TERRACE IL

LOCATIONS
HQ: PEPPER CONSTRUCTION COMPANY
643 N ORLEANS ST, CHICAGO, IL 606543690
Phone: 312 266-4700
Web: WWW.PEPPERCONSTRUCTION.COM

HISTORICAL FINANCIALS
Company Type: Private

Income Statement — FYE: September 30

	REVENUE ($mil)	NET INCOME ($mil)	NET PROFIT MARGIN	EMPLOYEES
09/20	737	10	1.4%	900
09/17	704	14	2.1%	—
09/16	805	20	2.5%	—
09/15	709	10	1.5%	—
Annual Growth	0.8%	(0.3%)	—	—

2020 Year-End Financials
Return on assets: 5.2%   Cash ($ mil.): 46
Return on equity: 20.2%
Current Ratio: 1.30

PEPPER CONSTRUCTION GROUP, LLC

Pepper Construction Group spices up the construction business with a little of this and a pinch of that. The company provides general contracting and construction management services for commercial office, education, entertainment, health care, and institutional clients, as well as waterworks projects. (Health care projects account for about 50% of Pepper's revenue.) Its client list includes UBS, Northwestern University, University of Notre Dame, Texas Heart Institute, Loyola University Medical Center, and NASA. Pepper Construction Group has divisions in Illinois, Indiana, Ohio, and Texas. Stanley F. Pepper founded the company in Chicago in 1927. The group is owned by his family and employees of the firm.

Operations
The company's Pepper Environmental Technologies unit provides environmental services. Green building has become a large part of Pepper Construction's operations. Its Green Team of certified professionals have helped construct more than 2.9 million sq. ft. of eco-friendly space. The Green Team has built the Apple Computer flagship store, HSBC Chicago North, and Kohl's Children's Museum.

The firm's Pepper-Lawson Waterworks group constructs water purification plants for municipal clients, including Houston and Missouri City, Texas.

Geographic Reach
Chicago-based Pepper Construction comprises four geographic divisions: Illinois; Indiana; Ohio; and Texas. Overall, the company is active in about 20 states, mostly in the central and northeastern states.

EXECUTIVES
General Vice President, Timothy F Sullivan Senior
Auditors: BKD LLP OAKBROOK TERRACE IL

LOCATIONS
HQ: PEPPER CONSTRUCTION GROUP, LLC
643 N ORLEANS ST, CHICAGO, IL 606543690
Phone: 312 266-4700
Web: WWW.PEPPERCONSTRUCTION.COM

PRODUCTS/OPERATIONS
Selected Operations
Pepper Construction Group, LLC (Chicago, Illinois)
Pepper Construction Co. (Chicago, Illinois)
Pepper Construction Co. of Indiana (Indianapolis, Indiana)
Pepper Construction Co. of Ohio, LLC (Dublin, Ohio)
Pepper Environmental Technologies, Inc. (Barrington, Illinois)
Pepper-Lawson Construction, LP (Houston, Texas)
Pepper-Lawson Waterworks, LLC (Houston, Texas)

COMPETITORS
GILBANE BUILDING COMPANY
H. J. RUSSELL & COMPANY
J.E. DUNN CONSTRUCTION GROUP, INC.
LECHASE CONSTRUCTION SERVICES, LLC
MCCARTHY BUILDING COMPANIES, INC.
MIRON CONSTRUCTION CO., INC.
O'NEIL INDUSTRIES, INC.
RUDOLPH AND SLETTEN, INC.
TDINDUSTRIES, INC.
THE HASKELL COMPANY

PERISHABLE DISTRIBUTORS OF IOWA, LTD.

LOCATIONS
HQ: PERISHABLE DISTRIBUTORS OF IOWA, LTD.
2741 SE PDI PL, ANKENY, IA 500213958
Phone: 515 965-6300
Web: WWW.CONTACTPDI.COM

HISTORICAL FINANCIALS
Company Type: Private

Income Statement — FYE: September 30

	REVENUE ($mil)	NET INCOME ($mil)	NET PROFIT MARGIN	EMPLOYEES
09/20	1,254	22	1.8%	1,100
09/16	1,179	23	2.0%	—
09/15	1,110	9	0.9%	—
09/11	911	15	1.7%	—
Annual Growth	3.6%	4.2%	—	—

2020 Year-End Financials
Return on assets: 5.8%   Cash ($ mil.): 74
Return on equity: 29.5%
Current Ratio: 1.20

HISTORICAL FINANCIALS
Company Type: Private

Income Statement — FYE: September 30

	REVENUE ($mil)	NET INCOME ($mil)	NET PROFIT MARGIN	EMPLOYEES
09/18*	1,346	38	2.9%	687
10/17	1,343	35	2.6%	—
10/16	1,307	33	2.6%	—
09/15	1,248	31	2.5%	—
Annual Growth	2.5%	7.3%	—	—

*Fiscal year change

2018 Year-End Financials
Return on assets: 25.9%   Cash ($ mil.): 15
Return on equity: 55.2%
Current Ratio: 1.30

PETER KIEWIT SONS', INC.

Kiewit is one of North America's largest construction and engineering companies. The company is active in building, industrial, mining, oil, gas, chemicals, power, transportation, water, and wastewater. It builds everything from roads and dams to high-rise office towers and power plants. Kiewit focuses on projects located throughout the US, Canada, and Mexico. It specializes in mine management, production, infrastructure construction, and maintenance, its mining experience includes constructing infrastructure, performing mine services or contract mining in coal, copper, diamond, gold, nickel, platinum, potash and rare earth mines throughout North America. Founded in 1884, Kiewit is owned by employees and Kiewit family members.

Operations

Kiewit provides engineering, construction, procurement, foundations, development services and decarbonization solutions.

Kiewit delivers more than 1,000 oil, gas and chemical projects. As a premier contractor in the North American power industry, Kiewit has installed more than 125,000 MW of capacity, and consistently ranks among the Engineering News-Record top five power contractors. Its diverse expertise includes renewable, hydrogen and fossil-fuel energy generation, energy storage of all types, carbon capture technologies as well as transmission and distribution. In addition, its successful track record includes the construction and upgrade of interstates; highways and bridges; rail lines and rail yards; urban mass transit systems; and airport runways, taxiways and associated facilities.

Geographic Reach

Based in Omaha, Nebraska, Kiewit operates across the US, Canada, and Mexico.

Sales and Marketing

Kiewit serves a diverse array of industries, including building, industrial, mining, oil, gas and chemical, power, transportation and water.

Company Background

The sons of Dutch immigrants, Peter and Andrew Kiewit founded masonry contractor Kiewit Brothers in 1884 in Omaha, Nebraska. Following the dissolution of the partnership in 1904 Peter continued as the company's sole proprietor. In 1931 ? 17 years after Peter's death ? his son Peter reorganized the business as Peter Kiewit Sons'.

HISTORY

Born to Dutch immigrants, Peter Kiewit and brother Andrew founded Kiewit Brothers, a brickyard, in 1884 in Omaha, Nebraska. By 1912 two of Peter's sons worked at the yard, which was named Peter Kiewit & Sons. When Peter Kiewit died in 1914, his son Ralph took over, and the firm took the name Peter Kiewit Sons'. Another son, Peter, joined Ralph at the helm in 1924 after dropping out of Dartmouth, and later took over.

During the Depression, Kiewit managed huge federal public works projects, and in the 1940s it focused on war-related emergency construction projects.

One of the firm's most difficult projects was top-secret Thule Air Force Base in Greenland, above the Arctic Circle. For more than two years 5,000 men worked around the clock, beginning in 1951; the site was in development for 15 years. In 1952 the company won a contract to build a $1.2 billion gas diffusion plant in Portsmouth, Ohio. It also became a contractor for the US interstate highway system (begun in 1956).

Peter Kiewit died in 1979, after stipulating that the largely employee-owned company should remain under employee control and that no one employee could own more than 10%. His 40% stake, when returned to the company, transformed many employees into millionaires. Walter Scott Jr., whose father had been the first graduate engineer to work for Kiewit, took charge. Scott made his mark by parlaying money from construction into successful investments.

When the construction industry slumped, Kiewit began looking for other investment opportunities, and in 1984 it acquired packaging company Continental Can Co. (selling off noncore insurance, energy, and timber assets). Continental was saddled with a 1983 class action lawsuit alleging that it had plotted to close plants and lay off workers before they were qualified for pensions. In 1991 Kiewit agreed to pay $415 million to settle the lawsuit. In the face of a consolidating packaging industry, the company sold Continental in the early 1990s.

In 1986 Kiewit loaned money to a business group to build a fiber-optic loop in Chicago; by 1987 it had launched MFS Communications to build local fiber loops in downtown districts. In 1992 Kiewit split its business into two pieces: the construction group, which was strictly employee-owned; and a diversified group, to which it added a controlling stake in phone and cable TV company C-TEC in 1993. That year Kiewit took MFS public; by 1995 it had sold all its shares, and the next year MFS was bought by telecom giant WorldCom.

In 1996 Kiewit assisted CalEnergy (now MidAmerican Energy) in a hostile $1.3 billion takeover of the UK's Northern Electric. Kiewit got stock in CalEnergy and a 30% stake in the UK electric company, all of which it sold to CalEnergy in 1998.

That year Kiewit spun off its telecom and computer services holdings into Level 3 Communications. Scott, who had been hospitalized the year before for a blood clot in his lung, stepped down as CEO, and Ken Stinson, CEO of Kiewit Construction Group, took over Peter Kiewit Sons'.

In 1999 Kiewit acquired a majority interest in Pacific Rock Products, a construction materials firm in Canada. Kiewit spun off its asphalt, concrete, and aggregates operations in 2000 as Kiewit Materials. Also that year the company created Kiewit Offshore Services to focus on construction for the offshore drilling industry. In 2001 the company acquired marine construction firm General Construction Company (GCC). The next year it expanded its offshore business further by buying a Canadian subsidiary from oil and gas equipment services company Friede Goldman Halter, which was trying to emerge from bankruptcy.

Kiewit made history in 2002 for the fastest completion of a project of its type when it completed the rebuilding of Webbers Falls I-40 Bridge in Oklahoma at the end of July. (The bridge had collapsed in May after being hit by a pair of barges, resulting in 14 fatalities.)

In 2004 Kiewit greatly increased its coal sales and reserves with the acquisition of the Buckskin Mine in Wyoming from Arch Coal.

Kiewit underwent a changing of the guard at the end of 2004, when 22-year veteran Bruce Grewcock took the reins as the company's fourth CEO since its founding. Stinson stayed on as the company's chairman.

In 2008 the group acquired TIC Holdings, a heavy industrial construction and engineering firm.

Through its Kiewit Power Engineers Co., the company was contracted by Plutonic Energy Corporation and GE Energy Financial Services to work on the 235 MW hydroelectric Toba Montrose project, one of British Columbia's largest renewable energy projects (completed around 2011).

In 2013 Kiewit entered the Australian market through a joint venture agreement that involves as $247 million engineer-procure-construct contract for a wet front end and ore wash plant situated at the Cloudbreak Mine in Northwest Australia. Fortescue Metals Group is the previous owner of Cloudbreak prior to the handover in early 2013.

Auditors : KPMG LLP OMAHA NEBRASKA

LOCATIONS

HQ: PETER KIEWIT SONS', INC.
3555 FARNAM ST STE 1000, OMAHA, NE 681313374
Phone: 402 342-2052
Web: WWW.KIEWIT.COM

Selected Locations
US
- Alaska
- Arizona
- Arkansas
- California
- Colorado
- Florida
- Georgia
- Hawaii
- Idaho
- Illinois
- Iowa
- Kansas
- Louisiana
- Maryland
- Massachusetts
- Minnesota
- Nebraska
- Nevada
- New Jersey
- New York
- North Carolina
- Oregon
- Tennessee
- Texas
- Utah
- Virginia
- Washington
- Wyoming

Australia
    Western Australia
Canada
    Alberta
    British Columbia
    Manitoba
    Newfoundland
    New Brunswick
    Ontario
    Quebec
    Saskatchewan

PRODUCTS/OPERATIONS

Selected Locations
US
Alaska
Arizona
California
Colorado
Florida
Georgia
Hawaii
Illinois
Iowa
Kansas
Maryland
Massachusetts
Minnesota
Nebraska
Nevada
New Jersey
New York
North Carolina
Oregon
Texas
Utah
Virginia
Washington
Wyoming
Canada
Alberta
British Columbia
Newfoundland
Ontario
Quebec
Mexico
Mexico City

Selected Subsidiaries and Affiliates
Aero Automatic Sprinkler
Cherne Contracting Corporation
Continental Fire Sprinkler Company
Kiewit Australia
Kiewit Bridge & Marine
Kiewit Building Group
Kiewit Energy Company.
Kiewit Engineering Group Inc.
Kiewit Infrastructure Co.
Kiewit Infrastructure South Co.
Kiewit Infrastructure West Co.
Kiewit Mining Group
Dry Valley/No. Rassmussen Ridge Mines
Buckskin Mining Company
San Miguel Mine
Walnut Creek Mining Company
Kiewit Offshore Services Ltd..
Kiewit Power Constructors Co.
Kiewit Power Engineers
Kiewit Texas Construction L.P.

COMPETITORS
BECHTEL GROUP, INC.
COLAS SA
FLUOR CORPORATION
KELLER GROUP PLC
OBAYASHI CORPORATION
PARSONS CORPORATION
PHILLIPS & JORDAN, INCORPORATED
SKANSKA USA CIVIL INC.
STERLING CONSTRUCTION COMPANY, INC.
TAKENAKA CORPORATION

HISTORICAL FINANCIALS
Company Type: Private

Income Statement — FYE: December 29

	REVENUE ($mil)	NET INCOME ($mil)	NET PROFIT MARGIN	EMPLOYEES
12/12	11,220	515	4.6%	14,700
12/11	10,381	790	7.6%	—
12/10	9,938	789	7.9%	—
Annual Growth	6.3%	(19.2%)	—	—

2012 Year-End Financials
Return on assets: 7.6%   Cash ($ mil.): 1,447
Return on equity: 13.2%
Current Ratio: 1.90

PETRO STAR INC.

Petro Star is an oil refining and fuel marketing shining star that brings heating fuel and energy (heating oil, diesel, and aviation and marine fuels) to the citizens of the communities in the vast, cold, and lonely expanses of the US' largest state, Alaska. It operates refineries at North Pole and Valdez and distributes fuels and lubricants throughout Interior Alaska, Dutch Harbor, Kodiak, and Valdez. Started in 1984 by a group of petroleum industry veterans, the company built its first refinery operations along the Trans-Alaska Pipeline at North Pole, Alaska. Petro Star is a subsidiary of Arctic Slope Regional Corp.

Operations
The company's divisions are Refining; Retail; Lubricants; Marine Fuel; Heating Fuel; Aviation; and Port of Alaska.

Refining operates two refineries: the 60,000 barrel-per-day Petro Star Valdez refinery which produces jet fuel, JP-8, JP-5, marine diesel, heating fuel and turbine fuel; and the North Pole refinery, approximately 22,000-barrel-per-day facility, producing heating fuel, kerosene, diesel, jet fuels, and asphalt base oil.

Its retail division is engaged in retail stores selling its products (North Pacific Fuel and Sourdough Fuel). It operates several gas stations and convenience stores throughout the state, offering fuel, food, groceries and propane sales for customer's convenience.

Petro Star Lubricants is a bulk lube repackaging company offering several product lines and provide technical services for all of the company's product lines.

Marine offers marine fueling as well as supplies such as pumps, hoses and nozzles.

Heating Fuel distributes locally produced heating and diesel fuel directly from the company's refineries in North Pole and Valdez to locations throughout Alaska.

Aviation is a supplier of jet fuel for the Ted Stevens International Airport for both commercial and corporate aircraft.

Petro Star distributes ultra low sulfur diesel, jet fuel and gasoline at Terminal 1 at the Port of Alaska.

Geographic Reach
Headquartered in Alaska, Petro Star operates in Kodiak, Dutch Harbor, Valdez, St Paul, Fairbanks, Anchorage, and an additional offices in Seattle.

Sales and Marketing
The company's customers include aviation, residential, commercial, industrial, marine, and military.

Company Background
The company has expanded through acquisitions, including fuel distribution firm Sourdough Fuel (in 1986), as well as the 1991 purchase of Alaska Lube and Fuel (now Petro Star Lubricants). Kodiak Sales (in 1997), and North Pacific Fuel (in 1998).

In 2008 Petro Star secured a $158.7 million aviation fuel contract from the Defense Logistics Agency.

LOCATIONS
HQ: PETRO STAR INC.
    3900 C ST STE 802, ANCHORAGE, AK 995035963
Phone: 907 339-6600
Web: WWW.PETROSTAR.COM

COMPETITORS
HOLLYFRONTIER CORPORATION
IDEMITSU KOSAN CO.,LTD.
Irving Oil Limited
MARTIN RESOURCE MANAGEMENT CORPORATION
PETROL OFISI ANONIM SIRKETI

HISTORICAL FINANCIALS
Company Type: Private

Income Statement — FYE: December 31

	REVENUE ($mil)	NET INCOME ($mil)	NET PROFIT MARGIN	EMPLOYEES
12/08	992	0	0.0%	300
12/03	291	3	1.2%	—
12/02	267	1	0.7%	—
12/01	279	3	1.1%	—
Annual Growth	19.9%	—	—	—

2008 Year-End Financials
Return on assets: —   Cash ($ mil.): 106
Return on equity: —
Current Ratio: 1.90

PETROCARD, INC.

LOCATIONS
HQ: PETROCARD, INC.
    730 CENTRAL AVE S, KENT, WA 980326109
Phone: 253 852-7801
Web: WWW.PETROCARD.COM

HISTORICAL FINANCIALS
Company Type: Private

Income Statement   FYE: March 31

	REVENUE ($mil)	NET INCOME ($mil)	NET PROFIT MARGIN	EMPLOYEES
03/12	1,173	0	0.1%	190
03/11	948	3	0.4%	—
03/10	791	3	0.4%	—
Annual Growth	21.7%	(50.7%)	—	—

2012 Year-End Financials
Return on assets: 0.6%   Cash ($ mil.): 1
Return on equity: 1.7%
Current Ratio: 1.00

PETROLEUM TRADERS CORPORATION

Petroleum Traders Corporation barters with fuel. The company provides wholesale gasoline, diesel fuel, and heating oil to fuel distributors, government agencies, and other large consumers of fuel such as businesses with vehicle fleets. The largest pure wholesale fuel distributor in the country, Petroleum Traders operates and trades in 44 US states. It supplies #1 and #2 low sulfur diesel fuels, biodiesel, high sulfur heating oil and kerosene, and conventional, ethanol, and reformulated blends of gasoline in regular, midgrade, and premium octane ratings.

Operations
Petroleum Traders focuses on supplying wholesale diesel and gasoline exclusively in the US, offering a range of turnkey wholesale diesel fuel and wholesale gasoline fuel services.

Sales and Marketing
The company provides discount fuel to commercial, government, and wholesale customers. In the commercial space it services the trucking, construction, railroad, mining, and manufacturing industries as well as utilities and private fleets.

Strategy
Petroleum Traders parlays its hedging experience into fuel cost management for its customers via firm pricing, cap programs, collars, and fuel swaps.

Company Background
The company was founded in 1979.

EXECUTIVES
Assistant Chief Executive Officer*, Vicki Himes
Auditors: BADEN GAGE & SHROEDER LLC FO

LOCATIONS
HQ: PETROLEUM TRADERS CORPORATION
7120 POINTE INVERNESS WAY, FORT WAYNE, IN 468047928
Phone: 260 432-6622
Web: WWW.PETROLEUMTRADERS.COM

COMPETITORS
ITOCHU ENEX CO., LTD.
J.A.M. DISTRIBUTING COMPANY
MERRIMAC PETROLEUM, INC.
RS ENERGY K.K.
SUN COAST RESOURCES, INC.

HISTORICAL FINANCIALS
Company Type: Private

Income Statement   FYE: June 30

	REVENUE ($mil)	NET INCOME ($mil)	NET PROFIT MARGIN	EMPLOYEES
06/21	1,241	12	1.0%	142
06/19	2,030	39	1.9%	—
06/18	1,815	11	0.6%	—
06/17	1,606	19	1.2%	—
Annual Growth	(6.2%)	(10.7%)	—	—

2021 Year-End Financials
Return on assets: 5.3%   Cash ($ mil.): 115
Return on equity: 7.3%
Current Ratio: 3.70

PGA TOUR, INC.

The PGA TOUR is the world's premier membership organization for touring professional golfers, co-sanctioning tournaments on the PGA TOUR, PGA TOUR Champions, Korn Ferry Tour, PGA TOUR Latinoamérica, and PGA TOUR Canada. Each PGA TOUR player has earned a position on the priority-ranking system that is used to select full-field open tournaments. Its major championships are the Masters Tournament, the Open Championship, THE PLAYERS Championship, and PGA Championship, U.S. Open. Worldwide, PGA TOUR tournaments are broadcast to nearly 215 countries and territories in about 30 languages. The PGA TOUR was formed in 1968 by a splinter faction of the PGA of America.

Geographic Reach
Headquartered in Florida, the PGA TOUR members hail from around the world. Its active international members are from nearly 30 countries and territories outside the US.

EXECUTIVES
V PRESS*, Charles L Zink
Public Relations Communications, Robert J Combs Senior V Press
OF PGA TOUR, Henry Hughes Senior V Press
Telecommunications PROD MEDIA, Donna G Orender Senior V Press
Finance, Ronald E Price Senior V Press
Vice Chairman, Will Mann V Press
OF, Jeff Monday V Press
Auditors: PRICEWATERHOUSECOOPERS LLP JA

LOCATIONS
HQ: PGA TOUR, INC.
100 TPC BLVD, PONTE VEDRA BEACH, FL 320823167
Phone: 904 285-3700
Web: WWW.PGATOUR.COM

COMPETITORS
AUGUSTA NATIONAL, INC.
CLUBCORP HOLDINGS, INC.
CONTINENTAL BASKETBALL ASSOCIATION
PROFESSIONAL BULL RIDERS, LLC
PROFESSIONAL DISC GOLF ASSOCIATION
TGC, INC.
THE ROYAL & ANCIENT GOLF CLUB OF ST. ANDREWS TRUST
TOWN SPORTS INTERNATIONAL HOLDINGS, INC.
UNITED STATES GOLF ASSOCIATION, INC.
WTA TOUR, INC.

HISTORICAL FINANCIALS
Company Type: Private

Income Statement   FYE: December 31

	REVENUE ($mil)	NET INCOME ($mil)	NET PROFIT MARGIN	EMPLOYEES
12/13	1,075	34	3.2%	3,563
12/06	894	3	0.3%	—
12/05	875	4	0.5%	—
12/04	802	3	0.4%	—
Annual Growth	3.3%	29.4%	—	—

2013 Year-End Financials
Return on assets: 1.6%   Cash ($ mil.): 149
Return on equity: 3.7%
Current Ratio: —

PHILADELPHIA CONSOLIDATED HOLDING CORP.

Because each industry has its own unique set of risks, Philadelphia Insurance Companies and its subsidiaries specialize in designing and underwriting commercial property/casualty insurance. Its niche clients include rental car companies (for that insurance they always want to sell you at the counter), not-for-profits, health and fitness centers, and day-care facilities. Its specialty lines include loss-control policies and liability coverage for such professionals as lawyers, doctors, accountants, dog groomers, and even insurance claims adjusters. Philadelphia Insurance Companies is a subsidiary of Tokio Marine Holdings.

Geographic Reach
Philadelphia Insurance Companies' operating subsidiaries, Philadelphia Insurance and Philadelphia Indemnity Insurance, sell and service policies through a network of independent agents and about 50 regional offices that stretch across the US. With its new-found backing from Tokio Marine, the insurer has access to broader distribution avenues in the US and overseas.

Sales and Marketing
In addition to commercial property and

casualty insurance, the company also sells personal coverage for collectible cars and homeowners flood insurance.

Strategy
Philadelphia Insurance Companies has been enhancing its information technology systems. The firm is working to upgrade its back-office infrastructure for more efficient handling of billing, claims, accounting, and data management functions.

LOCATIONS

HQ: PHILADELPHIA CONSOLIDATED HOLDING CORP.
1 BALA PLZ STE 100, BALA CYNWYD, PA 190041401
Phone: 610 617-7900
Web: WWW.PHLY.COM

PRODUCTS/OPERATIONS

Selected Products
Commercial and Personal Property/Casualty Insurance
    Adoption agencies
    Adult day care
    Amateur sports
    Antique collector car
    Apartments
    Auto leasing/rental program
    Boat dealers
    Bowling centers
    Builder's exchange
    Builders' risk
    Business auto fleet
    Camp operators
    Child care centers
    Consulting foresters
    Contractor environmental coverage
    Crime protection plus
    Entertainment
    Environmental
    Fairs and fairgrounds
    Festivals
    Film production
    Flood
    Golf and country clubs
    Health, fitness and wellness
    Home health care
    Homeowners association
    Hospice
    Hotels
    Life and business coaches
    Loss control
    Medical facilities and hospitals
    Motorsports
    Museums
    Non-profit and social service organizations
    Nursing homes
    Office parks
    Outdoor recreation
    Performing arts
    Pest control services
    Professional sports
    Public entities
    Real rstate dchedules
    Religious organizations
    RV parks and campgrounds
    Schools
    Security services (The Guardian)
    Shopping centers
    Special events
    Substance abuse rehabilitation facilities
    Temporary staffing agencies
    Volunteer fire department
    Zoos
Liability
    Accountants professional liability
    Allied Health professional liability
    Business owners
    Cyber security liability
    Employed lawyers professional liability
    Employment practices stand alone
    Excess liability
    Miscellaneous professional liability (Affinity Pro)

COMPETITORS

ADMIRAL INSURANCE COMPANY
APRIL
E-L Financial Corporation Limited
GREAT AMERICAN INSURANCE COMPANY
OHIO CASUALTY CORPORATION
SENTRY INSURANCE COMPANY
THE ERIE INSURANCE EXCHANGE ACTIVITIES ASSOCIATION, INC.
THE HANOVER INSURANCE COMPANY
TRAVELERS INSURANCE COMPANY LIMITED
UTICA MUTUAL INSURANCE COMPANY

HISTORICAL FINANCIALS
Company Type: Private

Income Statement — FYE: December 31

	ASSETS ($mil)	NET INCOME ($mil)	INCOME AS % OF ASSETS	EMPLOYEES
12/16	9,719	347	3.6%	1,374
12/15	9,047	323	3.6%	—
Annual Growth	7.4%	7.5%	—	—

PHOENIX CHILDREN'S HOSPITAL, INC.

Phoenix Children's Hospital (PCH) invests in the health of the next generation. Founded in 1983, one of the largest pediatric healthcare systems in the country provides a comprehensive range of medical services specifically for children and adolescents in the greater Phoenix area. The hospital has about 1,000 specialists who deliver care across more than 75 subspecialties, including emergency care, childhood cancers, hematology, neuroscience, heart disease, trauma, and orthopedics. It also operates a newborn intensive care unit (NICU) at its main campus. PCH has several pediatric outpatient care centers in surrounding Phoenix suburbs.

LOCATIONS

HQ: PHOENIX CHILDREN'S HOSPITAL, INC.
1919 E THOMAS RD, PHOENIX, AZ 850167710
Phone: 602 546-1000
Web: WWW.PHOENIXCHILDRENS.ORG

PRODUCTS/OPERATIONS

2014 Sales

	$ mil	% of total
Net patient service revenue	691.7	95
Net assets released from restrictions used for operations	10.2	2
Donations, gifts & contributions	8.3	1
Other operating revenue	15.3	2
Total	725.5	100

Selected Center of Excellence
Barrow Neurological Institute at Phoenix Children's Hospital
Center for Cancer and Blood Disorders
Center for Pediatric Orthopaedics
Level One Pediatric Trauma Center
Neonatal Intensive Care
Phoenix Children's Heart Center

COMPETITORS

ARROWHEAD REGIONAL MEDICAL CENTER
CHARLESTON AREA MEDICAL CENTER, INC.
CHILDREN'S HOSPITAL AND HEALTH SYSTEM, INC.
COVENANT MEDICAL CENTER, INC.
FLOYD HEALTHCARE MANAGEMENT, INC.
MILFORD REGIONAL MEDICAL CENTER, INC.
PHOEBE PUTNEY MEMORIAL HOSPITAL, INC.
TEXAS CHILDREN'S HOSPITAL
WELLMONT HEALTH SYSTEM
WELLSPAN HEALTH

HISTORICAL FINANCIALS
Company Type: Private

Income Statement — FYE: December 31

	REVENUE ($mil)	NET INCOME ($mil)	NET PROFIT MARGIN	EMPLOYEES
12/14	661	26	4.1%	3,000
12/13	655	31	4.9%	—
12/11	498	(5)	—	—
12/09	408	106	26.1%	—
Annual Growth	10.1%	(24.1%)	—	—

2014 Year-End Financials
Return on assets: 2.4%   Cash ($ mil.): 130
Return on equity: 8.8%
Current Ratio: 4.50

PHYSICIAN AFFILIATE GROUP OF NEW YORK PC

LOCATIONS

HQ: PHYSICIAN AFFILIATE GROUP OF NEW YORK PC
1400 PELHAM PKWY S BS37, BRONX, NY 104611138
Phone: 646 672-3651
Web: WWW.PAGNY.ORG

HISTORICAL FINANCIALS
Company Type: Private

Income Statement — FYE: June 30

	REVENUE ($mil)	NET INCOME ($mil)	NET PROFIT MARGIN	EMPLOYEES
06/19	745	21	2.8%	75
06/15	524	(0)	—	—
Annual Growth	9.2%	—	—	—

2019 Year-End Financials
Return on assets: 45.6%   Cash ($ mil.): 46
Return on equity: 45.6%
Current Ratio: —

PIEDMONT ATHENS REGIONAL MEDICAL CENTER, INC.

Piedmont Athens Regional Medical Center is a full-service health care facility with some 360 beds serving more than 15 counties in Athens and northeastern Georgia. The regional hospital provides general medical, surgical, and diagnostic services, as well as a wide range of specialty care in such areas as oncology, rehabilitation, pediatrics, and radiology. Piedmont Athens Regional is part of the not-for-profit Piedmont Healthcare, which operates about a dozen of hospitals, some 35 urgent care centers, and around 555 physician practice locations across Georgia.

Operations
Piedmont Athens Regional offers all major medical and surgical services including cancer care, cardiovascular care, neurology services, and orthopedic care. It has a Level 2 trauma center and a level 3 neonatal intensive care unit; it also offers women's care services, including a midwifery practice. The facility is the second-largest employer in the region with more than 3,300 employees, including physicians and healthcare professionals.

Geographic Reach
Located in Athens-Clarke County, Piedmont Athens Regional provides for the health care needs of people in a 17-county service area in northeast Georgia including the counties of Athens-Clarke, Banks, Barrow, Elbert, Franklin, Greene, Habersham, Hart, Jackson, Madison, Morgan, Oconee, Oglethorpe, Stephens, Taliaferro, Walton, and Wilkes.

Sales and Marketing
Company Background
Athens Regional Medical Center was established in 1919. It joined Piedmont Healthcare in October 2016.

EXECUTIVES
CMO*, Geoffrey Marx
Auditors : KPMG LLP GREENSBORO NC

LOCATIONS
HQ: PIEDMONT ATHENS REGIONAL MEDICAL CENTER, INC.
 1199 PRINCE AVE, ATHENS, GA 306062797
Phone: 706 475-7000
Web: WWW.PIEDMONT.ORG

PRODUCTS/OPERATIONS
Selected Services
Breast Health Center
Cancer Services
Diabetes Education
Emergency
Heart and Vascular
Home Health
Imaging Services
Labor and Delivery
Laboratory Services
Midwifery
Mind Body Institute
Occupational Health
Palliative Care
Pediatrics
Regional FirstCare
Rehabilitation
Sleep Disorders Center
Stroke Center
Surgery
Urgent Care
Women and Children
Wound Center

COMPETITORS
CONWAY REGIONAL MEDICAL CENTER, INC.
DEKALB MEDICAL CENTER, INC.
FIRSTHEALTH OF THE CAROLINAS, INC.
HEARTLAND REGIONAL MEDICAL CENTER
HOSPITAL AUTHORITY OF VALDOSTA AND LOWNDES COUNTY, GEORGIA
JEFFERSON HOSPITAL
NAVICENT HEALTH, INC.
NORTH MISSISSIPPI MEDICAL CENTER, INC.
RIVERVIEW HOSPITAL
UNITED HEALTH SERVICES HOSPITALS, INC.

HISTORICAL FINANCIALS
Company Type: Private

Income Statement — FYE: June 30

	REVENUE ($mil)	NET INCOME ($mil)	NET PROFIT MARGIN	EMPLOYEES
06/21	586	65	11.2%	3,000
06/20	502	10	2.0%	—
06/19	517	(21)	—	—
06/18	502	34	6.9%	—
Annual Growth	5.3%	23.7%	—	—

2021 Year-End Financials
Return on assets: 13.6%   Cash ($ mil.): 15
Return on equity: 32.2%
Current Ratio: 0.40

PIEDMONT HOSPITAL, INC.

Founded in 1905, Piedmont Healthcare is a private, not-for-profit organization that provides a hassle-free, unified experience. Every year, it cares for 3.4 million patients, has over 30 million visits to Piedmont.org, more than 450,000 appointments scheduled online by patients and over 100,000 virtual visits. Piedmont Healthcare is supported by a work force of more than 37,000 across some 1,400 locations and serving communities that comprise 80% of Georgia's population. This includes more than 20 hospitals, about 65 Piedmont Urgent Care centers, around 25 QuickCare locations, some 1,875 Piedmont Clinic physician practices and more than 2,800 Piedmont Clinic members. Piedmont Healthcare has provided $1.4 billion in uncompensated care and community benefit programming to the communities it serves over the past five years.

Operations
Piedmont Atlanta, the flagship hospital of Piedmont Healthcare, has grown into a 643-bed facility renowned for its high quality, patient-centered healthcare. Piedmont Athens Regional is one of northeast Georgia's largest not-for-profit hospitals, with 359-bed, acute care hospital and features a regional Level II trauma center and Level III neonatal ICU. Piedmont Newton is a 103-bed, acute-care, community hospital in Covington, Georgia offering 24-hour emergency services, women's services, a Level II Neonatal Intensive Care Unit (NICU), and general medical/surgical services. Piedmont Rockdale offers 24-hour emergency services, medical and surgical services and obstetrics/women's services including a Level III Neonatal Intensive Care Unit (NICU) and Laborist program.

Piedmont Healthcare provides a wide variety of services, including but not limited to heart and cancer treatment, transplant, primary care, neurology and neurosciences, women's services, emergency, breast health, extended care, imaging, rehabilitation, robotic surgery, urgent care and quick care and wound care and hyperbaric, among others.

Each year, it performs about 110,610 surgeries, completing some 490 organ transplants, and handling around 770,340 emergency department visits. It also sees about 1.2 million outpatients and around 20,100 infant deliveries annually.

Geographic Reach
Based in Georgia, Piedmont Healthcare serves communities across approximately 1.400 locations.

Sales and Marketing
Piedmont Healthcare serves approximately 3.4 million patients and communities that comprise 80% of Georgia's population.

Auditors : KPMG LLP ATLANTA GA

LOCATIONS
HQ: PIEDMONT HOSPITAL, INC.
 1968 PEACHTREE RD NW, ATLANTA, GA 303091281
Phone: 404 605-5000
Web: WWW.PIEDMONT.ORG

PRODUCTS/OPERATIONS
2014 Sales

	$ mil.	% of total
Net patient service revenue	1,595.3	96
Other revenue	62.1	4
Total	1,657.4	100

Selected Operations
Piedmont Atlanta
Piedmont Fayette Hospital (Fayetteville)
Piedmont Henry Hospital (Stockbridge)
Piedmont Mountainside Hospital (Jasper)
Piedmont Newnan Hospital (Newnan)
Piedmont Physicians Group (metropolitan Atlanta)

COMPETITORS
ALTRU HEALTH SYSTEM
COVENANT MEDICAL CENTER, INC.

EVANGELICAL COMMUNITY HOSPITAL
GUTHRIE HEALTHCARE SYSTEM
PHOEBE PUTNEY MEMORIAL HOSPITAL, INC.
PHOENIX CHILDREN'S HOSPITAL, INC.
SPARTANBURG REGIONAL HEALTH SERVICES DISTRICT, INC.
TAOS HEALTH SYSTEMS, INC.
THE LANCASTER GENERAL HOSPITAL
WELLSPAN HEALTH

HISTORICAL FINANCIALS
Company Type: Private

Income Statement — FYE: June 30

	REVENUE ($mil)	NET INCOME ($mil)	NET PROFIT MARGIN	EMPLOYEES
06/20	1,110	128	11.6%	6,419
06/16	918	60	6.5%	—
06/15	857	66	7.8%	—
06/10	689	75	11.0%	—
Annual Growth	4.9%	5.4%	—	—

2020 Year-End Financials
Return on assets: 7.3% Cash ($ mil.): 28
Return on equity: 17.5%
Current Ratio: 0.20

PIGGLY WIGGLY ALABAMA DISTRIBUTING CO., INC.

Auditors: DENT BAKER & COMPANY LLP BI

LOCATIONS
HQ: PIGGLY WIGGLY ALABAMA DISTRIBUTING CO., INC.
2400 J TERRELL WOOTEN DR, BESSEMER, AL 350202272
Phone: 205 481-2300
Web: WWW.PWADC.NET

HISTORICAL FINANCIALS
Company Type: Private

Income Statement — FYE: July 29

	REVENUE ($mil)	NET INCOME ($mil)	NET PROFIT MARGIN	EMPLOYEES
07/11	772	0	0.1%	500
07/10	837	0	0.0%	—
07/09	830	0	0.0%	—
Annual Growth	(3.5%)	85.6%	—	—

2011 Year-End Financials
Return on assets: 0.5% Cash ($ mil.): 4
Return on equity: 1.7%
Current Ratio: 1.70

PIH HEALTH WHITTIER HOSPITAL

LOCATIONS
HQ: PIH HEALTH WHITTIER HOSPITAL
12401 WASHINGTON BLVD, WHITTIER, CA 906021006
Phone: 562 698-0811
Web: WWW.PIHHEALTH.ORG

HISTORICAL FINANCIALS
Company Type: Private

Income Statement — FYE: September 30

	REVENUE ($mil)	NET INCOME ($mil)	NET PROFIT MARGIN	EMPLOYEES
09/19	651	59	9.2%	3,150
09/14	495	18	3.8%	—
09/13	491	81	16.7%	—
09/12	419	69	16.6%	—
Annual Growth	6.5%	(2.1%)	—	—

2019 Year-End Financials
Return on assets: 4.6% Cash ($ mil.): —
Return on equity: 8.5%
Current Ratio: 0.20

PIKEVILLE MEDICAL CENTER, INC.

Taking a nasty fall while hiking the rugged Appalachians will likely land you at Pikeville Medical Center (PMC). Serving patients in eastern Kentucky, the hospital boasts more than 260 beds and provides a full range of inpatient, outpatient, and surgical services. PMC's centers and departments handle a number of specialties, such as diagnostic imaging, echocardiogram, neurosurgery, cancer care, and bariatric surgery. Employing some 350 physicians, PMC also operates a rehabilitation hospital, a home health agency, and outpatient family practice and specialty clinics, as well as a physician residency program. PMC first opened on Christmas Day in 1924.

Operations
Pikeville, Kentucky-based PMC offers more than 400 services.

Strategy
PMC is rapidly expanding its services and facilities to keep pace with the needs of area residents. In recent years it has added such new services as pulmonary rehabilitation, plastic surgery, and orthopedic trauma. In addition, the hospital launched a $150 million expansion project that will add an 11-story outpatient center (including physician practices and surgery suites) and a 10-story parking garage. Additional expansion efforts have included opening new outpatient cancer, diagnostic, pain management, and primary care clinics.

An active participant in clinical trials and studies, PMC works to expand its research opportunities for patients and physicians. In 2013 the hospital began new treatment for patients with Paroxysmal Atrial Fibrillation (Afib) using Medtronic's Arctic Front Advance Cardiac Cryoballoon System.

Since 2012, when it inked a Medicaid contract with Coventry, PMC has contracts with all three providers: Coventry, Wellcare, and Kentucky Spirit. PMC become member of the Mayo Clinic Care Network in 2013. The agreement gives PMC providers access to Mayo Clinic resources, including its online point-of-care information system and its electronic consulting process that connects physicians with Mayo Clinic specialists on questions of diagnosis, therapy, or care management.

Auditors: PYA PC KNOXVILLE TENNESSEE

LOCATIONS
HQ: PIKEVILLE MEDICAL CENTER, INC.
911 BYPASS RD, PIKEVILLE, KY 415011602
Phone: 606 218-3500
Web: WWW.PIKEVILLEHOSPITAL.ORG

PRODUCTS/OPERATIONS
Selected Services
Bariatric Surgery
Breast Care Center
Critical Care
Diagnostics
Diabetes Education
Ear, Nose & Throat (Otolaryngology)
Emergency
Endocrinology
Family Practice
Gastroenterology
Gynecology/Obstetrics
Family Practice Clinic
Heart Institute
Heart Failure/Coumadin Clinic
Home Health
Home Medical Equipment
Inpatient
Infectious Disease
Laboratory Services
Leonard Lawson Cancer Center
Neonatology
Nephrology
Neurosurgery
Ophthalmology
Other Patient Services
Orthopedic Surgery
Palliative Care
Pediatrics
Pharmacy
Plastic & Reconstructive Surgery
Pulmonary Clinic
Radiology
Rehabilitation
Residency Program
Rheumatology
Sleep
Urology
Women and Childrens' Services
Wound Care Center

COMPETITORS
ARROWHEAD REGIONAL MEDICAL CENTER

BETHESDA HOSPITAL, INC.
NORTH FLORIDA REGIONAL MEDICAL CENTER, INC.
UNITED REGIONAL HEALTH CARE SYSTEM, INC.
YUMA REGIONAL MEDICAL CENTER

HISTORICAL FINANCIALS
Company Type: Private

Income Statement — FYE: September 30

	REVENUE ($mil)	NET INCOME ($mil)	NET PROFIT MARGIN	EMPLOYEES
09/20	568	17	3.0%	2,527
09/19	547	5	1.1%	—
09/18	524	(14)	—	—
09/16	489	29	5.9%	—
Annual Growth	3.8%	(12.3%)	—	—

2020 Year-End Financials
Return on assets: 2.4%   Cash ($ mil.): 277
Return on equity: 5.8%
Current Ratio: 3.00

PILKINGTON NORTH AMERICA, INC.

Pilkington North America has a clear view of the US glass market. The company manufactures and markets glass and glazing products primarily for the automotive and building industries. Benefits of its glass include fire protection, noise control, solar heat control, and thermal insulation. A majority of its sales come from automotive glass sold to the original equipment and replacement markets. More than a quarter of sales are made from building glass geared at homeowners and architects. A small but growing part of its business focuses on specialty glass used in solar energy conversion. Pilkington North America is a subsidiary of Pilkington plc, which operates as part of Japanese glass giant Nippon Sheet Glass.

Geographic Reach
Pilkington North America manages six float glass lines in the US (where molten glass is poured on a bed of molten tin to ensure flat surface and uniform thickness), more than half a dozen automotive glass fabrication facilities in the US, Canada, and Mexico, and a network of more than 100 US wholesale centers that distribute automotive replacement glass products.

Its six float glass lines including Rossford, Ohio (2); Laurinburg, North Carolina (2); Ottawa, Illinois (1); Lathrop, California (1). Products are shipped from its distribution centers in Columbus, Ohio and Phoenix, Arizona to external retailers and wholesale customers.

Sales and Marketing
The company provides glass products and glazing systems to automotive original equipment manufacturers of light vehicles, buses, trucks, and specialized and utility vehicles; and glass products and accessories for replacing and repairing windshields and other glass parts to automotive glass replacement aftermarket sectors. Pilkington North America also serves homeowners, architects, and other window manufacturers and offers its products to retailers and wholesalers.

Automotive products (57% OEMs and 43% for automotive glass replacement) account for 70% of total sales; architectural products account for the remaining 30%. Products are shipped from its distribution centers in Phoenix and Columbus, Ohio, to external retailers and wholesale customers.

Strategy
In line with its parent's strategy, a key focus for Pilkington North America's future is expanding its solar energy portfolio within its building products segment. The company anticipates an increase in volumes and that sales of solar energy glass will contribute a significant portion of those higher volumes. Although some of its float glass production lines were suspended during the economic crisis, some have since been converted into solar energy lines and are coming back on stream to support its expansion particularly in photovoltaics.

Product introductions are also a key part of Pilkington North America's growth strategy. In 2014 it introduced Pilkington MirroView 50/50, which enhances the standard MirroView's visual performance for a brightly lit environment, such as a store or showroom, and Pilkington OptiView Pro, a non-conductive anti-reflection coating especially designed for touch screen applications. In 2013 the company introduced Optiwhite which widens the color choice.

LOCATIONS

HQ: PILKINGTON NORTH AMERICA, INC.
811 MADISON AVE FL 3, TOLEDO, OH 436045688
Phone: 419 247-3731
Web: WWW.PILKINGTON.COM

PRODUCTS/OPERATIONS

Selected Products and Brands
Decoration
  Texture glass (18 pattern designs)
Fire protection
  Pyrodur (fire-resistant and radiant heat-protected glass)
  Pyrostop (fire-resistant insulating glass)
Glass systems
  Planar (structural glass system for architects)
  Profilit (exterior glazing glass)
Noise control
  Optiphon (laminated glass with high sound insulation)
Self-cleaning
  Activ Clear (clear float glass with self-cleaning properties)
Solar control
  Arctic Blue (tinted glass)
  Eclipse Advantage (solar control and thermal insulation glass)
  EverGreen (tinted glass)
  Solar-E (solar control and thermal insulation glass)
  SuperGrey (gray-colored solar control float glass)
Solar energy
  NSG TEC (coated glass for photovoltaic technologies)
  Sunplus (extra clear patterned glass for solar energy conversion)
  Optiwhite (extra clear float glass for solar energy conversion)
Special applications
  Mirropane (interior glass to create "infinity" mirror effects)
  TEC Glass (electrically conductive glass for flat panel displays, heated glass, and oven doors)
Thermal insulation
  Energy Advantage (energy-efficient window glass)
  OptiFloat (float glass)
  Spacia (medium thermal insulation glass)

COMPETITORS

AGC INC.
APOGEE ENTERPRISES, INC.
CARDINAL GLASS INDUSTRIES, INC.
GUARDIAN INDUSTRIES, LLC
NIPPON SHEET GLASS COMPANY, LIMITED
PITTSBURGH GLASS WORKS, LLC
QUANEX BUILDING PRODUCTS CORPORATION
SCHOTT CORPORATION
VIRACON, INC.
Vitro, S.A.B. de C.V.

HISTORICAL FINANCIALS
Company Type: Private

Income Statement — FYE: March 31

	REVENUE ($mil)	NET INCOME ($mil)	NET PROFIT MARGIN	EMPLOYEES
03/08	967	(11)	—	4,425
03/07	913	(17)	—	—
03/04	931	31	3.4%	—
Annual Growth	1.0%	—	—	—

2008 Year-End Financials
Return on assets: 12.3%   Cash ($ mil.): —
Return on equity: (-1.2%)
Current Ratio: 0.50

PIMA COUNTY

Auditors: STATE OF ARIZONA-DEBBIE DAVENP

LOCATIONS

HQ: PIMA COUNTY
130 W CONGRESS ST FL 6, TUCSON, AZ 857011317
Phone: 520 724-9999
Web: WEBCMS.PIMA.GOV

HISTORICAL FINANCIALS
Company Type: Private

Income Statement — FYE: June 30

	REVENUE ($mil)	NET INCOME ($mil)	NET PROFIT MARGIN	EMPLOYEES
06/17	873	17	2.0%	7,500
06/16	863	2	0.3%	—
06/13	789	(13)	—	—
Annual Growth	2.6%	—	—	—

2017 Year-End Financials
Return on assets: 0.4%   Cash ($ mil.): 521
Return on equity: 0.9%
Current Ratio: —

PINNACLE HEALTH HOSPITAL

Auditors : BAKER TILLY VIRCHOW KRAUSE LLP

LOCATIONS

HQ: PINNACLE HEALTH HOSPITAL
   4300 LONDONDERRY RD, HARRISBURG, PA 171095317
Phone: 717 782-3131
Web: WWW.PINNACLEHEALTH.ORG

HISTORICAL FINANCIALS
Company Type: Private

Income Statement — FYE: June 30

	REVENUE ($mil)	NET INCOME ($mil)	NET PROFIT MARGIN	EMPLOYEES
06/14	759	94	12.5%	4,800
06/13	733	105	14.4%	—
06/08	0	0	14.6%	—
06/05	0	0	—	—
Annual Growth	—	—	—	—

2014 Year-End Financials
Return on assets: 10.0% Cash ($ mil.): 1
Return on equity: 25.5%
Current Ratio: 0.30

PITT COUNTY MEMORIAL HOSPITAL, INCORPORATED

Vidant Medical Center is an acute health services facility that serves the vibrant community of Greenville, North Carolina, and surrounding areas. The 909-bed regional referral hospital's specialty divisions include Vidant Children's Hospital, East Carolina Heart Institute, a rehabilitation center, and the outpatient Vidant SurgiCenter. Other services include oncology, transplant, women's health, orthopedic, behavioral care, and home health and hospice care units. The center also serves as a teaching facility for East Carolina University's Brody School of Medicine. Vidant Medical Center (formerly Pitt County Memorial Hospital) is a member of University Health Systems of Eastern Carolina (dba Vidant Health).

Operations
In addition to serving as a primary teaching facility for the Brody School of Medicine, Vidant Medical Center provides clinical training for East Carolina University's allied health and nursing programs. About 2,000 students complete clinical programs at the medical center and its affiliated Vidant Health facilities each year.

Its subsidiary, PMI Inc., offers property management services.

Altogether, Vidant Medical Center serves more than 1.4 million people across its 29-county service area. Boasting a clinical staff of more than 500 physicians and 1,200 nurses, the medical center in 2013 tended to more than 46,000 inpatients and more than 275,000 outpatients. Its emergency department visits reached 121,000-plus in 2013.

Geographic Reach
Vidant Medical Center provides care to patients in a 29-county service territory in eastern North Carolina. It operates as a regional referral center for smaller community hospitals in the area, taking on complex care cases in its specialized fields of medicine.

Strategy
To enhance its service offerings to area residents, the Vidant Health organization regularly updates its facilities through capital improvement projects. In addition to basic equipment and infrastructure upgrades in 2011, the hospital completed phase one of an expansion project at the Vidant Medical Center that aims to improve the hospital's pediatric and cancer care capabilities.

To signify its mission to enhance the quality of life in its service territories, in 2012 University Health Systems of Eastern Carolina began operating as Vidant Health, and the Pitt County Memorial Hospital was renamed as Vidant Memorial Hospital.

Auditors : RSM US LLP MINNEAPOLIS MINNE

LOCATIONS

HQ: PITT COUNTY MEMORIAL HOSPITAL, INCORPORATED
   2100 STANTONSBURG RD, GREENVILLE, NC 278342832
Phone: 252 847-4100
Web: WWW.ECUHEALTH.ORG

PRODUCTS/OPERATIONS

Selected Services
Asthma Program (Pediatric)
Audiology
Behavioral & Mental Health
Cancer Care
Child Life
Children's Care
Children's Emergency Department
Children's Hospital
Community Health Programs
CyberKnife
Diagnostic Imaging
Diabetes
Emergency Services
Endoscopy Services
Gamma Knife

COMPETITORS

ATLANTIC HEALTH SYSTEM INC.
CAROMONT HEALTH, INC.
CONEMAUGH HEALTH COMPANY, LLC
GREATER BALTIMORE MEDICAL CENTER, INC.
HCA-HEALTHONE LLC
HOSPITAL SERVICE DISTRICT 1
SHAWNEE MISSION MEDICAL CENTER, INC.
SHELBY COUNTY HEALTH CARE CORPORATION
TRINITAS REGIONAL MEDICAL CENTER A NEW JERSEY NONPROFIT CORPORATION
UNIVERSITY OF VIRGINIA MEDICAL CENTER

HISTORICAL FINANCIALS
Company Type: Private

Income Statement — FYE: September 30

	REVENUE ($mil)	NET INCOME ($mil)	NET PROFIT MARGIN	EMPLOYEES
09/20	1,974	58	3.0%	15,000
09/18	1,201	131	10.9%	—
09/15	1,066	79	7.5%	—
09/14	1,025	79	7.8%	—
Annual Growth	11.5%	(5.0%)	—	—

2020 Year-End Financials
Return on assets: 2.4% Cash ($ mil.): 111
Return on equity: 4.8%
Current Ratio: 1.90

PITTSBURGH SCHOOL DISTRICT

Auditors : MAHER DUESSEL PITTSBURGH PEN

LOCATIONS

HQ: PITTSBURGH SCHOOL DISTRICT
   341 S BELLEFIELD AVE, PITTSBURGH, PA 152133552
Phone: 412 622-3500
Web: WWW.PGHSCHOOLS.ORG

HISTORICAL FINANCIALS
Company Type: Private

Income Statement — FYE: December 31

	REVENUE ($mil)	NET INCOME ($mil)	NET PROFIT MARGIN	EMPLOYEES
12/21	726	(0)	0.0%	1,770
12/20	715	3	0.5%	—
12/19	707	(21)	—	—
12/18	690	(19)	—	—
Annual Growth	1.7%	—	—	—

2021 Year-End Financials
Return on assets: — Cash ($ mil.): 16
Return on equity: —
Current Ratio: 2.50

PLACID HOLDING COMPANY

Auditors : HEIN & ASSOCIATES LLP DALLAS

LOCATIONS

HQ: PLACID HOLDING COMPANY
   1601 ELM ST STE 3900, DALLAS, TX 752014708
Phone: 214 880-8479

HISTORICAL FINANCIALS
Company Type: Private

Income Statement — FYE: December 31

	REVENUE ($mil)	NET INCOME ($mil)	NET PROFIT MARGIN	EMPLOYEES
12/13	4,929	47	1.0%	2
12/02	532	3	0.6%	—
12/01	579	18	3.1%	—
12/00	564	5	1.0%	—
Annual Growth	18.1%	17.5%	—	—

2013 Year-End Financials
Return on assets: 7.5%   Cash ($ mil.): 51
Return on equity: 12.8%
Current Ratio: 1.40

PLACID REFINING COMPANY LLC

A calm presence in the volatile oil and gas industry, Placid Refining owns and operates the Port Allen refinery in Louisiana, which converts crude oil into a number of petroleum products, including diesel, ethanol, gasoline, liquid petroleum gas, jet fuel, and fuel oils. Placid Refining's refinery has the capacity to process 80,000 barrels of crude oil per day. The company is one of the largest employers and taxpayers in West Baton Rouge Parish. Placid Refining, which is controlled by Petro-Hunt, distribute fuels across a dozen states in the southeastern US, from Texas to Virginia, and is a major supplier of jet fuel to the US military.

Auditors : HEIN & ASSOCIATES LLP DALLAS

LOCATIONS

HQ: PLACID REFINING COMPANY LLC
2101 CEDAR SPRINGS RD, DALLAS, TX 752012104
Phone: 214 880-8479
Web: WWW.PLACIDREFINING.COM

COMPETITORS

BIG WEST OIL PARTNERS, LP
CATLETTSBURG REFINING, LLC
Imperial Oil Limited
PETRO STAR INC.
SHELL MARTINEZ REFINING COMPANY

HISTORICAL FINANCIALS
Company Type: Private

Income Statement — FYE: December 31

	REVENUE ($mil)	NET INCOME ($mil)	NET PROFIT MARGIN	EMPLOYEES
12/13	4,929	47	1.0%	200
12/11	4,699	4	0.1%	—
12/10	3,686	39	1.1%	—
12/06	2,925	128	4.4%	—
Annual Growth	7.7%	(13.1%)	—	—

2013 Year-End Financials
Return on assets: 4.2%   Cash ($ mil.): 42
Return on equity: 1.0%
Current Ratio: 1.10

PLAINS COTTON COOPERATIVE ASSOCIATION

Plainly speaking, most of the US cotton used by textile mills worldwide starts with the Plains Cotton Cooperative Association (PCCA). The farmer-owned co-op markets millions of bales annually for members in Oklahoma, Kansas, and Texas. To obtain a competitive price for their cotton, PCCA takes advantage of Telmark LP's access to The Seam, an online cotton marketplace that continually updates cotton prices, buyer data, and more. The co-op operates cotton warehouses in Texas, Oklahoma, and Kansas. PCCA sold its textile and apparel operations in 2014 to focus exclusively on cotton marketing and warehousing. Formed in 1953, PCCA's customers include Replay, Urban Outfitters, and Abercrombie & Fitch.

Operations
PCCA is a member of the American Apparel Producers' Network, Amcot, the National Cotton Council of America, the National Council of Textile Organizations, the Texas Agricultural Coop Council, and The International Cotton Association.

Geographic Reach
Lubbock, Texas-based Plains Cotton Cooperative Association owns half a dozen cotton warehouses in Kansas, Oklahoma, and Texas. Its Telmark LP business is also headquartered in Lubbock.

Financial Performance
The cooperative, which distributed more than $22 million to its members, posted total net margins of $10.4 million from its fiscal 2012-2013 operations. Despite a small crop during the reporting period, PCCA saw its cotton marketing and warehouse divisions post profits. It was also helped by its IT division and support services. Feeling the drag of the US economy and unemployment, the co-op's textile and apparel division focused on cutting costs.

Strategy
To better focus on its core cotton marketing and warehousing businesses, PCCA sold its textile and apparel division to American Textile Holdings, LLC (AmTex) in June 2014. The sale gave AmTex control of all the operations of American Cotton Growers (ACG) denim mill in Littlefield, Texas, and Denimatrix S.A. in Guatemala.

Auditors : CROWE LLP DALLAS TEXAS

LOCATIONS

HQ: PLAINS COTTON COOPERATIVE ASSOCIATION
3301 E 50TH ST, LUBBOCK, TX 794044331
Phone: 806 763-8011
Web: WWW.PCCA.COM

PRODUCTS/OPERATIONS
Selected Sales and Services
Buying cotton
Cotton gins
   Gin bookkeeping
   Gin patronage
   Marketing and invoicing
   Scale ticket software
   Support and training
   Technology solutions
Cotton producers
   Agent gins
   Cash marketing
   marketing contracts
   Pool marketing
Warehousing

COMPETITORS

CALCOT, LTD.
PYXUS INTERNATIONAL, INC.
STAPLE COTTON COOPERATIVE ASSOCIATION
UNIVERSAL CORPORATION
WYNNSTAY GROUP P.L.C.

HISTORICAL FINANCIALS
Company Type: Private

Income Statement — FYE: June 30

	REVENUE ($mil)	NET INCOME ($mil)	NET PROFIT MARGIN	EMPLOYEES
06/16	892	23	2.7%	170
06/15	975	25	2.6%	—
Annual Growth	(8.6%)	(7.7%)	—	—

2016 Year-End Financials
Return on assets: 11.4%   Cash ($ mil.): —
Return on equity: 46.6%
Current Ratio: 1.50

PLAINS PIPELINE, L.P.

LOCATIONS

HQ: PLAINS PIPELINE, L.P.
333 CLAY ST STE 1600, HOUSTON, TX 770024101
Phone: 713 646-4100
Web: WWW.PLAINS.COM

HISTORICAL FINANCIALS
Company Type: Private

Income Statement — FYE: December 31

	REVENUE ($mil)	NET INCOME ($mil)	NET PROFIT MARGIN	EMPLOYEES
12/17	935	783	83.7%	200
12/16	780	621	79.6%	—
Annual Growth	19.9%	26.1%	—	—

2017 Year-End Financials
Return on assets: 8.9%   Cash ($ mil.): 8
Return on equity: 17.4%
Current Ratio: 0.40

PLAN INTERNATIONAL, INC.

Auditors: DYL & PERILLO INC PROVIDENCE

LOCATIONS

HQ: PLAN INTERNATIONAL, INC.
228 E 45TH ST FL 15, NEW YORK, NY 100173344
Phone: 401 738-5600
Web: WWW.PLAN-INTERNATIONAL.ORG

HISTORICAL FINANCIALS

Company Type: Private

Income Statement — FYE: June 30

	REVENUE ($mil)	NET INCOME ($mil)	NET PROFIT MARGIN	EMPLOYEES
06/20	612	(48)	—	21
06/18	660	33	5.0%	—
Annual Growth	(3.6%)	—	—	—

2020 Year-End Financials
Return on assets: (-17.8%)   Cash ($ mil.): 168
Return on equity: (-26.4%)
Current Ratio: 5.80

PLAN INTERNATIONAL, INC.

Auditors: DYL & PERILLO INC PROVIDENCE

LOCATIONS

HQ: PLAN INTERNATIONAL, INC.
155 PLAN WAY STE A, WARWICK, RI 028861099
Phone: 401 294-3693
Web: WWW.PLAN-INTERNATIONAL.ORG

HISTORICAL FINANCIALS

Company Type: Private

Income Statement — FYE: June 30

	REVENUE ($mil)	NET INCOME ($mil)	NET PROFIT MARGIN	EMPLOYEES
06/15	684	(5)	—	7
06/14	657	(5)	—	—
06/12	601	29	4.9%	—
06/10	531	93	17.6%	—
Annual Growth	5.2%	—	—	—

2015 Year-End Financials
Return on assets: (-2.2%)   Cash ($ mil.): 185
Return on equity: (-3.1%)
Current Ratio: 6.60

PLANO INDEPENDENT SCHOOL DISTRICT

EXECUTIVES

Associate Superintendent, Jim Hirsch
Auditors: WEAVER AND TIDWELL LLP DA

LOCATIONS

HQ: PLANO INDEPENDENT SCHOOL DISTRICT
2700 W 15TH ST, PLANO, TX 750757524
Phone: 469 752-8100
Web: WWW.PISD.EDU

HISTORICAL FINANCIALS

Company Type: Private

Income Statement — FYE: June 30

	REVENUE ($mil)	NET INCOME ($mil)	NET PROFIT MARGIN	EMPLOYEES
06/21	892	(38)	—	5,610
06/20	871	(61)	—	—
06/19	928	(74)	—	—
06/18	840	34	4.1%	—
Annual Growth	2.0%	—	—	—

2021 Year-End Financials
Return on assets: (-2.0%)   Cash ($ mil.): —
Return on equity: (-8.3%)
Current Ratio: —

PLY GEM HOLDINGS, INC.

Ply Gem makes and supplies exterior building materials used in home construction and renovation primarily in the US. Its products have included vinyl siding, aluminum windows and doors, stone veneer, and fence and railing. In addition to Variform (vinyl siding), its brands offer a broad selection of quality building products that includes nearly everything on the outside of a house. These products lead the industry as the #1 in windows, vinyl siding and metal accessories, with an unmatched portfolio, backed by industry-leading warranties. Every product is rigorously tested to ensure exceptional durability and performance for every region or climate. Limitless color, design and texture options are intended to work together to create custom curb appeal.

IPO

Operations

Ply Gem offers a wide array of products, including siding, windows, patio doors, stone, fence and railing, shutters and accents, gutters, as well as trim and moulding. The company's Home Design Visualizer is the ultimate tool for design inspiration and discovery. Its siding products have included vinyl, solar defense, insulated, steel, and aluminum lap siding, shake and shingle siding, and vertical siding. Customers can also choose from window styles offered by Ply Gem such as double hung, single hung, casement, as well as door styles including sliding, swinging, multi-sliding, and french doors.

Geographic Reach

The company is headquartered in North Carolina.

Mergers and Acquisitions

EXECUTIVES

Chief Accounting Officer, Bryan Boyle
Auditors: KPMG LLP RALEIGH NORTH CAROL

LOCATIONS

HQ: PLY GEM HOLDINGS, INC.
5020 WESTON PKWY STE 400, CARY, NC 275132322
Phone: 919 677-3900
Web: WWW.PLYGEM.COM

2017 Sales

	$ mil.	% of total
United States	1,849.9	90
Canada	202.8	10
Other foreign countries	3.6	—
Total	2,056.3	100

PRODUCTS/OPERATIONS

2017 Sales

	$ mil.	% of total
Windows & Doors	1,086.1	53
Sliding, Fencing, & Stone	970.2	47
Total	2,056.3	100

Selected Brands

Variform Siding
Napco Siding
Mastic Siding
Mitten Siding
Performance Siding
Georgia-Pacific
Canyon Stone
Simonton Windows
Great Lakes Window
Durabuilt
Leaf Relief
Leaf Relief Snap Tight
Leaf Smart
Leaf Logic
Ply Gem Shutters & Accents
Ply Gem Fence & Rail
Ply Gem Gutters
Ply Gem Roofing
Ply Gem Stone
Ply Gem Trim & Moulding
Ply Gem Windows & Doors

Selected Products

Fence & Rail
Gutters
Siding
Steel Siding
Stone Veneer
Trim
Windows and Doors

COMPETITORS

ANDERSEN CORPORATION
ASSOCIATED MATERIALS, LLC
BMC STOCK HOLDINGS, INC.
BUILDERS FIRSTSOURCE, INC.
INSTALLED BUILDING PRODUCTS, INC.
JELD-WEN HOLDING, INC.
MW MANUFACTURERS INC.
PELLA CORPORATION
THERMAL INDUSTRIES, INC.
WEATHER SHIELD MFG., INC.

HISTORICAL FINANCIALS
Company Type: Private

Income Statement   FYE: December 31

	REVENUE ($mil)	NET INCOME ($mil)	NET PROFIT MARGIN	EMPLOYEES
12/17	2,056	68	3.3%	9,000
12/16	1,911	75	3.9%	—
12/15	1,839	32	1.8%	—
12/14	1,566	(31)	—	—
Annual Growth	9.5%	—	—	—

2017 Year-End Financials
Return on assets: 5.2%   Cash ($ mil.): 71
Return on equity: 83.4%
Current Ratio: 1.70

POLK COUNTY

EXECUTIVES
County Manager, Bill Beasley
Vice Chairman*, Bill Braswell

LOCATIONS
HQ: POLK COUNTY
330 W CHURCH ST, BARTOW, FL 338303760
Phone: 863 534-6000
Web: WWW.POLK-COUNTY.COM

HISTORICAL FINANCIALS
Company Type: Private

Income Statement   FYE: September 30

	REVENUE ($mil)	NET INCOME ($mil)	NET PROFIT MARGIN	EMPLOYEES
09/18	602	48	8.0%	3,600
09/15	508	1	0.3%	—
09/12	593	(39)	—	—
09/09	589	(68)	—	—
Annual Growth	0.2%	—	—	—

2018 Year-End Financials
Return on assets: 1.0%   Cash ($ mil.): —
Return on equity: 1.3%
Current Ratio: —

POLK COUNTY SCHOOL DISTRICT

Auditors : CHERRY BEKAERT LLP ORLANDO F

LOCATIONS
HQ: POLK COUNTY SCHOOL DISTRICT
1915 S FLORAL AVE, BARTOW, FL 338307124
Phone: 863 534-0500
Web: WWW.POLKSCHOOLSFL.COM

HISTORICAL FINANCIALS
Company Type: Private

Income Statement   FYE: June 30

	REVENUE ($mil)	NET INCOME ($mil)	NET PROFIT MARGIN	EMPLOYEES
06/14	871	(5)	—	4,420
06/13	827	(40)	—	—
06/12	821	(42)	—	—
Annual Growth	3.0%	—	—	—

2014 Year-End Financials
Return on assets: (-0.4%)   Cash ($ mil.): 69
Return on equity: (-0.6%)
Current Ratio: —

POPULATION SERVICES INTERNATIONAL

Population Services International (PSI) goes far beyond the scope of its name. Founded in 1970 to promote global family planning, PSI has established social programs that use local networks in low-income regions to distribute such lifelines as insecticide-treated mosquito nets, iodized salt, snake boots, and insect repellent, along with condoms, contraceptives, and pregnancy test kits. The group prides itself on using business principals to confront health issues in more than 65 countries worldwide. It reportedly has averted 4.2 million unintended pregnancies, some 29 million malaria cases, and provided 1.8-plus million clients with of HIV testing and counseling. PSI is also active ensuring safe water supplies.

EXECUTIVES
Chief Human Resources Officer*, Brandon Guzzone
STRATEGY RESOURCES, Michael Holsher Senior V Press
Institute Director*, Mark Adam
Global Marketing Vice President*, Nikki Charman
Senior Vice President Cash*, Desmond Chavasse
Branch Director*, Karen Conley

LOCATIONS
HQ: POPULATION SERVICES INTERNATIONAL
1120 19TH ST NW STE 600, WASHINGTON, DC 200363605
Phone: 202 785-0072
Web: WWW.PSI.ORG

COMPETITORS
CELERA CORPORATION
CHILDREN'S HOSPITAL MEDICAL CENTER
SINGULEX, INC.
THE JACKSON LABORATORY
THE POPULATION COUNCIL INC

HISTORICAL FINANCIALS
Company Type: Private

Income Statement   FYE: December 31

	REVENUE ($mil)	NET INCOME ($mil)	NET PROFIT MARGIN	EMPLOYEES
12/13	584	4	0.8%	455
12/01	121	(0)	—	—
12/00	96	3	3.4%	—
Annual Growth	14.8%	2.9%	—	—

2013 Year-End Financials
Return on assets: 10.1%   Cash ($ mil.): 210
Return on equity: 0.8%
Current Ratio: 0.60

PORT NEWARK CONTAINER TERMINAL LLC

Port Newark Container Terminal handles boxed freight at one of the busiest ports in the US. In addition to moving containers to and from ships, Port Newark Container Terminal offers a rail terminal to accommodate intermodal freight transportation. The company operates under a long-term lease from the port's owner, The Port Authority of New York and New Jersey. Port Newark Container Terminal is owned by Ports America, Inc., a subsidiary of American International Group (AIG). AIG acquired Port Newark Container Terminal, through PineBridge (formerly AIG Investments) in 2007 as part of its purchase of the US port operations of DP World.

LOCATIONS
HQ: PORT NEWARK CONTAINER TERMINAL LLC
241 CALCUTTA ST, NEWARK, NJ 071143324
Phone: 973 522-2200
Web: WWW.PNCT.NET

COMPETITORS
APM TERMINALS NORTH AMERICA, INC.
CERES TERMINALS INCORPORATED
PORT OF FELIXSTOWE LIMITED
PORT OF HOUSTON AUTHORITY
VIRGINIA INTERNATIONAL TERMINALS, LLC

HISTORICAL FINANCIALS
Company Type: Private

Income Statement   FYE: December 31

	REVENUE ($mil)	NET INCOME ($mil)	NET PROFIT MARGIN	EMPLOYEES
12/21	595	237	39.9%	400
12/19	351	33	9.5%	—
12/18	298	30	10.1%	—
Annual Growth	26.0%	99.0%	—	—

2021 Year-End Financials
Return on assets: 39.7% Cash ($ mil.): 34
Return on equity: 116.7%
Current Ratio: 2.50

PORT OF LOS ANGELES

Auditors: MACIAS GINI & O'CONNELL LLP L

LOCATIONS

HQ: PORT OF LOS ANGELES
425 S PALOS VERDES ST, SAN PEDRO, CA 907313309
Phone: 310 732-3508
Web: WWW.PORTOFLOSANGELES.ORG

HISTORICAL FINANCIALS
Company Type: Private

Income Statement — FYE: June 30

	REVENUE ($mil)	NET INCOME ($mil)	NET PROFIT MARGIN	EMPLOYEES
06/21	572	128	22.5%	60
06/20	467	58	12.5%	—
06/19	506	168	33.3%	—
06/18	490	93	19.0%	—
Annual Growth	5.2%	11.3%	—	—

2021 Year-End Financials
Return on assets: 2.6% Cash ($ mil.): 1,012
Return on equity: 3.5%
Current Ratio: 6.20

PORTLAND GENERAL ELECTRIC COMP

LOCATIONS

HQ: PORTLAND GENERAL ELECTRIC COMP
33831 SE FARADAY RD, ESTACADA, OR 970238432
Phone: 503 630-6821

HISTORICAL FINANCIALS
Company Type: Private

Income Statement — FYE: December 31

	REVENUE ($mil)	NET INCOME ($mil)	NET PROFIT MARGIN	EMPLOYEES
12/21	2,415	245	10.2%	103
12/19	2,147	213	10.0%	—
12/17	2,009	187	9.3%	—
12/16	1,923	193	10.0%	—
Annual Growth	4.7%	4.9%	—	—

2021 Year-End Financials
Return on assets: 2.7% Cash ($ mil.): 45
Return on equity: 9.1%
Current Ratio: 1.00

PORTLAND PUBLIC SCHOOLS

Auditors: TALBOT KORVOLA & WARWICK LLP

LOCATIONS

HQ: PORTLAND PUBLIC SCHOOLS
501 N DIXON ST, PORTLAND, OR 972271876
Phone: 503 916-2000
Web: WWW.PPS.NET

HISTORICAL FINANCIALS
Company Type: Private

Income Statement — FYE: June 30

	REVENUE ($mil)	NET INCOME ($mil)	NET PROFIT MARGIN	EMPLOYEES
06/21	995	123	12.4%	5,244
06/20	973	358	36.8%	—
06/19	922	(133)	—	—
06/18	882	336	38.1%	—
Annual Growth	4.1%	(28.5%)	—	—

2021 Year-End Financials
Return on assets: 4.9% Cash ($ mil.): 363
Return on equity: 320.1%
Current Ratio: 6.20

POUDRE VALLEY HEALTH CARE, INC.

Providing health care is what this Poudre Valley is all about. The not-for-profit Poudre Valley Health System (PVHS) cares for residents of Colorado, western Nebraska, and southern Wyoming through the Poudre Valley Hospital and the Medical Center of the Rockies. With a total of about 440 beds, the two hospitals offer general medical and surgical services and trauma care. They also offer treatment centers for specialties including cancer, heart, brain, and spine disorders. PVHS is home to the Mountain Crest Behavioral Healthcare Center, which administers mental health and substance abuse treatment. PVHS is part of the Health District of Northern Larimer County; it is also part of University of Colorado Health.

Operations

The Poudre Valley Hospital features 270 patient beds, while the Medical Center of the Rockies has a capacity of about 170 beds. Beyond its primary hospital campuses, the health system also operates several outpatient clinics and a family medicine center that hosts a rural medicine residency program. Altogether, PVHS has more than 550 physicians practicing in more than 40 specialty fields.

In addition to its joint operating agreement with the University of Colorado Hospital, PVHS has formed collaborative care partnerships with local organizations including a local laser eye surgery center, numerous outpatient centers for rehabilitation, surgery, and infusion therapy, as well as home health care and home supply companies.

Geographic Reach

PVHS serves residents of Estes Park, Fort Collins, Greeley, and Loveland, Colorado, as well as Larimer and Weld Counties. The system also serves customers from Cheyenne and Laramie, Wyoming, and Scottsbluff, Nebraska.

Strategy

The organization has held a long tradition of partnering with numerous local organizations to expand its service offerings. To create a broader health organization for the Rocky Mountain region, PVHS formed a joint operating agreement with University of Colorado Hospital in 2012. Together, the systems are known as University of Colorado Health and are governed by a single board of directors. The hospitals continue to operate under their existing names.

Other growth efforts include the construction of a new $14.5 million emergency care center in 2012 and the opening of a new 12-bed women's and children's unit at Medical Center of the Rockies in 2013.

In 2013 it also opened the 36,000-sq.-ft. Indian Peaks Medical Center in Frederick at an estimated cost of $20 million to $30 million. It includes cardiology and diagnostics departments.

Company Background

The organization was founded in 1925. Since 1995, when PVHS reorganized as a private, not-for-profit health care organization, local property taxes that used to go straight to PVHS have been paid to the Health District of Northern Larimer County, which then uses them to fund PVHS' various activities.

Auditors: PLANTE & MORAN PLLC DENVER

LOCATIONS

HQ: POUDRE VALLEY HEALTH CARE, INC.
12401 E 17TH AVE STE B132, AURORA, CO 800452525
Phone: 970 495-7000
Web: WWW.UCHEALTH.ORG

PRODUCTS/OPERATIONS

Selected Services
Back, Neck and Spine Care
Cancer Care
Diabetes and Endocrinology
Hyperbaric Medicine
Imaging and Radiology
Laboratory Services
Orthopedics
Pain Care and Management
Seniors' Health
Weight and Metabolism
Women's Health
Wound Care

COMPETITORS

ASCENSION PROVIDENCE ROCHESTER HOSPITAL
HOSPITAL SERVICE DISTRICT 1
HOUSTON COUNTY HEALTHCARE AUTHORITY
KENNEDY HEALTH SYSTEM, INC.
VALLEY VIEW HOSPITAL ASSOCIATION

HISTORICAL FINANCIALS
Company Type: Private

Income Statement — FYE: June 30

	REVENUE ($mil)	NET INCOME ($mil)	NET PROFIT MARGIN	EMPLOYEES
06/20	1,266	209	16.5%	2,800
06/19	1,412	340	24.1%	—
06/16	523	92	17.7%	—
06/15	480	98	20.6%	—
Annual Growth	21.4%	16.2%	—	—

2020 Year-End Financials
Return on assets: 6.7%
Return on equity: 8.7%
Cash ($ mil.): 381
Current Ratio: 3.10

POWERSOUTH ENERGY COOPERATIVE

Several hundred thousand Alabamans and Floridians get their electric power courtesy of the work of PowerSouth Energy Cooperative, which provides wholesale power to its member-owners (16 electric cooperatives and four municipal distribution utilities). Its distribution members provide electric services to almost 417,200 customer meters in central and southern Alabama and western Florida. PowerSouth operates a more than 2,200-mile power transmission system and has more than 2,000 MW of generating capacity from interests in six fossil-fueled and hydroelectric power plants.

Geographic Reach
PowerSouth serves customers in Alabama (39 counties) and Florida (10 counties).

Operations
The company owns and operates six generation facilities and holds ownership interest in an additional facility. Its diverse generating fuel mix includes natural gas, coal, and water (hydro). It also has compressed air energy storage technology, and a disciplined fuel supply hedging program that minimizes the impact of fuel cost increases. In addition, PowerSouth maintains long-term purchased power agreements to ensure economic and reliable power supply for its members.

PowerSouth serves the wholesale energy needs of electric cooperatives and municipal electric systems in Alabama and northwest Florida, who in turn serve more than a million consumers. PowerSouth is dedicated to providing reliable energy at the lowest possible cost to its members.

Financial Performance
The company's revenues increased by 3% in 2013 primarily due to an increase in member revenues as a result of an increase in energy sales. The remaining increase was due to the surcharges added to the excess demand rate during 2013.

That year PowerSouth's net income decreased by 6% as the result of increased operating costs caused by higher distribution costs and administration and general expenses.

Its operating cash inflow increased to $63.5 million in 2013 (compared to $38.3 million in 2012) due to a rise in account receivables and inventories.

Strategy
To meet future demand and tightening environmental regulations, the company is looking to diversify and expand its power production assets, with an emphasis on cleaner energy plants. PowerSouth's long-term energy plans include a 20-year contract for 125 MW of nuclear power from two Vogtle Units being built by the Municipal Energy Authority of Georgia, near Augusta, and due to come onstream in 2016 and 2017. The company is also investing in wind power and biomass-to-energy initiatives.

Company Background
PowersSouth is owned and managed by it 20 distribution members.

The company once provided propane, but sold its Cooperative Propane unit in 2011 to focus on its core power businesses.

In 2008 Alabama Electric Cooperative changed its name to PowerSouth Energy Cooperative to better reflect its service territory (Alabama and Florida) and its opportunities for future growth.

Founded in 1941 as Alabama Electric Cooperative, the coop promotes a strong economic development program aimed at bringing industry into both Alabama and Florida.

Auditors : BKD LLP OKLAHOMA CITY OKLAH

LOCATIONS
HQ: POWERSOUTH ENERGY COOPERATIVE
2027 E THREE NOTCH ST, ANDALUSIA, AL 364212427
Phone: 334 427-3000
Web: WWW.POWERSOUTH.COM

PRODUCTS/OPERATIONS
View Archived What Charts | Edit 2013 Sales

	% of total
Electric Cooperatives	93
Municipalities	6
Other	1
Total	100

COMPETITORS
ASSOCIATED ELECTRIC COOPERATIVE, INC.
GEORGIA POWER COMPANY
INTERSTATE POWER AND LIGHT COMPANY
OGLETHORPE POWER CORPORATION
OMAHA PUBLIC POWER DISTRICT

HISTORICAL FINANCIALS
Company Type: Private

Income Statement — FYE: December 31

	REVENUE ($mil)	NET INCOME ($mil)	NET PROFIT MARGIN	EMPLOYEES
12/21	639	12	1.9%	640
12/20	547	12	2.3%	—
12/19	602	13	2.3%	—
12/18	612	12	2.0%	—
Annual Growth	1.5%	1.1%	—	—

2021 Year-End Financials
Return on assets: 0.5%
Return on equity: 3.2%
Cash ($ mil.): 221
Current Ratio: 1.30

PRAIRIE FARMS DAIRY, INC.

Prairie Farms Dairy is one of the largest and most successful dairy cooperatives in the Midwest and the South. With more than 700 dairy farmer/members, the cooperative offers a full line of retail and food service dairy products. It turns raw milk into fresh, fluid, cultured, and frozen dairy products under the Prairie Farms label. It also makes juices and ice cream novelties. The company's customers include food, drug, and convenience stores, mass merchandisers, schools, restaurants, and other food service operators. Located in Edwardsville, Illinois, it is the managing partner for joint ventures with smaller regional dairies. It makes its products at nearly 50 manufacturing plants and over 100 distribution facilities, which are located throughout the midwestern and southern areas of the US.

Operations
From its over 700 member farms, Prairie Farms sources milk products for its array of food products. It produces all varieties of milk, butter, cottage cheese, cream, ice cream, yogurt, and other diary-based products. It also goes outside its core to produce and sell teas, juices, and iced coffee.

In addition to manufacturing dairy foods, co-packing is a big part of Prairie Farms' operation. The company's PFD Supply and GMS Transportation non-dairy subsidiaries distribute products for fast-food chains.

Geographic Reach
Headquartered in Edwardsville, Illinois, Prairie Farms and its subsidiaries manufacture dairy products at nearly 50 plants and more than 100 distribution facilities in Arkansas, Illinois, Indiana, Iowa, Kansas, Kentucky, Michigan, Mississippi, Missouri, Nebraska, Oklahoma, Ohio, Tennessee, Texas, and Wisconsin.

Sales and Marketing
Prairie Farms' products are for sale through a variety of retail, grocery store,

foodservice, drug, club and dollar stores, mass merchandiser, and school locations in the same states in which it has production facilities. It sells its products under the Prairie Farms brand name, and the co-op also sells products through partners Hiland Dairy, East Side Jersey, Ice Cream Specialties, and Turner.

Company Background

The cooperative dates back to 1932, when Illinois farmers formed a statewide organization, Illinois Producers Creameries, to market and sell cream. In 1938 it became Prairie Farms Dairy.

Auditors : BKD LLP ST LOUIS MO

LOCATIONS

HQ: PRAIRIE FARMS DAIRY, INC.
3744 STAUNTON RD, EDWARDSVILLE, IL 620256936
Phone: 618 659-5700
Web: WWW.PRAIRIEFARMS.COM

Selected Areas of Distribution
Arkansas
Illinois
Indiana
Iowa
Kansas
Kentucky
Michigan
Mississippi
Missouri
Nebraska
Ohio
Oklahoma
Tennessee
Wisconsin

PRODUCTS/OPERATIONS

Branded Partners
Hiland Dairy Foods Company
Ice Cream Specialties,
Madison Farms Butter
Muller-Pinehurst Dairy
Turner Dairy

Selected Products
Butter
Cultured dairy products
    Cottage cheese (regular, low fat, and fat-free; small and large curd)
        Dips
        Sour cream
        Yogurt (regular, low fat and fat-free)
Fluid milk products
    Buttermilk
    Cream
    Egg nog (seasonal)
    Milk (regular, low fat, and fat-free)
    Flavored milk
Frozen desserts
    Frozen yogurt
    Ice cream (regular, low fat, and fat-free)
    Novelties
    Sherbet
Juices, drinks, and iced tea

COMPETITORS

AURORA ORGANIC DAIRY CORP.
BERKELEY FARMS, LLC
CRESUD S.A.C.I.F. y A.
DAIRYGOLD CO-OPERATIVE SOCIETY LTD
FOSTER DAIRY FARMS
HILAND DAIRY FOODS COMPANY, LLC
HORIZON ORGANIC DAIRY, LLC
MICHIGAN MILK PRODUCERS ASSOCIATION
NORTH PACIFIC CANNERS & PACKERS, INC.

ROBERTS DAIRY COMPANY, LLC

HISTORICAL FINANCIALS
Company Type: Private

Income Statement   FYE: September 30

	REVENUE ($mil)	NET INCOME ($mil)	NET PROFIT MARGIN	EMPLOYEES
09/13	1,721	14	0.8%	1,965
09/12	1,649	38	2.4%	—
09/11	1,607	28	1.7%	—
Annual Growth	3.5%	(28.9%)	—	—

2013 Year-End Financials
Return on assets: 1.9%   Cash ($ mil.): 12
Return on equity: 3.4%
Current Ratio: 1.20

PRATT CORRUGATED HOLDINGS, INC.

Auditors : GRANT THORNTON LLP ATLANTA

LOCATIONS

HQ: PRATT CORRUGATED HOLDINGS, INC.
1800 SARASOT BUS PKWY NE C, CONYERS, GA 300135775
Phone: 770 918-5678

HISTORICAL FINANCIALS
Company Type: Private

Income Statement   FYE: June 30

	REVENUE ($mil)	NET INCOME ($mil)	NET PROFIT MARGIN	EMPLOYEES
06/21	3,113	128	4.1%	222
06/20	2,649	75	2.9%	—
06/18	2,518	87	3.5%	—
06/17	2,360	65	2.8%	—
Annual Growth	7.2%	18.2%	—	—

2021 Year-End Financials
Return on assets: 7.8%   Cash ($ mil.): 247
Return on equity: 16.6%
Current Ratio: 1.40

PRATT INDUSTRIES, INC.

Pratt Industries (USA) doesn't mill around when it comes to recycling and caring for the environment. The company rivals the world's largest manufacturers of recycled paper and packaging and claims to be the 5th largest box manufacturer in the US and the world's largest, privately-held 100% recycled paper and packaging company. Pratt has a handful of operating divisions: recycling, mills, corrugating, converting, displays, packaging systems, and national accounts. Its products, which include container board and corrugated sheets, are sold to clients such as Rubbermaid and Pringles.

Operations

The company operates 32 sheet plants, 18 recycling centers, 16 corrugating plants, seven distribution centers, seven displaying facilities, four recycled paper mills, and one clean energy plant. It operates through the main divisions of Clean Energy, Converting, Corrugating, Display, Paper Mills, Recycling, Logistics, Specialty, and Strategic Services.

Geographic Reach

Pratt operates some 50 plants in more than 20 US states and Mexico.

Strategy

Pratt has strategically located its manufacturing facilities to reduce freight time and cost and to provide regional design and account management support. The locations enable it to react quickly and decisively to meet the needs of customers.

In 2015 Pratt Industries broke ground on its new $52 million corrugated box factory in Beloit, Wisconsin. The 350,000 sq. ft. facility, due for start-up in early 2016, will sit on a 56-acre site and produce 600 tons of recycled boxes a day at capacity.

Mergers and Acquisitions

In 2015 the company improved its footprint through the purchase of California-based food and agricultural packaging company, Robert Mann Packaging (RMP). Pratt paid $60 million for the privately-owned RMP group which has $150 million in annual sales and more than a dozen facilities in the western US and Mexico, including a 350,000 square-foot box-making plant in Salinas, California. The deal gave the company a nationwide footprint throughout the US with manufacturing sites stretching from New York to the West Coast.

Company Background

The company was founded in 1948 by Leon Pratt, grandfather of Anthony Pratt.

Auditors : GRANT THORNTON LLP ATLANTA

LOCATIONS

HQ: PRATT INDUSTRIES, INC.
4004 SMMIT BLVD NE STE 10, ATLANTA, GA 30319
Phone: 770 918-5678
Web: WWW.PRATTINDUSTRIES.COM

PRODUCTS/OPERATIONS

Selected Divisions
Converting
Corrugating
Displays
Mills
National Accounts
Packaging Systems
Recycling

Selected Products and Services
Bagging
    Merchandise bags
    Polypropylene bags
    Poly-tubing
    Seal-top bags
    Static shielded bags
Carton Closure/Sealing
    Adhesives
    Double coated tape

Duct tape
Filament tape
Foam tape
Foil tape
Masking tape
Poly-strapping
Pressure sensitive carton sealing tape
Staples
Steel Strapping
Teflon tape
Water activate carton sealing tape
Cushioning/Void Fill
   Air dunnage bags
   Bubble wrap
   Cellulose wadding
   Foam-N-Place
   Honeycomb
   Kraft wrap
   Loose fill foam
   Newsprint
   Polyethylene foam
   Polypropylene foam
Edge/Corner Protection
   Angleboard
   Anglewrap
   Cornerboard
   Form-A-Board
   Protect-A-Board
   Protect-A-Wrap
   Stackmaster
   Strap protectors
Labeling and Coding
   Cleaners
   Inks
   Labels
   Ribbons
Mailing and Shipping
   Mailers
   Packing list envelopes
   Shipping tubes and tags
Unitization
   Poly pallet covers
   Poly pallet shrink bags
   Poly top sheets
   Poly-strapping
   Shrink bundling
   Steel strapping
   Stretch film
Visual Packaging
   Blister packaging
   Clamshells
   Polyolefin shrinkfilm
   PVC shrink bands
   Skin packaging
   Skin packaging film

COMPETITORS

CRANE & CO., INC.
Cascades Inc
DS SMITH PLC
HOKUETSU CORPORATION
INTERNATIONAL PAPER COMPANY
INTERSTATE RESOURCES, INC.
JAMES CROPPER PUBLIC LIMITED COMPANY
Stora Enso Oyj
VICTORY PACKAGING, L.P.
WAUSAU PAPER CORP.

HISTORICAL FINANCIALS
Company Type: Private

Income Statement   FYE: June 30

	REVENUE ($mil)	NET INCOME ($mil)	NET PROFIT MARGIN	EMPLOYEES
06/21	3,064	225	7.3%	5,890
06/20	2,612	200	7.7%	—
06/18	2,498	200	8.0%	—
Annual Growth	7.0%	3.9%	—	—

2021 Year-End Financials
Return on assets: 7.4%   Cash ($ mil.): 707
Return on equity: 16.2%
Current Ratio: 2.40

PRECISION CASTPARTS CORP.

Precision Castparts Corp. (PCC) is the market leader in manufacturing large, complex structural investment castings, airfoil castings, forged components, aerostructures and highly engineered, critical fasteners for aerospace applications. In addition, PCC is the leading producer of airfoil castings for the industrial gas turbine. PCC also manufactures extruded seamless pipe, fittings, forgings, and clad products for power generation and oil & gas applications; commercial and military airframe aerostructures; and metal alloys and other materials to the casting and forging industries. The company is a subsidiary of Berkshire Hathaway. PCC was founded in 1947 by Joseph Cox.

Operations
PCC's operations include Investment Cast Products, Metals Products, Forged Products, and Airframe Products.

Its Investment Cast Products is the world leader in manufacturing high-quality, complex investment castings for aircraft engine, industrial gas turbine, airframe, and other applications, including the world's largest diameter investment cast components. Its PCC Structurals specializes in nickel-based superalloy, titanium, stainless steel, and aluminum investment castings for aerospace, land-based turbine, medical, and other applications. The PCC Airfoils manufactures hot section components including blades, vanes, shrouds, heat shields, and fairings.

PCC Metals Group aligns foremost leaders in alloy research: Special Metals Corporation and TIMET. PCC Energy Group is backed by their nearly two centuries of combined metallurgical expertise.

The Forged Products segment manufactures nickel-based, titanium, and steel alloy components for aerospace, industrial gas turbines, and general industrial markets, as well as extruded, seamless pipe for energy markets. In addition, the segment offers the largest range of nickel alloys and product forms for aerospace and other applications.

Airframe Products is one of the top manufacturers of engineered fasteners, fastening systems, metal components, and assemblies for aerospace, transportation, power generation, and general industrial markets. PCC Fastener Products offers one of the industry's broadest ranges of aerospace fasteners and precision components. The PCC Aerostructures manufactures world-class assemblies and components for the global aerospace market.

Geographic Reach
PCC is headquartered in Portland, Oregon.

Sales and Marketing
PCC serves the aerospace, power, and general industrial markets.

Strategy

Mergers and Acquisitions
PCC uses acquisitions to develop its businesses, expand internationally, provide low-cost manufacturing, and fund investment in technologies to add products and services.

Through new parent company Berkshire Hathaway, PCC in 2017 purchased Willhelm Schulz GmbH, a German maker of high-performance pipes catering mainly to the oil and gas industry. PCC is using the purchase as a springboard for future growth in Germany and Europe.

In 2016, PCC obtained Composites Horizons, an independent supplier of high temperature carbon and ceramic composite components, including ceramic matrix composites (CMC), for use in next-generation aerospace engines. The deal gave PCC the ability to offer its engine customers metallic and CMC material capability to meet a broader range of customer requirements.

Company Background
Oregon Saw Company was founded in 1949 and sold in 1953; its buyer wanted neither the future PCC nor a power tools unit, so the two became Omark Industries. In 1956 a buyer purchased the power tool business but wasn't interested in castings; that operation was spun off as Precision Castparts Corp.

In the early 1950s Oregon Saw developed a process for producing large parts by use of investment casting, making products that rivaled the strength of forged and machined parts at a fraction of the cost. After a two-year search, they landed their first aerospace customer -- Air Research Corp.

PCC went public in 1968. In 1976 the company acquired Centaur Cast Alloys (small investment castings, UK) to make parts for the European aerospace industry. By that time General Electric (GE) and Pratt & Whitney accounted for most of PCC's business.

To diversify, it added TRW's cast airfoils (used in aircraft engines and industrial gas turbines) division in 1986.

In 1997 PCC spent $437 million to acquire seven more companies that helped boost sales 75% from 1996 levels. The next year it purchased four metalworking companies that served industries other than aerospace.

In January 2016, the company was acquired by Berkshire Hathaway in a mega-deal valued at $37 billion.

HISTORY

The history of Precision Castparts Corp.

(PCC) is not as precise as its castings. The Oregon Saw Company was founded in 1949 and sold in 1953; its buyer wanted neither the future PCC nor a power tools unit, so the two became Omark Industries. In 1956 a buyer purchased the power tool business but wasn't interested in castings; that operation was spun off as Precision Castparts Corp.

In the early 1950s a group of Oregon Saw's casting employees developed a process for producing parts as large as 60 inches by use of investment casting, making products that rivaled the strength of forged and machined parts at a fraction of the cost. After a two-year search, they landed their first aerospace customer -- Air Research Corp. -- with many to follow. The higher operating temperatures generated by aircraft engines led the company to buy a vacuum furnace in 1959 to fabricate parts that could tolerate greater heat; two more vacuum furnaces were added and sales vaulted toward $10 million by 1967. PCC went public in 1968 and continued to grow. In 1976 the company acquired Centaur Cast Alloys (small investment castings, UK) to make parts for the European aerospace industry. By that time General Electric (GE) and Pratt & Whitney accounted for most of PCC's business. Edward Cooley, who had masterminded the company's growth since incorporation, forged ahead with plans to double production capacity.

In 1980 the airline industry crashed, but PCC's sales held at about $90 million. Structural airplane products soon picked up, and in 1984 the company bought two titanium foundries in France. To diversify, it added TRW's cast airfoils (used in aircraft engines and industrial gas turbines) division in 1986. That acquisition, renamed PCC Airfoils, increased PCC's annual sales by about 80%; sales reached $443 million by 1989.

The company broadened its offerings again in 1991 when it acquired Advanced Forming Technology, which made small, complex, metal-injection molded parts used in everything from adding machines to military ordnance. The early 1990s recession hit the airline industry and sales dropped. Cooley retired as chairman in 1994 and GE veteran William McCormick replaced him. The next year PCC acquired Quamco, Inc. (industrial tools and machines). In 1996 PCC flowed into the fluid management market with the acquisition of NEWFLO for about $300 million.

In 1997 PCC spent $437 million to acquire seven more companies that helped boost sales 75% from 1996 levels. The next year it purchased four metalworking companies that served industries other than aerospace. Having reduced dependence on sales to the aerospace industry to just over 50%, PCC began consolidating operations and closing plants to reduce costs.

The company continued to diversify through acquisitions in 1999, but it also expanded its aerospace operations with the purchase of Wyman-Gordon, a leading maker of advanced metal forgings for the aerospace market. PCC's 2000 acquisitions included the aerospace division of United Engineering Forgings and Germany-based Convey Engineering (heavy-duty valves). The next year the company bought the assets of Netherlands-based Wouter Witzel and the US's Drop Dies and Forgings Company (renamed Wyman-Gordon Cleveland). In 2002 PCC bought the rest of Western Australian Specialty Alloys (casting and forging alloys) for $27.6 million in cash and PCC shares.

In 2003 Precision Castparts' PCC Structurals unit reached a $400 million agreement with Rolls-Royce to supply large titanium and steel castings. That year the company acquired SPS Technologies, a producer of fasteners and other metal components for the aerospace, automotive, and industrial markets. In 2004 subsidiary SPS Aerospace Fasteners signed a four-year deal with Airbus worth about $72 million to supply collars, nuts, studs, and titanium pins to Airbus plants across Europe.

PCC acquired Air Industries Corporation in early 2005. In 2006 PCC bought Special Metals Corporation (SMC), a maker of nickel alloys and super alloys, for $295 million in cash and the assumption of $245 million in SMC debt. PCC intended to use SMC's product as raw materials for its own aircraft engine components. SMC also served the automotive, chemical, and power generation industries.

Later in 2006 PCC bought Shur-Lok Corporation, a manufacturer of aerospace fasteners, for about $110 million. The acquisition, combined with the 2005 purchase of Air Industries Corporation, helped to further PCC's desire to grow its airframe fasteners business.

Early in 2007 PCC completed the purchase of GSC, a leading maker of aluminum and steel structural investment casting for the aerospace, energy, and medical markets. It also acquired Cherry Aerospace, which expanded its fastener products portfolio.

In 2009 the company acquired Carlton Forge Works, which makes aircraft engines for Boeing and Airbus; California-based Arcturus Manufacturing (hammer forging operations) was included in the transaction. PCC also picked up Airdrome Holdings (fluid fittings), Fatigue Technology (cold expansion technology), and Hackney Ladish (forged pipe fittings) in 2009.

In late summer 2011, PPC purchased Primus International, a maker of complex metal industrial parts and assemblies. Its products (machined aluminum and titanium components used in aircraft wings, fuselages, and engine-related assemblies) cater to Boeing, Airbus, and other aerospace OEMs. The $900 million deal furthered the company's commitment to the global aerospace industry. In a similar vein, the company obtained Unison Engine Components (operating as Tru-Form Rings) from GE Aviation in mid-2011. Tru-Form made flash-welded and cold-rolled rings with jet engine as well as gas turbine applications.

PCC also acquired RathGibson, which makes tubing for the oil and gas, chemical/petrochemical, power-generation, and other markets, in 2012.

To expand both its Fasteners and Forged Products segments, PCC acquired the aerostructures and industrial products businesses of HÃ©roux-Devtek for about CAD$300 million (about $295.5 million) in 2012. Among other benefits, the acquisition expanded the company's product line for such OEMs as Lockheed, Bombardier, and Gulfstream. PCC also inked a deal to purchase the Synchronous Aerospace Group business of private investment firm Littlejohn & Co. in late 2012.

EXECUTIVES

CCO, Emi Donis
Auditors : DELOITTE & TOUCHE LLP PORTLAN

LOCATIONS

HQ: PRECISION CASTPARTS CORP.
5885 MEADOWS RD STE 620, LAKE OSWEGO, OR 970358647
Phone: 503 946-4800
Web: WWW.PRECAST.COM

PRODUCTS/OPERATIONS

Selected Products and Services
Fasteners
    Advanced forming technology
    E/One (for the disposal of residential sanitary waste)
    J&L fiber services (for pulp and paper industry)
    PCC Precision Tool Group
    SPS aerospace fasteners (for commercial/military aircraft)
    SPS engineered fasteners (high strength for automotive and construction applications)
Forged products
    Special Metals Corporation
    Wyman-Gordon Forgings
Investment Cast Products
    PCC Airfoils (high-temperature blades and vanes)
    PCC Structurals (structural investment castings)
    Specialty materials and alloys (alloys, waxes, and metal processing for investment casting)

COMPETITORS

ALLEGHENY TECHNOLOGIES INCORPORATED
BARNES GROUP INC.
EATON CORPORATION PUBLIC LIMITED COMPANY
GKN LIMITED
HITCHINER MANUFACTURING CO., INC.
IMI PLC
MILACRON HOLDINGS CORP.
RTI INTERNATIONAL METALS, INC.
SENIOR PLC
SPI/MOBILE PULLEY WORKS, INC.

HISTORICAL FINANCIALS
Company Type: Private

Income Statement — FYE: January 3

	REVENUE ($mil)	NET INCOME ($mil)	NET PROFIT MARGIN	EMPLOYEES
01/16*	7,002	817	11.7%	30,116
03/15	10,005	1,533	15.3%	—
03/14	9,616	1,784	18.6%	—
03/13	8,377	1,429	17.1%	—
Annual Growth	(5.8%)	(17.0%)	—	—

*Fiscal year change

2016 Year-End Financials
Return on assets: 4.0% Cash ($ mil.): 343
Return on equity: 7.0%
Current Ratio: 3.90

PREMIER HEALTHCARE ALLIANCE, L.P.

LOCATIONS
HQ: PREMIER HEALTHCARE ALLIANCE, L.P.
13034 BALNTYN CORP PL, CHARLOTTE, NC 282771498
Phone: 704 357-0022
Web: WWW.PREMIERINC.COM

HISTORICAL FINANCIALS
Company Type: Private

Income Statement — FYE: June 30

	REVENUE ($mil)	NET INCOME ($mil)	NET PROFIT MARGIN	EMPLOYEES
06/12	590	326	55.3%	199
06/11	679	311	45.8%	—
06/09	(1,830)	0	0.0%	—
Annual Growth	—	18233.3%	—	—

2012 Year-End Financials
Return on assets: 72.7% Cash ($ mil.): 129
Return on equity: 92.9%
Current Ratio: 5.30

PRESBYTERIAN HOSPITAL

LOCATIONS
HQ: PRESBYTERIAN HOSPITAL
200 HAWTHORNE LN, CHARLOTTE, NC 282042528
Phone: 704 384-4000

HISTORICAL FINANCIALS
Company Type: Private

Income Statement — FYE: December 31

	REVENUE ($mil)	NET INCOME ($mil)	NET PROFIT MARGIN	EMPLOYEES
12/09	688	68	10.0%	3,100
12/08	500	18	3.7%	—
Annual Growth	37.6%	270.7%	—	—

2009 Year-End Financials
Return on assets: — Cash ($ mil.): —
Return on equity: 10.0%
Current Ratio: —

PRESBYTERIAN MEDICAL CENTER OF THE UNIVERSITY OF PENNSYLVANIA HEALTH SYSTEM

LOCATIONS
HQ: PRESBYTERIAN MEDICAL CENTER OF THE UNIVERSITY OF PENNSYLVANIA HEALTH SYSTEM
51 N 39TH ST, PHILADELPHIA, PA 191042640
Phone: 215 662-8000
Web: WWW.PENNMEDICINE.ORG

HISTORICAL FINANCIALS
Company Type: Private

Income Statement — FYE: June 30

	REVENUE ($mil)	NET INCOME ($mil)	NET PROFIT MARGIN	EMPLOYEES
06/20	973	66	6.9%	1,370
06/15	546	(0)	0.0%	—
06/14	445	21	4.7%	—
06/13	429	7	1.7%	—
Annual Growth	12.4%	36.7%	—	—

2020 Year-End Financials
Return on assets: 8.2% Cash ($ mil.): 6
Return on equity: 12.9%
Current Ratio: —

PRINCE GEORGE'S COUNTY PUBLIC SCHOOLS

Auditors: CLIFTONLARSONALLEN LLP BALTIM

LOCATIONS
HQ: PRINCE GEORGE'S COUNTY PUBLIC SCHOOLS
14201 SCHOOL LN, UPPER MARLBORO, MD 207722866
Phone: 301 952-6000
Web: WWW.PGCPS.ORG

HISTORICAL FINANCIALS
Company Type: Private

Income Statement — FYE: June 30

	REVENUE ($mil)	NET INCOME ($mil)	NET PROFIT MARGIN	EMPLOYEES
06/14	1,932	(6)	—	22,000
06/13	1,966	43	2.2%	—
06/11	1,855	3	0.2%	—
06/07	1,627	13	0.8%	—
Annual Growth	2.5%	—	—	—

2014 Year-End Financials
Return on assets: (-0.4%) Cash ($ mil.): —
Return on equity: (-2.5%)
Current Ratio: —

PRINCE WILLIAM COUNTY PUBLIC SCHOOLS

Auditors: CHERRY BEKAERT LLP TYSONS COR

LOCATIONS
HQ: PRINCE WILLIAM COUNTY PUBLIC SCHOOLS
14715 BRISTOW RD, MANASSAS, VA 201123945
Phone: 703 791-7200
Web: WWW.PWCS.EDU

HISTORICAL FINANCIALS
Company Type: Private

Income Statement — FYE: June 30

	REVENUE ($mil)	NET INCOME ($mil)	NET PROFIT MARGIN	EMPLOYEES
06/13	1,048	23	2.3%	4,325
06/12	968	(18)	—	—
06/11	887	(66)	—	—
Annual Growth	8.7%	—	—	—

2013 Year-End Financials
Return on assets: 1.7% Cash ($ mil.): —
Return on equity: 1.9%
Current Ratio: —

PRISMA HEALTH-UPSTATE

From education and research to primary care and surgery, Upstate Affiliate Organization (dba Prisma Health-Upstate, formerly Greenville Hospital System) is out to keep residents of the "Golden Strip" (the corridor connecting Charlotte, North Carolina, and Atlanta) healthy. Originally founded in 1912, the system encompasses eight inpatient hospitals and more than 100 outpatient facilities. Its flagship facility is Prisma Health Greenville Memorial Hospital, a referral and academic medical center with more than 800 beds; other facilities include several smaller community hospitals, a nursing home, and a long-term acute care hospital. Greenville Hospital System merged with Palmetto Health in 2017; the combined system rebranded as Prisma Health in early 2019.

Operations

Prisma Health-Upstate offers a full range of services, including a primary care physician network, outpatient services, and home health care.

The system has teaching affiliations with Medical University of South Carolina and University of South Carolina Medical School, and nursing school affiliations with Clemson University and Bob Jones University. Prisma Health-Upstate offers residency programs in about a dozen specialties including internal medicine, OB-GYN, and vascular surgery. It also performs extensive medical research in partnership with pharmaceutical companies in areas including oncology, pediatric oncology, women's health, cardiology, and vascular disease.

Prisma Cancer Institute (formerly GHS Cancer Institute), a regional leader in cancer care, offers cancer treatment and prevention trials through the Community Clinical Oncology Program. It also offers Phase 1 clinical trials, genetic counseling, a blood and marrow transplant program and a number of patient-specific programs.

Financial Performance

GHS reported $2.1 billion in revenues in 2015, primarily from patient services. It posted $32 million in net income.

Strategy

In an effort to reduce unnecessary trips to the emergency room, Prisma Health-Upstate has been opening several MD360 urgent care clinics. By diverting patients away from the ER for after-hours and non-emergency health problems, GHS hopes to reduce health care costs and increase access to medical care.

Mergers and Acquisitions

In 2017, Greenville Hospital System joined forces with Palmetto Health to create South Carolina's largest health care system. The combined company rebranded itself as Prisma Health in early 2019. Greenville Hospital System became Prisma Health-Upstate.

EXECUTIVES

GOVERNANCE*, Joseph J Blake
Chief Nursing*, Carolyn Swinton
HEALTH INFO*, Mark Wess
CIO*, Rich Rogers

LOCATIONS

HQ: PRISMA HEALTH-UPSTATE
300 E MCBEE AVE STE 302, GREENVILLE, SC 296012899
Phone: 864 455-1120
Web: WWW.PRISMAHEALTH.ORG

PRODUCTS/OPERATIONS

2015 Sales

	$ mil	% of total
Net patient services	1,973.6	96
Other operating revenues	82.7	4
Total	2,056.3	100

Selected Operations

Baptist Easley Hospital (with Palmetto Health, Easley)
Greenville Memorial Hospital (tertiary academic and referral medical center)
Greer Memorial Hospital (Greer, acute care hospital)
Hillcrest Memorial Hospital (Simpsonville, general acute care hospital)
Laurens County Memorial Hospital (Clinton)
North Greenville Hospital (long-term acute care hospital)
Oconee Memorial Hospital (Seneca, inpatient and outpatient services)
Patewood Memorial Hospital (Greenville, inpatient elective hospital and outpatient center)

Selected Services

Behavioral Health
Cancer Institute
Children's Hospital
Heart & Vascular Institute
Medicine
Orthopaedics & Neurosurgery
Radiology
Rehabilitation
Surgery
Women's Health

COMPETITORS

AHS MEDICAL HOLDINGS LLC
CENTURA HEALTH CORPORATION
CHILDREN'S HEALTHCARE OF ATLANTA, INC.
CHILDREN'S HOSPITAL AND HEALTH SYSTEM, INC.
CHRISTIANA CARE HEALTH SYSTEM, INC.
COMMUNITY HOSPITAL OF THE MONTEREY PENINSULA
CONNECTICUT CHILDREN'S MEDICAL CENTER
MAIN LINE HEALTH SYSTEM
THE CHILDREN'S HOSPITAL OF PHILADELPHIA
TRIHEALTH, INC.

HISTORICAL FINANCIALS

Company Type: Private

Income Statement — FYE: September 30

	REVENUE ($mil)	NET INCOME ($mil)	NET PROFIT MARGIN	EMPLOYEES
09/13	1,001	80	8.1%	7,200
09/05	789	21	2.7%	—
09/04	789	21	2.7%	—
09/03	754	52	7.0%	—
Annual Growth	2.9%	4.4%	—	—

2013 Year-End Financials

Return on assets: —
Return on equity: 8.1%
Current Ratio: —
Cash ($ mil.): —

PRO PETROLEUM LLC

EXECUTIVES

Stockholder, B R Griffin

Auditors: GARRETT AND SWANN LLP LUBBOC

LOCATIONS

HQ: PRO PETROLEUM LLC
4710 4TH ST, LUBBOCK, TX 794164900
Phone: 806 795-8785
Web: WWW.PROPETROLEUM.COM

HISTORICAL FINANCIALS

Company Type: Private

Income Statement — FYE: December 31

	REVENUE ($mil)	NET INCOME ($mil)	NET PROFIT MARGIN	EMPLOYEES
12/15	1,063	5	0.5%	150
12/14	1,701	4	0.3%	—
12/13	1,815	12	0.7%	—
Annual Growth	(23.5%)	(35.6%)	—	—

2015 Year-End Financials

Return on assets: 4.1%
Return on equity: 12.5%
Current Ratio: 1.30
Cash ($ mil.): 33

PRODUCE ALLIANCE, L.L.C.

Auditors: MILLER COOPER & CO LTD DEE

LOCATIONS

HQ: PRODUCE ALLIANCE, L.L.C.
100 LEXINGTON DR STE 201, BUFFALO GROVE, IL 600896937
Phone: 847 808-3030
Web: WWW.PRODUCEALLIANCE.COM

HISTORICAL FINANCIALS

Company Type: Private

Income Statement — FYE: December 31

	REVENUE ($mil)	NET INCOME ($mil)	NET PROFIT MARGIN	EMPLOYEES
12/19	572	0	0.0%	75
12/18	504	0	0.1%	—
12/17	441	1	0.3%	—
12/16	381	2	0.7%	—
Annual Growth	14.5%	(56.8%)	—	—

2019 Year-End Financials

Return on assets: 0.4%
Return on equity: —
Current Ratio: 1.00
Cash ($ mil.): —

PRODUCTION TECHNOLOGIES, INC.

LOCATIONS

HQ: PRODUCTION TECHNOLOGIES, INC.
7651 WASHINGTON AVE S, EDINA, MN 554392417
Phone: 952 944-1076
Web: WWW.PTIMN.COM

HISTORICAL FINANCIALS
Company Type: Private

Income Statement   FYE: December 31

	REVENUE ($mil)	NET INCOME ($mil)	NET PROFIT MARGIN	EMPLOYEES
12/16	3,289	580	17.6%	25
12/15	3,488	719	20.6%	—
12/14	3,880	348	9.0%	—
12/11	4	0	9.8%	—
Annual Growth	280.1%	327.2%	—	—

2016 Year-End Financials
Return on assets: 30.8% Cash ($ mil.): —
Return on equity: 45.7%
Current Ratio: 2.70

PROMEGA CORPORATION

Promega is a global biotechnology company that provides tools to help researchers delve into the life sciences. The company sells more than 4,000 products that allow scientists to conduct various experiments in a range of life science work across areas such as cell biology; DNA, RNA and protein analysis; drug development; human identification; and molecular diagnostics. Promega has branches in around 15 countries around the world. The company sells its products directly and through over 50 distributors. Customers include academic, pharmaceutical, and clinical labs, as well as government agencies and energy and chemical companies.

Operations
Promega's products type includes cell biology, human identification, lab equipment and supplies, molecular diagnostics, nucleic acid analysis, and protein analysis.

Promega cell biology products include bioassays for biologics drug discovery, cell health assays, reagents to detect and quantify the activity of signaling pathways, energy metabolism assays, oxidative stress assays, and products to confirm the identity of cell lines. It also provides microplate readers optimized for use with its luminescence- and fluorescence-based assays.

Capillary electrophoresis (CE) and massively parallel sequencing (MPS) are two common methods used for human identification in forensic and paternity testing labs. In both methods, DNA is extracted from a variety of samples and specific regions of the DNA are examined to develop a unique genetic "fingerprint" for an individual. It also provides reagents, instrumentation, service and support for DNA extraction, quantification, STR amplification and analysis using capillary electrophoresis, and massively parallel sequencing approaches.

Promega offers GloMax luminometers, fluorometers and plate readers for data collection and analysis, the Maxprep/Maxwell liquid handler/extraction instrument combination for automating sample prep and nucleic acid purification, and HSM 2.0 devices for automating large-volume extractions in 50ml conical tubes. It also offers everyday supplies for molecular and cell biology experiments, including basic biochemical reagents and consumables such as plates, tubes, vacuum manifolds, magnetic stands, etc.

The company also offers a portfolio of reagents for nucleic acid purification, PCR, STR, genetic analysis and mutation detection for clinical research labs applying molecular techniques to the study of disease. It also offers customizable solutions that meet the stringent technical and quality requirements of molecular diagnostics labs.

Nucleic acid analysis includes molecular cloning enzymes, DNA ladders, DNA and RNA extraction kits, PCR enzymes and reagents, and products for NGS and Sanger sequencing.

Promega's unique portfolio of protein analysis laboratory products include mass spec proteases, protein purification tags/resins and fluorescent ligands, cell-free and cell-based protein expression systems, and novel methods for detecting and studying proteins at endogenous expression levels.

Geographic Reach
Headquartered in Madison, Wisconsin, Promega has branches in around 15 countries with a network of global distributors. It operates its manufacturing facilities through PBI in San Luis Obispo, California; PBS in Seoul; Promega BioSystems Sunnyvale in Sunnyvale, California; and Shanghai Promega Biological Products in Shanghai.

The company distributes its products in North America, Africa and the Middle East, Europe, Latin America, and the Asia/Pacific region.

Sales and Marketing
Promega's products are used in academic and government research, forensics, pharmaceuticals, clinical diagnostics, and agricultural and environmental testing. Promega also offers paternity testing kits and in vitro diagnostic test systems.

Company Background
Promega was founded in 1978 and is owned by investors and employees and led by founder and CEO William Linton.

Auditors : GRANT THORNTON LLP MILWAUKEE

LOCATIONS
HQ: PROMEGA CORPORATION
 2800 WOODS HOLLOW RD, FITCHBURG, WI 537115399
Phone: 608 274-4330
Web: WWW.PROMEGA.COM

PRODUCTS/OPERATIONS
Selected Product Categories
Cellular analysis
 Apoptosis
 Automation-robotics
 Cell viability
 Drug discovery
 Gene expression and reporter assays
 Immunological detection
 In-vitro toxicology
 Signal transduction
 Transfection
Genetic identity
Genomics
 Automation-robotics
 Cloning
 DNA and RNA purification
 Electrophoresis
 Food and GMO testing
 Genotype analysis
 In-vitro transcription
 Microarrays
 Plant biotechnology
 Reverse transcription and cDNA synthesis
 RNA interference
 Sequencing
Proteomics
 Electrophoresis
 Gene expression and reporter assays
 Mutagenesis
 Protein expression and analysis
 Protein interactions
 RNA interference
 Transfection

COMPETITORS
AFFYMETRIX, INC.
ALBANY MOLECULAR RESEARCH, INC.
BIOTROVE, INC.
BRICKELL BIOTECH, INC.
HALOZYME THERAPEUTICS, INC.
INTEGRATED DNA TECHNOLOGIES, INC.
LIFE TECHNOLOGIES CORPORATION
MEDIATECH, INC.
REPLIGEN CORPORATION
STRATEC SE

HISTORICAL FINANCIALS
Company Type: Private

Income Statement   FYE: March 31

	REVENUE ($mil)	NET INCOME ($mil)	NET PROFIT MARGIN	EMPLOYEES
03/21	878	323	36.9%	1,865
03/20	487	75	15.5%	—
03/17	386	55	14.3%	—
03/16	370	44	12.1%	—
Annual Growth	18.9%	48.5%	—	—

2021 Year-End Financials
Return on assets: 28.5% Cash ($ mil.): 105
Return on equity: 65.8%
Current Ratio: 3.70

PROVIDENCE HEALTH & SERVICES

Providence St. Joseph Health was established in 2016 from the merger of Providence Health & Services and St. Joseph Health System. The not-for-profit operates 50 hospitals and more than 800 clinics in seven states in the western US. Its facilities operate under such brands as Swedish Health Services, Hoag Memorial Hospital Presbyterian, and

Covenant Health . It provides health insurance through Providence Health Plans and offers subsidized housing for the low-income elderly and disabled. The young organization has also established the Institute for Mental Health and Wellness to improve access to quality mental health care around the nation.

Operations

In addition to its health care and housing operations, Providence St. Joseph operates a small Catholic university in Great Falls, Montana, called University of Great Falls, and a private high school -- aptly named Providence High School -- in Burbank, California.

Geographic Reach

The system has facilities in Alaska, California, Montana, New Mexico, Oregon, Texas, and Washington.

Providence Health International helps respond to health care needs in developing countries by shipping supplies to hospitals and clinics around the world, arranging for grants to cover the expense of sending volunteers overseas, and offering educational support to health professionals in foreign countries.

Strategy

Even as the organization struggles with higher charity care levels, it still has to work to invest in its infrastructure to keep its facilities up-to-date to expand to meet demand and to attract patients. For example, Providence Health embarked on a major campus expansion beginning at its Providence Alaska Medical Center to modernize the Newborn Intensive Care Unit (NICU), Prenatal and Mother Baby Units, and cardiac surgery program. The project increased the size of the NICU from 47 to 66 beds and added a number of cardiac operating rooms and surgical services. It expanded similar services at its Holy Cross Medical Center in California and is working to convert patient information to electronic patient medical records

In 2014 Providence Health opened the 3,000-sq.-ft. Providence Autism Center for Women and Children on Pacific Avenue in Everett.

That year Providence Sacred Heart Medical Center & Children's Hospital broke ground on an expansion and remodel of its adult cardiac intensive care unit (scheduled to open in 2016). The $19.2 million project includes the renovation and modernization of the existing 22-bed unit and the addition of 12 more critical care beds.

In 2016 Providence Health merged with fellow not-for-profit St. Joseph Health System , operator of nearly 20 hospitals in California, New Mexico, and Texas. The combination created a larger provider network of hospitals, physician groups, and outpatient centers, eliminating some overhead expenses in the process. Furthermore, by creating economies of scale, the new organization will be better positioned to negotiate with health plans.

EXECUTIVES

Chief Development Officer, Laurie Kelley
CDO, Mark Premo
Auditors : KPMG LLP SEATTLE WA

LOCATIONS

HQ: PROVIDENCE HEALTH & SERVICES
1801 LIND AVE SW, RENTON, WA 980573368
Phone: 425 525-3355
Web: WWW.PROVIDENCE.ORG

COMPETITORS

ADVENTIST HEALTH SYSTEM/SUNBELT, INC.
ADVENTIST HEALTHCARE, INC.
ALEXIAN BROTHERS HEALTH SYSTEM
COMMONSPIRIT HEALTH
DENVER HEALTH AND HOSPITALS AUTHORITY
DIGNITY HEALTH
NASSAU HEALTH CARE CORPORATION
SAINT LUKE'S HEALTH SYSTEM, INC.
ST. JOSEPH HEALTH SYSTEM
WHEATON FRANCISCAN SERVICES, INC.

HISTORICAL FINANCIALS
Company Type: Private

Income Statement   FYE: December 31

	REVENUE ($mil)	NET INCOME ($mil)	NET PROFIT MARGIN	EMPLOYEES
12/15	14,433	49	0.3%	130
12/12	280	14	5.3%	—
12/08	7,026	(156)	—	—
12/07	6,348	434	6.8%	—
Annual Growth	10.8%	(23.8%)	—	—

2015 Year-End Financials
Return on assets: 0.3%   Cash ($ mil.): 729
Return on equity: 0.6%
Current Ratio: 1.40

PROVIDENCE HEALTH & SERVICES - OREGON

Auditors : CLARK NUBER PS BELLEVUE WA

LOCATIONS

HQ: PROVIDENCE HEALTH & SERVICES - OREGON
1801 LIND AVE SW, RENTON, WA 980573368
Phone: 425 525-3355
Web: OREGON.PROVIDENCE.ORG

HISTORICAL FINANCIALS
Company Type: Private

Income Statement   FYE: December 31

	REVENUE ($mil)	NET INCOME ($mil)	NET PROFIT MARGIN	EMPLOYEES
12/19	3,823	946	24.8%	103,036
12/17	3,479	781	22.5%	—
12/09	2,057	57	2.8%	—
12/08	73	7	10.5%	—
Annual Growth	43.3%	54.9%	—	—

2019 Year-End Financials
Return on assets: 26.1%   Cash ($ mil.): 678
Return on equity: 31.5%
Current Ratio: 3.70

PSCU INCORPORATED

PSCU (Payment Systems for Credit Unions), the nation's premier payments CUSO, supports the success of 1,900 credit unions representing more than 5.4 billion transactions annually. PSCU's payment processing, risk management, data and analytics, loyalty programs, digital banking, marketing, strategic consulting and mobile platforms help deliver possibilities and seamless member experiences. Comprehensive, 24/7/365 member support is provided by contact centers located throughout the US. Founded in 1977, PSCU was formed by five leading credit union CEOs from GTE Federal Credit Union, Suncoast Schools Federal Credit Union, Pinellas County Teachers Credit Union, Publix Employees Federal Credit Union, and Railroad & Industrial Federal Credit Union.

Geographic Reach

Headquartered in Florida, PSCU operates three service centers located in Arizona, Nebraska and Michigan. TriVerity and The Loan has service center in Minnesota and its Lumin Digital has office located in California. PSCU also maintain office in Iowa.

Strategy

PSCU have invested more than $150 million over the last five years to support its 'digital first' strategy and are focused on the following areas as the company continue to optimize PSCU's operations and enhance the member experience. The focuses are: authentication; artificial intelligence; faster payments; and fintech/ open banking.

Mergers and Acquisitions

In 2022, PSCU acquired Juniper Payments, LLC from PITECO S.p.A. and two principal owners, who will continue with the company under PSCU. Headquartered in Wichita, Kan., Juniper Payments, LLC (Juniper) is the largest cloud-based non-bank third-party provider of inter-bank transaction and reporting systems in the US. Juniper will expand PSCU's value-added services for its financial institutions to support additional payments types. Through the acquisition, PSCU will add multi-tiered payments ? including ACH processing and domestic/ international wire remittance ? to its solutions set, as well as a virtual back-office payments gateway, member and business-originated instant payments and reporting, compliance, risk management and monitoring services.

Company Background

PSCU was formed in 1977 by leaders from Pinellas County Teachers Credit Union and the federal credit unions of GTE, Publix

Employees, Suncoast Schools, and Railroad and Industrial.

Auditors : PRICEWATERHOUSECOOPERS LLP TA

LOCATIONS

HQ: PSCU INCORPORATED
560 CARILLON PKWY, SAINT PETERSBURG, FL 337161294
Phone: 727 572-8822
Web: WWW.PSCU.COM

PRODUCTS/OPERATIONS

Selected Services
Advisors Plus
Credit Solutions
Debit Solutions
eCommerce Solutions
EMV
Prepaid Solutions
Risk Management Solutions
Total Member Care
Technology Tools
PSCU Partnerships/Sponsorships
Credit Union Cherry Blossom Run
Credit Union Student Choice
Filene Research Institute
Financial Service Center Cooperatives (FSCC)
Ongoing Operations
The Colonial Williamsburg Foundation

COMPETITORS

AMERICA FIRST CREDIT UNION
EQUIFAX INC.
ESL FEDERAL CREDIT UNION
FIRST DATA CORPORATION
HIGHER ONE HOLDINGS, INC.
MASTERCARD INCORPORATED
REGIONAL MANAGEMENT CORP.
SECURITY SERVICE FEDERAL CREDIT UNION
UNITED BANK CARD, INC.
VISA INC.

HISTORICAL FINANCIALS
Company Type: Private

Income Statement — FYE: September 30

	REVENUE ($mil)	NET INCOME ($mil)	NET PROFIT MARGIN	EMPLOYEES
09/20	582	37	6.4%	2,100
09/18	481	11	2.4%	—
09/16*	458	28	6.1%	—
12/12	377	38	10.2%	—
Annual Growth	5.6%	(0.4%)	—	—

*Fiscal year change

2020 Year-End Financials
Return on assets: 4.1%   Cash ($ mil.): 175
Return on equity: 13.7%
Current Ratio: 1.10

PUBLIC EMPLOYEE RETIREMENT SYSTEM, IDAHO

Auditors : EIDE BAILLY LLP BOISE IDAHO

LOCATIONS

HQ: PUBLIC EMPLOYEE RETIREMENT SYSTEM, IDAHO
607 N 8TH ST, BOISE, ID 837025518
Phone: 208 334-3365
Web: PERSI.IDAHO.GOV

HISTORICAL FINANCIALS
Company Type: Private

Income Statement — FYE: June 30

	REVENUE ($mil)	NET INCOME ($mil)	NET PROFIT MARGIN	EMPLOYEES
06/21	6,177	4,970	80.5%	62
06/20	1,362	243	17.9%	—
06/19	2,221	1,145	51.6%	—
06/18	2,160	1,157	53.6%	—
Annual Growth	41.9%	62.5%		

2021 Year-End Financials
Return on assets: 20.1%   Cash ($ mil.): 11
Return on equity: 20.2%
Current Ratio: —

PUBLIC HEALTH FOUNDATION ENTERPRISES INCORPORATED

LOCATIONS

HQ: PUBLIC HEALTH FOUNDATION ENTERPRISES INCORPORATED
13300 CRSSRADS PKWY N STE, LA PUENTE, CA 91746
Phone: 562 222-7861

HISTORICAL FINANCIALS
Company Type: Private

Income Statement — FYE: June 30

	REVENUE ($mil)	NET INCOME ($mil)	NET PROFIT MARGIN	EMPLOYEES
06/21	607	5	0.8%	6
06/20	137	1	0.8%	—
Annual Growth	341.0%	335.4%	—	—

2021 Year-End Financials
Return on assets: 2.5%   Cash ($ mil.): 8
Return on equity: 35.2%
Current Ratio: —

PUBLIC HOSPITAL DISTRICT 1 OF KING COUNTY

Auditors : KPMG LLP SEATTLE WASHINGTON

LOCATIONS

HQ: PUBLIC HOSPITAL DISTRICT 1 OF KING COUNTY
400 S 43RD ST, RENTON, WA 980555714
Phone: 425 228-3440
Web: WWW.VALLEYMED.ORG

HISTORICAL FINANCIALS
Company Type: Private

Income Statement — FYE: June 30

	REVENUE ($mil)	NET INCOME ($mil)	NET PROFIT MARGIN	EMPLOYEES
06/22	797	(59)	—	2,700
06/21	786	9	1.2%	—
06/19	694	12	1.7%	—
06/18	653	40	6.2%	—
Annual Growth	5.1%	—	—	—

2022 Year-End Financials
Return on assets: (-6.7%)   Cash ($ mil.): 76
Return on equity: (-26.3%)
Current Ratio: 1.10

PUBLIC UTILITY DISTRICT 1 OF CLARK COUNTY

There are no "we're No 1" signs waving at this publicly minded company's head office. Public Utility District No. 1 of Clark County (Clark Public Utilities) provides utility services to residents and businesses in Clark County, Washington. Clark Public Utilities transmits and distributes electricity to more than 184,100 customers; the company operates a 250-MW gas-fired power plant but purchases the bulk of its power from the Bonneville Power Administration. Clark Public Utilities also distributes water to more than 30,640 customers and collects and treats wastewater for the City of La Center, Washington.

Auditors : MOSS ADAMS LLP PORTLAND ORE

LOCATIONS

HQ: PUBLIC UTILITY DISTRICT 1 OF CLARK COUNTY
1200 FORT VANCOUVER WAY, VANCOUVER, WA 986633527
Phone: 360 992-3000
Web: WWW.CLARKPUBLICUTILITIES.COM

COMPETITORS

BOARD OF LIGHTS AND WATER
CITY OF FORT COLLINS
LINCOLN ELECTRIC SYSTEM
PUBLIC UTILITY DISTRICT NO 1 OF COWLITZ COUNTY
SOUTHERN MARYLAND ELECTRIC COOPERATIVE, INC.

HISTORICAL FINANCIALS
Company Type: Private

Income Statement — FYE: December 31

	REVENUE ($mil)	NET INCOME ($mil)	NET PROFIT MARGIN	EMPLOYEES
12/21	566	50	9.0%	325
12/19	479	28	5.9%	—
12/18	481	38	7.9%	—
12/17	502	45	9.1%	—
Annual Growth	3.1%	2.8%	—	—

2021 Year-End Financials
Return on assets: 4.1%
Return on equity: 8.8%
Current Ratio: 3.80
Cash ($ mil.): 349

PUBLIC UTILITY DISTRICT 1 OF SNOHOMISH COUNTY

Keeping its customers' safety is priority No. 1 at Public Utility District No. 1 of Snohomish County, Washington (Snohomish County PUD), which distributes electricity to over 360,000 electric customers in Washington State. The utility, the second largest PUD in the state, with over 2,200 sq. ml. service area, purchases most of its power supply from third parties (Bonneville Power Administration and other producers). It sells surplus power into the wholesale power transactions to balance its supply load. Snohomish County PUD also serves more than 21,000 water utility customers.

Operations
Snohomish County PUD's operations consist of three systems: the Electric System, the Generation System and the Water System.

The Electric System (about 95% of sales) is made up of electric transmission and distribution system.

The Generation System (some 5%) is composed of the company's Jackson Hydroelectric Project and four smaller hydroelectric projects.

The Water System (less than 5%) is made up of water distribution system.

Overall, around 90% of total sales came from its retail sales, while wholesale sales, and others account for the rest.

Geographic Reach
The company is headquartered in Everett, Washington.

Sales and Marketing
The PUD serves three categories of customers: Residential (around 305,915), Commercial (about 30,795), Industrial (nearly 75) and other (roughly 230).

The company offers a wide range of energy-efficiency solutions for business customers.

Financial Performance
PUD's revenue decreased from $695.8 million in 2018 to $685.7 million in 2019, which resulted from a decrease in wholesale sales and others.

Net income was $82.2 million, a 2% increase compared to the previous year.

Cash and cash equivalents at the end of the year were $45.6 million, 51% less compared to $45.6 million in the previous year. Cash provided by operating activities was $87.4 million. Financing activities used $142.3 million primarily from capital construction, while investing activities provided $5.6 million primarily from sale of special funds and investment securities.

Strategy
In 2019, the PUD completed its first Community Solar project, located at the home of the future Microgrid and Clean Energy Technology Center in Arlington. The 500-kilowatt array is the largest community solar project in the state.

With the launch of Community Solar, the PUD also awarded its final Planet Power solar energy grants to five community-focused and nonprofit organizations: Eagle Creek Elementary, Snohomish County Fire District No. 22, YMCA-Everett, Farmer Frog and Camp Killoqua.

Thanks to customer contributions to the Planet Power program through the years, an additional 329 kilowatts of solar energy has been added to the PUD's grid across 39 individual projects - 112 kilowatts in 2019 alone.

In addition to the hydropower resources available through Bonneville Power, the PUD continued to invest in its own hydroelectric projects. In 2019, the PUD completed the last of the capital improvements specifically identified in the new license for the Henry M. Jackson Hydroelectric Project near Sultan, which is capable of supplying power to over 53,000 homes. The PUD also continued to invest in and benefit from its four smaller projects at Woods Creek, Youngs Creek, Calligan Creek and Hancock Creek.

The PUD's other renewable energy resources include long-term contracts for wind projects in Central Washington and Oregon, and contracts with locally owned and operated biomass and biodigester facilities.

Company BackgroundIn 2013 solar energy capacity stood at two MW, enough to serve 170 homes. More than 350 PUD customers cover part of their electricity needs through their own solar energy units. The PUD's Solar Express program offers financial incentives and technical assistance for solar photovoltaic and solar hot water systems. In 2012 the company amended a power contract with Hampton Lumber (a fuel supplier since 2007) that will boost the level of biomass energy the utility will receive from the lumber company's Darrington plant. The new agreement will allow Snohomish County PUD to receive up to 2.5 MW of energy from Hampton Lumber, enough energy to power about 2,000 homes. Supported by $15.8 million in matching federal stimulus dollars, in 2011 Snohomish County PUD completed its first major project as part of a long-term upgrade of its electric grid with smart grid technology. The upgrade includes the installation of more than 160 miles of fiber optic cable, and connecting them to 62 substations, two radio sites and other utility buildings. The company began providing water utility service to parts of Snohomish County in 1946. Public Utility District No. 1 of Snohomish County began operating as power utility in 1949, providing publicly owned electric and water utility service to the residents of Snohomish County and Camano Island.

Auditors: BAKER TILLY MADISON WI

LOCATIONS
HQ: PUBLIC UTILITY DISTRICT 1 OF SNOHOMISH COUNTY
2320 CALIFORNIA ST, EVERETT, WA 982013750
Phone: 425 257-9288
Web: WWW.SNOPUD.COM

PRODUCTS/OPERATIONS
2014 Sales

	$ mil.	% of total
Retail sales	554.9	86
Wholesale sales	59.6	9
Other	30.6	5
Total	645.1	100

COMPETITORS
GREAT RIVER ENERGY
OMAHA PUBLIC POWER DISTRICT
PUBLIC SERVICE COMPANY OF NEW HAMPSHIRE
SACRAMENTO MUNICIPAL UTILITY DISTRICT
THE CITY OF SEATTLE-CITY LIGHT DEPARTMENT

HISTORICAL FINANCIALS
Company Type: Private

Income Statement — FYE: December 31

	REVENUE ($mil)	NET INCOME ($mil)	NET PROFIT MARGIN	EMPLOYEES
12/20	692	65	9.4%	879
12/19	685	82	12.0%	—
12/18	695	80	11.5%	—
12/17	686	75	11.1%	—
Annual Growth	0.3%	(5.0%)	—	—

2020 Year-End Financials
Return on assets: 2.9%
Return on equity: 4.1%
Current Ratio: 2.40
Cash ($ mil.): —

PUBLISHING OFFICE, US GOVERNMENT

The US Government Printing Office (GPO) keeps America informed in print and online. The GPO is the Federal government's primary centralized resource for gathering, cataloging, producing, providing, and preserving published information in all its forms. Part of the legislative branch, the GPO offers Congress, the courts, and other government agencies centralized services to enable them to easily produce printed documents according to uniform Federal specifications. The GPO also offers the publications for sale to the public and makes them available at no cost through the Federal Depository Library Program. The GPO is run like a business and requires payment from its government customers for services rendered.

EXECUTIVES

Acting Deputy, John Crawford
ACTING DEPUTY, John Crawford
Chief Public Relations Officer*, Gary Somerset
Acting CIO*, Tracee Boxley
CIO*, Sam Musa
Auditors : KPMG LLP WASHINGTON DC

LOCATIONS

HQ: PUBLISHING OFFICE, US GOVERNMENT
732 N CAPITOL ST NW, WASHINGTON, DC 204010002
Phone: 202 512-0000
Web: WWW.GPO.GOV

COMPETITORS

GSA OFFICE OF THE CIO
MANAGEMENT SERVICES, FLORIDA DEPARTMENT OF
NATIONAL ARCHIVES AND RECORDS ADMINISTRATION
U S OFFICE OF PERSONNEL MANAGEMENT
U.S. GENERAL SERVICES ADMINISTRATION

HISTORICAL FINANCIALS
Company Type: Private

Income Statement — FYE: September 30

	REVENUE ($mil)	NET INCOME ($mil)	NET PROFIT MARGIN	EMPLOYEES
09/20	915	(14)	—	1,880
09/19	937	51	5.5%	—
09/18	874	52	6.0%	—
09/17	874	58	6.7%	—
Annual Growth	1.6%	—	—	—

2020 Year-End Financials
Return on assets: (-1.3%)   Cash ($ mil.): 660
Return on equity: (-2.0%)
Current Ratio: 2.90

QUALITY OIL COMPANY, LLC

With more services than your average oil company, Quality Oil helps its customers get fueled up, cooled off, and well rested. And they can smoke if they want to. The company distributes fuel oil and propane to customers in the Winston-Salem area of North Carolina. Quality Oil provides air conditioning and heating equipment service, operates 47 convenience stores (Quality Marts), and about 20 service stations, and owns hotels in five southern states. In addition, the company operates 60 Quality Plus locations at which drivers can buy cigarettes at discount prices. The company also provides Right-a-Way oil change services at many of its gas stations.

Operations
In addition, the company's real estate unit (Quality Oil Real Estate) operates a diverse portfolio of retail and hotel sites, industrial units, residential subdivision developments, and a shopping center. Quality Marts and Quality Plus also provide heating and cooling and fleet fueling services.

Geographic Reach
Quality Oil owns and operates four Hampton Inns, two Hampton Inn & Suites, and one Homewood Suites in the Carolinas, Florida, Georgia, and Virginia. Affiliate Reliable Tank Line, LLC, transports petroleum products and provides fleet fueling services at 10 locations in North Carolina, northern South Carolina, eastern Virginia, and eastern Tennessee. Quality Oil Heating-Cooling has assets throughout North Carolina and parts of South Carolina, Virginia, Florida, and Tennessee and serves Forsyth County, Stokes County, Davie County, Davidson County, Yadkin County, Rowan County, and Iredell County.

Sales and Marketing
The company markets Shell oil products.

Strategy
To sharpen its competitive edge, in 2013 Quality Oil created a new department -- Retail Technology -- to maintain PDI Pricebook and POS Systems, and test and implement future technological developments.

To increase operational efficiency, in 2012 Quality Oil installed Professional Datasolutions Inc. (PDI) scanning software at all of its retail outlets.

Mergers and Acquisitions
To complement its existing oil and propane business, in 2012 Quality Oil acquired regional gas station and convenience store operator Horn Oil Co. in Mocksville, North Carolina.

Company Background
Expanding its store network, in 2011 the company opened Quality Mart locations #46 and #47 in Kernersville and Morrisville.

Quality Oil was founded in 1929 by Joe Glenn and Bert Bennett as a Shell oil products distributor, and is still owned and operated by descendants of the founders.

Auditors : BUTLER & BURKE LLP WINSTON-S

LOCATIONS
HQ: QUALITY OIL COMPANY, LLC
1540 SILAS CREEK PKWY, WINSTON SALEM, NC 271273705
Phone: 336 722-3441
Web: WWW.QUALITYOILNC.COM

PRODUCTS/OPERATIONS

Selected Brands
Hampton Inn
Quality Heating and Air Conditioning
Quality Mart
Quality Oil Appliance Sales and Service
Quality Oil Commercial Heating and On-Site Fueling
Quality Oil Fuel Oil
Quality Oil Gas Logs and Heaters
Quality Oil Propane
Quality Plus
Reliable Tank Line
Shell Oil products

Selected Mergers and Acquisitions
2012
Horn Oil Co. (Mocksville, North Carolina; gas station and convenience store operator)

COMPETITORS
CASTLE OIL CORPORATION
PETRO/CRYSTAL PETROLEUM CO., INC.
PETROLEUM MARKETERS, INCORPORATED
RICHLAND PARTNERS, LLC
SHIPLEY ENERGY COMPANY

HISTORICAL FINANCIALS
Company Type: Private

Income Statement — FYE: December 31

	REVENUE ($mil)	NET INCOME ($mil)	NET PROFIT MARGIN	EMPLOYEES
12/09	634	11	1.9%	1,000
12/08	806	27	3.4%	—
12/07	619	10	1.8%	—
12/06	542	15	2.8%	—
Annual Growth	5.4%	(8.1%)	—	—

2009 Year-End Financials
Return on assets: 9.9%   Cash ($ mil.): 11
Return on equity: 13.1%
Current Ratio: 0.90

R. DIRECTIONAL DRILLING & UNDERGROUND TECHNOLOGY, INC.

Auditors : KEN DUSSEAU PC

LOCATIONS

HQ: R. DIRECTIONAL DRILLING & UNDERGROUND TECHNOLOGY, INC.
  8560 N 77TH DR, PEORIA, AZ 853457969
Phone: 602 374-3173
Web: WWW.DRILLRDD.COM

HISTORICAL FINANCIALS
Company Type: Private

Income Statement — FYE: December 31

	REVENUE ($mil)	NET INCOME ($mil)	NET PROFIT MARGIN	EMPLOYEES
12/12	7,667	(1,040)	—	61
12/11*	7	2	29.9%	—
09/10	2	0	27.4%	—
Annual Growth	5174.7%	—	—	—

*Fiscal year change

2012 Year-End Financials
Return on assets: (-24.4%)   Cash ($ mil.): 416
Return on equity: (-48.7%)
Current Ratio: 1.30

R. E. MICHEL COMPANY, LLC

Blowing hot and cold is good for R.E. Michel. The company is one of the nation's largest wholesale distributors of heating, air-conditioning, and refrigeration (HVAC-R) equipment, parts, and supplies. The family-owned and operated firm offers more than 16,000 items through about 2 sales offices located across the Southern, Mid-Atlantic, and Northeastern regions of the country. R.E. Michel ships more than 20,000 items each day from its 900,000-sq.-ft. distribution center in Maryland. Its Exclusive Supplier Partnership (ESP) program offers customers inventory control, advertising, and marketing support. R.E. Michel was founded in 1935 as a supplier to the home heating oil burner industry.

Geographic Reach
The HVAC wholesaler maintains a handful of offices to cater to customers located in the Southern US, as well as in the Mid-Atlantic and Northeastern regions. Most recently opened offices reside in Ohio, California, Virginia, Florida, South Carolina, Arizona, and Tennessee.

Sales and Marketing
R.E. Michel uses up to 50 trailers to ship its more than 10,000 items each day. To this end, the company also ships more than 3,200 items via the United Parcel Service each week. As part of its business, it publishes a 1,300 page catalog that includes 20,000 catalog line items.

Auditors : CLIFTONLARSONALLEN LLP BALTIM

LOCATIONS
HQ: R. E. MICHEL COMPANY, LLC
  1 RE MICHEL DR, GLEN BURNIE, MD 210606408

Phone: 410 760-4000
Web: WWW.REMICHEL.COM

PRODUCTS/OPERATIONS
Selected Products & Services
Air conditioning & heating
Indoor air quality
Boilers
Water heating equipment
Hydronic & steam systems
Valves
Pipe & fittings
Fuel oil systems
Gas systems
Chemicals
Refrigeration equipment & supplies
Controls
Electrical supplies
Motors
Air handling products
Venting products
Duct, registers & grilles
Tools & test instruments
O.E.M. Parts

COMPETITORS
AIRECO SUPPLY, INC.
BAKER DISTRIBUTING COMPANY LLC
JOHNSTONE SUPPLY, INC.
KOCH AIR, LLC
MINGLEDORFF'S, INC.
NORTHERN TOOL & EQUIPMENT COMPANY, INC.
ORGILL, INC.
SLAKEY BROTHERS, INC.
THE HOME CITY ICE COMPANY
WATSCO, INC.

HISTORICAL FINANCIALS
Company Type: Private

Income Statement — FYE: December 31

	REVENUE ($mil)	NET INCOME ($mil)	NET PROFIT MARGIN	EMPLOYEES
12/20	999	57	5.7%	2,062
12/19	939	48	5.2%	—
12/18	898	37	4.1%	—
12/17	804	26	3.2%	—
Annual Growth	7.5%	29.8%	—	—

2020 Year-End Financials
Return on assets: 11.2%   Cash ($ mil.): 3
Return on equity: 17.8%
Current Ratio: 2.50

R. M. PARKS, INC.

Auditors : GUMBINER SAVETT INC SANTA MON

LOCATIONS
HQ: R. M. PARKS, INC.
  1061 N MAIN ST, PORTERVILLE, CA 932571686
Phone: 559 784-2384
Web: WWW.RMPARKSINC.COM

HISTORICAL FINANCIALS
Company Type: Private

Income Statement — FYE: October 31

	REVENUE ($mil)	NET INCOME ($mil)	NET PROFIT MARGIN	EMPLOYEES
10/18	571	0	0.0%	20
10/17	477	(0)	—	—
10/16	448	0	0.2%	—
10/15	534	0	0.2%	—
Annual Growth	2.3%	(73.9%)	—	—

2018 Year-End Financials
Return on assets: 0.1%   Cash ($ mil.): —
Return on equity: 0.2%
Current Ratio: 1.30

R. R. DONNELLEY & SONS COMPANY

RR Donnelley & Sons (RRD) is a leading global provider of multichannel business communications services and marketing solutions. It assists clients in developing and executing multichannel communication strategies that engage audiences, reduce costs, drive revenues and enhance compliance. Its content management offering, production platform, supply chain management, outsourcing capabilities and customized consultative expertise assists clients in the delivery of integrated messages across multiple media to highly targeted audiences at optimal times to their customers in virtually every private and public sector. Almost 70% of total revenue comes from US customers.

Operations
RRD's is divided into two reportable segments: Business Services and Marketing Solutions.

The Business Services segment, which accounts for nearly 80% of sales, includes all RRD's operations in Asia, Europe, Canada, and Latin America. The segment's product and services includes: Commercial printing products, Branded materials such as manuals, publications, brochures, business cards, flyers, post cards, posters, and promotional items, Packaging ranging from rigid boxes to in-box print materials for clients in consumer electronics, life sciences, cosmetics, and consumer packaged goods industries and others.

Marketing Solutions segment accounts for over 20% of sales and leverages integrated portfolio of data analytics, creative services and multichannel execution to deliver comprehensive, end-to- end solutions. It offers: Direct marketing, which includes audience segmentation, creative development, program testing, print production, postal optimization, and performance analytics for large- scale direct mail programs, Digital print and fulfillment, and other related services.

Geographic Reach

RRD, headquartered in Chicago, operates almost 120 facilities in the US and nearly 60 facilities in Asia, Europe, Canada, and Latin America.

The US accounts for almost 70% of the company's revenue while Asia accounts for over 20% and Europe contributes some 5%. Other countries and regions generate the remainder.

Sales and Marketing

RRD claims to have approximately 25,000 clients worldwide, including 92% of the Fortune 100, 79% of the Fortune 500 and 67% of the Fortune 1000.

RRD's products are distributed to end-users through US and foreign postal services, through retail channels, electronically or by direct shipment to client facilities. In cooperation with trusted logistics vendors, it manages the distribution of most client products it prints in the US and Canada to maximize efficiency and reduce costs for clients.

Financial Performance

Revenue in 2021 was $4.9 billion, an increase of 4% from 2020. Net sales increased $50.0 million due to favorable changes in foreign exchange rates and were unfavorably impacted by $6.5 million due to the Chile business closure in 2020. Net sales also increased due to higher volume reflecting strengthening demand for many of RRD's products and services and higher prices as the company attempts to recover inflationary cost increases.

Net income attributable to RRD common stockholders in 2021 was $3.7 million compared to $98.5 million from the prior year.

The company had $320.3 million in cash at the end of 2021. Cash generated by operations was $92.1 million. Cash provided by investing was $55.3 million, and cash used in financing was $75.3 million.

Strategy

The company's key strategic focus areas, which leverage its long-standing client relationships and comprehensive portfolio of capabilities, are as follows: driving profitable growth; extending their capabilities; expanding print and digital technology platforms; optimizing business performance; and disciplined capital allocation.

In driving profitable growth, the company intends to drive profitable growth in each of its core businesses and shift its portfolio mix toward higher growth segments.

The company intends to optimize its business performance by providing exceptional service and product quality to its clients while aggressively reducing its costs in order to improve margins and fund its transformation efforts.

RRD also aims to maintain a disciplined approach to capital allocation with an added focus on reducing its leverage, while also investing in its future through strategic capital investments and acquisitions.

Mergers and Acquisitions

In February 2022, Chatham Asset Management, a leading private investment firm, and RRD announced that they have completed a transaction in which affiliates of Chatham have acquired RRD for $10.85 per share in cash.

With the completion of the transaction, RRD expects its common stock will cease trading on the New York Stock Exchange before market open on February 28, 2022. In connection with the completion of the transaction, Thomas J. Quinlan has assumed the role of President and Chief Executive Officer of RRD.

Company Background

RR Donnelley was once even bigger than it is now, before it split itself up into three separate publicly traded companies in 2016. The breakup of the $11.7 billion conglomerate was conducted to "maximize shareholder value" by creating more focused companies. RR Donnelley kept the business communications and business process outsourcing holdings as the largest surviving entity with $7 billion in sales and 42,000 employees. The other two entities include LSC Communications, a $3.7 billion, 22,000-employee company serving magazine, catalog, and book publishers; and Donnelley Financial Solutions, which has 3,500 workers and $1.05 billion in sales and focuses on critical financial, investment ,and legal communications.

EXECUTIVES

CCO, Deborah L Steiner
CAO, Michael J Sharp
Auditors : DELOITTE & TOUCHE LLP CHICAGO

LOCATIONS

HQ: R. R. DONNELLEY & SONS COMPANY
35 W WACKER DR, CHICAGO, IL 606011723
Phone: 312 326-8000
Web: WWW.RRD.COM

2017 sales

	$ mil.	% of total
U.S	5,233	75
Asia	857.3	12
Europe	455	7
Other	394.3	6
Total	6,939.6	100

PRODUCTS/OPERATIONS

2017 Sales

	$ mil.	% of total
Variable Print	3,113.1	45
Strategic Services	1,765.7	25
International	2,060.8	30
Total	6,939.6	100

2017 Sales

	$ mil.	% of total
Product	5,326	77
Services	1,613.6	23
Total	6,939.6	100

Selected Operations

US print and related services
  Book (consumer, religious, educational and specialty, and telecommunications)
  Direct mail (content creation, database management, printing, personalization, finishing, and distribution in North America)
  Directories (yellow and white pages)
  Logistics (consolidation and delivery of printed products; expedited distribution of time-sensitive and secure material; print-on-demand, warehousing, and fulfillment services)
  Magazine, catalog, and retail inserts
  Short-run commercial print (annual reports, marketing brochures, catalog and marketing inserts, pharmaceutical inserts and other marketing, retail point-of-sale and promotional materials and technical publications)
International
  Business process outsourcing
  Global Turnkey Solutions (product configuration, customized kitting, and order fulfillment)

Selected Capabilities:
Digital
Print
Consulting & Execution
Logistics & supply chain
Industry solutions

COMPETITORS

ADVANCED XEROGRAPHICS IMAGING SYSTEMS, INC.
ELECTRONICS FOR IMAGING, INC.
IMAGELINX PLC
INNERWORKINGS, INC.
KIN AND CARTA PLC
LSC COMMUNICATIONS, INC.
MIMEO.COM, INC.
MULTI-COLOR CORPORATION
TARGET MEDIA PARTNERS INTERACTIVE, LLC
TTEC HOLDINGS, INC.

HISTORICAL FINANCIALS

Company Type: Private

Income Statement — FYE: December 31

	REVENUE ($mil)	NET INCOME ($mil)	NET PROFIT MARGIN	EMPLOYEES
12/21	4,963	4	0.1%	32,000
12/20	4,766	99	2.1%	—
12/19	6,276	(92)	—	—
12/18	6,800	(9)	—	—
Annual Growth	(10.0%)	—	—	—

2021 Year-End Financials
Return on assets: 0.1%   Cash ($ mil.): 280
Return on equity: —
Current Ratio: 1.40

R.C. WILLEY HOME FURNISHINGS

R.C. Willey Home Furnishings serves customers across the Western US with locations in Utah, Nevada, California, and Idaho. It sells furniture, appliances, electronics, and flooring. The company also sells mattresses. These products are sold under brand names Samsung, GE, Maytag, and LG, among others R.C. Willey is owned by the investment giant Warren Buffett of Berkshire Hathaway. Adding the buying power of the other home furnishings stores he owns across the nation, its huge buying power guarantees the lowest price on name-brand merchandise. The company was founded back in 1932 when Rufus Call Willey began selling appliances from the back of his red pickup truck.

Operations

The company is known for its large selection and reliable products such as furniture, appliances, electronics, flooring, and matresses under well-known brand names. It carries General Electric, Whirlpool, LG, Maytag, Sony, LG, Samsung, Serta, and Tempur-Pedic among others.

Geographic Reach

Salt Lake Utah-based, R.C. Willey operates about 15 stores in Utah, Nevada, Idaho, and California.

Sales and Marketing

A plus to R.C. Willey Home Furnishings customers, the company offers financing through its R.C. Willey Credit Card.

LOCATIONS

HQ: R.C. WILLEY HOME FURNISHINGS
  2301 S 300 W, SOUTH SALT LAKE, UT 841152516
Phone: 801 461-3900
Web: WWW.RCWILLEY.COM

PRODUCTS/OPERATIONS

Selected Products
Appliances
Electronics
Fitness
Flooring
Furniture
Mattresses

COMPETITORS

AMERICAN FURNITURE WAREHOUSE CO.
ASHLEY FURNITURE INDUSTRIES, LLC
BAER'S FURNITURE CO., INC.
BROWN JORDAN INC.
FRANCO MANUFACTURING CO. INC.
HOM FURNITURE, INC.
JORDAN'S FURNITURE, INC.
Leon's Furniture Limited
RAYMOURS FURNITURE COMPANY, INC.
SLUMBERLAND, INC.

HISTORICAL FINANCIALS
Company Type: Private

Income Statement — FYE: December 31

	REVENUE ($mil)	NET INCOME ($mil)	NET PROFIT MARGIN	EMPLOYEES
12/17	807	19	2.4%	3,401
12/16	800	26	3.3%	—
12/14	712	17	2.4%	—
12/13	664	15	2.3%	—
Annual Growth	5.0%	6.3%	—	—

2017 Year-End Financials
Return on assets: 2.1%   Cash ($ mil.): 62
Return on equity: 2.5%
Current Ratio: 4.10

RADY CHILDREN'S HOSPITAL AND HEALTH CENTER

EXECUTIVES

CMO*, Irvin A Kaufman
Auditors : LB KPMG LLP LOS ANGELES CA

LOCATIONS

HQ: RADY CHILDREN'S HOSPITAL AND HEALTH CENTER
  3020 CHILDRENS WAY, SAN DIEGO, CA 921234223
Phone: 858 576-1700
Web: WWW.RCHSD.ORG

HISTORICAL FINANCIALS
Company Type: Private

Income Statement — FYE: June 30

	REVENUE ($mil)	NET INCOME ($mil)	NET PROFIT MARGIN	EMPLOYEES
06/22	1,639	231	14.1%	4,033
06/21	1,336	593	44.4%	—
06/20	1,334	(20)	—	—
06/19	1,354	167	12.3%	—
Annual Growth	6.6%	11.4%	—	—

2022 Year-End Financials
Return on assets: 6.4%   Cash ($ mil.): 62
Return on equity: 9.4%
Current Ratio: 4.80

RADY CHILDREN'S HOSPITAL-SAN DIEGO

Rady Children's Hospital-San Diego handles the big injuries of pint-sized patients. Serving as the region's only pediatric trauma center, the nonprofit hospital boasts more than 520 beds. As part of its services, Rady Children's Hospital-San Diego offers comprehensive pediatric care, including surgical services, convalescent care, a neonatal intensive care unit, and orthopedic services. Across its service area the hospital also operates about 25 satellite centers that provide such primary and specialized care services as physical therapy and hearing diagnostics. Rady Children's Hospital, a teaching hospital affiliated with the University of California San Diego Medical School, was founded in 1954.

Operations

Rady Children's operates its own 36-bed emergency department -- The Sam S. and Rose Stein Emergency Care Center -- that each day sees up to 300 patients. It is the only regional emergency center solely dedicated and equipped to care for children. The hospital also operates California's only pediatric skilled nursing facility -- The Helen Bernardy Center -- to provide 24-hour care to disabled and medically fragile children in a homelike environment.

For treating non-life-or-limb-threatening injuries and illnesses, the hospital operates neighborhood urgent care centers in Escondido, La Mesa, Oceanside, and San Diego.

Through its medical school affiliation, Rady Children's engages in nearly 500 clinical trials in all pediatric specialties. It collaborates with University of California San Diego, the Sanford-Burnham Medical Research Institute, The Scripps Research Institute, the Salk Institute for Biological Studies, and St. Jude Children's Research Hospital. Specialized research facilities on campus include the Autism Discovery Institute, the Blair L. Sadler Center for Quality, and the Child and Adolescent Services Research Center.

The hospital operates a LEED-certified Acute Care Pavilion, which holds a neonatal intensive care unit, the Peckham Center for Cancer and Blood Disorders, and the Warren Family Surgical Center. It serves those suffering from eating disorders through its inpatient center to allow for intensive psychiatric therapy for patients with anorexia and bulimia and to aid families with home care.

In 2014, the hospital had 18,782 inpatient admissions, 230,383 outpatient visits, nearly 85,000 emergency department visits, and more than 54,000 urgent care visits. It performed about 20,000 surgeries.

Geographic Reach

Rady Children's Hospital serves as the pediatric medical center that caters to the California region of San Diego, Imperial, and southern Riverside counties. It has more than 30 offices throughout San Diego and southern Riverside counties, with satellite locations in Chula Vista, El Centro, Encinitas, Escondido, La Jolla, La Mesa, Murrieta, Oceanside, San Diego, and Solana Beach.

EXECUTIVES

CAO*, Jill Strickland

LOCATIONS

HQ: RADY CHILDREN'S HOSPITAL-SAN DIEGO
  3020 CHILDRENS WAY, SAN DIEGO, CA 921234223
Phone: 858 576-1700
Web: WWW.RCHSD.ORG

Selected Satellite Locations
Chula Vista
El Centro
Encinitas
Escondido
La Jolla
La Mesa
Murrieta
Oceanside
San Diego
Solana Beach

PRODUCTS/OPERATIONS

Selected Services
Allergy/Immunology
Attention Deficit Hyperactivity Disorder
Audiology/Hearing
Autism Discovery Institute
Behavioral Health
Brachial Plexus Clinic
Cancer & Blood Disorders
Cardiology
Cardiovascular Surgery
Celiac Disease Clinic
Center for Healthier Communities
Cerebral Palsy Center
Chadwick Center For Children & Families
Child & Adolescent Psychiatry Services (CAPS)
Child & Adolescent Services Research Center (CASRC)
Child Life Services
Children's Care Connection (C3)
Children's Hospital Emergency Transport (CHET)
Cleft Palate Clinic
Craniofacial Disorders
Critical Care
Cystic Fibrosis Center
Dental Surgery
Dermatology
Developmental Evaluation Clinic
Developmental-Behavioral Pediatrics
Developmental Screening & Enhancement Program (DSEP)
Developmental Services
Down Syndrome Center
Eating Disorders/
Medical-Behavioral Disorders Unit
Emergency Medicine
Endocrinology/Diabetes
Fatty Liver Clinic
Feeding Team
Gastroenterology, Hepatology & Nutrition
Genetics/Dysmorphology
Heart Institute
Helen Bernardy Center for Medically Fragile Children
Hematology/Oncology
HomeCare
Hospice
Infectious Diseases
Kawasaki Disease Clinic
Kidney/Liver Tranplant Program
Kidney Disease
Laboratory Services/Pathology
Liver Disease
Liver Transplant
Muscle Disease Clinic
Metabolic Medicine
Neonatology
Nephrology
Neurology
Neurosurgery
Newborn Screening Program
Nutrition Clinic
Occupational Therapy
Ophthalmology
Orthopedics
Otolaryngology/ENT
Pain Services
Palliative Care
Pediatric Surgery
Pediatrics & Hospital Medicine
Pharmacy Services
Physical Therapy
Prader-Willi Syndrome Clinic
Psychiatry
Pulmonary/Respiratory Medicine
Radiology
Rehabilitation Medicine
Rheumatology
Sleep Center
Speech/Language Pathology
Spiritual Care
Sports Medicine
Surgery
Toddler School (Alexa's PLAYC)
Trauma Center
Urgent Care
Urology
Weight & Wellness Center

COMPETITORS
ASCENSION SOUTHEAST MICHIGAN
METHODIST HOSPITAL OF SOUTHERN CALIFORNIA
NEWTON MEMORIAL HOSPITAL (INC)
ST. JUDE HOSPITAL
SUTTER BAY HOSPITALS

HISTORICAL FINANCIALS
Company Type: Private

Income Statement — FYE: June 30

	REVENUE ($mil)	NET INCOME ($mil)	NET PROFIT MARGIN	EMPLOYEES
06/21	1,254	449	35.8%	2,313
06/20	1,267	73	5.8%	—
06/19	1,300	208	16.0%	—
06/15	522	104	20.1%	—
Annual Growth	15.7%	27.5%	—	—

2021 Year-End Financials
Return on assets: 14.2%   Cash ($ mil.): 126
Return on equity: 22.3%
Current Ratio: 5.20

RALEIGH DUKE HOSPITAL GUILD

LOCATIONS
HQ: RALEIGH DUKE HOSPITAL GUILD
3400 WAKE FOREST RD, RALEIGH, NC 276097317
Phone: 919 954-3000
Web: WWW.DUKEHEALTH.ORG

HISTORICAL FINANCIALS
Company Type: Private

Income Statement — FYE: June 30

	REVENUE ($mil)	NET INCOME ($mil)	NET PROFIT MARGIN	EMPLOYEES
06/22	645	18	2.8%	600
06/21	609	84	13.9%	—
06/19	528	19	3.6%	—
06/18	478	22	4.6%	—
Annual Growth	7.8%	(4.8%)	—	—

2022 Year-End Financials
Return on assets: 4.3%   Cash ($ mil.): —
Return on equity: 5.3%
Current Ratio: 0.80

RALEY'S

Raley's is a third-generation family business that makes healthier food more accessible to everyone. The largest family-owned company in the greater Sacramento region operates about 130 supermarkets and superstores in northern California and Nevada. In addition to about 80 flagship Raley's Superstores, the company operates about 20 Bel Air Markets (in the Sacramento area), Nob Hill Foods (an upscale Bay Area chain with approximately 20 locations), and five discount warehouse stores under the Food Source banner in Northern California and Nevada. Raley's stores typically offer groceries, natural foods, and liquor, as well as in-store pharmacies. Tom P. Raley opened his first store Raley's grocery store in 1935.

Operations
In addition to supermarkets, Raley's pharmacy services offer immunizations, blood pressure screenings, translation services, and more.

Geographic Reach
The company is based in West Sacramento, California.

Mergers and Acquisitions
In late 2021, Raley's completed the purchase of West Sacramento, California-based The Raley's Companies, which operates approximately 124 supermarkets in northern California and Nevada under the Raley's, Bel Air, Nob Hill Foods, and Raley's O-N-E Market banners. Financial terms of the agreement were not disclosed.

Company Background
Raley's traces its roots to Placerville, California, and the 1935 opening of a grocery store by Tom Raley. The company has grown organically and through acquisitions; it acquired Bel Air Markets in 1992 and Nob Hill Foods in 1998. It remains family-owned.

EXECUTIVES
CTRL*, Ken Mueller
CAO*, Jennifer Warner

LOCATIONS
HQ: RALEY'S
500 W CAPITOL AVE, WEST SACRAMENTO, CA 956052696
Phone: 916 373-3333
Web: WWW.RALEYS.COM

2018 Stores

	No.
California	110
Northern Nevada	18
Total	128

PRODUCTS/OPERATIONS

2018 Stores

	No.
Supermarkets	
Raley's	78
Nob Hill	20
Bel Air	20
Food Source	8
Other	2
Total	128

COMPETITORS
CARDENAS MARKETS LLC
DEMOULAS SUPER MARKETS, INC.
DIERBERGS MARKETS, INC.

HAGGEN, INC.
REASOR"S LLC
SAVE MART SUPERMARKETS DISC
SHOPWELL, INC.
THE FRESH MARKET INC
UNITED SUPERMARKETS, L.L.C.
WHOLE FOODS MARKET, INC.

HISTORICAL FINANCIALS
Company Type: Private

Income Statement   FYE: June 30

	REVENUE ($mil)	NET INCOME ($mil)	NET PROFIT MARGIN	EMPLOYEES
06/12	3,162	(1)	0.0%	14,000
06/10	3,064	0	0.0%	—
06/09	0	0	—	—
Annual Growth	—	—	—	—

2012 Year-End Financials
Return on assets: (-0.2%)   Cash ($ mil.): 26
Return on equity: (-0.6%)
Current Ratio: 0.90

RAYMOND JAMES & ASSOCIATES INC

Does everybody love Raymond James & Associates (RJA)? Raymond James Financial hopes so. RJA is that company's primary subsidiary and one of the largest retail brokerages in the US. The unit provides brokerage, financial planning, investments, and related services to consumers. It performs equity and fixed income sales, trading, and research for institutional clients in North America and Europe. Its investment banking group provides corporate and public finance, debt underwriting, and mergers and acquisitions advice. RJA also makes markets for approximately 1,000 stocks, including thinly traded issues. Planning Corporation of America, a wholly-owned subsidiary of RJA, sells insurance and annuities.

Operations
RJA is engaged in most aspects of securities distribution and investment banking.

Geographic Reach
The company has more than 200 branches and satellite offices concentrated in the Mid-Atlantic, Midwest, Southeast, and Southwest portions of the US, in addition to ten institutional sales offices in Europe.

Sales and Marketing
RJA has many big name clients across dozens of industries. In 2013 Titan Medical announced that it has retained RJA to provide advisory services and present options, which could include a possible sale.

Strategy
In 2012 the company's parent completed its acquisition of Morgan Keegan & Co. and MK Holding, Inc. from Regions Financial Corporation. Some of the equity capital markets and fixed income operations of were integrated into RJA.

Auditors : KPMG LLP TAMPA FL

LOCATIONS
HQ: RAYMOND JAMES & ASSOCIATES INC
880 CARILLON PKWY, SAINT PETERSBURG, FL 337161100
Phone: 727 567-1000
Web: WWW.RAYMONDJAMES.COM

COMPETITORS
ALVAREZ & MARSAL HOLDINGS, LLC
D.A. DAVIDSON COMPANIES
DEERFIELD DUFF & PHELPS, LLC
JANNEY MONTGOMERY SCOTT LLC
KBW, LLC
MESIROW FINANCIAL HOLDINGS, INC
MORGAN JOSEPH TRIARTISAN LLC
RAYMOND JAMES FINANCIAL, INC.
SCOTT & STRINGFELLOW, LLC
WEDBUSH SECURITIES INC.

HISTORICAL FINANCIALS
Company Type: Private

Income Statement   FYE: September 30

	ASSETS ($mil)	NET INCOME ($mil)	INCOME AS % OF ASSETS	EMPLOYEES
09/17	9,917	198	2.0%	10,000
09/16	10,689	145	1.4%	—
09/15	7,893	167	2.1%	—
09/14	6,955	182	2.6%	—
Annual Growth	12.6%	2.8%	—	—

2017 Year-End Financials
Return on assets: 2.0%   Cash ($ mil.): 4195
Return on equity: 7.8%
Current Ratio: —

RAYMOURS FURNITURE COMPANY, INC.

Raymours Furniture is heating up the oft-chilly Northeast, doing business as Raymour & Flanigan. The company operates in several states through 94 retail stores, including nearly a dozen clearance centers. It sells furniture for just about every room in the house (bedroom, dining room, home office, living room), offering such pieces as bookcases, entertainment centers, headboards, mattresses, nightstands, recliners, sofas, and tables. Brands such as Broyhill, La-Z-Boy, Natuzzi, and Tempur Sealy are represented. Raymours is run by founding Goldberg family.

Operations
The company boasts 94 full-line showrooms, about a dozen clearance centers, 15 customer service centers, and four distribution centers in New York, New Jersey, Pennsylvania, Connecticut, Massachusetts, Delaware, and Rhode Island. Raymours also operates more than a dozen customer distribution centers. Its one warehouse property is located in Quakertown, Pennsylvania.

Geographic Reach
Based in New York, Raymours has become the largest furniture retailer in the Northeast. Through a contractor, it provides furniture delivery across the continental US.

Sales and Marketing
Raymours sells its furniture and accessories through its retail stores and online.

Strategy
Following significant expansion in 2008, Raymours has focused in recent years on expanding its presence on the Internet to entice more customers to shop. It added rugs and home decor items, such as lamps, throw pillows, wall art, and silk florals, to its online furniture catalog. It also extended its furniture delivery area to all states within the continental US through a partnership with a contracted delivery service.

Raymours also expanded its existing partnership with Kathy Ireland Worldwide (led by its namesake model-actress) by adding 10 upholstered pieces to its Kathy Ireland Home furniture collection. The Kathy Ireland pieces are sold exclusively through Raymours.

The company has been expanding its New York distribution center in Rockland County, spending some $46 million to purchase and renovate the 839,000-sq.-ft. facility, which will serve as its primary regional warehouse and distribution hub for the New York, New Jersey, and Connecticut areas.

In 2015, Raymours purchased the North Oaks Shopping Plaza. The majority of the complex, located at 1345 Route 1 South in North Brunswick, had been vacant for years. Raymours will become the plaza's new anchor.

Since 2013, Raymours has been prudently adding furniture showrooms in New York, one in Brooklyn in 2013 on Fulton Street and another in 2014 in Queens, which spans 22,000 sq. ft. on multiple levels.

Company Background
Founded in 1947 by brothers Arnold and Bernard Goldberg, Raymour & Flanigan is run by president and CEO Neil Goldberg and EVPs Michael and Steven.

Auditors : GREEN & SEIFTER SYRACUSE NEW

LOCATIONS
HQ: RAYMOURS FURNITURE COMPANY, INC.
7248 MORGAN RD, LIVERPOOL, NY 130904535
Phone: 315 453-2500
Web: WWW.RAYMOURFLANIGAN.COM

PRODUCTS/OPERATIONS
Selected Products
Accents
Area Rugs
Bedrooms

Dining Rooms
Entertainment
Home Decor
Home Office
Living Rooms
Mattresses
Youth Bedrooms

Selected Brands
Berkline
Bernhardt
Broyhill
Cindy Crawford Home
Kathy Ireland Home
La-Z-Boy
Natuzzi
Rowe
Sealy
Stanley Furniture
Stearns & Foster
Tempur-Pedic

COMPETITORS

ASHLEY FURNITURE INDUSTRIES, LLC
BAER'S FURNITURE CO., INC.
BOB'S DISCOUNT FURNITURE, LLC
CITY FURNITURE, INC.
FURNITURELAND SOUTH, INC.
JORDAN'S FURNITURE, INC.
KLAUSSNER FURNITURE INDUSTRIES, INC.
R.T.G. FURNITURE CORP.
ROOM & BOARD, INC.
SLEEPY'S REORGANIZATION, INC.

HISTORICAL FINANCIALS
Company Type: Private

Income Statement   FYE: December 29

	REVENUE ($mil)	NET INCOME ($mil)	NET PROFIT MARGIN	EMPLOYEES
12/07	881	30	3.4%	6,166
12/06	780	23	3.0%	—
12/05	655	21	3.2%	—
Annual Growth	16.0%	20.2%	—	—

2007 Year-End Financials
Return on assets: 13.5%   Cash ($ mil.): —
Return on equity: 38.1%
Current Ratio: 1.50

RDO CONSTRUCTION EQUIPMENT CO.

RDO Equipment sells and rents new and used trucks and heavy equipment to customers in the agriculture and construction industries. RDO Equipment operates more than 75 locations across the United States. It offers John Deere agriculture equipment, construction and forestry, and lawn and land, as well as Vermmer, Topcon, and other top brands. RDO also has partnerships in Africa, Australia, Mexico, Russia, and Ukraine, making it a total solutions provider and partner to customers around the globe. Ronald Offutt founded the family-owned and operated company in 1968.

Operations
The company offers new and used equipment, used agriculture and construction equipment. It offers heavy-duty equipment such as compact excavator, electric utility vehicle, mower-conditioner, tractor, disc mower, and more. These products are sold under brand names John Deere, Vermeer, Topcon, and other top brands such as Mazzotti, Spudnik, and Carlson Machine Control.

Geographic Reach
North Dakota-based RDO Equipment has over 75 stores across the US. Outside the US, the company operates through partnerships in Africa, Australia, Mexico, Russia, and Ukraine as RDO International.

Sales and Marketing
The company offers its products to industries such as agriculture, irrigation, technology, and construction.

Mergers and Acquisitions
I

Auditors : PRICEWATERHOUSECOOPERS LLP MI

LOCATIONS
HQ: RDO CONSTRUCTION EQUIPMENT CO.
225 BROADWAY N, FARGO, ND 581024800
Phone: 701 239-8700
Web: WWW.RDOEQUIPMENT.COM

PRODUCTS/OPERATIONS

Selected Brands
Hitachi
John Deete
Sakai
Topcon
Vermeer
Wirtgen

Selected Products
Balers
Chippers
Combines
Dozers
Drills
Excavators
Planters
Scrapers
Tractors
Trenchers
Wheel loaders

COMPETITORS
AGRI PACIFIC, INC.
FISHER AUTO PARTS, INC.
FLEETPRIDE, INC.
GREAT PLAINS MANUFACTURING, INCORPORATED
JOHN DEERE LIMITED
JOHN DEERE THIBODAUX, INC.
KUBOTA TRACTOR CORPORATION
SITEONE LANDSCAPE SUPPLY, INC.
SLOAN IMPLEMENT COMPANY, INC.
ZIEGLER INC.

HISTORICAL FINANCIALS
Company Type: Private

Income Statement   FYE: April 30

	REVENUE ($mil)	NET INCOME ($mil)	NET PROFIT MARGIN	EMPLOYEES
04/21	2,362	105	4.5%	1,500
04/20	2,242	48	2.1%	—
04/19	2,095	52	2.5%	—
Annual Growth	6.2%	41.8%	—	—

2021 Year-End Financials
Return on assets: 7.3%   Cash ($ mil.): 6
Return on equity: 20.5%
Current Ratio: 1.80

READING HOSPITAL

No, it's not a square on the game of Monopoly, but The Reading Hospital and Medical Center does treat patients in Berks County, Pennsylvania and the surrounding area. Operating as Reading Health System, the not-for-profit, 735-bed medical center provides acute care and rehabilitation programs, as well as behavioral and occupational health services. Specialty units include cancer, cardiovascular, weight management, diabetes, orthopedic, trauma (level II), and women's health centers. In addition to the main hospital, the Reading Health System includes Reading Health Rehabilitation Hospital and medical centers in nearby communities, as well as laboratory, imaging, and outpatient centers throughout its region.

Operations
The system also delivers academic clinical training through its School of Health Sciences and Residency programs and operates the 113-acre Highlands at Wyomissing retirement community.

Altogether, Reading Health System operates more than 45 locations with roughly 800 combined beds, including primary and specialty care centers operated by Reading Health Physician Partners, Reading Health Medical Services, and the Quick Care and Urgent Care organizations. It employs some 1,000 physicians and serves a population of more than 750,000 residents. The Reading Health System served about 124,400 emergency room patients during 2014; it also handled more than 31,000 inpatient discharges and 19,000 surgeries.

More than 90% of the company's revenues come from patient care services, while residential (rehabilitation) and other services account for the rest.

Geographic Reach
Reading Health System's main hospital campus is located on a 22-building campus on 36 acres in West Reading, Pennsylvania.

The system serves Berks County and the surrounding area.

Financial Performance
Reading Health System reported revenues of $901.1 million in fiscal 2014 (ended June), with net income of $62.8 million. Cash flow from operations totaled $30.2 million.

Strategy
Like most other hospitals, Reading Health System sees its fair share of uninsured or underinsured patients seeking care at the ER for problems that are often not

emergencies, which can put a strain on hospital finances. Reading works to divert these patients to its Quick Care and Urgent Care Centers to help reduce some of that burden. The organization is also working to increase the size of its primary care network.

Within the main hospital, Reading Health System is working to add new specialists such as interventional neuroradiologists and pediatric hospitalists, as well as physicians who specialize in cardiac revascularization and robotic surgery procedures. It is also working to modernize technologies, build new facilities, and expand partnerships with area health care organizations. For example, in 2013 it implemented its Reading HealthConnect electronic health record (EHR) system.

In addition, the network broke ground on a $354 million expansion at the main West Reading hospital campus. The facility, which is expected to open in 2016, will include new surgery and emergency treatment capacity and will add 150 private patient rooms; the project also includes conversion of existing rooms to private status. In 2015, Reading Health System opened a new family health care center; a new medical facility (featuring primary care physicians' offices, imaging services, and a laboratory) in Douglassville is also in the works.

Company Background
The Reading Hospital and Medical Center was founded in 1868 as The Reading Dispensary.

EXECUTIVES
CMO*, Ron Nutting
Auditors : PRICEWATERHOUSECOOPERS LLP PH

LOCATIONS
HQ: READING HOSPITAL
420 S 5TH AVE, READING, PA 196112143
Phone: 484 628-8000
Web: WWW.TOWERHEALTH.ORG

Selected Pennsylvania Operations
The Reading Health Dispensary (Reading)
The Reading Hospital (West Reading)
Reading Health Medical Services
Reading Health Medical Services at Muhlenberg (Reading)
Reading Health Medical Services at Northern Berks (Hamburg)
Reading Health Medical Services at Spring Ridge (Wyomissing)
Reading Health Medical Services at Wyomissing (Wyomissing)
Reading Health Medical Services at Wyomissing Plaza (Reading)
Reading Health Physicians
Reading Health Rehabilitation Hospital (Wyomissing)
QuickCare Centers (regional)
Urgent Care Centers (regional)

Selected Services
Audiology
Behavioral Health Services
Behavioral Medicine Pain Management
Center for Public Health
Chaplaincy Services
Chest Pain Center
Cleft Palate Clinic
Cochlear Implant Program
da Vinci Surgical System
Diabetes Center
Emergency Services
Epilepsy Monitoring Unit
Family Risk Assessment Program (FRAP)
HelpLine
Hospitalist Program
Infusion Center
Interventional Radiology
Laboratory Services
Library Services
Mammography Services
Nutrition Services
Occupational Health Services
Occupational Therapy
Pain Management
Palliative Care Program
Pediatrics - St' Chris Care
PET/CT Imaging
Physical Therapy
QuickCare -Reading Health Physician Network
Radiology Services
Rehabilitation Services
Respiratory Care
Senior Assessment Program
Sleep Center
Social Service
Speech and Hearing Center
Stroke Center
The Reading Hospital Home Care
Tobacco-Free Wellness Program
Travel Immunization Service
Women's Health Services
Wound Healing and Hyperbaric Medicine Center

COMPETITORS
KINGSBROOK JEWISH MEDICAL CENTER
LEHIGH VALLEY HEALTH NETWORK, INC.
NORTHSHORE UNIVERSITY HEALTHSYSTEM
UNIVERSITY HEALTH SYSTEMS OF EASTERN CAROLINA, INC.
WELLSTAR HEALTH SYSTEM, INC.

HISTORICAL FINANCIALS
Company Type: Private

Income Statement — FYE: June 30

	REVENUE ($mil)	NET INCOME ($mil)	NET PROFIT MARGIN	EMPLOYEES
06/09	675	42	6.2%	5,500
06/08	640	50	7.8%	—
06/06	(783)	0	0.0%	—
Annual Growth	—	—	—	—

2009 Year-End Financials
Return on assets: 5.4%   Cash ($ mil.): 43
Return on equity: 103.7%
Current Ratio: 1.80

READING HOSPITAL SERVICES INC

LOCATIONS
HQ: READING HOSPITAL SERVICES INC
6TH AND SPRUCE ST, READING, PA 19612
Phone: 610 988-8000

HISTORICAL FINANCIALS
Company Type: Private

Income Statement — FYE: June 30

	REVENUE ($mil)	NET INCOME ($mil)	NET PROFIT MARGIN	EMPLOYEES
06/21	1,263	187	14.8%	1
06/20	1,035	63	6.1%	—
06/08	24	(10)	—	—
06/03	0	0	81.7%	—
Annual Growth	53.4%	39.5%	—	—

2021 Year-End Financials
Return on assets: 17.7%   Cash ($ mil.): —
Return on equity: 286.3%
Current Ratio: 0.60

REALPAGE, INC.

RealPage is a leading global provider of software and data analytics to the real estate industry. The company's on-demand software platform is designed to make the property management process more efficient, enabling owners and managers of single- and multifamily rental properties to oversee their accounting, leasing, marketing, pricing, and screening operations from a single, shared database. It currently serves more than 19 million units around the world from offices in North America, Europe, and Asia. In 2021, RealPage was acquired by Thoma Bravo, a leading private equity investment firm focused on the software and technology-enabled services sector, in an all-cash transaction that valued RealPage at approximately $10.2 billion, including net debt.

Operations
RealPage provides a technology platform that enables real estate owners and managers to change how people experience and use rental space. Clients use the platform to gain transparency into asset performance, leverage data insights and monetize space to create incremental yields. It also provides commercial and mixed use property management solutions. RealPage has evolved its products from the desktop to the cloud, with many available both online and for mobile devices. The company's products manage everything from marketing to pricing and other property operations, such as Property Management, Sales and Marketing, Applicant Screening, Revenue Management, Spend Management, Utility Management, Renters Insurance, Resident Services, and Contact Center.

In addition, the company also offers Platform-as-a-Service through its RealPage Exchange, a comprehensive toolkit of integration services for third-party application providers and Infrastructure-as-a-Service, which reduces IT costs and improves integration performance and reliability to multifamily owners and operators.

Geographic Reach

Based in Richardson, Texas, RealPage has operations in Alabama, California, Illinois, Massachusetts, South and North Carolina, India, and the Philippines.

Sales and Marketing
Serving more than 19 million units globally, RealPage's suite of solutions benefits owners and managers of various rental property types, including conventional, affordable, commercial, military, student, single-family, multifamily, senior, and vacation housing.

Mergers and Acquisitions
In late 2021, RealPage entered into a definitive agreement to acquire HomeWiseDocs, a leading provider of data and document delivery services for the community association industry. RealPage plans to enhance its product portfolio and market reach with HomeWiseDocs' industry-leading solutions, significantly strengthening RealPage's position in the community association sector and positioning the combined company as the premier service provider in the industry.

In mid-2021, RealPage entered into a definitive agreement to acquire G5 Search Marketing (G5), a leading pure-play provider of digital marketing, advertising and analytics solutions to the real estate sector. RealPage plans to combine G5's industry-leading solutions with its end-to-end real estate platform, significantly accelerating RealPage's vision for marketing optimization and ultimately a better renter experience for its customers.

In early 2021, RealPage acquired WhiteSky Communications. WhiteSky provides managed communications services, enabling multifamily, student and other properties to provide managed bulk Internet, video, voice-over-internet protocol (VOIP) phone, and Wi-Fi services. With WhiteSky, residents of these properties regularly pay significantly less for high-speed, secure, community-wide Internet that can be provisioned in minutes instead of days. In addition, the opportunities for owners and operators to reap larger revenue shares than typically offered by phone and cable companies make managed bulk Internet the preferred choice for properties seeking to upgrade their resident service.

Company Background
RealPage was formed in 1998 to acquire Rent Roll, Inc., which marketed and sold on-premise property management systems for certain multifamily housing markets. Three years later, it released OneSite, its first on-demand property management system.

Auditors: ERNST & YOUNG LLP DALLAS TEX

LOCATIONS
HQ: REALPAGE, INC.
2201 LAKESIDE BLVD, RICHARDSON, TX 750824305
Phone: 972 820-3000

Web: WWW.REALPAGE.COM

PRODUCTS/OPERATIONS
2014 Sales

	$ mil.	% of total
On-demand	390.6	96
Professional & other	10.9	3
On-premise	3.1	1
Total	404.6	100

Products
Apartment Marketing
Contact Center
Electronic Payments
Market Research
Property Management
Renter's Insurance
Resident Portal
Resident Screening
Revenue Management
Spend Management
Utility Management
Vendor Credentialing
 Services
Business Intelligence
Client Portal
Housing Compliance
Professional Services
RealPage Exchange
RealPage Training
Support Services
Technology as a service
Technology Services
Vendor Services
 Solutions
Affordable
Conventional
Commercial
Single Family
Senior Living
Student Housing
Military Housing
Vacation Rentals

COMPETITORS
APPIAN CORPORATION
CALLIDUS SOFTWARE INC.
DEMANDWARE, INC.
EBIX, INC.
EGAIN CORPORATION
IMPERVA, INC.
INCONTACT, INC.
INFOR, INC.
OPOWER, INC.
WORKDAY, INC.

HISTORICAL FINANCIALS
Company Type: Private

Income Statement — FYE: December 31

	REVENUE ($mil)	NET INCOME ($mil)	NET PROFIT MARGIN	EMPLOYEES
12/20	1,158	46	4.0%	7,000
12/19	988	58	5.9%	—
12/18	869	34	4.0%	—
12/17	670	0	0.1%	—
Annual Growth	20.0%	397.1%	—	—

2020 Year-End Financials
Return on assets: 1.3%
Return on equity: 2.9%
Current Ratio: 1.20
Cash ($ mil.): 594

RECKSON OPERATING PARTNERSHIP, L.P.

EXECUTIVES
CAO, Matthew J Diliberto

LOCATIONS
HQ: RECKSON OPERATING PARTNERSHIP, L.P.
420 LEXINGTON AVE, NEW YORK, NY 101700002
Phone: 212 594-2700
Web: WWW.SLGREEN.COM

HISTORICAL FINANCIALS
Company Type: Private

Income Statement — FYE: December 31

	ASSETS ($mil)	NET INCOME ($mil)	INCOME AS % OF ASSETS	EMPLOYEES
12/18	7,009	199	2.8%	279
12/17	8,541	198	2.3%	—
12/16	8,754	313	3.6%	—
12/15	8,858	362	4.1%	—
Annual Growth	(7.5%)	(18.1%)	—	—

2018 Year-End Financials
Return on assets: 2.8%
Return on equity: 3.2%
Current Ratio: 3.00
Cash ($ mil.): 34

RECTOR & VISITORS OF THE UNIVERSITY OF VIRGINIA

The nation's third president, Thomas Jefferson founded the University of Virginia in 1819. Named Rector and Visitors of the University of Virginia, the university is known as UVA today. It boasts an enrollment of some 25,700 students throughout the university's over 10 graduate and undergraduate schools. One of the most prestigious public universities in the US, the school has been noted for its law program, business program, and its student-enforced conduct code (the Honor System). The school also includes the University of Virginia Health System, which trains future doctors and other health care workers at its Medical Center hospital.

Operations
UVA is an agency of the Commonwealth of Virginia, governed by the university's Board of Visitors. The university comprises three divisions: the Academic Division, the University of Virginia's College at Wise, and the Medical Center Division. Its College at Wise focuses on the humanities, arts, science, and professional disciplines, concentrating on instruction, research, and public service. The Medical Center Division offers both routine and ancillary patient services via its full-

service hospital and clinics.

The university, which has a 15:1 student-faculty ratio, employs some 3,000 full-time faculty and research staff supported by approximately 6,500 full-time staff members. It runs the College and Graduate School of Arts & Sciences, Darden School of Business, Frank Batten School of Leadership and Public Policy, McIntire School of Commerce, as well as the School of Architecture, School of Continuing & Professional Studies, and School of Data Science, among its schools. The university has approximately 17,000 undergraduates and some 8,700 graduate students.

It offers aerospace engineering, biology, comparative literature, health and wellbeing minor, criminal justice education, mechanical engineering and religious studies. The university also offers additional academic opportunities such as Air Force ROTC, Lifetime Physical Activity Options, Interdisciplinary Major Program and University Seminars.

Geographic Reach
The University of Virginia operates its more than 10 schools and medical center in Charlottesville while its College at Wise is in the Southwest Virginia town of Wise.

Sales and Marketing
The university caters to some 17,000 undergraduate students and some 8,700 graduate and professional students.

Strategy
In 2019, shortly after the University of Virginia marked its bicentennial, UVA President Jim Ryan shared a strategic vision for the University as a place both "great and good," offering a world-class educational experience while fulfilling its responsibility as an excellent and ethical partner to students, faculty, staff and surrounding communities.

The company's plan is built around four overarching goals. The first is to strengthen its foundation, which means supporting its students, faculty, and staff. The second is to cultivate the most vibrant community in higher education, in order to prepare its students to be servant-leaders in a diverse and globally connected world. The third is to enable discoveries that enrich and improve lives, and the fourth is to make UVA synonymous with service.

EXECUTIVES

FOR TREASURY MANAGEMENT, Jim Matteo
Auditors : WALTER J KUTCHARSKI RICHMOND

LOCATIONS

HQ: RECTOR & VISITORS OF THE UNIVERSITY OF VIRGINIA
1001 EMMET ST N, CHARLOTTESVILLE, VA 229034833
Phone: 434 924-0311
Web: WWW.VIRGINIA.EDU

PRODUCTS/OPERATIONS

Selected Schools
College and Graduate School of Arts & Sciences
Curry School of Education
Darden Graduate School of Business Administration
McIntire School of Commerce
School of Architecture
School of Continuing & Professional Studies
School of Engineering and Applied Science
School of Law
School of Medicine
School of Nursing

COMPETITORS

DELAWARE STATE UNIVERSITY
MARSHALL UNIVERSITY
MISSOURI STATE UNIVERSITY
PURDUE UNIVERSITY
THE COLLEGE OF WILLIAM & MARY
THE UNIVERSITY OF MEMPHIS
UNIVERSITY OF KANSAS
UNIVERSITY OF OKLAHOMA
UNIVERSITY OF THE PACIFIC
UNIVERSITY SYSTEM OF MARYLAND

HISTORICAL FINANCIALS
Company Type: Private

Income Statement — FYE: June 30

	REVENUE ($mil)	NET INCOME ($mil)	NET PROFIT MARGIN	EMPLOYEES
06/11	1,909	909	47.6%	13,300
06/10	524	97	18.6%	—
06/08	2,181	312	14.3%	—
06/07	2,121	1,114	52.5%	—
Annual Growth	(2.6%)	(5.0%)	—	—

2011 Year-End Financials
Return on assets: 11.4%   Cash ($ mil.): 324
Return on equity: 14.5%
Current Ratio: 1.40

REDEEMER HEALTH HOLY SYSTEM

LOCATIONS

HQ: REDEEMER HEALTH HOLY SYSTEM
1616 HUNTINGDON PIKE, JENKINTOWN, PA 190468001
Phone: 215 938-4000

HISTORICAL FINANCIALS
Company Type: Private

Income Statement — FYE: June 30

	REVENUE ($mil)	NET INCOME ($mil)	NET PROFIT MARGIN	EMPLOYEES
06/09	2,900	286	9.9%	1
06/99	0	(0)	—	—
Annual Growth	187.6%	—	—	—

2009 Year-End Financials
Return on assets: 73.5%   Cash ($ mil.): 47
Return on equity: 195.9%
Current Ratio: 0.80

REDNER'S MARKETS, INC.

Redner's Markets operates about 45 warehouse club-style supermarkets under the Redner's Warehouse Markets banner and more than a dozen Quick Shoppe convenience stores. Most of the company's stores are located in eastern Pennsylvania, but the regional grocer also operates several locations in Maryland and Delaware, having closed its one New York supermarket. Redner's Warehouse Markets house bakery, deli, meat, produce, and seafood departments, as well as in-store banks. The employee-owned company was founded by namesake Earl Redner in 1970. It is still operated by the Redner family, including chairman and CEO Richard and COO Ryan Redner.

Financial Performance
Redner's Markets rang up an estimated $865 million in sales in fiscal 2012 (ends September), up from about $859 million in sales the previous year.

Strategy
Redner's has been tinkering with its store portfolio, shuttering underperforming locations, including several in its core Pennsylvania market, while building new stores in existing and new markets. The regional chain has grown to four stores each in Delaware and Maryland since entering those markets in 2008, and 2005, respectively. Redner's is also growing its Web presence, doubling its online traffic in the first year of a digital shopper marketing program conducted in partnership with Google Shopping Network.

Auditors : RKL LLP WYOMISSING PENNSYLV

LOCATIONS

HQ: REDNER'S MARKETS, INC.
3 QUARRY RD, READING, PA 196059787
Phone: 610 926-3700
Web: WWW.REDNERSMARKETS.COM

2012 Warehouse Market Stores
No.
Pennsylvania 36
Delaware 4
Maryland 4
Total 44

PRODUCTS/OPERATIONS

2012 Stores

	No.
Redner's Warehouse Market	44
Quick Shoppe	14
Total	58

COMPETITORS

AHOLD U.S.A., INC.
ALBERTSONS COMPANIES, INC.
ASSOCIATED GROCERS OF NEW ENGLAND, INC.
ASSOCIATED WHOLESALE GROCERS, INC.
DEMOULAS SUPER MARKETS, INC.
FAREWAY STORES, INC.

SPARTANNASH COMPANY
UNIFIED GROCERS, INC.
URM STORES, INC.
WEIS MARKETS, INC.

HISTORICAL FINANCIALS
Company Type: Private

Income Statement   FYE: October 1

	REVENUE ($mil)	NET INCOME ($mil)	NET PROFIT MARGIN	EMPLOYEES
10/16*	864	4	0.6%	4,800
09/15	884	6	0.7%	—
09/14	902	1	0.2%	—
09/13	892	4	0.5%	—
Annual Growth	(1.1%)	1.8%	—	—

*Fiscal year change

2016 Year-End Financials
Return on assets: 3.0%   Cash ($ mil.): 56
Return on equity: 4.0%
Current Ratio: 3.40

REGAL ENTERTAINMENT GROUP

Regal Entertainment Group, a subsidiary of the Cineworld Group, operates one of the largest and most geographically diverse theatre circuits in the US, consisting of more than 7,200 screens in almost 550 theatres in more than 45 states along with American Samoa, the District of Columbia, Guam and Saipan. Provides bonus rewards through its Crown Club card, the company partners with Movietickets.com, Variety ? The Children's Charities, NCM ? America's Movie Network, World Travel Services, Will Rogers Institute, Fandango, Elavon and Patricia Neal Rehabilitation Center. The company was founded in 1989.

Operations
Regal Entertainment offers IMAX, RealD 3D, RPX, ScreenX, 4DX, Auro, Recliners and Dolby Atmos.

Geographic Reach
Tennessee-based Regal Entertainment operates in over 45 US states, the District of Columbia, Guam, Saipan, and American Samoa. The chain targets midsized metropolitan markets and suburban growth areas of larger cities. It has a large number of theaters in California, Florida, and New York.

Sales and Marketing
Regal Entertainment employs an interactive marketing program for specific films and concession items to increase attendance and consumption. Its Regal Crown Club loyalty program rewards frequent moviegoers with deals of concessions and more.

The company uses the internet, mobile and social media, print and multimedia advertising to promote its service. Regal Entertainment conducts special interactive marketing programs for specific films and concessions items.

Auditors: KPMG LLP KNOXVILLE TENNESSEE

LOCATIONS
HQ: REGAL ENTERTAINMENT GROUP
101 E BLOUNT AVE, KNOXVILLE, TN 379201632
Phone: 865 922-1123
Web: WWW.REGMOVIES.COM

PRODUCTS/OPERATIONS

2017 Sales

	$ in mils	% of total
Admissions	2,008.1	64
Concessions	930.2	29
Other	224.7	7
Total	3,163.0	100

Selected Operations
Cinemas
    Edwards Theatres
    Regal Cinemas
    United Artists Theatre Company
Theater advertising
    National CineMedia (20%)

COMPETITORS
AMC ENTERTAINMENT HOLDINGS, INC.
CARMIKE CINEMAS, LLC
CINEMARK HOLDINGS, INC.
CROWN MEDIA HOLDINGS, INC.
CinemaxX Holdings GmbH
Empire Theatres Limited
NATIONAL CINEMEDIA, INC.
READING INTERNATIONAL, INC.
SILVER CINEMAS ACQUISITION CO.
THE HOYTS CORPORATION PTY. LIMITED

HISTORICAL FINANCIALS
Company Type: Private

Income Statement   FYE: December 31

	REVENUE ($mil)	NET INCOME ($mil)	NET PROFIT MARGIN	EMPLOYEES
12/17	3,163	112	3.6%	25,359
12/16	3,197	170	5.3%	—
12/15*	3,127	153	4.9%	—
01/15	2,990	105	3.5%	—
Annual Growth	1.9%	2.2%	—	—

*Fiscal year change

2017 Year-End Financials
Return on assets: 999.9%   Cash ($ mil.): —
Return on equity: —
Current Ratio: 0.80

REGENTS OF THE UNIVERSITY OF MICHIGAN

Ranking among the top US public universities, Regents of the University of Michigan (or simply University of Michigan) boasts roughly 64,300 students in southeast Michigan. Its three campuses in Ann Arbor, Dearborn, and Flint offer more than 275 undergraduate and graduate degree programs in fields including architecture, education, law, medicine, music, and social work. The university has a student to faculty ratio of 15:1. The University of Michigan Health System includes three hospitals and more than 125 health clinics/centers.

Operations
The university has about 15 undergraduate schools and colleges offering architecture & urban planning; art & design; business; dental hygiene; education; engineering; information; kinesiology; literature, science, and the arts (LSA); music, theatre & dance; nursing; pharmacy; public health; and public policy. Its graduate programs include certificate, doctoral, and master's in the areas of anthropology, architecture, biophysics, business, chemical biology, and criminal study among others.

Geographic Reach
From its primary campuses in southeast Michigan, the university attracts students from more than 80 Michigan counties, some 50 states and about 140 countries.

Financial Performance
University's revenue for fiscal 2021 increased to $8.4 billion compared from the prior year with $8.0 billion.

Loss for fiscal 2021 decreased to $1.1 billion compared from the prior year with $1.4 billion.

Cash held by the company at the end of fiscal 2021 increased to $19.5 billion. Cash provided by noncapital financing activities was $900.9 million while cash used for operations and, capital and related financing activities were $331.3 million and $569.8 million, respectively.

Strategy
The University's long-term investment strategy combined with its endowment spending policy serves to insulate operations from expected volatility in the capital markets and provides for a stable and predictable level of spending distributions from the endowment. The success of the University's long-term investment strategy is evidenced by strong returns over sustained periods of time and the ability to limit losses in the face of challenging markets.

EXECUTIVES
AR Vice President*, Thomas A Baird
Research Vice President*, Rebecca Cunningham
Auditors : PRICEWATERHOUSECOOPERS LLP D

LOCATIONS
HQ: REGENTS OF THE UNIVERSITY OF MICHIGAN
500 S STATE ST, ANN ARBOR, MI 481091382
Phone: 734 764-1817
Web: WWW.UMICH.EDU

PRODUCTS/OPERATIONS

Selected Academic Units

Architecture and urban planning
Art and design
Business administration
Dentistry
Education
Engineering
Kinesiology
Law
Literature, science, and the arts
Medicine
Music
Natural resources and environment
Nursing
Pharmacy
Public health
Public policy
Social work

COMPETITORS

CASE WESTERN RESERVE UNIVERSITY
NORTHEASTERN UNIVERSITY
RECTOR & VISITORS OF THE UNIVERSITY OF VIRGINIA
THE UNIVERSITY OF NEW MEXICO
THE VANDERBILT UNIVERSITY
UNIVERSITY OF CALIFORNIA, SAN FRANCISCO
UNIVERSITY OF KANSAS
UNIVERSITY OF MISSOURI SYSTEM
UNIVERSITY OF OKLAHOMA
UNIVERSITY SYSTEM OF MARYLAND

HISTORICAL FINANCIALS
Company Type: Private

Income Statement — FYE: June 30

	REVENUE ($mil)	NET INCOME ($mil)	NET PROFIT MARGIN	EMPLOYEES
06/20	7,955	(0)	0.0%	34,624
06/19	7,989	522	6.5%	—
06/18	7,466	920	12.3%	—
Annual Growth	3.2%	—	—	—

2020 Year-End Financials
Return on assets: —
Return on equity: —
Current Ratio: 1.70
Cash ($ mil.): 1,284

REGIONAL CENTER OF THE EAST BAY, INC.

LOCATIONS

HQ: REGIONAL CENTER OF THE EAST BAY, INC.
500 DAVIS ST STE 100, SAN LEANDRO, CA 945772758
Phone: 510 618-6100
Web: WWW.RCEB.ORG

REGIONAL TRANSPORTATION AUTHORITY

EXECUTIVES

Department Executive Director, Joseph G Costello
Auditors : RSM US LLP CHICAGO ILLINOIS

LOCATIONS

HQ: REGIONAL TRANSPORTATION AUTHORITY
175 W JACKSON BLVD # 1650, CHICAGO, IL 606042711
Phone: 312 913-3200
Web: WWW.RTACHICAGO.ORG

HISTORICAL FINANCIALS
Company Type: Private

Income Statement — FYE: December 31

	REVENUE ($mil)	NET INCOME ($mil)	NET PROFIT MARGIN	EMPLOYEES
12/19	618	(102)	—	80
12/16	637	(99)	—	—
12/15	805	(77)	—	—
12/14	755	(3)	—	—
Annual Growth	(3.9%)	—	—	—

2019 Year-End Financials
Return on assets: (-12.1%)
Return on equity: —
Current Ratio: 1.70
Cash ($ mil.): 123

REGIONS HOSPITAL

Auditors : KPMG LLP MINNEAPOLIS MN

LOCATIONS

HQ: REGIONS HOSPITAL
8170 33RD AVE S, MINNEAPOLIS, MN 554254516
Phone: 952 883-6280
Web: WWW.HEALTHPARTNERS.COM

HISTORICAL FINANCIALS
Company Type: Private

Income Statement — FYE: June 30

	REVENUE ($mil)	NET INCOME ($mil)	NET PROFIT MARGIN	EMPLOYEES
06/20	547	37	6.9%	250
06/08	250	(2)	—	—
06/06	199	0	0.0%	—
06/05	184	0	0.0%	—
Annual Growth	7.5%	74.2%	—	—

2020 Year-End Financials
Return on assets: 12.5%
Return on equity: 999.9%
Current Ratio: —
Cash ($ mil.): 42

REGIONS HOSPITAL

Auditors : KPMG LLP MINNEAPOLIS MINNESO

LOCATIONS

HQ: REGIONS HOSPITAL
640 JACKSON ST, SAINT PAUL, MN 551012595
Phone: 651 254-3456
Web: WWW.REGIONSHOSPITAL..COM

HISTORICAL FINANCIALS
Company Type: Private

Income Statement — FYE: December 31

	REVENUE ($mil)	NET INCOME ($mil)	NET PROFIT MARGIN	EMPLOYEES
12/19	847	52	6.2%	47
12/17	790	47	6.0%	—
12/14	691	40	5.9%	—
12/09	515	17	3.4%	—
Annual Growth	5.1%	11.5%	—	—

2019 Year-End Financials
Return on assets: 5.4%
Return on equity: 8.5%
Current Ratio: 3.10
Cash ($ mil.): 184

HISTORICAL FINANCIALS
Company Type: Private

Income Statement — FYE: December 31

	REVENUE ($mil)	NET INCOME ($mil)	NET PROFIT MARGIN	EMPLOYEES
12/21	908	62	6.9%	414
12/20	819	52	6.4%	—
12/19	847	52	6.2%	—
12/14	636	40	6.4%	—
Annual Growth	5.2%	6.3%	—	—

2021 Year-End Financials
Return on assets: 5.5%
Return on equity: 8.4%
Current Ratio: 2.70
Cash ($ mil.): 298

REGIONS HOSPITAL FOUNDATION

If you live around the Twin Cities, Regions Hospital can help with your medical needs. The not-for-profit hospital has more than 450 beds and provides acute medical and emergency care services, as well as specialty programs in areas including behavioral health, rehabilitation, burn care, cancer, cardiovascular, orthopedic, pediatrics, and women's care. Regions Hospital is one of a handful of level I trauma centers in Minnesota and is also a teaching and residency center for the University of Minnesota Medical School. Regions Hospital is part of HealthPartners, which operates a network of medical centers and a health plan in the Twin Cities area.

Operations

In 2012 Regions Hospital operated at a

78% occupancy rate with some 25,000 inpatient visits. It also handled 78,000 emergency center visits, 13,000 surgeries, and some 2,500 births. It has about 650 physicians on its staff, plus another 800 affiliated doctors who are members of the HealthPartners Medical Group physician practice organization.

The hospital provided some $56 million in community benefits during 2012, including charity care and outreach programs.

Geographic Reach
Regions Hospital serves the St. Paul, Minnesota, metropolitan area, as well as patients from other areas across Minnesota and in western Wisconsin. It also sees visitors from other Midwest states.

Strategy
The hospital has expanded its facilities in recent years to meet the demands of a growing Twin Cities population and address certain underserved community health needs. For instance in 2012 Regions Hospital completed construction of a new $36 million eight-story inpatient mental health center with about 100 beds designed to replace its aging mental health facility. In addition, in 2009 the hospital wrapped up a $180 million expansion and renovation project that gave it a new 10-story patient tower with 20 new operating rooms, more than 35 private patient beds, and shell space for further expansion in the future.

In addition, the hospital looks to enhance services through new equipment and procedural offerings, as well as through partnerships with other area providers.

Company Background
Established in 1872, Regions Hospital became part of the HealthPartners network in 1993.

LOCATIONS
HQ: REGIONS HOSPITAL FOUNDATION
640 JACKSON ST, SAINT PAUL, MN 551012595
Phone: 651 254-3456
Web: WWW.REGIONSHOSPITAL.COM

PRODUCTS/OPERATIONS
Selected Specialties and Divisions
Behavioral Health
Birth Center
Breast Health Center
Burn Center
Cancer Care Center
Center for Dementia and Alzheimer's Care
Digestive Care Center
Emergency Center
Heart Center
Level I Trauma Center
Level I Pediatric Trauma Center
Neurosciences
Orthopedics
Palliative Care Unit
Rehabilitation Institute
Spine Center
Stroke Center
Surgery Center

COMPETITORS
ARKANSAS CHILDREN'S HOSPITAL
ASCENSION PROVIDENCE ROCHESTER HOSPITAL
BRONXCARE HEALTH SYSTEM
COMMUNITY HEALTH NETWORK, INC.
MEMORIAL HEALTH SERVICES

HISTORICAL FINANCIALS
Company Type: Private

Income Statement — FYE: December 31

	REVENUE ($mil)	NET INCOME ($mil)	NET PROFIT MARGIN	EMPLOYEES
12/12	581	36	6.3%	3,000
12/06	413	4	1.0%	—
12/05	430	12	2.8%	—
12/04	7	0	0.0%	—
Annual Growth	71.3%	320.5%	—	—

2012 Year-End Financials
Return on assets: 6.2%   Cash ($ mil.): 64
Return on equity: 6.3%
Current Ratio: 1.70

RESEARCH TRIANGLE INSTITUTE INC

Founded in 1958, Research Triangle Institute operates mainly under its trade name, RTI International (RTI), the not-for-profit enterprise conducts research in such areas as advanced technologies, environmental resources, and medicine. It provides such services and materials testing, as well as the software used in laboratories and research projects. Its experts hold degrees in more than 250 scientific, technical, and professional disciplines across the social and laboratory sciences, engineering, and international development fields. Serving the US federal government, other governments, businesses, foundations, universities, and for-profit companies, RTI offers analytical perspectives on public policy and has researchers working in offices around the world.

Operations
The company delivers independent, objective, and scientifically rigorous research, development, and technical services to support projects around the world.

Across its areas of practice (health, transformative research unit for equity, education and workforce development, energy research, justice research for policy, international development, and military support, among others), the company delivers comprehensive services and capabilities such as surveys and data collection, statistics and data science, evaluation, assessment, and analysis, program design and implementation, digital solutions for social impact, research technologies, drug discovery and development, analytical laboratory science, and engineering and technology R&D.

Geographic Reach
North Carolina-based RTI serves clients in more than 75 countries. RTI also offers multiple teleworking options to its worldwide staff members. RTI's regional offices in Asia, Africa, and Latin America and the Caribbean serve as operational hubs for projects throughout these regions. The company also maintains a wholly-owned subsidiary in India, RTI Health Solutions offices in Europe, and dozens of project-specific offices in many of the countries.

Sales and Marketing
The company's clients include government agencies, academia, foundations, global NGOs, and commercial companies. It maintains close ties with North Carolina State University, Duke University, North Carolina Central University, and the University of North Carolina at Chapel Hill.

Auditors : DELOITTE & TOUCHE LLP RALEIGH

LOCATIONS
HQ: RESEARCH TRIANGLE INSTITUTE INC
3040 CORNWALLIS RD, DURHAM, NC 277090155
Phone: 919 541-6000
Web: WWW.RTI.ORG

PRODUCTS/OPERATIONS
Selected Research Areas
Advanced technology research and development
Drug discovery and development
Economic and social
Education and training
Energy
Environmental
Health
International development
Laboratory and chemistry
Statistics
Survey

COMPETITORS
ABT ASSOCIATES INC.
DAI GLOBAL, LLC
IDC RESEARCH, INC.
LRN CORPORATION
NATIONAL ECONOMIC RESEARCH ASSOCIATES, INC.
NIELSEN CONSUMER INSIGHTS, INC.
POSITIVE EDGE STRATEGIES, INC
RESEARCH NOW GROUP, LLC
STATE AFFAIRS INC
WESTAT, INC.

HISTORICAL FINANCIALS
Company Type: Private

Income Statement — FYE: September 30

	REVENUE ($mil)	NET INCOME ($mil)	NET PROFIT MARGIN	EMPLOYEES
09/21	1,077	59	5.5%	3,117
09/20	912	25	2.8%	—
09/18	957	(1)	—	—
09/17	972	22	2.4%	—
Annual Growth	2.6%	27.0%	—	—

2021 Year-End Financials
Return on assets: 6.9%   Cash ($ mil.): 43
Return on equity: 12.0%
Current Ratio: 2.00

REX HEALTHCARE, INC.

Part of the UNC Health Care, UNC REX Healthcare is a not-for-profit health care provider that serves residents of Raleigh and the rest of Wake County, North Carolina. Founded in 1894, UNC REX Healthcare includes a medical staff of more than 1,100 physicians and 1,700 nurses, as well as primary and specialty care clinics throughout the area. Its facilities include an acute care hospital, five wellness centers and two skilled nursing facilities. Specialty centers and clinics provide services such as birthing, cancer treatment, same-day surgery, heart and vascular care, pain management, and sleep disorder therapy. UNC REX also provides home health and mobile emergency medical services. UNC HealthCare also includes affiliate UNC Hospitals.

Auditors : CLIFTON LARSON ALLEN LLP CHAR

LOCATIONS

HQ: REX HEALTHCARE, INC.
4420 LAKE BOONE TRL, RALEIGH, NC 276077505
Phone: 919 784-3100
Web: WWW.REXHEALTH.COM

PRODUCTS/OPERATIONS

Selected Specialty Services
Oncology
Heart and vascular
Surgical Services: Bariatric, Heartburn and GI
Orthopedic, Neuro and Spine
Rehabilitation
Emergency and Urgent Care
Women's Services
Wound Healing

COMPETITORS

ADVENTIST HEALTHCARE, INC.
LAKELAND REGIONAL MEDICAL CENTER, INC.
NATIONWIDE CHILDREN'S HOSPITAL
NORTHWESTERN MEMORIAL HEALTHCARE
ST. JOSEPH HEALTH SYSTEM
ST. LUKE'S EPISCOPAL-PRESBYTERIAN HOSPITALS
VISITING NURSE SERVICE OF NEW YORK
VITAS HEALTHCARE CORPORATION
WELLMED MEDICAL MANAGEMENT, INC.
WHITE COUNTY MEDICAL CENTER

HISTORICAL FINANCIALS
Company Type: Private

Income Statement — FYE: June 30

	REVENUE ($mil)	NET INCOME ($mil)	NET PROFIT MARGIN	EMPLOYEES
06/22	1,414	51	3.6%	5,500
06/20	1,180	(2)	—	—
06/13	731	8	1.2%	—
06/12	719	34	4.8%	—
Annual Growth	7.0%	3.9%	—	—

2022 Year-End Financials
Return on assets: 2.7%   Cash ($ mil.): 159
Return on equity: 5.1%
Current Ratio: 1.70

REX HOSPITAL, INC.

EXECUTIVES

Legal Affairs Vice President*, Tate Bombard
Medical Affairs Vice President, Linda Butler Md
REX HEALTHCARE FOUNDATION*, Sylvia Hackett
Operations, Chad T Lefteris Vpof
Patient Care Services Vice President*, Joel Ray
Physician SERVICES*, Bob Ricker
HOSPITALIST SERVICES*, Sean Tehrani

LOCATIONS

HQ: REX HOSPITAL, INC.
4420 LAKE BOONE TRL, RALEIGH, NC 276076599
Phone: 919 784-3100
Web: WWW.REXHEALTH.COM

HISTORICAL FINANCIALS
Company Type: Private

Income Statement — FYE: June 30

	REVENUE ($mil)	NET INCOME ($mil)	NET PROFIT MARGIN	EMPLOYEES
06/21	1,331	3	0.2%	3,500
06/20	0	(0)	—	—
06/16	904	106	11.8%	—
06/15	813	4	0.5%	—
Annual Growth	8.6%	(5.3%)	—	—

2021 Year-End Financials
Return on assets: 0.2%   Cash ($ mil.): 222
Return on equity: 0.3%
Current Ratio: 0.60

RHODE ISLAND HOSPITAL

LOCATIONS

HQ: RHODE ISLAND HOSPITAL
593 EDDY ST, PROVIDENCE, RI 029034923
Phone: 401 444-4000
Web: WWW.LIFESPAN.ORG

HISTORICAL FINANCIALS
Company Type: Private

Income Statement — FYE: September 30

	REVENUE ($mil)	NET INCOME ($mil)	NET PROFIT MARGIN	EMPLOYEES
09/14	1,016	(5)	—	6,400
09/13	1,048	49	4.7%	—
09/07	918	110	12.0%	—
Annual Growth	1.5%	—	—	—

2014 Year-End Financials
Return on assets: (-0.5%)   Cash ($ mil.): 32
Return on equity: (-1.2%)
Current Ratio: 1.70

RICH PRODUCTS CORPORATION

Rich Products is a family-owned food company which has grown from a niche maker of soy-based whipped toppings and frozen desserts to a leading global US frozen foods maker. The company has developed other products, such as toppings and icings, and Coffee Rich (non-dairy coffee creamer). It has expanded its product line to include frozen bakery and pizza doughs and ingredients for the food service and in-store bakery markets, plus appetizers, meals and snacks (Farm Rich), baked goods, ice cream cakes (Carvel), seafood (SeaPak), meatballs, and barbecue meat. With more than 4,000 product types, Rich Products has approximately 11,000 associates around the world.

Operations
Rich Products offers pizza, cake icing and sweet starters, beverage and finishing touches, desserts, bakery product and culinary solutions.

Geographic Reach
US-based, Rich Products has operations in over 100 countries worldwide, including in South Africa, Brazil, Mexico, China, India, the UK, Istanbul, the US and Canada.

Sales and Marketing
The company serves customers in foodservice, retail, in-store bakery, deli and prepared foods, among others. In addition to SeaPak, FarmRich, and Carvel, Rich Products' other consumer brands include F'real, Byron's, Jon Donaire, Casa Meatballs, Rich Whip, and more.

Mergers and Acquisitions
In mid-2021, Rich Products acquired Signature Breads, a decades-long leader in specialty breads and rolls. Rich Products will continue to produce key Signature Breads products like baguettes, ciabatta, and one-of-a-kind sandwich and dinner rolls, and the acquisition expands Rich's offerings in the par- and fully baked bread and roll categories.

EXECUTIVES

Vice Chairman, Mindy Rich
Executive Vice Chairman of the Board, William G Gisel Junior
Chief Human Resource Officer, Ed Moore
CIO, Yexi Liu

LOCATIONS

HQ: RICH PRODUCTS CORPORATION
1 ROBERT RICH WAY, BUFFALO, NY 142131701
Phone: 716 878-8000
Web: WWW.RICHS.COM

PRODUCTS/OPERATIONS

Selected Product Categories
Appetizers and snacks

Bakery products
BBQ
Breads and rolls
Cakes & desserts
Cooking creams
Gluten-free and all-natural
Meatballs and pasta
Pizza
Shrimp and seafood
Syrups and soaked cakes
Toppings and icings

Selected Consumer Brands
Byron's
Carvel
Casa
Coffee Rich
Farm Rich
Freal
French Meadow Bakery
Rich's
SeaPak

COMPETITORS

AZUMA FOODS INTERNATIONAL, INC. USA
Bakkavor Group ehf.
DAWN FOOD PRODUCTS, INC.
GORTON'S INC.
High Liner Foods Incorporated
LAKESIDE FOODS, INC.
PINNACLE FOODS FINANCE LLC
SHINING OCEAN, INC.
THAI UNION GROUP PUBLIC COMPANY LIMITED
THE HARRIS SOUP COMPANY

HISTORICAL FINANCIALS
Company Type: Private

Income Statement — FYE: December 31

	REVENUE ($mil)	NET INCOME ($mil)	NET PROFIT MARGIN	EMPLOYEES
12/12	2,858	0	0.0%	12,224
12/11	2,736	0	0.0%	—
12/10	2,465	0	0.0%	—
Annual Growth	7.7%	—	—	—

RICHARDSON INDEPENDENT SCHOOL DISTRICT

Auditors : HANKINS EASTUP DEATON TONN

LOCATIONS

HQ: RICHARDSON INDEPENDENT SCHOOL DISTRICT
400 S GREENVILLE AVE # 205, RICHARDSON, TX 750814100
Phone: 469 593-0000
Web: WEB.RISD.ORG

HISTORICAL FINANCIALS
Company Type: Private

Income Statement — FYE: June 30

	REVENUE ($mil)	NET INCOME ($mil)	NET PROFIT MARGIN	EMPLOYEES
06/22	557	253	45.5%	4,500
06/21	523	(42)	—	—
06/20	530	(70)	—	—
06/19	504	59	11.8%	—
Annual Growth	3.4%	62.2%	—	—

2022 Year-End Financials
Return on assets: 17.6% Cash ($ mil.): —
Return on equity: 276.6%
Current Ratio: —

RITE-HITE HOLDING CORPORATION

LOCATIONS

HQ: RITE-HITE HOLDING CORPORATION
195 S RITE HITE WAY, MILWAUKEE, WI 532041195
Phone: 414 355-2600
Web: WWW.RITEHITE.COM

HISTORICAL FINANCIALS
Company Type: Private

Income Statement — FYE: December 31

	REVENUE ($mil)	NET INCOME ($mil)	NET PROFIT MARGIN	EMPLOYEES
12/20	798	0	0.0%	1,000
12/19	767	0	0.0%	—
12/18	779	0	0.0%	—
12/05	274	0	0.0%	—
Annual Growth	7.4%	—	—	—

RIVER CITY PETROLEUM, INC.

Auditors : BFBA LLP SACRAMENTO CALIFOR

LOCATIONS

HQ: RIVER CITY PETROLEUM, INC.
3775 N FREEWAY BLVD # 101, SACRAMENTO, CA 958341926
Phone: 916 371-4960
Web: WWW.RCPFUEL.COM

HISTORICAL FINANCIALS
Company Type: Private

Income Statement — FYE: December 31

	REVENUE ($mil)	NET INCOME ($mil)	NET PROFIT MARGIN	EMPLOYEES
12/13	655	1	0.2%	55
12/12	579	1	0.2%	—
12/11	656	2	0.4%	—
Annual Growth	(0.1%)	(34.5%)	—	—

2013 Year-End Financials
Return on assets: 2.1% Cash ($ mil.): 4
Return on equity: 6.0%
Current Ratio: 1.30

RIVERSIDE HEALTHCARE ASSOCIATION, INC.

Extra! Extra! Read all about it! Residents of Newport News (and about a dozen other cities in Eastern Virginia) Turn to Riverside Health for Medical Care. The not-for-profit health care provider administers general, emergency, and specialty medical services from five hospitals, Riverside Regional Medical Center, Riverside Walter Reed Hospital, Riverside Tappahannock Hospital, and Riverside Shore Memorial Hospital, and Riverside Doctors Hospital, as well as a psychiatric hospital, a physical rehabilitation facility, and retirement communities. Riverside also operates physician offices and medical training facilities. Specialty centers provide home and hospice care, cancer treatment, and dialysis.

Operations
Combined, Riverside's hospitals (including rehabilitation and psychiatric) are home to nearly 1,000 beds. Its major hospitals include Riverside Regional Medical Center (450-bed flagship hospital); Riverside Walter Reed Hospital (67-bed acute care facility); Riverside Tappahannock Hospital (67-bed, serving the Northern Neck rural area); Riverside Shore Memorial Hospital (143-bed facility); and Riverside Doctors' Hospital Williamsburg (40 private rooms). It also operates specialty medical facilities, including a psychiatric hospital, a physical rehabilitation facility, and retirement communities.

Geographic Reach
It serves Eastern Virginia including cities of Gloucester, Hampton, Newport News, Poquoson, Richmond, Tappahannock, West Point, Williamsburg and Yorktown; Eastern Shore Area of Virginia; Counties of Essex, Gloucester, Isle of Wight, James City, King and Queen, King William, Lancaster, Mathews, Middlesex, New Kent, Northumberland, Richmond, and Surry.

Strategy

To keep up with demand, Riverside Health has been upgrading its older facilities and building new ones.

In 2013 the company opened a new hospital, the Doctors Hospital in Williamsburg. The 40 room hospital provides acute and emergency care, as well as specialty services including cardiology, neurology, and pulmonary care.

That year Riverside broke ground on the new Riverside Shore Memorial Hospital in Onley, which is expected to be completed in late 2015. It will have 57 private inpatient rooms, with the ability to add 12 more in the future.

In 2012 Riverside Walter Reed Hospital opened a new intensive care unit.

It is also investing in technology, physician expertise, and patient services. In 2013 Riverside Shore Medical Center at Metompkin converted to digital mammography equipment, offering patients a superior diagnostic tool to film mammograms.

Company Background

The original charter for Riverside dates back to 1915 when the company began as one hospital, founded by the community. In 1962, the hospital was relocated to the present site in central Newport News.

EXECUTIVES

Vice Chairman*, Jerold W Allen

Auditors : ERNST & YOUNG LLP RICHMOND V

LOCATIONS

HQ: RIVERSIDE HEALTHCARE ASSOCIATION, INC.
   701 TOWN CENTER DR # 1000, NEWPORT NEWS, VA 236064283
Phone: 757 534-7000
Web: WWW.RIVHS.COM

Selected Facilities -- Virginia
HOSPITALS
Riverside Behavioral Health Center (Hampton)
Riverside Doctors' Hospital (Williamsburg)
Riverside Regional Medical Center (Newport News)
Riverside Rehabilitation Institute (Williamsburg)
Riverside Tappahannock Hospital (Tappahannock)
Riverside Shore Memorial Hospital (Nassawadox)
Riverside Walter Reed Hospital (Gloucester)
RETIREMENT COMMUNITIES
Patriots Colony (Williamsburg)
Sanders (Gloucester)
Warwick Forest (Newport News)
SURGERY CENTERS
Doctors Surgery Center (Williamsburg)
Peninsula Surgery Center (Newport News)
Riverside Hampton Surgery Center (Hampton)

COMPETITORS

BAPTIST HEALTH CARE CORPORATION
BEACON MEDICAL GROUP, INC.
CAROMONT HEALTH, INC.
COLUMBIA HOSPITAL (PALM BEACHES) LIMITED PARTNERSHIP
HERITAGE VALLEY HEALTH SYSTEM, INC.
HOSPITAL AUTHORITY OF VALDOSTA AND LOWNDES COUNTY, GEORGIA
INSPIRA HEALTH NETWORK, INC.
MARTHA JEFFERSON HEALTH SERVICES CORPORATION
SOUTHCOAST HOSPITALS GROUP, INC.
WEST VIRGINIA UNITED HEALTH SYSTEM, INC.

HISTORICAL FINANCIALS

Company Type: Private

Income Statement   FYE: December 31

	REVENUE ($mil)	NET INCOME ($mil)	NET PROFIT MARGIN	EMPLOYEES
12/15	1,149	21	1.8%	8,000
12/14	1,059	(86)	—	—
12/13	1,017	101	10.0%	—
12/12	948	41	4.4%	—
Annual Growth	6.6%	(20.3%)	—	—

2015 Year-End Financials
Return on assets: 1.5%   Cash ($ mil.): 1
Return on equity: 2.9%
Current Ratio: 1.50

RIVERSIDE HOSPITAL, INC.

Riverside Hospital operates as Riverside Regional Medical Center, a 450-bed acute-care facility that serves the residents of Newport News, Virginia. Founded in 1916, the hospital moved to its current 72-acre campus in 1963, providing more than 30 medical specialties, including cancer treatment, cardiology, birthing, and diagnostic imaging. It specializes in cardiovascular and neurological surgeries and provides radiosurgery (radiation surgery) through a partnership with the University of Virginia Health System. Its emergency department is a 42-room Level II Trauma Center that treats more than 57,000 patients each year. Riverside Hospital is part of the Riverside Health System.

Operations

As part of its operations, Riverside Hospital operates a heart center, neonatal center, 18-bed neonatal intensive care unit, cancer care center, and radiosurgery center through a partnership with Chesapeake Regional and the University of Virginia Health System. Riverside Hospital works to prevent, diagnose, and treat diseases of the stomach, intestines, esophagus, pancreas, gall bladder, liver, and biliary tract through its Peninsula Gastroenterology & Riverside Endoscopy Center.

Geographic Reach

Riverside Hospital serves the health care needs of those who reside in and around Newport News, Virginia.

Auditors : ERNST YOUNG RICHMOND VA

LOCATIONS

HQ: RIVERSIDE HOSPITAL, INC.
   500 J CLYDE MORRIS BLVD, NEWPORT NEWS, VA 236011929
Phone: 757 594-2000
Web: WWW.RIVERSIDEONLINE.COM

PRODUCTS/OPERATIONS

Selected Services
Diagnostic Services
   Cardiac testing
   CT
   Digital mammography
   Electrocardiography
   Magnetic resonance imaging
   Nuclear medicine
   PET
   Ultrasound
Nutrition Services
   Radiosurgery Center
   Leksell Gamma Knife, Synergy S Radiosurgery
   Gastroenterology Procedures
   Colonoscopy and polypectomy
   Flexible sigmoidoscopy
   Upper endoscopic exams and therapy
   Endoscopic retrograde cholangiopancreatography (ERCP)
   Percutaneous endoscopic gastrostomy (PEG)
   Capsule/Cam (M2A) study of the small intestine
   Esophageal dilation
   Esophageal and anal manometry
   BRAVO pH study of the esophagus
Pulmonary Rehabilitation
Surgical Services

COMPETITORS

AKRON GENERAL MEDICAL CENTER
ASCENSION BORGESS HOSPITAL
HOSPITAL OF CENTRAL CONNECTICUT
METHODIST HOSPITAL OF SOUTHERN CALIFORNIA
SOUTH SHORE UNIVERSITY HOSPITAL

HISTORICAL FINANCIALS

Company Type: Private

Income Statement   FYE: December 31

	REVENUE ($mil)	NET INCOME ($mil)	NET PROFIT MARGIN	EMPLOYEES
12/18	618	61	10.0%	8,000
12/17	611	57	9.4%	—
12/16	636	65	10.3%	—
12/11	466	36	7.8%	—
Annual Growth	4.1%	7.9%	—	—

2018 Year-End Financials
Return on assets: 7.9%   Cash ($ mil.): (-39)
Return on equity: 8.9%
Current Ratio: 10.20

RIVERSIDE REGIONAL MEDIAL CENTER

EXECUTIVES

Principal, Debbie Davis

Vp of Ambulatory Care, Susan Mc Andrews

LOCATIONS

HQ: RIVERSIDE REGIONAL MEDIAL CENTER
   500 J CLYDE MORRIS BLVD, NEWPORT NEWS, VA 236011929
Phone: 757 856-7030
Web: WWW.RIVERSIDEONLINE.COM

HISTORICAL FINANCIALS
Company Type: Private

Income Statement   FYE: December 31

	REVENUE ($mil)	NET INCOME ($mil)	NET PROFIT MARGIN	EMPLOYEES
12/14	544	73	13.5%	1
12/08	301	0	0.2%	—
Annual Growth	10.4%	123.6%	—	—

2014 Year-End Financials
Return on assets: 13.1%   Cash ($ mil.): (-2)
Return on equity: 15.3%
Current Ratio: 6.90

RIVERSIDE UNIFIED SCHOOL DISTRICT

Auditors: NIGRO & NIGRO PC MURRIETA C

LOCATIONS

HQ: RIVERSIDE UNIFIED SCHOOL DISTRICT
3380 14TH ST, RIVERSIDE, CA 925013810
Phone: 951 788-7135
Web: WWW.RIVERSIDEUNIFIED.ORG

HISTORICAL FINANCIALS
Company Type: Private

Income Statement   FYE: June 30

	REVENUE ($mil)	NET INCOME ($mil)	NET PROFIT MARGIN	EMPLOYEES
06/21	668	(17)	—	3,740
06/19	592	(31)	—	—
06/18	540	(8)	—	—
06/17	513	75	14.7%	—
Annual Growth	6.8%	—	—	—

2021 Year-End Financials
Return on assets: (-1.3%)   Cash ($ mil.): 366
Return on equity: (-8.8%)
Current Ratio: 4.50

RIVERVIEW HOSPITAL

Riverview Hospital (which changed its operating name to Riverside Health in 2014) provides general medical and surgical care to residents in central Indiana. With about 155 beds and 300 physicians representing more than 35 medical specialties, the hospital is a full-service facility that offers specialty care in a number of areas, including heart disease, cancer, women's health, and orthopedics. Besides its main campus, Riverview operates several outpatient facilities, including an occupational health center, a community health clinic, and several rehab and fitness centers.

Operations
The Indiana hospital, which admits some 6,500 patients each year, provides family medicine, pediatrics, OB/GYN care, cardiac care, surgery, orthopedics and sports medicine, cancer care, interventional pain management, wound care, diabetes and endocrinology, internal medicine, and imaging, among other services. Also part of its operations, the health care facility runs a community health clinic, rehab and fitness centers, and an occupational health center.

Its Riverview Medical Group is a network of affiliated primary and specialty care doctors with 20 offices located throughout Hamilton and Tipton counties.

Geographic Reach
Riverview serves patients who reside in Indiana's Hamilton and Tipton Counties, particularly the service area north of Indianapolis in central Indiana. It has locations in Carmel, Cicero, Fishers, Noblesville, Sheridan, Tipton, and Westfield.

Strategy
To better reflect the organization's full scope of inpatient and outpatient services, in 2014 the hospital changed its name from Riverview Hospital to Riverview Health.

Expanding its services, in 2014 the hospital began building the Mugg-Z CafÃ©, an internet cafÃ© and gift shop for elders.

LOCATIONS

HQ: RIVERVIEW HOSPITAL
395 WESTFIELD RD, NOBLESVILLE, IN 460601434
Phone: 317 773-0760
Web: WWW.RIVERVIEW.ORG

PRODUCTS/OPERATIONS

Selected Services
Cancer Services
Diabetes and Endocrinology
Emergency Services
Heart and Vascular Services
Internal Medicine Services
Laboratory Services
Occupational Health Services
Orthopedic Services
Pediatric Services
Radiology and Imaging Services
Rehabilitation Services
Sleep Disorders Services
Surgery Services
Women's Health Services
Wound Care Services

COMPETITORS

BETHESDA HOSPITAL, INC.
CHILTON HOSPITAL
CONWAY REGIONAL MEDICAL CENTER, INC.
OHIO VALLEY MEDICAL CENTER, INCORPORATED
PORTER FOUNDATION, INC.

HISTORICAL FINANCIALS
Company Type: Private

Income Statement   FYE: December 31

	REVENUE ($mil)	NET INCOME ($mil)	NET PROFIT MARGIN	EMPLOYEES
12/18	574	2	0.4%	949
12/17	179	8	4.8%	—
12/16	171	1	1.1%	—
12/15	162	1	0.8%	—
Annual Growth	52.5%	16.4%	—	—

2018 Year-End Financials
Return on assets: 0.5%   Cash ($ mil.): 87
Return on equity: 0.8%
Current Ratio: 1.60

ROBERT BOSCH LLC

Robert Bosch LLC is your one-stop shop for German-engineered auto parts, appliances, and power tools. The company operates across four business sectors Mobility Solutions, Industrial Technology, Consumer Goods, and Energy and Building Technology. It offers customers a multitude of value-add, cross-sector solutions across a diversity of industry applications. The company provides outstanding products, and it utilizes expertise in sensor technology, systems integration, software and services, as well as its own IoT cloud, to offer each customer connected, cross-domain solutions from a single source. Active since 1906, Bosch LLC has grown to approximately 70 primary North American locations.

Operations
Robert Bosch LLC provides comprehensive expertise in vehicle technology with hardware, software, and services.

The Bosh mobility solutions web portal presents highlights from the areas of connected mobility, automated mobility, and powertrain and electrified mobility. It offers a wide range of spare parts to aftermarket and repair shops ? from new and exchange parts to repair solutions ? as well as repair shop equipment such as diagnostics software and hardware. In addition to service-training courses and partner programs for repair shops, Bosch also offers automobile competence and knowledge to service technicians all over the world. The company's eBike Systems develop, produce, and market products that fascinate people. Bosch Motorsport engineers' high performance solutions and provide access to Bosch technology for motorsport applications. In addition, Rober Bosch offers diagnostics software and hardware, training courses, and partner programs for repair shops.

Geographic Reach
Based in Farmington Hills, Michigan, Robert Bosch LLC has approximately 70 primary locations in the US, Canada, and Mexico.

EXECUTIVES

Managing Member, Markus Heyn

LOCATIONS

HQ: ROBERT BOSCH LLC
38000 HILLS TECH DR, FARMINGTON HILLS, MI 483313418
Phone: 248 876-1000
Web: WWW.BOSCH.US

PRODUCTS/OPERATIONS

2019 Sales

	% of total
Mobility Solutions	66
Consumer Goods	18
Industrial Technology	10
Energy and Building Technology	6
Other	3
Total	100

Selected Products
Automotive Technology
    Aftermarket
    Alternators
    Brake pads
    Car audio products
    Diesel parts
    Filters
    Fuel pumps
    Ignition products
    Oxygen sensors
    Spark plugs
    Spark plug wire sets
    Starters
    Wiper blades
    Original equipment
    Actuators
    Braking and chassis systems
    Car multimedia
    Electrical systems
    Electronic systems
    Powertrain systems - diesel
    Powertrain systems - gasoline
Consumer Goods and Building Technology
    Household appliances
    Cooktops
    Dishwashers
    Ovens
    Washers and dryers
    Power tools
    Angle grinders
    Belt sanders
    Circular saws
    Drill bits
    Drills
    Drywall drivers
    Impact wrenches
    Jigsaws
    Orbit sanders/polishers
    Planers
    Reciprocating saws
    Rotary hammers
    Routers
    Screwdriver bits and accessories
    Wet/dry vacuums
    Security Systems
    Access control
    Communications
    Fire detection
    Security management
    Video surveillance
    Thermotechnology
    Indoor climate control (heating and cooling, and hot water production)
Industrial Technology
    Drive and control
    Assembly
    Electric drives and controls
    Gears
    Hydraulics
    Linear motion
    Pneumatics
    Packaging
    Confectionary, cosmetics, and chemicals
    Packaging machines
    Packaging services
    Pharmaceuticals
    Production tools
    Air assembly tools
    Cordless assembly tools
    DC electric assembly tools
    Electric assembly tools
    Solar Energy
    Crystalline PV modules
    Solar cells
    Thin-film modules
    Wafers

COMPETITORS
BOSCH REXROTH CORPORATION
EAST PENN MANUFACTURING CO.
HITACHI AUTOMOTIVE SYSTEMS AMERICAS, INC.
KIMBALL ELECTRONICS GROUP, LLC
MAXWELL TECHNOLOGIES, INC.
PANASONIC CORPORATION
PRESTOLITE WIRE LLC
Robert Bosch Gesellschaft mit beschränkter Haftung
STRATTEC SECURITY CORPORATION
UNISON INDUSTRIES, LLC

HISTORICAL FINANCIALS
Company Type: Private

Income Statement   FYE: December 31

	REVENUE ($mil)	NET INCOME ($mil)	NET PROFIT MARGIN	EMPLOYEES
12/14	10,474	181	1.7%	1,532
12/10	6,810	326	4.8%	—
12/09	5,464	59	1.1%	—
Annual Growth	13.9%	25.1%	—	—

2014 Year-End Financials
Return on assets: 2.7%   Cash ($ mil.): 832
Return on equity: 13.0%
Current Ratio: 0.90

ROBERT W BAIRD & CO INC

Employee-owned Robert W. Baird & Co. brings mid-western sensibility to the high-flying world of investment banking. The company offers brokerage, asset management, and investment banking services to middle-market corporations, institutional clients, municipal, and wealthy individuals and families around the world. Its investment banking activities include underwriting and distributing corporate securities, mergers and acquisitions, capital advisory, equity capital markets and institutional sales and trading. The company advises clients on a range of other unique situations, such as fairness opinions, restructurings, takeover defenses and other special situations. Baird manages more than $355 billion in client assets. The company was founded in 1919.

Operations
Baird's Private Wealth Management offers opportunities for financial advisors and client relationship assistants. Its Asset Management business includes Baird Advisors and Baird Equity Asset Management. The company's Equity Capital Markets business is comprised of research, equity sales and trading, and investment banking, while Fixed Income Capital Markets unit consists of fixed income sales and trading and public finance.

Geographic Reach
Headquartered in Wisconsin, Baird has offices across the US, Europe and Asia.

Sales and Marketing
Baird primarily serves individuals, families and public entities throughout the US as well as corporations and institutions worldwide.

Company Background
Founded in 1919, Baird had been majority-owned by Northwestern Mutual since 1982. However, employees bought back the company's stock in a series of purchases that culminated in 2004.

LOCATIONS
HQ: ROBERT W BAIRD & CO INC
777 E WISCONSIN AVE FL 29, MILWAUKEE, WI 532025391
Phone: 414 765-3500
Web: WWW.RWBAIRD.COM

PRODUCTS/OPERATIONS
Business Groups
Asset Management
Equity Capital Markets
Fixed Income Capital Markets
Private Equity
Private Wealth Management

COMPETITORS
3I GROUP PLC
APAX PARTNERS HOLDINGS LTD
EVERCORE INC.
MACQUARIE GROUP LIMITED
MARTIN CURRIE LIMITED
NOMURA HOLDINGS, INC.
RAYMOND JAMES FINANCIAL, INC.
ROTHSCHILD & CO
SCHRODERS PLC
Vontobel Holding AG

HISTORICAL FINANCIALS
Company Type: Private

Income Statement   FYE: December 31

	ASSETS ($mil)	NET INCOME ($mil)	INCOME AS % OF ASSETS	EMPLOYEES
12/09	2,063	41	2.0%	2,000
12/08	1,080	36	3.4%	—
12/07	1,712	50	2.9%	—
Annual Growth	9.8%	(8.6%)	—	—

2009 Year-End Financials
Return on assets: 2.0%   Cash ($ mil.): 78
Return on equity: 11.2%
Current Ratio: —

ROBERT WOOD JOHNSON UNIVERSITY HOSPITAL, INC.

Robert Wood Johnson University Hospital (RWJUH) is the flagship facility of the Robert Wood Johnson Health System and Network. The medical center offers patients acute and tertiary care, including cardiovascular services, organ and tissue transplantation, pediatric care (at The Bristol-Myers Squibb Children's Hospital), Level I trauma care, cancer treatment (at the Cancer Hospital of New Jersey), women's health, and emergency medicine. Founded in 1884, the facility serves as a teaching center for the Robert Wood Johnson Medical School (RWJMS).

Operations
More than 9,000 physicians affiliated with RWJUH treat some 200,000 patients each year. The hospital handles some 283,00 inpatient admissions each year, as well as 700,000 emergency visits.

Other members of the Robert Wood Johnson Health System include Community Medical Center, Cooperman Barnabas Medical, Jersey City Medical Center, Monmouth Medical Center, Robert Wood Johnson University Hospital and Trinity Regional Medical Center.

Company Background
RWJUH was founded in 1884. In 2014, Somerset Medical Center was merged into RWJUH, adding more than 300 beds and providing RWJUH entry into the Somerset community.

RWJUH's parent company, Robert Wood Johnson Health System, merged with fellow New Jersey hospital system Barnabas Health in 2015, creating the largest hospital system in New Jersey. The combined entity began operating under the name RWJBarnabas Health.

EXECUTIVES

CMO*, Lewis Rubinson
Auditors : KPMG LLP SHORT HILLS NJ

LOCATIONS

HQ: ROBERT WOOD JOHNSON UNIVERSITY HOSPITAL, INC.
1 ROBERT WOOD JOHNSON PL, NEW BRUNSWICK, NJ 089011928
Phone: 732 828-3000
Web: WWW.RWJBH.ORG

PRODUCTS/OPERATIONS

Selected Services
Bariatric Surgery
Bloodless Surgery
Cardiothoracic Surgery
Colorectal Surgery
Comprehensive Sleep Disorders Center
Diabetes
Digestive Disorders
Emergency Department
Executive Health Program
Heart Transplantation
Injury Prevention
Kidney and Pancreas Transplantation
Lab Services (blood work and blood collection)
Level 1 Trauma Center
Neurosciences
    Clinical Neurosciences Center
    Deep Brain Stimulation for Movement Disorders
    Laser Ablation for Brain Tumor Treatment
    Neurosurgery
    New Jersey Brain Aneurysm & AVM Program
    Parkinson's Disease Information and Referral Center
    Stroke Center
    The Gamma Knife Center: Advanced Treatment for Brain and Spine
New Jersey Pain Institute at RWJUH
Orthopedic Surgery
Outpatient Radiology: University Radiology at Robert Wood Johnson
Palliative Care Program
Pastoral Care
Pelvic Floor and Incontinence Program
Physical and Occupational Therapy
Prostate Cancer Surgery
Radiation Oncology
    Gynecologic Brachytherapy
    Prostate Brachytherapy
    TomoTherapy
    Total Skin Electron Beam Therapy
Radiology (including CT, MRI and ultrasound)
Speech and Hearing Program
The Center for Wound Healing
The Limb Preservation Program
Therapeutic Apheresis
Thoracic Surgery
Vascular Surgery

COMPETITORS

BRONXCARE HEALTH SYSTEM
CHARLESTON AREA MEDICAL CENTER, INC.
HENRY FORD HEALTH SYSTEM
JOHN T. MATHER MEMORIAL HOSPITAL OF PORT JEFFERSON, NEW YORK, INC.
KALEIDA HEALTH
KENNEDY HEALTH SYSTEM, INC.
NORTHWELL HEALTH, INC.
SOUTHCOAST HEALTH SYSTEM, INC.
THE COOPER HEALTH SYSTEM
THE PENNSYLVANIA HOSPITAL OF THE UNIVERSITY OF PENNSYLVANIA HEALTH SYSTEM

HISTORICAL FINANCIALS
Company Type: Private

Income Statement   FYE: December 31

	REVENUE ($mil)	NET INCOME ($mil)	NET PROFIT MARGIN	EMPLOYEES
12/20	1,084	22	2.0%	4,674
12/19	1,451	(89)	—	—
12/18	1,337	(3)	—	—
12/17	1,249	(59)	—	—
Annual Growth	(4.6%)	—	—	—

2020 Year-End Financials
Return on assets: 1.4%   Cash ($ mil.): —
Return on equity: 3.2%
Current Ratio: 3.70

ROCHESTER CITY SCHOOL DISTRICT

EXECUTIVES

BOARD OF EDU*, Mary Adams
BOARD OF EDU*, Melisza Campos
BOARD OF EDU*, Cynthia Elliot
Board Manager*, Willa Powell
Auditors : FREEDMAXICK CPA PC ROCHEST

LOCATIONS

HQ: ROCHESTER CITY SCHOOL DISTRICT
131 W BROAD ST, ROCHESTER, NY 146141103
Phone: 585 262-8100
Web: WWW.RCSDK12.ORG

HISTORICAL FINANCIALS
Company Type: Private

Income Statement   FYE: June 30

	REVENUE ($mil)	NET INCOME ($mil)	NET PROFIT MARGIN	EMPLOYEES
06/13	708	74	10.6%	5,470
06/11	681	(19)	—	—
Annual Growth	1.9%	—	—	—

2013 Year-End Financials
Return on assets: 8.7%   Cash ($ mil.): 315
Return on equity: 123.6%
Current Ratio: —

ROCHESTER GAS AND ELECTRIC CORPORATION

Upstate New York residents count on Rochester Gas and Electric (RG&E) to keep the lights turned on. The regulated utility provides electricity to about 370,000 customers and natural gas to 306,000 customers. RG&E operates 22,500 miles of power transmission and distribution lines and has a generating capacity of approximately 400 MW from interests in fossil-fueled and hydroelectric power plants. RG&E and sister utility company New York State Electric & Gas (NYSEG) are subsidiaries of regional power and gas distribution player Avangrid).

Geographic Reach
RG&E's service territory contains a substantial suburban area and a large agricultural area in parts of nine counties including and surrounding the city of Rochester, New York, with a population of 1 million.

Financial Performance
The company operates under the Network business of IBERDROLA. The Network business accounted for 25% of

IBERDROLA's 2013 revenues; some 28% of Network sales came from US operations. IBERDROLA generated 10% of its total revenues from the US in 2013.

Strategy

To reduce its carbon emissions, RG&E, along with affiliate NYSEG is pushing green energy options, including a wind energy power program whereby residents can choose to have their power supply from wind generated sources.

In 2013 the company announced plans to retire its 18-MW Rochester 9 natural gas-fired combustion turbine, as it would be too expensive to repair the equipment failures that forced the unit offline that year.

Company Background

Between 2008 and the end of 2010, NYSEG or RG&E interconnected six landfill gas plants with a total of 26MW of generating capacity, three wind farms with 209 wind turbines (381 MW of generating capacity) in Wyoming and Steuben counties, a new 30 MW combined heat and power facility for Cornell University, and a lithium-ion battery energy storage facility for AES Corporation.

Auditors : KPMG LLP NEW YORK NY

LOCATIONS

HQ: ROCHESTER GAS AND ELECTRIC CORPORATION
89 EAST AVE, ROCHESTER, NY 146490002
Phone: 800 295-7323
Web: WWW.RGE.COM

COMPETITORS

ARIZONA PUBLIC SERVICE COMPANY
ARKANSAS ELECTRIC COOPERATIVE CORPORATION
GREAT RIVER ENERGY
NEW YORK POWER AUTHORITY
NSTAR LLC

HISTORICAL FINANCIALS
Company Type: Private

Income Statement			FYE: December 31
REVENUE ($mil)	NET INCOME ($mil)	NET PROFIT MARGIN	EMPLOYEES
12/17 850	83	9.8%	865
12/16 1,042	80	7.7%	—
12/10 982	54	5.5%	—
Annual Growth (2.0%)	6.3%	—	—

2017 Year-End Financials
Return on assets: 2.3%   Cash ($ mil.): —
Return on equity: 8.8%
Current Ratio: 1.20

ROCHESTER INSTITUTE OF TECHNOLOGY (INC)

The Rochester Institute of Technology (RIT) is a privately endowed university with nine colleges focused on providing career-oriented education to nearly 18,670 students. The school, which has a student-faculty ratio of about 13:1, offers approximately 85 bachelor's degree programs in art and design, business, engineering, science, and hospitality. RIT also confers more than 75 master's and eight doctorate degrees. The university's National Technical Institute for the Deaf is the first and largest technological college for learners who suffer from hearing loss. RIT, which traces its roots back to 1829, counts among its alumni the CEOs of Kodak and The Associated Press.

Operations

RIT's campus serves about 15,740 undergraduate and around 2,930 graduate students with help from its faculty and staff of more than 4,040. More than 900 deaf and hard-of-hearing students live, study, and work alongside hearing students on the RIT campus. Tuition runs more than $33,650 for general students and more than $17,275 for deaf and hard-of-hearing students.

RIT operates a campus in Dubai's Silicon Oasis, a not-for-profit global campus, technological-focused. The campus serves the university's goal of growing its reputation worldwide and expanding international opportunities for students. RIT Dubai offers undergraduate and graduate degree programs in engineering, business, information technology, and leadership.

Geographic Reach

Spanning some 1,300 acres in Rochester, New York, it has international campuses in China, Croatia, Dubai, and Kosovo. The university's students come from all 50 states and more than 100 nations around the world.

Strategy

RIT has acquired the former Radisson Hotel Rochester Airport, located next to its campus on Jefferson Road in Henrietta. RIT will renovate the entire facility and use it for housing students and university guests.

Auditors : PRICEWATERHOUSECOOPERS LLP RO

LOCATIONS

HQ: ROCHESTER INSTITUTE OF TECHNOLOGY (INC)
1 LOMB MEMORIAL DR, ROCHESTER, NY 146235698
Phone: 585 475-2411
Web: WWW.RIT.EDU

PRODUCTS/OPERATIONS

Selected Colleges
College of Applied Science and Technology
   School of Engineering Technology
   School of International Hospitality and Service Innovation
E. Philip Saunders College of Business
B. Thomas Golisano College of Computing and Information Sciences
Kate Gleason College of Engineering
College of Health Sciences and Technology
College of Imaging Arts and Sciences
   School for American Crafts
   School of Art
   School of Design
   School of Film and Animation
   School of Media Sciences
   School of Photographic Arts and Sciences
College of Liberal Arts
National Technical Institute for the Deaf
College of Science

Selected Graduate & Undergraduate Programs
Accounting
Applied Networking & Systems Administration
Applied Statistics
Biochemistry
Business
Civil Engineering Technology
Clinical Chemistry
Computer Integrated Machining Technology
Computer Science
Digital Imaging & Publishing Technology
Electrical/Mechanical Engineering Technology
Environmental Science
Finance
Glass & Glass Sculpture
Health Systems Administration
Healthcare Billing & Coding Technology
Imaging Arts: Photography
Industrial & Systems Engineering
Instruction Technology
Management
Medical Illustration
Metals/Jewelry Design
Ophthalmic Optical Finishing Technology
Print Media
Psychology
Service Leadership and Innovation
Voice Communication
Woodworking and Furniture Design

COMPETITORS

DELAWARE STATE UNIVERSITY
GRAND CANYON EDUCATION, INC.
NORTHEASTERN UNIVERSITY
PURDUE UNIVERSITY
Queen's University At Kingston
THE COLLEGE OF WILLIAM & MARY
UNIVERSITY OF NEW HAVEN, INCORPORATED
UNIVERSITY OF THE PACIFIC
VIRGINIA POLYTECHNIC INSTITUTE AND STATE UNIVERSITY
ZOVIO INC

HISTORICAL FINANCIALS
Company Type: Private

Income Statement			FYE: June 30
REVENUE ($mil)	NET INCOME ($mil)	NET PROFIT MARGIN	EMPLOYEES
06/18 579	203	35.2%	3,300
06/17 560	74	13.2%	—
06/12 490	16	3.4%	—
06/06 370	45	12.2%	—
Annual Growth 3.8%	13.4%	—	—

2018 Year-End Financials
Return on assets: 10.4%   Cash ($ mil.): 62
Return on equity: 14.2%
Current Ratio: —

ROCHESTER REGIONAL HEALTH

Auditors : FUST CHARLES CHAMBERS SYRACUS

LOCATIONS

HQ: ROCHESTER REGIONAL HEALTH
100 KINGS HWY S STE 2300, ROCHESTER, NY 146175503

Phone: 585 922-4000
Web: WWW.ROCHESTERREGIONAL.ORG

HISTORICAL FINANCIALS
Company Type: Private

Income Statement				FYE: December 31
	REVENUE ($mil)	NET INCOME ($mil)	NET PROFIT MARGIN	EMPLOYEES
12/18	2,189	38	1.8%	22,500
12/17	2,059	54	2.6%	—
Annual Growth	6.3%	(28.6%)	—	—

2018 Year-End Financials
Return on assets: 1.8% Cash ($ mil.): 170
Return on equity: 7.0%
Current Ratio: 1.60

ROCKFORD PUBLIC SCHOOLS

Auditors: BAKER TILLY US LLP OAK BROOK

LOCATIONS

HQ: ROCKFORD PUBLIC SCHOOLS
350 N MAIN ST, ROCKFORD, MI 493411092
Phone: 616 863-6320
Web: WWW.ROCKFORDSCHOOLS.ORG

HISTORICAL FINANCIALS
Company Type: Private

Income Statement				FYE: June 30
	REVENUE ($mil)	NET INCOME ($mil)	NET PROFIT MARGIN	EMPLOYEES
06/22	587	38	6.5%	895
06/19	104	50	48.7%	—
06/18	101	(10)	—	—
Annual Growth	55.1%	—	—	—

2022 Year-End Financials
Return on assets: 3.4% Cash ($ mil.): 320
Return on equity: 4.8%
Current Ratio: 2.80

ROPER ST. FRANCIS HEALTHCARE

CareAlliance Health Services (doing business as Roper St. Francis Healthcare) operates four hospitals -- the 370-bed Roper Hospital, the 200-bed Bon Secours St. Francis Hospital, the 85-bed Mount Pleasant Hospital, and the Roper Rehabilitation Hospital. Besides providing home health services, it also operates outpatient emergency, primary care, and diagnostic facilities. Roper St. Francis Healthcare serves Charleston, South Carolina, and surrounding communities. Its Roper St. Francis Physician Partners is one of the region's largest physician practices.

Operations

The health system comprises Roper Hospital, Bon Secours St. Francis Hospital, Roper St. Francis Mount Pleasant Hospital, Roper St. Francis Foundation, and Roper St. Francis Physicians Network. Altogether it boasts three acute care hospitals with 655-plus beds, one specialty hospital, 15 centers for outpatient services, three industrial medicine sites, five emergency rooms, and two urgent care centers.

Roper St. Francis Healthcare has a medical staff of some 800 physicians. The Roper St. Francis Physician Partners organization has more than 230 physicians who offer primary and specialty care including family practice, internal medicine, and pediatrics.

Geographic Reach
Altogether, Roper St. Francis Healthcare operates about 90 facilities in seven counties in the lowcountry region of South Carolina.

Strategy
The health system in 2014 signed an agreement with Trendlines Lab to collaborate on the development of new medical device inventions as well as low-cost solutions for clinical problems. The partnership will work to create devices that will address unmet needs identified by physicians and other health care providers.

Company Background
Roper St. Francis Healthcare was formed through the merger of Roper Hospital and Bon Secours St. Francis Hospital in 1998.

Roper St. Francis Physician Partners was formed through the 2009 combination of Roper St. Francis Physicians' Network and Lowcountry Medical Associates.

Auditors: DELOITTE & TOUCHE LLP CHARLO

LOCATIONS

HQ: ROPER ST. FRANCIS HEALTHCARE
125 DOUGHTY ST STE 760, CHARLESTON, SC 294035785
Phone: 843 724-2000
Web: WWW.RSFH.COM

Selected South Carolina Facilities
Hospitals
    Mt. Pleasant Hospital Campus - Mount Pleasant
    Roper Hospital Campus - Charleston
    Roper Rehabilitation Hospital
    St. Francis Campus - Charleston
Outpatient Centers
    After Hours Care - James Island
    Kiawah-Seabrook Medical & Urgent Care
    Roper Hospital Ambulatory Surgery - Berkeley
    Roper Hospital Ambulatory Surgery & Pain Management - James Island
    Roper Hospital Diagnostics & ER - Berkeley
    Roper Hospital Diagnostics & ER - Northwoods
    Roper Hospital Diagnostics - Farmfield
    Roper Hospital Diagnostics - Goose Creek
    Roper Hosptial Diagnostics - James Island
    Roper Hosptial Diagnostics - Kiawah-Seabrook
    Roper Hosptial Diagnostics - Moncks Corner
    Roper Hospital Imaging - Wesley Drive
    Roper Hospital Imaging - Wingo Way

COMPETITORS

ASCENSION SOUTHEAST MICHIGAN
GREATER LAFAYETTE HEALTH SERVICES, INC.
METHODIST LE BONHEUR HEALTHCARE
SAINT ELIZABETH REGIONAL MEDICAL CENTER
SOUTHERN ILLINOIS HEALTHCARE ENTERPRISES, INC.
ST. JOHN HEALTH SYSTEM, INC.
ST. JOSEPH HEALTHCARE FOUNDATION
ST. MARY'S HEALTH, INC.
ST. MARY'S MEDICAL CENTER, INC.
ST. VINCENT ANDERSON REGIONAL HOSPITAL, INC.

HISTORICAL FINANCIALS
Company Type: Private

Income Statement				FYE: December 31
	REVENUE ($mil)	NET INCOME ($mil)	NET PROFIT MARGIN	EMPLOYEES
12/14	793	(2)	—	6,000
12/09	682	56	8.3%	—
12/08	618	(51)	—	—
Annual Growth	4.3%	—	—	—

2014 Year-End Financials
Return on assets: (-0.3%) Cash ($ mil.): 54
Return on equity: (-0.7%)
Current Ratio: 1.30

ROUND ROCK INDEPENDENT SCHOOL DISTRICT (INC)

Auditors: WHITLEY PENN LLP AUSTIN TEX

LOCATIONS

HQ: ROUND ROCK INDEPENDENT SCHOOL DISTRICT (INC)
1311 ROUND ROCK AVE, ROUND ROCK, TX 786814941
Phone: 512 464-5000
Web: WWW.ROUNDROCKISD.ORG

HISTORICAL FINANCIALS
Company Type: Private

Income Statement				FYE: June 30
	REVENUE ($mil)	NET INCOME ($mil)	NET PROFIT MARGIN	EMPLOYEES
06/22	666	(156)	—	4,500
06/21	603	(196)	—	—
06/19	600	174	29.0%	—
Annual Growth	3.5%	—	—	—

2022 Year-End Financials
Return on assets: (-9.6%) Cash ($ mil.): 575
Return on equity: (-137.6%)
Current Ratio: —

ROUSE'S ENTERPRISES, L.L.C.

Auditors: TS KEARNS & CO THIBODAUX

LOCATIONS

HQ: ROUSE'S ENTERPRISES, L.L.C.
179 ROUSES DR, SCHRIEVER, LA 703953310
Phone: 985 447-5998
Web: WWW.ROUSES.COM

HISTORICAL FINANCIALS

Company Type: Private

Income Statement — FYE: December 29

	REVENUE ($mil)	NET INCOME ($mil)	NET PROFIT MARGIN	EMPLOYEES
12/10	691	24	3.5%	5,200
12/09	689	21	3.1%	—
12/06	247	11	4.8%	—
Annual Growth	29.4%	19.7%	—	—

2010 Year-End Financials
Return on assets: 15.7% Cash ($ mil.): 8
Return on equity: 25.8%
Current Ratio: 2.00

RTW RETAILWINDS, INC.

RTW Retailwinds (formerly New York & Company) caters to working women ages 25 to 49 looking for moderately priced apparel (jeans, dresses, and coordinates) and accessories (sunglasses, jewelry, and handbags). It offers proprietary branded fashions at more than 385 stores in about three dozen US states and online. The company sells merchandise under the New York & Company and Fashion to Figure names and has collaborations with celebrities such as Eva Mendes, Gabrielle Union, and Kate Hudson. RTW Retailwinds was founded in 1918 and filed for voluntary petitions for relief under Chapter 11 of the Bankruptcy Code in the United States Bankruptcy Court for the District of New Jersey in 2020.

Bankruptcy
In 2020, RTW Retailwinds and its subsidiaries have filed voluntary petitions for relief under Chapter 11 of the Bankruptcy Code in the United States Bankruptcy Court for the District of New Jersey (the Bankruptcy Court). The company has filed customary motions with the Bankruptcy Court that will authorize, upon Bankruptcy Court approval, the company's ability to maintain operations in the ordinary course of business, including, among other things.

Operations
RTW Retailwinds' stores average nearly 5,005 square feet and are located in shopping malls, lifestyle centers, outlet centers, and off-mall locations. The company offers an inclusive range of merchandise sizes: 00 to 20, XXS to XXL, petite, tall, and plus.

It sources some 95% of its merchandise from three countries ? China, Vietnam, and Indonesia.

Geographic Reach
New York-based RTW Retailwinds has stores in about 35 US states. Its largest markets include California (with more than 40 locations), Texas (about 35), Florida, New Jersey and Pennsylvania (about 25 each).

Sales and Marketing
In addition to store locations, RTW Retailwinds sells its merchandise exclusively at its retail locations and online at www.nyandcompany.com, www.nyandcompanycloset.com, www.fashiontofigure.com, and www.happyxnature.com. In 2020, the company discontinued its e-commerce business.

To compete in the competitive women's apparel and accessories arena, the company has been gradually increasing its spending on advertising and promotions. The company promotes its brands through direct mail, in-store marketing, digital marketing, email and text messaging programs, social media (Facebook, Instagram, Twitter, and Pinterest), public relations programs, and select advertising. The fashion chain targets women between the ages of 25 and 49.

Financial Performance
Net sales for fiscal year 2019 were $827.0 million, as compared to $893.2 million for fiscal year 2018. Contributing to the decrease in net sales was the Company's closing of 31 stores throughout fiscal year 2019, partially offset by growth in the eCommerce channel and sales from the new Fashion to Figure brand launched in the beginning of fiscal year 2018.

Net loss was $61.6 million for fiscal year 2019, as compared to net income of $4.2 million for fiscal year 2018.

Cash held by the company at the end of 2019 was $60.6 million compared to $95.5 million in the prior year. Cash used for operations, investing and financing activities were $24.5 million, $8.1 million and $2.2 million, respectively. Main uses of cash were capital expenditures and principal payment on capital lease obligations.

Strategy
The company's strategy focuses on: transformation into a digitally dominant retailer; evolve as a broader lifestyle brand; enhance brand awareness, increase customer engagement, and drive traffic; and drive eCommerce growth and expand omni-channel capabilities.

Prior to the impact of COVID-19, the company planned to accelerate its strategy to reposition itself as a digitally dominant retailer. With that, it anticipated the closure of 150 stores over the next 18 months as a component of the company's transformation to a digitally dominant portfolio of brands. If the company seeks protection under the bankruptcy laws as discussed above, it could close more than 150 stores, or it may close all of its stores. The reduction of non-productive selling square feet is an integral component of the company's goal to improve productivity and profitability across its chain of stores and online. Since the beginning of fiscal year 2014, the Company has closed 179 stores.

Company Background
RTW Retailwinds traces its history to its 1918 founding. The company operated as a subsidiary of Limited Brands for nearly 20 years, starting in 1985. In 2004 it went public as New York & Company. New York & Company changed its name to RTW Retailwinds in late 2018.

Auditors: BDO USA LLP NEW YORK NEW YO

LOCATIONS

HQ: RTW RETAILWINDS, INC.
330 W 34TH ST FL 9, NEW YORK, NY 100012406
Phone: 212 884-2000
Web: WWW.NYANDCOMPANY.COM

2018 Stores

	No.
California	45
New York	45
Texas	37
Florida	28
New Jersey	28
Pennsylvania	26
North Carolina	19
Virginia	19
Georgia	18
Illinois	18
Other states	128
Total	411

COMPETITORS

ARO LIQUIDATION, INC.
ASCENA RETAIL GROUP, INC.
AVENUE STORES, LLC
EXPRESS, INC.
FIVE BELOW, INC.
J. CREW GROUP, INC.
Lululemon Athletica Canada Inc
TAILORED BRANDS, INC.
THE CATO CORPORATION
THE FINISH LINE INC

HISTORICAL FINANCIALS

Company Type: Private

Income Statement — FYE: February 2

	REVENUE ($mil)	NET INCOME ($mil)	NET PROFIT MARGIN	EMPLOYEES
02/19	893	4	0.5%	1,460
02/18*	926	5	0.6%	—
01/17	929	(17)	—	—
Annual Growth	(1.9%)	—	—	—

*Fiscal year change

2019 Year-End Financials
Return on assets: 1.5% Cash ($ mil.): 95
Return on equity: 4.9%
Current Ratio: 1.40

RUDOLPH AND SLETTEN, INC.

Rudolph and Sletten ... the little-known tenth reindeer? More like the elves who built Santa's workshop. The firm is a mainstay of the California construction scene, especially Silicon Valley. It has built corporate campuses for Apple, Microsoft, and Wells Fargo, as well as Lucasfilm's Skywalker Ranch production facility. Rudolph and Sletten is one of the US' largest general building contractors, with site selection, design/build, and construction management capabilities. Key projects also include biotech labs, hospitals, and schools. Onslow "Rudy" Rudolph founded the company in 1959 and was joined by partner Kenneth Sletten in 1962. Rudolph and Sletten is a subsidiary of Tutor Perini Corporation.

Geographic Reach
Redwood City, California-based Rudolph and Sletten has regional offices in San Francisco, Sacramento, Irvine, San Diego, and Stockton, California. The firm is licensed to build in California, Arizona, Nevada, Washington, Colorado, Idaho, Oregon, Oklahoma, and Texas.

Sales and Marketing
Big name clients have included a number of prestigious institutions, such as Childrens Hospital Los Angeles, The University of Southern California, Genentech, and the Monterey Bay Aquarium. The company reports that more than 95% of its business comes from repeat customers.

Financial Performance
California is Rudolph and Slatten's largest market, representing an estimated $666 million in revenue in 2013.

Strategy
To capitalize on San Francisco's building boom, the firm hired several San Francisco construction veterans in early 2014 to expand its operations there. Rudolph and Sletten is currently working on projects in Mission Bay and the Financial District.

The firm is renowned for its green building practices, with nearly half the staff Leadership in Energy and Environmental Design (LEED)-accredited; it aims for 100% accreditation by 2013. Its own corporate headquarters was Gold LEED-certified based on its use of recycled materials, energy and water efficiency, and sustainable site. Other sustainable projects undertaken by Rudolph and Sletten include the Lawrence Berkeley National Laboratory and the NOAA Fisheries Services Southwest Science Center.

Auditors : DELOITTE & TOUCHE LLP LOS AN

LOCATIONS
HQ: RUDOLPH AND SLETTEN, INC.
2 CIRCLE STAR WAY FL 4, SAN CARLOS, CA 940706200

Phone: 650 216-3600

PRODUCTS/OPERATIONS
Major Markets
Biotechnology/pharmaceutical
Commercial office and corporate campuses
Education
Gaming and hospitality
Government
Health care
Industrial
Justice
Sports and entertainment
Technology

Selected Services
Estimating
Scheduling
Value engineering
Constructibility review
Building Information Modeling (BIM)
Construction
Construction management
Project management
Quality control
Disruption management
Commissioning
Self performed work
Sustainable cpnstruction
Safety

COMPETITORS
BECK INTERNATIONAL, LLC
JAYNES CORPORATION
M. A. MORTENSON COMPANY
MCCARTHY BUILDING COMPANIES, INC.
O'NEIL INDUSTRIES, INC.

HISTORICAL FINANCIALS
Company Type: Private

Income Statement — FYE: December 31

	REVENUE ($mil)	NET INCOME ($mil)	NET PROFIT MARGIN	EMPLOYEES
12/16	1,307	14	1.1%	700
12/15	940	7	0.7%	—
12/14	637	3	0.5%	—
12/13	665	(0)	0.0%	—
Annual Growth	25.2%	—	—	—

2016 Year-End Financials
Return on assets: 2.8%   Cash ($ mil.): —
Return on equity: 10.0%
Current Ratio: 0.90

RUSH UNIVERSITY MEDICAL CENTER

Auditors : DELOITTE & TOUCHE LLP CHICAG

LOCATIONS
HQ: RUSH UNIVERSITY MEDICAL CENTER
1620 W HARRISON ST, CHICAGO, IL 606123801
Phone: 312 942-5000
Web: WWW.RUSH.EDU

HISTORICAL FINANCIALS
Company Type: Private

Income Statement — FYE: June 30

	REVENUE ($mil)	NET INCOME ($mil)	NET PROFIT MARGIN	EMPLOYEES
06/17	2,267	302	13.3%	8,000
06/16	1,502	83	5.6%	—
06/15	1,408	(22)	—	—
06/14	1,969	208	10.6%	—
Annual Growth	4.8%	13.2%	—	—

2017 Year-End Financials
Return on assets: 7.9%   Cash ($ mil.): 99
Return on equity: 13.7%
Current Ratio: 0.90

RWJ BARNABAS HEALTH, INC.

RWJ Barnabas Health was formed by the merger of New Jersey health systems Barnabas Health and Robert Wood Johnson. It operates more than 10 acute care hospitals (including Monmouth Medical Center Southern Campus and Newark Beth Israel Medical Center), three acute care children's hospitals, a pediatric rehabilitation hospital with a network of outpatient centers, a freestanding 100-bed behavioral health center, two trauma centers, a satellite emergency department and ambulatory care center. RWJ Barnabas employs more than 9,000 physicians statewide and trains approximately 1,000 residents and interns each year. One of the New Jersey's largest private employer, RWJ Barnabas also operates the state's largest behavioral health network.

Operations
RWJ Barnabas also include geriatric centers, comprehensive home care and hospice programs, fitness and wellness centers, retail pharmacy services, medical groups, multi-site imaging centers, accountable care organizations, a burn treatment facility, medical groups, comprehensive cancer services and breast centers, and comprehensive cardiac surgery services, including a heart transplant center, a lung transplant center, and kidney transplant centers.

RWJ Barnabas treated over 3 million patients, had 2 million outpatient visits per year; performs some 283,000 inpatients and same day surgery patients and had 25,000 births.

Overall, patient service accounts for more than 90% of total revenue, while CARES Act grant and other revenue bring in the remaining some 10%.

Geographic Reach
Based in New Jersey, RWJ Barnabas has operations in eight counties serving five million people.

Financial Performance

The company's revenue in 2021 increased to $6.6 billion compared to $5.9 billion in the prior year.

Cash held by the company at the end of 2021 increased to $677.0 million. Cash provided by operations and financing activities were $195.7 million and $793.3 million, respectively. Cash used for investing activities was $433.6 million, mainly for purchases of investments.

EXECUTIVES

CPO*, Indu Lew
CSCDO*, Mark Manigan
Senior Vice President Cash, Stephen O'mahony

LOCATIONS

HQ: RWJ BARNABAS HEALTH, INC.
95 OLD SHORT HILLS RD, WEST ORANGE, NJ 070521008
Phone: 973 322-4000
Web: WWW.RWJBH.ORG

PRODUCTS/OPERATIONS

Selected Hospitals
Barnabas Health Behavioral Health Center
The Bristol-Myers Squibb Children's Hospital at RWJUH
Children's Hospital of New Jersey at Newark Beth Israel Medical Center
Clara Maass Medical Center
Jersey City Medical Center
Monmouth Medical Center
PSE&G Children's Specialized Hospital
Robert Wood Johnson University Hospital New Brunswick
Saint Barnabas Medical Center
The Unterberg Children's Hospital at Monmouth Medical Center

HISTORICAL FINANCIALS

Company Type: Private

Income Statement   FYE: June 30

	REVENUE ($mil)	NET INCOME ($mil)	NET PROFIT MARGIN	EMPLOYEES
06/21*	3,210	324	10.1%	34,000
12/20	5,900	940	15.9%	—
12/19	5,624	602	10.7%	—
12/18	5,351	9	0.2%	—
Annual Growth	(22.5%)	475.5%	—	—

*Fiscal year change

2021 Year-End Financials
Return on assets: 3.0%   Cash ($ mil.): 256
Return on equity: 6.3%
Current Ratio: 1.00

RYMAN HOSPITALITY PROPERTIES, INC.

Ryman Hospitality Properties (formerly Gaylord Entertainment) is a leading lodging and hospitality real estate investment trust that specializes in upscale convention center resorts and country music entertainment experiences. It includes the Gaylord Opryland Resort & Convention Center in Nashville, the Gaylord Palms Resort in Florida (close to Disney World), the Gaylord Texan Resort near Dallas, and the Gaylord National Resort and Convention Center in the Washington, DC, area. Ryman owned assets include a network of five upscale, meetings-focused resorts totaling over 9,915 rooms that are managed by Marriott under the Gaylord Hotels brand.

Operations

Ryman organized its operations into three principal business segments ? Hospitality, Entertainment, and Corporate and Other (no significant sales percentage) ? represented about 85%, and around 15%, respectively.

Its Hospitality segment includes the Gaylord Hotels branded hotels, the Inn at Opryland and the AC Hotel. Each of the Company's Gaylord Hotels properties is managed by Marriott pursuant to a management agreement for each hotel. The Entertainment segment includes the Grand Ole Opry, the Ryman Auditorium, WSM-AM, Ole Red, the General Jackson, the Wildhorse Saloon, Gaylord Springs, and the Company's investment in the Circle joint venture, among various others. Marriott manages the day-to-day operations of the General Jackson, Gaylord Springs and the Wildhorse Saloon pursuant to management agreements. The Corporate and Other segment includes operating and general and administrative expenses related to the overall management of the company which are not allocated to the other reportable segments, including certain costs for its retirement plans, equity-based compensation plans, information technology, human resources, accounting, and other administrative expenses.

Rooms accounts for some 35%, followed by food and beverage (some 30%); and the remaining accounts for entertainment and other hotel revenues.

Geographic Reach

Ryman Hospitality has properties in Tennessee, Maryland, Texas, Colorado and Florida. Its corporate office is located in Nashville, Tennessee.

Sales and Marketing

The company's advertising costs were $36.2 million, $23.0 million, and $53.2 million for 2021, 2020, and 2019, respectively.

Financial Performance

The company's revenue in 2021 increased by 79% to $939.4 million compared with $524.5 million in the prior year. The increase in its total revenues during 2021, as compared to 2020, is attributable to increases in its Hospitality segment and Entertainment segment revenues of $320.5 million and $94.4 million, respectively.

Net loss in 2021 decreased to $194.8 million compared with $460.8 million in the prior year, due to the increase in total operating expenses during 2021, as compared to 2020, is primarily the result of increases in Hospitality segment, Entertainment segment, and Corporate and Other segment expenses of $148.1 million, $39.5 million, and $9.8 million, respectively.

Cash held by the company at the end of fiscal 2021 increased to $163.0 million. Operating and financing activities provided $111.3 million and $261.7 million, respectively. Investing activities used $289.7 million, mainly for purchase of additional interest in Gaylord Rockies joint venture.

Strategy

The company's goal is to be the nation's premier hospitality REIT for group-oriented, destination hotel assets in urban and resort markets. To achieve this goal, the following strategies must be met.

Existing Hotel Property Design - Its Gaylord Hotels properties focus on the large group meetings market in the United States and incorporate meeting and exhibition space, signature guest rooms, food and beverage offerings, fitness and spa facilities and other attractions within a large hotel property so attendees' needs are met in one location. This strategy creates a better experience for both meeting planners and guests, and has led to its current Gaylord Hotels properties claiming a place among the leading convention hotels in the country.

Expansion of Hotel Asset Portfolio - While its short-term capital allocation strategy has focused on returning capital to stockholders through the payment of dividends, part of its long-term growth strategy includes acquisitions of other hotels, particularly in the group meetings sector of the hospitality industry, either alone or through joint ventures or alliances with one or more third parties. It intends to pursue attractive investment opportunities which meet its acquisition parameters, specifically, group-oriented large hotels and overflow hotels with existing or potential leisure appeal.

Continued investment in its existing properties. The company continuously evaluate and invest in its current portfolio, and consider enhancements or expansions as part of its long-term strategic plan. In 2021, Ryman completed its $158 million expansion of Gaylord Palms and the company also completed its renovation of all of the guestrooms at Gaylord National.

Leverage Brand Name Awareness - The company believes the Grand Ole Opry is one of the most recognized entertainment brands in the US. It promotes the Grand Ole Opry name through various media, including its WSM-AM radio station, the Internet and television, and through performances by the Grand Ole Opry's members, many of whom are renowned country music artists. As such, it has alliances in place with multiple distribution partners in an effort to foster brand extension. It believes that licensing its brand for products may provide an opportunity to increase revenues and cash flow with relatively little capital investment. It is continuously exploring additional products, such as television specials and retail products, through which it can capitalize on its brand affinity and awareness. To this end, it has invested in four Blake Shelton-themed multi-level bar, music venue and event spaces in Nashville, Orlando, Gatlinburg Tennessee, and Tishomingo Oklahoma, named after the Shelton hit "Ol' Red," and invested in Circle.

Short-Term Capital Allocation ? Prior to the COVID-19 pandemic, its short-term capital allocation strategy focused on returning capital to stockholders through the payment of dividends, in addition to investing in its assets and operations.

Mergers and Acquisitions
In late 2021, Ryman Hospitality Properties, Inc. reached an agreement with Stratus Properties Inc. (NASDAQ: STRS) to acquire Block 21, a mixed-use entertainment, lodging, office, and retail complex located in downtown Austin, Texas, for a total purchase price of $260 million. This acquisition allows Ryman to have a meaningful presence in two of the most dynamic music cities in this country and presents many opportunities to showcase the unique music cultures in each city to millions of fans through its Circle TV network.

HISTORY

The origins of Gaylord Entertainment can be traced back to the Oklahoma Publishing Co., a newspaper publishing company founded by Edward K. Gaylord, Ray Dickinson, and Roy McClintock in 1903. The publisher of The Daily Oklahoman, Oklahoma Publishing branched into radio in 1928 with the purchase of Oklahoma City radio station WKY. With its 1949 creation of Oklahoma City television station WKY-TV, Oklahoma Publishing made the leap into television.

Edward K. Gaylord died in 1974 at the age of 101, and his son, Edward L. Gaylord, was appointed CEO. Under his leadership, the company purchased Opryland USA in 1983 -- an acquisition that netted it the Grand Ole Opry, Opryland Themepark, and the Opryland Hotel. Opryland USA also launched country music cable network The Nashville Network that year.

In 1991 the increasingly diverse Oklahoma Publishing spun off its entertainment and broadcast holdings in the form of public company Gaylord Entertainment, which established its headquarters in Nashville, Tennessee. Gaylord Entertainment acquired a majority interest in cable music network Country Music Television (CMT) the same year. It later expanded CMT into Latin America, Asia, and the Pacific Rim. CMT also made a brief foray into Europe, but that initiative was ended in 1998.

Facing a consolidating entertainment and media landscape, Gaylord sold The Nashville Network and the US operations of CMT to Westinghouse (now CBS) in 1997. It also sold television station KSTW that year. The company expanded its reach into Christian music with the purchase of Word Entertainment, and its 1997 acquisition of Blanton Harrell Entertainment gave Gaylord a presence in artist management. Terry London was appointed CEO in 1997.

The company closed its Opryland theme park in 1998 in the face of declining attendance and broke ground at the same site for the Opry Mills entertainment, shopping, and restaurant complex (opened 2000). Gaylord also purchased a Nashville Ramada Inn in 1998 (later renaming it Radisson Hotel at Opryland). With its 1998 acquisition of Paris-based Pandora Investment, Gaylord branched into film distribution.

In 1999 the company formed Opryland Hospitality Group to oversee expansion of the Opryland hotel concept across the US. It also sold its last television station, KTVT in Dallas/Fort Worth, to CBS. Edward K. Gaylord II succeeded his father as chairman in 1999. That year the company launched its Internet division, GETdigitalmedia (later renamed Gaylord Digital), and moved online with the purchase of Christian Web sites Musicforce.com and Lightsource.com. Later the same year the company expanded its Internet presence with the purchase of Songs.com, a music Web site focused on independent artists. But in late 2000 the company announced it would close its Internet unit. Also in 2000 the company bought Corporate Magic, a firm focused on producing entertainment events for corporate audiences.

At the end of 2000, Gaylord sold Musicforce.com to Christian Book Distributors. Following that sale, it sold Lightsource.com to LifeAudio.com in early 2001. That year the company sold its film and television production units and announced a restructuring in order to cut costs. It also renamed Opryland Hotels to Gaylord Opryland while expanding into Texas and Florida. Colin Reed was appointed CEO in 2001.

Between 2001 and 2003 Gaylord Entertainment sold Word Entertainment to Warner Music Group, the Opry Mills shopping and restaurant complex to The Mills Corporation, the Acuff-Rose Music Publishing business to Sony/ATV, two of its Nashville radio stations to Cumulus Media, and its majority interest in the Oklahoma City Redhawks minor league baseball team.

Edward L. Gaylord officially retired from the company in 2003 at age 83. Also that year the company significantly expanded its hospitality business with the purchase of ResortQuest, a vacation and condominium property management firm. In 2004 the Gaylord family sold more than half its shares in the company, making Gabelli Funds the majority owner.

In 2005 Gaylord acquired 50% of Corporate Magic, a Dallas-based provider of production support for corporate meetings and events. It did so to support its meeting and convention facilities.

The company unloaded its minority interest in minor league hockey team the Nashville Predators in 2005. Two years later it sold ResortQuest to a subsidiary of Leucadia National Corp. for $35 million. Also in 2007 it sold its interest in sporting goods store operator Bass Pro Group. In 2008 the company opened the Gaylord National Resort and Convention Center in the Washington, DC, area. The property has some 2,000 rooms and approximately 450,000 square feet of meeting space.

Also in 2008 Gaylord terminated plans to acquire the Westin La Cantera Resort in San Antonio for about $253 million, citing a tough economic environment. In addition, the 2008 sale of its ResortQuest subsidiary, an online booking service in vacation rentals, property management, and resort real estate sales, fit the company's strategy of selling off assets that aren't related to its Grand Ole Opry or its operations in the meetings and convention market.

In 2009 the company responded to weak earnings by cutting approximately 500 jobs across all areas of the business. Gaylord reported steep dip in profits in 2010, primarily due to harsh flooding in Nashville, when the Cumberland River rose to historic levels, flowing over protective levees. The flood resulted in property damage and temporary closures at its properties in Nashville, causing lost revenues and an increase in expenses. Also in 2010 Gaylord sold its 50% stake in Corporate Magic back to that company's CEO.

The company changed its name to Ryman Hospitality Properties in 2012. It also converted to an REIT and sold the Gaylord brand to Marriott, which now manages Ryman's hotel properties and certain other entertainment holdings.

EXECUTIVES

Corporate Controller, Jennifer Hutcheson
Senior Vice President Asset Management, Patrick Chaffin
Auditors : ERNST & YOUNG LLP NASHVILLE

LOCATIONS

HQ: RYMAN HOSPITALITY PROPERTIES, INC.
1 GAYLORD DR, NASHVILLE, TN 372141207
Phone: 615 316-6000
Web: WWW.RYMANHP.COM

PRODUCTS/OPERATIONS

2015 Sales

	$ mil.	% of total
Hospitality	994.6	91
Entertainment (previously Opry and Attractions)	97.5	9
Total	1,092.1	100

2015 Sales

	$ mil.	% of total
Food and beverage	461.1	42
Rooms	404.5	37
Other hotel revenue	129.0	12
Entertainment (previously Opry and Attractions)	97.5	9
Total	1,092.1	100

Select Operations
Hospitality
    Gaylord Opryland Resort & Convention Center (Tennessee)
    Gaylord Palms Resort & Convention Center (Florida)
    Gaylord Texan Resort & Convention Center
    Radisson Hotel at Opryland (Tennessee)
Attractions
    Gaylord Springs Golf Links (golf club, Tennessee)
    General Jackson Showboat
    Grand Ole Opry
    Ryman Auditorium
    Wildhorse Saloon
    WSM-AM

COMPETITORS

AMERICAN VANTAGE COMPANIES
BOYD GAMING CORPORATION
CAESARS HOLDINGS, INC.
CARLSON, INC.
HILTON WORLDWIDE HOLDINGS INC.
HOST HOTELS & RESORTS, INC.
HYATT HOTELS CORPORATION
MARRIOTT INTERNATIONAL, INC.
MGM RESORTS INTERNATIONAL
SIX FLAGS ENTERTAINMENT CORPORATION

HISTORICAL FINANCIALS
Company Type: Private

Income Statement   FYE: December 31

	ASSETS ($mil)	NET INCOME ($mil)	INCOME AS % OF ASSETS	EMPLOYEES
12/16	2,405	159	6.6%	177,000
12/15	2,331	111	4.8%	—
12/14	2,413	126	5.2%	—
12/13	2,424	113	4.7%	—
Annual Growth	(0.3%)	12.0%	—	—

2016 Year-End Financials
Return on assets: 6.6%   Cash ($ mil.): 59
Return on equity: 43.3%
Current Ratio: —

S & B ENGINEERS AND CONSTRUCTORS, LTD.

S & B Engineers and Constructors (S&B) is one of the leading US-based contractors, providing its clients with true in-house engineering, procurement and direct-hire construction services to multiple industries. It primarily focuses on NGL fractionation, import / export terminals, pipelines, petrochemicals & polymers and refining. S&B is the leading American contractor when it comes to the execution of turnkey engineering, procurement and construction (EPC) of export terminals for ethane, propane and other natural gas liquids, as well as various refined products and petrochemicals. Founded in 1967, S&B remains a privately-held, family-owned company.

Operations
Its primary focus is on NGL fractionation, import / export terminals, pipelines, petrochemicals & polymers and refining.

It also has strong, recent experience with projects focused on converting natural gas liquids (NGLs) into high-value petrochemical feedstocks. This includes ethane cracking as well as propane dehydrogenation (PDH).

S&B has expertise in all major areas of an export terminal, such as product receiving, pre-processing, liquification, product loading (including barge, rail or truck), docks and jetties, products storage (including cryogenic, refrigerated and atmospheric tanks, as well as bullets and spheres) and associated utilities and offsites.

Geographic Reach
Houston-based S&B has offices in Texas (7), Louisiana (5), North Carolina, (1), South Carolina (1), Tennessee (1), Pennsylvania (1), and Missouri (1).

Sales and Marketing
The company primarily serves oil, gas and chemicals, energy, power, industrial, transportation, public works, federal and marine industries.

Auditors : ERNST & YOUNG LLP HOUSTON TX

LOCATIONS

HQ: S & B ENGINEERS AND CONSTRUCTORS, LTD.
7825 PARK PLACE BLVD, HOUSTON, TX 770874697
Phone: 713 645-4141
Web: WWW.SBEC.COM

Selected Locations
US
    Austin, TX
    Baton Rouge, LA (2)
    El Paso, TX
    Fort Worth, TX
    Freeport, TX
    Greenville, SC
    Houston
    Longview, TX
    McAllen, TX
    Monroe, LA
    New Orleans
    San Antonio
India
    Bangalore
    New Delhi

PRODUCTS/OPERATIONS

Selected Projects
Sulfur Tailgas Treating Unit, Blaine, WA
Crude Upgrade Project, El Segundo, CA
Pipeline Terminal Project, Los Angeles, CA
Refinery Revamp Project, Bakersfield, CA
Fractionation Expansion Project, Billings, MT
Gas Plant Project, Meeker, CO
SMR Project, Port Arthur, TX
ABF Program, BP Refinery, Texas City
Low Sulfur Gasoline & Diesel Projects, Houston, TX
Fine Paper Machine Project, Kingsport, TN

Selected Services
Construction
Engineering
Modules and skids
Plant services
Procurement
Project management

Selected Divisions
Ford, Bacon & Davis
S&B India
S&B Infrastructure
S&B Plant Services
S&B Power Division

COMPETITORS

ARB, INC.
BECHTEL GROUP, INC.
CHIYODA CORPORATION
Cno S/A
FURMANITE, LLC
HDR, INC.
LAGAN CONSTRUCTION LIMITED
ORION GROUP HOLDINGS, INC.
PC CONSTRUCTION COMPANY
TEAM, INC.

HISTORICAL FINANCIALS
Company Type: Private

Income Statement   FYE: December 31

	REVENUE ($mil)	NET INCOME ($mil)	NET PROFIT MARGIN	EMPLOYEES
12/18	679	0	0.0%	7,000
12/17	679	0	0.0%	—
12/16	950	0	0.0%	—
Annual Growth	(15.4%)	—	—	—

2018 Year-End Financials
Return on assets: —   Cash ($ mil.): 59
Return on equity: —
Current Ratio: 1.50

SACRAMENTO CITY UNIFIED SCHOOL DISTRICT

Auditors : CROWE LLP SACRAMENTO CALIFOR

LOCATIONS

HQ: SACRAMENTO CITY UNIFIED SCHOOL DISTRICT
5735 47TH AVE, SACRAMENTO, CA 958244528
Phone: 916 643-7400
Web: WWW.SCUSD.EDU

HISTORICAL FINANCIALS
Company Type: Private

Income Statement   FYE: June 30

	REVENUE ($mil)	NET INCOME ($mil)	NET PROFIT MARGIN	EMPLOYEES
06/21	760	7	1.0%	6,500
06/20	695	5	0.8%	—
06/19	690	(57)	—	—
06/18	635	(45)	—	—
Annual Growth	6.2%	—	—	—

SACRAMENTO MUNICIPAL UTILITY DISTRICT

The Sacramento Municipal Utility District (SMUD) doesn't want its name to be mud. One of the largest locally owned electric utilities in the US, SMUD serves more than 640,710 residential and commercial customer meters (a service area population of approximately 1.5 million) in California's Sacramento and Placer counties. SMUD is responsible for the acquisition, generation, transmission and distribution of electric power to its service area. It began serving Sacramento in 1946.

Operations
The utility operates more than 10,910 miles of transmission and distribution lines across its 900-sq.-mi. service area. It gets power from varied sources including hydropower, natural-gas-fired generators, renewable energy (such as solar and wind power), and purchases power on the wholesale market.

The company has installed some 600,000 smart meters at customer locations across its entire service area.

Geographic Reach
SMUD generates, transmits, and distributes electricity to a territory that includes Sacramento, Sacramento County, and a small portion of Placer and Yolo Counties.

Sales and Marketing
The company has over 640,710 customer contracts in some 1.5 million service area population.

Financial Performance
SMUD's revenue is $1.6 billion, similar to the previous year due to fluctuations in the company's segment revenues. Cash and cash equivalents at the end of the year were $308.1 million, 21% higher than in the previous year. Cash provided by operating activities was $415.9 million. Financing activities and investing activities used $313.7 million and $4.1 million, respectively. Main cash uses were repayments of commercial paper, construction expenditures, and purchases of securities.

Strategy
In 2019, SMUD continued its partnership with Habitat for Humanity by establishing a 2-year partnership to incentivize electrification and EV-ready homes and install rooftop solar. Building electrification programs resulted in a partnership with D.R. Horton to build more than 100 new all-electric homes. And through SMUD's Smart Homes Program, SMUD received commitments from local and national homebuilders to build approximately 1,900 new all electric homes by the end of 2022. SMUD has continued to grow its Greenergy program and is now one of the largest of its kind in the nation. Through its economic development program, SMUD played a key role in the attraction, retention and expansion of several companies in its service territory, which led to the creation of over 700 jobs.

As part of the hydro relicensing process, SMUD entered into long-term contracts to provide certain services to four different government agencies ? U.S. Department of Interior Bureau of Land Management, U.S. Department of Agriculture Forest Service, El Dorado County, and the California Department of Parks and Recreation. On Dec. 31, 2019 and 2018, the liability for these contract payments was $63.4 million and $58.8 million, respectively.

SMUD also has a long-term agreement with the Western Area Power Administration (WAPA) to purchase power generated by the Central Valley Project, a series of federal hydroelectric facilities operated by the U.S. Bureau of Reclamation.

Company Background
In 2012 SMUD announced that it is the leading utility in the US in terms of new homes which had solar panels installed during construction. The utility commenced the SMUD Solar Smart Homes program in 2006 and had constructed more than 1,000 homes with solar panels by 2012.

The company has been delivering power to customers in the region since 1946, but its history goes back to 1923, when citizens voted to create SMUD as a community-owned electric service. However, years of engineering studies, political battles and legal wrangling delayed SMUD's purchase of PG&E' s local electrical system.

In March 1946, the California Supreme Court denied PG&E's final petition to halt the sale, and nine months later SMUD finally began operations.

Auditors: BAKER TILLY US LLP MADISON

LOCATIONS
HQ: SACRAMENTO MUNICIPAL UTILITY DISTRICT
6201 S ST, SACRAMENTO, CA 958171818
Phone: 916 452-3211
Web: WWW.SMUD.ORG

PRODUCTS/OPERATIONS

2015 Sales

	% of total
Commercial & industrial	47
Residential	42
Wholesale power	6
Street lighting & other	5
Total	100

Selected Products and Services
Conservation programs
Customer billing programs
Diagnostic services
Electric vehicle charging stations
Energy assistance programs
Energy-efficient appliances and equipment
Energy management
Green energy programs
Power quality and environmental services
Security lighting
Shade trees for customers
Solar water heating
Surge protection
Tree trimming

COMPETITORS
CONSUMERS ENERGY COMPANY
GEORGIA POWER COMPANY
OMAHA PUBLIC POWER DISTRICT
PG&E CORPORATION
PINNACLE WEST CAPITAL CORPORATION
PPL ELECTRIC UTILITIES CORPORATION
PUBLIC SERVICE COMPANY OF NEW HAMPSHIRE
PUBLIC SERVICE ENTERPRISE GROUP INCORPORATED
PUBLIC UTILITY DISTRICT 1 OF SNOHOMISH COUNTY
TUCSON ELECTRIC POWER COMPANY

HISTORICAL FINANCIALS
Company Type: Private

Income Statement — FYE: December 31

	REVENUE ($mil)	NET INCOME ($mil)	NET PROFIT MARGIN	EMPLOYEES
12/21	1,790	339	19.0%	2,213
12/20	1,587	153	9.7%	—
12/19	1,559	78	5.1%	—
12/18	1,595	209	13.1%	—
Annual Growth	3.9%	17.5%	—	—

2021 Year-End Financials
Return on assets: 4.9%   Cash ($ mil.): 584
Return on equity: 14.8%
Current Ratio: 2.70

SADDLE BUTTE PIPELINE LLC

Auditors: HEIN & ASSOCIATES LLP DENVER

LOCATIONS
HQ: SADDLE BUTTE PIPELINE LLC
858 MAIN AVE UNIT 301, DURANGO, CO 813015496
Phone: 970 375-3150
Web: WWW.SBPIPELINE.COM

HISTORICAL FINANCIALS
Company Type: Private

Income Statement — FYE: December 31

	REVENUE ($mil)	NET INCOME ($mil)	NET PROFIT MARGIN	EMPLOYEES
12/12	689	656	95.2%	30
12/11	69	(10)	—	—
12/10	68	0	0.0%	—
Annual Growth	218.1%	9913.8%	—	—

2012 Year-End Financials
Return on assets: 425.5%   Cash ($ mil.): 144
Return on equity: 433.6%
Current Ratio: 50.40

2021 Year-End Financials
Return on assets: 0.6%   Cash ($ mil.): 297
Return on equity: —
Current Ratio: 3.50

SAINT AGNES MEDICAL CENTER

Protecting and caring for the vulnerable, Saint Agnes continues to ward off death for the patients at Saint Agnes Medical Center. The medical center provides health care to Valley residents of Fresno, California, through a 436-bed acute care hospital. Along with general surgery, the hospital offers a variety of services including asthma management, bariatric surgery (for which it has scored statewide accolades), cardiac rehabilitation, hospice care, and home care. The facility also runs an internal medicine physician residency and a nurses' residency program. Saint Agnes is part of Trinity Health, one of the largest Catholic health care systems in the US.

Operations
Saint Agnes Medical Center is a 436-bed medical campus that has some 2,600 staff members. The system typically logs more than 200 emergency department visits per day.

Geographic Reach
Saint Agnes Medical Center provides care to residents of California's Fresno, Madera, Kings, and Tulare counties.

Financial Performance
In fiscal 2017 (ended June), Saint Agnes Medical Center had operating revenues of $483 million.

Strategy
In 2017 Saint Agnes Medical Center established a graduate medical education program, which offers residency programs for internal medicine physicians and for nurses. As a teaching hospital, the facility is better positioned to attract physicians to its growing community, as well as training new ones who may stick around. Other programs in the works include family practice and emergency medicine physician residencies.

Company Background
The hospital system was established in 1929 by nine Holy Cross Sisters.

Saint Agnes Medical Center sponsors a number of community outreach programs throughout the Valley including adult day care, senior activity programs, health care clinics for the uninsured, and services for poor and homeless women.

LOCATIONS
HQ: SAINT AGNES MEDICAL CENTER
 1303 E HERNDON AVE, FRESNO, CA 937203309
Phone: 559 450-3000
Web: WWW.SAMC.COM

PRODUCTS/OPERATIONS
Selected Programs and Services
Cancer Services
Emergency Services
Endoscopy
Heart & Vascular
Home Health Care
Hospice
Imaging Services
Laboratory Services
Neuroscience
Occupational Health Center
Orthopaedics
Surgery
Palliative Care
Pulmonary Rehabilitation
Women's Services
Wound Care, Hyperbaric Medicine and Amputation Prevention

Selected Facilities
Breast Center
Cancer Center
The California Eye Institute at Saint Agnes
Child Development Center
Home Health and Hospice
Medical Library
Occupational Health Center
Outpatient Surgery North
Satellite Labs
Wound Care, Hyperbaric Medicine, and Amputation Prevention

COMPETITORS
FROEDTERT MEMORIAL LUTHERAN HOSPITAL, INC.
MERCY HEALTH - ST. RITA'S MEDICAL CENTER, LLC
SAINT JOSEPH HOSPITAL, INC
SAINT PETER'S UNIVERSITY HOSPITAL, INC.
THE JOHNS HOPKINS HEALTH SYSTEM CORPORATION

HISTORICAL FINANCIALS
Company Type: Private

Income Statement — FYE: June 30

	REVENUE ($mil)	NET INCOME ($mil)	NET PROFIT MARGIN	EMPLOYEES
06/21	601	67	11.2%	2,400
06/20	530	4	0.9%	—
06/18	513	35	6.9%	—
06/16	486	11	2.3%	—
Annual Growth	4.4%	43.0%	—	—

2021 Year-End Financials
Return on assets: 7.8%   Cash ($ mil.): 1
Return on equity: 11.3%
Current Ratio: 2.40

SAINT ALPHONSUS REGIONAL MEDICAL CENTER INC.

EXECUTIVES
CCO, Steven Nemerson
Auditors: DELOITTE & TOUCHE LLP DETROIT

LOCATIONS
HQ: SAINT ALPHONSUS REGIONAL MEDICAL CENTER INC.
 1055 N CURTIS RD, BOISE, ID 837061309
Phone: 208 367-2121
Web: WWW.SAINTALPHONSUS.ORG

HISTORICAL FINANCIALS
Company Type: Private

Income Statement — FYE: June 30

	REVENUE ($mil)	NET INCOME ($mil)	NET PROFIT MARGIN	EMPLOYEES
06/18	937	50	5.4%	40
06/15	37	(5)	—	—
06/14	29	(5)	—	—
06/11	0	(0)	—	—
Annual Growth	—	—	—	—

2018 Year-End Financials
Return on assets: 4.5%   Cash ($ mil.): 208
Return on equity: 6.8%
Current Ratio: 3.40

SAINT ALPHONSUS REGIONAL MEDICAL CENTER, INC.

Saint Alphonsus Regional Medical Center makes medical care its primary mission. The 384-bed hospital provides Boise, Idaho, and the surrounding region (including eastern Oregon and northern Nevada) with general, acute, and specialized health care services. Its facilities and operations include a level II trauma center, an orthopedic spinal care unit, an air transport service, and a home health and hospice division. Saint Alphonsus Regional Medical Center is part of Trinity Health's four-hospital Saint Alphonsus Health System, which serves Boise and Nampa in Idaho and Ontario and Baker City in Oregon. The Sisters of the Holy Cross founded the hospital in 1894.

Operations
Saint Alphonsus Regional Medical Center provides outpatient services through the 70 affiliated physician practices that make up the Saint Alphonsus Medical Group. It also operates the Saint Alphonsus Health Plaza, which provides urgent care and outpatient surgery, laboratory, rehabilitation, and primary care services.

The hospital also offers rural or homebound patients telemedicine services, through which remote physician visits are conducted using audio or video.

Geographic Reach
Saint Alphonsus Regional Medical Center serves a territory that includes portions of southwestern Idaho, northern Nevada, and eastern Oregon.

Strategy
Saint Alphonsus Regional Medical Center expands its facilities to improve medical care in its service territory. In 2014 it opened its newly expanded and renovated emergency department, which included a 30% increase in square footage. Also that year, it

became the first hospital in the region to utilize the EndoWrist Stapler technology on the da Vinci robotic system for minimally invasive surgeries.

LOCATIONS

HQ: SAINT ALPHONSUS REGIONAL MEDICAL CENTER, INC.
1055 N CURTIS RD, BOISE, ID 837061309
Phone: 208 367-2121
Web: WWW.SAINTALPHONSUS.ORG

COMPETITORS

ASCENSION PROVIDENCE HOSPITAL
GENESYS HEALTH SYSTEM
JEFFERSON HOSPITAL
MERCY HOSPITAL AND MEDICAL CENTER
MOSAIC HEALTH SYSTEM

HISTORICAL FINANCIALS
Company Type: Private

Income Statement — FYE: June 30

	REVENUE ($mil)	NET INCOME ($mil)	NET PROFIT MARGIN	EMPLOYEES
06/14	572	46	8.0%	3,500
06/13	545	43	7.9%	—
06/10	449	13	3.1%	—
Annual Growth	6.2%	35.2%	—	—

2014 Year-End Financials
Return on assets: 6.4%   Cash ($ mil.): 3
Return on equity: 10.6%
Current Ratio: 1.30

SAINT ELIZABETH MEDICAL CENTER, INC.

The primary teach hospital of Tufts University School of Medicine, St. Elizabeth's Medical Center provides health care services to residents in Allston, Boston, Brighton, Brookline, Newton, Watertown and Weston. St. Elizabeth Healthcare's programs include family medicine, cardiovascular care, women and infants' health, cancer care, neurology care, and orthopedics. St. Elizabeth's Medical Center was founded in 1868 by five laywomen members of the third order of St. Francis to care for women from Boston's South End. St. Elizabeth's is a member of Steward Health Care.

LOCATIONS

HQ: SAINT ELIZABETH MEDICAL CENTER, INC.
1 MEDICAL VILLAGE DR, EDGEWOOD, KY 410173403
Phone: 859 301-2000
Web: WWW.STELIZABETH.COM

Selected locations
St. Elizabeth Covington (Covington, Kentucky)
St. Elizabeth Edgewood (Edgewood, Kentucky)
St. Elizabeth Grant (Williamstown, Kentucky)
St. Elizabeth Ft. Thomas (St. Thomas, Kentucky)
St. Elizabeth Florence (Florence, Kentucky)
St. Elizabeth Falmouth (Falmouth, Kentucky)

COMPETITORS

AHS MEDICAL HOLDINGS LLC
CENTURA HEALTH CORPORATION
CHILDREN'S HEALTH CARE
CHILDREN'S HEALTHCARE OF ATLANTA, INC.
COOK CHILDREN'S HEALTH CARE SYSTEM
JOHNS HOPKINS ALL CHILDREN'S HOSPITAL, INC.
ST. FRANCIS HOSPITAL, ROSLYN, NEW YORK
ST. JOHN HEALTH SYSTEM, INC.
ST. MARY'S HEALTH CARE SYSTEM, INC.
ST. VINCENT ANDERSON REGIONAL HOSPITAL, INC.

HISTORICAL FINANCIALS
Company Type: Private

Income Statement — FYE: December 31

	REVENUE ($mil)	NET INCOME ($mil)	NET PROFIT MARGIN	EMPLOYEES
12/19	1,293	130	10.1%	6,227
12/14	633	45	7.1%	—
12/13	984	124	12.7%	—
12/08	623	(32)	—	—
Annual Growth	6.9%	—	—	—

2019 Year-End Financials
Return on assets: 6.0%   Cash ($ mil.): 69
Return on equity: 8.6%
Current Ratio: —

SAINT FRANCIS HEALTHCARE SYSTEM

Auditors: KERBER ECK & BRAECKEL LLP CAR

LOCATIONS

HQ: SAINT FRANCIS HEALTHCARE SYSTEM
211 SAINT FRANCIS DR, CAPE GIRARDEAU, MO 637035049
Phone: 573 331-3000
Web: WWW.SFMC.NET

HISTORICAL FINANCIALS
Company Type: Private

Income Statement — FYE: June 30

	REVENUE ($mil)	NET INCOME ($mil)	NET PROFIT MARGIN	EMPLOYEES
06/22	556	(122)	—	57
06/12	11	8	78.1%	—
Annual Growth	47.9%	—	—	—

2022 Year-End Financials
Return on assets: (-10.5%)   Cash ($ mil.): 68
Return on equity: (-13.8%)
Current Ratio: 1.30

SAINT FRANCIS HOSPITAL, INC.

LOCATIONS

HQ: SAINT FRANCIS HOSPITAL, INC.
6161 S YALE AVE, TULSA, OK 741361992
Phone: 918 502-2050
Web: WWW.SAINTFRANCIS.COM

HISTORICAL FINANCIALS
Company Type: Private

Income Statement — FYE: June 30

	REVENUE ($mil)	NET INCOME ($mil)	NET PROFIT MARGIN	EMPLOYEES
06/16	913	128	14.0%	4,000
06/15	877	171	19.6%	—
06/13	910	190	21.0%	—
06/12	838	157	18.7%	—
Annual Growth	2.2%	(5.0%)	—	—

2016 Year-End Financials
Return on assets: 5.6%   Cash ($ mil.): 312
Return on equity: 6.5%
Current Ratio: 8.90

SAINT JOSEPH HOSPITAL, INC

The goal of Saint Joseph Hospital (formerly Exempla Saint Joseph Hospital) is to give residents of the Mile High City exemplary care. The Denver acute care facility has nearly 400 licensed beds and specializes in areas including cardiovascular disease, cancer, orthopedics, pediatrics, neurology, diagnostics, and high-risk labor and delivery. The Catholic not-for-profit hospital sees about 50,000 emergency department visits annually and employs more than 1,300 physicians. The hospital also offers residency programs in family practice, internal medicine, obstetrics and gynecology, and general surgery. Catholic-sponsored Saint Joseph is part of SCL Health - Front Range.

Operations

Saint Joseph is one of the largest hospitals in the region. The medical center is a regional provider of critical cardiac care, neonatal ICU, orthopedic, and radiation oncology services. Its pediatric ward is a satellite facility of the Children's Hospital Colorado. The Saint Joseph campus also includes three outpatient care clinics that offer charity care, and the hospital conducts outreach programs in neighboring communities.

Altogether, the hospital admits some 20,000 inpatients per year and handles some 150,000 outpatient visits, more than 6,875 inpatients and 6,330 outpatient surgeries. As a not-for-profit entity, Saint Joseph contributes more than 10% of annual revenues to charity care and community service efforts.

Sales and Marketing

Saint Joseph maintains contracts with most Denver-area health plans and is a major admitting hospital for Kaiser Health Plan of Colorado.

Strategy

Saint Joseph has constructed a replacement facility for its aging hospital facilities. The new, $623 million medical center includes 365 beds (primarily in private patient rooms), as well as improved surgery, emergency, and diagnostic centers. The facility provides 826,143 square feet of new diagnostic, treatment and patient care spaces. The new facility specializes in heart and vascular care, cancer treatment, labor and delivery, respiratory health, orthopedics, and emergency care. The hospital was completed in the second half of 2014, with occupancy commencing in early 2015.

In 2013 Saint Joseph announced its intention to form a joint operating agreement with National Jewish Health. Together, the entities plan to collaborate on patient-centered health care methods, as well as education and research programs. The clinical operations of each organization would be jointly managed through the agreement, though the organizations will retain their respective assets.

The hospital is also involved in a federal pilot program designed to decrease the amount of unnecessary testing and treatments that can occur at hospitals by bundling service fees paid by Medicare; the program is managed by the Centers for Medicare and Medicaid Services. Such measures are part of the overall goal of the US health care industry to reduce medical spending.

Company Background

Saint Joseph Hospital merged with Lutheran Medical Center and Exempla Medical Group in 1997 to form Exempla Healthcare. The health network was co-sponsored by the Catholic-based Sisters of Charity of Leavenworth Health System (SCL Health System) and the Lutheran-sponsored Community First Foundation (CFF) until 2012 when SCL Health System acquired CFF's interest in the venture in a deal worth some $275 million. SCLHS had already gained operational oversight of all of the system's hospitals in late 2009.

Saint Joseph Hospital was founded in 1873 by SCL Health System. It was the first private hospital established in Colorado.

EXECUTIVES

CMO, Travis Sewalls

LOCATIONS

HQ: SAINT JOSEPH HOSPITAL, INC
1375 E 19TH AVE, DENVER, CO 802181114
Phone: 303 812-2000
Web: WWW.SCLHEALTH.ORG

PRODUCTS/OPERATIONS

Selected Services
Breast Care Center
Comprehensive Cancer Center
Community Outreach
Construction updates for exempla Saint Joseph Hospital
Electronic Medical Records
Emergency Care
Exemplea's Your Safety+Satisfaction
Family Medicine/Bruner Clinic
Heart Care
Home When Ready
Imaging Center
Intensive Care Unit
Medical Residency Programs
Midwife Practice
NICU-Neonatal Intensive Care Unit
Outpatient Physical Medicine + Rehab
Pediatric Care
Plastic and Reconstructive Surgery
Saint Christopher Inn
The Blood Donor Center
Weight Loss Surgery Center
Women's and Children's Services

COMPETITORS

MERCY HEALTH - ST. RITA'S MEDICAL CENTER, LLC
PROVIDENCE HEALTH & SERVICES-WASHINGTON
ST. AGNES HEALTHCARE, INC.
SWEDISH COVENANT HOSPITAL
THE PENNSYLVANIA HOSPITAL OF THE UNIVERSITY OF PENNSYLVANIA HEALTH SYSTEM

HISTORICAL FINANCIALS
Company Type: Private

Income Statement — FYE: December 31

	REVENUE ($mil)	NET INCOME ($mil)	NET PROFIT MARGIN	EMPLOYEES
12/19	614	48	7.9%	2,300
12/14	465	25	5.5%	—
12/13	490	51	10.5%	—
Annual Growth	3.9%	(1.1%)	—	—

2019 Year-End Financials
Return on assets: 5.8%   Cash ($ mil.): —
Return on equity: 8.3%
Current Ratio: 2.10

SAINT LOUIS UNIVERSITY

This university gives students a SLU of opportunities. Saint Louis University (SLU) is a Jesuit, Catholic school offering nearly 90 undergraduate, more than 100 graduate, and a host of professional degree programs through about a dozen schools and colleges, including a school of medicine and a campus in Madrid, Spain. Most programs require core classes in philosophy and theology. SLU has an enrollment of nearly 12,855 students. Its student-teacher ratio is 9:1. Saint Louis University was founded in 1818 by Reverend Louis William Du Bourg, Catholic Bishop of Louisiana.

Operations

In addition to its extensive educational programs, SLU's students and staff are involved in a number of research projects in areas including cancer, infectious disease, liver disease, aging and brain disorders, and heart/lung disease.

SLU also operates primary and specialty medical care clinics (some through its SLU Physicians organization) on its medical school campus. The university's School of Medicine is fully accredited by the Liaison Committee on Medical Education (LCME), the accrediting body for medical education in the US.

Geographic Reach

SLU's students hail from all 50 US states and more than 80 countries. In addition to its main campus in St. Louis, Missouri, the university operates a campus in Madrid, Spain.

Mergers and Acquisitions

Company Background

Saint Louis University was founded in 1818 by Reverend Louis William Du Bourg, Catholic Bishop of Louisiana.

Auditors: KPMG LLP COLUMBUS OH

LOCATIONS

HQ: SAINT LOUIS UNIVERSITY
3700 W PINE MALL, SAINT LOUIS, MO 631083306
Phone: 314 977-2500
Web: WWW.SLU.EDU

PRODUCTS/OPERATIONS

Colleges, Schools and Degree Granting Centers
Advanced Dental Education, Center for (CADE)
Arts and Sciences, College of
Business, John Cook School of
Education and Public Service, College of
Engineering, Aviation and Technology, Parks College of
Health Care Ethics, Albert Gnaegi Center for
Health Sciences, Doisy College of
Law, School of
Madrid, Spain Campus
Medicine, School of
Nursing, School of
Outcomes Research, Center for (SLUCOR)
Philosophy and Letters, College of
Professional Studies, School for
Public Health, School of
Social Work, School of

COMPETITORS

ABILENE CHRISTIAN UNIVERSITY
CREIGHTON UNIVERSITY
FAIRFIELD UNIVERSITY
GEORGETOWN UNIVERSITY (THE)
NEW MEXICO STATE UNIVERSITY
THE UNIVERSITY OF IOWA
THE UNIVERSITY OF NEW MEXICO
UNIVERSITY OF KANSAS
UNIVERSITY OF OKLAHOMA
UNIVERSITY OF SAN DIEGO

HISTORICAL FINANCIALS
Company Type: Private

Income Statement — FYE: June 30

	REVENUE ($mil)	NET INCOME ($mil)	NET PROFIT MARGIN	EMPLOYEES
06/10	750	28	3.8%	7,500
06/09	697	0	0.0%	—
06/08	633	(54)	—	—
Annual Growth	8.9%	—	—	—

2010 Year-End Financials
Return on assets: 1.7%   Cash ($ mil.): 141
Return on equity: 2.3%
Current Ratio: —

SAINT LUKE'S HEALTH SYSTEM, INC.

As a not-for-profit health system, St. Luke's is dedicated to providing high quality care to every person who comes through its doors. From its founding in 1902, to its establishment as a health system in 2006, to today, St. Luke's has long been a leader in quality care and a vital partner in addressing community health needs. St Luke's has eight medical centers, more than 1,000 beds in some 340 clinics and centers. It performs almost 42,800 surgeries and more than 8,100 births.

Operations
St. Luke's offers a heart transplant program treatment for complex brain and spinal cord diseases, advanced surgical care, and liver and kidney transplantation programs. Other specialized services include women's health, cancer treatment, rehabilitation, and home care.

St. Luke's Children's Hospital is the only children's hospital in Idaho. More than 150 skilled pediatricians and pediatric specialists work with referring physicians from around the region to provide high quality care. It has a staff of over 400 nurses, therapists, and other dedicated pediatric caregivers.

Geographic Reach
Based in Idaho, St. Luke's has operations Southern and Central Idaho, Eastern Oregon and Northern Nevada.

Strategy
St. Luke's is driven by its mission to improve the health of people in the communities it serves, which is grounded in its focus on population and community health. Company's strategy leads us to achieving its vision as it builds upon and enhance its reputation as the community's trusted partner in providing exceptional, patient-centered care.

St. Luke's strategy follows a clearly defined path: St. Luke are meeting people where they are on their health journey? improving health and lives by delivering exceptional performance and outcomes in quality, access and affordability.

Company Background
The predecessor to Saint Luke's Hospital was founded in 1882 by Episcopal priest Henry David Jardine.

EXECUTIVES
Interim Chief Executive Officer, Cliff A Robertson
Chief Quality Officer*, William C Daniel
Auditors : ERNST & YOUNG LLP KANSAS CITY

LOCATIONS
HQ: SAINT LUKE'S HEALTH SYSTEM, INC.
901 E 104TH ST, KANSAS CITY, MO 641314517

Phone: 816 932-2000
Web: WWW.SAINTLUKESKC.ORG

PRODUCTS/OPERATIONS
2015 Sales

	$ mil	% of total
Hospital	1,501.1	61
Other university	962.1	39
Total	2,463.2	100

Selected facilities
Anderson County Hospital (Garnett, Kansas)
Crittenton Children's Center (Kansas City, Missouri)
Hedrick Medical Center (Chillicothe, Missouri)
Saint Luke's Cushing Hospital (Leavenworth, Kansas)
Saint Luke's East (Lee's Summit, Missouri)
Saint Luke's Hospital (Kansas City, Missouri)
Saint Luke's Northland Hospital (Kansas City, Missouri)
Saint Luke's Northland Hospital (Smithville, Missouri)
Saint Luke's South (Overland Park, Kansas)
Wright Memorial Hospital (Trenton, Missouri)

Selected Services
Cancer services
Heart and vascular
Home care and hospice
Neuroscience
Surgical services
Transplant services
Women's and maternity services

COMPETITORS
CATHOLIC HEALTH SYSTEM, INC.
DENVER HEALTH AND HOSPITALS AUTHORITY
HENRY FORD HEALTH SYSTEM
KENNEDY HEALTH SYSTEM, INC.
PROVIDENCE HEALTH & SERVICES
SAINT JOSEPH HOSPITAL, INC
ST. JOHN'S HOSPITAL OF THE HOSPITAL SISTERS OF THE THIRD ORDER OF ST. FRANCIS
ST. LUKE'S HEALTH SYSTEM, LTD.
ST. VINCENT ANDERSON REGIONAL HOSPITAL, INC.
WILLIAM BEAUMONT HOSPITAL

HISTORICAL FINANCIALS
Company Type: Private

Income Statement — FYE: December 31

	REVENUE ($mil)	NET INCOME ($mil)	NET PROFIT MARGIN	EMPLOYEES
12/21	2,367	278	11.8%	5,111
12/20	2,153	156	7.3%	—
12/19	2,100	131	6.3%	—
12/18	1,901	42	2.2%	—
Annual Growth	7.6%	87.4%	—	—

2021 Year-End Financials
Return on assets: 7.8%   Cash ($ mil.): 668
Return on equity: 13.8%
Current Ratio: 2.40

SAINT LUKE'S HOSPITAL OF BETHLEHEM, PENNSYLVANIA

Auditors : WITHUMSMITHBROWN PC WHIPPANY

LOCATIONS
HQ: SAINT LUKE'S HOSPITAL OF BETHLEHEM, PENNSYLVANIA
801 OSTRUM ST, BETHLEHEM, PA 180151000
Phone: 484 526-4000
Web: WWW.SLHN.ORG

HISTORICAL FINANCIALS
Company Type: Private

Income Statement — FYE: June 30

	REVENUE ($mil)	NET INCOME ($mil)	NET PROFIT MARGIN	EMPLOYEES
06/22	1,406	117	8.3%	5,580
06/21	1,272	309	24.3%	—
06/20	982	40	4.2%	—
06/19	956	205	21.4%	—
Annual Growth	13.7%	(17.0%)	—	—

2022 Year-End Financials
Return on assets: 4.3%   Cash ($ mil.): 258
Return on equity: 13.0%
Current Ratio: 1.50

SAINT LUKE'S HOSPITAL OF KANSAS CITY

Auditors : ERNST & YOUNG LLP KANSAS CITY

LOCATIONS
HQ: SAINT LUKE'S HOSPITAL OF KANSAS CITY
4401 WORNALL RD, KANSAS CITY, MO 641113241
Phone: 816 932-2000
Web: WWW.SAINTLUKESKC.ORG

HISTORICAL FINANCIALS
Company Type: Private

Income Statement — FYE: December 31

	REVENUE ($mil)	NET INCOME ($mil)	NET PROFIT MARGIN	EMPLOYEES
12/18	803	4	0.5%	5,000
12/17	699	63	9.1%	—
12/16	641	26	4.1%	—
12/15	561	0	0.0%	—
Annual Growth	12.7%	198.0%	—	—

2018 Year-End Financials
Return on assets: 0.3%   Cash ($ mil.): 33
Return on equity: 0.5%
Current Ratio: 3.10

SAINT MARYS HOSPITAL

LOCATIONS
HQ: SAINT MARYS HOSPITAL
1216 2ND ST SW, ROCHESTER, MN 559021970

Phone: 507 255-5123
Web: WWW.MAYOCLINIC.ORG

HISTORICAL FINANCIALS
Company Type: Private

Income Statement   FYE: December 31

	REVENUE ($mil)	NET INCOME ($mil)	NET PROFIT MARGIN	EMPLOYEES
12/16	2,091	556	26.6%	3,250
12/15	1,963	503	25.6%	—
Annual Growth	6.6%	10.6%	—	—

2016 Year-End Financials
Return on assets: 27.3%   Cash ($ mil.): —
Return on equity: 33.4%
Current Ratio: 4.10

SAINT PAUL PUBLIC SCHOOLS, DISTRICT 625

Auditors : MALLOY MONTAGUE KARNOWSKI R

LOCATIONS

HQ: SAINT PAUL PUBLIC SCHOOLS, DISTRICT 625
360 COLBORNE ST, SAINT PAUL, MN 551023228
Phone: 651 767-8100
Web: WWW.SPPS.ORG

HISTORICAL FINANCIALS
Company Type: Private

Income Statement   FYE: June 30

	REVENUE ($mil)	NET INCOME ($mil)	NET PROFIT MARGIN	EMPLOYEES
06/21	790	30	3.9%	6,500
06/20	743	125	16.9%	—
06/19	732	(83)	—	—
06/18	711	17	2.5%	—
Annual Growth	3.6%	19.7%	—	—

2021 Year-End Financials
Return on assets: 2.2%   Cash ($ mil.): —
Return on equity: —
Current Ratio: 3.10

SALEM HEALTH

Salem Hospital serves the healthcare needs of residents in and around Oregon's Willamette Valley. The acute care hospital boasts about 455 beds and a medical staff of 440-plus physicians that represents some 45 specialty areas, such as oncology, joint replacement, obstetrics, diabetes, weight loss, and mental health, among others. The not-for-profit hospital offers a range of services from emergency and critical care to rehabilitation and community wellness programs. Its Center for Outpatient Medicine provides cancer care, outpatient surgery, and imaging services and has a sleep disorders center. Salem Hospital is part of Salem Health, which also includes West Valley Hospital and Willamette Health Partners.

Operations

The Oregon hospital also has a Family Birth Center that offers family-health education services and neonatal intensive-care services. Additionally, it provides space to community support services to benefit families.

Salem Hospital operates under the guidance of a 15-member volunteer Board of Trustees.

Strategy

As with many healthcare institutions in this age of reform, Salem Hospital is working hard to improve patient experience and the quality of healthcare it provides while reducing the cost of care and eliminating waste within its systems. It has been improving clinical documentation to ensure payments are received, standardizing care processes, improving scheduling of surgeries, leaving 30 open positions unfilled, and cutting another 30 positions.

Inspired by Toyota's lean production processes, the hospital entered into a five-year contract with John Black and Associates in 2010 to begin what it projects to be a transformation that will be accomplished incrementally over the next 20 years. Its goal is to improve care using a holistic, patient-centered approach and reduce waste in terms of waits, inventory, and other day-to-day processes.

Salem Hospital set a goal of becoming a Magnet hospital in 2003 and accomplished the feat in 2010. (Only 6% of hospitals in the US have achieved Magnet status.) Magnet certification is awarded to hospitals that meet a set of criteria that measures the quality and strength of their nursing staffs as set by the American Nurses' Credentialing Center, an affiliate of the American Nurses Association. Criteria includes patient outcomes, job satisfaction, and low turnover.

In 2009 the hospital opened a new patient tower. In 2010 it sold its money-losing home care department to LHC Group as a way of cutting operating costs.

Auditors : KPMG LLP PORTLAND OREGON

LOCATIONS

HQ: SALEM HEALTH
890 OAK ST SE, SALEM, OR 973013905
Phone: 503 561-5200
Web: WWW.SALEMHEALTH.ORG

PRODUCTS/OPERATIONS

Selected Services
Bariatrics
Cancer
Diabetes
Gynecology
Heart
Joint replacement
Neurosciences
Obstetrics
Orthopedics
Pain management
Psychiatric medicine
Psychology
Rehabilitation
Spine
Sleep
Stroke
Weight-loss surgery
Wound care

COMPETITORS

CKHS, INC.
GREENWICH PERINATOLOGY SERVICES, P.C.
JOHN T. MATHER MEMORIAL HOSPITAL OF PORT JEFFERSON, NEW YORK, INC.
JUPITER MEDICAL CENTER, INC.
KINGSBROOK JEWISH MEDICAL CENTER
NORTH SHORE UNIVERSITY HOSPITAL
NORTHSHORE UNIVERSITY HEALTHSYSTEM
TALLAHASSEE MEMORIAL HEALTHCARE, INC.
THE METROHEALTH SYSTEM
THE RUTLAND HOSPITAL INC ACT 220

HISTORICAL FINANCIALS
Company Type: Private

Income Statement   FYE: June 30

	REVENUE ($mil)	NET INCOME ($mil)	NET PROFIT MARGIN	EMPLOYEES
06/21	953	241	25.3%	3,400
06/20	864	75	8.7%	—
06/19	820	86	10.5%	—
06/18	773	99	12.8%	—
Annual Growth	7.2%	34.6%	—	—

2021 Year-End Financials
Return on assets: 11.8%   Cash ($ mil.): 36
Return on equity: 17.8%
Current Ratio: 1.10

SALT RIVER PROJECT AGRICULTURAL IMPROVEMENT AND POWER DISTRICT

One of the United States' largest government-owned utilities, Salt River Project (SRP) provides Phoenix with two types of currents: electric and water. Electricity comes from the Salt River Project Agricultural Improvement and Power District, a political subdivision of the State of Arizona. It operates the Salt River Project, a federal reclamation project, under contracts with the Salt River Valley Water Users' Association, including its obligations to the United States of America for the care, operation and maintenance of the project. The district owns and operates an electric system that generates, purchases, transmits and distributes electric power and energy, and provides electric service to residential, commercial, industrial and agricultural power users in parts of Maricopa,

Gila and Pinal counties. The district sells excess power to wholesale customers.

Operations
Staying true to its mission of providing water and electricity to SRP customers, the company owns or has stakes in about 15 major power generating plants fueled by diverse sources, including nuclear, fuel and steam. SPR also operates several dams along the Salt and Verde River and the canal system that produce electricity. SRP's portfolio of renewable energy sources includes solar, geothermal, wind, and biomass.

Some 85% of sales were generated from its retail electric.

Geographic Reach
Headquartered in Arizona, the company serves residential, commercial, industrial and agricultural power customers in a 2,900-square-mile service territory spanning parts of Maricopa, Gila, and Pinal counties in Arizona. In addition, the enterprise has mining loads in an adjacent 2,400-square-mile area in Gila and Pinal counties.

The SRP electric service area includes major portions of the cities of Apache Junction, Avondale, Chandler, Fountain Hills, Gilbert, Glendale, Guadalupe, Mesa, Paradise Valley, Peoria, Phoenix, Queen Creek, Scottsdale, Tempe, and Tolleson.

Sales and Marketing
SRP serves more than 1 million customers in the greater Phoenix metropolitan area.

Financial Performance
Operating revenues were $3.5 billion for fiscal year 2021 and $3.1 billion for fiscal year 2020, an increase of $354.1 million, or 11%. The increase in operating revenues was primarily due to increased retail electric and wholesale revenues.

In 2020, the company had a net income of $283.5 million, a $266.2 million increase from the previous year's net income of $17.3 million.

Strategy
SRP delivered a successful financial performance in FY21, including positive CNR results primarily driven by above-normal temperatures, strong customer growth and a focus on managing direct costs. Capital spending was 3% above budget as demand remained strong for new construction during the pandemic. Direct cost savings are 4% below the revised budget, or 8% below the original FY21 budget, due to initial expense reductions and continued savings throughout the fiscal year.

SRP reliably met customers' power needs during an intense summer that included an all-time system record peak demand and two major wildfires that threatened key transmission lines and other infrastructure. The entire West was dealing with these challenging conditions at the same time, critically stressing energy availability. SRP's customers continued to receive power during this period and throughout the year with a level of reliability among the best in the nation.

Company Background
SRP was founded in 1903 under the Natural Reclamation Act.

EXECUTIVES
Corporate Secretary, Stephanie Reed
Corporate Treasurer, Steven Hulet
Auditors : PRICEWATERHOUSECOOPERS LLP PH

LOCATIONS
HQ: SALT RIVER PROJECT AGRICULTURAL IMPROVEMENT AND POWER DISTRICT
 1500 N MILL AVE, TEMPE, AZ 852881252
Phone: 602 236-5900
Web: WWW.SRPNET.COM

PRODUCTS/OPERATIONS
2016 Sales
	$ mil.	% of total
Retail electric	2,749.1	90
Water	15.9	1
Other	282.3	9
Total	3,047.3	100

Selected Subsidiaries
Salt River Project Agricultural Improvement and Power District (electric utility)
 New West Energy Corporation (energy support services)
 Papago Park Center, Inc. (real estate facility management)
 SRP Captive Risk Solutions, Ltd. (domestic captive property, boiler, and machinery insurer)
Salt River Valley Water Users' Association

COMPETITORS
ALLETE, INC.
ARIZONA PUBLIC SERVICE COMPANY
GREAT RIVER ENERGY
IMPERIAL IRRIGATION DISTRICT
JACKSONVILLE ELECTRIC AUTHORITY
LOS ANGELES DEPARTMENT OF WATER AND POWER
NORTHWESTERN CORPORATION
ORLANDO UTILITIES COMMISSION (INC)
PUBLIC UTILITY DISTRICT 1 OF SNOHOMISH COUNTY
SACRAMENTO MUNICIPAL UTILITY DISTRICT

HISTORICAL FINANCIALS
Company Type: Private

Income Statement — FYE: April 30

	REVENUE ($mil)	NET INCOME ($mil)	NET PROFIT MARGIN	EMPLOYEES
04/21	3,475	577	16.6%	4,336
04/20*	3,121	126	4.1%	—
01/10	2,217	517	23.3%	—
04/05	2,251	362	16.1%	—
Annual Growth	2.7%	2.9%	—	—

*Fiscal year change

2021 Year-End Financials
Return on assets: 4.1%   Cash ($ mil.): 426
Return on equity: 9.7%
Current Ratio: 1.60

SAMARITAN HEALTH SERVICES, INC.

Auditors : KPMG LLP PORTLAND OREGON

LOCATIONS
HQ: SAMARITAN HEALTH SERVICES, INC.
 3600 NW SAMARITAN DR, CORVALLIS, OR 973305472
Phone: 541 768-5111
Web: WWW.SAMHEALTH.ORG

HISTORICAL FINANCIALS
Company Type: Private

Income Statement — FYE: December 31

	REVENUE ($mil)	NET INCOME ($mil)	NET PROFIT MARGIN	EMPLOYEES
12/21	1,431	48	3.4%	4,550
12/20	1,339	65	4.9%	—
12/19	1,233	32	2.6%	—
12/18	1,168	9	0.8%	—
Annual Growth	7.0%	75.1%	—	—

2021 Year-End Financials
Return on assets: 4.4%   Cash ($ mil.): 288
Return on equity: 9.0%
Current Ratio: 1.90

SAMARITAN'S PURSE

Auditors : DIXON HUGHES GOODMAN LLP CHA

LOCATIONS
HQ: SAMARITAN'S PURSE
 801 BAMBOO RD, BOONE, NC 286078721
Phone: 828 262-1980
Web: WWW.SAMARITANSPURSE.ORG

HISTORICAL FINANCIALS
Company Type: Private

Income Statement — FYE: December 31

	REVENUE ($mil)	NET INCOME ($mil)	NET PROFIT MARGIN	EMPLOYEES
12/20	894	224	25.1%	525
12/19	734	44	6.1%	—
12/18	709	22	3.1%	—
12/17	800	189	23.7%	—
Annual Growth	3.7%	5.7%	—	—

2020 Year-End Financials
Return on assets: 22.6%   Cash ($ mil.): 435
Return on equity: 24.3%
Current Ratio: 11.90

HOOVER'S HANDBOOK OF PRIVATE COMPANIES 2023

SAN ANTONIO INDEPENDENT SCHOOL DISTRICT FAC

Auditors: GARZA/GONZALEZ & ASSOCIATES S

LOCATIONS

HQ: SAN ANTONIO INDEPENDENT SCHOOL DISTRICT FAC
514 W QUINCY ST, SAN ANTONIO, TX 782125163
Phone: 210 554-2200
Web: WWW.SAISD.NET

HISTORICAL FINANCIALS
Company Type: Private

Income Statement — FYE: June 30

	REVENUE ($mil)	NET INCOME ($mil)	NET PROFIT MARGIN	EMPLOYEES
06/19	681	136	20.0%	7,600
06/16	659	43	6.5%	—
06/15	624	(14)	—	—
06/14	600	(110)	—	—
Annual Growth	2.6%	—	—	—

2019 Year-End Financials
Return on assets: 8.0%   Cash ($ mil.): 362
Return on equity: 88.9%
Current Ratio: —

SAN BERNARDINO CITY UNIFIED SCHOOL DISTRICT

Auditors: EIDE BAILLY LLP RANCHO CUCAMO

LOCATIONS

HQ: SAN BERNARDINO CITY UNIFIED SCHOOL DISTRICT
777 N F ST, SAN BERNARDINO, CA 924103017
Phone: 909 381-1100
Web: WWW.SBCUSD.COM

HISTORICAL FINANCIALS
Company Type: Private

Income Statement — FYE: June 30

	REVENUE ($mil)	NET INCOME ($mil)	NET PROFIT MARGIN	EMPLOYEES
06/21	900	130	14.5%	6,000
06/20	766	(56)	—	—
06/19	775	46	5.9%	—
06/18	712	27	3.8%	—
Annual Growth	8.1%	68.4%	—	—

2021 Year-End Financials
Return on assets: 7.0%   Cash ($ mil.): —
Return on equity: 52.8%
Current Ratio: —

SAN BERNARDINO COUNTY

EXECUTIVES
Chief Deputy*, Howard Ochi
Auditors: VAVRINEK TRINE DAY & CO LL

LOCATIONS

HQ: SAN BERNARDINO COUNTY
385 N ARROWHEAD AVE, SAN BERNARDINO, CA 924150103
Phone: 909 387-3841
Web: MAIN.SBCOUNTY.GOV

HISTORICAL FINANCIALS
Company Type: Private

Income Statement — FYE: June 30

	REVENUE ($mil)	NET INCOME ($mil)	NET PROFIT MARGIN	EMPLOYEES
06/20	4,008	223	5.6%	6,094
06/19	3,806	228	6.0%	—
06/16	3,186	165	5.2%	—
06/15	3,077	176	5.8%	—
Annual Growth	5.4%	4.8%	—	—

2020 Year-End Financials
Return on assets: 2.6%   Cash ($ mil.): 3,950
Return on equity: 6.0%
Current Ratio: —

SAN BERNARDINO COUNTY TRANSPORTATION AUTHORITY

Auditors: CROWE LLP COSTA MESA CALIFOR

LOCATIONS

HQ: SAN BERNARDINO COUNTY TRANSPORTATION AUTHORITY
1170 W 3RD ST FL 2, SAN BERNARDINO, CA 924101724
Phone: 909 884-8276
Web: WWW.GOSBCTA.COM

HISTORICAL FINANCIALS
Company Type: Private

Income Statement — FYE: June 30

	REVENUE ($mil)	NET INCOME ($mil)	NET PROFIT MARGIN	EMPLOYEES
06/22	672	158	23.6%	125
06/21	683	104	15.3%	—
06/20	553	20	3.7%	—
Annual Growth	10.3%	178.4%	—	—

2022 Year-End Financials
Return on assets: 10.4%   Cash ($ mil.): —
Return on equity: 14.0%
Current Ratio: 9.60

SAN DIEGO UNIFIED SCHOOL DISTRICT

Auditors: MAYER HOFFMAN MCCANN PC IRVIN

LOCATIONS

HQ: SAN DIEGO UNIFIED SCHOOL DISTRICT
4100 NORMAL ST, SAN DIEGO, CA 921032653
Phone: 619 725-8000
Web: WWW.SANDIEGOUNIFIED.ORG

HISTORICAL FINANCIALS
Company Type: Private

Income Statement — FYE: June 30

	REVENUE ($mil)	NET INCOME ($mil)	NET PROFIT MARGIN	EMPLOYEES
06/20*	1,972	(202)	—	17,000
08/19	0	0	0.9%	—
06/06	1,112	(2)	—	—
06/05	608	73	12.1%	—
Annual Growth	8.2%	—	—	—

*Fiscal year change

2020 Year-End Financials
Return on assets: (-3.2%)   Cash ($ mil.): —
Return on equity: —
Current Ratio: —

SAN JUAN UNIFIED SCHOOL DISTRICT

Auditors: CROWE HORWATH LLP SACRAMENTO

LOCATIONS

HQ: SAN JUAN UNIFIED SCHOOL DISTRICT
3738 WALNUT AVE, CARMICHAEL, CA 956083099
Phone: 916 971-7700
Web: WWW.SANJUAN.EDU

HISTORICAL FINANCIALS
Company Type: Private

Income Statement — FYE: June 30

	REVENUE ($mil)	NET INCOME ($mil)	NET PROFIT MARGIN	EMPLOYEES
06/21	658	98	14.9%	4,200
06/20	608	(142)	—	—
06/19	631	105	16.7%	—
06/18	620	(38)	—	—
Annual Growth	2.0%	—	—	—

2021 Year-End Financials
Return on assets: 6.8%   Cash ($ mil.): —
Return on equity: —
Current Ratio: —

SANFORD

Sanford (operating as Sanford Health) is one of the largest not-for-profit integrated health care systems in the US. It primarily serves rural areas through its network of about 45 regional and community hospitals in nine states including the Dakotas, Iowa, Minnesota, and Nebraska. The organization also operates about 300 local clinics and specialty outpatient practices. Specialist service include cancer, cardiology, vascular health, neurology, orthopedics, pediatrics, virology, and women's health. Sanford Health added more than 200 senior care locations in 24 states by acquiring Good Samaritan Society in 2019.

Operations

In addition to its 40-plus hospitals, Sanford's network includes about 200 senior living facilities (long-term care, assisted-living, and independent living centers) and 140 clinics. Altogether, the facilities in the Sanford Health network handle some 50,000 inpatient admissions and about 1.35 million outpatient visits each year. The network's 1,400 physicians provide care in more than 80 specialist fields.

Along with its health care facilities, Sanford Health also operates Sanford Laboratories, based in Sioux Falls and Rapid City, South Dakota. The system maintains Sanford Research, a not-for-profit research organization that draws upon the physicians of Sanford Health and researchers at the University of South Dakota. Sanford Research conducts some $100 million in research projects each year. Finally, the Sanford Health Plan is a not-for-profit health plan that serves individuals and employers across the system's region.

Geographic Reach

Sanford Health has hospital and clinic locations in communities in nine states including California, Iowa, Minnesota, Nebraska, North Dakota, Oklahoma, Oregon, and South Dakota. The company also operates about 200 senior care facilities in 24 states. It also has clinical affiliates in locations including Ghana, Africa; Karmiel, Israel; and Baja, Mexico.

Strategy

Growth plans for Sanford Health include the construction of hospital and clinic facilities in Minnesota and North Dakota and new health care and research facilities in South Dakota. A $700 million gift from local philanthropist T. Denny Sanford is enabling the establishment of several new facilities. That contribution is also supporting the organization's research programs in children's health and initiatives to find cures for conditions including breast cancer and type 1 diabetes.

In addition, Sanford Health expands by acquiring small community medical centers. The system is also growing by striking partnerships with small regional health care providers. In 2018 and 2019 it expanded in research and senior care by acquiring the Neuropsychiatric Research Institute and senior housing operator Good Samaritan Society.

The company agreed to merge with Iowa Health System, which operates as UnityPoint Health, in 2019, but the deal was terminated later that year. The transaction would have created a system with more than 75 hospitals in 26 states.

Mergers and Acquisitions

In early 2019 Sanford merged with senior health services provider The Evangelical Lutheran Good Samaritan Society. The transaction combined Sanford's hospital system with Good Samaritan's senior living facilities, creating an integrated health care, research, and insurance entity.

In 2018, Sanford Research absorbed Neuropsychiatric Research Institute, which focuses on eating disorders and obesity. With that acquisition, Sanford intends to establish a major research program in Fargo, North Dakota.

A deal to merge with Iowa Health System, which operates as UnityPoint Health, was canceled in 2019. The merger would have created a health network with about 75 hospitals in 26 states.

Company Background

Sanford was created from the 2009 merger of two Dakota health care legends: South Dakota's Sanford Health and North Dakota's MeritCare Health System. Both date back to the 1890s. Following the merger, the two units briefly kept their separate identities, but in 2010 organized under the Sanford Health-MeritCare name. The operating name was later shortened to Sanford Health.

Auditors : DELOITTE & TOUCHE LLP MINNEAP

LOCATIONS

HQ: SANFORD
  801 BROADWAY N, FARGO, ND 581023641
Phone: 701 234-6000
Web: WWW.SANFORDHEALTH.ORG

PRODUCTS/OPERATIONS

Selected Major Regional Medical Centers
Sanford Bemidji Medical Center (Bemidji, Minnesota)
Sanford Medical Center Bismarck (Bismarck, North Dakota)
Sanford Medical Center Fargo (Fargo, North Dakota)
Sanford USD Medical Center Sioux Falls (Sioux Falls, South Dakota)

COMPETITORS

ADVENTIST HEALTH SYSTEM/SUNBELT, INC.
ADVOCATE AURORA HEALTH, INC.
ADVOCATE HEALTH CARE NETWORK
BEAUMONT HEALTH
HOUSTON COUNTY HEALTHCARE AUTHORITY
IOWA HEALTH SYSTEM
LEGACY HEALTH
OHIOHEALTH CORPORATION
ORLANDO HEALTH, INC.
WILLIAM BEAUMONT HOSPITAL

HISTORICAL FINANCIALS

Company Type: Private

Income Statement — FYE: June 30

	REVENUE ($mil)	NET INCOME ($mil)	NET PROFIT MARGIN	EMPLOYEES
06/17	4,411	175	4.0%	50,000
06/16	4,231	108	2.6%	—
06/14	3	(11)	—	—
Annual Growth	939.2%	—	—	—

2017 Year-End Financials
Return on assets: 4.1%   Cash ($ mil.): 101
Return on equity: 7.1%
Current Ratio: 1.60

SANFORD BISMARCK

Auditors : EIDE BAILLY LLP MINNEAPOLIS

LOCATIONS

HQ: SANFORD BISMARCK
  300 N 7TH ST, BISMARCK, ND 585014439
Phone: 701 323-6000

HISTORICAL FINANCIALS

Company Type: Private

Income Statement — FYE: December 31

	REVENUE ($mil)	NET INCOME ($mil)	NET PROFIT MARGIN	EMPLOYEES
12/20	603	82	13.6%	2,781
12/09	3	0	16.4%	—
12/08	230	10	4.7%	—
12/06	218	3	1.5%	—
Annual Growth	7.5%	26.0%	—	—

2020 Year-End Financials
Return on assets: 28.4%   Cash ($ mil.): 3
Return on equity: 99.5%
Current Ratio: 1.90

SANFORD HEALTH

EXECUTIVES

CLINIC, Dan Blue Md
HEALTH SERVICES*, Ed Weiland
PLAN*, Ruth Krystopolski
Auditors : DELOITTE & TOUCHE LLP MINNEAP

LOCATIONS

HQ: SANFORD HEALTH
  1305 W 18TH ST, SIOUX FALLS, SD 571050401
Phone: 605 333-1720
Web: WWW.SANFORDHEALTH.ORG

HISTORICAL FINANCIALS
Company Type: Private

Income Statement — FYE: December 31

	REVENUE ($mil)	NET INCOME ($mil)	NET PROFIT MARGIN	EMPLOYEES
12/18*	4,819	141	2.9%	2,939
06/17	4,411	175	4.0%	—
06/16	4,231	114	2.7%	—
06/12	2,516	72	2.9%	—
Annual Growth	9.7%	10.1%	—	—

*Fiscal year change

2018 Year-End Financials
Return on assets: 3.3% Cash ($ mil.): 109
Return on equity: 5.3%
Current Ratio: 1.80

SANFORD HEALTH

Auditors: DELOITTE TAX LLP MINNEAPOLIS

LOCATIONS

HQ: SANFORD HEALTH
1305 W 18TH ST, SIOUX FALLS, SD 571050401
Phone: 605 333-1000

HISTORICAL FINANCIALS
Company Type: Private

Income Statement — FYE: June 30

	REVENUE ($mil)	NET INCOME ($mil)	NET PROFIT MARGIN	EMPLOYEES
06/17	3,741	138	3.7%	2
06/10	1,038	35	3.4%	—
Annual Growth	20.1%	21.4%	—	—

2017 Year-End Financials
Return on assets: 5.0% Cash ($ mil.): 78
Return on equity: 11.9%
Current Ratio: —

SANFORD NORTH

LOCATIONS

HQ: SANFORD NORTH
801 BROADWAY N, FARGO, ND 581023641
Phone: 701 234-2000
Web: WWW.SANFORDHEALTH.ORG

HISTORICAL FINANCIALS
Company Type: Private

Income Statement — FYE: June 30

	REVENUE ($mil)	NET INCOME ($mil)	NET PROFIT MARGIN	EMPLOYEES
06/10	677	(15)	—	7,200
06/08	112	2	2.0%	—
Annual Growth	145.1%	—	—	—

2010 Year-End Financials
Return on assets: (-10.8%) Cash ($ mil.): —
Return on equity: (-24.5%)
Current Ratio: 1.40

SANTA CLARA VALLEY TRANSPORTATION AUTHORITY

Auditors: EIDEBAILLY LLP MENLO PARK CA

LOCATIONS

HQ: SANTA CLARA VALLEY TRANSPORTATION AUTHORITY
3331 N 1ST ST, SAN JOSE, CA 951341906
Phone: 408 321-2300
Web: WWW.VTA.ORG

HISTORICAL FINANCIALS
Company Type: Private

Income Statement — FYE: June 30

	REVENUE ($mil)	NET INCOME ($mil)	NET PROFIT MARGIN	EMPLOYEES
06/21	568	90	15.9%	2,053
06/19	1,204	830	68.9%	—
06/17	16	(2)	—	—
06/16	19	(0)	—	—
Annual Growth	96.8%	—	—	—

2021 Year-End Financials
Return on assets: 1.2% Cash ($ mil.): —
Return on equity: 1.5%
Current Ratio: —

SAPP BROS., INC.

Need air in those 18 wheels? Sapp Bros Travel Centers (formerly Sapp Bros Truck Stops) has the usual air, gas, food, but also offers human conveniences such such as laundry rooms, mailbox rentals, private showers, and TV lounges. The company operates a chain of some 15 truck stops -- readily identifiable by the giant red-and-white coffeepot logo -- along interstate highways from Utah to Pennsylvania; with a concentration in Nebraska. Half of the locations also operate service centers, offering oil changes, new tires, and safety checks. Its sister company, Sapp Bros Petroleum, distributes fuels and lubricants to more than 200 retailers. The firm is run by CEO Bill Sapp, one of the four founding Sapp brothers.

Geographic Reach
Omaha-based Sapp Bros. has travel centers in eight states: Nebraska, Iowa, Utah, Colorado, Wyoming, Kansas, Illinois, and Pennsylvania.

Strategy
To raise its profile and rev up its business, Sapp Bros. in 2013 joined the roster of VP Racing Fuels's retail brand partners. The benefits of the affiliation include association with an attractive retail image, competitive credit card rates, and the ability to source unbranded fuel for its travel centers.

Auditors: KPMG LLP OMAHA NEBRASKA

LOCATIONS

HQ: SAPP BROS., INC.
9915 S 148TH ST, OMAHA, NE 681383876
Phone: 402 895-7038
Web: WWW.SAPPBROS.NET

2012 Locations

	No.
Nebraska	8
Iowa	2
Colorado	1
Illinois	1
Kansas	1
Pennsylvania	1
Utah	1
Wyoming	1
Total	16

COMPETITORS
ENGLEFIELD, INC.
GPM INVESTMENTS, LLC
HOLIDAY COMPANIES
RACETRAC PETROLEUM, INC.
RIP GRIFFIN TRUCK SERVICE CENTER, INC.

HISTORICAL FINANCIALS
Company Type: Private

Income Statement — FYE: September 30

	REVENUE ($mil)	NET INCOME ($mil)	NET PROFIT MARGIN	EMPLOYEES
09/21	1,128	21	1.9%	1,700
09/20	920	17	1.8%	—
09/19	1,194	4	0.4%	—
09/18	1,259	11	0.9%	—
Annual Growth	(3.6%)	21.7%	—	—

2021 Year-End Financials
Return on assets: 12.6% Cash ($ mil.): 2
Return on equity: 28.8%
Current Ratio: 1.30

SARASOTA COUNTY PUBLIC HOSPITAL DISTRICT

Sarasota County Public Hospital District, which does business as the Sarasota Memorial Health Care System, is a publicly owned hospital system serving residents in and around Sarasota on Florida's western coast. It is a full-service public health system, with two hospitals offering specialized expertise in heart, vascular, cancer, orthopedic and neuroscience services, as well as a state-of-the-art cancer care center and a network of outpatient centers, urgent care centers, laboratories, diagnostic imaging and physician practices, skilled nursing and rehabilitation among its many programs.

Operations

Sarasota Memorial Hospital-Sarasota Campus, with its flagship some 895-bed, acute-care hospital and 8-story Brian D. Jellison Cancer Institute Oncology Tower, is the only hospital in Sarasota County providing obstetrical services, pediatrics, Level III neonatal intensive care, psychiatric services for patients of all ages and a Level II Trauma Center.

The new Sarasota Memorial Hospital-Venice features some 110 private rooms, a 28-room Emergency Care Center, eight surgical suites, ten birthing suites and a pandemic-ready intensive care unit.

Sarasota Memorial receives some 44,280 inpatient visits and 1.2 million outpatient and physician visits each year.

Geographic Reach
Sarasota Memorial serves Florida's Sarasota County.

Sales and Marketing
Medicare and Medicaid combined account for some 70% of Sarasota Memorial's net patient service revenue. Self-pay and managed care and commercial make up the remainder.

Company Background
Sarasota Memorial was founded as a community hospital in 1925.

EXECUTIVES

NURSING*, Connie Andersen

LOCATIONS

HQ: SARASOTA COUNTY PUBLIC HOSPITAL DISTRICT
  1700 S TAMIAMI TRL, SARASOTA, FL 342393509
Phone: 941 917-9000
Web: WWW.SMH.COM

PRODUCTS/OPERATIONS

2016 Sales

	% of total
County Public Hospital District	
Sarasota Memorial Hospital	59
Corporate Division	2
Nursing & Rehabilitation Center	1
Charter Plan	-
SMH Health Care, Inc.	33
Physician Services, Inc.	5
Total	100

COMPETITORS

BRONXCARE HEALTH SYSTEM
FLOYD HEALTHCARE MANAGEMENT, INC.
NASSAU HEALTH CARE CORPORATION
OVERLAKE HOSPITAL MEDICAL CENTER
SALINAS VALLEY MEMORIAL HEALTHCARE SYSTEMS
SHANDS JACKSONVILLE MEDICAL CENTER, INC.
SHANDS TEACHING HOSPITAL AND CLINICS, INC.
TALLAHASSEE MEMORIAL HEALTHCARE, INC.
WELLMONT HEALTH SYSTEM
WELLSPAN HEALTH

HISTORICAL FINANCIALS
Company Type: Private

Income Statement   FYE: September 30

	REVENUE ($mil)	NET INCOME ($mil)	NET PROFIT MARGIN	EMPLOYEES
09/21	1,152	165	14.3%	7,000
09/20	986	154	15.7%	—
09/16	12	0	4.0%	—
09/15	590	131	22.3%	—
Annual Growth	11.8%	3.8%	—	—

2021 Year-End Financials
Return on assets: 5.9%   Cash ($ mil.): 65
Return on equity: 9.9%
Current Ratio: 0.60

SAVANNAH-CHATHAM COUNTY BOARD OF EDUCATION

Auditors: MAULDIN & JENKINS LLC SAVANN

LOCATIONS

HQ: SAVANNAH-CHATHAM COUNTY BOARD OF EDUCATION
  208 BULL ST, SAVANNAH, GA 314013843
Phone: 912 395-5534
Web: WWW.CHATHAMCOUNTYGA.GOV

HISTORICAL FINANCIALS
Company Type: Private

Income Statement   FYE: June 30

	REVENUE ($mil)	NET INCOME ($mil)	NET PROFIT MARGIN	EMPLOYEES
06/21	613	27	4.4%	4,800
06/20	587	41	7.1%	—
06/19	569	86	15.2%	—
06/18	525	41	7.8%	—
Annual Growth	5.3%	(12.9%)	—	—

2021 Year-End Financials
Return on assets: 1.9%   Cash ($ mil.): 129
Return on equity: 5.5%
Current Ratio: —

SAVE THE CHILDREN FEDERATION, INC.

Save the Children helps poor and malnourished children in some 15 US states and nearly 120 countries, focusing on such areas as health and nutrition, economic development, education, child protection, and HIV/AIDS. The humanitarian organization also participates in international disaster relief efforts, focusing on children and their families. Save the Children spends about 90% of its budget on program services, with the rest allocated to administration and fundraising. The group was founded in 1932, inspired by the international children's rights movement begun in the UK in 1919 by Eglantyne Jebb, founder of the British Save the Children Fund. It is a member of the International Save the Children Alliance.

Operations
Some 43% of the humanitarian organization's work is centered in Asia, with 34% in Africa. Save the Children spends the rest of its time in the US, Latin America, and the Middle East.

In 2012, alone, Save the Children helped 125 million girls and boys worldwide.

Geographic Reach
Save the Children operates programs in some 120 countries, including the US. It comprises 29 member organizations worldwide.

Financial Performance
The global aid organization's revenue declined by 3.5% in 2012 versus 2011, due largely to a 12% drop in private gifts, grants, and contributions, which account for nearly half of its total revenue. Save the Children directed 89% of its expenses to programs, which benefit children and allow the humanitarian organization to keep private costs (includes fundraising and management and general) at about 10% -- one of the best ratios for nonprofit organizations.

Strategy
With about 28% of its program services devoted to emergencies and 20% to education, Save the Children in 2014 partnered with The Malala Fund to help vulnerable Syrian and Jordanian children return to school. As part of the partnership, Save the Children is launching a pair of education projects. Another large portion of Save the Children's program services are focused on Health and Nutrition (25%) and Hunger & Livelihoods (10%).

Auditors: KPMG LLP NEW YORK NY

LOCATIONS

HQ: SAVE THE CHILDREN FEDERATION, INC.
  501 KINGS HWY E STE 400, FAIRFIELD, CT 068254861
Phone: 203 221-4000
Web: WWW.SAVETHECHILDREN.ORG

Selected Countries of Operation
Australia
Brazil
Canada
Denmark
Dominican Republic
Fiji
Finland
Germany
Guatemala
Honduras
Hong Kong
Iceland
India
Italy
Japan
Jordan
Korea
Lithuania

Mexico
Netherlands
New Zealand
Norway
Romania
South Africa
Spain
Swaziland
Sweden
Switzerland
United Kingdom
United States

COMPETITORS

AMERICARES FOUNDATION, INC.
BARNARDO'S
BRITISH RED CROSS SOCIETY
EASTER SEALS, INC.
FEEDING AMERICA
HELEN KELLER INTERNATIONAL
MARCH OF DIMES INC.
NATIONAL COUNCIL OF YOUNG MEN'S CHRISTIAN ASSOCIATIONS OF THE UNITED STATES OF AMERICA
UNITED STATES FUND FOR UNICEF
VOLUNTEERS OF AMERICA, INC.

HISTORICAL FINANCIALS
Company Type: Private

Income Statement — FYE: December 31

	REVENUE ($mil)	NET INCOME ($mil)	NET PROFIT MARGIN	EMPLOYEES
12/16	652	(7)	—	3,000
12/15	678	(10)	—	—
Annual Growth	(3.9%)	—	—	—

2016 Year-End Financials
Return on assets: (-2.8%)   Cash ($ mil.): 46
Return on equity: (-4.1%)
Current Ratio: 1.50

SCAI HOLDINGS, LLC

SCAI Holdings (dba SCA, or Surgical Care Affiliates) can stitch 'em up and move 'em out. The company operates one of the largest networks of outpatient surgery centers in the US. (Also known as ambulatory surgical centers, or ASCs, these facilities charge less than hospitals to perform routine surgeries.) SCA operates more than 200 surgery centers and surgical hospitals in about 35 states. The centers offer non-emergency day surgeries in orthopedics, ophthalmology, gastroenterology, pain management, otolaryngology (ear, nose and throat), urology, and gynecology. The company went public in 2013, but was acquired by insurance giant UnitedHealth in 2017 for some $2.3 billion.

EXECUTIVES
Chief Development Officer, Brian Mathis
Auditors : PRICEWATERHOUSECOOPERS LLP BI

LOCATIONS
HQ: SCAI HOLDINGS, LLC
510 LAKE COOK RD STE 200, DEERFIELD, IL 600155031
Phone: 847 236-0921
Web: WWW.SCA.HEALTH

PRODUCTS/OPERATIONS
2014 Sales by Payor
	% of total
Managed care & other discount plans	62
Medicare	20
Workers' compensation	10
Patients & other third-party payors	5
Medicaid	3
Total	100

2014 Sales
	$ mil	% of total
Net patient revenues	788.0	91
Management fee revenue	58.9	7
Other revenues	17.8	2
Total	864.7	100

COMPETITORS
ACADIA HEALTHCARE COMPANY, INC.
COMMUNITY HEALTH SYSTEMS, INC.
CONTINUCARE CORPORATION
HANGER, INC.
LHC GROUP, INC.
MERAKEY USA
PLANNED PARENTHOOD FEDERATION OF AMERICA, INC.
REHABCARE GROUP MANAGEMENT SERVICES, LLC
SELECT MEDICAL HOLDINGS CORPORATION
U.S. PHYSICAL THERAPY, INC.

HISTORICAL FINANCIALS
Company Type: Private

Income Statement — FYE: December 31

	REVENUE ($mil)	NET INCOME ($mil)	NET PROFIT MARGIN	EMPLOYEES
12/16	1,281	226	17.7%	5,248
12/15	1,051	273	26.0%	—
12/14	864	157	18.2%	—
12/13	802	52	6.6%	—
Annual Growth	16.9%	62.5%	—	—

2016 Year-End Financials
Return on assets: 8.5%   Cash ($ mil.): 131
Return on equity: 19.6%
Current Ratio: 1.30

SCHAUMBOND GROUP, INC.

EXECUTIVES
Pres-Ceo, Baohua Zheng
CPA, Kevin Hsu

LOCATIONS
HQ: SCHAUMBOND GROUP, INC.
225 S LAKE AVE STE 300, PASADENA, CA 911013009
Phone: 626 215-4998

HISTORICAL FINANCIALS
Company Type: Private

Income Statement — FYE: December 31

	ASSETS ($mil)	NET INCOME ($mil)	INCOME AS % OF ASSETS	EMPLOYEES
12/07	65	4	7.5%	550
12/06	50	4	9.6%	—
Annual Growth	28.2%	0.0%	—	—

2007 Year-End Financials
Return on assets: 7.5%   Cash ($ mil.): 14
Return on equity: 8.0%
Current Ratio: 8.20

SCHOOL BOARD OF BREVARD COUNTY

Auditors : MOORE STEPHENS LOVELACE PA

LOCATIONS
HQ: SCHOOL BOARD OF BREVARD COUNTY
2700 JDGE FRAN JMESON WAY, VIERA, FL 329406699
Phone: 321 633-1000
Web: WWW.BREVARDSCHOOLS.ORG

HISTORICAL FINANCIALS
Company Type: Private

Income Statement — FYE: June 30

	REVENUE ($mil)	NET INCOME ($mil)	NET PROFIT MARGIN	EMPLOYEES
06/14	626	7	1.2%	9,031
06/09	613	(19)	—	—
06/06	628	100	15.9%	—
06/05	564	43	7.8%	—
Annual Growth	1.2%	(18.0%)	—	—

2014 Year-End Financials
Return on assets: 0.7%   Cash ($ mil.): 64
Return on equity: 1.9%
Current Ratio: 2.40

SCHOOL BOARD OF BROWARD COUNTY, THE (INC)

EXECUTIVES
OF SCHOOLS, Doctor Vickie L Cartwright
Chief of Staff*, Jeffrey Moquin
Auditors : MSL PA ORLANDO FL

LOCATIONS
HQ: SCHOOL BOARD OF BROWARD COUNTY, THE (INC)
600 SE 3RD AVE, FORT LAUDERDALE, FL 333013125
Phone: 754 321-0000
Web: WWW.BROWARDSCHOOLS.COM

HISTORICAL FINANCIALS
Company Type: Private

Income Statement				FYE: June 30
	REVENUE ($mil)	NET INCOME ($mil)	NET PROFIT MARGIN	EMPLOYEES
06/21	3,069	111	3.6%	1,145
06/20	3,037	169	5.6%	—
06/19	2,924	167	5.7%	—
06/18	2,806	(65)	—	—
Annual Growth	3.0%	—	—	—

2021 Year-End Financials
Return on assets: 2.1%   Cash ($ mil.): 924
Return on equity: 35.5%
Current Ratio: 1.80

SCHOOL BOARD OF ORANGE COUNTY FLORIDA

Auditors: CHERRY BEKAERT LLP ORLANDO F

LOCATIONS
HQ: SCHOOL BOARD OF ORANGE COUNTY FLORIDA
445 W AMELIA ST LBBY, ORLANDO, FL 328011153
Phone: 407 317-3200
Web: WWW.ORANGECOUNTYFL.NET

HISTORICAL FINANCIALS
Company Type: Private

Income Statement				FYE: June 30
	REVENUE ($mil)	NET INCOME ($mil)	NET PROFIT MARGIN	EMPLOYEES
06/12	1,823	30	1.7%	25,000
06/11	1,895	24	1.3%	—
Annual Growth	(3.8%)	26.1%	—	—

2012 Year-End Financials
Return on assets: 0.6%   Cash ($ mil.): 194
Return on equity: 1.0%
Current Ratio: —

SCHOOL BOARD OF PALM BEACH COUNTY

LOCATIONS
HQ: SCHOOL BOARD OF PALM BEACH COUNTY
3300 FREST HL BLVD STE C, WEST PALM BEACH, FL 33406
Phone: 561 434-8000
Web: WWW.PALMBEACHSCHOOLS.ORG

HISTORICAL FINANCIALS
Company Type: Private

Income Statement				FYE: June 30
	REVENUE ($mil)	NET INCOME ($mil)	NET PROFIT MARGIN	EMPLOYEES
06/08	2,093	(68)	—	21,000
06/07	2,010	501	24.9%	—
06/05	1,656	(121)	—	—
06/04	1,290	61	4.8%	—
Annual Growth	12.9%	—	—	—

2008 Year-End Financials
Return on assets: (-1.4%)   Cash ($ mil.): 1,290
Return on equity: (-3.4%)
Current Ratio: —

SCHOOL DISTRICT 1 IN THE CITY AND COUNTY OF DENVER AND THE STATE OF COLORADO

Auditors: CLIFTONLARSONALLEN LLP GREENW

LOCATIONS
HQ: SCHOOL DISTRICT 1 IN THE CITY AND COUNTY OF DENVER AND THE STATE OF COLORADO
1860 N LINCOLN ST, DENVER, CO 802037301
Phone: 720 423-3200
Web: WWW.DPSK12.ORG

HISTORICAL FINANCIALS
Company Type: Private

Income Statement				FYE: June 30
	REVENUE ($mil)	NET INCOME ($mil)	NET PROFIT MARGIN	EMPLOYEES
06/12*	916	(100)	—	14,965
12/08	0	(0)	—	—
06/08	790	(38)	—	—
Annual Growth	3.8%	—	—	—

*Fiscal year change

2012 Year-End Financials
Return on assets: (-7.5%)   Cash ($ mil.): 348
Return on equity: —
Current Ratio: —

SCHWAB CHARITABLE FUND

Auditors: DELOITTE & TOUCHE LLP SAN FRA

LOCATIONS
HQ: SCHWAB CHARITABLE FUND
211 MAIN ST, SAN FRANCISCO, CA 941051905
Phone: 415 667-9131

HISTORICAL FINANCIALS
Company Type: Private

Income Statement				FYE: June 30
	REVENUE ($mil)	NET INCOME ($mil)	NET PROFIT MARGIN	EMPLOYEES
06/20	4,885	1,531	31.4%	26
06/18	3,465	1,549	44.7%	—
06/17	3,147	1,551	49.3%	—
06/16	2,018	819	40.6%	—
Annual Growth	24.7%	16.9%	—	—

2020 Year-End Financials
Return on assets: 8.9%   Cash ($ mil.): 29
Return on equity: 8.9%
Current Ratio: 1.60

SCL HEALTH - FRONT RANGE, INC.

Exempla aims to provide exemplary health care to residents in the Denver area. The Exempla medical network, operating as Exempla Healthcare, includes three hospitals: Exempla Saint Joseph Hospital (570 beds), Exempla Lutheran Medical Center (400 beds), and Good Samaritan Medical Center (more than 230 beds). It also operates the Exempla Physician Network, a chain of primary care clinics. The company employs more than 2,100 physicians. Among its specialties are cardiovascular services and surgeries, rehabilitation, cancer care, orthopedics, and women's and children's services. Exempla Healthcare is sponsored by the Catholic faith-based Sisters of Charity of Leavenworth Health System (SCL Health System).

Strategy
Exempla is investing in expansion of the facilities at Lutheran Medical Center. It is also constructing a new building for Saint Joseph Hospital that is set to open in 2015.

Company Background
Exempla Healthcare was formed in 1998, when Saint Joseph Hospital and Lutheran Medical Center combined.

Auditors: ERNST & YOUNG US LLP PHOENIX

LOCATIONS
HQ: SCL HEALTH - FRONT RANGE, INC.
2420 W 26TH AVE, DENVER, CO 802115306
Phone: 303 813-5000
Web: WWW.SCLHEALTH.ORG

PRODUCTS/OPERATIONS

2009 Revenues

	$ mil.	% of total
Exempla Saint Joseph Hospital	377.3	40
Exempla Lutheran Medical Center	302.6	32
Exempla Good Samaritan Medical Center	217.4	23
Exempla Physician Network	22.0	2
Colorado Lutheran Home & Exempla West Pines Behavioral Health	22.0	2
Exempla Lutheran Collier Hospice	6.7	1
Total	948.0	100

COMPETITORS

BAPTIST HEALTH SOUTH FLORIDA, INC.
FROEDTERT MEMORIAL LUTHERAN HOSPITAL, INC.
METHODIST LE BONHEUR HEALTHCARE
MULTICARE HEALTH SYSTEM
SAINT JOSEPH HOSPITAL, INC

HISTORICAL FINANCIALS
Company Type: Private

Income Statement — FYE: December 31

	REVENUE ($mil)	NET INCOME ($mil)	NET PROFIT MARGIN	EMPLOYEES
12/09	597	7	1.3%	5,300
12/05	472	30	6.5%	—
12/04	335	37	11.2%	—
12/02	267	27	10.1%	—
Annual Growth	12.2%	(16.2%)	—	—

2009 Year-End Financials
Return on assets: 0.9%   Cash ($ mil.): 53
Return on equity: 2.2%
Current Ratio: 0.40

SCOTT & WHITE MEMORIAL HOSPITAL

LOCATIONS

HQ: SCOTT & WHITE MEMORIAL HOSPITAL
2401 S 31ST ST, TEMPLE, TX 765080001
Phone: 254 724-2111
Web: WWW.BSWHEALTH.COM

HISTORICAL FINANCIALS
Company Type: Private

Income Statement — FYE: June 30

	REVENUE ($mil)	NET INCOME ($mil)	NET PROFIT MARGIN	EMPLOYEES
06/14*	832	87	10.5%	8,000
08/13	881	76	8.6%	—
08/10	902	41	4.6%	—
Annual Growth	(2.0%)	20.3%	—	—

*Fiscal year change

2014 Year-End Financials
Return on assets: 7.0%   Cash ($ mil.): 47
Return on equity: 8.1%
Current Ratio: 1.40

SCOTT AND WHITE HEALTH PLAN

The Scott & White Health Plan (SWHP) works to keep its members Safe & Well. The not-for-profit company provides health insurance plans and related services to more than 200,000 members across some 50 counties in and around Central Texas. Owned by the Scott & White network of hospitals and clinics, SWHP has employer-sponsored plans (including HMO, PPO, and consumer choice options) as well as several choices for individuals and families. It also offers COBRA, state-administered continuation plans, the Young Texan Health Plan for children, Medicare, and dental and vision benefits. The company began offering its services in 1982. Owner Scott & White is exploring a merger with Baylor Health Care System.

Auditors : ERNST & YOUNG US LLP INDIANAP

LOCATIONS

HQ: SCOTT AND WHITE HEALTH PLAN
1206 WEST CAMPUS DR, TEMPLE, TX 765027124
Phone: 254 298-3000
Web: WWW.BSWHEALTHPLAN.COM

PRODUCTS/OPERATIONS

Selected Products
Employer plans
Individual and family plans
Medicare plans
Vital Care programs

COMPETITORS

ALLWAYS HEALTH PARTNERS, INC.
CAPITAL DISTRICT PHYSICIANS' HEALTH PLAN, INC.
COMMUNITY HEALTH GROUP
HEALTH PARTNERS PLANS, INC.
NEW YORK STATE CATHOLIC HEALTH PLAN, INC.

HISTORICAL FINANCIALS
Company Type: Private

Income Statement — FYE: December 31

	REVENUE ($mil)	NET INCOME ($mil)	NET PROFIT MARGIN	EMPLOYEES
12/09	660	13	2.0%	426
12/08	621	(4)	—	—
12/07	586	8	1.4%	—
12/06	557	3	0.7%	—
Annual Growth	5.8%	54.1%	—	—

2009 Year-End Financials
Return on assets: 8.5%   Cash ($ mil.): 8
Return on equity: 18.4%
Current Ratio: 1.50

SCRIPPS HEALTH

Scripps Health is a $3.5 billion not-for-profit health system that serves the San Diego area through four acute-care hospitals. Altogether the health system treats more than 700,000 patients annually through more than 3,000 physicians. Its hospitals, along with several outpatient Scripps Clinic and Scripps Coastal Medical Center locations, is a network of integrated facilities with specialists from more than 60 medical and surgical specialist at some 30 outpatient centers and clinics. Scripps offers payer products and population health services through Scripps Accountable Care Organization, Scripps Health Plan and customized narrow network plans in collaboration with third-party payers. Scripps Health was founded in 1924 by philanthropist Ellen Browning Scripps.

Operations

Scripps Health offers cancer care, dermatology, heart care, neurology, OB-GYN, orthopedics, primary care, physical rehabilitation and Scripps Health Express. Primary care full range of services prevention, wellness and early detection services for diagnosis and treatment of injuries, illnesses and management of chronic medical conditions. Scripps Health Express provides offers same-day, walk-in care for minor illnesses and injuries seven days a week.

Scripps Health operates four emergency departments and three urgent care centers and is home to two of the region's five adult trauma centers: a Level I trauma center at Scripps Mercy Hospital, San Diego and Level II Trauma center at Scripps Memorial Hospital La Jolla.

Scripps Whittier Diabetes Institute is Southern California's leading diabetes center of excellence, committed to providing the best evidence-based diabetes screening, education and patient care in San Diego, including outpatient education, inpatient glucose management, clinical research, professional education, and community-based programs.

Geographic Reach

Based in San Diego, California, Scripps Health extends its operation from Chula Vista to Oceanside.

HISTORY

Scripps Health was founded by Ellen Browning Scripps in 1924 when the Scripps Memorial Hospital and Scripps Metabolic Clinic opened in La Jolla.

The network grew through the opening of Scripps Green Hospital in 1977, and the Scripps Memorial Hospital Encinitas campus was added through the purchase of San Dieguito Hospital the following year.

Scripps Mercy Hospital, which was first established in 1890 in San Diego, joined the Scripps network in 1995.

The Scripps Health system expanded once again when it acquired the Scripps Mercy Hospital Chula Vista campus in 2004.

EXECUTIVES

Chief Medical Officer, A Brent Eastman Md

Chief Development Officer*, John B Engle
CIO, Shane Thielman Corporate
CMO*, Ghazala Sharieff

LOCATIONS

HQ: SCRIPPS HEALTH
10140 CAMPUS POINT DR # 415, SAN DIEGO, CA 921211520
Phone: 800 727-4777
Web: WWW.SCRIPPS.ORG

Selected Facilities
Scripps Clinic (outpatient centers)
Scripps Coastal Medical Center (outpatient centers)
Scripps Green Hospital (La Jolla)
Scripps Memorial Hospital Encinitas
Scripps Memorial Hospital La Jolla
Scripps Mercy Hospital (San Diego)
Scripps Mercy Hospital Chula Vista

COMPETITORS

BANNER HEALTH
MEMORIAL HEALTH SERVICES
NORTHWELL HEALTH, INC.
ORLANDO HEALTH, INC.
PALOMAR HEALTH
PASADENA HOSPITAL ASSOCIATION, LTD.
SAINT JOSEPH HOSPITAL, INC
SOUTHCOAST HEALTH SYSTEM, INC.
UNIVERSITY HEALTH SYSTEM SERVICES OF TEXAS, INC.
UNIVERSITY HOSPITALS HEALTH SYSTEM, INC.

HISTORICAL FINANCIALS

Company Type: Private

Income Statement — FYE: September 30

	REVENUE ($mil)	NET INCOME ($mil)	NET PROFIT MARGIN	EMPLOYEES
09/15	2,943	371	12.6%	5,445
09/08	1,953	18	0.9%	—
09/07	1,781	223	12.6%	—
Annual Growth	6.5%	6.5%	—	—

2015 Year-End Financials
Return on assets: 8.3%
Return on equity: 12.0%
Current Ratio: 0.80
Cash ($ mil.): 464

SCRIPPS NETWORKS INTERACTIVE, INC.

Lifestyle TV is a livelihood for this company. Scripps Networks Interactive operates six lifestyle cable networks including Home & Garden Television (home building and decoration), the Food Network (culinary programs), DIY - Do It Yourself Network (home repair and improvement), the Cooking Channel (culinary how-to programming), and the Travel Channel (travel and tourism). The company additionally owns music channel Great American Country, and has minority interests in Asian Food Channel and regional sports network FOX Sports Net South. It also owns a 50% stake in UKTV. Trusts for the Scripps family own majority control of the company. In 2017 Discovery Communications agreed to buy Scripps Networks in a $14.6 billion deal.

Operations
Scripps Networks has two reportable segments: US networks and International Networks. Its US network segment accounts for almost 85% of total revenue.

Geographic Reach
Scripps Networks is based in Knoxville, Tennessee. The company has additional offices located in Atlanta, Chicago, Dallas, Detroit, Los Angeles, New York City, San Francisco, Miami, Chevy Chase, Maryland, and Washington DC. Scripps Networks maintains international offices in London, Milan, São Paulo, Sydney, the Philippines, and Singapore.

The company's Cooking Channel is available in Canada. HGTV is available in the Asia-Pacific region, the Middle East, North Africa, and New Zealand. Scripps Networks has also expanded Food Network across Latin America and Australia.

Sales and Marketing
Cable programmers such as Scripps Networks generate most of their revenue through advertising and carriage fees paid by cable system operators and satellite TV service providers. To help keep viewer loyalty and ratings high, the company targets its channels toward specific interests rather than airing programming for a general audience.

The company advertises its products through broadcast television networks, online and mobile outlets, radio programming, and print media. Scripps Networks spent $161.1 million on advertising and promotions in fiscal 2016.

Financial Performance
Scripps Networks reported about $3.4 billion in revenue for fiscal 2016. That was an increase of more than $400 million compared to the $3 billion the company reported for revenue the previous fiscal year. The increase was due to increased advertising sales and affiliate fee revenues.

Scripps Networks' net income was $673 million in fiscal 2016. That was an increase of about $67 million compared to the prior fiscal period when the company claimed a net income of $606 million, primarily as a result of an increase in total revenue.

The company ended fiscal 2016 with $948 million in cash from operating activities, which was an increase compared to fiscal 2015 when Scripps Networks ended the year with $814 million in cash from operations.

Strategy
Scripps Networks is focused on growing advertising revenues by increasing video plays and attracting more unique visitors to its websites through site enhancements and adding more video. Its strategy also includes trying to attract a broader audience through programming on national video streaming sites, developing new sources of revenue that capitalize on traffic growth at the company's own websites, and capitalizing on the movement of advertising dollars to mobile platforms.

The growth of the company's international business continues to be a strategic priority. Scripps Networks has expanded in Asia, Europe, and Latin America in recent years.

Mergers and Acquisitions

Auditors: DELOITTE & TOUCHE LLP CINCIN

LOCATIONS

HQ: SCRIPPS NETWORKS INTERACTIVE, INC.
9721 SHERRILL BLVD, KNOXVILLE, TN 379323330
Phone: 865 694-2700
Web: WWW.SCRIPPSNETWORKSINTERACTIVE.COM

2016

	$ in mil.	% of total
United States	2,884.4	85
Poland	443.3	13
Other International	73.5	2
Total	3,401.4	100

PRODUCTS/OPERATIONS

2016 sales

	$ in mil.	% of total
operating revenue		
U.S Networks	2,871.4	84
International Networks	557.0	16
Total	3,428.4	100

2016 sales

	$ in mil.	% of total
Advertising	2,416.4	71
Distribution	894.3	26
other	90.6	3
Total	3,401.4	100

Selected Operations
Lifestyle media
    Cooking Channel
    DIY Network
    Food Network (75%)
    Fox Sports Net South (7%)
    Great American Country
    HGTV (Home & Garden Television)
    Travel Channel (65%)
    UKTV (50%)
    Asian Food Channel (100%)
Interactive Services
    CookingChanneltv.com
    DIYNetwork.com
    FoodNetwork.com
    GACTV.com
    HGTV.com
    TravelChannel.com

COMPETITORS

AMC NETWORKS INC.
CABLEVISION SYSTEMS CORPORATION
COMCAST CORPORATION
DISCOVERY, INC.
FORMER CHARTER COMMUNICATIONS PARENT, INC.
GRIZZLY MERGER SUB 1, LLC
LIBERTY MEDIA CORPORATION
NEXSTAR MEDIA GROUP, INC.
SINCLAIR BROADCAST GROUP, INC.
TEGNA INC.

HISTORICAL FINANCIALS
Company Type: Private

Income Statement
FYE: December 31

	REVENUE ($mil)	NET INCOME ($mil)	NET PROFIT MARGIN	EMPLOYEES
12/17	3,561	814	22.9%	3,500
12/16	3,401	847	24.9%	—
12/15	3,018	778	25.8%	—
12/14	2,665	726	27.3%	—
Annual Growth	10.1%	3.9%	—	—

2017 Year-End Financials
Return on assets: 12.5% Cash ($ mil.): 130
Return on equity: 26.2%
Current Ratio: 3.10

SEACOR HOLDINGS INC.

SEACOR Holdings provides transportation and logistics services to support a wide range of business sectors. SEACOR has interests in domestic and international transportation and logistics. The company also has interests in crisis and emergency management services and clean fuel and power solutions. SEACOR acquired the capacity and operational expertise to tailor logistics solutions and deliver wherever its customers need them. Through well timed investments in diverse assets, technology and people, it has strengthened its business and enlarged its footprint. The company was founded in 1989. In 2021, SEACOR was acquired by American Industrial Partners (AIP) for $41.50 per share in cash.

Operations

SEACOR businesses are dedicated to ocean and inland transportation and logistics, crisis management, mitigation and recovery, and transforming energy use to cleaner alternatives. Its family of business includes Seabulk, Waterman, Seacor Island Lines, SCF, and Witt Obriens.

Seabulk provides safe and efficient marine logistics and infrastructure solutions, including ocean transportation, harbor and terminal services and vessel management.

Waterman provides global logistics and transportation to commercial and Government clients and has the capability and the creativity to ship efficiently and reliably worldwide. Its fleet includes US-Flag RORO vessels with heavy duty carrying capacity for tall and heavy cargoes, as well as purpose built PCTCs.

SEACOR Island Lines is the lifeline, providing integrated cargo transportation and logistics between the U.S. and the Bahamas and Turks and Caicos islands. With warehousing, terminal services and a fleet of specialized vessels, Island Lines provides integrated logistics solutions to businesses and communities.

SCF provides integrated river transportation and logistics. It provides customers with supply chain solutions using our fleet of barges and towboats, inland terminals and loading facilities, warehousing and storage distribution centers, fleeting operations, and shipyard and dock services.

Witt O'Brien's specializes in crisis and emergency management. Its mission is to make organizations as prepared and resilient as possible for all manner of man-made and natural disasters.

Geographic Reach

The company is headquartered in Fort Lauderdale, Florida and also has offices in new York, New York, and Houston Texas. It also has other operations in Washington, DC, as well as St, Louis, Missouri.

Mergers and Acquisitions

In mid-2021, SEACOR Holdings Inc. announced the completion of its acquisition of US Shipping Corp (USSC), a privately owned, leading, US-based provider of long-haul marine transportation for chemical and petroleum cargoes in the US coastwise trade, operating under the Jones Act. This strategic acquisition positions SEABULK, part of the SEACOR family of companies, as one of the largest Jones Act tanker operators with a fleet of 15 coastwise vessels ranging in size from 150,000 to 330,000 barrels of capacity. Terms of the transaction were not disclosed.

HISTORY

With only two vessels, SEACOR was founded in 1989 to service offshore oil rigs in the Gulf of Mexico. It quickly expanded its fleet by buying 36 vessels from midwestern utility holding company Nicor, which had diversified into oil services in the late 1970s.

When the Exxon Valdez oil spill prompted a 1990 federal law requiring energy companies to have cleanup plans, SEACOR was among the first to enter the safety business. In 1991 the company entered into a joint venture that operated safety standby vessels in the North Sea. By the time SEACOR went public in 1992, it had formed a similar joint venture in the US.

SEACOR expanded its Gulf operations throughout the 1990s. In 1994 it formed a joint venture with Transportación Maritima Mexicana to operate off the coast of Mexico. The company also gained some 165 ships by acquiring John E. Graham & Sons (1995) and McCall Enterprises (1996).

Also in 1996 SEACOR bought 45 offshore support vessels from the Netherlands' SMIT Internationale. As a result of the deal, the company changed its name to SEACOR SMIT Inc. in 1997. That year the firm created another joint venture to operate offshore Argentina, and SEACOR grabbed a 55% stake in Chiles Offshore, which began building two jack-up offshore drilling rigs.

SEACOR paid $37 million in 1998 for SMIT Internationale's 5% stake in the company. It also sold 34 vessels for $144 million (11 of these were chartered back to SEACOR) and accepted delivery of 10 new vessels. Also that year SEACOR invested in Globe Wireless, a marine telecommunications company concentrating on e-mail and data transfer. In 1999 SEACOR bought Kvaerner's Marinet Systems, which provides communications services to the shipping industry, with the intent of integrating its operations into Globe Wireless.

Chiles Offshore went public in 2000, and SEACOR retained a 27% stake. In 2001 SEACOR acquired UK shipping firm Stirling Shipping. The next year SEACOR sold its stake in Chiles Offshore to Ensco and acquired the remaining 80% of Tex-Air Helicopters, expanding its air support operations.

SEACOR SMIT changed its name in 2004 to SEACOR Holdings. That year SEACOR acquired Era Aviation, including its fleet of 128 helicopters, 16 aircraft, and 14 operating bases, from Rowan Companiesfor about $118 million.

In 2005 the company acquired former rival Seabulk International for $1 billion, including assumed debt. It sold its Globe Wireless unit two years later, exiting the maritime telecommunications business.

Expanding into US-based alcohol manufacturing, in 2012 the company acquired 70% of Illinois Corn Processing through an acquisition of a portion of its partner's interest.

Boosting it offshore support fleet, in 2011 SEACOR acquired 18 lift boats from Superior Energy for $142.5 million. It also bought eight foreign-flag roll-on/roll-off vessels and a 70% interest in an operating company engaged in the shipping trade between the US, the Bahamas, and the Caribbean.

To raise cash and in order to focus on its other core businesses, in 2011 SEACOR spun off its aviation unit (Era Group) which provides oil rig support helicopter and air medical transportation services. (Era accounted for 9% of SEACOR's 2010 revenues).

In 2012 the company merged its O'Brien's Response Management subsidiary with Witt Associates to create Witt O'Brien's, one of the US's top preparedness, crisis management, and disaster response and recovery organizations.

That year company sold a major portion of its environmental operations to equity firm J.F. Lehman & Company. The businesses sold included National Response Corporation (US oil spill response services), NRC Environmental Services Inc. (West Coast environmental and industrial services), and SEACOR Response Ltd. (international oil spill and emergency response services).

EXECUTIVES

CLO*, William C Long

Auditors: GRANT THORNTON LLP FORT LAUDE

LOCATIONS

HQ: SEACOR HOLDINGS INC.
2200 ELLER DR, FORT LAUDERDALE, FL 333163069
Phone: 954 523-2200
Web: WWW.SEACORHOLDINGS.COM

2016 Sales

	$mil.	% of total
United States	590.3	71
Europe, Primarily North Sea	82.7	10
Brazil, Mexico, Central and South America	64.8	8
Middle East and Asia	55.0	6
Africa, Primarily West Africa	37.8	5
Other	0.4	-
Total	831.0	100

PRODUCTS/OPERATIONS

2016 Sales

	$ mil.	% of total
Shipping Services	229.6	28
Offshore Marine Services	215.6	26
Inland River Services	167.6	20
ICP	177.4	21
Witt o'Brien's	42.9	5
Others	0.5	-
Eliminations and Corporate	(2.6)	-
Total	831.0	100

Selected Services

Alcohol manufacturing
Cargo delivery
Crew transportation
Helicopter and air medical services
Inland river barge transportation
Line handling (assisting tankers while loading)
Logistics services
Offshore construction support
Offshore maintenance work support
Oil spill response services
Salvage
Seismic data gathering support
Towing and anchor handling for drill rigs
Well stimulation support

COMPETITORS

BRISTOW HOLDINGS U.S. INC.
CROWLEY MARITIME CORPORATION
EURONAV MI II INC.
GULFMARK OFFSHORE, INC.
HORNBECK OFFSHORE SERVICES, INC.
INTERNATIONAL SHIPHOLDING CORPORATION
KAWASAKI KISEN KAISHA, LTD.
KEY ENERGY SERVICES, INC.
NIPPON YUSEN KABUSHIKI KAISHA
OVERSEAS SHIPHOLDING GROUP, INC.

HISTORICAL FINANCIALS

Company Type: Private

Income Statement   FYE: December 31

	REVENUE ($mil)	NET INCOME ($mil)	NET PROFIT MARGIN	EMPLOYEES
12/20	753	23	3.1%	2,195
12/19	799	34	4.3%	—
12/18	835	83	10.0%	—
12/17	577	81	14.1%	—
Annual Growth	9.3%	(34.2%)	—	—

2020 Year-End Financials

Return on assets: 1.5%   Cash ($ mil.): 65
Return on equity: 2.8%
Current Ratio: 2.20

SEALASKA CORPORATION

Sealaska Corporation is a native-owned investment firm active in natural resources, manufacturing, services, and gaming. The holding company owns land in southeastern Alaska, home to the Tlingit, Haida, and Tsimshian peoples. Sealaska core holdings include Sealaska Timber Corporation, Alaska Coastal Aggregates, Sealaska Constructors, Sealaska Environmental Services, and Colorado-based information technology services provider Managed Business Solutions. Subsidiary End-to-End Enterprises manages the company's gaming business. Sealaska's subsidiaries operate throughout North America and around the world. Its companies often win government contracts for construction, environmental, and engineering projects.

Operations

More than 60% of Sealaska's revenues came from its services segment during 2015, which includes subsidiary Sealaksa Environmental Services, Sealaksa Constructors, Sealaska Government Services, Sealaska Technical Services, Synergy Systems, and Managed Business Solutions.

Nearly 30% of Sealaska's revenues are earned by its natural resources business, which oversees land management and stewardship functions for all Sealaska lands. Sealaska owns about 290,000 acres of timberland, as well as the minerals rights to construction-grade aggregates on more than 565,000 acres. Sealaska Timber harvest timber and markets logs for the domestic and export markets.

The company's Investment Business Segment (5% of revenues) comprised the Majorie V. Young, Shareholder Permanent Fund, and the Investment and Growth Fund. Its Gaming segment is managed by its subsidiary End-to-End Enterprises.

Geographic Reach

Juneau-based Sealaska has offices through the US and several other countries, including Canada and Mexico, as well as Europe.

Financial Performance

Sealaska's annual revenues have fallen 65% since 2012 as its portfolio holdings (such as its civil construction business in Hawaii, and its natural resources business) haven't all fared well. The firm has rebounded from losses in 2013 however as it's sold off its less successful businesses and reduced costs.

The firm's revenue fell 10% to $109.4 million during 2015, with volatile markets causing a nearly $7 million decline in investment gains.

Revenue declines in 2015 caused Sealaska's net income to plunge 20% to $12 million, though operational improvements helped dampen the blow. The firm's services business in particular managed to grow its profits despite a small sales decline as it focused more on higher value added work. Sealaska's operating cash levels spiked nearly 80% to $18.62 million after adjusting its earnings for non-cash expenses such as investment losses.

Strategy

Sealaska continued in 2016 to target acquisitions in businesses operating in the natural foods and seafood, maritime services, environmental service, niche construction, and data analytics sectors. The company adopted a 2012-2017 plan designed to transform Sealaska into a financially sustainable and profitable company driven by its core cultural values. To that end, in 2013 the company sold its interest in its Nypro Kậnaak joint venture and the Sealaska Global Logistics business and exited the security guard services business (acquired in 2010), to support future acquisitions.

Company Background

Sealaska is the largest of 13 corporations formed under the Alaska Native Claims Settlement Act (ANCSA) of 1971, which promised some 44 million acres of land to Alaska natives. The company is owned by some 21,600 tribal member shareholders.

Subsidiary Haa AanÃ (meaning "our land") was established in 2009 as a way to promote the culture, social, and economic viability of Southeast Alaska. Haa AanÃ has assisted tribal members with their efforts to establish businesses such as a new oyster farms in southeastern Alaska. Haa AanÃ also promotes renewable energy initiatives such as a biomass heating system for commercial buildings. In 2012 Haa AanÃ launched a non-profit community development financial institution in order to provide financing and promote economic development.

Auditors: RSM US LLP ANCHORAGE ALASKA

LOCATIONS

HQ: SEALASKA CORPORATION
1 SEALASKA PLZ STE 400, JUNEAU, AK 998011276
Phone: 907 586-1512
Web: WWW.SEALASKA.COM

PRODUCTS/OPERATIONS

2014 Sales

	$ mil.	% of total
Services	81.1	67
Natural Resources	33.4	28
Investments	6.3	5
Gaming	0.2	-
Corporate & other	0.5	-
Total	121.5	100

Selected Subsidiaries

Alaska Coastal Aggregates
End-to-End Enterprises, LLC (gaming)
Haa Aaní, LLC
Managed Business Solutions (majority owned)
Sealaska Constructors, LLC
Sealaska Environmental Services
Sealaska Timber Corporation

COMPETITORS

C. Melchers GmbH & Co. KG
CARILLION PLC
FGX INTERNATIONAL HOLDINGS LIMITED
GUTHY-RENKER LLC
KIER GROUP PLC
REMINGTON OUTDOOR COMPANY, INC
RENEW HOLDINGS PLC.
TimberWest Forest Corp
WALT DISNEY COMPANY LIMITED(THE)
YAMAHA CORPORATION OF AMERICA

HISTORICAL FINANCIALS
Company Type: Private

Income Statement — FYE: December 31

	REVENUE ($mil)	NET INCOME ($mil)	NET PROFIT MARGIN	EMPLOYEES
12/20	697	71	10.3%	1,400
12/19	699	86	12.3%	—
12/18	429	69	16.1%	—
12/17	293	45	15.6%	—
Annual Growth	33.5%	16.2%	—	—

2020 Year-End Financials
Return on assets: 7.9%   Cash ($ mil.): 31
Return on equity: 15.2%
Current Ratio: 3.00

SEATTLE SCHOOLS DISTRICT NO. 1 OF KING COUNTY WASHINGTON

Auditors : PAT MCCARTHY OLYMPIA WA

LOCATIONS

HQ: SEATTLE SCHOOLS DISTRICT NO. 1 OF KING COUNTY WASHINGTON
   2445 3RD AVE S, SEATTLE, WA 981341923
Phone: 206 252-0000
Web: WWW.SEATTLESCHOOLS.ORG

HISTORICAL FINANCIALS
Company Type: Private

Income Statement — FYE: August 31

	REVENUE ($mil)	NET INCOME ($mil)	NET PROFIT MARGIN	EMPLOYEES
08/18	1,042	39	3.8%	4,650
08/06	553	4	0.8%	—
08/05	429	10	2.4%	—
Annual Growth	7.1%	11.0%	—	—

2018 Year-End Financials
Return on assets: 8.2%   Cash ($ mil.): 271
Return on equity: 24.0%
Current Ratio: —

SECURITY FINANCE CORPORATION OF SPARTANBURG

Folks looking for a little financial security just might turn to Security Finance Corporation of Spartanburg. Founded in 1955, the consumer loan company provides personal loans typically ranging from $100 to $600 (some states, however, allow loan amounts as high as $3,000). Customers can also turn to Security Finance for credit reports and tax preparation services. The company operates approximately 900 offices in more than 15 states that are marketed under the Security Finance, Sunbelt Credit, and PFS banner names. A subsidiary of Security Group, the financial institution also has locations operating as Security Financial Services in North Carolina and Longhorn Finance in Texas.

Operations
Security Finance boasts some 900 offices nationwide that operate under the Security Finance, Sunbelt Credit, and PFS names. The company specializes in offering consumers loans to individuals. It also provides consumer credit reports and assistance, as well as tax preparation services.

Geographic Reach
From its headquarters in South Carolina, Security Finance boasts offices in more than 15 states nationwide.

Company Background
Security Finance exited Colorado in 2010 after the state's attorney general general office filed a compliant that the company had been refinancing some consumer loans more than three times a year (the limit under Colorado law). The company agreed to repay acquisition fees that it had charged the customers for refinancing the loans.

Auditors : ELLIOTT DAVIS DECOSIMO LLC G

LOCATIONS

HQ: SECURITY FINANCE CORPORATION OF SPARTANBURG
   181 SECURITY PL, SPARTANBURG, SC 293075450
Phone: 864 582-8193
Web: WWW.SECURITYFINANCE.COM

Selected Locations
Alabama
Florida
Georgia
Idaho
Illinois
Louisiana
Missouri
Nevada
New Mexico
North Carolina
Oklahoma
South Carolina
Tennessee
Texas
Utah
Wisconsin

PRODUCTS/OPERATIONS

Selected Banners
Longhorn Finance (Texas)
PFS
Security Finance
Security Financial Services (North Carolina)
Sunbelt Credit

COMPETITORS

AMERICAN EXPRESS COMPANY
ATLANTICUS HOLDINGS CORPORATION
COGNITION FINANCIAL CORPORATION
CREDIT ACCEPTANCE CORPORATION
CREDIT HUMAN FEDERAL CREDIT UNION
GENERAL MOTORS FINANCIAL COMPANY, INC.
KINECTA FEDERAL CREDIT UNION
NELNET, INC.
REGIONAL MANAGEMENT CORP.
WORLD ACCEPTANCE CORPORATION

HISTORICAL FINANCIALS
Company Type: Private

Income Statement — FYE: December 31

	ASSETS ($mil)	NET INCOME ($mil)	INCOME AS % OF ASSETS	EMPLOYEES
12/16	625	70	11.3%	2,500
12/15	651	78	12.1%	—
12/14	648	83	12.8%	—
12/13	616	62	10.2%	—
Annual Growth	0.5%	4.1%	—	—

2016 Year-End Financials
Return on assets: 11.3%   Cash ($ mil.): 17
Return on equity: 20.6%
Current Ratio: —

SECURITY GROUP, INC.

Auditors : ELLIOTT DAVIS DECOSIMO LLC GR

LOCATIONS

HQ: SECURITY GROUP, INC.
   181 SECURITY PL, SPARTANBURG, SC 293075450
Phone: 864 582-8193
Web: WWW.SECURITYFINANCE.COM

HISTORICAL FINANCIALS
Company Type: Private

Income Statement — FYE: December 31

	ASSETS ($mil)	NET INCOME ($mil)	INCOME AS % OF ASSETS	EMPLOYEES
12/16	1,002	87	8.8%	2,500
12/15	1,020	97	9.6%	—
12/14	1,040	135	13.0%	—
12/13	1,263	107	8.5%	—
Annual Growth	(7.4%)	(6.4%)	—	—

2016 Year-End Financials
Return on assets: 8.8%   Cash ($ mil.): 35
Return on equity: 12.7%
Current Ratio: —

SECURITY HEALTH PLAN OF WISCONSIN, INC.

Security Health Plan of Wisconsin provides health insurance coverage and related services to some 200,000 members in more than 35 Wisconsin counties. Its managed network of providers includes more than 4,000 physicians, 40 hospitals, and health care facilities, as well as 55,000 pharmacies across the US. Security Health Plan provides policies for groups and individuals. Its products include HMO coverage plans and supplemental Medicare plans, as well as prescription drug and equipment coverage, disease management programs, and administration services for self-funded plans. Established in 1986, the company is the managed healthcare arm of Marshfield Clinic, which operates medical practices across the state.

Operations

Since it is affiliated with a medical care provider, Security Health Plan's coverage decisions are directly impacted by the practicing physician. The company's provider network consists of independent physician locations and parent Marshfield Clinic's more than 50 locations in Wisconsin.

In addition to HMO plans, the firm's comprehensive medical coverage plans include POS (point of service) and high-deductable offerings. Security Health Plan offers health care reimbursement accounts through third-party provider agreements with Employee Benefits Corporation and Diversified Benefits Services. In addition, the company provides community education and wellness programs.

Geographic Reach

Headquartered in the town of Marshfield, Security Health Plan serves the counties of Adams, Ashland, Barron, Bayfield, Burnett, Chippewa, Clark, Columbia, Dane, Douglas, Dunn, Eau Claire, Forest, Iron, Jackson, Juneau, Langlade, Lincoln, Marathon, Marquette, Monroe, Oneida, Pepin, Portage, Price, Rusk, Sauk, Sawyer, Shawano, Taylor, Trempealeau, Vilas, Washburn, Waupaca, Waushara, and Wood.

Sales and Marketing

Security Health Plan serves individuals, families, and small to large employer groups.

Strategy

Originally started in 1986 as an offshoot of the Greater Marshfield Community Health Plan, Security Health Plan's service territory has grown over the years. For instance, in 2012 the company extended its Advocare Medicare Advantage plan offering into several new counties. Security Health Plan also regularly adds primary care and specialty providers to its network to provide a broader range of accessible care services to its members, as well as to strengthen its operations in underserved regions. The company is also looking to enhance its IT systems to allow for greater information access, communication methods, and collaboration among its providers and members.

Auditors : KPMG LLP MINNEAPOLIS MN

LOCATIONS

HQ: SECURITY HEALTH PLAN OF WISCONSIN, INC.
1515 N SAINT JOSEPH AVE, MARSHFIELD, WI 544491343
Phone: 715 221-9555
Web: WWW.SECURITYHEALTH.ORG

COMPETITORS

CAPITAL DISTRICT PHYSICIANS' HEALTH PLAN, INC.
DEAN HEALTH PLAN, INC.
MINISTRY HEALTH CARE, INC.
SHERIDAN HEALTHCARE, INC.
U.S. HEALTHWORKS, INC.

HISTORICAL FINANCIALS
Company Type: Private

Income Statement — FYE: December 31

	REVENUE ($mil)	NET INCOME ($mil)	NET PROFIT MARGIN	EMPLOYEES
12/17	1,234	9	0.8%	1,006
12/09	814	27	3.4%	—
12/05	385	0	0.0%	—
12/04	369	17	4.7%	—
Annual Growth	9.7%	(4.4%)	—	—

2017 Year-End Financials
Return on assets: 2.8%   Cash ($ mil.): 159
Return on equity: 5.7%
Current Ratio: 1.10

SEMCO ENERGY, INC.

Alaska and Michigan have more in common than a cold climate. SEMCO ENERGY serves approximately 423,000 natural gas consumers in both states. The company's main subsidiary is utility SEMCO ENERGY Gas, which distributes gas to more than 290,000 customers in 24 Michigan counties. SEMCO's ENSTAR Natural Gas unit distributes gas to more than 133,000 customers in and around Anchorage, Alaska. The company's unregulated operations include propane distribution in Michigan and Wisconsin; pipeline and storage facility operation; and information technology outsourcing. In 2012 SEMCO ENERGY was acquired by AltaGas.

Auditors : ERNST & YOUNG LLP DETROIT MI

LOCATIONS

HQ: SEMCO ENERGY, INC.
1411 3RD ST STE A, PORT HURON, MI 480605480
Phone: 810 987-2200
Web: WWW.SEMCOENERGYGAS.COM

COMPETITORS

DELTA NATURAL GAS COMPANY, INC.
DTE GAS COMPANY
NORTHWESTERN CORPORATION
ONEOK PARTNERS, L.P.
SOUTHERN COMPANY GAS
SPIRE ALABAMA INC.
UNITIL CORPORATION
VECTREN CORPORATION
WISCONSIN GAS LLC
YANKEE GAS SERVICES COMPANY

HISTORICAL FINANCIALS
Company Type: Private

Income Statement — FYE: December 31

	REVENUE ($mil)	NET INCOME ($mil)	NET PROFIT MARGIN	EMPLOYEES
12/16	575	51	9.0%	500
12/14	674	51	7.6%	—
12/13	608	48	8.0%	—
12/12	582	41	7.2%	—
Annual Growth	(0.3%)	5.5%	—	—

2016 Year-End Financials
Return on assets: 3.2%   Cash ($ mil.): 4
Return on equity: 9.0%
Current Ratio: 1.20

SEMINOLE ELECTRIC COOPERATIVE, INC.

This Seminole is not only a native Floridian, but it has also provided electricity in the state since 1948. Seminole Electric Cooperative generates and transmits electricity for 10 member distribution cooperatives that serve 1.4 million residential and business customers in 42 Florida counties. Seminole Electric has more than 3,350 MW of primarily coal-fired generating capacity. The cooperative also buys electricity from other utilities and independent power producers, and it owns 350 miles of transmission lines. Some 90% of its power load uses the transmission systems of other utilities through long-term contracts.

Operations

Seminole Electric's primary resources include the 1,300 MW Seminole Generating Station and the 810 MW Richard J. Midulla Generating Station. The coop's renewable energy resources include waste-to-energy facilities, landfill gas-to-energy facilities, and a biomass facility. It also buys power, as needed, on the market.

Seminole Electric has more than 350 miles of transmission line.

Geographic Reach

The company serves customers in 45 counties in northeast, south central, and southeast Florida.

Financial Performance

In 2013 the coop's revenues declined by

1% due to lower rates and as well as a reduction in Member energy requirements and lower volumes sold to Non-Members.

Seminole Electric's net income increased by 48% in 2013 thanks to lower operating costs as a result of the absence of asset impairment costs and a drop in interest expenses.

The company's operating cash inflow increased to $86.05 million in 2013 (from $34.81 million in 2012) primarily due to improved net income and a change in working capital.

Strategy

The coop is seeking to respond to the State of Florida's push to get more power generation from renewable sources. In 2014 the company generating about 58% of its electricity from coal, 35% from natural gas, and 7% from green energy sources (up from 5.5% in 2011, making Seminole Electric one of the largest green energy providers in Florida).

Company Background

In 2012 it also made major environmental improvements to its main power plant, the coal-fired Seminole Generating Station. In 2011 Seminole Electric boosted its portfolio of purchased green energy to more than 140 MW (including 113 MW from waste-to-energy facilities).

Seminole Electric was formed in 1948 to aggregate the power demands of its members and is governed by a board of trustees representing the 10 member utilities. The cooperative built its first power plant in the 1970s.

Auditors : PRICEWATERHOUSECOOPERS LLP TA

LOCATIONS

HQ: SEMINOLE ELECTRIC COOPERATIVE, INC.
16313 N DALE MABRY HWY, TAMPA, FL 336181427
Phone: 813 963-0994
Web: WWW.SEMINOLE-ELECTRIC.COM

PRODUCTS/OPERATIONS

Members
Central Florida Electric Cooperative
Clay Electric Cooperative
Glades Electric Cooperative
Lee County Electric Cooperative
Peace River Electric Cooperative
Sumter Electric Cooperative
Suwannee Valley Electric Cooperative
Talquin Electric Cooperative
Tri-County Electric Cooperative
Withlacoochee River Electric Cooperative

COMPETITORS

ARKANSAS ELECTRIC COOPERATIVE CORPORATION
GREAT RIVER ENERGY
OMAHA PUBLIC POWER DISTRICT
POWERSOUTH ENERGY COOPERATIVE
WESTERN FARMERS ELECTRIC COOPERATIVE

HISTORICAL FINANCIALS

Company Type: Private

Income Statement FYE: December 31

	REVENUE ($mil)	NET INCOME ($mil)	NET PROFIT MARGIN	EMPLOYEES
12/18	1,083	21	1.9%	528
12/17*	1,067	23	2.2%	—
03/17	1,052	33	3.2%	—
12/16	1,067	20	1.9%	—
Annual Growth	0.7%	2.1%	—	—

*Fiscal year change

2018 Year-End Financials

Return on assets: 1.1%   Cash ($ mil.): 35
Return on equity: 5.4%
Current Ratio: 1.10

SENTARA HEALTHCARE

Sentara is an integrated, not-for-profit system of a dozen of hospitals in Virginia and Northeastern North Carolina, including a Level I trauma center, the Sentara Heart Hospital and the Sentara Healthcare Cardiovascular Research Institute, the Sentara Brock Cancer Center and the accredited Sentara Cancer Network, two orthopedic hospitals, and the Sentara Neurosciences Institute. The Sentara family also includes a medical group, Nightingale Regional Air Ambulance, home care and hospice, ambulatory outpatient campuses, advanced imaging and diagnostic centers, a clinically integrated network, the Sentara College of Health Sciences and the Optima Health Plan and Virginia Premier Health Plan serving 858,000 members in Virginia, and North Carolina.

Operations

With more than 3,800 medical staff, Sentara offers a wide range of medical services such as heart failure treatment, general surgery, imaging, joint replacement, maternity, home care, robotic surgery, transplant services, weight loss surgery, women's health and x-rays.

Geographic Reach

Based in Norfolk, Virginia, Sentara operates more than 100 care sites across Virginia and North Carolina.

Sales and Marketing

The company's Optima Health plan and Virginia Health plan serves more than 858,000 members.

Strategy

In 2021, Sentara Healthcare today announced a $10 million investment, called the Sentara Healthier Communities Fund, to improve the health of the communities the company serve and make a dramatic difference in the lives of its patients and neighbors.

The investment will be split into three areas of focus and will enhance capabilities for Sentara's partner universities and collaboration between the universities, health systems and community partners to improve public health: University Grants ($4 million total); Collaborative Grants (up to $3 million); and Community Grants (up to $3 million).

Company Background

Sentara Healthcare was founded in 1888 as Norfolk's 25-bed Retreat for the Sick. Norfolk General and Leigh Memorial merged in 1972.

Additional hospitals were acquired over the years including Hampton General Hospital (1988), Bayside Hospital (1991), Virginia Beach General Hospital (1998), Williamsburg Community Hospital (2002), Obici Hospital (2006), Potomac Hospital (2009), RMH Healthcare (2011), Martha Jefferson Hospital (2011), and Halifax Regional Health System (2013). Construction of the Sentara Princess Anne Hospital was completed in 2011.

In 2014, it acquired the assets and operations of Albemarle Hospital, Albemarle Physician Services, and Regional Medical Services through a 30-year capital lease agreement with Pasquotank County and Albemarle Hospital Authority. The businesses were combined into newly formed subsidiary SAMC.

EXECUTIVES

CDO*, Dana Beckton
Auditors : KPMG LLP NORFOLK VA

LOCATIONS

HQ: SENTARA HEALTHCARE
6015 PPLAR HALL DR STE 30, NORFOLK, VA 23502
Phone: 800 736-8272
Web: WWW.SENTARA.COM

PRODUCTS/OPERATIONS

Selected Hospitals
Charlottesville
    Martha Jefferson Hospital
    MJH Outpatient Care Center
    Health Services at Proffit Road
    Health Services at Spring Creek
    Sentara Home Care Services
    Optima Health
Hampton Roads
    Sentara CarePlex Hospital
    Sentara Heart Hospital
    Sentara Leigh Hospital
    Sentara Norfolk General Hospital
    Sentara Obici Hospital
    Sentara Princess Anne Hospital
    Sentara Virginia Beach General Hospital
    Sentara Williamsburg Regional Medical Center
    Orthopaedic Hospital at Sentara CarePlex
    Sentara Northern Virginia Medical Center
    Martha Jefferson Hospital
    RMH Healthcare
Harrisonburg
    RMH Healthcare
    Optima Health
Northern Virginia
    Sentara Northern Virginia Medical Center
    Sentara Lake Ridge
    Sentara Medical Group physicians

Sentara Home Care Services
Sentara Heart and Vascular Center
Optima Health

Selected Services
Cancer
Cardiac (Heart)
Digestive (Colorectal)
Home Care
Imaging
Maternity
Neurosciences
Rehabilitation
Seniors
Thoracic
Transplant
Trauma/Emergency Services
Urology
Vascular
Weight Loss Surgery
Women's

COMPETITORS

ATLANTIC HEALTH SYSTEM INC.
BAPTIST HEALTH SOUTH FLORIDA, INC.
CONCORD HOSPITAL, INC.
EASTERN MAINE HEALTHCARE SYSTEMS
INSPIRA HEALTH NETWORK, INC.
LEHIGH VALLEY HEALTH NETWORK, INC.
MEDSTAR HEALTH, INC.
POTOMAC HOSPITAL CORPORATION OF PRINCE WILLIAM
SOUTH MIAMI HOSPITAL, INC.
WEST FLORIDA REGIONAL MEDICAL CENTER, INC.

HISTORICAL FINANCIALS
Company Type: Private

Income Statement — FYE: December 31

	REVENUE ($mil)	NET INCOME ($mil)	NET PROFIT MARGIN	EMPLOYEES
12/20	8,861	738	8.3%	28,000
12/19	6,753	703	10.4%	—
12/17	5,297	580	11.0%	—
12/16	5,083	329	6.5%	—
Annual Growth	14.9%	22.4%	—	—

2020 Year-End Financials
Return on assets: 6.9% Cash ($ mil.): 1,315
Return on equity: 11.4%
Current Ratio: 1.60

SENTARA HOSPITALS - NORFOLK

Auditors: KPMG LLP NORFOLK VA

LOCATIONS

HQ: SENTARA HOSPITALS - NORFOLK
600 GRESHAM DR, NORFOLK, VA 235071904
Phone: 757 388-3000
Web: WWW.SENTARA.COM

HISTORICAL FINANCIALS
Company Type: Private

Income Statement — FYE: December 31

	REVENUE ($mil)	NET INCOME ($mil)	NET PROFIT MARGIN	EMPLOYEES
12/20	1,165	113	9.7%	2,459
12/17	877	63	7.2%	—
12/16	831	100	12.1%	—
12/15	791	92	11.7%	—
Annual Growth	8.1%	4.1%	—	—

2020 Year-End Financials
Return on assets: 15.4% Cash ($ mil.): 30
Return on equity: 21.6%
Current Ratio: 2.60

SERVANT FOUNDATION

Auditors: KELLER & OWENS LLC OVERLAND P

LOCATIONS

HQ: SERVANT FOUNDATION
7171 W 95TH ST STE 501, OVERLAND PARK, KS 662122254
Phone: 913 310-0279
Web: WWW.THESIGNATRY.COM

HISTORICAL FINANCIALS
Company Type: Private

Income Statement — FYE: March 31

	REVENUE ($mil)	NET INCOME ($mil)	NET PROFIT MARGIN	EMPLOYEES
03/21	641	239	37.4%	30
03/20*	405	60	15.0%	—
12/09	1	0	32.7%	—
06/08	0	(0)	—	—
Annual Growth	66.4%	—	—	—

*Fiscal year change

2021 Year-End Financials
Return on assets: 24.6% Cash ($ mil.): 6
Return on equity: 24.6%
Current Ratio: —

SERVCO PACIFIC INC.

Servco Pacific's business flows through an ocean's worth of enterprises. The company sells passenger vehicles (including Toyota, Subaru, Suzuki, and Chevrolet models) and commercial trucks through dealerships in Hawaii and Australia. In addition, Servco Home & Appliance wholesales kitchen and bath products to building professionals throughout the South Pacific; Servco Raynor Overhead Doors installs residential and commercial garage doors; Servco Insurance Services offers insurance coverage for businesses and individuals; and Servco School & Office Furniture outfits educational institutions and government agencies with desks, seating, and other furnishings. Servco Pacific was founded by Peter Fukunaga in 1919.

Operations
The diversified firm sells insurance through Servco Insurance Services (SIS) in Washington state. It clients are in the fishing, shipping, and cargo industries in several states, including Alaska. SIS also operates in Hawaii, where sister chains Servco Home & Appliance, Servco Forklift & Industrial Equipment, and Servco Automotive also operate. Sercvo Tire Company sells tires on Maui and in Honolulu.

Geographic Reach
Honolulu-based Servco Pacific has insurance offices in Seattle and Tacoma, Washington. Its other businesses operate in Hawaii (Kauai, Maui, Oahu, and the Big Island); and Australia (New South Wales, Queensland).

Financial Performance
The private company reports revenue of approximately $800 million annually.

Strategy
Servco Pacific, through its Australian subsidiary, has been expanding its Toyota dealer operations in recent years. During 2010 the company acquired majority stakes in Sunshine Toyota of Queensland and Dubbo City Toyota of New South Wales. It also purchased Pacific Toyota in Cairns in 2009. The deals have significantly grown Servco Pacific's business in Australia, part of a bid to strengthen its international presence; altogether, Servco Pacific owns five dealerships in the country. The firm started operating in Australia in late 2007 with the acquisition of a Toyota dealership in Brisbane. Closer to home, Servco is acquiring dealerships in Hawaii amid a influx of off-island businesses, including Lithia Motors, to Hawaii.

Mergers and Acquisitions
In February 2014, Servco acquired the assets of Maui's Island Subaru dealership in Kahului. The newly-acquired dealership will operate as Servco Subaru.

Auditors: ACUCITY LLP HONOLULU HAWAII

LOCATIONS

HQ: SERVCO PACIFIC INC.
2850 PUKOLOA ST STE 300, HONOLULU, HI 968194475
Phone: 808 564-1300
Web: WWW.SERVCO.COM

PRODUCTS/OPERATIONS

Selected Operations
Automotive
   Rex Tire and Supply
   Scion Dealers of Hawaii
   Subaru Dealers of Hawaii
   Suzuki Dealers of Hawaii
   Servco Australia
   Servco Chevy
   Servco Lexus
   Servco Truck & Commercial
   Toyota Dealers of Hawaii

Servco Home and Appliance Distribution
Servco Insurance Services
Servco Raynor Overhead Doors
Servco School and Office Furniture

COMPETITORS

ARNOLD CLARK AUTOMOBILES LIMITED
Controladora Mabe, S.A. de C.V.
FLEETPRIDE, INC.
HAIER AMERICA TRADING, L.L.C.
JVCKENWOOD USA CORPORATION
MIELE, INCORPORATED
OREGON SCIENTIFIC, INC.
PANASONIC CORPORATION OF NORTH AMERICA
RDO EQUIPMENT CO.
RUSSELL SIGLER, INC.

HISTORICAL FINANCIALS
Company Type: Private

Income Statement   FYE: December 31

	REVENUE ($mil)	NET INCOME ($mil)	NET PROFIT MARGIN	EMPLOYEES
12/18	1,802	66	3.7%	1,000
12/17	1,629	26	1.6%	—
12/16	1,435	29	2.1%	—
12/12	923	15	1.7%	—
Annual Growth	11.8%	27.1%	—	—

2018 Year-End Financials
Return on assets: 8.1%   Cash ($ mil.): 61
Return on equity: 24.9%
Current Ratio: 1.20

SES HOLDINGS, LLC

Auditors: KPMG LLP DALLAS TX

LOCATIONS
HQ: SES HOLDINGS, LLC
1820 N INTERSTATE 35, GAINESVILLE, TX 762402179
Phone: 940 668-1818
Web: WWW.SELECTENERGY.COM

HISTORICAL FINANCIALS
Company Type: Private

Income Statement   FYE: December 31

	ASSETS ($mil)	NET INCOME ($mil)	INCOME AS % OF ASSETS	EMPLOYEES
12/12	941	2	0.3%	1,700
12/11	1,019	131	12.9%	—
12/10	617	57	9.3%	—
Annual Growth	23.5%	(78.7%)	—	—

2012 Year-End Financials
Return on assets: 0.3%   Cash ($ mil.): 18
Return on equity: 0.6%
Current Ratio: 1.80

SEVENTY SEVEN ENERGY LLC

Seventy Seven Energy (formerly Chesapeake Oilfield Services) is a company that was spun off from Chesapeake Energy, one of the top onshore energy companies in the US. Chesapeake Energy reorganized six of its oilfield services subsidiaries into then Chesapeake Oilfield Services to create a new, publicly traded entity that offers drilling, hydraulic fracturing, and trucking services, as well as renting tools and manufacturing natural gas compressor equipment. It operates in onshore plays in the US. The company filed for Chapter 11 bankruptcy protection in 2016. In 2017 the company was bought by Patterson-UTI in a $1.76 billion stock deal, including debt.

Operations
The company conducts business through three operating segments: Hydraulic Fracturing, Drilling, and Oilfield Rentals.

The hydraulic fracturing segment (51% of Seventy Seven Energy's total revenues in 2015) operates through Performance Technologies, and provides high-pressure hydraulic fracturing services and other well stimulation services. This unit owns 11 hydraulic fracturing fleets with an aggregate of 440,000 horsepower, and six of these fleets are contracted in the Anadarko Basin and the Eagle Ford and Utica Shales. The fracturing process consists of pumping a fracturing fluid into a well at sufficient pressure to fracture the formation.

The drilling segment (38%) operates through Nomac Drilling, and provides land drilling services for oil and natural gas E&P activities.

The oilfield rentals segment (11%) operates through Great Plains Oilfield Rental, and provides premium rental tools and specialized services for land-based oil and natural gas drilling, completion and workover activities. It offers an extensive line of rental tools, including a full line of tubular products specifically designed for horizontal drilling and completion, with high-torque, premium-connection drill pipe, drill collars and tubing.

Geographic Reach
Seventy Seven Energy operates in the Anadarko and Permian Basins and the Eagle Ford, Haynesville, Marcellus, Niobrara, and Utica Shales.

Sales and Marketing
The company got 70% of its revenues from Chesapeake Energy (CHK) and its affiliates in 2015.

Financial Performance
In 2015 Seventy Seven Energy's net revenues decreased by 46%.

Drilling revenues decreased due to lower revenue days, driven by a drop in demand by non-CHK customers.

Hydraulic fracturing revenues declined due to a decrease in revenue per stage, driven by market pricing pressure.

Oilfield rental revenues decreased due to a decline in utilization and pricing pressure.

In 2015 Seventy Seven Energy's net loss grew by 2,675% due to lower revenues, loss on sale of a business, loss on sales of property and equipment, net, and impairment of goodwill.

Cash from operating activities increased by 7% due to the changes in the timing of collection of accounts receivable and the decline in overall operational activity.

Strategy
Chesapeake Energy decided to spin off its oilfield services in order to keep that activity separate from exploration and production. With exploration, production, and oilfield services under one umbrella, the company only had one customer - itself. By separating the oilfield services unit, Chesapeake Energy reduces its risk should exploration and production slow down, much as it did with natural gas drilling and the shift to natural gas liquids.

Nomac Drilling continued to upgrade its rig fleet in 2015, making 80% of its rig fleet capable of drilling on multi well pads. As one of the most active drillers in the United States, Nomac also continues to diversify its customer base, serving more than 20 different operators.

Seventy Seven Energy expects to spend $100 million in aggregate growth and maintenance capital expenditures in 2016. It also intends to explore opportunistic complementary acquisitions, particularly within the hydraulic fracturing segment.

In 2015 the company completed the previously disclosed sale of Hodges Trucking Company, L.L.C. to a wholly-owned subsidiary of Aveda Transportation and Energy Services Inc. for $42 million.

Company Background
The company was formed in October 2011 and filed to go public in April 2012 in an initial public offering seeking up to $862.5 million. It completed the spinoff in July 2014 and renamed the company, Seventy Seven Energy.

HISTORY

In 2011 Chesapeake Energy and its partners (including several joint ventures) accounted for about 94% of revenues, but the company's goal is to only provide about two-thirds of Chesapeake Energy's oilfield service needs.

With the 2011 reorganization, Chesapeake Oilfield Services took over a half dozen subsidiaries, including Compass Manufacturing, Great Plains Oilfield Rental, Hodges Trucking Company, Nomac Drilling, Oilfield Trucking Solutions, and Performance Technologies. The company generates the most revenue (about two-thirds of overall sales) from its drilling operations performed under Nomac Drilling. The majority of its rigs are contracted to Chesapeake Energy for use in the Anadarko Basin and the Marcellus Shale. The company is planning for more growth, in fact, Nomac Drilling ordered a dozen new rigs that can perform horizontal drilling in shale formations and other unconventional resource plays. All of the new rigs are expected to be delivered by May 2013.

Chesapeake Oilfield Services' second-largest segment is equipment rental offered through Great Plains Oilfield Rental, which accounted for almost 20% of sales in 2011. Great Plains Oilfield Rental offers drill pipe, drill collars, tubing, blowout preventers, frac and mud tanks, and it provides air drilling services and transfers water to wells for fracking. The rental segment also generates the highest margins since there's no operational costs involved. Oilfield trucking, offered through Hodges Trucking Company and Oilfield Trucking Solutions, accounted for about 10% of sales in 2011. The two companies own about 225 rig relocation trucks, almost 160 fluid hauling trucks, and 55 cranes and forklifts. And Compass Manufacturing, which can make 600 natural gas compressor units per year, accounted for about 5% of sales. Chesapeake Oilfield Services plans to have the company begin to manufacture other type of equipment used by its rental segment.

Its smallest operating segment is hydraulic fracturing services offered through Performance Technologies. Of course, hydraulic fracturing accounted for about 1% of sales in 2011 only because it began operations with four fleets in the fourth quarter. Chesapeake Oilfield Services plans to have eight fleets by 2013 and a dozen fleets by 2014.

Chesapeake Oilfield Services also took over the assets of Horizon Oilfield Services (bought in November 2011 for $17.5 million), Bronco Drilling (bought in June 2011 for $339 million), and Forrest Rig Company (bought in December 2010 for $84.5 million). Despite two acquisitions in 2011, the oilfield services segment topped the $1 billion mark in sales in 2011. The company also recorded a profit for the first time.

Prior to forming Chesapeake Oilfield Services, Chesapeake Energy's oilfield services subsidiaries were organized under COS Holdings, L.L.C. Should Chesapeake Oilfield Services successfully go public, it will own an interest in COS Holdings, L.L.C. Chesapeake Energy will still be the major shareholder and customer of both companies, with more than 50% of the voting power. Chesapeake Oilfield Services plans to use the proceeds from its IPO to pay off the predecessor company and to pay down debt.

Auditors : PRICEWATERHOUSECOOPERS LLP OK

LOCATIONS
HQ: SEVENTY SEVEN ENERGY LLC
  777 NW 63RD ST, OKLAHOMA CITY, OK 731167601
Phone: 405 608-7777
Web: WWW.PATENERGY.COM

PRODUCTS/OPERATIONS
SERVICES
Drilling
Pumping
Rentals
Selected Subsidiaries
Compass Manufacturing, L.L.C. (maufatures natural gas compression equipment)
Great Plains Oilfield Rental, L.L.C. (tool and equipment rental)
Hodges Trucking Company, L.L.C. (trucking services)
Nomac Drilling, L.L.C. (drilling services)
Oilfield Trucking Solutions, L.L.C. (trucking services)
Performance Technologies, L.L.C. (hydraulic fracturing)

2015 Sales
	in mil.	% of total
Drilling	436.4	38
Hydraulic fracturing	575.4	51
Oilfield rentals	76.5	7
Oilfield trucking	42.7	4
other operations	0.2	-
Total	1,131.2	100

COMPETITORS
BASIC ENERGY SERVICES, INC.
FORBES ENERGY SERVICES LTD.
Gibson Energy Inc
HALLIBURTON COMPANY
KEY ENERGY SERVICES, INC.
OCEANEERING INTERNATIONAL, INC.
PARKER DRILLING COMPANY
PATTERSON-UTI ENERGY, INC.
Precision Drilling Corporation
SUPERIOR ENERGY SERVICES, INC.

HISTORICAL FINANCIALS
Company Type: Private

Income Statement   FYE: December 31

	REVENUE ($mil)	NET INCOME ($mil)	NET PROFIT MARGIN	EMPLOYEES
12/15	1,131	(221)	—	1,700
12/14	2,080	(7)	—	—
Annual Growth	(45.6%)	—	—	—

2015 Year-End Financials
Return on assets: (-11.6%)   Cash ($ mil.): 130
Return on equity: (-186.3%)
Current Ratio: 2.10

SGT, LLC

Like its acronym name suggests, SGT (aka Stinger Ghaffarian Technologies) is used to taking military orders; in this case very specific, technical ones. An engineering services firm, SGT provides aerospace engineering, project management, IT systems development, and related services to NASA, the US Navy, the US Air Force, and other primarily military-related government entities through contracts. The company also offers science-related services such as earth, climate, and planetary modeling and analysis. SGT's facilities are located near airfields and other military facilities.

Geographic Reach
SGT operates a more than dozen offices including in Houston, Cleveland, and Los Angeles, White Sands (New Mexico), and Wallops Island (Virginia).

Sales and Marketing
The company serves the aerospace and aeronautics sectors in addition to civilian agencies and national security entities.

Strategy
SGT grows by signing contracts and working with other partners. In early 2017, it won a $45 million contract to support the National Oceanic and Atmospheric Administration (NOAA). Under the contract, SGT will support the National Mesonet Program, which brings non-federal meteorological data sources to NOAA for use in operations at weather forecast offices and numerical modeling information at the National Centers for Environmental Protection. To achieve this, SGT is working in partnership with Earth Networks, Weather Telematics, WeatherFlow, Synoptic Data Corp., Sonoma Technology Inc., Panasonic Avionics Corp., and the University of Oklahoma.

Company Background
SGT was founded in 1994 by Harold Stinger and Kam Ghaffarian.

EXECUTIVES
Chief Strategy Officer*, Charlie Goorevich
Chief Human Resources Officer*, Shelley Johnson
Auditors : GRANT THORNTON LLP MCLEAN VI

LOCATIONS
HQ: SGT, LLC
  7701 GREENBELT RD STE 400, GREENBELT, MD 207706521
Phone: 301 614-8600
Web: WWW.KBR.COM

COMPETITORS
ANALYTICAL GRAPHICS, INC.
JARDON & HOWARD TECHNOLOGIES, INCORPORATED
LOCKHEED MARTIN UK INTEGRATED SYSTEMS AND SOLUTIONS LIMITED
Maxar Technologies Ltd
NATIONAL SECURITY TECHNOLOGIES, LLC
POSITIVE EDGE STRATEGIES, INC
RAYTHEON BBN TECHNOLOGIES CORP.
ROSE INTERNATIONAL, INC.
SMARTRONIX, LLC
TYBRIN CORPORATION

HISTORICAL FINANCIALS
Company Type: Private

Income Statement   FYE: September 30

	REVENUE ($mil)	NET INCOME ($mil)	NET PROFIT MARGIN	EMPLOYEES
09/15	570	23	4.2%	2,300
09/13	416	15	3.7%	—
09/12	374	9	2.4%	—
09/08	292	8	2.8%	—
Annual Growth	10.0%	16.3%	—	—

2015 Year-End Financials
Return on assets: 20.1%   Cash ($ mil.): —
Return on equity: 69.0%
Current Ratio: 1.40

SHAMROCK FOODS COMPANY

Shamrock Foods Company is one of the nation's leading foodservice distributors with a strong presence in the western US. It primarily serves restaurants, healthcare facilities, military installations, catering companies, food banks, and hospitality customers by providing everyday staples such as meats, produce, dry goods, beverages, and supplies, as well as ethnic foods and artisanal, gourmet, and other specialty foods. Proprietary brands include Gold Canyon, Four Leaf Roasters, Markon, Jensen Foods, Pier 22 Seafood, and Rideglinc. Through Shamrock Farms, the company is also one of the largest family-owned and -operated dairies in the country. Founded in 1922, Shamrock Foods is still owned and operated by the founding McClelland family.

Operations
Shamrock Foods is now one of the top 10 largest foodservice distributors nationwide. Its products include high-quality meats, dairy, fruits and vegetables, beverages, dry goods and groceries, and kitchen supplies and equipment, among others.

Shamrock Foods' exclusive brands include Bountiful Harvest, Brickfire Bakery, Fair Meadow, ProPak, ProClean, ProWare, and Ridgeline Coffee Roasters. The company also works with national brands such as B&G Foods, Ecolab, Nestlé, Kellogg's, Kraft Heinz, Perdue, Schreiber, and more.

The company provides its customers with quality milk, beverage milk, half and half, heavy cream and cultures products through Shamrock Farms.

Geographic Reach
Headquartered in Phoenix, Arizona, Shamrock Foods has broadline distribution warehouses located in Phoenix, Arizona; Boise, Idaho; Denver, Colorado; Albuquerque, New Mexico; and Eastvale, California. In addition, the company also has systems distribution warehouses in Phoenix, Arizona; Denver, Colorado; Sacramento, California; and Portland, Oregon.

Sales and Marketing
Shamrock Foods serves in restaurants, healthcare, casinos and entertainment, lodging, schools and other industries.

EXECUTIVES
HRO, Vincent C Daniels
CMO, Ann M Ocana
CIO, Daniel J Saltich
Auditors : MAYER HOFFMAN MCCANN PC PHOEN

LOCATIONS
HQ: SHAMROCK FOODS COMPANY
3900 E CAMELBACK RD # 300, PHOENIX, AZ 850182615

Phone: 602 477-2500
Web: WWW.SHAMROCKFOODS.COM

PRODUCTS/OPERATIONS
Selected Products
Beverages
Center of the plate (meats)
Dairy
Cleaning supplies
Dry goods and groceries
Ethnic foods
Frozen foods
Paper and disposable products
Produce
Specialty
Supplies and equipment

COMPETITORS
FUTURE MANAGEMENT CORP.
KYOKUYO CO., LTD.
MAZZETTA COMPANY, LLC
ORE-CAL CORP.
PAMLICO PACKING CO., INC.
PHILLIPS FOODS, INC.
SEAFOOD SALES, INC.
SHERWOOD FOOD DISTRIBUTORS, L.L.C.
SIRNA & SONS, INC.
TRI-UNION SEAFOODS, LLC

HISTORICAL FINANCIALS
Company Type: Private

Income Statement — FYE: September 30

	REVENUE ($mil)	NET INCOME ($mil)	NET PROFIT MARGIN	EMPLOYEES
09/21	4,602	0	0.0%	5,300
09/20	3,894	0	0.0%	—
09/19	4,016	0	0.0%	—
Annual Growth	7.1%	—	—	—

SHANDS JACKSONVILLE HEALTHCARE, INC.

LOCATIONS
HQ: SHANDS JACKSONVILLE HEALTHCARE, INC.
655 W 8TH ST, JACKSONVILLE, FL 322096511
Phone: 904 244-0411
Web: WWW.UFHEALTHJAX.ORG

HISTORICAL FINANCIALS
Company Type: Private

Income Statement — FYE: June 30

	REVENUE ($mil)	NET INCOME ($mil)	NET PROFIT MARGIN	EMPLOYEES
06/21	823	64	7.9%	3,000
06/16	665	22	3.3%	—
06/13	522	(5)	—	—
06/12	515	(22)	—	—
Annual Growth	5.3%	—	—	—

2021 Year-End Financials
Return on assets: 9.1%
Return on equity: 23.6%
Current Ratio: 2.30
Cash ($ mil.): —

SHANDS JACKSONVILLE MEDICAL CENTER, INC.

Close to the shifting sands of the northern Florida coast, Shands Jacksonville Medical Center (doing business as UF Health Jacksonville) offers a range of services to the 19 counties it serves in Florida and southern Georgia. The 695-bed hospital includes a cardiovascular center, Level III neonatal intensive care unit, and a Level I trauma center. It also operates primary and specialty clinics in the Jacksonville area. The medical center is affiliated with the University of Florida and is the largest of seven hospitals in the Shands HealthCare family.

Operations
UF Health Jacksonville operates about 40 outpatient care centers. Overall, its facilities handle some 34,000 inpatient visits and 600,000 outpatient visits per year. The hospital's affiliation with the University of Florida (UF) includes collaborative treatment and research programs in areas including cancer, cardiovascular, neurology, orthopedic, and pediatric care.

Together with its UF colleagues and affiliates, UF Health Jacksonville provides a wide range of health care services across the continuum of care on an inpatient and outpatient basis. Backed by a team of more than 400 faculty physicians, it offers nearly 100 specialty services.

Geographic Reach
UF Health Jacksonville's facilities are located in Jacksonville, Florida, and surrounding areas of northeastern Florida and southeastern Georgia.

Financial Performance
The company's revenues increased by 3% in 2014 due to growth in net patient service revenues as a result of a growth in inpatient and outpatient volumes. Medicare accounted for 25% net patient revenues; Medicaid, 31%.

UF Health Jacksonville reported net income of $3 million in 2014 over a net loss in 2013 due to higher interest and a loss on the disposal of capital assets.

Operating cash flow in 2014 decreased by 8% due to higher payments to suppliers and vendors.

Strategy

UF Health Jacksonville has plans to build a second campus on the north side of Jacksonville to meet the needs of a growing community. It's also exploring ways to increase clinical efficiencies, such as implementing an electronic health record (EHR) system (with help from federal stimulus funding); it also is looking to maximize funding opportunities for its research programs.

The company is looking to develop a Health Science Center Medical Education on Jacksonville Regional Campus, including undergraduate, graduate, and health-related professions.

It also plans to build a 92-bed hospital wing for the North Campus which will provide greater access to more health care services for the center's residents, as well as those living in surrounding communities. Construction is scheduled to begin in 2015 with completion in 2017.

In 2015, UF Health North opened the six-story, 210,000-square-foot outpatient medical complex in North Jacksonville, which includes a 28-bed emergency room, advanced imaging, a midwife-led birth center, rehabilitation services and more than 20 specialty services.

Company Background

Founded in 1870 as the Duval Hospital and Asylum, UF Health Jacksonville started the first cancer program in Florida in 1948.

Auditors: CROWE LLP FORT LAUDERDALE

LOCATIONS

HQ: SHANDS JACKSONVILLE MEDICAL CENTER, INC.
655 W 8TH ST, JACKSONVILLE, FL 322096511
Phone: 904 244-0411
Web: WWW.UFHEALTHJAX.ORG

PRODUCTS/OPERATIONS

Selected Services
Cancer services
Cardiovascular services
Neuroscience services
Orthopaedic services
Pediatrics
Poison Center
Trauma and critical care services
Women and families

COMPETITORS

CHARLESTON AREA MEDICAL CENTER, INC.
NASSAU HEALTH CARE CORPORATION
ORLANDO HEALTH, INC.
TALLAHASSEE MEMORIAL HEALTHCARE, INC.
WELLMONT HEALTH SYSTEM

HISTORICAL FINANCIALS

Company Type: Private

Income Statement — FYE: June 30

	REVENUE ($mil)	NET INCOME ($mil)	NET PROFIT MARGIN	EMPLOYEES
06/16	663	23	3.6%	3,000
06/15	480	10	2.2%	—
06/10	592	19	3.2%	—
Annual Growth	1.9%	3.5%	—	—

2016 Year-End Financials
Return on assets: 4.0%   Cash ($ mil.): 68
Return on equity: 12.3%
Current Ratio: 2.50

SHANDS TEACHING HOSPITAL AND CLINICS, INC.

While its full name is Shands Teaching Hospital and Clinics, most people call it UF&Shands. The network, affiliated with the University of Florida, provides health care services to patients in north-central and northeast Florida. The UF Health network of hospitals and physician practices manages more than 3 million inpatient and outpatient visits each year and serves patients from more than 65 Florida counties, from around the nation and from more than 30 countries. Specialty services include oncology, pediatrics, cardiovascular, transplants, and neurological care. It also includes primary care and specialty practices throughout North Central and Northeast Florida, as well as Southeast Georgia.

LOCATIONS

HQ: SHANDS TEACHING HOSPITAL AND CLINICS, INC.
1600 SW ARCHER RD, GAINESVILLE, FL 326103003
Phone: 352 265-0111
Web: WWW.UFHEALTH.ORG

PRODUCTS/OPERATIONS

Selected Hospitals
UF Health Jacksonville (Jacksonville)
UF Health Physicians (Gainesville and Jacksonville)
UF Health Shands HomeCare and Shands Jacksonville Home Health (Gainesville and Jacksonville)
UF Health Shands Hospital (Gainesville)
UF Health Shands Psychiatric Hospital (Gainesville)
UF Health Shands Rehab Centers (Gainesville)
UF Health Shands Rehab Hospital (Gainesville

COMPETITORS

AMSURG CORP.
ASCENSION VIA CHRISTI HEALTH, INC
GUTHRIE HEALTHCARE SYSTEM
IPC HEALTHCARE, INC.
NORTHWELL HEALTH, INC.
SHANDS JACKSONVILLE MEDICAL CENTER, INC.
SWEDISH HEALTH SERVICES
TEXAS CHILDREN'S HOSPITAL
THE CLEVELAND CLINIC FOUNDATION
UNITED SURGICAL PARTNERS INTERNATIONAL, INC.

HISTORICAL FINANCIALS

Company Type: Private

Income Statement — FYE: June 30

	REVENUE ($mil)	NET INCOME ($mil)	NET PROFIT MARGIN	EMPLOYEES
06/21	2,235	231	10.3%	3,000
06/20	1,660	52	3.2%	—
06/19	1,651	66	4.0%	—
06/14	1,243	66	5.3%	—
Annual Growth	8.7%	19.6%	—	—

2021 Year-End Financials
Return on assets: 6.2%   Cash ($ mil.): —
Return on equity: 12.3%
Current Ratio: 1.50

SHARP HEALTHCARE

Sharp HealthCare is San Diego's leading health care provider and not for profit and dedicated delivering the highest quality patient-centered care and the latest medical technology and superior service. The network includes four acute-care hospitals (Sharp Chula Vista Medical Center, Sharp Coronado Hospital, Sharp Grossmont Hospital, and Sharp Memorial Hospital). With approximately 2,700 affiliated physicians and some 19,000 employees, Sharp HealthCare offers cancer treatment and heart and vascular care, endoscopy, mental health, orthopedics, and pregnancy and childbirth, plastic and reconstructive surgery, and hospice care. Sharp HealthCare was founded in 1957.

Operations

Sharp HealthCare operates four acute-care hospitals, three specialty hospitals, three affiliated medical groups and a full spectrum of facilities and services such as advance care planning, alcohol and drug dependency, bloodless medicines, cancer treatment, eating disorders, emergency and urgent care, heart and vascular care, internal medicine, laboratory services, plastic and reconstructive surgery, rehabilitation and physical therapy, senior care, weight loss surgery, and wound care and hyperbaric medicine, among others.

Geographic Reach

Sharp HealthCare is based in San Diego, California.

Sales and Marketing

Sharp HealthCare's health plan options provide coverage for employers of all sizes throughout its region and include valuable enhancements, such as interactive wellness resources, dental discounts and an exclusive global emergency services program.

Company Background

In 2011 the system doubled the capacity of Sharp Chula Vista Medical Center's emergency department at a cost of $12 million, and in 2012 the Chula Vista hospital opened a new cancer center.

The system began as a single hospital in 1955, named for a local pilot who died in WWII.

EXECUTIVES

Managing Member, Christopher Howard
Managing Member*, Michael Murphy
Managing Member*, Ann Pumpian
Managing Member*, Daniel L Gross
Managing Member*, Alison J Fleury
Managing Member*, William A Spooner
Managing Member, Carlisle Ky C Lewis Iii
Auditors : ERNST & YOUNG US LLP SAN DIEG

LOCATIONS

HQ: SHARP HEALTHCARE
  8695 SPECTRUM CENTER BLVD, SAN DIEGO, CA 921231489
Phone: 858 499-4000
Web: WWW.SHARP.COM

PRODUCTS/OPERATIONS

2014 Sales

	$ mil	% of total
Net patient revenue	1,806.3	62
Premium	1,024.6	35
Other	97.6	3
Total	2,928.5	100

Selected Programs and Services
Alcohol and drug dependency
Bloodless medicine
Cancer treatment
Complimentary and alternative medicine
Diabetes
Ear, nose, and throat
Eating disorders
Emergency and trauma
Endoscopy
Executive health
Eye care
Flu care
Health and wellness
Heart and vascular care
　　Heart valve surgery
Home care
Hospice
Integrative and complementary medicine
International patient services
Laboratory services
Men's health
Mental health
Neurology
Nutrition
Occupational health
Orthopedics
Pediatrics
Pregnancy and childbirth
Primary care and family health
Radiology and diagnostic imaging
Rehabilitation and physical therapy
Robotic surgery
Safety and injury prevention
Senior care and services
Skilled nursing
Sleep disorders
Stroke and neurology
Transplant
Travel medicine
Urgent care
Weight loss
　　Weight management support
　　Weight-loss surgery (bariatric)
Women's care
Worksite wellness
Wound care and hyperbaric medicine

Selected Facilities
Sharp Chula Vista Medical Center (340 beds)
Sharp Coronado Hospital (180 beds)
Sharp Grossmont Hospital (540 beds, La Mesa)
Sharp Mary Birch Hospital for Women & Newborns (170 beds, San Diego)
Sharp McDonald Center (20 beds, San Diego)
Sharp Memorial Hospital (675 beds, San Diego)
Sharp Mesa Vista Hospital (150 beds, San Diego)

COMPETITORS

BAPTIST HEALTH SYSTEM, INC.
IASIS HEALTHCARE LLC
MEDSTAR HEALTH, INC.
PASADENA HOSPITAL ASSOCIATION, LTD.
PEACEHEALTH
PRESBYTERIAN HEALTHCARE SERVICES
PROVIDENCE ST. JOSEPH HEALTH
SSM HEALTH CARE CORPORATION
THE CLEVELAND CLINIC FOUNDATION
VALLEY HEALTH SYSTEM

HISTORICAL FINANCIALS

Company Type: Private

Income Statement　　　　　　　　　　　FYE: September 30

	REVENUE ($mil)	NET INCOME ($mil)	NET PROFIT MARGIN	EMPLOYEES
09/19	1,680	(27)	—	14,000
09/14	1,234	(12)	—	—
09/13	1,158	(11)	—	—
09/09	897	(0)	—	—
Annual Growth	6.5%	—	—	—

2019 Year-End Financials
Return on assets: (-0.7%)　　Cash ($ mil.): 281
Return on equity: (-29.9%)
Current Ratio: 0.40

SHARP MEMORIAL HOSPITAL

The docs and the scalpels are sharp at Sharp Memorial Hospital. The flagship facility of Sharp HealthCare, the not-for-profit hospital has roughly 675 beds and is a designated trauma center for San Diego County. Specialties include cardiac care, women's health, multi-organ transplantation, and cancer treatment. It also provides skilled nursing, home health, and hospice services. Sharp Memorial Hospital first opened in 1955. Sharp HealthCare completed reconstruction efforts on the Sharp Memorial facility in 2009; the new hospital has improved inpatient, surgery, emergency, trauma, and intensive care facilities.

Operations

Along with a full range of inpatient services, Sharp Memorial's Outpatient Pavilion provides patients with cancer care, women's imaging, and endoscopy services. The center also conducts outpatient surgery procedures ranging from LASIK to orthopedic surgeries. More and more hospitals are adding outpatient services to their roster because they tend to be reimbursed at higher rates. The facility also provides patient education services, such as community health classes.

Sharp Memorial, which provides some $199 million in community benefits (including charity care and outreach efforts) each year, is affiliated with a number of other hospitals, clinics, and physician groups through its parent organization.

LOCATIONS

HQ: SHARP MEMORIAL HOSPITAL
  7901 FROST ST, SAN DIEGO, CA 921232701
Phone: 858 939-3636
Web: WWW.SHARP.COM

COMPETITORS

BETHESDA HOSPITAL., INC.
FROEDTERT MEMORIAL LUTHERAN HOSPITAL, INC.
HOLY SPIRIT HOSPITAL OF THE SISTERS OF CHRISTIAN CHARITY
MEMORIAL HEALTH SERVICES
NORTHWEST COMMUNITY HOSPITAL

HISTORICAL FINANCIALS

Company Type: Private

Income Statement　　　　　　　　　　　FYE: September 30

	REVENUE ($mil)	NET INCOME ($mil)	NET PROFIT MARGIN	EMPLOYEES
09/20	1,278	299	23.4%	3,500
09/18	1,306	247	19.0%	—
09/17	1,158	237	20.5%	—
09/16	1,200	290	24.2%	—
Annual Growth	1.6%	0.7%	—	—

2020 Year-End Financials
Return on assets: 8.6%　　Cash ($ mil.): 1
Return on equity: 10.1%
Current Ratio: 20.20

SHAWMUT WOODWORKING & SUPPLY, INC.

Shawmut Woodworking & Supply, which does business as Shawmut Design and Construction, provides beginning-to-end construction services, from preconstruction planning to post-construction quality assurance checks. The $1.3 billion national construction management firm has experience building retail, hotel, gaming, spa, sports, restaurant, education, banking, healthcare, and life science facilities. It also handles corporate interiors and high-end residential construction, and boasts expertise in cultural and historical preservation projects. The employee-owned company serves clients nationwide from offices in a handful of US states.

Operations

Shawmut's services include construction

management, lean construction, integrated project delivery, design/build, sustainable construction, virtual design and construction and MEP services.

Geographic Reach
Shawmut operates from offices in Boston, Massachusetts; New York; Chicago, Illinois; Los Angeles and Irvine California; Las Vegas, Nevada; Providence, Rhode Island; North Haven, Connecticut; Miami and West Palm Beach, Florida; and Springfield, Massachusetts.

Sales and Marketing
Shawmut serves a range of markets with varying needs, with projects involving corporate interiors, cultural and historic structures, healthcare and science, restaurants, retail, spas and health clubs, sports venues, and universities.

LOCATIONS
HQ: SHAWMUT WOODWORKING & SUPPLY, INC.
560 HARRISON AVE STE 200, BOSTON, MA 021182532
Phone: 617 622-7000
Web: WWW.SHAWMUT.COM

PRODUCTS/OPERATIONS
Selected Markets
Academic
Commercial
Corporate interiors
Cultural and historic
Gaming
Healthcare and science
Restaurants
Retail
Spas and healthclubs
Sports venues

Selected Services
Services
 Pre-Construction
  Master planning services
  Master project scheduling
  Lease review
  Value engineering
  Feasibility studies
  Green design services
  Drawing reviews
  Facilities audits and campus assessments
  Collaborative approach with architect/design team
  Comprehensive conceptual estimating
  BIM and virtual construction
  In-house M/E/P expertise
  Bid packages
  Constructability reviews
  Due diligence and site surveys
  Pre-qualification of subcontractors
  Management of permitting and approvals
  Development of specific phasing, schedules, and delivery methods
  Open book subcontractor bidding
  Logistics planning
  National purchasing power
 Construction
  Master project scheduling
  Weekly project team meetings
  Sites monitored by a Safety Manager
  Zero-tolerance safety program
  BIM and virtual construction services
  LEED documentation, certification, and green building techniques
  Permitting services
  Design/build services
  Communication with surrounding community
  Coordination of owner-supplied items and vendors
  Procurement solutions
  Schedule and budget controls
  24-hour/7 days-a-week emergency services
  Specialized services for program clients
  Indoor air quality management
  Construction and demolition waste recycling
  Customized waterproofing details
 Post-Construction
  Commissioning and close-out services
  O&M manuals and training
  Project services division
  1-year warranty walkthrough

COMPETITORS
BARTON MALOW COMPANY
DIMEO CONSTRUCTION COMPANY
GILBANE, INC.
HARDIN CONSTRUCTION COMPANY, LLC
HUNT CONSTRUCTION GROUP, INC.
LECHASE CONSTRUCTION SERVICES, LLC
LPCIMINELLI, INC.
THE MORGANTI GROUP INC
TISHMAN CONSTRUCTION CORPORATION
VJS CONSTRUCTION SERVICES, INC.

HISTORICAL FINANCIALS
Company Type: Private

Income Statement   FYE: November 30

	REVENUE ($mil)	NET INCOME ($mil)	NET PROFIT MARGIN	EMPLOYEES
11/14	957	7	0.7%	1,476
11/11	662	3	0.6%	—
11/09*	618	(21)	—	—
12/05	440	3	0.7%	—
Annual Growth	9.0%	9.9%	—	—

*Fiscal year change

2014 Year-End Financials
Return on assets: 2.4%   Cash ($ mil.): 74
Return on equity: 14.5%
Current Ratio: 1.20

SHAWNEE MISSION MEDICAL CENTER, INC.

Shawnee Mission Medical Center (SMMC) cares for Kansas City residents, primarily on the Kansas-side. The health care facility, located in the city's southwest suburbs, has some 500 inpatient beds. It also offers outpatient surgery and other health services in areas such as pediatrics, rehabilitation, oncology, and radiology. The medical center's emergency department receives some 50,000 visits each year. SMMC also operates satellite facilities, including the Shawnee Mission Outpatient Pavilion in nearby Lenexa, which offers emergency and outpatient diagnostic, general practice, and surgical care. SMMC is part of Adventist Health System.

Operations
SMMC handles some 20,000 inpatient admissions each year, as well as some 200,000 outpatient visits. Its staff includes about 700 physicians who specialize in about 50 fields of medicine. Specialist care centers include a Chest Pain Emergency Center and the Center for Women's Health. The hospital also provides primary and specialty care through the Shawnee Mission Physicians Group, including after-hours clinical care and cardiology and reproductive medicine services. SMMC delivers more babies per year than any other hospital in the metropolitan area.

Geographic Reach
SMMC is located on a more than 50-acre campus in Shawnee Mission (near Kansas City) in Johnson County, Kansas, and serves the surrounding area. The main hospital campus includes a free-standing surgery center, six physician practice buildings, a child-care center for associates, and a community health center.

Strategy
The SMMC organization looks at community needs to determine where it should grow. In 2013, the hospital opened a $44 million new birthing center to meet the growing need for obstetric services in the Kansas City area. The expansion effort tripled the size of the medical center's labor and delivery and postpartum rooms, allowing it to accommodate up to 5,000 births annually, and added a level III neonatal intensive care unit.

The facility is also adding to its technological abilities to better serve the community. In late 2014 it deployed the eMediTrack platform to help document and analyze data for compliance and accreditation readiness.

Company Background
SMMC is part of a network of more than 500 health care facilities sponsored by the Seventh-day Adventist Church.

LOCATIONS
HQ: SHAWNEE MISSION MEDICAL CENTER, INC.
9100 W 74TH ST, SHAWNEE MISSION, KS 662044004
Phone: 913 676-2000
Web: WWW.ADVENTHEALTH.COM

PRODUCTS/OPERATIONS
Selected Centers and Services
Bariatric Surgery
Behavioral Health
Britain Center (Cancer)
Center for Pain Medicine
CorporateCare
Diabetes
Emergency Services
Express Care
GI Services
Hand Specialty Center
HEALTHaware
Heart and Vascular Center
Home Health Care
Maternity
Holistic Care
Men's Health Program
Neurology
Nutrition and Weight Loss
Orthopedics
Plastic Surgery

Radiology
Rehabilitation Services
Reproductive Medicine
Robotic Surgery
Sleep Disorders Center
SM Outpatient Pavilion
SportsCare
Support Groups
Surgical Services
TherapyPlus
Transfer Center Urgent Care
Weight Loss Surgery
Women's Health
Wound Care Center

COMPETITORS

BLESSING HOSPITAL
COMMUNITY HOSPITALS OF CENTRAL CALIFORNIA
GREATER BALTIMORE MEDICAL CENTER, INC.
MEMORIAL HEALTH SERVICES
THE NEBRASKA MEDICAL CENTER

HISTORICAL FINANCIALS
Company Type: Private

Income Statement — FYE: December 31

	REVENUE ($mil)	NET INCOME ($mil)	NET PROFIT MARGIN	EMPLOYEES
12/19	546	66	12.2%	1,850
12/17	491	55	11.3%	—
12/16	454	54	12.0%	—
12/15	435	38	8.7%	—
Annual Growth	5.9%	15.1%	—	—

2019 Year-End Financials
Return on assets: 7.2%   Cash ($ mil.): 363
Return on equity: 9.7%
Current Ratio: 13.70

SHEA HOMES LIMITED PARTNERSHIP, A CALIFORNIA LIMITED PARTNERSHIP

Auditors : ERNST & YOUNG LLP LOS ANGELES

LOCATIONS

HQ: SHEA HOMES LIMITED PARTNERSHIP, A CALIFORNIA LIMITED PARTNERSHIP
655 BREA CANYON RD, WALNUT, CA 917893078
Phone: 909 594-9500

HISTORICAL FINANCIALS
Company Type: Private

Income Statement — FYE: December 31

	REVENUE ($mil)	NET INCOME ($mil)	NET PROFIT MARGIN	EMPLOYEES
12/13	930	125	13.5%	1,200
12/12	680	29	4.3%	—
12/99	1,793	184	10.3%	—
Annual Growth	(4.6%)	(2.7%)	—	—

2013 Year-End Financials
Return on assets: 8.4%   Cash ($ mil.): 206
Return on equity: 28.3%
Current Ratio: 1.30

SHELL MEDICAL PLAN

Auditors : PNCEWATERHOUSECOOPERS LLP PIT

LOCATIONS

HQ: SHELL MEDICAL PLAN
, PHOENIX, AZ 85072
Phone: 800 352-3705

HISTORICAL FINANCIALS
Company Type: Private

Income Statement — FYE: December 31

	REVENUE ($mil)	NET INCOME ($mil)	NET PROFIT MARGIN	EMPLOYEES
12/16	617	5	1.0%	2
12/15	571	(40)	—	—
12/13	536	6	1.2%	—
Annual Growth	4.8%	(1.6%)	—	—

2016 Year-End Financials
Return on assets: 10.1%   Cash ($ mil.): 58
Return on equity: 10.1%
Current Ratio: —

SHI INTERNATIONAL CORP.

SHI International is one of the world's largest transformational technology solutions providers. The company distributes scores of computer hardware and software products from suppliers such as Adobe, Cisco, Microsoft, VMware, Symantec, and Lenovo. It resells PCs, networking products, data storage systems, printers, software, and keyboards, among other items. SHI offers a range of professional services, including software licensing, asset management, managed desktop services, systems integration, and vocational training. The company serves corporate, government, and health care customers from approximately 35 offices across Australia, Canada, France, Hong Kong, Ireland, Singapore, the US, and the UK. SHI was founded in 1989 by Chairman Koguan Leo.

Operations
SHI helps companies achieve business goals through the use of technologies ranging from software licensing and end user computing devices to innovative cloud and edge solutions. The company provides foundational solutions that allow its customers to build resilient, agile technology-based answers to their most pressing business needs. These solutions include Integration Centers, IT Asset and Lifecycle Management, SHI Mobility, and Managed and Professional Services.

The company's popular product categories include laptops, desktop, tablets, printers, and monitors. Among its featured brands are Acer, Citrix, HP, LG, Nvidia, McAfee, and Samsung.

Geographic Reach
Based in Somerset, New Jersey, SHI has a global reach through approximately 35 offices worldwide, including its seven international offices in Australia, Canada, France, Hong Kong, Ireland, Singapore, and in the UK.

Sales and Marketing
SHI has some 5,000 experts from every area of IT operations, from volume licensing to security, data center to mobility and collaboration, supporting approximately 10 million end-users.

Strategy
In late 2021, SHI International launched SHI Complete, its new fully-managed IT service that helps small-and medium-sized businesses (SMBs) accelerate and optimize their IT transformation.

SHI Complete includes endpoint, cloud, network management, cybersecurity, and IT professional services into a single managed service so that SMB business leaders can take full advantage of the latest technologies and skills without having to take their eye off business growth or invest in a large in-house team.

With SHI Complete, experts at SHI can take full ownership of a customer organization's IT operations and ensure the right skills and strategies are leveraged to aid in scale and optimization efforts.

Auditors : COHN REZNICK LLP WHITE PLAINS

LOCATIONS

HQ: SHI INTERNATIONAL CORP.
290 DAVIDSON AVE, SOMERSET, NJ 088734145
Phone: 732 764-8888
Web: WWW.SHI.COM

PRODUCTS/OPERATIONS

Selected Products
Accessories
Peripherals
Hardware
Memory
Software

Selected Services
Cloud services
Computer vocational training services
Data center services
Events
Hardware services
Networking
POLARIS Software asset management
Storage
Strategic consulting
Webinars

COMPETITORS

CALYPSO TECHNOLOGY, INC.
GREENPAGES, INC.
LANYON SOLUTIONS, INC.

MARLABS INCORPORATED
PARAGON DEVELOPMENT SYSTEMS, INC.
PEAK RESOURCES, INC.
QUARK SOFTWARE INC.
QUEST MEDIA & SUPPLIES, INC.
SYNNEX CORPORATION
ZONES, LLC

HISTORICAL FINANCIALS
Company Type: Private

Income Statement — FYE: December 31

	REVENUE ($mil)	NET INCOME ($mil)	NET PROFIT MARGIN	EMPLOYEES
12/19	10,372	253	2.4%	5,000
12/18	9,767	245	2.5%	—
12/17	8,243	197	2.4%	—
12/16	7,268	104	1.4%	—
Annual Growth	12.6%	34.3%	—	—

2019 Year-End Financials
Return on assets: 10.4%
Return on equity: 36.9%
Current Ratio: 1.30
Cash ($ mil.): 63

SHOESTRING VALLEY HOLDINGS INC.

Andersen Construction Company focuses on commercial and industrial construction in the Western US. The group, which introduced concrete tilt-up construction to the Pacific Northwest, builds everything from parking structures to medical facilities, manufacturing plants, and industrial complexes. It also works on institutional projects for the government and education markets. Other projects include tenant improvements, seismic upgrades, and remediation construction. The company provides construction management (which accounts for 80% of its work), as well as general contracting and design/build delivery. It also offers startup and commissioning services. Chairman and CEO Andy Andersen founded the company in 1950.

Auditors : ALDRICH CPAS & ADVISORS LLP

LOCATIONS

HQ: SHOESTRING VALLEY HOLDINGS INC.
6712 N CUTTER CIR, PORTLAND, OR 972173933
Phone: 503 283-6712

PRODUCTS/OPERATIONS

Selected Services
Commercial development (acquisition, due diligence, financing, land entitlements, leasing, master planning, and permitting)
Construction management
Design/build
Estimating
General contracting
Green building
Preconstruction
Startup and commissioning

COMPETITORS

HOLDER CONSTRUCTION COMPANY

JACOBSEN CONSTRUCTION COMPANY, INC.
SWINERTON INCORPORATED
THE GEORGE SOLLITT CONSTRUCTION COMPANY
THE WEITZ COMPANY LLC

HISTORICAL FINANCIALS
Company Type: Private

Income Statement — FYE: December 31

	REVENUE ($mil)	NET INCOME ($mil)	NET PROFIT MARGIN	EMPLOYEES
12/21	735	7	1.1%	150
12/17	644	1	0.2%	—
01/16	582	0	0.2%	—
Annual Growth	4.0%	41.6%	—	—

2021 Year-End Financials
Return on assets: 3.3%
Return on equity: 20.7%
Current Ratio: 1.20
Cash ($ mil.): 33

SHRINERS HOSPITALS FOR CHILDREN

EXECUTIVES

CDO*, Stuart P Sullivan
Auditors : CBIZ MHM LLC CLEARWATER FL

LOCATIONS

HQ: SHRINERS HOSPITALS FOR CHILDREN
2900 N ROCKY POINT DR, TAMPA, FL 336071460
Phone: 813 281-0700
Web: WWW.SHRINERSCHILDRENS.ORG

HISTORICAL FINANCIALS
Company Type: Private

Income Statement — FYE: December 31

	REVENUE ($mil)	NET INCOME ($mil)	NET PROFIT MARGIN	EMPLOYEES
12/19	815	(87)	—	6,100
12/16	584	(269)	—	—
Annual Growth	11.8%	—	—	—

2019 Year-End Financials
Return on assets: (-0.9%)
Return on equity: (-1.0%)
Current Ratio: —
Cash ($ mil.): 33

SIERRA NEVADA CORPORATION

Sierra Nevada Corp. (SNC) is a trusted leader in solving the world's toughest challenges through advanced engineering technologies in Space Systems, Commercial Solutions, and National Security and Defense. The company's Dream Chaser spacecraft is set to become the next addition to the fleet of uncrewed cargo vehicles that ferry supplies to the International Space Station. The company also delivers tailored solutions to government and commercial customers, with applications in space exploration and satellites, aircraft integrations, navigation and guidance systems, threat detection and security, scientific research and infrastructure protection. SNC's subsidiaries and affiliates include Straight Flight, 3S, Deutsche Aircraft, Kutta Technologies Inc. & Kutta Radios Inc., 328 Support Services GmbH, and Sierra Space. The privately held company was founded in 1963.

Operations
SNC is a trusted leader in engineering answers to the world's toughest challenges, delivering customer-focused technologies and best-of-breed integrations in aerospace and defense. It creates the Dream Chaser spacecraft, a multi-mission space utility vehicle designed for transporting crew and cargo to Low-Earth orbit (LEO) destinations. It is also a world leader in Command, Control, Computers, Communications and Intelligence, Surveillance and Reconnaissance (C4ISR) that provides swift, flexible, and comprehensive solutions for the most difficult operational challenges. Its other solutions have included aircraft design, modification and support, rotary-wing integration and modernization, shooting star transport vehicle, cybersecurity, navigation, guidance and landing, satellite solutions, and electronic warfare systems.

Geographic Reach
SNC, based in Sparks, Nevada, operates from about 40 offices in across the US and at customer sites around the world. It has offices in England, Germany, and Turkey.

Sales and Marketing
Its existing supplier is Exostar.

Mergers and Acquisitions

Auditors : DELOITTE & TOUCHE LLP LOS ANG

LOCATIONS

HQ: SIERRA NEVADA CORPORATION
444 SALOMON CIR, SPARKS, NV 894349651
Phone: 775 331-0222
Web: WWW.SNCORP.COM

PRODUCTS/OPERATIONS

Business Units
Dream Chaser
Integrated ISR Solutions
Aircraft, Design, Modification and Support
Rotary-Wing Integration & Remanufacturing
Space Exploration
Cyber Security
Navigation, Guidance & Landing
Spacecraft & Satellite Solutions
Electronic Warfare Systems

COMPETITORS

ASTRONICS CORPORATION
BALL AEROSPACE & TECHNOLOGIES CORP.
BELL TEXTRON INC.
ESTERLINE TECHNOLOGIES CORPORATION

MARVIN ENGINEERING CO., INC.
MEGGITT DEFENSE SYSTEMS, INC.
NATIONAL AERONAUTICS AND SPACE ADMINISTRATION
ROCKWELL COLLINS, INC.
SPACE EXPLORATION TECHNOLOGIES CORP.
TEXTRON SYSTEMS CORPORATION

HISTORICAL FINANCIALS
Company Type: Private

Income Statement — FYE: December 31

	REVENUE ($mil)	NET INCOME ($mil)	NET PROFIT MARGIN	EMPLOYEES
12/14	1,481	0	0.0%	5,464
12/13	1,623	0	0.0%	—
12/12	1,400	0	0.0%	—
Annual Growth	2.9%	—	—	—

2014 Year-End Financials
Return on assets: —
Return on equity: —
Current Ratio: 1.50
Cash ($ mil.): 22

SIGNATURE FINANCIAL LLC

LOCATIONS
HQ: SIGNATURE FINANCIAL LLC
565 FFTH AVE AT 46TH ST 1 12 TH FLR, NEW YORK, NY 10017
Phone: 646 865-0767
Web: WWW.SIGNATURENY.COM

HISTORICAL FINANCIALS
Company Type: Private

Income Statement — FYE: December 31

	ASSETS ($mil)	NET INCOME ($mil)	INCOME AS % OF ASSETS	EMPLOYEES
12/18	47,364	505	1.1%	41
12/17	43,119	387	0.9%	—
12/16	39,047	396	1.0%	—
12/15	33,450	373	1.1%	—
Annual Growth	12.3%	10.6%	—	—

2018 Year-End Financials
Return on assets: 1.1%
Return on equity: 11.5%
Current Ratio: —
Cash ($ mil.): 432

SINAI HOSPITAL OF BALTIMORE, INC.

Sinai Hospital of Baltimore, part of the LifeBridge Health network, provides medical care in northwestern Baltimore. The 470-bed hospital is a not-for-profit medical center that includes such facilities as a heart center, a children's hospital, a cancer institute, and a rehab center. Other specialties include orthopedics, neurology, and women's care. Medical students from Johns Hopkins University and the University of Maryland do some of their training at the hospital. Sinai Hospital of Baltimore was founded in 1866 as the Hebrew Hospital and Asylum and became a subsidiary of LifeBridge when it merged with other area providers in 1998.

Operations
The Sinai Hospital of Baltimore handles about 26,000 inpatient admissions and some 75,000 emergency room visits per year. It also conducts about 20,000 inpatient and outpatient surgeries annually.

The medical center conducts a number of education and training programs, including residencies and fellowships, for about 400 medical students each year. It is a designated training site for the Johns Hopkins University's ambulatory and internal medicine clerkships.

Strategy
Sinai Hospital of Baltimore has completed several expansion efforts in recent years. In 2012 it opened a new dedicated inpatient hospice unit, as well as a new center for geriatric surgery. In addition, the 20-bed Friedman Neurological Rehabilitation Center was completed that year.

EXECUTIVES
Joint President, Neil Meltzer
Chief Medical Officer*, Daniel C Silverman

LOCATIONS
HQ: SINAI HOSPITAL OF BALTIMORE, INC.
2401 W BELVEDERE AVE, BALTIMORE, MD 212155270
Phone: 410 601-5678
Web: WWW.LIFEBRIDGEHEALTH.ORG

PRODUCTS/OPERATIONS
Selected Centers
Alvin & Lois Lapidus Cancer Institute at LifeBridge Health
Center for Joint Preservation and Replacement
Children's Hospital at Sinai
ER-7 Emergency Center
Heart Center at Sinai
International Center for Limb Lengthening
Krieger Eye Institute
Louis and Phyllis Friedman Neurological Rehabilitation Center
Rubin Institute for Advanced Orthopedics
Sandra and Malcolm Berman Brain & Spine Institute
Sinai Rehabilitation Center
The Spine Center at Sinai

Selected Services
Allergy and Immunology
Anesthesia
Cardiology
Cancer/Medical Oncology
Dermatology
Dialysis
Emergency Medicine
Endocrinology and Metabolism
Family Medicine
Gastroenterology
General Internal Medicine
Geriatric Medicine
Infectious Diseases
Nephrology (kidneys)
Pulmonary and Critical Care Medicine
Rheumatology (joints, tendons)
Neurology
Neurosurgery
Obstetrics and Gynecology
Ophthalmology (eye care)
Oral and Maxillofacial Surgery and Dentistry
Orthopedic Surgery
Otolaryngology (ear, nose & throat)
Pathology
Pediatrics
Pharmacy
Physical Medicine and Rehabilitation
Psychiatry
Radiation Oncology
Radiology
Surgery
Urology

COMPETITORS
CHILDREN'S HOSPITAL COLORADO
NEWYORK-PRESBYTERIAN/BROOKLYN METHODIST
SAINT PETER'S UNIVERSITY HOSPITAL, INC.
THE BROOKLYN HOSPITAL CENTER
THE JAMAICA HOSPITAL

HISTORICAL FINANCIALS
Company Type: Private

Income Statement — FYE: June 30

	REVENUE ($mil)	NET INCOME ($mil)	NET PROFIT MARGIN	EMPLOYEES
06/20	853	59	7.0%	4,497
06/19	803	41	5.1%	—
06/17	769	63	8.2%	—
06/16	690	26	3.9%	—
Annual Growth	5.4%	22.4%	—	—

2020 Year-End Financials
Return on assets: 9.4%
Return on equity: 55.0%
Current Ratio: 1.00
Cash ($ mil.): 74

SISTERS OF CHARITY OF LEAVENWORTH HEALTH SYSTEM, INC.

SCL Health is a faith-based, nonprofit healthcare organization dedicated to improving the health of the people and communities it serves, especially those who are poor and vulnerable. Founded by the Sisters of Charity of Leavenworth in 1864, its $2.8 billion health network provides comprehensive, coordinated care through eight hospitals, more than 150 physician clinics, and home health, hospice, mental health and safety-net services primarily in Colorado and Montana.

Geographic Reach
SCL Health has operations in Colorado and Montana.

Mergers and Acquisitions
In 2022, SCL Health and Intermountain Healthcare, two leading nonprofit healthcare organizations, have completed their merger, creating a model health system that provides high-quality, accessible, and affordable healthcare to more patients and communities

in Utah, Idaho, Nevada, Colorado, Montana, Wyoming, and Kansas. This combination employs more than 59,000 caregivers, operates 33 hospitals (including one virtual hospital), and runs 385 clinics across seven states while providing health insurance to one million people in Utah and Idaho. With the close of this merger, Intermountain Healthcare is the eleventh largest nonprofit health system in the US.

Company Background
In 2011 sponsorship of SCL Health was transferred from the Sisters of Charity of Leavenworth to Leaven Ministries, a new entity formed by the sisters and approved and recognized by the Catholic Church.

EXECUTIVES
CIO, Craig Richardville
Auditors : ERNST & YOUNG LLP DENVER CO

LOCATIONS
HQ: SISTERS OF CHARITY OF LEAVENWORTH HEALTH SYSTEM, INC.
500 ELDORADO BLVD # 6300, BROOMFIELD, CO 800213408
Phone: 303 813-5000
Web: WWW.SCLHEALTH.ORG

PRODUCTS/OPERATIONS
Selected Facilities
Clinics (primary and preventive health care services for low-middle income, uninsured population)
    Duchesne Clinic (Kansas City, KS)
    Marian Clinic (Topeka, KS)
    Marillac Clinic (Grand Junction, CO)
    Saint Vincent Clinic (Leavenworth, KS)
Hospitals
    Good Samaritan Medical Center, LLC (community hospital; Lafayette, CO)
    Lutheran Medical Center (community-based, acute care hospital; Wheat Ridge, CO)
    Saint Joseph Hospital (private teaching hospital; Denver, CO)
    Holton Community Hospital (managed; SCLHS affiliated hospital; Holton, KS)
    Holy Rosary Healthcare (acute care hospital and extended care facility; Miles City, MT)
    St. Francis Health Center, Inc. (holistic, family-centered, patient care programs; Topeka, KS)
    St. James Healthcare (acute care hospital; Butte, MT)
    St. Mary's Medical Center, Inc. (Grand Junction, CO)
    St. Vincent Healthcare (hospital with 31 outpatient clinics); Billings, MT)
Residential treatment
    Mount Saint Vincent Home (children's mental health treatment center)

COMPETITORS
CAPE COD HEALTHCARE, INC.
DIGNITY HEALTH
ENCOMPASS HEALTH CORPORATION
FAIRVIEW HEALTH SERVICES
LEGACY LIFEPOINT HEALTH, INC.
NORTHSHORE UNIVERSITY HEALTHSYSTEM
OVERLAKE HOSPITAL MEDICAL CENTER
THE LANCASTER GENERAL HOSPITAL
THE RUTLAND HOSPITAL INC ACT 220
UNIVERSAL HEALTH SERVICES, INC.

HISTORICAL FINANCIALS
Company Type: Private

Income Statement   FYE: December 31

	REVENUE ($mil)	NET INCOME ($mil)	NET PROFIT MARGIN	EMPLOYEES
12/21	3,159	278	8.8%	15,046
12/20	2,880	402	14.0%	—
12/19	2,844	390	13.7%	—
12/16	2,475	197	8.0%	—
Annual Growth	5.0%	7.0%	—	—

2021 Year-End Financials
Return on assets: 4.5%   Cash ($ mil.): 164
Return on equity: 6.9%
Current Ratio: 1.10

SKANSKA USA CIVIL INC.

Skanska USA Civil builds some of the world's largest cable-stayed bridges. Part of the US operations of Swedish engineering and construction giant Skanska, Skanska USA Civil focuses on infrastructure projects throughout the country. Along with sister firm Skanska USA Building, it is a market leader in the New York area, where it has worked on the Brooklyn Bridge, the AirTrain light-rail system, and the Roosevelt Island Bridge. It builds roads, tunnels, and rail systems, in addition to bridges and industrial and marine facilities, such as power and water filtration plants, gas-treatment plants, and dry docks.

Operations
Parent-company Skanska USA operates Skanska USA Civil and three sister business units with different specialties, such as Skanska USA Building, Infrastructure Development USA, and Commercial Development USA. The parent boasts a staff of nearly 11,000 US employees (as of mid-2016).

Among Skanska USA Civil's divisions is Bayshore Concrete, which produces precast concrete components for tunnel, bridge, dock, and pier construction. Bayshore Concrete's plant in Virginia focuses on East Coast shipments. Skanska Koch, which is based in New Jersey, has built or worked on some of the country's most recognizable structures, such as Yankee Stadium and the Brooklyn Bridge.

Another division, Underpinning & Foundation Skanska, is a heavy foundation contractor based in New York. It offers underpinning and pile-driving services for private and public projects that range from single-story buildings to skyscrapers.

Geographic Reach
While the firm's largest market is in its home state of New York, it serves the US from offices in California, Washington, Arizona, and Florida. Parent Skanska USA has 31 offices across the US and works on projects in nearly all 50 states, the District of Columbia, and Puerto Rico (as of mid-2016). The US is Skanska AB's largest market, accounting for 37% of its global revenue during 2015.

Sales and Marketing
Skanska USA Civil provides public and private clients with construction services in the civil, mechanical, industrial, marine, foundation and environmental sectors.

Financial Performance
Parent-company Skanska USA's revenue has been growing in recent years, and reached $7.1 billion in 2015.

Strategy
Parent Skanska USA ranked the third-largest building/manufacturing contractor by revenue and the third-largest heavy contractor by revenue on Engineering News-Record's rankings in 2015. The Skanska USA Civil division in particular has built a dominating presence on the East Coast since completing major projects such as the Meadowlands Football Stadium and Boston's Central Artery.

Skanska USA Civil in 2015 secured a contract with Competitive Power Ventures Holdings (CPV) to build the CPV Valley Energy Center in Wawayanda, New York with an order value of SEK 2.1 billion ($250 million); a new contract with MTA, New York City Transit to rebuild three rail stations in Brooklyn with an order value of SEK 670 million ($80 million); and a new joint-venture contract in California to improve State Route 58 near Hinkley, with Skanska USA's share of the order value worth SEK 640 million ($76 million).

Sister division Skanska USA Building in 2015 secured a SEK 750 million ($89 million) contract from existing customer, Tahoma School District, to construct a new high school and learning center in Maple Valley, Washington. That year the division also won a SEK 730 million ($87 million) contract to build Boeing's Commercial Airplane Decorative Paint Facility in Charleston, South Carolina.

Company Background
Civil construction, which is often publicly funded, was less affected by the economic downturn that hindered other construction segments, such as home building. However, Skanska is looking to diversify its business and become less dependent on public projects. In 2011 the company acquired US-based Industrial Contractors for $135 million. Industrial Contractors (integrated into Skanska US Civil) works on power and energy, commercial and light industrial, and heavy industrial projects.

Auditors : KPMG LLP NEW YORK NY

LOCATIONS
HQ: SKANSKA USA CIVIL INC.
7520 ASTORIA BLVD STE 200, EAST ELMHURST, NY 113701135

Phone: 718 340-0777
Web: USA.SKANSKA.COM

PRODUCTS/OPERATIONS

Selected Services
Commercial development
Construction management
Design-build
Financial services
Pharmaceutical validation
Pre-construction
Public-private validation
Self-performance
Operating Units
Bayshore Concrete Products
Industrial Construction Skanska
PCI Skanska
Skanska Koch
Underpinning & Foundation Skanska

COMPETITORS

BALFOUR BEATTY INFRASTRUCTURE, INC.
KELLER GROUP PLC
OBAYASHI CORPORATION
PETER KIEWIT SONS', INC.
TAKENAKA CORPORATION

HISTORICAL FINANCIALS
Company Type: Private

Income Statement — FYE: December 31

	REVENUE ($mil)	NET INCOME ($mil)	NET PROFIT MARGIN	EMPLOYEES
12/08	1,753	54	3.1%	5,200
12/07	1,611	52	3.2%	—
Annual Growth	8.8%	5.2%	—	—

2008 Year-End Financials
Return on assets: 6.1%   Cash ($ mil.): 172
Return on equity: 13.6%
Current Ratio: 1.50

SKANSKA USA CIVIL NORTHEAST INC.

LOCATIONS

HQ: SKANSKA USA CIVIL NORTHEAST INC.
7520 ASTORIA BLVD STE 200, EAST ELMHURST, NY 113701135
Phone: 718 340-0777

HISTORICAL FINANCIALS
Company Type: Private

Income Statement — FYE: December 31

	REVENUE ($mil)	NET INCOME ($mil)	NET PROFIT MARGIN	EMPLOYEES
12/08	816	51	6.3%	1,500
12/07	622	27	4.5%	—
12/06	467	17	3.7%	—
12/05	487	12	2.6%	—
Annual Growth	18.8%	59.9%	—	—

2008 Year-End Financials
Return on assets: 12.0%   Cash ($ mil.): 121
Return on equity: 25.1%
Current Ratio: 1.70

SKF USA INC.

SKF USA is a subsidiary of Swedish ball bearing giant AB SKF and a world leader in rolling bearings and related technologies including sealing solutions, lubrication systems and services. It also specializes in related services, from repair and rebuilding to consulting, logistics, and training. Its repair stations also provide bearing inspection, repair, and overhaul services. With hundreds of manufacturing, sales, and authorized distribution locations across the US, SKF USA's offerings are geared at a wide range of industries, including aerospace, automotive, construction, machine tooling, and alternative energy. Brand names include Alemite, Cooper, Kaydon, Lincoln, and Mityvac.

Operations
SKF USA offers application engineering, asset management services, condition based maintenance, mechanical maintenance, electric motor rebuilder, pump rebuilding, spindle repair and rebuild services, gearbox rebuilding, and aeronautic services.

For the auto industry, the SKF Vehicle Service Market serves the aftermarket for cars and commercial vehicles by providing high quality products and premium services to its customers.

Geographic Reach
Based in Lansdale, Pennsylvania, SKF USA has almost 30 manufacturing sites in the US, where it provides customized application engineering services through factories in Birmingham and Cleveland. The company additionally operates a technical Center in Plymouth, Michigan, that provides a range of engineering and testing services.

Sales and Marketing
SKF USA sells thousands of products and services through a network of over 4,000 US-based authorized distributors. For the auto industry, it serves the aftermarket for cars and commercial vehicles.

LOCATIONS

HQ: SKF USA INC.
890 FORTY FOOT RD, LANSDALE, PA 194464303
Phone: 267 436-6000
Web: WWW.SKF.COM

PRODUCTS/OPERATIONS

PRODUCTS
Actuation systems
Bearings, units & housings
Condition monitoring
Coupling systems
Linear motion
Lubrication solutions
Magnetic systems
Maintenance products
Power transmission
Seals
Test & measurement equipment
Vehicle aftermarket
SERVICES
Asset management services
Business consulting
Customer training
Engineering consultancy
Logistics
Mechanical maintenance
Remanufacturing & maintenance services
Service contracts

COMPETITORS

BARTON MALOW COMPANY
Bosch Rexroth AG
INA-Holding Schaeffler GmbH & Co. KG
INDUSTRIAL DISTRIBUTION GROUP, INC.
LEANLOGISTICS, INC.
MAHLE International GmbH
PRECISION PARTNERS, L.L.C.
PRIDGEON & CLAY, INC.
SOUTHCO, INC.
thyssenkrupp Materials Services GmbH

HISTORICAL FINANCIALS
Company Type: Private

Income Statement — FYE: December 31

	REVENUE ($mil)	NET INCOME ($mil)	NET PROFIT MARGIN	EMPLOYEES
12/14	3,138	155	5.0%	4,000
12/13	2,554	95	3.7%	—
12/12	2,397	138	5.8%	—
Annual Growth	14.4%	6.0%	—	—

2014 Year-End Financials
Return on assets: 3.8%   Cash ($ mil.): 29
Return on equity: 16.4%
Current Ratio: 2.40

SMDC MEDICAL CENTER

LOCATIONS

HQ: SMDC MEDICAL CENTER
502 E 2ND ST, DULUTH, MN 558051913
Phone: 218 726-4000

HISTORICAL FINANCIALS
Company Type: Private

Income Statement — FYE: June 30

	REVENUE ($mil)	NET INCOME ($mil)	NET PROFIT MARGIN	EMPLOYEES
06/21	663	62	9.4%	2,467
06/20	557	(15)	—	—
06/18	536	6	1.2%	—
06/17	504	0	0.0%	—
Annual Growth	7.1%	396.8%	—	—

2021 Year-End Financials
Return on assets: 5.7%   Cash ($ mil.): —
Return on equity: 30.6%
Current Ratio: 0.10

SMITHSONIAN INSTITUTION

One of the world's leading cultural institutions, the Smithsonian Institution houses some 155 million objects in about 20 museums, gardens, zoo and galleries, most of which are on the National Mall in Washington, DC. Admission to all but one of the Smithsonian's facilities is free. Some of its museums are Anacostia Community Museum, National Air and Space Museum, National Museum of African Art, National Museum of American History, National Postal Museum, Smithsonian American Art Museum and Smithsonian Institution Building (Castle).

Operations

The Smithsonian Institution Traveling Exhibition Service (SITES) organizes exhibitions on art, history and science and circulates them around the country. Each year, SITES travels around 60 exhibitions to hundreds of U.S. cities and towns in all 50 states and the District of Columbia, where they are viewed by millions of people.

Its research facilities includes the Archives of American Art, Smithsonian Conservation Biology Institute, Smithsonian Astrophysical Observatory, Smithsonian Environmental Research Center, Museum Conservation Institute, Smithsonian Libraries, Smithsonian Institution Archives, Smithsonian Tropical Research Institute and the Marine Station at Fort Pierce, Florida.

Geographic Reach

The Smithsonian Institution is located in Washington, DC.

Strategy

The company has a five-year strategic plan that was launched in 2017. The strategic plan has a number of goals which includes:

Be One Smithsonian - The company will work together as One Smithsonian to amplify the power of the stories it tells, increasing reach and impact. It will also view all of its exhibitions and spaces as an Institution-wide portfolio to be deployed strategically. Additionally, the company will be setting standards to create a seamless visitor experience across the Smithsonian by creating a unified customer relationship approach.

Catalyze new conversations and address complex challenges - The company will be magnifying its national and global reach through new collaborative approaches. It will also create new forums across the Smithsonian to proffer solutions to problems of national and global import.

Reach 1 billion people a year with a digital-first strategy - The company will create a digital laboratory to test and develop emerging museum-related digital technologies. The company will also be forging transformative strategic partnerships with major digital leaders, and create new digital platforms for scholars and educators to better access Smithsonian collections, research, and education resources.

Understand and impact 21st-century audiences - The company is working on learning how demographic changes, new learning styles, and new technologies affect the relevance of cultural institutions. It will also tell the complete American story, in person and online, in all of its museums, exhibits, and programs?and across them?with a focus on all Americans, nationally and locally.

HISTORY

English chemist James Smithson wrote a proviso to his will in 1826 that would lead to the creation of the Smithsonian Institution. When he died in 1829, he left his estate to his nephew, Henry James Hungerford, with the stipulation that if Hungerford died without heirs, the estate would go to the US to create "an Establishment for the increase and diffusion of knowledge among men." Hungerford died in 1835 without any heirs, and the US government inherited more than $500,000 in gold.

Congress squandered the money after it was received in 1838 but, perhaps feeling pangs of guilt, covered the loss. The Smithsonian was finally created in 1846, and Princeton physicist Joseph Henry was named its first secretary. That year it established the Museum of Natural History, the Museum of History and Technology, and the National Gallery of Art. The Smithsonian's National Museum was developed around the collection of the US Patent Office in 1858. The Smithsonian continued to expand, adding the National Zoological Park in 1889 and the Smithsonian Astrophysical Observatory in 1890.

The Freer Gallery, a gift of industrialist Charles Freer, opened in 1923. The National Gallery was renamed the National Collection of Fine Arts in 1937, and a new National Gallery, created with Andrew Mellon's gift of his art collection and a building, opened in 1941. The Air and Space Museum was established in 1946.

More museums were added in the 1960s, including the National Portrait Gallery in 1962 and the Anacostia Museum (exhibits and materials on African-American history) in 1967. The Kennedy Center for the Performing Arts was opened in 1971. The Collection of Fine Arts was renamed the National Museum of American Art, and the Museum of History and Technology was renamed the National Museum of American History in 1980.

The Smithsonian placed its first-ever contribution boxes in four of its museums in 1993.

A planned exhibit featuring the Enola Gay -- the plane that dropped the atomic bomb on Hiroshima -- created a firestorm in 1994 with critics charging that the exhibit downplayed Japanese aggression and US casualties in WWII. The original exhibit was canceled in 1995, the director of the Air and Space Museum resigned, and a scaled-down version of the exhibit premiered. In 2004 the exhibit attracted more protestors, prompting Smithsonian officials to evacuate and temporarily close the museum.

Large contributions from private donors continued in the 1990s; the Mashantucket Pequot tribe gave $10 million from its casino operations in 1994 for the Smithsonian's planned American Indian museum, and prolific electronics inventor Jerome Lemelson donated $10.4 million in 1995. The museum celebrated its sesquicentennial in 1996 amid news that $500 million in repairs were needed over the next 10 years.

California real estate developer Kenneth Behring gave the largest cash donation ever to the museum in 1997 -- $20 million for the National Museum of Natural History. Short of funds, the Smithsonian had to cut back on its 150th-anniversary traveling exhibit that year. The Smithsonian announced a $26 million renovation for the National Museum of Natural History in 1998. Two years later Behring quadrupled his record-breaking 1997 donation of $20 million by giving $80 million to the National Museum of American History. Catherine Reynolds withdrew most of her $38 million gift in 2002 after the Smithsonian Institution refused to implement her ideas for an exhibit at the National Museum of American History.

The National Museum of the American Indian opened on the National Mall in 2004.

Secretary Lawrence Small resigned under pressure in March 2007 amid criticism of his spending practices. CristiÁ¡n Samper, director of the Smithsonian's National Museum of Natural History, was named acting secretary. A report on the matter issued by the Smithsonian in June said its Board of Regents failed to provide the oversight that might have prevented Small's extravagant spending.

In July 2008 Wayne Clough became the 12th secretary of the Smithsonian.

Auditors : KPMG LLP WASHINGTON DISTRICT

LOCATIONS

HQ: SMITHSONIAN INSTITUTION
1000 JEFFERSON DR SW, WASHINGTON, DC 205600009
Phone: 202 633-1000
Web: WWW.SI.EDU

PRODUCTS/OPERATIONS

2016 Operating Revenue

	% of total
Federal appropriations	53
Contributions & private grants	18
Business activities	11
Government grants & contracts	8
Endowment	5
Other	5
Total	100

Selected Museums and Research Centers
Anacostia Community Museum

HOOVER'S HANDBOOK OF PRIVATE COMPANIES 2023

Arthur M. Sackler Gallery
Arts and Industries Building
Center for Folklife and Cultural Heritage
Conservation and Research Center
Cooper-Hewitt, National Design Museum (New York)
Freer Gallery of Art
Hirshhorn Museum and Sculpture Garden
National Air and Space Museum
National Museum of African Art
National Museum of American History
National Museum of Natural History
National Museum of the American Indian
National Museum of the American Indian - George Gustav Heye Center (New York)
National Science Research Center
National Portrait Gallery
National Postal Museum
National Zoological Park
Smithsonian American Art Museum
Smithsonian Astrophysical Observatory
Smithsonian Center for Latino Initiatives
Smithsonian Center for Materials Research and Education
Smithsonian Environmental Research Center (SERC)
Smithsonian Institution Building (The Castle)
Smithsonian Museum Conservation Institute
Smithsonian Tropical Research Institute

COMPETITORS

FIELD MUSEUM OF NATURAL HISTORY
ILLINOIS HISTORIC PRESERVATION AGENCY
J PAUL GETTY TRUST
NATIONAL GALLERY OF ART
NATIONAL GEOGRAPHIC SOCIETY
TEXAS STATE HISTORY MUSEUM FOUNDATION, INC
THE AMERICAN MUSEUM OF NATURAL HISTORY
THE ART INSTITUTE OF CHICAGO
THE METROPOLITAN MUSEUM OF ART
THE UNIVERSITY OF CHICAGO

HISTORICAL FINANCIALS
Company Type: Private

Income Statement   FYE: September 30

	REVENUE ($mil)	NET INCOME ($mil)	NET PROFIT MARGIN	EMPLOYEES
09/20	1,389	302	21.8%	6,100
09/19	1,375	180	13.1%	—
09/18	1,563	177	11.3%	—
09/17	1,514	153	10.1%	—
Annual Growth	(2.8%)	25.5%	—	—

2020 Year-End Financials
Return on assets: 5.0%   Cash ($ mil.): 886
Return on equity: 6.5%
Current Ratio: 1.20

SMMH PRACTICE PLAN, INC.

Auditors : KPMG LLP PITTSBURGH PA

LOCATIONS

HQ: SMMH PRACTICE PLAN, INC.
7175 SALTSBURG RD, PITTSBURGH, PA 152352252
Phone: 412 795-6069

HISTORICAL FINANCIALS
Company Type: Private

Income Statement   FYE: June 30

	REVENUE ($mil)	NET INCOME ($mil)	NET PROFIT MARGIN	EMPLOYEES
06/15	2,060	27	1.3%	26
06/14	2,005	570	28.4%	—
06/13	1,985	402	20.3%	—
06/12	1,976	(90)	—	—
Annual Growth	1.4%	—	—	—

2015 Year-End Financials
Return on assets: 4.8%   Cash ($ mil.): 49
Return on equity: 1.3%
Current Ratio: 0.60

SNAKE RIVER SUGAR COMPANY

Auditors : EIDEBAILLY LLP BOISE IDAHO

LOCATIONS

HQ: SNAKE RIVER SUGAR COMPANY
1951 S SATURN WAY STE 100, BOISE, ID 837092924
Phone: 208 383-6500
Web: WWW.AMALGAMATEDSUGAR.COM

HISTORICAL FINANCIALS
Company Type: Private

Income Statement   FYE: August 31

	REVENUE ($mil)	NET INCOME ($mil)	NET PROFIT MARGIN	EMPLOYEES
08/11	876	13	1.5%	2,500
08/10	839	18	2.2%	—
08/09	658	22	3.4%	—
Annual Growth	15.3%	(23.8%)	—	—

2011 Year-End Financials
Return on assets: 1.9%   Cash ($ mil.): 17
Return on equity: 4.8%
Current Ratio: 0.80

SNYDER'S-LANCE, INC.

Snyder's-Lance (formerly Lance) produces iconic brands that satisfy snackers across the globe with its one of the largest distribution networks in the business and an advanced research and development. Its wholesome snack products are sold under a variety of names, including Lance, Cape Cod, Tom's, Archway, Late July, Pretzel Crisps, Snack Factory, Stella Doro, and Snyder's brands at food retailers, mass merchants, and convenience and club stores in the US. International brands include Kettle Chips. Snyder's-Lance currently offers plant tours in its Hanover, Pennsylvania bakery and its Cape Cod Potato Chip factory in Hyannis, Massachusetts.

Operations
Synder's-Lance manufactures pretzels, sandwich crackers, kettle cooked chips, pretzel crackers, cookies, potato chips, tortilla chips, popcorn, nuts and other salty snacks. It operates under such brand names as Kettle, Pop Secret, Emerald, Krunchers, Jays, Eat Smart, and O-Ke-Doke, among others.

Geographic Reach
Snyder's-Lance is based in Charlotte, North Carolina.

HISTORY

A business deal gone awry stuck coffee dealer Philip Lance with 500 pounds of peanuts in 1913. Selling nickel bags of roasted peanuts and then peanut butter, Lance began packaging peanut-butter-and-cracker sandwiches. His son-in-law, Salem Van Every, joined him two years later to form Lance Packing. Lance introduced Toastchee in 1938 and by 1939, the year the firm became Lance, sales reached $2 million. The company began serving the institutional market in 1953 and began selling through vending machines the next year. Lance went public in 1961.

The family continued to run the company until 1973 when Van Every's grandson retired as CEO. After decades of serving mom-and-pop retailers, Lance found the snack market changing. Individual stores gave way to chains; Frito-Lay gobbled up grocery shelf space; and regional rival, Austin Quality Foods, nabbed sales in the new warehouse/club store market. Eventually the conservative company responded with an influx of new management, restructuring, and the advent of marketing.

Lance purchased Tamming Foods (sugar wafers) and Cape Cod Potato Chips (salty snacks) in 1999. Lance then signed an agreement with China Peregrine (now China Premium Food Corp) to export private-label snack foods to China. (Lance has since ceased distribution in China.)

In 2005 Lance's board of directors elected Bill Prezzano as chairman. David Singer, formerly EVP and CFO of Coca-Cola Bottling Co. Consolidated, was named president and CEO of the company. And in 2005, Lance purchased a Canadian sugar-wafer manufacturing plant from A&M Cookie Company Canada.

The $40 million acquisition of Tom's Foods in 2005 added four new bakery and potato chip manufacturing plants to the company's operations. Lance manufactures about 90% of its products; the remainder is purchased for resale.

While Frito-Lay dominates the snack-aisle grocery shelves, Lance's stronghold has been its company-owned vending machines placed in 15,000 locations such as break rooms and cafeterias. In order to concentrate on more profitable operations, in 2006 Lance began phasing out its vending-machine sales and ceased vending operations altogether in 2007. In addition the company joined the ranks of munchies makers that offer healthier products in 2007 with the $2 million purchase of a minority interest in Late July Products, a Massachusetts-based organic snack food maker (crackers, and sandwich crackers and cookies).

EXECUTIVES

CCO, John T Maples
Auditors : PRICEWATERHOUSECOOPERS LLP CH

LOCATIONS

HQ: SNYDER'S-LANCE, INC.
  13515 BALNTYN CORP PL, CHARLOTTE, NC 282772706
Phone: 704 554-1421
Web: WWW.CAMPBELLSOUPCOMPANY.COM

PRODUCTS/OPERATIONS

2015 Revenue

	$ mil	% of total
Branded products	1,155.4	70
Private brands	335.3	20
Other	165.7	10
Total	1,656.4	100

Selected Brands
Archway
Brent
Bugles
Cape Cod Potato Chips
Captain's Wafers
Choc-o-Lunch
Delicious
Diamond of California
Don Pablo's
EatSmart
Emerald
Grande
Jays
Kettle brand
KETTLE
Krunchers!
Lance
Nekot
Nipchee
Pop Secret
Pretzel Crisps
Sam's
Salerno
Snyder's of Hanover
Stella D'oro
Texas Pete
Thunder
Toastchee
Toasty
Tom's
Van-o-Lunch
Vista

COMPETITORS

Bahlsen GmbH & Co. KG
CSM BAKERY SOLUTIONS LLC
D F STAUFFER BISCUIT CO INC
GENERAL MILLS, INC.
INTERBAKE FOODS LLC
INVENTURE FOODS, INC.
MONDELEZ INTERNATIONAL, INC.
OTIS SPUNKMEYER HOLDINGS LLC
RIVIANA FOODS INC.
S-L SNACKS REAL ESTATE, INC.

HISTORICAL FINANCIALS
Company Type: Private

Income Statement — FYE: December 30

	REVENUE ($mil)	NET INCOME ($mil)	NET PROFIT MARGIN	EMPLOYEES
12/17	2,226	149	6.7%	6,100
12/16*	2,109	14	0.7%	—
01/15	1,620	192	11.9%	—
12/13	1,761	79	4.5%	—
Annual Growth	6.0%	17.2%	—	—

*Fiscal year change

2017 Year-End Financials
Return on assets: 4.1%   Cash ($ mil.): 18
Return on equity: 7.4%
Current Ratio: 1.60

SOCORRO INDEPENDENT SCHOOL DISTRICT

Auditors : GIBSON RUDDOCK PATTERSON LLC

LOCATIONS

HQ: SOCORRO INDEPENDENT SCHOOL DISTRICT
  12440 ROJAS DR, EL PASO, TX 799285261
Phone: 915 937-0100
Web: WWW.SISD.NET

HISTORICAL FINANCIALS
Company Type: Private

Income Statement — FYE: June 30

	REVENUE ($mil)	NET INCOME ($mil)	NET PROFIT MARGIN	EMPLOYEES
06/21	568	(166)	—	6,000
06/20	549	48	8.8%	—
06/19	509	120	23.7%	—
06/18	470	168	35.8%	—
Annual Growth	6.5%	—	—	—

2021 Year-End Financials
Return on assets: (-11.2%)   Cash ($ mil.): 396
Return on equity: (-135.4%)
Current Ratio: —

SOLSTICE HOLDINGS INC.

LOCATIONS

HQ: SOLSTICE HOLDINGS INC.
  7575 FULTON ST E, ADA, MI 493550001
Phone: 616 787-1000

HISTORICAL FINANCIALS
Company Type: Private

Income Statement — FYE: December 31

	REVENUE ($mil)	NET INCOME ($mil)	NET PROFIT MARGIN	EMPLOYEES
12/08	8,235	0	0.0%	14,000
12/07	7,168	0	0.0%	—
12/06	6,387	0	0.0%	—
Annual Growth	13.5%	—	—	—

2008 Year-End Financials
Return on assets: —   Cash ($ mil.): 1,072
Return on equity: —
Current Ratio: 1.10

SOUTH BROWARD HOSPITAL DISTRICT

South Broward Hospital District (dba Memorial Healthcare System) is a community-owned health services network that provides health service to residents of Florida's Broward and Palm Beach counties. The system's major hospitals include Memorial Regional Hospital, Memorial Hospital Pembroke, Memorial Hospital West, and Memorial Hospital Miramar. The hospitals have a combined capacity of roughly 1,980 licensed beds and provide services including diagnostic, emergency, surgical, and rehabilitative care. Memorial also operates a pediatric hospital, cardiac and vascular medicine institute, a cancer treatment center, and a center for women's health, as well as nursing home facilities (120 beds) and community clinics.

Operations
Memorial Regional Hospital and Memorial Regional Hospital South offer its community a variety of medical and surgical services. Joe DiMaggio Children's Hospital at Memorial provides a comprehensive array of pediatric services and is the leading children's hospital in Broward and Palm Beach counties. Memorial Hospital West, Memorial Hospital Miramar and Memorial Hospital Pembroke serve the communities of western Broward County and others in South Florida. Memorial Home Health Services, Memorial Manor nursing home and a variety of ancillary healthcare facilities round out the system's wide-ranging health services.

Geographic Reach
Memorial Healthcare System is based in Hollywood, Florida.

Financial Performance
For fiscal year 2022, the System's total operating revenue increased by 18% to $2.8 billion and operating expenses increased by 16%, resulting in operating income increasing by 144% from the prior year of $45.2 million to $110.4 million.

The company's cash at the end of 2021

was $239.2 million. Operating activities generated $121.7 million, while investing activities provided $14.5 million. Financing activities provided another $24.4 million.

EXECUTIVES

CSO, Matthew Muhart
CMO, Marc Napp
TRANSFORMATION, Nina Beauchesne
Auditors : RSM US LLP MIAMI FLORIDA

LOCATIONS

HQ: SOUTH BROWARD HOSPITAL DISTRICT
3501 JOHNSON ST, HOLLYWOOD, FL 330215421
Phone: 954 987-2000
Web: WWW.JDCH.COM

PRODUCTS/OPERATIONS

2015 Sales

	$ mil	% of total
Net patient service	1,630.8	92
Disproportionate share distribution	83.4	5
Other operating revenue	49.9	3
Total	1,764.1	100

Selected Facilities
Esther L. Grossman Women's Health & Resource Center
Memorial Cancer Institute
Memorial Hospital Miramar
Memorial Hospital Pembroke
Memorial Hospital West
Memorial Manor
Memorial Outpatient Center
Memorial Primary Care Center - Dania Beach
Memorial Primary Care Center - Hollywood
Memorial Primary Care Center - Miramar
Memorial Primary Care Center - West Hollywood
Memorial Regional Hospital
    Joe DiMaggio Children's Hospital
Memorial Regional Hospital South
Memorial Regional Hospital Fitness & Rehabilitation Center
Memorial Same Day Surgery Center
Memorial Urgent Care Center
Same Day Surgery Center at Memorial Hospital West

COMPETITORS

BAPTIST HEALTH SYSTEM, INC.
ELLIS HOSPITAL
GUTHRIE HEALTHCARE SYSTEM
MEMORIAL HEALTH SYSTEM OF EAST TEXAS
PHOEBE PUTNEY MEMORIAL HOSPITAL, INC.
SALINAS VALLEY MEMORIAL HEALTHCARE SYSTEMS
SARASOTA COUNTY PUBLIC HOSPITAL DISTRICT
SPARTANBURG REGIONAL HEALTH SERVICES DISTRICT, INC.
WELLMONT HEALTH SYSTEM
YAKIMA VALLEY MEMORIAL HOSPITAL ASSOCIATION

HISTORICAL FINANCIALS

Company Type: Private

Income Statement   FYE: April 30

	REVENUE ($mil)	NET INCOME ($mil)	NET PROFIT MARGIN	EMPLOYEES
04/21	2,339	283	12.1%	9,200
04/20	2,159	156	7.3%	—
04/19	2,148	165	7.7%	—
04/18	2,014	64	3.2%	—
Annual Growth	5.1%	63.7%	—	—

2021 Year-End Financials
Return on assets: 6.9%   Cash ($ mil.): 137
Return on equity: 10.6%
Current Ratio: 6.60

SOUTH CAROLINA PUBLIC SERVICE AUTHORITY (INC)

This company turns the lights on in South Carolina. South Carolina Public Service Authority, known as Santee Cooper (after two interconnected river systems), provides wholesale electricity to 20 cooperatives and two municipalities that serve more than 2 million customers in South Carolina. It directly retails electricity to more than 174,000 customers. One of the largest US state-owned utilities, Santee Cooper operates in all 46 counties in South Carolina and has stakes in power plants (fossil-fueled, nuclear, hydro, and renewable) that give it more than 5,180 MW of generating capacity. Its Santee Cooper Regional Water System also distributes water to customers in its service area.

Operations

Santee Cooper operates 5,029 miles of transmission lines and more than 2,841 miles of distribution lines. It also operates 105 transmission stations and 54 distribution substations. The company is the leading renewable energy producer in South Carolina.

Geographic Reach

In addition to supplying power to 20 cooperatives in all 46 counties in South Carolina, Santee Cooper also supplies power directly to 29 large industrial customers in 10 counties, Charleston Air Force Base, the town of Bamberg, and the City of Georgetown.

Sales and Marketing

The company serves more than 2 million customers in South Carolina. It directly retails electricity to more than 174,000 customers.

Financial Performance

In 2015 Santee Cooper's net revenues decreased by 6% to $1.9 billion compared due to lower kilowatt-hour sales (down 3%) and demand usage (down 2%).

The company's net income decreased by 73% to $34.4 million as the result of lower net revenues and higher electric maintenance expenses.

In 2015 Santee Cooper's operating cash inflow decreased by 77% to $237.6 million.

Strategy

With a eye toward getting 40% of its power from non-carbon emitting sources and conservation by 2020 the company has begun to invest heavily in nuclear, solar, wind, and other renewable energy sources.

In 2015 the company agreed to changes in its agreement with Westinghouse Electric, which acquired assets of a second partner in the V.C. Summer Nuclear Station plant construction consortium, giving Westinghouse more control over the project.

In 2014 Santee Cooper, in collaboration with Central Electric Power Cooperative and the state's electric cooperatives, agreed to buy the total energy output of Colleton Solar Farm, a utility-scale solar power farm being built by TIG Sun Energy, a subsidiary of the North Charleston-based InterTech Group. The solar array consists of 10,010 photovoltaic panels. Some panels are fixed while other panels follow the direction of the sun to maximize the production of solar energy.

South Carolina Resources, Santee Cooper, Central Electric Power Cooperative, and the state's electric cooperatives agreed in 2013 to build Colleton Solar Farm, the largest solar farm in the state (3,000 kilowatts of electricity).

Mergers and Acquisitions

In 2014 South Carolina Electric & Gas Company (SCE&G), principal subsidiary of SCANA Corporation, and Santee Cooper, announced an agreement for SCE&G to acquire from Santee Cooper a 5% ownership interest in the two new nuclear units, which are under construction at V.C. Summer Nuclear Station in Jenkinsville. Under the ownership agreement, SCE&G owns 55%; Santee Cooper, 45%. The 5% ownership interest would be acquired in three stages, with 1% to be acquired at the commercial operation date of the first new nuclear unit (late 2017 or the first quarter of 2018); an additional 2% to be acquired no later than the first anniversary of such commercial operation date; and the final 2% to be acquired no later than the second anniversary date of such commercial operation date.

Company Background

Santee Cooper is a government-owned entity.

Historically, the $48.2 million Santee Cooper project (55% federal loan and 45% federal grant), which connected the Santee and Cooper rivers and established hydroelectric dams and a transmission grid, began to generate electricity for the first time in 1942. It was founded in 1934.

HISTORY

In 2011, Santee Cooper dedicated a 311-kilowatt solar installation in Myrtle Beach, where it also has 2.4-kW wind turbine (the first utility-connected turbine on the state grid). Santee Cooper also contracted for power from biomass combustion and from anaerobic digestion on a livestock farm.

In late 2011, the US Nuclear Regulatory Commission conducted a final review of Santee Cooper's application for a license to build and operate two new nuclear units at

V.C. Summer Nuclear Station.

EXECUTIVES

Chief Financial, Kenneth W Lott Iii
PUBLIC AFFAIRS*, Pamela J Williams
Auditors : CHERRY BEKAERT LLP RALEIGH N

LOCATIONS

HQ: SOUTH CAROLINA PUBLIC SERVICE AUTHORITY (INC)
  1 RIVERWOOD DR, MONCKS CORNER, SC 294612998
Phone: 843 761-4121
Web: WWW.SANTEECOOPER.COM

PRODUCTS/OPERATIONS

2015 Sales

	$ mil.	% of total
Electricity	1,856.5	99
Water	8.1	-
Other	15.0	1
Total	1,879.6	100

COMPETITORS

ARIZONA PUBLIC SERVICE COMPANY
ARKANSAS ELECTRIC COOPERATIVE CORPORATION
DTE ELECTRIC COMPANY
DUKE ENERGY CORPORATION
GREAT RIVER ENERGY
NEXTERA ENERGY, INC.
SCANA CORPORATION
SEMINOLE ELECTRIC COOPERATIVE, INC.
STP NUCLEAR OPERATING COMPANY
THE SOUTHERN COMPANY

HISTORICAL FINANCIALS
Company Type: Private

Income Statement — FYE: December 31

	REVENUE ($mil)	NET INCOME ($mil)	NET PROFIT MARGIN	EMPLOYEES
12/19	1,722	(231)	—	1,748
12/17	1,756	90	5.2%	—
12/15	1,879	34	1.8%	—
12/13	1,816	65	3.6%	—
Annual Growth	(0.9%)	—	—	—

2019 Year-End Financials
Return on assets: (-2.0%) Cash ($ mil.): 311
Return on equity: (-11.2%)
Current Ratio: 1.70

SOUTH FLORIDA WATER MANAGEMENT DISTRICT LEASING CORP.

LOCATIONS

HQ: SOUTH FLORIDA WATER MANAGEMENT DISTRICT LEASING CORP.
  3301 GUN CLUB RD, WEST PALM BEACH, FL 334063007

Phone: 561 686-8800
Web: WWW.SFWMD.GOV

HISTORICAL FINANCIALS
Company Type: Private

Income Statement — FYE: September 30

	REVENUE ($mil)	NET INCOME ($mil)	NET PROFIT MARGIN	EMPLOYEES
09/10	595	(42)	—	1,200
09/08	910	(64)	—	—
09/06	947	51	5.4%	—
Annual Growth	(11.0%)	—	—	—

2010 Year-End Financials
Return on assets: (-0.8%) Cash ($ mil.): —
Return on equity: (-0.9%)
Current Ratio: 1.00

SOUTH NASSAU COMMUNITIES HOSPITAL

LOCATIONS

HQ: SOUTH NASSAU COMMUNITIES HOSPITAL
  1 HEALTHY WAY, OCEANSIDE, NY 115721551
Phone: 516 632-3000
Web: WWW.SOUTHNASSAU.ORG

HISTORICAL FINANCIALS
Company Type: Private

Income Statement — FYE: December 31

	REVENUE ($mil)	NET INCOME ($mil)	NET PROFIT MARGIN	EMPLOYEES
12/19	553	35	6.4%	2,800
12/18	461	(46)	—	—
12/17	451	(47)	—	—
12/16	437	(33)	—	—
Annual Growth	8.1%	—	—	—

2019 Year-End Financials
Return on assets: 4.5% Cash ($ mil.): 31
Return on equity: 11.8%
Current Ratio: 0.30

SOUTH SHORE HOSPITAL, INC.

EXECUTIVES

Clinical Vice President*, Edward Liao
ACUTE CARE Operations*, Timothy Quigley

LOCATIONS

HQ: SOUTH SHORE HOSPITAL, INC.
  55 FOGG RD, SOUTH WEYMOUTH, MA 021902455
Phone: 781 624-8000
Web: WWW.SOUTHSHOREHEALTH.ORG

HISTORICAL FINANCIALS
Company Type: Private

Income Statement — FYE: September 30

	REVENUE ($mil)	NET INCOME ($mil)	NET PROFIT MARGIN	EMPLOYEES
09/19	664	14	2.2%	2,375
09/18	575	10	1.9%	—
09/17	563	9	1.7%	—
09/16	558	17	3.1%	—
Annual Growth	6.0%	(5.1%)	—	—

2019 Year-End Financials
Return on assets: 2.2% Cash ($ mil.): 40
Return on equity: 4.4%
Current Ratio: 0.40

SOUTH TEXAS ELECTRIC COOPERATIVE, INC.

Auditors : BUMGARDNER MORRISON AND COMPAN

LOCATIONS

HQ: SOUTH TEXAS ELECTRIC COOPERATIVE, INC.
  2849 FM 447, VICTORIA, TX 779052931
Phone: 361 575-6491
Web: WWW.STEC.ORG

HISTORICAL FINANCIALS
Company Type: Private

Income Statement — FYE: December 31

	REVENUE ($mil)	NET INCOME ($mil)	NET PROFIT MARGIN	EMPLOYEES
12/21	550	18	3.3%	253
12/18	522	32	6.2%	—
12/17	495	26	5.4%	—
Annual Growth	2.7%	(9.0%)	—	—

2021 Year-End Financials
Return on assets: 1.3% Cash ($ mil.): 48
Return on equity: 4.4%
Current Ratio: 1.00

SOUTHCOAST HOSPITALS GROUP, INC.

When you feel more than a little physically washed up, get to one of the Southcoast Hospitals Group facilities. The not-for-profit company provides medical services in the southeastern corner of Massachusetts and in Rhode Island. Its primary facilities in Massachusetts are the Charlton Memorial Hospital (with about 330 beds) in Fall River, St. Luke's Hospital (420 beds) in New Bedford, and Tobey Hospital (65 beds) in Wareham, which provide acute medical care and specialty services including cardiology, neurology, orthopedics, and women's care. Southcoast Hospitals Group also operates about 20 ancillary facilities, including nursing and assisted-living facilities and home health and hospice agencies.

Auditors : DELOITTE TAX LLP JERICHO NY

LOCATIONS

HQ: SOUTHCOAST HOSPITALS GROUP, INC.
363 HIGHLAND AVE, FALL RIVER, MA 027203703
Phone: 508 679-3131
Web: WWW.SOUTHCOAST.ORG

COMPETITORS

BETHESDA HOSPITAL, INC.
HCA HEALTH SERVICES OF FLORIDA, INC.
MULTICARE HEALTH SYSTEM
THE JOHNS HOPKINS HEALTH SYSTEM CORPORATION
UNIVERSITY HEALTH SERVICES, INC.

HISTORICAL FINANCIALS
Company Type: Private

Income Statement — FYE: September 30

	REVENUE ($mil)	NET INCOME ($mil)	NET PROFIT MARGIN	EMPLOYEES
09/13	687	22	3.3%	3,853
09/12	704	49	7.0%	—
09/06	506	14	2.8%	—
09/04	445	13	3.1%	—
Annual Growth	4.9%	5.4%	—	—

2013 Year-End Financials
Return on assets: 6.9%   Cash ($ mil.): 6
Return on equity: 3.3%
Current Ratio: 0.60

SOUTHEAST PETRO DISTRIBUTORS, INC.

Auditors : JAMES MOORE & CO PL GAINE

LOCATIONS

HQ: SOUTHEAST PETRO DISTRIBUTORS, INC.
402 HIGH POINT DR STE A, COCOA, FL 329266600
Phone: 321 631-0245
Web: WWW.SOUTHEASTPETRO.COM

HISTORICAL FINANCIALS
Company Type: Private

Income Statement — FYE: December 31

	REVENUE ($mil)	NET INCOME ($mil)	NET PROFIT MARGIN	EMPLOYEES
12/11	553	5	1.0%	12
12/10	416	5	1.3%	—
12/09	331	4	1.5%	—
12/02	57	0	0.9%	—
Annual Growth	28.6%	29.8%	—	—

2011 Year-End Financials
Return on assets: 13.1%   Cash ($ mil.): 8
Return on equity: 35.4%
Current Ratio: 1.20

SOUTHERN BAPTIST HOSPITAL OF FLORIDA INC.

Auditors : ERNST & YOUNG LLP JACKSON F

LOCATIONS

HQ: SOUTHERN BAPTIST HOSPITAL OF FLORIDA INC.
800 PRUDENTIAL DR FL 3220, JACKSONVILLE, FL 322078202
Phone: 904 399-5620
Web: WWW.BAPTISTJAX.COM

HISTORICAL FINANCIALS
Company Type: Private

Income Statement — FYE: September 30

	REVENUE ($mil)	NET INCOME ($mil)	NET PROFIT MARGIN	EMPLOYEES
09/21	1,775	443	25.0%	4,000
09/20	1,465	33	2.3%	—
09/19	1,398	186	13.3%	—
09/18	1,234	209	17.0%	—
Annual Growth	12.9%	28.4%	—	—

2021 Year-End Financials
Return on assets: 10.8%   Cash ($ mil.): —
Return on equity: 17.2%
Current Ratio: 0.80

SOUTHERN CAL SCHOOLS VOL EMP BENEFITS ASSOC

EXECUTIVES

Prin, George McGregor
Auditors : ROSNER BROWN TOUCHSTONE & KELL

LOCATIONS

HQ: SOUTHERN CAL SCHOOLS VOL EMP BENEFITS ASSOC
8885 RIO SAN DIEGO DR # 327, SAN DIEGO, CA 921081624
Phone: 619 278-0021

HISTORICAL FINANCIALS
Company Type: Private

Income Statement — FYE: December 31

	REVENUE ($mil)	NET INCOME ($mil)	NET PROFIT MARGIN	EMPLOYEES
12/14	598	4	0.7%	9
12/13	551	5	1.0%	—
Annual Growth	8.6%	(29.1%)	—	—

2014 Year-End Financials
Return on assets: 6.6%   Cash ($ mil.): 38
Return on equity: 19.6%
Current Ratio: 2.30

SOUTHERN ILLINOIS HEALTHCARE ENTERPRISES, INC.

Southern Illinois Healthcare, a nonprofit health care system, operates the flagship 145-bed tertiary-care Memorial Hospital of Carbondale, as well as Herrin Hospital (with 114 beds) and St. Joseph Memorial Hospital (with 25 beds). The hospitals serve residents of across southern Illinois. The nearly 280-bed system provides services such as birthing, cardiac, cancer, and emergency care, as well as surgery and rehabilitation. Its cardiac care is offered through an affiliation with the Prairie Heart Institute at St. John's Hospital in Springfield, Illinois. The medical school at Southern Illinois University conducts its Family Practice Residency Program at Memorial Hospital of Carbondale.

Operations

Across its health system, Southern Illinois Healthcare employs more than 3,000 people. Physicians at its primary hospital, Memorial Hospital of Carbondale, represent nearly 40 medical specialties. It maintains the only dedicated pediatric unit in the region, as well as the largest birthing center with Level II Plus Special Care Nursery.

St. Joseph Memorial Hospital is a full-service, critical access hospital.

In addition to the patient hospitals, the system includes two clinics, two physician professional buildings, an urgent care clinic, and dedicated neurology, cancer, heart, sleep, and rehabilitation centers.

Geographic Reach

Most of Memorial Hospital of Carbondale's inpatient and outpatient visits come from residents of seven Illinois counties (Jackson, Franklin, Williamson, Perry, Johnson, Union, and Saline). St. Joseph Memorial Hospital serves the Murphysboro community.

Strategy

Teaming up to provide better care, independent not-for-profit health care organizations BJC HealthCare of St. Louis, CoxHealth of Springfield, Missouri, Memorial Health System of Springfield, Illinois., and Saint Luke's Health System of Kansas City, Missouri created The BJC Collaborative, L.L.C. (in 2012). Blessing Health System of Quincy and Southern Illinois Healthcare joined the Collaborative in 2013.

Company Background
During 2012, Southern Illinois Healthcare collaborated with community partners to conduct a Community Health Needs Assessment to spotlight health and quality of life issues in the communities served by Southern Illinois Healthcare.

Southern Illinois Healthcare was first established by four doctors in 1946 as the Southern Illinois Hospital Corporation.

Auditors : RSM US LLP SPRINGFIELD ILLIN

LOCATIONS

HQ: SOUTHERN ILLINOIS HEALTHCARE ENTERPRISES, INC.
1239 E MAIN ST STE C, CARBONDALE, IL 629013176
Phone: 618 457-5200

PRODUCTS/OPERATIONS

Selected Facilities
Herrin Hospital
Memorial Hospital of Carbondale
St. Joseph Memorial Hospital

Selected Services
Birthing Center
Cancer
Senior Renewal
Heart
Infusion Therapy
Neurosciences
Occupational Health
Pediatrics
Rehabilitation
Robotic-assisted Surgery
Sleep Medicine
Stroke
Surgical Services
Weight Loss Surgery
Wound Healing

COMPETITORS

FRANCISCAN HEALTH SYSTEM
METHODIST LE BONHEUR HEALTHCARE
NORTH MISSISSIPPI MEDICAL CENTER, INC.
ROBINSON HEALTH SYSTEM, INC.
SAINT ELIZABETH REGIONAL MEDICAL CENTER

HISTORICAL FINANCIALS
Company Type: Private

Income Statement — FYE: March 31

	REVENUE ($mil)	NET INCOME ($mil)	NET PROFIT MARGIN	EMPLOYEES
03/22	794	(33)	—	3,493
03/21	707	123	17.4%	—
03/20	696	(45)	—	—
03/19	685	22	3.2%	—
Annual Growth	5.1%	—	—	—

2022 Year-End Financials
Return on assets: (-2.5%)   Cash ($ mil.): 25
Return on equity: (-4.8%)
Current Ratio: 1.20

SOUTHERN ILLINOIS UNIVERSITY INC

Southern Illinois University (SIU) helps to train future doctors, dentists, and other other professionals. The university enrolls some 32,000 students at its two institutions -- Southern Illinois University at Carbondale (SIUC, which includes medical and law schools) and Southern Illinois University at Edwardsville (SIUE, which houses education, dental, and nursing schools) -- as well as smaller satellite centers. SIU offers associate, baccalaureate, master's, doctoral, and professional degrees. It also boasts a number of study abroad partnerships with international universities. Tracing its roots back to 1869, SIU is known for its extensive research programs.

Operations
Students across SIU's institutions hail from all 50 states and more than 100 countries. Combined, the campuses have some 2,600 faculty members and an annual budget of $870 million.

The Carbondale campus was chartered in 1869 as a teachers college, while the Edwardsville campus was founded in 1957. Most of the university's doctoral programs are housed at the SIUC campus, which conducts residencies through the School of Medicine. A majority of the institutions master's degrees are conferred at the SIUE campus.

Undergraduate and research programs are conducted at both primary SIU campuses. Students and faculty members participate in research programs in a number of fields, including biology, biodiversity, and molecular science. The university receives $78.5 million in research grants annually.

Geographic Reach
From its flagship campus in Carbondale, Illinois, SIU reaches to Edwardsville and to other parts of Southern Illinois, including Springfield, through satellite campus locations. Its satellite schools include SIU School of Medicine, SIU School of Dental Medicine, and SIU School of Nursing.

Financial Performance
SIU logged increases of 2% in fiscal 2012 as compared to 2011, pointing to a rise in student tuition and fees, private grants and contracts, and sales and services for the gains. Net income for the same reporting period rose 17% due to a boost in non-operating revenues attributable to increases in gifts and contributions, investment income, and payments on behalf of the university.

Strategy
As part of its focus, SIU is working to strengthen its undergraduate, graduate, and professional education. It's also concentrating on streamlining its administrative process while expanding its inter-campus and intra-campus collaboration through degree programs, international education, distributed learning, fundraising, and research opportunities for both students and faculty. SIU is also establishing partnerships with public and private sector groups.

LOCATIONS

HQ: SOUTHERN ILLINOIS UNIVERSITY INC
1400 DOUGLAS DR, CARBONDALE, IL 629014332
Phone: 618 536-3475
Web: WWW.SIU.EDU

COMPETITORS

DESALES UNIVERSITY
FAIRFIELD UNIVERSITY
NEW MEXICO STATE UNIVERSITY
SOUTH CAROLINA STATE UNIVERSITY
UNIVERSITY OF KENTUCKY

HISTORICAL FINANCIALS
Company Type: Private

Income Statement — FYE: June 30

	REVENUE ($mil)	NET INCOME ($mil)	NET PROFIT MARGIN	EMPLOYEES
06/22	631	30	4.8%	9,576
06/21	568	(7)	—	—
06/20	578	25	4.4%	—
06/19	581	28	4.9%	—
Annual Growth	2.8%	1.5%	—	—

2022 Year-End Financials
Return on assets: 2.4%   Cash ($ mil.): 69
Return on equity: 4.4%
Current Ratio: 1.90

SOUTHERN INDIANA GAS & ELECTRIC COMPANY

Auditors : DELOITTE & TOUCHE LLP INDIAN

LOCATIONS

HQ: SOUTHERN INDIANA GAS & ELECTRIC COMPANY
211 NW RIVERSIDE DR, EVANSVILLE, IN 477081251
Phone: 812 424-6411
Web: WWW.ACCESS2ENERGY.COM

HISTORICAL FINANCIALS
Company Type: Private

Income Statement — FYE: December 31

	REVENUE ($mil)	NET INCOME ($mil)	NET PROFIT MARGIN	EMPLOYEES
12/17	661	86	13.1%	779
12/16	692	95	13.9%	—
12/03	438	48	11.1%	—
12/02	693	59	8.6%	—
Annual Growth	(0.3%)	2.6%	—	—

2017 Year-End Financials
Return on assets: 3.8%   Cash ($ mil.): 2
Return on equity: 9.7%
Current Ratio: 1.80

SOUTHERN METHODIST UNIVERSITY INC

What do former first lady Laura Bush, actress Kathy Bates, and NFL Hall-of-Famer Doak Walker have in common? They're all graduates of Southern Methodist University (SMU). Founded in 1911 by what is now The United Methodist Church, SMU is a nonsectarian private institution offering undergraduate, graduate, and professional degrees in arts, business, engineering, humanities, law, science, and theology through eight schools. It's one of a handful of schools nationwide to offer an academic major in human rights. Nearly 12,375 students attend the university, which has a student-faculty ratio of 11:1. About 85% of full-time faculty hold the doctorate or highest degree in their fields.

Operations
The university offers more than 100 majors and 85 minors to choose from, as well as double and triple major opportunities and accelerated degree programs through eight schools. Some areas to study include accounting, advertising, art, business entrepreneurship, chemistry, data sciences, and earth sciences.

Geographic Reach
SMU is housed of some 130 buildings on about 235 acres, five miles north of downtown Dallas County. SMU's Taos campus is nearly 425 acres with about 30 buildings, located within the Carson National Forest and surrounded by the Sangre de Cristo Mountains. Students came from all 50 states, the District of Columbia and approximately 90 foreign countries. Students represent diverse economic, ethnic and religious backgrounds.

Financial Performance
The SMU endowment ended the fiscal year in 2019 (ended May), with a market value of $1.6 billion. Substantial endowment gifts of $25.7 million were received during the year, while endowment distributions of $81.0 million, an all-time high, provided support to the University.

EXECUTIVES
Vice President Business*, Chris Casey
EXTERNAL AFFAIRS*, Brad Cheves
Auditors : KPMG LLP DALLAS TX

LOCATIONS
HQ: SOUTHERN METHODIST UNIVERSITY INC
6425 BOAZ LN, DALLAS, TX 75205
Phone: 214 768-2000
Web: WWW.SMU.EDU

PRODUCTS/OPERATIONS
Selected Schools and Divisions
Annette Caldwell Simmons School of Education and Human Development
Bobby B. Lyle School of Engineering
Cox School of Business
Dedman College of Humanities and Sciences
Dedman School of Law
Meadows School of the Arts
Perkins School of Theology

COMPETITORS
COASTAL CAROLINA UNIVERSITY ALUMNI ASSOCIATION, INC.
COLLEGE OF SAINT BENEDICT
GWYNEDD MERCY UNIVERSITY
JOHNSON & WALES UNIVERSITY
NORWICH UNIVERSITY
OCCIDENTAL COLLEGE
PEPPERDINE UNIVERSITY
UNIVERSITY OF SAN FRANCISCO
UNIVERSITY OF ST ANDREWS
WAKE FOREST UNIVERSITY

HISTORICAL FINANCIALS
Company Type: Private

Income Statement — FYE: May 31

	REVENUE ($mil)	NET INCOME ($mil)	NET PROFIT MARGIN	EMPLOYEES
05/20	940	100	10.7%	2,200
05/18	652	96	14.7%	—
05/17	580	56	9.8%	—
05/13	563	115	20.5%	—
Annual Growth	7.6%	(2.0%)	—	—

2020 Year-End Financials
Return on assets: 2.9% Cash ($ mil.): 155
Return on equity: 3.9%
Current Ratio: —

SOUTHERN NATURAL GAS COMPANY, L.L.C.

Now here's a company that pipes in the goods that keep the South fueled, naturally. Southern Natural Gas operates an 7,600-mile long natural gas pipeline (SNG System), which serves major markets across the southeastern US. This system transports more than 3 billion cu. ft. of natural gas per day. The SNG pipeline system has about 60 billion cu. ft. of underground working natural gas storage capacity. Major customers include Atlanta Gas Light Company, Alabama Gas, Southern Company, and SCANA . Southern Natural Gas is a unit of El Paso Pipeline Partners.

EXECUTIVES
CAO, Rosa P Jackson

LOCATIONS
HQ: SOUTHERN NATURAL GAS COMPANY, L.L.C.
1001 LOUISIANA ST, HOUSTON, TX 770025089
Phone: 713 420-2600
Web: WWW.KINDERMORGAN.COM

COMPETITORS
FortisBC Energy Inc
GULF SOUTH PIPELINE COMPANY, LLC
ONEOK ENERGY SERVICES COMPANY, L.P.
Union Gas Limited
WESTERN MIDSTREAM OPERATING, LP

HISTORICAL FINANCIALS
Company Type: Private

Income Statement — FYE: December 31

	REVENUE ($mil)	NET INCOME ($mil)	NET PROFIT MARGIN	EMPLOYEES
12/17	606	143	23.7%	3
12/16	609	169	27.8%	—
Annual Growth	(0.6%)	(15.2%)	—	—

2017 Year-End Financials
Return on assets: 5.2% Cash ($ mil.): 3
Return on equity: 10.8%
Current Ratio: 0.90

SOUTHERN NEW HAMPSHIRE UNIVERSITY

Auditors : KPMG LLP BOSTON MA

LOCATIONS
HQ: SOUTHERN NEW HAMPSHIRE UNIVERSITY
2500 N RIVER RD, MANCHESTER, NH 031061018
Phone: 603 668-2211
Web: WWW.SNHU.EDU

HISTORICAL FINANCIALS
Company Type: Private

Income Statement — FYE: June 30

	REVENUE ($mil)	NET INCOME ($mil)	NET PROFIT MARGIN	EMPLOYEES
06/21	1,026	228	22.2%	1,000
06/20	997	124	12.5%	—
06/18	737	129	17.5%	—
06/16	0	0	—	—
Annual Growth	—	—	—	—

2021 Year-End Financials
Return on assets: 16.2% Cash ($ mil.): 386
Return on equity: 23.2%
Current Ratio: —

SOUTHERN NUCLEAR OPERATING COMPANY, INC.

The night the lights went out in Georgia, they should have called Southern Nuclear Operating Company. The company, a subsidiary of Southern Company since 1990, operates six nuclear power units at three plant locations, which combined, provide about 20% of the electricity used in Alabama and Georgia. Southern Nuclear's Joseph M. Farley Nuclear Plant began commercial operation in 1977. The Edwin I. Hatch Nuclear Plant and the Alvin W. Vogtle Electric Generating Plant are jointly owned by Southern Company's Georgia Power (50%), Oglethorpe Power (30%), the Municipal Electrical Authority of Georgia (18%), and the city of Dalton.

LOCATIONS

HQ: SOUTHERN NUCLEAR OPERATING COMPANY, INC.
42 INVERNESS CENTER PKWY, HOOVER, AL 352424809
Phone: 205 992-5000
Web: WWW.SOUTHERNCOMPANY.COM

COMPETITORS

China Energy Investment Corporation Limited
MASTEC, INC.
Marquard & Bahls AG
TISHMAN CONSTRUCTION CORPORATION
Wood Canada Limited

HISTORICAL FINANCIALS
Company Type: Private

Income Statement — FYE: December 31

	REVENUE ($mil)	NET INCOME ($mil)	NET PROFIT MARGIN	EMPLOYEES
12/16	922	0	0.0%	2,960
12/04	479	0	0.0%	—
12/03	441	0	0.0%	—
12/02	455	0	0.0%	—
Annual Growth	5.2%	—	—	—

2016 Year-End Financials
Return on assets: —   Cash ($ mil.): 14
Return on equity: 0.1%
Current Ratio: 1.00

SOUTHLAND INDUSTRIES

Southland Industries designs, builds, and maintains a variety of mechanical systems for facilities around North America. The mechanical engineering firm provides design, construction, fabrication, and maintenance of plumbing, process piping, fire protection, HVAC, and controls and automation systems. Southland Industries' clients are in the health care, life sciences, hospitality, industrial, education, data center, and government sectors. Projects include STAAT Mods ? Modular ICU Centers, Kaiser Downey Hospital, and International Airport Federal Inspection Services. Southland Industries was founded in 1949.

Operations
The company operates in four business units: Engineering, Construction, Envise and Energy.

Southland Engineering is a collaborative engineering partner that offers complete range of engineering services.

Its Southland Constructions offers integrated project delivery, design-build, design-assist, preconstruction, lean design and construction, manufactured and modular construction, building information modeling, mechanical construction, and fire protection installation.

Its Envise open platform provides building management solutions that improve facility through the usage of analytics, building automation, and equipment lifecycle management.

The company also has Southland Energy professionals that works to help the customers reduce both utility consumption and overall cost, without sacrificing its facilities operations.

Geographic Reach
Southland Industries has engineering offices in Washington, D.C. and Virginia. Its construction offices are in the Mid-Atlantic, Pacific Northwest, Northern California, Southern California, and Southwest regions.

Sales and Marketing
Southland Industries serves a wide variety of markets and industries, from pharmaceutical companies to casinos, educational institutions to retail centers as well as data center, government, hospitality, and industrial markets.

Company Background
Southland Industries is founded in 1949.

EXECUTIVES
Chief Human Resources Officer*, Lisa Hoffman Starr
Chief Commercial Officer*, Brian Boutte
Auditors : MOSS ADAMS LLP IRVINE CALIFO

LOCATIONS
HQ: SOUTHLAND INDUSTRIES
12131 WESTERN AVE, GARDEN GROVE, CA 928412914
Phone: 800 613-6240
Web: WWW.SOUTHLANDIND.COM

PRODUCTS/OPERATIONS

Selected Projects
Carl R. Darnall Army Medical Center
Kaiser Downey Hospital
MLK Hospital Renovation
Palo Alto Medical Foundation
UHS Temecula Hospital

Selected Services
Controls and automation
Energy analysis
Fire protection
HVAC
Planning and development
Plumbing
Process piping
Project management
Maintenance
Repair and retrofit

COMPETITORS
ALBERICI CORPORATION
CONTI LLC
GILBANE, INC.
HITT CONTRACTING, INC.
ISS TECHNICAL SERVICES HOLDINGS LIMITED
JOHN E. GREEN COMPANY
LORNE STEWART PLC
MCKINSTRY CO., LLC
MURPHY COMPANY MECHANICAL CONTRACTORS AND ENGINEERS
THE WALDINGER CORPORATION

HISTORICAL FINANCIALS
Company Type: Private

Income Statement — FYE: September 30

	REVENUE ($mil)	NET INCOME ($mil)	NET PROFIT MARGIN	EMPLOYEES
09/21	1,058	44	4.2%	2,150
09/11	407	61	15.0%	—
09/08	471	44	9.4%	—
09/07	(527)	0	0.0%	—
Annual Growth	—	—	—	—

2021 Year-End Financials
Return on assets: 9.8%   Cash ($ mil.): 185
Return on equity: 27.0%
Current Ratio: 1.50

SOUTHWEST RESEARCH INSTITUTE INC

Founded in 1947 by oilman and rancher Thomas Slick Jr., Southwest Research Institute (SwRI) is an independent, not-for-profit research and development institution that contracts to explore subjects in areas including automation and data systems, applied physics, space science and engineering, and chemistry. SwRI has about 2,700 scientists, engineers, and support staff at laboratories and offices in the US, China, and the UK. Customers include the private sector and government agencies. SwRI's Signature Science subsidiary researches national security, environmental management, and biotechnology.

Operations
SwRI provides contract research and development services to industrial and government clients. It keeps the scope of its work confidential and assigns patent rights arising from its sponsored research to the client.

The company operates through ten technical divisions, including Applied Physics, Applied Power; Chemistry & Chemical Engineering; Center for Nuclear Waste Regulatory Analyses; Defense & Intelligence Solutions and Intelligent Systems.

Geographic Reach
The company is based in Texas and has

operations in ten US states, including Colorado, Georgia and Maryland, as well as international locations in China and the United Kingdom.

Sales and Marketing

SwRI has eight market segments: automotive and transportation; biomedical and health; chemistry and materials; defense and security; earth and space; electronics and automation; energy and environment; and manufacturing and construction.

EXECUTIVES

Vice President Facilities, Paul Easley
Applied Physics Vice President, Kenneth Bennett Junior
Applied Power Vice President, Mary Massey
Vice-President Intelligent Systems, Steve Dellenback
Chemistry Vice President, Mike Macnaughton
FUELS LUBRICANTS Research, Steve Marty
Technical Vice President, Danny Deffenbaugh
Auditors : RSM US LLP SAN ANTONIO TEXAS

LOCATIONS

HQ: SOUTHWEST RESEARCH INSTITUTE INC
6220 CULEBRA RD, SAN ANTONIO, TX 782385100
Phone: 210 684-5111
Web: WWW.SWRI.ORG

PRODUCTS/OPERATIONS

Selected Technical Divisions
Aerospace Electronics and Information Technology
Applied Physics
Applied Power
Automation and Data Systems
Chemistry and Chemical Engineering
Engine, Emissions, and Vehicle Research
Fuels and Lubricants Research
Geosciences and Engineering
Mechanical Engineering
Signal Exploitation and Geolocation
Space Science and Engineering
Training, Simulation, and Performance Improvement

COMPETITORS

APPLIED RESEARCH ASSOCIATES, INC.
APTUIT, LLC
BURNS & MCDONNELL, INC.
ELECTRIC POWER RESEARCH INSTITUTE, INC.
GENERAL ATOMICS
GEOSYNTEC CONSULTANTS, INC.
HII MISSION DRIVEN INNOVATIVE SOLUTIONS INC.
INSTITUTE OF GAS TECHNOLOGY
MRIGLOBAL
S&ME, INC.

HISTORICAL FINANCIALS

Company Type: Private

Income Statement   FYE: September 24

	REVENUE ($mil)	NET INCOME ($mil)	NET PROFIT MARGIN	EMPLOYEES
09/21	725	52	7.2%	2,820
09/19	685	41	6.0%	—
09/18	583	38	6.6%	—
09/17	498	11	2.3%	—
Annual Growth	9.9%	46.5%	—	—

2021 Year-End Financials
Return on assets: 5.9%   Cash ($ mil.): 14
Return on equity: 7.7%
Current Ratio: 2.90

SPARROW HEALTH SYSTEM

Ailing residents of central Michigan fly to Sparrow Health System for care. The not-for-profit network's hospitals include the flagship Sparrow Hospital, Sparrow Hospital St. Lawrence, Sparrow Eaton Hospital, Sparrow Ionia Hospital, Sparrow Clinton Hospital, Sparrow Specialty Hospital, and Sparrow Carson Hospital. Sparrow Health performs about 23,000 surgeries in a year and 300 ER patients in a day. Sparrow Health provides inpatient and outpatient services, radiology, pharmacies, home care, hospice care, rehabilitation, lab and pet therapy through nearly 1,300 physicians in about 115 sites of care across mid-Michigan. Through its Mother Baby Center, Sparrow delivers about 4,000 babies annually.

Financial Performance

EXECUTIVES

CCO, Paul Entler
Auditors : PLANTE & MORAN PLLC GRAND RA

LOCATIONS

HQ: SPARROW HEALTH SYSTEM
1215 E MICHIGAN AVE, LANSING, MI 489121811
Phone: 517 364-5000
Web: WWW.SPARROW.ORG

PRODUCTS/OPERATIONS

Selected Services
Emergency room/Urgent Care
Laboratory
Medical Supply
Outpatient Rehabilitation
Pharmacy
Radiology

COMPETITORS

AVERA HEALTH
CARILION CLINIC
CKHS, INC.
DENVER HEALTH AND HOSPITALS AUTHORITY
FRANCISCAN ALLIANCE, INC.
MEDSTAR HEALTH, INC.
MEMORIAL HERMANN HEALTHCARE SYSTEM
NORTHSHORE UNIVERSITY HEALTHSYSTEM
THE CLEVELAND CLINIC FOUNDATION
UNIVERSITY HOSPITALS HEALTH SYSTEM, INC.

HISTORICAL FINANCIALS

Company Type: Private

Income Statement   FYE: December 31

	REVENUE ($mil)	NET INCOME ($mil)	NET PROFIT MARGIN	EMPLOYEES
12/21	1,505	147	9.8%	3,400
12/20	1,402	41	3.0%	—
12/19	1,340	99	7.4%	—
12/18	1,281	(57)	—	—
Annual Growth	5.5%	—	—	—

2021 Year-End Financials
Return on assets: 6.9%   Cash ($ mil.): 157
Return on equity: 12.8%
Current Ratio: 1.30

SPARTANBURG REGIONAL HEALTH SERVICES DISTRICT, INC.

Spartanburg Regional Health Services District (dba Spartanburg Regional Healthcare System or SRHS) provides a wide range of care options to northeast South Carolina. It operates Spartanburg Medical Center, Cherokee Medical Center, Pelham Medical Center, Spartanburg Hospital for Restorative Care, Ellen Sagar Nursing Center, Medical Group of the Carolinas, and Union Medical Center. The 745-bed Spartanburg Medical offers services including emergency, surgical, maternity, cancer, a Heart Center and inpatient rehabilitation. It houses the Gibbs Cancer Center & Research Institute, as well as centers specializing in heart, vascular, women's health, and outpatient care. SRHS also operates clinics, specialty outpatient centers, and long-term care, home health, rehabilitation, and hospice facilities. With approximately 700 physicians on staff, SRHS handles some 25,000 surgical procedures, delivers around 4,000 babies and has approximately 200,000 emergency center visits.

LOCATIONS

HQ: SPARTANBURG REGIONAL HEALTH SERVICES DISTRICT, INC.
101 E WOOD ST, SPARTANBURG, SC 293033040
Phone: 864 560-6000
Web: WWW.SPARTANBURGREGIONAL.COM

PRODUCTS/OPERATIONS

2014 Sales

	$ mil	% of total
Net patient service revenue	872.3	89
Premium revenue	73.4	7
Other operating revenue	36.4	4
Total	982.1	100

Selected Facilities
AccessHealth
Ellen Sagar Nursing Center in Union
Gibbs Cancer Center & Research Institute
Hospice Home
Medical Group of the Carolinas (MGC)
Pelham Medical Center in Greer
Regional HealthPlus (RHP)
Spartanburg Medical Center (SMC)
The Sports Medicine Institute
Union Medical Center

Selected Services
Bearden-Josey Center for Breast Health
Chest Pain Center
Comprehensive Pain Center
Congregational Nursing
Corporate Health
Emergency Center (Level I Trauma Center)
Emergency Medical Services (EMS)
Gibbs Cancer Center & Research Institute
Heart Center
Heart Wellness Program
Home Health
Hospice (Hospice Home)
Imaging and Laboratory Services
Neonatal Intensive Care Unit (Level III)
Neurology
Orthopaedic Services
Palliative Care Services
Pediatrics and Pediatric Intensive Care Unit
Rehabilitation Services
Robotic Surgery
Sleep Services
Stroke Center
Surgery (including minimally invasive)
Urology
Weight Loss Services
Women's Health
Wound Healing Center

COMPETITORS

FLOYD HEALTHCARE MANAGEMENT, INC.
GUTHRIE HEALTHCARE SYSTEM
NORMAN REGIONAL HOSPITAL AUTHORITY
NORTH MISSISSIPPI HEALTH SERVICES, INC.
NOVANT HEALTH, INC.
PHOEBE PUTNEY MEMORIAL HOSPITAL, INC.
SPECTRUM HEALTH SYSTEM
TENNESSEE WEST HEALTHCARE INC
WELLMONT HEALTH SYSTEM
WELLSPAN HEALTH

HISTORICAL FINANCIALS
Company Type: Private

Income Statement — FYE: September 30

	REVENUE ($mil)	NET INCOME ($mil)	NET PROFIT MARGIN	EMPLOYEES
09/20	1,468	18	1.3%	5,000
09/19	1,365	42	3.1%	—
09/18	1,147	28	2.5%	—
Annual Growth	13.1%	(19.1%)	—	—

2020 Year-End Financials
Return on assets: 1.2%
Return on equity: 20.3%
Current Ratio: 1.80
Cash ($ mil.): 348

SPECTRA ENERGY, LLC

Spectra Energy covers the spectrum of natural gas activities -- gathering, processing, transmission, storage, and distribution. The company, now part of Enbridge, operates more than 15,400 miles of transmission pipeline and has 305 billion cu. ft. of storage capacity in the US and Canada. Units include U.S. Gas Transmission, Texas Eastern Transmission, Natural Gas Liquids Division, and Market Hub Partners. It also has stakes in DCP Midstream, Maritimes & Northeast Pipeline, Gulfstream Natural Gas System, Spectra Energy Income Fund, and 75% of Spectra Energy Partners. Its Union Gas unit distributes gas to 1.5 million Ontario customers. In 2017, Spectra merged with Enbridge, creating the largest energy infrastructure company in North America.

Operations
Spectra Energy has managed its businesses in four reportable segments: Spectra Energy Partners, Distribution, Western Canada Transmission & Processing and Field Services.

Spectra Energy Partners provides transmission, storage and gathering of natural gas for customers in various regions of the Midwestern, northeastern and southeastern US and operates a crude oil pipeline system that connects Canadian and U.S. producers to refineries in the U.S. Rocky Mountain and Midwest regions. Spectra Energy Partners has accounted for about 50% of the company's revenue.

Distribution, about 30% of revenue, provides retail natural gas distribution service (its Union Gas unit distributes gas to 1.5 million customers in 400 communities in Ontario). It also provides natural gas transportation and storage services to other utilities and energy market customers.

Western Canada Transmission & Processing, about 20% of revenue, provides its customers with transportation services to move natural gas, natural gas gathering and processing services, and NGL extraction, fractionation, transportation, storage, and marketing services.

Field Services gathers, processes, treats, compresses, transports and stores natural gas; it also fractionates, transports, gathers, processes, stores, markets, and trades NGLs. Its DCP Midstream joint venture is 50% owned by Phillips 66. DCP operates in 17 US states.

Transportation, storage, and processing of natural gas have accounted for about two-thirds of Spectra Energy's revenue.

Geographic Reach
Spectra Energy's Spectra Energy Partners operates in northeastern and southeastern US and operates a crude oil pipeline system that connects Canadian and US producers to refineries in the Rocky Mountains and the Midwest. The Distribution segment serves natural gas customers in Ontario, Canada. Western Canada Transmission & Processing serves customers in western Canada and the northern US. Field Services gathers natural gas from the Mid-Continent, Rocky Mountain, East Texas-North Louisiana, Barnett Shale, Gulf Coast, South Texas, Central Texas, Antrim Shale, and Permian Basin.

All told, Spectra Energy has more than 100 facilities across North America.

Sales and Marketing
Spectra Energy's customers (end-users) purchase gas directly from suppliers or marketers, as well as through retail and wholesale outlets.

Financial Performance
Spectra Energy reported a 6% decline in revenue in 2016 to $4.9 billion from 2015. Each segment posted lower revenue for 2016. Lower energy prices were passed on to customers and warmer weather meant they used less energy. Revenue also was hurt by a weaker Canadian dollar. The Distribution segment did see some growth with additional customers and the Dawn Parkway Expansion Project.

The company's net income jump some 250% to $693 million in 2016 from 2015, mostly because of charges and costs the company had in 2015 but not 2016.

Spectra has cash flow from operations of about $2 billion in 2016, down from about $2.2 billion in 2015. The difference was driven by non-cash goodwill impairments in 2015, offset by higher earnings.

Strategy
Mergers and Acquisitions
Company Background
In 2012 Spectra Energy acquired one-third of DCP Sand Hills Pipeline and DCP Southern Hills Pipeline (NGL pipelines) from DCP Midstream for $459 million.

In 2012 Spectra Energy opened a new natural gas processing plant in Dawson Creek, British Columbia, part of its $1.5 billion investment strategy in infrastructure. That year it also signed a deal with BG Group to develop a pipeline from northeast British Columbia to serve BG Group's potential LNG export facility in Prince Rupert, on the northwest coast of the province.

To raise cash, in 2012 it sold a 38.76% interest in Maritimes & Northeast Pipeline to Spectra Energy Partners for $375 million.

In a move to boost its Gulf Coast natural gas storage position, in 2010 Spectra Energy acquired the Bobcat Gas Storage asset from Haddington Energy Partners and GE Energy Financial Service for about $540 million.

The company was founded in 2006.

EXECUTIVES
CAO, Dorothy M Ables
CDO, Guy G Buckley
CCO, Julie Dill
Auditors : DELOITTE & TOUCHE LLP HOUSTON

LOCATIONS
HQ: SPECTRA ENERGY, LLC
5400 WESTHEIMER CT, HOUSTON, TX 770565353

Phone: 713 627-5400
Web: WWW.SPECTRAENERGY.COM

2016 Sales

	$mil.	% of total
U.S.	2,461	50
Canada	2,455	50
Total	4,916	100

PRODUCTS/OPERATIONS

2016 Sales

	$ mil.	% of total
Spectra Energy Partners	2,533	52
Distribution	1,370	28
Western Canada Transmission & Processing	1,005	20
Others	8	—
Total	4,916	100

2016 Sales

	$ mil.	% of total
Transportation, storage and processing of natural gas	3,251	66
Distribution of natural gas	1,144	23
Transportation of crude oil	359	7
Sales of natural gas liquids	68	2
Other	94	2
Total	4,916	100

Selected Mergers and Acquisitions

2013
Express-Platte Pipeline System ($1.5 billion; pipeline moving crude oil from Western Canada to the US Rockies and Midwest refineries and markets)

2012
DCP Sand Hills Pipeline and DCP Southern Hills Pipeline ($459 million; 33.3%;NGL pipelines)

COMPETITORS

ATMOS ENERGY CORPORATION
DCP MIDSTREAM, LP
DTE GAS COMPANY
ENABLE MIDSTREAM PARTNERS, LP
ENERGY TRANSFER LP
ETP LEGACY LP
NEW JERSEY RESOURCES CORPORATION
ONEOK, INC.
SOUTHERN COMPANY GAS
TARGA RESOURCES CORP.

HISTORICAL FINANCIALS

Company Type: Private

Income Statement — FYE: December 31

	REVENUE ($mil)	NET INCOME ($mil)	NET PROFIT MARGIN	EMPLOYEES
12/16	4,916	1,020	20.7%	8,700
12/15	5,234	460	8.8%	—
Annual Growth	(6.1%)	121.7%	—	—

2016 Year-End Financials

Return on assets: 2.8%   Cash ($ mil.): —
Return on equity: 8.8%
Current Ratio: 0.50

SPIRE MISSOURI INC.

Auditors : DELOITTE & TOUCHE LLP ST LOU

LOCATIONS

HQ: SPIRE MISSOURI INC.
700 MARKET ST, SAINT LOUIS, MO 631011829
Phone: 314 342-0500
Web: WWW.SPIREENERGY.COM

HISTORICAL FINANCIALS

Company Type: Private

Income Statement — FYE: September 30

	REVENUE ($mil)	NET INCOME ($mil)	NET PROFIT MARGIN	EMPLOYEES
09/18	1,285	129	10.1%	2,271
09/17	1,171	113	9.6%	—
09/16	1,087	105	9.7%	—
09/15	1,416	105	7.4%	—
Annual Growth	(3.2%)	7.1%	—	—

2018 Year-End Financials

Return on assets: 3.5%   Cash ($ mil.): 2
Return on equity: 6.2%
Current Ratio: 0.50

SPIRIT REALTY CAPITAL, INC.

EXECUTIVES

CIO, Ken Heimlich
CLO, Jay Young

Auditors : ERNST & YOUNG LLP DALLAS TEX

LOCATIONS

HQ: SPIRIT REALTY CAPITAL, INC.
2727 N HARWOOD ST STE 300, DALLAS, TX 752012407
Phone: 972 476-1900
Web: WWW.SPIRITREALTY.COM

HISTORICAL FINANCIALS

Company Type: Private

Income Statement — FYE: December 31

	ASSETS ($mil)	NET INCOME ($mil)	INCOME AS % OF ASSETS	EMPLOYEES
12/17	7,263	77	1.1%	84
12/16	7,677	97	1.3%	—
12/14	8,017	(33)	—	—
12/13	7,231	1	0.0%	—
Annual Growth	0.1%	160.4%	—	—

2017 Year-End Financials

Return on assets: 1.1%   Cash ($ mil.): 8
Return on equity: 2.3%
Current Ratio: —

SPOHN INVESTMENT CORPORATION

Auditors : IT ERNST & YOUNG US LLP INDI

LOCATIONS

HQ: SPOHN INVESTMENT CORPORATION
600 ELIZABETH ST, CORPUS CHRISTI, TX 784042235
Phone: 800 756-7999

HISTORICAL FINANCIALS

Company Type: Private

Income Statement — FYE: June 30

	REVENUE ($mil)	NET INCOME ($mil)	NET PROFIT MARGIN	EMPLOYEES
06/20	811	(6)	—	80
06/19	828	8	1.1%	—
Annual Growth	(2.0%)	—	—	—

2020 Year-End Financials

Return on assets: (-0.8%)   Cash ($ mil.): 9
Return on equity: (-1.0%)
Current Ratio: 2.00

SPORTS, INC.

Auditors : JUNKERMIER CLARK CAMPANELLA

LOCATIONS

HQ: SPORTS, INC.
333 2ND AVE N, LEWISTOWN, MT 594572700
Phone: 888 538-3496
Web: WWW.SPORTSINC.US

HISTORICAL FINANCIALS

Company Type: Private

Income Statement — FYE: December 31

	REVENUE ($mil)	NET INCOME ($mil)	NET PROFIT MARGIN	EMPLOYEES
12/20	1,191	0	0.1%	38
12/19	983	0	0.0%	—
12/18	960	0	0.0%	—
12/17	913	0	0.0%	—
Annual Growth	9.3%	75.5%	—	—

2020 Year-End Financials

Return on assets: 0.3%   Cash ($ mil.): 3
Return on equity: 3.6%
Current Ratio: 1.10

SPRING BRANCH INDEPENDENT SCHOOL DISTRICT (INC)

Auditors : WHITLEY PENN LLP HOUSTON TEX

LOCATIONS

HQ: SPRING BRANCH INDEPENDENT SCHOOL DISTRICT (INC)
955 CAMPBELL RD, HOUSTON, TX 770242803
Phone: 713 464-1511
Web: WWW.SPRINGBRANCHISD.COM

HISTORICAL FINANCIALS
Company Type: Private

Income Statement — FYE: June 30

	REVENUE ($mil)	NET INCOME ($mil)	NET PROFIT MARGIN	EMPLOYEES
06/21	564	(56)	—	4,484
06/20	540	161	29.9%	—
06/19	582	22	3.9%	—
06/18	513	135	26.4%	—
Annual Growth	3.1%	—	—	—

2021 Year-End Financials
Return on assets: (-3.5%)   Cash ($ mil.): 41
Return on equity: (-31.0%)
Current Ratio: —

SPX FLOW, INC.

SPX Flow manufactures products for processing and transporting liquids that range from milk to oil. The company's products include pumps, valves, mixers, filters, air dryers, hydraulic tools, homogenizers, separators, and heat exchangers. It serves a wide range of end markets including food and beverage, chemical processing, compressed air, pharmaceutical, waste and water treatment, and mining. A short list of its brands include Bran + Luebbe, Lightnin, Johnson Pump, and Stone. SPX Flow has been a standalone company since 2015, with a heritage that dates back to the establishment of the Piston Ring Company in Michigan in 1912. In early 2022, SPX FLOW was acquired by Lone Star in an all-cash transaction valued at approximately $3.8 billion.

Operations
SPX FLOW offers a wide array of highly engineered infrastructure products with strong brands. Its product offering is concentrated in process technologies that perform mixing, blending, fluid handling, separation, thermal heat transfer, and other activities. It manufactures mixers, valves, separators, and heat exchangers to help produce customized solutions safely, sustainably, and consistently. In addition to the company's over 140,000 products, SPX FLOW has more than 800 patents and some 20 brands.

Geographic Reach
SPX Flow, based in Charlotte, North Carolina, operates in more than 30 nations and sales in more than 140 countries.

Sales and Marketing
SPX Flow partners with a range of customers. Some are in the mining and marine industries, and others are chemical and construction companies.

Mergers and Acquisitions
In 2021, SPX Flow completed the acquisition of UTG Mixing Group, the maker of Stelzer, Uutechnic, and Jamix mixing solutions for the chemical, food, metallurgical and fertilizer, environmental technology, water treatment and pharmaceuticals markets, for a cash consideration of ?0.60 per share. The addition of UTG's operations, based in Finland and Germany, will add technology, manufacturing capacity and technical expertise to SPX FLOW's already robust global portfolio of mixing and blending solutions, including Lightnin, Plenty and APV.

Company Background
SPX Flow was spun off from former parent SPX Corporation (as a separate, publicly-traded company) in 2015 to concentrate on its flow business. The flow-related business was developed in 1998 when SPX acquired Lightnin Mixers and merged with General Signal. It later added more flow-related businesses to its portfolio and began selling packaged solutions with complementary products.

By 2007, SPX's business reached annual revenue of more than $1.0 billion and the company began expanding internationally and organizing its business around the three global end markets of industrial, food and beverage, and power and energy.

EXECUTIVES

Non-Executive Chairman of the Board, Robert F Hull Junior
CIO, Kevin J Eamigh
President Global Manufacturing, Tyrone Jeffers V
Chief Human Resources Officer, Peter J Ryan
Auditors: DELOITTE & TOUCHE LLP CHARLOT

LOCATIONS

HQ: SPX FLOW, INC.
13320 BALNTYN CORP PL, CHARLOTTE, NC 282773607
Phone: 704 752-4400
Web: WWW.SPXFLOW.COM

2018 Sales

	$ mil.	% of total
United States	720.8	35
United Kingdom	218.6	10
China	154.6	7
France	109.2	5
Germany	94.1	5
Denmark	89.5	4
Other	703.3	34
Total	2,090.1	100

PRODUCTS/OPERATIONS

2018 Sales

	$ mil.	% of total
Food and Beverage	743.9	36
Industrial	755.8	36
Power and Energy	590.4	28
Total	2,090.1	100

Selected Products
Air dryers
Filters and dehydration equipment
Fluid mixers
Heat exchangers
High-integrity pumps
Metering systems
Valves

Selected Brands
APV (Gaulin and Rannie)
Bran & Luebbe
Copes-Vulcan
Delair
Deltech and Hankinson
Dollinger Filtration
Jemaco
Hankinson
Lightnin
M&J Valves
Pneumatic Products
Vokes
Waukesha Cherry-Burrell

COMPETITORS

CHART INDUSTRIES, INC.
DOVER CORPORATION
GOLD MEDAL PRODUCTS CO.
HEAT AND CONTROL, INC.
I.M.A. INDUSTRIA MACCHINE AUTOMATICHE SPA
JANEL CORPORATION
JOHN BEAN TECHNOLOGIES CORPORATION
KEY TECHNOLOGY, INC.
MECATHERM
REXNORD CORPORATION

HISTORICAL FINANCIALS
Company Type: Private

Income Statement — FYE: December 31

	REVENUE ($mil)	NET INCOME ($mil)	NET PROFIT MARGIN	EMPLOYEES
12/21	1,529	67	4.4%	5,000
12/20	1,350	6	0.5%	—
12/19	1,506	(93)	—	—
12/18	2,090	44	2.1%	—
Annual Growth	(9.9%)	14.5%	—	—

2021 Year-End Financials
Return on assets: 3.2%   Cash ($ mil.): 313
Return on equity: 6.5%
Current Ratio: 1.70

SRCTEC, LLC

LOCATIONS

HQ: SRCTEC, LLC
5801 E TAFT RD STE 7, SYRACUSE, NY 132123382
Phone: 315 452-8700
Web: WWW.SRCINC.COM

HISTORICAL FINANCIALS
Company Type: Private

Income Statement — FYE: September 30

	REVENUE ($mil)	NET INCOME ($mil)	NET PROFIT MARGIN	EMPLOYEES
09/10	583	42	7.3%	150
09/09	365	19	5.4%	—
Annual Growth	59.7%	115.0%	—	—

2010 Year-End Financials
Return on assets: 14.3%   Cash ($ mil.): 44
Return on equity: 7.3%
Current Ratio: 1.30

SSM HEALTH CARE CORPORATION

The mission of SSM Health began with five nuns who fled religious persecution in Germany in 1872 only to arrive in St. Louis in the midst of a smallpox epidemic. They formed their first hospital there in 1877. Today, the Midwest-based not-for-profit system, sponsored by the Franciscan Sisters of Mary, owns some 25 acute care hospitals more than 290 physician offices and other outpatient and virtual care services, ten post-acute facilities, comprehensive home care and hospice services, a pharmacy benefit company, a health insurance company and an accountable care organization. SSM Health's hospital operations are located primarily in Missouri, Wisconsin, Oklahoma and Illinois and its related businesses provide health related services in about 50 states.

Operations
SSM Health has some 11,000 physicians on its staff. The system has some 104,840 inpatient admissions and some 1.3 million outpatient visits each year.

Geographic Reach
Based in St. Louis, Missouri, SSM Health's facilities are located in Illinois, Missouri, Oklahoma, and Wisconsin.

Sales and Marketing
Managed care payments account for about half of SSM Health's net patient revenue, while Medicare accounts for about 25%, and Medicaid accounts for about 15%.

SSM Health advertising expenses were $21,085 and 22,851 in 2020 and 2019, respectively.

Financial Performance
Total operating revenues and other support for the year 2020 was $8.2 billion, a 4% increase from the previous year's revenue of $7.9 billion.

In 2020, the company had a net income of $397.7 million, a 24% increase from the previous year's net income of $319.5 million.

The company's cash at the end of 2020 was $820.9 million. Operating activities generated $1.1 billion, while investing activities used $688.8 million, primarily for purchase of assets limited as to use or restricted and short-term investments. Financing activities provided another $147.3 million.

Strategy
To satisfy the company's long-term rate-of-return objectives, SSMH relies on a total return strategy in which investment returns are achieved through both capital appreciation (realized and unrealized) and interest and dividend income. SSMH uses a diversified asset allocation to achieve its long-term return objectives within prudent risk constraints to preserve capital.

EXECUTIVES
CIO*, Sony Jacob
Auditors : DELOITTE & TOUCHE LLP ST LOU

LOCATIONS
HQ: SSM HEALTH CARE CORPORATION
10101 WOODFIELD LN # 120, SAINT LOUIS, MO 631322922
Phone: 314 994-7800
Web: WWW.SSMHEALTH.COM

PRODUCTS/OPERATIONS
Selected Facilities
Illinois
    St. Mary's Good Samaritan (joint sponsorship with Felician Services, two hospitals in Mt. Vernon and Centralia)
Missouri
    St. Francis Hospital & Health Services (Maryville)
    St. Mary's Health Center (Jefferson City)
    SSM Cardinal Glennon Children's Medical Center (St. Louis)
    SSM DePaul Health Center (Bridgeton)
    SSM St. Clare Health Center (St. Louis)
    SSM St. Joseph Health Center (St. Charles)
    SSM St. Joseph Health Center (Wentzville)
    SSM St. Joseph Hospital West (Lake St. Louis)
    SSM St. Mary's Health Center (Richmond Heights)
Oklahoma
    Bone & Joint Hospital (Oklahoma City)
    Shawnee Medical Center Clinic (Shawnee)
    St. Anthony Hospital (Oklahoma City)
    Unity Health Center (Shawnee)
Wisconsin
    Boscobel Area Health Care (managed, hospital and clinics, Boscobel)
    Columbus Community Hospital (affiliate, Columbus)
    Edgerton Hospital and Health Services (Edgerton)
    St. Clare Hospital (Baraboo)
    St. Clare Meadows Care Center (nursing home, Madison)
    St. Mary's Care Center (nursing home, Madison)
    St. Mary's Hospital (Madison)
    St. Mary's Janesville Hospital (Janesville)
    Stoughton Hospital (affiliate, Stoughton)
    Uplands Hill Health (affiliate, hospital and nursing care, Dodgeville)

COMPETITORS
IASIS HEALTHCARE LLC
INDIANA UNIVERSITY HEALTH, INC.
MERCY HEALTH
PEACEHEALTH
PROMEDICA HEALTH SYSTEMS, INC.
PROVIDENCE ST. JOSEPH HEALTH
ST. JOSEPH HEALTH SYSTEM
THE CLEVELAND CLINIC FOUNDATION
VALLEY HEALTH SYSTEM
WELLSPAN HEALTH

HISTORICAL FINANCIALS
Company Type: Private

Income Statement   FYE: December 31

	REVENUE ($mil)	NET INCOME ($mil)	NET PROFIT MARGIN	EMPLOYEES
12/17	6,497	245	3.8%	24,230
12/16	6,109	(30)	—	—
12/13	1,177	32	2.8%	—
Annual Growth	53.3%	65.9%	—	—

2017 Year-End Financials
Return on assets: 3.3%   Cash ($ mil.): 126
Return on equity: 10.5%
Current Ratio: 0.80

ST BARNABAS MEDICAL CENTER (INC)

Part of the RWJBarnabas Health system, Saint Barnabas Medical Center is a 600-bed, acute-care hospital that provides a full range of health services to residents of Livingston, New Jersey, and surrounding areas. The not-for-profit medical center provides general inpatient and outpatient care programs, as well as burn and perinatal care. It also houses units specializing in organ transplant, stroke care, cardiac surgery, and comprehensive cancer treatment. Its Institute for Reproductive Medicine and Science provides assisted reproductive technology services.

Operations
In combination with its satellite Saint Barnabas Ambulatory Care Center, the medical center serves about 300,000 outpatients per year. Saint Barnabas Medical Center is also a teaching affiliate of several regional schools, including the University of Medicine and Dentistry of New Jersey and Drexel University College of Medicine.

Company Background
New Jersey's first hospital, Saint Barnabas Medical Center was founded in 1865 in a private home.

EXECUTIVES
CAO, Franz Smith
Chief Human Resource Officer, Ruth Bash
Auditors : KPMG LLP NEW YORK NY

LOCATIONS
HQ: ST BARNABAS MEDICAL CENTER (INC)
94 OLD SHORT HILLS RD # 1, LIVINGSTON, NJ 070395668
Phone: 973 322-5000
Web: WWW.RWJBH.ORG

COMPETITORS
NEWARK BETH ISRAEL MEDICAL CENTER INC.
NEWYORK-PRESBYTERIAN/BROOKLYN METHODIST
SAINT AGNES MEDICAL CENTER
SAINT PETER'S UNIVERSITY HOSPITAL, INC.
ST. ANTHONY'S HOSPITAL, INC.

HISTORICAL FINANCIALS
Company Type: Private

Income Statement   FYE: December 31

	REVENUE ($mil)	NET INCOME ($mil)	NET PROFIT MARGIN	EMPLOYEES
12/20	858	55	6.5%	4,000
12/18	818	113	13.9%	—
12/17	818	113	13.9%	—
12/16	760	84	11.1%	—
Annual Growth	3.1%	(9.7%)	—	—

2020 Year-End Financials
Return on assets: 3.1% Cash ($ mil.): —
Return on equity: 5.1%
Current Ratio: 8.40

ST JOHN'S UNIVERSITY, NEW YORK

No university is an island, but one of St. John's campuses is on Manhattan Island. A private, co-educational Roman Catholic school, St. John's University offers undergraduate and graduate programs in more than 100 majors through five colleges, a law school, and a distance learning program. St. John's has more than 20,000 students at five campuses (Queens, Staten Island and Manhattan in New York City, one in Oakdale, New York, and one graduate center in Rome). The school has a 17-to-1 student-faculty ratio. More than 80% of its graduates reside in the New York region, including notable alumni such as former New York governors Hugh Carey and Mario Cuomo. The school was founded in 1870 by the Vincentian Community.

EXECUTIVES

FOR MISSION*, Bernard M Tracey
FOR ACADEMIC AFFAIRS*, Robert Mangione
Auditors : KPMG LLP GREENSBORO NC

LOCATIONS

HQ: ST JOHN'S UNIVERSITY, NEW YORK
  8000 UTOPIA PKWY, JAMAICA, NY 114399000
Phone: 718 990-6161
Web: HEALTHCARELAWSOCIETYSJLAW.WORDPRESS.COM

PRODUCTS/OPERATIONS

Selected Colleges and Schools
College of Pharmacy and Allied Health Professions
College of Professional Studies
The Peter J. Tobin College of Business
St. John's College of Liberal Arts and Sciences
St. John's Distance Learning
The School of Education
School of Law

COMPETITORS

ARKANSAS STATE UNIVERSITY
CLARKSON UNIVERSITY
DIPASQUA ENTERPRISES, INC.
THE CULINARY INSTITUTE OF AMERICA
THOMPSON HOSPITALITY CORPORATION

HISTORICAL FINANCIALS
Company Type: Private

Income Statement   FYE: May 31

	REVENUE ($mil)	NET INCOME ($mil)	NET PROFIT MARGIN	EMPLOYEES
05/20*	810	55	6.8%	3,310
12/16	0	(0)	—	—
Annual Growth	3132.6%	—	—	—

*Fiscal year change

2020 Year-End Financials
Return on assets: 3.7% Cash ($ mil.): 60
Return on equity: 5.9%
Current Ratio: —

ST LUKE'S HOSPITAL OF KANSAS CITY

LOCATIONS

HQ: ST LUKE'S HOSPITAL OF KANSAS CITY
  4401 WORNALL RD, KANSAS CITY, MO 641113220
Phone: 816 932-2000
Web: WWW.SAINTLUKESHEALTHSYSTEM.ORG

HISTORICAL FINANCIALS
Company Type: Private

Income Statement   FYE: December 31

	REVENUE ($mil)	NET INCOME ($mil)	NET PROFIT MARGIN	EMPLOYEES
12/13	647	11	1.8%	4
12/09	479	13	2.7%	—
Annual Growth	7.8%	(2.8%)	—	—

2013 Year-End Financials
Return on assets: 1.0% Cash ($ mil.): 34
Return on equity: 1.4%
Current Ratio: 0.40

ST LUKES-ROOSEVELT INSTITUTE

Auditors : ERNST & YOUNG US LLP INDIANAP

LOCATIONS

HQ: ST LUKES-ROOSEVELT INSTITUTE
  1111 AMSTERDAM AVE, NEW YORK, NY 100251716
Phone: 212 523-4000

HISTORICAL FINANCIALS
Company Type: Private

Income Statement   FYE: December 31

	REVENUE ($mil)	NET INCOME ($mil)	NET PROFIT MARGIN	EMPLOYEES
12/19	1,348	(22)	—	3
12/14	21	0	0.0%	—
Annual Growth	128.7%	—	—	—

2019 Year-End Financials
Return on assets: (-1.6%) Cash ($ mil.): 167
Return on equity: (-32.5%)
Current Ratio: 0.20

ST. CHARLES HEALTH SYSTEM, INC.

EXECUTIVES

Interim Chief Executive Officer, Steve Gordon

LOCATIONS

HQ: ST. CHARLES HEALTH SYSTEM, INC.
  2500 NE NEFF RD, BEND, OR 977016015
Phone: 541 382-4321
Web: WWW.STCHARLESHEALTHCARE.ORG

HISTORICAL FINANCIALS
Company Type: Private

Income Statement   FYE: December 31

	REVENUE ($mil)	NET INCOME ($mil)	NET PROFIT MARGIN	EMPLOYEES
12/19	1,002	168	16.8%	3,200
12/17	809	41	5.1%	—
12/13	631	40	6.4%	—
12/07	367	8	2.4%	—
Annual Growth	8.7%	27.8%	—	—

2019 Year-End Financials
Return on assets: 14.0% Cash ($ mil.): 52
Return on equity: 21.8%
Current Ratio: 0.50

ST. FRANCIS HOSPITAL, INC.

Auditors : DELOITTE TAX LP ATLANTA GA

LOCATIONS

HQ: ST. FRANCIS HOSPITAL, INC.
  1 SAINT FRANCIS DR, GREENVILLE, SC 296013955
Phone: 864 255-1000
Web: WWW.BONSECOURS.COM

ST. FRANCIS HOSPITAL, ROSLYN, NEW YORK

Sure, St. Francis Hospital can handle your gall bladder and sinus difficulties, but it's really on top of your heart problems. The hospital's Heart Center -- New York State's only specially designated cardiac center -- provides surgical, diagnostic, and treatment services. The 365-bed St. Francis Hospital also has centers for ENT (ear, nose, and throat), orthopedic, vascular, prostate, cancer, gastrointestinal, and general surgery services. As part of Catholic Health Services of Long Island, St. Francis opened its doors in 1954 to children and adults. It was originally established as St. Francis Hospital and Sanatorium for Cardiac Children in 1936.

Operations
St. Francis Hospital's Heart Center performs about 8,000 cardiac catheterizations, 3,000 coronary angioplasties, and about 1,500 open-heart operations every year. The center's DeMatteis Center for Cardiac Research and Education works to develop improved techniques for heart disease diagnosis, including conducting clinical trials through partnerships with device and equipment makers, and provides patient education and fitness programs.

Geographic Reach
St. Francis Hospital is located in Roslyn, New York. In addition, it has satellite New York locations in Greenvale (DeMatteis Center for Cardiac Research and Education), West Islip (South Bay Cardiovascular Center), and Hicksville (Bishop McHugh Health Center), as well as administrative offices in Port Washington.

Strategy
St. Francis Hospital has expanded in recent years to keep up with growing patient demand. It opened the Bishop McHugh Health Center to provide outpatient primary care services for uninsured and underinsured patients in 2012.

The hospital completed its largest expansion project to date in 2009 with the construction of the $190 million Nancy and Frederick DeMatteis Pavilion; the project increased the hospital's clinical space by about 40% and added 85 beds.

EXECUTIVES
Public Relations, Linda Cavallo-miller
Patient Care Vice President, Ann Cella R.n.
SERVICE RISK MGMT, Lynn Taylor Esq
Auditors : PRICEWATERHOUSECOOPERS LLP NE

LOCATIONS
HQ: ST. FRANCIS HOSPITAL, ROSLYN, NEW YORK
100 PORT WASHINGTON BLVD, ROSLYN, NY 115761347
Phone: 516 562-2000
Web: WWW.CHSLI.ORG

PRODUCTS/OPERATIONS
Selected Services
Anesthesiology
Breast Surgery
Cardiology
Cardiothoracic Surgery
Diabetes Care Center
Emergency Medicine
Gastroenterology
General Surgery
Hematology/Oncology
Nephrology
Neurology
Orthopedic Surgery
Otolaryngology
Podiatry
Psychiatry
Pulmonary Medicine
Radiology
Rehabilitation
Urology
Vascular Services
Women's Center

COMPETITORS
CHILDREN'S HEALTH CARE
CHILDREN'S HEALTH CLINICAL OPERATIONS
CHILDREN'S HEALTHCARE OF ATLANTA, INC.
CHILDREN'S HOSPITAL AND HEALTH SYSTEM, INC.
JOHNS HOPKINS ALL CHILDREN'S HOSPITAL, INC.

HISTORICAL FINANCIALS
Company Type: Private

Income Statement — FYE: December 31

	REVENUE ($mil)	NET INCOME ($mil)	NET PROFIT MARGIN	EMPLOYEES
12/15	614	37	6.2%	2,184
12/08	385	28	7.4%	—
12/04	366	47	12.9%	—
12/02	(828)	0	0.0%	—
Annual Growth	—	152.0%	—	—

2015 Year-End Financials
Return on assets: 3.9%   Cash ($ mil.): 34
Return on equity: 5.5%
Current Ratio: —

HISTORICAL FINANCIALS
Company Type: Private

Income Statement — FYE: August 31

	REVENUE ($mil)	NET INCOME ($mil)	NET PROFIT MARGIN	EMPLOYEES
08/19	652	69	10.6%	2,105
08/14	534	60	11.3%	—
Annual Growth	4.1%	2.9%	—	—

2019 Year-End Financials
Return on assets: 11.0%   Cash ($ mil.): 230
Return on equity: 22.6%
Current Ratio: 8.70

ST. JOHN HEALTH SYSTEM, INC.

St. John Health System aims to bring health into the lives of the ill. The not-for-profit system provides health care services to residents of Tulsa and surrounding areas in northeastern Oklahoma and southern Kansas. In addition to flagship facility St. John Medical Center, it owns or manages eight other community hospitals, as well as urgent care and long-term care facilities. St. John Health System provides primary and specialty medical care through OMNI Medical Group, and offers health insurance through CommunityCare health plan. Established in 1926 by the Sisters of the Sorrowful Mother, the health system is part of Marian Health.

Operations
Facilities owned, managed, or sponsored by St. John Health System include hospitals Oklahoma State University Medical Center, St. John Sapulpa, St. John Owasso, St. John Broken Arrow, Pawhuska City Hospital, Sedan City Hospital, Nowata Hospital, and Jane Phillips Medical Center. The company's senior living facilities include Franciscan Villa, Frances Streitel Villa, Heartsworth House, and Rosewood Terrace.

Strategy
St. John Health System will periodically add services to its offerings to meet community demand. In early 2011 St. John Health opened the St. John Weight Management Institute to offer its patients weight loss options including bariatric surgery. The health system's newest hospital, St. John Broken Arrow near Tulsa, was constructed in 2009.

In 2012 Marian Health entered talks with another Catholic health system operator, Ascension Health, over the possibility of merging St. John Health System and other Marian organizations into the Ascension organization.

LOCATIONS
HQ: ST. JOHN HEALTH SYSTEM, INC.
1923 S UTICA AVE, TULSA, OK 741046520
Phone: 918 744-2180
Web: WWW.STJOHNHEALTHSYSTEM.COM

PRODUCTS/OPERATIONS
Selected Facilities and Operations -- Oklahoma
CommunityCare (health plan)
Jane Phillips Medical Center (Bartlesville)
Nowata Hospital
Oklahoma State University Medical Center (managed facility in Tulsa)
OMNI Medical Group (physicians group)
Pawhuska City Hospital
Regional Medical Laboratory (clinical lab testing)
Sedan City Hospital
St. John Broken Arrow Hospital
St. John Medical Center (Tulsa)

St. John Owasso Hospital
St. John Physicians
St. John Sapulpa Hospital

COMPETITORS

CANYON RANCH ENTERPRISES, LLC
CORPORATE FITNESS WORKS, INC.
FITCORP CENTER MANAGEMENT CORP.
FRANCISCAN HEALTH SYSTEM
GOLD'S GYM INTERNATIONAL, INC.
GREATER LAFAYETTE HEALTH SERVICES, INC.
HEALTHTRAX, INC.
LIFESTYLE FAMILY FITNESS II, INC.
ST. VINCENT ANDERSON REGIONAL HOSPITAL, INC.
VIRGIN ACTIVE LIMITED

HISTORICAL FINANCIALS

Company Type: Private

Income Statement — FYE: June 30

	REVENUE ($mil)	NET INCOME ($mil)	NET PROFIT MARGIN	EMPLOYEES
06/14*	1,056	79	7.5%	4,011
09/12	977	74	7.7%	—
09/11	895	17	2.0%	—
Annual Growth	5.7%	64.9%	—	—

*Fiscal year change

2014 Year-End Financials
Return on assets: 5.2%
Return on equity: 9.9%
Current Ratio: 1.70
Cash ($ mil.): 44

ST. JOHN HOSPITAL AND MEDICAL CENTER

St. John Hospital & Medical Center is part of the larger Detroit area-based St. John Health regional health care system. Besides providing acute and trauma care, the 770-bed teaching hospital operates specialized cancer and pediatric centers, a hip and knee center, an inpatient mental health unit, and a Parkinson's Disease clinic. It also operates the only emergency trauma center on Detroit's East Side. The hospital was established in 1952 and has grown to include a 200-physician medical team that specializes in more than 50 medical and surgical fields. It boasts 34,000 admissions; 14,500 surgical visits; and more than 126,500 emergency center visits each year.

Operations

Its emergency center is a Level II Trauma Center that boasts Chest Pain Center and Heart Failure Center accreditations. St. John Hospital also operates a large inpatient pediatric unit, PICU, and Level III NICU or Level II Special Care Nursery. The hospital runs the Van Elslander Cancer Center.

Strategy

St. John Hospital expanded its operations by opening the Elaine E. Blatt Endoscopy Department and a new pediatric burn treatment room, both in 2012. It also expanded its mammography service capabilities with the purchase of Lakeshore Mammograph, giving it more than a dozen new mammography sites across southeastern Michigan. In addition St. John Hospital opened a new cardiac catheterization lab that brought new diagnostic options to patients in the Michigan Blue Water Area.

LOCATIONS

HQ: ST. JOHN HOSPITAL AND MEDICAL CENTER
28000 DEQUINDRE RD, WARREN, MI 480922468
Phone: 313 343-4000
Web: WWW.STJOHNPROVIDENCE.ORG

PRODUCTS/OPERATIONS

Selected Services and Operations
Alternative Health
Breast Care
Breast Feeding (Lactation) Consultation
Cracchiolo Inpatient Rehabilitation Center
Diabetes Education and Care
Diagnostic and Imaging Services
Echocardiogram
Emergency
Heart and Vascular Care
Hip and Knee Center
Minimally Invasive Surgery
Minor Emergency
Neonatal Intensive Care Unit (NICU)
Obstetrics
Oncology (cancer)
Parkinson's Movement Disorder Clinic
Pediatrics
Physical Therapy
Spine Center
TravelCare
Urgent Care
Wound Care

COMPETITORS

AKRON GENERAL MEDICAL CENTER
MERCY HOSPITAL AND MEDICAL CENTER
MERCY HOSPITAL SOUTH
ST. ANTHONY'S HOSPITAL, INC.
THE JAMAICA HOSPITAL

HISTORICAL FINANCIALS

Company Type: Private

Income Statement — FYE: June 30

	REVENUE ($mil)	NET INCOME ($mil)	NET PROFIT MARGIN	EMPLOYEES
06/15	753	36	4.8%	5,000
06/09	638	1	0.3%	—
06/05	0	0	—	—
06/03	1,642	9	0.6%	—
Annual Growth	(6.3%)	12.0%	—	—

2015 Year-End Financials
Return on assets: 3.0%
Return on equity: 6.1%
Current Ratio: 2.20
Cash ($ mil.): 1

ST. JOHN PROVIDENCE PHYSICIANS-CMG

Auditors: DELOITTE TAX LLP DETROIT MI

LOCATIONS

HQ: ST. JOHN PROVIDENCE PHYSICIANS-CMG
8444 ENGLEMAN, CENTER LINE, MI 480151567
Phone: 586 755-2400
Web: WWW.FATHERMURRAYVHC.COM

HISTORICAL FINANCIALS

Company Type: Private

Income Statement — FYE: June 30

	REVENUE ($mil)	NET INCOME ($mil)	NET PROFIT MARGIN	EMPLOYEES
06/09	1,562	(1)	—	317
06/08	15	(0)	—	—
Annual Growth	9831.8%	—	—	—

2009 Year-End Financials
Return on assets: (-24.4%)
Return on equity: (-293.2%)
Current Ratio: 2.10
Cash ($ mil.): —

ST. JOHN'S HOSPITAL OF THE HOSPITAL SISTERS OF THE THIRD ORDER OF ST. FRANCIS

Truck-struck Homer Simpson might use his last gasp trying to blurt out "St. John's Hospital of the Hospital Sisters of the Third Order of St. Francis-Springfield" to his ambulance driver, but he might be better off using the hospital's more common name, St. John's. D'oh! The 440-bed St. John's Hospital serves residents of central and southern Illinois with general and specialized health care services. The teaching hospital, affiliated with Southern Illinois University's School of Medicine, has centers devoted to women and children's health, trauma, cardiac care, cancer, orthopedics, and neurology. It also operates area health clinics. Founded in 1875, St. John's is part of the Hospital Sisters Health System.

Operations

The facility is Hospital Sisters Health System's flagship hospital. It has grown to boast about 700 physicians, podiatrists, and dentists from more than 30 specialties. In addition to educating medical students through Southern Illinois University's School of Medicine, St. Johns also supports those working on careers in nursing through its own nursing school, St. John's College. It also offers courses in pharmacy, pathology, respiratory therapy, and electroneurodiagnostics (brain disorder diagnostics) professions.

St. John's physicians perform more than 15,000 surgical procedures each year. It also receives some 54,000 emergency department visits and helps deliver about 2,000 babies annually.

Financial Performance
In 2014, revenue fell 26% to $450 million; this was primarily due to an 89% decline in contributions, investments, and foundation assets.

Strategy
The hospital has been expanding its offerings to provide more specialized services to area residents. Recent additions include 3-D mammographies and expanded children's surgical services. St. John's is also focused on improving access to health care through technology such as telemedicine. In 2014 it partnered with Greenville Regional Hospital to provide advanced treatment to stroke patients at their home hospital through STAT Stroke TeleMedicine.

Other strategic initiatives at the hospital include increasing doctor and nurse retention rates, growing nursing school enrollment rates, and increasing patient satisfaction scores. Part of its efforts to reach more patients has led St. John's to open new outpatient health centers in areas near the main hospital facility. The hospital has also renovated its main buildings, including the revamp of its day surgery and intermediate care departments.

Auditors : CROWE HORWATH LLP CHICAGO IL

LOCATIONS
HQ: ST. JOHN'S HOSPITAL OF THE HOSPITAL SISTERS OF THE THIRD ORDER OF ST. FRANCIS
800 E CARPENTER ST, SPRINGFIELD, IL 627691000
Phone: 217 544-6464
Web: WWW.HSHS.ORG

PRODUCTS/OPERATIONS
2014 Sales

	$ mil	% of total
Amount generated for taking care patients excluding provision	427.5	95
Other contributions	20.7	5
Other	1.4	-
Total	449.6	100

Selected Services
AthletiCare
Behavioral Health Services
Birth Center
Cancer Institute
Center for Living
Children's Hospital
Connect
Emergency/Trauma Care
Gastroenterology
Health Centers | Priority Care
Home Health
Hospice
Intensive Care Unit
Lab
Neurosciences Institute
Orthopedics
Pain Management Center
Prairie Heart Institute
Radiology
Regional Wound Care Center
Sleep Center
Stroke Treatment
Surgery | daVinci
TherapyCare | Rehab
Third Age Living
Women's Services

COMPETITORS
ASCENSION PROVIDENCE ROCHESTER HOSPITAL
FROEDTERT MEMORIAL LUTHERAN HOSPITAL, INC.
SAINT JOSEPH HOSPITAL, INC
SAINT PETER'S UNIVERSITY HOSPITAL, INC.
THE PENNSYLVANIA HOSPITAL OF THE UNIVERSITY OF PENNSYLVANIA HEALTH SYSTEM

HISTORICAL FINANCIALS
Company Type: Private

Income Statement   FYE: June 30

	REVENUE ($mil)	NET INCOME ($mil)	NET PROFIT MARGIN	EMPLOYEES
06/20	574	(11)	—	3,000
06/16	494	3	0.7%	—
06/15	501	3	0.8%	—
06/14	500	10	2.1%	—
Annual Growth	2.3%	—	—	—

2020 Year-End Financials
Return on assets: (-1.7%)   Cash ($ mil.): 28
Return on equity: (-11.1%)
Current Ratio: 0.40

ST. JOSEPH HEALTH SYSTEM

St. Joseph Health System has earned a medal for decades by caring for patients on the West Coast and, more recently, the South Plains. The health care network includes 16 acute care hospitals, home health agencies, hospice care, outpatient services, skilled nursing facilities, community clinics, and physician organizations throughout California and in eastern New Mexico and West Texas. In its primary market of California, the health system has some 2,900 beds at 10 hospitals. Its Covenant Health System unit operates in Texas and New Mexico with about 1,200 beds in its network of some 50 primary care facilities. St. Joseph is merging with fellow not-for-profit Providence Health & Services.

Operations
In 2013, the system discharged more than 142,000 patients and had more than 4 million outpatient and 513,000 emergency department visits.

Geographic Reach
The network operates acute care hospitals, home health agencies, urgent care centers, and other health care delivery organizations throughout California and in eastern New Mexico and West Texas. Based in Irvine, St. Joseph serves 10 communities in its operating regions.

Sales and Marketing
Government payments accounted for 44% of net patient revenue in 2013, while private payers accounted for 42%.

Financial Performance
Revenue increased 14% to $5.6 million due to an increase in patient service earnings. Net income decreased 83%, though, to $353 million as salary and benefits expenses increased. Operating cash flow fell 38% to $327 million that year.

Strategy
Already one of the largest health systems on the West Coast, St. Joseph continues to grow, thanks principally to its proficient fundraising.

The system invests regularly in network and facility expansion efforts. In 2013 it formed an affiliation with Hoag Memorial Hospital Presbyterian, which operates two hospitals in Orange County. The Hoag operations are being combined with five of St. Joseph's area hospitals to form a new network called Covenant Health Network. The affiliated facilities will provide comprehensive care in the region, while retaining their respective identities and religious affiliations.

In 2014 St. Joseph entered a collaborative care initiative with Cigna to improve access to health care and enhance care coordination.

In 2015 the system agreed to merge with Providence Health & Services, which operates more than 30 hospitals in five western states. The combination will create a larger provider network of hospitals, physician groups, and outpatient centers, eliminating some overhead expenses in the process. Furthermore, by creating economies of scale, the new organization will be better positioned to negotiate with health plans.

Company Background
St. Joseph Health System traces its roots back to 1920 when St. Joseph Hospital in Eureka, California, was first established. The health care system was officially organized in 1982 as it expanded and took on additional health care facilities. The system is a ministry of The Sisters of St. Joseph of Orange, which itself was organized in 1912.

EXECUTIVES
STRAT, Annette M Walker
Regional, Kevin Klockenga
Auditors : ERNST & YOUNG LLP IRVINE CA

LOCATIONS
HQ: ST. JOSEPH HEALTH SYSTEM
3345 MICHELSON DR STE 100, IRVINE, CA 926120693

Phone: 949 381-4000
Web: WWW.STJHS.ORG

Selected Operations
Northern California
    Petaluma Valley Hospital
    Queen of the Valley Medical Center (Napa)
    Redwood Memorial Hospital (Fortuna)
    St. Joseph Home Care Network (Sonoma)
    St. Joseph Hospital (Eureka)
    Santa Rosa Memorial Hospital
Southern California
    Mission Hospital (Mission Viejo)
    Mission Hospital Laguna Beach
    St. Joseph Hospital (Orange)
    St. Jude Medical Center (Fullerton)
    St. Mary Medical Center (Apple Valley)
West Texas/Eastern New Mexico
    Covenant Health System
    Artesia General Hospital (New Mexico)
    Covenant Hospital Levelland (Texas)
    Covenant Hospital Plainview (Texas)
    Covenant Medical Center (Lubbock, TX)
    Nor-Lea General Hospital (Lovington, NM)
    Roosevelt General Hospital (Portales, NM)

PRODUCTS/OPERATIONS

2014 Sales

	$ mil	% of total
Net patient service, net of provision for doubtful accounts	4,275.2	76
Premium	1,130.6	20
Other	225.9	4
Total	5,631.7	100

COMPETITORS

ADVENTIST HEALTHCARE, INC.
AMEDISYS, INC.
COMMONSPIRIT HEALTH
GENTIVA HEALTH SERVICES, INC.
LHC GROUP, INC.
NORTHWESTERN MEMORIAL HEALTHCARE
PEACEHEALTH
SPECTRUM HEALTH SYSTEM
STEWARD HEALTH CARE SYSTEM LLC
VITAS HEALTHCARE CORPORATION

HISTORICAL FINANCIALS
Company Type: Private

Income Statement   FYE: June 30

	REVENUE ($mil)	NET INCOME ($mil)	NET PROFIT MARGIN	EMPLOYEES
06/13	4,955	2,082	42.0%	5,400
06/10	4,268	268	6.3%	—
Annual Growth	5.1%	98.1%	—	—

2013 Year-End Financials
Return on assets: 3.6%   Cash ($ mil.): 329
Return on equity: 42.0%
Current Ratio: 0.80

ST. JOSEPH HOSPITAL OF ORANGE

If you're feeling green or blue in Orange County, St. Joseph Hospital of Orange is there to help get back to feeling pink and rosy. The California hospital provides general medical and surgical services, as well as specialty care such as women's health, mental health services, oncology, cardiology, and physical rehabilitation. Part of the St. Joseph Health System, the hospital provides primary care and specialty outpatient services through a network of affiliated physician practices. It also operates low-income and mobile clinics. The hospital has about 468 beds and a medical staff of some 1,000.

Operations
In addition to physician group affiliates St. Joseph Hospital Affiliated Physicians and St. Joseph Heritage Medical Group, the hospital also partners with the Childrens Hospital of Orange County to help expand pediatric care throughout the region. The hospital has more than 20,100 inpatient discharges and about 290,400 outpatient visits a year.

Geographic Reach
St. Joseph Hospital serves Orange County, California and the greater Los Angeles metropolitan area.

Strategy
St. Joseph Hospital has been working to expand its community outreach programs related to cancer through a number of projects including offering improved access to clinical trials; providing better overall access to cancer care; and implementing measures to garner support for the implementation of cancer electronic health records. St. Joseph Hospital is using stimulus money and about a $3 million award from the National Cancer Institute Community Cancer Centers Program to help fund its various projects.

Company Background
The company was founded in 1929 by the Sisters of St. Joseph of Orange.

EXECUTIVES

Chief of Staff*, Martin J Feldman

LOCATIONS

HQ: ST. JOSEPH HOSPITAL OF ORANGE
  1100 W STEWART DR, ORANGE, CA 928683891
Phone: 714 633-9111
Web: WWW.SJO.ORG

PRODUCTS/OPERATIONS

Selected Services
Bariatric Surgery
Behavioral Health
Cancer
Nasal & Sinus Center
Heart & Vascular Center
Kidney Dialysis Center
Maternity
Orthopedic Services
Sleep Disorders Center

COMPETITORS

JOHN C. LINCOLN HEALTH NETWORK
MERCY HEALTH - ST. RITA'S MEDICAL CENTER, LLC
SAINT JOSEPH HOSPITAL, INC
ST. JOHN'S HOSPITAL OF THE HOSPITAL SISTERS OF THE THIRD ORDER OF ST. FRANCIS
ST. VINCENT ANDERSON REGIONAL HOSPITAL, INC.

HISTORICAL FINANCIALS
Company Type: Private

Income Statement   FYE: June 30

	REVENUE ($mil)	NET INCOME ($mil)	NET PROFIT MARGIN	EMPLOYEES
06/18	627	40	6.5%	3,300
06/17	655	29	4.5%	—
06/16	599	11	2.0%	—
06/15	567	2	0.5%	—
Annual Growth	3.4%	144.6%	—	—

2018 Year-End Financials
Return on assets: 5.2%   Cash ($ mil.): 17
Return on equity: 14.4%
Current Ratio: 1.20

ST. JOSEPH HOSPITAL, INC.

LOCATIONS

HQ: ST. JOSEPH HOSPITAL, INC.
  1375 E 19TH AVE, DENVER, CO 802181114
Phone: 303 837-7111
Web: WWW.SCLHEALTH.ORG

HISTORICAL FINANCIALS
Company Type: Private

Income Statement   FYE: December 31

	REVENUE ($mil)	NET INCOME ($mil)	NET PROFIT MARGIN	EMPLOYEES
12/19	614	48	7.9%	2,400
12/16	530	(49)	—	—
12/15	498	37	7.5%	—
Annual Growth	5.4%	6.8%	—	—

2019 Year-End Financials
Return on assets: 5.8%   Cash ($ mil.): —
Return on equity: 8.3%
Current Ratio: —

ST. JOSEPH'S HEALTH PARTNERS LLC

St. Joseph's Healthcare System takes care of northern New Jersey. The system includes St. Joseph's Regional Medical Center, a tertiary teaching hospital with about 650 beds that includes the 120-bed St. Joseph's Children's Hospital. The regional hospital boasts a state-designated trauma center and provides such specialty services as cardiology, oncology, obstetrics, behavioral health, and neurology. The system also operates St. Joseph's Wayne Hospital, a community medical center with about 230 beds. Other operations include St. Vincent's Nursing Home, a home health agency, and a community clinic network. St. Joseph's Healthcare System is sponsored by the Sisters of Charity of Saint Elizabeth.

Operations

With a total of some 1,400 physicians and more than 1,000 beds, the St. Joseph's Healthcare facilities serve more than 1.6 million patients each year. The St. Joseph Regional facility handled some 1.3 million inpatient and outpatient visits, as well as 123,000 emergency room visits, while the St. Joseph's Wayne center saw 680,000 patients including 27,000 ER visitors.

Geographic Reach

St. Joseph's facilities are located in Cedar Grove, Paterson, Totowa, and Wayne in northern New Jersey.

Financial Performance

Revenue rose by 2% in fiscal 2013 to $714 million from $700 million in 2012. Income grew $110 million to $89 million from a net loss in 2012.

Medicare accounts for about 34% of net patient revenues while Medicaid accounts for 8%.

Strategy

The St. Joseph's Wayne and St. Joseph's Regional centers are undergoing a multi-year facility improvement project that boasts a total cost of some $250 million. The first phase was completed in 2009 and expanded St. Joseph's Regional outpatient services in areas including neurology, orthopedics, ophthalmology, and pediatrics. And the facility completed a new lobby and conference center in 2010. In 2012 its St. Joseph's Children's Hospital completed expansion efforts on its emergency and MRI facilities; it also opened a new birth defects center and launched a telemedicine suite through a partnership with St. Jude Children's Research Hospital. At the St. Joseph's Wayne facility, a new cardiac catheterization lab was added in 2012.

In addition, in 2012 the St. Joseph's Children's Hospital added a new specialist facility to serve residents of Paramus and nearby communities. In 2012, St. Joseph's Children's Hospital in Tampa opened its new Steinbrenner Children's Emergency/Trauma Center.

Company Background

St. Joseph's Healthcare traces its roots to the 1867 opening of the St. Joseph's Hospital by the Sisters of Charity of Saint Elizabeth.

EXECUTIVES

CMO, Philip Falcone
Auditors : ERNST & YOUNG LLP ISELIN NJ

LOCATIONS

HQ: ST. JOSEPH'S HEALTH PARTNERS LLC
703 MAIN ST, PATERSON, NJ 075032621
Phone: 973 569-6006

Web: WWW.STJOSEPHSHEALTH.ORG

PRODUCTS/OPERATIONS

Selected Facilities
St. Joseph's Regional Medical Center (Paterson)
    St. Joseph's Children's Hospital (Paterson)
St. Joseph's Wayne Hospital (Wayne)
St. Vincent's Nursing Home (Cedar Grove)
Visiting Health Services of New Jersey, Inc. (Totowa)

Selected Services
Blood Bank/Donation
Care Management/Social Work
Clinical and Educational Services
Driver Rehabilitation Program
Food and Nutrition Services
Identifying Obstacles
Information Technology
Laboratory Services
Mission Services
Pain Management Services
Pain Medicine Center
Palliative Care
Pathology/Laboratory
Pharmacy Services
Radiology
Rehabilitation
Swallowing Center
Telemedicine
Telemedicine Programs at St. Joseph's
Transfer Center

COMPETITORS

CATHOLIC HEALTH SYSTEM, INC.
CHI ST. LUKE'S HEALTH BAYLOR COLLEGE OF MEDICINE MEDICAL CENTER CONDOMINIUM ASSOCIATION
ST LUKE'S HOSPITAL
ST. DAVID'S HEALTHCARE PARTNERSHIP, L.P., LLP
ST. JOSEPH'S HOSPITAL HEALTH CENTER
ST. LUKE'S HEALTH SYSTEM, LTD.
ST. LUKE'S HOSPITAL OF DULUTH
ST. MARY'S HEALTH, INC.
ST. VINCENT ANDERSON REGIONAL HOSPITAL, INC.
ST. VINCENT'S HEALTH SYSTEM, INC.

HISTORICAL FINANCIALS

Company Type: Private

Income Statement				FYE: December 31
	REVENUE ($mil)	NET INCOME ($mil)	NET PROFIT MARGIN	EMPLOYEES
12/19	827	(4)	—	9,832
12/18	808	(22)	—	—
12/17	0	0	—	—
12/16	796	(13)	—	—
Annual Growth	1.3%	—	—	—

2019 Year-End Financials
Return on assets: (-0.5%)   Cash ($ mil.): 60
Return on equity: (-2.3%)
Current Ratio: 2.60

ST. JOSEPH'S HOSPITAL HEALTH CENTER

With about 450 inpatient beds, St. Joseph's Hospital Health Center serves the residents of 16 central New York counties. The not-for-profit hospital system provides general, emergency, and surgical care, as well as specialty services in areas such as obstetrics, cardiology, dialysis, and wound care. In addition to its inpatient facilities, the organization operates a home health agency, a nursing school, medical and dental residency programs, and several outpatient care centers. Its Franciscan Companies affiliate offers some ancillary services, including the provision of medical supplies, home health equipment, and senior services. St. Joseph's Hospital Health Center was founded in 1869 and became part of Trinity Health in 2015.

Operations

With a total of some 800 physicians, St. Joseph's Hospital Health Center admits some 28,000 inpatients each year. It also handles some 957,000 emergency room visits and about 640,000 outpatient visits annually. The hospital provides about $22 million in charity and community care each year as well.

Geographic Reach

St. Joseph's Hospital Health Center's service territory includes the New York counties of Broome, Cayuga, Chenango, Cortland, Delaware, Herkimer, Jefferson, Lewis, Madison, Oneida, Onondaga, Oswego, Otsego, St. Lawrence, Tioga, and Tompkins.

Financial Performance

In 2013 revenue rose 7% to $626 million as patient and other revenue grew. Net income also improved, by 33%, due to better investment returns.

Strategy

St. Joseph's Hospital Health Center is conducting a massive $220 million expansion program at its main campus. The first phase opened in 2011 and includes a larger emergency room facility with chest pain and psychiatric units. The hospital broke ground on the second phase of the project in 2012. The program will add a new patient tower, surgery facilities, a sterilization center, and an intensive care unit. In 2013 it opened a sleep center and a new surgical suite at the hospital. The following year St. Joseph's expanded its primary care center in west Syracuse and launched it electronic health record system.

Mergers and Acquisitions

In 2013 the center purchased Upstate Surgical Group creating a general surgery group in St. Joseph's ambulatory surgery group.

In late 2010 St. Joseph's Hospital Health Center boosted its physician network significantly by acquiring North Medical, a physician practice organization that operates five practices: Family Physicians, Urgent Care, Orthopedics & Rehabilitation, The Women's Place, and Living Proof Longevity Centre. Its practices are home to about 80 physicians and mid-level practitioners.

EXECUTIVES

CMO*, Joseph W Spinale
CSO*, Mark E Murphy

Information Technology Vice President*, Charles Fennell
INTEGRITY*, Jennifer Bolster
MISSION INTEGRATION*, Deborah Welch

LOCATIONS

HQ: ST. JOSEPH'S HOSPITAL HEALTH CENTER
301 PROSPECT AVE, SYRACUSE, NY 132031899
Phone: 315 448-5882
Web: WWW.SJHSYR.ORG

PRODUCTS/OPERATIONS

Selected Services
Centers of Excellence
    Cardiac Services
    The Center for Orthopedic and Spine Care
    Vascular Services
    Women and Children's Services
    Wound Care
    Home Care
    Dialysis
    Bariatric (Weight Loss) Services
Other Services and Centers
    Aesthetic Services
    Behavioral Health
    da Vinci Robotic Surgery
    Emergency Services
    Imaging
    Infusion (CPEPCNY)
    Interventional Radiology
    Medical Equipment
    Obstetric Services
    Palliative Care
    Pharmacy
    Physical Medicine & Rehabilitation
    Pulmonary Services
    Sleep Laboratory
    Social Adult Day Care
    Surgical Services
    Urology Services
Outpatient Services
    Dental Services
    Family Medicine Center
    Obstetrics and Gynecology
    Pediatric Office
    Physician Health
    Primary Care
    Westside Family Health Center

COMPETITORS

MERCY HOSPITAL SOUTH
MULTICARE HEALTH SYSTEM
ST LUKE'S HOSPITAL
ST. AGNES HEALTHCARE, INC.
ST. LUKE'S HOSPITAL OF DULUTH

HISTORICAL FINANCIALS
Company Type: Private

Income Statement — FYE: June 30

	REVENUE ($mil)	NET INCOME ($mil)	NET PROFIT MARGIN	EMPLOYEES
06/21*	632	28	4.5%	3,300
12/15	542	(2)	—	—
12/14	523	0	0.1%	—
12/09	436	5	1.2%	—
Annual Growth	3.1%	14.9%	—	—

*Fiscal year change

2021 Year-End Financials
Return on assets: 5.9%   Cash ($ mil.): 11
Return on equity: 129.5%
Current Ratio: 1.10

ST. JOSEPH'S HOSPITAL, INC.

EXECUTIVES

CMO*, Peter Charvat
Chief Medical Officer*, Sowmya Viswanathan

LOCATIONS

HQ: ST. JOSEPH'S HOSPITAL, INC.
3001 W DR MRTN LTHER KING, TAMPA, FL 336076307
Phone: 813 554-8500
Web: WWW.BAYCARE.ORG

HISTORICAL FINANCIALS
Company Type: Private

Income Statement — FYE: December 31

	REVENUE ($mil)	NET INCOME ($mil)	NET PROFIT MARGIN	EMPLOYEES
12/14	872	141	16.2%	300
12/09	719	75	10.4%	—
12/08	663	29	4.5%	—
12/06	565	63	11.2%	—
Annual Growth	5.6%	10.6%	—	—

2014 Year-End Financials
Return on assets: 11.0%   Cash ($ mil.): —
Return on equity: 12.5%
Current Ratio: 5.40

ST. JOSEPH'S UNIVERSITY MEDICAL CENTER INC

LOCATIONS

HQ: ST. JOSEPH'S UNIVERSITY MEDICAL CENTER INC
703 MAIN ST, PATERSON, NJ 075032621
Phone: 973 754-2000
Web: WWW.STJOSEPHSHEALTH.ORG

HISTORICAL FINANCIALS
Company Type: Private

Income Statement — FYE: December 31

	REVENUE ($mil)	NET INCOME ($mil)	NET PROFIT MARGIN	EMPLOYEES
12/19	821	(8)	—	6,000
12/18	798	(12)	—	—
12/16	763	(12)	—	—
12/15	752	60	8.0%	—
Annual Growth	2.2%	—	—	—

2019 Year-End Financials
Return on assets: (-1.0%)   Cash ($ mil.): 59
Return on equity: (-4.5%)
Current Ratio: 2.70

ST. JUDE HOSPITAL

St. Jude Medical Center gets sickly Southern Californians on their feet again. The faith-based, not-for-profit acute care facility, with some 385 beds, serves the residents of Orange County. The medical center provides an onsite cancer center (the Virginia K. Crosson Cancer Center) and a heart institute that offers cardiac surgeries and rehabilitation programs. It also provides inpatient and outpatient physical rehabilitation services and a variety of community outreach programs. Established by the Sisters of St. Joseph of Orange religious order in the 1950s, St. Jude Medical Center is part of the St. Joseph Health System.

Operations

Beyond the medical center's campus, St. Jude operates its Heritage Medical Group with outpatient locations throughout its region. The medical group includes specialists in plastic surgery, rheumatology, and gastroenterology. Altogether, St. Jude employs some 700 physicians. It handles more than 17,000 inpatient admissions each year, as well as 13,000 surgeries, 2,000 births, and 54,000 emergency room visits.

The organization spends some $47 million in community benefits, including outreach and charity care. Its mobile and fixed-site community clinics offer medical, dental, and preventative care services for low-income residents.

Geographic Reach

St. Jude serves residents in communities in California's Orange County, including Brea, Buena Park, Fullerton, La Habra, Placentia, and Yorba Linda.

Strategy

St. Jude is expanding its facilities through the construction of a new, $312 million patient tower schedule to open in late 2014. The Northwest Tower will feature private patient rooms, as well as enhanced surgical and data management capabilities. Other improvement measures include technology upgrades, such as a new neurovascular surgical system added in 2012.

In October 2011 St. Jude Medical Center closed its 12-bed pediatric unit and redirected patients younger than 16 to nearby Children's Hospital of Orange County. St. Jude's NICU (neonatal intensive care unit) remains open and the hospital continues to provide emergency and outpatient services to children.

LOCATIONS

HQ: ST. JUDE HOSPITAL
101 E VALENCIA MESA DR, FULLERTON, CA 928353809
Phone: 714 871-3280
Web: WWW.STJUDEMEDICALCENTER.ORG

COMPETITORS
ASCENSION SOUTHEAST MICHIGAN
MERCY HOSPITAL SOUTH
MULTICARE HEALTH SYSTEM
ST. JOSEPH'S HOSPITAL HEALTH CENTER
ST. LUKE'S HOSPITAL OF DULUTH

HISTORICAL FINANCIALS
Company Type: Private

Income Statement — FYE: June 30

	REVENUE ($mil)	NET INCOME ($mil)	NET PROFIT MARGIN	EMPLOYEES
06/18	557	50	9.1%	2,600
06/17	544	45	8.3%	—
06/16	490	4	0.9%	—
06/15	458	8	2.0%	—
Annual Growth	6.8%	77.9%	—	—

2018 Year-End Financials
Return on assets: 5.4%   Cash ($ mil.): (-10)
Return on equity: 9.9%
Current Ratio: 3.80

ST. LOUIS CHILDREN'S HOSPITAL

LOCATIONS
HQ: ST. LOUIS CHILDREN'S HOSPITAL
 1 CHILDRENS PL FL 2, SAINT LOUIS, MO 631101081
Phone: 314 454-6000
Web: WWW.STLOUISCHILDRENS.ORG

HISTORICAL FINANCIALS
Company Type: Private

Income Statement — FYE: December 31

	REVENUE ($mil)	NET INCOME ($mil)	NET PROFIT MARGIN	EMPLOYEES
12/20	779	120	15.5%	2,959
12/18	668	65	9.8%	—
12/17	609	62	10.2%	—
12/16	563	58	10.3%	—
Annual Growth	8.4%	20.2%	—	—

2020 Year-End Financials
Return on assets: 20.4%   Cash ($ mil.): —
Return on equity: 25.3%
Current Ratio: 1.70

ST. LUKE'S HEALTH NETWORK, INC.

St. Luke's University Hospital (formerly St. Luke's Hospital - Bethlehem Campus) serves residents of Pennsylvania's Lehigh Valley with primary, specialty, and emergency care services. The not-for-profit teaching hospital has about 480 acute-care beds. Its medical specialties include trauma, oncology, cardiology, orthopedics, neurology, open-heart surgery, radiology, and robotic surgery. The medical center also operates outpatient surgery centers and general physician care clinics, and it operates home health and community wellness programs. St. Luke's University Hospital was founded in 1872 and is part of the St. Luke's University Health Network.

Auditors : PRICEWATERHOUSECOOPERS LLP P

LOCATIONS
HQ: ST. LUKE'S HEALTH NETWORK, INC.
 801 OSTRUM ST, BETHLEHEM, PA 180151000
Phone: 610 954-4000
Web: WWW.SLHN.ORG

PRODUCTS/OPERATIONS
Selected Services
Cancer Center
Children's health
Diagnostic and Treatment Centers
Emergency
Heart Center
Neuroscience
Orthopaedics
Radiology/Imaging
Regional Breast Center (Center Valley)
Urgent Care Centers
Women's Imaging & Health Centers

COMPETITORS
COMMUNITY GENERAL HOSPITAL OF GREATER SYRACUSE
JEFFERSON COUNTY HMA, LLC
LIFEBRIDGE HEALTH, INC.
REGINA MEDICAL CENTER
RIVERVIEW HOSPITAL
SAINT LUKE'S HOSPITAL OF BETHLEHEM, PENNSYLVANIA
SALINE MEMORIAL HOSPITAL AUXILIARY
SAMARITAN REGIONAL HEALTH SYSTEM
ST DAVID'S SOUTH AUSTIN MEDICAL CENTER
TAS-CSEMCB, INC.

HISTORICAL FINANCIALS
Company Type: Private

Income Statement — FYE: June 30

	REVENUE ($mil)	NET INCOME ($mil)	NET PROFIT MARGIN	EMPLOYEES
06/22	2,969	(49)	—	2,958
06/19	2,116	59	2.8%	—
06/18	1,844	159	8.6%	—
06/17	1,521	121	8.0%	—
Annual Growth	14.3%	—	—	—

2022 Year-End Financials
Return on assets: (-1.4%)   Cash ($ mil.): 268
Return on equity: (-4.6%)
Current Ratio: 1.20

ST. LUKE'S HEALTH SYSTEM, LTD.

Founded in 1902, St. Luke's Health System is a not-for-profit health system and offers an emergency department, advanced inpatient and outpatient surgery, mother-baby services, diagnostics form x-ray to MRI, state of the art cancer treatment, critical care, a chest pain center and more. Its flagship facility is St. Luke's Boise Medical Center, which also includes a full-service children's hospital and primary and specialty physician clinics.

Operations
St. Luke's hospitals has eight hospitals and about 340 clinics & centers. The network also sees about 858,000 outpatients, 8,120 newborns, 42,790 surgeries, more than 1,000 beds, and over 52,000 hospital admissions.

St. Luke's Boise is the largest health care provider and the flagship hospital of St. Luke's Health System, providing access to highly skilled specialists, nurses, and staff within a friendly campus designed for healing. In additions, it is nationally recognized for quality and patient safety, and proud to be designated a Magnet hospital, the gold standard for nursing care.

Geographic Reach
St. Luke's has Idaho operations in Boise, Caldwell, Eagle, Fruitland, Jerome, Ketchum, McCall, Mountain Home, Nampa, and Twin Falls.

Strategy
St. Luke's strategy follows a clearly defined path:

Quality ? The company will work to advance its position as the go-to provider for consumers by delivering safe, effective care and an exceptional patient experience;

Access ? The company will evolve the way it delivers care to best meet the health needs of the people it serves when, where and how they deserve; and

Affordability ? The company will ensure the cost of high-quality health care is reasonable in the communities it serves, that it is understandable, and that it creates certainty for health care.

Company Background
In 2011 St. Luke's completed a $130 million project to rebuild the St. Luke's Magic Valley Medical Center. The new hospital building had about 190 beds and expanded emergency, cancer, and cardiac centers. The health system was also working to expand its Boise Medical Center's heart and vascular and pediatric departments, as well as its system-wide MSTI facilities.

The health system has also expanded its outpatient network to include new family practice, emergency care, and urgent care clinics in recent years. The network opened a

St. Luke's Nampa emergency care clinic and medical complex in 2012. In addition to updating its facilities, the St. Luke's Health System was working to upgrade its information technology assets.

St. Luke's added its fifth and sixth acute care hospitals in 2010 and 2011 when the 15-bed St. Luke's McCall (formerly McCall Memorial Hospital) and 25-bed St. Luke's Jerome (formerly St. Benedicts Medical Center) hospitals joined the health network through affiliation and merger agreements.

The health system was formed in 2006 when the three hospitals of the old St. Luke's Regional Medical Center network (Boise, Meridian, and Wood River) merged with Magic Valley Regional Medical Center, a former county facility in Twin Falls, Idaho.

EXECUTIVES

INTERIM CHIEF HUMAN RESOURCES OFFICER, Erin Simms

Auditors : DELOITTE & TOUCHE LLP BOISE

LOCATIONS

HQ: ST. LUKE'S HEALTH SYSTEM, LTD.
190 E BANNOCK ST, BOISE, ID 837126241
Phone: 208 381-2222
Web: WWW.STLUKESONLINE.ORG

PRODUCTS/OPERATIONS

Selected Idaho Facilities
St. Luke's Boise Medical Center (Boise)
    St. Luke's Children's Hospital
St. Luke's Clinics (multiple locations)
St. Luke's Eagle Urgent Care (Eagle)
St. Luke's Jerome Medical Center (Jerome)
St. Luke's Magic Valley Medical Center (Twin Falls)
St. Luke's McCall Memorial Hospital (McCall)
St. Luke's Meridian Medical Center (Meridian)
St. Luke's Mountain States Tumor Institute (multiple locations)
St. Luke's Wood River Medical Center (Hailey/Ketchum)

COMPETITORS

CATHOLIC HEALTH SYSTEM, INC.
CHI ST. LUKE'S HEALTH BAYLOR COLLEGE OF MEDICINE MEDICAL CENTER CONDOMINIUM ASSOCIATION
SAINT LUKE'S HEALTH SYSTEM, INC.
ST LUKE'S HOSPITAL
ST. DAVID'S HEALTHCARE PARTNERSHIP, L.P., LLP
ST. JOHN'S HOSPITAL OF THE HOSPITAL SISTERS OF THE THIRD ORDER OF ST. FRANCIS
ST. LUKE'S HOSPITAL OF DULUTH
ST. MARY'S HEALTH CARE SYSTEM, INC.
ST. VINCENT ANDERSON REGIONAL HOSPITAL, INC.
THE PUBLIC HEALTH TRUST OF MIAMI-DADE COUNTY

HISTORICAL FINANCIALS
Company Type: Private

Income Statement — FYE: September 30

	REVENUE ($mil)	NET INCOME ($mil)	NET PROFIT MARGIN	EMPLOYEES
09/21	3,347	337	10.1%	7,891
09/20	3,059	171	5.6%	—
09/19	2,894	91	3.2%	—
09/18	2,602	34	1.3%	—
Annual Growth	8.7%	114.7%	—	—

2021 Year-End Financials
Return on assets: 9.7%   Cash ($ mil.): 110
Return on equity: 20.2%
Current Ratio: 0.90

ST. LUKE'S HOSPITAL & HEALTH NETWORK

LOCATIONS

HQ: ST. LUKE'S HOSPITAL & HEALTH NETWORK
801 OSTRUM ST, BETHLEHEM, PA 180151000
Phone: 484 526-4000
Web: WWW.SLHN.ORG

HISTORICAL FINANCIALS
Company Type: Private

Income Statement — FYE: June 30

	REVENUE ($mil)	NET INCOME ($mil)	NET PROFIT MARGIN	EMPLOYEES
06/16	648	47	7.4%	75
06/15	602	38	6.4%	—
Annual Growth	7.6%	24.9%	—	—

2016 Year-End Financials
Return on assets: 5.1%   Cash ($ mil.): 43
Return on equity: 130.2%
Current Ratio: 1.30

ST. LUKE'S REGIONAL MEDICAL CENTER, LTD.

LOCATIONS

HQ: ST. LUKE'S REGIONAL MEDICAL CENTER, LTD.
190 E BANNOCK ST, BOISE, ID 837126241
Phone: 208 381-5500
Web: WWW.STLUKESONLINE.ORG

HISTORICAL FINANCIALS
Company Type: Private

Income Statement — FYE: September 30

	REVENUE ($mil)	NET INCOME ($mil)	NET PROFIT MARGIN	EMPLOYEES
09/20	1,586	89	5.6%	4,500
09/19	1,583	114	7.2%	—
09/14	1,255	31	2.5%	—
09/13	1,121	(19)	—	—
Annual Growth	5.1%	—	—	—

2020 Year-End Financials
Return on assets: 3.6%   Cash ($ mil.): —
Return on equity: 3.9%
Current Ratio: 8.40

ST. LUKE'S UNIVERSITY HEALTH NETWORK

Auditors : PRICEWATERHOUSECOOPERS LLP BA

LOCATIONS

HQ: ST. LUKE'S UNIVERSITY HEALTH NETWORK
801 OSTRUM ST, BETHLEHEM, PA 180151000
Phone: 610 954-4000
Web: WWW.SLHN.ORG

HISTORICAL FINANCIALS
Company Type: Private

Income Statement — FYE: June 30

	REVENUE ($mil)	NET INCOME ($mil)	NET PROFIT MARGIN	EMPLOYEES
06/22	2,969	(49)	—	71
06/21	211	0	0.0%	—
06/19	51	0	0.0%	—
06/18	147	0	0.0%	—
Annual Growth	111.6%	—	—	—

2022 Year-End Financials
Return on assets: (-1.4%)   Cash ($ mil.): 268
Return on equity: (-4.6%)
Current Ratio: 1.20

ST. MARY'S HEALTH, INC.

St. Mary's Medical Center of Evansville is a 433-bed hospital serving Indiana's River City. It is the primary facility in regional St. Mary's Health System, which is in turn part of Ascension Health. The Evansville hospital provides emergency, trauma, diagnostic, surgical, and rehabilitative services, as well as specialized cancer, cardiac, orthopedic, and neurological services. With a total of some 750 physicians, St. Mary's Health System also includes St. Mary's Hospital for Women & Children (100 beds, adjacent to the main hospital) and St. Mary's Warrick (a 25-bed hospital in Boonville, Indiana), as well as specialty outpatient, surgical, cancer, and home health units in surrounding areas of southern Indiana.

Operations

St. Mary's Medical Center of Evansville admits some 17,000 inpatients annually. It also handles around 64,000 emergency room visits and performs approximately 4,700 inpatient and 18,000 outpatient surgeries each year.

Company Background

St. Mary's Medical Center of Evansville was originally a Marine Hospital built by the US government. When the government shuttered its doors, city business leaders bought the building in 1872 and partnered with the Daughters of Charity to operate a community hospital.

Auditors : DELOITTE TAX LLP INDIANAPOLIS

LOCATIONS

HQ: ST. MARY'S HEALTH, INC.
3700 WASHINGTON AVE, EVANSVILLE, IN 477140541
Phone: 812 485-4000
Web: HEALTHCARE.ASCENSION.ORG

PRODUCTS/OPERATIONS

Selected Services
Breast Center
Cancer Care Services
Children's Health Care Services and Programs
Community Outreach Services
Convenient Care Centers
Diabetic Foot Clinic
Diabetes Services
Emergency Services Department
Endoscopy Suite
Foundation
Heart Services
Home Health Services
Hospitalists
Imaging/Radiology
Infusion Center
Laboratory Services
LifeFlight
Medical Equipment
Mental Health Services
Neurosciences & Stroke Care
Occupational Medicine Services
Orthopedic Healthcare
Palliative Care
Pastoral Care
Quality and Patient Safety
Rehabilitation Services
Respiratory Care
Senior Services
Sleep Disorders Center
Surgical Services
Trauma Services
Volunteers & Auxiliary
Weight Management Center
Women's Services and Programs
Women's Wellness Center

COMPETITORS

MERCY HOSPITAL SOUTH
ST. ANTHONY'S HOSPITAL, INC.
ST. JOSEPH'S HOSPITAL HEALTH CENTER
ST. JUDE HOSPITAL
ST. LUKE'S HOSPITAL OF DULUTH

HISTORICAL FINANCIALS
Company Type: Private

Income Statement   FYE: June 30

	REVENUE ($mil)	NET INCOME ($mil)	NET PROFIT MARGIN	EMPLOYEES
06/15	574	52	9.2%	3,500
06/13	468	48	10.4%	—
06/11	0	0	—	—
Annual Growth	—	—	—	—

2015 Year-End Financials
Return on assets: 6.4%   Cash ($ mil.): 12
Return on equity: 9.1%
Current Ratio: 2.80

ST. PETER'S HEALTH CARE SERVICES

Auditors : DELOITTE & TOUCHE LLP ROCHEST

LOCATIONS

HQ: ST. PETER'S HEALTH CARE SERVICES
315 S MANNING BLVD, ALBANY, NY 122081707
Phone: 518 525-1550
Web: WWW.SPHP.COM

HISTORICAL FINANCIALS
Company Type: Private

Income Statement   FYE: June 30

	REVENUE ($mil)	NET INCOME ($mil)	NET PROFIT MARGIN	EMPLOYEES
06/17	1,327	37	2.9%	6,000
06/16	552	39	7.1%	—
06/15	527	44	8.5%	—
06/14	509	21	4.1%	—
Annual Growth	37.6%	21.7%	—	—

2017 Year-End Financials
Return on assets: 2.7%   Cash ($ mil.): 124
Return on equity: 4.4%
Current Ratio: 2.60

ST. PETER'S HEALTH PARTNERS

St. Peter's Health Partners (formerly St. Peter's Health Care Services) is a not-for-profit health care system that serves northeastern New York. It includes health networks Seton Health and Northeast Health. Its primary facility, St. Peter's Hospital, has more than 440 acute-care beds and a medical staff of more than 600 physicians. Specialty services include emergency medicine, cancer and cardiovascular care, and women's health. St. Peter's also operates community health clinics, long-term care facilities, mental health centers, and home health and hospice agencies. Founded by the Religious Sisters of Mercy in 1869, St. Peter's operates from more than 125 locations and is a subsidiary of Catholic Health East.

Operations
St. Peter's Health Partners is the parent company for four hospitals: St. Peter's Hospital, the Albany Memorial and Samaritan Hospitals of Northeast Health, and Seton's St. Mary's Hospital. It also includes the Sunnyview Rehabilitation Hospital, the Community Hospice, and the Eddy Visiting Nurses Association, which provides skilled nurses for home health and senior services.

Strategy
To better serve Troy and Rensselaer counties, St. Peter's Health Partners has undertaken a 13-year, $150-million master facilities plan for Samaritan and St. Mary's Hospitals. The project includes constuction, renovation and modernization of inpatient facilites at Samaritan and outpatient facilities at St. Mary's. The project aims to fulfill a promise of the 2011 merger with Seton Health and Northeast Health: to improve health care facilities and programs in Troy.

Auditors : DELOITTE & TOUCHE LLP ROCHEST

LOCATIONS

HQ: ST. PETER'S HEALTH PARTNERS
315 S MANNING BLVD, ALBANY, NY 122081707
Phone: 518 525-1111
Web: WWW.SPHP.COM

PRODUCTS/OPERATIONS

Selected Operations
Albany Memorial Hospital
The Community Hospice
Eddy Visiting Nurses Association
Samaritan Hospital (Troy)
St. Mary's Hospital (Troy)
St. Peter's Hospital (Albany)
Sunnyview Rehabilitation Hospital (Schenectady)

COMPETITORS

FRANCISCAN HEALTH SYSTEM
GREATER LAFAYETTE HEALTH SERVICES, INC.
SAINT FRANCIS HOSPITAL AND MEDICAL CENTER FOUNDATION, INC.
ST. MARY'S HEALTH CARE SYSTEM, INC.
ST. VINCENT ANDERSON REGIONAL HOSPITAL, INC.

HISTORICAL FINANCIALS
Company Type: Private

Income Statement   FYE: June 30

	REVENUE ($mil)	NET INCOME ($mil)	NET PROFIT MARGIN	EMPLOYEES
06/20	1,446	(10)	—	4,000
06/18	1,337	6	0.5%	—
Annual Growth	4.0%	—	—	—

2020 Year-End Financials
Return on assets: (-0.7%)   Cash ($ mil.): 13
Return on equity: (-1.2%)
Current Ratio: 1.60

ST. TAMMANY PARISH SCHOOL BOARD

LOCATIONS

HQ: ST. TAMMANY PARISH SCHOOL BOARD
321 N THEARD ST, COVINGTON, LA 704332835
Phone: 985 892-2276
Web: WWW.STPSB.ORG

HISTORICAL FINANCIALS

Company Type: Private

Income Statement   FYE: June 30

	REVENUE ($mil)	NET INCOME ($mil)	NET PROFIT MARGIN	EMPLOYEES
06/21	578	(10)	—	5,000
06/20	522	31	6.1%	—
06/19	511	5	1.1%	—
Annual Growth	6.3%	—	—	—

2021 Year-End Financials
Return on assets: (-1.0%)   Cash ($ mil.): 224
Return on equity: —
Current Ratio: —

ST. VINCENT HOSPITAL OF THE HOSPITAL SISTERS OF THE THIRD ORDER OF ST. FRANCIS

Auditors : CROWE HORWATH LLP CHICAGO IL

LOCATIONS

HQ: ST. VINCENT HOSPITAL OF THE HOSPITAL SISTERS OF THE THIRD ORDER OF ST. FRANCIS
    835 S VAN BUREN ST, GREEN BAY, WI 543013526
Phone: 920 433-0111
Web: WWW.HSHS.ORG

HISTORICAL FINANCIALS

Company Type: Private

Income Statement   FYE: June 30

	REVENUE ($mil)	NET INCOME ($mil)	NET PROFIT MARGIN	EMPLOYEES
06/20	585	16	2.7%	2,360
06/19	567	29	5.1%	—
06/16	505	(35)	—	—
06/15	480	29	6.0%	—
Annual Growth	4.0%	(11.2%)	—	—

2020 Year-End Financials
Return on assets: 2.0%   Cash ($ mil.): 47
Return on equity: 2.9%
Current Ratio: 1.10

STAN BOYETT & SON, INC.

LOCATIONS

HQ: STAN BOYETT & SON, INC.
    601 MCHENRY AVE, MODESTO, CA 953505411
Phone: 209 577-6000

Web: WWW.BOYETT.NET

HISTORICAL FINANCIALS

Company Type: Private

Income Statement   FYE: December 31

	REVENUE ($mil)	NET INCOME ($mil)	NET PROFIT MARGIN	EMPLOYEES
12/08	656	0	0.1%	170
12/07	559	0	0.0%	—
12/06	475	0	0.1%	—
12/05	416	0	0.1%	—
Annual Growth	16.4%	28.4%	—	—

2008 Year-End Financials
Return on assets: 3.3%   Cash ($ mil.): 2
Return on equity: 17.6%
Current Ratio: 1.00

STANFORD HEALTH CARE

Stanford Health Care, along with Stanford Health Care Tri-Valley and Stanford Medicine Partners, is part of the adult health care delivery system of Stanford Medicine. As Stanford University's primary medical teaching facility, the 615-bed Stanford Hospital specializes in such areas as cardiac care, cancer treatment, neurology, surgery, and organ transplant. Stanford Health Care is part of the Stanford Medicine organization, which also includes the nearby Stanford University School of Medicine and Lucile Packard Children's Hospital (named for the wife of Hewlett-Packard co-founder David Packard).

Operations

Stanford Health Care delivers clinical innovation across its inpatient services, specialty health centers, physician offices, virtual care offerings, and health plan programs. It handles some over 72,530 adult and around 16,315 pediatric emergency visits, around 2 million outpatients and nearly 695,265 video visits during the year. The organization boasts such specialized clinics as the Byers Eye Institute, the Stanford Comprehensive Cancer Center, the Stanford Center for Marfan Syndrome and Aortic Disorders, and the California VitreoRetinal Center. It also operates centers for orthopedic, brain, blood and marrow transplant, and other specialist procedures.

Educational programs include medical and graduate student training, as well as residency and fellowship programs. The organization also conducts research in medical and biological fields.

Additionally, the system owns stakes in physician network University HealthCare Alliance, radiation therapy facility Stanford Emanuel Radiation Oncology Center, and health care advocacy firm CareCounsel.

Geographic Reach

Stanford Health Care has five locations in California.

EXECUTIVES

CDO*, Erica Yabokla
CMO, Norman Rizk Md
Auditors : PRICEWATERHOUSECOOPERS LLP SA

LOCATIONS

HQ: STANFORD HEALTH CARE
    300 PASTEUR DR, STANFORD, CA 943052200
Phone: 650 723-4000
Web: WWW.STANFORDHEALTHCARE.ORG

PRODUCTS/OPERATIONS

2014 Sales

	$ mil.	% of total
Net patient service revenue	2,839.4	95
Premium revenue	60.0	2
Other revenue	98.9	3
Total	2,998.3	100

Selected Services
Heart Center
Neurosciences
Orthopaedics
Sports Medicine
Stanford Cancer Center
Surgical Services
Transplant

COMPETITORS

ALBERT EINSTEIN HEALTHCARE NETWORK
CHARLESTON AREA MEDICAL CENTER, INC.
CHILDREN'S HOSPITAL MEDICAL CENTER
DUKE UNIVERSITY HEALTH SYSTEM, INC.
MASS GENERAL BRIGHAM INCORPORATED
NORTHWELL HEALTH, INC.
SWEDISH COVENANT HOSPITAL
THE CLEVELAND CLINIC FOUNDATION
THE PENNSYLVANIA HOSPITAL OF THE UNIVERSITY OF PENNSYLVANIA HEALTH SYSTEM
UNIVERSITY HOSPITALS HEALTH SYSTEM, INC.

HISTORICAL FINANCIALS

Company Type: Private

Income Statement   FYE: August 31

	REVENUE ($mil)	NET INCOME ($mil)	NET PROFIT MARGIN	EMPLOYEES
08/20	5,567	104	1.9%	14,100
08/18	4,910	456	9.3%	—
08/17	4,454	450	10.1%	—
08/15	3,570	372	10.4%	—
Annual Growth	9.3%	(22.4%)	—	—

2020 Year-End Financials
Return on assets: 1.1%   Cash ($ mil.): 1,642
Return on equity: 2.4%
Current Ratio: 1.60

STANFORD HEALTH SERVICES

Auditors : PRICEWATERHOUSECOOPERS LLP BO

LOCATIONS

HQ: STANFORD HEALTH SERVICES
    300 PASTEUR DR, STANFORD, CA 943052200

Phone: 650 723-4000
Web: WWW.STANFORDCHILDRENS.ORG

HISTORICAL FINANCIALS
Company Type: Private

Income Statement				FYE: August 31
	REVENUE ($mil)	NET INCOME ($mil)	NET PROFIT MARGIN	EMPLOYEES
08/11	2,510	415	16.6%	4
08/10	2,141	186	8.7%	—
Annual Growth	17.2%	123.2%	—	—

2011 Year-End Financials
Return on assets: —   Cash ($ mil.): 395
Return on equity: 16.6%
Current Ratio: 0.50

STAPLE COTTON COOPERATIVE ASSOCIATION

Referred to as Staplcotn, the Staple Cotton Cooperative has been a staple of its member-producers' business lives since 1921. One of the oldest and largest cotton marketing co-ops in the US, it provides domestic and export marketing, cotton warehousing, and agricultural financing to some 9,730 members in 47 states. As of 2011, the co-op handles nearly 14,000 farm accounts in 10 states. Staplcotn's inventory is consigned by member-producers and averages from 2.5 million to 3 million bales of cotton a year. The co-op operates though 15 warehouses serving the mid-south and southeastern US, to supply more than 25% of the cotton consumed by the US textile industry, as well as the needs of textile mills overseas.

LOCATIONS

HQ: STAPLE COTTON COOPERATIVE ASSOCIATION
214 W MARKET ST, GREENWOOD, MS 389304329
Phone: 662 453-6231
Web: WWW.STAPLCOTN.COM

PRODUCTS/OPERATIONS

Selected Services
Cotton services
    Loans
        Mill Sales Program
Marketing
Stapldiscount
Warehouse

COMPETITORS

CALCOT, LTD.
PLAINS COTTON COOPERATIVE ASSOCIATION
PYXUS INTERNATIONAL, INC.
UNIVERSAL CORPORATION
WYNNSTAY GROUP P.L.C.

HISTORICAL FINANCIALS
Company Type: Private

Income Statement				FYE: August 31
	REVENUE ($mil)	NET INCOME ($mil)	NET PROFIT MARGIN	EMPLOYEES
08/13	1,138	5	0.5%	312
08/12	1,236	8	0.7%	—
08/11	963	875	90.8%	—
Annual Growth	8.7%	(91.7%)	—	—

2013 Year-End Financials
Return on assets: 2.5%   Cash ($ mil.): 33
Return on equity: 5.3%
Current Ratio: 1.80

STATE OF ALABAMA

Auditors: RONALD L JONES MONTGOMERY A

LOCATIONS

HQ: STATE OF ALABAMA
300 DEXTER AVE, MONTGOMERY, AL 361043741
Phone: 334 242-7100
Web: WWW.ALABAMA.GOV

HISTORICAL FINANCIALS
Company Type: Private

Income Statement				FYE: September 30
	REVENUE ($mil)	NET INCOME ($mil)	NET PROFIT MARGIN	EMPLOYEES
09/21	31,016	3,945	12.7%	37,659
09/20	26,307	836	3.2%	—
09/19	23,698	677	2.9%	—
09/18	22,258	(34)	—	—
Annual Growth	11.7%	—	—	—

2021 Year-End Financials
Return on assets: 5.3%   Cash ($ mil.): 10,789
Return on equity: 10.0%
Current Ratio: —

STATE OF ALASKA

Auditors: KRIS CURTIS CPA CISA JUNEAU

LOCATIONS

HQ: STATE OF ALASKA
120 4TH ST, JUNEAU, AK 998011162
Phone: 907 465-3500
Web: WWW.AKLEG.GOV

HISTORICAL FINANCIALS
Company Type: Private

Income Statement				FYE: June 30
	REVENUE ($mil)	NET INCOME ($mil)	NET PROFIT MARGIN	EMPLOYEES
06/19	12,421	2,275	18.3%	4,300
06/18	12,318	2,779	22.6%	—
06/17	12,693	3,224	25.4%	—
Annual Growth	(1.1%)	(16.0%)	—	—

2019 Year-End Financials
Return on assets: 2.2%   Cash ($ mil.): —
Return on equity: 2.7%
Current Ratio: —

STATE OF ARIZONA

EXECUTIVES

General, Terry Goddard Attor
Auditors: LINDSEY PERRY CPA CFE PHOENI

LOCATIONS

HQ: STATE OF ARIZONA
1700 W WASHINGTON ST FL 7, PHOENIX, AZ 850072808
Phone: 602 542-4331
Web: WWW.AZ.GOV

HISTORICAL FINANCIALS
Company Type: Private

Income Statement				FYE: June 30
	REVENUE ($mil)	NET INCOME ($mil)	NET PROFIT MARGIN	EMPLOYEES
06/20	37,221	611	1.6%	34,161
06/19	34,554	1,496	4.3%	—
06/18	32,354	539	1.7%	—
06/17	31,295	385	1.2%	—
Annual Growth	6.0%	16.7%	—	—

2020 Year-End Financials
Return on assets: 1.1%   Cash ($ mil.): 8,771
Return on equity: 1.9%
Current Ratio: 1.50

STATE OF ARKANSAS

EXECUTIVES

Chief of Staff*, Morril Harriman
Auditors: ROGER A NORMAN JD CPA CFE

LOCATIONS

HQ: STATE OF ARKANSAS
4 CAPITOL MALL RM 403A, LITTLE ROCK, AR 722011013
Phone: 501 682-2345
Web: PORTAL.ARKANSAS.GOV

HISTORICAL FINANCIALS
Company Type: Private

Income Statement				FYE: June 30
	REVENUE ($mil)	NET INCOME ($mil)	NET PROFIT MARGIN	EMPLOYEES
06/21	22,391	1,077	4.8%	28,272
06/20	19,761	724	3.7%	—
06/19	13,821	997	7.2%	—
06/18	17,966	40	0.2%	—
Annual Growth	7.6%	199.7%	—	—

2021 Year-End Financials
Return on assets: 3.0%   Cash ($ mil.): 4,734
Return on equity: 5.4%
Current Ratio: 3.40

STATE OF CALIFORNIA

Auditors: MICHAEL S TILDEN CPA SACRAM

LOCATIONS

HQ: STATE OF CALIFORNIA
STATE CAPITAL, SACRAMENTO, CA 95814
Phone: 916 445-2864
Web: WWW.CA.GOV

HISTORICAL FINANCIALS
Company Type: Private

Income Statement — FYE: June 30

	REVENUE ($mil)	NET INCOME ($mil)	NET PROFIT MARGIN	EMPLOYEES
06/16	255,725	4,798	1.9%	208,580
06/16	255,725	4,798	1.9%	—
Annual Growth	—	—	—	—

2016 Year-End Financials
Return on assets: 1.4%   Cash ($ mil.): —
Return on equity: —
Current Ratio: 1.60

STATE OF COLORADO

Auditors: DIANNE E RAY CPA DENVER CO

LOCATIONS

HQ: STATE OF COLORADO
200 E COLFAX AVE STE 91, DENVER, CO 802031716
Phone: 303 866-5000
Web: WWW.COLORADO.GOV

HISTORICAL FINANCIALS
Company Type: Private

Income Statement — FYE: June 30

	REVENUE ($mil)	NET INCOME ($mil)	NET PROFIT MARGIN	EMPLOYEES
06/17	22,949	(240)	—	81,349
06/16	23,139	(295)	—	—
06/13	18,658	788	4.2%	—
06/12	17,586	472	2.7%	—
Annual Growth	5.5%	—	—	—

2017 Year-End Financials
Return on assets: (-0.5%)   Cash ($ mil.): 5,708
Return on equity: (-1.4%)
Current Ratio: 2.20

STATE OF DELAWARE

Auditors: CLIFTONLARSONALLEN LLP BALTIM

LOCATIONS

HQ: STATE OF DELAWARE
860 SILVER LAKE BLVD #1, DOVER, DE 199042402
Phone: 302 744-4101
Web: WWW.DELAWARE.GOV

HISTORICAL FINANCIALS
Company Type: Private

Income Statement — FYE: June 30

	REVENUE ($mil)	NET INCOME ($mil)	NET PROFIT MARGIN	EMPLOYEES
06/21	10,960	539	4.9%	25
06/20	8,513	535	6.3%	—
06/19	8,124	371	4.6%	—
06/17	7,368	(351)	—	—
Annual Growth	10.4%	—	—	—

2021 Year-End Financials
Return on assets: 2.5%   Cash ($ mil.): 619
Return on equity: —
Current Ratio: —

STATE OF GEORGIA

Auditors: GREG S GRIFFIN

LOCATIONS

HQ: STATE OF GEORGIA
206 WSHNGTON ST 111 STATE, ATLANTA, GA 30334
Phone: 404 656-1776
Web: WWW.GEORGIA.GOV

HISTORICAL FINANCIALS
Company Type: Private

Income Statement — FYE: June 30

	REVENUE ($mil)	NET INCOME ($mil)	NET PROFIT MARGIN	EMPLOYEES
06/21	55,707	5,578	10.0%	67,139
06/19	45,109	1,235	2.7%	—
06/17	42,410	1,167	2.8%	—
06/16	40,422	1,513	3.7%	—
Annual Growth	6.6%	29.8%	—	—

2021 Year-End Financials
Return on assets: 5.6%   Cash ($ mil.): 8,132
Return on equity: 12.8%
Current Ratio: —

STATE OF HAWAII

Auditors: ACCUITY LLP HONOLULU HAWAII

LOCATIONS

HQ: STATE OF HAWAII
201 MERCHANT ST STE 1805, HONOLULU, HI 968132963
Phone: 808 695-4620
Web: PORTAL.EHAWAII.GOV

HISTORICAL FINANCIALS
Company Type: Private

Income Statement — FYE: June 30

	REVENUE ($mil)	NET INCOME ($mil)	NET PROFIT MARGIN	EMPLOYEES
06/21	13,450	312	2.3%	44,201
06/20	12,091	(244)	—	—
06/19	11,744	57	0.5%	—
06/18	11,316	(39)	—	—
Annual Growth	5.9%	—	—	—

2021 Year-End Financials
Return on assets: 0.8%   Cash ($ mil.): 3,791
Return on equity: —
Current Ratio: —

STATE OF IDAHO

Auditors: APRIL RENFRO CPA MANAGER BO

LOCATIONS

HQ: STATE OF IDAHO
700 W JEFFERSON ST, BOISE, ID 837200001
Phone: 208 334-2100
Web: WWW.IDAHO.GOV

HISTORICAL FINANCIALS
Company Type: Private

Income Statement — FYE: June 30

	REVENUE ($mil)	NET INCOME ($mil)	NET PROFIT MARGIN	EMPLOYEES
06/21	12,566	1,664	13.2%	18,407
06/20	9,664	600	6.2%	—
06/19	8,615	157	1.8%	—
06/18	8,403	542	6.5%	—
Annual Growth	14.4%	45.3%	—	—

2021 Year-End Financials
Return on assets: 6.3%   Cash ($ mil.): 1,012
Return on equity: 8.8%
Current Ratio: —

STATE OF ILLINOIS

Auditors: WILLIAM G HOLLAND

LOCATIONS

HQ: STATE OF ILLINOIS
207 STATE HOUSE, SPRINGFIELD, IL 627060001
Phone: 217 782-6830

HISTORICAL FINANCIALS
Company Type: Private

Income Statement — FYE: June 30

	REVENUE ($mil)	NET INCOME ($mil)	NET PROFIT MARGIN	EMPLOYEES
06/13	62,451	1,596	2.6%	59,659
06/12	58,747	(522)	—	—
06/11	55,157	869	1.6%	—
Annual Growth	6.4%	35.5%	—	—

2013 Year-End Financials
Return on assets: 2.1%   Cash ($ mil.): 11,764
Return on equity: —
Current Ratio: —

STATE OF INDIANA

Auditors: PAUL D JOYCE CPA INDIANAPOL

LOCATIONS

HQ: STATE OF INDIANA
200 W WA ST STE 201, INDIANAPOLIS, IN 462042731

Phone: 317 232-4567
Web: WWW.STATE.IN.US

HISTORICAL FINANCIALS
Company Type: Private

Income Statement — FYE: June 30

	REVENUE ($mil)	NET INCOME ($mil)	NET PROFIT MARGIN	EMPLOYEES
06/20	38,553	375	1.0%	33,000
06/19	36,469	986	2.7%	—
06/18	33,877	408	1.2%	—
06/17	32,576	(78)	—	—
Annual Growth	5.8%	—	—	—

2020 Year-End Financials
Return on assets: 0.5% Cash ($ mil.): —
Return on equity: 1.1%
Current Ratio: —

STATE OF IOWA

Auditors: MARLYS K GASTON CPA DES MOI

LOCATIONS

HQ: STATE OF IOWA
1007 E GRAND AVE RM 105, DES MOINES, IA 503199003
Phone: 515 281-5211
Web: WWW.IOWA.GOV

HISTORICAL FINANCIALS
Company Type: Private

Income Statement — FYE: June 30

	REVENUE ($mil)	NET INCOME ($mil)	NET PROFIT MARGIN	EMPLOYEES
06/21	21,950	1,083	4.9%	24,304
06/20	19,439	348	1.8%	—
06/19	18,006	471	2.6%	—
06/18	17,093	(79)	—	—
Annual Growth	8.7%	—	—	—

2021 Year-End Financials
Return on assets: 2.6% Cash ($ mil.): 7,668
Return on equity: 3.9%
Current Ratio: 3.10

STATE OF KANSAS

EXECUTIVES

Chief Information Technology Officer*, Lee Allen
Auditors: CLIFTONLARSONALLEN LLP GREENW

LOCATIONS

HQ: STATE OF KANSAS
534 S KANSAS AVE STE 1210, TOPEKA, KS 666033403
Phone: 785 354-1388
Web: PORTAL.KANSAS.GOV

HISTORICAL FINANCIALS
Company Type: Private

Income Statement — FYE: June 30

	REVENUE ($mil)	NET INCOME ($mil)	NET PROFIT MARGIN	EMPLOYEES
06/21	19,473	1,186	6.1%	22,375
06/20	15,721	278	1.8%	—
06/19	14,988	794	5.3%	—
06/18	14,322	895	6.3%	—
Annual Growth	10.8%	9.8%	—	—

2021 Year-End Financials
Return on assets: 3.3% Cash ($ mil.): 5,774
Return on equity: 5.3%
Current Ratio: —

STATE OF LOUISIANA

Auditors: DARYL G PURPERA CPA CFE BA

LOCATIONS

HQ: STATE OF LOUISIANA
900 N 3RD ST FL 4, BATON ROUGE, LA 708025236
Phone: 225 342-0991
Web: WWW.LOUISIANA.GOV

HISTORICAL FINANCIALS
Company Type: Private

Income Statement — FYE: June 30

	REVENUE ($mil)	NET INCOME ($mil)	NET PROFIT MARGIN	EMPLOYEES
06/21	37,825	1,454	3.8%	47,937
06/20	32,178	560	1.7%	—
06/19	30,034	1,386	4.6%	—
06/18	28,849	829	2.9%	—
Annual Growth	9.4%	20.6%	—	—

2021 Year-End Financials
Return on assets: 2.1% Cash ($ mil.): 11,997
Return on equity: 8.4%
Current Ratio: —

STATE OF MAINE

Auditors: POLA A BUCKLEY CPA CISA/MAR

LOCATIONS

HQ: STATE OF MAINE
1 STATE HOUSE STA, AUGUSTA, ME 043330001
Phone: 207 287-3531
Web: WWW.MAINE.GOV

HISTORICAL FINANCIALS
Company Type: Private

Income Statement — FYE: June 30

	REVENUE ($mil)	NET INCOME ($mil)	NET PROFIT MARGIN	EMPLOYEES
06/21	12,227	1,040	8.5%	12,000
06/20	9,868	44	0.4%	—
06/19	8,155	357	4.4%	—
06/18	7,798	110	1.4%	—
Annual Growth	16.2%	111.3%	—	—

2021 Year-End Financials
Return on assets: 5.0% Cash ($ mil.): 2,721
Return on equity: 18.6%
Current Ratio: 2.20

STATE OF MARYLAND

EXECUTIVES

Chief of Staff, Matthew Clark
Auditors: CLIFTON LARSON ALLEN LLP BALT

LOCATIONS

HQ: STATE OF MARYLAND
45 CALVERT ST STE 1, ANNAPOLIS, MD 214011994
Phone: 410 767-6356
Web: WWW.MARYLAND.GOV

HISTORICAL FINANCIALS
Company Type: Private

Income Statement — FYE: June 30

	REVENUE ($mil)	NET INCOME ($mil)	NET PROFIT MARGIN	EMPLOYEES
06/21	48,269	2,850	5.9%	58,020
06/20	40,437	381	0.9%	—
06/19	38	1	3.2%	—
06/18	35,653	314	0.9%	—
Annual Growth	10.6%	108.5%	—	—

2021 Year-End Financials
Return on assets: 3.4% Cash ($ mil.): 9,767
Return on equity: 128.5%
Current Ratio: —

STATE OF MICHIGAN

Auditors: DOUG A RINGLER CPA CIA LAN

LOCATIONS

HQ: STATE OF MICHIGAN
111 S CAPITOL AVE, LANSING, MI 489331555
Phone: 517 373-7910
Web: WWW.MICHIGAN.GOV

HISTORICAL FINANCIALS
Company Type: Private

Income Statement — FYE: September 30

	REVENUE ($mil)	NET INCOME ($mil)	NET PROFIT MARGIN	EMPLOYEES
09/18	54,684	832	1.5%	55,416
09/17	52,459	702	1.3%	—
09/16	52,181	168	0.3%	—
Annual Growth	2.4%	122.5%	—	—

2018 Year-End Financials
Return on assets: 1.1% Cash ($ mil.): 11,188
Return on equity: 3.5%
Current Ratio: 2.70

STATE OF MINNESOTA

EXECUTIVES

State Treasurer, Carol C Johnson
Auditors : LORI LEYSEN CPA/SCOTT TJOMSLA

LOCATIONS

HQ: STATE OF MINNESOTA
130 STATE CPTOL 75 REV DR, SAINT PAUL, MN 551550001
Phone: 651 201-3400
Web: VALIDATE.PERFDRIVE.COM

HISTORICAL FINANCIALS
Company Type: Private

Income Statement — FYE: June 30

	REVENUE ($mil)	NET INCOME ($mil)	NET PROFIT MARGIN	EMPLOYEES
06/21	50,689	3,875	7.6%	35,217
06/19	41,741	1,040	2.5%	—
06/17	37,751	793	2.1%	—
Annual Growth	7.6%	48.6%	—	—

2021 Year-End Financials
Return on assets: 4.6%   Cash ($ mil.): 20,793
Return on equity: 9.2%
Current Ratio: 2.70

STATE OF MISSISSIPPI

Auditors : STEPHANIE C PALMERTREE CPA

LOCATIONS

HQ: STATE OF MISSISSIPPI
501 NW ST STE 1301 WLFOL, JACKSON, MS 39201
Phone: 601 359-3100
Web: WWW.MISSISSIPPI.GOV

HISTORICAL FINANCIALS
Company Type: Private

Income Statement — FYE: June 30

	REVENUE ($mil)	NET INCOME ($mil)	NET PROFIT MARGIN	EMPLOYEES
06/21	20,826	1,761	8.5%	27,775
06/20	17,717	492	2.8%	—
06/19	16,887	773	4.6%	—
06/18	16,518	(9)	—	—
Annual Growth	8.0%	—	—	—

2021 Year-End Financials
Return on assets: 4.3%   Cash ($ mil.): 1,945
Return on equity: 8.3%
Current Ratio: 2.60

STATE OF MISSOURI

Auditors : THOMAS A SCHWEICH JEFFERSON

LOCATIONS

HQ: STATE OF MISSOURI
301 W HIGH ST RM 570, JEFFERSON CITY, MO 651011517
Phone: 573 751-4013
Web: WWW.MO.GOV

HISTORICAL FINANCIALS
Company Type: Private

Income Statement — FYE: June 30

	REVENUE ($mil)	NET INCOME ($mil)	NET PROFIT MARGIN	EMPLOYEES
06/20	27,080	962	3.6%	51,488
06/19	25,748	309	1.2%	—
06/18	25,326	110	0.4%	—
06/17	24,769	(153)	—	—
Annual Growth	3.0%	—	—	—

2020 Year-End Financials
Return on assets: 1.6%   Cash ($ mil.): 4,652
Return on equity: 2.7%
Current Ratio: —

STATE OF MONTANA

EXECUTIVES

Lieutenant Governor*, Kristen Juras
Auditors : CINDY JORGENSON CPA HELENA

LOCATIONS

HQ: STATE OF MONTANA
1301 E 6TH AVE FL 2, HELENA, MT 596013875
Phone: 406 444-3111
Web: WWW.MT.GOV

HISTORICAL FINANCIALS
Company Type: Private

Income Statement — FYE: June 30

	REVENUE ($mil)	NET INCOME ($mil)	NET PROFIT MARGIN	EMPLOYEES
06/19	6,740	509	7.6%	418
06/18	6,228	95	1.5%	—
06/17	5,921	(195)	—	—
06/16	5,558	(89)	—	—
Annual Growth	6.6%	—	—	—

2019 Year-End Financials
Return on assets: 2.8%   Cash ($ mil.): 2,578
Return on equity: 4.3%
Current Ratio: —

STATE OF NEBRASKA

Auditors : KRIS KUCERA CPA CFE LINCOLN

LOCATIONS

HQ: STATE OF NEBRASKA
521 S 14TH ST STE 400, LINCOLN, NE 685082707
Phone: 402 471-2311
Web: WWW.NEBRASKA.GOV

HISTORICAL FINANCIALS
Company Type: Private

Income Statement — FYE: June 30

	REVENUE ($mil)	NET INCOME ($mil)	NET PROFIT MARGIN	EMPLOYEES
06/21	13,356	1,621	12.1%	18,653
06/20	10,006	354	3.5%	—
06/19	9,322	401	4.3%	—
06/18	8,643	(108)	—	—
Annual Growth	15.6%	—	—	—

2021 Year-End Financials
Return on assets: 5.2%   Cash ($ mil.): 2,580
Return on equity: 6.5%
Current Ratio: —

STATE OF NEVADA

EXECUTIVES

Chief of Staff, Gerald Gardner
State Controller, Kim Wallin
Auditors : EIDE BAILLY RENO NEVADA

LOCATIONS

HQ: STATE OF NEVADA
101 N CARSON ST STE 1, CARSON CITY, NV 897014752
Phone: 775 684-5670
Web: WWW.NV.GOV

HISTORICAL FINANCIALS
Company Type: Private

Income Statement — FYE: June 30

	REVENUE ($mil)	NET INCOME ($mil)	NET PROFIT MARGIN	EMPLOYEES
06/21	13,855	872	6.3%	14,790
06/20	11,924	73	0.6%	—
06/16	10,436	301	2.9%	—
06/15	9,446	(144)	—	—
Annual Growth	6.6%	—	—	—

2021 Year-End Financials
Return on assets: 2.9%   Cash ($ mil.): —
Return on equity: 6.4%
Current Ratio: —

STATE OF NEW HAMPSHIRE

Auditors : KPMG LLP BOSTON MASSACHUSETT

LOCATIONS

HQ: STATE OF NEW HAMPSHIRE
107 N MAIN ST, CONCORD, NH 033014951
Phone: 603 271-1110
Web: WWW.NH.GOV

HISTORICAL FINANCIALS
Company Type: Private

Income Statement   FYE: June 30

	REVENUE ($mil)	NET INCOME ($mil)	NET PROFIT MARGIN	EMPLOYEES
06/21	7,599	449	5.9%	12,280
06/20	6,398	(116)	—	—
06/19	5,955	110	1.9%	—
06/18	5,874	145	2.5%	—
Annual Growth	9.0%	45.6%	—	—

2021 Year-End Financials
Return on assets: 3.6%   Cash ($ mil.): 1,780
Return on equity: 10.6%
Current Ratio: 1.90

STATE OF NEW YORK MORTGAGE AGENCY

The State of New York Mortgage Agency (SONYMA, pronounced "Sony Mae") is a public benefit corporation of the State of New York that makes homebuying more affordable for low- and moderate-income residents of the state. SONYMA has two program divisions: Its single-family programs and financing division provides low-interest rate mortgages to first-time homebuyers with low and moderate incomes through the issuance of mortgage revenue bonds, while its mortgage insurance fund provides mortgage insurance and credit support for multi-family affordable residential projects and special care facilities throughout the state.

Operations
SONYMA is overseen by a board of directors comprised of the State Comptroller, Director of the Budget, Commissioner of Housing and Community Renewal, and four appointees of the Governor, Temporary President of the Senate, and Speaker of the Assembly. Operations of the agency rest with the president/CEO, who also serves in this capacity for the New York State Housing Finance Agency, the State's other major housing finance entity. The two agencies are jointly operated out of a New York City headquarters office, plus regional offices in Albany, Buffalo, and Long Island.

SONYMA receives no direct operating support from the State. All of its programs and operations are supported by agency funds, consisting of mortgage income, application fees, insurance premiums, and investment proceeds. The agency uses proceeds from the sale of tax-exempt and taxable bonds to finance the purchase of homes statewide through a network of lenders.

Financial Performance
SONYMA's operations -- specifically its volume of mortgage originations -- were impacted in fiscal 2011 by the ongoing weakness in the US real estate market and disruptions in the international capital markets. Mortgage reservations in 2011 were down 26% from 2010. This was offset partially by a low-interest rate environment, which provided opportunity to refund outstanding SONYMA bonds, lowering the agency's cost of borrowing and somewhat improving its financial condition.

Strategy
SONYMA is developing a program with the New York State Higher Education Services Corporation (HESC) to offer education loans to eligible students attending colleges and universities in the state.

Auditors : ERNST & YOUNG LLP NEW YORK N

LOCATIONS
HQ: STATE OF NEW YORK MORTGAGE AGENCY
641 LEXINGTON AVE FL 4, NEW YORK, NY 100224503
Phone: 212 688-4000
Web: HCR.NY.GOV

COMPETITORS
AMERICUS MORTGAGE CORPORATION
DITECH HOLDING CORPORATION
FIRST MORTGAGE CORPORATION
NATIONSTAR MORTGAGE HOLDINGS INC.
PNMAC HOLDINGS, INC.

HISTORICAL FINANCIALS
Company Type: Private

Income Statement   FYE: October 31

	ASSETS ($mil)	NET INCOME ($mil)	INCOME AS % OF ASSETS	EMPLOYEES
10/19	5,936	392	6.6%	221
10/18	5,324	147	2.8%	—
10/17	5,228	34	0.7%	—
10/16	5,187	63	1.2%	—
Annual Growth	4.6%	83.2%	—	—

2019 Year-End Financials
Return on assets: 6.6%   Cash ($ mil.): 6
Return on equity: 13.2%
Current Ratio: 7.30

STATE OF NORTH CAROLINA

EXECUTIVES
Chief of Staff*, Kristi Jones
Auditors : BETH A WOOD CPA RALEIGH NO

LOCATIONS
HQ: STATE OF NORTH CAROLINA
20301 MAIL SERVICE CTR, RALEIGH, NC 276990300
Phone: 919 715-1411
Web: WWW.NC.GOV

HISTORICAL FINANCIALS
Company Type: Private

Income Statement   FYE: June 30

	REVENUE ($mil)	NET INCOME ($mil)	NET PROFIT MARGIN	EMPLOYEES
06/19	48,977	836	1.7%	69,869
06/18	46,551	208	0.4%	—
06/17	45,371	1,172	2.6%	—
06/16	44,395	1,501	3.4%	—
Annual Growth	3.3%	(17.7%)	—	—

2019 Year-End Financials
Return on assets: 0.7%   Cash ($ mil.): 16,804
Return on equity: 1.2%
Current Ratio: —

STATE OF NORTH DAKOTA

EXECUTIVES
CAO*, Jodee Hanson
Auditors : JOSHUA C GALLION BISMARCK N

LOCATIONS
HQ: STATE OF NORTH DAKOTA
600 E BOULEVARD AVE # 101, BISMARCK, ND 585050660
Phone: 701 328-4905
Web: WWW.ND.GOV

HISTORICAL FINANCIALS
Company Type: Private

Income Statement   FYE: June 30

	REVENUE ($mil)	NET INCOME ($mil)	NET PROFIT MARGIN	EMPLOYEES
06/19	7,860	1,955	24.9%	8,800
06/17	6,408	172	2.7%	—
06/16	5,667	(1,080)	—	—
06/15	7,902	1,203	15.2%	—
Annual Growth	(0.1%)	12.9%	—	—

2019 Year-End Financials
Return on assets: 5.8%   Cash ($ mil.): 1,010
Return on equity: 7.7%
Current Ratio: —

STATE OF OKLAHOMA

Auditors : GARY A JONES CPA CFE OKLAH

LOCATIONS
HQ: STATE OF OKLAHOMA
421 NW 13TH ST STE 220, OKLAHOMA CITY, OK 731033784
Phone: 405 521-2342
Web: WWW.OK.GOV

HISTORICAL FINANCIALS
Company Type: Private

Income Statement   FYE: June 30

	REVENUE ($mil)	NET INCOME ($mil)	NET PROFIT MARGIN	EMPLOYEES
06/21	24,377	2,290	9.4%	37,613
06/20	19,511	27	0.1%	—
06/19	19,784	1,636	8.3%	—
06/18	17,805	602	3.4%	—
Annual Growth	11.0%	56.1%	—	—

2021 Year-End Financials
Return on assets: 4.1%   Cash ($ mil.): 11,144
Return on equity: 6.4%
Current Ratio: 3.00

STATE OF OREGON

EXECUTIVES
State Secretary*, Bev Clarno
Auditors : OFFICE OF THE SECRETARY OF STA

LOCATIONS
HQ: STATE OF OREGON
900 COURT ST NE STE 160, SALEM, OR 973014046
Phone: 503 378-3111
Web: WWW.OREGON.GOV

HISTORICAL FINANCIALS
Company Type: Private

Income Statement   FYE: June 30

	REVENUE ($mil)	NET INCOME ($mil)	NET PROFIT MARGIN	EMPLOYEES
06/21	36,855	3,614	9.8%	36,176
06/20	28,755	(409)	—	—
06/19	28,230	2,142	7.6%	—
06/18	26,037	874	3.4%	—
Annual Growth	12.3%	60.5%	—	—

2021 Year-End Financials
Return on assets: 5.1%   Cash ($ mil.): 15,514
Return on equity: 9.9%
Current Ratio: 4.40

STATE OF RHODE ISLAND

Auditors : DENNIS E HOYLE CPA PROVIDEN

LOCATIONS
HQ: STATE OF RHODE ISLAND
82 SMITH ST STE 102, PROVIDENCE, RI 029031121
Phone: 401 222-2080
Web: WWW.RI.GOV

HISTORICAL FINANCIALS
Company Type: Private

Income Statement   FYE: June 30

	REVENUE ($mil)	NET INCOME ($mil)	NET PROFIT MARGIN	EMPLOYEES
06/19	7,547	(49)	—	13,535
06/17	7,012	215	3.1%	—
06/16	6,860	(10)	—	—
06/15	6,787	160	2.4%	—
Annual Growth	2.7%	—	—	—

2019 Year-End Financials
Return on assets: (-0.3%)   Cash ($ mil.): 1,905
Return on equity: (-1.9%)
Current Ratio: 2.10

STATE OF SOUTH CAROLINA

Auditors : GEORGE L KENNEDY III COLUMB

LOCATIONS
HQ: STATE OF SOUTH CAROLINA
1205 PENDLETON ST, COLUMBIA, SC 292013756
Phone: 803 734-2100
Web: WWW.SC.GOV

HISTORICAL FINANCIALS
Company Type: Private

Income Statement   FYE: June 30

	REVENUE ($mil)	NET INCOME ($mil)	NET PROFIT MARGIN	EMPLOYEES
06/15	21,191	224	1.1%	67,816
06/14	20,459	613	3.0%	—
06/13	19,706	944	4.8%	—
Annual Growth	3.7%	(51.2%)	—	—

2015 Year-End Financials
Return on assets: 0.4%   Cash ($ mil.): 3,814
Return on equity: 0.9%
Current Ratio: —

STATE OF SOUTH DAKOTA

EXECUTIVES
State Auditor*, Rich Sattgast
Auditors : MARTIN L GUINDON CPA PIERRE

LOCATIONS
HQ: STATE OF SOUTH DAKOTA
500 E CAPITOL AVE, PIERRE, SD 575015001
Phone: 605 773-3378
Web: BHR.SD.GOV

HISTORICAL FINANCIALS
Company Type: Private

Income Statement   FYE: June 30

	REVENUE ($mil)	NET INCOME ($mil)	NET PROFIT MARGIN	EMPLOYEES
06/21	5,968	620	10.4%	8,256
06/20	4,349	179	4.1%	—
06/19	3,945	71	1.8%	—
06/18	3,828	87	2.3%	—
Annual Growth	16.0%	92.3%	—	—

2021 Year-End Financials
Return on assets: 4.2%   Cash ($ mil.): 2,795
Return on equity: 5.7%
Current Ratio: —

STATE OF TENNESSEE

Auditors : DEBORAH V LOVELESS CPA DIRE

LOCATIONS
HQ: STATE OF TENNESSEE
312 ROSA L PARKS AVE, NASHVILLE, TN 372431102
Phone: 615 741-2001
Web: WWW.TN.GOV

HISTORICAL FINANCIALS
Company Type: Private

Income Statement   FYE: June 30

	REVENUE ($mil)	NET INCOME ($mil)	NET PROFIT MARGIN	EMPLOYEES
06/18	32,194	902	2.8%	37,737
06/16	30,452	1,162	3.8%	—
Annual Growth	2.8%	(11.9%)	—	—

2018 Year-End Financials
Return on assets: 1.5%   Cash ($ mil.): 11,868
Return on equity: 2.0%
Current Ratio: —

STATE OF TEXAS

EXECUTIVES
Chief of Staff*, Luis Saenz
Deputy Chief of Staff*, David Whitley
Deputy Chief of Staff*, Jordan Hale
Auditors : LISA R COLLIER CPA CFE CID

LOCATIONS
HQ: STATE OF TEXAS
1100 SAN JACINTO BLVD, AUSTIN, TX 787011935
Phone: 512 463-2000
Web: WWW.TEXAS.GOV

HISTORICAL FINANCIALS
Company Type: Private

Income Statement — FYE: August 31

	REVENUE ($mil)	NET INCOME ($mil)	NET PROFIT MARGIN	EMPLOYEES
08/17	115,336	1,882	1.6%	144,175
08/15	107,351	1,992	1.9%	—
08/14	109,861	8,184	7.4%	—
08/13	0	0	—	—
Annual Growth	—	—	—	—

2017 Year-End Financials
Return on assets: 0.6%   Cash ($ mil.): 29,217
Return on equity: 1.1%
Current Ratio: 1.90

STATE OF UTAH

Auditors: OFFICE OF THE STATE AUDITOR

LOCATIONS

HQ: STATE OF UTAH
350 N STATE ST STE 200, SALT LAKE CITY, UT 841140002
Phone: 801 538-1000
Web: WWW.UTAH.GOV

HISTORICAL FINANCIALS
Company Type: Private

Income Statement — FYE: June 30

	REVENUE ($mil)	NET INCOME ($mil)	NET PROFIT MARGIN	EMPLOYEES
06/21	19,735	1,934	9.8%	29,821
06/20	15,501	1,117	7.2%	—
06/19	14,316	696	4.9%	—
06/18	13,582	986	7.3%	—
Annual Growth	13.3%	25.2%	—	—

2021 Year-End Financials
Return on assets: 3.2%   Cash ($ mil.): 9,548
Return on equity: 4.2%
Current Ratio: —

STATE OF VERMONT

EXECUTIVES

Chief of Staff*, Liz Miller

LOCATIONS

HQ: STATE OF VERMONT
109 STATE ST STE 4, MONTPELIER, VT 056090003
Phone: 802 828-1452
Web: WWW.VERMONT.GOV

HISTORICAL FINANCIALS
Company Type: Private

Income Statement — FYE: June 30

	REVENUE ($mil)	NET INCOME ($mil)	NET PROFIT MARGIN	EMPLOYEES
06/21	7,942	583	7.3%	8,795
06/20	6,091	38	0.6%	—
06/19	5,868	(13)	—	—
06/18	5,790	144	2.5%	—
Annual Growth	11.1%	59.1%	—	—

2021 Year-End Financials
Return on assets: 4.5%   Cash ($ mil.): 2,239
Return on equity: 38.2%
Current Ratio: 2.50

STATE OF WASHINGTON

EXECUTIVES

Lieutenant Governor*, Denny Heck
Chief of Staff*, Mary Alice Heuschel
Auditors: PAT MCCARTHY OLYMPIA WA

LOCATIONS

HQ: STATE OF WASHINGTON
106 LEGISLATIVE BUILDING, OLYMPIA, WA 985040001
Phone: 360 902-4111
Web: WWW.WA.GOV

HISTORICAL FINANCIALS
Company Type: Private

Income Statement — FYE: June 30

	REVENUE ($mil)	NET INCOME ($mil)	NET PROFIT MARGIN	EMPLOYEES
06/19	50,993	264	0.5%	57,659
06/18	49,114	2,692	5.5%	—
06/17	46,269	1,100	2.4%	—
06/16	43,294	1,096	2.5%	—
Annual Growth	5.6%	(37.8%)	—	—

2019 Year-End Financials
Return on assets: 0.2%   Cash ($ mil.): 17,528
Return on equity: 1.0%
Current Ratio: —

STATE OF WEST VIRGINIA

EXECUTIVES

Chief of Staff*, Brian Abraham
Auditors: ERNST & YOUNG LLP CHARLESTON

LOCATIONS

HQ: STATE OF WEST VIRGINIA
1900 KANAWHA BLVD E, CHARLESTON, WV 253050009
Phone: 304 558-2000
Web: WWW.WV.GOV

HISTORICAL FINANCIALS
Company Type: Private

Income Statement — FYE: June 30

	REVENUE ($mil)	NET INCOME ($mil)	NET PROFIT MARGIN	EMPLOYEES
06/19	12,469	649	5.2%	19,357
06/17	11,650	(2)	0.0%	—
06/16	11,147	(231)	—	—
06/15	11,175	(159)	—	—
Annual Growth	2.8%	—	—	—

2019 Year-End Financials
Return on assets: 2.2%   Cash ($ mil.): 6,813
Return on equity: 5.0%
Current Ratio: 3.20

STATE OF WISCONSIN

Auditors: JOE CHRISMAN MADISON WISCONS

LOCATIONS

HQ: STATE OF WISCONSIN
115 E CAPITOL, MADISON, WI 537020021
Phone: 608 266-1212
Web: WWW.WISCONSIN.GOV

HISTORICAL FINANCIALS
Company Type: Private

Income Statement — FYE: June 30

	REVENUE ($mil)	NET INCOME ($mil)	NET PROFIT MARGIN	EMPLOYEES
06/21	38,601	1,607	4.2%	35,522
06/20	33,421	627	1.9%	—
06/19	31,683	693	2.2%	—
06/17	28,874	474	1.6%	—
Annual Growth	7.5%	35.6%	—	—

2021 Year-End Financials
Return on assets: 2.0%   Cash ($ mil.): 16,418
Return on equity: 4.0%
Current Ratio: —

STATE UNIVERSITY OF NEW YORK

SUNY days are ahead for many New Yorkers seeking higher education. With an enrollment of more than 460,000 students, The State University of New York (SUNY) is vying with California State University System for the title of largest university system in the US. Most students are residents of New York State. Students come from all 50 states as well as 160 countries. SUNY maintains 64 campuses around the state, including four university centers, about two dozen university colleges, 30 community colleges, and a handful of technical colleges, as well as medical centers. The system has a student-teacher ratio of about 16:1.

Operations

The school offers more than 7,500

undergraduate programs of study -- including engineering, business, literature, medicine, agriculture, performing arts, and human services. SUNY also offers about 400 study abroad programs.

HISTORY

The State University of New York was organized in 1948, but it traces its roots back to several institutions founded in the 19th century. In 1844 the New York state legislature authorized the creation of the Albany Normal School, which was charged with educating the state's secondary school teachers. Two years later, the University of Buffalo was chartered to provide academic, theological, legal, and medical studies. More normal schools later were founded between 1861 and 1889 in Brockport, Buffalo, Cortland, Fredonia, Geneseo, New Paltz, Oneonta, Oswego, Plattsburgh, and Potsdam.

In the early 1900s the state established several agricultural colleges, including schools in Canton (1907), Alfred (1908), Morrisville (1910), Farmingdale (1912), and Cobleskill (1916). New York also set up several schools as units of Cornell University, including colleges of veterinary medicine (1894), agriculture (1909), home economics (1925), and industrial and labor relations (1945).

After WWII, veterans began to fill US colleges and universities, taking advantage of the GI Bill to secure a college education. The legislature set up SUNY in 1948 to consolidate 29 institutions under a single board of trustees charged with meeting the growing demand. The board coordinated the state colleges into a single body and established four-year liberal arts colleges, professional and graduate schools, and research centers. During the 1950s and 1960s new campuses were created at Binghamton, Stony Brook, Old Westbury, Purchase, and Utica/Rome, and enrollment began to take off, jumping from 30,000 in 1955 to 63,000 in 1959.

By the early 1970s SUNY had more than 320,000 students at 72 institutions. But budget constraints later that decade led to higher tuition, reduced enrollment goals, and employment cutbacks. In 1975 eight New York City community colleges were transferred to City University. SUNY's enrollment began growing again during the 1980s, reaching more than 400,000 by 1990. Early in the decade, the institution began implementing SUNY 2000, a plan that called for increasing access to education and diversifying undergraduate studies. Following his election in 1994, Governor George Pataki proposed more than $550 million in cuts to the SUNY system.

In 1997 John Ryan replaced Thomas Bartlett as chancellor. The following year SUNY became the exclusive sponsor of The College Channel, a guide to colleges and college life aimed at high school juniors and seniors and broadcast by PRIMEDIA's Channel One. In 1999 the governor's budget director, Robert King, was named chancellor to replace the retiring Bartlett. King challenged SUNY administrators and the state to increase levels of funding to help keep the university competitive against other top-flight institutions. In 2000 SUNY faced rising budget shortfalls at its teaching hospitals, in part because money was being siphoned off to other areas. That year King announced a set of initiatives to raise an additional $1.5 billion in federal research grants and $1 billion in private donations over five years.

King retired as the university's chancellor in June 2005. Nancy Zimpher became the university's first female chancellor in 2009. The university had been without a permanent leader since 2007 when John Ryan resigned.

EXECUTIVES

INTERIM CHANCELLOR, John B Clark
ACADEMIC AFFAIRS, Peter D Salins
OF THE UNIVERSITY, John O'connor
Vice-Chancellor Finance, Brian Stenson
Business Industry Relations, R Wayne Diesel
Auditors : KPMG LLP ALBANY NEW YORK

LOCATIONS

HQ: STATE UNIVERSITY OF NEW YORK
353 BROADWAY, ALBANY, NY 122462915
Phone: 518 320-1100
Web: WWW.SUNY.EDU

COMPETITORS

AUBURN UNIVERSITY
CALIFORNIA STATE UNIVERSITY SYSTEM
NEW YORK UNIVERSITY
NORTHWESTERN UNIVERSITY
PRESIDENT AND FELLOWS OF HARVARD COLLEGE
SUNY COLLEGE AT BROCKPORT
THE CITY UNIVERSITY OF NEW YORK
THE OHIO STATE UNIVERSITY
THE REGENTS OF THE UNIVERSITY OF CALIFORNIA
UNIVERSITY OF WISCONSIN SYSTEM

HISTORICAL FINANCIALS

Company Type: Private

Income Statement — FYE: June 30

	REVENUE ($mil)	NET INCOME ($mil)	NET PROFIT MARGIN	EMPLOYEES
06/12	5,961	(374)	—	88,024
06/06*	4	(2)	—	—
10/05	0	0	—	—
Annual Growth	—	—	—	—

*Fiscal year change

2012 Year-End Financials

Return on assets: (-2.5%) Cash ($ mil.): 1,642
Return on equity: —
Current Ratio: 1.50

STATEN ISLAND UNIVERSITY HOSPITAL

Staten Island University Hospital (SIUH) ferries health care services to residents of New York City's fastest growing borough and surrounding areas at its two medical campuses. Established in 1861, SIUH maintains about 715 beds and is a teaching affiliate of the State University of New York's Brooklyn Health Science Center. Its larger north campus includes units specializing in cardiology, pathology, cancer, blood-related diseases, burn treatment, trauma, and women's health. The south campus site offers specialty programs such as sleep medicine, geriatric psychiatry, and substance abuse services. A member of Northwell Health, SIUH employs approximately 1,200 physicians.

Operations

SIUH's Heart Institute of Staten Island, located on the north campus, is a joint venture between the hospital and Richmond University Medical Center. The Heart Institute specializes in cardiac diagnostics and "beating heart" surgeries.

The hospital operates several general physician practice and specialty health clinics on Staten Island. It also provides a home visit program and hospital-based hospice services.

SIUH is an affiliate of the SUNY Health Science Center at Brooklyn; its campuses serve as clinics for the Hofstra North Shore-LIJ School of Medicine, which SIUH owns in partnership with Hofstra University.

In 2013 SIUH had nearly 3,000 births, nearly 45,000 hospital discharges, about 126,000 emergency department visits, and more than 16,000 ambulatory surgeries.

LOCATIONS

HQ: STATEN ISLAND UNIVERSITY HOSPITAL
475 SEAVIEW AVE, STATEN ISLAND, NY 103053436
Phone: 718 226-9000
Web: WWW.NORTHWELL.EDU

PRODUCTS/OPERATIONS

Selected Services
Behavioral Health
Cancer Services
Cardiac Services
Cardiovascular and Thoracic Surgery
Medical Services including Endocrinology, Gastroenterology, Nephrology, and Pulmonary
Neuroscience and Spine Services
Orthopedic Services
Pediatrics
Rehabilitation Medicine
Surgical Services including General Surgery, Colorectal, Head & Neck, and Urology
Trauma and Burn Services
Women's Health

Selected Centers of Care

Center for Bariatric Surgery
Comprehensive Breast Center
Heart Institute
Institute of Sleep Medicine
Level III Perinatal Center
New York Head & Neck Institute at Staten Island
University Hospital
Regional Burn Center
Stroke Center
The Elizabeth A. Connelly Emergency and Trauma Center
The Sanford R. Nalitt Institute for Cancer and Blood Related Diseases; Children's Cancer Center

COMPETITORS

CHILDREN'S HOSPITAL COLORADO
PITT COUNTY MEMORIAL HOSPITAL, INCORPORATED
PRIME HEALTHCARE SERVICES - GARDEN CITY, LLC
PRINCETON HEALTHCARE SYSTEM HOLDING INC.
TAS-CSEMCB, INC.

HISTORICAL FINANCIALS
Company Type: Private

Income Statement — FYE: December 31

	REVENUE ($mil)	NET INCOME ($mil)	NET PROFIT MARGIN	EMPLOYEES
12/18	934	(33)	—	5,700
12/17	891	69	7.8%	—
12/16	871	57	6.6%	—
12/15	850	41	4.9%	—
Annual Growth	3.2%	—	—	—

2018 Year-End Financials
Return on assets: (-3.1%)   Cash ($ mil.): 34
Return on equity: (-6.7%)
Current Ratio: 3.50

STEPHEN GOULD CORPORATION

Others can worry about what's inside -- Stephen Gould Corporation concentrates on the package. The company provides a full range of packaging-related design and printing services for customers worldwide. Its products include gift packaging, point-of-purchase displays, product merchandising, and retail and industrial packaging. Stephen Gould Corporation also provides graphic design and package-engineering services, as well as assembly and fulfillment. The company was originally founded in 1939 by Stephen Gould, David Golden, and Leonard Beckerman.

Geographic Reach
Stephen Gould Corporation operates from about 40 facilities; branches are located primarily in the US (more than 20 states), but also in China, Ireland, Malaysia, and Mexico.

LOCATIONS
HQ: STEPHEN GOULD CORPORATION
35 S JEFFERSON RD, WHIPPANY, NJ 079811043
Phone: 973 428-1500
Web: WWW.STEPHENGOULD.COM

PRODUCTS/OPERATIONS
Selected Products and Services
Products
  Aerospace reusable cases
  Corrugated containers
  Gift packaging
  Industrial packaging
  Point of sale packaging
  Protective packaging
Services
  Creative services
  Logistics & facilities
  Package design & engineering

COMPETITORS

GRAPHIC PACKAGING HOLDING COMPANY
GREEN BAY PACKAGING INC.
INTERSTATE RESOURCES, INC.
MPS LANSING, INC.
NORTHERN TECHNOLOGIES INTERNATIONAL CORPORATION
PACKAGING CORPORATION OF AMERICA
SONOCO PRODUCTS COMPANY
TAYLOR CORPORATION
TRICORBRAUN INC.
WESTROCK COMPANY

HISTORICAL FINANCIALS
Company Type: Private

Income Statement — FYE: December 31

	REVENUE ($mil)	NET INCOME ($mil)	NET PROFIT MARGIN	EMPLOYEES
12/21	951	18	1.9%	512
12/20	782	11	1.4%	—
12/19	757	5	0.8%	—
12/16	665	11	1.8%	—
Annual Growth	7.4%	9.1%	—	—

2021 Year-End Financials
Return on assets: 4.6%   Cash ($ mil.): 11
Return on equity: 16.5%
Current Ratio: 2.20

STEVENS TRANSPORT, INC.

Staying cool is a must for Stevens Transport. An irregular-route, refrigerated truckload carrier (or reefer), Stevens hauls temperature-controlled cargo throughout the US, covering the 48 contiguous states. Through alliances Stevens also covers every province in Canada and every state in Mexico. The company operates a fleet of about 2,000 Kenworth and Peterbuilt tractors and 3,500 Thermo King refrigerated trailers from a network of more than a dozen service centers. Partnerships with railroads allow Stevens to arrange intermodal transport of temperature-controlled cargo. The company also provides third-party logistics services. Stevens Transport was founded in 1980.

Operations
The company owns 49% of B2B Transport, which provides an array of transportation related services to large, mid-sized, and small companies throughout North America.

Geographic Reach
Stevens Transport maintains its operations across Canada, Mexico, and the US through its partnerships with BNSF, Norfolk Southern, CSX, and Union Pacific. It has 13 logistics offices located in Canada and throughout the US.

Sales and Marketing
Stevens has provided refrigerated shipping services for such big names as General Mills, Kraft Foods, M&M Mars, Procter & Gamble, and Wal-Mart.

Strategy
Even in a US economy ripe with unpredictable fuel costs and a decline in consumer confidence, one thing has always worked in Stevens' favor: people will always need their food. The company has managed to maintain a steady growth rate by keeping costs down, updating the technology of its trucking equipment, and maintaining an efficient operating structure. Along these lines, in 2012 it implemented new mobile computing platforms across its fleet of tractors to enhance its customer services and optimize productivity.

Auditors : SADDOCK & CO PLLC DALLAS T

LOCATIONS
HQ: STEVENS TRANSPORT, INC.
9757 MILITARY PKWY, DALLAS, TX 752274805
Phone: 972 216-9000
Web: WWW.STEVENSTRANSPORT.COM

PRODUCTS/OPERATIONS
Selected Services
Intermodal
International
Logistics
Truckload

COMPETITORS

A. DUIE PYLE INC.
ABF FREIGHT SYSTEM, INC.
C.R. ENGLAND, INC.
CASESTACK LLC
CELADON GROUP, INC.
KLLM TRANSPORT SERVICES, LLC
KNIGHT TRANSPORTATION, INC.
NEW PRIME, INC.
PATRIOT HOLDING CORP.
ROEHL TRANSPORT, INC.

HISTORICAL FINANCIALS
Company Type: Private

Income Statement — FYE: December 31

	REVENUE ($mil)	NET INCOME ($mil)	NET PROFIT MARGIN	EMPLOYEES
12/15	668	87	13.0%	2,100
12/12	607	85	14.0%	—
12/11	566	76	13.5%	—
12/08	550	0	0.0%	—
Annual Growth	2.8%	505.7%	—	—

2015 Year-End Financials
Return on assets: 13.0%   Cash ($ mil.): 152
Return on equity: 16.3%
Current Ratio: 4.60

STEWARD HEALTH CARE SYSTEM LLC

Steward Health Care System is the largest private, tax-paying hospital operator in the country. With a total of more than 7,900 beds, Steward Health operates about 40 hospitals in nine states and the country of Malta including Holy Family Hospital, Norwood Hospital, St. Elizabeth's Medical Center, St. Joseph's Medical Center, and Jordan Valley Medical Center. Several of the hospitals are affiliated with Boston-area medical schoolss. Steward Health serves its patients through a closely integrated network of hospitals, multispecialty medical groups, urgent care centers, skilled nursing facilities and behavioral health centers.

Operations

Steward Health is a community-based care organization that offers a full range of health care services. Its operations include integrated network physicians, about 40 hospital campuses, more than 25 affiliated urgent care providers, more than 105 preferred skilled nursing facilities, and other services.

The system's network includes Steward Health Care Network, Steward Medical Group, Steward Urgent Care and Steward Insurance Plans.

With more than 12 million patient encounters per year, Steward Health Care Network is comprised of physicians who provide care for approximately 2.2 million patients annually. Steward Medical Group provides more than 6 million patient encounters per year. Steward Urgent Care network includes multiple affiliated and owned urgent care centers. The network includes affiliations with Doctors Express, Prima CARE, Compass Medical, Hawthorn Medical, Health Express, All Care Medical, and others. The system also partners with Steward Health Choice, which covers approximately 680,000 lives in three states.

Geographic Reach

Headquartered in Dallas, Steward Health currently operates nearly 40 hospitals across Arizona, Arkansas, Florida, Louisiana, Massachusetts, Ohio, Pennsylvania, Texas, and Utah.

Sales and Marketing

Serving over 800 communities, Steward Health has more than 43,000 health care professionals who care for more than 12 million patients annually.

Company Background

The company changed its name from Caritas Christi to Steward Health after being acquired by Cerberus Capital Management in 2010; it had previously been operated by the Catholic Archdiocese of Boston. The acquisition by Cerberus was worth some $895 million and provided operational funding and capital for hospital improvement projects; it also helped pay down debt obligations. As a result of the transaction, Steward Health became a for-profit corporation; however, a stipulation of the deal mandated that the health system's hospitals retain their pastoral and charitable care policies. The sale to Cerberus was not the first attempt by the Archdiocese of Boston to sell the ailing Caritas Christi system, which had been suffering from financial troubles for several years prior to the deal.

LOCATIONS

HQ: STEWARD HEALTH CARE SYSTEM LLC
 1900 N PEARL ST STE 2400, DALLAS, TX 752012470
Phone: 469 341-8800
Web: WWW.STEWARD.ORG

Services
Behavioral Health Services
Centers for Cancer Care
Center for Advanced Cardiac Surgery
Centers for Cardiac and Vascular Care
Centers for Weight Control
Home Care and Hospice
MAKOplasty® Services
Maternity Services

Selected Hospitals

Arizona
 Mountain Vista Medical Center (Mesa)
 St. Luke's Medical Center (Phoenix)
 Tempe St. Luke's Hospital
Arkansas
 Wadley Regional Medical Center at Hope
Colorado
 Pikes Peak Regional Hospital & Surgery Center (Woodland Park)
Florida
 Rockledge Regional Medical Center
 Sebastian River Medical Center
Louisiana
 Glenwood Regional Medical Center (West Monroe)
Massachusetts
 Carney Hospital (Dorchester)
 Good Samaritan Medical Center (Brockton)
 Holy Family Hospital (Methuen)
 Morton Hospital (Taunton)
 Nashoba Valley Medical Center (Ayer)
 New England Sinai Hospital (Stoughton)
 Norwood Hospital
 Quincy Community Care Network
 Saint Anne's Hospital (Fall River)
 St. Elizabeth's Medical Center (Brighton)
Ohio
 Northside Regional Medical Center (Youngstown)
 Trumbull Regional Medical Center (Warren)
Pennsylvania
 Easton Hospital
 Sharon Regional Medical Center
Texas
 Southwest General Hospital (San Antonio)
 The Medical Center of Southeast Texas (Port Arthur)
 The Medical Center of Southeast Texas -- Victory Campus (Beaumont)
Utah
 Davis Hospital and Medical Center (Layton)
 Jordan Valley Medical Center (West Jordan)
 Mountain Point Medical Center (Lehi)

COMPETITORS

ALMOST FAMILY, INC.
AMEDISYS, INC.
ASCENSION HEALTH
GENTIVA HEALTH SERVICES, INC.
LEGACY LIFEPOINT HEALTH, INC.
LHC GROUP, INC.
OPTION CARE HEALTH, INC.
SISTERS OF CHARITY OF LEAVENWORTH HEALTH SYSTEM, INC.
ST. JOSEPH HEALTH SYSTEM
TIVITY HEALTH, INC.

HISTORICAL FINANCIALS

Company Type: Private

Income Statement — FYE: September 30

	REVENUE ($mil)	NET INCOME ($mil)	NET PROFIT MARGIN	EMPLOYEES
09/07	1,240	30	2.5%	37,000
09/06	1,220	47	3.9%	—
09/05	27	2	8.0%	—
Annual Growth	572.6%	272.9%	—	—

2007 Year-End Financials
Return on assets: 3.6%   Cash ($ mil.): 73
Return on equity: 10.8%
Current Ratio: 1.10

STEWART'S SHOPS CORP.

I scream, you scream, we all scream for Stewart's ice cream -- especially if we live in upstate New York or Vermont, home to some 330 Stewart's Shops. The chain of convenience stores sells more than 3,000 products across 30-plus counties. They include dairy items, groceries, food to go (soup, sandwiches, hot entrees), beer, coffee, gasoline, and, of course, ice cream. In addition to its retail business, the company owns about 100 rental properties, including banks, hair salons, and apartments, near its stores. Stewart's Shops, formerly known as Stewart's Ice Cream Company, was established in 1945. The founding Dake family owns about two-thirds of the company; employee compensation plans own the rest.

Operations

The convenience store chain, which spans New York and Vermont, offers consumers milk, ice creams, coffee, to-go foods, beer, gasoline, and groceries. As part of its business, Stewart's Shops also acquires and develops (preferably adjacent) properties the likes of shops, banks, hair salons, and apartments that it then leases or sells.

Stewart's Shops makes its own dairy products, including its ice cream in more than 50 flavors that are hand-dipped and packaged. Recognized for its quality products, the company relies on a group of about 45 farmers in New York to supply its milk.

The vertically-integrated company, which makes about 75% of the items it sells, also offers private-label goods and national brands in its stores. Its private-label brands extend far beyond dairy products to include soda, chips, bread, and juices.

Geographic Reach
Based in New York, Stewart's Shops operates a chain of convenience stores across upstate New York and in Vermont.

Sales and Marketing
Stewart's Shops serves consumers through its New York and Vermont shops; two-thirds of its stores sell gas.

Strategy
The convenience store operator regularly extends its reach. In 2014 it's focused on Syracuse, New York, following several store openings in 2013 in Keeseville, Herkimer, Rotterdam, and Heuvelton, New York. The latter shops boast an expanded cooler, walk-in beer cave, and seating.

The company is also investing in environmentally friendly facilities. In 2013, for instance, it had 2,400 solar panels installed at its manufacturing and distribution center. Stewart's Shops anticipates that the effort will save nearly $40,000 a year in energy costs at the plant after about a 5-year period.

It enlisted the help of Paragon Software in 2014 to automate the planning of daily and seasonal deliveries. In turn, Stewart's Shops aims to lower mileage, reduce fuel usage, and improve truckload efficiencies.

Auditors : BST & CO CPAS LLP ALBANY NEW

LOCATIONS
HQ: STEWART'S SHOPS CORP.
 2907 STATE ROUTE 9, BALLSTON SPA, NY 120204201
Phone: 518 581-1201
Web: WWW.STEWARTSSHOPS.COM

PRODUCTS/OPERATIONS
Selected Products
Beverages
Coffee
Ice Cream
Food to go
Gasoline
Groceries
Milk

COMPETITORS
GPM INVESTMENTS, LLC
HOLIDAY COMPANIES
HOUCHENS INDUSTRIES, INC.
RED APPLE GROUP, INC.
SHEETZ, INC.
THE FRESH MARKET INC
THE JONES COMPANY
THE SPINX COMPANY LLC
TOWN PUMP, INC.
WEGMANS FOOD MARKETS, INC.

HISTORICAL FINANCIALS
Company Type: Private

Income Statement — FYE: January 2

	REVENUE ($mil)	NET INCOME ($mil)	NET PROFIT MARGIN	EMPLOYEES
01/22	2,164	164	7.6%	5,500
01/21*	1,667	166	10.0%	—
12/19	1,699	124	7.3%	—
12/17	1,542	92	6.0%	—
Annual Growth	8.8%	15.3%	—	—

*Fiscal year change

2022 Year-End Financials
Return on assets: 17.4%   Cash ($ mil.): 114
Return on equity: 22.2%
Current Ratio: 4.00

STILLWATER MINING COMPANY

Stillwater Mining has staked a claim to one of the few significant sources of platinum and palladium outside South Africa and Russia. The company extracts, processes, and refines platinum group metals (PGMs) -- platinum, palladium, and associated minerals -- at mines and a smelter in Montana. PGMs are used in catalytic converters for automobiles, as well as in jewelry and other applications. Stillwater Mining also owns exploratory properties of PGM and copper in Canada and copper and gold in Argentina. It produces about 404,000 ounces of palladium and 120,000 ounces of platinum annually. By-products include copper, gold, nickel, and silver. In 2016 Sibanye Gold bid $2.2 billion to buy the company.

Operations
Stillwater produces palladium, platinum, and associated metals (PGMs) through two segments: PGM Recycling (54% of sales) and Mine Production (46%).

The company operates the Stillwater and East boulder mines in Montana, as well as concentrating plants at both sites to upgrade ore to a concentrate. In addition, it operates a smelter, refinery, and laboratory in Columbus, Montana, to refine the concentrate to a PGM-rich filter cake. It also recycles spent catalyst material at the smelter and refinery to recover PGMs.

In addition to its producing mines, Stillwater holds the Blitz and Graham Creek development projects in Montana. It also owns a PGM-copper deposit in Ontario, Canada, which is in the permitting process, as well as the Altar porphyry copper-gold deposit in Argentina.

Financial Performance
Increased metal prices worldwide boosted Stillwater's revenues to $1.04 billion in 2013, up 30% from the previous year. Stillwater's PGM Recycling segment revenue increased due to a spike in recycling ounces sold and an increase in combined average realization on recycling sales.

However, after posting net income of $55 million in 2012, Stillwater suffered a net loss of $270 million in 2013. This was due to a large impairment charge of $461 million it paid in 2013 related to properties in Argentina and Marathon (in Ontario, Canada). Stillwater saw an increase of $46 million in operating cash flow from 2012 to 2013 due to higher prices for its products.

EXECUTIVES
Vice President Safety Health & Human Resources*, Kristen K Koss
Mine Operations Vice President*, Dee L Bray
Auditors : KPMG LLP BILLINGS MONTANA

LOCATIONS
HQ: STILLWATER MINING COMPANY
 536 E PIKE AVE, COLUMBUS, MT 590197616
Phone: 406 373-8700
Web: WWW.SIBANYESTILLWATER.COM

PRODUCTS/OPERATIONS
2016 Sales

	$ mil.	% of total
Mine production	405.0	57
PGM recycling	305.9	43
All others	0.4	-
Total	711.3	100

2016 Sales

	$ mil.	% of total
Palladium	410.6	58
Platinum	247.0	35
Rhodium	21.2	3
Other minerals	32.5	4
Total	711.3	100

COMPETITORS
ANGLO PACIFIC GROUP PLC
BARRICK TZ LIMITED
BHP GROUP PLC
COEUR MINING, INC.
Kinross Gold Corporation
Nexa Resources
POLYMETAL INTERNATIONAL PLC
RIO TINTO PLC
VEDANTA RESOURCES LIMITED
WEATHERLY INTERNATIONAL PUBLIC LIMITED COMPANY

HISTORICAL FINANCIALS
Company Type: Private

Income Statement — FYE: December 31

	REVENUE ($mil)	NET INCOME ($mil)	NET PROFIT MARGIN	EMPLOYEES
12/15	726	(23)	—	1,432
12/14	943	68	7.3%	—
12/13	1,039	(302)	—	—
Annual Growth	(16.4%)	—	—	—

2015 Year-End Financials
Return on assets: (-1.9%)   Cash ($ mil.): 147
Return on equity: (-2.6%)
Current Ratio: 8.70

STOCKTON UNIFIED SCHOOL DISTRICT

Auditors : CROWE LLP SACRAMENTO CALIFOR

LOCATIONS
HQ: STOCKTON UNIFIED SCHOOL DISTRICT
 56 S LINCOLN ST, STOCKTON, CA 952033100
Phone: 209 933-7000
Web: WWW.STOCKTONUSD.NET

HISTORICAL FINANCIALS
Company Type: Private

Income Statement — FYE: June 30

	REVENUE ($mil)	NET INCOME ($mil)	NET PROFIT MARGIN	EMPLOYEES
06/21	709	54	7.7%	3,000
06/20	618	(22)	—	—
06/19	602	8	1.3%	—
06/18	536	(24)	—	—
Annual Growth	9.8%	—	—	—

2021 Year-End Financials
Return on assets: 4.0%   Cash ($ mil.): —
Return on equity: 137.3%
Current Ratio: —

STORMONT-VAIL HEALTHCARE, INC.

EXECUTIVES

Medical Service Division Vice President*, Deb Yocum
Patient Care Services Vice President*, Carol Perry
Faculty Management Vice-President*, David Cuningham
Chief Compliance Officer*, Kevin Steck
Auditors : RSM US LLP DAVENPORT IOWA

LOCATIONS

HQ: STORMONT-VAIL HEALTHCARE, INC.
1500 SW 10TH AVE, TOPEKA, KS 666041301
Phone: 785 354-6000
Web: WWW.STORMONTVAIL.ORG

HISTORICAL FINANCIALS
Company Type: Private

Income Statement — FYE: September 30

	REVENUE ($mil)	NET INCOME ($mil)	NET PROFIT MARGIN	EMPLOYEES
09/21	872	123	14.2%	4,500
09/20	784	56	7.2%	—
09/19	768	34	4.4%	—
09/18	719	88	12.4%	—
Annual Growth	6.6%	11.6%	—	—

2021 Year-End Financials
Return on assets: 10.8%   Cash ($ mil.): 202
Return on equity: 16.9%
Current Ratio: 2.10

STRACK AND VAN TIL SUPER MARKET INC.

One of Chicagoland's leading grocery chains, Strack & Van Til operates more than 35 supermarkets in and around Chicago and northern Indiana. Stores operate under the banners of Strack & Van Til, Town & Country Food Market, and Ultra Foods. The regional grocery chain offers fresh and packaged foods and has delicatessen and bakery divisions in each of its stores. Its websites offer weekly circulars and coupons, as well as feature recipes, cooking videos, meal planners, and food-related articles. The company is owned by Chicago-based grocery distributor Central Grocers, which also operates supermarkets under the Berkot's and Key Market banners. In 2017 Central Grocers filed for Chapter 11 bankruptcy protection and put Strack & Van Til up for sale as part of the filing.

Strategy

Strack & Van Til and its regional rivals are facing increased competition from national chains, including Wal-Mart and Trader Joe's, moving into the market, while taking advantage of the woes of smaller ones. Rather than retreat, the grocery chain is pursuing a growth strategy, acquiring seven stores in its market area in late 2012. (With Safeway-owned Dominick's Supermarkets on the block, its stores are in play.) It is also investing in its existing stores and stocking more organic foods, to compete with the likes of Whole Foods. The company is revamping supermarkets in Valpariso, Hobart, and Chesterton, was well as an Ultra Foods store in Highland, Strack's supermarkets in Munster and Schereville, and an Ultra in Lansing, are slated for upgrades as well.

Wal-Mart, which had been expanding aggressively in the Chicago suburbs, has begun opening supercenters and smaller Walmart Express stores within the city limits. Its arrival has sparked fierce price competition among area grocers. Other relative newcomers to the Illinois grocery market include Roundy's, and non-traditional grocery chains, such as SuperTarget stores and limited-assortment ALDI. To take on nationwide retailers, Strack & Van Til bands together with other independent stores as members of the Central Grocers cooperative. The combined buying power helps the stores to offer competitive pricing and product selection.

In late 2013 the grocery chain launched a new marketing campaign, I'm a Strack & Van Til Shopper , to appeal to a wide audience while maintaining the company's value proposition.

Mergers and Acquisitions

In December 2012 Strack & Van Til acquired seven grocery stores from Indiana-based WiseWay Supermarkets. Four of the stores were converted to the Strack & Van Til banner, while three became Ultra Foods stores. Like Strack & Van Til, WiseWay was also supplied by Central Grocers.

Auditors : MCGLADREY & PULLEN LLP CHICAG

LOCATIONS

HQ: STRACK AND VAN TIL SUPER MARKET INC.
2244 45TH ST, HIGHLAND, IN 463222629
Phone: 219 924-7588
Web: WWW.STRACKANDVANTIL.COM

COMPETITORS
D'AGOSTINO SUPERMARKETS, INC.
DIERBERGS MARKETS, INC.
GRISTEDE'S FOODS, INC.
SUPER CENTER CONCEPTS, INC.
UNITED SUPERMARKETS, L.L.C.

HISTORICAL FINANCIALS
Company Type: Private

Income Statement — FYE: August 1

	REVENUE ($mil)	NET INCOME ($mil)	NET PROFIT MARGIN	EMPLOYEES
08/10	961	15	1.7%	2,000
08/09	995	13	1.4%	—
Annual Growth	(3.4%)	16.1%	—	—

2010 Year-End Financials
Return on assets: 7.7%   Cash ($ mil.): 10
Return on equity: 12.9%
Current Ratio: 1.40

SUASIN CANCER CARE INC.

Auditors : ERNST & YOUNG US LLP SAN DIEG

LOCATIONS

HQ: SUASIN CANCER CARE INC.
1301 PUNCHBOWL ST, HONOLULU, HI 968132402
Phone: 512 583-0205

HISTORICAL FINANCIALS
Company Type: Private

Income Statement — FYE: June 30

	REVENUE ($mil)	NET INCOME ($mil)	NET PROFIT MARGIN	EMPLOYEES
06/15	1,003	50	5.0%	4
06/14	851	31	3.7%	—
06/13	856	109	12.8%	—
Annual Growth	8.2%	(32.4%)	—	—

2015 Year-End Financials
Return on assets: 3.4%   Cash ($ mil.): 29
Return on equity: 7.9%
Current Ratio: 0.30

SUFFOLK CONSTRUCTION COMPANY, INC.

Suffolk Construction Company provides construction services from top to bottom. The company kicks off the building process with pre-construction services and follows through with design/build, and construction management. Suffolk Construction builds for both the public and private organizations in the science and technology, health care, education, government, and commercial sectors, operating in the Northeast, South, and West Coast regions of the US. Founded in 1982, the privately-held firm is owned by president and CEO John Fish, whose family has been in construction for four generations.

Operations
Suffolk Construction provides value throughout the entire project lifecycle by leveraging its core construction management services with vertical service lines that include real estate capital investment, design, self-perform construction services, technology start-up investment, and innovation research/development. Some projects have included 78 Haight housing development in San Francisco, a ground-up construction of Agua Caliente Casino Resort & Spa, luxury boutique hotel Alila Marea Beach Resort, and the construction of construction of two modern hotel Aloft and Element Hotels on D Street.

Geographic Reach
Boston-based Suffolk Construction operates nationwide across the Northeast, South, and West Coast regions.

Sales and Marketing
Suffolk Construction offers its services for projects in the assisted living, aviation and transportation, commercial, education, entertainment, government, healthcare, hospitality, non-profit, residential, retail, and science and technology sectors.

The company has also worked on projects for federal and local governments. In the past, Suffolk has built for the Army Corps of Engineers, the US Marine Corps, and US Navy.

Company Background
Already a successful builder in the New England area, Suffolk Construction has expanded nationally in the past through acquisitions. In 2009, it bought Massachusetts-based William A. Berry & Son, creating Suffolk's Berry Division, which specializes in health care and biomedical projects.

Suffolk Construction also acquired The Dietze Construction Group based in Ashburn, Virginia, in 2010. The deal strengthened Suffolk's position in the Mid-Atlantic region and expanded its ability to serve the government, health care, education, science/technology, and commercial sectors. Giving the company a boost in the West, Suffolk Construction acquired Southern California-based ROEL Construction in 2011.

EXECUTIVES
CMO*, Lea Stendahl

LOCATIONS
HQ: SUFFOLK CONSTRUCTION COMPANY, INC.
 65 ALLERTON ST, BOSTON, MA 021192923
Phone: 617 445-3500
Web: WWW.SUFFOLK.COM

PRODUCTS/OPERATIONS
Selected Services
Building information modeling
Construction management
Design/build
General contracting
Preconstruction
Sustainable building

COMPETITORS
BECK INTERNATIONAL, LLC
DOSTER CONSTRUCTION COMPANY, INC.
GILBANE BUILDING COMPANY
GILBANE, INC.
HENSEL PHELPS CONSTRUCTION CO.
LECHASE CONSTRUCTION SERVICES, LLC
SWINERTON INCORPORATED
THE HASKELL COMPANY
THE PIKE COMPANY INC
THE WEITZ COMPANY LLC

HISTORICAL FINANCIALS
Company Type: Private

Income Statement   FYE: August 31

	REVENUE ($mil)	NET INCOME ($mil)	NET PROFIT MARGIN	EMPLOYEES
08/15	2,500	0	0.0%	2,536
08/14	1,761	0	0.0%	—
08/13	1,825	0	0.0%	—
Annual Growth	17.0%	—	—	—

2015 Year-End Financials
Return on assets: —   Cash ($ mil.): 126
Return on equity: —
Current Ratio: 1.10

SUMMA HEALTH SYSTEM

Summa Health is one of the largest integrated healthcare delivery systems in the state. Formed in 1989 with the merger of Akron City and St. Thomas Hospitals, this nonprofit system now encompasses a network of hospitals, community-based health centers, a health plan, a multi-specialty group practice, an accountable care organization, research and medical education, and a foundation. Summa serves more than one million patients each year in comprehensive acute, critical, emergency, outpatient and long-term/home care settings. Outpatient care is extended throughout Summit, Portage and Medina counties in multiple community health centers.

Operations
Summa Health has more than 1,300 licensed beds at at Summa Health System ? Akron, Barberton and St. Thomas campuses and Summa Rehab Hospital.

Geographic Reach
Akron-based Summa Health serves customers in five counties in northeastern Ohio.

Financial Performance
Summa reported revenues of about $1.6 billion in 2012. The organization estimates that it makes a $2.8 billion business impact on the Ohio economy, as well as a $99 million impact on the state government's revenue.

Strategy
Summa has conducted growth efforts in recent years to expand its presence and service offerings in the region through organic growth efforts and partnership formations. For instance, the organization opened a new Summa Rehab Hospital through a partnership with Vibra; the $25 million facility consists of a 70,000-sq. ft. freestanding medical building. The Summa network also invested in expanding new emergency care clinics in Green and Medina, and it consolidated its home health and hospice organizations to improve profitability.

Also in 2012, Summa formed a joint management services organization with two affiliated physician organizations: Community Health Care and Pioneer Physicians Network. Together the organizations aim to streamline clinical processes.

In 2013 Summa also entered talks to form a partnership with hospital group Catholic Health Partners (CHP). The strategic partnership would give CHP a minority stake in the Summa network. Through the deal, Summa hopes to expand its strategic initiatives and strengthen its finances.

Summa invests heavily in the latest technology, continually seeking out the latest treatment options for some of today's most serious medical conditions.

Company Background
The company was formed in 1989 through the merger of Akron City Hospital and St. Thomas Hospital.

EXECUTIVES
CIO, Tanya Arthur
Auditors: RSM US LLP CLEVELAND OHIO

LOCATIONS
HQ: SUMMA HEALTH SYSTEM
 1077 GORGE BLVD, AKRON, OH 443102408
Phone: 330 375-3000
Web: WWW.SUMMAHEALTH.ORG

PRODUCTS/OPERATIONS
2012 Payers

	% of total
Medicare	47
Commercial/Managed care/Other	31
Medicaid	15
Self-pay	7
Total	100

Selected Ohio Facilities
Hospitals
 Akron City Hospital (Akron)
 Barberton Hospital (Barberton)
 Cuyahoga Falls General Hospital (aka Western Reserve Hospital, Cuyahoga Falls)
 Robinson Memorial Hospital (affiliate, Ravenna)
 St. Thomas Hospital (Akron)
 Wadsworth-Rittman Hospital (Wadsworth)
Other facilities
 Crystal Clinic Orthopaedic Center (Akron)

Natatorium Rehabilitation and Wellness Center (Cuyahoga Falls)
Summa Health Center at Cuyahoga Falls (Cuyahoga Falls)
Summa Health Center at Green (Uniontown)
Summa Health Center at Lake Medina
Summa Health Center at Western Reserve (Hudson)
Summa Health Center at White Pond/Park West (Akron)
Summa Rehabilitation Services at White Pond (Akron)
Summa Wellness Institute at Western Reserve (Hudson)
Specialty Surgery Center (Akron)

COMPETITORS

ADVOCATE AURORA HEALTH, INC.
ADVOCATE HEALTH CARE NETWORK
BEAUMONT HEALTH
DUKE UNIVERSITY HEALTH SYSTEM, INC.
MASS GENERAL BRIGHAM INCORPORATED
MERCY HEALTH
NASSAU HEALTH CARE CORPORATION
NORTHWELL HEALTH, INC.
UNIVERSITY HEALTH SYSTEMS OF EASTERN CAROLINA, INC.
UNIVERSITY HOSPITALS HEALTH SYSTEM, INC.

HISTORICAL FINANCIALS
Company Type: Private

Income Statement — FYE: December 31

	REVENUE ($mil)	NET INCOME ($mil)	NET PROFIT MARGIN	EMPLOYEES
12/21	1,668	163	9.8%	7,431
12/20	1,462	(208)	—	—
12/09	168	6	3.8%	—
12/08	1,264	(75)	—	—
Annual Growth	2.2%	—	—	—

2021 Year-End Financials
Return on assets: 7.0% Cash ($ mil.): 104
Return on equity: 15.1%
Current Ratio: 1.30

SUN COAST RESOURCES, INC.

Sun Coast Resources, Inc. is one of the largest wholesale petroleum marketers in the nation. Licensed in over 50 states with 18 locations in Texas, Oklahoma, and Louisiana, the company offer a vast array of products and services. The company has an extensive truck fleet (more than 1,000 vehicles) and delivers gasoline and diesel fuels, marine and aviation fuels, and lubricants. It also provides oilfield transportation and services, onsite and fleet fueling, petroleum tanks, and generator fueling services. Sun Coast was founded in 1985 by president and CEO Kathy Lehne.

Operations

Sun Coast carries a full line of Chevron oils and lubricants and is one of Chevron's largest lubricant distributors in the US. Other Sun Coast services include additive packages, bulk storage and warehousing, a computerized fleet tracking system, and customized schedule and deliveries. The company has of bulk fuel storage, fuel and lubricant tanks, including skid tanks, aviation certified tanks, emergency ISO tanks, and others. Its truck fleet includes bobtails, lowboys, lube trucks, pick-ups, roll-backs, and vacuum trucks.

Its transport trucks are capable of hauling approximately 7,500 gallons of diesel fuel, and approximately 8,600 gallons of gasoline. Sun Coast's lubricant trucks are capable of hauling bulk lubricants as well as drums, totes and other packaged products.

The company's products include aviation gasoline (avgas), gasoline, jet fuel, kerosene, marine diesel, ultra-low sulfur diesel fuel, and Chevron, Conoco, Mystik, Royal Purple, 76, and TOTAL lubrication products. It also offers services card lock service, filtration and fluid purification, fleet fueling and mobile on-site fueling, spill response, and other services.

Geographic Reach

Sun Coast owns and operates more than 15 offices in Arkansas, New Mexico, Mississippi, Oklahoma, Texas, and Louisiana. It markets its products over 50 US states.

Sales and Marketing

Sun Coast Resources, Inc. supplies Chevron, ConocoPhillips, CITGO, Mystik, Royal Purple, 76, Meropa and TOTAL lubricants to oil and gas operators across the country.

Company Background

It expanded into Louisiana in 2012 with the purchase of St. Martin Oil and Gas, which operated a small fleet of fuel transportation trucks from two bulk storage facilities in St. Martinville and Denham Springs.

Further expanding its portfolio, in 2012 the company acquired assets from bankrupt SMF Energy, including its wholly owned affiliate H&W Petroleum Co. Properties included more than 100 fuel trucks and support vehicles previously used by SMF's mobile refueling operations outside of Texas, and about 100 fuel and chemical transportation and support vehicles from H&W, its Lufkin blending facility, and fuel storage tanks across Texas.

That year Sun Coast further expanded its branded and unbranded fuel and lubricant distribution business by buying Houston-based ADA Resources.

In 2011 the company bought the commercial fuel and disaster response businesses of Cypress, Texas-based Roy Moffitt Customized Fueling.

LOCATIONS

HQ: SUN COAST RESOURCES, INC.
6405 CAVALCADE ST BLDG 1, HOUSTON, TX 770264315
Phone: 713 844-9600
Web: WWW.SUNCOASTRESOURCES.COM

PRODUCTS/OPERATIONS

Selected Products
Petroleum Products
  Aviation gasoline
  High sulfur diesel fuel
  Jet fuel
  Kerosene
  Lubricants
  Marine fuels
  Mid-grade fuel
  Low sulfur diesel fuel
  Premium low sulfur diesel fuel
  Premium unleaded gasoline
  Unleaded gasoline
Oils and Lubricants
  Automatic transmission fluid
  Chain oils
  Food-grade oils
  Fuel Additives
  Gear oils
  Greases
  Heat transfer oils
  Hydraulic oils
  Metal-working oils
  Motor oils
  Refrigeration oils
  Solvents and chemicals

Selected Mergers and Acquisitions
2012
St. Martin Oil and Gas (Louisiana; fuel transportation and storage)
SMF Energy (fuel trucks and support vehicles)
ADA Resources (Houston, Texas; branded and unbranded fuel and lubricant distribution)
2011
Roy Moffitt Customized Fueling (Cypress, Texas; Commercial fuel and disaster response businesses)

COMPETITORS

BENIT FUEL SALES & SERVICE INC.
COMPANHIA BRASILEIRA DE PETROLEO IPIRANGA
CRYSTAL FLASH, INC.
LIQUID TRANSPORT CORP.
MANSFIELD OIL COMPANY OF GAINESVILLE, INC.
PAKISTAN STATE OIL COMPANY LIMITED
SOUTHERN COUNTIES OIL CO.
TRANSMONTAIGNE LLC
TRUMAN ARNOLD COMPANIES
U.S. VENTURE, INC.

HISTORICAL FINANCIALS
Company Type: Private

Income Statement — FYE: December 31

	REVENUE ($mil)	NET INCOME ($mil)	NET PROFIT MARGIN	EMPLOYEES
12/07	1,064	2	0.3%	1,649
12/06	864	7	0.8%	—
12/05	867	13	1.6%	—
12/04	697	3	0.4%	—
Annual Growth	15.1%	(2.7%)	—	—

2007 Year-End Financials
Return on assets: 2.3% Cash ($ mil.): —
Return on equity: 13.4%
Current Ratio: 3.30

SUN MAR MANAGEMENT SERVICES

LOCATIONS
HQ: SUN MAR MANAGEMENT SERVICES
3050 SATURN ST STE 201, BREA, CA 928216278
Phone: 714 577-3880

HISTORICAL FINANCIALS
Company Type: Private

Income Statement				FYE: March 31
	REVENUE ($mil)	NET INCOME ($mil)	NET PROFIT MARGIN	EMPLOYEES
03/09*	742	0	0.1%	500
12/08	6	(0)	—	—
Annual Growth	—	—	—	—

*Fiscal year change

2009 Year-End Financials
Return on assets: 73.9%   Cash ($ mil.): —
Return on equity: —
Current Ratio: 0.80

SUN VALLEY ENERGY, INC.

EXECUTIVES
Managing Member, Margaret Nivens
Auditors: BATES CARTER & CO LLP GAINES

LOCATIONS
HQ: SUN VALLEY ENERGY, INC.
1181 ESTATES DR, GAINESVILLE, GA 305011803
Phone: 770 540-3935

HISTORICAL FINANCIALS
Company Type: Private

Income Statement				FYE: December 31
	REVENUE ($mil)	NET INCOME ($mil)	NET PROFIT MARGIN	EMPLOYEES
12/21	575	0	0.1%	3
12/20	326	0	0.2%	—
Annual Growth	76.2%	(15.0%)	—	—

2021 Year-End Financials
Return on assets: 8.9%   Cash ($ mil.): 4
Return on equity: 16.3%
Current Ratio: 2.20

SUNDT CONSTRUCTION, INC.

Auditors: MAYER HOFFMAN & MCCANN

LOCATIONS
HQ: SUNDT CONSTRUCTION, INC.
2620 S 55TH ST, TEMPE, AZ 852821903
Phone: 480 293-3000
Web: WWW.SUNDT.COM

HISTORICAL FINANCIALS
Company Type: Private

Income Statement				FYE: September 30
	REVENUE ($mil)	NET INCOME ($mil)	NET PROFIT MARGIN	EMPLOYEES
09/18	1,432	0	0.0%	1,000
09/17	1,134	0	0.0%	—
09/16	813	0	0.0%	—
09/13	895	0	0.0%	—
Annual Growth	9.8%	—	—	—

2018 Year-End Financials
Return on assets: —   Cash ($ mil.): 140
Return on equity: —
Current Ratio: 1.70

SUNKIST GROWERS, INC.

Sunkist Growers is one business that is least susceptible to an outbreak of scurvy among its employees. America's oldest continually operating citrus cooperative, the company is owned by California and Arizona citrus growers who farm some 300,000 acres of citrus trees. Sunkist offers traditional and organic fresh oranges, lemons, limes, grapefruit, and tangerines worldwide. The co-op, which operates some 20 packing facilities, also makes juice and cut fruit packaged in jars. Fruit that doesn't meet fresh market standards is turned into oils and peels for use in food products made by other manufacturers. Sunkist's customers include food retailers and manufacturers and foodservice providers worldwide.

Operations
The cooperative's seasonal citrus includes Meyer lemons, mandarin oranges, Clementine oranges, blood oranges, and tangelos. Sunkist is one of the most recognized brand names in the world.

Through some 40 licensing agreements, the Sunkist name appears on more than 600 beverages and other products -- from vitamins to candy to soda to pistachios. It offers Sunkist Fruit Gems (gummie candies), made for the company by the Jelly Belly Candy Company.

Some 45% of Sunkist's fresh fruit sales revenues come from markets outside the US, as well as more than 20% of its processed products revenues. To maintain its reach abroad, Sunkist works with the US government and the governments of foreign countries to open new markets that are off limits to Western citrus growers.

Geographic Reach
California-based Sunkist operates in the Americas, Europe, the Middle East, and Asia Pacific.

Sales and Marketing
Sunkist regularly advertises worldwide to encourage use of its citrus products and build its brand. Additionally, the company leverages television to get its name out, such as its alliance with the NBC motivational weight loss competition The Biggest Loser.

Sunkist, which has operated a centralized sales organization since 2009, sells its products primarily to food retailers and manufacturers, as well as to foodservice providers worldwide. The company is the largest marketing cooperative in the global fruit and vegetable industry.

Financial Performance
Gross annual sales of Sunkist-brand products exceed $1.2 billion worldwide.

Strategy
The company has been focused on market and portfolio expansion and getting the most from its citrus juice and oils and for-profit businesses. It is working to extend its reach to new markets, such as India, the Middle East, and Eastern Europe, where its core product has not historically been traded. To reach beyond citrus and expand its products portfolio, Sunkist is concentrating on table grapes. Through a pilot program with its existing citrus growers, the company markets Sunkist-branded California table grapes grown by them.

It also worked in recent years to improve the productivity of its Tipton juice processing plant. To this end, Sunkist in 2012 entered a 50:50 joint venture agreement with fellow juice processor Ventura Coastal. Under the name Ventura Coastal LLC, the entity operates the Ventura Coastal plant in Visalia and the Sunkist plant in Tipton. Beginning in 2013 Sunkist also partnered with Greene River Marketing to sell its Florida citrus in promising domestic and export markets.

The 2011-2012 growing season got off to a late start, thanks to slow maturing fruit. Its navel orange crop grew to a manageable 88 million cartons as compared to a challenging 93-million-carton crop the previous year. Lemons started slowly, as well, but both demand and price picked up. Protected groves fared well during the year while unprotected ones -- those outside the traditional growing areas -- did not. More susceptible to the cold, mandarins crops have suffered.

HISTORY

Sunkist Growers was founded in the early 1890s as the Pachappa Orange Growers, a group of California citrus farmers determined to control the sale of their fruit. Success attracted new members, and in 1893 the Southern California Fruit Exchange was born. The name "Sunkissed" was coined by an ad copywriter in 1908, and it was soon reworked into "Sunkist" and registered as a trademark, becoming the first brand name for a fresh produce item. Eventually the co-op renamed itself after its popular brand: It became Sunkist Growers in 1952. Sunkist began licensing its trademark to other companies in the early 1950s.

As early as 1916, efforts to increase citrus consumption included designing and marketing glass citrus juicers and encouraging homemakers to "Drink an Orange." The co-op also promoted the practice of putting lemon slices in tea or water and funded early research on the health benefits of vitamins (vitamin C in particular). In 1925 tissue wrappers gave way to stamping the Sunkist name directly on each piece of fruit.

Although Sunkist pioneered bottled orange juice in 1933, its juice marketing efforts were never as successful as those of its Florida competitors. Florida oranges are drippy and dowdy and thus better suited for juicing. Capitalizing on this aspect, Florida growers dominated the market for fresh and frozen juice.

In 1937 Congress created a system of citrus shipment quotas and limits (known as "marketing orders") that ultimately proved most beneficial to large citrus cooperatives. By the early 1990s the marketing order system was under political attack, and in 1992 the Justice Department filed civil prosecution against Sunkist, alleging that the co-op had reaped unfair extra profits by surpassing its lemon shipment limits. In 1994, after much legal wrangling, the quotas were abolished and the Justice Department dropped its case against Sunkist.

Inconveniently warm weather and increasing competition from imported citrus marked the harvests of 1996. That year the co-op had trouble maintaining discipline among its members; some undercut Sunkist price levels, while others flooded the market to sell their fruit at the higher early market prices, creating a supply surplus. Also that year the co-op relinquished the marketing of all Sunkist juices in North America to Florida-based Lykes Bros. in a licensing agreement.

The co-op agreed in 1998 to distribute grapefruit from Florida's Tuxedo Fruit, providing Sunkist with a winter grapefruit supply and increasing its year-round consumer a-peel. Also in 1998 Russell Hanlin, Sunkist president and CEO since 1978, was succeeded by Vince Lupinacci. Lupinacci, who had held positions with Pepsi and Six Flags, became the first person from outside the citrus business to hold Sunkist's top post.

In 1998 the company sold 90 million cartons of fresh citrus -- the greatest volume in its history -- despite increased competition from imported Latin American, South African, and Spanish crops, a damaging California freeze, and the ill effects of El NiÃ±o . The next year production was almost halved because of adverse weather.

Lupinacci resigned in 2000, citing personal and family reasons. Chairman emeritus James Mast then took the helm as acting president. Although the company grew its market through exports to China in 2000, its profits were squeezed that year by increasing foreign competition, a citrus glut, and lessened demand. In mid-2001 Jeff Gargiulo replaced Mast as Sunkist's president and CEO.

In 2003 Sunkist formed a joint venture with strawberry shipper Coastal Berry Co. to market strawberries under the Sunkist label year-round. (Coastal Berry's president and CEO John Gargiulo and Sunkist's former president and CEO Jeff Gargiulo are brothers.) Also that year, Sunkist began offering pre-cut bagged fruit to retail customers and restaurants in order to keep up with a changing market and consumer demand.

In retrospect, 2006 was an eventful year for Sunkist. The co-op's largest producer and 16-year-member Paramount Citrus Association left the organization. In addition, chairman and CEO David Krause stepped down and president Jeff Gargiulo left the company. Krause was replaced as chairman by Nicholas Bozick, president of produce grower/packer Richard Bagdasarian, Inc. Sunkist veteran and former president of Fruit Growers Supply Company, Timothy Lindgren was appointed president and CEO. And, citing expense as the determining factor, the co-op discontinued marketing berries (strawberries, blueberries, and raspberries) in 2006. Lindgren retired in 2008; he was replaced by EVP Russ Hanlin.

Auditors : MOSS ADAM LLP STOCKTON CALIF

LOCATIONS

HQ: SUNKIST GROWERS, INC.
27770 ENTERTAINMENT DR, VALENCIA, CA 913551092
Phone: 661 290-8900
Web: WWW.SUNKIST.COM

PRODUCTS/OPERATIONS

Selected Products
Fresh fruit
  Grapefruit
    Melo Golds
    Oro Blancos
    Pummelos
    Sweeties
    Texas Rio Star
    Western
  Lemons
    Eurkea/Lisbon
    Meyer
  Limes
    Key
    Persian
  Mandarins
    Clementine
    Honey
    Royal
    Satsuma
    Shasta Gold
  W. Murcott
  Oranges
    Cara Cara
    Moro
    Navel
    Valencia
  Tangelos
    Minneola
    Orlando
  Tangerines
    Dancy
    Fairchild
    Pixie
Packaged fruit
  Beverage concentrates
  Carbonated beverages (under license)
  Chilled fruit jellies (under license)
  Fruit juice
  Fruit juice drinks
  Fruit snacks (under license)
  Powdered fruit drinks
  Vitamins (under license)

COMPETITORS

DOLE FOOD COMPANY, INC.
DOVEX FRUIT COMPANY
FRESH KIST PRODUCE, LLC
FYFFES LIMITED
GRIMMWAY ENTERPRISES, INC.
JACK BROWN PRODUCE, INC.
MAYRSOHN INTERNATIONAL TRADING CO., INC.
NATIONAL GRAPE CO-OPERATIVE ASSOCIATION, INC.
Oppenheimer, David and Company I, LLC
THE WONDERFUL COMPANY LLC

HISTORICAL FINANCIALS

Company Type: Private

Income Statement   FYE: October 31

	REVENUE ($mil)	NET INCOME ($mil)	NET PROFIT MARGIN	EMPLOYEES
10/18	1,359	2	0.2%	500
10/17	1,299	9	0.7%	—
10/16	1,207	7	0.6%	—
Annual Growth	6.1%	(37.6%)	—	—

2018 Year-End Financials
Return on assets: 1.2%   Cash ($ mil.): 31
Return on equity: 2.0%
Current Ratio: 1.40

SUNOCO PIPELINE L.P.

LOCATIONS

HQ: SUNOCO PIPELINE L.P.
4041 MARKET ST, UPPER CHICHESTER, PA 190143121
Phone: 610 859-5700

HISTORICAL FINANCIALS
Company Type: Private

Income Statement   FYE: December 31

	REVENUE ($mil)	NET INCOME ($mil)	NET PROFIT MARGIN	EMPLOYEES
12/17	804	1,419	176.6%	6
12/16	1,070	796	74.4%	—
Annual Growth	(24.9%)	78.2%	—	—

2017 Year-End Financials
Return on assets: 17.6%   Cash ($ mil.): —
Return on equity: 19.8%
Current Ratio: 0.10

SUNTORY INTERNATIONAL

Suntory USA, established in the 1960s on the other side of the globe from its parent, Japanese trading giant Suntory Holdings Limited, imports Suntory products to the US market from its New York headquarters. Well-known offerings include wine, beer, and distilled spirits, such as Yamazaki Single Malt Whisky and Zen Green Tea and Midori Melon liqueurs. Other operations handled by Suntory USA include a soft drink bottling business (Pepsi Bottling Ventures), a winery, various restaurants, and its parent's bottled water division, Suntory Water Group, once the second-largest bottled water producer in the US. Altogether, Suntory USA comprises 17 companies, contributing 4% of its parent's 2013 revenue.

Auditors : PRICEWATERHOUSECOOPERS LLP NE

LOCATIONS
HQ: SUNTORY INTERNATIONAL
4141 PARKLAKE AVE STE 600, RALEIGH, NC 276122380
Phone: 917 756-2747

PRODUCTS/OPERATIONS
Selected Products & Brands
Beer & Happoshu
  Diet Draft Happoshu
  Hop's Draft Happoshu
  Jokki Beer
  Kinmugi Beer
  Magnum Dry Happoshu
  Malt's Beer
  The Premium Malt's Beer
Cocktails
  Calori
  Cocktail Bar
  Cocktail Calori
  Ginza Cocktail
  Super Chu-hi
Distilled Spirits
  Barley Shochu Wanko
  Daijuhyo Ko-rui Shochu
  HAKUSHU Blended Whiskey
  Hanauta Shochu Nanco
  HIBIKI Blended Whiskey
  KAKUGBIN Whiskey
  Ko-otsu Blended Shochu
  Kyogetsu GREEN
  Midori Melon liqueur
  Otsu-rui Sochu
  Suntory Shirofuda Whiskey
  Sweet Potato Shochu Wanco
  YAMAZAKI Single Malt Whiskey
  Zen Green Tea liqueur
Wine
  Akadama Sweet Wine
  Delica Maison Delicious Wine
  Sankaboshizai Mutenka Wine
  Tomi no oka Wine
  Tomi Wine
  Yukisaibai Budo no Oishii Wine

COMPETITORS
ASAHI GROUP HOLDINGS,LTD.
Clearly Canadian Beverage Corporation
HALEWOOD INTERNATIONAL LIMITED
HORNELL BREWING CO., INC.
JFC INTERNATIONAL INC.
KOKUBU GROUP CORP.
PRINCES LIMITED
RADICO KHAITAN LIMITED
Tingyi (Cayman Islands) Holding Corp.
WHITTARD TRADING LIMITED

HISTORICAL FINANCIALS
Company Type: Private

Income Statement   FYE: December 31

	REVENUE ($mil)	NET INCOME ($mil)	NET PROFIT MARGIN	EMPLOYEES
12/10	790	60	7.7%	2,199
12/09	13	5	42.0%	—
Annual Growth	5928.4%	1002.2%	—	—

2010 Year-End Financials
Return on assets: 8.1%   Cash ($ mil.): 60
Return on equity: 13.8%
Current Ratio: 1.50

SUPERIOR COMMUNICATIONS, INC.

EXECUTIVES
Legal Counsel*, Jennifer Ju
Stockholder*, Michael Cavanah
OF CREDIT & PAYABLES RECEIVABLES*, Ava Cheung
CMO*, Scott Shanks
Auditors : PRICEWATERHOUSECOOPERS LLP IR

LOCATIONS
HQ: SUPERIOR COMMUNICATIONS, INC.
5027 IRWINDALE AVE # 900, IRWINDALE, CA 917062187
Phone: 877 522-4727
Web: WWW.SUPERIORCOMMUNICATIONS.COM

HISTORICAL FINANCIALS
Company Type: Private

Income Statement   FYE: December 31

	REVENUE ($mil)	NET INCOME ($mil)	NET PROFIT MARGIN	EMPLOYEES
12/14*	734	6	0.9%	273
06/13	296	2	0.7%	—
12/12	1,365	0	0.0%	—
Annual Growth	(26.7%)	7565.4%	—	—

*Fiscal year change

2014 Year-End Financials
Return on assets: 2.2%   Cash ($ mil.): 25
Return on equity: 73.8%
Current Ratio: 1.10

SUTTER BAY HOSPITALS

Sutter West Bay Hospitals (doing business as California Pacific Medical Center, or CPMC) is a health care complex located in the heart of hospital-heavy San Francisco. The private, not-for-profit center's four area campuses (California, Davies, Pacific, and St. Luke's) offer acute and specialty care, including obstetrics and gynecology, cardiovascular services, pediatrics, neurosciences, orthopedics, and organ transplantation. With more than 1,300 beds between its campuses, the center also conducts professional education and biomedical, clinical, and behavioral research. CPMC is part of the West Bay Region division of the Sutter Health hospital system.

Operations

CPMC's Sutter Health West Bay Region also includes Novato Community Hospital, Sutter Lakeside Hospital, and Sutter Medical Center of Santa Rosa. In addition to acute medical services, CPMC also provides outpatient services at clinics in the San Francisco area, operates home health and hospice organizations, and conducts health education and charity care programs.

In 2011 CPMC's Research Institute conducted more than 200 clinical trials, including studies on aging, cancers, epilepsy, diabetes, cardiovascular disease, osteoporosis, organ transplantation and more. That year CPMC's Kidney and Pancreas Transplant Program performed the first ever single-hospital, five-way kidney swap transplant in California. CPMC's Joint Replacement Center is one of the leading joint replacement centers in the Bay Area, performing roughly 1,200 hip, knee, shoulder and elbow procedures per year. It has 1,859 CPMC Medical Staff (including St. Luke's) and 109 medical residents and fellows.

That year the healthcare system reported about 619,400 outpatient visits and 30,300 inpatient cases.

Geographic Reach
CPMC serves patients from San Francisco, Marin, San Mateo, Oakland, Berkeley, Palo Alto, Santa Rosa, San Jose. and the Bay Area.

Strategy
In order to meet California's seismic construction standards, CPMC plans to renovate or rebuild most of its hospital campuses, which are among the oldest medical centers in the San Francisco area. Its $2.5 billion reorganization plan includes the construction of a new 550-bed Cathedral Hill Campus that will include a full acute care hospital plus specialized women's and children's departments. CPMC also plans to rebuild and downsize the St. Luke's campus and convert the Pacific and California campuses into ambulatory care clinics. Reconstruction efforts at the Davies campus will include a new patient pavilion and a new Davies Neurosciences Institute for expanded neurological care. Major construction projects began in 2011 and will extend through 2015.

In 2010 the company sold its outpatient kidney dialysis operations to DaVita to focus on core operations.

Company Background
In 2007 parent Sutter Health merged St. Luke's Hospital into California Pacific to help keep the ailing St. Luke's afloat; St. Luke's provides care to many of San Francisco's low-income patients. CPMC had announced plans to turn St. Luke's into an outpatient facility in 2007; however, the company rescinded those plans after San Franciscans objected to the proposal.

Auditors: ERNST & YOUNG LLP SACRAMENTO

LOCATIONS
HQ: SUTTER BAY HOSPITALS
475 BRANNAN ST STE 130, SAN FRANCISCO, CA 941071731
Phone: 415 600-6000
Web: WWW.CPMCRI.ORG

PRODUCTS/OPERATIONS
Selected Hospitals
California Campus (aka Children's Hospital of San Francisco)
Davies Campus (aka Davies Medical Center or Franklin Hospital)
Pacific Campus (aka Presbyterian Medical Center)
St. Luke's Campus (aka St. Luke's Hospital)

COMPETITORS
JOHN MUIR HEALTH
METHODIST HOSPITAL OF SOUTHERN CALIFORNIA
RADY CHILDREN'S HOSPITAL-SAN DIEGO
ST. JUDE HOSPITAL
ST. LUKE'S HOSPITAL OF DULUTH

HISTORICAL FINANCIALS
Company Type: Private

Income Statement — FYE: December 31

	REVENUE ($mil)	NET INCOME ($mil)	NET PROFIT MARGIN	EMPLOYEES
12/11	1,616	67	4.1%	3,597
12/09	1,245	159	12.8%	—
12/08	830	168	20.3%	—
Annual Growth	24.9%	(26.5%)	—	—

2011 Year-End Financials
Return on assets: 4.3%
Return on equity: 6.6%
Current Ratio: 1.20
Cash ($ mil.): 76

SUTTER BAY MEDICAL FOUNDATION

The Palo Alto Medical Foundation (PAMF) is a not-for-profit, multi-specialty physician group providing medical and outpatient care mostly in the San Francisco Bay Area. It operates through five divisions serving distinct geographical areas: The Palo Alto Medical Clinic and the Camino Medical Group serve Silicon Valley and the East Bay; the Dublin Center and Fremont Center serve Alameda County; the Santa Cruz Medical Foundation; and the Mills-Peninsula Division. An affiliate of Sutter Health, PAMF's more than 1,200 doctors cover dozens of medical specialties; its facilities also provide outpatient surgery, diagnostic imaging, and women's services. Additionally, PAMF houses a Research Institute for medical research.

Operations
The medical foundation operates more than 50 medical centers, including primary care clinics, surgery hospitals, urgent care centers, and physical therapy and weight management clinics. Specialty care services include pediatrics, neurology, gynecology, and oncology. Its divisions use advanced electronic health record technologies to provide its patients with a coordinated network of care that includes more than 40 different locations and access to hundreds of specialists, including rare specialties such as gynecologic oncology and pediatric neurology.

In addition, PAMF's Research Institute has 140 active clinical studies being pursued by 25 research staff members, 18 research associates, 7 clinical research staff members, and one postdoctoral fellow.

PAMF's signature innovative project at its Innovation Center is linkAges, a community-based, multigenerational service exchange network designed to engage and activate existing resources within communities to improve the health and well-being of seniors and family caregivers.

Geographic Reach
PAMF's approximately 1,200 affiliated physicians and 5,400 employees serve about 850,000 patients at more than 40 different locations, including medical centers and clinics in Alameda, San Mateo, Santa Clara, and Santa Cruz counties. The group serves communities in and around Dublin, Fremont, Mountain View, Oakland, Palo Alto, San Francisco, San Jose, San Mateo, and Santa Cruz.

Strategy
To meet increased demand, the company is expanding its facilities. In 2013 PAMF broke ground on a new primary care medical clinic in Santa Cruz. The 18,000-sq.-ft. building, which houses family medicine, internal medicine, pediatric physicians, and urgent care services, opened in 2014. Other newly opened locations include an urgent care center at Mills Health Center in San Mateo, an outpatient medical center in San Carlos, and an outpatient surgery center in Fremont.

Additionally, to meet current and forecasted demand for primary and specialty medical care in the South Bay, PAMF is adding two more medical sites in Los Gatos, including a 40,000-sq.-ft. medical center (to house primary care, urgent care, diagnostic imaging, radiology and laboratory services) which is expected to open in 2015. PAMF is also opening its first location in Danville; that facility will be an expanded medical center by the end of the year.

The company launched its Care-A-Van mobile medical clinic in 2013. The mobile facility provides primary and wellness services including annual checkups, blood work, and vaccinations.

Company Background
PAMF was founded in 1930.

Auditors: ERNST & YOUNG LLP ROSEVILLE

LOCATIONS
HQ: SUTTER BAY MEDICAL FOUNDATION
795 EL CAMINO REAL, PALO ALTO, CA 943012302
Phone: 650 321-4121
Web: WWW.MYCAMINOMEDICAL.ORG

Selected locations
ALAMEDA COUNTY
Castro Valley Primary Care Center
Castro Valley Women's Health Center
Dublin Center
Fremont Center
Livermore Center
SAN MATEO COUNTY
Menlo Park Surgical Hospital
Portola Valley Women's Health Center
Redwood City Center
Redwood City Women's Health Center
Redwood Shores Health Center
San Carlos Center Family Medicine
SANTA CLARA COUNTY
Gynecologic Oncology (Los Gatos)
Gynecologic Oncology (Mountain View)
Los Altos Center
Mountain View Center
Nephrology (Palo Alto)
Nephrology (San Jose)
OB/Gyn (Sunnyvale)
Palo Alto Center
Plastic Surgery

Santa Clara Center
Sleep Disorder Center
Sunnyvale Center
Currently closed and renovations being planned
SurgiCenter (Mountain View)
Vision Care Center
West Valley Center
SANTA CRUZ COUNTY
Main Clinic
Neurology
Neurosurgery
Physical Medicine & Rehabilitation
Scotts Valley
Watsonville
Westside Office

COMPETITORS

BAPTIST MEMORIAL HEALTH CARE SYSTEM, INC.
BOSTON MEDICAL CENTER CORPORATION
MONMOUTH MEDICAL CENTER INC.
SIERRA VIEW DISTRICT HOSPITAL LEAGUE, INC.
THE MASSACHUSETTS GENERAL HOSPITAL

HISTORICAL FINANCIALS

Company Type: Private

Income Statement — FYE: December 31

	REVENUE ($mil)	NET INCOME ($mil)	NET PROFIT MARGIN	EMPLOYEES
12/21	3,061	(12)	—	1,168
12/01*	322	5	1.6%	—
10/00	198	23	11.9%	—
Annual Growth	13.9%	—	—	—

*Fiscal year change

2021 Year-End Financials

Return on assets: (-0.6%)
Return on equity: (-1.0%)
Current Ratio: 1.50
Cash ($ mil.): 261

SUTTER HEALTH

Sutter Health provides coordinated care to more than 3 million Californians and its integrated network invests heavily in research and pilot programs that fuel advancement in patient's care and medical research across the country. The Northern California, not-for-profit health care system is one of the nation's largest, with about 4,165 acute care beds. After being formed through the merger of Sutter Health and California Healthcare System, Sutter Health now caters to residents of more than 100 communities from the San Francisco Bay Area, Central Valley, Greater Sacramento Valley, Marin County, Sierra foothills and Santa Cruz.

Operations

Sutter Health affiliates provide allergy care, health education, home health care, hospice care, senior services and geriatric care, fertility services, primary care, and other specialized health care services.

Sutter Health has around 25 hospitals, more than 4,165 licensed general acute care beds, about 35 ambulatory surgery centers, and more than 12,000 physicians.

Sutter Health and Stanford Medicine create a partnership to expand access to coordinated, state-of-the-art cancer services for patients and their families in the East Bay. The Stanford Medicine | Sutter Health Cancer Collaborative, an integrated, multidisciplinary outpatient cancer center, will provide an integrated and comprehensive suite of cancer-related services to seamlessly coordinate early detection, cancer care and support programs.

Geographic Reach

Sutter Health is based in Sacramento, California.

Company Background

Although it traces its roots back to the 1800s, Sutter Health was officially formed through the 1996 merger of Sacramento's Sutter Health and the Bay Area's California Healthcare System.

EXECUTIVES

Chief Medical Officer, Gordon Hunt Md

LOCATIONS

HQ: SUTTER HEALTH
2200 RIVER PLAZA DR, SACRAMENTO, CA 958334134
Phone: 916 733-8800
Web: WWW.SUTTERHEALTH.ORG

Selected Hospitals
Alta Bates Summit Medical Center (Berkeley, Oakland)
California Pacific Medical Center (San Francisco)
Eden Medical Center (Castro Valley)
Kahi Mohala (Ewa, HI)
Marin General Hospital (Greenbrae)
Memorial Hospital Los Banos (Los Banos)
Memorial Medical Center (Modesto)
Menlo Park Surgical Hospital
Mills-Peninsula Health Services (Burlingame)
Novato Community Hospital (Novato)
Sutter Amador Hospital (Jackson)
Sutter Auburn Faith Hospital (Auburn)
Sutter Coast Hospital (Crescent City)
Sutter Davis Hospital (Davis)
Sutter Delta Medical Center (Antioch)
Sutter Lakeside Hospital (Lakeport)
Sutter Maternity & Surgery Center of Santa Cruz
Sutter Medical Center (Sacramento)
Sutter Medical Center of Santa Rosa
Sutter Roseville Medical Center
Sutter Solano Medical Center (Vallejo)
Sutter Tracy Community Hospital (Tracy)

PRODUCTS/OPERATIONS

2018 Sales

	$ mil.	% of total
Patient service revenue	10,957	86
Premium revenue	1,383	11
Contributions	6	-
Other	351	3
Total	12,697	100

Selected Services
Allergy Care
Alzheimer's and Brain Health
Arthritis and Rheumatology
Asthma Care
Back and Spine Services
Behavioral Health Care
Bioethics Services
Cancer Services
Cosmetic Surgery
Dermatology Services
Diabetes Services
Ear, Nose, and Throat Services
Emergency Services
Endocrinology
Fertility Services
Gastroenterology
Gynecology and Women's Health
Health Education
Heart and Vascular Services
Holistic and Integrative Medicine
Home Health and Hospice Care
Imaging
Kidney Disease and Nephrology
Lab and Pathology
Liver Care
Neuroscience
Occupational Health
Orthopedic Services
Palliative Care and Advanced Illness Management
Pediatric Services
Physical Therapy and Rehabilitation
Podiatric Services
Pregnancy and Childbirth Services
Primary Care
Pulmonary Care
Reconstructive Plastic Surgery
Senior Services and Geriatric Care
Surgical Services
Transplant Services
Urgent Care
Urology
Vision Care
Weight Loss Services
Long-Term Care Centers
Irene Swindells Alzheimer's Residential Care Center, San Francisco
Sutter Oaks Nursing Center, Sacramento
Sutter Senior Care PACE Program, Sacramento
Cancer Centers
Alta Bates Summit Comprehensive Cancer Center, Berkeley and Oakland
California Pacific Medical Center, San Francisco
Dorothy E. Schneider Cancer Center at Mills-Peninsula Health Services, Burlingame
Eden Medical Center, Castro Valley
Memorial Regional Cancer Center, Modesto
Sutter Auburn Faith Hospital, Auburn
Sutter Cancer Center, Sutter Medical Center, Sacramento
Sutter Cancer Center, Sutter Roseville Medical Center, Roseville
Sutter Solano Cancer Center, Vallejo
Programs listed above are approved by the American College of Surgeons' Commission on Cancer.
Research Institutes
California Pacific Medical Center, San Francisco
Palo Alto Medical Foundation Research Institute, Palo Alto
Sutter Health Institute for Research and Education, San Francisco
Sutter Institute for Medical Research, Sacramento
Home Health and Hospice Services
Coming Home Hospice
Cohen Cormier Home Attendant & Care Management
Sutter Auburn Faith VNA & Hospice
Sutter Care at Home
Sutter Coast Home Care
Sutter Infusion & Pharmacy Services / Emeryville and Sacramento
Sutter Lakeside Home Medical Services
Sutter Lifeline / Sacramento
Sutter North Home Health Agency
VNA of the Central Valley
VNA of Santa Cruz County
Express Medical Clinics
Sutter Express Care (Three locations in Sacramento & Placer counties)

COMPETITORS

ALLINA HEALTH SYSTEM
AMEDISYS, INC.
INTEGRIS HEALTH, INC.
LHC GROUP, INC.
NORTHSHORE UNIVERSITY HEALTHSYSTEM
PRESBYTERIAN HEALTHCARE SERVICES
PROVIDENCE ST. JOSEPH HEALTH
SISTERS OF CHARITY OF LEAVENWORTH HEALTH SYSTEM, INC.

THE LANCASTER GENERAL HOSPITAL
THE RUTLAND HOSPITAL INC ACT 220

HISTORICAL FINANCIALS
Company Type: Private

Income Statement   FYE: December 31

	REVENUE ($mil)	NET INCOME ($mil)	NET PROFIT MARGIN	EMPLOYEES
12/21	14,225	1,958	13.8%	48,000
12/20	13,220	82	0.6%	—
12/19	13,304	189	1.4%	—
12/18	12,697	(447)	—	—
Annual Growth	3.9%	—	—	—

2021 Year-End Financials
Return on assets: 9.6%   Cash ($ mil.): 735
Return on equity: 17.2%
Current Ratio: 3.20

SUTTER HEALTH PLAN

Auditors: ERNST & YOUNG LLP SACRAMENTO

LOCATIONS
HQ: SUTTER HEALTH PLAN
2700 GATEWAY OAKS DR # 120, SACRAMENTO, CA 958334337
Phone: 916 643-1197
Web: WWW.SUTTERHEALTHPLUS.ORG

HISTORICAL FINANCIALS
Company Type: Private

Income Statement   FYE: December 31

	REVENUE ($mil)	NET INCOME ($mil)	NET PROFIT MARGIN	EMPLOYEES
12/21	592	(1)	—	25
12/20	573	14	2.4%	—
12/19	518	25	4.8%	—
12/18	429	(16)	—	—
Annual Growth	11.3%	—	—	—

2021 Year-End Financials
Return on assets: (-0.6%)   Cash ($ mil.): 81
Return on equity: (-1.8%)
Current Ratio: 1.50

SUTTER HEALTH SACRAMENTO SIERRA REGION

Auditors: ERNST & YOUNG US LLP SAN DIEG

LOCATIONS
HQ: SUTTER HEALTH SACRAMENTO SIERRA REGION
2200 RIVER PLAZA DR, SACRAMENTO, CA 958334134
Phone: 916 733-8800
Web: WWW.SUTTERHEALTH.ORG

HISTORICAL FINANCIALS
Company Type: Private

Income Statement   FYE: December 31

	REVENUE ($mil)	NET INCOME ($mil)	NET PROFIT MARGIN	EMPLOYEES
12/13	1,884	148	7.9%	4,000
12/11	1,752	(16)	—	—
12/09	1,453	154	10.6%	—
12/02	4,634	322	6.9%	—
Annual Growth	(7.9%)	(6.8%)	—	—

2013 Year-End Financials
Return on assets: 8.6%   Cash ($ mil.): 69
Return on equity: 30.8%
Current Ratio: 0.30

SUTTER ROSEVILLE MEDICAL CENTER

LOCATIONS
HQ: SUTTER ROSEVILLE MEDICAL CENTER
1 MEDICAL PLAZA DR, ROSEVILLE, CA 956613037
Phone: 916 781-1000
Web: WWW.SUTTERROSEVILLE.ORG

HISTORICAL FINANCIALS
Company Type: Private

Income Statement   FYE: December 31

	REVENUE ($mil)	NET INCOME ($mil)	NET PROFIT MARGIN	EMPLOYEES
12/17	669	126	18.9%	1,700
12/16	628	121	19.3%	—
12/15	558	74	13.3%	—
12/12	484	95	19.6%	—
Annual Growth	6.7%	5.9%	—	—

2017 Year-End Financials
Return on assets: 35.4%   Cash ($ mil.): —
Return on equity: 129.3%
Current Ratio: 3.70

SUTTER VALLEY HOSPITALS

LOCATIONS
HQ: SUTTER VALLEY HOSPITALS
2200 RIVER PLAZA DR, SACRAMENTO, CA 958334134
Phone: 916 733-8800

HISTORICAL FINANCIALS
Company Type: Private

Income Statement   FYE: December 31

	REVENUE ($mil)	NET INCOME ($mil)	NET PROFIT MARGIN	EMPLOYEES
12/20	3,735	168	4.5%	405
12/19	3,614	12	0.3%	—
12/17	80	1	2.4%	—
12/16	83	8	10.3%	—
Annual Growth	158.5%	110.4%	—	—

2020 Year-End Financials
Return on assets: 6.4%   Cash ($ mil.): 120
Return on equity: 14.3%
Current Ratio: 1.40

SUTTER VALLEY MEDICAL FOUNDATION

Auditors: ERNST & YOUNG LLP ROSEVILLE

LOCATIONS
HQ: SUTTER VALLEY MEDICAL FOUNDATION
2700 GATEWAY OAKS DR, SACRAMENTO, CA 958334337
Phone: 916 887-7122
Web: WWW.SUTTERHEALTH.ORG

HISTORICAL FINANCIALS
Company Type: Private

Income Statement   FYE: December 31

	REVENUE ($mil)	NET INCOME ($mil)	NET PROFIT MARGIN	EMPLOYEES
12/20	1,666	242	14.5%	700
12/19	1,651	23	1.4%	—
12/18	1,556	(2)	—	—
12/09	505	(21)	—	—
Annual Growth	11.5%	—	—	—

2020 Year-End Financials
Return on assets: 26.9%   Cash ($ mil.): 398
Return on equity: 54.9%
Current Ratio: 2.00

SWEDISH HEALTH SERVICES

Swedish Health Services, doing business as Swedish Medical Center, is the largest not-for-profit health provider in the greater Seattle area. Swedish Medical operates five acute care hospitals; it also runs two ambulatory care centers and a network of more than 100 primary and specialty care offices in the greater Puget Sound region. Swedish Medical is affiliated with Providence St. Joseph Health, a Catholic, not-for-profit organization with about 35 hospitals in five states. Swedish's perform procedures such as robotic-assisted surgery and personalized treatment in cardiovascular care, cancer care, neuroscience, orthopedics, high-risk obstetrics, pediatric specialties, organ transplantation and clinical research.

EXECUTIVES

CMO*, Jaya Kumar

Auditors : ERNST & YOUNG US LLP SAN FRAN

LOCATIONS

HQ: SWEDISH HEALTH SERVICES
747 BROADWAY, SEATTLE, WA 981224379
Phone: 206 386-6000
Web: WWW.SWEDISH.ORG

PRODUCTS/OPERATIONS

Selected Washington Facilities
Ballard Campus (Seattle)
Cherry Hill Campus (Seattle)
Edmonds Campus (Edmonds)
First Hill Campus (Seattle)
Issaquah Campus (Issaquah)
Mill Creek Campus (ambulatory center in Everett)
Redmond Campus (ambulatory center in Redmond)

Selected Institutes and Services
Cancer Institute
Emergency Services
Heart and Vascular Institute
Neuroscience Institute
Orthopedic Institute
Pediatric Specialty Care
Primary Care
Pregnancy and Childbirth
Surgical Services
Transplant Program
Women's Health

COMPETITORS

AMSURG CORP.
ATRIUS HEALTH, INC.
BILLINGS CLINIC
DAVITA MEDICAL MANAGEMENT, LLC
NORTHWELL HEALTH, INC.
SHANDS TEACHING HOSPITAL AND CLINICS, INC.
SWEDISH COVENANT HOSPITAL
TEXAS CHILDREN'S HOSPITAL
THE CLEVELAND CLINIC FOUNDATION
THE MASSACHUSETTS GENERAL HOSPITAL

HISTORICAL FINANCIALS

Company Type: Private

Income Statement   FYE: December 31

	REVENUE ($mil)	NET INCOME ($mil)	NET PROFIT MARGIN	EMPLOYEES
12/17	2,438	(9)	—	2,279
12/16	1,278	(2)	—	—
12/15	1,240	56	4.6%	—
12/14	1,127	79	7.1%	—
Annual Growth	29.3%	—	—	—

2017 Year-End Financials
Return on assets: (-0.3%) Cash ($ mil.): 51
Return on equity: (-1.2%)
Current Ratio: —

SWEETWATER UNION HIGH SCHOOL DISTRICT

Auditors : CROWE LLP SACRAMENTO CALIFOR

LOCATIONS

HQ: SWEETWATER UNION HIGH SCHOOL DISTRICT
1130 FIFTH AVE, CHULA VISTA, CA 919112812
Phone: 619 691-5500
Web: WWW.SWEETWATERSCHOOLS.ORG

HISTORICAL FINANCIALS

Company Type: Private

Income Statement   FYE: June 30

	REVENUE ($mil)	NET INCOME ($mil)	NET PROFIT MARGIN	EMPLOYEES
06/21	641	97	15.2%	3,521
06/20	589	38	6.5%	—
06/19	601	22	3.8%	—
06/18	553	(17)	—	—
Annual Growth	5.0%	—	—	—

2021 Year-End Financials
Return on assets: 5.9% Cash ($ mil.): —
Return on equity: 47.7%
Current Ratio: —

SWINERTON BUILDERS

Swinerton Builders, a subsidiary of Swinerton, focuses on commercial and sustainable construction and renovation projects. Operating primarily in the western US, its interiors group offers interior tenant finishes and remodeling, working on such projects as high-tech and lab renovations, hospitals, retail facilities, and seismic upgrades. The employee-owned company's building group focuses on new construction and retrofitting for such projects as the San Francisco Museum of Modern Art, a Lockheed Martin launch vehicle assembly plant in Colorado, and the Bay Bridge toll operations building in San Francisco. Swinerton Builders operates from offices in California, Colorado, Hawaii, Texas, New Mexico, and Washington.

Operations

As part of its business, Swinerton Builders is involved in high-tech and lab renovations, hospitals, retail facilities, and seismic upgrades, as well as new construction and retrofitting projects.

Swinerton Builders also constructs many buildings to meet environmental standards. Green projects have ranged from fire stations and retail outlets to college facilities and hotels. Swinertons' own corporate offices in California are solar powered.

Geographic Reach

The building arm of Swinerton serves the western US through offices in California, Colorado, Hawaii, Texas, Oregon, and Washington. Its offices are located across California as well as in Austin, Texas; Denver, Colorado; Portland, Oregon; Seattle Washington; and Honolulu, Hawaii.

Sales and Marketing

Swinerton Builders serves a variety of sectors, involving: critical facilities, education, government, healthcare, hospitality, interiors, multi-family residential, native American, and renewable energy projects. Its clients have included NASA, the Federal Aviation Administration, Bureau of Indian Affairs, and several military and governmental entities, including the US Air Force, US Army, US Department of Agriculture, US Department of Homeland Security, and the US National Park Service.

Strategy

Swinerton Builders continues to work on high-value projects around the country. In 2015, after being selected from a two-phase, best value selection process, the company secured a contract to lead the design-build construction project of a $46 million parking building (with some 1,795 parking spaces) at the Denver International Airport (DIA) in Colorado.

The company's Swinerton Renewable Energy unit, which builds and offers services to the solar utility industry, expanded its capabilities in 2013 by adding comprehensive operations and maintenance (O&M) services for any solar facility across North America. The unit also launched a monitoring platform, named SOLV, to manage all the operational needs of customers with solar utility plants.

EXECUTIVES

CAO, John T Capener

Auditors : CLIFTONLARSONALLEN LLP WALNUT

LOCATIONS

HQ: SWINERTON BUILDERS
2001 CLAYTON RD STE 700, CONCORD, CA 945202792
Phone: 415 421-2980
Web: WWW.SWINERTON.COM

PRODUCTS/OPERATIONS

Selected Services
BIM/VD&C
Corporate Services
Critical Facilities
General Contracting
Government Construction
Management & Consulting
Preconstruction
Renewable Energy
Sustainable Construction/LEED

COMPETITORS

ALBERICI CORPORATION
BERGELECTRIC CORP.
BIG-D CONSTRUCTION CORP.
CLAYCO, INC.
DAVID EVANS AND ASSOCIATES, INC.
GILBANE, INC.

JOSEPH JINGOLI & SON, INC.
LECHASE CONSTRUCTION SERVICES, LLC
ROSENDIN ELECTRIC, INC.
WALBRIDGE ALDINGER LLC

HISTORICAL FINANCIALS
Company Type: Private

Income Statement — FYE: December 31

	REVENUE ($mil)	NET INCOME ($mil)	NET PROFIT MARGIN	EMPLOYEES
12/19	4,272	46	1.1%	76
12/18	3,541	38	1.1%	—
12/17	3,306	39	1.2%	—
12/16	3,664	53	1.5%	—
Annual Growth	5.2%	(4.8%)	—	—

2019 Year-End Financials
Return on assets: 3.3%   Cash ($ mil.): 243
Return on equity: 14.6%
Current Ratio: 1.30

SWINERTON INCORPORATED

Swinerton is building up the West just as it helped rebuild San Francisco after the 1906 earthquake. One of the largest contractors in California, the construction group builds commercial, industrial, and government facilities, including resorts, subsidized housing, public schools, soundstages, hospitals, and airport terminals. Through its subsidiaries (including Swinerton Builders), Swinerton offers general contracting and design/build services, as well as construction and program management. The firm also provides property management for conventional, subsidized, and assisted living residences, and is active in the renewable energy sector. The 100% employee-owned company traces its roots to 1888.

Operations
Swinerton has a special renewable energy division (Swinerton Renewable Energy) focused on solar and wind projects.

For North American solar power facilities, the company also offers comprehensive operations and maintenance (O&M) services, which include performance monitoring and alerting, parts management, service ticketing, reporting, preventive and corrective maintenance, warranty administration, and site maintenance (including vegetation mitigation and module washing).

Swinerton also has a special division to handle government construction projects, delivering large-scale, complex design and construction services for government agencies. Through the division, Swinerton has worked on federal courthouses and administrative buildings, training centers, VA hospitals, and military housing projects.

Geographic Reach
San Francisco-based Swinerton has more than a dozen offices throughout California, Colorado, Hawaii, Texas, Oregon, and Washington.

Financial Performance
With the California construction market experiencing some of the strongest growth the industry has seen since 2008, Swinerton posted nearly $1.8 billion in revenue in 2013, about $1.4 billion of which was rung up in California.

Strategy
Swinerton's renewable energy division has been busy with a series of projects and new services coming to the fold in recent years. In 2014, Duke Energy awarded Swinerton a contract to develop a pair of 20-megawatt solar farms, called the Pumpjack and Wildwood solar power projects, which will power some 10,000 households in central California once they're completed. In 2013, the company began offering comprehensive operations and maintenance (O&M) services for any North American solar facility.

The company also continues to work on other projects in recent years. In 2014, it started building the five-story, 117,000-square-foot building on behalf of the developer Breevast, which secured a 12-year lease agreement on the building with file-sharing service provider Dropbox. In 2013, it started work on Telecom Real Estate Services' Block Data Center in Las Vegas, with the goal of turning an existing warehouse facility into a Tier III modular data center. That year it also began construction on Chevron's 340,000 square-foot office complex and campus in Midland, Texas.

As one of the top waste-reducing companies in California, Swinerton employs green building construction and design practices to conserve resources, reduce waste, and create healthier environments. The company's own headquarters building in San Francisco received Gold LEED-EB (Leadership in Energy & Environmental Design for Existing Buildings) -- a top certification from the U.S. Green Building Council. Swinerton also built the LEED platinum rated NASA Ames Research Center Sustainability Base, the greenest government building in history.

EXECUTIVES
CAO, John T Capener
Auditors: CLIFTONLARSONALLEN LLP WALNUT

LOCATIONS
HQ: SWINERTON INCORPORATED
  2001 CLAYTON RD FL 7 FLR 7, SAN FRANCISCO, CA 94107
Phone: 415 421-2980
Web: WWW.SWINERTON.COM

PRODUCTS/OPERATIONS
Selected Companies and Divisions
Cameron Swinerton
Harbison-Mahony-Higgins Builders, Inc. (HMH, general contracting)
Swinerton Builders (general contracting)
Swinerton Government Services
Swinerton Management & Consulting (property assessment)
Swinerton Property Services (property management)
William P. Young Construction (engineering and civil construction)

Selected Projects
100 Montgomery
AECOM
Agilent Technologies
Andaz Wailea Resort & Villas
Avaya Research & Development
Bank of New York Mellon Newport Beach
Bank of New York Mellon San Francisco
Bright Horizons Colorado
Bright Horizons South Lake Union
Bruceville | 19.15 MWdc
Cache Creek Casino Resort
CalSTRS Office Headquarters
Caltech Solar Project | 1.10 MWdc
Cathedral of the Blessed Sacrament
Christopher High School
Cinépolis Del Mar
City Center Plaza and Entry Upgrades
City Target at the Metreon
CNET Headquarters
Columbia 3 | 11.06 MWdc Columbia Sportswear
de Young Museum
Delta Airlines Sky Club
Dillard | 12.03 MWdc

COMPETITORS
GILBANE BUILDING COMPANY
HOLDER CONSTRUCTION COMPANY
J.E. DUNN CONSTRUCTION COMPANY
KITCHELL CORPORATION
MCKINSTRY CO., LLC
MIRON CONSTRUCTION CO., INC.
ROSENDIN ELECTRIC, INC.
SWINERTON BUILDERS, INC.
THE RUHLIN COMPANY
THE WEITZ COMPANY LLC

HISTORICAL FINANCIALS
Company Type: Private

Income Statement — FYE: December 31

	REVENUE ($mil)	NET INCOME ($mil)	NET PROFIT MARGIN	EMPLOYEES
12/18	3,631	36	1.0%	900
12/17	3,365	31	0.9%	—
12/16	0	0	—	—
Annual Growth	—	—	—	—

2018 Year-End Financials
Return on assets: 2.5%   Cash ($ mil.): 230
Return on equity: 14.3%
Current Ratio: 1.30

TA CHEN INTERNATIONAL, INC.

Auditors: CHEN & FAN ACCOUNTANCY COPR

LOCATIONS
HQ: TA CHEN INTERNATIONAL, INC.
  5855 OBISPO AVE, LONG BEACH, CA 908053715
Phone: 562 808-8000
Web: WWW.TACHEN.COM

HISTORICAL FINANCIALS
Company Type: Private

Income Statement — FYE: December 31

	REVENUE ($mil)	NET INCOME ($mil)	NET PROFIT MARGIN	EMPLOYEES
12/17	1,257	32	2.6%	803
12/14	1,178	27	2.3%	—
12/13	904	8	1.0%	—
Annual Growth	8.6%	38.0%	—	—

2017 Year-End Financials
Return on assets: 3.2% Cash ($ mil.): 3
Return on equity: 7.8%
Current Ratio: 6.10

TACOMA PUBLIC SCHOOLS

Auditors: PAT MCCARTHY OLYMPIA WA

LOCATIONS
HQ: TACOMA PUBLIC SCHOOLS
601 S 8TH ST, TACOMA, WA 984054614
Phone: 253 571-1000
Web: WWW.TACOMASCHOOLS.ORG

HISTORICAL FINANCIALS
Company Type: Private

Income Statement — FYE: August 31

	REVENUE ($mil)	NET INCOME ($mil)	NET PROFIT MARGIN	EMPLOYEES
08/21	565	481	85.2%	3,700
08/20	554	(75)	—	—
08/19	544	(57)	—	—
08/18	495	(50)	—	—
Annual Growth	4.4%	—	—	—

2021 Year-End Financials
Return on assets: 23.8% Cash ($ mil.): 4
Return on equity: 107.0%
Current Ratio: —

TALEN ENERGY SUPPLY, LLC

EXECUTIVES
Managing Member, Ralph Alexander
Auditors: PRICEWATERHOUSECOOPERS LLP HO

LOCATIONS
HQ: TALEN ENERGY SUPPLY, LLC
1780 HUGHES LANDING BLVD # 800, THE WOODLANDS, TX 773804014
Phone: 888 211-6011

HISTORICAL FINANCIALS
Company Type: Private

Income Statement — FYE: December 31

	REVENUE ($mil)	NET INCOME ($mil)	NET PROFIT MARGIN	EMPLOYEES
12/20	1,726	(664)	—	4,981
12/19	2,597	(8)	—	—
12/18	2,714	(37)	—	—
12/16	3,913	(352)	—	—
Annual Growth	(18.5%)	—	—	—

2020 Year-End Financials
Return on assets: (-7.8%) Cash ($ mil.): 279
Return on equity: (-42.6%)
Current Ratio: 1.40

TALLGRASS ENERGY, LP

Tallgrass Energy holds 22.5% of (and manages) Tallgrass Equity, which itself owns (through Tallgrass MLP GP, LLC) all of Tallgrass Energy Partners' (TEP) incentive distribution rights, and a 1.4% general partner interest in TEP. Tallgrass Equity owns a 32.75% limited partner interest in TEP. TEP's business consists of the Tallgrass Interstate Gas Transmission (TIGT) system (in Colorado, Kansas, Missouri, Nebraska, and Wyoming); the Trailblazer Pipeline (Colorado, Wyoming, and Nebraska); a 66.7% membership interest in Tallgrass Pony Express Pipeline; the Casper and Douglas natural gas processing plants; and the West Frenchie Draw natural gas treating facility. It went public in 2015.

IPO
Tallgrass Energy raised $1.2 billion in its May 2015 IPO. It used the proceeds buy a 22.5% stake in Tallgrass Equity. As a result of the offering, Kelso & Co., the Energy & Minerals Group, and Tallgrass Energy company executives and directors reduced their collective holdings in the company from 99% to 77%.

Strategy
The company looks to TEP's stable, fee-based cash flow and strong potential for future distribution growth to directly benefit the company as a result of Tallgrass Energy's interest in Tallgrass Equity.

Auditors: PRICEWATERHOUSECOOPERS LLP DE

LOCATIONS
HQ: TALLGRASS ENERGY, LP
4200 W 115TH ST STE 350, LEAWOOD, KS 662112733
Phone: 913 928-6060
Web: WWW.TALLGRASS.COM

COMPETITORS
BREITBURN ENERGY PARTNERS LP
COLUMBIA PIPELINE GROUP, INC.
ENABLE OKLAHOMA INTRASTATE TRANSMISSION, LLC
ENERGY TRANSFER LP
ENLINK MIDSTREAM PARTNERS, LP
ETP LEGACY LP
EV ENERGY PARTNERS, L.P.
MERIT ENERGY COMPANY, LLC
TARGA PIPELINE PARTNERS LP
THE WILLIAMS COMPANIES INC

HISTORICAL FINANCIALS
Company Type: Private

Income Statement — FYE: December 31

	REVENUE ($mil)	NET INCOME ($mil)	NET PROFIT MARGIN	EMPLOYEES
12/18	793	467	59.0%	800
12/17	655	223	34.1%	—
12/16	605	243	40.2%	—
Annual Growth	14.5%	38.7%	—	—

2018 Year-End Financials
Return on assets: 7.9% Cash ($ mil.): 9
Return on equity: 21.1%
Current Ratio: 0.70

TARRANT COUNTY HOSPITAL DISTRICT

If Fort Worth residents are searching for health care, they need look no further than Tarrant County Hospital District (dba JPS Health Network). Founded in 1906 in Fort Worth, Texas, the network's flagship facility, John Peter Smith Hospital, has approximately 540 beds and provides specialty services including orthopedics, cardiology, and women's health. JPS Health Network also includes behavioral health treatment center Trinity Springs Pavilion and the JPS Diagnostic & Surgery Hospital of Arlington. The company provides family medical, dental, and specialty care through dozens of health care centers in northern Texas.

Operations
JPS Hospital is a member of the Council of Teaching Hospitals and Health Systems (COTH).

Sales and Marketing
The health system carries a Level 1 Trauma designation across the spectrum of health care specialties, meaning it is the referral hospital of choice for patients who are terribly injured.

Strategy
The health system works to improve the health of Tarrant County as a whole by training health care workers and physicians about working outside the hospital walls and within the community. The institution sponsors programs that are accredited through the Accreditation Council for Graduate Medical Education (ACGME), American Osteopathic Association, (AOA), and the Council on Podiatric Medical Education (CPME).

JPS Health Network opened JPS Medical Home Southeast Tarrant, a primary and specialty care facility, in 2014. The following year, the system relocated its Pain Management Clinic to a renovated site in Fort Worth.

EXECUTIVES

Interim Chief Financial Officer*, Randy Rogers
Auditors : BKD LLP DALLAS TX

LOCATIONS

HQ: TARRANT COUNTY HOSPITAL DISTRICT
1500 S MAIN ST, FORT WORTH, TX 761044917
Phone: 817 921-3431
Web: WWW.JPSHEALTHNET.ORG

Primary Locations -- Texas
Ambulatory Surgery Center (Fort Worth)
Cardiology Center (Fort Worth)
Enrollment & Eligibility Center (Fort Worth)
Family Medicine & Surgical Specialty Center (Fort Worth)
Healing Wings AIDS Center (Fort Worth)
John Peter for Cancer Care (Fort Worth)
JPS Urgent Care Center (Fort Worth)
Lifespan Family Medicine & Pediatrics (Fort Worth)
Patient Care Pavilion (Fort Worth)
Professional Building-Medicine Clinic (Fort Worth)
Trinity Springs Pavilion for Psychiatric Services (Fort Worth)

PRODUCTS/OPERATIONS

Selected Services
Behavioral Services
Cancer
Cardiology
Dental
Geriatrics
Healing Wings HIV/AIDS Center
Orthopedics and Sports Medicine
Robotic Surgery
School-Based Health Centers
Sexual Assault Nurse Examiner Program
Stroke / Neurosciences
Surgical Services
Trauma Services
Women's Services

COMPETITORS

ASCENSION PROVIDENCE HOSPITAL
ATLANTIC HEALTH SYSTEM INC.
BAPTIST MEMORIAL HEALTH CARE SYSTEM, INC.
BRYAN MEDICAL CENTER
JOHN C. LINCOLN HEALTH NETWORK
NEBRASKA METHODIST HEALTH SYSTEM, INC.
PITT COUNTY MEMORIAL HOSPITAL, INCORPORATED
PRIME HEALTHCARE SERVICES - GARDEN CITY, LLC
SHELBY COUNTY HEALTH CARE CORPORATION
THE UNIVERSITY OF VERMONT MEDICAL CENTER INC.

HISTORICAL FINANCIALS
Company Type: Private

Income Statement — FYE: September 30

	REVENUE ($mil)	NET INCOME ($mil)	NET PROFIT MARGIN	EMPLOYEES
09/21	982	327	33.3%	3,000
09/20	868	198	22.9%	—
09/19	673	32	4.9%	—
09/18	632	(3)	—	—
Annual Growth	15.8%	—	—	—

2021 Year-End Financials
Return on assets: 18.6%   Cash ($ mil.): 198
Return on equity: 23.7%
Current Ratio: 3.90

TARRANT COUNTY TEXAS (INC)

Auditors : DELOITTE & TOUCHE LLP DALLAS

LOCATIONS

HQ: TARRANT COUNTY TEXAS (INC)
100 E WEATHERFORD ST, FORT WORTH, TX 761960206
Phone: 817 884-1111
Web: WWW.TARRANTCOUNTY.COM

HISTORICAL FINANCIALS
Company Type: Private

Income Statement — FYE: September 30

	REVENUE ($mil)	NET INCOME ($mil)	NET PROFIT MARGIN	EMPLOYEES
09/21	895	55	6.2%	3,945
09/19	687	19	2.9%	—
09/18	650	(10)	—	—
09/17	625	(20)	—	—
Annual Growth	9.4%	—	—	—

2021 Year-End Financials
Return on assets: 1.7%   Cash ($ mil.): —
Return on equity: 3.2%
Current Ratio: —

TAUBER OIL COMPANY

Tauber Oil is a family-owned company that markets refined petroleum products, carbon black feedstocks, natural gas, natural gas liquids, crude oil, petrochemicals, and refined products. The company is one of the US's leading suppliers of feedstocks for reforming and olefin cracking. It also has oil and gas exploration and production operations. Subsidiary Tauber Petrochemical was created to beef up the company's international petrochemical business. The Houston-based company serves major and independent oil companies, major petrochemical producers and consumers, and small- to medium-sized end-users. Tauber Oil, which is owned by David and Richard Tauber, maintains a fleet of more than 500 rail cars to supply its customers.

Auditors : MOHLE ADAMS HOUSTON TEXAS

LOCATIONS

HQ: TAUBER OIL COMPANY
55 WAUGH DR STE 700, HOUSTON, TX 770075837
Phone: 713 869-8700
Web: WWW.TAUBEROIL.COM

PRODUCTS/OPERATIONS

Selected Products:
Natural Gas Liquids
 Butane
 Ethane
 Isobutane
 Propane
Petrochemicals
 Benzene
 Methanol
 MTBE
 Styrene monomer
 Toluene
 Xylene
Refined
 Aviation jet fuel
 Kerosene
 Low sulfur diesel
 No. 2 fuel oil

COMPETITORS

BP FRANCE
CHEVRON PIPE LINE COMPANY
IDEMITSU KOSAN CO.,LTD.
ITOCHU ENEX CO., LTD.
MOTIVA ENTERPRISES LLC
PETROBRAS AMERICA INC.
RS ENERGY K.K.
TEXON DISTRIBUTING L.P.
THE KENAN ADVANTAGE GROUP INC
TRANSMONTAIGNE LLC

HISTORICAL FINANCIALS
Company Type: Private

Income Statement — FYE: December 31

	REVENUE ($mil)	NET INCOME ($mil)	NET PROFIT MARGIN	EMPLOYEES
12/14	4,831	10	0.2%	135
12/13	4,769	16	0.3%	—
12/12	5,088	21	0.4%	—
Annual Growth	(2.6%)	(29.0%)	—	—

2014 Year-End Financials
Return on assets: 2.7%   Cash ($ mil.): 15
Return on equity: 6.9%
Current Ratio: 1.50

TECHNIP USA, INC

LOCATIONS

HQ: TECHNIP USA, INC
13460 LOCKWOOD RD, HOUSTON, TX 770446444
Phone: 281 591-4000

HISTORICAL FINANCIALS
Company Type: Private

Income Statement — FYE: December 31

	REVENUE ($mil)	NET INCOME ($mil)	NET PROFIT MARGIN	EMPLOYEES
12/08	1,377	111	8.1%	4,346
12/04	609	(1)	—	—
12/97	225,116	0	0.0%	—
Annual Growth	(37.1%)	79.2%	—	—

2008 Year-End Financials
Return on assets: 10.7%   Cash ($ mil.): 205
Return on equity: 26.5%
Current Ratio: 1.20

TECUMSEH PRODUCTS COMPANY LLC

Named for the legendary Shawnee chief, Tecumseh Products makes a line of hermetically sealed compressors and heat pumps for residential and commercial refrigerators and freezers, water coolers, air conditioners, dehumidifiers, and vending machines. The company's line of scroll compressor models are suited for demanding commercial refrigeration applications and consist primarily of reciprocating and rotary designs. Tecumseh sells its products to OEMs and aftermarket distributors in more than 100 countries worldwide, with more than 80% of its sales generated outside of the US. In mid-2015, Tecumseh agreed to be acquired by affiliates of Mueller Industries and Atlas Holdings for $123 million.

Geographic Reach
Tecumseh's products are manufactured in about a dozen plants in the US, Brazil, France (five facilities), and India (two facilities); assembly plants are located in Canada, Malaysia, and Mexico. Some of the company's facilities are made possible through joint ventures; one such venture is Song Jiang in China.

Sales and Marketing
The company serves 1,600 customers including Whirlpool and Electrolux, which together generate about 12% of the company's business. In 2014 almost 45% of the sales from its Brazilian location were made to its three largest customers. The company sells its products in 97 countries primarily through its own sales staff as well as independent sales representatives and authorized wholesale distributors. It markets its products under brand names that include Celseon, Tecumseh, Wintsys, Masterflux, Silensys, and Vector.

Financial Performance
Tecumseh has suffered four straight years of declining revenues and two straight years of net losses. Revenues fell 12% from $824 million in 2013 to $724 million in 2014 as the company posted a net loss of $33 million in 2014.

The decrease in revenue for 2014 was primarily due to a 8% drop in sales of compressors used in commercial refrigeration and aftermarket applications, a 23% decrease in sales of compressors for air conditioning applications, and a 13% drop in sales for compressors used in household refrigeration and freezer applications. Tecumseh was also negatively affected by a competitive pricing environment in Brazil and soft market conditions in North America throughout 2014.

Strategy
Focused on growing internationally, Tecumseh has invested in research and development engineering laboratories in North America, Europe, South America, and India. It also partners with R&D facilities at universities throughout the globe to provide life science research on how its products interface with the environment.

HISTORY
Master toolmakers Ray Herrick (friend and advisor to Henry Ford and Thomas Edison) and Bill Sage founded the Michigan-based company in 1930 as Hillsdale Machine & Tool. Its first products included small tools, toys, and car and refrigerator parts. By 1933 Herrick controlled the company. The next year the company bought a facility in Tecumseh, Michigan, where it began mass-producing car and refrigerator parts. The company changed its name to Tecumseh Products in 1934 and went public in 1937.

By the end of the 1930s, Tecumseh was a major producer of hermetic compressors. In 1941 its focus shifted to WWII efforts, and it began making anti-aircraft projectile casings and aircraft engine parts. Herrick's son Kenneth began working for Tecumseh in 1945. Two years later, a company-made compressor was used in the first home window air-conditioning unit.

Tecumseh bought two Ohio companies in 1950 and 1952, and introduced an AC compressor for cars in 1953. Two years later the company bought compressor designer Tresco, and hired Joseph Layton as Tecumseh's president and CEO. Tecumseh gained entry into the gasoline engine market with the purchase of Wisconsin's Lauson Engine (1956) and Power Products (1957). Acquisitions in the 1960s allowed Tecumseh to tap into the power-train market.

LOCATIONS
HQ: TECUMSEH PRODUCTS COMPANY LLC
5683 HINES DR, ANN ARBOR, MI 481087901
Phone: 734 585-9500
Web: WWW.TECUMSEH.COM

2014 Sales

	$ mil.	% of total
Europe	191.3	26
South America		
Brazil	182.8	25
Other countries	45.6	6
North America		
US	125.8	18
Other countries	15.7	2
Asia		
India	105.0	14
China	13.0	2
Other countries	5.9	1
Middle East & Africa	39.3	6
Total	724.4	100

PRODUCTS/OPERATIONS

2014 Sales

	% of total
Commercial refrigeration	62
Household refrigerator & freezer	19
Residential & specialty air conditioning	19
Total	100

Selected Products
Compressors (all hermetically sealed)
    Reciprocating (for air conditioning and commercial refrigeration)
    Rotary (for room and mobile air conditioning)
    Scroll (especially designed for demanding commercial refrigeration applications)
    Highlighted Products
    A Legend Reborn
    Tecumseh "K" Kits

COMPETITORS
AAON, INC.
ANTHONY, INC.
BRIGGS & STRATTON CORPORATION
BRISTOL COMPRESSORS INTERNATIONAL, LLC
DAIKIN INDUSTRIES, LTD.
DOVER CORPORATION
GOODMAN MANUFACTURING COMPANY, L.P.
LENNOX INTERNATIONAL INC.
TRANE INC.
WHIRLPOOL CORPORATION

HISTORICAL FINANCIALS
Company Type: Private

Income Statement   FYE: December 31

	REVENUE ($mil)	NET INCOME ($mil)	NET PROFIT MARGIN	EMPLOYEES
12/14	724	(32)	—	4,800
12/13	823	(37)	—	—
12/12	854	22	2.6%	—
Annual Growth	(7.9%)	—	—	—

2014 Year-End Financials
Return on assets: (-8.3%)   Cash ($ mil.): 42
Return on equity: (-21.8%)
Current Ratio: 1.40

TEKNOR APEX COMPANY

Teknor Apex offers a wide-ranging portfolio of chemicals and synthetic polymers. The company's six business divisions provide colorants (through its Teknor Color unit), vinyl compounds, thermoplastic elastomers, engineering thermoplastics, chemicals for the polyvinyl chloride (PVC) plasticizer market, and garden hoses. The company's compounds are used for building and construction, consumer products, industrial manufacturing, electrical and electronic devices, medical tools, packaging, and vehicular components. Founded in 1924 by Alfred A. Fain and his son-in-law Albert Pilavin, Teknor invented the first plasticized (flexible) PVC.

Operations
Teknor Apex operates via six business segments.

The company's Teknor Color unit offers standard and custom colorants for polymers, including olefins, styrenics, polyethylene terephthalate (PET), engineering thermoplastics, and thermoplastic elastomers.

Teknor's vinyl products include flexible and rigid polyvinyl chloride (PVC), fire-resistant plenum PVC, PVC elastomers, PVC blends (including rigid blends), chlorinated PVC, PVC film, and halogen-free flame retardant.

The company's Thermoplastic Elastomers lineup comprises styrenic block copolymer (SBC) compounds, polyolefin blends (TPE-O or TPO), thermoplastic vulcanizates (TPE-Vs or TPVs), polyurethane compounds (TPE-U or TPU), and other specialty blends.

Through its Engineering Thermoplastics business, Teknor offers 80 automotive OEM-approved nylon compounds or a custom formulated ETP.

The company's Chemicals segment produces esters for the PVC plasticizer market. It currently manufactures both traditional and specialty proprietary plasticizers and additives, which are used internally by the company's compounding divisions.

Teknor also sells hoses under brands like ZeroG, Neverkink, Flexalloy, and Apex.

Geographic Reach
Pawtucket, Rhode Island-based Teknor Apex has about 10 US manufacturing plants (including one manufacturing plant and sales office) in California, Kentucky, Massachusetts, the Carolinas, Rhode Island, Tennessee, Texas, and Vermont. In addition, the company has plants and sales offices in Belgium, Germany, Netherlands, China, and Singapore.

Sales and Marketing
Teknor Apex serves a diverse client base, including building and construction firms, consumer goods producers, electrical and electronics companies, industrial manufacturers, healthcare providers, packaging companies, and vehicle fabricators.

Mergers and Acquisitions
In late 2021, Teknor Apex acquired Lanier Color Company, located in Gainesville, GA, USA. Lanier Color is a leading supplier of color concentrates and specialty compounds for the thermoplastics industry with a focus in the building and construction market. The acquisition of Lanier expands Teknor Apex's portfolio to now include PVC color concentrates while adding to its specialty compounds offerings specific to the building and construction market.

In mid-2021 Teknor Apex acquired Dorum Color Company's dry color business. Dorum Color, located in Akron, Ohio, is a leading supplier of dry color in North America with a singular focus on the rotational molding market. The deal is structured as an asset purchase and customers will be supplied from Teknor's Henderson, Kentucky Facility. The acquisition expands the company's dry color portfolio.

Company Background
The company was founded in 1924 as a tire distributor and retreader by Alfred Fain in 1924. Fain's grandson now leads the privately held company.

Auditors : PICCERELLI GOLSTEIN & COMPANY

LOCATIONS
HQ: TEKNOR APEX COMPANY
505 CENTRAL AVE, PAWTUCKET, RI 028611900
Phone: 401 725-8000
Web: WWW.TEKNORAPEX.COM

PRODUCTS/OPERATIONS
Selected Products and Services
Vinyl
FLEXIBLE PVC COMPOUNDS
Apex Flexible PVC
FireGuard LS FR PVC
Flexalloy PVC Elastomers
Apex PVC Blends
RIGID PVC COMPOUNDS
Apex Rigid PVC
AquaGuard CPVC
Apex Rigid PVC Blends
CALENDERED PVC FILM
Apex Calendered PVC Film
Thermoplastic Elastomers (TPE)
TPS, TPV, TPO AND TPU COMPOUNDS
Medalist Medical TPEs
Monprene
Sarlink
Elexar
Engineering Thermoplastics
POLYAMIDES
Chemlon
Creamid
Polyolefins
HalGuard LS HFFR Compounds
Colorants / Masterbatches
Teknor Color
Color Store
Esters
TruVis Esters
Garden Hose

COMPETITORS
DYNEON LLC
E. T. HORN COMPANY
IP CORPORATION
JOYCE LESLIE INC
LANXESS CORPORATION
MILLER WASTE MILLS, INCORPORATED
PRIMEX PLASTICS CORPORATION
TICONA POLYMERS, INC.
TOTAL PLASTICS RESOURCES LLC
WASHINGTON PENN PLASTIC CO., INC.

HISTORICAL FINANCIALS
Company Type: Private

Income Statement — FYE: July 31

	REVENUE ($mil)	NET INCOME ($mil)	NET PROFIT MARGIN	EMPLOYEES
07/14	996	50	5.0%	2,863
07/05	574	0	0.0%	—
Annual Growth	6.3%	—	—	—

2014 Year-End Financials
Return on assets: 6.8%
Return on equity: 5.0%
Current Ratio: 2.40
Cash ($ mil.): 74

TEKSYSTEMS, INC.

TEKsystems, a subsidiary of staffing giant Allegis, provides IT consulting and staffing services from locations in North America, Europe, and Asia. Considered one of the nation's largest IT staffing firms, the company places more than 80,000 technical professionals each year who work in a variety of fields including telecommunications, construction and engineering. TEKsystems has more than 100 locations serving about 6,000 clients. TEKsystems is an Allegis Group company.

Operations
TEKsystems is an industry in full-stack technology services, talent services and real-world application. It offers services such as cloud enablement, data analytics and insights, DevOps and automation, digital experience, enterprise applications, modern enterprise management, risk and security, telecom design, implementation and operations.

Geographic Reach
Headquartered in Hanover, Maryland, the company has more than 100 locations throughout North America, Europe, and Asia.

Sales and Marketing
The company is working with over 6,000 customers, including 80% of the Fortune 500. It serve various industries primarily communications, financial services, healthcare services, and government. Additional industries the company serves are aerospace and defense, food and beverage, agriculture, automotive, among others.

Auditors : PRICEWATERHOUSECOOPERS LLP BA

LOCATIONS
HQ: TEKSYSTEMS, INC.
7437 RACE RD, HANOVER, MD 210761112
Phone: 410 540-7700
Web: WWW.TEKSYSTEMS.COM

PRODUCTS/OPERATIONS
SELECTED SERVICES
IT STAFFING SOLUTIONS
Communications Staffing Services
Digital Services
End User Services
IT Applications Staffing Services
IT Direct Placement Services
Network Infrastructure Staffing Services
TEKsystems Staffing Quality Process
Time and Expense
IT SERVICES
Applications Services
Education Services
Global Delivery Network
Infrastructure Services
Project Governance
IT TALENT MANAGEMENT EXPERTISE
Local Market
Selected Markets Served
Communications
Financial services
Government
Information technology
Expertise

COMPETITORS
APEX SYSTEMS, LLC
CENERGY INTERNATIONAL SERVICES, INC.
GUIDANT GLOBAL, INC.
MANPOWER UK LIMITED
MANPOWERGROUP INC.
OASIS OUTSOURCING HOLDINGS, INC.
PROFESSIONAL SERVICE INDUSTRIES, INC.
PROTIVITI INC.
R C M TECHNOLOGIES, INC.
TECHNISOURCE, INC.

HISTORICAL FINANCIALS
Company Type: Private

Income Statement   FYE: December 31

	REVENUE ($mil)	NET INCOME ($mil)	NET PROFIT MARGIN	EMPLOYEES
12/20	4,815	0	0.0%	2,900
12/19	4,927	0	0.0%	—
12/18	4,677	0	0.0%	—
12/17	4,350	0	0.0%	—
Annual Growth	3.4%	—	—	—

2020 Year-End Financials
Return on assets: —
Return on equity: —
Current Ratio: 2.80
Cash ($ mil.): 12

TEMPLE UNIVERSITY HEALTH SYSTEM, INC.

Temple University Health System (TUHS) is a network of academic and community hospitals associated with the Temple University School of Medicine. It provides primary, secondary, and tertiary care to residents in the Philadelphia County (Pennsylvania) area. The system includes 722-bed Temple University Hospital (a Level 1 trauma center) and a pair of community-based hospitals that provide acute and emergency care as well as the Jeanes Hospital and TUH-Episcopal Campus (home to a 120-bed behavioral health unit). TUHS supports programs in cardiology, organ transplantation, and oncology. In late 2019 the health system agreed to sell the Fox Chase Cancer Center to Philadelphia-based Thomas Jefferson University.

Operations
The $1.4-billion academic health system comprises Temple University Hospital, TUH-Episcopal Campus, TUH-Northern Campus, Fox Chase Cancer Center, Jeanes Hospital, Temple Transport Team, and Temple Physicians. It's affiliated with Temple University School of Medicine. Bermuda-based TUHS Insurance Company, Ltd. is a captive insurance company established to reinsure the professional liability claims of TUHS subsidiaries.

It offers everything from specialized cardiac care and spinal rehabilitation to a lung care center, a burn center, and stroke treatments.

Medicare and Medicaid account for 65% of net patient revenues.

Geographic Reach
Temple University Health System serves the residents of Philadelphia.

Sales and Marketing
TUHS markets itself through TV commercials and print and billboard advertising.

Financial Performance
In fiscal 2012 revenue rose by 37% to $1.35 billion vs. 2011. It attributes the double-digit gains to increases in net patient service revenue, research revenue, and other revenue. The system logged $107 million in net income during the reporting period as compared to a net loss in 2011.

Strategy
TUHS concentrates on adding services and expanding its geographic reach. It added Fox Chase Cancer Center in 2012; opened the women's care center in Elkins Park, Pennsylvania, in 2012; opened a third urgent care facility in Jenkintown, Pennsylvania, in 2013; and expanded into new markets by opening the Temple Health Center City facility.

EXECUTIVES

FOR PUBLIC AFFAIRS*, William T Bergman
Auditors : DELOITTE & TOUCHE LLP PHILADE

LOCATIONS

HQ: TEMPLE UNIVERSITY HEALTH SYSTEM, INC.
2450 W HUNTING PARK AVE, PHILADELPHIA, PA 191291302
Phone: 215 707-2000
Web: WWW.TEMPLEHEALTH.ORG

COMPETITORS
BAYLOR COLLEGE OF MEDICINE
BRONXCARE HEALTH SYSTEM
CHARLESTON AREA MEDICAL CENTER, INC.
OREGON HEALTH & SCIENCE UNIVERSITY MEDICAL GROUP
ROBERT WOOD JOHNSON UNIVERSITY HOSPITAL, INC.
SUNY DOWNSTATE MEDICAL CENTER
UNIVERSITY OF ALABAMA AT BIRMINGHAM
UNIVERSITY OF CALIFORNIA, SAN FRANCISCO
UNIVERSITY OF MISSOURI SYSTEM
UNIVERSITY OF VIRGINIA MEDICAL CENTER

HISTORICAL FINANCIALS
Company Type: Private

Income Statement   FYE: June 30

	REVENUE ($mil)	NET INCOME ($mil)	NET PROFIT MARGIN	EMPLOYEES
06/12	1,004	(48)	—	7,573
06/11	994	45	4.6%	—
06/09	0	(0)	—	—
Annual Growth	1819.9%	—	—	—

2012 Year-End Financials
Return on assets: (-5.1%)
Return on equity: (-22.0%)
Current Ratio: 2.30
Cash ($ mil.): 103

TEMPLE UNIVERSITY- OF THE COMMONWEALTH SYSTEM OF HIGHER EDUCATION

Temple University provides education and training services to approximately 40,000 undergraduate, graduate and professional students are enrolled in its more than 500 academic programs across the Philadelphia university's over 15 schools. Its Health Sciences Center includes Temple University Hospital and schools that teach medicine and dentistry. Part of Pennsylvania's Commonwealth System of Higher Education, Temple has eight different campuses in the Philadelphia area, as well campuses in Tokyo and Rome and offers study abroad programs in various locations. Dr. Russell Conwell founded the university in 1884; it was incorporated as Temple University in 1907.

Operations
Temple Health comprises the health, education and research activities carried out by the affiliates of Temple University Health System and the Lewis Katz School of Medicine at Temple University. The Lewis Katz School of Medicine at Temple University (LKSOM) is one of the nation's leading medical schools. It has attained a national reputation for training humanistic clinicians and biomedical scientists.

Together Temple's libraries hold more than four million bound volume equivalents, care for thousands of special collections of rare books and primary archival sources and provide a full range of services for faculty, students and community members.

Geographic Reach
Temple's main campus is located in North Philadelphia.

Strategy

Auditors : DELOITTE & TOUCHE LLP PHILADE

LOCATIONS

HQ: TEMPLE UNIVERSITY-OF THE COMMONWEALTH SYSTEM OF HIGHER EDUCATION
1801 N BROAD ST, PHILADELPHIA, PA 191226003
Phone: 215 204-1380
Web: WWW.TEMPLE.EDU

Selected Campuses
Philadelphia
   Ambler
   Center City
   Fort Washington
   Harrisburg
   Main
   Podiatric Medicine
   Health Sciences Center

International
Japan
Rome, Italy

COMPETITORS
ADELPHI UNIVERSITY
DESALES UNIVERSITY
HAMPTON UNIVERSITY
IDAHO STATE UNIVERSITY
LOYOLA UNIVERSITY OF CHICAGO
MISSOURI STATE UNIVERSITY
PHILADELPHIA UNIVERSITY
THE UNIVERSITY OF IOWA
UNIVERSITY OF ARKANSAS SYSTEM
UNIVERSITY OF SAN FRANCISCO

HISTORICAL FINANCIALS
Company Type: Private

Income Statement — FYE: June 30

	REVENUE ($mil)	NET INCOME ($mil)	NET PROFIT MARGIN	EMPLOYEES
06/22	3,943	197	5.0%	9,061
06/21	3,722	553	14.9%	—
06/20	3,628	154	4.3%	—
06/13	2,635	192	7.3%	—
Annual Growth	4.6%	0.3%	—	—

2022 Year-End Financials
Return on assets: 3.2%   Cash ($ mil.): 772
Return on equity: 5.1%
Current Ratio: 3.90

TENASKA ENERGY, INC.

LOCATIONS
HQ: TENASKA ENERGY, INC.
14302 FNB PKWY, OMAHA, NE 681544446
Phone: 402 691-9500
Web: WWW.TENASKA.COM

HISTORICAL FINANCIALS
Company Type: Private

Income Statement — FYE: December 31

	REVENUE ($mil)	NET INCOME ($mil)	NET PROFIT MARGIN	EMPLOYEES
12/07	654	0	0.0%	300
12/05	10,020	0	0.0%	—
Annual Growth	(74.4%)	—	—	—

2007 Year-End Financials
Return on assets: —   Cash ($ mil.): 142
Return on equity: —
Current Ratio: 1.70

TENERITY, INC.

Through its partners and affiliations, Affinion Group aims to make fans of its customers' customers. The company operates membership and loyalty programs on behalf of corporate clients seeking to strengthen their ties to consumers. It specializes in launching a variety of media services -- through direct mail and the Internet -- and packaging these benefits to its clients' customers. Programs overseen include AutoVantage, Buyers Advantage, and Travelers Advantage. Overall, the group offers its programs to some 65 million members worldwide through more than 5,700 partners.

Geographic Reach
The company has offices in Europe, South Africa, and the US. Most recently, Affinion expanded its footprint into Brazil and into Turkey. However, the company gets about 80% of its revenue from US.

Sales and Marketing
Affinion provides its customer engagement and loyalty solutions through retail and wholesale arrangements, with its marketing partners, in addition to its direct to consumer marketing efforts. Under a retail arrangement, it usually markets products to a marketing partner's customers by using that marketing partner's brand name and customer contacts. Under a wholesale arrangement, the marketing partner bears the expense to market products and services to its customers, collects revenue from the customer, and typically pays us a monthly fee per end-customer.

Marketing partners have included Citibank, JPMorgan Chase, Royal Bank of Scotland, and Wells Fargo. Revenues generated from Wells Fargo accounted for 15.3% of total revenues in fiscal 2012.

Affinion also markets its products through direct efforts such direct mail, online marketing, point-of-sale marketing, and telemarketing.

Financial Performance
In fiscal 2012 the company reported revenue of about $1.49 billion, down by 2.6%, compared to the $1.53 billion it reported in revenue for fiscal 2011. The decline in revenue was attributed to decreases in revenue from membership products along with declines in revenue from insurance and package products.

Strategy
The company intends to continue its growth in international markets through both organic initiatives, including geographic expansion, as well as the continued evaluation of strategic acquisitions that strengthen its customer engagement solutions, grow its distribution capabilities, or enhance its scale.

Affinion sees substantial opportunities to add new marketing partners in the retail, financial, travel, Internet, cable, telecom, and utilities industries, in both North America and Europe.

Mergers and Acquisitions
In 2012 Affinion extended its geographic reach in Europe with the acquisition of a majority stake in Back-Up, a leading concierge service. Affinion has accelerated its entry into that growing market through the formation of a partnership with Boyner Holding Company, one of the most respected and successful brands currently serving Turkish consumers.

EXECUTIVES
Chief Digital Officer, Rachel Bicking

LOCATIONS
HQ: TENERITY, INC.
6 HIGH RIDGE PARK, STAMFORD, CT 069051327
Phone: 203 956-1000
Web: WWW.CXLOYALTY.COM

2012 Sales

	$ mil.	% of total
US	1,191	80
UK	117	8
Other countries	186	12
Total	1,495	100

PRODUCTS/OPERATIONS
Selected Membership Products and Services
AutoVantage
Buyers Advantage
CompleteHome
CardCops
Everyday Privileges Gold
Everyday Values
Great Fun
Great Options
HealthSaver
Hot-Line
ID Secure
IdentitySecure
Just For Me
PC SafetyPlus
Privacy Guard
Shoppers Advantage
Travelers Advantage

Selected Partners
American Express
Bank of America
Choice Hotels
HSBC
JPMorgan Chase
TransWorld Entertainment
Wells Fargo

COMPETITORS
BAZAARVOICE, INC.
BORDERFREE, INC.
CONSUMER TECHNOLOGY ASSOCIATION
COUNCIL OF BETTER BUSINESS BUREAUS, INC.
DIRECT MARKETING ASSOCIATION, INCORPORATED
DIRECT SELLING ASSOCIATION (INC)
INDUSTRIAL SUPPLY ASSOCIATION
REACHLOCAL, INC.
SHELL FOUNDATION
TBA GLOBAL LLC

HISTORICAL FINANCIALS
Company Type: Private

Income Statement — FYE: December 31

	REVENUE ($mil)	NET INCOME ($mil)	NET PROFIT MARGIN	EMPLOYEES
12/18	699	303	43.3%	3,860
12/17	953	(24)	—	—
12/16	969	16	1.7%	—
Annual Growth	(15.0%)	331.4%	—	—

TERRACON CONSULTANTS, INC.

Employee-owned Terracon Consultants (Terracon) provides geotechnical, environmental, construction material evaluation, pavement engineering and construction management, and facilities engineering services. One of the nation's top design firms, the company serves the agriculture, oil & gas, telecommunications, commercial development, and transportation sectors, as well as government clients. The company has more than 175 offices in all 50 US states. It helps its customers comply with new building codes and environmental regulations, assess environmental hazards, and tackle the problem of aging structures.

Operations
Terracon provides practical solutions to environmental, facilities, geotechnical, and materials engineering challenges. Environmental services include asbestos and lead services, brownfields and site redevelopment, environmental management systems, regulatory compliance, and solid waste planning and design among others. It also provides facility engineering including building enclosure condition assessments, MEP consulting, engineering diagnostics, structural analysis and design, geotechnical consulting, construction monitoring & support, and construction material evaluation.

Geographic Reach
Kansas-based Terracon has operations throughout the US.

Sales and Marketing
Terracon serves a variety of industries, including agriculture, aquatics, commercial/retail, disaster response, federal, financial, healthcare, industrial, oil & gas, power generation/transmission, telecommunications, and transportation/infrastructure.

Some of its agricultural partners include Agriliance LLC, Cenex/Harvest States, Helena Chemical Company, Murphy Family Farms, Seaboard Farms, United Agri Products, Terra Industries, as well as its government clients such as US Air Force, US Department of Agriculture, NASA, Department of Commerce, and Federal Highway Administration.

Company Background
The company was founded in Iowa in 1965 as a joint venture between Shive, Hall and Hattery (civil consulting), Soil Testing Services (geotechnical testing), and Gerald Olson, P.E. (the company's founder and a project engineer).

Terracon is owned by its employees. The firm was ranked 51st on the Employee Ownership 100, the list of the top 100 largest majority employee-owned companies in the US in 2012.

Auditors: BKD LLP KANSAS CITY MISSOURI

LOCATIONS
HQ: TERRACON CONSULTANTS, INC.
10841 S RIDGEVIEW RD, OLATHE, KS 660616456
Phone: 913 599-6886
Web: WWW.TERRACON.COM

PRODUCTS/OPERATIONS
Selected Services
Materials
Special InspectionsOn-site Observation and MonitoringConstruction Quality Control and Quality Assurance ProgramsField and Laboratory Testing and AnalysisDesign and Review of Concrete, Grout and Asphaltic Concrete MixesStructural Steel Nondestructive TestingDeep Foundation Nondestructive Testing (NDT)Forensic Investigation and Evaluation of In-place MaterialsDiving Services
Geotechnical
    Subsurface exploration and testing
    Foundation analysis and design
    Soil stabilization
    Groundwater control
    Pavement design
Environmental
    Site assessment
    Industrial hygiene and occupational safety
    Regulatory compliance
    Solid waste planning and design
Facilities
    Roof/waterproofing consulting
    Foundation/structural consulting
    Life cycle cost analysis
    Peer reviews
    Seismic risk assessments
    Construction administration

Selected Markets
Agriculture
Commercial/Retail
Energy
Federal
Financial
Industrial
Telecommunications
Transportation/Infrastructure

COMPETITORS
ARCADIS U.S., INC.
CBRE HEERY, INC.
EISNERAMPER LLP
ENVIRONMENTAL RESOURCES MANAGEMENT LIMITED
ESCALENT, INC.
PARSONS BRINCKERHOFF GROUP LLC
PENNONI ASSOCIATES INC.
PROTIVITI INC.
S&ME, INC.
WESTON SOLUTIONS, INC.

2018 Year-End Financials
Return on assets: 44.5% Cash ($ mil.): 84
Return on equity: —
Current Ratio: 1.00

HISTORICAL FINANCIALS
Company Type: Private

Income Statement   FYE: December 31

	REVENUE ($mil)	NET INCOME ($mil)	NET PROFIT MARGIN	EMPLOYEES
12/21	907	29	3.2%	4,000
12/20	818	23	2.9%	—
12/19	804	21	2.7%	—
12/18	751	22	2.9%	—
Annual Growth	6.5%	10.0%	—	—

2021 Year-End Financials
Return on assets: 9.2% Cash ($ mil.): 4
Return on equity: 17.2%
Current Ratio: 2.40

TESLA ENERGY OPERATIONS, INC.

Ready to get off the grid? SolarCity can help. The company sells, installs, finances, and monitors turnkey solar energy systems that convert sunlight into electricity. Its systems, either mounted on a building's roof or the ground, are used by residential, commercial, and government customers such as eBay, Intel, Wal-Mart, and Homeland Security. SolarCity doesn't manufacture its systems but uses solar panels from Trina Solar, Yingli Green Energy, and Kyocera Solar, and inverters from Power-One, SMA Solar Technology, and Schneider Electric. In late 2016, SolarCity was acquired by Tesla Motors in a deal worth $2.6 billion.

Operations
SolarCity's main selling point is that it offers renewable energy for less than traditional utility companies. While customers feel good about choosing an alternative energy source, they're also usually saving money. Much of the costs associated with new installation and monthly fees are offset by SolarCity's investment funds. To date, the company has formed more than 20 investment funds and raised more than $1.5 billion from banks and other companies such as Credit Suisse, Google, PG&E Corporation, and U.S. Bancorp. (Two funds, however, are being audited by the IRS.) SolarCity also depends on federal and state tax rebates and credits to lower costs and create incentives for fund investors. For example, the federal government offers a tax credit of 30% to install solar power through 2016. (After 2016, the tax credit will fall to 10%.)

Electricity is sold under long-term contracts; generally customers agree to a 20-year term. Customers are either signed up as leases or power purchase agreements. Lease customers pay a fixed monthly rate while the rate for power purchase agreement customers depends on the amount of electricity the solar energy system produces. The vast majority of its customers (some 90%) "rent" the solar installations instead of buying them outright, in order to keep SolarCity in charge of the product warranty.

Geographic Reach
California-based SolarCity serves customers in 16 states and the District of Columbia. Its offices and warehouses reside in Arizona, California, Colorado, Connecticut, Hawaii, Maryland, Massachusetts, Nevada, New Jersey, New York, Oregon, Texas, Canada, and China. The company earned over 75% of its revenue collectively from California, Arizona, Colorado, Hawaii, and New York.

Sales and Marketing
The company's client list includes residential customers, commercial entities such as Wal-Mart, eBay, Intel, and Safeway, and government entities such as the U.S. Military. SolarCity sells its products and services through a direct outside sales force from 64 sales offices in 16 states and Washington, DC. (Most states have one sales office, but its home state of California has 12.) It also has a call center.

Financial Performance
Fast-growing SolarCity is posting impressive revenue gains, but no profits yet. Indeed, the solar services company reported $255 million in sales in 2014, an increase of 56% versus 2013. The company credited the double-digit gain for 2014 to a major increase in the installation and operation of solar energy systems under lease and power purchase agreements in new and existing markets, along with an increase in sales of solar energy systems and components. SolarCity's net loss for 2014 was fueled by an increase in sales and marketing costs and interest expenses.

Strategy
SolarCity installs about one of every four solar energy systems in the US, but is still hungry for more. The company's products and services are available through home-improvement-retail-giant The Home Depot. Also, in 2014, the company partnered with electronics retailer Best Buy to offer its products and services through some 60 Best Buy stores in California, Arizona, Hawaii, New York, and Oregon. SolarCity also partners with more than 100 homebuilders, including Pulte, and Del Webb. Other channel partners include Tesla Motors, Viridian Energy, Honda, Acura, and BMW.

While residential customers are important to the company, going forward SolarCity is seeking to install larger solar energy systems for businesses and government customers. The company is also growing its business through acquisitions.

Mergers and Acquisitions
In mid-2014, SolarCity acquired Silevo, a solar panel technology and manufacturing company. The acquisition helped to manage the company's supply chain and control the design and manufacturing of solar cells and photovoltaic panels that are a key component of its solar energy systems. The deal also enabled SolarCity to utilize and combine Silevo's technology with economies of scale to achieve significant cost reductions.

Company Background
SolarCity was founded in 2006 by CEO Lyndon Rive and his brother, COO and CTO Peter Rive. The Rives are cousins of non-executive chairman Elon Musk, a notable entrepreneur who co-founded PayPal and also heads Tesla Motors and SpaceX.

Auditors: ERNST & YOUNG LLP LOS ANGELES

LOCATIONS
HQ: TESLA ENERGY OPERATIONS, INC.
3055 CLEARVIEW WAY, SAN MATEO, CA 944023709
Phone: 888 765-2489
Web: WWW.SOLARCITY.COM

PRODUCTS/OPERATIONS
2013 Sales
	$ mil.	% of total
Operating leases	82.8	51
Solar energy system	81.0	49
Total	163.8	100

Selected Products and Services
Products
　Solar energy systems (panels, inverters, and mounting racks)
Services
　Energy efficiency upgrades
　Home energy evaluations

COMPETITORS
AMERESCO, INC.
AMERICAN DG ENERGY INC.
ANDALAY, INC.
ISS TECHNICAL SERVICES HOLDINGS LIMITED
JOHNSON CONTROLS, INC.
Just Energy Group Inc
LIME ENERGY CO.
MURPHY COMPANY MECHANICAL CONTRACTORS AND ENGINEERS
PEPCO ENERGY SERVICES, INC.
SSE PLC

HISTORICAL FINANCIALS
Company Type: Private

Income Statement　　　　　　　　　FYE: December 31

	REVENUE ($mil)	NET INCOME ($mil)	NET PROFIT MARGIN	EMPLOYEES
12/16	730	(820)	—	12,000
12/15	399	(768)	—	—
12/14	255	(375)	—	—
12/13	163	(151)	—	—
Annual Growth	64.6%	—	—	—

2016 Year-End Financials
Return on assets: (-9.0%)　Cash ($ mil.): 290
Return on equity: (-42.5%)
Current Ratio: 0.50

TEXAS AROMATICS, LP

Auditors: WEAVER & TIDWELL LLP HOUS

LOCATIONS
HQ: TEXAS AROMATICS, LP
3555 TIMMONS LN STE 700, HOUSTON, TX 770276450
Phone: 713 520-2900
Web: WWW.TEXASAROMATICS.COM

HISTORICAL FINANCIALS
Company Type: Private

Income Statement　　　　　　　　　FYE: December 31

	REVENUE ($mil)	NET INCOME ($mil)	NET PROFIT MARGIN	EMPLOYEES
12/18	567	5	0.9%	21
12/17	470	9	2.0%	—
12/16	449	11	2.6%	—
12/15	531	10	2.0%	—
Annual Growth	2.2%	(20.4%)	—	—

2018 Year-End Financials
Return on assets: 7.4%　Cash ($ mil.): 27
Return on equity: 13.6%
Current Ratio: 2.20

TEXAS CHILDREN'S HOSPITAL

Texas Children's Hospital (TCH) is one of the nation's best, largest and most comprehensive specialty pediatric hospitals, with more than 4.3 million patient encounters annually. Founded in 1954, the not-for-profit hospital provides full-service medical care for children, conducts extensive research, and trains pediatric medical professionals. Part of the Texas Medical Center complex, it has clinical facilities for every ailment ranging from psychological troubles to surgery and physical rehabilitation, as well as specialized heart, cancer, and neurological care. TCH is the primary pediatric training facility for Baylor College of Medicine.

Operations
TCH comprises Jan and Dan Duncan Neurological Research Institute; the Feigin Tower for pediatric research; Texas Children's Pavilion for Women, a comprehensive obstetrics/gynecology facility focusing on high-risk births; Texas Children's Hospital West Campus, a community hospital in suburban West Houston; and Texas Children's Hospital's The Woodlands, the first hospital devoted to children's care for communities north of Houston. In addition, the organization also created Texas Children's Health Plan, the nation's first HMO for children; has the largest pediatric primary care network in the country, Texas Children's Pediatrics; Texas Children's Urgent Care clinics that specialize in after-hours care tailored specifically for children; and a global health program that's channeling care to children and women all over the world.

The hospital prides itself on providing a strong and supportive culture to empower its more than 3,500 nurses. It provides care in more than 40 pediatric specialties and has multiple locations across Houston. Additionally, research at Texas Children's Hospital, spans more than 800 active clinical trials, over 800,000 square feet of laboratory space, and one of the largest and most diverse pediatric patient populations in the country. With funding of more than $115 million annually, over 120 TCH's and Baylor College of Medicine principal investigators are conducting over 1,000 clinical, basic sciences, and translational research projects at any given moment.

TCH encounters more than 4.3 million patients annually.

Geographic Reach
TCH has more than 10 locations across the greater Houston area. Its medical providers see patients at its hospitals in the Texas Medical Center, Katy in West Houston, and The Woodlands.

Texas Children's Hospital is located in Houston, Texas.

Auditors : IT CROWE LLP DALLAS TX

LOCATIONS
HQ: TEXAS CHILDREN'S HOSPITAL
6621 FANNIN ST, HOUSTON, TX 770302399
Phone: 832 824-1000
Web: WWW.TEXASCHILDRENS.ORG

PRODUCTS/OPERATIONS

2014 Sales

	$ in mil	% of total
Net patient revenue	1,530.6	60
Premium revenue	876.8	34
Medicaid & other supplemental reimbursement	59.4	2
Net assets released from restrictions for operations	28.2	1
Grants	21.9	1
Other income	41.8	2
Total	2,558.7	100

2014 Net Patient Revenue

	% of total
Managed care	61
Medicaid managed care	15
Medicaid	13
Self-pay	6
Commercial	5
Total	100

Selected Serives
Bariatric/weight control services
Certified trauma center
Chemotherapy
Dental services
Heart catheterization—diagnostic (child)
Genetic testing/counseling
HIV-AIDS services
Heart catheterization—treatment (child)
Kidney dialysis
Chemotherapy
Physical rehabilitation
Psychiatric services (Child/adolescent services, Consultation and Outpatient care)
Sleep center
Sports medicine
Urgent-care center
Women's health center
Wound management services

COMPETITORS
ANN & ROBERT H. LURIE CHILDREN'S HOSPITAL OF CHICAGO
ARKANSAS CHILDREN'S HOSPITAL
BILLINGS CLINIC
BOSTON MEDICAL CENTER CORPORATION
CHARLESTON AREA MEDICAL CENTER, INC.
CHILDREN'S HOSPITAL & RESEARCH CENTER AT OAKLAND
H. LEE MOFFITT CANCER CENTER AND RESEARCH INSTITUTE HOSPITAL, INC.
SHANDS TEACHING HOSPITAL AND CLINICS, INC.
SWEDISH HEALTH SERVICES
THE MASSACHUSETTS GENERAL HOSPITAL

HISTORICAL FINANCIALS
Company Type: Private

Income Statement　　　　　　　　FYE: September 30

	REVENUE ($mil)	NET INCOME ($mil)	NET PROFIT MARGIN	EMPLOYEES
09/19	2,601	181	7.0%	6,000
09/15	1,546	96	6.3%	—
09/14	1,383	70	5.1%	—
09/13	1,229	78	6.4%	—
Annual Growth	13.3%	14.9%	—	—

2019 Year-End Financials
Return on assets: 3.2%　　Cash ($ mil.): 56
Return on equity: 4.3%
Current Ratio: 0.50

TEXAS CHRISTIAN UNIVERSITY INC

Home of the Horned Frogs (the school mascot), Texas Christian University (TCU) offers bachelor's, master's, and doctorate degrees in approximately 220 fields of study. More than 11,000 undergraduate and graduate students attend the university's ten colleges and schools the cover fields of study ranging from liberal arts to engineering to business. TCU has nearly 700 full-time faculty members and a student-to-faculty ratio of 13:1. It also has one of the NCAA's top football programs. TCU is affiliated with the Disciples of Christ, a Protestant denomination.

Operations
The TCU academic programs are organized under ten schools in fields including liberal arts, communication, education, fine arts, science and engineering, nursing and health, and business. It offers more than 115 bachelors, approximately 65 masters, and nearly 40 doctoral degrees.

Tuition, fees, room and board and books cost about $66,600 per year for undergraduate and nearly $50,540 for graduate/professional.

Geographic Reach
TCU's campus takes up about 295 acres about five miles from downtown Fort Worth.

Strategy
TCU's strategy includes fostering a diverse and inclusive university for all; promoting academic excellence and elevating its academic profile and reputation through focused and dynamic academic planning; providing a highly engaging and inclusive its student experience, and recruiting and retaining a diverse world-class workforce; and telling compelling stories of TCU and its students, faculty, and staff.

Company Background
Brothers Addison and Randolph Clark established the school in 1873 as Addran Male and Female College (the school changed its name to Texas Christian University in 1902).

Auditors : GRANT THORNTON LLP DALLAS TE

LOCATIONS
HQ: TEXAS CHRISTIAN UNIVERSITY INC
2800 S UNIVERSITY DR, FORT WORTH, TX 761290001
Phone: 817 257-7000
Web: WWW.TCU.EDU

PRODUCTS/OPERATIONS

Selected Colleges and Schools
AddRan College of Liberal Arts
College of Communication
College of Education
College of Fine Arts
College of Science and Engineering
Harris College of Nursing and Health Sciences
John V. Roach Honors College
Neeley School of Business
Relationship with Brite Divinity School

COMPETITORS
BALL STATE UNIVERSITY
CLEVELAND STATE UNIVERSITY
LAFAYETTE COLLEGE
OAKLAND UNIVERSITY
THE UNIVERSITY OF NORTH CAROLINA AT CHARLOTTE
TRUSTEES OF BOSTON COLLEGE
UNIVERSITY OF LYNCHBURG
UNIVERSITY OF SAN DIEGO
UNIVERSITY OF SAN FRANCISCO
WILLAMETTE UNIVERSITY

HISTORICAL FINANCIALS
Company Type: Private

Income Statement　　　　　　　　FYE: May 31

	REVENUE ($mil)	NET INCOME ($mil)	NET PROFIT MARGIN	EMPLOYEES
05/22	684	346	50.6%	3,400
05/21	545	443	81.3%	—
05/20	562	(47)	—	—
05/19	558	26	4.8%	—
Annual Growth	7.0%	135.4%	—	—

2022 Year-End Financials
Return on assets: 8.1%　　Cash ($ mil.): 16
Return on equity: 11.0%
Current Ratio: —

TEXAS COUNTY AND DISTRICT RETIREMENT SYSTEM

Auditors: KPMG LLP AUSTIN TX

LOCATIONS

HQ: TEXAS COUNTY AND DISTRICT RETIREMENT SYSTEM
901 S MO PAC EXPY STE V50, AUSTIN, TX 787465776
Phone: 512 328-8889
Web: WWW.TCDRS.ORG

HISTORICAL FINANCIALS
Company Type: Private

Income Statement — FYE: December 31

	ASSETS ($mil)	NET INCOME ($mil)	INCOME AS % OF ASSETS	EMPLOYEES
12/16	26,387	1,761	6.7%	108
12/15	24,654	(182)	—	—
12/14	24,832	0	0.0%	—
12/10	18,116	2,178	12.0%	—
Annual Growth	6.5%	(3.5%)	—	—

2016 Year-End Financials
Return on assets: 6.7% Cash ($ mil.): 25
Return on equity: 6.7%
Current Ratio: —

TEXAS DEPARTMENT OF HOUSING & COMMUNITY AFFAIRS

LOCATIONS

HQ: TEXAS DEPARTMENT OF HOUSING & COMMUNITY AFFAIRS
221 E 11TH ST, AUSTIN, TX 787012410
Phone: 512 475-3800
Web: TDHCA.STATE.TX.US

HISTORICAL FINANCIALS
Company Type: Private

Income Statement — FYE: August 31

	REVENUE ($mil)	NET INCOME ($mil)	NET PROFIT MARGIN	EMPLOYEES
08/21	1,190	0	0.0%	370
08/20	287	4	1.7%	—
08/19	265	0	0.3%	—
08/18	99	7	8.0%	—
Annual Growth	128.9%	(58.6%)	—	—

2021 Year-End Financials
Return on assets: — Cash ($ mil.): 45
Return on equity: 0.1%
Current Ratio: 1.30

TEXAS DEPARTMENT OF TRANSPORTATION

Bob Wills saw Miles and Miles of Texas, and the Texas Department of Transportation (TxDOT) makes sure that we do too. TxDOT builds and maintains interstate, US, and state highways, as well as farm-to-market roads throughout the state. It also oversees public transportation systems in the state. The aviation division helps local governments manage funds for airport development. In 2009 the agency transferred some its responsibilities, including issuing license plates and vehicle titles, to the newly created Texas Department of Motor Vehicles. The governor-appointed, five-member Texas Transportation Commission oversees TxDOT's work. The agency dates back to the Texas Highway Department, created in 1917.

Operations

The Texas Department of Transportation is divided into 25 districts that each supervise the construction and maintenance of state highways in their jurisdictions. These districts are further divided into four administrative regions that provide such services as information technology, purchasing, accounting, and project management support for the districts. A major Texas city is included in each of the four regions.

Current TxDOT projects include widening Interstate 35 to six lanes throughout Central Texas and reconstructing the State Loop 12/State Highway 114 interchange to improve traffic conditions in the Dallas/Fort Worth area.

EXECUTIVES

Deputy Executive Director, Marc D Williams Pe
Chief of Staff, Richard Mcmonagle
Auditors: CROWE LLP DALLAS TEXAS

LOCATIONS

HQ: TEXAS DEPARTMENT OF TRANSPORTATION
150 E RIVERSIDE DR, AUSTIN, TX 787041202
Phone: 512 463-8588
Web: WWW.TXDOT.GOV

COMPETITORS

ARIZONA DEPARTMENT OF TRANSPORTATION
HNTB CORPORATION
MASSACHUSETTS DEPARTMENT OF TRANSPORTATION
MISSOURI DEPARTMENT OF TRANSPORTATION
NEW YORK DEPARTMENT OF TRANSPORTATION
OHIO DEPARTMENT OF TRANSPORTATION
TENNESSEE DEPARTMENT OF SAFETY
TRANSPORTATION, SOUTH CAROLINA DEPARTMENT OF
TRANSPORTATION, WEST VIRGINIA DEPARTMENT OF
VERMONT AGENCY OF TRANSPORTATION

HISTORICAL FINANCIALS
Company Type: Private

Income Statement — FYE: August 31

	REVENUE ($mil)	NET INCOME ($mil)	NET PROFIT MARGIN	EMPLOYEES
08/21	12,965	734	5.7%	14,720
08/20	12	(0)	—	—
08/19	12,069	1,107	9.2%	—
08/18	10,993	1,123	10.2%	—
Annual Growth	5.7%	(13.2%)	—	—

2021 Year-End Financials
Return on assets: 0.5% Cash ($ mil.): 9,619
Return on equity: 0.7%
Current Ratio: 3.60

TEXAS EASTERN TRANSMISSION, LP

Auditors: DELOITTE & TOUCHE LLP HOUSTO

LOCATIONS

HQ: TEXAS EASTERN TRANSMISSION, LP
5400 WESTHEIMER CT, HOUSTON, TX 770565353
Phone: 713 627-5400
Web: WWW.SPECTRAENERGY.COM

HISTORICAL FINANCIALS
Company Type: Private

Income Statement — FYE: December 31

	REVENUE ($mil)	NET INCOME ($mil)	NET PROFIT MARGIN	EMPLOYEES
12/17	1,389	347	25.0%	700
12/16	1,350	329	24.4%	—
12/12	956	406	42.5%	—
Annual Growth	7.8%	(3.1%)	—	—

2017 Year-End Financials
Return on assets: 4.2% Cash ($ mil.): —
Return on equity: 9.5%
Current Ratio: 0.60

TEXAS HEALTH HARRIS METHODIST HOSPITAL FORT WORTH

Harris Methodist Fort Worth Hospital is the largest and busiest hospital in Fort Worth. It is a private, not-for-profit, almost 730-bed tertiary care hospital serving the residents of Tarrant County and nearby communities in Texas. Harris Methodist provides both inpatient and outpatient care through its main medical center and on-site health clinics. Specialized services include emergency medicine, trauma care, orthopedics, occupational health, women's health, oncology, and rehabilitation. Its Harris Methodist Heart Center has about 100 beds. The hospital is the flagship facility of the Texas Health Resources hospitals system.

Operations

Harris Methodist, also known as Texas Health Harris Methodist Hospital Fort Worth, serves as a regional referral center. The hospital employs a medical staff of about 1,000 physicians.

Sales and Marketing

To promote its services to area residents, Harris Methodist uses a range of marketing avenues including print, television, online, radio, and outdoor advertising.

Strategy

To meet the growing needs of Fort Worth area residents, in 2012 Harris Methodist launched a $58 million construction project to add a new emergency care center adjacent to the medical center campus. The 75,000-sq. ft. center, scheduled for completion in 2014, will increase the hospital's emergency room capacity from about 60 beds to 90 beds. A sky bridge will connect the new emergency care center to the main hospital.

Mergers and Acquisitions

To further expand outpatient services, in 2012 Harris Methodist acquired the Clear Fork Surgery Center (now named Texas Health Outpatient Surgery Center Fort Worth). The ambulatory surgery center is located on the Harris Methodist hospital campus and was previously operated through a venture with Symbion and a group of physicians. The center performs about 10,000 procedures per year.

Company Background

The organization opened its doors in 1930 the leadership of Dr. Charles Harris and the Methodist Church.

EXECUTIVES

CMO*, Joseph Prosser

LOCATIONS

HQ: TEXAS HEALTH HARRIS METHODIST HOSPITAL FORT WORTH
    1301 PENNSYLVANIA AVE, FORT WORTH, TX 761042122
Phone: 817 250-2000
Web: WWW.TEXASHEALTH.ORG

PRODUCTS/OPERATIONS

Selected Centers and Services
Breast Center
Breastfeeding Resource Center
Business Health Services
Cancer
Complementary or Alternative Medicine
Diabetes
Emergency, Trauma Services
Executive Health Program
Fitness Center
Heart and Vascular
Gastroenterology
Home Health
Hospitalist Program
Imaging
Infertility
Mobile Health Unit
Neurosciences
Occupational Health
Orthopedics
Outpatient Physical Therapy
Respiratory
Weight Loss
Texas Health Physician Offices Saginaw
Palliative Care
Rehabilitation
Sports Medicine
Primary Stroke Center
Surgery
Texas Health Physician Offices Keller
Vascular and Interventional Radiology
Women and Infants
Wound Care

COMPETITORS

BEAUFORT MEMORIAL HOSPITAL
HOSPITAL AUTHORITY OF VALDOSTA AND LOWNDES COUNTY, GEORGIA
METHODIST HEALTHCARE SYSTEM OF SAN ANTONIO, LTD., L.L.P.
METHODIST HOSPITALS OF DALLAS
ST. JOSEPH'S HOSPITAL HEALTH CENTER

HISTORICAL FINANCIALS

Company Type: Private

Income Statement — FYE: September 30

	REVENUE ($mil)	NET INCOME ($mil)	NET PROFIT MARGIN	EMPLOYEES
09/20*	787	49	6.3%	3,500
12/17	843	55	6.5%	—
12/15	770	55	7.1%	—
Annual Growth	0.4%	(2.0%)	—	—

*Fiscal year change

2020 Year-End Financials
Return on assets: 4.3%   Cash ($ mil.): —
Return on equity: 13.2%
Current Ratio: 1.10

TEXAS HEALTH RESOURCES

Texas Health Resources (THR) is a faith-based, nonprofit health system that cares for more patients in North Texas than any other provider. THR serves North Texas through primary care and specialty physician practices, hospitals, outpatient facilities, urgent care centers, home health and preventive and fitness services. It has about 30 acute care and short-stay hospitals, including owned, managed, and joint venture facilities. THR also operates outpatient and surgical centers and physicians' offices, and it maintains affiliations with imaging, diagnostic, rehabilitation facilities, and home health agencies. THR's network includes more than 6,400 doctors and more than 4,100 licensed beds.

Operations

Texas Health Medial Associates offers primary services (family care, illness care, disease management, screening and testing) and specialist services (gastroenterology, general surgery, OB/GYN, pediatrics, rheumatology and ENT).

With about 1,075 physicians and other medical professionals in 250-plus locations, Texas Health Physicians Group offers extensive network of primary care including family care and internal medicine.

Geographic Reach

THR has operations in about 15 counties throughout North Texas, including Collin, Dallas, Ellis, Grayson, Henderson, Johnson, Kaufman, Parker, Rockwall, Somervell, Tarrant and Wise.

Sales and Marketing

THR serves more than 7 million residents of North Texas.

Financial Performance
Company Background

THR was formed in 1997 by the merger of Harris Methodist Health System, Presbyterian Healthcare System, and Arlington Memorial Hospital Foundation. In 2008 the organization rebranded its hospitals, unifying them all under the Texas Health Resources name.

THR had originally been the minority shareholder in a venture with Triad Hospitals to own Presbyterian Hospital of Denton. However, THR grew dissatisfied when Triad was acquired by Community Health Systems in 2007. After a long legal tussle, THR paid $100 million to acquire the hospital outright in 2009 and changed its name to Texas Health Presbyterian Hospital Denton. Texas Health Presbyterian found itself the focus of international media attention in 2014 when it treated the first case of Ebola on US soil.

Auditors : KMPG LLP DALLAS TEXAS

LOCATIONS

HQ: TEXAS HEALTH RESOURCES
   612 E LAMAR BLVD STE 400, ARLINGTON, TX 760114125
Phone: 682 236-7900
Web: WWW.TEXASHEALTH.ORG

PRODUCTS/OPERATIONS

Selected Facilities and Affiliates
Acute Care and Specialty Hospitals
    Texas Health Arlington Memorial
    Texas Health Harris Methodist Hospital Fort Worth
    Texas Health Huguley Hospital Fort Worth South
    Texas Health Presbyterian Hospital Dallas
    Texas Health Presbyterian Hospital Flower Mound
    Texas Health Presbyterian Hospital Rockwall
    Texas Health Center for Diagnostics & Surgery Plano
    Texas Heath Heart & Vascular Hospital Arlington
    USMD Hospital at Arlington
    USMD Hospital at Fort Worth
Affiliates
    Envision Imaging of North Fort Worth
    Texas Rehabilitation Partners
    Two Forest Imaging Dallas
    Southwest Diagnostic Imaging Center

COMPETITORS

ADVENTIST HEALTH SYSTEM/SUNBELT, INC.
BANNER HEALTH
BAPTIST HEALTH SOUTH FLORIDA, INC.
BEAUMONT HEALTH
HOUSTON COUNTY HEALTHCARE AUTHORITY
MEMORIAL HERMANN HEALTHCARE SYSTEM
OHIOHEALTH CORPORATION
ORLANDO HEALTH, INC.
SANFORD
VALLEY BAPTIST MEDICAL CENTER - BROWNSVILLE

HISTORICAL FINANCIALS
Company Type: Private

Income Statement — FYE: December 31

	REVENUE ($mil)	NET INCOME ($mil)	NET PROFIT MARGIN	EMPLOYEES
12/17	4,688	869	18.6%	21,277
12/13	718	285	39.8%	—
12/09	334	2	0.9%	—
12/06	2,287	2,299	100.5%	—
Annual Growth	6.7%	(8.5%)	—	—

2017 Year-End Financials
Return on assets: 9.8%   Cash ($ mil.): 435
Return on equity: 14.2%
Current Ratio: 1.60

TEXAS STATE UNIVERSITY SYSTEM

EXECUTIVES

FOR Finance, Claire Jackson

LOCATIONS

HQ: TEXAS STATE UNIVERSITY SYSTEM
601 COLORADO ST, AUSTIN, TX 787012904
Phone: 512 463-1808
Web: WWW.TSUS.EDU

HISTORICAL FINANCIALS
Company Type: Private

Income Statement — FYE: August 31

	REVENUE ($mil)	NET INCOME ($mil)	NET PROFIT MARGIN	EMPLOYEES
08/18	862	190	22.0%	3,196
08/17	854	145	17.1%	—
08/16	846	126	14.9%	—
Annual Growth	1.0%	22.9%	—	—

2018 Year-End Financials
Return on assets: 5.3%   Cash ($ mil.): 522
Return on equity: 13.1%
Current Ratio: 1.50

TEXAS WORKFORCE COMMISSION

The Texas Workforce Commission (TWC) supports economic development in the Lone Star State by developing its workforce. The state government agency with 28 regional workforce boards offers a number of services benefiting employers (recruiting, retention, and outplacement services) and workers (training and job-search resources). The agency also provides support services such as child care for targeted groups, employment and training services for veterans, publishes labor law and labor market information, and administers the state's unemployment insurance program. Texans receive most of TWC's services for free; the agency is funded primarily by the federal government.

Strategy

TWC has received over $2.8 million in a DOL grant award to fund the Apprenticeship Texas State Expansion Grant project, which has realigned agency services to support the expansion and implement Registered Apprenticeship as a leading talent development strategy. Target industries include Information Technology, Advanced Manufacturing, Aerospace and Defense, STEM, Finance and Energy. The project will serve 634 apprentices with a focus on women in apprenticeship, youth, and individuals with disabilities, veterans, Native Americans, and persons of color, among others.

EXECUTIVES

Interim Executive Director, Ed Serna

LOCATIONS

HQ: TEXAS WORKFORCE COMMISSION
101 E 15TH ST STE 122, AUSTIN, TX 787780001
Phone: 512 463-2222
Web: WWW.TEXASWORKFORCE.ORG

PRODUCTS/OPERATIONS

Program / Service
Adult Education & Literacy
Appeals
Apprenticeship
Career Schools & Colleges
Child Care Services
Choices
Civil Rights
Employment Services
Foreign Labor Certification
Labor Law
Labor Market & Career Information
Noncustodial Parent Choices
Rapid Reemployment Services
Self Sufficiency
Senior Community Service Employment Program
Skills Development
Skills for Small Businesses
Skills for Veterans
Supplemental Nutrition Assistance Program
Employment & Training
Trade Adjustment Assistance
Unemployment Benefits
Unemployment Tax
Veterans' Services
Workforce Investment Act

COMPETITORS

KANSAS DEPARTMENT OF LABOR
RHODE ISLAND DEPT OF LABOR AND TRAINING
WORKFORCE COMMISSION, LOUISIANA
WORKFORCE DEVELOPMENT, WISCONSIN DEPARTMENT OF
WORKFORCE INNOVATION, FLORIDA AGENCY FOR

HISTORICAL FINANCIALS
Company Type: Private

Income Statement — FYE: August 31

	REVENUE ($mil)	NET INCOME ($mil)	NET PROFIT MARGIN	EMPLOYEES
08/21	2,885	288	10.0%	4,600
08/20	2,276	495	21.8%	—
08/19	1,898	46	2.5%	—
08/18	1,822	134	7.4%	—
Annual Growth	16.5%	29.1%	—	—

2021 Year-End Financials
Return on assets: 56.0%   Cash ($ mil.): 223
Return on equity: 95.4%
Current Ratio: 2.20

THE ADMINISTRATORS OF THE TULANE EDUCATIONAL FUND

Auditors: DELOITTE & TOUCHE LLP NEW ORL

LOCATIONS

HQ: THE ADMINISTRATORS OF THE TULANE EDUCATIONAL FUND
6823 SAINT CHARLES AVE, NEW ORLEANS, LA 701185665
Phone: 504 865-5000
Web: WWW.TULANE.EDU

HISTORICAL FINANCIALS
Company Type: Private

Income Statement — FYE: June 30

	REVENUE ($mil)	NET INCOME ($mil)	NET PROFIT MARGIN	EMPLOYEES
06/16	924	(63)	—	5,500
06/15	1,054	40	3.9%	—
06/10	738	48	6.5%	—
06/09	737	0	0.0%	—
Annual Growth	3.3%	—	—	—

2016 Year-End Financials
Return on assets: (-2.7%)   Cash ($ mil.): 22
Return on equity: (-4.5%)
Current Ratio: —

THE AEROSPACE CORPORATION

A not-for-profit company, the Aerospace Corporation provides space-related research, development, and advisory services, primarily for US government programs. Aerospace addresses complex problems across the space enterprise and other areas of national and international significance through agility, innovation, and objective technical leadership. The Aerospace Corporation was established in 1960 and operates in around 20 locations across about a dozen states.

Operations
Space exploration, development, and security are increasingly important elements of national policy and strategy. Aerospace is providing nonpartisan research and strategic analysis to decision makers, and advancing innovative technical solutions.

Aerospace is dedicated to delivering mission success from an enterprise perspective, supporting its government customers with continuous engagement and a unique perspective that spans across a broad range of mission areas.

Geographic Reach
The Aerospace Corporation's headquarters, with engineering and laboratory facilities, is located in El Segundo, California. Major regional offices are located in Chantilly, Virginia and Colorado Springs, Colorado.

Company Background
Founding of The Aerospace Corporation in 1960, the progress of the corporation's work in support of the U.S. Air Force paralleled the advances that the country witnessed in the fields of science and technology.

Auditors : DELOITTE & TOUCHE LLP LOS ANG

LOCATIONS
HQ: THE AEROSPACE CORPORATION
2310 E EL SEGUNDO BLVD, EL SEGUNDO, CA 902454609
Phone: 310 336-5000
Web: WWW.AERO.ORG

PRODUCTS/OPERATIONS
Selected Services
Civil and Commercial
CORDS
Cyber Security
Labs
Launch Support
Mission Assurance
Systems Engineering
Technical Resources

COMPETITORS
AMERICAN INSTITUTES FOR RESEARCH IN THE BEHAVIORAL SCIENCES
AMERICAN SOCIETY FOR TESTING AND MATERIALS
ARGON ST, INC.
EPSILON SYSTEMS SOLUTIONS, INC.
EXELIS INC.
NOBLIS, INC.
SRI INTERNATIONAL
THE JACKSON LABORATORY
THE MITRE CORPORATION
WOODS HOLE OCEANOGRAPHIC INSTITUTION

HISTORICAL FINANCIALS
Company Type: Private

Income Statement — FYE: September 30

	REVENUE ($mil)	NET INCOME ($mil)	NET PROFIT MARGIN	EMPLOYEES
09/19	1,111	57	5.1%	3,920
09/15	916	(15)	—	—
09/14	881	5	0.6%	—
09/13	868	0	0.0%	—
Annual Growth	4.2%	149.2%	—	—

2019 Year-End Financials
Return on assets: 8.0%   Cash ($ mil.): 82
Return on equity: —
Current Ratio: 1.50

THE AMALGAMATED SUGAR COMPANY LLC

The Amalgamated Sugar Company, with roots reaching back to 1915, turns beets into sweets. It's the second-largest US sugar producer, processing sugar beets grown on about 180,000 acres in Idaho, Oregon, and Washington. The company manufactures granulated, coarse, powdered, and brown consumer sugar products marketed under the brand White Satin. It also makes products for retail grocery chains under private labels. The sugar company produces beet pulp, molasses, and other beet by-products for use by food and animal-feed manufacturers. Since 1997 Amalgamated Sugar has been owned by the Snake River Sugar Company, a cooperative that comprises sugar beet growers in Idaho, Oregon, and Washington.

Operations
The Amalgamated Sugar Company processes up to 1.6 billion pounds of sugar each year. Along with processing the cooperative's crops, the company provides its owner-farmers with agronomy advice and services, runs workshops and seminars, operates a co-op store, and sells used equipment.

The company's key management team is employed on a contract basis. A seven-member Management Committee oversees the management team. The committee comprises members of the cooperative's board of directors.

Geographic Reach
The Idaho-based company's sugar beets, which are grown in Idaho, Oregon, and Washington, are processed through the three sugar processing facilities it operates in Idaho. The Amalgamated Sugar Company's warehouses and bulk transfer stations are strategically located from the Midwest to the West Coast.

Sales and Marketing
The Amalgamated Sugar Company markets its sugar primarily in the nation's North Central, Intermountain, and Northwest regions. The company competes with not only cane sugar refiners, but also manufacturers of other forms of sweeteners, such as regular and high fructose corn syrup (HFCS), and non-nutritive, high intensity sweeteners the likes of aspartame.

Financial Performance
The Amalgamated Sugar Company generates some 90% of its annual sales through the sale of refined sugar. The balance of its revenue comes from animal feed derived from beet pulp and molasses and other by-products as a result of sugar beet processing.

Strategy
The industry's return to the use of real sugar in soft drinks and other beverages has become a boon for The Amalgamated Sugar Company. To this end, Pepsi Bottling Ventures has tapped the sugar beet processor to supply the bottler with granulated sugar. During the past few decades, more beverage makers have moved to using lesser-expensive high fructose corn syrup (HFCS) to sweeten their beverages as a way to cut costs and boost profits, but the shift spurred by consumers to return to sugar-sweetened drinks has become profitable for sugar processors the likes of The Amalgamated Sugar Company.

Auditors : EIDE BAILLY LLP BOISE IDAHO

LOCATIONS
HQ: THE AMALGAMATED SUGAR COMPANY LLC
1951 S SATURN WAY STE 100, BOISE, ID 837092924
Phone: 208 383-6500
Web: WWW.AMALGAMATEDSUGAR.COM

PRODUCTS/OPERATIONS
Selected Products
Bakers' special sugar
Brown sugar
Dark brown sugar
Extra-fine granulated sugar
Fine granulated sugar
Gel gran granulated sugar
Industrial coarse sugar
Powdered sugar, 10x and 12x
Sugar packets
Sugar standards
Type 50 medium invert sugar
Type O liquid sucrose (66.5 brix)
Type O liquid sucrose (67.5 brix)

COMPETITORS
AMERICAN CRYSTAL SUGAR COMPANY
C&H SUGAR COMPANY, INC.
Coöperatie Koninklijke Cosun U.A.
FLORIDA CRYSTALS CORPORATION
IMPERIAL SUGAR COMPANY
MICHIGAN SUGAR COMPANY
SOUTHERN MINNESOTA BEET SUGAR COOPERATIVE
THE WESTERN SUGAR COOPERATIVE
UNITED STATES SUGAR CORPORATION
UNITED SUGARS CORPORATION

HISTORICAL FINANCIALS
Company Type: Private

Income Statement — FYE: December 31

	REVENUE ($mil)	NET INCOME ($mil)	NET PROFIT MARGIN	EMPLOYEES
12/13	953	62	6.6%	1,500
12/12	907	14	1.6%	—
12/11	886	46	5.3%	—
Annual Growth	3.7%	16.0%	—	—

2013 Year-End Financials
Return on assets: 8.0%
Return on equity: 54.7%
Current Ratio: 0.90
Cash ($ mil.): 1

THE AMERICAN ENDOWMENT FOUNDATION

Auditors : MALONEY NOVOTNY LLC CANTON O

LOCATIONS

HQ: THE AMERICAN ENDOWMENT FOUNDATION
5700 DARROW RD STE 118, HUDSON, OH 442365026
Phone: 330 655-7552
Web: WWW.AEFONLINE.ORG

HISTORICAL FINANCIALS
Company Type: Private

Income Statement — FYE: December 31

	REVENUE ($mil)	NET INCOME ($mil)	NET PROFIT MARGIN	EMPLOYEES
12/16	848	349	41.2%	5
12/15	640	335	52.3%	—
12/12	133	86	64.7%	—
12/11	68	42	61.6%	—
Annual Growth	65.4%	52.6%	—	—

2016 Year-End Financials
Return on assets: 23.9%
Return on equity: 24.3%
Current Ratio: 21.30
Cash ($ mil.): 70

THE ANDREW W MELLON FOUNDATION

Recipients of funds from The Andrew W. Mellon Foundation don't take the organization for granted. One of the leading charitable foundations in the US, the organization provides about $280 million annually in grants, including awards in five core areas: including higher education and scholarship, performing arts, and museums and art conservation. Recent grant recipients include the Detroit Symphony Orchestra, Oberlin College, and the Metropolitan Museum of Art. The foundation was created in 1969 when Paul Mellon and Ailsa Mellon Bruce, the son and daughter of banking titan Andrew W. Mellon, merged their charitable foundations (Old Dominion Foundation and Avalon Foundation).

Auditors : PRICEWATERHOUSECOOPERS LLP NE

LOCATIONS

HQ: THE ANDREW W MELLON FOUNDATION
140 E 62ND ST, NEW YORK, NY 100658124
Phone: 212 838-8400
Web: WWW.MELLON.ORG

COMPETITORS

Artsmarketing Services Inc
JOHN LAING LIMITED
THE UNIVERSITY OF CINCINNATI FOUNDATION
The Governors of the University of Calgary
UNIVERSITY OF READING

HISTORICAL FINANCIALS
Company Type: Private

Income Statement — FYE: December 31

	REVENUE ($mil)	NET INCOME ($mil)	NET PROFIT MARGIN	EMPLOYEES
12/19	782	435	55.6%	70
12/18	54	(285)	—	—
12/17	980	655	66.9%	—
12/16	487	151	31.1%	—
Annual Growth	17.1%	42.2%	—	—

2019 Year-End Financials
Return on assets: 6.2%
Return on equity: 6.4%
Current Ratio: —
Cash ($ mil.): 9

THE ASSOCIATED PRESS

The Associated Press (AP) is an independent global news organization dedicated to factual reporting. AP is the most trusted source of fast, accurate, unbiased news in all formats and the essential provider of the technology and services vital to the news business, with news bureaus in some 250 locations. It provides some 2,000 stories per day, as well as 70,000 videos and 1 million photos per year. It works with organizations of all sizes across a broad spectrum of industries. A group of New York newspapers founded the AP in 1846 in order to chronicle the US-Mexican War more efficiently.

Operations
The AP offers services such as live and location services, branded content services, production services, advertising services, and operates through its media solutions including news production system, editorial planning, and events planning.

Geographic Reach
The Associated Press is headquartered in New York City and has an office in London. The AP also operates in some 250 locations in 100 countries.

Sales and Marketing
The company works with companies across all industries to provide engaging stories that resonate with their target audiences and customers. It caters to industries such as news and media (broadcasters, digital publishers, newspapers, production houses, OTT), brands and agencies (local and global brands such as finance, technology, travel, health, pharma, and creative agencies), and institutions (governments, NGO's, researchers, universities and colleges).

HISTORY

The Associated Press traces its roots to 1846, when New York Sun publisher Moses Yale Beach agreed to share news arriving by telegraph about the Mexican-American War with four other New York newspapers. The cooperative news gathering effort was later established as the AP, which began selling wire reports to other papers and started creating regional associations. Adapting to changing technologies and public interests, AP began covering sports, financial, and public interest stories in the 1920s and was selling news reports to radio stations in the 1940s. Advancements during WWII included using transatlantic cable and radio-teletype circuits to deliver news and photos.

In the late 1960s AP and Dow Jones introduced services to improve business and financial reporting. AP improved photo delivery, reception, and storage in the 1970s with the advent of Laserphoto and the Electronic Darkroom. It began transmitting news by satellite and offering color photographs to newspapers in the 1980s. In 1985 Louis Boccardi took over the job as president and CEO of AP.

AP adjusted to the media-heavy culture of the 1990s by launching the APTV international news video service and the All News Radio network in 1994. It then moved onto the Internet with The WIRE in 1996 and began offering online access to its Photo Archive in 1997. It bought Worldwide Television News in 1998, combining it with APTV to form AP Television News Limited (APTN). The following year it purchased the radio news contracts of UPI after the rival organization announced it was getting out of broadcast news.

In 2000 AP created an Internet division, AP Digital, to focus on marketing news to online providers. The cooperative continued its Internet focus the following year, launching AP Online en Español (news for Spanish-language websites) and AP Entertainment Online (multimedia entertainment news for websites). Also that year AP bought the Newspaper Industry Communication Center from the Newspaper Association of America.

In 2002 the company launched an

expanded editorial partnership with Dow Jones Newswires, increasing the amount of financial news distributed on AP wires. Later that year it acquired Capitolwire, a provider of state government news. Boccardi stepped down as CEO in 2003, handing the reins to former USA TODAY publisher Tom Curley.

AP relocated in 2004 from Rockefeller Plaza (its home for 65 years) to a new headquarters on the west side of Manhattan that features a 105,000-sq.-ft. newsroom and serves as a central hub of digital news streams.

The organization moved to strengthen its sports information coverage in 2005, merging its AP MegaSports operation with News Corporation's STATS, Inc. to form STATS, LLC, a 50-50 joint venture that provides sports-related information, content, and statistical analysis.

The following year AP launched The Online Video Network (OVN) service to provide news video to AP member and customer websites. The co-op responded to the harsh economy by cutting costs in 2008 with consolidation of its print, broadcast, and digital sales and marketing units. It continued its cost-cutting efforts in 2009 when it cut some 90 jobs, instituted a hiring freeze, and bought out about 100 employees.

Auditors : ERNST & YOUNG LLP NEW YORK N

LOCATIONS

HQ: THE ASSOCIATED PRESS
200 LIBERTY ST FL 19, NEW YORK, NY 102811105
Phone: 212 621-1500
Web: WWW.AP.ORG

PRODUCTS/OPERATIONS

Selected Products and Services
AP Digital News (Internet and wireless news delivery)
AP Images (photo services)
AP Mobile (mobile applications)
APTN (AP Television News, international television news service)
ENPS (electronic news production system)
Online Video Network (video content distribution)

COMPETITORS

AGENCE FRANCE PRESSE
BLOOMBERG L.P.
BUSINESS WIRE, INC.
COMTEX NEWS NETWORK, INC.
DOW JONES & COMPANY, INC.
MARKETWATCH, INC.
PR NEWSWIRE ASSOCIATION LLC
REACH PLC
THE NEW YORK TIMES COMPANY
THE PRESS ASSOCIATION LIMITED

HISTORICAL FINANCIALS
Company Type: Private

Income Statement — FYE: December 31

	REVENUE ($mil)	NET INCOME ($mil)	NET PROFIT MARGIN	EMPLOYEES
12/16	556	1	0.3%	3,533
12/15	568	183	32.3%	—
12/14	604	140	23.3%	—
Annual Growth	(4.0%)	(89.4%)	—	—

2016 Year-End Financials
Return on assets: 0.4% Cash ($ mil.): 24
Return on equity: —
Current Ratio: 0.60

THE BIG TEN CONFERENCE INC

EXECUTIVES
CLO*, Anil Gollahalli
Auditors : RSM US LLP CHICAGO IL

LOCATIONS

HQ: THE BIG TEN CONFERENCE INC
5440 PARK PL, ROSEMONT, IL 600183732
Phone: 847 696-1010
Web: WWW.BTAA.ORG

HISTORICAL FINANCIALS
Company Type: Private

Income Statement — FYE: June 30

	REVENUE ($mil)	NET INCOME ($mil)	NET PROFIT MARGIN	EMPLOYEES
06/20	768	41	5.4%	25
06/16	483	(10)	—	—
06/15	448	12	2.8%	—
06/14	338	2	0.6%	—
Annual Growth	14.6%	64.6%	—	—

2020 Year-End Financials
Return on assets: 12.6% Cash ($ mil.): 62
Return on equity: 21.2%
Current Ratio: —

THE BLOOMBERG FAMILY FOUNDATION INC

Auditors : GELLER & COMPANY LLC NEW YORK

LOCATIONS

HQ: THE BLOOMBERG FAMILY FOUNDATION INC
909 3RD AVE, NEW YORK, NY 100224731
Phone: 212 205-0100
Web: WWW.BLOOMBERG.ORG

HISTORICAL FINANCIALS
Company Type: Private

Income Statement — FYE: December 31

	REVENUE ($mil)	NET INCOME ($mil)	NET PROFIT MARGIN	EMPLOYEES
12/15	1,194	736	61.7%	2
12/14	1,328	1,048	79.0%	—
12/13	809	538	66.5%	—
12/09	452	279	61.8%	—
Annual Growth	17.6%	17.5%	—	—

2015 Year-End Financials
Return on assets: 10.3% Cash ($ mil.): 73
Return on equity: 10.3%
Current Ratio: —

THE BOARD OF EDUCATION OF FAYETTE COUNTY

Auditors : STROTHMAN AND COMPANY LOUISVI

LOCATIONS

HQ: THE BOARD OF EDUCATION OF FAYETTE COUNTY
450 PARK PL, LEXINGTON, KY 405111829
Phone: 859 381-4141

HISTORICAL FINANCIALS
Company Type: Private

Income Statement — FYE: June 30

	REVENUE ($mil)	NET INCOME ($mil)	NET PROFIT MARGIN	EMPLOYEES
06/21	631	45	7.3%	5,800
06/13	431	35	8.2%	—
06/12	422	(63)	—	—
06/11	415	49	11.8%	—
Annual Growth	4.3%	(0.7%)	—	—

2021 Year-End Financials
Return on assets: 4.7% Cash ($ mil.): 152
Return on equity: —
Current Ratio: —

THE BOLDT GROUP INC

Auditors : SCHENCK SC APPLETON WISCONSI

LOCATIONS

HQ: THE BOLDT GROUP INC
2525 N ROEMER RD, APPLETON, WI 549118623
Phone: 920 739-7800
Web: WWW.BOLDT.COM

HISTORICAL FINANCIALS
Company Type: Private

Income Statement — FYE: December 31

	REVENUE ($mil)	NET INCOME ($mil)	NET PROFIT MARGIN	EMPLOYEES
12/18	1,046	(11)	—	1,500
12/17	989	0	0.0%	—
12/16	1,022	17	1.7%	—
12/15	978	0	0.0%	—
Annual Growth	2.2%	—	—	—

2018 Year-End Financials
Return on assets: (-3.8%)   Cash ($ mil.): 39
Return on equity: (-30.9%)
Current Ratio: 1.10

THE BOND FUND OF AMERICA INC

LOCATIONS
HQ: THE BOND FUND OF AMERICA INC
333 S HOPE ST FL 55, LOS ANGELES, CA 900713061
Phone: 213 486-9200

HISTORICAL FINANCIALS
Company Type: Private

Income Statement — FYE: December 31

	REVENUE ($mil)	NET INCOME ($mil)	NET PROFIT MARGIN	EMPLOYEES
12/20	1,280	19,792	1546.2%	2
12/19	1,320	1,099	83.2%	—
12/18	1,140	1,775	155.6%	—
12/17	866	1,056	122.0%	—
Annual Growth	13.9%	165.6%	—	—

2020 Year-End Financials
Return on assets: 17.8%   Cash ($ mil.): 68
Return on equity: 28.2%
Current Ratio: —

THE BRIGHAM AND WOMEN'S HOSPITAL INC

It took three of Boston's oldest and most prestigious hospitals to form the health care behemoth that is Brigham and Women's Hospital. The Harvard-affiliated facility has nearly 800 beds and includes the Dana-Farber/Brigham and Women's Cancer Center, a partnership between the hospital and the Dana Farber Cancer Institute. Other specialty units focus on cardiology, neurology, transplants, and obstetrics. In addition to being a teaching hospital for Harvard Medical School, Brigham and Women's Hospital conducts research and clinical trials to help advance medical care. It's a top recipient of research grants from the National Institutes of Health and is a founding member of the Partners HealthCare System.

Operations
Brigham and Women's Hospital employs more than 3,000 physicians, fellows, and residents and almost as many nurses. Inpatient admissions reach 46,000 and ambulatory visits have grown to more than 3.5 million.

Brigham and Women's Hospital also operates the 150-bed Faulkner Hospital, which is located near the main campus and offers acute care and specialty services, including psychiatry and orthopedics. In addition, Brigham and Women's operates satellite physician offices, including primary and rehabilitation care.

The hospital is also known for performing the first full face transplant in the US. Brigham and Women's doctors performed the surgery in 2011 on a man whose face was severely burned when his head touched a high voltage line. Sponsored by the Department of Defense, the surgery was part of the military's efforts to expand research on innovative medical procedures.

Strategy
The hospital system has positioned itself to do remarkable work, such as a face transplant, through its continued focus on research. Brigham and Women's research institute: The Biomedical Research Institute at BWH spends on average $500 million annually to conduct research in a whole host of fields, including tissue engineering, emergency medicine, genomics, and infectious disease (to name a few).

In 2014 Brigham and Women's Hospital opened the Ann Romney Center for Neurologic Diseases, which will conduct medical research on five complex neurologic diseases, including multiple sclerosis (MS), Alzheimer's disease, Lou Gehrig's disease (ALS), Parkinson's disease, and brain tumors.

Company Background
The hospital was formed through the 1980 merger of Peter Bent Brigham Hospital, Robert Breck Brigham Hospital, and Boston Hospital for Women.

EXECUTIVES
Senior Vice President Cash*, Sonali Desai

LOCATIONS
HQ: THE BRIGHAM AND WOMEN'S HOSPITAL INC
75 FRANCIS ST, BOSTON, MA 021156106
Phone: 617 732-5500
Web: WWW.BRIGHAMANDWOMENS.ORG

COMPETITORS
BAYLOR UNIVERSITY MEDICAL CENTER
CHILDREN'S HEALTHCARE OF ATLANTA, INC.
DANA-FARBER CANCER INSTITUTE, INC.
SAINT PETER'S UNIVERSITY HOSPITAL, INC.
ST. JOHN'S HOSPITAL OF THE HOSPITAL SISTERS OF THE THIRD ORDER OF ST. FRANCIS
THE CHILDREN'S HOSPITAL CORPORATION
THE CHRIST HOSPITAL
THE UNIVERSITY OF CHICAGO MEDICAL CENTER
VHS HARPER-HUTZEL HOSPITAL, INC.
WOMAN'S HOSPITAL FOUNDATION

HISTORICAL FINANCIALS
Company Type: Private

Income Statement — FYE: September 30

	REVENUE ($mil)	NET INCOME ($mil)	NET PROFIT MARGIN	EMPLOYEES
09/20	2,282	(208)	—	8,376
09/17	2,128	55	2.6%	—
09/16	1,938	94	4.9%	—
09/15	1,811	60	3.4%	—
Annual Growth	4.7%	—	—	—

2020 Year-End Financials
Return on assets: (-5.8%)   Cash ($ mil.): 461
Return on equity: (-26.7%)
Current Ratio: 1.20

THE BROAD INSTITUTE INC

EXECUTIVES
CSO*, Todd Golub
CDO*, Justine Levin
CCO*, Clare Midgley
CPO*, Andy Porter
Auditors: PRICEWATERHOUSECOOPERS LLP BO

LOCATIONS
HQ: THE BROAD INSTITUTE INC
415 MAIN ST, CAMBRIDGE, MA 021421027
Phone: 617 714-7000
Web: WWW.BROADINSTITUTE.ORG

HISTORICAL FINANCIALS
Company Type: Private

Income Statement — FYE: June 30

	REVENUE ($mil)	NET INCOME ($mil)	NET PROFIT MARGIN	EMPLOYEES
06/22	1,040	143	13.8%	800
06/21	1,323	754	57.0%	—
06/20	551	53	9.6%	—
06/19	551	53	9.6%	—
Annual Growth	23.6%	39.5%	—	—

2022 Year-End Financials
Return on assets: 5.3%   Cash ($ mil.): 882
Return on equity: 7.3%
Current Ratio: 3.00

THE CHARLES STARK DRAPER LABORATORY INC

The Charles Stark Draper Laboratory (also known as Draper Lab) is a nonprofit engineering innovation company that serves the nation's interests and security needs; advances technologies at the intersection of government, academia, and industry; cultivates the next generation of innovators; and solves the most complex challenges. Multidisciplinary teams drawn from a broad and deep talent pool of 1,200 engineers. The not-for-profit corporation develops enabling guidance, navigation and control (GN&C) system solutions that provide our customers with needed mission capability in both defense and civil applications. It also designs and develops devices with precision electronics to collect and process data in a variety of formats, fusing data in heterogeneous formats.

Operations

Draper Lab's business areas include Strategic Systems, National Security, Space, and Commercial.

The Strategic Systems develop, test and deliver the world's most accurate and reliable guidance, navigation & control systems; radiation-hardened electronics; precision sensors and cyber resilience to drive mission success.

Through National Security, Draper collaborates with customers from pioneering precision guidance for munitions, designing autonomy architecture for unmanned undersea vehicles, advancing celestial navigation technology, developing algorithms for geospatial intelligence analysis, devising both hardware and software cyber security for embedded systems and more.

Draper engineers solutions that enable space exploration from advanced and autonomous guidance, navigation, and control to fault-tolerant computing and software design.

Commercial areas include three areas of emphasis and dozens more sectors relying on Draper This includes Biomedical Solutions, Automotive, and Environmental Solutions.

Geographic Reach

Headquartered in Cambridge, Massachusetts, Draper Lab maintains operations in Huntsville, Alabama; Cambridge, and Road Pittsfield, Massachusetts; Houston, Texas; Cape Canaveral, and St. Petersburg, Florida; Reston, Virginia; and Washington, D.C.

Company Background

The organization was founded in 1932 by MIT professor Charles Stark Draper as a teaching lab.

Auditors: GRANT THORNTON LLP BOSTON MA

LOCATIONS

HQ: THE CHARLES STARK DRAPER LABORATORY INC
555 TECHNOLOGY SQ, CAMBRIDGE, MA 021393539
Phone: 617 258-1000
Web: WWW.DRAPER.COM

PRODUCTS/OPERATIONS

Selected Research Areas
Biomedical engineering
   Tissue engineering
   Sensor development
Space systems
   Military space systems
   Planetary exploration
   Scientific spacecraft
   Space transportation
Special operations
   Robotics
   Small, low-power electronics
   Surveillance systems
Strategic systems
   Inertial guidance systems
Tactical systems
   Precision engagement systems
   Manned/unmanned systems
   Missile defense

COMPETITORS

BALL AEROSPACE & TECHNOLOGIES CORP.
CHARLES RIVER LABORATORIES INTERNATIONAL, INC.
KBR WYLE SERVICES, LLC
LANDAUER, INC.
NATIONAL INSTRUMENTS CORPORATION
NEOGENOMICS, INC.
PRECIPIO, INC.
QUALITY INSPECTION SERVICES, INC.
ROBIN A TECHNOLOGY REALISATIONS PLC
UNDERWRITERS LABORATORIES INC.

HISTORICAL FINANCIALS

Company Type: Private

Income Statement   FYE: July 31

	REVENUE ($mil)	NET INCOME ($mil)	NET PROFIT MARGIN	EMPLOYEES
07/16*	676	36	5.5%	1,800
06/14	522	28	5.4%	—
06/13	542	17	3.2%	—
06/12	514	(20)	—	—
Annual Growth	7.1%	—	—	—

*Fiscal year change

2016 Year-End Financials
Return on assets: 6.0%   Cash ($ mil.): 51
Return on equity: 9.7%
Current Ratio: 1.50

THE CHARLOTTE-MECKLENBURG HOSPITAL AUTHORITY

The medical facilities under the watchful eye of the Charlotte-Mecklenburg Hospital Authority care for the injured and infirmed. As the largest health care system in the Carolinas, the organization, operating as Carolinas HealthCare System (CHS), owns or manages more than 30 affiliated hospitals. It also operates long-term care facilities, research centers, rehabilitation facilities, surgery centers, home health agencies, radiation therapy facilities, and other health care operations. Collectively, CHS facilities have more than 6,400 beds, and affiliated physician practices employ more than 1,700 doctors. The network's flagship facility is the 875-bed Carolinas Medical Center in Charlotte, North Carolina.

HISTORY

Carolinas HealthCare System has expanded its network through acquisitions and affiliations. In 2006 it purchased the 100-bed Lincoln Medical Center (now named Carolinas Medical Center-Lincoln), which the company had already been managing for several years. In 2007 it acquired the 460-bed NorthEast Medical Center (now Carolinas Medical Center-NorthEast). Carolinas HealthCare made improvements at both facilities, including a complete reconstruction of the Lincoln campus and an eight-story patient tower addition at the NorthEast campus.

In 2008 and 2009 Carolinas HealthCare entered management services partnerships with AnMed Health (Anderson, South Carolina), Cannon Memorial Hospital (Pickens, South Carolina), St. Luke's Hospital (Columbus, North Carolina), Stanly Regional Medical Center (Albemarle, North Carolina), and Scotland Health Care System (Laurinburg, North Carolina).

EXECUTIVES

CMO*, Michael Parkerson
Senior Vice President Cash*, Andy Crowder
Auditors: KPMG LLP CHARLOTTE NORTH CAR

LOCATIONS

HQ: THE CHARLOTTE-MECKLENBURG HOSPITAL AUTHORITY
1000 BLYTHE BLVD, CHARLOTTE, NC 282035812
Phone: 704 863-6000
Web: WWW.ATRIUMHEALTH.ORG

PRODUCTS/OPERATIONS

2010 Revenue

	% of total
Tertiary & acute care services	72
Physicians' services	16
Post-acute care services	3
Specialty services	2
Other services & non-operating activities	7
Total	100

Selected Hospitals and Health Care Pavilions
AnMed Health Medical Center
AnMed Health Rehabilitation Hospital
AnMed Health Women's and Children's Hospital
Anson Community Hospital
Bon Secours/St. Francis Hospital
Cannon Memorial Hospital

Carolinas Medical Center
Carolinas Medical Center - Kannapolis (health care pavilion)
Carolinas Medical Center - Lincoln
Carolinas Medical Center - Mercy
Carolinas Medical Center - NorthEast
Carolinas Medical Center - Pineville
Carolinas Medical Center - Steele Creek (health care pavilion)
Carolinas Medical Center - Union
Carolinas Medical Center - University
Carolinas Medical Center - Waxhaw (health care pavilion)
Carolinas Rehabilitation
Carolinas Rehabilitation - Mount Holly
Cleveland Regional Medical Center
CMC - Randolph
Columbus Regional Healthcare System
Crawley Memorial Hospital
Grace Hospital
Kings Mountain Hospital
Levine Children's Hospital
MedWest - Harris
MedWest - Haywood
MedWest - Swain
Roper Hospital
Roper St. Francis - Mount Pleasant Hospital
Scotland Memorial Hospital
Stanly Regional Medical Center
St. Luke's Hospital
Valdese Hospital
Wallace Thomson Hospital
Wilkes Regional Medical Center

COMPETITORS

BAPTIST HEALTH SOUTH FLORIDA, INC.
CAPITAL DIVISION, INC.
COLUMBUS REGIONAL HEALTHCARE SYSTEM, INC
MERCY HEALTH PARTNERS, INC.
NORTH MISSISSIPPI MEDICAL CENTER, INC.
QHG OF SOUTH CAROLINA, INC.
SENTARA HEALTHCARE
SOUTHWEST MISSISSIPPI REGIONAL MEDICAL CENTER
UNITED HEALTH SERVICES HOSPITALS, INC.
WEST FLORIDA REGIONAL MEDICAL CENTER, INC.

HISTORICAL FINANCIALS
Company Type: Private

Income Statement — FYE: December 31

	REVENUE ($mil)	NET INCOME ($mil)	NET PROFIT MARGIN	EMPLOYEES
12/19	7,510	1,223	16.3%	62,000
12/18	6,228	(69)	—	—
Annual Growth	20.6%	—	—	—

2019 Year-End Financials
Return on assets: 9.7%
Return on equity: 16.0%
Current Ratio: 1.10
Cash ($ mil.): 377

THE CHEROKEE NATION

LOCATIONS

HQ: THE CHEROKEE NATION
17675 S MUSKOGEE AVE, TAHLEQUAH, OK 744645492
Phone: 918 453-5000

HISTORICAL FINANCIALS
Company Type: Private

Income Statement — FYE: September 30

	REVENUE ($mil)	NET INCOME ($mil)	NET PROFIT MARGIN	EMPLOYEES
09/16	541	1	0.4%	5,500
09/15	511	(15)	—	—
09/05	226	15	6.7%	—
09/04	203	14	6.9%	—
Annual Growth	8.5%	(15.3%)	—	—

2016 Year-End Financials
Return on assets: 0.1%
Return on equity: 0.1%
Current Ratio: —
Cash ($ mil.): 313

THE CHILDREN'S HOSPITAL CORPORATION

The Children's Hospital Corporation, dba Boston Children's Hospital, is dedicated to improving and advancing the health and well-being of children around the world through its life-changing work in clinical care, biomedical research, medical education and community engagement. The medical center is Harvard Medical School's main teaching hospital for children's health care, and it is the world's largest pediatric research center. Its nursing department partners with more than 25 schools of nursing throughout Massachusetts and New England. It maintains relationships with Brigham and Women's Hospital, Massachusetts General Hospital and many other hospitals in caring for its patients. It has more than 1,100 scientist for its research community.

Operations
With more than 40 clinical departments and about 260 specialized clinical programs, Boston Children's is one of the largest pediatric medical centers in the US. It provides a complete range of health care services for children of all ages, and in some cases, it can offer fetal interventions and treatments for adults.

Dana-Farber/Boston Children's Cancer and Blood Disorders Center, an integrated pediatric hematology and oncology program through Dana-Farber Cancer Institute and Boston Children's Hospital, provides ? in one specialized program.

Geographic Reach
Boston Children's Hospital has satellite locations and affiliates throughout Massachusetts. In addition to its main campus in Boston, it has satellites in Lexington, North Dartmouth, Peabody, and Waltham; doctors' offices in Brockton, Milford, Norwood, and Weymouth; and affiliates in Beverly, Fall River, Milford, New Bedford, South Weymouth, and Winchester.

EXECUTIVES

CIO*, Heather Nelson
Auditors : ERNST & YOUNG LLP BOSTON MA

LOCATIONS

HQ: THE CHILDREN'S HOSPITAL CORPORATION
300 LONGWOOD AVE, BOSTON, MA 021155737
Phone: 617 355-6000
Web: WWW.CHILDRENSHOSPITAL.ORG

PRODUCTS/OPERATIONS

Selected Services
Major centers
  Brain Center
  Cancer and Blood Diseases Center
  Heart Center
  Orthopedic Center
  Transplant Center
Other Services
  Airway, breathing and lungs
  Allergies and asthma
  Anatomy and function
  Bone, joint, and muscle
  Brain and nervous system
  Cancer and blood disorders
  Common childhood health topics and conditions
  Craniofacial anomalies
  Diet and nutrition
  Digestive, metabolic and renal disorders
  Ears, nose and throat
  Emergency medicine and trauma
  Eyes and vision
  Genetic disorders and birth defects
  Heart, blood and circulation
  International patient care
  Medical tests
  Newborns
  Psychiatric (mental) conditions
  Reproductive and urinary conditions
  Skin and vascular
  Viruses and infections

COMPETITORS

CHILDREN'S HOSPITAL MEDICAL CENTER
CHILDRENS HOSPITAL & MEDICAL CENTER
CIVEO U.S. HOLDINGS LLC
GOLDBERG LINDSAY & CO. LLC
HYATT HOTELS CORPORATION
JOHN D AND CATHERINE T MACARTHUR FOUNDATION
JOHNSON & WALES UNIVERSITY
ST LAWRENCE UNIVERSITY (INC)
THE CHENEGA CORPORATION
THE CHILDREN'S HOSPITAL OF PHILADELPHIA

HISTORICAL FINANCIALS
Company Type: Private

Income Statement — FYE: September 30

	REVENUE ($mil)	NET INCOME ($mil)	NET PROFIT MARGIN	EMPLOYEES
09/21	2,013	75	3.7%	8,000
09/20	1,267	(38)	—	—
09/19	2,046	136	6.7%	—
09/14	1,514	111	7.3%	—
Annual Growth	4.2%	(5.4%)	—	—

2021 Year-End Financials
Return on assets: 1.0%
Return on equity: 1.5%
Current Ratio: 6.60
Cash ($ mil.): 1

THE CHILDREN'S HOSPITAL OF ALABAMA

Auditors : DELOITTE & TOUCHE LLP BIRMIN

LOCATIONS

HQ: THE CHILDREN'S HOSPITAL OF ALABAMA
1600 7TH AVE S, BIRMINGHAM, AL 352331711
Phone: 205 939-9100
Web: WWW.CHILDRENSAL.ORG

HISTORICAL FINANCIALS
Company Type: Private

Income Statement — FYE: December 31

	REVENUE ($mil)	NET INCOME ($mil)	NET PROFIT MARGIN	EMPLOYEES
12/21	796	200	25.2%	3,329
12/20	682	25	3.7%	—
12/18	733	17	2.4%	—
12/17	736	113	15.4%	—
Annual Growth	2.0%	15.3%	—	—

2021 Year-End Financials
Return on assets: 9.6% Cash ($ mil.): 281
Return on equity: 11.9%
Current Ratio: 8.00

THE CHILDREN'S HOSPITAL OF PHILADELPHIA FOUNDATION

Auditors : PRICEWATERHOUSECOOPERS LLP PH

LOCATIONS

HQ: THE CHILDREN'S HOSPITAL OF PHILADELPHIA FOUNDATION
3401 CIVIC CENTER BLVD, PHILADELPHIA, PA 191044319
Phone: 215 590-1000
Web: WWW.CHOP.EDU

HISTORICAL FINANCIALS
Company Type: Private

Income Statement — FYE: June 30

	REVENUE ($mil)	NET INCOME ($mil)	NET PROFIT MARGIN	EMPLOYEES
06/22	3,679	6	0.2%	10,000
06/21	328	160	48.9%	—
06/20	189	(16)	—	—
06/13	195	97	49.8%	—
Annual Growth	38.6%	(26.2%)	—	—

2022 Year-End Financials
Return on assets: 0.1% Cash ($ mil.): 329
Return on equity: 0.1%
Current Ratio: 2.30

THE CHILDRENS HOSPITAL LOS ANGELES

Childrens Hospital Los Angeles (CHLA) is dedicated to treating the youngest critical care patients in the region. The about 570-bed hospital specializes in treating seriously ill and injured children, from its neonatal intensive care unit to its pediatric organ transplant center. CHLA's pediatric specialists also provide care at its ambulatory care center in Arcadia and through about 40 off-site practice sites. The hospital's pediatric specialties include cancer, kidney failure, and cystic fibrosis care. CHLA serves more than 107,000 children every year. It is one of only 12 children's hospitals in the nation (and the only one in California) ranked in all 10 pediatric specialties by U.S. News & World Report .

Operations
The CHLA medical staff includes about 600 physicians, most of which are members of the CHLA Medical Group. Its emergency department treats some 71,000 patients and the hospital sees more than 343,000 outpatients annually. Nearly 50% of its patients are under the age of four. CHLA is also the only freestanding level I Pediatric Trauma Center in LA County approved by the Committee on Trauma of the American College of Surgeons and among only 5% of US hospitals to be designated as a Magnet Hospital by the American Nurses Credentialing Center.

It is also a teaching hospital through its affiliation with the Keck School of Medicine of the University of Southern California and is home to the Saban Research Institute which conducts biomedical research into pediatric diseases. CHLA's training programs include 575 medical students, 85 full-time residents, three chief residents, and 98 fellows.

Financial Performance
Revenue decreased 7% to $803 million in 2014 due to a decline in net patient service revenue. Also that year, the company reported a net loss of $30 million due to the decline in revenue and higher operating expenses.

Strategy
CHLA is expanding its facilities to keep up with demand. In 2015, it opened the doors of a new outpatient center in Encino.

Company Background
Although it sometimes operates as Children's Hospital Los Angeles, the absent apostrophe in the legal Childrens Hospital of Los Angeles name is no accident. The intentional spelling honors the original incorporation documents filed in 1901, when the institution was founded as Childrens Hospital Society of Los Angeles.

EXECUTIVES
CIO*, Steven R Garske
CDO*, Alexandra Carter
Auditors : DELOITTE & TOUCHE LLP LOS ANG

LOCATIONS

HQ: THE CHILDRENS HOSPITAL LOS ANGELES
4650 W SUNSET BLVD, LOS ANGELES, CA 900276062
Phone: 323 660-2450
Web: WWW.CHLA.ORG

COMPETITORS
ANN & ROBERT H. LURIE CHILDREN'S HOSPITAL OF CHICAGO
ARKANSAS CHILDREN'S HOSPITAL
CHILDREN'S HEALTH CLINICAL OPERATIONS
CHILDREN'S HEALTHCARE OF ATLANTA, INC.
CHILDREN'S HEALTHCARE OF CALIFORNIA
CHILDREN'S HOSPITAL AND HEALTH SYSTEM, INC.
JOHNS HOPKINS ALL CHILDREN'S HOSPITAL, INC.
TEXAS CHILDREN'S HOSPITAL
THE CHILDREN'S MERCY HOSPITAL
The Hospital For Sick Children

HISTORICAL FINANCIALS
Company Type: Private

Income Statement — FYE: June 30

	REVENUE ($mil)	NET INCOME ($mil)	NET PROFIT MARGIN	EMPLOYEES
06/22	1,384	(116)	—	3,000
06/20	1,325	47	3.6%	—
06/19	1,485	216	14.6%	—
06/18	1,393	247	17.8%	—
Annual Growth	(0.2%)	—	—	—

2022 Year-End Financials
Return on assets: (-4.5%) Cash ($ mil.): 71
Return on equity: (-6.7%)
Current Ratio: 1.90

THE CHRIST HOSPITAL

Perched on the hilltop of Mt. Auburn, The Christ Hospital oversees the health of ailing residents throughout Greater Cincinnati. Along with the flagship 555-bed hospital, the organization operates in more than 100 locations throughout the area. An extensive network of approximately 1,200 physicians and 600 volunteers, the Christ Hospital offers specialized care in a variety of fields, including cardiac care, cancer treatment, kidney transplantation, spine treatment, and orthopedics. The not-for-profit hospital also provides an internal medicine residency program, a family medicine residency program, and a school of nursing. The Christ Hospital conducts research through its Lindner Research Center.

EXECUTIVES
Chief Marketing*, Jenny Collopy
Auditors : ERNST & YOUNG US LLP CINCINNA

LOCATIONS
HQ: THE CHRIST HOSPITAL
  2139 AUBURN AVE, CINCINNATI, OH 452192989
Phone: 513 585-2000
Web: WWW.THECHRISTHOSPITAL.COM

PRODUCTS/OPERATIONS
Selected Services
Cancer Services
Comprehensive Medicine
Heart & Vascular
Orthopaedics & Sports Medicine
Primary Care
Spine
Women's Health

COMPETITORS
CAPITAL HEALTH SYSTEM, INC.
FRANKLIN SQUARE HOSPITAL CENTER, INC.
HOSPITAL SERVICE DISTRICT 1
MERCY HOSPITAL AND MEDICAL CENTER
MERITER HEALTH SERVICES, INC.
ST. ANTHONY'S HOSPITAL, INC.
TEXAS HEALTH PRESBYTERIAN HOSPITAL DALLAS
THE BROOKDALE HOSPITAL MEDICAL CENTER
THE UNIVERSITY OF CHICAGO MEDICAL CENTER
TRIHEALTH, INC.

HISTORICAL FINANCIALS
Company Type: Private

Income Statement — FYE: June 30

	REVENUE ($mil)	NET INCOME ($mil)	NET PROFIT MARGIN	EMPLOYEES
06/20	1,050	8	0.8%	4,000
06/18	742	95	12.9%	—
06/17	929	14	1.5%	—
06/16	681	90	13.2%	—
Annual Growth	11.4%	(44.4%)	—	—

2020 Year-End Financials
Return on assets: 0.6%   Cash ($ mil.): 202
Return on equity: 1.5%
Current Ratio: 1.20

THE CITY OF SEATTLE-CITY LIGHT DEPARTMENT

City of Seattle - City Light Department (Seattle City Light) keeps guitars humming and coffee grinders running in the Seattle metropolitan area. The US's 10th largest municipally owned power company, Seattle City Light transmits and distributes electricity to almost 1 million residential, commercial, industrial, and government customers and owns hydroelectric power plants with more than 1,800 MW of generation capacity. The utility also purchases power from the Bonneville Power Administration and other generators, and it sells power to wholesale customers.

Operations
The company owns and operates generating, transmission, and distribution facilities and supplies electricity to 408,000 customer meters in Seattle and certain surrounding communities. It also supplies electrical energy to other City agencies at rates prescribed by City ordinances.

Geographic Reach
The Seattle City Light service area includes all of the City of Seattle, portions of the cities of Burien, Tukwila, SeaTac, Shoreline, Lake Forest Park and Renton, as well as parts of unincorporated King County.

Financial Performance
Seattle City Light reported a revenue increase of 5% (to $842.2) in 2013 primarily due to increased retail power revenues stemming from a 4% rate increase and a 1.2% Bonneville Power Administration pass-through rate adjustment.

It net income increased that year due to higher retail power sales, rate stabilization account unearned revenue transferred-in, power related revenues, and capital contributions. These were partially offset by higher expenses for generation, customer service, administrative and general, taxes, depreciation, interest, and lower investment earnings.

In 2013, Seattle City Light's operating cash inflow decreased to $229.7 (from $243.5 million in 2012) was due to higher tax paid and increased cash paid to a supplier.

Strategy
The company's long term objective is to continue to secure reliable, low-cost, and environmentally-sensitive power for its customers. To lower costs the utility is pushing its customers to conserve by taking green energy options such as installing more energy-efficient appliances and by buying renewable energy credits (allowing customers to pay for slightly higher costs of integrating renewable energy into the region's power grid).

Seattle City Light's six-year strategic plan, adopted in 2012, calls for an annual rate increase of 4.7% to pay for expanding Seattle City Light's infrastructure and services, including building its first electric substation for 30 years.

In 2013 the company added two new service request types to the 'Find It, Fix It' smartphone app, enabling Smartphone to report illegal dumping and streetlight outages, in addition to its existing features for reporting abandoned vehicles, graffiti, potholes and parking enforcement issues.

That year Seattle City Light and the Seattle Aquarium announced the start of construction for the largest solar array at any aquarium on the West Coast as part of the utility's Community Solar and Green Up programs. The $330,000 system will cover a large portion of the south side of the Seattle Aquarium's roof. Most of its 247 solar panels will produce electricity on behalf of City Light customers who want to buy solar power through the utility's Community Solar program. The rest of the panels are being installed as a demonstration project through the utility's voluntary Green Up renewable energy program with the electricity produced helping to power the Aquarium's operations.

Company Background
Evolving from several neighborhood electric companies that began serving Seattle in 1886, Seattle City Light was created in 1910 to power the city's streetlights. In 2005 the electric utility became the first in the US to become greenhouse gas neutral in its power generation.

EXECUTIVES
Interim Chief Financial Officer*, Brian Brunfield
Auditors : BAKER TILLY VIRCHOW KRAUZE LLP

LOCATIONS
HQ: THE CITY OF SEATTLE-CITY LIGHT DEPARTMENT
  700 5TH AVE STE 3200, SEATTLE, WA 981045065
Phone: 206 684-3200
Web: WWW.SEATTLE.GOV

PRODUCTS/OPERATIONS
2013 Sales

	% of total
Non-residential	63
Residential	37
Total	100

COMPETITORS
DUKE ENERGY FLORIDA, LLC
FAYETTEVILLE PUBLIC WORKS COMMISSION
GEORGIA POWER COMPANY
NEW YORK POWER AUTHORITY
OMAHA PUBLIC POWER DISTRICT
ORLANDO UTILITIES COMMISSION (INC)
PINNACLE WEST CAPITAL CORPORATION
PUBLIC SERVICE COMPANY OF NEW HAMPSHIRE
PUBLIC UTILITY DISTRICT 1 OF SNOHOMISH COUNTY
SACRAMENTO MUNICIPAL UTILITY DISTRICT

HISTORICAL FINANCIALS
Company Type: Private

Income Statement — FYE: December 31

	REVENUE ($mil)	NET INCOME ($mil)	NET PROFIT MARGIN	EMPLOYEES
12/21	1,109	198	17.9%	1,600
12/18	991	162	16.4%	—
12/17	989	120	12.2%	—
12/16	903	85	9.4%	—
Annual Growth	4.2%	18.5%	—	—

2021 Year-End Financials
Return on assets: 3.5%   Cash ($ mil.): —
Return on equity: 9.8%
Current Ratio: 1.70

THE CLEVELAND CLINIC FOUNDATION

The not-for-profit Cleveland Clinic Foundation operates about 20 hospitals in Ohio, Florida, Abu Dhabi, Toronto, and London. Combined, the foundation's hospitals have more than 6,000 beds. Its flagship location is its namesake Cleveland Clinic Health System, an academic medical center in Cleveland, Ohio. The system specializes in cardiac care, digestive disease treatment, and urological and kidney care, along with education and research opportunities. It has an international care center, children's hospital, and an outpatient center; it also contains research and educational institutes covering clinical drug research, ophthalmic studies, and cancer research, as well as physician and scientist training programs.

Operations

The Cleveland Clinic operates approximately 225 outpatient facilities in northern Ohio. These include outpatient family health centers, ambulatory surgery centers, physician offices, specialized cancer centers, and wellness centers.

Altogether, the medical centers known as the Cleveland Clinic Health System include about 6,500 beds and employ more than 5,050 full-time physicians. Cleveland Clinic handles almost 304,000 hospital admissions and more than 10.2 million outpatient visits each year. In 2021, it had more than 259,000 surgical cases.

Geographic Reach

In addition to its primary campus, Cleveland Clinic operates regional hospitals and numerous family and specialty health centers in northeastern Ohio. It operates a handful of facilities in Florida and several brain clinics in Nevada.

Internationally, it operates a health and wellness center in Canada and manages health centers in the United Arab Emirates and London.

Its corporate headquarters is located in Cleveland, Ohio.

Financial Performance

Company's revenue for fiscal 2021 increased to $12.4 billion compared from the prior year with $10.6 billion.

Cash held by the company at the end of fiscal 2021 decreased to $782.4 million. Cash provided by operations and investing activities were $885.8 million and $168.8 million, respectively. Cash used for financing activities were $1.4 billion, mainly for purchases of investments.

Strategy

The company invests in alternative investments to increase the investment portfolio's diversification. The asset allocation of the portfolio is broadly diversified across global equity and global fixed income asset classes and alternative investment strategies and is designed to maximize the probability of achieving the company's long-term investment objectives at an appropriate level of risk, while maintaining a level of liquidity to meet the needs of ongoing portfolio management.

Company Background

Cleveland Clinic Foundation traces its roots to 1921 when a group of Cleveland doctors teamed up to improve medical care and education. Its main campus has conducted breakthrough medical innovations through its history, such as the first face transplant in 2008, and it is regularly named to the US News & World Report's list of America's Best Hospitals.

EXECUTIVES

Chief Strategy Officer, Josette Beran
Chief Business Development Officer, Semih Sen
Research, Lara Jehi
CIO, Matthew Kull
Auditors : ERNST & YOUNG LLP CLEVELAND

LOCATIONS

HQ: THE CLEVELAND CLINIC FOUNDATION
9500 EUCLID AVE, CLEVELAND, OH 441950002
Phone: 216 636-8335
Web: WWW.CLEVELANDCLINIC.ORG

Selected Facilities
Ashtabula County Medical Center (Ashtabula, Ohio; management contract)
The Cleveland Clinic (Cleveland, Ohio)
    Cleveland Clinic Children's Hospital
    Cleveland Clinic International Center
Cleveland Clinic Canada (Toronto)
Cleveland Clinic Children's Hospital for Rehabilitation (Shaker Campus in Cleveland, Ohio)
Cleveland Clinic Family Health Centers (multiple locations in northeast Ohio)
Cleveland Clinic Florida (Weston, Florida)
Cleveland Clinic Florida (West Palm Beach, Florida)
Cleveland Clinic Lou Ruvo Center for Brain Health (Elko, Nevada)
Cleveland Clinic Lou Ruvo Center for Brain Health (Las Vegas, Nevada)
Cleveland Clinic Lou Ruvo Center for Brain Health (Reno, Nevada)
Euclid Hospital (Euclid, Ohio)
Fairview Hospital (Cleveland, Ohio)
Hillcrest Hospital (Mayfield Heights, Ohio)
Lakewood Hospital (Lakewood, Ohio)
Lutheran Hospital (Cleveland, Ohio)
Marymount Hospital (Garfield Heights, Ohio)
Medina Hospital (Medina, Ohio)
Richard E. Jacobs Health Center (Avon, Ohio)
South Pointe Hospital (Warrensville Heights, Ohio)

Selected Institutes
Cleveland Clinic Institutes
    Anesthesiology and Pain Management
    Bariatric and Metabolic
    Cancer Center/Taussig Cancer Institute
    Cleveland Clinic Children's and Pediatric
    Dermatology and Plastic Surgery
    Digestive Disease and Surgery
    Emergency Services
    Endocrinology and Metabolism
    Genomics
    Head and Neck
    Heart and Vascular
    Imaging
    Medicine
    Neurological
    Nursing
    Orthopaedic and Rheumatologic
    Pathology and Laboratory Medicine
    Respiratory
    Urology and Kidney
    Wellness
Special Expertise Institutes
    Arts and Medicine
    Body Donation
    Patient Experience
    Philanthropy
    Professional Staff Affairs
    Quality and Patient Safety
    Research

PRODUCTS/OPERATIONS

2018 Sales

	$ mil.	% of total
Net patient service revenue		
Self-pay	4,465.6	50
Managed care & commercial	2,871.7	32
Medicare	649.4	7
Medicaid	45.1	1
Other	895.8	10
Total	**8,927.6**	**100**

COMPETITORS

CARILION CLINIC
FAIRVIEW HEALTH SERVICES
INDIANA UNIVERSITY HEALTH, INC.
MCLAREN HEALTH CARE CORPORATION
NORTHSHORE UNIVERSITY HEALTHSYSTEM
NORTHWELL HEALTH, INC.
PROMEDICA HEALTH SYSTEMS, INC.
PROVIDENCE ST. JOSEPH HEALTH
UNIVERSITY HOSPITALS HEALTH SYSTEM, INC.
WELLSPAN HEALTH

HISTORICAL FINANCIALS

Company Type: Private

Income Statement   FYE: December 31

	REVENUE ($mil)	NET INCOME ($mil)	NET PROFIT MARGIN	EMPLOYEES
12/21	12,440	2,420	19.5%	44,000
12/20	10,627	1,482	14.0%	—
12/19	10,559	2,239	21.2%	—
12/18	8,927	176	2.0%	—
Annual Growth	11.7%	139.4%	—	—

2021 Year-End Financials
Return on assets: 10.0%   Cash ($ mil.): 667
Return on equity: 15.5%
Current Ratio: 1.20

THE CLEVELAND ELECTRIC ILLUMINATING COMPANY

The Cleveland Electric Illuminating Company (CEI) has a glowing reputation. The utility, commonly referred to as The Illuminating Company, distributes electricity to a base population of about 1.8 million inhabitants in a 1,600 sq. ml. area of northeastern Ohio. CEI has 33,210 miles of distribution lines. In 2010 the utility met 4,420 MW of hourly maximum generating demand from interests in fossil-fueled and nuclear power plants (which are operated by fellow FirstEnergy subsidiaries). It also engages in wholesale energy transactions with other power companies. CEI is also a competitive retail electric service provider in Ohio alongside sister companies Ohio Edison and Toledo Edison.

Auditors: PRICEWATERHOUSECOOPERS LLP CL

LOCATIONS

HQ: THE CLEVELAND ELECTRIC ILLUMINATING COMPANY
  76 S MAIN ST, AKRON, OH 443081812
Phone: 800 589-3101
Web: WWW.FIRSTENERGYCORP.COM

COMPETITORS

DUKE ENERGY FLORIDA, LLC
INDIANA MICHIGAN POWER COMPANY
NEXTERA ENERGY, INC.
OHIO EDISON COMPANY
THE SOUTHERN COMPANY

HISTORICAL FINANCIALS
Company Type: Private

Income Statement — FYE: December 31

	REVENUE ($mil)	NET INCOME ($mil)	NET PROFIT MARGIN	EMPLOYEES
12/16	928	37	4.0%	897
12/10	1,221	73	6.0%	—
12/09	1,676	(10)	—	—
12/08	1,815	284	15.7%	—
Annual Growth	(8.0%)	(22.4%)	—	—

2016 Year-End Financials
Return on assets: 0.9%   Cash ($ mil.): —
Return on equity: 2.7%
Current Ratio: 0.90

THE COMMUNITY HOSPITAL GROUP INC

JFK Medical Center plays a central role in health care in central New Jersey. The medical center is an acute care facility with some 500 beds and 950 physicians providing emergency, surgical, trauma, and other inpatient services. The hospital includes the JFK New Jersey Neuroscience Institute, which treats stroke and other neurological conditions, and the JFK Johnson Rehabilitation Institute, which treats traumatic injuries. JFK Medical Center also offers diagnostic imaging, cancer care, senior and hospice care, and family practice services. It is also a teaching hospital, affiliated with several area universities. The hospital is part of the JFK Health System.

Strategy

To expand its capacity for emergency services, JFK Medical Center launched construction of a new ER pavilion in 2013. The project includes the addition of a three-story structure above the existing ER facilities. To keep pace with cutting-edge medical technologies, the hospital has also made recent investments in upgrades to its diagnostic imaging, cardiac catheterization, and wound healing equipment.

Auditors: BAKER TILLY

LOCATIONS

HQ: THE COMMUNITY HOSPITAL GROUP INC
  98 JAMES ST STE 400, EDISON, NJ 088203902
Phone: 732 321-7000

PRODUCTS/OPERATIONS

Selected Centers and Affiliates
Adult Medical Day Program
Haven Hospice
JFK at Home
JFK Dental Clinic
JFK Family Medicine Center
JFK Hartwyck Nursing, Convalescent and Rehabilitation Centers
JFK Johnson Rehabilitation Institute (JRI)
JFK Mediplex Surgery Center
JFK New Jersey Neuroscience Institute
JFK Medical Center Muhlenberg Campus/JFK-Muhlenberg Snyder Schools
Whispering Knoll Assisted Living

COMPETITORS

BAPTIST HOSPITAL OF MIAMI, INC.
CENTRAL SUFFOLK HOSPITAL
CONEMAUGH HEALTH COMPANY, LLC
LONG BEACH MEDICAL CENTER
THE BROOKDALE HOSPITAL MEDICAL CENTER

HISTORICAL FINANCIALS
Company Type: Private

Income Statement — FYE: December 31

	REVENUE ($mil)	NET INCOME ($mil)	NET PROFIT MARGIN	EMPLOYEES
12/17	551	(13)	—	3,000
12/16	532	28	5.3%	—
12/14	467	(3)	—	—
12/10	427	(17)	—	—
Annual Growth	3.7%	—	—	—

2017 Year-End Financials
Return on assets: (-4.9%)   Cash ($ mil.): 39
Return on equity: (-46.5%)
Current Ratio: 1.40

THE CONLAN COMPANY

Auditors: SMITH ADCOCK & COMPANY LLP A

LOCATIONS

HQ: THE CONLAN COMPANY
  1800 PARKWAY PL SE # 1010, MARIETTA, GA 300678293
Phone: 770 423-8000

Web: WWW.CONLANCOMPANY.COM

HISTORICAL FINANCIALS
Company Type: Private

Income Statement — FYE: December 31

	REVENUE ($mil)	NET INCOME ($mil)	NET PROFIT MARGIN	EMPLOYEES
12/18	953	40	4.2%	391
12/17	930	40	4.3%	—
12/16	772	41	5.3%	—
12/15	589	13	2.3%	—
Annual Growth	17.3%	42.9%	—	—

2018 Year-End Financials
Return on assets: 16.3%   Cash ($ mil.): 93
Return on equity: 90.9%
Current Ratio: 1.20

THE COOPER HEALTH SYSTEM A NEW JERSEY NON-PROFIT CORPORATION

Cooper Health System, also known as Cooper University Health Care is the leading academic health system in South Jersey and provides access to primary, specialty, tertiary, and urgent care, all within one complete health system. Cooper includes South Jersey's only Level I trauma center (Cooper University Hospital), which is the busiest trauma center in the Philadelphia region. Cooper is also home to a leading cancer center (MD Anderson Cancer Center at Cooper), the only Level II pediatric trauma center in the Delaware Valley (Children's Regional Hospital at Cooper), three urgent care centers, and more than 100 outpatient offices from Southeastern Pennsylvania to the Jersey Shore, including large regional hubs in Camden, Cherry Hill, Voorhees, Willingboro, and Sewell. Cooper University Health Care receives more than 1.6 million patient visits annually, and treats patients from all 50 states and 35 countries.

Auditors: ERNST & YOUNG LLP ISELIN NJ

LOCATIONS

HQ: THE COOPER HEALTH SYSTEM A NEW JERSEY NON-PROFIT CORPORATION
  1 COOPER PLZ, CAMDEN, NJ 081031461
Phone: 856 342-2000
Web: WWW.COOPERHEALTH.ORG

PRODUCTS/OPERATIONS

2013 Net Patient Revenue

	%of total
HMO	34
Commercial	27
Medicare	19
Blue cross	13
Self-pay	3
Medicaid	4
Total	100

Selected Services
Adult Health Institute
Bariatric and Metabolic Surgery Center
Joint Replacement and Reconstruction Program
Manual Physical Therapy Program
Musculoskeletal Ultrasound
Neuromuscular Program
Orthopaedic Trauma Program
Otology/Neurotology
Pituitary Tumor and Neuroendocrine Program
Podiatry
Pulmonary Medicine
Rhinology / ENT Allergy / Skull-Base Surgery
Spine Center
Sports Medicine
Urogynecology
Urology
Women's Heart Program

COMPETITORS
CHARLESTON AREA MEDICAL CENTER, INC.
ELLIS HOSPITAL
HENRY FORD HEALTH SYSTEM
KALEIDA HEALTH
NORTHWELL HEALTH, INC.
NORTON HEALTHCARE, INC.
ORLANDO HEALTH, INC.
ROBERT WOOD JOHNSON UNIVERSITY HOSPITAL, INC.
THE PENNSYLVANIA HOSPITAL OF THE UNIVERSITY OF PENNSYLVANIA HEALTH SYSTEM
UNIVERSITY HEALTH SYSTEM SERVICES OF TEXAS, INC.

HISTORICAL FINANCIALS
Company Type: Private

Income Statement — FYE: December 31

	REVENUE ($mil)	NET INCOME ($mil)	NET PROFIT MARGIN	EMPLOYEES
12/20	1,545	73	4.7%	4,900
12/19	1,439	105	7.3%	—
12/18	1,292	54	4.2%	—
12/17	1,197	33	2.8%	—
Annual Growth	8.9%	29.7%	—	—

2020 Year-End Financials
Return on assets: 3.9%   Cash ($ mil.): 582
Return on equity: 7.7%
Current Ratio: 2.10

THE CORE GROUP LTD

Auditors : MAYER HOFFMAN MCCANN PC PHO

LOCATIONS
HQ: THE CORE GROUP LTD
6320 RESEARCH RD, FRISCO, TX 750333774
Phone: 602 494-0800
Web: WWW.CORECONSTRUCTION.COM

HISTORICAL FINANCIALS
Company Type: Private

Income Statement — FYE: December 31

	REVENUE ($mil)	NET INCOME ($mil)	NET PROFIT MARGIN	EMPLOYEES
12/21	1,148	20	1.8%	451
12/20	1,151	20	1.8%	—
12/19	1,004	14	1.4%	—
12/18	1,000	17	1.7%	—
Annual Growth	4.7%	4.8%	—	—

2021 Year-End Financials
Return on assets: 6.1%   Cash ($ mil.): 70
Return on equity: 36.6%
Current Ratio: 1.20

THE COUNTY OF BUCKS

EXECUTIVES
Interim Chief Operating Officer*, Leader Brian Hessenthaler
Auditors : ZELENKOFSKE AXELROD LLC JAMIS

LOCATIONS
HQ: THE COUNTY OF BUCKS
55 E COURT ST FL 5, DOYLESTOWN, PA 189014318
Phone: 215 348-6424
Web: WWW.BUCKSCOUNTY.GOV

HISTORICAL FINANCIALS
Company Type: Private

Income Statement — FYE: December 31

	REVENUE ($mil)	NET INCOME ($mil)	NET PROFIT MARGIN	EMPLOYEES
12/21	662	(36)	—	2,500
12/19	549	(42)	—	—
12/18	549	16	3.0%	—
12/17	514	(27)	—	—
Annual Growth	6.5%	—	—	—

2021 Year-End Financials
Return on assets: (-2.8%)   Cash ($ mil.): 292
Return on equity: (-7.7%)
Current Ratio: —

THE DANBURY HOSPITAL

Auditors : ERNST & YOUNG LLP HARTFORD C

LOCATIONS
HQ: THE DANBURY HOSPITAL
24 HOSPITAL AVE, DANBURY, CT 068106077
Phone: 203 739-7000
Web: WWW.NUVANCEHEALTH.ORG

HISTORICAL FINANCIALS
Company Type: Private

Income Statement — FYE: September 30

	REVENUE ($mil)	NET INCOME ($mil)	NET PROFIT MARGIN	EMPLOYEES
09/20	599	18	3.1%	3,000
09/19	741	24	3.4%	—
09/18	636	1	0.3%	—
Annual Growth	(2.9%)	223.4%	—	—

2020 Year-End Financials
Return on assets: 2.1%   Cash ($ mil.): 157
Return on equity: 4.9%
Current Ratio: 1.40

THE DAVID AND LUCILE PACKARD FOUNDATION

One of the wealthiest philanthropic organizations in the US, The David and Lucile Packard Foundation primarily provides grants to not-for-profit entities. The foundation focuses on operating in three areas: conservation and science; children, families, and communities; and population. The David and Lucile Packard Foundation boasts approximately $4.6 billion in assets. In 2009, the organization committed $100 million for the expansion of the Lucile Packard Children's Hospital at Stanford. The late David Packard (co-founder of Hewlett-Packard) and his wife, the late Lucile Salter Packard, created the foundation in 1964. Their children run the organization.

Auditors : PRICEWATERHOUSECOOPERS LLP

LOCATIONS
HQ: THE DAVID AND LUCILE PACKARD FOUNDATION
300 2ND ST, LOS ALTOS, CA 940223621
Phone: 650 917-7167
Web: WWW.PACKARD.ORG

COMPETITORS
BILL & MELINDA GATES FOUNDATION
CARNEGIE CORPORATION OF NEW YORK
HEWLETT, WILLIAM AND FLORA FOUNDATION (INC)
THE RALPH M PARSONS FOUNDATION
UNIVERSITY OF WISCONSIN FOUNDATION

HISTORICAL FINANCIALS
Company Type: Private

Income Statement — FYE: December 31

	REVENUE ($mil)	NET INCOME ($mil)	NET PROFIT MARGIN	EMPLOYEES
12/10	701	412	58.8%	85
12/09	398	74	18.8%	—
12/06	809	587	72.6%	—
12/05	0	0	69.6%	—
Annual Growth	302.5%	289.2%	—	—

2010 Year-End Financials
Return on assets: 6.7%   Cash ($ mil.): 213
Return on equity: 6.8%
Current Ratio: 2.00

THE DCH HEALTH CARE AUTHORITY

The DCH Healthcare Authority is concerned with the Druid City's health. The company, which does business as DCH Health System, provides health services to residents of Tuscaloosa and several other communities in Western Alabama. Its flagship facility is the 580-bed DCH Regional Medical Center, a full-service teaching hospital located near the University of Alabama campus. DCH Health System also includes the Northport, and Fayette medical centers, which together houses more than 385 acute-care beds. The hospitals offer a full range of inpatient and outpatient services, including primary, diagnostic, emergency, surgical, rehabilitative, and home health care.

Operations
Several of the system's hospitals operate specialty centers. For instance, DCH Regional has cancer and cardiology clinics, while the Northport Medical Center has specialty rehabilitation and mental health departments. In addition, Fayette Medical Center houses a 120-bed nursing home.

Geographic Reach
The company's headquarters is located at Tuscaloosa, Alabama along with DCH Regional Medical Center.

Strategy
Employees of the DCH Health System give their time and talents in service to others in West Alabama at work and in their community. Throughout the year, customers will see DCH employees volunteering their time to support community events that benefit organizations such as the March of Dimes, the American Heart Association and the American Cancer Society.

DCH Health System employees and physicians are out in their schools, churches, malls and at civic organizations sharing practical information on how to stay healthy. DCH sponsors health fairs and free screenings, including an annual prostate screening and a breast screening and education program.

Many support groups that help people in the community with special needs are supported by DCH, and DCH supports education by participating in the Adopt-A-School program. DCH Health System Hospitals shows their support for the community by providing health care to individuals who cannot afford it. The citizens of Tuscaloosa County have helped DCH meet its mission of service. Of the county's 3-cent sales tax, 7% is set aside for DCH Regional Medical Center to help pay for health care for indigent patients from Tuscaloosa County. DCH provides 17 dollars in care to the indigent for every dollar it receives.

Company Background
The "DCH" in the organization's name stands for Druid City Hospital, the name of the system's first hospital, which opened in 1923. Druid City is a nickname for Tuscaloosa.

Auditors: MORRISON & SMITH LLP TUSCALO

LOCATIONS
HQ: THE DCH HEALTH CARE AUTHORITY
809 UNIVERSITY BLVD E, TUSCALOOSA, AL 354012029
Phone: 205 759-7111
Web: WWW.DCHSYSTEM.COM

PRODUCTS/OPERATIONS
Selected Alabama Facilities
DCH Regional Medical Center (Tuscaloosa)
Fayette Medical Center (Fayette)
Northport Medical Center (Northport)
Pickens County Medical Center (Carrollton)

COMPETITORS
ATLANTIC HEALTH SYSTEM INC.
CONEMAUGH HEALTH COMPANY, LLC
HOSPITAL SERVICE DISTRICT 1
HOUSTON COUNTY HEALTHCARE AUTHORITY
KENNEDY HEALTH SYSTEM, INC.
LOMA LINDA UNIVERSITY MEDICAL CENTER
PITT COUNTY MEMORIAL HOSPITAL, INCORPORATED
SHELBY COUNTY HEALTH CARE CORPORATION
STAMFORD HEALTH SYSTEM, INC.
THE PUBLIC HEALTH TRUST OF MIAMI-DADE COUNTY

HISTORICAL FINANCIALS
Company Type: Private

Income Statement   FYE: September 30

	REVENUE ($mil)	NET INCOME ($mil)	NET PROFIT MARGIN	EMPLOYEES
09/21	566	(9)	—	4,683
09/20	534	18	3.4%	—
09/19	547	26	4.8%	—
09/18	520	6	1.3%	—
Annual Growth	2.9%	—	—	—

2021 Year-End Financials
Return on assets: (-1.3%)   Cash ($ mil.): 102
Return on equity: (-2.2%)
Current Ratio: 1.80

THE DREES COMPANY

The Drees Company is a big homebuilder in Cincinnati and one of the nation's top private builders. Drees targets first-time and move-up buyers with homes that are priced from about $100,000 to more than $1 million. Drees also builds condominiums, townhomes, and patio homes. Its homes portfolio ranges from its former Zaring Premier Homes luxury division to the company's more financially accessible and modest Marquis Homes division. Drees is active in Florida, Indiana, Kentucky, Maryland, North Carolina, Ohio, Tennessee, Texas, Virginia, and Washington, DC. The family-owned firm was founded in 1928.

Operations
In addition to home building, architecture, energy efficiency upgrades, and design services, Drees also provides new construction financing solutions through its subsidiary and mortgage lending business, First Equity Mortgage, which has closed more than $1 billion in loans.

Geographic Reach
Headquartered in Fort Mitchell, Kentucky, Drees operates across nearly 10 states in cities including Cincinnati and Cleveland, Ohio; Indianapolis; Nashville; Raleigh, North Carolina; Jacksonville, Florida; Austin, Houston and Dallas, Texas; and the Greater Washington, DC area.

Sales and Marketing
In recent years, Drees has concentrated on the fast-growing "move up" segment market, targeting home buyers looking to upgrade into larger houses.

In 2012, Drees converted its longtime Zaring Premier Homes luxury brand name to its flagship Drees Homes brand. While the move required rebranding in the greater Cincinnati area, Drees is banking on its brand reputation and recognition. It also allowed the residential homebuilder to consolidate its advertising, sales, and marketing efforts.

Financial Performance
While full details of the private company could not be found, Drees' CEO, David Drees, announced in July 2013 that he expected the company to reach $629 million in revenue by April 1, 2014.

Looking further back, Drees had revenues as high as $1.2 billion in 2006, which slid dramatically following the financial crisis to $490 million in revenue in 2010. To its benefit, Texas markets -- specifically Austin and Dallas -- remained active throughout the recession. Drees was also helped by entering the recession with a relatively low debt load of $364 million. By March 2013, Drees had sold land to generate cash flow and reduced its debt to $125 million.

Strategy
Ranked among the top 25 largest national homebuilders by BUILDER Magazine, Drees has been steadily expanding over the past few years to capitalize on an improving housing market.

In recent years, Drees has concentrated on the fast-growing and lucrative "move up" segment of the homebuyer's market, targeting home owners that are looking to upgrade to larger houses with higher-end amenities. In late 2014, the company landed a $100 million contract to build 237 homes in three Cincinnati-based residential communities, with the average house priced between $307,000 and $360,000. In September 2014, the company entered its first ever foray into the Houston, Texas market, with plans to price its houses there for more than $300,000 -- prime pricing to lure these "move up" buyers.

Company Background

A family-operated enterprise since its founding by immigrant Theodore Drees in 1928, the company is run by the third generation of the Drees family.

Auditors: DELOITTE & TOUCHE LLP CINCINN

LOCATIONS

HQ: THE DREES COMPANY
515 S CAPITL OF TEXAS HWY, WEST LAKE HILLS, TX 787464314
Phone: 859 578-4200
Web: WWW.DREESHOMES.COM

Selected Locations
Florida
   Jacksonville
Indiana
   Indianapolis
Kentucky
   Fort Mitchell
Maryland
   Frederick
North Carolina
   Raleigh
Ohio
   Cincinnati
   Cleveland
   Dayton
Tennessee
   Nashville
Texas
   Austin
   Dallas
Washington, DC

COMPETITORS

D.R. HORTON, INC.
KB HOME
LENNAR CORPORATION
PULTEGROUP, INC.
WILLIAM LYON HOMES

HISTORICAL FINANCIALS

Company Type: Private

Income Statement   FYE: March 31

	REVENUE ($mil)	NET INCOME ($mil)	NET PROFIT MARGIN	EMPLOYEES
03/16	722	31	4.3%	549
03/15	669	36	5.4%	—
03/14	683	35	5.3%	—
03/13	584	19	3.3%	—
Annual Growth	7.3%	17.6%	—	—

2016 Year-End Financials
Return on assets: 6.5%   Cash ($ mil.): 10
Return on equity: 14.1%
Current Ratio: 1.90

THE EMPIRE DISTRICT ELECTRIC COMPANY

Empire District Electric (EDE) light ups the middle of the US. The utility transmits and distributes electricity to a population base of more than 450,000 (about 217,000 customers in southwestern Missouri and adjacent areas of Arkansas, Kansas, and Oklahoma. It also supplies water to three Missouri towns and natural gas throughout most of the state. EDE's interests in fossil-fueled and hydroelectric power plants give it a generating capacity of 1,377 MW; it also wholesales power. The company also provides fiber-optic services. In early 2017 the company was bought by an Algonquin Power & Utilities unit in a C$3.2 billion (US$2.3 billion) deal.

Operations

EDE operates its businesses in three segments: electric, gas and other. The electric segment serves an area of 10,000 sq. ml., located principally in southwestern Missouri, and also includes smaller areas in southeastern Kansas, northeastern Oklahoma, and northwestern Arkansas. It also provides water service to three towns in Missouri.

Coal-fired generating units 1 and 2 at the Iatan Plant are jointly-owned by KCP&L (a subsidiary of Great Plains Energy), Missouri Joint Municipal Electric Utility Commission, Kansas Electric Power Cooperative and EDE, with EDE's share of ownership being 12% in each plant. The Plum Point Energy Station is a 670-MW, coal-fired generating facility near Osceola, Arkansas, of which EDE owns 50 MW of capacity.

EDE's natural gas operations distribute natural gas through The Empire District Gas Company. Its principal gas utility properties consist of about 87 miles of transmission mains and approximately 1,160 miles of distribution mains.

EDE's other segment consists of its fiber optics business (which it also uses in its own utility operations).

In 2013 the company generated about 90% of its revenue from its electric segment.

Geographic Reach

The company serves customers in Arkansas, Kansas, Missouri, and Oklahoma.

Sales and Marketing

EDE supplies retail electric service to 119 incorporated communities (and to various unincorporated areas) and wholesale service to four municipally owned distribution systems. The largest urban area it serves is the city of Joplin, Missouri, and its immediate vicinity, with a population of 160,000. Its three largest classes of customers are residential, commercial and industrial, which provided 43%, 30%, and 15%, respectively, of its electric operating revenues in 2013. The company derived about 90% of its retail electric revenues from Missouri.

Its gas operations serve 44,000 customers in northwest, north central and west central Missouri. It provides natural gas distribution to 48 communities and 377 transportation customers. The largest urban area it serves, is the city of Sedalia with a population of more than 20,000. Residential and commercial provided 63%, and 27% respectively, of its gas operating revenues in 2013.

EDE also has 118 fiber customers.

Financial Performance

The company's revenues increased by 7% in 2013, due to improved revenues across all of its segments. Electric sales increased due to higher electric rates, a growth in customers, and colder weather (which increased demand). However, commercial sales decreased, due to a net unbilled sales adjustment recorded in 2012; Industrial sales decreased due to operating reductions by several large industrial customers; and it wholesale sales decreased due to the closure of a large dairy facility in Monett, Missouri.

EDE's gas retail sales and revenues increased due to the colder weather; and other revenues also increased due to a growth in Southwest Power Pool transmission revenues in 2013.

The company's net income increased by 14% in 2013, primarily due to higher revenues, and as well as an increased allowance for equity funds used during construction.

EDE has seen growth in revenues since 2009, however it decreased in 2012 due to lower demand as a result of milder winter temperatures that year. The company has seen a healthy growth in cash flow from operations since 2009.

Strategy

The company has been boosting its generating capacity, including through its partial ownership in the Plum Point Energy Station in Arkansas and through several wind farm contracts. Total property additions for the three years ending in 2013 totaled $398 million and retirements during the same period totaled $39 million.

Seeking to boost its revenues to cover maintenance and expansion costs, in 2013 EDE filed for rate increases for its Arkansas and Missouri electric customers.

In 2013 the company filed an Integrated Resource Plan with the Missouri Public Service Commission to introduce additional demand-side management programs to help its customers use energy more efficiently.

Company Background

In May 2011 EDE's power system suffered extensive damage as as a result of the major tornado that tore through Joplin, Missouri. Initial damage reports from the Joplin tornado included the loss of 130 transmission poles.

Mild weather and the global recession suppressed demand and revenues in 2009, but lower gas and power costs helped EDE post an increase in operating income for that year. Cooler-than-normal winter weather and warmer-than-usual summer weather, and a rate increase, helped to boost power usage and lifted the company's revenues in 2010. A shrinking gas customer base due to depressed economic conditions led to lower gas revenues that year. Lower expenses allowed EDE to report an overall improved net income position in 2010.

EXECUTIVES

ELECTRIC*, Kelly S Walters
GAS*, Ronald F Gatz

LOCATIONS

HQ: THE EMPIRE DISTRICT ELECTRIC COMPANY
602 S JOPLIN AVE, JOPLIN, MO 648012337
Phone: 417 625-5100
Web: WWW.EMPIREDISTRICT.COM

PRODUCTS/OPERATIONS

Selected Subsidiaries
EDE Holdings, Inc. (nonregulated operations)
 Empire District Industries, Inc. (fiber-optic services)
The Empire District Gas Company

COMPETITORS

AMERICAN WATER WORKS COMPANY, INC.
ARTESIAN RESOURCES CORPORATION
BRISTOL WATER HOLDINGS UK LIMITED
ESSENTIAL UTILITIES, INC.
INTERSTATE POWER AND LIGHT COMPANY
LOS ANGELES DEPARTMENT OF WATER AND POWER
MISSISSIPPI POWER COMPANY
NORTHWESTERN CORPORATION
ORLANDO UTILITIES COMMISSION (INC)
SAN ANTONIO WATER SYSTEM

HISTORICAL FINANCIALS

Company Type: Private

Income Statement — FYE: December 31

	REVENUE ($mil)	NET INCOME ($mil)	NET PROFIT MARGIN	EMPLOYEES
12/17	584	36	6.3%	749
12/16	568	64	11.3%	—
12/15	605	56	9.3%	—
12/14	652	67	10.3%	—
Annual Growth	(3.6%)	(18.2%)	—	—

2017 Year-End Financials
Return on assets: 1.5%
Return on equity: 4.4%
Current Ratio: 1.20
Cash ($ mil.): 5

THE EVANGELICAL LUTHERAN GOOD SAMARITAN SOCIETY

The Evangelical Lutheran Good Samaritan Society strives to be a good neighbor to all, particularly to the elderly people in need of housing and health care. The not-for-profit organization owns or leases some 200 senior living facilities, including nursing homes, assisted living facilities, and affordable housing projects for seniors. Through its facilities, it also provides home health care services, outpatient rehabilitation, adult day care, and a variety of other services, such as specialized units for people with Alzheimer's disease and related dementias. Good Samaritan Society merged with hospital system Sanford Health in early 2019.

Operations

In 2013 the society owned or leased 177 continuum of care communities, and 34 home care, hospice, and private duty agencies (and controlled 29 operating affordable housing and senior housing with services projects). TELGSS managed 10 facilities owned by others and held minority stakes in a handful of joint ventures.

Geographic Reach

Outside its home state of South Dakota, TELGSS serves more than 27,000 clients across its 240 locations nationwide. It operates in Arizona, New Mexico, Texas, Florida, Colorado, Arkansas, Tennessee, Kentucky, West Virginia, Ohio, Indiana, Iowa, Wisconsin, Kansas, Nebraska, North Dakota, Minnesota, Montana, Idaho, Oregon, Washington, and Hawaii.

Financial Performance

The society's revenue has risen steadily for the past five years. Revenues increased by 2% to $972 million in 2013 from $954 million in 2012 due to higher Housing and Services and other revenues. Rehabilitation/skilled care activities contributed about 80% of total revenues.

Net income decreased by 76% to $7.7 million in 2013 due to an increase in housing and services and administrative expenses. A higher loss on disposal and impairment of property also contributed to the decline in net income.

Strategy

TELGSS' innovation strategy is to create and implement new products and services that respond to the changing needs of its clients.

In this regard, TELGSS has embraced the digital age by offering home telehealth services (the remote delivery of health care between a patient and his or her physician). Telehealth aims to reduce health care costs by eliminating the need to import expensive specialists to remote areas, allowing patients to more actively participate in their health care, and letting doctors to more accurately track patient medication compliance.

The health care society is also using a technology called WellAWARE through a partnership with Philips Lifeline and Honeywell HomMed. It uses sensor monitoring to keep tabs on the subscriber's daily routine. If there are blips in that routine (for example the patient does not get out of bed) a clinician can intervene more quickly. The system is made of small wireless sensors that use infrared light beams to detect motion; major declines in a subscriber's activity level or a fall can also trigger the detectors to call 911.

TELGSS has expanded its operations in recent years, boosting its number of locations by nearly 10. The health services provider opened a new campus in Fairfield Glade, Tennessee, with 30 rehabilitation and skilled care beds, 24 assisted living units, and 42 senior living apartments and cottages. In Hastings, Nebraska, it also added a pair of housing locations, including a 40-unit tax credit project, and a tax renovation of a 51-unit facility in Omaha. It's extending its reach in South Dakota, as well, by breaking ground on a new Good Samaritan Society in St. Martin Village near Rapid City, South Dakota.

TELGSS collaborates with the Mayo Clinic and other members of the Healthy Aging and Independent Living Consortium on OpenIDEO.com, exploring how to help patients maintain well-being and thrive as they age. In this context, in 2013 the company reported that it had developed three Services@Home agencies (serving more than 300 clients) during the last three years in Hot Springs Village (Arkansas), Loveland (Colorado), and Sioux Falls (South Dakota).

Company Background

Founded in 1922, TELGSS opened its first Good Samaritan center in 1923 as a home for disabled children.

Auditors: CLIFTON LARSON ALLEN LLP MINN

LOCATIONS

HQ: THE EVANGELICAL LUTHERAN GOOD SAMARITAN SOCIETY
4800 W 57TH ST, SIOUX FALLS, SD 571082239
Phone: 866 928-1635
Web: WWW.GOOD-SAM.COM

COMPETITORS

BENEDICTINE HEALTH SYSTEM
CONSULATE MANAGEMENT COMPANY, LLC
DIVERSICARE HEALTHCARE SERVICES, INC.
IASIS HEALTHCARE LLC
LIFE CARE CENTERS OF AMERICA, INC.
MANOR CARE, INC.
MIAMI JEWISH HEALTH SYSTEMS, INC.
NATIONAL HEALTHCARE CORPORATION
THE ENSIGN GROUP INC
THE RUTLAND HOSPITAL INC ACT 220

THE FINISH LINE INC

The Finish Line sells performance and casual footwear and apparel through more than 900 Finish Line stores and JD branded shops inside Macy's department stores across the US. Its core Finish Line stores are bigger than those of competitors and offer a wider array of clothing, accessories, and other merchandise, including jackets, backpacks, sunglasses, and watches. Finish Line offers big brand names (such as adidas, NIKE, and Timberland) and also markets its own private-label line of T-shirts, socks, and other basics. The company also sells athletic shoes and apparel online. It is a subsidiary of European sports retailer JD Sports Fashion.

Operations
Finish Line delivers the EPIC FINISH by providing the most desirable sneakers, latest trends, and exclusives from the best brands, such as Champion, Nike, Jordan, adidas, Puma, Vans, and Converse, among others.

Geographic Reach
Indianapolis-based Finish Line operates in more than 45 states and in Puerto Rico.

Sales and Marketing
Nearly all of Finish Line's merchandise is shipped directly from suppliers to its different retail stores, where the company processes and ships the merchandise by contract and common carriers to its stores/shops or directly to customers. The company also sell products online through its official website. In addition, the company employs approximately 13,000 associates.

Company Background
In 1976 boyhood friends Alan Cohen (a lawyer) and David Klapper (a retailer) founded Athletic Enterprises, the Indiana franchisee for The Athlete's Foot. By 1981 they had all The Athlete's Foot stores that the state's big malls could hold -- about a dozen. To expand beyond those confines, the pair teamed up with Dave Fagin and Larry Sablosky and formed The Finish Line.

EXECUTIVES

HISTORICAL FINANCIALS
Company Type: Private

Income Statement — FYE: December 31

	REVENUE ($mil)	NET INCOME ($mil)	NET PROFIT MARGIN	EMPLOYEES
12/15	1,011	(33)	—	24,000
12/13	979	0	0.0%	—
12/07	841	17	2.1%	—
12/06	836	44	5.3%	—
Annual Growth	2.1%	—	—	—

2015 Year-End Financials
Return on assets: (-1.9%) Cash ($ mil.): 17
Return on equity: (-4.5%)
Current Ratio: 2.30

INFORMATION
Albert J Sutera
CMO, John J Hall
Auditors: ERNST & YOUNG LLP INDIANAPOLI

LOCATIONS
HQ: THE FINISH LINE INC
3308 N MITTHOEFER RD, INDIANAPOLIS, IN 462352332
Phone: 317 899-1022
Web: STORES.FINISHLINE.COM

PRODUCTS/OPERATIONS
Selected Brands
adidas
Asics
Brooks
Lacoste
Mizuno
New Balance
NIKE
Pastry
Puma
Reebok
Saucony
The North Face
Timberland
Under Armour

Selected Products
Accessories
  Athletic equipment
  Athletic socks
  Backpacks
  Gym bags
  Headbands and sweatbands
  Shoe care
  Shoe insoles and liners
  Shoe laces
  Sunglasses
  Watches
Fan
  High school
  MLB
  NBA
  NCAA
  NFL
  Kids
  Shoes
  Clothing
Men's
  Caps
  Hats
  Jackets
  Jerseys
  Pants
  Shoes
  Shorts
  Socks
  Sweatshirts/fleece
  Tanks
  T-shirts
  Workout clothing
Women's
  Caps
  Hats
  Jackets
  Jerseys
  Pants
  Shoes
  Shorts
  Socks
  Sweatshirts/fleece
  Tanks
  T-shirts
  Team clothing
  Workout clothing

COMPETITORS
CALERES, INC.
DEBENHAMS PLC
DICK'S SPORTING GOODS, INC.
FOOT LOCKER, INC.
GENESCO INC.
HIBBETT SPORTS, INC.
RTW RETAILWINDS, INC.
SHOE CARNIVAL, INC.
TAILORED BRANDS, INC.
THE BUCKLE INC

HISTORICAL FINANCIALS
Company Type: Private

Income Statement — FYE: February 25

	REVENUE ($mil)	NET INCOME ($mil)	NET PROFIT MARGIN	EMPLOYEES
02/17	1,844	(18)	—	13,500
02/16	1,888	21	1.2%	—
02/15	1,820	79	4.4%	—
Annual Growth	0.7%	—	—	—

2017 Year-End Financials
Return on assets: (-2.4%) Cash ($ mil.): 90
Return on equity: (-4.0%)
Current Ratio: 2.20

THE FIRST DISTRICT ASSOCIATION

LOCATIONS
HQ: THE FIRST DISTRICT ASSOCIATION
101 S SWIFT AVE, LITCHFIELD, MN 553552800
Phone: 320 693-3236
Web: WWW.FIRSTDISTRICT.COM

HISTORICAL FINANCIALS
Company Type: Private

Income Statement — FYE: September 30

	REVENUE ($mil)	NET INCOME ($mil)	NET PROFIT MARGIN	EMPLOYEES
09/18	556	14	2.6%	150
09/17	609	19	3.2%	—
09/16	553	19	3.5%	—
09/15	615	13	2.2%	—
Annual Growth	(3.3%)	2.2%	—	—

2018 Year-End Financials
Return on assets: 7.8% Cash ($ mil.): —
Return on equity: 12.6%
Current Ratio: 0.90

THE FISHEL COMPANY

The Fishel Company reels in revenues by laying out lines. The company (also known as Team Fishel) provides engineering, construction, management, and maintenance services for electric and gas utility and communications infrastructure projects. The aerial and underground utility contractor designs and builds distribution networks for telecommunications, cable and broadband television, gas transmission and distribution, and electric utilities throughout the US. It also counts municipalities, state and federal agencies, universities, commercial building owners, financial services companies, health care providers, manufacturers and residential real estate developers among its clients.

Operations

The company's products and services include Structured Cabling Systems, Data Center build-outs, Wireless Networks, and Building Security and Automation. It has installed more than 16,000 communications networks for the healthcare, financial education, manufacturing, logistics, and government sectors.

Geographic Reach

The Fishel Company is licensed to do business in some two dozen states. It operates from 32 offices located in about 15 states, including Arkansas, Arizona, California, Florida, Georgia, Kentucky, Nevada, New Mexico, Ohio, Oklahoma, Pennsylvania, Tennessee, Texas, and Virginia.

Sales and Marketing

The company's power customers include American Electric Power, Arizona Public Service, Arkansas Valley Electric, Dayton Power & Light, Dominion Virginia Power, Duke Energy, Entergy, and First Electric Cooperative, among others.

In addition to utilities and power coops, the company serves other markets including Repair and Planning, Broadband, Broadband Network Services, Enterprise Solutions, and Advanced Technology Services.

Strategy

Fishel Company is tracking its business to a Vision 2020 initiative, which has a three-pronged goal of customer development, operational excellence, and teammate development. Its customer development focus involves natural gas distribution, power transmission and distribution (T&D) construction, and fiber network installation. Operational excellence goals are centered on bidding and pricing, project management, and being accident-free. Its teammate management focus comprises leadership development, performance management, workforce planning, and continuous improvement.

The company has strategic business relationships with TE Connectivity, Andrews Wireless, Belden, Commscope, Corning Cable Systems, Legrand, Ortronics, Leviton, Nexans Berktek OASIS, and Panduit.

Company Background

Kenneth Fishel founded the firm in 1936 as an underground contractor for telephone companies.

Auditors: CROWE LLP COLUMBUS OHIO

LOCATIONS

HQ: THE FISHEL COMPANY
1366 DUBLIN RD, COLUMBUS, OH 432151093
Phone: 614 274-8100
Web: WWW.TEAMFISHEL.COM

Selected Locations
Arizona
Arkansas
California
Florida
Georgia
Kentucky
Nevada
New Mexico
Ohio
Oklahoma
Pennsylvania
Tennessee
Texas
Virginia

PRODUCTS/OPERATIONS

Selected Services
Emergency restoration, repair & maintenance
Fiber overbuilds
GPS survey
Network installation
Permitting
Project management
Right of way
Site Design
Utility construction

Selected Markets
Commercial, industrial, advanced logistics
Electric Distribution & Transmission
Financial & health care
Gas distribution & transmission pipeline
Telecom & broadband cable
Wireless backhaul

COMPETITORS

ACUATIVE CORPORATION
ALTURA COMMUNICATION SOLUTIONS, LLC
AR UTILITY SPECIALISTS, INC
BARAN TELECOM, INC.
G4S SECURE INTEGRATION LLC
GARNEY HOLDING COMPANY
GLOBECOMM SYSTEMS INC.
HENKELS & MCCOY, INC
MAVERICK CONSTRUCTION CORP.
MICHELS CORPORATION

HISTORICAL FINANCIALS

Company Type: Private

Income Statement — FYE: December 31

	REVENUE ($mil)	NET INCOME ($mil)	NET PROFIT MARGIN	EMPLOYEES
12/21	636	60	9.6%	2,512
12/19	540	36	6.8%	—
12/17	434	29	6.8%	—
12/16	341	8	2.6%	—
Annual Growth	13.2%	46.6%	—	—

2021 Year-End Financials
Return on assets: 16.8%
Return on equity: 55.2%
Current Ratio: 1.50
Cash ($ mil.): 55

THE FORD FOUNDATION

As one of the nation's largest philanthropic organizations, the Ford Foundation can afford to be generous. The foundation offers grants to individuals and institutions worldwide that work to meet its goals of strengthening democratic values, reducing poverty and injustice, promoting international cooperation, and advancing human achievement. The Ford Foundation's charitable giving has run the gamut from A (Association for Asian Studies) to Z (Zanzibar International Film Festival). The foundation has an endowment of about $10 billion. Established in 1936 by Edsel Ford, whose father founded the Ford Motor Company, the foundation no longer owns stock in the automaker or has ties to the founding family.

Operations

The foundation, which is governed by an international board of trustees, makes grants in all 50 US states and supports programs in more than 50 countries.

It boasts about 10 regional offices in Latin America, Africa, the Middle East, and Asia.

Geographic Reach

Based in New York, the Ford Foundation is a grantmaking foundation that primarily serves the US but also global programs.

Strategy

The Ford Foundation's programs address several social justice issues, including democratic and accountable government, freedom of expression, access to education, economic fairness and opportunity, sexuality and reproductive rights, sustainable development, social justice, metropolitan opportunity, and human rights.

A small portion of its endowment is set aside for social investing. The foundation's funds typically finance critical projects, set new business models, and develop sustainable organizations. By investing $1 million or more in initiatives, the Ford Foundation's investment strategy aims to make a noteworthy impact and encourage other investors to also fund projects.

HISTORY

Henry Ford and his son Edsel gave $25,000 to establish the Ford Foundation in Michigan in 1936, followed the next year by 250,000 shares of nonvoting stock in the Ford Motor Company. The foundation's activities were limited mainly to Michigan until the deaths of Edsel (1943) and Henry (1947) made the foundation the owner of 90% of the automaker's nonvoting stock (catapulting the endowment to $474 million, the US's largest).

In 1951, under a new mandate and president (Paul Hoffman, former head of the Marshall Plan), the Ford Foundation made broad commitments to the promotion of world peace, the strengthening of democracy, and the improvement of education. Early education program grants overseen by University of Chicago chancellor Robert Maynard Hutchins ($100 million between 1951 and 1953) helped establish major international programs (e.g., Harvard's Center for International Legal Studies) and the National Merit Scholarships.

Under McCarthyite criticism for its experimental education grants, the foundation in 1951 granted $550 million to noncontroversial recipients such as liberal arts colleges and not-for-profit hospitals. Public TV support became a foundation trademark that year when the organization's money set up the Radio and Television Workshop.

The Ford family and the Ford Foundation held sole ownership of the Ford company until 1956, when the company offered shares of its stock to the public. The foundation sold some 22% of its Ford Motor Company shares that year, and shed the rest over the next 20-plus years.

The 1950s saw the beginning of international work; begun in Asia and the Middle East (1950) and extended to Africa (1958) and Latin America (1959), the programs focused on education and rural development. The foundation also supported the Population Council and research in high-yield agriculture with The Rockefeller Foundation.

The Ford Foundation targeted innovative approaches to employment and race relations in the early 1960s. McGeorge Bundy (former national security adviser to President John Kennedy), named president of the foundation in 1966, increased the activist trend with grants for direct voter registration; the NAACP; public-interest law centers serving consumer, environmental, and minority causes; and housing for the poor.

The early 1970s saw support for black colleges and scholarships, child care, and job training for women, but by 1974 inflation, weak stock prices, and overspending had eroded assets. Programs were cut, but continued support for social-justice issues led the conservative Henry Ford II to quit the board in 1976.

Under lawyer Franklin Thomas (named president in 1979), The Ford Foundation established the nation's largest community development support organization, Local Initiatives Support. Thomas, the first African-American to lead the foundation, was a catalyst in a series of meetings between white and black South Africans in the mid-1980s.

Thomas stepped down in 1996, and new president Susan Berresford, formerly EVP, consolidated the foundation's grant programs into three areas: Asset Building and Community Development; Peace and Social Justice; and Education, Media, Arts, and Culture. In the late 1990s Ford was surpassed by various other foundations, and it had to relinquish its 30-year title as the biggest charitable organization in the US.

In 2000 the foundation announced its largest grant ever, the 10-year, $330 million International Fellowship Program to support graduate students studying in 20 countries.

After the September 11, 2001, terrorist attacks, the foundation joined other philanthropic organizations in providing disaster relief. It made grants of $10 million in New York and more than $1 million in Washington, DC.

Berresford retired in early 2008 after 12 years as president of the foundation. She was succeeded by Luis UbiÃ±as, formerly a director at McKinsey & Company.

LOCATIONS

HQ: THE FORD FOUNDATION
320 E 43RD ST FL 4, NEW YORK, NY 100174890
Phone: 212 573-5370
Web: WWW.FORDFOUNDATION.ORG

PRODUCTS/OPERATIONS

Selected Core Issues
Democratic and accountable government
Economic fairness
Education opportunity and scholarship
Freedom of expression
Human rights
Metropolitan opportunity
Sexuality and reproductive health rights
Social justice philanthropy
Sustainable development

COMPETITORS

Bertelsmann Stiftung
CALIFORNIA COMMUNITY FOUNDATION
JOSEPH DROWN FOUNDATION
LEGAL SERVICES CORPORATION
ROCKEFELLER FOUNDATION
THE MAUREEN AND MIKE MANSFIELD FOUNDATION
THE ROBERT WOOD JOHNSON FOUNDATION
THE UCLA FOUNDATION
UNITED WAY WORLDWIDE
W. K. KELLOGG FOUNDATION

HISTORICAL FINANCIALS

Company Type: Private

Income Statement — FYE: December 31

	ASSETS ($mil)	NET INCOME ($mil)	INCOME AS % OF ASSETS	EMPLOYEES
12/15	12,114	(270)	—	556
12/14*	12,400	(7)	—	—
09/11	10,344	(5)	—	—
09/09	10,234	0	0.0%	—
Annual Growth	2.8%	—	—	—

*Fiscal year change

2015 Year-End Financials
Return on assets: (-2.2%)   Cash ($ mil.): 126
Return on equity: (-2.3%)
Current Ratio: 3.60

THE FRESH MARKET INC

The Fresh Market is a specialty grocery retailer that operates about 160 full-service upscale specialty grocery stores in over 20 US states, from Florida to New York. As the name suggests, the chain specializes in perishable goods, including fruits and vegetables, meat, and seafood. The initial 14,000-square-foot store differentiated itself from conventional supermarkets with a farmer's market atmosphere. It is a destination for those looking to discover the best including convenient, restaurant-quality meals, hand-picked produce, premium baked goods, fresh-cut flowers, custom-cut meats and carefully curated offerings. The company was founded by husband-and-wife team Ray and Beverly Berry, who opened their first store in 1982.

Operations

The Fresh Market's departments include produce, meat, seafood, bakery, grocery and dairy, deli and cheese, wine and beer, coffee, candy, bulk, floral and gifts, and private label.

The company sources produce from around the corner and around the world. Its fruits and veggies are carefully curated for optimal flavor and nutrition. Premium Choice beef is tender and savory, due in large part to having superior marbling, and includes only the top 10% of all beef in the US. Offering high quality chicken and turkey, the company's meat selections also include lean pork, made-in-store gourmet burgers and a range of specialty meat and superior cuts.

The Fresh Market's seafood department offers a great selection of fresh fish and shellfish, including customer favorites like seasonal Alaskan salmon, wild-caught sashimi-grade tuna and its succulent cocktail shrimp that are cooked in-shell with absolutely no preservatives. It provides the freshest, most flavorful live shellfish offerings including mussels to clams and oysters. In addition, the company also features a range of prepared seafood including marinated & stuffed fish, breaded shrimp, smoked salmon, and its ultimate crab cakes.

The company's deli and cheese department offers delicious charcuterie, deli meats and cheeses, imported and specialty cheese and a tasty selection of gourmet entrees, salads and sides for any occasion. Wine and beer department offers a beautiful assortment of chilled whites and rosÃ© wines. Coffee department offers a wide variety of coffee beans from across the globe. Its custom roasts include special flavors like Molten Chocolate, rich decaffeinated blends and customer favorites like Jamaican Blue Mountain Blend and the company's limited-edition seasonal coffees.

The Fresh Market's candy department offers extensive variety of candies, including chocolate bars, Jelly Belly jelly beans, and gummi bears. Its confection perfection includes exquisite treats from Godiva and Vosges. Its bulk department is a wonderful source for nuts, seeds, snack mixes, dried fruits and more. Floral and gifts department offers custom gift baskets.

Geographic Reach

Headquartered in Greensboro, North Carolina, the company currently operates nearly 160 stores in over 20 states across the US. Its stores are located in Alabama, Connecticut, Delaware, Florida, Georgia, Illinois, Louisiana, and some other states.

Sales and Marketing

In addition to its website, the company connects with its customers through social media platforms such as Facebook, Twitter, Pinterest, YouTube and Instagram.

Auditors : ERNST & YOUNG LLP CHARLOTTE

LOCATIONS

HQ: THE FRESH MARKET INC
300 N GREENE ST STE 1100, GREENSBORO, NC 274012171
Phone: 336 272-1338
Web: WWW.THEFRESHMARKET.COM

2016 Stores

	No.
Florida	45
North Carolina	22
Virginia	16
Georgia	15
Illinois	9
Tennessee	9
South Carolina	9
Alabama	6
Indiana	5
Louisiana	5
New York	5
Ohio	5
Pennsylvania	5
Maryland	4
Connecticut	3
Kentucky	3
New Jersey	3
Arkansas	2
Wisconsin	2
Delaware	1
Massachusetts	1
Mississippi	1
New Hampshire	1
Oklahoma	1
Total	**178**

COMPETITORS

E.H.BOOTH & CO.,LIMITED
FLOWERS FOODS, INC.
HOUCHENS INDUSTRIES, INC.
KINGS SUPER MARKETS, INC.
KUM & GO, L.C.
SCHNUCK MARKETS, INC.
SHEETZ, INC.
SPROUTS FARMERS MARKET, INC.
WEGMANS FOOD MARKETS, INC.
WHOLE FOODS MARKET, INC.

HISTORICAL FINANCIALS

Company Type: Private

Income Statement — FYE: January 31

	REVENUE ($mil)	NET INCOME ($mil)	NET PROFIT MARGIN	EMPLOYEES
01/16	1,857	65	3.5%	12,600
01/15	1,753	63	3.6%	—
01/14	1,511	50	3.4%	—
01/13	1,329	64	4.8%	—
Annual Growth	11.8%	0.7%	—	—

2016 Year-End Financials

Return on assets: 11.3%   Cash ($ mil.): 60
Return on equity: 18.0%
Current Ratio: 1.10

THE GEISINGER CLINIC

EXECUTIVES

CLO, David J Felicio Esq

LOCATIONS

HQ: THE GEISINGER CLINIC
100 N ACADEMY AVE, DANVILLE, PA 178229800
Phone: 570 271-6211
Web: WWW.GEISINGER.ORG

HISTORICAL FINANCIALS

Company Type: Private

Income Statement — FYE: June 30

	REVENUE ($mil)	NET INCOME ($mil)	NET PROFIT MARGIN	EMPLOYEES
06/20	1,625	(194)	—	12,000
06/18	1,290	(163)	—	—
06/15	991	(12)	—	—
06/14	849	(3)	—	—
Annual Growth	11.4%	—	—	—

2020 Year-End Financials

Return on assets: (-40.5%)   Cash ($ mil.): 52
Return on equity: (-88.1%)
Current Ratio: 0.70

THE GEORGE WASHINGTON UNIVERSITY

The George Washington University is the largest institution of higher education in the District of Columbia. The private, coeducational university's approximately 12,500 undergraduate and 15,300 graduate students are scattered across its primary campus at Foggy Bottom as well as its campuses in Mount Vernon and Ashburn, Virginia. With nearly 1,225 non-medical and nearly 1,270 medical faculty staff, the school's student-teacher ratio is about 13:1. Its academic programs, spread across some 10 schools, run the gamut from business to law to medicine. Notable alumni include former First Lady Jacqueline Kennedy Onassis, former SEC Chairman Mary Schapiro, and former US Secretary of State Colin Powell.

Operations

George Washington University has students enrolled in a range of disciplines, from forensic science and creative writing to international affairs and computer engineering, as well as medicine, public health, the law, and public policy.

It runs the Columbian College of Arts & Sciences, Corcoran School of the Arts & Design, School of Business, Graduate School of Education & Human Development, School of Engineering & Applied Science, as well as the Elliott School of International Affairs, GW Law, School of Media & Public Affairs, School of Medicine & Health Sciences, School of Nursing, Graduate School of Political Management, College of Professional Studies, Milken Institute School of Public Health, Trachtenberg School of Public Policy & Public Administration.

About 45% of its total sales come from student tuition fees, nearly 20% from patient care and approximately 15% from grants and contracts including indirect cost recoveries. It also generates a small amount from endowments, medical education agreements, auxiliary enterprises, contributions, and investments.

Geographic Reach

The George Washington University's students come from all 50 US states, Washington, DC, Guam, Puerto Rico, Virgin Islands, and nearly 140 countries.

Financial Performance

The company's revenue for fiscal 2021 decreased to $1.57 billion compared from the prior year with $1.69 billion.

Cash held by the company at the end of fiscal 2021 decreased to $280.1 million. Operating, investing, and financing activities used $11.0 million, $277.8 million, and $127.6 million, respectively. Main cash uses were unrealized gain on investments; purchases of investments; and payments of proceeds from borrowings on lines of credit.

Company Background

Chartered by the US Congress in 1821 as The Columbian College in the District of Columbia, the university adopted its present name in 1904.

Auditors : PRICEWATERHOUSECOOPERS LLP MC

LOCATIONS

HQ: THE GEORGE WASHINGTON UNIVERSITY
1918 F ST NW, WASHINGTON, DC 200520042
Phone: 202 994-6600
Web: WWW.GWU.EDU

PRODUCTS/OPERATIONS

Selected Schools

College of Professional Studies
Columbian College of Arts and Sciences
Elliott School of International Affairs
George Washington School of Business
George Washington University Law School
Graduate School of Education and Human Development
Graduate School of Political Management
School of Engineering and Applied Science
School of Media and Public Affairs
School of Medicine and Health Sciences
School of Public Health and Health Services

COMPETITORS

DRAKE UNIVERSITY
DUKE UNIVERSITY
GEORGETOWN UNIVERSITY (THE)
NORTH CAROLINA STATE UNIVERSITY
THE AMERICAN UNIVERSITY
THE UNIVERSITY OF CHICAGO

THE WASHINGTON AND LEE UNIVERSITY
UNIVERSITY OF CINCINNATI
UNIVERSITY OF ILLINOIS
UNIVERSITY OF SOUTHERN CALIFORNIA

HISTORICAL FINANCIALS
Company Type: Private

Income Statement   FYE: June 30

	REVENUE ($mil)	NET INCOME ($mil)	NET PROFIT MARGIN	EMPLOYEES
06/13	1,177	59	5.0%	5,000
06/06	921	146	15.9%	—
06/05	832	115	13.8%	—
Annual Growth	4.4%	(7.9%)	—	—

2013 Year-End Financials
Return on assets: 1.7%   Cash ($ mil.): 224
Return on equity: 3.1%
Current Ratio: —

THE GEORGETOWN UNIVERSITY

Georgetown University is the oldest Catholic university in the US. The institution's 17,400 undergraduate and graduate students are instructed by more than 2,340 faculty members (representing both full- and part-time) in nine schools ranging from the university's renowned Law Center to the Edmund A. Walsh School of Foreign Service and the Georgetown School of Medicine. The system has a student-teacher ratio of about 10:1. The university is also home to the Georgetown University Medical Center, and has forged numerous ties with its neighboring institutions in the Washington, DC, community.

Operations
The Georgetown University Medical Center provides a variety of medical services to area residents, in addition to serving as a teaching and research facility for the university. The medical center has several specialty medicine and research programs through a partnership with MedStar's Georgetown University Hospital, including Huntington disease care and brain development studies. Georgetown's research institutes are working to discover new medical treatments, including potential breast cancer therapies. The university receives some $179 million in research funding each year.

Geographic Reach
Georgetown University's main campus (54 buildings, including the medical center) is located on about 100 acres on the banks of the Potomac in Washington, DC. It also has locations in downtown Washington, DC, and in Arlington, Virginia.

Internationally, Georgetown University operates a School of Foreign Service campus in Qatar. The university also has study abroad programs in Argentina, Turkey, China, Chile, Italy, and England, and a nursing study program with the Australian Catholic University.

Financial Performance
Georgetown University reported about $1.12 billion in revenues in fiscal 2014, virtually flat with the previous year. Its earnings come from student tuition and fees, grants and contracts, auxiliary activities, and other sources. In fiscal 2015, undergraduate tuition was $46,200 per student (up from $44,280 in fiscal 2014 and $42,360 in fiscal 2013).

Strategy
Georgetown University expands and upgrades its facilities periodically to keep pace with modern technologies and appeal to a variety of students.

To expand its outreach programs, Georgetown University built a new location for its School of Continuing Studies in downtown Washington, DC. The new campus, located near the Law Center, opened in late 2013 and extends the reach of the university's presence downtown as it works to expand beyond its historical campus. It also officially launched its McCourt School of Public Policy in 2013.

It also launches new degree programs, such as the MIDP (master's of international development policy) and the Master of Science in Global Health.

Company Background
In 2010, Georgetown University received its largest philanthropic gift ever when it was granted a nearly $90 million endowment to support medical research at the university's medical center from a charitable trust established by the will of the late Harry Toulmin in 1965.

Georgetown University was founded in 1789 by John Carroll, the nation's first Catholic bishop. At the time of its founding, Georgetown University's historic campus was located in Georgetown, Maryland; the location is now part of the Washington, DC, metropolitan area. Among Georgetown University's alumni are President Bill Clinton, basketball great Patrick Ewing, and former US Surgeon General Antonia Novello.

EXECUTIVES
CIO*, H David Lambert
Auditors: PRICEWATERHOUSECOOPERS LLP MC

LOCATIONS
HQ: THE GEORGETOWN UNIVERSITY
  37TH AND O ST NW, WASHINGTON, DC 200570001
Phone: 202 687-0100
Web: WWW.GEORGETOWN.EDU

PRODUCTS/OPERATIONS
Selected Schools
Edmund A. Walsh School of Foreign Service
Georgetown College
Graduate School of Arts and Sciences
Law Center
McCourt School of Public Policy
Robert E. McDonough School of Business
School of Medicine
School of Nursing and Health Studies
School for Summer and Continuing Education

COMPETITORS
LOYOLA UNIVERSITY OF CHICAGO
MARSHALL UNIVERSITY
NORTHWESTERN UNIVERSITY
THE GEORGE WASHINGTON UNIVERSITY
THE UNIVERSITY OF CHICAGO
UNIVERSITY OF CINCINNATI
UNIVERSITY OF MISSOURI SYSTEM
UNIVERSITY OF OKLAHOMA
UNIVERSITY OF SOUTHERN CALIFORNIA
UNIVERSITY SYSTEM OF MARYLAND

HISTORICAL FINANCIALS
Company Type: Private

Income Statement   FYE: June 30

	REVENUE ($mil)	NET INCOME ($mil)	NET PROFIT MARGIN	EMPLOYEES
06/22	1,591	(34)	—	9,700
06/21	1,274	756	59.4%	—
06/20	1,341	(128)	—	—
06/19	1,330	(77)	—	—
Annual Growth	6.2%	—	—	—

2022 Year-End Financials
Return on assets: (-0.6%)   Cash ($ mil.): 211
Return on equity: (-1.5%)
Current Ratio: —

THE GOLUB CORPORATION

Supermarket operator The Golub Corporation offers tasty come-ons such as table-ready meals, gift certificates, automatic discount cards, and a hotline where cooks answer food-related queries. Golub operates about 130 Price Chopper supermarkets, Market 32 and Market Bistro banners in six states in the northeastern US (New York is its largest market).

Geographic Reach
Golub's Price Chopper chain is active in six US states. New York accounts for more than 60% of its locations, while Massachusetts and Vermont each contribute more than 10%. It also has locations in Connecticut, Pennsylvania, and New Hampshire.

Sales and Marketing
The company sells its products in its stores and online.

Company Background
Like many other retailers, the company is experimenting with new formats. In May 2012 it opened its first small-format store, known as Price Chopper Limited. The 19,000-square-foot store (about a third of the size of a typical Price Chopper supermarket) is located in a residential neighborhood in downtown Saratoga Springs, New York. The "Limited" store offers an edited selection of Price

Chopper's most popular products, a bakery, full-service meat, deli, and seafood departments, and a cafe with eat-in or take-out meals.

In fall 2011 Price Chopper launched a new online ordering and home delivery program called Price Chopper Shops4U . The service charges a service fee of $10, with an additional $6 fee for delivery. Customers can either pick up their orders at the store or have them delivered.

Brothers Bill and Ben Golub founded the company in 1932.

EXECUTIVES

Distribution Vice President, Robert Doyle
CONSUMER SERVICES, Mona J Golub
CAO, Leo Taylor

LOCATIONS

HQ: THE GOLUB CORPORATION
  461 NOTT ST, SCHENECTADY, NY 123081812
Phone: 518 355-5000
Web: WWW.PRICECHOPPER.COM

2013 Stores

	No.
New York	81
Massachusetts	16
Vermont	15
Connecticut	8
Pennsylvania	8
New Hampshire	4
Total	132

COMPETITORS

AHOLD U.S.A., INC.
BED BATH & BEYOND INC.
CASEY'S GENERAL STORES, INC.
COSTCO WHOLESALE CORPORATION
REASOR"S LLC
SHOPWELL, INC.
SPARTANNASH COMPANY
SUPERVALU INC.
VILLAGE SUPER MARKET, INC.
WAKEFERN FOOD CORP.

HISTORICAL FINANCIALS

Company Type: Private

Income Statement — FYE: April 24

	REVENUE ($mil)	NET INCOME ($mil)	NET PROFIT MARGIN	EMPLOYEES
04/16	3,427	8	0.2%	19,500
04/15	3,476	21	0.6%	—
Annual Growth	(1.4%)	(60.5%)	—	—

2016 Year-End Financials

Return on assets: 1.2% Cash ($ mil.): 22
Return on equity: 13.3%
Current Ratio: 0.70

THE HEALTH CARE AUTHORITY OF THE CITY OF HUNTSVILLE

Health Care Authority of the City of Huntsville ensures that residents get the medical attention they need. TheÂ volunteer board consists of nine members that governs the more than 880-bed Huntsville Hospital, one of the largest medical centers in Alabama with a staff of more than 650 physicians, as well as other medical facilities. Huntsville Hospital is also a teaching facility for the University of Alabama-Birmingham. The Health Care Authority of the City of Huntsville provides a list of nominees for board members to the City Council, which decides who is appointed to the board.

Auditors : DIXON HUGHES GOODMAN LLP BIRM

LOCATIONS

HQ: THE HEALTH CARE AUTHORITY OF THE CITY OF HUNTSVILLE
  101 SIVLEY RD SW, HUNTSVILLE, AL 358014421
Phone: 256 265-1000
Web: WWW.HUNTSVILLEHOSPITAL.ORG

COMPETITORS

CATHOLIC HEALTH SYSTEM OF LONG ISLAND, INC.
HEALTH PARTNERS PLANS, INC.
NORTHWESTERN MEDICAL FACULTY FOUNDATION
UNIVERSITY OF MICHIGAN HEALTH SYSTEM
UT MEDICAL GROUP, INC.

HISTORICAL FINANCIALS

Company Type: Private

Income Statement — FYE: June 30

	REVENUE ($mil)	NET INCOME ($mil)	NET PROFIT MARGIN	EMPLOYEES
06/19	1,700	218	12.9%	14,000
06/18	1,524	53	3.5%	—
06/17	1,407	46	3.3%	—
06/07	591	49	8.3%	—
Annual Growth	9.2%	13.3%	—	—

2019 Year-End Financials

Return on assets: 11.7% Cash ($ mil.): 88
Return on equity: 16.4%
Current Ratio: 1.40

THE HENRY M JACKSON FOUNDATION FOR THE ADVANCEMENT OF MILITARY MEDICINE INC

EXECUTIVES

CIO*, Rizwan Jan
Auditors : BDO USA LLP MCLEAN VA

LOCATIONS

HQ: THE HENRY M JACKSON FOUNDATION FOR THE ADVANCEMENT OF MILITARY MEDICINE INC
  6720A ROCKLEDGE DR # 100, BETHESDA, MD 208171888
Phone: 240 694-2000
Web: WWW.HJF.ORG

HISTORICAL FINANCIALS

Company Type: Private

Income Statement — FYE: September 30

	REVENUE ($mil)	NET INCOME ($mil)	NET PROFIT MARGIN	EMPLOYEES
09/21	581	16	2.8%	2,300
09/20	492	0	0.2%	—
09/19	495	(8)	—	—
09/13	441	12	2.9%	—
Annual Growth	3.5%	3.2%	—	—

2021 Year-End Financials

Return on assets: 5.7% Cash ($ mil.): 56
Return on equity: 10.2%
Current Ratio: 2.40

THE HERTZ CORPORATION

EXECUTIVES

CIO, Timothy M Langley-hawthorne
CAO, Alexandra D Brooks
Auditors : ERNST & YOUNG LLP TAMPA FLOR

LOCATIONS

HQ: THE HERTZ CORPORATION
  8501 WILLIAMS RD, ESTERO, FL 339283325
Phone: 239 301-7000
Web: WWW.HERTZ.COM

HISTORICAL FINANCIALS
Company Type: Private

Income Statement — FYE: December 31

	REVENUE ($mil)	NET INCOME ($mil)	NET PROFIT MARGIN	EMPLOYEES
12/17	8,803	332	3.8%	23,000
12/16	8,803	(488)	—	—
12/15	10,535	276	2.6%	—
Annual Growth	(8.6%)	9.7%	—	—

2017 Year-End Financials
Return on assets: 1.7% Cash ($ mil.): 1,072
Return on equity: 21.8%
Current Ratio: —

THE INCOME FUND OF AMERICA INC

Auditors: DELOITTE & TOUCHE LLP COSTA

LOCATIONS
HQ: THE INCOME FUND OF AMERICA INC
1 MARKET PLZ, SAN FRANCISCO, CA 941051101
Phone: 415 421-9360

HISTORICAL FINANCIALS
Company Type: Private

Income Statement — FYE: July 31

	REVENUE ($mil)	NET INCOME ($mil)	NET PROFIT MARGIN	EMPLOYEES
07/20	4,332	18,019	415.9%	7
07/19	4,050	160	4.0%	—
07/18	4,050	2,343	57.9%	—
07/16	3,577	6,660	186.2%	—
Annual Growth	4.9%	28.3%	—	—

2020 Year-End Financials
Return on assets: 13.6% Cash ($ mil.): 31
Return on equity: 14.2%
Current Ratio: —

THE INSTITUTE OF ELECTRICAL AND ELECTRONICS ENGINEERS INCORPORATED

The Institute of Electrical and Electronics Engineers (IEEE) has about 409,655 members, including nearly about 125,990 students in over 160 countries. The IEEE is the world's largest technical professional organization dedicated to advancing technology for the benefit of humanity. IEEE and its members inspire a global community through its highly cited publications, conferences, technology standards, and professional and educational activities. It sponsors some 2,000 annual conferences and publishes nearly a third of the world's technical literature, including journals, magazines, and conference proceedings. The IEEE was formed in 1963 in a combination of the American Institute of Electrical Engineers (founded in 1884) and the Institute of Radio Engineers (founded in 1912). Majority of its members were in the US.

Operations
Periodicals contribute approximately half of IEEE's total revenue. The remaining revenue comes from conferences, memberships, standards, public imperatives and others.

The Institute offers membership for terms of one year. The Institute satisfies its performance obligation and recognizes revenue evenly over the membership term as its members simultaneously receive and consume the benefits over that timeframe. Periodicals revenues primarily include subscriptions and online products and content. Media revenue primarily includes advertising space sold in newsletters and periodicals. Conference revenues primarily include registration and sponsorships, and also includes the conference proceedings and published articles related to respective conferences.

Geographic Reach
Based in New York, the company has its presence in USA (over 35% of total members), India (some 15%), China (about 10%), Canada and Japan (less than 5% each) and Other. Overall, the organization is known across 160 countries.

Sales and Marketing
The company has about 409,655 members, as well as nearly 125,990 student members.

Financial Performance
The company reported a revenue of 464.3 million, a decrease of $2.7 million, or 0.6%, from 2020. Mainly impacted due to pandemic related cancellation of planned large in person conferences and events.

The company's cash at the end of 2021 was $17.4 million. Operating activities generated $131.4 million, while investing activities used $132.3 million, primarily for purchases of investments. Financing activities used another $1.9 million, primarily for change in cash overdraft.

EXECUTIVES
Staff Director Financial Services*, Thomas Lynch
Auditors: GRANT THORNTON LLP ISELIN NE

LOCATIONS
HQ: THE INSTITUTE OF ELECTRICAL AND ELECTRONICS ENGINEERS INCORPORATED
445 HOES LN, PISCATAWAY, NJ 088544141
Phone: 212 419-7900
Web: IEEESHUTPAGES.S3-WEBSITE-US-WEST-2.AMAZONAWS.COM

2013 Members

	% of total
US	47
India, China & Pacific Rim	18
Canada	3
Other regions	32
Total	100

PRODUCTS/OPERATIONS
2013 Sales

	$ mil.	% of total
Periodicals	157.6	38
Conferences	153.9	37
Memberships & public imperatives	67.6	17
Standards	32.2	8
Other income	1.4	-
Total	412.7	100

Selected IEEE Societies
Aerospace and Electronic Systems
Antennas and Propagation
Broadcast Technology
Circuits and Systems
Communications
Computational Intelligence
Electromagnetic Compatibility
Geoscience and Remote Sensing

COMPETITORS
AMERICAN CANCER SOCIETY, INC.
AMERICAN CHEMICAL SOCIETY
AMERICAN LIBRARY ASSOCIATION
AMERICAN MEDICAL ASSOCIATION
BLUE CROSS AND BLUE SHIELD ASSOCIATION
EXPONENT, INC.
HOWARD HUGHES MEDICAL INSTITUTE
RELX PLC
THE BRITISH DENTAL INDUSTRY ASSOCIATION
UNITED KINGDOM ACCREDITATION SERVICE

HISTORICAL FINANCIALS
Company Type: Private

Income Statement — FYE: December 31

	REVENUE ($mil)	NET INCOME ($mil)	NET PROFIT MARGIN	EMPLOYEES
12/19	563	80	14.3%	1,068
12/17	494	34	6.9%	—
12/16	480	22	4.7%	—
12/09	338	18	5.5%	—
Annual Growth	5.2%	15.7%	—	—

2019 Year-End Financials
Return on assets: 9.8% Cash ($ mil.): 117
Return on equity: 14.1%
Current Ratio: —

THE JAMAICA HOSPITAL

Jamaica Hospital Medical Center has been operating in the Queens Borough of New York since before the nation of Jamaica even was born. The hospital serves Queens and eastern Brooklyn with general medical, pediatric, psychiatric, and ambulatory care services. The facility has about 430 beds. Its specialty services include a coma recovery unit, a dialysis center, a psychiatric emergency department, a rehabilitation center, as well as a traumatic brain injury recovery unit. The hospital also operates a nursing home with more than 220 beds, as well as family practice, ambulance, and home health services. Jamaica Hospital Medical Center is a subsidiary of MediSys Health Network.

Operations

Jamaica Hospital Medical Center treats some 130,000 patients annually through its emergency department, which contains a level I regional trauma center. The hospital also handles about 2,000 births each year in its labor and delivery wing.

In addition to acute care services, the hospital is a teaching facility associated with several educational organizations including Cornell University's Weill Medical College, the Mount Sinai School of Medicine, and St. George's University School of Medicine. It provides residency and training programs in areas including dentistry, podiatry, physician assistant, and osteopathic medicine. Some of its residency programs are conducted in partnership with other regional health centers including the New York Hospital and the Montefiore Medical Center.

The Ambulatory Care Centers include a Sleep Clinic, where sleep disorders in adults and children are evaluated and treated.

In 2014, the hospital had nearly 120,000 patients were treated in the Emergency Department; 300,000 patients were seen in the Ambulatory Care Centers (with locations at the main campus and also at the offsite centers in the community); and some 2,904 deliveries were performed.

Geographic Reach

Jamaica Hospital Medical Center serves a population greater than 1.2 million in Queens and eastern Brooklyn.

Strategy

To improve care for area residents, Jamaica Hospital Medical Center has expanded its sleep medicine division to include a new sleep disorder diagnosis center for adults and children. The hospital has also expanded its community care provisions through partnerships with area businesses and organizations.

Upgrading its technology, in 2015 the company introduced da Vinci Robot Now at its Flushing location.

Company Background

Jamaica Hospital Medical Center was founded in 1892.

Auditors: PRICEWATERHOUSECOOPERS LLP NE

LOCATIONS

HQ: THE JAMAICA HOSPITAL
8900 VAN WYCK EXPY FL 4N, RICHMOND HILL, NY 114182897
Phone: 718 206-6290
Web: WWW.JAMAICAHOSPITAL.ORG

PRODUCTS/OPERATIONS

Selected Centers and Services
Advanced Center for Psychotherapy
Allergy and Immunology
Ambulatory Care
Anesthesia
Cardiology
Clinical Services
Corporate Health
Critical Care Medicine
Dental
Dermatology
Dialysis-Island Rehabilitation
Emergency Medicine
Family Medicine
Gastroenterology
Home Health
Infectious Disease
Lupus Center
MediSys Family Care Centers
Nephrology
Neurology
Nursing
OB-GYN
Oncology
Orthopedic Surgery
Palliative Care
Pathology
Pediatrics
Podiatry
Prehospital Care
Psychiatry
Pulmonary Medicine
Radiology
Rehabilitation
Rheumatology
Surgery
TCU
The Brady Institute
Trump Pavilion~Jamaica Hospital Nursing Home
Women's Health
Women's Health Center

COMPETITORS

MERCY HOSPITAL AND MEDICAL CENTER
NEWYORK-PRESBYTERIAN/BROOKLYN METHODIST
PHELPS MEMORIAL HOSPITAL ASSOCIATION
THE BROOKDALE HOSPITAL MEDICAL CENTER
WINTER HAVEN HOSPITAL, INC.

HISTORICAL FINANCIALS

Company Type: Private

Income Statement — FYE: December 31

	REVENUE ($mil)	NET INCOME ($mil)	NET PROFIT MARGIN	EMPLOYEES
12/21	896	18	2.0%	3,251
12/20	845	35	4.2%	—
12/19	623	11	1.8%	—
12/18	739	15	2.1%	—
Annual Growth	6.6%	4.9%	—	—

2021 Year-End Financials
Return on assets: 6.1%
Return on equity: 123.8%
Current Ratio: 1.30
Cash ($ mil.): 23

THE JOHNS HOPKINS HEALTH SYSTEM CORPORATION

Named after philanthropist Johns Hopkins, the Johns Hopkins Health System (JHHS) gifts Baltimore residents with an array of health care services. The health system is an affiliate of world-renowned Johns Hopkins Medicine and oversees six hospitals: All Children's Hospital, Johns Hopkins Hospital, Bayview Medical Center, Howard County General Hospital, Sibley Memorial Hospital, and Suburban Hospital. The not-for-profit teaching hospitals offer inpatient and outpatient health services that include general medicine, emergency/trauma care, pediatrics, maternity care, senior care, and numerous specialized areas of medicine. JHHS also operates community health and satellite care facilities.

Operations

JHHS facilities handle 2.8 million patient encounters each year, including 115,000 inpatient admissions and 350,000 emergency room visits. In addition to the six Johns Hopkins Medicine hospitals (which combined house more than 2,600 beds), the JHHS organization includes four surgery centers, two dozen primary care clinics associated with the Johns Hopkins Community Physicians practice organization, and a home health care services agency. JHHS offers unified shared services to its members, including advertising, purchasing, finance, legal, and other administrative functions.

The Johns Hopkins name is well-known for health care, but is probably equally as well-known for its medical education and research initiatives. The health system's hospitals are affiliated with Johns Hopkins University, offering physicians-in-training a whole host of residency options.

Geographic Reach

The JHHS inpatient and outpatient facilities are located throughout Maryland and the Washington DC-area, as well as in Florida. The system operates a handful of outpatient surgery and imaging centers as well. The group's hospitals serve visitors from all over the world.

Strategy

The organization regularly expands through small to large construction efforts, as well as through acquisitions. For example, it has acquired two hospitals (All Children's Hospital in Florida and Sibley Memorial Hospital in Washington, DC) since 2010.

EXECUTIVES

Medical Affairs Vice President*, Beryl Rosenstein
Corporate Secretary*, Hannah Jones

Auditors : PRICEWATERHOUSECOOPERS LLP B

LOCATIONS

HQ: THE JOHNS HOPKINS HEALTH SYSTEM CORPORATION
600 N WOLFE ST, BALTIMORE, MD 212870005
Phone: 410 955-5000
Web: WWW.HOPKINSMEDICINE.ORG

PRODUCTS/OPERATIONS

Selected Facilities
All Children's Hospital (St. Petersburg, FL)
Bayview Medical Center (Baltimore, MD)
Howard County General Hospital (Columbia, MD)
Johns Hopkins at Cedar Lane (Columbia, MD)
Johns Hopkins at Greenspring Station (Lutherville, MD)
Johns Hopkins at Odenton (Odenton, MD)
Johns Hopkins at White Marsh (White Marsh, MD)
Johns Hopkins Hospital (Baltimore, MD)
Johns Hopkins Outpatient Center (Baltimore, MD)
Sibley Memorial Hospital (Washington, DC)
Suburban Hospital (Bethesda, MD)

COMPETITORS

ALEGENT CREIGHTON HEALTH
ASCENSION SOUTHEAST MICHIGAN
ATLANTIC HEALTH SYSTEM INC.
BETHESDA HOSPITAL, INC.
FROEDTERT MEMORIAL LUTHERAN HOSPITAL, INC.
GREATER BALTIMORE MEDICAL CENTER, INC.
LAFAYETTE GENERAL MEDICAL CENTER, INC.
MEDSTAR HEALTH, INC.
PRIME HEALTHCARE SERVICES - GARDEN CITY, LLC
SUBURBAN HOSPITAL, INC.

HISTORICAL FINANCIALS
Company Type: Private

Income Statement — FYE: June 30

	REVENUE ($mil)	NET INCOME ($mil)	NET PROFIT MARGIN	EMPLOYEES
06/22	8,155	(0)	0.0%	13,000
06/21	7,807	1,434	18.4%	—
06/20	7,110	(306)	—	—
06/19	6,826	(59)	—	—
Annual Growth	6.1%	—	—	—

2022 Year-End Financials
Return on assets: —
Return on equity: —
Current Ratio: 1.40
Cash ($ mil.): 945

THE LANCASTER GENERAL HOSPITAL

Lancaster General Health is a not-for-profit health system with a comprehensive network of care, including more than 300 primary-care and specialty physicians; outpatient and Urgent Care services; and four hospitals with a total of nearly 800 licensed beds: Lancaster General Hospital, Women & Babies Hospital, Lancaster Rehabilitation Hospital, and Lancaster Behavioral Health Hospital. Its membership in Penn Medicine brings together the strengths of a world-renowned, not-for-profit academic medical center and a nationally recognized, not-for-profit community health care system.

LOCATIONS

HQ: THE LANCASTER GENERAL HOSPITAL
555 N DUKE ST, LANCASTER, PA 176022207
Phone: 717 544-5511
Web: WWW.LANCASTERGENERALHEALTH.ORG

PRODUCTS/OPERATIONS

2014 Sales

	$ million	% of total
Net patient services revenue, less provision for bad debts	920.3	95
Medical services	10.6	4
Other revenue	35.4	1
Other	2.9	—
Total	969.2	100

Selected Specialties
Cardiology
Emergency medical
Intensive care
Neurology
Oncology
Radiology
Rehabilitation
Urology

COMPETITORS

ALLINA HEALTH SYSTEM
ALTRU HEALTH SYSTEM
BRONXCARE HEALTH SYSTEM
COMMUNITY HEALTH NETWORK, INC.
COVENANT MEDICAL CENTER, INC.
INTEGRIS HEALTH, INC.
OVERLAKE HOSPITAL MEDICAL CENTER
SOUTHCOAST HEALTH SYSTEM, INC.
THE RUTLAND HOSPITAL INC ACT 220
WELLSPAN HEALTH

HISTORICAL FINANCIALS
Company Type: Private

Income Statement — FYE: June 30

	REVENUE ($mil)	NET INCOME ($mil)	NET PROFIT MARGIN	EMPLOYEES
06/16	958	122	12.8%	7,000
06/15	920	110	12.1%	—
06/14	867	(13)	—	—
06/13	823	(15)	—	—
Annual Growth	5.2%	—	—	—

2016 Year-End Financials
Return on assets: 14.5%
Return on equity: 28.6%
Current Ratio: 2.50
Cash ($ mil.): 23

THE LANE CONSTRUCTION CORPORATION

Lane likes people to be in the fast lane. For more than a century, the heavy civil contractor and its affiliates have been widening, paving, and constructing lanes for highways, bridges, runways, railroads, dams, and mass transit systems in the eastern and southern US. The group also produces bituminous and precast concrete and mines aggregates at plants and quarries in the northeastern, mid-Atlantic, and southern US. Additionally, it sells and leases construction equipment. Founded in 1902, Lane Construction has offices in more than 20 states and is owned by descendants of Lane and employees.

Operations
Lane Construction specializes in heavy civil construction services and products in the transportation, infrastructure, and energy industries. During the past decade, Lane Construction has participated in more than 70 design-building projects with a combined value of more than $4 billion.

Beyond its construction projects, Lane operates divisions that manufacture bituminous and precast concrete, with mine aggregates at 70 plants and 12 quarries throughout the U.S.

Lane's business divisions are spread across the US, and include: Civil Wall Solutions, Cold River Materials, Prestress of the Carolinas, Senate Asphalt, Virginia Paving Company, and Virginia Sign & Lighting Company.

Lane affiliates include New Hampshire-based Cold River Materials, Senate Asphalt of Washington, D.C., and Virginia Paving and Virginia Sign & Lighting Co., among about a half a dozen others. In 2013 its Rea Contracting division in the Carolinas changed its name to Lane Construction Corp.

Geographic Reach
Lane Construction has offices in more than 20 US states, including Florida, Illinois, Maine, North Carolina, Pennsylvania, Texas, and Virginia. While most of Lane's projects take place along the East Coast, it also operates in the South/Southwest, and has international operations -- under the Lane Worldwide Infrastructure, Inc. name -- in the Middle East.

Financial Performance
While full financials of the privately-held company were not available, Lane Construction has posted annual revenues of more than $1 billion since 2010.

Strategy
The company continues to work for both public and private entities on a variety of high-value projects. In early 2015, the contractor was working on a joint-venture project with Skanska and Granite Construction Company on the $2.3 billion "I-4 Ultimate project," which involves design, build, finance, operating, and maintenance work on 21 miles of Interstate 4 from Orange County to Seminole County in Florida.

Also as of early 2015, Lane reported that it recently completed its $1.5-billion construction project on the I-495 Express Lanes in Virginia in one of the largest public-private joint ventures in the US. The same team also completed a $722 million expansion and improvement project on 29 miles of the I-95 Express (high occupancy toll road) lanes in Virginia. Both of these Virgina-based projects were completed ahead of schedule.

Auditors: KPMG LLP HARTFORD CT

LOCATIONS

HQ: THE LANE CONSTRUCTION CORPORATION
90 FIELDSTONE CT, CHESHIRE, CT 064101212
Phone: 203 235-3351
Web: WWW.LANECONSTRUCT.COM

PRODUCTS/OPERATIONS

Selected Projects
Airports
Bridges
Design-Build
Federal
Heavy Civil
Highways
Public Private Partnerships
Plants & Paving
Rail
Specialty Paving

Selected Divisions
Civil Wall Solutions
Cold River Materials Prestress of the Carolinas
Senate Asphalt
Sunquip
Sunrise Materials
Virginia Paving Company
Virginia Sun & Lighting Company
Wardwell
White Bros.

COMPETITORS

AUSTIN INDUSTRIES, INC.
CIANBRO CORPORATION
EDWARD KRAEMER & SONS, INC.
FLATIRON CONSTRUCTION CORP.
FREESEN INC.
GLENN O. HAWBAKER, INC.
GRANITE CONSTRUCTION INCORPORATED
SKANSKA USA CIVIL INC.
TRAYLOR BROS., INC.
WORD CONSTRUCTORS, L.L.C.

HISTORICAL FINANCIALS
Company Type: Private

Income Statement — FYE: December 31

	REVENUE ($mil)	NET INCOME ($mil)	NET PROFIT MARGIN	EMPLOYEES
12/18	847	76	9.0%	3,500
12/17	1,476	18	1.3%	—
12/16	1,196	39	3.3%	—
12/15	1,115	(16)	—	—
Annual Growth	(8.7%)	—	—	—

2018 Year-End Financials
Return on assets: 7.6%   Cash ($ mil.): 136
Return on equity: 15.2%
Current Ratio: 1.80

THE MARY IMOGENE BASSETT HOSPITAL

EXECUTIVES

CCO, Steven Heneghan
STATEGY & TRANSFORMATION, Lisa Betrus
Chief of Staff, Cailin Purcell
Senior Vice President Cash, Reginald Knight
Senior Vice President Cash, Denise Robinson

LOCATIONS

HQ: THE MARY IMOGENE BASSETT HOSPITAL
1 ATWELL RD, COOPERSTOWN, NY 133261394
Phone: 607 547-3456
Web: WWW.BASSETT.ORG

HISTORICAL FINANCIALS
Company Type: Private

Income Statement — FYE: December 31

	REVENUE ($mil)	NET INCOME ($mil)	NET PROFIT MARGIN	EMPLOYEES
12/19	604	0	0.0%	3,200
12/17	547	4	0.8%	—
12/16	443	5	1.3%	—
12/15	412	(2)	—	—
Annual Growth	10.0%	—	—	—

2019 Year-End Financials
Return on assets: 0.1%   Cash ($ mil.): 2
Return on equity: 0.1%
Current Ratio: 0.70

THE MASSACHUSETTS GENERAL HOSPITAL

Founded in 1811, Massachusetts General Hospital (Mass General), is the original and largest teaching hospital of Harvard Medical School. Mass General provides comprehensive primary care and medical specialty services to some 200,000 adult and pediatric patients in about 15 locations throughout Greater Boston. Its specialized medical departments include cancer, cardiology and heart surgery; neurology and neurosurgery; and diabetes and endocrinology. As a leading research facility, Mass General hosts a number of clinical drug and device trials and has an annual research budget of more than $1 billion.

Operations
Mass General Hospital for Children provides a full spectrum of care ? from primary care to a broad range of specialty and subspecialty pediatric services ? for newborns, children and adolescents from New England and around the world.

The Mass General Brigham connects a full continuum of care across a system of academic medical centers, community and specialty hospitals, a health insurance plan, physician networks, community health centers, home care, and long-term care services.

Additionally, Mass General operates as one of the largest hospital-based research networks in the nation, consisting of more than 30 clinical departments and centers and conducting some 1,200 clinical trials at any given time. With Harvard Medical School, Mass General offers about 30 residency programs, 140 fellowship programs, and continuing medical education programs.

Geographic Reach
Mass General's main hospital is located in downtown Boston and includes nearly 30 buildings housing inpatient and ambulatory care services located in Andover, Boston, Charlestown, Chelsea, Danvers, Everett, Foxborough, Revere, and Waltham.

Sales and Marketing
Mass General offers high-quality, coordinated care for patients and families via phone, video, email, and mobile applications.

Financial Performance
Strategy

EXECUTIVES

Co-Vice President, Joseph Betancourt

LOCATIONS

HQ: THE MASSACHUSETTS GENERAL HOSPITAL
55 FRUIT ST, BOSTON, MA 021142696
Phone: 617 726-2000
Web: WWW.MASSGENERAL.ORG

Selected Research Centers
AIDS
Cancer
Cardiovascular research
Computational and integrative biology
Cutaneous biology
Human genetics
Medical imaging
Neurodegenerative disorders
Photomedicine
Regenerative medicine
Reproductive biology
Systems biology
Transplantation biology

COMPETITORS

BAPTIST MEMORIAL HEALTH CARE SYSTEM, INC.
BILLINGS CLINIC
BOSTON MEDICAL CENTER CORPORATION
CATHOLIC HEALTH SYSTEM OF LONG ISLAND, INC.
FROEDTERT MEMORIAL LUTHERAN HOSPITAL, INC.
LAHEY HEALTH SYSTEM, INC.
SWEDISH HEALTH SERVICES
TEXAS CHILDREN'S HOSPITAL
THE CHILDREN'S HOSPITAL CORPORATION
THE CHILDREN'S HOSPITAL OF PHILADELPHIA

HISTORICAL FINANCIALS
Company Type: Private

Income Statement — FYE: September 30

	REVENUE ($mil)	NET INCOME ($mil)	NET PROFIT MARGIN	EMPLOYEES
09/20	2,954	51	1.8%	10,156
09/14	2,201	186	8.5%	—
09/13	2,274	148	6.5%	—
09/12	2,281	267	11.7%	—
Annual Growth	3.3%	(18.6%)	—	—

2020 Year-End Financials
Return on assets: 1.0%   Cash ($ mil.): 588
Return on equity: 1.8%
Current Ratio: 1.20

THE MEDICAL COLLEGE OF WISCONSIN INC

EXECUTIVES

Chief Development Officer*, Mitchell R Beckman
CPO*, Adrienne Mitchell
Auditors: LB PRICEWATERHOUSECOOPERS LLP

LOCATIONS

HQ: THE MEDICAL COLLEGE OF WISCONSIN INC
8701 WATERTOWN PLANK RD, MILWAUKEE, WI 532263548
Phone: 414 456-8296
Web: WWW.MCW.EDU

HISTORICAL FINANCIALS

Company Type: Private

Income Statement — FYE: June 30

	REVENUE ($mil)	NET INCOME ($mil)	NET PROFIT MARGIN	EMPLOYEES
06/20	1,286	68	5.3%	4,700
06/19	1,258	79	6.3%	—
06/15	1,036	107	10.4%	—
Annual Growth	4.4%	(8.8%)	—	—

2020 Year-End Financials
Return on assets: 2.7%   Cash ($ mil.): 117
Return on equity: 3.8%
Current Ratio: 0.50

THE MEDICAL UNIVERSITY OF SOUTH CAROLINA

Established in 1824, the Medical University of South Carolina (MUSC) provides Charleston with a wide range of health-related services including medical care, training, and research. MUSC has approximately 3,000 full- and part-time students and 850 residents each year through its six schools, which cover medical, pharmacy, nursing, dental, health professional, and graduate training. The MUSC Health organization includes the MUSC Medical Center in Charleston, which has some 2,500 beds and includes a children's hospital and a psychiatric institute, as well as the University Medical Associates physician practice organization.

Operations

MUSC has extensive research facilities and programs in areas including bioengineering and translational sciences. The university also participates in drug discovery clinical trial research programs. Its technology transfer program allows small start-up companies to license or purchase research programs that are nearing commercial development stages.

MUSC's key areas of research include cancer, addiction sciences, drug discovery, health disparities, inflammation and fibrosis, neuroscience, oral health, rehabilitation and stroke.

MUSC Health, MUSC's clinical health system, is dedicated to delivering the highest quality patient care available while training generations of competent, compassionate health care providers to serve the people of South Carolina and beyond. It comprises some 2,500 beds, more than 100 outreach sites, the MUSC College of Medicine, and the physicians' practice plan and more than 300 telehealth locations.

Geographic Reach

MUSC is located in Charleston, South Carolina.

Mergers and Acquisitions

In mid-2021, Medical University of South Carolina (MUSC) finalized the acquisition of Providence Health and KershawHealth, which are currently part of LifePoint Health for approximately $75 million. The acquisition includes three community hospitals, a freestanding emergency department (FSED) and affiliated physician practice locations serving communities in the Midlands. Providence Health serves Columbia, SC, and the surrounding region, with two full-service hospitals and a freestanding emergency room. KershawHealth is a full-service medical center located in Camden, SC, which has been an affiliate of MUSC Health.

Company Background

MUSC was created by an act of South Carolina's General Assembly in 1824. It is historically recognized as the first medical school in the South.

Auditors: KPMG LLP GREENSBORO NC

LOCATIONS

HQ: THE MEDICAL UNIVERSITY OF SOUTH CAROLINA
171 ASHLEY AVE, CHARLESTON, SC 294258908
Phone: 843 792-2123
Web: LIBRARY.MUSC.EDU

COMPETITORS

ALBANY MEDICAL CENTER
CHARLESTON AREA MEDICAL CENTER, INC.
DUKE UNIVERSITY HEALTH SYSTEM, INC.
MASS GENERAL BRIGHAM INCORPORATED
NASSAU HEALTH CARE CORPORATION
NORTHWELL HEALTH, INC.
REGENTS OF THE UNIVERSITY OF MICHIGAN
THE RUTLAND HOSPITAL INC ACT 220
THE WASHINGTON UNIVERSITY
UNIVERSITY OF CALIFORNIA, SAN FRANCISCO

HISTORICAL FINANCIALS

Company Type: Private

Income Statement — FYE: June 30

	REVENUE ($mil)	NET INCOME ($mil)	NET PROFIT MARGIN	EMPLOYEES
06/18	992	4	0.4%	5,500
06/17	914	9	1.0%	—
06/13	780	26	3.3%	—
06/09	836	3	0.4%	—
Annual Growth	1.9%	1.8%	—	—

2018 Year-End Financials
Return on assets: 0.3%   Cash ($ mil.): 322
Return on equity: 3.8%
Current Ratio: 3.70

THE METHODIST HOSPITAL

Houston Methodist (formerly The Methodist Hospital) owns and operates eight Houston-area medical centers, including the flagship location, which has roughly 985 operating beds and is known for innovations in urology and neurosurgery, among other specialties. Other hospitals include Houston Methodist Baytown, Houston Methodist Clear Lake, Houston Methodist Sugar Land, Houston Methodist The Woodlands, Houston Methodist West, Houston Methodist Willowbrook, and Houston Methodist Continuing Care. Together, the hospitals have more than 1,555 beds and employ more than 5,250 physicians. In addition to hospitals, the organization operates emergency care, imaging, outpatient, and rehab centers and manages a physician organization of around 775.

Operations

The health system has been recognized for high performance in several specialty areas, including cancer, diabetes, nephrology, pulmonology, and geriatrics. It's also been lauded for its specialties in cardiology and heart surgery, endocrinology, gastroenterology and GI surgery, gynecology, neurology and neurosurgery, orthopedics, and urology.

The hospital has educational and research affiliations with Cornell University's Weil Cornell Medical College, the New York-Presbyterian Hospital, University of Houston, Texas Annual Conference of the United Methodist Church, Texas A&M, and other organizations.

The 440,000-square-foot Houston Methodist Research Institute Translational Research Building, provides the technology and support its doctors need to effectively and efficiently bring cures through all stages of clinical trials and to all patients around the world. The Research Institute includes open laboratory space designed to house some 90 principal investigators, over 20 core facilities to enhance interdisciplinary research, and two Good Manufacturing Practice (GMP) facilities to prepare clinical-grade radiopharmaceuticals, biological agents and small molecules.

Geographic Reach
Based in Houston, Texas, and operates mostly in and around Houston, Texas, Houston Methodist has hospitals and medical facilities in Sugar Land, the Woodlands, Baytown, Nassau Bay, Clear Lake, and Katy.

Its Houston Methodist Global Health Care Services has operations in Dubai, UAE; Riyadh, KSA; Guadalajara, Mexico City, and Monterrey, Mexico; Guatemala City, Guatemala; Guayaquil, Ecuador; Managua, Nicaragua; Montevideo, Uruguay; San Salvador, El Salvador; and Tegucigalpa, Honduras.

Sales and Marketing
Partner with more than 450 companies representing several industries, population sizes and locations, Houston Methodist's programs provide financial and medical assistance to more than 150,000 patients every year.

EXECUTIVES
OF TREASURY*, Mike V Giblin

Auditors : DELOITTE & TOUCH LLP HOUSTON

LOCATIONS
HQ: THE METHODIST HOSPITAL
  6565 FANNIN ST, HOUSTON, TX 770302892
Phone: 713 441-2340
Web: WWW.HOUSTONMETHODIST.ORG

PRODUCTS/OPERATIONS
Selected Houston-Area Hospitals
Houston Methodist Hospital - Texas Medical Center (Houston)
Houston Methodist Sugar Land Hospital
Houston Methodist Willowbrook Hospital (Houston)
Houston Methodist West Hospital (Houston)
Houston San Jacinto Methodist Hospital (Baytown)
Houston Methodist St. John Hospital (Texas)
Houston Methodist St. Catherine Hospital (Texas)

Selected Services
Cancer / Oncology
Diabetes / Endocrinology
Digestive Diseases
Ear, Nose & Throat
Emergency Care
Heart & Vascular
Imaging / Radiology
Internal Medicine
Neurology
Neurosurgery
Obstetrics & Gynecology
Ophthalmology
Oral and Maxillofacial Surgery & Dentistry
Orthopedics & Sports Medicine
Otolaryngology Head & Neck Surgery
Pathology & Genomic Medicine
Plastic & Reconstructive Surgery
Psychiatry
Rehabilitation
Robotic Surgery
Transplant
Urology
Weight Management
Wellness

COMPETITORS
METHODIST HEALTHCARE SYSTEM OF SAN ANTONIO, LTD., L.L.P.
METHODIST HOSPITAL OF SOUTHERN CALIFORNIA
METHODIST HOSPITALS OF DALLAS
METHODIST LE BONHEUR HEALTHCARE
RIVERSIDE HEALTHCARE ASSOCIATION, INC.
RIVERVIEW HOSPITAL
SOUTHERN ILLINOIS HEALTHCARE ENTERPRISES, INC.
ST. MARY'S HEALTH, INC.
SUTTER BAY HOSPITALS
TEXAS HEALTH HARRIS METHODIST HOSPITAL FORT WORTH

HISTORICAL FINANCIALS
Company Type: Private

Income Statement — FYE: December 31

	REVENUE ($mil)	NET INCOME ($mil)	NET PROFIT MARGIN	EMPLOYEES
12/18	4,496	291	6.5%	15,000
12/17	3,887	531	13.7%	—
Annual Growth	15.7%	(45.2%)	—	—

2018 Year-End Financials
Return on assets: 3.2%
Return on equity: 4.4%
Current Ratio: 1.10
Cash ($ mil.): 246

THE METROHEALTH SYSTEM

Founded in 1837, MetroHealth System is redefining health care by going beyond medical treatment to improve the foundations of community health and well-being: affordable housing, a cleaner environment, economic opportunity and access to fresh food, convenient transportation, legal help and other services. MetroHealth has an academic medical center to research and for teaching and caregivers. Each active physicians holds an appointment at Case Western Reserve University Schools of Medicine. Its main campus hospital houses the Cleveland Metropolitan School District's Lincoln-West School of Science & Health, the only high school in America located inside a hospital.

Operations
MetroHealth has more than 600 doctors and 1,700 nurses. Services include behavioral health, vascular surgery, orthopedics, burn care, and pediatrics. The system also operates outpatient clinics, a regional rehabilitation clinic, a heart and vascular center, two skilled nursing centers, an outpatient center, and a medical- and surgical subspecialties. MetroHealth is home to Cuyahoga County's most experience in Level I Adult Trauma Center and Ohio's only adult and pediatric trauma burn center.

Geographic Reach
MetroHealth operates four hospitals, four emergency departments and more than 20 health centers and 40 additional sites throughout Cuyahoga County.

Sales and Marketing
The system serves more than 300, 000 patients, and two thirds of whom are uninsured or covered by Medicare or Medicaid.

Company Background
MetroHealth has been serving the medical needs of the Greater Cleveland community since 1837. It has been a major affiliate of Case Western Reserve University since 1914.

Auditors : RSM US LLP CLEVELAND OHIO

LOCATIONS
HQ: THE METROHEALTH SYSTEM
  2500 METROHEALTH DR, CLEVELAND, OH 441091900
Phone: 216 398-6000
Web: WWW.METROHEALTH.ORG

Selected Locations
J. Glen Smith Health Center (In partnership with the City of Cleveland, Cleveland)
MetroHealth Asia Town Health Center (Cleveland)
MetroHealth Beachwood Health Center (Beachwood, Ohio)
MetroHealth Broadway Health Center (Cleveland)
MetroHealth Brooklyn Health Center (Cleveland)
MetroHealth Buckeye Health Center (Cleveland)
MetroHealth Center for Sleep Medicine South Campus (Independence, Ohio)
MetroHealth Center for Sleep Medicine West Campus (Westlake, Ohio)
MetroHealth Lakewood Health Center (Lakewood)
MetroHealth Lee-Harvard Health Center (Cleveland)
MetroHealth Medical Center, Main Campus (Cleveland)
MetroHealth Old Brooklyn Campus (Cleveland)
MetroHealth Pepper Pike Health Center (Pepper Pike, Ohio)
MetroHealth Premier Health Center (Westlake, Ohio)
MetroHealth Rehabilitation Institute of Ohio (Cleveland)
MetroHealth Strongsville Health Center (Strongsville, Ohio)
MetroHealth West 150th Health and Surgery Center (Cleveland)
MetroHealth Westlake Health Center (Westlake)
MetroHealth West Park Health Center (Cleveland)
The Elisabeth Severance Prentiss Center for Skilled Nursing Care at MetroHealth (Cleveland)
Thomas F. McCafferty Health Center (In partnership with the City of Cleveland, Cleveland)

PRODUCTS/OPERATIONS
MetroHealth System Departments and Services
Aamoth Family Pediatric Wellness Center
Adolescent Clinic (Teen Health)
Advanced Gynecology (Center for Advanced Gynecology)
Advantage (MetroHealth Advantage)
Allergy & Immunology Clinic
Allergy Services (Department of Ear, Nose & Throat)
Amigas Unidas Program
Anesthesiology
Art Therapy
Arthritis Center (Rheumatology)
Audiology
Bariatric Surgery (Weight Loss Surgery Program)
Behavioral Health (Child and Teen Mental Health Services)
Birth Control Procedures
Birthing Services
Bone Health and Surgery (Orthopaedics
BREAST Program (Community Breast Cancer Outreach)
Burn Care Center
Cancer Care Center
Cardiology, Cardiovascular (Heart & Vascular Center)

Center for Advanced Gynecology
Center for Behavioral Health (Child and Teen Mental Health Services)
Centers for Community Health
Center for Sleep Medicine
Cerebrovascular
Childbirth Education
Child Life and Education
Children's Health (Pediatrics)
Children's Health Specialties
Closing the Gap (MetroHealth Buckeye Health Center)
Comprehensive Care Program (Services for Children with Special Needs)
Concussion Clinic
Cosmetic Dermatology
Dentistry and Oral Health
Dermatology
Diabetes Self-Management Program
Digital Mammogram
Ear, Nose, and Throat (ENT/Otolaryngology)
Emergency Medicine/Emergency Department
Endocrinology
Endoscopy Suite (Gastroenterology)
ExpressCare (MetroExpressCare)
Family Medicine Clinic at MetroHealth Medical Center
Fertility Services
Freedom From Smoking
Gastroenterology and Endoscopy Suite
Genetics Clinic
Geriatrics (Senior Health & Wellness Center)
Gynecology
Gynecology, Advanced (Center for Advanced Gynecology)
Gynecologic Oncology
Hand Center
Heart & Vascular Center
Hematology and Oncology (Cancer Care Center)
High-Risk Pregnancy Services
Hospital Medicine
Immunology (Allergy & Immunology Clinic)
Infectious Disease
Infertility Clinic
Infusion Therapy (Allergy & Immunology Clinic)
Internal Medicine Clinic at MetroHealth Medical Center
Internal Medicine and Pediatrics (Med-PEDS)
Kids' Health (Pediatrics
Kids' Korner Free Daycare Service at MetroHealth Medical Center
Latina Clinic: English | En espa?ol
LGBT Pride Clinic (At Thomas F. McCafferty Health Center Health Center)
Life Flight (Metro Life Flight)
Long-Term/Skilled Nursing Care
Maternal-Fetal Medicine (High-Risk Pregnancy Services)
Medicine (Department of Medicine)
Mental Health (Psychiatry)
Metro Life Flight
MetroHealth Advantage
MetroExpressCare
MetroHealth Rehabilitation Institute of Ohio
MetroHealth Select Health Plan
MetroHealth Simulation Center
Mi MetroHealth, Mi Comunidad
MyChart
Neonatology, Neonatal Intensive Care Unit (NICU)
Nephrology
Neurology
Neurosciences
Northeast Ohio Chapter of the National Spinal Cord Injury Association (NSCIA)
Northeast Ohio Regional Spinal Cord Injury System (NORSCIS)
Nose, Ear, and Throat (ENT, Otolaryngology)
Nursing
Nutrition
Obstetrics
Obstetrics and Gynecology
Occupational Medicine
Oncology (Cancer Care Center)
Opthalmologic (Eye) Surgery
Oral Health (Dentistry)
Oral and Maxillofacial Surgery
Orthopaedics

Osteopathic Medicine
Otolaryngology (Ear, Nose, and Throat)
Pain Management
Palliative Care
Pastoral Care
Pathology
Pediatrics
Permanent Birth Control Procedures
Pharmacy
Pregnancy Resources
Pride Clinic (At Thomas F. McCafferty Health Center Health Center)
Psychiatry (Behavioral/Mental Health)
Pulmonary and Critical Care
Quality Indicators
Radiology
Rehab, Rehabilitation Services (MetroHealth Rehabilitation Institute of Ohio)
Reiki
Reproductive Endocrinology and Infertility Clinic
Rheumatology (Arthritis Center)
Select Health Plan
Senior Health and Wellness Center
Simulation Center
Skeletal (Orthopaedics)
Skilled Nursing/Long-Term Care
Sleep Medicine, Sleep Studies
Spanish-language Information
Special Needs Services for Children (Comprehensive Care)
Spine Center
Stroke, Stroke & Cerebrovascular Center
Surgery
Throat (Otolaryngology, ENT)
Teen Health
Trauma, Burns, and Critical Care
Travel Clinic
Urgent Care (MetroExpressCare)
Urology
Vascular Health and Surgery (Heart & Vascular Center
Weight Loss Surgery Program (Bariatric Surgery)
X-ray (Radiology)

COMPETITORS

ARKANSAS CHILDREN'S HOSPITAL
CKHS, INC.
DENVER HEALTH AND HOSPITALS AUTHORITY
JERSEY CITY MEDICAL CENTER (INC)
JUPITER MEDICAL CENTER, INC.
KINGSBROOK JEWISH MEDICAL CENTER
NORTH SHORE UNIVERSITY HOSPITAL
NORTHSHORE UNIVERSITY HEALTHSYSTEM
READING HOSPITAL
SALEM HEALTH

HISTORICAL FINANCIALS
Company Type: Private

Income Statement — FYE: December 31

	REVENUE ($mil)	NET INCOME ($mil)	NET PROFIT MARGIN	EMPLOYEES
12/15	888	37	4.2%	7,700
12/13	813	41	5.1%	—
12/09	673	58	8.7%	—
Annual Growth	4.7%	(7.1%)	—	—

2015 Year-End Financials
Return on assets: 3.6% Cash ($ mil.): 4
Return on equity: 20.0%
Current Ratio: 1.10

THE MICHAELS COMPANIES INC

The Michaels Companies is one of the US' leading arts and crafts retailer with more than 1,275 Michaels stores across the country and in Canada. In addition to its retail outlets, the company also owns multiple brands that allow it to collectively provide arts, crafts, framing, floral, home dÃ©cor, and seasonal merchandise to hobbyists and do-it-yourself home decorators. It serves customers through digital platforms including Michaels.com and Michaels.ca. In early 2021, the company was acquired by Apollo Global Management at an equity value of approximately $3.3 billion.

Operations
Michaels offers arts, crafts, framing, floral, wall dÃ©cor, and seasonal merchandise.

In addition, the company also owns Artistree, a manufacturer of high-quality custom and specialty framing merchandise.

Geographic Reach
Based in the US, Michaels operates more than 1,275 stores in about 50 states and Canada.

Sales and Marketing
The company serves customers through digital platforms.

Mergers and Acquisitions
In 2016 Michaels Companies acquired Lamrite West, an international wholesale and retail supplier of arts and crafts, for $150 million. The acquisition added a business to the Michaels portfolio enhances its private brand development capabilities, accelerates its direct sourcing initiatives, and strengthens its business-to-business capabilities.

Company Background
Michael Dupey founded Michaels arts and crafts store in 1973 by converting a Ben Franklin variety store in Dallas that was owned by his father. With dad footing the bill, Dupey opened several other stores in Texas, and by the early 1980s Michaels operated 11 stores.

Dupey wanted to buy the company from his father; the two could not agree on a price, however, so dad sold the chain in 1983 to Peoples Restaurants, which operated the Bonanza Steakhouse chain. With 16 stores mostly in Texas, Peoples Restaurants spun off Michaels in 1984 to its shareholders.

In the mid-2000s private equity firms Bain Capital and Blackstone Group took the company private; it went public again in 2014.

HISTORY

Michael Dupey founded Michaels arts and crafts store in 1973 by converting a Ben Franklin variety store in Dallas that was owned by his father. With dad footing the bill, Dupey opened several other stores in Texas, and by the early 1980s Michaels operated 11 stores.

Dupey wanted to buy the company from his father; the two could not agree on a price, however, so dad sold the chain in 1983 to Peoples Restaurants, which operated the Bonanza Steakhouse chain and was run by brothers Sam and Charles Wyly (now vice chairman and chairman, respectively). As part of the deal, Dupey was paid $1.2 million and was given ownership of two Dallas stores plus royalty-free licensing rights to Michaels stores in North Texas.

With 16 stores mostly in Texas, Peoples Restaurants spun off Michaels in 1984 to its shareholders. Michaels then acquired Montiel, a Colorado-based retailer with 13 stores. The next year the company acquired six retailers. In 1987 Michaels acquired Moskatel's, a 28-store chain based in California. By 1988 the company operated nearly 100 stores in 14 states.

Michaels had achieved the mass to attract the attention of big investors, and in 1989 it agreed to a $225 million LBO engineered in part by Acadia Partners, an investment group headed by Robert Bass. The group was unable to raise the junk-bond debt financing needed to acquire the company, and the deal fell apart in early 1990; Michaels took a $4 million charge for its effort.

That year the company hired Dupey, who had built his own Michaels-MJDesigns chain in the meantime, to assist it in selecting and marketing merchandise; it fired him in 1991, beginning a stormy relationship that played out in court. The company continued to open new stores and had 140 outlets by the end of 1991.

In 1992 Michaels began a drive to become the first national arts and crafts chain. It opened stores in new markets, including Iowa, Ohio, Oklahoma, Virginia, and Washington, and made its debut in Toronto.

Two years later Michaels acquired several chains in the West, including Oregon Craft & Supply, H&H Craft & Floral Company, and Treasure House. Its biggest acquisition that year, however, was its $92 million purchase of 101-store Leewards Creative Crafts, which gave it a total of 360 stores in 38 states. In 1995 Michaels acquired 71 Aaron Brothers specialty framing and art supply stores.

Ironically, the company's far-reaching expansion did not include its birthplace. After a three-year court battle proving even the crafts business has an ugly side, in 1996 Michaels was awarded the right to operate stores in its home market, the Dallas-Fort Worth area, and Dupey's Michaels-MJDesigns stores removed the Michaels name from its signs. (Dupey, in turn, was permitted to sell his assets without first getting right of approval from Michaels.)

Lowe's veteran Michael Rouleau became CEO of Michaels in 1996. Struggling to knit together its acquisitions, Michaels lost $31 million in fiscal 1997, its second straight loss. Rouleau refined the chain's merchandise (reducing noncore items like party supplies) and expanded its distribution system.

The company opened 50 Michaels stores and relocated 14 in 1998. Michaels bought 16 stores (mainly in Maryland and Virginia) from bankrupt MJDesigns in 1999. To serve florists, interior decorators, and others, Michaels acquired a Dallas store in 2000, Star Wholesale Florist, and began operating it as Star Decorators' Wholesale Warehouse.

Michaels continued its expansion plans in 2001 and 2002, adding more than 140 Michaels stores and 33 Aaron Brothers locations. Also in 2002 Michaels opened three Village Crafts stores in smaller markets to test retailing 80% of its typical selection within half the square footage. The next year it opened another eight Village Craft stores, but decided to use the Michaels name for this concept.

In June 2003 the company opened its first of two test stores in the Dallas-Fort Worth area. Called ReCollections, the stores are dedicated to helping "scrappers" make and compile scrapbooks. The second ReCollections opened in October 2003. Also in 2003 Michaels opened another Star Decorators' Wholesale Warehouse, in Atlanta.

An additional 45 Michaels stores, seven Aaron Brothers stores, and six ReCollections locations were opened in 2004.

In March 2006, Michaels Companies put itself up for sale. Concurrently, CEO Michael Rouleau retired after a decade with the company and was replaced by a pair of senior executives -- Jeffrey N. Boyer and Gregory A. Sandfort -- who were named co-presidents of Michaels Companies. In late October the company was taken private (and thus delisted from the New York Stock Exchange) by Bain Capital Partners, LLC and The Blackstone Group in a deal that valued the firm at more than $6 billion.

In June 2007 Brian Cornell, a former Safeway and PepsiCo executive, joined Michaels Companies as its new CEO. In late 2007 and early 2008 the company closed all 11 of its Recollections and several Star Decorators Wholesale shops. The company said the move was made to focus on its core retail stores.

In March 2009 Cornell resigned to join SAM'S CLUB as its new chief executive. He was succeeded by John Menzer, a former Wal-Mart executive. In October the company opened its first store in Manhattan, as it tests an expansion into big cities. In July 2012 Menzer resigned as CEO of the company after suffering a stroke in April.

As it right-sized its retail footprint, Michaels Companies lured its crafty shoppers online by expanding its web-based offerings. In late 2010 it acquired an online scrapbooking application developed by Chicago-based ScrapHD. The application enables users to create digital scrapbooks that can be printed at home and bound into a book. Added to the MiDesign section of Michaels Companies' website, the application was relaunched in 2011.

The company went public again in 2014.

EXECUTIVES

Chief Operating Officer Sales, Patrick Venezia
Chief Compliance Officer, Tim Cheatham
Executive Stores Vice President, J Robert Koch
CAO, James E Sullivan
Auditors : ERNST & YOUNG LLP DALLAS TEX

LOCATIONS

HQ: THE MICHAELS COMPANIES INC
3939 W JOHN CARPENTER FWY, IRVING, TX 750632909
Phone: 972 409-1300
Web: WWW.MICHAELS.COM

2018 Sales

	$ mil.	% of total
US	4,783.9	91
Canada	488.0	9
Total	5,271.9	100

PRODUCTS/OPERATIONS

2018 Sales

	$ mil.	% of total
General crafts	2,604.9	50
Home décor and seasonal	1,230.0	23
Framing	801.1	15
Papercrafting	635.9	12
Total	5,271.9	100

Brands
Wilton
Elmer's
Darice
Aaron Brothers
Crayola

Selected Merchandise
General crafts
    Apparel crafts
    Bakeware
    Beads
    Books and magazines
    Doll-making items
    Jewelry-making supplies
    Needlecraft items (knitting, needlepoint, embroidery, cross-stitch, crochet, rug-making, quilts, afghans)
    Paper crafting
    Plaster
    Rubber stamp supplies
    Scrapbooking supplies
    Wall décor (candles, containers, baskets, potpourri, other home decorating items)
    Wood and woodcraft items
Art supplies
    Acrylics
    Adhesives
    Brushes
    Canvases and other painting surfaces
    Easels
    Finishes
    Memory book materials
    Oil paints
    Pastels
    Sketch pads
    Stenciling materials
    Water colors
Picture framing
    Backing materials
    Custom framing
    Framed art

Glass
Mat boards
Photo albums
Ready-made frames
Silk and dried floral
Artificial plants
Dried flowers
Floral arranging supplies
Silk flowers and plants
Seasonal items
Artificial trees
Candles
Christmas crafts
Gift-making supplies
Lights and ornaments
Wreaths
Hobby, party, and candles
Candle-making supplies
Paint-by-number kits
Party supplies (paper party goods, balloons, gift wrap, candy-making supplies, cake-decorating supplies)
Plastic model kits
Plush toys
Soap-making supplies
Wedding supplies (favors, flowers, headpieces, cake-decorating supplies)

COMPETITORS

A.C. MOORE ARTS & CRAFTS, INC.
AMERICAN GIRL BRANDS, LLC
BUILD-A-BEAR WORKSHOP, INC.
HOBBY LOBBY STORES, INC.
LOWE'S COMPANIES, INC.
OTCI CORP.
TARGET CORPORATION
TOYS "R" US LIMITED
TOYS "R" US, INC.
WH SMITH PLC

HISTORICAL FINANCIALS

Company Type: Private

Income Statement   FYE: January 30

	REVENUE ($mil)	NET INCOME ($mil)	NET PROFIT MARGIN	EMPLOYEES
01/21*	5,271	294	5.6%	45,000
02/20	5,072	272	5.4%	—
12/19	5,072	272	5.4%	—
02/19	5,271	319	6.1%	—
Annual Growth	0.0%	(3.9%)	—	—

*Fiscal year change

2021 Year-End Financials
Return on assets: 6.5%   Cash ($ mil.): 1,194
Return on equity: —
Current Ratio: 1.30

THE MIDDLE TENNESSEE ELECTRIC MEMBERSHIP CORPORATION

Middle Tennessee Electric Membership Corporation's service territory is smack dab in the middle of Tennessee. The utility cooperative distributes electricity to 190,750 residential and business customers (member/owners) in four counties (Cannon, Rutherford, Williamson, and Wilson), via more than 10,470 miles of power lines connected to 34 electric distribution substations. Middle Tennessee Electric purchases its power supply from the Tennessee Valley Authority. The corporation is Tennessee's largest electric cooperative and the sixth largest in the US.

Geographic Reach
The cooperative serves customers in Cannon, Rutherford, Williamson, and Wilson counties. According to a US Census report, three of Tennessee's five fastest growing counties (Rutherford, Williamson, and Wilson) are in Middle Tennessee Electric's service area, which also includes three of Tennessee's top five fastest-growing cities -- LaVergne, Smyrna, and Franklin.

Strategy
To harness green energy as a way to limit fossil fuel power sources and reduce carbon emissions, the utility cooperative is installing solar panels for customers. In 2012 the company completed a 850-panel solar field next to the City of Franklin's water plant. That year Middle Tennessee Electric had 70 solar projects operating across its service area and 30 more in the planning stages.

Company Background
Middle Tennessee Electric was formed in 1936 as part of a national rural electrification push.

EXECUTIVES

OF ENGNRNG*, Keith Thomason
Vice Chairman*, Tom Purkey
Auditors: WINNETT ASSOCIATES PLLC SHELB

LOCATIONS

HQ: THE MIDDLE TENNESSEE ELECTRIC MEMBERSHIP CORPORATION
555 NEW SALEM HWY, MURFREESBORO, TN 371293590
Phone: 615 890-9762
Web: WWW.MTE.COM

COMPETITORS

CLAY ELECTRIC COOPERATIVE, INC.
MISSISSIPPI COUNTY ELECTRIC COOPERATIVE, INC.
PEDERNALES ELECTRIC COOPERATIVE, INC.
RAPPAHANNOCK ELECTRIC COOPERATIVE
SOUTHERN MARYLAND ELECTRIC COOPERATIVE, INC.

HISTORICAL FINANCIALS

Company Type: Private

Income Statement   FYE: December 31

	REVENUE ($mil)	NET INCOME ($mil)	NET PROFIT MARGIN	EMPLOYEES
12/19*	618	0	0.0%	410
06/16	542	10	1.9%	—
06/13	524	27	5.3%	—
06/12	510	19	3.8%	—
Annual Growth	2.4%	—	—	—

*Fiscal year change

2019 Year-End Financials
Return on assets: —   Cash ($ mil.): 40
Return on equity: —
Current Ratio: 1.30

THE MITRE CORPORATION

A private, not-for-profit organization, the MITRE Corporation provides consulting, engineering, and technical research services primarily for agencies of the federal government. In addition to its two primary research facilities in Massachusetts and Virginia, MITRE also has additional sites across the country and around the world. It also manages several federally funded research and development centers serving organizations such as the Department of Defense, the Federal Aviation Administration, the Internal Revenue Service, and the Department of Veterans Affairs. MITRE was founded in 1958 by former MIT researchers.

Operations
MITRE brings innovative ideas into existence in areas as varied as artificial intelligence, intuitive data science, quantum information science, health informatics, space security, policy and economic expertise, trustworthy autonomy, cyber threat sharing, and cyber resilience.

The company operates federally funded research and development centers (FFRDCs), unique organizations that assist the US government with scientific research and analysis; development and acquisition; and systems engineering and integration. It also has an independent research program that explores new and expanded uses of technologies to solve its sponsors' problems.

Geographic Reach
The company has primary research facilities in Bedford, Massachusetts and McLean, Virginia.

Sales and Marketing
MITRE works in the public interest across federal, state and local governments, as well as industry and academia.

Strategy
In early 2022, MITRE and the Washington Metropolitan Area Transit Authority (Metro) announced a collaboration that is designed to strengthen Metro's Safety Management System (SMS).

Over the course of a three-year contract, MITRE will work with Metro to assess their safety culture, develop a plan to improve their safety data analytics, and deploy a secure Voluntary Safety Reporting Program (VSRP). The VSRP will produce data that can be integrated with other Metro safety information to continuously improve their data-driven safety risk management. Once implemented, the VSRP will lower barriers to safety and hazard reporting and elevate Metro's safety protocols.

Establishing Metro's safety culture baseline will formalize leadership's understanding of where the agency is and where it needs to go in terms of maturing their safety culture. The reporting program will provide Metro employees with the ability to report safety hazards voluntarily and confidentially.

Company Background

The MITRE Corporation was chartered in 1958 as a private, not-for-profit company to provide engineering and technical guidance for the federal government. Since then, MITRE has operated at the intersection of advanced technology and vital national concerns. The company grown to serve a variety of government agencies at the highest levels through the operation of federally funded research and development centers (FFRDCs).

EXECUTIVES

Chief Human Resources Officer, Julie Gravallese

LOCATIONS

HQ: THE MITRE CORPORATION
 202 BURLINGTON RD, BEDFORD, MA 017301420
Phone: 781 271-2000
Web: WWW.MITRE.ORG

COMPETITORS

ADVANCIA CORPORATION
ALTARUM INSTITUTE
AMERICAN INSTITUTES FOR RESEARCH IN THE BEHAVIORAL SCIENCES
HEALTH RESEARCH, INC.
NOBLIS, INC.
SRI INTERNATIONAL
STG LLC
THE BROOKINGS INSTITUTION
THE RAND CORPORATION
UNITED STATES DEPARTMENT OF COMMERCE

HISTORICAL FINANCIALS
Company Type: Private

Income Statement — FYE: October 5

	REVENUE ($mil)	NET INCOME ($mil)	NET PROFIT MARGIN	EMPLOYEES
10/08	1,234	22	1.8%	7,000
10/07	1,113	23	2.1%	—
Annual Growth	10.9%	(4.6%)	—	—

2008 Year-End Financials
Return on assets: —   Cash ($ mil.): 36
Return on equity: 1.8%
Current Ratio: 0.80

THE NATURE CONSERVANCY

The Nature Conservancy is a global conversation organization. The mission of The Conservancy is to conserve the lands and waters on which all life depends. The Conservancy conducts its activities throughout the United States, Canada, Latin America, the Caribbean, Europe, Africa, Asia, and the Pacific. It preserves the diversity of Earth's wildlife by saving more than 125 million acres of land, and 100 marine areas in every US state and over 70 countries worldwide. The Nature Conservancy has grown to become one of the most effective and wide-reaching environmental organizations in the world. The Nature Conservancy was founded in 1951.

Operations

The Nature and Conservancy gets around 45% of its support and revenues from dues and contributions, followed by investment income with about 35%, the Government contributions, as well as land sales and gifts, each with around 5%, and the rest comes from investments and other income.

The Nature Conservancy is urgently taking on the dual threats of biodiversity loss and the climate crisis, maximizing resilience and benefits for communities. It includes tackle climate change, protects land and water, provides food and water sustainably, and build healthy cities.

Geographic Reach

Based in Arlington, Virginia, The Nature Conservancy operates in more than 70 countries worldwide and all 50 US states. The organization works in Africa, the Asia-Pacific region, the Caribbean, Europe, Canada, India, and the Americas.

Auditors : PRICEWATERHOUSECOOPERS LLP MC

LOCATIONS

HQ: THE NATURE CONSERVANCY
 4245 FAIRFAX DR STE 100, ARLINGTON, VA 222031650
Phone: 703 841-5300
Web: WWW.NATURE.ORG

Selected Areas of Operation
Africa
Australia
Asia & the Pacific Islands
Caribbean
Central America
Europe
North America
South America

PRODUCTS/OPERATIONS

2014 Support & Revenue

	mil.	% of total
Dues & contributions	560.4	50
Investment income	235.2	22
Land sales & gifts	138.5	12
Government grants	120.7	11
1Other income	59.5	5
Total	1,114.3	100

2014 Dues & Contributions

	%
Individuals	37
Foundations	28
Bequests	23
Other organizations	6
Corporations	6
Total	100

COMPETITORS

AMERICAN FARMLAND TRUST (THE)
CONSERVATION INTERNATIONAL FOUNDATION
COOPERATIVE FOR ASSISTANCE AND RELIEF EVERYWHERE, INC. (CARE)
DUCKS UNLIMITED, INC.
NATIONAL AUDUBON SOCIETY, INC.
NATIONAL PARK FOUNDATION (INC)
NATURAL RESOURCES DEFENSE COUNCIL, INC.
THE CONSERVATION FUND, A NONPROFIT CORPORATION
THE NATIONAL TRUST FOR PLACES OF HISTORIC INTEREST OR NATURAL BEAUTY
WORLD WILDLIFE FUND, INC.

HISTORICAL FINANCIALS
Company Type: Private

Income Statement — FYE: June 30

	REVENUE ($mil)	NET INCOME ($mil)	NET PROFIT MARGIN	EMPLOYEES
06/19	992	118	11.9%	3,400
06/16	803	(8)	—	—
06/14	949	201	21.2%	—
06/13	859	106	12.4%	—
Annual Growth	2.4%	1.7%	—	—

2019 Year-End Financials
Return on assets: 1.5%   Cash ($ mil.): 193
Return on equity: 1.8%
Current Ratio: —

THE NEBRASKA MEDICAL CENTER

Cornhuskers take note: If health care is what you seek, The Nebraska Medical Center aims to please. The not-for-profit health system provides tertiary care at two campuses in Omaha, University Hospital and Clarkson Hospital, that collectively house about 680 licensed beds. The medical center, the largest health care facility in Nebraska, is the primary teaching facility of the University of Nebraska Medical Center (UNMC). It also serves as a designated trauma facility for eastern Nebraska and western Iowa, and provides highly specialized care, including organ transplantation. Its Clarkson West Medical Center campus houses outpatient surgery facilities, an emergency room, and doctors' offices.

Operations

The system has more than 1,000 physicians. In 2013, it had some 51,000 emergency department visits, more than 24,500 inpatient admissions, and about 428,000 outpatient visits.

In addition to University Hospital and Clarkson Hospital, Nebraska Medical Center operates a network of 40 specialty and primary care clinics in and around Omaha. The health system's Centers of Excellence include its Cancer Center, Heart Center, Neurological Sciences, Transplant Center, and Women's Health.

Geographic Reach

In addition to serving the residents of Omaha, the Nebraska Medical Center serves as a designated trauma facility for patients in eastern Nebraska and western Iowa.

Strategy

Like most other health care providers, the Nebraska Medical Center is looking for ways to cut costs in the face of decreasing reimbursements from federal payers (such as Medicare and Medicaid) and as pressure from health care reform mounts and hospitals are required to implement expensive digital record-keeping and physician order entry systems. One way that Nebraska Medical Center has sought to reduce its expenses it by signing up with companies such as Medassets to receive sourcing and group purchasing (GPO), medical device, and clinical consulting services for items used most by its physicians and for its pharmacy services.

The medical center and its sponsoring university are looking to expand its medical facilities to keep pace with a growing and aging population. UNMC is developing a new cancer center at the medical center's Omaha campus. Plans include three facilities - a multidisciplinary outpatient clinic, a 98-lab research tower, and a hospital tower with 108 beds dedicated to oncology patients. The project (estimated to cost $370 million) is expected to create 1,200 new jobs by 2020 and pump $100 million annually into Nebraska's economy.

The system is also working with UNMC to add a new outpatient center to the university's midtown campus. The Lauritzen Outpatient Center will feature 10 operating rooms, including four dedicated to opthalmic surgical procedures.

Auditors : KPMG LLP OMAHA NE

LOCATIONS

HQ: THE NEBRASKA MEDICAL CENTER
987400 NEBRASKA MED CTR, OMAHA, NE 681980001
Phone: 402 552-2000
Web: WWW.NEBRASKAMED.COM

PRODUCTS/OPERATIONS

Selected Services
Cancer Center
General Health Services
Heart and Vascular Services
Neurological Sciences
Transplantation

COMPETITORS

ATLANTICARE HEALTH SYSTEM INC.
CENTRASTATE HEALTHCARE SYSTEM INC
COMMUNITY HOSPITALS OF CENTRAL CALIFORNIA
FAIRFIELD MEDICAL CENTER
FLAGSTAFF MEDICAL CENTER, INC.
GREATER BALTIMORE MEDICAL CENTER, INC.
SHAWNEE MISSION MEDICAL CENTER, INC.
TALLAHASSEE MEMORIAL HEALTHCARE, INC.
UNIVERSITY HOSPITALS HEALTH SYSTEM, INC.
WELLSTAR HEALTH SYSTEM, INC.

HISTORICAL FINANCIALS
Company Type: Private

Income Statement — FYE: June 30

	REVENUE ($mil)	NET INCOME ($mil)	NET PROFIT MARGIN	EMPLOYEES
06/17	1,389	74	5.4%	4,100
06/16	1,119	60	5.4%	—
Annual Growth	24.1%	22.1%	—	—

2017 Year-End Financials
Return on assets: 5.2%   Cash ($ mil.): 67
Return on equity: 9.0%
Current Ratio: 2.40

THE NEW JERSEY TRANSIT CORPORATION

Government-owned New Jersey Transit (NJ TRANSIT) is the nation's third largest provider of bus, rail, and light rail passenger transportation services. Its systems connect major points in New Jersey and provide links to the neighboring New York City and Philadelphia metropolitan areas. Overall, the NJ TRANSIT service area spans about 5,325 sq. miles. One of the largest transportation companies of its kind in the US, NJ TRANSIT operates a fleet of around 2,220 buses, approximately 1,230 trains, and about 95 light rail vehicles. Collectively, the agency's passengers make nearly 270 million trips a year. NJ TRANSIT also administers several publicly funded transit programs for people with disabilities, senior citizens and people living in the state's rural areas who have no other means of transportation.

Operations

Aside from bus, rail, and light rail passenger transportation services, NJ TRANSIT also supports and encourages the use of personal vehicles, such as bicycles, e-bikes, e-scooters, Segways, and hoverboards, by providing accommodations for customers using personal vehicles to the greatest extent possible.

Geographic Reach

NJ TRANSIT is headquartered in New Jersey.

Sales and Marketing

NJ TRANSIT has an application where customers can plan and buy tickets for the company's services. The company also offers deals and discounts to its customers including students, with its promotional partners.

Company Background

NJ TRANSIT was founded in 1979 by the New Jersey legislature.

EXECUTIVES

CCO*, Christine Baker
Acting CIO*, Christopher Montgomery
Auditors : DELOITTE & TOUCHE LLP PARSIPP

LOCATIONS

HQ: THE NEW JERSEY TRANSIT CORPORATION
1 PENN PLZ E, NEWARK, NJ 071052245
Phone: 973 491-7000
Web: WWW.NJTRANSIT.COM

COMPETITORS

CAPITAL METROPOLITAN TRANSPORTATION AUTHORITY
FIRSTGROUP AMERICA, INC.
HARRIS COUNTY, METROPOLITAN TRANSIT AUTHORITY OF
LOS ANGELES COUNTY METROPOLITAN TRANSPORTATION AUTHORITY
NEW YORK CITY TRANSIT AUTHORITY
ORANGE COUNTY TRANSPORTATION AUTHORITY
REGIONAL TRANSPORTATION DISTRICT
SOUTHEASTERN PENNSYLVANIA TRANSPORTATION AUTHORITY
STUDENT TRANSPORTATION OF AMERICA, INC.
WASHINGTON METROPOLITAN AREA TRANSIT AUTHORITY

HISTORICAL FINANCIALS
Company Type: Private

Income Statement — FYE: June 30

	REVENUE ($mil)	NET INCOME ($mil)	NET PROFIT MARGIN	EMPLOYEES
06/18	1,056	(67)	—	1,000
06/04	583	256	44.0%	—
06/03	569	482	84.7%	—
Annual Growth	4.2%	—	—	—

2018 Year-End Financials
Return on assets: (-0.9%)   Cash ($ mil.): 80
Return on equity: (-1.9%)
Current Ratio: 0.90

THE NEW SCHOOL

When James Lipton asks you what your favorite swear word is, you know you've made it. The New School's drama department (formerly called The Actor's Studio) was made famous by the cable show Inside the Actors Studio, which features Lipton interviewing movie and television stars. TheÂ school offers degrees in theater for playwriting, directing, and acting, and has taught "Method" acting to grads such as Marlon Brando and Robert De Niro. It is also home to Parsons The New School for Design and has schools devoted to general studies, liberal arts, social research, management and urban policy, and music. More than 10,500Â traditional students andÂ 5,600 continuing education students are enrolled at The New School.

Operations

The New School offers more than 90 degree and diploma programs and majors to a population of undergraduate and graduate students who come from all 50 states and more than 100 foreign countries (about one-quarter of its students hail from international locations). It boasts small class sizes and a student-teacher ratio of about 10:1.

The New School for Public Engagement is the university's founding division and is composed of five schools: Milano School of International Affairs, Management, and Urban Policy; School of Language Learning and Teaching; School of Media Studies; School of Undergraduate Studies; and School of Writing. It has since added six divisions: Drama, Jazz, Lang, Mannes, Parsons, and Social Research.

Financial Performance
The New School's 2011 revenue grew by more than 5% vs. 2010. Net income increased 13% over the same period.

Strategy
Parsons' new academic center in Paris is slated to open in fall 2013. The Paris site will offer students a program that addresses the global nature of contemporary art and design practice, and reflects Europe's culture and philosophy.

The New School was founded in 1919 by a group of university professors and intellectuals in New York City as place for students wanting to explore their creativity and engage in deep thought while studying liberal arts. Dozens of years later, The New School has gained a reputation for its unconventional teaching methods, as well as for being the home of many world-renowned institutes including the think tank, The World Policy Institute. It also hosts the annual National Book Awards, which has helped establish the careers of some of the country's most recognized authors including Richard Powers and Jonathan Franzen.

Auditors : KPMG LLP NEW YORK NY

LOCATIONS
HQ: THE NEW SCHOOL
66 W 12TH ST, NEW YORK, NY 100118871
Phone: 212 229-5600
Web: WWW.NEWSCHOOL.EDU

PRODUCTS/OPERATIONS
Selected Schools
Eugene Lang College The New School for Liberal Arts
Mannes College The New School for Music
Milano The New School for Management and Urban Policy
The New School for Drama
The New School for General Studies
The New School for Jazz and Contemporary Music
The New School for Public Engagement
The New School for Social Research
Parsons The New School for Design

COMPETITORS
ART CENTER COLLEGE OF DESIGN
BARD COLLEGE
THE UNIVERSITY OF CHICAGO
THE WASHINGTON AND LEE UNIVERSITY
UNIVERSITY OF CALIFORNIA, BERKELEY

HISTORICAL FINANCIALS
Company Type: Private

Income Statement — FYE: June 30

	REVENUE ($mil)	NET INCOME ($mil)	NET PROFIT MARGIN	EMPLOYEES
06/20	558	(20)	—	855
06/19	427	20	4.8%	—
06/18	411	28	7.0%	—
06/16	370	(15)	—	—
Annual Growth	10.9%	—	—	—

2020 Year-End Financials
Return on assets: (-1.6%)   Cash ($ mil.): 6
Return on equity: (-3.6%)
Current Ratio: 0.10

THE NEW YORK AND PRESBYTERIAN HOSPITAL

The New York and Presbyterian Hospital is one of the most comprehensive, integrated academic health care delivery systems, and affiliated with two renowned medical schools, Weill Cornell Medicine and Columbia University of Vagelos College of Physician and Surgeons, New Presbyterian is consistently recognized as leader of medical education, groundbreaking research, and innovative, patient-centered clinical care. New York and Presbyterian Hospital have 2,600 beds, 6,500 affiliated physicians, and four major division: New York and Presbyterian Hospital, NewYork-Presbyterian Regional Hospital Network, NewYork-Presbyterian Physician Services, and NewYork-Presbyterian Community and Population Health. Formed in 1998 by the merger of The New York Hospital and The Presbyterian Hospital.

Operations
With some 2,600 beds and more than 6,500 affiliated physicians and 20,000 employees, NewYork-Presbyterian sees more than 2 million visits annually, including close to 15,000 infant deliveries and more than 310,000 emergency department visits.

NewYork-Presbyterian medical groups connect expert doctors with patients close to home to expand coordinated care and healthcare services across the regions we proudly serve. Its medical groups in Brooklyn, Queens, Westchester and Hudson Valley increase access to a wide range of primary and specialty care services, and include Weill Cornell Medicine and Columbia physicians.

NewYork-Presbyterian Community and Population Health, encompassing ambulatory care network sites and community health care initiatives, including NewYork Quality Care, the Accountable Care Organization jointly established by NewYork-Presbyterian, Weill Cornell, and Columbia.

Geographic Reach
NewYork- Presbyterian Hospital is based in New York.

Company Background
NewYork-Presbyterian Hospital was formed through the 1998 merger of the New York Hospital (founded in 1771) and the Presbyterian Hospital (founded in 1868). New York Hospital was known for advancing care in areas including women's health and surgery, while the Presbyterian Hospital was known for its pediatric division and its cancer center.

Auditors : ERNST & YOUNG LLP NEW YORK N

LOCATIONS
HQ: THE NEW YORK AND PRESBYTERIAN HOSPITAL
525 E 68TH ST, NEW YORK, NY 100654870
Phone: 212 746-5454
Web: WWW.NYP.ORG

PRODUCTS/OPERATIONS
2016 Patient Mix

	% of total
Medicare Managed	9
Medicare FFS	22
Medicaid Managed	23
Medicaid FFS	7
Managed Care and Other	37
Self-Pay	1
Workers Comp	1
Total	100

Selected Services
Cancer
Children's Health
Digestive
Geriatrics
Heart
Mens Health
Neuroscience
Orthopedic
Psychiatry
Rehabilitation Medicine
Transplant
Vascular
Womens Health

COMPETITORS
BEAUMONT HEALTH
CAREGROUP, INC.
CATHOLIC HEALTH SYSTEM, INC.
CATHOLIC MEDICAL CENTER
MONTEFIORE NYACK HOSPITAL FOUNDATION, INC.
PROSPECT WATERBURY, INC.
SAINT JOSEPH HOSPITAL, INC
THE BROOKLYN HOSPITAL CENTER
THE UNIVERSITY OF VERMONT MEDICAL CENTER INC.
WILLIAM BEAUMONT HOSPITAL

HISTORICAL FINANCIALS
Company Type: Private

Income Statement — FYE: December 31

	REVENUE ($mil)	NET INCOME ($mil)	NET PROFIT MARGIN	EMPLOYEES
12/21	9,859	1,578	16.0%	23,709
12/20	9,115	(382)	—	—
12/18	8,483	526	6.2%	—
12/17	5,616	762	13.6%	—
Annual Growth	15.1%	19.9%	—	—

2021 Year-End Financials
Return on assets: 8.0% Cash ($ mil.): 455
Return on equity: 14.3%
Current Ratio: 1.70

THE NORTH CAROLINA MUTUAL WHOLESALE DRUG COMPANY

Auditors: THOMAS KNIGHT TRENT KING AN

LOCATIONS

HQ: THE NORTH CAROLINA MUTUAL WHOLESALE DRUG COMPANY
816 ELLIS RD, DURHAM, NC 277036019
Phone: 919 596-2151
Web: WWW.MUTUALDRUG.COM

HISTORICAL FINANCIALS
Company Type: Private

Income Statement — FYE: March 31

	REVENUE ($mil)	NET INCOME ($mil)	NET PROFIT MARGIN	EMPLOYEES
03/10	1,035	0	0.0%	160
03/09	1,024	0	0.1%	—
03/08	1,007	1	0.2%	—
Annual Growth	1.4%	(64.1%)	—	—

2010 Year-End Financials
Return on assets: 0.2% Cash ($ mil.): 53
Return on equity: 0.8%
Current Ratio: 1.20

THE OHIO STATE UNIVERSITY WEXNER MEDICAL CENTER

Auditors: PRICEWATERHOUSECOOPERS LLP CO

LOCATIONS

HQ: THE OHIO STATE UNIVERSITY WEXNER MEDICAL CENTER
410 W 10TH AVE, COLUMBUS, OH 432101240
Phone: 614 293-8000
Web: WEXNERMEDICAL.OSU.EDU

HISTORICAL FINANCIALS
Company Type: Private

Income Statement — FYE: June 30

	REVENUE ($mil)	NET INCOME ($mil)	NET PROFIT MARGIN	EMPLOYEES
06/19	3,433	39	1.2%	35,000
06/18	3,106	137	4.4%	—
06/16	2,628	126	4.8%	—
Annual Growth	9.3%	(31.9%)	—	—

2019 Year-End Financials
Return on assets: 1.0% Cash ($ mil.): 987
Return on equity: 6.2%
Current Ratio: 4.40

THE ORANGE COUNTY PUBLIC SCHOOL DISTRICT

EXECUTIVES

Chief of Staff, Bridget Williams
Interim CAO, Doreen Concolino
Auditors: CHERRY BEKAERT LLP ORLANDO F

LOCATIONS

HQ: THE ORANGE COUNTY PUBLIC SCHOOL DISTRICT
445 W AMELIA ST, ORLANDO, FL 328011128
Phone: 407 317-3200
Web: WWW.OCPS.NET

HISTORICAL FINANCIALS
Company Type: Private

Income Statement — FYE: June 30

	REVENUE ($mil)	NET INCOME ($mil)	NET PROFIT MARGIN	EMPLOYEES
06/20	2,661	(26)	—	24,000
06/19	2,646	95	3.6%	—
06/18	2,506	107	4.3%	—
06/17	2,341	(25)	—	—
Annual Growth	4.4%	—	—	—

2020 Year-End Financials
Return on assets: (-0.4%) Cash ($ mil.): 377
Return on equity: (-0.6%)
Current Ratio: —

THE PARSONS CORPORATION

Industrial construction giant Parsons provides engineering, construction, and other services for corporate, institutional, and government projects worldwide. The company designs and builds structures; provides environmental remediation services including hazardous materials cleanup; and adds improvements to airports, rail systems, bridges, and highways. Parsons developed significant expertise and differentiated capabilities in key areas of cybersecurity, missile, intelligence, defense, C5ISR, space, geospatial, and connected communities. North America accounts for nearly 85% of revenue. The company was founded in 1944 by Ralph M. Parsons.

Operations
The company operates in two reporting segments: Critical Infrastructure and Federal Solutions.

The Federal Solutions segment serves the defense, environmental, intelligence, and security markets. It provides critical technologies, including cybersecurity; missile defense systems; C5ISR; space launch, ground systems and operations; geospatial intelligence; signals intelligence; nuclear and chemical waste remediation; and engineering services. The segment accounts for about 50% of total revenue.

Its Critical Infrastructure segment (roughly 50%) provides integrated design and engineering services for complex physical and digital infrastructure around the globe.

Geographic Reach
Centreville, Virginia-based, Parsons has operations in more than 35 states and about 15 countries. North America accounts for nearly 85% of revenue, Middle East accounts for about 15% of revenue, and the rest of the world generates the remaining.

Sales and Marketing
The company serves a diverse global customer base including federal, state, municipal and industry customers, and private sector infrastructure owners, such as the transportation authorities for the cities of Los Angeles, New York, and Paris, the state of New Jersey, AMTRAK, CSX, Metrolinx (Ontario, Canada), Riyadh Metro, Dubai Roads and Transportation Authority (Dubai RTA), and the Abu Dhabi Municipality.

Financial Performance
Revenue for the year ended December 31, 2021 compared to the prior year decreased $258.2 million to $3.7 billion. This decrease was primarily due to a decrease in revenue in its Critical Infrastructure segment of $234.3 million and a decrease in our Federal Solutions segment of $23.8 million.

In 2021, the company had a net income of $89 million, a 25% decrease from the previous year's net income of $118.9 million.

The company's cash at the end of 2021 was $343.9 million. Operating activities generated $205.6 million, while investing activities used $240.9 million, mainly for payments for acquisitions. Financing activities used another $106.5 million, primarily for repayments of borrowings.

Strategy
Parsons' growth strategy is to create the future of national security and critical infrastructure, while moving up the value

chain as a solutions integrator and software provider. The future is full of possibility, and the defense, intelligence, and critical infrastructure markets are where the company can collectively shape what tomorrow will look like. Its goal is to help create a safer, healthier, more sustainable, more connected and more secure world.

Mergers and Acquisitions

In mid-2021, Parsons acquired Echo Ridge LLC (Echo Ridge), a privately-owned company, for $9.0 million in cash. Echo Ridge adds position, navigation, and timing devices; modeling, simulation, test, and measurement tools; and deployable software defined radio products and signal processing services to Parsons' space portfolio.

In 2021, Parsons acquired Virginia-based BlackHorse Solutions, Inc., a privately-owned company, for $205.0 million. The strategic acquisition expands Parsons' capabilities and products in next-generation military, intelligence, and space operations, specifically in cyber, electronic warfare, and information dominance.

HISTORY

Ralph Parsons, the son of a Long Island fisherman, was born in 1896. At age 13 he started his first business venture, a garage and machine shop, which he operated with his brother. After a stint in the US Navy, Parsons joined Bechtel as an aeronautical engineer. The company changed its name to Bechtel-McCone-Parsons Corporation in 1938. However, Parsons later sold his shares in that company and left in 1944 to start his own design and engineering firm, the Ralph M. Parsons Co., after splitting with partner John McCone (who later headed the CIA).

Parsons Co. expanded into the chemical and petroleum industries in the early 1950s. During that decade it oversaw the building of several natural gas and petroleum refineries overseas, including the world's largest, in Lacq, France.

In the early 1960s the company began working in Kuwait, which later proved to be one of its biggest markets. By 1969 Parsons had built oil refineries for all of the major oil companies, designed launch sites for US missiles, and constructed some of the largest mines in the world. In 1969 the company went public. With annual sales of about $300 million, it ranked second only to Bechtel in the design and engineering field. Ralph Parsons died in 1974.

The company built oil and gas treatment and production plants in Alaska in the 1970s and reorganized itself into The Parsons Corporation and RMP International in 1978. It went private in 1984 as The Parsons Corporation, taking advantage of a new tax law that favored corporations with employee stock ownership plans (ESOPs). Not all employees were happy, though. Several groups sued, maintaining that the plan disproportionately benefited executives, and that the buyout left the ESOP with all of the debt but no decision-making power. A Labor Department investigation later exonerated Parsons executives.

Parsons had just finished work on a power plant in Kuwait when Iraq invaded in 1990. Several employees were detained by the Iraqis but were released shortly before the Persian Gulf War. Two years later the company returned to Kuwait to rebuild some of the country's demolished infrastructure.

In 1995 Parsons acquired Gilbert/Commonwealth, an engineering company that specializes in designing nuclear power plants as part of an effort to bolster Parsons' ability to compete for power plant projects in industrializing countries. That year Parsons was awarded a contract to help build the Seoul International Airport, one of the largest airport projects in the world.

James McNulty, who had led the company's infrastructure and technology group, replaced Leonard Pieroni as CEO in 1996 after Pieroni died in the Bosnia plane crash that also claimed the life of US Secretary of Commerce Ronald Brown. Later that year a Parsons-led consortium won a $164.5 million contract for infrastructure projects in Bosnia.

Parsons restructured in 1997 to focus on energy, transportation, and infrastructure projects. A Parsons/Inelectra joint venture won a $150 million construction contract in 1998 to develop Cerro Negro's heavy oil production facilities in Venezuela, and the next year Parsons was chosen to manage construction of a $5 billion refinery in Bahrain, a $1.4 billion gas plant in Saudi Arabia, and a $1 billion polyethylene project in Abu Dhabi.

Parsons partnered with TRW in 2000 to create TRW Parsons Management & Operations to bid on the DOE's Yucca Mountain site in Nevada, a potential repository for the US's high-level radioactive waste and spent nuclear fuel. It also was awarded a three-year contract to help rebuild the war-torn Serbian province of Kosovo and the next year was awarded a similar contract for Bosnia-Herzegovina.

In 2001 the company won a US Federal Aviation Agency contract to upgrade air traffic control towers and other equipment and systems, a contract that had been held by rival Raytheon since 1988. Parsons also strengthened its 80-year-old bridge division by acquiring bridge engineering firm Finley McNary. That year the company's joint venture with construction giant Fluor was awarded a contract to design and engineering work for the first offshore oil field in Kazakhstan.

In 2002 Parsons completed construction of the Parsons Fabrication Facility as a part for the US Army's push for alternative methods of chemical weapons disposal. The facility was designed to test process systems for chemical weapon and bulk agent disposal.

Also that year Parsons won a contract from Dallas Area Rapid Transit (DART) to provide systems engineering and construction management services for the second phase of the buildout for the light-rail system, the largest expansion of its kind in North America. In 2003 it also won a contract for final design and construction management of the first light-rail system in Charlotte, North Carolina. In 2004 the Parsons' joint venture with Kellogg Brown & Root won a controversial defense contract for oil field and refinery engineering, construction, and maintenance in Iraq.

Another project for Parsons was the design and engineering support for construction of Carquinez Bridge near San Francisco, the first major suspension bridge to be built in the US in more than 35 years.

Parsons' Infrastructure & Technology Group subsidiary sold its Cultural Resources group to Versar in 2005. The following year it was selected to provide engineering management support for Russia's Chemical Weapons Destruction Complex.

The company ran into trouble in war-torn Iraq in 2007. The army cancelled the remainder of a $70 million contract to build 20 hospitals in Iraq, due to performance problems with the construction. The company maintained (and an investigation supported) that the problems stemmed from mismanagement by the Army Corps of Engineers. It then lost a $99 million contract to build a prison in northern Iraq.

In 2009 the company acquired analytic services provider McMunn Associates, which did work for the Department of Defense, Department of Energy, and other government agencies.

EXECUTIVES

CLO, Michael R Kolloway
Chief Human Resource Officer, Susan Balaguer
Auditors : PRICEWATERHOUSECOOPERS LLP LO

LOCATIONS

HQ: THE PARSONS CORPORATION
5875 TRINITY PKWY STE 300, CENTREVILLE, VA 201201971
Phone: 703 988-8500
Web: WWW.PARSONS.COM

PRODUCTS/OPERATIONS

Selected Markets and Services
Parsons Commercial Technology
    Advanced manufacturing
    Commercial facilities
    Data management services
    Educational facilities
    Entertainment
    Health care
    Industrial environmental remediation
    Life sciences
    Mission critical facilities
    Telecommunications
    Vehicle inspection and compliance
    Wireless telecommunications systems

Parsons Infrastructure and Technology
    Community relations
    Construction
    Construction management
    Design
    Engineering
    Estimating
    Operations
    Operator training
    Procurement
    Program management
    Start-up and operations
Parsons Transportation
    Aviation
    Bridges
    Highways
    Railroads
    Revenue collection and management systems
    Systems engineering
    Transportation consumer services
    Transportation planning
    Tunneling
    Urban Transit
Parsons Water and Infrastructure
    Biosolids management
    Combined sewer overflows
    Construction/Construction management
    Desalination and membrane technology
    Design-build
    Emergency response support
    Environmental planning and restoration
    Master planning
    Ocean outfalls
    Operations and maintenance
    Storm water management
    Utility tunneling
    Wastewater collection systems
    Wastewater treatment
    Water resources
    Water supply and pipelines

COMPETITORS

BECHTEL GROUP, INC.
CACI INTERNATIONAL INC.
CATAPULT TECHNOLOGY, LTD.
CMTSU LIQUIDATION, INC
JACOBS ENGINEERING GROUP INC.
LEIDOS HOLDINGS, INC.
MANTECH INTERNATIONAL CORPORATION
PETER KIEWIT SONS', INC.
SCIENCE APPLICATIONS INTERNATIONAL CORPORATION
THE KEYW HOLDING CORPORATION

HISTORICAL FINANCIALS

Company Type: Private

Income Statement   FYE: December 31

	REVENUE ($mil)	NET INCOME ($mil)	NET PROFIT MARGIN	EMPLOYEES
12/18	3,560	239	6.7%	15,500
12/15	846	28	3.4%	—
Annual Growth	61.4%	102.7%	—	—

2018 Year-End Financials
Return on assets: 9.2%   Cash ($ mil.): 280
Return on equity: —
Current Ratio: 1.50

THE PENNSYLVANIA HOSPITAL OF THE UNIVERSITY OF PENNSYLVANIA HEALTH SYSTEM

Early to bed, early to rise may have made Ben Franklin healthy, wealthy, and wise. But for those not so healthy, he (along with Dr. Thomas Bond) found it wise to establish Pennsylvania Hospital, the nation's first such medical institution. The hospital is now a part of the University of Pennsylvania Health System (UPHS) and offers a comprehensive range of medical, surgical, and diagnostic services to the Philadelphia County area. Housing some 520 beds, Pennsylvania Hospital offers specialized care in areas such as orthopedics, vascular surgery, neurosurgery, and obstetrics; it is also a leading teaching hospital and a center for clinical research.

Operations
Pennsylvania Hospital has an average of about 29,000 inpatient admissions per year, including 5,200 births, as well as 115,000 outpatient and emergency care visits. The medical center has more than 800 physicians on its medical staff. In addition to its extensive medical care services, the company conducts medical training programs through its relationship with the University of Pennsylvania School of Medicine. Medical and clinical research programs are conducted with the school and with other research entities including government agencies. The hospital also collaborates with other UPHS entities, including the Penn Presbyterian Medical Center and the Hospital of the University of Pennsylvania. The medical center also provides educational services across academic programs, inlcuding Clinical Psychology Internship Program, Medicine, OB/GYN, Pathology, Radiology, Sports Medicine Fellowship, Surgery, and Vascular Surgery Fellowship.

Financial Performance
For the fiscal year 2014 (ended June 30) Pennsylvania Hospital's revenues increased by 8.4%, with a 9% increase in net patient service revenues 94% of total revenues); offset by a 1% decline in other revenues.

The company's net loss for the year decreased by 38% due to higher revenues and a decline in employee benefits paid.

Strategy
To improve the quality of care in the region, UPHS is expanding specialist programs at its facilities.

In 2014 Pennsylvania Hospital opened its new Well Mother & Baby Unit, which will represent Philadelphia's first all-private maternity suite unit. The new unit is part of Pennsylvania Hospital's $61 million long-range facility master plan and expands the company's offerings by providing private rooms to all of their maternity patients, along with an array of obstetrical services, from conception to discharge from the hospital following childbirth.

In 2013 UPHS expanded the orthopedic surgery program at Pennsylvania Hospital. The medical center is also enhancing services in fields including stroke care and women's health.

Company Background
The hospital was founded in 1751 by Benjamin Franklin and Dr. Thomas Bond to care for the sick-poor and insane of Philadelphia.

Auditors: LB PRICEWATERHOUSECOOPERS LLP

LOCATIONS

HQ: THE PENNSYLVANIA HOSPITAL OF THE UNIVERSITY OF PENNSYLVANIA HEALTH SYSTEM
 800 SPRUCE ST, PHILADELPHIA, PA 191076130
Phone: 215 829-3000
Web: WWW.PENNMEDICINE.ORG

PRODUCTS/OPERATIONS

Selected Centers
ALS Center
Birthing Suite
Center for Bloodless Medicine and Surgery
Crisis Response Center
CyberKnife
Diabetes Education Center
Joan Karnell Cancer Center
Pain Management Center
Parkinson's Disease and Movement Disorders Center
Penn Comprehensive Neurosciences Center
Penn Orthopaedic Institute
Penn Center for Voice
Sports Medicine and Rehabilitation Center
Sleep Disorders Center
Vascular Center
Women's Imaging Center

Selected Services
Behavioral health
Heart and vascular
Neonatology
Neurosurgery
Obstetrics (including high-risk maternal and fetal services)
Orthopedics
Otorhinolaryngology (ENT)
Urology
Vascular medicine/surgery

COMPETITORS

BRONXCARE HEALTH SYSTEM
CHARLESTON AREA MEDICAL CENTER, INC.
CHILDREN'S HOSPITAL & RESEARCH CENTER AT OAKLAND
KALEIDA HEALTH
PASADENA HOSPITAL ASSOCIATION, LTD.
ROBERT WOOD JOHNSON UNIVERSITY HOSPITAL, INC.
SAINT JOSEPH HOSPITAL, INC
SWEDISH COVENANT HOSPITAL
TEXAS CHILDREN'S HOSPITAL
THE CHILDREN'S HOSPITAL OF PHILADELPHIA

HISTORICAL FINANCIALS
Company Type: Private

Income Statement   FYE: June 30

	REVENUE ($mil)	NET INCOME ($mil)	NET PROFIT MARGIN	EMPLOYEES
06/20	678	2	0.4%	2,200
06/15	579	21	3.7%	—
06/14	534	(2)	—	—
06/10	485	27	5.7%	—
Annual Growth	3.4%	(20.8%)	—	—

2020 Year-End Financials
Return on assets: 0.3%   Cash ($ mil.): —
Return on equity: 0.5%
Current Ratio: —

THE PENNSYLVANIA STATE UNIVERSITY

The Pennsylvania State University system is one of the top of the world universities. Penn State has an enrollment of nearly 100,000 students. It offers more than 275 undergraduate programs at 20 campuses. The school's oldest and largest campus, with about half of the system's undergraduate students, is at University Park in central Pennsylvania. Other sites include the Penn State College of Medicine in Hershey, Pennsylvania, and the Dickinson School of Law in Carlisle, Pennsylvania.

Operations
It's more than 275 undergraduate programs include majors such as agriculture and natural resources, biological science, business, engineer, humanities and language, and social science. Penn State offers more than 190 graduate major programs, several stand-alone graduate minor programs, and approximately 100 undergraduate certificates and 20 two-year associate degrees. Some majors include accounting, aerospace engineering, anatomy, architectural engineering, art, and astrobiology.

Geographic Reach
Its two dozen campuses are located throughout Pennsylvania including in Abington, Altoona, Behrend, Berks, Carlisle, Great Valley (School of Graduate Professionals), Wilkes-Barre, University Park (largest Penn State campus), and York.

Company Background
Chartered in 1855 to apply scientific principles to farming, Penn State has conferred almost 800,000 degrees since its founding.

The university's storied football program was hit in 2012 with a four year postseason ban, the significant reduction of scholarships, the vacating of 112 wins and a $60 million fine, all stemming from the school's handling of the child molestation scandal involving former coach Jerry Sandusky. However, in 2015 the NCAA reversed its decision on the vacating of wins, restoring the late head coach Joe Paterno as the winningest coach in major college football history.

Auditors: DELOITTE & TOUCHE LLP PHILADE

LOCATIONS
HQ: THE PENNSYLVANIA STATE UNIVERSITY
201 OLD MAIN, UNIVERSITY PARK, PA 168021503
Phone: 814 865-4700
Web: WWW.PSU.EDU

PRODUCTS/OPERATIONS
Selected Colleges
College of Agricultural Sciences
College of Arts and Architecture
Smeal College of Business
College of Communications
College of Earth and Mineral Sciences
College of Education
College of Engineering
College of Health and Human Development
College of Information Sciences and Technology
School of International Affairs
School of Law
College of the Liberal Arts
College of Medicine
School of Nursing
Eberly College of Science
Graduate School
Schreyer Honors College

Selected Campuses
Penn State Abington Penn State Altoona
Penn State Beaver
Penn State Berks
Penn State Brandywine
Penn State DuBois
Penn State Erie, The Behrend College
Penn State Fayette, The Eberly Campus
Penn State Greater Allegheny
Penn State Harrisburg
Penn State Hazleton
Penn State Lehigh Valley
Penn State Mont Alto
Penn State New Kensington
Penn State Schuylkill
Penn State Shenango
Penn State Wilkes-Barre
Penn State Worthington Scranton
Penn State York

COMPETITORS
CLEVELAND STATE UNIVERSITY
CORNELL UNIVERSITY
MICHIGAN STATE UNIVERSITY
NORTH CAROLINA STATE UNIVERSITY
PURDUE UNIVERSITY
THE RUTGERS STATE UNIVERSITY
THE TRUSTEES OF THE UNIVERSITY OF PENNSYLVANIA
UNIVERSITY OF KANSAS
UNIVERSITY SYSTEM OF MARYLAND
WAYNE STATE UNIVERSITY

HISTORICAL FINANCIALS
Company Type: Private

Income Statement   FYE: June 30

	REVENUE ($mil)	NET INCOME ($mil)	NET PROFIT MARGIN	EMPLOYEES
06/22	7,867	(14)	—	44,000
06/21	7,275	2,444	33.6%	—
06/20	6,795	(712)	—	—
06/19	6,576	583	8.9%	—
Annual Growth	6.2%	—	—	—

2022 Year-End Financials
Return on assets: (-0.1%)   Cash ($ mil.): 1,058
Return on equity: (-0.1%)
Current Ratio: 2.80

THE PEPPER COMPANIES INC

Auditors: BKD LLP OAKBROOK TERRACE IL

LOCATIONS
HQ: THE PEPPER COMPANIES INC
643 N ORLEANS ST, CHICAGO, IL 606543608
Phone: 312 266-4703

HISTORICAL FINANCIALS
Company Type: Private

Income Statement   FYE: September 30

	REVENUE ($mil)	NET INCOME ($mil)	NET PROFIT MARGIN	EMPLOYEES
09/20	1,255	20	1.6%	1,100
09/17	1,119	22	2.0%	—
09/16	1,179	21	1.8%	—
09/11	1,177	10	0.9%	—
Annual Growth	0.7%	7.9%	—	—

2020 Year-End Financials
Return on assets: 4.5%   Cash ($ mil.): 82
Return on equity: 15.3%
Current Ratio: 1.30

THE PRESIDENT AND FELLOWS OF HARVARD COLLEGE

Auditors: PRICEWATERHOUSECOOPERS LLP B

LOCATIONS
HQ: THE PRESIDENT AND FELLOWS OF HARVARD COLLEGE
600 ATLANTIC AVE, BOSTON, MA 022102211
Phone: 617 495-1502
Web: WWW.WEBMEDIAUNIVERSITY.COM

HISTORICAL FINANCIALS
Company Type: Private

Income Statement   FYE: June 30

	REVENUE ($mil)	NET INCOME ($mil)	NET PROFIT MARGIN	EMPLOYEES
06/14	4,408	4,607	104.5%	11,500
06/13	4,214	1,056	25.1%	—
06/12	4,037	(1,446)	—	—
06/09	0	0	—	—
Annual Growth	—	—	—	—

2014 Year-End Financials
Return on assets: 7.2%   Cash ($ mil.): 87
Return on equity: 104.5%
Current Ratio: —

THE PRIDDY FOUNDATION

LOCATIONS

HQ: THE PRIDDY FOUNDATION
807 8TH ST STE 1010, WICHITA FALLS, TX 763013310
Phone: 940 723-8720
Web: WWW.PRIDDYFDN.ORG

HISTORICAL FINANCIALS
Company Type: Private

Income Statement — FYE: December 31

	REVENUE ($mil)	NET INCOME ($mil)	NET PROFIT MARGIN	EMPLOYEES
12/13	8,791	3	0.0%	4
12/12	3	(4)	—	—
12/10	32	27	86.7%	—
12/09	0	0	—	—
Annual Growth	—	—	—	—

2013 Year-End Financials
Return on assets: 2.5% Cash ($ mil.): 14
Return on equity: 2.5%
Current Ratio: —

THE PUBLIC HEALTH TRUST OF MIAMI-DADE COUNTY

Jackson Memorial Hospital is the flagship facility of the Jackson Health System (JHS). It has roughly 1,150 beds and offers a wide variety of services, including burn treatment, trauma, pediatrics, rehabilitation, obstetrics, and transplants. The system also includes two neighborhood community hospitals?Jackson South, Jackson North, and Jackson West? along with Holtz Children's Hospital, Jackson Behavioral Health Hospital, the Christine E. Lynn Rehabilitation Center for The Miami Project to Cure Paralysis at UHealth/Jackson Memorial, two nursing homes and a network of UHealth/Jackson Urgent Care centers, physician practices, and clinics. Jackson Memorial Hospital and JHS are overseen by The Public Health Trust of Miami-Dade County.

Operations

Jackson Memorial Hospital's Ryder Trauma Center is Miami-Dade County's only adult and pediatric Level 2 trauma center. Holtz Children's Hospital is one of the largest children's hospitals in the state and one of three in the US that specializes in pediatric multi-organ transplants.

Company Background

The Public Health Trust was created in 1973 by the Board of County Commissioners as an independent governing body to provide leadership for joint planning between Jackson Health System, the University of Miami Miller School of Medicine, Miami-Dade County, and other private and community organizations. Today, the Public Health Trust is considered the hospital system's governing board, picking its CEO and overseeing the system's operations.

EXECUTIVES

Chief Financial Innovation*, Mark Knight
Chief Human Resources Officer*, Julie Staub

LOCATIONS

HQ: THE PUBLIC HEALTH TRUST OF MIAMI-DADE COUNTY
1611 NW 12TH AVE, MIAMI, FL 331361005
Phone: 305 585-1111
Web: WWW.JACKSONHEALTH.ORG

COMPETITORS

ASCENSION PROVIDENCE ROCHESTER HOSPITAL
ATLANTIC HEALTH SYSTEM INC.
HOSPITAL SERVICE DISTRICT 1
KENNEDY HEALTH SYSTEM, INC.
LOMA LINDA UNIVERSITY MEDICAL CENTER
PHELPS MEMORIAL HOSPITAL ASSOCIATION
SHELBY COUNTY HEALTH CARE CORPORATION
ST LUKE'S HOSPITAL
THE DCH HEALTH CARE AUTHORITY
THE UNIVERSITY OF CHICAGO MEDICAL CENTER

HISTORICAL FINANCIALS
Company Type: Private

Income Statement — FYE: September 30

	REVENUE ($mil)	NET INCOME ($mil)	NET PROFIT MARGIN	EMPLOYEES
09/18	1,166	206	17.7%	12,990
09/17	1,160	184	15.9%	—
09/15*	883	200	22.7%	—
06/05	0	0	—	—
Annual Growth	—	—	—	—

*Fiscal year change

2018 Year-End Financials
Return on assets: 8.8% Cash ($ mil.): 308
Return on equity: 33.2%
Current Ratio: 1.30

THE QUEEN'S HEALTH SYSTEMS

EXECUTIVES

CIO, Harold Moscho
Auditors: KPMG LLP HONOLULU HI

LOCATIONS

HQ: THE QUEEN'S HEALTH SYSTEMS
1301 PUNCHBOWL ST, HONOLULU, HI 968132402
Phone: 808 691-5900
Web: WWW.QUEENS.ORG

HISTORICAL FINANCIALS
Company Type: Private

Income Statement — FYE: June 30

	REVENUE ($mil)	NET INCOME ($mil)	NET PROFIT MARGIN	EMPLOYEES
06/17	1,279	173	13.6%	8,000
06/15	118	7	6.0%	—
06/11	24	3	14.2%	—
06/10	25	5	22.4%	—
Annual Growth	75.2%	63.1%	—	—

2017 Year-End Financials
Return on assets: 6.9% Cash ($ mil.): 80
Return on equity: 11.3%
Current Ratio: 4.90

THE REGENTS OF THE UNIVERSITY OF COLORADO

The University of Colorado System spans four campuses and some 60,000 students. The Boulder campus, home to about 30,000 students, provides more than 2,500 courses in 150-plus fields through nine colleges and schools. The University of Colorado at Denver has an enrollment of more than 14,000 and has 120 study programs at a dozen schools, and its nearby Anschutz Medical Campus serves more than 500,000 patients annually. The smallest campus, University of Colorado at Colorado Springs, has six colleges with about 10,000 students and offers nearly 60 undergraduate, graduate, and doctoral degree programs. The system, which began in Boulder as the University of Colorado in 1876, boasts more than 4,000 faculty members.

Operations

In addition to its primary campuses in the cities of Boulder, Denver, and Colorado Springs, The University of Colorado System operates the Anschutz Medical Campus, which has an enrollment of about 3,500 students.

The university system has an annual budget of more than $2.9 billion. It receives a number contracts and grants through its extensive research programs, which also serve as teaching and training programs for its students. Areas of research include science, technology, and health care.

The University of Colorado System boasts a number of noteworthy faculty members, including Nobel Laureates John Hall, Eric Cornell, Carl Wieman, and Thomas Cech, all of which earned honors in either physics or chemistry.

Geographic Reach

The University of Colorado System serves some 60,000 students across several University of Colorado campuses in Boulder, Denver, and Colorado Springs. It's known for its leadership in higher education and research in the Rocky Mountain region.

Financial Performance

The University of Colorado System has enjoyed rising revenue in recent years due to organic growth.

Auditors : BKD LLP DENVER COLORADO

LOCATIONS

HQ: THE REGENTS OF THE UNIVERSITY OF COLORADO

3100 MAR ST STE 481 572 U, BOULDER, CO 803090001

Phone: 303 735-6624

Web: WWW.UCDENVER.EDU

PRODUCTS/OPERATIONS

Selected Campuses

University of Colorado - Boulder
University of Colorado - Colorado Springs
University of Colorado - Denver
University of Colorado Anschutz Medical Campus

COMPETITORS

HAMPTON UNIVERSITY
IDAHO STATE UNIVERSITY
NEW MEXICO STATE UNIVERSITY
NORTH CAROLINA STATE UNIVERSITY
NORTHERN ILLINOIS UNIVERSITY
SOUTH CAROLINA STATE UNIVERSITY
THE UNIVENSITY OF IOWA
UNIVERSITY OF ILLINOIS
UNIVERSITY OF VERMONT & STATE AGRICULTURAL COLLEGE
WILLAMETTE UNIVERSITY

HISTORICAL FINANCIALS

Company Type: Private

Income Statement — FYE: June 30

	REVENUE ($mil)	NET INCOME ($mil)	NET PROFIT MARGIN	EMPLOYEES
06/21	4,139	1,169	28.3%	12,980
06/20	4,239	584	13.8%	—
06/18	3,833	(197)	—	—
06/17	3,728	77	2.1%	—
Annual Growth	2.6%	97.3%	—	—

2021 Year-End Financials

Return on assets: 12.7% Cash ($ mil.): 351
Return on equity: 30.5%
Current Ratio: 5.60

THE RESEARCH FOUNDATION FOR THE STATE UNIVERSITY OF NEW YORK

The Research Foundation of State University of New York (The Research Foundation) collects and administers research and education grants from state and federal governments, corporations, and foundations on behalf of the 24-campus State University of New York, known as SUNY. The foundation has formed several affiliated divisions -- including Long Island High Technology Incubator and NanoTech Resources -- to operate research facilities, encourage scientific collaboration, and otherwise facilitate research for the university. It facilitates research for studies such as engineering and nanotechnology; physical sciences and medicine; life sciences and medicine; social sciences; and computer and information sciences.

Operations

The foundation manages SUNY's research portfolio. Research Foundation administrators help SUNY faculty, students and staff through every step of the research grant process, allowing them to focus on their work and ensuring compliance with university, grant sponsor and government requirements.

The Research Foundation protects SUNY's intellectual property (SUNY ranks among the nation's top faculty to commercialize their inventions for the public good).

The organization makes strategic investments to maximize the collective impact of SUNY research to drive investment and job growth. SUNY's Networks of Excellence assemble scientists and scholars from all campuses to collaborate on research projects in areas ranging from advanced manufacturing and energy to health and the humanities.

The Research Foundation is an integral partner in the execution and administration of the START-UP NY initiative to transform SUNY campuses and university communities across the state into tax-free communities for new and expanding businesses.

The organization funds its operations primarily from recoveries of indirect costs provided from grants and contracts.

Geographic Reach

The Research Foundation comprises a central office and operating units at 31 campus locations across New York State.

Financial Performance

The Research Foundation reported $1 billion in revenues in 2014 compared to $1.07 billion in 2013. The primary reason for the decline was due to decreased sales from federal grants and contracts, private grants and contracts, and investment income.

Investment income/loss included dividends and interest, realized and unrealized gains and losses, and equity adjustments from the foundation's investment in the Brookhaven Science Associates partnership.

The organization's net income decreased by $30 million in 2014 due to lower revenues and increased other program expenses.

Net cash provided by the operating activities increased by $127.7 million due to changes in interest payments on capital debts and other payments.

Strategy

In 2014, Iliad Neurosciences, a company focused on the development of innovative approaches to diagnosing and treating Autism Spectrum Disorders entered into an Exclusive License Agreement with The Research Foundation for The State University of New York. Under this deal, Iliad will provide a new biomarker to identify an abnormality in folate transport to the brain associated with susceptibility to Autism Spectrum Disorders. . The identification of this defect could lead to a targeted therapy that may improve the transport of folate to the brain in children and to the fetus in pregnant women who test positive for the folate receptor autoantibody.

Company Background

The Research Foundation was established in 1951, just three years after SUNY itself.

Auditors : KPMG LLP ALBANY NY

LOCATIONS

HQ: THE RESEARCH FOUNDATION FOR THE STATE UNIVERSITY OF NEW YORK

35 STATE ST, ALBANY, NY 122072826

Phone: 518 434-7000

Web: WWW.RFSUNY.ORG

PRODUCTS/OPERATIONS

2014 Revenues

	% of total
Federal grants & contracts	50
Private grants & contracts	23
State grants & contracts	17
Investments	2
Inventions & licenses	2
Local grants & contracts	2
Investment income	0
Gifts, capital gifts & grants	0
Other	4
Total	100

COMPETITORS

HEALTH RESEARCH, INC.
HOWARD HUGHES MEDICAL INSTITUTE
THE JACKSON LABORATORY
THE ROCKEFELLER UNIVERSITY
WHITEHEAD INSTITUTE FOR BIOMEDICAL RESEARCH

HISTORICAL FINANCIALS

Company Type: Private

Income Statement — FYE: June 30

	REVENUE ($mil)	NET INCOME ($mil)	NET PROFIT MARGIN	EMPLOYEES
06/21	1,300	52	4.0%	15,000
06/20	1,572	422	26.8%	—
06/13	1,079	42	3.9%	—
06/12	1,114	12	1.2%	—
Annual Growth	1.7%	16.7%	—	—

2021 Year-End Financials

Return on assets: 3.6% Cash ($ mil.): 159
Return on equity: 7.9%
Current Ratio: 0.80

THE RUDOLPH/LIBBE COMPANIES INC

The corporate model of a conglomerate composed of independent, unrelated businesses is not for The Rudolph/Libbe Companies. The group of companies can build or oversee real estate projects (general contractor Rudolph/Libbe Inc.); perform mechanical, electrical, and structural work (GEM Industrial); and then represent those properties in the market (RLWest Properties). Operating in the Ohio/Michigan corridor, the group provides site selection, design/build, and construction management. Its portfolio includes industrial, retail, municipal, residential, educational, health care, and mixed-use projects. Fritz and Phil Rudolph and their cousin Allan Libbe founded flagship subsidiary Rudolph/Libbe Inc. in 1955.

Auditors : REHMANN ROBSON TOLEDO OH

LOCATIONS

HQ: THE RUDOLPH/LIBBE COMPANIES INC
6494 LATCHA RD, WALBRIDGE, OH 434659788
Phone: 419 241-5000

COMPETITORS

BARTON MALOW COMPANY
CIANBRO CORPORATION
CLAYCO, INC.
GILBANE, INC.
GRAY CONSTRUCTION, INC.
GRAYCOR, INC.
H AND M CONSTRUCTION CO., INC.
KELTBRAY GROUP (HOLDINGS) LIMITED
LECHASE CONSTRUCTION SERVICES, LLC
Stuart Olson Inc

HISTORICAL FINANCIALS
Company Type: Private

Income Statement — FYE: December 31

	REVENUE ($mil)	NET INCOME ($mil)	NET PROFIT MARGIN	EMPLOYEES
12/18	573	16	2.8%	600
12/17	567	20	3.5%	—
12/16	502	23	4.8%	—
12/15	425	16	3.8%	—
Annual Growth	10.5%	(0.2%)	—	—

2018 Year-End Financials
Return on assets: 7.4%   Cash ($ mil.): 16
Return on equity: 25.9%
Current Ratio: 1.30

THE SAINT CLOUD HOSPITAL

Auditors : MCGLADREY LLP MINNEAPOLIS MN

LOCATIONS

HQ: THE SAINT CLOUD HOSPITAL
1406 6TH AVE N, SAINT CLOUD, MN 563031900
Phone: 320 251-2700
Web: WWW.CENTRACARE.COM

HISTORICAL FINANCIALS
Company Type: Private

Income Statement — FYE: June 30

	REVENUE ($mil)	NET INCOME ($mil)	NET PROFIT MARGIN	EMPLOYEES
06/21	1,117	151	13.5%	4,957
06/20	931	55	5.9%	—
06/18	864	39	4.5%	—
06/16	756	3	0.5%	—
Annual Growth	8.1%	113.0%	—	—

2021 Year-End Financials
Return on assets: 8.9%   Cash ($ mil.): 94
Return on equity: 15.1%
Current Ratio: 2.40

THE SALVATION ARMY

LOCATIONS

HQ: THE SALVATION ARMY
100 CENTER PL, NORCROSS, GA 30093
Phone: 770 441-6200
Web: SOUTHERNUSA.SALVATIONARMY.ORG

HISTORICAL FINANCIALS
Company Type: Private

Income Statement — FYE: September 30

	REVENUE ($mil)	NET INCOME ($mil)	NET PROFIT MARGIN	EMPLOYEES
09/09	830	(220)	—	16,168
09/08	533	(336)	—	—
09/07	1,185	318	26.9%	—
Annual Growth	(16.3%)	—	—	—

2009 Year-End Financials
Return on assets: (-6.7%)   Cash ($ mil.): 89
Return on equity: (-8.6%)
Current Ratio: 1.30

THE SALVATION ARMY

EXECUTIVES

1st Assistant Treasurer*, D Sue Foley
Legal*, Richard D Allen
PROPERTY*, Jorge E Diaz
PROPERTY, Adolph M Orlando Second
Auditors : GRANT THORNTON LLP NEW YORK

LOCATIONS

HQ: THE SALVATION ARMY
440 W NYACK RD OFC, WEST NYACK, NY 109941739
Phone: 845 620-7200
Web: WWW.SACONNECTS.ORG

HISTORICAL FINANCIALS
Company Type: Private

Income Statement — FYE: September 30

	REVENUE ($mil)	NET INCOME ($mil)	NET PROFIT MARGIN	EMPLOYEES
09/16	859	(224)	—	10,447
09/12	1,034	207	20.0%	—
09/09	782	(96)	—	—
09/08	288	(463)	—	—
Annual Growth	14.6%	—	—	—

2016 Year-End Financials
Return on assets: (-5.4%)   Cash ($ mil.): 122
Return on equity: (-9.7%)
Current Ratio: 0.30

THE SAVANNAH COLLEGE OF ART AND DESIGN INC

With more than 12,000 students, Savannah College of Art and Design (SCAD) in Georgia is a private, nonprofit, accredited university with students from across the US and more than 100 countries. It has undergraduate degrees in arts and fine arts as well as master's degrees in a range of subjects. The institution offers courses of study in 40-plus majors including fields such as architecture, interior and graphic design, fashion, film and television, painting, dance, and art history. The school also offers certificates in digital publishing, digital publishing management, historic preservation, interactive design, and typeface design and more than 60 other minors.

Operations
Annual tuition runs at about $30,000. The institution employs about 700 full- and part-time faculty members.

The school's most popular majors include animation, fashion graphic design, illustration, and photography. In addition to regular coursework, SCAD provides online distance education courses.

Geographic Reach
SCAD has campuses in Atlanta and Savannah, Georgia, as well as in Hong Kong and Lacoste, France. Students at the college hail from all 50 US states and more than 100 international countries.

Company Background
The school was founded in 1978 and has taken an active role in restoring architectural landmarks in Savannah.

Auditors : MAULDIN & JENKINS LLC ATLANTA

LOCATIONS

HQ: THE SAVANNAH COLLEGE OF ART AND DESIGN INC
126 E GASTON ST, SAVANNAH, GA 314015604

Phone: 912 525-5000
Web: WWW.SCAD.EDU

COMPETITORS

ART CENTER COLLEGE OF DESIGN
HOLLINS UNIVERSITY CORPORATION
PHILADELPHIA UNIVERSITY
RHODE ISLAND SCHOOL OF DESIGN
THE UNIVERSITY OF HARTFORD

HISTORICAL FINANCIALS
Company Type: Private

Income Statement — FYE: June 30

	REVENUE ($mil)	NET INCOME ($mil)	NET PROFIT MARGIN	EMPLOYEES
06/20	587	152	25.9%	1,200
06/10	314	10	3.2%	—
06/09	283	21	7.7%	—
Annual Growth	6.9%	19.3%	—	—

2020 Year-End Financials
Return on assets: 11.7%   Cash ($ mil.): 158
Return on equity: 14.7%
Current Ratio: 0.70

THE SCHOOL BOARD OF MIAMI-DADE COUNTY

Auditors: RSM US LLP MIAMI FLORIDA

LOCATIONS

HQ: THE SCHOOL BOARD OF MIAMI-DADE COUNTY
1450 NE 2ND AVE, MIAMI, FL 331321308
Phone: 305 995-1000

HISTORICAL FINANCIALS
Company Type: Private

Income Statement — FYE: June 30

	REVENUE ($mil)	NET INCOME ($mil)	NET PROFIT MARGIN	EMPLOYEES
06/21	4,458	141	3.2%	9
06/20	4,120	(41)	—	—
06/19	3,948	(14)	—	—
06/18	3,868	(46)	—	—
Annual Growth	4.8%	—	—	—

2021 Year-End Financials
Return on assets: 2.1%   Cash ($ mil.): 585
Return on equity: —
Current Ratio: 2.10

THE SCHOOL DISTRICT OF OSCEOLA COUNTY FLORIDA

Auditors: SHERRILL F NORMAN CPA TALLA

LOCATIONS

HQ: THE SCHOOL DISTRICT OF OSCEOLA COUNTY FLORIDA
817 BILL BECK BLVD, KISSIMMEE, FL 347444492
Phone: 407 870-4600
Web: WWW.OSCEOLASCHOOLS.NET

HISTORICAL FINANCIALS
Company Type: Private

Income Statement — FYE: June 30

	REVENUE ($mil)	NET INCOME ($mil)	NET PROFIT MARGIN	EMPLOYEES
06/21	853	164	19.3%	6,250
06/19	787	25	3.2%	—
06/18	695	13	2.0%	—
06/17	638	117	18.4%	—
Annual Growth	7.5%	8.9%	—	—

2021 Year-End Financials
Return on assets: 9.1%   Cash ($ mil.): 232
Return on equity: 18.5%
Current Ratio: —

THE SCHOOL DISTRICT OF PHILADELPHIA

Auditors: CHRISTY BRADY CPA PHILADELPH

LOCATIONS

HQ: THE SCHOOL DISTRICT OF PHILADELPHIA
440 N BROAD ST, PHILADELPHIA, PA 191304090
Phone: 215 400-4000
Web: WWW.PHILASD.ORG

HISTORICAL FINANCIALS
Company Type: Private

Income Statement — FYE: June 30

	REVENUE ($mil)	NET INCOME ($mil)	NET PROFIT MARGIN	EMPLOYEES
06/18	3,473	210	6.1%	21,065
06/17	3,250	220	6.8%	—
06/16	3,064	23	0.8%	—
06/11	2,930	(259)	—	—
Annual Growth	2.5%	—	—	—

2018 Year-End Financials
Return on assets: 5.7%   Cash ($ mil.): 190
Return on equity: —
Current Ratio: —

THE SCHOOL DISTRICT OF WEST PALM BEACH COUNTY

Auditors: RSM US LLP WEST PALM BEACH F

LOCATIONS

HQ: THE SCHOOL DISTRICT OF WEST PALM BEACH COUNTY
3300 FREST HL BLVD STE A3, WEST PALM BEACH, FL 33406
Phone: 561 434-8747
Web: WWW.BELIEVERSACADEMYINC.ORG

HISTORICAL FINANCIALS
Company Type: Private

Income Statement — FYE: June 30

	REVENUE ($mil)	NET INCOME ($mil)	NET PROFIT MARGIN	EMPLOYEES
06/21	2,752	298	10.8%	10,156
06/18	2,307	136	5.9%	—
06/17	2,146	78	3.7%	—
06/16	1,986	64	3.2%	—
Annual Growth	6.7%	36.0%	—	—

2021 Year-End Financials
Return on assets: 5.5%   Cash ($ mil.): —
Return on equity: 16.9%
Current Ratio: —

THE SCOULAR COMPANY

The Scoular Company buys, sells, stores, handles, processes and transports agricultural products (mainly grains) worldwide. It gets the mainstays of farming ? corn, millet, rye, peas and lentils, soybeans, and wheat ? where they need to go. The company transports these products via rail, truck and barge shipping partners. Scoular's other divisions offer fishmeal products for farm-animal, pet, and aquaculture feeds; ingredients for food manufacturers; and renewable fuels, as well as a host of risk management, logistics and product-related services. Scoular has more than 100 locations locally and internationally.

Operations

Scoular facilitates solutions for its customers at every step in the agricultural supply chain. It provides solutions for grains, food ingredients, animal feed ingredients, pet food ingredients, international trades and transportation.

The company has the network, confidence and creativity to make connections between farmers, processors, manufacturers, facilities, shippers and carriers worldwide. When it comes to animal feed, the company delivers flexible and valuable nutrition solutions whether it is for a dairy, feedmill or another animal feed manufacturer. Scoular's indirect, wholly owned and independently operated subsidiary, Petsource, provides comprehensive freeze-dried pet food manufacturing capabilities for ultimate quality control.

Scoular's grain products include barley, flaxseed, soybean, and sunflower seeds, among others. Other products include fats and oils, fibers, flours, sweeteners and more.

Geographic Reach

In addition to the company's headquarters in Omaha, Nebraska, and corporate offices in Overland Park, Kansas and Minneapolis, Minnesota, Scoular has more than 100 locations around the world.

Sales and Marketing

Scoular serves farmers, grain processors, animal feed manufacturers, aquafeed manufacturers, pet food manufacturers, food, beverage and supplement manufacturers, distilleries and renewable energy producers.

Strategy

Scoular, in mid-2021, created a new division to lead its businesses in the early stages of development and to serve as an incubator for strategic investment opportunities. Scoular Senior Vice President Ed Prosser will lead the new division, called "Emerging Businesses". The Emerging Businesses Division will include business activities focusing on biofuels, renewable energy, carbon markets, investments in agricultural technology, such as Roger LLC, and other future growth ventures.

Company Background

George Scoular founded the George Scoular Grain & Lumber Company in Nebraska in 1892. It was family-owned until 1967 when it was sold to a group of grain industry executives. It grew through acquisitions and partnerships over the following decades.

EXECUTIVES

CIO, Jeff Schreiner
Chief Human Resource Officer, Kurt Peterson
Auditors : KPMG LLP OMAHA NEBRASKA

LOCATIONS

HQ: THE SCOULAR COMPANY
13660 CALIFORNIA ST, OMAHA, NE 681545233
Phone: 402 342-3500
Web: WWW.SCOULAR.COM

COMPETITORS

BUNGE NORTH AMERICA, INC.
CARGILL, INCORPORATED
CHS INC.
Cofco Corporation
DEBRUCE GRAIN, INC.
E D & F MAN HOLDINGS LIMITED
LAND O'LAKES, INC.
LANSING TRADE GROUP, LLC
RICELAND FOODS, INC.
THE GAVILON GROUP LLC

HISTORICAL FINANCIALS
Company Type: Private

Income Statement   FYE: May 31

	REVENUE ($mil)	NET INCOME ($mil)	NET PROFIT MARGIN	EMPLOYEES
05/21	6,004	53	0.9%	730
05/20	4,612	32	0.7%	—
05/19	4,226	23	0.6%	—
Annual Growth	19.2%	51.3%	—	—

2021 Year-End Financials
Return on assets: 3.6%   Cash ($ mil.): —
Return on equity: 14.0%
Current Ratio: 1.20

THE SIMONS FOUNDATION INC

LOCATIONS

HQ: THE SIMONS FOUNDATION INC
160 5TH AVE FL 7, NEW YORK, NY 100107037
Phone: 646 654-0066
Web: WWW.SIMONSFOUNDATION.ORG

HISTORICAL FINANCIALS
Company Type: Private

Income Statement   FYE: December 31

	ASSETS ($mil)	NET INCOME ($mil)	INCOME AS % OF ASSETS	EMPLOYEES
12/21	5,183	744	14.4%	475
12/20	4,324	134	3.1%	—
12/19	4,000	302	7.6%	—
12/18	3,651	283	7.8%	—
Annual Growth	12.4%	37.9%	—	—

2021 Year-End Financials
Return on assets: 14.4%   Cash ($ mil.): 297
Return on equity: 17.4%
Current Ratio: —

THE SOUTHEASTERN CONFERENCE

Auditors : BARFIELD MURPHY SHANK & SMITH

LOCATIONS

HQ: THE SOUTHEASTERN CONFERENCE
2201 RICHARD ARRINGTN JR, BIRMINGHAM, AL 352031103
Phone: 205 949-8960
Web: WWW.SECSPORTS.COM

HISTORICAL FINANCIALS
Company Type: Private

Income Statement   FYE: August 31

	REVENUE ($mil)	NET INCOME ($mil)	NET PROFIT MARGIN	EMPLOYEES
08/21	833	0	0.1%	30
08/20	728	32	4.4%	—
08/19	720	23	3.3%	—
08/16	639	17	2.7%	—
Annual Growth	5.5%	(47.1%)	—	—

2021 Year-End Financials
Return on assets: 0.1%   Cash ($ mil.): 403
Return on equity: 0.5%
Current Ratio: —

THE ST LUKE'S-ROOSEVELT HOSPITAL CENTER

Auditors : ERNST & YOUNG US LLP INDIANAP

LOCATIONS

HQ: THE ST LUKE'S-ROOSEVELT HOSPITAL CENTER
1111 AMSTERDAM AVE, NEW YORK, NY 100251716
Phone: 212 523-4000
Web: WWW.MOUNTSINAI.ORG

HISTORICAL FINANCIALS
Company Type: Private

Income Statement   FYE: December 31

	REVENUE ($mil)	NET INCOME ($mil)	NET PROFIT MARGIN	EMPLOYEES
12/19	1,348	(22)	—	6,000
12/16	901	53	5.9%	—
12/15	859	61	7.1%	—
12/14	1,160	(17)	—	—
Annual Growth	3.0%	—	—	—

2019 Year-End Financials
Return on assets: (-1.6%)   Cash ($ mil.): 167
Return on equity: (-32.5%)
Current Ratio: 1.80

THE STAMFORD HOSPITAL

EXECUTIVES

CMO, Sharon Kiely
Auditors : ERNST & YOUNG LLP HARTFORD

LOCATIONS

HQ: THE STAMFORD HOSPITAL
1 HOSPITAL PLZ, STAMFORD, CT 069023602
Phone: 203 325-7000
Web: WWW.STAMFORDHEALTH.ORG

HISTORICAL FINANCIALS
Company Type: Private

Income Statement — FYE: September 30

	REVENUE ($mil)	NET INCOME ($mil)	NET PROFIT MARGIN	EMPLOYEES
09/21	819	90	11.0%	2,000
09/20	655	11	1.7%	—
09/19	608	(44)	—	—
09/18	574	3	0.7%	—
Annual Growth	12.6%	184.4%	—	—

2021 Year-End Financials
Return on assets: 6.4%   Cash ($ mil.): 207
Return on equity: 15.1%
Current Ratio: 1.60

THE SUNDERLAND FOUNDATION

LOCATIONS

HQ: THE SUNDERLAND FOUNDATION
5700 W 112TH ST STE 320, LEAWOOD, KS 662111759
Phone: 913 319-6194
Web: WWW.SUNDERLAND.ORG

HISTORICAL FINANCIALS
Company Type: Private

Income Statement — FYE: December 31

	REVENUE ($mil)	NET INCOME ($mil)	NET PROFIT MARGIN	EMPLOYEES
12/18	1,552	1,429	92.1%	7
12/10	6	2	35.2%	—
12/09	2	(2)	—	—
Annual Growth	105.9%	—	—	—

2018 Year-End Financials
Return on assets: 95.8%   Cash ($ mil.): 542
Return on equity: 95.8%
Current Ratio: —

THE SUNDT COMPANIES INC

Sundt has put its stamp on the Southwest. Through Sundt Construction and other subsidiaries, The Sundt Companies offers preconstruction, construction management, general contracting, and design/build services for commercial, government, and industrial clients. Projects include commercial buildings, military bases, light rails, airports, and schools. It builds mostly in Arizona, Nevada, California, New Mexico, and Texas. Sundt has overseen some notable projects including the development of the top-secret town of Los Alamos, New Mexico (where the first atomic bomb was built) and the relocation of the London Bridge to Arizona. Sundt Companies was formed in 1998 as a holding company for various company interests.

Operations
The Sundt Companies performs its work through various divisions: Industrial; concrete; building; heavy civil; and federal. The building division is divided into geographic regions: California; Southwest; and Texas; as well as a Federal Division.

Strategy
Like its peers, Sundt is dealing with the lingering effects of the construction downturn that greatly impacted the Southwest. (The company lost more than $750 million in government projects due to state budget constraints.) Indeed, Sundt anticipates that it may be 2015 before it sees a strong economy for construction. In the meantime, the firm has relied on a healthy backlog of projects and diversification efforts to sustain its business. To that end, it entered new geographic markets in 2012, including New Mexico, where it is building new dorms at New Mexico State University. It also recently began construction of new schools in El Paso, Texas, its first in the city. The firm formed a new Criminal Justice Specialization group in 2012 to win courthouse and detention facility work.

Sundt also has focused on making investments in improving technology used in the preconstruction and construction process. It also grew its self-perform work capabilities when it acquired Foley Masonry and Tile Inc. in 2010. Also that year Sundt opened a new office in San Antonio as part of the company's growth plan. The company expanded once again in 2011. It opened new offices to support projects in New Mexico, North Carolina, and Texas.

Auditors : MAYER HOFFMAN & MCCANN

LOCATIONS

HQ: THE SUNDT COMPANIES INC
2015 W RIVER RD STE 101, TUCSON, AZ 857041687
Phone: 520 750-4600
Web: WWW.SUNDT.COM

PRODUCTS/OPERATIONS

Selected Projects
Aviation
Commercial buildings
Concrete construction
Courthouses
Federal government
Hospitality
Hospitals & health care
Infrastructure & site development
Juvenile detention facilities
K-12 schools
Mining
Mission critical/Data center
Municipal buildings
Parking structures
Power plants & alternative energy
Prisons
Research & development facilities
Residential
Retail
Roads & bridges
Student housing & dormitories
Universities & community colleges
Water & wastewater treatment

Selected Services
Build-to-suit
Construction manager at risk (CMAR)
Construction/program manager
Design-bid-build/general contractor (DBB)
Preconstruction
Self-perform contracting

COMPETITORS
H. J. RUSSELL & COMPANY
MIRON CONSTRUCTION CO., INC.
SWINERTON INCORPORATED
THE TURNER CORPORATION
TURNER CONSTRUCTION COMPANY

HISTORICAL FINANCIALS
Company Type: Private

Income Statement — FYE: September 30

	REVENUE ($mil)	NET INCOME ($mil)	NET PROFIT MARGIN	EMPLOYEES
09/18	1,432	0	0.0%	1,800
09/17	1,134	0	0.0%	—
09/16*	813	0	0.0%	—
06/16	0	0	—	—
Annual Growth	—	—	—	—

*Fiscal year change

2018 Year-End Financials
Return on assets: —   Cash ($ mil.): 82
Return on equity: —
Current Ratio: 1.30

THE TOWN OF SMITHTOWN

Auditors : BONADIO & CO LLP NEW YORK

LOCATIONS

HQ: THE TOWN OF SMITHTOWN
99 W MAIN ST, SMITHTOWN, NY 117872603
Phone: 631 360-7600
Web: WWW.SMITHTOWNNY.GOV

HISTORICAL FINANCIALS
Company Type: Private

Income Statement — FYE: December 31

	REVENUE ($mil)	NET INCOME ($mil)	NET PROFIT MARGIN	EMPLOYEES
12/21	639	3	0.6%	400
12/20	115	(5)	—	—
12/19	112	4	3.7%	—
12/18	105	(4)	—	—
Annual Growth	82.1%	—	—	—

2021 Year-End Financials
Return on assets: 0.4%   Cash ($ mil.): 146
Return on equity: 0.9%
Current Ratio: —

THE TRUSTEES OF COLUMBIA UNIVERSITY IN THE CITY OF NEW YORK

EXECUTIVES

Interim Priest*, John H Coatsworth
Auditors: PRICEWATERHOUSECOOPERS LLP NE

LOCATIONS

HQ: THE TRUSTEES OF COLUMBIA UNIVERSITY IN THE CITY OF NEW YORK
202 LOW LIB 535 W 116 ST, NEW YORK, NY 10027
Phone: 212 854-9970
Web: WWW.COLUMBIA.EDU

HISTORICAL FINANCIALS

Company Type: Private

Income Statement — FYE: June 30

	REVENUE ($mil)	NET INCOME ($mil)	NET PROFIT MARGIN	EMPLOYEES
06/22	5,827	(1,192)	—	13,200
06/21	5,195	3,332	64.1%	—
06/20	5,201	271	5.2%	—
06/13	3,738	1,048	28.0%	—
Annual Growth	5.1%	—	—	—

2022 Year-End Financials
Return on assets: (-5.1%)
Return on equity: (-6.5%)
Cash ($ mil.): 714
Current Ratio: —

THE TRUSTEES OF PRINCETON UNIVERSITY

Princeton University is a vibrant community of scholarship and learning that stands in the nation's service and the service of humanity. As one of the eight elite Ivy League schools in the Northeastern US, Princeton is a research university that offers students degrees across around 35 departments and about 55 interdisciplinary certificate programs. It boasts around 8,360 students (around 5,295 undergraduate and some 3,065 graduate students). The highly selective school, which enjoys an undergraduate student-faculty ratio of 5:1. Nobel Prize winners associated with Princeton include Woodrow Wilson, writer Toni Morrison, and physicist Richard Feynman. One of the nation's wealthiest universities, Princeton has an endowment of more than $37 billion.

Operations

The Princeton campus comprises seven residential colleges that are organized by grade level (freshmen, sophomores, juniors, and seniors).

The university, which is supported by some 1,295 faculty members that include visitors and part-time appointments, encourages students to explore many disciplines and to develop a deep understanding in one area of concentration. Students apply to Princeton University, not to individual departments, programs or schools. Once enrolled, students may pursue either the Bachelor of Arts (AB) or the Bachelor of Science in Engineering (BSE). Within these degree programs, students can choose from among over 35 concentrations (computer science offers both AB and BSE) and over 50 interdepartmental certificate programs. The AB includes concentrations in Public Policy (Princeton School of Public and International Affairs) and the School of Architecture. Princeton also has a large research base, with some $400 million in funding per year, primarily from federal grants.

Geographic Reach

Located in Princeton, New Jersey, Princeton's campus includes over 200 campus buildings that cover about 600 acres.

Company Background

Founded in 1746 as the College of New Jersey, Princeton is the fourth-oldest college in the nation. In 1756 the college was moved to Nassau Hall, which served as the temporary capitol of the US in 1783 and is still part of the Princeton campus.

Auditors: PRICEWATERHOUSECOOPERS LLP N

LOCATIONS

HQ: THE TRUSTEES OF PRINCETON UNIVERSITY
1 NASSAU HALL, PRINCETON, NJ 085442001
Phone: 609 258-3000
Web: WWW.PRINCETON.EDU

PRODUCTS/OPERATIONS

Select Councils, Institutes and Centers
Bendheim Center for Finance
Center for Migration and Development
Center for the Study of Religion
Council of the Humanities
Council on Science and Technology
Davis Center for Historical Studies
James Madison Program in American Ideals and Institutions
Lewis-Sigler Institute for Integrative Genomics
Liechtenstein Institute on Self-Determination
Princeton Environmental Institute (PEI)
Princeton Institute for International and Regional Studies (PIIRS)
Princeton Institute for the Science and Technology of Materials (PRISM)
Princeton Writing Program
Program of Freshman Seminars in the Residential Colleges
Program in Law and Public Affairs
Program in Neuroscience
University Center for Human Values

COMPETITORS

DREW UNIVERSITY
LAFAYETTE COLLEGE
PRESIDENT AND FELLOWS OF HARVARD COLLEGE
THE COLLEGE OF WILLIAM & MARY
THE UNIVERSITY OF CHICAGO
THE WASHINGTON AND LEE UNIVERSITY
TRUSTEES OF BOSTON COLLEGE
UNIVERSITY OF CINCINNATI
UNIVERSITY OF DELAWARE
UNIVERSITY OF GEORGIA

HISTORICAL FINANCIALS

Company Type: Private

Income Statement — FYE: June 30

	REVENUE ($mil)	NET INCOME ($mil)	NET PROFIT MARGIN	EMPLOYEES
06/22	2,357	(1,275)	—	6,000
06/21	2,162	10,983	507.9%	—
06/20	2,173	383	17.7%	—
06/19	2,146	677	31.6%	—
Annual Growth	3.2%	—	—	—

2022 Year-End Financials
Return on assets: (-2.9%)
Return on equity: (-3.3%)
Cash ($ mil.): 27
Current Ratio: —

THE TURNER CORPORATION

The Turner Corporation, a subsidiary of German construction giant HOCHTIEF, is the leading general building and construction management firm in the US (as ranked by Engineering News-Record), ahead of rivals Bechtel and Fluor. The firm operates primarily through subsidiary Turner Construction, and has worked on notable projects such as Madison Square Garden, the UN headquarters, Yankee Stadium, the Taipei 101 Tower, and the 68,000-seat open-air stadium for the San Francisco 49ers. Known for its large projects, also offers services for midsized and smaller projects and provides interior construction and renovation services.

Operations

Turner works on more than 1,500 projects in a year totaling $8 billion in volume. The group has divisions dedicated to serving the aviation, health care, biotechnology, public assembly, sports, education, justice, and industrial sectors. Its homeland security group was established in order handle a growing demand for security systems and protection. The unit installed detection equipment in some 450 airports throughout the US. Turner Corporation also has an arm specializing in green building, with a focus on Leadership in Energy and Environmental Design (LEED) -certified projects. Turner Green Building has more than 400 LEED projects and green projects either completed or in progress.

Turner Corporation has subsidiaries providing auxiliary operations. Turner's risk management department offers contract review, project safety, and claims handling.

Turner Logistics handles procurement and supply chain management for projects, and Turner Facilities Management Solutions offers ongoing operations services. Also, the Turner School of Construction Management provides training for local subcontractors.

Geographic Reach

Dallas-based Turner Corporation boasts a network of offices across the US (with most in California and Ohio) and Canada (Vancouver and Toronto), with an global presence in 20 countries in Europe, Africa, East Asia, India, Latin America, and the Caribbean.

Sales and Marketing

Turner works on variety of projects from several sectors. It's known for its work in the categories of healthcare, education, offices, commercial properties, cultural facilities, sports facilities, and hotels. The company is also a leader in the green building category.

Strategy

With the construction market rebounding from the economic downturn, Turner is looking to high-growth markets in the US and overseas. As of early 2015, it was working on more than 1,900 projects, 80% of which were Education, Commercial, or Interior project-related. Some of these projects included the 17,000 sq. ft- interior remodel for Salesforce's Vancouver office; the 325,000 sq. ft- construction of the LEED-Certified RAND Corporation Headquarters in Santa Monica, California; and the 25,000-seat Charlotte Coliseum event arena for the City of Charlotte, North Carolina.

The company has also been making moves to expand its business abroad in recent years. In 2012, for example, Turner partnered with one of India's largest real estate developers, Sahara Prime City Ltd., to form Sahara Turner, which would lead the development and construction of multiple townships across the country with an approximate value of $2.5 billion by 2017. It also purchased a majority stake in Clark Builders, Canada, to capitalize on the country's growing construction market.

Turner often partners with fellow US-based HOCHTIEF subsidiary Flatiron, which specializes in civil engineering. Examples of the teamwork are the expansions of airports in San Diego and Sacramento.

HISTORY

At the turn of the century, an engineer and devout Quaker named Henry Chandlee Turner was convinced that a new type of steel-reinforced concrete (called the Ransome system) would change the construction industry. With this conviction and with the help of his partner, D. H. Dixon, Turner bought the rights to the technology for $25,000 and in 1902 founded Turner Construction Company.

One of the company's early projects was building the stairways for New York's first subway stations. As the Ransome method proved to be successful, Turner's reputation grew. Defense contracts during WWI raised Turner's take to $35 million in 1918.

Before the Depression, Turner was building high-rises, hotels, and stadiums. During the economic crash that started in 1929, the company survived by building retail stores, churches, and public buildings, a strategy it would employ successfully in later recessions.

Henry Turner retired in 1941. His brother Archer Turner managed the company during most of the war effort. As WWII raged, more than 80% of the company's work was defense-related. Projects included building and managing a submarine base in Oak Ridge, Tennessee, during the development of the atomic bomb.

In 1947 Henry C. Turner Jr., the founder's son, became president, and within four years he had led the company to more than $100 million in sales. By the time he stepped down as chairman in 1970, the firm had built skyscrapers, futuristic airports, and such landmarks as Madison Square Garden and the United Nations Secretariat and Plaza in New York City. Turner went public in 1969.

Howard S. Turner (the final family member to head the business) led the company during the 1970s. The company extended its global presence, opening offices in more countries, including Iran, Pakistan, and the United Arab Emirates. Turner also developed construction management services.

In 1984 The Turner Corporation was formed as a holding company for the construction company and the subsidiaries created or acquired as a result of diversification. Property development was one of these activities, but by 1987 Turner had begun to dispose of its real estate holdings. It did not move quickly enough, however, and when the real estate market crashed, Turner was caught with a large portfolio.

As commercial projects slowed, Turner sought work in more sectors, including public works and amusement projects (aquariums, arenas, hospitals, and universities). By 1994 these areas accounted for 70% of business. In 1993, as the building slump continued, Turner began a cost-cutting plan, which included laying off workers and closing offices. That year the company set up an $8.5 million restructuring reserve, and as the real estate market eased into recovery, Turner sold more of its real estate holdings.

In 1996 Turner won a contract to build a 10,000-seat arena in Salt Lake City to be used for the 2002 Winter Olympics. In 1997 Turner contracted to renovate 811 schools and build two campuses in California's San Fernando Valley, and in 1998 it was chosen to manage the construction of the Kansas City Motor Speedway.

Profits were recovering quickly. Nonetheless, in 1999 the company agreed to be acquired by German construction giant HOCHTIEF in a $370 million deal that ended Turner's joint venture with Switzerland's Karl Steiner. The company also relocated its corporate headquarters to Dallas that year to take advantage of the construction boom in the US Southwest.

In 2000 Turner created three new business groups to serve the aviation, pharmaceutical, and sports sectors. By the next year Turner's sports group was working on 17 projects. In 2001 the company was a member of the construction team that responded to the September 11 devastation at Ground Zero in New York City.

The next year the company celebrated its 100th anniversary with an exhibit at the National Building Museum in Washington, DC; the exhibit featured drawings and photos of some of Turner's notable projects during the past century. In 2003 Turner Construction acquired the assets of Tompkins Builders, the third-largest construction company in the Washington, DC, area, from former rival J.A. Jones Construction Co.

Turner Construction, which celebrated its 100th anniversary in 2002, has ranked among the leading general builders in the US since WWI. For 80 of the 100 years, the group had a Turner among its senior executives. Howard S. Turner was the last member of the family to serve in the company's senior ranks. The company's appointment of Peter Davoren in 2003 as president of Turner Construction reflected the rise of a new generation of leaders for the unit. Davoren was additionally appointed chairman and CEO in 2007.

Turner Construction announced in 2008 that it had signed the contract on its 15,000th major project.

Auditors : DELOITTE & TOUCHE LLP PRINCET

LOCATIONS

HQ: THE TURNER CORPORATION
66 HUDSON BLVD E, NEW YORK, NY 100012189
Phone: 212 229-6000
Web: WWW.TURNERCONSTRUCTION.COM

PRODUCTS/OPERATIONS

Selected Related Companies
E. E. Cruz (infrastructure)
Flatiron Construction Corp. (transportation construction, civil engineering)
Clark Builders (51%, Canada)

Selected Markets Served
Aviation
Commercial
Cultural and entertainment
Data center
Education
Government
Green building
Health care
Infrastructure
Industrial
Interiors
Pharmaceutical
Public Assembly
Religious
Research and development

Residential/hotel
Sports

Selected Services
Building information modeling
Building maintenance
Construction management
Design-build
Design-build/finance
Facilities management
General construction
Lean construction
Logistics
Medical planning and procurement
Preconstruction consulting
Program management
Project management

COMPETITORS

GILBANE BUILDING COMPANY
H. J. RUSSELL & COMPANY
MCCARTHY BUILDING COMPANIES, INC.
MIRON CONSTRUCTION CO., INC.
PARSONS CORPORATION
Skanska AB
THE PIKE COMPANY INC
THE SUNDT COMPANIES INC
TISHMAN CONSTRUCTION CORPORATION
TURNER CONSTRUCTION COMPANY

HISTORICAL FINANCIALS
Company Type: Private

Income Statement — FYE: December 31

	REVENUE ($mil)	NET INCOME ($mil)	NET PROFIT MARGIN	EMPLOYEES
12/15	10,523	107	1.0%	5,000
12/14	10,560	95	0.9%	—
12/13	9,522	80	0.8%	—
12/12	8,575	74	0.9%	—
Annual Growth	7.1%	12.9%	—	—

2015 Year-End Financials
Return on assets: 2.9% Cash ($ mil.): 880
Return on equity: 16.5%
Current Ratio: 1.00

THE UCLA FOUNDATION

Helping to make La-La Land a little more erudite, The UCLA Foundation raises, manages, and disperses funds to help support the tripartite education, research, and service mission of UCLA. With more than $1 billion in assets, the organization funds the aforementioned purposes, as well as campus improvements and special programs. About half of the foundation's gifts received are provided by foundations; corporations and alumni each account for some 15% of gifts. The UCLA Progress Fund, predecessor of the foundation, was established in 1945 by the school's alumni association.

Auditors : PRICEWATERHOUSECOOPERS LLP PH

LOCATIONS
HQ: THE UCLA FOUNDATION
10889 WILSHIRE BLVD # 11, LOS ANGELES, CA 900244201

Phone: 310 794-3193
Web: WWW.UCLAFOUNDATION.ORG

COMPETITORS
Bertelsmann Stiftung
CALIFORNIA COMMUNITY FOUNDATION
JOSEPH DROWN FOUNDATION
THE FORD FOUNDATION
THE ROBERT WOOD JOHNSON FOUNDATION

HISTORICAL FINANCIALS
Company Type: Private

Income Statement — FYE: June 30

	ASSETS ($mil)	NET INCOME ($mil)	INCOME AS % OF ASSETS	EMPLOYEES
06/21	5,049	239	4.7%	317
06/18	3,539	336	9.5%	—
06/17	3,050	346	11.4%	—
Annual Growth	13.4%	(8.8%)	—	—

2021 Year-End Financials
Return on assets: 4.7%   Cash ($ mil.): 9
Return on equity: 5.2%
Current Ratio: 1.30

THE UNITED ILLUMINATING COMPANY

EXECUTIVES
Information Technology Vice President*, W Marie Zanavich

Auditors : KPMG LLP STAMFORD CT

LOCATIONS
HQ: THE UNITED ILLUMINATING COMPANY
180 MARSH HILL RD, ORANGE, CT 064773629
Phone: 203 499-2000
Web: WWW.UINET.COM

HISTORICAL FINANCIALS
Company Type: Private

Income Statement — FYE: December 31

	REVENUE ($mil)	NET INCOME ($mil)	NET PROFIT MARGIN	EMPLOYEES
12/17	921	105	11.4%	920
12/16*	866	84	9.7%	—
06/00	344	34	10.0%	—
Annual Growth	5.6%	6.4%	—	—

*Fiscal year change

2017 Year-End Financials
Return on assets: 3.3%   Cash ($ mil.): —
Return on equity: 11.3%
Current Ratio: 0.50

THE UNIVERSITY OF CENTRAL FLORIDA BOARD OF TRUSTEES

The University of Central Florida (UCF, whose mascot is a stylized knight) is part of the State University System of Florida. Boasting an enrollment of more than 69,000 students, UCF offers more than 220 degree programs through a dozen colleges. Areas of study include psychology, health sciences, biomedical sciences, nursing, computer science, mechanical engineering, biology, integrated business, finance, and hospitality management. In addition to its main campus, UCF operates more than a dozen locations throughout Central Florida.

Operations

The University offers about a hundred bachelor's, 90 master's, around 30 research doctorates, three professional doctorates and three specialist degree programs. The university's research programs annually attract more than $192 million in funding.

In addition to more traditional areas of study, the university also boasts the Florida Interactive Entertainment Academy, where graduate students learn video-game development, including art, programming, and production. The academy is funded jointly by the State of Florida and UCF.

Geographic Reach

UCF is located on a 1,400-acre campus in Orlando. Through its main campus and its satellite locations, UCF serves around a dozen of county service areas including Brevard, Citrus, Flagler, Indian River, Lake, Levy, Marion, Orange, Osceola, Polk, Seminole, Sumter, and Volusia. Its students hail from all 50 US states and nearly 150 international countries. The university also conducts study abroad programs in about 35 countries.

Strategy

UCF leverages innovative learning, discovery and partnerships, fostering social mobility while developing the skilled talent needed to advance industry for its region, state and beyond.

The university partnered with Adobe in late 2020. UCF specifically is working with Adobe on a digital reading project that aims to reduce information overload. The project is part of Adobe's continuing efforts toward creating products that empower people to change the world, such as its recent collaboration with a UCF-spin-off, the nonprofit Limbitless Solutions Inc.

UCF has also added a new physical therapy program solely focused on pain. The 12-week summer course debuted in 2019 and teaches students about the physical, psychological and social aspects of pain management. The course helps students apply and understand the new, overall wellness model of patient care. UCF also added a new hybrid-class format called BlendFlex. The new class strategy includes some face-to-face and online components and has been added to the lineup of fully online and face-to-face classes.

Company Background

The school was founded in 1963 as Florida Technological University and held its first classes five years later. UCF changed its name to the current moniker in 1978.

EXECUTIVES

Vice Chairman, Alex Martins
Auditors : SHERRILL F NORMAN CPA TALLA

LOCATIONS

HQ: THE UNIVERSITY OF CENTRAL FLORIDA BOARD OF TRUSTEES
4000 CENTRAL FLORIDA BLVD, ORLANDO, FL 328168005
Phone: 407 823-2000
Web: WWW.UCF.EDU

PRODUCTS/OPERATIONS

Selected Colleges and Schools
Burnett Honors College
College of Arts and Humanities
College of Business Administration
College of Education
College of Engineering and Computer Science
College of Graduate Studies
College of Health and Public Affairs
College of Medicine
College of Nursing
College of Optics and Photonics
College of Sciences
Interdisciplinary Studies
Rosen College of Hospitality Management

COMPETITORS

BOISE STATE UNIVERSITY
DESALES UNIVERSITY
FAIRFIELD UNIVERSITY
GEORGIA INSTITUTE OF TECHNOLOGY
KENT STATE UNIVERSITY
MISSOURI STATE UNIVERSITY
NEW MEXICO STATE UNIVERSITY
NOVA SOUTHEASTERN UNIVERSITY, INC.
SOUTH CAROLINA STATE UNIVERSITY
THE UNIVERSITY OF IOWA

HISTORICAL FINANCIALS
Company Type: Private

Income Statement — FYE: June 30

	REVENUE ($mil)	NET INCOME ($mil)	NET PROFIT MARGIN	EMPLOYEES
06/21	570	(23)	—	6,500
06/08	374	108	28.9%	—
06/07	382	152	40.0%	—
Annual Growth	2.9%	—	—	—

2021 Year-End Financials
Return on assets: (-1.0%)   Cash ($ mil.): 16
Return on equity: (-2.1%)
Current Ratio: 5.20

THE UNIVERSITY OF CHICAGO MEDICAL CENTER

The University of Chicago Medical Center (UCMC) is a not-for-profit academic medical health system based on the campus of the University of Chicago in Hyde Park, and with hospitals, outpatient clinics and physician practices throughout Chicago and its suburbs. UCMC include the acute care Bernard A. Mitchell Hospital, the Comer Children's Hospital, a women's health and maternity facility, and an outpatient care center. Established in 1927 (and dedicated on Halloween of that year) the complex includes the affiliated University of Chicago Pritzker School of Medicine and forms the clinical arm of The University of Chicago Division of Biological Sciences. UCMC houses around 810 beds.

Operations

Its Bernard A. Mitchell Hospital includes helicopter transportation operations, emergency level-one pediatric trauma services, and regional burn and peri-natal units. The over 170-bed Comer Children's Hospital offers disease care, education, and research, as well as expanded newborn intensive care services.

UCMC sees some about 485,430 outpatient encounters and around 75,840 emergency room visits per year. The hospital is one of the largest providers of uncompensated care in Illinois, providing millions of dollars in charity care every year.

The Gwen and Jules Knapp Center for Biomedical Discovery works on discovery programs for a variety of medical conditions including diabetes, cancer, and pediatrics.

Geographic Reach

UCMC is located in Chicago, Illinois. Centered in historic, tree-lined Hyde Park, where the medical center complex is located on the University of Chicago campus, UChicago Medicine also has dozens of outpatient clinics around the Chicago area, including locations in downtown Chicago, the south suburbs and Northwest Indiana.

UChicago Medicine comprises the University of Chicago Medical Center, Pritzker School of Medicine, the Biological Sciences Division and Ingalls Memorial, a community-based hospital and outpatient facility in Harvey.

UChicago Medicine's outpatient facilities are conveniently located throughout the region, from the Magnificent Mile, River East and the South Loop in the heart of Chicago to Orland Park, Tinley Park, Flossmoor, Calumet City and South Holland in the south suburbs.

Company Background

The University of Chicago was founded in 1890 and expanded into medicine in 1898. Under then-University President William Rainey Harper, the University of Chicago temporarily became affiliated with the Rush Medical College with "the distinct purpose" of establishing a medical school when funds became available, according to Harper's Decennial address in 1902.

In 1916, the University of Chicago Board of Trustees set aside $5.3 million for construction, equipment and an endowment for an expansion into health care. However, World War I put a halt to the development. The project resumed in 1921, eventually reaching completion in 1927. By that time, costs had skyrocketed to nearly five times the original estimate.

EXECUTIVES

Co-Vice President, Maia Hightower
Auditors : KPMG LLP CHICAGO ILLINOIS

LOCATIONS

HQ: THE UNIVERSITY OF CHICAGO MEDICAL CENTER
5841 S MARYLAND AVE, CHICAGO, IL 606371443
Phone: 773 702-1000
Web: WWW.UCHICAGOMEDICINE.ORG

PRODUCTS/OPERATIONS

Selected Services
Cancer
Endocrinology
Gastroenterology
Geriatrics
Heart
Kidney disease
Neurosciences
Orthopaedics
Respiratory disease
Surgery
Transplantation
Women's services

Selected Facilities
Bernard A. Mitchell Hospital
Center for Care and Discovery
Chicago Lying-in Hospital (Maternity and Women's Hospital)
Comer Children's Hospital
Duchossois Center for Advanced Medicine (outpatient care and diagnostics)
Gwen and Jules Knapp Center for Biomedical Discovery
LaRabida Children's Hospital (affiliated facility)
Mercy Hospital (affiliated facility)
University of Chicago Pritzker School of Medicine
Weiss Memorial Hospital (affiliated facility)

COMPETITORS

ASCENSION PROVIDENCE ROCHESTER HOSPITAL
ASCENSION SETON
EISENHOWER MEDICAL CENTER
JERSEY CITY MEDICAL CENTER (INC)
LOMA LINDA UNIVERSITY MEDICAL CENTER
LONG BEACH MEDICAL CENTER
OUR LADY OF THE LAKE HOSPITAL, INC.
THE CHILDREN'S HOSPITAL CORPORATION
THE CHRIST HOSPITAL
WASHINGTON HOSPITAL CENTER CORPORATION

HISTORICAL FINANCIALS
Company Type: Private

Income Statement — FYE: June 30

	REVENUE ($mil)	NET INCOME ($mil)	NET PROFIT MARGIN	EMPLOYEES
06/22	2,985	(90)	—	9,346
06/21	2,789	519	18.6%	—
06/20	2,547	(53)	—	—
06/19	2,387	27	1.2%	—
Annual Growth	7.7%	—	—	—

2022 Year-End Financials
Return on assets: (-2.2%)   Cash ($ mil.): 60
Return on equity: (-4.1%)
Current Ratio: 1.30

THE UNIVERSITY OF DAYTON

More than 11,600 students make the University of Dayton one of the nation's largest Catholic universities and the largest private university in Ohio. The institution offers more than 80 undergraduate and 50 graduate and doctoral programs. Students are recruited on a national basis and from foreign countries. The student population more than 8,300 undergraduate and more than 3,000 graduate students. It has a student-to-faculty ratio of 14:1. Well-known alumni include the late author and columnist Erma Bombeck and Super Bowl-winning NFL coaches Jon Gruden and Chuck Noll.

Operations
The university academic units include College of Arts and Sciences, School of Business Administration, School of Education and Health Sciences, School of Engineering, and School of Law. Its program has included accounting, aerospace engineering, art history, biochemistry, biology, chemistry, communication, economics, finance, and music.

Geographic Reach
The university is located in Dayton, Ohio.

Strategy
Partnerships and Exchanges seeks, builds and maintains relationships with institutions and organizations all over the world for the purpose of increasing direct global opportunities for UD faculty, staff, students and partners abroad. Partnerships and Exchanges support activities that include education abroad programs, joint international research, dual degree agreements, faculty mobility to teach and achieve professional development, and other special enrollment programs.

Company Background
The University of Dayton was founded in 1850 by the Society of Mary (the Marianists).

Auditors : RSM US LLP DAYTON OHIO

LOCATIONS
HQ: THE UNIVERSITY OF DAYTON
300 COLLEGE PARK AVE, DAYTON, OH 454690002
Phone: 937 229-2919
Web: WWW.UDAYTON.EDU

COMPETITORS
DREW UNIVERSITY
NORTHERN ILLINOIS UNIVERSITY
THE GEORGE WASHINGTON UNIVERSITY
THE TRUSTEES OF PRINCETON UNIVERSITY
THE UNIVERSITY OF CHICAGO
TRUSTEES OF BOSTON COLLEGE
UNIVERSITY OF CINCINNATI
UNIVERSITY OF FLORIDA
UNIVERSITY OF WYOMING
WILLAMETTE UNIVERSITY

HISTORICAL FINANCIALS
Company Type: Private

Income Statement — FYE: June 30

	REVENUE ($mil)	NET INCOME ($mil)	NET PROFIT MARGIN	EMPLOYEES
06/20	747	29	4.0%	4,500
06/19	774	30	4.0%	—
06/16	521	(11)	—	—
Annual Growth	9.4%	—	—	—

2020 Year-End Financials
Return on assets: 1.7%   Cash ($ mil.): 69
Return on equity: 2.4%
Current Ratio: 0.50

THE UNIVERSITY OF IOWA

The University of Iowa is one of America's premier public ressearch university. Founded in 1847, the University of Iowa has some 31,205 students (and a student-faculty ratio of approximately 15:1) at its Iowa City campus. It is home to a dozen colleges spanning more than 200 areas of study, including distinguished programs in physics, astronomy, speech and hearing sciences, nursing, and creative writing. Its Writers' Workshop was the nation's first creative writing advanced degree program. It also includes programs in law, engineering, teaching, and medicine, as well as the affiliated University of Iowa Hospitals and Clinics health care organization.

Operations
University of Iowa comprises a dozen schools, the largest being the undergraduate College of Liberal Arts and Sciences. Other undergraduates enroll in schools of business, medicine, education, law, engineering, nursing, and pharmacy, while the dentistry, public health, and graduate schools provide graduate education programs.

Geographic Reach
University of Iowa is located in Iowa City, Iowa.

Sales and Marketing
The university caters around 31,205 students of which, about 21,610 is enrolled on undergraduate programs. Majority of its students came from white or unknown race.

Company Background
Among the University of Iowa's notable alumni are Al Jarreau, John Irving, Flannery O'Connor, Gene Wilder, and Tennessee Williams.

EXECUTIVES
Student Life Vice President, Sarah Hansen
Medical Affairs Vice President, J Brooks Jackson
Operations, Rod Lehnertz
OF UI CENTER FOR ADVANCEMENT, Lynette Marshall
Auditors : MARLYS K GASTON CPA DES MOI

LOCATIONS
HQ: THE UNIVERSITY OF IOWA
125 N MADISON ST, IOWA CITY, IA 52242
Phone: 319 335-3500
Web: WWW.UIOWA.EDU

PRODUCTS/OPERATIONS
Selected Colleges
College of Dentistry
College of Education
College of Engineering
College of Law
College of Liberal Arts and Sciences
College of Nursing
College of Pharmacy
College of Public Health
Graduate College
Henry B. Tippie College of Business
Roy J. and Lucille A. Carver College of Medicine

COMPETITORS
CALIFORNIA STATE UNIVERSITY, FRESNO
CLEMSON UNIVERSITY
DRAKE UNIVERSITY
FAIRFIELD UNIVERSITY
IDAHO STATE UNIVERSITY
JAMES MADISON UNIVERSITY
SOUTH CAROLINA STATE UNIVERSITY
SUNY AT BINGHAMTON
THE UNIVERSITY OF HARTFORD
UNIVERSITY OF ILLINOIS

HISTORICAL FINANCIALS
Company Type: Private

Income Statement — FYE: June 30

	REVENUE ($mil)	NET INCOME ($mil)	NET PROFIT MARGIN	EMPLOYEES
06/21	3,757	471	12.6%	17,000
06/16	2,859	253	8.9%	—
06/11	2,067	253	12.3%	—
Annual Growth	6.2%	6.4%	—	—

2021 Year-End Financials
Return on assets: 5.3%   Cash ($ mil.): 227
Return on equity: 9.0%
Current Ratio: 1.20

THE UNIVERSITY OF IOWA

Auditors: MARLYS K GASTON CPA DES MOI

LOCATIONS

HQ: THE UNIVERSITY OF IOWA
2660 UCC, IOWA CITY, IA 52242
Phone: 319 335-2119
Web: WWW.UIOWA.EDU

HISTORICAL FINANCIALS
Company Type: Private

Income Statement — FYE: June 30

	REVENUE ($mil)	NET INCOME ($mil)	NET PROFIT MARGIN	EMPLOYEES
06/18	3,176	588	18.5%	44
06/17	2,950	144	4.9%	—
Annual Growth	7.7%	308.5%	—	—

2018 Year-End Financials
Return on assets: 8.6%   Cash ($ mil.): 145
Return on equity: 13.6%
Current Ratio: 1.10

THE UNIVERSITY OF KANSAS HOSPITAL AUTHORITY

LOCATIONS

HQ: THE UNIVERSITY OF KANSAS HOSPITAL AUTHORITY
4000 CAMBRIDGE ST, KANSAS CITY, KS 661608501
Phone: 913 588-5000
Web: WWW.KANSASHEALTHSYSTEM.COM

HISTORICAL FINANCIALS
Company Type: Private

Income Statement — FYE: June 30

	REVENUE ($mil)	NET INCOME ($mil)	NET PROFIT MARGIN	EMPLOYEES
06/15	1,362	156	11.5%	2,661
06/02	321	6	2.0%	—
Annual Growth	11.8%	28.1%	—	—

2015 Year-End Financials
Return on assets: 9.4%   Cash ($ mil.): 140
Return on equity: 17.3%
Current Ratio: 2.00

THE UNIVERSITY OF NORTH CAROLINA

Tar heels can sink their feet into academia and athletics at The University of North Carolina. The system of 17 universities, including the flagship University of North Carolina at Chapel Hill campus, counts more than 220,000 undergraduate and graduate students across its campuses. It offers degrees in more than 200 disciplines. The university system, chartered in 1789, is home to medical schools, a teaching hospital, law schools, a veterinary school at NC State, a school of pharmacy, nursing programs, schools of education, schools of engineering, and a school for the arts. In addition, the system also operates the NC School of Science and Mathematics, a public residential high school for gifted students.

Operations
The university system comprises 17 public institutions that grant baccalaureate degrees. It also operates a public residential high school for gifted students under the name NC School of Science and Mathematics.

Each year, the university graduates more than 30,000 students.

Geographic Reach
The University of North Carolina system serves students worldwide. Of its enrollment, the system attracts far more in-state students than out-of-state students.

Financial Performance
Revenue for fiscal 2014 was $1.9 billion.

Strategy
To extend its reach, The University of North Carolina partners with half a dozen affiliates. They include UNC Center for Public Television, The North Carolina Arboretum, The North Carolina State Approving Agency, The North Carolina Center for International Understanding, The North Carolina State Education Assistance Authority, and The University of North Carolina Press.

In 2013 the system adopted a five-year strategic plan entitled "Our Time, Our Future." The plan's goals were designed to set priorities, allocate resources, plan programs, and refine academic missions.

EXECUTIVES
Vice Chairman*, Wendy Murphy
Auditors: SHARPE PATEL CPA CHARLOTTE N

LOCATIONS

HQ: THE UNIVERSITY OF NORTH CAROLINA
910 RALEIGH RD, CHAPEL HILL, NC 275143916
Phone: 919 962-2211
Web: WWW.NORTHCAROLINA.EDU

PRODUCTS/OPERATIONS
Selected Institutions
Appalachian State University
East Carolina University
Elizabeth City State University
Fayetteville State University
NC A&T State University
North Carolina Central University
NC State University
UNC Asheville
UNC Chapel Hill
UNC Charlotte
UNC Greensboro
UNC Pembroke
UNC Wilmington
UNC School of the Arts
Western Carolina University
Winston-Salem State University
NC School of Science and Mathematics

COMPETITORS
CONNECTICUT STATE UNIVERSITY SYSTEM
HAMPTON UNIVERSITY
MARSHALL UNIVERSITY
MISSOURI STATE UNIVERSITY
SOUTH CAROLINA STATE UNIVERSITY
SOUTHERN POLYTECHNIC STATE UNIVERSITY FOUNDATION, INC
THE UNIVERSITY OF NORTH CAROLINA AT CHARLOTTE
UNIVERSITY OF ILLINOIS
UNIVERSITY OF SAN FRANCISCO
WILLAMETTE UNIVERSITY

HISTORICAL FINANCIALS
Company Type: Private

Income Statement — FYE: June 30

	REVENUE ($mil)	NET INCOME ($mil)	NET PROFIT MARGIN	EMPLOYEES
06/13	1,838	267	14.6%	55,000
06/12	0	(0)	—	—
06/06	30	(9)	—	—
Annual Growth	79.3%	—	—	—

2013 Year-End Financials
Return on assets: 3.3%   Cash ($ mil.): 520
Return on equity: 5.9%
Current Ratio: 5.00

THE UNIVERSITY OF NORTH CAROLINA HEALTH SYSTEM

University of North Carolina Hospitals (UNCH) is at the heart of the UNC Health Care System (UNC HCS). The medical center provides acute care to the Tar Heel State through North Carolina Memorial Hospital, North Carolina Children's Hospital, North Carolina Neurosciences Hospital, and North Carolina Women's Hospital. Combined, the facilities have more than 800 beds. Specialties include cancer treatment at the North Carolina Cancer Hospital, organ transplantation, cardiac care, orthopedics, wound management, and rehabilitation. Not-for-profit UNC HCS is owned by the state of

North Carolina and is affiliated with the UNC-Chapel Hill School of Medicine.

Operations
UNCH operates under the umbrella of UNC HCS.

UNC HCS already extends beyond Chapel Hill and into the greater Triangle area through its network of primary care and specialty physician practices located in Orange, Wake, Durham, Chatham, and Lee counties. The system treats some 800,000 people at UNC HCS practices and clinics annually.

UNCH handles more than 37,000 patients each year and delivers 3,500 babies annually.

North Carolina Children's offers 150 inpatient beds and a comprehensive children's outpatient center. Every year provides specialty care to more than 70,000 children from all 100 North Carolina counties. The North Carolina Cancer Hospital is the clinical home of the UNC Lineberger Comprehensive Cancer Center. The state's only public cancer hospital, the North Carolina Cancer Hospital treats patients from every county in North Carolina, with more than 135,000 patient visits a year.

Geographic Reach
UNCH not only serves patients from all North Carolina counties, with about a third coming from the Research Triangle area, it also serves patients from neighboring states.

Strategy
Being one of the primary health care providers in the area, UNC HCS is nearly always expanding its services and service areas either through acquisitions or new construction.

In 2015 UNCH filed a petition with state regulators seeking the ability to add 42 acute-care beds at its Chapel Hill campus. If approved, UNC estimates it will cost the hospital $17 million and would be completed by mid-2018.

UNC HCS planned to open a new 86-bed acute-care hospital in Hillsborough in 2015, as part of an effort to reduce pressure on its Chapel Hill campus. The construction of the hospital will cost about $200 million. The new facility will offer an emergency department, outpatient surgery and a range of inpatient services to our patients in Alamance and Western Orange counties.

Dedicated cancer care and cancer research is another area in which UNC HCS is expanding. It opened a North Carolina Cancer Hospital at Rex Hospital in 2014.

The system is also building an Imaging Research Building, expected to open in 2013 to house the Biomedical Research Imaging Center and serve as a state resource for handling the acquisition, processing, analysis, storage, and retrieval of scientific images.

In 2013, UNC HCS established the first stage of its Hillsborough campus with the opening of a 60,000-square-foot medical office building. The building includes hospital services such as imaging, laboratory, pharmacy and medical and surgical oncology.

Company Background
In 2011 the hospital opened a new wing of the Newborn Critical Care Unit in the North Carolina Children's Hospital that houses 10 new patient beds, bringing the number of beds in the unit to 58.

UNCH was founded in 1952 under the name North Carolina Memorial Hospital. In 1989, the North Carolina General Assembly created UNCH.

Auditors : BETH A WOOD CPA RALEIGH NO

LOCATIONS
HQ: THE UNIVERSITY OF NORTH CAROLINA HEALTH SYSTEM
101 MANNING DR, CHAPEL HILL, NC 275144220
Phone: 919 966-5111
Web: WWW.UNCHEALTHCARE.ORG

PRODUCTS/OPERATIONS
Selected Facilities
North Carolina Cancer Hospital (Chapel Hill)
   UNC Lineberger Comprehensive Cancer Center
North Carolina Children's Hospital (Chapel Hill)
North Carolina Memorial Hospital (Chapel Hill)
North Carolina Neurosciences Hospital (Chapel Hill)
North Carolina Women's Hospital (Chapel Hill)

COMPETITORS
BEAUFORT MEMORIAL HOSPITAL
CATHOLIC HEALTH SYSTEM, INC.
CHILDREN'S HOSPITAL COLORADO
INDIANA UNIVERSITY HEALTH BALL MEMORIAL HOSPITAL, INC.
LHH CORPORATION
MEMORIAL HOSPITAL CORPORATION
PASADENA HOSPITAL ASSOCIATION, LTD.
THE EAST ALABAMA HEALTH CARE AUTHORITY
THE UNIVERSITY OF CHICAGO MEDICAL CENTER
UNIVERSITY HEALTH SYSTEM SERVICES OF TEXAS, INC.

HISTORICAL FINANCIALS
Company Type: Private

Income Statement   FYE: June 30

	REVENUE ($mil)	NET INCOME ($mil)	NET PROFIT MARGIN	EMPLOYEES
06/21	2,397	516	21.5%	6,000
06/16	1,551	87	5.6%	—
06/15	1,385	110	8.0%	—
Annual Growth	9.6%	29.2%	—	—

2021 Year-End Financials
Return on assets: 12.8%   Cash ($ mil.): 107
Return on equity: 53.5%
Current Ratio: 1.00

THE UNIVERSITY OF TEXAS HEALTH SCIENCE CENTER AT SAN ANTONIO

LOCATIONS
HQ: THE UNIVERSITY OF TEXAS HEALTH SCIENCE CENTER AT SAN ANTONIO
7703 FLOYD CURL DR, SAN ANTONIO, TX 782293901
Phone: 210 567-7000
Web: WWW.UTHSCSA.EDU

HISTORICAL FINANCIALS
Company Type: Private

Income Statement   FYE: August 31

	REVENUE ($mil)	NET INCOME ($mil)	NET PROFIT MARGIN	EMPLOYEES
08/11	767	62	8.2%	4,000
08/05	289	56	19.6%	—
08/04	289	56	19.6%	—
Annual Growth	15.0%	1.5%	—	—

2011 Year-End Financials
Return on assets: 4.3%   Cash ($ mil.): 99
Return on equity: 4.9%
Current Ratio: 1.60

THE UNIVERSITY OF TOLEDO

One of Ohio's 14 state universities, The University of Toledo (UT) is the third-largest by operating budget. It enrolls more than 20,200 students and offers more than 270 programs of study, including master's degree and doctoral programs. The university has a student-to-faculty ratio of 19:1. Its about 15 colleges focus on subjects ranging from visual and performing arts to business and innovation, as well as education, engineering, law, medicine, nursing, pharmacy, languages, and chemistry. The school also operates the University of Toledo Medical Center.

Operations
The University of Toledo Medical Center, affiliated with UT provides advanced care and healing in a patient-centered environment. It has access to the latest clinical trials and medical research and committed to teaching the next generation of health-care professionals.

The UT Medical Center features a Level I trauma center and extensive medical training programs on UT's Health Science Campus. It provides treatments for strokes and cancer that are unique within the state. Other specialties include kidney transplants and cardiology.

Geographic Reach
UT students come from more than 40 US states and about 85 international countries. The school has an extensive distance learning program. In addition to the main campus in Toledo, UT operates several satellite centers in Toledo (including the Health Science Campus, the Scott Park Campus, and the Center for the Visual Arts facility) and the Lake Erie Research and Education Center in Oregon, Ohio.

Financial Performance
Strategy
UT continues to work on its five-year strategic plan that ends in 2022, which includes promoting student success and academic excellence; improving research, scholarship, and creative activities; taking care of faculty, staff, and alumni; and improving the university's fiscal positioning and infrastructure, among others.

Company Background
UT and the Medical University of Ohio merged in 2006. UT is accredited by the Higher Learning Commission of the North Central Association of Colleges and Schools.

UT was established in 1872 and became a member of the state university system in 1967.

Auditors : CLIFTONLARSONALLEN LLP TOLEDO

LOCATIONS
HQ: THE UNIVERSITY OF TOLEDO
2801 W BANCROFT ST, TOLEDO, OH 436063390
Phone: 419 530-4636
Web: WWW.UTOLEDO.EDU

COMPETITORS
BAYLOR COLLEGE OF MEDICINE
CREIGHTON UNIVERSITY
IDAHO STATE UNIVERSITY
KENT STATE UNIVERSITY
THE UNIVERSITY OF IOWA
UNIVERSITY OF BIRMINGHAM
UNIVERSITY OF ILLINOIS
UNIVERSITY OF MIAMI
UNIVERSITY OF MISSOURI SYSTEM
UNIVERSITY OF OKLAHOMA

HISTORICAL FINANCIALS
Company Type: Private

Income Statement FYE: June 30

	REVENUE ($mil)	NET INCOME ($mil)	NET PROFIT MARGIN	EMPLOYEES
06/18	716	55	7.8%	7,000
06/17	728	(62)	—	—
Annual Growth	(1.6%)	—	—	—

2018 Year-End Financials
Return on assets: 4.7%
Return on equity: 176.9%
Current Ratio: 1.20
Cash ($ mil.): 40

THE UNIVERSITY OF UTAH

The University of Utah (U of U) is the state's oldest and most comprehensive institution of higher education and is the flagship institution of the state system of higher education. Founded in 1850 as the University of Deseret, the U of U has a total enrollment of more than 34,000 undergraduate and graduate students, with a student-to-faculty ratio of some 17:1. It offers over 100 major subjects at the undergraduate and graduate level at about 20 colleges and schools; its business, science, humanities, and engineering departments are the university's largest. It also offers medical, nursing, and pharmacy programs, as well as health and social science research programs. U of U confers nearly 8,950 baccalaureate, masters, and doctoral degrees annually.

Operations
The university includes an academic health system, University of Utah Health Care, which includes the U of U School of Medicine and the University of Utah Hospitals and Clinics. The University of Utah School of Medicine combines teaching, research, and clinical expertise to train future physicians for the rapidly changing world of medicine. With a faculty of more than 1,000 physicians and researchers and more than 20 clinical and basic science departments, the School of Medicine trains the majority of Utah physicians, MD degrees, physician assistant training, residencies, fellowship specialty training, degrees in public health, degrees in medical laboratory science, and science and research. U of U also includes institutes that conduct research programs in a variety of fields ? including health, math, fine arts, and engineering ? as well as technology commercialization projects.

Nearly 55% of total sales were generated from patient services, about 25% from sales and services, approximately 10% of sales from grants and contracts, and the remainder came from tuition and fees and auxiliary.

Geographic Reach
The 1,500 acre campus is located along the foothills of the Wasatch Mountains, the westernmost branch of the Rockies, overlooking Salt Lake City. U of U's international students hail from more than 130 countries which some are from Latin American, Bosnian, Pacific Islander, and Sri Lankan communities.

Financial Performance
In 2021, the university's total operating revenue for the year was $4.1 billion. The university's net position was $851.7 million.

The university's cash at the end of 2021 was $2.1 billion. Operating activities used $59.2 million. Investing activities used another $27.3 billion.

Strategy
The University diversifies assets among several investment managers of varying investment strategies. Diversification is an effective means of maximizing return while mitigating risk. In mid-2021, the University held more than 5% of its total investments in the Federal Home Loan Bank and the Federal Agricultural Mortgage Corporation. These investments represent 5.5%, and 5.2%, respectively, of the University's total investments.

EXECUTIVES
CSO*, Marlon Lynch
Chief Safety Officer*, Keith Squires
Auditors : OFFICE OF THE UTAH STATE AUDIT

LOCATIONS
HQ: THE UNIVERSITY OF UTAH
201 PRESIDENTS CIR, SALT LAKE CITY, UT 841129049
Phone: 801 581-7200
Web: WWW.UTAH.EDU

PRODUCTS/OPERATIONS
2015 Sales

	$ mil.	% of total
Patient services, net	1,816.3	53
Sales and services	740.2	21
Grants and contracts	362.6	10
Tuition and fees, net	304.0	9
Auxiliary and other	237.3	7
Total	3,460.4	100

Selected Colleges
College of Architecture and Planning
College of Education
College of Engineering
College of Fine Arts
College of Health
College of Humanities
College of Law
College of Mines and Earth Sciences
College of Nursing
College of Pharmacy
College of Science
College of Social and Behavioral Sciences
College of Social Work
David Eccles School of Business
Graduate School
Honors College
School of Medicine

COMPETITORS
CASE WESTERN RESERVE UNIVERSITY
PURDUE UNIVERSITY
Queen's University At Kingston
RECTOR & VISITORS OF THE UNIVERSITY OF VIRGINIA
REGENTS OF THE UNIVERSITY OF MICHIGAN
ROCHESTER INSTITUTE OF TECHNOLOGY (INC)
THE COLLEGE OF WILLIAM & MARY
UNIVERSITY OF KANSAS
UNIVERSITY OF OREGON
UNIVERSITY OF THE PACIFIC

THE UNIVERSITY OF VERMONT MEDICAL CENTER INC

The University of Vermont Medical Center (formerly Fletcher Allen Health Care) provides medical care in the Green Mountain State. The company operates an academic medical center in alliance with the University of Vermont College of Medicine. The not-for-profit health system serves residents of Vermont and northern New York through three primary hospital campuses in Chittenden County, Vermont, over 65 outpatient practices and 100-plus clinics, programs and services. UVM Medical Center is Vermont's only Level 1 Trauma Center, with the state's sole Neonatal Intensive Care Unit.

Operations

UVM Medical Center is part of an integrated health network across Vermont and northern New York that includes its UVM Health Network partners: UVM Health Network - Central Vermont Medical Center (Berlin, VT), UVM Health Network - Champlain Valley Physicians Hospital (Plattsburgh, NY), UVM Health Network - Elizabethtown Community Hospital (Elizabethtown, NY) UVM Health Network - Alice Hyde Medical Center (Malone, NY), UVM Health Network - Porter Medical Center (Middlebury, VT), the UVM Health Network Medical Group and Home Health & Hospice (formerly the Visiting Nurse Association of Chittenden and Grand Isle counties). It also maintains affiliation with Canton-Potsdam Hospital (Potsdam, NY) and Inter-Lakes Health (Ticonderoga, NY).

The UVM Medical Center in alliance with the University of Vermont College of Medicine is Vermont's academic medical center and one of approximately 130 centers in the country.

Geographic Reach

UVM Medical Center serves 1 million people who live in Vermont and Northern New York.

Company Background

The hospital system was created through the 1995 merger of the Fanny Allen Hospital (which opened in 1894), the Medical Center Hospital of Vermont (or Mary Fletcher Hospital, founded in 1876), and the University Health Center (formed in 1971). The hospitals are now known as Fanny Allen Campus, Medical Center Campus, and UHC Campus.

Fletcher Allen Health Care completed the implementation of an electronic health records (EHR) system that connects patient records at all of its facilities in 2010.

Auditors: PRICEWATERHOUSECOOPERS LLP BO

LOCATIONS

HQ: THE UNIVERSITY OF VERMONT MEDICAL CENTER INC
111 COLCHESTER AVE, BURLINGTON, VT 054011473
Phone: 802 847-0000
Web: WWW.UVMHEALTH.ORG

PRODUCTS/OPERATIONS

Selected Services
Cancer Care
Heart & Vascular
Orthopedics
Primary Care
Urgent Care
Women's Health

COMPETITORS

ALBERT EINSTEIN HEALTHCARE NETWORK
ASCENSION PROVIDENCE HOSPITAL
ATLANTIC HEALTH SYSTEM INC.
GREATER BALTIMORE MEDICAL CENTER, INC.
HACKENSACK MERIDIAN HEALTH, INC.
KENNEDY HEALTH SYSTEM, INC.
MARSHFIELD CLINIC HEALTH SYSTEM, INC.
PITT COUNTY MEMORIAL HOSPITAL, INCORPORATED
TRINITAS REGIONAL MEDICAL CENTER A NEW JERSEY NONPROFIT CORPORATION
WILLIAM BEAUMONT HOSPITAL

HISTORICAL FINANCIALS

Company Type: Private

Income Statement — FYE: September 30

	REVENUE ($mil)	NET INCOME ($mil)	NET PROFIT MARGIN	EMPLOYEES
09/20	1,033	35	3.4%	7,000
09/18	1,363	68	5.1%	—
09/17	1,246	129	10.4%	—
09/16	1,181	85	7.2%	—
Annual Growth	(3.3%)	(19.6%)	—	—

2020 Year-End Financials
Return on assets: 2.0%   Cash ($ mil.): 194
Return on equity: 3.8%
Current Ratio: 1.70

THE UNIVERSITY OF VIRGINIA

HISTORICAL FINANCIALS

Company Type: Private

Income Statement — FYE: June 30

	REVENUE ($mil)	NET INCOME ($mil)	NET PROFIT MARGIN	EMPLOYEES
06/13*	2,907	186	6.4%	18,000
12/08	0	0	0.0%	—
06/08	22	(10)	—	—
Annual Growth	164.4%	—	—	—

*Fiscal year change

2013 Year-End Financials
Return on assets: 3.7%   Cash ($ mil.): 486
Return on equity: 4.8%
Current Ratio: 3.60

LOCATIONS

HQ: THE UNIVERSITY OF VIRGINIA
1215 LEE ST, CHARLOTTESVILLE, VA 229080816
Phone: 434 924-0000
Web: WWW.UVAHEALTH.COM

HISTORICAL FINANCIALS

Company Type: Private

Income Statement — FYE: June 30

	REVENUE ($mil)	NET INCOME ($mil)	NET PROFIT MARGIN	EMPLOYEES
06/19	2,915	350	12.0%	453
06/18	2,788	544	19.5%	—
Annual Growth	4.5%	(35.6%)	—	—

2019 Year-End Financials
Return on assets: 2.7%   Cash ($ mil.): 149
Return on equity: 3.9%
Current Ratio: 1.00

THE VALLEY HOSPITAL INC

The Valley Hospital is second to none when it comes to its Same-Day Service program. More than one-third of the company's annual patients experience its longstanding continuum of one-day service; fully half the surgeries performed are same-day. The not-for-profit hospital is a 450-bed facility providing general and emergency services to residents of New Jersey's Bergen County. The hospital belongs to the Valley Health System, which also includes subsidiaries Valley Home Care and Valley Health Medical Group, and is an affiliate member of NewYork-Presbyterian Healthcare. The Valley Hospital, New Jersey's second busiest, has more than 800 physicians on its medical staff.

Operations

The Valley Hospital is well known for its cardiology, cancer, maternity, and neonatal care programs (including its neonatal ICU). Its key services also include emergency care, orthopedics, and neurosciences. The hospital's emergency department treated more than 75,000 patients in 2013. That year the hospital also admitted more than 49,240 patients and the delivered almost 3,200 babies.

The Valley Hospital's cardiac service includes a full range of diagnostic and interventional cardiac treatment services, including cardiac surgery, coronary angioplasty and electrophysiology studies. The hospital is also known for its work in lung cancer diagnosis and treatment, radiation oncology (including tomotherapy), chemotherapy and infusion, GYN oncology, prostate cancer care, and other clinical and support services.

Geographic Reach

The hospital serves more than 440,000

people in 32 towns in Bergen County and surrounding communities.

Strategy
The medical system is looking to improve its facilities and technology in order to keep up with demand. The Valley Hospital is the first and only hospital in northern New Jersey to offer brain and spinal surgery with a state-of-the-art O-armÂ® surgical imaging system, purchased through a $1 million grant from The Bolger Foundation.

In 2012 The Valley Hospital Valley became the first hospital in northern New Jersey to offer the latest breast imaging technology -- 3D breast tomosynthesis.

That year it also enhanced its capacity to perform minimally invasive surgery with the acquisition of the robotic da VinciÂ® Surgical System funded by a $1.6 million donation from The Bolger Foundation.

In 2012 the hospital opened a new Women's and Children's Resource Center to coordinate wide range of services for women and their families.

LOCATIONS
HQ: THE VALLEY HOSPITAL INC
223 N VAN DIEN AVE, RIDGEWOOD, NJ 074502736
Phone: 201 447-8000
Web: WWW.VALLEYHEALTH.COM

PRODUCTS/OPERATIONS
Selected Services
Adoption Screening and Evaluation Program
Ambulatory Infusion Center
Anticoagulation Management Service
Autism Services
Auxiliary
Barrett's Esophagus Center
Bariatric Surgery
Bereavement Services
Biplane
Bladder Cancer Care
Breast Center
Cancer Care
Capsule Endoscopy
Cardiac MRI
Cardiac Rehabilitation
Cardiac Surgery
Cardiology
Center for Childbirth
Kireker Center for Child Development
Center for Metabolic and Weight Loss Surgery
Center for Family Education
Center for Women's Heart Health
Center for Youth Fitness
Clinical Trials, Oncology
Clinical Trials, Cardiology
Colonoscopy
Community Resources
Complementary Medicine
Concussion Management Program
Continence Services
Cosmetic Laser Treatment
Critical Care
Diabetes Support Services
Diagnostic Imaging
Doula Program
Emergency Services
Emergency Services, Pediatric
Employee Recognition
Endoscopic Ultrasound
Epilepsy Monitoring Program, Adult
Epilepsy Center, Pediatric
ERCP
Esophagogastroduodenoscopy (EGD)
Extended Care

COMPETITORS
DOCTORS HOSPITAL OF AUGUSTA, LLC
GOOD SAMARITAN HOSPITAL MEDICAL CENTER
LHH CORPORATION
VALLEY HEALTH SYSTEM, INC.
WOMAN'S HOSPITAL FOUNDATION

HISTORICAL FINANCIALS
Company Type: Private

Income Statement — FYE: December 31

	REVENUE ($mil)	NET INCOME ($mil)	NET PROFIT MARGIN	EMPLOYEES
12/20	739	161	21.8%	2,900
12/19	860	113	13.2%	—
12/18	695	128	18.4%	—
12/17	657	80	12.2%	—
Annual Growth	4.0%	26.2%	—	—

2020 Year-End Financials
Return on assets: 7.7%
Return on equity: 12.3%
Current Ratio: 0.50
Cash ($ mil.): 12

THE VANDERBILT UNIVERSITY

The Vanderbilt University was founded in 1873 with a $1 million grant from industrialist Cornelius Vanderbilt. Since then, the university's endowment has grown to approximately $6.9 billion, making the Nashville school a haven for its more than 12,300 students and nearly 4,360 full-time faculty members. Boasting a 7:1 student-faculty ratio, Vanderbilt offers undergraduate and graduate programs in areas such as education and human development, divinity, engineering, and the arts and sciences. The university operates some 10 schools and colleges. Vanderbilt's Owen Graduate School of Management and its medical school regularly rank near the top in national surveys.

Operations
Top-ranked in both academics and financial aid, Vanderbilt offers residential undergraduate experience, with programs in the liberal arts and sciences, engineering, music, education and human development. The university also is home to nationally and internationally recognize graduate schools of law, education, business, medicine, nursing and divinity, and offers robust graduate-degree programs across a range of disciplines.

Vanderbilt is closely affiliated with the nonprofit Vanderbilt University Medical Center (VUMC), which manages more than 2 million patient visits yearly and collaborates closely with the university through education and research. Its home to an acute care hospital, an adults' and children's hospital, and several clinics, as well as the university's medical school, research facilities, and nursing programs.

Geographic Reach
Its approximately 340.7 acres campus is located a mile and a half southwest of downtown Nashville, Tennessee and it has about 180 buildings. Vanderbilt Dyer Observatory, located about nine miles from campus, also is listed on the National Register of Historic Places.

Strategy
Vanderbilt University aspires to shape the future of higher education and to foster the creation of knowledge that together improves the human condition. Vanderbilt has four foundational principles frame its aspirations as one of the world's great teaching and research universities. Its strategic initiatives include offering students a rich and diverse intellectual community that educates the whole person and cultivates lifelong learning; investing in multi- and inter-disciplinary programs to lead in defining and addressing important problems facing society, while pursuing new and exciting opportunities; building distinctive and distinguished programs that develop and offer effective solutions to pressing health and healthcare problems; and transforming education models through technology and research.

Company Background
During its first 40 years of existence, Vanderbilt was under the auspices of the Methodist Episcopal Church, South. The Vanderbilt Board of Trust severed its ties with the church in 1914 after a dispute with the bishops over who would appoint university trustees.

EXECUTIVES
CDO, Stephanie Oberhausen
Auditors : PRICEWATERHOUSECOOPERS LLP N

LOCATIONS
HQ: THE VANDERBILT UNIVERSITY
2301 VANDERBILT PL, NASHVILLE, TN 372350002
Phone: 615 322-7311
Web: WWW.VANDERBILT.EDU

PRODUCTS/OPERATIONS
Selected Schools and Colleges
Blair School of Music
College of Arts and Science
Divinity School
Graduate School
Law School
Owen Graduate School of Management
Peabody College of Education and Human Development
School of Engineering
School of Medicine
School of Nursing

COMPETITORS
PURDUE UNIVERSITY
RECTOR & VISITORS OF THE UNIVERSITY OF VIRGINIA
REGENTS OF THE UNIVERSITY OF MICHIGAN

THE QUEEN'S UNIVERSITY OF BELFAST
THE RUTGERS STATE UNIVERSITY
UNIVERSITY OF KANSAS
UNIVERSITY OF MISSOURI SYSTEM
UNIVERSITY OF OKLAHOMA
UNIVERSITY OF SOUTHERN CALIFORNIA
UNIVERSITY SYSTEM OF MARYLAND

HISTORICAL FINANCIALS
Company Type: Private

Income Statement   FYE: June 30

	REVENUE ($mil)	NET INCOME ($mil)	NET PROFIT MARGIN	EMPLOYEES
06/17	1,311	374	28.6%	21,000
06/16	1,270	(569)	—	—
06/15	4,121	131	3.2%	—
Annual Growth	(43.6%)	68.9%	—	—

2017 Year-End Financials
Return on assets: 5.5%   Cash ($ mil.): 935
Return on equity: 6.5%
Current Ratio: —

THE WALSH GROUP LTD

Operating through subsidiaries Walsh Construction, Walsh Canada, and Archer Western Contractors, The Walsh Group provides design/build, general contracting, and construction services for industrial, public, and commercial projects. The family-owned company offers complete project management services, from demolition and planning to general contracting and finance. The company is involved in the construction of highways, water treatment facilities, airports, hotels, convention centers, correctional facilities, and commercial, industrial, and residential buildings. Walsh operates out of roughly 20 offices in North America. The company was founded in 1898 by Matthew Myles Walsh.

Operations
Walsh Group offers seamlessly integrated services to plan, finance, build, operate and maintain the full life-cycle of a project including preconstruction, design-build, public-private partnerships, operations & maintenance, logistics, lean construction, sustainability, self-performance and building information modelling (BIM).

Geographic Reach
Walsh Group operates in about 20 regional offices across the US and Canada, each strategically located to support maximum quality and responsiveness to a growing customer base. Walsh Construction, Archer Western, and Walsh Canada headquarters are located in Chicago, Illinois; Atlanta, Georgia; and in Toronto, Ontario, respectively.

Sales and Marketing
Walsh Group mostly works on projects in the commercial building, transportation, aviation, water, industrial, and power sectors. These include wastewater and water treatment plants, rapid transit, highway and bridgework, educational facilities, warehouse/distribution facilities, athletic facilities, correctional facilities, and offices.

Financial Performance
One of America's largest private companies, Walsh Group reported its annual revenue grew 12% to $4.6 billion during 2014, up from $4.1 billion in 2013. Its annual revenues are up nearly 30% since 2007, and have more than doubled since 2004, when they were at $1.95 billion.

Company Background
The company was founded in the year 1898 by Matthew Myles Walsh. In 2012 Walsh Group acquired California-based R&L Brosamer, which specializes in heavy highway and other transportation projects. R&L Brosamer often works on projects for Bay Area Rapid Transit, California Department of Transportation, and Los Angeles World Airports. The deal helped Walsh strengthen its presence in California and bordering states, including Nevada and Arizona.

In 2011 Walsh was awarded its first overseas embassy project, a $200 million contract to build the New American Embassy at Oslo, Norway.

Auditors: WOLF & COMPANY LLP OAKBROOK T

LOCATIONS
HQ: THE WALSH GROUP LTD
929 W ADAMS ST, CHICAGO, IL 606073021
Phone: 312 563-5400
Web: WWW.WALSHGROUP.COM

PRODUCTS/OPERATIONS
Projects
Airports
Athletic facilities
Bridges
Conference centers
Correctional facilities
Data centers
Educational facilities
Entertainment
Government
Health care
High rise residential
Highways and bridges
Hotels
Interiors
Laboratories
Parking garages
Renovations
Retail centers
Senior housing
Treatment plants
Warehouse and distribution

COMPETITORS
ALBERICI CORPORATION
BRASFIELD & GORRIE, L.L.C.
GILBANE BUILDING COMPANY
GILBANE, INC.
HENSEL PHELPS CONSTRUCTION CO.
MCCARTHY BUILDING COMPANIES, INC.
SWINERTON INCORPORATED
THE PIKE COMPANY INC
TUTOR PERINI CORPORATION
WALBRIDGE ALDINGER LLC

HISTORICAL FINANCIALS
Company Type: Private

Income Statement   FYE: December 31

	REVENUE ($mil)	NET INCOME ($mil)	NET PROFIT MARGIN	EMPLOYEES
12/10	3,462	186	5.4%	5,000
12/09	3,316	191	5.8%	—
12/08	3,534	203	5.8%	—
Annual Growth	(1.0%)	(4.4%)	—	—

2010 Year-End Financials
Return on assets: 11.9%   Cash ($ mil.): 656
Return on equity: 27.9%
Current Ratio: 1.80

THE WASHINGTON UNIVERSITY

Washington University is a national hub for important research and business development, especially in the fields of biotechnology and plant science. Founded in 1853 by William Green leaf Eliot Jr., the independent university offers 300+ academic programs such as accounting, biology, chemistry, dance, economics, french and more. It has about 3,645 faculty members. The university has 14,500 full time students and students and faculty are from more than 100 countries. More than 6,000 graduate and professional students study at the university. The affiliated Washington University Medical Center is an acute-care hospital that also provides educational training and research services.

EXECUTIVES
Interim CIO*, Stephanie Reel
CCO*, Dedric Carter
Auditors: PRICEWATERHOUSECOOPERS LLP ST

LOCATIONS
HQ: THE WASHINGTON UNIVERSITY
1 BROOKINGS DR, SAINT LOUIS, MO 631304899
Phone: 314 935-5000
Web: WWW.WUSTL.EDU

PRODUCTS/OPERATIONS
2015 Sales

	$ mil	% of total
Patient service	985.4	36
Grants	368.5	14
Tuition & fees	356.2	13
Endowment spending distribution	266.2	10
Gifts	186.3	7
Educational	162.0	6
Others	382.7	14
Total	2,707.4	100

Selected Schools and Colleges
College of Arts & Sciences
    Graduate School of Arts & Sciences
    University College and Summer School (Arts & Sciences)

George Warren Brown School of Social Work
Sam Fox School of Design & Visual Arts
School of Engineering & Applied Science
School of Law
School of Medicine
Olin Business School

COMPETITORS

ARIZONA STATE UNIVERSITY
BOISE STATE UNIVERSITY
CASE WESTERN RESERVE UNIVERSITY
CLARK ATLANTA UNIVERSITY INC
NEWCASTLE UNIVERSITY
SOUTH DAKOTA STATE UNIVERSITY
THE MEDICAL UNIVERSITY OF SOUTH CAROLINA
UNIVERSITY OF KENTUCKY
UNIVERSITY OF OREGON
WRIGHT STATE UNIVERSITY

HISTORICAL FINANCIALS
Company Type: Private

Income Statement — FYE: June 30

	REVENUE ($mil)	NET INCOME ($mil)	NET PROFIT MARGIN	EMPLOYEES
06/22	4,435	(1,705)	—	9,600
06/21	3,837	5,981	155.9%	—
06/20	3,749	719	19.2%	—
06/19	3,544	554	15.7%	—
Annual Growth	7.8%	—	—	—

2022 Year-End Financials
Return on assets: (-999.9%)   Cash ($ mil.): —
Return on equity: (-999.9%)
Current Ratio: —

THE WHITING-TURNER CONTRACTING COMPANY

The Whiting-Turner Contracting provides construction management, general contracting, and design/build, and integrated services, primarily for large commercial, institutional, and infrastructure projects conducted across the US. A key player in retail construction, the employee-owned company also undertakes such projects as biotech cleanrooms, theme parks, historical restorations, senior living residences, educational facilities, stadiums, and corporate headquarters. Its clients include the US Marine, FedEx Ground, IBM, Costco, Las Vegas City Hall, Yale University, Stanford University, and NASA Langley Research Center Headquarters Building, among others. Operates from more than 50 locations across the US, Whiting-Turner Contracting was founded by G.W.C. Whiting and LeBaron Turner in 1909.

Operations

Whiting-Turner provides construction supplies and services that include masonry, metals, wood and plastics, thermal and moisture protection, doors and windows, finishes, specialties, equipment, furnishings, special construction, conveying systems, mechanical, and electric products. Other supplies and services include office equipment, office supplies, office furniture, office signage, cleaning, catering delivery, and flowers.

Geographic Reach

The Baltimore-based company has over 50 offices in Arizona, California, Delaware, Florida, Georgia, Maryland, New York, Ohio, Pennsylvania, Texas, and Virginia, among others.

Sales and Marketing

The company works on projects across a wide range of industries related to arts and entertainment, education, federal and military, healthcare, industrial, office, retail, multi-family residential, sports and fitness, transportation, and utilities, among other fields.

Company Background

G.W.C. Whiting and LeBaron Turner, classmates at MIT, founded the company in 1909 to build sewer lines.

LOCATIONS

HQ: THE WHITING-TURNER CONTRACTING COMPANY
  300 E JOPPA RD STE 800, BALTIMORE, MD 212863047
Phone: 410 821-1100
Web: WWW.WHITING-TURNER.COM

Selected Locations
Maryland - Baltimore (Headquarters)
California - Irvine
California - Los Angeles
California - Pleasanton
California - Sacramento
California - San Diego
Colorado - Denver
Connecticut - New Haven
Delaware - Newark
District of Columbia
Florida - Ft. Lauderdale
Florida - Orlando
Florida - Tampa
Georgia - Atlanta
Maryland - Cambridge
Massachusetts - Boston
Missouri - Kansas City
Nevada - Las Vegas
New Jersey - Bridgewater
New York - White Plains
North Carolina - Charlotte
North Carolina - Raleigh
Ohio - Cleveland
Pennsylvania - Allentown
Texas - Dallas
Texas - Houston
Texas - San Antonio
Virginia - Chantilly
Virginia - Norfolk
Virginia - Richmond

PRODUCTS/OPERATIONS

Selected Services
Construction management
  Agency
  At-risk
Design/build
General contracting
Preconstruction

Selected Markets
Biotechnology and pharmaceutical
Cleanroom and high-technology
Education
Entertainment
Federal/military
Food/beverage distribution
Health care
Historical restoration
Industrial and manufacturing
Interiors
Life sciences
Lodging and hospitality
Mission critical facilities
Mixed use
Offices and headquarters
Parking garages
Restaurants
Retail
Senior living
Sports
Sustainable
Technology
  Microelectronics
  Nano
Theme parks
Utilities
Warehouse and distribution

COMPETITORS

ADOLFSON & PETERSON, INC.
DAVID E. HARVEY BUILDERS, INC.
DPR CONSTRUCTION, INC.
HUNT CONSTRUCTION GROUP, INC.
JAYNES CORPORATION
LAYTON CONSTRUCTION COMPANY, LLC
MANHATTAN CONSTRUCTION COMPANY
MESSER CONSTRUCTION CO.
PERERA CONSTRUCTION & DESIGN INC.
RIVER CITY CONSTRUCTION, L.L.C.

HISTORICAL FINANCIALS
Company Type: Private

Income Statement — FYE: December 31

	REVENUE ($mil)	NET INCOME ($mil)	NET PROFIT MARGIN	EMPLOYEES
12/16	5,522	90	1.6%	4,560
12/15	5,729	80	1.4%	—
12/14	6,347	75	1.2%	—
Annual Growth	(6.7%)	9.8%	—	—

2016 Year-End Financials
Return on assets: 3.6%   Cash ($ mil.): 26
Return on equity: 11.4%
Current Ratio: 1.40

THEDACARE, INC.

ThedaCare is one of the leading nonprofit providers in northeast and central Wisconsin. It consists of seven hospitals, including Appleton Medical Center, Theda Clark Medical Center, New London Family Medical Center, Shawano Medical Center, and ThedaCare Medical Center in Waupaca; three dozen physician clinics; and community health and wellness programs. The hospitals provide pain management, neurology and stroke, behavioral health, orthopedics and cardiovascular services. ThedaCare also operates long-term care and assisted living facilities and provides occupational health and emergency transport services.

Operations
The health system operates seven hospitals and some three dozen physician locations.

Its offers ThedaCare's Heritage, Peabody Manor and Juliette Manor Communities ? choose from independent living, assisted living, or skilled care units, all on the same campus. It manages 24-hour emergency response system and on-site nursing staff.

Its clinical services include primary care, cancer and blood disorders, cardiovascular, orthopedics, and more; as well as support services such as senior living, diabetic support, and home medical equipment, among others.

Geographic Reach
Neenah, Wisconsin-based, ThedaCare serves in seven hospitals and nearly three dozen clinics, care centers and health services located in Berlin, Fox Cities, New London, Shawano, Waupaca, and Wild Rose.

Auditors : CLIFTONLARSONALLEN LLP MINNEA

LOCATIONS
HQ: THEDACARE, INC.
3 NEENAH CTR, NEENAH, WI 549563070
Phone: 920 454-4156
Web: WWW.THEDACARE.ORG

PRODUCTS/OPERATIONS
Selected Facilities and Programs
Appleton Medical Center
The Heritage Community (senior living)
ThedaCare Medical Center-New London
Peabody Manor (senior living)
Riverside Medical Center
Shawano Medical Center
Theda Clark Medical Center
ThedaCare at Home
ThedaCare at Work (occupational health services)
ThedaCare Behavioral Health
ThedaCare Physicians

COMPETITORS
ATLANTIC HEALTH SYSTEM INC.
ATLANTICARE HEALTH SYSTEM INC.
BORGESS HEALTH ALLIANCE, INC.
FLAGSTAFF MEDICAL CENTER, INC.
HACKENSACK MERIDIAN HEALTH, INC.
HCA-HEALTHONE LLC
JFK HEALTH SYSTEM, INC.
MEDSTAR HEALTH, INC.
SILVER CROSS HOSPITAL AND MEDICAL CENTERS
UNIVERSITY HEALTH SYSTEMS OF EASTERN CAROLINA, INC.

HISTORICAL FINANCIALS
Company Type: Private

Income Statement — FYE: December 31

	REVENUE ($mil)	NET INCOME ($mil)	NET PROFIT MARGIN	EMPLOYEES
12/20	1,031	110	10.7%	7,000
12/19	1,057	126	12.0%	—
12/18	995	(1)	—	—
12/17	909	88	9.7%	—
Annual Growth	4.3%	7.8%	—	—

2020 Year-End Financials
Return on assets: 6.9%
Return on equity: 10.2%
Current Ratio: 6.60
Cash ($ mil.): 76

THOMAS JEFFERSON UNIVERSITY

Thomas Jefferson University, founded in 1824 as the Jefferson Medical College, is today a national doctoral research university and a pioneer in transdisciplinary, professional education. Home of the Sidney Kimmel Medical College and the Kanbar College of Design, Engineering and Commerce, Jefferson is a preeminent academic institution delivering high-impact education in over 200 undergraduate and graduate programs to 8,400 students across ten colleges. The university's academic offerings now include architecture, business, design, engineering, fashion, health, medicine, science, social science and textiles. Student-athletes compete as the Jefferson Rams in the NCAA Division II Central Atlantic Collegiate Conference.

Operations
TJU conducts research and offers undergraduate and graduate instruction through the Sidney Kimmel Medical College, the Jefferson College of Nursing, the Jefferson College of Pharmacy, the Jefferson College of Health Professions, the Jefferson College of Population Health, the Jefferson College of Biomedical Sciences, the Jefferson College of Rehabilitation Sciences, the Kanbar College of Design, Engineering and Commerce, the School of Continuing and Professional Studies, the College of Architecture and the Built Environment, and the College of Science, Health and the Liberal Arts.

TJUH System, Abington Health, Aria Health System, Kennedy Health System and Magee Rehabilitation Hospital are integrated healthcare organizations that provide inpatient, outpatient and emergency care services through acute care, ambulatory care, rehabilitation care, physician and other primary care services for residents of the Greater Philadelphia Region. Jefferson Health includes 18 hospitals, 3,876 licensed beds, 3,500 physicians and practitioners and 9,600 nurses. It has more than 50 outpatient and urgent care locations and about 6.2 million outpatients each year.

Overall, net patient services account for about 80% of revenue, while grants and contracts, tuition and fees, investment income and other revenue account for the remaining some 20% of revenue.

Geographic Reach
TJU is located in Philadelphia, Pennsylvania, with additional campus locations in the Greater Philadelphia Region and Atlantic City, New Jersey.

Financial Performance
The company had a revenue of $5.7 billion in 2021, a 7% increase from the previous year's revenue of $5.3 billion.

The company's cash at the end of 2021 was $301.5 million. Operating activities generated $238.3 million, while investing activities used $561.2 million, mainly for purchases of investments. Financing activities used another $176.7 million, primarily for repayment of long-term obligations.

Company Background
Thomas Jefferson University was founded in 1824 as Jefferson Medical College. In 1877, Thomas Jefferson University Hospital was established and Jefferson Medical College became the second medical school in the country with a separate teaching hospital. In 1891 the school established the Jefferson Hospital Training College for Nurses, and in 1967 the College of Allied Health Sciences.

Thomas Jefferson University was officially established in 1969. In 1991, the NCI-designated Sidney Kimmel Cancer Center was established, and in 2006 the university had renamed and added the Schools of Nursing and Health Professions. Two years later, the Schools of Pharmacy and Population Health were formed. In 2014, the Sidney Kimmel Foundation bestowed a $110 million gift to Jefferson ? the largest gift in its history ? and Jefferson Medical College became Sidney Kimmel Medical College at Thomas Jefferson University.

In 2015 Thomas Jefferson University merged with Abington Health, a Philadelphia health care organization with two hospitals and several clinics. The merger gave Abington access to the university's educational and training facilities and expands the university's reach to the Philadelphia suburbs. In 2016 the organization's medical operations combined forces with Aria Health, which now operates as Aria -- Jefferson Health.

Jefferson and Philadelphia University merged in 2017 and kept the Thomas Jefferson name. (Philadelphia University was founded in 1884 as the Philadelphia Textile School.)

EXECUTIVES
CIO*, Alfred Salvato
Auditors : PRICEWATERHOUSECOOPERS LLP PH

LOCATIONS
HQ: THOMAS JEFFERSON UNIVERSITY
1020 WALNUT ST STE 1, PHILADELPHIA, PA 191075567
Phone: 215 955-6000
Web: WWW.JEFFERSON.EDU

PRODUCTS/OPERATIONS
Selected Research Centers and Institutes
Center for Translational Medicine
Daniel Baugh Institute
Delaware Health Science Alliance
Farber Institute for Neuroscience

Jefferson Coordinating Center for Clinical Research
Jefferson Vaccine Center
Kimmel Cancer Center

Selected Colleges and Schools
Sidney Kimmel Medical College
Jefferson Graduate School of Biomedical Sciences
Jefferson School of Health Professions
Jefferson School of Nursing
Jefferson School of Pharmacy
Jefferson School of Population Health

COMPETITORS

AUGUSTA UNIVERSITY
BAYLOR COLLEGE OF MEDICINE
GEORGETOWN UNIVERSITY (THE)
HAMPTON UNIVERSITY
LOYOLA UNIVERSITY OF CHICAGO
SAINT FRANCIS UNIVERSITY
THE UNIVERSITY OF IOWA
THE UNIVERSITY OF TOLEDO
UNIVERSITY OF SOUTHERN CALIFORNIA
VIRGINIA COMMONWEALTH UNIVERSITY

HISTORICAL FINANCIALS
Company Type: Private

Income Statement — FYE: June 30

	REVENUE ($mil)	NET INCOME ($mil)	NET PROFIT MARGIN	EMPLOYEES
06/17	3,951	700	17.7%	10,625
06/16	136	8	6.5%	—
Annual Growth	2788.6%	7723.4%	—	—

2017 Year-End Financials
Return on assets: 12.0%   Cash ($ mil.): 259
Return on equity: 23.1%
Current Ratio: 3.20

THOMAS JEFFERSON UNIVERSITY HOSPITALS, INC.

Named after the "Man of the People," Thomas Jefferson University Hospitals (dba Jefferson Health) serves the people of the Keystone State with a medical staff of more than 1,200 and some 1,550 beds. The system provides acute, tertiary, and specialty medical care from a dozen hospitals, nearly 20 outpatient centers, and about 10 urgent care centers. The hospital also administers cardiac care at the Jefferson Heart Institute, which provides everything from minimally invasive surgical procedures to heart transplants. Additionally, Jefferson Health operates as the teaching hospital for Thomas Jefferson University.

Operations
As part of its operations, Jefferson Health offers several premier programs to its patients as well as 35 different specialties. The system performed Delaware Valley's first liver transplant and designated a kidney transplant center for live and deceased donor transplants. In addition to transplantation, it provides surgical services, heart and vascular, digestive diseases, and bones and joints, in addition to its Kimmel Cancer Canter and Jefferson Hospital for Neuroscience. In 2014 the health system logged more than 470,000 outpatient visits, 45,000 admissions, and about 115,000 emergency room visits.

Geographic Reach
Through a handful of locations, Jefferson Health provides health care services to the residents of Philadelphia and the Delaware Valley. It shares a 13-acre campus with Thomas Jefferson University.

Strategy
In October 2017, Jefferson Health merged with New Jersey-based Kennedy Health, which operated three hospitals. The transaction followed closely on the heels of Jefferson's mergers with Aria Health and Abington Health.

In 2015, Jefferson Health added a new feature to its telemedicine program, JeffConnect, called On-Demand Virtual Care, which allows patients to connect with an emergency medicine physician via computers and mobile devices.

That year the Philadelphia 76ers partnered with the Rothman Institute and Jefferson Health. The Rothman Institute will provide the Official Orthopedics & Urgent Care of the Philadelphia 76ers, as well as the Official Team Physicians; Jefferson Health became an official hospital of the Philadelphia 76ers.

In 2014 the system opened the Jefferson Angioplasty Center, the outpatient practice for Jefferson's interventional cardiologists. It is co-located with the Vascular Center allowing for streamlined consultations and convenience, as the two specialties often see the same patients.

That year it also introduced genomic analyses of breast cancer in-house using the Prosigna Breast Cancer Prognostic Gene Signature Assay, significantly reducing turn-around time for test results and allowing patients to begin effective treatment sooner.

Company Background
Thomas Jefferson University Hospital was founded in 1825.

LOCATIONS
HQ: THOMAS JEFFERSON UNIVERSITY HOSPITALS, INC.
111 S 11TH ST, PHILADELPHIA, PA 191074824
Phone: 215 955-6000
Web: WWW.JEFFERSONHEALTH.ORG

PRODUCTS/OPERATIONS
Selected Services
Cancer
Diabetes & Endocrinology
Ear, Nose & Throat
Gastroenterology
Geriatrics
Gynecology
Nephrology
Orthopedics
Pulmonology
Rehabilitation
Urology

Selected University Locations
Jefferson at the Navy Yard
Jefferson Medical College
Jefferson College of Graduate Studies
Jefferson Radiology
Jefferson School of Health Professions
Jefferson School of Nursing
Jefferson School of Pharmacy
Jefferson School of Population Health
Jefferson Voorhees

COMPETITORS

BAYLOR UNIVERSITY MEDICAL CENTER
CAPITAL HEALTH SYSTEM, INC.
KENNEDY HEALTH SYSTEM, INC.
MERCY HOSPITAL AND MEDICAL CENTER
MERCY HOSPITAL SOUTH
SAINT JOSEPH HOSPITAL, INC
ST. ANTHONY'S HOSPITAL, INC.
TEXAS HEALTH PRESBYTERIAN HOSPITAL DALLAS
THE CHRIST HOSPITAL
WASHINGTON HOSPITAL CENTER CORPORATION

HISTORICAL FINANCIALS
Company Type: Private

Income Statement — FYE: June 30

	REVENUE ($mil)	NET INCOME ($mil)	NET PROFIT MARGIN	EMPLOYEES
06/16	1,495	76	5.1%	4,701
06/15	1,456	42	2.9%	—
06/14	1,510	51	3.4%	—
06/10	1,250	49	4.0%	—
Annual Growth	3.0%	7.7%	—	—

2016 Year-End Financials
Return on assets: 4.4%   Cash ($ mil.): 57
Return on equity: 8.7%
Current Ratio: 3.20

THOMPSON CREEK METALS COMPANY USA

Thompson Creek Metals has branched out from only mining molybdenum at its Thompson Creek site in Idaho to holding a diversified North American portfolio that also includes copper, gold, and silver assets. The company still obtains most of its sales (97%) from producing molybdenum, a metal used to strengthen steel and make it corrosion-resistant. It operates the Thompson Creek mine and mill in Idaho and owns 75% of the Endako mine in British Columbia (Japan's Sojitz owns 25%). Thompson Creek has a metallurgical facility in Pennsylvania and holds exploration assets in British Columbia and in the Yukon and Nunavut territories. It controls about 449 million pounds of molybdenum proved and probable reserves.

Operations
The company splits its activities into three main segments: US Operations

Molybdenum, Canadian Operations Molybdenum, and Copper-Gold (Development). Its US Operations segment includes mining, milling, roasting, and sale of molybdenum products from the Thompson Creek Mine and Langeloth facility. The Canadian Operations includes these activities from its 75%-owned Endako mine. Its Copper-Gold segment includes development expenditures from the Mt. Milligan project.

Geographic Reach

Although Thompson Creek operates primarily in North America, it sells to customers worldwide.

Financial Performance

In 2011 the company generated sales of $669.1 million, up about 13% from the previous year due to higher sales volumes and higher average molybdenum prices. These higher volumes and prices were offset by the company's higher operating expenses for its waste stripping activities at the Thompson Creek mine in the latter half of 2011.

However, on the strength of its sales, the company posted a net income for 2011 of $292.1 million, a jump of nearly 157% from the previous year.

Except for spike in 2008 revenues, Thompson Creek reported a downward trend in revenues from 2007 to 2010 primarily due to weak prices and lower production, but gained momentum in 2011. The spike in 2008 is attributable to the sales volumes in 2008 which were higher than 2007 primarily due to increased production levels.

Strategy

The company ranked as the fifth-largest producer of molybdenum in the Western world in 2011. Its flagship project, the open-pit molybdenum mine at the Thompson Creek property in Idaho, is its principal producing property (75% of molybdenum production). The company has produced more than 25 million pounds of molybdenum at its Thompson Creek mine annually since 1983.

Its majority-controlled Endako molybdenum mine in British Columbia is also a producing property. The company expanded its Endako property, starting up a new mill in 2012. It expects production at the Endako Mine to be as much as 16 million pounds of molybdenum per year.

Thompson Creek also is developing the Mt. Milligan project, an open-pit mine and copper flotation processing plant in British Columbia. The project has an estimated annual production of 81 million pounds of copper and 194,000 ounces of gold over the life of the mine. Commercial production is slated to commence in late 2013.

An underground copper, molybdenum, and silver exploration project is underway at the Berg property in British Columbia. The company also has two joint venture exploration projects, the Howard's Pass lead and zinc project (Yukon) and the Maze Lake gold project (Nunavut).

HISTORY

Things began looking up in 2010 after Thompson Creek acquired exploration company Terrane Metals in a deal worth $625 million. The move diversified Thompson Creek's commodity exposure to copper and gold through Terrane's flagship Mt. Milligan project in central British Columbia, while giving it further growth prospects through Terrane's Berg project, a copper-molybdenum-silver project, also in BC. By the end of 2010, the company's proved and probable reserves for it Mt. Milligan project totaled 2.1 billion pounds of contained copper and 6 million ounces of contained gold.

Auditors : KPMG LLP DENVER COLORADO

LOCATIONS

HQ: THOMPSON CREEK METALS COMPANY USA
26 W DRY CREEK CIR # 225, LITTLETON, CO 801208064
Phone: 303 761-8801

COMPETITORS

ASARCO LLC
FREEPORT-MCMORAN INC.
First Quantum Minerals Ltd
Inmet Mining Corporation
Teck Resources Limited

HISTORICAL FINANCIALS

Company Type: Private

Income Statement				FYE: December 31
	REVENUE ($mil)	NET INCOME ($mil)	NET PROFIT MARGIN	EMPLOYEES
12/14	806	(124)	—	1,700
12/13	434	(215)	—	—
12/12	401	(546)	—	—
Annual Growth	41.8%	—	—	—

2014 Year-End Financials
Return on assets: (-4.4%)   Cash ($ mil.): 265
Return on equity: (-14.0%)
Current Ratio: 2.50

THRUWAY AUTHORITY OF NEW YORK STATE

Leaving Manhattan or Brooklyn to shuffle off to Buffalo? The New York State Thruway Authority oversees a 641-mile toll road system and a 524-mile canal system. The authority's toll road system, known as the Governor Thomas E. Dewey Thruway, is the largest in the US. It crosses the state from New York City to Buffalo, and more than 80% of the population of New York State lives along the corridor formed by the Thruway's 426-mile main line. Other arms of the Thruway connect with toll roads and other highways in neighboring states. TheÂ New York State Canal Corporation oversees the state's canal system of five lakes andÂ four canals,Â which connect bodies of water such as the Hudson River withÂ Lake Champlain.

Auditors : TOSKI & CO CPAS PC WILLI

LOCATIONS

HQ: THRUWAY AUTHORITY OF NEW YORK STATE
200 SOUTHERN BLVD, ALBANY, NY 122092018
Phone: 518 436-2700
Web: THRUWAY.NY.GOV

COMPETITORS

Aleatica, S.A.B. de C.V.
OHIO TURNPIKE AND INFRASTRUCTURE COMMISSION
TRANSURBAN HOLDINGS LIMITED
WEST NIPPON EXPRESSWAY COMPANY LIMITED
YUEXIU TRANSPORT INFRASTRUCTURE LIMITED

HISTORICAL FINANCIALS

Company Type: Private

Income Statement				FYE: December 31
	REVENUE ($mil)	NET INCOME ($mil)	NET PROFIT MARGIN	EMPLOYEES
12/10	674	(127)	—	2,840
12/09	640	(129)	—	—
12/08	598	(129)	—	—
Annual Growth	6.1%	—	—	—

2010 Year-End Financials
Return on assets: (-2.3%)   Cash ($ mil.): 203
Return on equity: (-6.1%)
Current Ratio: 0.80

TMH PHYSICIAN ORGANIZATION

LOCATIONS

HQ: TMH PHYSICIAN ORGANIZATION
6565 FANNIN ST STE D200, HOUSTON, TX 770302703
Phone: 713 441-4182

HISTORICAL FINANCIALS

Company Type: Private

Income Statement				FYE: December 31
	REVENUE ($mil)	NET INCOME ($mil)	NET PROFIT MARGIN	EMPLOYEES
12/19	693	6	0.9%	51
12/18	600	0	0.1%	—
12/17	532	(0)	—	—
12/15	413	0	0.2%	—
Annual Growth	13.8%	71.2%	—	—

2019 Year-End Financials
Return on assets: 6.7%   Cash ($ mil.): 1
Return on equity: —
Current Ratio: 0.50

TMV CORP.

EXECUTIVES

Senior Vice President Business Development*,
Martin E Titus

LOCATIONS

HQ: TMV CORP.
14302 FNB PKWY, OMAHA, NE 681545212
Phone: 402 691-9500

HISTORICAL FINANCIALS

Company Type: Private

Income Statement — FYE: December 31

	REVENUE ($mil)	NET INCOME ($mil)	NET PROFIT MARGIN	EMPLOYEES
12/07	10,309	0	0.0%	91
12/05	9,470	0	0.0%	—
12/04	0	0	—	—
12/03	4,940	0	0.0%	—
Annual Growth	20.2%	—	—	—

TOLEDO PROMEDICA HOSPITAL

One of the region's largest acute-care facilities, The Toledo Hospital provides medical care to the residents of northwestern Ohio and southeastern Michigan. Boasting nearly 800 beds, the facility offers several specialties and services, including the Jobst Vascular Center, which provides cardiac and vascular services in conjunction with The University of Michigan. The Toledo Hospital, which shares a medical complex with the Toledo Children's Hospital, also operates trauma, emergency, outpatient, arthritis, sleep disorder, and women's health centers. The Toledo Hospital is a member of Toledo-based ProMedica Health System, a mission-based, not-for-profit healthcare organization formed in 1986.

Operations

The health care facility has expanded its footprint in Toledo in recent years. Besides its primary hospital, it operates a stroke unit, the Jobst Vascular Center, a medical complex with the Toledo Children's Hospital, and centers devoted to trauma, emergencies, arthritis, sleep disorders, and women's health. The Toledo Hospital and the Toledo Children's Hospital operate the Renaissance, a 10-story medical complex that has enabled the pair to expand capacity with private rooms, intensive and intermediate care units, and pediatric hematology and oncology services.

Geographic Reach

The Toledo Hospital serves the residents of a 27-county area consisting of northwest Ohio and southeast Michigan.

Strategy

To address the needs of area residents, The Toledo Hospital in late 2012 rolled out a program that makes a cardiologist available 24 hours a day, seven days a week. It's the only hospital in the region to provide this service. In early 2012 the hospital opened a 20-bed stroke unit and a new 15-bed neuro intensive care unit on a newly developed floor of its Renaissance tower.

LOCATIONS

HQ: TOLEDO PROMEDICA HOSPITAL
2142 N COVE BLVD, TOLEDO, OH 436063895
Phone: 419 291-4000
Web: WWW.PROMEDICA.ORG

PRODUCTS/OPERATIONS

Selected Services
Arthritis and Osteoporosis Center
Bariatric Surgery
Behavioral Health and Psychiatric Services
Breast Care Center
Cancer Care
Critical Care
Diabetes
Dialysis
Emergency Services
Endoscopy Services
Fertility Services
Heart Care
Hemophilia Outpatient Clinic
Hyperbaric Medicine
Laboratory Services
Lactation Services
Maternal - Fetal Medicine
Mom & Me Boutique
Neurology
Neurophysiology
OccuHealth
Orthopaedics
Outpatient Surgery
Palliative Care
Radiology / Imaging Services
Rehabilitation Services
Respiratory Care
Sleep Medicine
Surgical Services
Trauma Services
Urology / Nephrology
Vascular Services
Women's Services

COMPETITORS

BILLINGS CLINIC
CATHOLIC HEALTH SYSTEM OF LONG ISLAND, INC.
MONMOUTH MEDICAL CENTER INC.
NOVANT MEDICAL GROUP, INC.
WENATCHEE VALLEY MEDICAL GROUP, P.S.

HISTORICAL FINANCIALS

Company Type: Private

Income Statement — FYE: December 31

	REVENUE ($mil)	NET INCOME ($mil)	NET PROFIT MARGIN	EMPLOYEES
12/17	854	(115)	—	5,586
12/14	745	20	2.8%	—
12/09	635	19	3.0%	—
12/08	548	33	6.1%	—
Annual Growth	5.0%	—	—	—

2017 Year-End Financials
Return on assets: (-8.1%)   Cash ($ mil.): 83
Return on equity: (-35.3%)
Current Ratio: 0.30

TOM LANGE COMPANY, INC.

Tom Lange Company wants you to eat your veggies. One of the largest purchasers and distributors of fresh fruits and vegetables in the US, Tom Lange supplies its comestibles to clients in the retail, wholesale, and food service trades. The company also provides third party logistics services specializing in truckload freight movement. The company was founded in 1960 as a three-man operation in St. Louis, Missouri, Tom Lange has grown to encompass 35 offices in the US and Canada. Produce subsidiaries include Seven Seas, M&M Marketing, and Seven Seas Fruit.

Auditors: KERBER ECK & BRAECKEL LLP SP

LOCATIONS

HQ: TOM LANGE COMPANY, INC.
500 N BROADWAY STE 1320, SAINT LOUIS, MO 631022100
Phone: 314 934-2800
Web: WWW.TOMLANGE.COM

COMPETITORS

Dominion Citrus Income Fund
FRESHPOINT, INC.
GIUMARRA BROS. FRUIT CO., INC.
VAL-PRO, INC.
VESTEY FOODS LIMITED

HISTORICAL FINANCIALS

Company Type: Private

Income Statement — FYE: August 31

	REVENUE ($mil)	NET INCOME ($mil)	NET PROFIT MARGIN	EMPLOYEES
08/21	609	11	1.9%	160
08/20	578	6	1.1%	—
08/19	0	(0)	—	—
Annual Growth	20079.1%	—	—	—

2021 Year-End Financials
Return on assets: 11.1%   Cash ($ mil.): 20
Return on equity: 21.0%
Current Ratio: 1.80

TORAY TCAC HOLDING USA INC.

LOCATIONS

HQ: TORAY TCAC HOLDING USA INC.
365 S HOLLAND DR, PENDERGRASS, GA 305674625

Phone: 706 693-2226
Web: WWW.TENCATEGEO.US

HISTORICAL FINANCIALS
Company Type: Private

Income Statement   FYE: December 31

	REVENUE ($mil)	NET INCOME ($mil)	NET PROFIT MARGIN	EMPLOYEES
12/13	613	0	0.0%	1,500
12/12	626	0	0.0%	—
12/11	178	0	0.0%	—
Annual Growth	85.2%	—	—	—

2013 Year-End Financials
Return on assets: —   Cash ($ mil.): 8
Return on equity: —
Current Ratio: 3.00

TORRANCE HEALTH ASSOCIATION, INC.

Auditors: ERNST & YOUNG LLP LOS ANGELE

LOCATIONS

HQ: TORRANCE HEALTH ASSOCIATION, INC.
3330 LOMITA BLVD, TORRANCE, CA 905055002
Phone: 310 325-9110
Web: WWW.TORRANCEMEMORIALIPA.ORG

HISTORICAL FINANCIALS
Company Type: Private

Income Statement   FYE: June 30

	REVENUE ($mil)	NET INCOME ($mil)	NET PROFIT MARGIN	EMPLOYEES
06/21	913	132	14.6%	3,500
06/20	187	(22)	—	—
06/19	186	(3)	—	—
06/18	76	(4)	—	—
Annual Growth	129.1%	—	—	—

2021 Year-End Financials
Return on assets: 9.1%   Cash ($ mil.): 32
Return on equity: 19.7%
Current Ratio: 1.70

TORRANCE MEMORIAL MEDICAL CENTER

Back in 1925 Jared Sydney Torrance founded Torrance Memorial Medical Center in the southern California town that also bears his name. The not-for-profit medical center now includes approximately 610 beds, surgical suites, clinical and diagnostic labs, and specialist centers for cancer, metabolic, heart, and other conditions. It is one of three burn centers in Los Angeles. Torrance Memorial Medical Center reaches beyond its walls and into the community with hospice care and home health care. The hospital also provides nursing residency programs, and it offers staffing support services to physicians offices in the area.

Auditors: ERNST & YOUNG LLP LOS ANGELES

LOCATIONS

HQ: TORRANCE MEMORIAL MEDICAL CENTER
3330 LOMITA BLVD, TORRANCE, CA 905055002
Phone: 310 325-9110
Web: WWW.TORRANCEMEMORIAL.ORG

PRODUCTS/OPERATIONS

Selected Centers and Services
Bariatric Surgery Program
Blood Donor Center
Breast Diagnostic Center
Burn Center
Cancer Institute
Cardiovascular Institute
Chemical Dependency
Diabetes
Eating Disorders Program
Emergency Care
Endoscopy Center and GI Lab
Home Health
Hospice
Laboratory Testing (includes Outpatient Lab)
Maternal Child Health Services
Nuclear Medicine
Orthopedics
Palliative Care
Pediatrics
Pharmacy
Radiation Oncology
Radiology
Rehabilitation
Sleep Disorders Center
Stroke Center
Surgical Services
Transitional Care Unit
Urgent Care
Wound Center

COMPETITORS

ASCENSION PROVIDENCE HOSPITAL
BAPTIST MEMORIAL HEALTH CARE SYSTEM, INC.
CATHOLIC MEDICAL CENTER
EISENHOWER MEDICAL CENTER
HOSPITAL SERVICE DISTRICT 1
MEMORIAL HEALTH SERVICES
PHELPS MEMORIAL HOSPITAL ASSOCIATION
SHELBY COUNTY HEALTH CARE CORPORATION
UPPER CHESAPEAKE HEALTH FOUNDATION, INC.
WHITE MEMORIAL MEDICAL CENTER

HISTORICAL FINANCIALS
Company Type: Private

Income Statement   FYE: June 30

	REVENUE ($mil)	NET INCOME ($mil)	NET PROFIT MARGIN	EMPLOYEES
06/21	724	76	10.6%	3,500
06/20*	695	23	3.4%	—
03/20	503	15	3.1%	—
06/19	681	35	5.2%	—
Annual Growth	3.1%	46.8%	—	—

*Fiscal year change

2021 Year-End Financials
Return on assets: 5.9%   Cash ($ mil.): 12
Return on equity: 11.7%
Current Ratio: 1.70

TOWN OF HEMPSTEAD

Auditors: PKF O'CONNOR DAVIES LLP HAUP

LOCATIONS

HQ: TOWN OF HEMPSTEAD
1 WASHINGTON ST, HEMPSTEAD, NY 115504921
Phone: 516 489-5000
Web: WWW.HEMPSTEADNY.GOV

HISTORICAL FINANCIALS
Company Type: Private

Income Statement   FYE: December 31

	REVENUE ($mil)	NET INCOME ($mil)	NET PROFIT MARGIN	EMPLOYEES
12/21	616	118	19.2%	2,052
12/20	710	53	7.5%	—
12/19	588	5	0.9%	—
12/18	549	48	8.8%	—
Annual Growth	3.9%	34.7%	—	—

2021 Year-End Financials
Return on assets: 7.7%   Cash ($ mil.): 328
Return on equity: —
Current Ratio: 2.30

TOWN OF NORTH HEMPSTEAD

EXECUTIVES

OF TAXES*, Ann M Galante
Auditors: PKF O'CONNOR DAVIES LLP HARR

LOCATIONS

HQ: TOWN OF NORTH HEMPSTEAD
220 PLANDOME RD, MANHASSET, NY 110302399
Phone: 516 627-0590
Web: WWW.NORTHHEMPSTEADNY.GOV

HISTORICAL FINANCIALS
Company Type: Private

Income Statement   FYE: December 31

	REVENUE ($mil)	NET INCOME ($mil)	NET PROFIT MARGIN	EMPLOYEES
12/21	565	(31)	—	574
12/20	152	0	0.1%	—
12/19	152	7	4.7%	—
12/18	145	4	2.9%	—
Annual Growth	57.2%	—	—	—

2021 Year-End Financials
Return on assets: (-0.7%)   Cash ($ mil.): 346
Return on equity: (-1.4%)
Current Ratio: —

TOWNSHIP OF WOODBRIDGE

Auditors : LERCH VINCI & HIGGINS LLP F

LOCATIONS

HQ: TOWNSHIP OF WOODBRIDGE
1 MAIN ST STE 1 # 1, WOODBRIDGE, NJ 070953352
Phone: 732 634-4500
Web: TWP.WOODBRIDGE.NJ.US

HISTORICAL FINANCIALS

Company Type: Private

Income Statement — FYE: June 30

	REVENUE ($mil)	NET INCOME ($mil)	NET PROFIT MARGIN	EMPLOYEES
06/21*	549	17	3.3%	800
12/20	0	0	58.3%	—
06/20	479	11	2.3%	—
06/19	477	14	3.0%	—
Annual Growth	7.3%	12.3%	—	—

*Fiscal year change

2021 Year-End Financials
Return on assets: 2.3%   Cash ($ mil.): 157
Return on equity: 4.2%
Current Ratio: —

TRAMMO, INC.

Trammo, Inc. is a leading global commodity merchandiser engaged in the marketing, trading, distribution and transportation of wide variety of commodity products, including being a market leader in anhydrous ammonia, sulfur, sulfuric acid, nitric acid and petroleum coke. Trammo was founded by Ronald P. Stanton in 1965 with the intention of specializing in the international trade of ammonia. Trammo remains privately held and manages its operations through its headquarters in New York City and offices worldwide.

Operations

Anhydrous ammonia is an alkaline compound consisting of nitrogen and hydrogen which is transported worldwide in gaseous or liquid form on board pressurized or refrigerated vessels. These vessels (gas carriers) are also used in transporting liquefied petroleum gas (LPG). Only around 18 million metric tons are available for international marketing and seaborne trade, out of more than 200 million metric tons of ammonia produced annually worldwide.

Sulfur is a by-product of oil and gas production and refining, with this involuntary production accounting for up to 95% of traded volume. Annual production is about 70 million metric tons of sulfur of which about 40%-45% is available for seaborne trade.

Sulfuric acid is a key element in the production of fertilizer (phosphates and ammonium sulfate) which is its primary use (approximately 65% of total consumption). Sulfuric acid is also used in the mining industry for leaching of copper, nickel, uranium, and other elements from ores (approximately 15% of total consumption). It is also is used in various industrial processes (approximately 20% of total consumption), including the production of titanium dioxide for dyes and pigments, the production of other industrial chemicals, water treatment, the production of cellulose, paper and rubber, and in the food and glass industries. Sulfuric acid is one of the most widely used chemical commodities, its total worldwide annual production is approximately 265 million metric tons.

Nitric acid used predominantly as an intermediate for fertilizer production (mainly ammonium and calcium ammonium nitrate) and for the production of nitro-containing organic intermediates.

Petroleum coke ("petcoke") is a by-product of crude oil refining. The coking processes produce "green coke" which is then further processed into two main products, calcined petcoke and fuel grade petcoke. Annual production is around 140 million metric tons (MT). Calcined petcoke (approximately 25% of production) is used for making anodes for aluminum smelting, the dioxide industry, and production of steel and titanium whiles Fuel grade petcoke (approximately 75% of production) makes up most of the petcoke traded internationally.

Geographic Reach

Headquartered in New York, NY, Trammo owns and operates ammonia terminals in Meredosia and Niota, Illinois and a nitric acid production facility in North Bend, Ohio.

Company Background

In 2013 Transammonia changed its name to Trammo to more accurately represent the broad spectrum of products and services it provides.

In 2010 the company's bulk carriers division entered the commodity shipping business. TA Bulk Carriers operates a fleet of 15 to 20 vessels, which trade worldwide but focus on the handysize market (25,000-35,000 metric tons deadweight) in the Atlantic basin. In 2010 it transported about 2.9 million metric tons of cargo, primarily fertilizers and grains.

Ronald Stanton founded the company in 1965 as an international ammonia trader. It branched into fertilizer merchandising and trading in 1967, LPG trading in 1978, and petrochemicals trading in 1987.

EXECUTIVES

CRO, James H Benfield
Co-Vice President, Robert Lovett Senior
Chief Business Officer, Donald V Madden
CAO, Nicholas J Wilson
CIO, Benjamin A Tan

Auditors : RSM US LLP NEW YORK NY

LOCATIONS

HQ: TRAMMO, INC.
8 W 40TH ST FL 12, NEW YORK, NY 100182307
Phone: 212 223-3200
Web: WWW.TRAMMO.COM

PRODUCTS/OPERATIONS

Major SubsidiariesSea-3 (liquefied propane)Trammo Gas (LPG)Trammo Gas International, Inc. (LPG transportation for third parties.Trammo Petroleum (crude oil and oil products)Trammochem (petrochemicals)Fertilizers and CommoditiesNitrogen BasedAnhydrous AmmoniaAmmonium NitrateAmmonium SulfateCalcium Ammonium NitrateNitrogen, Phosphorus, Potassium (NPK) CompoundsUreaUrea Ammonium Nitrate SolutionsPhosphate BasedDiammonium PhosphateMonoammonium PhosphateNPK CompoundsSingle Super PhosphateTriple Super PhosphateSulphur BasedLump/Formed/Molten SulphurSulphuric AcidPotash BasedMuriate of PotashNPK CompoundsSulphate of PotashCarbon BasedCoalPetroleum CokePetrochemicalsBenzeneEthanolGasoline Blend ComponentsMethanolOlefinsStyrene MonomerTolueneXylenes and IsomersLPGButaneEthaneIso ButaneNatural GasolinePropane

COMPETITORS

AIRGAS, INC.
ASHLAND GLOBAL HOLDINGS INC.
BRENNTAG NORTH AMERICA, INC.
IDEMITSU KOSAN CO.,LTD.
Marquard & Bahls AG
NEXEO SOLUTIONS HOLDINGS, LLC
SASOL LTD
SOJITZ CORPORATION
UNIVAR SOLUTIONS INC.
UNIVAR SOLUTIONS USA INC.

HISTORICAL FINANCIALS

Company Type: Private

Income Statement — FYE: December 31

	REVENUE ($mil)	NET INCOME ($mil)	NET PROFIT MARGIN	EMPLOYEES
12/21	4,161	82	2.0%	184
12/20	1,786	21	1.2%	—
12/19	2,267	22	1.0%	—
12/18	3,212	(12)	—	—
Annual Growth	9.0%	—	—	—

2021 Year-End Financials
Return on assets: 9.1%   Cash ($ mil.): 113
Return on equity: 33.9%
Current Ratio: 1.50

TRC COMPANIES, INC.

TRC Companies is a leading global consulting, engineering and construction company that provides environmentally focused and digitally powered solutions. The company provides engineering, construction, and remediation services for power and utilities, industrial, transportation, real estate, water and government. Services include operation and consulting, filed services and inspection, engineering, and procurement and construction, among others. It also offers an Exit Strategy Program in which it assumes complete responsibility for a contaminated site's closure and cleanup. In late 2021, TRC was acquired by the private equity firm Warburg Pincus from New Mountain Capital. The company was incorporated in Connecticut in 1969.

Operations

TRC services are planning, field services and inspection, engineering, procurement and construction, operations and consulting, environmental, health and safety management, regulatory and environmental compliance, remediation and materials management and emergency management and response.

The company's electrical and power services include reliable and efficient energy solutions (including distributed energy and microgrids, power distribution engineering, protection and control, substations, telecommunications and transmission engineering), delivering power engineering solutions and partnering to improve utility operations. It provides end-to-end engineering and project execution services that help customers to construct or expand pipeline systems, compressor and pump stations, terminals, underground and surface storage and infield gathering and production facilities. Furthermore, TRC solutions include pipeline integrity, routing and siting, conceptual studies and substations, among others.

The company's projects include Scattergood Power Plant Decommissioning, Humboldt Bay Power Plant Decommissioning, New York Power Authority Poletti RE POWER, Emergency Preparedness ? Gas Utility ERPs and FEMA ICS Integration and Designing, Building and Deploying ESRI UN for a Midstream Service Provider, among others.

Geographic Reach

TRC is based in Connecticut. It operates a network of more than 150 offices located throughout the US, Canada, the UK and China. In the US, the company operates in approximately 40 states including Alabama, California, Indiana, Louisiana, Massachusetts, Montana, New Jersey, and many others.

Sales and Marketing

The company collaborates with its clients to design tangible solutions. The company has diverse clients in different industries such as oil and gas, industrial, transportation, real estate, water, government, education, healthcare and residential, among others.

Mergers and Acquisitions

In mid-2022, TRC Companies announced the expansion of its engineering and design capabilities with the acquisition of Draper Aden Associates (DAA). DAA has built a reputation of excellence as a full-service consulting and engineering firm with locations in Virginia and North Carolina and long-standing client relationships across the Mid-Atlantic region. DAA works closely with major Utility companies to support resiliency across their operations. Additionally, they provide engineering, energy related design and mapping services, water and wastewater design services, construction inspection and materials testing as well as surveying and environmental services across multiple key markets. Terms were not disclosed.

In early 2022, TRC Companies nnounced the expansion of its Air Management capabilities with the acquisition of United Sciences Testing, Inc. (USTI), who provides emissions audits and testing services to utility and industrial clients within the Great Lakes and Midwest regions of the US. The acquisition of USTI's technical experts add strength to its offerings geographically and expand its ability to support our client's energy transformation and ESG goals. Terms were not disclosed.

Also in early 2022, TRC Companies announced the expansion of its power & renewable energy and coastal engineering capabilities with the acquisition of ESS Group (ESS), a Northeast based firm widely recognized for its reputation as a best-in-class provider of Power and Renewable Energy, Coastal Engineering, and Water Resource Management expertise. The acquisition of ESS further expands and strengthens TRC's ability to support its client's ESG and Climate programs. Terms were not disclosed.

In mid-2021, TRC Companies announced the expansion of its digital capabilities with the acquisition of Quatric, a Montreal, QC and Quincy, MA-based company that provides engineering services and technology solutions to electric and gas utilities. The acquisition of Quatric further strengthens the company's investment in digital technologies and is part of its broader strategy as the company continues its development as a leading provider of technology-enabled solutions to the company's clients.

In early 2021, TRC Companies acquired EMI Consulting (EMI), a Seattle-based company that consults on the strategic development of clean energy solutions including energy efficiency, demand management, decarbonization and customer engagement. The acquisition reinforces the company's strategic growth objectives and strengthens its well-established ability to deliver innovative, integrated solutions for a wide range of advanced energy projects and programs.

Company Background

Incorporated in Connecticut in 1969, TRC has spent half a century providing cutting edge professional services in the engineering and consulting realm. From humble beginnings as The Research Corporation of New England, a meteorological and air quality analysis firm, TRC quickly expanded into the power, infrastructure and oil and gas markets and now serves as a tech-enabled consulting firm.

HISTORY

TRC was born as Travelers Research Center, a unit set up in 1953 by Travelers Insurance to do meteorological and industrial hygiene research. In 1969 Travelers (now part of Citigroup) spun off TRC Companies, which prospered as government spending on the environment and pollution control increased. It became a free-standing public entity in 1976. When the government began cutting back during the 1980s, TRC started courting the commercial market.

In 1994 TRC expanded, acquiring Environmental Solutions and Mariah Associates. It increased its international interests, forming joint ventures in 1995 and 1996 to help with the remediation of Poland's horrendous pollution.

Sales fell in 1996 and 1997, the result of a weak market and stiff competition in the environmental services industry. TRC responded with a major cost-cutting effort. In 1997 chairman and CEO Vincent Rocco and president Bruce Cowen resigned amid an investigation into options exercised by the two executives that the company's board had not authorized. Richard Ellison, head of the TRC Environmental Solutions subsidiary, was named chairman, president, and CEO.

Also in 1997 TRC teamed up with insurer American International Group to introduce a service called the Exit Strategy Program, in which TRC is paid to take full responsibility -- including liability risks -- for a contaminated site's closure and remediation.

In 1998 the company sold its Monitoring Instruments for the Environment subsidiary for about $2.7 million. The next year TRC embarked on a major buying spree: It purchased Alton Geoscience, which specialized in installation, removal, and replacement of fuel tanks; A&H Engineers, a transportation consulting and engineering firm in New York City; and Vectre, which provided brownfield remediation services in New Jersey. The company also landed an Exit Strategy contract to clean up a Superfund site in Maine.

Continuing to grow through acquisitions in 2000, TRC acquired Texas-based Hunter Associates, North Carolina-based Triange Environmental, and California-based Lowney Associates. Also that year the TRC twice scored big with its Exit Strategy product: a $103 million contract with Consolidated Edison to clean up a site in New York City and a $21 million contract with Lockheed Martin to clean up sites in California, Massachusetts, and New Jersey.

TRC kept on snapping up companies in 2001. The company bought Engineered Automation Systems, which provided electrical, mechanical, and environmental controls, and ECON, a provider of environmental services to the oil and gas companies that was to take on Exit Strategy business in the Gulf Coast region. The company also bought two infrastructure engineering companies, LandCon and CSM, that were to be combined with Hunter Associates.

The next year, eager to expand its outsourcing operations for the power industry, TRC acquired engineering firm E/PRO, which had experience in the US Northeast in the licensing of hydroelectric plants, as well as in designing, constructing, and managing other power utilities. TRC also completed its acquisition of transportation infrastructure firm SITE-Blauvelt Engineers, which targeted mid-Atlantic states.

In 2002 the group expanded westward by acquiring California-based environmental planning, training, and compliance management firm Essex Environmental. It also enhanced its Midwestern operations by buying Novak Engineering, a power transmission and distribution planning and design firm. In 2004 the group won a contract from the Department of Defense to design an "intelligent building" system to optimize energy use and detect threats within the Pentagon.

Ellison retired as president and CEO effective January 1, 2006 but remained chairman. Christopher Vincze, who had been COO, took over as president and CEO.

But TRC began to broaden its reach nationally in all segments of its business in 2010. Since 2010 the company has been marketing its energy and infrastructure services on a national basis, and its environmental services are being integrated into its national platform. Its national platform is linked to TRC's corporate sales and marketing organization.

Pursuing strategic acquisitions, in 2011 TRC continued acquired Alexander Utility Engineering, a San Antonio-based engineering and design firm that specializes in services to the electric utility and communications utility markets. The deal for Alexander, which posted earnings of about $3 million in 2010, expands TRC's engineering presence in the Texas market and advances its growth strategy. That same year, TRC acquired the environmental business of RMT Inc., a subsidiary of Alliant Energy Corp. The deal expands TRC's growth in the solar, wind, and geothermal energy markets. The company also picked up environmental consulting company The Payne Firm.

On the heels of acquiring RMT and Payne, the company formed a strategic partnership with California-based environmental consulting group EORM to acquire its eastern region operations, based in Danvers, Massachusetts. The deal enhances TRC's environmental management, sustainability, and safety operations, as well as broadens its geographic reach.

Broadening its geographic coverage, in 2012 the company opened an office in London.

In 2013 TRC acquired GE Air Emissions Testing for $3.2 million.

EXECUTIVES

Chief Strategy Officer, Jim Stephenson
Auditors : DELOITTE & TOUCHE LLP HARTFOR

LOCATIONS

HQ: TRC COMPANIES, INC.
21 GRIFFIN RD N, WINDSOR, CT 060951590
Phone: 860 298-9692
Web: WWW.TRCCOMPANIES.COM

PRODUCTS/OPERATIONS

2016 Sales

	% of total
Environmental	45
Energy	33
Infrastructure	12
Pipeline	10
Total	100

2016 Sales

	$ mil.	% of total
Net services	465.1	97
Insurance recoverable and others	16.0	3
Total	481.1	100

Selected Customers
AES Enterprises
ASARCO
Burlington Northern Santa Fe (BNSF)
Connecticut Resources Recovery Authority
Consolidated Edison
Duke Energy
El Paso Energy
Environmental Protection Agency
Exxon Mobil
Goodyear Tire & Rubber
Kinder Morgan
PG&E Corporation
Sempra Energy
State Departments of Transportation/Power Authorities
  California
  Louisiana
  Massachusetts
  New Hampshire
  New Jersey
  New York
  Pennsylvania
  Texas
  West Virginia

Selected Subsidiaries
Alexander Utility Engineering
Center Avenue Holdings
Cubix Corporation
Environomics Southwest
Hunter Associates
Site-Blauvelt Engineers, Inc.
Site Construction Services
TRC Engineers, Inc.
TRC Environmental Corporation
TRC Solutions, Inc.
Vectre Corporation

COMPETITORS

ARCADIS U.S., INC.
EXPRESS SERVICES, INC.
FIRCROFT ENGINEERING SERVICES LIMITED
KELLY SERVICES, INC.
KFORCE INC.
MANPOWERGROUP INC.
Stantec Inc
TECHNISOURCE, INC.
TETRA TECH, INC.
TRUEBLUE, INC.

HISTORICAL FINANCIALS
Company Type: Private

Income Statement — FYE: June 30

	REVENUE ($mil)	NET INCOME ($mil)	NET PROFIT MARGIN	EMPLOYEES
06/21	738	(16)	—	4,865
06/20	711	(58)	—	—
06/19	693	(30)	—	—
06/18	590	(48)	—	—
Annual Growth	7.8%	—	—	—

2021 Year-End Financials
Return on assets: (-1.5%)   Cash ($ mil.): 87
Return on equity: (-7.6%)
Current Ratio: 1.50

TRI STAR ENERGY, LLC

EXECUTIVES

Managing Member, John B Jewell Iii
Auditors : LATTIMORE BLACK MORGAAN & CA

LOCATIONS

HQ: TRI STAR ENERGY, LLC
1740 ED TEMPLE BLVD, NASHVILLE, TN 372081850
Phone: 615 313-3600
Web: WWW.TRISTARTN.COM

HISTORICAL FINANCIALS
Company Type: Private

Income Statement — FYE: December 31

	REVENUE ($mil)	NET INCOME ($mil)	NET PROFIT MARGIN	EMPLOYEES
12/11	730	3	0.5%	500
12/10	635	4	0.7%	—
12/09	547	0	0.0%	—
Annual Growth	15.5%	399.7%		

2011 Year-End Financials
Return on assets: 3.1%   Cash ($ mil.): —
Return on equity: 7.4%
Current Ratio: 0.70

TRIBOROUGH BRIDGE & TUNNEL AUTHORITY

Auditors : DELOITTE & TOUCHE LLP NEW YOR

LOCATIONS

HQ: TRIBOROUGH BRIDGE & TUNNEL AUTHORITY
ROBERT MSES BLDG RNDLLSI RANDALLS, NEW YORK, NY 10035
Phone: 212 360-3000

HISTORICAL FINANCIALS
Company Type: Private

Income Statement   FYE: December 31

	REVENUE ($mil)	NET INCOME ($mil)	NET PROFIT MARGIN	EMPLOYEES
12/21	2,194	(194)	—	1,500
12/20	1,660	672	40.5%	—
12/19	2,094	485	23.2%	—
12/18	1,999	453	22.7%	—

Annual Growth   3.1%   —   —   —

2021 Year-End Financials
Return on assets: (-1.5%)   Cash ($ mil.): 217
Return on equity: —
Current Ratio: 3.10

TRICON INTERNATIONAL, LTD.

EXECUTIVES
Business Director, Shi Weimin
Global Director, Sanjay Moolji
Auditors: BDO USA LLP HOUSTON TEXAS

LOCATIONS
HQ: TRICON INTERNATIONAL, LTD.
777 POST OAK BLVD STE 550, HOUSTON, TX 770563315
Phone: 713 963-0066
Web: WWW.TRICONENERGY.COM

HISTORICAL FINANCIALS
Company Type: Private

Income Statement   FYE: December 31

	REVENUE ($mil)	NET INCOME ($mil)	NET PROFIT MARGIN	EMPLOYEES
12/21	10,239	205	2.0%	451
12/20	5,790	49	0.9%	—
12/19	7,393	10	0.1%	—

Annual Growth   17.7%   339.3%   —   —

2021 Year-End Financials
Return on assets: 9.2%   Cash ($ mil.): —
Return on equity: 58.1%
Current Ratio: 1.20

TRINITY HEALTH CORPORATION

One of the largest not-for-profit, Catholic health care systems in the US, Trinity Health runs roughly 90 acute care hospitals and approximately 130 continuing care facilities in more than 20 US states. Beyond traditional health services, Trinity Health also provides health and wellness care including independent retail location Urgent Care Centers, specialty pharmacies providing specialized medicines for chronic care or other debilitating conditions, and an Outreach Lab where it able to send and receive lab work. Its home-based care offerings include companion care, remote patient monitoring, and hospice. The company employs approximately 6,800 physicians and clinicians.

Operations
Its Trinity Health Pharmacy Services provides specialty medications for complex, chronic, and rare diseases. Its highly-trained pharmacists and specialized care team take great care to provide guidance on drug interactions, allergies, and therapy management to each patient as well as provide customized education, follow-up, and side effect management.

Trinity Health's Military and Veterans Health Care Program is committed to providing convenient access to high-quality health services to meet the specific needs of military service members, veterans, and their family members.

Net patient service brings roughly 85% of Trinity Health's total revenue while capitation and premium and other revenue accounts for the remaining revenue.

Geographic Reach
Based in Livonia, Michigan, Trinity Health operates in more than 20 states including in Alabama, California, Florida, Georgia, Idaho, and Illinois.

Sales and Marketing
Medicare accounts for about 40% of net patient service revenues, Blue Cross accounts for some 20%, Medicaid for around 15%, while uninsured, commercial and other represents more than 20%.

Strategy
Xealth, the leader in enabling digital health at scale, in late 2021, announced that Trinity Health invested in the company. Trinity is one of 15 health system investors for the company, bringing the total Series B funding to $25 million. This support demonstrates continued provider consensus in adopting digital health in a way that best engages both clinicians and patients.

Company Background
Trinity Health was established in 2013 from the merger of Catholic Health East and the former Trinity Health organization.

The predecessor Trinity Health organization was formed through the 2000 merger of Mercy Health Services and Holy Cross Health System. Holy Cross was founded in 1979 but traces its roots to the founding of the Congregation of the Sisters of the Holy Cross in 1841; Mercy Health was founded in 1976 but originates with the Sisters of Mercy establishing operations in Iowa and Michigan in the 1860s and 1870s.

Catholic Health East was formed through the 1998 merger of three health ministries: Franciscan Sisters of Allegany Health System (tracing its roots to 1883 in Boston), Eastern Mercy Health System (1847, Pittsburgh), and Sisters of Providence Health System (1892; Holyoke, Massachusetts).

In 2015 New York-based St. Joseph's Hospital Health Center joined the Trinity hospital system.

Auditors: DELOITTE & TOUCHE LLP DETROIT

LOCATIONS
HQ: TRINITY HEALTH CORPORATION
20555 VICTOR PKWY, LIVONIA, MI 481527031
Phone: 734 343-1000
Web: WWW.TRINITY-HEALTH.ORG

Selected Facilities
California
    Saint Agnes Medical Center (Fresno)
Idaho and Oregon
    Saint Alphonsus Medical Center - Baker City
    Saint Alphonsus Medical Center - Nampa
    Saint Alphonsus Medical Center - Ontario
    Saint Alphonsus Regional Medical Center (Boise)
Indiana
    Saint Joseph Regional Medical Center (South Bend)
    Saint Joseph Regional Medical Center (Plymouth)
Illinois
    Loyola University Health System (Chicago)
    Loyola University Medical Center
    Loyola Gottlieb Memorial Hospital
    Mercy Hospital & Medical Center (Chicago)
Iowa and Nebraska
    Mercy Health Network (Clinton, Des Moines, Dubuque, Dyersville, Mason City, New Hampton, and Sioux City, Iowa; Oakland, Nebraska)
Maryland
    Holy Cross Hospital (Silver Spring)
Michigan
    Mercy Health Partners (Muskegon)
    Mercy Hospital (Cadillac)
    Mercy Hospital (Grayling)
    Saint Joseph Mercy Health System (Ann Arbor)
    Saint Mary's Health Care (Grand Rapids)
Ohio
    Mount Carmel Health System (Columbus)

PRODUCTS/OPERATIONS

2014 Net Patient Revnue

	% of total
Medicare	38
Blue Cross	20
Medicaid	13
Uninsured	4
Commercial and other	25
Total	100

2014 Sales

	% of total
Net patient service revenuel less provision for bad debts	87
Capitation and premium revenue	5
Other revenue	8
Total	100

COMPETITORS
ADVOCATE AURORA HEALTH, INC.
ADVOCATE HEALTH CARE NETWORK
ASCENSION HEALTH
BANNER HEALTH
COMMONSPIRIT HEALTH
IASIS HEALTHCARE LLC
IPC HEALTHCARE, INC.
NOVANT HEALTH, INC.
PROVIDENCE ST. JOSEPH HEALTH
UPMC

HISTORICAL FINANCIALS
Company Type: Private

Income Statement				FYE: June 30
	REVENUE ($mil)	NET INCOME ($mil)	NET PROFIT MARGIN	EMPLOYEES
06/19	2,046	38	1.9%	51,220
06/15	1,375	19	1.4%	—
Annual Growth	10.4%	18.8%	—	—

2019 Year-End Financials
Return on assets: 0.4% Cash ($ mil.): 49
Return on equity: 37.4%
Current Ratio: 0.80

TRINITY HEALTH OF THE MID-ATLANTIC REGION

Auditors: DELOITTE & TOUCHE LLP DETROI

LOCATIONS

HQ: TRINITY HEALTH OF THE MID-ATLANTIC REGION
3805 WEST CHESTER PIKE # 10, NEWTOWN SQUARE, PA 190732329
Phone: 610 567-6000
Web: WWW.TRINITYHEALTHMA.ORG

HISTORICAL FINANCIALS
Company Type: Private

Income Statement				FYE: June 30
	REVENUE ($mil)	NET INCOME ($mil)	NET PROFIT MARGIN	EMPLOYEES
06/18	745	64	8.7%	8,050
06/15	88	10	11.8%	—
Annual Growth	103.6%	83.7%	—	—

2018 Year-End Financials
Return on assets: 11.0% Cash ($ mil.): —
Return on equity: 18.6%
Current Ratio: 1.70

TRINITY HEALTH-MICHIGAN

Auditors: DELOITTE & TOUCHE LLP DETROIT

LOCATIONS

HQ: TRINITY HEALTH-MICHIGAN
20555 VICTOR PKWY, LIVONIA, MI 481527031
Phone: 810 985-1500
Web: WWW.STJOESHEALTH.ORG

HISTORICAL FINANCIALS
Company Type: Private

Income Statement				FYE: June 30
	REVENUE ($mil)	NET INCOME ($mil)	NET PROFIT MARGIN	EMPLOYEES
06/20	2,599	124	4.8%	4,540
06/18	3,595	303	8.4%	—
06/14	2,474	102	4.2%	—
06/13	2,475	138	5.6%	—
Annual Growth	0.7%	(1.5%)	—	—

2020 Year-End Financials
Return on assets: 3.0% Cash ($ mil.): —
Return on equity: 4.8%
Current Ratio: —

TRINITY MOTHER FRANCES HEALTH SYSTEM FOUNDATION

Trinity Mother Frances Health System Foundation (dba Trinity Mother Frances Hospitals and Clinics) hasÂ a complicated name but a simple mission: to improve patient health. Consisting of threeÂ general hospitals, several specialist facilities,Â and a large physicians' group, Trinity Mother Frances serves northeastern Texas. Its largest acute-care facility is Mother Frances Hospital-TylerÂ with more thanÂ 400 beds, offering comprehensive medical, surgical, trauma,Â andÂ cardiovascular care.Â Two smaller hospitalsÂ in JacksonvilleÂ and Winnsboro provide emergency, diagnostic, surgery, and select specialty services. The Trinity Clinic is a multi-specialty physician group that includes 300 doctors inÂ 36 community clinics.

Operations

Trinity Mother FrancesÂ Hospitals and Clinics' specialty facilities include the freestanding Trinity Mother FrancesÂ Rehabilitation Hospital in Tyler, which has 75 beds andÂ is operatedÂ through a joint venture with HealthSouth.Â It also operates the Tyler ContinueCARE Hospital, a long-term acute care hospital located within the Mother Frances Hospital-Tyler, as well as several urgent care centers.

Strategy

In 2010 the network added the 35-bed Mother Frances Hospital-WinnsboroÂ facility when it took over control of the Texas Health Presbyterian Hospital Winnsboro from Texas Health Resources. The transfer was made to align the Winnsboro hospital with the main Tyler facility, where the majority ofÂ specialized cases from Winnsboro were already being transferred.

The networkÂ also added a freestanding 72-bed cardiac facility, the Louis and Peaches Owen Heart Hospital, in Tyler. The first phase of the center was added to the existing Mother Frances Hospital-Tyler facilities in 2010; the second stage is a six-story freestanding towerÂ adjacent to the Tyler hospital. Construction on the tower started in early 2011,Â and was completed by the end ofÂ 2012.

Additionally, Trinity Mother Frances Hospitals and Clinics is investing in information technology initiatives. It began installing electronic health record (EHR) systems at its facilities during 2012 as part of the US government's health care improvement initiatives.

Company Background

Trinity Mother Frances Hospitals and Clinics was established by the 1995 merger of Mother Frances HospitalÂ and the Trinity Clinic, both founded in the 1930s.

Auditors: ERNST & YOUNG LLP DALLAS TX

LOCATIONS

HQ: TRINITY MOTHER FRANCES HEALTH SYSTEM FOUNDATION
800 E DAWSON ST, TYLER, TX 757012036
Phone: 903 531-5057

PRODUCTS/OPERATIONS

Selected Locations
DirectCARE (urgent care, multiple sites)
Louis and Peaches Owen Heart Hospital, Tyler
Mother Frances Hospital-Jacksonville
Mother Frances Hospital-Tyler
Mother Frances Hospital-Winnsboro
Trinity Clinics (physician practices, multiple sites)
Trinity Mother Frances Rehabilitation Hospital-Tyler
Tyler ContinueCARE Hospital

Selected Services
Anesthesiology
Audiology
Bariatric Surgery Center
Cancer
Cardiac Services
Cardiothoracic Surgery
Critical Care Intensivists
Ear, Nose & Throat
Emergency Medicine
Endocrinology
Gastroenterology, Hepatology and Endoscopy
Family Medicine
General Surgeons
Genetics
Hospitalists
Imaging, Radiology, Mammography
Internal Medicine
Neonatology
Neuroscience Institute
Obstetrics & Gynecology
Occupational Medicine - Health At Work
Ophthalmology, Optometry & Optical Services
Orthopedics
Pain Medicine
Pediatrics
Physical Medicine and Rehabilitation
Plastic Surgery
Podiatry
Psychiatry
Rehabilitation Hospital
Rheumatology
Sleep Medicine
Sports Medicine
Surgery Services
Trauma Services
Urgent Care
Urology Institute & Continence Center

Vascular Institute
Women & Children
WoundCARE

COMPETITORS

ASCENSION SETON
DIMENSIONS HEALTH CORPORATION
HOLY CROSS HOSPITAL, INC.
MERCY HOSPITAL AND MEDICAL CENTER
THE PUBLIC HEALTH TRUST OF MIAMI-DADE COUNTY

HISTORICAL FINANCIALS
Company Type: Private

Income Statement — FYE: June 30

	REVENUE ($mil)	NET INCOME ($mil)	NET PROFIT MARGIN	EMPLOYEES
06/13	653	21	3.3%	3,551
06/10	603	19	3.3%	—
06/09	(901)	0	0.0%	—
Annual Growth	—	1364.1%		

2013 Year-End Financials
Return on assets: 3.1%   Cash ($ mil.): 47
Return on equity: 7.2%
Current Ratio: 1.50

TRUMAN ARNOLD COMPANIES

Truman Arnold Companies (TAC) is one of the largest independent fuel wholesalers and aviation service providers in the US. Its energy business markets and sells more than 2.7 billion gallons of fuel to customers in industries like energy retail, trucking, utilities, mining, and construction. The company supplies refined products like gasoline, diesel, biodiesel, ethanol renewable fuels, and Diesel Exhaust Fluid (a non-hazardous product). TAC also serves the aviation industry by selling aviation fuel and providing Fixed Base Operations (aircraft fueling, hangar space, and transport) through over 15 locations in the US. TAC was founded in 1964 by Truman Arnold.

Operations
TAC operates through TACenergy, TAC Air, TAC Private Hangars, Keystone Aviation, and TAC Investments.

TACenergy sells an annual fuel volume of more than 2.7 billion gallons through a vast terminal supply network. This segment also provides a 24/7 logistics call center, a bulk trading desk, and a real-time inventory intelligence service (matching inventory supply with trading prices) that helps minimize fuel costs for customers.

TAC Air is the company's aviation division, which sells competitively priced aviation fuel and provides Fixed Base Operation services including ground handling, aircraft fueling, hangar space, aircraft maintenance, cargo handling, and de-icing.

Through Keystone Aviation, the company also provides private charter flights, aircraft management, and aircraft maintenance.

TAC Private Hangars is a secure, protected environment, operating 24/7/365. Each location provides hangar and connected office space, conference room/meeting space, private terminal and gate access, secured parking, ground services and fueling.

TAC Investments manage the company's capital by investing in a wide pool of assets.

Geographic Reach
TAC is headquartered in Dallas, Texas. TAC Air has FBO in over 15 locations including Arkansas, Colorado, Connecticut, Kentucky, and Louisiana, among others.

Sales and Marketing
TACenergy sells branded retail fuel to a range of customers including gasoline and diesel retailers, industrial users, transportation, oil & gas, waste disposal & recycling, trucking, government agencies, utilities, mining, and construction, as well as other commercial user or reseller of fuel. The company has a vast terminal supply network with outlets across the continent, plus a 24/7 logistical call center.

Strategy
TAC Investments manages the capital of the TAC balance sheet. We carefully invest in a diverse pool of assets that in turn produces an above-average risk-adjusted return, while expanding and supporting the TAC balance sheet by mitigating risk. This extensive and diverse pool of assets provides the foundation for TAC's purchasing power across all divisions.

In late 2020, The Arnold Companies is expanding its presence into New York with the addition of its 16th FBO location, TAC Air - BUF, at Buffalo Niagara International Airport. Acquiring Prior Aviation assets associated with its fixed base operations, TAC Air also plans to maintain the 120 associates supporting these operations. The full range of FBO services, including fuel, hangar and aircraft handling, as well as supporting the market's commercial airlines with into-plane fuel, charter handling, cargo services, de-icing and airline maintenance, will be offered by TAC Air.

Mergers and Acquisitions
In 2021, TAC acquired the assets of Gemini Air Group at Arizona's Scottsdale Airport (KSDL), Arizona, Dallas-based The TAC has established a Keystone Aviation operation there. Additionally, it created TAC Private Hangars, which will manage more than 65,000 sq ft of upscale private hangar and office space at KSDL.

In late 2020, TAC Air, a division of TAC, is expanding its presence into New York with the addition of its 16th FBO location, TAC Air - BUF, at Buffalo Niagara International Airport. Acquiring Prior Aviation assets associated with its fixed base operations, TAC Air also plans to maintain the 120 associates supporting these operations. The full range of FBO services, including fuel, hangar and aircraft handling, as well as supporting the market's commercial airlines with into-plane fuel, charter handling, cargo services, de-icing and airline maintenance, will be offered by TAC Air.

Company Background
Truman Arnold Companies was founded in 1964 as a Texas-based Conoco Distributor. It once operated a chain of 125 Road Runner convenience stores in eight states, before selling this network to Total Petroleum in 1989. It revived the brand in 2003. The company presently focuses on fuel marketing and providing aviation services, doing business under the TAC business name.

Auditors: THOMAS & THOMAS PLLC TEXARKAN

LOCATIONS

HQ: TRUMAN ARNOLD COMPANIES
100 CRESCENT CT STE 1600, DALLAS, TX 752016915
Phone: 903 794-3835
Web: WWW.THEARNOLDCOS.COM

COMPETITORS

COMPANHIA BRASILEIRA DE PETROLEO IPIRANGA
MACQUARIE INFRASTRUCTURE CORPORATION
MANSFIELD OIL COMPANY OF GAINESVILLE, INC.
MAXUM PETROLEUM HOLDINGS, INC.
PS ENERGY GROUP, INC.
SOUTHERN COUNTIES OIL CO.
SUN COAST RESOURCES, INC.
TEXON DISTRIBUTING L.P.
TRANSMONTAIGNE LLC
WORLD FUEL SERVICES CORPORATION

HISTORICAL FINANCIALS
Company Type: Private

Income Statement — FYE: September 30

	REVENUE ($mil)	NET INCOME ($mil)	NET PROFIT MARGIN	EMPLOYEES
09/17	2,119	18	0.9%	550
09/16	1,525	18	1.2%	—
09/15	1,595	17	1.1%	—
Annual Growth	15.2%	2.4%	—	—

2017 Year-End Financials
Return on assets: 5.6%   Cash ($ mil.): 3
Return on equity: 12.3%
Current Ratio: 1.20

TRUMAN MEDICAL CENTER, INCORPORATED

Truman Medical Center (also known as Truman Medical Centers/University Health) provides primary and mental health care at two not-for-profit hospitals in the Kansas City (Missouri) area. Its Hospital Hill runs one of the busiest emergency rooms in Kansas City and is known for treatments related to asthma, diabetes, obstetrics, ophthalmology, weight management, and women's health. TMC Lakewood, a 110-bed hospital, is a leading academic medical center providing a range of health care services to the greater Kansas City metropolitan area, including uninsured patients. The Lakewood Family Birthplace delivers more than 1,500 babies annually.

Auditors : BKD LLP KANSAS CITY MO

LOCATIONS

HQ: TRUMAN MEDICAL CENTER, INCORPORATED
2301 HOLMES ST, KANSAS CITY, MO 641082640
Phone: 816 404-1000
Web: WWW.UNIVERSITYHEALTHKC.ORG

PRODUCTS/OPERATIONS

Truman Medical Center Hospital Hill
Asthma Center
The Birthplace
Cardiovascular Center
Chiropractic Services KC CORE
Dental Maxillofacial Surgery
Diabetes Center
Emergency Care
Eye Clinic
Eye Foundation
GI Gastrointestinal
Hospital Hill Medical Pavilion
Infectious Disease Clinic
Oncology
Orthopaedics
Pulmonary Fibrosis
Radiology Services
Rehabilitation Services
Sickle Cell Disease Center
Sleep Center
Trauma Services
TruMed Clinic
Weight Management
Women's Care Breast Center
Women's Health Services
TMC Lakewood
Family Medicine Center
Lakewood Family Birthplace
Chiropractic Services
Counseling Services Lakewood
Dental Services
Dental Services Elks Mobile
GI Gastrointestinal
Emergency Medicine
Eye Care Center
Lakewood Medical Pavilion
Longterm Care Center
Medical Detox
Orthopaedic Services
Outpatient Surgery Center
Podiatry
Rehabilitation Services
Sports Medicine
Women's Health Services

COMPETITORS

ARKANSAS CHILDREN'S HOSPITAL
DENVER HEALTH AND HOSPITALS AUTHORITY
FROEDTERT MEMORIAL LUTHERAN HOSPITAL, INC.
JUPITER MEDICAL CENTER, INC.
MERCY HEALTH - ST. RITA'S MEDICAL CENTER, LLC
NORTH FLORIDA REGIONAL MEDICAL CENTER, INC.
THE NEBRASKA MEDICAL CENTER
WELLSTAR HEALTH SYSTEM, INC.
WINTER HAVEN HOSPITAL, INC.
YAKIMA VALLEY MEMORIAL HOSPITAL ASSOCIATION

HISTORICAL FINANCIALS
Company Type: Private

Income Statement — FYE: June 30

	REVENUE ($mil)	NET INCOME ($mil)	NET PROFIT MARGIN	EMPLOYEES
06/21	736	50	6.8%	3,000
06/20	693	(21)	—	—
06/19	666	13	2.0%	—
06/18	562	22	4.0%	—
Annual Growth	9.4%	30.7%	—	—

2021 Year-End Financials
Return on assets: 10.3% Cash ($ mil.): 24
Return on equity: 32.1%
Current Ratio: 0.50

TRUSTEES OF BOSTON COLLEGE

Operating in the city of Boston, Boston College (BC) enrolls some 15,075 students. It has a student-teacher ratio of 10:1. BC offers degrees in more than 50 fields of study through its eights schools and colleges on three campuses. Some programs include biology, chemistry, economics, geology, philosophy, and theology. The university also has more than 35 research centers, including the Institute for Scientific Research, and the Center for International Higher Education. BC is one of the oldest Jesuit Catholic universities in the nation and has the largest Jesuit community in the world.

Operations
BC offers a variety of graduate degree programs in the humanities, social sciences, and natural sciences lead to Ph.D., M.A., and M.S. degrees. It includes Classical Studies, Earth and Environmental Sciences, Geophysics, History, Philosophy and Theology, Physics, Political Science, Psychology, and Sociology.

The university is home to more than 35 centers and institutes designated for research and teaching. Research opportunities, including participation in faculty research projects, exist for both undergraduate and graduate students. It also houses eight libraries with nearly 3 million volumes.

The cost of tuition stood at $70,143.

Geographic Reach
The university has campuses in Brighton, Chestnut Hill and Newton, Massachusetts.

Company Background
The university was founded by Jesuits in 1863. During its first seven decades, BC was an exclusively undergraduate institution that served sons of the Irish working class. Its liberal arts emphasis was on the Greek and Latin classics, English and modern languages, and philosophy and religion. Development into the college it is today did not begin until the 1920s when the Graduate School of Arts and Sciences, the Law School, and the Evening College (known today as the James A. Woods, S.J., College of Advancing Studies) were inaugurated. All classes became co-educational in the 1970s, and today BC has a fairly equal split among male and female students.

Auditors : PRICEWATERHOUSE COOPERS LLP

LOCATIONS

HQ: TRUSTEES OF BOSTON COLLEGE
140 COMMONWEALTH AVE, CHESTNUT HILL, MA 024673800
Phone: 617 552-8000
Web: WWW.BC.EDU

PRODUCTS/OPERATIONS

Selected Colleges and Schools
Carolyn A. and Peter S. Lynch School of Education
College of Arts and Sciences
Graduate School of Arts and Sciences
Graduate School of Social Work
James A. Woods, S.J. College of Advancing Studies
School of Law
School of Theology and Ministry
Wallace E. Carroll School of Management
William F. Connell School of Nursing

COMPETITORS

ABILENE CHRISTIAN UNIVERSITY
DREW UNIVERSITY
THE COLLEGE OF WILLIAM & MARY
THE TRUSTEES OF PRINCETON UNIVERSITY
THE WASHINGTON AND LEE UNIVERSITY
TRINITY COLLEGE
UNIVERSITY OF DELAWARE
UNIVERSITY OF SAN DIEGO
VALDOSTA STATE UNIVERSITY
WILLAMETTE UNIVERSITY

HISTORICAL FINANCIALS
Company Type: Private

Income Statement — FYE: May 31

	REVENUE ($mil)	NET INCOME ($mil)	NET PROFIT MARGIN	EMPLOYEES
05/21	889	1,274	143.2%	2,493
05/20	865	(41)	—	—
05/18	835	169	20.2%	—
05/17	798	279	34.9%	—
Annual Growth	2.7%	46.2%	—	—

2021 Year-End Financials
Return on assets: 19.8% Cash ($ mil.): 20
Return on equity: 26.3%
Current Ratio: —

TRUSTEES OF DARTMOUTH COLLEGE

Part of the esteemed Ivy League, Dartmouth College is a private, four-year liberal arts college with an enrollment of more than 6,000 students. The university has an undergraduate college (offering about 40 programs) and graduate schools of business, engineering, and medicine, plus graduate programs in the arts and sciences. Its student-teacher ratio is about 6:1. It is also home to a number of centers and institutes including Children's Hospital at Dartmouth; Dartmouth Center on Addiction, Recovery, andÂ Education; and Center for Digital Strategies. Notable alumni include Daniel Webster, Robert Frost, Theodore "Dr. Seuss" Geisel, and Nelson Rockefeller.

Operations

Dartmouth is located on a 270-acre campus located in Hanover, New Hampshire.Â It also conducts study-abroad programs in about 20 countries. Through its collective institutes and graduate schools, the college conducts a number of research programs in areas including security, capitalism, energy, and infectious disease. Altogether it has about 50 research-focused groups, centers, and institutes and attracts more than $200 million in sponsored research funding per year.

Financial Performance

For fiscal year 2011, Dartmouth reported revenues of some $763 million. Operating expenses for fiscal 2011 were some $738 million. Dartmouth has an endowment of some $3.5 billion.

Company Background

Dartmouth is the nation's ninth oldest college, founded in 1769 by Reverend Eleazar Wheelock, a Congregational minister from Connecticut. Land forÂ its campus in Hanover, New Hampshire, was conveyed by a charter from King George III; it was the last institution of higher education established in the US under colonial rule.

Auditors : PRICEWATERHOUSECOOPERS LLP BO

LOCATIONS

HQ: TRUSTEES OF DARTMOUTH COLLEGE
6001 PARKHURST HALL # 207, HANOVER, NH 037553529
Phone: 603 646-1110
Web: HOME.DARTMOUTH.EDU

PRODUCTS/OPERATIONS

Selected Divisions
Admissions and Financial Aid
Advancement Office
Campus Planning and Facilities
Dean of the College
Faculty of the Arts & Sciences
Finance and Administration
Geisel School of Medicine
President's Office
Provost's Office
Thayer School of Engineering
The Trustees of Dartmouth College
Tuck School of Business

COMPETITORS

DESALES UNIVERSITY
FORDHAM UNIVERSITY
HOWARD UNIVERSITY (INC)
LAFAYETTE COLLEGE
PRESIDENT AND FELLOWS OF HARVARD COLLEGE
ST LAWRENCE UNIVERSITY (INC)
THE COLLEGE OF WILLIAM & MARY
THE PRESIDENT AND TRUSTEES OF COLBY COLLEGE
TRUSTEES OF BOSTON COLLEGE
YALE UNIVERSITY

HISTORICAL FINANCIALS
Company Type: Private

Income Statement — FYE: June 30

	REVENUE ($mil)	NET INCOME ($mil)	NET PROFIT MARGIN	EMPLOYEES
06/22	1,007	(273)	—	5,000
06/21	1,028	2,858	277.9%	
06/20	909	411	45.2%	
06/17	1,369	691	50.5%	
Annual Growth	(6.0%)	—	—	—

2022 Year-End Financials
Return on assets: (-2.4%)   Cash ($ mil.): 384
Return on equity: (-2.8%)
Current Ratio: —

TRUSTEES OF INDIANA UNIVERSITY

Founded in 1820, Indiana University is one of the top public research universities in the world. With a population of some 71,000 degree-seeking undergraduate students, 19,000 students in graduate program, and 7,200 international students from about 155 countries. The university's flagship institution IU-Bloomington; regional campuses in Fort Wayne, Gary, Kokomo, New Albany, Richmond, and South Bend; and an urban campus in Indianapolis that is operated with Purdue University. The university has about 21,000 faculty and professional and support staff. It has 200 research centers and institutes and offers 380 overseas study programs in more than 70 countries.

Operations

The university offers more than 200 undergraduate majors and more than 300 graduate programs; it also boasts more than 380 study-abroad programs.

Indiana University has more than 725,000 total living alumni and the university charged undergraduate tuition and fees of $11, 2020 for residents and $37,600 for non-residents.

Indiana University-Purdue University Indianapolis (IUPUI) is considered number 1 nonprofit management graduate program, number 1 environmental policy and management graduate program, ranking and campus statistics in university by US News and World Report. With more than 15 schools and degrees granted in more than 255 academic programs and 95 Purdue university academic program.

Geographic Reach

The university has major campuses in Bloomington and Indianapolis, and regional campuses in Gary, Kokomo, New Albany, Richmond, and South Bend.

Company Background

An 1820 statute created the Indiana Seminary, the predecessor to Indiana University. In 1828 the legislature changed the name of the institution to Indiana College, and in 1838 it established Indiana University.

Auditors : PAUL D JOYCE CPA STATE EXAM

LOCATIONS

HQ: TRUSTEES OF INDIANA UNIVERSITY
107 S INDIANA AVE, BLOOMINGTON, IN 474057000
Phone: 812 855-4848
Web: WWW.INDIANA.EDU

PRODUCTS/OPERATIONS

2015 Sales

	$ mil	% of total
Student fees	1,118.9	51
Auxiliary enterprises	318.7	14
Federal grants & contracts	293.9	13
Non-governement grants & contracts	136.5	6
Sales and services of educational units	39.4	2
State & local grants & contracts	21.1	1
Other revenue	279.1	13
Total	2,207.6	100

COMPETITORS

CLEVELAND STATE UNIVERSITY
MARSHALL UNIVERSITY
OAKLAND UNIVERSITY
OHIO UNIVERSITY
PURDUE UNIVERSITY
THE RUTGERS STATE UNIVERSITY
VIRGINIA POLYTECHNIC INSTITUTE AND STATE UNIVERSITY
WAYNE STATE UNIVERSITY
WICHITA STATE UNIVERSITY
WILLAMETTE UNIVERSITY

HISTORICAL FINANCIALS
Company Type: Private

Income Statement — FYE: June 30

	REVENUE ($mil)	NET INCOME ($mil)	NET PROFIT MARGIN	EMPLOYEES
06/16	2,256	105	4.7%	16,000
06/15	2,207	138	6.3%	—
06/14	2,195	201	9.2%	—
06/13	2,146	189	8.8%	—
Annual Growth	1.7%	(17.7%)	—	—

2016 Year-End Financials
Return on assets: 2.0%   Cash ($ mil.): 345
Return on equity: 2.8%
Current Ratio: 1.60

TRUSTEES OF THE ESTATE OF BERNICE PAUAHI BISHOP

Kamehameha Schools provides an education fit for a king ... or queen. The private charitable trust was founded and endowed by Princess Bernice Pauahi Bishop, great granddaughter and last royal descendant of Kamehameha the Great. One of the largest independent schools in the US, Kamehameha educates more than 5,000 elementary, middle school, and high school students, many of whom board at one of its three Hawaii campuses. In addition, it operates some 30 preschools with a total enrollment of about 1,500. Kamehameha Schools is also the largest private property owner in the state of Hawaii, and uses the proceeds from its real estate operations to support its schools.

Auditors: ERNST & YOUNG US LLP SAN DIEG

LOCATIONS

HQ: TRUSTEES OF THE ESTATE OF BERNICE PAUAHI BISHOP
567 S KING ST STE 200, HONOLULU, HI 968133002
Phone: 808 523-6200
Web: WWW.KSBE.EDU

COMPETITORS

ELWYN OF PENNSYLVANIA AND DELAWARE
IMAGINE SCHOOLS, INC.
MILTON HERSHEY SCHOOL
NOBEL LEARNING COMMUNITIES, INC.
THE GIRLS' DAY SCHOOL TRUST

HISTORICAL FINANCIALS
Company Type: Private

Income Statement — FYE: June 30

	REVENUE ($mil)	NET INCOME ($mil)	NET PROFIT MARGIN	EMPLOYEES
06/20	548	14	2.7%	1,500
06/15	767	333	43.5%	—
06/14	915	482	52.7%	—
06/13	519	109	21.1%	—
Annual Growth	0.8%	(24.8%)	—	—

2020 Year-End Financials
Return on assets: 0.2% Cash ($ mil.): 36
Return on equity: 0.2%
Current Ratio: 0.80

TRUSTEES OF THE UNIV OF PENNA RETIREE MED AND DEATH BENEFITS TRUST

Auditors: PRICEWATERHOUSECOOPERS LLP PH

LOCATIONS

HQ: TRUSTEES OF THE UNIV OF PENNA RETIREE MED AND DEATH BENEFITS TRUST
3451 WALNUT ST, PHILADELPHIA, PA 191046205
Phone: 215 898-8967

HISTORICAL FINANCIALS
Company Type: Private

Income Statement — FYE: June 30

	REVENUE ($mil)	NET INCOME ($mil)	NET PROFIT MARGIN	EMPLOYEES
06/21	9,337	1,773	19.0%	4
06/20	44	14	33.7%	—
06/18	54	28	52.4%	—
06/17	42	22	53.6%	—
Annual Growth	284.1%	196.4%	—	—

2021 Year-End Financials
Return on assets: 5.7% Cash ($ mil.): 2,126
Return on equity: 7.8%
Current Ratio: 0.60

TRUSTEES OF TUFTS COLLEGE

Tufts University wants to light up the minds of New England scholars. The school offers undergraduate and graduate degrees in areas such as education, engineering, psychology, art, English, music, and medicine. The university enrolls some 11,000 students and has 1,300 faculty members, and it offers classes in 70 fields at three campuses in Massachusetts (Boston, Medford/Somerville, and Grafton). It also has an international campus in Talloires, France. Tufts University's Fletcher School of Law and Diplomacy is the oldest continuous international relations graduate program in the country. The school is also home to New England's only Veterinary School.

Operations
Tufts University has a number of research programs at all three campuses, including clinical studies in medical, dental, veterinary, and nutritional fields. It also has research programs in areas such as biology, engineering, and technology, many of which are funded through grants and fellowship funds.

Financial Performance
Tufts University has an endowment of about $1.1 billion.

Strategy
Tufts University is working to expand the resources its School of Medicine. In 2012 it moved to add a new medical research lab to study serious infectious diseases (such as tuberculosis) within the Biomedical Research and Public Health Building. It also expanded the Cummings School of Veterinary Medicine by adding a new clinic for the care and study of pets with obesity problems. The university also expands by adding new degree programs, such as a doctorate in mamalian genetics in 2011.

Company Background
Tufts was founded in 1852 through a land donation by Boston-area businessman Charles Tufts to the Universalist Church. The school adopted its motto, Pax et Lux (Peace and Light), in 1857.

EXECUTIVES

Human Relations Vice President*, Kathe Cronin
Auditors: PRICEWATERHOUSECOOPERS LLP BO

LOCATIONS

HQ: TRUSTEES OF TUFTS COLLEGE
169 HOLLAND ST STE 318, SOMERVILLE, MA 021442401
Phone: 617 628-5000
Web: WWW.TUFTS.EDU

PRODUCTS/OPERATIONS

Schools & Colleges
Cummings School of Veterinary Science
Graduate School of Arts & Sciences
The Fletcher School
Friedman School of Nutrition Science and Policy
Sackler School of Graduate Biomedical Sciences
School of Arts & Sciences
School of Dental Medicine
School of Engineering
School of Medicine
Tisch College of Citizenship and Public Service

COMPETITORS

HAMPTON UNIVERSITY
SUNY, UNIVERSITY AT BUFFALO
THE JOHNS HOPKINS UNIVERSITY
THE UNIVERSITY OF IOWA
UNIVERSITY OF MIAMI

HISTORICAL FINANCIALS
Company Type: Private

Income Statement — FYE: June 30

	REVENUE ($mil)	NET INCOME ($mil)	NET PROFIT MARGIN	EMPLOYEES
06/21	1,033	805	78.0%	4,100
06/20	1,118	32	2.9%	—
06/15	914	(25)	—	—
06/14	965	68	7.1%	—
Annual Growth	1.0%	42.3%	—	—

2021 Year-End Financials
Return on assets: 16.6% Cash ($ mil.): 90
Return on equity: 23.0%
Current Ratio: —

TRUVEN HOLDING CORP.

Auditors: PRICEWATERHOUSECOOPERS LLP NE

LOCATIONS

HQ: TRUVEN HOLDING CORP.
100 PHOENIX DR STE 100 # 100, ANN ARBOR, MI 481082600
Phone: 734 913-3000

HISTORICAL FINANCIALS
Company Type: Private

Income Statement — FYE: December 31

	REVENUE ($mil)	NET INCOME ($mil)	NET PROFIT MARGIN	EMPLOYEES
12/15	610	(75)	—	2,110
12/14	544	(37)	—	—
12/13	492	(344)	—	—
12/12	241	(54)	—	—
Annual Growth	36.2%	—	—	—

2015 Year-End Financials
Return on assets: (-6.4%) Cash ($ mil.): 14
Return on equity: —
Current Ratio: 0.80

TSVC, INC.

Auditors: BKD LLP KANSAS CITY MO

LOCATIONS

HQ: TSVC, INC.
10841 S RIDGEVIEW RD, OLATHE, KS 660616456
Phone: 913 599-6886
Web: WWW.TSVCONTRACTING.COM

HISTORICAL FINANCIALS
Company Type: Private

Income Statement — FYE: December 31

	REVENUE ($mil)	NET INCOME ($mil)	NET PROFIT MARGIN	EMPLOYEES
12/21	907	49	5.4%	4,000
12/20	818	44	5.5%	—
12/18	751	30	4.1%	—
Annual Growth	6.5%	16.9%	—	—

2021 Year-End Financials
Return on assets: 9.9% Cash ($ mil.): 7
Return on equity: 16.1%
Current Ratio: 3.20

TUDOR INVESTMENT CORPORATION

Auditors: ERNST & YOUNG LLP NEW YORK N

LOCATIONS

HQ: TUDOR INVESTMENT CORPORATION
200 ELM ST STE 200 # 200, STAMFORD, CT 069023826
Phone: 203 863-6700
Web: WWW.TUDOR.COM

HISTORICAL FINANCIALS
Company Type: Private

Income Statement — FYE: December 31

	ASSETS ($mil)	NET INCOME ($mil)	INCOME AS % OF ASSETS	EMPLOYEES
12/15	831	222	26.7%	291
12/14	819	(80)	—	—
12/13	905	486	53.7%	—
12/11	624	187	30.0%	—
Annual Growth	7.4%	4.4%	—	—

2015 Year-End Financials
Return on assets: 26.7% Cash ($ mil.): 15
Return on equity: 47.5%
Current Ratio: —

TUFTS MEDICAL CENTER, INC.

Auditors: DELOITTE & TOUCHE LLP BOSTON

LOCATIONS

HQ: TUFTS MEDICAL CENTER, INC.
800 WASHINGTON ST, BOSTON, MA 021111552
Phone: 617 636-2254
Web: WWW.TUFTSMEDICALCENTER.ORG

HISTORICAL FINANCIALS
Company Type: Private

Income Statement — FYE: September 30

	REVENUE ($mil)	NET INCOME ($mil)	NET PROFIT MARGIN	EMPLOYEES
09/20	732	38	5.2%	3,800
09/17	681	12	1.8%	—
09/16	646	14	2.3%	—
Annual Growth	3.2%	26.8%	—	—

2020 Year-End Financials
Return on assets: 3.4% Cash ($ mil.): 27
Return on equity: 22.1%
Current Ratio: 1.10

TURNER CONSTRUCTION COMPANY INC

Turner Construction is a North America-based, international construction services company and is a leading builder in diverse market segments. With more than 1,500 dedicated staff, Turner provides construction services and technical expertise for commercial and multifamily buildings, airports, and stadiums, as well as correctional, educational, entertainment, and manufacturing facilities. Turner currently manages more than $50 billion dollar of work on projects totaling more than 50 million square meters worldwide. The company is also a leader in sustainable or green building practices. Founded in 1902 by Henry Turner, the company is the main operating unit of The Turner Corporation, which is a subsidiary of German construction group HOCHTIEF.

Operations
The Turner Engineering Group provides skill, oversight, and analysis to Turner project teams in order to optimize project design, offer solutions to design-related challenges, and add value for its clients. Its Technical Reviews are focused on individual trade disciplines, such as curtainwall or foundations, though they may include multiple building elements. Risk Analyses are focused on key aspects of project delivery, beginning with a thorough review of site conditions and significant design elements. Other components of risk are typically catalogued and prioritized in a Risk Register, a process that includes a thorough review of contractual requirements. Operations and Systems are evaluated during individual site inspections and construction method reviews in order to provide input on project execution.

As part of HOCHTIEF's Americas division, Turner works alongside other contractors in the US and Canada such as Flatiron, its subsidiary E.E. Cruz, SourceBlue and Clark Builders.

Geographic Reach
Headquartered in New York, Turner Construction has offices across North America and with a presence in more than 60 countries in Latin America and the Caribbean, India, Europe, Southeast Asia, and the Middle East.

Sales and Marketing
Turner Construction works on projects in industries including aviation, transportation, commercial, entertainment, government, green building, manufacturing, pharmaceutical, research & development, retail, and sports.

Company Background
Notable projects in Turner Construction's history include the World War II Memorial in Washington, DC, the John F. Kennedy Memorial Library in Boston, and the Rock and Roll Hall of Fame. Turner also built the new Yankee Stadium in New York. The company reached a milestone in 2008 by inking its 15,000th major contract.

Auditors: DELOITTE & TOUCHE LLP PRINCET

LOCATIONS

HQ: TURNER CONSTRUCTION COMPANY INC
375 HUDSON ST FL 6, NEW YORK, NY 100143667
Phone: 212 229-6000
Web: WWW.TURNERCONSTRUCTION.COM

PRODUCTS/OPERATIONS

Selected Services
Turner Engineering Group
Design+Build
Turner Logistics: Procurement Services
Medical Planning and Procurement

Building Information Modeling (BIM)
Lean Construction

COMPETITORS

ALBERICI CORPORATION
GILBANE BUILDING COMPANY
H. J. RUSSELL & COMPANY
HKS, INC.
MCCARTHY BUILDING COMPANIES, INC.
MIRON CONSTRUCTION CO., INC.
TAKENAKA CORPORATION
THE PIKE COMPANY INC
THE SUNDT COMPANIES INC
THE TURNER CORPORATION

HISTORICAL FINANCIALS
Company Type: Private

Income Statement FYE: December 31

	REVENUE ($mil)	NET INCOME ($mil)	NET PROFIT MARGIN	EMPLOYEES
12/14	10,516	96	0.9%	5,000
12/13	9,488	76	0.8%	—
12/12	8,552	70	0.8%	—
Annual Growth	10.9%	17.2%	—	—

2014 Year-End Financials
Return on assets: 2.8% Cash ($ mil.): 188
Return on equity: 14.1%
Current Ratio: 1.10

TURNPIKE COMMISSION, PA

Whether you're headed to Valley Forge or Gettysburg or to Philadelphia or Pittsburgh, a driving trip through Pennsylvania might mean spending time on some of the 545-plus miles of highway operated by the Pennsylvania Turnpike Commission. The toll road's main section runs from the Delaware River to the Pennsylvania-Ohio border, where it connects with the Ohio Turnpike. The Pennsylvania Turnpike also includes northeastern and western extensions. The system includes about 60 toll collection facilities and some 15 service plazas. Opened in 1940, it's known as America's First Superhighway. The Pennsylvania Turnpike Commission consists of five gubernatorial appointees and the state secretary of transportation.

Auditors : SB & COMPANY LLC OWINGS MILL

LOCATIONS

HQ: TURNPIKE COMMISSION, PA
700 S EISENHOWER BLVD, MIDDLETOWN, PA 170575529
Phone: 717 939-9551
Web: WWW.PATURNPIKE.COM

COMPETITORS

ARIZONA DEPARTMENT OF TRANSPORTATION
MISSOURI DEPARTMENT OF TRANSPORTATION
OHIO DEPARTMENT OF TRANSPORTATION
TEXAS DEPARTMENT OF TRANSPORTATION
TRANSPORTATION, SOUTH CAROLINA DEPARTMENT OF

HISTORICAL FINANCIALS
Company Type: Private

Income Statement FYE: May 31

	REVENUE ($mil)	NET INCOME ($mil)	NET PROFIT MARGIN	EMPLOYEES
05/22	1,507	(462)	—	2,200
05/21	1,231	(583)	—	—
Annual Growth	22.4%	—	—	—

2022 Year-End Financials
Return on assets: (-4.3%) Cash ($ mil.): 318
Return on equity: —
Current Ratio: 2.20

TURTLE & HUGHES, INC

Turtle & Hughes is one of the nation's largest independent electrical and industrial distributors. The company's exhaustive lineup is sold through two divisions: Electrical Distribution, which operates in about 20 branches and provides electrical services and solutions backed by a commitment to technical and product expertise, and Turtle & Hughes Integrated Supply (THIS), which has proven its leadership in the industrial supply market by partnering with global companies to reduce their total cost of ownership. Family-owned, the company is led by its first non-family CEO, Kathleen Shanahan.

Operations
Turtle & Hughes is organized into two divisions: the Electrical Distribution division provides electrical services and solutions backed by a commitment to technical and product expertise, and Turtle & Hughes Integrated Supply (THIS), which has proven its leadership in the industrial supply market by partnering with global companies to reduce their total cost of ownership.

It offers products such as automation, cable strays and struts, conduit and conduit fittings, electrical boxes and covers, fasteners, and hardware. It also offers alarms, security and signaling, batteries, fuses, blocks and holders, and heat cables, among others.

Geographic Reach
Turtle & Hughes, headquartered in Linden, New Jersey, operates through about 20 branches across the US.

Sales and Marketing
The company serves industries including automotive, aerospace, facility maintenance, oil & gas, medical devices, pharmaceutical, building materials, food & beverages and consumer products.

Company Background
Turtle & Hughes was founded in 1923 as an electrical supply house.

Auditors : EISNERAMPER LLP ISELIN NJ

LOCATIONS

HQ: TURTLE & HUGHES, INC
1900 LOWER RD, LINDEN, NJ 070366586
Phone: 732 574-3600
Web: WWW.TURTLE.COM

PRODUCTS/OPERATIONS

Selected Products
Datacom categories
    Anchors and fasteners
    Burial products/innerduct
    Cabinets and enclosures
    Cable management
    Cable tray/ladder rack
    Category rated and coax cable
    Connectivity
    Fiber-optic cable
    Hand tools
    Outside plant
    Power protection
    Raceway and duct systems
    Safety
    Security fencing
    Splices, connectors, and lugs
    Tools, testers, and safety
Electrical categories
    Alarms, annunciators, and signals
    Anchors and plugs
    Automation products
    Ballasts and transformers
    Batteries and flashlights
    Box enclosures
    Breakers, panels, and switchgears
    Cable trays and struts
    Conduit fittings
    Cord connectors
    Dimming controls
    Electrical tools
    Emergency lighting
    Enclosures
    Fans
    Fluorescent lighting
    Fuse holders and terminal blocks
    Generators
    Groundings
    Heat shrink
    Heating
    High-bay lighting
    Incandescent lighting
    Lamps
    Limit, temp., and proximity switch
    Lugs and terminals
    Metering equipment
    Motor control
    Motors, AC and DC drivers
    Outdoor lighting
    Pole line products
    Programmable controls
    Relays
    Strut/channel
    Test equipment
    Time clocks
    Transformers
    Wire, cable, and cord
    Wiring accessories
    Wiring devices
Industrial categories
    Adhesives and tapes
    Brushes and brooms
    Carbide tools
    Cutting fluid/lubricant
    Cutting tools
    Fasteners
    Hand tools
    Hoist, chain, and accessories
    Industrial abrasives
    Janitorial paper supplies
    Ladders
    Locks

Lubricating devices
Material handling
MRO supplies
Paint/markets
Pipe hangers
Pipe, valves, and fittings
Pneumatics
Pneumatic tools
Power tools
Safety equipment
Saw blades
Shim/shim stock
Solenoid valves
Strut/channel
Tooling accessories

COMPETITORS

BERRY COMPANIES, INC.
BILLOWS ELECTRIC SUPPLY COMPANY, INC.
BROCK WHITE COMPANY, LLC
FOXWORTH-GALBRAITH LUMBER COMPANY
GALCO INDUSTRIAL ELECTRONICS, INC.
ORSCHELN FARM AND HOME LLC
RICE LAKE WEIGHING SYSTEMS, INC.
SPAHN & ROSE LUMBER CO.
STONEWAY ELECTRIC SUPPLY CO.
TAP ENTERPRISES, INC.

HISTORICAL FINANCIALS
Company Type: Private

Income Statement — FYE: September 30

	REVENUE ($mil)	NET INCOME ($mil)	NET PROFIT MARGIN	EMPLOYEES
09/21	758	11	1.6%	900
09/19	758	21	2.8%	—
09/18	754	20	2.7%	—
09/17	671	18	2.7%	—
Annual Growth	3.1%	(10.1%)	—	—

2021 Year-End Financials
Return on assets: 4.1%   Cash ($ mil.): 12
Return on equity: 12.6%
Current Ratio: 2.00

U.S. GENERAL SERVICES ADMINISTRATION

The U.S. General Services Administration (GSA) manages the rental of more than 65 million square feet of real estate in US government-owned properties. In addition to acting as the government's landlord in obtaining office space for over a million federal workers, the GSA also manages properties and supplies equipment, telecommunications, and information technology products to its customer agencies. It spends around $85 billion annually for goods and services supporting about 8,300 buildings and more than 226,000 vehicles. The agency operates through divisions including the Federal Acquisition Service and Public Buildings Service. The GSA was established in 1949 to streamline the administrative work of the federal government.

Operations
GSA comprises the Federal Acquisition Service (FAS), the Public Buildings Service (PBS), and Staff Offices. In addition, it operates over 10 staff offices and two independent offices.

Through a network of service providers, FAS delivers information technology products and services, telecommunications services, travel and transportation management, motor vehicles and fleet services and issues nearly 6 million charge cards on average.

PBS operates within two divisions? workspace acquisition and property management. It acquires space for the federal government through new construction and leasing and leases almost 370 million square feet of workspace in more than 8,300 buildings, over 500 of which are on the National Register of Historic Places. PBS also manages the disposal of unused properties.

The GSA Staff Offices support the enterprise and are funded through either the Working Capital Fund or annual appropriations. It ensure GSA is prepared to meet its customers' needs on a day-to-day basis as well as in crises.

Overall, Acquisition Services Fund (ASF) accounts for over 60% of sales while Federal Buildings Fund (FBF) accounts for around 40%.

Geographic Reach
Headquartered in Washington, DC, the US General Services Administration provides services and support to more than 60 Federal departments and agencies. It delivers goods and services across the country and overseas through more than 10 regional offices located in major US cities.

Sales and Marketing
The company's FBF top customers are US department of Justice and US Department of Homeland Security with over 15% each, while ASF top customer is the US Department of Defense which accounts for about 70%.

Financial Performance
The company's revenue in 2021 increased to $31.7 billion compared to $29.0 billion in the prior year.

Strategy
The company's strategic goals are save taxpayer money through better management of Federal real estate; establish GSA as the premier provider of efficient and effective acquisition solutions across the Federal Government; improve the way Federal agencies buy, build, and use technology; and design and deliver expanded shared services within GSA and across the Federal Government to improve performance and save taxpayer money.

Company Background
The U.S. General Services Administration was established by President Harry Truman in 1949 to streamline the administrative work of the federal government. It consolidated the National Archives Establishment, the Federal Works Agency, the Public Buildings Administration, the Bureau of Federal Supply, the Office of Contract Settlement, and the War Assets Administration into one federal agency delivering and managing supplies and providing workplaces for federal employees.

GSA's original mission was to dispose of war surplus goods, manage and store government records, handle emergency preparedness, and stockpile strategic supplies for wartime.

EXECUTIVES

Acting Administrator*, Timothy Horne
CIO*, Casey Coleman

LOCATIONS

HQ: U.S. GENERAL SERVICES ADMINISTRATION
1800 F ST NW RM 6100, WASHINGTON, DC 204050001
Phone: 202 501-0450
Web: WWW.GSA.GOV

PRODUCTS/OPERATIONS

2018 Sales

	$mil.	% of total
Federal Buildings Fund		
Building Operations-Leased	6,420	26
Building Operations-Government Owned	5,261	21
Acquisition Services Fund		
Assisted Acquisition Services	7,043	29
Travel, Transportation, and Logistics	2,060	8
Information Technology	1,786	7
General Supplies and Services	1,300	5
Professional Services and Human Capital	87	-
Other Programs	113	1
Other Funds		
Working Capital Fund	657	3
Other General	37	
Eliminations	(921)	-
Total	23,843	100

Selected Products and Services Facilities & Construction Construction Related Materials Facility Related Materials Facility Related Services Human Capital Administrative Services Human Capital and Training Solutions Human Resources System General Support Services Industrial Products & Services Basic Materials Environmental Protection Equipment [Fire/Rescue/Safety] Hardware & Tools Industrial Products [Install/Maintenance/Repair/Build] Machinery & Components Test & Measurement Supplies Information Technology Cloud Computing Services Cybersecurity Products and Services Data Center Services Hardware Products and Services Software Products and Services Telecommunications and Network Services Office Management Furniture Office Equipment Office Supplies Professional Services Professional Services Schedule One Acquisition Solution for Integrated Services Security & Protection Security Services Security Systems Security Animals and Related Services Transportation & Logistics Services Vehicle Buying Vehicle Leasing Travel & Lodging Relocation

COMPETITORS

CENTRAL MANAGEMENT SERVICES, ILLINOIS DEPARTMENT OF
CONDUENT INCORPORATED

GENERAL SERVICES, CALIFORNIA DEPARTMENT OF
LIBERATA UK LIMITED
MANAGEMENT SERVICES, FLORIDA DEPARTMENT OF
MANTECH INTERNATIONAL CORPORATION
PUBLIC BUILDING SERVICE OFFICE OF CHIEF
FINANCIAL OFFICER (PF)
PUBLISHING OFFICE, US GOVERNMENT
SERCO INC.
U S OFFICE OF PERSONNEL MANAGEMENT

HISTORICAL FINANCIALS
Company Type: Private

Income Statement — FYE: September 30

	REVENUE ($mil)	NET INCOME ($mil)	NET PROFIT MARGIN	EMPLOYEES
09/16	20,457	290	1.4%	13,000
09/15*	38,976	486	1.2%	—
12/05	0	0	—	—
Annual Growth	—	—	—	—

*Fiscal year change

2016 Year-End Financials
Return on assets: 0.7%   Cash ($ mil.): —
Return on equity: 0.9%
Current Ratio: —

U.S. VENTURE, INC.

Privately held US Venture, Inc. is a North American leader in the distribution of fuel and transportation products. US Oil, its division, transports more than 2 million of fuel daily via pipelines, rail, light oil-barges, and trucks. The division maintains over 8 million BOE in storage capacity and has access to nearly 200 terminals. Through US AutoForce, the company is also a top distributor of tires and car parts to independent tire retailers, auto repair shops, and dealerships. The company's Lubricants division maintains a competitive business as well, set up to blend and market chemical products to automotive, industrial, and metalworking industries. Through the GAIN Clean Fuel brand, US Venture also sells clean biofuels.

Operations
US Venture has seven business divisions.

US Oil is a leading distributor of branded and unbranded refined products in the US and Canada. It transports more than 1 million gallons of energy products daily. US Oil also engages in energy trading.

Tires, car parts, and lubricants are distributed through the US AutoForce division, another industry leader. Its portfolio includes more than 30 tire brands, lubricant, and many branded car parts (mostly brakes, chassis, repair equipment, and exhausts).

US Lubricants blends and distributes lubricants under its THRIVE brand for automotive, industrial, and metalworking needs. It also provides support services like mobile filtration systems, oil analysis lab services, and fluids storage and handling systems.

US GAIN division supplies compressed natural gas (CNG) and renewable natural gas (RNG) to more than 50 fueling stations.

Breakthrough provides innovative transportation and supply chain strategies for the world's leading shippers. IGEN build excise tax software that meets the needs of the motor fuel industry.

US Petroleum Equipment supplies quality new, used, and rebuilt petroleum related equipment such as gasoline pumps, dispensers, and other related supplies "installing confidence" throughout Wisconsin, Northern Illinois, and Upper Michigan.

IGEN is an excise tax software designed to streamline tax filing in the motor fuel and tobacco industries.

Geographic Reach
Headquartered in Appleton, Wisconsin, US Venture operates throughout North America. US Oil handles fuel supply in the Midwest with over 30 terminals, and nearly 200 third-party terminal partners. The company has a concentration of fuel, tires, car parts, and convenience store services in the Midwest. It distributes fuels, car parts, and lubricants in North America.

Sales and Marketing
The US Oil division distributes products from a-dozen major oil brands including BP, Shell, Exxon, Mobil, Marathon, Citgo, Sunoco, Clark, and Phillips 66. It offers flexible pricing, and fixed-fuel contracts, and commodity trading. Traded products include gasoline, ethanol, biodiesel, jet fuels, propane, and butane.

Together with US Lubricants, it serves the agricultural, construction, forestry, marine, and mining industries. US Lubricants also supplies its products to automotive dealerships, repair shops, lube shops, and tire centers, and customers in commercial transportation, as well as industrial and metalworking lubricants.

Company Background
U.S. Oil was established in 1951 as Schmidt Oil by the sons of local fuel distributor, Albert Schmidt. The company changed its name to U.S. Venture in 2010 to reflect the company's increasingly diverse portfolio of entrepreneurial businesses. It has remained family-owned since its inception and today it is one of the largest privately held companies in Wisconsin.

Auditors : DELOITTE & TOUCHE LLP MILWAU

LOCATIONS
HQ: U.S. VENTURE, INC.
  425 BETTER WAY, APPLETON, WI 549156192
Phone: 920 739-6101
Web: WWW.USVENTURE.COM

PRODUCTS/OPERATIONS

Selected Operations
U.S. AutoForce (exhaust pipe manufacturing and autoparts distribution)
U.S. Lubricants (motor oil and related products)
U.S. Oil (gasoline, fuel oil, and natural gas)
U.S Gain (compressed natural gas)

COMPETITORS
ALON USA ENERGY, INC.
CITGO PETROLEUM CORPORATION
GEORGE E. WARREN LLC
J. D. STREETT & COMPANY, INC.
JOHN CRANE INC.
MARTIN MIDSTREAM PARTNERS L.P.
MIDSTREAM MAGELLAN PARTNERS L P
NOCO ENERGY CORP.
SOUTHERN COUNTIES OIL CO.
TRANSMONTAIGNE LLC

HISTORICAL FINANCIALS
Company Type: Private

Income Statement — FYE: July 31

	REVENUE ($mil)	NET INCOME ($mil)	NET PROFIT MARGIN	EMPLOYEES
07/15	8,076	173	2.1%	1,673
07/14	9,088	49	0.5%	—
07/13	7,346	47	0.6%	—
Annual Growth	4.9%	91.7%	—	—

2015 Year-End Financials
Return on assets: 16.9%   Cash ($ mil.): 13
Return on equity: 53.2%
Current Ratio: 1.70

UAW RETIREE MEDICAL BENEFITS TRUST

EXECUTIVES
Board of Trustees, Robert Naftaly
Auditors : DELOITTE TAX LLP DETROIT MI

LOCATIONS
HQ: UAW RETIREE MEDICAL BENEFITS TRUST
  200 WALKER ST STE 400, DETROIT, MI 482074229
Phone: 313 324-5900
Web: WWW.UAWTRUST.ORG

HISTORICAL FINANCIALS
Company Type: Private

Income Statement — FYE: December 31

	ASSETS ($mil)	NET INCOME ($mil)	INCOME AS % OF ASSETS	EMPLOYEES
12/18	60,352	1,176	1.9%	94
12/17	63,225	88	0.1%	—
12/16	58,966	(1,839)	—	—
Annual Growth	1.2%	—	—	—

2018 Year-End Financials
Return on assets: 1.9%   Cash ($ mil.): 5014
Return on equity: 2.1%
Current Ratio: 17.70

UC HEALTH, LLC.

From its flagship University of Cincinnati Medical Center to its state-of-the-art West

Chester Hospital, UC Health provides cancer care, dental care, surgery, transplant, trauma care and women's health. UC Health includes University of Cincinnati Medical Center, West Chester Hospital, Daniel Drake Center for Post-Acute Care, UC Gardner Neuroscience Institute, Lindner Center of HOPE, Bridgeway Pointe, and University of Cincinnati Physicians. The not-for-profit UC Health was formed in 2010 as collaboration between University of Cincinnati Physicians, University of Cincinnati Medical Center and West Chester Hospital.

Geographic Reach
UC Health has more than 40 locations across Ohio, Kentucky, and Indiana.

Company Background
Formerly known as The Health Alliance of Greater Cincinnati, the company changed its name to UC Health in 2010 after a number of its hospital members left the system and the University of Cincinnati took control of the remaining operations. Rumors of dissolution had swirled around the organization since its members began jumping ship starting in 2007.

Four of the organization's founding hospitals ultimately left the system: The 175-bed Fort Hamilton Hospital (now part of Kettering Health Network) and the 210-bed Jewish Hospital (now part of Catholic Healthcare Partners) departed in 2010. Two other hospitals (St. Luke's and Christ Hospital) broke off from the alliance after a long legal struggle in 2007.

EXECUTIVES
Co-Vice President*, Michael Legg
CMO*, Evaline Alessandrini
Auditors: DELOITTE TAX LLP CINCINNATI

LOCATIONS
HQ: UC HEALTH, LLC.
3200 BURNET AVE, CINCINNATI, OH 452293019
Phone: 513 585-6000
Web: WWW.UCHEALTH.COM

PRODUCTS/OPERATIONS
Selected Ohio Facilities
Drake Center (Cincinnati)
Linder Center of HOPE (Mason)
UC Health Surgical Hospital (West Chester)
University of Cincinnati Physicians (Cincinnati)
University of Cincinnati Medical Center (Cincinnati)
West Chester Hospital (West Chester)

COMPETITORS
BEACON MEDICAL GROUP, INC.
CAREGROUP, INC.
CATHOLIC HEALTH SYSTEM, INC.
CONTINUUM HEALTH PARTNERS, INC.
HMH HOSPITALS CORPORATION
JEWISH HOSPITAL & ST. MARY'S HEALTHCARE, INC.
MAINEHEALTH SERVICES
MERCY HEALTH PARTNERS, INC.
MERITER HEALTH SERVICES, INC.
WASHINGTON HOSPITAL CENTER CORPORATION

HISTORICAL FINANCIALS
Company Type: Private

Income Statement — FYE: June 30

	REVENUE ($mil)	NET INCOME ($mil)	NET PROFIT MARGIN	EMPLOYEES
06/18	1,661	40	2.5%	10,000
06/17	1,586	73	4.7%	—
06/10	138	(81)	—	—
06/09	102	0	0.0%	—
Annual Growth	36.3%	—	—	—

2018 Year-End Financials
Return on assets: 2.5%   Cash ($ mil.): 76
Return on equity: 4.9%
Current Ratio: 4.70

UCH-MHS

Memorial Hospital tries to keep good health more than a memory for the patients in its care. The hospital is a 520-bed general hospital which provides a range of children's and adult health-care services and specialties, including cardiac care, cancer treatment, trauma care, women's services, pediatric medicine, and rehabilitation. The hospital has about 700 physicians on its medical staff. Memorial Hospital also includes the 100-bed Memorial Hospital North and Children's Hospital Colorado, as well as outpatient clinics throughout the Colorado Springs area. In 2012 it became an affiliate of University of Colorado Health.

Operations
In 2013 alone, the Memorial Hospital Auxiliary gave more than $76,000 to Memorial Hospital to assist with equipment purchases and education to 17 different departments.

Geographic Reach
The hospital system has more than a dozen facilities throughout the Pikes Peak region of Colorado.

Strategy
In 2013 Memorial Hospital doubled the number of physicians in its medical group, hiring specialists in cardiology, oncology, thoracic surgery, neuroscience, trauma, breast surgery and other areas. That year it also secured achieved Primary Stroke Center Accreditation and Chest Pain Center Accreditation with PCI, two distinguished designations of quality.

UCHealth spent about $37 million in 2013 on new technology, repairs, and other improvements at Memorial Hospital. In 2013 Memorial Hospital introduced new electronic medical records system allows patients to access lab results, consult with physicians, make appointments, and conduct other medical-related activities online.

Company Background
In 2012 the hospital was named as the Official Hospital of the Colorado Springs US Olympic Training Center.

Memorial Hospital has been working to reduce expenses by increasing operational efficiencies. The health system was recognized by Thomson Reuters in 2010 for its efficiency measures, as it cut spending by $35 million in three years. The company considered converting itself into an independent not-for-profit to allow for further financial flexibility and expansion outside of the Colorado Springs area.

In order for Memorial Hospital to become an independent operation, it would have had to exit the Public Employees Retirement Association (PERA), the retirement fund currently responsible for its employee pensions. The two organizations were at odds over how much Memorial Hospital should have to pay in order to exit the fund. PERA estimated that about $245 million would cover Memorial Hospital's obligations to the fund; Memorial Hospital's estimate was between $25 and $50 million. The disparity led Memorial Hospital to table plans to exit PERA indefinitely.

The hospital system was established in 1904.

Auditors: PLANTE & MORAN PLUG DENVER

LOCATIONS
HQ: UCH-MHS
1400 E BOULDER ST, COLORADO SPRINGS, CO 809095533
Phone: 719 365-5000
Web: WWW.UCHEALTH.ORG

COMPETITORS
EISENHOWER MEDICAL CENTER
JOHN T. MATHER MEMORIAL HOSPITAL OF PORT JEFFERSON, NEW YORK, INC.
MISSION HOSPITAL, INC.
PROSPECT WATERBURY, INC.
SAINT JOSEPH HOSPITAL, INC

HISTORICAL FINANCIALS
Company Type: Private

Income Statement — FYE: June 30

	REVENUE ($mil)	NET INCOME ($mil)	NET PROFIT MARGIN	EMPLOYEES
06/21	1,150	128	11.2%	2,438
06/20	1,037	49	4.8%	—
06/19	1,051	97	9.3%	—
06/16	693	25	3.7%	—
Annual Growth	10.6%	38.1%	—	—

2021 Year-End Financials
Return on assets: 12.2%   Cash ($ mil.): 27
Return on equity: 35.5%
Current Ratio: 1.10

UFCW & EMPLOYERS TRUST LLC

Auditors: HEMMING MORSE CPA'S AND CONSUL

LOCATIONS

HQ: UFCW & EMPLOYERS TRUST LLC
  1000 BURNETT AVE STE 200, CONCORD, CA 945202058
Phone: 925 609-9068
Web: WWW.UFCWTRUST.COM

HISTORICAL FINANCIALS
Company Type: Private

Income Statement — FYE: December 31

	REVENUE ($mil)	NET INCOME ($mil)	NET PROFIT MARGIN	EMPLOYEES
12/14	553	33	6.0%	4
12/13	544	16	3.0%	—
Annual Growth	1.7%	107.2%	—	—

2014 Year-End Financials
Return on assets: 14.2%   Cash ($ mil.): 81
Return on equity: 26.2%
Current Ratio: 40.60

UFCW & EMPLOYERS TRUST LLC

Auditors: VAVRINEK TRINE DAY & CO LLP S

LOCATIONS

HQ: UFCW & EMPLOYERS TRUST LLC
  1000 BURNETT AVE STE 110, CONCORD, CA 945205713
Phone: 800 552-2400
Web: WWW.UFCWTRUST.COM

HISTORICAL FINANCIALS
Company Type: Private

Income Statement — FYE: December 31

	ASSETS ($mil)	NET INCOME ($mil)	INCOME AS % OF ASSETS	EMPLOYEES
12/18	460	10	2.3%	200
12/17	455	18	4.1%	—
Annual Growth	1.0%	(44.2%)	—	—

2018 Year-End Financials
Return on assets: 2.3%   Cash ($ mil.): 43
Return on equity: 3.0%
Current Ratio: 127.80

UGI UTILITIES, INC.

EXECUTIVES

FIN STRATEGY, Kirk R Oliver
CAO, Ann P Kelly

LOCATIONS

HQ: UGI UTILITIES, INC.
  1 UGI DR, DENVER, PA 175179039
Phone: 800 276-2722
Web: WWW.UGI.COM

HISTORICAL FINANCIALS
Company Type: Private

Income Statement — FYE: September 30

	REVENUE ($mil)	NET INCOME ($mil)	NET PROFIT MARGIN	EMPLOYEES
09/18	1,092	148	13.6%	1,520
09/17	887	116	13.1%	—
Annual Growth	23.1%	28.3%	—	—

2018 Year-End Financials
Return on assets: 4.6%   Cash ($ mil.): 10
Return on equity: 13.6%
Current Ratio: 0.50

UMASS MEMORIAL HEALTH CARE INC AND AFFILIATES GROUP RETURN

Auditors: FEELEY & DRISCOLL PC BOSTON

LOCATIONS

HQ: UMASS MEMORIAL HEALTH CARE INC AND AFFILIATES GROUP RETURN
  306 BELMONT ST 120, WORCESTER, MA 016041004
Phone: 508 334-5106
Web: WWW.UMMHC.ORG

HISTORICAL FINANCIALS
Company Type: Private

Income Statement — FYE: September 30

	REVENUE ($mil)	NET INCOME ($mil)	NET PROFIT MARGIN	EMPLOYEES
09/13	2,613	51	2.0%	500
09/10	2,594	65	2.5%	—
Annual Growth	0.2%	(7.7%)	—	—

2013 Year-End Financials
Return on assets: 2.4%   Cash ($ mil.): 156
Return on equity: 5.8%
Current Ratio: 0.80

UMASS MEMORIAL MEDICAL CENTER, INC.

Auditors: PRICEWATERHOUSECOOPERS LLP BO

LOCATIONS

HQ: UMASS MEMORIAL MEDICAL CENTER, INC.
  55 LAKE AVE N, WORCESTER, MA 016550002
Phone: 508 334-1000

HISTORICAL FINANCIALS
Company Type: Private

Income Statement — FYE: September 30

	REVENUE ($mil)	NET INCOME ($mil)	NET PROFIT MARGIN	EMPLOYEES
09/16	1,621	(130)	—	29
09/15	1,332	60	4.5%	—
09/14	1,258	19	1.6%	—
09/13	1,183	68	5.8%	—
Annual Growth	11.1%	—	—	—

2016 Year-End Financials
Return on assets: (-10.4%)   Cash ($ mil.): 124
Return on equity: (-83.3%)
Current Ratio: 1.20

UMASS MEMORIAL MEDICAL CENTER, INC.

Auditors: PRICEWATERHOUSECOOPERS LLP B

LOCATIONS

HQ: UMASS MEMORIAL MEDICAL CENTER, INC.
  365 PLANTATION ST STE 185, WORCESTER, MA 016052379
Phone: 508 334-1000
Web: WWW.UMMHEALTH.ORG

HISTORICAL FINANCIALS
Company Type: Private

Income Statement — FYE: September 30

	REVENUE ($mil)	NET INCOME ($mil)	NET PROFIT MARGIN	EMPLOYEES
09/21	2,176	38	1.7%	50
09/20	2,005	237	11.8%	—
09/19	1,856	16	0.9%	—
09/18	1,712	87	5.1%	—
Annual Growth	8.3%	(24.2%)	—	—

2021 Year-End Financials
Return on assets: 2.6%   Cash ($ mil.): 190
Return on equity: 7.9%
Current Ratio: 1.10

UNIFIED SCHOOL DISTRICT 259

Auditors: ALLEN GIBBS & HOULIK LC W

LOCATIONS

HQ: UNIFIED SCHOOL DISTRICT 259
  903 S EDGEMOOR ST, WICHITA, KS 672183337
Phone: 316 973-4000
Web: WWW.USD259.ORG

UNIPRO FOODSERVICE, INC.

UniPro Foodservice knows there's strength in numbers. As the largest US food service cooperative, its members include more than 650 independent member companies that provide food and food-related products to more than 800,000 food service customers, including health care and educational institutions, military installations, and restaurants. UniPro provides training, collective purchasing, and marketing materials to all distributors. Its products -- which include dry groceries and frozen and refrigerated foods -- are sold under the brand names CODE, ComSource, Nifda, and Nugget. Suppliers include Kraft Foods, Reynolds Food Packaging, Solo Cup, Tyson Foods, and Unilever Foodsolutions.

Operations
The cooperative's Multi-Unit Group (MUG), formed in 1985 to service multi-unit food service operators, include some of the largest member distributors in the UniPro network. MUG members are like a one-stop shop for multi-unit operators, offering fresh produce, paper products, and small wares from a single source in an effort to improve efficiency.

Geographic Reach
The Atlanta-based cooperative operates through more than 900 distribution centers across the US. Beyond the US, it has distribution operations in Canada, Mexico, the Bahamas, Australia, Costa Rica, Guam, and Japan.

Sales and Marketing
Progressive Group Alliance, a business unit, distributes and supplies partners with sales, marketing, and advice to customers. Brands include Alliance Pro (non-food), Coral Princess (seafood), GourMates (condiments), Harvest Gold (cheese, butter, and dairy-related products), and Premium Recipe (prepared entrees, salsas, and sauces).

Financial Performance
While privately-owned Unipro Foodservice doesn't report its financial results, collectively the cooperatives ring up an estimated $64 billion in sales annually.

Strategy
To enhance its members' competitiveness at home and abroad, in 2013 UniPro formed a strategic alliance with Technomic, a leading research and consulting firm to the food service industry. As part of the partnership, UnPro joined the steering committee of Technomic's Foodservice Category Management Institute.

Auditors: HA&W LLP ATLANTA GEORGIA

LOCATIONS
HQ: UNIPRO FOODSERVICE, INC.
2500 CUMBERLAND PKWY SE, ATLANTA, GA 303393942
Phone: 770 952-0871
Web: WWW.UNIPROFOODSERVICE.COM

PRODUCTS/OPERATIONS
Selected Suppliers
Cargill Foodservice
Durable Packaging International
Handgards, Inc.
Kraft Foods
Reynolds Foodservice Packaging
Solo Cup Company
Unilever Foodsolutions

COMPETITORS
ALPHA OMEGA DISTRIBUTORS, LTD.
ASSOCIATED GROCERS OF FLORIDA, INC.
B&G FOODS, INC.
BOAR'S HEAD PROVISIONS CO., INC.
CONSUMERS PACKING CO., INC.
CRAWSHAW GROUP PLC
KEHE DISTRIBUTORS, LLC
QUIRCH FOODS, LLC
SHERWOOD FOOD DISTRIBUTORS, L.L.C.
US FOODS HOLDING CORP.

HISTORICAL FINANCIALS
Company Type: Private

Income Statement — FYE: December 31

	REVENUE ($mil)	NET INCOME ($mil)	NET PROFIT MARGIN	EMPLOYEES
12/12	987	(0)	0.0%	140
12/11	881	0	0.0%	—
12/10	657	0	0.0%	—
Annual Growth	22.5%	—	—	—

2012 Year-End Financials
Return on assets: (-0.2%)   Cash ($ mil.): 6
Return on equity: (-3.5%)
Current Ratio: 1.00

HISTORICAL FINANCIALS (UniPro)
Company Type: Private

Income Statement — FYE: June 30

	REVENUE ($mil)	NET INCOME ($mil)	NET PROFIT MARGIN	EMPLOYEES
06/20	730	42	5.8%	5,406
06/19	688	13	1.9%	—
06/18	668	119	17.8%	—
06/17	632	15	2.4%	—
Annual Growth	4.9%	40.8%	—	—

2020 Year-End Financials
Return on assets: 3.2%   Cash ($ mil.): —
Return on equity: 22.7%
Current Ratio: —

UNIQUE DESIGNS, INC.

Auditors: PRAGER METIS CPAS LLC NEW YO

LOCATIONS
HQ: UNIQUE DESIGNS, INC.
425 MEADOWLANDS PKWY # 2, SECAUCUS, NJ 070941817
Phone: 212 575-7701

HISTORICAL FINANCIALS
Company Type: Private

Income Statement — FYE: March 31

	REVENUE ($mil)	NET INCOME ($mil)	NET PROFIT MARGIN	EMPLOYEES
03/22	579	8	1.5%	1
03/21	349	5	1.7%	—
03/16*	65	0	0.5%	—
12/14	0	0	—	—
Annual Growth	—	43.9%	—	—

*Fiscal year change

2022 Year-End Financials
Return on assets: 3.0%   Cash ($ mil.): 1
Return on equity: 7.0%
Current Ratio: 2.10

UNITED CONCORDIA LIFE AND HEALTH INSURANCE COMPANY

LOCATIONS
HQ: UNITED CONCORDIA LIFE AND HEALTH INSURANCE COMPANY
4401 DEER PATH RD, HARRISBURG, PA 171103907
Phone: 717 260-7081

HISTORICAL FINANCIALS
Company Type: Private

Income Statement — FYE: December 31

	REVENUE ($mil)	NET INCOME ($mil)	NET PROFIT MARGIN	EMPLOYEES
12/15	680	34	5.1%	1
12/14	731	57	7.9%	—
Annual Growth	(6.9%)	(39.8%)	—	—

2015 Year-End Financials
Return on assets: 10.3%   Cash ($ mil.): 54
Return on equity: 14.3%
Current Ratio: 1.10

UNITED COOPERATIVE

LOCATIONS
HQ: UNITED COOPERATIVE
N7160 RACEWAY RD, BEAVER DAM, WI 539169315
Phone: 920 887-1756
Web: WWW.UNITEDCOOPERATIVE.COM

HISTORICAL FINANCIALS
Company Type: Private

Income Statement   FYE: December 31

	REVENUE ($mil)	NET INCOME ($mil)	NET PROFIT MARGIN	EMPLOYEES
12/17	644	49	7.7%	358
12/16	630	41	6.6%	—
12/15	579	41	7.1%	—
12/14	577	57	10.0%	—
Annual Growth	3.7%	(4.7%)	—	—

2017 Year-End Financials
Return on assets: 8.0%
Return on equity: 12.1%
Current Ratio: 2.20
Cash ($ mil.): 22

UNITED DAIRYMEN OF ARIZONA

Its name says it all: United Dairymen of Arizona (UDA) is a group of Arizona-based dairy farmers united together to stabilize and strengthen the market for milk products. Supplied by some 90-member producers, the cooperative's plant has the capacity to process 10 million pounds of milk per day, about 90% of the milk in the state. Products include sweet cream and butter, fluid and condensed skim milk, and non-fat dry milk, among others. Customers include onsite cheese maker Schreiber Foods, fluid milk processors, and supermarket chains throughout The Grand Canyon State. UDA also makes dried lactose powder for food manufacturers. Started in 1960, the co-op was formed through a merger of two dairy associations.

Operations
UDA's Arizona-based manufacturing plant operates around the clock, often serving as a balancing plant for other area processors. Its capacity handles a broad line of milk products, shifting milk production according to dairy supply and market demand. The plant is the nation's largest supervised kosher milk facility with a weekly production capacity of more than 500 metric tons of kosher powder. UDA also produces blended dry products as part of a joint venture.

UDA's operations include providing emergency repair, preventative maintenance, installation, and transportation services, and related supplies to members. Since 2007, the co-op's service and supply division share a facility in Texas, too.

Geographic Reach
Based in Arizona, United Dairymen of Arizona serves other companies in the state as well as the US kosher niche. It exports products overseas.

Sales and Marketing
To its benefit, UDA enjoys long-term relationships with fluid milk processors, which enables it to rely on a steady market for about 30% of its fluid milk. Schreiber Foods, based in Tempe, Arizona, buys another 30% of its products.

Strategy
While UDA's business is concentrated in Arizona, its member interests cross both eastern California and Texas. Beyond the US, UDA has benefited from export assistance to sell cheese to customers in Asia, North Africa, and the Middle East. As a member of DairyAmerica (which is controlled by California Dairies), UDA further extends its international reach by selling non-fat dry milk, skim milk powder, and other products on the auction block known as GlobalDairyTrade, developed by Fonterra.

The only milk marketing co-op in Arizona, UDA is focused on improving production, processing, and marketing opportunities for member-producers. To that end, it strategically joins with other daily cooperatives to expand global trade of dairy products and promote legislation that addresses issues such as surplus of milk, low prices, and volatile markets.

Auditors: HERBEIN & COMPANY INC READI

LOCATIONS
HQ: UNITED DAIRYMEN OF ARIZONA
2008 S HARDY DR, TEMPE, AZ 852821211
Phone: 480 966-7211
Web: WWW.UDA.COOP

PRODUCTS/OPERATIONS
Selected Products and Services
Products
  Dried
  Dry milk blends
  Kosher powder
  Lactose powder
  Milk protein concentrate
  Nonfat dry milk
  Fluid
  Butter
  Cream
  Condensed skim milk
  Skim milk
Services
  Emergency repair
  Installation
  Preventative maintenance
  Transportation
Supplies
  Chemical
  Equipment
  Pharmaceutical

COMPETITORS
CALIFORNIA DAIRIES, INC.
DAIRY CREST GROUP LIMITED
GRANAROLO SPA
HILAND DAIRY FOODS COMPANY, LLC
MEIJI CO., LTD.

HISTORICAL FINANCIALS
Company Type: Private

Income Statement   FYE: September 30

	REVENUE ($mil)	NET INCOME ($mil)	NET PROFIT MARGIN	EMPLOYEES
09/11	825	21	2.6%	190
09/10	612	12	2.0%	—
09/09	812	2	0.3%	—
Annual Growth	0.8%	203.7%	—	—

2011 Year-End Financials
Return on assets: 16.2%
Return on equity: 32.4%
Current Ratio: 1.40
Cash ($ mil.): 30

UNITED FOOD AND COMMERCIAL WORKERS UNIONS AND FOOD EMPLOYERS BEN FUND

Auditors: VAVRINEK TRINE DAY & CO LLP S

LOCATIONS
HQ: UNITED FOOD AND COMMERCIAL WORKERS UNIONS AND FOOD EMPLOYERS BEN FUND
6425 KATELLA AVE, CYPRESS, CA 906305246
Phone: 714 220-2297
Web: WWW.SCUFCWFUNDS.COM

HISTORICAL FINANCIALS
Company Type: Private

Income Statement   FYE: March 31

	REVENUE ($mil)	NET INCOME ($mil)	NET PROFIT MARGIN	EMPLOYEES
03/18	581	(13)	—	15
03/17	593	2	0.5%	—
03/12	512	(34)	—	—
03/11	460	(74)	—	—
Annual Growth	3.4%	—	—	—

2018 Year-End Financials
Return on assets: (-4.2%)
Return on equity: (-7.0%)
Current Ratio: 161.40
Cash ($ mil.): 45

UNITED HEALTH SERVICES HOSPITALS, INC.

United Health Services Hospitals (UHS Hospitals) can service injuries from a slip in the snow or a slipped disc to health that's just plain slipping. The organization operates Binghamton General Hospital (about 200 beds), Wilson Medical Center (some 280 beds), and a group of primary and specialty care clinics in upstate New York. Specialty services include cardiology, dialysis, neurology, rehabilitation, pediatrics, and psychiatry. The Wilson Medical Center serves as a teaching hospital offering residency and fellowship programs. UHS Hospitals is a subsidiary of United Health Services, which operates a network of affiliated hospitals, clinics, long-term care centers, and home health agencies in the region.

Geographic Reach
Binghamton General is located in Binghamton, New York, while Wilson Medical Center is located in Johnson City, New York, both within the boundaries of Broome County. UHS Hospitals also operates primary and specialty care clinics in Broome, Chenango, Delaware, and Tioga counties in upstate New York.

Strategy
United Health Services Hospitals is investing in equipment upgrades and facility improvements at Binghamton General to help the facility remain at the forefront of medical technology and services. Wilson Medical Center, which acts as a regional referral center in areas including emergency medicine, newborn care, neurology, and heart surgery, has also been the subject of enhancement measures. The hospital recently completed construction of the new Decker Center for Advanced Medical Treatment, which offers high-tech diagnostic and acute care services.

Auditors : FUST CHARLES CHAMBERS LLP SYR

LOCATIONS

HQ: UNITED HEALTH SERVICES HOSPITALS, INC.
10-42 MITCHELL AVE, BINGHAMTON, NY 139031617
Phone: 607 762-2200
Web: WWW.NYUHS.ORG

COMPETITORS

ASCENSION SOUTHEAST MICHIGAN
ATLANTIC HEALTH SYSTEM INC.
CENTEGRA HEALTH SYSTEM
FIRSTHEALTH OF THE CAROLINAS, INC.
NYU WINTHROP HOSPITAL

HISTORICAL FINANCIALS
Company Type: Private

Income Statement — FYE: September 30

	REVENUE ($mil)	NET INCOME ($mil)	NET PROFIT MARGIN	EMPLOYEES
09/22*	633	(13)	—	5,000
12/21	792	46	5.8%	—
12/20	753	(1)	—	—
12/19	732	32	4.5%	—
Annual Growth	(4.7%)	—	—	—

*Fiscal year change

2022 Year-End Financials
Return on assets: (-1.8%) Cash ($ mil.): —
Return on equity: (-5.4%)
Current Ratio: 3.20

UNITED HOSPITAL INCORPORATED

LOCATIONS

HQ: UNITED HOSPITAL INCORPORATED
333 SMITH AVE N, SAINT PAUL, MN 551022344
Phone: 651 241-8000
Web: WWW.ALLINAHEALTH.ORG

HISTORICAL FINANCIALS
Company Type: Private

Income Statement — FYE: December 31

	REVENUE ($mil)	NET INCOME ($mil)	NET PROFIT MARGIN	EMPLOYEES
12/20	626	2	0.5%	3,400
12/14	503	30	6.0%	—
Annual Growth	3.7%	(32.4%)	—	—

2020 Year-End Financials
Return on assets: 0.1% Cash ($ mil.): —
Return on equity: 0.5%
Current Ratio: 1.30

UNITED SPACE ALLIANCE, LLC

United Space Alliance (USA) is a space-race heavyweight; the Houston-based prime contractor has run NASA's 173,000 pound Shuttles -- Discovery, Atlantis, and Endeavour. USA, a joint venture between Lockheed Martin and Boeing, was formed in response to NASA's move to consolidate multiple Space Shuttle contracts under a single entity. It is now wrapping up those contracts. USA has supported mission operations, astronaut and flight controller training, flight software development, Shuttle payload integration, and vehicle processing, launch, and recovery. It also has led training and planning for the International Space Station. USA served the Johnson and Kennedy Space Centers, and Marshall Space Flight Center.

Operations
The company has consolidated more than 30 heritage contracts which supported the Space Shuttle Program (including the Space Flight Operations contract, the Space Program Operations Contract, and the Integrated Mission Operations Contract).

Geographic Reach
Based in Houston, the company has another location in Titusville, Florida.

Strategy
The company served as NASA's primary partner in human space operations for the management of the Space Shuttle fleet and worked together for 55 Space Shuttle missions and more than 35 International Space Station increments.

In 2014 the company had no active contracts and will not pursue future contracts. The company is currently operating in an administrative capacity to close-out its managed government contracts (a process that will take a further about 5-7 years).

Company Background
In 2012 NASA awarded a one-year extension of the Integrated Mission Operations Contract to USA to continue providing mission and flight crew operations support for the International Space Station and Exploration Programs. The deal includes a further option for 2014. Throughout 2012 and 2013, however, USA laid off waves of workers that resided in its former Space Shuttle program.

The launch of space shuttle Atlantis in July 2011 marked the end of NASA's 30-year Space Shuttle program. The shuttles have transported astronauts, launched, recovered, and repaired satellites, as well as driven new research, and built and stocked the International Space Station with parts and provisions.

The joint venture was formed in 1996.

Auditors : PRICEWATERHOUSECOOPERS LLP HO

LOCATIONS

HQ: UNITED SPACE ALLIANCE, LLC
3700 BAY AREA BLVD # 100, HOUSTON, TX 770582783
Phone: 281 282-2592
Web: WWW.UNITEDSPACEALLIANCE.COM

PRODUCTS/OPERATIONS

Selected Capabilities
Flight software
Ground operations and processing
GSA (General Services Administration) services
Integrated logistics
Integration and program management
Mission operations
Safety

COMPETITORS

ARINC INCORPORATED
Bilfinger SE
ENGLOBAL CORPORATION

HNTB CORPORATION
INSITU, INC.
JACOBS ENGINEERING GROUP INC.
NATIONAL AERONAUTICS AND SPACE ADMINISTRATION
SIERRA NEVADA CORPORATION
SPACE EXPLORATION TECHNOLOGIES CORP.
VALINAR, LLC

HISTORICAL FINANCIALS
Company Type: Private

Income Statement — FYE: December 31

	REVENUE ($mil)	NET INCOME ($mil)	NET PROFIT MARGIN	EMPLOYEES
12/07	1,859	168	9.0%	8,000
12/06	1,920	146	7.6%	
Annual Growth	(3.2%)	14.8%	—	—

2007 Year-End Financials
Return on assets: 60.5% Cash ($ mil.): 57
Return on equity: —
Current Ratio: 1.00

UNIVERSITY COMMUNITY HOSPITAL, INC.

University Community Health (doing business as Florida Hospital Tampa Bay Division) is a 1,000-bed regional health care system with four locations spanning the Hillsborough, Pinellas, and Pasco counties of Florida. It oversees a network of eight hospitals in Florida's Tampa Bay area. Its four general hospitals -- three located in Tampa and one in nearby Tarpon Springs -- collectively house some 860 beds and provide emergency, surgical, and acute medical care, as well as provide outpatient services. The system also includes a specialty heart hospital, a women's hospital, and a long-term acute care hospital. Florida Hospital Tampa Bay Division is part of the Adventist Health System.

Strategy

As part of the Adventist Health System's network, the system has access to a broader, statewide network of physicians and specialists, as well as enhanced administrative and technological services organization.

In 2012 Florida Hospital Tampa Bay Division opened Florida Hospital Wesley Chapel and began work on three major construction projects including a new full-service Emergency Department (ED), expanding The Women's Center, and exterior and interior upgrades to the main hospital which should add a total of 54,000 sq. ft. to the scope of Florida Hospital Tampa.

Company Background

Its original name of University Community Health (UCH) reflected its proximity to the University of South Florida. UCH teamed up with Adventist Health in 2007 to build Wesley Chapel Medical Center. Buoyed by the success of the venture, in 2010 UCH and Adventist Health reached an accord and UCH became a member of Adventist Health.

LOCATIONS
HQ: UNIVERSITY COMMUNITY HOSPITAL, INC.
3100 E FLETCHER AVE, TAMPA, FL 336134613
Phone: 813 971-6000
Web: WWW.ADVENTHEALTH.COM

PRODUCTS/OPERATIONS
Selected Centers
Diabetes and Endocrinology Institute
Don Lau Family Center for Cancer Care
Florida Hospital Pepin Heart Institute
Occupational Health Service
Orthopedic Care Center
Pediatric Care Center
Sleep Center
The Women's Center
Wound Healing Institute

Selected Hospitals
Florida Hospital at Connerton
Florida Hospital Carrollwood
Florida Hospital North Pinellas
Florida Hospital Pepin Heart Institute
Florida Hospital Tampa
Florida Hospital Wesley Chapel
Florida Hospital Zephyrhills
Long Term Acute Care

COMPETITORS
ADVENTIST HEALTH SYSTEM/SUNBELT, INC.
BAPTIST HEALTH SOUTH FLORIDA, INC.
HEALTH FIRST, INC.
THE PUBLIC HEALTH TRUST OF MIAMI-DADE COUNTY
WEST FLORIDA REGIONAL MEDICAL CENTER, INC.

HISTORICAL FINANCIALS
Company Type: Private

Income Statement — FYE: December 31

	REVENUE ($mil)	NET INCOME ($mil)	NET PROFIT MARGIN	EMPLOYEES
12/19	761	62	8.2%	8,000
12/17	688	66	9.6%	—
12/16	483	39	8.2%	—
12/15	460	38	8.4%	—
Annual Growth	13.4%	12.5%	—	—

2019 Year-End Financials
Return on assets: 5.5% Cash ($ mil.): 209
Return on equity: 9.2%
Current Ratio: 4.90

UNIVERSITY HEALTH CARE, INC.

University Health Care wants to give patients a passport to good health. The company, which does business as Passport Health Plan, provides managed Medicaid insurance services to about 150,000 members throughout 16 counties in Kentucky. Offerings include HMO, Medicare Advantage, and children's health plans. University Health Care was founded in 1997 by a group of affiliated providers including the University of Louisville Medical Center, Jewish Hospital and St. Mary's HealthCare, and the Louisville/Jefferson County Primary Care Association. The health plan has an administration partnership with the AmeriHealth Mercy organization, a Medicaid managed care joint venture between AmeriHealth and Mercy Health System.

Auditors: MOUNTJOY CHILTON MEDLEY LLP L

LOCATIONS
HQ: UNIVERSITY HEALTH CARE, INC.
312 S 4TH ST STE 700, LOUISVILLE, KY 402023046
Phone: 502 585-7900

COMPETITORS
ALLWAYS HEALTH PARTNERS, INC.
ASCENSION VIA CHRISTI HEALTH, INC
HEALTH PARTNERS PLANS, INC.
MINISTRY HEALTH CARE, INC.
UNIVERSITY OF MICHIGAN HEALTH SYSTEM

HISTORICAL FINANCIALS
Company Type: Private

Income Statement — FYE: December 31

	REVENUE ($mil)	NET INCOME ($mil)	NET PROFIT MARGIN	EMPLOYEES
12/14	1,299	114	8.8%	165
12/00	330	3	1.2%	—
12/99	284	5	2.0%	—
12/98	809	0	0.0%	—
Annual Growth	3.0%	—	—	—

2014 Year-End Financials
Return on assets: 31.8% Cash ($ mil.): 140
Return on equity: 52.2%
Current Ratio: —

UNIVERSITY HEALTH SYSTEM SERVICES OF TEXAS, INC.

As the hospital system of the Bexar County Hospital District, University Health System serves residents of San Antonio and the surrounding region. University Hospital is proud to serve as the region's only Level I trauma center for both adults and children. Its network of health care services includes dozens of primary, specialty and walk-in centers, mobile health units, and an academic hospital that has earned its place among the top in the nation and recognized as the most preferred hospital in San Antonio. In addition to its hospital and network of health centers, University Health also includes Community First Health Plans, University Medicine Associates, University Health Foundation, and UT Health San Antonio. The company was founded in 1917 with the opening of the Robert B. Green Memorial Hospital.

Operations

The system, which has over 1,120 physicians, also operates preventive care centers, including the Texas Diabetes Institute, which provides treatment, research, and education for diabetes patients and health care professionals. The University Transplant Center performs a range of procedures, such as kidney, liver, and lung transplants. The Harlandale Independent School District school-based Health Center is a collaboration with Harlandale ISD that helps keep students healthy and learning.

University Health System's emergency department is the busiest in the area, taking in nearly 70,000 visits annually.

As part of its operations, University Health System is joint owner of San Antonio AirLIFE, which provides emergency air medical transport services aboard its fleet of Bell 430 helicopters.

University Health System provides health insurance through its Community First Health Plans, a not-for-profit HMO with thousands of members in Bexar and surrounding counties.

Geographic Reach

Headquartered in San Antonio, Texas, the company has over 45 locations across Texas.

Company Background

University Health System was founded in 1968.

Auditors: BKD LLP DALLAS TEXAS

LOCATIONS

HQ: UNIVERSITY HEALTH SYSTEM SERVICES OF TEXAS, INC.
4502 MEDICAL DR STOP 85-1, SAN ANTONIO, TX 782294402
Phone: 210 358-4000
Web: WWW.UNIVERSITYHEALTH.COM

PRODUCTS/OPERATIONS

2013 Sales

	$ in mil	% of total
Net patient services revenue	462.1	60
Premium revenue	261.7	34
Other revenue	49.3	6
Total	773.1	100

2013 Net Patient Revenue

	% of total
Medicare	22
Medicaid	21
Self-Pay including CareLink	37
Commercial insurance	19
Other	100
Total	

Selected Locations
University Hospital
University Health Care
Texas Diabetes Institute
University Family Health Centers

Selected Medical Services
Audiology
Blood Bank
Breast Health
Cancer

Cardiology
Craniosynostosis
Diabetes
ExpressMed
Emergency Center
Endoscopy
Epilepsy
Gynecology
Health Education
Hepatology
HIV/AIDS
Mammography
Maternal-fetal Medicine
Men's Health
Neurosciences
Newborn Services
NICU
Obstetrics
Outpatient Surgery
Pharmacy Services
Pediatrics
Primary Care
Rehabilitation
Respiratory Care
Robot Assisted Surgery
Stroke
Texas Diabetes Institute
Transcatheter Aortic Valve Replacement
Transplant Center
Trauma Center
Vascular
Women's Health

COMPETITORS

CHARLESTON AREA MEDICAL CENTER, INC.
COMMUNITY HOSPITALS OF CENTRAL CALIFORNIA
DALLAS COUNTY HOSPITAL DISTRICT
EAST TEXAS MEDICAL CENTER REGIONAL HEALTHCARE SYSTEM
NORTHEAST GEORGIA HEALTH SYSTEM, INC.
NORTHWELL HEALTH, INC.
ORLANDO HEALTH, INC.
THE NEBRASKA MEDICAL CENTER
UNIVERSITY HEALTH SYSTEMS OF EASTERN CAROLINA, INC.
UNIVERSITY HOSPITALS HEALTH SYSTEM, INC.

HISTORICAL FINANCIALS

Company Type: Private

Income Statement — FYE: December 31

	REVENUE ($mil)	NET INCOME ($mil)	NET PROFIT MARGIN	EMPLOYEES
12/21	1,976	292	14.8%	3,998
12/20	1,780	249	14.0%	—
12/19	1,610	150	9.3%	—
12/18	1,488	95	6.4%	—
Annual Growth	9.9%	45.2%	—	—

2021 Year-End Financials
Return on assets: 7.3%   Cash ($ mil.): 206
Return on equity: 15.4%
Current Ratio: 3.80

UNIVERSITY HOSPITAL

EXECUTIVES

Chief Human Resource Officer, Gerard A Garcia
CAO, Annette D Hastings
CCO, Danette L Slevinski

CIO, Richard T Tunnell
Vice Chairman, James M Orsini Md
Auditors: KPMG LLP NEW YORK NY

LOCATIONS

HQ: UNIVERSITY HOSPITAL
150 BERGEN ST STE 1, NEWARK, NJ 071032406
Phone: 973 972-4300
Web: WWW.UHNJ.ORG

HISTORICAL FINANCIALS

Company Type: Private

Income Statement — FYE: June 30

	REVENUE ($mil)	NET INCOME ($mil)	NET PROFIT MARGIN	EMPLOYEES
06/21	635	(6)	—	3,620
06/20	576	(48)	—	—
Annual Growth	10.2%	—	—	—

2021 Year-End Financials
Return on assets: (-0.8%)   Cash ($ mil.): 144
Return on equity: —
Current Ratio: 1.60

UNIVERSITY HOSPITALS HEALTH SYSTEM, INC.

University Hospitals Health System (UHHS) is on a mission to teach, research, and administer good health throughout northeastern Ohio. Its flagship facility University Hospitals of Cleveland (UHC), which operates as University Hospitals Case Medical Center (UHCMC), is a more than 1,000-bed tertiary care center serving Cleveland and other parts of northeastern Ohio. The teaching hospital, which is affiliated with Case Western Reserve University, is also home to Rainbow Babies & Children's Hospital, Seidman Cancer Center, and MacDonald Women's Hospital. the not-for-profit UHHS is also home to community hospitals, outpatient health and surgery centers, mental health facilities, and senior care centers.

Operations

UHHS' eight community hospitals, some of which are operated through affiliation agreements, provide a full range of specialty and general acute care from anesthesia to vascular surgery. Along with those, the system operates urgent care and neighborhood medical centers throughout the region. The UH Extended Care Campus includes a specialty hospital, outpatient rehabilitation, and extended care facility. UHHS also operates home health, occupational health, wellness, and managed care (health plan) divisions. The UHHS facilities have a total of some 1,800 beds.

Altogether, the network's facilities

handle some 65,000 inpatient visits per year, as well as 5.8 million outpatient procedures and 206,000 emergency room visits. It delivered more than 5,200 babies and conducted more than 60,000 surgeries in 2013.

In addition to conducting education and training programs for Case Western Reserve University School of Medicine students, UHHS partners with the university to operate the Center for Clinical Research and Technology. The center is the largest biomedical research facility in Ohio and focuses on translational research, which connects laboratory research to clinical bedside care.

UHHS' physician network consists of 1,700 physicians and 3,000 affiliated members. The system provided $270 million for community benefit and provided $253 million for research in 2013.

The hospital system is affiliated with three Cleveland-area health care providers: St. John Medical Center, UH Rehabilitation Hospital (a joint venture with Center Healthcare), and Southwest General.

Geographic Reach

UHHS operates about 30 health centers and outpatient office buildings, as well as more than 100 physician practice locations, across the northeastern Ohio region. It serves 16 counties.

Financial Performance

UHHS' revenues increased by 4% to $2.3 billion in 2013 due to higher patient service revenues.

Operating income increased by 21% $78.6 million that year due to a change in fair value of derivative instruments and a growth in investment income, partially offset by higher operating expenses.

UHHS' operating cash flow decreased by $143 million in 2013 due a change in beneficial interest in foundation and perpetual trusts, pension liability adjustments, and a change in operating assets and liabilities.

Strategy

The medical system is expanding by installing smaller regional and community hospitals and additional specialty care units within its larger facilities, including a neonatal intensive care unit, emergency care center, and a cancer care center within UH Case Medical.

To strengthen its clinical capabilities, it also expanded its established areas of excellence and developed new areas to improve access, it has forged new hospital partnerships. To enhance care in the communities served by its new partners, UHHS has opened satellites of some of its centers of excellence, initially for cancer care, cardiac care, pediatrics, and women's health. Pursuant to the growth strategy it has added two community hospitals that are now UHHS' largest: 387-bed UH Elyria Medical Center (formerly EMH Healthcare), and 332-bed UH Parma Medical Center (formerly The Parma Community General Hospital).

The company also plans to break ground on a $28 million state-of-the-art outpatient health center and freestanding emergency department in Broadview Heights with a projected completion date in late 2016. In 2013 University Hospitals Seidman Cancer Center expanded to Parma Community General Hospital, providing integrated cancer care to residents in Parma and surrounding communities.

To expand in another neighboring community, the system launched renovation of an office building that became the UH Solon Health Center in 2013. It also opened a new outpatient center, the UH Aurora Health Center, in 2012.

UHHS is also in the process of implementing an electronic health records (EHR) system across its facilities. The EHR system could make the network eligible for certain government incentives if they meet government guidelines for "meaningful use."

On the research front, in 2014 UHHS Case Medical Center conducted a Phase 3 clinical trial to evaluate the safety and effectiveness of an investigational medicine called LMTX in people with a type of dementia known as behavioral-variant Frontotemporal Dementia (previously known as Pick's Disease).

Company Background

UHHS completed construction of the UH Ahuja Medical Center, a new community hospital, in 2011.

The company was founded in 1866.

Auditors : DELOITTE TAX LLP CINCINNATI

LOCATIONS

HQ: UNIVERSITY HOSPITALS HEALTH SYSTEM, INC.
3605 WARRENSVILLE CTR RD, SHAKER HEIGHTS, OH 441229100
Phone: 216 767-8900
Web: WWW.UHHOSPITALS.ORG

PRODUCTS/OPERATIONS

Selected Facilities
Main Campuses
    Case Medical Center
    MacDonald Women's Hospital
    Rainbow Babies & Children's Hospital
    Seidman Cancer Center
Community Hospitals
    Ahuja Medical Center
    Bedford Medical Center (UH Regional Hospitals)
    Conneaut Medical Center
    Elyria Medical Center
    Geauga Medical Center
    Geneva Medical Center
    Parma Medical Center
    Richmond Medical Center (UH Regional Hospitals)

COMPETITORS

AVERA HEALTH
CARILION CLINIC
FRANCISCAN ALLIANCE, INC.
INDIANA UNIVERSITY HEALTH, INC.
LEHIGH VALLEY HEALTH NETWORK, INC.
MERCY HEALTH
NORTHWELL HEALTH, INC.
PASADENA HOSPITAL ASSOCIATION, LTD.
THE CLEVELAND CLINIC FOUNDATION
UNIVERSITY HEALTH SYSTEMS OF EASTERN CAROLINA, INC.

HISTORICAL FINANCIALS

Company Type: Private

Income Statement   FYE: December 31

	REVENUE ($mil)	NET INCOME ($mil)	NET PROFIT MARGIN	EMPLOYEES
12/17	580	33	5.7%	30,099
12/12	2,266	54	2.4%	—
12/09	1,938	110	5.7%	—
12/08	1,800	(153)	—	—
Annual Growth	(11.8%)	—	—	—

2017 Year-End Financials
Return on assets: 0.8%   Cash ($ mil.): 184
Return on equity: 1.6%
Current Ratio: 0.20

UNIVERSITY MEDICAL CENTER INC

LOCATIONS

HQ: UNIVERSITY MEDICAL CENTER INC
530 S JACKSON ST, LOUISVILLE, KY 402021675
Phone: 502 562-3000
Web: WWW.UOFLHEALTH.ORG

HISTORICAL FINANCIALS

Company Type: Private

Income Statement   FYE: June 30

	REVENUE ($mil)	NET INCOME ($mil)	NET PROFIT MARGIN	EMPLOYEES
06/21	713	13	1.9%	2,000
06/20	435	45	10.4%	—
06/19	607	23	3.8%	—
06/18	487	(72)	—	—
Annual Growth	13.5%	—	—	—

2021 Year-End Financials
Return on assets: 1.9%   Cash ($ mil.): 156
Return on equity: 4.7%
Current Ratio: 2.00

UNIVERSITY MEDICAL CENTER MANAGEMENT CORPORATION

Auditors : LAPORTE APAC METAIRIE LA

LOCATIONS

HQ: UNIVERSITY MEDICAL CENTER MANAGEMENT CORPORATION
2000 CANAL ST, NEW ORLEANS, LA 701123018

Phone: 504 903-3000
Web: WWW.LCMCHEALTH.ORG

HISTORICAL FINANCIALS
Company Type: Private

Income Statement   FYE: December 31

	REVENUE ($mil)	NET INCOME ($mil)	NET PROFIT MARGIN	EMPLOYEES
12/19	731	5	0.7%	2,000
12/18	675	1	0.2%	—
12/16	448	(65)	—	—
Annual Growth	17.7%	—	—	—

2019 Year-End Financials
Return on assets: 1.1%   Cash ($ mil.): 86
Return on equity: —
Current Ratio: 2.80

UNIVERSITY OF ALABAMA

Auditors : PRICEWATERHOUSECOOPERS LLP BI

LOCATIONS
HQ: UNIVERSITY OF ALABAMA
  301 ROSE ADMIN BLDG, TUSCALOOSA, AL 354870001
Phone: 205 348-7840
Web: EDUCATION.UA.EDU

HISTORICAL FINANCIALS
Company Type: Private

Income Statement   FYE: September 30

	REVENUE ($mil)	NET INCOME ($mil)	NET PROFIT MARGIN	EMPLOYEES
09/20	870	166	19.2%	3,950
09/19	906	55	6.1%	—
09/18	875	188	21.6%	—
09/17	833	224	26.9%	—
Annual Growth	1.5%	(9.4%)	—	—

2020 Year-End Financials
Return on assets: 3.3%   Cash ($ mil.): 156
Return on equity: 7.2%
Current Ratio: 1.30

UNIVERSITY OF ALABAMA HEALTH SERVICES FOUNDATION, P.C.

Auditors : PRICEWATERHOUSECOOPERS LLP BI

LOCATIONS
HQ: UNIVERSITY OF ALABAMA HEALTH SERVICES FOUNDATION, P.C.
  500 22ND ST S STE 100, BIRMINGHAM, AL 352333110
Phone: 205 731-9600

HISTORICAL FINANCIALS
Company Type: Private

Income Statement   FYE: September 30

	REVENUE ($mil)	NET INCOME ($mil)	NET PROFIT MARGIN	EMPLOYEES
09/21	859	75	8.8%	3,205
09/20	779	12	1.6%	—
09/19	705	(19)	—	—
09/18	668	12	1.9%	—
Annual Growth	8.7%	81.0%	—	—

2021 Year-End Financials
Return on assets: 7.1%   Cash ($ mil.): 58
Return on equity: 15.7%
Current Ratio: 1.00

UNIVERSITY OF ARKANSAS SYSTEM

Calling "Wooo, Pig, Sooie," at anyone in The University of Arkansas System (UA) is not an insult. The system encompasses more than a dozen schools, institutes, and campuses throughout the state, including five universities, a college of medicine, a math and science high school, and the Clinton School of Public Service, started in 2004 by former president Bill Clinton and offering the only Master of Public Service degree in the country. UA, which has an enrollment of more than 60,000, hails the razorback, or hog, as its mascot. "Wooo, Pig, Sooie" or "hog calling" is the school's cheer at sporting events. Its student-teacher ratio is 19:1; it has about 17,000 employees.

Operations
The flagship University of Arkansas campus in Fayetteville offers students undergraduate, graduate, and law degrees through about nine schools. Areas of study include architecture, agriculture, food, and life sciences, arts and sciences, business, education and health, engineering, and law. UA's Global Campus provides long-distance education online and via video streaming. Along with undergraduate training, the Global Campus offers professional degrees and career training.

Other system facilities include five community colleges, two law schools, and divisions of architecture, archeology, and criminal justice.

Financial Performance
Revenue increased about 1% in 2013, from $1.8 billion to $1.82 billion, due to record enrollment and increases in other revenue.

Strategy
In order to keep students coming to UA year after year, the system regularly improves it classroom offerings as well as it facilities. To that end, the university is building a $60 million performing arts center and a $20 million admissions building on the site of its former Bryce Hospital in Tuscaloosa.

Company Background
The Arkansas General Assembly established UA in Fayetteville in 1871 as the Arkansas Industrial University, and under the the Morrill Act of 1862, it became the state land-grant institution and first state-assisted college in Arkansas. On opening day, January 22, 1873, there were four teachers and eight students.

EXECUTIVES
CDO*, W Cody Decker
Interim Chief Financial Officer*, Chaundra Hall
Communications*, Carrie Phillips
Auditors : ROGER A NORMAN JD CPA CFE

LOCATIONS
HQ: UNIVERSITY OF ARKANSAS SYSTEM
  2404 N UNIVERSITY AVE, LITTLE ROCK, AR 722073608
Phone: 501 686-2500
Web: WWW.UASYS.EDU

PRODUCTS/OPERATIONS
Selected Campuses
Arkansas Archeological Survey
Arkansas School for Mathematics, Sciences, and the Arts (high school)
Clinton School of Public Service
Cossatot Community College of the University of Arkansas
Criminal Justice Institute
Division of Agriculture
Phillips Community College of the University of Arkansas
University of Arkansas Community College at Morrilton
University of Arkansas, Fayetteville
University of Arkansas at Fort Smith
University of Arkansas at Little Rock
University of Arkansas for Medical Sciences
University of Arkansas at Monticello
University of Arkansas at Pine Bluff
Winthrop Rockefeller Institute

COMPETITORS
AUBURN UNIVERSITY
DESALES UNIVERSITY
DUKE UNIVERSITY
GWYNEDD MERCY UNIVERSITY
KENT STATE UNIVERSITY
MARSHALL UNIVERSITY
MISSOURI STATE UNIVERSITY
RECTOR & VISITORS OF THE UNIVERSITY OF VIRGINIA
SYRACUSE UNIVERSITY
UNIVERSITY OF OREGON

HISTORICAL FINANCIALS
Company Type: Private

Income Statement   FYE: June 30

	REVENUE ($mil)	NET INCOME ($mil)	NET PROFIT MARGIN	EMPLOYEES
06/21	2,635	222	8.5%	14,025
06/20	2,449	85	3.5%	—
06/19	2,515	153	6.1%	—
06/18	2,402	139	5.8%	—
Annual Growth	3.1%	17.0%	—	—

2021 Year-End Financials
Return on assets: 4.1%   Cash ($ mil.): 705
Return on equity: 7.6%
Current Ratio: 3.50

UNIVERSITY OF CALIFORNIA

LOCATIONS

HQ: UNIVERSITY OF CALIFORNIA
1500 OWENS ST STE 320, SAN FRANCISCO, CA 941582335
Phone: 415 353-2057
Web: WWW.UCSF.EDU

HISTORICAL FINANCIALS

Company Type: Private

Income Statement — FYE: September 30

	REVENUE ($mil)	NET INCOME ($mil)	NET PROFIT MARGIN	EMPLOYEES
09/22*	38,895	(4,397)	—	28
06/19	13,353	(426)	—	—
Annual Growth	42.8%	—	—	—

*Fiscal year change

2022 Year-End Financials
Return on assets: (-4.2%)
Return on equity: (-973.7%)
Current Ratio: 1.40
Cash ($ mil.): 1,080

UNIVERSITY OF CALIFORNIA, DAVIS

University of California, Davis (UC Davis) is top tier public research university. The school, one of 10 University of California campuses, offers a wide variety of agricultural programs; its Viticulture and Enology department provides professional education for aspiring winemakers. Located between Sacramento and San Francisco, UC Davis also has colleges and professional schools in biology, engineering, education, law, business, medicine, and veterinary medicine, and it is recognized for its research programs. Offering about 105 academic majors and some 100 graduate degrees throughout its six schools, UC Davis enrolls approximately 38,445 undergraduate, graduate and professional students, and it has a student-faculty ratio of 21:1.

Operations

UC Davis comprises four colleges: Agricultural and Environmental Sciences; Biological Sciences; Engineering; and Letters and Science. The university also operates six professional schools: Education; Law; Management; Medicine; Veterinary Medicine; and the Betty Irene Moore School of Nursing.

UC Davis Health is an academic health system includes one of the country's best medical schools, a nationally ranked 627-bed acute-care teaching hospital, a 1,000-member physicians' practice group and the Betty Irene Moore School of Nursing. It is home to a National Cancer Institute-designated comprehensive cancer center, an international institute for neurodevelopmental disorders, a leading-edge stem cell program, and a top-ranked comprehensive children's hospital and other nationally prominent centers.

It also has access to more than 10 million items in the university's library, including books, journals, music and maps, in print and digital formats.

Geographic Reach

Spanning approximately 5,300 acres, the campus borders the city of Davis, the state capital is 20 minutes away, and destinations such as the San Francisco Bay Area, Lake Tahoe and the Napa Valley are within a two-hour drive. UC Davis has satellite campuses in San Ramon and Sacramento, as well as related educational facilities elsewhere in California and in Nevada.

Company Background

The school was originally known as the University Farm School, and accepted its first students at its new campus in the town of Davisville (later changed to Davis) in 1909. The California Legislature in 1905 authorized the establishment of a state agricultural college; the school that became UC Davis was administratively tied to UC Berkeley for decades, before gaining its status as an independent university in 1959.

LOCATIONS

HQ: UNIVERSITY OF CALIFORNIA, DAVIS
1 SHIELDS AVE, DAVIS, CA 956168500
Phone: 530 752-1011
Web: WWW.UCDAVIS.EDU

COMPETITORS

AUBURN UNIVERSITY
GEORGETOWN UNIVERSITY (THE)
IDAHO STATE UNIVERSITY
MISSOURI STATE UNIVERSITY
NATIONAL UNIVERSITY
THE REGENTS OF THE UNIVERSITY OF CALIFORNIA
THE UNIVERSITY OF IOWA
UNIVERSITY OF CINCINNATI
UNIVERSITY OF MISSOURI SYSTEM
UNIVERSITY OF SOUTHERN CALIFORNIA

HISTORICAL FINANCIALS

Company Type: Private

Income Statement — FYE: June 30

	REVENUE ($mil)	NET INCOME ($mil)	NET PROFIT MARGIN	EMPLOYEES
06/11*	2,697	360	13.4%	17,741
12/08	0	0	9.6%	—
06/08	14	0	6.1%	—
Annual Growth	474.6%	644.1%	—	—

*Fiscal year change

2011 Year-End Financials
Return on assets: 6.5%
Return on equity: 10.4%
Current Ratio: 2.50
Cash ($ mil.): 1,114

UNIVERSITY OF CALIFORNIA, LOS ANGELES

As a public research university, University of California, Los Angeles (UCLA) boasts an undergraduate and graduate population of about 45,900 students. It's also the second-oldest university in the system (after Berkeley), founded in 1919. UCLA's campus extends about 420 acres at the base of the Santa Monica mountains. UCLA offers more than 120 graduate and professional programs, ranging from an extensive selection of business and medical programs to degrees in 40 different languages. UCLA curriculum features more than 3,900 courses, 130 majors and 90 minors for undergraduates.

Geographic Reach

UCLA is located in beautiful Westwood, minutes from Hollywood and the downtown city center of Los Angeles.

Company Background

UCLA was founded in 1919 offering two-year undergraduate teacher-training programs. The school started offering graduate programs in 1933 followed by its first Ph.D. program in 1938. Over the years, the university has celebrated hundreds of milestones and the accomplishments of past graduates. Some of these include alumnus Ralph Bunche '27, who became the first person of color to win the Nobel Peace Prize; the first open-heart surgery to be performed in the western US in 1956; hosting the gymnastics and tennis competitions for the 1984 Olympics; and the first genetically-targeted breast cancer treatment in 1998. In 1969, UCLA became the first node on the ARPANET, the technical foundation of the Internet, and university professor Leonard Kleinrock sent the first message on the Internet.

LOCATIONS

HQ: UNIVERSITY OF CALIFORNIA, LOS ANGELES
405 HILGARD AVE, LOS ANGELES, CA 900959000
Phone: 310 825-4321
Web: WWW.UCLA.EDU

PRODUCTS/OPERATIONS

Selected Colleges and Schools
Anderson School of Management
College of Letters and Science
David Geffen School of Medicine at UCLA
Graduate School of Education and Information Studies
Fielding School of Public Health
Henry Samueli School of Engineering and Applied Science
Herb Alpert School of Music
Luskin School of Public Affairs
School of Dentistry
School of Law
School of Nursing

School of the Arts and Architecture
School of Theater, Film and Television
Semel Institute for Neuroscience and Human Behavior

COMPETITORS

CALIFORNIA STATE UNIVERSITY, SACRAMENTO
GEORGE MASON UNIVERSITY
MOREHOUSE COLLEGE (INC.)
NORTHWESTERN UNIVERSITY
QUINNIPIAC UNIVERSITY
THE CALIFORNIA STATE UNIVERSITY, NORTHRIDGE FOUNDATION
THE LELAND STANFORD JUNIOR UNIVERSITY
THE OHIO STATE UNIVERSITY
THE UNIVERSITY OF CHICAGO
UNIVERSITY OF SOUTHERN CALIFORNIA

HISTORICAL FINANCIALS
Company Type: Private

Income Statement — FYE: June 30

	REVENUE ($mil)	NET INCOME ($mil)	NET PROFIT MARGIN	EMPLOYEES
06/22	3,353	(244)	—	3,326
06/17	6	0	2.5%	—
Annual Growth	248.8%	—	—	—

2022 Year-End Financials
Return on assets: (-3.9%)   Cash ($ mil.): 1,631
Return on equity: —
Current Ratio: 3.50

UNIVERSITY OF CALIFORNIA, SAN FRANCISCO FOUNDATION

Auditors: SEILER LLP REDWOOD CITY CA

LOCATIONS

HQ: UNIVERSITY OF CALIFORNIA, SAN FRANCISCO FOUNDATION
220 MONTGOMERY ST STE 500, SAN FRANCISCO, CA 941043412
Phone: 415 476-6922
Web: GIVING.UCSF.EDU

HISTORICAL FINANCIALS
Company Type: Private

Income Statement — FYE: June 30

	REVENUE ($mil)	NET INCOME ($mil)	NET PROFIT MARGIN	EMPLOYEES
06/18	628	332	53.0%	73
06/99	33	39	117.7%	—
Annual Growth	16.6%	11.8%	—	—

2018 Year-End Financials
Return on assets: 15.2%   Cash ($ mil.): 395
Return on equity: 18.0%
Current Ratio: —

UNIVERSITY OF CHICAGO

LOCATIONS

HQ: UNIVERSITY OF CHICAGO
1414 E 59TH ST, CHICAGO, IL 606372916
Phone: 773 753-2270
Web: WWW.UCHICAGO.EDU

HISTORICAL FINANCIALS
Company Type: Private

Income Statement — FYE: June 30

	REVENUE ($mil)	NET INCOME ($mil)	NET PROFIT MARGIN	EMPLOYEES
06/13	3,091	182	5.9%	2
06/11	3,056	1,052	34.4%	—
Annual Growth	0.6%	(58.4%)	—	—

2013 Year-End Financials
Return on assets: 1.9%   Cash ($ mil.): 45
Return on equity: 2.9%
Current Ratio: 0.20

UNIVERSITY OF CINCINNATI

The University of Cincinnati (UC) is a research institution offering undergraduate, graduate, and professional education from its campuses in Ohio including UC Blue Ash College and UC Clermont College. The university enrolls approximately 46,700 students and has around 15 colleges. Academic offerings include business, law, medicine, engineering and applied science, pharmacy, and music. The institution offers about 415 other degree programs and more than 260 minors and certificates. UC was founded in 1819 and became a state university in 1977; the school has an endowment of approximately $1.6 billion. Notable alumni include former US president William Howard Taft and architect Michael Graves.

Operations
The university has a combined faculty and staff of more than 16,705 and a student teacher ratio of approximately 16.1. It consists of nine research and campus locations in the Greater Cincinnati region with an impact and reach that extends from the local to the global. This includes strategic partnerships in subject areas like engineering, economics, humanities and business administration with the University of Bordeaux, France; Ludwig Maximilian University, Germany; Chongqing University, China; Hong Kong Polytechnic University; Future University, Egypt, and many more, including institutional partnerships with about 45 colleges and universities in Europe alone. The largest employer in the region, UC has an annual economic impact of approximately $4.2 billion.

Geographic Reach
The university has nearly 120 facilities on around 475 acres land located in Cincinnati, Ohio. It attracts students from all 50 states and to nearly 115 countries.

Sales and Marketing
The university caters to around 46,710 students with a student-teacher ratio of 16:1.

Company Background
UC traces its history all the way back to 1819 when Cincinnati College and the Medical College of Ohio were chartered. In 1870, the city established the University of Cincinnati, which later absorbed Cincinnati College and the Medical College of Ohio. In 1906, UC created the first cooperative education program in the world. In 1977 UC joined the University System of Ohio. Today, UC is classified as a research university (meaning it has "Very High Research Activity") by the Carnegie Commission and is ranked as one of America's top 25 public research universities by the National Science Foundation.

Auditors: BKD LLP CINCINNATI OHIO

LOCATIONS

HQ: UNIVERSITY OF CINCINNATI
2600 CLIFTON AVE, CINCINNATI, OH 452202872
Phone: 513 556-6000
Web: WWW.UC.EDU

PRODUCTS/OPERATIONS

Selected Colleges & Schools
Clermont College (regional campus)
College-Conservatory of Music
College of Allied Health Sciences
College of Applied Science
College of Business
College of Design, Architecture, Art, & Planning
College of Education, Criminal Justice, and Human Services
College of Engineering
College of Law
College of Medicine
College of Nursing
James L. Winkle College of Pharmacy
McMicken College of Arts & Sciences
Raymond Walters College (regional campus)
School of Social Work

COMPETITORS

AUSTIN COLLEGE
GEORGETOWN UNIVERSITY (THE)
HAMPTON UNIVERSITY
MICHIGAN STATE UNIVERSITY
NORTHWESTERN UNIVERSITY
PRESIDENT AND FELLOWS OF HARVARD COLLEGE
THE TRUSTEES OF PRINCETON UNIVERSITY
THE UNIVERSITY OF CHICAGO
UNIVERSITY OF SOUTHERN CALIFORNIA
UNIVERSITY OF TEXAS AT EL PASO

HISTORICAL FINANCIALS
Company Type: Private

Income Statement FYE: June 30

	REVENUE ($mil)	NET INCOME ($mil)	NET PROFIT MARGIN	EMPLOYEES
06/11	1,198	48	4.1%	14,600
06/07	594	112	18.9%	—
06/06	557	20	3.6%	—
Annual Growth	16.6%	19.2%	—	—

2011 Year-End Financials
Return on assets: 1.1%   Cash ($ mil.): 83
Return on equity: 1.5%
Current Ratio: —

UNIVERSITY OF COLORADO

Auditors: CLIFTON LARSON ALLEN LLP GRE

LOCATIONS
HQ: UNIVERSITY OF COLORADO
1800 N GRANT ST STE 800, DENVER, CO 802031187
Phone: 303 831-6192
Web: WWW.COLORADO.EDU

HISTORICAL FINANCIALS
Company Type: Private

Income Statement FYE: June 30

	REVENUE ($mil)	NET INCOME ($mil)	NET PROFIT MARGIN	EMPLOYEES
06/19	4,097	427	10.4%	8,921
06/13	2,774	308	11.1%	—
06/12	2,641	141	5.4%	—
Annual Growth	6.5%	17.1%	—	—

2019 Year-End Financials
Return on assets: 5.6%   Cash ($ mil.): 179
Return on equity: 20.6%
Current Ratio: 1.20

UNIVERSITY OF COLORADO HEALTH

Auditors: PLANTE & MORAN PLL DENVER C

LOCATIONS
HQ: UNIVERSITY OF COLORADO HEALTH
12401 E 17TH AVE, AURORA, CO 800452548
Phone: 720 848-1031
Web: WWW.COLORADO.EDU

HISTORICAL FINANCIALS
Company Type: Private

Income Statement FYE: June 30

	REVENUE ($mil)	NET INCOME ($mil)	NET PROFIT MARGIN	EMPLOYEES
06/21	5,781	1,807	31.3%	7,593
06/20	5,055	485	9.6%	—
06/19	4,952	773	15.6%	—
06/18	4,341	747	17.2%	—
Annual Growth	10.0%	34.2%	—	—

2021 Year-End Financials
Return on assets: 16.3%   Cash ($ mil.): 582
Return on equity: 24.0%
Current Ratio: 0.90

UNIVERSITY OF COLORADO HOSPITAL AUTHORITY

University of Colorado Hospital Authority, doing business as UCHealth, operates the University of Colorado Hospital (UCH) in Aurora, Colorado. The facility is a teaching institution for -- you guessed it -- the University of Colorado. UCH is a 400-bed community hospital that includes a number of specialty care facilities, including centers specializing in oncology, respiratory care, and endocrinology. The facility also conducts medical training and research programs in partnership with the University of Colorado's Denver School of Medicine. In addition, UCHealth operates 10 primary care clinics in the Denver metropolitan area.

Operations
UCH is located on the University of Colorado's Anschutz Medical Campus, along with other health care providers and the University of Colorado's primary medical school campus, in Aurora, Colorado. Its Anschutz Inpatient Pavilion includes ICU, operating, imaging, pharmacy, and other care facilities. It also includes the Anschutz Cancer Pavilion, which not only offers cancer treatment but also conducts research; Rocky Mountain Lions Eye Institute for ophthalmic care; and a rehabilitation department offering addiction treatment services.

While UCH's operations are closely tied to the University of Colorado, UCH is governed by the UCH Authority, a separate legal entity.

Strategy
UCHealth has upgraded its facilities in recent years to provide state-of-the art medical care and educational and research resources. Among its recent projects has been a $20 million renovation and expansion of the Anschutz Cancer Pavilion, the addition of a brain tumor treatment lab to the Anschutz Outpatient Pavilion, and the construction of a new 12-story emergency department tower.

In 2015, the authority broke ground on another project -- the construction of a new $12.3 million emergency center at its Harmony Campus in Fort Collins, Colorado. It also acquired a majority stake in a dozen freestanding emergency rooms in Colorado that are operated by Adeptus Health. The facilities (plus two more under construction) operated under the First Choice banner but were rebranded as UCHealth ER.

LOCATIONS
HQ: UNIVERSITY OF COLORADO HOSPITAL AUTHORITY
4200 E 9TH AVE, DENVER, CO 802203706
Phone: 720 848-0000
Web: WWW.CUANSCHUTZ.EDU

COMPETITORS
BATON ROUGE GENERAL MEDICAL CENTER
BAYLOR COLLEGE OF MEDICINE
EISENHOWER MEDICAL CENTER
HOSPITAL SERVICE DISTRICT 1
KENNEDY HEALTH SYSTEM, INC.
LOMA LINDA UNIVERSITY MEDICAL CENTER
POUDRE VALLEY HEALTH CARE, INC.
THE UNIVERSITY OF CHICAGO MEDICAL CENTER
UNIVERSITY HEALTH SYSTEM SERVICES OF TEXAS, INC.
UPPER CHESAPEAKE HEALTH FOUNDATION, INC.

HISTORICAL FINANCIALS
Company Type: Private

Income Statement FYE: June 30

	REVENUE ($mil)	NET INCOME ($mil)	NET PROFIT MARGIN	EMPLOYEES
06/10	795	151	19.1%	4,200
06/09	1	0	0.0%	—
06/05	464	1	0.2%	—
Annual Growth	11.4%	169.7%	—	—

2010 Year-End Financials
Return on assets: 12.0%   Cash ($ mil.): 22
Return on equity: 24.3%
Current Ratio: 1.30

UNIVERSITY OF DELAWARE

Delaware brings up images of many things, our first president, that famous river, and now the private University of Delaware (UD). The school's flagship campus in Newark has an enrollment of roughly 17,000 undergraduate and close to 4,000 graduate students. The school also has four auxiliary campuses around the state. UD offers almost 150 undergraduate degrees, about 120 master's programs, and more than 50 doctoral programs, as well as associate's and dual graduate programs through seven academic schools. Among its instructors are well-known authors, scientists, artists, and Nobel Laureates.

Operations

UD is a Land Grant, Sea Grant, and Space Grant institution, meaning the school is eligible for government grants in each of these areas. The Carnegie Foundation for the Advancement of Teaching also classifies UD as a research university with very high research activity -- a designation given to less than 3% of US colleges and universities. UD ranks among the nation's top 100 universities in federal research and development support for science and engineering. The university even has its own 146-foot research vessel (named the Hugh R. Sharp) for undersea exploration.

The school has a student-teacher ratio of about 15:1. It has roughly 1,130 faculty members, nearly 80% of which are tenured. Almost 90% have doctorate or terminal professional degrees in their field. (A terminal degree is also referred to as a Ph.D and refers to the fact that no higher degree can be obtained on that track.)

UD's 2012-13 tuition and fees were $11,682 (in-state) and $28,772 (out-of-state).

Geographic Reach

The university has campuses in Dover, Georgetown, Lewes, Newark, and Wilmington.

Financial Performance

The school reported a 5% increase in revenues in 2012 as the result of an increase in tuition and fees, contributions, and sales and services of auxiliary enterprises.

However, UD's net income dropped by 118% in 2012 over 2011 due to higher expenses and a larger net realized and unrealized loss and an increase in a post-retirement benefit obligation.

In 2012 the university was supported by $1.21 billion endowment.

Company Background

UD got its start in 1743 as a private academy and was chartered by the state of Delaware in 1833. In athletics, the school began NCAA Division I competition for men in 1973 and for women in 1982. US Vice President Joe Biden and his wife Jill are both UD graduates.

EXECUTIVES

Interim Chief DIVERSITY, Fatimah Conley
Auditors : KPMG LLP PHILADELPHIA PA

LOCATIONS

HQ: UNIVERSITY OF DELAWARE
210 S COLLEGE AVE, NEWARK, DE 197165200
Phone: 302 831-2107
Web: WWW.UDEL.EDU

PRODUCTS/OPERATIONS

Selected Schools and Colleges
Agriculture and Natural Resources
Arts and Sciences
Business and Economics
Earth, Ocean, and Environment
Education and Human Development
Engineering
Health Sciences
25 Most Popular Majors (2011)
Biological Sciences
Nursing
Finance
Psychology
Elementary Teacher Education
Exercise Science
Mechanical Engineering
Accounting
English
Chemical Engineering
Criminal Justice
Political Science
Civil Engineering
Marketing
Hotel, Restaurant & Institutional Management
History
Human Services
Communication Interest
International Relations
Fashion Merchandising
Business Administration
Dietetics
Communication
Management
Pre-Veterinary Medicine & Animal Biosciences

COMPETITORS

BROWN UNIVERSITY IN PROVIDENCE IN THE STATE OF RHODE ISLAND AND PROVIDENCE PLANTATIONS
JOHN CARROLL UNIVERSITY
KANSAS STATE UNIVERSITY
MONTANA STATE UNIVERSITY, INC
RECTOR & VISITORS OF THE UNIVERSITY OF VIRGINIA
THE COLLEGE OF WILLIAM & MARY
THE WASHINGTON AND LEE UNIVERSITY
TRUSTEES OF BOSTON COLLEGE
TRUSTEES OF CLARK UNIVERSITY
The Governing Council of The University of Toronto

HISTORICAL FINANCIALS
Company Type: Private

Income Statement — FYE: June 30

	REVENUE ($mil)	NET INCOME ($mil)	NET PROFIT MARGIN	EMPLOYEES
06/20	1,312	(19)	—	3,600
06/19	1,069	60	5.7%	—
06/18	1,023	139	13.7%	—
06/17	992	159	16.1%	—
Annual Growth	9.8%	—	—	—

2020 Year-End Financials
Return on assets: (-0.5%)   Cash ($ mil.): 211
Return on equity: (-0.8%)
Current Ratio: 0.40

UNIVERSITY OF DENVER

Want a mile-high education? Colorado Seminary, which does business as University of Denver (DU), offers graduate and undergraduate degrees in more than 300 fields of study, including law, political science, humanities, education, engineering, and psychology. About 12,000 undergraduate and graduate students from across the US and more than 80 countries are enrolled at the school. Founded in 1864, the university has a student-to-faculty ratio of 11:1. DU is located on a 125-acre campus. Former Secretary of State Condoleezza Rice, former Interior Secretary Gale Norton, and former Coors Brewing CEO Peter Coors attended DU.

Operations

The university offers over 100 undergraduate degree programs in schools from Daniels College of Business, Daniel Felix Ritchie School of Engineering and Computer Science, Josef Korbel School of International Studies, Morgridge College of Education, and Sturm College of Law. It also offers over 120 programs across more than 10 schools and colleges, ranging from business, entrepreneurship and international politics to the natural and social sciences.

Geographic Reach

Based in Denver, the university's students study international economics in Prague, work on sustainable development in Thailand and use their spring breaks to provide medical relief in Central America.

Strategy

Despite campus growth, between 2006 and 2015, the University shrank its carbon footprint by 27% due to the use of carbon offsets and vehicles fueled by compressed natural gas (CNG). It operates the only CNG fueling station on a Colorado university campus.

Company Background

Founded in 1864 as the Colorado Seminary, only six years after the founding of Denver City in what was then the Colorado Territory.

Auditors : CLIFTONLARSONALLEN LLP ENGLEW

LOCATIONS

HQ: UNIVERSITY OF DENVER
2199 S UNIVERSITY BLVD, DENVER, CO 802104700
Phone: 303 871-3014
Web: WWW.DU.EDU

PRODUCTS/OPERATIONS

Selected Schools and Programs
Undergraduate Schools and Colleges
  Daniels College of Business
  Division of Natural Sciences & Mathematics
  Division of Arts, Humanities and Social Sciences
  Josef Korbel School of International Studies
  Morgridge College of Education
  School of Engineering and Computer Science
  University College
  Women's College
Graduate and Professional Programs
Daniels College of Business
Divisions of Arts, Humanities and Social Sciences
Divisions of Natural Sciences and Mathematics
Graduate School of Professional Psychology (GSPP)
Graduate School of Social Work (GSSW)
Graduate Tax Program
Interdisciplinary Degree Programs
Josef Korbel School of International Studies
Morgridge College of Education (MCE)
School of Engineering and Computer Science
The Sturm College of Law
University College

COMPETITORS

LAFAYETTE COLLEGE
MISSOURI STATE UNIVERSITY
THE UNIVERSITY OF NORTH CAROLINA AT CHARLOTTE
UNIVERSITY OF ARKANSAS SYSTEM
UTAH STATE UNIVERSITY

HISTORICAL FINANCIALS

Company Type: Private

Income Statement — FYE: June 30

	REVENUE ($mil)	NET INCOME ($mil)	NET PROFIT MARGIN	EMPLOYEES
06/20	716	(11)	—	1,400
06/19	521	43	8.4%	—
06/17	467	86	18.6%	—
06/16	458	9	2.2%	—
Annual Growth	11.8%	—	—	—

2020 Year-End Financials
Return on assets: (-0.6%)
Return on equity: (-0.8%)
Current Ratio: 0.50
Cash ($ mil.): 87

UNIVERSITY OF FLORIDA

Founded in 1853, the University of Florida (UF) is one of the largest in the country, with over 53,370 students and around 5,370 faculty and library staff members. UF is a major land-grant research university encompassing 2,000 acres in Gainesville, Florida. The university's around 15 colleges offer more than 300 undergraduate and graduate degree options, plus a comprehensive array of courses, including education, law, medicine, psychology, and philosophy. It is also a member of the Association of American Universities, a confederation of the top research universities in North America. A founding member of the Southeastern Conference, UF's athletic teams (the Florida Gators) are typically ranked nationally.

Operations

UF is active in research and operates approximately 180 research institutes and centers including the Center for Aquatic and Invasive Plants (IFAS), Emerging Pathogens Institute, and the Biomedical Sciences Research & Training (CBMSRT). It has research collaborations with the likes of Scripps Florida, Moffitt Cancer Center, and Sanford Burnham Prebys Medical Discovery Institute. Altogether, UF receives about $960 million in research grants annually.

UF also has extensive health education programs, including nursing and pharmacy colleges.

Geographic Reach

The University is headquartered in Gainesville, Florida.

Company Background

UF's alumni include Robert Cade, the inventor of Gatorade; best-selling mystery novelist Michael Connelly; actress Faye Dunaway; and former US Senator and Florida Governor Bob Graham. Other UF alumni include two Nobel Prize winners and three NASA astronauts.

Auditors: SHERRILL F NORMAN CPA TALLAH

LOCATIONS

HQ: UNIVERSITY OF FLORIDA
300 SW 13TH ST, GAINESVILLE, FL 326110001
Phone: 352 392-3261
Web: WWW.UFL.EDU

PRODUCTS/OPERATIONS

Selected Colleges
College of Agricultural and Life Sciences
College of Dentistry
College of Design, Construction, and Planning
College of Education
College of Engineering
College of Health and Human Performance
College of Journalism and Communications
College of Liberal Arts and Sciences
College of Medicine
College of Nursing
College of Pharmacy
College of Public Health and Health Professions
College of the Arts
College of Veterinary Medicine
Levin College of Law
Warrington College of Business Administration

COMPETITORS

EASTERN VIRGINIA MEDICAL SCHOOL
NEW MEXICO STATE UNIVERSITY
NORTH CAROLINA STATE UNIVERSITY
THE GEORGE WASHINGTON UNIVERSITY
THE RUTGERS STATE UNIVERSITY
THE UNIVERSITY OF IOWA
UNIVERSITY OF ILLINOIS
UNIVERSITY OF MIAMI
UNIVERSITY OF OKLAHOMA
UNIVERSITY OF SOUTHERN CALIFORNIA

HISTORICAL FINANCIALS

Company Type: Private

Income Statement — FYE: June 30

	REVENUE ($mil)	NET INCOME ($mil)	NET PROFIT MARGIN	EMPLOYEES
06/21	2,081	218	10.5%	5,106
06/20	2,019	(15)	—	—
06/15	1,735	261	15.1%	—
06/12	3,939	64	1.6%	—
Annual Growth	(6.8%)	14.6%	—	—

2021 Year-End Financials
Return on assets: 4.0%
Return on equity: 10.3%
Current Ratio: 4.40
Cash ($ mil.): 11

UNIVERSITY OF GEORGIA

Located in the quintessential college town of Athens, The University of Georgia (UGA) offers a wide range of degree programs to nearly 35,000 students. Forest resources, veterinary medicine, and law are a few of the school's academic programs. UGA, which also runs 170-plus study-abroad and exchange programs, administers the prestigious Peabody Awards, which honors media achievements, and boasts one of the nation's largest map collections. Famous alumni include former US Senator Phil Gramm, TV journalist Deborah Norville, and former PBS president Pat Mitchell. The University of Georgia was chartered by the State of Georgia in 1785 and graduated its first class in 1804.

Operations

As part of its business, UGA offers nearly two dozen bachelor's degrees in about 140 fields and roughly 35 master's degrees in nearly 140 fields. Its doctorate or professional degrees cover a broad spectrum of disciplines, such as law, pharmacy, veterinary medicine, and 90 other areas. The university has a student-teacher ratio of about 12:1.

Sales and Marketing

The university sources 80% of its students from the Peach State. Since 1851, 25 Georgia governors have graduated from UGA. The institution also boasts nine Pulitzer Prize recipients, 17 presidents or provosts of US colleges and universities, and four members of the National Academy of Sciences.

Strategy

Despite its annual endowment of more than $50 million, UGA has logged decreases in state appropriations in recent years due to overall declines in Georgia's budget. The result spurred UGA to cut its budget, increase undergraduate tuition fees, institute a "Special Institutional" mandatory fee of $200 per semester, reduce employer health insurance contributions, and increase energy conservation measures. Going forward, UGA has also not ruled out the possibility of hiking tuition further, citing that an increase of up to 30% would help to replace all of the state funding the university has lost due to the recession.

EXECUTIVES

Head Volunteer*, B J Garrett
Auditors: GREG S GRIFFIN

LOCATIONS

HQ: UNIVERSITY OF GEORGIA
424 E BROAD ST, ATHENS, GA 306021535
Phone: 706 542-2471
Web: WWW.UGA.EDU

PRODUCTS/OPERATIONS

Selected Schools and Colleges
Agricultural and Environmental Sciences
Arts and Sciences, Business
Ecology
Education
Environment and Design
Family and Consumer Sciences
Forest Resources
Graduate School

Journalism and Mass Communication
Law
Pharmacy
Public Health
Public and International Affairs
Social Work
Veterinary Medicine
The GHSU/UGA Medical Partnership
Engineering

COMPETITORS

AUBURN UNIVERSITY
MARSHALL UNIVERSITY
NORTH CAROLINA STATE UNIVERSITY
PURDUE UNIVERSITY
RECTOR & VISITORS OF THE UNIVERSITY OF VIRGINIA
THE COLLEGE OF WILLIAM & MARY
THE TRUSTEES OF PRINCETON UNIVERSITY
THE WASHINGTON AND LEE UNIVERSITY
UNIVERSITY OF DELAWARE
UNIVERSITY OF OKLAHOMA

HISTORICAL FINANCIALS
Company Type: Private

Income Statement — FYE: June 30

	REVENUE ($mil)	NET INCOME ($mil)	NET PROFIT MARGIN	EMPLOYEES
06/21	1,548	489	31.6%	17,800
06/20	1,067	(22)	—	—
06/19	1,094	72	6.7%	—
06/18	997	111	11.2%	—
Annual Growth	15.8%	63.7%	—	—

2021 Year-End Financials
Return on assets: 8.2%   Cash ($ mil.): 306
Return on equity: 17.4%
Current Ratio: 3.10

UNIVERSITY OF HAWAI'I OF MANOA

LOCATIONS

HQ: UNIVERSITY OF HAWAI'I OF MANOA
2500 CAMPUS RD, HONOLULU, HI 968222217
Phone: 808 956-7700
Web: WWW.HAWAII.EDU

HISTORICAL FINANCIALS
Company Type: Private

Income Statement — FYE: June 30

	REVENUE ($mil)	NET INCOME ($mil)	NET PROFIT MARGIN	EMPLOYEES
06/18	772	51	6.7%	8
06/11	871	139	16.0%	—
Annual Growth	(1.7%)	(13.2%)	—	—

2018 Year-End Financials
Return on assets: 1.2%   Cash ($ mil.): 122
Return on equity: —
Current Ratio: 2.10

UNIVERSITY OF HAWAII SYSTEM

With a reach that extends across half a dozen islands, the University of Hawai'i System consists of three university campuses, seven community college campuses, and several job training and research centers. The public higher education system has an enrollment of more than 60,000 students, about 85% of which are Hawaii residents. It offers more than 600 different doctorate, graduate, undergraduate, and associate degrees, as well as professional certificates, in more than 200 fields of study. The University of Hawai'i was founded in 1907 as the College of Agriculture and Mechanic Arts in Honolulu, incidentally while Hawaii was still a US territory.

Operations

Among its university campuses and community college campuses, the University of Hawai'i boasts locations in Manoa, Hilo, West O'ahu, Hawai'i, Honolulu, Kapi'olani, Kaua'i, Leeward, Maui, and Windward.

Strategy

The university has invested time and money in its information technology efforts. In 2012 the University of Hawai'i broke ground on a new Information Technology Center, a six-story building on the Manoa campus. The center offers the university a centralized facility for its system-wide Information Technology Services (ITS) division and serves as the new home of the university's enterprise information and communications technology systems.

The University of Hawai'i tackled a multi-pronged strategy in 2012 and exceeded its goals. It increased degree attainment for native Hawaiians at the university, degrees and certificates of achievement earned, disbursement of Pell Grants, going rates of public and private high schools to its campus, extramural fund support, degrees in STEM Fields, and non-state revenue streams.

To this end, a physicist at the University of Hawai'i at Manoa's John A. Burns School of Medicine partnered with colleagues from the US and Germany to provide the necessary research to provide a foundation for KinetiCor Inc. KenetiCor in 2013 received $700,000 in its first round of venture financing that helped the company launch formally. It's initially focused on commercializing the motion correction technology for Magnetic Resonance Imaging that was invented by Thomas Ernst, the university's Manoa physicist.

Auditors: ACCUITY LLP HONOLULU HAWAI'

LOCATIONS

HQ: UNIVERSITY OF HAWAII SYSTEM
2444 DOLE ST, HONOLULU, HI 968222399
Phone: 808 956-8111

Web: WWW.HAWAII.EDU

Selected Campuses
Manoa
Hilo
West O'ahu
Hawai'i
Honolulu
Kapi'olani
Kaua'i
Leeward
Maui
Windward

COMPETITORS

FLORIDA INTERNATIONAL UNIVERSITY
KENT STATE UNIVERSITY
NOVA SOUTHEASTERN UNIVERSITY, INC.
THE UNIVERSITY OF CHICAGO
UNIVERSITY OF ILLINOIS
UNIVERSITY OF LIVERPOOL
UNIVERSITY OF MIAMI
UNIVERSITY OF SOUTHAMPTON
UNIVERSITY SYSTEM OF MARYLAND
VILLANOVA UNIVERSITY IN THE STATE OF PENNSYLVANIA

HISTORICAL FINANCIALS
Company Type: Private

Income Statement — FYE: June 30

	REVENUE ($mil)	NET INCOME ($mil)	NET PROFIT MARGIN	EMPLOYEES
06/21	728	(70)	—	12,000
06/18	772	51	6.7%	
06/17	771	33	4.3%	
Annual Growth	(1.4%)	—	—	

2021 Year-End Financials
Return on assets: (-1.8%)   Cash ($ mil.): 296
Return on equity: —
Current Ratio: 2.60

UNIVERSITY OF HOUSTON SYSTEM

The University of Houston System plays an essential role in meeting the higher education needs of the Houston metropolitan area and Texas as the region's largest provider of comprehensive university services. The university system serves more than 75,000 students at four Houston-area universities. Flagship institution the University of Houston was founded in 1927 and offers about 275 undergraduate and graduate academic programs; it also conducts a number of research programs. Also under the system's umbrella are the University of Houston-Clear Lake, the University of Houston-Downtown, the University of Houston-Victoria, as well as a handful of learning centers in the area. The system was established in 1977.

Operations

The system includes the University of Houston, UH-Clear Lake, UH-Downtown and UH-Victoria, and instructional sites in Katy, Northwest Houston, Pearland and Sugar Land. Also at the University of Houston is

Houston Public Media, home to KUHT-TV8, Houston's PBS station and the nation's first educational television station; KUHF-88.7, Houston's National Public Radio station; and KUHF 88.7 HD-2, Houston's digital classical music stream.

The University of Houston is the largest university in Houston and the third largest in the state. It is a nationally competitive, comprehensive research university offering undergraduate, graduate, doctoral, distance and continuing education studies programs. The oldest of the UH System universities, it is the flagship of the UH System. It has been recognized as a Tier One institution by the Carnegie Foundation for its high level of research activity.

The University of Houston-Clear Lake is a Hispanic Serving Institution offering more than 90 degree programs across four colleges and has an alumni base of more than 75,000.

The University of Houston-Downtown is the second-largest university in Houston and the most ethnically diverse university in the state. It is a four-year institution located in the central business district, providing valuable opportunities for student internships at major corporations.

The University of Houston-Victoria is an undergraduate and master's university. UHV offers more than 80 academic programs, with concentrations in business; education and health professions; liberal arts and social sciences; and natural and applied sciences, along with one of the most dynamic online educational programs in the state.

Geographic Reach

The UH System includes the University of Houston, UH-Clear Lake, UH-Downtown and UH-Victoria, and instructional sites in Katy, Northwest Houston, Pearland and Sugar Land.

Sales and Marketing

UH System serves more than 75,000 students.

LOCATIONS

HQ: UNIVERSITY OF HOUSTON SYSTEM
4302 UNIVERSITY DR, HOUSTON, TX 772042011
Phone: 713 743-0945
Web: WWW.UHSYSTEM.EDU

PRODUCTS/OPERATIONS

Selected Colleges and Schools
University of Houston
    C.T. Bauer College of Business
    College of Education
    College of Liberal Arts and Social Sciences
    College of Natural Sciences and Mathematics
    College of Optometry
    College of Pharmacy
    College of Technology
    Conrad N. Hilton College of Hotel and Restaurant Management
    Cullen College of Engineering
    Gerald D. Hines College of Architecture
    Graduate College of Social Work
    Honors College
    Law Center
University of Houston-Clear Lake
    School of Business
    School of Education
    School of Human Sciences and Humanities
    School of Science and Computer Engineering
University of Houston-Downtown
    College of Business
    College of Humanities and Social Sciences
    College of Public Service
    College of Sciences and Technology
University of Houston-Victoria
    School of Arts and Sciences
    School of Business Administration
    School of Education and Human Development
    School of Nursing

COMPETITORS

AUSTIN COLLEGE
BOARD OF REGENTS OF THE UNIVERSITY OF NEBRASKA
CALIFORNIA STATE UNIVERSITY, EAST BAY
FLORIDA INTERNATIONAL UNIVERSITY
HAMPTON UNIVERSITY
SAN JOSE STATE UNIVERSITY
TEXAS TECH UNIVERSITY SYSTEM
THE UNIVERSITY OF CHICAGO
UNIVERSITY OF HAWAII SYSTEMS
UNIVERSITY OF LOUISVILLE

HISTORICAL FINANCIALS

Company Type: Private

Income Statement   FYE: August 31

	REVENUE ($mil)	NET INCOME ($mil)	NET PROFIT MARGIN	EMPLOYEES
08/15	605	41	6.9%	12,608
08/14	742	46	6.2%	—
08/13	1	81	6095.0%	—
08/12	688	132	19.3%	—
Annual Growth	(4.2%)	(31.9%)	—	—

2015 Year-End Financials
Return on assets: 6.1%   Cash ($ mil.): (-73)
Return on equity: 6.9%
Current Ratio: -0.20

UNIVERSITY OF IOWA HOSPITALS AND CLINICS

EXECUTIVES

Interim Chief Operating Officer, John N Kastanis
Auditors : KPMG LLP DES MOINES IOWA

LOCATIONS

HQ: UNIVERSITY OF IOWA HOSPITALS AND CLINICS
200 HAWKINS DR, IOWA CITY, IA 522421009
Phone: 319 356-1616
Web: WWW.UIHC.ORG

HISTORICAL FINANCIALS

Company Type: Private

Income Statement   FYE: June 30

	REVENUE ($mil)	NET INCOME ($mil)	NET PROFIT MARGIN	EMPLOYEES
06/21	2,158	201	9.3%	7,638
06/20	1,939	99	5.1%	—
06/19	1,834	111	6.1%	—
06/18	1,666	296	17.8%	—
Annual Growth	9.0%	(12.1%)	—	—

2021 Year-End Financials
Return on assets: 7.0%   Cash ($ mil.): 6
Return on equity: 10.3%
Current Ratio: 1.40

UNIVERSITY OF LOUISIANA SYSTEM FOUNDATION

Auditors : DARYL G PURPERA CPA CFE BA

LOCATIONS

HQ: UNIVERSITY OF LOUISIANA SYSTEM FOUNDATION
1201 N 3RD ST STE 7300, BATON ROUGE, LA 708025243
Phone: 225 342-6950
Web: WWW.ULSYSTEM.EDU

HISTORICAL FINANCIALS

Company Type: Private

Income Statement   FYE: June 30

	REVENUE ($mil)	NET INCOME ($mil)	NET PROFIT MARGIN	EMPLOYEES
06/21	903	248	27.5%	4,500
06/20	927	43	4.7%	—
06/19	942	28	3.0%	—
06/18	930	101	10.9%	—
Annual Growth	(1.0%)	34.9%	—	—

2021 Year-End Financials
Return on assets: 7.7%   Cash ($ mil.): 222
Return on equity: —
Current Ratio: 2.20

UNIVERSITY OF LOUISVILLE

Living up to its mandate to be a leading metropolitan research university, the University of Louisville (U of L) has hit a few out of the park. The U of L completed the first self-contained artificial heart implant and the first successful hand transplant at its University of Louisville Hospital.Â The health care focused university offers associate, baccalaureate, master's, professional, and doctorate degrees in some 170 fields of study including medicine, dentistry, nursing, and public health, as well as arts and sciences, education, business, law, music, social work, and engineering. It has more than 22,000 students enrolled in about a dozen colleges and schools on three campuses.

Geographic Reach

U of L's main campus, the 290-acre Belknap Campus, houses seven of the university's 12 colleges and schools and is located three miles from downtown Louisville. The U of L Health Sciences Center (housing the health-related schools) is located in downtown Louisville, while the Shelby Campus is in eastern Jefferson County.

Strategy

Despite its focus on health care, pressures on the health care industry (including the high cost of running a full-service hospital) prompted the school to explore a possible merger of the U of L Hospital with two other state health care providers, Saint Joseph Health Care and Jewish Hospital & St. Mary's HealthCare (JHSMH), in 2010. However, U of L was ultimately left out of the deal (completed in 2012) after Kentucky's governor voiced concerns over the potential loss of control over the U of L Hospital, which operates as a regional safety net medical care provider.

Company Background

The origins of the University of Louisville date back to 1798 with a meeting to establish Jefferson Seminary, which didn't open its doors until 1813 and closed 16 years later. Subsequent incarnations eventually led to the creation of the University of Louisville in 1846.

Notable alumni include author Sue Grafton, US Senator Christopher Dodd, and William Akers, inventor of the SPF sun protection rating system.

Auditors : CLIFTONLARSONALLEN LLP ST LO

LOCATIONS

HQ: UNIVERSITY OF LOUISVILLE
2301 S 3RD ST, LOUISVILLE, KY 402922001
Phone: 502 852-5555
Web: WWW.LOUISVILLE.EDU

PRODUCTS/OPERATIONS

Selected Colleges and Schools
Arts & Sciences
Brandeis School of Law
Business
Dentistry
Education & Human Development
Kent School of Social Work
Medicine
Music
Nursing
Public Health & Information Sciences
School of Interdisciplinary and Graduate Studies
Speed School of Engineering

COMPETITORS

GEORGETOWN UNIVERSITY (THE)
NORTHWESTERN UNIVERSITY
QUINNIPIAC UNIVERSITY
THE GEORGE WASHINGTON UNIVERSITY
THE UNIVERSITY OF CHICAGO
THE UNIVERSITY OF TEXAS SYSTEM
UNIVERSITY OF MISSISSIPPI
UNIVERSITY OF MISSOURI SYSTEM
UNIVERSITY OF OKLAHOMA
UNIVERSITY OF SOUTHERN CALIFORNIA

HISTORICAL FINANCIALS
Company Type: Private

Income Statement — FYE: June 30

	REVENUE ($mil)	NET INCOME ($mil)	NET PROFIT MARGIN	EMPLOYEES
06/21	850	64	7.6%	6,275
06/18	717	3	0.4%	—
06/12	559	(36)	—	—
06/11	591	32	5.4%	—
Annual Growth	3.7%	7.2%		

2021 Year-End Financials
Return on assets: 3.9%   Cash ($ mil.): 206
Return on equity: 6.6%
Current Ratio: 2.00

UNIVERSITY OF MARYLAND MEDICAL SYSTEM CORPORATION

The University of Maryland Medical System (UMMS) is a university-based regional health care system focused on serving the health care needs of Maryland. The UMMS, one of the largest employers in the Baltimore area, has more than 2,485 acute care beds and attends to such specialties as trauma care, cancer, cardiac, women's, vascular and neuroscience services, orthopedic rehabilitation, and pediatric care. University of Maryland Medical Center, the system's teaching hub, is one of the oldest academic hospitals in the US. In addition to its hospitals, UMMS also includes community clinics to address mental health, rehabilitation, and primary care.

Operations

UMMC's members' hospitals include the University of Maryland Medical Center, Baltimore Washington Medical Center, UM Rehabilitation & Orthopedic Institute, UM Capital Region Health, Mt. Washington Pediatric Hospital, UM Shore Health System, University of Maryland St. Joseph Medical Center, and Upper Chesapeake Health, among others.

University of Maryland Medical Center, which houses about 805 beds, is staffed entirely by physicians who double as faculty members at the University of Maryland School of Medicine (SOM), the system's longtime partner. The hospital contains additional specialty facilities dedicated to such areas as pediatrics, cancer treatment, cardiac disease, diabetes, organ transplants, Parkinson's disease, and shock trauma.

Aside from its integral partnership with SOM, UMMS has in recent years been bolstering its network of member hospitals to reach new markets in Maryland. Its affiliate, University of Maryland Upper Chesapeake Health, owns a pair of hospitals in northeastern Maryland (UM Upper Chesapeake Medical Center and UM Harford Memorial Hospital).

Geographic Reach

Based in Maryland, UMMS provides primary and specialty care at more than 150 locations across the state.

Company Background

The system's flagship hospital began on its present site in 1823 as Baltimore Infirmary. It later was known for many years as University Hospital until Maryland's legislature changed it from a state-run, single-building facility to a private, not-for-profit medical system in 1984. In short order, UMMS began expanding, mainly by adding existing hospitals.

EXECUTIVES

Chief of Staff*, Kara Bowman
EXTERNAL AFFAIRS*, Kristin Jones Bryce
Auditors : ERNST & YOUNG LLP BALTIMORE

LOCATIONS

HQ: UNIVERSITY OF MARYLAND MEDICAL SYSTEM CORPORATION
250 W PRATT ST, BALTIMORE, MD 212012423
Phone: 410 328-8667
Web: WWW.UMMS.ORG

PRODUCTS/OPERATIONS

Selected Facilities and Affiliates
Baltimore Washington Medical Center
Chester River Health System
Civista Medical Center
Kernan Orthopaedics and Rehabilitation
Maryland General Hospital
Mt. Washington Pediatric Hospital
Shore Health System
    Dorchester General Hospital
    The Memorial Hospital at Easton
University of Maryland Medical Center
    Marlene and Stewart Greenebaum Cancer Center
    R Adams Cowley Shock Trauma Center
    University of Maryland Hospital for Children
University of Maryland St. Joseph Medical Center
University Specialty Hospital
Upper Chesapeake Health
    Harford Memorial Hospital
    Upper Chesapeake Medical Center

COMPETITORS

ASCENSION PROVIDENCE ROCHESTER HOSPITAL
FIRSTHEALTH OF THE CAROLINAS, INC.
HOSPITAL SERVICE DISTRICT 1
KENNEDY HEALTH SYSTEM, INC.
LOMA LINDA UNIVERSITY MEDICAL CENTER
MERITER HEALTH SERVICES, INC.
THE CHILDREN'S HOSPITAL CORPORATION
THE UNIVERSITY OF CHICAGO MEDICAL CENTER
WASHINGTON HOSPITAL CENTER CORPORATION

YORK HOSPITAL

HISTORICAL FINANCIALS
Company Type: Private

Income Statement FYE: June 30

	REVENUE ($mil)	NET INCOME ($mil)	NET PROFIT MARGIN	EMPLOYEES
06/22	4,893	(81)	—	12,000
06/21	4,769	428	9.0%	—
06/20	4,364	70	1.6%	—
06/19	4,235	36	0.9%	—
Annual Growth	4.9%	—	—	—

2022 Year-End Financials
Return on assets: (-1.2%) Cash ($ mil.): 244
Return on equity: (-2.5%)
Current Ratio: 1.00

UNIVERSITY OF MARYLAND, COLLEGE PARK

EXECUTIVES

Acting Chief, Cynthia Edmunds
Auditors : CLIFTONLARSONALLEN LLP BALTIM

LOCATIONS

HQ: UNIVERSITY OF MARYLAND, COLLEGE PARK
PATUXENT BLDG 010, COLLEGE PARK, MD 207420001
Phone: 301 405-1000
Web: WWW.UMD.EDU

HISTORICAL FINANCIALS
Company Type: Private

Income Statement FYE: June 30

	REVENUE ($mil)	NET INCOME ($mil)	NET PROFIT MARGIN	EMPLOYEES
06/21	1,258	57	4.5%	8,871
06/18	1,369	100	7.3%	—
06/17	15	1	12.6%	—
Annual Growth	198.8%	131.4%	—	—

2021 Year-End Financials
Return on assets: 1.6% Cash ($ mil.): 793
Return on equity: 2.7%
Current Ratio: 2.40

UNIVERSITY OF MASSACHUSETTS INCORPORATED

The University of Massachusetts (UMass) has been expanding across the commonwealth since its founding in 1863. About 75,000 students are enrolled each year. The university's flagship campus is in Amherst, with 31,600 students and over 200 distinct academic programs including highly ranked programs in business computer science, health care and social science and largest public research university in New England. UMass is the third-largest research university in Massachusetts and the fourth-largest research university in New England, behind only Harvard, MIT and Yale with a record $687 million in annual research and development.

Operations
The tuition and fees accounts for about 40% of the revenue, grant and contract is about 30%, other operating revenue is almost 25%, and followed by auxiliary, with more than 5% of the revenue.

The system's Boston and Dartmouth campuses are renowned for their academic programs. UMass Boston is nationally recognized as a model of excellence for urban public research universities. Boston's distinguished intellectual contributions span the social sciences, education, health and wellness. UMass Dartmouth distinguishes itself as a variant university dedicated to engaged learning and innovative research and offers students high-quality academic programs through undergraduate majors and professional and doctorial programs, including the state state's only public law school.

Geographic Reach
University of Massachusetts is a world class public research university system with four comprehensive undergraduate and graduate campuses located in rural, urban, suburban and urban areas. The University of Massachusetts has more than 90 core research facilities across the state that are available to researchers from government, academia, and industry on a fee-for-service basis.

Sales and Marketing
University of Massachusetts offers about hundred degree programs at four undergraduate/graduate degree program on its website.

Financial Performance
Company's revenue for fiscal 2021 increased to $2.3 billion compared from the prior year with $2.4 billion.

Net loss for fiscal 2021 increased to $1.1 billion compared from the prior year with $1.0 billion.

Cash held by the company at the end of fiscal 2021 decreased to $353.9 million. Cash provided by financing activities was $1.1 billion, while cash used for operations and investing activities were $586.0 million and $367.0 million, respectively.

Mergers and Acquisitions
In 2021, University of Massachusetts has taken control of Brandman University, a California-based network of schools for adult learners, and rebranded it as UMass Global and plans to expand its online education offerings. The acquisition came after the end of a yearlong partnership between UMass and Brandman's former parent, Chapman University. Brandman serves about 22,000 students spreads across 25 locations and online as part of Chapman University.

Company Background
Notable UMass alumni include entertainer Bill Cosby, singer Natalie Cole, and former General Electric CEO Jack Welch.

EXECUTIVES

Vice Chairman*, Peter Levine
CCO Development*, Thomas Chumura
Auditors : KPMG LLP BOSTON MA

LOCATIONS

HQ: UNIVERSITY OF MASSACHUSETTS INCORPORATED
1 BEACON ST, BOSTON, MA 021083107
Phone: 617 287-7000
Web: WWW.MASSACHUSETTS.EDU

PRODUCTS/OPERATIONS

Selected Colleges and Schools
College of Engineering
College of Humanities and Fine Arts
College of Natural Sciences and Mathematics
College of Social and Behavioral Sciences
Commonwealth College
Graduate School
School of Education
School of Management
School of Nursing
School of Public Health and Health Sciences

COMPETITORS

FAIRFIELD UNIVERSITY
FGS-WI, LLC
GINCOP, INC.
NEW MEXICO STATE UNIVERSITY
QUAD/GRAPHICS INC.
SOUTH CAROLINA STATE UNIVERSITY
THE SHERIDAN GROUP INC
TOPPAN PRINTING CO., LTD.
Torstar Corporation
WALSWORTH PUBLISHING COMPANY, INC.

HISTORICAL FINANCIALS
Company Type: Private

Income Statement FYE: June 30

	REVENUE ($mil)	NET INCOME ($mil)	NET PROFIT MARGIN	EMPLOYEES
06/20	2,426	(39)	—	13,196
06/18	2,468	77	3.1%	—
06/17	2,442	325	13.3%	—
06/16	2,403	129	5.4%	—
Annual Growth	0.2%	—	—	—

2020 Year-End Financials
Return on assets: (-0.5%) Cash ($ mil.): 86
Return on equity: (-1.6%)
Current Ratio: 1.70

UNIVERSITY OF MINNESOTA PHYSICIANS

EXECUTIVES

CAO*, Rachel Croson
Auditors : KPMG LLP MINNEAPOLIS MN

LOCATIONS

HQ: UNIVERSITY OF MINNESOTA PHYSICIANS
720 WASHINGTON AVE SE # 200, MINNEAPOLIS, MN 554142924
Phone: 612 884-0600
Web: WWW.MPHYSICIANS.ORG

HISTORICAL FINANCIALS

Company Type: Private

Income Statement — FYE: June 30

	REVENUE ($mil)	NET INCOME ($mil)	NET PROFIT MARGIN	EMPLOYEES
06/20	702	27	3.9%	200
06/15	482	10	2.2%	—
06/14	490	23	4.8%	—
06/13	452	12	2.8%	—
Annual Growth	6.5%	12.0%	—	—

2020 Year-End Financials
Return on assets: 10.6%   Cash ($ mil.): 147
Return on equity: 23.2%
Current Ratio: 1.10

UNIVERSITY OF MISSISSIPPI MEDICAL CENTER

EXECUTIVES

INTEGRITY, Stacy Baldwin

LOCATIONS

HQ: UNIVERSITY OF MISSISSIPPI MEDICAL CENTER
2500 N STATE ST, JACKSON, MS 392164500
Phone: 601 984-2150
Web: WWW.UMC.EDU

HISTORICAL FINANCIALS

Company Type: Private

Income Statement — FYE: June 30

	REVENUE ($mil)	NET INCOME ($mil)	NET PROFIT MARGIN	EMPLOYEES
06/20	1,375	(72)	—	9,000
06/18	1,252	(87)	—	—
06/17	1,204	(78)	—	—
Annual Growth	4.5%	—	—	—

2020 Year-End Financials
Return on assets: (-3.7%)   Cash ($ mil.): 385
Return on equity: —
Current Ratio: 1.90

UNIVERSITY OF MISSISSIPPI MEDICAL CENTER

LOCATIONS

HQ: UNIVERSITY OF MISSISSIPPI MEDICAL CENTER
2500 N STATE ST, JACKSON, MS 392164500
Phone: 601 984-5670
Web: WWW.UMC.EDU

HISTORICAL FINANCIALS

Company Type: Private

Income Statement — FYE: June 30

	REVENUE ($mil)	NET INCOME ($mil)	NET PROFIT MARGIN	EMPLOYEES
06/14	1,042	30	2.9%	20
06/13	940	23	2.5%	—
Annual Growth	10.9%	29.9%	—	—

2014 Year-End Financials
Return on assets: 8.9%   Cash ($ mil.): 176
Return on equity: 2.9%
Current Ratio: 2.20

UNIVERSITY OF MISSOURI HEALTH CARE

EXECUTIVES

Interim Chief Executive Officer, Nim Chinniah
OF, Ann Toellner
Chief Compliance Officer, Matt Frederiksen-england
Auditors : KPMG LLP

LOCATIONS

HQ: UNIVERSITY OF MISSOURI HEALTH CARE
1 HOSPITAL DR, COLUMBIA, MO 652015276
Phone: 573 882-4141
Web: WWW.MUHEALTH.ORG

HISTORICAL FINANCIALS

Company Type: Private

Income Statement — FYE: June 30

	REVENUE ($mil)	NET INCOME ($mil)	NET PROFIT MARGIN	EMPLOYEES
06/16	749	62	8.4%	5,000
06/15	696	64	9.3%	—
06/08	0	0	1.0%	—
Annual Growth	140.0%	212.1%	—	—

2016 Year-End Financials
Return on assets: 5.9%   Cash ($ mil.): 27
Return on equity: 10.0%
Current Ratio: 1.40

UNIVERSITY OF MISSOURI SYSTEM

The University of Missouri (UM) is one of the nation's largest higher education institutions. Founded in 1839, UM educates more than 70,000 students at four campuses and through a statewide extension program with activities in every county of the state. Serving nearly 115 counties, the university's campuses are UM-Columbia UM-Kansas City, UM-St. Louis and the Missouri University of Science and Technology. MU Extension is a partnership of the University of Missouri campuses, Lincoln University, the people of Missouri through county extension councils, and the National Institute for Food and Agriculture of the US Department of Agriculture. Collectively, the UM System is a $3.0 billion enterprise that represents one of the greatest assets of the state of Missouri.

Operations

In addition to its university campuses, the University of Missouri System operates the University of Missouri HealthCare, which encompasses University Hospital and Clinics, Women's and Children's Hospital, Ellis Fischel Cancer Center, Rusk Rehabilitation Center, Missouri Psychiatric Institute, Missouri Orthopaedic Institute, and University Physicians. It also operates three academic schools at MU: School of Health Professions, School of Medicine and Sinclair School of Nursing. Its hospitals and clinics provide high-risk obstetrics, orthopaedic surgery, neurosciences, and cardiovascular care, among other services. It also has the region's only Level I Trauma Center.

In addition, patient medical services account for approximately 45%, tuition and fees generate about 20%, other auxiliary enterprises provide nearly 15%, state appropriations and grants and contracts bring in about 10% each and others represent the remaining less than 5%.

EXECUTIVES

Interim CIO*, Beth Chancellor

Auditors: BKD LLP KANSAS CITY MISSOUR

LOCATIONS

HQ: UNIVERSITY OF MISSOURI SYSTEM
321 UNIVERSITY HALL, COLUMBIA, MO 652113020
Phone: 573 882-2712
Web: WWW.UMSYSTEM.EDU

PRODUCTS/OPERATIONS

Selected Campuses
University of Missouri-Columbia
University of Missouri Health System (Columbia)
UM-Kansas City
UM-St. Louis
Missouri University of Science and Technology (Rolla)

Selected Colleges and Schools
College of Agriculture, Food and Natural Resources
    School of Natural Resources
College of Arts and Sciences
    School of Music
College of Education
    School of Information Science and Learning Technologies
College of Engineering
College of Human Environmental Sciences
    School of Social Work
College of Veterinary Medicine
Graduate School
    Harry S Truman School of Public Affairs
School of Health Professions
School of Journalism
School of Law
School of Medicine
Sinclair College of Nursing
Trulaske College of Business
    School of Accountancy

COMPETITORS

AUBURN UNIVERSITY
CREIGHTON UNIVERSITY
KENT STATE UNIVERSITY
MARSHALL UNIVERSITY
MISSOURI STATE UNIVERSITY
RECTOR & VISITORS OF THE UNIVERSITY OF VIRGINIA
REGENTS OF THE UNIVERSITY OF MICHIGAN
UNIVERSITY OF KANSAS
UNIVERSITY OF OKLAHOMA
UNIVERSITY SYSTEM OF MARYLAND

HISTORICAL FINANCIALS

Company Type: Private

Income Statement — FYE: June 30

	REVENUE ($mil)	NET INCOME ($mil)	NET PROFIT MARGIN	EMPLOYEES
06/18	2,851	267	9.4%	30,282
06/16	2,702	108	4.0%	—
06/13	2,404	221	9.2%	—
Annual Growth	3.5%	3.8%	—	—

2018 Year-End Financials
Return on assets: 3.1%   Cash ($ mil.): 360
Return on equity: 5.5%
Current Ratio: 1.30

UNIVERSITY OF NEVADA, RENO

Auditors: GRANT THORNTON LLP SAN JOSÉ

LOCATIONS

HQ: UNIVERSITY OF NEVADA, RENO
1664 N VIRGINIA ST, RENO, NV 895570002
Phone: 775 784-1110
Web: WWW.UNR.EDU

HISTORICAL FINANCIALS

Company Type: Private

Income Statement — FYE: June 30

	REVENUE ($mil)	NET INCOME ($mil)	NET PROFIT MARGIN	EMPLOYEES
06/21	1,162	318	27.4%	1,500
06/19	391	22	5.8%	—
06/18	366	51	13.9%	—
06/07	262	(212)	—	—
Annual Growth	11.2%	—	—	—

2021 Year-End Financials
Return on assets: 6.2%   Cash ($ mil.): 206
Return on equity: 10.8%
Current Ratio: 4.60

UNIVERSITY OF NEW MEXICO

The University of New Mexico (UNM) is most renowned for its schools of medicine, law, and education. Students also attend one of the school's four branches located around the northern part of the state at Gallup, Los Alamos, Rio Rancho, Taos, and Valencia. Through its schools and colleges, the university offers about 95 bachelor's degrees, around 70 master's degrees, more than 35 doctorate degrees, as well as professional practice programs in law, medicine, and pharmacy.

Operations

The University of New Mexico offers a wide variety of academic programs through twelve Colleges and Schools. These academic options include more than 215 degree and certificate programs, including about 95 baccalaureate, around 70 masters and over 35 doctoral degrees.

Colleges and Schools have included Anderson School of Management, College of Arts & Sciences, College of Education, College of Fine Arts, Graduate Studies, Honors College, College of Nursing, College of Pharmacy, College of Population Health, College of University Libraries & Learning Sciences, School of Architecture and Planning, School of Engineering, School of Law, School of Medicine, and University College.

Geographic Reach

UNM's main campus is located in Albuquerque. Satellite campuses are in Gallup, Los Alamos, Rio Rancho, Taos, and Valencia.

Company Background

UNM was founded in 1889.

Auditors: MOSS ADAMS LLP ALBUQUERQUE

LOCATIONS

HQ: UNIVERSITY OF NEW MEXICO
1800 ROMA BLVD NE, ALBUQUERQUE, NM 871310001
Phone: 505 277-0111
Web: GALLUP.UNM.EDU

PRODUCTS/OPERATIONS

2013 Sales

	% of sales
Clinical operations	42
Grants & contracts	21
Sales & services	16
Tuition & fees	10
Patients services	8
Other	3
Total	100

Schools and Colleges
Anderson School of Management
College of Arts & Sciences
College of Education
College of Fine Arts
College of University Libraries & Learning Sciences
Honors College
School of Architecture & Planning
School of Engineering
School of Law
School of Public Administration
University College

COMPETITORS

CREIGHTON UNIVERSITY
DESALES UNIVERSITY
MARQUETTE UNIVERSITY
NEW MEXICO STATE UNIVERSITY
NORTHEASTERN UNIVERSITY
RECTOR & VISITORS OF THE UNIVERSITY OF VIRGINIA
REGENTS OF THE UNIVERSITY OF MICHIGAN
UNIVERSITY OF CALIFORNIA, SAN FRANCISCO
UNIVERSITY OF MISSOURI SYSTEM
UNIVERSITY OF OKLAHOMA

HISTORICAL FINANCIALS

Company Type: Private

Income Statement — FYE: June 30

	REVENUE ($mil)	NET INCOME ($mil)	NET PROFIT MARGIN	EMPLOYEES
06/21	2,316	(0)	0.0%	18,362
06/20	2,050	629	30.7%	—
06/19	1,913	(137)	—	—
06/18	1,826	(181)	—	—
Annual Growth	8.2%	—	—	—

2021 Year-End Financials
Return on assets: —   Cash ($ mil.): 591
Return on equity: (-0.1%)
Current Ratio: 2.40

UNIVERSITY OF NORTH CAROLINA AT CHAPEL HILL

The University of North Carolina at Chapel Hill (UNC-Chapel Hill) has the education market cornered. One of the three original points making up North Carolina's Research Triangle (along with Duke University and North Carolina State University), Carolina is the flagship campus of the University of North Carolina (UNC) system. The institution is consistently among the top-ranked research schools in the US. It enrolls some 29,000 students and offers more than 250 undergraduate, graduate, and professional programs including law and medicine. It has 3,200 full-time faculty members.

Operations

The university includes 15 schools and colleges, as well as an adult learning center for continuing education programs. Its degree offerings include more than 100 master's degrees and about 70 doctorate programs.

UNC-Chapel Hill conducts extensive research programs in a variety of fields at its five health science schools (medicine, dentistry, pharmacy, nursing, and public health), its patient care facilities (operated through the University of North Carolina Hospitals affiliate), and its scientific teaching divisions (at the College of Arts and Sciences). The university attracted some $770 million in research grants and contracts during 2012. Funding sources include the National Institutes of Health. Research funding at UNC-Chapel Hill makes up more than half of awards for the entire UNC system.

Geographic Reach

UNC-Chapel Hill is located on a 730-acre campus that holds about 300 buildings. The university attracts students from all 50 US states and more than 145 international countries. It also has study abroad opportunities.

Financial Performance

UNC-Chapel Hill reported $2.5 billion in total revenues in 2012. Operating revenues make up the majority of earnings ($1.7 billion) from activities including student tuition, fees, federal grants and contracts, and patient services. Non-operating revenues include state appropriations, non-capital grants and gifts, and investment income. Operating expenses ran at about $2.4 billion for 2012, and the university had a budget for fiscal 2013 of some $2.5 billion.

Strategy

To expand its international education opportunities, in 2013 UNC-Chapel Hill formed a dual-degree partnership with Tsinghua University in China. The partnership offers business administration executive master's degrees.

Company Background

Chartered in 1789, Carolina is the oldest public university in the US. Notable alumni include author Thomas Wolfe and President James K. Polk, as well as athlete Michael Jordan and journalist Charles Kuralt.

EXECUTIVES

Vice-Chancellor Finance*, Richard L Mann

Vice-Chancellor Finance*, Roger Patterson
Auditors : BETH A WOOD CPA RALEIGH NO

LOCATIONS

HQ: UNIVERSITY OF NORTH CAROLINA AT CHAPEL HILL
  104 AIRPORT DR, CHAPEL HILL, NC 275995023
Phone: 919 962-1370
Web: WWW.UNC.EDU

PRODUCTS/OPERATIONS

Selected Schools, Colleges, and Centers
College of Arts and Sciences
Eshelman School of Pharmacy
Friday Center for Continuing Education
General College
Gillings School of Global Public Health
Graduate School
Kenan-Flagler Business School
School of Dentistry
School of Education
School of Government
School of Information and Library Science
School of Journalism and Mass Communication
School of Law
School of Medicine
School of Nursing
School of Social Work

Selected Academic Departments
African and AfroAmerican Studies
Air Force ROTC
Anthropology
Army ROTC
Art
Biology
Chemistry
Classics
Communication Studies
Dramatic Art
Economics
English and Comparative Literature
Exercise and Sport Science
Geography
History
Marine Sciences
Music
Nutrition
Pharmacology
Philosophy
Political Science
Psychology
Religious Studies
Sociology
Surgery

COMPETITORS

MARSHALL UNIVERSITY
MICHIGAN STATE UNIVERSITY
MISSOURI STATE UNIVERSITY
NORTH CAROLINA STATE UNIVERSITY
RECTOR & VISITORS OF THE UNIVERSITY OF VIRGINIA
THE RUTGERS STATE UNIVERSITY
THE UNIVERSITY OF NORTH CAROLINA AT CHARLOTTE
TRUSTEES OF INDIANA UNIVERSITY
UNIVERSITY OF KENTUCKY
WILLAMETTE UNIVERSITY

HISTORICAL FINANCIALS
Company Type: Private

Income Statement
FYE: June 30

	REVENUE ($mil)	NET INCOME ($mil)	NET PROFIT MARGIN	EMPLOYEES
06/19	2,073	229	11.0%	12,204
06/17	1,773	95	5.4%	—
06/11	1,704	391	23.0%	—
06/08	281	149	53.1%	—
Annual Growth	19.9%	3.9%	—	—

2019 Year-End Financials
Return on assets: 8.0% Cash ($ mil.): 240
Return on equity: 378.1%
Current Ratio: 2.10

UNIVERSITY OF NORTH TEXAS SYSTEM

Auditors : BKD LLP FORT WORTH TEXAS

LOCATIONS

HQ: UNIVERSITY OF NORTH TEXAS SYSTEM
  1302 TEASLEY LN, DENTON, TX 762057946
Phone: 940 565-2281
Web: WWW.UNTSYSTEM.EDU

HISTORICAL FINANCIALS
Company Type: Private

Income Statement
FYE: August 31

	REVENUE ($mil)	NET INCOME ($mil)	NET PROFIT MARGIN	EMPLOYEES
08/21	709	66	9.3%	537
08/20	668	(20)	—	—
08/19	657	(83)	—	—
08/18	654	79	12.2%	—
Annual Growth	2.7%	(6.0%)	—	—

2021 Year-End Financials
Return on assets: 2.3% Cash ($ mil.): 262
Return on equity: 8.6%
Current Ratio: 1.20

UNIVERSITY OF OREGON

This school's got all its ducks in a row. As one of the largest schools in the state, the University of Oregon (UO) has an enrollment of about 22,760 students and some 2,095 faculty members. It offers its students eight different schools and colleges, plus a graduate college, with fields of study range from the arts and journalism to business and law. Part of the Oregon University System, UO also offers development services, an honors program, research institutes, and continuing education courses. The school's athletic department organizes around 15 sports activities including lacrosse and football; the teams are called The Ducks.

Operations
UO has a student-to-teacher ratio of 16:1, and an average class size of 20. Course offerings range across lecture, discussion, seminar, activity, laboratory, independent study, and independent research formats, and UO has a total of more than 300 undergraduate programs, more than 80 graduate subject areas and more than 30 research centers and institutes. The university's most popular majors for undergraduates include accounting, architecture, art, biology, business administration, chemistry, education, economics, english, environmental science, human physiology, journalism, political science, public relations, and sociology. Its freshman retention success rate is nearly 90%.

Geographic Reach
UO is located at some 295-acre campus in Eugene, Oregon, that includes about 80 buildings. It also has a satellite campus in Portland. Students come to UO from all 50 US states (plus Washington, DC, and two US territories), as well as about 100 foreign countries. More than half of students are Oregon residents. A number of students also participate in more than 300 study abroad and internship programs in approximately 90 international locations.

Company Background
The Oregon State Legislature created the university in 1872 and students first enrolled in 1876.

Auditors : MOSS ADAMS LLP PORTLAND ORE

LOCATIONS

HQ: UNIVERSITY OF OREGON
1585 E 13TH AVE, EUGENE, OR 974031657
Phone: 541 346-1000
Web: WWW.UOREGON.EDU

PRODUCTS/OPERATIONS

Colleges and Schools
Charles H. Lundquist College of Business
College of Arts and Sciences
College of Education
Graduate School
Robert D. Clark Honors College
School of Architecture and Allied Arts
School of Journalism and Communication
School of Law
School of Music and Dance

COMPETITORS

BPP HOLDINGS LIMITED
COLORADO STATE UNIVERSITY
DESALES UNIVERSITY
GROSSMONT UNION HIGH SCHOOL DISTRICT
SCHOOL FACILITIES CORPORATION
IMAGINE SCHOOLS, INC.
NOBEL LEARNING COMMUNITIES, INC.
NORTHEASTERN UNIVERSITY
SAN DIEGO COUNTY OFFICE OF EDUCATION
STRIDE, INC.
THE GIRLS' DAY SCHOOL TRUST

HISTORICAL FINANCIALS
Company Type: Private

Income Statement FYE: June 30

	REVENUE ($mil)	NET INCOME ($mil)	NET PROFIT MARGIN	EMPLOYEES
06/22	871	158	18.2%	7,971
06/21	692	(16)	—	—
06/20	741	329	44.4%	—
06/18	740	(8)	—	—
Annual Growth	4.2%	—	—	—

2022 Year-End Financials
Return on assets: 5.2% Cash ($ mil.): 233
Return on equity: 11.1%
Current Ratio: 1.60

UNIVERSITY OF PITTSBURGH-OF THE COMMONWEALTH SYSTEM OF HIGHER EDUCATION

The University of Pittsburgh (Pitt for short) operates its flagship campus in the Oakland neighborhood of Pittsburgh. More than 35,000 graduate and undergraduate students attend the main campus, as well as four regional campuses. Pitt Panthers pursue degrees in about 400 disciplines, including arts and sciences, business, law, medicine, and engineering. The school has a student-teacher ratio of 14:1. Pitt is also affiliated with the UPMC health system, which operates about 20 hospitals, numerous clinics, and an insurance company. Pitt was founded in 1787, making it one of the oldest universities in the US.

Operations
Pitt is considered a leading US public research university, and as such spends more than $700 million annually on research projects. Pitt is recognized for its work in about a dozen disciplines including computer modeling, philosophy, the humanities, international studies, aging, neuroscience, bioengineering, commercial innovation, education, national preparedness, drug discovery, translational medicine, and nanoscience. It was at Pitt that Jonas Salk developed the polio vaccine at what is now known as Salk Hall.

Notable Pitt alumni include Academy Award winner Gene Kelly, Nobel Peace Prize winner Wangari Maathai, Pulitzer Prize winner Michael Chabon, and US Senator Orrin Hatch.

Geographic Reach
In addition to the main campus in Pittsburgh, which houses 17 schools, colleges, and a center for social and urban research, Pitt has regional campus locations in Bradford, Greensburg, Johnstown, and Titusville.

Financial Performance
Pitt reported revenues of some $2 billion in 2014. Most of the university's revenues come from grants and contracts, followed by student tuition and fees, commonwealth appropriation, endowment distributions, and other sources of income.

Strategy
In addition to providing high quality education programs for its students, Pitt works to engage in research, scholarly, and artistic projects that advance global learning. It also works to collaborate with government agencies and businesses to advance science, medicine, and technology, seeking active partners as well as funding provider to further its programs.

EXECUTIVES

CIO*, Jeffer Choudhry
Auditors : KPMG LLP PITTSBURGH PENNSYL

LOCATIONS

HQ: UNIVERSITY OF PITTSBURGH-OF THE COMMONWEALTH SYSTEM OF HIGHER EDUCATION
4200 5TH AVE, PITTSBURGH, PA 152600001
Phone: 412 624-4141
Web: WWW.PITT.EDU

PRODUCTS/OPERATIONS

Selected Schools and Colleges
The John A. Swanson School of Engineering
The Joseph M. Katz Graduate School of Business
  College of Business Administration
Kenneth P. Dietrich School of Arts and Sciences
  College of General Studies
School of Dental Medicine
School of Education
School of Health and Rehabilitation Sciences
School of Information Sciences
School of Law
School of Medicine
School of Nursing
School of Pharmacy
School of Public and International Affairs
School of Public Health
School of Social Work
University Center for International Studies
University Honors College

COMPETITORS

DESALES UNIVERSITY
DRAKE UNIVERSITY
DUKE UNIVERSITY
FLORIDA A & M UNIVERSITY
SYRACUSE UNIVERSITY
THE JOHNS HOPKINS UNIVERSITY
THE UNIVERSITY OF HARTFORD
THE UNIVERSITY OF IOWA
UNIVERSITY OF CALIFORNIA, SAN DIEGO
UNIVERSITY OF ILLINOIS

HISTORICAL FINANCIALS
Company Type: Private

Income Statement — FYE: June 30

	REVENUE ($mil)	NET INCOME ($mil)	NET PROFIT MARGIN	EMPLOYEES
06/21	2,502	1,548	61.9%	9,607
06/20	2,352	(168)	—	
06/19	2,352	111	4.8%	—
06/18	2,276	381	16.8%	—
Annual Growth	3.2%	59.5%	—	—

2021 Year-End Financials
Return on assets: 16.0% Cash ($ mil.): 76
Return on equity: 23.6%
Current Ratio: —

UNIVERSITY OF SAN FRANCISCO INC

University of San Francisco (USF) is one of 27 Jesuit Catholic colleges and universities in the US. The main USF campus sits on 55 acres near Golden Gate Park in San Francisco. The school, which was formed in 1855 as St. Ignatius Academy, enrolls more than 10,000 undergraduate and graduate students combined. USF operates five schools and colleges, including the College of Arts and Sciences, School of Management, and School of Nursing and Health Professions as well as the School of Law and the School of Education (both of which enroll graduate students only). Tuition, fees, and room and board average a total of more than $68,470 per year for a traditional undergraduate student.

Operations
University of San Francisco (USF) offers more than 40 majors and 70 minors in the College of Arts and Sciences, School of Management, and School of Nursing and Health Professions. It has some 470 full-time faculty members and nearly 670 part-time faculty members and a student/faculty ratio of 13:1.

USF's more than 10,000 student enrollment includes more than 5,850 undergraduates and more than 4,215 grad students (including law students). The independent, private, not-for-profit university is one of the nation's most ethnically diverse schools. More than 55% of its students are Asian, African-American, Latino, Native Hawaiian/Pacific Islander, or multi-ethnic.

In addition to its main campus, the university has additional locations -- in downtown San Francisco, Orange County, Pleasanton, Sacramento, Santa Rosa, and South Bay -- that offer programs for working students wanting to advance existing careers, switch career paths, or acquire new professional skills.

Geographic Reach
University of San Francisco (USF), located in San Francisco, California, has a significant international student population: nearly 15% of its student body comes from outside the US.

USF offers a study abroad program with options in more than 40 countries.

Strategy
To keep up with growth, USF opened a campus in downtown San Francisco at 101 Howard Street. The university also changed the name of its school of nursing to the School of Nursing and Health Professions to reflect the institution's commitment and expansion of its master of public health degree.

Company Background
The University of San Francisco's founding president, Anthony Maraschi, S.J., arrived in San Francisco as an Italian immigrant in 1854. The next year, he borrowed $11,500 to build a Jesuit church and school on the south side of Market Street. The original college, known as St. Ignatius Academy, opened its doors to its first class in 18585. The State of California granted the college a charter in 1859.

St. Ignatius College was renamed the University of San Francisco in 1930. The university became fully co-educational, welcoming women to all programs, in 1964.

Auditors : PRICEWATERHOUSECOOPERS LLP BO

LOCATIONS
HQ: UNIVERSITY OF SAN FRANCISCO INC
2130 FULTON ST, SAN FRANCISCO, CA 941171050
Phone: 415 422-5555
Web: WWW.USFCA.EDU

PRODUCTS/OPERATIONS
Selected Schools and Colleges
College of Arts
College of Sciences
School of Education
School of Law
School of Management
School of Nursing

COMPETITORS
CALIFORNIA STATE UNIVERSITY, MONTEREY BAY
GWYNEDD MERCY UNIVERSITY
LAFAYETTE COLLEGE
MARSHALL UNIVERSITY
MISSOURI STATE UNIVERSITY
OAKLAND UNIVERSITY
THE COLLEGE OF WILLIAM & MARY
TRUSTEES OF BOSTON COLLEGE
UNIVERSITY OF THE PACIFIC
WILLAMETTE UNIVERSITY

HISTORICAL FINANCIALS
Company Type: Private

Income Statement — FYE: May 31

	REVENUE ($mil)	NET INCOME ($mil)	NET PROFIT MARGIN	EMPLOYEES
05/21	571	117	20.6%	1,200
05/20	554	34	6.2%	—
05/17	417	50	12.1%	—
Annual Growth	8.2%	23.6%	—	—

2021 Year-End Financials
Return on assets: 7.8% Cash ($ mil.): 117
Return on equity: 11.1%
Current Ratio: 0.60

UNIVERSITY OF SOUTH ALABAMA

When you go by the moniker USA and the campus beauty queen wins the Miss USA title year after year (the Pi Kappa Phi Miss USA pageant, that is) you're standing on hallowed ground. In this case it's the ground of the University of South Alabama, situated on the upper Gulf Coast. The school's crown jewel is its College of Medicine and other facilities, including USA Medical Center, USA Knollwood Hospital, and USA Children's and Women's Hospital. USA also offers degrees in Health, Arts and Sciences, Business, Education, Engineering, Nursing, Computer and Information Sciences, Continuing Education and Special Programs, and the Graduate School. More than 14,880 students call the USA home.

Operations
USA offers 41 different bachelor programs, 31 masters programs, and 10 doctoral programs.

Financial Performance
The school reported an 8% increase in revenues in 2012 thanks to higher tuition and fee rates and an increase in student enrollment and credit hours taken, and a rise in net patient service revenues (29% of total 2012 revenues). Other operating revenues also increased in 2012 thanks to higher revenues from the Electronic Health Records Incentive Program.

USA reported net income in 2012 of $38 million (versus a net loss in 2011) due to decline in operating loss, and an increase in non-operating revenues (primarily from higher investment returns and state appropriations).

The university saw an increase in revenues between 2010 and 2012 largely due to organic growth.

Strategy
USA is pushing to expand and strengthen its development program and increase student enrollment. In 2013 the school received a gift of $250,000 from alumni

Dr. and Mrs. Steven H. Stokes to start a new Center for Environmental Resiliency.

Company Background
Founded in 1963, USA has graduated more than 75,000 students, including 18,200 teachers and school administrators (including 85% of Mobile's public school teachers).

Auditors : KPMG LLP JACKSON MISSISSIPPI

LOCATIONS

HQ: UNIVERSITY OF SOUTH ALABAMA
307 N UNIVERSITY BLVD, MOBILE, AL 366883053
Phone: 251 460-6101
Web: WWW.SOUTHALABAMA.EDU

PRODUCTS/OPERATIONS

USA Colleges and Schools
Arts and Sciences
Auburn University School of Pharmacy at USA
Computing
Continuing Education and Special Programs
Education
Engineering
Mitchell College of Business
Medicine
Nursing
Pat Capps Covey College of Allied Health Professions

COMPETITORS

DELAWARE STATE UNIVERSITY
MONTANA STATE UNIVERSITY, INC
WEST VIRGINIA UNIVERSITY
YOUNGSTOWN STATE UNIVERSITY
ZOVIO INC

HISTORICAL FINANCIALS
Company Type: Private

Income Statement — FYE: September 30

	REVENUE ($mil)	NET INCOME ($mil)	NET PROFIT MARGIN	EMPLOYEES
09/21	860	126	14.6%	5,403
09/20	782	124	15.9%	—
09/18	653	(0)	—	—
09/17	662	47	7.2%	—
Annual Growth	6.8%	27.4%	—	—

2021 Year-End Financials
Return on assets: 6.5%   Cash ($ mil.): 207
Return on equity: 36.8%
Current Ratio: 1.50

UNIVERSITY OF SOUTH FLORIDA

The University of South Florida (USF) is the fastest-rising university in America. The school has more than 50,000 students at three campuses in Tampa, St. Petersburg, and Sarasota/Manatee. It offers some 180 undergraduate, graduate, specialty, and doctoral degree programs through about 15 colleges, including Arts and Sciences, Business, Education, Engineering, Marine Science, Pharmacy, and Public Health. USF also offers graduate certificates, continuing education courses, and teacher certifications, and it is a major research institution among US universities. USF was founded in 1960; its mascot is the bull.

Operations
The university has about 2,145 teaching faculty members and maintains a 22:1 student-to-faculty ratio. USF's core offerings include an extensive health sciences program, including medical, nursing, pharmacy, and public health colleges, grouped under the USF Health banner. The health organization also includes patient care facilities such as family care practices, emergency clinics, and Alzheimer's centers.

USF Health also hosts medical research programs in areas such as neurological conditions, cardiovascular care, pediatrics, infectious disease, and biotechnology. The university also has research programs in a range of science, engineering, and arts fields.

Geographic Reach
USF has more than 4,690 international students, or about 10% of the total student population. The university's campuses in Florida encompass over 1,560 acres. The main Tampa campus includes the USF Health facilities and health-related schools.

Sales and Marketing
The university caters to over 50,000 students.

Auditors : SHERRILL F NORMAN CPA TALLA

LOCATIONS

HQ: UNIVERSITY OF SOUTH FLORIDA
4202 E FOWLER AVE, TAMPA, FL 336208000
Phone: 813 974-2011
Web: WWW.USF.EDU

PRODUCTS/OPERATIONS

2013 Revenue

	% of total
Contracts & grants	26
Student financial aid	26
Tuition	16
General revenue	14
Auxiliary enterprises	11
Intercollegiate athletics	3
Lottery	2
Concessions & fees	2
Total	100

Selected Colleges
The Arts
Arts & Sciences
Behavioral & Community Sciences
Business
Education
Engineering
Global Sustainability
Honors College
Marine Science
Medicine
Nursing
Pharmacy
Public Health
University College (graduate school)

COMPETITORS

CLARK ATLANTA UNIVERSITY INC
FAIRFIELD UNIVERSITY
NEW MEXICO STATE UNIVERSITY
SOUTH CAROLINA STATE UNIVERSITY
SOUTH DAKOTA STATE UNIVERSITY
THE JOHNS HOPKINS UNIVERSITY
THE UNIVERSITY OF IOWA
THE WASHINGTON UNIVERSITY
UNIVERSITY OF FLORIDA
UNIVERSITY OF KENTUCKY

HISTORICAL FINANCIALS
Company Type: Private

Income Statement — FYE: June 30

	REVENUE ($mil)	NET INCOME ($mil)	NET PROFIT MARGIN	EMPLOYEES
06/21	795	(23)	—	16,165
06/20	821	(95)	—	—
06/19	849	4	0.5%	—
06/18	871	36	4.1%	—
Annual Growth	(3.0%)	—	—	—

2021 Year-End Financials
Return on assets: (-0.9%)   Cash ($ mil.): 70
Return on equity: (-2.9%)
Current Ratio: 6.20

UNIVERSITY OF TENNESSEE

Whether you want to learn the art of aviation or get ready for a career in public service, the University of Tennessee System (UT) is here to help. The 200-year-old school provides undergraduate, graduate, and professional academic programs to about 50,000 students; programs include business, engineering, law, pharmacy, medicine, and veterinary medicine. It has a student-teacher ratio of about 16:1. Campuses include the flagship Knoxville location, as well as the Health Science Center at Memphis, the Space Institute at Tullahoma, the statewide Institute for Public Service, and the Institute of Agriculture. Other UT System campuses are located in Chattanooga and Martin. UT was founded in 1794 as Blount College.

Financial Performance
UT's funding comes from gifts, grants, and contracts (about 30%), state appropriations (roughly 28%), tuition and fees (20%), and a handful of auxiliary enterprises and independent operations (the remainder).

Company Background
Notable alumni include former Senate Majority Leader Howard Baker, Nobel Prize-winning economist James Buchanan, and author Cormac McCarthy.

LOCATIONS

HQ: UNIVERSITY OF TENNESSEE
1331 CIRCLE PARK DR, KNOXVILLE, TN 379163801
Phone: 865 974-2303
Web: WWW.UTK.EDU

PRODUCTS/OPERATIONS

Selected Colleges, Schools, and Institutes
College of Agricultural Sciences and Natural Resources
College of Allied Health Sciences
College of Architecture and Design
College of Arts and Sciences
College of Business Administration
College of Communication and Information
College of Dentistry
College of Education, Health, and Human Sciences
College of Engineering
College of Graduate Health Sciences
College of Health Science Engineering
College of Law
College of Medicine
College of Nursing
College of Pharmacy
College of Social Work
College of Veterinary Medicine
Graduate School of Medicine
School of Art
School of Music
Space Institute

COMPETITORS

DESALES UNIVERSITY
DRAKE UNIVERSITY
GWYNEDD MERCY UNIVERSITY
HOWARD UNIVERSITY (INC)
OKLAHOMA STATE UNIVERSITY
QUINNIPIAC UNIVERSITY
SYRACUSE UNIVERSITY
THE JOHNS HOPKINS UNIVERSITY
UNIVERSITY OF ARKANSAS SYSTEM
WILLIAM PATERSON UNIVERSITY

HISTORICAL FINANCIALS
Company Type: Private

Income Statement — FYE: June 30

	REVENUE ($mil)	NET INCOME ($mil)	NET PROFIT MARGIN	EMPLOYEES
06/12	1,092	60	5.5%	12,000
06/11*	1,034	296	28.7%	—
12/08	1	0	0.0%	—
Annual Growth	847.7%	—	—	—

*Fiscal year change

2012 Year-End Financials
Return on assets: 1.6%   Cash ($ mil.): 357
Return on equity: 2.3%
Current Ratio: 1.50

UNIVERSITY OF UTAH HEALTH HOSPITALS AND CLINICS

University of Utah Health is the only academic medical center in the state of Utah and the Mountain West and provides patient care for the people of Utah, Idaho, Wyoming, Montana, western Colorado, and much of Nevada. It also serves as the training ground for the majority of the state's physicians, nurses, pharmacists, therapists, and other health care professionals. Its system is comprised of five hospitals and twelve community health care centers, as well six schools and colleges, including the colleges of Health, Nursing, and Pharmacy, the Eccles Health Sciences Library, and the schools of Dentistry and Medicine. The University Hospital provides care in areas including surgery, emergency care, cardiology, radiology, and organ transplant services; it also houses centers for medical education, training, and research. It is headquartered in Salt Lake City, Utah.

LOCATIONS

HQ: UNIVERSITY OF UTAH HEALTH HOSPITALS AND CLINICS
50 N MEDICAL DR, SALT LAKE CITY, UT 841320001
Phone: 801 581-2121
Web: HEALTHCARE.UTAH.EDU

COMPETITORS

BAPTIST HOSPITAL OF MIAMI, INC.
CENTRASTATE HEALTHCARE SYSTEM INC
FROEDTERT MEMORIAL LUTHERAN HOSPITAL, INC.
HOLY SPIRIT HOSPITAL OF THE SISTERS OF CHRISTIAN CHARITY
LEHIGH VALLEY HEALTH NETWORK, INC.
ST. ANTHONY'S HOSPITAL, INC.
THE CHILDREN'S HOSPITAL OF PHILADELPHIA
TRIHEALTH, INC.
UNITED REGIONAL HEALTH CARE SYSTEM, INC.
VHS HARPER-HUTZEL HOSPITAL, INC.

HISTORICAL FINANCIALS
Company Type: Private

Income Statement — FYE: June 30

	REVENUE ($mil)	NET INCOME ($mil)	NET PROFIT MARGIN	EMPLOYEES
06/14	1,282	20	1.6%	4,200
06/06	0	(0)	—	—
06/05	0	(0)	—	—
Annual Growth	126.0%	—	—	—

2014 Year-End Financials
Return on assets: 2.0%   Cash ($ mil.): 179
Return on equity: 4.5%
Current Ratio: 2.30

UNIVERSITY OF VERMONT & STATE AGRICULTURAL COLLEGE

The University of Vermont (UVM) boasts scenic views and comprehensive secondary education. the university offers more than 100 majors through its seven undergraduate colleges, as well 46 master's programs and 21 doctoral programs at its Graduate College and College of Medicine. UVM has an enrollment of more than 12,820 students, including undergraduate, graduate, medical, and continuing education program participants. The university also conducts research programs in areas including translational science, cancer care, and transportation. UVM, a public land grant university, has more than 1,360 faculty members.

Operations
UVM comes from Universitas Veridis Montis, which is Latin for "University of the Green Mountains." Its campus consists of more than a dozen dining facilities -- including a pair of convenience stores and Cyber Cafe -- and nearly 40 residence halls for on-campus students. Off-campus, UVM offers a research park, four research farms, nine natural areas (including the summit of Mount Mansfield), and the Rubenstein Ecosystem Science Laboratory in the Leahy ECHO Center for Lake Champlain.

Geographic Reach
The UVM campus, which spans 460 acres in Burlington, Vermont, enrolls students from nearly all US states. The university also provides education to some 350 international students from more than 50 countries.

Financial Performance
As a public land grant university, UVM draws a portion of its budget from the state of Vermont. Other sources of income include student tuition and fees, charitable gifts, and returns on investment funds. The university's office of technology commercialization brings in some income by licensing out research discoveries to spinoff entities.

Strategy
To attract and retain a quality student population, UVM regularly conducts construction and renovation efforts on its campus facilities in areas ranging from academics and recreation to research and athletics.

Furthermore, UVM seeks to provide more flexible education options for students, including expanding its onlinep rograms.

Company Background
UVM is the fifth oldest university in the New England area after Harvard, Yale, Dartmouth, and Brown. It's the first institution of higher education to declare public support for the freedom of religion and the first university to admit women and African-Americans into Phi Beta Kappa honor society.

Notable alumni include education philosopher John Dewey and film producer Jon Kilik.

Ira Allen founded the university in 1791, the same year that Vermont became the 14th state. Located in between the Adirondack and Green mountain ranges, UVM's motto is the Latin phrase Universitas Viridis Montis, or University of the Green Mountains.

Auditors: KPMG LLP COLCHERSTER VERMON

LOCATIONS

HQ: UNIVERSITY OF VERMONT & STATE AGRICULTURAL COLLEGE
85 S PRSPECT ST WTRMAN BL, BURLINGTON, VT 054050001

Phone: 802 656-3131
Web: MED.UVM.EDU

PRODUCTS/OPERATIONS

Selected Colleges and Schools
College of Agriculture and Life Sciences
College of Arts and Sciences
College of Education and Social Services
College of Engineering and Mathematical Sciences
College of Medicine
College of Nursing and Health Sciences
Continuing Education
Graduate College
Honors College
Rubenstein School of Environment and Natural Resources
School of Business Administration

COMPETITORS

NEW MEXICO STATE UNIVERSITY
SOUTH CAROLINA STATE UNIVERSITY
THE UNIVERSITY OF IOWA
UNIVERSITY OF ILLINOIS
VILLANOVA UNIVERSITY IN THE STATE OF PENNSYLVANIA

HISTORICAL FINANCIALS

Company Type: Private

Income Statement — FYE: June 30

	REVENUE ($mil)	NET INCOME ($mil)	NET PROFIT MARGIN	EMPLOYEES
06/22	691	5	0.8%	3,710
06/21	647	188	29.2%	—
06/20	661	23	3.6%	—
06/19	650	39	6.1%	—
Annual Growth	2.1%	(49.0%)	—	—

2022 Year-End Financials
Return on assets: 0.3%   Cash ($ mil.): 237
Return on equity: 0.9%
Current Ratio: 3.80

UNIVERSITY OF VIRGINIA

Auditors: MARTHA S MAVREDES RICHMOND

LOCATIONS

HQ: UNIVERSITY OF VIRGINIA
2400 OLD IVY RD FL 2, CHARLOTTESVILLE, VA 229034827
Phone: 434 982-5522
Web: WWW.COOPERCENTER.ORG

HISTORICAL FINANCIALS

Company Type: Private

Income Statement — FYE: June 30

	REVENUE ($mil)	NET INCOME ($mil)	NET PROFIT MARGIN	EMPLOYEES
06/21	3,027	3,715	122.8%	51
06/20	2,946	208	7.1%	—
Annual Growth	2.7%	1684.5%	—	—

2021 Year-End Financials
Return on assets: 20.4%   Cash ($ mil.): 344
Return on equity: 28.9%
Current Ratio: 1.20

UNIVERSITY OF WASHINGTON INC

The University of Washington (UW) is one of the world's preeminent public universities. Founded in 1861 as the Territorial University of Washington, UW has smaller branches in Tacoma and Bothell in addition to its main campus in downtown Seattle. The university, whose mascot is a Husky, offers 1,800 undergraduate courses each quarter. It also operates four hospitals: University of Washington Medical Center, Harborview Medical Center, Northwest Hospital, and Valley Medical Center.

Operations

University of Washington confers some 18,200 bachelor's, master's, doctoral, and professional degrees each year. Around 20 of its undergraduate and graduate received Fulbright Student awards. The school's some bachelor degree fields include biology, psychology, political science, economics, and communications.

The school's annual sponsored grant and contract research funding exceeds $1.63 billion.

Geographic Reach

The UW is a multi-campus university in Seattle, Tacoma and Bothell, Washington.

Financial Performance

Operating revenues increased $339 million, or 6%, in 2021. Revenue from patient services increased $115 million as fewer non-emergent and elective procedures were cancelled during the year due to the COVID pandemic compared to 2020, resulting in higher volumes and revenue.

Profit for fiscal 2021 increased to $7.9 billion compared from the prior year with $5.9 billion.

Cash held by the company at the end of fiscal 2021 decreased to $137.4 million. Cash used for operations and investing activities were $307.0 million and $368.7 million, respectively. Cash provided by financing activities was $668.9 million.

Strategy

The ability to increase profitability will depend, in part, on successfully executing UW Medicine strategies. In general, these strategies are intended to improve financial performance through the reduction of costs and streamlining how clinical care is provided, as well as mitigating the negative reimbursement trends experienced within the market. With a continued focus on patient volumes shifting from inpatient to outpatient settings due to technological advancements and demand for care that is more convenient, affordable and accessible as well as the industry-wide migration to value-based payment models as government and private payers shift risk to providers, UW Medicine's focus is on successfully managing costs and care.

Auditors: KPMG LLP SEATTLE WASHINGTON

LOCATIONS

HQ: UNIVERSITY OF WASHINGTON INC
4300 ROOSEVELT WAY NE, SEATTLE, WA 981054718
Phone: 206 543-4444
Web: WWW.WASHINGTON.EDU

PRODUCTS/OPERATIONS

Selected Colleges and Schools
College of Arts and Sciences
College of Built Environments
College of Education
College of Engineering
College of the Environment
Evans School of Public Affairs
The Graduate School
Information School
Michael G. Foster School of Business
School of Dentistry
School of Law
School of Medicine
School of Nursing
School of Pharmacy
School of Public Health
School of Social Work

COMPETITORS

CORNELL UNIVERSITY
PURDUE UNIVERSITY
THE RUTGERS STATE UNIVERSITY
TRUSTEES OF BOSTON UNIVERSITY
TRUSTEES OF INDIANA UNIVERSITY
UNIVERSITY OF KENTUCKY
UNIVERSITY OF NORTH CAROLINA AT CHAPEL HILL
VIRGINIA POLYTECHNIC INSTITUTE AND STATE UNIVERSITY
WAYNE STATE UNIVERSITY
WICHITA STATE UNIVERSITY

HISTORICAL FINANCIALS

Company Type: Private

Income Statement — FYE: June 30

	REVENUE ($mil)	NET INCOME ($mil)	NET PROFIT MARGIN	EMPLOYEES
06/22	6,570	472	7.2%	27,228
06/21	5,841	2,001	34.3%	—
06/20	5,511	343	6.2%	—
06/19	5,485	481	8.8%	—
Annual Growth	6.2%	(0.6%)	—	—

2022 Year-End Financials
Return on assets: 2.6%   Cash ($ mil.): 162
Return on equity: 5.7%
Current Ratio: 1.60

UNIVERSITY OF WISCONSIN HOSPITALS AND CLINICS AUTHORITY

The University of Wisconsin Hospitals and Clinics Authority (UW Hospitals and Clinics) has the last word when it comes to the health of Badger Staters. The centerpiece of the authority is the UW Hospitals and Clinics medical campus which is home to a nearly 1,490-bed hospital, the American Family Children's Hospital, a cancer clinic, and a small inpatient psychiatric ward, as well as Level I adult and pediatric trauma centers. Serving more than 600,000 patients each year with approximately 1,750 physicians at seven hospitals and more than 80 outpatient sites, the hospital administers cancer treatment, heart and stroke care, organ transplantation, and a host of other medical services. The UW Hospitals and Clinics organization also operates area health clinics that provide general and specialty outpatient care and emergency room services.

Financial Performance

In fiscal 2014 revenue increased 8% to $1.3 billion on an increase of net patient service revenues (which grew 7.7% that year). Net income rose 24% to $108 million due to an increase of non-operating revenue (grants, gifts, and donations, for example). Cash flow from operations fell 20% to $141 million as more was paid out to suppliers and employees.

UW Hospitals and Clinics is an independent not-for-profit organization and receives no state funding, with the exception of reimbursement for care of Medicaid patients.

EXECUTIVES

Chief Nurse*, Rudy Jackson

CSO*, Carey Gehl

CCO*, Peter D Newcomer

External Affairs Vice President, Jay Robaidek Senior

Auditors : RSM US LLP MINNEAPOLIS MINNE

LOCATIONS

HQ: UNIVERSITY OF WISCONSIN HOSPITALS AND CLINICS AUTHORITY
   600 HIGHLAND AVE, MADISON, WI 537920001
Phone: 608 263-6400
Web: WWW.UWHEALTH.ORG

PRODUCTS/OPERATIONS

Selected Services
Adult Primary CareFamily MedicineGeriatricsInternal MedicinePrimary CareWomen's Health and WellnessAdult Specialty CareAllergy, Asthma and ImmunologyAudiologyBehavioral Health Services (Addiction)Blood and Bone Marrow TransplantBreast Care ServicesBurn CenterCancer (UW Carbone Cancer Center)Cardiothoracic SurgeryCardiovascular MedicineColon and Rectal SurgeryCosmetic Surgery (Transformations)Dermatology (Skin Care)Digestive Health ServicesEar, Nose and Throat (ENT, Otolaryngology)Pediatric Primary Care Family MedicinePediatric and Adolescent MedicinePrimary CarePediatric Specialty CareAdolescent Alcohol/Drug Assessment Intervention ProgramAmerican Family Children's HospitalBehavioral PediatricsChild ProtectionDevelopmental PediatricsGenetics and MetabolismNeonatologyPediatric Allergy, Asthma and ImmunologyPediatric AudiologyOther ServicesChild LifeHospital SchoolKohl's Safety CenterPet TherapyPositive Image CenterSpiritual Care Services

COMPETITORS

CHARLESTON AREA MEDICAL CENTER, INC.
CHILDREN'S HOSPITAL AND HEALTH SYSTEM, INC.
INTERMOUNTAIN HEALTH CARE, INC.
LEGACY HEALTH
LEHIGH VALLEY HEALTH NETWORK, INC.
MONTEFIORE MEDICAL CENTER
READING HOSPITAL
SWEDISH COVENANT HOSPITAL
UNIVERSITY HOSPITALS HEALTH SYSTEM, INC.
WELLSTAR HEALTH SYSTEM, INC.

HISTORICAL FINANCIALS

Company Type: Private

Income Statement — FYE: June 30

	REVENUE ($mil)	NET INCOME ($mil)	NET PROFIT MARGIN	EMPLOYEES
06/22	4,027	(27)	—	1,350
06/21	2,337	435	18.6%	—
06/20	2,075	202	9.8%	—
06/19	3,396	231	6.8%	—
Annual Growth	5.9%	—	—	—

2022 Year-End Financials
Return on assets: (-0.4%)   Cash ($ mil.): 1,014
Return on equity: (-0.9%)
Current Ratio: 2.10

UNIVERSITY OF WISCONSIN MEDICAL FOUNDATION, INC.

UW Medical Foundation provides administrative services to faculty physicians at the University of Wisconsin School of Medicine and Public Health. The foundation, a not-for-profit entity, is a physician practice organization that works in cooperation with the UW Hospital and Clinics and other medical offices and clinics throughout the Badger State. The foundation coordinates clinical sites and provides technical and professional staffing services, as well as administrative support for legal, marketing, information technology, and logistics functions.

Operations

UW Medical Foundation provides support services for more than 1,200 member doctors located at about 45 physician practices and 60 clinical outreach locations. It also helps clinical practices with quality initiatives. The foundation provides some $200 million in charity care each year. Its community activities include sponsoring health outreach events and donating safety products to low-income families.

Physicians in the organization provide services across a number of medical specialties, including oncology, gastroenterology, women's health, kidney care, orthopedics, respiratory therapy, and urology.

Company Background

The organization has expanded over time: UW Medical Foundation merged with Physicians Plus Medical Group in 1998 and with the University Community Clinics in 2003.

Auditors : MCGLADREY LLP PALOS HILLS IL

LOCATIONS

HQ: UNIVERSITY OF WISCONSIN MEDICAL FOUNDATION, INC.
   7974 UW HEALTH CT, MIDDLETON, WI 535625531
Phone: 608 821-4223
Web: WWW.UWHEALTH.ORG

COMPETITORS

BAYLOR COLLEGE OF MEDICINE
LOMA LINDA UNIVERSITY
OREGON HEALTH & SCIENCE UNIVERSITY MEDICAL GROUP
THE UNIVERSITY OF IOWA
UNIVERSITY OF VIRGINIA MEDICAL CENTER

HISTORICAL FINANCIALS

Company Type: Private

Income Statement — FYE: June 30

	REVENUE ($mil)	NET INCOME ($mil)	NET PROFIT MARGIN	EMPLOYEES
06/21	824	34	4.2%	3,200
06/20	785	7	1.0%	—
06/19	796	2	0.3%	—
06/18	784	40	5.2%	—
Annual Growth	1.7%	(5.1%)	—	—

2021 Year-End Financials
Return on assets: 4.1%   Cash ($ mil.): 353
Return on equity: 9.0%
Current Ratio: 1.20

UNIVERSITY OF WISCONSIN SYSTEM

The University of Wisconsin System (UW System) is one of the largest public university systems in the US. Across its vast operations there are almost 13 four-year universities, about 26 branch campuses, and a statewide extension program that reaches every Wisconsin county. The UW System has more than 165,000 students and approximately 40,000 faculty and staff members. Its two main campuses are UW at Madison and UW at Milwaukee, which offer hundreds of undergraduate and graduate programs including doctoral and professional degrees. The university was founded in 1848 by the state of constitution.

Operations

The UW Systems operating revenue comes from: Tuition and fees, generating about 40% of revenue; Federal grants and contract (nearly 20%); State, local, & private grants and contracts (accounts for more than 10%); Sales and services of educational activities (accounts for some 10%); Sales and service of auxiliaries account for more than 10%, and all other operating revenues account for about 15%. The UW Systems is the largest systems of public higher education in the country, with 13 universities across 26 campuses and statewide extension network with offices in every country.

Geographic Reach

One of the nation's largest public universities, the UW System boasts offices and campuses in every county in Wisconsin.

Financial Performance

Total operating revenue for 2020 was $3.7 billion, a 2% dip from the previous year's total operating revenue.

In 2020, the company had a net income of $5.4 billion, a 1% increase from the previous year's net income.

The company's cash at the end of 2020 was $1.9 billion. Investing activities provided $41.5 million, while operating activities used $1.2 billion. Net cash provided by noncapital financing activities generated $1.6 billion.

Strategy

In early 2021, The University of Wisconsin System launched a new precollege pipeline initiative to help guide high school students in preparing for, applying to, and enrolling in one of its 13 universities. The initiative involves placing student coaches and recruiters in a select number of regional high schools.

The initial investment of $1 million will be equally divided among five universities ? UW Oshkosh, UW-Parkside, UW-Platteville, UW-Stout, and UW-Whitewater.

In addition to raising the profile of UW institutions across the state, this effort is intended to create a more robust pipeline to the UW System by engaging students earlier in the college-going process and providing additional hands-on support, including for students who may be the first in their families to pursue a university education. Strong partnerships between UW universities and local high schools, their high school counselors, and community organizations that serve young people will be a hallmark of this important effort.

Each of the universities that receives funding will use it to develop and implement precollege activities and programs that best serve the needs of the students in their respective areas.

Company Background

The University of Wisconsin System was created in 1971 through the merger of the University of Wisconsin (established 1848) and Wisconsin State Universities (originating in 1857 as the Normal Schools).

HISTORY

When Wisconsin became a state in 1848, its constitution called for the establishment of a state university. A board of regents was named, and it first established a preparatory school because regents felt Wisconsin's secondary schools were not advanced enough to prepare students for university studies. The school began classes in 1849 with 20 students in the Madison Female Academy Building. The University of Wisconsin's first official freshman class began studies in the fall of 1850. A campus was established a mile west of the state capitol in Madison. By 1854, when it held its first commencement (with two graduates), the school had 41 students.

Enrollment dipped during the Civil War (all but one of the school's senior class joined the army) but soon rebounded, and by 1870 the university had almost 500 students. Meanwhile, it established a school of agriculture (1866) and a school of law (1868). The state established normal schools (teachers' colleges) in Platteville (1866), Whitewater (1868), Oshkosh (1871), and River Falls (1874).

There was also a teachers' course for women at the university in Madison. However, when John Bascom became president in 1874, he transformed the university into a truly coeducational institution, putting women "in all respects on precisely the same footing" with the men.

While the university at Madison remained Wisconsin's primary seat of learning, the state continued to establish normal schools. It opened institutions in Milwaukee (1885), Superior (1893), Stevens Point (1894), La Crosse (1909), and Eau Claire (1916). The nine normal schools eventually became a system of state colleges called Wisconsin State Universities.

The university at Madison also continued to grow, and by the late 1920s it had almost 9,000 students. WWII brought a drop in enrollment, but afterward it took off, jumping from about 7,000 in 1945 to over 22,000 by the late 1950s. The University of Wisconsin-Milwaukee branch was founded in 1956. Other branch campuses were established in Green Bay (1965) and Kenosha (1968).

The Madison campus became a focal point for student protests during the Vietnam War. Events came to a head in 1970 when President Fred Harrington resigned during a four-day standoff between students and the National Guard. War protesters also placed a bomb outside Sterling Hall, which housed the Army Math Research Center; the explosion killed one student and injured three others.

The state legislature merged the University of Wisconsin and the Wisconsin State Universities in 1971 to create The University of Wisconsin System.

EXECUTIVES

University Relations Vice President*, Jeff Buhrandt

Academic Vice President, Johannes Britz Int Sr

Auditors : PLANTE & MORAN PORTAGE MI

LOCATIONS

HQ: UNIVERSITY OF WISCONSIN SYSTEM
1220 LINDEN DR, MADISON, WI 537061525
Phone: 608 262-2321
Web: WWW.WISCONSIN.EDU

PRODUCTS/OPERATIONS

Selected Four-Year Campuses
UW-Eau Claire
UW-Green Bay
UW-La Crosse
UW-Madison
UW-Milwaukee
UW-Oshkosh
UW-Parkside
UW-Platteville
UW-River Falls
UW-Stevens Point
UW-Stout
UW-Superior
UW-Whitewater

Selected Two-Year Colleges
UW-Baraboo/Sauk County
UW-Barron County
UW-Fond du Lac
UW-Fox Valley
UW-Manitowoc
UW-Marathon County
UW-Marinette
UW-Marshfield/Wood County
UW-Richland
UW-Rock County
UW-Sheboygan
UW-Washington County
UW-Waukesha

COMPETITORS

CALIFORNIA STATE UNIVERSITY SYSTEM
NORTHWESTERN UNIVERSITY
REGENTS OF THE UNIVERSITY OF MINNESOTA
STATE UNIVERSITY OF NEW YORK
THE UNIVERSITY OF CHICAGO
THE UNIVERSITY OF TEXAS SYSTEM
TRUSTEES OF BOSTON COLLEGE
UNIVERSITY OF DELAWARE
UNIVERSITY OF MAINE SYSTEM
VALDOSTA STATE UNIVERSITY

HISTORICAL FINANCIALS

Company Type: Private

Income Statement — FYE: June 30

	REVENUE ($mil)	NET INCOME ($mil)	NET PROFIT MARGIN	EMPLOYEES
06/18	3,613	203	5.6%	3,190
06/17	3,702	(20)	—	—
Annual Growth	(2.4%)	—	—	—

2018 Year-End Financials
Return on assets: 2.2%   Cash ($ mil.): 1,868
Return on equity: 3.7%
Current Ratio: 4.00

UNIVERSITY SYSTEM OF MARYLAND

The University System of Maryland (USM) operates one of the largest public university systems in the country, serving approximately

171,000 students through a dozen institutions, including Towson University, University of Maryland Global Campus, and Bowie State University. USM comprises eleven degree-granting institutions, one research entity and an administrative unit. Its degree-granting institutions provide a full range of undergraduate, graduate, professional and continuing education opportunities for students. Its research entity conducts basic and applied research, and transfers new technology to constituencies. The administrative unit includes the System Chancellor and staff who support the Board.

Operations
USM has nearly 1,000 buildings, including approximately 20 libraries. The University of Maryland, College Park (UMCP), USM's flagship institution and preeminent public research university.

Across its system of more than 10 institutions and three regional higher education centers, more than 213,000 USM students, faculty, and staff are engaged in innovative scholarship, teaching, and research that drives economic growth and strengthens communities throughout the state.

Geographic Reach
USM's headquarters is located in Baltimore, Maryland. It also has office locations in Adelphi, Annapolis, and Columbia.

Company Background
Notable University of Maryland alumni include Muppet creator Jim Henson, news anchor Connie Chung, Seinfeld creator Larry David, and football legend Norman "Boomer" Esiason.

EXECUTIVES
Vice Chairman, Barry P Gossett
Auditors : SB & COMPANY LLC OWINGS MILL

LOCATIONS
HQ: UNIVERSITY SYSTEM OF MARYLAND
3300 METZEROTT RD, ADELPHI, MD 207831651
Phone: 301 445-2740
Web: WWW.USMD.EDU

Selected Institutions
Bowie State University
Coppin State University
Frostburg State University
Salisbury University
Towson University
University of Baltimore
University of Maryland, Baltimore
University of Maryland, Baltimore County
University of Maryland, College Park
University of Maryland Eastern Shore
University of Maryland University College
University of Maryland Center for Environmental Science

Selected Schools and Colleges
College of Agriculture and Natural Resources
School of Architecture, Planning, and Preservation
College of Arts and Humanities
College of Behavioral and Social Sciences
Robert H. Smith School of Business
College of Chemical and Life Sciences
College of Computer, Mathematical and Physical Sciences
College of Education
A. James Clark School of Engineering
The Graduate School
Philip Merrill College of Journalism
College of Information Studies
School of Public Health
School of Public Policy
Office of Undergraduate Studies

COMPETITORS
DUKE UNIVERSITY
KENT STATE UNIVERSITY
MARSHALL UNIVERSITY
RECTOR & VISITORS OF THE UNIVERSITY OF VIRGINIA
REGENTS OF THE UNIVERSITY OF MINNESOTA
THE TRUSTEES OF THE UNIVERSITY OF PENNSYLVANIA
UNIVERSITY OF KANSAS
UNIVERSITY OF MISSOURI SYSTEM
UNIVERSITY OF OKLAHOMA
UNIVERSITY OF SOUTHERN CALIFORNIA

HISTORICAL FINANCIALS
Company Type: Private

Income Statement — FYE: June 30

	REVENUE ($mil)	NET INCOME ($mil)	NET PROFIT MARGIN	EMPLOYEES
06/21	3,454	111	3.2%	28,000
06/18	3,601	338	9.4%	—
06/17	3,515	355	10.1%	—
Annual Growth	(0.4%)	(25.2%)	—	—

2021 Year-End Financials
Return on assets: 1.0%   Cash ($ mil.): 2,681
Return on equity: 1.6%
Current Ratio: 3.10

UNIVERSITY SYSTEM OF NEW HAMPSHIRE

The University of New Hampshire (UNH) is a liberal arts college that serves about 12,600 undergraduate and more than 2,200 graduate students. The institution offers more than 100 majors and academic programs of study at nine colleges and schools. The student-faculty ratio is 20:1. UNH is the flagship institution of the University System of New Hampshire. In 2007 the university graduated its first international class in Seoul under a program run by its Whittemore School of Business and Economics. Founded in 1866 as the New Hampshire College of Agriculture and the Mechanic Arts, UNH is a designated land-grant, sea-grant, and space-grant chartered school.

Operations
UNH's most popular bachelor's programs include business administration, undeclared liberal arts, psychology, English, and communication, followed by mechanical engineering, biology, biomedical science, civil engineering, and political science.

The University System of New Hampshire includes Keene State College, Plymouth State University, and Granite State College, in addition to UNH.

Geographic Reach
In addition to its main campus in Durham, UNH has a campus in Manchester, and its School of Law is in Concord. Almost 60% of the school's student body comes from within state, with a concentration of others coming from the northeastern region of the US. UNH is developing new academic programs, expanding its online courses and opportunities, and creating new international initiatives for faculty and students in Costa Rica, Chile, Ghana, India, South Korea, and China.

Strategy
UNH is engaged in a strategic plan to support its growth through 2020. Its plan for creating a learning-centered environment includes such initiatives as establishing a New Venture Fund to promote collaborative research and teaching opportunities; developing new programs to support independent research and scholarship; commercializing UNH's intellectual capital; and promoting diversity and inclusiveness, as well as international opportunities. It also includes making major capital investments in technology to build a high-capacity cyber-infrastructure and a learning portal to promote interdisciplinary collaboration; renovating, restoring, and adding on to facilities; and constructing a new center for the arts.

Auditors : CLIFTONLARSONALLEN LLP QUINCY

LOCATIONS
HQ: UNIVERSITY SYSTEM OF NEW HAMPSHIRE
5 CHENELL DR STE 301, CONCORD, NH 033018522
Phone: 603 862-1800
Web: WWW.USNH.EDU

PRODUCTS/OPERATIONS
Selected Colleges and Schools
College of Engineering and Physical Sciences
College of Health and Human Services
College of Liberal Arts
College of Life Sciences and Agriculture
The Graduate School
Thompson School of Applied Science
University of New Hampshire at Manchester
University of New Hampshire School of Law
Whittemore School of Business and Economics
Special Academic Opportunities
Graduate Research Conference
Hamel Center for Undergraduate Reasearch
Honors program
International research opportunities program
Student internships
Study abroad
Undergraduate research opportunities program

COMPETITORS
CLEMSON UNIVERSITY
RENSSELAER POLYTECHNIC INSTITUTE
SUNY AT BINGHAMTON
THE UNIVERSITY OF HARTFORD
VILLANOVA UNIVERSITY IN THE STATE OF PENNSYLVANIA

HISTORICAL FINANCIALS
Company Type: Private

Income Statement — FYE: June 30

	REVENUE ($mil)	NET INCOME ($mil)	NET PROFIT MARGIN	EMPLOYEES
06/22	707	(36)	—	16,000
06/21	633	161	25.5%	—
06/20	642	(1)	—	—
Annual Growth	4.9%	—	—	—

2022 Year-End Financials
Return on assets: (-1.6%)   Cash ($ mil.): 110
Return on equity: (-2.3%)
Current Ratio: 1.70

UOFL HEALTH, INC.

Auditors: BLUE & CO LLC WESTERVILLE

LOCATIONS

HQ: UOFL HEALTH, INC.
530 S JACKSON ST, LOUISVILLE, KY 402021675
Phone: 502 562-3000
Web: WWW.UOFLHEALTH.ORG

HISTORICAL FINANCIALS
Company Type: Private

Income Statement — FYE: June 30

	REVENUE ($mil)	NET INCOME ($mil)	NET PROFIT MARGIN	EMPLOYEES
06/21	1,935	87	4.5%	10,000
06/20	1,109	212	19.1%	—
Annual Growth	74.5%	(59.0%)	—	—

2021 Year-End Financials
Return on assets: 7.6%   Cash ($ mil.): 163
Return on equity: 15.3%
Current Ratio: 1.80

UPMC

UPMC is a world-renowned health care provider and insurer. It is an international health care leader ? pioneering groundbreaking research, treatments, and clinical care. UPMC operates approximately 40 academic, community, and specialty hospitals, some 800 doctors' offices and outpatient sites, employs 4,900 physicians, and offers an array of rehabilitation, retirement, and long-term care facilities in western and central Pennsylvania, Maryland, New York, and around the globe. As a leading academic medical center with world-class clinical expertise and a growing, financially sound health insurance company, UPMC offers a seamless experience for patients across a continuously expanding geographic footprint.

Operations
UPMC provides a wide range of clinical services such as aesthetic plastic surgery, behavioral and mental health, cancer, diabetes, endocrine surgery, fitness and wellness, general surgery, and heart and vascular, among others.

Geographic Reach
UPMC's primary operating territory is the Pittsburgh area and western and central Pennsylvania, Maryland, and New York. Outside the US, UPMC operates health care facilities in Ireland, Italy, Kazakhstan, and China.

Its headquarters is in Pittsburgh, Pennsylvania.

Company Background
UPMC traces its roots to 1893, when Louise Lyle, the wife of a Presbyterian minister, founded its predecessor. The hospital was incorporated as Presbyterian Hospital of Pittsburgh two years later. In 1930, the hospital joined forces with the University of Pittsburgh and broke ground on a new location, which opened its doors in 1938.

EXECUTIVES

CCO*, Janilee Johnson
SVCS, Leslie Davis
Chief Innovation Officer*, Derek Angus
Physician SERVICES*, Joon Lee
CMO*, Donald Yealy
Auditors: ERNST & YOUNG LLP PITTSBURGH

LOCATIONS

HQ: UPMC
200 LOTHROP ST, PITTSBURGH, PA 152132536
Phone: 412 647-8762
Web: WWW.UPMC.COM

Selected Pennsylvania Facilities
Children's Hospital of Pittsburgh of UPMC
Magee-Womens Hospital of UPMC (Pittsburgh)
UPMC Bedford Memorial (Everett)
UPMC East (Pittsburgh)
UPMC Hamlot (Erie)
UPMC Horizon (Greenville and Shenango Valley)
UPMC McKeesport (McKeesport)
UPMC Mercy (Pittsburgh)
UPMC Montefiore (Pittsburgh)
UPMC Northwest (Seneca and Oil City)
UPMC Passavant (McCandless and Cranberry)
UPMC Presbyterian (Pittsburgh)
UPMC Shadyside (Pittsburgh)
UPMC St. Margaret (Pittsburgh)
UPMC Western Psychiatric Institute and Clinic (Pittsburgh)

PRODUCTS/OPERATIONS

2018 Sales

	$ mil.	% of total
Net patient services	8,823	47
Insurance enrollment	8,492	45
Other	1,462	8
Total	18,777	100

2018 Sales by Segment

	$ mil.	% of total
Health Services	11,881	57
Insurance Services	9,005	43
Adjustments	(2,109)	-
Total	18,777	100

Selected Services
Behavioral and Mental Health Services
Cancer
COPD and Emphysema Center
Dermatology
Diabetes and Endocrinology
Ear, Nose and Throat
Emergency Medicine
Family/Primary Care Medicine
Gastroenterology
Geriatrics
Heart and Vascular
Imaging Services
Kidney Disease
Liver
Neurology
Ophthalmology
Pain Medicine
Pathology
Pediatrics
Pulmonology and Respiratory
Rehabilitation
Rheumatology
Sports Medicine
Stroke Care
Thyroid
Urology
Women's Health
Wound Healing Services

COMPETITORS

BANNER HEALTH
IASIS HEALTHCARE LLC
INDIANA UNIVERSITY HEALTH, INC.
MASS GENERAL BRIGHAM INCORPORATED
NORTHWELL HEALTH, INC.
NOVANT HEALTH, INC.
PROVIDENCE ST. JOSEPH HEALTH
THE CLEVELAND CLINIC FOUNDATION
TRINITY HEALTH CORPORATION
WELLMONT HEALTH SYSTEM

HISTORICAL FINANCIALS
Company Type: Private

Income Statement — FYE: December 31

	REVENUE ($mil)	NET INCOME ($mil)	NET PROFIT MARGIN	EMPLOYEES
12/21	24,366	1,857	7.6%	80,000
12/20	23,093	1,113	4.8%	—
12/19*	20,609	462	2.2%	—
06/15	614	326	53.1%	—
Annual Growth	69.2%	28.2%	—	—

*Fiscal year change

2021 Year-End Financials
Return on assets: 8.0%   Cash ($ mil.): 930
Return on equity: 16.5%
Current Ratio: 1.00

UPMC MAGEE-WOMENS HOSPITAL

LOCATIONS

HQ: UPMC MAGEE-WOMENS HOSPITAL
300 HALKET ST, PITTSBURGH, PA 152133108
Phone: 412 641-1000
Web: WWW.UPMC.COM

HISTORICAL FINANCIALS
Company Type: Private

Income Statement   FYE: June 30

	REVENUE ($mil)	NET INCOME ($mil)	NET PROFIT MARGIN	EMPLOYEES
06/16	838	92	11.1%	2,300
06/15	823	62	7.6%	—
06/00	7	7	98.8%	—
Annual Growth	33.9%	16.8%	—	—

2016 Year-End Financials
Return on assets: 17.7%   Cash ($ mil.): 1
Return on equity: 19.0%
Current Ratio: 9.40

UPMC PINNACLE HOSPITALS

Auditors : PARENTEBEARD LLC YORK PA

LOCATIONS

HQ: UPMC PINNACLE HOSPITALS
409 S 2ND ST STE 1C, HARRISBURG, PA 171041612
Phone: 717 782-5678
Web: WWW.UPMC.COM

HISTORICAL FINANCIALS
Company Type: Private

Income Statement   FYE: June 30

	REVENUE ($mil)	NET INCOME ($mil)	NET PROFIT MARGIN	EMPLOYEES
06/21	1,355	176	13.0%	4,500
06/20	1,130	61	5.4%	—
06/10	559	14	2.5%	—
06/09	538	0	0.0%	—
Annual Growth	8.0%	—	—	—

2021 Year-End Financials
Return on assets: 17.7%   Cash ($ mil.): 3
Return on equity: 24.1%
Current Ratio: 1.30

UPMC PRESBYTERIAN SHADYSIDE

Auditors : ERNST & YOUNG LLP PITTSBURGH

LOCATIONS

HQ: UPMC PRESBYTERIAN SHADYSIDE
200 LOTHROP ST MH-N739, PITTSBURGH, PA 152132536
Phone: 412 647-2345
Web: WWW.UPMC.COM

HISTORICAL FINANCIALS
Company Type: Private

Income Statement   FYE: June 30

	REVENUE ($mil)	NET INCOME ($mil)	NET PROFIT MARGIN	EMPLOYEES
06/10	8,046	276	3.4%	8,200
06/09	1,723	83	4.8%	—
06/06	1,627	0	0.0%	—
Annual Growth	49.1%	—	—	—

2010 Year-End Financials
Return on assets: 3.5%   Cash ($ mil.): 158
Return on equity: 9.1%
Current Ratio: 0.80

UPSTATE NIAGARA COOPERATIVE, INC.

Auditors : DOPKINS & COMPANY LLP BUFFALO

LOCATIONS

HQ: UPSTATE NIAGARA COOPERATIVE, INC.
368 PLEASANT VIEW DR, LANCASTER, NY 140861316
Phone: 716 892-3156
Web: WWW.UPSTATENIAGARA.COM

HISTORICAL FINANCIALS
Company Type: Private

Income Statement   FYE: December 31

	REVENUE ($mil)	NET INCOME ($mil)	NET PROFIT MARGIN	EMPLOYEES
12/21	1,239	34	2.8%	1,400
12/18	903	22	2.5%	—
Annual Growth	11.1%	14.2%	—	—

2021 Year-End Financials
Return on assets: 7.1%   Cash ($ mil.): 45
Return on equity: 14.3%
Current Ratio: 1.60

URM STORES, INC.

URM Stores is a leading wholesale food distribution cooperative serving more than 160 grocery stores in the Northwest. Its member-owner stores operate under a variety of banners, including Family Foods, Harvest Foods, Super 1 Foods, Trading Co. Stores, and Yoke's Fresh Market. It also owns the Rosauers Supermarkets chain. In addition to grocery stores, URM supplies 1,500-plus restaurants, hotels, and convenience stores; it also offers such services as merchandising, store development consulting, and technology purchasing. The cooperative was founded in 1921 as United Retail Merchants. The business is privately owned by its members.

Operations
The company's Spokane, Washington-based Peirone Produce distribution subsidiary supplies fresh produce, including organic produce, as well as specialty items source from Arizona, California, Florida, Mexico, and Texas. In addition to groceries and produce, URM Stores sells insurance to its members and food service customers through URM Insurance Agency. Insurance products include business insurance for stores and personal lines of coverage for owns and their employees.

Geographic Reach
Regional wholesaler URM Stores supplies stores and other customers in much of eastern Washington, northern Idaho, Oregon, and Montana.

Financial Performance
URM Stores rings up sales of about $775 million, employs more than 2,700 people, and has assets exceeding $100 million.

Strategy
In 2010 the company moved its Spokane, Washington-based Peirone Produce distribution subsidiary into a larger facility boasting 70,000 sq. ft. of warehouse space and 7,000 sq. ft. of office space. It is equipped with about 15 docks for loading outgoing trucks and another dozen docks for unloading incoming trucks. The facility is more than twice the size of Peirone's previous building, which had nearly 10 docks total. Because of the larger space and greater number of docks, Peirone Produce said it has been able to improve its productivity.

Auditors : BDO USA LLP SPOKANE WA

LOCATIONS

HQ: URM STORES, INC.
7511 N FREYA ST, SPOKANE, WA 992178043
Phone: 509 467-2620
Web: WWW.URMSTORES.COM

PRODUCTS/OPERATIONS

Selected Banners
CenterPlace Market
Family Foods
Harvest Foods
Trading Co. Stores
Rosauers Supermarkets
Super 1 Foods
Yoke's Fresh Market

COMPETITORS

ASSOCIATED FOOD STORES, INC.
ASSOCIATED GROCERS OF NEW ENGLAND, INC.
ASSOCIATED WHOLESALE GROCERS, INC.
CASESTACK LLC
CENTRAL GROCERS, INC.
CERTCO, INC.
HOUCHENS INDUSTRIES, INC.
SPARTANNASH COMPANY
THE HOME CITY ICE COMPANY
UNIFIED GROCERS, INC.

HISTORICAL FINANCIALS
Company Type: Private

Income Statement   FYE: August 2

	REVENUE ($mil)	NET INCOME ($mil)	NET PROFIT MARGIN	EMPLOYEES
08/08*	932	8	0.9%	2,100
07/07	859	7	0.8%	—
07/06	799	4	0.6%	—
Annual Growth	8.0%	41.0%	—	—

*Fiscal year change

2008 Year-End Financials
Return on assets: 3.8%   Cash ($ mil.): 2
Return on equity: 11.0%
Current Ratio: 1.20

US HEALTHCARE SYSTEM

Auditors : DELOITTE TAX LLP DETROIT MI

LOCATIONS

HQ: US HEALTHCARE SYSTEM
  3200 BURNET AVE, CINCINNATI, OH 452293019
Phone: 513 585-1821
Web: WWW.UCHEALTH.COM

HISTORICAL FINANCIALS
Company Type: Private

Income Statement   FYE: June 30

	REVENUE ($mil)	NET INCOME ($mil)	NET PROFIT MARGIN	EMPLOYEES
06/18	1,695	52	3.1%	10
06/17	1,583	25	1.6%	—
06/15	1,482	80	5.5%	—
06/13	4	(0)	—	—
Annual Growth	224.3%	—	—	—

2018 Year-End Financials
Return on assets: 3.2%   Cash ($ mil.): 48
Return on equity: 6.4%
Current Ratio: 0.60

USG CORPORATION

USG Corporation is a market leader in wallboard and gypsum products in North America. It is a top seller of wallboard, gypsum fiberboard, and construction plaster products that are used for finishing interior walls, ceilings, and floors. The company is also a major North American supplier of building-related performance materials, ceiling grid, and acoustic tiles. Recognized brands include Sheetrock, Durock, Fiberock, and Donn. Its products are used to build some of the world's most iconic structures, such as the Freedom Tower in New York, Burj Khalifa in Dubai, and Lotte Tower in Seoul. In 1902, some 30 independent gypsum rock and plaster manufacturing companies merged to consolidate their resources and form the United States Gypsum Company.

Operations

The USG Corporation's business is comprised of two divisions that help its customers design the spaces they live, work and play.

Its Gypsum Division is home to the iconic products like Sheetrock brand drywall and joint treatment that made it synonymous with high-quality building materials and solutions, as well as innovative products and systems that simplify work, speed up the construction process and reduce the number of people required on job sites.

Its Ceilings Division includes products from traditional grid suspension ceiling systems, the industry's first integrated acoustical drywall system and specialty products that inspire thoughtful designs.

Geographic Reach

Headquartered in Chicago, Illinois, USG Corporation operates about 50 manufacturing locations in the US and some parts of Canada, as well as in Mexico/Latin America.

Sales and Marketing

The company serves construction markets around the world with wall, ceiling, flooring, sheathing, and roofing products.

Company Background

In 1901 a group of 35 companies joined to form U.S.G., the largest gypsum producing and processing business in the industry. In 1915, the company began producing lime, followed by paint manufacturing in 1924.

By 1931 it was producing insulating board and metal lath fields. When the company bought Masonite in 1984, its changed its name to USG the next year.

In 2019, the company is expected to bt acquired by Germany-based company Knauf.

HISTORY

In 1901 a group of 35 companies joined to form U.S.G., the largest gypsum producing and processing business in the industry. Sewell Avery became CEO in 1905 (he led U.S.G. until 1951). U.S.G. began producing lime in 1915. It became United States Gypsum (U.S. Gypsum) in 1920 and began making paint in 1924. By 1931 it was producing insulating board and metal lath fields. It also added two lime businesses and two gypsum concerns.

The company bought Masonite in 1984 and changed its name to USG the next year. It acquired Donn (remodeling materials) in 1986 and DAP (caulk and sealants) in 1987.

Auditors : DELOITTED & TOUCHE LLP CHICAG

LOCATIONS

HQ: USG CORPORATION
  550 W ADAMS ST, CHICAGO, IL 606613665
Phone: 312 436-4000
Web: WWW.USG.COM

2018 Sales

	$ mil.	% of total.
US	2,871	81
Canada	448	13
Other Foreign	211	6
Geographic transfers	(194)	-
Total	3,336	100

Subsidiaries
United States Gypsum Company
USG Interiors, LLC
USG Foreign Investments, Ltd.
USG Netherlands Global Holdings B.V.
CGC Inc.
USG Latin America, LLC.
USG Holding de Mexico, S.A. de C.V.
USG Mexico, S.A. de C.V.

PRODUCTS/OPERATIONS

2018 Sales (by Segment)

	$ mil.	% of total
US Wallboard and Surfaces	1,927	54
US Performance Materials	392	11
US Ceilings	541	15
Canada	448	13
Other	252	7
Eliminations	(224)	-
Total	3,336	100

COMPETITORS

ARMSTRONG WORLD INDUSTRIES, INC.
ASSOCIATED MATERIALS, LLC
BLUELINX HOLDINGS INC.
CORNERSTONE BUILDING BRANDS, INC.
JELD-WEN HOLDING, INC.
KNAUF INSULATION, INC.
LOUISIANA-PACIFIC CORPORATION
LafargeHolcim Ltd
OWENS CORNING
Q.E.P. CO., INC.

HISTORICAL FINANCIALS
Company Type: Private

Income Statement   FYE: December 31

	REVENUE ($mil)	NET INCOME ($mil)	NET PROFIT MARGIN	EMPLOYEES
12/17	3,204	88	2.7%	7,300
12/16	3,017	510	16.9%	—
Annual Growth	6.2%	(82.7%)	—	—

2017 Year-End Financials
Return on assets: 2.3%   Cash ($ mil.): 394
Return on equity: 4.8%
Current Ratio: 2.40

USS-UPI, LLC

US and Korean steel manufacturing interests come together in the form of USS-POSCO Industries (UPI), a 50/50 joint venture between United States Steel (US Steel) and POSCO. The company operates a steel plant (formerly owned by US Steel) in Pittsburg, Northern California. It manufactures flat-rolled steel sheets in various forms: cold-rolled steel, galvanized steel, and tinplate. In addition, USS-POSCO churns out iron oxide, which is used to make hard and soft ferrites. UPI sells its products to more than 150 customers in more than dozen states throughout the western US. End products include office furniture, computer cabinets, metal studs, cans, culverts, and metal building materials.

Operations
UPI's main product lines include cold rolled sheet, galvanized sheet, hot rolled pickled and oiled sheet, and tin plate. It has the capacity to produce about 1.5 million tons of product per year.

Geographic Reach
The company markets its products primarily in the western US.

Sales and Marketing
UPI ships steel products to more than 150 customers across North America. The company sells its products to a wide range of manufacturers whose end products include automotive parts, computer cabinets, culverts, food packaging, metal buildings, metal studs, and office furniture. About 1/3 of UPI's product line is tinplate for the canning industry.

Strategy
Its Korean co-owner supplied high quality raw materials for use at the plant. In order to stay competitive in the face of cheaper steel imports, UPI jettisoned non-core product lines to focus on steel sheet and tin. However, strong competition and poor market prices forced the company in 2011 to introduce furloughs at the plant and enforce temporary shutdowns of the facility.

Company Background
The company rebounded from a major fire in 2001. In 2010 UPI invested heavily in remediation measures to clean up soil and groundwater impacted by its plant activities.

US Steel teamed up with POSCO (then Pohang Iron & Steel Company) in 1986 as part of a major reorganization of the aging Pittsburg plant, which first opened in 1910.

Auditors : KPMG LLP SACRAMENTO CALIFOR

LOCATIONS
HQ: USS-UPI, LLC
900 LOVERIDGE RD, PITTSBURG, CA 945652808
Phone: 800 877-7672
Web: WWW.USSUPI.COM

PRODUCTS/OPERATIONS

Selected Steel Products
Cold Rolled Annealed
Hot Dipped Galvanized
Hot Rolled Pickled and Oiled
Tinplate

COMPETITORS
A. FINKL & SONS CO.
CALIFORNIA STEEL INDUSTRIES, INC.
Chongqing Iron & Steel Company Limited
NIPPON STEEL CORPORATION
NLMK, PAO
NUCOR CORPORATION
REPUBLIC STEEL
STEEL TECHNOLOGIES LLC
Samuel, Son & Co., Limited
Wugang Group Co., Ltd.

HISTORICAL FINANCIALS
Company Type: Private

Income Statement — FYE: December 31

	REVENUE ($mil)	NET INCOME ($mil)	NET PROFIT MARGIN	EMPLOYEES
12/15	648	(4)	—	1,326
12/08	1,198	11	1.0%	—
12/07	998	(40)	—	—
12/06	1,034	14	1.4%	—
Annual Growth	(5.1%)	—	—	—

2015 Year-End Financials
Return on assets: (-1.5%)   Cash ($ mil.): —
Return on equity: —
Current Ratio: 0.90

UTAH STATE UNIVERSITY

Utah State University (USU) has more than 40 academic departments at colleges of agriculture, arts, business, education and human services, engineering, science, natural resources, and humanities and social sciences. It offers about 170 bachelor's degree programs and more than 140 graduate degree programs. Biology, elementary education, mechanical and aerospace engineering, and business administration are among the university's most popular majors. About 29,000 students attend its main campus in northern Utah, its three branch campuses, or extension facilities located across the state. USU was established in 1888 as an agricultural college.

Operations
USU has a student-to-faculty ratio of 18:1. Alumni of the university include Greg Carr, founder of the Greg C. Carr Foundation, and Charlie Denson, former president of NIKE.

Geographic Reach
USU students hail from all 50 US states and some 80 international countries. The university's students have the opportunity to study abroad through partnerships with 140 other institutions located around the world. USU's main campuses or branch offices in Utah are located in Brigham City, Logan, San Juan, Tooele, and Uintah Basin.

Financial Performance
Revenues increased at USU by 4% to some $340 million due to increased income from tuition and fees, higher enrollment, and increased state appropriations. The gain was offset by decreases in gifts, grants, and contracts. Net income fell 41% to $68 million due to higher operating expenses from salary, benefit, and other costs.

Strategy
To expand its facilities and meet growing student needs, USU is adding a new school of business building and a new athletics center to its main campus. The university recently completed construction of a new $47 million agricultural building on the main campus, as well as a new administration building on the USU Eastern campus. In addition, USU is building a new distance education building on its Logan campus.

To further expand resources for students, USU began offering a Master of Business Administration (MBA) program at the Brigham Young University's Idaho campus in 2013.

EXECUTIVES
Vice President Business, Ronald S Godfrey
Auditors : OFFICE OF THE STATE AUDITOR S

LOCATIONS
HQ: UTAH STATE UNIVERSITY
1000 OLD MAIN HL, LOGAN, UT 843221000
Phone: 435 797-1000
Web: WWW.USU.EDU

COMPETITORS
MISSOURI STATE UNIVERSITY
NEW MEXICO STATE UNIVERSITY
SOUTH CAROLINA STATE UNIVERSITY
SOUTH DAKOTA STATE UNIVERSITY
WILLAMETTE UNIVERSITY

HISTORICAL FINANCIALS
Company Type: Private

Income Statement — FYE: June 30

	REVENUE ($mil)	NET INCOME ($mil)	NET PROFIT MARGIN	EMPLOYEES
06/21	560	187	33.4%	700
06/20	559	77	13.9%	—
06/19	537	94	17.5%	—
06/18	461	39	8.7%	—
Annual Growth	6.7%	67.4%	—	—

2021 Year-End Financials
Return on assets: 8.5%   Cash ($ mil.): 136
Return on equity: 11.5%
Current Ratio: 2.40

UTI, (U.S.) HOLDINGS, INC.

EXECUTIVES
Pres-Ceo, Christopher Dale
Treas*, Clinton Smith
Vice Pres*, Mary Anne Henry
Asst Treas*, Matthew Tachouet
Asst SEC*, Kristen Galbreath
Vice Pres-SEC*, Lance Damico
Quality Assurance Supervisor, Jason Dugas
Auditors : DELOITTE & TOUCHE LLP LOS AN

LOCATIONS
HQ: UTI, (U.S.) HOLDINGS, INC.
400 SW 6TH AVE STE 906, PORTLAND, OR 972041634
Phone: 503 953-1300

HISTORICAL FINANCIALS
Company Type: Private

Income Statement — FYE: January 31

	REVENUE ($mil)	NET INCOME ($mil)	NET PROFIT MARGIN	EMPLOYEES
01/10	3,567	45	1.3%	5,981
01/08	534	12	2.3%	—
Annual Growth	158.3%	91.3%	—	—

2010 Year-End Financials
Return on assets: 20.5% Cash ($ mil.): 350
Return on equity: 1.3%
Current Ratio: 1.20

VAL VERDE UNIFIED SCH DIS

LOCATIONS
HQ: VAL VERDE UNIFIED SCH DIS
975 MORGAN ST, PERRIS, CA 925713103
Phone: 951 940-6100
Web: WWW.VALVERDE.EDU

HISTORICAL FINANCIALS
Company Type: Private

Income Statement — FYE: June 30

	REVENUE ($mil)	NET INCOME ($mil)	NET PROFIT MARGIN	EMPLOYEES
06/21	583	21	3.6%	1,500
06/20	525	41	7.9%	—
06/19	527	(15)	—	—
06/18	529	30	5.8%	—
Annual Growth	3.3%	(11.7%)	—	—

2021 Year-End Financials
Return on assets: 2.1% Cash ($ mil.): —
Return on equity: 6.5%
Current Ratio: —

VALLEY CHILDREN'S HEALTHCARE FOUNDATION

LOCATIONS
HQ: VALLEY CHILDREN'S HEALTHCARE FOUNDATION
9300 VALLEY CHILDRENS PL, MADERA, CA 936368761
Phone: 559 353-3000
Web: WWW.VALLEYCHILDRENS.ORG

HISTORICAL FINANCIALS
Company Type: Private

Income Statement — FYE: September 30

	REVENUE ($mil)	NET INCOME ($mil)	NET PROFIT MARGIN	EMPLOYEES
09/19	793	159	20.0%	2,800
09/18	698	122	17.6%	—
09/17	604	121	20.1%	—
09/16	601	83	13.9%	—
Annual Growth	9.7%	23.9%	—	—

2019 Year-End Financials
Return on assets: 9.0% Cash ($ mil.): 31
Return on equity: 12.1%
Current Ratio: 1.30

VALLEY CHILDREN'S HOSPITAL

Auditors: MOSS ADAMS LLP STOCKTON CA

LOCATIONS
HQ: VALLEY CHILDREN'S HOSPITAL
9300 VALLEY CHILDRENS PL, MADERA, CA 936368762
Phone: 559 353-3000
Web: WWW.VALLEYCHILDRENS.ORG

HISTORICAL FINANCIALS
Company Type: Private

Income Statement — FYE: September 30

	REVENUE ($mil)	NET INCOME ($mil)	NET PROFIT MARGIN	EMPLOYEES
09/20	614	93	15.2%	1,800
09/19	771	41	5.4%	—
09/15	575	24	4.3%	—
09/13	542	103	19.0%	—
Annual Growth	1.8%	(1.4%)	—	—

2020 Year-End Financials
Return on assets: 5.1% Cash ($ mil.): 87
Return on equity: 7.2%
Current Ratio: 1.20

VALLEY CHILDRENS HEALTH CARE

LOCATIONS
HQ: VALLEY CHILDRENS HEALTH CARE
5085 E MCKINLEY AVE, FRESNO, CA 937271964
Phone: 559 454-1601
Web: WWW.VALLEYCHILDRENS.ORG

HISTORICAL FINANCIALS
Company Type: Private

Income Statement — FYE: September 30

	REVENUE ($mil)	NET INCOME ($mil)	NET PROFIT MARGIN	EMPLOYEES
09/21	749	177	23.6%	18
09/20	763	98	13.0%	—
Annual Growth	(1.8%)	79.1%	—	—

2021 Year-End Financials
Return on assets: 7.9% Cash ($ mil.): 178
Return on equity: 11.2%
Current Ratio: 1.30

VALLEY HEALTH SYSTEM GROUP RETURN

Auditors: VALLEY HEALTH SYSTEM WINCHEST

LOCATIONS
HQ: VALLEY HEALTH SYSTEM GROUP RETURN
220 CAMPUS BLVD STE 310, WINCHESTER, VA 226012889
Phone: 540 536-4302

HISTORICAL FINANCIALS
Company Type: Private

Income Statement — FYE: December 31

	REVENUE ($mil)	NET INCOME ($mil)	NET PROFIT MARGIN	EMPLOYEES
12/17	904	32	3.6%	8
12/13	625	22	3.7%	—
12/12	628	46	7.4%	—
12/09	538	45	8.5%	—
Annual Growth	6.7%	(4.2%)	—	—

2017 Year-End Financials
Return on assets: 2.3% Cash ($ mil.): 65
Return on equity: 3.9%
Current Ratio: 0.40

VALUE DRUG COMPANY

Value Drug Company (Value Drug) sees a great deal of value in keeping independent pharmacies competitive. The company is a purchasing cooperative of hundreds of independent drugstores that provides wholesale pharmaceutical distribution services to its members, primarily in the central Pennsylvania area. Its products include pharmaceuticals and non-prescription medications, medical equipment, health and beauty aids, nutritional supplies and other health care-related products. The company works with some of the world's largest pharmaceutical makers. Value Drug was founded in 1934 and incorporated in 1936. The company is led by president Greg Drew, a former Rite-Aid executive.

Operations

The company is not just a pharmaceutical wholesaler but it also provides retail and specialty pharmacy services, long-term care pharmacy support, and immunization service offerings. Value Drug offers more than 25,000 products including brand, generic, injectable, and specialty pharmaceuticals, over-the-counter products, home health care, long-term care supplies, health, beauty and wellness, as well as seasonal and everyday gifts. Value Drug also participates in such retail initiatives as the federal 340B Drug Discount Program, an adult immunization tracking program, and competitive generic sourcing program OptiSource.

Geographic Reach

Value Drug is located in Duncansville, Pennsylvania.

Sales and Marketing

Value Drug customers include pharmacists and business owners. It offers a variety of marketing tools for its customers such as store signage and consumer email communications to physician marketing support for CP specialty pharmacy services. Value Drug provides valuable resources that help generate traffic and its customer's increase sales.

Strategy

Value Drug is committed to providing transparency in its pricing and optimizing manufacturer relationships and purchasing power to improve buying conditions for its members. Value Drug also takes note of the changing consumer and independent pharmacy owners' needs. The company has assembled a diverse portfolio of programs and services that satisfy both the customer's need for convenience and low-cost healthcare and the pharmacist's need to increase growth, efficiency, and profitability.

Value Drug strives to keep independent pharmacies independent. Its Value Buy/Sell Program was established to assist those seeking to sell their business, as well as those looking for new ownership or expansion opportunities. Through its partnership with PRS, members have access to industry-leading buying, selling and transferring services, while its partnership with Sykes & Co. provides members with access to accounting, tax and advisory services.

Value Drug also provides resources that help generate traffic and increase sales in pharmacies. It offers a variety of marketing tools to help its members stay top-of-mind with patients and customers in their communities. Through Value Drug's partnerships with leading suppliers, clients can purchase high-quality apparel and promotional products featuring the clients' pharmacy's logo and brand designs.

Company Background

Value Drug Company was founded in 1934. Value Drug Company was then incorporated in 1936. The first warehouse occupied was located at 5th Avenue and 24th Street. In 1970, Drenning Trucking Co. was the first delivery service. In 2015, Value Drug introduces the ValueDrugHub mobile app, the first pharmaceutical wholesaler to provide a mobile app for order receiving and discrepancies.

Auditors : HILL BARTH & KING LLC WEXFOR

LOCATIONS

HQ: VALUE DRUG COMPANY
195 THEATER DR, DUNCANSVILLE, PA 166357144
Phone: 814 944-9316
Web: WWW.VALUEDRUGCO.COM

COMPETITORS

AMERISOURCEBERGEN CORPORATION
AUSTRALIAN PHARMACEUTICAL INDUSTRIES LTD
CARDINAL HEALTH, INC.
J M SMITH CORPORATION
Mediq B.V.
OMNICARE, INC.
PFIZER LIMITED
PRIME THERAPEUTICS LLC
SUZUKEN CO., LTD.
THE HARVARD DRUG GROUP L L C

HISTORICAL FINANCIALS

Company Type: Private

Income Statement — FYE: March 31

	REVENUE ($mil)	NET INCOME ($mil)	NET PROFIT MARGIN	EMPLOYEES
03/22	955	1	0.1%	200
03/21	1,010	1	0.2%	—
03/20*	1,156	0	0.1%	—
12/18	1,034	(0)	0.0%	—
Annual Growth	(2.6%)	—	—	—

*Fiscal year change

2022 Year-End Financials
Return on assets: 0.8% Cash ($ mil.): 6
Return on equity: 7.4%
Current Ratio: 1.50

VAN ATLAS LINES INC

The main subsidiary of Atlas World Group, moving company Atlas Van Lines provides transportation of household goods throughout the US and between the US and Canada. The company is one of the largest movers in the US. Atlas Van Lines also offers specialized transportation services for such cargo as trade show materials, fine art, electronics, pianos, store fixtures, and even individual cars and motorcycles. It operates through a network of some 500Â agents in the US and about 150 in Canada -- independent companies that use the Atlas brand in assigned geographic territories and cooperate on interstate moves. Atlas Van Lines was formed in 1948 by a group of 33 small moving companies.

EXECUTIVES

CIO*, David C Smith

LOCATIONS

HQ: VAN ATLAS LINES INC
1212 SAINT GEORGE RD, EVANSVILLE, IN 477112364
Phone: 812 424-4326
Web: WWW.ATLASVANLINES.COM

COMPETITORS

ARPIN MOVING, INC.
ATLAS WORLD GROUP, INC.
PICKFORDS LIMITED
UNITED VAN LINES, LLC
VAN WHEATON LINES INC

HISTORICAL FINANCIALS

Company Type: Private

Income Statement — FYE: December 31

	REVENUE ($mil)	NET INCOME ($mil)	NET PROFIT MARGIN	EMPLOYEES
12/08	696	19	2.8%	606
12/06	58	2	4.3%	—
12/05	59	3	6.5%	—
Annual Growth	127.4%	71.0%	—	—

2008 Year-End Financials
Return on assets: 9.3% Cash ($ mil.): (-2)
Return on equity: 12.5%
Current Ratio: 2.40

VANDERBILT UNIVERSITY MEDICAL CENTER

Founded in 1874, Vanderbilt University Medical Center (VUMC) is one of the largest academic medical centers in the Southeast. VUMC has a total of about 1,615 licensed hospital beds at Vanderbilt University Hospital, Vanderbilt Psychiatric Hospital, Vanderbilt Bedford Hospital, Vanderbilt Tullahoma-Harton Hospital, Vanderbilt Stallworth Rehabilitation Hospital, Vanderbilt Wilson County Hospital and Monroe Carell Jr. Children's Hospital at Vanderbilt. VUMC is a Level 1 Trauma Center and Burn Center in the region. Its world-leading academic departments and centers make scientific discoveries, advance clinical care and train the next generation of health care professionals through more than 100 residency and fellowship programs.

Operations

Through the Vanderbilt Health Affiliated Network, VUMC works with more than 60 hospitals and 5,000 clinicians across Tennessee and 5 neighboring states to share best practices and bring value-driven and cost-effective health care to the Mid-South.

VUMC performs more than 70,000 surgical cases and had more than 130,000 emergency department visits.

Geographic Reach
VUMC is based in Nashville, Tennessee.

Mergers and Acquisitions
In 2021, Vanderbilt University Medical Center acquired of Tennova Healthcare-Shellbyville and Tennova Healthcare-Harton hospitals and their related businesses, including physician clinic operations and outpatient services, from subsidiaries of Community Health Systems Inc. (CHS). With the acquisition of the hospitals in Shelbyville and Tullahoma, and the partnership with Tennova Healthcare-Clarksville, VUMC is expanding its ability to serve the communities of Middle Tennessee. Terms of the transactions will remain confidential.

Auditors: ERNST & YOUNG LLP NASHVILLE

LOCATIONS

HQ: VANDERBILT UNIVERSITY MEDICAL CENTER
1211 MEDICAL CENTER DR, NASHVILLE, TN 372320004
Phone: 615 322-5000
Web: WWW.VANDERBILTHEALTH.COM

PRODUCTS/OPERATIONS

Selected Facilities
Annette and Irwin Eskind Biomedical Library
Bill Wilkerson Center for Otolaryngology and Communication Sciences
Comprehensive Spine Center
Dayani Center for Health and Wellness
Monroe Carell Jr. Children's Hospital at Vanderbilt
Orthopaedic Institute
School of Medicine
School of Nursing
Sports Medicine Center
Stallworth Rehabilitation Hospital
Transplant Center
Vanderbilt Center for Better Health
The Vanderbilt Clinic
Vanderbilt Heart and Vascular Institute
Vanderbilt Psychiatric Hospital
Vanderbilt University Hospital
Vanderbilt-Ingram Cancer Center

COMPETITORS

CHARLESTON AREA MEDICAL CENTER, INC.
DUKE UNIVERSITY HEALTH SYSTEM, INC.
NORTHWELL HEALTH, INC.
THE CHILDREN'S HOSPITAL OF PHILADELPHIA
THE NEBRASKA MEDICAL CENTER
TRINITAS REGIONAL MEDICAL CENTER A NEW JERSEY NONPROFIT CORPORATION
UNIVERSITY HOSPITALS HEALTH SYSTEM, INC.
UNIVERSITY OF VIRGINIA MEDICAL CENTER
WILLIAM BEAUMONT HOSPITAL
YORK HOSPITAL

HISTORICAL FINANCIALS
Company Type: Private

Income Statement — FYE: June 30

	REVENUE ($mil)	NET INCOME ($mil)	NET PROFIT MARGIN	EMPLOYEES
06/20	4,930	182	3.7%	19,000
06/18	4,086	98	2.4%	—
06/17	3,894	264	6.8%	—
Annual Growth	8.2%	(11.5%)	—	—

2020 Year-End Financials
Return on assets: 3.5% Cash ($ mil.): 1,182
Return on equity: 13.0%
Current Ratio: 1.20

VANGUARD CHARITABLE ENDOWMENT PROGRAM

EXECUTIVES

Chief Development Officer, David Ryder
Auditors: PRICEWATERHOUSECOOPERS LLP PH

LOCATIONS

HQ: VANGUARD CHARITABLE ENDOWMENT PROGRAM
2670 WARWICK AVE, WARWICK, RI 028894269
Phone: 888 383-4483
Web: WWW.VANGUARDCHARITABLE.ORG

HISTORICAL FINANCIALS
Company Type: Private

Income Statement — FYE: June 30

	REVENUE ($mil)	NET INCOME ($mil)	NET PROFIT MARGIN	EMPLOYEES
06/13	1,117	608	54.4%	22
06/12	908	424	46.7%	—
06/11	890	402	45.2%	—
06/10	490	15	3.2%	—
Annual Growth	31.6%	239.7%	—	—

2013 Year-End Financials
Return on assets: 16.8% Cash ($ mil.): 14
Return on equity: 16.9%
Current Ratio: —

VCC, LLC

Auditors: HOGAN TAYLOR LLP LITTLE ROCK

LOCATIONS

HQ: VCC, LLC
1 INFORMATION WAY STE 300, LITTLE ROCK, AR 722022197
Phone: 214 574-4500
Web: WWW.VCCUSA.COM

HISTORICAL FINANCIALS
Company Type: Private

Income Statement — FYE: December 31

	REVENUE ($mil)	NET INCOME ($mil)	NET PROFIT MARGIN	EMPLOYEES
12/18	779	0	0.0%	350
12/17*	682	0	0.0%	—
06/16	261	0	0.0%	—
Annual Growth	43.8%	—	—	—

*Fiscal year change

2018 Year-End Financials
Return on assets: — Cash ($ mil.): 39
Return on equity: —
Current Ratio: 1.00

VCU HEALTH SYSTEM AUTHORITY

Auditors: ERNST & YOUNG LLP RICHMOND V

LOCATIONS

HQ: VCU HEALTH SYSTEM AUTHORITY
1250 E MARSHALL ST, RICHMOND, VA 232985023
Phone: 804 828-9000
Web: WWW.VCUHEALTH.ORG

HISTORICAL FINANCIALS
Company Type: Private

Income Statement — FYE: June 30

	REVENUE ($mil)	NET INCOME ($mil)	NET PROFIT MARGIN	EMPLOYEES
06/19	3,895	140	3.6%	7,399
06/18	3,399	162	4.8%	—
06/17	3,014	309	10.3%	—
06/05	899	47	5.3%	—
Annual Growth	11.0%	8.0%	—	—

2019 Year-End Financials
Return on assets: 3.6% Cash ($ mil.): 408
Return on equity: 5.5%
Current Ratio: 2.20

VEONEER, INC.

Auditors: ERNST & YOUNG AB STOCKHOLM

LOCATIONS

HQ: VEONEER, INC.
26360 AMERICAN DR, SOUTHFIELD, MI 480346116
Phone: 248 223-0600
Web: WWW.VEONEER.COM

HISTORICAL FINANCIALS
Company Type: Private

Income Statement — FYE: December 31

	REVENUE ($mil)	NET INCOME ($mil)	NET PROFIT MARGIN	EMPLOYEES
12/21	1,657	(385)	—	7,543
12/19	1,902	(522)	—	—
12/18	2,228	(294)	—	—
Annual Growth	(9.4%)	—	—	—

2021 Year-End Financials
Return on assets: (-22.0%) Cash ($ mil.): 423
Return on equity: (-45.1%)
Current Ratio: 1.70

VIBRANTZ CORPORATION

Ferro is a leading producer of specialty materials that are sold to a broad range of manufacturers who, in turn, make products for many end-use markets. With nearly 50 manufacturing plants worldwide, the company make various colorants, including ceramic glazes, pigments, and porcelain enamels. It also produces electronics, and color (such as conductive metals and pastes used in solar cells), and polymer and ceramic engineered materials. Its products are used in construction and by makers of appliances, autos, building and renovation, electronics, sanitary, packaging, consumer products and household furnishings. The company gets more than 65% of its revenue from international customers.

Operations
Ferro's products fall into two general categories: functional coatings (about 65% of revenue), which perform specific functions in the end products and manufacturing processes of its customers; and color solutions (about 35%), which provide performance and aesthetic characteristics to its customers' products which include frits, porcelain and other glass enamels, glazes, stains, decorating colors, pigments, inks, polishing materials, dielectrics, electronic glasses, and other specialty coatings.

Geographic Reach
Ohio-based Ferro owns manufacturing plants in Belgium, China, Colombia, France, Germany, Mexico; Cleveland, Ohio; and Penn Yan, New York. In addition, the company leases manufacturing facilities in the UK, Germany, Japan, Israel, and Turkey.

The US is the largest market accounting for about 35% of revenue. Germany is the second largest market accounting for about 15% of revenue and the other countries account for the remaining 50% of revenue.

Sales and Marketing
Ferro serve a diverse set of industries, including automotive, construction, appliances, healthcare, food and beverage, information technology, energy and defense. It primarily sells its products directly to customers, but also uses indirect sales channels, such as agents and distributors.

Financial Performance
During the year ended December 31, 2021, net sales increased $167.3 million, or 17% to $1.1 billion, compared with 2020. Net sales increased by $123.9 million and $43.4 million in Functional Coatings and Color Solutions, respectively.

In 2021, the company had a net income of $150.5 million, a 242% increase from the previous year's net income of $44 million.

The company's cash at the end of 2021 was $71.5 million. Investing activities generated $490.7 million, while operating activities used $61.3 million, mainly for accounts receivable. Financing activities used another $538.1 million for principal payments on term loan facility.

Company Background
Ferro Corporation was incorporated in Ohio in 1919 as an enameling company. It eventually transformed into a producer of specialty materials for a broad range of manufacturers serving the end-use markets.

Auditors: DELOITTE & TOUCHE LLP CLEVELA

LOCATIONS
HQ: VIBRANTZ CORPORATION
6060 PARKLAND BLVD # 250, MAYFIELD HEIGHTS, OH 441244225
Phone: 216 875-5600
Web: WWW.FERRO.COM

2018 Sales

	$ mil.	% of total
United States	379.9	24
Spain	305.1	19
Other international	927.4	57
Total	1,612.4	100

PRODUCTS/OPERATIONS
2018 Sales

	$ mil.	% of total
Performance Coatings	733.9	46
Performance Colors and Glass	487.5	30
Color Solution	391	24
Total	1,612.4	100

PRODUCTS
PERFORMANCE COATINGS
Fine Ceramics
Porcelain Enamel
Structural Ceramics
Tile Coatings
Vetriceramici
PERFORMANCE COLORS AND GLASS
Automotive
Decoration
Electronic
Industrial
PIGMENTS, POWDERS & OXIDES
Liquid Colors & Dispersions
Metal Powders
Nubiola
Pigments
Surface Technologies

COMPETITORS
AVIENT CORPORATION
ArcelorMittal Dofasco G.P.
BODYCOTE PLC
CARDOLITE CORPORATION
GENERAL MAGNAPLATE CORPORATION
KOLORFUSION INTERNATIONAL, INC.
MATERIAL SCIENCES CORPORATION
MATERION CORPORATION
METOKOTE CORPORATION
MINERALS TECHNOLOGIES INC.

HISTORICAL FINANCIALS
Company Type: Private

Income Statement — FYE: December 31

	REVENUE ($mil)	NET INCOME ($mil)	NET PROFIT MARGIN	EMPLOYEES
12/21	1,126	150	13.4%	3,585
12/20	958	44	4.6%	—
12/19	1,018	7	0.7%	—
12/18	1,612	80	5.0%	—
Annual Growth	(11.3%)	23.0%	—	—

2021 Year-End Financials
Return on assets: 11.7% Cash ($ mil.): 71
Return on equity: 27.5%
Current Ratio: 1.80

VICTORY INTERNATIONAL GROUP, LLC

LOCATIONS
HQ: VICTORY INTERNATIONAL GROUP, LLC
14748 PIPELINE AVE STE B, CHINO HILLS, CA 917096024
Phone: 949 407-5888
Web: WWW.VICTORYINTLGROUP.COM

HISTORICAL FINANCIALS
Company Type: Private

Income Statement — FYE: December 31

	REVENUE ($mil)	NET INCOME ($mil)	NET PROFIT MARGIN	EMPLOYEES
12/20	896	62	6.9%	230
12/07	87	1	1.4%	—
Annual Growth	19.5%	35.2%	—	—

2020 Year-End Financials
Return on assets: 7.3% Cash ($ mil.): 260
Return on equity: 10.8%
Current Ratio: 2.90

VIRGINIA COLLEGE BUILDING AUTHORITY

LOCATIONS
HQ: VIRGINIA COLLEGE BUILDING AUTHORITY
101 N 14TH ST, RICHMOND, VA 232193665
Phone: 804 225-2142
Web: TRS.VIRGINIA.GOV

HISTORICAL FINANCIALS
Company Type: Private

Income Statement — FYE: June 30

	ASSETS ($mil)	NET INCOME ($mil)	INCOME AS % OF ASSETS	EMPLOYEES
06/21	1,937	(290)	—	2
06/20	1,693	(285)	—	—
06/19	2,339	(209)	—	—
06/18	2,141	(145)	—	—
Annual Growth	(3.3%)	—	—	—

VIRGINIA COMMONWEALTH UNIVERSITY

Virginia Commonwealth University (VCU) serves the common interests of its more than 30,000 enrolled students. The university offers more than 200 certificate, undergraduate, graduate, and doctoral programs through its 15 schools. Spread across two campuses in Richmond: Monroe Park and Medical College of Virginia (MCV), which includes the Schools of Allied Health, Dentistry, Medicine, Nursing, Pharmacy, and Public Health. Specialty facilities include the VCU Medical Center and a branch campus of the School of the Arts in Qatar. Founded in 1917 as the Richmond School of Social Work and Public Health, in 1968 the school merged with the Medical College of Virginia to form VCU.

EXECUTIVES

University Relations Vice President*, Grant J Heston
Auditors : MARTHA S MAVREDES RICHMOND

LOCATIONS

HQ: VIRGINIA COMMONWEALTH UNIVERSITY
912 W FRANKLIN ST, RICHMOND, VA 232849040
Phone: 804 828-0100
Web: WWW.VCU.EDU

COMPETITORS

ADELPHI UNIVERSITY
AUGUSTA UNIVERSITY
EAST CAROLINA UNIVERSITY
HAMPTON UNIVERSITY
IDAHO STATE UNIVERSITY
JAMES MADISON UNIVERSITY
SAINT FRANCIS UNIVERSITY
THE UNIVERSITY OF IOWA
THE UNIVERSITY OF TOLEDO
THOMAS JEFFERSON UNIVERSITY

HISTORICAL FINANCIALS
Company Type: Private

Income Statement — FYE: June 30

	REVENUE ($mil)	NET INCOME ($mil)	NET PROFIT MARGIN	EMPLOYEES
06/21	775	157	20.3%	11,000
06/20	784	49	6.3%	—
06/18	763	12	1.7%	—
06/17	760	84	11.1%	—
Annual Growth	0.5%	16.9%	—	—

2021 Year-End Financials
Return on assets: 7.0%   Cash ($ mil.): 128
Return on equity: 16.6%
Current Ratio: 2.40

VIRGINIA DEPARTMENT OF TRANSPORTATION

EXECUTIVES

Acting Deputy Secretary*, John W Lawson

LOCATIONS

HQ: VIRGINIA DEPARTMENT OF TRANSPORTATION
1401 E BROAD ST, RICHMOND, VA 232192052
Phone: 804 786-2701
Web: WWW.VIRGINIADOT.ORG

HISTORICAL FINANCIALS
Company Type: Private

Income Statement — FYE: June 30

	REVENUE ($mil)	NET INCOME ($mil)	NET PROFIT MARGIN	EMPLOYEES
06/10	3,240	473	14.6%	10,737
06/06	3,047	410	13.5%	—
06/05	0	0	—	—
06/04	2,857	56	2.0%	—
Annual Growth	2.1%	42.7%	—	—

2010 Year-End Financials
Return on assets: 2.3%   Cash ($ mil.): 2,013
Return on equity: 2.7%
Current Ratio: —

VIRGINIA HOUSING DEVELOPMENT AUTHORITY

Though Virginia is famous for its Civil War-era plantations, these historic estates represent a lifestyle out of reach for most. For Virginians seeking a more modest homestead, there's the Virginia Housing Development Authority (VHDA). The not-for-profit quasi-government agency, founded by the Virginia General Assembly in 1972, provides developers of rental properties and low- to moderate-income borrowers with low interest rate loans to renovate or purchase houses and apartments across the state. Its loan products are offered by more than 140 authorized lenders throughout Virginia. The VHDA is self-supporting, issuing bonds to raise capital.

Auditors : KPMG LLP RICHMOND VIRGINIA

LOCATIONS

HQ: VIRGINIA HOUSING DEVELOPMENT AUTHORITY
601 S BELVIDERE ST, RICHMOND, VA 232206504
Phone: 804 780-0789

COMPETITORS

FLORIDA HOUSING FINANCE CORPORATION
IMH FINANCIAL CORPORATION
MMA CAPITAL HOLDINGS, INC.
RHODE ISLAND HOUSING AND MORTGAGE FINANCE CORPORATION
STATE OF NEW YORK MORTGAGE AGENCY

HISTORICAL FINANCIALS
Company Type: Private

Income Statement — FYE: June 30

	ASSETS ($mil)	NET INCOME ($mil)	INCOME AS % OF ASSETS	EMPLOYEES
06/16	8,024	171	2.1%	300
06/15	8,070	176	2.2%	—
06/14	8,014	132	1.7%	—
Annual Growth	0.1%	13.7%	—	—

2016 Year-End Financials
Return on assets: 2.1%   Cash ($ mil.): 1027
Return on equity: 5.7%
Current Ratio: 1.40

VIRGINIA INTERNATIONAL TERMINALS, LLC

Virginia International Terminals (VIT) operates marine terminals and an inland port on behalf of the Virginia Port Authority (VPA), a state agency. Established in 1982, VIT's marine terminals handle containerships and other vessels in Newport News, Norfolk, and Portsmouth. The terminals are linked by rail to the Virginia Inland Port in Front Royal, which serves as an intermodal container transfer facility conveying cargo from ships to trucks and vice versa. CenterPoint Properties, investment firm The Carlyle Group, and terminal operator Carrix Inc. bid to create a public-private partnership with VIT. The Transportation Secretary dismissed the bids in late 2010, after cargo activity started improving.

Auditors : PB MARES LLP HARRISONBURG V

LOCATIONS

HQ: VIRGINIA INTERNATIONAL TERMINALS, LLC
601 WORLD TRADE CTR, NORFOLK, VA 23510
Phone: 757 440-7120
Web: WWW.VIT.ORG

COMPETITORS

CARRIX, INC.
PORT NEWARK CONTAINER TERMINAL L.L.C.
PORT OF SEATTLE
SOUTH CAROLINA STATE PORTS AUTHORITY
SSA MARINE, INC

HISTORICAL FINANCIALS

Company Type: Private

Income Statement — FYE: June 30

	REVENUE ($mil)	NET INCOME ($mil)	NET PROFIT MARGIN	EMPLOYEES
06/20	619	(27)	—	400
06/19	551	(1)	—	—
06/18	521	16	3.1%	—
06/17	478	(7)	—	—
Annual Growth	9.0%	—	—	—

2020 Year-End Financials
Return on assets: (-14.1%)   Cash ($ mil.): 54
Return on equity: (-26.7%)
Current Ratio: 1.60

VIRGINIA MASON MEDICAL CENTER

EXECUTIVES

CIO*, Suzanne Anderson
Auditors : KPMG LLP SEATTLE WA

LOCATIONS

HQ: VIRGINIA MASON MEDICAL CENTER
1100 9TH AVE, SEATTLE, WA 981012756
Phone: 206 223-6600
Web: WWW.VMFH.ORG

HISTORICAL FINANCIALS

Company Type: Private

Income Statement — FYE: December 31

	REVENUE ($mil)	NET INCOME ($mil)	NET PROFIT MARGIN	EMPLOYEES
12/20	1,118	47	4.3%	5,000
12/19*	1,156	29	2.5%	—
03/19	274	10	4.0%	—
12/18	1,101	(16)	—	—
Annual Growth	0.8%	—	—	—

*Fiscal year change

2020 Year-End Financials
Return on assets: 3.3%   Cash ($ mil.): 205
Return on equity: 8.5%
Current Ratio: 1.60

VIRGINIA POLYTECHNIC INSTITUTE & STATE UNIVERSITY

Virginia Polytechnic Institute and State University, more commonly known as Virginia Tech, is the state's largest university, enrolling some 37,000 students each year. The university offers some 110 undergraduate degree programs and around 170 master's and doctoral degree programs through nine colleges and a graduate school. It has a student-teacher ratio of 14 to 1. The school's most popular majors include agriculture, business, biology, communications, medicine, and engineering. Virginia Tech, which was formed in 1872, serves the surrounding community through outreach and education programs.

Operations
The school charges some $32,274 tuition and fees for in-state undergraduates and $31,622 tuition and fees for out-of-state students.

Virginia Tech manages a research portfolio of nearly $500 million. Research is focused on new developments in agriculture, biotechnology, energy management (including fuel-cell technology and power electronics), computer science and communication technology, and other fields.

Geographic Reach
Virginia Tech has about 215 buildings, a 2,600-acre main campus in Blacksburg (and a nearby 1,800-acre agricultural research farm), off-campus educational facilities in Alexandria, Arlington, Falls Church, Leesburg, Manassas, and Middleburg, and a study-abroad site in Switzerland. It has eleven Agricultural Research and Extension Centers across Virginia.

Company Background
Virginia Tech was founded as a land-grant college in 1872.

EXECUTIVES

Com Operations Vice President*, Sherwood G Wilson
FOR ADVANCEMENT*, Charles D Phlegar
Auditors : STACI A HENSHAW RICHMOND VI

LOCATIONS

HQ: VIRGINIA POLYTECHNIC INSTITUTE & STATE UNIVERSITY
300 TURNER ST NW STE 4200, BLACKSBURG, VA 240616100
Phone: 540 231-6000
Web: WWW.VT.EDU

PRODUCTS/OPERATIONS

Selected Colleges
College of Agriculture and Life Sciences
College Architecture and Urban Studies
College of Engineering
College of Liberal Arts and Human Sciences
College of Natural Resources and Environment
College of Science
Pamplin College of Business
Virginia-Maryland Regional College of Veterinary Medicine

COMPETITORS

DELAWARE STATE UNIVERSITY
GEORGIA INSTITUTE OF TECHNOLOGY
NORTHEASTERN UNIVERSITY
PURDUE UNIVERSITY
ROCHESTER INSTITUTE OF TECHNOLOGY (INC)
TRUSTEES OF INDIANA UNIVERSITY
UNIVERSITY OF OREGON
UNIVERSITY OF THE PACIFIC
WEST VIRGINIA UNIVERSITY
WRIGHT STATE UNIVERSITY

HISTORICAL FINANCIALS

Company Type: Private

Income Statement — FYE: June 30

	REVENUE ($mil)	NET INCOME ($mil)	NET PROFIT MARGIN	EMPLOYEES
06/21	1,162	300	25.8%	6,866
06/20	1,188	120	10.2%	—
06/19	1,160	130	11.2%	—
06/18	1,279	181	14.2%	—
Annual Growth	(3.2%)	18.2%	—	—

2021 Year-End Financials
Return on assets: 8.9%   Cash ($ mil.): 273
Return on equity: 16.5%
Current Ratio: 1.30

VIRGINIA PREMIER HEALTH PLAN, INC.

Auditors : KPMG LLP MC LEAN VA

LOCATIONS

HQ: VIRGINIA PREMIER HEALTH PLAN, INC.
600 E BROAD ST STE 400, RICHMOND, VA 232191800
Phone: 804 819-5164
Web: WWW.VIRGINIAPREMIER.COM

HISTORICAL FINANCIALS

Company Type: Private

Income Statement — FYE: December 31

	ASSETS ($mil)	NET INCOME ($mil)	INCOME AS % OF ASSETS	EMPLOYEES
12/20*	741	71	9.6%	165
06/19	438	(51)	—	—
06/18	405	(14)	—	—
06/15	319	(0)	—	—
Annual Growth	15.1%	—	—	—

*Fiscal year change

2020 Year-End Financials
Return on assets: 9.6%   Cash ($ mil.): 32
Return on equity: 18.3%
Current Ratio: 0.80

VIRTU FINANCIAL LLC

EXECUTIVES

CAO, Anthony Manganiello
Auditors : DELOITTE & TOUCHE LLP NEW YOR

LOCATIONS

HQ: VIRTU FINANCIAL LLC
165 BROADWAY, NEW YORK, NY 100061404
Phone: 212 418-0100
Web: WWW.VIRTU.COM

HISTORICAL FINANCIALS
Company Type: Private

Income Statement — FYE: December 31

	ASSETS ($mil)	NET INCOME ($mil)	INCOME AS % OF ASSETS	EMPLOYEES
12/14	3,324	190	5.7%	18
12/13	3,963	182	4.6%	—
Annual Growth	(16.1%)	4.3%	—	—

2014 Year-End Financials
Return on assets: 5.7%   Cash ($ mil.): 75
Return on equity: 89.5%
Current Ratio: —

VIRTUA-WEST JERSEY HEALTH SYSTEM, INC.

Auditors : GRANT THORNTON LLP PHILADELPH

LOCATIONS

HQ: VIRTUA-WEST JERSEY HEALTH SYSTEM, INC.
1000 ATLANTIC AVE, CAMDEN, NJ 081041132
Phone: 856 246-3000

HISTORICAL FINANCIALS
Company Type: Private

Income Statement — FYE: December 31

	REVENUE ($mil)	NET INCOME ($mil)	NET PROFIT MARGIN	EMPLOYEES
12/19	843	117	13.9%	4,100
12/17	919	207	22.6%	—
12/04	399	29	7.4%	—
12/03	354	6	1.8%	—
Annual Growth	5.6%	20.0%	—	—

2019 Year-End Financials
Return on assets: 5.0%   Cash ($ mil.): 62
Return on equity: 8.2%
Current Ratio: 0.20

VIZIO, INC.

VIZIO offers HDTVs and sound bars on its webstore, online across dozens of retailers, and in thousands of brick and mortar stores throughout the US. The company also offers a portfolio of innovative sound bars that deliver consumers an elevated audio experience, as well as Universal SmartCast TV remotes and sound bar display remotes. VIZIO sells many of its low-priced electronics through top discount chains including Amazon, Best Buy, Costco, Sam's Club, Target, and Walmart. Thanks to its low prices, VIZIO ranked as the #1 American-based sound bar brand.

Operations

The company designs a collection of televisions, sound bars, and the SmartCast smart TV platform with the consumer's desires in mind, and has been rated America's Fastest Growing TV Brand with Quantum Dot and America's Fastest Growing Sound Bar Brand with Dolby Atmos. In addition, it offers remote controls and built-in bluetooth for streaming music wirelessly.

The company partners with Inscape and generates more comprehensive TV viewing data and helps companies gain a deeper and more accurate understanding of their audience.

Sales and Marketing

VIZIO offers other businesses to showcase contents or applications in VIZIO platform. The company markets its products through retailers such as Nebraska Furniture Mart, Dell.com, Fred Meijer, B&H Photo, and Meijer, among others.

Company Background

The company was founded by William Wang in 2002 and initially sold its TVs at membership retailers such as Costco Wholesale, BJ's Wholesale Club, and Sam's Club. It then extended its reach to discount retailers Wal-Mart and Sears.

The TV maker entered the market for smart TVs, which are integrated with internet functionality, when it shipped its first model during the second half of 2011.

VIZIO entered the PC market in mid-2012 with a new line of laptops and desktops starting at about $890. By combining its entertainment know-how with the power of the latest Intel Core processors, VIZIO hopes to set a new standard for the Windows experience. The line consists of the VIZIO Thin + Light, Notebook, and All-in-One PC.

LOCATIONS

HQ: VIZIO, INC.
39 TESLA, IRVINE, CA 926184603
Phone: 855 833-3221
Web: WWW.VIZIO.COM

PRODUCTS/OPERATIONS

Selected Products
Cables and other accessories
Blue-ray disc players
HDTVs
HD home theater systems
Headphones
Internet routers
Personal computers
Tablet computers
Smartphones
Speakers

COMPETITORS

EMERSON RADIO CORP.
FUNAI ELECTRIC CO., LTD.
Loewe AG
MARSHALL AMPLIFICATION PLC
PIONEER CORPORATION
POLK AUDIO, LLC
SHARP CORPORATION
SKULLCANDY, INC.
Samsung Electronics Co., Ltd.
UNIVERSAL ELECTRONICS INC.

HISTORICAL FINANCIALS
Company Type: Private

Income Statement — FYE: December 31

	REVENUE ($mil)	NET INCOME ($mil)	NET PROFIT MARGIN	EMPLOYEES
12/08	2,006	10	0.5%	398
12/07	1,929	7	0.4%	—
12/06	671	1	0.2%	—
12/04	46	0	1.0%	—
Annual Growth	155.8%	115.7%	—	—

2008 Year-End Financials
Return on assets: 3.2%   Cash ($ mil.): 42
Return on equity: 0.5%
Current Ratio: 0.90

VNS CHOICE

Auditors : KPMG LLP HARTFORD CT

LOCATIONS

HQ: VNS CHOICE
220 E 42ND ST FL 3, NEW YORK, NY 100175806
Phone: 212 609-7235
Web: WWW.VNSHEALTHPLANS.ORG

HISTORICAL FINANCIALS
Company Type: Private

Income Statement — FYE: December 31

	REVENUE ($mil)	NET INCOME ($mil)	NET PROFIT MARGIN	EMPLOYEES
12/19	1,863	55	3.0%	651
12/14	1,388	(72)	—	—
12/13	1,299	(90)	—	—
12/09	419	4	1.0%	—
Annual Growth	16.1%	29.1%	—	—

2019 Year-End Financials
Return on assets: 11.7%   Cash ($ mil.): 124
Return on equity: 165.6%
Current Ratio: 7.90

W.S. BADCOCK CORPORATION

W.S. Badcock furnishes homes down in Dixie and beyond. As one of the largest privately-owned furniture retailers in the US, the company sells furniture for every room in the house. It sells its furniture and accessories through more than 300 stores that operate under the banner names Badcock Home Furnishing Centers and Badcock &more. Aside from its e-commerce site, Badcock's stores network extends to nearly 10 southeastern states. Stores also carry appliances, lawn equipment, electronics, mattresses, rugs, bedding, lighting, wall art, and other decorative accessories. The company was founded by Henry S. Badcock in 1904 as a general mercantile store. Today it is in its fourth generation of family management.

Geographic Reach
Headquartered in Mulberry, Florida, with more than 1,200 corporate employees, W.S. Badcock operates primarily in the southeastern US. Its operations span the states of Georgia, Alabama, Mississippi, Tennessee, and the Carolinas, expanding into Virginia, West Virginia, and Kentucky.

Strategy
Through the company's dealer business model, more than 80% of Badcock's stores are individually owned. As part of the model, the company does not require a franchise fee but instead consigns merchandise to the dealers. As opposed to the typical franchise system startup, this consignment method aims to allow for a quicker startup along with the benefits of business ownership.

Already established in half a dozen states, Badcock has been expanding its store network in Virginia, Kentucky, and West Virginia. Despite a slowdown in its expansion plans amid the recession and downturn in furniture retailing, the company aims to grow its stores network again throughout the Southeast.

EXECUTIVES
Executive Strategy Vice President, Henry C Badcock
Auditors : KPMG LLP TAMPA FL

LOCATIONS
HQ: W.S. BADCOCK CORPORATION
190 NW PHOSPHATE BLVD, MULBERRY, FL 338602327
Phone: 863 425-4921
Web: WWW.BADCOCK.COM

PRODUCTS/OPERATIONS
Selected Products
Accessories
Appliances
Electronics
Furniture
Mattresses

COMPETITORS
AMERICAN SIGNATURE, INC.
Brick Ltd, The
CITY FURNITURE, INC.
NEBRASKA FURNITURE MART, INC.
OFS BRANDS HOLDINGS INC.
R.T.G. FURNITURE CORP.
RAYMOURS FURNITURE COMPANY, INC.
SLEEPY'S REORGANIZATION, INC.

THE CARTER-JONES LUMBER COMPANY
W. B. MASON CO., INC.

HISTORICAL FINANCIALS
Company Type: Private

Income Statement — FYE: June 30

	REVENUE ($mil)	NET INCOME ($mil)	NET PROFIT MARGIN	EMPLOYEES
06/21	901	86	9.6%	1,689
06/19	874	38	4.4%	—
Annual Growth	1.6%	50.8%	—	—

2021 Year-End Financials
Return on assets: 10.7% Cash ($ mil.): 108
Return on equity: 18.6%
Current Ratio: 5.00

WAKE COUNTY PUBLIC SCHOOL SYSTEM

EXECUTIVES
Vice Chairman*, Chris Heagarty

LOCATIONS
HQ: WAKE COUNTY PUBLIC SCHOOL SYSTEM
5625 DILLARD DR, CARY, NC 275189226
Phone: 919 431-7343
Web: WWW.WCPSS.NET

HISTORICAL FINANCIALS
Company Type: Private

Income Statement — FYE: June 30

	REVENUE ($mil)	NET INCOME ($mil)	NET PROFIT MARGIN	EMPLOYEES
06/10	1,224	13	1.1%	17,000
06/09	1,425	(7)	—	—
06/08	1,374	(1)	—	—
Annual Growth	(5.6%)	—	—	—

2010 Year-End Financials
Return on assets: 0.5% Cash ($ mil.): 91
Return on equity: 0.5%
Current Ratio: 1.40

WAKE FOREST UNIVERSITY HEALTH SCIENCES

Auditors : KPMG LLP GREENSBORO NC

LOCATIONS
HQ: WAKE FOREST UNIVERSITY HEALTH SCIENCES
250 HOSPITAL DR, LEXINGTON, NC 272926842
Phone: 336 248-5161
Web: WWW.WAKEHEALTH.EDU

HISTORICAL FINANCIALS
Company Type: Private

Income Statement — FYE: June 30

	REVENUE ($mil)	NET INCOME ($mil)	NET PROFIT MARGIN	EMPLOYEES
06/21	1,283	396	30.9%	209
06/18	1,002	43	4.4%	—
Annual Growth	8.6%	108.6%	—	—

2021 Year-End Financials
Return on assets: 19.1% Cash ($ mil.): 177
Return on equity: 32.6%
Current Ratio: 0.70

WAKE, COUNTY OF NORTH CAROLINA

EXECUTIVES
County Manager, David Ellis
County Manager*, Duane Holder
County Manager*, Ashley Jacobs
County Manager*, Emily Lucas
Vice Chairman*, Phil Matthews
Auditors : ELLIOT DAVIS PLLC RALEIGH N

LOCATIONS
HQ: WAKE, COUNTY OF NORTH CAROLINA
300 S SALISBURY ST # 1700, RALEIGH, NC 276011751
Phone: 919 856-6160
Web: WWW.WAKEGOV.COM

HISTORICAL FINANCIALS
Company Type: Private

Income Statement — FYE: June 30

	REVENUE ($mil)	NET INCOME ($mil)	NET PROFIT MARGIN	EMPLOYEES
06/18	1,377	67	4.9%	3,700
06/16	1,291	(297)	—	—
06/15	0	—	—	—
Annual Growth	—	—	—	—

2018 Year-End Financials
Return on assets: 3.5% Cash ($ mil.): —
Return on equity: —
Current Ratio: —

WAKEFERN FOOD CORP.

Wakefern Food is the largest retailer-owned cooperative in the nation with approximately 50 member companies who independently own and operate more than 360 supermarkets across the northeastern US. The cooperative offers more than $10 billion in purchasing power and provides unmatched support services, including private label brand development, advertising support, category management, engineering services, store quality assurance and inspections, health and wellness services, marketing, retail store development, pharmacy support services and media and public relations. The members' stores operate under the Fairway Market, ShopRite, The Fresh Grocer, Price Rite Marketplace, Gourmet Garage and Dearborn Market banners. Wakefern was founded by eight independent grocers in 1946.

Operations

From supplying virtually everything in center store, from general merchandise to beauty aids, along with produce, frozen foods, meats, and dairy, Wakefern provides outstanding service that enables its wholesale customers to deliver constant value to consumers. In addition to a milk processing and distribution facility and a seafood processing plant, wholesale customers can benefit from a wide range of capabilities offered through Wakefern, including transportation, quality assurance, category management, merchandising support services, technical support and store development.

Readington Farms, Wakefern's wholly-owned subsidiary, is a high volume, multi-product line producer of Bowl & Basket milk and spring water, orange juice, iced teas, and drinks for Wakefern banner brands ShopRite and Price Rite Marketplace. The cooperative's unique brand offerings include Wholesome Pantry, Bowl & Basket, and Paperbird.

Geographic Reach

Based in Keasbey, New Jersey, Wakefern's member retailers own and operate more than 360 retail supermarkets in Connecticut, Delaware, Maryland, Massachusetts, New Jersey, New York, Pennsylvania, Rhode Island, and New Hampshire.

Sales and Marketing

Wakefern has a network of more than 70,000 associates. The company markets its brand through its website.

Company Background

In 1946, in an effort to assist struggling independent grocers, a sales representative from Del Monte Foods introduced cooperative buying to eight independent grocers from Newark, New Jersey. By the end of that year, each grocer having invested $1,000, Wakefern Food Corp. was officially founded.

HISTORY

Wakefern Food was founded in 1946 by seven New York- and New Jersey-based grocers: Louis Weiss, Sam and Al Aidekman, Abe Kesselman, Dave Fern, Sam Garb, and Albert Goldberg. The company got its name by taking the first letters of the last names of five of the original founders (Weiss, Sam and Al Aidekman, Kesselman, and Fern). Like many cooperatives, the association sought to lower costs by increasing its buying power as a group.

They each put in $1,000 and began operating a 5,000-sq.-ft. warehouse, often putting in double time to keep both their stores and the warehouse running. The shopkeepers' collective buying power proved valuable, enabling the grocers to stock many items at the same prices as their larger competitors.

In 1951 Wakefern members began pooling their resources to buy advertising space. A common store name -- ShopRite -- was chosen, and each week co-op members met to decide which items would be sale priced. Within a year, membership had grown to over 50. Expansion became a priority, and in the mid-1950s co-op members united in small groups to take over failed supermarkets. One such group, called the Supermarkets Operating Co. (SOC), was formed in 1956. Within 10 years it had acquired a number of failed stores, remodeled them, and given them the ShopRite name.

During the late 1950s sales at ShopRite stores slumped after Wakefern decided to buck the supermarket trend of offering trading stamps (which could then be exchanged for gifts), figuring that offering the stamps would ultimately lead to higher food prices. The move initially drove away customers, but Wakefern cut grocery prices across the board and sales returned. The company did embrace another supermarket trend: stocking stores with nonfood items.

The co-op was severely shaken in 1966 when SOC merged with General Supermarkets, a similar small group within Wakefern, becoming Supermarkets General Corp. (SGC). SGC was a powerful entity, with 71 supermarkets, 10 drugstores, six gas stations, a wholesale bakery, and a discount department store. Many Wakefern members opposed the merger and attempted to block the action with a court order. By 1968 SGC had beefed up its operations to include department store chains as well as its grocery stores. In a move that threatened to break Wakefern, SGC broke away from the co-op, and its stores were renamed Pathmark.

Wakefern not only weathered the storm, it grew under the direction of chairman and CEO Thomas Infusino, elected shortly after the split. The co-op focused on asserting its position as a seller of low-priced products. Wakefern developed private-label brands, including the ShopRite brand. In the 1980s members began operating larger stores and adding more nonfood items to the ShopRite product mix. With its number of superstores on the rise and facing increased competition from club stores in 1992, Wakefern opened a centralized, nonfood distribution center in New Jersey.

In 1995, 30-year Wakefern veteran Dean Janeway was elected president of the co-op. The company debuted its ShopRite MasterCard, co-branded with New Jersey's Valley National Bank, in 1996. The following year the co-op purchased two of its customers' stores in Pennsylvania, then threatened to close them when contract talks with the local union deteriorated. In 1998 Wakefern settled the dispute, then sold the stores.

The company partnered with Internet bidding site Priceline in 1999, offering customers an opportunity to bid on groceries and then pick them up at ShopRite stores. Big V, Wakefern's biggest customer, filed for Chapter 11 bankruptcy protection in 2000 and said it was ending its distribution agreement with the co-op. In July 2002, however, Wakefern's ShopRite Supermarkets subsidiary acquired all of Big V's assets for approximately $185 million in cash and assumed liabilities.

Infusino retired in May 2005 after 35 years with Wakefern Food. He was succeeded by former vice chairman Joseph Colalillo. The cooperative added to its footprint in 2007 when it acquired about 10 underperforming retail locations from Stop & Shop. The stores, located mostly in South Jersey, were rebranded under the ShopRite banner.

Auditors: KPMG LLP SHORT HILLS NJ

LOCATIONS

HQ: WAKEFERN FOOD CORP.
5000 RIVERSIDE DR, KEASBEY, NJ 088321209
Phone: 908 527-3300
Web: WWW.WAKEFERN.COM

COMPETITORS

ASSOCIATED WHOLESALE GROCERS, INC.
C&S WHOLESALE GROCERS, INC.
DEMOULAS SUPER MARKETS, INC.
EDEKA ZENTRALE Stiftung & Co. KG
HAGGEN, INC.
SPARTANNASH COMPANY
SUPERVALU INC.
THE GREAT ATLANTIC & PACIFIC TEA COMPANY, INC.
VILLAGE SUPER MARKET, INC.
WM MORRISON SUPERMARKETS P L C

HISTORICAL FINANCIALS

Company Type: Private

Income Statement — FYE: September 27

	REVENUE ($mil)	NET INCOME ($mil)	NET PROFIT MARGIN	EMPLOYEES
09/14	11,871	5	0.0%	3,500
09/13	11,455	0	0.0%	—
09/12	11,010	5	0.0%	—
Annual Growth	3.8%	0.0%	—	—

2014 Year-End Financials
Return on assets: 0.3% Cash ($ mil.): 128
Return on equity: 2.7%
Current Ratio: 0.80

WAKEMED

If you wake up in a hospital in Wake County, North Carolina, you may be at one of WakeMed health system's facilities. WakeMed is a network of medical centers including three acute care hospitals and a physical rehabilitation hospital, outpatient and emergency clinics, rehabilitation facilities, skilled nursing centers, laboratories, physicians' offices, and home care service agencies. Its hospitals, the WakeMed Raleigh Campus, WakeMed North Hospital, WakeMed Cary Hospital, as well as WakeMed Rehabilitation Hospital, include specialty divisions such as heart care, stroke, trauma, critical care, diabetes, asthma, and children's and women's centers. Combined, its facilities offer more than 940 beds. WakeMed also conducts research and medical training programs.

Auditors : PLANTE & MORAN PLLC GRAND RA

LOCATIONS

HQ: WAKEMED
3000 NEW BERN AVE STE G10, RALEIGH, NC 276101231
Phone: 919 350-8000
Web: WWW.WAKEMED.ORG

PRODUCTS/OPERATIONS

Selected North Carolina Facilities
Blue Ridge Surgery Center (Raleigh)
Brier Creek Healthplex (Raleigh)
Knightdale Medical Building (Knightdale)
WakeMed Apex Healthplex (Apex)
WakeMed Brier Creek Medical Park (Raleigh)
WakeMed Cary Hospital (Cary)
WakeMed Clayton Medical Park (Clayton)
WakeMed Fuquay-Varina Outpatient and Skilled Nursing Facility (Fuquay-Varina)
WakeMed Garner HealthPlex (Garner)
WakeMed Home Health (Raleigh)
WakeMed North Healthplex (Raleigh)
WakeMed Raleigh Campus (Raleigh)
    WakeMed Rehab Hospital (Raleigh)
WakeMed Wake Forest Road Outpatient Rehab Center (Raleigh)
WakeMed Zebulon/Wendell Outpatient and Skilled Nursing Facility (Zebulon)

COMPETITORS

ARROWHEAD REGIONAL MEDICAL CENTER
BETHESDA HOSPITAL, INC.
CAROMONT HEALTH, INC.
CHRISTUS SPOHN HEALTH SYSTEM CORPORATION
FIRSTHEALTH OF THE CAROLINAS, INC.
HUNTINGTON HOSPITAL DOLAN FAMILY HEALTH CENTER, INC.
KENNESTONE HOSPITAL AT WINDY HILL, INC.
MARION COMMUNITY HOSPITAL, INC.
MULTICARE HEALTH SYSTEM
SUBURBAN HOSPITAL, INC.

HISTORICAL FINANCIALS
Company Type: Private

Income Statement — FYE: September 30

	REVENUE ($mil)	NET INCOME ($mil)	NET PROFIT MARGIN	EMPLOYEES
09/21	1,481	34	2.3%	16,933
09/15	1,065	(32)	—	—
Annual Growth	5.7%	—	—	—

2021 Year-End Financials
Return on assets: 2.3%   Cash ($ mil.): 62
Return on equity: 5.8%
Current Ratio: 4.50

WALSH CONSTRUCTION COMPANY

Auditors : WOLF & COMPANY LLP OAKBROOK

LOCATIONS

HQ: WALSH CONSTRUCTION COMPANY
5960 N BROADWAY ST, CHICAGO, IL 606603524
Phone: 312 563-5400
Web: WWW.WALSHCONSTRUCTION.COM

HISTORICAL FINANCIALS
Company Type: Private

Income Statement — FYE: December 31

	REVENUE ($mil)	NET INCOME ($mil)	NET PROFIT MARGIN	EMPLOYEES
12/10	1,627	35	2.2%	3,000
12/09	1,711	56	3.3%	—
12/08	1,847	68	3.7%	—
Annual Growth	(6.2%)	(27.7%)	—	—

2010 Year-End Financials
Return on assets: 4.7%   Cash ($ mil.): 281
Return on equity: 14.1%
Current Ratio: 1.50

WALTON CONSTRUCTION - A CORE COMPANY, LLC

EXECUTIVES

Managing Member, James K Jacobs

LOCATIONS

HQ: WALTON CONSTRUCTION - A CORE COMPANY, LLC
2 COMMERCE CT, NEW ORLEANS, LA 701233225
Phone: 504 733-2212

HISTORICAL FINANCIALS
Company Type: Private

Income Statement — FYE: December 31

	REVENUE ($mil)	NET INCOME ($mil)	NET PROFIT MARGIN	EMPLOYEES
12/08	695	0	0.0%	700
12/07	626	0	0.0%	—
12/06	0	0	—	—
12/05	0	0	—	—
Annual Growth	—	—	—	—

2008 Year-End Financials
Return on assets: 15.8%   Cash ($ mil.): 4
Return on equity: —
Current Ratio: 1.20

WALTON FAMILY FOUNDATION INC

LOCATIONS

HQ: WALTON FAMILY FOUNDATION INC
125 W CENTRAL AVE RM 218, BENTONVILLE, AR 727125248
Phone: 479 273-5605
Web: WWW.WALTONFAMILYFOUNDATION.ORG

HISTORICAL FINANCIALS
Company Type: Private

Income Statement — FYE: December 31

	REVENUE ($mil)	NET INCOME ($mil)	NET PROFIT MARGIN	EMPLOYEES
12/09	740	368	49.8%	7
12/08	421	244	58.0%	—
12/00	244	190	78.0%	—
Annual Growth	13.1%	7.6%	—	—

2009 Year-End Financials
Return on assets: 20.2%   Cash ($ mil.): 24
Return on equity: 20.2%
Current Ratio: —

WASHINGTON HEALTHCARE PHYSICIANS, MARY

Auditors : PBMARES LLP FREDERICKSBURG V

LOCATIONS

HQ: WASHINGTON HEALTHCARE PHYSICIANS, MARY
2300 FALL HILL AVE # 101, FREDERICKSBURG, VA 224013342
Phone: 540 741-1100
Web: WWW.MARYWASHINGTONHEALTHCARE.COM

HISTORICAL FINANCIALS
Company Type: Private

Income Statement — FYE: December 31

	REVENUE ($mil)	NET INCOME ($mil)	NET PROFIT MARGIN	EMPLOYEES
12/19*	734	28	3.9%	15
06/18	328	1	0.4%	—
12/16	610	30	5.0%	—
12/15	584	17	3.1%	—
Annual Growth	5.9%	12.6%	—	—

*Fiscal year change

2019 Year-End Financials
Return on assets: 6.1%   Cash ($ mil.): —
Return on equity: 17.7%
Current Ratio: 0.50

WASHINGTON HOSPITAL CENTER CORPORATION

Washington Hospital Center (doing business as MedStar Washington Hospital Center) may be the official hospital of the Washington Redskins, but you don't have to be a professional football player to make use of the facility's services. The hospital, at the heart of the MedStar Health system, serves some 500,000 patients living in and around the nation's capital each year. Washington Hospital Center has 912 beds and includes specialized care centers for cancer, cardiovascular conditions, and stroke. Other offerings include organ transplantation, a regional burn treatment center, and emergency air transportation. MedStar Washington also conducts clinical research and offers educational residency and fellowship programs.

Operations

MedStar Washington has about 1,350 doctors and dentists on staff; many of whom are involved in Washington Hospital Center's 520 clinical research studies. The hospital is affiliated with the medical schools of The George Washington University, Georgetown University, Johns Hopkins, and several other regional educational institutions. Its Cardiac Ventricular Assist Device program is accredited by The Joint Commission.

The hospital is also home to MedSTAR, one of the country's top shock-trauma and medevac programs, and also operates the region's only adult burn center.

MedStar Washington has some 390,000 outpatient and 37,000 inpatient visits each year. It also provides care for some 3,500 births and some 87,000 emergency department visits.

Strategy
Company Background

Washington Hospital Center was created through the merger of three regional hospitals: Emergency, Garfield, and Episcopal Eye, Ear and Throat. The actual idea of the Hospital Center was conceived in 1943, but it took nearly 15 years for funding, planning, and construction to be completed.

LOCATIONS

HQ: WASHINGTON HOSPITAL CENTER CORPORATION
110 IRVING ST NW, WASHINGTON, DC 200103017
Phone: 855 546-1686
Web: WWW.MEDSTARHEALTH.ORG

COMPETITORS

ASCENSION PROVIDENCE ROCHESTER HOSPITAL
BEACON MEDICAL GROUP, INC.
CONTINUUM HEALTH PARTNERS, INC.
HAMOT HEALTH FOUNDATION
MERITER HEALTH SERVICES, INC.
MILES HEALTH CARE, INC
STAMFORD HEALTH SYSTEM, INC.
THE CHILDREN'S HOSPITAL OF PHILADELPHIA
THE UNIVERSITY OF CHICAGO MEDICAL CENTER
TRIHEALTH, INC.

HISTORICAL FINANCIALS
Company Type: Private

Income Statement — FYE: June 30

	REVENUE ($mil)	NET INCOME ($mil)	NET PROFIT MARGIN	EMPLOYEES
06/16	1,166	35	3.1%	5,637
06/15	1,121	23	2.1%	—
06/14	1,107	22	2.1%	—
06/08	1,028	14	1.4%	—
Annual Growth	1.6%	12.3%	—	—

2016 Year-End Financials
Return on assets: 6.6% Cash ($ mil.): —
Return on equity: 10.6%
Current Ratio: 1.20

WASHINGTON SUBURBAN SANITARY COMMISSION (INC)

Washington Suburban Sanitary Commission (WSSC) provides water and wastewater services in Maryland's Montgomery and Prince George's counties, just outside the nation's capital. WSSC serves around 474,000 customers, representing 2 million residents, in an area of about 1,000 square miles. The agency draws water from the Potomac and Patuxtent rivers and maintains three reservoirs. The commission also operates two water filtration plants, six wastewater treatment plants, and some 11,000 miles of sewer and water main lines, including a network of nearly 5,600 miles of fresh water pipeline and over 5,400 miles of sewer pipeline. WSSC was established in 1918.

EXECUTIVES

Internal Auditor*, Mel Schwartz
Auditors: BCA WATSON RICE LLP WASHINGTO

LOCATIONS

HQ: WASHINGTON SUBURBAN SANITARY COMMISSION (INC)
14501 SWEITZER LN, LAUREL, MD 207075901
Phone: 301 206-8000
Web: WWW.WSSCWATER.COM

COMPETITORS

ARTESIAN RESOURCES CORPORATION
COLORADO SPRINGS UTILITIES
DEE VALLEY GROUP LIMITED
DENVER BOARD OF WATER COMMISSIONERS
PENNSYLVANIA - AMERICAN WATER COMPANY
SAN ANTONIO WATER SYSTEM
SJW GROUP
SOUTHERN WATER SERVICES LIMITED
THE YORK WATER COMPANY
VEOLIA WATER NORTH AMERICA OPERATING SERVICES, LLC

HISTORICAL FINANCIALS
Company Type: Private

Income Statement — FYE: June 30

	REVENUE ($mil)	NET INCOME ($mil)	NET PROFIT MARGIN	EMPLOYEES
06/22	837	149	17.9%	2,000
06/21	749	49	6.6%	—
06/20	749	23	3.2%	—
06/19	742	139	18.8%	—
Annual Growth	4.1%	2.3%	—	—

2022 Year-End Financials
Return on assets: 1.5% Cash ($ mil.): 30
Return on equity: 2.9%
Current Ratio: 0.90

WASHOE COUNTY SCHOOL DISTRICT

LOCATIONS

HQ: WASHOE COUNTY SCHOOL DISTRICT
425 E 9TH ST, RENO, NV 895122800
Phone: 775 348-0200
Web: WWW.WASHOESCHOOLS.NET

HISTORICAL FINANCIALS
Company Type: Private

Income Statement — FYE: June 30

	REVENUE ($mil)	NET INCOME ($mil)	NET PROFIT MARGIN	EMPLOYEES
06/21	759	2	0.4%	7,000
06/19	713	(95)	—	—
06/18	683	190	27.8%	—
06/17	640	57	8.9%	—
Annual Growth	4.4%	(52.4%)	—	—

2021 Year-End Financials
Return on assets: 0.1% Cash ($ mil.): —
Return on equity: —
Current Ratio: 3.60

WELCH FOODS INC., A COOPERATIVE

Welch Fooods is a co-op owned by more than 700 American farming families across the country who bring their best to every harvest. The company produces the Welch's brand grape and white grape juices. Its beverage line includes sparkling juices and cocktails. Welch supplies fresh grapes and snacks as well as preserved offerings (jellies, jams, and spreads). Its products are made from Concord and Niagara grapes grown at family farms across the US. The company was

HOOVER'S HANDBOOK OF PRIVATE COMPANIES 2023

founded in 1849 by Ephraim Bull when he grows the first Concord grape on his farm in Massachusetts.

Operations
Welch Foods offers juices, fruit jams, jellies, spreads, and cocktails primarily made from grapes. It also offers snacks from fresh fruit slushies to gummy snacks to frozen mixed fruit.

Geographic Reach
Massachusetts-based Welch Foods has vineyards in Cincinnati, Ohio; Grandview, Washington; Lawton, Michigan; North East, Pennsylvania; Rogers, Arizona; and Westfield, New York.

Financial Performance
National Grape Cooperative and Welch Foods's sales grew to $608.5 million in 2014. Volume grew 4% during the year, with its Bottled 100% Juice product leading the way with 11% growth, though all core product categories showed market share and volume growth. Spread sales grew by 7% during the year, while refrigerated juices grew by 8%.

The cooperative's net proceeds jumped significantly to $84 million in FY2014, the second highest level in its history, according to the company.

Company Background
In 1869 Dr. Thomas Bramwell Welch pasteurized Concord grape juice to create a non-alcoholic alternative to wine for his church. The beverage was a hit at the World's Fair in Chicago in 1893 and by 1923 Concord grape jelly was introduced.

The farmers who grew grapes for Welch's took ownership of the company and began operating it as a co-op in 1952.

EXECUTIVES
CMO, David Eisen

LOCATIONS
HQ: WELCH FOODS INC., A COOPERATIVE
575 VIRGINIA RD, CONCORD, MA 017422761
Phone: 978 371-1000
Web: WWW.WELCHS.COM

PRODUCTS/OPERATIONS
Selected Brands and Products
BAMA
   Jams, jellies, and preserves
   Peanut butter
Welch
   Bottled and canned juices
   Dried fruit
   Fresh table grapes
   Frozen juices
   Fruit juice bars
   Jams, jellies, and preserves
   Pourable concentrated juices
   Refrigerated juices
   Single-serve juices

COMPETITORS
BELL-CARTER FOODS, LLC
BIRDS EYE FOODS, INC.
MOTT'S LLP
NATIONAL GRAPE CO-OPERATIVE ASSOCIATION, INC.
ODWALLA, INC.
REED'S, INC.
SENECA FOODS CORPORATION
SUNKIST GROWERS, INC.
THE J M SMUCKER COMPANY
TROPICANA PRODUCTS, INC.

HISTORICAL FINANCIALS
Company Type: Private

Income Statement   FYE: August 31

	REVENUE ($mil)	NET INCOME ($mil)	NET PROFIT MARGIN	EMPLOYEES
08/16	600	83	14.0%	1,000
08/15	609	81	13.3%	—
08/14	609	76	12.6%	—
08/13	608	65	10.7%	—
Annual Growth	(0.5%)	8.8%	—	—

2016 Year-End Financials
Return on assets: 20.6%   Cash ($ mil.): 7
Return on equity: 233.2%
Current Ratio: 1.40

WELLMONT HEALTH SYSTEM

At Wellmont Health System, wellness is paramount. Wellmont Health System provides general and advanced medical-surgical care to residents of northeastern Tennessee and southwestern Virginia. The health system consists of about a dozen owned and affiliated hospitals that collectively have more than 1,000 licensed beds. One of its facilities is a rehabilitation hospital operated in partnership with HealthSouth. The system's Holston Valley Medical Center features a level I trauma center and a level III neonatal intensive care unit (NICU). Wellmont also operates numerous ancillary facilities, including an assisted living center, a mental health clinic, home health care and hospice agencies, and outpatient centers.

Operations
Today, Wellmont is one of the region's largest employers with a staff of more than 6,500 medical professionals. Nearly 600 physicians deliver care at Wellmont's facilities that include eight hospitals in Tennessee and Virginia. Other facilities include an outpatient surgery center, a child development center, a cancer center, urgent care centers, and a health network of physicians that include occupational health providers. The hospital also offers urgent care transportation with its Wellmont One Air Transport.

Wellmont is the only health system in Tennessee to offer two major trauma centers (at Holston Valley Medical Center in Kingsport and Bristol Regional Medical Center in Bristol).

Sales and Marketing
Medicare payments accounted for nearly 85% of Wellmont's net patient revenue in fiscal 2013 (ended June); Medicaid and TennCare (Tennessee's state Medicaid program) each accounted for nearly 10%.

Financial Performance
Revenue increased 1% to $798 million in fiscal 2013 (ended June) on higher net patient revenue. However, patient volumes were mixed: Some categories declined while others increased. For example, emergency department visits dropped 7% as more patients chose to visit the system's more affordable urgent care centers.

Net income rose significantly that year, increasing 79% to $47 million. This was due to a change in net unrealized gains on investments and a change in the funded status of benefit plans. Cash flow from operations fell 5% to $74 million.

Strategy
Wellmont has expanded by opening new outpatient facilities, including a new physical therapy clinic in 2013, and by acquiring existing medical facilities. For example, in 2015 it agreed to buy out Adventist Health in their partnership owning Takoma Regional Hospital in Tennessee. The system also expands its service territory by partnering with other area care providers.

In 2014, the company migrated to a new electronic medical records (EMR) system, replacing its four existing EHR platforms.

Mergers and Acquisitions
In 2015 Wellmont announced plans to merge with a neighboring health system, Mountain States Health Alliance. By combining operations, the two systems hope to better provide care for communities in northeast Tennessee as well as Virginia, Kentucky, and North Carolina. The states of Tennessee and Virginia have to approve the transaction.

Company Background
Founded in 1996, Wellmont has grown over the years primarily through acquisitions including Lee Regional Medical Center, Mountain View Regional Medical Center, and Takoma Regional Hospital (through a partnership with Adventist Health).

EXECUTIVES
CMO*, Dale Sargent
Auditors: KPMG LLP NASHVILLE TENNESSEE

LOCATIONS
HQ: WELLMONT HEALTH SYSTEM
1905 AMERICAN WAY, KINGSPORT, TN 376605882
Phone: 423 230-8200
Web: WWW.BALLADHEALTH.ORG

PRODUCTS/OPERATIONS
Selected Facilities
Bristol Regional Medical Center (Bristol, Tennessee)
Hancock County Hospital (Sneedville, Tennessee)
Hawkins County Memorial Hospital (Rogersville, Tennessee)
HealthSouth Rehabilitation Hospital of Kingsport (HealthSouth partnership; Kingsport, Tennessee)
Holston Valley Medical Center (Kingsport, Tennessee)

Lee Regional Medical Center (Pennington Gap, Virginia)
Lonesome Pine Hospital (Big Stone Gap, Virginia)
Mountain View Regional Medical Center (Norton, Virginia)
Takoma Regional Hospital (Greeneville, Tennessee)

Selected Services
Cancer Care
Children
Diabetes
Emergency and Trauma
Family Medicine
Hearing Services
Heart Care
Home Care
Hospice
Hospitalists
Marsh Regional Blood Center
Neurology
Occupational Medicine
Orthopedics
Palliative Care
Psychiatry
Radiology
Rehabilitation and Therapy
Sleep Medicine
Stroke Care
Surgical Services
Weight Loss
Women's Health

COMPETITORS

ALLINA HEALTH SYSTEM
EAST TEXAS MEDICAL CENTER REGIONAL HEALTHCARE SYSTEM
NORTHWELL HEALTH, INC.
NORTON HEALTHCARE, INC.
NOVANT HEALTH, INC.
SALINAS VALLEY MEMORIAL HEALTHCARE SYSTEMS
THE RUTLAND HOSPITAL INC ACT 220
UNIVERSITY HOSPITALS HEALTH SYSTEM, INC.
WELLSPAN HEALTH
WELLSTAR HEALTH SYSTEM, INC.

HISTORICAL FINANCIALS
Company Type: Private

Income Statement — FYE: June 30

	REVENUE ($mil)	NET INCOME ($mil)	NET PROFIT MARGIN	EMPLOYEES
06/21	807	91	11.4%	6,114
06/17	908	53	5.9%	—
Annual Growth	(2.9%)	14.4%	—	—

2021 Year-End Financials
Return on assets: 19.3% Cash ($ mil.): —
Return on equity: 47.6%
Current Ratio: 0.70

WELLS REAL ESTATE INVESTMENT TRUST II

Auditors : DELOITTE & TOUCHE LLP ATLANT

LOCATIONS
HQ: WELLS REAL ESTATE INVESTMENT TRUST II
1 GLENLAKE PKWY STE 1200, ATLANTA, GA 303287267
Phone: 404 465-2200
Web: WWW.WELLSREITII.COM

HISTORICAL FINANCIALS
Company Type: Private

Income Statement — FYE: December 31

	REVENUE ($mil)	NET INCOME ($mil)	NET PROFIT MARGIN	EMPLOYEES
12/12	576	48	8.3%	9
12/11	613	56	9.2%	—
Annual Growth	(5.9%)	(15.2%)	—	—

2012 Year-End Financials
Return on assets: — Cash ($ mil.): —
Return on equity: 8.3%
Current Ratio: 0.10

WELLSPAN MEDICAL GROUP

Auditors : ERNEST & YOUNG LLP BALTIMORE

LOCATIONS
HQ: WELLSPAN MEDICAL GROUP
140 N DUKE ST, YORK, PA 174011170
Phone: 717 851-6515
Web: WWW.WELLSPAN.ORG

HISTORICAL FINANCIALS
Company Type: Private

Income Statement — FYE: June 30

	REVENUE ($mil)	NET INCOME ($mil)	NET PROFIT MARGIN	EMPLOYEES
06/20	567	(13)	—	709
06/16	375	(43)	—	—
06/15	336	(36)	—	—
06/14	251	(25)	—	—
Annual Growth	14.5%	—	—	—

2020 Year-End Financials
Return on assets: (-10.3%) Cash ($ mil.): —
Return on equity: (-53.3%)
Current Ratio: 0.70

WESCO AIRCRAFT HOLDINGS, INC.

Incora, formerly Wesco Aircraft and Pattonair, is a leading, independent distributor and global provider of innovative supply chain solutions. Beginning with a strong foundation in aerospace and defense, Incora also utilizes its supply chain expertise to serve automotive, healthcare, energy, electronics, pest control, industrial equipment manufacturing, marine, pharmaceuticals and beyond. Incora incorporates itself into customers' businesses, managing all aspects of supply chain from procurement and inventory management to logistics and on-site customer services. With more than 644,000 SKUs, the company serves more than 8,400 customers globally.

Operations

Incora divides its operations across five main product lines: hardware, chemicals, electronic components, tooling, machined and fabricated parts, and other products. The company sources its inventory from over 7,000 suppliers.

Geographic Reach

The company is headquartered in Fort Worth, Texas, with a global footprint that includes about 70 locations in more than 15 countries.

Sales and Marketing

Incora markets its products and services to a diverse range of industries such as aerospace, automotive, pharmaceuticals, deference and more. The company also sales its products through online eCommerce store.

EXECUTIVES

CCO*, Declan Grant
PEOPLE DIVERSITY*, Kevin Erickson
CCO*, Dave Fawcett
CIO*, Ryan Worobel
Auditors : PRICEWATERHOUSECOOPERS LLP LO

LOCATIONS

HQ: WESCO AIRCRAFT HOLDINGS, INC.
2601 MEACHAM BLVD STE 400, FORT WORTH, TX 761374213
Phone: 817 284-4449
Web: WWW.INCORA.COM

2016 Sales

	$ mil.	% of total
North America	1,185.3	80
Rest of World	292.1	20
Total	1,477.4	100

2016 Sales

	$ mil.	% of total
United States of America	1,087.7	74
United Kingdom	195.5	13
Other foreign counties	194.2	13
Total	1,477.4	100

PRODUCTS/OPERATIONS

2016 Sales

	$ mil.	% of total
Hardware	711.2	48
Chemicals	600.1	41
Electronic components	105.2	7
Bearings	34.7	2
Machined parts and other	26.2	2
Total	1,477.4	100

PRODUCTS
HARDWARE
Blind fasteners
Bolts and screws
Clamps
Hi lok pins and collars
Hydraulic fittings
Inserts
Lockbolts and collars
Nuts
Panel fasteners
Rivets
Springs
Valves
Washers
CHEMICALS
Adhesives
Cleaners and cleaning solvents

Coolants and metalworking fluids
Industrial gases
Lubricants
Oil and grease
Paints and coatings
Sealants and tapes
ELECTRONIC COMPONENTS
Circuit breakers
Connectors
Interconnect accessories
Lighted products
Relays
Switches
Wire and cable
BEARINGS
Airframe control bearings
Ball bearing
Bushings
Needle roller bearings
Precision bearings
Rod ends
Spherical bearings
OTHER PRODUCTS
Brackets
Installation tooling
Milled parts
Shims
Stampings
Turned parts
Welded assemblies

COMPETITORS

ATLAS VENTURE, INC.
CONDUENT INCORPORATED
CTS CORPORATION
EVERTEC, INC
FASTENAL COMPANY
INA-Holding Schaeffler GmbH & Co. KG
INNERWORKINGS, INC.
JANUS CAPITAL GROUP INC.
MASTEC, INC.
RECALL CORPORATION

HISTORICAL FINANCIALS

Company Type: Private

Income Statement — FYE: September 30

	REVENUE ($mil)	NET INCOME ($mil)	NET PROFIT MARGIN	EMPLOYEES
09/19	1,696	21	1.3%	3,527
09/18	1,570	32	2.1%	—
09/17	1,429	(237)	—	—
09/16	1,477	91	6.2%	—
Annual Growth	4.7%	(38.4%)	—	—

2019 Year-End Financials
Return on assets: 1.2% Cash ($ mil.): 38
Return on equity: 3.0%
Current Ratio: 3.60

WESLEY MEDICAL CENTER, LLC

LOCATIONS

HQ: WESLEY MEDICAL CENTER, LLC
550 N HILLSIDE ST, WICHITA, KS 672149976
Phone: 316 962-2000
Web: WWW.WESLEYMC.COM

HISTORICAL FINANCIALS

Company Type: Private

Income Statement — FYE: December 31

	REVENUE ($mil)	NET INCOME ($mil)	NET PROFIT MARGIN	EMPLOYEES
12/17	608	80	13.3%	40
12/16	555	56	10.3%	—
12/15	545	60	11.1%	—
12/14	520	88	17.0%	—
Annual Growth	5.3%	(3.0%)	—	—

2017 Year-End Financials
Return on assets: 17.2% Cash ($ mil.): —
Return on equity: 29.7%
Current Ratio: 6.50

WEST PENN POWER COMPANY

LOCATIONS

HQ: WEST PENN POWER COMPANY
76 S MAIN ST BSMT, AKRON, OH 443081817
Phone: 800 686-0021
Web: WWW.FIRSTENERGYCORP.COM

HISTORICAL FINANCIALS

Company Type: Private

Income Statement — FYE: December 31

	REVENUE ($mil)	NET INCOME ($mil)	NET PROFIT MARGIN	EMPLOYEES
12/17	1,009	110	11.0%	11
12/16	1,020	116	11.4%	—
Annual Growth	(1.1%)	(5.0%)	—	—

2017 Year-End Financials
Return on assets: 4.1% Cash ($ mil.): —
Return on equity: 13.6%
Current Ratio: 1.60

WEST VIRGINIA UNIVERSITY HOSPITALS, INC.

West Virginia University Hospitals (WVUH) has West Virginians covered. The health care system's 530-bed main campus includes the Ruby Memorial Hospital, the WVU Children's Hospital, and the behavioral health Chestnut Ridge Center, as well as outpatient care centers.Â Other services include centers for eye and dental care, cancer treatment, and family medicine. WVUH's facilities serve as the primary teaching locations for the West Virginia University's health professions schools. Cheat Lake Physicians is the physicians group associated with the health system. WVUH is a member of the West Virginia United Health System.

Strategy

To increase its capacity for patient services, WVUH launched a $230 million project to build a new tower addition at its main Ruby MemorialÂ Hospital facility in 2012. The project will add about 115 general inpatient beds.

WVUH is also working to expand its community outreach capabilities and lower the cost of inpatient care through technology initiatives. The health system is adding a number of tele-health services, including psychiatry and stroke programs that allow patients to communicate with doctors via video conferencing systems. These services especially help residents living in rural settings.

Auditors : DIXON HUGHES GOODMAN LLP CHAR

LOCATIONS

HQ: WEST VIRGINA UNIVERSITY HOSPITALS, INC.
1 MEDICAL CENTER DR, MORGANTOWN, WV 265061200
Phone: 304 598-4000
Web: WWW.WVUCANCER.ORG

COMPETITORS

DALLAS COUNTY HOSPITAL DISTRICT
GREATER BALTIMORE MEDICAL CENTER, INC.
PITT COUNTY MEMORIAL HOSPITAL, INCORPORATED
THE NEBRASKA MEDICAL CENTER
UNIVERSITY HEALTH SYSTEMS OF EASTERN CAROLINA, INC.

HISTORICAL FINANCIALS

Company Type: Private

Income Statement — FYE: December 31

	REVENUE ($mil)	NET INCOME ($mil)	NET PROFIT MARGIN	EMPLOYEES
12/20	1,452	57	3.9%	6,267
12/18	1,193	(39)	—	—
12/12	1,386	96	6.9%	—
12/06	0	0	—	—
Annual Growth	—	—	—	—

2020 Year-End Financials
Return on assets: 2.9% Cash ($ mil.): 229
Return on equity: 6.5%
Current Ratio: 2.10

WEST VIRGINIA UNITED HEALTH SYSTEM, INC.

West Virginia United Health System (WVUHS) helps residents in the Mountain State stay on top of their health.Â The systemÂ operates United Hospital Center (in Clarksburg), as well asÂ hospitals inÂ the West Virginia University Hospitals (WVUH) system, including City Hospital (Martinsburg),

Jefferson Memorial Hospital (Ranson), and WVUH's home hospital in Morgantown.Â In addition, WVUHS operates WVUH's Cheat Lake physicians ambulatory center, as well as a network of about a dozen primary care clinics located throughout central and northern West Virginia. Combined, the system's hospitals and clinics have more than 1000 beds and treat approximately 1.4 million patients annually.

Auditors : DIXON HUGHES GOODMAN LLP CHAR

LOCATIONS

HQ: WEST VIRGINIA UNITED HEALTH SYSTEM, INC.
1 MEDICAL CENTER DR, MORGANTOWN, WV 265061200
Phone: 304 598-4000
Web: WWW.WVUMEDICINE.ORG

PRODUCTS/OPERATIONS

Selected facilities
Barbour Country Family Medicine
Bridgeport Physicians Care
Chestnut Ridge Center
City Hospital
Doddridge Family Medicine
Elk Memorial Clinic
Harrisville Medical Center
Jefferson Memorial Hospital
Lumberport Family Medicine
Oakland Family Medicine Center
Pennsboro Medical Center
Pinewood Medical Center
Shinnston Healthcare Clinic
United Hospital Center
United Summit Center
WVU Hospitals

COMPETITORS

BAYCARE HEALTH SYSTEM, INC.
CAPITAL DIVISION, INC.
GENESIS HEALTH SYSTEM
HERITAGE VALLEY HEALTH SYSTEM, INC.
MARTHA JEFFERSON HEALTH SERVICES CORPORATION
MERCY HEALTH NETWORK, INC.
MILES HEALTH CARE, INC
MOUNTAIN STATES HEALTH ALLIANCE
NORTH MISSISSIPPI HEALTH SERVICES, INC.
RIVERSIDE HEALTHCARE ASSOCIATION, INC.

HISTORICAL FINANCIALS
Company Type: Private

Income Statement — FYE: December 31

	REVENUE ($mil)	NET INCOME ($mil)	NET PROFIT MARGIN	EMPLOYEES
12/20	3,122	213	6.8%	7,000
12/19	2,770	238	8.6%	—
12/17	2,172	132	6.1%	—
12/16	1,877	103	5.5%	—
Annual Growth	13.6%	20.0%	—	—

2020 Year-End Financials
Return on assets: 5.2%   Cash ($ mil.): 729
Return on equity: 11.8%
Current Ratio: 2.00

WEST VIRGINIA UNIVERSITY

LOCATIONS

HQ: WEST VIRGINIA UNIVERSITY
1501 UNIVERSITY AVE, MORGANTOWN, WV 265055523
Phone: 304 293-0111
Web: WWW.WVU.EDU

HISTORICAL FINANCIALS
Company Type: Private

Income Statement — FYE: June 30

	REVENUE ($mil)	NET INCOME ($mil)	NET PROFIT MARGIN	EMPLOYEES
06/21	775	127	16.5%	565
06/20	797	45	5.8%	—
Annual Growth	(2.8%)	178.0%	—	—

2021 Year-End Financials
Return on assets: 5.0%   Cash ($ mil.): 107
Return on equity: 10.3%
Current Ratio: 1.50

WEST VIRGINIA UNIVERSITY

West Virginia University (WVU) is the intellectual home of more than 29,000 Mountaineers (the school's mascot) and the state's preeminent institution of higher learning. WVU offers more than 180 bachelor's, master's, doctoral, and professional degree programs through some 15 colleges and schools. The university's clinical psychology and forestry programs have been recognized nationally and it boasts 100% post-graduate job placement for its nursing, pharmacy, and mining engineering majors. WVU also runs a two-year, residential school, Potomac State College, in Keyser, West Virginia.

Operations
Its 1,099 acres campus university offers a joint petroleum and natural gas engineering major. It also operates eight experimental farms and four forests throughout the state, in addition to WVU Jackson's Mill State 4-H Camp and Lifelong Learning Center near Weston. Some 93% of its full-time faculty have earned doctorates or first-professional degrees in their disciplines. More than 800 students traveled to another country for study abroad courses in the 2011-12 academic year. Undergraduate tuition and fees for the 2012-13 year was reported as $9,808.

WVU is an independent operating unit of the West Virginia Higher Education Fund.

Geographic Reach
The university's main campus is in Morgantown. It also has divisional campuses in Charleston, Keyser, Martinsburg, and Montgomery.

Financial Performance
The university reported a 4% increase in revenues in 2012 due to a growth in capital grants and gifts revenue, tuition, and fees, as well as revenues from auxiliary enterprise, gifts, and other sources. Capital grants and gifts increased by $55.9 million thanks to a donation of a master license agreement from Siemens PLM for educational software. Tuition and fees increased by $19.9 million in 2012 thanks to a fee rate hike and an increase in non-resident student enrollment. Auxiliary revenues grew by $12.2 million due to an increase in revenues from room and dining services, auxiliary fees, and athletics revenues. Organic growth has lifted the company's revenues since 2009.

Net income increased by 51% in 2012 due to a growth in other net non-operating revenues of $3.2 million as a result of a settlement agreement in the amount of $7.2 million, partially offset by operating revenues.

Strategy
In addition to WVU's campus-based activities, the university is focusing on expanding its online and distance learning options to increase educational access and research activities.

Company Background
WVU was founded in 1867 as a public land-grant institution. It one of only 11 schools in the US that are land-grant, doctoral research universities with a comprehensive medical school.

EXECUTIVES

Advisor TO THE, Jay Cole Special
Auditors : CLIFTONLARSONALLEN LLP PLYMOU

LOCATIONS

HQ: WEST VIRGINIA UNIVERSITY
1500 UNIVERSITY AVE, MORGANTOWN, WV 26506
Phone: 304 293-2545
Web: WWW.WVU.EDU

PRODUCTS/OPERATIONS

Selected Colleges and Schools
Benjamin M. Statler College of Engineering and Mineral Resources
College of Business and Economics
College of Creative Arts
College of Education and Human Services
College of Law
College of Physical Activity and Sport Sciences
Davis College of Agriculture, Natural Resources, and Design
Eberly College of Arts and Sciences
Perley Isaac Reed School of Journalism
Potomac State College of WVU
School of Dentistry
School of Medicine
School of Nursing
School of Pharmacy
School of Public Health
WVU Institute of Technology

COMPETITORS

DELAWARE STATE UNIVERSITY
IOWA STATE UNIVERSITY OF SCIENCE AND TECHNOLOGY
MONTANA STATE UNIVERSITY, INC
PURDUE UNIVERSITY
THE UNIVERSITY OF MEMPHIS
TRUSTEES OF INDIANA UNIVERSITY
UNIVERSITY OF NEW ORLEANS
VIRGINIA POLYTECHNIC INSTITUTE AND STATE UNIVERSITY
WAYNE STATE UNIVERSITY
YOUNGSTOWN STATE UNIVERSITY

HISTORICAL FINANCIALS
Company Type: Private

Income Statement — FYE: June 30

	REVENUE ($mil)	NET INCOME ($mil)	NET PROFIT MARGIN	EMPLOYEES
06/22	856	0	0.0%	6,245
06/18	808	41	5.1%	—
06/17	783	8	1.1%	—
Annual Growth	1.8%	(45.8%)	—	—

2022 Year-End Financials
Return on assets: —   Cash ($ mil.): 137
Return on equity: —
Current Ratio: 1.40

WESTCHESTER COUNTY HEALTH CARE CORPORATION

EXECUTIVES
1st*, Mitchell Hochberg
Auditors: GRANT THORNTON LLP NEW YORK

LOCATIONS
HQ: WESTCHESTER COUNTY HEALTH CARE CORPORATION
100 WOODS RD, VALHALLA, NY 105951530
Phone: 914 493-7000
Web: WWW.WESTCHESTERMEDICALCENTER.ORG

HISTORICAL FINANCIALS
Company Type: Private

Income Statement — FYE: December 31

	REVENUE ($mil)	NET INCOME ($mil)	NET PROFIT MARGIN	EMPLOYEES
12/21	1,869	44	2.4%	12,252
12/20	1,536	(65)	—	—
12/19	1,718	12	0.7%	—
12/18	1,641	(10)	—	—
Annual Growth	4.4%	—	—	—

2021 Year-End Financials
Return on assets: 2.1%   Cash ($ mil.): 236
Return on equity: —
Current Ratio: 1.20

WESTERN FARMERS ELECTRIC COOPERATIVE

Power also comes sweeping down the plain in Oklahoma thanks to the Western Farmers Electric Cooperative. Led by its coal- and natural gas-fueled generating plants -- three in Anadarko, one in Mooreland, and one in Hugo (all in Oklahoma) -- the generation and transmission co-op produces more than 1,845 MW of capacity. It pipes power over 3,700 miles of transmission lines to two-thirds of rural Oklahoma, and parts of New Mexico. It also operates 264 substations and 59 switch stations. Western Farmers Electric Cooperative, which is owned by its member distribution cooperatives, supplies 22 distribution co-ops and Altus Air Force base, which serve a total of a half million members.

Operations
The company maintains a well-balanced and diversified portfolio of generation resources reflecting a mix of technologies and fuel types. In 2013 coal represented 33% of Western Farmers Electric Cooperative's energy production, with natural gas at 12 percent. Power generated from wind resources represents about 14% of the coop's energy mix, hydro, 7%. Economy purchases, energy imbalance purchases, and contract power, (primarily natural gas), made up the balance.

Geographic Reach
Western Farmers Electric Cooperative's members consist of 22 distribution cooperatives (serving customers in Kansas, Oklahoma, New Mexico, and Texas) and the Altus Air Force Base in Oklahoma.

Financial Performance
In 2013 the company's revenues increased by 15% to $525.3 million due to a 7.7% energy sales increase. (Its average MWh sales growth rate of 5.5% over the past three year is above the national average). Western Farmers Electric Cooperative also gets a small amount of off-system sales from three of its four New Mexico members. Power sales increased $64 million in 2013 due to higher MWh sales, a slight increase in wholesale power rates, and a 40% rise in natural gas prices.

Western Farmers Electric Cooperative's net income increased by 61% in 2013 due to higher sales and an increase in noninterest income.

That year the company's operating cash inflow increased to $53.3 million (compared to $21.2 million in 2012) primarily due to higher net income and increased coal and oil inventory.

Strategy
Western Farmers Electric Cooperative has diversified its fuel mix to meet green energy regulations and boasts one of the state's largest renewable energy portfolios. The diversity in generation mix helps reduce exposure to changing market conditions, helping to keep rates competitive.

In 2013 the company signed a purchase with Apex Clean Energy, through its subsidiary Balko Wind, LLC, for 100 MW of wind energy from the Balko Wind Project. With this agreement, Apex has sold all the capacity of 300 MW project, which will produce enough electricity to power over 110,000 U.S. homes. This new site represents the fifth Oklahoma wind farm development that is a part of an ongoing commitment to diversify Western Farmers Electric Cooperative's portfolio of generation sources.

That year it also entered into a purchase and sale agreement with community-wind developer, National Renewable Solutions, to acquire the development assets for the Broadview Wind Projects in New Mexico. The two projects with a combined 19.8 MW capacity, will each sell power over the next 20 years to Western Farmers Electric Cooperative. This wind farm site is in the service territory of Western Farmers Electric Cooperative member Farmers' Electric Cooperative.

In 2012 the company teamed up with Enel Green Power, which that year began operating the 150-MW Rocky Ridge Wind Project in Kiowa and Washita counties, Oklahoma. The energy generated by the wind farm will be bought by Western Farmers Electric Cooperative.

In 2012 Calpine Corporation agreed to supply Western Farmers Electric Cooperative with electric generation capacity and power (up to 280 MW) from Calpine's gas-fired Oneta Energy Center from June 2014 through 2035.

Company Background
Growing its geographic coverage, in late 2010 Western Farmers Electric Cooperative added four New Mexico-based cooperatives (Farmers', Central Valley, Lea County and Roosevelt County, with a total of 400 MW of load) to its membership.

Responding to a growing demand for power, in 2009 the power co-op completed an expansion project at its gas-fueled Anadarko plant, adding some 145 MW of power generating capacity.

Western Farmers Electric Cooperative was organized in 1941 by western Oklahoma rural electric distribution cooperatives in order to secure power generation and distribution at an affordable rate. The co-op began generating power in 1950.

Auditors: KPMG LLP OKLAHOMA CITY OK

LOCATIONS
HQ: WESTERN FARMERS ELECTRIC COOPERATIVE
701 NE 7TH ST, ANADARKO, OK 730052297

Phone: 405 247-3351
Web: WWW.WFEC.COM

COMPETITORS

ARKANSAS ELECTRIC COOPERATIVE CORPORATION
ASSOCIATED ELECTRIC COOPERATIVE, INC.
GREAT RIVER ENERGY
SEMINOLE ELECTRIC COOPERATIVE, INC.
TRI-STATE GENERATION AND TRANSMISSION ASSOCIATION, INC.

HISTORICAL FINANCIALS
Company Type: Private

Income Statement — FYE: December 31

	REVENUE ($mil)	NET INCOME ($mil)	NET PROFIT MARGIN	EMPLOYEES
12/18	715	14	2.0%	378
12/17	686	13	2.0%	—
12/16	655	24	3.7%	—
12/15	671	31	4.6%	—
Annual Growth	2.2%	(22.8%)	—	—

2018 Year-End Financials
Return on assets: 1.0%   Cash ($ mil.): 14
Return on equity: 3.9%
Current Ratio: 1.10

WESTERN GOVERNORS UNIVERSITY

EXECUTIVES

Senior Vice President Technology, David Morales
Auditors : TANNER LLC SALT LAKE CITY UT

LOCATIONS

HQ: WESTERN GOVERNORS UNIVERSITY
4001 S 700 E STE 700, SALT LAKE CITY, UT 841072533
Phone: 801 428-5213
Web: WWW.WGU.EDU

HISTORICAL FINANCIALS
Company Type: Private

Income Statement — FYE: June 30

	REVENUE ($mil)	NET INCOME ($mil)	NET PROFIT MARGIN	EMPLOYEES
06/20	922	40	4.3%	530
06/19	855	62	7.3%	—
06/15	381	25	6.8%	—
06/14	297	24	8.3%	—
Annual Growth	20.8%	8.4%	—	—

2020 Year-End Financials
Return on assets: 7.7%   Cash ($ mil.): 48
Return on equity: 16.0%
Current Ratio: 0.40

WESTERN OREGON UNIVERSITY

LOCATIONS

HQ: WESTERN OREGON UNIVERSITY
345 MONMOUTH AVE N, MONMOUTH, OR 973611329
Phone: 503 838-8000
Web: WWW.WOU.EDU

HISTORICAL FINANCIALS
Company Type: Private

Income Statement — FYE: June 30

	REVENUE ($mil)	NET INCOME ($mil)	NET PROFIT MARGIN	EMPLOYEES
06/08	1,251	80	6.4%	706
06/06*	0	(0)	—	—
12/05	1	0	30.1%	—
06/04	1	0	22.9%	—
Annual Growth	483.6%	324.8%	—	—

*Fiscal year change

2008 Year-End Financials
Return on assets: —   Cash ($ mil.): 355
Return on equity: 6.4%
Current Ratio: 0.70

WGL HOLDINGS, INC.

WGL Holdings, owners of the regulated Washington Gas Light Company, sells natural gas to more than 1 million customers in the District of Columbia, Maryland, and Virginia. Whether the company is distributing clean natural gas safely to a customer's home, providing electric power through renewable wind energy, or installing energy-efficient systems for the federal government, its vision is consistent and clear throughout its business: to be the preferred source of clean and efficient energy solutions.

Operations
WGL Holdings is the parent company of Washington Gas, WGL Energy, WGL Midstream, and Hampshire Gas. Washington Gas, its leading subsidiary, has provided safe, reliable natural gas service to customers in the D.C. area and serves more than one million customers in the District of Columbia, Maryland, and Virginia. Its unregulated subsidiaries provide energy-related services to residential and commercial customers, including government organizations.

Geographic Reach
Headquartered in Pittsburgh, Pennsylvania, WGL Holdings primarily operates in Washington, DC, Maryland, and Virginia.

Sales and Marketing
WGL sells and delivers natural gas and/or electricity directly to residential and commercial customers. Washington Gas has some 1 million customers in the District of Columbia, Maryland, and Virginia.

Strategy
Company Background
WGL was established in the year 2000 as a Virginia corporation. On January 25, 2017, WGL entered into an Agreement and Plan of Merger (Merger Agreement) to combine with AltaGas Ltd., a Canadian Corporation (AltaGas). On July 6, 2018, the merger was consummated between AltaGas, WGL, and Wrangler Inc. (Merger Sub), a newly formed indirect wholly owned subsidiary of AltaGas.

EXECUTIVES

Corporate Secretary, Leslie T Thornton
CAO, William R Ford
CRO, Louis J Hutchinson Iii

LOCATIONS

HQ: WGL HOLDINGS, INC.
1000 MAINE AVE SW, WASHINGTON, DC 200243494
Phone: 202 624-6011
Web: WWW.WGL.COM

PRODUCTS/OPERATIONS

2018 Sales

	$ mil.	% of total
Retail energy marketing	1,009.7	42
Utility	1,248.1	53
Commercial energy services	79.8	3
Midstream energy services	40.6	2
Eliminations	(36.4)	-
Total	2,341.8	100

2018 Sales

	$ mil.	% of total
Non-utility	1,112.3	47
Utility	1,229.5	53
Total	2,341.8	100

Selected Subsidiaries
Hampshire Gas Company (underground natural gas storage)
Wrangler SPE LLC
Washington Gas Light Company (natural gas utility)
Washington Gas Resources Corp. (nonregulated business holding company)
  Washington Gas Energy Services, Inc. (retail energy services)
  Washington Gas Energy Systems, Inc. (commercial energy systems and HVAC services)

COMPETITORS

ATMOS ENERGY CORPORATION
Algonquin Power & Utilities Corp
AltaGas Ltd
CENTERPOINT ENERGY, INC.
EVERSOURCE ENERGY
FIRSTENERGY CORP.
NEW JERSEY RESOURCES CORPORATION
NORTHWEST NATURAL GAS COMPANY
PIEDMONT NATURAL GAS COMPANY, INC.
SPIRE INC.

HISTORICAL FINANCIALS
Company Type: Private

Income Statement — FYE: September 30

	REVENUE ($mil)	NET INCOME ($mil)	NET PROFIT MARGIN	EMPLOYEES
09/18	2,341	21	0.9%	1,586
09/17	2,354	177	7.6%	—
09/16	2,349	168	7.2%	—
09/15	2,659	132	5.0%	—
Annual Growth	(4.2%)	(45.8%)	—	—

2018 Year-End Financials
Return on assets: 0.3%
Return on equity: 1.2%
Current Ratio: 0.60
Cash ($ mil.): 57

WHEATON FRANCISCAN SERVICES, INC.

Wheaton Franciscan Services, Inc. (WFSI) is the not-for-profit parent company for more than 100 health care, housing, and social service organizations in Colorado, Illinois, Iowa, and Wisconsin. Also known as Wheaton Franciscan Healthcare, WFSI operates about 15 hospitals including Affinity Health System, Rush Oak Park Hospital, and United Hospital System, with more than 1,600 beds total. WFSI also includes long-term care centers, home health agencies, and physician offices. Its Franciscan Ministries division provides affordable housing units including assisted-living facilities and low-income dwellings. The health system is sponsored by The Franciscan Sisters, Daughters of the Sacred Hearts of Jesus and Mary.

Operations
Many of WFSI's hospitals are operated in partnership with other area providers. For instance, the Affinity Health System in Wisconsin is jointly sponsored by Wheaton Franciscan Sisters and Ministry Health Care, while the Rush Oak Park Hospital in Illinois is operated through a partnership between WFSI and the Rush System for Health.

The health system partners with the YMCA of Milwaukee to try to address chronic health concerns of area residents. The two organizations converted a local YMCA campus into the YMCA Healthy Lifestyle Village. The center offers health screenings, health education, outpatient therapy, and fitness services. WFSI and the YMCA have more Healthy Lifestyle Village campuses planned for other locations within their service areas.

The organization had a total of 1,656 beds and 2,620 housing units at the end of 2014.

In fiscal 2013, WSFI delivered more than 8,000 babies and had more than 330,000 emergency department visits. It reported more than 1,580,000 outpatient visits and some 64,000 hospital admissions. It employs more than 500 physicians and has some 2,000 affiliated physicians.

Geographic Reach
WFSI operates in Wisconsin, Iowa, Colorado, and Illinois.

Financial Performance
The not-for-profit system's revenues were flat in fiscal 2014 at $1.8 billion. Net income totaled $184 million.

Strategy
To increase the scope of specialty health care services it can provide to the community, WFSI recruits new physicians and specialists to the Wheaton Franciscan Medical Group. The system also works to improve communication among its physicians and facilities by adding electronic health record (EHR) systems.

In 2013, the system opened a new 80,000-sq.-ft. outpatient center specializing in neurology services.

Company Background
The Franciscan Sisters, Daughters of the Sacred Hearts of Jesus and Mary (also known as the Wheaton Franciscan Sisters) founded WSFI in 1983 as a holding company for their ministry operations. The health system traces its roots back to the founding of the St. Mary's Hospital in Racine, Wisconsin, in 1882.

EXECUTIVES
Vice Chairman, Michael Mack
Auditors : KPMG LLP CHICAGO IL

LOCATIONS
HQ: WHEATON FRANCISCAN SERVICES, INC.
400 W RIVER WOODS PKWY, GLENDALE, WI 532121060
Phone: 414 465-3000
Web: WWW.MYWHEATON.ORG

PRODUCTS/OPERATIONS
Selected Operations
Franciscan Ministries, Inc. (housing in Colorado, Illinois, Iowa, and Wisconsin)
Illinois
    Marianjoy Rehabilitation Hospital (Wheaton)
    Rush Oak Park Hospital (affiliate, Oak Park)
Iowa (Wheaton Franciscan Healthcare of Iowa)
    Covenant Medical Center (Waterloo)
    Mercy Hospital (Oelwein)
    Sartori Memorial Hospital (Cedar Falls)
Wisconsin
    Affinity Health System (partnership with Minstry Health Care)
    Calumet Medical Center (Chilton)
    Mercy Medical Center (Oshkosh)
    St. Elizabeth Hospital (Appleton)
    Wheaton Franciscan Healthcare of Southeast Wisconsin
    All Saints Hospital (two campuses in Racine)
    Elmbrook Memorial Hospital (Brookfield)
    Franklin Hospital (Franklin)
    St. Francis Hospital (Milwaukee)
    St. Joseph Hospital (Milwaukee)
    Wisconsin Heart Hospital (Wauwatosa)
    United Hospital System, Inc. (affiliated system)
    Kenosha Medical Center (Kenosha)
    St. Catherine's Medical Center (Pleasant Prairie)

COMPETITORS
ASCENSION HEALTH
CENTRASTATE HEALTHCARE SYSTEM INC
CORIZON HEALTH, INC.
DEAN HEALTH SYSTEMS, INC.
GEISINGER HEALTH

HISTORICAL FINANCIALS
Company Type: Private

Income Statement — FYE: June 30

	REVENUE ($mil)	NET INCOME ($mil)	NET PROFIT MARGIN	EMPLOYEES
06/14	1,754	128	7.3%	18,000
06/13	1,763	177	10.1%	—
06/12	1,723	(112)	—	—
Annual Growth	0.9%	—	—	—

2014 Year-End Financials
Return on assets: 5.5%
Return on equity: 11.4%
Current Ratio: 1.30
Cash ($ mil.): 58

WHITE PLAINS HOSPITAL MEDICAL CENTER

Auditors : ERNST & YOUNG US LLP NEW YORK

LOCATIONS
HQ: WHITE PLAINS HOSPITAL MEDICAL CENTER
41 E POST RD, WHITE PLAINS, NY 106014607
Phone: 914 681-0600
Web: WWW.WPHOSPITAL.ORG

HISTORICAL FINANCIALS
Company Type: Private

Income Statement — FYE: December 31

	REVENUE ($mil)	NET INCOME ($mil)	NET PROFIT MARGIN	EMPLOYEES
12/17	620	40	6.5%	2,000
12/16	460	23	5.1%	—
12/15	389	23	6.1%	—
12/14	353	8	2.3%	—
Annual Growth	20.7%	70.9%	—	—

2017 Year-End Financials
Return on assets: 5.9%
Return on equity: 10.1%
Current Ratio: 1.00
Cash ($ mil.): 45

WHOLE FOODS MARKET, INC.

Whole Foods Market is the world's #1 natural and organic foods grocery store chain. The company operates more than 535 retail and non-retail stores throughout the US, Canada, and the UK. Its product categories include bakery, beauty and body care, beer, bulk, catering, cheese, floral, grocery, meat, prepared foods, produce, seafood, wellness and supplements, and wine. Most of the food and other items the stores sell are free of pesticides, preservatives, sweeteners, and cruelty. Founded in Austin, Texas in 1980, Whole Foods pioneered the supermarket concept in natural and organic foods retailing.

Geographic Reach

Headquartered in Austin, Texas, Whole Foods operates nearly 515 store in the US, about 15 stores in Canada, and more than five stores in the UK. It has regional offices in North Atlantic (Connecticut, Maine, Massachusetts, New Hampshire, and Rhode Island), Mid-Atlantic (Maryland, New Jersey, Pennsylvania, Virginia, and Washington, DC), Northeast (Connecticut, New Jersey, and New York), Southeast (Alabama, Florida, Georgia, Mississippi, North Carolina, South Carolina, and Tennessee), Midwest (Illinois, Indiana, Iowa, Kentucky, Michigan, Minnesota, Missouri, Ohio, Wisconsin, and Ontario, Canada), Southwest (Arkansas, Louisiana, Oklahoma, and Texas), Rocky Mountain (Colorado, Kansas, Missouri, Nebraska, New Mexico, Utah, and El Paso, Texas), North Pacific (British Columbia, Oregon, and Washington), North California (North California, Northern Nevada, and Idaho), Southern Pacific (Arizona, Southern California, Southern Nevada, and Hawaii), and the UK.

Sales and Marketing

Whole Foods spent $113 million on advertising in 2017, versus $96 million in 2016 and $89 million in 2015.

Financial Performance

Whole Foods has seen its revenue rise over the last five years, yet increasing availability of fresh foods and new distribution channels industry-wide has had a negative impact on comparable store sales.

In fiscal 2017 (ended September), revenue was $16 billion, up 2% over 2016. Although transaction count declined, basket size increased over the previous year, and the company opened more than 30 new stores. Whole Foods' net income decreased by more than 50% to $245 million that year due to more than $150 million in merger-related expenses and about $95 million for store closures, relocations, and lease terminations (more than three times 2016 and 2015 combined).

In 2017 cash from operating activities was $1.14 billion, up almost 2% from the previous year.

Company Background

Whole Foods was incorporated in 1978. The company opened its first store in 1980.

During the 1990s, the company acquired other grocers and food establishments including Wellspring Grocery, Mrs. Gooch's, Fresh Fields, Bread of Life, and Merchant of Vino. It acquired national grocer Wild Oats Markets in 2007

The company was acquired by Amazon.com in 2017.

HISTORY

With a $10,000 loan from his father, John Mackey started SaferWay Natural Foods in Austin, Texas, in 1978. Despite struggling, Mackey dreamed of opening a larger, supermarket-sized natural foods store. Two years later SaferWay merged with Clarksville Natural Grocery, and Whole Foods Market was born. Led by Mackey, that year it opened an 11,000-sq.-ft. supermarket in the counterculture hotbed of Austin. The store was an instant success, and a second store was added 18 months later in suburban Austin.

The company slowly expanded in Texas, opening or buying stores in Houston in 1984 and Dallas in 1986. Whole Foods expanded into Louisiana in 1988 with the purchase of like-named Whole Food Co., a single New Orleans store owned by Peter Roy (who served as the company's president from 1993 to 1998). Sticking to university towns, Whole Foods added another store in California the next year and acquired Wellspring Grocery (two stores, North Carolina) in 1991. In 1992 it debuted its first private-label products under the Whole Foods name. Seeking capital to expand even more, the company raised $23 million by going public in early 1992 with 12 stores.

Every competitor in the fragmented health foods industry became a potential acquisition, and the chain began growing rapidly. In 1992 Whole Foods bought the six-store Bread & Circus chain in New England. The next year it added Mrs. Gooch's Natural Foods Markets (seven stores in the Los Angeles area). Its biggest acquisition came in 1996, when it bought Fresh Fields, the second-largest US natural foods chain (22 stores on the East Coast and in Chicago). Although the purchase hurt profits in 1996, sales surpassed $1 billion for the first time in fiscal 1997 as Whole Foods neared 70 stores. In 1997 it introduced the less-expensive 365 private label and acquired the Granary Market (Monterey, California) and Bread of Life (two stores, South Florida) natural foods supermarkets.

Capitalizing on the growing popularity of nutraceuticals (natural supplements with benefits similar to pharmaceuticals), the company paid $146 million in 1997 for Amrion, a maker of nutraceuticals and other nutritional supplements (merged with subsidiary WholePeople.com in 2000). It capped the year by buying coffee roaster Allegro Coffee. (Both companies are based in Boulder, Colorado, home of its former main rival, the smaller Wild Oats.) Also in 1997 Whole Foods acquired the six-store Merchant of Vino natural foods and wine shop chain to foster the development of its wine departments.

In 1998 Whole Foods opened its first store in Boulder -- a 39,000-sq.-ft. superstore with amenities such as a juice bar and a prepared foods section. At year's end, Roy resigned as president and was replaced by Chris Hitt. In 1999 Whole Foods bought four-store Boston-area chain Nature's Heartland.

In 2000 Whole Foods merged its online operations (wholefoods.com) with its direct marketing and nutritional supplement unit (Amrion) to form Wholepeople.com. Later that year the company merged Wholepeople.com with lifestyle marketing firm Gaiam; Whole Foods received a minority stake in Gaiam and started selling food online through Gaiam.com.

Hitt resigned in mid-2001, and Mackey took over his duties. Later that year Whole Foods acquired the three upscale Harry's Farmers Market stores in Atlanta; the sale did not include the Harry's In A Hurry stores, which later shut down.

In 2002 Whole Foods crossed the border into Canada. Its first foreign store opened in downtown Toronto that May.

Mackey was named Entrepreneur of the Year in 2003 by consulting firm Ernst & Young. That year Whole Foods acquired Select Fish, a Seattle-based seafood processor and distributor, and opened a seafood distribution facility in Atlanta.

In 2004 Whole Foods opened a 59,000-sq.-ft. store in the new Time Warner Center in Manhattan. The new store, which includes a 248-seat cafe, sushi bar, wine shop, and gourmet bakery, is the largest supermarket in New York City. That year the company acquired the UK organic-food retailer Fresh & Wild for $38 million.

To support its rapid growth, in 2004 Whole Foods Market expanded its number of operating regions from eight to 10 by separating the Southwest region into the Southwest and Rocky Mountain regions, and the Northern Pacific region into the Northern California and Pacific Northwest region. The company announced the opening of its first Gluten-Free Bakehouse, a dedicated gluten-free baking facility located outside Raleigh, North Carolina. Overall, the company opened 12 new stores in 2004.

In January 2005 Whole Foods launched the Animal Compassion Foundation, an independent, non-profit organization dedicated to the compassionate treatment of livestock. The company moved that month to its new corporate headquarters across the street from its old location in downtown Austin. Its new flagship store opened its doors in March at the same location. In October Whole Foods increased its number of operating regions from 10 to 11 by separating the North Atlantic region into the North Atlantic and Tri-State regions. Overall in fiscal 2005 the company opened a dozen new stores, including its first in Nebraska and Ohio. In

2006 the company acquired a store in Portland, Maine, and converted it to the Whole Foods Market banner.

In August 2007 Whole Foods acquired its main competitor -- Boulder, Colorado-based Wild Oats Markets -- in a deal valued at about $565 million (plus $106 million in debt). In early October the company sold 35 Henry's Farmers Market and Sun Harvest stores to a subsidiary of Los Angeles-based Smart & Final for about $166 million. The stores, in California and Texas, were acquired with Wild Oats.

The company launched a bi-monthly magazine called Whole Foods Market Magazine at its midwestern stores in 2008. On the heels of its disappointing third-quarter results in August 2008, shares of the company's stock fell to a six-year low and Whole Foods suspended its dividend. Blaming the poor economy, the company announced the layoffs of some 50 employees at its Austin headquarters in August 2008. Overall, in fiscal 2008 the company introduced about 300 new private-label items.

For the first time in its 29-year history, Whole Foods reported negative same-store sales in the quarter ended December 2008 as traffic in its stores fell.

In March 2009 the company reached a settlement in its long-running dispute with the FTC over its acquisition of Wild Oats in 2007. Whole Foods agreed to sell 32 stores, including 19 Wild Oats locations that had already been closed. In exchange, the FTC dropped its crusade to undo the merger. In December 2009 John Elstrott was named chairman of Whole Foods Market after Mackey voluntarily relinquished the chairmanship, which he had held since 1980. In May 2010 Walter Robb, formerly co-president of the company, was promoted to co-CEO of Whole Foods, a title he now shares with Mackey.

Auditors : ERNST & YOUNG LLP AUSTIN TEX

LOCATIONS

HQ: WHOLE FOODS MARKET, INC.
550 BOWIE ST, AUSTIN, TX 787034644
Phone: 512 477-4455
Web: WWW.WHOLEFOODSMARKET.COM

PRODUCTS/OPERATIONS

Selected Product Categories
Bakery
Body care
Educational products
Floral
Grocery
Household products
Meat and poultry
Nutritional supplements
Pet products
Prepared foods
Produce
Seafood
Specialty (beer, wine, cheese)
Textiles

COMPETITORS

7-ELEVEN, INC
ALBERTSONS COMPANIES, INC.
DELHAIZE AMERICA, LLC
FAIRWAY GROUP HOLDINGS CORP.
GNC HOLDINGS, INC.
PUBLIX SUPER MARKETS, INC.
SPARTANNASH COMPANY
THE GREAT ATLANTIC & PACIFIC TEA COMPANY, INC.
THE KROGER CO
US FOODS HOLDING CORP.

HISTORICAL FINANCIALS
Company Type: Private

Income Statement — FYE: September 24

	REVENUE ($mil)	NET INCOME ($mil)	NET PROFIT MARGIN	EMPLOYEES
09/17	16,030	245	1.5%	95,000
09/16	15,724	507	3.2%	—
09/15	15,389	536	3.5%	—
09/14	14,194	579	4.1%	—
Annual Growth	4.1%	(24.9%)	—	—

2017 Year-End Financials
Return on assets: 3.7%   Cash ($ mil.): 322
Return on equity: 7.1%
Current Ratio: 1.60

WILBUR-ELLIS HOLDINGS II, INC.

Wilbur-Ellis is a leading US privately- and family-owned international distribution business with sales over $3 billion. Through its agribusiness division, Wilbur-Ellis sells fertilizer, herbicides, insecticides, seed, and farm machinery in North America. The Connell division exports and distributes food ingredients and specialty chemicals throughout the Pacific Rim. Its nutrition division serves international customers in the livestock, pet food, and aquaculture industries. Additionally, Wilbur-Ellis new division, Nachurs Alpine Solutions sells liquid fertilizer into turf, specialty, international, and private label markets. Wilbur-Ellis was founded in 1921 by Brayton Wilbur Sr., Floyd Ellis and Thomas Franck.

Operations

Wilbur-Ellis' Agribusiness division is one of the top marketers and distributors of agricultural products in the US. Connell is the largest marketer and distributor of specialty chemicals and ingredients. The Nutrition division offers a full range of solutions that include customized vitamins and mineral packages, forage, animal proteins, grains, vegetables and value-added alternative feeds derived from food processing.

Geographic Reach

The San Francisco-based company has agribusiness operations in the West, Southwest, and Midwest regions on the US. Connell has some 50 offices in nearly 20 countries across the Asia/Pacific and the US. Connell's major leadership hubs are in Singapore, Bangkok, Hong Kong and San Francisco. The Nutrition division has operations in North America, and in Japan and New Zealand.

Sales and Marketing

The Connel sells ingredients and specialty chemicals to the coatings, food, personal care, plastics, paper, construction, and other industries. Nachurs Alpine's products sold into oil and gas markets, transportation and mining markets and industrial chemical markets are all sold under the NASi brand.

Auditors : PRICEWATERHOUSECOOPERS LLP SA

LOCATIONS

HQ: WILBUR-ELLIS HOLDINGS II, INC.
345 CALIFORNIA ST FL 27, SAN FRANCISCO, CA 941042644
Phone: 415 772-4000
Web: WWW.WILBURELLIS.COM

PRODUCTS/OPERATIONS

Selected Products and Services
Agribusiness Division
    Agricultural chemicals
    Fertilizers
    Fungicides
    Herbicides
    Insecticides
    Machinery
    Pesticides
    Seed protectants
    Seed treatments
    Sprayers
    Supply-chain management
Connell Bros. Division
    Industrial chemicals
Feed Division
    Aquaculture products
    Feed ingredients
    Food oils
    Forage products
    Pet food
Professional Products
    Forestry
    Fungicides
    Herbicides
    Golf
    Fungicides
    Landscape
    Fungicides
    Nursery/Greenhouse
    Fungicides
    Vegetation Management
    Selective and nonselective growth regulators

COMPETITORS

ARMITAGES PET PRODUCTS LIMITED
BEARCOM GROUP, INC.
BENEFIT COSMETICS LLC
BRENNTAG NORTH AMERICA, INC.
FRESHPOINT, INC.
GORDON FOOD SERVICE, INC.
JAFRA COSMETICS INTERNATIONAL, INC.
KENT CORPORATION
SALLY BEAUTY HOLDINGS, INC.
TRACTOR SUPPLY COMPANY

HISTORICAL FINANCIALS
Company Type: Private

Income Statement — FYE: December 31

	REVENUE ($mil)	NET INCOME ($mil)	NET PROFIT MARGIN	EMPLOYEES
12/11	2,812	0	0.0%	4,600
12/10	2,342	0	0.0%	—
12/09	0	0	—	—
12/00	1,100	0	0.0%	—
Annual Growth	8.9%	—	—	—

WILLIAM BEAUMONT HOSPITAL

Beaumont Health System is an eight-hospital regional health system with more than 3,337 beds and more than 5,000 physicians along with numerous community-based medical centers throughout suburban Detroit (in Oakland, Macomb, and Wayne counties). Additional facilities include nursing homes, a home health care agency, a research institute, and primary and specialty care clinics, as well as rehabilitation, cardiology, and cancer centers. Beaumont is the exclusive clinical teaching site for the Oakland University William Beaumont School of Medicine; it also has affiliations with Michigan State University College of Osteopathic Medicine and Wayne State University School of Medicine.

Operations
The system draws on a rich history of pioneering medical research to serve the health needs of southeastern Michigan and advance healing techniques nationwide.

Beaumont holds a Level I trauma designation in Oakland and Macomb counties. The system's Children's Hospital has more than 80 pediatric subspecialists. Its research institute has more than 1,000 active clinical studies, including interventional clinical research trials.

A teaching hospital, Beaumont has 40 residency and fellowship programs with more than 450 participants. The system is also the exclusive clinical partner of William Beaumont School of Medicine, providing more than 1,500 physicians to the school's faculty.

In fiscal 2014, the system had more than 103,000 admissions, some 9,700 infant births, more than 250,000 emergency department visits, and more than 2.3 million outpatient visits.

Financial Performance
In 2014, Beaumont's annual revenues totaled $2.5 billion.

Strategy
The system expands its care offerings by partnering with other service providers (such as insurance groups), adding new facilities to its network, and by taking advantage of government initiatives to modernize its systems. For example, in 2015 Beaumont opened a breast care and imaging services center in Trenton, Michigan.

In 2014, Beaumont merged with hospital operators Oakwood Healthcare and Botsford Hospital, creating a $3.8 billion not-for-profit organization that can provide improved care services across their communities. For example, patients will benefit from having a single electronic health record across all of the system's sites.

Company Background
The health system traces its roots to Dr. William Beaumont, an army doctor who conducted groundbreaking research on the human digestive system on Mackinac Island, Michigan, in the 1820s. The first Beaumont Hospital was opened in Royal Oak in 1955; the Troy facility was opened in 1977; and its third hospital in Grosse Pointe was acquired in 2007 from Bon Secours Health System.

EXECUTIVES
MED, Ananias Diokno Md
Vice Chairman, Mark Shaevsky

LOCATIONS
HQ: WILLIAM BEAUMONT HOSPITAL
3601 W 13 MILE RD, ROYAL OAK, MI 480736712
Phone: 947 522-1177
Web: WWW.BEAUMONT.ORG

COMPETITORS
ASCENSION PROVIDENCE ROCHESTER HOSPITAL
BEAUMONT HEALTH
CHARLESTON AREA MEDICAL CENTER, INC.
HENRY FORD HEALTH SYSTEM
KENNEDY HEALTH SYSTEM, INC.
NORTHWELL HEALTH, INC.
ORLANDO HEALTH, INC.
ROBERT WOOD JOHNSON UNIVERSITY HOSPITAL, INC.
THE PENNSYLVANIA HOSPITAL OF THE UNIVERSITY OF PENNSYLVANIA HEALTH SYSTEM
UNIVERSITY HEALTH SYSTEM SERVICES OF TEXAS, INC.

HISTORICAL FINANCIALS
Company Type: Private

Income Statement — FYE: December 31

	REVENUE ($mil)	NET INCOME ($mil)	NET PROFIT MARGIN	EMPLOYEES
12/17	1,473	71	4.9%	18,050
12/16	1,396	118	8.5%	—
12/15	1,300	142	10.9%	—
Annual Growth	6.5%	(29.1%)	—	—

2017 Year-End Financials
Return on assets: 3.8%   Cash ($ mil.): 175
Return on equity: 3.9%
Current Ratio: 12.30

WILMINGTON TRUST COMPANY

LOCATIONS
HQ: WILMINGTON TRUST COMPANY
1100 N MARKET ST STE 1300, WILMINGTON, DE 198901100
Phone: 302 651-1000
Web: WWW.WILMINGTONTRUST.COM

HISTORICAL FINANCIALS
Company Type: Private

Income Statement — FYE: December 31

	ASSETS ($mil)	NET INCOME ($mil)	INCOME AS % OF ASSETS	EMPLOYEES
12/17	4,960	30	0.6%	1,818
12/16	3,685	17	0.5%	—
12/15	1,928	36	1.9%	—
Annual Growth	60.4%	(9.0%)	—	—

2017 Year-End Financials
Return on assets: 0.6%   Cash ($ mil.): 4386
Return on equity: 5.7%
Current Ratio: —

WINCO HOLDINGS, INC.

Auditors: KPMG LLP BOISE ID

LOCATIONS
HQ: WINCO HOLDINGS, INC.
650 N ARMSTRONG PL, BOISE, ID 837040825
Phone: 208 377-0110

HISTORICAL FINANCIALS
Company Type: Private

Income Statement — FYE: March 28

	REVENUE ($mil)	NET INCOME ($mil)	NET PROFIT MARGIN	EMPLOYEES
03/09	4,104	225	5.5%	14,000
03/08	3,515	132	3.8%	—
03/07	2,976	106	3.6%	—
Annual Growth	17.4%	45.5%	—	—

2009 Year-End Financials
Return on assets: 15.2%   Cash ($ mil.): 146
Return on equity: 24.4%
Current Ratio: 1.30

WIPRO, LLC

Auditors: DELOITTE HASKINS & SELLS LLP

LOCATIONS
HQ: WIPRO, LLC
300 TRI STATE INTL # 320, LINCOLNSHIRE, IL 600694416

Phone: 732 509-1502
Web: WWW.WIPRO.COM

HISTORICAL FINANCIALS
Company Type: Private

Income Statement   FYE: March 31

	REVENUE ($mil)	NET INCOME ($mil)	NET PROFIT MARGIN	EMPLOYEES
03/18	585	(45)	—	800
03/13	120	(17)	—	—
Annual Growth	37.1%	—	—	—

2018 Year-End Financials
Return on assets: (-4.8%)   Cash ($ mil.): 22
Return on equity: (-20.4%)
Current Ratio: 0.70

WISCONSIN MILWAUKEE COUNTY

EXECUTIVES

District Attorney*, John Chisholm
Clerk of Courts*, John Barrett
County Executive*, Scott Walker
Auditors : BAKER TILLY VIRCHOW KRAUSE

LOCATIONS

HQ: WISCONSIN MILWAUKEE COUNTY
  901 N 9TH ST STE 306, MILWAUKEE, WI 532331425
Phone: 414 278-4211
Web: COUNTY.MILWAUKEE.GOV

HISTORICAL FINANCIALS
Company Type: Private

Income Statement   FYE: December 31

	REVENUE ($mil)	NET INCOME ($mil)	NET PROFIT MARGIN	EMPLOYEES
12/20	941	45	4.9%	4,400
12/19	877	16	1.9%	—
12/18	851	2	0.3%	—
12/17	852	5	0.7%	—
Annual Growth	3.4%	100.3%	—	—

2020 Year-End Financials
Return on assets: 1.9%   Cash ($ mil.): —
Return on equity: —
Current Ratio: 3.50

WORLD WIDE TECHNOLOGY HOLDING CO., LLC

Auditors : ERNST & YOUNG LLP ST LOUIS

LOCATIONS

HQ: WORLD WIDE TECHNOLOGY HOLDING CO., LLC
  1 WORLD WIDE WAY, SAINT LOUIS, MO 631463002

Phone: 314 919-1400
Web: WWW.WWT.COM

HISTORICAL FINANCIALS
Company Type: Private

Income Statement   FYE: December 31

	REVENUE ($mil)	NET INCOME ($mil)	NET PROFIT MARGIN	EMPLOYEES
12/14	6,702	88	1.3%	7,052
12/13	6,392	77	1.2%	—
12/12	5,041	67	1.3%	—
Annual Growth	15.3%	14.2%	—	—

2014 Year-End Financials
Return on assets: 6.4%   Cash ($ mil.): 109
Return on equity: 38.0%
Current Ratio: 1.20

WORLD WIDE TECHNOLOGY, LLC

World Wide Technology (WWT) is a global technology solution provider that primarily provides such IT services as network design and installation, systems and application integration, and license consulting. It works with the world's trusted brands such as Cisco, VMware, NetApp, Dell Technologies, Red Hat and several others, but also include emerging tech players like Tanium and Dedrone. WWT serves businesses in the retail, oil and gas, financial services, life sciences, energy and utilities industries, as well as public sectors. With more than 300 labs, the company has over 200 technology partners in the Advanced Technology Center (ATC). WWT was founded in 1990.

Operations
WWT provides consulting, ATC lab, application, automation and orchestration, supply chain and integration, infrastructure, EA+, and strategic staffing services.

The company partner with the world's leading technology manufacturers and maintain the highest levels of certification to bring hardware and software solutions. These manufacturers can be evaluated in one environment, its ATC, and range from Silicon Valley heavyweights like Hewlett Packard Enterprise, Microsoft, Intel, Nvidia, Apple, Okta, and Veritas, among others.

Geographic Reach
Headquartered in St. Louis, Missouri, WWT has more than 20 facilities throughout the world and more than 4 million-sq. ft. of warehouse, distribution, and integration space worldwide. It also has integration labs in the US, Europe and Asia Pacific and sales offices and distribution centers around the world.

Sales and Marketing
WWT serves customers in energy and utility, financial, global service provider, healthcare, life sciences, and manufacturing industries.

Financial Performance
WWT has around $14.5 billion in annual revenue.

Strategy
World Wide Technology plans to hire at least 1,000 new employees in 2022, on top of the roughly 1,000 net new employees the solution provider superstar onboarded in the previous year.

World Wide Technology prefers to grow organically versus via acquisitions as the company continues its successful strategy of doubling both top line and bottom line revenue every five years.

Auditors : BURDS & KUNTZ PC SAINT LOUIS

LOCATIONS

HQ: WORLD WIDE TECHNOLOGY, LLC
  1 WORLD WIDE WAY, SAINT LOUIS, MO 631463002
Phone: 314 569-7000
Web: WWW.WWT.COM

PRODUCTS/OPERATIONS

Selected Services
IT Products and Solutions
  Facilities Infrastructure
  Integration and Staging
  Leasing
  Managed Services
  Order Management and Reporting
  Pre-Sales Support
  Value Added Reseller
Professional Services
  Configuration
  Implementation
  Planning and Design
  Training
Supply Chain Services
  Business Process Outsourcing
  Logistics/Warehousing
  Material Planning and Scheduling
  Outsourced Procurement
  Supplier Management

COMPETITORS

ACCRUENT, LLC
AMAX ENGINEERING CORPORATION
ATTRONICA COMPUTERS, INC.
CONTINENTAL RESOURCES, INC.
DAIWABO INFORMATION SYSTEM CO., LTD.
DEMATIC CORP.
KORBER SUPPLY CHAIN US, INC.
PC SPECIALISTS, INC.
PROSYS INFORMATION SYSTEMS, INC.
WESTCON GROUP, INC.

HISTORICAL FINANCIALS
Company Type: Private

Income Statement   FYE: December 31

	REVENUE ($mil)	NET INCOME ($mil)	NET PROFIT MARGIN	EMPLOYEES
12/15	5,927	95	1.6%	2,286
12/14	5,057	95	1.9%	—
12/13	4,545	77	1.7%	—
Annual Growth	14.2%	10.7%	—	—

2015 Year-End Financials
Return on assets: 5.7%   Cash ($ mil.): 46
Return on equity: 18.8%
Current Ratio: 1.40

WORLEY & OBETZ, INC.

Auditors: HOROVITZ RUDOY & ROTEMAN LLC

LOCATIONS

HQ: WORLEY & OBETZ, INC.
85 WHITE OAK RD, MANHEIM, PA 175458550
Phone: 717 665-6891
Web: WWW.WORLEYOBETZ.COM

HISTORICAL FINANCIALS

Company Type: Private

Income Statement — FYE: August 31

	REVENUE ($mil)	NET INCOME ($mil)	NET PROFIT MARGIN	EMPLOYEES
08/17	677	2	0.4%	68
08/16	584	1	0.3%	—
08/15	520	2	0.4%	—
08/14	466	1	0.4%	—
Annual Growth	13.2%	14.0%	—	—

2017 Year-End Financials

Return on assets: 3.0%
Return on equity: 16.3%
Cash ($ mil.): —
Current Ratio: 1.50

WTG GAS PROCESSING, L.P.

LOCATIONS

HQ: WTG GAS PROCESSING, L.P.
211 N COLORADO ST, MIDLAND, TX 797014607
Phone: 432 682-4349
Web: WWW.WESTTEXASGAS.COM

HISTORICAL FINANCIALS

Company Type: Private

Income Statement — FYE: December 31

	REVENUE ($mil)	NET INCOME ($mil)	NET PROFIT MARGIN	EMPLOYEES
12/07	588	85	14.5%	25
12/06	498	64	13.0%	—
12/05	484	69	14.4%	—
12/04	342	39	11.5%	—
Annual Growth	19.7%	29.2%	—	—

2007 Year-End Financials

Return on assets: 29.8%
Return on equity: 37.2%
Cash ($ mil.): 45
Current Ratio: 2.90

XMED OXYGEN & MEDICAL EQUIPMENT, LP

LOCATIONS

HQ: XMED OXYGEN & MEDICAL EQUIPMENT, LP
15230 SURVEYOR BLVD, ADDISON, TX 750014338
Phone: 972 416-5502
Web: WWW.FIXMYPWC.COM

HISTORICAL FINANCIALS

Company Type: Private

Income Statement — FYE: December 31

	REVENUE ($mil)	NET INCOME ($mil)	NET PROFIT MARGIN	EMPLOYEES
12/18	4,060	227	5.6%	24
12/08	3	0	7.2%	—
12/06	0	0	—	—
12/05	4	0	11.7%	—
Annual Growth	68.6%	59.3%	—	—

2018 Year-End Financials

Return on assets: 19.1%
Return on equity: —
Cash ($ mil.): 13
Current Ratio: 1.00

YAKIMA VALLEY MEMORIAL HOSPITAL ASSOCIATION INC

Whether you're a major yakker or quiet as a mouse, Yakima Valley Memorial Hospital serves the health care needs of patients of all types. The health provider's acute-care hospital, skilled-nursing facilities, and outpatient specialty treatment facilities serve patients in and around Yakima in Washington State. The hospital has about 225 beds and provides a variety of services such as heart care, orthopedics, pediatrics, cancer treatment, women's health, and mental health care. It also offers sleep and wound care and provides home health and hospice services. The organization is a not-for-profit group governed by a board of directors.

Operations

Yakima Valley Memorial Hospital sees about 15,000 inpatients each year, as well as 77,000 emergency room visits and 3,100 births. It serves a total of more than 130,000 patient per year.

The organization provides a full range of inpatient and outpatient services that include critical care, surgery, diagnostics, cancer care, heart care, orthopedics, a family birthplace, a neonatal intensive care unit, pediatrics, physical therapy, and psychiatric care. Its Children's Village provides care for kids with special health or development needs. Other specialty units include the Garden Village skilled nursing center and the Cottage in the Meadow hospice facility. The organization also runs a community education program and a maternal health preventative care program.

Among its staff are 330 physicians representing 35 medical specialties.

Geographic Reach

In addition to its main 26-acre campus in Yakima, Washington, the organization has 15 locations throughout Yakima County.

Financial Performance

During 2012 the hospital provided $73.7 million in Community Benefits (22% more than in 2011). Included in this number was more than $33 million to cover a shortfall from Medicare funding. Net patient revenue in 2012 was $286 million.

Strategy

Yakima Valley Memorial Hospital is upgrading its infrastructure and its technologies to better serve area residents. In 2013, for instance, it added digital breast screening systems to its mammography center, and in 2012 the facility invested $1.3 million to replace aging beds.

In 2013 the hospital announced that it was looking for a partner to help it with several challenges, including Medicare reimbursement cuts, state Medicaid funding woes, and the high costs of health information technology. The three prospective groups (which submitted proposals) included Virginia Mason Medical Center in Seattle; Seattle-based Swedish Health Services and Renton-based Providence Health & Services; and Vancouver (Washington)-based PeaceHealth and the University of Washington Medicine Medicine in Seattle.

Company Background

Yakima Valley Memorial Hospital was founded in 1950.

Auditors: KPMG LLP SEATTLE WA

LOCATIONS

HQ: YAKIMA VALLEY MEMORIAL HOSPITAL ASSOCIATION INC
2811 TIETON DR, YAKIMA, WA 989023761
Phone: 509 249-5129
Web: WWW.YAKIMAMEMORIAL.ORG

PRODUCTS/OPERATIONS

Selected Services and Locations

16th Avenue Pavilion
Apple Valley Family Medicine
Cardiac Rehabilitation and Wellness Center
Cascade Surgical Partners
Children's Village
Family Medicine of Yakima
Garden Village
Home Health and Hospice
Memorial Cornerstone Medicine
Memorial Hospitalist Program
Memorial's Valley Imaging
North Star Lodge Cancer Center

'Ohana Mammography Center
Pacific Crest Family Medicine
Selah Family Medicine
Sleep Center at Memorial
Surgi-Center at Memorial
The Springs Rehabilitation and Occupational Medicine
Water's Edge Pain Relief Institute
Yakima Gastroenterology Associates
Yakima Internal Medicine
Yakima Neurosurgery Associates
Yakima Plastic Surgery Associates
Yakima Vascular Associates

COMPETITORS

FROEDTERT MEMORIAL LUTHERAN HOSPITAL, INC.
MERCY HEALTH - ST. RITA'S MEDICAL CENTER, LLC
MULTICARE HEALTH SYSTEM
PROVIDENCE HEALTH & SERVICES-WASHINGTON
WELLSTAR HEALTH SYSTEM, INC.

HISTORICAL FINANCIALS
Company Type: Private

Income Statement — FYE: December 31

	REVENUE ($mil)	NET INCOME ($mil)	NET PROFIT MARGIN	EMPLOYEES
12/21	550	3	0.6%	1,150
12/20	517	11	2.3%	—
12/19	500	9	2.0%	—
12/18	470	(12)	—	—
Annual Growth	5.4%	—	—	—

2021 Year-End Financials
Return on assets: 0.7%   Cash ($ mil.): 52
Return on equity: 1.1%
Current Ratio: 1.20

YALE NEW HAVEN HEALTH SERVICES CORPORATION

Yale New Haven Health System is Connecticut's leading healthcare system. The company operates Yale-New Haven Hospital, Greenwich Hospital, Bridgeport Hospital, and Lawrence & Memorial Hospital and has a contract relationship with The Westerly Hospital in Rhode Island (Northeast Medical Group), as well as children's, cancer, psychiatric care hospitals. In addition, Yale New Haven Health Services operates outpatient facilities and provides such managed care services as network contracting, as well as disease management programs. Yale New Haven Health System had 153,005 inpatient discharges annually, 3.6 million outpatient encounters and accumulated total assets of approximately $6.5 billion.

Operations
Through its Yale-New Haven, Bridgeport, Greenwich, Lawrence & Memorial, and Northeast Medical Group delivery networks, the company provides comprehensive, cost effective, advanced patient care. The company's clinical services include primary and preventive care, specialty, acute care, rehabilitation, skilled nursing and coordination of home care.

Yale New Haven Health System, in affiliation with the Yale School of Medicine and other universities and colleges, educates health professionals and advances clinical care.

The 501-bed Bridgeport Hospital serves more than 23,000 inpatients and nearly 350,000 outpatients a year.

The 206-bed Greenwich Hospital is a community teaching hospital. Lawrence & Memorial Hospital is a 280-bed general and acute care hospital serving parts of Connecticut, New York, and Rhode Island.

Northeast Medical Group is a not-for-profit multispecialty medical foundation. Its Westerly Hospital (served by the Yale New Haven Health System) is a 60-bed, not-for-profit acute care community hospital serving southern Rhode Island and southeastern Connecticut.

Geographic Reach
Yale New Haven Health System serves patients in Southern Connecticut, Southwestern Rhode Island, and parts of New York's Westchester County.

Company Background
Yale New Haven Health System was formed in 1996.

Auditors: KPMG LLP PHILADELPHIA PA

LOCATIONS
HQ: YALE NEW HAVEN HEALTH SERVICES CORPORATION
789 HOWARD AVE, NEW HAVEN, CT 065191300
Phone: 203 688-4242
Web: WWW.YNHH.ORG

PRODUCTS/OPERATIONS
Selected Facilities
Bridgeport Hospital (Bridgeport, Connecticut)
Greenwich Hospital (Greenwich, Connecticut)
Yale-New Haven Hospital (New Haven, Connecticut)
  Yale-New Haven Children's Hospital
  Yale-New Haven Psychiatric Hospital
  Smilow Cancer Hospital at Yale-New Haven

COMPETITORS
ASCENSION SOUTHEAST MICHIGAN
BAPTIST HEALTH SYSTEM, INC.
BEAUMONT HEALTH
BRONSON HEALTH CARE GROUP, INC.
CARE NEW ENGLAND HEALTH SYSTEM
FREEMAN HEALTH SYSTEM
MEDSTAR HEALTH, INC.
NEW MILFORD HOSPITAL, INC.
PASADENA HOSPITAL ASSOCIATION, LTD.
WESTERN CONNECTICUT HEALTH NETWORK, INC.

HISTORICAL FINANCIALS
Company Type: Private

Income Statement — FYE: September 30

	REVENUE ($mil)	NET INCOME ($mil)	NET PROFIT MARGIN	EMPLOYEES
09/20	742	(1)	—	52,768
09/19	657	0	0.0%	—
09/15	449	19	4.4%	—
09/13	427	35	8.2%	—
Annual Growth	8.2%	—	—	—

2020 Year-End Financials
Return on assets: (-0.1%)   Cash ($ mil.): 564
Return on equity: (-0.3%)
Current Ratio: 0.80

YALE NEW HAVEN HOSPITAL, INC.

Yale-New Haven Hospital (YNHH) is the flagship member of the Yale New Haven Health System. It provides tertiary care in more than 100 medical specialties to residents of southwestern Connecticut. The not-for-profit hospital has around 1,540 beds on two campuses. Its main location includes the Yale-New Haven Children's Hospital and the Yale-New Haven Psychiatric Hospital. Its Smilow Cancer Hospital provides the very best cancer care available. YNHH provides cardiac and cancer care, performs organ transplants, and offers a variety of outpatient clinics. Yale New Haven Hospital was founded as the General Hospital Society of Connecticut in 1826.

Operations
YNHH offers heart and vascular services, cancer (oncology), transplantation, pediatrics, neurosciences, obstetrics, and digestive health, to name a few.

A key component of the main hospital facility is the Smilow Cancer Hospital, which conducts cancer care and research in partnership with Yale University's Cancer Center. In addition to Smilow, it also operates the Yale New Haven Children's Hospital and Yale New Haven Psychiatric Hospital.

Geographic Reach
The company is headquartered in New Haven, Connecticut.

LOCATIONS
HQ: YALE NEW HAVEN HOSPITAL, INC.
20 YORK ST, NEW HAVEN, CT 065103220
Phone: 203 688-4242
Web: WWW.YNHH.ORG

PRODUCTS/OPERATIONS
Selected Services
Ambulatory (outpatient) services
Bariatric surgery
Blood draw stations
Dental center
Diabetes and endocrinology
Diagnostic radiology

Ear, nose, and throat
Emergency services
Endocrine surgery
Gastroenterology
Geriatrics
Kidney disease
Maternity
Psychiatry
Pulmonology
Urology

COMPETITORS

CHARLESTON AREA MEDICAL CENTER, INC.
COVENANT MEDICAL CENTER, INC.
EVANGELICAL COMMUNITY HOSPITAL
INDIANA UNIVERSITY HEALTH, INC.
MILFORD REGIONAL MEDICAL CENTER, INC.
MISSION HOSPITAL, INC.
PROMEDICA HEALTH SYSTEMS, INC.
THE CARLE FOUNDATION HOSPITAL
THE CLEVELAND CLINIC FOUNDATION
THE LANCASTER GENERAL HOSPITAL

HISTORICAL FINANCIALS
Company Type: Private

Income Statement — FYE: September 30

	REVENUE ($mil)	NET INCOME ($mil)	NET PROFIT MARGIN	EMPLOYEES
09/20	2,923	49	1.7%	30,278
09/19	3,266	258	7.9%	—
09/15	2,388	107	4.5%	—
09/14	2,360	120	5.1%	—
Annual Growth	3.6%	(13.9%)	—	—

2020 Year-End Financials
Return on assets: 1.5%   Cash ($ mil.): 325
Return on equity: 2.5%
Current Ratio: 3.70

YALE UNIVERSITY

What do former President George W. Bush and actress Meryl Streep have in common? They are Yalies. Yale University is one of the nation's most prestigious private liberal arts institutions, as well as one of its oldest (founded in 1701). Yale comprises an undergraduate college, a graduate school, and more than a dozen professional schools. Programs of study include architecture, law, medicine, and drama. Its 12 residential colleges (a system borrowed from Oxford) serve as dormitory, dining hall, and social center. The school has around 12,000 students and nearly 4,000 faculty members.

Operations
Yale's graduate students, of which there are more than 6,500, outnumber its more than 5,300 undergrads. Undergraduate tuition runs at around $42,000 per year, plus $13,000 in room and board. Graduate tuition is about $35,000 per year. The university has some 4,000 faculty members.

The university has extensive research programs affiliated with its graduate school and its graduate-level professional schools, which cover architecture, art, divinity, drama, engineering and applied science, forestry and environmental studies, law, management, medicine, music, nursing, and public health.

Yale also operates the Yale University Press, which publishes works of academics and professionals, including e-books and traditional books. It published 475 titles during 2012 and has produced about 9,000 titles in total.

Geographic Reach
Yale's facilities cover a total of 1,100 acres, including a 340-acre central campus with 260 buildings in New Haven, Connecticut; a 140-acre West Campus on the edge of New Haven; and 600 acres of athletic fields and natural preserve areas outside of town. Yale's students come from all 50 US states and about 110 foreign countries.

Financial Performance
Sales for Yale have grown over the last five years, and the university showed a 1% increase in revenues to more than $2.8 billion in 2012 due to higher student income, grants and contracts (for research and training programs), medical service revenues, and other income sources. Endowment income and grants and contracts are the largest source of revenue.

Yale's annual operating budget is about $2.7 billion.

Yale's roughly $19 billion endowment ranks as one of the largest in the US. Yale's Endowment grew about 9% in 2010, producing a gain of $1.4 billion.

Company Background
Yale was founded in 1701 through the vision of a group of colonial clergymen who began planning for a university in the 1640s. It was named Yale College in 1718 after a Welsh merchant, Elihu Yale, who made a sizable donation to the institution.

EXECUTIVES

General Vice President*, Dorothy Robinson
Auditors : PRICEWATERHOUSECOOPERS LLP

LOCATIONS

HQ: YALE UNIVERSITY
105 WALL ST, NEW HAVEN, CT 065118917
Phone: 203 432-2550
Web: WWW.YALE.EDU

PRODUCTS/OPERATIONS

Colleges and Schools
Graduate School of Arts and Sciences
Professional schools
   School of Architecture
   School of Art
   Divinity School
   School of Drama
   School of Engineering & Applied Science
   School of Forestry & Environmental Studies
   Law School
   School of Management
   School of Medicine
   School of Music
   School of Nursing
   School of Public Health
   Institute of Sacred Music
Yale College (undergraduate studies)

Residential Colleges
Berkeley College
Branford College
Calhoun College
Davenport College
Ezra Stiles College
Jonathan Edwards College
Morse College
Pierson College
Saybrook College
Silliman College
Timothy Dwight College
Trumbull College

COMPETITORS

BALL STATE UNIVERSITY
NORTHEASTERN UNIVERSITY
PURDUE UNIVERSITY
Queen's University At Kingston
THE COLLEGE OF WILLIAM & MARY
THE PRESIDENT AND TRUSTEES OF COLBY COLLEGE
THE RUTGERS STATE UNIVERSITY
TRUSTEES OF BOSTON COLLEGE
TRUSTEES OF BOSTON UNIVERSITY
The Governing Council of The University of Toronto

HISTORICAL FINANCIALS
Company Type: Private

Income Statement — FYE: June 30

	REVENUE ($mil)	NET INCOME ($mil)	NET PROFIT MARGIN	EMPLOYEES
06/19	4,105	(15)	—	11,000
06/18	3,848	3,270	85.0%	—
06/17	3,647	2,447	67.1%	—
Annual Growth	6.1%	—	—	—

2019 Year-End Financials
Return on assets: —   Cash ($ mil.): 709
Return on equity: —
Current Ratio: —

YATES GROUP, INC.

E-Z Mart Stores aims to make filling gas tanks and stomachs EZR for small-town America. The regional convenience store chain operates about 295 stores across four neighboring states, including Arkansas, Louisiana, Oklahoma, and Texas. Rather than build its own stores, the company usually expands through acquisitions. In addition to the standard hot dogs, sodas, coffee, and cigarettes, most E-Z Mart locations also offer Shell, Conoco, Phillips 66, or CITGO gasoline. E-Z Mart was founded in 1970 by Jim Yates in Nashville, Arkansas. Yates died in 1998 when the plane he was piloting crashed, leaving his daughter Sonja Hubbard at the company's helm as CEO.

Geographic Reach
Ranked #35 on Convenience Store News ' "Top 100 Convenience Stores Report," E-Z Mart is a regional c-store chain that primarily serves Texas and Arkansas, as well as Oklahoma and Louisiana.

Sales and Marketing
Aiming to offer the chain's customers access to updated fuel prices, a list of

locations, and in-store promotions, among other items, E-Z Mart partnered with OpenStore by GasBuddy to roll out a new E-Z Mart website and mobile app. The fully integrated mobile app enables consumers to send feedback from their mobile phones and receive time-sensitive electronic mobile coupons.

Strategy

While E-Z Mart has trimmed its store count during the past decade or so, including exiting markets such as Missouri, it continues to make strategic acquisitions. Like other convenience store operators seeking to boost in-store sales, E-Z Mart is expanding its food and beverage offering, adding fresh-brewed iced tea to all of its stores and installing freezers. Outside, the company has a deal with Redbox to place its movie rental kiosks outside of E-Z Mart stores.

Auditors : BKD LLP FORT SMITH ARKANSAS

LOCATIONS

HQ: YATES GROUP, INC.
 2015 GALLERIA OAKS DR, TEXARKANA, TX 755034618
Phone: 903 336-6246
Web: WWW.CONOCOPHILLIPS.COM

2014 Stores

	No.
Texas	96
Arkansas	95
Oklahoma	80
Louisiana	18
Total	289

COMPETITORS

GPM INVESTMENTS, LLC
RACETRAC PETROLEUM, INC.
SHEETZ, INC.
THE JONES COMPANY
THE PANTRY INC

HISTORICAL FINANCIALS
Company Type: Private

Income Statement — FYE: December 31

	REVENUE ($mil)	NET INCOME ($mil)	NET PROFIT MARGIN	EMPLOYEES
12/16	786	16	2.1%	2,100
12/15	827	16	2.0%	—
12/14	1,026	19	1.9%	—
12/13	1,003	15	1.5%	—
Annual Growth	(7.8%)	3.2%	—	—

2016 Year-End Financials
Return on assets: 7.9%   Cash ($ mil.): 7
Return on equity: 12.6%
Current Ratio: 1.30

YORK HOSPITAL

York Hospital, operating as WellSpan York Hospital, takes its name from the community whose health it seeks to preserve. Part of WellSpan Health, the medical center has about 570 beds and serves residents of York and surrounding area of south-central Pennsylvania. It is a regional leader in cardiovascular and orthopedic care and has programs in other specialty areas, including oncology, behavioral health, and geriatrics. Additionally, WellSpan York Hospital operates a Level 1 trauma center, offers outpatient surgery, emergency, home health, and diagnostic imaging services. It is also has teaching and research programs. The hospital was founded in 1880.

Operations

WellSpan York Hospital has been recognized as a top 100 US hospital by US News for more than five years in a row. It is also recognized for its cardiovascular and orthopedic programs. The center employs about 700 doctors.

The hospital's education programs include five allied health schools and seven residency programs. Affiliated organizations include the medical schools of Drexel University, Pennsylvania State University, and University of Maryland.

Strategy

WellSpan York Hospital is working to improve its specialist programs to meet the growing medical needs of area residents. In 2011 for instance, it collaborated with technology firm Cerner and pharmaceuticals firm Hospira to form an infusion management program for its intensive care unit; the program aims to reduce infusion-related errors. In addition, it launched a urinary catheter removal protocol to reduce infection rates, and it implemented an aortic valve replacement program (making it one of three facilities in Pennsylvania to offer the open-heart surgery alternative).

LOCATIONS

HQ: YORK HOSPITAL
 1001 S GEORGE ST, YORK, PA 174033645
Phone: 717 851-2345
Web: WWW.WELLSPAN.ORG

COMPETITORS

ATLANTIC HEALTH SYSTEM INC.
KENNEDY HEALTH SYSTEM, INC.
LONG BEACH MEDICAL CENTER
MAINEHEALTH
OHIOHEALTH CORPORATION

HISTORICAL FINANCIALS
Company Type: Private

Income Statement — FYE: June 30

	REVENUE ($mil)	NET INCOME ($mil)	NET PROFIT MARGIN	EMPLOYEES
06/20	1,163	15	1.4%	6,200
06/18	1,063	181	17.0%	—
06/16	990	17	1.8%	—
06/15	925	82	9.0%	—
Annual Growth	4.7%	(28.3%)	—	—

2020 Year-End Financials
Return on assets: 0.7%   Cash ($ mil.): 249
Return on equity: 1.2%
Current Ratio: 1.20

ZEN-NOH GRAIN CORPORATION

Auditors : KPMG LLP NEW ORLEANS LOUISIA

LOCATIONS

HQ: ZEN-NOH GRAIN CORPORATION
 1127 HWY 190 E SERVICE RD, COVINGTON, LA 704334929
Phone: 985 867-3500
Web: WWW.ZGCUSA.COM

HISTORICAL FINANCIALS
Company Type: Private

Income Statement — FYE: May 31

	REVENUE ($mil)	NET INCOME ($mil)	NET PROFIT MARGIN	EMPLOYEES
05/22	12,392	186	1.5%	250
05/21*	9,771	211	2.2%	—
03/21	9,771	211	2.2%	—
05/20	5,930	44	0.7%	—
Annual Growth	44.6%	105.0%	—	—

*Fiscal year change

2022 Year-End Financials
Return on assets: 6.5%   Cash ($ mil.): 36
Return on equity: 19.9%
Current Ratio: 1.20

Hoover's Handbook of Private Companies

Index of Executives

Index Of Executives

A

Ables, Dorothy M 517
Abraham, Brian 538
Acheson, Eleanor D 378
Adam, Mark 437
Adams, Mary 467
Adzick, Susan 337
Akhavan, Chris 241
Albanese, Craig 386
Albright, Todd R 191
Alessandrini, Evaline 638
Alexander, Ralph 554
Allen, Herbert 226
Allen, Jerold W 464
Allen, Lee 534
Allen, Mike 12
Allen, Richard D 604
Allred, Mark 82
Almaraz, Frank 143
Almquist, Jeff 177
Aloma, Angel 227
Alsobrooks, Angela 238
Ambrozie, Tony 61
Andersen, Connie 485
Andersen, Paul 271
Anderson, Selynto 308
Anderson, Suzanne 676
Andrews, Susan Mc 464
Angeloro, Vincent 241
Angus, Derek 667
Anschutz, J Barron 109
Antonovich, Michael D 171
Apperson, Kevin 335
Arlt, Tim 381
Arnold, Thomas G 219
Arroliga, Alejandro 69
Arroyo, Quemuel 352
Arthur, Lavone 69
Arthur, Tanya 544
Aske, Jennings 386
Aspillaga, Marea 61
Attor, Terry Goddard 532
Austin, Pam 59

B

Badcock, Henry C 678
Badlani, Sameer 220
Baird, Thomas A 459
Baker, Christine 596
Baker, Emily A 127
Baker, Ron 285
Balaguer, Susan 599
Baldwin, Dennis 101
Baldwin, Stacy 656
Ball, Calvin 271
Barcala, Cheryl 140
Barchi, Daniel 386
Barnard, Keith 226
Barrett, John 692

Bartolo, Anthony F 56
Barton, Jeffrey 326
Bartschat, Michael 292
Barwood, Marlene A 286
Bash, Ruth 520
Battenfield, Keith 110
Baty, Darren 272
Beasley, Bill 437
Beauchesne, Nina 510
Beautz, Janet K 177
Beckman, Mitchell R 590
Beckton, Dana 494
Bello, Adam J 173
Bellone, Steven 178
Benfield, James H 625
Benfield, Stephanie Stuckey 128
Bensema, David J 62
Beran, Josette 574
Bergman, William T 558
Bernardes, Ricardo 100
Betancourt, Joseph 589
Betrus, Lisa 589
Bicking, Rachel 559
Biscardi, Joseph 1
Bjorck, Meredith W 265
Blake, Joseph J 444
Board, Bruce Leino 246
Board, George Cowden Iii 71
Bolster, Jennifer 527
Bombard, Tate 462
Bonewell, Fred 143
Bonilla, Emily 174
Boss, Jane 102
Bouet, Vivan 143
Boutte, Brian 515
Bowman, Kara 654
Boxley, Tracee 449
Boyington, Sheila 253
Boyle, Bryan 436
Boynton, Timothy J 306
Brandt, Tim 26
Braswell, Bill 437
Braveman, Peter E 109
Bray, Dee L 542
Brekke, Stein-erling 217
Brodsky, Stephen 418
Brooks, Alexandra D 585
Brooks, Harley 415
Brown, Jeff 126
Brown, Jocelyn 365
Brown, Marcus V 215
Brown, Michael 176
Brown, Michael G 136
Browne, Lori M 229
Broyles, Rob 226
Bruce, Karla 219
Bruhl, Elise 137
Brunfield, Brian 573
Bryan, Alex 6
Bryce, Kristin Jones 654
Buckley, Guy G 517
Buescher, John 336
Buhrandt, Jeff 665

Buhrow, Jason 272
Bumb, Duane 137
Bunnell, Ron 59
Buretta, Sheri 124
Burke, Courtney 16
Burke, Yvonne Brathwaite 171
Burnett, Don 168
Burnette, Don 168
Bush, Tim 183
Buster, Bob 175
Byrne, Bobbie 210

C

Cagle, R Jack 170
Cahill, Patricia 165
Call, Valerie Mc 130
Callahan, Emily 35
Callender, Robert G 387
Campbell, Barbara 331
Campos, Melisza 467
Campos, Tony 177
Cannady, David 89
Cantrell, Mike 168
Capener, John T 552
Capener, John T 553
Carpenter, Dan 280
Carraway, Barbara O 130
Carrigan, Gerry 398
Carson, Crystal 154
Carson, Keith 166
Carter, Alexandra 572
Carter, Dedric 618
Cartwright, Doctor Vickie L 486
Casey, Chris 514
Catena, Cornelio 153
Cavallo-miller, Linda 522
Cavanah, Michael 548
Cepero, Monica 167
Cerrai, Francesco 137
Chaffin, Patrick 473
Chambers, Matthew 69
Chambolle, Thomas 88
Chancellor, Beth 656
Chancellor, James 285
Chandra, Subodh 130
Charette, Gary C 40
Charman, Nikki 437
Charvat, Peter 527
Chavasse, Desmond 437
Cheatham, Tim 593
Cheung, Ava 548
Cheves, Brad 514
Chinn, Bruce 117
Chinniah, Nim 656
Chisholm, John 692
Choudhry, Jeffer 659
Chumura, Thomas 655
Clark, John B 539
Clark, Matthew 534
Clark, Rodney 292

Clark, Talisa R 168
Clarkson, Daniel J 49
Clarno, Bev 537
Co, Erin Niewinski 373
Co, Gary Richardson 373
Co, Nora K Carr 249
Coatsworth, John H 608
Cogen, Jeff 173
Cohen, Evan 376
Colanero, Stephen A 30
Colbert, Michael B 173
Cole, Rischa 207
Coleman, Casey 636
Collingsworth, J M 357
Collopy, Jenny 573
Concolino, Doreen 598
Conley, Fatimah 650
Conley, Karen 437
Constantine, Dow 171
Constantine, Tom 57
Cooke, Julie 49
Cooper, Mark 110
Coorigan, Micheal 201
Coosvp, Lisa Getzfrid 257
Cordero, Maribel Gomez 174
Corporate, Kiera Page 394
Corporate, Shane Thielman 489
Costello, Joseph G 460
Couchman, Glen 69
Coulombe, Stephen 88
Cox, Chris A 30
Cox, Colby 214
Craig, David 170
Crawford, John 449
Crawford, John 449
Cronin, Kathe 633
Croson, Rachel 656
Cross, Jeffrey D 33
Crowder, Andy 570
Crowther, Chip 79
Cruz, Dimitri J 215
Cuningham, David 543
Cunningham, Rebecca 459
Curran, Laura 173
Currier, Rand 245
Curry, Ken 381

D

D'agosta, Jeffrey 375
Dadlani, Sunil 50
Dale, Christopher 670
Damico, Lance 670
Daniel, William C 479
Daniels, Vincent C 498
Dant, Joe 210
Davis, Brian 210
Davis, Debbie 464
Davis, Leslie 667
Davis, Robert 179
Day, Edwin 176

Index Of Executives

Deaupre, Paul 242
Decker, W Cody 646
Decolli, Debbie 137
Deere, Joshua 30
Deering, Michael 319
Deffenbaugh, Danny 516
Dehring, Timothy A 399
Dejaco, Lynn 253
Dekle, Christopher 219
Dellenback, Steve 516
Demarco, Nick 137
Dempsey, June 360
Depies, Lori 231
Desai, Sonali 569
Desjarlais, Roger 171
Diamond, Robert 295
Diana, Edward A 174
Diaz, Jorge E 604
Dickson, Rebecca T 167
Diehm, Russell C 90
Diesel, R Wayne 539
Diganci, Todd 224
Diliberto, Matthew J 457
Dill, Julie 517
Dillon, Tim 271
Dimauro, Vincent A 169
Dodson-reed, Candace 271
Doerr, David M 12
Doig, David 118
Dole, Rodney 177
Donheiser, Gail 241
Donis, Emi 442
Dooley, Charles 178
Dorchester, Wendy 318
Doyle, Robert 585
Drew, Joel 102
Ducatman, Barbara 72
Dugas, Jason 670
Dunham, Kara 112
Dunley, Pamela 210

E

Eamigh, Kevin J 519
Easley, Paul 516
Edelstein, Gara 241
Edmunds, Cynthia 655
Edwards, Carladenise 260
Eisen, David 682
Eklund, Andrea 280
Elder, Larry 79
Elliot, Cynthia 467
Ellis, David 678
Ellison, Seth 314
Elrich, Marc 366
Emery, Karen 43
Engle, John B 489
Englehart, Michael 369
Entler, Paul 516
Erickson, Kevin 683
Esparza, Ryan 284
Esq, David J Felicio 583
Esq, Lynn Taylor 522
Estby, Rebecca 149
Etheridge, Felicia 143
Evans, Michael E 270

F

Fabrication, John Higgins Pres 226
Faerber, Craig 30
Fagan, Cathlyn 398
Falcone, Philip 526
Falk, Kathleen 168
Fansler, Janet 306
Faulkner, Jennifer 386
Fawcett, Dave 683
Fay, Kristine 308
Feldman, Martin J 525
Fennell, Charles 527
Feuer, Bradley A 65
Fick, Daniel 272
Finley, Wayne 170
Fleury, Alison J 500
Flores, Jeanne 109
Flores, Rose 137
Flynn, Rachel 219
Fogarty, Kevin 304
Foley, D Sue 604
Ford, Gary 350
Ford, William R 687
Foster, David 209
Fowlkes, Steven H 221
Frampton, Marcus 15
Fredell, Thomas 191
Frederiksen-england, Matt 656
Freeman, Dena 341
Fretwell, Betsy 133

G

Galante, Ann M 624
Galbreath, Kristen 670
Galindo, Susan 395
Galioto, Frank 137
Garcia, Adrian 170
Garcia, Gerard A 644
Gardner, Gerald 535
Garrett, B J 651
Garske, Steven R 572
Garsys, Lucia 170
Gatz, Ronald F 579
Gaudette, Kevin 231
Gay, Caroline 306
Gehl, Carey 664
Geisler, Heather 260
George, Kimberly D 21
Gibb, Matthew 158
Giblin, Mike V 591
Gil, Ryan 341
Gilkie, Jennifer 190
Gingrich, Christopher 304
Glavey, Patrick 374
Glick, Barry 28
Glieberman, Bernard 270
Goar, Michael 359
Godfrey, Ronald S 670
Goldberg, Michael 226
Gollahalli, Anil 568
Golub, Mona J 585
Golub, Todd 569
Gonick, Lev 44
Goorevich, Charlie 497

Gordon, Steve 521
Gossett, Barry P 666
Gould, Dixon 191
Graniere, Rick 341
Grant, Declan 683
Gravallese, Julie 595
Grayless, Robert 169
Green-cheatwood, Toni 81
Green, Kylenne 277
Greener, Fred 79
Gridley, Maryanne 201
Griffin, B R 444
Griffin, Caroline 201
Griffin, J Timothy 378
Gross, Daniel L 500
Grunau, Paul W 41
Guge, Brett 100
Guiley, Thomas E 201
Gutierrez, Laline 341
Guzzone, Brandon 437

H

Haas, John J 198
Hackett, Sylvia 462
Hackney, James R 399
Haggerty, Scott 166
Haidar, Wael 89
Haigis, Kevin 188
Hakim, Veronique 352
Hale, Jordan 537
Hall, Chaundra 646
Hall, John J 580
Hallian, Terence 126
Halsey, Casey S 282
Halsey, Casey S 283
Hamilton, Tiffany 418
Hammond, John 166
Hampton, Tonya Jackman 260
Hanerkson, David 148
Hansen, Sarah 612
Hanson, Bryan C 161
Hanson, Jodee 536
Harmon, Eric 158
Harness, Carl 170
Harper, Ed 353
Harriman, Morril 532
Harris, Roger 378
Harris, Toi B 342
Harrison, Brandon 98
Hartfield, Nicholas 394
Harvey, Anne 137
Hassanein, Ahmed 305
Hastings, Annette D 644
Hausman, Rick 233
Haverkamp, Michael F 79
Hawkins, Ronald E 316
Heagarty, Chris 678
Heck, Denny 538
Heimlich, Ken 518
Helmer, Richard 412
Hemstreet, Tim 320
Heneghan, Steven 589
Henry, Brent L 332
Henry, Mary Anne 670
Hensing, John 59

Hernandez, Catherine 294
Herpich, Peter M 65
Herrera, Dennis 126
Herron, Dallas 144
Hessenthaler, Leader Brian 576
Heston, Grant J 675
Heuschel, Mary Alice 538
Heydlauff, Dale E 33
Heyn, Markus 465
Hicks, Juanita 87
Hickson, Nina 128
Hightower, Maia 611
Hilal, Nabil 42
Hill, Bryan 219
Hill, Thomas W 221
Himes, Vicki 429
Hinton, Angela 128
Hirsch, Jim 436
Hobson, David 210
Hochberg, Mitchell 686
Hodges, Ernest M 221
Hodnett, David 58
Holder, Duane 678
Hoody, Dan 260
Hopkins, Denver 184
Horne, Timothy 636
Horwedel, Gregory 170
Houchens, Steve 133
Hough, David 260
Howard, Christopher 500
Hsu, Kevin 486
Hudson, Bill 278
Hughes, David P 295
Hughes, Michael P 295
Hulet, Steven 481
Hunn, Robert 341
Huntzicker, James 177
Hutcheson, Jennifer 473
Hylander, Kenneth 378

I

Iannarelli, Rocco 386
Igoe, Paul G 204
Ii, John Tavaglinoe 175
Ii, Joseph T Giglia 217
Ii, Odie Donald 128
Iii, Carlisle Ky C Lewis 500
Iii, John B Jewell 627
Iii, Kenneth W Lott 511
Iii, Louis J Hutchinson 687
Int, Thomas Jeitschko 356
ior, Sister Bernice Coreil D.c. Sen 45
Ishmael, Cheryl 201
Itambo, Eric 147

J

Jackson, Claire 565
Jackson, J Brooks 612
Jackson, Jimmy L 168
Jackson, Rosa P 211
Jackson, Rosa P 514
Jackson, Rudy 664

Index Of Executives

Jacob, Sony 520
Jacobs, Ashley 678
Jacobs, James K 680
Jacobs, Kathleen E 389
Jahn, Timothy 62
Jakosky, Donn 419
James, Letitia 135
Jan, Rizwan 585
Jared, David 147
Jehi, Lara 574
Jensen, Claus Torp 343
Johnson, Carol C 535
Johnson, Frank 129
Johnson, Gary 42
Johnson, Janilee 667
Johnson, Michael 177
Johnson, Michael 177
Johnson, Robbie 63
Johnson, Rodney D 191
Johnson, Shelley 497
Johnson, Tracy 224
Jolley, Burke 292
Jones, Hannah 587
Jones, Kristi 536
Jones, Michael 121
Jones, Stephen 64
Joslyn, Scott 318
Jouvenal, Joe 336
Ju, Jennifer 548
Judge, Julie 335
Junior, Alan R Crain 216
Junior, Alfred W Young 198
Junior, Alphonso Jefferson 167
Junior, Kenneth Bennett 516
Junior, Norman J Beauchamp 356
Junior, Robert Campbell 212
Junior, Robert F Hull 519
Junior, Robert Hale 245
Junior, William G Gisel 462
Junior, William J Gilbane 239
Junior, Woodrow Myers 84
Juras, Kristen 535

K

Kafer, Ann 248
Kanary, Maryann 67
Kane-williams, Edna 2
Karr, Michael 419
Kastanis, John N 653
Kaufman, Irvin A 452
Keck, Sharon J 12
Kelley, Laurie 446
Kelly, Ann P 639
Kelton, Justin 336
Kenney, Jim 137
Kent, Geoff 279
Kepler, Jody 363
Kersey, Frances 136
Kiely, Sharon 606
Kiley, Krystal 223
Kimbrough, Bradly 338
Kinder, Richard D 379
King, Michael 275
Kinsey, Armond 50
Kirchoff, Bob 163

Kitchen, Carol 248
Klass, Cheryl 295
Kleiman, Joel 174
Klockenga, Kevin 524
Knabe, Don 171
Knight, Mark 602
Knight, Reginald 589
Koch, J Robert 593
Koenecke-grant, Carol 119
Kolloway, Michael R 599
Koss, Kristen K 542
Kottman, Bill 210
Koza, Eric 56
Krausz, Keira 405
Krystopolski, Ruth 483
Kuhn, Rebecca 59
Kull, Matthew 574
Kulper, Michael 1
Kumar, Jaya 552

L

Labrecque, Rachel S 42
Lai-bitker, Ellis 166
Lalor, William 57
Lambert, H David 584
Lance, Jean Fitterer 59
Langford, Stephen 73
Langley-hawthorne, Timothy M 585
Lawson, John W 675
Lazarus, Anne 137
Leblanc, Stephen 190
Lee, Joon 667
Lee, William 126
Leeming, Rosemary 236
Legg, Michael 638
Legrand, Jeff 226
Lehnertz, Rod 612
Leichtner, Scott J 241
Leighty, Scott 50
Leonard, Christopher 219
Leonardi, Phil 398
Lester, Jeff 104
Levin, Justine 569
Levine, Peter 655
Lew, Indu 472
Ley, James 177
Ley, James 177
Li, Celina 406
Liang, Janet 294
Liao, Edward 511
Libertino, John 306
Libonate, Mark 49
Lindsay-wood, Elizabeth 251
Liu, Yexi 462
Llechu, Armando 308
Locke, Jace D 216
Long, William C 490
Lopez, Jorge 343
Lortz, Andre 113
Lovelace, Rob 103
Lucas, Emily 678
Luke, Richard 376
Lurker, Nancy 404
Lyash, Jeff 68
Lynch, Marlon 615

Lynch, Thomas 586

M

Machen, Robert 35
Mack, Michael 688
Macnaughton, Mike 516
Madden, Donald V 625
Majni, J Christopher 338
Maltbie, John L 176
Manganiello, Anthony 677
Mangione, Robert 521
Manigan, Mark 472
Mann, Chris 185
Mann, Richard L 658
Mantz, Constantine A 1
Maples, John T 509
Marchiniak, Jenny 327
Marquardt, Jane 326
Marshall, Jay 272
Marshall, Lynette 612
Martinez, Lisa 308
Martinez, Mike 128
Martins, Alex 611
Marty, Steve 516
Marx, Geoffrey 431
Mason, Debby D 351
Mason, Jo 158
Massey, Mary 516
Mastro, Mary Lou 210
Mathis, Brian 486
Matis, Greg 278
Matteo, Jim 458
Matthews, Phil 678
Mauriello, Susan 177
May, Lee 168
Mbanda, Laurent 156
Mccarley, Kirk 178
Mccoy, Daniel P 166
Mccuskey, Kenneth D 189
Mcghee, Craig 123
McGregor, George 512
Mckey, William 166
Mcmillan, Lee 2
Mcmonagle, Richard 563
Md, A Brent Eastman 488
Md, Ananias Diokno 691
Md, Bruce H Hamory 236
Md, Dan Blue 483
Md, Gordon Hunt 550
Md, James M Orsini 644
Md, Linda Butler 462
Md, Norman Rizk 531
Md, Steve Keuer 123
Medeiros, Karen 239
Meffert, Walt 363
Meltzer, Neil 504
Merkel, Michael T 114
Midgley, Clare 569
Mielak, Gary 210
Miley, Nate 166
Miller, Liz 538
Mitchell, Adrienne 590
Moffa, Dominic 236
Molina, Gloria 171
Molinaro, Marcus J 206

Mollet, Chris 210
Monahan, Elizabeth F 198
Montgomery, Christopher 596
Moolji, Sanjay 628
Moore, Christine 174
Moore, Ed 462
Moore, Lena 61
Moquin, Jeffrey 486
Morales, David 687
Moranishi, Susan 166
Morris, Brad 2
Morris, Victor 93
Moscho, Harold 602
Mueller, Ken 453
Muhart, Matthew 510
Murphy, Karen 236
Murphy, Mark E 526
Murphy, Michael 500
Murphy, Wendy 613
Musa, Sam 449
Myers, Adam 84
Myers, Michael 336

N

Naese, Marc 419
Naftaly, Robert 637
Nakagawa, Roger T 96
Nakamoto, David 133
Napp, Marc 510
Nelson, Deana 306
Nelson, Heather 571
Nelson, Melissa 132
Nemerson, Steven 476
Nerland, Paul 169
Newcomer, Peter D 664
Newmyer, Joyce 6
Nienen, Marge 121
Nigrin, Daniel 326
Nissen, James A 426
Nivens, Margaret 546
Njau, Caroline 119
Noble, Walt 372
Novick, Steve 138
Nunez, Diana 138
Nutting, Ron 456

O

O'connell, Tim 141
O'connor, John 539
O'hearn, Patricia 140
O'mahony, Stephen 472
O'nan, Stephen B 114
Oberhausen, Stephanie 617
Ocana, Ann M 498
Ochi, Howard 482
Ockers, Thomas 241
Odegaard, Richard 247
Oh, Joyce 251
Oliver, Kirk R 639
Omalley, Ed 392
Orr, Mark 248
Orson, Marshall D 193

Index Of Executives

Oswald, Kathy 260
Ouchida, Michael 275

P

Parchinski, Kathleen 217
Parija, Soubhagya 386
Parkerson, Michael 570
Pascuzzi, Steve 185
Patel, Ketul J 264
Patrick, Ryan 134
Patry, Dean 40
Patterson, L Brooks 174
Patterson, Roger 658
Patton, Robin Van 156
Paxton, Stuart 310
Payton, Robert 210
Pe, Marc D Williams 563
Peacor, Melissa S 175
Penney, Robert 110
Perez, Maripaz 202
Permet, Robert 368
Perrin, Maria 265
Perry, Carol 543
Perry, Karl E 59
Pesgens, Suzanne 304
Peters, Len 389
Peterson, Kurt 606
Peterson, Mark 30
Peterson, Richard D 113
Petizio, Robert 167
Petti, Filippo 398
Phillips, Carrie 646
Phlegar, Charles D 676
Pierce, Tera 138
Pirie, Ellen 177
Pirro, Nicholas J 174
Pittman, Steuart 166
Pizzo, Kristine 386
Plam, Kathleen 132
Poenitske, Jason P 405
Poloncarz, Mark 169
Pond, Ayoka 63
Porter, Andy 569
Pottorff, Gary W 399
Powell, Willa 467
Powrie, Raymond 104
Pratt, Marcel S 137
Precinct, Rodney Ellis 170
Premo, Mark 446
Prendergast, Mark 245
Press, Donna G Orender Senior V 429
Press, Henry Hughes Senior V 429
Press, Jeff Monday V 429
Press, Michael Holsher Senior V 437
Press, Robert J Combs Senior V 429
Press, Ronald E Price Senior V 429
Press, Will Mann V 429
Price, John Wiley 168
Prinner, John 245
Prosser, Joseph 564
Pulomena, John 357
Pumpian, Ann 500
Purcell, Cailin 589
Purkey, Tom 594

Q

Quigley, Timothy 511
Quinn, Brian 356

R

R.n., Ann Cella 522
Ramirez, Shanna 143
Ramsey, Tom 170
Rash, Matthew P 42
Rassmussen, Anne 423
Ray, Joel 462
Reardon, Aaron 177
Rebsamen, C B 308
Reed, Glenn 270
Reed, Stephanie 481
Reed, Susan 167
Reel, Stephanie 618
Renne, Louise 126
Reyes, Alejandro 270
Riazi, Atefeh 343
Rice, David 61
Rich, Mindy 462
Richardville, Craig 505
Richter, John 145
Ricker, Bob 462
Ristuben, Steve 134
Rivinius, Jessica 354
Robbins, Kenneth B 255
Robertson, Cliff A 479
Robertson, Steve 255
Robinson, Denise 589
Robinson, Dorothy 695
Rodriguez, Yolanda 270
Rogers, Randy 555
Rogers, Rich 444
Rojek, Kenneth J 393
Romm, Sylvia 50
Rosenstein, Beryl 587
Roth, Colin 223
Rothermel, Paige 84
Rousseau, Jean M 178
Rubinson, Lewis 467
Rull, Arlyn 355
Ryan, John 188
Ryan, Michael 398
Ryan, Peter J 519
Ryder, David 673

S

S, Mary Beth Claus 386
Saenz, Denise 180
Saenz, Luis 537
Saffer, Lori Polep 161
Salins, Peter D 539
Saltich, Daniel J 498
Salvato, Alfred 620
Sandeen, Mark 11
Sanodo, Raquel 271
Sargent, Dale 682
Sattgast, Rich 537
Scanlon, John 110
Schaffner, Rick 73
Schleper, Denny 146
Schmidt, Barry 248
Schooler, Rick 308
Schreiner, Jeff 606
Schutter, George 243
Schwartz, James 166
Schwartz, Mel 681
Schwartz, Raphe 120
Scott, Emily Allinder 68
Scp, Katrina R Redmond 209
Seard-mccormick, Ellicia 219
Second, Adolph M Orlando 604
Sederstrom, Nneka O 260
Seger, Clint 81
Sellers, Thomas 251
Sen, Semih 574
Senior, Bruce Mc Donald Md 93
Senior, Doctor Brent Powers 315
Senior, Greg G Maxwell 117
Senior, J Craig Baker 33
Senior, Jared W Heald 218
Senior, Jay Robaidek 664
Senior, Jill C Anderson 386
Senior, Robert Lovett 625
Senior, Timothy F Sullivan 426
Senior, William H Dunn 283
Serna, Ed 565
Sewalls, Travis 478
Sewell, Collin 274
Shaevsky, Mark 691
Shanks, Scott 548
Sharieff, Ghazala 489
Sharp, Michael J 451
Sharpe, Anita 137
Shaw, Harold H 334
Shaw, Jennifer 87
Sheikh, Sana 245
Siddiqui, Omer 192
Siegert, Nancy L 360
Sielak, George 43
Silverman, Daniel C 504
Silverman, Deven 394
Simms, Erin 529
Singh, Gagan 336
Siplin, Victoria P 174
Sleeth, Shaun 336
Slevinski, Danette L 644
Smith, Christopher 337
Smith, Clinton 670
Smith, David A 375
Smith, David C 672
Smith, Franz 520
Smith, Jeffrey V 176
Snyder, Thomas G 135
Sola, Lester 355
Solomon, Lesley 188
Somerset, Gary 449
Special, Frederick Khouri Evp 227
Special, Jay Cole 685
Speed, Kevin 56
Spinale, Joseph W 526
Spooner, William A 500
Spradley, Suzanne 392
Squires, Keith 615
Sr, Johannes Britz Int 665
Stadtler, Dj 378
Stanley, Stephen E 42
Stanwood, Michael 226
Starr, Lisa Hoffman 515
Staub, Julie 602
Steck, Kevin 543
Steele, Gail 166
Stehlik, Christine 241
Steinberger, Eric 50
Steiner, Deborah L 451
Stendahl, Lea 544
Stenson, Brian 539
Stephenson, Jim 627
Stevens, Jon I 86
Stewart, James 57
Stewart, Louis 139
Stone, Jeff 175
Stoner, Roberta B 257
Strickland, Jill 452
Stringer, Scott 135
Stuart, Cindy 264
Stulac-motzel, Wendy Chief Ambulatory Population 260
Stutzman, Paul 245
Sullivan, James E 593
Sullivan, Stuart P 503
Sumar, Nageeb 225
Sutera, Albert J 580
Sutton, Patricia A 7
Swift, Micheal A 177
Swinton, Carolyn 444
Szczuk, Jason 89

T

Tachouet, Matthew 670
Talarico, Nick 199
Tan, Benjamin A 625
Tatum, Demitrios 172
Taylor, Larry 145
Taylor, Leo 585
Taynton, Philis 177
Tedesco, James 167
Tehrani, Sean 462
Teixeira, Kay 327
Testerman, Christopher R 174
Therady, Agnes 229
Thomason, Keith 594
Thompson, Jeff 231
Thompson, Matt 271
Thompson, Robert 246
Thornton, Leslie T 687
Tilton, David 236
Titus, Martin E 623
Toellner, Ann 656
Tomasky, Susan 33
Tracey, Bernard M 521
Tunnell, Richard T 644
Turner, Mike 248
Turner, William 312
Tuten, Steve 285
Tweedy, Robyn 381

U

Uribe, Mayra 174

Index Of Executives

V

V, Gary Delanois Senior 1
V, Gregory A Beck 114
V, Todd S Werner Junior 7
V, Tyrone Jeffers 519
Vadakumcherry, Sebastian 15
Vajda, Devit 151
Valdez, Armando 150
Vanderlaan, Meg 375
Vaughn, D Blayne 405
Venable, Jerry 295
Venezia, Patrick 593
Vincent, Suzanne M 292
Vipperman, Robert 21
Viswanathan, Sowmya 527
Vithoulkas, John A 170
Vlatkovich, Mychal 134
Voss, Zeb 352
Vpof, Chad T Lefteris 462

W

Wagner, Harvey L 351
Wagner, Harvey L 425
Walders, William 257
Waldman, Eyal 340
Walker, Algernon 130
Walker, Annette M 524
Walker, Scott 692
Wallin, Kim 535
Walsh, Meghan 260
Walters, Kelly S 579
Ward, Doris M 126
Warne, Teresa A 32
Warner, Elizabeth 103
Warner, Jennifer 453
Warren, Jim 225
Weber, Del B 410
Weber, Emily 339
Weiland, Ed 483
Weimin, Shi 628
Weinfurter, Daniel 192
Weitz, Ron 169
Welch, Deborah 527
Werblo, Jackelyn E 92
Wess, Mark 444
Weston, Marc A 189
Westrick, Karl J 327
Whitley, David 537
Widerlite, Paula 323
Williams, Bridget 598
Williams, Pamela J 511
Wilson, Nicholas J 625
Wilson, Nicole H 174
Wilson, Sherwood G 676
Windhaus, Donna 79
Wingo, Bill 293
Wise, Bonnie M 170
Wise, Deanna 59
Wolfe, Stephen 322
Woo, Melissa 356
Wormoudt, Mardi 177
Worobel, Ryan 683
Wright, Lori 419
Wskeland, Oddgeir 217

Y

Yabokla, Erica 531
Yaroslavsky, Zev 171
Yealy, Donald 667
Yocum, Deb 543
Young, Jay 518
Young, Terrance 249
Yudd, Charles 320

Z

Zacariassen, Christian 378
Zanavich, W Marie 610
Zappa, Michael 184
Zheng, Baohua 486
Ziffer, Jack A 61
Zink, Charles L 429